Canada

Andrea Schulte-Peevers, Becca Blond, Kerryn Burgess, Pete Cruttenden,
John Lee, Mark Lightbody, Graham Neale, Matt Phillips, Lisa Roberts,
Aaron Spitzer, Justine Vaisutis, Ryan Ver Berkmoes

Contents

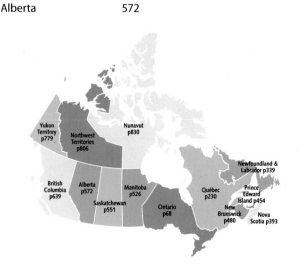

Yukon Territory p779
Northwest Territories p806
Nunavut p830
Newfoundland & Labrador p339
British Columbia p639
Alberta p572
Saskatchewan p551
Manitoba p526
Québec p230
Prince Edward Island p454
Ontario p68
New Brunswick p480
Nova Scotia p393

Destination Canada

The Creator must have been in an especially good mood when designing Canada. There are big-shouldered mountains chiseled into rugged splendor by glaciers and the elements. Across the prairies, fields of golden wheat wave gently in the wind, sheltered by a cerulean sky. The cry of the loon and the howl of the wolf drift over vast expanses of wilderness where nature still grandstands, raw, pristine and fierce. Pathways off the beaten track lead you to grazing moose and burly bears, while the skies are darkened by gargantuan skeins of Canada geese. Rainforests, serpentine coastlines, a gazillion streams, the eternal blanket of arctic ice and even a small desert – all are parts of the vast and unique natural patchwork that is Canada.

This is a country whose boundless menu of activities and sights allows you to calibrate your itinerary to whatever level of adventure you choose. In the summer you can raft fierce rapids or paddle along placid streams, venture on a wilderness trek, or cycle around quiet islands or down steep mountains. The cities too are treasure troves of experiences. Dive with wolf eels and octopuses in Vancouver, explore Toronto's ethnic neighborhoods, indulge in Montréal's superb cuisine scene or trace colonial history in St John's. In winter it's off to schuss down the slopes of Whistler or Mont Tremblant, to warm your spirits (or imbibe them) at an outdoor carnival or spend a steamy night at Québec City's unique Ice Hotel.

No matter where you travel in the world's second-largest country, you'll find exceptionally hospitable and friendly people and a delightful hotchpotch of cultures. Watch Scottish bagpipers on parade in Nova Scotia, croon French chansons in Québec, tempt your senses at Vancouver's Chinatown or attend a First Nations powwow in Saskatchewan. Just don't go looking for archetypal Canadians; they're as elusive as the mythical Bigfoot.

EDDIE BRADY

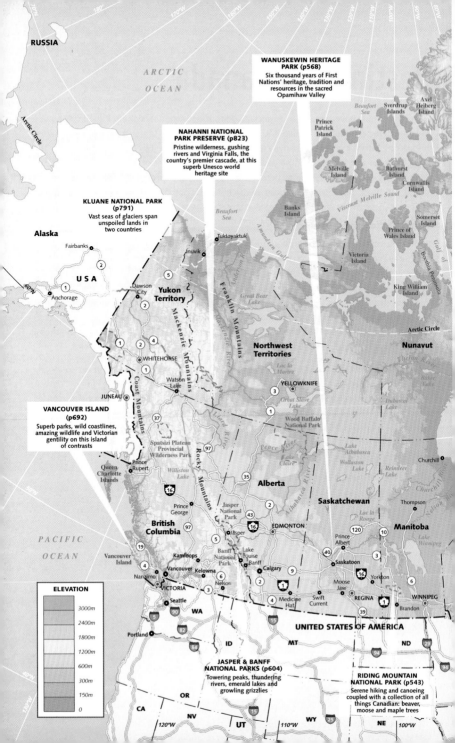

WANUSKEWIN HERITAGE PARK (p568)
Six thousand years of First Nations' heritage, tradition and resources in the sacred Opamihaw Valley

NAHANNI NATIONAL PARK PRESERVE (p823)
Pristine wilderness, gushing rivers and Virginia Falls, the country's premier cascade, at this superb Unesco world heritage site

KLUANE NATIONAL PARK (p791)
Vast seas of glaciers span unspoiled lands in two countries

VANCOUVER ISLAND (p692)
Superb parks, wild coastlines, amazing wildlife and Victorian gentility on this island of contrasts

JASPER & BANFF NATIONAL PARKS (p604)
Towering peaks, thundering rivers, emerald lakes and growling grizzlies

RIDING MOUNTAIN NATIONAL PARK (p543)
Serene hiking and canoeing coupled with a collection of all things Canadian: beaver, moose and maple trees

ELEVATION

3000m
2400m
1800m
1200m
600m
300m
150m
0

RUSSIA

ARCTIC OCEAN

Arctic Circle

Alaska

Fairbanks

USA

Anchorage

Inuvik

Tuktoyaktuk

Dawson City

Yukon Territory

WHITEHORSE

Watson Lake

JUNEAU

Prince Rupert

Queen Charlotte Islands

Spatsizi Plateau Provincial Wilderness Park

Williston Lake

Prince George

British Columbia

Kamloops

Kelowna

Vancouver Island

Vancouver

Nanaimo

VICTORIA

Seattle

WA

Portland

OR

CA

NV

UT

Beaufort Sea

Banks Island

Great Bear Lake

Mackenzie River

Franklin Mountains

Mackenzie Mountains

Anderson River

Amundsen Gulf

Victoria Island

Prince of Wales Island

King William Island

Somerset Island

Bothia Peninsula

Prince Patrick Island

Melville Island

Bathurst Island

Cornwallis Island

Axel Heiberg Island

Sverdrup Islands

Viscount Melville Sound

Gulf of

Northwest Territories

YELLOWKNIFE

Great Slave Lake

Lac la Martre

Wood Buffalo National Park

Liard River

Peace River

Lake Claire

Athabasca River

Lake Athabasca

Wollaston Lake

Reindeer Lake

Churchill

Nunavut

Arctic Circle

Thelon River

Dubawnt Lake

Baker Lake

Lac la Ronge

Churchill

Thompson

Alberta

Jasper National Park

Jasper

Banff National Park

Lake Louise

Banff

Calgary

Nelson

Medicine Hat

Swift Current

Saskatchewan

Prince Albert

Saskatoon

Moose Jaw

REGINA

Yorkton

Brandon

WINNIPEG

Manitoba

Lake Winnipeg

Nelson River

PACIFIC OCEAN

Coast Mountains

Rocky Mountains

UNITED STATES OF AMERICA

ID

MT

WY

ND

NE

EDMONTON

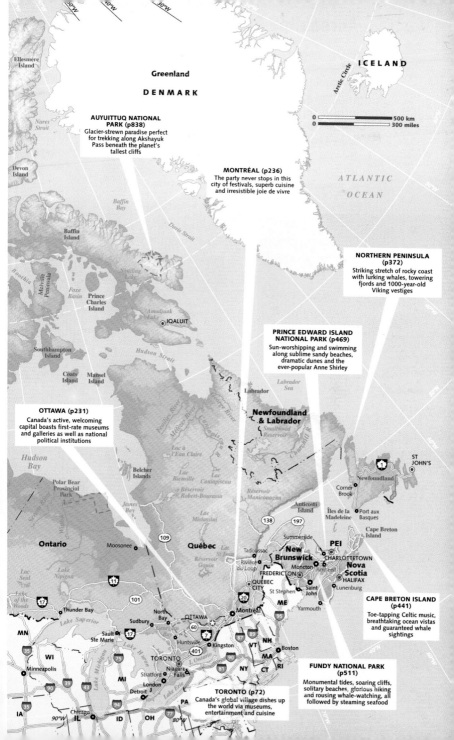

ICELAND

Greenland

DENMARK

AUYUITTUQ NATIONAL PARK (p838)
Glacier-strewn paradise perfect for trekking along Akshayuk Pass beneath the planet's tallest cliffs

MONTRÉAL (p236)
The party never stops in this city of festivals, superb cuisine and irresistible joie de vivre

ATLANTIC OCEAN

NORTHERN PENINSULA (p372)
Striking stretch of rocky coast with lurking whales, towering fjords and 1000-year-old Viking vestiges

PRINCE EDWARD ISLAND NATIONAL PARK (p469)
Sun-worshipping and swimming along sublime sandy beaches, dramatic dunes and the ever-popular Anne Shirley

OTTAWA (p231)
Canada's active, welcoming capital boasts first-rate museums and galleries as well as national political institutions

Newfoundland & Labrador

CAPE BRETON ISLAND (p441)
Toe-tapping Celtic music, breathtaking ocean vistas and guaranteed whale sightings

FUNDY NATIONAL PARK (p511)
Monumental tides, soaring cliffs, solitary beaches, glorious hiking and rousing whale-watching, all followed by steaming seafood

TORONTO (p72)
Canada's global village dishes up the world via museums, entertainment and cuisine

0   500 km
0   300 miles

Canada's magical outdoors will motivate even committed couch potatoes. You can swim at **Prince Edward Island National Park** (p469), paddle the **Yukon River** (p786) or sea kayak around the islands of Québec's **Mingan Archipelago National Park** (p311). There's excellent hiking, including in Saskatchewan's **Prince Albert National Park** (p570), with its white-pelican colony, bison and Grey Owl's cabin. The arctic air will lash your skin while you're dog-sledding near **Yellowknife** (p811), spotting polar bear in **Churchill** (p545), Manitoba, or whale-watching in Newfoundland's **Witless Bay Ecological Reserve** (p356).

GRANT DIXON

Cross the Arctic Circle while hiking in Auyuittuq National Park (p838), Nunavut

GLENN VAN DER KNIJFF

Hit the slopes at 2010 Winter Olympic venue, Whistler-Blackcomb (p687)

Kayak the serene waters and explore the islands of Clayoquot Sound (p718), Vancouver Island, a Unesco world-biosphere reserve

MICHAEL LAANELA

Many of Canada's cities are intriguing mixes of history, culture and the ingenuity of the people who built them. You can savor the wild west spirit in **Calgary** (p590), especially at the famous Calgary Stampede. In the Yukon, **Dawson City** (p798) takes you back to the Klondike gold-rush era, while **Charlottetown** (p458) on Prince Edward Island, considered Canada's birthplace, cherishes its colonial pedigree. It's impossible not to be smitten by historic **Québec City** (p278), with its dramatic bluff-top location above the St Lawrence River. The country's oldest city, though, is Newfoundland's **St John's** (p345), whose delightful web of crooked lanes reflects its fishing village origins.

STEPHEN SAKS

Tempt your tastebuds at Granville Island Public Market (p672), Vancouver

Admire Victorian architecture on Rue St-Denis, Plateau Mont-Royal (p247), Montréal

GEORGI G SHABLOVSKY

Escape the city as you stroll the shores of Toronto Island (p82), Toronto

CHERYL CONLON

In Canada, nature has been as creative and prolific as Picasso in his prime. Feast your eyes on floating icebergs at **Brimstone Head** (p368) in Newfoundland or find inspiration among the lush forests of Ontario's **Killarney Provincial Park** (p171), as did the famous Group of Seven painters. Travel off the beaten path to the roaring **Virginia Falls** (p823) in the Northwest Territories, the paradisiacal **Soper River** (p837) in Nunavut, or the rugged **Queen Charlotte Islands** (p768) in British Columbia. More easily accessible are the lacy fjords and flat-top mountains of **Gros Morne National Park** (p373) in Newfoundland, and the wildlife-filled wilderness of **Riding Mountain National Park** (p543) in Manitoba.

Wonder at the surreal, azure waters of Peyto Lake (p607), Banff National Park

Explore the unusual formations of eroded 'flowerpots' at Hopewell Rocks (p513), New Brunswick

Disappear in the spray of Niagara Falls on a Maid of Mist boat tour (p122)

Getting Started

Canada has excellent tourism infrastructure that makes traveling a pleasure. From backpackers to jetsetters, all travelers will find their needs and expectations met. Room and transportation reservations are a good idea in summer and around holidays. One thing to keep in mind is the country's immense scale. If you're like most people, you're traveling to get away from daily stresses, so don't try to pack too much into your itinerary and do consider limiting your explorations to one or two regions in depth.

WHEN TO GO

There are reasons to visit Canada at any time of year, but most people arrive in summer when temperatures are pleasant and much of the action moves outdoors. Just what constitutes 'summer,' though, varies by region. In southern Canada, it generally refers to the period between Victoria Day (late May) and Labour Day (early September). In the northern regions, however, summer starts as late as mid-June and ends, often abruptly, with the first snowfall in early to mid-September.

In most areas, March to May and September to October bring fewer tourists and often surprisingly pleasant weather. Fall, which finds forests cloaked in a spectacular mantle of color, is a great time to visit.

For more information, see Holidays (p854) and Climate Charts (p849).

Canadian winters are long, cold and dark. With most outlying attractions closed, your explorations are pretty much limited to the ski resorts and cities. Québec City, Toronto and Winnipeg are among those cities hosting big winter carnivals. City museums generally remain open in those months, and the ballet, opera and symphony season is in full swing as well.

COSTS & MONEY

Canada is fairly inexpensive, although regional variations exist. In general, Ontario, Alberta and British Columbia are more costly than other provinces, but not as bad as the three northern territories (Yukon Territory, Northwest Territories and Nunavut). Your dollar will stretch furthest in Québec, the Maritimes, Manitoba and Saskatchewan. Discounts are widely available to children, students and seniors throughout the country.

In most regions, you can live quite comfortably on about $80 to $100 per day; double that and you'll be living it up. For mere survival, you'll need to budget about $50, but this will mean camping or sleeping in hostels, riding buses, preparing your own meals or eating take-out snacks and fast food, and limiting your entertainment.

Comfortable mid-range accommodations start at around $70 for a double room, usually including breakfast. Many properties have special

---

DON'T LEAVE HOME WITHOUT...

- Checking the visa (p861) and border-crossing (p863) requirements, as these may change
- Valid travel insurance (p854)
- Bug spray (p881)
- Your driver's license and registration papers, plus adequate liability insurance (p872)
- Car, hotel or camping reservations (p842), especially when traveling in summer
- This book and an open mind

'family' rooms or can supply sleeping cots for a small fee. In some places, children under a certain age pay nothing if staying in their parents' room without requiring extra bedding.

A full restaurant meal with wine or beer generally costs between $20 and $30, plus tax of 7% to 17% and a tip. The bill is lower if you stick to cafés and casual restaurants and skip alcoholic drinks. Rental cars cost from $30 to $40 a day for a compact, not including gas.

Taxes are added to nearly all goods and services, but you can get at least a portion of them back through the Visitor Rebate Program (p857). For tipping guidelines, see p857.

LONELY PLANET INDEX

Liter/US gallon of gas: $0.84/3.17

Liter of bottled water: $0.90

Bottle of Molson Canadian: $2

Souvenir T-shirt: $10

Cup of coffee and a donut: $2

HOW MUCH?

Hotel double room: $70-120

Pack of cigarettes: $5-7

Roll of 36-exposure print film: $6.50

Movie ticket: $8-9

Newspaper: $1

TRAVEL LITERATURE

To get you in the mood for your trip, consider reading some of these titles written by travelers who have visited Canada before you.

Part history, part adventure tale, *Maps & Dreams: Indians and the British Columbia Frontier* is Hugh Brody's colorful account of the ancient ways of a small band of Beaver nation Aboriginals in northwest Canada and their clash with modern civilization.

Jonathan Waterman takes a similar focus in *Arctic Crossing*, a personal journey through the Northwest Passage and into Inuit territory where he observes the progress, failures and history of the embattled Inuit people.

The Inuit referred to Victoria Jason as *Kabloona in the Yellow Kayak* (*kabloona* means 'stranger'), which became the title of this grandmother's compelling book about her 7500km paddling expedition from Churchill, Manitoba, to Tuktoyaktuk on the Beaufort Sea from 1991 to '94.

Humor, magic and sly literary conceits make David McFadden's *Great Lakes Suites*, a collection of vignettes about trips he took around Lakes Erie, Huron and Ontario, hallucinogenically funny and poignantly insightful.

Humorous at times, scholarly at others, *Rediscovering the Great Plains* by Norman Henderson is an engaging travel memoir recounting the author's adventures while exploring Saskatchewan's Qu'Appelle River Valley via horse, canoe and dogsled.

In *Wilderness Journey*, Ian and Sally Wilson weave a fascinating blend of their own travel adventures and tales from voyageur life as they follow in the footsteps of fur traders in Saskatchewan and Manitoba.

Finally, *Sacre Blues: An Unsentimental Journey Through Québec*, by Taras Grescoe, is an often laugh-out-loud book that introduces us to the hilarious and maddening foibles of the Québécois. Linguistics, unsavory lust for *poutine* and the province's reputation as 'Canada's smoking section' are all artfully skewered by the author's dry wit.

INTERNET RESOURCES

An American's Guide to Canada (www.icomm.ca/emily/) A sassy look at the critical differences between the USA and its northern neighbor (eg which one has more donut shops per capita).

Canada's Cultural Gateway (www.culture.ca) All the facts about Canada, including what Mounties actually do out there on the prairies.

Canadian Tourism Commission (www.travelcanada.ca) From Alberta to the Yukon, this official tourist information site is packed with details on all aspects of travel to and within Canada.

CIA World Factbook (www.cia.gov/cia/publications/factbook/geos/ca.html) About as dry as a martini, but packed with useful and frequently updated data about geopolitical, demographic, economic and other aspects of Canada.

Government of Canada (http://canada.gc.ca) The mother of all Canada websites, with links to everything from the latest immigration rules to the lyrics of *O Canada* (the national anthem).

Lonely Planet (www.lonelyplanet.com) Canada travel news and summaries, the Thorn Tree bulletin board, and SubWWWay links to more web resources.

TOP TENS
CANADA ON CELLULOID

Grab a bowl of popcorn and get in the mood for your Canadian adventure with one (or some) of these flicks made by Canada's top directors. Many have won international acclaim, including coveted Oscars, Golden Globes and Palmes d'Or.

- *Mon oncle Antoine* (1971) Director: Claude Jutra
- *The Apprenticeship of Duddy Kravitz* (1974) Director: Ted Kotcheff
- *Videodrome* (1983) Director: David Cronenberg
- *I've Heard the Mermaid Singing* (1987) Director: Patricia Rozema
- *Jesus de Montréal* (1989) Director: Denys Arcand
- *33 Short Films About Glenn Gould* (1993) Director: François Girard
- *Hard Core Logo* (1996) Director: Bruce McDonald
- *The Sweet Hereafter* (1997) Director: Atom Egoyan
- *Hollywood North* (2003) Director: Peter O'Brian
- *Les Invasions barbares* (2003) Director: Denys Arcand

GREAT CANADIAN READS

Storytelling opens a window on the culture and psyche of a country's people. Prepare for your trip by reading these works by some of Canada's finest writers. See p42 for reviews of some of them.

- *The Anciens Canadien* (1863) Philippe Aubert de Gaspé Sr
- *Anne of Green Gables* (1908) Lucy Maud Montgomery
- *Wild Geese* (1925) Martha Ostenso
- *The Tin Flute* (1945) Gabrielle Roy
- *The Stone Angel* (1964) Margaret Laurence
- The Deptford Trilogy: *Fifth Business* (1970), *The Manicore* (1972) and *World of Wonders* (1975) Robertson Davies
- *The Wars* (1977) Timothy Findley
- *In the Skin of a Lion* (1987) Michael Ondaatje
- *Cat's Eye* (1989) Margaret Atwood
- *Whylah Falls* (1990) George Elliott Clarke

PARTY IN THE STREETS

Canadians know how to let their hair down. There's almost always something interesting going on around the country and in summer, cities such as Montréal never seem to stop having fun. Here's our list of favorites, but see p852 for more.

- Winter Carnival (Québec City, Québec; p287) February
- Yukon Quest (Whitehorse, Yukon; p786) February
- Stratford Festival (Stratford, Ontario; p142) April to November
- Calgary Stampede (Calgary, Alberta; p597) July
- Festival International de Jazz (Montréal, Québec; p253) July
- Great Northern Arts Festival (Inuvik, Northwest Territories; p827) July
- Klondike Days (Edmonton, Alberta; p583) July
- Festival Acadien (Caraquet, New Brunswick; p523) August
- Toronto International Film Festival (Toronto, Ontario; p96) September
- Oktoberfest (Kitchener, Ontario; p137) October

Itineraries
CLASSIC ROUTES

CENTRAL CORRIDOR
Two weeks / Toronto to Québec City

Book-ended by two of Canada's great cities, this route offers some of Canada's best culture, cuisine and character. Start in tantalizing **Toronto** (p72), filled with world-class architecture, museums, restaurants, nightclubs and parks. Take a day trip to **Niagara Falls** (p121), then head east to lovely **Quinte's Isle** (p200). Catch the ferry to Adolphustown, then retrace history along the Loyalist Parkway into **Kingston** (p201) with its well-preserved town center. Then follow the St Lawrence River northeast to **Gananoque** (p207). Stop at **Upper Canada Village** (p209), a recreated 1860s town, before heading to **Ottawa** (p213). Get your culture fix at the many museums and sample the bustling café and nightlife scene before your next stop, **Montréal** (p236). Be seduced by the city's blend of French joie de vivre, British tradition and North American can-do spirit. There are great sights and even better restaurants to give your stomach a workout. Once you've had your fill, swing over to the **Laurentians** (p265) to hike, cycle or canoe yourself back into shape. End your trip in **Québec City** (p278). Its charming old town, walled and dramatically positioned on a bluff, will leave you with sweet memories long after you've returned home.

Prepare for a roller-coaster of urban and rural delights on this 1450km journey across two great provinces that never has you far from a major lake or river. It can be 'done' in 10 days, but add a few more and you'll connect more deeply with this fascinating land and its people.

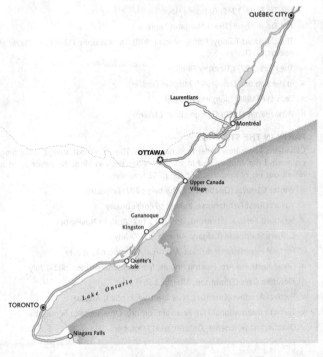

BEST OF THE WEST
Three to four weeks / British Columbia & Alberta

Start with a couple of days in dynamic **Vancouver** (p647), where you'll be spoiled for choice by superb sights and western Canada's best cuisine scene. Hop on a ferry to **Victoria** (p693), fill up with tea and crumpets, then rent a car and head north. On Vancouver Island you can sea kayak and dive off **Quadra Island** (p724), hike and boat in **Strathcona Provincial Park** (p725), absorb First Nations culture at **Alert Bay** (p727) and spot orcas off **Port McNeill** (p727) and **Port Hardy** (p728). Port Hardy is also where you'll catch the ferry for an unforgettable journey through the **Inside Passage** (p728) to **Prince Rupert** (p764), past ice-coated mountain peaks and rugged islands draped in dense forest. Grab binoculars for close-ups of eagles, whales, porpoises, seals and other wildlife. Prince Rupert is the jumping-off point to the mist-shrouded and mysterious **Queen Charlotte Islands** (p768), with their unique ecosystems, old-growth forest and ancient aboriginal villages and totems. If you've got an extra five days, this is a must-do. Otherwise, it's time to board VIA Rail's *Skeena*, which chugs past rivers, lakes and glacier-edged mountains on its two-day journey from Prince Rupert to **Jasper** (p622), where you should rent another car. The national parks of Jasper and **Banff** (p609) form the dramatic core of the Canadian Rockies. You'll want to spend several days hiking, horse-back riding, kayaking and otherwise exploring the great outdoors. Wild-life encounters are guaranteed. From there, head west back into British Columbia for more spectacular mountain scenery in **Yoho** (p757), **Glacier** (p756) and **Mt Revelstoke** (p756) national parks. Finally, work your way back to Vancouver via the lake-studded **Okanagan Valley** (p739), famous for its fruit orchards and wineries.

Vancouver, the Inland Passage and the Rocky Mountains: prepare to feast on a smorgasbord of scenic delights on this 3000km traipse around British Columbia and Alberta. Allow at least three weeks for this epic journey by boat, car and train.

ROADS LESS TRAVELED

ALASKA HIGHWAY
Two weeks / Dawson Creek to Fairbanks

A marvel of engineering, the Alaska Hwy meanders through a vast land shaped by forest, tundra, muskeg and ice fields. Your adventure starts in **Dawson Creek** (p778), a pint-sized town and one-time railroad terminus some 360km northeast of Prince George. Snap a picture of yourself at the Mile Zero sign and hit the road. You'll soon leave the prairies behind as you reach the foothills of the Rockies. **Fort St John** and **Fort Nelson** (p778) are good supply stops for the upcoming trio of provincial parks. First up is **Stone Mountain Provincial Park** (p778), a jumble of steep mountains and U-shaped valleys inhabited by moose, caribou, stone sheep, mountain goats and other critters. Further north, **Muncho Lake Provincial Park** (p778) is named for its jaw-droppingly beautiful lake, the color of which ranges from the blue of Cameron Diaz' eyes to cloverleaf green. After a day on the trail, a soak in the natural hot tubs at **Liard River Hot Springs Provincial Park** (p778) is in order. The highway enters the Yukon at **Watson Lake** (p790), famous for its bizarre 'forest' of 50,000 signposts. If you're ready for a bit of civilization, you'll find it in **Whitehorse** (p783). Enjoy its museums and the historic SS *Klondike* sternwheeler. Ready for more wilderness? A highlight awaits in **Kluane National Park** (791), home to the world's largest nonpolar ice fields and soaring mountains, including Canada's tallest mountain, Mt Logan (5959m). The highway enters Alaska shortly after **Beaver Creek** (p793), from where it's about another 450km to Fairbanks. For background information on the Alaska Hwy, see p789.

Open roads, big skies, breathtaking scenery and enough wildlife to give you that safari feeling are what await you on this legendary 2451km road trip from northern British Columbia to Alaska via the Yukon. Resist the temptation to race through it: nature's true charms don't reveal themselves at high speeds.

TRANS-CANADA HIGHWAY

**Three weeks to two months /
Newfoundland to British Columbia**

The world's longest highway is technically a patchwork of several provincial roads. Scenic stretches alternate with mundane ones; many of the fine sights require detours off the highway. For the full low-down, see www.transcanadahighway.com.

From **St John's** (p345), Canada's oldest city, the Trans-Canada Hwy traverses Newfoundland, then resumes after a ferry ride in Sydney on beautiful **Cape Breton Island** (p441), Nova Scotia. Continue to New Brunswick (or detour via **Prince Edward Island**, p454), then follow the Saint John River via **Fredericton** (p484) to Québec's **Gaspé Peninsula** (p319). Following the mighty St Lawrence River, the highway reaches romantic **Québec City** (p278) and metropolitan **Montréal** (p236) before plunging into Ontario near **Ottawa** (p213). From there, follow in the footsteps of fur traders to **Sudbury** (p179) and **Sault Ste Marie** (p187), the gateway to the Algoma wilderness that inspired the Group of Seven painters. Savor the superb stretch of road skirting Lake Superior to **Thunder Bay** (p194). The highway then enters the prairie flatlands of Manitoba and Saskatchewan, only briefly enlivened by **Winnipeg** (p530) and quirky **Moose Jaw** (p560) with its Prohibition-era smuggling tunnels. The Rockies offer a dramatic change of scenery as the highway meanders through **Calgary** (p590) and **Banff** (p609) in Alberta before entering British Columbia at **Yoho National Park** (p757) and reaching its highest point (1643m) at Kicking Horse Pass. The mountains eventually give way to river country. The most memorable section leads through the **Fraser River Canyon** (p736) from where it's only a quick jaunt to **Vancouver** (p647) and the ferry to **Victoria** (p693).

So you want bragging rights to having done the world's longest road trip? This 7821km belt of asphalt cinched around the country's girth from St John's, Newfoundland, to Victoria, British Columbia, should do the trick. Pack patience, curiosity and an open mind.

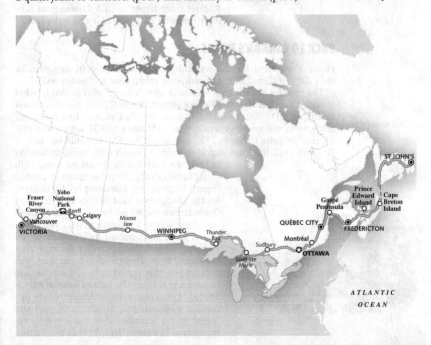

TAILORED TRIPS

ROAD RAVES

Canada has some of the world's most spectacular drives. In Newfoundland, the **Viking Trail** (p372) is an epic coastal road taking you past fjord-laced Gros Morne National Park and the L'Anse aux Meadows Viking settlement. Another ocean drive is along Nova Scotia's **Cabot Trail** (p444), which loops around Cape Breton Highlands National Park, revealing vistas of surreal beauty while whales patrol offshore. To get off the beaten track, head to eastern Québec where Rte 132 loops around the rugged coast of the **Gaspé Peninsula** (p319), punctuated by cliffs, waterfalls and villages. In Ontario, the **Lake Superior Shore** (p191) swoops and dips from Sault Ste Marie to Thunder Bay past rocky shores and forests. Canada's northernmost road, the gravelly **Dempster Hwy** (p803), leads quite literally to the 'edge of the world.' Mountains, valleys, rivers and tundra of primordial beauty accompany you as you cross the Arctic Circle en route from Dawson City, Yukon to Inuvik in the Northwest Territories. Also in the Yukon is the breathtaking **Top of the World Hwy** (p803), which winds from Dawson City to the Alaskan border. In Alberta, the **Icefields Parkway** (p606) is the country's most famous mountain road. It carves through the Rockies from Jasper to Lake Louise, past achingly beautiful lakes, icefields and waterfalls.

BACK TO CANADA'S ROOTS

Fierce Norsemen, fur traders, indigenous warriors, gold diggers...the early days of Canada were tumultuous, calamitous and waaay wild.

The first Europeans to see Canada were Vikings who settled in what is now **L'Anse aux Meadows National Historic Site** (p377) in Newfoundland in around AD 1000. Though this is technically Canada's first European settlement, that credit generally goes to **St John's** (p345), which was 'discovered' by John Cabot in 1497 and settled in 1528. It would be another 80 years until the founding of the oldest *French* settlement, **Québec City** (p278), the only North American town with intact fortifications. To see an entire re-created French fortress, visit **Louisbourg** (p449) in Nova Scotia. Discussions held at Province House in **Charlottetown** (p458) on Prince Edward Island paved the way to Canadian union. The fledgling country soon turned its attention to the vast west, an idea that met with resistance from the local Métis. Their leader, Louis Riel, was captured in the 1885 Battle of Batoche and hanged a year later. The **Batoche National Historic Site** (p571) re-creates the settlement where this conflict took place. A decade later, gold was found in the Klondike River, still vividly remembered in **Dawson City** (p798) in the Yukon.

The Authors

ANDREA SCHULTE-PEEVERS Coordinating Author, Québec

Canada has loomed large in Andrea's imagination ever since her mom casually mentioned that part of her German family had emigrated there generations ago. She has since explored some of the finest corners of the 'Great White North,' including Vancouver and the Rockies. For this book, she was able to indulge her passion for food and good living while researching Montréal and southern Québec. A veteran Lonely Planet author, Andrea makes her home in Los Angeles with her husband David and her cat, Mep the Fierce. She's still looking for those elusive relatives....

The Coordinating Author's Favorite Trip

Of my many trips to Canada, one to the Rockies packed the most wallop. Banff and Jasper National Parks (p604) were love at first sight, with their beautiful lakes fringed by robust crags. Then there was that elk scattering a busload of tourists like nine-pins, black bear dancing on a golf course and a wild-eyed horse charging down a cliff-side trail with me hanging on for dear life. Vancouver (p647) was also a joy – strolling Stanley Park, sipping chowder at the Granville Island Public Market and doing dim sum in Chinatown. For great food, though, nothing beats Montréal (p236). I love the easygoing spirit, the French influence and the fun shopping. For future trips I've got my eye on the Inside Passage (p728) and polar bear–watching in Churchill (p545).

BECCA BLOND Alberta

In her spare time Becca likes to take cross-country road trips in her old blue Toyota, so she jumped at the opportunity to drive up north and check out Alberta for this book. Once 'in country' (following a little trouble at the border), the beauty of western Canada brought back fond memories of family vacations in the region, including camping next to grizzly bear and long glacier hikes. When not on the road for Lonely Planet, Becca calls Boulder, Colorado, home.

KERRYN BURGESS Ontario

Kerryn graduated with a degree in journalism from the Royal Melbourne Institute of Technology. So armed, she worked as an intern in the Australian parliament, traveled around the world, and moved to Ontario to work as a media monitor. Here she spent weekdays in a Toronto office transcribing interviews with Canadian politicians and weekends hiking the Niagara Escarpment. Kerryn joined Lonely Planet in 1999, and is the managing editor for the Americas region. She researched the Georgian Bay & Lakelands and Northern Ontario areas of this guide.

PETE CRUTTENDEN   British Columbia
Born in the remote reaches of Western Australia, Pete has always felt an affinity for isolated places and natural beauty. He found British Columbia absolutely blessed with both – his advice: get out and see it all if you possibly can. Pete has also traveled though Australia's central deserts, and into the northern reaches of Australia's eastern and western coasts while working on other Lonely Planet guides. When not traveling, he rides his bike, plays indoor soccer, edits university texts and travel guides, and writes restaurant reviews.

JOHN LEE   British Columbia
Born and raised in the UK, John moved to Canada's West Coast in 1993 and became a full-time freelance travel writer soon after finishing his graduate degree at the University of Victoria. His work has appeared in more than 70 publications around the world, including the *Los Angeles Times*, *Travel + Leisure*, *Globe and Mail* and the *London Observer*. He specializes in writing about Canada and the UK, but his all-time favorite journey was on the Trans-Siberian Railway. John wrote about Vancouver and Canada's culinary traditions for this book.

MARK LIGHTBODY   Ontario, Québec, New Brunswick
Mark took his first breath in Montréal. He grew up there and nearly drowned in the Eastern Townships. Nearby he had his first drink and first kiss, and like much in Québec, they too were memorable. Mark studied in Ontario and now lives in Toronto. He travels extensively across central and eastern Canada, for pleasure and on assignment. While relishing the cities and towns between the Bay of Fundy and Thunder Bay, he also explores the outdoors with gusto. Mark has contributed to numerous previous editions of this book, and ventured to Eastern Ontario, regional Québec and New Brunswick this time around.

GRAHAM NEALE   Manitoba, Saskatchewan, Ontario
While other high-school graduates backpacked to Europe or tropical destinations, Graham left his native Vancouver to test his fortitude against prairie winters in Saskatoon. He lasted two years and considered himself a true 'prairie folk,' much to the guffaws of true prairie folk. He never forgot the things he saw or people he met in the most underrated part of North America. Writing about Saskatchewan and Manitoba for this book gave Graham the chance to add personality to places not on everyone's to-do list, while writing about Southwestern Ontario was a chance to say, 'Get off Hwy 401 and enjoy.'

MATT PHILLIPS   Prince Edward Island, Newfoundland & Labrador

After growing up on Canada's west coast, with his head in the sky and his toes in the sea, Matt has managed to use kayaks, canoes, ATVs, helicopters, sailboats, a few pairs of size 13s and even a hovercraft to discover some of his country's nethermost regions and meet some interesting characters. He's even spent time exploring deep beneath its surface. With his penchant for isolated beauty and his love of a good laugh, surely nowhere was better for Matt to do a little research and writing than Newfoundland, Labrador and Prince Edward Island.

LISA ROBERTS   Nova Scotia

A Newfoundlander, Lisa has lived in Guatemala and Mexico. Now appreciating the charms of traveling close to home, she was thrilled to research Nova Scotia from her home base in Halifax. Lisa adopted her Saturday morning ritual of coffee and croissants at the Halifax Brewery Market more than a decade ago as an undergrad at Dalhousie University, and would happily write a travel guide just for first-time market-goers. Lisa is a frequent contributor to CBC Radio in Halifax, and owns an old house with a sweet little garden in that city's North End.

AARON SPITZER   Northwest Territories, Nunavut

Aaron has a thing for bad latitudes. He was born and raised in Indiana and at age 13 took his first airline flight – to Yellowknife, in the Northwest Territories. A decade later he moved to the polar region for good, and now lives in Whitehorse. He has worked as a kayak guide in Alaska, a newspaper editor in Antarctica and Nunavut, and a television news producer and reporter in the Northwest Territories and the Yukon. He wrote the Nunavut chapter and much of the Northwest Territories chapter of this book.

JUSTINE VAISUTIS   Ontario

Justine's addiction to the nomadic lifestyle began in South Africa and South Korea, where she lived as a little tacker. Her obsession was augmented after a road trip up the US coast culminating in a Vancouver winter and love for all things Canadiana. Back in the real world, she completed an arts degree in Third World Development Studies, but decided it was more enjoyable to save the world by writing about it, and embarked on the noble career of a travel writer. For this book she updated Toronto, Stratford and the Niagara region of Southwestern Ontario.

RYAN VER BERKMOES
Yukon, Northwest Territories

Ryan wrote the Yukon chapter and the Sahtu and Western Arctic sections of the Northwest Territories chapter, areas he also covered for a previous edition of this book. Ryan also spent a good part of 2003 up north researching Lonely Planet's *British Columbia*, which includes a large section on the Yukon. Always a big fan of Canada's wild north, Ryan is prone to phrases like 'It's incredible up there, eh?' when extolling the virtues of one of the world's great destinations.

CONTRIBUTING AUTHORS

Sam Benson is the author of Lonely Planet's *Toronto*, which was adapted for the Ontario chapter of this guide. As a travel writer, Sam has taken readers from the mountains of Whistler to the wine country of the Niagara Peninsula, and finds herself sidetracked often by the Megacity's funky fashion, fusion food and film festivities.

Bruce Dowbiggin wrote the sports section of the Culture chapter (p34). Bruce is an award-winning sports journalist and national sports commentator based in Calgary. His columns regularly feature in the *Calgary Herald*. He is the author of several books on hockey and frequently hosts TV and radio programs, including for the CBC.

Will Ferguson wrote about Canada's national psyche in the Culture chapter (p34). Will was born and raised in the hamlet of Fort Vermilion, a former fur-trading post in northern Alberta. He is the author of several humorous books of memoirs and social commentary, including *How to Be a Canadian: Even If You Already Are One*, *Why I Hate Canadians* and *Bastards & Boneheads: Our Glorious Leaders, Past and Present*.

Dr David Goldberg The Health chapter (p878) is adapted from material written by Dr Goldberg, who completed his training at Columbia-Presbyterian Medical Center in New York City. He is an infectious diseases specialist and the editor-in-chief of www.mdtravelhealth.com.

Cleo Paskal wrote the Cirque du Soleil boxed text in the Culture chapter (p34). She is cowriter of the Emmy-award winning TV series *Cirque du Soleil: Fire Within*.

Margo Pfeiff wrote about Canada's lifestyle, multiculturalism, population and religion in the Culture chapter (p34). She is a Montréal-based journalist who's lived a pan-Canadian lifestyle. She grew up in British Columbia, then moved to Québec and frequently traveled to – plus developed a passion for – Canada's north. Her work has appeared in the *Globe and Mail*, *National Post* and *Los Angeles Times*, among other publications.

Jennie Punter wrote about Canada's arts scene in the Culture chapter (p34). For years Jennie wrote about theater, classical music and visual arts, before moving to Toronto to become a rock 'n' roll scribe. Today she regularly reviews films for the *Globe and Mail*, is a contributing editor to *FLARE* magazine and works in documentary film and TV.

Snapshot

Canadians are certainly not fans of radical change. They showed this to be so once again at the polls in June 2004, when they voted to keep center-left Liberals in power for a fourth consecutive term, albeit as a minority government. To push through his legislative agenda, Prime Minister Paul Martin has been forced to work with other parties, such as the left-leaning New Democratic Party and the separatist Bloc Québecois. Alas, Canadian minority governments don't usually survive long, so don't be surprised if somebody else is at the helm by the time you read this.

A major challenge for whoever's in power is how to reconcile the divergent interests of Canada's provinces and territories. The only shared sentiment seems to be that the federal government is too powerful and insensitive to their particular needs. This tension is greatest in predominantly francophone Québec, which periodically threatens to secede from confederation (see p32). But frequent grumbling can also be heard from the western provinces and territories, which desire more control over their vast natural resources. Even the mild-mannered Maritimes are bickering about federal claims to fishing and mineral rights off their shores.

One topic discussed at dinner tables around the country is the state of the nation's much-cherished but ailing universal health care system. To be sure, the quality of care is high and getting treatment for minor ailments easy. But try seeing a specialist or getting a hip replacement and you could be on a waiting list for months. Frustration runs so high there's talk of allowing those with deep pockets to pay for private health care, effectively creating a two-tiered system not unlike what exists in the USA.

Unlike their southern neighbors, Canadians are remarkably pragmatic – and progressive – when dealing with controversial social issues. Same-sex marriage, for instance, became legal in Ontario in 2003 and in British Columbia, Québec, the Yukon, Manitoba and Nova Scotia in 2004, spurring the Liberals to draft legislation to extend rights nationwide. The measure, which enjoys support from most parties, has been presented to the Canadian Supreme Court; a decision was expected in late 2004.

Pot is another hot-button issue. Although medical marijuana became legal in 2001, recreational use is still a felony. Most parties support decriminalizing (ie imposing lower penalties for) possession of small quantities of marijuana. However, they stop short – for now – of complete legalization, even though the right-leaning Fraser Institute calculated that such a move could net $2 billion in tax revenue.

Internationally, Canada is committed to cooperation. It signed the Kyoto Protocol, does its part in the war on terrorism and sent troops to Afghanistan. But its refusal to support the invasion of Iraq has strained its relationship with the USA. Seemingly more interested in keeping peace than making war, over 125,000 of Canada's military personnel serve as UN peacekeepers worldwide, more than any other nation's.

Ties between the USA and Canada remain strong, especially on the economic front. With over 80% of Canadian exports going to the USA and more than 70% of imports coming from the USA, the economies are inextricably linked. The US economic slump was severely felt in Canada, and outbreaks of Severe Acute Respiratory Syndrome (SARS), West Nile Virus and mad cow disease in 2003 hampered the rebound. Figures were looking more promising at press time. Forecasters expect the Canadian economy to grow strongly.

FAST FACTS

Population: 31.83 million

Inflation: 2.5%

Unemployment: 7.3%

Gross domestic product: $1.2 trillion

Average family income: $73,200

Average hourly wage: $18.40

Life expectancy: women 83.5 years, men 76.6 years

Length of Trans-Canada Hwy: 12,860km

Percentage of Canadians who speak only French: 13.3%

Number of Canadians who identify as Aboriginal: more than 1 million

History

Canada's human history began between 40,000 and 25,000 years ago, toward the end of the last Ice Age. The earliest ancestors of Canada's present-day Aboriginal peoples were most likely hunter-nomads who migrated from Asia over a land bridge linking Siberia and Alaska in pursuit of caribou, elk, bison and other animals. As the earth warmed and the glaciers retreated, these immigrants slowly began to spread all across the Americas.

About 4500 years ago, a second major wave of migration from Siberia brought the ancestors of the Inuit to Canada. They regarded the entire North, from Alaska to Greenland, as promising real estate. These early Inuit were members of the Dorset Culture, which was named after Cape Dorset on Baffin Island, where its remains were first unearthed. Around AD 1000 a separate Inuit culture, the whale-hunting Thule of northern Alaska, began making its way east through the Canadian Arctic as far as Greenland. As these people spread, they absorbed or replaced the Dorset Culture. The Thule are the direct ancestors of the modern Inuit.

When the first European explorers and fishers arrived in Canada in the late 15th century, Aboriginal peoples had spread into six major geographic locations within what are now Canada's borders. On the mild Pacific coast, tribes including the Haida and Nootka lived in independent villages where they enjoyed an abundant supply of fish, game and berries, built cedar-plank houses, and carved elaborate totem poles and canoes.

To the east, the Plains First Nations, which includes the Sioux and the Blackfoot, occupied the prairies from Lake Winnipeg to the Rocky Mountain foothills. Primarily buffalo hunters, they cunningly killed their prey by driving them over cliffs, such as at Head-Smashed-In Buffalo Jump (p632) in southern Alberta. The buffalo provided both sustenance and the hides used for tipis and clothes.

Present-day southern Ontario and the area along the St Lawrence River was home to the Iroquoian-speaking peoples, who were divided into the Five Nations, the Huron, the Erie and the Neutral confederacies. Although often at war with each other, they were a rather sophisticated lot who built sturdy longhouses, lived in large farming communities and traded with other tribes.

Life was a lot harsher for the Northeast Woodlands peoples, who lived in the chilly boreal forest stretching across northern Canada. These tribes include the Algonquin and Mi'kmaq in the Maritimes, the Innu in Québec and Labrador, and the Cree and Ojibwe in northern Ontario and Manitoba. The extinct Beothuk of Newfoundland also belonged to this group (see the boxed text on p371). Living in small nomadic bands, they were primarily hunters of caribou, moose, hare and other animals, which they caught using snares and traps.

Survival was even more of a challenge for the arctic tribes such as the Inuit and Dene. Skilled whale and big-game hunters migrated seasonally,

The Illustrated History of Canada by Craig Brown (ed), written in a readable and conversational style, is a superb resource for learning about all facets of the country's fascinating past.

Olive Patricia Dickason's *Canada's First Nations: A History of Founding Peoples from Earliest Times* is the definitive survey of Aboriginal peoples and how they have shaped Canadian history from precolonial times to the present.

In *Canadian History for Dummies*, best-selling author Will Ferguson uses his irreverent, opinionated and energetic style to take you on an entertaining cruise through his country's wild and wacky past. Yes, history can be fun.

TIMELINE

Before 25,000 BC	Around AD 1000
Humans arrive in North America from Asia via the Bering Strait	Vikings wash ashore at L'Anse aux Meadows in Newfoundland

---

HOW CANADA GOT ITS NAME

When naming Canada, the Fathers of Confederation briefly considered calling it 'Dominion of Borealia' (from the Latin for 'north') as a counterpart to the Dominion of Australia (from the Latin for 'south'). It was Jacques Cartier who first used the word 'Canada' to describe France's newest 'possession,' taking his cue from *kanata*, a Huron-Iroquois word for 'village' or 'settlement.' Although the name quickly appeared on maps, it wasn't officially used until 1791, when the Province of Québec was divided into the colonies of Upper and Lower Canada. In 1841, the two Canadas were united under one name, the Province of Canada. At the time of Confederation in 1867, the new country assumed the official name of the Dominion of Canada.

The beaver, the maple tree and the maple leaf are all official symbols of Canada. The country's official colors are red and white. *O Canada*, composed by Calixa Lavallée in 1880, only became Canada's national anthem in 1980. Until then, the British anthem *God Save the Queen* had been used.

---

traveling by canoe or dogsled. Winters were spent in igloos or simple wooden structures.

WHEN WORLDS COLLIDE

The first Europeans to wash up on Canadian shores were the Vikings, a tribe of adventurous seafarers hailing from Iceland and Greenland. From about AD 1000 they poked around the eastern shores of Canada, establishing winter settlements and way-stations for repairing ships and restocking supplies, such as the one preserved at L'Anse aux Meadows (p372) in Newfoundland. The local tribes did not exactly roll out the welcome mat for these intruders, who eventually tired of the hostilities and withdrew. There would be no more visits from the outside for another three or four centuries.

The action began heating up again in the late 15th century. In 1492, backed by the Spanish crown, Christopher Columbus went searching for a western sea route to Asia and instead stumbled upon some small islands in the Bahamas. Other European monarchs, excited by his 'discovery,' quickly sponsored expeditions of their own. In 1497, Giovanni Caboto, better known as John Cabot, sailed under a British flag as far west as Newfoundland and Cape Breton. Although there's no evidence of where he first made landfall, the village of Bonavista in eastern Newfoundland usually gets the nod.

Cabot didn't find a passage to China, but he did find cod, then a much-coveted commodity in Europe. In short order, hundreds of boats were shuttling between Europe and the fertile new fishing grounds. Whalers from northern Spain soon followed. Many of these mariners began trading with the Aboriginal peoples, giving them pots, beads and iron axes in exchange for furs.

By the time the French got into the game, the hunt was on not only for the Northwest Passage but also for gold. Spanish conquistadors had found immeasurable treasure among Aztec and Inca civilizations, and King François I hoped for similar riches in the frosty North. In 1534 he dispatched explorer Jacques Cartier, who found only 'stones and horrible rugged rocks' while probing around the coast of Labrador.

In *Cod: A Biography of the Fish that Changed the World*, Mark Kurlansky takes an engaging look at the role this humble fish has played in shaping world history and how its popularity threatens its very survival today.

Black Robe (1991): Based on the novel by Brian Moore, this movie follows a young Jesuit missionary on his journey to Québec, where he intends to introduce the Huron to his Christian God. It's brutally realistic, raw and filled with despair.

1534	1608
Jacques Cartier lands in what is now Québec and claims it for France	Samuel de Champlain founds the first permanent settlement at Québec City

Nevertheless, when he reached the Gulf of St Lawrence, Cartier went ashore at today's Gaspé (p325) and dutifully claimed the land for France. He had friendly encounters with the local Iroquois, only to seize two of the chief's sons and spirit them back to Europe. To his credit, he returned them a year later when sailing up the St Lawrence River as far as Stadacona, present-day Québec City, and Hochelaga, today's Montréal. Here he got wind of a land called Saguenay that was full of gold and silver. The rumor prompted Cartier's third voyage, in 1541, but alas, the mythical land remained elusive. To learn more about Canada's great explorers, starting with Jacques Cartier, see www.civilisations.ca/vmnf/explor/explcd_e.html.

In *The People of New France* Allan Greer skillfully and insightfully zeroes in on the many struggles the adventuresome colonists faced, without forgetting to include the perspective of those upon whose lives they intruded.

THE BIRTH OF NEW FRANCE

The French king's explorer having found neither treasure nor a passage to Asia, King François I got bored with his distant colony for a while. A few decades later all that changed, oddly enough because of a fashion trend. Felt hats were becoming all the rage and, as the cognoscente knew, there were no finer hats than those made from beaver pelts. With beavers all but extinct in the Old World, the demand for a fresh supply was strong.

In 1588, the French crown granted the first trading monopoly in Canada, only to have this claim promptly challenged by other merchants. The race for control of the fur trade was on. The economic value of this enterprise and, by extension, its role in shaping Canadian history, cannot be underestimated. It was the main reason behind the country's European settlement, at the root of the struggle for dominance between the French and the British, and the source of strife and division between Aboriginal groups.

Get more details about the events and people that shaped New France with the handy timeline published at www.republiquelibre.org/cousture/NVFR2.HTM.

In order to gain control of the distant lands, the chief order of business was to put some European bodies on the ground. In the summer of 1604, a group of French pioneers established a tentative foothold on Île Ste-Croix, then moved to Port-Royal (today's Annapolis Royal) in Nova Scotia the following spring. Exposed and difficult to defend, neither site made a good base for controlling the inland fur trade. As the would-be colonists moved up the St Lawrence River, they finally came upon a spot their leader, Samuel de Champlain, considered more promising. And so the settlement of Québec (which means 'Where the River Narrows' in Algonquian) sprang into existence in 1608. 'New France' had become a reality.

Champlain was aware that the survival of his struggling colony depended on good relations with the local Aboriginal tribes who supplied the beavers that the French were eager to trade. However, the territory along the St Lawrence River was hotly contested by the Five Nations and the Huron Confederacy, and Champlain had to decide which tribe to support. He chose the Huron Confederacy, and quickly made himself popular by blowing away three Iroquois leaders with his fancy firearms during an initial skirmish. The French were in. Things weren't all plain sailing for the settlers: when Champlain died in 1635, his colony, after 32 years of settlement, numbered no more than 300 people. Intermittent fighting with the Iroquois continued, and in 1649

1752	1763
Canada's first newspaper, the weekly *Halifax Gazette*, is published	France cedes its Canadian colonies to Britain in the Treaty of Paris

TRADING ON TRADITION

No matter where you travel in Canada, chances are at some point you'll be doing some shopping at a department store called The Bay. These stores are all that's left of the once mighty Hudson's Bay Company (HBC), which for a couple of centuries controlled the fur trade across a vast stretch of wilderness in northern and western Canada. Founded by royal charter in 1670, it is considered Canada's first corporation and is one of the world's oldest corporations in continuous operation.

Its original purpose was to ensure the British got their hands on as many beaver furs as they could. They did so by enlisting numerous Aboriginal tribes to trap the animals and bring their pelts to a string of coastal trading posts called 'factories.' These were overseen from company headquarters, York Factory (p548), in a strategic spot at the mouth of the Nelson River in what is now Manitoba. In exchange, the trappers received metal tools, hunting gear and other coveted items.

The HBC experienced a brief setback after 1682, when its French founders Radisson and Des Groseilliers, frustrated with the slow pace of further exploration, defected back to the king of France and set up the competing La Compagnie du Nord. The French captured some of the HBC's factories but were eventually forced by the Treaty of Utrecht to renounce all claims to the HBC's territories.

After selling all of its land to the Dominion of Canada in the late 19th century, the HBC survived by opening a series of retail stores, including The Bay, especially in the west, and later became involved in the oil business. Despite protests from animal rights activists, HBC stores continue to sell furs. If fur isn't your thing, another traditional item still sold at The Bay stores is the company's legendary 'point blanket.' Warm and durable, these blankets were an important item in the fur trade. Each blanket was rated on its size and weight according to a point system, with each point worth one beaver pelt in exchange. To this day, the length of an indigo blue line woven into the side of each blanket indicates the number of points. Beaver pelts, however, are no longer accepted as payment.

Learn more about the fascinating history of the Hudson's Bay Company and its role in Canadian history at www.hbc.com/hbc/e_hi/default.htm, or read *Empire of the Bay: The Company of Adventurers That Seized a Continent* by Peter C Newman, a blustering account of the legendary company, from its fur-trading origins to today's department stores.

it led to the dispersal and near-extermination of the Huron peoples. The 'Great Peace' didn't come until 1701.

CONTROL & CONFLICT

The French maintained their fur trade monopoly for several decades, but in 1670 the British began mounting a formidable challenge. They caught a lucky break when a pair of disillusioned French explorers, Radisson and Des Groseilliers, confided that the best fur country actually lay to the north and west of Lake Superior, which was easily accessible via Hudson Bay. King Charles I quickly formed the Hudson's Bay Company (see the boxed text above) and granted it a trade monopoly over all the lands whose rivers and streams drained into the bay. This vast territory, called Rupert's Land, encompassed about 40% of present-day Canada, including Labrador, western Québec, northwestern Ontario, Manitoba, most of Saskatchewan and Alberta and part of the Northwest Territories.

1818	1858
Canada's border is defined as the 49th Parallel from Lake of the Woods to the Rocky Mountains	Gold is discovered in British Columbia

Meanwhile, in the south, the British had booted the Dutch out of the Hudson River Valley. Finding themselves hemmed in, the French sought to expand their territory inland, moving beyond the Great Lakes to the western prairies and south along the Mississippi to the Gulf of Mexico. But events in Europe soon took over local apirations for expansion. Being on the losing side in the War of the Spanish Succession (1701–14), France – in the 1713 Treaty of Utrecht with Britain – was forced to officially recognize British claims to Hudson Bay and Newfoundland and to give up all of Nova Scotia (then called Acadia) except for Cape Breton Island.

A few decades later another European conflict, the Seven Years' War, once again pitted Britain and France against each other. Hostilities spilled over into North America in what is known as the French and Indian War, which began in 1754. This time the British set out to beat the French for good. After several years of fighting, the tide turned in their favor with the capture of Louisbourg, the famous fortress on Cape Breton Island. This gave the British control of the strategically important entrance to the St Lawrence River. The following year, they besieged Québec, eventually scaling the cliffs in a surprise attack and quickly defeating the stunned French. It was one of Canada's bloodiest and most famous battles, and left both commanding generals dead. At the Treaty of Paris (1763) France handed Canada over to Britain.

GROWING PAINS

Managing the newly acquired territory presented quite a challenge to the British. To quell uprisings by Aboriginal tribes, such as the attack on Detroit by Ottawa Chief Pontiac, the British government issued the Royal Proclamation of 1763. The proclamation prevented colonists from settling west of the Appalachian Mountains and regulated purchases of aboriginal land. Though well-intentioned, the proclamation was largely ignored.

The other big headache for the British was managing the French Canadians. Tensions quickly rose when the new rulers imposed British law, which heavily restricted the rights of Roman Catholics, including the rights to vote and hold office. However, British hopes that this discriminatory policy would launch a mass exodus and make it easier to anglicize the remaining settlers did not pan out. The French were there to stay.

Meanwhile, the first rumblings of revolution could be heard from the American colonies to the south. The British governor, Guy Carleton, wisely reasoned that winning the political allegiance of the French was more valuable than turning them into tea drinkers. This led to the passage of the Québec Act of 1774. The Act confirmed French Canadians' right to their religion, allowed them to assume political office and restored the use of French civil law. Indeed, during the American Revolution (1775–83) most French Canadians refused to take up arms for the American cause, although not many willingly defended the British either.

After the Revolution, the English-speaking population exploded with the northward migration of some 50,000 settlers from the newly inde-

For a treasure trove of historical resources as well as biographies of hundreds of famous Canadians, look no further than www .collectionscanada.ca.

Even if you missed CBC's excellent TV series *Canada: A People's History*, the show's companion site at http://history.cbc.ca/ history traces each of the 17 episodes in great detail.

pendent American colonies. Although called United Empire Loyalists due to their presumed allegiance to Britain, many settlers were probably motivated more by the prospect of cheap land than by actual love of king and crown. The vast majority ended up in Nova Scotia and New Brunswick, while a smaller group settled along the northern shore of Lake Ontario and in the Ottawa River Valley (forming the nucleus of what became Ontario). About 8000 moved to Québec, thereby creating the first sizeable anglophone community in this French-speaking bastion.

ROAD MAP TO UNITY

Partly in order to accommodate the interests of Loyalist settlers, the British government passed the Constitutional Act of 1791, which divided the colony into Upper Canada (today's southern Ontario) and Lower Canada (now southern Québec). Lower Canada retained French civil laws, but both provinces were governed by the British criminal code.

Each colony was directed by a governor installed by the British crown. The governor in turn appointed the members of his 'cabinet,' then called the Executive Council. The legislative branch consisted of an appointed Legislative Council and an elected Assembly, which ostensibly represented the interests of the colonists. In reality, though, the Assembly held very little power, since the governor could veto its decisions. Not surprisingly, this was a recipe for friction and resentment. This was especially the case in Lower Canada, where an English governor and an English-dominated Council held sway over a French-dominated Assembly.

Rampant cronyism made matters even worse. Members of the conservative British merchant elite dominated the Executive and Legislative Councils and showed little interest in French-Canadian matters. Called the Family Compact in Upper Canada and the Château Clique in Lower Canada, their ranks included brewer John Molson and university founder James McGill. The groups' influence grew especially strong after the War of 1812, an ultimately futile attempt by the USA to take over its northern neighbor.

In 1837, frustration over these entrenched elites finally reached a boiling point. Parti Canadien leader Louis-Joseph Papineau and his Upper Canadian counterpart, Reform Party leader William Lyon Mackenzie, launched open rebellions against the government. Although both uprisings were quickly crushed, the incident signaled to the British that the status quo wasn't going to cut it any longer. They dispatched John Lambton, the Earl of Durham, to investigate the causes of the rebellion. Although fundamentally racist and controversial even then, nearly all the recommendations in Durham's report were adopted in the Union Act of 1840.

The earl correctly identified ethnic tensions as the root cause of the rebellion, calling the French and British 'two nations warring in the bosom of a single state.' He then lived up to his reputation as 'radical Jack' by asserting that French culture and society were inferior and obstacles to expansion and greatness. Only assimilation of British laws,

DID YOU KNOW?

Delegates to the Charlottetown Conference in 1864 had to sleep on their steamships because the circus was in town and all of the inns were fully booked.

In *1867: How the Fathers Made a Deal*, Christopher Moore introduces us to the major players that cobbled Canada into confederation, and to the ideas and values that inspired them.

1885	1885
Canada's first national park opens in Banff, Alberta, and the Canadian Pacific Railway is completed	Métis leader Louis Riel hanged for treason

language and institutions would quash French nationalism and bring long-lasting peace to the colonies.

With this goal in mind, Lower and Upper Canada were renamed Canada West and Canada East, then merged into the Province of Canada and henceforth piloted by a single legislature, the new Parliament of Canada. Each ex-colony had the same number of representatives, which wasn't exactly fair to Lower Canada, the population of which was much larger. On the plus side, the new system brought responsible government (ie the government became accountable to the elected representatives of the Assembly) that severely restricted the governor's powers and eliminated nepotism.

While most British Canadians welcomed the new system, the French were less than thrilled. If anything, the union's underlying objective of destroying French culture, language and identity made Francophones cling together even more tenaciously. The provisions of the Act left deep wounds that still haven't fully healed today.

Thus the united province was not exactly built on solid footing. The decade or so following unification was marked by political instability as one government replaced another in fairly rapid succession. Meanwhile, the USA had grown into a self-confident economic powerhouse, while British North America was still a loose patchwork of independent colonies. The American Civil War (1861–65) and the USA's purchase of Alaska from Russia in 1867 raised fears of annexation. As it became clear that only a less volatile political system would stave off these challenges, the movement toward federal union began to gain momentum.

Confederation was first discussed at the Charlottetown Conference, held at Province House in Charlottetown, Prince Edward Island (PEI), in September 1864. The group that would go down in history as the 'Fathers of Confederation' included delegates from Nova Scotia, New Brunswick, the Province of Canada and PEI (only Newfoundland and British Columbia did not attend). It took two more meetings – one in Québec City, the other in London – before parliament passed the British North America Act in 1867. It gave birth to the modern, self-governing state of Canada – the Dominion of Canada – uniting Ontario, Québec, Nova Scotia and New Brunswick with Ottawa as its capital. PEI didn't join until 1873. The day the Act became official, July 1, is celebrated as Canada's national holiday; it was called 'Dominion Day' until it was renamed 'Canada Day' in 1982.

HOW THE WEST WAS WON

One of the first priorities of the infant dominion was to bring the remaining land and colonies into the confederation. Under its first prime minister, John A Macdonald, the government in 1869 acquired vast Rupert's Land, which had essentially been held in trust by the Hudson's Bay Company, for the paltry sum of £300,000 (about $11.5 million in today's money). Now called the Northwest Territories, the land was only sparsely populated, mostly by Plains First Nations and several thousand Métis (may-*tee*), a racial blend of Cree, Ojibwe or Saulteaux and French- Canadian or Scottish fur traders, who spoke

The Last Spike: The Great Railway 1881–1885 by popular Canadian historian Pierre Berton is an engagingly written account of this epic engineering feat and the people who made it happen.

DID YOU KNOW?

Singer-songwriter Gordon Lightfoot honored the epic construction of the railroad with his popular *Canadian Railroad Trilogy.*

1913	1922
Immigration to Canada crests, with more than 400,000 people coming ashore this year	Joseph-Armand Bombardier invents the snowmobile in his workshop at Valcourt, Québec

THE REHABILITATION OF LOUIS RIEL

Rebel, murderer, traitor – Métis leader Louis Riel has been called many things. But a growing number of Canadians prefer to see him as a hero who defended the rights of the oppressed against an unjust government. Statues of Riel now stand on Parliament Hill in Ottawa and outside the Manitoba Legislature in Winnipeg, where his boyhood home (p535) and grave have become places of pilgrimage. The University of Saskatchewan in Saskatoon has named its campus theater, student center and pub after Riel. The government's 1998 Statement of Reconciliation to Canada's Aboriginal peoples included an apology for Riel's execution. In 2002, after broadcasting a re-enactment of Riel's trial, the Canadian Broadcasting Corporation (CBC) conducted a straw poll among its viewers: 87% of them returned a 'not guilty' verdict.

French as their main language. Their biggest settlement was the Red River Colony around Fort Garry (today's Winnipeg).

The Canadian government immediately clashed with the Métis people over land-use rights, causing the latter to form a provisional government led by the charismatic Louis Riel (see the boxed text above). Riel sent the Ottawa-appointed governor packing and, in November 1869, seized control of Upper Fort Garry, thereby forcing Ottawa to the negotiating table. However, with his delegation already en route, Riel impulsively and for no good reason executed a Canadian prisoner he was holding at the fort. Although the murder caused widespread uproar in Canada, the government was so keen to bring the West into the fold it agreed to most of Riel's demands, including special language and religious protections for the Métis. As a result, the then-pint-sized province of Manitoba was carved out of the Northwest Territories and entered the dominion in July 1870. Macdonald sent troops after Riel but he narrowly managed to escape to the USA. He was formally exiled for five years in 1875.

British Columbia (BC), created in 1866 by merging the colonies of New Caledonia and Vancouver Island, was the next frontier. The discovery of gold along the Fraser River in 1858 and in the Cariboo region in 1862 had brought an enormous influx of settlers to such goldmine boomtowns as Barkerville and Williams Lake (p776). Once the gold mines petered out, though, BC was plunged into poverty. In 1871 it joined the dominion in exchange for the Canadian government assuming all its debt and promising to link it with the East within 10 years via a transcontinental railroad.

The construction of the Canadian Pacific Railway is one of the most impressive chapters in Canadian history. Macdonald rightly regarded the railroad as crucial in truly unifying the country, spurring immigration and stimulating business and manufacturing. It was a costly proposition, made even more challenging by the rough and rugged terrain the tracks had to traverse. To entice investors, the government offered major benefits, including vast land grants in western Canada. The final spike on the railroad was driven at Craigellachie, BC, on November 7, 1885.

To bring law and order to the 'wild west,' in 1873 the government created the North-West Mounted Police (NWMP), which later became

Reminiscences of the North-West Rebellions, online at http://wsb .datapro.net/rebellions/ index.html, is an often-compelling personal account of the two Métis rebellions led by Louis Riel in 1869 and 1885. It was written by Major Charles A Boulton, a Canadian army officer who lived through both of them.

Halfbreed by Maria Campbell is the haunting account of a Métis woman born in 1940s Saskatchewan and her struggles to overcome isolation, poverty and discrimination.

Early 1960s	**1962**
Québec's 'Quiet Revolution' brings fundamental change	Canada becomes the third nation in space, after the Soviet Union and the USA

the Royal Canadian Mounted Police (RCMP). Nicknamed 'Mounties,' they still serve as Canada's national police force. Although they were effective, the NWMP couldn't prevent trouble from brewing on the prairies. With the buffalo – their main livelihood – all but gone, the Plains First Nations had been forced to sign a series of treaties relegating them to reserves with each person getting 52 acres of land. They also got some cash; hunting, trapping and fishing rights; and the promise of schools, tools and ammunition. It may have sounded like a good deal at the time, but much of the help never arrived and before long the Plains First Nations realized how much they had given up. Slowly they began to challenge their status.

Meanwhile, many Métis had moved to Saskatchewan and settled in Batoche (p571) along the South Saskatchewan River. As in Manitoba, they quickly clashed with government surveyors over land issues. In 1884, after their repeated appeals to Ottawa had been ignored, they coaxed Louis Riel out of exile to represent their cause. Rebuffed, Riel responded the only way he knew: by forming a provisional government and leading the Métis in revolt. Riel had the backing of the Cree, but times had changed: with the railroad nearly complete, government troops arrived within days. Riel surrendered in May 1885. In November, he was hanged for treason.

COMING OF AGE
Canada rang in the 20th century on a high note. Industrialization was in full swing, gold had been discovered in the Yukon, and Canadian resources – from wheat to lumber – were increasingly in demand. In addition, the completion of the Canadian Pacific Railway had opened the floodgates to immigration.

Between 1885 and 1914 about 4.5 million people arrived in Canada. This included large groups of Americans and Eastern Europeans, especially Ukrainians, who went to work cultivating the prairies. Optimism reigned: a buoyant Prime Minister Wilfrid Laurier said 'The 19th century was the century of the United States. I think we can claim that it is Canada that shall fill the 20th century.' It was only natural that this new-found self-confidence would put the country on track to autonomy from Britain. The issue took on even greater urgency with the outbreak of WWI in 1914.

Canada – as a member of the British Empire – found itself automatically drawn into the conflict. In the first years of the war, more than 300,000 volunteers were shipped to the European battlefields. As the war dragged on and thousands of soldiers returned in coffins, recruitment ground to a halt. The government, intent on replenishing its depleted forces, introduced the draft in 1917. It proved to be a very unpopular move, to say the least, especially among French Canadians. Animosity toward Ottawa was already at an all-time high as a result of the government abolishing bilingual schools in Manitoba and restricting the use of French in schools in Ontario. The conscription issue was to fan the flames of nationalism even more. Thousands of Québecois took to the streets in protest and the issue left Canada divided and Canadians distrustful of their government.

Did some of your ancestors emigrate to Canada? A good place to start your genealogical quest is at www.genealogy.gc.ca.

Octobre (1994): Controversial and provocative Québecois filmmaker Pierre Falardeau takes an intense look at the terrorist abduction and murder of Pierre Laporte during the 1970 October Crisis from the viewpoint of the kidnappers.

1976	1979
Montréal hosts the Olympic Games	Chris Haney and Scott Abbott invent the Trivial Pursuit board game

By the time the guns of WWI fell silent in 1918, most Canadians were fed up with sending their sons and husbands to fight and die in distant wars for Britian. Under the government of William Lyon Mackenzie King, an eccentric fellow who communicated with spirits and worshipped his dead mother, Canada began asserting its independence. Mackenzie King made it clear that Britain could no longer automatically draw upon the Canadian military, started signing treaties without British approval, and sent a Canadian ambassador to Washington. This forcefulness ultimately led to the Statute of Westminster, passed by the British Parliament in 1931. The Statute formalized the independence of Canada and other Commonwealth nations, although Britain retained the right to pass amendments to those countries' constitutions. This right was removed only with the 1982 Canada Act, which was signed into law by Queen Elizabeth II on Parliament Hill in Ottawa on April 17. Today, Canada is a constitutional monarchy with a parliament consisting of an appointed upper house, or Senate, and an elected lower house, the House of Commons. The British monarch remains Canada's head of state, although this is predominantly a ceremonial role and does not effectively diminish the country's sovereignty. Within Canada, the appointed governor general is the monarch's representative.

TAKING STEPS TOWARDS HEALING

Canada never experienced the all-out massacres that marred the clash of Europeans and Native Americans in the USA. Nevertheless, its Aboriginal population has still suffered discrimination, loss of territory and civil rights violations throughout the country's history.

In 1990, aboriginal frustration over these issues reached a boiling point with the Oka Crisis (see the boxed text on p265), a violent standoff between the government and a band of Mohawk activists. The crisis focused national attention on aboriginal human rights violations and outstanding land claims. To find out more about the crisis, see *Rocks at Whiskey Trench* (2000), the fourth is a series of documentaries by filmmaker Alanis Obomsawin about the event that shook Canada.

In the aftermath of Oka, a Royal Commission on Aboriginal Peoples issued a report recommending a complete overhaul of relations between the government and indigenous peoples. Slow to respond at first, in 1998 the Ministry of Indian and Northern Affairs issued an official Statement of Reconciliation that accepted responsibility for past injustices toward Aboriginal peoples. It specifically apologized for the policy of removing children from their families and educating them in underfunded government schools in the name of assimilation. Most importantly, though, it pledged to give indigenous peoples greater control over their land, resources, government and economy. You can read the entire Statement of Reconciliation at www.ainc-inac .gc.ca/gs/rec_e.html, or find out about Gathering Strength, the government's 'aboriginal action plan,' at www.ainc-inac.gc.ca/gs/index_e.html.

Recent high-profile developments include the creation of Nunavut in 1999, which gave 28,000 people – mostly Inuit – control over about one-fifth of Canadian soil. And in 2000, the Nisga'a tribe of northwestern British Columbia won self-government and the right to manage its land and resources. Hundreds more land claims have since been filed.

An excellent first stop for finding out about Aboriginal peoples in contemporary Canadian society is www.aboriginalcanada.gc.ca, a comprehensive portal to online resources, treaties, organizations and more.

A 'DISTINCT' SOCIETY

The period after WWII brought another wave of economic expansion and immigration, especially from Europe. The 1950s were a time of unprecedented wealth, and the middle class mushroomed. The only province left behind was Québec. For a quarter of a century, it remained in the grip of ultra-conservative Maurice Duplessis and his Union Nationale party, with support from the Catholic church and business interests. Only after Duplessis' death in 1959 and the election of a Liberal government did the province finally begin to modernize, secularize and liberalize in what is called the 'Quiet Revolution.' This included expanding the public sector, investing in public education and nationalizing the provincial hydroelectric companies.

The Essential Trudeau weaves a complex pastiche of one of Canada's boldest, most outspoken and influential prime ministers through his own writings, speeches and interviews, selected and introduced by Ron Graham.

Still, progress wasn't swift enough for radical nationalists who claimed that Québec's independence was the only way to ensure francophone rights. Even French premier Charles de Gaulle seemed to join the cause, (in)famously proclaiming '*Vive le Québec libre!*' at Montréal's Town Hall during a 1967 state visit to Canada. The federal government under Lester B Pearson was so incensed at de Gaulle's remark that it officially admonished him, causing him to cut short his Canadian visit. The following year René Lévesque founded the sovereignist Parti Québecois (PQ).

The situation got very tense during the October Crisis in 1970, when the most radical wing of the separatist movement, the Front de Libération du Québec (FLQ; Québec Liberation Front), kidnapped Québec's labor minister Pierre Laporte and a British trade official in an attempt to force the independence issue. Prime Minister Pierre Trudeau declared a state of emergency and called in the army to protect government officials. Two weeks later, Laporte's body was found in the trunk of a car. The murder discredited the FLQ in the eyes of many erstwhile supporters and the movement quickly faded away.

Lévesque's PQ won the 1976 Québec provincial election and quickly pushed through a bill that made French the province's sole official language. His 1980 referendum on secession, however, was resoundingly defeated, with almost 60% voting *non*. The issue was put on the back burner for much of the 1980s.

Lévesque's successor, Robert Bourassa, agreed to a constitution-led solution – but only if Québec was recognized as a 'distinct society' with special rights. In 1987 Prime Minister Brian Mulroney unveiled an accord that met most of Québec's demands. To take effect, the so-called Meech Lake Accord needed to be ratified by all 10 provinces and both houses of parliament by 1990. Dissenting premiers in three provinces eventually pledged their support but, incredibly, the accord collapsed when a single member of Manitoba's legislature refused to sign. Mulroney and Bourassa drafted a new, expanded accord, but the separatists picked it apart and it too was trounced. The rejection sealed the fate of Mulroney, who resigned the following year, and of Bourassa, who left political life a broken man.

Relations between Anglos and Francophones hit new lows, and support for independence was rekindled. Only one year after returning to power in 1994, the PQ, under Premier Lucien Bouchard, launched a

1982	1984
Queen Elizabeth II signs the Canada Act, giving Canada complete sovereignty	Cirque du Soleil is founded in Québec by a group of Canadian street performers

second referendum. This one was a real cliff-hanger: Québecois decided by 52,000 votes – a razor-thin majority of less than 1% – to remain within Canada.

The voices of separatism seemed silenced, especially after the PQ lost its decade-long grip on power to Jean Charest's Liberals in the 2003 Québec elections. However, if the national elections of 2004 are any indication, the tide may be turning once again. The Bloc Québecois (the federal version of the Parti Québecois) received 48.8% of the vote, while the scandal-plagued Liberals received only 33.9%. Separatism, it seems, is likely to stay at the top of Québec's – and by extension, Canada's – agenda for some time to come.

Canadian Government apologizes to Aboriginal peoples	Nunavut is created in the eastern Arctic

The Culture

THE NATIONAL PSYCHE Will Ferguson

O Canada! The Great White North. A vast and empty land, where pale people in small villages huddle together for warmth.

O Canada! An urban miracle. A dynamic, postmodern entity. A land of shining towers and hermetically sealed shopping centers.

So which is it? Is Canada a northern frontier or a sleek urban nation?

The answer: it is both, and it is neither. Yes, the landscape of Canada is epic and awe-inspiring, but the people are mostly urban dwellers. Indeed, with more than 80% of its population living in cities, Canada is one of the most urbanized nations on earth. But – and this is very important – urban does not mean 'inner city,' and it certainly doesn't mean 'edgy' or 'gritty.' It means, simply, that most Canadians do not live in romantic rustic settings, amid log cabins and howling timber wolves.

It can be quite misleading, this use of the word 'urban' to describe Canada. The truth is, it is the smaller, quieter cities – along with the sleepy suburban communities that surround large centers – that make up a major part of Canada's 'urban reality.' Places such as Moose Jaw, Red Deer, Orillia, Summerside – they are all part of that misleading statistic, that urbanite 80%. This is something that many desperately hip Canadian commentators, yearning for a 'concrete jungle,' New York–style identity have never figured out: Canada is urban, but not in the way they think.

Historically, Canada's three great themes are:

- Keeping the Americans out.
- Keeping the French in.
- Trying to get the Aboriginals to somehow disappear.

For visitors, the first of these is often the most apparent. You cannot discuss Canada without discussing the USA, because the most overwhelming fact about Canada is not – as many believe – the weather. No. It isn't the bone-chill of winter that defines Canada; it is instead the looming, almighty presence of the United States.

In Canada, we live in the shadow of the USA, and like anything attempting to grow in the shade, it can be a struggle. In the purest sense, the very definition of Canadian is 'not American.' Canadians rejected the American Revolution and turned back armed invasions from the south at several crucial moments. As a country, we have fought long and hard for the right to be *not* American. Nonetheless, America is ever-present. Canada is swamped by US pop culture to a degree that Europeans cannot even begin to fathom: it spills over our borders, it fills our airwaves and magazine stands. It is everywhere, but it is not ours.

In this role of 'overwhelmed observers,' Canadians have become attuned to subtle nuances and small differences (a great deal of Canadian nationalism seems to spring from the fact that we say 'zed' while Americans say 'zee').

We have learned that being inundated by American culture doesn't have to be a form of indoctrination; it can also be a form of inoculation. We are always aware of who we are not, even as we grope toward defining who we are. Mexico, the other bookend to the American Dream, at least has a linguistic barrier to protect it; in Canada, the French language buffers less than a quarter of the population.

Will Ferguson was born in Fort Vermilion, Alberta. He is the author of humorous books including *How to Be a Canadian: Even If You Already Are One; Why I Hate Canadians;* and *Bastards & Boneheads: Our Glorious Leaders, Past and Present.* In *Beauty Tips from Moose Jaw* he hobnobs with polar bears in Churchill, searches for a lost kingdom in Québec and gets mugged by moose in Newfoundland.

Canadian author and artist Douglas Coupland, who coined the term 'Generation X,' provides an affectionate, quirky tribute to his homeland in a pair of art books, *Souvenir of Canada* (2001) and *Souvenir 2* (2004).

Beyond Canada's binary code of French and English are the echoes of a previous world, one that existed long before the arrival of Europeans: that of the Aboriginals. Canadians are very good at pretending that the third-world conditions on their aboriginal reserves don't exist. (The classic Canadian denial is to say, 'Yes, but the Americans were much worse in the way they treated their indigenous population!' This alibi – 'But it's worse in the States!' – is used to excuse everything from our treatment of Canada's indigenous peoples to the staggering inefficiency of our public Medicare system.)

Keep in mind that Canada was founded on very different principles than those of the USA. Canada chose evolution over revolution. Where the USA enshrined 'life, liberty, and the pursuit of happiness' as its team motto – and the French, veering even further into vacuous (but powerful) catchphrases, came up with '*liberté, égalité, fraternité*' – Canadians chose a less romantic, more pragmatic trio of beliefs: peace, order, and good government. These core values, these three primary goals, are enshrined in the Canadian constitution. They represent Canada's mission statement.

Canada was the first country in the world, in 1985, to pass a national multicultural act and the first to establish a federal department of multiculturalism. Today, 40% of Canadians claim their origins are in places other than Britain or France, and you can find swaths of hyphenated Canadians (Chinese-Canadians, Italian-Canadians, African-Canadians) in every region and every province. A former premier of Manitoba, Gary Filmon, summed it up: 'Canada has an Aboriginal past, a bilingual present and a multicultural future.'

Author and photographer Matt Jackson spent four years hitchhiking across Canada from the Pacific to the Atlantic and up to the Yukon. Read about his journey at www .mattjackson.ca.

LA BELLE VIE IN LA BELLE PROVINCE *Margo Pfeiff*

A long history struggling for their place in North America, a sense of linguistic isolation in a sea of English, and a wealth of francophone musicians, writers and filmmakers who connect with their audiences have created a strong, rich Québecois culture.

Québec's Francophones know who they are; they are Quebecers first and Canadians second. Although they narrowly voted *non* in the 1995 referendum on separation, they have always felt they are a nation, not a province, and as a result the parliament building in Québec City is the Assemblée Nationale and the province-run parks are called Parcs National.

Bilingualism is on the rise in Québec, especially in Montréal and Québec City. The drill is that you'll likely be greeted with '*Bonjour.*' Answering 'Hi' signals a switch to English. Continue in French and you may be hit with *joual* – a working-class dialect of Québecois French that can be difficult to understand. Outside the main cities of Québec, few people speak English.

Quebecers live up to some of their stereotypes as Canada's heaviest gamblers and smokers. Happily, Québec is also the home of the three-hour, wine-drenched lunch where conversation is less likely to be about money than about love, vacations or culture. There is a palpable anything-goes, love-of-life vibe in Québec, an innate sensuality about the place. There is more eye contact between the sexes and it's easier to start a conversation with a stranger in a café than in anglophone Canada. Politics and lifestyle are more liberal than in the rest of the country, too.

Little gets in the way of having a good time, not even the weather, which Quebecers rarely grumble about though they have plenty of fodder. Winters are brutally cold, but a cozy indoor social life takes over and snowmobile, cross-country and downhill ski trails are busy. In the brutally hot, humid summer, life moves outdoors with a continuous string of food, comedy, music and cultural festivals, which see downtown cores cordoned off to traffic, and sound stages on street corners. And if Quebecers can't get away to weekend cottages, they can always vacation in 'Balconville' with a barbecue, a deck chair and a cold one with which to toast *la belle vie*.

It has been argued that adopting a philosophy of multiculturalism actually divides people, creating a splintered society of separate solitudes. But this assumes that ethnic identity and national values are incompatible, that one cannot be both Italian and Canadian at the same time. As though adding 'Italian' to the mix will somehow water down one's identity. This is a crude form of either/or thinking; life is far more complex than that. Hyphens don't limit our view of the world – they expand it.

Canada is built on top of fault lines: historical, cultural and linguistic. In situations like this, a nation either descends into warring tribal factions, or it learns to be tolerant, inclusive and flexible. It is a remarkable feat, but Canada has managed to turn all of these contradictions and internal inconsistencies – the constant pressure that comes from living next to the USA, the deep cracks that shift below our feet: French, English, Aboriginal, multiethnic – to its advantage. In Canada, the art of strategic compromise is a matter of national survival.

Canada may not be a US-style melting pot, and it may not be an edgy, urban nation. But it is very much an open society. It is a meeting place of ideas, of people, of possibilities. As anthropologist Claude Levi-Strauss noted, 'All great civilizations are basically crossroads civilizations.'

LIFESTYLE Margo Pfeiff

Canadians are stereotyped as a nice, polite pack of unarmed Americans in winter clothes with no sense of humor. While we are generally nice and polite, don't schlep Glock pistols and wear our toques (hats) out of necessity, we actually have produced internationally acclaimed comedians from Jim Carrey to Mike Myers, as well as Montréal's world-class Just for Laughs Festival (p253). Our differences with Americans may be subtle, but they are significant.

A typical Canadian family of mum, dad and 1.5 kids will live on an average annual salary of $60,000. More often than not, both parents work. Their children will go on to postsecondary education in numbers unrivaled in any other country (with female students vastly outnumbering males), creating the most highly educated population in the world. Peek into a Canadian home and you're likely to see all the latest electronic gadgets, and a car or two in the garage, but living standards are more modest than in the USA due to a lower per capita income and some of the highest rates of taxation in the world. These factors also contribute to a 'brain drain' of skilled Canadians to the USA, where there is often more opportunity for career advancement and earnings.

Although 'average,' this portrait of the archetypal mother, father and children living together now represents only 44% of all families in Canada, a figure falling every year. The number of single-parent families has been growing, as it has for common-law relationships, especially in predominantly Roman Catholic Québec. There, 30% of couples live together unwed, a proportion comparable to Sweden. Nationally, twice as many Canadians live in common-law relationships as Americans. Same-sex marriage was legalized in mid-2003 by more than a few Canadian provinces and territories, although same-sex divorce – an area of federal jurisdiction – has not yet been sanctioned. Currently, same-sex couples comprise only 0.5% of legal unions in Canada, and adoptions by same-sex parents are not uncommon.

Canadian tolerance of alternative lifestyles extends to marijuana use, which has already been legalized for medicinal purposes. The government has made several largely unsuccessful attempts at growing

DID YOU KNOW?

Trivial Pursuit, the electric light bulb, the zipper, the snowmobile (called a Ski-Doo), instant mashed potatoes and antigravity suits were all invented by Canadians.

Margo Pfeiff is a Montréal-based journalist who lives a pan-Canadian lifestyle, having grown up in British Columbia, moved to Québec and frequently traveled to – plus developed a passion for – Canada's far north. Her work has appeared in the *Globe and Mail*, *National Post* and *Los Angeles Times*, among other publications.

In *O Canada! Travels in an Unknown Country* (1992), British travel writer Jan Morris succinctly pins down the vast cultural differences, diverse lifestyles and idiosyncrasies of 10 Canadian cities.

marijuana to meet that demand. A federal bill to legalize possession of marijuana for personal use is in the works, but pot arrests have already dropped 30% as police turn a blind eye to those who possess small quantities of the drug. Three million Canadians, or just over 12% of the population, claim to have used cannabis at least once in the previous year.

Leisure-loving Canadians work about three weeks less per year than Americans, and less than Australians, too. During the two-month summer school break, many kids spend a week or two in camp learning outdoor skills, languages and sports. On weekends or for vacations, families head to lakes and beaches in a campervan or to a cabin in the woods in 'cottage country' outside major cities. Canadians are known for winter sports, especially skiing and hockey, which is popular in arenas year-round, on outdoor rinks and lakes during winter, and on suburban streets throughout the summer where goals are set up in the middle of the road.

But Canadians are much more likely to watch hockey than to play it; almost half of all Canadians, including children, are overweight or obese. Canadian participation in organized sports and physical activity is 34%, ahead of both the USA and Australia, but even in the most active province, British Columbia (where Vancouver has the country's highest life-expectancy), only one in four adults does enough exercise to obtain cardiovascular benefit. Although Canadians prefer beer over wine and are not excessive in their consumption of either, they do overindulge in doughnuts: Canadians consume three times as many doughnuts per

DID YOU KNOW?
More than 10 million Canadians (over 40% of the population) admit to having tried marijuana at least once in their lifetime.

NUNAVUT *Margo Pfeiff*

For the first time since 1949, when Newfoundland joined the Confederation, on April 1, 1999 Canadian mapmakers were sent back to the drawing board to change the national boundaries to create Nunavut ('Our Land' in Inuktitut). The largest of Canada's provinces and territories, Nunavut is run by the smallest population; outnumbered nearly 30 to 1 by caribou, Nunavut's 45,070 people reside in a statistically solitary 0.01 persons per square kilometer.

Getting to know the Inuit is not as easy as getting to know the 15% of the population of Nunavut who are 'southerners'; the Inuit you're likely to befriend will have had extensive contact with non-Inuit people, working as interpreters or with government departments. The culture is so vastly different that misunderstandings frequently occur.

Although they live in houses with flushing toilets and drive ATVs (4WD vehicles), the Inuit are still very much connected with their nomadic past. The Inuktitut language remains strong, with 65% of adults and children speaking it regularly at home. Some social customs are very traditional, especially in the far-flung hamlets. Inuit don't knock before entering a residence and will often simply get up to leave without saying goodbye, and this is not considered rude.

Children are allowed free rein, as the Inuit do not believe in scolding or disciplining them. In a land where there can be no darkness or no daylight for months on end, adhering to a clock is difficult. Kids play outside all 'night' long in summer and will join their parents on hunting trips during the school year, which sometimes affects their southern education. Adults do not force traditional knowledge on their children, whom they feel could not use it in a modern society, and they may sometimes be at a loss to help youngsters survive in a contemporary Canadian landscape.

It helps to know that many of the grandfathers and grandmothers you come across in a hamlet might have only come in 'off the land' in the late 1960s, after growing up on the move while living in summer camps and winter igloos. Considering the cultural transformation from a nomadic hunter-gatherer existence to satellite dishes and KFC in less than a half-century, most anthropologists and others agree the Inuit are not doing badly at all.

Check out www.canoe
.ca for information on
current events, arts and
lifestyle for Anglophones
in Canada; the French
site (www.canoe.qc.ca)
focuses on Québecois
culture.

capita as Americans – more than anyone else in the world, in fact – especially at the ubiquitous Tim Hortons franchises.

Canadians are proud that gun ownership is restricted, and point to a low violent crime rate as the result. At present, the homicide rate nationally is at its lowest since 1967. Crimes of all kind have been falling and Toronto, the biggest city, recently came in with the country's third-lowest crime rate. Vancouver has Canada's highest break-and-enter rate, a problem fuelled by a high rate of drug addiction, particularly in downtown Vancouver's east side, where drug dealing and taking is openly carried out before the eyes of an overwhelmed city police force.

Canadians are world-savvy, avid travelers. They frequently hop across one of the 125 US border crossings for a weekend or even a day trip to shop and fill up on cheaper gasoline. In winter, flocks of retired Canadians, nicknamed 'snowbirds,' flock south for months on end to warm destinations, particularly the southern USA. Canadians are also keen globetrotters. More than 25% of Canadians travel to countries other than the USA (compared to fewer than 10% of Americans who travel overseas), the most popular destination being Mexico, which recently outpaced the UK, followed by France and Cuba.

News, culture and social
commentary from the
Great White North, with
an emphasis on politics,
can be found at www
.mapleleafweb.com.

Canadians see themselves as something like North America's Kiwis: reserved, embarrassed by flag-waving nationalism, green and peace-loving with a social conscience. Canadians may not have the sense of history of the UK, or the bravado and self-assuredness of the Aussies, but it's just a matter of time before it's realized that in its own quiet, polite way, Canada is cool. And not just in terms of climate.

POPULATION Margo Pfeiff

Canada is one of the most urbanized nations on earth, with almost 80% of the county's population of more than 30 million people living in towns of 10,000 people or more. But it's as if Canadians are huddled for warmth in the south of the country, with roughly 90% of the population residing within 160km of the US border. More than half the population lives in the eastern provinces of Ontario and Québec. Once you head north, the population dwindles along with the number of trees, and it's clear why Canada averages only 3.3 souls per square kilometer, which is only slightly more crowded than Australia.

DID YOU KNOW?

Canada's total population
is approximately the
same as the cities of New
York and Los Angeles
combined.

Historically, Canadians have always been on the move within the country's borders. While balmy weather in British Columbia (BC) draws winter-weary Canadians from farther east, there is a reverse flow of those taking promotions in the country's biggest city, Toronto. It's almost a tradition for the Maritimes' young people to leave their unemployment-plagued home provinces to find work in central or western Canada. Jobs and reasonable housing in Calgary have recently created a boom, which has made it the country's fastest growing city.

SPORTS Bruce Dowbiggin

Advice to visitors: Canadians will want you to believe that they're a peace-loving nation. 'War was foreign to Canadian thinking, but peace-keeping was the natural role for us to play' is how historian JL Granatstein describes our cultivated self-image. To casual observers, Canada is the beige of nations, neutral to the core, with conscientious objectors. Just not when it comes to sports.

Judging by the games it has brought to the world, Canada will stomp on your head, snap your spine and pull out your still-beating heart if it gets half a chance. Then it will take you for a friendly beer afterward. The only two team sports in the world that do not eject a player for fighting in the course of a game (hockey and lacrosse) are products of the 'True North, Strong and Free.'

How to explain? In a country that has had more makeovers than Joan Rivers, that shelters and encourages a host of minorities, Canadian sports – and hockey in particular – is one of the few remaining vestiges of a frontier nation of voyageurs (travelers), *courieurs de bois* (trappers) and men of the deep (miners). Our famed Mounties may have been reduced to a musical ride in Ottawa, but for Canadians who remember a nation that was always first to join up for a world war, sport is a ride on the wild side.

The first thing you need to know about Canadian sports is: don't ever, ever call the national passion *ice* hockey. This will instantly draw surveillance by security officials. The game is simply hockey. And in a nation that can't agree about anything, everyone agrees about hockey. From September to June, the fastest sport in the world holds Canadians in its thrall. When Canada's men won the Olympic gold medal in 2002, almost 11 million Canadians watched on TV; when the women won their gold, almost 8 million tuned in. Which is somewhat surprising, because no Canadian team in the National Hockey League (NHL) – the world's elite loop – has won the top prize, the Stanley Cup, for more than a decade. When Calgary came within a goal of winning the hallowed Cup in 2004, the nation nearly ground to a halt. A federal election was moved to the back pages and restaurants closed on game nights for lack of customers.

While there are millions from coast to coast who play hockey, the focus is on the NHL and the Cup, donated in the 1880s by colonial governor-general, the Earl of Stanley (thank God it wasn't the Earl of Sandwich). Lord Stanley saw hockey as a gentleman's game, and would spin in his mausoleum back in Blighty were he to see how vicious and pitiless the game has become. While the violence has been curtailed somewhat, a top scrapper can still fight 30 times a year while playing hockey. And players occasionally end up in court for the more outrageous fouls with sticks, fists and helmets.

Of course, hockey is a brilliant, exciting game, even when the rough stuff doesn't get in the way. Tickets to matches are expensive, but outside of Toronto and Vancouver they're usually easy to obtain. Incidentally, hockey could be said to have replaced lacrosse as Canada's national sport. Developed by Canada's First Nations and played on solid, not frozen, ground, lacrosse is no less ferocious or skillful a sport. Lacrosse is similar to soccer, but it's played with a small rubber ball and sticks that have woven leather baskets for catching and carrying the ball. Until very recently lacrosse was in danger of disappearing from the public consciousness, but the sport seems to be experiencing a renaissance with a new pro league.

The gore doesn't end with hockey and lacrosse. Canada has its own version of North American football, the Canadian Football League (CFL), with nine teams from Montréal to Vancouver. While the Canadian version is played by 12 men and on a bigger field than its American counterpart, it's no less hard-hitting. November's Grey Cup (donated by – you guessed it – another Brit on loan to Canada during the 19th century) is the annual championship game and cause for a national drinking fest. The libations are easier to understand when you remember that game-time temperatures have dipped as low as -10°C.

Bruce Dowbiggin is an award-winning sports journalist and national sports commentator based in Calgary. His columns regularly feature in the *Calgary Herald*. He is the author of several books on hockey and frequently hosts TV and radio programs, including for the CBC.

Slap Shot (1977), directed by George Roy Hill, is a cult film for all Canadians and hockey fans, in which profane humor and bloody violence collide as Paul Newman stars as the coach of a minor-league hockey team.

The Stick: A History, a Celebration, an Elegy (2003) by Bruce Dowbiggin toasts one of Canada's most beloved icons: the hockey stick.

CURLING *Bruce Dowbiggin*

To its fans it's the 'roaring game.' To detractors, it's frozen shuffleboard. But curling is the yin to hockey's yang in Canadian sports culture.

A Canadian sport that actually eschews fighting, curling requires players to slide polished granite stones to a target at the other end of a long sheet of ice. Closest to the center wins a point in this sport that originated in Scotland. The name 'curling' comes from the way the stones curl in or out as they spin due to the friction between ice and stone. Players use a broom to affect how much curl a stone will get. Honestly. I'm not making this up.

To win a national championship in the Brier (men) or the Tournament of Hearts (ladies), competitors must first make it out of their own home rinks and work up through the ranks each year. While some have said it's just a poor excuse to drink when the golf courses are shut, curling's top events draw millions of TV viewers and provide great parties at the rink. Appreciating this unassuming game is key to understanding Canada's modest, self-effacing side. Just before hockey punches you in the mouth.

As befits the topographical stew that is Canada, you can thoroughly amuse yourself in the great outdoors year-round, with skiing, paddling, cycling, hiking or diving (see p845 for information on these activities). And if you like to fly or cast, the rivers, lakes and streams of the east, west and north have unsurpassed fishing. Whether it's angling for arctic char in the wilderness, salmon off Vancouver Island or fly fishing in the heart of downtown Calgary, there's a memory just for you. In winter, you can ice fish. Don't worry, it's OK to say 'ice' fishing. Just no 'ice' hockey, OK?

Take a virtual tour of the Hockey Hall of Fame, complete with a 3-D experience of the immortal Stanley Cup, at www.hhof.com.

MULTICULTURALISM Margo Pfeiff

Unlike the USA, which has a 'melting pot' tradition of preferring immigrants to blend into the existing American fabric, Canada prides itself on its multiculturalism, a word coined here in the 1960s. Tolerant of ethnic differences, every major city has a Greektown, Little Italy, Chinatown or Little Punjab. While nearly 60% of the country is English-speaking, in a broad swath through Québec and New Brunswick over 20% of the population have French as their mother tongue. Dotted throughout are the remaining areas of Allophones, representing languages from Icelandic to Urdu.

Just over 1.3 million people consider themselves to be Aboriginal, representing just over 3% of the total population, second only to New Zealand's Maori population in terms of Aboriginal make-up of the national population. The majority of Aboriginal people live in the prairie provinces and northern Canada, with one-half residing in urban areas. Aboriginal peoples include First Nations (those of North American Indian descent), as well as Métis (those with 'mixed blood' ancestry) and Inuit. One-third of the Aboriginal population is under the age of 14, as birth rates for Aboriginal people are almost twice the national average. As in other nations, such as Australia, the suicide rate, which is six times higher than for the rest of the population, is an alarming indicator of social crisis.

Zacharias Kunuk's *Atanarjuat* (Fast Runner; 2001; www.atanarjuat .com) is a mystical Inuit-language film about vengeance among people divided by a shaman. Set in Nunavut, it won the 2002 Cannes' Camera d'Or award.

Multiculturalism has been a defining characteristic of Canada since Europeans first landed here. The French were the first to arrive, with the English on their heels. Asians immigrated to build the transcontinental railway in the 1800s, and by the time of the most recent census in 2001, the country had become home to 200 different ethnic groups speaking 100 languages.

BC has a long history of accepting Japanese, Chinese and South Asian immigrants, and more recently large numbers of people from Eastern Europe and Iran have settled there. The prairie provinces traditionally attracted Ukrainians in large numbers. Ontario, which has sizable Caribbean and Russian populations, is also home to 60% of Canada's Muslims, who now make up 2% of the Canadian population. Québec encourages French-speaking immigrants from Tunisia, Morocco, Vietnam and Haiti. Although immigrants have moved into all regions of the country, nearly three-quarters migrate to just the three biggest metropolitan areas: Vancouver, Montréal and Toronto, the last of which receives the biggest share.

Since the late 1980s, Canada has received more immigrants per capita than the USA, and foreign-born Canadians now make up 18% of the population, the highest level in 70 years – only in Australia is the proportion higher. In the USA, only about 10% of citizens are foreign-born. Canada's percentage of visible minorities continues to increase, with the largest group being more than one million Chinese. Projections show that by 2016, visible minorities will account for one-fifth of Canada's population. Increased immigration in recent years has changed the face of Canada's schools; nearly one in five students in Toronto and Vancouver are new arrivals and roughly half of them speak no English or French. In fact, according to the 2001 census, fewer than 20% of Canadians are actually bilingual in English and French.

Considering the numbers and diversity, there is relatively little racial strife in Canada, but as in any multicultural country there are some ongoing problems with interracial conflicts. There has also been controversy about Canada's refugee process. Many Canadians feel the system is too lenient on visitors who arrive in Canada and declare themselves refugees, which grants them a government-subsidized existence while they await a hearing on their status, which can take months or sometimes even years. Some refugees disappear into the system or illegally skip to the USA. International people-smuggling rackets often target Canada because the coastline is vast and penalties are less severe than in the USA. The racketeers coach their human cargo on how to declare refugee status, but often their ultimate destination is America, a quick (but illegal) trip over the border.

RELIGION Margo Pfeiff

Although seven out of every 10 Canadians identify themselves as either Roman Catholic or Protestant, immigration has made Islam the country's fastest-growing religion. In Canada, two-thirds of Muslims actively practice their faith, while only one-fifth of Christians regularly attend religious services. More Canadians are reporting no religion, and in modern Québec, once devoutly Catholic, church attendance is at an all-time low. Buddhism is booming, however, and there are many retreats, some of the best-known of which are in the Maritime provinces; New York City–born Tibetan Buddhist guru Ane Pema Chödrön has established a center in Cape Breton (see p445). Canada also has its share of obscure, fringe sects, from the radical Russian Doukhobours (see the boxed text on p563), who have a history of stripping naked and burning down their houses, to the Solar Temple sect that committed mass suicide in the Laurentian Mountains outside Montréal. Québec is also home base for the flamboyant Raelians, who believe humans were created by aliens and made unsubstantiated claims in 2002 to have cloned a human baby.

Inuit people are the subject of *Nanook of the North* (1922), a silent classic filmed in Canada by American director Robert J Flaherty.

DID YOU KNOW?

Gaelic is more often spoken in Nova Scotia, one of Canada's eastern provinces, than in Scotland.

ARTS Jennie Punter

For years Jennie Punter wrote about theater, classical music and visual arts, before moving to Toronto to become a rock 'n' roll scribe. Today she regularly reviews films for the *Globe and Mail*, is a contributing editor of *Flare* magazine and works in documentary film and TV.

'The medium is the massage.' The famous phrase coined by renowned communication theorist and Canadian Marshall McLuhan retains its provocative thrust 50 years on, when 25% of Canadian households' cultural expenditure goes toward cable or satellite TV services. And when it's -40°C, who wouldn't cuddle up with a good hockey game, a world-class documentary or a couple of hours of hilarious homespun comedy on the tube?

Lest that send the message that Canada is a nation of couch spuds, consider where the other 75% goes. Canadians enthusiastically support the arts with their participation, pocketbooks (spending around $2.4 billion on books and $1 billion on movie tickets annually) and, perhaps more begrudgingly, tax dollars.

Government funding of emerging and established artists and an array of arts organizations blossomed in the 1960s and '70s, firmly establishing a culture of professionalism that helped develop both domestic and international audiences for Canadian talent while keeping the big bad wolf (the USA) from blowing the house down.

While dominant 19th- and early 20th-century archetypes such as 'the wilderness,' 'the idea of north' and stories of rural life can still be found among Canada's creative output, overall the arts in Canada are a true reflection of the 'global village' (see the boxed text below).

Literature

Storytelling in Canada began with its indigenous peoples, whose living oral traditions are a vibrant part of the country's literary history, contemporary writing and spoken-word scenes. In the modern world, literature is the creative endeavor by which Canada has most effectively defined and distinguished itself and, in the last two decades, revealed its rich diversity of urban and rural voices. Canadian writers are an industrious bunch – read the jacket of a novel by any established author (say, Michael Ondaatje's *The English Patient*, Margaret Atwood's *Surfacing* or Austin Clarke's *The Polished Hoe*) and he or she will probably also be described as a poet, visual artist, teacher, filmmaker, or radio host – and Canadian readers are darn proud of them.

Canuck Chicks and Maple Leaf Mamas: Women of the Great White North (2002) by Ann Douglas is a boisterous romp through two centuries of Canadian 'herstory'; browse excerpts online at www.canuckchicks.com.

The 20-year-old International Festival of Authors (p96), held along Toronto's Harbourfront, is one of the world's premier literary events. The festival website (www.readings.org) links to other festivals and writers' groups (including French-language events) across Canada. The Word On The Street Book and Magazine Fair (www.thewordonthestreet.ca), held in late September, is a coast-to-coast affair during which city streets close for celebration. In most urban centers, chains such as Chapters/Indigo and independent bookstores frequently hold author readings and display

---

THE ORACLE OF THE ELECTRONIC AGE *Sam Benson, author of Lonely Planet's* Toronto

One of the great cultural critics hailing from Canada was Marshall McLuhan, a commentator who preached on the 20th-century explosion of electronic media and its ability to hypnotize us into passivity. His most famous book, *The Medium is the Massage* (1967), propelled McLuhan to the forefront of 1960s counterculture. John Lennon, Yoko Ono and other pilgrims came to visit him during his tenure as the director of the University of Toronto's Centre for Culture and Technology. Today McLuhan is best remembered for his outlandish wordplay, evidenced by statements such as 'the future of the book is the blurb,' and his prediction that TV would unite us all in one global village.

local writers prominently; browsers will find an array of collections such as *Breathing Fire: Canada's New Poets* (1998) and *An Anthology of Canadian Native Literature in English* (1998) on the shelves.

The Canadian Broadcasting Corporation's (CBC) Radio One (www .cbc.ca) broadcasts literary news and interviews authors throughout its daytime programs. Perhaps inspired by Oprah's Book Club, on which Ann-Marie MacDonald's debut epic *Fall On Your Knees* (1996) and Rohinton Mistry's masterful *A Fine Balance* (2001) featured in the same season, the CBC introduced its *Canada Reads* series. In 2004, panelists and listeners chose to read Saskatchewan novelist and short-story writer Guy Vanderhaeghe's *The Last Crossing*, a wonderful yarn set in the 1800s in which two brothers go searching for a missing third brother in western Canada. The CBC's shortlist included several literary luminaries and their most recent or acclaimed works – Margaret Atwood *(Oryx and Crake)*, Mordecai Richler *(Barney's Version)*, Margaret Laurence *(The Diviners)*, Robertson Davies *(Fifth Business)*, Alice Munro *(The Love of a Good Woman: Stories)* and Carol Shields *(Unless: A Novel)*, as well as science fiction writer Robert J Sawyer *(Calculating God)* and recent Booker Prize winner Yann Martel *(Life of Pi)*.

Strong regional literary scenes are reflected in Canada's abundance of small presses, many of which were founded in the 1960s; these include Les Editions d'Acadie (New Brunswick), VLB éditeur (Montréal), Toronto's House of Anansi and Coach House, and BC's Arsenal Pulp and Theytus Books, the latter an Aboriginal-owned and -run publishing company. The 1960s was an exciting era in Canadian poetry, too, when George Bowering was at the center of a progressive west coast movement and acclaimed concrete poet bp Nichol was a member of Toronto's influential Four Horsemen sound poetry group.

Translation is also considered an art in Canada. The finest French-Canadian literature can be read in English. Roger Lemelin's classic *La Famille Plouffe* (1948), the second of three thematically linked novels about the evolution of Québecois society, was adapted for TV by Denys Arcand. Manitoba-born Gabrielle Roy's *The Tin Flute* (1945) was the first Canadian book to win a major literary prize in France. From Montréal, Monique Proulx is one of Québec's most beloved contemporary writers.

Almost 100 years old now, Lucy Maud Montgomery's *Anne of Green Gables*, about a feisty red-haired orphan, remains an international classic and a focal point of tourism on Prince Edward Island (p473).

Cinema & TV

Established in 1939, the National Film Board of Canada (NFB; www .nfb.ca) was the country's filmmaking hub for two decades and, with its regional studios across the country, remains a respected institution for documentaries and animation. To date, the NFB remains the Canadian entity with the most Oscar nominations. Experimental animation pioneer Norman MacLaren made trippy jazz-fueled shorts (*Begone Dull Care;* 1949) and the stop-motion Cold War classic *Neighbours* (1952), while Cordell Barker (*The Cat Came Back;* 1988), Richard Condie (*The Big Snit;* 1985) and Wendy Tilby (*When the Day Breaks;* 1999) are among the more recent Oscar nominees. Visitors to NFB Mediatheques in Montréal and Toronto can program their own free private-viewing film festivals (see the NFB website for more information).

In both filmmaking and TV, Canada boasts many of the finest storytellers in documentary – from pioneer Pierre Perrault and cinema verité

Louis Riel: A Comic Strip Biography (2003) by Chester Brown, an unusual graphic novel that is also a powerful landmark work, tells the fascinating story of Manitoba's charismatic 19th-century Métis leader.

Vancouver (2003) by David Cruise and Alison Griffiths is a sprawling, artfully told and character-rich historical novel that incorporates First Nations mythology. It begins in 13,477 BC and ends in 21st-century Vancouver's downtrodden east-side streets.

For background on the stars of the Great White North and cool trivia about Canadian film, check out www .northernstars.ca.

master Allan King *(Warrendale, Dying at Grace)* to counterculture chronicler Ron Mann *(Comic Book Confidential, Grass)*, director-activists Alanis Obomsawin and Nettie Wild, experimentalist Peter Mettler and a string of newcomers whose work often premieres at Toronto's Hot Docs (www.hotdocs.ca), the largest international documentary film festival in North America. Mark Achbar's *The Corporation* (2003), an exploration of corporate evils, was a hot documentary in 2004.

Hundreds of big-budget Hollywood films, TV series and movies-of-the-week are shot in Canada, which is attractive to foreign filmmakers for its locations, studio facilities, top-notch crews, tax breaks and the advantageous exchange rate. Much of *The X-Files* was shot in and around Vancouver, while Toronto's Queen St E was retro-fitted for Ron Howard's *Cinderella Man* in 2004, and Casa Loma (p87) has been a popular location for several films such as *X-Men* (2000). Both cities vie for the title of 'Hollywood North,' but there is also plenty of action in Québec, where Old Montréal frequently stands in for Paris, as well as Halifax (where part of Canadian-born James Cameron's *Titanic* was filmed) and Alberta. City and regional film commissions regularly post information on their websites about what's shooting in their areas.

Over 95% of Canada's annual box office returns are for Hollywood or foreign films, but the stats are different in Québec, where 20% of ticket sales are for Canadian-made films. Claude Jutra's *Mon Oncle Antoine* (1971), a moving coming-of-age story with plenty of snow, often tops Best Canadian Films lists (for our recommendations, see p11).

When it comes to Québecois cinema, Jean-Pierre Lefevre is an independent maverick who encouraged many young directors, including Denys Arcand, who recently won an Oscar for *Le Invasions barbares* (The Barbarian Invasions; 2003). Francois Girard makes films in both English and French, including the must-see *Thirty Two Short Films About Glenn Gould* (1993). Other filmmakers of note include Jean-François Pouliot *(La Grande séduction;* 2003), Léa Pool *(Lost and Delirious;* 2001) and newcomer Philippe Gagnon *(Premier juillet, le film;* 2004).

Anglophone directors abound, too. *The Rowdyman* (1972) was an early hit for beloved Newfoundland actor Gordon Pinsent, who has starred in many films and the popular TV series *Due South* (about Mounties) and *Power Play* (about hockey). Directors Norman Jewison *(In the Heat of the Night, Moonstruck, The Hurricane)* and David Cronenberg *(The Fly, Naked Lunch)* are highly regarded cinema veterans, while the films of Atom Egoyan *(Ararat,* the Oscar-nominated *Sweet Hereafter* and *Exotica),*

Deepa Mehta (the wedding comedy *Bollywood/Hollywood),* Winnipeg's Guy Maddin *(The Saddest Music in the World,* about a one-legged beer baroness), Jeremy Podeswa *(The Five Senses),* Jamaican-born Clément Virgo *(Love Come Down),* Lynn Stopkewich *(Kissed)* and Gary Burns *(A Problem With Fear)* are worthy DVD rentals. The ubiquitous Don McKeller *(Last Night, The Red Violin)* has written for and acted in films by many of the aforementioned directors. Peter Wellington's award-winning *Luck* (2003) stars indie darling Sarah Polley, who is a budding filmmaker herself. Vancouver's Trent Carlson *(The Delicate Art of Parking;* 2003) and Toronto's Sudz Sutherland *(Love, Sex and Eating the Bones;* 2003) are two exciting new directorial talents.

Held in September, the Toronto International Film Festival (p96) is one of the world's premiere cinema events, where Hollywood and the Canadian and foreign film industries do business and host screenings (which are frequently sold out) of films from the four corners of the globe. Excellent fall film festivals are hosted by Vancouver (p666), Montréal (p253); and in Halifax (p404) the Ottawa Animation Festival (www.awn .com/ottawa) is another world-class event.

For credit-watchers, Howard Shore and Michael Danna are two of the finest (and busiest) film-score composers working today.

Music

Canadian fans are as avid, loyal and adventurous as they come, so it's no surprise that the sounds of Canada are as diverse as its people, from Six Nations hip-hop (Ontario's Tru Rez Crew) to cowboy swing in the urban jungle (Toronto's The Sadies) to retro soul out on the prairies (Winnipeg's Remy Shand).

Summer travelers, especially those visiting Canada's urban centers, will undoubtedly encounter musical celebrations of some sort, or visitors can plan to catch international events such as the Festival International de Jazz (p253) in Montréal; the Winnipeg Folk Festival (p536); the country's largest classical event, Festival Vancouver (p666); the Canadian Aboriginal Music Awards, part of the annual Canadian Aboriginal Festival (p96), held in Toronto; or farther-flung gems such as the Dawson City Music Festival (p801).

From the iconoclasm of classical pianist Glenn Gould to the turntable eccentricities of Montreal DJ Kid Koala, from the prolific road map of country legend Stompin' Tom Connors to the sonic embrace of Lillith-tour founder Sarah McLachlan, from the sublime choral works of composer Healy Willan to the virtuoso antics of Cape Breton fiddler Ashley MacIsaac, Canada has produced more than its fair share of internationally acclaimed innovators and icons.

Canadian musicians have been a hit south of the border for decades. Guy Lombardo and his Royal Canadians played the famous New York radio New Year's Eve broadcast (1931–62), Paul Anka made teeny-boppers swoon in the '50s (and wrote the lyrics to 'My Way'), and jazz giant Oscar Peterson painted an indelible portrait of the landscape with his piano trio 'Canadiana Suite' (1964). In the early '60s, Montréal singer Ginette Reno began her ascent to becoming one of the most beloved entertainers in Canada and abroad.

Influential folk-oriented singer-songwriters and *chansonniers* (cabaret singers) emerged in French and English Canada in the 1960s and '70s, and many of them still make vital music: Joni Mitchell, Leonard Cohen, Gordon Lightfoot, Neil Young, Bruce Cockburn, Kate and Anna McGarrigle, Gilles Vignault and Daniel Lavoie. Renowned for backing Bob Dylan, The Band created their own rock 'n' roll legacy, with member Robbie Robertson addressing his Mohawk heritage in solo and producing projects. Winnipeg's The Guess Who churned out hits around the same time, including its much-covered 1970 hit single, 'American Woman.'

DID YOU KNOW?

Although born in Beirut, Lebanon, Keanu Reeves grew up in Toronto.

To link to the latest Canadian sounds, try www.maplemusic.com (self-explanatory, eh?) and www.distribution select.ca, a Québec distributor of francophone musicians.

TOP FIVE UNOFFICIAL CANADIAN NATIONAL ANTHEMS

- 'The Hockey Song' (Stompin' Tom Connors)
- 'Lovers in a Dangerous Time' (performed by writer Bruce Cockburn or the Barenaked Ladies, take your pick)
- 'Mon Pays' (Gilles Vignault)
- 'Snowbird' (Anne Murray)
- 'Takin' Care of Business' (Bachman-Turner Overdrive)

Daniel Lanois became 'the most important producer to emerge in the eighties,' according to *Rolling Stone,* by working with U2, Bob Dylan and Robbie Robertson. He explored his French-Canadian roots on solo albums, while rocker Bryan Adams was Canada's most radio-friendly export of the decade. From Vancouver, DOA secured its place in the punk pantheon, while Skinny Puppy's industrial soundscapes delighted goths everywhere. From Toronto, Jane Siberry's rarified storytelling aesthetic spawned legions of Sibheads, power trio Rush made intelligent, progressive platinum rock and Dream Warriors put Canada on the hip-hop map. Grammy-winning Alberta native kd lang was dubbed the next Patsy Cline, then blazed her own trail, famously coming out in an interview in the *Advocate* in 1992 and turning her considerable pipes to the art of interpretation – on *Hymns of the 49th Parallel* (2004), she croons tunes by some classic Canadian recording artists.

The innovative mixed-media web portal www.cbcradio3.com is like listening to a hip non-commercial radio station while reading a culture-themed magazine, all produced by the coolest kids in school.

Despite grappling with the same issues facing many countries (declining sales, illegal downloading), Canada's popular music industry thrives, thanks in part to the enterprising spirit of an array of independent companies and the major labels' commitment to sustaining and developing Canadian rosters. The continuing vitality of cable TV stations MuchMusic, MusiquePlus and Bravo, along with regulations stipulating that more than a quarter of music-radio programming must feature Canadian content (called CanCon), ensure that music written and/or performed by Canadians is constantly in the public eye. Since 1971 CanCon has been the source of considerable cultural debate: in its early days, some pundits charged that it bred mediocrity, but now they're asking 'Is it still needed?'

In the late '90s, mainstream airwaves around the world were ruled by Québec-bred pop diva Céline Dion, country crossover queen Shania Twain and confessional rock songstress Alanis Morissette, while the domestic celebrity of popsmiths Barenaked Ladies (all male) has

---

THROATSINGING *Aaron Spitzer*

Among Canada's profusion of peoples, the Inuit stand out. Canadian Inuit and their brethren in Siberia, Alaska and Greenland number just 150,000 souls, but they've contributed disproportionately to global culture. Inuit dreamed up the igloo, devised the ultrapopular kayak, and churn out world-renowned lithographs and soapstone carvings. Now, Inuit *kattajjaq* – throatsinging – is winning big-time recognition.

Throatsinging, most commonly associated with pastoralists in Mongolia, Tuva and Tibet, has become something of a world music fad. It's a vocal style that must be heard to be believed, involving contortions of the diaphragm, throat and mouth to conjure guttural, otherworldly voices. In the Americas, only the Inuit throatsing. For them, *kattajjaq* was traditionally a game, played by women to while away the polar night. Two *kattajjaqiit* would face one another, arm in arm, each using the other's mouth as an echo chamber. One would kick off the cadence, employing throaty inhalations and exhalations to imitate sounds from nature. Her partner would answer in the off-beat, trying to match noises and keep pace with the quickening tempo. Whoever laughed or stumbled, lost.

In the 20th century, killjoy missionaries forbade throatsinging, but the surreal art was kept alive by a few transgressors. Now elderly, they've passed *kattajjaq* to a burgeoning crop of younger singers. Their mesmerizing music can be heard on various collections of aboriginal music (try searching Inukshuk Productions' catalogue at www.inukshukproductions.ca), on the albums of the Nunavut duo Tudjaat, and as backing vocals on two recent Björk albums, including the 2004 release *Medulla*.

Aaron Spitzer is a former Nunavut newspaper editor who still lives north of 60.
He also wrote the Nunavut chapter of this guidebook.

finally translated into international recognition. More recently, the eclectic grooves of Victoria's Nelly Furtado and Napanee teen rocker Avril Lavigne have made international splashes, while retro jazz pianist-singer Diana Krall returned to Vancouver Island to write intimate original tunes for *The Girl in the Other Room* (2004). Roots-rock fueled Blue Rodeo, Cowboy Junkies and The Tragically Hip boast two decades of musical evolution and devoted fandom, while Ron Sexsmith, Kathleen Edwards, Ford Pier, Sarah Harmer, Stefie Shock and newcomer Marie-Elaine Thibert have put their individual stamps on Canada's singer-songwriter tradition.

Some of the coolest contemporary made-in-Canada acts include Nova Scotian rapper Buck 65; BC bands Hot Hot Heat and the New Pornographers; Ontario's Hawksley Workman, Sum 41, Broken Social Scene and Feist; Québec's Lhasa (who sings in three languages), Sam Roberts, Les Trois Accords and the Stills; and Nunavut singer-songwriter Lucie Idlout.

Visual Arts

In Canada, painting, sculpture and other visual arts encompass an array of expression. Major galleries exhibit the strengths of their permanent collections and host traveling exhibitions from home and abroad. Visitors to Canada's major cities will find artist-run centers, storefront gallery strips, such as Toronto's Queen St W (p112), collections of regionally-focused art, such as Regina's MacKenzie Art Gallery (p556), and specialized collections such as the Alex Colville collection in Ottawa's National Gallery (p216). City visitors may also bump into outdoor sculpture or one of Canada's annual photography festivals, such as Contact (www .contactphoto.com) in Toronto. Travelers taking the back roads will discover plenty of local creativity, too.

Influenced by landscape painter Tom Thomson (1877–1917), the Toronto-based Group of Seven (p117) created iconic images of the rugged Canadian wilderness, which can be seen at the National Gallery in Ottawa, the Art Gallery of Ontario (p84) in Toronto and the McMichael Collection (p116) of Canadian art in Kleinberg, just outside Toronto. The influence of abstract artist Paul-Émile Borduas (1905–60), a French-Canadian painter whose work can be seen at the Musée d'Art Contemporain (p242), and the Automatiste movement (1941–54) still resounds, while Painters Eleven, Les Plasticiens and Regina Five are renowned Canadian groups that pushed artistic boundaries in the 1950s and '60s. Jean-Paul Riopelle, Betty Goodwin and Michael Snow are among the many contemporary Canadian artists of international renown. Winnipeg-born Jane Cardiff and George Bures Miller won a special jury prize at the Venice Biennale, one of the oldest and most prestigious competitive art exhibitions in the world, in 2003.

The shared history of aboriginal and nonaboriginal cultures in Canada is most immediately perceived through the visual arts. In the mid-19th century, Paul Kane and Cornelius Krieghoff both painted aboriginal subjects; works by them can be seen at the Royal Ontario Museum (p86) and the National Gallery. Emily Carr (p699) visited First Nations villages in northern BC and her vivid paintings of totem poles, architecture and nature, some of which are displayed at the Vancouver Art Gallery (p655), are inspired by aboriginal art and spirituality – 'Indian art broadened my seeing,' she wrote in her posthumously published 1946 autobiography. Since the mid-20th century there has been strong appreciation of and a market for aboriginal art, in particular Inuit sculpture. Some aboriginal

DID YOU KNOW?

Thirty-five per cent of music played on radio stations and a whopping 50% of programming on most TV channels must be Canadian content (endearingly known as CanCon).

Even if you skip the nation's capital, you can still examine more than 10,000 works from the permanent collection of the National Gallery of Canada online at http://cybermuse .beaux-arts.ca.

artists work in a collective environment, while others pursue a more individualistic path – look for Norval Morriseau's colorful paintings of Ojibwe legends; influential west-coast artist Bill Reid's awe-inspiring sculptures, some of which are on display at the University of British Columbia's Museum of Anthropology (p658) in Vancouver; works by Saskatchewan-born Edward Poitras; and younger artists such as Mari-anne Nicholson and Brian Jungen.

Theater & Dance

Mondo Canuck (1996) by former CBC radio host Geoff Pevere is the definitive encyclopedia of Canadian pop culture.

While ancient performance traditions inform the work of many companies in Canada's vibrant aboriginal theatre scene – Native Earth Performing Arts (www.nativeearth.ca), based in Toronto, is a key mover – many plays focus on contemporary life in the context of sociopolitical issues. The in-ternational success of Manitoba-born Tomson Highway (who wrote the award-winning *Rez Sisters* in the 1980s) has inspired a new generation of exciting playwrights, such as Darrell Dennis *(Tales of an Urban Indian)*.

Professional theater in Canada first arose in the mid-20th century when novelist Robertson Davies (1913–95) became English-speaking

---

THE WHOLE WORLD LOVES A QUÉBECOIS ACCORDION PLAYER *Cleo Paskal*

Montréal's mixture of European-style artistic pretension and American-style marketing (backed up by those useful government subsidies) has created a unique media environment. But argu-ably the most famous entertainment empire in the city was started by an accordion player and a few of his buddies.

In 1982, Québecois busker Guy Laliberté and some stilt-walking pals set up a street performers' festival in the overtly quaint, artsy town of Baie St Paul (p298), just up the coast from Québec City. It was a hit. That gave them the momentum to apply for a government grant to hold another festival in conjunction with the 450th anniversary of Jacques Cartier's arrival. They got it, and in 1984 Cirque du Soleil (www.cirquedusoleil.com) was born.

Laliberté spent some time in Europe, in part training with the European masters at the Swiss circus Knie (www.knie.ch). He and his team were influenced by the grace they found in the differ-ent performance traditions in Europe and Asia. The new Montréal-based circus wanted to create a melding of old-world sensibilities and new-world salesmanship. They were as much influenced by the Gesamtkunstwerk of Wagner (in which several art forms are combined to produce a work of art for the stage) as by the showmanship of PT Barnum.

After a few local successes with very little financial return, they took to the road. In the best circus tradition, according to Laliberté: 'We had no money to put gasoline in our truck to come back if we failed down there. We said, we live or die in Los Angeles.'

Fast forward: Cirque's original handful of employees now number 2500. They have nine shows running, three permanently based in Las Vegas, one at Walt Disney World in Orlando, and five on tour. They have produced CDs, feature films, an IMAX movie, an Emmy-award-winning behind-the-scenes series, and have plans for much, much more.

Cirque's latest show, the Las Vegas–based *Zumanity*, is pushing boundaries of a different sort, bringing artsy eroticism to vacationing Midwesterners. So far, Cirque has had an unerring feel for the balance between pretension and excitement, and *Zumanity* sales are doing well. Some people would say it lets husbands from Omaha justify taking their wives to see a bit of flesh in the name of culture.

Meanwhile, Normand Latourelle, another of the original founders of Cirque, has just launched *Cavalia* (www.cavalia.net), a reinvention of the traditional horseshow. Featuring more than 30 horses, and with a theme of 'man's relationship with the horse, and their evolution together,' it hopes to do for horseback riding what Cirque did for somersaults. And so far the show, performed under North America's largest touring big top, is selling out. The circus is back in town.

Cleo Paskal is a cowriter of the Emmy-award winning TV series Cirque du Soleil: Fire Within.

TRAIL MARKER: INUKSHUK

When traveling in Canada's arctic regions, if a pile of rocks by the side of the road does not look like it got there through forces of nature, it is probably an Inukshuk, an arrangement of boulders that roughly resembles a human figure and is used to mark locations of significance, to aid navigation in the treeless tundra of the North and to scare caribou in the direction of hunters lying in wait for prey. Also a symbol of welcome, Inukshuk have been guiding travelers for centuries.

Canada's leading playwright/director. Gratien Gélinas' *Tit-Coq* ushered in Québec's modern theater era, and large-scale companies such as Montréal's Theatre du Nouveau Monde and major festivals such as Ontario's Stratford Festival (p143) were founded. By the 1960s, professional theaters existed in most cities, but Canadian talent remained under-utilized. During the '70s alternative movement, hundreds of small, artist-driven professional theaters focused on Canadian work and some of the country's best-known playwrights, including Michel Tremblay, Sharon Pollock and George F Walker, first gained prominence.

Today, from the visual masterpieces of Québec-born innovator Robert Lepage (1957–) to the sprawl of summertime fringe festivals (see www .fringetoronto.com/history.html£caff for listings), and touristy stalwarts such as the Shaw Festival (p131), Canada is a theater cornucopia. Toronto claims North America's second-largest theater scene, offering Broadway-style musicals, adventurous repertory companies such as Soulpepper, veterans such as the Canadian Stage Company and multicultural ensembles including Buddies in Bad Times Theatre (p110), a groundbreaking queer theatrical company.

Canada's vibrant dance culture is also diverse. The Toronto-based National Ballet of Canada, Montréal's Les Grandes Ballet Canadiens (p262) and the Royal Winnipeg Ballet are the country's premier companies. Modern dance flowered late in the 1970s, particularly in Montréal, where the influence of solo pioneer Margie Gillis still reverberates. Montréal-based La La La Human Steps captured the international scene in the '80s and continues its ground-breaking work today, while Toronto's annual fFIDA International Dance Festival (www.ffida.org) presents the latest in contemporary moves.

Traditions brought to Canada by early settlers, for example highland dancing, as well as the dance styles of more recent immigrant groups (eg Ukrainian, Afro-Caribbean and Indian), are represented by amateur and professional ensembles, many of whom perform during cultural festivals. Internationally recognized troupes that defy categorization are Toronto's Red Sky Performance (www.redskyperformance.com), which produces original works that connect world indigenous cultures by fusing dance, music, masks and storytelling, and Cirque du Soleil (opposite).

Architecture

Travelers to Canada will spot distinct regional architecture, from wood-framed fishing cottages in the Maritimes to Montréal triplexes and the grain elevators of the prairies (see p554), to name just a few. Québec City's Old Town, Nova Scotia's Lunenberg (p411) and Ontario's Niagara-on-the-Lake (p129) are just a few of the country's well-preserved, historical architecture areas. Many of Canada's 19th-century buildings, such as Montréal's Basilique Notre Dame (p240), Ottawa's

Parliament Buildings (p215), the famous Fairmont Banff Springs hotel (p616) and Victoria's Empress Hotel (p703) can be appreciated for much more than their functions.

Montréal's Expo '67 introduced a new era of modernism in Canadian architecture; some of its structures still stand (p248). Douglas Cardinal's beautifully designed Canadian Museum of Civilization (p227) in Gatineau (Hull), just across the bridge from Ottawa, draws inspiration from the architect's Métis heritage; more recently, Cardinal also designed the National Museum of the American Indian in Washington, DC. Although the CN Tower (p83) remains Toronto's most famous landmark, Mies van der Rohe's starkly elegant Toronto-Dominion Centre is a favorite. Toronto is also awash in 21st-century architecture, notably by international celebrities Daniel Libeskind, who is working on the crystal addition to the Royal Ontario Museum (p86), and Frank Gehry, who is transforming the Art Gallery of Ontario (p84), which happens to be just a few blocks from his childhood home.

Environment

The evolution of Canada into one of the world's most prosperous nations is inextricably tied to its land and the mind-boggling riches it has yielded – and still yields today. The first explorers came looking for gold, but instead found coastal waters thick with cod and forests fecund with beaver, resources that fed fashion trends and the appetites of wealthy Europeans. The fur trade in particular became the backbone of the country's early economy; the question of who would control it was at the heart of the conflict between the French and the British. Later generations, moving westward, found fertile soil in the prairies and gold in the Klondike. Today, it's oil in Alberta, natural gas in the Arctic and diamonds in the Northwest Territories that help fatten the gross national product.

Centuries of exploitation have left some scars, but there's no question that Canada is still one darn beautiful country. Its many different landscapes – rainforest to alpine glaciers, prairies to the Arctic, and even a tiny pocket of desert – support an immeasurable wealth and diversity of wildlife. It's still possible to experience vast stretches of pristine wilderness, sometimes not much different than when the first humans barreled across the Bering Strait thousands of years ago. Then there is the vast system of national and provincial parks that protects places where Nature has been at her most creative. These are playgrounds to cherish and explore.

THE LAND

A quick glance at a map of the world is all you need in order to know that Canada is one behemoth of a country. In fact, at nearly 10 million sq km, it's the second largest after Russia. But unlike its massive neighbor across the North Pole, Canada's shape has the delicacy of an intricately fashioned piece of lacework due, largely, to water. It's surrounded by oceans on three sides; its coastline, if stretched out, would reach halfway to the moon. In fact, Canada's coastline is the world's longest, at over 202,000km. Islands larger than many European countries – Baffin, Vancouver and Newfoundland among them – hem in the vast mainland, and the world's largest freshwater lake island, Manitouline Island in Lake Huron, is also here. And thanks to a couple of million rivers and lakes, Canada is the repository of 20% of the world's fresh water.

Much of this water fills the dips and dents of the massive Canadian Shield, a vast horseshoe-shaped region of Precambrian rock chiseled and gouged by glaciers and erosion over hundreds of millions of years. This vast mosaic of forests, lakes, bogs and tundra occupies nearly half the country's landmass south of the tree line, stretching all the way from Labrador to Ontario, then to Saskatchewan and the Arctic Ocean. It's a rugged, cool and remote land that's more popular with birds and beaver than with people. In addition to Aboriginals, many of those living here are miners and loggers who exploit the enormous wealth of natural treasures, including nickel, copper, silver, gold and diamonds.

About 90% of Canada's population is squished into a more hospitable 300km-wide ribbon running parallel to the 6500km-long border with the USA. In the Pacific region, coastal British Columbia has the most temperate climate, but is often drenched by rains. The Yukon, to the north, has 20 of the country's highest mountains, including the highest, Mt Logan (5959m). Along with Alberta, the Yukon is part of the Cordillera region, which is also defined by other mountain ranges, most famously

The Green Lane (www .ec.gc.ca) is the gateway to a gazillion pages maintained by the government's Environment Canada.

Grey Owl: Three Complete & Unabridged Canadian Classics (1931–35) unites three of the best works by one of Canada's earliest conservationists, a British aristocrat whose love and respect for nature developed while living with the Ojibwe tribe in Saskatchewan.

CANADIAN WORLD HERITAGE SITES

For more information on world heritage sites, visit Unesco's website (http://whc.unesco.org).

▪ **Canadian Rocky Mountains Parks** (Alberta/British Columbia, 1984, 1990; p604 and p752) Magic mountain scenery includes Banff, Jasper, Kootenay and Yoho National Parks and several provincial parks.

▪ **Dinosaur Provincial Park** (Alberta, 1979; p631) A fossil site with bones from 35 species of dinosaurs, some 75 million years old.

▪ **Gros Morne National Park** (Newfoundland, 1987; p373) Superb mosaic of coastal lowland, alpine plateau, fjords, glacial valleys, sheer cliffs, waterfalls and pristine lakes.

▪ **Head-Smashed-In Buffalo Jump** (Alberta, 1981; p768) A precipice where herds of bison leapt to their deaths when chased by Aboriginal hunters.

▪ **Historic District of Québec City** (Québec, 1985; p278) A fine example of a fortified colonial city with perfectly intact ramparts.

▪ **Kluane National Park & Reserve** (Yukon, 1979; p791) Untamed land with the world's largest nonpolar icefields and Canada's highest peak, Mt Logan (5959m).

▪ **L'Anse aux Meadows National Historic Site** (Newfoundland, 1978; p377) Vestiges of an 11th-century Viking village, the continent's oldest European settlement.

▪ **Nahanni National Park Reserve** (Northwest Territories, 1978; p823) Deep canyons, pristine forest, huge waterfalls and the fierce South Nahanni River, tops for whitewater journeys.

▪ **Old Town Lunenburg** (Nova Scotia, 1995; p411) The best surviving example of a planned British colonial settlement in North America.

▪ **Parc de Miguasha** (Québec, 1999; p329) The world's most outstanding fossil site for lobe-finned fish, an important evolutionary link.

▪ **SGaang Gwaii** (Anthony Island; Gwaii Haanas National Park Reserve, British Columbia, 1981; p769) Totem poles stare eerily out to sea on this island off the Queen Charlotte Islands.

▪ **Waterton Lakes National Park** (Alberta, 1995; p634) An exceptional variety of plants and mammals in prairies, forests and alpine and glacial features.

▪ **Wood Buffalo National Park** (Alberta, 1983; p638) North America's largest population of wild bison and a whooping crane nesting place.

the Canadian Rockies. Going east, the land soon flattens into the prairies, which take you into skies as wide as Jim Carrey's smile. The great plains of southern Manitoba, Saskatchewan and parts of lower Alberta are among the world's great breadbaskets.

The Canadian Shield puts an abrupt end to the fertile ranges of the prairies. Across the shield, in southern Ontario and Québec, is an area defined as the Great Lakes–St Lawrence Lowlands. It is home to about half the country's population, most living in Toronto, Montréal and Ottawa.

The nonprofit Canadian Wildlife Federation is working hard to protect Canada's wild species and spaces. Find out more at www.cwf-fcf.org.

Eastern Canada culminates in the Appalachian region, which embraces hilly and wooded New Brunswick, Newfoundland, Nova Scotia and Prince Edward Island, all with deeply indented coastline that provides for some fine fishing.

Finally, capping it all off like froth on a cappuccino, is the Artic region, the country's final frontier of perpetually frozen, primordial beauty.

WILDLIFE
Animals

A trip to Canada is a thrilling experience when it comes to watching animals in the wild. Just about anywhere you travel, you're likely to come across wildlife in the flesh, from the lumbering moose to the majestic bear, the quick-footed deer and the plodding turtle.

LAND MAMMALS

No other animal has shaped the history of Canada more than the beaver, whose coveted pelt brought the first permanent European settlers to these shores. North America's largest rodent has a beefy body, webbed hind feet and a long, muscular tail that serves as a rudder when swimming. The axiom 'busy as a beaver' is well justified: skilled loggers and engineers, they each cut down up to 200 trees per year and build elaborate 'lodges,' dams and canals. They live in forests throughout the country and are most active between dusk and dawn. If you're lucky, you might spot one paddling across a stream or lake with its head just above the water.

The porcupine is Canada's second-largest rodent. This curious, slow-moving animal is covered in up to 30,000 quills, which form a formidable defense mechanism. When under threat, the porcupine vigorously lashes its tail, thereby dislodging loose quills as if throwing them. It feeds mainly on bark and tree buds, and used to be a staple of the aboriginal diet. The quills are sometimes used in aboriginal decorative work.

The white-tailed deer can be found anywhere from Cape Breton in Nova Scotia to the Great Slave Lake in the Northwest Territories. Its bigger relative, the caribou, is unusual in that both males and females sport enormous antlers. Barren-ground caribou, which feed on lichen and spend most of the year on the tundra from Baffin Island to Alaska, are the most common. Some Inuit hunt caribou for hides and food, and it occasionally shows up on menus as far south as Montréal, Toronto and Vancouver.

One of the biggest deer species is the elk *(wapiti)*, a formidable creature whose 'bugling' roars can scare the bejeezus out of you. Their relatively small herds roam around western Canada, especially the Kootenays and Vancouver Island in BC, although quite a few also hang out in the national parks of Banff and Jasper, and Waterton Lakes, Riding Mountain and Prince Albert.

Still more humungous is the moose, whose skinny, ballerina-like legs support a hulking body with a distinctive shovel-like snout. Males grow a spectacular rack of antlers every summer, only to discard it in November. You'll spot moose foraging near lakes, muskegs and streams as well as in the forests of the western mountain ranges in the Rockies and the Yukon. Newfoundland has grown a huge moose population since they were first introduced there in the early 1900s.

Neither moose nor elk are generally aggressive, and they will often generously pose for photographs. They can be unpredictable, though, so don't startle them. During mating season (September), the males can become belligerent, so stay in your car.

The huge, heavy-shouldered, shaggy bison (buffalo) that once roamed the prairies in vast herds now exists only in parks. It is said that there were once as many as 70 million bison in North America. Their herds would often take days to pass by a single point. Their 19th-century slaughter – often by chartered trainloads of 'sportsmen' who left the carcasses to rot – is one of the great tragedies of the North American west, affecting the very survival of Aboriginal peoples. To see the largest herd, visit Wood Buffalo National Park (p821) in the Northwest Territories. Smaller herds roam the national parks of Waterton Lakes and Elk Island (p589) in Alberta, Prince Albert in Saskatchewan and Riding Mountain in Manitoba.

Considering a visit to Churchill for a polar bear 'buggy tour'? Be sure to check out the website of Dennis the Bear Man at www.polarbearcam.com.

Never Cry Wolf (1983), directed by Carroll Ballard, is a beautifully filmed and well-acted dramatization of the true story of Canadian biologist Farley Mowat that turns the mythology of the 'big bad wolf' on its head.

DID YOU KNOW?

If anyone ever serves you polar bear liver for dinner, watch out: they might be trying to kill you! A few bites and you'd quickly succumb to 'death by vitamin A,' dangerous concentrations of which are stored within the bear's liver.

BEAR NECESSITIES *Becca Blond*

The Canadian Rockies are home to the endangered grizzly bear and the smaller black bear (although black bear are sometimes brown and some grizzlies almost black). You can tell the bear apart by looking for certain distinguishing characteristics: the grizzly has a dish-shaped face, smaller and more rounded ears and a prominent shoulder hump.

Although some people have an inordinate fear of being hurt by bear, it's actually far more dangerous to be a bear than it is to be a human in this region. In Banff National Park alone, 90% of known grizzly-bear deaths have occurred within 0.4km of roads and buildings, with most bear either being killed by cars or by wardens when bear and people get mixed up.

Bear are intelligent opportunists who quickly learn that humans come with food and tasty garbage. Unfortunately, once this association is learned, a bear nearly always has to be shot. Remember: a fed bear is a dead bear. Never feed these majestic animals. Always use bear-proof bins (provided at campgrounds) to properly store your food, and keep your campground tidy by picking up all scraps. Parks Canada's *You're in Bear Country* pamphlet provides useful information on these and other matters.

Bear are also creatures that can sprint the length of a football field in six seconds. Although such encounters are rare, bear will readily attack if their cubs are around or if they feel surprised or threatened. Your best defenses against surprising a bear are to remain alert, avoid hiking at night (when bear feed) and be careful traveling in places where visibility is obscured.

If you do encounter a bear and it doesn't see you, move a safe distance downwind and make noise to alert to your presence. If the bear sees you, slowly back out of its path, avoid eye contact, speak softly and wave your hands above your head slowly. Never turn your back to the bear and never kneel down. If a bear charges, do not run and do not scream (which may frighten the bear and make it more aggressive), because the bear may only be charging as a bluff. Drop to the ground, crouch face down in a ball and play dead, covering the back of your neck with your hands and your chest and stomach with your knees. Do not resist the bear's inquisitive pawing – it may get bored and go away.

If a bear attacks you in your tent at night, you're likely dealing with a predatory bear that perceives you as a food source. In this extremely rare scenario, you should fight back aggressively with anything you can find; don't play dead.

But as we said before, the likelihood of being attacked by one of these animals is extremely small, and you shouldn't spend too much time thinking about it. It's more useful to think about the impact you have on the park's wildlife. Give the bear, and other animals, the respect they deserve and the space they need. If you see one on the side of the road, consider not stopping. If you do decide to pull over, move on after a few minutes. If simple steps are taken to minimize bear–human encounters it will help ensure future generations have the chance to see wildlife that is still truly wild.

If you're lucky enough to spot a bear in the wild, it'll most likely be a black bear. (Keep your distance, though; for more, see the boxed text above.) About half a million of these furry critters patrol the forests and bushland just about everywhere except Prince Edward Island, southern Alberta and southern Saskatchewan.

Ursus arctos horribilis, better known as the grizzly bear, makes its home on the higher slopes of the Rocky and Selkirk Mountains of British Columbia, Alberta and the Yukon. It stands up to a fearsome 3m tall and has a distinctive hump between its shoulders. Grizzlies are solitary animals with no natural enemies except humans. Although they enjoy an occasional snack of elk, moose or caribou, they usually fill their bellies with berries and other vegetation.

The fiercest member of the bear family, the polar bear, weighs less than 1kg at birth but grows to be as heavy as a Volkswagen (up to 800kg). Pretty much the only place to observe them is from late September to early November in Churchill, Manitoba (p548), one of their major maternity denning grounds. For more information about these fascinating creatures, see p549.

Another formidable predator is the wolf, which can be every bit as fierce and cunning as is portrayed in fairytales, although they rarely attack humans. Wolves hunt in packs and aren't afraid to take on animals much larger than themselves, including moose and bison. They're still fairly common in sparsely populated areas between Labrador and the Yukon. If you're out in the bush, you may hear them howling at the moon (see p168 for information about organized wolf howls in Algonquin Provincial Park, Ontario).

DID YOU KNOW?

The moose's name comes from the Algonquian word *moz*, which means 'twig eater.'

MARINE MAMMALS

There is only one creature in the water that fears no enemy other than humans: the killer whale (orca), so named because its diet includes seals, belugas and other whales. Their aerodynamic bodies, signature black-and-white coloration and incredible speed (up to 40km/h) make them the Ferraris of the aquatic world. They're most commonly seen around Vancouver Island (p699) and along the Inside Passage (p697) to Alaska.

Other whale species frolic in eastern waters such as around the Fundy Isles in New Brunswick, the tip of Digby Neck and the north shore of Cape Breton Island in Nova Scotia, and off Cape Spear in Newfoundland. Belugas are the smallest, typically measuring no more than 4.5m and weighing about one ton. They are chatty fellows who squeak, groan and peep while traveling in closely-knit family pods. Blue whales are the planet's largest animals, reaching up to 27m in length and weighing as much as 30 elephants. Each one eats about 40 tons of krill per day. Finbacks aren't much smaller; they're easily identified by the asymmetrical coloring of the lower jaw – white or yellowish on the right side and black on the left side. Humpbacks average 15m and typically weigh 30 tons. They have distinctive dorsal protuberances and a finely serrated tail. Minkes can grow to 10m and are likely to approach boats, delighting passengers with acrobatics as they hurl themselves out of the water.

Can't tell a warbler from a woodpecker? Fear not. Consult the *Sibley Field Guide to Birds of Eastern North America* (2000) by David Sibley, a comprehensive, beautifully illustrated and, above all, portable companion for bird-watchers. Also available for western North America.

BIRDS

Canadian skies are home to 462 bird species, with BC and Ontario boasting the greatest diversity. The most famous feathered resident is the common loon, Canada's national bird. It's a waterbird whose mournful yet beautiful call often rings out across quiet backcountry lakes early or late in the day. The great blue heron, one of the country's largest birds, is a timid fellow that's an amazing sight on take-off.

What's all the flap about? Well, if you're a Canada goose, it can be up to 1000km a day. Flying in their distinctive V formation, some of these geese have made the trip from northern Québec to the USA in a single day! Now that's something to crow about...

The true ruler of the sky, though, is the bald eagle, whose wingspan can reach more than 2m. It was Canadian banker Charles Broley who first connected the dots between DDT and the plummeting population of these regal birds. That was in the late 1940s, and things have been looking way up since then.

Plants

Canada is a forest nation. Trees cover nearly half of the country, providing living space to roughly two-thirds of the estimated 140,000 species of plants, animals and microorganisms living in Canada. Stretching from coast to coast and from the US border to the arctic tree line, they are highly diversified and have adapted to the soil, climate and weather conditions.

In the far north are the frost-molded landscapes of the arctic tundra, a word derived from the Finnish *tunturia* and, quite appropriately, meaning 'treeless plain.' It may look barren, but there's actually plenty of growing going on, with more than 1700 types of plants thriving during the short summer season, most of them lichen, mosses and low shrubs – there are even some wildflowers.

Further south, tundra transitions to taiga, better known as boreal forest, named after Boreas, the Greek god of the north wind. This giant green belt dappled with bogs, fens, marshes, lakes, rivers and wetlands is the country's largest forest ecosystem, stretching for about 5000km from the Yukon to Labrador. Cold-tolerant conifers such as pine, fir and spruce thrive in this harsh climate of long winters and short but warm summers. On the southern edge of the boreal forest you'll sometimes see a few deciduous trees – mostly white birch and poplar.

Keep track of the progress of the Trans Canada Trail and find out about routes in each of the provinces and territories at www .tctrail.ca.

In eastern Canada, the Acadian forest in the Maritime provinces and the Laurentian forest in Québec both support eclectic flora. Pines, including the majestic wine pine, and spruces tickle the leaves of maples, oaks, birches and other hardwoods that supply Canada's famous autumn colors.

In Ontario is the parkland zone, which marks the transition between the eastern forests and the prairies. Trembling aspen is the dominant tree.

Manitoba, Saskatchewan and Alberta are best known for their flat prairie grasslands, now mostly covered in cultivated grains. Short, mixed and tall grasses once blanketed this region but, except for a few protected pockets, these are a thing of the past.

BC has the most diverse vegetation in the country. The Rocky Mountain forests consist of subalpine species such as Engelmann spruce, alpine

TRANS CANADA TRAIL

Imagine a single trail almost half as long as the earth is round and connecting three of the world's four major oceans. That would be the Trans Canada Trail (TCT), an 18,078km-long ribbon winding from Cape Spear in Newfoundland to Victoria on Vancouver Island in British Columbia. An offshoot will head north from Calgary through the Yukon to Tuktoyaktuk in the Northwest Territories, with a branch extending east through Nunavut to Chesterfield Inlet on Hudson Bay. It will be the longest such trail in the world, linking millions of people, hundreds of communities and dozens of landscapes. Its entire length will take about 300 days to cycle, 500 days to ride on horseback or 1000 days to walk.

It was the country's 125th birthday in 1992 that inspired this ambitious idea. The now-disbanded organization in charge of the celebrations wanted to leave a lasting legacy, and provided enough seed money to launch the project in 1994. Everyone was asked to pitch in, including ordinary people who can 'buy' 1m of trail for a $50 donation. This entitles them to have their name inscribed on one of dozens of Trail Pavilions along the route. So far almost 200,000 people have immortalized themselves in this fashion.

The TCT is knitted together from existing and new trails. Much of it, including all of the Newfoundland and Prince Edward Island sections, will run along former railway tracks. It's designed to be used year-round; by hikers, cyclists and horseback riders in summer and by cross-country skiers and snowmobile enthusiasts when temperatures drop. For now, the TCT remains a work in progress. Completion of the first phase is expected in the fall of 2005, when the trail's span from east to west coast will be open to hikers and cyclists.

fir and larches, with lodgepole pine and aspen at higher elevations. In the rainforest-like climate of the Pacific Coast, the trees soar skyward. There are ancient, gigantic western red cedar, Douglas fir, western hemlock and Sitka spruce species. Some are more than 1000 years old, making them veritable Methuselahs of the tree world.

NATIONAL, PROVINCIAL & TERRITORIAL PARKS

It all began in Banff. In 1883, three railroad workers discovered a cave with steamy hot springs on the eastern slopes of the Rocky Mountains. Two years later, the springs and 26 sq km of spectacular mountain scenery surrounding them became Canada's first national park. Today, Banff National Park has grown in size to 6641 sq km and ranks among the most popular of the 42 national parks administered by **Parks Canada** (☎ 888-773-8888; www .parkscanada.ca; ☽ 8am-8pm Eastern Standard Time), a federal government agency. Each park preserves a place of outstanding natural beauty, unique geographical features or historical significance – and sometimes all three.

Great Canadian Parks (www.greatcanadian parks.com) has excellent background information and useful planning tips for dozens of the country's finest national and provincial parks.

The parks can be as tiny as the 8.7-sq-km St Lawrence Islands National Park in Ontario or as gigantic as Wood Buffalo National Park in the Northwest Territories and Alberta, which at 44,807 sq km is slightly bigger than Denmark. Taken together, the parks represent about 2.2% of Canada's total land area and cover all types of natural highlights, from islands to mountains, cliffs to glaciers and fjords to forests. All parks protect various species of wildlife and act as natural laboratories for researchers and scientists.

Canada's national parks are extremely popular, particularly in summer, and in an effort to keep them from being loved to death, Parks Canada regulates them with varying degrees of strictness. Most have interpretive centers staffed by knowledgeable rangers who can supply maps and publications and help you plan your trip. Depending on the park, you can rent canoes, kayaks, boats, bicycles and other equipment. Practically all parks maintain a network of hiking trails suitable for all levels of fitness. Multiday backcountry treks usually require registration and may be subject to quotas. Popular winter activities include cross-country skiing and snowshoeing. Accommodations are usually limited to camping, although some parks also have shelters and lodges. For general information about camping, see p843.

Northern Wild (2001), edited by David Boyd, is an anthology of essays in which Canada's finest nature writers explore their relationship with – and love for – the wilderness with humor, insight and passion

Parks Canada also administers 150 national historic sites. For day-use only, these sites preserve various icons of Canadian history, including forts, pioneer homesteads, archaeological sites and battlefields.

Most parks and historic sites charge admission, usually $3.50 to $7 per day per person, with discounts for seniors, children and families. If you'll be visiting a lot of parks, a National Pass, good for unlimited visits in a calendar year, may be a wise investment. Passes are valid either at 28 national parks ($45/22/38/89 per adult/child/senior/family), 74 national historic sites ($35/18/29/69) or both ($59/29/49/119). Various multiday regional passes, such as the Viking Trail Pass and the East Coast Pass, are available as well. Expect fees to increase in coming years to compensate for federal budget cuts.

Each province also runs its own system of parks and reserves. There are literally hundreds of them, mostly used for recreation but also, to a certain extent, to protect wildlife and historic sites. Many are just as spectacular as the national parks. The best-organized provincial parks offer similar infrastructure to their national cousins, including interpretive centers, equipment rental and campgrounds. There's usually a small admission charge, although many parks are free. Parks in the territories tend to be

THE BEST OF CANADA'S NATIONAL PARKS

Park	Location	Features	Activities	Best time to visit	Page
Auyuittuq	Nunavut	pristine glacier-carved arctic wilderness; beluga whales, walrus, seals, caribou, lemmings, arctic hare	hiking, climbing	mid-Jul & mid-Aug	p838
Banff	Alberta	majestic mountains, hot springs, historic sites; moose, elk, bear, bison, wolves, deer	hiking, climbing, canoeing, kayaking, rafting, skiing	year-round	p604
Bruce Peninsula	Ontario	rugged cliffs, forest, lakes; wildflowers, orchids, black bear, rattlesnakes	swimming, hiking, canoeing, fishing, diving	Jun-Sep	p155
Cape Breton Highlands	Nova Scotia	steep headlands, coastal wilderness, Acadian forests; moose, woodland caribou, bald eagles, whales	hiking, cycling, cross-country skiing	summer & fall	p444
Elk Island	Alberta	endangered aspen parkland; bison, moose, deer, elk, birds	bird-watching, hiking, cross-country skiing	year-round	p589
Fundy	New Brunswick	beaches, sandstone cliffs, world's highest tides; black bear, moose, beaver, peregrine falcons	hiking, cycling, swimming	summer & fall	p511
Glacier	British Columbia	glacier-shrouded mountains; endangered mountain goats & caribou, grizzly bear	hiking, ski touring, caving, mountaineering, fishing	Aug & Sep	p752
Gros Morne	Newfoundland & Labrador	deep fjords, golden flat-top mountains; moose, caribou, whales, seals	hiking, kayaking, cross-country skiing	late Jun–early Oct	p373
Kluane	Yukon	giant icefields, mountains & valleys; Dall sheep, grizzly & black bear, moose, caribou, goats, eagles, peregrine falcons	hiking, mountain biking, fishing	May–early Oct	p791

small, simple and inexpensive to visit; they are often used for overnight camping, although facilities may be basic.

ENVIRONMENTAL ISSUES

When it comes to nature, few countries are as well endowed as Canada, with its myriad rivers, lakes, forests and wilderness areas, the world's longest coastline and bountiful wildlife. Canadians value and cherish these assets and are among the world's staunchest supporters of the environment. Yet individual attitudes are at serious odds with the country's environmental performance as a whole.

According to a study published by the Organization for Economic Cooperation and Development (OECD), which compares the environmental track record of 26 industrialized nations, Canada is among the three worst offenders in terms of greenhouse gas emissions, water and energy consumption, energy efficiency, logging and nuclear waste generation.

Canada's Green Party (www.greenparty.ca), founded in 1983, scored 4.3% of the popular vote in the 2004 national elections, almost quintupling its 2000 showing. Alberta and British Columbia offered the strongest support, Manitoba the least.

Park	Location	Features	Activities	Best time to visit	Page
Mauricie	Québec	lake & forest area: moose, black bear, beaver, otter, wolves, snowshoe hare	hiking, canoeing, cross-country skiing	year-round	p277
Nahanni	Northwest Territories	remote mountain & river wilderness; grizzly & black bear, mountain goats, moose, Dall sheep, wolves	flightseeing, kayaking, rafting	mid-Jun– mid-Sep	p823
Pacific Rim Reserve	British Columbia	coastal lowlands & rainforests; bald eagles, black bear, leatherback turtles, cougar	hiking, kayaking	Jun–Sep	p716
Prince Albert	Saskatchewan	boreal forest, historic sites; white pelicans, bison	hiking, swimming, canoeing, cycling, fishing, cross-country skiing	year-round	p569
Prince Edward Island	Prince Edward Island	dramatic coastline, sand dunes & beaches, red sandstone cliffs; piping plover, red fox		summer & fall	p469
Wapusk	Manitoba	remote lowland wilderness; polar bear, beluga whales, snow geese	wildlife-watching	Jul-Nov	p547
Waterton Lakes	Alberta	mountain meets prairie; cougar, grizzly & black bear, elk, wildflowers	hiking, boat tours, cycling, cross-country skiing	spring-fall	p634
Wood Buffalo	Northwest Territories	boreal plains; bison, whooping cranes, ducks, geese, eagles, moose, caribou, lynx, bear, wolves	canoeing, fishing, hiking, boating	spring, summer & fall	p821
Yoho	British Columbia	mountain peaks, waterfalls, river valleys, glacial lakes, fossil beds	waterfall-viewing, hiking, cycling, cross-country skiing	summer, fall & winter	p752

Canada's environment is under attack, and the warning signs are everywhere. One of the most troubling is that the country is getting warmer. Between 1949 and 2000, the average annual temperature increased by 0.9°C. Not so bad, you say? Think again. Even such a modest increase is changing fish migration patterns (sockeye salmon have been spotted in the Arctic), creating insect infestations in BC's forests and causing extreme weather conditions such as droughts in the prairies and ice storms in the Maritimes.

Another major concern is the threat to wildlife, primarily as a result of deforestation, the spread of exotic species and the loss of wetlands. According to the Committee on the Status of Endangered Wildlife in Canada (Cosewic), some 456 species are currently at risk of extinction. The list includes most whale species, whooping cranes and Atlantic cod, which was essentially fished to death off the coasts of Newfoundland and Labrador. Even the mighty polar bear is not immune. With the sea ice in

Sierra Club Canada (www.sierraclub.ca) has been active in conservation issues since 1963. Local chapters organize hikes (usually free) that are open to nonmembers.

ARRIVE PREPARED, LEAVE NO TRACE

If you're planning an adventure in Canada's wilderness, it's essential that you do so responsibly. One thoughtless gesture – hiking off-trail through fragile soil or building an illegal fire – can take years for nature to repair. The cumulative effect of millions of feet in Canada's parks every year is taking its toll in many wilderness areas.

Most hiking and camping advice is common sense. First, know what you are getting into. Find out what weather to expect and pack accordingly, even if you're just going for a few hours. Get trail maps and talk to a park ranger about trail conditions, dangers and closures. Also ask a ranger to confirm that your abilities, equipment and plans match the needs of your trip.

Once in the wild, do everything possible to minimize your impact. Stick to established trails and campgrounds. Be particularly sensitive to areas around lakes, rivers and the like: don't wash yourself or your dishes in streams or rivers, and camp at least 80m from them. Use a gas stove for cooking or make fires in established fire pits only. When you leave, take out everything you brought in and remove every trace of your visit.

Conduct yourself as if you were a guest in someone's house – which in fact you are. Observe wildlife from a distance, but do not approach or feed it. If you find cultural or historic artifacts, leave them untouched. And finally, be aware and respectful of other visitors. Human noise travels far and is the fastest way to spoil a whole valley's worth of solitude.

For more information and advice, visit the Leave No Trace Center website (www.lnt.org).

Hudson Bay melting ever earlier, they are put on an involuntary diet as they have has less time to fatten up on seals for the winter.

Canada's full environmental track record is unveiled in *Canada vs the OECD*, a comprehensive study by the University of Alberta that compares the country's performance with other industrialized nations. Download the report from www.environmental indicators.com.

As in other industrialized nations, Canada's environmental needs frequently run counter to economic interests. In northern Alberta, oil is being coaxed from oil sands, a messy process that requires huge amounts of energy and poisons the atmosphere with greenhouse gases. Nearby, plans are underway for a controversial 1220km-long pipeline, the Mackenzie Gas Project, to be tunneled beneath the wilderness of the Northwest Territories. In eastern Canada, acid rain is killing trees and polluting rivers and lakes because the soil there lacks the alkalinity needed to neutralize the acids raining down from the industrial corridors along the US–Canadian border. The OECD report put it bluntly: Canada's economy is among the dirtiest and least efficient in the industrialized world.

It's hard to imagine that things used to be even worse, but there is at least some progress on several fronts. Many Canadians breathe cleaner air now than 25 years ago (exceptions include population-dense southern Ontario and southern Québec), recycling of paper and glass is increasing, sewage treatment has improved and municipal waste has been reduced. In addition, more forests are being replanted, while the amount of land set aside for parks and wilderness areas has doubled since 1973.

Ostensibly, the Canadian government seems committed to doing all it can to reduce the greenhouse effect and other environmental problems. Canada signed the Kyoto Protocol (unlike its southern neighbors and over the objections of industry) and there's a huge bureaucracy dedicated to the environment. But meeting the Kyoto Protocol requirements is proving to be a tall order for a country that gobbles up more energy per capita than even the USA. The government hopes that its new climate-change plan (www.climatechange.gc.ca) will get the job done, but environmentalists remain doubtful. They're skeptical that proposed measures, such as improving vehicle fuel efficiency, creating cleaner gasoline, investing in renewable energies and imposing stricter industrial emission standards, will be enough to bring Canada's environmental performance on a par with most people's needs and desires.

Learn more about the intriguing boreal forest, its role in averting global warming and the threats to its survival posed by industry, in Daniel Gawthrop's *Vanishing Halo* (1999).

Food & Drink John Lee

Once accurately described as a culinary backwater where the creation of a new maple syrup dish warranted national headlines, Canada has earned its place at the international food-and-drinks table in recent years. It's done so via the emergence of world-class restaurant scenes in Montréal, Toronto and Vancouver; the celebration of some truly interesting and diverse regional dishes across the country; and the globally recognized maturing of its wine production at the same time as its craft-brewing sector flourishes like never before.

For visitors, this means that eating and imbibing in Canada can now be a highlight rather than simply a refueling necessity, although it still takes some creative exploration to indulge in the best tastes of the nation. Whatever part of Canada you arrive in, make sure you take the time to uncover a few local dishes – mercifully, not all of them are served with maple syrup.

A true taste of the west coast, *Pacific Flavours Guidebook & Cookbook* (2001) by Virginia Lee features dozens of contemporary indigenous recipes along with a clutch of wine recommendations and insightful BC restaurant profiles.

STAPLES & SPECIALTIES

Canada offers an enticing smorgasbord of regional specialties that together make up a national menu of provincially inspired soul food. These cuisines directly reflect the climate, local produce and cultural influences of each region.

The main dish of the Maritime provinces is lobster, boiled in the pot and served with a little butter, and the main place to get stuck into it is at a community hall lobster supper on Prince Edward Island (p471). Dip into some mussels, potato salad and hearty seafood chowder while you're waiting for your kill to arrive at the table, but don't eat too much;

ISLAND CHEFS COOK UP A SCENE

While Victoria will always be Canada's spiritual home of dainty afternoon teas, a radical band of young city chefs is creating a culinary scene that goes way beyond Earl Grey and crumpets. And they're doing it with an unusual collective approach that showcases Vancouver Island's cornucopia of indigenous foods.

Launched in 1999, the Island Chef's Collaborative (ICC) brings together Victoria's culinary auteurs, each dedicated to sourcing and serving high-quality, mostly organic foods from local farmers, fishers and foragers. These chefs, many of whom are in their 30s, work closely with purveyors, enjoying in return a wealth of unique ingredients for their bold seasonal menus. These flavorful ingredients include Cowichan Valley duck, Salt Spring Island mussels, dozens of locally foraged mushrooms and fruit such as tayberries, salmonberries and marionberries.

But while they work together to share resources, produce and suppliers, these chefs remain diverse and competitive when it comes to cooking up the goods. Sean Brennan's approach at Brasserie L'Ecole (p704), for example, is pure, country-style cooking served in a casual atmosphere. His classic peasant dishes include creamed chanterelles on toast with shallots and a little bacon.

In contrast, over at Spinnakers Brewpub & Restaurant (p705) – a local gourmet brewpub legend that has been producing its own beers and vinegars for years – chef Ken Hueston is all about comfort food and revealing the region's unique flavors to visitors. Among his popular dishes, the seasonal paysan-style platter is a seafood celebration of Salt Spring Island clams, Tofino swimming scallops and Queen Charlotte Islands salmon.

Victoria now has the second-highest number of restaurants per capita of any city in North America, after San Francisco.

you'll need to leave room for the bulging fruit pie that'll come your way afterward.

Nova Scotia visitors should save their appetites for Digby scallops and Lunenberg sausage, while the favored food of Newfoundland and Labrador (see p352) combines rib-sticking dishes of cod cheeks, cod tongues and snow crab, which is bigger than lobster and has sweeter meat.

Along with broiled Atlantic salmon, the French-influenced region of New Brunswick has *poutine râpée* (potatoes stuffed with pork and boiled for a few hours), which has been filling the bellies of locals for decades.

Québec, where fine food seems to be the raison d'être for many, is the center of French-Canadian cuisine. Montréal is the nation's fine-dining capital, but there's an appreciation of food at all levels here that includes hearty pea soups, exquisite cheeses and tasty pâtés sold at markets. Of course, there's also *poutine* (gravy and cheese curds poured liberally over the best fries in Canada; see p313) and smoked-meat sandwiches the size of boxing gloves. Snackers will also want to chew on a few oven-warm Montréal-style bagels – the finest in Canada.

Ontario – especially Toronto – is a melting pot of international cuisines. Head south to the Niagara Peninsula and you'll find some of Canada's finest wines cohabiting with restaurants that fuse contemporary approaches and traditional local ingredients, such as lake fish. Maple syrup is a super-sweet flavoring of choice here, and it's found in decadent desserts such as beavertails (sugary pastries with rich toppings).

Far from the bounty of the seas, the prairie provinces of Manitoba, Saskatchewan and Alberta have their own winning culinary ways. The latter, Canada's cowboy country, is the fine steak capital. There's a historic Eastern European influence in Manitoba, where immigrant Ukrainians have made staples of pierogies and spicy sausages. Meat-lovers on a low-fat kick should try some lean bison meat. Head to Saskatchewan for dessert, though. The province's fruit pies are its most striking culinary asset, especially when prepared with tart Saskatoon berries.

British Columbians have traditionally fed themselves from the sea and the fertile farmlands of the interior. The Okanagan Valley's peaches, apples and berries, best purchased from roadside stands throughout the region, are the staple of many summer diets (see p739), but it's seafood that attracts the foodies, who tuck into juicy wild salmon and Tofino swimming scallops, as well as tender Salt Spring Island lamb and carrots grown so close to the sea you can taste the salt.

Nunavut, in the Arctic Circle, may be Canada's newest territory, but it has a long history of aboriginal food that's a true culinary adventure for most travelers. Served in some restaurants (but more often in family homes – make friends with locals and they may invite you for a home-prepared feast), regional specialties include arctic heather-smoked char and a cornucopia of raw and cooked delicacies featuring caribou, arctic hare and polar bear.

An ever-expanding feast of traditional and reinvented Newfie recipes submitted by locals can be found at www .wordplay.com/cuisine; favorites include barbecued caribou ribs, stuffed moose heart and Newfoundland molasses cake.

TRAVEL YOUR TASTEBUDS

Some unusual foods you may taste on your travels include Prince Edward Island's Solomon Gundy, a marinated herring and chopped-meat combo, and Newfoundland's legendary seal flipper pie. Fiddleheads, the fresh shoots of a nutritious wild plant, are often served like vegetables in New Brunswick, while BC is home to scores of distinctive mushroom varieties, many foraged and served at restaurants. In Nunavut, frozen raw char served like a Popsicle with soy sauce for dipping is a true favorite.

DRINKS

While most visitors quickly come across the innocuous beer produced en masse by Labatt and Molson, Canada's brewery giants, a little digging uncovers a thriving microbrewery scene dripping with fantastic ales, bitters and lagers.

While midsized breweries like Sleemans in Ontario, Moosehead in New Brunswick, Big Rock in Alberta and Okanagan Springs in BC produce some easy-to-find, highly quaffable beers, it's the smallest brewmasters that offer up the real taste treats. Nowhere is that more evident than in BC, whose craft-brewing scene is one of the best in North America. Here you should hunt around for the dark, chocolaty or downright earthy tastes of beer from local producers such as Storm, Philips, Crannög and Gulf Islands Brewery. It's a similar story in Québec, whose popular bottled microbrews are generally stronger than their BC counterparts and are frequently adorned with labels bearing colorful satanic imagery.

Canada's wines are gaining even greater kudos than its beer, with BC's Okanagan Valley region (p745) and southern Ontario's Niagara Peninsula (p131) area developing some excellent wineries, many of which are worth visiting. The Niagara Peninsula wine region, which has a climate similar to that of Northern California, is home to over three dozen wineries. Among Canada's prominent wine labels are Inniskillin and Stoney Ridge from Ontario and Mission Hill, Quails Gate and the new First Nations winery Nk'Mip Cellars in BC. There are also many boutique wineries worth checking out in Nova Scotia, southern Québec and on Vancouver Island. Make sure you try some ice wine (see p133) during your visit; the sweet dessert tipple, made from grapes frozen on the vine, is a specialty.

> Canadian Beer Index (www.realbeer.com/canada) is a searchable database of beer, brewpubs and microbreweries. Vote for your favorite brew and check out upcoming events across the country.

> Canada's more than 300 wineries and thousands of wine varieties are explored at the Wines of Canada website (www.winesofcanada.com), which uncovers history, regional varietals and award-winning vintages.

CELEBRATIONS

Food and drink are a big part of celebrating in Canada, where summer barbecues, autumn's Thanksgiving Day, Christmas get-togethers in winter and spring's Easter holidays traditionally feature large family feasts with plenty of meat dishes, salad bowls, giant desserts and beer and wine. International dishes feature in public celebrations across the country, for example to mark Chinese New Year in Vancouver and St Patrick's Day in Montréal.

Several Canadian regions showcase their cuisines with annual festivals dedicated to signature dishes and restaurant scenes. Recommended are Quebec City's giant Gastronomy Festival (www.festivalgastronomie quebec.com) in April, and the wine-and-dine feature of Montréal's Festival Montréal en Lumière (www.montrealhighlights.com) in February. In that same month, BC visitors can partake of two new annual events: the wildly popular Dine Out Vancouver (www.tourismvancouver.com/dining/dineout.cfm) and Dine Around Victoria (www.tourismvictoria.com/dinearound), when top local restaurants show off their skills with two- or three-course tasting menus ($15 to $25).

Wine lovers are spoilt for choice when it comes to festivals. Among the many held each year, few will want to miss September's Niagara Wine Festival (p133) in Ontario.

> The culinary bounty of La Belle Province is vividly brought to life in A Taste of Quebec (2001) by Julian Armstrong, a collection of regional traditional and contemporary recipes that concisely profiles more than 100 dishes.

WHERE TO EAT & DRINK

Canada abounds with places to eat, and even small towns usually offer everything from cheap-and-cheerful diners to North Americanized international cuisines and a couple of upmarket gourmet options. There are also many family-oriented, midpriced options for those traveling with kids. While there are many variations, most restaurants open for lunch (usually between 11.30am and 3pm) and dinner from 5pm (some fancy establishments only open for dinner). Mid-range and family restaurants often stay open all day. Closing times vary greatly and often depend on how busy the restaurant is on the day. For information on meal prices, see p853.

The Chef's Table (2000) by Lucy Waverman et al records the creations of top Toronto chefs, with background color on the city's culinary scene; part of the profits go to Second Harvest, a local charity.

Service is generally excellent at Canadian bars and restaurants. See p856 for information on taxes, and opposite for information on tipping. Solo travelers are welcomed at cafés, resto-bars and sushi joints, where there are often counters to perch at. Fine-dining establishments are generally welcoming of individual diners, but family-oriented eateries may make you feel less comfortable.

Quick Eats

The best-value meals on the run are found in covered and outdoor street markets, but shopping-mall food courts – particularly in Toronto and Vancouver – often have excellent, independent multiethnic operators serving fast, heaped, fresh-cooked dishes for just a few dollars.

VEGETARIANS & VEGANS

While two of Canada's biggest cities – Toronto and Vancouver – feature vegetarian options on most menus and have dozens of dedicated eateries for noncarnivores, the rest of the country is a little hazy in understanding the concept. BC is the nation's most vegetarian-friendly province, but you will almost certainly be met with blank stares in many Québec restaurants when you ask if a menu item is vegetarian. Expect similar responses in the Maritimes and on the prairies, where seafood and meat are a way of life. In these regions, strict adherents should limit themselves to any vegetarian-only eateries they can find, since 'vegetarian' menu items in mainstream restaurants may have been prepared with meat stock or lard, or cooked alongside meat. Not surprisingly, vegans can expect an even rougher ride. The VegeDining website (www.vegdining.com) has listings of vegetarian restaurants across the country.

Check out www.eatsmart.web.net, the Ontario Healthy Restaurant Program's online searchable directory of eateries offering healthy food options and wheelchair access.

WHINING & DINING

The majority of Canadian restaurants are ready, willing and able to deal with families, offering crayons, booster seats and child-adept servers. Special kids menus usually rely heavily on breaded chicken and fries, macaroni and cheese, and brightly colored minipizzas. As an alternative, ask for a half-order of something more nutritious from the adult menu. Servers often work extra hard to keep kids happy, so consider adding a few dollars to your tip to reward exemplary service in the face of adversity.

DID YOU KNOW?

Canada is the doughnut-eating capital of the world, consuming more of those sweet treats per capita than any other nation.

Families with screaming children or even ones who are fairly well behaved will not feel comfortable at the finest establishments, where menu options may be severely limited and unsympathetic fellow diners may send dirty looks your way.

HABITS & CUSTOMS

Canadians usually follow the North American tradition of eating morning breakfast, midday lunch and early evening dinner, although late dinners (from 8pm) are common in Québec. On weekends, many restaurants serve brunch from 10am, sometimes until as late as 4pm. Canadians are sociable eaters so it's common for restaurants to be noisier than their European counterparts. And following the US style, eating fries or pizza

DOS & DON'TS

Do...

- Tip around 15% (pretax) in restaurants and bars with good table service.
- Make reservations for popular restaurants, especially top-end establishments.
- Take a bottle of wine if you're invited to a dinner party at someone's home.

Don't...

- Tip the full 15% unless the service has been good.
- Tip if a gratuity has been automatically added to your bill – a growing and annoying practice.
- Arrive at a barbecue without a contribution (eg beer, dessert, fruit plate).

with one's fingers is very common – in fact, other diners will know you are from overseas if you eat your pizza with a knife and fork.

Expect the generally high standards of North American restaurant and bar service to apply in Canada, although there are some regional variations. Meals in Québec restaurants always take longer than in other parts of Canada because there is a tradition of savoring the food and enjoying the company. This can be frustrating if you're on a schedule, but it's best to sit back, relax and go with the flow: you'll enjoy the meal more. If you're in a hurry at any restaurant in Canada, it's worth mentioning this when you order because it will usually expedite your meal. Table service is common at most pubs, although you can still order at the bar. Don't forget to tip your table server, and consider dropping some change in the bar-server's pot if you stick around for a few beers. See above for tips on tipping.

Most areas of Canada impose some form of smoking ban in public places like bars and restaurants. These bans, which are policed with varying degrees of severity, operate in cities including Toronto, Edmonton, Saskatoon, Vancouver, Victoria, Winnipeg, Waterloo and Ottawa; Nunavut, the Northwest Territories, PEI and Nova Scotia have also adopted widespread smoking bans. But many establishments have outdoor smoking patios or smokers' rooms if you can't make it through the night without your nicotine.

COOKING COURSES

Cuisine tourism has been spreading like wildfire across Canada in recent years. Among the more educational options are classes in Ontario and BC.

Toronto is stuffed with a plethora of cooking course options, but among the best for dabblers of all skill levels are those offered by **Great Cooks** (☎ 416-861-4727; www.greatcooks.ca), which regularly delves into traditional techniques as well as hot trends in one of Canada's leading restaurant cities. Away from the city, in Ontario's Niagara Peninsula wine region, the popular Wine Country Cooking School (p132) offers a wide variety of hands-on one-day and longer residential courses showcasing the area's wine and agricultural bounties.

Vancouver's Barbara-Jo's Books to Cooks (p662) offers an ever-changing roster of short cooking classes, many of which are led by renowned local chefs. These can book up months in advance, so call ahead for reservations. If you aren't lucky enough to secure a place in a course, you can always buy a copy of *Great Chefs Cook at Barbara-Jo's*, which includes recipes,

Part wine-primer, part cookbook, part travel guide, *A Year in Niagara: the People and Food of Wine Country* (2002) by Kathleen Sloan-McIntosh is a fascinating, colorful account that includes dozens of recipes from local chefs and vineyards.

DID YOU KNOW?

Canadian electrical engineer Thomas Ahearn reputedly invented the electric cooking range, in 1882. It was first installed in Toronto's Windsor Hotel.

hints and anecdotes from more than 40 top chefs who have taught classes at the shop.

Those interested in the cornucopia of distinctive produce grown on Vancouver Island should take the fascinating educational farm tour of the Cowichan Valley run every Sunday from the **Aerie Resort** (☎ 250-743-7115; www.aerie.bc.ca; 600 Ebedora Lane, Malahat). After touring local producers, wineries and cheese purveyors with a local chef, the gathered ingredients are prepared for a sumptuous dinner.

EAT YOUR WORDS

Want to know your *poutine* from your *patates*? A *tourtière* from a *tarte au sucre*? Get behind the cuisine of French Canada by getting to know the language. For pronunciation guidelines, see p885.

Useful Phrases

I'd like to reserve a table.
Je voudrais reśerver une table.   zher voo-dray ray-zair-vay ewn ta-bler

I have a reservation.
J'ai une réservation.   zhay oon ray-zair-va-syon

A table for (two), please.
Une table pour (deux), s'il vous plaît.   oon ta-bler poor (der) seel voo play

Do you have a specialty?
Avez-vous une spécialité?   avay-voo oon spay-sya-lee-tay

I'm a vegetarian.
Je suis végétarian/végétarienne. (m/f)   zher swee vay-zhay-ta-ryun/ay-zhay-ta-ryen

Do you have a kids' menu?
Avez-vous un menu pour enfants?   avay-voo un mer-new poor on-fon

Where are the restrooms?
Où sont les toilettes?   oo son lay twa-let

Food Glossary

BASICS
beurre (ber) – butter
fromage (fro-mazh) – cheese
jigs dinner – Newfoundland dish of boiled salt beef and vegetables
lait (lay) – milk
pain (pun) – bread
pierogies (pye-ro-zhee) – savory miniparcels of potato, cheese, meat and/or onion
salade (sa-lad) – salad
soupe (soop) – soup

MEATS
jambon (zhom-bon) – ham
peameal bacon – sweet pickle-cured boneless pork loin rolled in a cornmeal coating
porc (por) – pork
poulet (poo-lay) – chicken
saucisse (so-sees) – sausage
tourtière (toor-tyair) – meat pie

FRUIT & VEGETABLES
champignon (shom-pee-nyon) – mushroom
citron (see-tron) – lemon
fraise (frez) – strawberry
patates frites (pa-tat freet) – French fries
poutine (poo-teen) – fries served under gravy and cheese curds

DESSERTS
beavertail – sugary pastry served with rich toppings
butter tart – rich pastry with hyper-sweet filling
gâteau (ga-to) – cake
Nanaimo bar – rich chocolate brownie with creamy layer
Timbits – 'doughnut holes' served at Tim Hortons coffee shops

DRINKS
bière (bee-yair) – beer
BYOB – bring your own bottle; some restaurants, especially in Québec, encourage you to bring your own bottle of wine, beer etc.
café (ka-fay) – coffee
eau (o) – water
ice wine – sweet dessert wine made from grapes frozen on the vine
jus (zhew) – juice
pint – a large glass of beer (rarely a pint in volume)
sleeve – a medium-sized glass of beer
vin (vun) – wine

ONTARIO

Ontario

CONTENTS

Canada's second-largest province is bound by the arctic shores of Hudson Bay in the north and tempered by the lush banks of the Great Lakes in the south. The influence of these contrasting bodies of water on Ontario's climate and dramatic landscape are extreme. Shimmering lakes, dense tracts of forest, sublime beaches, undulating hills peppered with vineyards, hidden canyons and seemingly deserted farmlands all find their own plots in the province. But they leave enough room for the country's largest city, Toronto, as well as its capital, Ottawa. Add to the mix the spectacular and unforgettable Niagara Falls, and you get an idea of just a smidgeon of the diversity on offer here.

Most of Ontario's population resides in the south, where bearable winters and steamy summers provide hospitable conditions. Between the two large cities, visitors are lured by a series of small towns and historic settlements, each reflecting Ontario's country flavor in their own way. In the north, wilderness parks and isolation offer respite from civilization and provide opportunities to see the northern transitional and boreal forests. The resource-based cities of Sudbury, Sault Ste Marie and Thunder Bay are also good starting points for trips around the more rugged areas of Ontario, from the Lake Superior shore as far north as legendary James Bay, with one of the province's oldest settlements, Moosonee.

Year round, Ontario celebrates its diversity in style through a smorgasbord of events. Thespians and literary gluttons will enjoy Stratford's Shakespeare festival or the Shaw Festival in Niagara-on-the-Lake. Connoisseurs of a different activity – beer drinking – can immerse themselves in Kitchener's Oktoberfest, and Toronto's festival calendar is so full that the city seems to be in a constant state of celebration.

HIGHLIGHTS

- Bring out your inner artist while adventuring in exquisite **Killarney** (p171) and **Algonquin** (p166) Provincial Parks
- Overdose on the multiethnic milieu of **Toronto** (p72) or the cultural confluence of **Ottawa** (p213)
- Catch the *Polar Bear Express* to the outpost of **Moosonee** (p179), then let yourself be guided by the Mushkegowuk Cree
- Get sprayed by the thundering cascades of **Niagara Falls** (p121)
- Find an oasis of solitude and tranquility on **Pelee Island** (p149), Canada's southernmost land
- Shuffle gingerly in the treetops at **Haliburton Forest** (p212)

Moosonee ★

Algonquin Provincial Park
Killarney Provincial Park
Ottawa
Haliburton Forest
Toronto
Niagara Falls
Pelee Island

- POPULATION: 12,234,000
- PROVINCIAL CAPITAL: TORONTO
- AREA: 1,076,395 SQ KM

ONTARIO

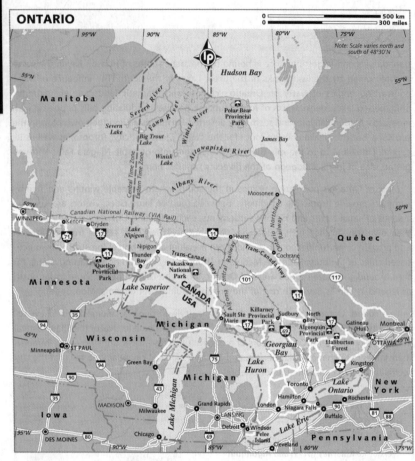

History

When Europeans staggered into this region, they found it settled and occupied by several aboriginal nations. The Algonquin and Huron tribes first dominated the southern portion of the province, but by the time of European exploration and trade in the early part of the 18th century, the Iroquois Confederacy, also known as the Five Nations, dominated the area south of Georgian Bay and east to Québec. The Ojibwe covered the lands north of the Great Lakes and west to the Cree territory of the prairies in what is now Alberta and Saskatchewan.

The first Europeans to see much of Ontario were French explorers and traders in the 17th century, as they set up forts to facilitate trade and to provide a link with the Mississippi River. It wasn't until the arrival of the British Loyalists, around 1775, that any large-scale settlement began. After the War of 1812, British immigrants began to settle in still larger numbers, and by the end of the nineteenth century, farms, industries and cities were growing markedly. At the end of each of the world wars, immigration boomed.

Ontario is now Canada's most populous province, and it is the first choice of immigrants from across the globe, with Toronto proving a powerful draw thanks to its strong economy and well-established support services for immigrants.

Climate

Ontario covers a distance of 1730km between its most northern and southern points. As a result, there's plenty of room for variation in the weather. In the north, the climate is generally continental, with bitterly cold winters and mild summers. Southern Ontario's climate is constantly influenced by cold air from the arctic north meeting warm water transported from the Great Lakes and the Gulf of Mexico. This creates substantial precipitation for much of the year (between September and February the humidity lingers around 70%) and a far milder climate than in the north, particularly during winter.

That said, the entire province receives heavy snowfall during winter. January is the coldest month of the year, with averages of around -4°C on the Niagara Peninsula and -18°C in the northerly areas of the province.

In the south, where most of the province's population lives, winter snow melts rapidly with the coming of spring. As summer draws closer, the strip of land bordering the USA gets increasingly hot and sticky, particularly the Niagara Peninsula. July is the warmest month, averaging around 23°C in southwestern Ontario and 19°C in eastern Ontario.

National & Provincial Parks

Ontario has six of Canada's national parks. In the south, the lucid waters of Georgian Bay are home to the Georgian Bay Islands National Park (p162), the Bruce Peninsula National Park (p156), and Canada's premier national marine conservation area, Fathom Five National Marine Park (p156).

Point Pelee National Park (p149) sits on the southernmost point of the Canadian mainland. In the north, Pukaskwa National Park (p193), Ontario's only wilderness national park, maintains stunning views of Lake Superior.

St Lawrence Islands National Park (p208) is Canada's smallest national park. Encompassing more than 20 islands, this water-based park lures day-trippers and visitors traversing the province.

Add 104 **provincial parks** (☎ 800-668-2746; www .ontarioparks.com) and you start to get an idea of Ontario's vast wilderness. Many of the provincial parks have hiking and camping facilities. Campsites for up to six people cost an average of $25 per night, ranging from those without electricity or showers (from $18.50) to those with excellent locations, showers and electricity (up to $30 per night). You can make reservations over the telephone by calling **Ontario Parks** (☎ 888 668 7275) or book online at www.ontarioparks.com/english/ reservations.html. There is a $12 booking fee on top of the cost of your campsite. Reservations for most parks are strongly recommended as sites go quickly, particularly over weekends and holidays.

Getting There & Away

Ontario is well-connected to the rest of Canada by plane, train and automobile.

AIR

Most Canadian airlines and major international carriers arrive at Canada's busiest airport, Lester B Pearson International Airport in Toronto. Air Canada and WestJet service the province well, connecting both Toronto and Ottawa with just about anywhere in the country. Both CanJet and Jetsgo also offer budget airfares, albeit to fewer Canadian destinations. First Air and Canadian North connect Ottawa with Iqaluit in Nunavut daily (from $625 one-way, three hours). For contact details for all these airlines, see p869.

BUS

Heading west, Greyhound Canada (p870) has connections between Toronto and Winnipeg in neighboring Manitoba (adult/child $190/95, 31 hours, four daily) and, if you've got the stamina, Vancouver ($360/180, 65 to 70 hours, four daily) in British Columbia. Unless you're doing these journeys in small stints, competitive airfares will provide a quicker and more economical option. Traveling east, Greyhound Canada connects Ottawa and Montréal ($34/17, two to 2½ hours) frequently.

Heading across the border, Greyhound (p867) operates services between Toronto and Buffalo ($32/16, 2½ to three hours, seven daily), Detroit ($62/31, 5½ hours, five daily Monday to Saturday, two daily Sunday) and New York ($114/69, 10 to 12 hours, five daily).

TRAIN

VIA Rail (p875) trains service the Ontario–Québec City corridor, with connections from Windsor all the way through to Montréal.

ONTARIO IN...

Five days

Hit the ground running in **Toronto** (below), delving into the multicultural neighborhoods and the Harbourfront's atmosphere. Spend two days exploring the museums, galleries, parks, shops and world-class eateries, but save enough energy for a show or live gig.

On day three be humbled by **Niagara Falls** (p121) before winding your way through the vineyards and villages of the **Niagara Peninsula** (p131).

On day four head northeast to **Ottawa** (p213) to sample the city's cultural offerings. Stop in historic **Kingston** (p201) or picnic in one of the many provincial parks along the way.

One week

With more time you can travel west and lose yourself in beautiful **Algonquin Provincial Park** (p166). This semi-wilderness teems with lakes, hiking trails and so many activities you'll have difficulty choosing.

Two weeks

In two weeks you have time to explore the magnificent beaches and resorts circling **Georgian Bay** (p153), traverse a stretch of the **Bruce Trail** (p156) on the **Bruce Peninsula** (p155), and visit unique **Fathom Five National Marine Park** (p156).

Give the speedometer a workout on the Trans-Canada Hwy and discover **Lake Superior's** (p191) pristine wilderness. Continue to **Thunder Bay** (p194) and into sparsely populated **northern Ontario** (p172), then catch the wilderness train to **Moosonee** (p178), one of Ontario's oldest European settlements.

This trip can either be done in a long haul, with only one stop and change of train in Toronto, or in stages, as VIA Rail services numerous stations in between. VIA Rail also provides services beyond northern Ontario into Manitoba.

Getting Around

BUS

Greyhound Canada (p870) covers southern Ontario fairly well, but services are not fast, while Ontario Northland (p871) services northern Ontario. See the Getting There & Around sections of specific destinations in this chapter for details.

CAR & MOTORCYCLE

If you're driving in Ontario, remember you can turn right on a red light after first having made a full stop.

TRAIN

VIA Rail (p875) has services along the Toronto–Ottawa corridor, as well as from Toronto up through northern Ontario to Longlac.

Ontario Northland (☎ 800-461-8558; www.ontc .on.ca) operates train and bus routes through-

out northern Ontario. Their *Northlander* service connects Toronto with Cochrane, from where buses take passengers to Hearst and Kapuskasing. The *Polar Bear Express* runs from Cochrane to Moosonee in northern Ontario. Ontario Northland also has services out of Sudbury.

TORONTO

☎ 416 / pop 2.8 million

Like hypnotized subjects, visitors from all walks of life converge on this diverse city, sample a shot of its global infusion and walk away enriched, if not a little gobsmacked. 'TO' (*tee*-oh, or 'T dot' in hip-hop culture) breaks conventions on a daily basis and thrives in its constant evolution. That's Toronto in a nutshell: fiercely proud, enlightened and always going against the cultural grain.

Toronto, Ontario's capital, is Canada's largest city. In fact, the sizes of its population, government and budget are greater than those of some Canadian provinces. In addition to being a primary focus for English-Canadian arts and culture, Toronto is well entrenched as the nation's financial, communications and business hub. It has the busiest Canadian port on the Great Lakes and is a major center for banking, manufacturing and publishing. Also, the city has been called Hollywood North – you may well wander unexpectedly into a movie shoot.

Diversity is what Toronto rightly uses to define its character. Since WWII this 'icebox' city has been melted by waves of Portuguese, Greek, Italian, Latin-American, Chinese, Southeast Asian, Indian and Caribbean immigrants, their transplanted cultures largely undiminished by translation. Tolerance is a reigning virtue.

Toronto's concrete and steel downtown is manageably small and safe, and numerous compact neighborhoods and ethnic communities flare out from the core. Much of it can be easily explored on foot, from the spicy corners of the city's markets to the beachfront boardwalks.

Today, as summer festivals seize you with their fervor, and Toronto's living mosaic of historical and ethnic neighborhoods inspire wanderlust, it's difficult to imagine the city was once tagged 'Toronto the Good' for its well-documented stiffness. Piety has since made way for invention, and now restaurants and cafés sport outdoor patios for half the year, club-goers and barflies party till late, and all manner of fashions and subcultures coexist.

HISTORY

In the 17th century, present-day Toronto was Seneca Aboriginal land. Étienne Brûlé, on a trip with Samuel de Champlain in 1615, was the first European to see the site. The Aboriginals did not particularly relish the visit. The chilly reception, ongoing suspicion and ill will temporarily impeded further French development. It wasn't until around 1720 that the French established a fur-trading post and mission in what's now the city's west end.

In 1793 the British took over and John Simcoe, lieutenant governor of the new Upper Canada, chose the site as the capital (which had formerly been at Niagara-on-the-Lake) and founded a town that became known as York. During the War of 1812, the American forces reached Fort York on April 27, 1813, and after a short struggle overcame British and Ojibwe troops. The

Americans looted and razed York, but held it for only six days before Canadian troops kicked them out and chased them all the way back to the US political headquarters in Washington.

In 1834, with William Lyon Mackenzie as the first mayor, York was renamed Toronto, an Aboriginal name meaning 'meeting place.' The Victorian city, controlled by conservative politicians, became known as 'Toronto the Good,' a tag that only began to fade in the 1970s. Religious restraints (it was illegal to hire a horse on Sunday) and strong anti-vice laws were largely responsible. Not all that long ago, curtains were drawn in department-store windows on Sunday, because window-shopping was considered sinful, and movies couldn't be screened on the holy day.

Like many big cities, Toronto had a great fire; in 1904 about five hectares of the inner city burned, leveling 122 buildings. Amazingly, no one was killed. By the 1920s Bay St was booming, in part because gold, silver and uranium mines had been discovered in northern Ontario.

In 1941, 80% of the population was Anglo-Celtic. But the city began to change after WWII. Close to one million immigrants have arrived since then. Italians make up the largest non-British ethnic group. But since the 1970s Portuguese, Chilean, Greek, Southeast Asian, Chinese and West Indian immigrants have rolled into the city in waves. This influx of new tongues, customs and food has livened up a place once thought to be a hopeless case of one-dimensional Anglo reserve.

In 1998 when five cities were incorporated into the Megacity, Toronto became the largest city in Canada and the fifth largest in North America. That's certainly a long way from its beginnings as the second-choice capital after pastoral Niagara.

ORIENTATION

Downtown Toronto's grid-style layout, with nearly all the streets running north–south and east–west, means it's easy to stay oriented.

Yonge St (pronounced young), the main north–south artery, runs about 18km from Lake Ontario north to the city boundary, Steeles Ave, and beyond. The central downtown area is bounded by Front St to the

TORONTO IN...

One Day

Start at **Harbourfront** (p78), strolling along the shores of Lake Ontario and taking in the galleries and gardens at the **York Quay Centre** (p78). Then hop on a ferry to **Toronto Islands** (p82). In the afternoon, head up to **Bloor-Yorkville** (p86) via the **Art Gallery of Ontario** (p84) before tucking into a seafood lunch at **Mövenpick's Bistretto & La Pêcherie** (p104). Spend a couple of hours window-shopping in the nearby boutiques.

Start the evening with a drink at **Madison Avenue Pub** (p107) and then treat yourself to any number of flavors in the restaurants along **Queen West** (p105). Top it all off with a **live show** (p107).

Two Days

On day two, head to the **Royal Ontario Museum** (p86), then lunch at the **St Lawrence Market** (p101) in unique **Baldwin Village** (p83). In the afternoon explore Toronto's underbelly on our **walking tour** (p91). That evening, attend an intimate jazz set at **Montréal Bistro & Jazz Club** (p108) and nibble on late-night *mezes* (Greek tapas) and drinks at **Danforth Ave** (p105) in Greektown.

Four Days

On your third day, visit the spectacular **Niagara Falls** (p121). Overnight there, then spend a day meandering through the picturesque countryside and wineries of the **Niagara Peninsula Wine Country** (p131).

south, Bloor St to the north, Spadina Ave to the west and Jarvis St to the east. Street names change from 'East' to 'West' at Yonge St, and the street numbers begin there.

Lester B Pearson International Airport is 27km west of downtown. At the southern end of the downtown area is Union Station where long-distance trains arrive and depart. Heading north on Yonge St, long-distance buses operate out of the Metro Toronto Coach Terminal which is in the **Dundas Sq** area. You can't miss this block; it's dominated by the Eaton Centre, a large shopping complex. Just west of here is Toronto City Hall.

Due west, Toronto shows off its multi-cultural roots via the diverse smells, colors, flavors and architecture of **Chinatown** and bohemian **Baldwin Village**.

Running parallel to Yonge St, University Ave is Toronto's widest street and the route of most major parades. The lit beacon atop the Canada Life Building, near the corner of University Ave and Queen St, is a guide to the weather. The light at the top is color-coded: green means clear, red means cloudy, flashing red means rain, and flashing white means snow. University Ave heads north to the University of Toronto (UT) and surrounds Queens Park. Near to UT is **The Annex**, a student neighborhood. To the east is upmarket **Bloor-Yorkville**.

To the west of the UT campus, occupying a few narrow streets west of Spadina Ave, between College St and Dundas St W, **Kensington Market** represents multicultural Toronto at its most authentic. Influenced by immigrants from Hungary, Italy, Portugal, Ukraine, China, Latin America, East and West India, Korea, Vietnam, Malaysia and Thailand this historic market neighborhood still draws new immigrants every day, along with plenty of bohemians, punks and anarchists who make it their home.

Surrounding Kensington Market, **Little Italy** and **Queen West** don't have any sights to speak of, but are exemplary of the distinct community identities essential to the vibe of present-day Toronto. In either neighborhood you can expect to shop avariciously, dine deliciously and rock out or shake your booty all night long.

The five cities surrounding and adjacent to the relatively small area of Toronto proper amalgamated in 1998. This enlarged Toronto has been dubbed the Megacity. The urban sprawl beyond the new city boundaries is known as the Greater Toronto Area (GTA).

Maps

Lonely Planet's color, fold out *Toronto City Map* has a handy street index and a laminated write-on, wipe-off surface. Ontario Tourism (p77) provides free provincial maps that are handy for excursions. **MapArt** (www.mapart.com) publishes an excellent series of affordable maps covering central Toronto, the GTA and southwestern Ontario; they're sold at many bookstores and newsstands.

INFORMATION
Bookstores

Toronto has more than its fair share of independent bookstores, most of which are found around downtown and The Annex, a student-dominated neighborhood.

Chapters Books & Magazines (Map pp80-1; ☎ 416-920-9299; 110 Bloor St W; ☺ 9am-10pm Sun-Thu, 9am-11pm Fri & Sat; subway Bay) Four-storey corporate juggernaut.

Glad Day Books & Magazines (Map pp80-1; ☎ 416-961-4161, 877-783-3725; 598A Yonge St; subway Wellesley) Canada's oldest queer bookstore, stocking 'everything under the rainbow.'

Open Air Books & Maps (Map pp80-1; ☎ 416-363-0719; 25 Toronto St; subway King) Great for travel guides and maps plus books on nature, camping and outdoor activities.

Pages Books & Magazines (Map pp80-1; ☎ 416-598-1447; 256 Queen St W; ☺ 9:30am-10pm Mon & Wed, 9:30-11pm Thu & Fri, 10am-11pm Sat, 11am-8pm Sun; streetcar 501) Arguably Toronto's finest independent bookstore with a smorgasbord of magazines, small-press editions, nonfiction and new literature.

TheatreBooks (Map pp80-1; ☎ 416-922-7175; www .theatrebooks.com; 11 St Thomas St; subway Bay) Original scripts, music, film, dance, drama theory, plus screenwriting software, DVDs and videos. Events feature readings by playwrights, actors and movie critics.

This Ain't the Rosedale Library (Map pp80-1; ☎ 416-929-9912; 483 Church St; ☺ 10am-10pm Sun-Thu, 10am-11pm Fri & Sat; subway Wellesley) A lesbigay community institution, this bookstore sells novels, modern first editions, nonfiction titles, children's books and piles of magazines.

Toronto Women's Bookstore (Map pp80-1; ☎ 416-922-8744, 800-861-8233; 73 Harbord St; streetcar 510) Nonprofit bookstore selling diverse titles by women authors from equally diverse backgrounds.

Cultural Centers

Alliance Française (Map pp80-1; ☎ 416-922-2014; www.alliance-francaise.ca; 24 Spadina Rd; subway Spadina)
Italian Cultural Institute (Map pp80-1; ☎ 416-921-3802; www.iicto-ca.org/istituto1.htm; 496 Huron St; subway Spadina)

Japan Foundation (Map pp80-1; ☎ 416-966-1600; www.japanfoundationcanada.org; 2nd fl, Colonnade, 131 Bloor St W; admission usually free; ☺ closed Sun; subway Bay, Museum) Japanese cultural centre offering temporary multimedia exhibitions and special events, some of which require advance reservations.

Spanish Centre (Map pp80-1; ☎ 416-925-4652; www .spanishcentre.com; 40 Hayden St; subway Bloor-Yonge)

Emergency
Police, Fire & Ambulance (☎ 911)
Police (☎ 416-808-2222, TDD 416-467-0493) For nonemergencies.
SOS Femmes (☎ 416-487-6794, 800-287-8603)
Toronto Rape Crisis Centre (☎ 416-597-88-8808, TTY 416-597-1214)

Internet Access

Toronto's cheapest Internet cafés are found along Yonge St, Bloor St, in The Annex and along Spadina Ave in Chinatown. Rates start at $2 per hour.

Chapters Books & Magazines (Map pp80-1; ☎ 416-920-9299; 110 Bloor St W; per hr $5; ☺ 9am-10pm Sun-Thu, 9am-11pm Fri & Sat; subway Bay)

Grey Region Comics (Map pp80-1; ☎ 416-975-1718; 550 Yonge St; per hr $6; ☺ 9am-midnight; subway Wellesley)

Kinko's (Financial District; Map pp80-1; ☎ 416-363-2705; 357 Bay St; per 30min $7.50; ☺ 24hr; subway Queen); The Annex (Map pp80-1; ☎ 416-928-0110; 459 Bloor St W; per 30min $7.50; ☺ 24hr; subway Spadina)

Media

CIUT (89.5FM; www.ciut.fm) 'Real Radio' from the UT campus; tune in to the 'Radio Music Gallery' (10am Friday).
Edge (102.1 FM; www.edge.ca) Toronto's premier new-rock station, with breaking music news.
Eye Weekly (www.eye.net) Free alternative weekly, focused on arts and entertainment.
Globe & Mail (www.globeandmail.ca) Elder statesman of the national daily newspapers.
Now Toronto (www.nowtoronto.com) Outstanding alternative weekly, free every Thursday.
Toronto Life (www.torontolife.com) Upmarket lifestyle, dining, arts and entertainment monthly magazine.
Toronto Star (www.thestar.com) Toronto's daily newspaper.
Toronto Sun (www.canoe.com/NewsStand/Toronto Sun/home.html) Sensationalist news and good sports coverage.
Where Toronto (www.where.ca/toronto) The most informative of the free glossy tourist magazines.
Xtra! (www.xtra.ca) Toronto's free, gay-oriented alternative biweekly.

ONTARIO

TORONTO

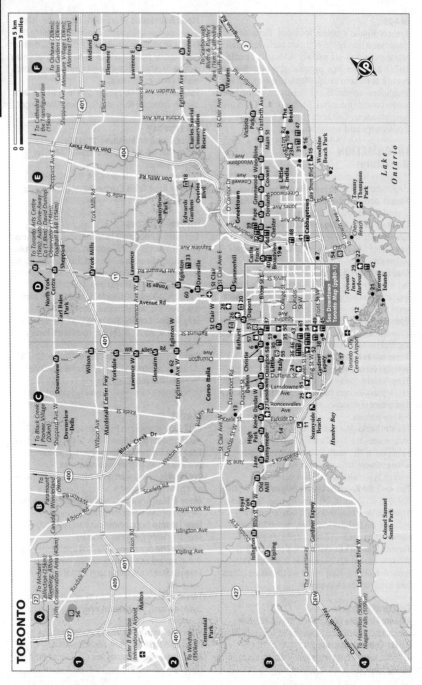

Medical Services

Ambulatory Care Centre (ACC; Map pp80-1; ☎ 416-323-6400; 76 Grenville St; ☻ 24hr; subway Queens Park) Non-emergency medical services for women and families.

Dental Emergency Clinic (Map pp76-7; ☎ 416-485-7121; 1650 Yonge St; ☻ 8am-midnight; subway St Clair)

Hassle-Free Clinic (Map pp80-1; ☎ 416-922-0566 for women, 416-922-0603 for men; 2nd fl, 556 Church St; subway Wellesley) Drop-in and appointment-only hours for STD/HIV testing and reproductive health services.

Hospital for Sick Children (Map pp80-1; ☎ 416-813-1500, Telehealth line 866-797-0000; www.sickkids .on.ca; 555 University Ave; subway Queens Park) Affectionately known as 'Sick Kids', this hospital specializes in treating children. There's no emergency room.

Mount Sinai Hospital (Map pp80-1; ☎ 416-596-4200, emergency room 416-586-5054; www.mtsinai.on.ca; 600 University Ave; ☻ 24hr; subway Queens Park)

Shoppers Drug Mart (Map pp80-1; ☎ 416-961-2042; 360 Bloor St; ☻ 24hr; subway Spadina) Multiple branches around town.

Toronto General Hospital (Map pp80-1; ☎ 416-340-3111, emergency room 416-340-3946; www.uhn.ca; 200 Elizabeth St; ☻ 24hr; subway Queens Park)

Money

Foreign currency exchange is available from the numerous banks littering Yonge St.

American Express (Map pp80-1; ☎ 416-967-3411; Holt Renfrew Centre, 50 Bloor St W; subway Bloor-Yonge)

Money Mart (Map pp80-1; ☎ 416-920-4146; 617 Yonge St; ☻ 24hr; subway Wellesley) Less than stellar rates plus high fees, but at least this place is open around the clock.

Thomas Cook Bloor-Yorkville (Map pp80-1; ☎ 416-975-9940; 1168 Bay St; subway Bloor-Yonge); Financial District (Map pp80-1; ☎ 416-366-1961; 10 King St E)

Post

There are dozens of postal branches inside stores all around the city.

Main Post Office (Map pp80-1; ☎ 416-506-0911, 800-267-1177; 595 Bay St, Toronto, ON, M5G 2C0; ☻ 9am-5pm Mon-Sun; streetcar 505) General delivery/poste restante available. There is also a **branch** (Map pp80-1; ☎ 416-214-2353; 31 Adelaide St E; ☻ 8am-5:45pm Mon-Fri; subway Queen) with shorter queues for general services.

Tourist Offices

Ontario Tourism (Map pp80-1; ☎ 416-314-0944, 800-668-2746, French 416-314-0956, 800-268-3736; www .ontariotravel.net; subway level, Eaton Centre, 220 Yonge St; ☻ 10am-9pm Mon-Fri, 9:30am-7pm Sat, noon-5pm Sun) Staffed by knowledgeable and multilingual folk. Plenty of brochures and information on the rest of Ontario are available.

Tourism Toronto (Map pp80-1; ☎ 416-203-2600, 800-499-2514; www.torontotourism.com; 207 Queens Quay W; ☻ 8:30am-5pm Mon-Fri) You can pop in for information or contact one of their telephone agents; after hours use the automated touch-tone information menu.

Travel Agencies

STA Travel Bloor-Yorkville (Map pp80-1; ☎ 416-925-5800; 200 Bloor St W; subway Museum); The Annex (Map pp80-1; ☎ 416-593-7240; 258B College St; streetcar 506)

Travel CUTS Union Station (Map pp80–1; ☎ 416-365-0545; 65 Front St W; subway Union); The Annex (Map pp80–1; ☎ 416-979-2406; 187 College St; streetcar 506) Good bargains for under 26ers.

DANGERS & ANNOYANCES

Downtown east of Yonge St (basically anywhere from the Gardiner Expressway north to Carlton St), women walking alone after dark are likely to be mistaken for prostitutes by curb-crawling johns. Late at night, everyone should avoid the southern section of Jarvis St, between Carlton and Queen Sts, especially the area around Allan Gardens.

Because many social service agencies have recently closed, there is an increasing number of homeless people and youths begging on the streets. Keep in mind that homeless people are more likely to be victims of assault or harassment than perpetrators.

Although violent crime rates are steadily falling, property theft has increased slightly. Police estimate that at least 73 gangs operate in Toronto. Biker wars that have racked Québec have made their way into Ontario. If you see biker gangs out on the highway, give them a wide berth.

Frostbite can be a problem in winter – the average temperature in January is several degrees below zero, and the wind-chill factor lowers it substantially. When this is the case, radio stations broadcast warnings and advise how long it is safe to stay outside. This is your cue to scuttle below ground into Toronto's PATH system (p91). For more on avoiding and treating exposure, see p880.

SIGHTS

The glut of Toronto's sights can be found in the scenically refurbished Harbourfront and nearby financial district, both at the southern end of downtown. Galleries, waterparks, sports stadiums, gardens and historical sights mingle there. Just offshore are the Toronto Islands, where folk head to soak up the peace and admire the skyline views.

Many of Toronto's oldest and best-preserved buildings sit just east of Union Station in the neighborhood of Old York.

North from the lake, modernity and history mix around Dundas Sq, with shopping centers, office blocks, museums and majestic theatres all occupying their own plots.

TORONTO BY THE NUMBERS

- Canadian immigrants who settle in Toronto: 1 out of every 4
- Tibetan Buddhist temples in the Megacity: 3
- Unemployment rate: 8.6%
- Number of municipal beaches: 14
- Percentage of the US population within a day's drive of Toronto: 50%
- Number of bridges: 535
- Population density per square kilometer: 3800
- Total length of city sidewalks: 7060km
- Median family income: $64,000
- Estimated number of visitors during Pride Week: 1 million

This spirited atmosphere continues well into the domain of UT and The Annex, where you'll find gracious old mansions, eccentric markets and even a faux castle. On the eastern side of this district you land smack bang in Toronto's ritzy Bloor-Yorkville, where excellent museums and galleries offer their visual wares alongside designer shops.

Harbourfront

At the foot of Yonge and York Sts are Lake Ontario and the redeveloped waterfront area called Harbourfront. Once a run-down district of warehouses, factories and docklands, the area now teems with folk of all ages milling about the restaurants, theaters, galleries, artists' workshops, stores, condominiums and parkland all along Queens Quay. Ferries (p115) for the Toronto Islands dock here.

YORK QUAY CENTRE

Throughout the summer, particularly on weekends, the **Harbourfront Centre** (Map pp80–1; ☎ 416-973-3000, box office 416-973-4000; www.harbourfront.on.ca; 235 Queens Quay W; ☽ most galleries open Tue–Sun; streetcar 509, 510) puts on a kaleidoscopic variety of performing arts shows, many especially for kids and some free. Performances sometimes take place on the covered outdoor concert stage beside the lake.

Also outside are the unusual **Artists' Gardens**; pick up a brochure at the Harbourfront Centre information desk by the box office.

Admission is free to all the indoor galleries, which include the **Photo Passage** and the **Craft Studio** (☎ 416-973-4963; ☺ 10am-6pm Tue & Sun, 10am-8pm Wed-Sat), where artists blow hot glass, mold clay, weave textiles, design jewelry and teach classes.

West of the Harbourfront center is the **Power Plant** (Map pp80-1; ☎ 416-973-4949; www.the powerplant.org; 231 Queens Quay W; adult/child under 12/student/senior $4/free/2/2, admission free 5-8pm Wed; ☺ noon-6pm Tue-Sun, noon-8pm Wed; streetcar 509, 510), a gallery that celebrates contemporary Canadian art, one artist at a time. Its focus is painting, sculpture and large-scale installations. Free talks by visiting artists and curators, and tours led by the gallery director, will enhance your appreciation.

QUEEN'S QUAY TERMINAL

This refurbished 1926 **warehouse** (Map pp80-1; ☎ 416-203-0510; www.toronto.com/queensquay; 207 Queens Quay W; ☺ most shops open 10am-6pm; streetcar 509, 510) is filled with skylights, arts-and-crafts shops and the Premier Dance Theatre. It's a picturesque beginning for a harborfront stroll, which would not be complete without the vociferous ticket sellers hawking harbor cruises outside (see p94).

TORONTO MUSIC GARDEN

Delicately strung along the western harbourfront, this **garden** (Map pp80-1; 475 Queens Quay W; admission free; ☺ dawn-dusk; streetcar 509, 510) was designed in collaboration with cellist Yo-Yo Ma. It expresses Bach's *Suite No 1 for Unaccompanied Cello* through landscape, with an arc-shaped grove of conifers, a swirling path through a wildflower meadow and a grass-stepped amphitheatre where free concerts are held. Contact the Harbourfront Centre box office in York Quay Centre (opposite) for performance schedules.

ONTARIO PLACE

This 40-hectare **recreation complex** (Map pp76-7; ☎ 416-314-9900, 866-663-4386; www.ontarioplace.com; 955 Lake Shore Blvd W; grounds admission before/after 5pm $13/5; ☺ 10am-4pm Jun, 10am-8pm Jul & Aug, 10am-6pm Sat & Sun late May & Sep) is built on three artificial islands and poses the best fun you can have beating the summer heat. A 'Play All Day' pass (adult/child $29/15) entitles you to most of the thrill rides and attractions, including **Soak City** waterpark and walk-up seating at the **Cinesphere**, where 70mm IMAX films are shown on a six-story-high curved screen. Parents should know about the H2O Generation Station, a popular children's soft-play climbing area where you can let 'em go nuts. Additional attractions, such as the human-sized **MegaMaze** and House of Blues concerts at the **Molson Amphitheatre** (Map pp80-1; ☎ 416-260-5600), must be paid for separately. On rainy days, many of the activities, restaurants and rides do not operate.

A free red trolley operates between the clock tower on the Front St side of Union Station and Ontario Place, running every half-hour from 8:30am to 7pm on weekends. Otherwise, take the streetcar to Exhibition Place and trek through the grounds and over Lakeshore Bridge.

EXHIBITION PLACE

Each year these historic **grounds** (Map pp76-7; ☎ 416-263-3600; off Lake Shore Blvd W, btwn Strachan Ave & Dufferin St; streetcar 509, 511) are revived for their original purpose, the Canadian National Exhibition (p96). During 'The Ex' millions of visitors flood the midway for carnival rides, lumberjack competitions and home-grown fun. The beaux-arts Victory statue over Princes' Gate has flown aloft since 1927, when Canada celebrated its 60th birthday.

Other events held at Exhibition Place throughout the year include the Molson Indy (p95) and a variety of spectator sports and indie design shows. At other times the grounds are often bereft of visitors.

FORT YORK

Established by the British in 1793 to protect the town of York (as Toronto was then known), this hoary **fort** (Map pp76-7; ☎ 416-392-6907; Garrison Rd, off Fleet St W east of Strachan Ave; admission & tours adult/child $5/3; ☺ 10am-5pm Jun-Aug, 10am-4pm Sep-May, closed mid-Dec–early Jan, tours hourly; streetcar 509, 511) was almost entirely destroyed during the War of 1812 when a small band of Ojibwe warriors and British troops couldn't stop the US fleet.

Today a handful of the original log, stone and brick buildings have been restored. In summer, men decked out in 19th-century British military uniforms carry out marches and drills and fire musket volleys, but kids much prefer running around the fort's embankments with wooden rifles. If you get lost looking for the fort, just look for the old Union Jack waving in the breeze.

ONTARIO

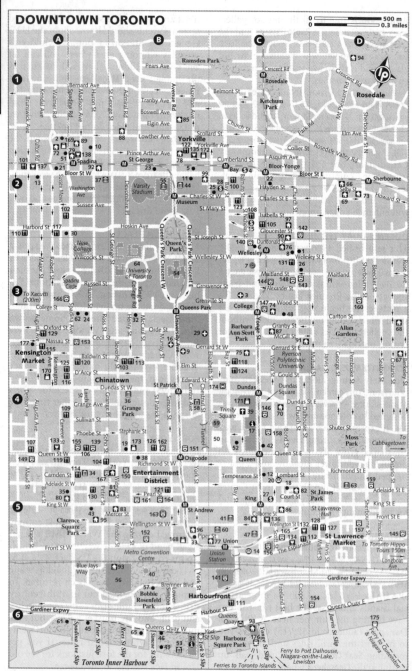

DOWNTOWN TORONTO

STEAM WHISTLE BREWING

This **microbrewery** (Map pp80-1; ☎ 416-362-2337, 866-240-2337; www.steamwhistle.ca; 255 Bremner Blvd; admission free, 30min tours $4; 🕑 noon-6pm Mon-Sat, tours hourly 1-4pm; streetcar 509, 510) specializes in a crisp European-style Pilsner. In fact, that's all they make! During snappy tours of the premises, guides will actually blow the railway roundhouse's historic steam whistle. Tours include free tastings at the brewery's retail store and a souvenir glass or bottle opener. Call to check

INFORMATION
- 519 Community Centre **1** C3
- Alliance Française **2** A2
- Ambulatory Care Centre **3** C3
- American Express **4** C2
- Chapters Books & Magazines **5** B2
- Glad Day Books & Magazines **6** C3
- Grey Region Comics **7** C3
- Hassle-Free Clinic **8** C3
- Hospital for Sick Children **9** B4
- Italian Cultural Institute **10** A2
- Japan Foundation **11** B2
- Kinko's **12** C5
- Kinko's **13** A2
- Main Post Office **14** C5
- Money Mart **15** C2
- Mount Sinai Hospital **16** B3
- Ontario Tourism **17** C4
- Open Air Books & Maps **18** C5
- Pages Books & Magazines **19** B4
- Post Office **20** C5
- Shoppers Drug Mart **21** A2
- Spanish Centre **22** C2
- STA Travel **23** B2
- STA Travel **24** A3
- TheatreBooks **25** C2
- This Ain't the Rosedale Library **26** C3
- Thomas Cook **27** C5
- Thomas Cook **28** C2
- Toronto General Hospital **29** B3
- Toronto Women's Bookstore **30** A2
- Tourism Toronto **31** B6
- Travel CUTS **32** B3
- Travel CUTS **33** B5
- University of Toronto-St George Campus **64** B3
- Wheel Excitement **65** B6
- York Quay Centre (see 46)

SIGHTS & ACTIVITIES (pp78-94)
- 401 Richmond **34** A5
- Art at 80 **35** A5
- Art Gallery of Ontario **36** B4
- Bata Shoe Museum **37** A2
- Chum/Citytv Complex **38** B5
- Church of the Holy Trinity **39** C4
- CN Tower **40** B6
- Design Exchange **41** C5
- Elgin & Winter Garden Theatre Centre **42** C4
- Europe Bound Outfitters **43** A5
- Gardiner Museum of Ceramic Art **44** B2
- Great Lakes Schooner Company (see 31)
- Grey Line Tours (see 174)
- Harbourfront Boating Centre **45** A6
- Harbourfront Canoe & Kayak Centre (see 45)
- Harbourfront Centre **46** B6
- Hockey Hall of Fame **47** C5
- Maple Leaf Gardens **48** C3
- Mariposa Cruise Lines (see 31)
- Molson Amphitheatre **49** B6
- Nathan Phillips Square **50** C4
- Native Canadian Centre of Toronto **51** A2
- Old City Hall **52** C4
- Power Plant **53** B6
- Provincial Legislature **54** B3
- Queen's Quay Terminal (see 31)
- Royal Ontario Museum **55** B2
- Skydome **56** B6
- Steam Whistle Brewing **57** B6
- Textile Museum of Canada **58** B4
- Toronto City Hall **59** C4
- Toronto Dominion Gallery of Inuit Art **60** C5
- Toronto Music Garden **61** A6
- Toronto Public Library – Lillian H Smith Branch **62** A3
- Toronto Tours Ltd (see 31)
- Toronto's First Post Office **63** D5

SLEEPING (pp96-101)
- 1871 Historic House **66** D2
- Albert's Inn **67** D4
- Amsterdam Guesthouse **68** D3
- Au Petit Paris **69** D2
- Bond Place Hotel **70** C4
- Canadiana Backpackers Inn **71** B5
- Casa Loma Inn **72** A2
- Clarion Hotel and Suites Selby **73** D2
- Days Inn Toronto Downtown **74** C3
- Delta Chelsea Toronto Downtown **75** C4
- Dundonald House **76** C3
- Fairmont Royal York **77** C5
- Four Seasons **78** B2
- Global Guesthouse **79** A2
- Global Village Backpackers **80** A5
- Holiday Inn on King **81** B5
- Hostelling International Toronto **82** C5
- Hôtel Le Germain **83** B5
- Hotel Victoria **84** C5
- Howard Johnson Inn **85** B1
- Le Royal Meridien King Edward **86** C5
- Les Amis Bed & Breakfast **87** C3
- Lowther House **88** B2
- Madison Manor **89** A2
- Mansion **90** C2
- Neill-Wycik College Hotel **91** C3
- Quality Hotel **92** A2
- Renaissance Toronto Hotel at SkyDome **93** B6
- Robin's Nest **94** D1
- SoHo Metropolitan Hotel **95** A5
- Strathcona Hotel **96** B5
- Victoria's Mansion Inn & Guesthouse **97** C2
- Westin Harbour Castle **98** C6
- Windsor Arms **99** B2

EATING (pp101-6)
- Bloor St Diner **100** C2
- By the Way **101** A2
- Cora Pizza **102** A2
- Eating Garden **103** B4
- Fez Batik **104** A5
- Fire on the East Side **105** C2
- Fresh by Juice for Life **106** A4
- Fressen **107** A4
- Friendly Thai **108** C2
- Furama Cake & Dessert Garden **109** A4
- Harbord Fish & Chips **110** A2
- Harbour Sixty Steakhouse **111** C6
- Jamie Kennedy Wine Bar **112** C5
- Jodhpore Club **113** B4
- Jules Restaurant Tarterie **114** A5
- Jumbo Empanadas **115** A4
- Kim Thanh **116** A4
- Kubo DX (see 41)
- Latitude **117** A2
- Le Commensal **118** C4
- Le Gourmand **119** A5
- Lee Garden **120** A4
- Marche Mövenpick (see 47)
- Mata Hari Grill (see 103)
- Monsoon **121** B5
- Mövenpick's Bistretto & La Pêcherie **122** B2
- Okonomi House **123** C2
- Oro **124** C4
- Phõ' Hu'ng **125** A4
- Phõ' Hu'ng (see 23)
- Queen Mother Café **126** B4
- St Lawrence Market & Hall **127** D5
- Sen5es (see 95)
- Spring Rolls **128** D5
- Streams of Blessings Fish Shack **129** A3
- YYZ Restaurant & Wine Bar **130** A5
- Zelda's **131** C3

DRINKING (pp106-7)
- C'est What **132** C5
- Cameron House **133** A4
- Esplanada Bier Markt **134** C5
- Hemingway's **135** B2
- Irish Embassy Pub & Grill **136** C5
- James Joyce Traditional Irish Pub **137** A2
- Madison Avenue Pub **138** A2
- nia (see 132)
- Woody's/Sailor (see 143)

ENTERTAINMENT (pp107-12)
- 360 **139** A4
- 5ive **140** C3
- Air Canada Centre **141** C6
- B-Side (see 104)
- Babylon **142** C2
- Black Eagle **143** C3
- Buddies in Bad Times Theatre **144** C3
- Canadian Opera Company (see 156)
- Canadian Stage Company **145** D5
- Canon Theatre **146** C4
- Cinemathique Ontario (see 36)
- Cineplex Odeon Carlton **147** C3
- Cineplex Odeon Varsity (see 100)
- Crews/Tango/Zone **148** C3
- Element **149** A5
- Famous Players Paramount **150** B5
- Four Seasons Centre **151** B4
- Glenn Gould Studio **152** B5
- Grossman's **153** A3
- Guvernment **154** D6
- Horseshoe Tavern **155** A4
- Hummingbird Centre for the Performing Arts **156** C5
- Lorraine Kimsa Theatre for Young People **157** D5
- Massey Hall **158** C4
- Montréal Bistro & Jazz Club **159** D5
- Phoenix **160** D3
- Princess of Wales Theatre **161** B5
- Rex **162** B4
- Roy Thomson Hall **163** B5
- Royal Alexandra Theatre **164** B5
- St Lawrence Centre for the Arts **165** C5
- Silver Dollar Room **166** A3
- System Soundbar **167** A5
- Tallulah's Cabaret (see 144)
- Toronto Symphony Orchestra (see 163)
- Wild Oscar's (see 148)

SHOPPING (pp112-3)
- Arctic Nunavut (see 31)
- Bay of Spirits Gallery **168** B5
- Cedar Basket **169** A2
- Courage My Love **170** A4
- Eaton Centre **171** C4
- Guild Shop **172** B2
- John Fluevog **173** B4

TRANSPORT (pp113-16)
- Metro Toronto Coach Terminal **174** C4
- New Frontier Rent-a-Car (see 81)
- Seaflight Hydrofoils **175** D6
- Toronto Island Ferries **176** C6
- Wheels 4 Rent **177** A3

hours and tour schedules, which are subject to change.

Toronto Islands

The Toronto Islands were once an immense sandbar, stretching 9km out into the lake from the foot of present-day Woodbine Ave. On April 13, 1858, however, a hurricane-force storm cut through the sandbar and created the Gap (now known as the Eastern Channel), forming Toronto's jewel-like islands. All the islands are now connected to each other by bridges or footpaths. The islands are only accessible by a 10-minute ferry ride (see p115).

CENTRE ISLAND PARK

From the ferry terminal, head past the information booth and first aid station to quaint **Centreville Amusement Park** (Map pp76-7; ☎ 416-203-0405; www.centreisland.ca; grounds admission free, rides 75¢, day-pass $17-23; ☯ 10:30am-5pm Mon-Fri & 10:30am-8pm Sat & Sun late May–early Sep, weekends only early May–mid-May & early Sep–mid-Sep, weather permitting). Scattered across a few hundred acres are an antique carousel, goofy golf course, miniature train rides, sky gondola and even a petting zoo, **Far Enough Farm**.

Head south over the bridge toward the splashing fountains and gardens, where you'll find an English-style hedge maze and ticket booths for tram tours (30-minute ride per adult/child/concession $5/2/4) of the island. To the east is a boathouse where canoes, kayaks and paddleboats can be rented ($15 to $25 per hour). On the south shore are changing rooms, lockers (rental $2), snack bars, bicycle rentals and a pier leading out into the lake.

HANLAN'S POINT

At the western end of Centre Island, by the Toronto City Centre Airport (TCAA) is this sporty **point** (Map pp76-7), named after world champion sculler 'Ned' Hanlan, a member of the first family to settle here year-round. Interestingly, the point was once known as the 'Coney Island of Canada.' Babe Ruth hit his first professional home run here in 1914 while playing minor-league baseball – the ball drowned in Lake Ontario.

Following the paved paths past picnic tables and barbecue pits brings you near Hanlan's Point Beach, the best of the islands. Popular for years, especially with gay men, the 'clothing optional' status of this beach was finally legalized by the city council in 1999. Civic-minded island volunteers distribute 'naked-beach etiquette' flyers to new arrivals. Officially, the beach is only supervised during July and August.

WARD'S ISLAND

At the western end of Ward's Island is a Frisbee golf course and a groovy children's fort, both free. An old-fashioned boardwalk runs all along the south shore of the island, passing the back gate of the Rectory (p101) café.

Old York

Historically speaking, the old town of York comprises just 10 square blocks. But today it extends east of Yonge St all the way to the Don River, and from Queen St south to the waterfront Esplanade. This is an excellent area to see the remains of Toronto's past.

DISTILLERY HISTORIC DISTRICT

This rousing **complex** (Map pp76-7; ☎ 416-866-8687; www.thedistillerydistrict.com; 55 Mill St; admission free; ☯ 10am-6pm Tue-Sun, later in summer; streetcar 503, 504), at the 1832 Gooderham and Worts distillery, is full of cobblestone streets and Victorian warehouses converted into galleries, artists' studios, design shops, coffee houses and restaurants – even a brewery. The self-guided audio tours aren't very riveting, so join one of the more lively guided tours ($5 to $6) departing from the visitors' center on Trinity St, just south of the main gates. Tours (which require a minimum of six people) run on demand. Booking is mandatory.

ST LAWRENCE MARKET & HALL

Old York's **market** (Map pp80-1; ☎ 416-392-7120; www.stlawrencemarket.com; South Market, 2 Front St E; admission free; ☯ 8am-6pm Tue-Thu, 8am-7pm Fri, 5am-5pm Sat; streetcar 504) has been a neighborhood meeting place for over two centuries. The restored **South Market** building, which houses specialty food vendors (see p101), dates back to Toronto's 1845 city hall.

Inside the old council chambers upstairs, the **Market Gallery** (☎ 416-392-7604; admission free; ☯ 10am-4pm Wed-Fri, 9am-4pm Sat, noon-4pm Sun) is now the city's exhibition hall, with displays of paintings, photographs, documents and historical artifacts.

On the opposite side of Front St, the **North Market** comes alive with a Saturday farmers' market and an antiques market on Sunday. After being sadly neglected, it was rebuilt around the time of Canada's 100th birthday in 1967.

A few steps further north, the glorious **St Lawrence Hall** (1849), topped by a clock tower that can be seen for blocks, is considered one of the city's finest examples of Victorian classicism.

TORONTO'S FIRST POST OFFICE

Dating from the 1830s, the old **post office** (Map pp80-1; 416-865-1833; www.townofyork.com; 260 Adelaide St E; admission by donation; 9am-4pm Mon-Fri, 10am-4pm Sat & Sun; streetcar 503, 504) is now a living museum. After you have written your correspondence with a quill pen and ink, costumed staff will seal the letter with wax and send it postmarked 'York-Toronto 1833' for a small fee. Self-guided tour pamphlets are available by the front door, where a gift shop sells Victorian-style writing materials. At the back of the old-fashioned reading room are interesting historical displays about the old town of York and a model of Toronto c 1873. Famous folks such as William Lyon Mackenzie and the Baldwins once rented postal boxes here. To find the post office, look for the British and Canadian flags flying out front, just west of the Bank of Upper Canada building.

Downtown Toronto

This area covers several boroughs in downtown Toronto. The area around Union Station, known as the **Financial District**, is kept busy night and day with briskly pacing executives, disoriented tourists and folk heading to hockey games (p111) at Air Canada Centre. West of the Financial District, occupying two blocks of King St W, between John St and Simcoe St, is Toronto's **Entertainment District** (nicknamed Clubland).

Heading north on Yonge St, **Dundas Sq** is the city's newest public space with an outdoor concert stage right in the heart of downtown. It's often better known for the nearby landmark, **Eaton Centre**, which sprawls between Queen and Dundas Sts. Both are located south of the main Yonge St strip and east of the Queen St shopping district.

West of Dundas Sq, occupying one short block of Baldwin St between Beverly and McCaul Sts, is shady **Baldwin Village**. The village has Jewish roots, but the bohemian air comes from counterculture US exiles who decamped here during the Vietnam War. Today Baldwin St resembles a Manhattan-esque movie set, complete with Italian sidewalk cafés.

Heading further west will land you in Toronto's vibrant **Chinatown**, which occupies a chunk of Spadina Ave between College and Queen Sts. A brilliant vermilion twin dragon gate stands on Spadina Ave, just north of Dundas St W, marking the epicenter.

North of Dundas Sq, the main **Yonge St strip** falls between College and Bloor Sts. Often called the 'longest road in the world,' it's peppered with shops and entertainment, although it may seem to be the start of the world's longest, most unrelenting strip of porn theaters, exotic-dance venues and XXX lingerie boutiques. One long block east is Church St, Toronto's gay quarter. The rainbow flag–festooned **Church-Wellesley Village** has its epicenter at the intersection of Church and Wellesley Sts.

CN TOWER

The **Canadian National Tower** (Map pp80-1; 416-868-6937; www.cntower.ca; 301 Front St W; main observation deck adult/child 4-12/senior $19/14/17, Sky-Pod deck extra $5; 10am-10pm, later in summer; subway Union) is the highest freestanding structure (553m) in the world, and most visitors feel obligated to take a gander at this city icon. Its primary function is radio and TV communications, but relieving tourists of as much cash as possible is another priority. Glass elevators whisk you up the outside to observation decks at the top. For extra thrills, one deck has a glass floor, and the other is a windy, vertigo-inducing outside platform. On a clear day, you can see for about 160km, and at night the tower provides a spectacular view of the city lights. If it's hazy, however, you won't be able to see a thing. Summer queues for the elevator can be up to two hours long – going up *and* coming back down. For those with reservations at the award-winning revolving restaurant, **360** (416-362-5411; prix fixe dinner adult/child $65/37.50; dinner year-round, lunch May-Dec), the elevator ticket price is waived.

ONTARIO

ART GALLERY OF ONTARIO

The collections of the **AGO** (Map pp80-1; ☎ 416-979-6648; www.ago.net; 317 Dundas St W; adult/youth 6-15/student/senior/family $12/6/9/9/25, admission free 6-8:30pm Wed; ☟ 11am-6pm Tue-Fri, 11am-8:30pm Wed, 10am-5:30pm Sat & Sun; streetcar 505) are excellent, and unless you have a lot of stamina, you'll need more than one trip to see them all. Highlights include rare Québecois religious statuary, First Nations and Inuit carvings, and major Canadian works by Emily Carr (p699) and the Group of Seven (p117). The museum is known for its Henry Moore sculpture pavilion, which has benches with sit-down listening stations (one recounts the controversy over City Hall's acquisition of Moore's work).

Looking out onto its own park, the **Grange** (☎ 416-977-0414; admission included with AGO ticket) is a restored Georgian house that's part of the AGO. There's authentic mid-19th-century furniture, and staff in period dress present life in a 'gentleman's residence' of the time, staying in character without so much as a snicker. The Grange may be open shorter hours than the AGO.

For schedules of free gallery tours, art play for kids, special events and films at the Cinematheque Ontario (p109), call ☎ 416-979-6649, check at the information desk or go to the museum's website, which also has updates on Transformation AGO, a project of extensive gallery renovations and expansion overseen by famed architect Frank Gehry, whose childhood home is nearby.

HOCKEY HALL OF FAME

In a gorgeous, gray stone rococo Bank of Montreal building (c 1885), this hockey **shrine** (Map pp80-1; ☎ 416-360-7765; www.hhof .com; lower concourse, BC Pl, 30 Yonge St; adult/child under 3/youth 4-13/senior $12.50/free/8; ☟ 10am-5pm Mon-Fri, 9:30am-6pm Sat, 10:30am-5pm Sun, to 6pm daily during summer; subway Union) gives fans everything they could possibly want. You can attempt to stop Wayne Gretzky's winning shot (in virtual reality) or have your photo taken with hockey's biggest prize – the one and only Stanley Cup. After being overwhelmed by interactive multimedia exhibits and nostalgic hockey memorabilia, even visitors unfamiliar with the game may come to an understanding of Canada's passion for one of the fastest (and most violent!) sports.

ELGIN & WINTER GARDEN THEATRE CENTRE

A restored masterpiece, the **theater** (Map pp80-1; ☎ 416-314-2871; www.heritagefdn.on.ca; 189 Yonge St; tours adult/student/senior $7/6/6; ☟ tours usually given at 5pm Thu & 11am Sat; subway Queen) represents the last operating double-decker theater in the world. In 1913 the breathtaking Winter Garden was built as the flagship for a vaudeville chain that never really took off, while the downstairs Elgin was converted into a movie house in the 1920s.

The Ontario Heritage Foundation saved both theaters from demolition in 1981. During a $29-million restoration, bread dough was used to uncover original rose-garden frescoes, the Belgian-made carpeting was replaced and the beautiful foliage hanging from the ceiling of the Winter Garden was replaced, leaf by painstaking leaf. New seats were bought from Chicago's infamous Biograph Theater.

Entertaining public tours, which are worth every penny, are given by the same passionate volunteers who staff the theaters' ongoing restoration efforts. See p110 for box office information.

TORONTO DOMINION GALLERY OF INUIT ART

Housed inside a Toronto-Dominion Centre tower, this **gallery** (Map pp80-1; ☎ 416-982-8473; ground fl & mezzanine, Maritime Life Tower, Toronto-Dominion Centre, 79 Wellington St W; admission free; ☟ 8am-6pm Mon-Fri, 10am-4pm Sat & Sun; subway St Andrew) provides an exceptional insight into Inuit culture. The gallery contains outstanding aboriginal carvings and sculptures in stone and bone.

CHUM/CITYTV COMPLEX

At the corner of John St, this **complex** (Map pp80-1; ☎ 416-599-7339; www.mztv.com; 277 Queen St W; museum admission adult/student/senior/family $6/4/4/18; ☟ museum tours noon, 2pm & 4pm Mon-Fri; streetcar 501) includes a public video booth, the infamous **Speakers Corner**. Anyone can step inside and, for just a loonie ($1), record themselves saying or doing pretty much anything. Creative and controversial segments are broadcast on Canada's original reality TV show, *Speakers Corner*. At the adjacent studios of MuchMusic, the Canadian version of MTV, you might see pop stars dashing from their limos as teen fans cheer à la Beatlemania; every Wednesday afternoon, kids decked out in full-on club gear wait in line to get picked as dancers on *Electric Circus*. Above the east parking lot, a CityPulse news truck spins its wheels as it crashes out of the Citytv studio walls. At the back of the logo shop, almost opposite McCaul St, the **MZTV Museum** displays vintage TV sets.

CITY HALL

Much-maligned **City Hall** (Map pp80-1; ☎ 416-392-7341; www.city.toronto.on.ca; 100 Queen St W; admission free; ✹ 8:30am-4:30pm Mon-Fri; subway Queen) was Toronto's first advance into architectural modernity. Its twin clamshell towers, and the flying saucer–style structure between them at the bottom, were completed in 1965 to Finnish architect Viljo Revell's award-winning design. Frank Lloyd Wright called it a 'head marker for a grave,' and in a twist of fate Revell died before construction was finished. When sculptor Henry Moore first offered to sell *The Archer,* located in the gardens, from his own personal collection and at a low price, the city council (unbelievably) refused. Ask for a self-guided tour pamphlet (available in eight languages) at the information desk in the lobby.

Out front is Nathan Phillips Sq, a meeting place for skaters, demonstrators and office workers on their lunch breaks. In summer, look out for a farmers' market (held from 10am to 2:30pm Wednesday), free concerts and special events. The fountain pool becomes a popular ice-skating rink during winter. Don't feel intimidated if you are a novice – you won't be alone. Immigrants from around the world are out there gingerly making strides toward assimilation.

On the other side of Bay St is **Old City Hall** (1899). It was the definitive work of Toronto architect EJ Lennox, the same man who built Casa Loma (p87). Lennox was chastised for inscribing his name just below the eaves here. Now housing court rooms, this distinctive Romanesque hall has an off-center bell tower, painted murals and an allegorical stained-glass window. First-floor exhibits are open to the public.

SKYDOME

As technically awe-inspiring as CN Tower, this **sports stadium** (Map pp80-1; ☎ 416-341-2770; www.skydome.com; 1 Blue Jays Way; 1hr tours adult/child 5-11/youth 12-17 $12.50/7/8.50; ✹ tour schedules vary, French-language tours Jul & Aug; subway Union) opened in 1989 and had the world's first fully retractable dome roof. Made mostly of concrete, this feat of engineering moves at a rapid 22m per minute, taking just 20 minutes to completely open. That beats Montréal's Olympic Stadium, which opened once and failed to ever do so again.

Tours are pricey for what you get. After watching a 10-minute introductory film, the tour sprints up to a box suite, takes in the view from the stands and press section, and briefly walks through a locker room (without athletes). Did you know that eight 747s would fit on the playing field and that the stadium uses enough electricity to light the province of Prince Edward Island?

A cheap seat to a Blue Jays game (p111) is the least expensive way to see the SkyDome. Rooms overlooking the field can be rented at the SkyDome's own hotel, the Renaissance Toronto (p98).

Before leaving, look for the faces of Michael Snow's *Audience* sculptures gazing back at you from their perch high up on SkyDome's northern exterior.

TEXTILE MUSEUM OF CANADA

Although obscurely situated, this small **museum** (Map pp80-1; ☎ 416-599-5321; www.textilemuseum.ca; 55 Centre Ave; adult/student/family $8/6/22, admission by donation 5-8pm Wed; ✹ 11am-5pm Tue-Fri, 11am-8pm Wed, noon-5pm Sat & Sun; gallery tours usually 2pm Sun; subway St Patrick) will delight anyone with the slightest interest in handmade textiles and tapestries. Exhibits draw upon a permanent collection of almost 10,000 items from Latin America, Africa, Europe, Southeast Asia and India, as well as contemporary Canada. Workshops teach batik, weaving, knitting and more.

DESIGN EXCHANGE

A streamlined moderne building, the **Design Exchange** (Map pp80-1; ☎ 416-363-6121; www.dx.org; 234 Bay St; admission free, surcharge for special exhibitions; ✹ 10am-6pm Mon-Fri, noon-5pm Sat & Sun; subway King) served as the original Toronto Stock Exchange from 1937, and its opening pushed Toronto ahead of Montréal as Canada's financial center. Note the art deco stone friezes and the medallions on the stainless steel doors depicting toilers in the nation's industries. Inside are eye-catching temporary exhibits of contemporary industrial design and a unique gift shop.

ONTARIO

401 RICHMOND

Admirers have called this sprawling **arts complex** (Map pp80-1; ☎ 416-595-5900; www.401richmond .net; 401 Richmond St W; admission free; ☯ most galleries Tue–Sat; streetcar 510) a 'city within a city,' and it certainly lives up to the moniker. Inside an early 20th-century lithographer's warehouse, 401 Richmond is bursting with diverse contemporary art and design galleries for painters, holographers, photographers, printmakers, sculptors, milliners and other arty folks. It has a glass elevator, ground-floor artists' café and roof garden, too. After your visit, swing by **Art at 80** (Map pp80-1; 80 Spadina Ave; ☯ Tue–Sat), another varied contemporary gallery complex, just two blocks away.

MAPLE LEAF GARDENS

This hallowed **hockey arena** (Map pp80-1; 60 Carlton St; subway College) was home to the Toronto Maple Leafs for over half a century, starting with the opening game against the Chicago Blackhawks in 1931. Although the Leafs lost that game, they went on to win nearly a dozen Stanley Cup championships and play a record-breaking number of sold-out seasons before moving to the **Air Canada Centre** (p111) in 1999. Over the years, Elvis Presley, Frank Sinatra and the Beatles all performed at Maple Leaf Gardens.

Rumors that this much-loved piece of city history was to be torn down are only partly true. Stirring up mixed emotions, the Gardens are to be turned into a fairly substantial grocery store, which will also sell 'non-food offerings.' Although this seems a sad postscript for hockey fans, much of the exterior of the building will remain intact and development will be done in conjunction with Heritage Toronto.

Bloor-Yorkville

Once Toronto's version of Greenwich Village or Haight-Ashbury, the old counter-cultural bastion of **Yorkville** has become the city's *trés* glamorous shopping district, done up with art galleries, towering condos, glitzy nightspots, exclusive restaurants and outdoor cafés. Yet antiques shops in well-preserved Victorian houses and atmospheric Old York Lane provide glimpses of yesteryear.

Bloor-Yorkville officially stretches from Yonge St west to Avenue Rd and beyond it into The Annex. Its southern boundary is

---

> **TOP FIVE PLACES TO ESCAPE THE CROWDS**
>
> ▪ **Toronto Music Garden** (p79) Harbourfront
>
> ▪ **Toronto Dominion Gallery of Inuit Art** (p84) Financial District
>
> ▪ **Church of the Holy Trinity** (p92) Dundas Sq
>
> ▪ **Roof Garden at 401 Richmond** (left) Chinatown
>
> ▪ **Gardiner Museum of Ceramic Art** (opposite) Bloor-Yorkville

---

along fashionable Bloor St, with the neighborhood's northern edge at curvaceous Davenport Rd.

ROYAL ONTARIO MUSEUM

The multidisciplinary **ROM** (Map pp80-1; ☎ 416-586-5549; www.rom.on.ca; 100 Queen's Park; adult/child 5-14/student/senior $15/10/12/12, admission free 4:30-9:30pm Fri, surcharge for special exhibitions; ☯ 10am-6pm Mon–Thu & Sat, 10am-9:30pm Fri, 11am-6pm Sun; subway Museum) was Canada's largest museum even before it embarked upon Renaissance ROM, an ambitious building project due to be completed in late 2005. After renovations are complete, the museum will boast a panoramic restaurant, eye-catching 'crystal' galleries overlooking Bloor St and new space for international traveling exhibitions.

Meanwhile the museum remains open. ROM's collections are weighty, filling five floors with natural science, ancient civilization and art exhibits. The Chinese temple sculptures, **Gallery of Korean Art** and costumery and textile collections are some of the best in the world. Kids will be mesmerized by the dinosaur rooms, Egyptian mummies and a replica of an immense bat cave found in Jamaica. Also worth searching out are four towering cedar **crest poles** carved by First Nations tribes in British Columbia; the largest (85m) was shipped from the West Coast by train, then lowered through the museum roof, leaving only centimeters to spare. Other highlights include the **Institute of Contemporary Culture**, where temporary media and design exhibits might feature Frank Lloyd Wright furniture or modern photography.

All of this said, a quick walk-through satisfies most visitors and the best time to visit is on Friday night, when admission is free and there's always a lively special event. If you're driving, ask at the front desk for discount parking vouchers valid at the 9 Bedford Rd municipal lot.

BATA SHOE MUSEUM

This innovative **museum** (Map pp80-1; ☎ 416-979-7799; www.batashoemuseum.ca; 327 Bloor St W; adult/child 5-14/student/senior/family $6/2/4/4/12, admission free from 5pm Thu; ☷ 10am-5pm Tue-Wed, Fri & Sat, 10am-8pm Thu, noon-5pm Sun; subway St George), designed by famed architect Raymond Moriyama to resemble a stylized shoebox, stands on fashion-conscious Bloor St. It has much more to offer than you might at first imagine. Over 10,000 'pedi-artifacts' from every corner of the globe were hunted down by Sonja Bata, of the same family that founded Canada's famous shoe company. Children and adults will gaze in fascination at the museum's 19th-century French chestnut-crushing clogs, aboriginal polar boots and famous modern pairs worn by Elton John, Indira Gandhi and Pablo Picasso.

Beginning with a replica set of footprints almost four million years old, the permanent exhibits cover the evolution of the shoe-making craft, as well as human footwear, both gruesome and gorgeous, with a focus on how shoes have signified social status throughout human history. Regularly changing exhibitions on special topics are just as thoughtfully curated. On the 3rd floor you can peek through glass windows at curators restoring shoes. The museum's website lets you view some of the treasures online.

GARDINER MUSEUM OF CERAMIC ART

This small **museum** (Map pp80-1; ☎ 416-586-8080; www.gardinermuseum.on.ca; 111 Queen's Park; adult/student/senior/family $10/6/6/24, admission free 1st Tue each month; ☷ 10am-6pm Mon, Wed & Fri, 10am-8pm Tue & Thu, 10am-5pm Sat & Sun; subway Museum) was founded by philanthropists who were passionate collectors themselves. The museum's excellent collections of ceramics are spread over two floors and cover several millennia of art history, focusing on pre-Columbian wares from Mexico, Central and South America, Italian Renaissance majolica, 17th-century English tavern ware

and blue-and-white Chinese porcelain designed for export to European markets.

On certain days you can take a guided tour or drop in at the Clay Pit for hands-on pottery demonstrations; call for schedules. The museum gift shop has free exhibitions by contemporary Canadian potters that are well worth browsing. Note the museum is closed for renovations until fall 2005.

University of Toronto & The Annex

Founded in 1827, the prestigious University of Toronto (UT) is Canada's largest university, with almost 40,000 full-time students and over 10,000 faculty and staff. Its venerability is obvious after just a quick wander around the central St George campus with its distinct college quadrangles.

West and north of the UT campus lies **The Annex**, a residential neighborhood populated primarily by students and professors. It overflows with pubs, organic grocery stores, global-minded eateries and spiritual venues.

CASA LOMA

Literally the 'House on a Hill,' this mock medieval-style **castle** (Map pp76-7; ☎ 416-923-1171; www.casaloma.org; 1 Austin Tce; adult/child 4-13/youth 14-17/senior $12/6.75/7.50/7.50; ☷ 9:30am-5pm, last entry 4pm, gardens free 4pm-dusk Tue May-Oct; subway Dupont) proudly juts up above The Annex proper. It's best reached on foot via the scenic Baldwin Steps, leading up from Spadina Ave, north of Davenport Rd, past flowering gardens with benches. Casa Loma's towers offer views of the city that rival those from CN Tower and self-guided audio tours (available in eight languages) lead you through the sumptuous interior.

The eccentric 98-room mansion was built after 1910 for Sir Henry Pellat, a wealthy financier whose fortunes derived from his exclusive contract to provide Toronto with electricity. The conservatory where the Pellats did their entertaining is lit by an Italian chandelier with electrical bunches of grapes. Rugs are done in the same patterns as Windsor Castle. Sir Henry later lost everything he had in land speculation, and he and his wife were forced to move out.

SPADINA HOUSE

This gracious **mansion** (Map pp76-7; ☎ 416-392-6910; www.toronto.ca/culture/spadina.htm; 285 Spadina Rd; grounds admission free, tours adult/child 6-12/youth 13-18/

senior $6/4/5/5; noon-5pm Tue-Sun May-Aug, noon-4pm weekdays Sep-Dec, Sat & Sun only Jan-Apr; subway Dupont) was built in 1866 as a country estate. It's still lit by Victorian gaslights, and the impressive interior contains fine furnishings and art collected over three generations.

Begin with a short film shown in the basement, near historical exhibits, then hear all about the history of the Austin family and the neighborhood on the tour, which points out 1905 Tiffany lamps and a stunning art nouveau frieze in the billiards room. The grounds include a stunning apple orchard (host to afternoon teas, strawberry festivals and summer musical concerts) and beautiful Edwardian and Victorian gardens.

PROVINCIAL LEGISLATURE

The seat of Ontario's **provincial legislature** (Map pp80-1; ☎ 416-325-7500; www.ontla.on.ca; Queen's Park, north of College St; admission free; tours usually 10am-4pm Mon-Fri year-round, also 9am-4pm Sat & Sun in summer, legislature usually in session Mon-Thu Mar-Jun & Sep-Dec; subway Queen's Park) resides in an 1893 pinkish sandstone building in Queen's Park. You'll usually find a few stray demonstrators writing up sandwich boards and determinedly picketing the front steps.

Free tours of the legislative building depart frequently from the information desk (call or go online for schedules) but you can attend a session of the adversarial legislative assembly for free. Security regulations are in full force, so you can't smoke, write, read or even applaud as the honorable members heatedly debate such pressing issues as snowmobile safety.

UNIVERSITY OF TORONTO – ST GEORGE CAMPUS

At **UT** (Map pp80-1; ☎ 416-978-2011, visitor information 416-978-5000; www.utoronto.ca; Nona Macdonald Visitors' Centre, 25 King's College Circle; admission free; tours usually weekday mornings & afternoons, also weekend mornings Sep-May; streetcar 506, 510) campus life focuses on the grassy expanse of **King's College Circle**, where students study on blankets, kick soccer balls around and dream of graduation day in domed **Convocation Hall**.

Dating from 1919, sociable **Hart House** (☎ 416-978-2452; www.harthouse.utoronto.ca; 7 Hart House Circle) is an all-purpose art gallery, music performance space, theater, student lounge and café. The **Soldiers' Tower**, a memorial to

students who gave their lives during WWI and WWII, is next door. A nearby mid-19th-century Romanesque Revival building houses the **UT Art Centre** (☎ 416-978-1838; www .utoronto.ca/artcentre; 15 King's College Circle; admission free; noon-6pm Tue-Fri, noon-4pm Sat Sep-Jun, noon-6pm Tue-Fri Jun-Aug), a contemporary art gallery for Canadian and world culture.

You'll also find thought-provoking exhibitions south of King's College Circle inside the boldly designed **Eric Arthur Gallery** (☎ 416-978-5038; www.ald.utoronto.ca; 230 College St; admission free; usually 9am-5pm Mon-Fri, noon-5pm Sat), curated by the university's faculty of landscape, architecture and design.

Free university walking tours of the historic St George campus cover many of these sights. Student tour guides may also tell you of the haunted love triangle involving the stonemasons who worked on the neo-Romanesque University College, then point out how the campus' old cannons aim toward the Provincial Legislature buildings, which are only a stone's throw (or one good shot) east of campus.

NATIVE CANADIAN CENTRE OF TORONTO

This **community center** (Map pp80-1; ☎ 416-964-9087; www.ncct.on.ca; 16 Spadina Rd; schedules vary; subway Spadina) hosts Thursday night drum socials, seasonal powwows and elders' cultural events that promote harmony and conversation between tribal members and non–First Nations peoples. You can also drop by the Toronto Native Community History Project, or make reservations to join one of the 'Great Indian Bus Tours' of Toronto to get a better understanding of the area's aboriginal history.

East Toronto

The district east of Parliament St to the Don River was settled by Irish immigrants fleeing the potato famine of 1841. It became known as **Cabbagetown** because the sandy soil of the area provided ideal growing conditions for cabbages. Since the 1970s there has been considerable gentrification of this once run-down area, although it's still a haven for artists. Today Cabbagetown has possibly the richest concentration of fine Victorian architecture in North America, and it's worth a stroll to peek at some of the beautifully restored houses and their carefully tended gardens.

TOMMY THOMPSON PARK

Often still known as the Leslie St Spit, this **park** (Map pp76-7; ☎ 416-661-6600; www.trca.on.ca; cnr Leslie St & Unwin Ave; admission free; ⏰ 9am-6pm Apr-Oct, 9am-4:30pm Sat, Sun & holidays Nov-Mar; streetcar 501, 502, 503, then bus 83) is an accidental wilderness; converted by the Toronto & Region Conservation Authority from landfill to a phenomenal wildlife success. It is one of the world's largest nesting places for ring-billed gulls, as well as being a haven for terns, black-crowned night heron and other colonial water birds.

Summer schedules of free interpretive programs and guided walks, which often have an ecological angle, are posted at the front gate. Songbirds fly in during the spring and fall migrations; in winter, you'll observe several species of owl here, including the great horned and snowy varieties. At the end of the path that traverses the park from the entrance gate there is a lighthouse and skyline views of the city.

The park is popular with cyclists and in-line skaters – the Martin Goodman Trail (p90) passes the park. To get to the park by public transport, take any streetcar east along Queen St to Jones Ave, then transfer to the 83 Jones bus southbound. Get off at Commissioners St, from where it's a 500m walk south to the park's main gate. Note this bus does not run on Sunday or some holidays. Call the conservation authority for information on van shuttles from the gate into the park between early May and mid-October.

RIVERDALE FARM

This **farm** (Map pp76-7; ☎ 416-392-6794; www .friendsofriverdalefarm.com; 201 Winchester St; admission free; ⏰ 9am-6pm May-Oct, 9am-5pm Nov-Apr, farmers' market 3:30-7pm Tue May-Oct; streetcar 506) is the site of the original Toronto Zoo, where prairie wolves used to howl at night and scare the Cabbagetown kids. It's now run as a working farm museum, with two barns to wander through, a summer wading pool and pens of waterfowl and other animals, some of which may be petted. It's a great place to head with kids in tow.

The Beaches

To residents, 'The Beach' is a rather wealthy, mainly professional neighborhood down by the lakeshore. To everyone else, it's part of The Beaches – meaning the suburb, the beaches themselves and the parklands along Lake Ontario.

BEACHES & PARKS

Of all the **beaches** (Map pp76-7; ☎ 416-392-8186; www.city.toronto.on.ca; ⏰ dawn-dusk; streetcar 501), **Kew Beach** is the most popular section of sand. A boardwalk runs by the **Silverbeach Boathouse**, which doesn't actually have boats but does rent sports equipment and beach toys during summer. Adjacent **Kew Gardens** offers rest rooms, snack bars, a skate rink, a lawn bowling club and benches for kicking back; at the west end near Woodbine Beach, there's an excellent Olympic-sized public swimming pool (p91). The Martin Goodman Trail (p90) leads past **Ashbridge's Bay Park**, where you'll find a lighthouse and the historic **Leuty Life Saving Station**. Off Queen St, **Glen Stewart Ravine** is a patch of wilder green leading north to Kingston Rd.

Greater Toronto Area

Many of the towns surrounding Toronto have been incorporated into the Megacity, which is just as monstrous as it sounds, at least when it comes to navigation by visitors. Reaching these areas can often be rewarding, but it'll take a large chunk of your day if you don't have a car. Some of the must-do attractions for families traveling with younger children (see p92) are located in the outskirts, and one of the historic sites will suffice for a good day out.

HIGH PARK

The city's biggest **park** (Map pp76-7; ☎ 416-392-1111; www.city.toronto.on.ca; 1873 Bloor St W; admission free; ⏰ dawn-dusk; subway High Park, streetcar 501, 506, 508) is a popular escape, whether for a little picnicking, cycling, skating or sitting in the flower gardens and watching the sunset. Near the northern gates are tennis courts and an outdoor swimming pool. In the park's south are the refreshing **Hillside Gardens** overlooking **Grenadier Pond**, where people ice-skate in winter. A road continues downhill past the animal paddocks (a small children's zoo) to **Colborne Lodge** (☎ 416-392-6916; Colborne Lodge Dr; adult/child under 13/youth 13-18/senior $3.50/2.50/2.75/2.75; ⏰ noon-5pm May-Sep, noon-4pm Tue-Sun Oct-Dec, Sat & Sun only Jan-Apr), a Regency-style cottage built in 1836.

SCARBOROUGH BLUFFS

A few kilometers east of The Beaches, these **cliffs** (☎ 416-392-8186; off Kingston Rd/Hwy 2, Scarborough; admission free; ☒ dawn-dusk) of glacial deposits (commonly known as till) tower over the lakeshore. When Elizabeth Simcoe came here in 1793, she named this spot Scarborough after the town in Yorkshire, England, also famed for its cliffs. If you want to be atop the cliffs (and you do), there are several parks that will give you access to footpaths, sweeping views of the bluffs and panoramas of Lake Ontario, as well as ways of getting down to the water.

From Kingston Rd (Hwy 2), turn south at Cathedral Bluffs Dr to reach an excellent vantage point, **Cathedral Bluffs Park**. It's the highest section of the bluffs (at 98m). At the top of the cliffs, erosion has created oddly beautiful formations resembling cathedral spires, at the same time revealing full-profile evidence of five different glacial periods. On-street parking is severely limited here.

Below, in the lake itself, landfill has been used to form **Bluffer's Park** (☎ 416-338-3278; Brimley Rd; admission free; ☒ Jul & Aug; subway Victoria Park, then bus 12), a boat-mooring and recreational area for walking and beach activities. Access to Bluffer's Park is from Brimley Rd, running south off Kingston Rd, less than 1km west of Cathedral Bluffs Dr. It's a 10-minute walk south of the nearest bus stop.

ACTIVITIES

Torontonians are passionate about the active life, and we don't just mean hockey. Outdoor activities are definitely where it's at, with folks cycling, blading and running along lakeshore trails, hiking up the city's river ravines and paddling on Lake Ontario during summer. In winter, ice-skating is a favorite pastime. Don't be surprised if you see hard-core enthusiasts cycling when there's snow on the sidewalks, or hockey players skating on artificial ice in the middle of July.

Cycling & In-Line Skating

For cyclists, in-line skaters and runners, the **Martin Goodman Trail** is the place to go. This paved recreational trail stretches from The Beaches along the downtown Harbourfront to the Humber River in the west end. Along the way you can connect to the paved and single-track mountain bike trails of the **Don Valley** system at Cherry St. On the Toronto Islands (p82) the boardwalk on the south shoreline and all of the interconnecting paved paths are car-free zones. For a challenge, you can also cycle or skate around hilly High Park (p89).

If you fancy a longer trek, the Martin Goodman Trail is part of the Lake Ontario Waterfront Trail (p201), which stretches 350km from east of Toronto to near Niagara-on-the-Lake, where you can pick up the paved recreational trail alongside the Niagara Parkway (p124).

A recreational cycling club, the **Toronto Bicycling Network** (☎ 416-760-4191; http://tbn.on.ca), is an excellent informational resource, with organized rides open to nonmembers ($5). Check the website or call for in-line skating events. **Toronto's Community Bicycling Network** (Map pp76-7; ☎ 416-504-2918; www.communitybicyclenetwork.org; Queen West, 761 Queen St W; streetcar 501) runs BikeShare (www.bikeshare.org). For $25 per year, members can borrow a single-speed yellow bike from any of a dozen centrally located hubs for up to three days. Note that wearing bike helmets is compulsory for under-18s in Toronto.

There are more bicycle and skate rentals in Toronto:

Beaches Cyclery (Map pp76-7; ☎ 416-699-1461; 1882 Queen St E)

Centre Island Bicycle Rental (Map pp76-7; ☎ 416-203-0009; Toronto Island Park; bicycles/tandems per hr $6/13; ferry Centre I)

Europe Bound Outfitters (Map pp80-1; ☎ 416-205-9992; www.europebound.com; 383 King St W; streetcar 504) Rents mountain bikes and tandems with helmets.

High Park Cycle & Sports (Map pp76-7; ☎ 416-614-6689; 2878 Dundas St W; subway Keele)

Wheel Excitement (Map pp80-1; ☎ 416-260-9000; 249 Queens Quay W; bicycles & in-line skates per hr/day $12/27; ☒ 10am-6pm Mon-Fri, 10am-7pm Sat & Sun late Apr-Oct; streetcar 509, 510)

Water Sports

People tend not to swim in Lake Ontario, even though the city has more than a dozen lifeguarded beaches, open in July and August. Water quality is often poor, especially after rainstorms, and the city periodically closes its public beaches due to toxic levels of pollution. Before swimming, check with **Toronto's Beach Water Quality Hotline** (☎ 416-392-7161; www.city.toronto.on.ca/beach) or keep your eyes and ears tuned to TV news announcements.

Free outdoor swimming can be found at the municipal pool in **High Park** (☎ 416-392-0695) or at **Gus Ryder Pool** (Map pp76-7; ☎ 416-392-6696), aka Sunnyside, on Lake Shore Blvd south of High Park. West of The Annex, the pool at **Christie Pitts Park** (Map pp76-7; 750 Bloor St W; ☎ 416-392-0745) has water slides, and there is the Olympic-sized **DD Summerville Pool** (Map pp76-7; ☎ 416-392-0740; Woodbine Park) at The Beaches.

There is **windsurfing** at The Beaches too; rentals are available in the Ashbridge's Bay area at the western edge of the Beach boardwalk; contact the **Toronto Windsurfing Club** (www.torontowindsurfingclub.com) for details.

Sailboat, kayak and canoe rental and lessons are available at:

Harbourfront Boating Centre (Map pp80-1; ☎ 416-203-3000; 283 Queens Quay W) Rents sailboats and powerboats.

Harbourfront Canoe & Kayak Centre (Map pp80-1; ☎ 416-203-2277, 800-960-8886; www.paddletoronto .com; 283A Queens Quay W; canoes per hr/day $15/40, kayaks $18/50, tandem kayaks $30/65; streetcar 509, 510) Also offers private and group lessons; has a sailing school for people with disabilities.

Ice Skating

In winter there are scenic places to ice skate downtown, including **Nathan Phillips Sq** (Map pp80-1; ☎ 416-338-7465; 100 Queen St W; ☒ 10am-10pm; subway Osgoode) outside City Hall and at the Harbourfront Centre (p78; ☒ 10am-10pm Sun-Thu, 10am-11pm Fri & Sat), both with artificial ice rinks open mid-November to March, weather permitting. Admission is free; rental skates cost from $6. Following cold weather there's a natural ice rink at High Park's Grenadier Pond (p89).

The Toronto Bicycling Network (opposite) organizes group skates (nonmembers $5) every Friday between December and March, with dinner afterward.

WALKING TOUR

When the weather outside is frightening, head for Toronto's underground **PATH** (www .city.toronto.on.ca/path) system, an accidental labyrinth of mostly subterranean corridors connecting many of the sights downtown, skyscrapers and shops. This 5km walk, which is best tackled in winter, will take about 2½ hours, not counting any dawdling over steaming cups of coffee and fast-fuel doughnuts.

WALK FACTS

Start Union Station
Finish Trinity Sq
Distance 5km
Duration 2½ hours

Start at **Union Station** (1; p114). Follow the SkyWalk signs over the railroad tracks to the **CN Tower** (2; p83), and then to **SkyDome** (3; p85). Retrace your steps to Union Station, then cross under Front St to the **Fairmont Royal York** (4; p98). Enter the hotel, then turn around to look up above the doors at a fresco landscape of Canadian history, from arctic Inuit to voyageurs in their canoes.

Back inside the basement concourse of Union Station, head for the double doors at the back leading to the **Air Canada Centre** (5; p111), which has interesting architectural displays near the Bay St entrance.

Retrace your steps to Union Station one last time, then follow the color-coded arrows to **BC Place** (6) and the **Hockey Hall of Fame** (7; p84). Pass through Commerce Court en

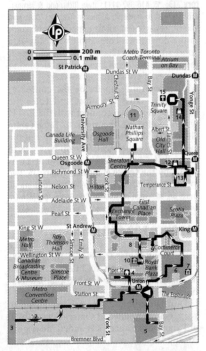

route to the **Toronto-Dominion Centre** (8; TD Centre; cnr Wellington & York Sts). After passing the electronic stock market displays, turn left toward 220 Bay St, but instead go up the escalators into the **Design Exchange** (9; p85). Back below the TD Centre, follow the signs for the Maritime Life Tower to visit the **Toronto Dominion Gallery of Inuit Art** (10; p84).

Backtrack to the TD Centre, then start looking for signs that point toward Exchange Tower, the Richmond-Adelaide Centre, the Sheraton Centre Toronto and finally, **City Hall** (11; p85). Pop your head up above ground to see the ice-skaters on Nathan Phillips Sq (p91), the weather beacon on the Canada Life Building to the west and the clock tower of Old City Hall to the east.

Back underground on the PATH, follow the signs for the **Bay** (12; ☎ 416-861-9111; 176 Yonge St; 10am-9pm Mon-Fri, 9:30am-7pm Sat, noon-6pm Sun; subway Queen) department store. Walk through the department store basement, diverting right toward the parking garage and Bay-Adelaide Centre. Walk up the stairs and exit onto Temperance St, from where it's a quick dash to the **Cloud Forest Conservatory** (13; ☎ 416-392-1111; btwn Richmond & Temperance Sts, east of Yonge St; admission free; 10am-3pm Mon-Fri; subway Queen), an unexpected sanctuary in the downtown core. Built vertically as a 'modernist ruin,' it has exposed steel, creeping vines, a waterfall and a mural depicting the trades of construction workers.

After warming up inside the conservatory, walk across the street and enter the Bay once more to reconnect with the PATH system, following the signs to **Eaton Centre** (14; p112). Walk to the northern end of the mall and take the escalators up by Ontario Tourism (p77) two levels to finish at Trinity Sq, by the **Church of the Holy Trinity** (15; Map pp80-1; ☎ 416-598-4521; www.holytrinitytoronto.org; 10 Trinity Sq; admission by donation; 10am-3pm Mon-Fri, services 9am & 10:30am Sun, noon Wed; subway Queen).

TORONTO FOR CHILDREN

Special events for children take place throughout the year; two of the best are the Milk International Children's Festival of the Arts (p95) and the Canadian National Exhibition (p96).

During summer it's easy (if expensive) to keep 'em entertained at Ontario Place (p79) or Paramount Canada's Wonderland (right). At any time of year, interactive exhibits at

the Ontario Science Centre (below) and Royal Ontario Museum (p86) are winners. Explore the Harbourfront (p78), Toronto Islands (p82), The Beaches (p89) and High Park (p89). Then give your little city slickers a taste of rural life at Riverdale Farm (p89) or Black Creek Pioneer Village (below).

Paramount Canada's Wonderland (☎ 905-832-7000; events line ☎ 905-832-8131; www.canadas-wonderland.com; Hwy 400/Rutherford Rd, Vaughan; 1-day pass adult/child 3-6/senior $45/26/26; 10am-10pm in summer, Sat & Sun only late Apr–late May & early Sep–early Oct) A state-of-the-art amusement park with over 60 rides, including killer roller coasters and the Cliffhanger super-swing, which slams through walls of water and allows riders to experience zero gravity. Wonderland also has an exploding 'volcano,' a 20-hectare water park (bring a bathing suit), Nickelodeon Central and Hanna-Barbera Land for the young 'uns. Queues can be lengthy, except on overcast days, and most rides operate rain or shine.

Wonderland is about a 45-minute drive northwest of downtown Toronto on Hwy 400. Exit at Rutherford Rd, about 10 minutes north of Hwy 401. Alternatively, from Yorkdale subway station, catch a **GOTransit** (☎ 416-869-3200; www.gotransit.com) Wonderland Express bus ($4.25).

Ontario Science Centre (Map pp76-7; ☎ 416-696-3127; tickets 416-696-1000; www.ontariosciencecentre.ca; 770 Don Mills Rd; adult/child 4-12/youth 13-17/senior $14/8/10/10; 10am-5pm; subway Eglinton, then bus 34) At this excellent, ever-evolving museum you can climb a rock wall, catch a criminal with DNA fingerprinting and race an Olympic bobsled, all in one day. Within the walls of this architectural extravaganza are over 800 interactive, high-tech science exhibits and live demonstrations that will wow most kids (and even some adults).

Combined discount tickets with Omnimax films are available. Check the museum's website for special family events, including theme-night sleepovers (reservations required). The center is located in a small ravine on the corner of Eglinton Ave E and Don Mills Rd.

Black Creek Pioneer Village (☎ 416-736-1733, 888-872-2344 ext 5400; www.blackcreek.ca; 1000 Murray Ross Pkwy, Downsview; adult/child 5-14/student/senior $11/7/10/10; 10am-4pm May-Dec; subway Finch, then bus 60) Toronto's most popular historical attraction for families re-creates rural life in

19th-century Ontario. Here workers in period costume care for farm animals, play fiddlin' folk music and demonstrate country crafts and skills using authentic tools and methods. Shops sell the artisans' handiwork, which consists of everything from tin lanterns to fresh bread to woven throw rugs. Holidays are often the best time to visit; traditional Victorian Christmas celebrations start in mid-November. The village is on the southeast corner of Steeles Ave and Jane St, a 40-minute drive northwest of downtown.

For entertainment, drop by storytime at the **Toronto Public Library – Lillian H Smith Branch** (Map pp80-1; ☎ 416-393-7753; www.tpl.toronto.on.ca; 239 College St; admission free; ☑ 10am-8:30pm Mon-Thu, 10am-6pm Fri, 9am-5pm Sat, also 1:30-5pm Sun Sep-Jun; streetcar 506, 510) or attend a performance at the innovative **Lorraine Kimsa Theatre for Young People** (Map pp80-1; ☎ 416-862-2222; www.lktyp.ca; Old York, 165 Front St E; tickets $18-28; bus 75).

An excellent online resource for parents is www.helpwevegotkids.com/gui/index.asp, which lists everything child-related in Toronto, including last-minute babysitters and daycare programs.

QUIRKY TORONTO

Toronto has its fair share of the weird and wonderful, all of which adds to the spectacle and flavor of this diverse city.

From late July to early August, rhythm from well south of the border infiltrates the city's pores during **Caribana** (☎ 877-673-2742; www.caribana.com). This Caribbean festival culminates in a weekend of reggae, steel drum and calypso music and dance with a huge carnival parade along Lake Shore Blvd W, featuring outrageous costumes à la Rio. It can take five hours or more in passing – that's some party!

For a real gas, drop by Canada's first **O₂ Spa Bar** (Map pp76-7; ☎ 416-322-7733, 888-206-0202; www.o2spabar.com; 2044 Yonge St; ☑ noon-6pm Sun-Tue, 11am-9pm Wed-Fri, 10am-9pm Sat; subway Davisville). Modeled after Japan's 'I-need-a-boost' stations, patrons are hooked up to pure oxygen hoses for 20 minutes ($20). You can even add a flavor (grapefruit, anyone?). Private lounge rooms have mood lighting and reclining leather seats.

A good night out with a twist you won't find elsewhere is ready and waiting at **Cineforum** (Map pp76-7; ☎ 416-603-6643; 463 Bathurst St; adult/child under 15/youth under 24 $20/5/10; streetcar 506,

511), where Torontonian character Reg Hartt showcases classic and avant-garde films in the front room of his Victorian row house. Animation retrospectives are his specialty, as are rare Salvador Dali prints. Come prepared for entertainingly idiosyncratic lectures, sometimes delivered while the movies are playing. You'll see ads wrapped around telephone poles advertising upcoming features, and you'll need to bring your own food and drink.

Alternatively you could head to **Theatre Passe Muraille** (Map pp76-7; Theater Beyond Walls; ☎ 416-504-7529; www.passemuraille.on.ca; 16 Ryerson Ave; tickets $20-35, previews $16; streetcar 501), an alternative theater housed in the old Nasmith's Bakery & Stables buildings. Since the 1960s, its cutting-edge productions have focused on radical new plays (over 400 of 'em so far) with contemporary Canadian themes. Ask about post-performance chats with the cast and producers, usually held on the first Tuesday evening after the show opens.

If you're looking for an unusual gift, you're bound to find something at **Come As You Are** (Map pp76-7; ☎ 416-504-7934, 877-858-3160; www.comeasyouare.com; 701 Queen St W; ☑ 11am-7pm Mon-Wed, to 9pm Thu & Fri, to 6pm Sat, noon-5pm Sun; streetcar 501). Catering to both sexes and all kinds of orientations, Canada's pioneering co-op sex shop sells books, toys, videos and DVDs. You may even be inspired to sign up for a workshop on erotic photography or Bondage 101!

Gifts of an entirely different nature can be found at **Beguiling** (Map pp76-7; ☎ 416-533-9168; www.torontocomics.com; 601 Markham St; ☑ 11am-7pm Mon-Thu & Sat, to 9pm Fri, noon-6pm Sun; subway Bathurst). It's the kind of crowded, mixed-up place that Robert Crumb would drop by (in fact, he has). Be mesmerized by original 'zines, indie comics, pop culture books, limited edition artworks and posters. Check the website for city-wide events. While you're in the vicinity, duck into **Suspect Video & Culture** (Map pp76-7; ☎ 416-588-6674; www.suspectvideo.com; 605 Markham St; ☑ noon-11pm Mon-Sat, noon-10pm Sun; subway Bathurst), *the* place to buy or rent eclectic, independent and rare videos and DVDs, or purchase alternative books, 'zines, comics and bizarre toys.

Lastly, popping into one of Toronto's quirky institutions – **Honest Ed's** (Map pp76-7; ☎ 416-537-1574; 581 Bloor St W; ☑ 10am-9pm Mon-Fri, 10am-6pm Sat, 11am-6pm Sun; subway Bathurst) is always good fun. Inside this colorful, gaudy discount-shopping emporium giant signs say things like 'Don't just stand there, buy something' and 'Only our floors are crooked!' In business for over 50 years, it's now quite a spectacle, with marquee lights reminiscent of a three-ring circus. You won't believe the queues before opening time. Owner Ed Mirvish has earned kudos as Toronto's most beloved theater impresario, too.

TOURS
Boat
Several companies run boat tours around the harbor and Toronto Islands between about May and September. Most boats depart from Harbourfront at Yonge St Slip and York St Slip, at the foot of York St. For shorter harbor excursions, you can often just show up and buy a ticket at the quay, though reservations are recommended for brunch and dinner cruises.

The following are recommended:

Great Lakes Schooner Company (Map pp80-1; ☎ 416-203-2322, 800-267-3866; www.greatlakesschooner .com; 90-min cruise adult/child/senior $20/11/18; ☼ 1-3 departures Jun–Labour Day; streetcar 509, 510) Tours in the authentic 1930s trading schooner *Kajama*. Moored behind the Power Plant, but there's often a seasonal ticket kiosk beside Queen's Quay Terminal. Discounts available for online bookings.

Mariposa Cruise Lines (Map pp80-1; ☎ 416-203-0178, 800-976-2442; http://mariposacruises.com; Queen's Quay Terminal, 207 Queens Quay W; 1hr tours adult/child/ senior $16.50/11.50/15; ☼ 5 departures daily; streetcar 509, 510) Also offers leisurely three-hour dinner cruises ($65). Sunday brunch cruises sail between May and September.

Toronto Tours Ltd (Map pp80-1; ☎ 416-868-0400; www.torontotours.com; 145 Queens Quay W; 1hr harbor cruise adult/child 2-12 $20/10; ☼ departures 10am-6pm Apr-Nov; streetcar 509, 510) Departures every half-hour. Also offers one-hour evening cruises during June, July and August.

Keep in mind that ferries to and from the Toronto Islands offer spectacular views of the city that are cheap in comparison with the private boat tours.

Bus
Bus tours around Toronto are convenient, but with TTC (p115) day passes being so cheap, a do-it-yourself tour also makes sense. For tours of Niagara Peninsula Wine Country, see p133. If you're looking for something organized, or you want to get to Niagara Falls, try:

Gray Line Tours (Map pp80-1; ☎ 416-594-3310, 800-353-3484; www.grayline.ca; departs Metro Toronto Coach Terminal, 610 Bay St; 2-day pass adult/child under 12/senior $34/18/30; ☼ departures hourly; subway Dundas) Two-hour, double-decker bus tours of central Toronto. Buy tickets for these hop-on, hop-off tours on board the bus. Passengers who book in advance can request pick-ups from downtown hotels and hostels.

JoJo Tours (☎ 416-201-6465, 888-202-3513; http:// home.interlog.com/~jojotour/; day tours $50; ☼ May-Oct) Niagara Falls tours including a stop at a winery and Niagara-on-the-Lake.

Moose Travel (☎ 888-816-6673; www.moosenetwork .com; day tours from $50; ☼ May-Oct) Niagara Falls tours.

ROMBus (☎ 416-586-5797; www.rom.on.ca/explore/ publicprograms/rombus.php; full-day tours $80) Monthly tours arranged around historical, cultural and architectural themes organized by the Royal Ontario Museum.

Toronto Hippo Tours (Map pp80-1; ☎ 416-703-4476, 877-635-5510; www.torontohippotours.com; 151 Front St W; 90 min tours adult/child 3-12/youth/ senior $35/23/30/30; ☼ hourly departures 11am-6pm May-Nov) Amphibious buses take passengers on narrated tours of downtown before splashing into the city's harbor.

Walking & Cycling
Most folk's favorite way to experience Toronto is on foot or by bicycle. The following add informative commentary to their tour itineraries:

A Taste of the World (☎ 416-923-6813; www.toronto walksbikes.com; 2¼hr tours adult/child/senior $15/9/13, 3½hr tours $35/22/30; ☼ year-round) Quirky, well-qualified guides lead off-beat walking and cycling tours of Toronto's nooks and crannies. Reservations recommended.

Civitas City Walks (☎ 416-966-1550; http://ourworld .compuserve.com/homepages/civitas; 2hr tours adult/ child under 12 $12/free; ☼ May-Oct) Offers three walks, focusing on either colonial, Victorian or modern architecture.

Heritage Toronto (☎ 416-338-3886; www.heritage toronto.org; ☼ usually weekends late Apr–mid-Oct) Excellent historical, cultural and nature walks led by museum docents and neighborhood historical society members. The free tours last from 1½ to three hours. Reservations not required.

ROMWalks (☎ 416-586-8097; www.rom.on.ca; ☼ usually Sun afternoons & Wed evenings May–mid-Sep) Volunteers from the Royal Ontario Museum lead free, one- to two-hour historical and architectural walking tours, rain or shine.

FESTIVALS & EVENTS

JANUARY–FEBRUARY

WinterCity Festival (☎ 416-338-0338; www.toronto
.ca/special_events; late Jan–mid-Feb) Toronto defies
the winter shackles with this city-wide celebration of
culture, cuisine and the arts. Many of the events are free.

APRIL

Hotdocs (☎ 416-203-2155; www.hotdocs.ca) North
America's largest documentary film festival screens more
than 100 docos from around the globe and supports the
industry through network, development and marketing
opportunities for film makers.

MAY

Doors Open Toronto (☎ 416-961-1698; www.doors
open.org) Toronto's architectural treasures open their
doors to the public.

**Milk International Children's Festival of the
ARTS** (☎ 416-973-4000; www.harbourfront.on.ca/milk)
Around Victoria Day weekend, the Harbourfront Centre
belongs to kids reveling in international puppetry, theatre,
dance, musical performances, art workshops, outdoor
games and storytelling.

JUNE

North by Northeast (NXNE; ☎ 416-863-6963; www
.nxne.com; mid-Jun) A $25 wristband gets you into
any of 400 new music shows at over two dozen clubs, all
squeezed into this independent music and film festival over
one long weekend.

Pride Week (☎ 416-927-7433; www.pridetoronto.com;
late Jun) Toronto's most flamboyant event celebrates
all varieties of sexuality, climaxing with an out-of-the-closet
Dyke March and an outrageous Pride Parade. Pride's G-spot
is in the Church–Wellesley Village and most events are free.

Queen's Plate (end Jun) The year's major horse race
and one of North America's oldest (held since 1859) is run
at Woodbine Racetrack.

Caravan (late Jun–early Jul) A nine-day cultural exchange between ethnic groups, offering music, dance and
food native to their homelands. A passport ($25) entitles
you to visit 25 ethnic pavilions around the city.

Toronto Downtown Jazz Festival (www.tojazz.com;
late Jun–early Jul) For 10 days (and nights) jazz,
blues and world beats blaze in the streets, nightclubs and
concert halls of the city centre, with musical workshops,
film screenings and harbor cruises.

JULY

Molson Indy (☎ 416-966-6202, 866-670-4639; www
.molsonindy.com; mid-Jul) Drivers from the international circuit compete in front of large crowds during the
two days of practice and qualifying trials, with the big race
on the third day at Exhibition Place. You'll hear the noise
pollution everywhere.

GAY & LESBIAN TORONTO

Toronto is a major center for gay and lesbian life, with numerous businesses and bars catering
specifically to the queer community. During Pride Week (above), about a million visitors descend
on the city. The focus of the action is the **Church–Wellesley Village**, spread along Church St north
and south of Wellesley St E, where a busy residential/commercial mix draws crowds for strolling and people-watching on weekends. Other gay-friendly neighborhoods include The Annex,
Kensington Market, Queen West and Cabbagetown.

Gay nightlife venues are abundant and although men's bars and clubs vastly outnumber
lesbian venues, grrrls should take heart because Toronto is home to drag kings, women-
only bathhouse nights and queer reading series. See p110 for more drinking spots and
entertainment options.

In 2003 Toronto became the first city in North America to legalize same-sex marriage. Apply
at **City Hall** (Map pp80-1; ☎ 416-363-9248, 416-363-0316; City Clerk's Office, 100 Queen St W; license $110;
8:30am-4:15pm Mon-Fri) In September 2004, an Ontario Court also recognized the first legal
same-sex divorce. Although the Divorce Act (a federal law) remains unchanged at the time of
writing, the ruling signifies another historic step towards equality for same-sex couples.

See p854 for gay and lesbian resources in Canada. Other helpful local resources in Toronto:
519 Community Centre (Map pp80-1; ☎ 416-392-6874; www.the519.org; Church-Wellesley Village, 519
Church St; subway Wellesley)
Glad Day (p75)
Lesbian & Gay Immigration Task Force (☎ 416-925-9872 ext 2211; www.legit.ca)
This Ain't the Rosedale Library (p75)
Toronto Women's Bookstore (p75)
Xtra! (p75)

Beaches International Jazz Festival (☎ 416-698-2152; www.beachesjazz.com; ☑ mid-Jun) Going strong for more than 15 years, this high-caliber jazz festival puts on free performances around the city.

AUGUST
Canadian National Exhibition (CNE; www.theex.com) Claiming to be the oldest (from about 1879) and largest annual exhibition in the world, the Ex presents over 700 agricultural shows, lumberjack competitions, outdoor concerts, carnival games and rides at Exhibition Place. This is topped by an air show and fireworks for two weeks prior to, and including, Labour Day.

SEPTEMBER & OCTOBER
Toronto International Film Festival (TIFF; ☎ 416-968-3456; www.bell.ca/filmfest) Toronto's prestigious 10-day celebration is one of the world's best film festivals and a major cinematic event. Usually held in September, it lasts about a week and a half and features films of all lengths and styles, as well as gala events and stars. You can obtain tickets for individual screenings or buy all-inclusive packages. Tickets sell out very quickly.
International Festival of Authors (☎ 416-973-4000; www.readings.org) The festival brings over 100 acclaimed authors from Canada and abroad to the Harbourfront Centre for readings, panel discussions, lectures, awards and book signings.

NOVEMBER
Canadian Aboriginal Festival (☎ 519-751-0040; www.canab.com; ☑ late Nov) A multiday celebration of dancing, drumming, artisan crafts, new films and traditional teachings.

SLEEPING
Booking good-value accommodation is likely to be the thorniest issue in planning your trip to Toronto. Reservations outside the deep-freeze winter months are mandatory because decent options are likely to be full every night from Victoria Day through to the last vestiges of summer. Bookings also limit the sting of wildly fluctuating hotel tariffs – many places charge double or triple the off-peak rates during summer and on major holidays. Some hostels, guesthouses and B&Bs may not charge tax, but hotels certainly will, so be prepared.

Downtown offers historic hotels, boutique digs and lakefront properties, albeit at higher prices than almost any other neighborhood. But you don't have to spend all your dough to be close to the action. Guesthouses and B&Bs are prolific in eastern To-

ronto, the gay neighborhood centered on the Church-Wellesley Village, and among the quiet, leafy residential districts surrounding the University of Toronto campus. If you don't mind spending slightly more time on public transport, it's worth seeking out one of the many travelers' favorites in the Greater Toronto Area.

Toronto's popular B&B industry caters to most budgets. Many B&Bs require a two-night minimum stay. A great place to start looking online is www.bbcanada.com, which has nearly 100 listings in the city. A few independent B&B operators belong to the **Toronto Guild of Bed & Breakfasts** (www.torontoguild .com). Booking agencies are another way to save time and money. Reliable agencies:
Bed & Breakfast Homes of Toronto Association (☎ 416-363-6362; www.bbcanada.com/associations/toronto2)
Downtown Toronto Association of Bed and Breakfast Guest Houses (☎ 416-410-3938; www.bnbinfo.com)

Harbourfront & Toronto Islands
Toronto Island Bed & Breakfast (Map pp76-7; ☎ 416-203-0935, fax 416-203-2646; 8 Lakeshore Ave, cnr 3rd St; d with shared bathroom incl breakfast from $60; ferry Ward's Island) For unforgettably unique acommodation, take the ferry over to Ward's Island, then walk about 300m toward the south shore, turn left and look for this quaint white clapboard house. Rooms fill up quickly during summer. Rates include the use of bicycles.

Westin Harbour Castle (Map pp80-1; ☎ 416-869-1600, 800-937-8461; www.westin.com; 1 Harbour Sq; d from $250; streetcar 509, 510; P ⍟) On the waterfront, the 1000-room Westin is popular with business travelers and families. Some standard rooms enjoy lake views and the hotel's revolving restaurant overlooks Lake Ontario and the Toronto Islands.

Old York
BUDGET
Hostelling International Toronto (HI Toronto; Map pp80-1; ☎ 416-971-4440, 877-848-8737; www.hihostels .ca; 76 Church St; dm $23-28, d $70-80, monthly rates incl taxes $520-675; ☑ reception 24hr; streetcar 504 King) This award-winning hostel gets votes for renovations that include a rooftop deck, electronic key locks and air-conditioning. Beds in quad rooms may not cost any more than those in larger dormitories, so ask when making reservations. Check the website for Hostelling

International cardholder discounts around town.

TOP END

Le Royal Meridien King Edward (Map pp80-1; ☎ 416-863-9700, 800-543-4300; www.lemeridien-king edward.com; 37 King St E; d from $260; subway King; (P)) The glorious 'King Eddy' is Toronto's oldest hotel, named for King Edward VII, who gave it the royal seal of approval over a century ago. This grand dame was built by Toronto architect EJ Lennox; today it's a showpiece of baroque plasterwork, marble and etched glass. Standard rooms are well priced (including twice-daily maid service), especially on weekends.

Downtown Toronto

BUDGET

Canadiana Guesthouse & Backpackers (Map pp80-1; ☎ 416-598-9090, 877-215-1225; www.canadianalodging .com; 42 Widmer St; dm incl taxes $22-28, s/d incl taxes $50/65; ⏱ reception 8am-midnight; streetcar 504 King) This friendly, air-conditioned property occupies a few charming Victorian townhouses in the Entertainment District; it has only a few dozen dorm beds and a couple of private rooms. Although the hostel regularly fills up with European travelers, you're more likely to find an empty bed here than elsewhere.

Global Village Backpackers (Map pp80-1; ☎ 416-703-8540, 888-844-7875; www.globalbackpackers.com; 460 King St W; dm incl taxes $22-28, d incl taxes $56-60; ⏱ reception 24hr; streetcar 504 King, 511 Spadina) This kaleidoscopically colored independent hostel was once the Spadina Hotel, where Jack Nicholson, the Rolling Stones, Leonard Cohen and the Tragically Hip stayed. It's in an optimal location and even has its own bar, hence the party atmosphere.

MID-RANGE

Hotel Victoria (Map pp80-1; ☎ 416-363-1666, 800-363-8228; www.hotelvictoria-toronto.com; 56 Yonge St; d incl breakfast $100-60; subway King) This early 20th-century place is one of the best small hotels downtown. Refurbished throughout, it still maintains a few old-fashioned features, such as its fine lobby. The multilingual, 24-hour reception staff warmly welcomes all guests. Rates include free health club privileges.

Delta Chelsea Toronto Downtown (Map pp80-1; ☎ 416-595-1975, 877-814-7706; www.deltachelsea.com; 33 Gerrard St W; d from $110; subway College; (P) (R)) Who says one hotel can't be all things to all

people? With nearly 1600 rooms, Toronto's largest and arguably best-value hotel bustles with tourists, business travelers and families. If you're traveling with children, you'll appreciate apartment-style suites stocked with cookie jars, bunk beds and alphabet fridge magnets. Breakfast is often available in the skyline lounge, Deck 27.

Dundonald House (Map pp80-1; ☎ 416-961-9888, 800-260-7227; www.dundonaldhouse.com; 35 Dundonald St; s/tw/d incl breakfast from $85/110/135; subway Welles-ley; (P)) Voted a community favorite, this striking black-gabled house has stained glass windows and flower gardens. Guest amenities include a sauna and fitness room, complimentary bicycles and, for an added fee, shiatsu massage. Accommodations range from no-frills single or twin bedrooms up to $175 for a double with bay windows and a private balcony.

Les Amis Bed & Breakfast (Map pp80-1; ☎ 416-928-1348; www.bbtoronto.com; 31 Granby St; s/d with shared bathroom incl breakfast & taxes from $70/90; subway College) Run by a Parisian couple, this cheery B&B offers full, gourmet vegetarian (or vegan) breakfasts. Air-conditioned rooms have futon beds. The only drawback is its slightly sketchy location, despite being just steps from Eaton Centre. French, German and Japanese are spoken. Gay and lesbian travelers are welcome.

ONTARIO

Victoria's Mansion Inn & Guesthouse (Map pp80-1; ☎ 416-921-4625; www.victoriasmansion.com; 68 Gloucester St; d $100-30; subway Wellesley; P Q) Award-winning Victoria's Mansion can accommodate travelers for short and long-term stays in a renovated 1880s heritage building; studio suites have kitchenettes. The owners are known to be personable.

Strathcona Hotel (Map pp80-1; ☎ 416-363-3321, 800-268-8304; www.thestrathconahotel.com; 60 York St; d from $115; subway St Andrew) Convenient to Union Station, this familiar face offers all the usual amenities (including Web TV), and yet, for the downtown area, is reasonably priced. Guests enjoy discounts at the fitness and racquet club next door.

Other recommendations:

Mansion (Map pp80-1; ☎ 416-963-8385; www.the mansion.ca; 46 Dundonald St; d incl breakfast $70-100; subway Wellesley; P) Above-average ambience with rooms with Victorian, Edwardian or Regency decor.

Days Inn Toronto Downtown (Map pp80-1; ☎ 416-977-6655, 800-329-7466; www.daysinn.com; 30 Carlton St; d from $80; subway College; P ⚘) Reliable and convenient, with good fitness facilities.

Bond Place Hotel (Map pp80-1; ☎ 416-362-6061, 800-268-9390; www.bondplacehoteltoronto.com; 65 Dundas St E; d from $90; subway Dundas; P) Modest high-rise with good summer rates and even better winter ones. Wheelchair-accessible.

TOP END
Fairmont Royal York (Map pp80-1; ☎ 416-368-2511, 866-540-4489; www.fairmont.com/royalyork; 100 Front St W; d from $210; subway Union; P ⚘) This place has accommodated rock stars to royal guests since 1929. Built opposite Union Station by the Canadian Pacific Railway, its mock-chateau style adds character to Toronto's skyline. Rooms exude richness and style, with rates that rise depending on demand.

Hôtel Le Germain (Map pp80-1; ☎ 416-345-9500, 866-345-9501; www.germaintoronto.com; 30 Mercer St; d $200-500, ste $475-900; streetcar 504 King; P) Hip and harmonious, this hotel is just a short walk from the Entertainment District and SkyDome. Clean lines, soothing spaces and Zen-inspired materials all deliver a promised 'ocean of well-being.' Guests are pampered with Aveda bath products, in-room Bose stereos, a rooftop terrace and a lobby library with a cathedral ceiling.

Renaissance Toronto Hotel at SkyDome (Map pp80-1; ☎ 416-341-7100, 800-468-3571; www.renaissance hotels.com; 1 Blue Jays Way; d/ste from $220/295; subway

---

WHAT A SCORE!

The SkyDome hotel became notorious when, during one of the first Blue Jays baseball games, a couple in one of the upperfield side rooms – forgetfully or rakishly – became involved in some sporting activity of their own with the lights on, much to the crowd's amusement. Such a scoring performance was later repeated at another game. After that, the hotel insisted on guests signing waivers that stipulated there would be no more such free double plays.

Union; P ⚘) Only 70 of the most expensive rooms overlook the playing field; if you request one, be prepared for floodlights and SkyDome noise at all hours. Mostly covered walkways (very handy in winter) connect this upmarket chain hotel with Union Station.

Holiday Inn on King (Map pp80-1; ☎ 416-599-4000, 800-263-6364; www.hiok.com; 370 King St W; d from $145; streetcar 504; P ⚘) Near the Theatre Block, this dazzlingly white hotel seems to have been airlifted straight off Waikiki Beach. Standard rooms enjoy lake or city views, while the seasonal rooftop pool gazes onto CN Tower. Children under age 20 stay and eat free when accompanied by a parent. Visit the website for great Internet-only deals.

Bloor-Yorkville
MID-RANGE
Toronto Downtown Bed & Breakfast (Map pp76-7; ☎ 416-921-3533; www.tdbab.com; 57 Chicora Ave; d/ste incl breakfast from $130/220; bus 5; P) This lovely, gay-owned place is a quick bus ride north of Yorkville. Enjoy fresh-baked cookies by the fireplace, or relax with a movie borrowed from the video and DVD library. Breakfast varies from continental to a full, hot gourmet meal by a French-trained chef.

Quality Hotel (Map pp80-1; ☎ 416-968-0010, 877-424-6423; www.qualityinn.com; 280 Bloor St W; d from $115, ste from $140; subway St George; P) This high-rise chain hotel has a prime location near the museums and shopping. Especially good value are newer rooms that come with cathedral ceilings and king-sized beds, and the one-bedroom executive suites. Another perk is free admission to a nearby health club.

Howard Johnson Inn (Map pp80-1; ☎ 416-964-1220, 800-446-4656; www.hojo.com; 89 Ave Rd; d incl breakfast from $120; subway Bay; P) Next to Hazelton

Lanes shopping center, HoJo offers the cheapest acommodation in ritzy Yorkville. Standard-issue rooms have down-to-earth wood and brick decor.

TOP END

Windsor Arms (Map pp80-1; ☎ 416-971-9666; www .windsorarmshotel.com; 18 St Thomas St; ste from $300; subway Bay; 🖳) The Windsor Arms is an exquisite piece of Toronto history. The 1927 neo-gothic mansion boasts a grand entrance, stained glass windows, nearly faultless services and an on-site spa. With a price tag of up to $2000, the luxury suites boast 24-hour butler service.

Four Seasons (Map pp80-1; ☎ 416-964-0411, 800-819-5053; www.fourseasons.com/toronto; 21 Avenue Rd; d from $300; subway Bay) Some of the city's most costly rooms are found at the Four Seasons in the heart of Yorkville. Everyone here looks quite glamorous, particularly during the film festival when stars adopt this as their favorite hotel. Even 'moderate' rooms have antique writing desks and marble bathrooms, while superior rooms and suites have walk-out balconies. Also worth mentioning is the indoor/outdoor pool, unique boutiques and five-star contemporary French cuisine at Truffles restaurant.

University of Toronto & The Annex
BUDGET

Castlegate Inn (Map pp76-7; ☎ 416-323-1657; www .castlegateinn.com; 203 Spadina Rd; s & d incl breakfast $60-100, weekly rates from $275; subway Dupont; 🅿) This casual inn is one of the best budget travel bargains in Toronto. Owned by avid travelers, it occupies three apartment houses, all within striking distance of the UT campus and Yorkville. If you're sensitive to noise, request a quiet upper-floor room facing away from the street. Continental breakfast and limited parking are free.

Global Guesthouse (Map pp80-1; ☎ 416-923-4004; singer@inforamp.net; 9 Spadina Rd; s/d with shared bathroom $52/62, s/d with private bathroom $62/72; subway Spadina) This old-fashioned brick Victorian with beautiful carved gables and a balcony sits just north of Bloor St. Decently spacious rooms with cable TVs fill up quickly and include shared telephone and kitchenette access.

MID-RANGE & TOP END

Lowther House (Map pp80-1; ☎ 416-323-1589, 800-265-4158; www.lowtherhouse.ca; 72 Lowther Ave; d incl breakfast $90-160; subway St George; 🅿) Equidistant from Yorkville, several museums and UT's St George campus is this restored century-old Victorian mansion that lures guests with its gardens and common-area fireplace. You'll be spoilt in a suite with a marble double Jacuzzi or a sun room. French spoken.

Madison Manor (Map pp80-1; ☎ 416-922-5579, 877-561-7048; www.madisonavenuepub.com; 20 Madison Ave; d incl breakfast $90-195; subway Spadina; 🅿) Guests at this boutique inn enjoy daytime billiards parlor privileges at the nearby Madison Avenue Pub (p107). All rooms have a bathroom, air-conditioning and Internet access; a few have fireplaces or balconies, too. Continental breakfast is served.

Casa Loma Inn (Map pp80-1; ☎ 416-924-4540; casalomainn@sympatico.ca; 21 Walmer Rd; s/d from $80/90; subway Spadina; 🅿) When it's all lit up at night, this breathtaking turn-of-the-20th-century Victorian inn seems like a pint-sized version of its namesake (p87). Each of the 23 rooms has a TV, fridge, microwave and air-conditioning.

Beverley Place (☎ 416-977-0077, fax 416-599-2242; 235 Beverley St; r incl breakfast $65-120) This three-storey Victorian dating from 1877 has many of its original features, including wonderfully high ceilings. The entire place is furnished and decorated with interesting antiques and collectibles. The 'Queen Room' (with an impressive bed) costs more, as does the 3rd-floor, self-contained apartment with its own balcony and city view.

Kensington Market

The friendly, no-frills **College Hostel** (☎ 416-929-4777; www.affordacom.com; 280 Augusta Ave; dm $22-28, s/d with shared bathroom incl taxes from $50/60; streetcar 506; 🅿) may not have the safest location in bohemian Kensington Market, but backpackers rave about the perks: free lockers, free breakfast, free Internet, free local calls and an on-site sushi bar.

East Toronto
BUDGET

Neill-Wycik College Hotel (Map pp80-1; ☎ 416-977-2320, 800-268-4358; www.neill-wycik.com; 96 Gerrard St E; s/d/f/tr with shared bathroom $40/60/65/80; 🕑 May-Aug; subway College) This favorite has private bedrooms with telephones inside apartment-style suites that share a kitchen/lounge and bathroom. There are laundry facilities, lockers, TV lounges, a student-run cafeteria serving breakfast and incredible views from the rooftop sundeck. The building isn't air-conditioned and there are no fans, so be prepared to sweat it out in mid-summer.

Amsterdam Guesthouse (Map pp80-1; ☎ 416-921-9797; www.amsterdamguesthouse.com; 209 Carlton St; s/d with shared bathroom from $55/65; streetcar 506) This polished Victorian house is not at all stuffy, and has a rear balcony with bird's-eye views of downtown. The simple rooms have air-conditioning and cable TV. Although not large, the rooms are clean and comfy. Look for the flags flying out front.

MID-RANGE

Clarion Hotel & Suites Selby (Map pp80-1; ☎ 416-921-3142, 800-446-4656; www.hotelselby.com; 592 Sherbourne St; d/ste incl breakfast from $110/200; subway Sherbourne; P) During the 1920s Ernest Hemingway resided at this turreted Victorian mansion while he worked as a reporter for the *Toronto Star* before heading to Paris. Standard rooms are nothing special, except for the bargain rates, but two-room suites with high ceilings and fireplaces are found inside the original mansion. It's worth asking the friendly manager for weekend and multinight discounts.

Albert's Inn (Map pp80-1; ☎ 416-929-9525; pimblett@attcanada.ca; 263 Gerrard St E; s/d from $65/85, ste $195; streetcar 505, 506; P) This jovial place sits above a restaurant and pub. It's run by a quirky English gentleman who used to work at London's Mayfair Hotel – he describes his sense of humor as 'Monty Python,' so be prepared. Each room (some are without a bathroom) has air-conditioning, TV and a telephone, while the Balmoral Suite has a working fireplace and kitchen. The owner's other property, called **Pimblett's B&B** (www.pimbletts-rest.com), is resplendent with antiques, a library and mahogany fireplace.

1871 Historic House (Map pp80-1; ☎ 416-923-6950; www.1871bnb.com; 65 Huntley St; s/d incl breakfast from $70/80; subway Sherbourne; P) What other property can claim both Buffalo Bill Cody and John Lennon as one-time guests? In this historic Victorian home, which displays its art and antiques in sunny common areas, all rooms are without a bathroom, but the coach house suite has its own whirlpool.

Au Petit Paris (Map pp80-1; ☎ 416-928-1348; www.bbtoronto.com/aupetitparis; 3 Selby St; s/d incl breakfast from $85/110; subway Sherbourne; P) An exquisite bay-and-gable Victorian home with hardwood floors and modern decor.

TOP END

Robin's Nest (Map pp80-1; ☎ 416-926-9464, 877-441-4443; www.robinsnestbandbtoronto.com; 13 Binscarth Rd; d incl breakfast $125-225; subway Rosedale, then bus 82; P) This luxurious, restored, five-star 1892 heritage home (it looks like a mansion) is your best shot at feeling like a million bucks. The 'Tree Tops Suite' comes with mansard ceilings, an antique chesterfield and views of the formal garden. Breakfast is served on the veranda or on a silver tray delivered straight to your room.

The Beaches

Accommodating the Soul (Map pp76-7; ☎ 416-686-0619, 866-686-0619; www.bbcanada.com/6127.html; 114 Waverley Rd; d incl breakfast $95-125; streetcar 501; P) A short walk from the lakefront, this early 20th-century home boasts antiques and delicious gardens, and will delight travelers looking for tranquility. Some rooms have shared bathrooms, and full hot breakfasts are served. It's gay-owned.

Greater Toronto Area

Bonnevue Manor (Map pp76-7; ☎ 416-536-1455; bonne@interlog.com; 33 Beaty Ave, west of Jameson Ave; d incl breakfast from $100; streetcar 501, 504, 508; P) Often voted one of the city's best B&Bs, this gay-owned hostelry is inside a restored 1890s redbrick mansion that has lovely hand-crafted architectural details. Over a dozen guest rooms have warm-colored decor.

Red Door Bed & Breakfast (Map pp76-7; ☎ 416-604-0544; www.reddoorbb.com; 301 Indian Rd, south of Bloor St W; s/d incl breakfast from $90/115; subway Keele; P) Near Roncesvalles Village, a predominantly Eastern European neighborhood, this B&B is just a short walk from High Park. Run by an artistic and musical couple, there's a grand piano in the living room, and some French is spoken. Every room has air-conditioning; the Oak Suite also has a sofa bed and a fireplace. Full hot breakfasts are served.

Toadhall Bed & Breakfast (☎ 905-773-4028; www.225toadhall.ca; 225 Lakeland Cres, Richmond Hill; s/d incl breakfast $95/125; P) It's worth trekking north of the city center to stay in a solar-powered home on the shores of Lake Wilcox, which offers swimming, canoeing and windsurfing in fair weather. Although there is no air-conditioning, you can count on cool lake breezes and the owners also have a greenhouse. Gourmet breakfasts emphasize organic fare (vegetarian by request).

Drake Hotel (Map pp76-7; ☎ 416-531-5042; www
.thedrakehotel.ca; 1150 Queen St W, east of Dufferin St; d
$120-190, ste $220-250; streetcar 501) This century-
old hotel has been revamped for a cool $5
million. It presides beyond the edge of the
Queen West strip. Beckoning to bohemians, artists and indie musicians, it has even
lured famed chef David Chrystian into its
kitchens. Artful rooms come with vintage
furnishings, throw rugs, flat-screen TVs
and high-speed Internet access.

Other recommendations:

Beaconsfield (Map pp76-7; ☎ 416-535-3338; www
.bbcanada.com/771.html; 38 Beaconsfield Ave, east of
Dufferin St; d with shared bathroom incl breakfast $85, ste
$135-70; streetcar 501; P) Victorian-style boutique hotel
with a beautiful garden.

Grayona Tourist Home (Map pp76-7; ☎ 416-535-
5443, 800-354-0244; 1546 King St W, east of Roncesvalles
Ave; s/d with shared bathroom $60/80; streetcar 504; P)
Fridges, TVs and telephones in every room. A good choice
for families.

EATING

America calls itself a 'melting pot,' but Canadians prefer the term 'mixed salad' for
themselves. The metaphor is never more apt
than when applied to the Megacity's eclectic
dining scene. Torontonians have known the
secret to good cuisine for decades – fusion is
the future of food. So it's no surprise to find
miso or Thai lemongrass sprinkled across the
contemporary bistro menus here, but keep in
mind the lingering British influences, too. A
pint with lunch and afternoon high teas are
still much-loved traditions.

You'll find high-powered restaurants in
the Financial District, many traditional places
in Old York, and a new world of choices in
Baldwin Village. A glut of good eateries catering to all tastebuds and wallets compete
for hungry tummies around Kensington
Market, Little Italy and Queen West.

Harbourfront

Harbour Sixty Steakhouse (Map pp80-1; ☎ 416-777-
2111; 60 Harbour St; dinner $27-50; lunch Mon-Fri, din-
ner daily; streetcar 509, 510) Inside the stately 1917
Toronto Harbour Commission building, an
opulent baroque dining room glows with
brass lamps. Sink into a gold brocade ban-
quette and order from a variety of steaks,
sterling salmon or seasonal Florida stone-
crab claws and broiled Caribbean lobster
tail. The only sour note? Side dishes are

somewhat overpriced. Arrive early to get
started on an award-winning wine list of European and New World vintages, then stay
late and linger over chocolate soufflé with
Grand Marnier crème anglaise.

Toronto Islands

Rectory (Map pp76-7; ☎ 416-203-2152; 102 Lakeshore
Ave; meals $4-16; lunch Wed-Sun, till 8pm Fri & Sat; ferry
Ward's I) Charmingly set beside the boardwalk
on Ward's Island (p82), this cozy art gallery
and café serves light meals, apple cider and
weekend brunch in the garden. Reservations
are recommended for brunch and dinner,
although you can always stop by for a quick
snack and some liquid refreshment.

Old York
BUDGET

St Lawrence Market (Map pp80-1; ☎ 416-392-7120;
South Market, 2 Front St E; 8am-6pm Tue-Thu, 8am-
7pm Fri, 5am-5pm Sat; streetcar 503, 504) Classical
musicians often play at the city's beloved
indoor market, where you'll be amazed by
the range and quality of produce, baked
goods and imported foodstuffs. Faves include Carousel Bakery, Future Bakery, St
Urbain for Montréal-style bagels and, on
the lower level, Mustachio's chicken sandwiches that are said to be 'about as big as your
head.' Toronto's historic farmers' market
(since 1803) is held in the North Market,
starting at 5am every Saturday.

MID-RANGE

Spring Rolls (Map pp80-1; ☎ 416-365-7655; 85 Front St E;
mains $7-13; lunch & dinner; streetcar 503, 504) Spring
Rolls has settled into a new dining space bedecked with Chinese warriors, Buddhas and
a shark aquarium. Bowls of Vietnamese *bún*
(rice vermicelli), spicy Sichuan noodles and
pad thaï (stir-fried noodles) are followed by
grilled sea bass and banana fritters. An energetic after-work crowd often unwinds at
sidewalk tables.

TOP END

Montréal Bistro & Jazz Club (Map pp80-1; ☎ 416-363-
0179; 65 Sherbourne St; mains $10-23; lunch Mon-Fri,
dinner Mon-Sat) This jazz club does not rate its
food in second place. Heavily influenced
by Québecois cooking, the chefs whip up
seafood cocotte, grilled Atlantic salmon and
roast lake duck, all served at tête-à-tête tables
lit by boudoir lamps.

ONTARIO

Downtown Toronto

BUDGET

Phở Hu'ng (Map pp80-1; ☎ 416-593-4274; 350 Spadina Ave; mains $6-10; ☻ lunch & dinner; streetcar 510) This is an authentic Vietnamese restaurant in Chinatown that cooks up an array of delicious soups with fresh greens. It's so authentic in fact that certain dishes may be a touch too daring for some (what, don't you like pork intestines and blood?). A fair-weather bonus is the patio. It has another **branch** (Map pp80-1; ☎ 416-963-5080; 2nd fl, 200 Bloor St W; subway Museum) in Bloor-Yorkville.

Le Gourmand (Map pp80-1; ☎ 416-504-4494; 152 Spadina Ave; meals $5-10; ☻ breakfast, lunch & dinner Mon-Fri, 9am-6pm Sat, 9am-4pm Sun; streetcar 510, 501) A nirvana for foodies, this upmarket grocery store stocks Napa Valley mustards and rare chocolates made in Mexico. Peruse the deli case and pastry shelves, or pop by for a foamy cappuccino and dish of homemade gelato. As for breakfast, can we tempt you with a warm chocolate-banana-nut bread pudding topped by fresh fruit, cream and maple syrup?

Le Commensal (Map pp80-1; ☎ 416-596-9364; 655 Bay St, entrance off Elm St; buffet $2 per 100g; ☻ lunch & dinner; subway Dundas) Cafeteria-style Le Commensal sells fresh salads, hot main dishes with international flavors and desserts naturally sweetened with maple syrup or fruit nectars. Everything is strictly vegetarian and most dietary restrictions can be easily accommodated; only a few dishes border on bland. Expect to pay about $10 for a fair-sized meal, before drinks and taxes. Beer, wine and herbal tea are also sold.

Other Chinatown cheap eats:

Furama Cake & Dessert Garden (Map pp80-1; ☎ 416-504-5709; 248-50 Spadina Ave; items from $1; ☻ lunch & dinner; streetcar 510) Lotus seed cakes and curried buns for pocket change.

Kim Thanh (Map pp80-1; ☎ 416-979-7928; 336 Spadina Ave; items from $1; ☻ lunch & dinner; streetcar 510) Specializes in *bánh mì* (Vietnamese sub sandwich) with meat or tofu filling.

MID-RANGE

Marche Mövenpick (Map pp80-1; ☎ 416-863-0108; street level, BC Place, 42 Yonge St; buffet lunch $10, mains $8-25; ☻ breakfast, lunch & dinner; subway Union) An innovative market-style restaurant dreamt up in Switzerland, Mövenpick will satisfy anyone's taste buds. Wander between the fresh-food stations, filling up your tray with such treats as Atlantic salmon and potato *rösti*, Belgian waffles topped with cherries, signature maple ice cream or fresh juices, baked goods and salads. It's great fun for kids, but watch the price stamps on your check-out card because they add up quickly.

Kubo DX (Map pp80-1; ☎ 416-368-5826; 234 Bay St; dim sum lunch $10, mains $9-14; ☻ lunch & dinner Mon-Fri; subway King) Inside Design Exchange (p85), sharply styled Kubo offers a happy sight for artistic eyes, quick gastronomic pleasures and a lot of laughter upon reading the menu. Snack on 'Dumb & Dumplings' with spicy soy dipping sauce or the 'Grill of a Lifetime' steak wrap with orange-peppercorn marinade and fiery onions.

Fez Batik (Map pp80-1; ☎ 416-204-9660; 129 Peter St; mains $12-16; ☻ lunch & dinner; streetcar 501) Flowery murals bedeck the walls, and the patio sprawls into the lap of the Entertainment District. A tame menu belies the crazy come-on, showing Italian pastas, Asian main dishes and Southwestern sandwiches. Order a flourless mocha torte or maple butter tart for that perfect pre-clubbing sugar rush. By night patrons scoff dinner to underground hip-hop.

Fire on the East Side (Map pp80-1; ☎ 416-960-3473; 6 Gloucester St; dinner $12-22; ☻ lunch & dinner Wed-Sun, from 10am Sat & Sun; subway Wellesley) A stone's throw from Yonge St, this ultrachic dining room feels just like someone's living room. A haywire fusion kitchen works variations on African, Caribbean, French Acadian and Cajun themes, bouncing from spicy crab cakes to jalapeño-vodka pasta. Desserts are homemade.

Mata Hari Grill (Map pp80-1; ☎ 416-596-2832; 39 Baldwin St; lunch $8-10, dinner mains $11-18; ☻ lunch Mon-Fri, dinner daily; streetcar 505) A romantic hideaway makes perfect sense on Baldwin Street. Revel in a cozy nook with gilt mirrors and richly colored fabrics before diving into fiery beef *rendang* or 'Chicken Kapitan' curry, an authentic Nyonya (Straits Chinese) dish. The desserts are inspired, and so is the list of ice wines and imported beers.

Queen Mother Café (Map pp80-1; ☎ 416-598-4719; 208 Queen St W; mains $8-19; ☻ lunch & dinner; subway Osgoode) This Queen St institution is beloved for its cozy, dark wooden booths and surprisingly good pan-Asian dim sum, as well as Canadian comfort food. Kids are welcome, albeit on the patio.

Zelda's (Map pp80-1; ☎ 416-922-2526; 542 Church St; mains $7-17; ☻ lunch & dinner; subway Wellesley) Zany

Zelda's has a winning combination of familiar food, crazy cocktails and a spacious outdoor patio. A diverse Church-Wellesley crowd adores the brash, colorful and queer atmosphere, especially on drag queen and leather theme nights.

Lee Garden (Map pp80-1; ☎ 416-593-9524; 331 Spadina Ave; mains $8-12; ☺ dinner; streetcar 510) Longstanding, casual Lee Garden offers an unusually varied menu of Cantonese comfort fare and seafood. It's open late – but you should expect to join the queue of regulars, who rave about the blackboard specials.

Fresh by Juice for Life (Map pp80-1; ☎ 416-599-4442; 336 Queen St W; items $4-8; ☺ 8:30am-6:30pm Mon-Fri, 9am-6:30pm Sat, 10:30am-6:30pm Sun; streetcar 501, 510) Everything is made fresh at this city fave. A wholesome and tasty menu includes kaleidoscopic salads and 'Free Tibet' rice bowls, plus smoothies, shakes and 'vital fluids' to cure whatever ails. There are other branches in **The Annex** (Map pp76-7; ☎ 416-531-2635; 521 Bloor St W; subway Bathurst) and **Queen West** (Map pp76-7; ☎ 416-913-2720; 894 Queen St W; streetcar 501).

Good pick-me-up lunches in the form of crepes, quiches and salads can be had at **Jules Restaurant Tarterie** (Map pp80-1; ☎ 416-348-8886; 147 Spadina Ave; meals $6-13; ☺ lunch Mon-Sat, dinner Mon-Fri; streetcar 510, 501), or if Thai, Malay and Indonesian are your gastronomic preference, try **Friendly Thai** (Map pp80-1; ☎ 416-924-8424; 678 Yonge St; mains $7-13; ☺ lunch & dinner; subway Wellesley).

Other spicy sensations:
Eating Garden (Map pp80-1; ☎ 416-595-5525; 41-3 Baldwin St; mains $8-15; ☺ lunch & dinner; streetcar 505) Classics such as fresh seafood in garlic appear next to inventive dishes showing pan-Asian flair.

Jodhpore Club (Map pp80-1; ☎ 416-598-2502; 33 Baldwin St; weekday lunch buffet $8, mains $7-13; ☺ lunch Mon-Sat, dinner daily; streetcar 505) Spicy curries, from the beaches of Goa up into the Himalayas. Excellent lunch buffet.

TOP END

The truly divine **Sen5es** (Map pp80-1; ☎ 416-961-0055; 318 Wellington St W; breakfast & lunch $5-17, dinner $32-45; ☺ dinner Wed-Sun, lounge 5pm-1am; streetcar 510) is a catering extravaganza that reigns over the ground floor of the SoHo Metropolitan Hotel (p97). In the sun-drenched, airy café, you can breakfast on an impeccable cappuccino and croissant with chocolate butter, while the sleek modern dining room harbors a chef's table, offering lobster ravioli or an ocean hot plate with citrus-ginger dipping sauce

at night. Take your dinner in the lounge to sample from the same amazing menu for under $25 per plate.

Monsoon (Map pp80-1; ☎ 416-979-7172; 100 Simcoe St; dinner $20-36; ☺ lunch Mon-Fri, dinner Mon-Sat; subway St Andrew) Clean Zen lines and mid-century modern designs mix harmoniously in this lounge below street level. Monsoon's tasting menu ($88/60 with/without wine pairings) goes all out, listing the likes of halibut seared in ginger-sake sauce or Bangkok bouillabaisse along with lemongrass sorbet to refresh your palate between glorious courses. Diners canoodle in romantic pockets.

Oro (Map pp80-1; ☎ 416-597-0155; 45 Elm St; pastas $18-22, dinner $25-45; ☺ lunch Mon-Fri, dinner Mon-Sat; subway Dundas) A showpiece for the contemporary Canadian food creations of chef Dario Tomaselli, elegant Oro successfully grazes the outer limits of culinary creativity. Plates of tuna sashimi with kumamoto oyster and oven-roasted bluenose sea bass and wild mushroom ravioli are followed by similarly sensational sweets. Fresh-cut flowers rest atop polished tables, and contemporary art hangs on the walls.

YYZ Restaurant & Wine Bar (Map pp80-1; ☎ 416-599-3399; 345 Adelaide St W; mains $26-33; ⊙ dinner; streetcar 510, 504) Formerly of Mercer Street Grill, chef Chris Zielinski has reincarnated his daring fusion fare at this mod 1960s-style moon lounge, which stole its name from Toronto's airport abbreviation. A recent 'winterlicious' menu featured sweet potato–chipotle–lime soup paired with pan-seared Atlantic salmon and scallops, plus a side of sesame-encrusted sushi rice, all crowned by a royal coconut and banana mousse.

Bloor-Yorkville
MID-RANGE & TOP END
Bloor Street Diner (Map pp80-1; ☎ 416-928-3105; Manulife Centre, 55 Bloor St W; breakfast & lunch $6-14, dinner $15-21; ⊙ breakfast, lunch & dinner; subway Bloor-Yonge) This swanky place belies its humble-sounding name with banquettes, starched tablecloths, formal table service by attentive waitstaff and a Parisian-style patio. You may even catch stars dining here during the film festival. The steak and rotisserie fare are as distinguished as the bistro's wine list.

Okonomi House (Map pp80-1; ☎ 416-925-6176; 23 Charles St W; mains $6-13; ⊙ lunch & dinner; subway Bloor-Yonge) The authentic Okonomi House is one of the only places in Toronto, let alone North America, dishing up *okonomiyaki*, a savory Japanese cabbage pancake filled with your choice of meat, seafood or vegetables. It's perfect cold-weather food, as Toronto's police force can testify.

Mövenpick's Bistretto & La Pêcherie (Map pp80-1; ☎ 416-926-9545; 133 Yorkville Ave; mains $13-45; ⊙ brunch Sat & Sun, lunch & dinner daily; subway Bay) Another branch of the Mövenpick empire, this restaurant has everyone raving about its seafood. A daily-changing menu is written on a chalkboard, which waitstaff will hoist over to your table before launching into descriptions of the day's mouth-watering fare. Vegetarian dishes can be made to order. Although the atmosphere is smart, it's also family-friendly, especially inside the casual street level.

University of Toronto & The Annex
BUDGET
Cora Pizza (Map pp80-1; ☎ 416-922-1188; 656 Spadina Ave; ⊙ lunch & dinner; streetcar 510) Students and locals rave about the gourmet toppings and inventive combinations on these pizzas. They're heavenly on a winter day.

MID-RANGE
By the Way (Map pp80-1; ☎ 416-967-4295; 400 Bloor St W; mains $7-11; ⊙ breakfast, lunch & dinner; subway Bathurst, Spadina) A fixture in The Annex, this neighborhood bistro has a daily-changing menu of Mediterranean and New World fusion dishes, with plenty of creative choices for vegetarians. Service is A+ and the wine list features Niagara ice varietals and labels from as far away as Oregon and Australia. But why do people forsake the cozy booths inside for the claustrophobic patio?

Latitude (Map pp80-1; ☎ 416-928-0926; 89 Harbord St; mains $12-20; ⊙ lunch daily, dinner Tue-Sat; streetcar 510) An Uruguayan chef takes care with pan–Latin American fare, and although the menu occasionally speaks of Asia, there's always fried yucca or plantains on the side. Looking for a romantic tree-draped back patio? Walk straight back past the intimate wine bar.

Harbord Fish & Chips (Map pp80-1; ☎ 416-925-2225; 147 Harbord St; meals $6-10; ⊙ lunch & dinner; bus 94) This fish-and-chip shack wins big smiles for its generous portions of haddock and halibut, all freshly fried. Get yours wrapped in newspaper, or eat at outdoor picnic tables while your laundry spins at Coin-O-Rama across the street.

Kensington Market
BUDGET
Jumbo Empanadas (Map pp80-1; ☎ 416-977-0056; 245 Augusta Ave; items $3-6; ⊙ lunch Mon-Sun, dinner Mon-Sat; streetcar 510) They're not kidding – real Chilean empanadas (beef, chicken, cheese or vegetable) and savory corn pie with beef, olives and eggs always sell out early in the day. The bread and salsas are also homemade.

MID-RANGE
Streams of Blessings Fish Shack (Map pp80-1; ☎ 416-597-2364; 285 Augusta Ave; mains $6-12; ⊙ lunch & dinner; streetcar 506) A reggae-style seafood kitchen, Streams of Blessings boasts chilled-out couches and a few tables, but the ace-in-the-hole is the food: Jamaican-style fish (fried whole and peppered with incendiary hot sauce), red snapper stew served with a side of plantains and vegetarian coconut bun sandwiches.

Little Italy
MID-RANGE
Bar Italia (Map pp76-7; ☎ 416-535-3621; 582 College St; meals $7-25; ⊙ lunch & dinner Mon-Sun, from 10:30 Sat &

Sun; streetcar 506) Trendsetters come and go, but Bar Italia remains a place to be seen, as well as to relax. Grab an excellent sandwich or lightly done pasta, with a lemon gelato and a rich coffee afterward, and you could while the entire afternoon or evening away. Seats on the convivial sidewalk patio are scarcely ever free.

TOP END

Xacutti (Map pp80-1; ☎ 416-323-3957; 503 College St; small plates $8-15, large plates $20-35; ⊙ brunch & lunch Sat & Sun, dinner Tue-Sat; streetcar 506) Swirls of chocolate brown and jet black come alive with saffron accents, as befits such exotic twists on regional Indian cooking as Goan-spiced duck, or hot tikka baked salmon with tamarind sauce. In a hurry? You won't believe your good luck: the kitchen offers prepared take-out meals.

Queen West
BUDGET

Dufflet Pastries (Map pp76-7; ☎ 416-504-2870; 787 Queen St W; items from $2; ⊙ 10am-7pm Mon-Sat, noon-6pm Sun; streetcar 501) Dufflet's desserts appear at Toronto's most prestigious restaurants; bite into tasty little temptations like sugar cookies, tarts or sinful chocolate cakes here.

MID-RANGE

Cantena (Map pp76-7; ☎ 416-703-9360; 181 Bathurst St; dinner $12-22; ⊙ dinner daily, 10:30am-4:30pm Sat & Sun; streetcar 501, 511) Glorious Cantena hides on an unsavory street corner. Who would suspect that its motto is 'Damn fine food. Kick-ass cocktails'? Or that the ultra-creative menu lives up to its promises? A tapas-style dinner menu of platters, meant to be shared by up to four people, is a steal, and on weekends there's the Hangover Helper brunch (served until 4:30pm).

Fressen (Map pp80-1; ☎ 416-504-5127; 478 Queen St W; mains $12-18; ⊙ brunch Sat & Sun, dinner daily; streetcar 501) The city's epitome of haute vegetarian (and vegan) dining, smiling service and high-backed wooden booths make for an enjoyable night out here, even for carnivores. A strong and stylish organic menu picks among the world's cuisines, depending on what's seasonal when you visit.

Red Tea Box (Map pp76-7; ☎ 416-203-8882; 696 Queen St W; lunch or afternoon tea $15-25; ⊙ 10am-6pm Mon & Wed-Thu, 10am-7pm Fri & Sat, noon-5pm Sun; streetcar 501) This jewel-like place has authentic

South Asian flair. Hand-woven Thai textiles drape the walls and people are willing to queue for their monthly changing *bentō* boxes, which reveal a fusion of taste-bud temptations. Everything's gorgeous, and seasonally inspired. The afternoon tea is exotic and inviting. Reservations are not accepted.

Authentic gems:

Jalapeño's (Map pp76-7; ☎ 416-216-6743; 725 King St W; mains $9-15; ⊙ lunch & dinner; streetcar 504) Superb regional Mexican specialties like chicken *molé poblano* (spicy sauce with a hint of chocolate).

Terroni (Map pp76-7; ☎ 416-504-0320; 720 Queen St W; meals $6-12; ⊙ breakfast, lunch & dinner; streetcar 501) Traditional southern Italian grocery store and deli.

TOP END

Susur (Map pp76-7; ☎ 416-603-2205; 601 King St W; mains $35-45, tasting menu $70-110; ⊙ dinner Mon-Sat; streetcar 504, 511) Star chef Susur Lee will take you on a whimsical journey with his elaborate tasting menus, which race from Europe to the New World to Asia and back again. Each plate is a magical study in contrasts, complemented by an imaginative wine list. Even vegetarians will find a bounty of culinary goodness here. Make reservations at least several weeks in advance.

East Toronto
MID-RANGE

Real Jerk (Map pp76-7; ☎ 416-463-6055; 709 Queen St E; mains $5-12; ⊙ lunch Mon-Fri, dinner daily; streetcar 501, 502, 503, 504) This renowned Caribbean kitchen serves classic jerk (preserved, thinly sliced meat) chicken, oxtail or goat curries, 'rasta pasta' and Red Stripe beer. Inside it feels just like a huge beach bar, with reggae beats, tropical decor and Jamaican flags hanging everywhere.

Ouzeri (Map pp76-7; ☎ 416-778-0500; 500A Danforth Ave; mezes $5-10, mains $12-20; ⊙ lunch & dinner; subway Chester) Sophisticated mezes and seafood endear this friendly place to local families. Roasted eggplant with a Greek salad and a cold beer will cost around $15. There's live traditional Greek music some nights.

Yer Ma's Kitchen (Map pp76-7; ☎ 416-778-1804; 141 Danforth Ave; mains $8-20; ⊙ dinner, closed Mon; subway Broadview) Dora Keogh's pub serves amazing Irish fare from an open country-style kitchen at the back. Salmon, potato and green onion cakes served with chili sour cream are unforgettable. Handwritten menus are put out in the bar from 5pm until

ONTARIO

whenever the kitchen runs out of food, but you're usually safe arriving before 9pm.

Other recommendations:

Silk Road Café (Map pp76-7; ☎ 416-463-8660; 341 Danforth Ave; mains $7-12; ❧ lunch Tue-Sat, dinner daily; subway Chester) Get your noodle fix here with hot Japanese sake or cool Chinese plum wine.

Rashnaa (Map pp76-7; ☎ 416-929-2099; 307 Wellesley St E; mains $6-10; ❧ lunch & dinner; streetcar 506) Unbeatable prices and imaginative dishes like South Indian devil curries and Sri Lankan 'String Hopper Rotty.'

ΠAN (Map pp76-7; ☎ 416-466-8158; 516 Danforth Ave; mezes $5-13, mains $13-23; ❧ dinner; subway Chester) Traditional Greek mezes and delights.

TOP END

Café Brussel (Map pp76-7; ☎ 416-465-7363; 124 Danforth Ave; mains $24-30; ❧ dinner Tue-Sat; subway Broadview) This neck of the woods may be known as Greektown, but diners don't seem to mind the Belgian invasion. Mussels ($18 per kg with *frites*) are served 32 ways, from Tahiti to Provençale style. European, Québecois and Belgian microbrews are on hand, while a notable wine list includes more than 600 labels.

The Beaches
MID-RANGE

White Bros Fish Co (Map pp76-7; ☎ 416-694-3474; 2248 Queen St E; meals $5-15; ❧ dinner Tue-Sun, lunch Fri; streetcar 501) A fraternal feeling suffuses this storefront, which we'll crown the king of all The Beaches' fish-and-chip shops. Cheery tables fill up fast as diners demand hearty chowders, citrus seafood salads, grilled calamari, blackened fish and divine scallops. Kids are part of the decor here.

Beacher Café (Map pp76-7; ☎ 416-699-3874; 2162 Queen St E; mains $8-18; ❧ breakfast, lunch & dinner; streetcar 501) Looking like a seaside house out of a Virginia Woolf novel, this long-running café has a sought-after sidewalk patio. Particularly good are the egg and pancake brunches; at other times the burgers, salads and seafood are reasonable. Splashes of local artwork change monthly.

Greater Toronto Area
TOP END

Celestin (Map pp76-7; ☎ 416-544-9035; 623 Mt Pleasant Rd; mains $28-45; ❧ dinner Tue-Sat; subway St Clair, then bus 74) Chef Pascal Ribreau's imaginative French cooking triumphs inside a converted bank, where tantalizing *amuse-bouche* (amusements for the mouth) precede artful

mains of succulent lamb shanks, baked Atlantic salmon with homemade gnocchi or veal sweetbreads. Celestin's atmosphere induces serenity; it has widely spaced tables and superb service by waitstaff who know all about the wines cellared away in the old bank vault.

DRINKING

Considering its British heritage, it's odd that Toronto has so many out-of-the-box pub chains with names starting with a generic 'Duke' or 'Bishop' and ending with Newcastle, Firkin or something just as predictable, instead of watering holes with genuine character.

Never fear, however, the city has candidates for punters seeking a genuine Toronto drinking hole. Pubs are popular in Old York and The Annex, particularly the latter where they also function as venues of procrastination for UT students. On Little Italy's swank College St, porto bars are fast outnumbering martini lounges, while new bohemians favor Queen West. Other watering holes are found Downtown.

Legislation has been passed in Toronto which bans smoking in all bars, pool halls, bingo halls, casinos and racetracks. Smoking is still permitted in restaurants, dinner theatres and bowling alleys but only in designated smoking rooms.

C'est What (Map pp80-1; ☎ 416-867-9499; 67 Front St E, Old York; streetcar 504) Over 30 whiskeys and two dozen Canadian microbrews are on hand at this modern pub near the St Lawrence Market. An in-house brewmaster has created a velvety Coffee Porter that is heavenly. Feel free to drink your way across the nation here.

Irish Embassy Pub & Grill (Map pp80-1; ☎ 416-866-8282; 49 Yonge St, Old York; subway King) Calling themselves 'Ambassadors of Irish Hospitality,' this smart-looking pub is loved by all. It holds court inside a distinguished Victorian edifice with stained glass windows and glowing lamps. A convivial crowd stops by for after-work drinks, footy matches on satellite TV and hearty gourmet pub fare, including ale-battered halibut and Irish stew.

Amsterdam Brewing Co (Map pp76-7; ☎ 416-504-6886; 600 King St W, Queen West; ❧ 11am-11pm Mon-Sat, 11am-6pm Sun; streetcar 504, 511) Toronto's first microbrewery makes cheery batches of cold-filtered beers, including a Belgian-style framboise, Irish stout, Dutch amber ale and the 'Avalanche' (a stunningly strong lager). The signature 'Nut Brown Ale' utilizes four different Canadian and international malts, including a chocolate variety from Belgium.

Madison Avenue Pub (Map pp80-1; ☎ 416-927-1722; 14-18 Madison Ave, The Annex; subway Spadina) The elegant Madison is built out of three Victorian houses, where antique-looking lamps light the curtained upper floors at night. Wander the elephantine interior, where you'll find a fireplace, jukebox, darts, billiards, live piano music (Thursday to Saturday) and a specialty bar stocking imported beers and scotch. Did we mention there are five patios, too?

Gladstone Hotel (Map pp76-7; ☎ 416-531-4635; 1214 Queen St W, Queen West; streetcar 501) A down-at-heel historic hotel on Queen West reveals Toronto's avant-garde arts scene. It's best known for the Melody Bar, a place for karaoke (9pm to 2am Wednesday to Saturday). Other spaces, namely the Art Bar and the Gladstone Ballroom, are taken over by off-beat DJs, 'earresponsible' musicians and odd events like nouveau vaudeville or a 'Pedal to the Metal' craft fair. Cover charge varies (usually $10 or less).

Lion on the Beach (Map pp76-7; ☎ 416-690-1984; 1958 Queen St E, The Beaches; streetcar 501) An expansive pub that spills out onto the sidewalk (lyin' on the beach – get it?). There's a respectably long list of beers and hearty pub grub, such as bangers and mash or fried rainbow trout, to keep everyone satisfied. Children are welcome.

Castro's Lounge (Map pp76-7; ☎ 416-699-8272; 2116 Queen St E, The Beaches; streetcar 501) An attitude-free zone near the Beach, this bohemian bar has lots of Canadian microbrews, vintage posters and hardwood tables, around which cluster the local literati, conspiracy theorists, political activists and slacker hangers-on. Occasionally the bar hosts spoken word events and live music.

Hemingway's (Map pp80-1; ☎ 416-968-2828; 142 Cumberland St, Bloor-Yorkville; subway Bay) Equal parts sports pub, singles' bar and jazz venue, Hemingway's is undeniably a Yorkville hot spot. Its heated double-deck rooftop patio makes for a vivacious night out with upwardly mobile Torontonians.

More watering holes:

Cobalt (Map pp80-1; ☎ 416-923-4456; 426 College St, Little Italy; streetcar 506) A heavy dose of ambience with an eclectic vibe.

Esplanade Bier Markt (Map pp76-7; ☎ 416-862-7575; 58 The Esplanade, Old York; streetcar 504) The beer menu covers Belgium to South Africa to Trinidad, with over 150 varieties.

James Joyce Traditional Irish Pub (Map pp80-1; ☎ 416-324-9400; 386 Bloor St W, The Annex; subway Spadina) A student favorite with live folk music.

ENTERTAINMENT

Toronto's nightlife artfully keeps everyone busy long after dark, and there's plenty of entertainment going on during the daylight hours, too. Whether it's a Mad Bastard Cabaret (p108), indie film festival, legendary Second City comedy, world-class concert, radical Canadian theater, a slate of live local bands or a simple brewpub, you'll have no trouble finding it here. There are free outdoor festivals and concerts going on nearly every weekend, especially in summer (see p95).

The city's most encyclopedic entertainment guide is inside the free alternative weekly *Now*, while *Xtra!* and *eye* stay on top of the club, alt-culture and live-music beats. All three daily newspapers provide weekly entertainment listings, too. Glossy *Toronto Life* magazine publishes a monthly 'what's on' guide.

For an added booking fee, **Ticketmaster** (☎ 416-870-8000; www.ticketmaster.ca) sells tickets for major concerts, sports games, theater and performing arts events. Buy tickets online or at various city outlets, including Sky-Dome. **TO Tix** (☎ 416-536-6468 ext 40; www.totix.ca; 1 Dundas St E, Dundas Sq; ☺ noon-6pm Tue-Sat; subway Dundas) sells half-price and discount same-day rush tickets. The classified sections of newspapers and alternative weeklies also list tickets available for every event in town.

Live Music

Live music thrives in Toronto, and whether you're tuned to rock, reggae, jazz, blues, hip-hop, folk or classical, there are venues small and large fuelling your passion all over town. Expect to pay anywhere from nothing to a few dollars on weeknights; up to $20 or more for breakthrough weekend acts. Under-19s are usually not admitted to bars or clubs where alcohol is served, except during all-ages shows.

Mega-tours stop at SkyDome, the Air Canada Centre and the Molson Amphitheatre at Ontario Place. Major independent concert halls are **Phoenix** (Map pp80-1; ☎ 416-323-1251;

410 Sherbourne St; streetcar 506) and Koolhaus inside the Guvernment (p111).

ROCK, JAZZ & BLUES

Local bands often get their first gigs at **360** (Map pp80-1; ☎ 416-593-0840; 326 Queen St W; streetcar 501), the former Royal Canadian Legion hall. Full slates of live shows almost nightly feature indie rock bands, from renowned Canadian acts to bizarrely named unknowns.

Horseshoe Tavern (Map pp80-1; ☎ 416-598-4753; 370 Queen St W; streetcar 501) Past its 50th birthday, the legendary Horseshoe with its long-ass country-and-western bar is still showcasing 'roots, rock and alt nu music.' The Police played here to an almost empty house on their first North American tour; Sting did an encore in his underwear. Tuesday is usually a no-cover music night.

nia (Map pp80-1; ☎ 416-867-9499; 19 Church St; ☺ from 9:30pm; streetcar 504) This slender music lounge catapults a new act onto the stage nearly nightly. Open your ears to Toronto's singer-songwriters or international pop, roots, rock, funk, ambient and world grooves. Even the Barenaked Ladies have played here.

Rex (Map pp80-1; ☎ 416-598-2475; 194 Queen St W; streetcar 501) Make a beeline for the Rex Hotel, which has risen out of its down-at-the-heel past to become a renowned venue for live jazz and blues. Over a dozen different Dixieland, experimental and other local and international acts knock over the joint each week. Drinks are cheap, and the cover is never more than $6.

Silver Dollar Room (Map pp80-1; ☎ 416-763-9139; 486 Spadina Ave; streetcar 506, 510) True blues reign supreme at the legendary Silver Dollar, where big-name touring acts from down south (ie Detroit and Chicago) kick up ticket prices, sometimes above $30 on weekends. There's no cover charged for midweek bluegrass jams and Saturday afternoon shows.

Montréal Bistro & Jazz Club (Map pp80-1; ☎ 416-363-0179; 65 Sherbourne St; streetcar 503, 504) Top-notch local and international jazz cats play in front of the petite table lamps at elegant Montréal Bistro. For a really romantic night out you can top it off with dinner here (p101). Monday is for one-off events, while headliners perform Tuesday through Saturday.

Healey's (Map pp76-7; ☎ 416-703-5882; 178 Bathurst St, Queen West; ☺ 8pm-2am Tue-Sat; streetcar 501) This 300-person club has an idiosyncratic line-up of rock, as well as blues, soul and roots music. Stop by when owner Jeff Healey, a Canadian music icon, audiophile and radio DJ, gets up on stage with his house band. Tuesday open-jam nights and Saturday matinees have no cover.

Cameron House (Map pp80-1; ☎ 416-703-0811; 408 Queen St W; streetcar 501) Get down with soul, R&B, acid jazz and other alt-music at this veteran Queen West venue. Artists, musicians, dreamers and slackers – all types – fill the front and back rooms here. On Sunday evenings, Mad Bastard Cabaret ('accordion singing about love, lust and Spain') is a big draw, and so are live swing music nights.

Lee's Palace (Map pp76-7; ☎ 416-532-1598; 529 Bloor St W; subway Bathurst) Lee's Palace has set the stage for Dinosaur Jr, Buffalo Tom and the Cure. When Nirvana played here in 1990, Kurt Cobain started an infamous bottle-throwing incident. With booming acoustics, it's a viable alt-rock concert venue.

Grossman's (Map pp80-1; ☎ 416-977-7000; 379 Spadina Ave; streetcar 510) Inside a grubby 1940s tavern near Kensington Market, the emphasis is on singin' the blues, but acoustic rock and folk acts also appear. Incidentally, Dan Akroyd first worked on *The Blues Brothers* routine here. Grossman's has music nightly – the Sunday night jam session has been raising the roof for nearly two decades – but rarely a cover charge.

CLASSICAL, OPERA & WORLD MUSIC

The main classical performance season starts in September and runs straight through until spring. Roy Thomson Hall and Massey Hall also present a world of music, from opera tenors to chamber groups to the Girls Choir of Harlem.

Canadian Opera Company (Map pp80-1; ☎ 416-363-8231, 800-250-4653; www.coc.ca; tickets $40-175) In business for over half a century, Canada's national opera company can claim to have invented surtitles, where text translations visible to the audience are projected over a proscenium arch. Advance tickets sell out quickly; check the website about a month before opening night for details. Performances are currently held at the **Hummingbird Centre for the Performing Arts** (Map pp80-1; ☎ 416-393-7476; 1 Front St E; ☺ box office 10am-6pm Mon-Fri, 10am-1pm Sat; subway Union) but will be moved to the new **Four Seasons Centre for the Performing Arts** (Cnr Queen St & University Ave) once construction is finished in 2006.

Glenn Gould Studio (Map pp80-1; ☎ 416-205-5555; http://glenngouldstudio.cbc.ca; Canadian Broadcasting Centre, 250 Front St W; tickets $15-40; ☺ box office 11am-6pm Mon-Fri, during summer 11am-5pm Tue-Thu; streetcar 504) Free noontime concerts are given in the Glenn Gould Studio, where the soundtrack for *Schindler's List* was recorded. You'll need to purchase advance tickets for highly esteemed evening concerts of classical and contemporary music by soloists, chamber groups, choirs and symphony orchestras between September and June. Young international artists are often featured.

Harbourfront Centre (Map pp80-1; ☎ box office 416-973-4000; www.harbourfront.on.ca; 235 Queens Quay W; ☺ box office 1-8pm Tue-Sat; streetcar 509, 510) The vibrant Harbourfront Centre puts on a variety of world-class musical performances throughout the year, including Sunday family shows (adult/family $8/20) and free outdoor summer concerts in the Toronto Music Garden (p79).

Toronto Symphony Orchestra (TSO; Map pp80-1; ☎ 416-593-4828; www.tso.on.ca; customer service center box office; 212 King St W; tickets $30-100; ☺ box office 10am-6pm Mon-Fri, noon-5pm Sat; subway St Andrew) A range of classics, Cole Porter-era pops and new music from around the world are presented by the TSO at **Roy Thomson Hall** (Map pp80-1; ☎ 416-872-4255; www.roythomson.com; 60 Simcoe St; ☺ box office 10am-6pm Mon-Fri, noon-5pm Sat; subway St Andrew), **Massey Hall** (Map pp80-1; www.masseyhall.com; 178 Victoria St; subway Queen) and the Toronto Centre for the Arts. Younger patrons aged 15 to 29 can buy 'tsoundcheck' (www.tsoundcheck.com) tickets for $10; these tickets usually go on sale the Monday of the performance week.

Cinemas

Ticket prices start at $7/4 for adults/children at indie and arthouse cinemas, doubling to $14/8.50 at commercial monoliths.

Cinematheque Ontario (Map pp80-1; ☎ 416-968-3456; www.bell.ca/cinematheque; Art Gallery of Ontario, 317 Dundas St W; ☺ closed late Aug & Sep; subway St Patrick) The popular Cinematheque Ontario screens world cinema, independent films and retrospectives of famous directors, sometimes introduced by film critics and Canadian authors. Nonmembers can purchase tickets at the box office 30 minutes before the

day's first screening. Be quick – tickets sell quickly.

Cineplex Odeon Varsity (Map pp80-1; ☎ 416-961-6303; 2nd fl, Manulife Centre, 55 Bloor St W; subway Bloor-Yonge) Screening a range of movies, from Hollywood blockbusters to small-budget indie releases, this state-of-the-art multiplex has VIP theaters, with extra leg room, tableside refreshment service and smaller screens (but excellent sound). In downtown, **Cineplex Odeon Carlton** (Map pp80-1; ☎ 416-598-2309; 20 Carlton St; subway College) attracts a more diverse crowd by screening major independent films and some truly bizarre offerings.

Bloor Theatre (Map pp76-7; ☎ 416-516-2330; www.bloorcinema.com; 506 Bloor St W; subway Bathurst) This art-deco theater with a two-tiered balcony screens a wonderfully varied schedule of new releases, art-house flicks, shorts, documentaries and vintage films. Buy an annual membership card ($4) and pay just $4 per movie.

Famous Players Paramount (Map pp80-1; ☎ 416-368-5600, IMAX 416-368-6089; 259 Richmond St W; subway Osgoode) This gargantuan multiplex features new releases and the latest in IMAX technology, including 3D. It's always screening a dozen movies or more, with some offbeat picks found among bigger mainstream releases.

More flick picks:

Docks Drive-In Theatre (Map pp76-7; ☎ 416-461-3625; www.thedocks.com; 11 Polson St; ☺ Apr-Sep) Waterfront complex accommodating cars and nonmotorists. Double bills feature first-run blockbusters.

Greektown's Music Hall (Map pp76-7; ☎ 416-778-8272; www.festivalcinemas.com; 147 Danforth Ave; subway Broadview) Part of the Festival Cinemas group.

Theater

Toronto is a playground for first-rate theater. Big-time Broadway musicals have their try-outs, indefinite runs and encore engagements year-round on downtown's Theatre Block and near Dundas Sq. Upstart companies favor smaller venues around Harbourfront and in the Distillery Historic District. The main season runs from September through June. Go to www.onstagetoronto.ca or check newspapers and alternative weeklies for current listings.

Tickets for major productions are sold through **TicketKing** (☎ 416-872-1212, 800-461-3333; www.ticketking.com). For half-price tickets,

ONTARIO

go to TO Tix (p107) or inquire about 'rush' tickets at theater box offices.

Canadian Stage Company (Map pp80-1; ☎ 416-368-3110; www.canstage.com; 26 Berkeley St; tickets $25-50; ☺ box office 10am-6pm Mon-Sat; streetcar 503, 504) Contemporary CanStage produces top Canadian and international plays by the likes of David Mamet and Stephen Sondheim. Plays are staged at its own theater and the **St Lawrence Centre for the Arts** (Map pp80-1; ☎ 416-366-7723, 800-708-6754; 27 Front St E, Old York; subway Union).

Dream in High Park (Map pp76-7; ☎ 416-367-1652 ext 500; 1873 Bloor St W, High Park; admission by donation $15; ☺ 8pm Tue-Sun Jul & Aug; streetcar 506) From July until Labour Day, CanStage's wonderful mid-summer presentation of Shakespeare happens under the stars in High Park. Show up early and take a blanket. Admission is 'pay what you can', but donations are appreciated.

Buddies in Bad Times Theatre (Map pp80-1; ☎ 416-975-8555; www.buddiesinbadtimestheatre.com; 12 Alexander St; tickets around $20; subway College) This innovative venue for lesbigay and Canadian theater hosts original plays, contemporary dance and music. It's tiny – there are only 300 seats for the main stage.

Elgin & Winter Garden Theatre Centre (Map pp80-1; ☎ 416-872-5555; www.mirvish.com; 189 Yonge St, Dundas Sq; tickets $25-100; ☺ box office 11am-5pm Mon, 11am-8pm Tue-Sat, noon-2pm Sun; subway Queen) The restored Elgin & Winter Garden Theatre stages high-profile productions. Nearby, the **Canon Theatre** (Map pp80-1; ☎ 416-872-1212, 800-461-3333; 244 Victoria St; tickets $25-120; ☺ box office 10:30am-6pm Mon, 10:30am-8pm Tue-Sat, 11am-3pm Sun), a 1920s-era Pantages vaudeville hall, is a hot ticket for musicals such as *The Producers*.

Royal Alexandra Theatre (Map pp80-1; ☎ 416-872-1212, 800-461-3333; www.mirvish.com; Theatre Block, 260 King St W; tickets $25-100; ☺ box office 10:30am-6:30pm Mon-Tue, 10:30am-8:30pm Wed-Sat, 11am-7pm Sun; streetcar 504) Familiarly known as the 'Royal Alex' and found on Toronto's Theatre Block, it's one of the most impressive theaters in the city. Nearby is the lavish **Princess of Wales Theatre** (Map pp80-1; 300 King St W; ☺ box office 10:30am-6:30pm Mon-Fri). At either theater, you can catch splashy Broadway musicals.

Factory Theatre (Map pp76-7; ☎ 416-504-9971; www.factorytheatre.ca; 125 Bathurst St, Queen West; tickets $20-35, previews $12; ☺ box office noon-8pm Tue-Sat; streetcar 511) In an off-the-beaten-path Victorian home, this innovative theater company

premieres Canadian and international plays, as well as new playwrights' scribblings during the independent **SummerWorks Theatre Festival** (☎ 416-410-1048; www.summerworks.ca).

Gay & Lesbian Venues

For a bevy or 10 and far too much good fun, head to one or more of the following venues, many of which are in the Church–Wellesley Village.

Woody's/Sailor (Map pp80-1; ☎ 416-972-0887; www.woodystoronto.com; 465-7 Church St; subway Wellesley) On any given night, Woody's sells more beer than any other bar in the country. The city's most popular gay bar complex has a full bag of special tricks, from drag shows to leather events to billiards tables, and DJs spin nightly. It has even made cameo appearances on the TV series *Queer as Folk*.

El Convento Rico (Map pp76-7; ☎ 416-588-7800; 750 College St; ☺ Thu-Sun; streetcar 506) Inside a former church, this queer Latin dance palace sees as much straight as gay clientele these days, but drag shows still triumphantly go on stage Friday and Saturday night.

5IVE (Map pp80-1; ☎ 416-964-8685; 5 St Joseph St; ☺ Wed-Sun; subway Wellesley) Electronica and progressive house music dominate this upmarket gay spot, where go-go boys shine like angels and women clubbers are in the mix. Avoid a cover charge before midnight some nights, or attend 'Sunday morning worship' starting after dawn until noon.

Babylon (Map pp80-1; ☎ 416-923-2626; 533 Church St; subway Wellesley) A hip martini lounge (with hundreds of imaginative varieties to choose from), Babylon rises inside an elegant Church–Wellesley Village brownstone. Lie back upon couches upstairs where beautiful boys languorously swirl jewel-colored cocktails.

Crews/Tango/Zone (Map pp80-1; ☎ 416-972-1662; 508 Church St; subway Wellesley) An elevated front patio is perfect for people-watching. Women kick up the heat at Tango, next door to the men's bar Crews (nice pun!) and cabaret-style the Zone. Show up for drag queen and king shows, or when DJs spin, usually on weekends. Nearby Victorian-style **Wilde Oscar's** (Map pp80-1; ☎ 416-921-8142; 518 Church St) pub draws a genial, mostly male crowd.

Black Eagle (Map pp80-1; ☎ 416-413-1219; 457 Church St; subway Wellesley) Leather, uniform and denim men go here, where strict dress codes are in full effect. Seriously raunchy theme nights include free clothes checks at the door.

Nightclubs

No matter whether it's a big-floored dance club or a hole-in-the-wall underground spot, what's in and what's not changes in the blink of an eye. Cover charges of $5 to $12 apply on weekends, although early birds and women may get in free some nights. Most clubs open their doors around 9pm or 10pm (some don't really get going until even later) and close around 4am.

Mainstream dance clubs crowd 'Clubland', the area of the Entertainment District between Queen and King Sts W, mostly along the smaller streets of Duncan, John and Peter. The whole area is jammed on weekends; check out the beautiful people queuing and find a club that suits your taste. In Church–Wellesley Village, many bars have DJ nights. Alternative dance clubs lie along Queen West. Restaurants, bars and lounges in Little Italy are also known for their nightlife grooves. Yorkville offers a few dance floors.

System Soundbar (Map pp80-1; ☎ 416-408-3996; 117 Peter St; 🖂 Wed-Sat; streetcar 510) Resident house and drum 'n' bass DJs drive a powerful vibe, with guest appearances by UK and European DJs. Diversity is key for the crowd, with ravers, club prowlers and dance divas dying for progressive and trance grooves.

Element (Map pp80-1; ☎ 416-359-1919; 553 Queen St W; streetcar 501) It's not just another pretty hipster bar – bi-level Element imports local and international DJs. Expect to hear progressive house, techno and trance tunes. It's an open-minded spot.

Hooch (Map pp76-7; ☎ 416-703-5069; 817 Queen St W; streetcar 501) Upstairs from the Gypsy Co-op restaurant, this lounge heats up many nights of the week, often with no cover, for DJs spinning soul, jazz, house, drum 'n' bass and more. Think of rare grooves and hipster moves. Its sister, **B-Side** (Map pp80-1), over at the Entertainment District's Fez Batik (p102) has a 'jazzanova' vibe and resident DJs.

Guvernment (Map pp80-1; ☎ 416-869-0045; www .theguvernment.com; 132 Queens Quay E; 🖂 usually Thu-Sat; bus 6, 75) For a diversity of venues, nothing beats the 4500-sq-ft Guv. Some say it's too mainstream, but DJs spin hip-hop, R&B, progressive house and trance music to satisfy all appetites. The rooftop skyline

views are as impressive as the Arabian fantasy lounge and art-deco bar.

Matador (Map pp76-7; ☎ 416-533-9311; Greater Toronto, 466 Dovercourt Rd, west of Ossington Ave; 🖂 1:30am-5:30am Fri & Sat; streetcar 506) For three decades there has been after-hours madness on the huge dance floor of the Matador, just west of Little Italy. Live bands play honky-tonk and classic rock, though the owner once wrangled Leonard Cohen into a surprise show.

Other recommendations:

Docks (Map pp76-7; ☎ 416-469-5655; www.thedocks .com; 11 Polson St, off Cherry St; 🖂 Thu-Sun) Multiple nightclubs on a lakeshore entertainment complex. Peaks during summer.

Tallulah's Cabaret (Map pp80-1) Inside Buddies in Bad Times Theatre (p110), this popular club lures a mixed and unpretentious crowd.

Sports

Torontonians enjoy their spectator sports as much as any large city, with the big drawcards being baseball and hockey. SkyDome stadium is home to the **Blue Jays** (☎ 416-341-1234, 888-654-1000; www.bluejays.com; tickets from $7; 🖂 regular season Apr-Sep) of Major League Baseball's American League. They won the World Series in 1992 and 1993 – the only times that baseball's top prize has been won by a non-US team. Tickets can be bought with a credit card by phone, online or through Ticketmaster (p107). You'll pay a booking fee. You can buy tickets for cash at the SkyDome box office near Gate 9. The cheapest seats are a long way above the field. Instead, try the 500-level seats (from $22) behind home plate. The **Toronto Argonauts** (☎ 416-341-2700; www.argonauts.ca; tickets $15-50; 🖂 regular season Jun-Oct) of the fast-paced professional Canadian Football League (CFL) also play at SkyDome. Over the past 130 years, Toronto's football team has brought home more Grey Cup championships than any other city in Canada. You should bring a jacket, as things cool off at night when SkyDome's roof is open.

From September to April, the **Toronto Maple Leafs** (☎ 416-815-5500; www.mapleleafs.com; tickets $30-400; 🖂 regular season Oct-Apr) of the National Hockey League play at the **Air Canada Centre** (ACC; Map pp80-1; ☎ 416-977-1641; Bay St at Lake Shore Blvd), also known as The Hangar. Every game is pretty well sold out in advance, but a limited number of same-day tickets go on sale through Ticketmaster (p107) at 10am and then later at the ACC's ticket wicket starting around 5pm. Hockey tickets are costly, with even the 'cheap' seats going for $30.

During hockey season, the **Toronto Raptors** (☎ 416-815-5500; www.nba.com/raptors; tickets from $11; ☽ regular season Oct-Apr) of the National Basketball Association also play at the ACC. Single-game tickets, which can cost hundreds of dollars, are sold through Ticketmaster (p107).

Lacrosse (p39) may not be what you first think of when it comes to Canadian sports, but the 10-team National Lacrosse League (www.nll.com) has been building momentum for two decades. Toronto's lacrosse team, **Toronto Rock** (☎ 416-596-3075 ext 223; www .torontorock.com; tickets $10-50; ☽ regular season Jan-Apr) is red hot, having won the league's championship title in 2003. They too play at the ACC.

Woodbine Racetrack (Map pp76-7; ☎ 888-675-7223; www.woodbineentertainment.com; 555 Rexdale Blvd, Rexdale; admission free, binocular rentals $2; ☽ live races held Mar-Nov; ℗) features thoroughbreds and harness racing and is home to the prestigious Queen's Plate. It's northwest of downtown Toronto off Hwy 427, near Hwy 27. By public transport, take the subway to Kipling, then catch the direct express Woodbine shuttle bus that picks patrons up before post time (usually 12:05pm, except 6:45pm for Wednesday races) and returns them 20 minutes after the last race.

SHOPPING

Shops dot every part of the city, but you'll find concentrations of stores in huge malls like the **Eaton Centre** (Map pp80-1; ☎ 416-598-8560; 220 Yonge St; ☽ 10am-9pm Mon-Fri, 9:30am-7pm Sat, noon-6pm Sun; subway Queen, Dundas) or neighborhoods like **Kensington Market**, where TO's young bohemians buy their Rastafarian and retro clothing, along with superhero lunchboxes. On the same side of town, eclectic **Queen West** has the lion's share of radical music and clothing shops, many operated by vintage collectors or designers themselves. West of UT's St George campus, students frequent The Annex for its specialized bookstores, second-hand music shops and a hodgepodge of artistic shops, especially along Harbord St and on Markham St (aka Mirvish Village).

Chichi Bloor-Yorkville is the city center's most exclusive shopping district. This day-spa mecca was once 'Flower Power' central for hippies during the 1960s. Nothing is free here nowadays, least of all 'love' from the haughty sales clerks. Fine art and antiques dealers set up shop on Yorkville's laneways. The beauty of the pieces – and their accompanying price tags – will make you gasp.

Downtown, the underground PATH (p91) shops are literally bargain basements for discount clothing, everyday goods and services. Canadian and international design shops line King St W between Jarvis and Parliament Sts, an area known as the Design Strip. Also near downtown, the burgeoning Distillery Historic District is a major draw, with its design shops, art galleries and craft studios all inside a Victorian-era factory. Pre-loved bargains can be found at St Lawrence Market (p101), which hosts an antique and flea market every Sunday. Artisan shops abound around York Quay Centre (p78) on Harbourfront, while outdoors outfitters can be found on King St, west of the Theatre Block. Fringe shops to suit all tastes reside on the Yonge St strip and in the Church–Wellesley Village.

Aboriginal Art & Canadian Crafts

Arctic Nunavut (Map pp80-1; ☎ 416-203-7889, 800-509-9151; ground fl, Queen's Quay Terminal, 207 Queens Quay W; ☽ 10am-6pm; streetcar 509, 510) Carved Inukshuk figurines, handcrafted jewelry, embroidered vests, arctic-related books, polar footwear, videos and DVDs are all sold here. Proceeds from sales benefit the Nunavut Development Corporation, which supports artists from Canada's Aboriginal-run territory.

Bay of Spirits Gallery (Map pp80-1; ☎ 416-971-5190; 156 Front St W; ☽ 10am-6pm Mon-Fri, 11am-5pm Sat; subway Union) This is one of the only galleries in Toronto to see works by West Coast First Nations artists. This atmospheric art gallery specializes in high-quality aboriginal carvings and prints, as well as handcrafted jewelry, blankets and embroidered goods. Be aware that some less-expensive items (and maybe even some more expensive ones) are not made in Canada (see p859).

Guild Shop (Map pp80-1; ☎ 416-921-1721; 118 Cumberland St; subway Bay) The Ontario Crafts Council has been promoting artisans for over 70 years. Ceramics, jewelry, glassworks, prints and carvings make up most of the displays, but you could also catch a special exhibition of Pangnirtung weaving or Cape Dorset graphics. Staff are knowledgeable about First Nations art.

Cedar Basket (Map pp80-1; ☎ 416-964-9087; 16 Spadina Rd; ☺ 10am-6pm Mon-Wed & Fri, 10am-8pm Thu, 10am-4pm Sat; subway Spadina) The nonprofit gift shop of the Native Canadian Centre (p88) sells original works by First Nations artists, including beaded moccasins, bone choker necklaces, porcupine quill boxes, dreamcatchers, pottery, carvings and jewelry. It also carries aboriginal music CDs.

Fashion

John Fluevog (Map pp80-1; ☎ 416-581-1420; www .fluevog.com; 242 Queen St W; ☺ 11am-7pm Mon-Wed, 11am-8pm Thu & Fri, 10am-7pm Sat, noon-6pm Sun; streetcar 501) Creating one-of-a-kind shoes with attitude, this Vancouver-based designer claims '50s furniture and anything vintage as his inspirations. The website has previews of Fluevog's latest whimsies, costing up to a few hundred dollars per fantastic pair. Shoes come as tough-girl chunky or sex-kitten pointy as you like, with equally hip selections for men.

Courage My Love (Map pp80-1; ☎ 416-979-1992; 14 Kensington Ave; ☺ 11:30am-6pm Mon-Fri, 11am-6pm Sat, 1-5pm Sun; streetcar 505, 510) Vintage clothing stores have been around Kensington Market for decades, but Courage My Love amazes fashion mavens with its second-hand slip dresses, retro pants and white dress shirts in a cornucopia of styles. The beads, buttons, leather goods and silver jewelry are handpicked.

Annie Thompson Studio (Map pp76-7; ☎ 416-703-3843; 674 Queen St W; ☺ 11am-6pm Tue-Sat, 1-5pm Sun; streetcar 501) Internationally famous designer Annie Thompson's shop sells local clothing creations with a bold, yet relaxed urban modish look for both sexes. Her motto: 'Personality is a terrible thing to waste.' Pieces are individually numbered like limited-edition artwork.

Preloved (Map pp76-7; ☎ 416-504-8704; 613 Queen St W; ☺ 11am-6pm Mon-Wed, 11am-7pm Thu & Fri, 10am-7pm Sat, noon-6pm Sun; streetcar 501) Movie stars are among the many devotees of Preloved's one-of-a-kind clothing re-designs of brave new cuts of vintage clothing. An aloha shirt might become a skirt, or a chrysanthemum kimono could be made into pajama pants – it's all original work here.

GETTING THERE & AWAY
Air

Most Canadian airlines and international carriers arrive at Canada's busiest airport, **Lester B Pearson International Airport** (Map pp76-7; ☎ 416-247-7678, Terminal 3 ☎ 416-776-5100), located about a 27km drive northwest of downtown Toronto. Terminal assignments are subject to change, so call ahead or check the airport entrance signs carefully.

Air Canada and WestJet compete heavily and match fares between Toronto and Ottawa (from $54), Montréal (from $90), Halifax (from $125), Calgary (from $150), Edmonton (from $175), Vancouver (from $194) and Victoria (from $300).

On the Toronto Islands, small **Toronto City Centre Airport** (Map pp76-7; ☎ 416-203-6942) is used by regional airlines, helicopter companies, charter and private flights.

Boat

From Toronto, speedy **Seaflight Hydrofoils** (Map pp80-1; ☎ 416-504-8825, 877-504-8825; 249 Queens Quay W) operates 70-minute boat trips to Queenston dock, along the Niagara Parkway. Fares (one way/round-trip $40/70) include a shuttle bus to either Niagara Falls or Niagara-on-the-Lake. Make reservations three to five days ahead. With advance notice, bicycles can be accommodated at no extra charge.

Bus

Long-distance buses operate from the **Metro Toronto Coach Terminal** (Map pp80-1; ☎ 416-393-7911; 610 Bay St; subway Dundas), which has coin lockers and a **Travellers' Aid Society** (☎ 416-596-8647) help desk. When making reservations, always ask for a direct or express bus. Advance tickets do not guarantee a seat.

Greyhound Canada connects Toronto with much of southwestern Ontario, including Niagara Falls (adult/child $27/14, 1½ hours, frequently), Hamilton ($19.50/10, six daily Monday to Friday, one daily Saturday), and London ($34.50/17.50, 2¼ hours, five to 10 daily). West of Toronto, Greyhound Canada travels from Toronto to Sudbury ($66/33, five hours, four daily), Sault Ste Marie ($125/65, 10¾ hours, five daily) and Thunder Bay ($180/90, 20 hours, four daily). It also operates the route to Ottawa ($73/37, 5¼ hours, frequently) and Montréal ($88/44, eight hours, frequently), Kitchener ($21/11, 1¾ hours, frequently) and Peterborough ($27/13.50, 1¾ hours, frequently). See p71 for information about cross-border Greyhound buses to and from the USA. Fares offered by Coach Canada (p871) to Niagara Falls, Montréal, and New York City are comparable to Greyhound's.

Adjacent to the main coach terminal, on its western side, is the bus station for (among other runs) **GO Transit** (☎ 416-869-3200, 888-438-6646; www.gotransit.com), a government line that services many of the nearby surrounding towns, stopping frequently along the way. It's mainly used by commuters, but does go a relatively long way west of Toronto (to Hamilton, for example).

Car & Motorcycle

Toronto is served by expressways from all four directions. Expect congestion. Along the lake, the Gardiner Expressway runs west into Queen Elizabeth Way (QEW). QEW goes to Hamilton and Niagara Falls. Just at the city's western border is Hwy 427, which runs north to the airport. Highway 401 runs east–west above the downtown area; east to Kingston and Montréal, and west to Windsor, which is across the border from Detroit, Michigan. The often bumper-to-bumper segment of Hwy 401 between Hwy 427 and Yonge St has been called the busiest stretch of road in North America after California's Santa Monica Freeway. On the eastern side of the city, the Don Valley Parkway connects Hwy 401 to the Gardiner Expressway at the southern edge of the city.

Major international car-rental agencies (p873) have reservation desks at Pearson airport, as well as several citywide offices. Smaller independent agencies offer lower rates, but may have fewer (and perhaps older) cars available. **New Frontier Rent-A-Car** (Map pp80-1; ☎ 416-979-5678, 800-567-2837; www.newfrontiercar.com; Holiday Inn on King, 370 King St W; streetcar 504) and **Wheels 4 Rent** (Map pp80-1; ☎ 416-585-7782; www.wheels4rent.ca; 77 Nassau St; streetcar 510) rent compact cars from around $26 per day excluding taxes.

For long-distance trips, drive-away cars are an option – about half a dozen agencies are listed in the Yellow Pages (under Automobile). One is **Auto Drive-Away Co** (☎ 416-225-7754; www.torontodriveaway.com; 5803 Yonge St), which has cars for Canadian and US destinations. Also check the newspaper classified ads in either the *Toronto Sun* or the *Toronto Star* and the travel ads in *Now*.

Train

Grand **Union Station** (Map pp80-1; ☎ 416-869-300; 140 Bay St) downtown has currency exchange booths and a **Travellers' Aid Society** (☎ 416-366 7788) help desk, but no left-luggage lockers.

VIA Rail services are excellent along the so-called Québec–Windsor corridor, an area of heavy traffic stretching from Québec City to Windsor (just across the US–Canada border from Detroit, Michigan). There are frequent daily departures for Kingston (adult/child $58/29, 2¼ hours), Ottawa ($85/43, about four hours) and Montréal ($92/46, about 4½ hours), but fewer on weekends. VIA Rail also services Sudbury Junction ($93/47, seven hours, once daily on Tuesday, Thursday and Saturday), which is about 10km from the center of Sudbury town. Other cities that can be reached by VIA Rail include Niagara Falls ($24/13, two hours) and London ($40/20, two to three hours).

Ontario Northland (☎ 416-314-3750) runs the *Northlander* train to northern Ontario destinations, including Huntsville, North Bay and Temagami, and the *Polar Bear Express* to Moosonee. For the latter, take the Northlander to Cochrane (adult/child $130/65, 10½ hours, once daily except Saturday) and make connections there.

Amtrak trains link Toronto's Union Station with Buffalo (adult/child $26/13, four hours), Chicago ($75/33, 14 hours) or New York City ($75/33, 14 hours), with stops or other possible connections along the way. Reservations are needed for all trains.

GO Transit trains (p116) also use the station.

GETTING AROUND
To/From the Airport

Airport Express (☎ 905-564-3232, 800-387-6787; www.torontoairportexpress.com) operates a 24 hour express bus service that connects Lester B Pearson International Airport with the Metro Toronto Coach Terminal and major downtown hotels, including the Westin Harbour Castle, Fairmont Royal York and the Delta Chelsea Toronto Downtown. Buses depart every 20 to 30 minutes; the one-way trip takes an hour to 90 minutes, depending on traffic. A one-way/round-trip ticket costs $16/27 (cash or credit card);

students and seniors receive 10% off one-way fares.

If you're not carrying heavy luggage, the cheapest way to Pearson is via TTC (right) subway and bus. At the time of writing, the fastest route was to take the Bloor–Danforth subway line west to Kipling station, then transfer to the No 192 Airport Rocket bus (5:30am to 2am daily); allow at least an hour for the trip from downtown ($2.25). Night buses to the airport include the TTC's westbound No 300A Bloor-Danforth bus (every 15 minutes), which connects the airport with central Toronto in about 45 minutes.

A metered taxi from central Toronto to Pearson takes about 45 minutes, depending on traffic, and costs around $45. Fares from the airport are strictly regulated by drop-off zone, starting at $38 to downtown. If you're driving yourself, avoid using Hwy 401 during morning and evening rush hours; instead, take the Gardiner Expressway west from Spadina Ave and go north on Hwy 427. Parking at the airport garage costs $2.25 to $3.25 per half hour. Long-term parking at an off-site lot costs $13 per day or $59 per week, with free terminal shuttles available.

Boat

During summer, **Toronto Islands ferries** (Map pp80-1; ☎ 416-392-8193; www.city.toronto.on.ca/parks/island/ferry.htm; adult/child $6/3.50) run approximately every 30 minutes from 8am to 11pm. The journey only takes 10 to 15 minutes, but queues can be long on weekends and holidays, so show up early. Ferry services are greatly reduced the rest of the year, running approximately every 45 minutes daily. During winter, ferries service only Ward's Island. The ferry dock is at the foot of Bay St, off Queens Quay, just west of the Westin Harbour Castle.

Car & Motorcycle

Parking is expensive in Toronto – usually $2.50 to $3.50 per half hour, with an average daily maximum of $10 or more (or a flat rate of around $5 after 6pm). Cheapest are the Toronto Parking Authority's municipal lots, which are scattered around the downtown area and marked by green signs. They cost the same as metered street parking, which (if you can find any) is usually $2 per hour. Some metered spaces may have a central payment kiosk for an entire row. Purchase

the appropriate amount of time using cash or a credit card and be sure to display the receipt on your dashboard. Note it's not free to park next to a broken meter – it's illegal. Residential streets have only severely restricted on-street parking.

Traffic is generally horrendous around the edges of town, and except for during winter, construction never ends. Always budget extra time for delays. All vehicles must stop behind the rear doors of streetcars while they are loading or unloading passengers. Pedestrians use painted crosswalks with flashing lights to cross the street, and traffic must stop for them.

Highway 407, running east–west from Markham to Mississauga for about 40km just north of the city, is an electronic toll road. Cameras record your license plate and the time and distance traveled. If you don't have a prepaid electronic gizmo on the car, a bill is mailed to you (bills are sent out of province and to some US states).

Public Transportation

The **Toronto Transit Commission** (TTC; www.toronto.ca/ttc) provides Toronto with a good subway, bus and streetcar system. There's a 24 hour information line (☎ 416-393-4636). The regular adult fare is $2.25 (cash), or 10 tickets (or tokens) for $18. Day passes ($7.50) are also available. Tickets or tokens are available in the subway and at some convenience and corner variety stores. Once one fare is paid, you can transfer to any other bus, subway or streetcar within one hour at no extra charge. One ticket can get you anywhere the system goes. Get a transfer from the driver, or in the subway from the machine inside the turnstiles.

The subway system is clean and fast. There is one east–west line, which goes along Bloor St/Danforth Ave, and two north–south lines, one up Yonge St and one along Spadina Ave. The aboveground Scarborough RT train line connects the subway with the northeastern part of the city, from the Victoria Park stop to the Scarborough Town Centre. The Harbourfront LRT car runs above and below ground from Union Station (on Front St) to Harbourfront, along Queens Quay W to Spadina Ave and back again. The subway runs from 6am (except on Sunday, when it starts at 9am) until about 1:30am. Bus hours vary; some run late, but are infrequent.

ONTARIO

Streetcars are slower than the subway, but they stop more often (usually every block or two). Streetcars display their route number and final destination on both the front and rear cars. They usually operate from 5am until 1:30am, with reduced service on weekends. Routes are numbered in the 500s and streetcars roll on St Clair Ave and College, Dundas, Queen and King Sts (all of which run east–west). Bathurst St and Spadina Ave streetcars mainly run north–south, then turn west at the lakefront toward the Canadian National Exhibition grounds (511 Bathurst) or east toward Union Station (510 Spadina). The 509 Harbourfront streetcar travels from Union Station along Lake Shore Blvd west to the CNE grounds.

GO Transit (☎ 416-869-3200) trains leave Union Station from 7am to 11:30pm daily, serving the suburbs of Toronto east to Whitby and west to Hamilton. Fares are on an honor system; ticket inspection is random. Service is fast and steady throughout the day and frequent during weekday rush hours.

Taxi

Metered fares start at $2.75; add $1.25 for each additional kilometer, depending on traffic. Taxi stands are commonly found outside hotels, museums, shopping malls and entertainment venues.

Reliable companies include **Crown Taxi** (☎ 416-750-7878, 877-750-7878), **Diamond Taxicab** (☎ 416-366-6868) and **Royal Taxi** (☎ 416-777-9222; www.royaltaxi.ca), which has a fleet of wheelchair-accessible taxis.

AROUND TORONTO

Within an approximate 1½ hour drive of Toronto are a large number of small towns that were once centers for local farming communities. Some of the country's best land is here, but working farms are giving way to urban sprawl, and many of the old downtown areas are now surrounded by modern housing developments.

Still, desperate city dwellers make day trips around this district popular, especially on Sundays. There is still some nice rolling landscape and a few conservation areas (essentially parks), which are used for walking or picnicking. Quite a few of the towns attract antique hunters, and art galleries and craft shops are plentiful.

Northwest of Toronto, **Caledon**, set in the Caledon Hills, is one of the larger and closer examples. Not far southwest of Caledon, **Terra Cotta** is one of the closest points to Toronto for access to an afternoon's walk along part of the Bruce Trail (p156), which runs for 780km north to south. The **Hockley Valley** area, near Orangeville, provides more of the same. The **Credit River** has trout fishing, and in winter the area is not bad for cross-country skiing (see p159), although the hills aren't high enough for downhill skiing.

McMichael Canadian Art Collection

In Kleinburg, this excellent **gallery** (☎ 905-893-1121, 888-213-1121; www.mcmichael.com; 10365 Islington Ave, Kleinburg; adult/child under 5/student/senior/family $15/free/12/12/30; ☺ 10am-4pm Nov-Apr, 10am-5pm May-Oct) is a must-see for anyone interested in First Nations and modern Canadian art.

Advertising itself as 100% Canadian, the gallery exhibits work by the country's best-known painters, collectively termed the Group of Seven (see the boxed text opposite). Many visitors are equally captivated by the Inuit and British Columbian First Nations prints, photography and carvings, which are not as easily found at museums in downtown Toronto. Special changing exhibitions may feature photography or one particular artist or school of work.

The gallery's rustic handcrafted wooden buildings (including painter Tom Thomson's cabin, which was moved from Rosedale Ravine) are set among walking trails that crisscross conservation-area wetlands.

Apart from this main attraction, Kleinburg is also home to numerous antique shops, small galleries, craft shops and places for a nosh, as well as the Kortright Centre for Conservation (opposite). The town is 18km north from the corner of Islington Ave and Hwy 401 in Toronto. To get there by car, go north up Hwy 427 to Hwy 27 and continue north. Turn right at Nashville Rd.

Public transportation is limited and a little awkward, but can be used. There is no service, though, on weekends or holidays. First, take the Toronto subway west to Islington on the east–west line. From there, catch bus No 37D north for around 35 minutes to Steeles Ave. At the intersection of Steeles and Islington Aves, transfer to the Rte 13 York Region Transit bus. The only one of these of any use for those wishing to visit the gallery is at 8:45am, so you must make this connection. The bus will take you to the gallery gate in about 20 minutes, from where it's a 10-minute walk in. On the way back, bus No 13 leaves at about 5pm or 6pm. To check details, call **York Region Transit** (☎ 905-762-2100, 866-668-3978; www.yorkregiontransit.com).

David Dunlap Observatory

Just north of the Toronto city limits, this **observatory** (☎ 905-884-2672; www.astro.utoronto.ca/DDO; 123 Hillsview Dr, Richmond Hill; tours adult/child 7-12/senior $6/4/4; ☺ call for schedules) offers 40-minute introductory talks on modern astronomy, followed by a bit of stargazing through Canada's biggest optical telescope (the reflector measures 1.9m) if skies are clear.

Tickets are sold on a first-come, first-served basis (cash only) and children under seven years old are not permitted, due to safety concerns. On some clear-sky nights, the Royal Astronomical Society of Canada brings its own telescopes and sets up informal (and free!) viewing for the public outside, too.

To reach the observatory, drive for about 30 minutes up Bayview Ave past 16th Ave

to Hillsview Dr, turn left onto Hillsview Dr and drive 1km west until you see the white dome on your left. Alternatively, take the TTC Yonge line subway north to Finch station. Walk underground to a nearby transit terminal and catch the **York Region Transit** (☎ 905-762-2100, 866-668-3978; www.yorkregiontransit .com) No 91 Bayview bus, which stops upon request at Hillsview Dr, from where it's a 1km walk to the observatory. The entire trip costs $2.25, with a free transfer from the subway station.

Local Conservation Areas

Southern Ontario is urban. To offset this somewhat, the government has designated many conservation areas – small nature parks for walking, picnicking and (sometimes) fishing, swimming and cross-country skiing. The **Toronto and Region Conservation Authority** (☎ 416-661-6600; www.trca.on.ca) is responsible for the development and operation of these areas, most of which are difficult to reach without a vehicle.

The quality and characteristics of the areas vary quite markedly. While some protect noteworthy geographic areas, others are

---

THE MAGNIFICENT SEVEN

The Group of Seven comprised a number of painters who came together in 1920 to celebrate the Canadian landscape in a new and vital way.

Fired by an almost adolescent enthusiasm, this men's group used paintbrushes to explore and capture on canvas the rugged wilderness of Canada. The energy they felt then can be seen today in some stunning paintings – vibrant, light-filled canvases of Canada's mountains, lakes, forests and townships.

This gung-ho group of painterly talent spent a lot of time traipsing the wilds of northern Ontario, capturing the landscape through the seasons and under all weather conditions. Their favorite subjects included Algonquin Provincial Park, Georgian Bay, Lake Superior and Algoma. The Algoma Central Railway even converted an old boxcar into living quarters for the painters – a freight train would deposit them on a siding for a week or more, and the intrepid painters would set off, on foot or by canoe, to paint from morning till night.

The original seven members (the group later expanded to become the Canadian Group of Painters) were Franklin Carmichael, Lawren Harris, AY Jackson, Frank Johnston (later replaced by AJ Casson), Arthur Lismer, JEH MacDonald and FH Varley. Although he died before the group was officially formed, painter Tom Thomson was considered by other members as the group's leading light.

An experienced outdoorsman, Thompson drowned in 1917, just as he was producing some of his most powerful work. His deep connection to the land can be clearly seen in his vivid paintings. While the group took studios in Toronto (they sketched outside but produced finished work indoors), Thompson preferred working and living in his small rustic shack out back. As soon as the winter ice broke, he'd be off to the great north.

The best places to see work by the Group of Seven are the McMichael Collection (opposite), the Art Gallery of Ontario (p84) and the National Gallery of Canada (p216) in Ottawa.

ONTARIO

more historic in emphasis. Generally, they are not wild areas, and some are not even pretty, but they are close to major centers and do offer some relief from concrete. Tourism Toronto has a list of those around Toronto and within a 160km radius of town.

One place that makes a good, quick escape on a nice summer day is the large **Albion Hills Conservation Area** (☎ 905-880-4855, Hwy 50; admission $4; ⓨ 9am-dusk). It's primarily a quiet, wooded area with walking trails. In winter, it allows for decent cross-country skiing. It's on the west side of town; take Indian Line (by the airport) north. It becomes Hwy 50, which then leads to the park.

Also in this region, near Kleinburg, is the **Kortright Centre for Conservation** (☎ 905-832-2289, 9550 Pine Valley Dr, Woodbridge; adult/child $5/3; ⓨ 10am-4pm). There are trails here, too, but it's more of a museum, with displays and demonstrations on resources, wildlife and ecology. It's wheelchair-accessible.

West of Toronto, near Milton, there are two conservation areas to consider visiting. **Crawford Lake** (☎ 905-854-0234, Steeles Ave, at Guelph Line; adult/child $6/3.50; ⓨ 10am-4pm May-Oct) is one of the most interesting in the entire system. The deep, cool and pretty glacial lake set in the woods is surrounded by walking trails. Details on its formation and unique qualities are given in the well-laid-out interpretive center. Also on-site is a reconstructed 15th-century Iroquoian longhouse village. Crawford Lake is 5km south of Hwy 401, down a road called Guelph Line. There is a snack bar and some picnic tables at the site. The Bruce Trail (p156) also runs through the park.

In about the same general area is the **Mountsberg Conservation Area** (☎ 905-854-2276; Millburough Line; adult/child $4.50/3.25; ⓨ 10am-4pm). To reach it, exit south off Hwy 401 at Guelph Line and continue to the No 9 Sideroad. Travel west to Town Line and turn north for 3.2km. It's 19km west of the town of Milton. The site provides a series of country-related educational programs throughout the year. One of the best is the maple-syrup/sugaring-off demonstration put on each spring; it explains in detail the history, collection and production of this Canadian specialty. If you've got kids, they can climb, scale, and slide to the point of exhaustion in the Cameron Playbarn, which is great for the car ride home.

Cathedral of the Transfiguration

This Slovak Byzantine Catholic **cathedral** (☎ 905-887-5706; 10350 Woodbine Ave), straight up Hwy 404 from Toronto in the village of Gormley (near the town of Markham), is one of Canada's largest, standing 62.7m high to the tip of its copper-topped spire. Although built in 1987, it has the style and grandeur of a European church constructed centuries ago. Actually this 1000-seat church is based on a smaller version found in the Czech Republic. One of the impressive features is the French-made main bell, ringing in at 16,650kg, second in size only to the one in Sacré Coeur in Paris. It's also the first cathedral in the western hemisphere to be blessed by a pope – John Paul II did the honors. Call ahead to check opening hours.

Cullen Gardens & Miniature Village

About a 45-minute drive east from Toronto on Hwy 401, in the town of Whitby, is a 10-hectare site of carefully tended **gardens** (☎ 905-668-1600, 300 Taunton Rd W; adult/child/senior/family $12.50/5.50/9/40; ⓨ 9am-8pm Jun-Aug, 10am-6pm Apr & May, 10am-6pm Sep-Jan), which are interspersed with miniature models. A path, which will take two or three hours to walk if you're looking at all the impressive detail, winds through the gardens past a miniature village, modern suburban subdivision, farms and a cottage country scene. The buildings, people and activities portrayed offer, in a sense, a glimpse of life in southern Ontario. The floral aspect of the gardens – although colorful and quite extensive – should not be confused with botanical gardens but rather be viewed as the setting for the various scenes. The park appeals to a variety of people, particularly children.

The gardens are off Hwy 12, about 5km north along Hwy 401. When hunger strikes, there is a pleasant picnic and snack area (bring your own food) or a fairly pricey sit-down restaurant.

Parkwood Estate

In Oshawa, about 40km east of downtown Toronto on Hwy 401, you'll stumble across the **estate** (☎ 905-433-4311; www.parkwoodestate .com; 270 Simcoe St N; admission $6; ⓨ 10:30am-4:30pm Tue-Sun Jun-Aug, 1:30-4:30pm Tue-Sun Sep-May) of RS McLaughlin, who once ran the Canadian division of General Motors. The property consists of a 55-room mansion with antique furnishings, set amid large gardens. The admission price includes a tour. Afternoon tea is served outside during summer and in the conservatory during winter. Call for hours and closing days – they vary.

SOUTHWESTERN ONTARIO

Ontario south and west of Toronto has a long history of aboriginal settlement, agricultural importance, industrial development and urban sprawl. Today, it's primarily used as a conduit between Toronto and the USA (either Detroit to the west or New York State to the south) but those who dare venture off Hwy 401 or the QEW will take delight in the region's storied heritage, limestone and red-brick buildings, tree-lined boulevards, green pastures and sandy shorelines.

The standout highlight is the thunderous, mist-spraying Niagara Falls. On the way there from Toronto, you'll arch around Lake Ontario. Known as the 'Golden Horseshoe,' the continuous strip of urbanization suddenly gives way to the fruit-growing and wine-producing lands of the Niagara Peninsula between Lakes Ontario and Erie.

Farther west, sandier soil suits the growing of other crops, but also lends itself to the sandy beaches on the north shore of Lake Erie and east shore of Lake Huron. Kitchener and London serve as centers for the mixed farming of their regions and Windsor – like Detroit, Michigan (its counterpart across the river) – is a hub for auto manufacturing.

The area is heavily populated and the USA is close by, so attractions and parks do get busy in summer.

HAMILTON
☎ 905 / pop 490,000
As the center of Canada's iron and steel industry Hamilton is, calling a spade a spade, 'Steeltown.' It's a heavily industrialized city between Toronto and Niagara, but there are concerted clean-up efforts, and quite a few

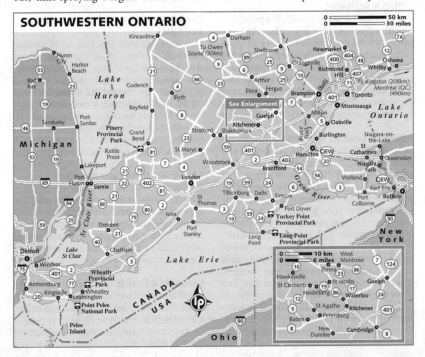

SOUTHWESTERN ONTARIO

green spaces have found their way in and around the city. The Niagara Escarpment runs through the southern part of town, giving decent views of Lake Ontario.

Orientation & Information

Hamilton sits at the southwestern end of Lake Ontario and marks the split between the Niagara-bound QEW and Hwy 403, which meets Hwy 401 to Detroit.

In town, westbound King St and eastbound Main St are the one-way major arteries; King St has most of the downtown shops and restaurants. Jackson Sq, between York, King, Bay and James Sts, is a large complex including restaurants, shopping centers, the Farmer's Market and Copps Coliseum. James St heads south through town toward the Niagara Escarpment.

Downtown has the **tourist office** (☎ 905-546-2666, 800-263-8590; www.hamiltonundiscovered.com; 34 James St S; ☼ 9am-5pm, closed Sun Sep-May). Look for other busy summer-only visitors' centers around the city, such as at the Royal Botanical Gardens or the African Lion Safari.

Sights & Activities

The Hamilton area has some of the province's top attractions, and the city's efforts to clean up its act means there are plenty of good parks and multi-use trails. The **Escarpment Rail Trail** (8km), parts of the Trans Canada Trail (p56) and the Lake Ontario Waterfront Trail (p201) are some of the more-traveled, and the tourist office has an excellent trail map for **walking** and **cycling**.

ROYAL BOTANICAL GARDENS

With nearly 1000 hectares of flowers, natural park and a wildlife sanctuary, these **gardens** (☎ 905-527-1158; 680 Plains Rd W; www.rbg.ca; adult/senior & child $8/7; ☼ 9am-dusk) are only one of six in the world to be designated 'royal.' During spring, the rock garden is a highlight, with three hectares of rare trees and shrubs, waterfalls, ponds and 125,000 spring-flowering bulbs. Think a rose is a rose? Think again. From June to October, thousands of roses, including many antique varieties, bloom in the Centennial rose garden. The arboretum is best in May when a mammoth collection of lilacs is in full bloom. The sanctuary is home to birds, deer, fox, muskrat and coyote with trails winding through marsh and wooded ravines.

AFRICAN LION SAFARI

About 1000 animals and birds roam this vast, cageless **animal park** (☎ 905-623-2620, 800-461-9453; RR1, Cambridge; adult/child/senior $23/19/21; ☼ 10am-5:30pm late Jun–Labour Day, 10am-4pm Mon-Fri & 10am-5pm Sat & Sun May-Jun & Labour Day–early Oct). It's possible to get terrifyingly close to lions, giraffes, monkeys and other animals. You can drive through, but if you think bird droppings on your car are bad, use the park tour bus ($5) instead. Kids love this zoo, which is 25km north of Hamilton, and it's far more enlightening than a traditional one.

DUNDURN CASTLE

A boxy, column-fronted, 36-room mansion, this **castle** (☎ 905-546-2872; 610 York Blvd; adult/child/student/family $10/5/8/18; ☼ noon-4pm, closed Mon Sep-May) once belonged to Sir Allan Napier McNab, prime minister from 1854 to 1856. It sits on a cliff overlooking the harbor and is furnished in mid-19th-century style. Also on-site is a **military museum** (☼ 1-5pm Tue-Sun) with weapons and uniforms dating from the War of 1812.

CANADIAN FOOTBALL HALL OF FAME & MUSEUM

Despite worldwide mockery of 'Canadian Football,' nothing stops Canadian sports fans from having a huge amount of pride and enthusiasm for their fast-paced brand of football. The **Football Hall of Fame & Museum** (☎ 905-528-7566, 58 Jackson St W; admission $3; ☼ 10am-4pm Tue-Sat) puts more than 100 years of history on display through equipment, photos and the Grey Cup – the Canadian Football League's (CFL's) top prize.

CANADIAN WARPLANE HERITAGE MUSEUM

This spacious **museum** (☎ 905-679-4183; 9280 Airport Rd; adult/child/family $10/8/30; ☼ 9am-5pm) is in an impressive building near the airport. It has a collection of over two-dozen vintage planes, all in flying condition, celebrating Canada's aviation history.

Festivals & Events

A full-costumed reenactment (☎ 905-662-8458; adult/youth $5/2) of a battle between British and US soldiers in the War of 1812 is held at Stoney Creek Battlefield Park, 8km south of town in mid-June.

Sleeping & Eating

Highway 403 and the QEW are dotted with plenty of chain and standard motels, which are considerably cheaper than accommodations in Toronto or Niagara-on-the-Lake.

Two blocks west of the Convention Centre is the pedestrian-only Hess Village, with cobblestone streets, eateries with wrought-iron fences and outdoor patios.

Entertainment

The 15-time Grey Cup champion **Hamilton Tiger-Cats** (☎ 905-527-1508; www.ticats.ca; ⊙ Jul-Nov) have been playing football since 1869. These days they play against their main rival, Toronto, and other teams in the CFL at **Ivor Wynn Stadium** (75 Balsam Ave). Tickets are available through **Ticketmaster** (⊙ 905-481-4444; www .ticketmaster.ca; tickets $13-47).

Getting There & Away

WestJet uses **John C Munro Hamilton International Airport** (YHM; ☎ 905-679-1999; 9300 Airport Rd), 10km south of town, as a major hub for flights to other parts of Canada.

Coach Canada, Greyhound Canada and Toronto-bound Go Transit commuter buses and trains run from the **GO Centre** (☎ 905-529-0196; 36 Hunter St E), three blocks south of the center of town.

WELLAND CANAL AREA

The historic Welland Canal, connecting Lake Ontario to Lake Erie, is a shipping bypass of Niagara Falls. A series of eight locks along the 42km-long canal overcomes the difference of about 100m in the lakes' water levels. Built between 1914 and 1932 it's now in its fourth incarnation. It's part of the St Lawrence Seaway that allows shipping into the industrial heart of North America from the Atlantic Ocean.

Between Hamilton and the Niagara River, **St Catharines** is the major town of the Niagara fruit- and wine-producing district. Remnants of the first three canals (built in 1829, 1845 and 1887) can be seen at various points in town. At **Lakeside Park**, along the waterfront in **Port Dalhousie** (dal-oo-zey), the still-visible early canals opened into Lake Ontario. This old harbor area is now a blend of the new and historic, with a reconstructed wooden lock, the oldest and smallest jail in the province and a lighthouse set alongside contemporary bars and restaurants. Hikers and walkers will

enjoy parts or all of the 45km **Merritt Trail**, a walk following the Welland Canal from Port Dalhousie to Port Colborne.

For a more up-to-date look at the canal, the **Welland Canals Centre** (☎ 905-984-8880; 1932 Government Rd; ⊙ 11am-4pm) at lock three, just outside St Catharines, has a viewing platform close enough to almost touch the building-sized ships as they wait for the water levels to rise or fall. Shipping schedules and a computer display of the stages of the locks tell you when the next boat will be here. Also here is the **St Catharines Museum** (adult/child/student/senior $4.25/2.50/3.25/4), with enthusiastic costumed interpreters and exhibits on the canal and its construction.

The town of **Welland** has become known for its more than two-dozen painted **murals** depicting scenes from the history of the area and the canal. They can be seen around town on the sides of buildings, with the heaviest concentration along Main St E. A pamphlet on the paintings can be picked up at **Tourism of Welland Niagara** (☎ 905-735-8696; 800 Niagara St N; ⊙ 9am-6pm Mon-Fri).

Port Colborne, where the canal meets Lake Erie, contains the eighth lock – one of the largest in the world – in **Lock Eight Park**, south of Main St. The quiet, good-looking town has a boardwalk promenade along the canal with shops and restaurants good for an afternoon or evening meal.

NIAGARA FALLS

Spanning the Niagara River between Ontario and upper New York, these thundering falls are one of Canada's top tourist destinations, drawing over 13 million people annually. Although there are hundreds of waterfalls that are taller, in terms of sheer volume Niagara Falls are hard to beat: the equivalent of more than a million bathtubs full of water goes over every minute.

The falls themselves are certainly impressive, particularly the Canadian Horseshoe Falls. They look good by day and by night, when colorful spotlights flicker across the misty foam. Even in winter, when the flow is partially hidden and the edges frozen solid – like a freeze-framed film – it's quite a spectacle. (But, as one reader warned, the mist freezes on contact!)

Very occasionally the falls stop altogether. The first recorded instance of this occurred on the morning of Easter Sunday 1848, when an ice jam completely cut off the flow of water. It caused some to speculate that the end of the world was nigh; some residents even took the opportunity to scavenge the riverbed beneath the falls.

It is said that Napoléon's brother rode from New Orleans in a stagecoach with his new bride to view the falls, and it's been a honeymoon attraction ever since. The town is sometimes humorously but disparagingly called a spot 'for newlyweds and nearly deads' (it's recently been called Viagra Falls).

Supplementing the falls, the city has a jaw-dropping array of artificial attractions, which – together with the casino, hotels, restaurants and flashing lights – produce a sort of Canadian Las Vegas.

Orientation

The town of Niagara Falls is split into two main sections: the older commercial area, where locals go about their business, and the other, largely tacky (but fun) part around the falls, which has been developed for visitors. The latter also has pretty green areas that offer some contrast to the built-up tourist area.

In the 'normal' part of town, also known as downtown, Queen St and Victoria Av are the main streets. The area around Bridge St, near the corner of Erie Av, has both the train and bus stations, with hostels nearby. Generally there is little to see or do in this part of town.

About 3km south along the river are the falls and all the trappings of the tourist trade: restaurants, hotels, shops and attractions. In the vicinity of the falls, the main streets are busy Clifton Hill, Falls Av, Centre St, Victoria Av and Ferry St.

Going north along the river is scenic parkland, which runs from the falls downstream about 20km to Niagara-on-the-Lake. Many of the B&Bs are between the two main sections of town.

Information

Accessible Niagara (www.accessibleniagara.com) Advice for the mobility-impaired.

Discover Niagara (www.discoverniagara.com) Online travel deals and an events calendar.

Greater Niagara General Hospital (☎ 905-358-0171; 5546 Portage Rd) 24 hour emergency room.

Info Niagara (www.infoniagara.com) Privately run website has helpful links.

Niagara Parks Commission (☎ 905-371-0254, 877-642-7275; www.niagaraparks.com; ☽ 9am-4pm, to 11pm in peak summer season) Runs information desks (open daily) at Maid of the Mist Plaza and Table Rock Information Centre.

Ontario Tourism Travel Centre (☎ 905-358-3221; 5355 Stanley Av; ☽ 8:30am-6pm, later in summer) On the western outskirts of town. Look here for free tourist booklets containing maps and discount coupons for attractions and rides.

Post Office (☎ 905-356-4845; Cnr Queen St & St Clair Ave)

Sights & Activities
THE FALLS & AROUND

On the US side of the river, the pretty **Bridal Veil Falls** (often referred to as the American Falls) crash onto mammoth rocks that have fallen due to erosion. The grander, more powerful **Horseshoe Falls**, on the Canadian side, plunge into the **Maid of the Mist pool**, which is indeed misty and clouds views of the falls from afar. An excellent and free vantage point is the observation deck of the souvenir shop of the Table Rock Information Centre by the falls. To get close to the falls (and to get unobstructed photos), arrive early in the morning before the crowds or take a Maid of the Mist boat trip.

Less than 1km south of Horseshoe Falls, the **Niagara Parks Greenhouse** (7145 Niagara Parkway; admission free; ☽ 9:30am-5pm) provides year-round floral displays. Opposite, rusting away in the upper rapids of the river, the **Old Scow** is a steel barge that has been lodged on rocks and waiting to be washed over the falls since 1918.

The best of the four major tour services is **Maid of the Mist** (☎ 905-358-0311; www.maidofthemist.com; 5920 Niagara Parkway; adult/child $13/8; ☽ 9:45am-4:45pm Mon-Fri, to 5:45pm Sat & Sun Apr–late Oct, to 7:45pm daily in summer), which has been taking brave passengers close to the falls for a view from the bottom since 1846. It's loud and wet and lots of fun. Everyone heads for the boat's upper deck, but views from either end of the lower deck are just fine, too. Departures are every 15 minutes, weather permitting.

From Table Rock Information Centre, you can **Journey Behind the Falls** (☎ 905-354-1551; 6650 Niagara Parkway; adult/child $10/6; ☽ 9am-5:30pm Mon-Fri, to 7:30pm Sat & Sun) by donning a plastic poncho and walking through rock-cut tunnels halfway down the cliff side – as close as you can get to the falls without getting in

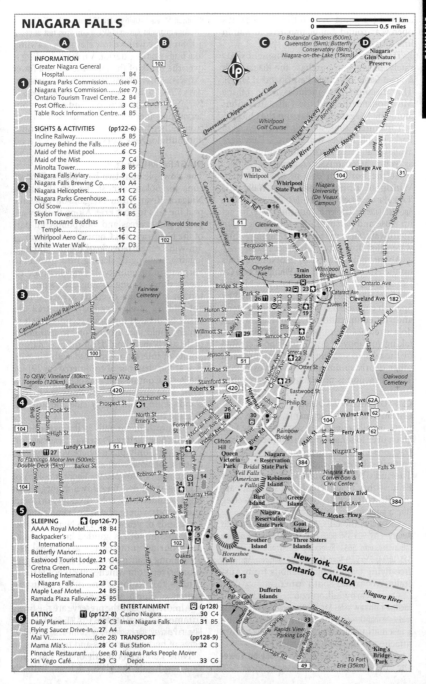

NIAGARA FALLS

| 0 | | 1 km |
| 0 | | 0.5 miles |

INFORMATION
Greater Niagara General
Hospital...........................**1** B4
Niagara Parks Commission......(see 4)
Niagara Parks Commission......(see 7)
Ontario Tourism Travel Centre..**2** B4
Post Office..............................**3** C3
Table Rock Information Centre..**4** B5

SIGHTS & ACTIVITIES (pp122-6)
Incline Railway.......................**5** B5
Journey Behind the Falls.........(see 4)
Maid of the Mist pool..............**6** C5
Maid of the Mist....................**7** C4
Minolta Tower........................**8** B5
Niagara Falls Aviary................**9** C4
Niagara Falls Brewing Co.......**10** A4
Niagara Helicopters...............**11** C2
Niagara Parks Greenhouse.....**12** C6
Old Scow.............................**13** C6
Skylon Tower........................**14** B5
Ten Thousand Buddhas
Temple.............................**15** C2
Whirlpool Aero Car...............**16** C2
White Water Walk..................**17** D3

SLEEPING (pp126-7)
AAAA Royal Motel........**18** B4
Backpacker's
International..............**19** C3
Butterfly Manor.........**20** C3
Eastwood Tourist Lodge.**21** C4
Gretna Green..............**22** C4
Hostelling International
Niagara Falls............**23** C3
Maple Leaf Motel.......**24** B5
Ramada Plaza Fallsview.**25** B5

EATING (pp127-8)
Daily Planet..............**26** C3
Flying Saucer Drive-In...**27** A4
Mai Vi.....................(see 28)
Mama Mia's..............**28** C4
Pinnacle Restaurant.....(see 8)
Xin Vego Café............**29** C3

ENTERTAINMENT (p128)
Casino Niagara...........**30** C4
Imax Niagara Falls.......**31** B5

TRANSPORT (pp128-9)
Bus Station...............**32** C3
Niagara Parks People Mover
Depot....................**33** C6

To Botanical Gardens (500m);
Queenston (5km); Butterfly
Conservatory (8km);
Niagara-on-the-Lake (15km)

Niagara
Glen Nature
Preserve

Church's Ln

Queenston-Chippawa Power Canal

Whirlpool
Golf Course

Niagara Parkway

Recreational Trail

Robert Moses Pkwy

Lewiston Rd

McKoon
Ave

College Ave

The
Whirlpool

Whirlpool
State Park

Niagara
University
(De Veaux
Campus)

Canadian National Railway

Stanley Ave

River Rd

11

16

Highland Ave

11th St

Thorold Stone Rd

Glenview
Ave

15

Ferguson St

Buttrey St

Chrysler
Ave

Train
Station

Whirlpool
Bridge

Ontario Ave

Cataract Ave

Cleveland Ave 182

Main St

Lockport Rd

Bridge Ave

Park St

32   23

26   3

19

Queen St

Fairview
Cemetery

Homewood Ave

Huron St

Morrison St

Willmott St

29

Jepson St

McRae St

Stamford St

Roberts St

Valley Way

St Lawrence Ave

Ellis

Simcoe St

20

Seneca Ave

22

21

Eastwood St

Otter St

Palmer Ave

Robert Moses Parkway

Portage Rd

Oakwood
Cemetery

Drummond Rd

Portage Rd

100

To QEW; Vineland (30km);
Toronto (120km)

Bellevue St

Valley Way

2

420

Kitchener St

1

North St
Emery St

Forsythe
St

Frederica St

Cook St

High St

104

10

27

Lundy's Lane

51

To Flamingo Motor Inn (500m);
Double Deck (5km)

Barker St

Woodland
Blvd

Corwin Ave

Franklin Ave

Robinson Ave

Allendale Ave

Clark Ave

Buchanan Ave

Main St

Murray St

Dixon St

Dunn St

102

Oakes
Dr

Allanthus Ave

Stanley
Ave

Ferry St

Prospect St

420

Walnut Ave

Lewis Ave

McGrail Ave

Ellen Ave

Victoria Ave

18

28

30   9

Clifton
Hill

River Rd

Oak St

Buttrey St

7

Philip St

John St

Newman Hiram St

Pine Ave 62A

Walnut Ave 62

Ferry Ave 62

104

Rainbow
Bridge

Niagara
Reservation
State Park 384

Robinson St

Queen
Victoria
Park

Bridal
Veil Falls
(American
Falls)

Niagara
Falls St

Niagara Falls
Convention &
Civic Center

Rainbow Blvd

Buffalo Ave

384

Murray Hill

Murray St

14

24

31

Fallsview Blvd

Bird
Island

Green
Island

Niagara
Reservation
State Park

Robinson
Island

Goat
Island

Three Sisters
Islands

25

4

5

6

Brother
Island

Horseshoe
Falls

13

12

Par 3 Golf
Course

New York USA
Ontario CANADA

Dufferin
Islands

Niagara River

33

Rapids View
Parking Lot

Recreational Trail

Upper Rapids Blvd

King's
Bridge
Park

To Fort
Erie (35km)

49

a barrel (or going over to the US side). It's open year-round, but be prepared to wait in line for your brief turn in the spray.

Tickets to the above can be bought separately, or you can purchase the **Niagara Falls & Great Gorge Adventure Pass** (adult/child $32/19). This discount pass includes Maid of the Mist, Journey Behind the Falls, attractions along the Niagara Parkway and the Queenston historical sites, as well as the Niagara Parks People Mover shuttle buses. Passes are available at Table Rock Information Centre as well as at various attractions.

At the northern end of town, next to Whirlpool Bridge, **White Water Walk** (4330 Niagara Parkway; adult/child 6-12 $6/3; ☺ 10am-5pm late Apr–Oct, later in summer) is another way to get up close and personal, this time on a 325m boardwalk suspended above raging white water, just downstream from the falls.

About 4.5km north of Horseshoe Falls on the Niagara River is the **Whirlpool Aero Car** (☎ 888-255-1321; 3850 Niagara Parkway/River Rd; adult/child 6-12 $10/6; ☺ hours vary). It was designed by Spanish engineer Leonardo Torres Quevedo and started operation in 1916. Here a gondola stretches 550m between two outcrops, taking you above a deadly whirlpool created by the falls, so you can peer at logs, tires and other debris spinning in the eddies below. This attraction is not wheelchair accessible.

CLIFTON HILL & AROUND

Clifton Hill is a street name, but the term more usually refers to a slope near the falls given over to sense-bombarding artificial attractions in Disney-like concentration. You name it – Ripley's Believe It or Not, Madame Tussaud's Wax Museum, Criminals Hall of Fame – they're all here. In most cases, paying the entrance fee will leave you feeling like a sucker.

Closer to the falls, the jungly **Niagara Falls Aviary** (☎ 905-356-8888, 866-994-0090; www.niagara fallsaviary.com; 5651 River Rd; adult/child 6-12/senior $15/10/14; ☺ 9am-9pm May-Oct, to 5pm Nov-Apr) has free-flying tropical bird exhibits from Australia, Africa and South America.

On a nearby hilltop reached via a quaint **incline railway** (rides $1; ☺ 9am-5pm Apr–mid-Oct, to midnight mid-Oct–Mar) meant for tourists, there's a fascinating **museum** of Niagara Falls history attached to the IMAX Niagara Falls.

Adjacent to the IMAX is **Skylon Tower** (☎ 905-356-2651, 877-475-9566; www.skylon.com; 5200 Robinson St; adult/child under 13/senior $9.50/5.50/8.50; ☺ 8am-midnight Apr–mid-Oct, 11am-9pm rest of year), a 158m spire with yellow elevators crawling like bugs up the exterior. Virtually lording it over the brink of the falls, the **Minolta Tower** (☎ 905-356-1501, 800-461-2492; adult/child 6-18/senior/ family $7/5/5/20, day & night return ticket adult/child 6-18 $9/7; ☺ hours vary) has indoor and outdoor observation galleries. On clear days, the views from either tower stretch as far as Toronto and Buffalo, New York.

NIAGARA PARKWAY

The slow, pleasant two-lane **Niagara Parkway** runs for 56km, almost the length of the Niagara River, from Niagara-on-the-Lake past the falls to Fort Erie. Along the way are parks, picnic areas and viewpoints, all part of the Niagara Parks Commission system. A 3m-wide paved **recreational trail** for cycling, jogging, walking or skating runs parallel to Parkway in its entirety. It's excellent for either a short or long cycling excursion. The terrain is flat, the riverside scenery pleasant and it's rarely very busy. The trail can easily be divided into four sections, each of which would take around one to two hours of leisurely pedaling. Historic and natural points of interest are marked with plaques. Ask at the chamber of commerce (p129) for the Parks Commission's excellent *Recreation Trail Map*. In season, fabulous fresh fruit stands selling cold cherry cider pop up beside the trail.

Just north of the falls is the exceptional **Niagara Glen Nature Preserve** (admission free; ☺ 24hr), the only place where you can gain a sense of what the area was like before the arrival of Europeans. There are 4km of walking trails winding down a gorge, past huge boulders, icy cold caves, wildflowers and woods where the falls were situated thousands of years ago. The Niagara Parks Commission offers guided nature walks daily during summer for a nominal fee. Take along your own water, as the Niagara is one river from which you do not want to drink – this region is one of the industrial centers of North America.

Almost opposite the preserve are the finely trimmed **Botanical Gardens** (☎ 905-356-8554; 2565 Niagara Parkway; admission free; ☺ dawn-dusk) with 100 acres of herbs, vegetables and trees.

Nine kilometers north of the falls, you can step inside the glass-enclosed **Butterfly**

Conservatory (☎ 905-358-0025; 2405 Niagara Parkway; adult/child 6-12 $8.50/4; ☺ 9am-5pm, later in summer) where more than 50 species make their way out of chrysalides and flutter about more than 130 species of flowers and plants. Since this is also a breeding facility, you can see new butterflies being released, usually around 9:30am, each morning. There's also an outdoor butterfly garden.

QUEENSTON

In Queenston village, a quaint, sleepy historic throwback just before the Lewiston Bridge to the USA, is the historic **Mackenzie Heritage Printery & Newspaper Museum** (☎ 905-262-5676; 1 Queenston St, Queenston; adult/child 6-12 $2.50/1.50; ☺ 10am-4pm May–mid-Oct), where William Lyon Mackenzie once edited the hell-raising *Colonial Advocate*.

Nearby, the **Laura Secord Homestead** (☎ 905-262-4851; 29 Queenston St, Queenston; adult/child 6-12 $2.50/1.50; ☺ 10am-4pm May–mid-Oct) honors one of Canada's best-known heroines (partly because of the chocolate company that bears her name), who lived here during the War of 1812. At one point during the war, she hiked nearly 30km to warn the British soldiers of impending attack by the USA – even though she was a US citizen by birth. The house can be visited and the rose garden out front is said to have been planted by Laura herself.

Further north, **RiverBrink Gallery** (☎ 905-262-4510; www.riverbrink.org; 116 Queenston St, Queenston; adult/child under 12/senior $5/free/4; ☺ 10am-5pm Wed-Sun Victoria Day–Thanksgiving) is the home of the Samuel E Weir Collection of Canadian art, which includes early landscapes of the Niagara Peninsula and works by the Group of Seven (p117). Weir had the house built as a live-in gallery and library in 1916 to house his remarkably extensive art, book and antique collection. He formed a foundation to administer the estate for public access, provided that he was buried in the front lawn (which, in due time, he was).

A little farther along the Niagara Parkway is **Queenston Heights Park**, a national historic

---

DAREDEVILS

Surprisingly, more than a few people who have gone over Niagara Falls, suicides aside, do live to tell about it. A schoolteacher named Annie Taylor first devised the successful padded-barrel method in 1901, promoting a rash of barrel stunters that continued into the 1920s.

The 1980s was a particularly busy period, with five stunt people taking the plunge, all successfully. One of them said he did it to show teenagers there were thrills available without drugs (yeah, right). Perhaps the most unfortunate crusader of this era was Karl Soucek. In 1984 he completed the trip in a bright red barrel at the Horseshoe Falls. Only six months later he died in another barrel stunt at the Houston Astrodome, which certainly says something about tempting fate.

Also during the '80s, two locals successfully took the plunge lying head to head in the same barrel. After tumbling over the falls they emerged from their vessel with only minor injuries. In fact they refused medical attention, which made their subsequent journey to the Niagara Parks Police Office all the more expedient.

The first stuntman of the 1990s, witnessed and photographed by startled visitors, went over the edge in a kayak. He was so confidant he made dinner reservations for that night. Unfortunately, he's now paddling the great white water in the sky. The US citizen who tried to jet ski over the falls in 1995 might have made it – if his rocket-propelled parachute had opened.

Another American, Kirk Jones, became the first person in recorded history to survive a trip over the falls unaided during 2003. During his court appearance his brother claimed "he [Kirk] didn't really have a lot going for him." The judge agreed and ordered Jones never to return to Canada except for court appearances. Life picked up for Jones soon afterwards when a Texas circus lured him with the irresistible opportunity to be 'the world's greatest stuntman.' Jones accepted his destiny and the position.

Only one person who took the trip over the falls accidentally has had the good fortune to survive. He was a seven-year-old boy from Tennessee who surged over from a tipped boat upstream in 1960 and did it without breaking even a bone. But there's no need to go to such extremes yourself when IMAX Niagara Falls (p128) allows everyone to try the plunge – virtually, that is.

ONTARIO

site known for its towering **monument** to Major General Sir Isaac Brock, 'Saviour of Upper Canada.' The winding stairwell inside takes you up over 50m to see a fabulous view. Self-guided walking tours of the hillside recount the 1812 Battle of Queenston Heights, a significant British victory that helped Canada resist becoming part of the USA.

The southern end of the Bruce Trail (p156), which extends 780km to Tobermory on Georgian Bay, is in Queenston. There are numerous access points in the Niagara and Hamilton areas.

Quirky Niagara Falls

If the tourist bustle is messing with your inner sanctum, you'll find tranquility at the totally out-of-context but intriguing **Ten Thousand Buddhas Temple** (☎ 905-371-2678, 4303 River Rd; admission free; ☼ 9am-5pm, main temple open Sat & Sun only). Visitors are welcome to view various sculptures and artworks from China and to enjoy the calm environment.

Tranquility of a different sort altogether waits at the bottom of a good brew at **Niagara Falls Brewing Co** (☎ 905-356-2739; 6863 Lundy's Lane; tours free, reservations required; ☼ call for hours). Tours include a sample of the famous Eisbock (German for 'ice ram') beer.

Tours

If you're cashed up, you can snatch aerial photographs and a bird's-eye view of the falls with **Fly Niagara** (☎ 877-359-2924; www .flyniagara.com; 30-min flights adult/child $100/75). All passengers get window seats and your trip is fully narrated. Flights leave from Niagara District Airport, which is north of the falls, on the corner of Airport Rd and Niagara Stone Rd. You can do the same thing in a chopper with **Niagara Helicopters** (☎ 905-357-5672; www.niagarahelicopters.com; 3731 Victoria Ave; 10-min flights adult/child 2-11 $100/55; ☼ 9am-sunset, weather permitting).

Closer to terra firma, **Double Deck** (☎ 905-374-7423; www.doubledecktours.com; 3957 Bossert Rd; tours adult/child from $22/12; ☼ 9am Apr-Oct) offers sightseeing tours on red British double-decker buses. You can stay on or get off at will, even taking two days to complete the tour.

See p94 for companies offering day tours to Niagara Falls from Toronto, and p133 for tours of the Wine Country leaving from Niagara Falls.

Festivals & Events

Illuminating the falls has been a tradition since 1860, when the tightrope walker, the Great Blondin, first carried flares and shot off fireworks. Every night of the year, colored spotlights are turned on the falls, and in summer there are weekend fireworks.

Spring Festival Opening with the Maid of the Mist Parade, this festival celebrates the colors and scents of spring with a feast of concerts, fireworks and events from mid-May to late June.

Niagara Wine & Food Classic (☎ 905-356-6061, 800-563-2557; Queen Victoria Park; ☼ mid-Sep) A gastronomic celebration to welcome the autumn wine harvest. Some of the region's top wines are paired with sublime cuisine.

Art by the Falls (☎ 905-227-7248; admission $3; ☼ early Oct) About 100 artists, designers and craftspeople from all over Canada are lured to Niagara Falls to demonstrate their skills.

Winter Festival of Lights (www.discoverniagara.com) A season of day and night events including concerts, car shows and even cheerleading championships held between late November and mid-January. The undisputed highlight is a series of spectacular nighttime light displays set up along a 36km route.

Sleeping

Accommodations are plentiful, but can be completely booked up. In summer, on weekends and for holidays (Canadian and US), prices spike sharply. Many B&Bs (peruse some of them online at www.bbniagarafalls .com) are found along River Rd, midway between the falls area and the old downtown. If you haven't made a reservation, just look for vacancy signs.

BUDGET

Backpacker's International Inn (☎ 905-357-4266, 800-891-7022; 4219 Huron St, cnr Zimmerman Ave; dm/d $29/50) This independent hostel is housed inside a grand 19th-century home. Upstairs rooms, which are like those in a small European hotel, are particularly charming. Rates include taxes, morning coffee and a muffin. Guests have use of kitchen facilities and bicycles can be rented.

Hostelling International Niagara Falls (☎ 905-357-0770, 888-749-0058; 4549 Cataract Ave; dm $19) Set in a former commercial building in the old town, this popular hostel can squish in around 90 people. Fortunately the facilities, including a sizeable kitchen, laundry rooms, lockers and a large lounge, are good. It's in a convenient spot, close to the train and bus stations, and you can rent bicycles. Linen rental is available for $2 per person.

MID-RANGE

Gretna Green (☎ 905-357-2081, 5077 River Rd; r incl breakfast $95-125; **P**) This comely B&B has four rooms with private baths, TVs and air-conditioning. Breakfast is of the full English variety (which can just about render you comatose) and the friendly English host is a plus. Occasionally pick-up service from the train and bus stations is offered. This is a good option for families.

Eastwood Tourist Lodge (☎ 905-354-8686, www .theeastwood.com; 5359 River Rd; r incl breakfast $110-140, ste incl breakfast $150-175; ☼ May-Dec; **P**) This striking 1891 house with balconies overlooking the river has been opening its doors to visitors since the 1960s. The stately exterior belies an industrious and professional air within. Each of the numerous rooms is spacious and has air-conditioning, cable TV, telephones and an en suite. English, German and Spanish are spoken.

Flamingo Motor Inn (☎ 905-356-4646, 800-738-7701; www.flamingomotorinn.com; 7701 Lundy's Lane; d peak/off-peak from $70/50) Of the colony of motels lining Lundy's Lane, Flamingo stands out in kitsch style. Enticements include waterbeds, saunas and heart-shaped Jacuzzis – very saucy. If you're just looking for a good night's sleep, the accommodating rooms also offer phones, cable TVs and comfy beds.

Maple Leaf Motel (☎ 905-354-0841, fax 905-354-2074; 6163 Fallsview Blvd; d $40-100) Tucked away in a quiet pocket, this low-key, friendly motel is a peaceful retreat. Towering maple trees surround the property and spotless rooms include TVs and air-conditioning.

AAAA Royal Motel (☎ 905-354-2632; www.domain fortune.com/royalmotel; 5284 Ferry St; d from $55; 🛢) This central motel is very near the lights of Clifton Hill and is less than a 30-minute walk to the falls. The rooms are plain but fine (no phones), and there is a small pool. It's close to a glut of restaurants.

TOP END

Butterfly Manor (☎ 905-358-8988; www.vaxxine. com/bb/bflymnr.htm; 4917 River Rd; d incl breakfast $80-110) This beautiful, award-winning B&B has six commodious rooms, one of which has an open fireplace – it's divine in winter. During summer you'll appreciate the air-conditioning and all year round the break-fast smells are delicious. French, Italian, German and Spanish are spoken.

Ramada Plaza Fallsview (☎ 905-356-1501, 800-272-6232; www.ramada.com; 6732 Fallsview Blvd; d $130-200, ste $180-350) New and flashy, this four-star number has rates to match the spectacular views. Perched 150m above the Niagara gorge inside the Minolta Tower, all rooms have the little touches like hair dryers, fridges, tea and coffee makers and TVs.

Eating

Finding food in Niagara Falls is no problem, but be prepared for quantity rather than quality. For cuisine a cut above, you're better off heading to the wine country.

BUDGET

Daily Planet (☎ 905-371-1722; 4573 Queen St; meals $5-10; ☼ breakfast, lunch & dinner) This is a great place to escape the tourist crowds and grab a hearty meal. The fare is pub grub and Mexican-accented snacks, all complimented well by a good brew. It's in the slow part of old downtown, but that doesn't stop folk kicking up their heels and dancing from time to time.

Flying Saucer Drive-In (☎ 905-356-4553; 6768 Lundy's Lane; meals $4-16; ☼ breakfast, lunch & dinner) For 'out of this world' fast food, you can't miss this diner out on the Lundy's Lane motel strip. Famous 99¢ breakfast specials are served until noon, but heftier meals in the way of steaks, seafood, fajitas, burgers and hot dogs are also on-board.

MID-RANGE

Mama Mia's (☎ 905-354-7471; 5719 Victoria Ave; mains $12-16; ☼ lunch & dinner) There is an abundance of Italian eateries around town, but this one has been serving up tasty and authentic pastas, seafood and carnivorous delights since the 1960s. The atmosphere is relaxed and friendly and this is a good place to cart your kids along to.

Mai Vi (☎ 905-358-0697; 5713 Victoria Ave; dishes $9-16; ☼ dinner) The food (and the presentation) in this neat little Vietnamese place is absolutely outstanding. It could hold its own in any big city. Just close your eyes and jab the menu – from *pho* to rice plates, vermicelli noodles and crispy duck – you can't go wrong.

Xin Vego Café (☎ 905-353-8346; 4939 Victoria Ave; dishes $8-15; ☼ lunch & dinner Wed-Sun) This vegetarian restaurant is an oasis in Niagara Falls' concrete cuisine jungle. The innovative menu has an eclectic spread of dishes with Thai and Japanese influences. Even die-hard carnivores may have trouble tasting the difference between the veggie pork and the real thing.

TOP END

You can enjoy superb views and dinner to match at both **Revolving Restaurant** (mains $30-70; ☺ lunch & dinner) in the Skylon Tower and the **Pinnacle Restaurant** (mains $20-45; ☺ lunch & dinner) within Minolta Tower. Both serve exquisite fare, with an emphasis on seafood.

Entertainment

On Clifton Hill, the immensely successful **Casino Niagara** (☎ 800-563-2557; www.casinoniagara .com; 5705 Falls Ave; ☺ 24hr; free shuttle buses run from hotels & attractions all over town) never closes.

IMAX Niagara Falls (☎ 905-374-4629; www.imax niagara.com; 6170 Fallsview Blvd; adult/child 4-12/senior $12/6.50/8.50) shows somewhat outdated 45-minute shows about the history of the falls running almost continuously, alternating with French versions and other current IMAX features.

Getting There & Away

BOAT

Speedy Seaflight Hydrofoils (p113) runs services between Toronto and the Queenston dock, from where a complimentary shuttle service to Niagara Falls is available.

BUS

The **bus station** (☎ 905-357-2133; 4555 Erie Ave) is away from the falls area in the older part of town, across the street from the train station. Greyhound Canada buses depart frequently for Toronto ($20, 1½ to two hours) as well as to Buffalo, New York ($5.50, one to 1½ hours, two to three departures daily) with Greyhound.

Casino Niagara (☎ 416-599-8892, 877-361-2888; www.itripmate.com) shuttles passengers by bus from Toronto to Niagara Falls daily. Passengers must be over 19 (ID required), and round-trip tickets cost $18. Note you must board a return bus from the casino within 24 hours. Call or check the website for schedules and pick-up information. Advance reservations are recommended.

Niagara Airbus (☎ 905-374-8111, 800-268-8111; www.niagaraairbus.com) is a door-to-door serv-ice with frequent connections to and from airports in Toronto (adult/child $55/25, 1½ hours) and Buffalo, New York ($57/23, 1½ hours).

TRAIN

VIA Rail runs trains from Toronto ($23.50, two hours, twice daily). The Niagara Falls **train station** (☎ 888-842-7245; 4267 Bridge St) is opposite the bus station.

Getting Around

Walking is best for getting around the central falls area, where many sights are concentrated. To visit outlying sights along the Niagara Parkway, other transport is needed.

CAR & MOTORCYCLE

Driving in and around the center is nothing but a costly headache. Follow the signs to one of the several parking districts and stash the car for the day. There is limited metered parking around town, but pay parking lots (from $5 per 30 minutes, or $13 per day) are plentiful. The huge Rapids View parking lot, which is also the depot for the Niagara Parks People Mover (see below), is a little over 3km south of the falls off River Rd.

PUBLIC TRANSPORTATION

Operated by the Niagara Parks Commission, the **Niagara Parks People Mover** (day pass adult/child $6/3; ☺ departs every 20min 9am-11pm Mar-Oct) is an economical and efficient bus system. The depot is in the huge Rapids View parking lot. Day passes can be purchased at most stops. Shuttles follow a 15km path from the Rapids View parking lot north past the Horseshoe Falls, Rainbow and Whirlpool Bridges, Whirlpool Aero Car and, during peak season, to Queenston village.

Niagara Transit (☎ 905-356-1179; www.niagara transit.com; shuttle rides adult/child $3/1, day pass for 1 adult & 2 children $6; ☺ mid-May–Nov, departures every 30min 9-1:30am in peak season) provides a shuttle bus service around town. One route, the Red Line, goes around Clifton Hill and other falls attractions, then up Lundy's Lane to the motels and back. The Blue Line runs from the downtown bus and train stations to the falls area attractions, by the Table Rock Information Centre and down the Niagara Parkway to the Rapids View parking lot, then loops back around up Portage Rd and Stanley Ave. The Green Line goes from Rainbow Bridge north to Whirlpool Aero Car, then back down River Rd past the B&Bs to Clifton Hill. Out of season, Niagara Transit's regular city buses (adult/child $2.25/1) must be used.

NIAGARA-ON-THE-LAKE

Originally a Neutral Indians village, this small town 20km downstream (north) from Niagara Falls was founded by Loyalists from New York State after the American Revolution. It later became the first capital of the colony of Upper Canada.

Today it's considered one of the best-preserved 19th-century towns in North America. The lakeside location, tree-lined streets and old houses make Niagara-on-the-Lake a nice place to see before or after the falls, although stampedes of tour buses tend to dampen the town's charm. It's best to avoid the main street and stroll down the side streets for a taste of former quiet times in a small, prosperous Ontario town.

Orientation & Information

Queen St is the main street. On the eastern side of the downtown area, toward Niagara Falls, King St crosses Queen St at large Simcoe Park. Beyond that, Queen St becomes Picton St.

Niagara-on-the-Lake Chamber of Commerce (☎ 905-468-1950; www.niagaraonthelake.com; 26 Queen St, cnr King St; ⏰ 10am-7:30pm Apr-Oct; 10am-5pm Nov-Mar) At the helpful visitors' information center, staff can book acommodation for you for free.

Sights & Activities

Aside from the acclaimed George Bernard Shaw Festival (see the boxed text on p131), this town only warrants a brief stop.

Queen St teems with shops of the ye olde variety selling antiques, British-style souvenirs and homemade fudge. The people at wonderful **Greaves Jams & Marmalades** (☎ 905-468-7831; 55 Queen St, cnr Regent St; ⏰ 9:30am-6pm Sun-Thu, to 6:30pm Fri & Sat) are f urth-generation jam-makers. Further east is the Victorian-era **Niagara Apothecary** (☎ 905-468-3845; 5 Queen St; admission by donation; ⏰ noon-6pm mid-May–early Sep), a museum fitted with great old cabinets, remedies and jars.

The **Niagara Historical Society Museum** (☎ 905-468-3912; www.niagara.com/~nhs; 43 Castlereagh St, cnr Davy St; adult/child/student/senior $5/1/2/3; ⏰ 10am-5:30pm May-Oct, 1-5pm Nov-Apr), south of Simcoe Park, has a vast collection relating to the town's past, ranging from First Nations artifacts to Loyalist and War of 1812 collectibles. The Chamber of Commerce can provide you with the *Historic Guide*, a free pamphlet outlining in brief the town's history and providing a self-guided walking tour.

At the southeastern edge of town, restored **Fort George** (☎ 905-468-4257; www.niagara .com/~parkscan; $8/5/6.50; off Niagara Parkway; adult/child/senior $8/5/6.50; ⏰ 10am-5pm Apr-Oct) dates from 1797. The fort was the site of important battles during the War of 1812, changing hands between the British and US forces a couple of times. Within the walls

---

O BROTHER, WHERE ART THOU?

What do Irish Republicans, African Americans, Mohawk tribes and Québec radicals have in common? They all hate the British – or at least they did during the mid-19th century. Although the resultant Fenian raids (tacitly approved but not acknowledged by the USA) are a side note to Canadian history, their epic goals are worth recounting.

A series of border incursions organized by the Fenian brotherhood, made up of Irish Americans loyal to the Republican cause, had as their goal the harassment of British forces and the eventual capture of Canada's major cities, Toronto and Montréal. Why? The fiendish Fenian brethren planned to hold both cities hostage until Britain agreed to free Ireland. Veteran fighters from the US Civil War, including a company of African-American soldiers, along with 500 Mohawk warriors and French sympathizers in Montréal, rallied to the cause.

Everything went tragicomically awry when the raids began in 1866. Although one detachment of Fenians quickly overran Fort Erie, a deadly combination of fever outbreak, poor planning, and even laziness on the part of the brethren – along with efficient spying by British military scouts – stopped the major brunt of the attack. When those Fenians at Fort Erie attempted to retreat across the Niagara River, they were arrested by a US warship, convicted and sentenced in a New York court, then quietly released. Prisoners-of-war taken to Toronto fared far worse; nearly two dozen were executed. Nevertheless, the Fenian border raids continued sporadically into 1871.

are the officers' quarters, a working kitchen, the powder magazine and storage houses. Ghost tours, skills demonstrations and battle re-enactments occur throughout the summer. Tucked behind the fort is **Navy Hall**, at the water's edge. Only one building remains of what was a sizable supply depot for British forts on the Great Lakes during the 18th century. It was destroyed during the War of 1812. The US **Fort Niagara** is across the river.

Back in town are the **Butler's Barracks** (admission free). First used by the British at the end of the War of 1812 as a storage and barracks site, the Canadian military has since used the location to train troops for both World Wars and for the Korean War.

Tours

Niagara Wine Tours (☎ 905-468-1300, 800-680-7006; www.niagaraworldwinetours.com; 92 Picton St; tours per person $55-120; Apr-Oct) Offers various bicycle tours of the area's wineries, including tastings. Bikes are also available for rent ($25/day). See p133 for more Wine Country tours.

Whirlpool Jet (☎ 905-468-4800, 888-438-4444; www.whirlpooljet.com; 61 Melville St; 45-min tours adult/youth 6-14 $54/44; Apr–mid-Oct) Thrills passengers with a 29km trip through the rapids of the lower Niagara River – bring a change of clothes! Reservations are required.

Sleeping

Although there are over 300 B&Bs in town, acommodation here is generally expensive and often booked out. When the Shaw Festival is on, lodging is even tighter, so plan ahead.

Amberlea Guest House (☎ 905-468-3749, 285 John St; r incl breakfast $95) It's a little farther out (six blocks from Queen St), but this Tudor-style cottage is still accessible to the town center. Set in a tranquil pocket, all rooms are tastefully furnished and very comfortable. You can enjoy the colorful garden, thick with foliage, from the deck. Rooms contain TVs and some have fireplaces.

School Master's House (☎ 905-468-1299; www.schoolmastershouse.com; 307 Mississauga St; d $125-185) Dating from 1818, this grand dame of the town was once the teaching grounds for many United Empire Loyalists. Set on an expansive block, the vintage facade now contains just enough mod-cons to cater to the comfort-needy without detracting from the building's charm. All rooms come with TVs, VCRs, fridges and hair dryers, but the fireplaces are original. Guests can also rent bicycles to explore the surrounding area.

Prince of Wales Hotel (☎ 905-468-3246, 888-669-5566; www.vintageinns.com; 6 Picton St, cnr King St; d $225-375, ste $425-475;) Opposite Simcoe Park, this elegant Victorian hotel was built in 1864 and much of the interior has retained its period charm. An abundance of frills and floral prints seem to cater particularly to honeymooners, but it's the perfect spot for anyone looking to indulge. Features include a spa and an excellent restaurant.

Also recommended:

Carol's Saltbox (☎ 905-468-5423, 223 Gate St; d incl breakfast with shared/private bathroom from $95/110)

Henry & Irene's Guest House (☎ 905-468-3111; 285 William St; r incl breakfast $75-85)

Eating

A few blocks from Queen St, Queen's Royal Park makes a good place for a picnic along the water.

Escabeche (☎ 905-468-3246, 888-669-5566; 6 Picton St, cnr King St; dinner $22-35; breakfast, lunch & dinner) The fine-dining room at the opulent Prince of Wales Hotel takes its food seriously as it does every other fine detail. Seafood features strongly on the contemporary menu, which offers taste inventions such as smoked trout, pancetta and potato cakes, followed by poached Atlantic salmon fillet with lemongrass potatoes and plum soy. Leave room for dessert – you've been warned.

Fans Court (☎ 905-468-4511; 135 Queen St; mains $13-20; lunch & dinner Tue-Sun) A menu graced with Cantonese, Szechwan and pan-Asian dishes distinguishes this fine eatery from its neighbors in this most Anglo of towns. If your taste buds are yearning for a change along the lines of Singapore beef or sizzling lemon chicken then you're definitely in the right place. Bamboo and fans adorn the interior, and during summer you can dine al fresco in the courtyard.

Epicurean (☎ 905-468-0288; 84 Queen St; lunch $6-9, dinner $17-21; lunch daily, dinner Wed-Sun) By day this welcoming lunch cafeteria dishes up fresh and tasty sandwiches and salads. The ambience is upped a notch at night when the cafeteria gives way to a stylish bistro. The menu follows suit, offering meals the likes of grilled salmon, leek and mushroom ragu with pancetta and capers.

A SHAW THING

In 1962, a lawyer and passionate dramatist, Brian Doherty, led a group of residents in eight performances of George Bernard Shaw's *Candida* and 'Don Juan in Hell' from *Man and Superman*. Doherty chose Shaw because he was 'a great prophet of the 20th century,' and because Shaw 'was the only outstanding playwright writing in English, with the obvious exception of Shakespeare, who produced a sufficient number of plays to support a festival.'

Doherty's passion did indeed infiltrate the performance and the first season blossomed what is now the internationally respected **Shaw Festival** (☎ 905-468-2172, 800-511-7429; www.shawfest .com; tickets $20-77; ☺ box office 9am-8pm). After more than 40 years of growth, the festival lures a global audience and critical acclaim from late June to late July each year. Visionary art direction has infused a variety of works and playwrights and aside from an opening Shaw showstopper, you'll be treated to Victorian drama, plays of continental Europe, US drama, musicals, mystery and suspense plays and classics from the pens of Oscar Wilde, Virginia Woolf, Noel Coward and George Walker.

In 1985 the festival academy was established, primarily as a vehicle for the exchange of skills among the festival's ensemble of actors. Since then it has expanded to include various educational programs: there are specialized seminars held through the season and, on selected Saturdays, informal Lunchtime Conversations, where the public can join in discussions with members of the Shaw Festival company.

Ten to 12 plays are performed every season in three theaters around town – the Court House Theatre, the Festival Theatre and the Royal George Theatre, a onetime vaudeville house and cinema. All three theaters are within walking distance of the town center. The Niagara Historical Society Museum (p129) has also established day programs of arts and crafts for children during matinee performances, just in case they're a tad young for the literary analysis.

The best seats in the house on Saturday night at the Festival Theatre will set you back $77. Cheaper rush seats go on sale at 9am on the day of performance, but are not available for Saturday shows. Students and seniors can get good reductions on some matinees, and weekday matinees are the cheapest. Under 30s also get discounts at the Festival Theatre and there are lunchtime one-act plays for $20.

Tickets can be bought from the box office from mid-April through mid-January. If you're planning to see a play, call the toll-free telephone number from anywhere in Canada or the USA well in advance and ask for the Shaw Festival guide, or check the Internet site, which has all the details, the year's performances and other useful information, as well as ticket order forms.

Getting There & Around

There are no direct buses between Toronto and Niagara-on-the-Lake. From Toronto, you must go to St Catharines or Niagara Falls, then transfer. **Charterways Bus Lines** (☎ 905-688-9600) runs a service from St Catharines to Fort George. During summer the **Niagara-on-the-Lake Shuttle Bus** (☎ 905-685-5463; one way/round trip $10/15; two to three departures daily May-Sep) transfers folks to and from Niagara Falls. Taxis to Niagara Falls charge about $35.

A high-speed hydrofoil (p113) runs between Toronto docks and Queenston, south of Niagara-on-the-Lake, with a shuttle bus to town included in the fare.

Cycling is a fine way to explore the area, and bicycles can be rented by the hour, half day or full day at Niagara Wine Tours.

NIAGARA PENINSULA WINE COUNTRY

If it seems strange to find winemaking here in the Great White North, remember that the Niagara Peninsula sits on the 43rd parallel, similar in latitude to northern California and further south than Bordeaux, France. The moderate microclimate created by Lake Ontario and the Niagara escarpment, and mineral-rich soil, have contributed significantly to the area's viticultural success. Since the 1980s, Niagara's cottage industry has really grown up and international award-winning vintners are now capably turning out international-caliber vintages.

Information

The best way to explore the region is with wheels and at least two drivers. You'll need several days to enjoy the spectacle of the

FORT ERIE

South from Niagara Falls, the Niagara Park-way continues to the town of Fort Erie. Situated where the Niagara River meets Lake Erie, across from Buffalo, New York, it's connected to the USA by the Peace Bridge. The town is best visited for the reconstruction of historic **Fort Erie** (☎ 905-871-0540; 350 Lakeshore Rd; adult/child $6.50/4; ☺ 10am-6pm May-Nov), first built in 1764 and also known as the Old Stone Fort. The USA seized it in 1814 before retreating. At the fort, a museum, military drills and uni-formed soldiers can be seen. Take the worthwhile guided tour; it's included in the price.

countryside, alternating between driving and tasting roles. Area tourist offices have lists of the 30-some wineries and their locations. Official wine route maps and helpful guide booklets are freely available at many wineries' tasting rooms, or check out www.winesofontario.org.

Sights & Activities

The following drive hits the Niagara Peninsula's highlights, both for quality and style, taking in wineries and farm stands on the way to Niagara-on-the-Lake.

Coming from Toronto on the QEW, after about an hour turn right onto Roberts Rd and you'll find **Kittling Ridge Estate Winery & Spirits** (☎ 905-945-9225; www.kittlingridge.com; 297 South Service Rd, Grimsby; ☺ 10am-6pm Mon-Sat, 11am-5pm Sun), which looks rather like a factory. But just one taste of its award-winning ice and late-harvest wines will win you over. Free tours are given at 2pm daily (also at 11:30am on weekends from June to September).

Continue east on the service road, then cut south onto what eventually becomes rambling Hwy 81. Around Beamsville, look out for the photogenic **Peninsula Ridge Estates Winery** (☎ 905-563-0900; www.peninsularidge.com; 5600 King St W, Beamsville; ☺ 10am-6pm, tours 11:30am & 3pm). The new wines taste unfinished, but the log-cabin tasting room and hilltop setting are beautiful.

Highway 81 meanders east past Cherry Ave, where you can turn right to **Lakeview Cellars Estate Winery** (☎ 905-562-5685; www.lakeviewcellars.on.ca; 4037 Cherry Ave, Vineland; ☺ 10am-5:30pm),

known for its ice wine varietals, including a special cabernet franc version.

Further east is **Vinelands Estates Winery** (☎ 905-562-7088, 888-846-3526; www.vineland.com; 3620 Moyer Rd; ☺ 10am-5pm, restaurant 11:30am-5pm, to 10pm May-Oct), the original source of viticulture in the Niagara region. Like an elder statesman, Vinelands impresses everyone with its gray stone buildings. Almost all the wines here are excellent, especially the pinot gris. Tours are given at 3pm daily (weekends only November to April).

Back on Hwy 81, continue east through the rolling countryside to Jordan, best known for its **Creekside Estate Winery** (☎ 877-262-9463; www.creeksideestatewinery.com; 2170 4th Ave, Jordan Station; ☺ 10am-6pm), just east of town, where you can tour the underground cellars and stroll along nature trails.

Heading back east on Hwy 81 for about 30 minutes, you'll enter the Niagara-on-the-Lake region. Take a left onto Four Mile Creek Rd, which will take you to **Hillebrand Estates Winery** (☎ 905-468-1723, 800-572-8412; www.hillebrand.com; 1249 Niagara Stone Rd, Niagara-on-the-Lake; ☺ 10am-6pm). This place mostly ferments wines made for the mass market, not connoisseurs. For those who've never visited a winery before, however, its introductory tours (given hourly) and tasting bar presentations are recommended. The presentations cost $5 and teach you how to identify regional taste and aroma essences.

Further north, near Lake Ontario, **Konzelmann Estate Winery** (☎ 905-935-2866; www.konzelmannwines.com; 1096 Lakeshore Rd, Niagara-on-the-Lake; ☺ 10am-6pm Mon-Sat, noon-6pm Sun) is one of the oldest wineries in the region and the only one to take full advantage of the lakeside microclimate. The late-harvest vidal tastes of golden apples, and the ice wines, helped along by freezing winter winds off the lake, are superb. Tours are given at 2pm from May to September.

Next on the right is the **Strewn** (☎ 905-468-1229; www.strewnwinery.com; 1339 Lakeshore Rd, Niagara-on-the-Lake; ☺ 10am-6pm), already producing medal-winning vintages and home to the popular **Wine Country Cooking School** (☎ 905-468-8304; www.winecountrycooking.com), where one-day, weekend and weeklong classes offer pure indulgence. At the winery, tours are given at 1pm daily; special ice wine tours require reservations.

Closer to Niagara-on-the-Lake, **Sunnybrook Farm Estate Winery** (☎ 905-468-1122; www .sunnybrookfarmwinery.com; 1425 Lakeshore Rd, Niagara-on-the-Lake; ☒ 10am-6pm) specializes in unique Niagara fruit and berry wines, such as spiced apple and blackberry.

After passing congested Niagara-on-the-Lake, the wine route continues down the Niagara Parkway to **Reif Estate Winery** (☎ 905-468-7738; www.reifwinery.com; 15608 Niagara Parkway, Niagara-on-the-Lake; ☒ 10am-6pm). Situated between Line 2 and Line 3 Rds, this well-established winery has ice wines; tours are given at 1:30pm daily from May to October. Nearby, award-winning **Inniskillin** (☎ 905-468-2187, 888-466-4754; www.icewine.com; Line 3, cnr Niagara Pkwy, Niagara-on-the-Lake; ☒ 11am-5:30pm) is a master of the ice wine craft. Tours are given at 10:30am and 2:30pm daily (weekends only November to April); self-guided tours are available anytime.

Tours

See p130 for Wine Country tours departing from Niagara-on-the-Lake.

Crush on Niagara (☎ 905-562-3373, 866-408-9463; www.crushtours.com; tours $95-125) Small-group van tours departing from various pick-up points in the Niagara region.

Niagara Airbus (☎ 905-374-8111, 800-268-8111; www .niagaraairbus.com; tours from Niagara-on-the-Lake $35, from Niagara Falls $50-85, from Toronto $95-135) Stops at well-known wineries; some itineraries include vineyard tours, lunch and shopping in Niagara-on-the-Lake.

Festivals & Events

Niagara Icewine Festival (☎ 905-688-0212; www .grapeandwine.com) A 10-day event held in mid-January throughout the Niagara region, showcasing wines from Ontario's best vineyards.

Niagara Wine Festival (☎ 905-688-0212; www.grape andwine.com) A week-long event in mid-September celebrating the region's finest produce off the vine.

Niagara New Vintage Festival (☎ 905-688-0212; www.grapeandwine.com) Mid-June to late July.

Sleeping & Eating

This picturesque region offers some excellent dining and acommodation alternatives to Niagara Falls' glitzy concrete hotels and the concentration of indistinguishable B&Bs in Niagara-on-the-Lake.

Colonist House B&B (☎ 905-563-7838; colonist@vax xine.com; 4924 King St, Beamsville; d incl breakfast $110) This quaint B&B oozes charm from the picket fence out front to the antique-filled guest rooms. Sunlight floods through ample windows throughout the house and cooked breakfasts including homemade bread, fresh fruit and coffee to tempt even choosy eaters.

Keaton Manor B&B (☎ 905-688-3625; keatonmanor bbb@sympatico.ca; 1590 Regional Rd 81, St Catharines; r incl breakfast $95-125; ☒) In its heyday some 170 years ago, this manor was a tavern complete with grand ballroom. Today the manor is a spacious and comfortable B&B set in eight acres of stunning woodland. The on-site

---

LIQUID GOLD

Niagara's regional wineries burst onto the scene at Vinexpo 1991 in Bordeaux, France. In a blind taste test, judges awarded one of the coveted gold medals to an Ontario ice wine, and international attendees' mouths fell open. These specialty vintages, with their arduous harvesting and sweet, yet multidimensional taste, continue to draw aficionados and the curious to the Niagara Peninsula wine country.

A certain percentage of grapes are left on the vines after the regular harvest season is finished. The vines are then covered with netting to protect them from birds. If storms and mold do not destroy them, the grapes grow ever more sugary and concentrated until three days of consistent, low winter temperatures (-8°C) freeze them entirely during December or January.

When this happens, rapid harvesting of the fragile icy grapes must be done carefully by hand in the predawn darkness so that the sun doesn't melt the ice inside and dilute the resulting grape juice. The grapes are subsequently pressed and aged in barrels for several months, even up to a year. After decanting, the smooth ice vintages taste intensely of apples, or even more exotic fruit, and pack quite an alcoholic kick.

Why are ice wines so expensive? It takes 10 times the usual number of grapes to make just one bottle of ice wine. This, combined with labor-intensive production methods and the high risk of crop failure, often drives the price well above $40 per 375mL bottle. Late-harvest wines picked earlier in the year may be less costly (and less sweet), but just as full-flavored and aromatic.

pond attracts swans and turtles, and foodies will love the chef-prepared breakfasts.

Vinelands Estates Winery (☎ 905-562-7088, 888-846-3526; www.vineland.com; 3620 Moyer Rd; r incl breakfast $135) This excellent winery has a small but gracious B&B with a self-contained kitchen. The **restaurant** (meals $15-40; ☺ lunch & dinner) has unbeatable views of the vineyards and cooks up exotic inventions such as eastern spice-cured salmon, foie gras torchon with rich brioche and lime-pickled jumbo shrimp. There are also a few vegetarian options on the menu.

Peninsula Ridge (☎ 905-563-0900; 5600 King St W, Beamsville; mains $28-38, tasting menu $75; ☺ lunch & dinner Wed-Sun) If you're looking for divine gastronomy, make a beeline for Peninsula's stylish dining room. Guests are served superb infusions such as grilled tuna loin with roasted red pepper, Jerusalem artichoke and niçoise olives or roasted wild boar tenderloin with spinach and ricotta ravioli. The five-course tasting menu is utter indulgence.

Angel Food Café (☎ 905-945-5522; 43 Main St E, Grimsby; mains $11-19; ☺ lunch & dinner Mon-Sat) Boasting multicultural flavors good enough to rival any restaurant in Toronto, Angel Food Café sizzles up Szechwan Atlantic salmon, Louisiana blackened catfish and a delectable *pad thai*. Creative pastas cater to vegetarians and you can consume the good stuff in classy surrounds.

Gables Restaurant (☎ 905-945-1997; 13 Mountain St, Grimsby; mains $10-20; ☺ lunch & dinner) The chef at this family-friendly restaurant has chosen a safe rather than imaginative route, but no one's complaining about hearty meals of grilled salmon fillet with a zesty cucumber salsa or New Zealand spring lamb with a dijon mustard and herb crust. Vegetarians and kids are also well catered for here.

Also recommended:

Bonnybank (☎ 905-562-3746; nnt@vaxxine.com; RR1, Vineland Station; r incl breakfast $90-120) Stately Tudor house in a gorgeous wilderness setting. Call for directions.

Olde Fashioned Lunch Box (☎ 905-562-7669; 4630 Victoria Ave; meals $4-10; ☺ 8am-8pm Tue-Sun) Outstanding homemade sandwiches and burgers.

Getting There & Away

By car, the journey from Toronto to this neck of the woods takes between one and 1½ hours. Take the QEW heading southwest toward Niagara Falls and stay on it as it travels westbound past Hamilton. Vineland, which is the central area in the region, is about 90km from Toronto. The official Wine Route is signposted at various exits off the QEW, on rural highways and along backcountry roads.

See p133 for organized tours to the region.

BRANTFORD & AROUND

☎ 519 / pop 110,000

When a town can lay claim to the location of a prosperous Mohawk village, invention of the telephone and birthplace of the greatest hockey player ever, you know it's got plenty going on. Surrounded by farmland and bisected by the Grand River, Brantford has an old limestone downtown.

Bordering the southeast city limits, the Six Nations–New Credit District has been a First Nations' center for centuries. Captain Joseph Thayendanegea Brant led the Six Nations people here from upper New York State in 1784 and established a village that long served the district's First Nations tribes. Evidence of European settlement and industrial growth along the Grand in the following centuries is seen in the Victorian houses and limestone buildings throughout the region.

Information

Tourism Brantford (☎ 519-751-9900, 800-265-6299; www.brantford.ca; 399 Wayne Gretzky Pkwy; ☺ 9am-8pm Mon-Fri, to 9pm Sat, to 5pm Sun) In a new building, including a mini-museum, off Hwy 403.

Sights

Captain Brant's tomb is on the grounds of the tiny **Her Majesty's Chapel of the Mohawks** (☎ 519-758-5444; 291 Mohawk St; suggested donation $2; ☺ 10am-6pm Jul–Labour Day, 1-5pm Wed-Sun Labour Day–Jul), best visited on sunny afternoons when light streams through the stained-glass windows. On-site of the original village, it's the oldest Protestant church in Ontario and the world's only Royal Indian Chapel.

A replica 17th-century Iroquois village with a longhouse, **Kanata** (☎ 519-752-1229; www.kanatavillage.net; 440 Mohawk St; admission $4; ☺ 8:30am-3:30pm Mon-Fri, 10am-4pm Sat & Sun) is set within a huge forested area. Authentic exhibits and authentic demonstrations teach First Nations' traditions.

Put down your cell phone and pay homage. Alexander Graham Bell changed communication when he completed the first telephone at **Bell Homestead National Historic Site** (☎ 519-756-6220; www.bellhomestead.ca; 94 Tutela Heights; admission $2; ☺ 9:30am-4:30pm Tue-Sun) on July 26th, 1874. This was Bell's first North American home, and it contains his other inventions and furnishings.

With exhibits proudly showcasing 28 athletes at a time, the true centerpiece at **Brantford Sports Hall of Recognition** (☎ 519-756-9900; 254 North Park St; free; ☺ 9am-9pm Mon-Fri, 9am-4pm Sat, 11am-6pm Sun) is Wayne 'The Great One' Gretzky's permanent display. Gretz learned and honed his game for countless hours on the backyard hockey rink of his Brantford home as a kid before he shattered record books and impressed the world with his skills.

Southeast of Brantford is **Six Nations–New Credit** (otherwise known as the Six Nations of the Grand River Reserve, or Ohsweken) a well-known aboriginal community. Established in the late 18th century, it gives visitors a glimpse of traditional and contemporary First Nations culture. 'The Gathering Place,' **Odrohekta** (☎ 519-758-5444; www.sixnationstourism.com; cnr Hwy 54 & Chiefswood Rd; ☺ 9am-430pm) is the visitor's center and has information as well as a small, museum-like collection. For custom tours of the reserve and its Band Council House (the seat of all decision making), phone ahead to make an appointment. Across the street, **Chiefswood National Historic Site** (☎ 519-752-5005; admission $3; ☺ 10am-3pm Tue-Sun May-Oct) is the home of Mohawk poet E Pauline Johnson, whose writing reflected a blend of European and aboriginal cultures.

Festivals & Events

The **Grand River Powwow** (☎ 519-445-4061; www.gr powwow.com; adult/child $10/2; ☺ late Jul) is a major two-day event held in late July with hundreds of colorful dancers, traditional drumming and singing, as well as aboriginal foods and crafts sales.

Getting There & Away

Brantford's **bus station** (☎ 519-756-5011; 64 Darling St) is downtown. Greyhound Canada connects to Toronto ($24, one to two hours), London ($20, 1½ hours) and (via Hamilton) Niagara Falls ($29, four hours).

GUELPH

☎ 519 / pop 106,000

Guelph is a mid-sized town where attractive brick houses that would make the Three Little Pigs proud flank tree-lined streets. A university town and home of Sleeman's Brewery, Guelph is a nice place to live and a great place to hang out, kick back and enjoy.

West of Toronto – just north of Hwy 401 – the downtown area is overseen by the dominant stone-faced look of **Church of Our Lady**. Covered Old Québec St and outdoor Wyndam St are the main shopping areas, and Wyndam St is a good place for lunch or a drink.

Worthwhile shows occur in the seven galleries of the **Macdonald Stewart Art Centre** (☎ 519-837-0010; 358 Gordon St; admission free; ☺ noon-5pm Tue-Sun), specializing in Inuit and other Canadian art. The park outside features abstract (gravity-defying cubes) and random (metal faces) works of art.

The birthplace of John McCrae, **McCrae House Museum** (☎ 519-836-1482; 108 Water St; adult/ concession $4/3; ☺ 1-5pm, closed Sat Sep-Apr) is a living museum that puts his life on display. McCrae was a Canadian soldier and author of 'In Flanders Fields' – an antiwar poem written during WWII, read by all Canadian school kids.

Undoubtedly the only place where a bunch of jackasses will warm even the hardest of hearts, the **Donkey Sanctuary of Canada** (☎ 519-836-1697; www.donkeysanctuary.ca; 6981 Puslinch Concession Rd; admission by donation; ☺ 9am-4pm Wed & Sun May-Nov) is off Hwy 6 north from Hwy 401. It's a peaceful, pastoral refuge for formerly abused and neglected donkeys who've become enamored with carefree living and are now happy, gentle and amusing animals. In other words: it's 'jackass-tic.'

Cornerstone (☎ 519-827-0145; 1 Wyndham St N; mains $6-9; ☺ 8-1am) A well-worn and well-used vegetarian place that's just as comfortable serving morning coffee and granola as it is hosting late-night pints and pizzas. On some evenings acoustic guitar is featured, but if you want quiet, the outside seating is great on warm summer evenings.

Latino's (☎ 519-836-3431; 51 Cork St E; mains $7-10; ☺ lunch & dinner, closed Sun) This family-run place with a welcoming atmosphere serves some incredibly good Chilean food at bargain prices. Everything is homemade; you can't go wrong, from the soups to the *ceviche* to the enchiladas.

KITCHENER-WATERLOO

☎ 519 / pop 277,000

Referred to as 'Kitchener,' 'Waterloo,' 'K-W' (but *not* 'kay-dub') or 'Kitchener and Waterloo,' these two cities located an hour west of Toronto have formed a symbiotic relationship rather than doing battle for visitors and residents. In the heart of rural southern Ontario, K-W acts as more than a hub for the surrounding Amish and Mennonite farming communities, and it's worth a day trip from Toronto or a stop in your journey along the Trans-Canada Hwy.

Kitchener's original name, Berlin, points to its German settlement. The Old World culture is still evident today, coming to the forefront during the huge Oktoberfest. Kitchener's old stone architecture is juxtaposed against the modern dot-com construction in Waterloo, and two universities bring youthful energy to the area.

Orientation & Information

Kitchener is the southern city and, being nearly three times the size of Waterloo, serves as the true downtown center for the area. The main throughway, King St, runs roughly north–south (it's King St W and E in Kitchener, King St N and S in Waterloo) and only the signs that welcome you to Waterloo (northbound) or Kitchener (southbound) indicate that you've even changed cities.

'Uptown' in Waterloo, along King St N from Bridgeport Rd to William St, is a district full of brick buildings and is less compact than Kitchener's 'downtown,' with diverse shops, restaurants and bars near the University of Waterloo.

KW Tourism (☎ 519-745-3536, 800-265-6959; www .kw-visitor.on.ca; 191 King St W; 8am-6pm Mon-Fri, 10am-4pm Sat & Sun) Maps and information.

Sights & Activities

Downtown Kitchener provides a nice walk through tree-lined streets featuring old-world architecture and new-world creations such as ultra-modern **City Hall** (200 King St W). Uptown Waterloo is a great place to kick back and hang out with locals. Most of K-W's major sites are a five- to 20-minute drive from downtown.

KW Tourism has a list of **nature walks** and **cycling routes** that are great in the blooming summertime or color-changing autumn. Again, most are just outside town.

KITCHENER MARKET

The **farmers' market** (☎ 519-741-2287; 300 King St E; www.kitchenermarket.ca; 7am-2pm Sat, also 8am-2pm Wed May-Oct) has been open downtown since 1839, although it has recently moved into new digs. Bread, jam, cheese, sausages and produce cultivated and created by the mainly Amish and Mennonite farmers are sold alongside handicrafts such as quilts, rugs, clothes and handmade toys. There are also conventional farmers selling their wares, but the Mennonite or Amish farmers of Eastern European ancestry live much as their grandparents did in the 19th century (see the boxed text on p139). It makes you think twice, considering that everything has been made from scratch without the help of machines. The new market building is shared with the florists, cafés and delis of the **Market Shops** (10am-6pm Mon-Fri, 7am-6pm Sat).

DOON HERITAGE CROSSROADS

This re-creation of a pioneer **settlement** (☎ 519-748-1914; 10 Huron Rd; adult/child/senior/family $6/3/4/15; 10am-4:30pm May-Dec, Mon-Fri only Labour Day–Dec 23, closed Dec 23–Apr) c 1914 chronicles the times when technological advances such as motors and electricity began to change lives in Waterloo. Costumed volunteers walking the old boardwalks that connect the general store, workshops and other buildings will take you back to that time. There is also a model of an original Russian Mennonite village and a replica of an 1856 railway.

JOSEPH SCHNEIDER HAUS

This Heritage Canada **site** (☎ 519-742-7752; 466 Queen St S; adult/child/senior/family $2.25/1.25/1.50/5; 10am-5pm July & Aug, 10am-5pm Wed-Sat & 1-5pm Sun Sep-Jun), one of the first homes built in the area, has been restored to depict life in the 1800s. Originally built for a prosperous Mennonite from Pennsylvania, its original architecture is amazing, as are the demonstrations of day-to-day chores and skills from that time.

KITCHENER-WATERLOO ART GALLERY

This **gallery** (☎ 519-579-5860; www.kwag.on.ca; 101 Queen St N; admission free; 10am-5pm Mon-Sat, 1-5pm Sun) in the Centre in the Square performance hall has a 3500-piece collection of art with a local focus, but which also includes work from around the world.

WOODSIDE NATIONAL HISTORIC SITE

A stone-built **mansion** (☎ 519-571-5684; 528 Wellington St N; adult/child/senior/family $3.50/1.75/3/8.75; 🕙 10am-5pm late May–Dec) in a lush, green garden preserves the 100-year-old home of Canada's 10th prime minister, William Lyon Mackenzie King. Not only has the building been restored and furnished in upper-class 1890s style, but the piano-playing, costumed tour leaders bring the era to life.

HOMER WATSON HOUSE & GALLERY

In the former **home** (☎ 519-748-4377; 1754 Old Mill Rd; suggested donation $2; 🕙 noon-4:30pm Tue-Sun Apr-Dec) of one of Canada's first notable landscape painters, this small, specialized museum has various pieces relating to Homer's life and work.

Kitchener-Waterloo For Children

The **Waterloo Regional Children's Museum** (☎ 519-749-9387; www.wrcm.ca; 10 King St W; admission $7; 🕙 10am-5pm Mon-Sat, noon-5pm Sun, closed Mon Sep-May) has been playing around downtown since it opened in 2003, and has been well received by the young and not-so-young. Hands-on displays have different themes every month to teach and play, while the permanent display featuring K'nex building block creations is a big hit.

Sportsworld (☎ 519-653-4442, 800-393-9163; www .sportsworld.on.ca; 100 Sportsworld Dr) and **Bingemans Park** (☎ 519-744-1555, 800-667-0833; www.bingemans .com; 1380 Victoria St N) are massive entertainment parks containing, among other diversions, waterslides, wave pools, go-karts, video arcades and restaurants.

Festivals & Events

Ontario Mennonite Relief Sale (☎ 519-745-8458; www.ontario-mennonite-relief-sale.org; 🕙 last weekend May) In New Hamburg, 19km west of Kitchener-Waterloo, a pancake breakfast, sale of Mennonite food and an auction of wonderful handmade quilts and wall coverings is held, all to raise money for the needy worldwide.

Uptown Waterloo Jazz Festival (☎ 519-885-1921; www.uptownwaterloojazz.ca; 🕙 mid-July) Big-time jazz, small-town environment.

Waterloo Busker Carnival (☎ 519-747-8769; www .waterloo-buskers.com; 🕙 late Aug) Street performers

from around the world entertain and dazzle; a must-see if you're in the area.

Oktoberfest (☎ 519-570-4267, 888-294-4267; www .oktoberfest.ca; 🕙 early–mid-Oct) This nine-day Bavarian festival – the biggest of its kind in North America and said to be the largest outside of Germany – is K-W's favorite event, and that of many others as well, since it brings in about 500,000 people each year. German food, music, dancing and, of course, *biergartens* are part of the festivities that culminate in a huge parade. Accommodations during the festival should be reserved well in advance. For getting around, there is a free festival bus, in addition to city buses.

Sleeping

There are plenty of motels on Victoria St N west of King St or along King St E, south of downtown towards Hwy 401. KW Tourism office can help with finding B&Bs, as can the **Waterloo Region Bed & Breakfast Association** (www.bbcanada.com/associations/wrabba).

Morning Crescent (☎ 519-743-4557, 877-743-4557; www.morningtoncres.ca; 11 Sunbridge Cres; s/d with bathroom $110-20; P 🖳 🐾) In an unassuming house in a quiet neighborhood a restful stay awaits. The Coach Room with its fireplace and carved wood furniture, including headboard, is a favorite. The backyard pool and hot-tub are refreshing and relaxing.

Walper Terrace Hotel (☎ 519-745-4321, 800-265-8749; www.walper.com; 1 King St W; s/d $100/110; P) Complete renovations to the interior have given this heritage property modern style, while keeping its old-world charisma. The exterior's smooth stone walls and intricate carvings define strength; the dark wood and new green carpets inside bring comfort. The rooms aren't spacious, but they've preserved old-time charm.

Eating

Make sure to hit the farmer's market (see opposite) if you're in town at the right time. Thanks to Kitchener's European heritage, you'll find a few Euro-style delis on (and just off) King St downtown, including **Fiedlers** (☎ 519-745-8356; 197 King St E; 🕙 closed Sun & Mon), which is stacked full of cheeses, rye breads, sausages and salamis.

Williams Coffee Pub (mains $4-8; 🕙 6:30am-2am Mon-Sat, 7:30-1am Sun); Kitchener (☎ 519-744-7199; 198 King St W); Waterloo (☎ 519-725-4432; 33 University Ave E) is a regional chain where university crowds go for good coffee or a fresh soup, salad and sandwich meal. Grab a newspaper and settle in, or have a game of chess out front on the sidewalk.

Howl at the Moon (☎ 519-744-8191; 320 King St W; mains $5-15; ☯ 11am-late) This wood-and-terracotta pub and bar has a fun, semi-formal look and an informal attitude. The wraps and sandwiches are bursting with fresh ingredients, plus the kids' menu makes it good for families. Daily food and drink specials and the patio make this an enjoyable spot for lunch.

Café Mozart (☎ 519-578-4590; 45 Queen St S; desserts $3-6; ☯ 8am-6pm) A little – or very large, if you wish – piece of the land of chocolate is here for you to enjoy. After the nose gets a whiff, the mouth will soon be munching on pastries, cakes or something covered with chocolate.

Concordia Club (☎ 519-745-5617; 429 Ottawa St S; lunch $7, dinner mains $10-17; ☯ lunch & dinner, also brunch Sun) For solid German fare, go where the locals go and get your fill of schnitzel. Dark wood, low ceilings, red linen and loud conversation genuinely compliment the menu. There's live entertainment – polka, if you like – on Friday and Saturday night, and the *biergarten* in summer.

Drinking

There are plenty of down-to-earth places catering to the university kids looking to grab a pint. *Echo* is a free weekly, available from bookstores and most restaurants around town, with good club listings. A collection of clubs, bars and lounges lives downtown on **King St W**, north of Water St.

Still Bar & Grill (☎ 519-743-5657; 125 King St W) The Still has a huge, glassed-in front patio complete with a sand volleyball pit. It's open, airy and dark inside the brick building, so take your fancy of where to enjoy a beer, of which there are more than a dozen on tap.

Sammy's Garage (☎ 519-744-7661; 400 King St W; ☯ closed Tue-Thu) Sammy's is K-W's party club. The old tow-truck in front reminds those who work hard to play hard. Touring DJs often spin here on weekends.

Entertainment

K-W has recently focused on its arts and culture scene.

Theatre&Company (☎ 519-571-0928; www.theatre andcompany.org; 27 King St W; adult $22-33, student $15-25) This theater puts on some fantastically quirky and whimsical productions, mainly by Canadian playwrights.

Centre in the Square (☎ 519-579-5860, 800-265-8977; www.centre-square.com; 101 Queen St N; tickets $30-50) This performance hall hosts live musical acts (sometimes held with the Kitchener-Waterloo Symphony), comedy and Broadway productions.

Getting There & Around

If you're driving, take the Rte 8 exit from Hwy 401, about an hour west of Toronto. If you want someone else to drive, the **bus station** (☎ 519-741-2600; 15 Charles St W) is a five-minute walk from downtown. Greyhound Canada runs frequently to Toronto ($21, 1½ to two hours) and makes four daily trips to London, Ontario ($21, 1½ to two hours).

THE PUB CRAWL

Four fine historic country taverns dating from 1875 or earlier are found west of K-W for your pint-sloshing pleasure. Remember to designate a nondrinking driver as you make the trip to these outlying communities.

- **Blue Moon** (☎ 519-634-8405; 1677 Snyders Rd E; ☯ 11:30am-late) Take Hwy 8 west from Kitchener to Petersburg to this Georgian-style inn built in 1848; a great place for live blues.

- **EJ's** (☎ 519-634-5711; 39 Snyder Rd W; ☯ 11:30am-late, closed Mon) Take Hwy 8 west to Baden to find hand-painted tin ceiling tiles, an 1891-built oak bar and ornamental beer taps in an old brick building. It also has a patio for sunny afternoons.

- **Kennedy's Country Tavern** (☎ 519-747-1313; 62 Erb Rd West; ☯ 11am-late) Take Hwy 8 east from Baden; turn left onto Rte 12 (north) to St Agatha to this Irish bar with a lively atmosphere and honest pints.

- **Olde Heidelberg Restaurant & Brewpub** (☎ 519-699-4413; 2 King Street; ☯ 11:30am-late) Take Rte 12 (north) from St Agatha; turn right onto Township Rd 6 (north) to Heidelberg. In the heart of a German settlement, Bavarian beer is brewed on the premises of this pub.

The **train station** (cnr Victoria & Weber Sts) is an easy walk north of downtown. VIA Rail trains serve Toronto and London daily; schedules vary.

Grand River Transit (☎ 519-585-7555; www.grt.ca; tickets $2.25) has extensive service in the K-W area. The No 7 bus heads up and down King St about every 10 minutes.

ST JACOBS

To really immerse yourself in the Mennonite lifestyle, drive 6km north of Waterloo along King St N to St Jacobs. The original 19th-century buildings that line the small historic village's streets mostly house arts-and-crafts and gift shops. Don't be surprised if you pass a horse and buggy along the way. The **Mennonite Story** (☎ 519-664-3518; 1408 King St; admission $3; 🕑 11am-5pm Mon-Sat & 1:30-5pm Sun Apr-Dec, 11am-4:30pm Sat & 2-4:30pm Sun Jan-Mar), in the **visitors center**, has very good interpretive exhibits on the Mennonites and their history.

At the **Maple Syrup Museum & Antique Market** (☎ 519-664-1232; cnr Front & King Sts; admission free; 🕑 10am-6pm Mon-Sat, 12:30-5:30pm Sun), on the 3rd floor of the Country Mill, you can learn about the production of that Canadian specialty and staple of pancake breakfasts – maple syrup – as well as its historical significance to the area.

St Jacobs Farmers' Market & Flea Market (☎ 519-747-1830, 800-265-3353; Farmer's Market Rd; 🕑 7am-3:30pm Thu & Sat, also 8am-3pm Tue summer), about 2km south of the village, is the quintessential country market, complete with horse-and-buggy sheds. Avoid the tendency to write this off as a tourist trap and know that hordes of people, even locals, come here for the quality produce, smoked meat, cheese, baked treats and crafts. Adding to the experience, cattle are auctioned next door at the Livestock Exchange. Across the street, **Waterloo Market** (🕑 7am-2pm Sat) is less busy and presented with less fanfare, but still has local products.

ELMIRA

About 8km north of St Jacobs up Hwy 86, Elmira is a more real, working, country Mennonite town. In spring, it hosts the **Maple Syrup Festival** (☎ 519-669-2605; www.elmiramaplesyrup.com; 🕑 1st Sat in Apr) with street activities and pancake breakfasts – it's considered Ontario's biggest and best.

THE MENNONITES

Most people see Mennonites as black-clothed, carriage-riding, traditional farmers eschewing modern life. And while basically true, these characteristics are only part of the story.

A 16th-century Protestant sect from Switzerland was forced to move around Europe due to religious disagreements. During a stay in Holland they decided on a name for themselves, derived from one of their Dutch leaders, Menno Simons. Another leader, William Penn, promised religious freedom and prosperity in the rural settings of what is now known as Pennsylvania Dutch country in the USA. Word of cheaper land and more of it in southern Ontario drew many Mennonites north in the late 19th century.

Ontario has several groups of Mennonites. The 'plain' group is known for simple clothes and simple living. The Old Order Mennonites are the strictest and most rigid in their practices and beliefs. Similar to the Amish, even buttons on clothes are considered a vanity. They don't worship in a church but hold services in undecorated houses within the community.

Benjamin's (☎ 519-664-3731; fax 519-664-1513; 1430 King St N; r $90-130), a renovated 1852 inn that sits right in the village, has rustic, comfortable furnishings and bright, open rooms. Traditional pasta, seafood and steak meals are served in the charming country **dining room** (lunch $10-15, dinner mains $17-27), which has a stone fireplace.

Stone Crock Bakery (☎ 519-664-3612; 1402 King St N; 🕑 6:30am-6pm Mon-Sat, 12:30-5:30pm Sun) has pies, muffins, breads and scones fresh from the oven that taste as good as they smell. If you prefer a heartier lunch, **Vidalia's Market Dining** (☎ 519-664-2575; 1398 King St; mains $4-10; 🕑 11am-9pm) next door is an indoor market café with food stands.

CENTRE WELLINGTON

☎ **519 / pop 187,000**

Set on the Grand River, surrounded by rolling green hills and pastures and dotted with willows, maples and oaks, the natural setting of Wellington County compliments the area's historical buildings and farms.

ONTARIO

O(LD) CANADA

For a nice local drive and a trip through the past, take an afternoon to explore some of the timeless sites in the area. Head north along King St from Kitchener to **St Jacobs** (p139). Then head east on Rte 17 through patchwork farmlands to Rte 23 and turn left. Taking another left on Covered Bridge Dr allows you to rekindle youthful romance or start a new one at the **Kissing Bridge**, constructed in 1889 and the only covered bridge remaining in Ontario. Drive over the bridge and follow the road to Rte 86, then turn left. Stop in **Elmira** (p139) or keep driving west on Rte 86, hanging a left onto Rte 10 and heading south to **Hawkesville** to see its blacksmith's shop. From there, Rte 10 goes south to the Mennonite town of **St Clements**, where you can stop and shop at interesting stores. Leave town by taking Rte 15 west and turn left onto Township Rd 6, then another left onto Rte 12 to **St Agatha** with its dramatically impressive church steeple. Keep going on Rte 12 through **Petersburg**, where you'll turn left onto Rte 8 to return to Kitchener.

The folks of the main towns of Elora and Fergus, close to each other and connected by Rte 18, were proactive in keeping their old buildings original rather than replacing them with contemporary structures, and local owners have done their bit to keep them looking as good as old.

Information

Information Centre (☎ 519-843-5140, 877-242-6353; www.ferguselora.com; 400 Tower St S; ☯ 10am-5pm Mon-Fri, noon-4pm Sat & Sun) There's a well-stocked and informative tourist office in Fergus.

Sights

WELLINGTON COUNTY MUSEUM & ARCHIVES

Between Fergus and Elora, this excellent stone-walled, red-roofed House of Industry-turned-House of Refuge provided shelter for aged and homeless for almost a century before becoming a **museum** (☎ 519-846-0916; Rte 18; adult/child $3/2; ☯ 9:30am-4:30pm Mon-Fri, 1-5pm Sat & Sun) in 1957. It passionately displays and informs on local history. Recognized as a national historic site, it's perched on a hill overlooking the river, a symbolic reminder of the region's agricultural roots, but inside there's an obvious pride for other aspects of the area's history. Only a portion of the 4,000 artifacts are displayed in the 12 galleries; the centerpiece is the recreated WWII trench with mannequins cast from descendants of actual Wellington County residents who fought in the war.

ELORA GORGE CONSERVATION AREA

A scenic wonder not far from Elora, this **gorge** (☎ 519-846-9742; Wellington City Rd; adult/child $3.75/2; ☯ late-Apr–mid-Oct) is a deep limestone canyon through which the Grand River flows. Easy walks lead to cliff views, caves and the Cascade waterfalls – a sheet of water spilling and splashing over a stepped cliff. **Tubing** (admission $2, rentals $12) down the slow-flowing river is a fun way to spend a warm afternoon. It's also a good place to camp.

Activities

There are many parks and conservation areas located along the sections of the river south of Wellington, all offering access and information. Canoeing is possible in many places. **Adventure Paddling** (☎ 519-827-6849; www.adventurepaddling.com) will help you with gear and trips. Other spots in the river have swimming facilities and walking trails. A dozen blocks east of Elora along Mill St E, the clear waters and limestone walls of the **Elora Quarry Conservation Area** make it a popular swimming hole. There's a change room and it's a very scenic place for kids of all ages to float and soak on a hot day. For more information, contact **Grand River Country** (☎ 800-267-3399; www.grandrivercountry.com).

Whether you want to cruise through the towns or ride through the pastures, **Salem Cyclery** (☎ 519-846-8446; www.salemcyclery.ca; 320 Erb St) will rent bikes or put together getaway escapes.

Festivals & Events

Reminessence Festival (☎ 519-843-4852; www.remfest.com; ☯ mid-Jun) From sock hops to bell-bottoms as Wellington remembers the '50s, '60s and '70s.
Elora Festival (☎ 519-846-0331, 800-265-8977; www.elorafestival.com; ☯ mid-Jul–mid-Aug) Annual classical and folk music festival with some concerts held at the quarry. On a lit-up floating stage in pastoral surroundings is an impressive way to spend a warm summer evening.

Fergus Scottish Festival and Highland Games

(☎ 519-787-0099; www.fergusscottishfestival.com; 550 Belysyde Ave E; day/weekend $14/37; ☺ mid-Aug) For two days, if it's not Scottish, it's doesn't count. Tug-of-Wars, caber tossing, bagpipes, Celtic music, kilts, haggis and hugely popular Scotch nosing, or tasting ($35), take place in one of North America's largest bonny and g'eat celebrations.

Elora Fergus Studio Tour (☺ late Sep or early Oct) Popular weekend self-guided tours visit local artisans' workshops.

Sleeping

Grand River Guesthouse (☎ 519-846-5980; www.grand riverguesthouse.com; 94 Water St, Elora; r $90-100) This redbrick country home is set within thick forest, yet it has excellent views of the river and Elora across the water. Pastel-colored rooms and comfy, bright beds let you sleep deep, but the full breakfasts in the sunny kitchen won't have you sleeping too late.

Elora Mill Inn (☎ 519-846-5356; www.eloramill.com; 77 Mill St W, Elora; r $165-250) The five-story building with limestone walls and huge wooden beams literally on the edge of the river serves only as a general reminder of the industrious mill it used to be; the dark and luxurious restoration inside has given it a new image. Stoically relaxing, the inn ensures your stay here will be a comfortable reflection on Wellington's relationship with history.

Elora Gorge Conservation Area's **campground** (☎ 519-846-9742, 866-668-2267; www.grand river.ca; Wellington City Rd; tent/RV sites $24/28) has 550 sites – usually full during the summer, especially on holiday weekends – that can be reserved (for a $9 fee).

Eating

Elora's shaded seclusion by the river offers some relaxing eateries.

Desert Rose Café (☎ 519-846-0433; 130 Metcalfe St, Elora; mains $6-10; ☺ lunch & dinner) This local fave has recently gone completely vegetarian while retaining its Mexican and Greek menu. It's hard to go wrong with the moussaka or black bean chili, but whatever your tastes, the atmosphere is earthy and wholesome.

Shepherd's Crook (☎ 519-846-5775; 8 Mill St W, Elora; mains $8-10; ☺ 11am-late) Overlooking the river and the pedestrian bridge that crosses it, enjoy a ploughman's lunch or Guinness-baked meat pie at this English pub.

Elora Mill Inn (☎ 519-846-5356; 77 Mill St W, Elora; lunch/dinner $10/27) In the darkly-colored, formal dining room in the inn, light lunches include sandwiches and salads. Dinner is a serious affair as Atlantic salmon and veal medallions show up on the menu.

Riversedge Café (☎ 519-787-9303; Queen St W, Fergus; mains $5-8; ☺ lunch & dinner, closed Mon & Tue) With a nice location in Fergus behind the Market Building and a patio over the river, this place is great for a sandwich, burger or one of the vegetarian pasta dishes and an afternoon in the sun.

Shopping

Plenty of small stores in Elora's Geddes St and Fergus's St Andrews St offer crafts, jewelry, paintings and pottery, much of which is produced by the numerous local craftspeople. The central **Fergus Market** (☎ 519-843-5221; ☺ 9am-5pm Sat & Sun), off Bridge St, is in a historic brick building with lots of gift and artisan's shops.

Getting There & Away

Greyhound Canada stops at the **Highland Inn** (280 Bridge St) in Fergus – have a beer while you wait – and **Little Katy Variety Store** (☎ 519-846-5951; 185 Geddes St) in Elora on Monday, Wednesday and Friday mornings and Tuesday, Thursday, Saturday and Sunday evenings for trips to Toronto ($24, two hours).

STRATFORD

Surrounded by farmland, Stratford distinguishes itself from typical slow-paced, rural Ontario with a consciously pretty aesthetic and world-famous Shakespeare festival. Many of the numerous older buildings in the attractive, architecturally interesting downtown have been restored. Stratford's Avon River, with its swans and green lawns, together with the town's theaters, help Stratford deliberately and successfully resemble Stratford-upon-Avon in England.

Orientation & Information

Queen's Park and the Festival Theatre are at the east end of town, just north of Ontario St. From the park, Lakeside Dr runs along the river back into town and meets York and Ontario Sts near the courthouse. Almost everything is within walking distance of the visitor information center.

Stratford Public Library (☎ 519-271-0220; 19 St Andrew St; ☺ 1-9pm Mon, 9:30am-9pm Tue-Thu, 9:30am-6pm Fri & Sat) Free Internet access.

THESPIAN FESTIVITIES

Sir Alec Guinness played Richard III on opening night of the celebrated **Stratford Festival** (☎ 519-273-1600, 800-567-1600; www.stratford-festival.on.ca; Festival Theatre, Queen's Park, 55 Queen St; tickets $20-105), which began humbly in a huge tent at Queen's Park beside the Avon River. The festival, which recently celebrated its 50th season, has achieved international acclaim; the productions are first-rate and feature respected actors.

Aside from the plays, there are a number of other interesting programs, and some are free (for others, a nominal fee is charged and reservations are required). Among them are post-performance discussions with the actors, backstage tours, costume warehouse tours, lectures and luncheons, music concerts and dramatic readings by famous authors.

Surprisingly, the festival season runs from April to November. There are four theaters – all in town – that stage contemporary and modern drama and music, operas and, of course, works by the Bard. Mainstage productions take place at the Festival Theatre, with its round, protruding stage in modern Elizabethan style. The Avon Theatre is the secondary venue, seating more than 1000 theatergoers. The Tom Patterson Theatre is smaller than the Avon, with just under 500 seats. Attached to the Avon is the newly built Studio Theatre, an intimate 260-seat repertory venue.

Tickets go on sale to the general public in early January, and by show time nearly every performance is sold out. Spring previews and fall end-of-season shows are discounted up to 50%. Students and seniors also qualify for reduced rates at some shows.

Tourism Stratford (☎ 519-271-5140, 800-561-7926; www.city.stratford.on.ca; 47 Downie St; ⏰ 9am-5pm Mon-Fri)

Tourism Stratford Visitor Information Center (York St & Lakeside Dr; ⏰ 9am-5pm May-Oct) Beside the river, off York St.

Sights & Activities

Even though the play's the thing, pretty Stratford lures visitors with other pleasant ways to pass the time. The Avon River flows peacefully beside the town and adds to its charm. On the river just west of the Tourism Stratford Visitor Information Center, the **Shakespearean Gardens** (admission free; ⏰ dawn-dusk) are on the site of an old wool mill on the waterfront. Near the bridge, look for a bust of Shakespeare. You can get food to feed the mute, black swans (popcorn is easier to digest than bread) at the visitor information centre.

The **Stratford-Perth Museum** (☎ 519-271-5311; www.cyg.net/~spmuseum; Discovery Centre, 270 Water St; adult/child 6-12/youth 13-18 $4.50/2/4; ⏰ 10am-5pm Tue-Sat, noon-5pm Sun-Mon, 10am-4pm Tue-Sat Sep-Apr, closed weekends Jan & Feb), beside the Festival Theatre, has collections of early-20th-century Canadiana and special historical and cultural exhibitions.

Neighboring **Queen's Park** has good footpaths leading from the Festival Theatre and following the river past Orr Dam and a stone bridge, dating from 1885, to the formal **English flower garden**.

In a renovated 1880s Victorian pump house you'll find **Gallery Stratford** (☎ 519-271-5271; www.gallerystratford.on.ca; 54 Romeo St N; adult/student/senior $10/8/8; ⏰ 1-4pm Tue-Sun, 10am-4pm Sat mid-Jan–early-Mar & mid-Nov–mid-Dec, 10am-4pm daily mid-Mar–mid-Apr & mid-Sep-early Nov, 9am-5pm May-early Sep) near Confederation Park. Featured inside the gallery are shows of innovative contemporary art, emphasizing Canadian works and festival themes.

The city center, with its almost too-quaint shops and eateries, is ideal for ambling. Just about everything is close to Ontario St, where **Gallery Indigena** (☎ 519-271-7881; www.galleryindigena.com; 69 Ontario St; ⏰ noon-4pm Sun & Mon, 10am-5:30pm Tue-Sat) specializes in Canadian aboriginal art. Various bookshops sell festival-themed volumes. Queen's Park and the Festival Theatre are at the east end of town, just north of Ontario St. From the park, Lakeside Dr runs along the river back into town and meets York and Ontario Sts near the Perth County Courthouse, one of the town's most distinctive landmarks. A few blocks southeast along Downie St is the old-fashioned **City Hall**, a strikingly symmetrical construction in Queen Anne Revival style at the corner of Wellington St. Brief tours of the building are given at 11am on Friday during July and August.

Don't miss out on a walk along the river, where the park, lawns and theaters have been laid out in a soothing manner.

Tours

You can take in the parks, swans, grand houses and even grander gardens on 30-minute **boat tours** that depart from downstairs behind the Tourism Stratford Visitor Information Center. Canoes, kayaks and paddleboats can also be rented there (per hour $15 to $25).

Free **history walks** depart from Tourism Stratford (opposite) at 9:30am Saturday from May until October, weather permitting, and also on weekdays during July and August. With one of the descriptive maps available, you could do your own walking tour. One map, put out by the local architectural conservation committee, details some of the history and architecture of the downtown area.

Festivals & Events

This town's most celebrated event is the Stratford Festival (see the boxed text opposite).

Stratford Garden Festival (www.stratfordgarden festival.com; admission $7; ☉ mid-March) A four-day horticultural extravaganza, featuring a diversity of flora from around the world in numerous gardens. Guest speakers and presentations appear throughout.

Stratford Summer Music (☎ 800-567-1600; www .stratfordsummermusic.ca; tickets free–$25; ☉ late-Jul) Ten days of classical, cabaret and theatrical music, with acclaimed musicians from around Canada converging to perform.

Sleeping

Because of the number of visitors lured to town by the theaters, lodging is, thankfully, abundant. By far the majority of rooms are in B&Bs and the homes of residents with a spare room or two. In addition, in the higher price brackets there are several well-appointed, traditional inns in refurbished, century-old hotels. Particularly useful for B&B accommodation is the **Stratford Festival Visitor Accommodation Bureau** (☎ 519-273-1600, 800-567-1600; www.stratfordfestival.ca; d from $50).

BUDGET

Stratford Fairgrounds (☎ 519-271-5832; www.strat fordfairgrounds.com; 20 Glastonbury Dr; tent sites $16, RV sites $18-20; ☉ Apr-Oct) These grounds play host to a farmers' market and a number of other events, but during summer they offer a central camping ground with good facilities.

MID-RANGE

Bentley's Inn (☎ 519-271-1121, 800-361-5322; www .bentleys-annex.com; 99 Ontario St; ste $80-195) This modern, dark-wood furnished inn houses commodious bi-level suites and lofts. Skylights, kitchenettes and period furnishings are standard in the stylish rooms and there's a hint of Shakespeare about the decor.

Queen's Inn (☎ 519-271-1400, 800-461-6450; www .queensinnstratford.ca; 161 Ontario St; d $70-135, whirlpool ste $200) This historic inn with a wide range of rooms near Waterloo St dates from the mid-19th century and is the oldest hotel in town. Management wrote the book on service. Prices are cut by up to half between November and April, and good weekend packages are available. Many of the rooms are larger than some apartments (and feature more amenities).

Acrylic Dreams (☎ 519-271-7874; 66 Bay St; r incl breakfast $105-140) This renovated 1879 cottage has polished wooden floorboards and pleasant country decor. Antiques are scattered throughout and some rooms have cable TV. The full vegetarian breakfasts are an absolute feast.

Rosecourt Motel (☎ 519-271-6005, 888-388-5111; www.rosecourtmotel.com; 599 Erie St; r incl breakfast $70-135) Close to town and with an appealing retro feel befitting its 1949 roots, this motel offers generic but comfortable, spotless rooms. Each has a patio and some are fully self-contained. Breakfast here is continental.

TOP END

Annex Inn (☎ 519-271-1407; 38 Albert St; d $125-250) Operated by the same folks as Bentley's Inn, this attachment features luxury suites with an emphasis on fine furnishings, right down to the bed linen. Large windows fill the suites with ample sunlight and inside you'll find gas fireplaces, stereos and whirlpools.

Mercer Hall Inn (☎ 519-271-1888, 888-816-4011; www.mercerhallinn.com; 108 Ontario St; d $95-170, ste $125-200) Another fine choice, with liberal luxuries for the price tag, Mercer Hall Inn has uniquely artistic rooms with handcrafted furniture. Some also contain kitchenettes, electric fireplaces or whirlpools. Bookshelves, CD racks and a DVD library are stocked with Canadiana.

ONTARIO

Eating

Stratford may be small, but its culinary diversity should impress even hardened city slickers. Sophisticated and global menus grace several restaurants and even the cafés are cultured.

BUDGET

Tango Coffee Bistro (☎ 519-271-9202; 104 Ontario St; meals $4-10; ☣ 8am-8pm) The aromatic coffee will draw addicts of the bean through this place's doors, but it would be a shame to leave without sampling the tasty and filling sandwiches, calzones and pizzas on offer here. The artistic environment is accented by fine art for sale and live music on Friday and Saturday night. Fair-trade coffee blends include a light-roasted 'Sleepy Monk.'

York St Kitchen (☎ 519-273-7041; 41 York St; meals $5-15; ☣ breakfast, lunch & dinner) This small eatery dishes up excellent home-style cooking with a classy edge. Try the Middle Eastern tabbouleh with lamb, mint and pine nuts, spicy seafood couscous or vegetarian Asian noodle salad with peanut sauce and tofu, and you'll see where we're coming from. Simpler fare such as sandwiches and picnic plates are just as tasty.

MID-RANGE

Down the Street Bar & Café (☎ 519-273-5886; 30 Ontario St; lunch $8-12, dinner mains $18-25; ☣ lunch & dinner) With gilt mirrors and whiffs of Parisian cafés, this place offers pre-theater dining, microbrews and wines by the glass. The menu is multicultural and after the food supplies have been exhausted the bar steps in as one of Stratford's core nightlife venues.

Old Prune (☎ 519-271-5052; 151 Albert St; lunch $8.50-20, prix fixe dinner $65, cooking class $45; ☣ lunch Wed-Sun, dinner Tue-Sun) From November until March, the famous Stratford Chef's School trains at this Edwardian house, where tables overlook a tranquil garden. Expect fresh, often organic and innovative contemporary food with just a hint of Québecois cuisine. Make reservations.

Principal's Pantry (☎ 519-272-9914; basement, Discovery Centre, 270 Water St; meals $8-20; ☣ lunch & dinner) Across from the Festival Theatre, this dining room's proceeds support youth and community service projects. It's a family-orientated restaurant with simple, healthy fare. Hearty tortillas, pies and quiches hit the spot and it's very kid friendly. Wheelchair access is good.

Stratford's Olde English Parlour (☎ 519-271-2772; 101 Wellington St; meals $6-15; ☣ lunch & dinner) This historic 1870s inn dishes up sophisticated pub grub – baked green apple risotto with a citrus and tomato compote sits alongside peppercorn and herb–crusted rack of lamb on the menu. Carnivores, vegetarians and seafood gluttons are all well catered for here.

TOP END

Church Restaurant (☎ 519-273-3424; 70 Brunswick St, cnr Waterloo St; lunch $8-25, dinner $20-55, prix fixe dinners from $70; ☣ lunch & dinner Tue-Sun, Belfry Bar 9pm-midnight Fri & Sat) The grand dame of Stratford's culinary scene maintains its reputation with dishes such as pan-roasted elk striploin or seared diver-caught scallops with crab spring risotto, truffle and mascarpone sabayon. It's inside the old Christ Church (1874), with organ and altar still intact. Reservations are essential.

Getting There & Away

For select summer weekend matinees, direct buses depart Toronto's **Yorkdale Mall** (Map pp76-7; subway Yorkdale) at 10am, returning from Stratford at 7pm (round trip $35); contact the Festival Theatre box office (p142) to check schedules and make reservations. Infrequent Greyhound Canada buses from Toronto ($22, three hours) require a transfer in Kitchener.

VIA Rail runs two daily trains to Toronto ($30, 2½ hours). Trains also go west to London or Sarnia, with connections for Windsor.

LONDON

☎ 519 / pop 336,500

When you've got the Thames River, Hyde Park and Oxford St all in one place, that's London calling; but this town halfway between Toronto and Detroit really doesn't have enough resemblance for even the very confused to ask, 'Do you mean London, England or London, Ontario?'

London is a quiet, clean and conservative town important to the Lake Erie area. It blends a fair bit of industry, manufacturing and agriculture with one of the country's largest universities. There's a relatively built-up downtown with plenty of green spaces and pleasant streets surrounding it.

ONTARIO

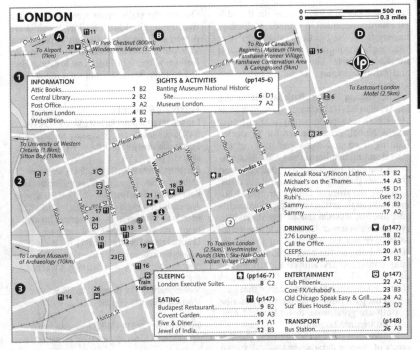

Orientation & Information

East–west Dundas St and north–south Richmond St converge at the center of the downtown area. The northern end of Richmond St is the hip strip, with a host of shops, eateries and cafés. There are some shady tree-lined streets and elegant Victorian houses around the edges of the downtown area.

Attic Books (☎ 519-432-7277; 240 Dundas St; ☺ closed Sun) There are floor-to-ceiling shelves of well-perused books here.

Central Library (☎ 519-661-4600; 261 Dundas St; ☺ 9am-9pm Mon-Thu, 9am-6pm Fri, 9am-5pm Sat) Excellent and modern with a mini art gallery; free ½hr Internet express terminals.

Post Office (☎ 800-267-1177; 515 Richmond St)

Tourism London (☎ 519-661-5000, 800-265-2602; www.londontourism.ca) Downtown (267 Dundas St; ☺ 8:30am-4:30pm Mon-Fri; 10am-5pm Sat & Sun) Shares its location with the Canadian Medical Hall of Fame and its interesting – or gory – displays of brains, hearts and bones; Wellington (696 Wellington Rd S; ☺ 10am-1pm & 2-6pm Wed-Sun)

Webst@tion (☎ 519-645-4998; 211 Dundas St; per hr $4) Internet access.

Sights & Activities

An educational and research facility affiliated with the university, the **London Museum of Archaeology** (☎ 519-473-1360; 1600 Attawandaron Rd; www.uwo.ca/museum; adult/child/senior $3.50/1.50/3; ☺ 10am-4:30pm) displays materials and artifacts spanning 11,000 years of aboriginal history in Ontario. **Lawson Prehistoric Indian Village** (☺ May-Sep) is an active dig of a 500-year-old village that is being reconstructed as the site is being excavated.

Relive London's history at the 30-building **Fanshawe Pioneer Village** (☎ 519-457-1296; www.fanshawepioneervillage.com; 2609 Fanshawe Park Rd; adult/child/student/family $5/3/4/15; ☺ 10am-4:30pm Tue-Sun May-Thanksgiving) on the eastern edge of the city. Costumed blacksmiths, farmers and craftspeople perform their trades in true 19th-century-pioneer-village-life fashion. Dine at the tearoom or bring your own picnic. The adjoining **Fanshawe Conservation Area** is a conservation and recreation area with swimming, walking and picnicking areas.

The **Royal Canadian Regiment Museum** (☎ 519-660-5102; www.rcrmuseum.ca; Canadian Forces Base, cnr Oxford & Elizabeth Sts; admission free; ☺ 10am-4pm

Tue-Fri, noon-4pm Sat & Sun) focuses on the oldest infantry regiment in Canada. It displays history from the North-West Rebellion of 1885 right through both World Wars and the Korean War. The extensive dioramas and exhibits display weapons, medals and uniforms.

The **Banting Museum National Historic Site** (☎ 519-673-1752; 442 Adelaide St N; adult/child/senior $4/free/3; ☷ noon-4pm Tue-Sat) is in the house where Nobel Prize winner Sir Frederick Banting lived and developed the method for extracting insulin in the 1920s. The museum outlines the history of diabetes, and chronicles Banting's medical contributions.

Telling the story of London from 1826 to today through artifacts, maps, documents and photos, **Museum London** (☎ 519-661-0333; www.londonmuseum.on.ca; 421 Ridout St N; suggested donation $3; ☷ noon-5pm Tue-Sun) is an impressive glass building on the riverbank. It also contains contemporary and classic art pieces, all made by local artists. Next door, Eldon House is London's oldest residence that puts you in the past, rather than trying to describe it. Both are great ways to understand how London became London.

London is a great walking town. The **University of Western Ontario** (☎ 519-661-2111; 1151 Richmond St) has an immaculate riverside campus, or pick up the map-brochure from the Tourism London office for the self-guided Downtown Discovery Trail – a walk through London's diverse history. Also grab *London's Walking Map* for some great nature walks in the area. The **Sifton Bog** is a unique ecology in southern Ontario. It's an acid bog that is home to a range of unusual plants and animals, including lemmings, shrews, the carnivorous sundew plant and nine varieties of orchid. **Westminster Ponds** is an area of woods, bogs and ponds south of town that supports a variety of wildlife, including foxes and herons. There is a viewing tower, and a boardwalk around some sections of the large undeveloped area.

A well done re-creation of a small 1000-year-old Iroquois longhouse community is found at **Ska-Nah-Doht Indian Village** (☎ 519-264-2420; 8348 Longwoods Rd; admission $3; ☷ 9am-4:30pm, closed weekends Labour Day–Victoria Day), 32km west of the city. The village structures are encircled by a maze that kids love to get lost in. A museum contains artifacts thousands of years old and recounts the area's history.

Outside the walls, crops have been planted that the original First Nations would have grown and there are also burial platforms. The site is in the wooded Longwoods Rd Conservation Area. From London, take Hwy 402 to interchange 86 and then follow Hwy 2 west.

Festivals & Events

London International Airfest (☎ 519-473-6444; www.londonairshow.com; ☷ late Jun) Snowbirds put on a show; planes and jets are on the go; hot air balloons, at night they glow.

Bluesfest International (☎ 519-851-6202; www.thebluesfest.com; ☷ mid-Jul) Big names sing the blues.

Home County Folk Festival (☎ 519-432-4310; www.homecounty.ca; ☷ mid-Jul) Free event in Victoria Park where fairly big names take to the stage over four days. Dance, crafts and inexpensive food also feature.

London Fringe Theatre Festival (☎ 519-434-0606; www.londonfringe.on.ca; ☷ early–mid-Aug) Three-week event featuring theater, busker and music acts all over downtown.

Shakespeare on the Thames (☎ 519-661-5500; admission by donation; ☷ mid-Aug–late-Aug) The name says it all.

Western Fair (☎ 519-438-3247; www.westernfair.com; ☷ mid-Sep) A 10-day agricultural and amusement fair.

Sleeping

The **London & Area B&B Association** (☎ 519-851-9988; www.londonbb.ca) has a list of places, averaging $50 for singles and $65 to $75 for doubles. Wellington Rd south of town to Hwy 401 and the commercial zone of Dundas St E, heading east to Hwy 2, are predictable motel strips.

Pink Chestnut (☎ 519-673-3963; 1035 Richmond St; r $50-80; P) The best thing about this B&B is the location between the university and downtown. The second-best thing about it is the antique-filled, comfortable rooms. The 1920s house is on a pleasant street and has a certain British charm.

Eastcourt London Motel (☎ 519-451-5520, 866-316-5449; 1585 Dundas St E; r $50-60; P ☲) Nothing fancy here, just clean and basic rooms.

London Executive Suites (☎ 519-679-3932, 800-265-5955; 362 Dundas St; www.les-hotel.com; ste $70-100; P ☲) This former apartment building just on the outside of downtown has spacious rooms with balconies and kitchens. No surprises, just comfy mattresses, solid furniture and good views from the upper floors.

Windermere Manor (☎ 519-858-1391; www.winder meremanor.com; 200 Collip Circle; r/ste $115/140; **P**) Set on a green hill overlooking the Thames, downtown and the university, this is a manor in every sense of the word. It's close enough to walk downtown, the scenery is nice enough to want to and you'll be rested enough so you can.

Fanshawe Conservation Area & Campground (☎ 519-451-2800; 1424 Clarke Rd; tent/RV sites $23/29; ⊙ late-Apr–mid-Oct) There is convenient camping within the city limits at this campground near Fanshawe Pioneer Village.

Eating

Richmond Row – Richmond St north of Dufferin to Oxford St – is lined with cafés and various casual eateries. Colorful, semi-permanent diner wagons are found around town. **Sammy** (items $3-6; ⊙ 10am-6pm); Downtown (cnr Richmond & Carling Sts); Train Station (cnr Richmond & York Sts) proffers cheap, fresh souvlaki and falafels.

A good place to start the day is **Rubi's** (☎ 519-679-2800; 391 Richmond St; items $2-5; ⊙ breakfast & lunch), a little brick-walled café filled with Londoners. **Five & Diner** (☎ 519-433-1081; 650 Richmond St; mains $6-9; ⊙ 7am-9pm) is a throwback, with glistening chrome and tableside jukeboxes; it's fun for any meal.

Covent Garden (☎ 519-439-3921; 130 King St; ⊙ 8am-6pm Mon-Thu & Sat, to 7:30pm Fri, 11am-4pm Sun) This huge barn-shaped brick market in the center of downtown is an excellent place to whet and satisfy any appetite. There's a permanent collection of delis, bakeries, produce shops and world cuisine eateries as well as seasonal vendors. Buskers frequently perform outside and it always has the buzz of a high-quality marketplace.

Mexicali Rosa's/Rincon Latino (☎ 519-645-2078; 120 Dundas St; dishes $5-9; ⊙ 8am-10pm) Popularity has allowed this London favorite to upgrade from hole-in-the-wall to linen, comfortable chairs and more seating amid bright colors and Mexican vigor. What hasn't changed is the menu; excellent, dirt-cheap authentic Salvadoran food is prepared with flair and care. From Mexican omelettes to genuine tamales, everything is good.

Budapest Restaurant (☎ 519-439-3431; 346 Dundas St; mains $9-15; ⊙ lunch & dinner) Amidst traditional decor and textiles, this tavern-style restaurant has been serving up Hungarian and European goulash and schnitzels since the 1950s.

Mykonos (☎ 519-434-6736; 572 Adelaide St N; mains $10-17; ⊙ lunch & dinner) For excellent Greek food and an authentic atmosphere, try this restaurant on the east side of town. Main courses include a range of vegetarian dishes and lots of seafood. There's an outdoor patio and Greek music in the evenings.

Jewel of India (☎ 519-434-9268; 390 Richmond St; mains $5-11) In this small, quaint restaurant, with curtains in the windows and candles on the tables, the spicy and curried dishes are exquisite. Popular are the five-course lunch specials, from soup to dessert, for under $7.

Michael's on the Thames (☎ 519-672-0111; 1 York St; mains $15-30; ⊙ lunch & dinner Mon-Fri, dinner only Sat & Sun) Fine dining (primarily steak and seafood) can be enjoyed in this oak-furnished dining room. Michael's also serve pasta and other dishes – roast duck is a specialty – in an incredibly peaceful and intimate location overlooking the Thames River.

Drinking

276 Lounge (☎ 519-645-4880; 276 Dundas St) In ultra-fancy Old City Hall restaurant is this ultra-chic lounge and martini bar with live DJs and house music.

Call the Office (☎ 519-432-2263; 216 York St) Safe dive bar with cheap drinks and alternative live bands.

CEEPS (☎ 519-432-1425; 671 Richmond St) For good times, this no-nonsense bar has been a perennial favorite for London's party-hearty crowd.

Honest Lawyer (☎ 519-433-4913; 228 Dundas St) A long, narrow place with a beer-colored hue and a fun crowd to get you in the mood for knocking back a few.

Entertainment

London is known as a great blues town. A good option is **Old Chicago Speak Easy & Grill** (☎ 519-434-6600; 153 Carling St).

Club Phoenix (☎ 519-963-1448; 441 Richmond St) is London's newest club, housed in the old Bank of Montreal building. The Phoenix is as good a party bar as it is a dance club, and it hosts martini nights and keg stands (often both at the same time) with authority. Cheap drinks are served before 11pm. **Core FX/Ichabod's** (☎ 519-434-5698; 335 Richmond St) is another bar and dance club that attracts college-age crowds.

Getting There & Around

London International Airport (YXU; ☎ 519-452-4015; 1750 Crumlin Rd) services airlines that fly to Toronto, as well as to limited Canadian and US destinations.

Greyhound Canada uses the **bus station** (☎ 519-434-3991; 101 York St) to run eight daily buses to Toronto ($32, 2½ hours) and four to Windsor ($30, 2½ hours).

From the **train station** (☎ 519-672-5722; cnr York & Richmond Sts), VIA Rail serves Toronto ($50, two hours) at least half a dozen times a day, with two trips going via Stratford. In the other direction, trains go to Chicago via Sarnia ($30, one hour) or Windsor ($60, two hours).

London Transit Commission (☎ 519-451-1347) has extensive service around town.

ST THOMAS

St Thomas is a small farming community with a well-maintained downtown of fine Victorian architecture, 20km south of London on the way to the Lake Erie shoreline.

For the kid in everyone is the **Elgin County Railway Museum** (☎ 519-631-6284; 225 Wellington St; admission $2; ☉ 10am-5pm late-May–Labour Day), an old brick warehouse full of rolling stock. An old 1930s steam locomotive is on display as well as real cabooses, and there is some interesting rail history to be learned.

Unfortunately, St Thomas does have a deep, dark story to tell. Hearts were broken around the world when the famous circus elephant Jumbo was hit by a train here and met his end in 1885. A life-sized **statue** at the west end of town pays tribute to the poor beast.

LAKE ERIE SHORELINE

From the Welland Canal to the Detroit River, the Lake Erie shore boasts sandy beaches, diverse ecologies, peaceful parks and little reason to question why so many have summer cottages here. The industrial era and the environmental ignorance of the early 20th century resulted in heavy pollution of Lake Erie (shallowest of the five Great Lakes) but more recent environmental sensitivity has brought the waters back from the brink. It is now not only safe but also enjoyable to swim these waters: they get quite warm and improbably turquoise in some places. Lake Erie also supports commercial fishing and the local restaurants specialize in Erie perch and walleye, the local catches.

Port Dover & Around

Port Dover is a summer beach town with an incredibly laid-back aura. The **Visitor Centre** (☎ 519-583-1314; 19 Market St W; ☉ 9am-noon & 1-5pm Mon-Fri) loans coaster bikes for free.

The **Port Dover Harbour Museum** (☎ 519-583-2660; 44 Harbour St; admission by donation; ☉ 1-4:30pm Mon, 10am-4:30pm Tue-Fri, noon-4pm Sat & Sun) is a cute little old fishing house detailing the lake's fishing industry. Near the water, but off the main tourist area, it's full of maritime trinkets.

Southwest along the coast, **Turkey Point Provincial Park** (☎ 519-426-3239; Rte 10; admission per person $8.50, sites $23.35; ☉ mid-May–early Oct) and **Long Point Provincial Park** (☎ 519-586-2133; Hwy 59; admission/site $8.50/23.25; ☉ mid-May-early Oct) are popular day-use and camping parks. Long Point Provincial Park is located on a spit, so the beaches are excellent and the swimming is top rate. Turkey Point Provincial Point is good for ornithologists and nature lovers as it's a spot where migrating birds stop to rest.

Standard rooms in the white building near the beach in town are what you'll find at the **Erie Beach Hotel** (☎ 519-583-1391; 19 Walker St; r from $80). The pub serves the usual, along with a few seafood dishes, and the formal dining room is all about the perch and shrimp.

Port Stanley

Port Stanley has a very tiny, but very attractive downtown and an agreeable atmosphere that doesn't care to be overly pretentious. There is a fine summer program at the **Port Stanley Festival Theatre** (☎ 519-782-4353; 302 Bridge St). The **Port Stanley Terminal Rail** (☎ 519-782-3730, 877-244-4478; www.pstr.on.ca; 309 Bridge St; adult/child $10/5.50; ☉ noon, 1:30pm & 3pm July–Labour Day, weekends May-Oct) uses a 14km portion of the historic London and Port Stanley Railroad track for one-hour trips.

Leamington & Around

Lakeside Leamington is Ontario's tomato capital and a major ketchup producer – the Heinz factory is a big employer in town and its production lines go *over* the street. The small downtown area attracts a lot of visitors for clothes and antiques shopping. Leamington is 25km south of Hwy 401 and, along with neighboring Kingsville, serves as a gateway to Pelee Island.

East of Leamington, **Wheatley Provincial Park** (☎ 519-825-4659; Hwy 3; admission $9.50, tent & RV sites $26-30; ☺ mid-Apr–early Oct) has good camping despite much of the beach being swept away in a violent storm in 1998. The park does get fairly busy during bird migration periods.

Southeast of town, **Point Pelee National Park** (☎ 519-322-2365; 407 Robson Rd; admission $5), on the southernmost point of mainland Canada, is known for the thousands of birds that stop during spring and autumn migrations. The fall migration of monarch butterflies is a delightful spectacle of swirling black and orange. The region also contains some plants found nowhere else in the country, such as the prickly pear cactus. There are numerous nature trails, a 1.5km boardwalk through the marsh, forest areas and sandy beaches within the park. **Hillman Marsh**, on the shoreline north of Point Pelee, offers good bird-watching.

Pelee Island Winery (☎ 519-733-6551, 800-597-3533; www.peleeisland.com; 455 Seaclid Dr; ☺ 9am-6pm Mon-Sat, 11am-5pm Sun) offers tours, including a trip down to the huge wooden cellar doors and tastings at its production facilities in Kingsville, just west of Leamington. The grapes actually come from Pelee Island, so the name isn't a fraud and quite a variety of wines are produced here, including Canadian sparkling wine.

Pelee Island

A flat, limestone, North American–shaped oasis sits in the blue waters of Lake Erie. Covered in ridiculously richly-colored green fields and forests and outlined by white sandy beaches, Pelee Island is fast becoming a big attraction in southern Ontario.

INFORMATION

Visitor information centers in the area will help you plan your Pelee visit, as will www .pelee.com. During midsummer, ferries and accommodations should be booked in advance. Note there is no bank or ATM on the island.

SIGHTS & ACTIVITIES

Tranquility takes center stage here and the chaos of the modern world seems much further than a 1½-hour ferry ride away. The **glacial grooves** on the southeastern corner of the island remind us how slowly time moves and the long, skinny, sandy spit – absolutely the southernmost point of Canada – on the southern **Fish Point Nature Reserve** reminds us how remote this place is. The 1833 **lighthouse** on the northeastern corner of the island indicates its history, and the fun had on patios, in shops and at wineries around the island brings modern verve.

Enjoy the fruits of the island on the green lawn during a tour and tasting at Pelee Island Winery's **Wine Pavillion** (☎ 519-724-2469; www.peleeisland.com; 20 East West Rd; adult/child/senior $5/free/4; ☺ 10am-6pm mid-May–mid-Oct). Far less productive, but a worthwhile visit, are the atmospheric abandoned ruins of **Vin Villa Winery** and grounds and the old lighthouse.

SLEEPING & EATING

Pelee's popularity has brought a lot of B&B and cottage activity to the island. Most cottages only rent out by the week and most properties take advantage of the western side's fantastic sunsets or northern side's ferry terminal convenience.

Tin Goose Inn (☎ 519-724-2223, 877-737-5557; www .goose.on.ca; r/ste $100/175) A yellow house with smallish rooms but loads of color sits behind a picket fence at the end of a boardwalk. Wooded seclusion and a short walk from the east coast beaches only magnify Pelee's serenity.

Pelee Island Hotel & Pub (☎ 519-724-9994; www .peleeislandhotel.com; 1085 West Shore Rd; mains $6-22, r with/without lake view $130/100) On the western side of the island, near the dock, the steep, dramatic-roofed building watches over the lake. Inside the pub, the central bar, standard tables and chairs and wood-paneled walls don't scream fanciness, but you'd be crazy not to enjoy your perch sandwich at a picnic table or bar stool on the patio anyway. The multilevel deck means there is no bad seat for the sunsets. Rooms at the inn are standard and pretty small, but they're cheaper on weekdays.

Scudder Beach Bar & Grill (☎ 519-724-2902; 325 North Shore Rd; mains $6-15) This place serves food fresh off the grill all week long, but if you're on the island on Sunday afternoon, head to the outdoor barbecue at Scudder's. It's right at the ferry dock and the patio means plenty of good times.

There is camping on the east side of the island and though wooded **East Park Campground** (☎ 519-724-2931; sites $15) is basic, it's on the beach, very quiet and little used.

GETTING THERE & AROUND
From Leamington and Kingsville, **Ontario Ferries** (☎ 800-661-2200, 519-326-2154 in Leamington; www.bmts.com/~northland/pelee/pelee.html; adult/child/youth/senior $7.50/free/3.75/6.25, car/bicycle/motorcycle $16.50/3.75/8.25; ☼ Apr–mid-Dec) run to the island; the ferry schedule depends on the day and season, and reservations are a good idea. From Pelee Island, ferries also connect to Sandusky, Ohio (adult/child/youth/senior $13.75/free/6.75/11.25, car/bicycle/motorcycle $30/6.50/14.50). **Pelee Flyer** (☎ 519-733-4611, 888-467-3533; www.peleeflyer.com; adult/child $15/12, bike $5; ☼ May–mid-Oct) is a new hydrofoil that zips to the island from Kingsville in 22 minutes.

Bicycles can be rented at **Comfortech Bicycle Rentals** (☎ 519-724-2828; west dock; per day $20).

Amherstburg
South of Windsor, where the Detroit River flowing from Lake St Clair runs into Lake Erie, sits small, historic Amherstburg.

On grassy hills along the river stand the impeccable brick buildings of the **Fort Malden National Historic Site** (☎ 519-736-5416; 100 Laird Ave; admission $4; ☼ 10am-5pm May 1-Oct 31), a British fort built in 1840. Beginning with the arrival of the fur traders, the area was the focal point for a lot of tension among the French, First Nations and English and, later, the Americans. Here, during the War of 1812, General Brock (together with his ally, Shawnee Chief Tecumseh) discussed plans to take Detroit.

For one of the best historical displays about the Underground Railroad, a gateway to freedom for thousands of former black slaves in pre-Civil War USA, **John Freeman Walls Historic Site** (☎ 519-258-6253; www.undergroundrailroadmuseum.com; ☼ 10am-5pm) is the place. The original log cabin built by Walls, a fugitive slave from North Carolina, in 1876 was an actual terminal for others searching for freedom, and there are other original buildings as well.

Learn about black settlement of the Windsor area at the **North American Black Historical Museum** (☎ 519-736-5433, 800-713-6336; www.blackhistoricalmuseum.com; 277 King St W; adult/child/family $5.50/4.50/20; ☼ 10am-5pm Wed-Fri, 1-5pm Sat & Sun late-Apr–Nov). The Nazrey African Methodist Episcopal Church, a national historic site, was built by former slaves and played a role in the Underground Railroad as a terminal. There are also general displays on black history in North America.

Park House Museum (☎ 519-736-2511; www.parkhousemuseum.com; 214 Dalhousie St; admission $3; ☼ 10am-4pm Jun-Aug, 11am-4pm Mon-Fri Sep-May) is the oldest house in town, and the only one not *from* town. It was built on the other side of the river, ferried across in 1799 and is now furnished in 1850s style.

WINDSOR
☎ 519 / pop 208,000
Windsor, laying claim as the only Canadian city *south* of mainland USA, sits at the southwestern tip of Ontario, across the Detroit River from Detroit, Michigan. Like its US counterpart, Windsor is primarily a car-making city; unlike Detroit, Windsor's downtown is cute, neat and clean with an abundance of parks and gardens, especially along the river.

Of course, there are also the obligatory border-town currency exchange outlets, immigration lawyer offices and Cuban cigar shops, but the safe core, late-night bars and younger drinking age make Windsor quite the fun spot on summer nights. The city also served as a terminal on the Underground Railroad (see above).

Orientation & Information
The lively central area is around the junction of Riverside and Ouellette Sts.
Convention & Visitors Bureau of Windsor, Essex Country and Pelee Island (☎ 519-255-6530,

800-265-3633; www.visitwindsor.com; 333 Riverside Dr; 8:30am-4:30pm Mon-Fri) Has information on Windsor and the area; there is also a kiosk inside Casino Windsor.

Ontario Travel Information Centre (☎ 800-265-3633; 8:30am-8pm Jun-Aug, 8:30am-4:30pm Sep-May) Downtown (☎ 519-973-1338; 110 Park St E); Bridge (☎ 519-973-1310; 1235 Huron Church Rd) Has offices near the Detroit-Windsor Tunnel entrance and the foot of the Ambassador Bridge.

Sights & Activities

The huge, posh **Casino Windsor** (☎ 519-258-7878; www.casinowindsor.com; 445 Riverside Dr W; 24hr) and hotel complex overlooking the river has served as a massive injection into Windsor's tourism and renewal. An 18m-high waterfall and fountains and the hourly water show grab your attention when you first walk in. The sounds and sights of 5¢ to $100 slot machines and $5 to $25 gaming tables draw you to the real action. It's a lively place anytime of day as people arrive by the busload from across the river. The minimum age for entry is 19 years.

The whiskey was here long before the gambling. Distributed to 151 countries, Canadian Club has come from **Walkerville Distillery** (☎ 519-561-5499, 800-447-2609; cnr Riverside Dr & Walker Rd; adult/child/senior $8/free/6; 11am-6pm, Fri-Sun only Jan-Mar) since 1858. There is a tour of the processes where you can taste the splendors of this drop.

The distinctive concrete and glass **Art Gallery of Windsor** (☎ 519-977-0013; www.artgallery ofwindsor.com; 401 Riverside Dr W; admission $2; noon-5pm Wed & Thu, to 9pm Fri, 11am-5pm Sat & Sun) faces the Detroit skyline and contains an awesome permanent collection focused on Canadian works.

You can see good views of the Detroit skyline, which are particularly striking on a clear night, from anywhere along Riverside Dr, especially **Dieppe Gardens** (cnr Ouellette & Riverside Sts). Check out the 3-D art at **Odette Sculpture Park**, almost under the Ambassador Bridge.

Festivals & Events

Windsor-Detroit International Freedom Festival (☎ 519-252-6274; Jul 1-4) Combines Canada's July 1 national holiday with the July 4 celebrations in the USA along the riverfront for an event of parades, concerts and dances, ending in one of the continent's largest fireworks displays.

NO MORE BETS

In the spring of 2004, Casino Windsor went through a fairly bitter labor dispute with its 3,500 casino workers, who went on a 41-day strike. Not only did the Casino itself lose about $1 million in gambling revenue per day, the estimated 12,750 daily casino visitors stayed home or went elsewhere. The resulting effect on Windsor was a dramatic change from fun town to ghost town and showed just how closely the success of Windsor the city is tied to the casino. The casino is slowly approaching its usual number of visitors, bringing people back to the city, and there is little doubt what Windsor's number one attraction is.

Sleeping & Eating

There are a ton of places to sleep in Windsor and reservations aren't crucial. Chain hotels and local motels dominate Huron Church Rd, leading off the Ambassador Bridge. Prices are higher on weekends but drop outside of summer.

There's no shortage of eateries on and around happening Ouellette St, which runs down to Riverside Dr. In the heart of the city, **Coffee Exchange** (☎ 519-253-1923; 341 Ouellette St; 7am-9pm) is a great local café with comfy couches. It's good to go for your morning coffee and bagel or lunchtime sandwich.

Nisbet Inn (☎ 519-256-0465; www.nisbetinn.ca; 131 Elliott St W; mains $7-11, s/d $65/75) This place primarily serves as an old-country, traditional English pub with imported beer on tap and good pub fare to enjoy by the fireplace or on the patio, but in keeping true to the 'inn' part, it's also a B&B with four rooms – shared bath – upstairs. It's central to anything you'll want to do in Windsor.

Cadillac Motel (☎ 519-969-9340, 888-541-3333; www.cadillacmotel.com; 2498 Dougall St; r $65-90;) The drive-up motel is close to downtown and convenient to the bridge. It's got spaciously pleasant rooms, all recently renovated.

Plunkett's Bistro (☎ 519-252-3111; 28 Chatham St E; mains $9-20; 11am-late) The menu covers the map from burgers to *pad thai* to chorizo and goat cheese chicken, but they don't make anything they can't handle. This is the spot where Windsorites who aren't into the casino go for fun (Thursday night is reserved for 'singles' parties), drinks at the horseshoe bar and good food.

Spago Trattoria e Pizzeria (☎ 519-252-9099; 614 Erie St E; mains $7-13; ☺ lunch & dinner) You'll get true Italian tastes and energy here. If you're not in the mood for delicious pasta, they make some outstanding pizzas in the wood-fired oven. If you're in the mood for delicious pasta and a little more quietness, the more formal **Spago Ristorante Italiano** (☎ 519-252-2233; 690 Erie St E; mains $8-15) is up the street.

Getting There & Away

Detroit-Windsor is a major international border crossing, via either the famous and expansive **Ambassador Bridge** (toll $4/US$2.75), or the convenient **Detroit-Windsor Tunnel** (toll $3.50/US$2.50) that runs between downtowns.

The **bus station** (☎ 519-254-7577; 44 University Ave) is downtown near the tunnel. Greyhound Canada runs four daily buses through London ($34, two hours) to Toronto ($67, five hours). US-bound trips to places such as Chicago ($75, seven to nine hours) will transfer from Greyhound Canada to Greyhound in Detroit.

VIA Rail runs frequent trains to Toronto ($85, four hours) via London ($46, two hours) from the **train station** (☎ 519-256-5511; cnr Walker & Wyandotte Sts), 3km east of the downtown core near the river.

LAKE HURON SHORELINE

Lake Huron has some of the cleanest waters of the Great Lakes and it's wide enough that from its eastern shore, the sun actually sets on the waterline.

In the town of Dresden, about 100km northeast of Windsor, is **Uncle Tom's Cabin Historic Site** (☎ 519-683-2978; www.uncletomscabin .org; 29251 Uncle Tom's Rd; adult/child/student/family $6.25/4.50/5.25/20; ☺ 10am-5pm Mon-Sat, noon-5pm Sun, closed Mon & Tue Sep-Jun). Uncle Tom was the fictional protagonist and title of the book written by Harriet Beecher Stowe in 1852, based on real-life hero Reverend Josiah Henson. The site displays articles relating to the story and the Underground Railroad.

On the southern shore of Lake Huron, across the Bluewater Bridge from Port Huron, Michigan (a border crossing good for avoiding Windsor's traffic), is industrial **Sarnia**. Acting as the hub of Chemical Valley, an oil-and-chemical production and refining complex, it's the natural home of the

Oil Museum of Canada (☎ 519-834-2840; Hwy 21; adult/child/senior $5/3/4; ☺ 10am-5pm, closed Sat & Sun Nov-May) A re-creation of the first commercial oil well in North America is here along with original buildings from the boom times that followed.

Fans of geology will appreciate the 350-million-year-old concretions at **Kettle Point**, 40km northeast of Sarnia. Laypeople may just see a bunch spherical rocks. Some of these calcite formations, which sit on beds of softer shale, are nearly 1m in diameter. The rare kettles are found in other countries, but are often underground, and this collection is considered top rate.

Farther up the coast, south of Grand Bend, is **Pinery Provincial Park** (☎ 519-243-2220; Hwy 21; admission $12, tent/RV sites $23/30), with 10km of beaches and lots of trails winding through the wooded sections and sand dunes make it a good place to camp at any of the 1000 sites.

Acting as the regional center, **Goderich** could possibly be your new favorite southwestern Ontario town. The distinctive circular main street with the county courthouse and green parks in the center serves as a bulls-eye for attractiveness: beauty and history radiate from there. Grab the self-guided *Architectural Heritage Tour* from **Tourism Goderich** (☎ 519-524-6600, 800-280-7637; www.town .goderich.on.ca; ☺ 9am-7pm late Mar–Labour Day, 9am-4:30pm Labour Day–late-May) or the *Visitor's Guide* and use the map to take a walk along the beach boardwalks, making sure to be on the bluffs to take in the amazing sunsets.

Walk along the wooden floorboards at **Huron County Museum** (☎ 519-524-2686; 110 North St; adult/student $5/3; ☺ 10am-4:30pm Mon-Sat, 1pm-4:30pm Sun) for an excellent look at general history and pioneer days. Displays include everything from old furniture and china to an old steam engine and a tank. **Governor's House & Historic Gaol Museum** (☎ 519-524-6971; 181 Victoria St; admission $5; ☺ 10am-4:30pm late-May–Labour Day) is an octagonal building which served as the courthouse and jail for almost 130 years imposingly set on the bluffs on the lakeshore.

The nearby village of **Blyth** is home to some of the most preferred summer theater in the province. The **Blyth Festival** (☎ 877-862-5984; www.blythfestival.com; ☺ Jul-Sep) features primarily Canadian plays, from outdoor pioneer performances to indoor gut-busting comedies.

GEORGIAN BAY & LAKELANDS

Cold, deep, majestic Georgian Bay dwarfs many of the world's bodies of freshwater, even though it's only one part of one of the Great Lakes. The deeply indented, irregular shoreline along the eastern side, with its myriad islands, is trimmed by slabs of pink granite barely supporting wind-bent pine trees. The works of the country's best-known painters, the Group of Seven, provide the icons of this region, perhaps none more so than AJ Casson's *White Pine*.

The region's place in the collective imagination shares space with its status as the playground of southern Ontario. From the Victoria Day weekend in late May onwards, Torontonians take part in the annual ritual of negotiating and dividing 'cottage time' between factions of families that have owned the same lakeside retreat for generations. They then pack their swimming costumes and make the annual pilgrimage

northward. In peak season – July and August – it seems most of the province is here to escape the southwestern heat and smog. In September and October leaf-peepers tour the region for its showy display of autumn foliage, and in January and February skiing, snowmobiling and ice fishing are at their peak.

Summer is the best time for most activities, and very small towns and communities such as Tobermory, Britt and Killarney are nearly deserted outside the stretch from Victoria Day to Thanksgiving in mid-October. In other places some attractions, accommodations and restaurants close out of season, but the towns are large enough to support activity year-round.

This section is ordered loosely anticlockwise around Georgian Bay and the surrounding area, starting with the Lake Huron beach resort of Southampton, then up the Bruce Peninsula to Tobermory. The Tobermory–Manitoulin Island ferry is one way to reach the Trans-Canada Hwy (Hwy 17) across northern Ontario. Alternatively, you can drive around the eastern side of

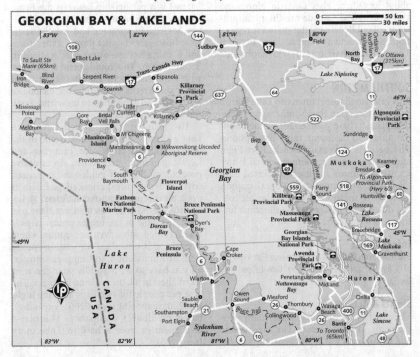

GEORGIAN BAY & LAKELANDS

ONTARIO

Georgian Bay; if you're starting in Toronto the difference in time required is not significant.

Inland from the east shore, the region between the towns of Gravenhurst and Huntsville is referred to as Muskoka, and constitutes establishment country cottage, some of it very exclusive, although this is not readily apparent to travelers. (For a surreptitious peek at 'millionaires row' on Lake Muskoka, you can take a boat cruise from Gravenhurst or Bracebridge.)

BARRIE

Barrie, 90km north of Toronto, is not worth visiting in its own right but is the unofficial gateway to most of the Georgian Bay area. There's a large **Ontario Travel Information Centre** (☎ 705-725-7280, 800-668-2746; 21 Molson Park Dr; ☺ 8am-8pm mid-Jun–Aug, 8:30am-5pm Apr–mid-May & Sep-Nov, to 6pm mid-May–mid-Jun, 7am-5pm Dec-Mar) just south of Barrie at Hwy 400.

On Friday afternoon and Sunday or Monday night, especially on holiday weekends in summer, expect a slow drive between Toronto and Barrie (up to 1½ hours) or just about anywhere else. Ontario Northland and Greyhound Canada are the main providers of public transportation in the region. Both have frequent express buses between Toronto and Barrie ($21, 1½ hours, one hourly).

SOUTHAMPTON

Of all the small resort towns on Lake Huron or south Georgian Bay, Southampton is the best place to base yourself for a beach holiday that also has some rainy-day options. The beaches at Wasaga Beach, Port Elgin and Sauble Beach are longer, much better known and more intensely marketed than the one at Southampton, but Southampton is only a 15-minute drive from the last two. For details of the Lake Huron shoreline further south, see p152.

Information

Southampton Chamber of Commerce (☎ 519-797-2215, 888-757-2215; 201 High St; ☺ 10am-4:30pm Tue-Sat)

Sights & Activities

The beaches are the only reason many people come to Lake Huron. The sand is fine and the water is warm and generally safe for young children. In summer there's always something (markets, carnivals, bingo games) going on.

Bruce County Museum (☎ 519-797-2080, 866-318-8889; www.brucecounty.on.ca/museum; 69 Victoria St N; admission by donation; ☺ 9am-5pm Mon-Fri) has an extensive collection of artifacts relating to shipwrecks. At the time of research the museum was building a new center at an adjacent site, with completion scheduled for late 2005.

Taking a tour with the **Marine Heritage Society** (☎ 519-797-5862, 888-797-5862; tours $20) is the only way to visit Chantry Island, which is a sanctuary for migratory birds and the site of a scenic lighthouse. The island is just offshore from Southampton, and the tour includes the lighthouse keeper's quarters and historic gardens as well as the lighthouse itself. Trips run twice daily from May to July, and three times a day from August to September, weather permitting. Departures are from the south side of the mouth of the Saugeen River, right in town.

The **Chantry Island Institute** (www.chantryisland.com) is a partnership between the Bruce County Museum and the Marine Heritage Society. In summer and fall the institute hosts short workshops, expeditions and evening lectures at various locations in Southampton. You could spend a Saturday with an archaeologist learning about Great Lakes shipwrecks ($85); the cost includes a lecture and an expedition to the island. Book through the museum.

The Saugeen River, which flows into Lake Huron at Southampton, is one of the best-established routes for canoeing and kayaking in southern Ontario. An extensive program of short self-guided and organized trips aimed at inexperienced paddlers is available through **Thorncrest Outfitters** (☎ 519-797-1608, 888-345-2925; www.thorncrestoutfitters.com; 193 High St). One of the most popular trips is a self-guided soft-adventure option where everything is organized for you, including B&B acommodation and luggage transfer; all you have to do is paddle your canoe or kayak. Best of all, there are no portages! The cost per couple for two days and one night is $220 (canoeing) or $260 (kayaking), based on double occupancy. Thorncrest also operates from a base in Tobermory (see p156).

Sleeping

Stewart House (☎ 519-797-5094; 48 Victoria St N; r $65) This B&B isn't elegant (check out the proudly displayed beer bottle collection), but the rooms are among the cheapest in town and it's all clean and comfortable.

Cedar Court Motel (☎ 519-797-3777, 888-945-5598; www.cedarcourt.ca; 243 Huron St S; r $80-85) This welcoming motel is super-close to the beach on a quiet street. All rooms are spacious and have kitchenettes.

Southampton Inn (☎ 519-797-5915, 888-214-3816; www.thesouthamptoninn.com; 118 High St; ste $120) This inn has the personality of a B&B with the spaciousness of hotel suites – every bedroom has a private sitting room – making it great for extended stays. The family suites in the basement can be configured for three people or more.

Chantry Breezes (☎ 519-797-1818, 866-242-6879; www.chantrybreezes.on.ca; 107 High St; s/d $110/130) The yoga studio here makes this B&B our favorite place to stay in Southampton. Classes cost $15 per person, when the owner has time to give them in between whipping up breakfasts of fresh local produce. Lactose and wheat intolerances are catered for. It's all so healthy and contemporary, you'd hardly know you were in a historic home.

Eating

Duffy's Famous Fish & Chips (☎ 519-797-5972; 151 High St; fish & chips $8.25; ✓ 11:30am-9pm Mon-Sat & noon-8pm Sun) The name says it all: this eat-in restaurant is the best place in town for deep-fried goodness.

Southampton Inn Cafe (☎ 519-797-5915, 888-214-3816; 118 High St; mains $7-10; ✓ noon-5pm Mon-Sat) Eat in at the small, bright café, or get a prepared meal to take to the beach: sandwiches, light pastas and poached salmon all feature.

Grosvenor's (☎ 519-797-1226; 124 Grosvenor St; mains $24-30; ✓ dinner Mon-Sat) Grosvenor's does classic French and Italian things to local produce – lamb from nearby Wiarton is crusted with herbs and served with mint jus; veal from Kincardine is served with mushroom ravioli and Marsala demiglace. For tastes of one of these and six other courses, choose the tasting menu ($60/85 without/with matched wines). The dining room feels homey rather than designer, but has crisp white napery.

Getting There & Away

From Toronto's international airport **Grey Bruce Airbus** (☎ 519-389-4433; www.greybruceairbus.com) connects to Southampton ($53, three hours, four daily). From downtown Toronto, **Can-ar** (☎ 905-738-2290, 800-387-7097; www.can-arcoach.com) operates a bus service to Port Elgin ($35, 4½ hours, one daily), from where you can catch a taxi the last 10km to Southampton for about $13.

BRUCE PENINSULA

The Bruce, as it's known, is an 80km-long limestone outcrop at the northern end of the Niagara Escarpment. On one side of the peninsula are the cold, clear waters of Georgian Bay, and on the other are the much warmer waters of Lake Huron. Rocky shorelines, sandy beaches, cliffs and green woodlands rise out of the lakes. The peninsula has attracted a growing artistic community, drawn by the lack of development compared to the rest of southern Ontario.

The main base for travelers is Tobermory, a pretty, unpretentious village on the tip of the peninsula. Activity centers on the harbor area known as Little Tub, which bustles in summer and is all but deserted in the off-season. Most travelers barrel along Hwy 6 from Wiarton, a straight, boring stretch of road, and head directly to Tobermory, but it's worth exploring the back roads for a taste of the rural, often rugged scenery that makes the Bruce so special.

Information

Bruce County Tourism (☎ 800-268-3838; ✓ 8:30am-4:30pm Mon-Fri) A telephone service providing information; there's no walk-in office.

Tobermory Chamber of Commerce (☎ 519-596-2452; www.tobermory.org; Hwy 6, Tobermory; ✓ 9am-5pm)

Sights

From Hwy 6 just south of the Bruce Peninsula National Park boundary, take Dyer's Bay Rd to the quaint village of **Dyer's Bay**, parts of which are reminiscent of Cape Cod, with pretty clapboard houses and shoreline scenery. Follow the road northeast for a scenic drive with Georgian Bay on one side and the limestone cliffs of the Niagara Escarpment on the other. The road is slow going and mostly unsealed past Dyer's Bay. It ends 7km past Dyer's Bay at **Cabot Head Lighthouse** (admission by donation; ✓ May-Thanksgiving). There is a small museum inside the lighthouse, and you can climb to the top for views over Georgian Bay. There are other more accessible lighthouses on the peninsula, but the journey and isolation are part of the attraction here.

The best-known, most visited feature of **Fathom Five National Marine Park** is **Flowerpot Island**, named after the 'flowerpots' of the area: top-heavy, precarious-looking rock formations created by wave erosion. Several boat tours visit the island from Tobermory, including the **MV Seaview III** (☎ 519-596-2950, 800-640-2092; www.seaview.on.ca; Little Tub, Tobermory; tours adult/child $20/12.50). The tour includes time off the boat on the island. Trips run six times daily in summer and depending on demand and the weather in May, June, September and October.

Activities

HIKING

Some of the best features of the peninsula – the Niagara Escarpment, 1000-year-old cedars and many orchid species – are protected and made accessible by the **Bruce Peninsula National Park** (☎ 519-596-2233; day use per vehicle $7.50; ☺ May-Thanksgiving). The center of most activity in the park is the **Cyprus Lake Campground & Visitor Centre** (☎ 519-596-2263; Cyprus Lake Rd; ☺ 8am-4:30pm), where you can obtain information on hiking trails. The Cyprus Lake area has good short, easy hikes, ranging from about 1km to 5km in length. The park takes in the best section of the Bruce Trail along the shoreline cliffs.

KAYAKING

Kayaking all day, comfortable B&B accommodation every night and organic food – does life get any better than this? The **Paddling Gourmet** (☎ 519-596-8343; www.paddlinggourmet .com; 129 Bay St, Tobermory) runs trips on Georgian Bay in the national marine park at a relaxed, flexible pace in groups of up to six people. Many travelers come as much for the eating as for the paddling, not that lolling about is compulsory – owner 'Jungle Jane' imparts as much enthusiasm as her moniker suggests. A one-day trip costs $110, and a three-day trip $350. Instruction and equipment are included, and trips can be customized.

Thorncrest Outfitters (☎ 519-596-8908, 888-345-2925; www.thorncrestoutfitters.com; Hwy 6, Tobermory) runs one-day kayaking trips on the inland lakes of the Bruce (they're much calmer than Georgian Bay) for $90. These trips are aimed at beginners and include plenty of instruction. Thorncrest also offers day trips

---

BRUCE TRAIL

Southern Ontario's best-loved footpath is the Bruce Trail, all 780km of it. Tobermory marks the northern end of the trail, which edges along the Niagara Escarpment from Queenston on the Niagara River to the tip of the Bruce Peninsula. You can hike for an hour, a day or a week; whichever section of the trail you choose will give you an understanding of why the escarpment is a Unesco world biosphere reserve. This designation recognizes that the area balances the protection of significant ecosystems with surrounding development. Much of the Bruce Trail is characterized to some extent by the 'development' aspect: it passes over private and public land including farmland and patches of forest easily accessible from (and regularly crossed by) rural roads.

In contrast, the most rugged and spectacular stretch of the trail is the portion between Dyer's Bay and Tobermory, most of which is protected as part of the Bruce Peninsula National Park. If you're so inclined, a highlight of backcountry camping along this route in summer is skinny-dipping until long after the sun goes down against a usually private backdrop of brilliant blue Georgian Bay, quiet pebble beaches or warmer inland lakes.

If you prefer a comfortable bed after a long day of hiking, and the convenience of having your luggage transported for you, get in touch with **Home to Home** (☎ 888-301-3224; www .hometohomenetwork.ca), a network of Bruce Peninsula B&Bs catering to hikers.

The **Bruce Trail Association** (☎ 800-665-4453; www.brucetrail.org) publishes a detailed guide ($35) to the entire route; it's available in major bookstores in the area. The association's website is an excellent source of information for planning a day trip, and includes directions for driving to some of the best short hikes.

on Georgian Bay for the same price. For independent paddling, you can rent just about anything through Thorncrest.

SCUBA DIVING

Tobermory is the scuba diving capital of Ontario and offers some of the best wreck diving in North America. Visibility in the area is almost always exceptionally good, but the water is really, really cold. Some of Canada's oldest shipwrecks lie submerged in the marine park, which has a **Diver Registration & Visitor Centre** (☎ 519-596-2233) in the Little Tub area of Tobermory.

G&S Watersports (☎ 519-596-2200; www.gswater sports.com; 8 Bay St S, Tobermory) offers gear rentals, certification courses (from $475 to $675 for open-water certification) and 'discovery' dives for beginners ($150).

CYCLING

Flat, quiet backroads and the scale of the area make the Bruce ideal for self-guided cycling trips. A good place to rent a bike is Jolley's Alternative Wheels (p158) in Owen Sound. Alternatively, if you want everything organized for you, contact **Georgian Shores Cycle Tours** (☎ 519-371-1773; 810 10th St, Owen Sound). Each night is spent at a B&B and meals, luggage shuttles and experienced guides are included in the prices. Choose from trips of two days ($350), three days ($525) or five days ($850), or add Manitoulin Island as well for a six-day tour ($975). The distance covered each day is 50km to 60km. To rent a bike, add $30 to $75. Women-only tours are available too.

Sleeping

In summer it's absolutely essential to book accommodations in advance. The options listed here are in Tobermory.

Cha Mao Zah (☎ 519-596-2708; www.indiancarver .com; 7111 Hwy 6, Tobermory; camping per tipi $30-75, cabins $50-75) Cha Mao Zah features camping in canvas tipis (which sleep from two to eight people; you can't set up your own tent here). The rustic but comfortable cedar cabins are suitable for one or two people, and bathrooms are in a separate building. Outside July and August, Cha Mao Zah often caters to school groups.

Cedar Vista Motel (☎ 519-596-2395; www.cedar vistamotel.com; Hwy 6, Tobermory; r $75-85) Neat and quiet, this motel is within walking distance

of the main part of Tobermory, on the highway away from the water.

Innisfree (☎ 519-596-8190; www.bbcanada.com/ innisfree; 46 Bay St, Tobermory; r $90) Innisfree is a refreshing inn-style B&B. The individually decorated rooms have wide views over the harbor, and some have direct access to a deck.

Grandview (☎ 519-596-2220; www.grandview-tober mory.com; Bay St, Tobermory; r $100-120) The Grandview offers comfortable motel-style acommodation and a well-known restaurant.

Camping is available in the **Bruce Peninsula National Park** (☎ 519-596-2233; ☼ May-Thanksgiving; backcountry/campground sites $8/22). You can book backcountry sites at **Cyprus Lake Campground & Visitor Centre** (☎ 519-596-2263; Cyprus Lake Rd; ☼ 8am-4:30pm); reservations for campgrounds must be made through **Parks Canada** (☎ 877-737-3783; www.pccamping.ca).

Eating

Harvest Moon Bakery (☎ 519-592-5742; 3927 Hwy 6; ☼ 9:30am-4:30pm Fri-Wed mid-Jun–mid-Sep) Hemp flour features in some of the organic goods produced so lovingly at this bakery and sculpture garden, which employs wwoofers (willing workers on organic farms) to help out with the chores. The fruit pies ($8.50), butter tarts and savory pastries can be enjoyed outdoors with a fair trade coffee. The bakery is 10km north of Ferndale on the west side of Hwy 6.

Craigie's (☎ 519-596-2867; Little Tub, Tobermory; fish & chips $9; ☼ 8am-9pm May-Oct) Craigie's has been serving fish and chips to Tobermory since 1932, so by now they've got it just about perfect: super-fresh, and crumbed rather than battered.

Rocky Raccoon Cafe (☎ 519-795-7586; 967 Dyer's Bay Rd, Dyer's Bay; ☼ noon-9pm May-Oct) It rocks! Best eats: Indian maple spice bread ($2), Tibetan *momos* (steamed dumplings; $8) and locally smoked ribs ($20). If the farmer down the road has a glut of strawberries, expect a feast. There's a terrific range of local brews, including Bruce County Lager from the microbrewery in nearby Neustadt. The café has a pressed-metal ceiling and warm ambience. You won't want to leave, but you might feel better about it knowing that the owners have another café on Manitoulin Island (p185). Reservations recommended.

Stone Orchid (☎ 519-596-2800; 7078 Hwy 6, Tobermory; mains $14-21) For Indonesian food, quirky decor and a bit of shopping on the side (Indonesian artifacts), it has to be the Stone Orchid. The restaurant is open for both lunch and dinner, but the Indonesian options are served only for dinner; lunch is standard family-restaurant fare.

Grandview (☎ 519-596-2220; Bay St, Tobermory; mains $22-27) Locals recommend the Grandview for a special night out. Much of the appeal comes from the harbor view: this is the best dining location on the peninsula, especially if you get an outside table. Dinner choices, mostly old world style, include roast duck with cherries and brandy ($25) and local fish ($23).

Getting There & Away
The Bruce Peninsula is accessible by bus only on Friday, Saturday and Sunday from late June to early September, when **Laidlaw Transit** (☎ 519-376-5712, 519-376-5375) runs services between Owen Sound and Tobermory ($20, 1½ hours, one daily).

For travel between the Bruce Peninsula and Manitoulin Island (p184), the Chi-Cheemaun ferry is operated by **Ontario Ferries** (☎ 800-265-3163; www.ontarioferries.com; ☼ early May–mid-Oct). It connects Tobermory with South Baymouth (adult/child/car one way $12.50/6/27, 1¾ hours). From late June to early September there are four crossings daily, and from early May to late June, and early September to mid-October, two daily. It's not uncommon to have to wait for a crossing, so reservations are strongly suggested.

OWEN SOUND
In its early days as a shipping center, Owen Sound rocked with brothels, bars and merchant seamen. As the largest city on Georgian Bay (population 22,000) it still bustles year-round with easily accessible natural attractions, good museums, a thriving artistic community and an acclaimed festival of folk music. The Sydenham River lends the city a peaceful feel where it drifts through the centre.

Information
Owen Sound Visitor Information Centre (☎ 519-371-9833, 888-675-5555; www.owensound.ca; 1155 1st Ave W; ☼ 9am-6pm Mon-Sat, to 7pm Fri & 11am-5pm Sun Victoria Day–Thanksgiving, 9am-5pm Mon-Fri & 11am-5pm Sat & Sun Jan–Victoria Day, 9am-5pm Mon-Fri, 11am-5pm Sat & Sun Thanksgiving-Dec)

Sights & Activities
The **Tom Thomson Memorial Art Gallery** (☎ 519-376-1932; www.tomthomson.org; 840 1st Ave W; admission by donation; ☼ 10am-5pm Mon-Sat, noon-5pm Sun Jun-Sep, 11am-5pm Tue-Fri, noon-5pm Sat & Sun Sep-Jun) displays the work of Tom Thomson, a contemporary of the Group of Seven (see the boxed text on p117) and one of Canada's best-known painters, as well as the work of other Canadian painters. Thomson grew up here, and many of his works were done nearby. The gallery also shows touring exhibitions and works from its collection of contemporary Canadian art.

Grey Roots (☎ 519-376-3690; www.greyroots.com; 102599 Grey Rd 18; adult/child $6/3.50; ☼ 10am-4pm Sun-Thu, to 7pm Fri & Sat) consists of the museum, cultural collections and tourism services of the whole county. At the time of research this brand-new center was weeks away from opening, and its hours and displays were still being finalized. Plans included artifacts illustrating the area's agricultural and fishing heritage.

Hometown hero Billy Bishop, who became a flying ace in WWI, is honored at the former Bishop family home, now the **Billy Bishop Heritage Museum** (☎ 519-371-0031; www.billybishop.org; 948 3rd Ave W; adult/student $4/2; ☼ 10am-4pm Jul & Aug, noon-4pm Tue-Sun Sep-Jun, closed Jan & weekends in Feb). The museum, which is designated a national historic site, illustrates Canada's aviation history as well as Bishop's career.

There are seven scenic **waterfalls** in the county, including three set in conservation areas very close to Owen Sound. You could explore them by bike, available for rent at **Jolley's Alternative Wheels** (☎ 519-371-1812; www.alternativewheels.com; 939 2nd Ave E; per day $25; ☼ 8am-5pm Tue-Fri, 10am-5pm Sat).

Festivals & Events
Summerfolk Music Festival (☎ 519-371-2995, 866-528-8225; www.summerfolk.org; ☼ Aug) This major North American festival runs for three days in mid- to late August. International and local musicians come to perform in Kelso Park, right along the water, and attendances can number 12,000. Tickets start at $68.

Sleeping
Diamond Motor Inn (☎ 519-371-2011; 713 9th Ave E; r $60-70) A pleasant no-frills choice, this motel has bright rooms with cooking facilities. It's on the edge of town.

Raven-Croft House (☎ 519-372-0640; www.bb canada.com/ravencroft; 883 7th Ave E; r $65-85) This 1880 home is immaculately decorated, but thankfully still feels like the B&B we'd like to live in, not a museum piece. The owner particularly likes having families to stay, and can configure the rooms accordingly. There's a guest sitting room with a fireplace and library.

Butchart Estate (☎ 519-371-0208, 877-280-2403; www.butchartestate.com; 919 5th Ave E; s/d $99/109; 🖳) When the Butchart family of Butchart Gardens fame (p708) first emigrated to Canada from Scotland they settled in Owen Sound, and this Queen Anne home is part of their local legacy. More recent owners added an indoor pool and a hot tub. This is among the town's most luxurious B&B accommodations – pure elegance.

Eating

Marketside (☎ 519-371-7666; 813 2nd Ave E; mains $4-7; 🕙 10am-5:30pm Mon-Sat, to 7pm Fri) Marketside's posters and friendly staff make it a quasi community centre – get a celebrant for your gay commitment ceremony or information on the next peace seminar with your curried lentil soup ($4 for the soup).

Grey Heron (☎ 519-371-8141; 229 9th St E; dinner mains $12-20; 🕙 lunch Mon-Fri, dinner Mon-Sat) Could this be the only restaurant in the country that hosts Scrabble games on Tuesday afternoon? Create your own ambience by placing 'quirky' on a triple word score, because the bland decor doesn't lend much. The food gets 50 bonus points: try a bison burger made from locally raised buffalo ($9).

Norma Jean's Bistro (☎ 519-376-2232; 243 8th St E; dinner mains $14-21) Marilyn would have felt welcome here – her namesake is warm and inviting, and no steam vent would have blown her skirt up while she had a drink at the bar. According to the menu the Garbo burger ($5) wants to be alone: it features just lettuce, pickle and tomato.

Drinking

Some of the founding mothers of Canada's temperance movement lived in Owen Sound, and it wasn't until 1972, after 66 long years

---

SKIING & SNOWBOARDING NORTH OF TORONTO

Ontario probably isn't the first place that comes to mind when you think of skiing and boarding in Canada. The province whose highest point towers to 693m can't compete with British Columbia and Alberta when it comes to vertical drop. But there's still great cross-country skiing to be had just about everywhere: most hiking trails can be skied in winter, and provincial parks are popular places to experience a wild winter wonderland from skis.

For alpine skiing and boarding, the resort with the most vertical drop (216m), the most lifts (12) and the best après-ski options is Blue Mountain (p160). Three other top choices cluster close to each other off Hwy 400 just north of Barrie, all within 1½ hours of Toronto by car. All offer rentals (from $30 per day), lessons and beginner packages and operate every day. As they say around here, it beats the pants off down-hilling in Saskatchewan and if you lose control it's not as far to the bottom as at Whistler. The ski season runs from about mid-December to about mid-March, but it varies from year to year depending on the weather. The resorts stay open for as long as they can. Peak season is January and February.

Horseshoe Valley (☎ 705-835-2790; www.horseshoeresort.com; lift passes $27-44) This resort has 35km of cross-country trails, a tubing park and eight lifts leading to dozens of runs for skiers and snowboarders. The number of lifts means the lines move quickly, even on busy days. It's also got a hotel, a spa, several eateries, a fireside lounge and night skiing until 10pm. From Hwy 400, turn east onto Horseshoe Valley Rd; the resort is 6km from the highway. Bus packages from Toronto cost around $60, including lift pass.

Mt St Louis–Moonstone (☎ 705-835-2112; www.mslm.on.ca; lift passes $30-44) Mt St Louis–Moonstone has only two lifts, but it has steeper terrain (around 160m vertical drop) and longer runs than Horseshoe Valley. No accommodations or night skiing, though. From Hwy 400, take Mt St Louis Rd to the west and you're almost there.

Snow Valley Resorts (☎ 705-721-7669; www.skisnowvalley.com) This is a great option if you're traveling as a family or spending extended time in Toronto. Pricing isn't set up for one-off trips, but the packages are good value: six one-night tickets cost $79, and six one-day tickets $149. It's 'low-profile,' physically and figuratively (the flattest of the three), with eight lifts and night skiing all week. No accommodations. From Hwy 400, take Hwy 26 northwest to the resort off Snow Valley Rd.

without a drink, that the town voted to allow the sale of alcohol. Now many of the restaurants and pubs serve one of Ontario's most popular microbrews, Creemore Springs, made just down the road in Creemore.

Jazzymyn's (☎ 519-371-7736; 261 9th St E) Best visited for cozy ambience, colorful decor, a great selection of draft beers (including Creemore) and occasional live music in an intimate space. On Tuesday night there's an open Celtic jam session.

Shopping

Owen Sound Artists' Co-op (☎ 519-371-0479; 279 10th St E) The co-op features the work of more than 30 regional artists. Photography, weaving, knitting, basketwork, pottery and jewelry are all represented, and the quality is very high. It's almost unfair to single out individual works, but the decorated gourds ($85 to $160) are exquisite. Each one takes over a year to make, including growing time.

Owen Sound Farmers' Market (☎ 519-371-3433; www.owensoundfarmersmarket.ca; 114 8th St E; ☒ 7am-12:30pm Sat) This farmers' market is one of the oldest in Ontario, and it's the best place to buy seasonal local produce. You'll likely find honey, apples, maple syrup and baked goods among the bounty.

Getting There & Away

Greyhound Canada buses connect Owen Sound with Barrie ($27, 2¼ hours, three daily).

COLLINGWOOD & BLUE MOUNTAIN

Collingwood is the nearest town to the massive development of Blue Mountain resort, under construction by Intrawest, the same folks who brought you Whistler in British Columbia and Mont-Tremblant in Québec. At the time of research completion was scheduled for 2010, but already there are plenty of dining and accommodation options on the mountain open in summer and winter.

Collingwood itself, about 10 minutes from the resort area, has a historic town centre and scenic surroundings, with the highest sections of the Niagara Escarpment nearby, and Georgian Bay lapping at the edges of town. The area that includes Collingwood, the resort and the surrounding hills is known collectively as the Blue Mountains.

Information

Blue Mountain (☎ 705-445-0231; www.bluemountain .ca) Centralized number and website provide information on all aspects of the resort.

Georgian Triangle Tourism Association (☎ 705-445-7722; www.georgiantriangle.com; 30 Mountain Rd, Collingwood; ☒ 9am-5pm)

Sights & Activities

Blue Mountain skiing and snowboarding is the best in Ontario in terms of vertical drop (216m) and the number of lifts (12), four of them high-speed. There are three terrain parks, multiple pipes and half-pipes and more than 30 runs rated from beginner to double black diamond. Lift tickets (valid from 9am to 4:30pm) cost $49 for adults and $29 for youths and seniors. Half-day and evening tickets are available for slightly less, and all are reduced early and late in the season (up to mid-December and after mid-March). For the same price as an adult ticket, you can get a beginner package that includes some lifts, a lesson and ski rentals; add $10 for the snowboard package. In summer, the resort offers loads of activity packages in the surrounding area: mountain biking, sailing, climbing, hiking and windsurfing, for example. For details on all these activities contact **Activity Central** (☎ 705-443-5522, 800-955-6561; www .blueactivities.com; ☒ 8:30am-6pm, to 8:30pm Jul & Aug & mid-Dec–mid-Mar), which has a storefront in the village to the side of the Grand Georgian hotel, near the landmark Starbucks.

To escape the summer crowds call **Free Spirit Tours** (☎ 705-444-3622; www.freespirit-tours .com), which specializes in rock climbing along the Niagara Escarpment; prices start at $40 for half a day of climbing. Hiking, cycling and kayaking trips are also available.

Sleeping

In Collingwood, budget-oriented motels dominate. At Blue Mountain there are many condo-style choices similar to the Grand Georgian, all offering luxurious accommodation and resort facilities starting at $130 per room midweek; for details, contact Blue Mountain.

Moores Motel (☎ 705-445-2478; www.mooresmotel .com; Hwy 26, Collingwood; r $65-80) A few construction workers from the resort call this place home, and it's homey and quiet, if a little shabby at the edges. It's west of Collingwood, close to the resort.

Beild House (☎ 705-444-1522; www.beildhouse.com; 64 3rd St, Collingwood; r $115-35) Indulge in an afternoon cooking school, spa treatment or rose petals scattered on your pillow in this frilly 1909 B&B.

Blue Mountain Inn (☎ 705-445-0231; www.blue mountain.ca; r $155-90) When this place was built people were still skiing on planks of wood. The inn was synonymous with Blue Mountain from the 1940s until the developers came along. It's still 50% family owned, and feels a little more personal than the new places close by.

Grand Georgian (☎ 705-445-0231; www.bluemoun tain.ca; r $130-240) The Grand Georgian has all the luxuries you expect in new resort accommodations: hot tubs, games room, fireplaces, a gym, and skiing from your door. It's in the village at the heart of the resort action.

Eating

Grandma Lambe's (☎ 519-538-2757; Hwy 26; ☾ 8am-6pm Sat-Thu, to 7pm Fri) Grandma Lambe's is not in Collingwood; in fact it's roughly 35km to the west on Hwy 26, between Thornbury and Meaford. But of the many roadside places in southern Ontario that sell fresh produce and baked goods, this one is worth U-turning for. The aroma of cinnamon, cooked fruit and pastry is overwhelming in the best way, and the store is a delicious jumble of maple syrup vintages, bushels of vegetables and tables piled with pies, buns and jellies.

Terracotta Restaurant (☎ 705-445-4623; 100 Pine St, Collingwood; mains $14-19) Outmoded decor in the dining room belies admirable attention to detail in the kitchen and a contemporary menu: mod Canadian with nods to Italy, for example, in the form of duck breast on porcini risotto cake with honey balsamic jus ($17).

Copper Blues (☎ 705-446-2643; Blue Mountain; lunch mains $10-12, dinner mains $22-25) The resort-trendy, bustling, brick-walled space features an extensive wine list and protein-rich mains: typically chargrilled rack of lamb with a pistachio and mustard cream sauce ($24).

Getting There & Around

Greyhound Canada connects Collingwood with Barrie ($19, one hour, three daily) on the Owen Sound route. **Ace Cabs** (☎ 705-445-3300) can drive you between Collingwood and Blue Mountain ($15, 15 minutes).

MIDLAND

The small commercial center of Midland is the most interesting of the Huronia region's towns. The Huron-Ouendat first settled this area, and developed a confederacy to encourage cooperation among the neighboring Aboriginal peoples. The established Huron-Ouendat settlements attracted French explorers and, more critically, Jesuit missionaries. The Jesuits' legacy forms th basis of several of Midland's contemporary attractions.

Information

Midland Chamber of Commerce (☎ 705-526-7884, 800-263-7745; 208 King St; ☾ 9am-5pm Mon-Fri, 11am-4pm Sat & Sun)

Sights & Activities

A short walk from downtown, Little Lake Park contains **Huronia Museum & Huron-Ouendat Village** (☎ 705-526-2844; www.huroniamuseum.com; 549 Little Lake Park Rd; adult/youth/senior $6/4.50/5.50; ☾ 9am-6pm Jul & Aug, 9am-5pm Sep-Jun, closed Sun Jan-Mar). The village is a replica of 500-year-old Huron-Ouendat settlement (from before the French Jesuits arrived on their soul-saving mission). The museum has a few aboriginal artifacts and lots of more modern memorabilia (check out the Slenderizer, c 1958). Admission covers both sites.

For a good complement to the village, visit **Ste-Marie among the Hurons** (☎ 705-526-7838; www.saintemarieamongthehurons.on.ca; Hwy 12; adult/student $11/9.50; ☾ 10am-5pm May-Thanksgiving). This historic site 5km from Midland reconstructs the 17th-century Jesuit mission, and costumed guides answer questions. Graphic depictions of the deaths by torture of some of the missionaries were etched into the minds of older Canadians by now-discarded history books. The **Martyrs' Shrine** (☎ 705-526-3788; adult/child $3/free; ☾ 8:30am-9pm Victoria Day–Thanksgiving), opposite the Ste-Marie complex, is a monument to six missionaries and is the site of pilgrimages each year. In 1984 even the pope showed up.

Right beside the Ste-Marie site, the **Wye Marsh Wildlife Centre** (☎ 705-526-7809; admission $7; ☾ 10am-6pm Jul & Aug, 10am-4pm Sep-Jun) provides boardwalks, trails and an observation deck over the marsh and its birdlife, including the much-trumpeted trumpeter swans, back from the brink of extinction. Guided walks are offered free with admission, and canoe tours through the marsh cost $5.

Midland is also known for its **murals**, which are painted on more than 30 buildings downtown. The murals were painted between 1990 and 2001 as part of a program to improve the business area, and depict local historical and modern scenes in fine detail.

From the town dock, 2½-hour boat tours cruise the inside passage to Georgian Bay and the islands around Honey Harbor aboard the *Miss Midland*. They're operated by **Midland Tours** (☎ 705-549-3388, 888-833-2628; www.midlandtours.com; adult/student/family $20/15/50; ☽ Victoria Day–Thanksgiving) and depart at 1.45pm daily, with extra departures on weekends from June to August.

Sleeping & Eating

Park Villa (☎ 705-526-2219, 888-891-1190; 751 Yonge St; r $90) This large, reliable motel has been recently renovated. The location is handy to downtown.

Galerie Gale (☎ 705-526-8102; www.galeriegale .com; 431 King St; r $75-105) This Tudor-style B&B is elegant yet invitingly eclectic, featuring abstract artwork by one of the owners, a full-time artist. There is a separate lounge area for guests, and the house is within walking distance of downtown.

Little Lake Inn (☎ 705-526-2750, 888-297-6130; www.littlelakeinn.com; 669 Yonge St; r $115-125) This B&B is in a modern home with fantastic lake views. Each room has a whirlpool, and the owner is happy for guests to use her Internet access. Old-fashioned hospitality with contemporary comforts.

Globe Delicatessen & Coffee Place (☎ 705-526-7960; 478 Elizabeth St; mains $5-7; ☽ 9:30am-4pm Mon-Wed, to 5pm Thu & Fri, 9:30am-3pm Sat) This glorious deli is unusual in the region, but steeped in tradition. One group of German women who emigrated to Canada in the 1950s have been coming here for lunch every Friday for 30 years. Goulash with spaetzle is served every Tuesday ($7), and the other specials change regularly.

Riv Bistro (☎ 705-526-9432; 249 King St; mains $7-15; ☽ lunch Mon-Fri year-round, dinner May-Oct, Sat & Sun Nov-Apr) Great food with a Mediterranean slant is the norm at this small but classy eatery.

Cellarman's Ale House (☎ 705-526-8223; 337 King St; mains $8-17) This dark, intimate British-style pub even has an intimate location, tucked away off King St. Snuggle up with a steak and kidney pie ($8) and a beer, and enjoy live Celtic music some evenings.

Getting There & Away

Greyhound Canada buses connect Barrie with Midland ($19, one hour, two daily).

PENETANGUISHENE

Little 'Penetang,' as it's usually known, reels in gazillions of boaters and fishers baited by the waters around the 30,000 islands that dot Georgian Bay between Penetang and Parry Sound. **Georgian Bay Islands National Park** (☎ 705-756-2414, 888-773-8888; www.pc.gc.ca/pn-np/on/ georg; ☽ mid-May–Thanksgiving) encompasses 59 of the islands, and is accessible only by boat.

Penetang is one of three towns from which you can explore the waterways on a boat tour. From the dock area, cruises on the **Georgian Queen** (☎ 705-549-7795, 800-363-7447; www.georgian baycruises.com; adult/student $20/15; ☽ May-Aug) sail daily during June and August. In May, tours are held daily on Saturday and Sunday only. Compared with the cruises from Midland (p161), these ones are longer (three hours), go past more islands, and happen on a bigger boat, so you're less likely to feel queasy. For the biggest boat of all, head to Parry Sound for the *Island Queen* (p170).

Discovery Harbour (☎ 705-549-8064; Church St; adult/student $5.50/4.50; ☽ 10am-5pm Jul & Aug, 10am-5pm Mon-Fri Victoria Day–Jun) is a reconstructed naval base north of the town center. The original base was built by the British after the War of 1812 in case the American forces came back for more, but they didn't. It features reconstructed ships, and there are daily sailing programs aboard two of these. Admission prices include a guided tour.

Just north of Penetang, **Awenda Provincial Park** (☎ 705-549-2231; Awenda Park Rd; day use per vehicle $9.50; ☽ mid-May–mid-Oct) is small but worthy. It's attractive to day visitors for its four fine beaches connected by easy trails.

Penetang is only minutes up the road from Midland, which is your best bet for overnight stays. Greyhound Canada connects Penetanguishene with Barrie ($14, 1¼ hours, three daily).

ORILLIA

At the north end of Lake Simcoe, Orillia has a strong boating culture, being a major link in the Trent-Severn Waterway (see p210). From town, pleasure craft cruise the canal and Lake Couchiching. The town gets a lot of tourist traffic, being on Hwy 11 and close to Hwy 400.

Information

Tourist office (☎ 705-326-4424; 150 Front St S)

Sights

Orillia was the home of humorist Stephen Leacock, whose *Sunshine Sketches of a Little Town* was based on the place. In 1928 he built a house that is now the **Leacock Museum** (☎ 705-329-1908; www.leacockmuseum.com; 50 Museum Dr; adult/child $5/4; ☯ 10am-5pm Jun-Aug, 10am-5pm Mon-Fri May & Sep). In late July the museum hosts the Leacock Summer Festival, a well-regarded literary festival; tickets to readings cost $5 to $10.

The historic **Orillia Opera House** (☎ 705-326-8011; www.operahouse.orillia.on.ca; 20 Mississaga St W) hosts productions including those of the popular **Sunshine Festival Theatre Company** (☎ 800-683-8747; www.sunshinefestival.ca), whose season runs from June to December and features the likes of *Cats* and *Oklahoma!*

The **Island Princess** (☎ 705-325-2628; www .orilliacruises.com; adult $12-16, child $6-8; ☯ mid-Jun–Thanksgiving) leaves from the dock at 2:15pm daily, with up to four cruises a day in July and August. Lunch and dinner cruises cost roughly double the prices listed here, and reservations are required for these. If you're only going to do one cruise while you're in the area and it's dramatic scenery you seek, the cruises on Georgian Bay departing from Midland (p161), Penetanguishene (opposite) and Parry Sound (p169) are a better bet.

Aboriginal-owned **Casino Rama** (☎ 888-817-7262; Rama Rd; admission free; ☯ 24hr) is also a stage for the touring circuit: think Drew Carey, Pat Boone and Air Supply.

Sleeping

HI Orillia Home Hostel (☎ 705-325-0970; fax 705-325-9826; 198 Borland St E; dm members/nonmembers $16/20) It's a good idea to insist on seeing one of the rooms before you check in, because they will be too small or stuffy for some travelers' comfort. Good luck – you'll need all your powers of persuasion if our experience is anything to go by.

Bayview Inn (☎ 705-330-0290, 866-543-8996; 341 Atherley Rd; r $70-80) This motel is comfortable, clean and cheerfully predictable – right down to some noise from the busy road outside.

Cranberry House (☎ 705-326-6871, 866-876-5885; cranberryhouse@encode.com; 25 Dalton Cres S; r $100-125) Dalton Cres feels like the set for a wholesome, family-friendly movie, probably one with Christmas involved. Every (modern) house on the street is impeccably groomed on the outside, and Cranberry House is no exception. Inside, the owner can't do enough to help her guests.

Stone Gate Inn (☎ 705-329-2535, 877-674-5542; www.stonegateinn.com; 437 Laclie St; r $110-140) Orillia's newest and most luxurious hotel acommodation offers stylish rooms incongruously surrounded by parking lots and the Beer Store.

Eating

La Mezzaluna Cafe and Art Gallery (☎ 705-329-4684; 133 Mississaga St E; mains $6-9; ☯ 8:30am-8pm

---

SNOWMOBILING IN ONTARIO

The stereotypical snowmobiler is a hard-drinkin', hard-ridin' man who likes the outdoors most when it's whizzing by at high speed, but women and families are active in recreational clubs across Ontario as well. Rising insurance costs are changing the demographic of the sport, and snowmobilers are perceived by some parts of the travel industry as wallets with motors. Snowmobiling has a severe-injury rate about three times higher than that of either snowboarding or skiing (when a snowmobiler takes on a tree or a not-quite-frozen lake at 90km/h, nature usually wins).

Ontario's system of recreational snowmobile trails is the longest in the world at 46,000km. Throughout the province thousands of motels and lodges cater to this subculture, and it's not uncommon to see motels advertising snowmobile parking with video security. Orillia's casino has an area set aside for the purpose. Also in Orillia, **Cottage Country Tours** (☎ 705-325-0111, 800-298-2979; 452 Jamieson Dr) provides short snowmobile tours starting at $150 for 2½ hours, ranging up to $315 for a day; rates include all gear. For this and other winter activities, the peak season is January and February.

For more information on snowmobiling in the province, visit the website of the **Ontario Federation of Snowmobile Clubs** (www.ofsc.on.ca).

Tue-Fri, 8:30am-4pm Sat & Mon, 10am-4pm Sun) With its wooden floors, pressed-metal ceilings and espresso coffee this café will make you want to linger even though the food is better at other places on the same street.

Picasso's (☎ 705-326-8254, 888-214-8776; 121 Mississaga St E; lunch mains $8-12, dinner mains $22-36; ☽ lunch Tue-Fri, dinner Tue-Sat) Picasso's *Weeping Woman* would not have wept here, unless it were for pleasure at finding a French-Canadian bistro in Orillia. She might have started with the creamy French lentil soup with duck breast ($8), then cried out for more of the Ontario lamb rack with Dijon crust and port reduction ($34). And if she were vegetarian she'd have plenty of choices, including tomato and goat cheese napoleon ($8).

Cosmo's Ristorante (☎ 705-327-8330; 90 Mississaga St E; pasta $11-18; mains $15-24; ☽ lunch Tue-Fri, dinner Tue-Sat) Almost everything about Cosmo's hangs together: the formal service, the Italian crooner on the stereo. But what's that sports screen doing above the bar? Never mind, because even the spaghetti with meatballs ($11), that old standby, is made special with fresh herbs.

Getting There & Away
Ontario Northland buses connect Orillia with Toronto ($24, two hours, four daily) on the Sudbury route.

GRAVENHURST
Once a logging and shipping centre, Gravenhurst still feels more like a working town than nearby Bracebridge (20km away), which is the pick of the two for overnight stays.

Gravenhurst Chamber of Commerce (☎ 705-687-4432; www.gravenhurstchamber.com; 685 Muskoka Rd N; ☽ 8:30am-4:30pm Mon-Fri) provides visitor information.

Muskoka Fleet (☎ 705-687-6667; www.muskokafleet .com; 820 Bay St; ☽ Victoria Day–Thanksgiving) offers sightseeing cruises on two very different boats. The *Segwun* is a much-loved restored steamboat that, in a previous incarnation, delivered mail to Muskoka resorts and villages not served by railways in the days before cars. The *Wenonah II* is a bigger, old-style but newly built diesel ship. Both offer various cruises incorporating an optional breakfast, brunch, lunch or dinner (cruises from $22, with food from $35). 'Millionaires row' cruises take in a shoreline of grand summer homes.

Bethune Memorial House (☎ 705-687-4261; 235 John St N; admission $3; ☽ 10am-5pm mid-May–Oct) honors Canadian doctor Norman Bethune, who traveled throughout China in the 1930s as a surgeon and educator. Outside summer, hours are changeable.

In summer, thousands flock to **Music on the Barge** (☎ 705-687-3412; Gull Lake Park; admission by donation) to hear big-band numbers, jazz or country and western. Shows start at 7:30pm each Sunday from late June to late August.

Gravenhurst Opera House (☎ 705-687-5550, 888-495-8888; Muskoka Rd S) presents a busy season of professional theater through July and August.

Another draw is the especially good **farmers' market** (☎ 705-684-8731; Gull Lake Park; ☽ 9am-2pm Wed mid-May–early Oct) where you can pick up smoked trout, organic produce and local crafts.

At the time of research, work had just begun on a massive Gravenhurst waterfront development called **Muskoka Wharf**. A heritage and interpretive center, restaurants, accommodations, galleries and a pavilion for the farmers' market were to feature, and could make the town's restaurant scene more inviting. The completion date was unknown; for updates, visit the town's official website (www.gravenhurst.ca).

Ontario Northland runs buses between Toronto and Gravenhurst ($31, 2½ hours, six daily) on the North Bay route. The stopping point in Gravenhurst is the **train station** (☎ 705-687-2301; 150 2nd Ave). Ontario Northland also operates trains on the same route ($33, 2½ hours, six weekly).

BRACEBRIDGE
Bracebridge has instant appeal. Its natural beauty comes from its setting right on the Muskoka River, and there are more than 20 waterfalls in the town and surrounding area, including the 16m Bracebridge Falls in the centre of town. This power source for the nearby mills helped the area to prosperity.

Information
Bracebridge Visitor Centre (☎ 705-645-5231; 1 Manitoba St; ☽ 9am-5pm Mon-Fri, 10am-4pm Sat year-round, also noon-4pm Sun May-Sep)

Sights & Activities
Bracebridge Falls come as a surprise in such a developed area. They're right at the visitor

centre, and paved paths along the river lead to viewpoints. **Muskoka Falls**, also known as South Falls, are about 6km south of town off Hwy 11. With a height of 33m, they're the highest in Muskoka. **Wilson's Falls** and **High Falls**, both just north of town, are very impressive, and there are walking trails in the area. All the falls are at their most thunderous in spring.

Bracebridge and the whole Muskoka area are dotted with the studios of artists working in many different media. Landscape painting, jewelry, ceramics and woodwork are especially well represented, and many artists open their studios to the public by appointment or during annual self-guided studio tours. These typically run for a weekend and enable you to visit for free as many places as you can drive to during the two days. The **Muskoka Autumn Studio Tour** (www.muskoka.com/tour) happens each September. In Bracebridge, a good point of contact for information on the studios is the **Arts Council of Muskoka** (☎ 705-646-9511; www.artscouncilofmuskoka.com; 111 Manitoba St).

Muskoka Cottage Brewery (☎ 705-646-1266, 800-881-4229; www.muskokabrewery.com; 13 Taylor Rd) offers free tours of its operations hourly on Friday and Saturday in July and August. Tours last 20 minutes, and conclude with tastings of the four brews (a great cream ale, two lagers and a dark ale) in the retail store on site, which is open all year during business hours.

The **Lady Muskoka** (☎ 705-646-2628, 800-263-5239; www.ladymuskoka.com; adult/child $18/9; ☺ Victoria Day–Thanksgiving) offers cruises of the Muskoka River and Lake Muskoka several times daily in July and August, and less often in other months. Brunch/dinner cruises cost $28/45 for adults and half that for children. Cruises last 2¾ hours and take in the lake's 'millionaires row' of sumptuous summer homes. They depart from Riverside Inn off Ecclestone Dr.

The most peaceful way to explore Muskoka's lakes and rivers is by kayak or canoe, both available for rent at **Muskoka Outfitters** (☎ 705-646-0492; www.muskokaoutfitters.com; 60 Manitoba St; ☺ 9am-6pm Mon-Sat, noon-5pm Sun). The staff here also run regular short guided trips between late June and August, specializing in sea kayaking. A day of paddling including instruction, gear rental and lunch costs $80. Organized winter options include ice climbing; shopfront hours are shorter then.

Sleeping

Riverview B&B (☎ 705-645-4022, 888-998-9961; 420 Beaumont Dr; s $35-40, d $70-80) True to its name, this place has river views, and for solo travelers the value for money is exceptional.

Wellington Motel (☎ 705-645-2238; 265 Wellington St; r $90-100) Considering its location near the highway, the Wellington feels quiet and secluded. It's fairly new, and the rooms have standard-issue equipment plus video players.

Pine Lodge (☎ 705-385-2271; www.pinelodgeinn .com; 10 Muskoka Rd, Port Sydney; s $105-120, d $140-160) Pine Lodge is great for families, with huge communal areas and homey furnishings. It's very easy-going with nothing too fancy, within sight of the water in a rural area about 15 minutes by car north of Bracebridge, halfway to Huntsville. Rates include dinner and breakfast; costs vary widely depending on group size and length of stay.

Bay House (☎ 705-645-7508; www.bbmuskoka .com/bayhouse; 2 Dominion St; r $115-168) What you're paying for here is the setting. It doesn't come any more perfect than this, almost on the water, surrounded by trees. The B&B is modern, there's a separate guest lounge, and breakfasts are extra special (orange and walnut French toast with honey orange sauce, for example).

Inn at the Falls (☎ 705-645-2245, 877-645-9212; www.innatthefalls.net; 1 Dominion St; s $100-160, d $110-170) The inn is a local landmark and a destination in itself. The building dates from the 1870s, and the 'estate' now includes six neighboring houses as well. The communal areas are charmingly decorated in period style, and some of the bedrooms are magnificent – you'll need a set of stairs to reach the king bed in the William Mullock room. Fortunately, one is provided. The inn has its own restaurant and pub.

Eating

Marty's Coffeehouse (no ☎ ; 5 Manitoba St; mains $5-8) Butter tarts are ubiquitous across Canada. But don't form an opinion on them until you've tried Marty's version ($2.25). This is the butter tart at its evolutionary peak, with perfectly flaky pastry and a molten, caramelized middle. Bite, then suck, then follow with an espresso chaser. This cozy café with hardwood floors also offers soup and sandwiches.

Fox & Hounds (☎ 705-645-2245, 877-645-9212; 1 Dominion St; mains $11-16) The low-ceilinged, faux-English pub at the Inn at the Falls offers typical pub fare in an atypically classy setting. Head out the back for a great Muskoka patio.

Riverwalk (☎ 705-646 0711; 1 Manitoba St; lunch mains $9-17, dinner mains $25-30) Riverwalk brings together a stunning falls-side setting and a seasonal menu that capitalizes on local produce. Maple syrup from the region features in the house-cured Atlantic salmon on yucca root ($13), and local chanterelles are a highlight of the seared duck breast with balsamic-glazed peaches ($29).

Inn at the Falls (☎ 705-645-2245, 877-645-9212; 1 Dominion St; mains $25-35) The formal dining room at the inn features water views from a setting that's elevated both literally and figuratively. The dinner menu is small but special: seared medallions of Ontario elk with roasted garlic, wild mushrooms and saffron-truffle cream sauce ($25) were one of four choices when we visited.

Drinking

Old Station (☎ 705-645-9776; 88 Manitoba St) On summer evenings this is the most happening place in town. The patio overlooks the main drag – perfect for post-kayak recovery sessions, and recommended by local outfitters. Settle in with a pint of Muskoka ale from the brewery just over the road.

Getting There & Away

Ontario Northland buses connect Bracebridge with Toronto ($33, 2¾ hours, six daily) on the North Bay route.

HUNTSVILLE

Muskoka's largest town has a pleasant, historic feel. It's not much of a travel destination in itself, but it is the last major place for supplies west of Algonquin and it can be used as a base for day trips into the park.

The **chamber of commerce** (☎ 705-789-4771; 8 West St N; ☾ 9am-5pm Mon-Fri, 10am-3pm Sat) provides visitor information.

Heritage Place (☎ 705-789-7576; www.muskoka heritageplace.org; 88 Brunel Rd; adult/child/family $18/16/60; ☾ May-Oct), spread over 90 acres, has two museums, a pioneer village and a steam train, which give some historical perspective to the region.

During the first three weeks of July, Huntsville hosts a **Festival of the Arts** (☎ 705-788-2787, 800-663-2787; www.huntsvillefestival.on.ca) featuring classical music, jazz, theater, dance and literary events around town.

Algonquin Retreat B&B (☎ 705-789-4115; 7 Forestview Dr; r $60-95) has very friendly, welcoming hosts, and you'll be sharing close quarters with them. The house is in a treed residential area.

A dated but attractive choice is **Sunset Inn Motel** (☎ 705-789-4414, 866-874-5360; www.sunsetinn motel.com; 69 Main St W; r $100), which is clean and comfortable, with rooms set well back from the highway, overlooking the water.

King William Inn (☎ 705-789-9661, 888-995-9169; www.kingwilliaminn.com; 23 King William St; r $100-130), which has new-looking furnishings, is one of the better independent motels in town.

Double Scotts Michelle's Pub (☎ 705-788-3014; 34 Main St E; mains $6-8) – is it a café or is it a pub? It doesn't matter when you get free cookies at the bar in a quirky, narrow space.

Foodies may bypass **Louis's II Restaurant** (☎ 705-789-5704; 24 Main St E; dinner mains $6-12; ☾ 7am-9pm) because they don't know that beyond the vinyl booths and fake plants lies fresh trout, simply pan-friend, with a salad of mixed greens ($12). Whatever you order, have it with mashed potato and gravy. Great comfort food.

River Bend (☎ 705-788-9484; 8 Park Dr; lunch mains $8-12, dinner mains $18-28), outside the town centre, is well worth seeking out for its bistro fare and waterside setting. The quinoa, the smoked-tomato pasta and the goat cheese salad are good vegetarian choices, but roast duck and braised lamb shanks feature too.

Ontario Northland runs buses between Huntsville and Toronto ($41, 3¼ hours, six daily) on the North Bay route. The stopping point is **Huntsville Travel** (☎ 705-789-6431; 3 Main St E). It also operates trains on the same route ($43, three hours, six weekly).

ALGONQUIN PROVINCIAL PARK (WEST)

Algonquin is one of Canada's best-known parks, and Ontario's oldest and largest. It was established in 1893 and comprises about 7800 sq km of semiwilderness: a vast landscape of forests, cliffs, rivers, bogs and thousands (thousands!) of lakes. Along with Killarney and the Temagami wilderness region, Algonquin is one of Ontario's most

---

HOW TO FIND SECLUSION IN ALGONQUIN

Algonquin's popularity can't be overstated. The park's excellent facilities are a boon to young families and adventurers of all levels of experience who want easy access to the outdoors and a sociable camping experience. This can mean a very, very busy Hwy 60 corridor.

If it's seclusion you seek, try these tips:

- For drive-in camping, book a site at one of the 'satellite' campgrounds away from Hwy 60. Kiosk, Brent and Achray campgrounds are all accessible via Hwy 17 north of the park. You'll have to drive a lot further, but it's worth it for the secluded feel.

- Avoid starting your canoe trip at Canoe Lake or Opeongo Lake. If you do start at Opeongo Lake, take a water taxi up the lake to avoid a long paddle and to get you into wilder areas.

- Even if you've done only a little backcountry camping, don't be afraid to aim for a canoe-in campsite. Some are only a few kilometers from Hwy 60, no more than an hour's paddle.

- Don't go in mid-June, because getting away from the blackflies is as important as getting away from the crowds.

- Do go in September, when the thickest crowds have left.

- Do go midweek.

- Don't let any of this put you off going!

---

easily accessible outdoor gems, a must-see for canoeists and hikers.

Orientation

The one major road through the park, Hwy 60, runs across its southern edge, via Huntsville. This corridor is 'lined' (relatively) with campgrounds, hiking trails and lodges. Lesser used roads make the park accessible from the west, north and east. For information on the eastern end of the park, see p212.

Away from all those areas with road access is the vast interior, which is accessible only via about 2000km of charted canoe routes and some hiking trails. Locations within the park are usually described in terms of their distance from the 'west gate,' which is not really a gate at all, but rather a point that marks the western boundary of the park on Hwy 60.

Information

The park is open year-round. You can take Hwy 60 through the park for free, but to stop you must pay the day-use fee ($12 per vehicle). The Hwy 60 corridor has cell phone coverage for a couple of kilometers on each side of the road, as well as some payphones.

Algonquin Visitor Centre (☎ 613-637-2828; www .algonquinpark.on.ca; Hwy 60; ☼ 10am-5pm mid-Apr–Oct, to 9pm mid-Jun–Sep, 10am-4pm Sat & Sun Nov– mid-Apr) This world-class visitor center is worth a visit in its own right. Displays and dioramas illustrate the park's wildlife, history and geology in ways that will appeal equally to adults and children, and the viewing platform gives spectacular views. The center also has a bookstore and a cafeteria. It's 43km inside the west gate. Opening hours vary almost by the week, but are never shorter than those given here.

Information Centre (☎ 705-633-5572; www.algon quinpark.on.ca; Hwy 60; ☼ 8am-4:30pm) You can also talk to park staff at this smaller center, just inside the west gate.

Sights

The opportunities for **wildlife-watching** in Algonquin are superb, even (or particularly) on Hwy 60. Along this road you're almost certain to see moose, especially in spring when the animals are attracted to the salt left over from winter de-icing. Deer, beavers, otters, mink and many bird species can be seen if you choose the right time of day, especially if you're gliding along a river in a canoe.

The excellent **Logging Museum** (☎ 613-637-2828; Hwy 60; admission free; ☼ 9am-5pm mid-May–mid-Oct) has extensive exhibits and interpretation of the park's logging heritage. The displays are spread along a 1km trail that remains open even when the reception area, bookstore and theater are closed. The museum is located 55km from the park's west gate, just inside the east gate.

DON'T BE A LONE WOLF

Algonquin Provincial Park is very active in wolf research, and public wolf howls are an incredible way to experience the presence of wolves. Wolves will readily respond to human imitations of their howling, so park staff conduct communal 'howling sessions' some Thursday nights in August. These events are highly organized, and you could be one of 2000 or more people standing beside their cars in the darkness waiting for park naturalists to initiate the howling. There is no guarantee that a wolf howl will be held on any particular night or in any particular place – it all depends on the presence of wolves in a location somewhere near Hwy 60. Wolf howls are announced only on the days they are actually held, so check the bulletin boards or phone the visitor center on a Thursday in August.

Activities

If you have only one wilderness adventure while you're in Ontario, consider making it a canoe trip in Algonquin. No park is better set up for novice paddlers, because the outfitters are used to helping people who don't really know where to start but want to give it a go.

Summer weekends are especially busy and a quota system at each canoe-route access point has been established, so book ahead. Many people begin their trip at Canoe Lake or Opeongo Lake, which are super-convenient, but you might have to queue to launch. Water taxis can whisk you up Opeongo Lake, avoiding a long, rough paddle and getting you into the wilder areas (make reservations through Algonquin Outfitters). The further in you get by portaging, the more solitude you'll find.

Hiking in the park is also popular, and there are 140km of trails, including many short ones off or near Hwy 60 that can be enjoyed as part of a day trip.

Outfitters located in and around the park offer rentals of just about everything you might need to get going, from canoes ($18 to $33), packed food ($25 per person) and tents ($12) to sleeping bags, sleeping pads and stoves ($3 to $6 each). All prices are per day. Those most conveniently located:

Algonquin North Wilderness Outfitters (☎ 705-744-3265; www.algonquinnorth.com; Hwy 17) This outfitter isn't on Hwy 60, it's on Hwy 17 at Hwy 630; great for more secluded northern access.

Algonquin Outfitters (☎ 705-635-2243, 800-469-4948; www.algonquinoutfitters.com) At four locations in and around the park: Oxtongue Lake, Huntsville, Opeongo Lake and Brent. Rents everything you could need; highly recommended.

Canoe Algonquin (☎ 705-636-5956; Hwy 518 E, Kearney) Located north of Huntsville; putting in at the nearby western access points gets you to a peaceful setting almost instantly.

Portage Store (☎ 705-633-5622; www.portagestore .com; Hwy 60) Located 14km inside the park's west gate.

Tours

The outfitters offer some guided trips, particularly Algonquin Outfitters, whose trips have an excellent reputation. However, that's not the main focus of most outfitters. The operators listed here offer everything from three-day trips aimed at beginners ($300 to $400) to customized remote adventures that last as long as your stamina allows. All have their own lodge base. For help with choosing, see p174.

Call of the Wild (☎ 416-200-9453, 800-776-9453; www.callofthewild.ca)

Canadian Wilderness Trips (☎ 416-960-2298; www .canadianwildernesstrips.com)

Northern Edge Algonquin (☎ 800-953-3343; www .algonquincanada.com)

Voyageur Quest (☎ 416-496-3605, 800-794-9660; www.voyageurquest.com)

Sleeping & Eating

Within the park itself, you have four main choices: camp at one of 11 campgrounds accessible by car, camp in the backcountry (accessible only by canoe or hiking), stay in one of the park service's yurts (basic tent-like roofed structures), or sleep in comfort at one of the three top-end resorts. Along with the cafeteria at the information centre, the resorts are the only places in the park where you can buy meals. Outside the park boundaries there are many choices, mostly motels, cottages and family-style resorts, along or near Hwy 60, many of which have attached restaurants. If you're not camping and budget is a big consideration, consider staying in Huntsville (p166), which is close enough to allow day trips (it's 43km from the west gate). It's also the best place for self-caterers to stock up on supplies.

BUDGET

To make camping and yurt reservations you must contact the centralized reservation service for **Ontario Parks** (☎ 519-826-5290, 888-668-7275; www.ontarioparks.com), not Algonquin itself. Some sites are available on a first-come, first-served basis, but reservations are strongly recommended. Car camping costs from $22 to $30 per site, the yurts cost $65 and backcountry camping costs $9 per person.

Wolf Den (☎ 705-635-9336; www.wolfdenbunkhouse .com; 3429 Hwy 60, Oxtongue Lake; dm $18, s/d $50/54) This backpacker hostel has great facilities and a good buzz. Most of the beds are in log cabins. It's a five minute drive west of the park.

MID-RANGE

Blue Spruce Resort (☎ 705-635-2330; www.blues pruce.ca; Hwy 60; r $115-130, cottages per week $850-1130) Everything at Blue Spruce is superbly presented: even the smallest rooms are enormous and have full kitchens. Kids are well catered for, with cribs, play pens and high chairs available for rent. Blue Spruce is 7km west of the park.

Dwight Village Motel (☎ 705-635-2400; www.dw ightvillagemotel.com; 2801 Hwy 60; r $110) The friendliness of the owners sets this place apart. The rooms are small, but very modern and spotlessly clean. It's 25km west of the park right on the highway, just east of the village of Dwight.

Lakewoods Cottage Resort (☎ 705-635-2087; www.lakewoods-resort.net; Oxtongue Lake Rd; cottages $80-180) The cottages here are basic, spacious and well equipped with furniture you won't have to tip-toe around. Each one sleeps a different number of people, from two to eight. In July and August the minimum stay is one week. It's roughly 10km west of the park.

Algonquin Inn (☎ 705-635-2434, 800-387-2244; www .algonquininn.com; Hwy 60, Oxtongue Lake; r $100, cottages per week $1000-1200) This is more of a big motel than an inn, so the atmosphere isn't electric, but the rooms with water views are pleasant. The complex is 11km west of the park.

TOP END

All of these resorts, the only permanent accommodations inside the park, include breakfast and dinner in their rates. Prices given here are based on double occupancy.

The dining rooms are open to nonguests; none of them is licensed, but it's fine to bring your own alcohol. All operate from mid-May to mid-October.

Bartlett Lodge (☎ 705-633-5543; www.bartlett lodge.com; cabins per person $205) One especially interesting cabin sets this place apart: 'Sunrise' is totally solar powered. Bartlett Lodge is accessed by boat (provided for you) from a point 23km inside the west gate. For nonguests, breakfast costs $14, dinner from $45.

Arowhon Pines (☎ 705-633-5661; www.arowhon pines.ca; r per person $190, cabins per person $245-315) While Bartlett Lodge is wonderfully secluded, Arowhon is made private by being well north of Hwy 60; the turn-off is 15km inside the west gate. It has a spectacular dining room and a very good reputation for its food; reservations are not necessary for lunch ($25) but they are for dinner (around $45).

Killarney Lodge (☎ 705-633-5551; www.killarney lodge.com; Hwy 60; r per person $200, cabins per person $215-270) The bright paintwork is what first strikes guests: some like it; others find it a little incongruous in a provincial park. The lodge is 33km inside the west gate.

Getting There & Away

The park's west gate is 43km from Huntsville. **Hammond Transportation** (☎ 705-645-5431; www.hammondtransportation.com) runs a shuttle service in July and August between Huntsville and the park ($28, three weekly). It connects with Ontario Northland buses to and from Huntsville on Monday, Wednesday and Friday. Buses depart **Huntsville Travel** (☎ 705-789-6431; 3 Main St E) at 1:15pm, and stop in the park at Oxtongue Lake (near the west gate), the Portage Store (14km inside the west gate) and the Lake of Two Rivers (32km inside the west gate), leaving the Lake of Two Rivers at 2:30pm to return to Huntsville.

PARRY SOUND

Parry Sound, like Midland and Penetanguishene, is very busy in summer as a base for boaters exploring the 30,000 islands area of Georgian Bay. It's the largest (population 6500) of the small towns between southern Georgian Bay and Sudbury.

Information

Parry Sound Visitor Information Centre (☎ 705-378-5105; Hwy 69; ☼ 10am-5pm Sun-Fri, to 6pm Sat Victoria Day–Thanksgiving, 9am-4pm Mon-Sat &

10am-4pm Sun Thanksgiving–Victoria Day) On the east side of the highway about 12km south of town.

Sights & Activities

The **Charles W Stockey Centre** (☎ 705-746-4466; www.charleswstockeycentre.com; 2 Bay St) incorporates the **Bobby Orr Hall of Fame** (10am-6pm Tue-Sat, noon-6pm Sun; adult/child $8/6). For the uninitiated, Bobby Orr was a superb ice-hockey player born in Parry Sound, a Boston Bruins defenseman in the 1960s and '70s who changed the role of that position forever with his offensive prowess. At this huge shrine to the great man you can strap on the pads and face an automated puck-firing machine, play air hockey or announce a game.

An adventurous way to explore the area's waterways is on a paddling trip with **White Squall** (☎ 705-342-5324; www.whitesquall.com; 53 Carling Bay Rd, Nobel; 9am-5:30pm Apr-Thanksgiving, to 8pm Fri Jul & Aug), based about 18km northwest of Parry Sound. One of the owners has been described as the father of kayaking in Ontario, so you couldn't be in better hands. This company runs an extensive program of short trips on Georgian Bay, priced at around $53 for half a day, and $105 to $120 for a full day. Longer trips ($600 to $730) have themes such as yoga, geology, photography, gourmet food or astronomy. In Parry Sound itself you can get information from the company's **retail store** (☎ 705-746-4936; 19 James St; 9:30am-5:30pm Mon-Sat). Many of White Squall's staff are as passionate about roots and folk music as they are about paddling, and you can buy some of the hard-to-find tracks listed on p180 at the store.

If you're less adventurous, you can cruise the 30,000 islands on the 550-passenger **Island Queen** (☎ 705-746-2311, 800-506-2628; 9 Bay St; adult/child $25/12.50; Jun-Thanksgiving). Trips push off at 2pm daily, with extra (10am) departures in July and August. Another option is the little tugboat **MV Chippewa III** (☎ 705-746-6064, 888-283-5870; www.georgianbaycruise.com; 99 Champaigne St; Jun-Oct). It operates a less regular schedule of lunch cruises (adult/child $28/14 plus lunch) and dinner cruises (adult/child $48/22.50).

Parry Sound hosts a nationally renowned annual festival of classical music, the **Festival of the Sound** (☎ 705-746-2410, 866-364-0061; www.festivalofthesound.on.ca; mid-Jul–early Aug). Individual ticket prices start at $16, and 'festival passports' start at $375.

For information on two provincial parks close to Parry Sound, see p172.

Sleeping & Eating

Trapper's Choice (☎ 705-746-9491; 50 Joseph St; r $75) Roomy, quiet and sweet-smelling, Trapper's Choice passes all the tests of a decent budget motel.

Victoria Manor (☎ 705-746-5399; www.solutionsforu.com/victoria; 43 Church St; s/d with shared bathroom $75/85, ste $110) This Victorian B&B has a tenderly kept garden and spacious rooms with some period furnishings. There is a lounge area for guests, and it's all within walking distance of the centre of town.

Country Gourmet (☎ 705-746-5907; 65 James St; mains $4-7; 7am-4pm Mon-Fri, 8am-4pm Sat) Parry Sound's best bakery has date squares, brownies and cinnamon buns big enough to share ($1.75), light meals like spanakopita ($7), ample seating and espresso coffee.

Wellington's (☎ 705-746-1333; 105 James St; mains $6-16) Memorabilia lines the walls of this cozy, low-ceilinged pub where the menu is full of happy pub-meal surprises. The vegetarian nutburger is made with brown rice, peanuts, wheatgerm and alfalfa ($6.25), and pastas can be prepared as usual or with rice noodles or soba noodles. Meat options such as the Canadian burger ($9.50) are juicy good.

Getting There & Away

Ontario Northland buses connect Parry Sound with Toronto ($45, 3¾ hours, three daily) on the Sudbury route.

BRITT

Britt is a peaceful, tiny place bypassed by almost everyone driving up or down Hwy 69 between Parry Sound and Killarney. Its history is as a sawmill town, but in more recent years its stand-out country inn, the **Little Britt Inn** (☎ 705-383-0028, 888-383-4555; www.zeuter.com/~lilbritt; Hwy 526; r $105-125), has built a reputation among foodies who are prepared to travel to far-flung places for regional food. Not that it's an earnest grain-fed-everything sort of place – the kids' menu in the more casual downstairs restaurant features fried liver with onions, broccoli and green olives, priced according to the noisiness of the kids. Upstairs, game is a specialty, and the seasonal menu might include smoked duck breast ($19) or bacon-wrapped elk tenderloin ($23). The inn has just four very spacious rooms, and the whole place has water views.

In laid-back Britt, activities are an afterthought to eating and reclining, but you can take a very exclusive little boat tour on Georgian Bay with **Barron Tours** (☎ 705-383-0448). Cruise wherever you like with up to five other people for around $75 per hour (not per person).

Britt is about 70km north of Parry Sound and 5km west of Hwy 69.

KILLARNEY PROVINCIAL PARK

Killarney (☎ 705-287-2900; Hwy 637; day use per vehicle $9.50) is often called the jewel in the Ontario Parks system. The Group of Seven artists had a cabin near the Hwy 6 access point (west of the park) and were instrumental in the park's establishment. It was in Killarney that AJ Casson painted the iconic *White Pine*, and in summer the park runs a program of painting and other activities aimed at promoting the park through artistic awareness.

Killarney's achingly beautiful scenery comprises birch and pine forest edged by the magnificent La Cloche Mountains. Its lakes have astoundingly clear water with remarkable visibility, partly as a result of acid rain. By the late 1970s some of the lakes were essentially devoid of life, but recovery is underway as a result of reductions in smelter emissions coming out of Sudbury and other areas.

Orientation & Information

The center of the action is the George Lake Campground Information Centre. At the time of research, planning was underway for a new interpretive and visitor center in the campground area, to be called La Cloche Wilderness Centre; completion was scheduled for late 2005. The tiny village of Killarney, which serves the park, is outside the park boundary at the end of Hwy 637.

Activities

The park's 100km **La Cloche Silhouette Trail** was named after Franklin Carmichael's painting *La Cloche Silhouette*. The trail is one of the best backcountry hikes within a five-hour drive of Toronto, and is like walking through a series of Group of Seven canvases, with sapphire lakes, pine trees growing at impossible

angles and gleaming white cliffs. The trail as a whole is rugged and not for inexperienced hikers, but the first stretch from the west trailhead near the information center to Acid Lake is more moderate and can be done as a day trip. This hike is 4km each way and you should allow three to four hours for the round trip. Several short walks (2km to 4km) start near the information center too.

For canoeing and kayaking you can rent everything you need locally, or join a guided trip with Killarney Outfitters. Wild Women Expeditions (p181) and Sundog Outfitters & Retreat Centre (p182) occasionally run trips here too. Canoe rentals cost from $20 to $33 per day; kayak rentals range from $23 to $56. The following outfitters serve the George Lake Campground area and will deliver canoes and kayaks to several locations:

Killarney Kanoes (☎ 705-287-2197, 888-461-4446; www.killarneykanoes.com) These outfitters with a credit card number and they'll give you a combination for one of their canoes kept on-site at locations that include George Lake.

Killarney Outfitters (☎ 705-287-2828, 800-461-1117; www.killarney.com; Hwy 637) The storefront location is 5km west of the George Lake Campground. Associated with Killarney Mountain Lodge, it offers themed and customized guided trips based at the lodge or with camping. These cost from $95 for a day trip to $800 for four days.

Sleeping & Eating

Killarney is one of Ontario's few parks with a 'wilderness' classification and has no powered campsites, even at George Lake. The total number of campsites is low, so make reservations as far in advance as you can. For all reservations for the campground (sites $26) and backcountry (per person $9), contact **Ontario Parks** (☎ 519-826-5290, 888-668-7275; www.ontarioparks.com). The other places listed here are in the village of Killarney.

Sportsman's Inn (☎ 705-287-2411, 800-282-1913; www.sportsmansinn.ca; Channel St; r $50-85) You can spend a long summer evening admiring the passing parade of cruising boats if you book a 2nd-floor balcony room. The 3rd-floor rooms have shared bathrooms and a certain amount of dilapidated charm. The bar and dining room at this landmark old waterfront place in the centre of town are open to nonguests. The grilled fish ($19) is simple but good, and comes with fresh asparagus if it's in season.

BUT KILLARNEY IS ALWAYS FULL!

You've planned your summer trip around visiting the 'jewel' in the Ontario Parks system but you just can't get a reservation. Don't despair – consider these two contrasting, less high-profile parks also located off Hwy 69 along the east side of Georgian Bay. For camping reservations in either, contact **Ontario Parks** (☎ 519-826-5290, 888-668-7275; www.ontarioparks.com).

Killbear Provincial Park (☎ 705-342-5492; day use per vehicle $9.50, campsites $18.50-24; ☷ Victoria Day–Thanksgiving) Camping in this very accessible park is a great introduction to classic Group of Seven scenery, especially those rugged rocky shores and easily anthropomorphized lonely pine trees. Killbear has 880 campsites, but most of them are unpowered so things are relatively quiet. There are great day hikes and lookout points but no backcountry camping. The park is about half an hour from Parry Sound by car, off Hwy 69 northwest of town.

Massasauga Provincial Park (☎ 705-378-0685; backcountry sites $9; ☷ May–late Oct) Sorry hikers, this one's only for canoeists and kayakers. You could paddle around the park's hundreds of windswept islands and mainland lakes all summer long and still see only a tenth of them. Massasauga has parking for campers only, so day visits are not possible, and all access to the 135 backcountry campsites is by water. It covers a vast area south of Parry Sound. For advice on planning a trip here, call the park or talk to the folks at White Squall (p170) in Parry Sound.

Killarney Mountain Lodge (☎ 705-287-2242, 800-461-1117; www.killarney.com; d per person $150-170, cabins per person incl dinner $140-200; ☷ mid-May–Thanksgiving) The lodge attracts a steady stream of guests who arrive by floatplane or by yacht. The carousel lounge, built in 1958, features panoramic views. Its furnishings (and those of the bedrooms) haven't changed much in the past five decades and now have retro appeal – it all makes you want to order a brandy Alexander. The dining room serves 'comfort food' such as meatballs ($16.50), panfried fish ($18.50) and vegetarian lasagne ($15.50); it's open to nonguests.

Herbert Fisheries (fish & chips $8.50; ☷ 11am-6:30pm Jun–mid-Sep, to 8pm Jul & Aug, 11am-6:30pm Fri-Sun May & mid-Sep–Thanksgiving) Traveling to Killarney and not having fish and chips outdoors down at the dock would be like going to Munich's Oktoberfest and not drinking the beer. This place is so popular that in summer you might have to wait two hours to receive your order. But readers have testified that it's worth it, and we agree.

Getting There & Away

The park is 60km east of Hwy 69 along Hwy 637. It is not accessible by public transportation.

NORTHERN ONTARIO

Canada specializes in provinces large enough that anywhere else in the world they'd be individual countries. Ontario is one of those. And northern Ontario is only a part of it, with only 4% of the province's population. Yet it's bigger than France and Germany put together, a vast area that registers only distantly in the consciousness of most southern Ontarians. It has few roads, few people and even fewer jobs. The fortunes of the region's cities and small communities still rise and fall with cyclical changes in the demand for whatever natural resources their area provides (nickel in Sudbury, grain transport through Thunder Bay, logging almost everywhere), although the larger centers have diversified to avoid the precarious one-industry-town scenario.

Northern Ontario's highway towns have been described as passing lanes on the Trans-Canada Hwy (Hwy 17). But venture off the highways (you don't have to detour far) and it's a completely different story.

One subculture takes the form of hundreds of remote lodges catering mainly to hunters and anglers, many accessible only by floatplane. Another, the one of most interest to travelers, is for adventurers who love to kayak, canoe or hike: the area's remoteness means an outdoor paradise of wild rivers, too many lakes to count (someone once reached a million then gave up) and exceptional national and provincial parks. The Temagami area, Mississagi Provincial Park, Lake Superior Provincial Park and Pukaskwa National Park are very special, wild places that make Algonquin (although it's a must-see) seem like a metropolis. If you're inexperienced in the outdoors, you can find organized adventure travel with an ecotourism focus well established in the care of a small number

NORTHERN ONTARIO

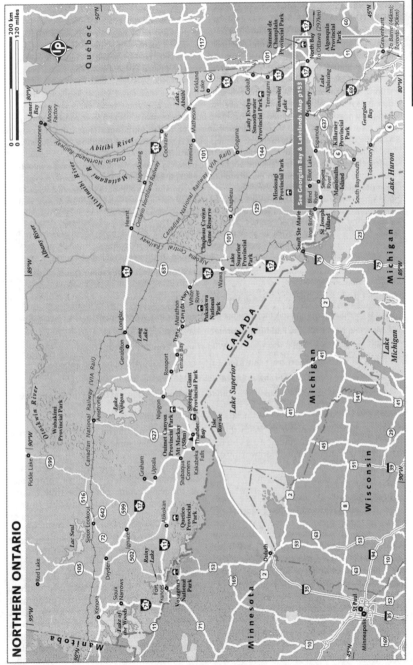

ONTARIO

HOW TO FLOAT YOUR BOAT

Ontario has more surface area composed of water than any other province in Canada (around 16%), and northern Ontario and the Georgian Bay area in particular are awash with numerous lakes and rivers. Canoeing and kayaking are extraordinarily popular activities here – if you've already mountain-biked in Utah, skied in Switzerland and hiked in Tasmania, then you've come to the right place.

In Ontario almost anyone can and will rent you a canoe for a day. For anything longer than that, it pays to hook up with an experienced tour operator or outfitter (who will organize everything you need for a self-guided trip, including boats, tents, stove, packed food, route planning, even insect repellent). You should plan well ahead for guided trips; some longer trips run only a couple of times a year. An excellent starting point is the website for **Paddling Ontario** (www.paddlingontario.com), an alliance of adventure travel providers.

To help you choose, we've selected our favorite paddling centers. Many of them have a wilderness lodge that's an ecotourism destination in itself. You won't find manicured lawns, minigolf or room service at all of them, and some have shared indoor or outhouse bathrooms. You will find small owner-operated businesses, some of the most enthusiastic guides in the country, and an experience that will sustain you long after you return home:

- Best ecolodge base and organic food: **Smoothwater Outfitters and Ecolodge** (p176), Temagami
- Most extensive set-up for self-guided trips: **Algonquin Outfitters** (p168), Algonquin
- Best Algonquin lodge-based trips: **Northern Edge Algonquin** and **Voyageur Quest** (p168), Algonquin
- Best Lake Superior specialists: **Naturally Superior Adventures** (p192), Wawa
- Best Canadian roots and folk music before and after your trip: **White Squall** (p170), Parry Sound
- Most laid-back pace: the **Paddling Gourmet** (p156), Tobermory
- Best female energy and onsite massage: **Wild Women Expeditions** (p181), Sudbury
- Least remote trips: **Thorncrest Outfitters** (p154 and p156), Southampton and Tobermory
- Most remote trips: **Canoe Frontier Expeditions** (p198), Pickle Lake
- Quintessential 'ecotourism' experience: **Sundog Outfitters and Retreat Centre** (p182), Sudbury

of owner-operators (see above). With their advice or on one of their guided trips you're virtually guaranteed an expedition worthy of *several* group emails to home.

For the most remote experience of all, and the opportunity to be a part of the growing Aboriginal-guided travel scene, you can take a train to Moosonee and then a boat or helicopter to the distant island of Moose Factory.

When you've seen enough rocks and trees, the landscape that's inspired the, er, 'imagination' of at least two songwriters who've penned tracks called 'Rocks and Trees' (see p180), make a beeline for Sudbury, Sault Ste Marie or Thunder Bay for their museums, galleries and nightlife (spending time in the region's small towns makes the big cities' excellent restaurants seem even better).

Travel in northern Ontario is highly seasonal. In May some visitor centers are still closed. From around June, blackflies and mosquitoes can make outdoor activity a nightmare for a few weeks in some areas as the leaves come out – the time of year varies from place to place and year to year, so check locally by phoning a tour operator before planning a trip. The best months to visit (unless you're a winter adventurer made entirely of steel) are July and August.

This section is organized in line with the two highway routes through the region. Highways 17 and 11 intersect at North Bay. From North Bay, Hwy 11 runs north and west for 995km until it rejoins Hwy 17 at Nipigon. Highway 17 runs west from North Bay, from where it's 1010km to Nipigon. The two highways split again west of Thunder Bay.

NORTH BAY

North Bay bills itself as 'just north enough to be perfect,' which begs the question 'perfect for what?' It's north enough to make an impression on Torontonians and north enough for the big pub on the main street to have moose heads mounted on the wall. With a population of 55,000 it's a logical stop on the Trans-Canada Hwy or en route to the magnificent Temagami wilderness area.

Orientation & Information

Main St is the main street; south of town it becomes Lakeshore Dr. The downtown area is between Cassells and Fisher Sts.

North Bay Chamber of Commerce (☎ 705-472-8480, 800-387-0516; Hwy 11; ☺ 9am-5pm) Near the junction with Hwy 17, this place is 5km south of downtown.

Sights & Activities

North Bay has had a stable sort of history compared to the dramatic busts of the surrounding single-industry towns, but it had also missed the excitement of the booms – until the Dionne identical quintuplets came along. Born in 1934, the five girls became Canada's most famous multiple-birth story, an overnight tourist attraction during the peak of the Depression. Beside the tourist office on the North Bay bypass, the **Dionne Quints Museum** (☎ 705-472-8480; 1757 Seymour St N; adult/child $3/1.75; ☺ 9am-5pm mid-May–Jun, to 7pm Jul & Aug, 9am-4pm Sep–Thanksgiving) contains artifacts from their early years. (Their later years don't make such a happy story – growing up in something like a zoo isn't the healthiest start.)

Samuel de Champlain Provincial Park (☎ 705-744-2276; Hwy 17; day-use per vehicle $9.50), 50km east of North Bay, is a small but very beautiful park set in a rugged, rocky landscape featuring white pines. The park protects parts of the Mattawa River on a historical route long used for trading before the voyageurs (traders) arrived and tackled the rapids here. The centerpiece of the hands-on **Voyageur Heritage Centre** (☺ 8:30am-4pm Mon-Fri Victoria Day–Thanksgiving, also 1-4pm Sat & Sun Jul & Aug) is a giant birchbark canoe of the type the fur traders used on their 2000km journey to Fort William on Lake Superior. In July and August the park offers daily guided tours in 8.6m canoes along the most interesting section of the river. The six-hour trip departs at 10am and costs $25/15 for adults/children;

shorter tours are also available. The park has some quite rugged hiking trails (considering there's no backcountry camping), up to 9km in length, and offers the same sort of pristine wilderness as Algonquin, with not nearly as many people.

The **Chief Commanda II** (☎ 705-494-8167, 866-660-6686; www.georgianbaycruise.com; Memorial Dr; ☺ Victoria Day–Sep) takes up to 300 passengers on cruises across Lake Nipissing among the Manitou Islands (adult/child $14/8.50), to the upper French River (adult/child $20/10) or to Callander Bay at sunset (adult/child including dinner $48/40).

Sleeping & Eating

The bulk of accommodations are in motels, with many along Lakeshore Dr in the south end of town; the big chains are a good bet. For reservations for camping (sites $18 to $28) at Samuel de Champlain Provincial Park, contact **Ontario Parks** (☎ 519-826-5290, 888-668-7275; www.ontarioparks.com).

Gray's Log House (☎ 705-495-2389; www.grayslog house.com; 5270 Hwy 63; s/d $75/85) One of the owners stitched the quilt you'll be sleeping under, and she can sell you one too. Gray's Log House is billed as a B&B, but the 1870 log cabin in a rural area feels more like the hideaway you wish your family owned. Self-caterers can prepare meals in the fully equipped guests' kitchen. Build an extra night into your itinerary, because you won't want to leave – it's the most peaceful, welcoming haven for miles around.

Birches & Breezes B&B (☎ 705-498-6253; birches andbreezes@sympatico.ca; 2105 Northshore Rd; s/d $75/85) This new house with water frontage has luxuriously appointed rooms. The 'bay room' overlooking Grassy Bay is our favorite, but the 'birches' room with its sleigh bed is fine too. Birches & Breezes is about 30 minutes out of town on a rural road.

Moose (☎ 705-472-8834; 134 Main St E; mains $7-15) You know you've hit north when you find moose heads mounted on the hewn-timber walls. Food at the cozy Moose is the same as at equivalent pubs down south: burgers ($8), Caesar salad ($4) and chicken wings ($0.60 each).

Kabuki House (☎ 705-495-0999; 349 Main St W; lunch mains $8-11, dinner mains $22-26) Kabuki House is not formal, but it feels very special, with exquisite Japanese artworks on the walls in a series of small rooms. For our taste, dinner lacked the finesse we might have associated with the setting and the prices, but lunch is very good value.

Churchill's (☎ 705-476-7777, 866-314-1115; 631 Lakeshore Dr; lunch mains $12-20, dinner mains $28-38) If you're thinking of proposing to someone while you're in North Bay, do it at Churchill's, where intimate, candlelit rooms invite whispers and shy glances. And if he says no, console yourself with the seared scallops with sesame basmati rice and wasabi lime sauce ($36).

Getting There & Away

Between Toronto and North Bay, Ontario Northland runs buses ($62, five hours, five daily) and trains ($63, five hours, six weekly). Greyhound Canada connects North Bay with Sudbury ($27, 1¾ hours, three daily) and Ottawa ($66, 5½ hours, two daily). The terminus for all services is the **train station** (☎ 705-495-4200; 100 Station Rd).

TEMAGAMI

Temagami is a small town (population 1000) north of North Bay on Lake Temagami. More importantly, the name refers to the wilderness of the area, renowned internationally for its old-growth forests of red and white pines, its archeological sites and pictographs, its interconnected system of canoe routes, and scenery that includes waterfalls and some of the province's highest terrain.

Information

Temagami Tourist Information (☎ 800-661-7609; 7 Lakeshore Dr; ☻ 8:30am-5pm Mon-Fri Sep-Jun, to 7pm Jul & Aug)

Sights & Activities

The Temagami group of provincial parks includes **Lady Evelyn Smoothwater Provincial Park**, which has Ontario's highest point, Ishpatina Ridge (693m). The park has no facilities, and its campsites are accessible only by canoe. Information on the area can be obtained from **Finlayson Point Provincial Park** (☎ 705-569-3205, 800-667-1940; day use per vehicle $9.50; ☻ mid-May–mid-Sep), which does have facilities for visitors; it's 2km south of the town of Temagami.

There is a huge range of activities synonymous with two of the most interesting places to stay in Temagami. Many guests of Smoothwater use the ecolodge to segue into a self-guided canoe trip where everything

is organized for you: canoe rentals, packed food, route consultation and so on. Rates start at $75 per person per day. In winter, cross-country skiing and snowshoeing are Smoothwater's focus. From Northland Paradise Lodge, rates for privately guided photography trips start at $100 per day for up to four people, then $25 for each extra person.

The trips offered by **Wolf Within Adventures** (☎ 705-569-3557; www.wolfwithin.ca) are a unique way to experience winter in Temagami. Guided dog-sledding trips entail instruction in dog handling, harnessing and driving techniques before you head off on the sleds through the forests and across now-frozen lakes. Weekend trips cost from $350, and run with a minimum of just two people and a maximum of eight. Customized longer trips are also available. On an adventurous eight-night trip ($1550), group members have much more involvement in setting up camp each night and feeding the huskies. This is one of the best opportunities you'll have to learn about traditional methods of travel and survival in temperatures of -50°C. Travelers always come away full of affection for the dogs. These options operate between December and March. In summer, Wolf Within runs two-week canoe trips of around 120km in the Temagami area for around $1450.

Close to the town of Temagami, half an hour by car further north, the tiny town of **Cobalt** makes a fascinating highway detour. Silver mining was responsible for its boom, which lasted about 20 years from 1903, when its population exploded to 20,000. Now, even in a region littered with small-town reminders of the 'busts,' its ghost-town poignancy stands out, and it's designated as a national historic site.

Sleeping & Eating

Smoothwater Outfitters & Ecolodge (☎ 705-569-3539; www.smoothwater.com; dm/r $25/95) Smoothwater is a wonderful place to stay, but it's so much more than that. This inspiring ecolodge hosts regular courses and retreats in yoga, painting, breadmaking, regional cuisine, photography, even making furniture from twigs. Acommodation is in peaceful private rooms furnished with quilts, artwork and twig furniture, or in the basic bunkrooms. Meals featuring organic regional produce are served at a big communal table.

For information on Smoothwater's outfitting services, see p176.

Northland Paradise Lodge (☎ 705-569-3791; www.northland-paradise.com; Stevens Rd; d $75) During research we interrupted the owner butchering a moose that had just met its end on the highway. The lodge caters to a hunting, fishing and snowmobiling crowd, but the semiprofessional photographer who owns it is busiest guiding trips for clients who want to shoot pictures, not animals. The motel-style rooms are basic and comfortable, with full kitchen facilities. No need to cook extra for the owner – he eats only wild game. The lodge is within walking distance of the train station on the shores of a lake.

Getting There & Away

Ontario Northland connects Temagami with North Bay by bus ($17, 1¼ hours, two daily) and train ($17, 1½ hours, six weekly).

COCHRANE

In summer, little Cochrane's main reason for being is the *Polar Bear Express*, which sets out here on its journey through northern wilderness to Moosonee. The enormous train station dominates the town (population 5700), and if you stand on the long platform under an enormous sky as the sun sets you can get the sense that you're soon heading off on a frontier adventure.

Information

Cochrane Tourist Association & Board of Trade
(☎ 705-272-4926, 800-354-9948; 3 3rd Ave; ☯ 9am-4pm Mon-Fri)

Sights & Activities

The **Polar Bear Express** (☎ 800-268-9281, 705-272-4228; www.polarbearexpress.ca; adult/child $96/48; ☯ Tue-Sun late Jun–late Aug) is the best known of the two trains that depart Cochrane. It caters primarily to tourists, departing at 8:30am and returning the same day. The trip takes 4½ hours each way, so if you return the same day you'll have time for only a quick peek around Moosonee and Moose Factory.

A slower local train, the **Little Bear** (adult/child $96/48), also operated by Ontario Northland, caters to a mix of tourists, locals, trappers, geologists and hardcore paddlers (one car is specifically designed to transport canoes). It's a flagstop train, meaning it stops wherever anyone wants to get on or off. The *Little*

Bear operates three days a week year-round, and doesn't return the same day. Reservations are required for both trains.

Despite the name of the train, there are no polar bears living in the wild in the region. But at the time of research, Cochrane was abuzz with news of the imminent arrival of the town's newest residents, three polar bears to be housed at the **Polar Bear Conservation & Education Habitat** (www.polarbearhabitat.ca; 1 Drury Park Rd; adult/child/student $20/12/18). The site features a natural setting and a bear hospital with maternity ward; it's hoped that the facility will be used for breeding, but it all depends on the bears' cooperation. The same location incorporates a new **Heritage Village**, an assortment of buildings replicating life in Cochrane in the early 1900s when the town was established, with costumed staff. Admission covers both attractions. Operating hours had not been established at the time of research, but the site was likely to open daily year-round.

The **Railway & Pioneer Museum** (☎ 705-272-4361; 210 Railway St; admission $3; ☯ 9am-5pm Jun-Aug) features loads of railway memorabilia and displays on pioneer life. The Tim Horton section is not about the now-famous doughnut stores but about the hometown hero and Maple Leafs hockey player who started the franchise. This section of the museum is expected to move to the new Tim Horton Event Centre, a community recreation complex scheduled for completion by late 2005.

Sleeping & Eating

When the *Polar Bear Express* is running, you absolutely must book acommodation in advance. At all times of the year, keep in mind that you don't come this far north for the food. All the family-style restaurants dish out huge servings of burgers and steak for between $10 and $20. Smoking is not unknown in some of the eating places here, even when it's technically not allowed (further south you'd be lynched for lighting up).

Commando Motel (☎ 705-272-2700; fax 705 272-5036; 80 7th Ave; r $60) For no-frills, basic rooms the Commando is a good choice; it's right across from the train station.

Station Inn (☎ 705-272-3500, 800-265-2356; r $90-100) Go one better than staying near the train station – stay on top of it! This modern, pleasant, charmless place is unbeatably convenient. It has its own restaurant.

Best Western Swan Castle Inn (☎ 705-272-5200, 800-265-3668; 189 Railway St; r $110) The main difference between the Swan Castle and the Station Inn is that this big, newish chain motel is opposite the train station.

Betty's B&B (☎ 705-272-4085; Hwy 11; r $60-140) Betty's is one woman's fantasy, but Barbie and Ken would feel right at home here. The exterior architecture has touches of gingerbread house style, and the honeymoon suite (fully soundproof) is magnificent in its own way, with an enormous whirlpool and a throne-like toilet right in the bedroom. It's 10km south of town.

Spinning Wheel Restaurant & Tavern (☎ 705-272-4777; 105 3rd St; mains $10-20) Spin out a summer evening here in a big space with faux plants, fairy lights, a sports screen and plenty of beer.

Getting There & Away

Between Cochrane and North Bay, Ontario Northland runs buses ($64, 6¼ hours, two daily) and trains ($67, 5¼ hours, six weekly). All services arrive at and depart from the **train station** (☎ 705-272-4228).

MOOSONEE & MOOSE FACTORY

Moosonee and Moose Factory sit near the tundra line, and are as far north as most people ever get in eastern Canada. Aim further north than this and you'll need to arrange an expedition involving floatplanes, canoes, snowmobiles, dogsleds or snowshoes. The railway reached Moosonee only in 1932, about 30 years after it was established by Révillon Frères (known today as Revlon) as a trading post. From Moosonee a quick boat trip across the river takes you to the island of Moose Factory, which is not an industrial site that churns out the large hairy beasts on a production line, but a small settlement and the site of a Hudson's Bay Company trading post founded in 1672.

While you're pondering having come so far north by train, consider that 300 years ago, when so many furs were changing hands, the main access was *from* the north via Hudson and James Bays. For far longer the Mushkegowuk Cree have called the area home. The population varies seasonally, but is about 2800 in Moosonee and 2500 in Moose Factory.

Information

Both Moosonee and Moose Factory have ATMs.

Moose Factory Tourism Association (☎ 705-658-6200) A useful telephone information service.

Sights & Activities

In Moosonee, the **Révillon Frères Museum** (☎ 705-336-2625; 50 Révillon St N; admission free; 🕙 9am-5pm Sat-Thu Jun-Aug) documents the Hudson's Bay Company's rival, the North West Company. Nearby, the **Ministry of Natural Resources Interpretive Centre** has displays on the regional geography and fauna.

In Moose Factory, the **Cree Cultural Interpretive Centre** features indoor and outdoor exhibits of artifacts, including bone tools, traditional toys, and dwellings from the pre-contact era. At the time of research it had closed indefinitely because of vandalism, but was going to reopen, probably in late 2005, and there were plans to expand and upgrade the whole operation.

The **Moose Factory Centennial Museum** (admission free; 🕙 Jul & Aug) displays maps, furs and the Hudson's Bay Staff House, which dates from the early 1700s. Moosehide altar cloths and Cree prayer books are a feature of the 1860 St Thomas' Anglican Church.

At the time of research the Moose Cree First Nation was constructing the **Washow James Bay Wilderness Centre** (www.moosecree.com/economic-development/tourism-initiatives/washow/index), scheduled for completion during 2005. This activity center and acommodation base in an even more remote area about 70km east of Moosonee is designed to take travelers back in time. Satellite villages surround the main center, some with bark-construction dwellings typical of the pre-contact era, and others featuring contact-era canvas tipis. Guests travel between the main base and the villages by canoe, and activities in the area might include demonstrations of trapping and fishing. Practical details and prices had not been established at the time of research, so check the website for the latest information.

Tours

Moose Cree Outdoor Discoveries & Adventures (☎ 705-658-4619; www.moosecree.com/economic-develop ment/tourism-initiatives/mcoda) run by the Moose Cree First Nation, offers customized trips incorporating cultural activities (storytelling and traditional foods, for example) along with canoeing in summer and snowshoeing in winter. The company can organize absolutely anything you want to do, given enough notice, so it's impossible to give prices; it depends on whether you're one person or many, and whether you want a one-day island tour or a weeklong wilderness expedition. The trips offer a unique opportunity to experience something beyond what many train passengers see.

Two Bay Tours (☎ 705-336-2944; www.twobay.com) operates the packages offered through Ontario Northland (the train service that gets you here), and if you want to take its bus tour of Moosonee and Moose Factory (adult/child $22/11) you should arrange it at the train station in Cochrane before you depart. Other options include well-established one-day excursions on the *Polar Princess* boat with a bus tour of Moose Factory ($52/26); short Fossil Island tours ($18/9); and twilight Moosonee bus tours ($11).

Sleeping & Eating

Be sure to reserve accommodations before you arrive.

Cree Village Ecolodge (☎ 705-658-6400, 888-273-3929; www.creevillage.com; Moose Factory; r $95-135) By far the most interesting place to stay is the Cree-owned and operated ecolodge, designed and furnished to reflect traditional Cree values. The environmental sensitivity of the design extends to the organic wool and cotton used in the carpets, blankets and bed linen, organic soaps in every room, and some composting toilets. Breakfast, lunch and dinner are available to nonguests as well as guests, and are served in the Shabotowan Great Hall. Game is a specialty: choose hunter's pizza topped with caribou ($13), caribou stew ($16), or chicken if you're chicken.

Tamarack Suites (☎ 705-336-2496; Moosonee; $100) Each cedar-built suite here has two bedrooms and a fully equipped kitchen, so it's great for self-caterers.

Tidewater Provincial Park (☎ 705-336-1209, 705-272-4365; tent sites $18.50; ⌖ mid-Jun–Aug) This park is between the mainland and Moose Factory, accessible by water taxi. It has no facilities so you must be self-sufficient.

Polar Bear Lodge (☎ 705-336-2345; www.polarbearlodge.com; Moosonee; s/d $94/100, lunch main $6, dinner mains $14) The outside looks like a high school but the inside is comfortable. In the dining room, basic meals of pork chops, chicken or steak are served.

Getting There & Around

Moosonee and Moose Factory are not accessible by car. For information on the trains from Cochrane, see p178. Water taxis and freighter canoes shuttle between Moosonee and Moose Factory (adult/child $3.50, 10 minutes, 2km). During fall freeze-up (about three weeks from late November) and spring thaw (one to four weeks from late April or early May) Moose Factory is accessible only by helicopter, which can be arranged through Moose Cree Outdoor Discoveries & Adventures for around $30 per person per trip. In winter the river becomes an ice bridge.

COCHRANE TO NIPIGON

Hunters, anglers and truckers make up most of the visitors to the few towns along the desolate 615km stretch of Hwy 11 between Cochrane and Nipigon, Ontario's most northerly major road. The road has few passing lanes and is often closed by blizzards in winter. The only reason for travelers to use it is to save time between Cochrane and Thunder Bay, and the towns with the best choice of motels are Kapuskasing and Hearst. Hearst is the northern terminus of the Algoma Central Railway (p187) and the westernmost point of Ontario Northland's train services to and from North Bay ($100, 10 hours, one daily). It's best known as a moose-hunting center. Tiny Longlac has places to stay and is a logical stopping point distance-wise, but ranks especially high on the scale of godforsakeness. Nipigon is where Hwy 11 meets Hwy 17, which in contrast is the best route for accessing northern Ontario's wilderness highlights (see p191).

SUDBURY

Sudbury started out as a temporary railway construction town, but boomed because of nickel (which it's been supplying to the world for more than 100 years), platinum, palladium, copper, gold, tellurium, selenium and sulfur. Inco Ltd, one of the world's largest nickel producers, is the town's biggest employer, and strong demand for nickel in China and Japan combined with low output in Russia have seen the city doing well in the first decade of the 21st century. But demand is always cyclical, and Sudbury has

TOP 10 SONGS ABOUT NORTHERN ONTARIO

The first thing you should pack for an extended trip to Canada is not a warm sweater or bear spray but a big pile of CDs, because if you're going to see much of the country you'll be spending a lot of time in the car, train or bus. Many of Canada's best songwriters impart a strong sense of place through their lyrics: the tracks listed here in ascending order of poignancy are about, or really should have been about, northern Ontario.

- 'It Ain't Easy Being a Moose' by 19 James. The long-suffering protagonist spends his whole goofy life trying to dodge blackflies, mosquitoes and highway traffic, but alas… ouch. If CBC Radio One put this track on high rotation the government could scrap the moose-hazard signs on the Trans-Canada Hwy.

- 'Rocks and Trees' by Wendell Ferguson. Warning: this track is highly addictive; it's possibly the only tune ever to rhyme 'proliferous' with 'coniferous.' It's from *I Pick Therefore I Jam*; don't miss Ferguson's follow-up release, *Happy Songs Sell Records, Sad Songs Sell Beer*.

- 'Rocks and Trees' by the Arrogant Worms. See the pattern? If you don't now, you will when you travel Hwy 17 or 11. While Ferguson cheerfully contends that he can't take any more of this landscape, the zany Worms' version (same title, different song) could be Canada's alt-comedy national anthem, or northern Ontario's call to arms if ever it decides to secede.

- 'Sudbury Saturday Night' by Stompin' Tom. Canada's king of country is probably best known for 'The Hockey Song,' a sporting anthem guaranteed to transmit earworm (listen just once and it will live in your brain for weeks). The best antidote is *Souvenirs*, a compilation of 25 similarly catchy ditties including 'Sudbury Saturday Night,' which has a good chance of outmaneuvering 'The Hockey Song' for mental airplay.

- 'The Wreck of the Edmund Fitzgerald' by Gordon Lightfoot. This ballad by the boomer generation's favorite troubadour has helped make the *Edmund Fitzgerald* perhaps the most famous of the ships to have gone down in the notorious gales of November on Lake Superior.

- 'White Squall' by Stan Rogers. Folk legend Stan Rogers' contribution to the 'tragic death by drowning' genre is a less epic, more personal tale of the sadness left behind when a young, eager sailor takes the lakes for granted.

- 'A Town Called What the Fuck' by Kevin Closs. The lyrics from Ontario folk-fest fave Kevin Closs are atypically cynical, but they might resonate as you travel Hwy 17. Closs counts John Denver, Bruce Cockburn and Stan Rogers among his strongest influences.

- 'Mill Towns' by David Francey. This carefully crafted narrative from one of Canada's best songwriters recalls generational change in company towns. Try the whole Juno-winning roots album, *Far End of Summer*, between Wawa and Nipigon on Hwy 17.

- 'One Hand on the Radio' by Aengus Finnan. This meditative a capella piece is a tribute to the radio announcer whose voice keeps the protagonist company as he drives through the night. The Dublin-born balladeer lives in Ontario and has toured extensively in remote communities in Canada.

- *Waiting for the Cage* by the Grievous Angels. It's not a single track but an entire album dedicated to life in mining towns (singer-songwriter Chuck Angus lives in Cobalt, p176). The Grievous Angels specialize in grit (other albums include *One Job Town* and *22 Trailer Park*); the line-up on *Waiting for the Cage* features guitar, fiddle, piano and accordion.

diversified to help protect itself against the busts that inevitably follow the booms; it's now a world center for the development of specialty mining technology.

Sudbury has long had a reputation for ugliness. The rough, rocky landscape was debased for years by the felling of trees used to fuel early methods of extracting nickel, and by the clouds of sulphurous fumes that followed. The result was a bleak, moonscapelike setting.

The worst of these characteristics have been (continue to be) reversed. In 1971 Inco built a superstack to scatter emissions from its operations, and in the early 1990s the city received a UN award for its efforts at land reclamation. Sudbury's still no botanical garden: it has plenty of the grimy sprawl typical of industrial cities, and the staff at nearby Killarney Provincial Park can provide travelers with information about the whole area's ongoing recovery from the effects of acid rain. But it's come a long way, and within an hour of downtown are two excellent ecolodge-type operations that make great bases for exploring the surrounding hills, forests and lakes.

Some sophisticated eating and entertainment options help put to rest the stereotype of the bingo-playing 'Sudbury Saturday Night' immortalized by country singer Stompin' Tom (see the boxed text opposite).

Orientation & Information

The main streets downtown are Elm St (running east–west) and Durham St (going north–south). The main area runs along Elm St from Notre Dame Ave to Lorne St, but all the major attractions are widely dispersed.

Cybernet Cafe (☎ 705-674-0958; cnr Elm St & Notre Dame Ave; per 30min/hr $3/5; ☷ 8am-9pm Mon-Wed, to 11pm Thu & Fri, 9am-11pm Sat, 10am-6pm Sun) Located inside a shopping center; in the evening, entry is directly off the street corner.

Rainbow Country Travel Association (☎ 705-522-0104, 800-465-6655; 1984 Regent St S; ☷ 8:30am-8pm Jun-Aug, 8:30am-4:30pm Mon-Fri, 10am-6pm Sat Sep-May) Ten kilometers south of town.

Sights

SCIENCE NORTH

The huge **science center** (☎ 705-523-4629, 800-461-4898; www.sciencenorth.ca; 100 Ramsey Lake Rd; adult/child $16/13; ☷ 9am-5pm May & Jun, 9am-6pm Jul & Aug, 10am-4pm Sep-Apr) is a major regional attraction conspicuously housed in two snowflake-shaped buildings built into a rocky outcrop on the edge of Lake Ramsey. Inside, you pass through a tunnel within the 2.5-billion-year-old Canadian Shield to the several levels of exhibits. The best thing about it is that almost everything is 'hands-on' and you could spend hours testing out the bed of nails, gauging your fitness level, wandering through a gallery of live butterflies and patting a tarantula. The display on research conducted at the Sudbury Neutrino Observatory, which is offsite and 2km underground, is fascinating. Major exhibits

change regularly, as do films screened in the Imax cinema (adult/student $8/6.50).

DYNAMIC EARTH

In northern Ontario nearly every little town has some form of mining museum, but **Dynamic Earth** (☎ 705-523-4629, 800-461-4898; www.dynamicearth.ca; Big Nickel Rd; adult/child $16/13; ☷ 9am-5pm May & Jun, 9am-6pm Jul & Aug, 10am-4pm Sep–mid-Nov & Apr) is in a league of its own. This huge attraction incorporates an underground tour (with a simulated dynamite blast), hands-on exhibits relating to earth sciences and a rock gallery. There's plenty of interactive stuff to keep young kids as well as adults interested. The site's Big Nickel (a 9m-high five-cent coin) is actually made of stainless steel, whose main component is nickel.

COPPER CLIFF MUSEUM

This **museum** (☎ 705-674-3141 ext 2460; Power St, Copper Cliff; admission free; ☷ 11am-4pm Tue-Sun Jun-Aug) occupies a pioneer log cabin in Copper Cliff. It's filled with furnishings and tools from the early 20th century. Some of the interest lies in getting here if you come via the back roads: Copper Cliff is the area where Inco has its mammoth operations, roughly 6km west of the city center.

FLOUR MILL HERITAGE MUSEUM

Similar in style to Copper Cliff Museum, this **museum** (☎ 705-673-3141 ext 2460; 245 St Charles St; admission free; ☷ 10am-4pm Tue-Sat, 11am-4pm Sun Jun-Sep) is sited in a 1903 clapboard house with period implements, artifacts and furnishings. It tells the story of the three flour silos on Notre Dame Ave.

ART GALLERY OF SUDBURY

This **art gallery** (☎ 705-675-4871; 251 John St; admission free; ☷ noon-5pm Tue-Sun) is housed in a historic mansion. It features changing art shows, often focusing on the work of local artists. There is also a permanent display of articles relating to the region's history.

Activities

Wild Women Expeditions (☎ 705-866-1260, 888-993-1222; wildwomenexp.com) is based roughly 45km west of Sudbury near Nair Centre, and operates a great program of activities on site: fly-fishing, yoga, vocal workshops, herbal retreats, arts events and stacks more, all for women only. The pace is relaxed, with loads of time for reading, seeing the on-site massage therapist, or just hanging out in the wilderness setting. All these events run on specific dates over several days, and include acommodation and all meals. The acommodation consists of basic cabins with outhouse bathrooms. Away from its base, in summer the company runs guided kayaking trips, cycling tours on Manitoulin Island, and canoe trips in Temagami, Killarney, Mississagi and other areas. Canoe trips typically cost around $360 for three nights, including all gear, food and accommodations.

Sundog Outfitters & Retreat Centre (☎ 705-855-0042, 888-266-1103; www.sundogoutfitters.com) is roughly 45km northwest of Sudbury near Dowling, in a wilderness setting on Lake Simmons. Sundog offers guided canoe trips ranging from four days to six days ($450 to $700) on the nearby Spanish River and in Killarney Provincial Park; prices cover all gear, food and accommodations. You will be guided by one of the proprietors themselves.

Outfitting for self-guided canoe trips costs around $75 per day, including food, and many canoeists stay at the center for the first and last nights of their trip. Sundog also runs occasional workshops loosely themed as 'sustainable living' (straw-bale construction or building an outdoor oven, for example), and outdoor wilderness yoga retreats ($390 for three nights). You can tour the set-up for a small donation ($3 is suggested) if you call in advance.

Festivals & Events

Cinéfest (☎ 705-688-1234; www.cinefest.com; ⏺ mid-Sep) For all those films you couldn't get tickets to at the Toronto International Film Festival, your best bet is Cinéfest, Canada's fourth-largest film festival. Industry types head to Sudbury to party after the big one in Toronto.

Northern Lights Festival Boréal (☎ 705-674-5512; www.nlfb.on.ca; ⏺ early Jul) This mega music fest held in Bell Park features rising stars and established acts from around the country – watch for Kevin Closs and the Arrogant Worms (see p180).

Sleeping

Plentiful chain motels dominate the accommodations scene in Sudbury, and they're a good bet if you want something utterly predictable. They're all clearly signed from all highways leading into town, and all charge from $70 to $100 per room.

Four Sisters Motel (☎ 705-670-0071; 1077 Lorne St; r $45-65) Don't let the name fool you into thinking this is anything like Wild Women, because it's simply a no-frills budget motel.

Belmont Inn (☎ 705-673-1131; www.belmontinn .com; 340 York St; r $60) This excellent alternative to the chain motels has a quiet, appealing feel, well-appointed rooms, and some nice touches in the foyer, such as free magazines and newspapers.

Days Inn (☎ 705-674-7517, 800-329-7666; 117 Elm St W; r $90) Renovated rooms, all mod-cons and a central location characterize this branch of the franchise.

Parker House Inn (☎ 705-674-2442, 888-250-4453; www.bbcanada.com/sudburyparkerhouse; 259 Elm St; s $80-125, d $90-140) Our favorite place to stay downtown is an elegant, welcoming inn with a rabbit warren of individually decorated rooms in several buildings, all centrally located. You'll love the crystal chandelier in the main entrance.

If you call the owners of Sundog Outfitters & Retreat Centre (left) in advance you can arrange to stay without participating in the activities, if space permits. Accommodations ($35 to $60 per person) consist of floored, canvas-walled tents with mostly bunk beds and outhouse bathrooms. Similarly, Wild Women Expeditions (p181) might be able to fit female travelers in around a group booking. The cost is about $200 per person for two nights including all meals.

Eating

Cafe Matou Noir (☎ 705-673-6718; 86 Durham St; mains $4-7; ⏺ 8am-3pm Mon-Sat) In the back of the browse-worthy Black Cat Too magazine store, this little eating area serves up light lunches and breakfast specials such as scrambled eggs on a muffin ($2).

Books & Beans (☎ 705-673-7823; 113 Durham St; ⏺ 8am-5pm Mon-Fri) Overheard: 'Like, when I was arrested it was cool, you know?' When we visited, activists were comparing arrests and planning their next campaign over the lentil soup ($2.60). Join in or bury your face in something from the piles of second-hand books and sip surreptitiously on a latte. There's a small menu of sandwiches ($4) and a vast menu of beverages at this quirky coffee shop.

Sudbury Sapporo Ichibang (☎ 705-673-2233; 79 Cedar St; lunch mains $9-10, dinner mains $13-16; ⏰ 11am-9pm Mon-Fri, 5-9pm Sat) This casual, charming Japanese restaurant serves the sushi, teriyaki and noodles you'd expect.

Parker House Inn (☎ 705-674-2442, 888-250-4453; 259 Elm St; mains $10-12; ⏰ 11am-10pm Mon-Wed, 11am-11pm Thu & Fri, 10am-11pm Sat, 10am-10pm Sun) If you don't like the first dining room you come to, that's OK: choose from one of five other areas after you've placed your order at the counter. There's a patio, a garden room and several warm, cozy spaces with wooden floors and cute lamps. The weekend brunch menu is fabulous, and you could linger over the newspapers for hours. In the evening the warm ambience is still there, but meal choices are a little less special, and might include salmon with lemon hollandaise and rice ($10), served to cool vocal jazz.

Respect Is Burning (☎ 705-675-5777; 82 Durham St; mains $10-20) Regional Italian food comes to the big city, where the citrus-marinated, chargrilled tuna steak with a Sicilian sauce of tomatoes, capers, olives and white wine suits the no-carbs set ($18). For the rest of us there's the 'Son of Satan' pizza, featuring jalapeno peppers, spicy salami and a wicked crust ($16). This hip megaspace feels intimate despite its size and bustle factor, and the bar is good for a stylish drink even if you're not eating.

Ristorante Verdicchio (☎ 705-523-2794; 1351 Kelly Lake Rd, West End Business Park; pasta $16-18, mains $19-34; ⏰ lunch Mon-Fri, dinner Mon-Sat) Start with the wine list. Its 35 magnificent pages embrace only Italian wines, organized by region, with explanatory notes on each region. The contemporary menu is driven by luxury ingredients, not innovative techniques: ravioli of smoked salmon and snow crab ($18) is typical. The decor won't win awards and neither will the industrial-park location (no, you're not lost), but the impeccable service might.

Entertainment

Towne House Tavern (☎ 705-674-6883; 206 Elgin St) Heaps of Canada's bands-that-have-made-it played here on their way up, including the Tea Party. It's still the best place in the region to hear local and visiting indie acts. Cover varies according to who's playing, but it's more than when this place was a lumberjack hangout in the 1920s. It's

grungy and it's in a seedy part of town. Naturally.

Zig's (☎ 705-673-3873; 54 Elgin St) Sudbury's gay/lesbian/bisexual bar has pool tables, a quiet lounge area, a big dance floor and regular karaoke. Go through the unmarked door then down the stairs. Straight-friendly.

11th Hour Lounge (☎ 705-675-5777; 82 Durham St) After 11pm each Saturday the lower level of Respect Is Burning changes gear and transforms into a loungy drinking space with a DJ or original live music.

100 Georges (☎ 705-675-2155; 50 Cedar St) It started life as a blues bar, but the blues you'll hear now are being pumped out by cover bands. The slick, cavernous space works as a restaurant by day and a crowded, popular club by late night.

Getting There & Around

Air Canada and Bearskin Airlines serve the airport in the northeast corner of the city, where all the major car-rental chains are represented. Bearskin connects Sudbury with Toronto, Ottawa, North Bay, Sault Ste Marie and Thunder Bay.

Ontario Northland and Greyhound Canada use the same **bus depot** (☎ 705-524-9900; 854 Notre Dame Ave) about 3km north of the downtown core. Ontario Northland runs between Sudbury and Toronto ($62, six hours, three daily), as does Greyhound ($66, five hours, three daily). Greyhound Canada also connects Sudbury with Sault Ste Marie ($54, 4½ hours, four daily) and North Bay ($27, 1¾ hours, three daily).

Sudbury train station (☎ 800-361-1235; cnr Minto & Elgin Sts) is centrally located, but the only train that uses it is the one that traverses miles of nothingness all the way to White River ($88, nine hours, three weekly). Except for Chapleau, the 'destinations' it serves are not covered in this book.

Most trains use **Sudbury Junction train station** (☎ 800-361-1235; Lasalle Blvd), which is about 10km northeast of the town center. VIA Rail trains connect Sudbury Junction with Toronto ($93, 6¾ hours, three weekly) and stations west to Winnipeg ($348, 31 hours, three weekly). There is no direct train service east to Ottawa; you must go via Toronto.

From the downtown **transit center** (☎ 705-675-3333; cnr Notre Dame Ave & Elm St), city buses ($2.25) run regularly to main attractions.

LUMBERJACK FOR A DAY

A trip along Hwy 17 between Sudbury and Sault Ste Marie reveals a string of mining and timber towns. You could blink and miss them and not be missing too much at all. But even (or especially) if you're a tree-hugging type, consider a contrasting and instructive introduction to the wilderness that makes all the driving worthwhile.

First, stop at Espanola (70km west of Sudbury), a pulp-and-paper town physically and economically dominated by **Domtar Ltd** (☎ 800-663-6342). Free 1½-hour tours run twice a week from mid-June to the end of August, and will give you some sense of the significance of forestry in northern Ontario. The tours include visits to the pulping operations and paper-making section, and afterwards you can walk around the trails outside the facility, which was used as a prisoner of war camp during WWII. Wear sturdy shoes; children must be over 12.

Blind River (100km west of Espanola) is a highway pit stop and home to one of several small museums on the route, the **Timber Village Museum** (☎ 705-356-7544; Hwy 17; admission $2; ☺ 10am-5pm Jul & Aug, 10am-4pm Mon-Fri Apr-Dec). It's stuffed full of artifacts that lack written commentary, but its highlight is three videos related to logging. Two were filmed by the lumber company concerned, and consist of rare archival footage of the day-to-day lives of lumberjacks in Algonquin Provincial Park and Blind River in the 1930s and 1950s. Another, produced by the Ministry of Natural Resources, is a re-creation of a 1932 winter logging camp in northern Ontario.

MANITOULIN ISLAND

The world's largest freshwater island, Manitoulin Island is a rural region of farms, villages and summer cottages. From Espanola to the island's Little Current, Hwy 6 winds across La Cloche Peninsula and over the North Channel across white quartzite and granite outcrops, with stunning views of countless bays, lakes and inlets (boaters put the 225km North Channel in the same league as the Mediterranean and the Caribbean as a cruising destination). The island includes the unceded aboriginal reserve of Wikwemikong. There is little sense of being on an island because it's so big, about 140km long and 40km wide. Almost all of the island's attractions, accommodations and eating places are seasonal, and the season is sharply defined by the ferry schedule.

Information

Manitoulin Tourism Association (☎ 705-368-3021; www.manitoulintourism.net; Hwy 6, Little Current; ☺ 10am-4pm May-Oct) The association also has an un-staffed booth at the South Baymouth ferry dock, open from the first to last ferry sailing each day. It organizes small volunteer-run offices in Gore Bay and Manitowaning. Hours for these depend on the availability of volunteers (at least 10am to 4pm), and dates coincide with the ferry schedule.

Sights

The **Ojibwe Cultural Foundation** (☎ 705-377-4902; www.ojibwe.on.ca; cnr Hwys 540 & 551, M'Chigeeng; admission free ☺ 9am-5pm Mon-Fri, 9am-3pm Sat & Sun

Jul & Aug, 9am-4pm Mon-Fri Sep-Jun) is not to be missed. It has very well curated changing exhibits on the Anishnaabe people of Manitoulin, the North Channel and the north shore of Lake Huron (the Ojibwe, Odawa and Potawatami). At the time of research, a photo exhibit illustrated the painful story of children forcibly taken from their families in these areas and sent to residential schools in the mainland town of Spanish. The art gallery here displays high-quality paintings and drawings, and there is a gift shop.

Very close by (500m east of Hwy 551), and also part of M'Chigeeng First Nation, is **Nimkee Art Gallery & Native Crafts** (☎ 705-377-5450; Hwy 540, M'Chigeeng; ☺ 10am-6pm Jun-Oct; admission free). This gallery features the owner's works in oil and acrylic on media including birchbark and rawhide, and some local pottery, quillwork and carvings. In the same area, **Kasheese Studios** (☎ 705-377-4141; cnr Hwys 540 & 551; ☺ 10am-6pm Victoria Day–Thanksgiving) highlights a more eclectic mix of work by a wider range of local Aboriginal artists.

Activities
CYCLING & KAYAKING

Manitoulin is great for cycling because nearly all the roads feel like backroads. **Bike Manitoulin** (☎ 705-377-5017; www.bikemanitoulin .com) organizes self-guided cycling trips. For $400, the owner will set you up with meals, B&B accommodations, maps, baggage transfer and vehicle support for a weekend (two nights). Groups usually consist of six to eight cyclists. Most people bring their own bikes, but you can rent one for $20 per day. Day trips, including lunch, cost $30 plus bike rental. In contrast, guides accompany the Manitoulin tours offered by Georgian Shores Cycle Tours (p157). These trips start in Owen Sound and include ferry transfers.

Bike Manitoulin also offers a kayaking option that combines paddling with peddling. The kayak component is guided, with several nights of camping. This five-day trip costs $795.

HIKING & SWIMMING

For natural beauty, the north of the island between Meldrum Bay and Little Current has some of the best scenery. The **Cup and Saucer Trail**, near the junction of Hwy 540 and the Bidwell Rd 18km southwest of Little Current, leads to the highest point on the island (351m), which has marvelous views over the North Channel. A little further west, on Hwy 540 near the cute village of Kagawong, is the popular beauty spot of **Bridal Veil Falls**. Manitoulin's largest beach is west of the ferry landing at the village of **Providence Bay**. A quieter beach backed by dunes can be found at **Carter Bay**, also on the southeastern shore.

Festivals & Events

'Wiky,' as Wikwemikong is known, hosts a huge **powwow** on the first weekend in August. Many of the events are competitive, with prize money for the best dancers, drummers and Anishinabemowin language speakers, among other things. Weekend passes cost $15. For information contact the **Wikwemikong Heritage Organization** (☎ 705-859-2385; www.wikwemikongheritage.ca).

Sleeping

Happy Acres B&B (☎ 705-859-3453, 800-203-9028; www.fobba.com/happyacres/; Hwy 6; s/d $40/50; ☼ May-Thanksgiving) A friendly young family runs this B&B in a big, homey farmhouse about 8km north of South Baymouth.

Huron Motor Lodge (☎ 705-859-3131; Hwy 6, South Baymouth; r $85, cottages $90-135; ☼ May-Oct) The ferry departure point is right across the road from this well-presented motel. The exterior sparkles, the interior is plain and the cottages are spacious.

Shaftesbury Inn (☎ 705-368-1945; 19 Robinson St, Little Current; s $90-115, d $105-155) The Shaftesbury Inn is a warm, welcoming B&B-style inn with homey rooms and a very European restaurant.

Eating

Rocky Raccoon Cafe (☎ 519-282-8111; 24 Water St, Gore Bay; mains $8-20; ☼ noon-9pm May-Oct) The owners are passionate about local produce, so the menu changes all the time depending on what's in season but always shows some Indian and Nepali influences. Tibetan *momos* (steamed dumplings; $8) come in meaty or vegetarian versions. No, it's not a chain, but yes, it's run by the same folks who have another fabulous place by this name in Tobermory. Reservations recommended.

Garden's Gate (☎ 705-859-2088; Hwy 542; mains $12-18; ☼ lunch & dinner May-Oct) The crafty tearoom setting doesn't do justice to the quality of the food here. The whitefish is so fresh you have to feel sorry for it, and the vegetarian choices, such as the spinach patties with a tomato-based sauce, are a touch quirky. Fairtrade coffees and Ontarian microbrews feature too. It's 14km from South Baymouth.

Shaftesbury Inn (☎ 705-368-1945; 19 Robinson St, Little Current; mains $18-25; ☼ dinner May-Oct) Cleanse any brown rice and tofu from your system with a hearty Old World meat dish like Hungarian goulash, German beef roulade or Wiener schnitzel.

Entertainment

De-ba-jeh-mu-jig Theatre Group (☎ 705-859-2317; www.debaj.ca) The summer season of one of Canada's foremost aboriginal theater events runs for about a month from mid- or late July in Wikwemikong, and if you can plan your trip to coincide with it, it's sure to be a highlight.

Manitoulin Island Dark Sky Association (www.manitoulindarksky.com) There's so little going on in Manitoulin in the evening that the lack of 'bright lights, big city' entertainment options has helped give rise to this group of stargazers, which aims to keep the nights dark for stargazing; it coordinates occasional astronomy nights. Some municipalities on the island have agreed to use lighting systems that don't produce 'sky glow.'

Getting There & Around

The island is accessible from the north via a toll-free swing bridge across the North

ONTARIO

DEER TRAIL

Deer Trail is the name given to a scenic touring route that incorporates Elliot Lake and other features. Coming west along Hwy 17 from Sudbury, turn right onto Hwy 108 at Serpent River. The half-loop rejoins Hwy 17 at Iron Bridge for a total of about 130km. The scenery is far more rugged than anything you'll see along Hwy 17, and passes waterfalls, trailheads offering access to old-growth forest, and Mississagi Provincial Park. The road is narrow and hilly in parts, and you should allow up to three hours of driving time plus stops.

Channel. In summer, the bridge closes for 15 minutes every hour on the hour to allow shipping traffic through the channel. For information on the ferry from the south, see p158. There is no land-based public transportation to or around Manitoulin.

ELLIOT LAKE

What do you get if you combine a city that exists solely because of uranium with a magnificent natural setting? In the case of Elliott Lake, you get one big retirement village. The first uranium mining claim in the area was staked in 1953 and the town came into being soon afterwards, growing at an explosive rate through the 1950s to become a wild place with stacks of mobile homes, a police shack and a fire shack. A series of booms and busts ended when the last uranium mine closed in 1996, and today the city has capitalized on its location by reinventing itself as a retirement center.

Elliot Lake is not only notably orderly and prosperous, it's also strikingly dull (unless you're scouting for somewhere to retire) in a friendly, bizarre, benign sort of way. Movie buffs, think *Pleasantville* meets early *Dogville*. For self-equipped paddlers and hikers, though, it's a gateway to one of Ontario's best relatively undiscovered parks.

The **Elliott Lake Welcome Centre** (☎ 705-848-7737, 800-661-6192; Hwy 108; ☙ 9am-8pm Victoria Day–Aug, 9am-5pm Mon-Sat Sep–Victoria Day) provides visitor information.

In the same building is the **Nuclear & Mining Museum** (☎ 705-848-2084; Hwy 108; ☙ 9am-7pm Jun-Aug, 9am-5pm Mon-Fri Sep–May). Here mining company Rio Algom presents an extensive display on the uranium mine decommissioning process, and a GIS database provides visitors with access to information on environmental monitoring. The town's pride is evident in a collection of newspaper articles from the 1950s, and you can get up close and personal with animal traps, beaver pelts and stuffed and mounted animals. Extensive literature presents the environmental case for fur trapping.

Elliot Lake has no motels or B&Bs. Of the three hotels, the best is the **Fireside Inn** (☎ 705-461-3711; www.firesideinn.org; 220 Ontario Ave; r $80), which has lake-view rooms and a cavernous, popular sports bar and restaurant where specials include Jamaican jerk chicken ($7).

MISSISSAGI PROVINCIAL PARK

Of all the Ontario parks with easy road access, **Mississagi** (☎ 705-848-2806, 705-865-2021; Hwy 639; day use per vehicle $9.50; backcountry sites $7.50, campsites $18.50-20; ☙ Victoria Day–Thanksgiving), 25km north of Elliot Lake, has a stronger sense than most of being a secluded retreat. Its campsites don't have electricity, and some of its few facilities (the gatehouse and toilets) are solar-powered.

Mississagi doesn't attract the same crowds that Algonquin does, yet it offers some comparable forested splendor. In ecological terms its 4900 hectares are in a transition zone, and maples, yellow birches, white birches and trembling aspens all thrive. Over billions of years, wave action on some lakes has resulted in a geological feature known as ripple rock.

Some of the park's canoe routes, which are up to 80km long, start right near the campground on Semiwite Lake. Canoe rentals are available at the park office for $20/30 per half/full day. Wild Women Expeditions (p181) runs guided canoe trips here.

For hikers, the relatively easy **Hallenburg trail** is just over 7km long and has a gorgeous view over the lake; it's one of several shorter choices. The 22km McKenzie loop is a two-day backcountry route with awesome ridgetop views.

For camping reservations, call **Ontario Parks** (☎ 519-826-5290, 888-668-7275; www.ontario parks.com). If you want a real bed head to **Laurentian Lodge** (☎ 705-848-0423; www.laurentian lodge.com; Hwy 108; r $70-100, 6-bed cottages per week $1090-1340). The lodge is 30km north of Elliott Lake, just outside the park in a wilderness setting. Its vast size gives it a conference-type atmosphere, but in summer almost all guests are families. The cottages and motel-style rooms offer plenty of privacy and lake views worthy of a superlative – most have decks right over the water. The park is not accessible by public transportation.

ST JOSEPH ISLAND

St Joseph Island is a sleepy, woodsy little place where folks wave as you drive by. If you've lived here for at least two generations, you might almost start to qualify for 'local' status.

The island's main attraction is the **Fort St Joseph National Historic Site** (☎ 705-246-2664; www .parkscanada.gc.ca/joseph; Hwy 548; adult/child $3.50/1.75; ☺ 10am-5pm Victoria Day–Thanksgiving). The British fort ruins date from the turn of the 18th century and are staffed by workers in period costume. The reception center displays aboriginal, military and fur-trade artifacts.

The island also produces a high proportion of Ontario's maple syrup, and in March and April when the sap is running many producers offer tours. **Thompson's Maple Products** (☎ 705-246-2970; www.thompsonisland.com/maple; 1733 Hilton Rd, Hilton Beach) stays open year-round. It sells maple syrup, maple butter and maple candies from the house whenever the owners are at home, and offers free tours in spring.

Better accommodations and restaurants than those on the island are found in Sault Ste Marie, 50km west. The island is reached by a toll-free bridge off Hwy 17.

SAULT STE MARIE

'The Soo,' as the city is called, sits strategically where Lake Huron and Lake Superior meet. The rapids of the St Mary's River were traditionally fished by the Ojibwe, and later presented an obstacle to the fur traders; now, close to the downtown area, a series of canals and locks enables huge freighters to navigate the last 'steps' of the St Lawrence Seaway system that stretches westward from the Atlantic Ocean to Lake Superior. Aside from the busy port, resource-based industries are major, but declining, employers. Diversification has come in the form of call centers and relo-

cating some provincial government offices from Toronto to the Soo.

Of all the northern cities, Sault Ste Marie offers the most instant gratification to travelers, the highlight being the Tour Train.

Orientation & Information

Sault Ste Marie's downtown area is compact and cheery, with pretty much everything of interest on or near Queen St. The International Bridge connects Sault Ste Marie with its twin of the same name in Michigan, USA.

Ontario Travel Information Centre (☎ 705-945-6941; 261 Queen St W; ☺ 8am-6pm mid-May–mid-Jun, to 8pm mid-Jun–Aug, 8:30am-6pm Sep–mid-Oct, 8:30am-5pm mid-Oct–mid-May)

Sights

ALGOMA CENTRAL RAILWAY & AGAWA CANYON

The Agawa Canyon is a rugged wilderness area accessible only via the **Algoma Central Railway** (ACR; ☎ 705-946-7300, 800-242-9287; www.algoma centralrailway.com). The 500km rail line, which runs due north from town to Hearst, goes through a scenic area of mountains, waterfalls, valleys and forests. The route was constructed from 1899 to bring raw materials into the industrial plants of Sault Ste Marie, and about 20 years later the Group of Seven artists shuttled along the line immortalizing its scenery on canvas from their boxcar studio: the results include Frank Johnston's *Canyon* and *Agawa* and JEH MacDonald's *Algoma Waterfall* and *Agawa Canyon*.

The **Tour Train** (www.agawacanyontourtrain.com; ☺ mid-Jun–mid-October) operates one-day round-trips to the canyon at 8am daily. The cost for adults/children is $59/20 until early September (summer fares), and $78/47 from then onwards (autumn fares). The trip is spectacular in autumn, when the forests turn brilliant reds and yellows. Normally, the colors are at their peak in the last two weeks of September and in early October. Meals and snacks are available onboard, and a two-hour stopover allows for a quick walk on the canyon floor before the trip back to Sault Ste Marie at 1:30pm.

On irregular weekends from late December to early March the so-called **Snow Train** runs the canyon route for $59/30. Although

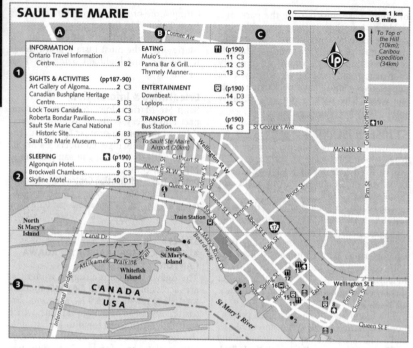

SAULT STE MARIE

INFORMATION
Ontario Travel Information
Centre...................................1 B2

SIGHTS & ACTIVITIES (pp187-90)
Art Gallery of Algoma.................2 C3
Canadian Bushplane Heritage
Centre....................................3 D3
Lock Tours Canada.......................4 C3
Roberta Bondar Pavilion...........5 C3
Sault Ste Marie Canal National
Historic Site........................6 B3
Sault Ste Marie Museum.............7 C3

SLEEPING (p190)
Algonquin Hotel........................8 D3
Brockwell Chambers.................9 C3
Skyline Motel..............................10 D1

EATING (p190)
Muio's.......................................11 C3
Panna Bar & Grill........................12 C3
Thymely Manner.......................13 C3

ENTERTAINMENT (p190)
Downbeat.................................14 D3
Loplops.....................................15 C3

TRANSPORT (p190)
Bus Station...............................16 C3

the winter scenery is spectacular, you can't get off the train – it's too cold and there's too much snow.

A regular train runs the full length of the line beyond the canyon over less impressive flat, forested lakelands, various bridges and northern muskeg to the town of Hearst (p179). It's a flagstop train (it stops wherever someone wants to get on or off) and entails at least one night in Hearst if you're returning to Sault Ste Marie. Between the canyon and Hearst the line is dotted with lodges catering largely to anglers, hunters and groups. In winter the same route serves mostly snowmobilers. The return cost between Sault Ste Marie and Hearst is $160/95.

Both the tour train and the regular train cater to hardcore paddlers seeking access to canoe routes in Lake Superior Provincial Park (p191) and other areas, and canoes can be taken on board. Among the companies offering guided packages is Naturally Superior Adventures (p192). Some of its river canoe trips use the railway to access remote areas, while its land packages include the train trip to the canyon area, a

guided 13km overnight hike, and optional meals. Prices range from $175 to $400, and this option is highly recommended if you want to get away from the hordes of daytrippers.

All trains depart from the **train station** (129 Bay St), which also sells tickets.

SAULT STE MARIE CANAL NATIONAL HISTORIC SITE

You can stroll any time around North and South St Mary's Island, which is protected as a **national historic site** (☎ 705-941-6262; 1 Canal Dr). The often continuous lake traffic (about 80 freighters a day in summer) can be watched from a viewing stand or from anywhere along the locks for no charge, but the boats are a long way out, mainly using the American locks. The Canadian lock, built in 1895, is the oldest and is used only for recreational vessels.

On South St Mary's Island the **Attikamek walking trail**, which winds through the woods and under the International Bridge, make a nice retreat, with views of the shorelines, rapids and ships.

SEEING STARS IN SAULT STE MARIE

While you're in the Soo, step outside on a clear night and look up at the stars. That's how it all started for the city's favorite daughter and Canada's first female astronaut, Roberta Bondar. Even as a young girl Bondar wanted to be a 'spaceman,' so she clipped a coupon from the back of a cereal box and sent away for a free space helmet, only to receive a one-dimensional cut-out by return mail. She was devastated – but not deterred.

Besides getting top marks at high school, she was athlete of the year in her graduation year. At university she earned a degree in zoology and agriculture while getting her pilot's license and coaching the archery team. Continuing her education, she bagged a master's degree in experimental pathology, then a doctorate in neurobiology and (just to stay well-rounded) finished off her medical degree. For fun, she parachuted and got her scuba-diving certification. At last count she was up to six earned degrees and 29 honorary ones, on top of being chancellor of Peterborough's Trent University.

Of course when the National Research Council of Canada decided to begin a space program, Bondar put her hand up, along with 4300 other Canadians. She was one of the six picked. As a payload scientist on board the shuttle *Discovery* in 1992, she studied the effects of weightlessness on the human body.

Upon returning to terra firma, she wrote a book about her experiences, *Touching the Earth*, which included many of her own photographs. She now earns a living through photography and as a motivational speaker based in Toronto. Her *Passionate Vision: Discovering Canada's National Parks* is a good travel souvenir. In *Canada: Landscape of Dreams*, her photographs accompany the words of famous Canadians discussing what the country means to them. Bondar's latest photography project, in progress at the time of research, features portraits of female astronauts.

Bondar's still strongly connected with her home town and very proud of it (the feeling is mutual). The Canadian Bushplane Heritage Centre displays artifacts from her *Discovery* mission, and the Roberta Bondar Pavilion in the waterfront area is named after her. If you catch her summering in the family cottage just northwest of the city, she might even autograph one of those books for you.

A good way to appreciate the significance of the locks and canals is on a commentated cruise with **Lock Tours Canada** (☎ 705-253-9850, 877-226-3665; www.locktours.com; adult/child $23.50/12; ☽ Victoria Day–Thanksgiving). These depart from behind the Roberta Bondar Pavilion off Foster Dr. There are several trips daily from June to August, and fewer at other times. The two-hour tour goes through both the Canadian and American locks and is the only way to see the latter from Canada.

CANADIAN BUSHPLANE HERITAGE CENTRE

Even if your interest in commercial flying focuses on the free toothpaste, you'll find plenty of information to fascinate at the **bushplane museum** (☎ 705-945-6242, 877-287-4752; 50 Pim St; adult/student/child $10.50/5/2; ☽ 9am-6pm mid-May–mid-Oct, 10am-4pm mid-Oct–mid-May). The 20-minute film about the role of bushplanes in the development of northern Ontario is a great introduction to the region, and you might leave seeing bush pilots as folk heroes of the communities they serve. A jiving soundtrack captures the sense of adventure associated with the main form of transportation in the huge areas of the province that are beyond the reach of roads and railways. There are loads of aircraft at various stages of restoration on display, and the whole place is run by fanatical volunteers who are happy to share a yarn about any aspect of flight.

ART GALLERY OF ALGOMA

The **art gallery** (☎ 705-949-9067; www.artgalleryof algoma.on.ca; 10 East St; admission by donation; ☽ 10am-5pm Mon-Sat) has two rooms of changing exhibits that often features artists from the region.

SAULT STE MARIE MUSEUM

For a good introduction to the region, it's worth visiting the **museum** (☎ 705-759-7278; 690 Queen St E; adult/student $5/3; ☽ 10am-8pm Mon-Sat &

12:30-4:30pm Sun Jun-Sep, 9:30am-4:30pm Tue-Sat Oct-May). Displays focus on Aboriginal peoples, the fur trade that changed their lives, and the local logging and mining industries. An exhibit about Hudson's Bay Company blankets explains the way the blankets were used in trade: a so-called one-point wool blanket, which was big enough to keep a child warm, was worth one beaver pelt (see the boxed text on p25).

Activities

Caribou Expeditions (☎ 800-970-6662; www.caribou-expeditions.com; 1021 Mission Rd, Goulais) is based about 35km north of Sault Ste Marie and runs an extensive program of kayaking trips in the area, including expeditions in Lake Superior Provincial Park and Pukaskwa National Park.

Sleeping

Algonquin Hotel (☎ 705-253-2311, 888-269-7728; www.hihostels.ca/saultstemarie; 864 Queen St E; r $25) Locals may tell you they've always thought of the Algonquin as kind of seedy, and it does have a mildly decrepit air. But when we visited we found the rooms clean, quiet and a steal at this price. It's HI-affiliated but has no backpacker-type facilities or atmosphere.

Skyline Motel (☎ 705-942-1240, 800-461-2624; www.skylinemotel.ca; 232 Great Northern Rd; r $65-75) Each room here has a hairdryer, an iron and an ironing board, unusual in a budget motel. It's not flash but it's clean, quiet and comfortable.

Top o' the Hill (☎ 705-253-9041, 800-847-1681; www.bbcanada.com/69.html; 40 Broos Rd; s $65, d $85-125) The manicured garden is a feature of this secluded B&B atop a hill about 10 minutes by car from downtown. The house has a formal feel but children are welcome. To reach it from the intersection of Great Northern Rd and Hwy 550 (also called Second Line East), go west on Hwy 550 for 7.4km, then turn north onto Broos Rd.

Brockwell Chambers (☎ 705-949-1076; www.bbcanada.com/1218.html; 183 Brock St; s $75-115, d $85-125) As you sip a complimentary glass of wine by the fireplace near the shelves of leather-bound books it's easy to imagine you're the bank manager for whom this grand house was built in 1905. Everything here is supremely elegant; children can't be accommodated.

Eating

Muio's (☎ 705-254-7105; 685 Queen St E; mains $5-12; ☺ 7am-9pm) Time almost stood still at Muio's c 1950 – it's a homespun diner with old chandeliers, a few booths, and breakfasts blissfully packed with carbs and cholesterol. The eggs, thick slabs of Canadian back bacon, toast, coffee and homefries ($4.50) are a better bet than lunch or dinner.

Thymely Manner (☎ 705-759-3262; 531 Albert St E; mains $14-28) Of the many Italian options in town, this one has the most innovative pastas and the best salads.

Panna Bar & Grill (☎ 705-949-8484; 472 Queen St E; lunch mains $6-12, dinner mains $15-23) Panna occupies a slick, white, contemporary space and has food and service to match. Continue the 'white' theme with an appetizer of baked goat cheese ($9) and some of the best homemade bread this side of Toronto.

Entertainment

If all you're after is cheap beer, you could join the hordes who cross the International Bridge to drink in Michigan, where you'll pay less than half what you'll pay on the Canadian side of the river. But the Soo has two much better nightlife options of its own.

Loplops (☎ 705-945-0754; www.loplops.com; 651 Queen St E; ☺ 4pm-late Wed-Fri, 7pm-late Sat) Loplops' owners have thrown their hearts into every aspect of this intimate, stylish little space, from their choice of local materials used in construction (check out the steel bar) to the great range of wines available by the glass. Come for a quiet drink, or for one of the regular evenings of folk, jazz or other events by local and visiting artists.

Downbeat (☎ 705-256-8844; 740 Queen St E; ☺ 8pm-late Mon-Thu & Sat, 4pm-late Fri) Velour-covered couches, low lighting and grandma's kitchen chairs equal retro-groove chic, and a small stage regularly hosts eclectic indie acts.

Getting There & Around

Air Canada and Bearskin Airlines serve Sault Ste Marie airport, which is about 13km west of town on Hwy 550, then 7km south on Hwy 565. All the major car-rental chains are represented here. Flights connect the city with Toronto and Sudbury.

The **bus station** (☎ 705-949-4711; 73 Brock St) is downtown. Greyhound Canada buses run between Sault Ste Marie and Sudbury ($54, 4½ hours, four daily).

LAKE SUPERIOR SHORE

The Lake Superior shore is one of those drives you must do before you die, comparable in spectacle to Alberta's Icefields Parkway (p606) and Nova Scotia's Cabot Trail (p444). Between Sault Ste Marie and Thunder Bay, Hwy 17 flirts with the shoreline, swooping up and down through dramatic rock cuttings and inlets. Presiding over the whole remote, undeveloped area is awesome Lake Superior, traditionally known to the Ojibwe as Gitche Gumee (Big Sea Water). This body of freshwater, the largest in the world by surface area, is sometimes benign, but often brutal. From a kayak you can see down 10m through pure, clear water, but as you paddle you must always show your respect for the water spirit Misshepezhieu (mish-ih-puh-*shoo*). For when Superior gets angry there are disastrous shipwrecks, none more a part of Canadian folklore than the *Edmund Fitzgerald*, an ore carrier sunk with all souls lost in 1975, and immortalized by Gordon Lightfoot (see the boxed text on p180).

The Lake Superior shore is not a short, concentrated drive. The distance from Sault Ste Marie to Thunder Bay is 690km, and while the highway dances most of its dwindling towns have as much appeal as a slow number with a great-uncle. Sailors used to say it was better to go on half rations than to have to stop in Marathon, and in Terrace Bay the roadhouse diner features TV screens in each booth. It's a long haul, and you'll probably feel faintly dissatisfied at the ratio of effort to reward if you speed through.

To really appreciate this area, you must leave the highway and explore it on foot, by sea kayak or by canoe (for some good starting points, see the boxed text on p174). A guided trip virtually guarantees an extraordinary wilderness experience bookended by plenty of creature comforts and some of the best food in the north. Then there's the map-speck of Rossport (p193), which in the most charming way has not much at all, and that's the whole point.

If you're still on a mission to get across the country as fast as possible, the towns with the most facilities (banks, plenty of motels and more than roadhouse restaurants) are Wawa (p192) and Marathon, although you'll find other motels and roadhouse diners at sparse intervals.

LAKE SUPERIOR PROVINCIAL PARK

The best feature of the shoreline drive between Sault Ste Marie and Thunder Bay is **Lake Superior Provincial Park** (☎ 705-856-2284; Hwy 17; day use per vehicle $9.50; backcountry sites $7.50, campsites $18-30), which is characterized by sheer cliffs, stately boulders, misty forests and long, empty beaches that could have been lifted from the Caribbean. The 1556-sq-km park comprises a mix of southern and northern forests. Some arctic alpine plants grow in the microclimate around the lake, particularly on the 200m cliffs near iconic **Old Woman Bay** (so named because it is said you can see the face of an old woman in the cliffs). The park is in one of the wettest areas in Ontario, and the coast is often enveloped in mist or fog, which lends it a primeval, spooky air.

The **visitor center** (☎ 705-882-2026; Hwy 17; ☺ 9am-9pm Jul-Aug) is situated in the Agawa Bay campground area, roughly 25km north of the park's southern boundary. At the time of research the center was brand new and had not established its long-term opening hours.

If you have only a day and you want to see the park's cultural highlight, head to the Agawa Rock pictographs. These images, painted in red ochre probably bound with fish oil, record the stories of generations of Ojibwe, although their full significance is unknown. The pictographs are estimated to be 150 to 400 years old. The site is roughly 16km north of the southern boundary of the park, just west off Hwy 17. A moderate, 500m walking trail leads from the parking area to the rock ledge where, if the lake is calm, the images can be viewed.

The park's headline hike is the 65km **coastal trail**, a steep, rugged, difficult route that takes five to seven days. There are five road access points, so you can also do a shorter section. The trail features hard climbs, spectacular vistas and sandy beaches, as well as the pictographs site.

Ten other hikes are accessible from Hwy 17. The diverse **Orphan Lake trail** is a moderate 8km loop featuring maple and birch forest, lake lookouts, a pebble beach and the Baldhead River. Group of Seven member Lawren Harris painted in this area. Access is from the west side of Hwy 17, a few kilometers north of the Katherine Cove day-use area.

For canoeists, the eight charted inland routes range from the 16km Fenton-Treeby loop, suitable for novices, to challenging routes accessible only via the Algoma Central Railway (p187). On Lake Superior itself, kayaking is growing in popularity. The main outfitter and tour operator serving the park is Naturally Superior Adventures (p192) in nearby Wawa. Its five-day coastal trip ($990) is suitable for newish kayakers, while inland canoe trips range from $460 to $870. Caribou Expeditions (p190) runs an extensive program of guided kayaking trips in the park: its four-day novice trip ($660) is popular.

The three campgrounds are just off Hwy 17. Bookings must be made through **Ontario Parks** (☎ 519-826-5290, 888-668-7275; www.ontario parks.com).

Moose are a road hazard in much of northern Ontario, but the park has a particularly high concentration of the animals, so take care on the highway.

WAWA

Wawa's name is an Ojibwe word meaning 'wild goose' and was bestowed on the town because of the thousands of geese that stop over on Lake Wawa during migrations. The area was once known as Michipicoten (Great Bluff), but it's just as well the town finally settled on Wawa, because it would have been hard to make a big bluff into a big statue of the sort northern Ontario specializes in. As things stand, a 9m-high steel goose marks the edge of town; the goose competes for landmark status with the stuffed moose on the veranda of Young's General Store. Michipicoten First Nation, west of the town center, retains the name.

From 1725 the area was the site of several fur-trading posts, being located at the crossroads of long-established trade routes north to Hudson Bay and east to Montréal. Later on the economic mainstays were iron ore and gold, but the iron mine closed in 1998 and there is only one active gold mine left in the area. Outdoor tourism has taken up some of the slack left by the decline of resource industries, and the small town (population 3700) is a supply center for the regional parks, as well as a base for remote fly-in fishing operations in the north.

Information

Visitor Information Centre (☎ 705-856-2244, 800-367-9292; 200 Mission Rd; ☺ 8am-8pm Jul & Aug, 9am-6pm Victoria Day–Jun & Sep-Thanksgiving)

Activities

Naturally Superior Adventures (☎ 705-856-2939, 800-203-9092; www.naturallysuperior.com) has a lodge 8km southwest of Wawa from which it runs an extensive program of kayaking and canoeing trips. Unlike some operators in the remote parts of Ontario it has frequent departures, so you might not have to plan things very far in advance to find a trip to suit your experience. Guided day trips ($95) depart several times a week, while relaxed weekend kayaking trips ($300) feature an afternoon of instruction, one night at the lodge, and paddling on Lake Superior, with one night of beach camping. These trips are suitable for total beginners. For self-guided paddlers, kayaks and canoes are available for rent for $35 to $50 per day.

Not all the company's adventures involve spending all day on the water. Workshops in landscape painting, wilderness photography and personal growth ($435 to $1145) are lodge-based, and will give you a taste of the Superior seascape from the lodge's picture windows as well as outdoors.

A few kilometers south of Wawa, west of the highway, easy road access leads to **Silver Falls** or **High Falls**. High Falls has a popular picnic area, and the two sets of falls are linked by a short section of the long-distance Voyageur Trail.

Sleeping & Eating

Rock Island Lodge (☎ 705-856-2939, 800-203-9092; www.naturallysuperior.com; campsites $15, r $70; ☺ Apr-Nov) Naturally Superior Adventures' lodge is a welcoming retreat even if you're not participating in the activities. The three big rooms are basic but comfortable and have water views, as does the lounge area. Meals can be arranged, and you can use the kitchen.

Mystic Isle Motel (☎ 705-856-1737, 800-667-5895; www.mysticisle.com; Hwy 17; r $65) Mystic Isle is right on the highway, but it has a tranquil location perched on a hill, surrounded by trees.

Wawa Motor Inn (☎ 705-856-2278, 800-561-2278; www.wawamotorinn.com; 100 Mission Rd; r $95) The rooms here are particularly well fitted out, and the motel has its own restaurant with a cozy fireplace.

Kinniwabi Pines (☎ 705-856-7302, 800-434-8240; Hwy 17; mains $14-17) What would you expect to find lurking behind the facade of a standard highway motel in remote northern Ontario? Food from Trinidad, mon! Stewed catfish ($17) and spicy baked pork with rice ($15) hiding at the bottom of an eclectic Chinese and pan-European menu attest to the owner's heritage.

Getting There & Away

Greyhound Canada buses connect Wawa with Sault Ste Marie ($41, three hours, three daily).

CHAPLEAU

Chapleau is a small logging center (population 2800) and gateway to the largest crown game preserve in the western hemisphere. For information, contact the **tourist office** (☎ 877-774-7727; 34 Birch St; ☯ 8:30am-4:30pm Mon-Fri) or the **Centennial Museum & Information Centre** (705-864-1122; 94 Monk St; ☯ 9am-4pm May-Aug).

An abundance of provincial parks protect the area's waterways; they include **Missinaibi Provincial Park** (☎ 705-234-2222, 705-864-1710; day use per vehicle $7, campsites $22-24; ☯ early May–mid-Sep) in the middle of the game preserve.

Get set for extreme adventure: **Missinaibi Headwaters Outfitters** (☎ 705-864-2065; www.missi naibi.com; Racine Lake), based in the preserve, runs trips on 20 arctic watershed rivers. There's plenty of whitewater for the experienced paddler; for self-guided trips outfitting costs $90 per person per day. Guided trips in remote areas cater to all levels of experience.

VIA Rail trains connect Chapleau with Sudbury ($53, 5¼ hours, three weekly).

PUKASKWA NATIONAL PARK

Pukaskwa (*puk-ah-sah*; ☎ 807-229-0801; www.parks canada.ca/pukaskwa; Hwy 627; day use adult/child $4.50/2.25; backcountry sites $5-8, campsites $21-23) shares many of the same natural features as Lake Superior Provincial Park, minus the highway through the middle: the Hattie Cove area on the northern tip, where the park office and sole campground are located, is as far as you can get by car. There's cell phone coverage in the Hattie Cove area if you site yourself carefully, and one outdoor payphone at the park office.

Pukaskwa features an intact predator–prey ecosystem. Caribou used to be the dominant prey animal but they are now in decline; the park is the southernmost mainland location in which they occur naturally. Estimates of the park's population vary between nine and 30, and park staff consider themselves lucky to sight one. Caribou are very wary of people, but Roberta Bondar (see the boxed text on p189) spent several days in Pukaskwa taking photos for *Passionate Vision: Discovering Canada's National Parks* and captured a caribo·ı on film, more evidence that there's nothing she can't do.

If you have only one day to experience the park and you're physically fit, the must-do hike is the one from the Hattie Cove area to White River, culminating in a 30m-long, 23m-high **suspension bridge** over the river. It's the best photo op for miles around, with all the cachet of backcountry hiking but less of the weight to carry. It's a rugged walk of 7.5km each way, and you can expect wet conditions underfoot.

That walk constitutes just a part of the **coastal trail** (60km one way). As for all remote hikes, be prepared: Pukaskwa is known for its dramatic changes in weather, which bring spectacular lighting effects and skies worthy of Armageddon.

Pukaskwa offers challenging canoeing, including the Pukaskwa River wilderness route and the less difficult, more accessible White River, a 72km trip. For kayakers, there are plenty of coastal possibilities, but you should plan to be windbound about one day in three. Naturally Superior Adventures (opposite) offers a guided 14-day adventure ($1730) from Hattie Cove south down the coast and back to its lodge for experienced kayakers, and canoe and kayak rentals. Caribou Expeditions (p190) is another Lake Superior specialist operating in Pukaskwa: its five-day kayaking trip costs $1025.

You'll probably need a boat shuttle service if you're doing any extended hiking or paddling. Contact **McCuaig Marine Services** (☎ 807-229-0193, mccuaigk@onlink.net), which can pick you up or drop you off anywhere along the coast.

ROSSPORT

Rossport is the best place on Lake Superior to do precisely nothing, in a setting reminiscent of a model miniature village, minus the kitsch, plus the quaintness. It features no signage, no fast-food stores, no motels, and hardly any people – the permanent population numbers roughly 100. What it does have is a lakeshore setting and some of the most inviting and unusual accommodations between Sault Ste Marie and Thunder Bay. Everything mentioned here is about one minute's walk from everything else, including the picture-book churches, the tiny caboose museum and a gift shop, Rossport's only nod to commerce. Rossport was founded as a railway stop, and when freight trains pass through today the entire village rumbles.

At **Rossport Inn** (☎ 877-824-4032; www.rossport inn.on.ca; 6 Bowman St; s/d $62/68, cabins $85; ☼ May-Oct) it's hard to know who or which is more charming – the 'old salt' who runs the place, or the historic 1884 inn, with its wooden floors, Hudson's Bay Company blankets, layers of quilts and sloping ceilings.

Gothic cathedrals inspired the design of the utterly contemporary rooms at **Serendipity Guest House** (☎ 807-824-2890; www.serendipity gardens.ca; 8 Main St; r $100), which was almost new at the time of research. The co-owner designed and built the place himself: each room features white pine and maple woodwork and bold colors. Serendipity's **café** (☼ 11am-8pm; lunch mains $9-12, dinner mains $22) captures the mood of Rossport through its big picture windows overlooking the lake; like the guesthouse it's open year-round.

Willows Inn B&B (☎ 807-824-3389; www.bbontario .com/thewillowsinn; 1 Main St; r $80-125; ☼ May-Oct) in the renovated schoolhouse has a homey atmosphere, and one room is wheelchair-accessible.

The turn-off to Rossport from Hwy 17 is blessedly easy to miss, so slow down and look carefully for the sign.

OUIMET CANYON PROVINCIAL PARK

About 33km west of Nipigon and 65km northeast of Thunder Bay, this **park** (☎ 807-977-2526; admission by donation; ☼ Victoria Day–Thanksgiving) is like nothing you will see from the highway. It protects an awesome canyon 3km long and 150m wide and deep, with walls that are virtually perpendicular. Fences and viewing stations have been built right at the sheer edges for heart-pounding views. The canyon was scoured out during the last Ice Age, and the microclimate at the bottom supports some rare arctic alpine plants. A 1km trail meanders around the top; camping is not allowed. Ouimet Canyon is 12km off Hwy 17 to the northwest.

SLEEPING GIANT PROVINCIAL PARK

Part of the Sibley Peninsula, this **park** (☎ 807-977-2526; Hwy 587; day use per vehicle $9.50, backcountry sites $7.50, campsites $22-30) arcs 35km into Lake Superior. Its distinctive profile can be seen from far in the distance, and sheer cliffs rising 240m out of the lake offer sensational views. The visitor center and campground are at Marie Louise Lake in the south of the peninsula.

The park is large and rugged enough to offer backcountry camping, yet compact enough to seem easily manageable, and it's great for day trips from Thunder Bay, which is about 45km from the northern boundary. The **Kabeyun trail** takes a minimum of two days, and follows the dramatic west coast of the peninsula. Shorter hikes feature viewpoints, bogs, lakes and forests. You're almost sure to see white-tailed deer. Its also common to see porcupines and red foxes.

At the very end of the peninsula where the sealed road deteriorates sits the tiny, remote community of **Silver Islet**, looking almost like a Newfoundland outport. From the mid-1800s this was the site of the world's richest silver mine; now there's a seasonal general store and a museum-worthy collection of houses and cottages.

For camping reservations, contact **Ontario Parks** (☎ 519-826-5290, 888-668-7275; www .ontarioparks.com).

THUNDER BAY

Thunder Bay reveals its charms very, very slowly. Some travelers never see past the two bleak downtown areas and the even drearier malls and expressways between them. The urban mess is a fascinating contrast with the magnificent natural setting on which the city has almost turned its back, at least in town-planning terms. But Thunder Bay is home to a strong arts scene and the largest Finnish population outside Helsinki, which adds diversity to the eating and entertainment options.

Because Thunder Bay is so far west in its time zone, there's still light in the sky at 11pm in midsummer.

History

In 1679 the French built a fort in the area, which has traditionally been occupied by the Ojibwe, but they soon abandoned it. After the American Revolution the British built a fur-trading post here, and in 1803 things really took off when the location became the headquarters of the North West Company (beaver-pelt central). Soon afterwards it became known as Fort William. This was the first of two settlements that would become fierce rivals. The second started as a landing place five kilometers north, and eventually became known as Port Arthur.

Around the same time as Port Arthur settled on a name (1882), and mining had become the region's most important industry, the Canadian Pacific Railway arrived, and soon the first shipment of wheat from the prairies chugged in from the west. So began the area's heyday as a grain transporter. All the grain being shipped eastward stopped here before the trip to the Atlantic via Lake Superior and the St Lawrence seaway. Terminals, grain elevators and other storage and cargo handling facilities still stretch along 45km of central waterfront, although the boom times are over now that a lot of grain heads west from the prairies instead of east.

It was only in the late 1960s that Fort William and Port Arthur voted to amalgamate, and after a bit of squabbling over the name, Thunder Bay came into being in 1970. Thunder Bay today is essentially a blue-collar town in slow economic decline, although its redneck reputation is readily challenged. Early in the 21st century it was designated a 'cultural capital of Canada' for a year, which meant an injection of federal cash for public artworks and events.

Orientation

Thunder Bay still has two distinct downtown areas, but the names Port Arthur and Fort William have been largely and loosely replaced by Thunder Bay North and Thunder Bay South respectively. When the two towns merged, the area between them sucked most of the life out of their centers and moved it to the area in between, which is now a wasteland of fast-food outlets and the Intercity Mall.

In Thunder Bay North, shops, restaurants and hotels cluster in the area bordered by Red River Rd, Cumberland St, John St and Algoma St. In Thunder Bay South, the main streets are May St and Victoria Ave. The two core areas are connected principally by Fort William Rd and Memorial Ave.

Information

Pagoda information center (☎ 807-684-3670; cnr Red River Rd & Water St; ☼ 9am-5pm May-Sep) This is the most central source of visitor information.

Tourism Thunder Bay (☎ 807-983-2041, 800-667-8386; Hwy 17; ☼ 8:30am-8:30pm mid-Jun–Aug, 9am-5pm Sep–mid-Jun) This information center is about 6km east of town.

Sights

OLD FORT WILLIAM HISTORICAL PARK

Thunder Bay's feature attraction is this **historical park** (☎ 807-473-2344; www.fwhp.ca; adult/child/family $10/8/31; ☼ 10am-5pm mid-May–mid-Jun, to 6pm mid-May–mid-Oct). From 1803 to 1821, Fort William was the headquarters of the North West Company. Here the Ojibwe and the voyageurs did their fur trading, and settlers and explorers arrived from the east. In 1821, after much haggling and hassling, the company was absorbed by its chief rival, the Hudson's Bay Company, and Fort William declined in importance as a trading center.

The old fort settlement, with 42 historic buildings spread over 50 hectares, re-creates some aspects of the early, thriving days of the fur trade through buildings, tools, artifacts and documents. Workers in period dress demonstrate skills and crafts, perform historical reenactments and answer questions.

The site is southwest of Thunder Bay, past the airport off Broadway Ave.

THUNDER BAY MUSEUM

This small historical **museum** (☎ 807-623-0801; 425 Donald St E; admission $3, free Sat; ☼ 1-5pm Tue-Sun) is well curated, and has enough educational value to keep adults interested and children entertained. The chronology moves through prehistory, Ojibwe ways of life, fur trading and European settlement, with the focus on the 1800s and 1900s. It's a good introduction to the region.

THUNDER BAY ART GALLERY

Contemporary aboriginal art is featured at this **gallery** (☎ 807-577-6427; www.tbag.ca; 1080 Keewatin St, Confederation College; adult/student $3/1.50, free Wed; ☼ noon-8pm Tue-Thu, noon-5pm Fri-Sun). Norval Morrisseau, one of Canada's best-known aboriginal painters, was born in Thunder Bay, and some of his work is on view. Traveling exhibitions from the region and the rest of Canada are also shown.

MT MACKAY

Mt Mackay is the tallest mountain in the area's northwestern mountain chain, rising to about 350m. Its lookout, which offers good views of Thunder Bay, is part of the **Fort William First Nation** (☎ 807-622-3093; www.fwfn.com; Mission Rd; per vehicle $5; ☼ 9am-10pm mid-May–early Oct). To reach the area from Thunder Bay South, take James St south off Arthur St over the river to City Rd, and follow the signs. A walking trail leads from the viewing area to the top of the mountain.

KAKABEKA FALLS

A spectacular 40m-high waterfall is the feature of **Kakabeka Falls Provincial Park** (☎ 807-473-9231; admission $7-9.50 per car), 25km west of Thunder Bay off Hwy 17. It's most impressive in spring, when the water in the river is at its highest, or after heavy rains. Walkways lead around and across the falls.

TERRY FOX LOOKOUT & MEMORIAL

Outside Tourism Thunder Bay, the landmark **memorial** honors the Canadian who, in the early 1980s while dying of cancer, ran halfway across the country to raise money for cancer research. After having one leg amputated, he made it from Newfoundland to Thunder Bay, raising millions and becoming a national hero before finally succumbing.

Activities

Wabakimi Canoe Outfitters & Ecolodge (☎ 807-767-2022; www.wabakimi.com; Dog Lake Rd), based northeast of town off Hwy 527 N, offers canoe rentals, outfitting and customized guided trips. Themed possibilities include ecology, geology or wildlife (the founder is a biologist with a particular interest in caribou). The company's focus is the remote **Wabakimi Provincial Park** (☎ 807-475-1634), and it has an ecolodge on the edge of the park near Armstrong, which is about 250km north of Thunder Bay.

Festivals & Events

JUNE

Thunder Bay Children's Festival (☎ 807-343-2324; www.tbcf.net; ☼ mid-Jun) Hands-on, interactive events for kids are the focus of this three-day festival based at the community auditorium. Canadian and international performers and artists in many disciplines provide entertainment.

Superiorfinn Junahhus Arts Festival (☎ 807-964-2941; ☼ on or around Jun 21) Thunder Bay's Finnish community are the experts on celebrating the summer solstice and Finnish heritage here in the land of the almost-midnight sun. The action centers on Finlandia Hall and Bay St for one day.

Thundering Women Festival (☎ 807-625-0328; www.thunderingwomen.ca; ☼ late Jun) Music and all sorts of artsy activities feature at this three-day women-oriented festival based in Chippewa Park.

JULY

Thunder Bay Blues Festival (☎ 807-684-3509, 800-463-8817; www.tbayblues.ca; ☼ early Jul) The blues fest down at the waterfront runs for three days of outdoor shows and jamming.

Thunder Bay Fringe Festival (☎ 807-344-1343; www.tbfringe.com; ☼ early Jul) Emerging and established performers fringe it up at various indoor and outdoor venues for a week.

Great Rendezvous (☎ 807-473-2344; www.fwhp.ca; ☼ mid-Jul) For three days Fort William Historical Park hosts a re-creation of the annual meeting of the Ojibwe, North West Company employees, voyageurs and other traders.

Ojibway Keeshigun (☎ 807-473-2344; www.fwhp.ca; ☼ late Jul) Also held at Fort William, this aboriginal heritage festival features drumming, singing and dancing for a weekend.

AUGUST

Festa Italiana (☎ 807-345-5511; www.italiancc.com; ☼ early Aug) For two days the Italian community takes its turn at celebrating the best of its food, music and dance. The heart of the action is the Italian Cultural Centre.

Sleeping

All these options are in and around the northern core, except for the international hostel.

Thunder Bay Backpackers Inn (☎ 807-683-3995, 866-424-5687; hostelscanada2002@yahoo.ca; 139 Machar Ave; dm $20, s/d $23/46) The basement sauna ($8 per person) is a nice touch in this happily messy hostel in a centrally located residential street. You can self-cater in the cute 1950s kitchen before retiring to one of the cramped dorms. The inn is about 3km from the Greyhound Canada bus station.

Thunder Bay International Hostel (☎ 807-983-2042; www.thunderbayhostel.com; 1594 Lakeshore Dr; campsites $13, dm $20) This hostel occupies a house, a cabin and even an old bus in a rural setting 18km east of town. Kids will love the bus, which can sleep a family of up to six.

ONTARIO

Superior Motel (☎ 807-345-1408; 446 Cumberland St N; r $50-60) The main-road setting is unglamorous, but spacious rooms, Scandinavian quilts and ample natural light, especially on the upper level, make the Superior a bargain.

McVicar Manor (☎ 807-344-9300; www.bbcanada .com/3918.html; 146 Court St N; r $70-120) Sumptuousness without fuss characterizes this B&B, a grand manor built in 1906 for a coal merchant. Even the smallest room is bigger than most hotel suites, and unlike hotel suites all rooms have the tasteful, personal touch of the young owners. Ask them what unionists did to the manor in the 1960s. It involved a bomb, but we don't want to scare you off, because if you're only going to stay at one B&B in northern Ontario, you should make it this one. Babies can't be accommodated; if you're traveling with children, inquire in advance about whether the manor is an appropriate choice.

Prince Arthur Waterfront Hotel (☎ 807-345-5411, 800-267-2675; www.princearthur.on.ca; 17 Cumberland St N; r/ste $90/160) The Prince Arthur occupies a landmark historic building downtown, but the rooms are motel-style and don't have any sense of history. The water views from the upper levels are good.

Eating

For Caribou and Bistro One, respectively the city's hippest and most exclusive eating spaces, look in the unlikely semi-industrial area bordered by Harbour Expressway, Balmoral St, Fort William Rd and the McIntyre River. Yes, you're in the right place – go forth boldly.

Hoito Restaurant (☎ 807-345-6323; 314 Bay St; ☻ 7am-8pm Mon-Fri, to 8pm Sat & Sun; mains $4-10) You'll think you've stumbled into a staff cafeteria in Finland – in fact that's how the Hoito started in 1918, providing affordable meals to Finnish bushworkers when they came to the city. At this Thunder Bay institution breakfast is served until 7:30pm, and dinner starts at 10:45am, but we would happily eat the sandwich of salted raw salmon on rye ($4.25) for every meal for a week. Once you've eaten here it's hard to go anywhere else.

Aurora Grille (☎ 807-346-4477; 45 Court St S; lunch mains $10-12, dinner mains $16-22) You won't find dried cherries, gorgonzola cheese and smoked bacon ($11) on a pizza anywhere other than at this huge, bustling place, which has a wood-fired oven and a diverse menu.

Giorg Ristorante (☎ 807-623-8052; 114 Syndicate Ave N; mains $15-20; ☻ lunch Fri, dinner Tue-Sat) This stylish Italian dinner favorite in Thunder Bay South has an open-plan kitchen, a seasonal menu and very special pasta.

Caribou Restaurant & Wine Bar (☎ 807-628-8588; 727 Hewitson St; lunch mains $10-15, dinner mains $24-28; ☻ lunch Thu & Fri, dinner daily) Caribou occupies an Ikea-look space with lots of pale wood, loud music and the best pizza in town ($12).

Bistro One (☎ 807-622-2478; 555 Dunlop St; appetizers $9-11, mains $25-30) Choose favorites such as lamb rack with gorgonzola butter and roast potatoes ($30), or more upbeat sea bass with leeks, shiitakes and anchovy cream ($28). The most memorable parts of an evening here are the low-lit, intimate sense of occasion and the exemplary service.

Drinking

Cronos Cafe (☎ 807-622-9700; 433 Syndicate Ave S; mains $4-8; ☻ 11am-7pm Mon-Fri, noon-7pm Sat) The best place for chilling out over an espresso is tucked away in an otherwise desolate corner of the southern downtown area. Cool jazz, a big bookcase and local art set the serene scene.

Dragonfly Lounge (☎ 807-345-2600; 170 Algoma St N) Hidden away in a residential area above a Chinese restaurant called Ma's is a hip, dark, loungy little bar with quirky ornaments, intimate corners and a DJ some nights.

Madhouse Tavern Grill (☎ 807-344-6600; 295 Bay St) It's a little forbidding from the street, but head on in: this is the kind of neighborly pub where you can feel almost as comfortable ordering a pot of tea as a pint of Heineken. It's great any time of day or night, and has pool tables, squashy couches and magazines as well as a good menu.

Entertainment

Magnus Theatre (☎ 807-345-5552; www.magnus .on.ca; 10 Algoma St S; adult $25-32, student $14-32) This professional theater company has premiered some now-classic Canadian works, but it also draws on international repertoire to perform six plays each season. Previews cost only $18; entry to the theater is off Waverley St.

Thunder Bay Symphony (☎ 807-345-4331; www .tbso.ca) The symphony's season runs from October to May in at least four venues, including the 1500-seat performing arts center called the Community Auditorium.

Kanga's (☎ 807-344-6761; 379 Oliver Rd; ☺ 7am-10pm Mon-Fri, 8am-11pm Sat & Sun) Saunas are hugely popular in Thunder Bay, and Kanga's is a lot like a public swimming complex. There's no nudity in the public areas, but each sauna is private, and each includes its own changing room – you rent one to suit the size of your group. Or you can go alone and feel completely comfortable; you'll still have a room to yourself. Use of the public hot tub is included in the price, which starts at $11 per person. On Friday nights, Kanga's is a huge social event, the hottest (even steamiest) entertainment in town, and you should book.

Armani's (☎ 807-626-8002; 513 Victoria Ave E) After all that culture and sweating, if it's a nightclub you seek you'll find it and a young crowd at Armani's in the southern downtown area.

Getting There & Away

Thunder Bay is served by Air Canada, WestJet and Bearskin Airlines. The airport is about a 15-minute drive southwest of the city, at the junction of Hwy 17 and Hwy 61. Flights connect the city with Sudbury, Sault Ste Marie, Toronto and Winnipeg.

Greyhound Canada buses run to and from Sault Ste Marie ($123, nine hours, three daily) and Winnipeg ($108, 10 hours, three daily). The Greyhound Canada **bus depot** (☎ 807-345-2194; 815 Fort William Rd) lies between the two downtown areas near the Intercity Mall.

Getting Around

Car rental chains are well represented at the airport. The major hotels, including the Prince Arthur Waterfront Hotel, offer airport shuttles for their guests. The 'Arthur' city bus route goes from the Thunder Bay South area to the airport ($2); catch it anywhere on Arthur St.

Thunder Bay Transit (☎ 807-684-3744; www .thunderbay.ca) covers all areas of the city and the bus drivers are helpful, which is just as well because Thunder Bay can be hard to navigate, being so big. Buses have two main hubs: the **Thunder Bay North terminal** (cnr May & Miles Sts) and the **Thunder Bay South terminal** (cnr Water & Camelot Sts). One-way trips cost $2.25.

THUNDER BAY TO MANITOBA

Beyond Kakabeka Falls the traffic thins and the highway is not as scenic as it is east of Thunder Bay. At Shabaqua Corners, the highway forks. From here the northern route along Hwy 17 is the quickest way to Winnipeg, Manitoba. The southern route (Hwy 11 and Hwy 71) is less traveled and more scenic but slower. Signs mark the beginning of a new time zone (you save an hour going west).

Almost limitless fishing camps and lodges dominate the region – lots of folks and visitors around here live to fish, and as you pass through service stations might try to lure you by offering free minnows with your tank of gas.

A world apart from the angling culture, and far from either of the highway routes, is the tiny settlement of **Pickle Lake**, and one of the last frontiers for canoeists, the aptly named **Canoe Frontier Expeditions** (☎ 866-285-8618; www.canoefrontier.com) – just in case the rest of northern Ontario isn't north enough for you. Similarly remote is **Goldseekers Canoe Outfitting & Wilderness Expeditions** (☎ 800-591-9282; www.goldseekers.net), based in the gold-rush town of Red Lake. Both virtually guarantee the trip of a lifetime as far from civilization as you can get in eastern Canada.

Northern Route

Ignace and **Dryden** have plenty of motels and basic restaurants but no compelling reason to stop. The biggest and best place to pause is **Kenora**, a pulp-and-paper town that's also a hub for much of the local tourist activity, which consists mainly of summer vacation cottages and fishing and hunting trips. Avoid the bypass to go through town and take in the pretty setting along the convoluted shores of the area known as Lake of the Woods.

The **visitor center** (☎ 807-467-4637, 800-535-4549; 1500 Hwy 17 E; ☺ 8am-5pm Mon-Fri, 9am-5pm Sat & Sun) is about five minutes east of the centre of Kenora. Main St and Front St, along the water, are the main centers of activity.

The **Lake of the Woods Museum** (☎ 807-467-2105; www.lakeofthewoodsmuseum.ca; 300 Main St S, Memorial Park; adult/child $2/1; ☺ 10am-5pm Jul & Aug, 10am-5pm Tue-Sat Sep-Jun) features the aboriginal and industrial history of the area, and highlights the period around the start of the 20th century when Kenora changed rapidly.

Serenity on the River (☎ 807-543-3107; Oldford Rd; dm $25), well northwest of town, is a backpacker hostel with water frontage. To reach it from the bypass, turn north onto Hwy 596, go right on Olson Rd, then go left on Oldford Rd, and the house is 2km along on the right.

Motel options along the highway include **Whispering Pines** (☎ 807-548-4025; Hwy 17 E; r $50-60), 10km east of town, across the street from a beach. **Days Inn** (☎ 807-468-2003; 920 Hwy 17 E; r $90-100), south of downtown, features an indoor waterslide. Restaurants cluster on Main St.

Greyhound Canada connects Kenora with Thunder Bay ($86, 6½ hours, four daily) and Winnipeg ($34, two hours, four daily).

Southern Route

Once an iron-mining town, **Atikokan** has plenty of motels and lodges. It's the supply center for **Quetico Provincial Park** (☎ 807-597-4602, 807-597-2735; day use per vehicle $7-12, camping per person campground $22-28, backcountry $13-16), a huge park mostly undeveloped but for one campground. The park is famous for its remote canoe routes (1500km of them). **Canoe Canada Outfitters** (☎ 807-597-6418; www .canoecanada.com), based in Atikokan, provides both self-guided and guided trips into this internationally known, protected, pristine wilderness.

Fort Frances is a busy point for crossing the border into the USA, and both sides of the border are also popular outdoor destinations. The **Fort Frances Museum** (☎ 807-274-7891; www.fort-frances.com/museum; 259 Scott St; admission free; ☉ 10am-5pm mid-Jun–Aug, 10am-5pm Mon-Sat Sep–mid-Jun) offers a historical introduction to the area.

Kay-Nah-Chi-Wah-Nung (☎ 807-483-1163; Shaw Rd; admission $7; ☉ 10am-6pm Jun-Sep, 10am-5pm Wed-Sun Oct-May) is a sacred Ojibwe site 50km west of Fort Frances on Hwy 11 at Emo. This site is historically significant as an early habitation location and as Canada's largest ancient ceremonial burial center.

Sioux Narrows, about 80km south of Kenora on the eastern side of Lake of the Woods, is a resort town, and many cottages, lodges, motels, campgrounds and houseboats are available for rent in the area.

EASTERN ONTARIO

Eastern Ontario is an arrowhead-shaped region north of Toronto, pointing east toward Montréal. Within this accessible southern triangle are a varied range of highlights including – from north to south – internationally known Algonquin Provincial Park, the historic lakeside city of Kingston and lazy, pastoral Quinte's Isle, which features one of Ontarians' favorite parks. The northern area is primarily lake-filled cottage country. The less-inhabited Haliburton Highlands is a quiet region of lovely, rolling forested hills. The Kawartha Lakes have intriguing aboriginal sights, and the verdant Thousand Islands decorate the St Lawrence River between Ontario and upstate New York.

Also throughout Eastern Ontario are some fine provincial parks that are perfect for hiking, canoeing, swimming and camping. More than a handful of pretty, laid-back resort towns swell with activity through the summer months.

Surprisingly, there is still no major highway running directly between Toronto and Ottawa. Rural, two-lane Hwy 7 is the route most used (at least for part of the

---

TEMPTED WITH APPLES

The **Apple Route** winds along Lake Ontario on Hwy 2 from Port Hope east to Trenton. Before Hwy 401 was built, this meandering, two-lane strip of asphalt, running through the main streets of countless towns, was the main route between Toronto and Montréal. That was then a two-day trip, necessitating a stop around Kingston. Today much of the highway's adjacent land remains rural and much of it is dedicated to apple orchards. The lake moderates the climate and protects the orchards from brutal frosts.

Colborne has the **Apple Blossom Tyme Festival** in spring and Brighton, at the other end, celebrates the harvest during **AppleFest** weekend. Along the road, look for pick-your-own orchards, always fun for the whole family. Saturday morning farmers' markets are found in Port Hope, Cobourg, Belleville, Brighton and Trenton. For more information call ☎ 866-277-5378 or check out www.appleroute.com.

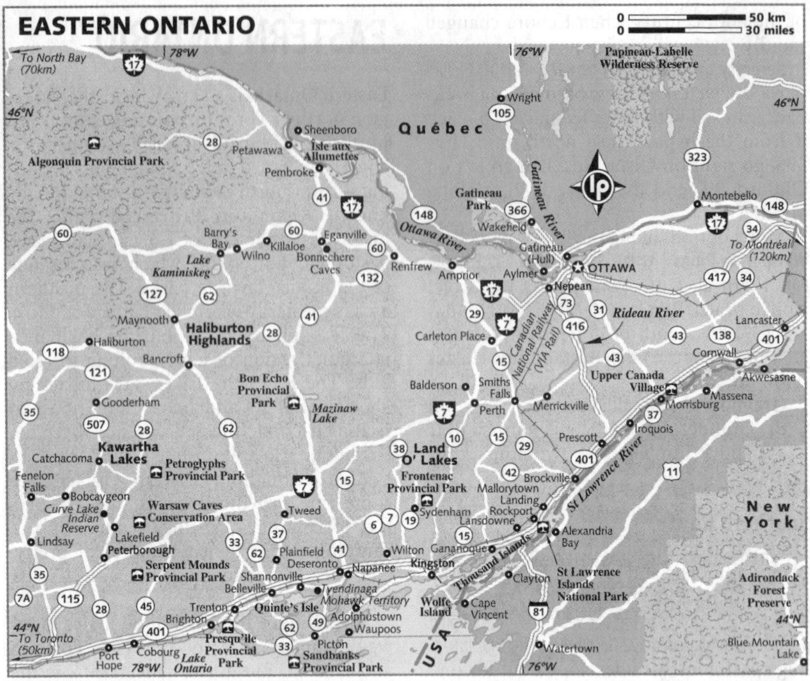

trip) and its green, winding course makes a pleasing alternative to the major highways. But it is not fast: expect the trip to take five hours.

The following places in Eastern Ontario are arranged to roughly follow three east–west routes; Hwy 401, in the south, along the St Lawrence River; Hwy 7 in the middle; and then a more northerly path.

PRESQU'ILE PROVINCIAL PARK

South of Brighton, this **park** (☎ 613-475-4324; day use per vehicle $8, tent/RV sites $25-30) on Lake Ontario west of Trenton, lures carefree beach-goers with its broad stretch of sand, but bird-watchers make up a sizable portion of the visitors too. The adjacent marsh is home to many species and is a migration pit stop to many more in spring and autumn.

QUINTE'S ISLE

The irregularly shaped island provides a quiet, pastoral retreat from the bustle of much of southern Ontario. The rolling farmland is reminiscent of Prince Edward Island, and in fact, Quinte's Isle is also known as Prince Edward County. Many of the little towns were settled in the 18th and 19th centuries. The island has been somewhat rediscovered and is slowly being developed for visitors and as a burgeoning new wine district. That said, it remains unspoiled and bucolic.

Following the shoreline of Lake Ontario, Hwy 33, the **Loyalist Parkway** retraces the steps of the British Loyalists who settled here after fleeing the American Revolution. It runs for 94km from Trenton to Kingston, passing over Quinte's Isle. To continue at Glenora, Quinte's Isle, catch the continuously running, five-minute, free and panoramic ferry to Adolphustown.

Orientation & Information

Small but active **Picton** is the only town of any size on the island and has one of the six district museums. The **chamber of commerce** (☎ 613-476-2421, 800-640-4717; www.pecchamber.com; 116 Main St; 🕑 9am-5pm May-Oct, 9am-5pm Mon-Fri Nov-Apr) has detailed maps of the island and walking tour guides, and will help with booking B&Bs and bike rentals.

Sights & Activities

Surrounded by apple orchards, the boutique **Waupoos Winery** (☎ 613-476-8338; Country Rd 8; admission free; ☽ 11am-5pm, Wed-Sun mid-May–mid-Oct), with its patio overlooking the vines and lake makes an enjoyable, intoxicating stop. It's one of six on the island.

Traffic is light on most roads, which lead past large old farmhouses and cultivated fields. The St Lawrence River is never far away, and many routes offer good views. The island is popular for **cycling** – it's generally flat, and some of the smaller roads are well shaded. The excellent **strawberry-picking** in late June draws many visitors.

Immensely popular **Sandbanks Provincial Park** (☎ 613-393-3319; Country Road 12; day use per vehicle $8, tent/RV sites $25/30; ☽ Apr–late Oct), is divided into two sections: the Outlet (with an irresistible strip of sandy beach) and the Sandbanks (containing most of the area's sand dunes, some over three stories high). The unvisited, undeveloped section at the end of the beach is good for walking and for exploring the dunes and backwaters. It's recommended – it's unlike anywhere else in Ontario.

Near Glenora, **Lake on the Mountain** is really nothing more than a picnic site, but merits a stop to see the unusual lake with no apparent source. It sits on one side of the road at a level actually higher than that of the pavement, while just across the street is a terrific view over Lake Ontario and some islands hundreds of meters below. A plaque outlines the local Mohawk legends.

Tyendinaga Mohawk Territory, just off Quinte's Isle, re-enacts the original coming in full tribal dress in mid-May. The **Native Renaissance II Gallery & Shop** (☎ 613-396-3255; Hwy 49, Deseronto; ☽ daily) has a sizable collection of aboriginal arts and crafts and a section where new ones are created.

Sleeping

Though the full gamut of lodgings is available, the area is best known for camping. This is a favorite summer destination, so reserve in advance. Each of the island's towns have attractive, country-style B&Bs.

Sandbanks Provincial Park is one of the most popular parks in the province; reservations – or good luck – are essential. For camping reservations, contact **Ontario Parks** (☎ 519-826-5290, 888-668-7275; www.ontarioparks .com). The park is booked months in advance

through midsummer, but there are always some first-come first-served sites too. Arrive early in the morning for one. From mid-August, there are more openings.

Picton Harbour Inn (☎ 613-476-2186, 800-678-7906; www.pictonharbourinn.com; 33 Bridge St; r $100-110) All the simple rooms at this unassuming, two-level hotel at the edge of Picton face the water. Main St is walkable and the restaurant is ideal for breakfast.

Entertainment

The restored **Regent Theatre** (☎ 877-411-4761; www.theregenttheatre.org; 224 Main St) hosts a good series of summer plays, concerts and readings.

KINGSTON

☎ 613 / pop 113,000

Kingston is one of Canada's most charming and best-preserved towns. Known fittingly as 'Limestone City' for its many distinctive 19th-century buildings made of local graystone, it has an appealing historic air. Side streets lined with redbrick Victorian houses and impressive churches supplement the

---

LAKE ONTARIO WATERFRONT TRAIL

Launched in 1995, after years of work by provincial and local governments, community groups and conservation authorities, the 325km Lake Ontario Waterfront Trail stretches from Quinte West through Toronto to Stony Creek on the far western edge of Lake Ontario. When completed it will run from Niagara-on-the-Lake to Gananoque and measure 650km.

Suitable for walking, cycling and even in-line skating (although not all sections are surfaced), the trail links 184 natural areas, 160 parks and dozens of museums, galleries and historic sites. It runs through 28 cities, towns and villages. Hundreds of organized activities, from sidewalk sales to jazz festivals, occur along the trail during summer.

The **Waterfront Regeneration Trust** (☎ 416-943-8080; www.waterfronttrail.org; 372 Richmond St W, Toronto) can provide maps and information on trail events, or ask at local tourist offices. A waterfront trail map book is available at **Mountain Equipment Co-op** (☎ 416-340-2667; www.mec.ca; 400 King St W, Toronto).

architectural interest. High-rises and modern developments are limited in the central core. The attractive waterfront, which is filled with pleasure boats, adds to the genteel atmosphere.

Once a fur-trading depot, Kingston later became the principal British military post west of Québec and was briefly the national capital. Much evidence remains of its waterfront defense and indeed, the contemporary military is still very much a presence.

The city is also home to Queen's University, founded in 1841, so a youthful, educated vitality is brought to the mix. Paradoxically, Kingston has a national reputation as a home to several large, (in)famous prisons.

Built strategically where Lake Ontario flows into the St Lawrence River, Kingston is a convenient stopping-off point almost exactly halfway between Montréal and Toronto, and it's not difficult to spend an interesting and enjoyable day (or even three) in and around town.

Orientation

Kingston lies a few kilometers south of Hwy 401. Princess St, the main street, runs east through town to the waterfront on Lake Ontario.

At the bottom of Princess St, Ontario St runs along the harbor by the start of the Cataraqui River/Rideau Canal to Ottawa. This is the older, much-restored area, based around the massive landmark of City Hall. Kingston Tourism, Victoria Battery and Shoal Tower (in Confederation Park), one of the four Martello towers in the city, are also here. There are views east across the mouth of the canal to the Royal Military College. The compact core is easily walkable.

King St leads out along the lake's shore toward the university. Here you'll see many fine 19th-century houses and parklands.

Information

Fort Henry Information Centre (☎ 613-542-7388; ☻ 10am-5pm May-Sep) Away from the city center at the fort, near the junction of Hwys 2 and 15.
Hotel Dieu Hospital (☎ 613-544-3310;166 Brock St; ☻ emergency room 8am-10pm) Centrally located.
Indigo (☎ 613-546-7650; 259 Princess St; ☻ 9am-10pm Mon-Sat, 10am-6pm Sun) Wide-ranging bookstore with a café that even serves wine.

Kingston Tourism (☎ 613-548-4415, 888-855-4555; www.kingstoncanada.com; 209 Ontario St; ☻ 9am-8pm Jun-Sep, 9am-5pm Mon-Fri & 10am-4pm Sat & Sun Sep-Jun) Across from City Hall in Confederation Park.
Post Office (☎ 613-530-2260; 120 Clarence St; ☻ 9am-4pm Mon-Fri)
Town Crier (☎ 613-544-7122; 350 King St E; per 30min $2; ☻ 7:30am-7pm) Excellent café with good Internet access.

Sights

Conveniently, most sites are found around the central, historic downtown.

FORT HENRY NATIONAL HISTORIC SITE

This restored British **fortification** (☎ 613-542-7388; www.forthenry.com; Fort Henry Dr; adult/student/child $11/8.75/5.50; ☻ 10am-5pm late May-Oct), dating from 1832, dominates the town from its hilltop perch and is the city's prime attraction. The beautiful structure is brought to life by colorfully uniformed guards trained in military drills, artillery exercises and the fife-and-drum music of the 1860s. Inside the fort, you can peek into a fully furnished officer's room and the commandant's quarters among other things. Admission includes a guided tour.

The soldiers put on displays throughout the day; the best is the 3pm Garrison Parade. Special events occur almost monthly.

MARINE MUSEUM OF THE GREAT LAKES

Kingston was long a center for shipbuilding, and the **museum** (☎ 613-542-2261; 55 Ontario St; museum $5.25, museum, ship and pump-house museum $6.75; ☻ museum 9am-6pm Jun-Oct, 10am-4pm Mon-Fri Apr-Jun, ship Mar–Labour Day) is on the site of the shipyard. In 1678, the first vessel built on the Great Lakes was constructed here. Among the yard's list of credits are ships built during the War of 1812. The museum details these and other aspects of the Great Lakes' history. The 3000-ton icebreaker *Alexander Henry* can be boarded. In fact, you can sleep on board – it's operated as a B&B/hostel.

PUMP HOUSE STEAM MUSEUM

The one-of-a-kind, completely restored, steam-run **pump house** (☎ 613-542-2261; 23 Ontario St; admission $5.25; ☻ 10am-5pm May–Labour Day) was first used in 1849. It now contains several engines and some scale models, all run on steam. Train buffs will also want to see the model trains from around the world.

KINGSTON

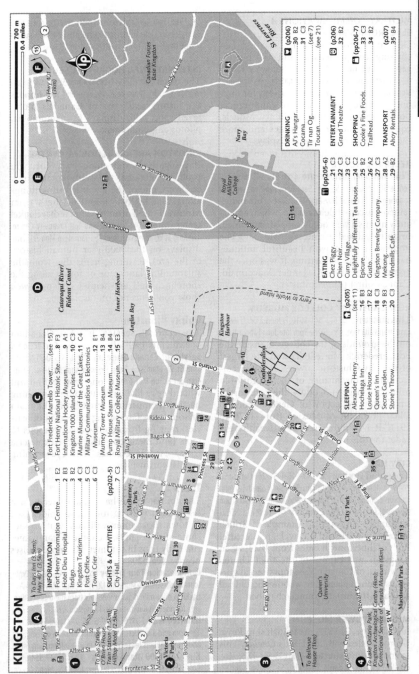

INFORMATION
Fort Henry Information Centre..............1 E2
Hotel Dieu Hospital..............................2 B3
Indigo...3 B2
Kingston Tourism..................................4 C3
Post Office..5 C3
Town Crier..6 C3

SIGHTS & ACTIVITIES (pp202-5)
City Hall...7 C3
Fort Frederick Martello Tower..........(see 15)
Fort Henry National Historic Site..........8 F3
International Hockey Museum................9 A1
Kingston 1000 Island Cruises.............10 C3
Marine Museum of the Great Lakes....11 C4
Military Communications & Electronics
   Museum..12 E1
Murney Tower Museum.......................13 B4
Pump House Steam Museum................14 B4
Royal Military College Museum...........15 E3

SLEEPING (p205)
Alexander Henry............................(see 11)
Hochelaga Inn....................................16 B3
Louise House.......................................17 B2
Queen's Inn..18 C3
Secret Garden.....................................19 B3
Stone's Throw......................................20 C3

EATING (pp205-6)
Chez Piggy..21 C3
Chien Noir...22 C3
Curry Village.......................................23 C3
Delightfully Different Tea House..........24 C2
Epicure..25 C2
Gusto..26 A2
Kingston Brewing Company.................27 C3
Mekong...28 A2
Windmills Café....................................29 B2

DRINKING (p206)
AJ's Hangar...30 B2
Cocamo..31 C3
Tir nan Og......................................(see 7)
Toucan...(see 21)

ENTERTAINMENT (p206)
Grand Theatre......................................32 B2

SHOPPING (pp206-7)
Cooke's Fine Foods..............................33 C3
Trailhead...34 B2

TRANSPORT (p207)
Ahoy Rentals.......................................35 B4

MILITARY COMMUNICATIONS & ELECTRONICS MUSEUM

Despite the driest of names, this is a fascinating, comprehensive, and well put together **museum** (☎ 613-541-5395; Hwy 2 East on the military base; admission by donation; ☻ 8am-4pm Mon-Fri, 11am-5pm Sat & Sun; mid-May–Sep) for anyone interested in all types of communication technology or things military. Models, equipment, life-sized vignettes and more make up the chronological displays.

BELLEVUE HOUSE

This **national historic site** (☎ 613-545-8666; 35 Centre St; admission $3; ☻ 9am-6pm Jun-Sep, reduced hr spring & fall, closed Nov-Apr) is a superbly maintained Tuscan-style mansion, which apparently means a very oddly shaped, balconied, brightly painted architect's field day. The impressive place with beautiful antiques has a lovely garden setting. It was once the home of Sir John Alexander Macdonald, Canada's first prime minister.

ROYAL MILITARY COLLEGE MUSEUM

This **museum** (☎ 613-541-5010; Frederick Dr off Hwy 2 East; admission free; ☻ 10am-5pm late Jun–Labour Day), on the grounds of the college, is inside the Fort Frederick Martello Tower, the largest of the city's historic towers. It has a collection on the history of the century-old military college and, oddly, the noteworthy small arms collection of General Porfirio Diaz, president of Mexico from 1876 to 1911. It was purchased by a wealthy ex-cadet for this museum.

CITY HALL

The grand **City Hall** (☎ 613-546-4251; 261 Ontario St; ☎ 9am-4pm Mon-Fri, also 11am-3pm Sat & Sun Jul & Aug, tours on demand Mon-Fri Jun-Sep, also 11am-3pm Sat & Sun Jul & Aug) is one of the country's finest classical buildings – an excellent example of British Renaissance Tuscan Revival architecture! Built of limestone, it dates from 1843, when Kingston was capital of the then United Provinces of Canada. Free tours reveal gorgeous stained glass, fine woodwork, old jail cells and the ornate council chamber.

MURNEY TOWER MUSEUM

Just offshore, in 1812, the British ship *Royal George* battled with the USA's *Oneida*. This round **defense structure** (☎ 613-544-9925; Macdonald Park, cnr of Barrie St & King St E; admission $3; ☻ 10am-5pm Jun-Sep) from 1846 was part of the early riverside fortifications and now houses local and military historical artifacts.

INTERNATIONAL HOCKEY MUSEUM

The **center** (☎ 613-544-2355; Alfred St at York St; admission $4; ☻ 10am-4pm mid-Jun–mid-Sep) honors the history and stars of Canada's most-loved sport with displays of memorabilia, photos and equipment.

KINGSTON ARCHAEOLOGICAL CENTRE

If you've been out along Hwy 401, you probably noticed the sedimentary rock outcrops, one of the few interesting things along that highway's entire length from Montréal to Toronto. The **archaeological center** (☎ 613-542-3483; behind Tett Creativity Centre, 370 King St W; admission free; ☻ 9am-4pm Mon-Fri) has displays on the 8000-year human history of the area, featuring items dug from the surrounding landscape or found along the shoreline. Staff are helpful and may well show you items not on display.

Quirky Kingston

'Correctional Service' is what Canadian bureaucrats call jails, and the **Correctional Service of Canada Museum** (☎ 613-530-3122; 555 King St W; admission free; ☻ 9am-4pm Mon-Fri, 4pm Sat & Sun May-Sep) is one way to find out what they're like without doing something nasty. The museum, across from the main prison, has a fascinating collection of articles, ranging from confiscated weapons to tools (and methods – like carved cafeteria trays) used in escapes. The eye-opening visit is worthwhile.

Tours

The tourist office has a pamphlet with a self-guided walking tour of the older part of town. Boat tours will take you around some of the islands; a couple of companies run daily trips in summer. For more cruises nearby, see p208.

Confederation Tour Trolley (☎ 613-548-4453; 50min tours adult/senior & student $12/9; ☻ mid-May–Sep) A trackless mini-train departs regularly from the tourist office area for rides around the central Kingston area.

Haunted Walk (☎ 613-549-6366; 2hr tours $12; ☻ 8pm mid-Jun–Oct) Tours featuring stories of hangings and grave robbers leave from the tourist information office.

Kingston 1000 Island Cruises (☎ 613-549-5544; 1 Brock St) Has several cruises leaving from the *Island Queen* dock, on Ontario St at the foot of Brock St. The 1½-hour trip ($17) aboard the *Island Belle* takes you around the interesting Kingston shoreline with commentary on noteworthy sites. Throughout the summer there are two or three trips a day. There are also three-hour cruises ($22) and dinner or sunset sails on the *Island Queen* showboat.

Festivals & Events

Call the tourist office for details.

Kingston Buskers Rendezvous (Jul) Three days always filled with surprises.

Kingston Jazz Festival (613-545-0761; www .kingstonjazz.com; Sep) Bops the town in various locations for a week.

Sleeping

Kingston offers a full range of choices from camping to deluxe B&Bs. Motels are strung along Princess St and along Hwy 2 on each side of town. The tourist office can help with finding more choices.

BUDGET

Alexander Henry (613-542-2261; www.marmus.ca; 55 Ontario St; r $32-90; May-Oct; P) In summer, a unique B&B experience is this moored, retired 64m icebreaker. The ship is part of the downtown Marine Museum of the Great Lakes. Beds are in the former crew's quarters, and a continental breakfast is served from the galley. Wander all over the ship, it hasn't been gentrified at all – the vessel is plain, simple and functional, and the 19 rooms are pretty much like those on a working ship. This partially explains the good prices, from hostel bunks to the captain's quarters.

Louise House (613-531-8237 ext 400; kingston@ hihostels.ca; 329 Johnson St; dm $18, s/d incl breakfast $35/50; May–late Aug; P) This summer-only HI hostel is downtown. The rest of the year this 1847 house is a university residence.

Hilltop Motel (613-542-3846; 2287 Princess St; r $35-55) This fine budget place is clean, quiet and friendly. The rooms are small and modest but it's just a few minutes' drive from downtown.

Lake Ontario Park (613-542-6574; fax 613-542-6574; King St W; campsites $20) Only 4km from downtown, this convenient campground is operated by the city's parks department. It's west, out along King St, and is green and reasonably quiet. There's a small (weedy) beach. A city bus runs from downtown right to the campground from Monday to Saturday until 7:30pm (Friday until 10:30pm).

MID-RANGE

Stone's Throw (613-544-6089; www.astonesthrow .ca; 21 Earl St; r $65-$130) Morphed out of one of the city's 200-year-old limestone houses are three comfortable rooms with private or semi-private bathrooms. Breakfast is included. The patio overlooks the lake and you can walk downtown.

Queen's Inn (613-546-0429, 866-689-9177; www .queensinn.ca; 125 Brock St; r $79-150) Historic and central, the Queen's, dating from 1839, is one of the oldest hotels in the country but now offers modern facilities and services in its 17 rooms. There's an onsite restaurant and sports bar at this stone place in the heart of downtown.

O'Brien House (613-542-8660; 39 Glenaire Mews; s/d with shared bathroom $60/80, r $95; P) Up near the train station, northwest of the downtown area, this well-established homey Irish place is a little less costly than the city norm even with the breakfast. The owners seem to particularly like overseas visitors. There are reduced rates for children. Coffee and tea are available all day.

Days Inn (613-546-3661; www.daysinnkingston .com; 33 Benson St; r $110-120; P) Close to Hwy 401 but just a few minutes' drive into town, this chain is convenient. The fitness center helps, too.

TOP END

Hochelaga Inn (613-549-5534; www.hochelagainn .com; 24 Sydenham St; r $150-190) Some places are simply worth the money. Heck, the must-be-seen-to-be-believed exterior here is nearly worth the price. The 1880s Victorian gem, in the swish Sydenham neighborhood, with antique-filled rooms and an elegant breakfast room, is one-of-a-kind.

Secret Garden (613-531-9884, 877-723-1888; www.the-secret-garden.com; 73 Sydenham St; r $110-160; P) Also in Sydenham is this substantial Victorian mansion, with seven finely decorated guest rooms and a pleasant garden patio. Step into a lost era.

Eating
BUDGET

Epicure (613-536-5389; 291 Princess St; mains under $8; 8am-late) Amid increasingly yuppified downtown Kingston is this bit of funk, grit and fun, where you can read the paper, quaff a beer and wolf down a breakfast or sandwich any time of day. The menu is short but well prepared and boasts a few French-inspired items. On weekend mornings, the double-vision special of two-egg benedict and a pitcher of beer ($10) may come in handy.

Delightfully Different Tea House (☎ 613-546-0236; 222 Wellington St; mains under $8; ☒ 8am-4pm Mon-Fri, 10am-4pm Sat) Tucked on the corner, this grandma-like cottage turns out excellent low-cost fresh sandwiches, salads and bagels for lunch, or muffins and the like for breakfast. Include the distinctive Moroccan peanut tomato soup with a meal. There's a wide variety of teas – and you pick the pot.

MID-RANGE

Windmills Café (☎ 613-544-3948; 184 Princess St; lunch/dinner mains $8/15; ☒ 9am-9pm, closed Sun) Contemporary Windmills serves very good vegetarian and meat dishes amid café-for-grownups surroundings. The healthful, creative menu has an international twist and may include items such as Thai shrimp salad or warm goat-cheese torte. Wine is served.

Mekong (☎ 613-549-5902; 394 Princess St; mains under $10; ☒ 11am-11pm) Students and members of the local Vietnamese community enjoy this spotless place with great food at absurd prices. How about spicy chicken, chopped spring roll, a heap of veggies and peanuts with vermicelli for $7? There are plenty of hearty *pho*s (soups) that can make a meal, too.

Gusto (☎ 613-536-5175; 425 Princess St; lunch $8-14, dinners $16-26; ☒ 11-1am) This stylish place at the corner of Division St is one of the city's in spots. The design, the food and even the customers are all very well turned out and the bar features martinis. The menu is primarily Italian fare with such classics as veal *scaloppini*.

Curry Village (☎ 613-542-5010; 169A Princess St; lunch/dinner mains $8/10; ☒ 11:30am-2pm & 5pm-9:30pm Mon-Sat, 2-9pm Sun) Upstairs, this long-running spot features *biryanis*, tandooris and a range of curries – and even classic but hard-to-find mulligatawny soup. Service can be slow but your meal will be freshly cooked.

Kingston Brewing Company (☎ 613-542-4978; 34 Clarence St; mains $8-14; ☒ 11am-2am) This pub brews its own ales and lagers (try its Dragon's Breath Ale) and also has a good selection of non-house brands. It also makes its own wines and ciders, the first in Canada

to do so, and smokes its own ribs! Hey, this is truly a hands-on operation! There are inexpensive tavern-style munchies and, interestingly, a daily curry.

TOP END

Chien Noir (☎ 613-549-5635; 69 Brock St; lunch/dinner mains $10/25; ☒ 11:30am-10pm) Urbane, sleek and modern in design, this French-style bistro delivers the gastronomic goods. Steak *frites* is a favorite but there's duck confit and mussels too and an excellent value daily prix fixe. There's a decision-cramping brunch menu on weekends, too.

Chez Piggy (☎ 613-549-7673; 68 Princess St; lunch/dinner mains $12/22; ☒ 11:30am-2pm, 6-10pm) For a splurge, this is the city's best-known restaurant. It's in a renovated early-19th-century building down a small alley, with a pretty courtyard, off King St between Brock and Princess Sts. Although it's been a local go-to spot since 1979, standards have never slipped. The innovative menu includes pastas, scallops and salmon. There is also a Sunday brunch with some unique items.

Drinking & Entertainment

The Kingston Brewing Company is a great watering hole, as is **Toucan** (☎ 613-544-1966; 76 Princess St), an Irish pub, down the alley near King St, which sometimes has live music but always has cold beer.

Cocama (☎ 613-544-1428; 178 Ontario St; cover charge applies) This huge dance floor down near the waterfront is styled after the Limelight in New York City.

AJ's Hangar (☎ 613-547-3657; 393 Princess St) Students enjoy the multilevels offering a mix of live rock, pool tables and dancing.

Grand Theatre (☎ 613-530-2050; 218 Princess St) The city's premier venue presents theater, the symphony, concerts and comedy.

Tir nan Og (☎ 613-544-7474; 200 Ontario St) Most nights this Irish oasis serves up live Celtic music with no cover charge.

Shopping

The middle of town in the 19th century was Brock St, and many of the original shops still stand along it. It's worth a stroll. Take a look in **Cooke's Fine Foods** (☎ 613-548-7721; 61 Brock St), a gourmet shop with old, wooden counters and a century-old pressed-metal ceiling. There are lovely aromas and a curious assortment of goods and shoppers, including local professors drinking the fresh coffee at the back of the store.

For quality outdoor/camping equipment and supplies, check out **Trailhead** (☎ 613-546-4757; 237 Princess St).

On Tuesday, Thursday, Saturday and Sunday, a small, open-air market takes place downtown, behind City Hall on King St. Get some flowers for your room.

Getting There & Away

The **bus terminal** (☎ 613-547-4916; 175 Counter St) is a couple of kilometers south of Hwy 401, east off Division St. Service to Toronto is frequent throughout the day (at least eight trips), ditto for Ottawa, slightly less frequently to Montréal. Services also go to some smaller centers, such as Pembroke and Cornwall. The one-way fare to Toronto is $47 (three hours), Ottawa $35 (2½ hours) and Montreal $48 (3 hours).

For car rental, try **Discount** (☎ 613-384-6002; 1654 Bath Rd), which offers pick-up and drop-off.

The train station is a long way northwest from the downtown area. VIA Rail runs five daily trains to Montréal ($71, 2¼ hours), four to Ottawa ($44, two hours) and eight to Toronto ($72, 2¼ hours).

Getting Around

For information on getting around by bus, call **Kingston Transit** (☎ 613-546-0000). To get to town from the bus terminal, there is a city bus stop across the street. Buses depart 15 minutes before and after the final bus. From the train station, city bus No 1 stops on the corner of Princess and Counter Sts, just a short walk from the bus station.

Cyclists will be happy to note that the Kingston area is generally flat, and both Hwys 2 and 5 have paved shoulders. Rentals are available at **Ahoy Rentals** (☎ 613-539-3202; 23 Ontario St). If you're driving, the parking lot on Ontario St at Earl St is best.

WOLFE ISLAND

The free mini-cruise on the car ferry from Kingston to Wolfe Island is a delightful jaunt. The 20-minute trip affords views of the city, the fort and a few of the Thousand Islands. Wolfe Island, the largest in the chain at 30km by 11km, lies halfway to the USA and is basically flat farmland, although many of its inhabitants now work in town.

There is not a lot to see on the island, but the 150-year-old **General Wolfe Hotel** (☎ 613-385-2611; 800-353-1098; www.generalwolfehotel.com; r $55-$115) just a short walk from the dock will give you an excuse to visit. The highly regarded dining room serves French/nouvelle cuisine. The prix fixe is $33; à la carte is pricier.

For a quiet night camping, there's **Hi-Lo Hickory** (☎ 613-385-2430, 877-996-7432; fax 613-385-1424; 260 Hogan Rd; tent & RV sites $20-24). It's about 12km east of the Kingston ferry terminal and has a beach.

On the Kingston side, the ferry terminal is at the intersection of Ontario and Barrack Sts. The ferry runs continuously every hour or so from 6am to 1am daily, taking about 50 vehicles at a time. From Wolfe Island, another ferry links to Cape Vincent, New York, but a toll is charged on this segment if you have a car.

GANANOQUE

Pleasant, easy-going Gananoque (gan-an-awk-way) is the gateway to the Thousand Islands. It is also the area's commercial center and offers the best visitor amenities. Bustling in summer, the waterfront is lined with some tourist-oriented shops in replica 19th-century architecture.

For information on lodging or activities, the **chamber of commerce** (☎ 613-382-3250, 800-561-1595; www.1000islandsgananoque.com; 10 King St E; 9am-5pm May-Oct, 9am-5pm Mon-Fri, 10am-4pm Sat & Sun Nov-Apr) is well-informed.

Several operators provide cruises; ask for details before selecting – some make stops, others don't, and there are long and short trips. **Gananoque Boat Line** (☎ 613-382-2144; www.ganboatline.com; 6 Water St, off King St; 1hr tours adult/child $14/7, 3hr tours $20/7, castle $22/7 May-Sep) has trips of varying lengths and stopovers at Boldt Castle are permitted. For island/cruise details, see p208.

You can also organize your own boat trips through **Houseboat Holidays** (☎ 613-382-2842; www.gananoque.com/hhl; RR3, Gananoque; midweek/weekend/weekly rates from $850/650/1350).

Misty Isles Lodge (☎ 613-382-4232; www.mistyisles.ca; 25 River Rd, Lansdowne) rents kayaks and offers tours, instruction and camping packages.

Gananoque sports an abundance of memorable upmarket and architecturally eye-catching inns. **Victoria Rose Inn** (☎ 613-382-3386, 888-246-2893; www.victoriaroseinn.com; 279 King St W; d incl breakfast $120-210) Once the mayor's house, this monument of Victorian splendor has a glassed-in veranda overlooking garden terraces and a dining room for evening meals to complement the comfortable, spacious rooms.

Gananoque Inn (☎ 613-382-2165, 800-465-3101; www.gananoqueinn.com; 550 Stone St S; r from $155) is right at the water's edge. The old carriageworks B&B has been welcoming guests since 1896. Everything in town is minutes away by foot.

Stone Cottage (☎ 613-382-3554; www.bbcanada .com/4425.html; 340 Garden St; r incl breakfast $50-95) is less expensive, but hosts Wilma and Jim, who have been running B&Bs for years, make up for any possible lack of luxury. They are knowledgeable about the area and provide good advice.

Thousand Islands Playhouse (☎ 613-382-7020; www.1000islandsplayhouse.com; 550 Stone St) has, since 1983, presented a quality line-up of mainly light summer theater.

THOUSAND ISLANDS

Stretching from Kingston to Mallorytown Landing, this pretty region actually boasts 1800 islands dotting the river between the two national mainlands. It's a sedate, summery area with some low-key attractions, Loyalist history and lazy boat cruises.

Between Gananoque and Mallorytown Landing, the narrow, slow-paced **Thousand Islands Parkway** dips south of Hwy 401 and runs along the river for 35km before rejoining the highway. It makes a scenic, recommended side trip. The route offers picnic areas and good views out to many of the islands from the pastoral strip of shoreline. There is an art colony in the area, and in autumn, many of the studios are open. The **Bikeway** bicycle path extends the full length of the parkway.

Close to Lansdowne is a busy bridge to New York State. The **Skydeck** (☎ 613-659-2335; Hill Island; adult/child $8/5; ☽ 8:30am-dusk mid-Apr–Oct) is a 125m observation tower between the bridge spans. Its three decks provide great views over the river area and there's a restaurant.

The Thousand Islands are graced by numbers of grand summer mansions, some better described as castles. They stand as monuments to the lavish lifestyles of wealthy tycoons who popularized the resort area in the late 19th and early 20th centuries.

Nearby Rockport is a cruise center. Heritage 1000 Island Cruises (p204) utilizes two of the area's last vintage vessels, one from 1929, the other 1959. One cruise has a stopover option at gorgeous, rambling Boldt Castle (admission $5), never finished because the woman for whom it was intended died. **Rockport Boat Line** (☎ 613-659-3402, 800-563-8687; 23 Front St; tours $14; ☽ May-Nov) runs two vessels cruising daily (on the hour from July to October) including a look-see past the castle. **1000 Island Cruises** (☎ 800-353-3157; Boathouse Country Inn, 17-19 Front St; tours adult/student $20/18 with castle stop) offers three cruises, one with a stopover at the castle. Passengers stopping at the castle are subject to US customs regulations, and non-Canadians may need a passport and visa. The autumn cruises with multicolored leaves as a backdrop are justly popular.

St Lawrence Islands National Park (☎ 613-923-5261; backcountry sites $13), the smallest in the system, is a gentle, green archipelago, consisting of 17 islands scattered along 80km of river. Park headquarters at Mallorytown Landing has an interpretive and information center, walking trail and beach. The center is open all year, but access to the islands is only from Victoria Day to Labour Day. Many of the islands have picnicking, and 13 islands offer backcountry campsites accessible only by water taxis or rented boats.

BROCKVILLE

Attractive Brockville, with its many old stone buildings, mansions and classic-looking main street is one of the best stops along the river. The courthouse and jail in the town center date from 1842. During summer, many of the finest buildings are lit up, accentuating the slight resort flavor of this casual river port by the Thousand Islands.

Brockville Museum (☎ 613-342-4397; 5 Henry St; adult/child $4/3; ☽ 10am-5pm Mon-Sat, 1-5pm Sun May-Oct; 10am-5pm Mon-Fri Nov-Apr), in the historic Beecher House, provides a look at the area's history. **Fulford Place National Historic Site** (☎ 613-498-3003; 287 King St E; adult/child $5/4; ☽ 11am-4pm Wed-Sun Jun-Sep; 11am-4pm Sat & Sun Oct-May) is a 35-room Edwardian mansion from the 1900s.

1000 Islands Cruises (☎ 613-345-7333, 800-353-3157; Broad St; 1hr tours adult/child/student/senior $12/7/11/11; 2½hr tours $20/12/18/18; mid-May–mid-Oct) offers two to four cruises that tour the islands daily, the longer trip stopping at Singer Castle, which wouldn't be out of place in Scotland. It was built with funds from the Singer Sewing Machine Co. Note it is in the USA (have your papers in order!). Admission is $20 or there's a free video tour to watch on the premises.

Pine St Inn (☎ 613-498-3866; dunnwithflair@hotmail .com; 92 Pine St; d incl breakfast $75) is a fine 1870 brick home, close to the pub and the cruise departure dock, with a porch made for kickin' back and watching the river flow.

PRESCOTT

Another 19th-century town, Prescott has the International Bridge to Ogdensburg, New York State and, more interestingly, **Fort Wellington National Historic Site** (☎ 613-925-2896; adult/child $4/2.50; ✆ 10am-7pm May-Sep). The original fort was built during the War of 1812. It was rebuilt in 1838 and served militarily until the 1920s. Some original fortifications remain, as does a blockhouse and the officers' quarters from the 1830s. During summer, guides in costume supplement the interpretive displays. In the third week of July, the fort hosts the country's largest military pageant, which includes mock battles in full regalia.

Colonel's Inn (☎ 613-925-1288, 888-718-5588; www.bbcanada.com/colonelsinn; 408 East St; d $60-100; ⊛) is a lovely historic stone house off the main street downtown, near the fort.

MORRISBURG

Tiny Morrisburg is known far and wide for it's quality historic site, **Upper Canada Village** (☎ 613-543-4328, 800-437-2233; adult/student $17/11; ✆ 9:30am-5pm mid-May–mid-Oct). This detailed re-creation of a country town from the 1860s consists of about 40 buildings, and costumed workers bring the past to life. There's a blacksmith's shop, sawmill, working farm and inn (with meals) all set by the river and requiring at least several hours to fully explore. Without transportation, the village can be reached aboard buses running between Ottawa and Cornwall and on some Montréal to Toronto trips.

The **Inn by the Park** (☎ 613-543-0660; www .bbcanada.com/5298.html; 22 Sir James Morris Dr; d $60) is a quiet, Spanish-style B&B peacefully set by the river. There are also about half a dozen motels and campgrounds.

Highway 2 along the river is slow but provides a more scenic trip than Hwy 401. **Parks of the St Lawrence** (☎ 613-543-3704, 800-437-2233) government agency, based in Morrisburg, runs Upper Canada Village, the nearby **Upper Canada Migratory Bird Sanctuary** and Fort Henry, in Kingston, as well as many of the area campgrounds and parks.

CORNWALL

Cornwall is the last large city in Ontario along the St Lawrence Valley and has the Three Nations Bridge to Massena, New York, a busy entry point. In the 1870s Thomas Edison helped set up the first factory lit by electricity here.

On Cornwall Island, the Akwesane Mohawk reserve has the **Ronatahonni Cultural Centre** (☎ 613-932-9452; admission free; ✆ 8am-4pm Mon-Fri), focusing on Iroquois culture with artifacts and a replica longhouse.

The **Long Sault Parkway** connects a series of parks and beaches along the river.

PETERBOROUGH

For those traveling the more northerly route through Eastern Ontario, Peterborough is a good base for exploring the Kawartha Lakes region. It's a mid-sized, green university town with the Otonabee River drifting by and through a large hydraulic lock.

The **tourist office** (☎ 800-461-6424; www.theka warthas.net; 175 George St N; ✆ 8:30am-8pm Mon-Sat, 10am-4pm Sun Jul & Aug, 9am-5pm Mon-Fri, 9am-4pm Sat Sep-Jun) helps with planning your town or district visit.

The **Canadian Canoe Museum** (☎ 705-748-9153; 910 Monaghan Rd; adult/family $6.50/18; ✆ 10am-5pm May-Oct; 10am-4pm Mon-Fri, 1-4pm Sat & Sun Nov-May) is excellent. Re-opened in 2004, it has a fabulous collection with 200 canoes and kayaks as well as related exhibits in the attractive, well-designed space.

Ten kilometers southeast of town is **Lang Pioneer Village** (☎ 705-295-6694; Hwy 7 to County Rd 34; adult/child $6/3; ✆ noon-5pm Sun-Fri, 1-4pm Sat late May–early Sep), with costumed workers, demonstrations and 20 buildings dating from 1800 to 1900.

Highway 7 has motels and the old central area has good restaurants and some B&Bs. **St Veronus** (☎ 705-743-5714; 129 Hunter St W; ✆ 11am-1am) is a combination Belgian beer temple and café/restaurant that merits investigation.

KAWARTHA LAKES

Many of the towns across this vacation region have a good restaurant or two and, usually, a couple of antique dealers. **Bobcaygeon**, **Fenelon Falls** and **Lindsay** are worth dropping into. Hiking and canoe routes abound throughout the Kawarthas as do aboriginal sites. The tourist office at Peterborough (p) is the best source of information on the region.

About 900 Ojibwe reside at Curve Lake Indian Reserve, off Hwy 23, 34km north of Peterborough. **Whetung Ojibway Centre** (☎ 705-657-3661; admission free; ◷ 9am-5pm) has a vast collection of aboriginal crafts from around the country. The log building contains both new and old examples of aboriginal art, and the museum section has traditional pieces and valuable works from such artists as Norval Morrisseau. The shop sells both trinkets and quality work. The tearoom, open May to Thanksgiving, offers traditional foods such as buffalo burgers and corn soup.

Spirit Walks (☎ 800-461-6424) is an association of Aboriginals and area experts who put together ideas and tour packages focusing on the geography and cultural traditions of the First Nations people. Prices range widely ($10 to $100) depending on the destination and program. **Kawartha Kayaking** (☎ 877-877-2723; RR2, Lakefield) runs enjoyable kayak trips and packages around Stoney Lake suitable for novices. For example, a one-day kayak package with lunch and a lesson is $95.

The district has some intriguing parks as well. **Petroglyphs Provincial Park** (☎ 705-877-2552; off Hwy 28; admission $8.50; ◷ mid-May–Thanksgiving) has probably the best collection of prehistoric rock carvings in the country. Rediscovered in 1954, there are reportedly 900 figures and shapes carved into the park's limestone ridges, although only a fraction of that number is really discernable. Consequently, though interesting, it is not an overwhelming site. The area and small lake within the park remain important spiritual sites for the local Aboriginals. **Serpent Mounds Provincial Park** (☎ 705-295-6879; off Rte 34; admission $8.50; ◷ May-Oct), south of town, is the site of an ancient aboriginal burial ground. North on Rte 38, the **Warsaw Caves Conservation Area** (☎ 877-816-7604; ◷ mid-May–Oct) has hiking, swimming, camping and spelunking in eroded limestone tunnels and caves.

The **Central Ontario Loop Trail** (www.looptrail.com), a 450-km scenic recreational trail, much of it on abandoned rail lines, passes through Peterborough. It runs to Lindsay, Fenelon Falls, up to Haliburton and back south from Bancroft. The Peterborough tourist office can provide information on the trail.

TRENT-SEVERN WATERWAY

The **waterway** (☎ 800-663-2628; www.ftsw.com; ◷ mid-May–mid-Oct) cuts diagonally across cottage country, following rivers and lakes through or near many of the region's best-known resort areas, including the Kawartha Lakes and Lake Simcoe. It runs for 386km

---

THE LURE OF THE LURE

Eastern Ontario, most notably the Kawarthas and Haliburton Highlands, is a fishing paradise, drawing anglers from far and wide and many from across the US border. Bass, northern pike, delicious walleye (pickerel) and the near-mythic muskellunge (muskie) are the prime species in these relatively warm waters. Occasionally a prehistoric-looking sturgeon is pulled to the surface to the shock of all. But nothing compares to the fables concerning the muskie – like anglers jumping overboard when they get one in the boat, or, in utter fear, shooting it and thus sinking their means of transport.

Locals like to tell the story of the visiting angler who, while having a very successful day, wondered how he might find the same productive hole the following day. His partner said, 'let's mark the spot, we'll put an x on the floor of the boat.' The smirking response to that was, 'what a goofy idea, what if we don't get the same boat?'

Licenses ($24 to $37 per week) are mandatory and available from many bait and tackle shops or sports equipment stores. Also beware of seasons and catch limits. Many people now practice catch and release. Some regional marinas have daily boat and motor rentals, as do cottage resorts. If nothing else, you can always enjoy the haunting calls of the loon.

through 44 locks between Trenton on Lake Ontario and Georgian Bay on Lake Huron. Yachties and sailors of every description follow this old, aboriginal route each summer. Used a century ago for commerce, the system is now strictly recreational with flow regulated by 125 dams.

Several companies rent fully equipped houseboats by the weekend, the week or for longer periods. Some even have barbecues and can accommodate up to eight people (six adults), which makes not only for a good party but also for a more reasonably priced one. The trips are good for families, too, with separate sleeping rooms for the kids. **Egan Houseboat Rentals** (☎ 705-799-5745, 800-720-3426; www.houseboat.on.ca/welcome.htm; Egan Marine, RR4, Omemee), west of Peterborough on Rte 7, is recommended and well established. Being right by the Kawartha Lakes gives you the option of hanging around the lakes or going all the way to Lake Simcoe. Rates vary depending on type of boat and timing, but are from $1069 per four days mid-week. Count on using $25 worth of gas per day and $25 per day for insurance.

LAND O' LAKES

North and northeast of Kingston is a rocky, lake-filled region of small towns and summer cottages ideal for leisurely exploration. The area reveals a blend of rural life, history and nature. Fishing and camping possibilities are abundant.

In 2002 the roughly triangular area between Kingston, Westport and Brockville was declared Canada's 12th Unesco Biosphere Reserve. Called the Thousand Islands–Frontenac Arch reserve, it is the third-richest biodiversity region in Canada (after BC's Gulf Islands and Lake Erie's Carolinian forest).

One of the largest parks in eastern Ontario and popular with artists, **Bon Echo Provincial Park** (☎ 613-336-2228; Hwy 41; day use per car $8.50, tent & RV sites $24-30; ☿ late May–late Oct) is another good spot for canoeing. Some of the lakes are quite shallow and get very warm. There are walk-in and canoe-in campsites or roadside campgrounds with facilities. For camping reservations, contact **Ontario Parks** (☎ 519-826-5290, 888-668-7275; www.ontarioparks.com). At Mazinaw Lake, don't miss the extensive aboriginal **rock paintings** on granite cliffs.

Frontenac Provincial Park (☎ 613-376-3489; Rte 19; day use per car $9.50, backcountry sites $9) straddles both the lowlands of southern Ontario and the more northern Canadian Shield, so the flora, fauna and geology of the park are mixed. The park is designed for overnight hikers and canoeists – there are relatively few backcountry sites scattered throughout, accessible only by foot or water. Maps show trails and canoe routes.

The entrance and the information center are at **Otter Lake**, off Rte 19 north of Sydenham. The swimming is excellent, the bass fishing is pretty good, and there are no bears to worry about. **Frontenac Outfitters** (☎ 613-376-6220), near the main entrance, rents canoes.

RIDEAU CANAL

This 150-year-old, 200km-long canal/river/lake system connects Kingston with Ottawa through the Land O' Lakes, assisted by 47 locks. The historical route is ideal for boating with parks, small towns, lakes and many places to stop en route.

After the War of 1812, there was a fear that there could be yet another war with the Americans. The Duke of Wellington decided to link Ottawa and Kingston in order to have a reliable communications and supply route between the two military centers. Although the canal is just 200km in length, its construction was a brutal affair, involving as many as 4000 men battling malaria and the Canadian Shield, working against some of the world's hardest rock. The canal climbs 84m from Ottawa over the Shield, then drops 49m to Lake Ontario. And guess what? It never saw any military service.

The canal did prove useful later in the century for shipping goods, but it is now used mainly for recreation. Roads run parallel with much of the canal, so walking or cycling is also possible. **Houseboat Holidays** rents houseboats for meandering along the canal. The boats sleep six to eight and come with all kitchen necessities.

The **Rideau Trail** is a 400km hiking trail system that links Kingston with Ottawa. It passes through Westport, Smiths Falls and many conservation areas, traversing forests, fields, marshes and some stretches of road along the way. Most people use the route for day trips, but longer trips are possible. The main trail is marked by orange triangles; side trails are marked by blue triangles. The

Rideau Trail Association (☎ 613-545-0823; www
.rideautrail.org) prints a map kit for the entire
route. Between Kingston and Smiths Falls
are numerous campsites, the rest of the way,
it's mainly roofed accommodations. Camping on private land is possible, but obtain
the owner's permission first.

SMITHS FALLS

Midway along the Rideau Canal system,
Smiths Falls makes a decent short stop. In
addition to several minor sights, it's a focal
point for the many boats using the canal.

Smiths Falls has become known as much
for the **Hershey Chocolate Factory** (☎ 613-283-
3300; 1 Hershey Dr; admission free; ☺ 9am-5pm) as for
its history or its canal location. A free tour
of the Canadian branch plant of this famous
US chocolate company is recommended. It
isn't acceptable to dive into the undulating
vats of liquid chocolate, but you can find
out how chocolate bars are created and then
start eating (discounts offered). Hershey Dr
is off Hwy 43 E – just follow your nose.
Tours are given on weekdays only, but you
can do a self-guided tour anytime.

The canal's locks can be viewed in the
middle of town, and the best of the three
small historical museums is the **Rideau Canal
Museum** (☎ 613-284-0505; 34 Beckworth St S; admission $3; ☺ 10am-4:30pm Victoria Day–mid-Oct), which
is housed in a 19th-century mill.

A TASTE OF THE COUNTRY

While exploring eastern Ontario keep an
eye out for some of the local specialties.
Cheese is made in the region, including
write-home-about cheddars. Two excellent
producers are **Mapledale** (☎ 613-477-2454)
in Plainfield and **Balderson** (☎ 613-267-
4492) in Perth. Lanark County is Ontario's
largest producer of maple syrup and spin-
off products. Also drop in to **Wheelers
Maple Products** (☎ 613-278-2090) near Balderson, northwest of Perth. Strawberries are
grown all over Quinte's Isle and blueberries
grow wild across the northern sections of
the region. Note though that many sellers
along Hwy 7 are actually selling cultivated
blueberries, despite their advertising. Wild
berries, while much smaller, are more intensely flavored. Lastly, look out for homemade jams and honeys.

HALIBURTON HIGHLANDS

Running northeast from the Kawartha
Lakes, the highlands present an irregular,
eye-pleasing landscape of woods and lakes.
Bancroft is well known for its minerals and
for the big gem festival held each August.
Examples of 80% of the minerals found in
Canada are dug up in this area.

The resortlike village of Haliburton is
the major supply center. Nearby, north on
Rte 7, the visitor's highlight is the privately-
managed **Haliburton Forest** (☎ 705-754-2198; www
.haliburtonforest.com). Its recommended 'Walk
in the Clouds' hike ($85) takes you on pulse-
quickening suspended planks (20m above
the ground) through the treetops while providing a bird's-eye view of the woods. A visit
to the Wolf Centre is included. New in 2004
is the six-person submarine for underwater
tours ($130). Ask about water clarity before
going under.

To the south, Hwy 507 between Catcha-
coma and Gooderham is perhaps the narrowest, oldest-looking highway in the province;
it often seems more like a country lane.

ALGONQUIN PROVINCIAL PARK (EAST)

The hilly eastern side of this renowned park
has some fine features, including Barron
Canyon, which makes a great canoeing destination, and numerous waterfalls. There's
a **campground** (☎ 705-633-5572; reservations 888-668-
7275; campsites $25) at the Achray access point
on Grand Lake as well as many backcountry
sites, including some beauties with a beach
just a 20-minute paddle away.

Algonquin Portage (☎ 613-735-1795; www.algo
nquinportage.com; 1352 Barron Canyon Rd; dm $24, break-
fast $6), west of **Pembroke** on Rte 28 (the road
to Achray), rents tents, sleeping bags and
canoes and has rustic accommodations, a
shuttle service, food and gas. **Esprit Rafting**
(☎ 800-596-7238) is based near Pembroke, on
the Ottawa River, east of Algonquin. It offers a one-day canoe trip down the Barron
Canyon in the park between May and October ($90).

Maynooth is a small logging community
about a 20-minute drive south of Algonquin's east gate. At **South Algonquin Backpackers
Hostel** (☎ 613-338-2080, 800-595-8064; www.hihostels
.ca; Hwy 62; dm/s/d $16/25/35) meals are available
in a nicely converted old Arlington hotel
and trips into the park are organized.

For more on the park, see p166.

EGANVILLE

Small but agreeable, this town is worth a stop to see the **Bonnechere Caves** (☎ 613-628-2283, 800-469-2283; Fourth Chute Rd; adult/child/youth $12/8/9 ☺ 10am-4pm late-May–Sep, Sat & Sun Sep–Oct). The caves and passages, 8km southeast of town, formed the bottom of a tropical sea about 500 million years ago. They contain animal fossils from long before the dinosaur age. Pathways lead through parts of the extensive system, past fossil banks and stalactites. You can see them on the interesting, humorous tours, which are included in admission. Kids and the nimble enjoy squeezing through some of the narrow, damp passages.

OTTAWA

☎ 613 / pop 785,000

Surprise! The nation's capital is coming into its own. Long stereotyped as a staid, white-bred government town, Ottawa is finally outgrowing those perceptions. With its 'Silicon Valley North' high-tech sector, burgeoning ethnic population, two universities, expanding nightlife, scrumptious international food and progressive outlook, it's a city that is looking ahead.

The areas in and around downtown are lively, there's tons to do, and the special events and festivals never seem to stop. An abundance of museums and cultural activities is another enticement that helps attract the five million tourists who arrive here each year.

The city core is blessed with substantial architecture trimmed by the confluence of the Ottawa and Rideau Rivers and edged by the Rideau Canal. The stately neoGothic Parliament Buildings act as a landmark. The gently rolling Gatineau Hills of Québec are visible to the north. And with generous green spaces, exceptional recreational trails and air unfouled by heavy industry you'll notice people walking, jogging and cycling everywhere.

You may be surprised by the amount of French you hear. Québec is just a stone's throw away, but also most federal government workers are required to be bilingual.

It all makes an enticing package. Ottawa a happening place? Who'd a thunk it?

HISTORY

The area's first inhabitants were the Algonquin Aboriginals, followed by French fur traders. After 1759, British settlers started arriving, and in 1826, British troops founded a permanent base in present-day Ottawa in order to build the Rideau Canal (linking the Ottawa River to Lake Ontario). First called Bytown, Ottawa was named after a local Aboriginal people in 1855. In 1857 Queen Victoria made it the capital (a compromise between Montréal and Toronto).

After WWII, Paris city planner Jacques Greber was charged with plans to beautify Ottawa. The pleasant city is now dotted with parks, and most of the land along the waterways is for recreational use. With ballooning government size, and the well paid staff to run it, the city took off.

Diversifying economics and an entrenched tolerance has meant steady growth for the city. With transplanted Canadians and newcomers from around the globe, the city is increasingly cosmopolitan.

ORIENTATION

Ottawa's central core is quite compact, and you can get around on foot. Downtown Ottawa is divided into eastern and western sections by the Rideau Canal. The unmistakable Parliament Buildings backing onto the Ottawa River mark the northern edge of downtown. To the east, over the canal, is the castle-like Château Laurier, a major landmark. In front of it is Confederation Sq, with the National War Memorial in its center. **Byward Market** is a few minutes' walk farther east. The market area is a dense, convivial four-block district of clubs, restaurants, cafés and shops anchored around the Market Square stalls and vendors. Look for the huge Rideau Centre, a three-level enclosed shopping mall with a walkway over the street. This is Rideau St, the main thoroughfare of Ottawa East.

South of the Parliament Buildings is the Sparks St pedestrian mall. Bank St is the main north–south commercial street with shops and restaurants. Gladstone Av roughly marks the southern boundary of the downtown area.

Of the four bridges to Gatineau, Québec, take Portage Bridge (off Wellington St) for downtown.

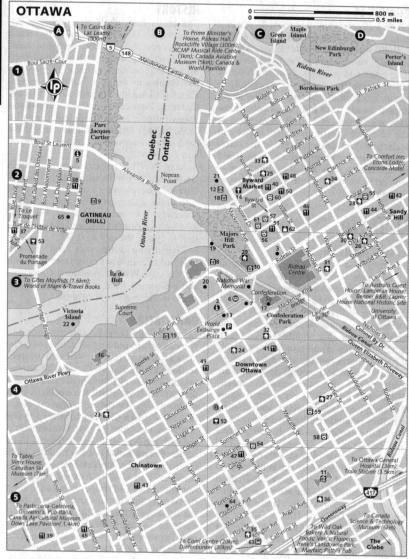

OTTAWA

To Casino du Lac Leamy (500m)

To Prime Minister's House, Rideau Hall; Rockcliffe Village (300m); RCMP Musical Ride Centre (3km); Canada Aviation Museum (5km); Canada & World Pavilion

To Comfort Inn; Econo Lodge; Concorde Motel

To Gîtes Moyfrids (1.6km); World of Maps & Travel Books

To Le Troquet

To Australis Guest House; Lampman House; Benner B&B; Laurier House National Historic Site

To Table; Vimy House; Canadian Ski Museum (7km)

To Pasticceria-Gelateria; Giovanni's; Pub Italia; Canada Agricultural Museum; Dows Lake Pavilion (1.4km)

To Ottawa General Hospital (3km); Train Station (3.5km)

To Corel Centre (20km); Diefenbunker (30km)

To Wild Oak Bakery & Natural Foods; Von's; Flippers; Irene's Lansdowne Park; Mayfair; Patty's Pub

To Canada Science & Technology Museum (6km)

INFORMATION

Sparks St mall has several banks and currency exchange outlets.

Accu-Rate Foreign Exchange (☎ 613-596-0612; 2nd fl, World Exchange Plaza, 111 Albert St; ⏱ 9am-5pm Mon-Fri) Handles traveler's checks.

Capital Infocentre (☎ 613-239-5000, 800-465-1867; www.capcan.ca; 90 Wellington St; ⏱ 8:30am-9pm mid-May–Sep, 9am-5pm Oct–mid-May) An efficient place opposite the Parliament Buildings. Park (free on weekends) in World Exchange Plaza (111 Albert St), one block south.

Chapters (☎ 613-241-0073; 47 Rideau St; ⏱ 9:30am-11pm Mon-Sat, 9:30am-10pm Sun) Extensive general bookstore.

Flat Planet (☎ 613-231-3528; 226 Bank St; per 30min $2; ⏱ 9am-11pm Mon-Fri, to midnight Sat & Sun) Internet access.

Main Post Office (☎ 613-844-1545; 59 Sparks St; ☟ 9am-4pm Mon-Fri)

Ottawa General Hospital (☎ 613-737-7777; 501 Smyth Rd; ☟ 24hr) Southeast of downtown; has an emergency room.

Travel Cuts (☎ 613-565-3555; 740 Bank St) One of several branches around town.

World of Maps and Travel Books (☎ 613-724-6776; 1235 Wellington St; ☟ 9am-6pm Mon-Fri, 9am-5pm Sat, noon-4pm Sun) Excellent selection of maps (including topographical ones) and guidebooks.

DANGERS & ANNOYANCES

Nearly around the clock, the Byward Market area of Ottawa is busy. Late at night, however, it gets a bit of an edge to it, with some drug and prostitution traffic. Walking alone in the quieter areas in the wee hours should be avoided.

SIGHTS

Ottawa's museums and attractions are often in a state of flux and are frequently closed, either being renovated, repaired, upgraded or moved. It can't hurt to call for their current status. Many are closed on Monday. Also note that admission at many may be free at least one day or evening every week (see the boxed text on p217).

A new site to ask about is the Portrait Gallery of Canada, being developed at 100 Wellington St, in the former US embassy. Also in the planning stages is a national his-

tory museum, slated for the former train station across from the War Memorial.

Many top attractions are clustered conveniently, in the city's central north end. See under Gatineau (p227) for more sites nearby, including the essential Museum of Civilization.

Parliament Hill

Federal government buildings dominate downtown Ottawa, especially those on Parliament Hill, off Wellington St near the canal. At the tourist office, pick up a free copy of the *Walking Tour of Parliament Hill*, which lists various details about the buildings.

The primary Parliament Building, **Centre Block** (☎ 613-239-5000, tours 613-996-0896; admission free; ☟ 9am-8pm Mon-Fri, 9am-5pm Sat & Sun), with its Peace Tower and clock, is most striking. Beside it are East and West Blocks, with their sharp, copper-topped roofing.

Inside Centre Block, the public can see the Commons and Senate when they're in session. Question Period in the House of Commons is a major attraction. It occurs early every afternoon and at 11am on Friday. Admission is on a first-come, first-served basis.

The interior of the building is all hand-carved limestone and sandstone. See the beautiful library with its wood and wrought iron. Free 20-minute tours run frequently, but reservations are required; be prepared

---

OTTAWA IN...

Two days

Start your visit with the changing of the guard and a tour at **Parliament Hill** (p215). In the afternoon see one of the major museums, say the **National Gallery** (below) or **Canadian Museum of Nature** (below). Browse **Bytown Market** (p223) and enjoy dinner there. On day two cross the river to Gatineau, see the **Museum of Civilization** (p227) and have lunch nearby. Back in Ottawa, toward evening, stroll Little Italy for a drink and dinner.

Four Days

Follow the two-day tour and then experience **Turtle Island Aboriginal Experience** (p217). Later in the day check on a special event or festival. For dinner, wander Chinatown followed by a pub downtown for some music. On day four, leave town for a side trip to **Wakefield** (p229) via the historic train or drive up the Ottawa River for a wet day **white-water rafting** (p229).

One Week

Follow the four-day itinerary and on the fifth day stay in town. See one of the other museums or **RCMP Musical Ride Centre** (p219) and then relax on an afternoon **boat cruise** (p220). In the evening see a show or a concert. For day six, explore wooded **Gatineau Park** (p228), walk a trail, visit **Mackenzie King Estate** (p228) and then hit the beach. On the last day see some countryside on a day trip to **Upper Canada Village** (p209) in Morrisburg on the St Lawrence River.

---

for tight security, including metal detectors. In summer, you can book tours at the conspicuous white tent; in winter, there's a reservation desk inside the building. The Peace Tower, accessed via an angled elevator and affording grand views, can be visited without the tour. Either way expect long waits.

At 10am daily in summer, see the colorful changing of the guard on the lawns. At night during summer, there's a free sound and light show on Parliament Hill – one version in English, the other in French.

Canadian Museum of Nature

South of the downtown area, this **museum** (☎ 613-566-4700; 240 McLeod St; adult/child/senior/family $8/3.50/7/18; 9:30am-5pm Fri-Wed, to 8pm Thu May–Labour Day, 10am-5pm Tue-Sun Labour Day–May; bus 5, 6 & 14) is housed in an attractive Victorian building. With one of Canada's foremost natural history collections, the four-storey museum fosters an appreciation of nature and includes a good section on dinosaurs from Alberta. Also excellent are the realistic mammal and bird dioramas depicting Canadian wildlife. Major temporary exhibits on specific mammal, mineral or ecological subjects are a feature.

The **Viola MacMillan Mineral Gallery** is amazing, with some of the largest gems and minerals you're ever likely to see. The simulated mine comes complete with a shaky elevator. The east coast tidal zone re-creation is also very realistic. A separate section of the museum is geared toward children, and there's a cafeteria.

National Gallery

Canada's premier **art gallery** (☎ 613-990-1985; 380 Sussex Dr; adult/youth/senior & student/family $6/3/5/12; 10am-6pm Fri-Wed, to 8pm Thu May–mid-Oct; 10am-5pm Wed-Sun, to 8pm Thu mid-Oct–Apr, closed public holidays in winter) is a must. It has an enormous collection of North American and European works in various media, all housed in an impressive building in the center of town. It's just a 15-minute walk from the Parliament Buildings.

The striking glass and pink granite gallery overlooking the Ottawa River was designed by Moshe Safdie, who also created Montréal's Habitat (a unique apartment complex) and Québec City's Musée de la Civilisation and renovated Ottawa's City Hall.

The numerous galleries, some arched and effectively colored, display classic and contemporary pieces, with an emphasis on Canadian artists. The US and European collections do, however, contain examples from nearly all the heavyweights. The gallery also presents changing exhibits and shows.

The thoughtful chronological display of Canadian painting and sculpture not only gives a history of Canadian art but also, in a real sense, provides an outline of the development of the country itself, beginning with the depictions of aboriginal life at the time the Europeans arrived. On Level 2 are the **Inuit Gallery** and works from the fine **photography collection**.

Two pleasant courtyards offer the eyes a rest. Between them sits one of the gallery's most unusual and appealing components, the beautifully restored 1888 **Rideau St Chapel**, which was saved from destruction and relocated from a few blocks away.

The complex is large; you'll need a few hours, and you'll still tire before seeing all the exhibits, let alone the changing film and video presentations, lectures and concerts. There's a decent café, a restaurant, and a very fine shop with gifts and books. Underneath the gallery are two levels of parking ($8.50 per day).

Canadian War Museum & Vimy House

This **museum** (☎ 613-776-8600; 330 Sussex Dr; adult/veteran/senior/family $4/free/$3/$9; ⊗ 9:30am-5pm Fri-Wed, to 8pm Thu May–mid-Oct; closed Mon mid-Oct–May) traces the country's military history and has Canada's largest collection of war-related items and art. The life-sized replica of a WWI trench is captivating. Renowned architect Raymond Moriyama has been selected to design the new war museum, which is scheduled to open in 2005, just west of Parliament Hill.

Enthusiasts should ask here about little-known **Vimy House** (☎ 613-776-8600; 221 Champagne Ave N; admission free; ⊗ 10am-4pm May-Oct, 10am-4pm Sat Oct-May), a warehouse for heavy artillery, which is west along Wellington St (about 12 minutes by car).

Canada Aviation Museum

With nearly 120 aircraft housed in a triangular building about the size of four football fields at Rockcliffe Airport, this is a top-rate **collection** (☎ 613-993-2010; 11 Aviation Parkway; adult/child/senior $6/3/4; ⊗ 9am-5pm Fri-Wed, to 9pm Thu May–Labour Day, 10am-5pm Fri, Tue & Wed, to 9pm Thu Labour Day–May) See planes ranging from the Silver Dart of 1909 and the Spitfire right through to the first turbo-powered Viscount passenger jet and modern jets. The Cessna Crane is the very one your author's father

(Alexander Lightbody) trained in for the RCAF. Other exhibits include video games and audiovisuals.

Call ahead to check opening hours, as they vary with attendance levels and the time of year. The museum is about 5km northeast (along Rockcliffe Parkway) from downtown, near the Canadian Forces base.

Turtle Island Aboriginal Experience

This intriguing **replica** (☎ 613-564-9494; Victoria Island off Portage Bridge; admission & 1hr tours $7; ⊗ 11am-6pm mid-Jun–Sep) of an Aboriginal village offers glimpses into the original culture of the area. The demonstrations, music and dancing, canoes and longhouse are informative and entertaining. A café offers traditional food. The $20 ticket including a two-hour village tour, a dance and lunch is good value. The highest priced option ($149) includes overnight camping in a tipi at Gatineau Lake. Turtle Island is within walking distance of downtown.

Bytown Museum & Ottawa Locks

Focusing on city history, **Bytown Museum** (☎ 613-234-4570; admission $5; ⊗ 10am-5pm Mon-Sat, 1-5pm Sun May–mid-Oct, hrs vary mid-Oct–Apr) is in the oldest stone building in Ottawa. It's east of Parliament Hill, beside the canal – go down the stairs from Wellington St. Used during construction of the canal to store equipment and money, it now contains artifacts and documents pertaining to local history.

The series of **locks** at the edge of the Ottawa River in the Colonel By Valley, between

---

OTTAWA FOR FREE

Sights such as Parliament Hill (p215), the National Gallery (opposite) and Canada & World Pavillion (p218) offer free admission all the time. Some of Ottawa's other sights offer free or discounted admission at least one day per week:

- **Canadian Museum of Nature** (opposite) Free after 5pm on Thursday.

- **Canadian War Museum** (left) Half-price admission on Sunday and free after 4pm Thursday.

- **Canada Aviation Museum** (left) Free after 5pm Thursday.

Château Laurier and the Parliament Buildings, marks the north end of the 198km Rideau Canal (p211), which runs to Kingston and the St Lawrence River. Colonel By, who was put in charge of constructing the canal, set up his headquarters here in 1826.

Royal Canadian Mint

The **mint** (☎ 613-993-8990; 320 Sussex Dr; adult & senior/family $2/8, tours $3 Mon-Fri, $1.50 Sat & Sun; ☺ 9am-9pm Mon-Fri, to 6pm Sat & Sun May–Aug, 9am-5pm daily rest of year). No longer producing day-to-day coinage, the mint strikes special-edition coins, commemorative pieces, bullion investment coins and the like. Founded in 1908 and renovated in the mid-1980s, this imposing stone building has always been Canada's major refiner of gold. Call to arrange 45-minute tours where you can see the process – from sheets of metal to bags of coins. Sorry, no free samples. The main circulation-coin mint is in Winnipeg, Manitoba (see p535).

Currency Museum

If you like to look at money, you can see lots more of it at the **museum** (☎ 613-782-8914; Bank of Canada, 245 Sparks St; admission free; ☺ 10:30am-5pm Mon-Sat, 1-5pm Sun, Jun-Aug; closed Mon Sep-May). Various displays tell the story of money through the ages across the globe, from whales' teeth to collectors' banknotes.

Canadian Museum of Contemporary Photography

Wedged between Château Laurier and the canal in a reconstructed railway tunnel, the **CMCP** (☎ 613-990-8257; 1 Rideau Canal; admission free; ☺ 10am-6pm Fri-Wed, to 8pm Thu May–mid-Oct, 10am-5pm Wed & Fri-Sun, to 8pm Thu mid-Oct–May) is the historic- and contemporary-photo museum. The museum houses the country's vast photographic archives.

Unfortunately, gallery space is limited, and you may want to check what's on before visiting. Exhibits are often, but not always, of Canadian work and may not be of very much interest to the casual viewer unacquainted with esoteric approaches to the photographic medium. For buffs, it's a must. Shows change quarterly.

Canada & World Pavilion

The newest of Ottawa's sites, the **pavilion** (☎ 613-239-5000; 50 Sussex Drive; admission free; ☺ 10am-5pm Wed-Mon May–mid-Jun & mid-Sep–Oct, to 6pm mid-Jun–mid-Sep) highlights the achievements and accomplishments of Canadians, both widely known and obscure. The interactive, high-tech exhibits are divided into themes of spirit, heart and mind and cover sports, arts, medicine – you name it. Most people will end up saying, 'well, whatdoyaknow?' at least once.

Canada Agricultural Museum

This government-owned **experimental farm** (☎ 613-991-3044; 930 Carling Ave at Prince of Wales Dr; adult/child $6/3; ☺ 9am-5pm Mar-Oct, hrs vary Nov-Feb), southwest of downtown, includes about 500 hectares of flowers, trees, shrubs and gardens. The site is used for research on all aspects of farming and horticulture. There are tours, or you can go walking on your own. The farm also has livestock and showcase herds of cattle, an observatory, a tropical greenhouse and an arboretum. The latter is good for walking or having a picnic and is also great in winter for tobogganing. Kids love the pigs and sheep. The farm can be reached on the city's network of cycling routes. The museum is closed in winter, but the barn is open all year.

Prime Minister's House & Rideau Hall

You can view the outside of the present prime minister's **house** (24 Sussex Dr) and take a peek at the property. For security reasons, there is no strolling around the grounds.

Rideau Hall (☎ 613-991-4422; 1 Sussex Dr; admission free; ☺ visitors center 9:30am-5:30pm May-Nov), the governor general's pad, was built in the early 20th century. There are free 45-minute walking tours of the residence, with stories of some of the goings-on over the years. Tours are offered through the day in summer, or you can stroll the grounds all year.

At the main gate, the small changing of the guard ceremony happens on the hour throughout the day from the end of June until the end of August.

Both houses are northeast along Sussex Dr. Rideau Hall is off Princess Dr, the eastern extension of Sussex Dr. Farther east along Sussex Dr, **Rockcliffe Village** is one of the poshest, most prestigious areas in the country. Behind the mansion doors live some very prominent Canadians and many foreign diplomats.

RCMP Musical Ride Centre

Even the Mounties have to practice, and this **center** (☎ 613-998-8199; 1 Sandrich Rd; admission free; grounds ⊙ 9am–4pm May–Oct, 10am–2pm Oct–Apr; bus No 7) is where the musical ride pageant is perfected. The public is welcome to watch the practice sessions and the other equestrian displays held from time to time. Call for practice time details and the sunset ride schedule; some practices have a full band and bright uniforms. Tours of the stables are given from 8:30am to 11am and 1:30pm to 3:30pm Monday to Friday during the summer season and the visitor information center is open year-round. If traveling by car, take Sussex Dr east to Rockcliffe Parkway. At Birch St, turn right to the grounds.

Laurier House National Historic Site

This **Victorian home** (☎ 613-992-8142; 335 Laurier Ave; admission $3.75; ⊙ 9am–5pm Mon-Sat, 1-5pm Sun Apr–mid-Oct, hrs vary mid-Oct–Mar), built in 1878, was the residence of two prime ministers, Wilfrid Laurier and the eccentric Mackenzie King. The home is beautifully furnished throughout – don't miss the study on the top floor. Each of the two prime ministers is represented by mementos and possessions.

It's best to visit in the early morning (that is, before the tour buses arrive); you'll have the knowledgeable guides all to yourself.

Cathedral-Basilica of Notre Dame

Built in 1839, this is one of the city's most impressive **houses of worship** (Guigues Ave; admission free; ⊙ 7am–6pm). A pamphlet available at the door outlines the many features, including carvings, windows, the organ and the neoGothic ceiling. The cathedral is across from the National Gallery, in the Byward Market area.

Supreme Court of Canada

This rather intimidating **structure** (☎ 613-995-5361; 301 Wellington St; admission free; ⊙ 9am-5pm Mon-Fri) is partially open to nonlitigants. Construction of the highest court of the land began in 1939 but was not completed until 1946. The grand entrance hall, which is 12m high, is certainly impressive. Visitors can stroll around the grounds, lobby and courtroom, and during summer a visit can include a free tour given by a law student (call for the schedule). During the rest of the year, reservations are required for tours.

National Archives of Canada

The mandate of this **institution** (☎ 613-995-5138; 395 Wellington St; admission free; ⊙ 9am-10pm) is to collect and preserve the documentation of Canada. The vast collection includes paintings, maps, photographs, diaries, letters, posters and even 60,000 cartoons and caricatures collected over the past two centuries. Changing exhibits are on view.

ACTIVITIES

In summer, there are canoe and rowboat rentals for trips along the canal at **Dows Lake Pavilion** (☎ 613-232-1001) at Dows Lake. The lake, a bulge in the Rideau Canal, is southwest of the downtown core; go south along Bronson Ave or Booth St.

The city has an excellent parks system, with a lot of inner-city green space. There are many **walking**, **jogging** and **cycling trails**, as well as picnic areas. You'll even find some **fishing**. The tourist office has a sheet, with map, of all the parks and a description of each as well as a cycling map. Ottawa is the best city in Canada for cyclists, with an extensive system of paths in and around town and through the parks. **Rent-A-Bike** (☎ 613-241-4140; bicycle per day $23; ⊙ May–Sep) offers bicycle rentals; it's in the rear parking lot at the Château Laurier (p222). Where the Rideau River meets the canal south of town (at the junction of Colonel By St and Hog's Back Rd) are the **Prince of Wales Falls** and walking and cycling paths. The falls, a popular picnic spot with an adjacent set of locks, are also known as Hog's Back Falls.

Surrounding the city on the east, south and west, and running adjacent to both sides of the Ottawa River and the Rideau Canal, is a broad strip of parkland known as the **Greenbelt** (☎ 613-239-5000). Within this area of woodlands, marsh and fields are nature trails, more cycle paths, boardwalks, picnic areas and conservation areas.

In winter, there's skiing as close as 20km from town, in the Gatineau Hills. Two resorts with variously graded hills are **Camp Fortune** (☎ 819-827-1717; 300 Chemin Dunlop, Chelsea) and **Mont Cascades** (☎ 819-827-0301; 448 Mont Cascades, Cantley). Further afield, **Mont Ste Marie** (☎ 819-467-5200; 76 Chemin de la Montagne, Lac Ste Marie) is higher and less crowded. Gatineau Park (p228) has excellent cross-country ski trails with lodges along the way. In warm weather, the park is good for walking and picnicking.

The Rideau Canal is well known for **ice-skating** in winter, with 5km of maintained ice. Rest spots on the way serve great doughnuts (known as beavertails) to go with the hot chocolate, although, judging by the prices, the beaver must be getting scarce. Ask at Capitol Infocenter (p214) about skate rentals.

OTTAWA FOR CHILDREN

Canada Science & Technology Museum (☎ 613-991-3044; 1867 St Laurent Boul; adult/child/senior/family $6/3/5/14; ♥ 9am-5pm May-Sep, 9am-5pm Tue-Sun Oct-Apr), on the corner of Russell Rd southeast of downtown, has all kinds of hands-on exhibits. Try things out, test yourself, watch physical laws in action and see optical illusions. Also on display are farm machines, trains, model ships and stagecoaches. The bicycle and motorcycle collections are good. Higher-tech exhibits include computers and communication technologies. Make sure you don't miss the incubator, with live chicks in various stages of hatching.

The large display on space technology is interesting, with an assortment of Canadian space artifacts. An astronomy section has films and slides about the universe; on clear nights, you can make reservations to take a peep through the large refracting telescope. Free parking.

A historic throwback, the 19th-century **Log Farm** (☎ 613-825-4352; 640 Cedarview Rd, Nepean; admission free; ♥ 10am-4pm Thu-Sun May-Sep, hrs vary Oct-Apr), complete with house, buildings and equipment, is 20km southwest of Parliament Hill. There are farm animals, trails and wagon rides; take a picnic. Special fee-based events take place throughout the year.

QUIRKY OTTAWA

A bizarre, little-known quirk worth seeing is the **stray-cat sanctuary**, with dollhouse-like shelters. It's on Parliament Hill between the West Block and Centre Block, toward the river. Some say loftily that it represents the Canadian ideal of welcoming and caring for the world's needy, but then again, maybe it's just nutty.

Another unique sight is **Diefenbunker** (☎ 613-839-0007; 3911 Carp Rd, Carp; adult/child $12/10; ♥ hrs vary), a secret underground fort built in the early 1960s as a military/government refuge and now reopened as a Cold War

museum. The huge, creepy shelter was built to house 300 personnel for 30 days in case of nuclear attack. Displays include air-raid sirens and bombs. It's about a 30-minute drive west of town, in the village of Carp. Admission includes a one-hour tour and parking.

The **Canadian Ski Museum** (☎ 613-722-3584; 2nd fl, Trailhead Bldg, 1960 Scott St; admission free; ♥ 9am-5pm Mon-Sat, 11am-5pm Sun) has a small, specialized exhibit with a collection of equipment, clothing, photographs and memorabilia outlining Canadian ski history.

TOURS

The HI Ottawa Jail (p221) hostel sometimes organizes trips in the region.

Amphibious Lady Dive (☎ 613-223-6211; Sparks St at Elgin St; 1hr tours adult/child $18/14; ♥ May-Oct) Uses an amphibious vehicle that does a road tour and then plunges into the Ottawa River.

Capital Double Decker & Trolley Tours (☎ 613-565-5463; Sparks St at Metcalfe St) offers a few different options. Note that the trolley is just a bus decorated to look that way, and that the vehicle is the only difference between the tours. The narrated tour ($25) lets you hop on and off at 16 stops, including some in Gatineau. The route takes at least two hours, but you have the day to do it – a good way to get around. There's also a sunset tour ($15) and a fall-colors trip ($22).

Gray Line (☎ 613-565-5463; Sparks St at Metcalfe St; 1½hr city tours $28; May-Nov) Tickets available at its street-corner kiosk. All bus tours depart from there, but there is hotel pick-up, too. It also offers longer tours of the region and beyond.

Haunted Walk (☎ 613-232-0344; kiosk Sparks St at Elgin St) has three unique walking tours, one outlining ghoulish and supernatural historical events ($14), one of the old jail ($12) and another of Château Laurier ($10).

Paul's Boat Lines (☎ 613-235-6781; Ottawa Locks; 1½hr Ottawa River tour; adult/child $15/8; 1¼hr Rideau Canal cruise adult/child $14/8; ♥ mid-May–Oct) For tickets and information, there's another dock at Rideau Canal, across from the National Arts Centre. The river trip is recommended.

FESTIVALS & EVENTS

Ottawa has more than 60 annual events:

Winterlude (♥ early Feb) This good and popular festival is held over three consecutive weekends of festivities, mainly around frozen Dows Lake and the canal. The ice sculptures are really worth seeing.

Canadian Tulip Festival (☎ 613-567-5757; www.tulipfestival.ca; ♥ late May) This event sees the city decorated with 200 types of tulips, mainly from Holland.

Festivities include parades, regattas, car rallies, dances, concerts and fireworks.

Festival Franco-Ontarien (☎ 613-741-1225; www .ffo.ca; ❂ Jun) This festival is good fun and an opportunity to see some of the country's French culture through music, crafts and more.

Pride Week Festival (☎ 613-238-2424; www.gay canada.com/ottawa-pride; ❂ Jul) After a week of gay and lesbian events, this festival culminates in a racy parade.

Ottawa International Jazz Festival (☎ 613-241-2633; www.ottawajazzfestival.com; ❂ late Jul) A 10-day festival featuring shows in Ottawa and Hull.

Central Canada Exhibition (❂ end Aug) A 10-day event with myriad displays, a carnival and entertainment at Lansdowne Park.

Ottawa Folk Festival (☎ 613-230-8234; www .ottawafolk.org; ❂ late Aug) This two-day music festival is increasingly popular.

SLEEPING

The city has an impressive array of lodgings in all price ranges. Acommodation choices are scattered through town and on the outskirts. Most of the places listed here are central and have parking, some at no additional cost. During summer, even with Parliament in recess, the city is busy and reservations are recommended. Business-oriented downtown hotels may offer summer specials. During the Winterlude festival in February is also a time to pre-book.

One good area for B&Bs is south of Rideau St, in and around the Sandy Hill district. This posh pocket is a neighborhood of heritage houses and architectural distinction. It's quiet and close to downtown too. The No 2 and No 7 buses run along Rideau St from downtown. Another good choice is the colorful Byward Market area. Gatineau has less convenient but generally lower cost B&Bs.

There are two main motel strips, one on each side of the downtown area. On the convenient east side, look along Rideau St and its extension, Montréal Rd.

Budget

Ottawa Backpackers Inn (☎ 613-241-3402, 888-394-0334; www.ottawahostel.com; 203 York St; dm/r $19/38; check-in 7am-midnight; P ▯) Right downtown in the market, this easygoing hostel is deservedly popular for it's atmosphere and management. There's a kitchen and room for 35 in this converted 19th-century house that's often full. There is one fully private

room. Take No 4 bus from the bus station or No 95 from the train.

HI Ottawa Jail (☎ 613-235-2595, 800-663-5777; www.hihostels.ca/ottawa; 75 Nicholas St; dm from $20, r members/nonmembers $52/56; ▯ P) The HI hostel in the old Ottawa jail – see the gallows at the back – is one of the best-known hostels in the country. It has a very good, central location near the Parliament Buildings. There are 150 beds in the restored building, most of them in old cells, so you can wake up behind bars. Take No 4 bus from the bus station or the No 95 bus from the train station.

Voyageur's Guest House (☎ 613-238-6445; www .bbcanada.com/1897.html; 95 Arlington Ave; s $39-49, d $54-59; P) There are eight clean rooms with shared bathrooms. Voyageur is on a quiet residential street, right behind the bus terminal and is the best low-priced place in town. It's simple but homey, convenient, and popular with international travelers. The managers here are always very welcoming.

YM-YWCA (☎ 613-237-1320; www.educom.on.ca/ ymca-ywca; 180 Argyle Ave; s/d shared bathroom $53/63, s/q with private bathroom $63/83; P) Amenities include a cafeteria and, while institutional, it's clean and well-run.

Concorde Motel (☎ 613-745-2112; fax 613-745-2112; 333 Montréal Rd, Vanier; r $45-55) Don't book a room for your mother and it ain't much to look at, but if the hostels are full or you're traveling on the cheap, this will do. Check along Carling Ave about 10km from downtown for other economical choices.

Camp Hither Hills (☎ 613-822-0509; terrym@bserve .com; 5227 Bank St, Hwy 31; tent & RV sites $18-23; ☺ mid-May–mid-Oct) For campers, this is the closest to town at 10km south of the city limits. There are other places to camp both east and west of town on Hwy 17 as well as in Gatineau Park (see p228), across the river in Québec.

Mid-Range

Auberge des Arts (☎ 613-562-0909, 877-750-3400; aubergedesarts@rogers.com; 104 Guigues Ave; s $65, d shared/private bathroom $75/100; ☐) This is a collectibles- and antique-filled home, but it's comfortable, not prissy at all, and has air-conditioning. English, French and Spanish are spoken, and the owner, Chantal, serves excellent healthful breakfasts.

L'Auberge du Marché (☎ 613-241-6610, 800-465-0079; http://members.rogers.com/aubergedumarche; 87 Guigues Ave; s $65, d shared/private bathroom $75/95) This modern, immaculate place with rooms in the private adjacent townhouse is a real bargain. There are three share-facilities rooms and one with private bathroom. Nicole gives you your own key to the separate entrance.

Gasthaus Switzerland Inn (☎ 613-237-0335, 888-663-0000; www.gasthausswitzerlandinn.com; 89 Daly Ave; r $108-148; ☐) This Swiss-style place enjoys one of the best locations in town, two blocks south of Rideau St and the market. The guesthouse has been created out of a large, old stone house and has 22 rooms, all with private bathrooms. Breakfast includes Swiss muesli, bread, cheese, eggs and coffee. The Swiss managers speak an impressive array of languages, including German and French.

Australis Guest House (☎ 613-235-8461; www .bbcanada.com/1463.html; 35 Marlborough St; s/d shared bathroom $65/75, s/t private bathroom $85/100) This comfy place is recommended for its excellent breakfasts and its helpful hosts, Carol and Brian. They offer a pick-up service from the train or bus station if arranged in advance. Marlborough St is south of Laurier, about a half-hour walk to the Parliament Buildings.

Albert House Inn (☎ 613-236-4479, 800-267-1982; www.albertinn.com; 478 Albert St; s $98, d $98-175; ☐) Downtown, Albert House, a mansion from 1875, features 17 well-appointed, richly-decorated rooms. The location is handy and you get all the comforts at this little hotel including an extensive breakfast menu.

Doral Inn (☎ 613-230-8055, 800-263-6725; www .doralinn.com; 486 Albert St; r from $95; ☐) This central, restored inn from 1879 with 40 rooms, recently taken over by Travelodge, retains its small hotel ambience and distinctive decor. Some housekeeping units (kitchenettes) are available and a free continental breakfast is included.

Business Inn (☎ 613-232-1121, 800-363-1777; www.thebusinessinn.com; 180 MacLaren St; s/d from $89/99; ☐ ☐) With 140 suites, from studios to two-bedrooms, this is a full-service operation, including full kitchens, restaurant, laundry and fitness center. It's also very central. Rates include continental breakfast.

Lampman House (☎ 613-241-3696, 877-591-4354; www.bbcanada.com/1239.html; 369 Daly Ave; r $80-95; ☐) This Victorian house with 12-foot ceilings and a rooftop deck is a good bargain. One room has a private bathroom. Daly Ave is two blocks south of Rideau St.

Benner's B&B (☎ 613-789-8320, 877-891-5485; www.bbcanada.com/benners; 541 Besserer St; d shared bathroom $85, d private bathroom $95-120) Comfortably and tastefully decorated, this 1910 house is one street south of Rideau St in the Sandy Hill District and just a 15-minute walk to downtown.

Reliable chain motels close to downtown:

Comfort Inn Downtown (☎ 613-746-4641, 888-891-1169; www.choicehotels.ca/cn480; 112 Montréal Rd; r $110; ☐) Recently renovated and only a five-minute drive to downtown. Continental breakfast and newspaper is thrown in.

Days Inn (☎ 613-789-5555, 888-789-4949; www .daysinn.ca; 319 Rideau St; d $110; ☐) Also upgraded, very close to Byward Market, walkable to downtown.

Econo Lodge (☎ 613-789-3781, 800-263-0069; fax 613-789-0207; 475 Rideau St; s from $90, d from $99; ☐) Also has a handy little breakfast shop.

Top End

Arc (☎ 613-238-2888, 800-699-2516; www.arcthehotel .com; 140 Slater St; r $135-425; ☐) The Arc is large for a boutique hotel with 112 rooms but truer than nearly all to the concept with a stunning minimal, elegant design throughout. Call it low-key, muted and restfully hip. There's even an in-house CD library and a player in each room. Now that's cool. There's a quiet bar and a restaurant with an outstanding reputation too.

Fairmont Château Laurier (☎ 613-241-1414, 800-441-1414; www.fairmont.com/laurier; 1 Rideau St; r $230-

400; P ♿) The classic, castle-like place by the canal is the city's best known hotel and is a landmark in its own right. You won't want for creature comforts and the location is pretty much the heart of Ottawa. If you scored at the casino, try the $1800 suite.

Lord Elgin Hotel (☎ 613-235-3333, 800-267-4298; www.lordelginhotel.ca; 100 Elgin St; r from $165; P) This stately old place from 1941, overhauled in 1991, has all the amenities and has seen its share of celebrity names over the decades. The location is ideal, with numerous restaurants and sites an easy walk away – there's even a Starbucks on the premises.

EATING

Recent years have been good to Ottawa's food scene. Increasing ethnic diversity and sophistication have resulted in a smorgasbord of gastronomic choices.

Bounteous Byward Market boasts 150 options in one condensed epicurean district. During the warm months, many of the eateries have outdoor tables lending a very festive aura. From here restaurants spill along Rideau St.

Downtown along Bank St and its side streets are still more places to eat. Southeast of downtown, The Glebe district, based along Bank St between Paterson Ave south to the canal, is a lively neighborhood with numerous pubs, restaurants, cafés and appealing shops. A stroll along the 800 block reveals a range of eating choices.

A stroll along Elgin St between Somerset and Frank Sts will also turn up numerous places to eat, outdoor patios, cafés, pubs and several nightspots.

Ottawa has a small but authentic Chinatown with numerous eateries within walking distance west of downtown. It's based around the corner of Bronson Ave and Somerset St W. A few blocks west around Booth St are numerous Vietnamese places. A little farther west, Preston St's Corso Italia, Ottawa's Little Italy, is absolutely lined with appealing Italian restaurants and patio umbrellas.

Budget

All through downtown and around the market, look for the chip wagons parked on the streets serving excellent fries and hamburgers. The adventurous can try *poutine*, fries with cheese curds and gravy, a passion in Québec.

Market Square (Byward Market Sq, cnr William & George Sts; meals under $8; ☇ lunch & dinner) Anchoring the market district, this market building is a fabulous place to be when hunger strikes. Aside from all the fresh produce and cheese there's an international array of quick take-out places offering Middle Eastern, Indian, breads and pastries, fruit salad, soup…the works. For dessert don't miss the stand at the corner of William and George selling beavertails – hot, flat doughnuts that first became popular when sold to skaters along the canal in winter.

Pho Bo Ga (☎ 613-230-2931; 784 Somerset W; mains $5-7; ☇ Mon-Sat 10am-10pm, Sun 10am-9pm) It's small and packed, but the menu is simple, sort of – 30 kinds of beef noodle soup and a few chicken choices. Throw in the greens, add some hot sauce, and it's a meal – filling and delicious.

Pasticceria-Gelateria Italiana (☎ 613-233-2104; 200 Preston St; desserts $5; ☇ 11am-11pm) What an amazing array of fresh pastries. Get a cappuccino and indulge. Have you ever seen a wedding-cake showroom? Well, don't let this chance melt away. If it's hot outside, get a fresh gelato.

Nate's (☎ 613-789-9191; 316 Rideau St; mains $5-9; ☇ 8am-9pm) This Jewish delicatessen, a local institution, is renowned for its low prices on basic food. The popular breakfast special is the cheapest in Canada ($3 for the works). Ask for the Rideau Rye – it's good bread for toast. Nate's also serves blintzes, latkes and smoked meat. The service is blindingly fast. It's open and busy on Sunday.

Wild Oat Bakery & Natural Foods (☎ 613-232-6232; 815 Bank St; under $8; ☇ 9am-7pm Mon-Fri, 9am-6pm Sat & Sun) With a warm homey atmosphere and great aromas, this café is a fine alternative to the major coffee chains. Tempt yourself with soups, salads, vegetarian tofu pies and the counter of sweets.

Mid-Range

Caribbean Flavours (☎ 613-237-9981; 881 Somerset St W; mains $8-15; ☇ noon-10pm Tue-Sun) At the edge of Chinatown, this small, comfortable find dishes up fabulous food from the islands. The plate-filling rotis of chicken, beef or goat make a delicious and substantial meal. Platters include soup, vegetables and rice. Unless your cell phone's speed dial is set for 911, don't order your food spicy; medium should suffice for most tastes. Wash it down with the excellent mouth-puckering ginger beer made on the premises. At meal's end, crunch one of the freshening cardamom seeds.

Zak's Diner (☎ 613-241-2401; 16 Byward St; mains $5-11; ⏰ 9am-9pm Sun-Thu, 24hr Fri & Sat) It's got the '50s diner look, but it's young, hip and friendly. The club sandwich is dynamite, and the shakes and breakfasts are renowned. Wraps are also on offer, so it's not a total time warp.

Pub Italia (☎ 613-232-2326; 434 Preston St; mains $12; ⏰ lunch & dinner) Mama mia, a cross between a trattoria and an Irish pub…and it works! It looks like a twisted Catholic sanctuary for food and drink. Enjoy the unusual atmosphere with pizzas, numerous pastas, and a range of British brews, either inside or on the patio. There's a fascinating array of bargain mussel dishes and live music on Thursday and Friday night.

Von's (☎ 613-233-3277; 819 Bank St; mains $7-16; ⏰ breakfast, lunch & dinner) This continental-style bistro with soft music is a good-value neighborhood spot perfect for a leisurely weekend omelette breakfast. Classic fare such as steak *frites* dominates the evening menu, supported by a wide salad selection.

Horn of Africa (☎ 613-789-0025; 364 Rideau St; mains $6-11; ⏰ 11am-11pm) This slightly tattered, local Ethiopian hangout warrants a visit for excellent exotic stews and dishes eaten with *injera*, an African pancake-like flatbread. Some vegetarian and spicy dishes are included with the lentil, chickpea and kebab combinations. Servers are gracious and helpful.

Royal Thai (☎ 613-562-8818; 272 Dalhousie St; dinner mains $12; ⏰ lunch & dinner) Some market eateries are based more on location than gastronomy, but the food here is the real deal. Awesome soups and dishes such as chicken in pandanus leaves, wonderful pineapple rice, curry red shrimp and of course, the peanut sauces and coconut milk, make this the best Thai in town.

Table (☎ 613-729-5973; 1230 Wellington; mains $10-17; ⏰ lunch & dinner) Meat-eaters beware, this could give vegetarian food a good name. Served buffet style and sold by the gram – don't take all heavy stuff! – this is health food with tastebuds in mind. Mainly organic and with vegan and raw choices for the hardcore, items include spinach wraps, stir fries, vegetarian lasagne and even pastries made right here.

Friday's (☎ 613-237-5353; 150 Elgin St; mains $15-22; ⏰ dinner daily, lunch Mon-Fri) Since 1972 the various dining rooms in this old mansion have marked special occasions and a big night out. Given the great location and posh surroundings, the meals are reasonably priced, especially the prix fixe for $28. Roast beef, with five different cuts offered, and steaks are the specialties but there is something for everyone. The upstairs piano bar is a fine place for a before- or after-dinner drink.

Mekong (☎ 613-237-7717; 637 Somerset St W; mains $8-16; ⏰ 11am-11pm) It doesn't look like much from the outside but, once past the entrance screen, this place is surprisingly smart. It's endorsed for good Vietnamese dishes, as well as Chinese, including fresh seafood.

Suisha Gardens (☎ 613-236-9602; 208 Slater St; mains $10-16; ⏰ lunch & dinner) Near the corner of Bank St is this highly recommended Japanese place. The food is excellent (though somewhat Westernized), the environment authentic and the service perfect. The best room is downstairs and to the left. Dinner for two is $50 before drinks, and prices are lower at lunch.

Roses Cafe (☎ 613-233-5574; 523 Gladstone Ave; mains $7-15; ⏰ dinner, lunch Mon-Fri) Good, cheap, mainly vegetarian Indian food is served at this small but well-established restaurant decorated with travel posters. The thali dinners, vegetarian or with meat, and the tasty *masala dosa* for lunch are recommended.

Royal Oak (☎ 613-236-0190; 318 Bank St; mains $9; ⏰ lunch & dinner) This is a friendly, good place for British beer, an excellent burger or a beef-and-Stilton pie.

THE AUTHOR'S CHOICE

Sweetgrass Aboriginal Bistro (☎ 613-562-3683; 108 Murray St; lunch/dinner $11/15-40; ⏰ lunch Mon-Fri, dinner Mon-Sat) One of very few restaurants across the country specializing in Aboriginal-style foods, this cozy, happening bistro offers a unique dining experience. Well-prepared items include buffalo, elk, pheasant, Atlantic salmon, rabbit pâté, bannock and corn soup. It's colorful, friendly, and manages the difficult trick of being upmarket yet relaxed. Aboriginal art adorns the walls and the open kitchen concept is uncommon in Canada for a place serving up this caliber of meal.

Top End

Flippers (☎ 613-232-2703; 819 Banks St; mains $15-28; ☺ dinner, lunch Tue-Sat) For years, this upstairs restaurant by the corner of 4th Av has satisfied seafood lovers. Ottawa is far from saltwater but this wood-stained and green room presided over by a mermaid does an admirable job with lobster, mussels, oysters and fresh fish.

Domus Café (☎ 613-241-6007; 87 Murray St; lunch/dinner mains $16/27; ☺ closed Sun dinner) If you're looking for a splurge but want substance, not just style, you've found it. The kitchen uses fresh, local, often organic produce in creating excellent Canadian regional nouveau meals that change with the seasons. You could start with lobster bisque, try the rainbow trout salad, and follow with halibut or duck. Other mains include marinated pork tenderloin and lamb sirloin. The room's soft yellows add to the dressy, sedate, elegant surroundings.

Giovanni's (☎ 613-234-3156; 362 Preston St; mains $20-40; ☺ dinner, lunch Mon-Fri) Since 1983 locals, along with numerous celebrities and sports stars, have been enjoying the refined experience here. Classic decor and top service combine with the menu featuring veal but also including seafood, steaks and typical, traditional Italian faves.

DRINKING

Hotel Lafayette (☎ 613-241-4747; Byward Market, York St) The 'Laff,' from 1849, is good for its cheap draft beer day or night. It's your old, basic, grubby hotel beer parlor, but its character attracts a wide cross section of people.

Patty's Pub (☎ 613-730-2434; 1186 Bank St) This Irish-themed pub is a comfortable local hangout with music from Thursday to Saturday and with a relaxing outdoor patio in summer.

Zoe's (☎ 613-241-1414; 1 Rideau St) is a classic piano bar in the Château Laurier.

ENTERTAINMENT

Express is the city's free entertainment weekly. *Capital Xtra* is similar but geared toward gay and lesbian readers. Both can be found around town from street boxes or in various cafés, restaurants, bars and music and book shops. Also check Thursday's *Ottawa Citizen* for complete club and entertainment listings.

Live Music

Cover charges vary at the city's music clubs.

Zaphod Beeblebrox (☎ 613-562-1010; 27 York St) Long-running, eclectic and popular with everything from New Age to rock to African music to rhythm and blues. Live bands play most nights, and prices are low. And you can't fault the selection of small-brewery beers.

Rainbow Bistro (☎ 613-241-5123; 76 Murray St) You can catch good live blues, reggae or folk upstairs at this much-appreciated club.

Manx Pub (☎ 613-231-2070; 370 Elgin St) This small, arty place offers single malts and microbrewery beers. There's often some good live weekend folk music with up-and-comers and cover charges are low.

Barrymores (☎ 613-233-0307; 323 Bank St) Rough and ready, this much-loved hangout features mainly live rock and metal on weekends. It looks like its abandoned, but that's cachet.

Irene's Pub (☎ 613-230-4474; 885 Bank St) Thankfully, no interior design work has been done at this funky, comfortable pub, which often has live Celtic, folk or blues to go with the great variety of imported beers.

Nightclubs

E18teen (☎ 613-244-1188; 18 York St) This is a cool hot spot for scotch and martinis in the Byward Market area.

Maxwell's (☎ 613-232-5771; 340 Elgin; $5) A fun feature at this dance club is the live swing band every Wednesday that draws admirably light-of-feet patrons.

Theater

National Arts Centre (NAC; ☎ 613-755-1111; www .nac-cna.ca; 53 Elgin St) This complex has theaters for drama and opera and is also home to the symphony orchestra. It also presents a range of concerts and variety acts. It's on the banks of the canal, in Confederation Sq.

Gay & Lesbian Venues

Lookout Bar (☎ 613-789-1624; 41 York St) The market contains this multitiered gay and lesbian fave.

Icon (☎ 613-235-4005; 366 Lisgar St) Actively-managed Icon always has something different happening at the lounge downstairs and dance bar upstairs, all catering to gays. Wednesday is karaoke night.

Cinemas
There are two repertory theaters showing two films a night: **Mayfair** (☎ 613-730-3403; 1074 Bank St; nonmembers $9) and **Bytown Cinema** (☎ 613-789-3456; 325 Rideau St; $9)

Sports
The Ottawa Senators play NHL hockey at the **Corel Centre** (☎ 613-599-0300, tickets 613-755-1166; Hwy 17, Kanata).

Lansdowne Park (☎ 613-580-2429; 1015 Bank St) is home to the **Renegades** (☎ 613-231-5608) of the Canadian Football League.

SHOPPING
Byward Market Square is at the corner of George and Byward Sts north of Rideau St. This old market building from the 1840s lends its name to the adjacent neighborhood. It's a colorful, bustling area where activity peaks on Saturday. Market Square is open every day from 9:30am to 6pm, while outdoor vendors set up around the building daily all year from about 6am. Farmers from west Québec and the Ottawa Valley sell vegetables, fruit and flowers, while specialty shops offer gourmet meat, seafood, baked goods and cheese. Crafts are also sold around the market building.

Bank St, south of the canal, between Euclid and Cameron Aves, has several antique and collectible shops as well as cafés where you can ponder your purchases.

GETTING THERE & AWAY
Air
Ottawa International Airport (☎ 613-248-2000; 50 Airport Rd) is 20 minutes south of the city and is, perhaps surprisingly, small. Main airlines serving the city include Air Canada, American Airlines, British Airways, Jetsgo, Northwest Airlines and KLM, US Airways and WestJet.

Bus
The **central bus station** (☎ 613-238-5900; 265 Catherine St, near Bank St) is a dozen blocks south of downtown. Greyhound Canada is the main bus company, and operates some routes under the name Midland Penetang Coach Lines in the Midland and Owen Sound area. One-way fares include Kingston ($38, 2½ hours), Toronto $62 (five hours), Montréal $33 (2½ hours) and Sudbury $88 (six to eight hours). There are seven buses daily to Toronto, some of which are express, and 15 daily for Montréal. Buses depart frequently for Kingston and Sudbury.

Car & Motorcycle
Discount (☎ 613-745-1546; 421 Gladstone St) charges $30 per day to rent compact cars. The major national chains (p873) have desks at the airport and around town.

Train
The **train station** (☎ 613-244-8289, 888-842-7245; 200 Tremblay Rd) is 7km southeast of downtown, near the junction of Alta Vista Rd and Hwy 417, just east of the Rideau Canal. VIA Rail operates four daily trains to Toronto ($99, four hours) and Montréal ($44, 1¾ hours). The fare to Kingston is $42 (two hours).

Trips west, for example to Sudbury, require a change of trains in Toronto, making them long trips.

GETTING AROUND
To/From the Airport
The cheapest way to get to the airport is by city bus. Take bus No 97 from the corner of Slater and Albert Sts. The ride takes 30 minutes.

You can also try the Airport Shuttle Bus (☎ 613-260-2359, per person $12), which leaves from many major hotels every half hour from about 5am to midnight. The ride takes about 25 minutes. The bus is not as frequent on weekends.

A taxi from the airport costs about $25.

Car & Motorcycle
There is free parking in World Exchange Plaza on weekends, and it's always the best place to park when visiting the downtown tourist office, one block away. Hourly metered parking can be found throughout downtown. Parking lots have daily rates of about $6; generally the municipal ones marked in green are cheapest. Sparks St downtown is closed to traffic.

Public Transportation
Ottawa and Hull operate separate bus systems. A transfer is valid from one system to the other, but may require an extra payment.

OC Transpo (☎ 613-741-4390) operates the Ottawa bus system, which tends to be volatile, with frequent changes in routes. Call for assistance – the agents are very helpful. The standard fare is $2.50 cash only but cheaper multiple tickets can be bought at corner stores around town. All Ottawa buses stop running by around midnight; most quit earlier.

AROUND OTTAWA
Gatineau (Hull)
☎ 819 / pop 230,000

Across the river in Québec, Gatineau is nearly as much the other half of Ottawa as it is a separate city. In late 2001, the name of Hull was changed to Gatineau as part of an administrative amalgamation of various towns. On the street, the central downtown will be called Hull for many years yet. The city has its share of ghastly-looking government offices, and workers cross the river in both directions each day, but the Gatineau side remains home to most of the area's French population. Away from the core, the cultural and architectural differences become more evident.

Gatineau is the main city of the region of Québec known as Outaouais (pronounced as though you were saying 'Ottawa' with a French accent). The Québec government has a booklet available at the tourist office outlining the region's attractions and activities, mostly of the outdoor variety. There are some huge parks and reserves within a few hours' drive of town.

ORIENTATION & INFORMATION
Promenade du Portage, easily found from either Portage Bridge or Alexandra Bridge, is the main downtown street.

The City Hall, known as Maison du Citoyen, is an attention-grabbing, dominating modern building with a 20m-high glass tower at 25 Rue Laurier. It contains an art gallery and a meditation center (what English-speaking bureaucracy would do that?).

Gatineau's tourist information office, **La Maison du Tourisme** (☎ 800-265-7822; 103 Rue Laurier at Boul St Laurent; ☯ 8:30am-5pm Mon-Fri, 9am-4pm Sat & Sun) is situated just over the Alexandra Bridge.

The Ottawa city bus and trolley tours include Gatineau in their circuits (p228).

Many of the Gatineau sites are on the Ottawa map.

SIGHTS
Canadian Museum of Civilization
The must-see **museum** (☎ 819-776-7000; www.civilization.ca; 100 Rue Laurier; adult/child/senior $10/6/7, half-price Sun; ☯ 9am-6pm, to 9pm Thu May-mid-Oct; 9am-5pm, to 9pm Thu mid-Oct-Apr; Ⓟ) is principally concerned with the history of Canada. It's in the large, striking complex with the copper domes on the riverbank opposite the Parliament Buildings. Allow the best part of a day to seriously explore the place.

Grand Hall, with its simulated forest and seashore, illuminates northwest coastal Aboriginal cultures and offers explanations with the extraordinary display of huge west coast totems.

Canada Hall presents 1000 years of Canadian history with displays and realistic re-creations tracing Canada's early beginnings, the story of the European founding, the voyages of the country's explorers, settlement and developments through to the 1880s. The Basque ship section, complete with the sound of creaking wood in the living quarters, brings to life the voyages undertaken to reach the New World. Also particularly good are the Acadian farm model and the replica of the early Québec town square.

Great Adventure provides kids with an entertaining and educational world tour complete with passport and includes some excellent interactive exhibits.

The fourth permanent exhibit, called **First People's Hall**, outlines Aboriginal history, culture and art from sea to sea to sea.

In addition, numerous evolving temporary shows and exhibits express and reveal specific aspects of what Canada is about.

Cineplus shows IMAX and OMNIMAX films. The ever-changing shows, despite hefty prices, are extremely popular so arrive early.

There is a good **cafeteria** that offers, among other things, sandwiches and a salad bar or economical full meals all served within view of the river and Parliament Hill. The museum bookstore and gift shop are worth a browse.

Casino du Lac Leamy
The other big site is the posh **gambling hall** (☎ 819-772-2100; 1 Boul du Casino; admission free; ☯ 11am-3am; Ⓟ) with docking facilities and a helipad – to get those high rollers!

The sizable casino complex is comparable to a Las Vegas–style resort, complete with a huge hotel, 1000-seat theater, flashy shows, conference center, high-class restaurant and abundant gambling facilities. The attire here is somewhat dressy. The casino is north of the center, off the third exit after going over Macdonald Cartier Bridge from Ottawa.

SLEEPING & EATING

The tourist office can help locate a B&B. Prices are lower than the Ottawa average. Motels can be found along Boul Alexandre Taché, which runs beside the river to the west of downtown Gatineau after you come across the bridge from Ottawa. There are also some business-oriented hotels downtown.

Gîtes Moyfrids (☎ 819-772-8557; www.bbcanada .com/moyfrids; 43 Millar St; s/d shared bathroom incl full breakfast $55/65) The owner at this quiet but central spot with a leafy garden speaks English, French, German and Norwegian.

Le Troquet (☎ 819-776-9595; 41 Rue Laval; mains under $14; ⏰ lunch & dinner) The atmosphere and excellent food make this almost like a quick budget trip to Paris. Lunch on broccoli soup, baguette with brie, tomatoes and Dijon mustard followed by café au lait all for $9.

Café Aubry (☎ 819-777-3700; 5 Rue Aubry; mains under $10; ⏰ lunch & dinner, closed Sun) This café/ bar serves light lunches and then heats up at night. It's located in a tiny pedestrian mall just off Promenade du Portage.

Café Henry Burger (☎ 819-777-5646; 69 Rue Laurier; dinner mains $36; ⏰ dinner, lunch Mon-Fri; P) Established in 1922, this is one of the oldest and most elegant restaurants in Canada. Keep an eye out for political movers and shakers. The expensive French menu changes with the seasons but always includes seafood and various meats.

DRINKING & ENTERTAINMENT

After 2am, when the Ontario bars are closed, real partygoers head across the river from Ottawa to Hull, where things are open until 3am and later. Narrow Rue Aubry, in the middle of downtown, has several nightspots, some with live music. **Le Bistro** (☎ 819-778-0968; Rue Kent, cnr Rue Aubry) attracts a casual and young crowd for music, food and drinks.

GETTING THERE & AWAY

The **Outaouais Bus System** (☎ 819-770-3242) has buses that operate along Rideau and Wellington Sts in Ottawa. From downtown Ottawa, bus Nos 8, 27 and 40 all go to Promenade du Portage.

A bicycle route over the Alexandra Bridge from Ottawa connects with a trail system that goes around much of central Gatineau and to Ruisseau de la Brasserie (Brewery Creek), a park area east of downtown.

Gatineau Park

Gatineau Park is a deservedly popular, 36,000-hectare area of woods and lakes in the Gatineau Hills of Québec, northwest of Hull. The **visitors' center** (☎ 819-827-2020; 33 Scott Rd; admission free; ⏰ 9am-5pm) is 12km from Ottawa's Parliament Hill, off Hwy 5. On weekends, some roads may be closed to cars; parking must be paid for at the more popular destinations.

The park is home to plenty of wildlife, including about 100 species of birds, and features 150km of hiking trails and 90km of cycling trails. **Lac Lapêche**, **Lac Meech** and **Lac Phillipe** have beaches for swimming (including a nude gay beach at Lac Meech) and thus are the most popular. The latter includes a **campground** (☎ reservations 819-456-3016; tent & RV sites $24), while there is canoe camping ($20) at Lac Lapêche, where canoes can be rented for $30 per day. You can fish in the lakes and streams, and the hiking trails are good for cross-country skiing in winter. Small **Pink Lake**, rimmed by a boardwalk, is pretty but off-limits for swimming.

Also in the park is **Mackenzie King Estate** (☎ 800-465-1867; per car $8; ⏰ 10am-5pm mid-May–mid-Oct), the summer estate of William Lyon Mackenzie King, who was prime minister in the 1920s, late 1930s and early 1940s. Here he indulged his hobby of collecting ruins, both genuine and fake. In 1941, King had bits of London's House of Commons brought over after the German blitz. His home, Moorside, is now a museum with a pleasant tearoom. An astute politician, King was interested in the occult and apparently talked to both his dead dog and deceased mother.

Occurring in September or October, **Fall Rhapsody** (☎ 800-465-1867; www.canadascapital.gc.ca/ gatineau) is a festival that celebrates the brief but colorful season when the leaves change –

a time when the maples and birches of the Gatineau Hills are having their last fling before winter. Activities during the two-week festival may include organized walks, orienteering events, art exhibits and brunches with live music. During Fall Rhapsody, there are cheap buses from Ottawa to various spots in Gatineau Park.

There is no public transportation to the park, but the Ottawa–Maniwaki bus route passes it.

Wakefield

Charming and scenic, historic Wakefield, just outside Gatineau Park, is a mix of heritage buildings, restaurants, cafés, lodgings and tourist-oriented shops. It's popular for day trips, but many stay longer.

Northwest of Gatineau Park, there are several outfitters who use a turbulent section of the Ottawa River for rafting adventures. The trips range from half-day to two-day adventures and run from roughly April to October. No experience is needed, and the locations are less than two hours from Ottawa. Book ahead for weekends, as the trips fill up. You may be able to get discounts for mid-week trips.

Recommended **Esprit Rafting** (☎ 800-596-7238; www.espritrafting.com; just off Hwy 148 in Davidson), just over the Québec border a few kilometers from Fort Coulonge, uses small, bouncy, 14-foot self-bailing rafts and provides pick-up and delivery from the Ottawa and Gatineau hostels. Esprit offers a one-day rafting trip with lunch ($100) and a whole range of other options, such as various canoe trips and kayaking courses. Good dormitory accommodations are available at its rustic Auberge Esprit lodge for $20, including breakfast and use of canoes and kayaks. You can also camp. All meals (the barbecue dinners are a treat) are offered.

Two other reliable organizations with comparable prices nearby are **Wilderness Tours** (☎ 800-267-9166) and **OWL Rafting** (☎ 800-461-7238), with both wild and mild trips, the latter being good for families; OWL's prices

start at $100 (over age 12) for six hours of rafting, a barbecue lunch and use of the resort facilities and equipment. Gentle float trips start at adult/child $65/45 with lunch and use of resort facilities. Both companies offer meals, camping and more expensive cabin accommodations, which should be booked ahead.

For more thrills, another option is a bungee jump ($87) or the high and fast rip ride ($30) at **Great Canadian Bungee** (☎ 819-459-3714, 877-828-8170; www.bungee.ca; Morrison's Quarry, Hwy 105), just south of Wakefield.

The **Hull-Chelsea Wakefield (HCW) Steam Train** (☎ 819-778-7246, 800-871-7246; www.steamtrain.ca; 165 Rue Deveault, north of central Gatineau; adult $39, adult during fall colors $45) connects Gatineau to Wakefield. The 1907 train travels alongside the park, making entertaining 64km one-day round trips daily from early May to mid-October. Reservations are recommended. In Wakefield, there's enough time for a meal or stroll and to watch the train get pushed around in the other direction by hand!

The HI **Gatineau Parc International Hostel** (☎ 819-459-3180/2113; carman@magma.ca; Carman Rd; dm $18-20) consistently gets great reviews, as does the affable, energetic, creative manager, Robert. It makes an excellent base for exploring the park and is a fine, always-evolving retreat in its own right. With 80 acres linked to the park, there is no end of outdoor possibilities here. Cycling, hiking, canoeing and cross-country skiing are all available (to really get into the bush, ask about the Haven). Other features are a sauna, fireplace, family rooms, music nights, restaurant and organic greenhouses. You may be able to get picked up after getting off the Voyageur Ottawa–Maniwaki bus; call for details.

Totally nondescript, the ragged **Black Sheep Inn (Mouton Noir)** (☎ 819-459-3228; 753 Riverside Dr; cover charge varies) has deservedly earned an incredible reputation for the bands it brings in and is a fabulous place to hear good music.

Québec

CONTENTS

Québec's appeal is, in the end, an intangible. Certainly, it is not known as 'La Belle Province' for nothing. Much of its geography is breathtaking. Canada's largest province encompasses windswept Arctic tundra in the north; wild boreal forests in the middle; rolling farmland in the south; and convoluted seascapes in the east.

Montréal deserves its reputation as a happening, hip amalgam of culture, style, diversity and unqualified presence. Captivating, historic Québec City is Canada's most European-flavored destination. And Québec's countless, bewitching small towns and villages remain alive, unsullied by the monotony of current building and business trends.

Still, more than anything, it is the leisurely pace, the joie de vivre and the ineffable way of life that most touches the visitor. For that, thanks goes to the province's people, the vast majority of whom speak French, making Québec unlike anywhere else in North America. Their unique, self-preserving culture manifests itself far beyond language into architecture, food, mores, music and religion. As you explore the province, savor that timeless air.

The Laurentians boast splendid mountains and year-round resorts. The Eastern Townships is a checkerboard of villages, farms, summer retreats and ski hills. Unspoiled Charlevoix is a sensory delight. The Gaspésie, with its rugged shoreline, wallops you with its splendor. Northern forests, home to huge untamed parks, provide accessible wilderness.

Québec may often be at odds with the rest of English-speaking Canada, but you won't be at odds with it.

HIGHLIGHTS

- Drink and dance in two languages in sociable **Montréal** (p260)
- Absorb the unique culture, history and charm of walled **Québec City** (p256)
- Get sprayed by whales in the Saguenay River fjord at **Tadoussac** (p302)
- Savor mouth-watering cuisine in idyllic **Charlevoix** (p296)
- Hike the stunning peaks above the tree line in **Parc de la Gaspésie** (p323)
- Swoosh the slopes at action-packed ski resorts such as **Mont-Tremblant** (p323)
- Hear the wolf's howl in the Laurentian's **Parc du Mont Tremblant** (p268)
- Sea-kayak amid the remote, sculpted islands of the **Mingan Archipelago National Park** (p311)

Mingan Archipelago National Park ★

Tadoussac ★   ★ Parc de la Gaspésie

Charlevoix ★

Parc du Mont Tremblant ★   ★ Québec City
Mont-Tremblant ★
★ Montréal

POPULATION: 7,510,000	PROVINCIAL CAPITAL: QUÉBEC CITY	AREA: 1,540,687 SQ KM

QUÉBEC

QUÉBEC

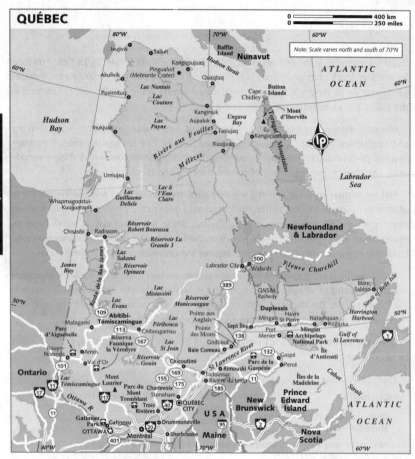

History

Québec has had a tumultuous history, and by Canadian standards, a very long and complicated one. Much of it is reflected in the architecture and preserved historical sites, so learning some of the province's colorful story comes painlessly with travel here.

At the time of European exploration, the entire region was fully settled and controlled by various Aboriginal groups, all of whom are resident today. Principal among them are the Mohawks along the St Lawrence River, the Cree above them, the Innu still further north and east, and the Inuit in the remote far north.

French explorer Jacques Cartier landed in what is now Québec City and Montréal in 1535 (see p24). Samuel de Champlain, also of France, first heard and recorded the word 'kebec' when he founded a settlement at Québec City some 70 years later, in 1608. Throughout the rest of that century, the French and English skirmished over control of Canada (see p25), but by 1759 the English, with a final battle victory on the Plains of Abraham at Québec City, established themselves as the winners in the Canadian colony sweepstakes. From that point on, French political influence in the New World waned.

When thousands of British Loyalists fled the American Revolution in the 1770s, the new colony divided into Upper (today's Ontario) and Lower (now Québec) Canada;

almost all the French settled in the latter region. Power struggles between the two language groups continued through the 1800s, with Lower Canada joining the Canadian confederation as Québec in 1867.

The 20th century saw Québec change from a rural, agricultural society to an urban, industrialized one, but one that continued to be educationally and culturally based upon the Catholic Church, which wielded immense power. About 90% of the population today is Roman Catholic, though the church's influence has declined sharply in recent decades.

The tumultuous 1960s brought the so-called 'Quiet Revolution,' during which all aspects of francophone society were scrutinized and overhauled. Intellectuals and extremists alike debated the prospect of independence from Canada, as Québecois began to assert their sense of nationhood. For more on the crisis of the '60s, see p32.

Formed in 1968, the pro-independence Parti Québecois came to power in 1976, headed by the charismatic René Lévesque. Since then, two referendums have returned 'No' votes on the question of separating from Canada. While the issue remains alive today, it is no longer topical. The notion of an independent Québec is less attractive

to a younger generation with more global concerns.

Québec in the new century remains something of a political enigma, nursing independence sentiments, but ultimately being more concerned with economic and day to day life issues. In 2004, for the first time, so-called allophones (people living in Québec whose first language is neither French or English) outnumbered Anglophones (those whose mother tongue is English). This is due to immigration, however many new arrivals speak either French or English as a second language. For example, people from Vietnam or Haiti often know some French.

Climate

Québec is a province of temperature extremes. Montréal and Québec City can go from 40°C to -40°C in six months. Generally, the summers are comfortably warm, although high humidity can make Montréal pretty steamy. Winters are very snowy, but usually bright, sunny and dry. The further north and east you travel, the cooler the summer days become, and even in midsummer a sweater may be required for evenings. By September, temperatures drop noticeably everywhere but in the southeast.

DISTINCT, NO DOUBT

Since the Québec separatism movement first began in the 1960s, there has been fretting both in and outside of the province over its distinctiveness, its 'distinct society' and how it needs protecting. Perhaps, but it doesn't take visitors long to note a cultural difference, and it doesn't seem to be diminishing.

Sixty percent of the time Québecois differ from the rest of Canada on questions of morality, personal tolerance and beliefs. They indicate they prefer people who seek happiness rather than hard work. On issues of abortion, homosexuality and sex education, Québecois rate more liberally overall, and Montréal has long been a gay-friendly city.

Québecois drink more than the Canadian average, they smoke everywhere, they gun through yellow lights, their couples argue in the streets, their bars stay open later. Women eating alone in restaurants won't be looked at askance, and menus often offer quarter liters of wine for solo diners. National surveys indicate that residents here are the most likely to play hooky from work. Not only that, the reason for their absenteeism is more likely than anywhere else in Canada to be that they wanted to have sex! Québec residents are most laissez-faire about allowing their own teenagers to sleep with their partners in the family home at young ages. And they are less concerned with marriage, with many couples living common-law. In a country with an alarmingly low birthrate, Québec's is lower still. At press time a survey showed Quebecers work fewer hours and sleep more than other Canadians – where do we sign up?

The province supports a flourishing independent French music and film industry. Concerns about a disappearing culture seem alarmist, *non*? And we haven't even gotten to politics...

FOUR LITTLE WORDS

Many tourists wonder what the three words written on Québec license plates, *Je me souviens*, mean. When they're told 'I remember,' they usually go silent. As far as license-plate slogans go, it's certainly not as straightforward as 'The Sunshine State.'

The phrase was first added to the provincial coat of arms way back in 1883. Author Eugène Taché, the architect of Québec City's Parliament Building, intended it to pronounce the peoples' hardships. It can be interpreted in various ways, but most agree that it infers, in a sense, the perceived marginalized status of Québec's French citizens, their believed victimization by colonization policies and denial of nationhood. In 1939, the provincial government officially adopted 'Je me souviens' as its slogan and it later appeared on the license plates.

The fourth word to be aware of is 'national' which, in a similar vein, gets inappropriately used by provincial bureaucrats. Upon arriving in Québec City, highway signs announce the 'national' capital. This is news in Ottawa and to the rest of the country. Similarly, the province has taken to calling its provincial parks 'national' parks. This is particularly confusing because there are indeed four true federal, national parks in Québec and almost 20 national historic sites. The vast majority of Québecois are not this petty.

National & Provincial Parks

The province's protected areas can be a highlight of any trip to Québec. Aside from preserving regions of remarkable beauty, they offer a host of invigorating activities, including canoeing, kayaking, rafting, hiking, cycling and camping in the wild. Full-moon hikes, campfire nature talks and historic demonstrations are fun as well. Forillon National Park (p324) and Saguenay (p304), Bic (p318), Mont-Tremblant (p268) and Gaspésie (p323) Provincial Parks are among those especially recommended.

Parks Canada (☎ 888-773-8888; www.parkscanada .ca) administers four national parks and 19 national historic sites in Québec. The historic sites, such as forts and lighthouses, are mostly day-use areas and reveal fascinating bits of history.

The **Société des Établissements de Plein Air du Québec** (Sépaq; ☎ 418-890-6527, 800-665-6527; www .sepaq.com) oversees Québec's enviable array of provincial parks and wildlife reserves. Confusingly, they refer to their parks as 'national.' The parks provide outstanding camping, wildlife viewing, eco-adventure and recreation. They range from beaches to bird sanctuaries to rugged gorges.

Réserve fauniques (wildlife reserves) conserve and protect the environment but also make these spaces publicly accessible. Hunters and fishers use the reserves (permits required) but more and more visitors are discovering them as less crowded alternatives to national and provincial parks.

The reserves offer the same gamut of activities but generally provide fewer services (information centers, canteens, guided tours etc).

Lastly, you may see the term 'Zec.' This is a '*zone d'exploitation contrôlée*,' or a semi-protected natural area. These are primarily regulated forest zones, often with rustic, basic camping permitted.

Getting There & Away

Québec is easily accessible by air, bus, car and train. It shares borders with the US states of New York, Vermont, New Hampshire and Maine. For border crossing information, see p863 and p861.

AIR

Québec's main airport is in Montréal, although Québec City is also busy. Carriers serving the province include Air Canada, Air Canada Tango and bargain airlines CanJet, Jetsgo and WestJet (see p868).

BUS

Greyhound Canada, Coach Canada, Acadian Lines and other bus companies connect the province with Ontario and Atlantic Canada in a seamless network (see p870). From the USA, Greyhound (p867) operates one daily bus service between Montréal and New York City.

CAR & MOTORCYCLE

Continental US highways link directly with their Canadian counterparts at numerous border crossings. These roads connect to the Trans-Canada Hwy (Hwy 40 within Québec), which runs directly through Montréal and Québec City. It's about 490km from Boston to Montréal, 540km from Toronto and 600km from New York City.

TRAIN
VIA Rail (p875) has fast and frequent services along the so-called Québec City–Windsor corridor, which includes a stop in Montréal. From the USA, Amtrak (p867) trains run once daily between Montréal and New York City.

Getting Around
AIR
Several small, regional carriers provide intra-provincial connections. For flights in the Far North there is First Air, Air Inuit and Air Creebec. Québecair Express covers the North Shore, Gaspésie and Îles de la Madeleine from Québec City and Montréal. For airline contact details, see p868.

BOAT
Ferries are an important means of travel around the province. There are numerous services across the St Lawrence River as well as to islands in the Gulf such as the Îles de la Madeleine, and along the remote Lower North Shore toward Labrador.

BUS
The province is well served by bus lines, including:
Voyageur (☎ 800-661-8747; www.greyhound.ca)
Orléans Express (☎ 888-999-3977; www.orleans express.com)
Limocar (☎ 866-700-8899; www.limocar.com)
Intercar (☎ 888-861-4592; www.intercar.qc.ca)
Autobus Viens (☎ 877-348-5599)
Autobus Maheux (☎ 888-797-0011; www.web diffuseur.qc.ca/maheux) Covers the northwest regions.

See the Getting There & Away sections of individual destinations in this chapter for specific trip details.

CAR & MOTORCYCLE
Highways throughout the province are good. In the far eastern and northern sections, slow, winding, even non-paved sections are typical and services may be few. For road conditions, a serious factor in winter, call ☎ 877-393-2363. Note that turning right at red lights is not permitted anywhere on the island of Montréal, in Québec City or anywhere else that signs indicate not to do so.

The ride-share agency **Allô Stop** (www.allostop .com) offers an inexpensive way to travel within

---

QUEBEC IN...

Five days
Start with two day's of **Montréal's** (p236) unique culture. On day three drive through the Laurentians to **Mont-Tremblant** (p268). On day four, let **Québec City** (p278) enchant you. Have a fabulous meal and sip café au lait amid the lively streets. Spend your last day absorbing the walled city's visible history.

Seven days
Follow the above but then ramble through **Charlevoix** (p296) en route to the **Saguenay River** (p312) for two days. Stop for lunch in **Baie St Paul** (p298) or **Pointe au Pic** (p300). Spend the last two nights in welcoming **Tadoussac** (p302). Go whale-watching, wander the shoreline or cruise the fjord.

Two weeks
Follow the five-day schedule but linger around **Québec City** (p278) on day six. Take a boat trip to fascinating **Gross Île** (p312) and consider a late afternoon in **St Jean Port Joli** (p313). Leave Québec City for a leisurely tour of **Charlevoix** (p296). On day nine arrive in **Tadoussac** (p302) for a two-night stay. On day 11 ferry across the St Lawrence to **Rivière du Loup** (p314). Start with a stop at **Parc du Bic** (p318) and then for the last days explore the **Gaspé Peninsula** (p319). Take a hike in **Parc de la Gaspésie** (p323), drive the spectacular shoreline and wind down in lovely **Percé** (p325).

Québec and to other provinces by linking up drivers and paying passengers headed in the same direction. Passengers pay $6 for a one-year membership, plus a portion of the ride cost to the agency; the rest goes to the driver. There are offices in Montréal, Québec City, Sherbrooke, Saguenay and Rimouski. See the Getting There & Away sections of those destinations for details.

TRAIN

VIA Rail connects Montréal and Québec City to the South Shore and Gaspésie.

MONTRÉAL

☎ 514 / pop 3.4 million

Picture this: Two elegant women sitting in a café. One speaking French, the other English except that – midway through her reply – the English speaker switches to French, which the French speaker answers in English. And so it goes in the uniquely bifurcated brains of those who call Montréal home and where the culture is as much of a mélange as is the language.

The food (oh, the food!), the fashions, the friendliness of the people and the very streets themselves are reflective of a city where two distinct cultures have managed to harmoniously blend and create a milieu that is a celebration of its people. This finds expression in the endless festivals and parties, in the wealth of its artistic and cultural venues and in the quality of life that would horrify Montréalers if it did not include daily feasts, time spent strolling or with family and endless talks in cafés over *je ne se quoi*.

In spring and summer, you can almost make out the strains of accordion music and the sweet songs of a Parisienne chanteuse lilting in the breeze. It is time to express style and color and to be seen as a savant. Streets bustle with a wonderfully nonchalant urgency that is only possible here. People are definitely going places, just not too fast.

Montréal is a city that embraces you. You need only perfect the 'double-cheek-kiss' and her spirit will lead you on to very personal and lovely explorations. It makes no sense at all to drive when the city core is so easily walked. And, *mon dieu!* Think of all the beauty you would miss if stuck in a car not plying the breezes on foot or by bicycle.

HISTORY

In May 1642, a small fleet of boats sailed up the St Lawrence River. The few dozen missionaries aboard had survived a cold winter crossing the fierce Atlantic Ocean from their native France. Finally they had reached the spot their fellow countryman, explorer Jacques Cartier, had stumbled across over a century earlier. Led by Paul Chomedey de Maisonneuve, the pioneers went ashore and began building a small settlement they called Ville-Marie in honor of the virgin. It would be the birthplace of Montréal.

Ville-Marie soon blossomed into a major fur-trading center and exploration base, despite fierce resistance from the local Iroquois. Skirmishes continued until the signing of a peace treaty in 1701. The city remained French until the 1763 Treaty of Paris, which saw France cede Canada to Great Britain. In 1775, American revolutionaries briefly occupied the city, but left after failing to convince the Québecois to join forces with them against the British.

Despite surrendering its pole position in the fur trade to Hudson Bay in the 1820s, Montréal boomed throughout the 19th century. Industrialization got seriously underway after the construction of the railway and the Canal de Lachine, which in turn attracted masses of immigrants. Other major milestones included the founding of McGill University in 1821, a stint as capital of the United Provinces of Canada (1844–49) and the opening of the Canadian Pacific Railway (CPR) headquarters in 1880.

After WWI the city sashayed through a period as 'Sin City' as hordes of Americans seeking fun flooded across the border to escape Prohibition. By the time mayor Jean Drapeau took the reins, Montréal was ripe for an extreme makeover. During his long tenure (1954–57, 1960–86), the city gained the metro system, many of downtown's high-rise offices, the underground city and the Place des Arts. Drapeau also twice managed to firmly train the world's spotlight on Montréal: in 1967 for the World Expo and in 1976 for the Olympic Games.

These days, Montréal is a self-confident, economically sound and vibrant city with more college students than Boston. It routinely ranks among the top 20 places to live on the planet, according to no less an authority than the UN.

ORIENTATION

Montréal is a vaguely arrow-shaped island about 40km long and 15km wide. Its most famous natural landmark is 233m-high Mont Royal which, on its southern side, is buttressed by the downtown business district. McGill University, major museums, the main tourist office, and the main train station are all here as well. Shopping is excellent along Rue Ste-Catherine Ouest, the main east–west drag, and in the **Underground City**. This ingenious 30km warren of subterranean passageways – which keeps you cool in summer and warm in winter – also provides access to restaurants, museums, movie theaters, offices and metro stations. Look for the blue signs at street level to know where to descend; down below it's all well signposted, although getting lost is part of the fun.

In the east, downtown is bounded by Boul St-Laurent, known simply as 'The Main.' Street names east of this major artery bear the Est (East) suffix, while those to the west include Ouest (West) in their name.

Heading south on Boul St-Laurent takes you to historic **Old Montréal**, anchored by bustling Place Jacques Cartier and the Basilique Notre Dame. Cute cobbled lanes lead to the waterfront and the **Old Port** where four major *quais* (piers) jut into the St Lawrence River. Looking south across the water,

you'll spot the two islands that make up the recreational expanse of Parc Jean-Drapeau. The **Pôle des Rapides** district, which hugs the southern shore of the Canal de Lachine, is just west of the Old Port.

On its way north from Old Montréal, Boul St-Laurent first passes through the city's small **Chinatown** before climbing up to the **Plateau Mont-Royal**, Montréal's hippest neighborhood with a huge concentration of bars, restaurants and boutiques. Still further north is **Little Italy**, another foodie mecca.

East of Boul St-Laurent, Rue Ste-Catherine leads to the **Quartier Latin**, home of the Central Bus Station with service to the airport and other destinations. The north–south Rue St-Denis, which bisects the Quartier, is another fun mile filled with myriad diversions. From here it's only a short walk further east along Rue Ste-Catherine to **The Village**, the hub of gay and lesbian life in Montréal.

The **Olympic Park** area is about 5km east of these central neighborhoods and best reached via Rue Sherbrooke.

For details about traveling between Montréal's airport and downtown, see p264.

Maps

The maps in this book should suffice when exploring central Montréal, but you can pick up a free map at the tourist offices

---

MONTRÉAL IN...

One Day

Start the day with our walking tour of **Old Montréal** (p240), then visit the city's birthplace at the **Musée d'Archéologie et d'Histoire Pointe-à-Callière** (p241). Work off lunch by scaling **Mont Royal** (p247) for panoramic city views, then spend the rest of the afternoon shopping along Rue Ste-Catherine and in the Underground City. Wrap up the day with dinner in the **Plateau Mont-Royal** (p247).

Two Days

Follow the one-day itinerary, then make **Olympic Park** (p248) the focus of your second day. In fine weather, follow up a visit to the **Biodôme** (p249) with a trip up the **Tour de Montréal** (p248). Or head straight to the **Jardin Botanique** (p249) for some blossom sniffing. Spend the afternoon soaking up the vibe of the Plateau Mont-Royal before heading to Little Italy for dinner.

Three Days

Follow the two-day itinerary, then start day three with a culture fix at the **Musée des Beaux Arts** (p242) before heading to the waterfront. Either rent a bicycle for a leisurely trip along the **Canal de Lachine** (p251), with a stop at **Marché Atwater** (p257) for picnic supplies, or board a jet boat for a bumpy ride on the **Lachine Rapids** (p253). After dinner in Old Montréal catch live jazz at **L'Escogriffe** (p261) or the **House of Jazz** (p261).

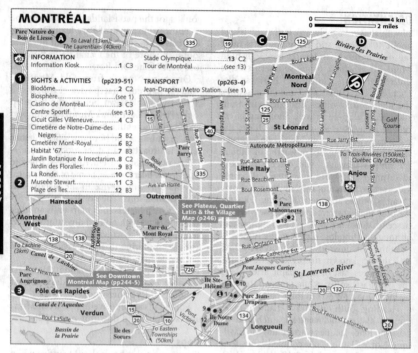

MONTRÉAL

0 — 4 km
0 — 2 miles

INFORMATION
Information Kiosk....................1 C3

SIGHTS & ACTIVITIES (pp239-51)
Biodôme..............................2 C2
Biosphère.........................(see 1)
Casino de Montréal................3 C3
Centre Sportif....................(see 13)
Cicuit Gilles Villeneuve...........4 C3
Cimetiére de Notre-Dame-des
 Neiges............................5 B2
Cimetiére Mont-Royal..............6 B2
Habitat '67........................7 B3
Jardin Botanique & Insectarium...8 C2
Jardin des Floralies..............9 B3
La Ronde..........................10 C3
Muséee Stewart...................11 C3
Plage des Îles...................12 B3

Stade Olympique...................13 C2
Tour de Montréal................(see 13)

TRANSPORT (pp263-4)
Jean-Drapeau Metro Station....(see 1)

(opposite), which includes a useful outline of the underground city. If you need more detail, try Lonely Planet's laminated Montréal map or those produced by MapArt, sold at convenience stores and bookshops.

INFORMATION
Bookstores
Chapters (Map pp244-5; ☎ 514-849-8825; 1171 Rue Ste-Catherine Ouest; ⏱ 9am-10pm Mon-Thu, to 11pm Fri & Sat, 10am-9pm Sun; metro Peel) Books galore, plus a coffee bar with Internet access.

Indigo (Map pp244-5; ☎ 514-281-5549; Place Montréal Trust, 1500 Ave McGill College; ⏱ 9am-11pm; metro Peel) Chapters' equally comprehensive sister store.

Ulysses (Map p246; ☎ 514-843-9447; 4176 Rue St-Denis; ⏱ 10am-6pm Mon-Wed, to 9pm Thu & Fri, 10am-5:30pm Sat, 11am-5:30pm Sun; metro Mont-Royal) Travel books and maps.

Cultural Centers
British Council (Map pp244-5; ☎ 514-866-5863; Bureau 4200, 1000 Rue de la Gauchetière Ouest, Bureau 4200; metro Bonaventure)

Goethe Institute (Map p246; ☎ 514-499-0159; 418 Rue Sherbrooke Est; metro Sherbrooke)

Emergency
Police, Ambulance & Fire (☎ 911)
Rape Crisis Center (☎ 514-934-4504)
Montréal Police Station (☎ 514-280-2222) For nonemergencies.

Internet Access
Battlenet 24 (Map pp244-5; ☎ 514-846-3333; 1407 Rue du Fort; per hr $3; ⏱ 24hr; metro Guy-Concordia)

Chapters (Map pp244-5; ☎ 514-849-8825; 1171 Rue Ste-Catherine Ouest; per hr $6 ⏱ 9am-10pm Mon-Thu, to 11pm Fri & Sat, 10am-9pm Sun; metro Peel)

Net 24 (Map pp244-5; ☎ 514-845-9634; 2157 Rue Mackay; per hr $4; ⏱ 24hr; metro McGill)

Netopia (Map p246; ☎ 514-286-5446; 1737 Rue St-Denis; per hr adult/student $5/4; ⏱ 24hr; metro Berri-UQAM)

Internet Resources
City of Montréal (www2.ville.montreal.qc.ca in French) Official city website.

Montréal Clubs (www.montreal-clubs.com) Keeps the finger on the pulse of Montreal's latest nightlife hotspots.

Tourism Montréal (www.tourism-montreal.org) Official website of the Montréal tourist office with reams of information and a last-minute hotel search function with guaranteed 10% discount.

Left Luggage

You'll find lockers and/or left-luggage stations (checkrooms) at the airport, in the central bus station and in the main train station. Expect to pay about $5 per piece per day.

Media

The *Montréal Gazette* is the main English-language daily newspaper with solid coverage of national affairs, politics and arts. The weekend edition has useful what's-on listings, although the free alternative weeklies, the *Mirror* and the *Hour*, are better sources. Published every Thursday, they're widely available in restaurants, bars and shops. Their French counterparts are *Voir* and *Ici*.

Medical Services

CLSC (Map pp244-5; ☎ 514-934-0354; 1801 Boul de Maisonneuve Ouest; metro Guy-Concordia) Walk-in community health center for minor ailments; costs $105 (cash only) per visit, not including tests.

Pharmaprix Pharmacy Mont-Royal (☎ 514-738-8464; 5122 Chemin de la Côte-des-Neiges; ☒ 24hr; metro Côte-des-Neiges) Downtown (Map pp244-5; ☎ 514-933-4744; 1500 Rue Ste-Catherine Ouest; metro Guy-Concordia) Check the Yellow Pages for additional branches.

Royal Victoria Hospital (Map pp244-5; ☎ 514-842-1231; 687 Ave des Pins Ouest; ☒ 24hr; metro McGill) McGill University–affiliated, with emergency room, and the best option for English-speaking patients; $520 per visit (admittance only).

Money

You'll find currency exchange counters at the airport, the train station, the main tourist office (right), the casino (p250; open 24 hours) and throughout the central city, especially along Rue Ste-Catherine.

American Express (Map pp244-5; ☎ 514-284-3300; 1141 Boul de Maisonneuve Ouest; ☒ 9am-5pm Mon-Fri; metro Peel)

National Bank of Canada Plateau Mont-Royal (Map p246; 4506 Rue St-Denis; metro Mont-Royal) Quartier Latin (Map p246; 801 Rue Ste-Catherine Est; metro Berri-UQAM) Check the Yellow Pages for additional branches.

Post

Main Post Office (Map pp244-5; ☎ 800-267-1177; 1250 Rue University; ☒ 8am-5:45pm Mon-Fri; metro McGill) The largest branch, but you'll find many other locations around town.

Station Place d'Armes (Map pp244-5; 435 Rue St-Antoine, Montréal, Québec H2Z 1H0) Have poste restante (general delivery) mail sent here.

Tourist Information

Montréal and Québec province maintain a central phone service for tourist information (☎ 514-873-2015, 877-266-5687).

Centre Infotouriste (Map pp244-5; www.bonjour quebec.com; Ste 100, 1255 Rue Peel; ☒ 8:30am-7:30pm Jun–early Sep, 9am-6pm mid-Sep–May; metro Peel) Information about Montréal and all of Québec. Free hotel, tour and car reservations, plus currency exchange.

Montreal Science Information Booth (Map pp244-5; King Edward Pier; ☒ 10am-5pm Sun-Thu, 10am-8pm Fri & Sat late Apr–late Jun, 10am-8pm Sun-Thu, to 8:30pm Fri & Sat late Jun–early Sep)

Montréal Tourist Office (Map pp244-5; www.tourism -montreal.org; 174 Rue Notre Dame Est; ☒ 9am-5pm Jan-Oct, to 7pm Jun–early Sep; metro Champ-de-Mars)

Old Port Information Kiosk (Map pp244-5; Quai Jacques Cartier; ☒ 10am-7pm Mon-Fri, to 8pm Sat & Sun early May–mid-Jun & mid–late Aug, 10am-10pm daily mid-Jun–mid-Aug, 10am-5pm Mon-Fri, to 7pm Sat & Sun Sep, closed Oct-Apr)

Québec Gay Chamber of Commerce (☎ 514-522-1885, 888-595-8110; www.infovillagegai.com in French)

Travel Agencies

American Express (Map pp244-5; ☎ 514-284-3300; 1141 Boul de Maisonneuve Ouest; ☒ 9am-5pm Mon-Fri; metro Peel)

Boutique Tourisme Jeunesse (Map p246; ☎ 514-844-0287; 205 Ave du Mont-Royal Ouest; ☒ 10am-6pm Mon-Wed, to 9pm Thu & Fri, 10am-5pm Sat) Run by Hostelling International; also sells books, maps, travel insurance and ISIC cards.

Voyages Campus (Map p246; ☎ 514-843-8511; www .travelcuts.com; 1613 Rue St-Denis; ☒ 10am-5pm Mon-Wed, to 8pm Thu & Fri, 10am-4pm Sat; metro Berri-UQAM) Known as Travel Cuts outside Québec; see the Yellow Pages for additional branches around town.

SIGHTS

Most visitors spend the bulk of their time scoping out the great museums and stores of downtown, enjoying the views from Mont Royal, or haunting the worn lanes of Old Montréal and the refurbished Old Port. Of the outer districts, the Olympic Park area and Lachine hold the greatest sight-seeing appeal. The Plateau, Quartier Latin and Village are the best neighborhoods for simply wandering and getting lost. In summer the meadows, pathways and attractions of Parc Jean-Drapeau are an easy getaway from the city bustle.

Note that most museums are closed on Monday. Custom-made for culture buffs, the Montréal Museum Pass ($39) is valid for three consecutive days and gets you admission to 30 museums plus unlimited use of the bus and metro system. It's available at the tourist offices, major hotels and the participating museums.

Old Montréal

The oldest section of the city is a warren of crooked cobblestone lanes flanked by colonial and Victorian stone houses filled with intimate restaurants, galleries and boutiques. A stroll around here will delight romantics and architecture fans, especially at night when the most beautiful facades are illuminated. And the waterfront is never far away.

Old Montréal is anchored by lively Place Jacques Cartier and dignified Place d'Armes, which are linked by busy Rue Notre Dame. The southern end of Place Jacques Cartier gives way to Rue St-Paul, the district's prettiest and oldest street.

BASILIQUE NOTRE DAME

Montréal's famous landmark, **Notre-Dame Basilica** (Map pp244–5; ☎ 514-842-2925; www.basiliquenddm.org in French; 110 Rue Notre Dame Ouest; adult/child $4/2; ☑ 8am-4:30pm Mon-Sat, 12:30-4:15pm Sun; metro Place d'Armes) is a visually pleasing if slightly gaudy symphony of carved wood, paintings, gilded sculptures and stained-glass windows. Built in 1829 on the site of an older and smaller church, it also sports a famous Casavant organ and the Gros Bourdon, said to be the biggest bell in North America. The interior looks especially impressive during an otherwise overly melodramatic **sound and light show** (adult/child $10/5) staged from Tuesday to Saturday nights.

The basilica made headlines in 1994 when singer Céline Dion got married under its soaring midnight-blue ceiling, and again in 2000 when Jimmy Carter and Fidel Castro shared pall-bearing honors at the state funeral of former Canadian Prime Minister Pierre Trudeau.

A popular place for regular Montréalers to tie the knot is the much smaller **Chapelle du Sacré Coeur** (Sacred Heart Chapel) behind the main altar. Rebuilt in a hotchpotch of historic and contemporary styles after a 1978 fire, its most eye-catching element is the floor-to-ceiling bronze altarpiece.

PLACE D'ARMES

The twin-towered Notre-Dame Basilica lords over this dignified square, where the early settlers once battled it out with the local Iroquois. A statue of Maisonneuve stands in the middle of the square, which is surrounded by some of Old Montréal's finest historic buildings. In fact, the **Old Seminary**, next to the basilica, is the city's oldest, built by Sulpician missionaries in 1685 and still occupied today.

Behind the templelike curtain of columns in the northwest corner lurks the **Bank of Montréal** (Map pp244–5; ☎ 514-877-6810; 119 Rue St-Jacques Ouest; admission free; ☑ 10am-4pm Mon-Fri; metro Place d'Armes). It harbors the head office of Canada's oldest bank, founded in 1817. The opulent marble interior is worth a gander and there's a small money museum as well.

Looming on the square's east side is the red sandstone **New York Life Building** (1888), which was the city's first skyscraper. Today it is dwarfed by the Art Deco **Aldred Building** (1931), which was intended to emulate the Empire State Building until the Great Crash of 1929 put an end to such lofty ambitions.

CENTRE D'HISTOIRE DE MONTRÉAL

This small **museum** (Map pp244–5; ☎ 514-872-3207; www2.ville.montreal.qc.ca/chm; 335 Place d'Youville; adult/concession $4.50/3; ☑ 10am-5pm Tue-Sun May-Aug & Wed-Sun Sep-Apr; metro Place d'Armes, Square Victoria) puts a human spin on city history in an engaging multimedia exhibit. You can listen to the tales of real people while sitting in a period kitchen or travel back in time while watching archival footage from the 1940s or '60s. For sweeping views, head to the rooftop.

PLACE JACQUES CARTIER & AROUND

Gently sloped Place Jacques Cartier in the heart of Old Montréal is a beehive of activity, especially in summer when it's filled with flowers, street musicians, vendors and visitors. The cafés and restaurants lining it are neither cheap nor good, but they do offer front-row seats for the action. There is a tourist office (p238) in the northwest corner.

At the square's north end stands the **Colonne Nelson** (Nelson's Column; Map pp244–5), a monument erected by the British to the general who defeated the French and Spanish fleet at Trafalgar. Nelson faces a small statue of Admiral Vauquelin across the street, put there as a riposte by the French.

Looking mightily majestic with its green copper roof and perky turret, the **Hôtel de Ville** (City Hall; Map pp244–5; ☎ 514-872-3355; 275 Rue Notre Dame Est; admission & tours free; 8:30am–4:30pm, tours mid-Jun–mid-Aug; metro Champ-de-Mars) towers above the square's northeast end. Modeled on the city hall of Tours, France, and completed in 1878, its grandeur reflects the city's 19th-century wealth and confidence. In 1967, French President Charles de Gaulle surprised everyone by proclaiming 'Vive le Québec libre!' ('Long live free Québec!') to cheering crowds from its balcony. These four little words were enough to fan the flames of separatism, straining relations with Ottawa for years. Inside, the **Hall of Honour**, adorned with scenes of rural Québec, is worth a closer inspection.

The petite palace across the street is the **Château de Ramezay** (Map pp244–5; ☎ 514-861-3708; www.chateauramezay.qc.ca; 280 Rue Notre Dame Est; adult/child/student/senior $7/4/5/6; 10am–6pm Jun-Sep, 10am–4:30pm Tue-Sun Oct–May; metro Champ-de-Mars), built in 1705 as the residence of Montréal governor Claude de Ramezay. During the American Revolution, Ben Franklin stayed here, fruitlessly attempting to convince the Canadians to join the cause. Now a museum of early Québec history, its web of rooms brims with an eclectic assortment of furniture, art and objects. The mahogany-paneled **Salle de Nantes** is a feast for the eyes, and there's a pretty garden as well.

OLD PORT   Map pp244–5

Montréal's Old Port has morphed into a park and fun zone paralleling the mighty St Lawrence River for 2.5km and punctuated by four grand *quais*. Locals and visitors alike come here for strolling, cycling and in-line skating. Cruise boats, ferries, jet boats and speedboats all depart for tours from various docks (p253). In winter, you can cut a fine figure on an outdoor ice-skating rink (p251).

Historical relics include the striking white **Clock Tower** (☎ 514-596-7678; Clock Tower Pier; admission free; 10am–9pm mid-Jun–mid-Aug, closed Oct–mid-May, call for hrs mid-May–mid-Jun & mid-Aug–Sep; metro Champ-de-Mars) on the port's northern end. Built in 1922 to honor sailors

who died in WWI, it affords commanding views of the river and city.

A perennial family favorite is the **Centre des Sciences de Montréal** (Montréal Science Centre; ☎ 514-496-4724; www.montrealsciencecentre.com; King Edward Pier; adult/child/teen & senior/family $10/7/9/30; 9:30am–5pm Sun-Thu, 10am–5pm Fri & Sat mid-Jun–mid-Sep, to 4pm daily mid-Sep–mid-Jun; metro Champ-de-Mars). There are plenty of buttons to push, knobs to pull and games to play as you make your way through the high-tech exhibition halls. The two permanent exhibits – Eureka! and Technocity – seek to unravel the mysteries of nature and technology, while the Immersion Movie Game is a collective video game projected onto giant screens.

The center also includes an IMAX cinema (p262) showing vivid nature and science films in 2-D or 3-D.

MUSÉE D'ARCHÉOLOGIE ET D'HISTOIRE POINTE-À-CALLIÉRE

Housed in a striking, contemporary building, the excellent **Museum of Archaeology and History** (☎ 514-872-9150; www.pacmuseum.qc.ca; 350 Place Royale; adult/child 6-12/student/senior $10/3.50/6/7.50; 10am–6pm Mon-Fri & 11am–6pm Sat & Sun late Jun–early Sep, 10am–5pm Tue-Fri & 11am–5pm Sat & Sun mid-Sep–mid-Jun; metro Place d'Armes) sits near the original landing spot of the early settlers and provides a good overview of the city's beginnings. Make time for the multimedia show before plunging underground into a maze of excavated foundations, an ancient sewerage system and vestiges of the first European cemetery. Artifacts and interactive stations help bring the past to life. The lookout tower and restaurant can be visited free of charge.

MARCHÉ BONSECOURS

The silvery dome standing sentinel over Old Montréal like a glamorous lighthouse belongs to **Bonsecours Market** (☎ 514-872-7730; 350 Rue St-Paul Est; 10am–9pm Mon-Sat, to 6pm Sun late Jun–early Sep, 10am–6pm daily Sep-Mar; metro Champ-de-Mars). After a stint as city hall, the neoclassical structure served as the city's main market hall until supermarkets drove it out of business in the 1960s. These days, the flower and vegetable stands have been replaced with fancy boutiques selling arts, crafts and clothing produced in Québec. This is not a bad place to pick up some quality souvenirs.

QUÉBEC

QUÉBEC

CHAPELLE NOTRE-DAME-DE-BONSECOURS   Map pp244–5

Also known as the **Sailor's Church** (☎ 514-282-8670; www.marguerite-bourgeoys.com; 400 Rue St-Paul Est; admission free, museum adult/child/senior & student $5/2/3; ☺ 10am-5pm Tue-Sun), Montréal's oldest stone church (1658) for centuries occupied a special spot in the heart of seamen who came here to pray for safe passage. Small ship models left here by grateful survivors still dangle from its ceiling. The adjoining **Musée Marguerite Bourgeoys** has exhibits about the chapel's history and the life of Marguerite Bourgeoys, who was Montréal's first teacher. There are fine harbor views from the tower.

Downtown   Map pp244–5

Montréal's modern downtown has a North American look, with wide thoroughfares chopping a forest of skyscrapers into a grid pattern. At street level you'll find some of the city's most beautiful churches, striking buildings, museums, green spaces and major shopping areas. You'll find an almost Latin spirit pervades the cafés, restaurants and bars, especially along Rue Crescent.

MUSÉE DES BEAUX ARTS

A must for art lovers, the **Museum of Fine Arts** (☎ 514-285-2000; www.mbam.qc.ca; 1380 Rue Sherbrooke Ouest; permanent collection admission free, special exhibitions adult/child/student & senior $12/3/6, half-price Wed after 5:30pm; ☺ 11am-5pm Tue-Sun, during special exhibitions to 9pm Wed; metro Guy-Concordia) has amassed several millennia's worth of paintings, sculpture, decorative arts, furniture, prints, drawings and photographs. European heavyweights include Rembrandt, Picasso and Monet, but the museum really shines when it comes to Canadian art. Highlights include works by Jean-Baptiste Roy-Audy and Paul Kane, landscapes by the Group of Seven and abstractions by Jean-Paul Riopelle. There's also a fair amount of Inuit and Amerindian artifacts and lots of fancy decorative knick knacks, including Japanese incense boxes and Victorian chests. The temporary exhibits are often exceptional.

Exhibits spread across the classical, marble-clad Michal and Renata Hornstein Pavilion and the crisp, contemporary Jean-Noël Desmarais Pavilion across the street.

MUSÉE D'ART CONTEMPORAIN

Canada's only major showcase of contemporary art, this **museum** (☎ 514-847-6226; www.macm.org; 185 Rue Ste-Catherine Ouest; adult/child under 12/student/senior $6/free/3/4, admission free 6-9pm Wed; ☺ 11am-6pm Tue & Thu-Sun, to 9pm Wed; metro Place des Arts) offers an excellent survey of Canadian, and in particular Québecois, creativity. All the local legends, including Jean-Paul Riopelle, Paul-Émile Borduas and Génévieve Cadieux, are well represented. There are great temporary shows, too. Free English-language tours run at 6:30pm Wednesday and at 1pm and 3pm on weekends.

CENTRE CANADIEN D'ARCHITECTURE

Architecture buffs should make a beeline to the **Canadian Centre for Architecture** (☎ 514-939-7026; www.cca.qc.ca; 1920 Rue Baile; adult/child under 12/student/senior $8/free/5/6, admission free 5:30-9pm Thu, students free all day Thu; ☺ 10am-5pm Tue, Wed & Fri-Sun, to 9pm Thu; metro Guy-Concordia). It combines a museum and a research institution in

---

MONTRÉAL TRIVIA

▪ Mont Royal is *not* a dormant volcano, despite what you may have read elsewhere.

▪ John Lennon wrote 'Give Peace a Chance' during his famous 1969 'bed-in for peace' with Yoko Ono in Suite 1742 of the Fairmont Le Reine Elizabeth (p255).

▪ Anna Leonowens, who inspired the movie *The King and I*, starring Yul Brynner and Deborah Kerr, is buried in Cimetière Mont Royal, north of Parc Mont Royal.

▪ IMAX technology, a Canadian invention, premiered here at Expo '67.

▪ Montréal is closer to the equator than Paris.

▪ Montréal has the only Hector Guimard–designed Art Nouveau metro entrance station in use outside Paris (it's on Square Victoria).

▪ The city has hosted the longest running St Patrick's Day parade in North America, since 1824.

one sleek, innovative complex that seamlessly integrates with the historic **Shaughnessy House**. Once the home of a wealthy businessman, the gray limestone treasure encapsulates 19th-century high-class living. The ritziest room is a lounge with intricate woodwork and a grand fireplace.

The center's galleries show prints, drawings, models and photos of remarkable buildings, both local and international. There's also a **sculpture garden** with a dozen or so works scattered about a terrace overlooking southern Montréal. It's especially impressive when illuminated at night.

Free English-language tours run at 7:30pm Thursday and at 1:30pm Friday, Saturday and Sunday.

MUSÉE MCCORD

Beaded headdresses, fine china, elegant gowns, letters, photographs and toys are among the more than 1.2 million objects forming the collection of the well-regarded **McCord Museum of Canadian History** (☎ 514-398-7100; www.mccord-museum.qc.ca; 690 Rue Sherbrooke Ouest; adult/child/student/senior $10/3/5.50/7.50; ☽ 10am-6pm Tue-Fri, 10am-5pm Sat & Sun year-round & Mon mid-Jun–early Sep; metro McGill). Changing and permanent exhibitions tell the history – and stories – of the people who built the country, zeroing in on the unique challenges they faced, from icy winters to multiculturalism. The museum is especially renowned for its **Notman Photographic Archives**, which offer an unparalleled visual record of Canada's evolution since 1840. Ask about guided tours and children's workshops.

CATHÉDRALE MARIE REINE DU MONDE

A beloved Montréal landmark, the **Cathedral of Mary Queen of the World** (☎ 514-866-1661; cnr Boul René Lévesque Ouest & Rue Mansfield; admission free; ☽ 7am-7:30pm Mon-Fri, 7:30am-8:30pm Sat, 8:30am-7:30pm Sun; metro Bonaventure) was completed in 1894 as a symbol of Catholic power in the heart of Protestant Montréal. Modeled after St Peter's Basilica in Rome, it exudes the same quiet majesty as the original despite being built on only one quarter of the area. A row of copper-clad saints presides over the entrance, while inside all eyes are drawn to the lavish altar canopy, a replica of Bernini's famous 'Baldacchino' in St Peter's. The most impressive chapel is the second one on the left, which is an extravaganza in marble and mosaic containing the tombs of the diocese's bishops.

CATHÉDRALE CHRIST CHURCH

An island of calm engulfed by commercialism, the Anglican **Christ Church Cathedral** (☎ 514-843-6577; 635 Rue Ste-Catherine Ouest; admission free; ☽ 7am-6pm; metro McGill) is a beautiful neo-Gothic confection that was so poorly engineered that it started sinking into the marshy ground shortly after its 1859 completion. To save the building, the original stone steeple eventually had to be replaced with the current aluminum version. In 1987, an amazing engineering feat saw the church temporarily supported by concrete stilts while a shopping mall was carved out directly underneath it.

The interior is well worth a look, most notably for the dizzyingly detailed altarpiece carved entirely from stone and honoring the fallen of WWI.

MCGILL UNIVERSITY

Sometimes called the 'Harvard of the North,' **McGill University** (Map pp244-5; ☎ 514-398-4455; www .mcgill.ca; 845 Rue Sherbrooke Ouest; metro McGill) counts six Nobel laureates, two Canadian prime ministers and William Shatner among its alumni. These days, some 30,000 students try to uphold the university's grand reputation, which is especially stellar in medicine and engineering. It was founded in 1821 with money and land donated by James McGill, a Scotland-born fur trader. The leafy campus with its Victorian edifices is a pretty place for a stroll or a picnic.

The university's **Musée Redpath** (☎ 514-398-4086; admission free; ☽ 9am-5pm Mon-Fri, 1-5pm Sat & Sun, closed Fri mid-Jun–early Sep) is one of the oldest museums in Canada, and it shows. Nevertheless, it has some interesting natural history exhibits, including a life-sized dinosaur skeleton and Egyptian mummies.

MONTRÉAL PLANETARIUM

The 20m-high dome of the **Montréal Planetarium** (☎ 514-872-4530; www.planetarium.montreal .qc.ca; 1000 Rue St-Jacques; adult/child/student & senior $7.75/4/6; ☽ 12:30-5pm Mon, 10am-5pm Tue-Thu, 10am-8:30pm Fri, 12:30-8:30pm Sat & Sun, closed Mon Sep-Jun; metro Bonaventure) opens a window on the universe during narrated 50-minute shows alternately in French and English. Call for the current schedule.

QUÉBEC

500 m
0.3 miles

SLEEPING ☐ (pp254-6)
Alternative Backpackers..............45 E5
Auberge Bonsecours.....................46 G5
Auberge Les Passants du Sans Soucy..47 F5
Castel Durocher.............................48 E2
Fairmont Le Reine Elizabeth........49 D4
HI Montréal International Youth
  Hostel.......................................50 B4
Hotel du Fort................................51 A3
Hotel Nelligan...............................52 F5
L'Abri du Voyageur.......................53 F3
Le Beau Soleil B&B...................(see 46)
Le Petit Prince..............................54 C4
Manoir Ambrose...........................55 C4
Montréal Y Hotel..........................56 C4

EATING ☐ (pp256-9)
Boustan..57 C3
Bronté..58 B3
Eggspectation...............................59 F5
Ferreira Café.................................60 D3
Gandhi..61 C5
Gibby's..62 E6
Le Commensal...............................63 D4
Marché de la Villette.....................64 C5
Olive & Gourmando.....................65 C5
Ong Ca Can..................................66 F3

S Le Restaurant.............................67 F5
Titanic..68 E5
Tokyo..69 E5
Wok Café......................................70 B3

DRINKING ☐ (p260)
Brutopia.......................................71 C4
Le Ste-Elisabeth............................72 G3
Sir Winston Churchill Pub.............73 C3

ENTERTAINMENT ☐ (pp260-2)
Altitude 737.................................74 D4
Bell Centre (Montréal Canadiens)...75 C4
Centaur Theatre............................76 F5
Foufounes Electriques...................77 F3
House of Jazz................................78 E2
IMAX..79 F6
Les Grands Ballet Canadiens.....(see 82)
Metropolis.....................................80 F3
Molson Stadium (Montréal
  Alouettes)..................................81 D2
Montréal Opera........................(see 82)
Orchestre Symphonique de
  Montréal..................................(see 82)
Place des Arts...............................82 F3
Pollack Concert Hall.....................83 D3
Upstairs...84 B4

SHOPPING ☐ (pp262-3)
Caban...85 D3
Centre Eaton................................86 D3
Cheap Thrills.................................87 D3
Galerie Le Chariot.........................88 F5
Guilde Canadienne des Métier
  d'Art Québec..............................89 D3
Ogilvy...90 C3
Parasuco.......................................91 C3

TRANSPORT (pp263-4)
Parc Jean-Drapeau Ferries.............92 G6
Pelletier Car Rental.......................93 B4
Station Aérobus............................94 D4

OTHER
AML Cruises..................................95 F6
Lachine Rapids Tours.....................96 H5
Le Bateau Mouche........................97 G6

0 — 200 m
0 — 0.1 miles

INFORMATION

Boutique Tourisme Jeunesse	1 B2
Centre d'Information Touristique du Village	2 C5
Goethe Institute	3 C4
National Bank of Canada	4 B2
National Bank of Canada	5 C5
National Bank of Canada	6 C5
Netopia	7 D1
Police	8 B5
Ulysse	9 B2
Voyages Campus	10 D1

SIGHTS & ACTIVITIES (pp239-51)

Georges Étienne Cartier Monument	11 A2
Maison des Cyclistes	12 A2
Observatoire de L'Est	13 A2

SLEEPING (pp254-6)

Anne Ma Soeur Anne	14 B3
Armor Manoir Sherbrooke	15 B4
Au Piano Blanc B&B	16 C2
Auberge de la Fontaine	17 C1
Auberge Maeva	18 C1
Couette et Café Cherrier	19 C4
Hôtel Le Jardin D'Antoine	20 D1
Pierre et Dominique B&B	21 B4
Shézelles B&B	22 C2
Turquoise B&B	23 D4

EATING (pp256-60)

Anise	24 A1
Area	25 C5
Au Pied de Cochon	26 C3
Buona Notte	27 B4
Café Santropol	28 A3
Chao Praya	29 B1
Cluny	30 A4
Est-Asie	31 D5
Fairmont Bagel	32 B1
L'Express	33 B3
La Chronique	34 B1
La Colombe	35 C3
La Paryse	36 D1
Le Commensal	37 D1
Le Jardin de Panos	38 B3
Le Roi du Plateau	39 B2
Les 3 Brasseurs	40 D1
Maestro SVP	41 B4
Med Grill	42 B4
Schwartz's	43 B3
Wilensky's Light Lunch	44 B1

DRINKING (p260)

Aigle Noir	45 C5
Edgar Hypertavern	46 D2
Else's	47 B3
Gogo Lounge	48 B3
Le St Sulpice	49 D1
Luba Lounge	50 A4
Pub Magnolia	51 D5
Sky Pub & Club	52 D5

ENTERTAINMENT (pp260-2)

Aria	53 B5
Café Campus	54 B4
Casa del Popolo	55 B1
Cinéma du Parc	56 A4
Ex-Centris Cinema	57 B4
L'Escogriffe	58 B2
Mado Cabaret	59 C5
National Film Board	60 D1
Stereo	61 C5
Tokyo Bar	62 B3
Unity II	63 C5

SHOPPING (pp262-3)

Eva B	64 B4
Revenge	65 B3

TRANSPORT (pp263-4)

Allô Stop	66 B2
Station Centrale de l' Autobus (Central Bus Station)	67 D2

Parc du Mont Royal

Montréalers are proud of their 'mountain,' **Mount Royal Park** (Map pp244-5; ☎ 514-872-6559, www.lemontroyal.qc.ca), the work of New York Central Park designer Frederick Law Olmsted. It's a sprawling, leafy playground that's perfect for cycling, jogging, horseback riding, picnicking and, in winter, cross-country skiing and tobogganing. In fine weather, enjoy panoramic views from the **Kondiaronk lookout** (Map pp244-5) near **Chalet du Mont Royal** (Map pp244-5), a grand old white villa that hosts big-band concerts in summer; or from the **Observatoire de l'Est** (Map pp244-5), a favorite rendezvous spot for lovebirds. It takes about 30 minutes to walk between the two. En route you'll spot the landmark 40m-high **Cross of Montréal** (1924; Map pp244-5), which is illuminated at night. It's there to commemorate city founder Maisonneuve who single-handedly carried a wooden cross up the mountain in 1643 to give thanks to God for sparing his fledgling village from flooding.

Less 'lofty' attractions include **Lac aux Castors** (Map pp244-5), or Beaver Lake, where you can rent paddleboats in summer and ice skates and sleds in winter. North of here are two vast cemeteries. The Catholic **Cimetière de Notre-Dame-des-Neiges** (Map p238) holds the remains of mayors, artists, clerics and *Titanic* victims. Further north, the protestant **Cimetière Mont-Royal** (Map p238) is smaller and more noted for its birdwatching than celebrity tombs.

On the park's northeastern edge, on Ave du Parc, stands the **Georges Étienne Cartier monument** (Map p246), which every Sunday draws hundreds of revelers for tribal playing and spontaneous dancing in what has been dubbed 'Tam Tam Sundays' (tam-tams are bongo-like drums). It's nothing less than an institution. If the noise doesn't show you the way there, just follow your nose towards whiffs of 'wacky tabaccy.' This is also a good spot to pick up some unusual handicrafts sold by local artisans.

Mont Royal can be entered via the steps at the top of Rue Peel. Bus Nos 80 and 129 make their way from the Place des Arts metro station to the Georges Étienne Cartier monument on Ave du Park. Bus No 11 from the Mont Royal metro stop traverses the park.

ORATOIRE ST-JOSEPH

Gigantic, domed **St-Joseph's Oratory** (☎ 514-733-8211; www.st-joseph.org; 3800 Chemin Queen Mary; admission free; ⏱ crypt & votive chapel 6am-9:30pm; metro Côte-des-Neiges) commands a spectacular hilltop setting just west of Parc du Mont Royal. The largest shrine anywhere honoring Jesus' father (St Joseph is also Canada's patron saint) has modest origins as a small chapel built in 1904 by a devoted monk named Brother André. André had a knack for healing people, which brought droves of people to the chapel in hopes of a miracle. As word spread, a larger structure was needed to accommodate the many pilgrims. Crutches left by the cured still fill a chapel illuminated by thousands of votives. Also on view: Brother André's heart. It was stolen in 1973 (who would do such a thing?) but 'miraculously' resurfaced a year later. André was beatified in 1982.

Plateau Mont-Royal

East of Parc du Mont Royal, the Plateau is Montréal's youngest, liveliest and artiest neighborhood. Originally a working-class district, it changed its stripes in the 1960s and '70s when writers, singers and other creative folk moved in. Among them was playwright Michel Tremblay whose unvarnished look at some of the neighborhood's more colorful characters firmly put the Plateau on the path to hipdom.

These days, many Montréalers dream of living here if only house prices would stop rising. As you stroll through its side streets, admiring the signature streetscapes with their winding staircases, ornate wrought-iron balconies and pointy Victorian roofs, you'll begin to understand why.

The Plateau is bordered roughly by Boul St-Joseph to the north and Rue Sherbrooke to the south, Mont Royal to the west and Ave de Lorimier to the east. The main drags are Boul St-Laurent ('The Main'), Rue St-Denis and Ave du Mont Royal, all lined by sidewalk cafés, restaurants, clubs and boutiques. Rue Prince Arthur, Montréal's quintessential hippie hangout in the 1960s, and Ave Duluth are alive with bring-your-own-wine eateries.

Though still part of the Plateau, the **Mile End** neighborhood in its northwestern corner has a different, more multicultural flair; it's where Hassidic Jews live side by side with immigrants from Portugal to Greece. Canadian novelist Mordecai Richler used Mile End as the setting for some of his novels, including *The Apprenticeship of Duddy Kravitz* which, in 1974, became a movie starring Richard Dreyfuss. The main streets are Rue Bernard, Ave Laurier, increasingly trendy Rue St-Viateur, Boul St-Laurent and Ave du Parc with its many authentic Greek restaurants. To the west, Mile End segues into the upmarket Outremont district favored by the upper-class French.

Little Italy

Montréal may be the closest thing to Paris in North America, but step into Little Italy and you'll think you're in Rome. The zest and flavor of the old country find their way into this lively district north of the Plateau, where the espresso seems stiffer, the pasta sauce thicker and the chefs plumper. Italian football games seem to be broadcast straight onto Boul St-Laurent, where the green-white-red flag is proudly displayed. Drink in the atmosphere on a stroll and don't miss the Marché Jean Talon (p259), which always hums with activity.

BREAK A LEG!

All great cities have distinctive architecture, and in Montréal it is found not in grandiose public buildings but in the charming wrought-iron outdoor staircases gracing many a Victorian brick and greystone, especially in the Plateau. Decorative they surely are, but whoever thought they'd be practical in a city smothered by ice and snow half the year must have been either a surgeon or a lawyer.

Well, not quite. It all goes back to the 19th century when the city fathers, in a noble effort to beautify the streetscape, passed a law requiring all residences to be fronted by a patch of green. Naturally, this meant less living space, a concept not warmly embraced by Montréalers. So they got around the issue in a wily fashion by banishing the interior staircase outside. It was an ingenious idea not only because it freed up valuable living space, but also because it saved in heating costs. And what's a little more shoveling anyway?

Quartier Latin

Irresistibly French in outlook and studenty in verve, the Quartier Latin is one of Montréal's most electric neighborhoods. The area blossomed with the arrival of the Université de Montréal in 1893, which drew several prestigious cultural institutions and the wealthy French bourgeoisie in its wake. The district fell out of fashion after the university relocated to a larger campus north of Mont Royal. Fortunes turned again when the Université de Québec was established in 1969, and the International Jazz Festival provided a further boost in the 1980s. Today the quarter bubbles 24 hours a day, anywhere in its densely packed rows of bars, trendy bistros, music clubs and record shops.

The Quartier Latin is a dwarf among Montréal neighborhoods, little over 1.5km square within the borders of Rue Sanguinet, Rue Sherbrooke, Rue St-Hubert and Boul René Lévesque. Old Montréal is just south of here, best reached via Rue St-Denis.

The Village

Over the past decade or so, Montréal's gay community has breathed new life into this once-derelict district. Today, gay-friendly doesn't even begin to describe The Village, hub of one of the world's most exuberant gay communities. People of all persuasions wander Rue Ste-Catherine and savor the joie de vivre in its cafés, bistros and discerning eateries. The nightlife is renowned for its energy, but during the day the streets bustle with workers from the big media firms nearby. August is the most frenetic time as hundreds of thousands of international visitors gather to celebrate Divers/ Cité, a major annual gay pride parade.

The spine of the (Gay) Village is Rue Ste-Catherine Est and its side streets between Rue St-Hubert in the west and Ave de Lorimier in the east.

Olympic Park & Around

Montréal hosted the 1976 Olympic summer games, which brought a host of attractions, including a beautiful botanical garden, to the area east of central Montréal, accessible from Rue Sherbrooke.

OLYMPIC PARK

The centerpiece of the sprawling Olympic Park is the multipurpose **Stade Olympique**

(Olympic Stadium; Map p238; ☎ 514-252-4141; www.rio
.gouv.qc.ca in French; 4141 Ave Pierre de Coubertin; tours
adult/child/senior & student $7/5/6; ⌚ 9am-6pm; metro
Viau), which seats up to 80,000 and today
hosts sporting events, concerts and trade
shows (see the boxed text on right).

On a nice day, it's well worth boarding
the bilevel funicular zooming up the **Tour de
Montréal** (Montréal Tower; Map p238; ☎ 514-252-4737;
adult/child/senior & student $12/6/9; ⌚ 10am-9pm Jun-
Sep, to 5pm Oct-May), the world's largest inclined
structure (190m at a 45-degree angle), for
360-degree views of the city, river and surrounding countryside from the glassed-in
observation deck.

Down below is the Centre Sportif (p251).

BIODÔME

In the former Olympic Velodrome, the
Biodôme (Map p238; ☎ 514-868-3000; www.biodome
.qc.ca; 4777 Ave Pierre de Coubertin; adult/child/student
& senior $11.75/6/9, combination ticket with the Jardin
Botanique/Insectarium $19/9.50/14; ⌚ 9am-6pm late
Jun–early Sep, 9am-5pm mid-Sep–mid-Jun; metro Viau)
beautifully re-creates four ecosystems teeming with plant and animal life. A guided
path leads to the hot and humid Tropical
Forest where the anacondas, caimans and
two-toed sloths draw the biggest crowds.
From there it's off to the more temperate Laurentian woodlands with trees that
change color in fall just like in the real
world. A giant aquarium and a rocky cliff
are at the heart of the Gulf of St Lawrence
section, although the penguins of the Polar
World habitat clearly steal the show.

A free shuttle runs between the Biodôme
and the Jardin Botanique.

JARDIN BOTANIQUE & INSECTARIUM

Opened in 1931, Montréal's **Botanical Garden** (Map p238; ☎ 514-872-1400; www.ville.montreal
.qc.ca/jardin; 4101 Rue Sherbrooke Est; adult/child/senior
& student May-Oct $11.75/6/9, Nov-Apr $8.75/4/6.75,
combination ticket with Biodôme $19/9.50/14; ⌚ 9am-
6pm mid-Jun–mid-Sep, 9am-9pm mid-Sep–Oct, 9am-5pm
Nov–mid-Jun; metro Pie-IX) is the world's third
largest after those in London and Berlin.
Some 22,000 species of plants grow in 30
outdoor gardens, including the tranquil
Japanese Garden, a symphony of stone and
water sprinkled with rhododendrons, water
lilies and bonsai trees. Other highlights include the First Nations Garden, the Chinese
Garden and the Rose Garden as well as 10

A MOST 'CRUMBLING' EXPERIENCE

Ask any Montréaler and you'll find that
scandal, indignation and tales of corrup-
tion envelop Montréal's Olympic Stadium,
known as the 'Big O' or, more recently, 'The
Big Owe.' Its architectural beauty, alas, was
not matched by sound engineering, and the
structure was fraught with disaster right
from the start. The original stadium roof
was intended to unfold like an umbrella,
pulled by cables attached to the Montréal
Tower. Alas, it never worked properly and
was eventually replaced by a static model.
The stadium too required a litany of repairs,
especially after a concrete beam collapsed
over spectators during a football game
(no one was injured). Montréalers are still
paying off an Olympic-sized mountain of
debt as the total cost, so far, has exceeded
$2 billion.

greenhouses filled with cacti, banana trees,
orchids and other tropical flowers.

Tickets also include a visit to the **Insectarium** with its intriguing collection of creepy
crawlies, most of them dead and mounted,
but there are also living species, including
tarantulas, bees and scorpions. Not to be
missed is the Butterfly House.

The best way to get around this huge place
is by hop-on, hop-off trolley that makes its
rounds every 20 minutes or so (summer
only). Free guided tours leave at 10am and
1:30pm daily except Wednesday from the
reception center (no tours in October). All
facilities are wheelchair-accessible.

Parc Jean-Drapeau

Occupying the site of the hugely successful
1967 World Fair, **Parc Jean-Drapeau** (Map p238;
☎ 514-872-6120; www.parcjeandrapeau.com) consists
of two islands surrounded by the St Lawrence: Île Ste-Hélène and Île Notre-Dame.
Although nature is the park's main appeal,
it's also home to a Vegas-sized casino, a
Formula One racetrack and an old fort
museum. In summer an **information kiosk**
(☎ 514-872-4537) opens near the metro stop
Jean-Drapeau.

Drivers should take Pont (Bridge)
Jacques Cartier for Île Ste-Hélène and Pont
de la Concorde for Île Notre-Dame. **Ferries**
(Map pp244-5; ☎ 514-281-8000; Quai Jacques Cartier;

QUÉBEC

mid-May–mid-Oct) shuttle pedestrians and bicycles to the park from the Old Port. Cyclists and in-line skaters can access the park by following the signs for Cité du Havre, then for Île Notre-Dame from the Canal Lachine bike path.

Bus No 167 runs between the islands.

ÎLE STE-HÉLÈNE   Map p238

The northern tip of the island is occupied by La Ronde (☎ 514-397-2000; www.laronde.com; adult/child $30/18; ☺ 10am-8pm late May–mid-Jun, to 10:30pm mid-Jun–early Sep; metro Jean-Drapeau), a giant amusement park. Owned by US-based Six Flags, the amusement park has a battery of bone-shaking thrill rides, including Le Splash, which will leave you soaked, Le Monstre, the world's highest wooden roller coaster, and Le Vampyre, a suspended coaster with five gut-wrenching loops. There's also a good assortment of kiddie rides, live shows and a mini-rail with good river and city views. In June and July, the park hosts the Mondial SAQ International Fireworks Competition on weekends (p253).

Near La Ronde stands an old fort built in the 19th century by the British to defend Montréal from an attack by the Americans. Inside the stone ramparts is the Musée Stewart (☎ 514-861-6701; www.stewart-museum.org; adult/child/student & senior $8/free/6; ☺ 10am-6pm mid-May–early Sep, 10am-5pm Wed-Sun mid-Sep–early May) where a collection of old maps, documents, navigational equipment, firearms and other artifacts traces the early days of Canada.

Walkways meander around the island, past gardens and among the old pavilions from the World's Fair. One of them, the American pavilion in the spherical Bucky Fuller dome, has become the Biosphère (☎ 514-283-5000; adult/child/senior & student $10/6/7.50; ☺ 10am-6pm Jun-Sep, noon-5pm Mon, Wed & Fri, 10am-5pm Sat & Sun Oct-May). Using hands-on displays, this center explains the Great Lakes–St Lawrence River ecosystem, which makes up 20% of the planet's fresh water reserves. There's a great view of the river from the Visions Hall.

ÎLE NOTRE-DAME   Map p238

Created from 15 million tons of earth and rock excavated when the metro was built, Île Notre-Dame is laced with canals and pretty garden walkways. The Grand Prix du Canada Formula One race (p253) is held each year on the Circuit Gilles Villeneuve, named after the Québec racecar driver who died in a crash in 1982. From mid-April to mid-November the smoothly paved track is open for cyclists and in-line skaters.

Throughout the year, the island's main draw is the huge, spaceshiplike Casino de Montréal (☎ 514-392-2746; 1 Ave du Casino; admission free; ☺ 24hr) in the former French pavilion from the World's Fair. You can challenge Lady Luck at 3000 slot machines and 115 gaming tables. Alcohol is not allowed on the floor and you must be 18 to enter. Bridges link the pavilion to the Jardin des Floralies, a lovely rose garden.

On the southern tip of the island, the Plage des Îles (opposite) draws thousands on hot summer days. Nearby is the Bassin Olympique, the former Olympic rowing basin, which now hosts the popular Dragon Boat Race & Festival in late July. Dragon boats are long, narrow boats adorned with a dragonhead and propelled by up to 50 paddlers.

HABITAT '67   Map p238

Between Old Montréal and Île Ste Hélène lies Cité du Havre, a narrow land-filled jetty built to protect the harbor from currents and ice. Here, for the 1967 World Fair, Moshe Safdie designed Habitat '67, an experimental housing complex. It's a hotchpotch of reinforced concrete cubes cleverly stacked at bizarre angles to provide privacy and views to each of the 150 units. Among the most sought-after living space in Montréal, each is now worth a fortune (around $750,000 for a 1250-sq-ft two-cube apartment).

Lachine

The western suburb of Lachine is worth a visit for its history, architecture and general ambience. Not touristy, it reveals a little of Montréal's roots and culture. The side streets behind the impressive College Ste Anne nunnery and City Hall, both along Boul St-Joseph, make for good wandering.

Completed in 1825, the Canal de Lachine stretches for 14.5km from the Old Port to Lac St-Louis and was built to circumvent the fierce Lachine Rapids of the St Lawrence River. The construction of the St Lawrence Seaway led to its closing to shipping in 1970, but its banks have since been transformed into a park that's terrific for cycling and walking. Since 2002, pleasure and sightseeing boats have plied its calm waters and a marina is being planned at the bottom of Rue Peel.

The **Fur Trade at Lachine Canal National Historic Site** (☎ 514-637-7433; www.parkscanada .gc.ca/fourrure; 1255 Boul St-Joseph; adult/child/senior $3.50/1.75/3; ☉ 1-5:30pm Mon, 10am-5:30pm Tue-Sun Apr–mid-Oct, 9:30am-5pm Wed-Sun mid-Oct–Nov; metro Angrignon, bus No 195), in an old stone house on the waterfront, tells the story of the fur trade in Canada. Lachine became the hub of Montréal's fur-trading operations because the rapids made further river navigation impossible before the canal was built.

Nearby, a **visitor center** (☎ 514-364-4490; 500 Rue des Iroquois; admission free; ☉ 9am-8pm mid-Jun–mid-Aug, reduced hrs mid-Aug–Nov & Apr–mid-Jun, closed Dec-Mar) runs guided tours and presents historical exhibits about the canal.

ACTIVITIES
Cycling & In-line Skating

In 2002 Montréal got the nod from *Bicycling* magazine as the best cycling city in North America, and deservedly so. With more than 300km of cycling and skating paths, pedaling possibilities are bountiful. One popular route parallels the Canal de Lachine (opposite) for 14.5km, starting in Old Montréal, passing a lot of history en route. Picnic tables are scattered along the way, so pick up some tasty victuals at the fabulous Marché Atwater (p257).

The smooth **Circuit Gilles Villeneuve** (Map p238) on Île Ste Hélène is another cool track. It's open and free to all from mid-April to mid-November except in mid-June when it hosts the Grand Prix du Canada Formula One car race.

For more ideas, stop by a bookstore, tourist office or any of these bicycle and in-line skate rental outlets:

Ça Roule Montréal (Map pp244-5; ☎ 514-866-0633; www.caroulemontreal.com; 27 Rue de la Commune Est, Old Port; bicycles per hr/24hrs $7.50/30, in-line skates for first/additional hr $9/4.50; ☉ 9am-8pm Apr-Oct)

La Maison des Cyclistes (Map p246; ☎ 514-521-8356, 800-567-8356; www.velo.qc.ca; 1251 Rue Rachel Est; ☉ 8:30am-8pm Mon-Fri, 9am-7pm Sat & Sun) Café, bookstore and rentals.

Vélo Aventure (Map pp244-5; ☎ 514-847-0666; www .veloaventure.com; Conveyor Pier, Old Port; bicycles per hr/8hr $7/22, in-line skates for first/additional hr $9/4.50; ☉ 9am-9pm Apr-Oct)

Ice Skating

Take to the ice any time the mood strikes at the gigantic **Atrium** (Map pp244-5; ☎ 514-395-0555; www.le1000.com; 1000 Rue de la Gauchetière Ouest; adult/child $5.50/3.50, skate rentals $4.50; ☉ 11:30am-8pm Tue-Thu, 10:30am-midnight Fri & Sat Oct-Apr, reduced hrs May-Sep), a state-of-the-art glass-domed indoor rink in Montréal's tallest tower; ask about kids' sessions and disco nights.

The **Patinoir du Bassin Bonsecours** (Map pp244-5; ☎ 514-496-7678; Parc du Bassin Bonsecours, Old Port; admission $3, skate rentals $6; ☉ 11am-6pm in winter, weather permitting) is one of Montréal's most popular outdoor skating rinks.

The **Lac aux Castors** (☎ 514-872-6559; Parc du Mont Royal; admission free, skate rentals $6; ☉ 9am-6pm in winter, weather permitting) is another excellent place for outdoor skating – it's nestled in the woods near a large parking lot and pavilion.

Swimming
Map p238

The best place to do laps is at Olympic Park's **Centre Sportif** (☎ 514-252-4622; 4141 Ave Pierre de Coubertin; adult/student $3.50/2.50; ☉ 6:30am-10pm Mon-Fri, 9am-6pm Sat & Sun), a huge indoor complex with six swimming pools, diving towers and a 20m-deep scuba pool.

On hot summer days, the **Plage des Îles** (☎ 514-872-6093; Île Notre-Dame; adult/child $7.50/3.75; ☉ 10am-7pm late Jun–late Aug), an artificial sandy beach, can be a cool place to go for a swim. You won't have much privacy on days when it reaches its 5000-person capacity. The water is filtered and treated with chemicals and is considered safe, clean and ideal for kids. Kayaks, pedal boats and other water sports equipment may be rented from the Water Sports Pavilion at the beach's north entrance.

WALKING TOUR

If the weathered walls and cobbled stones of Old Montréal could talk, they would spill stories teeming with fierce Iroquois, tenacious colonists, wily fur traders, high-powered bankers, wicked wenches, scheming generals and even the occasional ghost or two.

This tour travels 350 years back in time starting, quite appropriately, on **Place Royale (1)**, ground zero of Montréal history and the spot where the first settlers presumably landed in 1642. To get the full low-down, drop in at the nearby **Musée d'Archéologie et**

QUÉBEC

WALK FACTS

Start & Finish Place Royale
Distance 2km
Duration One hour, longer if you stop at the museums

d'Histoire Pointe à Callière (**2**; p241). If pushed for time, at least take the elevator to the tower for sweeping views of the gentrified Old Port (p241), Parc Jean-Drapeau (p249) and Habitat '67 (p250).

Turn left as you exit, then right on Rue St-François-Xavier past the columned old stock exchange which now houses the **Centaur Theatre** (**3**; p261). Turn right again on Rue Notre-Dame, walking past the **Old Seminary** (**4**; p240), the city's oldest building, to **Place d'Armes** (**5**; p240) where the Iroquois battled it out against early settlers led by Maisonneuve. That's him in bronze in the square's centre facing the famous **Basilique Notre Dame** (**6**; p240), a place of pilgrimage for fans of Jesus, architecture and Céline Dion, who got married here in 1994.

Following Rue Notre-Dame east leads past the **Palais de Justice** (**7**; Courthouse) whose modern design contrasts sharply with the domed 19th-century grandeur of the adjacent **Vieux Palais de Justice** (**8**; Old Courthouse) and the neoclassical elegance of the **Cour d'Appel du Québec** (**9**; Québec Appellate Court) across the street. A few steps more and you're in **Place Jacques Cartier** (**10**;

p240) whose cafés and vibrant street life make a good spot for a rest. The palace-like structure northeast of the square is the **Hôtel de Ville** (**11**; p241) where Montréal's mayor keeps his offices. The Hôtel faces the much smaller **Château de Ramezay** (**12**; p241), a former governor's mansion and now a museum.

Continue south on Rue St-Claude to Rue St-Paul and the domed **Marché Bonsecours** (**13**; p241), the former market hall turned boutique bastion. A stroll west on Rue St-Paul, Montréal's oldest street, takes you past more shops, restaurants, cafés and neat old buildings (many with charming courtyards) and eventually back to Place Royale.

MONTRÉAL FOR CHILDREN

Montréal offers plenty of diversions for the wee ones. Kids love animals, of course, making the Biodôme (p249) – home of porcupines, penguins and other local and exotic critters – a sure winner. Keep the momentum going by visiting the brigade of creepy crawlies at the nearby Insectarium (p249).

Budding scientists will have a field day at the Centre des Sciences de Montréal (p241), which has dozens of interactive stations and video games. Space travelers can catch a show at the Montréal Planetarium (p243) or head to the Cosmodôme Space Sciences Centre (p265) in nearby Laval where they can learn all about what

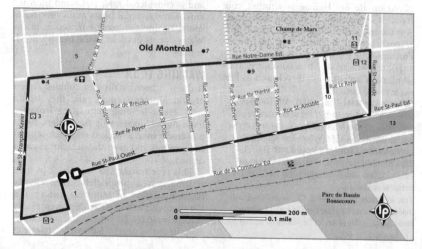

it takes to be an astronaut. Many museums have special kid-oriented workshops and guided tours.

On hot summer days, a few hours spent at the Plage des Îles (p250), a big beach on Île Notre Dame within Parc Jean-Drapeau, will go a long way towards keeping tempers cool. On nearby Île Sainte-Hélène awaits the La Ronde (p251) amusement park whose stomach-churning roller coasters and other diversions are especially thrilling for teens. There's ice skating all year long at the grand Atrium (p251), which offers special kids' sessions on Saturday mornings. In winter, you can take a spin on the frozen Lac aux Castors (p251) in Parc du Mont Royal or on the popular Patinoir du Bassin Bonsecours (p251) outdoor rink in Old Montréal.

Many hotels can provide referrals to reliable, qualified babysitting services.

TOURS
Boat
AML Cruises (Map pp254-5; ☎ 514-842-9300; www .croisieresaml.com; adult/child/senior & student $24/10/22; 11:30am, 2pm, 4pm) AML runs 90-minute tours taking in the Old Port and Île Ste-Hélène. Tours depart from Quai King Edward.

Lachine Rapids Tours (Map pp254-5; ☎ 514-284-9607; www.jetboatingmontreal.com; jet boats adult/child/teen $55/35/45, speed boats $22/16/18; 10am-6pm May-Oct) Prepare to get wet on jet boat tours of the Lachine Rapids departing from the Clock Tower Pier. The speedboat tours are bouncy half-hour jaunts around Parc des Îles leaving from Quai Jacques Cartier.

Le Bateau Mouche (Map pp254-5; ☎ 514-849-9952; www.bateau-mouche.com; 1hr tours adult/child/senior & student $17/9.50/16; 10am, 1:30pm, 3pm, 4:30pm) Leaving from Quai Jacques Cartier, cruises aboard climate-controlled, glass-roofed boats explore the Old Port and Parc Jean-Drapeau. A 90-minute version ($22.50/9.50/20.50) departs at 11:30am.

Bus
All tour buses depart from outside the Centre Infotouriste (Map pp254–5).

Autobus Viens/Impérial (☎ 514-871-4733; 3hr tours adult/child/student & senior $35/18/32; 9am, 10am, 1pm & 3pm May-Oct, 10am & 1pm Nov-Apr) This comprehensive tour takes you to all major Montréal sights, including Old Montréal (with half-hour tours of Basilique Notre Dame), Parc Drapeau and the Olympic Park. Their double-decker hop-on, hop-off tour ($31/16/26) makes nine stops; tickets are valid on two consecutive days.

Gray Line/Coach Canada (☎ 514-934-1222; www .grayline.com; late May–late Oct) This well-known tour operator runs 90-minute **Heart of Montréal** (adult/child $26/16; 10am & noon) tours that provide a basic overview of Old Montréal, Mont Royal and the downtown area. The six-hour **Deluxe Montréal** ($55/35; 11am) tour includes admission to the Tour de Montréal, Biodôme and Jardin Botanique.

Walking
Guidatour (☎ 514-844-4021; www.guidatour.qc.ca; adult/child/senior & student $14/6/12; tours 11am & 1:30pm late Jun–Sep) Guidatours' bilingual guides spice up historical tours of Old Montréal with colorful tales and anecdotes. Tours depart from the Basilique Notre Dame (Map pp254-5).

FESTIVALS & EVENTS
Montréal is known as the 'City of Festivals' and nary a week goes by without some type of celebration. During the peak summer season (June to August) entire neighborhoods may be closed to traffic.

Fête des Neiges (☎ 514-872-6120; www.fetedes neiges.com; late Jan) Fun and games in the snow over three consecutive weekends starting in Parc Jean-Drapeau.

Grand Prix of Canada (☎ 514-350-0000; www .grandprix.ca; Jun) The world's best drivers descend on Circuit Gilles Villeneuve on Île Notre Dame for North America's biggest Formula One event.

Le Mondial SAQ (☎ 514-397-2000; www.lemondial saq.com; mid-June–late July) This international fireworks competition features the world's best pyrotechnics in 10, 30-minute shows held at La Ronde once or twice a week during the competition.

Festival International de Jazz (☎ 514-871-1881, 888-515-0515; www.montrealjazzfest.com; early Jul) For 12 days the heart of downtown explodes in jazz and blues during 400 concerts, most of them outdoors and free.

Just for Laughs Festival (☎ 514-845-3155, 888-244-3155; www.hahaha.com; mid-Jul) Everyone gets giddy for two weeks at this international comedy festival with hundreds of shows, including free ones in the Quartier Latin.

Les FrancoFolies (☎ 514-876-8989, 888-444-9114; www.francofolies.com; from late Jul) This annual international showcase of French-language music and theater spotlights today's biggest stars and those on the rise over 10 days.

Festival des Films du Monde (☎ 514-848-3883; www.ffm-montreal.org; late Aug) Held over 10 days, this prestigious international film festival attracts stars, directors, producers and writers plus about half a million visitors.

'OUT' & ABOUT IN MONTRÉAL

Montréal is one of Canada's gayest cities with the rainbow flag flying especially proudly in **The Village** along Rue St-Catherine between Rue St-Hubert and Rue Dorion. Dozens of high-energy bars, cafés, restaurants, saunas and clubs flank this strip, turning it pretty much into a 24/7 fun zone. Also here is the **Centre d'Information Touristique du Village** (Map p246; ☎ 514-522-1885; www.infogayvillage.com; 576 Rue Ste-Catherine Est; ☒ 10am-6pm Mon-Fri), whose staff can help you plug into the current scene. The authoritative guide to the gay and lesbian scene is **Fugues** (www.fugues .com), a monthly free mag found throughout The Village. Gays and lesbians in need of help should contact the nonprofit **Gayline** (☎ 514-866-5090, 888-505-1010; www.gayline.qc.ca; ☒ 7-11pm).

The big event on The Village calendar is the **Divers/Cité Festival** (☎ 514-285-4011; www.diverscite .org), Montréal's version of Pride Week, usually held in late June or early July. It draws as many as one million people. Almost as much of a pull is the **Black & Blue Festival** (☎ 514-875-7226; www.bbcm .org) in October with major dance parties, cultural and art shows and a mega-party in the Olympic Stadium. In 2006, Montréal will host the **1st World Outgames** (www.montreal2006.org), a huge athletic and cultural event expected to draw more than 16,000 participants from around the world.

Bars and clubs worth checking out include the following:

- **Sky Pub & Club** (Map p246; ☎ 514-529-6969; 1474 Rue Ste-Catherine Est) Huge place with rooftop terrace complete with Jacuzzi and pool.

- **Aigle Noir** (Map p246; ☎ 514-529-0040; 1315 Rue Ste-Catherine Est) For the leather-and-fetish crowd.

- **Pub Magnolia** (Map p246; ☎ 514-526-6011; 1329 Rue Ste-Catherine Est) A hip lesbian bar.

- **Unity II** (Map p246; ☎ 514-523-2777; 1171 Rue Ste-Catherine Est; ☒ Fri-Sun) Sexy dance club humming with shirtless techno ravers, muscle queens and mellow straights.

- **Mado Cabaret** (p261).

SLEEPING

Montréal is busiest in summer when the festival season is in full swing and room reservations are essential. Old Montréal is great if you like being close to the waterfront, although accommodations here – mostly in the form of *auberges* (inns) and a brand-new crop of ultra-deluxe boutique hotels – does not come cheap. Prices are lower in the vibrant Plateau and Village neighborhoods, veritable B&B bastions that put you in the thick of the city's best nightlife. Most of the bigger hotels are west of here in downtown, close to the major museums and abundant shopping.

The following agencies can help book accommodations:

B&B Downtown Network (☎ 514-289-9749, 800-267-5180; www.bbmontreal.qc.ca)

Centre Infotouriste (p239)

Hospitalité Canada (☎ 514-287-9049, 866-665-1528; www.hospitality-canada.com)

Old Montréal   Map pp244–5

Alternative Backpackers (☎ 514-282-8069; www .auberge-alternative.qc.ca; 358 Rue St-Pierre; dm/r incl tax $19/55) A stylish option for the cash-strapped, this laid-back hostel in a nicely renovated 1875 building is like a muesli bar in designer wrapping. Original art abounds and organic breakfasts cost $3.50.

Le Beau Soleil B&B (☎ 514-871-0299; lebonseco urs@bellnet.ca; 355 Rue St-Paul Est; s $75-95, d $90-110) A spiraling outdoor staircase (vertigo sufferers beware) leads up to this bright B&B with good-sized, sunny rooms opposite Marché Bonsecours. Facilities are shared, and there's a little winter garden for socializing.

Auberge Bonsecours (☎ 514-396-2662; www .aubergebonsecours.com; 353 Rue St-Paul Est; s $95-160, d $160-250) This delightful retreat at the end of a flower-festooned courtyard has seven snug, air-conditioned rooms, including one suitable for the wheelchair-bound. Hand-painted aboriginal armoires and colorful canvases add cheerful touches, while the huge terrace invites sunbathing or post-sightseeing relaxing.

Auberge Les Passants du Sans Soucy (☎ 514-842-2634; www.lesanssoucy.com; 171 Rue St-Paul Ouest; r $140-175, ste $205) This classy property exudes refined, countrified ambience with oriental carpets, antiques and exposed stone walls. The lobby doubles as an art gallery.

Among Old Montréal's sleek boutique hotels, our favorite is the **Hotel Nelligan** (☎ 514-788-2040, 877-788-2040; www.hotelnelligan .com; 106 Rue St-Paul Ouest; r $210-450; P ⬚).

Downtown   Map pp244–5

BUDGET

HI Montréal International Youth Hostel (☎ 514-843-3317, 866-843-3317; www.hostellingmontreal.com; 1030 Rue Mackay; dm $23, r $58-68) Large, central and well organized, this hostel has dorms sleeping four to 10 people, plus several private rooms; all have air-conditioning and bathrooms. The big kitchen, café and common areas often buzz with activity, especially in summer when reservations are a must.

L'Abri du Voyageur (☎ 514-849-2922; www .abri-voyageur.ca; 9 Rue Ste-Catherine Ouest; r with shared bathroom $70-80, studio with bathroom $105-115) High ceilings, bare-brick walls and wooden floorboards infuse this popular abode in Montréal's rather tame 'red-light district' with an unexpected dose of charm. The large suites in a nearby building are great for groups and families.

MID-RANGE

Manoir Ambrose (☎ 514-288-6922; www.manoir ambrose.com; 3422 Rue Stanley; s $60-115, d $70-125; P) This smoke-free Victorian has 22 rooms dressed in appealing reds and pastels and outfitted with such modern amenities as wireless Internet access. Children under 10 don't pay a penny when staying with their parents.

Montréal Y Hotel (☎ 514-866-9942; www.ydesfem mesmtl.org; 1355 Boul René-Lévesque Ouest; s/d with shared bathroom $60/75, s/d $75/85; ⬚ women only) After a thorough makeover, this nonprofit place has shed its dowdy feel and now offers basic but appealing rooms to both men and women. Guests have access to a fridge, microwave and laundry facilities. Rooms with private bathroom also have TV and phone.

Another good choice in this price category is **Castel Durocher** (☎ 514-282-1697; www .casteldurocher.com; 3488 Rue Durocher; r $100-200; P ⬚ ⬚); the pool is off-site.

TOP END

Hotel du Fort (☎ 514-938-8333, 800-565-6333; www .hoteldufort.com; 1390 Rue du Fort; r $135-175, ste $175-275; P) Attentive staff, rooms with killer downtown views and a generous breakfast buffet are among the assets recommending this full-service hotel. There are restaurants and shopping just around the corner. Wheelchair-friendly.

Fairmont Le Reine Elizabeth (☎ 514-861-3511; www.fairmont.com; 900 Boul René-Lévesque; d from $220; P) Behind a decidedly functional exterior hides this giant den of luxury with a long guest list of celebs and dignitaries, including John Lennon (see the boxed text on p242).

Plateau Mont-Royal   Map p246

BUDGET

Auberge Maeva (☎ 514-523-0840; www.auberge maeva.com; 4755 Rue St-Hubert; dm/r incl breakfast & tax $20/50) Readers have warmly recommended this small hostel for its family-style ambience, generous breakfasts and central yet quiet location. Make new friends in the big kitchen and outdoor patio.

Another appealing budget choice is **Pierre et Dominique B&B** (☎ 514-286-0307; www.bbcanada .com/928.html; 271 Square St-Louis; r with shared bathroom $48-95).

MID-RANGE

Anne Ma Soeur Anne (☎ 514-281-3187; www.anne masoeuranne.com; 4119 Rue St-Denis; s $85-135, d $95-150) Mornings here start with buttery croissants delivered to your room and a fresh pot of coffee brewed right in your own small kitchen. Rooms, though smallish, feature clever beds that fold up to reveal a full dining table. The larger studios are great for families or small groups.

Couette et Café Cherrier (☎ 514-982-6848, 888-440-6848; www3.sympatico.ca/couette; 522 Rue Cherrier; s $70-85, d $85-105; P ⬚) This charismatic B&B offers an astonishing plethora of perks. Greet the day with a customized breakfast and English-language newspaper, unwind in the fireplace lounge or on the rooftop terrace, then retire to your room with cable TV, telephone and terry robe.

Au Piano Blanc (☎ 514-845-0315; http://aupiano blanc.ca; 4440 Rue Berri; r without/with bathroom $80/125) Owner Céline, a professional chanteuse (no, not *that* Céline!), has drenched her enchanting B&B in a rainbow of colors, giving it a pleasingly artsy touch. Two of the five freshly remodeled rooms have private bathrooms with romantic claw-foot tubs. This one's a keeper. Full guest-kitchen.

Shézelles B&B (☎ 514-849-8694; www.bbcanada .com/2469.html; 4272 Rue Berri; s/d $65/80, studio $140)

Paneled walls and a large fireplace make this B&B a bastion of warmth and hospitality. The giant basement suite sleeps up to six and comes with whirlpool, piano, full kitchen and separate entrance. It's truly a steal.

Armor Manoir Sherbrooke (☎ 514-285-0140, 800-203-5485; www.armormanoir.com; 157 Rue Sherbrooke Est; r $100-130; **P**) Behind the Victorian facade with a Rapunzel-style tower awaits this elegant, traditional hotel with a time-honored ambience and decent-sized rooms.

TOP END

Auberge de la Fontaine (☎ 514-597-0166, 800-597-0597; www.aubergedelafontaine.com; 1301 Rue Rachel Est; r $155-225, ste $205-290; **P**) This elegant inn located on the edge of Parc de la Fontaine dazzles with class, not glitz. Breakfast is a generous spread and you're free to raid the fridge for snacks and dessert. Room 21 is the nicest with a dual whirlpool tub and park-facing terrace. Guests in wheelchairs can be accommodated.

Quartier Latin & The Village   Map p246

Turquoise B&B (☎ 514-523-9943, 877-707-1576; www .turquoisebb.com; 1576 Rue Alexandre-DeSève; r with shared bathroom $60-90) On a quiet street, yet close to the heart of The Village, the Turquoise flaunts edgy urban charm tempered by the warmth of beautifully restored Victorian design details. The flower-filled garden with its own goldfish pond is an island of tranquility. It's gay-friendly.

THE AUTHOR'S CHOICE

Le Petit Prince (Map pp244-5; ☎ 514-938-2277, 877-938-9750; www.montrealbandb.com; 1384 Ave Overdale; r $180; **▢**) Beg, steal or lie to score one of the four rooms in this textbook-perfect B&B. The dynamic young owners, Robert and Jonathan, are impeccable and generous hosts with a knack for making everyone feel welcome. Hand-picked furniture and creative use of color give each room its unique feel; two have private balconies. Not only the romantically inclined will appreciate the blissful beds, whirlpools for two and hearty fireplaces. Breakfast is a full gourmet affair, whipped up in a cool kitchen with race-car red retro-style appliances. And yes, you can have breakfast in bed.

Hôtel Le Jardin D'Antoine (☎ 514-843-4506, 800-361-4506; www.hotel-jardin-antoine.qc.ca; 2024 Rue St-Denis; r $100-170; **P**) Right in the thick of the Quartier Latin action, this quiet hotel has various room types, most characterized by a flowery decorating scheme and super-sized bathrooms.

EATING

Montréalers are serious food freaks. The standard of cuisine is frighteningly high, with zero tolerance for limp lettuce, an uninspired sauce or lukewarm Atlantic char. And there are never, ever too many restaurants (there were more than 5000 at last count).

Downtown and especially the Plateau are a diner's nirvana. More than any other street, Boul St-Laurent epitomizes the city's culinary wealth. From boisterous soup parlors in Chinatown to Schwartz's smoked meat emporium to trendy Plateau gourmet temples, they're all along here. Still further north loom Mile End, the birthplace of the famous Montréal bagel, and Little Italy with its comfortable trattoria and not-to-be-missed Jean Talon Market.

Eateries with a policy of *apportez vôtre vin* (bring your own wine; BYOW) cluster along Rue Prince Arthur and Ave Duluth Est in the Plateau.

Old Montréal   Map pp244–5

BUDGET

Olive & Gourmando (☎ 514-350-1083; 351 Rue St-Paul Ouest; meals $5-10; ☯ 8am-6pm Tue-Sat, to 10pm Thu) This bustling corner café puts a premium on choice organic ingredients which turn up in delicious salads, sandwiches and hot lunches. Yummy country-style breads, too.

Marché de la Villette (☎ 514-807-8084; 324 Rue St-Paul Ouest; dishes $7-10; ☯ 9am-6pm) Gourmets on the run can stock up on foie gras ($250 per kg) and other deli items. Those with more time can rub shoulders with the locals during satisfying lunches concocted from regional products.

Titanic (☎ 514-849-0894; 445 Rue St-Pierre; mains $3.50-12; ☯ 7am-4:30pm Mon-Fri) This little labyrinthine café tucked away in a basement is a bit hard to spot. Make an effort, though, because the salads, pastas and creative sandwiches are definitely worth it.

TOP FIVE MONTRÉAL (TR)EATS

- **Au Pied de Cochon** (p258) – total indulgence, Montréal-style.
- **Bronté** (p258) – a perfect fusion of substance and style.
- **Chao Phraya** (p259) – taste-bud-tempting Thai.
- **Ferreira Café** (below) – Portuguese goes gourmet.
- **Schwartz's** (p258) – the quintessential smoked meat parlor.

MID-RANGE

Ghandi (☎ 514-845-5866; 230 Rue St-Paul Ouest; mains $12.50-20; ☺ lunch Mon-Fri, dinner daily) Curries are like culinary poetry at this elegant, kitsch-free Indian restaurant, which also does a mean tandoori duck and butter chicken. Portions are ample, fragrant and steamy, and the service is impeccable.

Tokyo (☎ 514-844-6695; 185 Rue St-Paul Ouest; meals $14-25; ☺ lunch Mon-Fri, dinner Mon-Sat) Sushi in its infinite varieties is clearly the star of the show at this popular sushi den, which serves up its fishy morsels in an ambience of Zen-like simplicity (translation: the decor ain't much to write home about). Reservations recommended.

Eggspectation (☎ 514-282-0119; 201 Rue St-Jacques; mains $9-15; ☺ 6am-5pm) Famous for its huge breakfast menu (including a dozen versions of eggs Benedict), this small chain also serves salads, pastas and chicken in a family-friendly ambience.

TOP END

Gibby's (☎ 514-282-1837; 298 Place d'Youville; mains $20-35; ☺ dinner) The setting alone, in a 200-year-old converted stable, offers eye-candy galore, but it's the food – especially expertly cut steaks – that truly shines. A drink in the bar is a perfect overture to an evening of fine dining. Reservations essential.

S Le Restaurant (☎ 514-350-1155; 125 Rue St-Paul Ouest; dinner mains from $25; ☺ 7am-11pm) An appetizing aroma streaming from the open kitchen greets you as you enter this cutting-edge chic restaurant where star chef Steve Lemieux gets creative with fresh meat, fish and seasonal vegetables. His famous yellow-tomato gazpacho is a veritable flavor bomb.

Downtown
BUDGET & MID-RANGE

Boustan (Map pp244-5; ☎ 514-843-3576; 2020 Rue Crescent; ☺ 11-4am) This little Lebanese joint scores high in popularity on the city's shwarma circuit. Its late hours make it a favorite with night owls in need of restoring balance to the brain between bars.

Buona Notte (Map p246; ☎ 514-848-0644; 3518 Boul St-Laurent; mains $10-23; ☺ lunch Mon-Sat, dinner daily) This humming place is a darling of the see-and-be-seen crowd. Because of – or despite – its clientele, it serves up excellent Italian and international fare. Reservations essential.

Marché Atwater (☎ 514-937-7754; 138 Ave Atwater; ☺ 8am-6pm Mon-Wed, 8am-9pm Thu & Fri, 8am-5pm Sat & Sun) This superb market brims with vendors selling mostly local and regional products, from perfectly matured cheeses to crusty breads, exquisite ice wines and tangy tapenades. It's all housed in a 1933 brick hall.

Ong Ca Can (Map pp244-5; ☎ 514-844-7817; 79 Rue Ste-Catherine Est; mains $8-13; ☺ lunch & dinner Tue-Sun) Despite its crisp white linens and intricate artwork, this bustling Vietnamese restaurant only looks pricey. The kitchen staff gets most things right, although the lemon grass rolls and anything involving beef get especially high marks from loyal patrons.

Wok Café (Map pp244-5; ☎ 514-938-1882; 1845 Rue Ste-Catherine Ouest; mains $7-10; ☺ lunch & dinner) The cucumber-green walls and framed posters add a touch of class to this unpretentious pan-Asian café where you can enjoy dim sum all day long or wolf down respectable *kung pao* chicken and other classics – hot, cheap and plentiful.

Le Commensal (Map pp244-5; ☎ 514-871-1480; 1204 Ave McGill College; dishes $1.69 per 100g; ☺ 11:30am-10pm) This small self-service vegetarian buffet chain offers plenty of healthy options for filling up on casseroles, salads and desserts. It's priced by weight, so don't load up on potatoes. There's another branch in the **Quartier Latin** (Map p246; ☎ 514-845-2627; 1720 Rue St-Denis).

TOP END

Ferreira Café (Map pp244-5; ☎ 514-848-0988; 1446 Rue Peel; mains $17-34; ☺ Mon-Sat) Munch complimentary olives while perusing the menu at this beautiful Portuguese restaurant. The chef, Marino Tavares, gives sardines, sea bass and snapper the gourmet treatment. There's also a superb port selection. Reservations essential.

QUÉBEC

THE AUTHOR'S CHOICE

Bronté (Map pp244-5; ☎ 514-934-1801; 1800 Rue Sherbrooke Ouest; mains $20-36; ☒ dinner Tue-Sat) Bronté is the kind of place where everything has perfect pitch. The look is 1920s supper club meets 21st-century techno parlor. Sensuous booths the color of French vanilla hem in the long dining room bathed in Kool-aid pink and orange accent lighting. Settle in and prepare for your taste buds to do cartwheels as you indulge in the culinary compositions of chef Joe Mercuri. Hip, young and a true artist in the kitchen, he knows how to turn market-fresh fare into beautiful dishes that will linger in your memory long after you've paid the bill. Even the desserts are worth the hip-expanding indulgence. Impeccable service, gorgeous tableware and a superb wine list. Reservations advised.

Plateau Mont-Royal   Map p246
BUDGET

Schwartz's (☎ 514-842-4813; 3895 Boul St-Laurent; meals $7-14; ☒ 9-12:30am Sun-Thu, to 1:30am Fri, to 2:30am Sat) Don't be deterred by the line that inevitably forms outside this legendary smoked meat parlor. Join the eclectic clientele – students to celebrities – at the communal tables and don't forget to order the pickles, fries and coleslaw.

Cluny (☎ 514-866-1213; 257 Rue Prince Arthur; mains $5-13; ☒ 8am-4pm Mon-Wed, 8am-8pm Thu & Fri) Day after day tables at this industrial-chic cafeteria fill up with hip patrons hungry for delectable *ciabatta* sandwiches, creative pastas and mountainous salads. Cluny, by the way, is the owner's dog.

Café Santropol (☎ 514-842-3110; 3990 Rue St-Urbain; mains $6-10; ☒ 11:30am-midnight) A groovy hangout perfect for reading, writing or just plain procrastinating while sinking your teeth into one of the legendary and often bizarre sandwiches. One percent of the profit is donated to local charities. There's a nice garden out back.

MID-RANGE & TOP END

La Colombe (☎ 514-849-8844; 554 Rue Duluth Est; meals $35; ☒ dinner Tue-Sun) At this humming, smoke-free place, a new menu takes shape every morning as owner-chef Moustapha scours Montréal's markets for the freshest

and choicest ingredients. It's all excellent, but whenever duck or veal are featured, go for it (BYOW).

Le Roi du Plateau (☎ 514-844-8393; 51 Rue Rachel Ouest; mains $9-20; ☒ dinner) Tables are squished together as tightly as the sardines on the big belching grill in this wildly popular Portuguese eatery, which lurks behind a ho-hum facade. Succulent and finger-lickin' good chicken is clearly the *roi* (king) of the menu.

Le Jardin de Panos (☎ 514-521-4206; 521 Rue Duluth Est; mains $12-21; ☒ lunch & dinner) The flower-filled back courtyard of this delightful Greek eatery will transport you straight to the Mediterranean. There's a solid selection of mains, although for a sampling of tastes and textures the mixed appetizer platter can't be beat (BYOW).

Maestro SVP (☎ 514-842-6447; 3615 Boul St-Laurent; mains $14-40; ☒ lunch Mon-Fri, dinner) A changing palette of 15 varieties of oysters are the specialty at this trendy bistro where tables are lit by a halo of halogen. If you're not into slimy mollusks, try the fried calamari, tangy tilapia or any of the pasta dishes.

Au Pied de Cochon (☎ 514-281-1114; 536 Rue Duluth Ouest; mains $12-25; ☒ dinner Tue-Sun) French-trained chef Martin Picard quickly captured the hearts and tummies of Montréal gourmets with his avant-garde interpretations of classic country fare. No animal is safe from his kitchen. If you're going to send your cholesterol levels through the roof, it might as well be with the foie gras *poutine*. It's non-smoking.

Med Grill (☎ 514-844-0027; 3500 Boul St-Laurent; meals around $50; ☒ dinner) The restaurant name is a misnomer, for the dishes at this chic boîte actually take global fusion to the nth degree. Spicy shrimp paired with Israeli couscous and caramelized Asian eggplant is a typically fanciful creation, gobbled up by a Rolls-Royce crowd of diners.

Mile End & Little Italy   Map p246
BUDGET

Fairmount Bagel (☎ 514-272-0667; 74 Ave Fairmount Ouest; bagels 50¢-$1.50; sandwiches $3.50-7; ☒ 24hr) The original Montréal bagel baker still churns them out 24/7, from the classic onion to the newfangled muesli, sun-dried tomato and pesto variations. Plenty of shmears for takeout as well.

La Maison du Bagel (☎ 514-276-8044; 263 Ave St-Viateur Ouest; bagels 50¢-$1.50, sandwiches $4-8; ⏲ 24hr) Also known as St Viateur bagel shop, this place is just as famous as Fairmount Bagel, if not quite as old. Try them both and judge for yourself which one is better. To get here take bus No 55.

Wilensky's Light Lunch (☎ 514-271-0247; 34 Ave Fairmount Ouest; dishes $2.50-5; ⏲ 9am-4pm Mon-Fri) Generations of meat-lovers have flocked to Moe Wilensky's corner joint to order 'The Special,' a pressed bologna sandwich. It has even been immortalized in Mordecai Richler's novel *The Apprenticeship of Duddy Kravitz*. Wash it down with a fountain cherry cola.

MID-RANGE

Marché Jean Talon (☎ 514-277-1588; 7075 Ave Casgrain; ⏲ 8am-6pm Mon-Wed, to 9pm Thu & Fri, 8am-5pm Sat & Sun; metro Jean Talon) The pride of Little Italy, this delightfully diverse market is perfect for putting together a picnic. A great stop is Marché des Saveurs, devoted entirely to Québec specialties like wine and cider, fresh cheeses, smoked meats and preserves.

Alep (☎ 514-270-6396; 199 Rue Jean Talon Est; mains $8-14; ⏲ dinner Tue-Sun; metro De Castelnau) A tantalizing mélange of cumin, coriander and other spices envelops the impressive dining room with decor inspired by the famous citadel in Alep, Syria. The Middle Eastern food here is tops. Make a meal from wonderful appetizers or try beef kebabs and fish dishes.

Chao Phraya (☎ 514-272-5339; 80 Ave Laurier Ouest; mains $10-17; ⏲ dinner) Blending a bouquet of exotic spices, the fine Thai food here is so perky it may get you off your Prozac. Standards such as *pad thai* and *tom ka* become standouts and there's plenty of meatless fare as well. Reservations recommended.

TOP END

Lucca (☎ 514-278-6502; 12 Rue Dante; mains $18-36; ⏲ lunch Mon-Fri, dinner Mon-Sat; metro Jean Talon) This hot little Italian number is on the speed dial of many Montréal foodies. The menu, put together daily from market-fresh ingredients and written on a chalkboard, ranges from classics to adventurous culinary spins. It's *la dolce vita*, Québec-style.

Anise (☎ 514-276-6999; 104 Ave Laurier Ouest; 6/9-course tasting menu $65/90; ⏲ dinner Wed-Sun) Master chef Racha Bassoul doles out modern takes on classic French cuisine at this stylish outpost with citrus-colored walls and carmine banquettes. Only hand-selected, seasonal ingredients find their destiny in such dishes as scallops and pan-fried foie gras, his interpretation of 'surf and turf'.

La Chronique (☎ 514-271-3095; 99 Ave Laurier Est; mains $20-30; ⏲ lunch Tue-Fri, dinner Tue-Sat) It's always a treat to discover what Belgian-born chef Marc de Canck has up his sleeve on any given night. It could be venison in leek sauce or sweetbreads paired with spicy chorizo, but most likely it'll be good. Reservations recommended.

Quartier Latin & The Village   Map p246

La Paryse (☎ 514-842-2040; 302 Rue Ontario Est; mains $7-10; ⏲ 11am-11pm Mon-Fri, noon-11pm Sat & Sun) Thick and juicy – the cooks at this smart little retro diner sure know how to get burgers right. Don't sulk if you're not a meat eater as there are plenty of tasty soups and tofu-based choices as well.

L'Express (☎ 514-845-5333; 3927 Rue St-Denis; mains $12-20; ⏲ 8-2am) This place is so fantastically French, you'd half expect to see the Eiffel Tower out the window, especially after guzzling too much of the excellent wines. The food's classic Parisian bistro – think steak *frites*, bouillabaisse, tarragon chicken – and so is the attitude. Reservations essential.

Les 3 Brasseurs (☎ 514-845-1660; 1658 Rue St-Denis; mains $9-14; ⏲ 11-1am or later) If you'd like to cap a day of sightseeing with belly-filling fare and a few pints of handcrafted beer, stop by this convivial brewpub with its stylized warehouse looks and rooftop terrace. The house specialty is 'Flamm's,' a French spin on pizza.

Est-Asie (☎ 514-598-1118; 1320 Rue Ste-Catherine Est; mains $11-21; ⏲ lunch Mon-Fri, dinner daily) The cool techno decor does little to distract diners from the exotic dishes at this place with its high hipster quotient. The menu hopscotches from Japan to Thailand to Vietnam and China, mostly with convincing results.

Area (☎ 514-890-6691; 1429 Rue Amherst; mains $20-30; ⏲ lunch Tue-Fri, dinner Tue-Sat) The black-on-black decor, fresh regional produce and an extensive wine list are the ingredients for success at this Village restaurant. The food is fusion at its finest and is often packed with flavors subtle and unexpected.

DRINKING

The best drinking strips are along the café-terrace-lined Rue Crescent in downtown, and the jazzy arteries of the Plateau – Boul St-Laurent, Rue St-Denis and Ave du Mont Royal. The bars along Rue Ste-Catherine in The Village are mostly gay but not exclusively so.

Brutopia (Map pp244–5; ☎ 514-323-9277; 1219 Rue Crescent; ☻ 3pm-3am Sun-Fri, noon-3am Sat) Boisterous and brick-lined Brutopia brews its own beer, including outstanding India Pale Ale, in sparkling copper vats right behind the bar. A friendly, young crowd invades nightly, not least for the live bands.

Sir Winston Churchill Pub (Map pp244–5; ☎ 514-288-0623; 1455 Rue Crescent; ☻ 11:30-3am) This is the original Crescent St watering hole, founded in 1967 by Johnny Vale, a one-time comrade of Che Guevara. The late local author Mordecai Richler used to knock back cold ones in the bar upstairs. Things get clamorous between 5pm and 8pm when it's two-for-one happy hour.

Gogo Lounge (Map p246; ☎ 514-286-0882; 3682 Boul St-Laurent) Drenched in psychedelic decor and retro furniture, this groovy outpost is a hipster fave, famous for its huge martini selection. All drinks are listed on old vinyl records. Dress nicely.

Le St Sulpice (Map p246; ☎ 514-844-9458; 1680 Rue St-Denis; ☻ 11-3am) On a hot summer night, a cool place to be is the huge beer garden of this always-bustling hangout. Great people-watching potential here, as well as in the café, with three terraces and a disco. Did we mention the place was huge?

Luba Lounge (Map p246; ☎ 514-288-5822; 2109 Rue Bleury; ☻ 9pm-3am) This intimate, unpretentious boîte with its complexion-friendly lighting and plush velvety sofas is great for chilling while being showered with hip-hop and electronica. The jam session on Monday nights is popular with aspiring lounge lizards.

Else's (Map p246; ☎ 514-286-6689; 156 Rue Roy Est; ☻ 8-3am) A quintessential neighborhood pub, Else's feels as comfortable as a hug from an old friend. You can quickly seep into the relaxed atmosphere with candlelit tables to chat over and finger food to thwart the munchies.

Edgar Hypertavern (Map p246; ☎ 514-521-4661; 1562 Ave du Mont Royal Est; ☻ 3pm-3am) Once a trashy dive, Edgar's has long been a place to come for a good time. The bar staff pours with a generous elbow and the eclectic medley of sounds is kept at conversation-friendly levels.

Le Ste-Elisabeth (Map p244–5; ☎ 514-286-4302; 1412 Rue Ste-Elisabeth; ☻ 4pm-3am Mon-Thu, from 6pm Sat & Sun) Microbrews, imported Euro beers and quality Scotch sing their sweet siren song to the low-key crowd of this popular pub. It's a pretty place with a lovely garden overlooked by an upstairs terrace.

ENTERTAINMENT

Not exactly slow-paced in the daytime, Montréal really bursts to life when the sun goes down. The nightlife is, simply speaking, Canada's best, as even Torontonians will grudgingly admit. The city's club scene is dynamic and exuberant with much of the action unfolding along Boul St-Laurent, Rue Ste-Catherine Est (in The Village) and, in the western part of town, Rue Crescent. Music lovers can easily get their fill from the extensive menu of jazz and classical to pop and New Age to world beats. And performing arts fans have plenty of theater and dance troupes of international renown from which to choose.

Tickets for major concerts, shows, festivals and sporting events are available from the box offices of individual venues or from **Admission** (☎ 514-790-1245, 800-361-4595; www.admission.com) or **Ticketmaster** (☎ 514-790-1111; www.ticketmaster.ca).

See Media (p239) for publications that help you keep the finger on the pulse of the latest happenings. For details about top clubs and the DJs du jour, pick up a copy of the glossy *ME* (Montréal Entertainment). For raves, check for flyers in record stores, bars and clubs. **Info-Arts Bell** (☎ 514-790-2787) is an information line for cultural events, plays and concerts. For details of particularly gay-friendly bars and clubs, see the boxed text on p254.

Nightclubs

Altitude 737 (Map pp244–5; ☎ 514-397-0737; 1 Place Ville-Marie; ☻ 5-7pm Wed, to 10pm Thu, to 3am Fri & Sat) This restaurant-bar-disco combo always promises 'high times' thanks to its location at the top of Montréal's tallest office tower. Alas, attitude reigns at this altitude, but the drinks prices are surprisingly fair and the buzz electric.

Tokyo Bar (Map p246; ☎ 514-842-6838; 3709 Boul St-Laurent; ⏰ 10pm-3am) Sink back into the comfy circular white leather booths, martini in hand, and cast your eyes over the impeccably wrapped crowd writhing to house, hip-hop and disco. If things get too hot, you could always get lost in translation on the rooftop terrace.

Stereo (Map p246; ☎ 514-286-0325; 858 Rue Ste-Catherine Est; ⏰ 3-10am Sat & Sun) The after-hours choice for years, this Village club owes its popularity to stellar in-house and imported DJs, an excellent sound system and good mix of gays, straights, students and drag queens. Things get pretty hot by 5am. No alcohol.

Aria (Map p246; ☎ 514-987-6712; 1280 Rue St-Denis; ⏰ 1:30-10am Sat & Sun) If you're sleepless in Montréal, greet the dawn at this ex-movie theater turned mega-club in the Quartier Latin. It's been hyped for its outta-this-world sound system and three floors of dancing to different sounds.

Also recommended:

Mado Cabaret (Map p246; ☎ 514-525-7566; 1115 Rue Ste-Catherine Est) Outrageous drag shows and standup comedy; Tuesday nights are the most rollicking.

Metropolis (Map pp244-5; ☎ 514-844-3500; 59 Rue Ste-Catherine Est; ⏰ 10pm-3am Fri & Sat) Art Deco cinema turned into Canada's largest dance club with dazzling sound and light shows.

Live Music
JAZZ, BLUES & ROCK

L'Escogriffe (Map p246; ☎ 514-842-7244; 4467a Rue St-Denis; ⏰ 6pm-1am) This smoky and intimate Plateau club serves up some wicked jazz every night. The Thursday jam session, featuring the Mile End Jazz Quartier, is an institution.

Café Campus (Map p246; ☎ 514-844-1010; 57 Rue Prince Arthur Est; ⏰ 8:30pm-3am Tue-Sun) This perennially popular student club packs 'em in with its eclectic line-up of local and international bands. Its famous Wednesday blues nights often attract fairly big-name talent. Themed nights include 'retro Tuesday' and 'Francophone Sunday.'

Casa del Popolo (Map p246; ☎ 514-284-3804; www.casadelpopolo.com; 4873 Boul St-Laurent; ⏰ from 11am) Low-key and funky, this café-bar cum art gallery cum performance venue usually has several events scheduled in three locations. The café serves fairtrade coffees and vegetarian fare. Check the website for full details.

House of Jazz (Map pp244-5; ☎ 514-842-8656; 2060 Rue Aylmer; ⏰ 11:30-1am) The former Biddle's may have been renamed since the death of its founder Charlie Biddle in 2003, but it remains a fixture on the Montréal jazz scene. With no cover charge, the place is often packed, so prepare to wait in line. Nice terrace and good food, too.

Upstairs (Map pp244-5; ☎ 514-931-6808; 1254 Rue Mackay; ⏰ noon-1am Tue-Fri, 5pm-1am Sat & Sun) Some mighty fine talent, both home-grown and imported, has tickled the ivories of the baby grand in this intimate jazz joint. Shows start at 9pm. Nice terrace and respectable dinner menu.

Foufounes Electriques (Map pp244-5; ☎ 514-844-5539; 87 Rue Ste-Catherine Est; ⏰ 3pm-3am) The graffiti-covered walls and industrial charm should tip you off that the 'Electric Buttocks' isn't exactly a mainstream kinda place. Punk, hardcore and grunge often rule the night at this two-decades-old alternative bastion. There's cheap beer and a nice terrace.

CLASSICAL   Map pp244–5

Opéra de Montréal (☎ 514-985-2258; Place des Arts) The Montréal Opera has delighted fans of Mozart, Wagner and Bizet for about 25 years. Productions are in the original language with surtitles.

Orchestre Symphonique de Montréal (☎ 514-842-9951; Place des Arts, Salle Wilfrid-Pelletier) One of Canada's most accomplished orchestras, the OSM has been helmed by such famous conductors as Otto Klemperer, Zubin Mehta and Charles Dutoit. Check for free summer concerts at the Basilique Notre Dame and the Olympic Park.

McGill Chamber Orchestra (☎ 514-487-5190) Founded in 1939, this fine chamber ensemble is one of Canada's oldest. Concert series are held in various venues, including the **Pollack Concert Hall** (555 Rue Sherbrooke Ouest) and the Place des Arts.

Theater & Dance

Centaur Theatre (Map pp244-5; ☎ 514-288-3161; 453 Rue St-François Xavier) Based in the beautiful Old Stock Exchange in Old Montréal, the Centaur ranks among the country's leading theater companies. Its repertoire ranges from Shakespeare classics to experimental fare by local English-language playwrights.

Cirque du Soleil (☎ 514-722-2234; www.cirquedu soleil.com) For the past two decades, this phenomenally successful troupe (see the boxed text on p48) has redefined what circuses are all about. Headquartered in Montréal, it usually inaugurates new shows in the city every year or two. Call or check with the tourist office.

Les Ballets Jazz de Montréal (☎ 514-982-6771; www.balletsdemontreal.com) This modern-dance troupe has earned a sterling reputation for showcasing its classically trained dancers in experimental forms. Performances take place at various venues around town.

Les Grands Ballets Canadiens (☎ 514-849-8681; www.grandsballets.qc.ca) Québec's leading ballet troupe stages four shows annually. They range from classical to modern programs and are both innovative yet accessible to general audiences.

Cinemas

Multiplex theaters showing Hollywood blockbusters abound, but plenty of art and indie houses survive as well. Look up what's showing where at www.cinema-montreal .com, with reviews and details of discount admissions.

Popular independent theaters include **Cinéma du Parc** (Map p246; ☎ 514-281-1900; 3575 Ave du Parc) and **Ex-Centris Cinema** (Map p246; ☎ 514-847-3536; 3530 Boul St-Laurent).

IMAX (Map pp244-5; ☎ 514-496-4629; adult/child/ teen & senior/family 2-D films $10/7/9/30, 3-D films $12/9/11/38; ⏲ 10am-9:30pm Sun-Thu, 10am-10:30pm Fri & Sat late Jun–late Sep, shorter hrs rest of year), part of the Centre des Sciences de Montréal (p241), is a great place to take the kids. Discounted tickets with museum admission and for double features are available.

THE AUTHOR'S CHOICE

National Film Board (Map p246; ☎ 514-283-9000; 1564 Rue St-Denis; ⏲ noon-9pm Tue-Sun) A paradise for serious cinephiles, the NFB hosts regular screenings from its 6000-film archive, but the real attraction is the **Cinérobothèque** – make your choice, and a robot housed in a glass-roofed archive pulls your selection from the stacks. Then settle back into individual, stereo-equipped chair units to watch your personal monitor (students/nonstudents per hr $2/3).

Sports

Hockey and Catholicism are regarded as national religions in Québec, but football also attracts a fair number of 'worshippers.'

Montréal Canadiens (Map pp244-5; ☎ 514-932-2582; www.canadiens.com; Bell Centre, 1200 Rue de la Gauchetière Ouest; tickets $23-160) Bell Centre is home base for this National Hockey League team and 24-time Stanley Cup winners (the last time in 1993). Although they have struggled in recent years, Montréalers still have a soft spot for the 'Habs' and games sell out routinely. After kick-off you might be able to snag a half-price ticket from the scalpers lurking by the entrance. Bring binoculars for the rafter seats.

Montréal Alouettes (Map pp244-5; ☎ 514-871-2255; www.montrealalouettes.com; Molson Stadium, Ave des Pins Ouest; tickets $20-75) This once-defunct Canadian Football League team is the unlikely hottie of the city's sports scene, especially since winning the league's Grey Cup trophy in 2002. They have sold out every game since 1999, so order tickets early.

SHOPPING

Hold on to your wallets! Montréal is shopping nirvana. Hardcore shoppers will inevitably end up on Rue Ste-Catherine Ouest, which is chock-a-block with department, chain and one-of-a-kind stores, plus multilevel malls like the **Centre Eaton** (Map pp244-5, ☎ 514-288-3710; Rue St-Catherine btwn Ave McGill College & Rue University; ⏲ 10am-9pm Mon-Fri, 9am-5pm Sat, 10am-5pm Sun). And that's just at street level. Head underground and you'll have hundreds more retailers displaying everything from tuberoses to tank tops.

For shopping at a more leisurely pace, head to the Plateau. Boul St-Laurent, Rue St-Denis and Ave du Mont Royal are famous for their unique boutiques hawking trendy must-haves. On Rue St-Paul in Old Montréal, the focus is on tourist-oriented trinket shops with some very respectable art galleries thrown into the mix. Antiques aficionados can easily spend a day scouring the shops along Rue Notre Dame Ouest between Ave Atwater and Rue Guy, known as Antique Alley.

Chabanel District (900 Boul St-Laurent; ⏲ 9am-1pm Sat) Bring cash, patience and a nose for bargains when visiting this eight-block expanse of factory outlets, importers and manufacturers. You'll find everything from skimpy thongs to fur coats and wedding dresses. Haggling is allowed, but returns are not. Some shops are open during the week and many close in January and July. Bus No 55 will get you there.

Revenge (Map p246; ☎ 514-843-4379; 3852 Rue St Denis) This hip outpost specializes in renowned Québecois fashion designers, including Jean-Claude Poitras and Marie Saint-Pierre. A dramatic mural by painter Claude Théberge adorns the walls.

Ogilvy (Map pp244-5; ☎ 514-842-7711; 1307 Rue Ste-Catherine) Dripping with tradition, this Victorian-era department store stocks all the top international labels. Be sure to visit the historic concert hall on the 5th floor. Since 1927, a kilt-clad bagpiper has roamed the store daily at noon.

Caban (Map pp244-5; ☎ 514-844-9300; 777 Rue Ste-Catherine) At this three-floor emporium of good taste you'll find everything for home and hearth, from sleek wine glasses to stylish lamps and fun tableware.

Galerie Le Chariot (Map pp244-5; ☎ 514-875-4994; 446 Place Jacques Cartier) This three-level gallery specializes in museum-quality Inuit art, primarily soapstone sculptures. Each piece has been authenticated by the Canadian government.

Guilde Canadienne des Métier d'Art Québec (Map pp244-5; ☎ 514-849-6091; 2025 Rue Peel; ☽ Mon-Sat) Founded in 1906, this gallery-like space presents only the finest in Canadian arts and crafts from around the country.

Parasuco (Map pp244-5; ☎ 514-284-2288; 1414 Rue Crescent) Made right here in Montréal, Parasuco has become one of Canada's hottest labels for jeans and casual wear. Their high-energy flagship store stocks all the latest styles.

Eva B (Map p246; ☎ 514-849-8246; 2013 Boul St-Laurent) The '60s, '70s and '80s are alive and well at this groovy retro boutique. Stock up on styles guaranteed to make you a standout at any party. Costume rentals, too.

Cheap Thrills (Map pp244-5; ☎ 514-844-8988; 2044 Rue Metcalfe) It's easy to lose track of time as you browse through this big selection of used books and music (CDs and some vinyl), both with a mainstream and offbeat bent and sold at bargain prices.

GETTING THERE & AWAY
Air
Both domestic and international airlines land at **Pierre Elliott Trudeau International Air-**port (YUL; ☎ 514-394-7377, 800-465-1213; www.admtl .com), formerly known as Dorval Airport, about 20km west of downtown. Facilities include lockers, a left-luggage office, ATMs and a currency exchange desk. Montréal's other airport, Mirabel, no longer handles passenger flights.

Bus
Buses to the airports and to Canadian and US destinations depart from the **Station Centrale de l'Autobus** (Central Bus Station; Map p246; ☎ 514-842-2281; 505 Boul de Maisonneuve Est).

Several bus operators offer services in all directions. See p264 for contact details for all these companies. Voyageur runs regular and express buses to Ottawa ($36, 2¼ hours, 20 daily), while Orléans Express serves Québec City ($39, 3¼ hours, up to 18 daily) as well as the Mauricie and Gaspésie regions.

Coach Canada offers the best deal to Toronto ($78, 6¾ hours, nine daily). Voyageur covers the same route but is slightly more expensive ($92). Greyhound has daily services to New York City ($97, eight hours, four daily). Limocar goes to the Laurentian resorts and the Eastern Townships.

Montréal is also a stop on the eastern Canada circuit run by Moose Travel Network (p875).

Car & Motorcycle
All the major international car-rental companies have branches at the airport, main train station and elsewhere around town. See p873 for general contact information.

If you need a car for a week or longer, try **Transtate Automarché** (☎ 514-631-0304; www .automarche.com in French; 475 Ave Dumont), near the airport, where seven-day rates start at $299, including tax, liability insurance and 1400km. **Pelletier Car Rental** (Map pp244-5; ☎ 514-281-5000; www.pelletierrentacar.com; 1163 Rue Mackay) is another reputable local company.

The ride-share agency **Allô Stop** (Map p246; ☎ 514-985-3032; 4317 Rue St-Denis) has an office in the Plateau. Sample fares are $15 to Québec City, $16 to Ottawa, $35 to Toronto and $65 to New York.

Train
Montréal's **Gare Centrale** (Central Train Station; Map pp244-5; 895 Rue de la Gauchetière Ouest) is the local hub for VIA Rail. The overnight service

between Montréal and Toronto is a treat aboard new modern and comfortable cars. Trains leave at 11:30pm nightly except Saturday, arriving around 8am; fares include breakfast. One-way sleeper-car fares start at $140.

Amtrak runs one train daily to/from New York City (US$62, nine hours).

GETTING AROUND
To/From the Airport

L'Aérobus (☎ 514-399-9877; www.autobus.qc.ca) runs shuttle buses from Montréal Trudeau to downtown every half-hour between 7am and 1am and in the opposite direction from 5am to 11pm (one-way/return $12/22). Buses stop after about 35 minutes at **Station Aérobus** (Map pp244-5; 777 Rue de la Gauchetière Ouest), from where a free minibus will ferry you anywhere you like in downtown. The buses stop about 10 minutes later at Station Centrale de l'Autobus (Map p246).

You can also make the trip on public transport using bus and metro, which is less convenient but cheaper. From outside the arrivals hall, catch bus No 204 Est to the bus transfer station at Gare Dorval (Dorval Train Station). Switch to bus No 211 Est and get off at the Lionel-Groulx metro station. Buses operate from 5am to 1am; the entire journey takes about an hour and costs $2.50.

Drivers heading into town should take Autoroute 13 Sud, which merges with Autoroute 20 Est; this in turn takes you into the heart of downtown, along the main Autoroute Ville Marie (the 720). The trip takes about 20 to 30 minutes when traffic runs smoothly, but up to one hour during peak times.

A taxi to/from Trudeau airport costs a flat rate of $31.

Car & Motorcycle

Though Montréal is fairly easy to navigate, public transportation is preferable to a car for getting around town. If you choose to drive, you'll find metered street parking (with meters set back from the curb) and public garages throughout the central area, especially underneath big hotels and shopping complexes. Expect to pay about $12 to $20 per day.

Note that turning right at red lights is illegal on the island of Montréal.

Public Transportation

Montréal has a modern and convenient bus and metro system run by **STM** (☎ 514-786-4636 automated 24hr infoline; www.stm.info). The metro is the city's subway system and runs quickly and quietly on rubber tires, just like the one in Paris. It operates until at least 12:30am. Some buses provide service all night.

One ticket can get you anywhere in the city. If you're switching between buses, or between bus and metro, get a free transfer slip, called a *correspondence*, from the driver; on the metro take one from the machines just past the turnstiles. Transfers are valid for 90 minutes only for travel in one direction.

Tickets cost $2.50 but are cheaper by the half-dozen ($11). There are also 'Tourist Cards' for $8/16 for one/three days and weekly cards for $18 (valid Monday to Sunday). Note that bus drivers won't give change.

Taxi

Flag fall is $2.75, then it's $1.30 per kilometer. You can flag down a cab on the street or order one by phone, for instance from **Taxi Diamond** (☎ 514-273-6331) or **Taxi Co-Op** (☎ 514-636-6666).

AROUND MONTRÉAL
Laval

☎ 450 / pop 350,000

Although primarily a dormitory community, the island of Laval – wedged between Montréal and the Laurentians – is not without charm.

One of the most beautiful spots for boating, canoeing and kayaking is the **Parc de la Rivière-des-Mille-Îles** (☎ 450-622-1020; www.parc-mille-iles.qc.ca; 345 Boul Ste-Rose; admission free; ☽ 9am-6pm). Straddling the Rivière des Mille Îles, the park embraces 10 islands where you can disembark on self-guided water tours. About 10km of the river (including calm inner channels) are open for paddling. You can rent canoes and kayaks (from $28 per day) or rowboats ($35 per day). If you'd rather not go it alone, join a nature tour run by **Amikayak** (☎ 450-667-4612; www.amikayak.com; 110 Rue Venise; 3hr tours adult/child from $49/25; ☽ May-Oct). In winter, the park is popular with cross-country skiing and skating enthusiasts.

From Montréal, take Hwy 15 north to exit 16, Boul Ste-Rose – the park is four

THE OKA CRISIS

In the summer of 1990, Oka was the scene of a major, armed confrontation between Mohawk people and the government. The conflict began in March when Oka's mayor decided to expand the city's golf course onto land the Mohawks considered sacred. It ended, after 78 days, with the Mohawks surrendering to a small battalion of Canadian soldiers. What started as a local conflict focused the nation's, and indeed the world's, attention on injustices and mistreatment perpetrated upon Aboriginal peoples throughout the country. In the wake of Oka, the federal government launched a commission to study the problem and instituted a variety of social programs. The golf course, by the way, was built elsewhere. (For more on aboriginal issues, see the boxed text on p31.)

blocks east of there. Alternatively, you can take the metro to Henri-Bourassa and transfer to bus No 72, which takes you to the park entrance.

For an 'out-of-this-world' experience, head to Laval's other major draw, the **Cosmodôme Space Sciences Centre** (☎ 450-978-3600; www.cosmodome.org; 2150 Hwy 15; adult/child & student/senior $10/6.50/7.50; ☯ 10am-6pm Jul & Aug, 10am-6pm Tue-Sun Sep-Jun). At this interactive museum of space technologies, you have the opportunity to touch a real moon rock, marvel at an original Apollo mission space suit and study rocket models, space shuttles and the solar system. There's a multimedia show, 'Reach for the Stars,' which simulates space travel with cool special effects on a 360-degree screen.

The center is about a 20-minute drive north from downtown Montréal on Hwy 15 (Autoroute des Laurentides). By public transportation, take bus No 60 or 61 from the Henri Bourassa metro station.

Oka

This small town, about 50km west of Montréal and technically part of the Laurentians (right), is known for **Abbaye Cistercienne d'Oka** (Cistercian Abbey; ☎ 450-479-8361; www.abbayeoka.com; 1600 Chemin d'Oka; adult/child $2/free; ☯ church 4am-8pm, store 10am-4:30pm Mon-Fri, 10am-4pm Sat). Founded by French monks in the 1880s, it is one of the oldest monasteries in North America and, quite possibly, soon to be a thing of the past. Only a few aged monks remain and the order is looking to sell the abbey and move to smaller digs. For now, though, you can visit the church of this beautifully located complex and pick up monk-made chocolates, cider and cheese in the little store.

The nearby **Parc d'Oka** (☎ 450-479-8365; www.sepaq.com/oka; 2020 Chemin Oka; adult/child $3.50/1.50; ☯ 9am-7pm), a beautiful expanse laced with hiking trails and hugging Lac des Deux Montagnes, offers a bunch of outdoor activities, including sailing, canoeing and swimming (equipment rental available). The 800-site **campground** (tent sites $18.50, RV sites partial/full hookup $23/33) draws swarms of campers. Some of the park is wheelchair-accessible.

There is no public transport to Oka. From Montréal, take Hwys 15 or 13 to Rte 640 westbound, which leads to Rte 344 and Oka.

THE LAURENTIANS

An easy drive north of Montréal, the Laurentians (Laurentides in French) are meant to be savored like a rich wine, not guzzled like a mug of ale. Despite encroaching development, this is a gentle, unhurried region of billowing hill country sprinkled with lakes, laced by rivers and freckled with villages dominated by their church spires. The scenery makes a perfect backdrop for myriad outdoor pursuits, from hiking to fishing, kayaking to swimming. For cyclists the 200km-long P'tit Train du Nord Linear Park is tailor-made for excursions short or long. In winter, it's the 'white gold' that beckons. Millions of ski hounds descend upon what is the largest concentration of ski resorts in North America. The two most famous are Mont St-Sauveur and Mont-Tremblant.

During peak times – in July, August, at Christmas and on winter weekends – prices soar and the roads can get frustratingly clogged. March and April is maple season, while fall finds the hills drenched in a coat of many colors. Many attractions are only open during the high season, roughly from May to October.

Orientation & Information

The Laurentians extend between 60km and 130km north of Montréal with nearly all towns lining up along Hwy 15, the Autoroute des Laurentides. The old Rte 117, running parallel to it, is slower but more scenic. It takes over north of Ste-Agathe-des-Monts where Hwy 15 ends.

Besides the tourist offices listed under individual towns, you'll find branches in many other Laurentian towns. Official hours are from 8:30am to 7pm between late June and early September and 9am to 5pm the rest of the year. Actual hours, though, may vary, depending on such factors as day of week, the weather and the visitor influx, so call ahead.

Association Touristique des Laurentides (Laurentian Tourist Association; ☎ 450-436-8532, 800-561-6673, reservation service 450-436-3507; www.laurentides .com; ☯ 9am-5pm) Regional tourist office; can answer questions on the phone, make room bookings and mail out information. Operates a free room reservation service.

La Maison du Tourisme des Laurentides (La Porte du Nord, exit 51 off Hwy 15; ☯ 8:30am-8pm late Jun—early Sep, 8:30am-5pm mid-Sep—mid-Jun) Information office maintained by the Laurentian Tourist Association with helpful staff and lots of maps and brochures, including the excellent *Official Tourist Guide*.

Getting There & Around

Limocar runs buses from Montréal's Central Bus Station to the Laurentians at least four times daily. Towns serviced include St-Sauveur ($17, 1½ hours) and Mont-Tremblant ($27, 2½ hours). Ski packages are available, including a round-trip fare and a one-day lift pass. They cost $46/52 for a weekday/weekend to St-Sauveur and $64/71 to Mont-Tremblant.

From May to October, **Autobus du P'tit Train du Nord** (☎ 819-275-3113; tickets $15-35) runs two buses daily between St Jérôme and Mont Laurier, stopping as needed. Bicycles are transported at no extra charge. For $9, it will transport your luggage between lodgings so you can hike or cycle without the added weight.

Drivers coming from Montréal should follow either Hwy 15 or the slower Rte 117.

ST-JÉRÔME

Some 43km north of Montréal, St-Jérôme is the official gateway to the Laurentians. Despite its administrative and industrial demeanor, it's worth a quick stop for its Byzantine-style **cathedral** (☎ 450-432-9741; 355 Rue St-George; admission free; ☯ 7:30am-4:30pm) and adjacent **Musée D'Art Contemporain** (☎ 450-432-7171; 185 Rue du Palais; admission free; ☯ noon-5pm Tue-Sun), which often presents superb exhibits featuring regional artists.

St-Jérôme is also the southern terminus of the **Parc Linéaire du P'tit Train du Nord** (☎ 450-436-8532; cycling/cross-country skiing permits $5/7, children free), a trail system built on top of old railway tracks and snaking 200km north to Mont Laurier, passing streams, rivers, rapids, lakes and great mountain scenery. In summer it's open to bicycles and in-line skates and you'll find rest stops, information booths, restaurants, B&Bs and bike rental and repair shops all along the way. Snow season lures cross-country skiers to the section between St-Jérôme and Val-David, while snowmobile aficionados rule between Val-David and Mont Laurier.

ST-SAUVEUR-DES-MONTS

St-Sauveur-des-Monts (or St-Sauveur, for short) is the busiest village in the Laurentians and is often deluged with day-trippers thanks to its proximity to Montréal (60km). A pretty church anchors Rue Principale, the attractive main street, flanked by restaurants, cafés and boutiques. **St Sauveur/Piedmont** (☎ 450-227-3417; www.tourismepdh.org in French; 605 Chemin des Frênes, Piedmont) is the local tourist office, and **Banque Nationale** (☎ 450-227-8445; 6 Rue de la Gare) has a branch in town. **Café Saint-Sau** (☎ 450-227-3124; inside Galerie des Monts mall, Block 1-2, 75 Rue de la Gare; per hr $8; ☯ 8am-9pm) has Internet access.

Sights & Activities

The **downhill skiing** (www.mssi.ca) is excellent here with about 100 runs for all levels of expertise crisscrossing the area's five major ski hills. St-Sauveur is famous for its night skiing, with many slopes open until 11pm. Lift tickets range from $27 to $43. Nearby Morin Heights has excellent **cross-country skiing** with over 150km of interconnecting trails.

In summer, the area's biggest ski mountain, Mont St-Sauveur, is transformed into the **Parc Aquatique** (Water Park; ☎ 450-227-4671; 350 Rue St-Denis; taller/shorter than 1.4m per day $29/24, half-day $23/20; ☯ 10am-7pm Jun—early Sep). Kids of all ages love getting wet in the wave pool, plunging down the wicked slides (including a couple starting near the mountaintop and reached by chairlift) or being pummeled on rafting rides.

For two weeks starting in late July, St-Sauveur's **Festival des Arts** (☎ 450-227-0427; www.artssaintsauveur.com) brings dozens of international dance troupes to town. Many performances are free.

Sleeping

Auberge Sous L'Edredon (☎ 450-227-3131; www .bbcanada.com/aubergesousledredon; 777 Rue Principale; r $75-140; 🏊) A pretty inn about 2km from the village center and close to a little lake and the Mont Habitant ski area. Some of the delightfully decorated rooms have fireplaces and private facilities.

Le Petit Clocher (☎ 450-227-7576; www.bbcanada .com/lepetitclocher; 216 Rue de l'Église; s/d $140/165) A gorgeous inn occupying a converted monastery on a little hillside above town. It has newly decorated rooms, many of which have extraordinary views.

Eating

Maestro (☎ 450-227-2999; 339 Rue Principale; mains $11-16; 🕑 dinner) Dishes at this popular restaurant are as inspired as the theatrical decor. Expect what is essentially Mediterranean cuisine with unusual flavor and texture pairings.

Papa Luigi (☎ 450-227-5311; 129 Rue Principale; mains $14-28; 🕑 dinner) Meals become culinary celebrations at this classic Italian restaurant whose relaxed mountain-lodge looks belie the upmarket service and quality.

Also recommended:

La Brûlerie des Monts (☎ 450-227-6157; 197 Rue Principale; meals $5-10; 🕑 7am-9pm) *The* place in town for breakfast and sandwiches, with a great terrace.

Chez Bernard (☎ 450-240-0000; 411 Rue Principale; dishes $6-15; 🕑 11am-7pm) Superb deli with local specialties, some homemade, plus full meals perfect for picnics.

VAL-DAVID

Val-David is a pint-sized village with an almost lyrical quality and a gorgeous setting along the Rivière du Nord and at the foot of the mountains. Its charms have made it a magnet for artists whose studios and galleries line the main street, Rue de L'Église. There is a **tourist information** (☎ 819-322-2900; www.valdavid.com; 2501 Rue de l'Église) in town.

Sights & Activities

From mid-June to mid-August, the **1001 Pots Festival** (☎ 819-322-6868; www.1001pots.com), a huge ceramic exhibit and sale, brings some 100,000 people to town. It's the brainchild of Japanese-Canadian artist Kinya Ishikawa whose utilitarian yet stylish pieces are displayed year-round at his **Atelier du Potier** (☎ 819-322-6868; 2435 Rue de L'Église; 🕑 10am-5pm Tue-Sun).

The great outdoors is Val-David's other main attraction. **Phénix Sports and Adventure** (☎ 819-322-1118; 2444 Rue de L'E'glise) and **Pause Plein Air** (☎ 819-322-6880; 1381 Rue de la Sapinière) rent bicycles, kayaks and canoes. Phénix also offers cycle-canoe packages on the Rivière du Nord.

Rock climbing is to Val-David what skiing is to other Laurentian villages, with more than 500 routes from easy walls to challenging cliffs. The mountain-climbing school **Passe Montagne** (☎ 819-322-2123; 1760 Montée 2e rang; 🕑 mid-Apr–mid-Oct) offers courses for beginning and experienced rock hounds from $60.

Sleeping & Eating

HI Le Chalet Beaumont (☎ 819-322-1972; www .chaletbeaumont.com; 1451 Rue Beaumont; dm member/ non-member $16/20, d with/without bathroom $60/50; 🖥) This fantastic HI hostel in an historic log cabin on a wooded hill has the look and amenities of a luxurious country retreat. Free sauna and Internet, communal kitchen and bar, bicycle and ski rentals and helpful, friendly staff.

Le Grand Pa (☎ 819-322-3104; 2481 Rue de L'Église; mains $8-18; 🕑 lunch & dinner) This convivial restaurant gets a winning mix of locals and visitors nibbling on toothsome wood-fired pizzas or tasty pasta dishes. A *chansonnier* serenades diners on Friday and Saturday nights. Big terrace.

La Vagabonde (☎ 819-322-3953; 1262 Chemin de la Rivière; 🕑 9am-6pm Wed-Sun) This popular café and bakery serves delicious handcrafted organic breads and pastries.

STE-AGATHE-DES-MONTS

Although no longer the elegant resort that once drew Queen Elizabeth II and Jacqueline Kennedy, Ste-Agathe-des-Monts still exudes some of the old-world Anglo-Saxon charm of the English settlers who built it up as a retreat in the 1890s. There's a **tourist information**

QUÉBEC

office (☎ 819-326-0457; www.sainte-agathe.org; 24 Rue St-Paul Est) in town, as well as a hospital with an emergency room, **Centre Hospitalier Laurentien** (☎ 819-324-4000; 234 Rue St-Vincent; ☯ 24hr).

The town's main asset is the beautiful **Lac des Sables**, which is accessible via three public beaches ($5) and perfect for basking in the sun. **Les Croisière Alouette** (☎ 819-326-3656; adult/child/student & senior $12/5/10; ☯ mid-May–mid-Oct) runs 50-minute narrated cruises during which you'll spot some of the glorious lakefront villas harkening back to the town's one-time grandeur.

Auberge Le St-Venant (☎ 819-326-7937; www.st-venant.com; 234 Rue St-Venant; r $100-150) This nine-room hotel has cozy rooms sheathed in cheerful colors and boasting lake views and private bathrooms. Amenities include cable TV and air-conditioning.

ST-FAUSTIN-LAC-CARRÉ

The gateway to the Mont-Tremblant region, St-Faustin has a couple of attractions in its own right. At the maple-sugar shack **Cabane à Sucre Millette** (☎ 819-688-2101; 1357 Rue St Faustin; adult/child $7/5; ☯ 11:30am-8pm Tue-Sun Mar-Apr, by reservation only May-Feb), you can see production in action – sap is still culled in horse-drawn carts – and sample the results.

The **Centre Touristique Éducatif des Laurentides** (☎ 819-326-1606; 5000 Chemin du Lac Cordon; adult/child/student $5.50/2.50/3.50; ☯ 8am-7pm mid-Jun–early Sep, 8am-5pm mid-Apr–mid-Jun & early Sep–mid-Oct) is a marvelous protected area and a great place to learn about local flora and fauna. The 35km trail network includes some wheelchair-accessible sections, and there are canoe and kayak rentals as well.

VILLE DE MONT-TREMBLANT

The Mont-Tremblant area is the crown jewel of the Laurentians, lorded over by the 960m-high eponymous mountain, dotted with pristine lakes and traversed by rivers. It's a hugely popular four-season playground, drawing ski bums from late October to mid-April, and hikers, bikers, golfers, water sports fans and other outdoor enthusiasts the rest of the year.

The area of Ville de Mont-Tremblant is divided into three sections: **Station Tremblant**, the ski hill and pedestrianized tourist resort at the foot of the mountain; **Mont-Tremblant Village**, a sweet and tiny cluster of homes and businesses about 4km southwest of here; and **St-Jovite**, the main town and commercial center off Rte 117, about 12km south of the mountain. A shuttle bus ($1, 6am to 8pm) connects all three.

Information

Au Grain de Café (☎ 819-681-4567; inside Homewood Suites par Hilton, Tremblant Resort; per 10min $3; ☯ hrs vary) Internet access.

Banque Nationale (☎ 819-425-4444; inside Country Inn & Suites, Station Tremblant; ☯ 10am-5pm)

Clinique Medicale Saint-Jovite (☎ 819-425-2728; 910 Rue de L'École, St-Jovite)

MAPLE SYRUP & THE SUGAR SHACK

Maple syrup is Canada's most recognized export, with three quarters of the world's total output hailing from Québec. It was Aboriginal tribes who taught Europeans how to make the sweet nectar and by the 19th century, cultivating the sap and transforming it into syrup had quickly become a local tradition.

Every summer, starches accumulate in sugar maple trees, which are native to North America. As soon as the mercury dips below zero, they turn into sucrose. To tap the sugar inside the tree, inventive types have come up with a system that sucks out the sap through a series of tubes called Sysvacs. These snake through a maple grove straight to machines that cook the juice into syrup. The different grades produced depend on how long it is cooked and to what temperature (to make taffy, for example, it must cook to 26°C above boiling point).

Sugar shacks became part of the Québecois experience in the early 20th century. They remain places to experience the maple tradition at its best. The 'taffy pull' is the most fun – you scoop up some snow, put it on a plate and have some steaming syrup from a piping cauldron poured onto it. The syrup hardens as it hits the snow, and it can then be twisted onto a Popsicle stick and sucked and chewed until you feel the need to do it all over again.

Sugar shacks are only open for a month or so, in February and March. A few are mentioned in this book (see for example above) but any tourist information office can recommend others.

Mont Tremblant Tourism (☎ 800-322-2932; www
.tourismemonttremblant.com) St-Jovite (☎ 819-425-3300;
48 Chemin de Brébeuf) Mont-Tremblant Village (☎ 819-
425-2434; 5080 Montée Ryan, cnr Rte 327) Station Tremblant
(☎ 819-681-3000 ext 46643; Place des Voyageurs)

Sights & Activities

Station Tremblant (☎ 819-681-3000, 888-736-2526;
www.tremblant.com; adult lift ticket full/half-day $54/44)
is among the top-ranked international ski
resorts in eastern North America according to *Ski* magazine and legions of loyal
fans. Founded in 1938, it sprang from the
vision of Philadelphia millionaire Joe Ryan
and has been seriously slicked up since
1991 when Intrawest, the Vancouver company responsible for putting Whistler on
the map, took over its administration. The
mountain has a vertical drop of 650m and
is laced with 94 trails and two snow parks
served by 13 lifts, including an express gondola. Ski rentals start at $28 per day.

A new summer attraction is the **downhill
luge track** (1/2/3 rides $10/16.50/21) that snakes
down the mountain for 1.4km; daredevils
can reach speeds up to 50km/h. The nearby
Activity Centre (☎ 891-681-4848; www.tremblant
activities.com) can arrange for a wide variety of
outdoor pursuits, from fishing to canoeing
to horseback riding.

The southern mountain base spills over
into a sparkling **pedestrian tourist village** with
big hotels, shops, restaurants and an un-
deniable patina of poshness. The cookie-
cutter architecture doesn't quite exude the
rustic European charm its planners sought
to emulate, but this seems of little concern
to the 2.5 million annual visitors milling
along its cobbled lanes year after year.

For 10 days every mid-July, the resort is
aswarm with music fans during the **Festival
International du Blues**, the country's biggest
blues festival. Contact Station Tremblant
for details.

Sleeping & Eating

HI Mont-Tremblant Hostel (☎ 819-425-6008; www
.hostellingtremblant.com; 2213 Chemin du Village, Mont-
Tremblant Village; members/non-members incl tax dm
$22/26.60, d $56/65; 🖳) This attractive hostel
right next to Lac Moore (free canoe rentals)
features a big kitchen and large party room
with bar, pool table and fireplace. The clean
and spacious rooms often fill to capacity,
especially in ski season.

Country Inn & Suites by Carlson (☎ 819-681-
5555, 800-461-8711; 1000 Chemin des Voyageurs, Station
Tremblant; r per person from $60; 🖳) You won't
miss many amenities from home in the
large and functional suites of this contemporary ski lodge. All have full kitchens.
Children under 17 stay free.

Auberge Le Lupin (☎ 819-425-5474, 877-425-5474;
www.lelupin.com; 127 Rue Pinoteau, Mont-Tremblant Village; r $80-130; 🖳) This 1940s log house offers
snug digs near Lac Tremblant beach. The
ski station is only 1km away.

Restaurant Lorraine (☎ 819-425-5566; 2000
Chemin du Village; mains $6-13; 🕑 6am-10pm) Pizza,
sandwiches, chicken and pasta are the staples at this unfussy feel-good kind of place
in Mont-Tremblant Village. There's a full
breakfast menu as well.

Microbrasserie La Diable (☎ 819-681-4606; mains
$10-20; 🕑 lunch & dinner) After a day of tearing
down the mountain, the hearty sausages,
burgers and pastas served at this lively
tavern at Station Tremblant fill the belly
nicely, as do the tasty homebrews.

PARC DU MONT TREMBLANT

Nature puts on a terrific show in **Parc du
Mont Tremblant** (☎ 819-688-2281; reservations
800-665-6527; www.parksquebec.com; Chemin du Lac
Supérieur; adult/child per day $3.50/1.75), the prov-
ince's biggest and oldest park – it opened
in 1894. Covering 1510 sq km of gorgeous
Laurentian lakes, rivers, hills and woods,
the park boasts rare vegetation (including
silver maple and red oak), hiking and biking trails and canoe routes. It is home to
foxes, deer, moose and wolves, and a habitat for more than 200 bird species, including a huge blue heron colony.

The park is divided into three sectors.
The most developed area is the **Diable sector**,
home to beautiful Lac Monroe. The main
entrance is but 28km northeast of Station
Tremblant. The year-round service center,
which also has equipment rentals, is another 11km from the entrance.

Diable's incredible trails range from an
easy 20-minute stroll past waterfalls to day-
long hikes that take in stunning views of
majestic valleys. You can also take your
bike out on some trails or rent canoes; a
highly rated canoe trip goes down the serpentine Rivière Diable. The gentle section
between Lac Chat and La Vache Noir is
perfect for families.

QUÉBEC

Further east, the **Pimbina sector** is a 10-minute drive from St-Donat. Here you'll also find an **information center** (✆ mid-May–mid-Oct & mid-Dec–Mar), canoe and kayak rentals and campgrounds with some amenities. Activities include swimming at Lac Provost and hiking and biking trails nearby. A highlight is the **Carcan Trail**, a 14.4km route to the top of the park's second-highest peak (883m), which passes waterfalls and lush scenery on the way.

Further east is the **L'Assomption sector**, accessible via the town of St-Côme. It is the most untamed part of the park, with more trails, secluded cottages and remote camping options. In winter, you can't access this sector by car, as snow covers the roads.

The wilder interior and eastern sections are accessible by dirt roads, some of which are old logging routes. The off-the-beaten-track areas abound in wildlife. With some effort, it's possible to have whole lakes to yourself, except for the wolves whose howls you hear at night. By late August, nights start getting cold and a couple of months later a blanket of snow adds a magic touch. That's when cross-country skiing and snowshoeing are popular activities in the Diable and Pimbina sectors.

Some of the park's many campgrounds (tent sites $18.50 to $23) come with amenities, but most are basic. Reservations are recommended in busy periods. Some of the nicest spots can only be reached by canoe. There's also lodging in primitive backpacker huts (per person $21) and cozy cabins (per person $29 to $43).

MONTRÉAL TO QUÉBEC CITY

The St Lawrence River forms the main natural link between Montréal and Québec City, which are also joined by Hwy 40, a four-lane expressway that can get you from one city to the other in less than three hours. The road passes through Trois-Rivières, the gateway to the Mauricie, a region that manages to celebrate both its industrial heritage and the treasures bestowed by nature. South of the river, Hwy 20 is another fast route connecting Montréal and Québec City. Along with Hwy 10, it provides access to the Eastern Townships, a slow-paced rural area whose charming villages offer glimpses of old-time Québec.

EASTERN TOWNSHIPS

Known romantically as the 'Garden of Québec,' this region is a lush mosaic of rolling hills, green farmland, lakes and woodland – fitting images for an extension of the US Appalachians. Also called 'Cantons-des-l'Est' and 'L'Estrie' by French speakers, the region begins 80km southeast of Montréal and stretches to the Vermont and New Hampshire borders. New Englanders will feel right at home with the covered bridges and round barns.

Spring is the season for 'sugaring off' – the tapping, boiling and preparation of maple syrup (see the boxed text on p268). Summer brings fishing and swimming in the numerous lakes; in fall the foliage dazzles with drop-dead gorgeous colors, and apple cider is served in local pubs. Cycling is extremely popular in the warmer months, with nearly 500km of trails taking in sumptuous landscapes. In winter, there's excellent downhill skiing in Bromont, Mont Orford and Sutton.

Originally the territory of Abenakis, the townships were settled in the aftermath of the 1776 American Revolution by New England Loyalists seeking to remain under the British crown. They were joined by successive waves of immigrants from Ireland and Scotland as well as French Canadians who today make up the vast majority of residents.

The district is also home to a fast-growing wine region that produces some respectable whites and an excellent ice wine, a dessert wine made from frozen grapes.

The layout of the Eastern Townships is conducive to exploring in zigzag rather than linear fashion. Distances between villages are short and getting lost on the country roads is just part of the fun and often leads to unexpected discoveries. Sherbrooke, the biggest town, is located at the junction of two major highways, Hwy 55 leading to Drummondville where it joins with Hwy 20 to Québec City, and Hwy 10 to Montréal.

Besides the tourist offices listed under individual towns, you'll find branches in many other townships, although some are only open from June to September. Official hours are from 10am to 6pm between June and

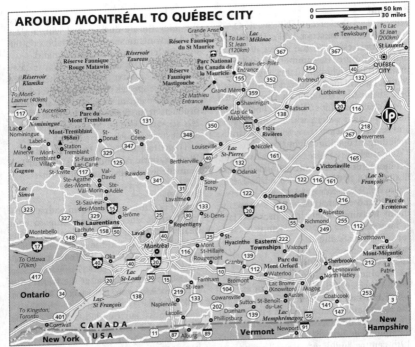

AROUND MONTRÉAL TO QUÉBEC CITY

September and from 10am to 5pm at other times. However, actual hours may vary, so it's best to call ahead. The **Eastern Townships Regional Tourism Office** (☎ 450-375-8774, 866-472-6292; www.easterntownships.cc; exit 68, Hwy 10) is at the turnoff for Granby/Bromont.

Getting There & Away

Coming from Montréal, Hwy 10 will take you straight to the Eastern Townships to just east of Sherbrooke where it continues as Rte 112. Coming from Québec City via Hwy 20, the fastest route is via Hwy 55 which you'll pick up near Drummondville.

Limocar operates bus service between Montréal's Station Centrale d'Autobus and Magog ($26, 1½ hours) and Sherbrooke ($30, 2½ hours) up to 15 times daily. Up to eight of these buses also stop in Granby ($18.50, one to 1½ hours), while Bromont is served twice daily ($21.50, 2¼ hours). From Friday to Monday, Limocar also has a service to Trois Rivières ($27, three hours) in the Mauricie region.

Autobus Viens operates a twice-daily bus service between Montréal's central bus sta-

tion and the townships of Sutton ($16, one hour) and Lac Brome ($17, 2¼ hours).

The ride-share organization **Allô Stop** (☎ 819-821-3637; 1204 Rue King Ouest) has a branch in Sherbrooke. Rides to Montréal/Québec City are $10/16.

Granby

The town isn't much, but you'll score big with your kids if you take them to the **Granby Zoo** (☎ 450-372-9113; www.zoodegranby.com; 525 Rue St-Hubert; adult/child 5-12 & senior $24/18; ⏰ 10am-7pm Jun-Aug, 10am-6pm Sat & Sun Sep–mid-Oct). The tigers, kangaroos, elephants and some 170 other species of finned, feathered and furry friends rarely fail to enthrall the little ones. If you think the cages are unpleasantly crammed, take comfort in the fact that plans are underway to bring the zoo into the 21st century. Tickets include admission to the **Parc Aquatique Amazoo**, a small water park with a churning wave pool and rides.

Granby is near exit 68 off Hwy 10. Limocar buses stop at Dépanneur Couche-Tard, 111 Rue St-Charles Sud.

Bromont

This town revolves around **Ski Bromont** (☎ 450-534-2200; www.skibromont.com; 150 Rue Champlain), a year-round resort on the slopes of 533m-high Mt Brome. In summer its 100km of marked trails, including 12 thrilling downhill routes, have made it a mecca for mountain bike aficionados (Bromont has even hosted world championships). Families flock to the hugely popular water park. In winter, skiers and snowboarders take over the 52 trails, including 30 open for night skiing.

On weekends from May to November, Bromont's other major attraction is its giant **flea market** (☎ 450-534-0440; 16 Rue Lafontaine; admission free; ☾ 9am-5pm Sat & Sun), just off Hwy 10, with more than 1000 vendors attracting thrifty treasure-hunters from near and far.

Limocar buses stop at Dépanneur Shefford, 624 Rue Shefford.

Lac Brome (Knowlton)

Lac Brome is the name of seven amalgamated towns orbiting the eponymous lake, with Knowlton on the southern shore being the largest and most attractive. First settled by Loyalists in 1802, the town still retains an upmarket British flair and numerous 19th-century buildings. A stroll around its cute downtown, which teems with quality boutiques, art galleries, cafés and restaurants, is a fun way to spend an hour or two. Pick up a free walking tour pamphlet from the Auberge Knowlton, which has been in business since 1849, making it the oldest continuously operating inn in the Eastern Townships. There is a **tourist office** (☎ 450-242-2870; 696 Chemin Lakeside; ☾ Jun–early Sep) on the northern lakeshore.

For more local history, drop in at the **Musée Historique du Comté de Brome** (☎ 450-243-6782; 130 Rue Lakeside; adult/child $5/2.50; ☾ 10am-4:30pm Mon-Sat, 11am-4:30pm Sun mid-May–mid-Sep), where exhibits include a recreated general store and courthouse and, incongruously, a WWI Fokker DVII plane.

Auberge Knowlton (☎ 450-242-6886; www.cclacbrome.qc.ca/AK; 286 Chemin Knowlton; d incl breakfast $110) is a landmark Victorian, in business since 1849, which has come a long way since the stagecoach days. Antique-style furniture meets modern amenities in the country-themed, spacious rooms. Breakfast is à la carte. Here you will also find **Le Relais** (☎ 450-242-2232; 286 Chemin Knowlton; mains lunch $9-14, dinner $17-28), a great place to try the juicy Brome duck paired with a glass of local wine. In summer, the tables on the upstairs terrace are much in demand.

Lac Brome is also famous for its tasty ducks, which have been bred here since 1912 on a special diet including soy and vitamins. You can pick up pâté and other products at the **Brome Lake Duck Farm** (☎ 450-242-3825; 40 Chemin Centre; ☾ 8am-5pm Mon-Fri, 10am-6pm Sat, 10am-5pm Sun).

To get to Lac Brome from Hwy 10, take Rte 243 south. Autobus Viens stops at Dépanneur Rouge, 483 Rue Knowlton.

Sutton

Sutton is a little Loyalist town with a pretty main street where you can shop to your heart's content or let your hair down during après ski partying in the many bars. There is Internet access at **Net Connect** (☎ 450-538-4198; 20 Place Sutton; per hr $5; ☾ 10am-5:30pm Mon-Sat) and information at the **tourist office** (☎ 450-538-8455; www.sutton-info.qc.ca; 11b Rue Principale Sud).

Sutton is surrounded by the Sutton Mountains, a string of velvety, round hills whose highest peak (Sommet Rond) rises to 968m. Not surprisingly, this makes Sutton a major winter sports hub with much of the action centered on **Mont Sutton** (☎ 450-538-2545; www.montsutton.com; 671 Chemin Maple; day ticket adult/child $44/25; ☾ 9am-4pm). You have 55 trails for plunging down the mountain; the longest run is 2.85km.

In summer, Sutton is prime hiking territory, especially in a conservation area called **Parc d'Environnement Naturel** (☎ 450-538-4085; adult/child day-fee $4/3; ☾ Jun-Oct) where 80km of trails have been carved through the thickly forested mountains. Backpackers can unfold their tents at three primitive campgrounds (the one at Lac Spruce is the nicest).

Inside a perfectly restored heritage building, **Auberge Le St-Amour** (☎ 450-538-6188, 888-538-6188; www.innsutton.com; s/d $70/105; ▯) is a pretty inn and a great place for a weekend escape or romantic interlude. Some of the pretty rooms have views of Mont Sutton and there's a good restaurant as well.

At **Le Bistro du 14** (☎ 450-538-2478; 14 Rue Principale; dishes $7-11; ☾ 9am-9pm late Jun–Oct, 10am-6pm Thu-Mon Nov-May), an airy upstairs bistro, you can watch owner Claudette prepare your meal right there in an open kitchen. It's a great spot for breakfast, light and healthy lunches or simply a coffee.

For a serious meal, book a table in the little cottage, **Le Gastronome** (☎ 450-538-2121; 6 Rue Principale; dishes $24-45; ☾ dinner), with its historic pressed metal ceiling and intriguing menu. How about the pan-seared caribou medallion with a purée of caramelized celery and carrots?

Sutton is 18km south of Knowlton via Rtes 104 and 215. Autobus Viens stops at the Esso gas station, 28 Rue Principale.

Valcourt

Valcourt would be a mere blip on the radar were it not for local resident Joseph Armand Bombardier, the father of the Ski-Doo (snowmobile) whose invention is a great source of pride to Canadians. At the **Musée J Armand Bombardier** (☎ 450-532-5300; www.musee bombardier.com; 1001 Ave J-A Bombardier; adult/student & senior $5/3; ☾ 10am-5pm May-Aug, 10am-5pm Tue-Sun Sep-Apr) you can see early models of his Ski-Doo (and amusing historic clips of how they looked in action), the original workshop and a collection of contemporary and vintage snowmobiles. Tours of the plant, which also churns out ATVs and Sea-Doos, are offered as well (for an additional $5/3).

To get to Valcourt, take exit 90 off Hwy 10, then follow Rte 243. There are no buses.

Magog

Magog occupies a prime spot on the north shore of **Lac Memphrémagog**, a banana-shaped lake that stretches south for 44km, all the way across the US border.

INFORMATION

CLSC Health Clinic (☎ 819-843-2572; 50 Rue St-Patrice Est)

La Petite Place (☎ 819-847-3067; 108 Place du Commerce; per hr $6; ☾ 8:30am-5pm Mon-Thu, to 7:30pm Wed-Fri, to 4pm Sat & Sun) Internet access; tucked into the basement, in the back of the parking lot.

Tourist office (☎ 819-843-2744; www.tourisme -memphremagog.com; 55 Rue Cabana) Off Rte 112.

SIGHTS & ACTIVITIES

There's a **beach** in Magog, but on hot summer days carving out space for your towel can be a tall order. Since the rest of the shore is largely in private hands, the lake is best explored from the water. **Club de Voile** (☎ 819-847-3181; Plage des Cantons) is among

several outfitters renting kayaks, sailboats and windsurfing equipment, while **Croisières Memphrémagog** (☎ 819-843-8068; adult/child $20/10; ☾ mid-May–Sep) offers 1¾–hour narrated cruises. Watch out for Memphré, the feisty yet elusive creature that lives, Nessie-style, at the lake bottom!

SLEEPING

À L'Ancestrale B&B (☎ 819-847-5555, 888-847-5507; www.ancestrale.com; 200 Rue Abbott; r incl breakfast $95-125; ☐) Wake up to a four-course gourmet breakfast at this intimate retreat whose four rooms are dressed in a romantic, countrified look and outfitted with refrigerators and coffee makers. It's central but on a quiet street.

Auberge du Centre d'Arts Orford (☎ 819-843-3981; 3165 Chemin du Parc; cabin per person $23, s/d $44/58) This inn on the woodsy grounds of the Centre d'Arts makes a good base for exploring Parc du Mont Orford. Rooms are basic but modern and comfortable. If you like roughing it, rent one of the rustic cabins (basically tiny permanent tents with shared facilities, summer only).

Also recommended:

Auberge Au Lion d'Or (☎ 819-843-6000, 877-843-6000; www.auliondor.com; 2240 Chemin du Parc; s $95-145, d $110-165; ☐ ☒) En route to Parc du Mont Orford with outdoor pool and gourmet restaurant.

La Belle Victorienne B&B (☎ 819-847-0476, 888-440-0476; www.bellevic.com; 142 Rue Merry Nord; d $95-125; ☐) A daintily elegant Victorian in central Magog.

EATING

Bistro Lady of the Lake (☎ 819-868-2004; mains $13-19; ☾ dinner Tue-Sun) The lakeside location is a major asset of this bustling eatery, which serves uncomplicated food for all tastes. In winter, its homemade brews draw a big après-ski crowd.

Auberge Georgeville (☎ 819-843-8683; 71 Rte 247; 5-course dinner $40; ☾ dinner) People flock from near and far for the good-value gourmet dinners at this hilltop Victorian inn (rooms from $235) on Lac Memphrémagog's eastern shore, about 25 minutes from downtown Magog. Many dishes feature such Québec products as caribou, Brome duckling and Gaspé crayfish. Reservations recommended.

For light vegetarian meals, try La Petite Place Internet café.

GETTING THERE & AWAY

Limocar buses stop at 768 Rue Sherbrooke.

Abbaye St-Benoît-du-Lac

About 12km south of Magog, on the western lakeshore, is the **Abbaye St-Benoît-du-Lac** (☎ 819-843-4080; www.st-benoit-du-lac.com; admission free; ☯ church 5am-9pm, gift shop 9-10:45am & 11:45am-4:30pm Mon-Sat Sep-Jun, to 6pm Jul & Aug), home to about 50 Benedictine monks. The complex is a striking blend of traditional and modern architecture, including a hallway awash in colorful tiles and a lofty church with exposed structural beams and brick walls. If you can, visit at 11am or 5pm (or Thursday at 7pm) when the monks practice Gregorian chant. Music CDs, cheeses and apple cider are among the products for sale in the gift shop.

Parc du Mont Orford

About a 10-minute drive north of Magog, **Parc du Mont Orford** (☎ 819-843-9855; 3321 Chemin du Parc; adult/child per day $3.50/1.50; ☯ year-round), home to snapping turtles and countless bird species, is fairly compact and often gets busy. Fitness freaks can peak-bag the park's two mountains, **Mont Chauve** (600m) and **Mont Orford** (853m), while water babies have three lakes in which to play. The biggest is Lac Stukely, which has a beach, camping, boat rentals and other infrastructure.

Winter activities include snowshoeing and cross-country skiing in the park as well as downhill skiing at the **Station de Ski Mont-Orford** (☎ 819-843-6548; www.orford.com; lift tickets adult/child $44/26; ☯ 9am-4pm). It offers a vertical drop of 540m and 54 slopes, mostly for beginners and intermediate skiers, plus a snow park with half-pipe and other fun features.

Just outside the park boundaries, the **Centre d'Arts Orford** (Orford Arts Center; ☎ 819-843-9871; 3165 Chemin du Parc; tickets $27-50) hosts the **Festival Orford**, a prestigious series of 40 to 50 classical concerts, from late June to mid-August.

North Hatley

North Hatley wins top honors as the cutest of all the cute Eastern Townships. It occupies an enchanting spot at the northern tip of the picture-perfect (and monsterless) Lac Massawippi, about 17km east of Magog.

Rich Americans have always loved it here, so much so, in fact, they started building their stately vacation homes as early as 1880. A Yankee influence still makes itself felt (there are as many cow paintings and scented candles here as anywhere in New England!) and Rue Principale is even sometimes referred to as 'Main St.' Many of the fancy homes have been converted into B&Bs, inns or gourmet restaurants, including the ultra-deluxe Auberge Hatley.

A great way to explore the delightful terrain surrounding North Hatley is on horseback; **Randonées Jacques Robidas** (☎ 819-563-0166) offers rides year-round.

Days begin with a delicious multicourse breakfast and end with creamy chocolates at **Tapioca B&B** (☎ 819-842-2743; www.tapioca.qc .ca; 680 Chemin Sherbrooke; r incl breakfast $115-155), backed onto a big, flower-filled garden. Rooms have private bathrooms and small balconies.

One of the region's top addresses, **Auberge Hatley** (☎ 819-842-2451, 800-336-2451; www.auberge hatley.com; 325 Chemin Virgin; r incl breakfast & dinner $290-590; ☐ ☒) is a member of the prestigious Relais & Chateau association and regularly counts dignitaries and celebrities among its guests. Rooms are all you could wish for, and the meals? To die for!

Pilsen (☎ 819-842-2971; 55 Rue Principale; mains $9-17; ☯ lunch & dinner) is the liveliest restaurant in town, famous for its salmon, both grilled and smoked, and upmarket pub fare. There's a nice riverside terrace and another facing the lake.

Like the Auberge Hatley, **Manoir Hovey** (☎ 819-842-2421; 575 Chemin Hovey; 3-course dinner $55; ☯ dinner) is another of the area's premier dining rooms where the emphasis is on refined Québecois fare prepared from fresh and local ingredients.

North Hatley is about 17km east of Magog along Rte 108. Coming from Sherbrooke, take Rte 243 to Rte 108. There is no bus service.

Sherbrooke

Sherbrooke is the region's largest city and its administrative and industrial capital. It has Internet access at **Presse Boutique Café** (☎ 819-822-2133; Rue Wellington Nord; per hr $6; ☯ 10am-11pm); the **Hospital Hôtel-Dieu** (☎ 891-346-1110; 580 Rue Bowen Sud) if you need medical services; a **National Bank of Canada** (☎ 819-563-7832; 3075 Boul Portland; ☯ 10am-3pm Mon & Tue, 10am-7pm Wed, 10am-8pm Thu, 10am-4pm Fri); and a **tourist office** (☎ 819-821-1919; www.tourisme sherbrooke.com; 3010 Rue King Ouest).

The historic center sits at the confluence of two rivers and is bisected by Rue Wellington and Rue King, the main commercial arteries. On weekend nights, raucous partying erupts in Rue Wellington's many bars and cafés. Quietly overlooking the action from its hilltop perch south of there is the **Cathédrale St-Michel** (☎ 819-563-9371; 130 Rue de la Cathédrale; admission free; ☾ 9am-noon & 2-4pm), a monumental granite edifice.

North of here, across the Rivière Magog on Rue Dufferin, are Sherbrooke's two major museums. The **Musée des Beaux-Arts** (☎ 819-821-2115; 241 Rue Dufferin; adult/student $6/5; ☾ 1-5pm Tue-Sun, to 9pm Wed) has a good permanent collection featuring works by regional artists and also stages temporary exhibits. Next door, the **Centre d'Interprétation de l'Histoire de Sherbrooke** (☎ 819-821-5406; 275 Rue Dufferin; adult/student $6/5; ☾ 9am-5pm Tue-Fri, 10am-5pm Sat & Sun late Jun–Sep, 9am-noon Tue-Fri, 1-5pm Tue-Sun Oct–mid-Jun) offers an engaging introduction to the town's history and rents out tapes for self-guided city tours on foot or by car ($10).

Further south, Rivière Magog flows into the pretty **Lac des Nations**, surrounded by a scenic paved trail perfect for walking, in-line skating and bicycling (rentals available).

For an interesting contrast to francophone Sherbrooke, swing by **Lennoxville**, which is as English as tea and crumpets, although only 5km south of the city center (take bus Nos 2 or 82). This is largely due to the dominant presence of the Anglican **Bishop's University** (☎ 819-822-9600; Rue du Collège), founded in 1843 and modeled after Oxford and Cambridge in England. The campus' architectural highlight is **St Mark's Chapel** (admission free; ☾ 8:30am-5pm), richly decorated with carved pews and stained-glass windows.

If you'd like to spend the night in Sherbrooke, you'll find several motels on Rue King Ouest.

Brasserie Daniel (☎ 819-346-7989; 380 Rue King Ouest; mains $13-26; ☾ lunch & dinner), with its huge, dimly lit dining room has been a local favorite for three decades. The menu is big on steaks and seafood, with a few token vegetarian dishes. It helps if you speak some French.

Sherbrooke lies along Hwy 10, about 25km northeast of Magog. The Limocar bus terminal is at 80 Rue du Depôt.

Coaticook

South of Sherbrooke lies a sweet and rural region of rolling valleys, painted barns, grain silos and covered bridges crossing brooks with names like Moe's or Niger. This is dairy country and with more than 300 farms it's no surprise that cows outnumber people here, earning the area the moniker of 'Québec's milk basin.' The **Festival du Lait** (Milk Festival) takes place in Coaticook, the regional hub, every August.

Coaticook is also home to the **world's longest suspended footbridge** (169m, as certified by no lesser authority than the *Guinness Book of World Records*). The 1887 original succumbed to flooding a few years ago, but its successor is just as impressive. The 50m-high bridge dangles above a craggy river-carved gorge and is easily spotted from the side of the road. If you want to cross it (not recommended for the vertigo-prone), you'll have to pay admission to the **Parc de la Gorge** (☎ 819-849-2331; 135 Rue Michaud; adult/child $7/4; ☾ year-round), which also gives access to hiking, biking and cross-country skiing trails.

Parc du Mont-Mégantic

At the heart of a scenic and delightfully uncrowded area, the **Parc du Mont-Mégantic** (☎ 819-888-2941; 189 Rte du Parc; day entry adult/child $3.50/1.50; ☾ 9am-11pm Jun-Aug, 9am-5pm Sep–May) holds mega-sized appeal for wilderness fans and stargazers. Encounters with moose, white-tailed deer, coyote and other wildlife are pretty much guaranteed as you roam the trails of this park.

The park's **AstroLab** (☎ 819-888-2941; www .astrolab.qc.ca; adult/child $10.50/8, summit tours day $13/10, night $19/13; ☾ noon-11pm late-Jun–late-Aug, noon-5pm Sat & Sun, also 8-11pm Sat late May–late Jun & late Aug–mid-Oct) is an astronomy research center that explains space through interactive exhibits and a multimedia show. A highlight is a tour of the observatory at the summit. Reservations are required.

The park is approximately 60km east of Sherbrooke along Rtes 108 and 212. There is no bus service.

MAURICIE

Mauricie is one of Québec's less-known regions, despite being in a strategic spot halfway between Montréal and Québec City. Stretching 300km from Trois-Rivières north to Lac St Jean, it follows the flow of the mighty St Maurice River, which for centuries has been the backbone of the area's industrial heritage. Logs were being driven down the river to the pulp and paper mills until as late as 1996. Centuries earlier, the region had given birth to the country's iron industry; the original forge is now a national historic site. Industry still dominates the lower region, but things get considerably more scenic after the river reaches La Mauricie National Park.

Trois-Rivières

Founded in 1634, Trois-Rivières is North America's second-oldest city north of Mexico, but you'd never know it: a roaring fire that swept through in 1908 left little of the city's historic looks. Still, the city center, right on the north shore of the St Lawrence River, is not without charms and some bona fide tourist attractions. The name, by the way, is a misnomer as there are only two, not three, streams here. There are, however, three branches of the St Maurice River at its mouth, where islands split its flow into three channels.

ORIENTATION

Rue Notre Dame and Rue des Forges, the main arteries in Trois-Rivières' compact downtown, are lined with cafés and bars. A riverfront promenade leads to the oldest section of town along Rue des Ursulines.

INFORMATION

Caisse Populaire (☎ 819-693-3833; 5700 Boul Jean XXII; ☪ 10am-2pm Mon-Sat, to 8pm Thu) The only currency exchange, about 2.5km north of downtown.

Hôpital St-Joseph (☎ 819-697-3333; 731 Rue Ste-Julie)

Le Bucafin Internet Café & Laundromat (☎ 819-376-2122; 920 Rue St-Maurice; per hr $2.50; ☪ 8:30am-10pm Mon-Fri, 9:30am-11pm Sat & Sun)

Main Post Office (Rue des Casernes, cnr of Rue des Ursulines)

Tourist Office (☎ 819-375-1122; 1457 Rue Notre Dame; ☪ 8am-8pm Jun–early Sep, 9am-5pm Mon-Fri, 10am-4pm Sat & Sun early Sep–Oct, 9am-5pm Mon-Fri Nov-May)

SIGHTS & ACTIVITIES

For a town its size, Trois-Rivières has an astonishing number of museums, even if many are only of moderate interest. Unquestionably the most intriguing is **En Prison** (In Prison; ☎ 819-372-0406; 200 Rue Laviolette; adult/child/student $6.50/2.50/4.50; ☪ 9:30am-6:30pm Jun-Aug, 10am-5pm Tue-Sun Sep-May), an exhibit housed in an 1822 prison that remained open for business until 1986. Ex-cons bring the harsh realities of the lock-up vividly to life during 90-minute tours (unfortunately in French only) that include a stop at dark and dank underground cells known as 'the pit.' The prison exhibit is affiliated with the adjacent **Musée Québecois de Culture Populaire** (☎ 819-372-0406; adult/child/student incl En Prison $9/6.50/7.50; ☪ 9:30am-6:30pm Jun-Aug, 10am-5pm Tue-Sun Sep-May), which has a renowned regional folk art collection and changing exhibits, often with a quirky pop culture bent.

For a slice of the town's religious history, stop at the **Musée des Ursulines** (☎ 819-375-7922; 734 Rue des Ursulines; adult/student $3/2; ☪ 1-5pm Wed-Sun Mar & Apr, 9am-5pm Tue-Fri & 1-5pm Sat & Sun May-Oct). The former hospital founded by Ursuline nuns in 1639 forms a pretty backdrop for the fine collection of textiles, ceramics, books and prints related to religion. Beautiful frescoes adorn the chapel.

Church fans should also make a beeline to the colossal **Cathédrale de l'Assumption** (☎ 819-374-2409; 362 Rue Bonaventure; admission free; ☪ 7am-noon & 2-5pm), a soaring neo-Gothic confection with exquisite sculpture and intricate Florentine stained-glass windows.

In nearby Cap de la Madeleine (take bus No 2), about 4km northeast of the center, the even grander **Sanctuaire Notre Dame du Cap** (☎ 819-374-2441; 626 Rue Notre Dame; admission free; ☪ 8:30am-8pm) looks like a spaceship on a launch pad. Up to 1660 worshippers can congregate underneath the dome while being serenaded by a giant Casavant organ. A Marian shrine with a miracle-performing statue draws believers year round.

About 7km northwest of the centre (take bus No 4), **Les Forges-du-Saint-Maurice** (☎ 819-378-5116; www.parkscanada.gc.ca/forges; 10,000 Boul des Forges; adult/child $4/2; ☪ 9:30am-5:30pm mid-May–early Sep, 9:30am-4:30pm Sep & Oct) is a national historic site preserving the 18th-century birthplace of the Canadian iron industry. Costumed guides take you around the grounds and into the blast furnace, while a sound-and-light show reveals the daily operations of Canada's first ironworks.

Croisières/Cruises (☎ 819-375-3000) runs various cruises – mostly 90-minute spins on the St Lawrence and St Mauricie Rivers ($14) – from the landing docks at the foot of Rue des Forges.

SLEEPING & EATING

L'Emerillon B&B (☎ 819-375-1010; www.gitescanada
.com/1949.html; 890 Terrasse Turcotte; r $65-105) This
is, hands-down, one of the classiest B&Bs
we've ever seen. A grand wooden staircase
leads to the four rooms, the nicest of which
features a heavenly four-poster bed and balcony with river views. There are two large
common rooms with a billiards table, telescope and piano.

Auberge Le Fleurvil (☎ 819-372-5195; www
.fleurvil.qc.ca; 635 Rue des Ursulines; s $65-85, d $80-120;
☐ ☎) Operated by a gregarious Harley afi-
cionado with a knack for decorating, this
enchanting inn fronts a lush garden with
pool. Most of the nine rooms have private
facilities.

Orangekaki Bistro & Bar (☎ 819-375-5358; 120
Rue des Forges; mains $10-22; ☺ lunch & dinner, brunch
Sat & Sun) This bustling spot, with its quasi-
industrial looks, is great for quaffing a cold
one or digging into heaped plates of food.
Mussels, prepared in nine different ways,
are a specialty.

Le Muscadin (☎ 819-691-9080; 60 Rue des Forges;
dishes $3-9; ☺ 9am-5:30pm Tue-Sat) At this stylish
deli, the homemade soups, quiches, sandwiches and other light fare are served with
a side of original art gracing the walls.

GETTING THERE & AWAY

Trois-Rivières lies about 150km northeast of
Montréal and 130km southwest of Québec
City and is easily accessible via Hwys 40
and 20 or Rtes 138 and 132.

The **bus station** (☎ 819-374-2944; 275 Rue St-
Georges) is located behind the Hôtel Delta.
Orléans Express runs eight daily buses to
Montréal ($27, 1½ to 2½ hours) and six
daily to Québec City ($26, 1¾ hours). Limo-
car operates services to/from Sherbrooke
in the Eastern Townships from Friday to
Monday ($27, three hours).

Shawinigan

There would be little reason to stop in
Shawinigan were it not for the unique **Cité
de l'Énergie** (City of Energy; ☎ 819-536-8516; www
.citedelenergie.com; 1000 Ave Melville; adult/child/student
$15/8/13, tours $7; ☺ 10am-6pm Jul & Aug, 10am-5pm
Tue-Sun Jun & Sep, last admission 2½ hrs before closing).
Built around a 1901 hydroelectric power
station and the country's oldest aluminum
smelter, it celebrates the region's industrial
legacy with lots of different exhibits and

experiences. You'll learn all about turbines,
electrochemistry, aluminum and pulp and
papermaking in a multimedia show and
exhibits. A 'walk-through comic book' will
have you racing along with scientists who
must save the environment through switching to nonpolluting hydrogen. There are
river and trolleybus cruises, a 115m-high
observation tower and the nightly **Kosmo-
gonia** (adult/child $37/18; ☺ Jul & Aug) spectacle
featuring musicians, dancers and acrobats.
Throughout the summer, the National Gallery of Canada moves into the aluminum
smelter with different world-class temporary exhibits. Most labeling is in English
and French, but the tours are in French
only (so far).

Shawinigan is about 40km north of Trois-
Rivières via Hwy 55. Orléans Express runs
two buses daily from Trois-Rivières ($10,
50 minutes).

Parc National du Canada de la Mauricie

Moose foraging by an idyllic lake, the
plaintive cry of a loon gliding across the
water, bear cubs romping beneath a pot-
pourri of birch, poplar, maple and other
trees waiting to put on a spectacular show
of color in the fall – these are scenes you
might quite possibly stumble across while
visiting **La Mauricie National Park** (☎ 819-538-
3232, 888-855-6673; www.pc.gc.ca/mauricie; adult/child
$5/2.50). What may well be Québec's best-
run and best-organized park is also among
its most frequented. The arresting beauty
of the nature here, whether seen from a
canoe or a walking trail, is everyone's eye
candy, but particularly suits those who
don't want to feel completely disconnected
from 'civilization.'

The park covers 550 sq km, straddling
northern evergreen forests and the more
southerly hardwoods of the St Lawrence
River Valley. The low, rounded Laurentian
Mountains, which are among the world's
oldest, are part of the Canadian Shield,
which covers much of the province. Between these hills lie innumerable small
lakes and valleys. The Canadian government created the park in 1970 to protect
some of the forest that the paper industry
was steadily chewing up and spitting out.
At one point, two sawmills were operating
in the park's current territory. But that's all
in the past now.

ORIENTATION & INFORMATION

The main entrance is at **St-Jean-des-Piles** (Hwy 55, exit 226), but there's another at **St-Mathieu** (Hwy 55, exit 217). Both are well indicated and double as **information centers** (⏰ 7am-10pm Jun–early Sep, 9am-4:30pm Sat-Thu, to 10pm Fri May & early Sep–Oct). They are connected by the 63km-long Rte Promenade, which runs through the park. St Mathieu is closed from late October until early May.

ACTIVITIES

The numerous **walking trails**, which can take you anywhere from a half-hour to five days to complete, offer glimpses of the indigenous flora and fauna, brooks and waterfalls (the **Chutes Waber** in the park's western sector are particularly worth the hike), as well as panoramic views onto delicate valleys, lakes and streams.

The longest trail, **Le Sentier Laurentien**, stretches over 75km of rugged wilderness in the park's northern reaches. Backcountry campsites are spaced out every seven to 10km. No more than 40 people are allowed on the trail at any time, making reservations essential. There's a fee of $39 and you must arrange for your own transport to cover the 30km from the trail's end back to the Route Promenade. Topographic maps are for sale at the park.

The park is excellent for **canoeing**. Five canoe routes, ranging in length from 14km to 84km, can accommodate everyone from beginners to experts. Canoe rentals ($20 per day) are available at three sites, the most popular being **Lac Wapizagonke**, which has sandy beaches, steep rocky cliffs and waterfalls. One popular day trip has you canoeing from the Wapizagonke campground to the west end of the lake, followed by a 7.5km loop hike to the Chutes Waber and back by canoe.

The most popular winter activity is **cross-country skiing**, with some 85km of groomed trails (adult/student/senior $8/4/7).

SLEEPING & EATING

Camping at designated sites costs $21 without electricity and $23 with it; camping in the wild during canoe trips costs $13 without a campfire permit, or $19 with one.

You can also sleep in four- to 10-person dorms in one of two **outdoor lodges** (☎ reservations 819-537-4555; per person $25). They are 3.5km

from the nearest parking lots, so you must come in by foot, bike, canoe or ski.

There are no restaurants in the park, so the best thing is to stock up on supplies in Trois-Rivières or Shawinigan before heading north.

QUÉBEC CITY

☎ 418 / pop 167,000

Everybody enjoys Québec City, known simply as Québec. Age, background and thickness of wallet don't matter. With historic character in the very air, a wonderful location perched on a cliff overlooking the St Lawrence River, cozy inns, fabulous eating and reasonable prices, how can you miss?

The city is the cradle and protector of French culture in North America and the heart that first beat the province's blood. Moreover, it is the jewel of the province. Since 1985, the entire old town has been placed on the UN's prestigious world heritage list. The central core is a living museum, each street a page in the book of French Canada's struggle for survival, even dominion, in British North America. The old part of Québec remains the only walled city in the USA and Canada.

Yet it is also a lively capital with a compact, vibrant downtown population of just 167,000 people. As a major tourist mecca, that number swells by some eight million visitors a year, 13% of them from outside Canada. Québec can hands-down lay claim to being the most 'European' city on the continent. Old Montréal shares this feeling to some degree, as does the French Quarter in New Orleans, but nowhere else in North America is the picture as complete.

Aside from its work as the center of government, the city also has an important port. In conjunction with Laval University, 'new-economy' high-tech enterprises are developing, particularly in such specialized fields as photonics, geomatics, biotechnology, nutraceuticals and software.

Although many residents are bilingual, the vast majority are French-speaking and 94% can claim French ancestors. But because this is primarily a tourist town – ranking with Banff and Victoria as one of the country's most-visited destinations – most service industry staff can, at a minimum, communicate in English.

HISTORY

One of the continent's earliest settlements, the site was already a Huron village called 'Stadacona' when French explorer Jacques Cartier landed in 1535 on his second voyage to the New World. He returned in 1541 to start a post upstream, but the plan failed, setting back France's colonial ambitions for 50 years. Explorer Samuel de Champlain finally founded the city for the French in 1608, calling it Kebec, from the Algonquian word meaning 'the river narrows here.'

The English successfully attacked in 1629, but Québec was returned to the French under a treaty three years later and it became the center of New France. Repeated English attacks followed. In 1759, General Wolfe led the British to victory over Montcalm on the Plains of Abraham. One of North America's most famous battles, it virtually ended the long-running conflict between Britain and France. In 1763, the Treaty of Paris gave Canada to Britain. In 1775, the American revolutionaries tried to capture Québec but were promptly pushed back. In 1864, meetings were held here that lead to the formation of Canada in 1867. Québec City became the provincial capital.

In the 19th century, the city lost its status and importance to Montréal. When the Great Depression burst Montréal's bubble in 1929, Québec City regained some stature as a government center. Some business-savvy locals launched the now-famous Winter Carnival in the 1950s to incite a tourism boom. Obviously, it's still working.

In 2001, the city was the site of the Summit of the Americas, which exploded into mass demonstrations against globalization. Images of authorities battling protesters were broadcast around the globe. In 2008, the city will celebrate the 400th anniversary of its founding. Hold on tight.

ORIENTATION

The city itself is surprisingly small, covering 93 sq km, with nearly all things of interest packed into one compact, walkable district.

Part of the city sits atop the cliffs of **Cap Diamant** (Cape Diamond), and part lies below. Québec is thus divided into **Haute Ville** (Upper Town) and **Basse Ville** (Lower Town), each with old and new sections. The Citadelle, a fort and landmark, stands on the highest point of Cap Diamant. Together, the 10 sq km of these historic upper and lower areas, within the stone walls, form the appealing **Vieux Québec** (Old Town).

The other major landmark is the splendid, dominating, copper-topped, castle-style Fairmont Le Château Frontenac hotel dating from 1892. Behind the château, a large boardwalk called the Terrasse Dufferin edges along the cliff, providing fabulous views across the river. Below Château Frontenac is **Old Lower Town**, the oldest section of the city.

The two main streets heading southwest from **Old Upper Town** are Boul René Lévesque and, to the south, Grande Allée, which eventually becomes Boul Wilfrid Laurier.

The wider area of Lower Town has the highways leading north, east and west. To the extreme southwest of the city are Pont de Québec or Pont Pierre Laporte, both bridges leading to the south shore.

To get oriented, Obsérvatoire de la Capitale (p286) gives views from 31 floors up.

If you're driving, your plan should be to get to Vieux Québec, then park the car for the duration of your stay. **Lévis**, both a suburb and a town in its own right, is seen directly across the river from Old Québec.

INFORMATION
Map pp282–3

Internet Access

Bibliothèque Collège de Jésuites (☎ 418-691-6492; 775 Rue St Jean) Provides unique, must-see, ecclesiastical (and free) Internet access. Get a no-cost temporary membership.

Centre Internet (☎ 418-692-3359; 52 Côte de Palais; ⏱ 10am-10pm)

Medical Services

Health Info (☎ 418-648-2626; ⏱ 24hr) For consultations with nurses.

L'Hôtel Dieu de Québec (☎ 418-525-4444; 11 Côte de Palais; ⏱ 24hr) A centrally located hospital with emergency services.

Money

Transchange International (☎ 418-694-6906; 43 Rue de Buade; ⏱ 8am-10pm May-Oct, 9am-5pm Nov-Apr) Currency exchange.

Tourist Information

Centre Infotouriste (☎ 418-649-2608, 800-363-7777; www.bonjourquebec.com; 12 Rue Ste Anne; ⏱ 8:30am-7:30pm Jun-Sep, 9am-5pm Oct-May) Busy provincial tourist office; also handles city inquiries. Tour operators also have counters here.

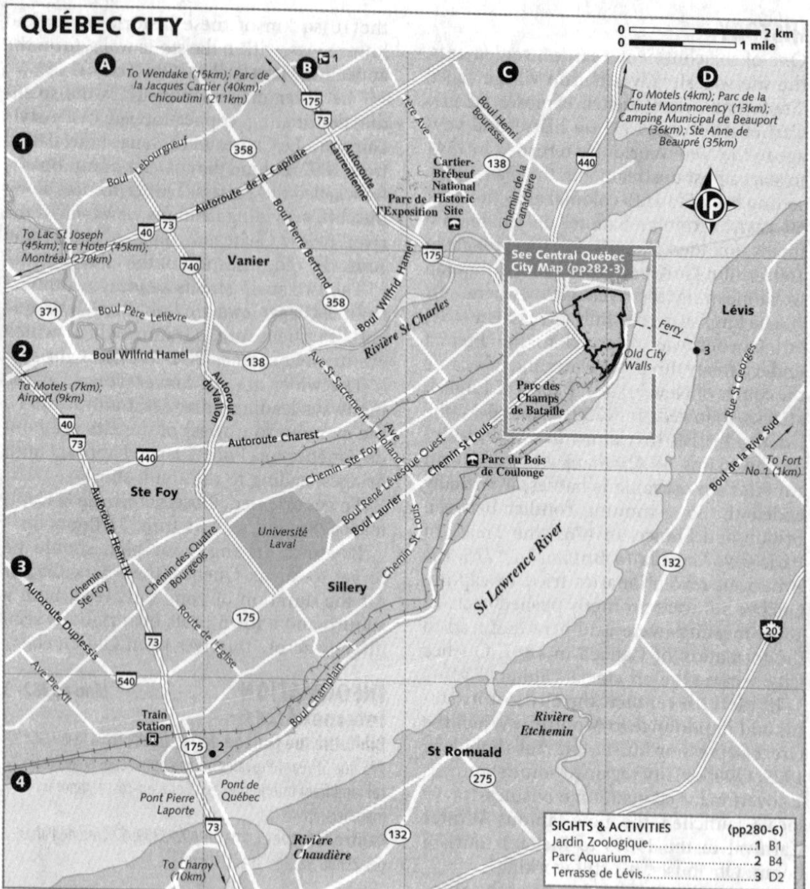
QUÉBEC CITY
0 2 km
0 1 mile
A
B
C
D
1
2
3
4
To Wendake (15km); Parc de la Jacques Cartier (40km); Chicoutimi (211km)
To Motels (4km); Parc de la Chute Montmorency (13km); Camping Municipal de Beauport (36km); Ste Anne de Beaupré (35km)
To Lac St Joseph (45km); Ice Hotel (45km); Montréal (270km)
To Motels (7km); Airport (9km)
To Fort No 1 (1km)
To Charny (10km)
Boul Lebourgneuf
Autoroute de la Capitale
Autoroute Laurentienne
Boul Pierre Bertrand
1ère Ave
Boul Henri Bourassa
Chemin de la Canardière
Cartier-Brébeuf National Historic Site
Parc de l'Exposition
Vanier
Boul Wilfrid Hamel
Boul Père Lelièvre
Rivière St Charles
See Central Québec City Map (pp282-3)
Old City Walls
Ferry
Lévis
Rue St Georges
Ave St Sacrément
Autoroute du Vallon
Autoroute Charest
Ave Holland
Chemin Ste Foy
Boul René Lévesque Ouest
Chemin St Louis
Parc des Champs de Bataille
Parc du Bois de Coulonge
Boul de la Rive Sud
Ste Foy
Autoroute Henri IV
Université Laval
Boul Laurier
Chemin St Louis
St Lawrence River
Chemin des Quatre Bourgeois
Chemin Ste Foy
Autoroute Duplessis
Route de l'Église
Sillery
Ave Pie XII
Boul Champlain
Train Station
Rivière Etchemin
St Romuald
Pont de Québec
Pont Pierre Laporte
Rivière Chaudière
SIGHTS & ACTIVITIES (pp280-6)
Jardin Zoologique 1 B1
Parc Aquarium 2 B4
Terrasse de Lévis 3 D2

Kiosk Frontenac A tourist information booth on Terrasse Dufferin facing the Château Frontenac; makes reservations for all city activities and is the starting point for some tours.

Québec City Tourist Office (☎ 418-641-6290; www.quebecregion.com; 835 Ave Wilfrid Laurier; 🕑 8:30am-7:30pm Jun 24–Labour Day, to 6:30pm Labour Day–mid-Oct, 9am-5pm Mon-Sat, 1-5pm Sun mid-Oct–late Jun) This official city information office is less crowded.

SIGHTS

Pretty much the entire walled city can be considered an attraction, with virtually every building holding some historic and/or architectural interest. Despite that, there are not many outstanding, must-see individual points of note.

Old Upper Town

Map pp282–3

FORTIFICATIONS OF QUÉBEC

The largely restored old wall is a national historic site. You can walk the complete 4.6km circuit on top of it all around the Old Town for free. From this vantage point, much of the city's history is within easy view. At the old Powder Building beside Porte St Louis, the **interpretation center** (☎ 418-648-7016; 100 Rue St Louis; adult/student $3.50/3; 🕑 9am-5pm mid-May–mid-Oct) provides information. It also runs guided 90-minute **walking tours** ($10, kids free with paying adult) from here and the Kiosk Frontenac on Terrasse Dufferin.

Beside the wall, two short blocks north of Porte St Jean, the **Parc d'Artillerie** (☎ 418-648-

4205; 2 Rue d'Auteuil; adult/student $3.50/3; ⏱ 10am-5pm Apr–mid-Oct) is another national historic site. Formerly housing French military headquarters and then a British garrison, this interpretation center includes a scale model of Québec in the year 1800 and a history lesson for kids.

LA CITADELLE

The dominating **Citadelle** (Fort; ☎ 418-694-2815; Côte de la Citadelle; adult/child/senior $8/4.50/7; ⏱ 9am or 10am–5pm or 6pm Apr-Sep, 10am-3pm Oct) was begun by the French in 1750, but completed by the British in 1820 after 30 years of work, and served as part of the defense system against invading Americans.

Today the Citadelle is the home base of Canada's Royal 22s (known in bastardized French as the Van Doos, from the French for 22, *vingt-deux*), a French regiment that developed quite a reputation in both world wars and the Korean War. The museum outlines the group's history and includes a guided tour of the Citadelle (which you aren't allowed to visit on your own). The **changing of the guard** ceremony takes place at 10am each day in the summer months. The **beating of the retreat**, which features soldiers banging on their drums at shift's end, happens at 6pm on Tuesday, Thursday, Saturday and Sunday during July and August. It's a small bit of Canadiana right in the heart of Québec.

BATTLEFIELDS PARK

This huge park runs southwest from the Citadelle. Its hills, gardens, monuments and trees are now perfect for strolling, cycling etc. But this was once a bloody battleground, the site of a conflict that determined the course of Canadian history. The part closest to the cliff is known as the **Plains of Abraham** – it was here in 1759 that the British finally defeated the French, with both generals, Wolfe of Britain and Montcalm of France, dying in the process.

Within the park are diverse sites. The reception center at the **Discovery Pavilion** (☎ 418-648-4071; 835 Ave Wilfred Laurier; admission free; ⏱ 9am-5:30pm) makes a good place to start. The staff offer park bus tours and sell ticket packages, which are worthwhile if you want to see multiple attractions. Also there is **Canada Odyssey** (www.odysseecanada.com; adult/child $7/5.50), a 75-minute multimedia show focusing on the famous battle.

National Battlefields Park Interpretive Centre (☎ 418-648-5641; adult/child $3.50/3; ⏱ 10am-5:30pm mid-May–mid-Oct, 10am-5:30pm Tue-Sun mid-Oct–mid-May) focuses on the dramatic history of the park with yet another multimedia show, and has soldiers' uniforms. It's west of Discovery Pavilion.

The standout museum in the park is really an art gallery. The worthwhile **Musée du Québec** (☎ 418-643-2150; www.mdq.org; admission free; ⏱ 10am-6pm Thu-Tue, Jun–Labour Day, 10am-5pm

QUÉBEC

QUÉBEC CITY IN...

Two Days

Jump right in with breakfast at **Casse Crêpe Breton** (p289). Start your explorations within the walls of Old Upper Town. See the **fortifications** (opposite), **Battlefields Park** (above) and the **Citadelle** (p281). After dinner at **aux Anciens Canadiens** (p290), stroll **Terrasse Dufferin** (p286). On day two, explore **Old Lower Town** (p284). Have a beer at **L'Oncle Antoine** (p291). Take the **ferry to Lévis** (p291) and return for dinner at a Lower Town **patio** (p290).

Four Days

Follow the first two days but postpone the Lévis ferry. On day three, delve into the Latin Quarter with visits to **Musée de l'Amérique Française** (p284) and the **Basilica Notre Dame** (p284). Have a café au lait at **Chez Temporel** (p290). Spend the afternoon beyond the historic old walls. Relax in **Parc du Bois de Coulonge** (p286). Wander Rue St Jean or Rue Cartier and stop for a leisurely dinner.

On day four, leave the city via ferry to **Lévis** (p294). Drive riverside Hwy 132 through St Michel de Bellechasse with lovely views to Île d'Orléans. From Berthier sur Mer take the cruise/tour to **Grosse Île** (p312). Visit **Montmagny** (p313), take in one of its specialized museums and enjoy a country meal before returning to Québec.

CENTRAL QUÉBEC CITY

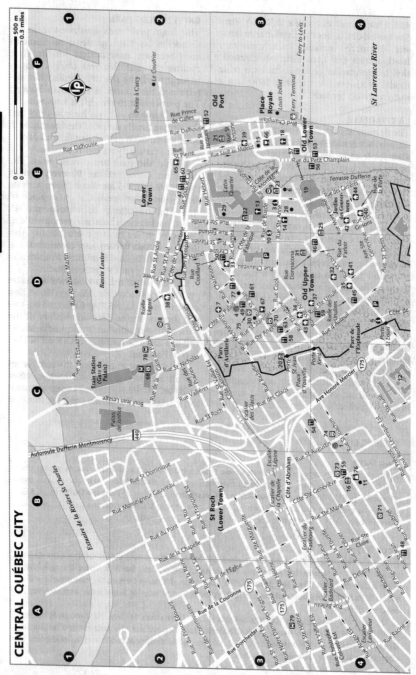

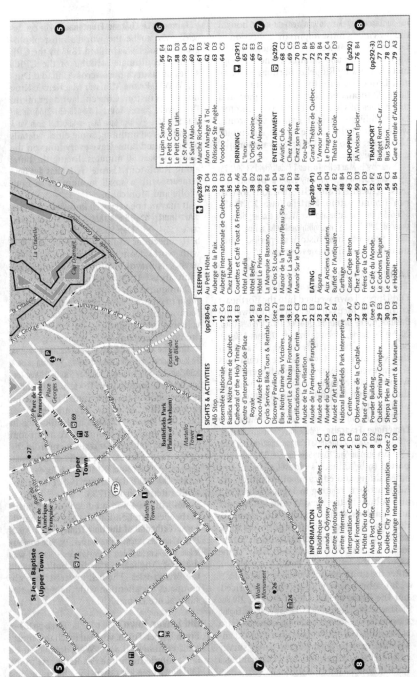

QUÉBEC

INFORMATION (pp280-6)
Bibliothèque Collège de Jésuites......	1 C4
Canada Odyssey........................	2 C5
Centre Infotouriste....................	3 E3
Centre Internet........................	4 D3
Interpretation Centre..................	5 D4
Kiosk Frontenac.......................	6 E3
L'Hôtel Dieu de Québec................	7 D3
Main Post Office.......................	8 D2
Post Office.............................	9 E3
Québec City Tourist Information...(see 2)	
Transchange International..............	10 D3

SIGHTS & ACTIVITIES (pp280-6)
Allô Stop...............................	11 B4
Assemblée Nationale...................	12 C4
Basilica Notre Dame de Québec........	13 E3
Cathedral of the Holy Trinity..........	14 E3
Centre d'Interpretation de Place Royale.	15 E3
Choco-Musée Érico.....................	16 B4
Cyclo Services Bike Tours & Rentals...	17 D2
Discovery Pavilion..................(see 2)	
Élise Notre Dame des Victoires........	18 E3
Fairmont Le Château Frontenac........	19 E3
Fortifications Interpretive Centre......	20 C3
Musée de la Civilisation...............	21 E3
Musée de l'Amérique Français.........	22 E3
Musée du Fort.........................	23 E3
Musée du Québec......................	24 A7
Musée d'Art Inuit.....................	25 E4
National Battlefields Park Interpretive Centre.	26 A7
Observatoire de la Capitale...........	27 C5
Place d'Armes..........................	28 E3
Powder Building.....................(see 5)	
Québec Seminary Complex..............	29 E3
Sherpa Plein Air.......................	30 D3
Ursuline Convent & Museum............	31 D3

SLEEPING (pp287-9)
Au Petit Hôtel.........................	32 D4
Auberge de la Paix....................	33 D3
Auberge Internationale de Québec.....	34 D3
Chez Hubert...........................	35 D4
Couettes et Café Toast & French.......	36 A6
Hôtel Acadia..........................	37 D4
Hôtel Belley..........................	38 D2
Hôtel Le Priori.......................	39 E3
La Marquise Bassano...................	40 E4
Le Clos St Louis......................	41 D4
Manoir de la Terrasse/Beau Site.......	42 E4
Manoir La Salle.......................	43 D3
Manoir Sur le Cap....................	44 E4

EATING (pp289-91)
Aspara.................................	45 D4
Aux Anciens Canadiens.................	46 D4
Buffet de l'Antiquaire.................	47 E2
Carthage..............................	48 B4
Casse Crêpe Breton....................	49 D3
Chez Temporel........................	50 D3
Fréres de la Côte.....................	51 D3
Le Café du Monde......................	52 F2
Le Cochons Dingue....................	53 E4
Le Commensal.........................	54 C3
Le Hobbit.............................	55 B4
Le Lupin Santé.......................	56 E4
Le Petit Cochon......................	57 E3
Le Petit Coin Latin...................	58 D3
Le St Amour..........................	59 D4
Le Saint Malo........................	60 E2
Marché Richelieu.....................	61 D3
Mon Manège à Toi....................	62 A6
Rôtisserie Ste Angèle.................	63 D3
Voodoo Grill.........................	64 C5

DRINKING (p291)
L'Inox.................................	65 E2
L'Oncle Antoine......................	66 E3
Pub St Alexandre.....................	67 D3

ENTERTAINMENT (p292)
Aviatic Club..........................	68 C2
Chez Maurice........................	69 C5
Chez son Père........................	70 D3
Fou-bar..............................	71 B4
Grand Théâtre de Québec..............	72 B5
L'Amour Sorcier......................	73 B4
Le Drague............................	74 C4
Théâtre Capitole.....................	75 D3

SHOPPING (p292)
JA Moisan Épicier....................	76 B4

TRANSPORT (pp292-3)
Budget Rent-a-Car....................	77 D3
Bus Station...........................	78 C2
Gare Centrale d'Autobus..............	79 A3

Tue-Sun Labour Day–May, to 9pm Wed year-round) houses the province's most important collection of Québecois art, as well as international paintings, sculpture and ceramics. The holdings include work by Riopelle, Borduas, Dallaire and Leduc. Be sure to look out for art by James Duncan and Cornelius Krieghoff and the statues of Québec's best-loved sculptor, Louis-Philippe Hébert (whose 22 bronze works adorn the facade of the Assemblée Nationale, p286). Ticket prices vary for special exhibitions.

Nearby is **Martello Tower 1** (adult/child $3.50/2.75; ⏱ 10am-5:30pm mid-Jun–early Sep), a British defense structure from 1812 that kids love to run around within. **Martello Tower 2** (☎ 418-649-6157; cnr Rue Taché and Ave Wilfred Laurier; dinner & show (BYOW) $35; ⏱ in English weekly Jul & Aug, call for dates) presents fun, historical, period whodunnit dinner-theater evenings.

LATIN QUARTER

The **Latin Quarter** refers to a section of the Old Upper Town wedged into the northeast corner. The focus of the area is the towering **Basilica Notre Dame de Québec** (☎ 418-694-0665; 20 Rue De Buade; admission free; ⏱ 7:30am-4:30pm). Samuel de Champlain erected a chapel on this site in 1633. Over the next centuries several ever-bigger replacements were built, with this last completed in 1925. The grandiose interior faithfully re-creates the spirit of the 18th century.

Next door is the excellent **Musée de l'Amérique Française** (Museum of French America; ☎ 418-692-2843; 2 Côte de la Fabrique; adult/student $5/3; ⏱ 10am-5pm Jul-Sep, 10am-5pm Tue-Sun Oct-Jun). Purported to be Canada's oldest museum, this entertaining and educational institution exhibits artifacts relating to French settlement and culture in the New World. It's not dry and employs some very creative, changing displays. The admission fee also covers some adjacent seminary buildings, with their religious artifacts, and quiet courtyards. If the gates to the left of the basilica are closed, enter the grounds at 9 Rue le l'Université.

It's a bit hokey and a little over-priced, but the **Musée du Fort** (☎ 418-692-2175; 210 Rue Ste Anne; adult/student/senior $7.50/4.50/5.50; ⏱ English shows on the hour 10am-5pm May-Oct, less frequently rest of year) model/diorama does give a quick, enjoyable, easy-to-grasp audio-visual survey of the city's battles and history, making a good introduction to it all.

Fairmont Le Château Frontenac (1 Rue des Carrières), said to be the world's most photographed hotel, was built in 1893 by the CPR as the penultimate striking of the CPR's series of luxury hotels across Canada. During WWII, Prime Minister MacKenzie King hosted Winston Churchill and Franklin Roosevelt here. **Tours** (☎ 418-691-2166; adult/child $7/4.50; ⏱ 10am-6pm May–mid-Oct, 1-5pm Sat & Sun mid-Oct–Apr) outlining some quirky details of the storied hotel leave every hour on the hour and last 50 minutes. Facing the hotel along Rue Mont Carmel is **Jardins des Gouverneurs**, with a small monument to both Wolfe and Montcalm.

It may not be very well known, but **Musée d'Art Inuit** (☎ 418-694-1828; 39 Rue St Louis; adult/student $6/4; ⏱ 9:30am-5:30pm) houses one of the best collections of Inuit art in the country, with works from northern Québec (Nunavik), Nunavut (Baffin Island) and other Inuit areas. Aside from simply displaying 450 unique works of art, the museum places them in context. Connected to the museum (conveniently!) is a stunning gallery selling valuable Inuit sculptures. But beware, these are not cheap trinkets or souvenirs.

Ursuline Convent & Museum (☎ 418-694-0694; 12 Rue Donnacona; adult/student $6/4; ⏱ 10am-noon & 1:30-5pm Tue-Sat, 1:30-5pm Sun May-Sep; 1-4:30pm Tue-Sun Oct-Apr), founded in 1641, is the oldest girls' school on the continent. The museum recounts the generally forgotten story of the Ursuline sisters' lives and influence in the 17th and 18th centuries. A new room houses intricate gold and silver embroidery. At the same address, the lovely **chapel** (admission free; ⏱ 10-11:30am & 1:30-4:30pm Tue-Sat, 1:30-4:30pm Sun May-Oct) dates from 1902 but retains some interiors from 1723.

Built in 1804 and modeled on St Martin in the Fields in London, the elegantly handsome **Cathedral of the Holy Trinity** (☎ 418-692-2193; 31 Rue des Jardins; admission free; ⏱ 9am-6pm May & Jun, 9am-8pm Jul & Aug, 10am-4pm Sep–mid-Oct) was the first Anglican cathedral built outside the British Isles. The bell tower, 47m-high, competes for attention with the nearby Basilica Notre Dame.

Old Lower Town   Map pp282–3

From Upper Town, you can reach this must-see area in several ways. Walk down Côte de la Canoterie from Rue des Remparts to the Old Port or edge down the charming and steep Rue Côte de la Montagne. About halfway down on the right there is a shortcut, the Break-Neck Stairs (Escalier Casse-Cou), which leads down to Rue du Petit Champlain. You can also take the **funicular** from Terrasse Dufferin ($1.50 each way).

Teeming **Rue du Petit Champlain** is said to be, along with Rue Sous le Cap, the narrowest street in North America, and is also one of the oldest. Look for the incredible wall paintings that feature on the 17th- and 18th-century buildings. There are murals and then there are these! Also keep an eye out for the numerous plaques, statues and street performers that add to the whole.

Place Royale, the central, principal square of Lower Town has 400 years of history behind it. When Samuel de Champlain founded Québec, it was this bit of shoreline that was first settled. In 1690, cannons placed here held off the attacks of the English naval commander Phips and his men. Today the name 'Place Royale' often generally refers to the district.

Built around the old harbor in Old Lower Town northeast of Place Royale, the **Vieux Port** (Old Port) is being redeveloped as a multipurpose waterfront area.

CENTRE D'INTERPRETATION DE PLACE ROYALE

This **interpretive center** (☎ 418-646-3167; 27 Rue Notre Dame; adult/student $4/3; ⌚ 10am-5:30pm late Jun–Oct) touts the area as the cradle of French history on the continent with a series of good participatory displays, one with costumes for kids. While here, pick up a brochure on the vaulted cellars (ancient stone basements), some of which can be visited for free, including the one right here, complete with costumed barrel-maker.

ÉGLISE NOTRE DAME DES VICTOIRES

Dating from 1688, **Our Lady of Victories Church** (☎ 418-692-1650; 32 Rue Sous le Fort; admission free; ⌚ 9:30am-4:30pm), a modest house of worship on the square, is the oldest stone church in the USA and Canada. It stands on the very spot where de Champlain set up his 'Habitation,' a small stockade, 80 years prior to the church's arrival. Inside are copies of works by Rubens and Van Dyck. Hanging from the ceiling is a replica of a wooden ship, the *Brézé*, thought to be a good-luck charm for ocean crossings and battles with the Iroquois.

MUSÉE DE LA CIVILISATION

The **Museum of Civilization** (☎ 418-643-2158; 85 Rue Dalhousie; adult/student $7/4, free Tue Sep-May; ⌚ 10am-7pm late Jun–early Sep, 10am-5pm Tue-Sun early Sep–late Jun) is striking architecturally, especially because it incorporates some preexisting buildings. The three permanent exhibits are unique and well worth seeing. One focuses on the cultures of Québec's Aboriginals, the second (Memories) offers a chronology of life in the province via the objects that defined the different eras. The third, new in 2004, traces the history of Québec through all aspects of time and place, both minor and major. The changing shows, often contemporary in concern, are generally much less successful.

Outside the Walls

There is life outside the walls, but few tourists and still fewer significant attractions. However, that doesn't mean these parts of the city need to be totally ignored. **St Jean Baptiste**, flanking Old Town to the west, and **St Roch** to the northwest of Old Town, are both worth exploring on foot.

The heart of the former, part of Upper Town, is **Rue St Jean**, which extends from the Old Town. Good restaurants, hip cafés and bars and interesting shops, some of which cater to a gay clientele, line it between Ave Dufferin and Rue Racine, but the down-to-earth ambience is proof that you're out of the tourist zone. From Rue St Jean, take any side street and walk downhill (northwest) to the narrow residential streets like Rue D'Aiguillon, Rue Richelieu or Rue St Olivier. Just as long, outside staircases are trademarks of Montréal architecture, so are these miniature, scrunched-together houses, some with very nice entrances, typical of Québec City's residential landscape.

Walking down Côte Ste Geneviève, you'll get to a steep staircase, the Escalier de la Chapelle, which takes you down to the Lower Town and to the interesting St Roch area. Traditionally a working class district for factory and naval workers, it's been slowly gentrifying. Sprouting along the main artery, **Rue St Joseph**, with its junk shops and secondhand clothes stores, are spiffy, trendy new restaurants and bars. Art galleries are appearing here and on **Rue St Vallier Est**.

OBSÉRVATOIRE DE LA CAPITALE

Back in Upper Town, the **Capital Observatory** (Map pp282-3; ☎ 418-644-9841; 1037 Rue de la Chevrotière; adult/student & senior $5/4; ☽ 10am-5pm Jun 24–mid-Oct, 10am-5pm Tue-Sun rest of year) offers great views from the 31st floor and should help you get your bearings. Bone up on local history by reading the information panels.

PARC DU BOIS DE COULONGE

Not far west of the Plains of Abraham (p281) lie the colorful gardens of this **park** (Map pp282-3; ☎ 418-528-0773; 1215 Chemin St Louis; admission free), a paean to the plant world and a welcome respite from downtown. Now open to the public, this woodland with extensive horticultural displays used to be the private property of a succession of Québec's and Canada's religious and political elite.

ASSEMBLÉE NATIONALE

Just across from the Porte St Louis is the **National Assembly** (Map pp282-3; ☎ 418-643-7239; Cnr Ave Honoré Mercier & Grande Allée Est; admission free; ☽ 9am-4:30pm late Jun–Sep, 9am-4:30pm Mon-Fri Sep–late Jun), the home of the Provincial Legislature. The National Assembly building is a Second Empire structure from 1886. Free tours are given in English and French. The facade of the building is decorated with 22 bronze statues of significant provincial historical figures.

CARTIER-BRÉBEUF NATIONAL HISTORIC SITE

On the St Charles River, north of the central walled section of the city, this **national historic site** (Map p286; ☎ 418-648-4038; 175 Rue de l'Espinay; adult/student $3.50/2.50; ☽ 10am-6pm mid-Jun–mid-Sep) marks where Cartier and his men were nursed through the winter of 1535 by First Nations people. There's a full-scale replica of Cartier's ship and a reproduction of an aboriginal longhouse in the park's green (but rather inauthentic-looking) riverside setting.

ACTIVITIES

Outside the Château Frontenac along the riverfront, 425m-long **Terrasse Dufferin** is a marvelous stroll with dramatic views over the river, perched as it is 60m high on a cliff. It's peppered with quality street performers vying for attention.

Cyclo Service (Map pp282-3; ☎ 418-692-4052; 160 Quai St André), inside the farmers' market, rents bikes and organizes excellent bike tours of the city and outskirts. The knowledgeable and fun guides frequently give tours in English. There are good cycling maps covering the vicinity.

Sherpa Plein Air (Map pp282-3; ☎ 418-640-7437; www.sherpapleinair.com; 1045 Rue St Jean) operates Navette Shuttle, an excellent, fairly-priced service taking people out of the city to sites such as Jacques Cartier Park and Cap Tormentine for hiking, birding and kayaking. Sherpa even rents and takes bikes. If you want to get out of town and get active, call these guys.

QUÉBEC CITY FOR CHILDREN

Certainly this town is about history, architecture and food. While much of the old walled city, including accommodations and restaurants, is geared to adults, this is not exclusively the case. Several restaurants listed in the Eating section are suitable for kids. There are good things to do with younger ones in the central core, while around the edges are other sites fully designed for kids' enjoyment.

In the historic area, walking the Fortifications (p280) suits all ages. The Citadelle (p281) ceremonies with uniformed soldiers, such as beating the retreat, are winners too. Dufferin Terrasse, with its view and abundance of buskers, always delights children. Place d'Armes and Place Royale are also good for street performers. And of course, what little one doesn't like to climb all over a cannon? The cheap ferry to Lévis (p292) and any boat cruise always appeals to the whole family as would a slow tour of Old Town in a horse-drawn *calèche* (p287).

Parc Aquarium (Map p280; ☎ 418-646-9328; 1675 Ave des Hôtels; adult/child/family $25/16/75; ☽ 10am-8pm Jun-Sep, 10am-5pm Sep-Jun) Newly upgraded with seals, polar bear and thousands of smaller species.

Jardin Zoologique (Map p280; ☎ 418-622-0312; 9300 Rue de la Faune; adult/child 3-5/child 6-12/child12-17/family $10/5/8/9/35; ☽ 10am-8pm Apr-Oct, 10am-4pm Oct-Apr) Specializes in birdlife with 300 species, reptiles, insects, themed gardens and a tropical greenhouse.

Choco-Musée Érico (Map pp282-3; ☎ 418-524-2122; 634 Rue St Jean; admission free; ☽ 10am-6pm Mon-Wed & Sat, 10am-9pm Thu & Fri, 11am-5pm Sun) Chocolate museum and store – get a history lesson, see the kitchen and then try to resist the gift shop!

TOURS

Guided walking tours can pack a lot of specialized knowledge into a short time. For example, on one tour a cannonball wedged into a tree right beside the sidewalk on Rue St Louis is pointed out as strollers pass blindly by.

Popular boat-tour operators such as MV *Louis Jolliet* and other vessels moored near Place Royale go downriver to Montmorency Falls and by Île d'Orléans. For city views, you can't beat the cheap ferry across to Lévis.

Calèches (horse-drawn carriages) give a nice ride but they can be expensive – $60 for about 40 minutes. Drivers do provide some commentary.

There are several recommended tour operators:

La Compagnie des Six Associes (☎ 418-692-3033; walking tours $16) Boasts a great staff and very good walking circuits like the ever-popular 'Vice and Drunkenness,' which creaks open the rusty door on the history of alcohol and prostitution in the city. Other tours, done in English and French, focus on epidemics, disasters and crimes. A cheery bunch, they are. Make reservations at the company's kiosk at the main tourist office.

Les Tours Adlard (☎ 418-692-2358; 2½hr walking tours $17) Also very well-informed, and can arrange private walks.

Old Québec Tours (☎ 418-664-0460; 2¼hr city driving tours $25) Offers a four-hour trip to Montmorency Falls and Île d'Orléans ($37) and other options, too. They'll pick you up at your hotel.

Paul Gaston l'Anglais (☎ 418-529-3422; 2hr walking tours $15) Affable archeologist Paul gives excellent, novel, thematically diverse walking tours (eg beer brewing, cemeteries of Old Québec, parks) when not zipping around town researching on his bike.

FESTIVALS & EVENTS

Winter Carnival (www.carnaval.qc.ca; ☉ Jan) This famous annual event, unique to Québec City, bills itself as the biggest winter carnival in the world, with parades, ice sculptures, a snow slide, boat races, dances, music and lots of drinking during the first half of February. Activities take place all over Old Town (many at the Parc de l'Esplanade), and the famous slide is on the Terrasse Dufferin behind the Château. If you want to go, organize the trip early, as accommodations fill up fast, and bring lots of warm clothes.

Fête Nationale de la St Jean Baptiste (www .snqc.qc.ca in French; ☉ Jun 23) On this night, Québec City parties hard. Originally a holiday honoring John the Baptist, this day has evolved into a quasi-political event celebrating Québec's distinct culture and nationalistic leanings. Major festivities on the Plains of Abraham start around 8pm.

Fête de Nouvelle France (Back to Colonial Times; ☎ 418-694-5560; ☉ Jul-Sep) Periodic re-enactments of the last days of the French regime are conducted at various locations.

Festival d'Été (Summer Festival; ☎ 888-992-5200; www.infofestival.com; ☉ early Jul) This festival features some 500 free shows, concerts, drama and dance performances. Most squares and parks in the Old Town host daily events, especially Parc de la Francophonie (behind Hôtel de Ville) at noon and in the evenings.

Les Grands Feux Loto-Québec (☎ 888-924-3473; ☉ late Jul) Major fireworks show at Chutes Montmorency.

Fiertè Québec (Gay Festival; ☎ 418-523-2003; ☉ early Sep) The celebrations end in a huge, outlandish parade.

SLEEPING

There are many, many places to stay in Québec City, and generally the competition keeps the prices down to a reasonable level. The best are the numerous, small European-style hotels scattered around Old Town. They offer character, convenience and a bit of romance. Motels close to town and larger downtown hotels tend to be expensive.

Outlying motels are concentrated primarily in two areas. Beauport, with some basics of below average cost, is just a 12-minute drive northeast of the city. To get there, go north along Ave Dufferin, then take Hwy 440 until the exit for Boul Ste Anne/Rte 138; head to the 500 to 1200 blocks. A bike trail from the city passes nearby.

A second area is west of the center on Boul Wilfrid Hamel (Rte 138). To get there, head west on Hwy 440 to the Henri IV exit. City buses run to these districts, so whether you have a car or not, they may be the answer if you find everything booked up downtown. The further you go, the further the prices drop. Prices generally are higher than usual for motels, averaging about $90 to $120 in the high season.

As you'd expect in such a popular city, the top choices are often full. Look for a room before 2pm or reserve ahead. Midsummer and during Winter Carnival are especially busy times, particularly weekends. Off-season prices drop markedly. Most rooms have been upgraded to include private bathrooms, unless otherwise noted here.

QUÉBEC

THE AUTHOR'S CHOICE

Hôtel Acadia (☎ 418-694-0280, 800-463-0280; www.hotelacadia.com; 43 Rue Ste Ursule; r $85-280; **P**) Formerly known as Maison Acadienne, this long-time visitor fave is carved out of three adjacent historic houses on Rue Ste Ursule, a convenient side street that is both easy on the eyes and quiet. The 41 rooms come in a range of sizes, features and prices, providing something for everyone, from small quarters without bathrooms to luxury spreads with fireplaces or whirlpools. Breakfast is served in a cute little alcove and there's a peaceful garden overlooking the old Ursuline convent.

Old Upper Town
Map pp282–3

BUDGET

HI Auberge Internationale de Québec (☎ 418-694-0775; www.aubergeinternationaledequebec.com; 19 Rue Ste Ursule; dm members/nonmembers $20/24, r with shared bathroom $50/54; 🖳) A friendly, lively place, this central hostel is happening and usually full in summer, despite its 283 beds. Rooms are off creaky, wooden-floored corridors that go on forever. The pleasant cafeteria serves three economical meals per day.

Auberge de la Paix (☎ 418-694-0735; www.aubergedelapaix.com; 31 Rue Couillard; dm incl breakfast $20; 🖳) Much smaller and quietly tucked away on a lovely street, the well-established, central hostel has room for 60 in 14 clean rooms spread over three floors. There is one double room, which is generally for families. There's a pleasant garden, too. Continental breakfast is served.

Manoir La Salle (☎ 418-692-9953; 18 Rue Ste Ursule; r with shared bathroom $55-65) One of the very few guesthouses not yet renovated, this old, simple place is unabashedly worn and basic, yet it's clean and the location is perfect. You may prefer the upstairs rooms to avoid having to go through the lobby to the bathroom, as guests on the ground floor do. Some kitchenettes are available.

MID-RANGE

Au Petit Hôtel (☎ 418-694-0965; aupetitehotel@sym patico.ca; 3 Ruelle des Ursulines; r $65-100; **P**) Sitting on a tranquil, dead-end lane and covered in bright awnings and flowers, this place practically beckons you in. The 16 plain, clean rooms are priced by size, each has a private bathroom and the ones across the street in the annex have air-conditioning.

La Marquise Bassano (☎ 418-692-0316, 877-692-0316; www.marquisedebassano.com; 15 Rue des Grisons; r $85-165; **P**) Rooms sporting canopy beds, claw-foot tubs or a rooftop deck are part of the allure of this fine, old home in a serene location. Young, gregarious owners Veronyc and Francis join guests for Friday happy hour. You won't stay in bed with the fresh-baked chocolate bread for breakfast!

Chez Hubert (☎ 418-692-0958; bheber@microtec.net; 66 Rue Ste Ursule; r/q incl breakfast $85/120; **P**) With four tasteful rooms that come with free parking, this is another top choice on this fine street. Rooms all have sinks in this house from 1886. Amiable Hubert's English has a few rough edges, but he has none.

Manoir de la Terrasse/Beau Site (☎ 418-694-1592; 4 & 6 Rue de la Porte; r $95-125) Very near the boardwalk, but quiet, the small rooms here represent good value. Some have their own balcony, there is a sedate little garden and a self-service basic continental breakfast.

Manoir Sur Le Cap (☎ 418-694-1987; www.manoir-sur-le-cap.com; 9 Ave Ste Geneviéve; r from $105; **P**) There are 14 rooms in this house by the boardwalk; some overlooking the park, the Château or the river. They're modern, but many have attractive stone or brick walls.

TOP END

Le Clos Saint Louis (☎ 418-694-1311, 800-461-1311; www.clossaintlouis.com; 69 Rue St Louis; r incl breakfast in low/high season from $155/215; **P**) It's hard to tell which trait is more evident here: the obvious care and work that the owners devote or simply the oozing, inherent, natural 1844 Victorian charm. For those wishing to splurge, this is unquestionably the premier place to spend a night. These rooms will awe the most jaded traveler. The 18 spacious, lavishly decorated rooms each come with a whirlpool tub in a beautifully tiled bathroom. You could pick your room blindfolded and love it, but try No 4. A good breakfast is served.

Fairmont Le Château Frontenac (☎ 418-692-1751, 800-441-1414; www.fairmont.com; 1 Rue des Carrières; r from $230; **P**) More than just a hotel, more than just a landmark, the castle-like château is the enduring symbol of Québec City. Historic and architectural details are revealed on tours! Even one of TV's *The Bachelor* episodes was filmed here in 2004. Room rates reach the stratosphere.

Old Lower Town   Map pp282–3

Hôtel Belley (☎ 418-692-1694; www.oricom.ca/belley; 249 Rue St Paul; r $85-135) A great place for the young and hip who still like their comfort and chic, this place offers spacious, impeccably decorated, though sparse rooms, with brick walls or wood paneling. On the 1st floor is a wonderful bar, the Belley Tavern.

Hotel Le Priori (☎ 418-692-3992, 800-351-3992; www.hotellepriori.com; 15 Rue Sault Au Matelot; r $180-220) At the opposite end of the top-end spectrum of Upper Town accommodations, Le Priori is one of the town's best-kept secrets. And history is nowhere in sight. Instead, this sleekly designed boutique-style hostelry is elegantly understated and stresses personal service. Both the slick bar and green outdoor dining area are gorgeous.

Outside the Walls

Most accommodations outside the walls are in motels.

Couettes et Café Toast & French (Map pp282–3; ☎ 418-523-9365; wwwquebecweb.com/toast&french; 1020 Ave Cartier; s/d $75/85) Away from the crowds but close to Grande Allée, this nice place offers tastefully decorated rooms. The owner takes special delight in guests who wish to perfect their French over morning toast and coffee.

Camping Municipal de Beauport (☎ 418-666-2228; 95 Rue Sérénité; tent/RV sites $20/24) This excellent campground north of Québec City is

green, peaceful and just a 15-minute drive from the Old Town. To get there, take Hwy 440 or Hwy 40 toward Montmorency, get off at exit 321 and turn north.

EATING

Restaurants are abundant and the quality is generally high. Central places pack in the crowds by serving an odd mix of high- and low-brow cuisine. Many of these places are not bad value for money and often boast unbeatable locations and festive atmospheres. But the less-obvious choices in all price ranges usually provide superior dining experiences. For the best bargains, get the *table d'hôte* (complete meal), especially at lunch.

Old Upper Town   Map pp282–3
BUDGET

Casse Crêpe Breton (☎ 418-692-0438; 1136 Rue St Jean; mains under $7; ☷ 8am-6pm) Tiny and unassuming, this find specializes in hot, fresh crêpes of every kind starting as low as $4. Some diners like to sit right up at the counter and watch the chef at work.

Le Petit Coin Latin (☎ 418-692-2022; 8½ Rue Ste Ursule; mains under $9; ☷ 7:30am-10:30pm) For a French-style breakfast, try this excellent, very European spot near Rue St Jean for croissants, muffins or eggs. In summer you can eat the low-priced lunch specials out on the patio.

CHILLIN' AT CANADA'S COOLEST HOTEL

Spending hundreds of dollars to sleep on a bed of ice might not sound too cool, but North America's first ice hotel has been a blistering success since opening in 2001.

It's hard to fathom, but everything here is made of ice: the reception desk, the pen you sign the guest book with, the sink in your room, your bed, dishes, even the shot glasses, which frequently come in handy.... Okay, not *everything* is made of ice. There are no ice hot tubs or ice fireplaces. But once inside, no one feels like nit-picking. Visitors say that the bed is not as frigid as it sounds, courtesy of thick sleeping bags laid on lush deer pelts.

Some 350 tons of ice go into the five-week construction of this perishable hotel. One of the most striking aspects is its size – over 3000 sq meters of frosty splendor. First impressions in the entrance hall are strangely overwhelming – tall, sculpted columns of ice support a ceiling where a crystal chandelier hangs, and carved sculptures, tables and chairs line the endless corridors.

The hotel is about a half-hour drive from central Québec City. It's located at Lac St Joseph's Station Écotouristique Duchesnay, and is convenient to icy activities – skiing, snowshoeing, dog-sledding, igloo-building and ice-fishing.

The ice hotel offers several packages, starting at $552 per double, including a welcome vodka, dinner and breakfast (with hot drink). If you're not staying, simply take the tour for $14. For information, contact **Ice Hotel** (☎ 418-875-4522, 877-505-0423; www.icehotel-cananda.com; 143 Rte Duchesnay, Ste Catherine de la Jacques Cartier). It's off exit 295 of Hwy 40, west of Québec City via Rte 367.

Chez Temporel (☎ 418-694-1813; 25 Rue Couillard; mains $5; ☺ 9am-11pm) Straight off a street in Paris, this out-of-the-way café makes its own croissants and perfect café au lait. There are sandwiches, soups and salads too.

For self-catering, **Marché Richelieu** (☎ 418-692-3647; 1097 Rue St Jean) offers breads from the in-house bakery, fruits, cheeses and even bottles of wine with screw-top lids.

MID-RANGE

Rôtisserie Ste Angèle (☎ 418-694-3339; 32 Rue Ste Angèle, mains $9-16; ☺ lunch Mon-Fri, dinner Mon-Sat) Totally charming, particularly the atticlike 2nd floor, this side-street restaurant with a patio features a range of chicken dishes, such as barbecue and coq au vin, but there's also salmon and other meat mains. A kids' menu is available.

Frères de la Côte (☎ 418-692-5445; 1190 Rue St Jean; lunch table d'hôte $15, mains $15; ☺ lunch & dinner) The quiet, cultivated ambiance here, trimmed by lacy curtains and brick walls, goes well with the menu of Québec specialties. One of those is a long tradition – horse meat. When in Rome, don't say neigh, say yea! If not, don't trot, there is duck, salmon and less adventurous chicken and pasta dishes.

Apsara (☎ 418-694-0232; 71 Rue d'Auteuil; mains $13; ☺ lunch Mon-Fri, dinner daily) I'm in Québec, so why would I want Asian food? Because, since 1982, this has been one of the best, tastiest and most consistently good places in town.

THE AUTHOR'S CHOICE

Aux Anciens Canadiens (☎ 418-692-1627; 34 Rue St Louis; mains $13-25; ☺ noon-9pm) Yes, it's on one of the busiest tourist strips in town. Regardless, the staff don't waver in their commitment. Housed in the historic Jacquet House, which dates from 1676, the always noteworthy kitchen relies on traditional country dishes and typical Québecois specialties. Here you can sample such provincial fare as apple wine, pea soup, duck or trout followed by dessert of maple-syrup pie. The special table d'hôte menu, offered from noon to 5:45pm, starts at the very fair price of $15 and includes a glass of wine or beer. The house's original rooms have been left intact, resulting in several small, intimate dining areas, and the wait staff wear historic garb.

The mix of Cambodian, Thai and Vietnamese plates utilizing lemongrass, spicy peanut sauces, rice and delicate noodles is outstanding. The upmarket room with soft Oriental music suits the kitchen's high standards.

TOP END

Le Saint Amour (☎ 418-694-0667; 48 Rue Ursule; mains $25-34; ☺ lunch Mon-Fri, dinner daily) What the heck, the exchange rate is pretty good and you might as well have one last memorable meal before getting back to reality. Look no further. First, the room itself, a soft courtyard bathed in natural light, whets the appetite. The chef, renowned for his foie gras, elevates his artfully presented creations to haute cuisine. The theme is nouvelle French. Lastly, all desserts are made on the premises and the service is attentive. PS – the lunch table d'hôte at $16 is a steal.

Old Lower Town   Map pp282–3

Rue St Paul is lined with restaurants and their outdoor tables.

BUDGET

Buffet de l'Antiquaire (☎ 418-692-2661; 95 Rue St Paul; mains under $7; ☺ 6am-9pm) One of the most 'real' spots in town, this frenetic but friendly diner serves up true, filling Québec home-cooking at a head-spinning pace. It's great for breakfast or a lunch of pork balls (no, not those balls) with rice, stew or chopped steak.

MID-RANGE

Le Lupin Sauté (☎ 418-692-5325; 52 Rue du Petit Champlain; mains $13-18; ☺ lunch & dinner) This very appealing, cozy restaurant amid the Lower Town street bustle specializes in country-cooking with many dishes incorporating rabbit, but is equally adept at salmon, duck and chicken. In fine weather, patrons enliven the flowery patio.

Le Café du Monde (☎ 418-692-4455; 84 Rue Dalhousie; mains $15-20; ☺ lunch & dinner daily, brunch Sat & Sun) Climb the stairs and voilà, you find yourself across the ocean overlooking boats plying the Seine, not the St Lawrence. Bright, airy and casually elegant (no need to dress up), this first-rate Parisian bistro is surprisingly affordable. It has been a local favorite for years. There is something for everyone on the authentic but extensive menu, from escargot with Pernod to venison, duck confit, pasta and local cheeses.

Le Cochons Dingue (☎ 418-694-0303; 41 Boul Champlain; mains $8-16; ⏰ 8am-1am) Since 1979, this ever-popular people's choice has been serving visitors and locals straight-ahead French standbys. From *café au lait en bôl* to *croque monsieur*, sandwiches, salads, mussels or quiche. It's all good day-to-day food and a very kid-friendly place to boot.

New **Le Petit Cochon** (☎ 418-694-0303; 6 Rue Cul-de-Sac), a hole-in-the-wall just around the corner from Le Cochons, is good for a quick pick-me-up of coffee and pastries.

TOP END

Le Saint Malo (☎ 418-692-2004; 75 Rue St Paul; lunch table d'hôte $9-13, dinner table d'hôte $20-26; ⏰ lunch Mon-Fri, dinner Mon-Sat) Among the cluster of restaurants on Rue St Paul, this one serves traditional French fare in an intimate, Old-World ambiance. The classic menu has been bringing them back for years; there's lamb, beef with Roquefort, fish and even a luscious bouillabaisse.

Outside the Walls

Beyond the walls, there are three main eating districts. Rue St Jean, away from the tourist haunts, houses numerous, inexpensive ethnic eateries, as do the adjacent side streets. Many have a bring-your-own-wine policy. Ave Cartier, running between Grande Allée Ouest and Boul René Lévesque Ouest, is also a busy hangout for residents. Lastly, west along Grande Allée from Old Town, you'll find a popular and lively strip of more than a dozen alfresco, economical, visitor-oriented restaurants complete with touts. All have complete lunch specials (from soup to coffee) for $8 to $11; at most places, dinners range from $13 to $23.

MID-RANGE

Le Hobbit (Map pp282-3; ☎ 418-647-2677; 700 Rue St Jean; mains $10-16; ⏰ 11:30am-10pm) Casual but with some atmosphere provided by brick walls and candles, this modest café serves very good value specials at lunch and dinner. The delicious steak *frites* for $10 is among the best deals in town. Various fresh pasta dishes and salads round out the menu.

Mon Manège à Toi (Map pp282-3; ☎ 418-649-0478; 102 Boul René Lévesque; mains $13-16; ⏰ lunch & dinner) The 2nd-floor dining room has a unique menu that features specialties and products from the Gaspé Peninsula. There's seafood,

including chowders and cod foie gras, but also sweetbreads. Look for the all-you-can-eat mussel specials too. Québec and Belgian beers wash it all down.

Le Commensal (Map pp282-3; ☎ 418-647-3733; 860 Rue St Jean; mains $16; ⏰ 11am-9:30pm) The appealing array of strictly vegetarian food including vegan and organic options is served cafeteria-style and sold by weight. Don't take all heavy stuff! There are also soups, salads and desserts. Bring your own wine.

Carthage (Map p280; ☎ 418-529-0576; 399 Rue St Jean; dinner mains $14; ⏰ lunch & dinner) This BYOW Tunisian restaurant offers couscous, meat and vegetarian specials, all lightly spiced. Tables and chairs fill the colorful room while at the tables by the windows patrons kneel on cushions in traditional Middle-Eastern style.

VooDoo Grill (Map pp282-3; ☎ 418-647-2000; 575 Grande Allée Est; mains $9-18; ⏰ lunch & dinner) Described by the owners as a 'restaurant/museum,' it's even more than that. An experience just to walk through, the complex merges two discos, a bar, a splendid dining room that stretches the concept of exotic decor, and a laid-back patio overlooking fashionable Grande Allée. Specialties include wok meals, huge Asian soups, mega-salads, and many meat dishes with, er, exotic sauces.

DRINKING   Map pp282-3

L'Inox (☎ 418-692-2877; 38 Rue St André; ⏰ 11am-1am) In the Old Port area, the city's only brewpub draws beer lovers to its pleasant outdoor patio. A must-visit, the spot includes a small museum where you can learn about the craft of beer-making. Then, until the wee hours, you can put that knowledge to practical use.

L'Oncle Antoine (☎ 418-694-9176; 29 Rue St Pierre; ⏰ 11am-late) Also at the port and set clandestinely in the stone cave-cellar of one of the city's oldest surviving houses (dating from 1754), this great tavern pours out excellent Québec microbrews (try the Barberie Noir stout or the strong Belgian-style Fin du Monde), several drafts *(en fût)* and various European beers.

Pub St Alexandre (☎ 418-694-7075; 1087 Rue St Jean; ⏰ 11am-3am) This oft-packed social center in the heart of the Upper Town strip has 200 kinds of beer (ever tried Lebanese, New Zealand or Portuguese beer?), single malts and an array of pub grub.

ENTERTAINMENT

Though Québec City is small, it's active after dark. The French entertainment paper *Voir*, published each Thursday, offers complete listings. Rue St Jean, and to a lesser degree Grand Allée and Ave Cartier, are the happening streets. Rue St Jean attracts the youngest crowd.

Nightclubs
Map pp282–3

Aviatic Club (☎ 418-522-3555; 450 Rue de la Gare du Palais; ☷ noon-3am) Though also known as a fine restaurant, the hip atmosphere make this dimly lit lounge with DJs a trendy hit into the wee hours. The setting in the sumptuously grand train station is part of the draw.

Chez Maurice (☎ 418-640-0711; 525 Grand Allée Est; ☷ 9pm-3am) This is a disco geared to dancing and set in a Victorian mansion. Changing themes geared to the young and fashionable include flashlight-only Thursday nights.

Gay & Lesbian Venues
Map pp282–3

Le Drague (☎ 418-649-7212; 815 Rue St Augustin; ☷ noon-late, shows 7:30pm, 9:30pm & 12:30am Sun) The city's gay and lesbian scene is pretty small, but this place is its star player: a multifaceted bar with three different rooms and vibes. The tavern has drag shows on Sunday. From Thursday to Saturday nights, there are two packed floors of dancing. The mostly male crowd spills out into an alleyway when things get really heated.

L'Amour Sorcier (☎ 418-523-3395; 789 Côte Ste Geneviève; ☷ 2pm-3am Thu-Sun) The tamer atmosphere at this café-bar is mainly enjoyed by lesbians, but gay men are welcome too.

Theater
Map pp282–3

Grand Théâtre de Québec (☎ 418-643-8131; 269 Boul René Lévesque Est) The city's main performing arts center presents classical concerts, dance and theater, all usually of top quality. The Opéra de Québec often performs here.

Théâtre Capitole (☎ 418-694-4444; 972 Rue St Jean) A smaller spot to catch performing arts, this theater/restaurant sometimes offers cabaret and musical revues.

Live Music
Map pp282–3

Chez son Père (☎ 418-692-5308; 24 Rue St Stanislas; ☷ noon-2am) One of the best *boîtes à chanson* (live, informal singer/songwriter club) for years, this spot boasts a great atmosphere. You can catch some newcomers here, plus occasional big-name concerts. The cover charge varies; sometimes its free.

Fou-Bar (☎ 418-522-1987; 525 Rue St Jean; ☷ 3pm-3am) Laid-back and with an eclectic mix of bands, this is one of the town's classics for good live music.

SHOPPING

Claustrophobically narrow and thick with gawkers, Rue de Tresor, by the Château, is nonetheless worth a browse for the (mostly) talented artists and their works, which are surprisingly affordable.

In Old Lower Town, Rue St Paul has about a dozen shops selling antiques, curiosities and old Québecois relics.

Farther along, at the waterfront, the Marché du Vieux Port (160 Quai St André) is the farmers' market where you can buy dozens of local specialties, from wines and ciders to honeys, chocolates, herbal hand creams and, of course, maple syrup products. It's open until 7pm daily but peaks on summer Saturday mornings when local area farmers come in and stalls are set up outside the building.

JA Moisan Épicier (Map pp282-3; ☎ 418-522-0685; 699 Rue St Jean) Established in 1871, this is considered the oldest grocery store in North America. A timelessness pervades the air wafting over the range of goods, which include maple products.

GETTING THERE & AWAY
Air

The airport is west of town off Hwy 40, near where north–south Hwy 73 intersects it. Air Canada Jazz offers daily flights to Montréal and the Îles de la Madeleine.

Boat

The **ferry** (☎ 418-644-3704) between Québec City and Lévis runs constantly – all day and most of the night. The one-way fare is $2.50/1.75 per adult/child and $5.60 per car. Fares are about 25% cheaper from October to March. It provides great views of the river, cliffs, Québec skyline and the Château Frontenac, even if the cruise lasts just 10 minutes. The terminal in Québec City is at Place Royale.

Bus

The **bus station** (Map pp282-3; ☎ 418-525-3000; 320 Rue Abraham Martin) is beside the main train station, Gare du Palais. Buses run to Montréal

($45, three to four hours) nearly every hour through the day and evening. Buses also regularly go to Rivière du Loup ($34, 3½ hours) and then on to Edmundston, New Brunswick ($48, five hours). The Intercar buses run up the north coast to Tadoussac ($43, four hours). Intercar runs up the north shore to Baie Comeau. Orléans Express covers the south shore to New Brunswick. USA-bound buses all go via Montréal (see p867).

Car & Motorcycle

All car rental agencies suggest booking two days ahead. **Kangouroute** (☎ 418-683-9000, 888-768-8388; Gare du Palais train station) is a local agency. **Budget** (Map pp282-3; ☎ 418-692-3660; 29 Côte du Palais) operates in town and at the airport. **Discount** (☎ 418-692-1244, 800-263-2355; Centre Infotourist, 12 Rue St Anne) often offers cheaper rates; call for locations.

Allô Stop (Map pp282-3; ☎ 418-522-0056; www.allostop.com; 665 Rue St Jean) gets drivers and passengers together for cheap rides to other parts of Québec. As an example, a ride to Montréal costs $15.

Motorcycles are not permitted within the walls of Old Town.

Taxi

In winter **Co-op Taxi** (☎ 418-525-5191) operates the Hiver Express taxis to the ski hills.

Train

Odd as it may seem, small Québec City has three **train stations** (☎ 418-692-3940, 800-361-1235), all with the same phone numbers. In Lower Town, the renovated and simply gorgeous **Gare du Palais** (Map pp282–3), complete with bar and café, is central and convenient, off Rue St Paul. Daily trains go to Montréal ($38, three hours) and destinations further west. Bus No 800 from Place d'Youville runs to the station.

The **Ste Foy station** (Map p280; 3255 Chemin de la Gare), southwest of the downtown area, is used by the same trains and is simply more convenient for residents who live on that side of the city.

The third station is inconveniently across the river in the town of **Charny**. Trains here mainly serve eastern destinations, such as the Gaspé Peninsula and the Maritimes, but some also go to Montréal. Buses connect to Ste Foy. Overnight trains go Moncton, New Brunswick ($148, 12 hours) every day except Tuesday. Some trains from downtown will connect to Charny.

GETTING AROUND
To/From the Airport

The only way to get between town and the airport is by taxi (about $27). Try **Taxi Coop** (☎ 418-525-5191).

Bicycle

Many bike paths run through and around the city. The tourist office sells a detailed map, *Greater Québec Cycling Trails*. Cyclo Services (p286) rents bikes.

Car & Motorcycle

In Québec City, driving isn't worth the trouble. You can walk just about everywhere, the streets are narrow and crowded, and parking is an exercise in frustration. But if you're stuck driving, the tourist office can give you a handy map of city-operated parking lots that don't gouge too much. The public lot beside Discovery Pavilion (p281) charges $6 per 12 hours. Better still are parking lots in St Roch, which charge about half the price as those in Upper Town. There are a few off Rue St Vallier Est. Parking there means a 10-minute hike (up lots of stairs), but you can buy yourself a treat with the money you save.

Public Transportation

A ride on the recommended city **bus system** (☎ 418-627-2511) costs $2.50 (or $6.30 for three tickets), with transfer privileges. The buses go out as far as Ste Anne de Beaupré on the North Shore. The central bus terminal, **Gare Centrale d'Autobus** (Map pp282-3; 225 Boul Charest Est), in Lower Town, will supply you with route maps and information.

Many buses serving the Old Town area stop in at Place d'Youville, just outside the wall on Rue St Jean. Bus No 800 goes to Gare Palais, the central long-distance bus and train station. Bus Nos 800 and 801 go from downtown to Laval Université.

AROUND QUÉBEC CITY

As charming as Old Québec may be, and as tempting as it may be to wander around for days, the larger Québec region is well worth exploring. Other than Lévis, the sights here are all on the north side of the river. The south side also possesses excellent, recommended places to visit, but their nature and location makes them more time-consuming and buses are not practical, so they are listed after the North Shore, starting on p312.

Lévis

A cross between a smallish town and a suburb of Québec City, Lévis doesn't offer must-sees for the visitor, but the ferry ride over makes a fine mini-cruise that features good views of Québec. In town, the main shops and restaurants are along Ave Bégin. **Tourisme Lévis** (☎ 418-838-6026; ☽ May-Oct), at the ferry landing, has a good package ($6) that includes return ferry and a 30-minute guided bus shuttle to several points of interest, including the following.

Near the ferry landing, the **Terrasse de Lévis**, a lookout point inaugurated in 1939 by King George VI and (the then future) Queen Elizabeth II, offers excellent vistas of Québec City and beyond from the top of the hill on Rue William-Tremblay.

Between 1865 and 1872, the British built three forts on the south shore cliffs to protect Québec. One, known as **Fort No 1** (☎ 418-835-5182; 41 Chemin du Gouvernement; adult/youth/family $3.50/3/8.75; ☽ 9am-5pm May-Aug, 1-4pm Thu-Sun Sep), has been restored and operates as a national historic site with guided tours. It's on the east side of Lévis in Lauzon.

Wendake

Small Wendake, about 15km northwest of the city via Hwy 73 (exit 154), attracts interest with its reconstructed Huron-Ouendat village, the curiously spelled **Onhoúa Chetek8e** (☎ 418-842-4308; 575 Rue Stanislas-Kosca; adult/student & child $8/7; ☽ 9am-5pm May-mid-Oct). The 'letter' 8 in Huron-Ouendat is pronounced 'oua,' like the 'wh' in 'what.'

A guided tour takes you into a traditional longhouse and into a sweat lodge, while you learn about liberal child-rearing practices and aboriginal beliefs in the meaning of dreams. Activities and shows (at additional cost) can make it a full day. Call ahead to make sure there are English-speaking guides on duty when you want to visit. An on-site restaurant serves bison, caribou, succotash and linguini (for the timid) for $14 to $28. The gift shop sells souvenirs and crafts, all done by locals. Bus No 72 runs from Québec ($2.50) and takes between 30 minutes and an hour, depending on traffic.

St Gabriel de Valcartier

St Gabriel de Valcartier, accessible via Rte 371 north from Wendake, has the popular **Village Vacances** (☎ 418-844-2200; 1860 Boul Valcartier), a mini-city that offers a gamut of family fun, especially the huge **Aqua Park** (adult/child $25/18; ☽ 10am-5pm early–late Jun, to 7pm late Jun–early Sep), which is packed to capacity on hot summer days. Horseback riding and rafting are also offered.

Stoneham

At Stoneham, the **Station Touristique** (Mountain Resort; ☎ 418-848-2411, 800-463-6888; 1420 Chemin du Hibou) offers an array of summer and winter activities in a friendly resort atmosphere with lodgings and restaurants. Stoneham is one of the province's main ski centers, switching to mountain biking and walking in summer.

Auberge du Jeune Voyageur (☎ 418-848-7650; jeune_voyageur@hotmail.com; 24 Montée des Cassandres; dm $20, s/d with shared bathroom $40/50) is a comfortable combo B&B/hostel, just north of the village of Stoneham that earns kudos as a lot of fun and has bike rentals and organized activities. It's a few minutes' drive from Parc de la Jacques Cartier.

Parc de la Jacques Cartier

This huge **wilderness park** (☎ 418-848-3169, 800-665-6527; www.sepaq.com; admission $3.50), just off Rte 175 about 40km from Québec City, is ideal for a quick escape. In less than an hour, you can be camping, hiking or biking along trails or canoeing along the long, narrow and exceptionally scenic Rivière Jacques Cartier. The only drawback is that the park's main road follows the river, and unless you go further inland, vehicles whiz by as you're canoeing.

Near the entrance to the park, an information center provides details of activities and services. Camping equipment, canoes and bikes are rented. Simple overnight cabins are scattered throughout the park, and there are campgrounds ($18 to $28). In winter, there's cross-country skiing with shelter huts along some routes. **Sherpa Plein Air** (☎ 418-640-7437) runs shuttles from Québec.

Going a little further north leads to the enormous **Réserve Faunique des Laurentides** (☎ 418-848-2422; Rte 175; admission $3.50) with much the same attractions, only wilder.

Île d'Orléans

An uncontestable highlight of the region, the island feels eons away from Québec City, even though the city is visible from many spots. This special tranquility has attracted hundreds of urbanites who keep summer or permanent homes here. Many others come for the day or weekend.

While no longer sleepy, the island is still primarily a pastoral farming region, with gentle landscapes and views across onto either shore. One road (60km) circles the island, with two more running north–south. Their edges are dotted with strawberry fields, orchards, cider-producers, windmills and arts and crafts workshops and galleries. Some of the villages contain houses that are up to 300 years old, and there are other wooden or stone cottages in the Normandy style. Other areas of the island seem like a well-off city suburb transplanted into a forest.

Information is available from the **tourist office** (☎ 418-828-9411, 866-941-9411; www.iled orleans.com; 490 Côte du Pont; 🕑 8:30am-7:30pm late Jun–Sep, 10am-5pm Oct–mid-Jun), which is visible as soon as you cross the bridge; it has helpful staff and bike rentals.

SIGHTS & ACTIVITIES

Visit **La Vignoble Isle de Bacchus** (☎ 418-828-9562; 1071 Chemin Royal), the island's only winery. The tours and tasting should be on your agenda and you can even spend the night.

In the other direction is **Domaine Steinbach** (☎ 418-828-0000; 2205 Chemin Royal). This combination apple orchard and cider house is another most charming place to stop – whether you sleep in the 300-year-old manor or not. The fine ciders, jams and vinaigrettes, on sale in the main house, are obviously made with affection. Sampling is encouraged.

SLEEPING & EATING

If you refuse to leave, the island is blessed with memorable places to sleep and eat. There's even a campground. It's an easy commute from here to Québec City if you've got a car.

Auberge le P'tit Bonheur (☎ 418-829-2588; 183-86 Côte Lafleur; dm $19) This hostel in a gorgeous stone manor lies in the middle of the south side at St Jean. It rents bikes and cross-country skis.

La Picardie (☎ 418-829-3832; fax 418-829-0502; 3547 Chemin Royal; s/d $55/75) This fine stone house with antique furnishings, a lovely view and very congenial hosts makes a good end to a day.

La Maison Vignoble (☎ 418-828-9562; d incl breakfast $85) A classic Québec farmhouse at the winery. Gaze at Montmorency Falls across the backyard, vineyards in the front. Life is tough.

Domaine Steinbach (☎ 418-828-0000; 2205 Chemin Royal; s/d $75/85) The rooms here are extremely comfortable, and the views across to Charlevoix' mountains are magnetic.

Le Moulin de St Laurent (☎ 418-829-3716, 888-629-3888; 754 Chemin Royal; lunch mains $11-21, dinner mains $14-26; 🕑 lunch & dinner May–mid-Oct) You'd be hard-pressed to find a more agreeable place to dine than this delightful, south shore ancestral stone house with tables inches from a waterfall. The well-prepared, diverse menu is continental with regional flourishes, such as wild boar and salmon.

Restaurant Les Ancêtres (☎ 418-828-2718; 391 Chemin Royal; mains $14-26; 🕑 dinner late May–Sep) Decisions, decisions… This is another wonderful place at which to eat. The gorgeous old house looks across the river and the inviting dining room features Québec specialties such as caribou or duck as well as seafood and lamb.

Parc de la Chute Montmorency

These waterfalls, about 7km east of Québec City, have been turned into a tourist trap. Yes, they are higher than Niagara Falls, but they're not nearly as impressive. They are perfectly visible from the main road and can be visited free. But be warned, parking, from May to November, costs $8.50! Inside the **park** (☎ 418-663-3330; 2490 Ave Royale) you can pay another hefty fee for the cable car or walk the 487 steps for free. Note, the cable car doesn't provide the best views – the suspended footbridge right above the falls does.

The park lies along Rte 138 in Beauport. To enter for free, either park your car at the church parking lot in neighboring Beauport, then walk 1km to the falls, or catch bus No 800 at Place d'Youville in Québec City and transfer at the Beauport terminal, taking bus No 50 to the top of the falls or No 53 to the bottom. You can also cycle here from Québec City.

Ste Anne de Beaupré

Here we have a case study in our ability to mix the sacred and the profane. It's intriguing in that it is one of the few remaining mega-attractions related not to nature, nor artificial diversions, but to faith. Now part quasi-religious theme park, Ste Anne is justly renowned for its immaculate and mammoth **basilica** (☎ 418-827-8227; 10018 Ave Royale; admission free; ☺ 8:30am-4:30pm). Since the mid-1600s, the village has been an important Christian site and the annual late-July pilgrimage draws thousands, turning all nearby space into a random, gypsy-like camp.

Inside the basilica, begun in the late 1920s, crutches surround the door, all cast off by the legions that have allegedly been healed. The church features impressive tile work, stained glass and ceiling mosaics, but TV monitors flashing instructions (eg 'Kindly Keep Silent') detract from the religious atmosphere. Not to mention the souvenir kiosk outside and the Blessings Bureau next door – line up to have a priest bless the Jesus keychain you've just bought. (Those holding up the line are evidently trying to slip in a spontaneous confession.) The gift shops selling Catholic imagery and polar-bear T-shirts, the popping flashbulbs and the inn opposite the Basilica designed like a chapel, stained glass included (but with useful inexpensive cafeteria), all add to the surreal atmosphere.

Nearby is the **Cyclorama of Jerusalem** (☎ 418-827-3101; 8 Rue Régina; adult/child $7/4; ☺ 9am-6pm late Apr–late Oct), not an indoor cycling track, but a enormous 360-degree painting of Jerusalem on the day Jesus died.

Intercar (☎ 418-525-3000 in Québec City) runs buses from the Québec City bus station up the north shore. The buses stop in town at the **Depanneur Oleo** (☎ 418-824-3624; 2 Rte de l'Église) store. There are three 30-minute trips daily ($7).

Mont Ste Anne

The slopes here, 50km from Québec, make it one of the province's top **ski resorts** (☎ 418-827-4561; 2000 Boul Beau Pré). Novices, expert skiers and snowboarders alike rave about its 50-plus trails with more than a dozen lifts. In summer, a scenic gondola glides to the mountain's summit. Bicycle and hiking trails wind up to and around the top. Throughout April there's a giant sugar shack set up here. For Nordic skiing, the village of St Ferreol les Neiges, 8km from Mont Ste Anne along Rte 360, has 224km of excellent trails.

The on-site water slides and walking trails at **Camping Mont Ste Anne** (☎ 418-827-5281; Rang St Julien; campsites $24-31) distinguish this large, green park east of Mt Ste Anne. It's one of several on Rte 138 going east from Québec City through the Ste Anne de Beaupré area.

The new Village Touristique (tourist village) in the resort has **condo rentals** (☎ 800-463-7775) year round.

The **Hiver Express** (☎ 418-525-5191) offers bus service to/from Québec City for skiers (p292).

Canyon Ste Anne

Some 6km northeast of Beaupré on Rte 138, in a deep chasm, are the 74m-high **waterfalls** (☎ 418-827-4057; 206 Rte 138; adult/child $6.50; ☺ 9am-5:30pm Jun 24–Sep, 9am-4:30pm May–Jun 24 & Sept-Oct). You can walk around and across them via a series of steps, ledges and bridges. Though busy, this is quite a pleasant spot – its less developed and more dramatic than the falls at Montmorency.

Cap Tourmente National Wildlife Area

Along the riverside beyond Cap Tourmente village off Rte 138 lies this **bird sanctuary** (☎ 418-827-4591; 570 Chemin du Cap Tourmente; adult/child $4/2; ☺ 9am-5pm). Flocks of snow geese arrive in spring and autumn, but many other species make these wetlands home.

CHARLEVOIX

This is life the way it was intended to be. For 200 years, this pastoral strip of hilly, flowery farmland wedged between northern wilderness and the river has been a summer retreat for the wealthy and privileged. Though vestiges of this remain and prices are higher than elsewhere, it's become a more democratic destination and the value per dollar rate is substantial. Unesco has classified the entire area a World Biosphere Reserve, which has resulted in worthwhile restrictions on the types of permitted developments, as well as a palpable sense of pride among residents.

Beyond Mont Ste Anne, the bucolic coastal district backed by mostly wooded mountains totals 6000 sq km yet is home to just 30,000 people, the bulk of whom can contentedly gaze out to the river. Aside from rolling hills, glacier-carved crevices, cliffs and jagged rock faces, the most unique geographical feature of the area is the immense valley from Baie St Paul to La Malbaie, formed by the impact of a prehistoric meteor. A space rock weighing 15 billion tons, with a diameter of about 2km, smashed into the earth in this area at 36,000km/hr some 350 million years ago. The point of impact was the present-day Mont des Éboulements, halfway between Baie St Paul and La Malbaie, some 10km inland. The crater left by the meteor measures 56km in diameter.

Charlevoix' perfect blend of nature and arts is supplemented by a culinary culture of serious distinction, known for incorporating local ingredients. Take advantage of the set, good-value *tables d'hôte* and you won't go through money as quickly as belt notches. Add to this the outstanding array of accommodations, intriguing history, a tradition of arts and crafts (studios, called *ateliers,* are ubiquitous) and superb outdoor possibilities and you'll soon understand why people rave about the region. Of course, there are the spas, and in fall the foliage is remarkable.

A ferry crosses the river to Charlevoix at St Semeon from Rivière du Loup. A Charlevoix driving route to consider is going along the river one way (Rte 362) and returning on the high road (Rte 138) inland, experiencing ear-popping hills en route.

LE MASSIF

Outside of Petite Rivière St Francois is **Le Massif** (☎ 418-632-5876, 877-536-2774; www.le massif.com; 1350 Rue Principale) perhaps the best, little-known ski center in the country. It offers the highest vertical drop (770m) and most snow (650cm) east of the Rockies and a fabulous view over the St Lawrence River. Perched at the top of the hill, the chalet serves up regional cuisine, not heatlamp burgers. It's about an hour's drive from Québec City.

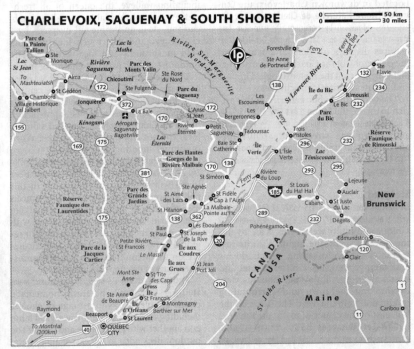

CHARLEVOIX, SAGUENAY & SOUTH SHORE

QUÉBEC

BAIE ST PAUL

The first glimpse of Baie St Paul as you arrive along Rte 138 from Québec City provides a hint of the area's enchantment. Nestled in the bay's valley, dominated by the church, its narrow old streets sing out, 'Come on down.' The town's main street, Rue St Jean Baptiste, is lined with historic houses, some of which have been converted into galleries and restaurants. Artists' studios and craft shops are scattered around the side streets. Cirque du Soleil (see the boxed text on p48) originated here.

Orientation & Information

The main streets get congested in peak season (July and August) as this is the busiest spot in the region.

Tourist office (☎ 418-435-4160, 800-667-2276; www.tourisme-charlevoix.com; 444 Boul Mgr de Laval; ☻ 9am-9pm Jun-Oct, 9am-5pm Nov-May) On Rte 138 just west of town.

Town Tourist Office (☎ 418-240-3218; 6 Rue St Jean Baptiste; ☻ 10am-6pm)

Sights

Located in downtown Charlevoix, the **Centre d'Histoire Naturelle de Charlevoix** (☎ 418-435-6275; admission by donation; ☻ 9am-5pm late May–mid-Oct, 10am-4pm Sat & Sun mid-Oct–late May) features displays on flora and fauna and the geography of the Charlevoix district, explaining in detail the meteorological impact and the area's seismic proclivities.

The two main public galleries in this art-rich town are the **Centre d'Art** (☎ 418-435-5654; 4 Rue Ambroise-Fafard; admission free; ☻ 10am-6pm) and, down the street, the architecturally attention-grabbing **Centre d'Exposition** (☎ 418-435-3681; 23 Rue Ambroise-Fafard; admission $3; ☻ 10am-6pm).

Sleeping

La Balcon Vert (☎ 418-435-5587; 22 Côte du Balcon Vert; tent site/dm/d $18/18/55; ☻ mid-May–mid-Oct) Unique and multifaceted, this is an involving place to spend the night. With its restaurant, bar, woodsy setting, chalets, dorms and campground, it's a retreat, hotel and hostel all in one. Enjoy the fabulous view overlooking the town and surrounding mountains from the deck. The site is up the hill, east of the center of town, off Rte 362.

Gîte Les Mésanges B&B (☎ 418-435-6273; gitemesange@caramail.com; 1067 Boul Mgr de Laval; s/d $70/75) You just want to stay here when you see it. Typically Québecois inside and out, all the rooms have private bathrooms and it's just 1km from the bustling core. All in all a great deal. We dare you not to take a picture.

Auberge La Muse (☎ 418-435-6839, 800-841-6839; www.lamuse.com; 39 Rue St Jean Baptiste; r $90-160) Yet another enticing, central place, this one is bright yellow and white, but it has an ace up its sleeve. Aside from the relaxing rooms and the showy garden out back, the French dining room here, featuring game and organic meats and open to nonguests, is outstanding.

Also recommended is **Au Gîte Germain Belanger** (☎ 418-435-3961; 2 Rue de Capitaine; d incl breakfast $50) with five rooms on a quiet, modest residential street a few minutes from the center.

Eating

Where to begin?

Mouton Noir (☎ 418-240-3030; Rue Ste Anne; table d'hôte $24-28; ☻ lunch & dinner) Since 1978, the Black Sheep has been home to refined dining in minimally-designed elegance. Fish, including walleye, the queen of all freshwater species, is available, as well as lamb, caribou, steak and more, all overseen by a critical eye and deft touch incorporating wild mushrooms and local produce. The outdoor *terrasse* (patio) is charming too.

L'Orange Bistro (☎ 418-240-1197; 29 Rue Fafard; dinner mains $12-16; ☻ lunch & dinner) The central, colorful, beckoning Victorian house with a fine patio surprises with its sophisticated menu of Charlevoix veal, smoked salmon, local cheeses and use of fresh herbs. Work off dinner shooting pool upstairs.

Le Saint Pub/Microbrasserie Charlevoix (☎ 418-240-2332; 2 Rue Racine; mains $9-13; ☻ 11am-2am) Beer lovers will be foamy at the mouth in this half-brewery, half-pub, where many meals are infused with the locally brewed malt (eg beer-marinated smoked meat, salads with beer vinaigrette). For $5, you can try four regional brews in sample sizes. Local cheeses are on the menu, too. The friendly atmosphere makes it a popular hangout.

Al Dente (☎ 418-435-6695; 30 Rue Leclerc; mains $10-17; ☻ 10am-10pm) The fresh, homemade pastas are blended with a range of choices including one with the renowned local lamb and another with goat cheese and olives. The outdoor deck adds to the casual allure here.

For an excellent coffee, **Café des Artistes** (☎ 418-435-5585; 25 Rue St Jean Baptiste; ☺ 8am-8pm) can't be beat.

Getting There & Away

The **bus station** (☎ 418-435-6569; 2 Rte de l'Équere) is at La Grignotte restaurant, about a 20-minute walk from downtown at Boul Mgr de Laval. Three Intercar buses a day go to/from Québec City ($17, 1¼ hours), with an extra Friday service. There are also three buses daily to/from La Malbaie ($8, 45 minutes) and beyond.

PARC DE GRANDS JARDINS

This **provincial park** (☎ 866-702-9202, reservations 800-665-6527; www.parcsquebec.com; adult/family $3.50/7; ☺ 8am-8pm Jun-Aug, 9am-5pm Sep-May) covers 310 sq km, much of it taiga. Excellent hiking and rugged topography are the lure at this gem. The hills frame well over 100 small lakes. Caribou may be spotted. The half-day trek up **Mont de Lac des Cynes** (Swan Lake Mountain) is an exceptional short hike. The tireless among you might want the challenge of one of the longest and most difficult continuous trails east of the Rockies, **La Traversée**, which stretches 100km from the Parc des Grands Jardins, snaking down the great valleys in the Parc des Hautes Gorges and winding up in the Parc du Mont Grands Fonds. An intermediate-level hiker needs about seven days for the full trek. You can rent canoes and kayaks and stay at primitive campsites ($19 to $24) or rustic, pioneer-style cottages ($43). Bring all necessary supplies.

To get to the park, take Rte 381 north of Baie St Paul; it's 30km to the visitors' center and 46km to the main entrance.

ÎLE AUX COUDRES

Quiet, rural Île aux Coudres is what many people disappointed in better-known Île d'Orléans are looking for. It's the kind of gentle, easygoing place where you go to spend an afternoon and end up staying for days. With warm breezes, sunny days and flowering roadsides, the essence of summer resides here. There are a few museums, but the real pleasures are in lazy walks along the beach, drives around the island and a leisurely meal. The road encircling the island is 26km.

The **tourist office** (☎ 418-438-2930; 21 Rue Royale Ouest; ☺ 9am-5pm May-Oct) is near the crossroads just beyond the port.

Sights & Activities

Before or after boarding the ferry in mainland **St Joseph de la Rive**, drop in to the good little **Musée Maritime** (☎ 418-635-1131; 305 Rue de l'Église; adult/child $4/free; ☺ 9am-5pm Jun 24–Sep, reduced hrs May, Jun, Sep, Oct). It details the region's maritime history, particularly the building of schooners, many crafted right here beginning in 1946. Visitors can climb aboard two beauties.

The **Musée de l'Île aux Coudres** (☎ 418-438-2753; 231 Chemin des Coudriers; adult/student $3.50/3; ☺ 8:30am-7pm May-Oct) makes a pleasant stop, with its antique-shop feel. It chronicles the island's settlement and features displays on local flora and fauna. At **Les Moulins** (☎ 418-438-2184; 36 Chemin du Moulin; adult/student $2.75/2; ☺ 10am-5pm May 24–mid-Oct) the windmill is still used to grind flour; fresh bread is made.

Cycling is popular and a shuttle runs from the ferry to the **bicycle rental shop** (☎ 418-438-2332, 877-438-2118) in July and August. They even offer four-person jalopy/rickshaw-like quadricycles complete with umbrellas!

For some sea kayaking, head to **Kayak de Mer** (☎ 418-438-4388, 866-438-8438; 3043 Chemins des Coudriers), on the south side of the island. Options range from rentals (half-day $30) to organized tours such as the 90-minute sunset trip. The more adventurous five-hour excursion includes lots of explanations about the island's marine and bird life.

Sleeping & Eating

There are half a dozen restaurants and even more places to stay, from campgrounds to B&Bs and motels.

Les Tournesols B&B (☎ 418-438-1201; 2527 Chemins des Courdiers; s/d with shared bathroom incl breakfast $50/65) Across the island from the ferry, this handsome stone house has four rooms, each with a sink. The owners have worked in the restaurant business so you can expect a breakfast worth getting up for.

Auberge La Coudière (☎ 418-438-2838, 888-438-2882; 2891 Chemin du Coudrier; s/d $75-100; mains $14-18; ☻) The mini, wood-lined complex here includes the inn, motel units and grand river/mainland views. There's a restaurant (open for breakfast and dinner) featuring regional foods.

Getting There & Away

Free **ferries** (☎ 418-438-2743) take 15 minutes and depart on the hour June to September, less frequently the rest of the year. They leave from the bottom of the precipitous hill in St Joseph de la Rive.

LES ÉBOULEMENTS

Many Québec residents seem to have a special place in their heart for this region. Indeed, the scenery here is sublime with farms running from the town's edge to the river. You may have to stop while a farmer leads cattle across the highway. Note the piles of wood used for the long winters and the many carving outlets. Also look for the unusual rock formations – these are the result of a powerful 1663 earthquake. And be sure to arrive hungry for a must-stop at **Les Saveurs Oubliées** (☎ 418-635-9888; 350 Rang St Godefroy; meals $40-50; ✆ 11am-9pm Wed-Mon Jun-Oct). You're right at the farm at this exquisite restaurant specializing in lamb and organic vegetables. The restaurant name means, justifiably, 'forgotten flavors.' Have a walk around the barn and then have a seat at the prize-winning table (BYOW). The lamb is served about 10 succulent ways; good luck deciding. The farm sells local products all day, but no lunch is served and dinner begins at 5:30pm. Reservations are essential.

POINTE AU PIC/LA MALBAIE

The community of La Malbaie is now an amalgamation of Pointe au Pic, La Malbaie and three other smaller, previously separate villages on both sides of the Rivière Malbaie. To prevent confusion and because they are still known by their previous names, they are referred to that way here. Pointe au Pic is on the west side of the river, La Malbaie on the east. But forget the politics; this is one of Charlevoix's most illustrious towns, with a rich history, quality tourist facilities and a major casino.

There is a **Tourist Office** (☎ 418-665-4454; 630 Boul de Comporté; ✆ 8:30am-9pm mid-Jun–Sep, 8:30am-4:30pm Mon-Fri Oct–mid-Jun) in La Malbaie.

Sights

Seemingly a small and insignificant village, **Pointe au Pic** was a holiday destination for the wealthy at the beginning of the 20th century, drawing the elite from as far away as New York. One of its famous residents was US president William Howard Taft, who had a summer home built here. Some of these large, impressive 'cottages' along Chemin des Falaises have now been converted into comfortable inns. Nature, art and the good life intersect somewhere here.

Attesting to the area's glory – past and present – is the splendor of the **Manoir Richelieu**. The sprawling, romantic hotel dating from 1928 got a $140 million facelift in 1999 and resembles Québec City's Château Frontenac. Employees are seen discreetly polishing doorknobs. Today, it's mainly filled with busloads of gamblers rabidly partaking of the adjacent, posh **casino** (☎ 418-665-5322; admission free; ✆ 10am or 11am–midnight or 3am), but it's still worth a look.

Most visitors will want to spend their visit in the hilly, concentrated district surrounding the Manoir. Part art gallery, part museum, the active (and enviably located) **Musée de Charlevoix** (☎ 10 Chemin du Havre; adult/student & senior $5/4; ✆ 10am-6pm Jun 24–Sep, 10am-5pm Tue-Fri & 1-5pm Sat & Sun Oct–Jun 24) portrays the life and times of Charlevoix through a variety of media.

Maison du Bootlegger (☎ 418-439-3711; 110 Ruisseau des Frênes, Ste Agnes; admission $5; ✆ 11am-8pm, mid-Jun–mid-Sep) In Ste Agnès is this totally unexpected hostelry in a conventional-looking farmhouse built in 1860. In 1933, during the prohibition period, the interior was surreptitiously modified by an American bootlegger. It's a marvel of secret doorways and hidden chambers to deter the morality squad. Tours reveal the house within a house. It also now features a crazy, party restaurant where the meals, based around barbecued meats, come with boisterous entertainment.

At **Cap à L'Aigle**, a little village 10km east of La Malbaie, are the brand new **Jardins** (gardens; ☎ 418-665-6060; 623 Rue St Raphael) with a lovely array of lilacs and four multicolored themed gardens.

Sleeping

There are many totally gorgeous places to spend a night. One very enticing strip of moderately priced B&Bs lines Rue du Quai right at the water's edge, tucked away from the rest of Pointe au Pic village. La Malbaie is less geared to visitors and has the more 'normal' day-to-day facilities, eating options and stores. There are still good accommodations however.

Auberge Chez Mona (☎ 418-665-6793, 877-665-6793; www.aubergemona.com in French; 40 Rue de Quai, Pointe au Pic; d $65-75) With just four rooms, all with private bathrooms, Mona's cute, flower-shrouded place has the added advantage of a very pleasing café downstairs.

L'Eau Berge (☎ 418-665-3003; www.quebecweb .com/leauberge; 315 Boul de Comporté, Pointe au Pic; d incl breakfast $70-110) Also in Pointe au Pic is the welcoming, neatly trimmed yellow house with the punny name and the air of a different era in its seven rooms. The two more expensive ones have a full bath.

Motel Murray Bay (☎ 418-665-2441; 40 Rue Laure-Conan, La Malbaie; r $45) This pedestrian but very clean, convenient and friendly place is the best bargain in the vicinity. It's right on the main road along the water on the way into Malbaie.

Camping des Chutes Fraser (☎ 418-665-2151; 500 Chemin de la Vallée, La Malbaue; tent & RV sites $17-27) This campground with a waterfall, up toward Mont Grand Fond park, is a good place to camp.

Eating

Le Passe Temps (☎ 418-665-7660; 245 Boul de Comporté, Pointe au Pic; mains $10-16; ☺ dinner) Sample some traditional French meals in a comfortable room with lots of natural wood yet not thin the wallet. Specialties are crêpes, savory and sweet, and fondue.

Auberge des Peupliers (☎ 418-665-4423, 888-282-3743; www.aubergedespeupliers; 381 Rue St Raphael, Cap a l'Aigle; mains $15-26; ☺ dinner) The dining room at this veranda-wrapped inn has long been revered. The chef uses local produce, fish and lamb.

Auberge des 3 Canards (☎ 418-665-3761; 115 Côte Bellevue, Pointe au Pic; mains $15-24; ☺ 5:30-9:30pm) Since the 1950s, the restaurant at this inn, perched on the hill, has enjoyed a reputation for top quality. It features fresh, regional cuisine with impeccable presentation and attentive service. Reservations are suggested.

PARC DES HAUTES GORGES DE LA RIVIÈRE MALBAIE

Enough with all the delicious eating. This **provincial park** (☎ 418-439-1227, 800-665-6527, reservations 866-702-9202; www.parcsquebec.com; adult/family $3.50/7; ☺ 7am-9pm May–mid-Oct) is still relatively unexplored, other than for the popular river cruise. A paved road reached it only in 2000. The 233-sq-km park boasts several unique features, including the highest rock faces east of the Rockies. Sheer rock plummets (sometimes 800m) to the calm Rivière Malbaie,

which snakes off at right angles at times. The river valley is one of Québec's loveliest.

There are several vigorous trails criss-crossing the park to be attacked by the fit and adventurous. One is a 4.5km walk straight up through several vegetation zones, from a maple grove to the permafrost.

A highlight is the boat **cruise** (adult/child $25/15; ☺ late May–mid-Oct) up the river squeezed between mountains, but this can easily (and more quietly) be accomplished in a canoe. Get tickets at the modest café.

Many people make it a day trip, but there is basic camping ($19 to $24). Canoes are rented, and with one the best beach campsites can be reached. Bring all required supplies.

To get here from Québec City, drive northeast along Rte 138, head north at St Hilarion and follow the signs (it's about a 35km drive from Rte 138); if you're in La Malbaie, head back west along Rte 138, then head north at the cutoff for St Aimé des Lacs and keep going to the park.

ST SIMÉON

This generally unremarkable town calls itself an ecological village, mainly because of **Les Palissades Centre Éco-forestier** (☎ 418-638-3333; 502 Rue St Laurent; adult/child $4/2.50; ☺ 9am-8pm Jun-Sep, 9am-6pm Thu-Sun Oct), 13km out of town. At this forest center, you can walk on 15km of trails with lookouts to admire the unusual geological formations. The new Via Ferrata is an adrenaline-cranking guided cliff walk using cables and mountaineering gear; no experience is required. There is now also a 400m climbing wall, not for the faint of heart.

The village is also a busy **ferry port** (☎ 418-638-2856) connecting Rivière du Loup, on the south shore of the St Lawrence. The hour-long ride runs from mid-April to January. Throughout the summer, there are four or five departures a day. The fare is $12/8 per adult/child and $31 per car. Save money by taking the first (8:30am) or last trip of the day. No reservations are taken, so arrive well before launch time.

BAIE STE CATHERINE

This attractive dot on the map is in many ways the poorer sister of Tadoussac (p302). A number of the activities offered in Tadoussac can also be arranged from here.

QUÉBEC

QUÉBEC

The main point of interest on this side of the Saguenay River fjord is the **Pointe Noire Observation Centre** (☎ 418-237-4383; Rte 138; admission $2; ⏰ 9am-6pm mid-Jun–mid-Oct), up the hill from the ferry landing. This whale-study post where the Saguenay and St Lawrence rivers meet features an exhibit, a slide show and films, plus an observation deck with a telescope for views over the confluence. The boardwalk is one of the best places to see belugas – you can often spy them in the Saguenay very close to shore, especially when the tide is coming in.

Some of the large whale-watching cruises that depart from Tadoussac also pick up passengers from Baie Ste Catherine's pier. **Groupe Dufour Croisières** (☎ 418-692-0222, 800-463-5250; 22 Quai St André; tours from $50) offers tours on boats carrying anywhere from 48 to 489 passengers. **AML** (☎ 800-563-4643; Baie Ste Catherine Pier) is another reliable mega-operator with a host of whale and fjord trips using a variety of vessels, including speedy Zodiacs. They moor here and in Tadoussac.

Azimut Aventure (☎ 418-237-4477, 800-843-1100; 185 Rte 138) is one of the best places to organize kayaking expeditions. This friendly, professional bunch tends to attract a clientele who are serious about their water sports. The range of possible excursions, lasting hours to days, includes a memorable two-day trip to L'Anse St Jean ($100). You can also rent kayaks ($35/day) and plan your own itinerary.

If it's very busy in Tadoussac, there are a few B&Bs here and a restaurant.

At the southern end of town, the free 10-minute ferry to Tadoussac runs across the Saguenay River. The boat departs every 20 minutes from 8am to 10pm weekdays and from 1pm to 8pm on Saturday; at all other times, it runs every 40 minutes.

SAGUENAY

The Saguenay River fjord landscape ranks among the most stunning and dramatic in the province. The river, fed by Lac St Jean, is 100km long, stretching from north of Chicoutimi to the captivating, winding village of Tadoussac. At places the cliffs, sometimes 500m high, tower majestically over the water. Formed during the last Ice Age, the fjord is the most southerly one in the

Northern Hemisphere. As deep as 270m in some places, the riverbed rises to a depth of only 20m at the fjord's mouth at Tadoussac. This makes the relatively warm, fresh waters of the Saguenay jet out atop the frigid, salt waters of the St Lawrence, leading to massive volumes of krill, which in turn leads to the visitor highlight of the area – whales – which feed on it. They and the entire waterway now enjoy protected status. Mysteriously, the krill levels are dropping, and so too are the number of whales.

There are two main areas of the Saguenay region. The first hugs the Saguenay River and consists of park and tiny, scenic villages along both sides. The second is the partially urban, industrialized section with mid-sized Chicoutimi as its pivot. Both depend on the same lifeline: the imposing, ever-present river fjord.

TADOUSSAC

Striking Tadoussac, with a population of fewer than 1000 people, explodes with life in the summer, when thousands of visitors arrive, coinciding with the return of the ocean's behemoth mammals. However, unlike other single-purpose tourist towns, Tadoussac has much more to offer, including walks along sand dunes, boat trips up the Rivière Saguenay, sea-kayaking expeditions and fabulous hiking. The picturesque town (marred somewhat by tacky whale-fin cruise advertising) also makes a good social spot, with central lodgings, souvenir shopping and several very informal bars where you can hang after a day's activities. All the sites and boat trips operate seasonally. From November to May Tadoussac downshifts to a crawl.

History

Tadoussac became the first fur-trading post in European North America in 1600, eight years before the founding of Québec City. The word *tatouskak,* in the Innu (Montagnais) language, means breast, and refers to the two, rounded hills by the fjord and bay. When the Hudson's Bay Company closed its doors in the mid-1850s, Tadoussac was briefly abandoned, only to be revived as a resort with the building of the prominent Hotel Tadoussac in 1864. The town was also reinvented as an important cog in the pulp and paper wheel, spun enthusiastically by British industrialist William Price.

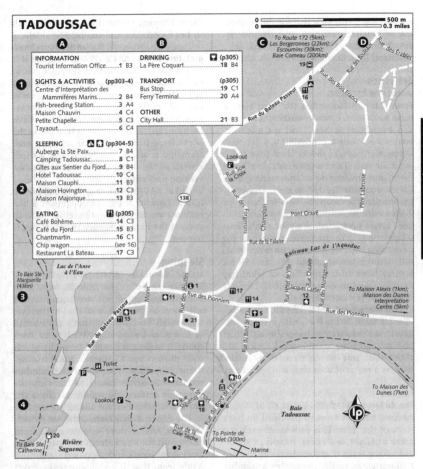

TADOUSSAC

0   500 m
0   0.3 miles

INFORMATION	
Tourist Information Office	1 B3

SIGHTS & ACTIVITIES	(pp303-4)
Centre d'Interprétation des Mammiféres Marins	2 B4
Fish-breeding Station	3 A4
Maison Chauvin	4 C4
Petite Chapelle	5 C3
Tayaout	6 C4

SLEEPING	(pp304-5)
Auberge la Ste Paix	7 B4
Camping Tadoussac	8 C1
Gîtes aux Sentier du Fjord	9 B4
Hotel Tadoussac	10 C4
Maison Clauphi	11 B3
Maison Hovington	12 C3
Maison Majorique	13 B3

EATING	(p305)
Café Bohème	14 C3
Café du Fjord	15 B3
Chantmartin	16 C1
Chip wagon	(see 16)
Restaurant La Bateau	17 C3

DRINKING	(p305)
La Père Coquart	18 B4

TRANSPORT	(p305)
Bus Stop	19 C1
Ferry Terminal	20 A4

OTHER	
City Hall	21 B3

QUÉBEC

Information

Café Bohème (☎ 418-235-1180; 239 Rue des Pionniers; ☼ 7am-11pm) Internet access upstairs.

Tourist information office (☎ 418-235-4744, 866-235-4744; www.tadoussac.com; 197 Rue des Pionniers; ☼ 8am-9pm Jun-Aug, 8:30am-5pm Mon-Fri Sep-May) In the middle of town with very patient staff who can help with accommodations.

Sights

The **Centre d'Interpretation des Mammiféres Marins** (CIMM; ☎ 418-235-4701; 108 Rue de la Cale Sèche; adult/child/senior/family $6.25/3/4/14; ☼ noon-5pm mid-May–mid-Jun & late Sep–late Oct, 9am-8pm mid-Jun–late Sep) gives visitors excellent background information on local sea creatures through videos and exhibits.

The mini-museum **Maison Chauvin** (☎ 418-235-4657; 157 Rue du Bord de l'Eau; adult/student $3/2; ☼ 9am-9pm mid-Jun–mid-Sep, 9am-5pm late May–mid-Jun & mid-Sep–early Oct) is a replica of the continent's first fur-trading post and offers some history on the first transactions between Aboriginals and Europeans. Exhibits are in French, but ask for an English guidebook.

Built in 1747 by the Jesuits, **Petite Chapelle** (☎ 418-235-4324; Rue du Bord de l'Eau; adult/child $2.50/1; ☼ 9am-9pm mid-Jun–mid-Oct) is one of the oldest wooden churches in the country. This small house of worship is also known as the Indian Chapel.

The provincial government operates a **fish-breeding station** (☎ 418-235-4569; 115 Rue du Bateau Passeur; adult/child $5/4; ☼ 10am-6pm mid-May–Aug) to provide fish for the restocking of Québec's salmon streams and rivers. You can see its operations and get a firsthand look at the fish.

Activities

WHALE-WATCHING

From May to November (the best time is June to October), **whale-watching** is the reason everybody is here, and it's phenomenal. Check out the possibilities carefully – you want to get the kind of tour that's right for you. Tickets are available all over town, but investigate at the marina dock where you can see the vessels. Generally the smaller the boat, the better. The zippy Zodiacs are recommended but young children aren't permitted. Wait for a calm day; whale-spotting is easier. The early morning or evening trips are quieter with fewer boats out. Expect to pay about $50 to $55 for a three-hour trip. Regardless of what trip you do, take lots of warm clothes. Nobody is ever too hot out there.

For the adventurous, **Tayaout** (☎ 418-235-1056; 148 Rue du Bord de l'Eau), offers some seakayaking whale-watching expeditions. Other voyages sight-see up the fjord. Prices are about the same for either option. Again, there is a range of boat sizes and specialties.

HIKING

Parc du Saguenay (☎ 418-235-4238, 877-272-5229; at the dunes) borders most of the fjord on both sides of the river. This provincial park is a hiker's delight, with over 100km of splendid hiking trails that sometimes open onto striking views of the fjord, plus a number of trailside refuges where you can spend the night. Trails begin right in town. By the dock, a short walking path, beginning and ending at the Rue du Bord de l'Eau, leads around the peninsula at Pointe de l'Islet park. Spying whales from the shore here is not rare.

Overlapping with the above, and extending to the Saguenay, Charlevoix and North Shore regions, with various entry points, **Saguenay-St Lawrence Marine Park** (☎ 418-235-4703, 877-272-5229; 182 Rue de l'Église) was the first conservation project in Québec to be jointly administered by the federal and provincial governments. This liquid park covers and protects 1138 sq km of water and coastline from the Baies des Ha! Ha! (near La Baie) to

the St Lawrence River, then stretches north to Les Escoumins and south to St Fidèle.

Parc du Saguenay's **Maison des Dunes Interpretation Centre** (☎ 418-235-4238; adult/child $4/2; ☺ 9am-5pm Jun–mid-Oct), 5km out of town at the end of Rue des Pionniers, is a fabulous spot. An exhibit explains why what everyone calls 'dunes' in the area are actually marine terraces, formed by waves, not wind, as dunes are. A 7km walking trail along the shore leads from town or short paths lead from the center to the beach and a small waterfall. The dunes are accessible without visiting the center.

At Lac de l'Anse à l'Eau, the 43km hiking trail to Baie Ste Marguerite begins; this trip requires overnighting in the refuge huts, so contact the Parc du Saguenay before heading out.

Sleeping

Maison Majorique (☎ 418-235-4372; 158 Rue du Bateau-Passeur; tent sites per person $8, dm/d $17/42) Famous and infamous are equally valid adjectives at this one-of-a-kind expansive, red-roofed hostel/house that's always full of energy and good vibes. With front-lawn sports, a well-used bar and casual banquet-style dinners for $7, there's always something happening. Ask about the minibus service that drives hikers to trails up the Saguenay, letting you walk back along the fjord, and other current adventure trips.

The annex, **Maison Alexis** (389 Rue des Pionniers; ☺ summer only), a three-minute drive from town, feels eons away from the busy center, nestled in woods and supposedly haunted. Aside from that, it's a quiet, creaky, great old place.

Auberge la Ste Paix (☎ 418-235-4803; 120 Rue Saguenay; d incl breakfast $65-70) This excellent out-of-sight choice is spacious and has a very congenial host and a great garden. The seven rooms come with a morning meal that gets the day off right.

Maison Hovington (☎ 418-235-4466; 285 Rue de Pionniers; r $75-95) The old-style Québec home from 1865 has five bedrooms, a very colorful living room, a terrific view and even a typical Québec double-swing on the lawn for unwinding. But there's that beautiful porch, too. Breakfast is buffet style.

Gîtes aux Sentier du Fjord (☎ 418-235-4934; 148 Coupe de l'Islet; d $65/70) Tucked away, totally hidden at the end of a dead-end street with a walking trail at the end of the driveway, is this inconspicuous B&B with five rooms.

Maison Clauphi (☎ 418-235-4303; 188 Rue des Pionniers; B&B s/d with shared bathroom $75/85, d $100) Choose among accommodations in a motel, B&B (rooms with shared bathroom) or a more luxurious suite.

Camping Tadoussac (☎ 418-235-4501; 428 Rue du Bateau Passeur; tent/RV sites $21/28) During summer, the 200 places here fill up nightly; arrive early in the morning to get one of the sandy sites. Enjoy the great view from the playground. The campground is by Rte 138, 2km from the ferry. If it's full, go to Les Bergeronnes further along the coast.

Hotel Tadoussac (☎ 418-235-4421; www.groupedu four.com; 165 Rue du Bord de l'Eau; d from $150) Looking somewhat like a sanatorium, this huge, seemingly out-of-place luxury resort was built in 1864 and has been renovated several times since. Meal plans are offered. A walk through the lobby and around the grounds is an experience. A pianist accompanies meals in the dining room.

Eating

Café Bohème (☎ 418-235-1180; 239 Rue des Pionniers; mains $4-9; ☼ 7am-11pm) A great hangout, this bohemian café serves healthful sandwiches, delicious soups, quiches and good breakfasts with fairtrade coffee. Most nights there is a film or a poetry reading or a talk by a naturalist or…

Café du Fjord (☎ 418-235-4626; 152 Rue du Bateau Passeur (Rte 138); lunch/dinner buffet $13/16; ☼ 11am-3pm & 6pm-11pm) A convivial atmosphere and succulent food help make this cabinlike space a winner. There is only a buffet (all you can eat or by weight), but the choice, seafood included, is sumptuous. After the restaurant closes, the bar keeps rocking until the wee hours.

Restaurant La Bateau (☎ 418-235-4427; 246 Rue des Forgerons; mains lunch/dinner $10/15; ☼ lunch & dinner) For Québec fare, try this amenable place with a great view, inside or out on the patio. Menu items include pea soup, *tourtière*, salmon pie, pork 'n' beans and for dessert sugar or raisin pie; provincial classics all!

Chantmartin (☎ 418-235-4733; 412 Rue du Bateau Passeur (Rte 138); mains $5-25; ☼ 8am-10pm) Despite an odd combination that looks almost like a truck stop, this place turns out very good pizzas for casual diners, as well as very well-prepared full dinners that may be caribou pâté followed by salmon wrapped in pastry. Go figure.

The fries from the **chip wagon** lcoated next door to Chantmartin are exceptional; say 'hello' to Claude.

Drinking

Le Père Coquart (☎ 418-235-1170; 115 Rue de l'Islet; ☼ 11am-midnight) Sample a number of Québec microbrews here by the glass, half-liter or pitcher.

Getting There & Away

Tadoussac is right off Rte 138. The 10-minute ferry from Baie Ste Catherine in Charlevoix is free and runs around the clock (p301). The terminal is at the end of Rue du Bateau Passeur.

Intercar (☎ 418-235-4653; 433 Rte 138) buses connect Tadoussac with Montréal ($88, 7½ hours) and Québec City ($43, four hours) twice a day and run as far north as Baie Comeau. The bus stop is opposite the campground at the Petro-Canada garage.

LES BERGERONNES

With two worthwhile attractions, an excellent campground and a couple of B&Bs, Les Bergeronnes provides a quiet alternative to the bustle of Tadoussac.

Archéo Topo (☎ 418-232-6695; 498 Rue de la Mer; adult/child $6/3; ☼ 10am-5pm late May–mid-Oct) is a research and exhibition center dedicated to archeological findings along the North Shore. Outside, trails lead down to the beach.

A few kilometers further east is the **Cap de Bon Désir Interpretation Centre** (☎ 418-232-6751; 162 Rue de l'Église; adult/child $5/2; ☼ 8am-8pm Jun-Aug, 9am-6pm Sep), run by Parks Canada. At this worthwhile stop, you'll find captivating marine life exhibits and scheduled activities, but the real attractions are the large rocks by the shore – seaside chairs from which it is often possible to spot passing whales.

Outside of **Les Escoumins**, 12km north of Les Bergeronnes on Rte 138, is Essipit, an Innu community. The **Essipit Centre** (☎ 418-233-2202, 888-868-6666; 1087 Rue de la Réserve; ☼ 10am-8pm late May–Oct) sells excellent local crafts and makes reservations for a campground and chalets. The center offers whale-watching cruises at slightly lower prices than in

Tadoussac. Blue whales are more likely to be seen in this area.

From Les Escoumins, a ferry ($13.50/8 per adult/child, $34 per car) goes to Trois Pistoles two or three times daily from mid-May to mid-October.

L'ANSE ST JEAN

Heading west up the fjord is a fine drive on either side of the river. There are more good stops on the south side, but perhaps the rugged topography is a bit better on the north, though access to the river is less frequent.

First stop on the south side is L'Anse St Jean, a lovely village tucked in the mountains that makes a good exploration base. Walk the Parc du Saguenay trails or get out on the water. There's also the marvelous view at L'Anse de Tabatière.

Among several cruise options is **Croisière Personnalisée Saguenay** (☎ 418-272-2739; 15 Rue du Faubourg) offering four types of cruises on a 7m motorboat, including some island exploration.

If you want to get your own paddles wet, head to **Fjord en Kayak** (☎ 418-272-3024; 359 Rue St Jean Baptiste; tours from $32), which offers great excursions that last from 1½ hours to five days, the latter with gourmet meals!

Perched atop a steep hill (even by car it's a challenge; if walking, prepare for a long, tough hike), **Auberge Chez Monika** (☎ 418-272-3115; 12 Chemin des Plateaux; dm $12) is an idyllic medicinal plant farm doubling as a hostel. Run like a commune by a multilingual herbalist and her students, the lodging includes a shared kitchen. It's 4.7km from Rte 170; follow the signs for the Centre Équestre (Equestrian Center), which is almost next door.

There is a range of choices at **Les Gîtes du Fjord** (☎ 418-272-3430, 800-561-8060; 354 St Jean Baptiste; r $65-160, ⬛), from a simple room to hillside cabins of varying sizes and amenities. It has its own quality restaurant.

You can hear the river gurgling across the street at **Auberge de Cévannes** (☎ 418-272-3180, 877-272-3180; Rue St Jean Baptiste; s/d $45/60), a little B&B by the covered bridge, a few minutes from the dock. There are several other very fine B&Bs in town, too.

Try some excellent provincial specialty foods at **Le Maringoinfre** (☎ 418-272-2385; 212 Rue St Jean Baptiste; mains $12-22; ☺ 5-11pm, May-Oct), such as smoked pork or caribou.

RIVIÈRE ÉTERNITÉ

The town itself might be rather moribund, but there's a lot going on nearby, including main entrances to both the Saguenay-St Lawrence Marine Park and Parc du Saguenay (p302). Contact the local **park information office** (☎ 418-272-1556, 877-272-5229; 91 Rue Notre Dame; ☺ 9am-6pm Jun 24–Sep, to 4pm Mon-Fri rest of year) about local trips, trails, kayak rentals and numerous guided activities.

A very rigorous hike, or rather a brutally long staircase, leads to an 8.5m-tall statue of the **Virgin Mary**. She looms ominously on one of the fjord's highest cliffs, protecting the sailors and boats below. It was erected in 1881 by Charles Robitaille, who had narrowly escaped death the previous winter after his horse crashed through the ice over the waters below the cliff. He vowed to honor the Virgin Mary for having saved his life and commissioned the work from Louis Jobin, a well-known sculptor. It took over a week to cart and assemble the towering figure.

Back in town, the **church** has a renowned collection of 250 Christmas manger vignettes. On Rte 170, don't miss the **Halte des Artistes**, a free, drive-through exhibit of wood sculptures on the west side of town.

CHICOUTIMI

This regional center is quite pleasant thanks in part to its pedestrianized port area, vital downtown and its young population (it's home to a university and Cégep, a junior college). Originally the site of a 1676 fur-trading post, it became a world pulp and paper capital in the early 20th century, along with Trois Rivières.

The staff at the **Tourist Office** (☎ 418-698-3167, 800-463-6565; 295 Rue Racine Est; ☺ 8:30am-4:30pm Mon-Fri) are unharried and helpful.

Sights & Activities

La Pulperie (☎ 418-698-3100; 300 Rue Dubuc; adult/student $10/6; ☺ 9am-6pm late Jun–early Sep) was once the world's biggest pulp mill. Although it no longer operates, a guided tour and exhibition explain the mill's history and its role in the city's development. The extensive tour includes most of the city's main sites, all concentrated in an area dubbed the 'Bassin.' Tours begin at the **Chambre de Commerce** (☎ 418-698-3100; 194 Rue Price Ouest).

The tour also features the **House of Arthur Villeneuve**, containing his famous depictions of the town and landscape. Villeneuve's former home has now become a museum, known not so much for the paintings it contains but for the painting it is. The entire house has been painted inside and out like a series of canvases in Villeneuve's bright, naive folk style.

The **Petite Maison Blanche** (Little White House), which held steady against a devastating flood of 1996 and which news photographs made famous, can also be seen on the same premises.

Sleeping

Auberge Centre Ville (☎ 418-543-0253; fax 418-693-1701; 104 Rue Jacques Cartier Est; d $45-65; P) This is a good, centrally located place with no frills.

Cégep (☎ 418-549-9520, 534 Rue Jacques Cartier Est; s/d without bedding $17/25, with bedding $21/29; P) This adequate college residence is 1.5km from the bus station. It's in the sinister gray building to the far left of the college's general entrance.

Eating

Numerous cafés, bistros and bars punctuate Rue Racine Est. Chain restaurants mainly lie on Boul Talbot and Boul Saguenay.

Au Café Croissant (☎ 418-545-7211; 406 Rue Racine Est; mains under $8; 8am-5pm Mon-Fri) Bustling and friendly, this cafeteria serves up healthful, tasty light meals to area workers.

Bistro La Cuisine (☎ 418-698-2822; 387A Racine Est; mains $16; 11am-10pm) Feast on mussels, pasta and burgers in a slick, relaxed atmosphere.

Getting There & Away

Intercar (☎ 418-543-1403; 55 Rue Racine Est) bus line connects to Québec City, Montréal, and Tadoussac. **L'Autobus L'Anse St Jean** (☎ 418-543-1403) runs a van down the Saguenay to L'Anse St Jean.

LAC ST JEAN

The Lac St Jean region refers to the ring of towns surrounding the lake of the same name, whose shoreline forms a wobbly circle 210km around. Fairly flat, the region is defined almost entirely by the 1053-sq-km lake. While exceedingly popular with French Québecois, the area seems overrated. It is much less scenic or interesting than other regions and may draw its appeal largely from

quasi-political reasons. Lac St Jean touts itself as the heart of Québec nationalism. That said, there are a few worthwhile sites and nibbles to enjoy as it also claims itself the province's blueberry and meat pie *(tourtiére)* capital. Certainly, if you see the chocolate-covered blueberries anywhere, go for them.

The 256km of cycling trails around the lake combine to form the **Véloroute des Bluets** (Blueberry Bike Trail), and nearly every town along the way has some facilities to make the trip easier – rental and repair shops, B&Bs that cater to cyclists and rest areas. For maps and a list of helpful stops along the way, contact the **Véloroute** (☎ 418-668-0849; 1671 Ave du Pont Nord) in Alma.

Mashteuiatsh is one of the best-organized aboriginal villages in the province. The **Musée Amérindien de Mashteuiatsh** (☎ 418-275-4842; 1787 Rue Amishk; adult/student $7/5; 10am-6pm mid-May–mid-Oct, 9am-noon & 1-4pm Mon-Fri rest of year) features good exhibits with multimedia displays on the history and way of life of the Pekukamiulnuatsh.

Village Historique Val Jalbert (☎ 418-275-3132; Rte 169; adult/child 7-14 $12/6; 9am-5pm mid-May–mid-Jun, Sep & Oct, 9am-7pm mid-Jun–Aug) is not a village per se but a ghost town come to life. It re-creates life at the beginning of the 20th century in a town revolving around the pulp and paper industry. Guides in period costume explain the history and really get into the act, singing old folk tunes and waving rulers like strict old schoolteachers.

Auberge Île du Repos (☎ 418-347-5649; 105 Rte Île du Repos; tent sites $16, member/nonmember dm $19/23, r from $64) takes up an entire little island between Ste Monique and Péribonka. This HI resort features hostel dorms, kitchen facilities, private chalet rooms, camping, a rather pricey restaurant, a bar with pricey live music and a beach with swimming in murky water. It's peculiarly popular with Québecois looking for some rest and recreation, though there's no public transportation here and the atmosphere depends a lot on the other guests.

STE ROSE DU NORD

On the Saguenay River's less-frequented north side, 45km from Chicoutimi, one of Québec's prettiest villages seamlessly blends in with the surrounding natural world. It's a pleasure to wander around here, letting the gentle pace of the village envelop you.

QUÉBEC

SAY A PRAYER FOR BATHTUB MARY

Despite dropping attendances and the declining influence of Québec's Roman Catholic Church, its iconography remains a pervasive part of the provincial landscape. Captivating, sometimes jarring images of the Virgin or a bloodied Jesus on the cross adorn both urban and rural settings. Inspirational statues embellish gardens, gaze out to sea and mark the entrances to villages. These religious expressions make a striking addition to the province's already considerable visual appeal.

One type to look out for is the so-called 'Bathtub Mary,' a folk-art tradition that occasionally graces the roadside. A traditional claw-foot bathtub is stood on end, usually one-quarter to one-half buried. With the arched top thus forming a sort of protective encasement, placed standing within the tub is a statue of Mary. Sometimes the edge of the tub is painted or otherwise adorned, and plants and flowers are grown around the bottom.

You can pitch your tent on a hill at **Camping Descente des Femmes** (☎ 418-675-2581; 154 Rue de la Montagne; tent sites $13-18) and wake up to a view over the village and onto the fjord. The showers and toilets are in a converted grange, and the owner's a hoot.

Pourvoirie du Cap au Leste (☎ 418-675-2000; Chemin du Cap à l'Est; s/d incl dinner from $100/160) is an outfitter offering dramatic views over a large stretch of the fjord. It organizes hiking, canoeing, kayaking, snowmobiling, snowshoeing and other activities. The onsite restaurant, open to nonguests, serves superb regional cuisine. It's at the end of a side road off Rte 172 between Ste Anne du Rose and St Fulgence.

NORTH SHORE

The Côte Nord (North Shore) comprises two large regions, Manicouagan (stretching to Godbout) and Duplessis (east to the Labrador border). Statistics here are a bit overwhelming. The two regions together encompass an awesome 328,693 sq km (the size of New Zealand, Belgium and Switzerland put together) and 1250km of coastline.

In this vast expanse live only some 107,000 hardy souls, almost all along the coast, making the area's population density a meager 0.3 persons per square kilometer.

The further east you go, the greater the distance between villages, the fewer the people, the deeper the isolation, and the wilder the nature. Inland is a no-man's land of hydroelectric power stations, outfitter resorts, dense forest and labyrinthine rivers. This part of the Canadian Shield was heavily glaciated, resulting in a jumble of lakes and rivers.

Highlights for visitors are the unique, awe-inspiring Mingan Archipelago National Park and, for those who have to push that bit extra, the remote, isolated villages such as Harrington Harbour clinging to the Lower North Shore.

BAIE COMEAU

This unattractive city owes its existence to Robert McCormick, former owner of the Chicago Tribune, who, in 1936, decided to build a colossal pulp and paper factory here. This enterprise necessitated harnessing the hydroelectric power of the Manicouagan and Outardes Rivers. This in turn begat other hydro-dependent industries like aluminum processing. The immense Reynolds Company still produces its famous foil here, among other products.

Baie Comeau is useful as a road gateway to/from Labrador (p386) and more and more intrepid, adventurous camper caravans are passing through each year on their Newfoundland circuit. Highway 389 runs north past the Manicouagan projects and then beyond to Wabush and Labrador City, on the border of Labrador. Along the way is a fascinating landscape with lake-filled barrens, tundra and the **Groulx Mountains**, about 120km northwest of the hydroelectric complex Manic Cinq, where the peaks reach as high as 1000m.

A year-round **ferry** (☎ 418-294-8593, 877-562-6560) makes the 2½-hour journey to Matane on the Gaspé Peninsula twice daily from mid-June to September, less frequently during other months ($13 per adult, $30 per car). Reservations are recommended.

GODBOUT

This tiny town occupies a lovely, sleepy, windswept spot on the St Lawrence. Originally a 17th-century trading post, it flourished thanks to its salmon-filled rivers, Godbout and Trinité. It remains one of the best spots in the province for salmon fishing.

The old general store serves as the **tourist information office** (☎ 418-568-7647; 100 Rue Pascal Comeau; ⏳ 9am-5pm Mon-Fri mid-Jun–mid-Sep), which has a small exhibit on local history and some great antiques. The **Musée Amérindien et Inuit** (☎ 418-568-7306; 134 Rue Pascal Comeau; adult/child $3/2; ⏳ 10am-7pm Jun-Sep) owns a nice collection of Inuit and aboriginal sculptures. If you feel like **swimming**, dive into the Rivière Godbout, at the western end of the village. The **Dépanneur Proprio** (☎ 418-568-7535; 156 Rue Pascal Comeau; s/d $30/40), a convenience store, sells fishing permits for non-residents and rents out plain, neat rooms on the 2nd floor.

There's a **ferry** (☎ 418-568-7575) that links Godbout with Matane (p322).

POINTE DES MONTS

This marks the point where the St Lawrence graduates from river to gulf. The 1830 lighthouse here, one of the oldest in Québec, has lorded over dozens of shipwrecks over the past century, despite its function. The 28m-tall lighthouse sits on a picturesque spit of land and has been converted into a **museum** (☎ 418-939-2400; www.pointe-des-monts .com; 1830 Chemin du Vieux Phare; admission $3; ⏳ 9am-5pm mid-Jun–mid-Sep) that explains the lives of the keepers and their families, who lived inside it. Various overnight accommodations (double including breakfast from $60) are available either in the lighthouse or a nearby log cabin or chalets. The on-site dining room serves first-rate local specialties, but only to guests. Inquire about the excellent dinner–room–sea-excursion packages (from $150), which could make an exotic, relaxing and fun stop. The owners have one stipulation for the couple package deals: you have to be in love or about to be!

POINTE AUX ANGLAIS

A few kilometers east of this tiny village lies a long public beach where people can pitch their tents in the wooded dunes for free and spend a day sighting whales offshore. The beach is sandy, sprawling and clean – one of the finest on the North Shore – and while there are no services whatsoever here (not even a toilet), you can shower for $4 at the nearby restaurant, **Le Routier de Pentecôte** (☎ 418-799-2600; 2767 Rte 138; s/d $35/45; ⏳ 6am-

9:30pm). You can also rent a cheap room here. There are two official campgrounds around the village of Rivière Pentecôte, 8km north of Pointe aux Anglais on Rte 138. The larger, which is able to accommodate RVs, is **Du Grand Ruisseau** (☎ 418-799-2116; Rte 138; tent & RV sites $14-21).

SEPT ÎLES

The last town of any size along the North Shore, Sept Îles boasts several worthwhile stops. Despite the rather distant location, this is Canada's second-busiest port as measured by tonnage.

The main **tourist office** (☎ 418-962-1238, 888-880-1238; 1401 Boul Laure Ouest; ⏳ 8am-9pm mid-Jun–Sep, reduced hrs rest of year) is open year-round. A smaller, seasonal office is at the port.

Sights

The Innu reserves, Uashat in the western sector of the city and Maliotenam 14km east, look rather colorless, but run well-organized enterprises, including the **Musée Shaputuan** (☎ 418-962-4000; 290 Boul des Montagnais; adult/student $3/2; ⏳ 9am-5pm late Jun–early Sep, 9am-5pm Mon-Fri & 1-5pm Sat early Sep–late Jun). The museum covers Montagnais (Innu) history, culture, traditions and superstitions. Temporary exhibits of local artists' work are also held in the circular exhibition hall, itself divided into four sections symbolizing the seasons.

Another worthwhile stop is **Le Vieux Poste** (☎ 418-968-2070; Boul des Montagnais; admission $2; ⏳ 9am-5pm late Jun–late Aug), an old fur-trading post built in 1661. It has been reconstructed as a walk-through series of buildings, each with its own exhibit to show the lifestyles of the hunters who used to call the forest home.

Activities

There is a small island archipelago off Sept Îles. The largest island, **Île Grande Basque**, is a pretty spot to spend a day, walking on the 12km of trails or picnicking on the coast. **La Petite Sirène** (☎ 418-968-2173; adult/child 6-13 yrs $15/9) runs 10-minute boat crossings from Sept Îles' port to/from the island 10 times a day and also organizes guided trips there. Tickets are available at the port, Parc du Vieux Quai, where other companies offer similar trips. For guided **kayaking** tours of the islands, contact **Vêtements des Îles** (☎ 418-962-7223; 637 Ave Brochu). Île du Corosol is a bird refuge.

QUÉBEC

Sleeping & Eating

You'll find several motels along Rte 138 (Boul Laure).

HI Le Tangon (☎ 418-962-8180; 555 Ave Cartier; www.hihostels.ca; tent sites $10, dm member/nonmember $16/20, s/d with shared bathroom $28/45) This HI hostel contains basement rooms with six to eight beds each; the private rooms on the 2nd floor often fill up with fishermen. The hostel area is fairly cramped, and there's little room to socialize, but it's very clean.

Le Gîte Les Tournesols (☎ 418-968-1910; www .7tournesols.com in French; 368 Ave Evangeline; s/d $60/ 80) Looking a lot like a big-city suburban home, this welcoming B&B with three bright rooms is located in one of the quiet parts of town.

Pub St Marc (☎ 418-962-7770; 588 Ave Brochu; mains $8-18; ☺ 11am-midnight) With a mellow ambiance, outdoor patio and long hours, this is a perfect spot for a casual but decent meal or just a couple of drinks. The pastas and salads are not bad at all.

Seafood is plentiful around town, too.

Getting There & Away

Intercar (☎ 418-962-2126; 126 Rue Mgr Blanche) runs a daily bus to/from Baie Comeau ($35, 3½ hours) and one to/from Havre St Pierre ($28, 2½ hours).

In Rimouski, **Relais Nordik** (☎ 418-723-8787, 800-463-0680; www.relaisnordik.com) operates a ferry that travels along the Lower North Shore to Blanc Sablon once a week. From Sept Îles, it leaves the Quai Mgr Blanche and travels to Île d'Anticosti (p319). Advance bookings are essential.

QNS&L Railway (☎ 418-962-9411; 100 Rue Retty) operates a twice-weekly train service to Labrador City (round-trip fare $116) and treats passengers to phenomenal scenery. Cutting through forests, the tracks pass over gorges, dip inside valleys, curve around waterfalls and rapids, slice through a section of mountain and jut along stretches of lakes, rivers, hills and forest as far as the eye can see. The train crosses a 900m-long bridge, 50m over Rivière Moisie and past the 60m-high Tonkas Falls. Buy tickets at Hôtel Sept Îles, 451 Rue Arnaud. A separate service runs once a week to Schefferville, 568km north, one of the province's most remote spots, though once a thriving mining town.

MINGAN

Immediately east of Sept Îles, the scenery changes dramatically. Villages cease to appear with regularity, the trees become progressively smaller, some hilltops lead to stretches of muskeg, and river after river reaches its destination, some by creeping humbly, others by tumbling forcefully into the St Lawrence, sometimes off a rocky cliff, sometimes in the torrents of stunning rapids.

Mingan is definitely worth a stop. Populated by a dynamic Innu community (who call it Ekuanitshit), the village occupies a lovely spot where wind and waves have carved out strange monoliths and figures by the coast. Not to be missed is the **Église Montagnaise** (☎ 418-949-2272; 15 Rue de l'Église; admission free; ☺ 8am-7pm), a little church with traditional motifs inside, which makes for a striking mix of Catholicism and aboriginal culture. A tipi form enshrines the crucifix, and the stations of the cross are painted on animal skin parchment.

HAVRE ST PIERRE

East of Mingan, the sizable fishing town of Havre St Pierre has a lot of charm, though its highly developed tourist industry feels out of place in this otherwise laid-back region. It's also an industrial zone, where iron oxide and titanium rich rock are extracted (in mines near Lac Allard) and then shipped to processing plants in Tracy-Sorel. If you're up early enough, you can catch the miners heading for their break-of-dawn train, which takes them 43km north to the mines.

Havre St Pierre was founded in 1857 by six Acadian families who left the Îles de la Madeleine and set up here in traditionally Inuit territory. At the **tourist information office** (☎ 418-538-2512; 957 Rue de la Berge; ☺ 9am-9pm mid-Jun–mid-Sep, 8am-5pm Mon-Fri rest of year), a small exhibit has been mounted in the old general store.

Auberge Boréale (☎ 418-538-3912; 1288 Rue Boréale; s/d $50/60), a large B&B in the eastern end of town, rents bikes and boasts a pretty sea view.

At **Auberge de la Minganie** (☎ 418-538-1538; 3908 Rte 138; tent site/dm $9/16), you can rent a canoe and immerse yourself in the surrounding serenity. The minus is that this hostel is inconveniently 17km west of town, there's no transportation (though the Intercar bus from Sept-Îles will stop if you ask and you'll have to walk the remaining 700m). The plus is that this isolated hostel sits on a beautiful, quiet bay, surrounded by trails through woods. Beds are in separate cabins, and there are laundry and kitchen facilities. In Havre St Pierre, the Intercar bus stops at a store, **Variétés Jomphe** (☎ 418-538-2033; 843 Rue de l'Escale).

MINGAN ARCHIPELAGO NATIONAL PARK

By far the region's main attraction, the park is a protected string of 40 main offshore islands stretching more than 85km from Longue Pointe de Mingan to 40km east of Havre St Pierre. The islands' distinguishing characteristics are the odd, erosion-shaped stratified limestone formations along the shores. They're dubbed 'flowerpots' for the lichen and small vegetation that grow on top. Perched there might be the goofy puffin (*macareux moine* in French), a striking cross between a parrot and penguin and one of some 200 bird species in the area.

The **visitor reception center** (☎ 418-538-5264; www.parkscanada.gc.ca; 975 Rue de l'Escale; admission $4.50; ◯ mid-Jun–Sep) has all kinds of information. Comparison shop for a variety of excursions at kiosks lined up by the marina. In general, the smaller the boat, the better the experience. Count on paying $35 to $55 per excursion. **Agaguk** (☎ 418-538-1588; 1062 Rue Boréale) is run by a young dynamic team that rents kayaks, canoes and bikes and does excellent guided kayak tours of the archipelago. For inexperienced paddlers, these guided trips are a great way to appreciate one of the country's best destinations for sea-kayaking. The topography, flora and fauna are exceptional.

Camping (tent sites $13) is allowed on some of the islands, but you must register first at the park's visitor reception center.

ÎLE D'ANTICOSTI

Only in the last few years has this island's 7943 sq km of nature begun to unfold its beauty before a slowly growing number of visitors. A French chocolate maker named Henri Menier (his empire turned into Nestlé) bought the island in 1895 to turn it into his own private hunting ground. With more than 120,000 deer on the island, it has long since been popular with hunters. Now parts have been turned into wildlife reserves and nature lovers are arriving too. It's a heavily wooded, cliff-edged island with waterfalls, canyons, caves and good salmon rivers.

But it is neither easy nor cheap to visit. **Port Menier**, inhabited mainly by employees of the wildlife reserve and those in the service industry, is the closest thing to a village on the island. It's from here that the island's lone road ventures to the interior. The **tourist office** (☎ 418-535-0250; Chemin des Forestiers; ◯ Jun-Sep) helps with all visitor matters. There are also a few restaurants and B&Bs in the area, but accommodations should be arranged before arrival.

Though it's possible to reach and tour the island yourself, it requires much planning. Nearly every visitor goes with one of the many small-group package tours. Get information at the Havre St Pierre tourist information office (opposite). The only regular transportation service is the once-weekly boat from Rimouski operated by Relais Nordik (p318).

NATASHQUAN

Natashquan is still getting used to its connection to the rest of the province. Route 138 joined Natashquan to Sept Îles in 1996, and it has been paved only since 1999. Romantics are drawn here for the experience of going to the end of the road and for the peaceful, windswept beauty. Others treat a trip here as a pilgrimage to the birthplace of Gilles Vigneault, a singer-songwriter of great stature in Québec.

There is the small **tourist information office** (☎ 418-726-3756; 33 Allée des Galets), but because the tourism infrastructure here is not well-developed, just ask around if you'd like to go on, say, a kayaking trip. Just like in the old days, things get done via word of mouth and people's genuine desire to be helpful.

Les Galets is a small collection of small white houses with bright red roofs huddled together on a small peninsula. Fishermen used to sort and dry their catch here. It's now an abandoned, lovely area. Aside from enjoying the endless, sandy beaches, you can hike some 15km of inland trails through isolated, peaceful woods full of waterfalls, lookouts and obscenely beautiful spots.

QUÉBEC

LOWER NORTH SHORE

The string of tiny villages in the far eastern corner of the province remains an enigma for most Québecois, mere names on the weather report. Because no roads connect them to the rest of the province and because you can only reach the towns via a weekly boat, the area represents too challenging a destination for all but the most determined. Snowmobilers can travel on a trail that links Natashquan with Blanc Sablon.

The Relais Nordik (p319) boat is the region's main lifeline, sailing every week (except mid-January to early April) from Rimouski and bringing supplies, curiosity-seekers and, for the brief period while the boat remains docked in each port of call, a few hours of fresh conversation for locals. During the two to three hours in each port, passengers can disembark and sniff around. Having a bicycle is a great idea. Most of the villages are spread around the ports, but even the inland ones can be visited by hopping a lift with friendly locals.

Kegasta is an anglophone village known for its crushed-seashell-covered roads. **Harrington Harbour**, the next town, is living eye candy. Considered one of Québec's 10 prettiest villages, this anglophone community has made much of its rocky terrain and small, wind-sheltered bay. All the brightly colored houses are perched atop rocks. A popular place to stop is **Amy's B&B and Craft Shop** (☎ 418-795-3376).

Blanc Sablon is the end of the line, 2km west of the Labrador border. A **ferry** (☎ 418-461-2056) links it to St Barbe in Newfoundland (less than an hour's ride), and a paved road connects it to several coastal villages in Labrador. A mainly anglophone fishing community lives in this historic area, where numerous archeological digs have turned up a European presence since the 16th century and an Aboriginal one stretching back more than 7000 years.

SOUTH SHORE

The South Shore, from just east of Lévis to the Lower St Laurent region (Bas St Laurent) to Ste Flavie at the start of the Gaspé Peninsula, offers an eclectic mix of worthwhile stops. Tourists often zip along in a rush, making only brief stops. But there

are fascinating islands to discover, a major woodcarving center, and a stunning, rugged shoreline park. Everybody ends up liking Rivière du Loup, and Rimouski has a new museum chronicling a little-known, *Titanic*-like tragedy.

To these attractions add the spectacular views across the St Lawrence River to Île d'Orléans and the mist-covered mountains beyond. Highway 20 to beyond Riviére du Loup is faster but the old Rte 132 is more scenic and goes through the heart of numerous riverside villages. Ferries cross the St Lawrence at Rivière du Loup and Trois Pistoles.

GROSS ÎLE

The small village of Berthier sur Mer founded in 1672 serves mainly as the departure point for the best boat tours to **Grosse Île National Historic Site** (☎ 418-248-8888, 800-463-6769; www.pc.gc.ca/ihn-nhs/qc/grossile; ☼ mid-May–mid-Oct). Times and prices are determined by the boat tour operators.

The island, which served as the major quarantine station for immigrants arriving from Europe from 1832 to 1937, is without a doubt one of the most interesting excursions in the province. It sheds much light on a little-known aspect of North American history. The tragic histories lived out on the island are cleverly, at times movingly, explained by guides. The tour includes visits to the disinfection chambers, the original hospital and living quarters of the immigrants, and the memorial burial area that holds the remains of 7500 people! Many of those who died were of Irish descent. In 1909, a 48-foot Celtic cross – the tallest in the world – was erected in their memory. You'll also be told about the 600 species of flora on the island (21 of them rare).

Croisières Lachance (☎ 418-259-2140, 888-476-7734; 110 Rue de la Marina; tours adult/child from $39/19) has two tours of differing duration departing from the marina one to four times daily from mid-May to mid-October. The price includes a round trip to Grosse Île, as well as a Parks Canada–guided excursion of the island.

Other tours cruise around the 21-island **Îles aux Grues** archipelago and stop at the main island, which is inhabited. Boat packages include a tour. See Montmagny (right) for more info. For either trip, wear warm clothing and comfortable shoes.

POUTINE, MAIS OUI

Visitors are often curious when seeing *poutine* on the ubiquitous Québec chip stand menu boards along with the bilingually named hamburgers and hotdogs. These oft-seen roadside trucks and trailers, called *cantines* or *casse croutes*, are an institution unto themselves. Québecois of every type love their fresh, homemade junk food and the high quality reflects their discriminatory expectations. Québec fries – fresh-cut, never frozen and served limp and greasy (if done right) – are certainly among the world's best.

Well now, the mysterious and much-adored *poutine* is a variation on these *frites*. Originating in the early 1980s and spreading across the province like a grease fire, this revered dish consists of the fries, upon which a layer of cheese curds has been sprinkled followed by a smothering dose of thick, brown gravy. If you've got the heart (and arteries), certainly give it a try. And then you can graduate to the embellished versions such as Italienne, with spaghetti!

The water in the St Lawrence here begins to get salty, and the concentration increases gradually further east.

Although backtracking a little toward Québec City, **Manoir de Beaumont** (☎ 418-833-5635; www.manoirdebeaumont.qbc.net; 485 Rue du Fleuve (Rte 132); r $65-75), a B&B perched on the hill overlooking the river and Île d'Orléans, is a real find and a bargain to boot. Each of the five restored, spacious rooms is handsomely decorated and the setting is peaceful.

MONTMAGNY

This first town of any size east of Lévis has a towering church and a couple of diverse things to consider. First, it is a good launching point for a visit to **Île aux Grues**. This is the only inhabited island in the 21-island archipelago, as well as the biggest (10km long). It has North America's largest unspoiled wetland on its eastern tip. Bird-watchers flock here and to Montmagny in spring and autumn, as snow geese, among others, stop nearby on their migration route. The island has a couple of walking trails. Two or three **ferries** (☎ 418-248-6869; free) leave daily from the marina in the center of town for the 25-minute crossing. Other commercial excursions to the archipelago are also possible.

In Montmagny is the **Centre Éducatif des Migrations** (Migration Educational Center; ☎ 418-248-4565; 45 Rue du Bassin Nord; adult/student $6/5; ☼ 10am-5pm Jun-Nov), an interpretive center with exhibits on migration, both bird and human. The first portion features a comprehensive display on snow geese. The second presents the history of European migration at Grosse Île and the surrounding south shore through a sound and light show.

The **Accordion Museum** (☎ 418-248-7927; 301 Boul Taché; adult/student $5/3.50; ☼ 10am-4pm mid-Jun–Sep) could well be unique. Though perhaps lacking in broad respect, the squeezebox has long been, and continues to be, a worthy instrument in the Gallic world. Displays outline its history and some famous players, and CDs are available. In September is the four-day **Carrefour**, an accordion-music festival with performances by musicians from around the globe.

A vine-covered, restored century home, **La Belle Epoque** (☎ 418-248-3373, 800-490-3373; 100 Rue St Jean; r $70-90, dinner mains $16; ☼ lunch & dinner Jun-Sep) has comfortable rooms and a very good dining room where meals can also be served outdoors in the pleasant courtyard.

ST JEAN PORT JOLI

Small but stretched out along the shore and based around a huge two-spired church right in the middle, St Jean is a famous center for the Québec art of woodcarving. Locals call it the world capital of wooden sculpture, and they can make a good case to support it.

There are scores of studios and shops and roadside examples. It's not hard to spend a couple of hours browsing around town. For a good introduction, see the fine showpieces of the woodcarvers' art at the **Musée des Anciens Canadiens** (☎ 418-598-3392; 332 Ave de Gaspé Ouest; adult/child $5/2.50; ☼ 8:30am-9pm Jul & Aug, 9am-5:30pm May, Jun, Sep & Oct). Ask for an English guide booklet. The museum displays work by some of the best-known local sculptors, past and present, and of course has a retail outlet.

Is **La Maison de l'Ermitage** (☎ 418-598-7553; www.bbcanada.com/ermitage; 56 Rue de l'Ermitage; r incl breakfast $60-95) an eye-catcher or what? The

3½-storied, multiturreted inn almost gestures to you. There are three bright rooms with bathrooms and one without.

More modest, **Maison Miville-Deschenes** (☎ 418-598-7833; 60 Ave de Gaspé Est; r $55-85) is still very attractive. The five rooms at this central house with the wide balcony each have a private bathroom, and there are homemade breakfasts.

Campgrounds lie in both directions outside town, with the closer ones to the east. Numerous motels line Rte 132.

Camping de la Demi Lieue (☎ 418-598-6108, 800-463-9558; 598 Hwy 132 Est; campsites $20-26; 🐾) is a huge campground (more than 300 sites) featuring a heated pool and all the amenities. At least you won't feel alone!

A veritable institution, **La Boustifaille** (☎ 418-598-3061; 547 Ave de Gaspé Ouest; mains $6-13; 🕑 lunch & dinner) is renowned far and wide. It serves Québecois food. After huge portions of pork ragout, meat tourtière and cheese quiche, topped off with maple syrup cake, you won't need to eat for several days. The adjacent theater puts on French variety shows.

Orléans Express buses stop in the center of town at the SOS convenience store across the street from the church. Two run between here and Québec City daily ($23, 2¼ hours) but won't leave enough time for a visit.

RIVIÈRE DU LOUP

Kind of in the middle of nowhere and known for nothing in particular, this mid-sized town has a powerful but ineffable seductiveness. Visitors often leave with a lingering attachment. Built on a rocky ridge (which gives it several extremely steep hills) at the mouth of the Rivière du Loup, and with views of the St Lawrence, part of the appeal is certainly physical. The busy winding central streets watched over by the silver church spire have a captivating appeal and the riverside sections of town are pleasingly arranged. Add to that the fine restaurants and the abundance of lodgings and a recharging stop is well in order. The city benefits from its position as gateway to the Maritime provinces (Edmundston in New Brunswick is 122km away) and a ferry connects to St Siméon, in the Charlevoix region. For these reasons, it does get very busy, even full, in high season.

There is a **Tourist Office** (☎ 418-862-1981; 189 Boul de l'Hôtel de Ville; 🕑 8:30am-4:30pm Mon-Fri) in town.

Sights

At the small **Parc des Chutes** (admission free), a few minutes' walk from downtown at the end of Rue Frontenac, picnic tables and a 2.3km trail offer a chance to admire the 30m waterfalls that power a small hydroelectric power station.

A short drive up to the hilly areas of town leads you to the tiny **Park de la Croix Lumineuse**, where an illuminated cross guards a nice lookout. To get there from downtown, take Rue Joly south to the underpass leading to Rue Témiscouata. Make a left on Chemin des Raymond, then turn left at Rue Alexandre, right at Rue Bernier and left at Rue Ste Claire.

Eccentricity is alive and well at **Les Carillons** (☎ 418-862-3346; 393 Rue Témiscouata; adult/child $5/2; 🕑 9am-8pm late Jun–early Sep, 9am-5pm early–late Jun & early Sep–early Oct), the self-proclaimed largest museum in the world dedicated to bells. Spread out over sprawling gardens are some 200 bells saved from metal smelters, the largest weighing 1000kg.

The lively **Musée du Bas St Laurent** (☎ 418-862-7547; 300 Rue St Pierre; adult/student $5/3; 🕑 10am-6pm early Jun–early Oct, 1-5pm Tue, Thu-Sun & 6-9pm Mon & Wed early Oct–early Jun), more a gallery than museum, shows local artists, but is best for the vast collection of early Québec photographs some of which are displayed in one room each year.

Activities

Offshore, a series of protected islands sport bird sanctuaries and provide habitat for other wildlife. The nonprofit group **La Société Duvetnor** (☎ 418-867-1660; 200 Rue Hayward), founded in 1979 by marine biologists keen to preserve the fragile ecosystem, offers a range of bird-watching and nature excursions that last anywhere from a few hours to several days. Sighting belugas is common. Trails wind around l'Île aux Lièvres. Prices range from $25 for a 90-minute trip to and around the Îles du Pot à l'Eau de Vie, to $35 ($20 for kids) for a day trip to Île aux Lièvres, and $50 to $180 for overnight stays in cottages or an old lighthouse, including meals. Basic camping is possible too. Boats leave from the marina.

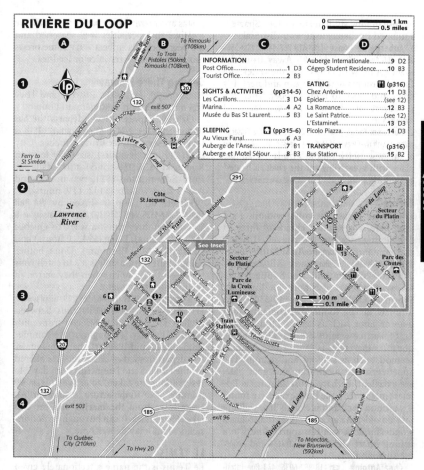

RIVIÈRE DU LOOP

0 — 1 km
0 — 0.5 miles

To Rimouski (108km)
To Trois Pistoles (50km); Rimouski (108km)

INFORMATION
Post Office................................1 D3
Tourist Office............................2 B3

SIGHTS & ACTIVITIES (pp314-5)
Les Carillons.............................3 D4
Marina.....................................4 A2
Musée du Bas St Laurent........5 B3

SLEEPING (pp315-6)
Au Vieux Fanal.........................6 A3
Auberge de l'Anse....................7 B1
Auberge et Motel Séjour.........8 B3

Auberge Internationale............9 D2
Cégep Student Residence......10 B3

EATING (p316)
Chez Antoine...........................11 D3
Epicier.................................(see 12)
La Romance.............................12 B3
Le Saint Patrice....................(see 12)
L'Estaminet..............................13 D3
Picolo Piazza...........................14 D3

TRANSPORT (p316)
Bus Station..............................15 B2

QUÉBEC

St Lawrence River

Côte St Jacques

Secteur du Platin

Parc des Chutes

Parc de la Croix Lumineuse

Secteur du Platin

Ferry to St Siméon

Train Station

Park

To Québec City (210km)
To Hwy 20
exit 503
exit 96
To Moncton, New Brunswick (592km)

For straight whale-watching trips there's **Croisières AML** (☎ 418-867-3361, 800-563-4643; 200 Rue Hayward; 3hr tours $50; ⏰ mid-Jun–mid-Oct). If you're crossing the river to Tadoussac, save your trip for there.

The **Petit Témis Interprovincial Linear Park** (☎ 418-868-1869) makes a scenic bike and walking trail, mainly flat, which runs along an old train track for the 135km from Rivière du Loup to Edmundston, New Brunswick. Bike rentals are available at the trailhead on Rue Fraser near the Petro-Canada gas station.

Sleeping
Accommodations are costly here and get full through summer. Many are closed in the off-season.

Auberge Internationale (☎ 418-862-7566; www .aubergeriviere-du-loup.qc.ca in French; 46 Boul de l'Hôtel de Ville; dm members/nonmembers from $16/20, d $25) The HI hostel is ensconced in this old, yellow house boasting a central location and a placid, welcoming atmosphere. It's open all year, cheap breakfasts are served and good activities are organized.

Auberge et Motel Séjour (☎ 418-862-9524, 866-862-9524; 150 Boul de l'Hôtel de Ville; r $45-60, motel $65-80; ⏰ seasonally) The simple no-nonsense choices here are conveniently located and you can't argue with the prices or the sunsets.

Cégep Student Residence (☎ 418-862-6903 ext 282; 325 Rue St Pierre; s/d $25/35) Clean and quiet, at least when school is out, this college housing might not give the most authentic picture of how students really live. Sparsely equipped kitchens are at your disposal.

Auberge de l'Anse (☎ 418-867-3463, 800-556-0406; 100 Anse au Persil; d $75-95) Away from the town center with views over the water, the 11 quiet rooms here are clean and neat. It's open mid-April to mid-October. There's a restaurant on site with regional fare and breakfasts.

Au Vieux Fanal (☎ 418-862-5255; 170 Rue Fraser; d without/with river view $85/100; ☒ seasonally; ☒) One of the best motels on the strip is this simple place with great views of the river, a heated swimming pool and charming owners.

Eating

There's no excuse for going without good food here. For a tough choice of three in one setting, head to the converted house that contains **La Romance/Le St Patrice/Epicier** (☎ 418-862-9895; 169 Rue Fraser). All are open daily for dinner and lunch Sunday to Friday; Epicier is also open for lunch on Saturday. La Romance (mains $30) is an intimate dining room with romantic fondues or game such as venison and buffalo. Le St Patrice (mains $20 to $26) on the house's other side, is fancier and features seafood, such as scallops and scampi. The appetizers, like local crab and goat pâté, are excellent. Perhaps most alluring is Epicier (mains $20), the least-expensive room. It's around back and is exactly like walking into an old-time grocery store. It also has a wonderful deck that transports diners to a fishing wharf. Get the steakfrites and enjoy the surroundings.

Chez Antoine (☎ 418-862-6936; 433 Rue Lafontaine; table d'hôte lunch/dinner $14/35, dinner mains $16-30; ☒ lunch Mon-Fri, dinner) Long-considered the best in town, it maintains its tradition. Specialties include Atlantic salmon, shellfish and fondue. In fine weather the *terrasse* completes a very enjoyable dining experience.

L'Estaminet (☎ 418-867-4517; 299 Rue Lafontaine; mains $6-13; ☒ 10am-midnight or 1am) You can feast on good salads, *panini* and pasta in a publike atmosphere, then wash them down with some 150 types of beer. Mussels with fries, the house specialty, start at $8.

Picolo Piazza (☎ 418-868-1671; 371 Rue Lafontaine; mains $9-18; ☒ lunch & dinner) Despite specializing in pizzas, make no mistake – this is quality cuisine with a Mediterranean nod. The

pastas and pizzas with a paper-thin crust are creative, the specialties well seasoned and the beer cocktails offbeat – try some brews mixed with cranberry juice or iced tea.

Getting There & Away

Highway 20 (exit 503), Rte 132 and Hwy 185 lead directly into Rivière du Loup.

Orléans Express arrives/departs the **bus station** (☎ 418-862-4884; 83 Boul Cartier). It has seven buses daily to/from Québec City ($37, 2½ to four hours), six daily to/from Rimouski ($26, 1¼ hours), three daily to/from Edmundston ($21, two hours) and two to/from Halifax ($142, 11½ hours).

Rivière du Loup is linked by **VIA Rail** (☎ 418-867-1525, 800-361-5390; Cnr Rue Lafontaine & Rue Fraserville) three times a week to Québec ($55, 3½ hours), Percé ($94, 10 hours) and Halifax ($140, 14½ hours). Don't bother going to the station unless it's to catch your train – it's only open when they arrive, in the middle of the night.

A **ferry service** (☎ 418-862-5094; 199 Rue Hayward; adult/child aged 5-11/car $12/8/31) runs between Rivière du Loup and St Siméon from mid-April to January. Throughout the summer (mid-July to mid-August), there are four or five departures a day. Discounts are offered for the earliest and latest trips each day. No reservations are taken, so arrive at least 90 minutes prior to departure in summer. All boats leave from the marina and the trip takes 65 minutes. It can be rough; a motion-sickness pill may be welcome.

LE TÉMIS

Le Témis is the name affectionately given to a region concentrated around its main geographical feature, the 40km-long Lac Témiscouata. It's relatively unexplored, and non–French speaking visitors are few.

Highway 185, with its pulp and paper mills and forests interspersed with farms, provides a foretaste of New Brunswick. If you take this route, you can say you've been to **St Louis du Ha! Ha!** Its odd name could come from the Hexcuewaska Aboriginal language, referring to something unexpected, or from a 15th-century French expression for 'dead end'; others say it reflects the exclamation of wonder the area's colonizers uttered upon seeing such beauty. Considering the town's relative lack of attractiveness, we'd vote for one of the former explanations.

Near **Cabano**, a number of motels with the typical Québec amenity, a bar, and some campgrounds are easily found. In Cabano itself, there are a couple of restaurants on the one main street near the edge of the lake. **Fort Ingall** (☎ 418-854-2375; 81 Chemin Caldwell; adult/child $6.50/4; ✆ 9:30am-6pm Jun-Sep) is a 1973 reconstruction of an 1839 British fort set up to keep out Americans who had set their sights on the south shores of the St Lawrence.

The brief ferry ride across the scenic lake from tiny Notre Dame du Lac is a fine summer diversion. The slender lake is nestled between green hills. From the other side, roads lead to **Auclair**, one part of a multivillage cooperative that, in the early 1970s, joined forces to stand up to the provincial government, which argued that providing essential services was prohibitively costly, and wanted to close the towns down. After winning their stay of execution, residents opened a number of mini-industries, including a potato seed producer, lumber mill, maple grove, medicinal herb garden and even a coffin builder.

Domaine Acer (☎ 418-899-2825; 65 Rte du Vieux Moulin, Auclair; guided visit $2; ✆ 9am-5pm mid-Mar–mid-Oct, to 6pm Jul & Aug) is a maple grove-cum-economuseum, where you can taste maple products, all made or even originated on the premises. Sample the country's first alcoholic beverages made from a maple sap base, including Val Ambré, called cleverly an aceritif, from acer, the Latin for maple. The stuff is heavenly. In the gift shop, also pick up some of the maple jelly, which is great on toast. There are English signs in the facility and some guides speak a bit of English.

ÎLE VERTE
Just east of Rivière du Loup, Hwy 20 ends and, except during its brief reappearance around Rimouski, you must continue on Rte 132. This is like being forced to have a good time. It's a slow, scenic ride, so relax and go with it.

If you're liking it and want something still slower, Île Verte, with a population of 39, should do the trick. This dreamy 11km-long slice of the past is a fave of birders and cyclists and also has the river's oldest lighthouse. It won't be long before the island's old ways disappear and summer cottages take over. There are a dozen mostly inexpensive, easy-going places to stay, including the lighthouse.

EXTRA SPECIAL SPECIALTY

Culinary Charlevoix is known, along with numerous gourmet delicacies, for its lamb. But tiny Île Verte has something for the table found nowhere else in North America – salt-water lamb. Dominique Caron, the island's last shepherd, began raising sheep in 1999. Unlike their counterparts elsewhere, they are raised and fed on salty meadows, spending four hours a day grazing on the flats during low tide. And that's a sight that distracts the most ardent bird- or whale-watcher. These sheep have more muscle and less fat than other sheep, and the meat is more tender and flavorful. Alas, it is not plentiful. Local restaurants, inns and B&Bs serve it, as does the Château Frontenac (p284) in Québec City (at higher prices).

A small **ferry** (☎ 418-898-2843) and costlier **water taxis** (☎ 418-898-2199) shunt over according to the tides. Consider renting a bike in L'Isle Vert and leaving the car. Reservations are recommended.

TROIS PISTOLES
In rendering homage to the Basque fishermen who used to fish in the St Lawrence centuries before the arrival of other Europeans, the **Parc de l'Aventure Basque en Amérique** (☎ 418-851-1556; 66 Ave du Parc; adult/student $6/3.50; ✆ 9am-8pm Jun–mid-Oct) opens the door onto a part of history few are familiar with. The exhibits are in French only, but an English booklet is available, and English tours can be booked in advance. On the first weekend in July, the museum hosts the International Basque Festival, with music, games and a small parade.

Behind the museum is a large *fronton*, a rectangular, marked court with a large wall on one end used to play a game of *pelote* Basque, one of the world's oldest ball games. With ball speed up to 300km/h, it's also the world's fastest ball and bat game. Visitors can try playing *pelote* for themselves by renting the court with equipment for $10 per hour.

Guided excursions to the offshore **Îles aux Basques** (☎ 418-851-1202; 11 Rue du Parc; per person $15; ✆ Jun–early Sep) touch upon the social history of the island as well as its present status as a protected bird sanctuary. **Les Écumeurs**

(☎ 418-851-9955, 888-817-9999) run three-hour whale and seal-watching trips in either Zodiacs or larger, covered boats ($45).

Up on a hill with views in all directions, **La Rose des Vents** (☎ 418-851-4926, 888-593-4926; 80 2nd Rang Ouest; s/d incl breakfast $50/70), a lovely, old place with a modified roofline has been completely renovated inside. Comfortable rooms come with substantial breakfasts.

Camping & Motel des Flots Bleus Sur Mer (☎ 418-851-3583; Rte 132, Rivière Trois Pistoles; tent/RV $18/22, s/d from $40/60), a campground 5km west of town on the banks of the Rivière Trois Pistoles, is a small, quiet affair with a neighboring bare-bones motel.

A passenger ferry operated by **Compagnie de Navigation des Basques** (☎ 418-851-4676, 866-851-4676; 11 Rue du Parc) runs to/from Les Escoumins on the North Shore two or three times daily from mid-May to mid-October. The fare is $14 per adult, $35 per car. Reservations are accepted, but you must be at the terminal 45 minutes before departure.

PARC DU BIC

One of the smaller provincial parks is nonetheless one of Québec's most striking, and a visit is highly recommended. At times the landscape can seem surreal, especially with thousands of eiders flying overheard.

The **park** (☎ 418-869-3333; 33 Rte 132; adult/child $3.50/1.50; ☼ mid-May–mid-Oct) covers 33 sq km of islands, bays, jagged cliffs, lush, conical mountaintops and rocky shores covered with plump gray and harbor seals. The plethora of activities here includes organized minibus tours, sea-kayaking expeditions, specialized walks, bicycle rental (per day $18) and hiking, biking and Nordic skiing. The hiking and sea-kayaking are superb. The trail to **Champlain Peak** rewards with splendid views, or simply take the shuttle. It is not hard to spend a day or even longer exploring. The friendly, flexible and knowledgeable staff at **Kayak Rivi-Air Aventure** (☎ 418-736-5252; 3257 Rte 132), in the park, offer good kayaking options, including sunset, half- and full-day outings ($32/37/70).

The park's campground is nice, but you'll learn too late that not only does the traffic noise from the nearby hills not stop all night, it gets louder by the fitful hour. Off-season when the park is closed visitors can walk in for free.

RIMOUSKI

Rimouski is a fairly large, growing industrial and oil-distribution town. Despite that, it's not an ugly place and the main street, Rue St Germain, which runs east and west from the principal cross street, Ave Cathédrale, is made lively in part by the sizable student population.

At the intersection of Rue St Germain and Ave Cathédrale is the Place des Veterans. There you'll find the helpful **tourist office** (☎ 418-723-2322; 50 Rue St Germain Ouest; ☼ 9am-8pm mid-Jun–Sep, reduced hrs rest of year).

Sights & Activities

Five kilometers east of town is the newly rebuilt and expanded **Musée de la Mer** (☎ 418-724-6214; 1034 Rue du Phare; adult/family $9.50/24; ☼ 10am-5pm Jun & late Aug–mid-Oct, 9am-7pm Jul–late Aug), which tells the dramatic yet astonishingly little-known story of the sinking of the *Empress of Ireland* in 1914. After the *Titanic*, it's the worst disaster in maritime history. In the 14 minutes it took for the ship to sink after being rammed inadvertently by a Norwegian ship, 1012 people lost their lives. The museum has the country's largest collection relating to the ship and a multimedia show on the sinking.

Across the street from the museum is **Pointe au Père Lighthouse National Historic Site** (admission is by the same ticket, and it's open the same hours as the museum) which has displays on navigating the river and diving to the *Empress*. A film reveals what the ship now looks like (it's still here underwater). The lighthouse itself can be climbed, too.

The wreck itself is considered one of the premier **scuba diving** sites in the world and draws international visitors. However, this is a dangerous dive. Know what you are doing; several curious, inexperienced divers have died. Currents, visibility and water temperature are serious challenges.

In town, a pretty stone church, dating from 1826, houses **Musée Régional de Rimouski** (☎ 418-724-2272; 35 Rue St Germain Ouest; adult/student $4/3; ☼ 10am-9pm Wed-Sat, 10am-6pm Sun-Tue Jun-Sep, noon-5pm Wed-Sun Oct-May), which is primarily a gallery of local, contemporary art.

For hiking, mountain biking and a view of a canyon and waterfalls from the province's highest suspended bridge (62m), head to **Le Canyon des Portes de l'Enfer** (☎ 418-735-6063;

Chemin Duchénier; admission $6.50) in St Narcisse de Rimouski, some 30km south of Rimouski along Rte 232.

Sleeping

Gîte Victoria (☎ 418-723-4483; 77 Rue St Pierre; s incl breakfast $50-65; d incl breakfast $60-75) Four quiet rooms in the city center, each decorated in tasteful, pseudo-Victorian style.

Auberge de la Vieille Maison (☎ 418-723-6010; 35 Rue St Germain Est; s/d with shared bathroom incl breakfast $60-75) Somewhere between a B&B and a hotel (you do get the morning meal), this large house styled after a country home features eight comfortable rooms, all with hardwood floors. Plus, it's right on the main street.

Cégep Residences (☎ 418-723-4636; 320 Rue St Louis; students s/d $18/25, nonstudents s/d $23/32, without bedding s/d $12/18) This college rents standard student rooms year-round, on a daily, weekly or monthly basis. The walls look solid enough, but noise comes straight through them like they aren't there. In summer, though, some floors are pretty quiet.

Motels can be found on Boul St Germain, Boul Ste Anne and along Rte 132.

Eating

Central Café (☎ 418-722-4011; 31 Rue de l'Évêché Ouest; mains $8-15; ⏱ lunch & dinner) Off the main street in this old, two-storey house is one of the town's best, economical nights out. The popular bistro with a fine *terrasse* has something-for-everyone Italian fare.

Le Crêpe Chignon (☎ 418-724-0400; 140 Ave de la Cathédrale; mains $6-11; ⏱ lunch & dinner) Small and cozy, with an inexpensive French menu, this bright light on the Rimouski dining scene serves delicious savory and dessert crêpes in a relaxed, friendly atmosphere.

La Brûlerie d'Ici (☎ 418-723-3424; 91 St Germain Ouest; ⏱ 8am-11pm) For hanging out, having a continental breakfast, a light snack or just getting decent coffee, this is the place.

Getting There & Away

BOAT

There's a **ferry** (☎ 418-725-2725, 800-973-2725) linking Rimouski with Forestville on the North Shore. From late April to early October, two to four boats make the 55-minute journey every day. The one-way fare is $15/10 per adult/child. A car is $35. Reservations are accepted.

The **Relais Nordik** (☎ 418-723-8787, 800-463-0680; www.relaisnordik.com in French; 17 Ave Lebrun) takes passengers on its weekly cargo ship en route to Sept Îles, Havre St Pierre and villages along the Lower North Shore. It departs Rimouski at noon Tuesday from early April to mid-January and gets to Blanc Sablon at 7pm Friday. There are different classes of cabins, and prices vary accordingly. For accommodations, meals (amazingly good) and transport in the basic, four-person cabin, the fare is $801 return. Reservations are best made months in advance, especially if you want to take a vehicle, for which the costs are exorbitant. All boats and ferries leave from the marina, off the highway, just north of the city. Motion-sickness pills are advisable and a bicycle is very handy at the stopovers.

BUS

Orléans Express buses leave from the **bus station** (☎ 418-723-4923; 90 Rue Léonidas) to Québec City ($43, four hours, seven daily), Rivière du Loup ($23, 1½ hours, five daily) and Gaspé ($40, four daily), and the south (nine hours, two daily) and north (seven hours, two daily) coasts of the peninsula.

CAR

Allô Stop (☎ 418-723-5248; www.allostop.com; 106 Rue St Germain Est; ⏱ 10am-5:30pm Sat-Wed, 10am-9pm Thu & Fri) hooks up drivers with those needing lifts to Québec City or Montréal. A ride to Québec costs just $15.

TRAIN

For VIA Rail services, the **train station** (☎ 800-835-3037; 57 Rue de l'Évêché Est) is only open when trains pull in, usually after midnight. Six trains a week go to/from Montréal ($90, eight hours).

GASPÉ PENINSULA

The rounded chunk of land that juts out north of New Brunswick into the Gulf of St Lawrence is known locally as 'La Gaspésie.' And what an inspiring, relatively neglected bit of paradise it is. Compared with its admittedly impressive kin, Cape Breton Island, it is less commercial, less developed, less busy and cheaper, and has even more jaw-dropping scenery.

QUÉBEC

East of Matane, the characteristic features of the region really become evident: the trees and woods thicken into forests, the towns dwindle in size, the St Lawrence River widens, eliminating glimpses of the other side, the wind picks up the salt air, and you sense remoteness more and more. The landscape, particularly on the north coast, also becomes breathtakingly spectacular, as rocky cliffs plunge into the sea and layers of mountains and hills stretch for miles. Little villages, punctuated by the silvery church spires glistening in the sun, crouch around coves.

The south coast of the Gaspé Peninsula along the Baie des Chaleurs, known as the bay side, is quite different from the north coast. The land is flatter and less rocky and the weather warmer. Despite the red, seaside cliffs, the landscape is not as impressive. There are a few English towns (residents have charming accents; they pronounce Gaspé 'Gaspee' and Percé 'Percy'!). For the traveler who struggles with French, these communities can make a *petit* respite!

The Gaspé has some of Québec's best hiking and possibilities for adventure tourism. Parc de la Gaspésie is stunningly rugged and Percé has one of the country's most magnificent landmarks. The inland area is virtually uninhabited.

Visitors will have no problem finding services, though tourism is less developed than elsewhere. One word of caution – the tourist season runs from about June to mid-September. Outside those times things seriously wind down, and from November to mid-May visitors are as rare as warm days.

STE FLAVIE

On Rte 132 in Ste Flavie, the large **Gaspésie information center** (☎ 418-775-2223, 800-463-0323; 357 Rte de la Mer; ⊙ 8am-8pm mid-Jun–mid-Sep, 8:30am-4:30pm rest of year) is a wealth of help. If you're here late in the season, pick up one of the pamphlets listing facilities that remain open until mid-October.

Ste Flavie's **Centre d'Art Marcel Gagnon** (☎ 418-775-2829; 564 Rte de la Mer; admission free; ⊙ 8am-11pm May-Sep, 8am-9pm Oct-Apr) is definitely worth a visit. It's an ever-evolving inn, restaurant and art school based around an exhibit of more than 80 life-sized concrete statues by prolific sculptor, painter and writer Marcel Gagnon. The figures, all with different faces, march out to sea, appearing and disappearing with the tide. Gagnon's studio/gallery displays and sells a range of work and now his son, Guillaume, is also creating works of his own. It's becoming a family industry, but it's all done so well who can whine?

The center includes a restaurant/café that is recommended and the **Auberge** (☎ 418-775-2829; 564 Rte de la Mer; s $50-90, d $60-100) for spending the night in a comfortable room by the water's edge. Breakfast is included. The restaurant has seafood mains from $13 to $19 and less expensive dishes, but with its location it's ideal for just a drink.

Captaine Homard (☎ 418-775-8046; 180 Rte de la Mer; mains $13-18, table d'hôte $25; ⊙ lunch & dinner), just west down the road, gets packed with locals and visitors. The very nice, nautically-themed dining room overlooking the river features seafood. When you roll out, Rte de la Mer also has half a dozen B&Bs.

INTERNATIONAL HIKING ON THE APPALACHIAN TRAIL

The continent's longest continuous hiking trail stretches from Mt Springer, Georgia, USA to Forillon National Park at the tip of the Gaspé Peninsula. It runs along the peaks and valleys of the Appalachian Mountains, one of the world's oldest chains, for a total of 4574km. The 946km Canadian segment was added to the well-established American trail in 2001 and though still not well known, forced a name change to the International Appalachian Trail (IAT).

The Canadian extension winds from Maine, through New Brunswick (274km), over Mt Carlton, its highest peak, and into Québec at the Matapédia Valley. It courses 672km through the scenic valley, north to Amqui then east through breath-taking Parc de la Gaspésie to coastal Mont St Pierre and along the Gulf, ending at the cliffs in Forillon.

Although there are portions that should be attempted only by experienced hikers, the trail is well marked with shelters and campsites along the way. For more details, log on to www .internationalat.org. You can order a Gaspé hiking trail map by calling ☎ 800-463-0323, clicking on www.tourisme-gaspesie.com or asking at major Gaspésie tourist offices. Information is also available at outfitters in Matapédia (p330) and park information offices.

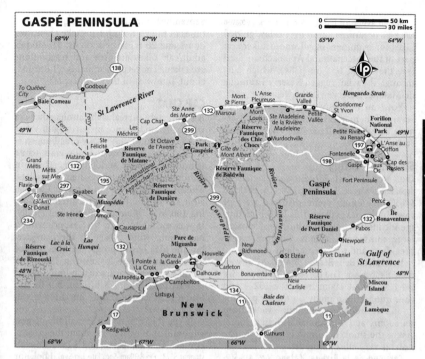

GASPÉ PENINSULA

QUÉBEC

While here, drop by the **Vieux Moulin** (☎ 418-775-8383; 141 Rte de la Mer; admission free; ◷ 9am-9pm) where rarely seen mead, a wine produced from honey, is made.

GRAND MÉTIS

One of the province's most revered attractions, the **Jardins de Métis** (☎ 418-775-2222; 200 Rte 132; adult/child/student $14/free/12; ◷ 8:30am-6pm Jun–mid-Oct) comprises 16 hectares (40 acres) of immaculately tended gardens boasting more than 2000 varieties of plants. Begun in 1910, the gardens are also known as the Reford Gardens (after Elsie Reford, who inherited the land from her uncle Lord Mount Stephen, founder of the CPR). Streams, paths and bridges add variety to the landscape, as does a 37-room mansion doubling as a museum. Various international floral exhibits also bloom here every summer. For a pick-me-up, there's a restaurant and café with afternoon teas served.

About 10km east of town are the villages of **Métis Beach** and **Métis sur Mer**, with nice sandy beaches. This area has tradition-

ally been a country retreat for bourgeois, wealthy English families. It's worth taking a detour through the towns to see the large houses with Anglo-Saxon signs positioned on their front lawns.

MATANE

Matane is a commercial fishing port famous for its shrimp. While not a particularly enticing town, you could do worse at meal time, especially during the **Festival de la Crevette** (Shrimp Festival), which takes place around June 20 every year.

A **tourist office** (☎ 418-562-1065; 968 Ave du Phare Ouest; ◷ 9am-6pm Jun-Sep) can be found here.

Sights & Activities

Salmon go up the river here to spawn in June and the observation center/dam/salmon ladder where fish can be seen is worth a peak before or after dinner. It's in the park at the top of Rue St Jerome. It's also possible to do some fishing right downtown. Take the Promenade des Capitaines road off Rte 132 and you'll see salmon anglers in action.

Absolu Aventure (☎ 418-566-5774; www.ecoaventure.com) organizes one- to 14-day guided hikes for beginners or advanced hikers on part of the International Appalachian Trail (see the boxed text on p284), which cuts through the wild, rugged Réserve Faunique de Matane. Reserve via the website.

You can buy fish, fresh or smoked, at several fish markets in town. Try **Poissonnerie Boréalis** (☎ 418-562-7001; 985 Ave du Phare Ouest; ⊙ 9am-6pm).

Sleeping & Eating

Chez Nicole (☎ 418-737-4896; www.giteetaubergedupassant.com/nicole; 3371 Rte 132 Ouest, St Ulrich; s/d $45/50). Although some distance west of town in the next village, this B&B is recommended for its quiet location, great sunsets, large comfortable rooms, fabulous megabreakfasts and overall excellent value.

Hotel Motel Belle Beach (☎ 418-562-2323; www.hotelbelleplage.com; 1310 Rue Matane sur Mer; s $65, d $69-$120) About 100m from Rte 132 – and thus quieter than many on the strip – this good riverside place offers fine views from its rooms and a reasonable dining room. Ask if the smoked salmon is available. The hotel is very close to the ferry terminal.

Camping de la Rivière Matane (☎ 418-562-3414; 150 Rte Louis Félix Dionne; tent & RV sites $13-19) Southwest of downtown, this place (with 144 sites) offers good, quiet camping in the woods. Follow the signs from the corner of Rue Parc Industriel and the Rte Louis Félix Dionne and proceed for 3km.

Le Rafiot (☎ 418-562-8080; 1415 Ave de Phare Ouest; seafood mains $13-16; ⊙ lunch Mon-Fri, dinner Mon-Sat) This yellow-and-white place on Rte 132 is a casual sort of pub with maritime-themed decor, plenty of seafood and good prices on shrimp dinners all summer long. There are also more standard, lower-cost brasserie items on the menu.

Getting There & Away

Buses (☎ 418-562-4085; 521 Rte 132) arrive at and depart from the Irving gas station, 1.5km east of the center of town. Two Orléans Express buses a day go to Gaspé ($48, 5¼ hours), and four a day go to Rimouski ($18, 1½ hours).

The **ferry terminal** (☎ 418-562-2500, 877-562-6560) provides the easternmost link to the North Shore. Passenger ferries carrying 126 cars run year-round to Baie Comeau and Godbout several times a day from May to

September. Service is less frequent other times of the year. Both trips take about two hours and 20 minutes and cost $13/30 per adult/car. Bikes are free and reservations are taken. The ferry terminal is off Rte 132, about 2km west of the town center.

CAP CHAT

A completely surreal sight awaits you here where the St Lawrence meets the gulf. After nearly 200km of *only* rocky coastline, scattered villages and forested hills, giant white windmills appear suddenly, perched on hilltops stoically twirling their propellers. This is the largest wind farm in Canada, with 133 of the dreamlike critters producing 100 MW of electricity, all used locally. It was meant to be a first experiment in harnessing wind power in the province, but the idea hasn't progressed much since the windmills were installed in 1988. The world's largest vertical axe windmill (110m) is here, too – alas, it's broken, but freeze-frame it in a photo and your friends will never know!

If you'd like to take a tour of the biggest windmill and learn more about the project, contact **Éole Cap-Chat** (☎ 418-786-5719; adult/student $5/3; ⊙ 8:30am-5pm late Jun-Sep). Look for the signs on Rte 132 just west of Cap Chat. English-language tours are available.

Right off Rte 132 east of the bridge at Cap Chat, **Camping Au Bord de la Mer** (☎ 418-786-2251; tent & RV sites $14-18) is a simple campground offering some nice views.

STE ANNE DES MONTS

A regional service center, Ste Anne is home to numerous restaurants, motels and shops. It's not one of the prettier highlights, but it is a good place to stock up before heading into Parc de la Gaspésie. The **tourist bureau** (☎ 418-763-7633; 96 Boul Ste Anne Ouest; ⊙ 9am-4:30pm Mon-Fri) is right on Rte 132. The Orléans Express bus stop is next door.

A converted school, **L'Échouerie** (☎ 418-763-1555; 295 1-ère Ave Est; dm $20) hostel offers a kitchen, a café, bike rental, transportation to Parc de la Gaspésie – the works. To get there from the bus stop, cross the street, go east to Rte de Parc, heading toward the church, then east along the river road. It's a 2km walk. The only hang-up is that it was for sale during research and its future was uncertain.

Ensconced in an old, Québec-style home with a typical red roof, **Gîte l'Estran** (☎ 418-763-3261; 43 1-ére Ave Est; s/d $50/60), a handsome and convenient B&B, is close to the wharf and church.

PARC DE LA GASPÉSIE

From Ste Anne des Monts, Rte 299 runs south to the outstanding, rugged **park** (☎ 418-763-3181, 866-727-2427; www.sepaq.com/Fr/Parcs/Gaspesie.htm; admission $3.50), 802 sq km of spectacular scenery dotted with lakes and two of the province's most beautiful mountain ranges, the Chic Choc and McGerrigle Mountains, which together include 25 of the 40 highest summits in Québec. One of the province's best camping spots is here, as well as some of the best hiking (the International Appalachian Trail passes through). What's more, the only herd of caribou south of the St Lawrence River lives in the park. If you're lucky, you'll see them in the distance, but stay on the paths to protect them and the fragile vegetation.

At the park's **Interpretation Centre** (☎ 418-763-7811; ☾ 8am-8pm early Jun–late Sep), the staff are extraordinarily helpful in planning a schedule to match your time and budget. They also rent hiking equipment.

Mont Jacques Cartier (1270m) is the highest peak in the Gaspésie. Hiking the mountain takes about 3½ hours roundtrip and makes for a very worthwhile excursion – the alpine scenery and views are fantastic, and it's fairly common to see some of the herd of woodland caribou munching on lichen near the barren peaks. Other fabulous walks include the strenuous, steep trek to the summit of **Mont Albert** and the less known, exhilarating half-day return trip up **Mont Xalibu** with alpine scenery, mountain lakes and a waterfall on the way. Morning and evening, moose often feed at **Lac Paul**.

Overnight **camping** tent and RV sites cost $24 in one of the four campgrounds. The busiest one is across the road from the Interpretation Centre, but try for a spot at the 39-site campground at Lac Cascapédia. Throughout the park, **chalets** start at $80 a day.

Gîte du Mont Albert (☎ 418-763-2288, 866-727-2477; www.parcsquebec.com; r $112, cottages $136-235; ☒) is a large, comfortable lodge next to the Interpretation Centre for those who like their nature spiced with luxury. The facili-

ties include the pool (open to campers, too) and a first-class restaurant – if you want to treat yourself, here's the place to do it.

A bus runs from the Ste Anne des Monts tourist information center to the Interpretation Centre. It leaves at 8am daily; the roundtrip fare is $7/4 adult/child. Another **shuttle** ($14 roundtrip) runs hikers to the La Galène campground, the closest to Mont Jacques Cartier. From there, another shuttle ($6) takes hikers the final 4km to the beginning of the hiking trail that leads up the mountain; that shuttle departs five times daily. The buses operate from June 24 to the end of September.

RÉSERVE FAUNIQUE DES CHIC CHOCS

The **reserve** (☎ 418-797-5214; admission $3.50) surrounds and bleeds into Parc de la Gaspésie. Mainly a site for hunting and fishing, it also attracts geological expeditions. The park's rangers offer a gem-collecting trip (adult/child under 14 $23/12). Agates are common. In general, the area is less impressive than the Parc de la Gaspésie. To reach the main entrance, go south on Rte 299, 12km past the Gîte du Mont Albert, then east for 1.5km on the Rte du Lac Ste Anne toward Murdochville.

MONT ST PIERRE

The scenery becomes ever more spectacular east of Ste Anne des Monts. The North Shore, across the St Lawrence, disappears from view, and the road winds around rocky cliffs and waterfalls, every curve unveiling a stretch of mountains cascading down to the sea.

Mont St Pierre appears after a dramatic bend in the road and features brilliant sunsets. The town takes its name from a 418m mountain with a cliff that people regularly fling themselves from: enthusiasts of **hang-gliding** and **para-gliding** come here in droves to enjoy one of the best spots on the continent for the sport. At the end of July, the international hang-gliding festival **Fête du Vol Libre** (☎ 418-797-2222) turns the skyline multicolored with hundreds of sails for 10 days. Near the eastern end of town, a rough road goes to the summit of Mont St Pierre, where there are takeoff stations and excellent views. If you're not hoofing it up the mountain – which takes an hour – you must have an ATV.

If you feel like running off a cliff, your best bet is to do it with **Pilot Yvon Volé** (☎ 418-797-2896; 34 Rue Prudent Cloutier). The tandem jump with Yvon costs a cool $100 for a 10- or 15-minute ride, but hey, you only live once.

Near the village of Mont Louis, just 6km east, the **Parc et Mer Mont Louis** (☎ 418-797-5270; 18 10-ème Rue Est; admission free; ☽ 8am-10pm late Jun–Sep) is a combination Internet café, restaurant and campground with a water's edge location.

Parc de la Gaspésie can be reached via rough, unpaved roads (watch for logging trucks!) from behind Mont St Pierre, but having a good map is helpful, as the routes are not marked well.

Motel Mont St Pierre (☎ 418-797-2202, 800-797-2202; puunik@glovetrotter.qc.ca; s/d $65/75) is a good choice among the limited options.

Auberge Les Vagues (☎ 418-797-2851; 84 Rue Prudent Cloutier; dm $16, s/d $25/42, motel rooms $35/45), a hostel/motel, has tiny rooms, but the place includes all you'll need, with a low-brow restaurant/bar and communal kitchen on the premises. The motel rooms have undergone slightly more renovations than the hostel accommodations.

The smaller of two campgrounds in Mont St Pierre, **Camping du Pont** (☎ 418-797-2951; 120 Rue Prudent Cloutier; tent site $16) is slightly more pleasant, though near the main road.

EAST OF MONT ST PIERRE

Eastbound, the landscape increases in majesty. Everybody finds their own favorite vistas and villages to marvel over and photograph. Watch for the viewpoints and picnic areas and be prepared for some strain on the engine and the brakes. **Ste Madeleine de la Rivière Madeleine** has a lighthouse with adjacent café to visit for a pit-stop. As the road winds and then dips into and out of towering green valleys around **Grande Vallée**, look for unusual, even playful, patterns etched by glaciers onto the planet's oldest rock. At L'Anse Pleureuse, turn south to **Murdochville** for tours (including going underground) of its impressive, yet somewhat unappealing, **copper mine** (☎ 418-784-3335; 345 Rte 198; adult/child $8/5; ☽ 9am-5pm mid-Jun–mid-Oct).

Petite Vallée is a particularly attractive village that bursts to life with the **Festival en Chanson** (☎ 418-393-2394; ☽ end Jun). Founded in 1982, this has become one of the most popular and important folk-song festivals

in the province, launching the careers of popular singers Daniel Boucher and Richard Séguin. It usually lasts about 10 days and, despite its status, has retained an intimate feel – kids and even the local butcher participate impromptu on stage.

So, you're thinking this is a peaceful area? Hard to imagine, but miniscule **St Yvon** was hit by a very wayward torpedo in WWII.

For those not visiting Forillon, Rte 197 runs south just past Petite Rivière au Renard, avoiding the end of the peninsula.

At **Cap des Rosiers**, the gateway to Forillon National Park, a **graveyard** on the cliff tells the town's history: how the English came from Guernsey and Jersey; how the Irish settlers were Kavanaghs, O'Connors etc; and how both groups mingled with the French. Generations later, the same names live on. The lighthouse is the highest in Canada.

FORILLON NATIONAL PARK

Well worth a stop for its rugged seaside terrain and wildlife, this **park** (☎ 418-368-5505; www.pc.gc.ca/pn-np/qc/forillon; adult/child/senior/family $5/2.25/4.25/12.50; ☽ reception 9am-9pm Jun–early Oct, park 24hr) lies at the extreme northeastern tip of the peninsula. Run by the ever-efficient Parks Canada, it offers a wealth of organized activities (at least one a day in English). In the woods, you might come across moose, deer, fox and an increasing population of black bear (many tourists report sightings – take precautions, see p54). The shoreline cliffs attract seabirds (including great blue herons), and whales and seals make frequent appearances offshore.

There are two main entrances with visitors' centers where you can pick up maps: one at L'Anse au Griffon (east of Rivière au Renard), on Rte 132, and another on the south side of the park at Fort Péninsule.

Sights & Activities

The north coast consists of steep limestone cliffs – some as high as 200m – and long pebble beaches. **Cap Bon Ami** showcases the best of this topography. You can do some whale-watching through the telescope there (and look for seals close to shore). In the north sector, beyond Cap des Rosiers, you'll find a great picnic area with a small, rocky beach. The south coast features more beaches, some sandy, with small coves. **Penouille Beach** is said to have the warmest waters.

The good trails that meander through the park range from easy, 30-minute walks to a rigorous 18km trek that takes six hours one way. The lovely hike to **Cap Gaspé** is gentle and provides seashore views. The International Appalachian Trail (see the boxed text on p320) ends in the park, where the Appalachians plunge into the sea.

Boat tours offer an opportunity for **whale-watching**.

Sleeping

HI Auberge de Gaspé (☎ 418-892-5153; www.gaspesie.net/aj-gaspe; 2095 Boul Grande Grève, Cap aux Os; dm $16/20, r members/nonmembers $21/25; � May-Nov) One of the most established HI hostels in the province features a fine view overlooking the bay. This friendly spot can accommodate 54 people. Breakfast and dinner are available, as are kitchen facilities.

Forillon Campgrounds (☎ 418-368-6050; tent/RV sites $21/23) The park contains 367 campsites in four campgrounds, and it often fills to capacity. Petit Gaspé is the most popular campground, as it is protected from sea breezes and has hot showers. The smallest campground (41 sites) is at Cap Bon Désir.

Getting There & Around

Transportation is very limited. The Orléans Express bus that runs along the north coast of the peninsula from Rimouski to Gaspé (p319) stops at the hostel throughout the summer. A drawback for those without vehicles is that this still leaves a prohibitive distance to any of the hiking trails and campgrounds. The hostel rents bikes and the bus driver may drop passengers within the park. A shuttle tools around the park stopping at Penouille ($1.50).

GASPÉ

After a few hundred kilometers of tiny villages, Gaspé may seem like a small metropolis. And after hours of stunning scenery, it also feels pretty mundane, even with the pleasant location at the end of the bay. Despite the anticlimax, it's a place to get some practicalities accomplished for you and your vehicle.

This was where Jacques Cartier first landed in June 1534. After meeting with the Iroquois of the region, he boldly planted a wooden cross and claimed the land for the king of France.

The **Musée de la Gaspésie** (☎ 418-368-1534; 80 Boul Gaspé; adult/student $4/3; � 9am-7pm late Jun–early Sep, 9am-5pm Tue-Fri & 1-5pm Sat & Sun early Sep–mid-Dec & mid-Jan–late Jun) depicts the lives of the region's settlers and features some maritime exhibits, crafts and a section on traditional foods. A newer exhibit details a naval battle out in the gulf during WWII. The site also familiarizes you with Cartier's voyages. Perhaps best are the unique six standing bronze plates outside comprising the descriptive **monument** (admission free; ☐ 24hr) commemorating his landing.

The **Site Historique Micmac de Gespeg** (☎ 418-368-6005; 783 Boul Pointe Navarre; adult/student $5/4; ☐ 9am-5pm mid-Jun–mid-Sep) teaches visitors about the traditional Mi'kmaq culture in a re-created village setting with a good gift shop. English tours are available.

Motel Adams (☎ 418-368-2244, 800-463-4242; www.moteladams.com; 20 Rue Adams; s/d from $60/70) has large rooms, an attached restaurant and bar and a central, easy to find location, making it a no brainer for a one-night stopover.

The central, regional college up the hill in a monumental edifice, **Cégep de la Gaspésie** (☎ 418-368-2749; 94 Rue Jacques Cartier; s/d $25/40), is worth checking for a cheap bed during the summer. There are laundry and kitchen facilities.

For a standout bite and delicious coffee, the homey, amenable **Café des Artistes** (☎ 418-368-2255; 249 Rue de Gaspé; mains $4-20; ☐ 8am-10:30pm), with atmosphere to spare, is miles away from the Tim Hortons across the street. And the bathrooms are nice enough to move into.

A small airport south of town links Gaspé with Montréal and the Îles de la Madeleine daily. For flights, contact Air Canada Jazz.

PERCÉ

The Supreme Being had a very good day when designing and laying down this bit of the planet. It's as though it was all neatly placed to engage and charm the human eye. Even the encroachment and developments of *Homo sapiens* have, with a few exceptions, somehow maintained the grand scheme.

The highlight, and to what the town owes its fortunes and glory, however modest, is a huge chunk of multihued limestone with a hole in it. The 88m-high, 475m-long **Rocher Percé** (Pierced Rock), one of Canada's best-known landmarks, is truly stunning; photos could never do its majesty justice.

QUÉBEC

Together with the many activities possible here, and the dense (by Gaspé standards) assortment of lodgings and eateries, it's certainly enough to warrant a multiday stay. Spring and fall make perfect visiting times but, even in the peak summer season, avoiding large concentrations of people is possible with some planning.

The **tourist office** (☎ 418-782-5448, 800-463-0323; 142 Rte 132; ☒ 9am-7pm late May–Nov) is in the middle of town.

Sights & Activities

The town's most famous attraction, **Rocher Percé**, is accessible from the mainland at low tide only (a timetable is posted at the tourist information office and by the stairs leading down to the rock). Signs warning of falling rocks should be taken seriously – each year, some 300 tons of debris detach from the big rock. In fact, there used to be two holes in it, but one arch came crashing down in 1845. To get there, take Chemin du Mont Joli to the end and descend the stairs. The park, which oversees the rock, charges $3.50 a day for a pass to all its other components including the interpretation center, Île Bonaventure and some of the surrounding waters.

The newly-moved **Centre d'Interprétation** (☎ 418-782-2240; 4 Rue du Quai; admission $3.50; ☒ 9am-5pm Jun–mid-Oct) is a good place to learn about the local flora, fauna and geology in bilingual exhibits.

The boat trips to green **Île Bonaventure**, an island bird sanctuary with more than 200,000 birds (including the continent's largest gannet colony) make for highly recommended excursions. Tour operators have booths and touts all over town, but you can also go to the dock and enquire at their offices. Ask whether you can disembark at the island, or just sail around it. The bigger boats can't get as close to the attractions.

Club Nautique de Percé (☎ 418-782-5403; 199 Rte 132) rents kayaks and offers kayak tours and dive trips. The pool here might suit those who don't wish to brave the seas.

Behind the town are some stimulating walks, for which the map from the tourist office is useful. Hike up to **Mont Ste Anne** to take in a great view and to see the cave along the 3km path, which begins behind the church. Another walking trail (3km) leads to the **Great Crevasse**, a deep crevice in the mountain near the Camping Gargantua campground.

Tours

Les Traversiers de l'Île (☎ 418-782-2750; 9 Rue du Quai) Offers good 90-minute cruises, and tours that give you time to walk the trails on the island. It's best to leave early (take a picnic) to make the most of the day and catch a late afternoon trip back. At $15, it's the world's best deal.

Taxi Percé (☎ 418-782-2102; 16 Rue St Michael) Gives tours around town hitting all the beauty spots such as La Grotte, Mont Ste Anne and Le Pic d'Aurore, which are difficult to reach without transportation.

GANNET GATHERING

Of the hundreds of bird species in Québec, none is closer to the hearts of Québecois than the northern gannet (Fou de Bassons). This may be due partially to their common trait of flying to Florida for the winter!

Île Bonaventure is home to 60,000 such birds, North America's largest colony. But it's not the sheer numbers or the noise that makes seeing them unforgettable. Adult gannets are of striking beauty, characterized by blazing white plumage highlighted by piercing blue eyes surrounded by a black patch and handsome gray-blue bills. During mating season, their heads turn pale yellow, as if glowing from within.

Mature gannets have a wingspan of about 2m, which is evident in their graceful flight, sometimes seeming never to require a single flap. Seeing them return to their life-long mate, evidently without a moment's confusion despite the mob, and then indulging in a little friendly caressing is both touching and amusing.

And then there is the bird's dive-bomb approach to hunting. They strike from a distance of about 20m, plunging straight down, sending spray all over the place, and then more often than not resurfacing from as deep as 5m with a mouthful of fish.

A visit to see them on the island (where you can get fabulously close and not disturb them) is a highlight of this already totally engaging day-trip. Other colonies exist on Île d'Anticosti and on the Îles de la Madeleine.

Sleeping

Accommodations here are fair bargains, although prices can spike sharply upward during midsummer, when visitor traffic is very heavy. But prices drop appreciably during the shoulder seasons. At the cheap end of the spectrum, numerous campgrounds, several with write-home-about views, lie close at hand. Booking ahead or finding a bed by early afternoon is recommended in high season. The tourist office can help you find a place if you're not having much luck.

There are three very good, convenient guesthouses with character on tranquil Rue de l'Église, right in the heart of town. They were built about 1910 and are open from May to October.

Gîte le Presbytère de Percé (☎ 418-782-5557; www.perce-gite.com; 47 Rue de l'Église; s incl breakfast $50-70, d $60-90) By the massive church and with a well-tended garden, the sizable, bright old place has rooms of varying sizes with gleaming hardwood floors sharing two full bathrooms.

Maison Ave House (☎ 418-782-2954; 38 Rue de l'Église; s/d with shared bathroom $30/40) And the prices just went up! The adorable owner of the Maison, Ethel, has been serving visitors for many years and is slowly winding down. The comfy, wood-lined rooms come with sinks.

La Maison Réhal (☎ 418-782-2910; http://pages.globetrotter.net/jaar001; 42 Rue de l'Église; s/d $50/60) From the outside, it's historic and subtle, featuring a wrap-around veranda. On the inside, its spic and span and totally renovated, but that doesn't prepare you for the decor, with its flowing curtains and valences and wild color schemes. If you don't like surprises, go to Holiday Inn – oops, there isn't one. The five different rooms come with continental breakfast.

Auberge du Gargantua Camping & Motel (☎ 418-782-2852; 222 Rte des Failles; tent & RV sites $20, motel s/d $60/75) Perched at the highest point around Percé, this complex features great views, nearby walking trails and, in the motel section, an excellent dining room. Far from the touristy center, 3km north of town off Rte 132, this is a great place.

La Maison Rouge (☎ 418-782-2227; rmasse@globetrotter.net; 125 Rte 132; dm/s/d $20/40/60) Another highly recommended choice, it comprises a converted red barn with three 10-bed rooms, plus a central, stately home with fine and spacious accommodations. The owners rent kayaks and encourage guitar-playing and building bonfires.

Hôtel La Normandie (☎ 418-782-2112, 800-463-0820; www.normandieperce.com; 221 Rte 132 Ouest; r $129-189). The classiest spot in town, the retreat-like Normandie amenities include the beach, room balconies, a dining room for seafood and expansive lawns with panoramas of Percé.

Motel Fleur de Lys (☎ 418-782-5380, 800-399-5380; www.gaspesie.com/fleurdelys; 248 Rte 132; s/d $80/90) Aside from being well-maintained, central and on the water, some of the units at the Fleur de Lys include handy, money-saving kitchenettes.

Eating

The following are open June to October. At other times, cross your fingers, there'll be one, maybe two places in town open.

La Maison du Pêcheur (☎ 418-782-5331; 155 Place du Quai; pizzas $13-23, mains $15-24; ☾ lunch & dinner) An obvious choice for a little splurge, this maritime-themed dining room serves 16 types of fantastic pizza (even octopus pizza!) baked in its Maplewood-heated stove, as well as other succulent dishes, particularly fish and seafood. The *table d'hôte* is a good buy. All this and a view of the rock to boot.

Les Fous de Bassans (☎ 418-782-2266; 162 Rte 132; mains $9-17; ☾ breakfast, lunch & dinner) This casual, long-running fave café just off the main street is recommended anytime – for just a coffee or a meal in the warm atmosphere. The menu includes seafood dishes and some vegetarian items.

Resto-bar Le Matelot (☎ 418-782-2569; 7 Rue de l'Église; mains $8-20; ☾ lunch & dinner) Good meals come with some ambiance at this candlelit place off the main street, which features seafood in the mid-price range (lobster's the specialty). They have a few tables out front. Later at night, you can just have a beer and catch the night's entertainment.

For picnic breads, try the **bakery** (9 Rue Ste Anne).

Getting There & Away

Orléans Express buses go twice daily in each direction. They both connect to Rimouski ($59, 8½ hours). A trip to Cap aux Os (Forillon National Park) requires a transfer in

Gaspé. During research the bus was stopping at the park in front of the tourist office, but a new location was planned.

VIA Rail serves the south side of the peninsula three times a week from Montréal (via Charny at Québec City). The one-way fare from Charny to Percé, a 12-hour ride, is $126. The station is 10km south of town at Anse à Beaufils. A taxi there costs about $13. The trains travel through the Matapédia Valley and along the south coast of the Gaspé.

NEW CARLISLE

One of the area's English towns, New Carlisle was founded by Loyalists and boasts some grand colonial homes. Three Protestant churches recall New England 19th-century architecture. René Lévesque, the provincial premier who worked the hardest for Québec separatism, was born here and lived at 16 Rue Sorel.

Hamilton House (☎ 418-752-6498; 115 Rue Gérard Lévesque; adult/student $4/3.50; ☯ 10am-4:30pm Jun-Sep) is a highlight of the area. Dating from 1852, it once housed the local member of parliament and his family. The two-story mansion has been lovingly stuffed to the brim with old photographs, scrapbooks, antiques and costumes of all kinds, placed thematically in the 14 rooms. Visits include a trip to the 'haunted basement.' Tea and scones are served in the sitting room most afternoons.

BONAVENTURE

A pleasant town founded by Acadians in 1791, Bonaventure boasts the region's most interesting attractions.

The **Musée Acadien** (☎ 418-534-4000; 95 Ave Port Royal; adult/student $5/4; ☯ 9am-6pm end Jun-early Oct; 9am-5pm Mon-Fri, 1-5pm Sun mid-Oct-mid-Jun) merits a visit. Its bilingual booklets explain some of the tragic yet fascinating Acadian history. The museum hosts great Acadian music evenings at 7:30pm on Wednesday.

Across the street, **Les Cuirs Fin de la Mer** (☎ 418-534-2926; 76 Rte 132 Est; ☯ 8am-8pm Jun 24-Sep, reduced hrs rest of year) is a must. It sells a range of nifty conversation-starting products made from fish skin. Cod, salmon, eel, shark – you name it. No, it doesn't smell; it's like leather, and is actually tanned in the basement. There are wallets, belts, ties, even a few skirts!

North of town, the **Grotte de St Elzéar** (☎ 418-534-4335, 800-790-2463; 198 Rte de l'Église; adult/child main cave $22/11, adventure cave $35/27; ☯ 8am-4pm Jun-mid-Oct) offers tours of one of Québec's oldest caves, one guided observational, the other spelunking on your own. You descend into the cool depths (it's one way to escape summer heat, but bring warm clothes!) and view the stalactites and stalagmites. English tours must be booked in advance. To get there, take Chemin de la Rivière and follow the signs.

The well-run outfit **Cime Aventure** (☎ 418-534-2333; www.cimeaventure.com; 200 Chemin Arsenault) leads a large variety of canoe/kayak trips – either a few hours along the scenic, tranquil Rivière Bonaventure (claimed to be Québec's cleanest) or several days around the tip of the Gaspésie. Excursions run from two hours ($25) to six days with one-day trips about $70. Cime Adventure's site has a camping-supply store (with vegetarian food), bike rental, a sauna and a campground. Take Chemin de la Rivière, which extends from Ave Grand Pré.

Bonaventure has some charming, if eccentric, places to stay and a good selection of eateries.

The specialty at **Auberge du Café Acadien** (☎ 418-534-4276; 168 Rue Beaubassin; s/d $50/60; mains $8-17; ☯ 9am-9pm) is the owners' smoked salmon (marinated in light maple sauce and smoked with maple wood). The delicious stuff comes alongside other excellent, Cajun-style meals in the restaurant. Upstairs has five comfortable guest rooms with shared bathroom.

Ask the owner of **Gîte du Foin Fou** (☎ 418-534-4413; 204 Chemin de la Rivière; s/d $40/55) why he calls his B&B 'Crazy Hay.' Answer: 'Because there's hay all around, and a nut in the middle – me!' There are creative surprises to be found everywhere in this spacious house that attracts a young, artistic, laid-back crowd.

Cime Aventure (☎ 418-534-2333; www.cimeaventure.com; 200 Chemin Arsenault tent/tipi sites $20/40) is one of the province's nicest campgrounds.

NEW RICHMOND

Nestled in the bay near the mouths of two rivers, New Richmond is another small Loyalist (read: English-speaking) center. The **British Heritage Village** (☎ 418-392-4487; 351 Boul Perron Ouest; adult/senior & student/family $10/7/$25; ☯ 9am-6pm Jun-Aug) re-creates a Loyalist village

Niagara-on-the-Lake (p129),
Ontario

CHRIS MELLOR

Walking track beside the Ottawa River (p219), Ottawa

CHRIS MELLOR

CN Tower (p83), Toronto

Niagara Falls (p121), Ontario

JON DAVISON

Place Royale (p285), Québec City

Restaurant on Rue du Petit Champlain (p285), Québec City

Mont-Tremblant (p268), Québec

Shops (p262) in downtown Montréal

of the late 1700s. As well as an interpretive center there are houses, a general store, a lighthouse and other buildings. The center also covers the influence of later Irish and Scottish immigrants.

CARLETON

With an active fishing wharf, fine scenic setting and good walking trails, Carleton is easily one of the best stops along the bay. The people of the Gaspésie come here for a day at the beach.

There's a seasonal **Tourist Office** (☎ 418-364-3544; 629 Boul Perron; ☼ 9am-5pm Jun-Sep) in the Hôtel de Ville. From the docks, boats depart for fishing or sightseeing excursions. At the **bird sanctuary** at the Baie du Barachois, right in the center of town, you can see herons, terns, plovers and other shore birds along the sandbar. Walking paths and a road also lead behind the town to the top of **Mont St Joseph** (555m), which provides fine views over the bay and across to New Brunswick. The blue metal-roofed oratory at the top can be visited – after the climb, the snack bar is a welcome sight.

Watch for the green awnings at the well-placed and economical **Gîte la Mer Montagne** (☎ 418-364-6474; www.bbcanada.com/3846.htm; 711 Boul Perron; s/d $55/65), with five rooms. Keep an eye on New Brunswick from the deck.

Set on a jutting spit of land in front of town, **Camping de Carleton** (☎ 418-364-3992; Pointe Tracadigash; tent & RV sites $15-20) gives you access to miles of beach. You can go swimming here, too. Rent canoes nearby to do some birding or just to explore the calm inner bay.

Le Marin (☎ 418-364-7602; 215 Rte de Quai; dinner mains $18-25; ☼ lunch Mon-Fri, dinner daily) is an inviting dockside eatery right on the water. It serves fresh seafood and other specialties using local ingredients. Since 1963, locals and visitors have been enjoying the food and view at **Le Héron** (☎ 418-364-3881; 561 Boul Perron (Rte 132); mains $3-19; ☼ 8am-midnight). It's got all the basics plus a kid's menu, seafood and even frog legs! You can't miss this large landmark in the middle of town.

Orléans Express buses stop at 561 Boul Perron; get tickets inside Le Héron. Buses go to Rimouski and Montréal twice daily. The **VIA Rail station** (☎ 800-361-5390; Rue de la Gare) is 1km from the center of town, back against the mountains.

PARC DE MIGUASHA

The small peninsula south of Rte 132, near Nouvelle, is renowned for its fossils, so much so that it is one of Canada's 13 Unesco world heritage sites. Evidently, no other fossil site does a better job of illustrating the Devonian period (342 to 395 million years ago) and its actually made to come alive. In this small region are 'the greatest number and best preserved specimens found anywhere in the world of the lobe-finned fishes that gave rise to the first four-legged, air-breathing terrestrial vertebrates – the tetrapodes.'

Inquire at the **information centre** (☎ 418-794-2475; 231 Rte Miguasha Ouest; adult/child/family $7.75/3.75/14.75, less for park only; ☼ 9am-6pm Jun–mid-Oct) about guided walks that take visitors through the museum and along a trail to the fossil-filled cliffs, where you can see fish and insects that existed here so long ago. Do not collect your own fossils!

POINTE À LA GARDE

There is no village here, just a castle. Yes, a castle; a modern, wooden one built by someone fulfilling a life-long dream to live in fairy-tale surroundings. It appears amid the trees as if from a storybook. Good news for others: it has been transformed into one of Québec's most memorable hotels. Ironically, the grandiose premises include a separate excellent, year-round HI hostel.

At **Chateau Bahia** (☎ 418-788-2048; 52 Boul Perron; dm $15-20, shared 3–5-bed r per person $24, d without/with bathroom $45/60; ☼ May-Oct), rooms come with their own staircase and balcony, allowing you your night in a castle tower – for a fraction of the price you might have to pay in Europe. For all rooms, breakfast is included. The on-site restaurant serves banquet-style dinners ($14) at 8:30pm, and these are stupendous. The Orléans bus will stop 100m from the door if you ask the driver.

POINTE À LA CROIX/LISTUGUJ

The bay now peters out in a swampy mix of mist-covered islands and weeds. Listuguj is the Mi'kmaw part of town, an area where they've lived for centuries. A bridge crosses over to Campbellton, New Brunswick. Some people live on New Brunswick time here (one hour ahead), as so many people work there, and businesses tend to accommodate both time zones.

A few kilometers west of the bridge the **Battle of the Restigouche National Historic Site** (☎ 418-788-5676; Rte 132; adult/child/senior/family $4/2.25/3.25/8.75; ⏱ 9am-5pm Jun–early Oct) details the 1760 naval battle of Restigouche, which finished off France's New World ambitions. The captivating interpretive center with simulated ship explains the battle's significance to the British and displays salvaged articles and even parts of a sunken French frigate.

MATAPÉDIA VALLEY

Between the village of Matapédia and the coast of the St Lawrence River lies this peaceful, pretty valley that's unlike any other portion of the Gaspésie. The broad-leafed maple and elm trees that cover the valley add a lot of color in autumn. The Rivière Matapédia is famous for its salmon fishing. Both Presidents Nixon and Carter forgot the world's cares casting a line here.

Matapédia

Somnolent, riverside Matapédia is a gateway for those embarking on the International Appalachian Trail (see the boxed text on p320). The tiny village also offers opportunities for some beautiful canoe/kayak expeditions. **Nature-Aventure** (☎ 418-865-2100; 9 Rue du Vieux Pont) leads a range of rugged and worthwhile paddles along either the Restigouche or Matapédia.

Causapscal

A pretty picture, the traditional look of the little town of Causapscal comes from a beautiful stone church and many older houses with typical Québecois silver roofs. Sometimes the odors of nearby sawmills make things unpleasant, but people generally come here to enjoy the outdoors. More than 25km of walking and observation trails meander through the surrounding hills. Salmon is king here, as you can tell by the outlandish salmon statue on the main road.

There are a couple of covered bridges south of town and, in the center, there's a pedestrian-only suspension bridge across the Matapédia – anglers go there to cast their lines where the Rivières Causapscal and Matapédia meet. If you want to try your luck at fishing, ask for details at the **tourist office** (☎ 418-756-6048; 53 Rue St Jacques;

⏱ 9am-4:30pm Mon-Sat Jun-Sep) or call the Québec government office (☎ 800-561-1616). Regulations are tight and all anglers require location-specific permits. They range in price from $10 to $250 a day and you gets what you pays for!

Regardless, check out the gorgeous **Matamjaw Historic Site** (☎ 418-756-5999; 53 Rue St Jacques; adult/senior & student/family $5/4.25/15; ⏱ 9am-5pm mid-Jun–Sep) for a glimpse of how the old-boys network did things when they wanted to fish. Admit it, you're envious.

If you want to linger, the **Auberge La Coulée Douce** (☎ 418-756-5720, 888-756-5270; www .lacouleedouce.com; 21 Rue Boudreau; s/d $75/85) up on the hill, is comfortable and has a dining room. Here you can listen to all manner of tall fishing tales.

The Orléans Express bus linking New Brunswick to the Lower St Lawrence stops at 122 Rue St Jacques.

ÎLES DE LA MADELEINE

Only higher temperatures and a few palm trees separate the world's island paradises from this string of isles in the Gulf of St Lawrence. These remote islands bewitch the visitor with their sense of isolation and unspoiled natural beauty. Where sandy beaches don't greet the waves, iron-rich red cliffs do. Wind and sea have molded them into fantastic shapes that seem to take on new forms in changing light; one never tires of looking at them.

In complement to the landscape's unusual hues, many of the island's houses and fishing boats sport smart, audacious colors. A can of paint goes a long way here, where small, modern villages are alight in purples, yellows, greens and reds. It's the kind of laid-back place where people don't lock their doors. The contented locals are not overly sociable or solicitous, but they're friendly and respectful of each other's privacy. About 95% of the population is francophone, but Anglophones with Scottish and Irish ancestry, descendants of shipwrecked sailors, live on Île d'Entrée and Grosse Île.

The Îles de la Madeleine (Magdalen Islands) are a dozen islands stretched out over some 100km, 105km from Prince Edward Island. Six of them are linked by long

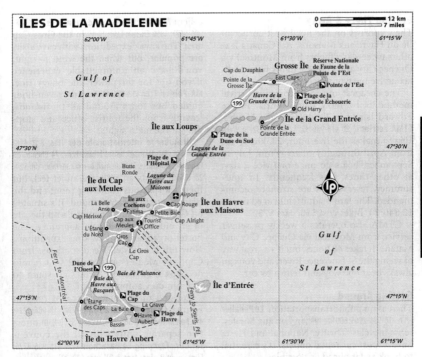

ÎLES DE LA MADELEINE

Gulf of St Lawrence

Cap du Dauphin
Pointe de la Grosse Île
Grosse Île
East Cape
Réserve Nationale de Faune de la Pointe de l'Est
Pointe de l'Est
Havre de la Grande Entrée
Plage de la Grande Échouerie
Old Harry
Île aux Loups
Île de la Grand Entrée
Pointe de la Grande Entrée
Plage de la Dune du Sud
Lagune de la Gande Entrée
Plage de l'Hôpital
Butte Ronde
Île du Cap aux Meules
Lagune du Havre aux Maisons
Airport
Île aux Cochons
La Belle Anse
Cap Rouge
Île du Havre aux Maisons
Cap Hérissé
Fatima
Petite Baie
Cap Alright
L'Étang du Nord
Cap aux Meules
Tourist Office
Gros Cap
Le Gros Cap
Gulf of St Lawrence
Dune de l'Ouest
Baie du Havre aux Basques
Baie de Plaisance
Île d'Entrée
L'Étang des Caps
Plage du Cap
La Baie
La Grave
Havre Aubert
Plage du Havre
Bassin
Île du Havre Aubert

Ferry to Montréal
Ferry to Souris PEI

QUÉBEC

sand spits and Rte 199. Except for Cap aux Meules, villages here are spread out and without traditional centers; the names refer more to regions than to towns.

Most surprising of all, in summer the place bubbles with life. Where the Gaspésie is overwhelmingly beautiful but socially limp, the islands are teeming with the energy of young, free-minded travelers (almost all French Québecois) who come here for days, even months. In fact, the place has been a magnet for artists, hippies and drifters since the 1960s, when they 'rediscovered' the islands. This influence continues to be felt with the current adventurous visitors into healthy foods, relishing the outdoors and letting it all hang out in bars livelier than you'd find on Rue St Denis in Montréal. Families and older couples come for more personal, private experiences.

Apart from the social scene, most of the islands' activities and sights revolve around the sea. Beach-strolling and exploring lagoons, tidal pools and cliff formations can take up days, but so can poking around the fishing villages and going on nature excursions. Swimming is possible in the open sea or, preferably, in some of the shallow lagoons. Beware of dangerous currents.

The sea and wind, which is nearly always very strong, create a powerful draw for kite- and windsurfing. The islands make a spectacular place for cycling – the main roads are paved and in good condition.

In July, look for the major sand castle contest on Havre Aubert and, at the end of August, the **Traditions Maritimes en Fête** with songs, shows and exhibits. In early spring, the controversial seal hunt causes friction.

Lodging is mostly in small B&Bs in people's homes, but there are also a couple of motels and campgrounds. The fresh seafood is memorable, especially the local mussels and lobster. A local specialty is *pot-en-pot*, a dish of mixed fish, seafood and sauce baked in a pie crust. The adventurous may want to try the dark, strong-tasting seal meat.

The islands fall in the Atlantic Time Zone, one hour ahead of mainland Québec.

Getting There & Away

The airport is on the northwest corner of Île du Havre aux Maisons. Air Canada Jazz offers twice-daily flights from Montréal via Québec City and Gaspé. Flights from Halifax arrive once or twice a week.

The cheapest and most common arrival method is by ferry from Souris, Prince Edward Island to Île du Cap aux Meules. **CTMA Ferries** (☎ 418-986-3278, 888-9863278; www .ctma.ca) makes the five-hour, 223km cruise from April through January. From July to September, boats go once or twice a day; at other times, less frequently. In midsummer, reservations are strongly recommended. The fare is adult/child aged five to 12 $40/20. Bikes cost $10, cars $75.

CTMA also operates a weekly passenger service from Montréal via Québec City and Matane. It takes 48 hours, but it's a great way of seeing the St Lawrence River, and you can always boat one way and return by car.

Getting Around

There is no public transportation. **Le Pédalier** (☎ 418-986-2965; 800 Rte 199), in Cap aux Meules, rents bicycles. Thrifty, National and Hertz have airport car rental outlets. It's essential to book as far ahead as possible.

ÎLE DU CAP AUX MEULES

Cap aux Meules is the busiest town on the islands and the commercial center of the archipelago. It's quite modern, which can be a little disconcerting for those seeking a quainter place. If you need supplies or to do some banking, do it here.

The **main tourist office** (☎ 418-986-2245, 877-624-4437; www.tourismeilesdelamadeleine.com; 128 Chemin du Débarcadère; ☼ 7am-9pm Jun 24–Sep, hrs vary rest of year) is near the ferry terminal, and has staff who can help find accommodations.

On the west side of the island lie the areas of **Fatima** and **L'Étang du Nord**, where you can see the red cliffs in their glory. At **La Belle Anse**, you can walk along the cliffs to gape at their patterns of erosion. At **Cap du Phare** (Cap Hérissé), the lighthouse is a popular place to watch sunsets. In the middle of the island, the high peak, **Butte du Vent**, offers a 360-degree panorama. At **Anse de l'Étang du Nord**, the harbor cuddles a concentration of boutiques and cafés.

Young, enthusiastic sportspeople who can ensure your outdoors thrills run the excellent **Aerosport Carrefour d'Aventures** (☎ 418-986-6677; 1390 Chemin Lavernière) in the Gros Cap area. The kayak expeditions with cave visits are popular, but when the wind is right, you'll have an unforgettable experience if you opt for the power kite buggy ride. **MA Poirier** (☎ 418-986-4467) runs seven-hour guided bus tours around all the islands, leaving from the tourist office and stopping at the main sights.

HI Auberge Internationale des Îles (☎ 418-986-4505; ilesdelamadeleine@hihostels.ca; 74 Chemin du Camping; campsites $15-20, member/nonmember dm $24/28, d $50) boasts an intimate, quiet feel, but there's a spacious gathering room and the islands' prettiest campground. It's situated on Gros Cap, a small peninsula on the site of an old marine biology laboratory. The hostel organizes sea-kayaking expeditions. Now *this* is a hostel! Head southeast from Cap aux Meules on Rte 199 to Chemin de Gros Cap. Follow Gros Cap south to Chemin du Camping.

Located on a quiet stretch of road in Fatima, **Chalet-Maison à Edgar** (☎ 418-986-5214; 49 Chemin Thorne; d $85-120, weekly $550-850) offers two separate units with all the conveniences. **Camping Le Barachois** (☎ 418-986-4726; Chemin du Rivage; tent & RV sites $17-23) is the islands' largest campground, but it still feels crowded.

Dropping into **Pas Perdus** (Lost Steps; ☎ 418-986-5151; 160 Chemin Principal; d $65; café meals $6-12; ☼ 7am-10pm) is a big part of the Magdalen experience, whether you sleep in the upstairs rooms or not (and they can be noisy when things get wild downstairs). The relaxed, bohemian, wood-paneled café is the center of the islands' youth-culture scene. At some point, everyone rolls through to have a drink at the bar, surf the Internet, read a book, or grab a shark burger ($6). Monday nights, locals kick the energy up a notch with the famous jam sessions.

Enjoy light, healthful meals in a relaxed atmosphere at **Café Théâtre Wendell** (☎ 418-986-6002; 185 Chemin Principal; mains $6-12; ☼ 11am-11pm), a perfect hangout in Cap aux Meules. It screens films most weekends at 9pm.

La Factrie (☎ 418-986-2710; 521 Chemin du Gros Cap; mains $8-20; ☼ lunch & dinner Mon-Sat) is in a lobster processing plant! Cafeteria-style, it serves up fresh seafood with no pretensions. Try the homemade soup ($4) and *coquilles* St Jacques ($6).

ÎLE DU HAVRE AUBERT

The archipelago's largest island lies south of Cap aux Meules, connected by long strings of sand at points barely wider than the road.

The liveliest area of **Havre Aubert** town is La Grave, an old section by the water at the southeastern tip of the island. Small craft and gift shops, some restaurants and many old houses line the main street. Here you feel the rustic charm of an old-time fishing community.

On any rainy day, the interesting **aquarium** (☎ 418-937-2277; 146 Chemin de la Grave; adult/child $5/3; ☼ 10am-6pm Jun–mid-Oct) is packed with visitors disturbed from their seaside activities. The 'petting pool' makes a popular stop.

The **Musée de la Mer** (☎ 418-937-5711; 1023 Rte 199; adult/child $4/2; ☼ 9am-6pm late Jun–Aug, 9am-5pm Mon-Fri & 1-5pm Sat & Sun Sep–late Jun) features displays on shipwrecks and the islands' transportation and fishing history.

A must-visit is the **Artisans du Sable** (☎ 418-937-2917; 907 Rte 199), a workshop and boutique specializing in creations made of sand.

La Maison de Camille (☎ 418-937-2516; 946 Chemin de la Grave; s/d $50/60), a B&B in the heart of La Grave, is a real charmer. A garden out back lines the waterfront, the wood-paneled interior exudes real warmth, and your barefooted host is a true winner (so laid-back that you might have to make your own breakfast).

Your island experience won't be complete without a visit to **Café de la Grave** (☎ 418-937-5765; 969 Rte 199; mains $8-12; ☼ opens 8:30am). This grand ex–general store has been transformed into a blissful café serving nachos, sandwiches, soups, salads, daily specials and *pot-en-pot*.

ÎLE DU HAVRE AUX MAISONS

Probably the most scenic of the islands, Havre aux Maisons is an explorer's paradise. Heading north from Cap aux Meules, take the first left from Rte 199 to Chemin de la Petite Baie and Chemin des Cyr, which curves around **Butte Ronde**, a steep, high hill worth the climb. Even more impressive is the east coast of the island, which you can see by following Chemin de la Pointe Basse and Chemin des Montants. Best approached from the north along Chemin des Montants, the landscape is ridiculously scenic, with rolling hills, isolated houses and a cute lighthouse guarding a dramatic view onto rocky cliffs and the rugged sea.

GROSSE ÎLE

Despite generations of isolation on the islands, many of the English residents here barely speak a word of French, a touchy subject for the francophone locals. Pointe de la Grosse Île, East Cape and Old Harry are the main communities. At Old Harry (named in honor of Harry Clark, who was for a long time the area's only inhabitant), walruses used to be slaughtered for oil. Sea Cow Lane is the site of the former walrus landing.

Gateway to the East Interpretation Center (☎ 418-985-2931; 56 Rte 199; admission free; ☼ 10am-6pm May-Sep) features an excellent exhibit on the rare flora and geological peculiarities of the islands. The center is near the salt mine, which excavates at a depth of more than 200m below sea level.

In Pointe de la Grosse Île, check out **Trinity Church**, known for its stained glass depicting Jesus, the fisherman. Through the windows you can see graves, piles of lobster traps, some solitary houses and then the sea – the island's world in microcosm.

At the **Council for Anglophone Magdalen Islanders** (☎ 418-985-2116; 787 Rte Principale; admission free; ☼ 8am-4pm Mon-Fri, 1-4pm Sat & Sun) in Old Harry, you can visit an old schoolhouse, which housed grades one through six for 52 years (take a look at what they had to use as a toilet!). About 16km north off La Grosse Île lies **Île Brion**, an ecological reserve that's home to 140 species of birds and much interesting vegetation.

POINTE DE L'EST

Linking Grosse Île and Île de la Grande Entrée this wild region boasts the archipelago's most impressive beach. **Plage de la Grande Échouerie**, a curving sweep of pale sand, extends for about 10km from Pointe Old Harry. Take the short road that begins near Old Harry's harbor.

ÎLE DE LA GRANDE ENTRÉE

This is a beautiful, isolated section of the archipelago less frequently visited than other areas.

Just past Old Harry, stop at **St Peter's by the Sea**, a lovely, peaceful little church overlooking the sea and bounded by graves of the Clark and Clarke families. On a breezy day, the inside offers a quiet stillness broken only by creaking rafters. The richly carved door honors drowned fishermen.

QUÉBEC

At **Club Vacances des Îles** (☎ 418-985-2833; 377 Rte 199), knowledgeable guides lead 2km to 10km nature walks ($5 to $10), ornithological kayak trips and cave exploration excursions ($30) where you swim, in a wetsuit, through caves and grottos, and even indulge in sensual mud baths! Tours in English are available, but ask first. The cafeteria is open to all, but the accommodations are for tour packages only.

One of the best restaurants on the islands is the unassuming but atmospheric **Délices de la Mer** (☎ 418-985-2831; 907 Chemin Principal; mains $7-16; ⏲ 8am-9pm) at the end of Rte 199. Sit with the fishermen and try the delicious chowder or cod.

FAR NORTH

Wherever you are in Canada, 'the North' or 'far North' are ambiguous terms. For the vast majority of people, two hours north of Montréal – or a few hours' drive north from almost any of the country's major cities – is considered the North. In Québec, certainly, straying more than a couple of hundred kilometers beyond the main population centers puts you in the land of the boreal forest. And yet, if you travel as far north as possible on the most remote route in the middle of nowhere, you might get halfway up the province.

The North, obviously, is an immense region, the most northerly sections of which are dotted with tiny Inuit and First Nations settlements accessible only by bush plane. The developed areas largely owe their existence to massive industrial operations – mining, forestry and hydroelectricity. While accessing the really far North (the Inuit communities in Nunavik) requires expensive flights, other areas of the Abitibi-Témiscamingue and James Bay regions can easily, with time, be reached by car and bus, and will provide a taste of Canada's True North.

ABITIBI-TÉMISCAMINGUE

What's it like up here? In over 65,140 sq km, the people barely outnumber the lakes. But despite the shortage of humans, this sparsely populated area occupies a special place in the Québecois imagination. The last area to be settled and developed on a major scale, it stands as a symbol of dreams and hardships.

The traditional land of the Algonquins, Abitibi-Témiscamingue is an amalgamation of two distinct areas, each named after different tribes. Témiscamingue, accessible only via northern Ontario and one long road south of Rouyn-Noranda, sees few tourists. It's more diversified in its vegetation and landscape, with valleys and the grand Lac Témiscamingue. Most of Abitibi's slightly more visited terrain is flat, which makes the stunning valleys and cliffs of Parc d'Aiguebelle all the more striking.

Abitibi-Témiscamingue was colonized following the usual pattern of resource exploitation. Before the 19th century, the only Europeans in the area were hunters and fur traders. Then forestry and copper mining brought more development. In the 1920s gold fever struck and thousands flooded the region in search of their fortune. Boomtowns bloomed around deposits. Many of these mines have now closed, with only the larger ones of Val d'Or (meaning Valley of Gold) and Rouyn-Noranda still surviving.

Today, this vast region of Québec retains an oddly exotic air, partially due to its remoteness. Generally, visitors are seeking solitude in its parks or are en route to still more epic northern destinations.

Réserve Faunique la Vérendrye

Relatively accessible, this immense **park** (☎ 819-736-7431, 800-665-6527; www.sepaq.com; Hwy 117; admission $3.50; ⏲ mid-May–mid-Sep) is best as a canoeing destination. Very satisfying circuit routes of varying lengths have been mapped and there are stunning campsites sprinkled around the lakes' edges. Even in a heat wave in midsummer, you may well have entire lakes virtually to yourself. And you don't need to be an expert or an athlete to enjoy the peace in this park. Aside from camping, there are chalets for rent. The waterfalls at Lac Roland are worth seeing. Though not evident, this is not a true wilderness as the central lakes are actually part of a massive reservoir and are very shallow.

The park is accessed at four points, all on Hwy 117. Coming from the Laurentians, **Le Domaine** (☎ 819-435-2541), 58km past the village of Grand Remous, has information, canoe rentals and services. Staff are so friendly you may receive an unexpected Christmas card!

During the 180km drive across the reserve from the south end to Val d'Or, there are no villages – make sure your tank is full.

Val d'Or

Born in 1933 around the Sigma gold mine, Val d'Or today looks like a mining boom-town of yesterday, with wide avenues and a main street (3-ème Ave) that one can easily imagine was frenzied in gold-rush days. That main street retains its traditional rough edge. The Sigma mine still operates, though it's no longer the city's economic engine. The **tourist office** (☎ 819-824-9646; 1070 3-ème Ave Est; ☺ 9am-5pm) is on Hwy 117 at the eastern end of town.

La Cité de l'Or (☎ 819-825-7616; 90 Ave Perreault; adult/student $25/20; ☺ underground tours 8:30am-5:30pm late Jun–early Sep) offers guided excursions 91m underground to show what gold mining's all about. On the same site is the **Village Minier de Bourlamaque** (adult/student $12/10), a restored mining village with 80 log houses. Call to reserve tours in advance, and don't forget to bring warm clothes if you're going underground.

Air Creebec flies into Val d'Or from Montréal. **Autobus Maheux** (☎ 888-797-0011; www.webdiffuseur.qc.ca/maheaux) covers the region with buses to Montréal (seven hours), Matagami (3½ hours), Rouyn-Noranda (1½ hours) and Chibougamau via Senneterre (six hours).

Parc d'Aiguebelle

As the Abitibi landscape can be a tad on the dull side, the stunning scenery in this **provincial park** (☎ 819-637-7322; 1737 Rang Hudson; admission $3.50; ☺ year-round) comes as a doubly pleasant surprise. Suddenly there are magnificent canyons and gorges, massive rocky cliffs with fascinating geological formations and excellent, rugged hiking trails (some 60km worth) flanked by trees 200 years old.

This small park (only 268 sq km) has three entrances – via Mont Brun (well marked on Hwy 117 between Val d'Or and Rouyn-Noranda; this is the closest to the suspended bridge), via Destor (off Rte 101 between Rouyn-Noranda and La Sarre) and via Taschereau (south from Rte 111 between La Sarre and Amos). There are lovely campgrounds (sites $21) near all three, as well as canoe and kayak rentals.

Rouyn-Noranda

The area's most interesting town is made up of two distinct sectors. At Noranda (in the city's northwest) the successful mines were set up; it was run, settled and organized by American and British industrialists. The French established Rouyn (in the southeast part of the city) as a frontier town; it was chock-full of brothels, bars, hotels and shops. To this day, you can see the difference between Rouyn's more helter-skelter setup and Noranda's elite, orderly feel.

Your first stop should be **Maison Dumulon** (☎ 418-797-7125; 191 Ave du Lac; tours $3; ☺ 9am-8pm late Jun–early Sep, 9am-5pm Mon-Fri early Sep–late Jun). The town's first general store and post office opened here in 1924, and it later turned into a residence, which has been charmingly transformed to re-create the look and feel of the old general store. On the fun guided tour, friendly staff in costume explain the town's interesting history. At the **tourist office** (☎ 418-797-3195; ☺ 9am-5pm Mon-Fri), also housed here, you can pick up free day parking permits.

For staying overnight, nondescript motels edge Ave Larivière.

Highway 117 runs right through Rouyn-Noranda. Autobus Maheux runs coaches from the **bus station** (☎ 418-762-2200; 52 Rue Horne) to Val d'Or and North Bay, Ontario.

JAMES BAY

Comprising 350,000 sq km (nearly 1½ times the size of the UK), James Bay (Baie James) is the largest administrative municipality in the world. Only 30,000 people live here, almost half of them Cree living on eight reserves separated by hundreds of kilometers.

This area truly represents Québec's final frontier, with the seeming endlessness of unpopulated boreal spruce forests giving way to the taiga, where trees become more visibly stunted the further north you go.

The near-mythic Rte de la Baie James ends at Radisson, a small village 1400km north of Montréal and 800km north of Amos. A 100km extension branches westward to Chisasibi, a Cree reserve near James Bay. This area is defined by the immense James Bay hydroelectric project, a series of hydroelectric stations that produce half of Québec's energy resources. It is to get a glimpse of these that many visitors make the trek.

QUÉBEC

While temperatures sporadically attain 30°C in July or August, it is essential to bring warm clothes for chilly evenings. The usual July daytime temperature is around 17°C. In winter – which can come as early as October – the temperatures are often below -15°C and can reach -40°C.

Most people access the region via Abitibi. Route 109 runs 183km north to Matagami, the last town before Rte 109 becomes the Rte de la Baie James and continues 620km to Radisson. To reach the eastern sector, where Chibougamau is the largest town, you're better off starting from the Lac St Jean region. From Chibougamou, a grueling 424km gravel road (Rte du Nord) joins the Rte de la Baie James at Kilometer 274. It's also possible to drive from Senneterre to Chibougamau (351km) on the paved Rte 113, passing through several Cree villages. The Chibougamou region is of little interest.

Matagami

For a dreary town in the middle of nowhere, this place sure feels busy. Since 1963, when the town was founded, it has been the site of a copper and zinc mine. It's also Québec's most northerly forestry center. Both of these industries are still going strong here, and shift workers are always coming and going. Plus, almost everyone driving through on Rte 109 on the way to Radisson stops here for the night.

Motel Le Caribou (☎ 819-739-4550; fax 819-739-4552; 108 Boul Matagami; s/d $60/65) is a bit more run-down than the hotel, but is fine for a night. The dingy bar in front draws long-faced, jowly clientele.

Hôtel-Motel Matagami (☎ 819-739-2501; 99 Boul Matagami; s/d $125/140) is considered the top place in town. It's decent enough and always seems to be crowded – mainly because of the restaurant, which is open from 5am to 10pm daily.

Every day but Saturday, the Autobus Maheux bus travels to/from Val d'Or (3½ hours) stopping at Hôtel-Motel Matagami.

Route de la Baie James

This road, an extension of Rte 109 to the James Bay hydroelectric projects, is paved, wide and kept in good shape.

At Kilometer 6, a **tourist office** (☎ 819-739-2030) operates 24 hours a day throughout the year. You must at least slow down here

and announce yourself through a speaker; for safety reasons, everyone traveling north is registered. It's worth stopping and going inside, however, as you can pick up several booklets and pamphlets that detail the geological and geographical features along the way and offer information about forest fires. There are bilingual information panels all along the road and emergency telephones at Kilometers 135, 201, 247, 301, 361, 444 and 504.

At Kilometer 37, you'll reach the route's only **campground** (☎ 819-739-4473).

Everyone needs to stop at Kilometer 381, the so-called Relais Routier, the only gas station and service stop on the road. It's open 24 hours a day. There's a **cafeteria** (☎ 819-638-7948) and a motel (single/double $55/80) of sorts.

Radisson

Named after explorer Pierre-Esprit Radisson, the village was set up in 1973 to house the workers on the James Bay hydroelectric project. It looks and feels larger than its population of 350 would suggest, partly because it was built to accommodate fluctuating numbers of workers (who work for eight days, then fly home for six) and because some families have decided to settle permanently here and create a real village.

The scenery around Radisson is spectacular, with views of the majestic Rivière La Grande from the built-up area around the larger-than-life LG2 hydroelectric power station (also called Robert Bourassa station), just outside town. The **tourist office** (☎ 819-638-8687; 198 Rue Jolliet; ☼ 8am-8pm Jun-Oct) is at the village's entrance. At other times, contact the **Town Hall** (☎ 819-638-7777; 101 Place Gérard Poirier).

Everyone who makes it here takes a free, guided tour of the power station (get details at the tourist office). The main offices of **Hydro Québec** (☎ 819-638-8486) are in the Pierre Radisson Complex. After an introduction to hydroelectricity, you'll be taken inside and outside the massive LG2. This, together with LG2A, the world's largest underground power station (as tall as a 15-story building but buried 140m deep in the bedrock), produces 25% of the province's energy and ranks among the top handful in size globally.

Eight power stations stretch out over the 800km length of Rivière La Grande; thus, the same water is used eight times, for a total energy output of 15,244 megawatts. It took 20 years, 185,000 laborers and 70 million work hours to complete construction at a cost of some $23.5 billion. The most impressive element is the Robert Bourassa spillway, backed by the enormous Réservoir Robert Bourassa, which is three times the size of Lac St Jean. Stretching out almost 1km in length, this 'giant staircase' of a spillway features a series of 10 steps blasted out from rock, each 10m high with a landing the size of two football fields.

There are several functional motels and **Camping Radisson** (☎ 819-638-8687; 198 Rue Jolliet) on a hill behind the tourist office.

Chisasibi

Located near where Rivière la Grande meets James Bay, 100km west of Radisson, Chisasibi is a Cree village well worth visiting. The surrounding environment, windswept taiga doused by the arctic breezes from James Bay, is haunting.

The town as it looks now has existed only since 1981. Before this, the residents lived on the island of Fort George, 10km from town, where the Hudson's Bay Company had set up a fur-trading post in 1837. A vestige of the old-fashioned way of life survives in the many tipis seen in backyards here – mainly these are used for smoking fish.

Margaret and William Cromarty (☎ 819-855-2800) offer excellent guided excursions of varying lengths to **Fort George**, where most of the original structures, including churches, schools and cemeteries remain. Traditional meals can be ordered. The **Mandow Agency** (☎ 819-855-3373; www.mandow.ca) also arranges fishing trips, canoe trips, cultural exchanges and winter activities. Email them with your desire and they may well be able to set it up.

The **Motel Chisasibi** (☎ 819-0855-2838; fax 819-855-2735; s/d $97/122) offers the only commercial accommodations.

LG1, another hydroelectric station, is 81km west of Radisson on the way to Chisasibi. While it's less monumental than Robert Bourassa (LG2), enough concrete went into its construction to pave a road from Montréal to Miami. Five lookouts near the complex provide stunning views of Rivière La Grande. Contact Hydro Québec in Radisson to take a tour of this station.

NUNAVIK

The territory of Nunavik stretches from the 55th to the 62nd parallel, bordered by Hudson Bay to the west, the Hudson Strait to the north and Ungava Bay and the Labrador border to the east. It's a tad smaller than France, yet fewer than 10,000 people live here in 14 villages. Hundreds of kilometers of tundra separate them from each other, with no roads to join them. Almost 90% of the population is Inuit; the remainder includes Cree, Naskapis and white Québecois.

There is a great geographic diversity. Even the tundra has many rich shades of beauty and the region is far from a desolate plain of snow and ice. In the southwest, beaches and sand dunes stretch as far as the eye can see. In the northeast, the formidable Torngat Mountains extend in a series of bare, rocky peaks and untamed valleys 300km along the border of Labrador. The province's highest peak, Mont d'Iberville (1652m), is here.

There are also five meteorite-formed craters in Nunavik (of the 144 known on Earth). The largest – indeed one of the largest on the planet – is called **Pingualuit**, a 1.4-million-year-old cavity with a diameter of 3.4km and a depth of 433m (the height of a 145-story building) in parts. The lake that's formed inside the crater contains water considered among the purest in the world. In terms of transparency, it's second only to Japan's Lake Masyuko. Pingualuit lies 88km southwest of Kangiqsujuaq.

Floating above this unusual terrain are the magical northern lights (aurora borealis), which can be seen an average of 243 nights each year.

Socially, the villages hold great interest. The Inuit are generally friendly and approachable. It's their adaptability that's helped them make such a radical transition in their lifestyles in so short a time. But the differences between Inuit communities and contemporary North American towns may give the unprepared a jolt of culture shock.

The villages range in population from 160 (Aupaluk) to 2050 (Kuujjuaq). Half the population is under 18, as you might guess by the sheer number of little ones running around. Everybody gets by all right here, money-wise, but some struggle with the serious social problems of domestic violence, drug abuse and alcoholism (even though most villages are 'dry').

Because Nunavik can only be accessed by plane, few casual tourists make the trip. Yet those willing to make their own local contacts can do independent travel. Be prepared for high prices for goods and services. On average, food prices are close to double what they are in Québec City.

After Inuktitut, the most widely-spoken language here is English. More youngsters are learning French than their parents did, but elders can rarely speak anything other than Inuktitut.

First Air provides (costly) service between Montréal and Kuujjuaq ($735 to $1070 one-way, 2¼ hours, daily). Air Inuit flies the same route as well as from Montréal to Puvirnituq ($1495, 3½ hours, daily). From there, flights go to other villages such as Kuujjuarapik-Whapmagoostui ($580, two hours, daily). Air Creebec flies to other communities.

Newfoundland & Labrador

CONTENTS

NEWFOUNDLAND & LABRADOR

Edged by 17,000km of dramatic, rocky coastline, and set at the crossroads of two mighty ocean currents, the mixing of which attracts 22 species of whales, dolphins and porpoises, Newfoundland and Labrador is an aquatic nirvana. Watching over the festivities are some of the world's largest seabird populations, and mountains of ice cruising majestically down Iceberg Alley.

Cartographers have always been unkind to the province, making it look as though it sits up in the Arctic. In fact, St John's is 300km further south than Vancouver. Countless idyllic fishing villages cling to the most precarious and stunning sections of shore; they are fascinating places to visit. Many of these villages are only accessible by boat and are some of the most remote settlements left in North America.

Parts of the province's interior are so barren and hostile that large sections remain virtually unexplored. Glaciers have sculpted this land and left erratics (boulders carried by glaciers) scattered like marbles on a playground. The glaciers interacted differently with the unique rocks of the Northern Peninsula, creating massive razor-sided fjords that rival any of those found in Scandinavia. The hiking and vistas here are nothing less than extraordinary.

Calling this diverse, historic land home are some of the warmest and funniest people on the continent. They've had more than their fair share of hardship over the centuries, including the collapse of fish stocks in the 1990s, but their infamous sense of humor lives on.

Newfoundland and Labrador's visiting season is short, with many services shut between October and May. Icebergs are most abundant from April through early July, while whales join the celebrations a little later and cavort until August.

HIGHLIGHTS

- Paddle through the exhaled mist of ocean giants at **Witless Bay Ecological Reserve** (p356)

- Stand atop one of flat earth's five dramatic corners at **Brimstone Head** (p368) and stick your nose deep into **Iceberg Alley** (p378)

- Ponder a move to Labrador in the charming island village of **Battle Harbour** (p388)

- Search for words and breath on a fjord-topping precipice at **Gros Morne National Park** (p373)

- Soak up the humor and history of North America's oldest city, **St John's** (p345)

- Experience the verdant 1000-year-old Viking site at **L'Anse aux Meadows National Historic Site** (p377), the discovery of which made Columbus toss in his grave

▪ POPULATION: 520,000	▪ PROVINCIAL CAPITAL: ST JOHN'S	▪ AREA: 404,520 SQ KM

NEWFOUNDLAND & LABRADOR

History
Evidence of Inuit and other Aboriginal groups in the province dates back over 10,000 years. Much later, but still 500 years ahead of Columbus, the Vikings landed and established a settlement in AD 1000.

The Vikings were long gone when John Cabot (Italian-born Giovanni Caboto) sailed around the shores of Newfoundland in 1497, under the employ of England's Henry VII. He returned to Bristol a hero, with news of finding a new and shorter route to Asia. For his troubles, the king rewarded him with the royal sum of £10. While Cabot was badly mistaken, his stories of cod stocks so prolific that one could nearly walk on water spread quickly throughout Europe.

Soon the French, Portuguese, Spanish and Basques were also fishing off Newfoundland's coast. There were no permanent settlements on the island, and the fishing crews returned to Europe with their bounties at the end of each season. The English fishers' primary base was St John's, while the French congregated around Placentia and the Port au Port Peninsula. In the end it was the War of the Spanish Succession and the 1713 Treaty of Utrecht that finally ceded all of Newfoundland to England.

Despite fighting so hard for the territory, England spent more than a century trying to stop English settlement here. Laws were passed against everything from farming and tree cutting to having a stove in a shelter. England believed settlements would be less valuable than the migratory fishery. The fishery was also the informal training ground of the mighty English navy. In the end, the persistence of Newfoundlanders won out, and their lives would thrive on the fishery until the late 20th century.

The province has a rich aviation history, too, having been a departure point or stopover in 40 pioneering transatlantic flights between 1919 and 1937, including those of Charles Lindbergh and Amelia Earhart.

Surprisingly, the province was the last to join Canada, doing so in 1949.

Climate
Newfoundland's weather is cool throughout the year, and Labrador's especially so, with arctic currents and north winds. Temperatures peak in June, July and August, which are the best times to travel. Precipitation is highly variable throughout the year, typically falling 15 days of every month. Fog and wind plague the coast much of the year.

National & Provincial Parks
Newfoundland and Labrador is home to two **national parks** (www.pc.gc.ca), Gros Morne National Park (p373), on the Northern Peninsula, and Terra Nova National Park (p362) in eastern Newfoundland. Gros Morne is a Unesco world heritage site and is known for its massive fjords and good hiking, while Terra Nova is famous for its serpentine shores and for water activities. If you plan on spending more than five days in a national park, ask about buying a season pass.

The province also has 14 **provincial parks** (☎ reservations 877-214-2267; www.gov.nf.ca/parks&reserves) spread along the rugged coasts. Vehicles entering parks are typically charged $5 for a day permit. Camping is possible at all parks except Chance Cove. Sites with flush toilets and hot showers are available in most parks for $13 per night. La Manche, Sir Richard Squires Memorial and Pinware Parks charge $10 per night for their sites with pit toilets and running water. Reservations should be made at least three days ahead by calling the toll-free number.

Six seabird ecological reserves, four fossil/geology ecological reserves and six rare plant/habitat ecological reserves have been established in the province. There are also large inland sections of the Avalon Peninsula and eastern Newfoundland that have been designated as wilderness reserves.

Opening dates vary among the provincial parks and reserves, but they typically open in mid-May and close in mid-September.

Language
Two hundred years ago Newfoundland and Labrador had the most homogeneous immigrant population in the New World. Coastal fishing families from Ireland and England made up almost the entire population. Since then, as a result of living in isolated outposts, their accents have evolved into almost 60 different dialects. Strong, lilting inflections, unique slang and colorful idiom pepper the language, sometimes confounding even residents – 'yes, bye.' The authoritative source is the *Dictionary of Newfoundland English,* but numerous slimmer volumes provide many fun, colorful examples.

NEWFOUNDLAND

0 ————— 100 km
0 ————— 60 miles

Note: Scale varies north and south of 49°N

Québec

Atlantic Time Zone
Eastern Time Zone

Strait of Belle Isle

Pinware River Provincial Park
Red Bay
Belle Isle
L'Anse aux Meadows National Historic Site
Forteau
L'Anse au Loup
Cape Onion
Pistolet Bay Provincial Park
Blanc Sablon
St Barbe
Main Brook
St Anthony

Eastern Time Zone

Port au Choix
432
Roddickton
Grey Islands
Northern Peninsula
430

ATLANTIC OCEAN

Table Point Ecological Reserve
Hawke's Bay

Portland Creek

Cow Head
The Arches
Fleur de Lys
La Scie
Change Islands
Brimstone Head

Gros Morne National Park
Baie Verte
Notre Dame Bay
Twillingate Island
Fogo Island

Rocky Harbour
Western Brook Pond
Baie Verte Peninsula
410
Springdale
Moreton's Harbour
Farewell
Dildo Run Provincial Park
Boyd's Cove

Woody Point
Norris Point
Trout River
Deer Lake
Lewisporte
340

Lark Harbour
1
330

Blow Me Down Provincial Park
Gander
320

Port au Port Peninsula
Corner Brook
Marble Mountain
Grand Falls-Windsor
Bonavista Bay

Lourdes
Cape St George
Stephenville
Port au Port West
Burnside
Bonavista

St George's Bay
Maelpaeg Lake
Bay du Nord Wilderness Reserve
Terra Nova National Park
Trinity

Barachois Pond Provincial Park
480
Head of Bay d'Espoir
360
Bonavista Peninsula
Grates Cove

Cape Anguille
Rose Blanche
Conne River
Clarenville
Conception Bay
Bay de Verde

Isle aux Morts
La Poile
Grand Bruit
Burgeo
Grey River
St Albans
Rencontre East
Heart's Content
70
Carbonear

Cape Ray
Petites
François
McCallum
Pool's Cove
Heart's Delight
210
Harbour Grace

John T Cheeseman Provincial Park
Port aux Basques
Ferry
Hermitage
Breton
Terrenceville
Bay L'Argent
Dildo
Brigus
ST JOHN'S
Cape Spear

Ramea
Fortune Bay
Argentia
Placentia
Avalon Peninsula
Bay Bulls
Witless Bay

Cabot Strait
South Coast Outports Ferry
Ile de Miquelon
Grand Bank
Marystown
Burin Peninsula
91
Placentia Bay
100
La Manche PP
Cape Broyle
Ferryland

Port aux Basques - North Sydney (NS) Ferry
St Pierre & Miquelon (FRANCE)
Fortune
Burin
St Lawrence
Point St
La Haye
Cape St Mary's
St Mary's Bay
Trepassey
10
Chance Cove Provincial Park
Cape Race

Argentia - North Sydney (NS) Ferry
Ile St Pierre
Marystown
St Mary's
Portugal Cove South

NEWFOUNDLAND & LABRADOR

Getting There & Away

AIR

While St John's is the most popular airport in the territory, Deer Lake is a great option if you will be centering your travels on the west coast. Note that there is no appreciable difference in cost in flying to St John's versus Deer Lake.

Air Canada has regular nonstop flights to St John's and Deer Lake from Halifax ($120 to $250), Montréal ($150 to $350) and Toronto ($150 to $350). Jetsgo has services between Toronto ($170 to $190) and St John's three times a week. Canjet serves both Deer Lake and St John's from Halifax (from $120) and Moncton (from $140). See p869 for airline contact details.

BOAT

Marine Atlantic (☎ 800-341-7981; www.marine-atlantic.ca) connects Port aux Basques, in western Newfoundland, and Argentia, on the Avalon Peninsula, with North Sydney in Nova Scotia. These massive ferries carry passengers and vehicles and are the most popular way to enter the province.

Reservations are recommended in midsummer. Generally one or two days' notice is sufficient unless you require a berth in a cabin, in which case the earlier you book, the better. Early-morning and late-night trips are usually less busy and, if you're walking or cycling, you shouldn't have any problems getting aboard. Boats offer entertainment areas with feature-length movies, video games, children's play areas complete with nursery facilities, and lounges with live music.

The Port aux Basques ferry (adult/child under 13 $27/13.50, per car/motorcycle $77/39) operates year-round, typically with two daily sailings during winter and three or four daily sailings between mid-June and mid-September. Departure times vary day-by-day. Daylight summer crossings take approximately six hours, while winter and night sailings are about seven hours. If you don't feel like sleeping in your chair, a four-berth cabin will set you back $99.

The Argentia ferry (adult/child under 13 $76/38, per car/motorcycle $158/79, 14 hours) leaves North Sydney at 6am Monday, 7am Wednesday and 4pm Friday mid-June to late September. It returns from Argentia at 11:59pm Monday, 7:30am Thursday and 8:30am Saturday. Four-berth cabins cost $138. Vehicle fares do not include drivers.

If you'll be arriving late, it would be wise to have a room booked in Port aux Basques or Placentia, which is near Argentia's terminal.

CAR & MOTORCYCLE
The only route into the province by road is through western Labrador via northern Québec (see p392).

TRAIN
There is one train in the province. It enters western Labrador from Sept-Îles, Québec, and travels to Labrador City (see p310).

Getting Around
Like Newfoundland's icebergs, you need to go with the flow here. Times and schedules

---

TOP FIVE FARCICAL PHRASES OF NEWFOUNDLAND

- lawnya vawnya: having a lot to eat at a great dance party
- lick for smatter: going blow for blow in fisticuffs
- nunny fudger: a person who dreams more of their upcoming dinner than the work at hand
- scurrifungeing: a thorough cleaning
- whizgigging: boisterous, silly laughing or being foolish

---

change often and seemingly without reason. Travel connections, if there are any, are not always smooth or convenient. For many visitors with a plan, this can be frustrating, annoying and challenging. But the rewards are well worth the trouble.

AIR
Provincial Airlines (☎ 800-563-2800; www.provincial airlines.ca) has substantial coverage of Newfoundland, and some Labrador services. **Air Labrador** (☎ 800-563-3042; www.airlabrador.com), based out of Happy Valley-Goose Bay, thoroughly covers Labrador.

BOAT
All ferry fares and schedules are compiled by the **Provincial Ferry Services** (www.gov.nl.ca /ferryservices). Each service has its own phone number with up-to-the-minute information; it's wise to phone before embarking.

Information on coastal ferry services for the Burin Peninsula, the islands of Notre Dame Bay, the south coast outports and the northern coast of Labrador are all found in the relevant sections later in this chapter.

Labrador Marine (☎ 866-535-2567) connects Newfoundland to Labrador. The MV *Apollo* (adult/child under 12 $10/5.25, per car/ motorcycle $20.50/10.25, two hours) runs between St Barbe in Newfoundland and Blanc Sablon, Québec, on the Labrador Straits between May and early January. From the beginning of July to mid-September, when things are at their busiest, the boat runs two or three times a day between 8am and 6pm; at other times service drops to once or twice daily. Schedules vary wildly day to day for this journey. Note that the ferry terminal in Blanc Sablon operates on Newfoundland Time and not Eastern Time, which the rest of Blanc Sablon follows.

Between mid-June and mid-September, Labrador Marine also runs a weekly vehicle and passenger service to Cartwright (adult/ child under 12 $66/33, per car/motorcycle $107/54, 24 hours) and Goose Bay (adult/ child under 12 $107/53.50, per car/motor-cycle $175/88, 46 hours, including a nine-hour stop in Cartwright) from Lewisporte. The boat leaves Lewisporte on Friday at 10am. You can also join the ferry for the Cartwright–Goose Bay leg only (adult/child under 12 $44/22, per car/motorcycle $72/37) at 7pm Saturday. The boat leaves Goose Bay at 6pm Tuesday for the return run to Lewisporte via Cartwright. There is a cafeteria on board and berths can be rented for the journey. A single berth in a shared room between Lewisporte and Goose Bay is $41.25, while a four-berth private cabin costs $165.

With the completion of Rte 510 to Cartwright from Blanc Sablon, Québec (on the Labrador Straits), the ferry service between Lewisporte and Cartwright may be discontinued in the near future.

BUS

There is only one cross-island bus route on Newfoundland, run by **DRL Coachlines** (☎ 709-738-8088; www.drlgroup.com/Coachlines/coachlines_new.html). One bus runs in each direction daily between St John's and Port aux Basques. It takes approximately 13½ hours to cover the 904km-long Hwy 1 and the 28 potential stops. Prices and times are provided in the Getting There & Away sections of relevant destinations.

The public bus network consists of a series of small, regional services that usually connect with one or more major points. Although not extensive, this system works pretty well and will get most people where they want to go. See specific destinations in this chapter for more information.

CAR & MOTORCYCLE

An ever-growing road network connects major towns and most of the regions of interest to visitors, but remains sketchy in some areas, such as Labrador. Winter snow and ice can also slow things down and hinder access to certain areas. The **Department of Transportation and Works** (☎ 709-729-2300; www.roads.gov.nl.ca) has the most current information and it is wise to check with it before heading through remote areas of the province.

Wildlife, especially moose, presents a real danger. There is more than one moose–vehicle collision a day in the province, and smacking into a beast the height of a horse and weighing 400kg, with 2m-wide antlers, is more wildlife than most people care for. Heed the warning signs, keep your speed down and travel during the day.

The rough winter weather and continual salting mean roads are almost completely devoid of markings by spring. Driving can be a little disconcerting before they are repainted in late May, especially in the cities.

Outside St John's, Corner Brook and a few large towns, such as Gander and Port aux Basques, the visitor traffic is light. The distances are so great they shock most people – this is magnified by the slow rate of travel, thanks to heavily contorted single-lane roads.

NEWFOUNDLAND & LABRADOR IN...

Four Days

Wake up before dawn in **St John's** (p345) and head to **Signal Hill** (p347) or **Cape Spear** (p348) to watch the sun rise over the Atlantic and its icebergs. Take your time wandering Water St and the colorful old section of town, stopping to gander at some of the historic sites or to enjoy a sumptuous meal at the **Duck Street Bistro** (p353).

After a couple of days of land-loving, kayak or cruise offshore to the stunning wildlife of the **Witless Bay Ecological Reserve** (p356). Wind along the Avalon's scenic roads and take in diminutive yet stunning villages such as **Brigus** (p358) and **Grates Cove** (p359).

One Week

Add a memorable stay in the historic and charming seaside communities of **Trinity** (p361) and **Bonavista** (p362), or head down the **Burin Peninsula** (p363), where a quick hop to the French territory of **St Pierre & Miquelon** (p365) and all its delicacies is possible. If coastal wilds pique your curiosity, venture into **Terra Nova National Park** (p362).

Two Weeks

Include a couple of days in the sublime setting of **Notre Dame Bay** (p368) before heading west to the mighty fjords of **Gros Morne National Park** (p373) and the monumental Viking history at **L'Anse aux Meadows National Historic Site** (p377).

ST JOHN'S

☎ 709 / pop 99,100

Encamped on the steep slopes of its protective harbor and under the omnipresent
shadow of Signal Hill sits Newfoundland
and Labrador's largest city and capital.
Despite those titles, slick bistros and the
odd glass tower, St John's is still a fishing
village at heart. Weather-torn ships line
its harbor, crooked colorful houses crowd
crooked streets, narrow alleys and endless
stairs climb its shores and the warmth of
the people is sweet and palpable. No level of
shyness on your part is more powerful than
the charm of Newfoundlanders and you'll
undoubtedly end up sharing a conversation
or a pint with one during your stay.

St John's is North America's oldest city
and Britain's first overseas colony, thus
earning it the distinction in many eyes of
being the birthplace of the British Empire.
Its possessive name is simply short for its
lifeblood, St John's Harbour.

HISTORY

Whether it was Cabot in the *Matthew* in
1497, or fishers who crossed an ocean to
harvest the seething seas of cod shortly
thereafter, it must have been a special sight
to sneak beneath the ominous cliffs of Signal Hill and discover this steeply arched,
protective harbor.

The harbor's grand reputation led to the
first European settlement here in 1528. Sir
Humphrey Gilbert landed in St John's 55
years later, and proudly claimed the land for
Queen Elizabeth I. It is not known what the
Spanish, Portuguese and French who were in
the harbor at the time thought of this. Gilbert
spent only a couple of weeks as governor
before he decided to head back to England;
he died when his ship sank en route.

The fact that St John's is such an excellent
natural harbor actually hindered its growth
during the late 1600s and most of the 1700s.
During this time the settlement was razed
and taken over several times as the French,
English and Dutch fought for it tooth and
nail. After Britain's ultimate victory on Signal Hill, things finally settled down in the
1800s and St John's started to take shape.

Since then four fires have brought the
city to its knees, the last in 1892. Each time

locals rebuilt with their pride and, more
importantly, their sense of humor, intact.

Despite the centuries of outward turmoil,
the harbor somehow steadfastly maintained
its position as the world trade center for
salted cod well into the 20th century. Today
its wharves still act as service stations to
fishing vessels from around the world.

ORIENTATION

While the streets of St John's can be confusing, it is extremely hard to get lost. The
massive landmark of Signal Hill to the
northeast is visible from much of the hilly
city, and simply walking downhill will inevitably take you to the harbor. One of the
oldest sections of the city sits on the harbor
at the base of Signal Hill. This small group
of houses is known as the Battery.

The main streets of St John's are Water
and Duckworth Sts, which run parallel to
each other and the waterfront. They are
lined with restaurants, shops and bars. At
the northeastern end of Water St is the
small Harbourside Park, with a monument
to Sir Humphrey Gilbert. Across the street,
a sharply rising park holds a war memorial
and benches with views.

The major cross-town route is Queen's Rd,
which turns into New Gower St to the south.
New Gower St continues south past City Hall
and the ceremonial 'Mile 0' of the Trans-
Canada Hwy (Hwy 1) before becoming Rte
2, which leads to the actual Hwy 1. Rennie's
Mill Rd heads northeast and connects with
Portugal Cove Rd, which passes the airport.

INFORMATION

Bookstores

Second Page Bookstore (☎ 709-722-1742; 363 Water
St) Perfect for a secondhand book or pristine A-Ha poster.
Wordplay (☎ 709-726-9193; 221 Duckworth St) A good
place to find local literary works.

Emergency

Police, Ambulance & Fire (☎ 911)
Royal Newfoundland Constabulary (☎ 709-729-
8000; 1 Fort Townshend St) For nonemergencies.

Internet Access

L'Association Francophone de St Jean (☎ 709-
726-4900; 96 Le Marchant Rd; ⏱ 9am-5pm Mon-Fri)
Free Internet access. **Wordplay** (☎ 709-726-9193; 221
Duckworth St; per hr $9) After surfing the Internet, check
out the art gallery and bookshop.

Medical Services

Health Sciences Complex (☎ 709-777-6300; 300 Prince Phillip Dr) 24-hour emergency room.

St Clares Mercy Hospital (☎ 709-777-5000; 154 LeMarchant Rd) 24-hour emergency room.

Water St Pharmacy (☎ 709-579-5554; 335 Water St) Sells maps of the Grand Concourse.

Money

CIBC (☎ 709-576-8800; 215 Water St)
Scotia Bank (☎ 709-576-6000; 245 Water St)

Post

Central Post Office (☎ 709-758-1003; 354 Water St)

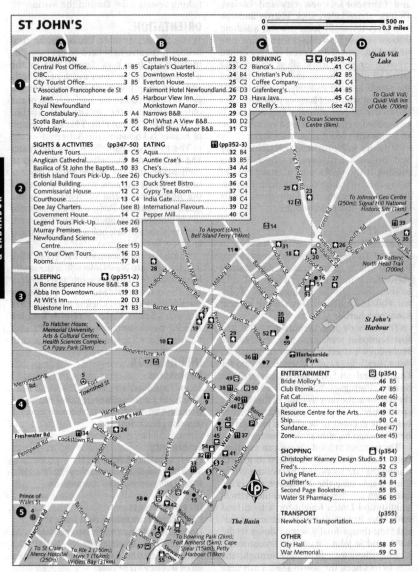

ST JOHN'S

INFORMATION
Central Post Office............................**1** B5
CIBC...**2** C5
City Tourist Office............................**3** B5
L'Association Francophone de St
Jean...**4** A5
Royal Newfoundland
Constabulary................................**5** A4
Scotia Bank..**6** B5
Wordplay...**7** C4

SIGHTS & ACTIVITIES (pp347-50)
Adventure Tours..............................**8** C5
Anglican Cathedral..........................**9** B4
Basilica of St John the Baptist....**10** B3
British Island Tours Pick-Up.....(see 26)
Colonial Building...........................**11** C3
Commissariat House.......................**12** C3
Courthouse.......................................**13** C4
Dee Jay Charters..........................(see 8)
Government House...........................**14** C2
Legend Tours Pick-Up................(see 26)
Murray Premises.............................**15** B5
Newfoundland Science
Centre...(see 15)
On Your Own Tours......................**16** B3
Rooms...**17** B4

SLEEPING (pp351-2)
A Bonne Esperance House B&B..**18** C3
Abba Inn Downtown.....................**19** B3
At Wit's Inn......................................**20** D3
Bluestone Inn...................................**21** B3

Cantwell House..................................**22** B3
Captain's Quarters.............................**23** C2
Downtown Hostel...............................**24** B4
Everton House.....................................**25** C2
Fairmont Hotel Newfoundland....**26** D3
Harbour View Inn...............................**27** D3
Monkstown Manor.............................**28** B3
Narrows B&B..**29** C3
Oh! What A View B&B.......................**30** D2
Rendell Shea Manor B&B................**31** C3

EATING (pp352-3)
Aqua...**32** B4
Auntie Crae's......................................**33** B5
Ches's...**34** A4
Chucky's..**35** C4
Duck Street Bistro.............................**36** C4
Gypsy Tea Room.................................**37** C4
India Gate...**38** C4
International Flavours........................**39** D2
Pepper Mill..**40** C4

DRINKING (pp353-4)
Bianca's..**41** C4
Christian's Pub....................................**42** B5
Coffee Company.................................**43** C4
Grafenberg's..**44** B5
Hava Java...**45** C4
O'Reilly's...(see 42)

ENTERTAINMENT (p354)
Bridie Molloy's....................................**46** B5
Club Etomik..**47** B5
Fat Cat..(see 46)
Liquid Ice..**48** C4
Resource Centre for the Arts.......**49** C4
Ship..**50** C4
Sundance.......................................(see 47)
Zone..(see 45)

SHOPPING (p354)
Christopher Kearney Design Studio.**51** D3
Fred's...**52** C3
Living Planet.......................................**53** C3
Outfitter's..**54** B4
Second Page Bookstore...................**55** B5
Water St Pharmacy...........................**56** B5

TRANSPORT (p355)
Newhook's Transportation.............**57** B5

OTHER
City Hall...**58** B5
War Memorial......................................**59** C3

Quidi Vidi Lake

To Quidi Vidi;
Quidi Vidi Inn
of Olde (700m)

To Ocean Sciences
Centre (8km)

To Johnson Geo Centre
(250m); Signal Hill National
Historic Site (1km)

To Battery;
North Head Trail
(700m)

To Airport (6km);
Bell Island Ferry (14km)

St John's
Harbour

Harbourside
Park

To Hatcher House;
Memorial University;
Arts & Cultural Centre;
Health Sciences Complex;
CA Pippy Park (2km)

Bonaventure Ave

Merrymeeting
Rd

Fort
Townshend St

Harvey Rd

Long's Hill

Freshwater Rd

Carter's Hill

Cookstown Rd

Pennywell Rd

Goodview St

Livingstone St

Lime St

Prince of
Wales St

The Basin

To St Clares
Mercy Hospital
(250m)

To Rte 2 (350m);
Hwy 1 (16km);
Witless Bay (31km)

To Bowring Park (2km);
Fort Amherst (5km); Cape
Spear (15km); Petty
Harbour (18km)

Tourist Information

City Tourist Office (☎ 709-576-8106; www.stjohns.ca; 348 Water St; 🕑 9am-4:30pm Mon-Fri early Sep–mid-Jun, Mon-Sun mid-Jun–early Sep) Staff are extremely knowledgeable about anything St John's–related. They'll do their best to answer your provincial questions, too. Nab a provincial or city roadmap here.

Newfoundland & Labrador Tourism (☎ 800-563-6353; www.gov.nl.ca/tourism/; Visitor Services Section, PO Box 8730, St John's, NF A1B 4K2) This helpful website and 24-hour information line are great sources of information for tourism in the province.

SIGHTS

St John's storied history and impressive physical settings seem inexorably entwined in many of the town's sights, making visits both educational and visually enthralling. Most sights are downtown or along the rocky coast within a 15-minute drive.

Signal Hill National Historic Site

Forever standing guard over St John's Harbour are the sheer, striated cliffs of the city's most famous landmark, Signal Hill. The glorious view alone is worth the trip. Thanks to its roles in military and communications history, the hill has been designated a **national historic site** (Signal Hill Rd; admission free; 🕑 24hr). There's a **Visitors Interpretive Centre** (☎ 709-772-5367; adult/child under 17/family $3.50/1.75/8.75; 🕑 8:30am-4:30pm, to 8pm mid-Jun–early Sep, closed weekends mid-Oct–mid-May) with a small museum featuring interactive displays on the site's history. If you plan to see Cape Spear the same day, grab an Eastern Newfoundland National Historic Sites Pass (adult/child under 17/family $5.50/3/14).

The last North American battle of the Seven Years' War took place here in 1762, and Britain's victory ended France's renewed aspirations for control of eastern North America. You can see some cannons and remains of the late 18th-century British battery at **Queen's Battery & Barracks** further up the hill. The diminutive castle topping the hill is **Cabot Tower** (admission free; 🕑 8:30am-5pm, to 9pm Jun–early Sep). It was built in 1900 to honor both John Cabot's arrival in 1497 and Queen Victoria's Diamond Jubilee. Here Italian inventor Guglielmo Marconi gleefully received the first wireless transatlantic message from Cornwall, England, in 1901. There are guides and displays in the tower; an amateur radio society operates a station from the tower in summer.

In midsummer, several dozen soldiers dressed as the 19th-century Royal Newfoundland Company perform a **tattoo** (admission $2; 🕑 11am & 3pm Wed-Sun Jul–mid-Aug) on O'Flaherty Field next to the visitors center. It wraps up with the firing of historic cannons.

An amazingly rewarding way to reach Cabot Tower is along the **North Head Trail** (1.7km) connecting the tower with the Battery section of town down on the harbor. The walk traces the cliffs and isn't something to attempt in icy, foggy or dark conditions. Let's just say it's a long way down.

Quidi Vidi

Over Signal Hill, away from town, is the tiny, picturesque village of **Quidi Vidi**. Here you'll find the oldest cottage in North America, **Mallard Cottage** (☎ 709-576-2266; 2 Barrows Rd; admission free; 🕑 10am-5pm May-Sep), which dates from the 1750s. It's now a national heritage site and a very cluttered antique/junk shop. Something is sure to charm you; profits go to maintenance.

Built in 1762 and still symbolically guarding the bay from up the hill is **Quidi Vidi Battery** (☎ 709-729-2977; Cuckhold's Dr; admission $3; 🕑 10am-5:30pm mid-Jun–Thanksgiving). Built by the French after they took St John's, the battery was quickly claimed by the British and remained in military service into the 1800s. Period-garbed interpreters dole out historical information.

Inland from the village, **Quidi Vidi Lake** is the site of the city-stopping St John's Regatta (p351) and the **Royal St John's Regatta Museum** (☎ 709-576-8921; cnr Lakeview Ave & Clancy Dr, off Forest Rd; admission free; 🕑 Jul & Aug) is on the 2nd floor of the boathouse at the lake. Opening hours vary. A popular trail leads around the lake.

Quidi Vidi Brewing (☎ 709-738-4040; 15 Barrows Rd; admission incl 1 beer & tastings $6; 🕑 noon-4pm Mon-Fri) is a microbrewery located in an old fish-processing plant on the tiny wharf. A recently developed brew uses melted icebergs.

A scenic 20-minute walk from atop Signal Hill will get you to the village. By car, take Forest Rd from the city and follow it past the lake until it turns into Quidi Vidi Village Rd. Locals prefer you to park on the outskirts of town and walk in.

NEWFOUNDLAND & LABRADOR

Cape Spear

A 15km drive southeast of town leads you to the most easterly point in North America. The coastal scenery at this spot is spectacular, and you can spot whales through much of the summer. The area is preserved as the **Cape Spear National Historical Site** (☎ 709-772-5367; Blackhead Rd; adult/senior/child under 17/family $3.50/1.75/1.75/8.75; ⊙ mid-Oct–mid-May) and includes an **interpretive center** (⊙ 9:30am-8pm mid-May–early Sep, 10am-6pm early Sep–mid-Oct), the refurbished 1835 **lighthouse** (⊙ 10am-6pm mid-Jun–mid-Oct) and the heavy gun batteries and magazines built in 1941 to protect the harbor during WWII. A trail leads along the edge of the headland cliffs, past 'the most easterly point' observation deck and up to the lighthouse. You can continue all the way to Maddox and Petty Harbour if you wish. You reach the cape from Water St by crossing the Waterford River south of town and then following Blackhead Rd for 11km.

Rooms

Historically, in the fishing villages of Newfoundland and Labrador, the word 'rooms' refers to shoreline buildings where catches were processed.

Years in the making, the **Rooms** (☎ 709-729-0917; www.therooms.ca; 9 Bonaventure Ave) is finally slated for opening in June 2005 and will be the new home of the provincial museum, art gallery and archives. The province's vibrant history will be told through artifacts, interactive exhibits and fun activities. The art gallery beneath the steeples will display pieces from its 5500-piece collection, while the natural-light gallery will house sculpture exhibits. The three steeples of this massive stone-and-glass complex now dominate St John's skyline.

Basilica of St John the Baptist

Built in 1855, the soaring twin spires of the **basilica** (☎ 709-754-2170; 200 Military Rd; admission free; ⊙ 8am-3pm Mon-Fri, 8am-6pm Sat, 8am-12:30pm Sun) pierce the sky and are visible all the way from Signal Hill. Its design marks the revival of classical architecture in North America. Restoration to bring the mighty facade of this national historic site back to its original grandeur began in 2004. Inside, 65 unique stained-glass windows illuminate the remarkable polychromatic Italianate

ceiling and its gold-leaf highlights. The honor of being named a 'basilica' was bestowed on the church by Pope Pius XII on its centennial anniversary. Free half-hour tours are offered 10am to 5pm Monday to Saturday in July and August, according to demand. If you'd like to learn more, ask about the **Basilica-Cathedral Museum**, which holds a small collection of sacred vessels, paintings and books.

Anglican Cathedral of St John the Baptist

Serving Canada's oldest parish (1699), the **Anglican cathedral** (☎ 709-726-5677; 22 Church Hill; admission free; ⊙ 10:30am-noon & 2-4:30pm Mon-Fri Jun-Sep) is one of the finest examples of ecclesiastical Gothic architecture in North America. Although originally built in the 1830s, all but its exterior walls were reduced to ashes by the Great Fire of 1892. It was rebuilt around the majestic stone skeleton in 1905. The Gothic ribbed ceiling, graceful stone arches and long, thin stained-glass windows are timeless marvels. A gargoyle dating from the 12th century stands guard over the south transept – a gift from the Diocese of Bristol. Students offer tours of this national historic site.

Johnson Geo Centre

The **centre** (☎ 709-737-7880; 175 Signal Hill Rd; adult/child under 17/family $6/3/15; ⊙ 9:30am-5pm Mon-Sat, 1-5pm Sun, closed Mon mid-Oct–May) opened in 2002 and hosts a fascinating underground exhibit on the wonders of Newfoundland's world-renowned geology. Preschoolers and professors will find it equally pleasing. Look for the large glass-encased entry en route to Signal Hill.

Fort Amherst

Across the Narrows from Signal Hill, and dwarfed by its massive cliffs, are the remains of a centuries-old **fort** (Fort Amherst Rd; admission free; ⊙ 24hr). You can almost touch the icebergs and whales from here, and the views along the rugged coast are incredible. You'll discover remnants of WWII gun batteries and a lighthouse (1810), the first in Newfoundland. Have a peak inside the **Lighthouse Tearoom and Museum** (☎ 709-754-0619; admission free; ⊙ noon-5pm Jul & Aug), reached by heading out of town on Water St, turning left at Blackhead Rd and following the signs.

Commissariat House

Near Gower St, this late-Georgian **mansion** (1820; ☎ 709-729-6730; King's Bridge Rd; admission $3; ☻ 10am-5:30pm mid-Jun–mid-Oct) was used by the supplies officer of the British military. It was later used as a church rectory, nursing home and children's hospital. The house has been restored to reflect the style of 1830 and contains many period pieces.

Government House

Set amongst a gorgeous stand of chestnut, maple and oak trees is the Palladian-style **Government House** (☎ 709-729-4494; Military Rd). Built at the same time as the White House, but at four times the cost, this austere mansion (1831) with its prominent corner quoins and window surrounds is home to the province's lieutenant governor. The interior of this national historic site maintains most of its original furnishings and has recently been opened for tours. They run Wednesday and Thursday at 10am, but you must book ahead.

Colonial Building

This regal **building** (☎ 709-729-3065; Military Rd) sits across from Government House and was the seat of the provincial legislature from 1850 to 1960. It's built of white limestone from Cork, Ireland, which crossed the mighty Atlantic as ships' ballast. If the door is open, have a peek inside.

CA Pippy Park

The dominant attraction of the northwestern edge of downtown is the feature-filled 1343-hectare **CA Pippy Park** (☎ 709-737-3655). Recreational facilities include walking trails, picnic areas, playgrounds and a campground. The park also has a snack bar. **Memorial University**, the province's only university, is here too.

The university's **botanical garden** (☎ 709-737-8590; admission $2; ☻ 10am-5pm May-Nov) is at Oxen Pond, at the western edge of the park off Mt Scio Rd. There's a cultivated garden and a nature reserve. Together, these and the park's **Long Pond** marsh provide visitors with an excellent introduction to the province's flora and varying natural habitats, including boreal forest and bogs. The bird-watching is good at Long Pond, and mammals such as moose can sometimes be spotted in the park.

The **Freshwater Resource Centre** (☎ 709-754-3474; Nagle's Pl; adult/child under 14/family $5/3/15; ☻ 9am-5pm, closed Wed Sep-Jun) is across the street from the campground in a hexagonal balconied building. Inside is the **Fluvarium**, a glass-sided cross-section of a 'living' river. Viewers can peer through large windows to observe the natural, undisturbed goings-on beneath the surface of Nagle's Hill Brook. Numerous brown trout and the occasional eel can be seen. If there has been substantial rain or high winds, all visible life is lost in the murkiness.

There's also a demonstration **fish hatchery**, and exhibits aimed at children that examine plants, insects and fish of freshwater ecosystems. Outside there are interpretive trails; it's possible to walk all the way to Quidi Vidi Lake from here. Opening times vary, but feeding time is scheduled at 4pm, and tours are offered hourly except at 4pm.

Murray Premises

The fully renovated **Murray Premises** (cnr Water St & Beck's Cove) is one of the oldest warehouses in the city. It was built in the 1840s, somehow dodged the fire of 1892 and today is a national historic site. Wander amongst its aged timbers and bricks. Tucked in the back behind the restaurants and shops is the **Newfoundland Science Centre** (☎ 709-754-0823; adult/student $6/4.25; ☻ 10am-5pm Mon-Fri, 10am-6pm Sat, noon-6pm Sun), a hands-on science experiment for kids. Exhibits change three times a year.

Ocean Sciences Centre

Right out of *20,000 Leagues Under the Sea*, this **research facility** (☎ 709-737-3708; Marine Lab Rd; admission free; ☻ 10am-5pm Jun–Labour Day) is operated by Memorial University and examines the life cycle of salmon, seal navigation, ocean currents and life in cold oceanic regions. The outdoor visitors' area consists of local sea life in touch tanks.

The center is about 8km north of town just before Logy Bay, at the end of Marine Lab Rd, on the ocean. From town, take Logy Bay Rd (Rte 30) and then follow Marine Dr.

Courthouse

At the bottom of Church Hill, looming over Water St, is the Romanesque Revival **courthouse** (Duckworth St). In 1988 it had a major facelift and now appears pretty much as it did when it first opened in 1904. While you're admiring its quirky, grand exterior, it's still a working courthouse, so besides some court theatrics, there's nothing of note inside.

Bowring Park

Southwest of town, this **park** (Waterford Bridge Rd) is a popular green haven with streams, meandering walkways and a massive duck pond – the lodge sells duck food ($1). The **Peter Pan statue** is a replica of the famous one in Kensington Gardens in London, England, and was made by the same sculptor. It's a memorial to Sir Edgar Bowring's godchild, who was one of 94 people killed in the shipwreck of the SS *Florizel* in 1918.

ACTIVITIES

Grand Concourse is an ambitious 95km-long network of trails all over town and linking St John's with the nearby Mt Pearl and Paradise via downtown sidewalks, trails, river corridors and old railway beds. The system, largely completed in 2000, is a clever piece of forward urban thinking. Most hiking is done in the CA Pippy Park and Quidi Vidi Lake areas. Maps ($1.74) are available from newsstands and **Water St Pharmacy** (☎ 709-579-5554; 335 Water St). Some street signs are color-coded to map trails, and signs and plaques can be seen all over town.

For information on kayaking around St John's, see p355.

ST JOHN'S FOR CHILDREN

St John's makes a pretty good place to keep the wee ones entertained, rain or shine. CA Pippy Park (p349) is a kids' haven, with a huge playground, lots of neat trails and of course, the Fluvarium. The ever-hungry ducks at Bowring Park (above) love company, as do the sea creatures at the Ocean Sciences Centre (p349). Just knowing a cannon will blast at the end of the tattoo should keep them riveted at Signal Hill (p347). The various boat tours (right) are also a great bet, but it may be wise to inquire if there are icebergs and whales in the area first.

For kids over 12, some kayaking (p355) is an adventurous way to spend the day. While geology may not initially spark their interest, the fact that the Johnson Geo Centre (p348) is underground may do the trick. Another rainy-day option is the science center (p349) at the Murray Premises.

QUIRKY ST JOHN'S

After visiting the historic sights and hearing the celebrated history of St John's, join Reverend Thomas Wyckham Jarvis Esq as he descends into the city's former darkest corners and explores the folklore and paranormal activity of North America's oldest city. Fun-loving locals, living along the tour's route, have been known to throw in a eerie moan or two! The **St John's Haunted Hike** (☎ 709-685-3444; $5; ⓨ 9.30pm Sun-Thu Jun–mid-Sep) is truly for the brave and for those with a penchant for believing.

TOURS
Boat

Adventure Tours (☎ 709-726-5000; Pier 7, Harbour Dr; 2hr tours adult/child under 13 $35/20; ⓨ 1pm May-Oct) Sail on the tall ship *Scademia* for some horizon-searching – calm days are best for whale spotting. Note that calm does not equate to warm on the water, so layer up.

Dee Jay Charters (☎ 709-753-8687; Pier 7, Harbour Dr; 2hr tours adult/child under 16 $30/15; ⓨ 10am, 2pm & 6pm Jun-Sep) This boat sneaks into Quidi Vidi and makes a run down to Cape Spear in search of icebergs in June and whales in July and August. Seabirds are always on the menu.

Bus

British Island Tours (☎ 709-738-8687; 2½hr tours adult/child under 16 $20/10; ⓨ 9:30am & 1:30pm May–early Oct) These tours aboard a double-decker bus include Signal Hill and Quidi Vidi. Pick-up is from the Fairmont Hotel Newfoundland.

Legend Tours (☎ 709-753-1497; 66 Glenview Tce; ⓨ Apr-Oct) This award-winning tour operator has various tours that cover St John's ($32), Cape Spear ($42) and the Marine Dr area ($69). The commentary is richly woven with humor, historical tidbits and information on the people and province. Legend also picks up from the Fairmont Hotel Newfoundland.

On Your Own Tours (☎ 709-753-5353; 112 Duckworth St; ⓨ May–mid-Oct) This outfit will design an itinerary for you – anything from a one-day walking tour to month-long adventures. It can organize car rentals and accommodations as well.

Walking

There are two good self-guided walking tours available from the tourist office (p347), as well as St John's Haunted Hike (see above).

FESTIVALS & EVENTS

St John's Day Celebration (☎ 709-576-8106; ⓨ Jun) Four days of celebratory concerts, parades, street dances and sporting events begin around June 18 to commemorate the city's birthday. Jazz, blues and children's concerts are featured.

Pippy Park Family Days Festival (☎ 709-729-3904; ☾ late Jul) Music, dance and fun activities for children are held in various areas of the verdant park for two days.

George Street Festival (☎ 709-576-8106; ☾ late Jul) The mighty George St becomes one big nightclub for a fabulous week of daytime and night time musical performances.

Provincial Folk Festival (☎ 709-576-8508; ☾ 1st weekend Aug) This wonderful three-day event takes place in Bannerman Park. It's an intimate festival celebrating traditional Newfoundland music, dancing and storytelling.

Royal St John's Regatta (☎ 709-576-8921; ☾ 1st Wed Aug) The streets are empty, the stores are closed and thousands migrate to the shores of Quidi Vidi Lake. This rowing regatta officially began in 1825 and is now the oldest continuously held sporting event in North America.

SLEEPING

While there are scores of tiny inns and B&Bs offering great value in the heart of St John's, the same can't be said of hotels and motels. Only the luxurious top-end hotels with harbor views have more to offer than their smaller counterparts. Parking is available at or near all accommodations.

Budget

Downtown Hostel (☎ 709-754-7658; 25 Young St; dm $23) It's a toss-up who has more character, the owner Carola or the building itself. She is a ball of helpful energy and laughs, while the sagging building literally hangs from the central chimney. Crooked homemade furniture resists the steeply plunging floors, and electrical cords and world maps adorn the walls.

Hatcher House (☎ 709-737-7933; Memorial University, Prince Phillip Dr; s/d nonstudent $33/54, s/d student $25/39; ☾ May-Aug) Although it takes a few phone calls (try office hours Monday to Friday) to get things sorted, this campus facility is a great budget option. Meals are available and there are buses to town – it's a 2km walk.

CA Pippy Park (☎ 709-737-3669; fax 709-737-3303; Nagles Place; tent sites $16, RV sites $22-24; ☾ May-Sep) Despite being conveniently close to town and the university, just off Allandale Rd at Higgins Line, this campground is quiet and surprisingly verdant. It fills up in summer, especially on weekends when there can be some partying.

Mid-Range

Cantwell House (☎ 709-754-8439, 888-725-8439; www.cantwellhouse.nf.net; 25 Queen's Rd; d incl breakfast $85) Take tea from a seat on Cantwell's deck and stare out over a colorful collage of row houses to the blue harbor below. A friendly atmosphere combines with a sense of privacy in Cantwell House's Victorian ambience.

Narrows B&B (☎ 709-739-4850, 866-739-4850; www.thenarrowsbb.com; 146 Gower St; s/d $75/$95) Warm colors mix with elegant trims and large wooden beds in the rooms of this welcoming B&B. There are modern amenities throughout and a gorgeous sitting room and balcony where guests can mingle and swap whale stories. The upper room has a fine harbor view and a pullout for children.

Oh! What A View B&B (☎ 709-576-7063; www.ohwhataview.com; 184 Signal Hill Rd; d incl breakfast $75-100) While it's a bit of a walk from town, the name says it all. Several common balconies take in the mesmerizing views below. The rooms are bright and modern, if a little on the small side. Ask for room No 8 with its Juliet balcony.

Everton House (☎ 709-739-1616, 866-754-1326; www.evertonhouse.com; 23 King's Bridge Rd; d incl breakfast $95-140, ste $220-250) Contemporary furnishings and bold colors fill the insides of this posh heritage home, while lush gardens and trees encircle it. Rod iron beds, lavish fabrics and plush flooring add to the ambience. Its luxurious suites are a great top-end choice.

At Wit's Inn (☎ 709-739-7420, 877-739-7420; www
.atwitsinn.ca; 3 Gower St; d incl breakfast $100-130; 🖳)
Polished floorboards, plasterwork ceilings,
ornate fireplaces, and beds you'll have trouble leaving make this inn memorable. The
living and dining rooms are as swank as
they are comfy.

Captain's Quarters (☎ 709-576-7173; www.cap
tainsquarters.ca; 2 King's Bridge Rd; r incl breakfast $80-
110) It's not as refined as the B&Bs and
inns, but this option is great for families
and usually has a room to spare when you
need one. It's across from Commissariat
House.

Other recommendations:

A Bonne Esperance House B&B (☎ 709-726-3835;
www.wordplay.com/bonne_esperance; 20 Gower St;
d $100-150)

Abba Inn Downtown (☎ 709-754-0058; www
.abbainn.com; 36 Queen's Rd; d incl breakfast $75-185)

Monkstown Manor (☎ 709-754-7324, 888-754-7377;
51 Monkstown Rd; s/d with shared bathroom incl breakfast
$60/70)

Top End

Harbour View Inn (☎ 709-722-3892, 866-722-3892;
www.harbourviewinn.net; 54 Water St; ste incl light breakfast $150-210) Situated on famous Water St,
this luxury hotel opened in 2004 and offers unobstructed views of St John's Harbour from every suite. Along with genteel
furnishings, there's in-floor heating, small
kitchen units and at least one large TV. The
smart sofas fold out for children and some
of the rooms are designed to be wheelchair
accessible.

Rendell Shea Manor B&B (☎ 709-738-7432,
877-738-7432; www.rendellshea.com; 82 Cochrane St; d
$140-230) Thank the Great Fire of 1892 for
sparing this historic home. It's set across
from Government House, and full of 19th-
century opulence. Superb architectural
details, grand canopy beds and fireplaces
embellish the rooms.

Fairmont Hotel Newfoundland (☎ 709-726-
4980; www.fairmont.com/newfoundland; 115 Cavendish Sq;
r $210-380) The imposing stone facade of this
sumptuous beast stands high at the end of
Duckworth St. Put on that signature bath-
robe, slide into your comfy chair and watch
the pulse of St John's Harbour below. Comfort is always guaranteed at the Fairmont.

EATING

The days of St John's being just a fish-and-
chips town are long gone. Although still
only a small city, the variety and quality of
its culinary arts will impress the closet critic
in anyone. Don't worry, though, you can
still get your fish-and-chippy.

Budget

International Flavours (☎ 709-738-4636; 4 Quidi Vidi
Rd; meals $8-9; ⏰ 11am-7pm Mon-Sat) Perhaps the
only thing sweeter than the curries is the Pa-
kistani owner, Talat. Each day she creates a
fabulous new meal.

Ches's (☎ 709-726-2373; 5-9 Freshwater Rd; meals
$5-8; ⏰ 9-2am Sun-Thu, 9-3am Fri & Sat) Ches's and
its fish-and-chips are an institution in Newfoundland. No frills, just cod that will melt
in your mouth.

HAVING A SCOFF

Having a 'scoff,' to use a local term for eating, can be a bit of an adventure across the province,
with many unfamiliar terms showing up on menus. Most of these unknown dishes have something
to do with the sea and are well worth sampling.

Cod tongues are actually the tender, fleshy bits between the lower jaws, while cod cheeks are
just that, cod cheeks. Scruncheons is a nice word to say, and one perfectly suited to fried bits of
pork fat. Fish cakes are a blend of cod, potato and onion mushed together and fried – delicious.
On the other hand, flipper pie is truly for the brave – the strong flavor of seal meat is definitely
an acquired taste.

Two of Newfoundland's favorite meals are fish 'n' brewis and jig's dinner. Fish 'n' brewis is a
blend of salted fish, onions, scruncheons and a unique near-boiled bread. Jig's dinner is a right
feast comprising potatoes, carrots, cabbage, greens, pea-and-bread pudding, salted beef, turkey,
chicken and occasionally moose.

To finish off your traditional meal, try figgy duff, a thick fig pudding that is boiled in a cloth
bag, or devour a doughboy, the provincial version of a dumpling.

When you're done eating you can rightfully say in local parlance, 'I'm full as an egg.'

Auntie Crae's (☎ 709-754-0661; 272 Water St; 🕙 8am-7pm) Come to this specialty food store for a cuppa joe, groceries, chowder or a sandwich. Relax with your goodies in Fishhook Neyle's Common Room. A band plays at Neyle's every Tuesday at noon.

Mid-Range

Pepper Mill (☎ 709-726-7585; 178 Water St; dinner mains $17-20; 🕙 lunch & dinner Mon-Sat) Welcoming and casual, this little place is renowned for its inspired seafood fare. You'll be hard-pressed not to order the prosciutto-wrapped cod fillet with melted brie. Or will it be the salmon marinated in single malt scotch? You can't go wrong here.

Gypsy Tea Room (☎ 709-739-4766; 195 Water St; dinner mains $15-18; 🕙 lunch & dinner) Heavy salsa and Latin music radiate in this edgy eatery. Finished with blackberry and port jus, the special duck confit served in a parmesan crisp with wild mushroom risotto is transcendent. When the kitchen closes, the volume increases and the bar takes over. It's also a creative place for weekend brunch.

India Gate (☎ 709-753-6006; 286 Duckworth St; mains $11-15; 🕙 lunch & dinner) This is the local Indian favorite. For $9 the weekday all-you-can-eat lunch special is a steal – it runs from 11:30am to 2:30pm. As with all Indian eateries, there are loads of vegetarian options.

Chucky's (☎ 709-579-7888; 10 King's Rd; mains $8-20; 🕙 lunch & dinner) A semester's worth of Newfoundland history is eclectically hung from Chucky's walls. Locals come here for traditional Newfoundland dishes. There's fish, caribou, moose and, if you're up for it, flipper pie.

Top End

Aqua (☎ 709-576-2782; 310 Water St; dinner mains $19-29; 🕙 lunch & dinner) This hip bistro's food speaks wonders, so sit back and enjoy. For a starter, savor the pistachio-crusted goat's cheese with raspberry-mango sauce and garlic crustini. The mains range from seafood to wild game – the caribou with warm bakeapple coulis is extraordinary.

Bianca's (☎ 709-726-9016; 171-3 Water St; mains $20-34; 🕙 lunch & dinner) Well-to-do's rave about the roasted rack of lamb and the Muscovy duck. Bianca's extensive wine list is world-class and unrivaled in St John's.

THE AUTHOR'S CHOICE

Duck Street Bistro (☎ 709-753-0400; 250 Duckworth St; dinner mains $15-20; 🕙 lunch & dinner) This gem on Duckworth St lurks behind a very ho-hum exterior. Head in and up the stairs to its warm and modest dining area and prepare for a treat. Sauces that can only be described as sublime grace creative pasta, crepe and wrap specials. Indulge in the catch of the day or try the vegetarian and vegan options that would impress even the most fervent carnivores. Throw in some Asian influence and you have, dollar for dollar, the best restaurant in St John's.

DRINKING

While pubs have been here for centuries, long enough to perfect their craft, a range of exciting young bars and lounges have found footholds on and around George St. So raise a pint to the lads, or sink into leather and sip a martini – it's your choice. Expect most bars and pubs to charge a small cover (about $5) on weekends or when there's live music.

Cafés are creeping in along Water St and you won't have a tough time finding a great chai latte or cappuccino.

Christian's Pub (☎ 709-753-9100; 23 George St) It's not the most polished pub in town, but it is perhaps the most friendly. There's no better man than Keith to make you an 'Honorary Newfoundlander' (see the boxed text on p354).

O'Reilly's (☎ 709-722-4853; 15 George St) Energy greets you at the door in this great Irish pub. The ever-popular open-mike night is on Tuesday, while dancing and live Celtic music take over on weekends.

Grafenberg's (☎ 709-722-7768; 390 Duckworth St) Relax with a martini and jazz in Grafenberg's rich atmosphere.

Bianca's (☎ 709-726-9016; 171-3 Water St) Peruse the city's finest wine, single-malt and imported beer selections from the luxurious depths of leather armchairs. Bianca's is also a top-end eating option (see left).

Quidi Vidi Inn of Olde (☎ 709-576-2223; 67 Quidi Vidi Village Rd, Quidi Vidi) This quirky yet beloved little pub sits just out of town in Quidi Vidi. If only the 2000 spoons on the wall could talk…

NEWFOUNDLAND & LABRADOR

IS YOU A SCREECHER?

In a province heralded for its humor, what better way to welcome visitors than with a little laugh. Within a few days of your arrival in St John's, you'll undoubtedly be asked by locals if you've been screeched, or in traditional Newfoundland slang, 'Is you a screecher?'

The process of screeching typically takes place in local pubs, involves a wee bit of rum, and is derived from the 1940s when new arrivals were given their rites of passage, and from pranks played on sealers heading to the ice for the first time.

Today, becoming an 'Honorary Newfoundlander' involves as much fun as embarrassment. You'll hear songs, you'll sing songs and you'll laugh yourself silly. You might even learn something!

Hava Java (☎ 709-753-5282; 216 Water St; 🕒 7:30am-11pm Mon-Fri, 9am-11pm Sat & Sun) The atmosphere at this place is refreshingly antifranchise; it just focuses on making the best coffee in town. If you need that leather lounger to truly enjoy your espresso, head to **Coffee Company** (☎ 709-576-3606; 204 Water St; 🕒 7:30am-11pm). You can also ward off sailor's scurvy with a fine fruit smoothie at **Auntie Crae's** (☎ 709-754-0661; 272 Water St; 🕒 8am-7pm).

ENTERTAINMENT

Staying entertained in St John's is a pretty easy thing to do. Perhaps because this is such an intimate city, word-of-mouth seems to be the major vehicle for entertainment information. Venues are close together – have a wander and enjoy.

Live Music

Ship (☎ 709-753-3870; 265 Duckworth St; cover $4-7) Attitudes and ages are checked at the door of this little pub, tucked down Solomon's Lane. You'll hear everything from jazz to indie, and even the odd poetry reading.

Fat Cat (☎ 709-739-5554; 5 George St; cover $5) Blues radiates from this cozy bar nightly during the summer.

Bridie Molloy's (☎ 709-576-5990; 5 George St; weekend cover $5) Adjacent to Fat Cat, this polished Irish pub hosts an older crowd and offers Irish and Newfoundland music six nights a week.

Nightclubs

St John's true nightclubs, which only open late on Friday and Saturday night, cater to energetic straight and gay crowds. Cover charges vary, but are typically between $5 and $10.

Club Etomik (☎ 709-579-1070; 13 George St) Packed with a young crowd, this cavernous nightclub reverberates with the latest dance music trends. Close by, **Sundance** (☎ 709-753-7822; cnr George & Adelaide Sts) offers similar surrounds.

Zone (☎ 709-754-2492; 216 Water St) This is the premier gay dance bar in Newfoundland. Straights are equally welcome.

Liquid Ice (☎ 709-754-2190; 186b Water St) If you like your house, drum and base or hip-hop, wade into this gay-friendly nightspot.

Theater

Arts & Culture Centre (☎ 709-729-3900, 800-663-9449; cnr Allandale Rd & Prince Phillip Dr) Live theater and dance performances are staged regularly.

Resource Centre for the Arts (☎ 709-753-4531; LSPU Hall, 3 Victoria St) Local playwrights' work is presented in this intimate environment.

Shakespeare by the Sea Theatre (☎ 709-576-0980; www.nfld.com/~sbts/menu.html; adult/child under 12/student $12/5/10; 🕒 6pm early Jul & late Aug) Live outdoor productions are presented at Bowring Park amphitheater. Note there are no advance sales.

SHOPPING

Music, jam and local art are just some of St John's fine wares. Explore the nooks and crannies of Water and Duckworth Sts and you'll find something with your name on it.

Fred's (☎ 709-753-9191; 198 Duckworth St; 🕒 9:30am-9pm Mon-Fri, 9:30am-6pm Sat, noon-5pm Sun) This is the premier music shop in St John's. It features brilliant local music such as Buddy Wasisname and The Other Fellers.

Christopher Kearney Design Studio (☎ 709-726-2508; 114 Duckworth St; 🕒 10:30am-5:30pm Mon-Sat) This talented goldsmith produces outstanding Labradorite jewelry.

Living Planet (☎ 709-739-6810; 116 Duckworth St) For quirky tourist T-shirts even locals are proud to wear.

Outfitter's (☎ 709-579-4453; 220 Water St) A camping and gear shop where you can purchase maps for the East Coast Trail.

GETTING THERE & AWAY
Air
For information on St John's inter-province air services, see p342.

Bus
The bus system is a little confusing, but if you can track things down, it can work fairly well. The **DRL Coachlines** (☎ 709-738-8088; www.drlgroup.com/Coachlines/coachlines_new.html) bus leaves St John's for Port aux Basques ($97, 13½ hours) and points west daily at 7:45am from Memorial University's Student Centre.

Newhook's Transportation (☎ 709-726-4876, in Placentia 709-227-2552; 13 Queen St, St John's) provides service down the southwestern Avalon Peninsula to Placentia, making a stop at the Argentia ferry terminal ($20, two hours, twice daily).

Car & Motorcycle
The preferred method of coming and going from St John's is by rental car. Nationwide companies such as Avis, Budget, Dollar, National and Hertz (see p873) have offices at the airport. While not at the airport, **Enterprise** (☎ 709-722-9480; 229 Kenmount Rd) offers the best rates. Its daily fee for new compact cars with 150 free kilometers per day and insurance is $69. **Rent-A-Wreck** (☎ 709-753-2277; 43 Pippy Pl) has used compact cars with 100 free kilometers per day, including insurance, for $74.

Share Taxi
Leaving once or twice a day, these large vans typically seat 15 and allow you to jump on or off at any point along their routes. **Molloy's Taxi** (☎ 709-722-4249) serves Trepassey ($15, two hours) daily except Sunday. **Fleetline Bus Service** (☎ 709-722-2608) provides daily service, except Sunday, to Carbonear ($15, 2½ hours) and the lower Conception Bay area. **Shirran's** (☎ 709-722-8032) daily service plies the Bonavista Peninsula, including a stop in Bonavista ($25, 3½ hours). **Foote's Taxi** (☎ 709-832-0491, 800-866-1181) travels down the Burin Peninsula as far as Fortune ($35, four hours).

GETTING AROUND
To/From the Airport
The new nautically inspired airport is 6km north of St John's on Portugal Cove Rd

(Rte 40). A government flat rate applies for trips from the airport to town. The official service is **Dave Gulliver Cabs** (☎ 709-722-0003), and depending on your destination it will cost either $17.50 or $20. Taxis from town to the airport run on meters and should cost around $14.

Car & Motorcycle
The city's one-way streets and unique intersections have the ability to confound even the most dedicated map reader. Thankfully, citizens are incredibly patient and the police are known for their sense of humor. A loonie will get you an hour at the parking meters that line Water and Duckworth Sts. **AP Parking Garage** (cnr Baird's Cove & Harbour Dr; ☎ 6:30am-11pm) charges $1 for 30 minutes or $9 for the day.

Public Transportation
The **Metrobus** (☎ 709-722-9400; www.metrobus .com; one-way fare $1.75, book of 10 tickets $15.75) has numerous routes that ply most of the city. Maps and schedules are online and in the Yellow Pages. Your best bets are the No 3, which circles town via Military Rd and Water St before heading to the university, and No 12, which runs between Quidi Vidi Lake and Bowring Park along Water St.

Taxi
Except for the trip from the airport, all taxis operate on government-standardized meters. A trip within town should cost around $5. **Dave Gulliver Cabs** (☎ 709-722-0003) and **Jiffy Cabs** (☎ 709-722-2222) both provide dependable service.

AROUND ST JOHN'S
North of St John's
Secluded and rocky, **Middle Cove** and **Outer Cove** sit just north of St John's on Rte 30 – they're perfect for a beach picnic. **Edge Outfitters** (☎ 709-782-5925; www.kayakjim.com; ☼ Jun-Aug) offers full-day trips ($110) that explore the rugged shores and hidden caves around Middle Cove.

North at the head of **Torbay Bight** is the enjoyably short **Father Troy Trail**, which hugs the shoreline. The view from **Cape St Francis** is worth the bumpy gravel road from Pouch Cove. There's an old battery and you may just luck out and see a whale or two.

West of St John's

West of town on Topsail Rd (Rte 60), just past Paradise, is **Topsail** and its panoramic views of Conception Bay and its islands.

The largest of Conception Bay's little landmasses is **Bell Island** – it makes an interesting day trip. West of St John's, it's about a 14km drive and 20-minute trip by **ferry** (☎ 709-895-6931; per passenger/car $3/5; ☼ hourly 6am-11pm). Bell Island has the distinction of being the only place on the continent to see enemy action in WWII. Its pier and 80,000 tons of iron ore were torpedoed by German U-boats in 1942 – at low tide, you can still see some of the aftermath. The island sports a pleasant mélange of beaches, coastal vistas, lighthouses and trails. Miners here used to work in shafts under the sea at the world's largest submarine iron mine. The **Iron Ore Mine & Museum** (☎ 709-488-2880; adult/child under 12 $7/3; ☼ 11am-7pm Jun-Sep) details the operation and gives visitors the chance to visit the underground shafts – dress warmly.

South of St John's

Its back lapping up against steep rocky slopes, **Petty Harbour** is filled with weathered boats, wharves and sheds on precarious stilts. Its obvious beauty has not gone unnoticed by movie production companies.

Take it all in from the scenic little deck at the **Orca Inn** (☎/fax 709-747-9676; Main Rd; s/d incl breakfast $60/65). Room Nos 3 and 4 both have great views.

In **Goulds**, at the junction of Rte 10 and the road to Petty Harbour in Bidgood's Plaza, is **Bidgood's** (☎ 709-368-3125; ☼ 9am-9pm Mon-Sat, noon-5pm Sun). This supermarket purveys traditional Newfoundland specialties that will either intrigue or repulse you. It has a religious following among locals who come to buy such delicacies as fresh seal flipper, caribou steak and moose in a jar. In season there's also fresh cod tongues, saltfish and lobster. For the more faint of heart, there are jars of the province's distinctive jams – try partridgeberry or the elite of the island's berries, bakeapple.

BAY BULLS & WITLESS BAY

This is a prime area for whale-, iceberg- and bird-watching. There is a **visitor information center** (☎ 709-334-2609; Rte 10; ☼ 9am-4:30pm mid-Jun–Sep, to 7pm Jul & Aug) in Witless Bay.

Four islands off Witless Bay and southward are preserved as the **Witless Bay Ecological Reserve** and represent one of the top seabird breeding areas in eastern North America. Every summer, more than a million pairs of seabirds gather to breed, including puffins, kittiwakes, storm petrels and the penguinlike murres.

Several companies run great trips to the islands between May and October. Beneath the sheer cliffs, the boats hug the shore, giving you an earful as well as an eyeful – the shrieks are both enthralling and cacophonous.

The best months for trips are June and July, when the humpback and minke whales arrive to join the birds' capelin (a type of fish) feeding frenzy. Screams of joy will overpower the din of the birds if just one humpback launches out of the water in a mighty breach. If you really hit the jackpot, in early summer an iceberg might be thrown in too.

Tours from Bay Bulls visit Gull Island, which has the highest concentration of birds. Further south, tours leaving Bauline East head to nearby Great Island, home to the largest puffin colony.

To no one's surprise, kayaking has also taken off in the area. You don't just see a whale in a kayak, you feel its presence. You can't miss the boat tour and kayak operators – just look for signs off Rte 10. Reservations are suggested.

Recommended tour companies:

Gatherall's (☎ 800-419-4253; Northside Rd, Bay Bulls; 1½hr tours adult/child under 17/student $48/20.50/36; ☼ May-Oct) A fast, large new catamaran gives you as much time at the reserve as O'Brien's. It's also more stable and a wise choice for people prone to seasickness.

O'Brien's (☎ 709-753-4850, 877-639-4253; south side of Bay Bulls; 2hr tours adult/child under 18/student $43/20/33; ☼ May-Sep) Daily departures regularly throughout the summer. A more expensive but exhilarating option is the two-hour tour in a high-speed zodiac ($75). You cover much more ground, get closer to shore and may just pop into a sea cave. Three-hour guided kayak tours are $58 and there's a shuttle service from St John's ($20).

Ocean Adventure Tours (☎ 709-334-3998; 1hr tours adult/child under 12 $20/15) These tours operate out of Bauline East, south of Torso Cove, and are only 10 minutes from Great Island.

Stan Cooke Sea Kayaking (☎ 709-579-6353, 888-747-6353; Harbour Rd, Cape Broyle; 4hr tours $69; ☼ May-Oct) Further south in Cape Broyle, Stan offers great guided tours for beginners and advanced paddlers.

AVALON PENINSULA

The Isthmus of Avalon, at points only 5km wide, connects this peninsula and half the province's population to the rest of Newfoundland and Labrador. Besides the concentration of people, it's home to four of the province's six seabird ecological reserves, one of its two wilderness reserves and 28 of its 41 national historic sites.

Tiny fishing villages seem to dot every crack and crevice along this magnificent coastline.

For hikers, the epic **East Coast Trail** stretches 520km from Cape St Francis all the way to Cape Race, making use of existing coastal trails and bucolic rural paths. It is part easy coastal walking, part tough wilderness trail. A 50km segment also connects with the 50km D'Iberville Trail in the Avalon Wilderness Reserve (right). The **East Coast Trail Association** (☎ 709-738-4453; www.eastcoasttrail.com) has loads of information. Maps are available at the **Outfitter's** (☎ 709-579-4453; 220 Water St) in St John's.

At Argentia, in the southwest, is the terminal for the ferry to Nova Scotia.

SOUTHEASTERN AVALON PENINSULA

The scenic Irish Loop, comprising Rtes 10 and 90, circles the southeastern section of the peninsula, which is known primarily for its wildlife, archeology and fog.

La Manche Provincial Park

Diverse bird life, along with beaver, moose and snowshoe hare, can be seen in this lush park only 53km south of St John's. A highlight is the 1.25km trail to the remains of La Manche, a fishing village that was destroyed in 1966 by a fierce winter storm. Upon arrival, you'll see the beautiful newly built suspension bridge dangling over the narrows – it's part of the East Coast Trail. The trail head is at the park's fire exit road.

There is excellent **camping** (☎ 709-685-1823; fax 709-729-1100; Rte 10; tent sites $10; ☉ mid-May–mid-Sep) at this park, with many sites overlooking the pond.

Ferryland

Ferryland, one of North America's earliest settlements, dates to 1621, when Sir George Calvert established the Colony of Avalon. A few Newfoundland winters later he was scurrying for warmer parts. He settled in Maryland and eventually became the first Lord Baltimore. Other English families arrived later and maintained the colony despite it being razed by the Dutch in 1673 and by the French in 1696.

The seaside surrounds of the **Colony of Avalon Archaeological Site** (☎ 709-432-3200; Rte 10; adult/child under 14/student/family $6/3/4/15; ☉ 10am–5pm mid-May–mid-Oct, 9am-7pm mid-Jun–early Sep) only add to the rich atmosphere. One can easily envisage life in the 17th century in this village huddled around an inner harbor. Archeologists are regularly at the site (8am to 4:30pm Monday to Friday), where everything from axes to bowls are being recovered. The **visitor center** houses interpretive displays and many of the artifacts that have been recovered and restored.

The village's former courthouse is now the small **Historic Ferryland Museum** (☎ 709-432-2155; Rte 10; admission $2; ☉ 9am-5pm Jun-Sep). It tells of Ferryland's survival and its role in colonizing the continent. The towering hill behind the museum was where settlers would climb to watch for approaching warships or to escape the Dutch and French incursions. After seeing the view from the summit, you'll understand why the settlers named the hill 'the Gaze.'

Once a convent, **Downs Inn** (☎ 709-432-2808, 877-432-2808; fax 709-432-2659; Rte 10; d with/without bathroom $75/65) has four rooms. A full breakfast is included, and everything is close by.

The owner of **Ferryland Cafe & Gifts** (☎ 709-432-2130; Rte 10; light meals $4-7; ☉ 9am-7pm), Rhonda, is a bundle of energy and so very proud of her shop. She should be – it's the best food around. It's just south of the visitor center on Rte 10.

Avalon Wilderness Reserve

Dominating the interior of the region is the 1070-sq-km **Avalon Wilderness Reserve** (☎ 709-635-4520; free permit required). Thanks to illegal hunting, this region's caribou population was as low as 100 in the 1980s. Twenty years later, there are countless thousands of caribou roaming the area. Permits for hiking and canoeing are available at La Manche Provincial Park (left).

Even if you don't trek into the wilds, you are still bound to see some caribou along Rte 10 between Chance Cove Provincial Park and St Stevens. Seeing one of these impressive beasts is a treat rarely experienced by those not living in the far north of Canada, Russia or Finland.

The southern coast is affectionately known as the manufacturer and distributor of fog in the province – Portugal Cove holds an unofficial world record for the most foggy days in a row.

Mistaken Point Ecological Reserve

This **ecological reserve** (☎ 709-635-4520) protects 620-million-year-old multicelled marine fossils – easily the oldest in North America. Some of these fossils are unique, and paleontologists are still struggling with names for them. Unesco is considering naming the reserve a world heritage site. It's reached by a treacherous 45-minute hike from the gravel road between Portugal Cove South and Cape Race. It was the lighthouse keeper at Cape Race who received the fateful last message from the *Titanic*.

Trepassey

Trepassey was the launching place of Amelia Earhart's transatlantic flight in 1928 – she was the first woman to cross the Atlantic by air. The diminutive **Trepassey Museum** (☎ 709-438-2779; Main Rd; admission by donation; 🕓 Jul & Aug) has local artifacts. Opening hours vary.

You'll find warm hospitality and crisp, clean rooms that feature simple pine furniture at **Northwest B&B** (☎ 709-438-2888, 877-398-2888; Rte 10, Trepassey; d incl light breakfast with/without bathroom $70/65).

Along Rte 90

The area from St Vincent's to St Mary's provides an excellent chance of seeing whales, particularly the humpback, which feeds close to shore. Halfway between the two villages is **Point La Haye Natural Scenic Attraction**, a dramatic arm of fine pebbles stretching across the mouth of St Mary's Bay – it's perfect for a walk.

Salmonier Nature Park (☎ 709-229-7888; Rte 90; admission free; 🕓 10am-6pm Jun–Labour Day, 10am-4pm Mon-Fri Labour Day–Jun) rehabilitates injured and orphaned animals for release back into the wild. A 2.5km trail through the woods takes you past indigenous fauna and natural enclosures with moose, caribou and beaver. There's an **interpretive center** and touch displays for children. The park is on Rte 90, 12km south of the junction with Hwy 1.

CONCEPTION BAY

Charming fishing villages stretch endlessly along Conception Bay's scenic western shore until they're met by the vast cliffs at land's end, near Bay Verte. Found amongst the bay's bright boats and fishing nets is Brigus, perhaps the most picturesque village in the province. Conception Bay sits a mere 80km from St John's. For information on share taxis from the capital, see p355.

Brigus

Resting on the water and surrounded by rock bluffs is the heavenly village of Brigus. Its idyllic stone-walled streams meander slowly past its delightful old buildings and colorful gardens before emptying into the serene Harbour Pond. Famous American painter Rockwell Kent lived here during WWI, before his eccentric behavior got him deported on suspicion of spying for the Germans in 1915. The path toward his old cottage makes for a great walk.

Robert Bartlett, the town's most famous son, is renowned as one of the foremost arctic explorers of the 20th century. He made more than 20 arctic expeditions, including one in 1909, when he cleared a trail in the ice that enabled US commander Robert Peary to make his celebrated dash to the North Pole. Bartlett's house, **Hawthorne Cottage** (☎ 709-528-4004; cnr Irishtown Rd & South St; adult/child under 17/family $3/2/7; 🕓 10am-6pm mid-May–mid-Oct), is a national historic site and museum.

Also in town is **Ye Olde Stone Barn Museum** (☎ 709-528-3391; 4 Magistrate's Hill; admission $1; 🕓 noon-6pm mid-Jun–Labour Day), which has a set of displays on Brigus' 200-year history.

Below the church, on the waterfront, is the **Brigus Tunnel**, which was cut through rock in 1860 so Robert Bartlett could easily access his ship in the deep cove on the other side.

In July and August, a **walking theater** (☎ 709-528-4817; 🕓 2:30pm Sun) presents Brigus' history with costumes, dancing and skits – a steal for $5. If you're here, you won't miss them. There are no advance sales.

The **Brittoner** (☎ 709-528-3412; fax 709-528-3412; 12 Water St; s/d incl breakfast $50/60; 🕓 May-Oct), an old-fashioned Victorian home, backs onto Harbour Pond – enjoy. The loft is perfect for families.

A clean, comfortable and child-friendly farmhouse, **Brookdale Manor** (☎ 709-528-4544; brookdalebb@hotmail.com; Farm Rd; s/d $50/60) is just out of the village. It's also wheelchair accessible.

Every perfect village needs a perfect eatery. At **North St Café** (☎ 709-528-1393; 29 North St; light meals $7; ☯ 10am-6pm Jun-Oct, to 8pm Jul & Aug), quiche, fish cakes, fine desserts and afternoon tea are all on order.

Hibbs Cove

Hibbs Cove, an attractive village at the end of the Port de Grave Peninsula, hosts the **Fishermen's Museum** (☎ 709-786-3912; admission $2; ☯ noon-6pm late Jun–early Sep). Inside are pictures and artifacts depicting the trade at the start of the 20th century.

Harbour Grace

A mixed crowd of historic figures has graced this large harbor over the past 500 years. Notables include the infamous pirate Peter Easton and the celebrated Amelia Earhart. Near the northern end of Water St, in the heritage district, there are two vastly different churches that are equally handsome. The cute redbrick customs house is now a small town **museum** (☎ 709-596-5465; Water St; admission $3; ☯ 10am-5pm Jun-Sep).

The citizens of Harbour Grace liked the look of the SS *Kyle* (1913) beached at the mouth of their harbor so much, they actually paid to have it restored instead of removed.

In 1932, four years after her flight from Trepassey, Amelia Earhart took off from **Harbour Grace Airfield** (☎ 709-596-5901; Earhart Rd) and became the first woman to cross the Atlantic solo.

North of Harbour Grace

The largest town north of Harbour Grace is Carbonear. Unfortunately, the most interesting thing about Carbonear itself is the remote island offshore. The windswept **Carbonear Island** has had a tumultuous history, with international battles, pirate intrigues and shipwrecks.

Farther up the coast, at **Northern Bay Sands Park** (☎ 709-584-3465; Rte 70; tent sites $11; ☯ May-Oct), jagged cliffs stand guard over a gorgeous beach. Day-use is $4 per vehicle. There's a great freshwater swimming area where the creek meets the sea.

Clinging to cliffs at the northern end of the peninsula are the remote and striking villages of **Bay de Verde** and **Grates Cove**. Hundreds of subtle 500-year-old rock walls line the hills around Grates Cove and have been declared a national historic site. Offshore, in the distance, is the inaccessible **Baccalieu Island Ecological Reserve** with its three million pairs of Leach's storm petrel – the largest such colony in the world.

TRINITY BAY

Thicker forests, fewer villages and subdued topography typify the shores of Trinity Bay and give the west coast of the peninsula a more serene feeling than its eastern shore. Whoever named the villages Heart's Desire, Heart's Delight and Heart's Content must have agreed.

Heart's Content

The **Cable Station Provincial Historic Site** (☎ 709-583-2160; Rte 80; admission $2.50; ☯ 10:30am-5:30pm late Jun–Thanksgiving) tells the story of the first permanent transatlantic cable that was laid here in 1866. The word 'permanent' is significant, because the first successful cable (connected in 1858 to Bull Arm, on Trinity Bay) failed shortly after Queen Victoria and US President James Buchanan christened the line with their congratulatory messages.

Dildo

Oh, to have been a fly on the wall when cable TV first introduced Dildo to the dildo… And yes, the road to Heart's Desire, Heart's Delight and Heart's Content goes through Dildo.

TOP FIVE WAYS TO IMPRESS A NEWFOUNDLANDER

- Know that heading 'up the shore' is actually moving south.
- Never look at your watch.
- Tell them your hometown when they ask, 'Where you longs to?'
- Visit Labrador.
- Know that it's bad luck to leave a building by a different door to the one you came in.

Joking aside, Dildo is a lovely village and its shore is a good spot for whale-watching. Pothead (no joke) whales come in by the pod, and humpbacks, a larger species, can also be seen in summer. The **Dildo Interpretation Centre** (☎ 709-582-2687; Front Rd; admission free; ☑ Jul-Sep) has exhibits on the area's 19th-century codfish hatchery, as well as the on-going Dorset Eskimo archeological dig on Dildo Island. Opening hours vary.

Two flawlessly restored houses comprise **Inn by the Bay** (☎ 709-582-3170; innbythebaydildo.com; 78 Front Rd; d incl breakfast $80-150; ☑ May-Dec), which is the most luxurious spot to stay on the northern Avalon. The views from George House and its palatial lawn are unbeatable. The elegant **Veranda Sunroom** (mains $14-17), and its view, is open to guests for dinner.

ARGENTIA

Argentia, 131km from St John's, hosts the terminal serving ferries to Nova Scotia (p342). **Newhook's Transportation** (☎ 709-227-2552, in St John's 709-726-4876; 13 Queen St, St John's) connects Argentia and Placentia with St John's by road. A provincial **information chalet** (☎ 709-227-5272; Rte 100; ☑ hrs vary to coincide with ferry sailings) is 3km from the ferry on Rte 100.

PLACENTIA

In the early 1800s, Placentia – then Plaisance – was the French capital of Newfoundland, and French attacks on the British at St John's were based here. Near to town, perched high above the shores, is **Castle Hill National Historic Site** (☎ 709-227-2401; adult/child under 17 $3.50/1.75; ☑ 10am-6pm mid-May–mid-Oct). Here, remains of French and British fortifications from the 17th and 18th centuries have panoramic views over Placentia and the surrounding waters.

The fascinating **graveyard** next to the Anglican church holds the remains of people of every nationality that has settled here since the 1670s. The **O'Reilly House Museum** (☎ 709-227-5568; 48 Orcan Dr; admission $2; ☑ 9am-8pm Mon-Fri, noon-8pm Sat & Sun mid-Jun–Aug), within a century-old Victorian home, gives you more of an inside look at the town and its past luxuries. Wander past the other notable buildings, including the **Roman Catholic church** and the **stone convent**. A boardwalk runs along the stone-skipper's delight of a beach.

The slightly old fashioned rooms of **Oceanview Efficiency Suites** (☎ 709-227-5151; fax 709-227-7700; Beach Rd; r $70) are spacious and have small kitchens. The rooms at the back grant you harbor views.

Another good option is the **Harold Hotel** (☎ 709-227-2107, 877-227-2107; Main St; tw/d $60/80). It's plain but central, and the **restaurant** (meals $6-14) serves great pizza.

CAPE ST MARY'S

Wander the tops of stratified and verdant precipices and gaze out over the crashing waves to the mystifying clouds of birds below. At the southeastern tip of the peninsula is **St Mary's Ecological Reserve**, one of the most accessible bird colonies on the continent. Visit the **interpretive center** (☎ 709-277-1666; adult/child under 18/family $5/2/10; ☑ 8am-7pm mid-Jun–mid-Sep, 9am-5pm mid-May–mid-Oct) and snag a map for the 1.4km trail to Bird Rock, the third-largest gannet-nesting site in North America. Its near-vertical cliffs provide ideal nesting conditions for nearly 70,000 seabirds, including kittiwakes, murres and razorbills. During summer, guides are present to answer questions.

EASTERN NEWFOUNDLAND

Two peninsulas reach awkwardly out to sea and form the eastern section of the island. The Bonavista Peninsula projects northward and is freckled with historic fishing villages, one of which claims to be the oldest town in North America. The waters here are rich in wildlife, and the shores are great for hiking. Contact the **Discovery Trail Tourism Association** (☎ 709-466-3845; www.thediscovery trail.org) for information on the peninsula's many trails. While Clarenville is the access point and service center for the area, there is not much besides the **provincial tourist office** (☎ 709-466-3100; 379 Hwy 1; 9am-6pm mid-May–Sep, 8am-8pm Jun–Aug). Preserving sections of the northern coast, and sitting across Clode Sound from the peninsula is Terra Nova National Park.

The massive and lightly populated Burin Peninsula juts southward into the Grand Banks and makes up the rest of eastern Newfoundland. The ferry for France – yes, France – departs from Fortune and heads to St Pierre and Miquelon (p365).

Character-filled shed, Prince Edward Island (p454)

Gros Morne National Park (p373),
Newfoundland

Prince Edward Island National
Park (p469), Prince Edward
Island

Fundy National Park (p511), New
Brunswick

Cabot Trail (p441), Cape Breton Island, Nova Scotia

Cape Breton Island (p441), Nova Scotia

Saint John River (p491), New Brunswick

L'Anse aux Meadows National Historic Site (p377), Newfoundland

TRINITY

You can't get lost in Trinity, yet most people try – walking aimlessly through its crooked seaside lanes, past its storybook heritage houses and gardens is simply that gratifying. Trinity has much to offer despite its size (its population is just 200) and sees more than its fair share of visitors in the summer.

First visited by Portuguese explorer Corte-Real in 1500 and established as a town in 1580, Trinity might be the oldest town on the entire continent.

Information

Post office (☎ 709-464-2240; 1 Garland Rd)
Royal Bank (☎ 709-464-2260; Rte 230)
Trinity Medical Clinic (☎ 709-464-3721) On the road out of town.

Sights & Activities

Trinity's major **historical sites** (☎ 709-464-3599, 709-464-2042; adult/child under 12 $7.50/free; ☼ 10am-5:30pm mid-Jun–mid-Oct) all have the same opening hours and a single admission charge.

The marvelous redbrick **Lester Garland House** (West St) was rebuilt to rekindle and celebrate cultural links between Trinity and Dorset, England – major trading partners in the 17th, 18th and 19th centuries. Next door the **Lester Garland Premises** (West St) have been restored to portray the port's general store, owned by the Ryan family from 1902 to 1952. The **Interpretation Centre** (West St) is back up the lane and tells of Trinity's fascinating history. Over 2000 pieces are displayed within the **Trinity Museum** (Church Rd), including the second-oldest fire wagon in North America, dating from 1811. Also on Church Rd is the **Hiscock House Provincial Historic Site**, which is a restored merchant's home, furnished to around 1910.

Further afield is **Fort Point**, where you'll find four cannons, the remains of the British fortification from 1745. There are 10 more British cannons in the water, all compliments of the French in 1762.

The **Skerwink Trail** (5km) is a fabulous loop that affords superb coastal vistas. It's accessible from the church in Trinity East, off Rte 230.

Tours

Atlantic Adventures (☎ 709-781-2255; Dock Lane; 2½hr tours $40; ☼ Jun-Sep) Several conventional whale-watching tours leave daily from the wharf near the Dock Restaurant.

Ocean Contact (☎ 709-464-3269; the Village Inn, Taverner's path; 3hr tours adult/child under 13/child 13-15 $55/35/45; ☼ mid-Jun–mid-Aug) This research organization is run by renowned scientist Dr Peter Beamish, and offers more than just whale-watching. Its state-of-the-art boat uses 'rhythm based communication' to interact with whales. Seeing a whale jump on cue is as mind-boggling as it is exhilarating. Reservations are recommended.

Trinity Walking Tours (☎ 709-464-3723; Clinch's Lane; adult/child $8/free; ☼ 10am) These entertaining and educational tours start behind Hiscock House.

Sleeping & Eating

For such a diminutive town, there are numerous fine inns and B&Bs. During the summer space gets tight, so it's wise to book ahead.

Village Inn (☎ 709-464-3269; beamish@oceancontact .com; Taverner's Path; s $70-80, d $75-85) This inn has classic country rooms with bright windows, antique furnishings and weathered floorboards. Ask Peter about his gift from Boris Yeltsin. The **dining room** (mains $8-15; ☼ breakfast, lunch & dinner) is open to nonguests (after 9am) and makes great traditional meals along with amazing partridgeberry pie and vegetarian options.

Artisann Inn & Campbell House B&B (☎ 709-464-3377, 877-464-7700; www.artisaninntrinity.com; High St; d $110-115, apt $135-225; ☼ May-Oct) The B&B is surrounded by flowers and looks over the ocean, while the colorful inn hovers over the sea on stilts.

Eriksen Premises (☎ 709-464-3698, 877-464-3698; www.trinityexperience.com; West St; d incl breakfast $85-110; ☼ mid-May–mid-Oct) This Victorian home offers elegance in accommodations and **dining** (mains $13-22; ☼ lunch & dinner).

Trinity Cabins (☎ 709-464-3657; fax 709-464-3764; Rte 239; 2-bedroom cabins $50-55; ☼ May-Oct) These rustic cabins date from 1948 and are said to have been the first tourist accommodations in the province. They have kitchens and, for the brave, there's a beach nearby. Ask for unit No 32.

Dock Restaurant (☎ 709-464-2133; Dock Lane; mains $7-15; ☼ breakfast, lunch & dinner) This scenic spot sits next to the wharf and prepares great chowder and seafood.

Entertainment

Alongside the Lester Garland Premises is the **Rising Tide Theatre** (☎ 888-464-3377; www .risingtidetheatre.com; Water St; matinee/evening tickets $10/14; ☼ Tue-Sun mid-Jun–mid-Oct), which hosts the 'Seasons in the Bight' theater festival and

NEWFOUNDLAND & LABRADOR

the celebrated **Trinity Pageant** (adult/child under 15 $10/free; ☺ 2pm Wed, Sat & Sun), an entertaining outdoor drama on the history of Trinity.

Fiddle and caller let loose at **Rocky's Place** (☎ 709-464-3400; High St) on Wednesday at 10pm. Learn some traditional dance, or relax and watch the show.

Getting There & Around
Trinity is 259km from St John's and is reached via Rte 230 off Hwy 1. See p355 for information on share taxis from St John's.

BONAVISTA
As the story goes, on June 24, 1497, John Cabot's first words upon seeing the New World were 'O buona vista!' ('Oh, happy sight!'). From all descriptions, this pleasant and charming place is where he first set foot in the Americas. Despite its early beginnings, it wasn't until the 1600s that Bonavista became a permanent village. The next century of its life would be filled with British and French battles for possession of the north shore.

Information
The nearest tourist office is in Clarenville (see p360).
Bonavista Community Health Centre (☎ 709-468-7881; Hospital Rd)
Post Office (☎ 800-267-1177; 28 Church St)
Scotiabank (☎ 709-468-1070; 1 Church St)

Sights & Activities
Ryan Premises National Historic Site (☎ 709-468-1600; Ryans Hill Rd; adult/senior/family $3.50/1.75/8.75; ☺ 10am-6pm mid-May–Thanksgiving) is a restored 19th-century saltfish mercantile complex evocatively honoring five centuries of commercial fishing in Newfoundland, through multimedia displays, interpretive programs, live music and theater.

An impressive full-scale replica of the ship on which Cabot sailed into Bonavista is at **Ye Matthew Legacy** (☎ 709-468-1493; Roper St; adult/child under 17/family $5.50/2.75/14.75; ☺ 10am-6pm Jun-Thanksgiving, to 8pm Jul–mid-Aug). The interpretation center opened in 2003 and gives an insight into the amazing vessel and the original's crossing.

Cape Bonavista Lighthouse (☎ 709-468-7444; Rte 230; adult/child under 13 $2.50/free; ☺ 10am-5:30pm mid-Jun–Thanksgiving) is a brilliant red-and-white striped lighthouse dating from 1843. The interior has been restored to the 1870s and is now a provincial historic site. A **puffin colony** lives just offshore; they put on quite a show when the sun is low.

At **Dungeon Park** (Cape Shore Rd; admission free), you can stand on the beach to the thunderous applause of the waves retreating through the rocks and stare out to distant sea stacks on this wave-hewn coast. Nowhere is the power of water more evident than at the Dungeon, a deep chasm, 250m in circumference, that was created by the collapse of two sea caves.

Other sights of interest in town are the **courthouse** (Church St), where the whipping post still stands, and the collection of buildings at the **Mockbeggar Property** (Mockbeggar Rd). Outside town near **Maberly** on Rte 238, there's an offshore island where thousands of puffins, kittiwakes and murres roost. Between Maberly and Little Catalina there is an excellent 17km coastal hiking trail.

Sleeping & Eating
Ocean Side Cabins (☎ 709-468-7771; randjabbott@nf.sympatico.ca; Cape Shore Rd; 1-/2-bedroom apt $65/75) The simple apartments sit beachside en route to Cape Bonavista. Unit Nos 1 to 4 are closest to the beach, with No 4 being wheelchair accessible. The **restaurant** (meals $8-12; ☺ breakfast, lunch & dinner) serves seafood dinners and the occasional stir-fry.

Butler's By the Sea B&B (☎ 709-468-2445; hbutler@thezone.net; 15 Butler Cres; d $75-100) Follow the superfluity of signs to this charming, roomy place.

Getting There & Around
Bonavista is a scenic 28km drive north of Trinity along Rte 230. **Shirran's** (☎ 709-722-8032) provides the most comprehensive bus service on the peninsula. Failing that, **Bonavista Cabs** (☎ 709-468-2457) and **Marsh Taxi** (☎ 709-468-7715) are viable options.

TERRA NOVA NATIONAL PARK
The waters of Clode and Newman Sounds cut deeply into remnants of the ancient Appalachian Mountains and provide a spectacular setting for this **park** (☎ 709-533-2801; Hwy 1; adult/child under 17/family per day $5/2.50/12.50, admission free mid-Oct–mid-May). Backing the craggy cliffs and endless sheltered inlets are lakes, bogs and hilly woods that together typify the regional geography. Moose, bear,

beaver and bald eagles roam this territory, while whales, otter and the occasional iceberg watch from the depths. For the visitor there is a full gamut of activities: canoeing, kayaking, hiking, camping, and even swimming in Sandy Pond.

Information

Marine Interpretation & Information Centre
(☎ 709-533-280; Hwy 1; ⏰ 9am-5pm May-Oct, to 9pm Jun-Sep) Oodles of park information and some interesting displays.

Sights & Activities

The Marine Interpretation & Information Centre at Salton's sits off Hwy 1, 240km east of St John's and 80km west of Gander. Aquariums, underwater cameras and touch tanks let you explore the ocean's secrets.

Terra Nova's 14 hiking trails total almost 100km. Highly recommended is the **Malady Head Trail** (5km), which climaxes at the edge of a headland cliff offering stunning views of Southwest Arm and Broad Cove. **Sandy Pond Trail** (3km) is an easy loop around the pond – your best place to spot a beaver. Pissing Mare Falls and shorebirds are seen along the **Coastal Trail** (9km).

Access to backcountry campgrounds is gained along sections of the epic **Outport Loop** (55km). The loop in its entirety is rewarding, but be warned: parts are unmarked – not to mention mucky. A compass, a topographical map and ranger advice are prerequisites for this serious route. It's possible to break it up using Ocean Watch Tours, which can drop you off during one of its tours.

The **Sandy Pond-Dunphy's Canoe Route** (10km) makes a great paddle and has only one small portage. From the end of Dunphy Pond, another portage gains you access to the waters of Pitts Pond. There are **canoe rentals** (☎ 709-677-2221; per hr/day $10/29; ⏰ 10am-6pm mid-Jun–Labour Day) at Sandy Point.

Sea kayaking is taking off in the park, and with over 200km of shoreline the possibilities are endless. It's possible to rent **kayaks** (single/double per day $45/55) from Terra Nova Adventures. At Burnside, 15km from the park's western gate, popular boat tours leave for the renowned **Beothuk archeological sites** of Bloody Reach and Beaches. Beaches contains the largest Beothuk settlement ever

discovered and the only Beothuk grave ever found. For information on Beothuk Aboriginal people, see the boxed text on p371.

Tours

Burnside Heritage Foundation (☎ 709-677-2474; 4½hr tours $35; ⏰ mid-Jun–early Sep) Fascinating boat tours to the famous archeological remains of the extinct Beothuk tribe. While waiting for the boat, you can visit the field laboratory and a museum ($2), open from 9am to 8pm.

Ocean Watch Tours (☎ 709-533-6024; ⏰ mid-May–Oct) Three-hour research trips (adult/child under 13 $45/22.50) allow you special interaction with the wildlife, including whales and – hold on – plankton! Tours leave at 9am from behind the Marine Interpretation Centre. The two-hour fjord tour ($35/17.50) is less science, more fun; it leaves at 1pm and 4pm.

Terra Nova Adventures (☎ 709-533-9797, 888-533-8687; ⏰ May-Oct) Next to Ocean Watch, popular 2½-hour kayak tours (adult/youth $45/35) leave at 10am and 1:30pm daily. There are also six- to seven-hour coastal tours ($119/95). All tours are subject to demand and reservations are advised.

Sleeping

Although Terra Nova has nearly 600 campsites, on summer weekends it's best to arrive early or book ahead by calling **Parks Canada** (☎ 866-533-3186; www.canadiancamping.ca). It's also possible to book online. There is a $10 fee for phone and online reservations.

Newman Sound Campground (tent sites $14, RV sites $17-26) This is the park's main campground. Also found here is **Newman Sound Service Center** (☎ 709-533-9133), with groceries, a laundromat and bicycle rentals.

Malady Head Campground (tent sites $17) This more basic campground is at the northern end of the park.

Backcountry camping (free permit required; tent sites per day/season $8/56) If you'd like to really get away from things, there are eight backcountry campsites. Half sit along the southern shore of Newman Sound and can be reached by paddling, hiking, water taxi or Ocean Watch Tours. The other half are inland and accessed primarily by canoe.

BURIN PENINSULA

This southern peninsula and its mighty Grand Banks underlying the Atlantic Ocean were the base for European fishing boats for almost 500 years. Today, fish stocks are low and fishing boats are few and far between.

It seems some people are still making a living at the sea though, as rumors are afloat of booze running from nearby St Pierre to the shores of the peninsula. In one coastal village, the man behind the counter of the government liquor store is affectionately known, to those who toast nightly to France, as the 'Maytag man' because he never has anything to do.

Information & Orientation

Although Marystown is the largest town on the peninsula, there's not much to see besides the **information center** (☎ 709-279-1887; Rte 210; 9am-9pm mid-Jun–early Sep, 9am-5pm Mon-Fri early Sep–mid-Jun).

Burin is the most attractive town on the peninsula, and has a gorgeous elevated boardwalk over the waters of its rocky shoreline. The town of St Lawrence is known for fluorite mining, scenic coastal hikes and a charming umbrella tree. In the town of Grand Bank, there's an interest-ing self-guided walk through the historic buildings and waterfront; each summer it's home to an entertaining theater festival. Just south is Fortune, the jumping-off point for St Pierre and Miquelon.

Sights

The Yugoslavia pavilion from Montréal's Expo '67 has come a long way to host the fine **Provincial Seamen's Museum** (☎ 709-832-1484; Marine Dr, Grand Bank; adult/child $2.50/free; 9am-5pm May-Oct). It deserves a visit. It depicts both the era of the banking schooner and the changes in the fishery over the years. Kids will adore the model sailing ships.

Burin Heritage Museum (☎ 709-891-2217; Seaview Dr, Burin; admission free; 9am-5pm May-Oct, to 8pm Jul & Aug) has displays in two historical homes telling of life's highs and lows in remote outports. There's also a small gallery for traveling art exhibits.

The **St Lawrence Miner's Museum** (☎ 709-873-2222; Rte 220, St Lawrence; admission free; 9am-

---

A NIGHT OF EQUALITY

In St Lawrence you'll see plenty of plaques and monuments about the wrecks and rescues of the USS *Truxton* and USS *Pollux*, but the most interesting story of all is lurking in the name of a wee child's playground.

It was February 18, 1942, when a vicious midnight storm smashed the USS *Truxton* and USS *Pollux* into the rocks near the village of St Lawrence. At this time the US Navy was segregated, with African Americans strictly working as servants to white officers.

Clinging to the deck of the *Truxton* as it broke up under him was African American Lanier Phillips. Born in 1923 and raised in the deep south, near Georgia, he had faced racism his entire life and knew nothing else. He had even watched the Ku Klux Klan burn down his school. Like the other five African Americans aboard, he knew he had two options: stick with a sinking ship in -22°C temperatures, or take his chances in the water and risk being lynched when he got to shore. Lanier was the only one of the six to risk shore. After fighting his way through the thick black bunker C oil coating the sea, he collapsed on a narrow stretch of beach. Daring locals used ropes to pull his limp body up the sheer 25m cliffs, and rushed him to a local home.

When he came to, he was naked in a tub and being incessantly scrubbed by white women. He may have been more afraid at this moment than when he jumped off the ship. This type of contact with white women would surely mean his death. After more scrubbing and hearing the women quizzically commenting on his curly hair and how the oil had amazingly stained his skin, he realized that the women had never seen an African American before. After some humorous explanations, he was soon dressed in the husband's clothing, tucked into bed and spoon-fed hot soup. His next realization was even more astounding than the first: these white people actually wanted him to live.

The next day his dream of equality was rudely interrupted when he was dragged from the house by the navy. However, his brief experience of St Lawrence's colorblindness changed his life and he became a lifetime activist against discrimination in the navy, and at home in Georgia. Phillips went on to become the first African-American navy sonar technician and still visits St Lawrence occasionally. He even donated money to build the little park that bears his name.

On the fateful night of the wreck, 203 men died, 185 were rescued, and one man was reborn.

4:30pm Jun–early Sep, to 9pm Jul & Aug) outlines St Lawrence's mining history and tells of its days as the world's largest producer of fluorite.

Just 3km from Fortune, **Fortune Head Ecological Reserve** (☎ 709-832-2810; off Rte 220; admission free; ☸ 24hr) protects fossils dating from the planet's most important period of evolution. Some 550 million years ago, in a span of only 25 million years, life on Earth evolved from simple organisms to complex animals.

Activities

The Burin Peninsula offers some interesting **hikes**, due in part to its varied coastline. Ask at Burin Heritage Museum about locating the **Captain Cook's Lookout** trailhead. It's about a 20-minute walk from town to the panoramic view. Off Pollux Cr in St Lawrence, the **Cape Trail** (4km) and **Chamber Trail** (2km) shadow the cliff edges and offer amazing vistas down to rocky shores and some famous WWII ship wrecks. Another good trail is the **Marine Hike** (6km) that traces Admiral's Beach near Grand Bank. It leaves from Christian's Rd off Rte 220.

Sleeping & Eating

There are some great places to stay on the peninsula, but they are spread thinly. Finding good restaurants is even harder, as people here don't eat out much. Don't worry – you should be starving yourself for the upcoming onslaught of fine French fare anyway. Only 8km from the ferry, Grand Bank is the perfect place to base your jump to France (right).

Sound of the Sea B&B (☎ 709-891-2115, 866-891-2115; www.soundofthesea.com; 16A Seaview Dr, Burin; d incl taxes $60-70) This old merchant's home overlooks the harbor and is only steps away from the town's beautiful boardwalk. The loft with a pullout sofa is perfect for families.

Heritage Square B&B (☎ 709-891-1353; gregr@ superweb.ca; Seaview Dr, Burin; s/d $50/65) This 1920s home is perched on a bluff overlooking the ocean and sits next to the Burin museum.

Thorndyke B&B (☎ 709-832-0820, 866-882-0820; www.thethorndyke.com; 33 Water St, Grand Bank; d with/ without bathroom $80/60; ☸ Jun-Sep) This gorgeous heritage home in Grand Bank is only seconds from the water and the views from its decks, antique-filled rooms and sunroom are timeless.

Sharon's Nook & The Tea Room (☎ 709-832-0618; Water St, Grand Bank; meals $5-8; ☸ 7am-10pm Mon-Sat, 11am-8pm Sun) This countrified eatery serves up great lasagna, chili and sandwiches, and heavenly cheesecake.

Getting There & Around

The Burin Peninsula is accessed via Rte 210 off Hwy 1. The drive from St John's to Grand Bank is 369km and takes just over four hours. **Foote's Taxi** (☎ 709-832-0491, 800-866-1181) travels from St John's down the Burin Peninsula as far as Fortune ($35, four hours).

It's possible to reach Pool's Cove on the south coast from Bay L'Argent via Rencontre on a passenger ferry (adult/student $8/4). Between November and mid-May, the boat leaves Bay L'Argent at 9:15am on Sunday and Friday for the three-hour trip. The return sailing leaves Pool's Cove the same day at 1:15pm. The rest of the year the boat leaves Bay L'Argent at 12:45pm on Monday, Thursday and Saturday and at 9:15am on Tuesday, Friday and Sunday. The return trips during this period leave at 8:45am Monday, Thursday and Saturday and at 1:15pm on Tuesday, Friday and Sunday. Confirm these schedules with **Provincial Ferry Services** (www.gov.nl.ca/ferryservices) or call ☎ 709-891-1050.

ST PIERRE & MIQUELON

Surrounded by the mighty Atlantic, just 16km offshore from the Burin Peninsula, the French *tricolore* stands tall and calls this archipelago home. Beneath this fluttering flag rests France's last North American possession, St Pierre and Miquelon. Although smaller than its neighbor Miquelon, St Pierre is the more populated and developed island, with most of its 5600 residents living in the town of St Pierre.

Citizens here take their national pride very seriously – some even feel it's their duty to maintain France's foothold in the New World. French cars, stereotypical French window displays and pastry shops line the colonial streets. Even the beautiful little blue placards that line Parisian streets stare out from St Pierre's walls, announcing street names. Locals kiss their hellos and pay for things in euros – this is definitely no cousin of Newfoundland.

CAPONE CONNECTION

The USA's Prohibition era and Al Capone came knocking in the 1920s and changed St Pierre overnight. Gone was the sleepy fishing harbor; in its place stood a booming port crowded with warehouses, each brimming with booze. Bottles were removed from their crates, placed in smaller carrying sacks and taken secretly to the US coast by rumrunners. The piles of Cutty Sark whiskey crates were so high on the docks, clever locals used the wood to both build and heat houses. Some of them remain and they are known as 'Cutty Sark cottages.'

Anecdotal evidence suggests the covert trade continues. St Pierre still imports enough alcohol to pickle each and every citizen a few times over, and there is a distinct and humorous lack of alcohol sales in areas on the Burin Peninsula. Some say St Pierre's spirits flow as far away as the mighty George St in St John's.

After they were discovered by the Portuguese in 1520, Jacques Cartier claimed the islands for France in 1536. At the end of the Seven Years' War in 1762, the islands were turned over to Britain, only to be given back 21 years later as a condition of the Treaty of Paris. Since then, peaceful (and not so peaceful) battles have erupted over the islands' fishing rights. Negotiations in the past 15 years have finally settled most of the conflict.

INFORMATION

While French is widely spoken, many people are bilingual. Canadian visitors need only official photo identification, while EU citizens and Americans need passports. Other nationalities should confirm with their French embassy if a visa is needed prior to arrival.

Note that time on the islands is half an hour ahead of Newfoundland Time, and that calling the islands is an international call, meaning you must dial ☎ 011 before the local number. The only calling cards that work on the islands are the ones bought there.

While merchants gladly accept the loonie, you'd be crazy not to indulge in some

euros from the ATMs. Prices are quoted in euros (€) and things are generally more expensive than in Newfoundland. You'll also likely need a round plug 220-volt electrical adapter.

Lastly, note that some stores are closed on Saturday afternoons, most are closed on Sunday and, apart from the odd restaurant, almost everything is closed between noon and 1:30pm.

The **St Pierre Tourist Office** (☎ 800-565-5118, off the islands 508-410-200; www.st-pierre-et-miquelon .com; Place du Général de Gaulle; ⏰ 7:30am-6pm Jun-Sep, 8:30am-noon & 1:30-5:30pm Mon-Fri Oct-May) provides a great map of the town and oodles of information.

SIGHTS & ACTIVITIES

In St Pierre, the best thing to do is just wander and soak it up. Pop into stores and partake of goods you'd usually have to cross an ocean for. Despite meticulous research, there is no clear winner on the best pastry shop in town. Unfortunately, you'll have to determine this yourself.

While pastries are important, allow enough time for the magical **Île aux Marins** (3hr tours adult/child €16/12; ⏰ 9am & 2pm May-Sep). This island museum comprises a beautiful abandoned village out in the harbor. A bilingual guide will walk you through colorful homes, a small schoolhouse museum and the grand church (1874). For details on this and other tour possibilities, see the tourist office.

If you're lucky you'll see some locals playing *pelote,* a distinctly Basque game, at the wall on Place Richard Briand. The huge **cemetery** (Ave Commandant Roger Birot), **L'Arche Museum** (rue du 11 Novembre) and **Héritage Museum** (Place du Général de Gaulle) are mildly interesting and give some added insight into the island's history.

Miquelon, 45km away, is visited less and is less developed. The village of **Miquelon,** centered on the church, is at the northern tip of the island. From nearby **l'Étang de Mirande**, a walking trail leads to a lookout and waterfall. From the bridge in town, a scenic 25km road leads across the isthmus to the wild and uninhabited island of **Langlade**. There are some wild horses and smaller animals such as rabbits, and around the rocky coast and lagoons you'll see seals and birds.

FESTIVALS & EVENTS

From mid-July to the end of August, folk dances are often held in St Pierre's square.

Bastille Day (�} Jul 14) The largest holiday of the year.

Basque Festival (�} mid-Aug) A week-long festival with plenty of music, marching and invigorating street fun.

SLEEPING & EATING

There are just over a dozen accommodations on St Pierre and Miquelon. Hotels are substantially more expensive than the inns *(auberges)*. Things get tight in summer, so book ahead. As with the rest of France, there is an abundance of great eateries – indulge.

Hotel Île de France (☎ 508-410-350; hotelile defrance@cheznoo.net; 6 rue Maître Georges Lefèvre, St Pierre; s/d €80/88) Spacious and simple rooms fill this centrally located hotel. It's home to a great **restaurant** (mains €8-17; �} noon-2pm & 7-10:30pm) serving traditional French fare and pizzas. The lunch specials (€10) are a delicious bargain.

Chez Hélène B&B (☎ 508-413-108; fax 508-415-402; 15 rue Beaussant, St Pierre; s/d with shared bathroom €40/45) This is the brightest of choices, with rooms looking out over the harbor. Room No 6 has a wee balcony for taking everything in.

Auberge Dupont (☎ 508-414-301; dupontpm@ cheznoo.net; 14 rue du Temple, St Pierre; s/d €40/50; 🖳) While a bit of a hike, Dupont is quiet and clean, and some rooms have great views. It's perfect for families.

Maxotel (☎ 508-416-457; girmaxro@cheznoo.net; 42 rue Sourdeval, Miquelon; 2-bedroom apt €54/61) The simple apartments that can sleep up to four people (€86) have kitchens and sit near the sea. It's a 10-minute walk from the wharf.

Le Cabestan (☎ 508-412-100; 1bis rue Marcel Bonin; mains €17-26; �} noon-2pm & 7-9pm Tue-Sun) The traditional Basque meals using hot peppers are superb. The crème brûlée is a divine way to end the meal.

Le Maringouin'fre (☎ 508-419-125; 22 rue Général Leclerc; meals €5-8; �} 11am-10:15pm) This is the perfect place for a cheaper meal or fantastic crepes.

GETTING THERE & AWAY
Air

Air Saint-Pierre (☎ 508-410-000; www.airsaintpierre .com) serves St John's (€94), Montréal (€353) and Halifax (€176), with three weekly fights each.

Boat

St Pierre Tours (☎ 709-832-0429; 800-563-2006; 5 Bayview St, Fortune) operates two ferries to St Pierre. From Fortune on Newfoundland, the MV *Maria Galanta* (adult/child under 11 $81/40.50, one hour) departs at 1:30pm Friday and Sunday from April to November and daily in July and August. It leaves St Pierre at 2:45pm. The MV *Arethusa* (same price as *Maria Galanta*, 1½ hours) makes trips Monday to Thursday and Saturday during May, June and September, leaving Fortune at noon and departing St Pierre at 2:45pm. During July and August, it offers one-day round-trips leaving Fortune at 7:30am and departing St Pierre at 2:45pm. While the MV *Arethusa* is slower, it offers outside seating and a better opportunity for whale-watching.

GETTING AROUND

The MV *Maria Galanta* serves Miquelon (adult/child €20/10, one hour) from St Pierre on Tuesday, Friday and Sunday. Other ferries ply the route to Langlade (€16 round-trip) and Île aux Marins (€3 round-trip).

Locamat Testeur (☎ 508-413-030; 10 rue Richerie) rents bicycles (per half/full day €10/13.50) and scooters (per half/full day €24/34).

On both St Pierre and Miquelon, bus tours can take you around the island. In a couple of days much can be seen on foot.

CENTRAL NEWFOUNDLAND

This vast, little-populated area is the largest geographic region of Newfoundland. Its convoluted northern shore is sprinkled with countless charming villages and is truly a provincial treasure.

The southern area is mostly inaccessible woodland dotted with lakes. One road leads down to the coast, through endless barren plateaus, and links many small remote villages to the rest of the province.

GANDER

Gander is at the crossroads of Hwy 1 and Rte 330, which leads to Notre Dame Bay. It is a convenient stopping point, but is one of the province's least attractive places. It's a suburb with no downtown.

NEWFOUNDLAND & LABRADOR

First came the airport, then came Gander. The site was chosen by the British in the 1930s because of its proximity to Europe and its fogless weather. Gander served the first regular transatlantic flights and then, during WWII, was a stopover for planes on their way to Europe. During the Cold War, the airport was an Aeroflot refueling stop and thousands of Russian, Cuban and Eastern Bloc citizens would jump ship here to claim asylum. Most recently, Gander gained attention for its hospitality to the thousands whose planes were rerouted here after the 2001 terrorist attacks in the USA.

There is a **tourist chalet** (☎ 709-256-7110; 9am-8pm mid-Jun–Sep, 9am-5pm Mon-Fri Oct–mid-Jun) on Hwy 1 at the central exit into town. **DRL Coachlines** (☎ 709-738-8088; www.drlgroup .com/Coachlines/coachlines_new.html) has its stop at the **airport** (☎ 709-651-3434). Buses leave for St John's ($45, 5¼ hours) at 5:02pm and Port aux Basques ($68, 8¼ hours) at 11:43pm.

For aviation fanatics, the **North Atlantic Aviation Museum** (☎ 709-256-2923; Hwy 1; adult/child $3/2; 9am-9pm Jul & Aug, 9am-5pm Mon-Fri Sep-Jun) has exhibits detailing Newfoundland's air contributions to WWII and the history of navigation. Just east on Hwy 1 is the sobering **Silent Witness Monument**, a tribute to 248 US soldiers whose plane crashed here in December 1985.

Sinbad's Hotel and Suites (☎ 709-651-2678, 800-563-8330; www.sinbadshotel.nf.ca; Bennett Dr; r $80-90) has clean, comfortable hotel rooms within the center of Gander. Its **restaurant** (mains $13-21; breakfast, lunch & dinner) is known as the best place to dine in town. Try the screeched salmon.

Irving West Hotel (☎ 709-256-2406; fax 709-651-3860; 1 Caldwell St; r $65-80;) is close to the highway and has simple standard rooms with balconies. There's a heated outdoor pool.

If you eat in Gander, it should be at **Giovanni's Café** (☎ 709-651-3535; 71 Elizabeth Dr; light meals $5-8; 7:30am-9pm Mon-Sat, 10am-9pm Sun) – coffee, wraps, sandwiches and salads.

NOTRE DAME BAY AREA

Numerous narrow bays drive deeply inland providing countless small coves and rock promontories for some 80 villages to cling to. Offshore is a cluster of islands, including Fogo, New World and Twillingate. If you visit them, you'll be rewarded with a peek deep into Iceberg Alley.

FLAT EARTH'S FIVE CORNERS

Despite the 'realistic' satellite photos, some traditionalists haven't been 'fooled' by the images of a round earth. Heading up their cause is the Flat Earth Society, which believes that myths about our spinning spherical world hurtling through space can only lead to our planet's inhabitants living a confused and disorientated life.

In 'reality,' the stable and calming flat earth is said to have five striking corners: Lake Mikhayl in Tunguska (Siberia); Easter Island; Lhasa (Nepal); the South Pacific island of Ponape; and Brimstone Head on Fogo Island, right here in Newfoundland. Climb up the craggy spine of Brimstone Head and stare off the abyss to earth's distant edge. You're guaranteed a stunning view of Iceberg Alley, and if you're lucky, you may catch a glimpse of that giant turtle the flat earth is riding on.

Fogo Island

Settled in the 1680s, Fogo Island is an intriguing place to poke around and some of its villages are charming despite their ruggedness.

Backed by rocky hills, the village of **Joe Batt's Arm** encircles a large bay; the view from one side of the bay to the other will remind you of fishing villages of centuries past.

Nearby is **Tilting**, perhaps the most engaging village on the island. The Irish roots run deep here and so do the accents. The inland harbor is surrounded by picturesque fishing stages and flakes, held above the incoming tides by weary stilts. There's also the great coastal **Turpin's Trail** (9km) that leaves from Tilting, near the beach at **Sandy Cove**.

On the opposite end of the island is the village of **Fogo** and the indomitable **Brimstone Head** (see the boxed text above). After you take in the mystical rock's view, do another great hike in town: the **Lion's Den Trail** (5km), which visits a Marconi radio site.

A small herd of caribou and some ponies roam freely on the island and under the watchful eye of Brimstone Head.

There is a great **folk festival** (☎ 709-266-2218) in July.

A heritage house has been converted into the small **Bleak House Museum** (☎ 709-226-2237; Rte 333; admission free; 10am-6pm Jul-Sep) in Fogo.

The town also has the reconstructed **School House Museum** (☎ 709-266-2237; off Main St; admission free; ☉ hrs vary Jul-Sep).

The village of **Little Seldom** has two refurbished buildings at the marina that house the **Marine Interpretation Centre** (☎ 709-627-3366; adult/student $2/1; ☉ 10am-5pm May-Oct) and its local heritage displays.

SLEEPING & EATING

Peg's B&B (☎ 709-266-2288; jengreene@yahoo.ca; 60 Main St, Fogo; d with/without bathroom $65/55) Nestled right in the heart of Fogo, this bright place offers up a friendly atmosphere and some harbor views.

Quiet Canyon Hotel (☎ 709-627-3477; fax 709-627-3382; Man O'War Cove; s/d $70/75) This is the only hotel on Fogo Island and while it lacks charm, it's clean and comfortable. It's right off the ferry terminal.

Beaches Bar & Grill (☎ 709-266-2750; 42 Main St, Fogo; mains $7-12; ☉ 11am-8pm) This pub-style place serves meals ranging from fish-and-chips to steak and seafood platters.

GETTING THERE & AWAY

Fogo is reached by ferry from Farewell. Four boats leave daily between 9am and 8:30pm for the hour-long trip. Some sailings stop at the Change Islands and take 20 minutes longer. The round-trip fare is $18.50 for car and driver, and $6.50 for additional passengers. Schedules vary, so check with **Provincial Ferry Services** (www.gov.nl.ca/ferryservices) or call ☎ 709-292-4300.

New World Island

From the mainland, causeways almost imperceptibly connect Chapel Island, tiny Strong's Island, New World and Twillingate Islands. At Newville the **visitors' center** (☎ 709-628-5343; Rte 340; ☉ 9am-6pm early Jun–Sep) has maps of the area and information on the fine district trails and walks.

Pretty **Dildo Run Provincial Park** (☎ 709-629-3350; Rte 340, Virgin Arm; tent sites $13; ☉ early Jun–mid-Sep) has fine camping and picnicking set in a wooded area by a bay. Due to currents, swimming is not recommended.

The western section of New World Island is far less visited. The small fishing villages clutch the rough, rocky edges of the sea and hold some of the area's older houses. A small trail starts at **Carter's Cove** and winds its way to an abandoned fishing village.

At Moreton's Harbour is the small **Moreton's Harbour Community Museum** (☎ 709-684-2507; admission free; ☉ 8am-10pm mid-Jun–Labour Day), in an old-style house furnished in much the manner it would have been when the town was a prosperous fishing center.

To the east, **Pike's Arm** has a similar **museum** (☉ 10am-6pm Mon-Sat late Jun–Sep) and sits close to a stepped trail that leads to a phenomenal **lookout**.

Twillingate Island

Actually consisting of two barely separated islands, North and South Twillingate, this area of Notre Dame Bay gets the most attention, and deservedly so. The two islands and their largest town, Twillingate, sit just north of New World Island and are reached from the mainland via several short causeways. It's stunningly beautiful, with every turn of the road revealing new ocean vistas, colorful fishing wharves or tidy groups of pastel houses perched on cliffs and outcrops. An influx of whales and icebergs every summer only adds to the mix. Places even sell ice from the icebergs, and you can get it in your drinks too. Twillingate's website (www.twillingate.com) and the tourist office in Newville (left) provide useful information on the area.

SIGHTS & ACTIVITIES

Without a doubt, your first stop on the island should be **Prime Berth** (☎ 709-884-2485; Walter Elliott Causeway; admission $4.50; ☉ 10am-5:30pm mid-Jun–mid-Sep). Run by an engaging fisherman, this private fishing museum, with its imaginative and deceivingly simple concepts, is brilliant, and fun for scholars and school kids alike.

The **Long Point Lighthouse** (☎ 709-884-2247; admission free; ☉ hrs vary) is a spectacular place, with dramatic views of the coastal cliffs. Travel up the winding steps, worn from lighthouse-keepers' footsteps since 1876, and gawk at the 360-degree view. This is an ideal vantage point for spotting icebergs in May and June, even occasionally into July.

The town of Twillingate's **museum** (☎ 709-884-2825; off Main St; admission $1; ☉ 10am-8pm late May–Oct) is housed in a former Anglican rectory and tells the history of the island since the first British settlers arrived in the mid-1700s. It also displays articles brought back from around the world by local sea captains, including a cabinet from India, a hurdy-gurdy from Germany and an Australian boomerang. Another room delves into the seal hunt and its controversy. There's a historic **church** next door.

In **Little Harbour**, en route to the town of Twillingate, a short trail leads to the secluded and picturesque **Jone's Cove**. Toward Durrell, the **Iceberg Shop** (☎ 709-884-2242; Main St; admission free; ✆ 9am-9pm May-Sep), with its iceberg interpretation center, ice cream and gregarious owner, is worth a peek.

Don't neglect to tour the exceptionally scenic **Durrell** and its **museum** (☎ 709-884-2780; admission $1; ☎ 9am-5pm Jun-Sep, to 8pm Jul & Aug), perched atop Old Maid Hill. Bring your lunch; there are a couple of picnic tables and a spectacular view.

TOURS

Twillingate Adventure Tours (☎ 709-884-5999, 888-447-8687; off Main St; adult/child $30/15; ✆ May-Sep) Great two-hour trips depart Twillingate's wharf every day to view icebergs and whales.
Twillingate Island Boat Tours (☎ 709-884-2242) Offers identical service to Twillingate Adventure Tours, leaving from the Iceberg Shop (Main St).

FESTIVALS & EVENTS

Traditional music and dance, some of which goes back to the 16th century, merrily take over the village of Twillingate. This **Fish, Fun & Folk Festival** (www.fishfunfolkfestival.com; ✆ late Jul) is fantastic and you'd do well to attend. There is also oodles of food and some interesting fishing exhibits.

SLEEPING

Despite having about a dozen accommodation options, Twillingate gets very busy in the summer. Book early if possible.
Paradise B&B (☎ 709-884-1999, 877-882-1999; fred.bridger@nf.sympatico.ca; 192 Main St; d $70; ✆ May–mid-Oct) Set on a bluff overlooking Twillingate's harbor, Paradise offers the best view in town. You can wander down to the beach below, or relax on a lawn chair and soak it all up. Oh, the rooms are comfy too. Angle for room No 1.
Harbour Lights Inn (☎ 709-884-2763; www.harbourlightsinn.com; 189 Main St; d incl light breakfast $80-95; ✆ May-Sep) South African hospitality greets you in this historical and popular home. It's located right on the harbor and has amenities like TVs and whirlpools.

Toulinguet Inn B&B (☎ 709-884-2080, 877-684-2080; www.toulinguetinn.ca; 56 Main St; s/d $65/70; ✆ May-Sep) Sit on the deck of this beautiful 1920s home and smell the fresh sea air. The views are just as great and the house is bright and roomy.
Beach Rock B&B (☎ 709-884-2292; www.bbcanada.com/beachrock; s/d $50/65; ✆ Apr-Oct) This modest, homey B&B south of Twillingate, in Little Harbour, aptly sits across from the beach. With some trails nearby, it's perfect for kids.

EATING

Anchor Inn (☎ 709-884-2776; off Main St; dinner mains $10-16; ✆ breakfast, lunch & dinner mid-May–Sep) The chef's special of succulent shrimp stir-fried with fresh vegetables is as superb as the dining room's ocean view.
R&J (☎ 709-884-5566, 709-884-5421; 110 Main St; meals $8-12; ✆ 8am-midnight) Be bold and sink your teeth into some fish 'n' brewis (see the boxed text on p352), or dine on shrimp, scallops and battered fish. Pizzas are also available.
All Around the Circle Dinner Theatre (☎ 709-884-5423; Crow Head; adult/child under 12 $26/13; ✆ 7pm Mon-Sat Jun–mid-Sep) Six of Newfoundland's best not only cook you a traditional meal, they also leave you in stitches with their talented performances. It's just south of the Long Point Lighthouse.

Lewisporte

Stretched out Lewisporte, known primarily for its ferry terminal, is the largest town on Notre Dame Bay. Other than the boats, there really isn't much reason to visit – though as a distribution center it does have all the goods and services.

The simple **Brittany Inns** (☎ 709-535-2533, 800-563-8386; www.brittanyinns.com; Main St; r $65-80) has 34 rather stark but clean rooms. Several have kitchenettes and all have oddly mismatched toilet-seat covers. Wheelchairs are welcome.
Oriental Restaurant (☎ 709-535-6993; 131 Main St; meals $5-10; ✆ 11am-11pm) is pretty straightforward, but you get a chance at a few vegetables – by now you know that finding veggies can be a challenge in these parts.

Due to new road construction, the future of the Lewisporte–Labrador ferry is in jeopardy. See p343 for ferry information. The **DRL Coachlines** (☎ 709-738-8088; www.drlgroup.com/

BEOTHUK ABORIGINALS

The Beothuks were the Aboriginal peoples of Newfoundland when Europeans first set foot in the New World. Due to their ceremonially ochre-coated faces, they were dubbed 'red men' by the arriving Europeans, a name soon applied to all of North America's indigenous peoples.

Seminomadic and known for their birch-bark canoes, these Algonquian-speaking people had a unique and ultimately deadly relationship with the Europeans. Due to the migratory fishery in Newfoundland, European settlements were abandoned in the winter, thus giving Beothuks access to metal tools and goods that they would otherwise have had to obtain by trading. This enabled the Beothuks to reduce their contact with Europeans and maintain their culture. Once permanent settlements took hold, however, and conflicts over land occurred, the Beothuks found themselves without any valuable European trading contacts. This forced them further into isolation, where resources were inadequate for their survival.

Before anybody had enough gumption or time to do anything about the situation, just two Beothuk women remained alive to leave behind what knowledge they could. Shanawdithit, the last known Beothuk, died in St John's in 1829.

Coachlines/coachlines_new.html) stops at Brittany Inns on Main St. Departures for St John's ($51, six hours) leave at 3:54pm and Port aux Basques ($65, 7½ hours) at 1:25pm.

GRAND FALLS-WINDSOR

The sprawl of two small pulp-and-paper towns has met and now comprises the community of Grand Falls-Windsor. The former entity of Grand Falls is more interesting for visitors and its town center, south of Hwy 1, is near the Exploits River along Church Rd and High St.

Information

Visitor information center (☎ 709-489-6332; Hwy 1; 9am-5:30pm late May–late Sep) Just west of town at exit 17.

Sights

The **Mary March Provincial Museum** (☎ 709-292-4522; Cromer Ave; adult/child/student $2.50/free/2; 9:30am-4:30pm May-Oct) is accessed from exit 18A S and is worth visiting. Exhibits concentrate on the recent and past histories of aboriginal peoples in the area, including the extinct Beothuk tribe (see above).

Set next to Rush Pond, not far from the visitors center, is Beothuk Park and the **Loggers' Life Provincial Museum** (☎ 709-486-0492; exit 17, Hwy 1; admission $2.50; 9am-4:30pm late May-Oct). Here you can experience the life of a 1920s logging camp – smells and all!

Overlooking Grand Falls is the **Salmonid Interpretation Centre** (☎ 709-489-7350; admission $3; 8am-dusk mid-Jun–mid-Sep). Exhibits delve into the Atlantic salmon, and there's an observation deck to watch the fish struggle upstream to spawn. Unfortunately, this all takes place under the shadow of the pulp mill. It's reached by crossing the river south of High St and following the signs.

Sleeping & Eating

Hill Road Manor B&B (☎ 709-489-5451, 866-489-5451; www.hillroadmanor.com; 1 Hill Rd; $70-85) Manor is right – this place is gorgeous! Elegant rooms, beds that will have you gladly oversleeping and a vibrant sunroom combine for a stylish and comfortable stay. Kids are welcome.

Hotel Robin Hood (☎ 709-489-5324; robin.hood@ nf.sympatico.ca; 78 Lincoln Rd; r incl light breakfast $80-90) Set back from the road in a nice stand of trees is this central option. The rooms are large but simple.

Royal Oak Restaurant (☎ 709-489-7878; dinner mains $16-23; lunch & dinner, closed Sun) A respected chef has leased this restaurant within the Hotel Robin Hood, and produces the finest fare in town. His pan-seared cod, fajitas and vegetarian options are all splendid.

Kelly's Pub & Eatery (☎ 709-489-9893; 18 Hill Rd; meals $7-10) Hidden neatly behind the smoky pub is this great countrified spot. It makes the best burgers in town and the stir-fries are not too shabby either.

Getting There & Away

DRL Coachlines (☎ 709-738-8088; www.drlgroup.com/ Coachlines/coachlines_new.html) has its bus stop at the **Highliner Inn** (☎ 709-489-5639; exit 17, Hwy 1 Service Rd). St John's ($56, 6½ hours) services leave at 3:15pm, and Port aux Basques' ($60, seven hours) leave at 2:14pm daily.

NEWFOUNDLAND & LABRADOR

CENTRAL SOUTH COAST

Route 360 runs 130km through the center of the province to the south coast. It's a long way down to the first settlements at the end of **Bay d'Espoir**, a gentle fjord. Note there is no gas station on the route, so fill up on Hwy 1. **St Alban's** is set on the west side of the fjord. You'll find a few motels with dining rooms and lounges around the end of the bay.

Farther south is a concentration of small fishing villages. The scenery along Rte 364 to Hermitage is particularly impressive, as is the scenery around **Harbour Breton**. It's the largest town in the region and huddles around the ridge of a gentle inland bay, with its back sheltered from the Atlantic.

Southern Port Hotel (☎ 709-885-2283; www .southernporthotel.com; Rte 360, Harbour Breton; r $75-80) opened its new digs in 2002, and they are quite a step up from the old place. Rooms are spacious and well appointed; even-numbered rooms have views. The hotel is wheelchair accessible. The **restaurant** (mains $7-15; ☽ breakfast, lunch & dinner) serves quality ribs, wraps and stir-fries.

Hickey's Bus Service (☎ 709-885-2523) has patchy service linking Harbour Breton with Grand Falls-Windsor. St Alban's is connected to Grand Falls-Windsor ($30, two hours) by bus (☎ 709-538-3429).

Government passenger ferries serve Hermitage, making the western south coast outports accessible, and Pool's Cove (p365), which links to the Burin Peninsula.

NORTHERN PENINSULA

Like an extended index finger from a clenched fist, the immense Northern Peninsula reaches outward from Newfoundland to the Labrador Sea's frigid waters. Its tip is marked by windswept and barren flatlands, along with Europe's first footsteps in the New World. The 1000-year-old Viking settlement of L'Anse aux Meadows is now an honored Unesco world heritage site. Over 250km south, another Unesco site punctuates the opposite end of this remarkable peninsula. Here, within the Long Range Mountains, sits Gros Morne National Park, with its astounding fjords and world-renowned geologic diversity.

The **Viking Trail** (Rte 430) that connects these two famous sites is an attraction in its own right, and makes the long journey an extraordinary one. Sights along the way include the remarkable rock formations at the Arches and Table Point Ecological Reserve, an old whaling station at Hawke's Bay and a national historic site at Port au Choix.

From the smallest of berries to the largest of whales, nature in this region will not fail to astonish you. Many people base their entire Newfoundland trip around this unique region and usually end up coming back for more, year after year. The ever-increasing number of people pouring into this area has meant an increase in tourist services over the years. Yet things can still fill up in the peak of summer. It can be a wet, cool place, with a lot of bugs, so if you're camping, be prepared for the odd night in a motel.

It's roughly a five- to six-hour drive from Deer Lake to St Anthony. Bus transportation is possible, if a bit irregular, along the entire route.

DEER LAKE

There's little in Deer Lake for the visitor, but it's a convenient jumping-off point for trips up the Northern Peninsula. Rocky Harbour (71km) is north on Rte 430, while Hwy 1 connects Deer Lake to Port aux Basques (268km) in the south and Gander (299km) to the east.

A **tourist chalet** (☎ 709-635-2202; ☽ 9am-7pm mid-May–Sep, 8am-8pm mid-Jun–Aug) sits right on Hwy 1.

If you have to spend the night in Deer Lake, **Driftwood Inn** (☎ 709-635-5115, 888-635-5115; www.driftwoodinn.net; 3 Nicholasville Rd; s/d $75-90) is a great option. It is quite hospitable. It also has a decent **restaurant** (meals $8-12; ☽ lunch & dinner) downstairs. It's about 2.5km from the Irving Big Stop, off exit 15 from Hwy 1.

The **DRL Coachlines** (☎ 709-738-8088; www.drl group.com/Coachlines/coachlines_new.html) bus stops in Deer Lake at the **Irving Big Stop** (☎ 709-635-2130) on Hwy 1. Note that DRL's bus is not synchronized with shuttle services (p381) heading up the Northern Peninsula from Corner Brook. If you call ahead, though, they may work things out for you.

For information about air services to Deer Lake, see p342. The airport is just off Hwy 1. Nationwide companies Avis, Budget and Hertz have services at the airport. For more information on rental-car companies and costs, see p873.

GROS MORNE NATIONAL PARK

Long one of Canada's treasures, **Gros Morne National Park** (☎ 709-458-2066; per day adult/child under 17/family $7.50/3.75/15; ☉ day use facilities mid-May–mid-Oct) became a world treasure in 1997, when Unesco granted it a world heritage designation. To visitors, the park's stunning flat-top mountains and deeply incised fjords are simply supernatural playgrounds. To geologists, this park is a blueprint for our planet; it has supplied them with evidence for theories such as plate tectonics. These attributes have earned the park the moniker 'Galapagos of Geology.' This, combined with the area's 4500 years of human occupation, played a major part in the UN designation.

Within this unique area, wildlife abounds and visitors are likely to see moose, caribou, whales and offshore seals.

Orientation

Several small fishing villages dot the shoreline and provide an interesting mix of culture and amenities. Rocky Harbour is the largest village and is quite central, as is Norris Point. On the south side of the divisive Bonne Bay is Woody Point, which has Tablelands and Green Gardens at its doorstep. Furthest south, at the end of Rte 431, is the quaint village of Trout River.

There is enough to do in and around the park to easily fill several days. Admission includes the trails, Discovery Centre and all day-use areas. It also goes toward the cost of a campsite.

Information

Discovery Centre (☎ 709-453-2127; Rte 431 near Woody Point; ☉ 9am-5:30pm, to 9pm Sun & Wed late May–mid-Oct) Has some interactive exhibits and a multimedia theater explaining the ecology, geology and human history of the area. There's also a helpful information desk, daily interpretive activities and a small café.

Main Visitor Center (☎ 709-458-2066; off Rte 430; ☉ 9am-4pm Mon-Fri May–late Oct, to 9pm late Jun–early Sep) Located 25km from the park's entrance on Rte 430, at the exit to Norris Point. As well as issuing day and backcountry permits, it has maps, books and an impressive interpretive area.

Park Entrance Kiosk (Rte 430; ☉ 10am-6pm mid-May–mid-Oct) By the park entrance near Wiltondale.

Sights

Dominating the southwest corner of the park are the unconquerable and eerie **Tablelands**.

They've practically been to hell and back, and yet still stand tall. This massive flat-topped massif was part of the earth's mantle before tectonics raised it from the depths and planted it squarely on the continent. Its rock is so unusual that plants can't even grow on it. You can view the barren, golden phenomenon up close on Rte 431, or catch it from a distance at the stunning **photography lookout** above Norris Point.

West of the Tablelands, dramatic volcanic sea stacks and caves mark the coast at **Green Gardens**.

At the wharf in Norris Point is the new **Bonne Bay Marine Station** (☎ 709-458-2550; adult/student $5/4; ☉ 10am-5pm Jun-Aug), a part of Memorial University and a world-class teaching and research facility. Every half-hour there are interesting interactive tours, and the aquariums display the marine ecological habitats in Bonne Bay. For kids, there are touch tanks and a rare blue lobster.

Further up the coast past Sally's Cove, waves batter the rusty and tangled remains of the **SS Ethie**. The story of this 1919 wreck, and the subsequent rescue, was inspiration for a famous folk song.

The Long Range Mountains continue to loom large over the Viking Trail as you head north along the coast. When you're hit with a sudden feeling of disbelief, you have reached **Western Brook Pond**, the park's premier fjord. Its sheer 700m cliffs plunge to the blue abyss and dramatically snake into the mountains. See p374 for information about the fantastic boat tours.

Only 20km north, the gentle, safe, sand-duned beach at **Shallow Bay** seems almost out of place – as if transported from the Caribbean by some bizarre current. The water, though, provides a chilling dose of reality, rarely getting above 15°C.

For history, visit the **restored fishing camp** (Rte 430; admission free; ☉ 10am-6pm early Jun–late Sep) at Broom Point, which depicts the inshore fishery of the 1960s. The three Mudge brothers and their families fished here from 1941 until 1975, when they sold the entire camp, including boats, lobster traps and nets, to the national park. Everything has been restored and is now staffed by guides.

At the **Lobster Head Cove Lighthouse** (Rte 430; admission free; ☉ 10am-6pm mid-May–mid-Oct) is an interpretive exhibit on 4000 years of human occupation along this coast. Outside, in the

NEWFOUNDLAND & LABRADOR

oodles of tidal pools, you can find some of the more interesting marine occupants of this rugged place.

Inquire at the visitor center about the interpretive programs, guided walks and evening presentations put on by park staff throughout summer.

Activities

HIKING

Nineteen maintained trails of varying difficulty snake through 100km of the park's most scenic landscapes and make for some of the best hikes in the province. The gem of the park's trail system is **James Callahan Gros Morne Trail** (16km) to the peak of Gros Morne, the highest point in the area at 806m. While there are sections with steps and boardwalks, this is a strenuous seven- to eight-hour hike, and includes a steep rock gully that must be climbed to the ridgeline of the mountain. Standing on the 600m precipice and staring out over 10 Mile Pond, a sheer-sided fjord, can only be described as sublime. A popular strategy is to backcountry camp at **Fern Gulch** along the trail, and scale the mountain without packs.

Green Gardens Trail (16km) is almost as scenic and challenging. The loop has two trailheads off Rte 431, with each one descending to Green Gardens along its magnificent coastline formed from lava and shaped by the sea. Plan on seven to 10 hours of hiking or book one of the three backcountry camping areas, all of them on the ocean, and turn the hike into an overnight adventure. A less strenuous day hike (9km) to the beach and back is possible from this trail's Long Pond Trailhead.

Shorter scenic hikes are the **Tablelands Trail** (4km), which extends to Winterhouse Brook Canyon; **Lookout Trail** (5km) near Woody Point, which loops to the site of an old fire tower above the tree line; and **Western Brook Pond Trail** (6km), the most popular trail in the park, which is an easy hike to the western end of the fjord and back.

Other overnight hikes include the **Stanleyville Trail** (4km), which visits an old logging camp where there is backcountry camping. Western Brook Pond Trail and **Snug Harbour Trail** (10km) can be combined for an 8km one-way hike to backcountry campsites in the famous fjord. Or book your passage on the tour boat and have it drop you off at the

head of Western Brook Pond, where there are several more backcountry campsites.

The granddaddies of the trails are the **Long Range Traverse** (35km) and **North Rim Traverse** (27km), serious multiday treks over the mountains. Permits and advice from park rangers are required. For backcountry campsite information, see opposite.

If you plan to do several trails, invest $12 in a copy of the *Gros Morne National Park Trail Guide*, a waterproof map of the park with trail descriptions on the back.

KAYAKING

Kayaking in the shadow of the Tablelands and through the spray of whales is truly something to be experienced. Gros Morne Adventure Guides provides rentals (single/double per day $50/60) for experienced paddlers and tours for novices.

SKIING

Many of the hiking trails are used as cross-country skiing trails in winter, but in recent years the park has undertaken an ambitious ski-trail construction program; many trails in the impressive 55km system were designed by Canadian Olympic champion, Pierre Harvey.

SWIMMING

Near Rocky Harbour is **Gros Morne Swimming Pool** (☎ 709-458-2350; Rte 430; adult/child $3/2; ☯ late Jun–Aug), with a 25m swimming pool and – wait for it – a hot tub! Opening hours vary.

The fearless can swim from the beaches at Shallow Bay and Trout River.

Tours

Atlantic Canada Adventure (☎ 709-458-3089; www.acatours.com; Norris Point) Offers guided hikes to your specifications. The two owners speak English, French, German and Italian.

Bon Tours (☎ 709-458-2730, 800-563-9887; Main St, Rocky Harbour; ☯ Jun-Sep) The Western Brook Pond boat tour (2½hr trip adult/child $35/16) at 10am, 1pm & 4pm is phenomenal. The dock is a 3km walk from Rte 430 and it's wise to reserve at least a day in advance. The Bonne Bay tour (2hr trip adult/child $30/12) leaves from Norris Point, with a stop at Woody Point. Ask about discounts for booking both tours.

Gros Morne Adventure Guides (☎ 709-458-2722, 800-685-4624; 9 Clarkes Lane, Norris Point; 2½hr tours adult/child/family $45/35/140) These popular half-day sea kayak tours of Bonne Bay leave daily. Full-day, multiday and Western Brook Pond trips are all on order, as are hiking, skiing and snowshoeing trips. Reservations are required.

Tableland Boat Tours (☎ 709-451-2101; Trout River; 2½hr tours adult/child $35/18; ☺ mid-Jun–mid-Sep) Runs daily up Trout River Pond past the Tablelands.

Festivals & Events

In Cow Head there is the perennially popular **Gros Morne Theatre Festival** (☎ 709-243-2899, 877-243-2899; various locations; tickets $9-17; ☺ Jun–mid-Sep). You'll leave giggling and tapping your toes. Reservations are recommended for both the indoor and outdoor performances.

Sleeping

While Rocky Harbour is central and has the most options, don't overlook staying in Norris Point or Woody River, especially if you will be visiting the southern half of the park.

Aunt Jane's Place B&B (☎ 709-453-2485; vmanor .grosmorne@nf.sympatico.ca; Water St, Woody Point; s/d with shared bathroom $40-60, d $70; ☺ mid-May–mid-Oct) This historic place oozes character, however you may be woken early in the morning by the heavy breathing of whales – so sorry.

Gros Morne Cabins (☎ 709-458-2020; www.gros morne.com/gros_morne_cabins; Main St, Rocky Harbour; 1-/2-bedroom cabins $100/150) While backed by tarmac, these cabins are fronted by nothing but ocean. Each of the 22 beautiful log cabins has a kitchen and pullout sofa for kids. Inquire next door at Endicott's variety store.

Sugar Hill Inn (☎ 709-458-2147; 888-229-2147; www.sugarhillinn.nf.ca; 115-119 Sexton Rd, Norris Point; d $75-130, ste $165-95; ☺ mid-Jan–Oct) Slide into the sauna or hot tub after a day in the Tablelands, then savor a gourmet meal in the scenic guests-only dining room (three-course dinner $35). All that's left to do is retire to a bit of luxury for a well-deserved snooze.

Wild Flowers Country Inn (☎ 709-458-3000, 888-811-7378; Main St, Rocky Harbour; d incl breakfast $100-120; ☺ May–mid-Oct) Nestled in trees off the main drag, this lovely home has some fine views and beautiful rooms with pine floors. No 4 has a wee balcony. Kids are welcome.

Bottom Brook Cottages (☎ 709-458-2236; fax 709-458-2799; Main St, Rocky Harbour; 2-bedroom cottage $90) Each of these simple little cottages has a kitchen, barbecue and balcony. There's also a nice adjacent brook and a fire pit for evening entertainment.

Terry's B&B (☎ 709-458-2373, 877-458-2373; Pierce's Lane, Norris Point; tw & d with shared bathroom $45, d $65-75; ☺ Jun-Sep) Terry's sits within a stone's throw of Bonne Bay's waters and is a low-key place to stay. Terry is a character; he's recently added a couple of larger rooms to his rambling home.

CAMPING

Within Gros Morne National Park are four developed **campgrounds** (☎ 800-414-6765; www.parkscanada.gc.ca/grosmorne; tent & RV sites without hookups $21). **Berry Hill** (☺ late Jun–mid-Sep), the largest, is most central; **Lomond** (☺ late May–mid-Oct) is closest to the southern park entrance; **Trout River** (☺ early Jun–late Sep) is closest to the Tablelands; and **Shallow Bay** (☺ early Jun–late Sep) has ocean swimming.

There's a primitive **campground** (sites without showers $13; ☺ all year) at Green Point. Numerous **backcountry campsites** ($8) are spread along trails; these sites must be reserved at the visitor center.

Eating

You'll have no problem finding fine eats while you're in the park, no matter where you stay.

Java Jack's (☎ 709-458-3004; Main St, Rocky Harbour; meals $7-18; ☺ 9am-9pm May-Oct, 7am-10pm Jul–Labour Day) Jack's is growing up – literally. Its days of simply providing Gros Morne's best coffees, wraps and soups are over. Now it also has a dining room upstairs where people can relish fine seafood, caribou and vegetarian fare.

Seaside Restaurant (☎ 709-451-3461; Main St, Trout River; dinner mains $13-20; ☺ lunch & dinner late May–mid-Oct) This well-regarded dining room sits squarely on the beach in Trout River. Grab a sandwich and chowder for lunch or delve into the scallop and shrimp dinners.

Old Loft Restaurant (☎ 709-453-2294; Water St, Woody Point; dinner mains $15-20; ☺ noon-7pm May-Oct, to 9pm Jul & Aug) Set on the water in Woody Point, this tiny place is popular for its traditional Newfoundland meals and seafood.

Earle's Video & Convenience (☎ 709-458-2577; Main St, Rocky Harbour; meals $6-12; ☺ 9am-11pm) Earle is an institution in Rocky Harbour. Besides selling groceries and renting videos, he has great pizza, moose burgers and traditional Newfoundland fare. There's a patio and, after all these years, a sit-down section.

NEWFOUNDLAND & LABRADOR

Getting There & Around

For shuttle and bus services to Rocky Harbour, Woody Point and Trout River from Corner Brook, see p381.

Run by Bon Tours (p374), the Bonne Bay Tour acts as a water taxi ($10, daily) between Woody Point and Norris Point (watch for whales). Times vary.

PORT AU CHOIX

If Port aux Choix wasn't a 13km detour off the Viking Trail, its riches would be much better known. It sits on a stark peninsula and is home to a large fishing fleet, quirky museum and a national historic site that bears its name.

Sights & Activities

The **Port au Choix National Historic Site** (☎ 709-861-3522; Point Richie Rd; adult/child under 17 $5.75/3; ☒ 9am-5pm Jun–mid-Oct, to 8pm mid-Jun–Aug) sits on ancient burial grounds of three different Aboriginal groups, dating back 4400 years. The modern visitors center tells of these groups' creative survival in the area and of one group's unexplained disappearance 3200 years ago. A highlight of the site is **Phillip's Garden**, a site with vestiges of Paleo-Eskimo houses.

The **Dorset Trail** (8km) makes an interesting way to visit the site. It leaves the visitor center and winds across the barrens through stunted trees, passing a Dorset Paleo-Eskimo **burial cave** before finally reaching Phillip's Garden. A shorter route leaves from Phillip Dr at the end of town. From here you hopscotch your way over the jigsaw of skeletal rock to the site 1km away.

If you continue, it's another 3km to the **Point Riche Lighthouse** (1871). A plaque next to the tower recounts the many French and English conflicts in the area between the 1600s and 1900s. In 1904, France relinquished its rights here in exchange for privilege in Morocco (ah yes, the days when all the world was a Monopoly board). The lighthouse is also accessible via the visitors center road.

At the edge of town is Ben Ploughman's capricious **Studio Gargamelle/Museum of Whales** (☎ 709-861-3280; Rte 430; adult/student $3/2; ☒ 9am-5pm Mon-Sat Jun–mid-Sep). His very engaging, knowledgeable and humorous manner complements the fascinating and ever-evolving whale museum he's creating. A highlight is the impressive whale skeleton that he's wiring together. Have a look at his artwork – *Crucifixion of the Cod* is a classic.

Sleeping & Eating

Jeannie's Sunrise B&B (☎ 709-861-2254, 877-639-2789; Fisher St; s/d $55/65; ☒) Staying with Jeannie is a sunrise indeed. And her breakfasts! Spacious and comfy rooms, a bright reading nook and Internet access all do the hospitality justice.

Sea Echo Motel (☎ 709-861-3777; seaecho@thezone.net; Fisher St; r $80-100, 2-bedroom apt $75) The three wood-lined apartments have some character, not to mention kitchens, living rooms and TVs – a steal.

The Anchor Café (☎ 709-861-3665; Fisher St; mains $10-16; ☒ lunch & dinner) You can't miss this place – the front half is the bow of a boat – and don't, because it has the best meals in town. The luncheon specials offer good value and the dinner menu has a wide array of sumptuous seafood.

ST BARBE TO STRAITSVIEW

As the Viking Trail nears St Barbe, the waters of the gulf quickly narrow and give visitors their first opportunity to see the desolate shores of Labrador. Ferries (p343) take advantage of this convergence and ply the route between St Barbe and the Labrador Straits. At Eddies Cove, the road sadly leaves the coast and heads inland towards the eastern shore. The northern tip of the peninsula has several diminutive fishing villages that provide perfect bases for your visit to L'Anse aux Meadows National Historic Site.

Sleeping

Sitting along the eastern shore of the peninsula's end, less than 10km south of the Viking Trail, are Straitsview, Gunners Cove and Quirpon, the jump-off point for Quirpon Island. The western shore, accessible from Rte 437, holds Pistolet Bay Provincial Park and Cape Onion.

Quirpon Lighthouse Inn (☎ 709-634-2285; 877-254-6586; www.linkumtours.com; Quirpon Island; s/d $200/300; ☒ May-Oct) Ever dreamed of being a lighthouse keeper on a remote speck of rock in the middle of raucous seas? Well here's your chance. You'll be without phone coverage and TV, so you'll have to make do with whales, waves and icebergs – good luck.

Tickle Inn (☎ 709-452-4321; www.tickleinn.net; Rte 437; ☺ Jun-Sep; s/d incl light breakfast $50/70; ☺ Jun-Sep) In Cape Onion, this delightful seaside inn, built in 1890, is surrounded by a white picket fence, oodles of grass and your own private beach. Sit in the parlor, feel the warmth of the Franklin woodstove and enjoy great home-cooked meals. The tickle question is up to you.

Valhalla Lodge B&B (☎ 709-623-2018, 877-623-2018; www.valhalla-lodge.com; Rte 436; s/d $60/80; ☺ mid-May–Oct) Set on a hill in Gunners Cove and overlooking the ocean, this lodge is only 5km from the Viking site. Put your feet up on the deck and watch icebergs in comfort. This very view inspired Pulitzer Prize–winning author E Annie Proulx as she wrote *The Shipping News* here.

Snorri Cabins (☎ 709-623-2241; www.snorricabins .com; Rte 436, Straitsview; 2-bedroom cabins $65-70; ☺ May-Nov) These cabins offer simple comfort and great value. They're perfect for families, with a full kitchen, sitting room and a pull-out sofa.

Dockside Motel (☎ 709-877-2444; info@dockside motel.nf.ca; Rte 430; s/d $70/75, 2-bedroom cabins $85) This place is literally next door to the ferry landing in St Barbe and has 15 rooms, 10 cabins and a restaurant.

Pistolet Bay Provincial Park (☎ 709-454-7580; Rte 437; tent & RV sites without hookups $13; ☺ early Jun–mid-Sep) This is a good place to stay if you're camping. There's a sandy beach, hot showers and laundry facilities, but be warned: the mosquitoes and blackflies have a really mean streak.

Eating

Fishermen's Galley (☎ 709-623-2431; Rte 436, St Lunaire-Griquet; meals $8-18; ☺ breakfast, lunch & dinner) Operated by a fisherman, and set on the water overlooking a distant tickle (still confused about tickles? This is a great place to ask), this large dining room serves great crab casseroles along with fajitas and vegetarian stir-fry.

Northern Delight (☎ 709-623-2220; Rte 436, Gunner's Cove; meals $9-13; ☺ breakfast, lunch & dinner late Apr–mid-Oct) Dine on a local favorite such as turbot cheeks and pan-fried cod, or just have a 'Newfie Mug-up' (bread, molasses and a strong cup of tea).

L'ANSE AUX MEADOWS NATIONAL HISTORIC SITE

While the unobtrusive and low-key approach taken by Parks Canada at this **Viking site** (☎ 709-623-2608; Rte 436; adult/child under 17/family $7/5.50/17.50; ☺ 9am-5pm Jun–mid-Oct, to 8pm mid-Jun–early Sep) makes it all the more special, don't let it undermine the site's monumental significance.

In an unspoiled, waterside setting – looking pretty much as it did in AD 1000 – are the remains of the settlement created by Vikings from Scandinavia and Greenland who became the first Europeans to land in North America, some 500 years before Columbus. Replicas of sod buildings complete with costumed docents, demonstrations and simulated fires almost transport you back in time.

Just landing here, after navigating the treacherous North Atlantic in small boats, says something of the Vikings' courage. The fact that they settled, constructed houses, fed themselves and even smelted iron out of the bog to forge nails, says something of their ingenuity and fortitude – all this from a group, led by Leif Eriksson, son of Eric the Red, who were only in their 20s.

Allow two or three hours to browse through the interpretive center and look at its artifacts, see the film and walk around the remains of eight original wood-and-sod buildings and the three reconstructions.

Also captivating is the story of Norwegian explorer Helge Ingstad, who rediscovered the site in 1960, ending years of searching. His tale and that of his wife, an archeologist, is told in the interpretive center. A short path behind the replica buildings leads to a small graveyard where the body of local inhabitant George Decker, who made Ingstad's day by pointing out the mounds in the terrain, lies.

Walking the 3km trail that winds through the barren terrain and along the coast that surrounds the interpretive center is also rewarding.

L'ANSE AUX MEADOWS

It's worth going to the top of the cape to pretty L'Anse aux Meadows village, with its hand-scribbled signs advertising iceberg ice.

On the way is the **Norstead** (☎ 709-623-2828; adult/family $7/14; Rte 436; ☺ 10am-6pm Jun-Sep), a commercial site set up to present Viking

NEWFOUNDLAND & LABRADOR

ICEBERG ALLEY

Whether it's your first or 40th sighting, nothing stops a conversation like the silent arrival of a luminous iceberg. Born from Greenland's glaciers and sculpted by the sea on their 1800-nautical-mile journey south, the icebergs that ply the Newfoundland waters are simply spellbinding.

Each year 10,000 to 40,000 new icebergs enter the Baffin and Labrador currents for their graceful three-year trip to Newfoundland's famed 'Iceberg Alley.' This stretch of sea runs along the north and east coast of Newfoundland and is strewn with bergs in late spring and early summer. Fogo and Twillingate Islands in Notre Dame Bay and St Anthony on the Northern Peninsula are some of the best places in the province to view these blue-and-white moving mountains. That said, even St John's is graced with a few hundred of the marvels each season.

While viewing an iceberg and feeling its chill is an astounding experience, there are other more subtle ways to enjoy these massive ice cubes. Locals harvest some smaller bergs, and if you ask in restaurants you may get some of the spirited ice along with your drink. You'll be stunned by both its antics and its longevity.

---

life as it was here 1000 years ago. There are four building re-creations, demonstrations on food, textiles etc, and a ship replica.

If you're totally captivated by the whole Viking experience, nearby is **Viking Boat Tours** (☎ 709-623-2100; Noddy Bay; 2½hr tours adult/child under 12 $40/25; ☑ 10am, 1pm & 4pm late May–mid-Sep), which offers boat tours ($30) on a replica Viking ship. You don't have to row, but you can't sail either; the Canadian Coast Guard won't allow it. So you motor around the bay looking at shipwrecks, icebergs and coastal scenery. Be prepared for cold and wet.

Relish the butternut squash soup, peruse a few vegetarian options or sink your teeth into some tender Labrador caribou tenderloin at **Norseman Gallery & Café** (☎ 709-623-2018; Rte 436; dinner mains $12-20; ☑ 9am-10pm Jun–mid-Oct). This is probably the best restaurant north of Gros Morne. Time your arrival for sunset – you won't regret it.

ST ANTHONY

Congratulations! You've made it to the end of the road; your windshield has helped control the insect population and you have seen two world heritage sites. After such grandeur, St Anthony may be a little anticlimactic. It's not what you'd call pretty, but it has a rough-hewn charm.

Grenfell is a big name around here. Sir Wilfred Grenfell was a local legend and, by all accounts, quite a man. This English-born and -educated doctor first came to Newfoundland in 1892 and, for the next 40 years, traveling by dog-sled and boat, built hospitals and nursing stations and organized much-needed fishing cooperatives along the coast of Labrador and around St Anthony.

Information
Grenfell Interpretation Centre (☎ 709-454-4011; West St, opposite the hospital; ☑ 9am-4pm Jul & Aug). Visitor information.

Sights & Activities
Grenfell Historic Properties (adult/family $6/12; ☑ 9am-5pm mid-May–Sep, to 8pm mid-Jun–Aug) subsume a number of local sites pertaining to Wilfred Grenfell. The **Grenfell Interpretation Centre** is an attractive and modern exhibit recounting the historic and sometimes dramatic life of Grenfell. Its handicraft shop has some high-quality carvings and artwork, as well as embroidered parkas made by locals – proceeds go to maintenance of the historic properties. Out back, near the **Dockhouse Museum** and new playground, try to spot the odd footprint from Grenfell's beloved dog-sled team in the exterior walls of the carpentry building.

Grenfell's beautiful mansion is now the **Grenfell Museum** (☎ 709-454-2281), located behind the hospital. Past the wraparound porch, dyed burlap walls and antique furnishings envelop memorabilia including a polar bear rug and, if rumors are correct, the ghost of Mrs Grenfell. Even the hardened caretaker is wary of being here alone.

The main road through town ends at **Fishing Point Park**, where a lighthouse and towering headland cliffs overlook the sea. The **Iceberg Alley Trail** and **Whale Watchers Trail** both lead to cliff-top observation platforms – the names say it all.

WESTERN NEWFOUNDLAND •• Corner Brook **379**

Tours

Northland Discovery Tours (☎ 709-454-3092; 2½hr tours adult/child $40/25; ⏰ 9am, 1pm & 4pm mid-May–mid-Oct) offer highly recommended cruises for whale- or iceberg-viewing that leave from a new dock behind the Grenfell Interpretation Centre on West St. The northerly latitude means St Anthony has the longest iceberg season in Newfoundland.

Sleeping & Eating

Fishing Point B&B (☎ 709-454-2009; l.budgell@nf .sympatico.ca; Fishing Point Rd; s/d with shared bathroom $50/60) This tiny, old-fashioned place clings to the rocks en route to the lighthouse and offers the best harbor view in St Anthony. Get up early, grab some coffee and watch the boats head out to sea.

Haven Inn (☎ 709-454-9100, 877-428-3646; www .haveninn.ca; 14 Goose Cove Rd; r $80-120) What it lacks in charm, it makes up in size and amenities. Some rooms have fireplaces and Jacuzzi tubs. In the **dining room** (meals $6-17; ⏰ 7am-9pm), you'll get a good view of the harbor, and some light fare like poached salmon with rice pilaf.

Vinland Motel (☎ 709-454-8843, 800-563-7578; vin land.motel@nf.sympatico.ca; West St; r $85-105) This is a sizable 43-room motel in the center of town.

Lightkeeper's Café (☎ 877-454-4900; Fishing Point Park; meals $8-20; ⏰ lunch & dinner mid-Jun–Sep) This little gem of an eatery sits in the shadow of the lighthouse and is often graced by the sight of icebergs and whales. A trip here is as obligatory as it is enjoyable. The chowder and scallops are legendary.

Leifburdir (☎ 877-454-4900; adult/child/teen $37/20/25; ⏰ 7:30pm mid-Jun–Sep) For a more social, zany meal, try the Leifburdir next door. You enter a sod house and find yourself at a Viking banquet complete with participatory skits and a full meal, including the likes of moose stew, stuffed salmon and desserts.

Entertainment

For some good, casual fun get to the **Legion** (☎ 709-454-2340; East St, leaving town) building on Wednesday night, when some local musicians play traditional stuff and snacks are available.

Getting There & Away

Flying to St Anthony is technically possible, but the airport is nearly an hour away. If you're leaving St Anthony by car, you have

two options: backtrack entirely along Rte 430, or try the new sections of Rte 432 that run down the east coast and Hare Bay. This will meet up with Rte 430 near Plum Point, between St Barbe and Port aux Choix.

The Viking Express (p381) bus picks up at the **Irving Station** (☎ 709-454-2601; Main St) across from the Vinland Motel on West St, leaving for Corner Brook ($52, seven hours) at 10am Sunday, Tuesday and Thursday.

WESTERN NEWFOUNDLAND

The western section of the province, below that mighty finger of a peninsula, offers a good mix of geography and history. To the north there's Corner Brook, Newfoundland's second-largest town, and the French region on the Port au Port Peninsula. To the south there is the broad, green, fertile Codroy Valley and the ferry town of Port aux Basques, which hangs on the jagged, rocky shore.

CORNER BROOK

As if washed here by a tidal wave, the town of Corner Brook is splashed up the hills at the eastern end of the Humber Arm's 40km-long waters. While the varied topography creates some fine vistas, one can't help but notice the plume of white gases rising from the town's lifeblood, its pulp and paper mill. On the bright side, it's perhaps the sunniest region of the province.

Orientation

The downtown area consists of Main St by Remembrance Square and up along maple-lined Park St toward the Heritage District, which has some nice shops and restaurants.

Information

Family Bookstore (☎ 709-639-9813; Corner Brook Mall, Maple Valley Rd; ⏰ 9:30am-6pm, to 9pm Wed-Fri, noon-5pm Sun) A tremendous selection of Newfoundland literature.
Post Office (☎ 709-637-8807; 14 Main St)
Public Library (☎ 709-634-0013; Sir Richard Squires Bldg, Mt Bernard Ave; ⏰ 1-8pm Mon & Tue, 10am-8pm Wed, 10am-5pm Thu-Sat) Free Internet access.
Tourist Office (☎ 709-639-9792; cnr Confederation Dr & West Valley Rd; ⏰ 9am-9pm mid-May–mid-Oct, 9am-5pm mid-Oct–mid-May) Just off Hwy 1 at exit 5. Has a craft shop.

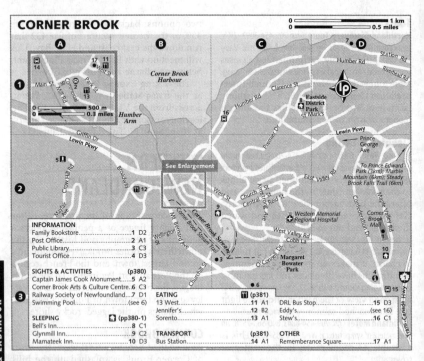

CORNER BROOK

0 ——— 1 km
0 ——— 0.5 miles

Corner Brook Harbour

Humber Arm

See Enlargement

INFORMATION
Family Bookstore..................1 D2
Post Office...........................2 A1
Public Library......................3 C3
Tourist Office......................4 D3

SIGHTS & ACTIVITIES (p380)
Captain James Cook Monument.....5 A2
Corner Brook Arts & Culture Centre..6 C3
Railway Society of Newfoundland.....7 D1
Swimming Pool.......................(see 6)

SLEEPING (pp380-1)
Bell's Inn............................8 C1
Glynmill Inn.........................9 C2
Mamateek Inn......................10 D3

EATING (p381)
13 West.............................11 A1
Jennifer's...........................12 B2
Sorento.............................13 A1

TRANSPORT (p381)
Bus Station.........................14 A1

DRL Bus Stop......................15 D3
Eddy's..............................(see 16)
Stew's.............................16 C1

OTHER
Rememberance Square...............17 A1

Sights & Activities

A tribute to Cook for his work in surveying the entire region in the mid-1760s, the **Captain James Cook Monument** (Crow Hill Rd, off Atlantic Ave), a national historic site, is northwest of downtown. Cook's names for many of the islands, ports and waterways, such as the Humber Arm and Hawke's Bay, remain today. His successes here paved the way for his more historic voyages to the South Pacific. What Cook would think about his cliff-top monument being overshadowed by its panoramic views is a good question to ponder – while enjoying the view! The route here is convoluted, but well-marked.

Within historic Humbermouth Station, the **Railway Society of Newfoundland** (☎ 709-634-5658; Station Rd, off Humber Rd; admission $2; ⏱ 10am-8pm mid-Jun–mid-Sep) has a handsome steam locomotive and some narrow-gauge rolling stock that chugged across the province from 1921 to 1939, as well as a photographic exhibit.

An arm of Memorial University, the **Corner Brook Arts & Culture Centre** (☎ 709-637-2580; University Dr) features a 400-seat performing arts facility and an **art gallery** (admission free; ⏱ 9am-5pm), which displays the works of local artists as well as touring exhibitions. Culture is fine, but many people head to the center for the **swimming pool** (☎ 709-637-2584; admission $3; ⏱ hrs vary).

Marble Mountain (☎ 709-637-7616; Hwy 1) is a major downhill ski center in the Humber Valley 8km east of town. When the white stuff has departed, the **Steady Brook Falls Trail** (500m) leads from the ski area's rear parking lot, behind the Petro-Canada station, to a cascade of water that tumbles more than 30m.

Another scenic walk is the **Corner Brook Stream Trail** (2km), which follows the stream's banks and part of Glynmill Pond. It starts in the parking lot of the Glynmill Inn on Cobb Lane.

Sleeping

Bell's Inn (☎ 709-634-1150, 888-634-1150; www.bellsinn.ca; 2 Ford's Rd; r incl breakfast $55-90) Warm Edinburgh hospitality and extremely comfortable surroundings grace this B&B, which is within walking distance of town. Room

Nos 1 and 4 have stunning views and there is even a playground for kids.

Glynmill Inn (☎ 709-634-5181, 800-563-4400; www .glynmillinn.ca; 1 Cobb Lane; d $95-115, ste $115-160) This large, classic Tudor-style inn was originally built for the engineers supervising the pulp mill's construction in the 1920s, at that time the largest project in the history of paper-making. Lawns, gardens and graciousness surround this elegant inn.

Mamateek Inn (☎ 709-639-8901, 800-563-8600; 64 Maple Valley Rd; r $85-100) This large, slightly dated hotel has views from even-numbered rooms; kids under 12 stay for free.

Prince Edward Park (☎ 709-637-1580; db.randell@ nf.sympatico.ca; North Shore Hwy; tent sites $12, RV sites $15-15; ☸ mid-Jun–early Sep) Set up your tent in the woods, just a five-minute drive from town. Take exit 7 off Hwy 1 and follow the signs.

Eating & Drinking

13 West (☎ 709-634-1300; 13 West St; dinner mains $20-30; ☸ lunch & dinner) Scallops, cashews, curried cream sauce and pineapple chutney collide with linguini for an unforgettable dish at this well-received bistro. Vegetarians will gleefully inspect their – gasp! – choices.

Jennifer's (☎ 709-632-7979; 48-50 Broadway; lunch buffet $6, dinner mains $10-18; ☸ lunch & dinner) This great place sits above a gift shop of the same name. It's known for its seafood, steak and incredible lunch buffet.

Sorento (☎ 709-639-3466; 18 Park St; mains $8-20; ☸ lunch & dinner) Enjoy great Italian food at this low-lit eatery. After dinner, slide into the swank contemporary jazz lounge for a drink or two.

Getting There & Away

Corner Brook is a major hub for bus services throughout Newfoundland. Most operators use the **bus station** (☎ 709-634-4710) in the center of town, adjacent to the Millbrook Mall shopping center. The exceptions are DRL, which stops at the **Confederation Dr Irving station** (☎ 709-634-7422) across from the visitor center; and Stew's and Eddy's, who share an office at 9 Humber Rd. Those hoping to make connections between these various stations will require a taxi. Reservations are essential for all services.

DRL Coachlines (☎ 709-738-8088; www.drlgroup .com/Coachlines/coachlines_new.html) buses heading eastward to St John's ($79, 10½ hours)

depart at 11:25am daily. At 5:55pm services leave for Port aux Basques ($32, three hours). **Stew's** (☎ 709-634-7777, 709-634-8281) runs a shuttle to Burgeo ($30, two hours) departing at 3pm, except Friday, when it leaves at 4pm. **Eddy's** (☎ 709-634-7777) travels to Stephenville ($13, 1¼ hours) four times daily. **Gateway** (☎ 709-695-3333, 888-695-3322) operates weekdays, departing for Port aux Basques ($30, three hours) at 3:45pm. Returns depart Port aux Basques at 8am.

Martin's (☎ 709-453-2207) shuttles operate weekdays, departing for Woody Point ($14, 1½ hours) and Trout River ($12, 1¼ hours) at 4:30pm. Returns depart Woody Point and Trout River at 9am. **Pittman's** (☎ 709-458-2084) shuttles operate weekdays, departing for Rocky Harbour ($15, 1½ hours) at 4:30pm. Returns depart Rocky Harbour at 9am.

The **Viking Express** (☎ 709-634-4710) bus to St Anthony ($52, seven hours) departs at 4pm Monday, Wednesday and Friday. Stops include Deer Lake ($7, 45 minutes) and Rocky Harbour ($15, two hours).

Around Corner Brook
BLOMIDON MOUNTAINS

Running along the south side of the Humber Arm are the **Blomidon Mountains**, raised from a collision with Europe some 500 million years ago. They're great for hiking, provide many vistas out to the Bay of Islands and have a resident caribou population. Some of the trails, especially ones up on the barrens, are not well marked, so topographical maps and a compass are essential. More details on the area can be found in Keith Nicol's *Best Hiking Trails in Western Newfoundland*.

One of the easiest and most popular trails begins at a parking lot on the left side of Rte 450 (500m from the Blow Me Down Brook bridge). The trail can be taken for an hour or so; for more avid hikers it continues well into the mountains, where you're on your own.

At **Blow Me Down Provincial Park** (☎ 709-681-2430; fax 709-681-2238; Rte 450; campsites $13; ☸ early Jun–mid-Sep), the beaches and scenery may keep you longer than expected. If you're heading to the park or the hiking trail near the Blow Me Down Brook bridge, follow Rte 450, which heads west from the south side of Corner Brook. You'll find the park near the end of the road, some 47km from town.

STEPHENVILLE

Stephenville is possibly the least appealing town in Newfoundland and, festival time aside, there is no compelling reason to stop. From mid-July to early August, however, the town is alive with theater during the **Stephenville Theatre Festival** (☎ 709-643-4882; www.stf.nf.ca). There's the Bard, Broadway and to stir the pot, some cutting-edge Newfoundland plays.

PORT AU PORT PENINSULA

The large peninsula west of Stephenville is the only French area of the province. It became known as the French Shore in the early 1700s. Today, the strongest culture is along the western shore between **Cape St George** and **Lourdes**. Here children still go to French school, preserving their dialect, which is now distinct from the language spoken in either France or Québec.

In **Port au Port West**, near Stephenville, the gorgeous **Gravels Trail** (3km) leads along the shore, passing secluded beach after secluded beach – each a stone-skipper's dream. Nearby is the massive and historic **Our Lady of Mercy Church** (☎ 709-648-2632; off Rte 460; admission free; ☉ 10am-5pm mid-Jun–Sep) – its intricacies will have you shaking your head. Just up the road in Felix Cove, stop at **Alpacas of Newfoundland** (☎ 709-648-9414; Rte 460) and stare deeply into the bewildering eyes of the llama's fluffiest relative.

BARACHOIS PROVINCIAL PARK

This popular **park** (☎ 709-649-0048; Hwy 1; tent & RV sites without hookups $13; ☉ mid-May–mid-Sep), sitting just south of Rte 480 on Hwy 1, is one of the few in the province to offer a backcountry experience. From the campground, the **Erin Mountain Trail** (4.5km) winds through the forest and up to the 400m peak, where there are backcountry campsites and excellent views of the surrounding area. Allow two hours for the climb.

Not so far away are a couple of leisurely nature trails and a nice swimming area.

PORT AUX BASQUES

Approaching Port aux Basques on the ferry from Nova Scotia, the 'Rock' can be quite a forbidding site at first. The houses stand gathered on the end of a rocky peninsula, as if they've been chased from the hostile barren land and are just waiting for the signal to jump. The apprehension wears off at the first sight of a Newfoundlander's smile, and soon you'll find the roughness of the place is its most appealing characteristic.

The narrow, winding roads of the town's old section sneak their way around the rocky outcrops and are edged with traditional wooden houses. A walk is gratifying and offers different views and angles at every turn.

Port aux Basques (sometimes called Channel–Port aux Basques) was named in the early 16th century by Basque fishers and whalers who came to work the waters of the Strait of Belle Isle, which separates Newfoundland from Québec. Today, the life and economy of Port aux Basques revolve around the terminal for the Marine Atlantic ferry.

Orientation & Information

When leaving the ferry, turn left after crossing the bridge and head southeast along Caribou Rd to reach the town center. The **tourist chalet** (☎ 709-695-2262; Hwy 1; ☉ 6am-8pm mid-May–Sep), with information on all parts of the province, is on Hwy 1 a few kilometers out of town on the way to St John's. Nearby, across Grand Bay Bottom, is the hospital and large shopping center. You'll find postal and banking services along the crooked roads in the old section of town.

Sights & Activities

Downtown, across from the town hall, is the two-story **Gulf Museum** (☎ 709-695-7604; 118 Main St; adult/family $4/7; ☉ 10am-7pm early Jul–late Aug). Most of the collection is maritime artifacts – many are from shipwrecks. The showpiece of the museum is the astrolabe, which was found by a diver off Isle aux Morts along the south coast from town in 1981. This striking brass navigational instrument, made in Portugal in 1628, is designed on a principle discovered by the ancient Greeks to allow for charting of the heavenly bodies. Variations on it have been used for nautical navigation since 1470. This astrolabe is in remarkable condition and is one of only about three dozen in the world.

To the west of town is **Grand Bay West Beach** (Kyle Lane). This long sweeping beach is backed by grassy dunes, which are breeding grounds for the endangered piping plover – have fun, but watch your step. The **Cormack**

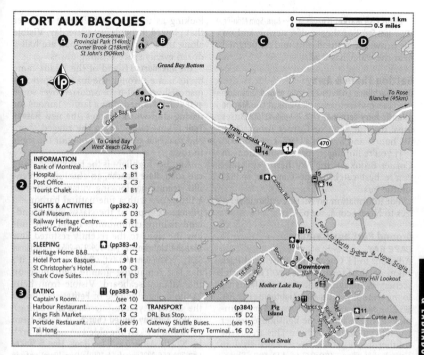

PORT AUX BASQUES

INFORMATION
Bank of Montreal.............................1 C3
Hospital...2 B1
Post Office......................................3 C3
Tourist Chalet.................................4 B1

SIGHTS & ACTIVITIES (pp382-3)
Gulf Museum...................................5 D3
Railway Heritage Centre..................6 B1
Scott's Cove Park............................7 C3

SLEEPING (pp383-4)
Heritage Home B&B.........................8 C2
Hotel Port aux Basques...................9 B1
St Christopher's Hotel....................10 C3
Shark Cove Suites..........................11 D3

EATING (pp383-4)
Captain's Room........................(see 10)
Harbour Restaurant.......................12 C2
Kings Fish Market..........................13 C3
Portside Restaurant...................(see 9)
Tai Hong.......................................14 C2

TRANSPORT (p384)
DRL Bus Stop................................15 D2
Gateway Shuttle Buses.............(see 15)
Marine Atlantic Ferry Terminal...16 D2

Trail (11km) leaves from here and flirts with the coast all the way to JT Cheeseman Provincial Park (p384).

The **Railway Heritage Centre** (☎ 709-695-7560; off Hwy 1; tours $2; ☼ 9am-9pm Jul & Aug) and **Scott's Cove Park** (Caribou Rd), with its restored boardwalk and new amphitheater, are also interesting stops.

Sleeping & Eating

With all the ferry traffic, reservations are a good idea unless you arrive very early in the day.

Shark Cove Suites (☎ 709-695-3831; fax 709-695-7919; 16 Currie Ave; 1-/2-bedroom apt $65/75) These massive 56- and 92-sq-meter apartments are perfect to sprawl out in after a long ocean voyage. With sofa beds, even the one-bedroom apartment is perfect for families.

St Christopher's Hotel (☎ 709-695-7034, 800-563-4779; www.stchrishotel.com; Caribou Rd; s $70-95, d $75-100) From this hilltop location, the hotel's odd-numbered rooms offer a fine view over the harbor. It's close to the boardwalk and also has a good restaurant, **Captain's Room** (meals $8-14; ☼ breakfast, lunch & dinner).

Hotel Port aux Basques (☎ 709-695-2171, 877-695-2171; www.hotelpab.com; 1 Grand Bay Rd; s $70-85, d $75-170) This comfortable, large hotel is just off Hwy 1 and lets kids stay for free. For those in need of some pampering, the luxury rooms will do the trick. The **Portside Restaurant** (meals $8-14; ☼ 7am-2pm & 5-8pm) within the hotel is one of the better places to eat in town.

Heritage Home B&B (☎ 709-695-3240; 11 Caribou Rd; d & tw with shared bathroom $55, ste $65; ☼ May-Oct) You can stay in bed at this five-room guesthouse almost until the ferry, literally across the street, blows its horn. This B&B is bright and comfortable, and the suite is suited to families.

Harbour Restaurant (☎ 709-695-3238; 121 Caribou Rd; meals $5-11; ☼ 7am-midnight, to 4am Sat & Sun) While you'll get better food at the hotels, you can't beat the harborside view here. It now serves pizzas and donairs (spiced beef in pita bread) to go along with the fried chicken and fish and chips.

Tai Hong (☎ 709-695-3116; High St; meals $7-11; ☼ 11am-11pm) Standard Chinese fare, served with fresh vegetables – a rarity in these parts.

NEWFOUNDLAND & LABRADOR

Kings Fish Market (Charles St; ☯ 8am-5pm Mon-Fr, 10am-4pm Sat) For those self-catering and on the prowl for seafood, this market perched near the water has it all.

Getting There & Away

DRL Coachlines (☎ 709-738-8088; www.drlgroup.com /Coachlines/coachlines_new.html) stops at the **Marine Atlantic ferry terminal** (☎ 709-695-4216). Buses leave daily at 8am for Corner Brook ($32, 3½ hours) and St John's ($97, 13½ hours).

If you're hoping to make connections in Corner Brook for the Northern Peninsula, you're best catching the Gateway (p381) shuttle bus.

For information on Marine Atlantic services to Nova Scotia, see p342.

Around Port aux Basques

CAPE RAY

Adjacent to JT Cheeseman Provincial Park 14km north of town is **Cape Ray**. The coastal scenery is engaging, and the road leads up to the windblown **Cape Ray Lighthouse** (☎ 709-695-2262; admission $2; ☯ 10am-9pm Jul & Aug) complex. If you're lucky, the lighthouse keeper will let you climb the tower. This area is the southernmost known Dorset Paleo-Eskimo site, dating from 400 BC to AD 400. Thousands of artifacts have been found here and some dwelling sites can be seen.

There are also some fine hikes in the surrounding areas. The Cormack Trail (p382) will eventually stretch north from here to Flat Bay near Stephenville. The **Table Mountain Trail** (12km) is more like a rugged road (don't even think about driving up it) and begins on Hwy 1 opposite the exit to Cape Ray. The hike leads to the top of a 518m plateau, where there are ruins from a secret US radar site and airstrip from WWII. It's not a hard hike, but allow three or four hours for it.

JT Cheeseman Provincial Park (☎ 709-695-7222; fax 709-695-9384; Rte 408; tent & RV sites without hookups $13; ☯ late May–mid-Sep) rests next to the beach and has great facilities thanks to its new comfort station.

SOUTH COAST

The often-ignored Rte 470, which heads east out of Port aux Basques for about 45km, is an ideal little side trip. Edging along the shore, the road rises and falls over the rounded, eroded windswept terrain,

looking as though it's following a glacier that plowed through just yesterday. Visible along the other side of the road are half a dozen evenly spaced fishing towns.

Isle aux Morts (Island of the Dead) came by its name through the many shipwrecks just offshore that have occurred over some 400 years. Named after a family famous for daring ship-wreck rescues, the new **Harvey Trail** (7km) twists along the rugged shore and makes a great walk. Look for the signs in town.

Another highlight is the last village along the road, **Rose Blanche**, an absolutely splendid, traditional-looking village nestled in a little cove with a fine natural harbor – a perfect example of the classic Newfoundland fishing community. From here follow the signs to the recently restored **Rose Blanche Lighthouse** (☎ 709-956-2052; adult/family $3/7; ☯ 9am-9pm May-Oct). Built in 1873, it's the last remaining granite lighthouse on the Atlantic seaboard. Visible from here, in the isolated village of **Petites** (inquire at the docks if you're interested in visiting), is the **Bethany United Church**. It dates from 1859 and is likely the oldest wooden church in North America. The **Hook, Line & Sinker** (☎ 709-956-2005; meals $6-10; ☯ 9am-10pm) café is right next door and is a delightful spot for lunch or dinner.

For those without a vehicle, **Gateway Transportation** (☎ 709-695-3333, 888-695-3322) offers flexible tours from Port aux Basques that visit Rose Blanche and the Codroy Valley for $120 (up to four people).

SOUTH COAST OUTPORTS

'Outport' is the name given to any of the tiny coastal fishing villages accessible only by boat. These little communities are some of the most remote settlements in North America. No longer self-sufficient from the sea alone, the outport communities are dwindling one by one as government pressure forces them to relocate to more accessible areas. The remaining outports, still grasping to the rocky southern coastline, harbor the rough life at its most traditional. Visiting them is perhaps the best place to witness the unique Newfoundland culture.

SIGHTS & ACTIVITIES

An anomaly along this stretch of coast is **Burgeo**. Perhaps one of Newfoundland's best-kept secrets, it rests in the middle of the south coast, and is connected to Hwy 1 via the seldom traveled 148km-long Rte 480. Climb the stairs to **Maiden Tea Hill** and look over the rocky hills, endless inlets and island-sprinkled coast. Its provincial park is home to 7km of magnificent sand, which likely comprises the best beach in the entire province.

The outports are great areas for remote camping and hiking. People have particularly raved about the trails around **François**.

SLEEPING & EATING

Accommodations are hassle-free in Burgeo, and along the way you should have little trouble lining up something, even if it's just with a family. The locals are very helpful and do see a few (not many) strangers passing through lugging backpacks. If you're concerned, the tourist information office in Port aux Basques (p382) could help, but informal boarding houses may not be registered with the tourism department.

Burgeo Haven B&B (☎ 709-886-2544, 888-603-0273; 111 Reach Rd, Burgeo; s/d with shared bathroom $60/75; ☾ mid-May–mid-Sep; ▢) This large house backs onto a large inlet and offers a serene setting. Stumble out the front door minutes before sunrise, walk across the street and up to Maiden Tea Hill, for a sight you shan't soon forget. The owners can also arrange accommodation for you in François.

Sandbanks Provincial Park (☎ 709-886-2331; fax 709-635-4541; off Rte 480; tent & RV sites without hookups $13; ☾ late May–mid-Sep) The endless beach reigns supreme in this beautiful provincial park. Two-thirds of the campsites are nestled in the forest, while the remainder are in a grassy area.

Blue Mountain Cabins (☎ 709-492-2753; cynthia billard@hotmail.com; Grand Bruit; s/d $65/70) There are just two cottages at this place in Grand Bruit. Meals are offered to guests at modest prices.

Gillett's Motel (☎ 709-886-1284; www.gilletts motel.ca; 1 Inspiration Rd, Burgeo; d $75) Another option in Burgeo is this recently renovated hotel. It's closest to the ferry, wheelchair accessible and has a nice **dining room** (meals $7-15).

ANY MUMMERS LOUD IN?

During the evenings of the 12 days of Christmas in the small coastal outports of Newfoundland, an unusual and magical centuries-old tradition takes place. Houses are stocked with Christmas cake and spirits for the boisterous few who call themselves mummers. These hilariously clad and disguised locals wander the lanes and by-paths, musical instruments in hand, and beat on every door, calling out, 'Any mummers loud in?' With gleeful anticipation, the door is opened and the festivities begin. The mummers' goal is a simple one: entertain, eat, drink, dance and get out, all before the hosts can guess who they are.

GETTING THERE & AWAY

The easiest way to access the south coast is via Rte 480 to Burgeo. Note there is not a gas station along the entire highway. Stew's (p381) bus service conveniently links Burgeo to Corner Brook, allowing coastal trips to start or end here.

If you have the time and patience, a trip across the south coast is incredibly rewarding. While the following ferries run all year, the route described below is from the schedule for mid-May through September. If hours are not given here, it is because departures are not regular. Schedules can change, so check with **Provincial Ferry Services** (www.gov.nl.ca/ferryservices) or call ☎ 709-292-4302.

Starting at Rose Blanche, ferries leave for Lapoile ($3.50, 1½ hours) and Grand Bruit ($4.25, 2½ hours) at 3:30pm daily (except Tuesday and Thursday). On the same days there are two boats from Lapoile to Grand Bruit ($3.25, one hour). From Grand Bruit to Burgeo ($5, three hours), boats only leave Tuesday at 8:45am. From Burgeo you have a couple of options. There is one daily ferry to Ramea ($3, 1½ hours) and one daily (except Tuesday and Thursday) ferry to Grey River ($4.25, 2½ hours). If you take the Ramea boat, your only options from there to Grey River ($3.25, 1½ hours) are on the 8am and 3:30pm sailings each Tuesday or Thursday. From Grey River there are daily (except Tuesday and Thursday) sailings to François ($3.75, two hours) at 4:30pm. Ferries leave François for McCallum ($3.74, 2½ hours) and Hermitage ($5.50, 4½ hours) at 7am Thursday. If you departed from McCallum your next chance to reach Hermitage (1½ hours) is the following Thursday at 9:45am.

At Hermitage, you'll have to suss out transportation back to Rte 360 and possible transportation via **Hickey's Bus Service** (☎ 709-885-2523). Or you could always go back the way you came!

LABRADOR

The land should not be called New Land, being composed of stones and horrible rugged rocks…I did not see one cartload of earth and yet I landed in many places…there is nothing but moss and short, stunted shrub. I am rather inclined to believe that this is the land God gave to Cain.

Jacques Cartier

A disappointed Jacques Cartier spoke these bitter words in 1534, after having explored 200km of Labrador's shores. Almost 5000 years later, this vast, rugged land, comprising over 293,000 sq km and stretching over 800km from the Strait of Belle Isle to Cape Chidley, is one of the last incompletely explored areas in Canada and one of the largest, cleanest natural areas anywhere.

The geological base of Labrador is the ancient Laurentian Shield – possibly the oldest unchanged region on earth. It's thought the land looks much the same as it did before life on the planet began – expect primeval-looking, undulating, rocky, puddled expanses with little vegetation. Four great caribou herds, including the world's largest (some 750,000 head), migrate across Labrador to their calving grounds each year.

Inuit and Innu have occupied Labrador for thousands of years, and until the 1960s the population was still limited to them and a few longtime European descendants known as 'liveyers.' They eked out an existence for centuries by fishing and hunting from their tiny villages that freckled the coast. The interior was virgin wilderness.

Despite the 2001 official governmental consolidation of Newfoundland with Labrador, the Labrador flag is still displayed, and the residents will long continue to consider themselves a breed apart. Over the past few decades, the economic potential of Labrador's vast natural resources has not gone unnoticed, and several of them have been tapped. Although deep in the interior and extremely isolated, projects like the massive iron-ore mines in Wabush and Labrador City and the hydroelectric dam at Churchill Falls are shaping the land around them and shifting the demographics and way of life for the Labrador population. These three cities and Happy Valley-Goose Bay, the home of a military base, are now home to half of Labrador's 28,000 people.

The northern coast of the province remains essentially unchanged, however, and is a great place to explore the Inuit and Aboriginal-influenced villages of Labrador. As in southern Newfoundland, a unique trip on the supply ferries is possible with some planning. Camping is an option all across Labrador but is mostly done in a van or camper as this is often a cold, wet and windy place. And the bugs can make you suicidal.

Note that Cartwright and Northern Labrador are on Atlantic Time, while the Labrador Straits (not including the Québec portion) are on Newfoundland Time (which is 30 minutes ahead of Atlantic Time). There is a one-hour time difference between Québec and Labrador City: Labrador City (on Atlantic Time) is one hour ahead of Québec (on Eastern Time).

LABRADOR STRAITS

Its stark cliffs lying 18km across the Strait of Belle Isle and visible from the Northern Peninsula of Newfoundland, this historic coast is Labrador's most accessible region. The first European settlement in Labrador occurred here, and many of the inhabitants are the descendants of the fishers who crossed from Newfoundland to fish in the rich strait centuries ago. Attractions include the desolate but awe-inspiring far north landscapes, icebergs, sea birds, whales and sunken 16th-century galleons at Red Bay.

Orientation & Information

Your first stop in Labrador Straits will not actually be in Labrador at all, as the ferry terminal and airport are both in Blanc Sablon, Québec. This remote region of La Belle Province is known as the Lower North

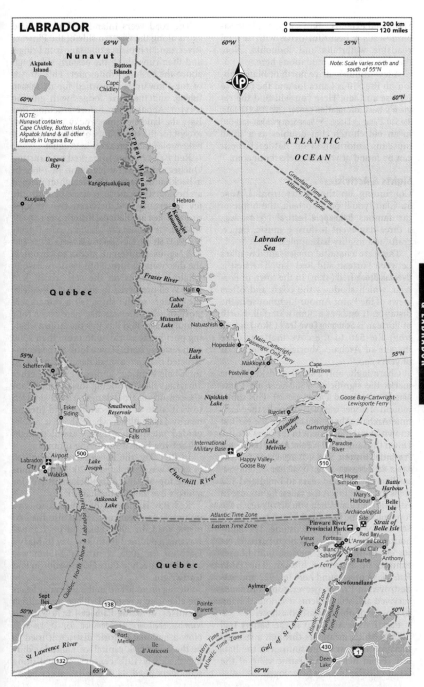

LABRADOR

0 ━━━━━ 200 km
0 ━━━━━ 120 miles

Note: Scale varies north and
south of 55°N

Nunavut

Akpatok
Island

Button
Islands

Cape
Chidley

NOTE:
Nunavut contains
Cape Chidley, Button Islands,
Akpatok Island & all other
Islands in Ungava Bay

*Ungava
Bay*

Kuujjuaq

Kangiqsualujjuaq

Torngat Mountains

Hebron

Kaumajet Mountains

*ATLANTIC
OCEAN*

Greenland Time Zone
Atlantic Time Zone

*Labrador
Sea*

Fraser River

Nain

*Cabot
Lake*

*Mistastin
Lake*

Natuashish

Québec

*Harp
Lake*

Hopedale

Nain-Cartwright
Passenger Only Ferry

Makkovik

Postville

Cape
Harrison

Schefferville

*Nipishish
Lake*

Rigolet

Goose Bay-Cartwright-
Lewisporte Ferry

Esker
Siding

*Smallwood
Reservoir*

Churchill
Falls

*International
Military Base*

*Hamilton
Inlet*

Cartwright

Paradise
River

*Lake
Melville*

Happy Valley-
Goose Bay

Airport

500

Labrador
City

Wabush

*Lake
Joseph*

Churchill River

510

Port Hope
Simpson

*Battle
Harbour*

*Atikonak
Lake*

Mary's
Harbour

**Belle
Isle**

Québec North Shore & Labrador Railroad

Atlantic Time Zone

Eastern Time Zone

Archaeological
Site

*Strait of
Belle Isle*

Pinware River
Provincial Park

Red Bay

Forteau

Vieux
Fort

L'Anse au Loup

Blanc
Sablon

L'Anse au Clair

St
Anthony

St Barbe

Ferry

Newfoundland

Sept
Îles

138

Aylmer

Pointe
Parent

Eastern Time Zone
Atlantic Time Zone

Gulf of St Lawrence

Atlantic Time Zone
Newfoundland Time Zone

132

St Lawrence River

Port
Menier

*Île
d'Anticosti*

430

1

Deer
Lake

Shore and extends 74km south of Blanc Sablon – it's a beautiful drive with several roadside waterfalls and lookouts. Note there are no accommodations here.

A few minutes' drive north of Blanc Sablon on Rte 510 is Labrador and the town of L'Anse au Clair. Here you will find the region's best **information center** (☎ 709-931-2013; Rte 510, L'Anse au Claire; 🕑 9am-5pm mid-Jun–mid-Oct) in an old church that doubles as a small museum. Information on Battle Harbour can be found at www.battleharbour.com.

Sights & Activities

Continuing up the straits from L'Anse au Clair, you'll pass Forteau, the home of the famous **Bakeapple Festival** (🕑 mid-Aug), a three-day event featuring music, dance, crafts and mighty bakeapples.

There are a handful of pleasant day-hikes between Forteau and Red Bay. The first is **Overfall Brook Trail** (4km) in the town of Forteau, which shadows the coast and offers views of the Point Amour Lighthouse in the distance. It ends at a 30m waterfall. North of Forteau is **Schooner Cove Trail** (3km), a trek from Rte 510 to the cove that was once the site of Archaic Aboriginals thousands of years ago.

Charmingly, only a small roadside plaque marks the significant 7500-year-old **L'Anse Amour Burial Mound** (L'Anse Amour Rd). This subtle mound of stones was placed here by the Maritime Archaic Aboriginals and is the earliest known burial monument in the New World. Down the same road is **Point Amour Lighthouse Provincial Historic Site** (☎ 709-927-5825; L'Anse Amour Rd; admission $2.50; 🕑 10:30am-5:30pm mid-Jun–Thanksgiving). Four years to build and 127 steps to climb, this is the tallest lighthouse in Atlantic Canada. When you dizzily reach the top, you will be bestowed with a spectacular 360-degree view of the coastline. The lighthouse keeper's house has been partially restored to the 1850s period and houses exhibits on maritime history. The HMS *Raleigh* went aground here in 1922 and was destroyed in 1926; however, some ordnance survived and still presents a serious danger, so beware of objects washed ashore.

Past L'Anse au Loup is the **Battery Trail** (2km), which meanders through a stunted tuckamore forest to the summit of the Battery. From here a panoramic view of the Strait of Belle Isle can be enjoyed.

The road veers inland at Pinware, and skirts along the western side of the Pinware River, until it crosses a one-lane iron bridge, and then runs along the eastern side, high above the rushing whitewater. This stretch of the Pinware is renowned for its **salmon fishing**, and there are lodges with guiding service. About 10km before reaching Red Bay, the land becomes rocky and barren, except for the superfluity of blueberries and bakeapples (and pickers) in August.

Red Bay's harbor is marked by a rusting Québec ship that ran aground in 1966. In a backhanded way, this freighter helped archeologists locate a treasure beneath the icy waters. Spread between two venues, brilliant **Red Bay National Historic Site** (☎ 709-920-2051; Rte 510, Red Bay; adult/child under 17/family $7/3.50/17.50; 🕑 9am-5pm mid-Jun–mid-Oct, to 8pm Jul & Aug) uses different media to chronicle the discovery of three 16th-century Basque whaling galleons on the sea bed in Red Bay. Well preserved in the ice-cold waters, the vestiges of the ships tell a remarkable story of what life was like here some four centuries ago. Red Bay was the largest whaling port in the world, with more than 2000 men residing here. Have a look at the reconstructed *chalupa* (a small Basque dingy used for whale hunting) and some of the other amazing relics, including the all-important 4½-century-old markings. You'd do well to visit some of the excavated land sites on nearby **Saddle Island**, where there is a self-guided interpretive trail. Careful though, it'll set you back a whopping toonie!

In Red Bay, the **Boney Shore Walking Trail** (4.6km) was completed in 2003 and climbs to the top of American Rockyman Hill for a bird's-eye view of the harbor.

Red Bay is the end of paved road, and up until a few years ago it was also the end of the road. In 2001, 80km of pink gravel was pushed inland from Red Bay to Mary's Harbour. In 2003, a further 245km was added, connecting Port Hope Simpson and Cartwright.

Sitting on an island in the Labrador Sea is the elaborately restored village and saltfish premises of **Battle Harbour** (☎ 709-921-6216; www.battleharbour.com; admission $5; 🕑 Jun-Sep). Now a national historic district, it used to be the unofficial 'capital' of Labrador during the early 19th century, when fishing schooners lined its docks. It's accessed by boat ($40 round-trip) from Mary's Harbour and you can come for the day or spend a few nights in one of the historic houses. Be warned: icebergs and the occasional pod of orcas may slow the boat's progress – apologies for the delay.

Tours

Experience Labrador (☎ 877-938-7444; www.experience labrador.com; Cartwright) offers customized multi-day kayaking trips ($225 per adult per day) along the remarkable northern coast – paddle the endless sands of the Wonderstrands that mesmerized the Vikings so long ago.

Sleeping & Eating

Battle Harbour Inn (☎ 709-921-6677; www.battlehar bour.com; Battle Harbour; dm/s/d incl 3 meals $57/125/175; ☽ Jun-Sep) Accommodations are spread among various heritage homes and cottages in this historic village.

Alexis Hotel (☎ 709-960-0228; info@alexishotel.ca; off Rte 510, Port Hope Simpson; d $80-130) A favorite of former US president George HW Bush, this recently renovated, luxurious fishing lodge is halfway between Blanc Sablon and the ferry in Cartwright. The scenic **dining room** (meals $5-13; ☽ breakfast, lunch & dinner) prepares everything from local fare to pizzas.

Northern Light Inn (☎ 709-931-2332, 800-563-3188; www.northernlightinn.com; 56 Main Rd, L'Anse au Clair; s/d $85/105) This modern and well-kept motel is your closest option to Blanc Sablon. The even-numbered rooms have views of the harbor and there are a couple of wheelchair-accessible suites. The **dining room** (meals $8-17; ☽ breakfast, lunch & dinner) is your best bet for food in town.

Seaview Cabins (☎ 709-931-2840; bradleyhancock@ hotmail.com; 33 Main St, Forteau; apt $80-90) The sofa beds make these comfortably furnished apartments a nice option for families. Large unit No 7 has the best view. Inquire at the **restaurant** (meals $6-16; ☽ breakfast, lunch & dinner) across the street. There's also a grocery store.

Riverlodge Hotel (☎ 709-921-6948; www.river lodgehotel.com; off Rte 510, Mary's Harbour; r $85-90) Some rooms are newer than others – unit Nos 258 to 261 are quite nice. This 15-room hotel also has a **restaurant** (meals $5-15; ☽ breakfast, lunch & dinner).

Cartwright Hotel (☎ 709-938-7414; www.cart wrighthotel.ca; 3 Airport Rd, Cartwright; r $80-100) This simple hotel has 10 rooms, a **dining room** (meals $5-15; ☽ 6am-10pm) and a lounge.

Getting There & Around

AIR

Provincial Airlines (☎ 800-563-2800; www.provincial airlines.ca) has scheduled flights to Blanc Sablon from St John's ($195) and St Anthony ($70). Note departure times in Blanc Sablon are on Eastern Time, which is 30 minutes behind the Labrador Straits (Newfoundland Time) in the winter and 90 minutes behind in the summer, as Blanc Sablon does not observe daylight saving time.

BOAT

For information on the Blanc Sablon to St Barbe ferry, see p343. For passenger ferries from Cartwright to the northern coast, see p390 and for vehicle ferries from Cartwright to Goose Bay and Lewisporte, see p343.

CAR & MOTORCYCLE

Those traveling by car should be aware that the road running down the coast from Blanc Sablon is not connected to farther destinations in Québec. South of Red Bay, Rte 510 is sealed and open all year. The government has been taking its time deciding whether to keep the long, and sometimes rough, gravel section heading north to Cartwright open in the winter. It's best to check ahead with the **Department of Transportation and Works** (☎ 709-729-2300; www.roads.gov.nl.ca).

Rental cars and trucks are available in Blanc Sablon from **Eagle River Rent-a-Car** (☎ 408-461-2040).

NORTHERN COAST

North of Cartwright up to Ungava Bay there are a half-dozen small, semitraditional communities and settlements accessible only by sea or air along the rugged, largely unspoiled mountainous coast.

Living off the land completely has pretty much disappeared, especially now that the fishing industry has all but gone belly up. While unemployment is high and many people rely on government funds, the lifestyle remains unchanged in many ways due simply to the isolation and the small size of the villages. The people are a determined lot – they have to be.

In 1993 on the shores of Voisey's Bay, near Nain, geologists discovered stunningly rich concentrations of copper, cobalt and especially nickel. After a decade of bickering between the government and the mining giant Inco Ltd, the massive project looks to be starting production in 2006. The mine is expected to pump $11 billion into the provincial economy over 30 years and will likely open up the north – for better or worse.

Sights & Activities

The first port of call on the north coast is **Makkovik**, an early fur-trading post and a traditional fishing and hunting community. Both new and old-style crafts can be bought.

Farther north in **Hopedale** visitors can look at the old wooden Moravian mission church (1782). This **national historic site** (☎ 709-933-3663; admission $5; ⏱ 8am-8pm Jun-Sep) also includes a store, residence, some huts and a museum collection.

Natuashish is a new town that was formed when the troubled village of Utshimassit (Davis Inlet) was relocated to the mainland in 2002. The move was made after a 2000 study showed that 154 of 169 youths surveyed had abused solvents (ie sniffed gasoline) and that 60 of them did it on a daily basis.

The last stop on the ferry is **Nain**, and it's the last town of any size as you go northward. Fishing has historically been the town's main industry, but this will change once production starts at Voisey's Bay nickel deposit. After the fishing season, hunting and trapping continue as they have for centuries. The Piulimatsivik-Nain Museum burned down in 1999, and most of the artifacts are now stored in the **mission house**. You may be able to get someone to open it up for you.

From Nain, you can try to arrange boat transportation to the **Tongat Mountains**, which are popular with climbers because of their altitude (some of the highest peaks east of the Rockies) and isolation. The **Kaumajet Mountains** also make for an out-of-this-world hiking experience – inquire at the Amaguk Inn.

Sleeping & Eating

The accommodations situation is a bit of an unknown; most travelers use the ferry as a floating hotel. For those wishing to get off and wait until the next boat, it usually means winging it for a room, as only Hopedale and Nain have official lodging.

Amaguk Inn (☎ 709-933-3750; fax 709-933-3764; Hopedale; s/d $95/105) This 12-room inn also has a **dining room** (meals $10-12), and a lounge where you can get a cold beer.

Atsanik Lodge (☎ 709-922-2910; fax 709-922-2815; Sand Banks Rd, Nain; s/d $115/125) This large lodge and its **restaurant** (meals $13-18) are your best bet in Nain.

Getting There & Away

Provincial Airlines (☎ 800-563-2800; www.provincial airlines.ca) serves most of the northern coast's villages from Goose Bay.

A passenger ferry plies this section of coast between mid-June and September. It leaves Cartwright at 7am Wednesday for its week-long return journey to Nain. After making an overnight stop in Goose Bay on Wednesday, the ferry leaves at 1pm Thursday and makes successive 90-minute stops in Makkovik (7:30am Friday), Postville (noon Friday), Hopedale (6pm Friday), Natuashish (7am Saturday) and Nain (12:30pm Saturday) before she hops back along the same route and pulls into Cartwright on Tuesday at 2pm. The round-trip to Nain costs $208 for adults and $100 for children, while a bunk in a shared cabin is $97 and a deluxe two-berth cabin is $840. Ticket and accommodation fares are based on nautical miles traveled, so you'll pay less if don't go as far north as Nain. There is a cafeteria onboard that serves four meals a day (you didn't forget about 'night lunch' did you?). Check for any schedule or cost changes with **Labrador Marine** (☎ 866-535-2567) before heading out.

CENTRAL LABRADOR

Making up the territorial bulk of Labrador, the central portion is an immense, very sparsely populated and ancient wilderness. Paradoxically, it also has the largest town in Labrador, Happy Valley-Goose Bay. The town has all the services, including hotels, but for the outsider there isn't a lot to see or do and it is very isolated. The remote, forested landscape attracts many anglers and hunters, however, and there are numerous fly-in possibilities for camping.

Goose Bay was established during WWII as a staging point for planes on their way to Europe, and has remained an aviation center. Today there is a Canadian military base used by pilots from both Canada and NATO for testing high-tech planes, in particular controversial low-flying jets that the Innu say disturb their way of life. The airport is also an official NASA alternate landing site for the space shuttle.

Sights & Activities

Officially opened by Queen Elizabeth II in 1997, the **Labrador Interpretation Centre** (☎ 709-497-8566; Hillview Dr, North West River; admission $3; ☺ 1-4pm Wed-Sun) is the provincial museum, which holds some of Labrador's finest works of art.

The **Northern Lights Building** (☎ 709-896-5939; 170 Hamilton River Rd; admission free; ☺ 10am-5:30pm Mon-Sat, to 9pm Thu & Fri) hosts a military museum, interesting lifelike nature scenes and simulated northern lights. Children, and the child in you, should check out the huge collection of model trains in the lower section of the building.

Labrador Heritage Society Museum (☎ 709-497-8779; off Rte 500; admission $2; ☺ 9am-5:30pm mid-Jun–Sep) outlines some of the history of the area through photographs, and includes a traditional trapper's shelter, samples of animal furs, some of the minerals found in Labrador and details on the ill-fated Wallace-Hubbard expedition into Labrador's interior. The museum, incorporating a 1923 Hudson's Bay Company store, is on the north side of town on the former Canadian Forces base.

Sleeping & Eating

Aurora Hotel (☎ 709-896-3398; www.aurorahotel.com; 382 Hamilton River Rd; r $85-120) Renovated in 2002, this hotel sits at the crossroads of the airport and sea port. The rooms are very comfortable and some are wheelchair accessible. Enjoy a caribou burger in the **restaurant** (meals $8-18; ☺ breakfast, lunch & dinner) or head to the lounge for some drinks.

Royal Inn & Suites (☎ 709-896-2456; royal.inn@nf.sympatico.ca; 3 Royal Ave; d incl light breakfast $65, ste $75-115) This hotel has just added some suites to round out its array of rooms. Some with kitchens are available.

TMT's B&B (☎ 709-896-4404; fax 709-896-2990; 451 Hamilton River Rd; r $35-55) Family atmosphere and home cooking wait for you at TMT's. It's also the cheapest lodging in town.

Getting There & Away

AIR

Provincial Airlines (☎ 800-563-2800; www.provincialairlines.ca) has daily flights serving Goose Bay from St John's ($240), and Deer Lake ($195). Air Canada (p869) has similar but more expensive services. **Air Labrador** (☎ 800-563-3042; www.airlabrador.com) serves Labrador's smallest communities from Goose Bay.

BOAT

For passenger ferry information between Goose Bay and Cartwright, see opposite. For Goose Bay vehicle- and passenger-ferry information from Cartwright and Lewisporte, see p343.

CAR & MOTORCYCLE

Your options by car from Happy Valley-Goose Bay are westward along the gravel of Rte 500 to Churchill Falls and then on to the twin cities of Labrador City and Wabush. The drive from Goose Bay to Labrador City takes about 10 hours. There are no services until Churchill Falls, so stock up. The road can also be very rough. Still, travelers have made it in passenger cars, though to quote one: 'I don't know that I'd do it again.' Before leaving, contact the **Department of Transportation and Works** (☎ 709-729-2300; www.roads.gov.nl.ca) for the latest conditions.

Trucks can be rented in Happy Valley-Goose Bay at the airport from **National** (☎ 709-896-5575), but due to conditions on Rte 500, you cannot buy insurance. If you plan on leaving the vehicle in Wabush, there's a painful $800 return fee.

WESTERN LABRADOR

Everything in this area of Labrador is oversized in the extreme. The landscape is massive and endless, the development projects are gargantuan and the celestial polychromatic artwork can take up the entire night sky.

Labrador City/Wabush

These twin mining cities, just 15km from Québec, represent modern, industrial Labrador and are generally referred to collectively as Labrador West. The largest open-pit iron ore mine in the world is in Labrador City, and another operates in Wabush. The towns have developed around the mine sites since they opened in the late 1950s.

INFORMATION

On Rte 500 west of Labrador City, a new complex hosts the **Labrador West Tourism office** (☎ 709-944-7631; ☺ 9am-5pm Mon-Fri, 9am-9pm daily mid-Jun–Labour Day).

SIGHTS & ACTIVITIES

In the same building as the tourist office is **Gateway Labrador** (☎ 709-944-5399; 1365 Rte

MAGNETIC PERFORMANCES

Thanks to the magnetic north pole being in northern Canada, the glowing fluorescent colors of the aurora borealis (northern lights) decoratively dance across the sky in this region two nights out of every three. While scientists state the lights are simply charged particles from the sun trapped in the earth's magnetic field, the Inuit believe that the shimmering lights are the sky people playing a game of ball. Others believe the lights are unborn children playing. The Ojibwe called the lights Waussnodae and believed them to be torches held by their dead grandfathers to light the way along the Path of Souls. The souls of the recently deceased walked this path, the Milky Way, to their final resting place.

Note that in summer, with its extremely long daylight hours, the show may only be visible in the wee hours of the morning.

500, Labrador City; adult/student $3/2.50; ⊗ 9am-9pm Jun–Labour Day, 9am-5pm Mon-Fri, noon-5pm Sat & Sun Sep-May) and its **Montague Exhibit Hall**, where 3500 years of human history and culture, including the fur trade, are represented with exhibits of intriguing artifacts and displays.

Just out of town the landscape has been sculpted by glaciers and is a vast expanse of low, rolling, forested mountains interspersed with areas of flat northern tundra. The **Wapusakatto Mountains** are just 5km from town, and parts have been developed for skiing. From Wabush, 39km east on Rte 500 is **Lac Grand Hermine Park** (☎ 709-282-5369; admission $3; ⊗ Jun–mid-Sep), with a beach and some fine scenery. The **Menihek hiking trail** (15km) goes through wooded areas with waterfalls as well as open tundra. Outfitters can take anglers to excellent **fishing** waters. In the winter this area is a training ground for the Canadian national Nordic ski team.

If big holes and trucks the size of apartment buildings lift your skirt, you can tour the **mines** (admission free; ⊗ 1:30pm Wed & Sun Jul-Sep) by contacting Labrador West Tourism (p391).

SLEEPING & EATING

Carol Inn (☎ 709-944-7736, 888-799-7736; carolinn@ crrstv.net; 215 Drake Ave, Labrador City; r $80) All 20 of the rooms at this place have kitchenettes and air-conditioning. There's also a fine **dining room** (meals $20-30; ⊗ dinner Tue-Sat), a **pub** (meals $8-12; ⊗ 8am-midnight) and a small pizza franchise.

Wabush Hotel (☎ 709-282-3221; www.wabushhotel .com; 9 Grenville Dr, Wabush; s/d $90/95) Centrally located in Wabush, this chalet-style 68-room hotel has spacious and comfortable rooms. The **dining room** (meals $8-20; ⊗ 6:30am-midnight) has a popular dinner buffet.

Tamarack B&B (☎ 709-944-6002; 835 Tamarack Dr; s/d with shared bathroom incl breakfast $40/60) This is a simple, homey B&B just off Rte 500 as you're coming from Goose Bay.

Breadbasket Bakery & Café (☎ 709-944-5355; carol Lake Shopping Centre, 208 Humber Ave; meals $5-10; ⊗ 7am-9pm Mon-Fri, 9am-9pm Sat & Sun) There are some nice chicken fajitas to go with the soups, salads and sandwiches.

GETTING THERE & AWAY

Air

Both Labrador City and Wabush are connected to the rest of the province by Air Canada and **Air Labrador** (☎ 800-563-3042; www .airlabrador.com).

Car & Motorcycle

Fifteen kilometers west from Labrador City along Rte 500 is Fermont, Québec. From there Rte 389 is mainly paved (with some fine gravel sections) and continues south 581km to Baie Comeau. See p391 for information on Rte 500 heading east.

National (☎ 709-944-2000) has an office in Wabush, but rental cars may not be driven on rough Rte 500.

Train

Western Labrador is accessible via a twice-weekly train link with Sept Îles, Québec (adult/child under 12 $64/32, round-trip $116). In Labrador City, the **train station** (☎ 709-944-8205) is at Airport Rd. Trains leave Wednesday at noon and Friday at 1pm. The trip takes eight hours and travels through some stunning wilderness. There is a snack car for light lunches.

Nova Scotia

CONTENTS

NOVA SCOTIA

In Nova Scotia, you're never more than 56km from the sea. Whatever your favorite sort of coastline, be it picturesque fishing villages, white-sand beaches, dramatic cliffs or extensive estuaries, you'll find it here. In years gone by, privateers chased tall ships into isolated coves in order to seize their booty and schooners raced along these shores. Today, lobster boats share the ocean with kayaks, the preferred means of exploring sheltered bays and offshore islands.

Many of Nova Scotia's most spectacular vistas are on Cape Breton Island, also renowned for its hospitality and music. Other beautiful areas of Nova Scotia are easily visited on short trips from Halifax. One of the most attractive cities in Canada, the capital city is immensely livable: you can crisscross the interesting sections on foot in an hour. It's a hotbed for music, art, filmmaking, beer brewing and, of course, beer drinking.

Halifax is also home to many of Nova Scotia's best festivals, including the Atlantic Jazz Festival in July. During the Stan Rogers Folk Festival, the population of Canso explodes 10-fold with devotees of folk music and songwriting, while the Evolve Festival gathers rock bands and eco-activists together for an August weekend in Antigonish.

Nova Scotia has a conservative side: it's the only province that still restricts shopping on Sundays, and a young woman was recently dethroned as princess of a local festival for spending nights at her boyfriend's place. But that conservatism is slowly being eroded by time and the influence of new Nova Scotians – a motley crew of Vietnam draft-dodgers, Buddhists, artists, university students and Maritimers – from New Brunswick, Prince Edward Island, or elsewhere in Nova Scotia – who want to try 'big city' life in Halifax.

HIGHLIGHTS

- Watch whales from your campsite in **Meat Cove** (p446)
- Enjoy buskers, boats and people-watching along the waterfront boardwalk in **Halifax** (p398)
- Forage the fossil-laden shoreline of **Parrsboro** (p433)
- Learn the difference between a march and a reel at the **Celtic Music Interpretive Centre** (p441) near Mabou, and then go dancing
- Discover the warm ocean waters and sandy beaches near **Tatamagouche** (p436)
- Sample French soldiers' rations or a general's feast c 1744 at **Louisbourg National Historic Site** (p449)
- Stroll through the perfectly preserved, British colonial streets of **Lunenburg** (p411) on your way to the harborfront, where captains of tall ships and lobster boats offer cruises with the best views of all

Meat Cove
Mabou
Louisbourg National Historic Site
Tatamagouche
Parrsboro
Halifax
Lunenburg

| POPULATION: 937,000 | PROVINCIAL CAPITAL: HALIFAX | AREA: 55,491 SQ KM |

History

From time immemorial, the Mi'kmaq First Nation lived throughout present-day Nova Scotia, which they divided into districts where different families each had hunting territory. When the French established the first European settlement at Port Royal in 1605, Grand Chief Membertou offered them hospitality and became a frequent guest of Samuel de Champlain.

That close relationship with the French led to considerable suspicions by the British after they gained control of Nova Scotia, and rewards were offered for Mi'kmaw scalps. The Mi'kmaq helped some French-speaking Acadians evade deportation, but starting in 1755 most were sent to Louisiana (where they became 'Cajuns') and elsewhere for refusing to swear allegiance to the British Crown (see the boxed text on p422).

Nova Scotia was repopulated by some 35,000 United Empire Loyalists retreating from the American Revolution, including a small number of African slaves owned by loyalists and also freed Black Loyalists. New England planters settled other communities and, starting in 1773, waves of Highland Scots uprooted by the clearances arrived in northern Nova Scotia and Cape Breton Island.

Most Nova Scotians trace their ancestry to the British Isles, as a look at the lengthy 'Mac' and 'Mc' sections of the phone book easily confirms. Acadians who managed to return from Louisiana after 1764 found their lands in the Annapolis Valley occupied. They settled instead along the French Shore between Yarmouth and Digby and, on Cape Breton Island, around Chéticamp and on Isle Madame. Today Acadians make up some 18% of the population, though not as many actually speak French. African Nova Scotians account for about 4% of the population. There are approximately 20,000 Mi'kmaq in 18 different communities concentrated around Truro and the Bras d'Or lakes on Cape Breton Island.

Different aspects of Nova Scotian history are captured in 27 excellent provincial museums. If you're likely to take in several, it's worth buying an annual pass (adult/family $38/75) available at all museums in Nova Scotia.

Climate

The ocean surrounding Nova Scotia tends to keep the weather moderate, with cooler temperatures nearer the coast than inland. Summer and autumn are usually sunny, although the eastern areas and Cape Breton Island are often windy. The entire southern coast from Shelburne to Canso is often wrapped in a morning fog, which may take until noon or later to burn off. Winters can be very snowy but, again, the ocean keeps temperatures from plunging.

National & Provincial Parks

There are enough parks in Nova Scotia to organize a month-long tour of the province around them. Kejimkujik National Park (p415) is best appreciated from a canoe, as it protects an inland network of lakes and portage routes. Hiking around in the fall is also enjoyable when the leaves turn color. The famous Cabot Trail wends its way through coastal mountains in Cape Breton Highlands National Park (p444), one of the most dramatic parks in Canada. Both national parks offer some services and rustic campsites year-round.

Cape Chignecto Provincial Park (p434), the largest and newest park, offers a true wilderness experience, with rugged hikes and backcountry camping amongst old-growth forest. It's open from Victoria Day weekend (late May) to mid-November.

Some 120 other **provincial parks** (www.parks.gov.ns.ca; campsites $14-18) include beaches, picnic parks and 20 well-dispersed campgrounds that open in late May or mid-June and close anytime from early September to mid-October. Reservations for campsites can be made by calling the individual park with a credit card after May 1. You can stay up to two weeks in any park. The campgrounds offer a range of sites, including some big enough for RVs, but there is no power and no water hookups. With no hum of generators, provincial parks are ideal for tenters.

Getting There & Away

AIR

Air Canada, CanJet, Jetsgo and Westjet (p869) have daily flights from Toronto to Halifax; round-trip fares range from $260 to $450 depending on the season. Air Canada also flies to Boston from Halifax ($350 to $600, 2¼ hours, twice daily).

NOVA SCOTIA

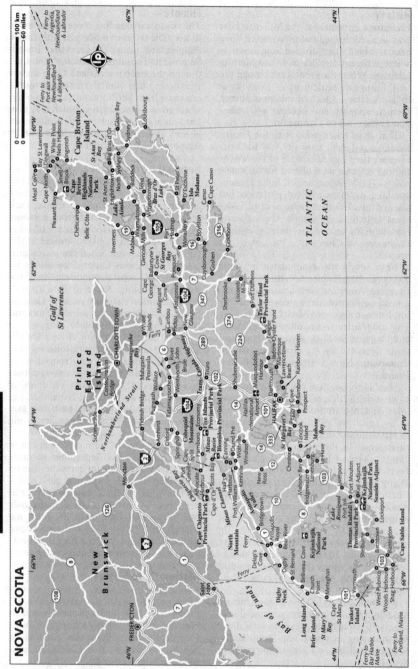

BUS

Acadian Lines (☎ 902-454-9321, 800-567-5151; www
.acadianbus.com) provides bus service through
the Maritimes with connections to the rest
of Canada and the USA. From Halifax,
destinations include Toronto ($168, 26
hours, daily), Montreal ($125, 18 hours,
twice daily) and Bangor, Maine ($80, 10½
hours, Thursday to Saturday), where there
are connections for Boston and New York.
All Acadian Lines prices include taxes, and
there are discounts for children five to 11
years (50%), students (15%) and seniors
(25%). **DRL Coachlines** (☎ 902-450-1987, 877-450-
1987; www.drlgroup.com) travels along the South
Shore from Halifax to Yarmouth ($40, 5½
hours, daily) with connections to the ferries
(below). There are discounts for students
(15%) and seniors (25%) and for purchasing return tickets.

BOAT

New Brunswick

Bay Ferries (☎ 888-249-7245; www.nfl-bay.com; adult/
child 3-10 yrs/child 11-17 yrs $35/15/20, car/bicycle $95/10)
has a three-hour trip from Saint John, New
Brunswick, to Digby. Off-season discounts
and various packages are available.

Newfoundland

Marine Atlantic (☎ 800-341-7981; www.marine
-atlantic.ca) operates ferries year-round to Port
aux Basques, Newfoundland, from North
Sydney (adult/child under 13 $27/13.50, per
car/motorcycle $77/39). Daytime crossings
take between five and six hours, overnight
crossings take up to eight hours. Cabins
and reclining chairs cost extra. In summer,
you can opt for a 14-hour ferry ride (adult/
child under 13 $76/38, per car/motorcycle
$158/79) to Argentia on Newfoundland's
east coast. Reservations are required for
either trip.

Prince Edward Island

Northumberland Ferries (☎ 902-566-3838, 800-
565-0201; adult/child under 12 $12.50/free, vehicle with
passengers $53) cruises between Wood Islands,
Prince Edward Island (PEI), and Caribou,
near Pictou, up to nine times daily. You
only pay when leaving PEI. The one-hour
crossing is a nice alternative to the Confederation Bridge (p458). No reservations are
required, but it's wise to show up half an
hour before the sailing.

USA

Ferries from the USA to southwestern
Nova Scotia have become destinations in
themselves, with casinos, spas and fine
dining. Bay Ferries operates the high-speed
catamaran **Cat** (☎ 888-249-7245; www.catferry
.com; adult/child 3-10 yrs/child 11-17 yrs US$55/25/35,
car/bicycle US$110/10; ☼ late May–mid-Oct) that
skates across the water from Bar Harbor,
Maine, to Yarmouth in less than three
hours. The **Scotia Prince** (☎ 866-412-5270;
www.scotiaprince.com; adult/child 5-12 yrs $US85/45,
car/bicycle US$120/15; mid-Apr–early Nov) takes 11
hours to travel from Portland, Maine, to
Yarmouth.

TRAIN

VIA Rail (p875) runs services between Montréal and Halifax (one-week advance purchase adult/child two to 11 years $121/60,
20 hours, daily except Tuesdays) with stops
in Amherst (advance purchase adult/child
$105/52, 16 hours from Montréal) and Truro
(advance purchase adult/child $112/56, 18
hours). Students pay the same as adults
with no need for advance purchase; adult
discount fares may sell out so it's best to
book as early as possible.

Getting Around

Renting a car is certainly the easiest way
to get around and can be more economical than taking the bus. Shuttle buses are
another alternative (see p407). Distances
are very manageable; you can easily stay in
the Annapolis Valley and do day trips to
the South Shore and vice versa. The longest
drive most people will do is the four-hour
haul to Cape Breton Island from Halifax.

The direct route to most places will be
on a 100-series highway (eg 101, 102, 103),
which have high speed limits and limited
exits. There is usually a corresponding
older highway (eg 1, 2, 3) that passes
through communities and has varying
speed limits, but none higher than 80km/h.
The Trans-Canada Hwy (Hwy 104/105)
cuts directly across the province from Amherst to Sydney without passing through
Halifax. Other backroads snake across
rural Nova Scotia, usually numbered 200
to 299 when traveling vaguely east–west
and 300 to 399 going north–south. You'll
find more potholes than gas stations along
these.

NOVA SCOTIA

NOVA SCOTIA IN...

Two Days

Start by walking along the harbor boardwalk in **Halifax** (below). If it's Saturday, detour into the **Halifax Farmers' Brewery Market** (p407) for coffee and cinnamon rolls, then see if the **Bluenose II** (p404) is in port and take a cruise under sail around the harbor. Spend an afternoon in the **Museum of Natural History** (p403), making sure to see the Butterfly Pavilion. Get an ice cream at **Dío Mío Gelato** (p406) and stroll around the **Public Gardens** (p402).

On the next day, drive along Hwy 3 to **Mahone Bay** (p411) and **Lunenburg** (p411).

One Week

Follow the two-day itinerary, then keep going south. Stroll along white-sand beaches near **Liverpool** (p415), hike the **Keji Adjunct** (p416) and take a kayaking tour out of **West Pubnico** (p419). Then head to **Wolfville** (p423) for fine dining and pastoral views, and on to **Annapolis Royal** (p425) to tour historic gardens and the Fort Anne graveyard by night.

Two Weeks

Follow the one-week itinerary, then drive to **Cape Breton Island** (p441). Take in a square dance at **Glencoe Mills** (p441), swim in warm ocean waters off **Inverness** (p442) and visit museums in **Chéticamp** (p442). Then explore **Cape Breton Highlands National Park** (p444), leaving time for whale-watching from **Meat Cove** (p446). Return to Halifax via the **Eastern Shore** (p451), taking an afternoon hike in **Taylor Head Provincial Park** (p452).

HALIFAX

☎ 902 / 360,000

The quality of life in Halifax persuades many talented folks who could make it in Toronto to stay right here. The ocean is nearby, the air is clean, and the pace is sane. People drawn to Halifax by its several universities contribute to the vibrant downtown scene. Few chain establishments compete with the unique restaurants and cafés that Haligonians flock to.

There's usually an ocean breeze on the Halifax waterfront, where a boardwalk leads several kilometers past museums, shops and restaurants. If there's too big a crowd, accessible wilderness can be found in Point Pleasant Park or on McNabs Island.

HISTORY

The Mi'kmaq called present-day Halifax Che-book-took, meaning 'the biggest harbor.' Its immense natural harbor made Halifax an easy choice for a British stronghold after Fortress Louisbourg was returned to the French under the 1748 Treaty of Aix-la-Chapelle. The town was founded in 1749 by General Cornwallis. German Lutherans, considered friendly 'foreign Protestants,' made up most of the original population. Halifax's second-oldest building is Brunswick St's Little Dutch Church, so-named because the British could not pronounce or spell 'Deutsch.' Cornwallis relocated many of the original German settlers to Lunenburg in 1753.

Halifax has always been an important base for the navy. During WWI and WWII, hundreds of ships massed in the extensive Bedford Basin before traveling in convoys across the North Atlantic. In 1917 the *Mont Blanc*, a French munitions ship carrying TNT and highly flammable benzol, collided with another ship. The 'Halifax Explosion,' the world's biggest man-made explosion prior to A-bombs being dropped on Japan in 1945, ripped through the city. More than 1900 people were killed and 9000 injured. Almost the entire northern end of Halifax was leveled and many buildings and homes that were not destroyed by the explosion burned to the ground when winter stockpiles of coal in the cellars caught fire.

ORIENTATION

The downtown area, three universities and older residential neighborhoods are contained on a compact peninsula cut off from mainland Halifax by an inlet called the North West Arm. Almost all sights of interest to visitors are concentrated in this area, making walking the best way to get around. Point Pleasant Park is at the extreme southern end of the peninsula, and the lively **North End** neighborhood – home to African Nova Scotians, art-school students and most of Halifax's gay bars – stretches from the midpoint to the northern extreme.

Two bridges span the harbor, connecting Halifax to Dartmouth and leading to highways north (for the airport) and east. The MacDonald Bridge at the eastern end of North St is closest to downtown. The airport is 40km northwest of town on Hwy 102.

INFORMATION
Bookstores
Trident Booksellers & Café (p406) has a fine selection of books, new and used.

Book Room (☎ 902-423-8271; 1546 Barrington St; ☘ 9am-7:30pm Mon-Fri, 9am-5pm Sat Jul-Sep, to 5:30pm Mon & Tue Oct-Jun) Around for nearly 160 years, it stocks a good selection of maps and travel guides, plus books by local authors.

Bookmark (☎ 902-423-0419; 5686 Spring Garden Rd; ☘ 9am-10pm Mon-Fri, 9am-6pm Sat, 11am-6pm Sun) Good selection of maps and travel guides.

John W Doull Bookseller (☎ 902-429-1652; 1684 Barrington St; ☘ 9:30am-6pm Mon & Tue, 9:30am-9pm Wed-Fri, 10am-9pm Sat) This secondhand store has more books than many libraries.

Mountain Equipment Co-op (☎ 902-421-2667; 1550 Granville St; ☘ 10am-9pm Mon-Fri, 9am-6pm Sat Jul & Aug, 10am-7pm Mon-Wed, 10am-9pm Thu & Fri, 9am-6pm Sat Sep-Jun) Topographical maps and guides to hiking, kayaking and biking in Nova Scotia.

Internet Access
Blowers St Paper Chase (☎ 902-423-0750; 5228 Blowers St; per hr $8; ☘ 8am-8pm Mon-Sat, 9am-8pm Sun) This cool café charges by the minute or the hour.

Halifax North Branch Memorial Library (☎ 902-490-5723; 2285 Gottingen St; ☘ 10am-9pm Tue-Thu, 10am-5pm Fri & Sat) Computers on a first-come, first-served basis.

Khyber Digital Media Centre (☎ 902-446-4053; http://khyberarts.ns.ca/kdmc; 1588 Barrington St; per hr $5; ☘ noon-8pm Tue-Fri, to 6pm Sat) Friendly staff here on the 2nd floor of the Khyber Centre for the Arts (p401) can help you upload video and audio; you can check email here.

Second Cup (☎ 902-429-0883; 5425 Spring Garden Rd; ☘ 7am-midnight) A half-hour of Internet access is free with any purchase at this café.

Internet Resources
Halifax Info (www.halifaxinfo.com) Details about festivals, sights and tours.

Studio Map (www.studiorally.ca) A guide to art and craft studios across the province, plus a shortlist of spot-on recommendations for eateries and B&Bs.

Media
The *Coast*, a free weekly publication available around town, is the essential guide for music, theater, film and events.

Medical Services
Family Focus (☎ 902-420-2038; 5991 Spring Garden Rd; consultation $60; ☘ 8:30am-9pm Mon-Fri, 11am-5pm Sat & Sun) Walk-in or same-day appointments.

Halifax Infirmary (☎ 902-473-3383/7605; 1796 Summer St; ☘ 24hr) For emergencies.

Money
Bank branches clustered around Barrington and Duke Sts change traveler's checks for a $3 fee.

Travelex (☎ 902-873-3612; Halifax International Airport; ☘ 6am-9pm) Charges $5.50 per transaction.

Post
Lawton's Drugs (☎ 902-429-0088; 5675 Spring Garden Rd; ☘ 8am-9pm Mon-Fri, 8am-6pm Sat, noon-5pm Sun) Post office inside.

Main Post Office (☎ 902-494-4670; 1680 Bedford Row; ☘ 7:30am-5:15pm Mon-Fri) Pick up mail sent to General Delivery, Halifax, NS B3J 2L3 here.

Tourist Information
Check out posters for performances and events on the bulletin boards just inside the door of the Halifax Public Library.

Tourism Nova Scotia (☎ 902-425-5781, 800-565-0000; www.novascotia.com) Operates visitor information centres in Halifax and six strategic locations across the province, plus a free booking service for accommodations, which is useful when rooms are scarce in mid-summer. It publishes the *Doers & Dreamers Guide* that lists places to stay, attractions and tour operators.

Visitor Information Centres (VICs) Downtown (☎ 902-490-5946; 1595 Barrington St; ☘ 8:30am-8pm Jul & Aug, 8:30am-7pm May, Jun & Sep, 8:30am-4:30pm Mon-Fri rest of year); Halifax International Airport (☎ 902-873-1223; ☘ 9am-9pm); Waterfront (☎ 902-424-4248; 1655 Lower Water St; ☘ 8:30am-8pm Jun-Sep, 8:30am-4:30pm Wed-Sun Oct-May)

SIGHTS
Historic Downtown
CITADEL HILL NATIONAL HISTORIC SITE
Canada's most visited national historic site, the huge **Citadel** (☎ 902-426-5080; off Sackville St;

HALIFAX

0 _____ 500 m
0 _____ 0.3 miles

INFORMATION
Blower's Paper Chase..............1 B4
Book Room............................2 B4
Bookmark..............................3 A5
Halifax Public Library.............4 B5
John W Doull Bookseller.........5 B4
Khyber Digital Media Center..(see 21)
Lawtons Drugs........................6 A5
Main Post Office.....................7 C3
Mountain Equipment Co-op....8 C4
Second Cup...........................9 B5
Venus Envy...........................10 B4
Visitor Information Centre......11 B4
Visitor Information Centre......12 C4

SIGHTS & ACTIVITIES (pp399-403)
Anna Leonowens Gallery.......13 B3
Art Gallery of Nova Scotia.....14 B3
Citadel Hill National Historic
Site....................................15 A4

City Hall...............................16 B3
Government House................17 C5
Halifax Public Gardens..........18 A5
Historic Properties................19 B2
HMCS Sackville.....................20 C3
Khyber Centre for the Arts....21 B4
Maritime Museum of the
Atlantic.............................22 C3
Mary E Black Gallery.............23 B4
Old Burying Ground..............24 C5
Old Town Clock....................25 A3
Pier 21 Centre......................26 D6
Province House.....................27 B3
St Paul's Church...................28 B3

SLEEPING (pp404-5)
Garden Inn B&B....................29 A6
Halliburton House Inn...........30 C5
HI Halifax Heritage House
Hostel...............................31 C6

Lord Nelson Hotel.................32 A5
Waverley Inn........................33 C6

EATING (pp405-6)
Bluenose II Restaurant..........34 B3
Café C'est Si Bon..................35 B3
Chives Bistro........................36 C4
Dharma Sushi.......................37 B4
Dio Mio Gelato.....................38 A5
Elephant's Eye Decor & Café.39 B3
Harbourside Market..............40 C2
Il Mercato............................41 A5
Mediteraneo Café.................42 C3
Old Triangle Irish Alehouse...43 C3
Ray's Falafal.........................44 B3
Rogue's Roost......................45 B5
Salty's.................................46 C2
Satisfaction Feast.................47 B4
Thirsty Duck Pub & Eatery....48 B5
Tribeca...............................49 B4

DRINKING (p406)
Argyle Bar & Grill..................50 B4
Dome..................................51 B3
Economy Shoe Shop.............52 B4
Henry House........................53 C6
Liquor Store.........................54 A6
Lower Deck..........................55 B2
Reflections Cabaret...............56 B4
Split Crow...........................57 B3
Trident Booksellers & Café....58 C6

ENTERTAINMENT (pp406-7)
Bearly's Bar & Grill................59 C6
Ginger's Tavern.....................60 B4
Halifax Metro Centre.............61 B3
Khyber Club.....................(see 21)
Neptune Theatre..................62 B4
Park Lane Cinemas................63 A5
St Matthew's United Church...64 C5

SHOPPING (p407)
Fireworks Gallery..................65 B4
Halifax Farmers Brewery
Market..............................66 C4

TRANSPORT (pp407-8)
Acadian Lines......................67 D6
Enterprise Rent-a-Car......(see 67)
Halifax Ferry Terminal...........68 C3

OTHER
Bluenose II...........................69 C3
Cable Wharf.........................70 C3
Impark.................................71 C6
Metro-Park...........................72 C4
Murphy's Company Store.......73 B3
Murphy's on the Water......(see 70)
Police Headquarters..............74 A3
Westin Hotel.........................75 D6

NOVA SCOTIA

To MacDonald
Bridge (1km);
Dartmouth (2km);
Airport (40km)

To St. George's
Round Church
(200m); Cornwallis
St. Baptist
Church (250m);
Little Dutch
Church (600m)

To Discount Car Rentals;
Club NRG; Club Vortex;
Mobey's Eatery;
Highlife Café (200m);
Marquee (200m); Halifax
Backpacker's Hostel (500m);
Fresh Start B&B (1.4km);
Maritime Command
Museum (1.4km);
Hydrstone Market (2km)

Scotia
Square Mall

Ferry to
Dartmouth

Ferry to
Woodside

Waterfront Boardwalk

To Museum of Natural
History; Halifax
Infirmary (200m)

To Family
Focus (500m)

To Point Pleasant
Park (750m)

Victoria
Park

To McNab's
Island (2.5km)

Cornwallis
Park

Train
Station

adult/child/senior/family $9/4.50/7.75/22.50 Jun-Aug, 30% discount May & mid-Sep–early Nov; ⊙ 9am-6pm Jul & Aug, 9am-5pm rest of year) is an oddly angled fort on top of Halifax's big central hill. Construction began in 1749 with the founding of Halifax; this version of the Citadel is the fourth, built from 1818 to 1861. Guided tours explain the fort's shape and history. The grounds inside the fort are open year-round, with free admission when the exhibits are closed.

KHYBER CENTRE FOR THE ARTS

This historic building was saved from demolition by community activists and converted into an artist-run **center** (☎ 902-422-9668; www.khyberarts.ns.ca; 1588 Barrington St; admission free; ⊙ 11am-5pm Tue, Wed, Fri & Sat, 11am-10pm Thu) with several galleries. There's also a digital media center (p399) and an entertainment venue (see Khyber Club, p406). It's a great place to touch base with emerging artists.

OTHER SIGHTS

At the corner of Barrington and Bishop, **Government House** has been the residence of the provincial lieutenant governor since 1807, when it was built for Governor John Wentworth. It's currently not open to the public. Across the street, the **Old Burying Ground** is the final resting place of some 12,000 people buried between 1749 and 1843. A display points out graves of historical significance.

After Charles Dickens visited the Nova Scotia legislature in 1842, he wrote 'it was like looking at Westminster through the wrong end of a telescope.' **Province House** (☎ 902-424-4661; 1726 Hollis St; guided tours free; ⊙ 9am-4pm Mon-Fri Sep-Jun, 9am-5pm Mon-Fri, 10am-4pm Sat & Sun Jul & Aug), which is a fine example of Georgian architecture, was the first legislature in a British colony to win local self-government.

The provincial **Art Gallery of Nova Scotia** (☎ 902-424-7542; www.agns.gov.ns.ca; 1723 Hollis St; adult/child 6-17 yrs/student/family $10/2/4/20, by donation 5-9pm Thu; ⊙ 10am-5pm Fri-Wed, 10am-9pm Thu) is housed in the impressive Dominion Building (c 1868), once used as the post office. Free tours are given at 2pm Sunday year-round, daily during July and August.

Off the pedestrian area on Granville St, the **Anna Leonowens Gallery** (☎ 902-494-8184; 1891 Granville St; admission free; ⊙ 11am-5pm Tue-Fri, noon-4pm Sat, show openings 5:30-7:30pm Mon) shows work by students and faculty of the Nova Scotia College of Art & Design, which occupies much of the Historic Properties. The gallery is named for the founder of the college, who was immortalized in *The King and I* for her relationship with the King of Siam.

Established in 1749 with the founding of Halifax, Anglican **St Paul's Church** (☎ 902-429-2240; 1749 Argyle St; admission free; ⊙ 9am-4pm Mon-Fri) once served parishioners from Newfoundland to Ontario. Designed by James Gibbs, a student of Sir Christopher Wren, it resembles St Peter's Church in London. Across the square, Halifax's **City Hall** is a true gem of Victorian architecture.

Mary E Black Gallery (☎ 902-424-4062; www.craft-design.gov.ns.ca; 1683 Barrington St; admission free; ⊙ 10am-9pm Mon-Thu, 10am-4pm Fri, 9am-5pm Sat & Sun), in the Nova Scotia Centre for Craft & Design, has changing exhibits by Nova Scotian craftspeople.

At the top of George St, at Citadel Hill, the **Old Town Clock** has been keeping time for 200 years. The inner workings arrived in Halifax in 1803 after being ordered by Prince Edward, the Duke of Kent.

Waterfront Boardwalk

HISTORIC PROPERTIES

The Historic Properties is a group of restored buildings at 1869 Upper Water St built between 1800 and 1905. Originally designed as huge warehouses for easy storage of goods and cargo, they now house shops, boutiques, restaurants and bars and are connected by the waterfront boardwalks. Artisans, merchants and buskers do business around the buildings in the summer.

The 1814 **Privateer's Warehouse** is the area's oldest stone building. The privateers were government-sanctioned and -sponsored pirates who stored their booty here. Among the other vintage buildings are the wooden **Old Red Store** – once used for shipping operations and as a sail loft – and **Simon's Warehouse**, built in 1854.

MARITIME MUSEUM OF THE ATLANTIC

Part of this impressive waterfront **museum** (☎ 902-424-7490; http://museum.gov.ns.ca/mma; 1675 Lower Water St; adult/child 6-17 yrs/senior/family $8/4/7/21, ½price Nov-Apr; ⊙ 9:30am-5:30pm Wed-Mon, to 8pm Tue Jun-Sep, 9:30am-5:30pm Mon & Wed-Sat, to 8pm Tue,

1-5:30pm Sun May & Oct, 9:30am-5pm Wed-Sat, to 8pm Tue, 1-5pm Sun Nov-Apr) was a chandlery, where all the gear needed to outfit a vessel was sold. You can smell the charred ropes, cured to protect them from saltwater, and try pumping a hand-operated foghorn. There's a wildly popular display on the *Titanic* and another on the Halifax Explosion. The 3-D film about the *Titanic* costs $3.50. Outside at the dock you can explore the CSS *Acadia*, a retired hydrographic vessel from England.

The last WWII corvette **HMCS Sackville** (adult/child $3/2; ☉ 10am-5pm Jun-Sep) is docked nearby and staffed by the Canadian Navy.

PIER 21 CENTRE

Pier 21 was to Canada what Ellis Island was to the USA. Between 1928 and 1971 over a million immigrants entered Canada through Pier 21. Their stories and the historical context that led them to abandon their homelands are presented in this **museum** (☎ 902-425-7770; http://pier21.ns.ca; 1055 Marginal Rd; adult/child/student/family $7.75/4.30/5.50/18; ☉ 9:30am-5:30pm May-Nov, 10am-5pm Tue-Fri, noon-5pm Sat Dec-Mar). Researchers fanned out across Canada to get first-hand testimonials from immigrants who passed through Pier 21. These moving videos are shown in screening rooms off a railcar; don't miss it – and bring your hanky.

North End

The North End has been a distinct neighborhood for almost as long as Halifax has existed. The town center was still within palisades in the early 1750s when the 'North Suburbs' became popular because of its larger building lots.

The Admiral of the British navy for all of North America was based in Halifax until 1819 and threw grand parties at Admiralty House, now the **Maritime Command Museum** (☎ 902-427-0550 ext 6725; 2725 Gottingen St; admission free; ☉ 9:30am-3:30pm Mon-Fri). Apart from the beautiful Georgian architecture, the museum is worth a visit for its eclectic collections: cigarette lighters, silverware and ships' bells, to name a few. One notable bell is a cracked specimen from the victorious *Shannon*, which took the USS *Chesapeake* in a famous skirmish of the War of 1812.

St George's Round Church (☎ 902-423-1059; http://collections.ic.gc.ca/churchandcommunity; 2222 Brunswick St), built in 1800 according to the design specifications of the Duke of Kent,

included separate seating areas for naval and civilian congregants. A rare circular Palladian church with a main rotunda 18m in diameter, it was damaged by fire in 1994. Tours are by arrangement. Tours of the 1756 **Little Dutch Church** (2405 Brunswick St), the second-oldest building in Halifax, can also be arranged through St George's. The **Cornwallis St Baptist Church** (5457 Cornwallis St) has been serving African Nova Scotians since the 1830s. Walk by on Sunday morning and hear the gospel music overflow its walls.

Halifax Public Gardens

At the corner of Spring Garden Rd and South Park St, these are considered the finest Victorian city gardens in North America. Walloped by Hurricane Juan (see the boxed text below), there's still an abundance of trees and flowerbeds. Oldies bands perform off-key concerts in the gazebo on Sunday afternoons in summer, tai chi practitioners go through their paces, and anyone who brings checkers can play on outside tables.

Point Pleasant Park

Some 39km of nature trails, picnic spots and the **Prince of Wales Martello Tower** – a round 18th-century defensive structure – are all found within this 75-hectare sanctuary. Trails around the perimeter of the park offer views of McNabs Island, the open ocean and the North West Arm. Bus No 9 along Barrington St goes to Point Pleasant, and there's ample free parking off Point Pleasant Dr.

HURRICANE JUAN

Haligonians didn't really believe the weather forecast on September 28, 2003. Despite hurricane warnings, many put their garbage out on the curb as usual or walked down to the waterfront to see the big waves. But Hurricane Juan hit Halifax with a vengeance, toppling hundreds of the stately, mature trees that line Halifax streets and killing two people. Enormous root systems lifted up sidewalks. Thousands spent the next week without power, some without water. The hurricane traced a path across Nova Scotia, exiting near Tatamagouche en route to Prince Edward Island. In Point Pleasant Park, Hurricane Juan destroyed 57,000 trees, or 70% of the total.

McNabs Island

This 400-hectare island in Halifax harbor has dunes, beaches, 30km of roads and trails, and abandoned military fortifications. Trails are maintained by a volunteer group which also offers information (see www.mcnabsisland.ca). Staff of the **McNabs Island Ferry** (☎ 902-465-4563; http://mcnabsisland .com; Government Wharf; round-trip ticket adult/senior & child $10/8; ☒ 24hr) will provide you with a map and an orientation to the island, plus firewood ($5) if you want to camp. The ferry runs from Fisherman's Cove in Eastern Passage, a short drive through Dartmouth. When the ferry staff are not too busy, they'll pick you up in Halifax for the same fare. Another option is the **harbor taxi** (☎ 902-830-3181; round-trip fare for up to 8 people $60), based at Cable Wharf.

Dartmouth

Founded in 1750, one year after Halifax, Dartmouth is Halifax's counterpart just across the harbor. It is more residential than Halifax, and the downtown area lacks the capital's charm and bustle.

However, Dartmouth does make for a cheap harbor cruise via the ferry, the oldest saltwater ferry system in North America, dating back to a 1752 rowboat. Alderney Gate houses the ferry terminal, the Dartmouth public library and Eastern Front Theatre (p407).

Dartmouth Heritage Museum (☎ 902-464-2300; www.dartmouthheritagemuseum.ns.ca; 26 Newcastle St; admission $2; ☒ 10am-5pm Tue-Sun mid-Jun–Aug, 1:30-5pm Wed-Sat Sep–mid-Jun) displays an eclectic collection in **Evergreen House**, the former home of folklorist Helen Creighton (who traversed the province in the early 20th century recording stories and songs). Tickets include admission on the same day to the 1786 **Quaker House** (59 Ochterloney St; ☒ 10am-5pm Tue-Sun Jun-Aug), the oldest house in the Halifax area, which was built by Quaker whalers from Nantucket who fled the American Revolution. Guides in costume lead visitors around the house, and there's a children's dress-up box.

ACTIVITIES
Cycling

Cycling is a great way to see sites on the outskirts of Halifax – you can take bikes on the ferries to Dartmouth or cycle over the MacDonald Bridge. **Velo Bicycle Club** (www.velo halifax.ca) organizes several rides each week; see the website.

Pedal & Sea Adventures (☎ 902-857-9319, 877-772-5699; www.pedalandseaadventures.com; per day/week incl tax $30/130) will deliver the bike to you, complete with helmet, lock and repair kit. They also lead good-value tours; one-/two-day trips including taxes and meals cost $95/225.

Hiking

There are both short and long hikes within the city, many accessible by public transit. See www.novatrails.com for detailed trail descriptions and directions to trailheads. There's also hiking in Point Pleasant Park (p402) and on McNabs Island (p403).

Kayaking

Ideally you'll do this further away from polluted Halifax harbor. But if you can't wait to get on the ocean, try **Sea Sun Kayak Adventures** (☎ 902-471-2732; www.paddlenovascotia.com; St Mary's Boat Club, 1741 Fairfield Rd, off Jubilee Rd), which offers enjoyable day-long tours ($75) of sites along the sheltered North West Arm. They also have a second location in Terrence Bay, a short drive from Halifax, that rents kayaks (half-/full day $35/50) and offers a range of other trips. Their 'Kayak Bus' will pick up paddlers.

HALIFAX FOR CHILDREN

Dartmouth Sportsplex (☎ 902-460-2600; www.dart mouthsportsplex.com; 110 Wyse Rd; ☒ 5:30am-10:30pm Mon-Fri, 6am-9pm Sat, 9am-10:30pm Sun, extended hrs Sep-Jun) A warm-water pool. Pirate's Cove (for children at least 1.22m tall) has three waterslides; call or check the website for opening hours.

Harbour Hopper Tours (☎ 902-490-8687; 55min tours adult/child under 7/child 8-15 yrs/family $23/8/14/66) Tours on the *Lark 5*, a seaworthy tour bus, cover the sights on land and water, leaving near Cable Wharf at the bottom of Prince St.

Museum of Natural History (☎ 902-424-7353; http://museum.gov.ns.ca/mnh; 1747 Summer St; adult/family $5/15 mid-Jun–mid-Oct, $3/9 late Oct–early Jun, free 5-8pm Wed year-round; ☒ 9:30am-5pm Mon-Sat, to 8pm Wed, 1-5pm Sun, to 5:30pm Thu-Tue Jun–mid-Oct) Daily summer programs introduce children to Gus the toad and demonstrate the cooking of bugs. Exhibits on history and the natural world will keep parents engaged, too. It's just a couple of blocks north of Spring Garden Rd or west of Citadel Hill.

TOURS

Murphy's on the Water (☎ 902-420-1015; 1751 Lower Water St) runs a range of tours on Halifax harbor, from two-hour tours to dinner cruises, including the popular Harbour Hopper Tours (see p403) and Halifax to Peggy's Cove ($70 including lunch). **Murphy's Company Store** (☎ 902-422-8972; 1903 Barrington St), off the Granville St pedestrian area, also sells tickets.

There are several other options on sea and land:

Bluenose II (☎ 902-634-1963, 800-763-1963; www .bluenose2.ns.ca; Lower Water St, near Maritime Museum; adult/child 3-12 yrs $20/10) This replica of the famous two-masted racing schooner, the *Bluenose*, seen on the back of Canada's 10¢ coin, runs harbor tours when it's in town.

Halifax Ghost Walk (☎ 902-466-1323; macrev@ns .sympatico.ca; adult/concession $8/5; 🕗 8pm) Two hours of pirate tales and ghost stories as you're guided from the Old Town Clock to the docks. Contact a VIC for details.

Salty Bear Adventure Tours (p875) A sociable budget alternative for touring the province.

FESTIVALS & EVENTS

Nova Scotia Multicultural Festival (www.mans.ns.ca; 🕗 late Jun) This weekend festival on the Dartmouth waterfront celebrates diversity with great performances and even better food.

Nova Scotia Tattoo (www.nstattoo.ca; 🕗 early Jul) Vast formations of Scottish bagpipers on parade.

Atlantic Jazz Festival (www.jazzeast.com; 🕗 mid-Jul) A full week of free outdoor jazz concerts each afternoon, and evening performances ranging from world music to classic jazz trios (tickets $15-30). Check out volunteering opportunities.

alFresco Film Festo (☎ 902-420-4528; www.atlantic film.com; waterfront boardwalk at Terminal Rd; tickets $5; 🕗 9pm Fri & Sat Jul & Aug) Presented by the Atlantic Film Festival, hundreds of film-lovers bring deck chairs and blankets to watch classic films projected onto a painted screen on a waterfront building. Come early to snag the limited seating.

Halifax International Busker Festival (www .buskers.ca; 🕗 early Aug) Comics, mimics, daredevils and musicians perform for waterfront crowds.

Atlantic Film Festival (www.atlanticfilm.com; tickets $9.50-15; 🕗 Sep) A week and a half of great flicks.

Grou Tyme Acadian Festival (www.groutyme.com; per day $5; 🕗 3rd week of Sep) Free Acadian entertainment from as far away as Louisiana.

SLEEPING
Budget

HI Halifax Heritage House Hostel (☎ 902-422-3863; www.hihostels.ca; 1253 Barrington St; member/nonmember dm $19/24, r $50/57; 🕗 check-in 2pm-midnight) This downtown HI hostel in a fine historic house has friendly staff and a spacious common kitchen. The 65 beds fill up in the summer; reserve ahead.

Halifax Backpackers Hostel (☎ 902-431-3170, 888-431-3170; www.halifaxbackpackers.com; 2193 Gottingen St; dm/d/f $20/50/65; P) This 36-bed North End hostel is bright, well run and has a common kitchen. Co-ed dorms hold no more than six beds. The storefront café is a community gathering-spot. Many city buses stop right in front, but solo female travelers may not like coming home at night to this rough-edged neighborhood.

Caroline's B&B (☎ 902-469-4665; 134 Victoria Rd; s/d $40/50; 🕗 Apr-Dec) This Dartmouth B&B is an economical alternative to staying in Halifax and it's close to both bus routes and the ferry. Three rooms share two bathrooms.

Shubie Campground (☎ 902-435-8328, 800-440-8450; www.shubiecampground.com; Jaybee Dr, off Waverley Rd) This privately run, municipality-owned Dartmouth campground is the only one accessible from Halifax on public transportation. A grassy field with little shade, facilities include showers and a laundromat.

Mid-Range

Garden Inn B&B (☎ 902-492-8577, 877-414-8577; www.gardeninn.ns.ca; 1263 South Park St; d/tw incl breakfast $110/120; P $6) This 1875 Victorian house has 23 air-conditioned rooms, two of which are wheelchair-accessible. A short walk from

> **THE AUTHOR'S CHOICE**
>
> **Halliburton House Inn** (☎ 902-420-0658; www.halliburton.ns.ca; 5184 Morris St; r incl breakfast $125-180; P) The first chief justice of Nova Scotia once lived in one of the three stately homes that make up this unique inn in a prime downtown location. Some of the smallest – and least expensive – rooms have balconies overlooking the garden patio. Service is excellent.

downtown, it backs onto an atmospheric graveyard. The self-serve breakfast has freshly baked goods.

Fresh Start B&B (☎ 902-453-6616, 888-453-6616; http://bbcanada.com/2262.html; 2720 Gottingen St; r incl breakfast $95; P ⌨) This beautifully restored, gay-friendly Victorian B&B is in a quiet part of the North End. Seven twin or queen-bed rooms all have shared bathrooms.

Waverley Inn (☎ 902-423-9346, 800-565-9346; www.waverleyinn.com; 1266 Barrington St; d incl breakfast $115-170; P ⌨) The 32 rooms at this slightly threadbare historic inn retain their mid-19th century charm.

Top End

Lord Nelson Hotel (☎ 902-423-5130, 800-565-2020; www.lordnelsonhotel.com; 1515 South Park St; d $155-235; P $12.50) This elegant 1920s hotel is across from Halifax Public Gardens. Off-season, a standard double room is $99. Use the in-house fitness center, or there are free passes to the YMCA next door.

EATING

Bars and pubs also serve food (see p406). Kitchens close around 10pm.

Budget

Ray's Falafel (☎ 902-492-0233; Scotia Square Mall, cnr Barrington & Duke Sts; meals $4-5; ⌚ 8am-6pm Mon-Wed, 8am-9pm Thu & Fri, 9am-6pm Sat) Ray's has been voted the best falafel in Halifax for 10 years running by readers of the *Coast*.

Bluenose II Restaurant (☎ 902-425-5092; 1824 Hollis St; meals $6-8; ⌚ 7am-10pm Mon-Fri, 8am-10pm Sat & Sun) The menu at this classic, busy diner ranges from Greek and Italian to full lobster dinners, and beer's on tap.

Medic Café (☎ 902-423-4403; 1571 Barrington St; meals $7-10; ⌚ 7am-9pm Sun-Thu, 7am-9pm Fri & Sat) Mediterranean entrées are served with

tabouli and hummus, along with seafood and sandwiches; there are breakfasts for $5 too.

Queen of Cups Teahouse (☎ 902-463-1983; 44 Ochterloney St; lunch $5-8, ⌚ 10am-5pm Mon-Sat, 11am-3pm Sun) Opposite Quaker Whaler House in Dartmouth, this teahouse has good healthy lunches of soup, salad or a sandwich, or try a lobster crepe ($12). Formal afternoon tea is arranged with 24-hour notice; call ahead for a tarot ($60) or tea-leaf ($20) reading.

Mid-Range

Harbourside Market (Historic Properties, 1869 Upper Water St; meals $9-12; ⌚ 7am-9pm Mon-Thu, 7am-10pm Fri, 7:30am-10pm Sat, 7:30am-9pm Sun) The nicest food court ever. Six separate cafeteria-style restaurants serve freshly made food from pizzas to seafood. Enjoy your meal on a deck overlooking the harbor. A brewpub offers a selection of lagers and ales.

Elephant's Eye Decor & Café (☎ 902-420-1225; 1727 Barrington St; meals $11-13; ⌚ 9:30am-5pm Mon-Wed, 9:30am-9pm Thu-Sat) This understated little gem offers a soup, crepe or vegetarian entree of the day, and a seafood dish of the day. The tea biscuits are perfect with butter and jam.

Il Mercato (☎ 902-422-2866; 5650 Spring Garden Rd; mains $10-20; ⌚ 11am-11pm) This long-standing Italian favorite doesn't take reservations; come early or late on weekends, or wait a short while.

Rogue's Roost (☎ 902-492-2337; 5435 Spring Garden Rd; mains $7-12; ⌚ 11am-1am Mon-Sat, noon-midnight Sun) This brewpub has oven-baked wraps that make for sizable, tasty meals.

Café C'est Si Bon (☎ 902-425-5799; 1717 Barrington St; lunch mains $7-9, dinner mains $10-15; ⌚ 7am-11pm Sun-Tue, to 2am Wed-Sat) This relaxed, pleasant café features local art and a menu of seafood, filled crepes and pastas. It's very popular for weekend brunch. There's often live music.

Old Triangle Irish Alehouse (☎ 902-492-4900; 5136 Prince St; mains $16-21; ⌚ 11am-midnight) This comfortable pub has veggie burgers and ploughman's lunches. Items on the kids' menu are $4.50; it's kids-free after 8pm.

Other recommendations:

Dharma Sushi (☎ 902-425-7785; 1576 Argyle St; meals $9-16; ⌚ lunch Mon-Fri, dinner Mon-Sat) The best of Halifax's many sushi restaurants.

Highlife Café (☎ 902-422-7050; 2011 Gottingen St; mains $10-17; ⌚ 11:30am-8:30pm Tue-Fri, 5-10pm Sat & Sun) Music, decor and flavors straight out of Ghana, just five minutes' walk north from Citadel Hill.

NOVA SCOTIA

THE AUTHOR'S CHOICE

Dío Mío Gelato (☎ 902-492-3467; 5670 Spring Garden Rd; meals $5-8; ☼ 8am-10pm Mon-Fri, noon-10pm Sat & Sun) Italian ice cream and fruit ices are concocted from all-natural ingredients, and nearby Halifax Public Gardens is the perfect place to enjoy them. For lunch, choose from three different veggie burgers or the healthy and flavorful salads and sandwiches.

Satisfaction Feast (☎ 902-422-3540; 1581 Grafton St; mains $9-15; ☼ lunch & dinner) Vegan and vegetarian dishes.

Thirsty Duck Pub & Eatery (☎ 902-422-1548; 5470 Spring Garden Rd; mains $7-14; ☼ 11am-midnight) Pub food tastes great when the sun is out and you're sitting on the roof.

Top End

Chives Bistro (☎ 902-420-9636; 1537 Barrington St; mains $17-26; ☼ dinner Mon-Sat) Chives stakes its reputation on seasonal, local ingredients. Enjoy sumptuous squash soups, grain-fed chicken and desserts with wild blueberries.

Salty's (☎ 902-423-6818; 1869 Upper Water St; lunch mains $10-16, dinner mains $20-26; ☼ lunch & dinner) So close to the water, part of this classy restaurant was washed away during Hurricane Juan. Now the ocean figures only on the plate with dishes such as blackened halibut and grilled salmon. The chowder is considered the best in Halifax.

Tribeca (☎ 902-492-4036; 1588 Granville St; tapas $8-15, mains $20-25; ☼ lunch & dinner) Tribeca appeals to a hip Halifax crowd with its exposed walls and black booths. Enjoy tasty tapas in the cozy bar.

DRINKING

Halifax rivals St John's, Newfoundland, for the most drinking holes per capita. The biggest concentration of attractive bars is on Argyle St, where temporary streetside patios expand the sidewalk each summer. Pubs and bars close at 12:30am, a few hours earlier on Sunday. The downtown **liquor store** (☎ 902-423-6716; 5440 Clyde St; ☼ 10am-10pm Mon-Thu, 10am-11pm Fri & Sat) is closed altogether on Sunday.

Economy Shoe Shop (☎ 902-423-8845; 1663 Argyle St) This has been the 'it' place to drink and people-watch in Halifax for almost a decade. On weekend nights actors and

journalists figure heavily in the crush. It's a pleasant place for afternoon drinks. The kitchen dishes out tapas ($6 to $10) until last call at 1:45am.

Henry House (☎ 902-423-5660; 1222 Barrington St) The most atmospheric pub in town is close to inns and hostels in the southern end of downtown. The basement is inviting and dark.

Argyle Bar & Grill (☎ 902-492-8844; 1575 Argyle St) The Argyle comes into its own each too-short summer, when the rooftop patio attracts a crowd for daiquiris.

Trident Booksellers & Café (☎ 902-423-7100; 1256 Hollis St; ☼ 8am-5pm Mon-Fri, 8:30am-5pm Sat, 11am-5pm Sun) This sedate café is the place to linger with your journal or novel.

Other recommendations:

Dome (☎ 902-422-5453; 1740 Argyle St) Dubbed the 'Liquordome,' with four establishments under one roof. 'The Attic' has live music; the others are nightclubs open until 3am.

Lower Deck (☎ 902-425-1501; Historic Properties, 1869 Upper Water St; cover $3) The broad plank tables are made for slamming pints on.

Reflections Cabaret (☎ 902-422-2957; 5184 Sackville St) A mainly gay disco that attracts a mixed crowd. It opens at 4pm, but the action really starts after 10pm and it stays open until 3am.

Split Crow (☎ 902-422-4366; 1855 Granville St) This drinking hole's history goes back as far as Halifax itself.

ENTERTAINMENT

Check out the *Coast* to see what's on.

Live Music

Halifax's music scene began in the mid-1990s when Nirvana's label signed local band Sloan. Halifax was declared the 'new Seattle' and everyone wore flannel. Since then, the town's live music scene has diversified, with folk, hip-hop, alternative country and rock gigs every weekend. The **Khyber Club** (membership $10, weekend cover $6; ☼ 5pm-1am Tue-Fri, 8pm-1am Sat), on the 1st floor of the Khyber Centre for the Arts (p401), is a happening venue with spoken word on Tuesday, hip-hop on Wednesday and pop, rock or folk musicians on weekends.

Marquee (☎ 902-429-3020; 2037 Gottingen St; cover $6-25) This is the choice venue for touring bands and big-name locals; shows start around 10:30pm. Up-and-coming musicians play downstairs in Hell's Kitchen. Admission to the Marquee gets you into Hell's Kitchen, but not vice versa.

Ginger's Tavern (☎ 902-425-5020; 1662 Barrington St; cover $5) This mellow venue showcases folk and alternative country acts.

Bearly's Bar & Grill (☎ 902-423-2526; 1269 Barrington St; cover $3) The best blues musicians in Atlantic Canada play here at incredibly low cover charges. Wednesday karaoke nights draw a crowd and some fine singers.

St Matthew's United Church (1479 Barrington St) This downtown church often hosts classical concerts. Prices are listed in the *Coast*.

Theater

The two professional theaters in Halifax – Neptune Theatre and Eastern Front Theatre – take a break in summer, with their last shows typically playing in May. However, Shakespeare by the Sea provides diversion through the summer.

Neptune Theatre (☎ 902-429-7070; www.neptune theatre.com; 1593 Argyle St) This downtown theater presents musicals and well-known plays on its main stage ($37), and edgier stuff in the studio ($20).

Eastern Front Theatre (☎ 902-463-7529; www .easternfront.ns.ca; Alderney Gate; tickets $20-25) In Dartmouth, Eastern Front debuts several works by Atlantic playwrights each year.

Shakespeare by the Sea (☎ 902-422-0295; www .shakespearebythesea.ca; Point Pleasant Park; suggested donation $10; ☻ Jun-Sep) Fine performances of the Bard's works at the Cambridge Battery, an old fortification, in the middle of the park. Check the website for a map and details.

Film

Park Lane Cinemas (☎ 902-423-4598; Park Lane Mall, Spring Garden Rd & Dresden Row) Hollywood flicks and occasional screenings of independent films.

Sports

Halifax Mooseheads junior hockey team plays at **Halifax Metro Centre** (☎ 902-451-1221; 5284 Duke St; tickets $13.50).

SHOPPING

Halifax Farmers' Brewery Market (☎ 902-492-4043; 1496 Lower Water St; ☻ 8am-1pm Sat Jan-May, 7am-1pm Sat May-Dec) North America's oldest farmers' market, in the 1820s Keith's Brewery Building, is the ultimate shopping experience. Head here to people-watch and buy organic produce, jewelry, clothes and crafts. Come early or late to avoid the crowds.

Fireworks Gallery (☎ 902-420-1735; 1569 Barrington St; ☻ 10am-5:30pm Mon-Thu & Sat, 10am-8pm Fri) Beautiful jewelry by resident goldsmiths is for sale; other pieces by artisans from across the Maritimes are on display. Prices vary widely.

Hydrostone Market (5515-47 Young St; ☻ 10am-6pm Tue-Fri, 10am-5pm Sat, noon-5pm Sun) was part of the reconstruction effort following the Halifax Explosion. The quaint row of shops, cafés and restaurants includes the **Bogside Gallery** (☎ 902-453-3063; ☻ 10am-6pm Mon, Tue & Fri, 10am-8pm Wed & Thu, 10am-5pm Sat, noon-5pm Sun), featuring fine crafts from Atlantic Canada.

GETTING THERE & AWAY

Air

Air Canada, Canjet, Westjet and Jetsgo all have multiple flights daily between Halifax and major Canadian cities such as Toronto ($450, 2½ hours), Montréal ($400, 1½ hours) and Ottawa ($400, 1¾ hours). Air Canada also flies between Halifax and other Maritime destinations (Saint John $500, 45 minutes, four times daily; Moncton $500, 40 minutes, four times daily) and to Boston ($700, 2¼ hours, twice daily). In summer, there's a daily flight to London ($900, 7¼ hours) via Saint John's, Newfoundland. All prices vary widely depending on sales and how far in advance the ticket is purchased. See p869 for information.

Bus

Acadian Lines (☎ 902-454-9321; www.acadianbus .com; 1161 Hollis St) terminal is at the VIA Rail station next to the Westin Hotel. Its buses travel daily to Truro and Amherst and connect to Montréal and New York. It also goes to Digby ($40, four hours), with stops throughout the Annapolis Valley, and to Sydney ($62, 6½ hours) stopping in Antigonish ($35, 3½ hours).

DRL (☎ 902-450-1987, 877-450-1987; www.drlgroup .com) serves all stops on the South Shore. The 4½-hour trip from Halifax to Yarmouth is $50.

Shuttle

Private shuttle buses compete with the major bus companies. They usually pick you up and drop you off and, with fewer stops, they also travel faster. The slight trade-off is a more cramped ride. **Cloud Nine Shuttle** (☎ 902-742-3992, 888-805-3335; www .thecloudnineshuttle.com) goes to Yarmouth ($50,

3½ hours), stopping along the South Shore each afternoon, returning to the Halifax area each morning. Airport pickup or drop-off is an extra $5. **Campbell's Shuttle Service** (☎ 800-742-6101; www.campbell-shuttle-service.com) charges $48 per person (per bicycle $5) to Yarmouth, as does **Amero's Shuttle** (☎ 888-283-2222; www.ameroshuttle.com), which travels through the Annapolis Valley; book several days ahead. **Try Town Transit** (☎ 877-521-0855, 902-521-0855) goes to Mahone Bay ($22, 50 minutes) and Lunenburg ($23, one hour).

Scotia Shuttle (☎ 902-435-9686, 800-898-5883; www.atyp.com/scotiashuttle) travels to Sydney on Cape Breton Island ($50, five hours, twice daily). MacLeod's Shuttle (☎ 902-539-2700, 800-471-7775) does this route once a day. **Inverness Shuttle Service** (☎ 902-945-2000, 888-826-2477) travels between Halifax and Inverness, Cape Breton Island (adult/student $40/35) every day but Saturday.

PEI Express Shuttle (☎ 902-462-8177, 877-877-1771; www.peishuttle.com) and **Go-Van** (☎ 866-463-9660) both charge $50 per person to Charlottetown, PEI, with early morning pickups; Go-Van charges $15 per bicycle. **Advanced Shuttle** (☎ 877-886-3322, 902-886-3322) and **Square One Shuttle** (☎ 902-436-3830, 877-675-3830; www.square1shuttle.ca) leave Halifax in the afternoon for Charlottetown; Advance Shuttle charges $10 per bicycle.

Train

One of the few examples of monumental Canadian train station architecture left in the Maritimes is found at 1161 Hollis St. Options with VIA Rail include overnight service to Montréal (one-week advance purchase adult/child two to 11 years $121/60, 20 hours, daily except Tuesdays).

GETTING AROUND
To/From the Airport

Halifax International Airport is 40km northeast of town on Hwy 102 toward Truro. **Airbus** (☎ 902-873-2091; one-way/return $12/20) runs between 5am and 11pm and picks up at major hotels. **Share-A-Cab** (☎ 902-429-5555, 800-565-8669; one-way $24) must be booked a day ahead. A taxi to or from the airport costs $38 to $44.

Car & Motorcycle

Pedestrians almost always have the right-of-way in Halifax. Watch out for cars stopping suddenly!

Outside the downtown core, you can usually find free on-street parking for up to two hours. Otherwise, try private **Impark** (1245 Hollis St; per hr/12hr $1/6) or the municipally owned **Metro-Park** (☎ 902-830-1711; 1557 Granville St; per hr/12hr $2/14). Halifax's parking meters are enforced from 8am to 6pm Monday to Friday.

It costs considerably more to rent a car at the airport than in town. All the major national chains (see p873) are represented there and also have offices in Halifax. **Enterprise Rent-a-Car** (☎ 902-492-8400; www.enterprise.com; 1161 Hollis St) has an office in the train station and at several other locations near downtown. It has some of the lowest rates. If you book far ahead, you can get a weekend rental for $10 a day, the best deal around. **Discount Car Rentals** (☎ 902-453-5153; www.discountcar.com; 2710 Agricola St) also has good deals, depending on availability. It's 1.25km north of the northwest corner of Citadel Hill.

Public Transportation

Metro Transit (☎ 902-490-6600; one-way fare $1.75, 20 tickets $30) runs the city bus system and the ferries to Dartmouth. Transfers are free when traveling in one direction within a short time frame. Maps and schedules are available at the ferry terminals and at the information booth in Scotia Square Mall.

Bus No 7 cuts through downtown and North End Halifax via Robie St and Gottingen St, passing both hostels. Bus No 1 travels Spring Garden Rd, Barrington St, and the south part of Gottingen St before crossing the bridge to Dartmouth. 'Fred' is a free city bus that loops around downtown every 30 minutes in the summer.

Taking the ferry to Dartmouth from the Halifax waterfront is a nice way of getting on the water, even if it's just for 12 minutes. Woodside, where another ferry goes in peak periods, is a good place to start a bike ride to Eastern Passage or Lawrencetown.

AROUND HALIFAX
Eastern Shore Beaches

When downtown dwellers venture over the bridge to Dartmouth on a hot summer's day, it's most likely en route to a beach. There are beautiful, long, white-sand beaches all along the Eastern Shore, and several are a reasonable drive from Halifax.

The water never gets very warm, but brave souls venture in for a swim or a surf, particularly if the fog stays offshore.

The closest – and therefore busiest – of the Eastern Shore beaches, **Rainbow Haven**, is 1km long. It has washrooms, showers, a canteen and a boardwalk with wheelchair access to the beach. Lifeguards supervise a sizable swimming area. To get there, take Portland St from downtown Dartmouth through Cole Harbour, where it becomes Cole Harbour Rd/Hwy 207, and turn right on Bissett Rd. Turn left at the end of Bissett Rd and then right at the beach entrance.

The most popular destination for surfers, **Lawrencetown Beach** faces directly south and often gets big waves compliments of hurricanes or tropical storms hundreds of kilometers away. The beach is 25km from Halifax, just a short distance beyond Rainbow Haven. Stay on Hwy 207 which begins to follow the coast after Cole Harbour and leads you right to the beach. It boasts a supervised swimming area, washrooms and a canteen. Rent surf equipment (cash only) from **Dacane Sports** (☎ 902-431-7873; surfboard/bodyboard/wetsuit rental per 24hr $25/15/20). Prebooked hour-long lessons ($69) include equipment rental for a day after the lesson. From the beach, it's just 8km along Crowell Rd to **Porters Lake Provincial Park** (☎ 902-827-2250; http://parks.gov.ns.ca; 1160 Crowell Rd; campsites $18), a campground on a peninsula and small island in Porters Lake, with 158 nicely separated, shady campsites. It's best to reserve for Friday or Saturday nights from mid-July to mid-August.

With more than 3km of white sand, **Martinique** is the longest beach in Nova Scotia. Even if you find the water too cold for a swim, this is a beautiful place to walk, watch birds or play Frisbee. Follow the signs for Hwy 7 from Dartmouth, drive about 40km, and then turn right onto East Petpeswick Rd in Musquodoboit Harbour.

Sambro

Just 18km south of Halifax, **Crystal Crescent Beach** is on the outskirts of the fishing village of Sambro. There are actually three beaches here in distinct coves; the third one out – toward the southwest – is clothing-optional and gay-friendly. An 8.5km **hiking trail** begins just inland and heads through barrens, bogs and boulders to Pennant Point. To get here, take Herring Cove Rd from the roundabout in Halifax all the way to Sambro, then follow the signs.

Prospect

As pretty as Peggy's Cove, Prospect doesn't attract a fraction of the tourist traffic. An undeveloped **trail** starts at the end of Indian Point Rd and leads 3km along the coast past plenty of perfect picnic spots. There's not a lot of room to park at the trailhead, so you may need to leave your vehicle on the roadside into the village.

Peggy's Cove

Canada's best-known fishing village lies 43km west of Halifax on Hwy 333. It dates from 1811 and has just 60 residents. They are literally lost in the crowd during the tourist season – Peggy's Cove is one of the most-visited attractions in the Maritimes. With its impressive granite shore and lighthouse, plus a small picture-perfect cluster of wharves and sheds, its easy to see why Peggy's Cove is a favorite.

It's best to visit before 10am in the summer as tour buses arrive in the middle of the day and create one of the province's worst traffic jams. There's a free parking area with washrooms and a **tourist information office** (☎ 902-823-2253; 109 Peggy's Cove Rd; ☻ 9am-7pm Jul & Aug, 9am-5pm mid-May–Jun, Sep & Oct) on the left as you enter the village. Across the street, the **de-Garthe Gallery** (☎ 902-823-2256; admission $2; ☻ 9am-5pm mid-May–Oct) has paintings by local artist William deGarthe (1907–83), who sculpted the magnificent 30m-high **Fishermen's Monument** into a rock face in front of the gallery.

The **lighthouse** is now a small post office with its own lighthouse-shaped stamp cancellation mark. A poignant **memorial** to those who perished aboard Swissair Flight 111 just offshore is off Hwy 333, about 1.8km north of the turnoff to Peggy's Cove.

Large **Wayside Camping Park** (☎ 902-823-2271; wayside@hfx.eastlink.ca; 10295 Hwy 333, Glen Margaret; tent/RV sites $20/30) is 10km north of Peggy's Cove, and 36km from Halifax, with lots of shady sites up on the hill. It's crowded in midsummer.

Lover's Lane Cottages on the Ocean (☎ 902-823-2670; www3.ns.sympatico.ca/lovers-lane; 8388 Hwy 333; r $65-100; ☻ Jun-Sep) is just 500m north of the Swissair Memorial; cottages are attractive and fully equipped.

Oceanstone Inn & Cottages (☎ 902-823-2160, 866-823-2160; www.oceanstone.ns.ca; 8650 Peggy's Cove Rd, Indian Harbour; r/cottage $85/175; 🖳) are just a short drive from Peggy's Cove, and are its tranquil antithesis. If you have limited time in Nova Scotia, this is a great place to experience one corner of it. Whimsically decorated cottages are a stone's throw from the beach. Guests can use paddleboats to venture to small islands and outcroppings, some with lighthouses. An award-winning **dining room** (mains $20-30; 🕙 dinner Sat & Sun May, Jun & Oct, daily Jul-Sep) offers scrumptious seafood dinners and appetizers (reservations recommended). The inn and cottages are open year-round, with great off-season specials and discounts.

Tea & Treasures (☎ 902-823-1908; 8369 Peggy's Cove Rd; lunch $5-8, dinner mains $8-15; 🕙 8am-6pm Jul-Oct, 8am-4pm May & Jun) offers basic home cooking and local crafts.

SOUTH SHORE

Highlights of this stretch of Nova Scotian coast south of Halifax include colorful, historic architecture in picturesque harbors and some beautiful beaches further south. The first third of the area, closest to Halifax, is cottage country for the city's elite and is quite popular with day-tripping tourists and locals. Highway 3 – labeled the 'Lighthouse Route' by tourism officials – can be slow as a result. Take this scenic route if you're not pressed for time and want to check out antique shops or artisans' wares en route. Travel times can be halved by taking Hwy 103 directly to the closest exit for your destination.

CHESTER

Overlooking Mahone Bay, the old village of Chester was established in 1759. It's had a colorful history as the haunt of pirates and Prohibition-era bathtub-gin smugglers. Over the past several decades, it's become a northern Martha's Vineyard: a choice spot for well-to-do Americans and Haligonians to have a summer home. There's a large **regatta** in the attractive harbor in mid-August.

Information
Tourist Office (☎ 902-275-4616; Hwy 3; 🕙 9am-7pm Jul & Aug, 10am-6pm Jun & Sep, 10am-5pm May & Oct) In the old train depot near the Chester turnoff.

Sights & Activities
A fine example of Georgian architecture from 1806, the **Lordly House Museum** (☎ 902-275-3842; 133 Central St; admission free; 🕙 10am-5pm Tue-Sat, 1-5pm Sun mid-May–mid-Oct) has three period rooms illustrating 19th-century upper-class life and Chester history. The museum is also an artists' studio.

Tancook Island (population 190) is a 45-minute ferry ride (return $5; four runs Monday to Friday, two on weekends; exact schedule at http://freepages.history.rootsweb.com/~tancook/ferry.htm) from Chester's government wharf. Walking trails crisscross the island. Settled by Germans and French Huguenots in the early 19th century, the island is famous for its sauerkraut. The last ferry from Chester each day overnights in Tancook Island.

Sleeping & Eating
Mecklenburgh Inn B&B (☎ 902-275-4638; www.mecklenburghinn.ca; 78 Queen St; s/d incl breakfast with shared bathroom $85/95, with private bathroom $125/135; 🕙 May-Dec) This casual four-room inn, built in 1890, has a breezy 2nd-floor veranda; some rooms have private adjacent balconies, most have private bathrooms.

Graves Island Provincial Park (☎ 902-275-4425; http://parks.gov.ns.ca; 3km northeast of Chester off Hwy 3; campsites $18) An island in Mahone Bay connected by a causeway to the mainland has 64 wooded and open campsites. RVs usually park in the middle of the area, but some shady, isolated tent sites are tucked away on the flanks of the central plateau. Graves Island is very popular in midsummer; it will be full Friday and Saturday nights.

Kiwi Café (☎ 902-275-1492; 19 Pleasant St; light lunches $6-9; 🕙 7:30am-4pm) A New Zealand chef prepares fabulous sandwiches and delicious breakfasts here.

Julien's Pastry Shop Bakery (☎ 902-275-2324; 43 Queen St near Pleasant St; sandwiches $4-5; 🕙 8am-5pm Tue-Sun) Julien's freshly baked French pastries are addictive.

Fo'c'sle Tavern (☎ 902-275-3912; Queen St at Pleasant St; mains $8-11; 🕙 11am-11pm Sun-Thu, to midnight Fri & Sat) This lively pub serves seafood and sandwiches with local sausage ($7.50).

Entertainment
Chester Playhouse (☎ 902-275-3933; www.chesterplayhouse.ns.ca; 22 Pleasant St; tickets about $20) This older theater space has great acoustics for

live performances. Plays or dinner theater are presented most nights, except Mondays, in July and August, with occasional concerts during spring and fall.

MAHONE BAY

Mahone Bay, on a bay with more than 100 islands, is a little piece of eye candy. About 100km from Halifax, it's a great base for exploring this section of the South Shore. There are many pleasant B&Bs and a good selection of restaurants, most on Main St.

Information

Jaberwocky Café & Booktrader (☎ 902-531-3310; 643 Main St; ✆ 10am-8pm Jun-Sep, 11am-5:30pm Thu-Mon Oct-May) Coffee and secondhand books.

Mahone Bay (www.mahonebay.com) Links to restaurants and accommodations.

VIC (☎ 902-624-6151; 165 Edgewater St; ✆ 10am-5pm Sat & Sun May, 9am-6pm Jun & Sep, 9am-7pm Jul & Aug, 10am-5pm Oct). Has walking-tour brochures.

Sights & Activities

In a row along Edgewater St, facing the waterfront, are three historic **churches** belonging to the Anglican, Lutheran and United denominations.

Settlers' Museum & Cultural Centre (☎ 902-624-6263; 578 Main St; admission free; ✆ 10am-5pm Tue-Sat, 1-5pm Sun Jun–mid-Oct) shows exhibits on the settlement of this area by 'Foreign Protestants' in 1754 and local architecture.

Amos Pewter (☎ 800-565-3369; www.amospewter .com; 589 Main St; admission free; ✆ 9am-6:30pm Mon-Sat, 10am-5:30pm Sun Jul & Aug, 9am-5:30pm Mon-Sat, noon-5:30pm Sun May, Jun, Sep & Oct) is both a museum demonstrating the art of pewter-making and a store where wares are sold.

Festivals & Events

On the weekend prior to the first Monday in August, the **Mahone Bay Wooden Boat Festival** (☎ 902-624-0348; www.woodenboatfestival.org) features workshops in boatbuilding and daily races of small craft.

Sleeping & Eating

Kip & Kaboodle Backpackers Hostel (☎ 902-531-5494, 866-549-4522; www.kiwikaboodle.com; Hwy 3; dm incl breakfast $25) This new hostel, 3km from the attractions of Mahone Bay's Main St and 7km from Lunenburg, has nine beds, an outdoor pool, and a superior location. Owners offer town pickup.

Red Door B&B (☎ 902-624-8479; www.bbcanada .com/7052.html; 381 Main St; s/d $70/80) This simple home is in a quiet location across from the liquor store, about 500m from the waterfront.

Fairmont House B&B (☎ 902-624-8089; www.fair monthouse.com; 654 Main St; s/d/ste $70/95/150) This attractive, comfortable wooden house near Government Wharf and the shops has two rooms and one suite, all with private bath. It's gay-friendly.

Mahone Bay B&B (☎ 902-624-6388, 866-239-6252; www.bbcanada.com/4078.html; 558 Main St; r incl breakfast $115-125) Enjoy a view of the three churches from this friendly 1860s shipbuilder's home. All comforts are included, from cable TV to bathrobes.

Mimi's Ocean Grill (☎ 902-624-1342; 662 Main St; lunch $12-15; dinner $18-25; ✆ lunch & dinner Thu-Tue May-Oct) Try Mahone Bay's most frequently recommended place to eat for nouvelle cuisine with Thai and Italian overtones.

Mug & Anchor (☎ 902-624-6378; 643 Main St; mains $7-14; ✆ 11am-12:30am). View Mahone Bay from the waterfront deck of this upmarket pub. The fish isn't deep-fried and there are some decent vegetarian options, plus a nice microbrew on tap.

Jo-Ann's Deli Market & Bake Shop (☎ 902-624-6305; 9 Edgewater St; ✆ 9am-6pm May-Oct) In the very heart of Mahone Bay, this is the place to come for organic veggies, sinfully rich cakes, pastries and other goodies.

Shopping

Main St, which skirts the harbor, is scattered with shops selling antiques, quilts, chocolates and pottery.

Suttles & Seawinds (☎ 902-624-6177; 446 Main St) This long-standing institution offers Nova Scotia–made quilts and unique gifts.

Moorings Gallery (☎ 902-624-6208; 575 Main St; ✆ 10:30am-5pm Mon-Sat, 1-5pm Sun Jun-Aug, 11am-5pm Thu-Sat, 1-5pm Sun May & Oct-Dec) This gallery features pottery, jewelry and fine art by Maritime artists and craftspeople.

LUNENBURG

This attractive town, known for the *Bluenose* sailing schooner built here in 1921, was the first British settlement outside Halifax. It's the region's only Unesco world heritage site, due to its well-preserved Old Town with dozens of beautiful homes and buildings. Look for the distinctive 'Lunenburg

Bump,' a five-sided dormer window on the 2nd floor that overhangs the 1st floor.

Lunenburg was settled largely by Germans, Swiss and Protestant French who were first recruited by the British as a workforce for Halifax. Many of the original settlers had been farmers, but they soon turned toward the sea. Lunenburg still has one of the major fishing fleets of the north Atlantic seaboard.

Be warned: even on a rainy Monday you're guaranteed to find considerable throngs of tourists in Lunenburg. The top-notch festivals draw even more visitors.

Information

Explore Lunenburg (www.explorelunenburg.ca) Local history and tourism information.

Lunenburg Public Library (☎ 902-634-8008; 19 Pelham St; ☺ 10am-6pm Tue, Wed & Fri, 10am-8pm Thu, 10am-5pm Sat) Free Internet access.

Lunenburg VIC (☎ 902-634-8100, 888-615-8305; 11 Blockhouse Hill Rd; ☺ 9am-6pm May-Oct, to 8pm Jul & Aug) Tourist brochures and help with accommodations.

Sights & Activities

The dragger *Cape Sable* and the fishing schooner *Theresa E Connor* are just two of the exhibits at the **Fisheries Museum of the Atlantic** (☎ 902-634-4794; http://fisheries.museum .gov.ns.ca; 68 Bluenose Dr; adult/child under 18/family $9/3/22; ☺ 9:30am-5:30pm early May–late Oct). The knowledgeable staff includes a number of

retired fishers who can give firsthand explanations of the fishing industry. An awesome aquarium on the 1st floor lets you get eye-to-eye with flounder, halibut and other sea creatures. Films screen regularly in the 3rd-floor theater.

Considered the finest example of Georgian architecture in the province, 1793 **Knaut-Rhuland House** (☎ 902-634-3498; 125 Pelham St; admission $3; ☺ 11am-5pm Tue-Sat, 1-5pm Sun early Jun–Sep) has costumed guides who point out its features.

Lunenburg Academy (97 Kaulbach St) is the huge black-and-white turreted hilltop structure visible on your way in from Halifax. Built entirely of wood in 1895 as a prestigious high school, it is now a public school. In July and August, it's home to the **Lunenburg Seaside Craft School** (☎ 902-634-3242; www.lunenburgcraftschool.com; 5-day course $435). Pre-registration is required for courses in basket weaving, paper art and a host of other crafts, but you can call to check for openings.

Captain Angus J Walters House (☎ 902-634-2020; 37 Tannery Rd; admission $2; ☺ 1-7pm Mon-Fri, 1-5pm Sat) was donated to the town by the descendants of Captain Walters, who skippered the famous *Bluenose*. It's dedicated to preserving the history of the man and the schooner.

Bicycles can be rented and repaired at the **Lunenburg Bike Barn** (☎ 902-634-3426; www.bike

---

NOVA SCOTIA

NOVA SCOTIA'S TOP FIVE CHILDREN'S ATTRACTIONS

- **Museum of Industry** (p439) Interactive displays; children can try their hand at a miniature assembly line or clamber over old locomotives.

- **Nova Scotia Museum of Natural History** (p403) Awesome staff help children get up close and personal with insects, frogs and other natural wonders. The museum chef will even fry up some worms to truly gross out and delight small visitors.

- **Ross Farm Museum** (☎ 902-689-2210; http://museum.gov.ns.ca/rfm; Rte 12, New Ross; adult/child under 17/family $6/2/15, admission free 9:30-11am Sun; ☺ 9:30am-5:30pm May-Oct, Wed-Sun only Nov-Apr) A 24-hectare, 19th-century farm with animals from kittens to oxen. Help out with milking the cows or other farm chores. New Ross is 26km north of Hwy 103 near Mahone Bay, but can also be reached easily from Halifax or Wolfville.

- **Shubenacadie Provincial Wildlife Park** (p431) More than 30 species of mammal, more than 60 kinds of birds, and a giant playground. There's baby-changing areas and picnic tables.

- **Upper Clements Parks** (☎ 902-532-7557, 888-248-4567; www.upperclementspark.com; 2931 Hwy 1; admission $8, rides $3, 10 tickets $20; ☺ 11am-7pm mid-Jun–early-Sep) This is the place to get your roller-coaster fix. There's a good range of gentler rides for small kids. It's 6km southwest of Annapolis Royal.

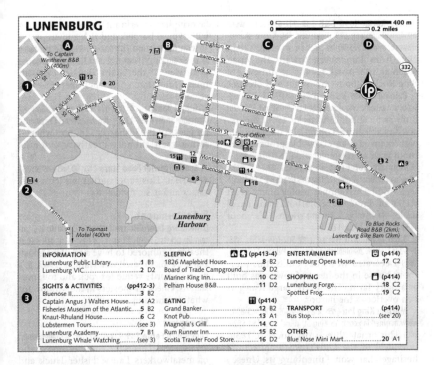

LUNENBURG

0 _____ 400 m
0 _____ 0.2 miles

INFORMATION		
Lunenburg Public Library	1	B1
Lunenburg VIC	2	D2

SIGHTS & ACTIVITIES	(pp412-3)	
Bluenose II	3	B2
Captain Angus J Walters House	4	A2
Fisheries Museum of the Atlantic	5	B2
Knaut-Rhuland House	6	C2
Lobstermen Tours	(see 3)	
Lunenburg Academy	7	B1
Lunenburg Whale Watching	(see 3)	

SLEEPING	(pp413-4)	
1826 Maplebird House	8	B2
Board of Trade Campground	9	D2
Mariner King Inn	10	C2
Pelham House B&B	11	D2

EATING	(p414)	
Grand Banker	12	B2
Knot Pub	13	A1
Magnolia's Grill	14	C2
Rum Runner Inn	15	B2
Scotia Trawler Food Store	16	D2

ENTERTAINMENT	(p414)	
Lunenburg Opera House	17	C2

SHOPPING	(p414)	
Lunenburg Forge	18	C2
Spotted Frog	19	C2

TRANSPORT	(p414)	
Bus Stop	(see 20)	

OTHER		
Blue Nose Mini Mart	20	A1

lunenburg.com; 579 Blue Rocks Rd; hybrid/tandem bikes per day $20/40), almost 2km east of town toward the small fishing community of Blue Rocks. On a small peninsula with no commercial development, this area is a cyclist's dream with few hills, great ocean views, and little vehicle traffic. Owner Merrill Heubach will gladly help you plan your trip.

Tours

Tours depart from the wharf adjacent to the Fisheries Museum on Bluenose Dr.

Bluenose II (☎ 902-634-1963, 800-763-1963; www .bluenose2.ns.ca; 2hr cruise adult/child 3-12 yrs $20/10) This classic replica of the *Bluenose* racing schooner is sometimes in Halifax and sometimes in Lunenburg. Clambering about the schooner when it's in port is free.

Lunenburg Whale Watching (☎ 902-527-7175; adult/child under 14 $42/30; ☀ Jun–mid-Oct) Offers three-hour trips that promise sightings of birds and seals as well as whales.

Lobstermen Tours (☎ 902-634-3434; www.lobster mentours.com; 45min tours adult/child $12/6) The two-hour tour includes hauling lobster pots and examining their contents in a touch tank. The mini-tour cruises around Lunenburg Harbor.

Festivals & Events

Boxwood Festival (www.boxwood.org; festival pass $50; ☀ last week Jul) Flautists and pipers from around the world put on stellar public concerts.

Lunenburg Folk Harbour Festival (☎ 902-634-3180; www.folkharbour.com; ☀ Aug) Singer-songwriters from Canada and beyond, plus traditional music and gospel.

Nova Scotia Folk Art Festival (www.nsfolkartfestival .com; ☀ 1st Sun in Aug)

Oktoberfest (☎ 902-634-3108; luntown@auracom .com; ☀ late Sep–early Oct) Five days of pints and schnitzel.

Sleeping

Make reservations as far ahead as possible, especially if you want to visit during a summer festival. Many of the inns and B&Bs inhabit large, gracious and historic properties; some open year-round and have off-season discounts.

Captain Westhaver B&B (☎ 902-634-4937; www3 .ns.sympatico.ca/westhaver.haus; 102 Dufferin St; s/d $55/65) This magnificent Lunenburg house has shared bathrooms. It's a short walk northwest of the center.

NOVA SCOTIA

Blue Rocks Road B&B (☎ 902-634-8033; www
.bikelunenburg.com; 579 Blue Rocks Rd; r with shared/
private bathroom $75/90) A great choice, less than
2km from Lunenburg toward the open
ocean and the small fishing community of
Blue Rocks. Rooms are bright and breezy.

Pelham House B&B (☎ 902-634-7113, 800-508-
0446; www.pelhamhouse.ca; 224 Pelham St; d/f $85/120)
Built as a captain's home in 1906, this relaxed establishment offers a laundry, private
bathrooms and an accessible ground-floor
room with a private veranda ($100).

Topmast Motel (☎ 902-634-4661, 877-525-3222;
www.topmastmotel.com; 92 Mason's Beach Rd; r $90, with
kitchen $105) This simple motel offers great
views of Lunenburg harbor from small
decks off the back of the rooms. It's about
1.5km from Old Town.

1826 Maplebird House (☎ 902-634-3863, 888-
395-3863; www.maplebirdhouse.ca; 36 Pelham St; d $95;
🔊) Decorated with cozy quilts, this four-
room house in the heart of town was built
as a dairy farm. The lovely, large rear garden overlooks the harbor.

Mariner King Inn (☎ 902-634-8509, 800-565-8509;
www.marinerking.com; 15 King St; d incl breakfast $120-
200) This ornate three-story house (c 1830)
is typical of the Old Town architectural
heritage that won Lunenburg its Unesco
designation.

Board of Trade Campground (☎ 902-634-
8100/3656; lbt@aliantzinc.ca; 11 Blockhouse Hill Rd; tent/
RV sites $18/$25; 🖳) The only budget option
in town, this campground, beside the VIC,
has great views and a lot of gravel RV sites.
Grassy tent sites are closely packed together
and lack shade.

Eating
Sampling the fish here is an absolute must.
Try some offbeat Lunenburg specialties.
Solomon Gundy is pickled herring with onions. Lunenburg pudding – pork and spices
cooked in the intestines of a pig – goes well
with Scotch and water. Fish cakes with rhu-
barb chutney are also popular.

Magnolia's Grill (☎ 902-634-3287; 128 Montague
St; mains $7-15; 🕑 lunch & dinner) This favorite of
local and traveling foodies is often busy.
Try one of the many soups of the day, from
creole-peanut to potato-leek, or the gently
spicy Tunisian vegetable stew. Seafood and
an extensive wine list are available.

Knot Pub (☎ 902-634-3334; 4 Dufferin St; meals
$6-10; 🕑 11am-midnight) This year-round local

favorite has sauerkraut and sausage, along
with typical burgers and fish and chips.

Rum Runner Inn (☎ 902-634-9200; 66 Montague
St; meals $8-25; 🕑 lunch & dinner) Enjoy the same
great view as the Grand Banker, but with
much finer fare. The chef specializes in
seafood.

Grand Banker (☎ 902-634-3300; rear entrance, 82
Montague St; meals $8-17; 🕑 lunch & dinner) Depends
on views of the Fisheries Museum wharf –
rather than culinary creativity – for its
success.

Scotia Trawler Food Store (☎ 902-634-4914; 266
Montague St) This supermarket has local delicacies and basic foodstuffs.

Entertainment
Lunenburg Opera House (☎ 902-634-4010; 290 Lincoln St; tickets $5-20) This rickety old 400-seat
theater is rumored to have a resident ghost.
Built as an Oddfellows Hall in 1907, it's
now a favorite venue for rock and folk musicians. Check the posters in the window for
what's coming up.

Shopping
Lunenburg Forge (☎ 902-634-7125; 146 Bluenose Dr;
🕑 10am-6pm) This is the summertime studio
of metalworkers Laurie Fisher Huck and
Christopher Huck (their winter studio is
in Mexico). Laurie created the whimsical
sea creatures that hang from Lunenburg's
street poles.

Spotted Frog (☎ 902-634-1976; 125 Montague St;
🕑 10am-8pm Jul & Aug, 10am-5pm rest of year) There's a
wide selection of Nova Scotian folk art here.

Getting There & Away
DRL Coachlines buses pull in at **Blue Nose
Mini Mart** (35 Lincoln St) on their way from Halifax ($25, two hours) to Yarmouth ($34, 2½
hours). For details and alternative shuttles,
see p407.

BRIDGEWATER
Bridgewater, an industrial town with a big
Michelin tire plant, is the largest center on
the South Shore. **Wile Carding Mill** (☎ 902-543-
8233; museum.gov.ns.ca/wcm; 242 Victoria Rd; adult/child
$2/1; 🕑 9:30am-5:30pm Mon-Sat, 1-5:30pm Sun Jun-Sep)
is an authentic water mill dating from 1860.
Carding is the straightening and untangling
of wool fibers in preparation for spinning.
This mill did in an hour what would otherwise take a woman a whole week.

LIVERPOOL

Liverpool was once ruled by British privateers who protected British trade routes from incursions by the USA during the War of 1812, and did the odd bit of plundering for their own coffers. It is well situated for exploring several gorgeous white-sand beaches, Kejimkujik National Park (68km north, see p415) and its Seaside Adjunct (15km southwest, see p416). **Privateer Days** (www.privateerdays.com), a celebration of piracy and history, is held in early July.

Information

Tourist Office (☎ 902-354-5421; 28 Henry Hensey Dr; ☑ 9am-7pm Jul & Aug, 10am-5pm Jun & early–mid-Sep) Near the river bridge, it has a walking-tour pamphlet and brochures of scenic drives.

Sights & Activities

Sherman Hines is behind a number of new cultural attractions in Liverpool. One of the Maritimes' most prolific photographers, and a wealthy Liverpudlian, his most ambitious venture is the **Rossignol Cultural Centre** (☎ 902-354-3067; www.rossignolculturalcentre.com; 205 Church St; adult/child/student $4/2/3; ☑ 10am-5:30pm Mon-Sat). It contains mini-museums of wildlife and folk art, outhouses and a couple of galleries. Admission includes entry to **Sherman Hines Museum of Photography & Galleries** (☎ 902-354-2667; www.shermanhinesphotographymuseum.com; 219 Main St; ☑ 10am-5:30pm Mon-Sat), where six galleries in the old town hall run the gamut of media.

Perkins House Museum (☎ 902-354-4058; http://museum.gov.ns.ca/peh; 105 Main St; adult/child $2/1; ☑ 9:30am-5:30pm Mon-Sat, 1-5:30pm Sun Jun–mid-Oct) displays articles and furniture from the colonial period. Built in 1766, it's the oldest house belonging to the Nova Scotia Museum. Next door, the **Queen's County Museum** (☎ 902-354-4058; www.queensmuseum.netfirms.com; 109 Main St; admission $1; ☑ 9:30am-5:30pm Mon-Sat, 1-5:30pm Sun Jun–mid-Oct, 9am-5pm Mon-Sat rest of year) has First Nations artifacts and more materials relating to town history, as well as some writings by early citizens.

At **Fort Point**, a cairn marks the site where Frenchman Samuel de Champlain landed in 1604. You can blow the hand-pumped foghorn in the **lighthouse** (☎ 902-354-5260; 21 Fort Lane, at the end of Main St; admission free; ☑ 10am-6pm mid-May–mid-Oct).

Hank Snow Country Music Centre (☎ 902-354-4675; www.hanksnow.com; 148 Bristol Ave; admission $3; ☑ 9am-5pm Mon-Sat, noon-5pm Sun late May–early Oct) sheds light on Nova Scotia's status as a northern Nashville. In the old train station, it captures the history of Snow, Wilf Carter and other crooners and yodelers.

Sleeping & Eating

Geranium House (☎ 902-354-4484; 87 Milton Rd; r $50) This B&B on a large wooded property next to the Mersey River has three rooms with shared bathroom and welcomes cyclists and families.

Lane's Privateer Inn (☎ 902-354-3456, 800-794-3332; www.lanesprivateerinn.com; 27 Bristol Ave; s/d incl breakfast $80/95) Originally the home of a swashbuckling privateer, this inn has been in the same family for three generations. It now has a bookshop and gourmet food store. Its cozy pub and dining room (open 7am to 10pm) offer seafood with surprising sauces and some Mexican dishes (mains $9 to $25). Try a pear and blue cheese salad.

Liverpool Pizzeria (☎ 902-354-2422; 155 Main St, near cnr Market St; lunch combos $7, pizzas $12-17; ☑ 8:30am-11pm Sun-Thu, to midnight Fri & Sat) This pleasant restaurant has a kids' menu.

Entertainment

Astor Theatre (☎ 902-354-5250; www.astortheatre.ns.ca; 59 Gorham St) The Astor is the oldest continuously operating performance venue in the province. Built in 1902 as the Liverpool Opera House, it presents films, plays and live music.

KEJIMKUJIK NATIONAL PARK

This inland park contains some of Nova Scotia's most pristine wilderness and best backcountry adventure opportunities. Less than 20% of Kejimkujik's 381 sq km is accessible by car; the rest is reached either on foot or by paddle. Canoeing is an ideal way to explore this area of glacial lakes; the park is well set up for extended, overnight paddles.

Information

Visitor Center (☎ 902-682-2772, 800-414-6765; www.parkscanada.gc.ca/keji; Hwy 8; adult/child/family $4.50/2.25/11.25; ☑ 8:30am-9pm mid-Jun–early Sep, to 4pm rest of year, closed weekends Nov-Mar) Get an entry permit and reserve backcountry sites here.

Activities

The main **hiking** loop is a 60km trek that begins at the east end of George Lake and ends at the Big Dam Lake trailhead. September to early October is prime hiking time; the bugs in the spring would drive you mad. A shorter loop, ideal for an overnight trek, is the 26km Channel Lake Trail that begins and ends at Big Dam Lake. More than a dozen lakes are connected by a system of portages, allowing canoe trips of up to seven days. A topographical map ($10) may be required for ambitious multiday trips. Rent canoes and other equipment in the park at **Jakes Landing** (☎ 902-682-5253; ☺ 8am-9pm Jun-Sep, off-season by appointment). One-hour hire of a kayak, bike or rowboat is $6, double kayak or canoe is $8; 24-hour hire is $30/33 and one-week hire is $125.

Sleeping & Eating

Forty-five backcountry campsites ($8 per person plus a $5 booking fee) are scattered among the lakes of Kejimkujik. You must book them in advance by calling or stopping at the park's visitor center. There's a 14-day maximum; you can't stay more than two nights at any site.

Raven Haven Hostel & Family Park (☎ 902-532-7320; www.annapoliscounty.ns.ca/rec/ravhav/hostel .htm; 2239 Virginia Rd off Hwy 8, South Milford; dm member/nonmember $16/18, tent/RV sites $16/19; ☺ mid-Jun–early Sep) This community-run HI hostel and small family campground is 25km south of Annapolis Royal and 27km north of the national park. The four-bed hostel is in a cabin near the beach. There are 15 campsites, including some private wooded ones. Canoes and paddleboats can be rented.

Jeremy's Bay Campground (☎ 902-682-2772, 800-414-6765; sites summer/winter $21/15) Its 360 campsites include a handful of walk-in sites near the shoreline. Thirty percent of the sites are assigned on a first-come, first-served basis. These will be taken by mid-afternoon Friday on any midsummer weekend. It costs $10 to reserve a site.

Whitman Inn (☎ 902-682-2226, 800-830-3855; www.whitmaninn.com; 12389 Hwy 8; r $70-90; ☺ Feb-Oct, dinner Wed-Mon; ☒) About 4km south of the park in Caledonia, this gracious older inn has a wide veranda and great facilities. Breakfast and picnic lunches ($7) are available for guests. Anyone is welcome for dinner (mains $13 to $20) from 6pm to 8pm July and August; call for hours the rest of the year.

SEASIDE ADJUNCT (KEJIMKUJIK NATIONAL PARK)

The 'Keji Adjunct' protects one of the last undeveloped oceanfront beach areas on the eastern seaboard between Port Joli and Port Mouton (ma-*toon*) Bay. The only access from Hwy 103 is along a 6.5km gravel road. Drinking water and bathrooms are available at the parking lot. From there, two mostly flat trails lead to the coast. **Harbour Rocks Trail** (5.2km return) follows an old cart road through mixed forest to a beach where seals are often seen. A loop trail around **Port Joli Head** is 8.7km return.

The Port Joli Basin contains **Point Joli Migratory Bird Sanctuary** with waterfowl and shorebirds in great numbers (*Nova Scotia Birding on the Lighthouse Route* is an excellent resource available at VICs). It's only easily accessible by kayak. The **Rossignol Surf Shop** (☎ 902-683-2550; www.surfnovascotia.com; 600 St Catherine's River Rd, Port Joli; half/full-day kayak rentals $30/45, tours $60/95) rents kayaks and offers guided tours.

Thomas Raddall Provincial Park (☎ 902-683-2664; www.parks.gov.ns.ca; campsites $18), across Port Joli Harbour from Keji Adjunct, has large, private campsites with eight walk-in ones. The forested campground extends out onto awesome beaches.

At time of research, a new community-run 20-bed hostel was nearing completion in Port Mouton. Contact Bill Heppell at pmhostel@eastlink.ca or ☎ 902-683-2262 to check on its status.

LOCKEPORT

An unpretentious fishing village set behind beautiful Crescent Beach, Lockeport is worth a detour from Hwy 103. The **Crescent Beach Centre** (☎ 902-656-3123; 157 Locke St; ☺ 9am-7pm Jul & Aug, 9am-4pm Jun & Sep, 10am-4pm Tue-Sat rest of year) has tourist information. Check out a memorial quilt for 17 local fishermen lost at sea in 1964. Follow the boardwalk to get to Crescent Beach itself. It's a nesting sight for the endangered piping plover, so dogs should always be on a leash and people should always be careful where they walk.

Little School Museum (29 Locke St; admission by donation; ☺ 10am-5pm Jul & Aug), just up from the beach, captures early local history. One room is restored as an 1890s village schoolroom, another has a collection of old fishing implements.

Five houses overlooking the harbor on South St are protected as a heritage streetscape. Built between 1836 and 1876 by descendants of town father Jonathan Locke, they show the distinct style of Colonial, Georgian and Victorian times.

A plaque at the far end of South St examines the history of the homes and the families who once lived there.

Hire surfboards and bodyboards at the Crescent Beach Centre (per hour/half-day/day $10/20/40, with wetsuit $20/30/50). Lockeport's back harbor, accessible via a long boardwalk, is a good site for **birding**.

Atwell's Restaurant & Pizzeria (☎ 902-656-3030; 24 Beech St; mains $7-14; 🕙 7am-9pm) is a basic, friendly place with seafood and sandwiches. **Striker's Café** (☎ 902-656-2695; 10 Beech St; meals $4-7; 🕙 11am-9pm Mon & Wed-Sat, 11am-2pm Tue) serves burgers and fish and chips in a ten-pin bowling alley.

SHELBURNE

One of the most attractive towns on the South Shore, Shelburne has 17 homes older than 1800 in its historic district, bounded by Water St and Dock St. These early buildings once housed Loyalists who retreated here from the American Revolution. In 1783 Shelburne was the largest community in British North America with 16,000 residents, many from the New York aristocracy who exploited the labor of Black Loyalists living in nearby Birchtown (p418). Shelburne's history is celebrated with **Founders' Days** during the last weekend of July.

Information

Tourist Office (☎ 902-875-4547; 31 Dock St; 🕙 8am-8pm Jul & Aug, 11am-5pm mid-May–Jun & Sep) Has copies of a self-guided historic district walking tour.

Sights & Activities

Four museums in the historic district relate Shelburne's history as a Loyalist community and a shipbuilding center. Admission to all four museums costs $8, a single admission is $3.

Built in 1784, **Ross-Thomson House** (☎ 902-875-3141; www.rossthomson.museum.gov.ns.ca; 9 Charlotte Lane; admission free 9:30am-noon Sun; 🕙 9:30am-5:30pm Jun–mid-Oct) and the store adjacent to it belonged to well-to-do Loyalist merchants who arrived from Cape Cod. Furniture, paintings and original goods from the store

are on display. The house is surrounded by authentic period gardens.

Another c 1787 Loyalist house is now the **Shelburne County Museum** (☎ 902-875-3219; cnr Maiden Lane & Dock St; 🕙 9:30am-5:30pm Jun–mid-Oct, 10am-noon & 2-5pm Mon-Fri rest of year) with a collection of Loyalist furnishings, displays on the history of the local fishery and a small collection of Mi'kmaw artifacts, including typical porcupine-quill decorative work.

The **Muir-Cox Shipyard** (☎ 902-875-1114; www.historicshelburne.com/muircox.htm; 18 Dock St; 🕙 9:30am-5:30pm Jun-Sep) has been in almost continuous operation since 1820, turning out barques, yachts and fishing boats. It's still active year-round, but the interpretive center is seasonal. Likewise, Shelburne dories (small open boats once used for fishing from a mother schooner) are still made to order at the **Dory Shop Museum** (☎ 902-875-3219; http://museum.gov.ns.ca/dory; 11 Dock St; 🕙 9:30am-5:30pm Jun-Sep) for use as lifeboats.

Ocean Breeze Kayak Adventures (☎ 902-875-2463; 18 Dock St; 🕙 9:30am-5:30pm Jun-Sep) rents kayaks (per half-/full-day $35/50) and bicycles (with helmet $20 per day) and guides tours (per half-/full-day $45/105) around Shelburne harbor.

There's a **trail** for hiking or biking the 6km to Birchtown (p418) across from Spencer's Garden Centre at the far south end of Main St.

Sleeping

Islands Provincial Park (☎ 902-875-4304; www.parks.gov.ns.ca; off Hwy 3; campsites $18) Across the harbor from Shelburne are 65 campsites in mature forest and a beach for swimming.

Loyalist Inn (☎ 902-875-2343; fax 902-875-1452; 160 Water St; r $55) This three-story wooden hotel once sheltered people traveling by stage coach. Live music in the bar downstairs can make it noisy, and female travelers might feel uncomfortable with the flimsy locks and proximity to the bar.

MacKenzie's Motel & Cottages (☎ 902-875-2842, 866-875-0740; www.mackenziesmotel.ns.ca; 260 Water St; r/cottages $65/85; 🐾) This motel has nice extras like an outdoor pool, small fridges and coffeemakers.

Cooper's Inn B&B (☎ 902-875-4656, 800-688-2011; www3.ns.sympatico.ca/coopers; 36 Dock St; r $100-145) Across from a rare working cooperage that still makes barrels for the fishing industry, this was once home to generations of coopers. Part of the building dates back to 1784 and was actually brought here from Boston. Now it's a comfortable, unique inn with six rooms. The smallest room opens directly into the heritage garden.

Eating

Charlotte Lane (☎ 902-875-3314; 13 Charlotte Lane; mains $12-25; ⊗ lunch & dinner Tue-Sat) People drive from Halifax to eat here, and then rave about it; evening reservations are highly recommended. Try salmon glazed with miso and mustard ($16) or chicken baked with camembert ($15). The chef is constantly revising an extensive annotated wine list.

Nellie Bly's Café (☎ 902-875-1220; 149 Water St; lunch mains $4-7, dinner mains $8-16; ⊗ 11am-9pm) This unpretentious spot serves seafood at very reasonable prices. Lunch offerings include quiche, sandwiches and salads.

Shelburne Pastry & Tea House (☎ 902-875-1164; 151 Water St; mains $7-14; ⊗ 10am-7pm Mon-Fri) Delicious fresh pasta usually features as the daily lunch special.

Drinking

Beandock (☎ 902-875-1302; 10 John St) Enjoy the view and the good coffee on the patio of this café, right on the water at the corner of Dock St.

Sea Dog Saloon (☎ 902-875-2862; 1 Dock St; ⊗ 11am-midnight Mon-Sat, noon-8pm Sun) The outdoor terrace overlooking Shelburne harbor is the best place to have a pint in town. There's also a full pub menu.

BIRCHTOWN

Just as Shelburne was once the largest settlement in British North America, so Birchtown was once the largest settlement of freed African slaves in North America. Named for British General Samuel Birch who signed the freedom papers of many Black Loyalists at the end of the American Revolution, it was home to close to 1500 freed Blacks in 1784 (see the boxed text below).

Black Loyalist Heritage Society Historical Site & Museum (☎ 902-875-1381, 888-354-0722; www.black loyalist.com; 104 Birchtown Rd; ⊗ 11am-6pm Tue-Fri, noon-6pm Sat, noon-5pm Sun) includes a museum, an old burial ground and a walking trail that leads to a 'pit house' which archeologists think was once a temporary shelter. There are also pleasant picnic areas and a **trail** for hiking or cycling the 6km to Shelburne (see p417).

BARRINGTON

Barrington was settled in 1760 by 50 families from Cape Cod. Several **museums** (☎ 902-637-2185; per museum adult/child $2/1; ⊗ 9:30am-5:30pm Mon-Sat, 1-5:30pm Sun Jun-Sep) are run by the local historical society. For years, church services of all faiths and community meetings happened in the New England–style meeting

---

AFRICAN NOVA SCOTIANS

A venerable and visible minority, African Nova Scotians' history is linked to most parts of the African Diaspora. After the American Revolution, about 3500 Black Loyalists were rewarded by the British with land for settlements near Shelburne, Halifax, Digby and Guysborough. Nine years later, in 1792, after barely surviving harsh winters and unequal treatment, 1200 of them boarded 15 ships bound for Sierra Leone, in West Africa, where they founded Freetown. Another 2000 from the USA settled in the Maritimes after the War of 1812, and still others came from the Caribbean in the 1890s to work in the Cape Breton Island coal mines.

While many Blacks escaped slavery by moving to Nova Scotia, they have not been treated as equals. Underfunded, segregated schools existed until the 1950s. In 1970 the City of Halifax forcibly removed residents of Africville from their homes on the shore of the Bedford Basin in order to build the MacKay Bridge; the community and its church were bulldozed and the people moved to cramped public housing projects in North End Halifax. Today, African Nova Scotians are underrepresented in high-school graduation ceremonies and overrepresented in courtrooms and prisons.

The United Baptist Church has been a pillar of this community almost since the beginning, something poet George Elliott Clarke writes about in *Whylah Falls,* an award-winning collection of linked poems set in an imagined settlement of Black Loyalist descendants. A self-guided tour of African heritage in Nova Scotia is available online (www.dal.ca/~bcichair/bheritage1a.html).

house, now the **Old Meeting House Museum** (http://museum.gov.ns.ca/omh; 2408 Hwy 3). Many town founders are buried in the graveyard next door. Interpreters at the **Barrington Woolen Mill Museum** (http://museum.gov.ns.ca/bwm; 2368 Hwy 3) demonstrate handspinning, dyeing and weaving in what was a thriving community enterprise in the late 19th century. The **Seal Island Light Museum** (2422 Hwy 3) is a replica of a lighthouse, including the original light.

BARRINGTON TO PUBNICO

At Barrington, you can choose to take the fast, not-very-scenic Hwy 103 to Yarmouth, or to meander along about 100km of interesting coastline via Hwy 3. If you stop and have a chat with locals – and local wharves are fine spots to stretch your legs – you'll notice two distinct accents in this small corner of Nova Scotia. In **Cape Sable Island** and **Woods Harbour** people speak with a Boston drawl, testament to the close relationship between this part of Nova Scotia and that US city. Then, starting in **Lower East Pubnico**, English is spoken with an Acadian French accent.

WEST PUBNICO

Not to be confused with Middle West Pubnico, Lower West Pubnico, East Pubnico (and its derivatives) or Pubnico proper, West Pubnico is an old Acadian community; for more on Acadians, see p422. **Le Village Historique Acadien** (☎ 902-762-2530; Old Church Rd; adult/child under 6/child 7-18 yrs $4/free/2; ◷ 9am-5pm mid-Jun–Sep) recreates an Acadian village, with a blacksmith shop, a timber-frame house and a fish store. Opposite the firehall, the **Musée Acadien & Archives** (☎ 902-762-3380; www.museeacadien.ca; 898 Hwy 335; admission $3; ◷ 9am-5pm Mon-Sat, 12:30-4:30pm Sun) displays household items, original maps and a collection of more than 300 cameras.

Seaclusion Kayak Adventures (☎ 902-648-8339; www.seaclusion.ca) is owned by Kendrick d'Entremont, a descendant of the founder of West Pubnico. Novice and experienced kayakers are well served by a range of tours, from kayaking introductions that touch on natural and cultural history (per half-/full-day $50/90) to multiday excursions to the nearby Tusket Islands (two-/three-day trips including meals $290/425), which are home to about 2000 wild sheep.

YARMOUTH

Yarmouth is the largest town in western Nova Scotia and the destination for ferries from Portland and Bar Harbor, Maine (see p397). It's been said that Yarmouth is too big to be cute and too small to be interesting. The main street boasts a staggering number of gift shops selling tacky trinkets and most restaurants close early. Nonetheless, there's a day's worth of interesting sights.

Information

About Yarmouth (www.aboutyarmouth.com) Has a calendar of events and accommodation and dining options.
VIC (☎ 902-742-5033; 228 Main St; ◷ 7:30am-9pm Jul & Aug, 7.30am-4:30pm May, Jun, Sep & Oct) Also has a money exchange counter.
Yarmouth Public Library (☎ 902-742-2486; 405 Main St; ◷ 10am-8pm Mon-Thu, 10am-5pm Fri, 10am-4pm Sat, 1-4pm Sun) Free Internet access.

Sights & Activities

First settled by New Englanders from Massachusetts in 1761, Yarmouth reached its peak of growth and prosperity in the 1870s. The Collins Heritage Conservation District protects many fine Victorian homes built around that time. Check at the VIC for a self-guided walking tour.

Yarmouth County Museum (☎ 902-742-5539; http://yarmouthcountymuseum.ednet.ns.ca; 22 Collins St; adult/student/family $3/2/6; ◷ 9am-5pm Mon-Sat, 2-5pm Sun Jun–mid-Oct, 2-5pm Tue-Sat mid-Oct–May), in a former church, contains five period rooms related to the sea. A combined admission ticket (adult/child/student/family $5/1/2/10) includes **Pelton-Fuller House** (◷ 9am-5pm, Mon-Sat, Jun-Oct) next door. It's a Victorian home typical of the heritage district, filled with period artwork, glassware and furniture.

Firefighters' Museum (☎ 902-742-5525; http://museum.gov.ns.ca/fm; 431 Main St; adult/family $3/6; ◷ 9am-9pm Mon-Sat, 10am-5pm Sun Jul & Aug, 9am-5pm Mon-Sat Jun & Sep, closed Sat other months) has fire engines from 1819 to 1935 and an exhibit where kids can pretend to fight a fire.

W Laurence Sweeney Museum (☎ 902-742-3457; 112 Water St; adult/family $3/7.50; ◷ 10am-6pm Mon-Sat late May–mid-Oct) shows the business of fishing, from catching to processing and selling.

Yarmouth Light (☎ 902-742-1433; Hwy 304; admission free; ◷ 9am-9pm Jul & Aug, 10am-3pm May, Jun, Sep & Oct) is at the end of Cape Forchu, a left on Hwy 304 from Main St. The lighthouse affords spectacular views.

NOVA SCOTIA

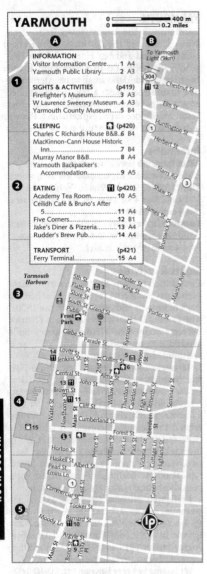

YARMOUTH 0 ___ 400 m / 0 ___ 0.2 miles

INFORMATION	
Visitor Information Centre........	1 A4
Yarmouth Public Library...........	2 A3

SIGHTS & ACTIVITIES	(p419)
Firefighter's Museum...............	3 A3
W Laurence Sweeney Museum..	4 A3
Yarmouth County Museum......	5 B4

SLEEPING	(p420)
Charles C Richards House B&B..	6 B4
MacKinnon-Cann House Historic Inn.......................	7 B4
Murray Manor B&B................	8 A4
Yarmouth Backpacker's Accommodation................	9 A5

EATING	(p420)
Academy Tea Room................	10 A5
Ceilidh Café & Bruno's After 5...........................	11 A4
Five Corners.......................	12 B1
Jake's Diner & Pizzeria...........	13 A4
Rudder's Brew Pub...............	14 A4

TRANSPORT	(p421)
Ferry Terminal.....................	15 A4

mean 'flophouse'! Two adjoining rooms can be a family room.

Murray Manor B&B (☎ 902-742-9625, 877-742-9629; www.murraymanor.com; 225 Main St; s/d incl breakfast $80/95; 🖳) Three rooms share a bathroom in this stately two-story house just a block from the ferry. Surrounded by a stone wall, this B&B is included on the heritage walking tour. It has Gothic windows on the 1st floor and low windows – called kneeling or praying windows – on the 2nd floor.

Charles C Richards House B&B (☎ 902-742-0042; www.charlesrichardshouse.ns.ca; 17 Collins St; r/ste $125/210) The owners of this Queen Anne Victorian mansion won a provincial award for returning a neglected rooming house to its former glory. Stained-glass windows abound, as do plants in the conservatory.

The same team brought another heritage property back to life: **MacKinnon-Cann House Historic Inn** (☎ 902-742-0042; www.mackinnon cannin.com; 27 Willow St; r $100-165) opened late in 2004. Restored antiques furnish seven elegant guest rooms.

Eating

The culinary choices are decidedly limited, especially if you prefer to eat after 7pm.

Rudders Brew Pub (☎ 902-742-7311; 96 Water St; pub menu $9-12, dinner mains $16-29) This 300-seat waterfront pub and restaurant brews up a mean ale on site, and has a wide-ranging menu. Drinks are poured until the wee hours on busy summer nights.

Ceilidh Café & Bruno's After 5 (☎ 902-742-0031; 276 Main St; lunch mains $4-9, dinner mains $13-18; 🕑 8am-5pm Mon & Tue, 8am-8pm Wed-Sun, 9am-9pm Wed-Sun Jul & Aug) Chef Bruno's restaurant serves up seafood in French sauces in the evenings; the popular café serves healthy sandwiches and salads and decadent desserts.

Academy Tea Room (☎ 902-749-0193; 113 Main St; sandwiches $7-8; 🕑 10am-4pm Tue-Sat) This is a nice alternative for a pot of tea ($2.50) or lunch. The menu of sandwiches includes interesting vegetarian creations and good deli meats.

Five Corners (☎ 902-742-7876; 624 Main St; mains $9-15; 🕑 11am-8pm, to 9pm Jul & Aug) This attractive restaurant is reasonably priced.

Jake's Diner & Pizzeria (☎ 902-742-8882; 322 Main St; lunches & dinners $5-7; 🕑 9am-midnight Sun-Wed, to 1am Thu, to 3am Fri & Sat) This friendly pizza joint is open till midnight or later.

Sleeping

Yarmouth Backpacker's Accommodation (☎ 902-749-0941; yarmouthbackpackers@hotmail.com; 6 Trinity Pl; dm/f $20/65) This c 1865 Italianate mansion has been turned into a hostel by a friendly Canadian-Australian couple, but follow their lead and don't use the term 'hostel' around town – it's locally understood to

Getting There & Away
DRL Coachlines and several shuttle bus companies travel from Yarmouth to Halifax ($50, 4½ hours). Yarmouth is also a jumping-off point to Maine via ferry (see p397).

ANNAPOLIS VALLEY & FRENCH SHORE

The Annapolis Valley is a popular daytrip destination. Highlights include views of the Bay of Fundy, historic farmhouses, and overflowing farmers' markets. Once the main breadbasket for colonial Canada, the Annapolis Valley still produces much of Nova Scotia's fresh produce and especially lots of apples. In more recent years, a number of wineries have also taken advantage of the sandy soil. Dykes protecting the rich agricultural land are evidence of hard work by early Acadians.

Highway 1 passes through all the major towns in the valley, but to really get into the countryside, try taking the smaller roads that run parallel to Hwy 1 (p424) where picture-perfect farms and orchards come into view. South of Digby along the coast of St Mary's Bay, Hwy 1 is scattered with small French-speaking Acadian communities, interspersed with beautiful views. Crafts are offered out of people's houses. The best among them are the quilts and the woodcarvings.

WINDSOR
A small town on the Avon River, Windsor was once the only British stronghold in this region. Today it seems to suffer from an abundance of history and a shortage of present. Check out the attractions in an afternoon and move on to the Wolfville area. Windsor is also the place to enjoy bluegrass music – think lots of fast banjo picking. Avon River Park (right) hosts two bluegrass festivals, one in June and one in July, and is a hangout for aficionados all summer long.

Orientation & Information
Highway 1 becomes Water St in town, and the main intersection is with Gerrish St. The helpful **tourist office** (☎ 902-798-2690; 31 Colonial Rd; ☿ 8:30am-6:30pm Jul & Aug, 9am-5pm Sat & Sun Jun, Sep & Oct) is just off exit 6 from Hwy 101. The dyke beside the tourist office offers a view of the tidal river flats.

Sights & Activities
Off King St, the **Fort Edward National Historic Site** (☎ 902-798-4706; admission free; ☿ 10am-6pm Mon-Sat, noon-4pm Sun Jul & Aug) preserves remnants of a British fort dating from 1750. It was used as one of the assembly stations during the expulsion of the Acadians. The grounds are accessible year-round.

The Victorian **Haliburton House** (☎ 902-798-2915; 414 Clifton Ave; adult/student $3/2; ☿ 9:30am-5:30pm Mon-Sat, 1-5:30pm Sun Jun–mid-Oct) was the home of Judge Thomas Chandler Haliburton (1796–1865), writer of the Sam Slick stories. Although they aren't read much now, many of Haliburton's expressions, such as 'quick as a wink' and 'city slicker,' are still used.

Windsor's claim as the birthplace of ice hockey is very much debated. The evidence is gathered at the **Windsor Hockey Heritage Society** (☎ 902-798-1800; 128 Gerrish St; admission free; ☿ 10am-5pm Mon-Sat).

An especially ornate Victorian house, the 1890 **Shand House Museum** (☎ 902-798-8213; adult/concession $3/2; ☿ 9:30am-5:30pm Mon-Sat, 1-5:30pm Sun Jun–mid-Oct) also offers historical displays and a great view from the tower room.

Sleeping & Eating
Meander In B&B (☎ 902-798-2514, 877-387-6070; www.bbcanada.com/meanderinbandb; 153 Albert St; s/d $55/70) This 1898 mansion in the center of town has three rooms with shared bathroom. There's evening tea with home-baked goods.

Avon River Park (☎ 902-684-3299; 955 Hwy 1, Mount Denson; tent/RV sites $10/16) This small campground, perched above the Avon River, is a great spot to watch the effect of the dramatic Bay of Fundy tides.

Spitfire Arms Alehouse (☎ 902-792-1460; 29 Water St; mains $7-11; ☿ 11am-midnight) This traditional pub is the best place to eat in town. There's live music on weekends.

Shopping
Signature Glass (☎ 902-792-1133; 43 Water St; ☿ 10am-5pm Mon-Fri, 10am-4pm Sat) Both a gallery and studio for glass artist Pam Kinsman, who hand paints and fires beautiful glass vases, teapots and sculptures.

NOVA SCOTIA

GRAND PRÉ

Grand Pré, 25km past Windsor at the outskirts of Wolfville, is now a very small English-speaking town. In the 1750s, however, it was the site of one of the most tragic but compelling stories in eastern Canada's history (see the boxed text on p422).

Sights & Activities

At **Grand Pré National Historic Site** (☎ 902-542-3631; 2205 Grand Pré Rd; admission $5.75; ☯ 9am-6pm May-Oct), a modern interpretive center explains the historical context for the deportation from Acadian, Mi'kmaw and British perspectives and traces the many routes Acadians took from and back to the Maritimes.

Beside the center, a serene **park** contains gardens and an Acadian-style stone church. There's also a bust of American poet Henry Wadsworth Longfellow who chronicled the Acadian saga in *Evangeline: A Tale of Acadie*, and a statue of his fictional Evangeline, now a romantic symbol of her people.

Beyond the park, you can see the farmland created when the Acadians built dykes along the shoreline as they had done in northwest France for generations. There are 1200 hectares below sea level here, protected by just over 9000m of dyke. It's a beautiful area and you'll easily understand why the Acadians didn't want to leave.

Sleeping & Eating

Evangeline Inn & Motel (☎ 902-542-2703, 888-542-2703; www.evangeline.ns.ca; 11668 Hwy 1; r $60-90) This 1950s motel has updated, comfortable rooms.

Grand Pré House B&B (☎ 902-542-4277; 273 Old Post Rd; s $60-70, d $75-95) The current owners bought this historic home from the original family and added a meditation hut and sauna. This charming, tranquil spot overlooks a horse pasture and the dykelands. There's no smoking.

Stirling's (☎ 902-542-2703; sandwiches $3-5; ☯ 7:30am-7pm) The restaurant on the same grounds as the Evangaline Inn & Motel is famous for homemade pie ($2.95).

Domaine de Grand Pré (☎ 902-542-1753; 11611 Hwy 1; mains $14-27; ☯ lunch & dinner) This restaurant on the grounds of Grand Pré Wines has a beautiful outdoor patio paved with fieldstones and shaded with grapevines. The food is Swiss influenced. Tours with wine tasting ($6) are given at 11am and 3pm daily.

Shopping

Tangled Garden (☎ 902-542-9811; 11827 Hwy 1; ☯ 10am-6pm) Impossible to classify, this is probably the best-smelling shopping experience in Nova Scotia. Buy a bottle of herb-infused vinegar or jelly to take away, or stroll the gardens and meditative labyrinth while licking herb-flavored ice cream.

THE ACADIANS

When the French first settled the area around the Minas Basin, they called the region Arcadia, a Greek and Roman term for 'pastoral paradise.' This became Acadia, and by the 18th century, the Acadians felt more connection with the land they worked than with the distant Loire Valley they'd come from.

To the English, however, they would always be French, with whom rivalry and suspicion was constant. The Acadians refused to take an oath of allegiance to the English king after the Treaty of Utrecht granted Nova Scotia to the British, considering it an affront to their Catholic faith. When hard-line lieutenant governor Charles Lawrence was appointed in 1754, he quickly became fed up with the Acadians and ordered their deportation. The English burned many villages and forced some 14,000 Acadians onto ships.

Many Acadians headed for Louisiana and New Orleans; others went to various Maritime points, New England, Martinique in the Caribbean, Santo Domingo in the Dominican Republic, or back to Europe. Nowhere were they greeted warmly with open arms. Some hid out and remained in Acadia. In later years many of the deported people returned but found their lands occupied. In Nova Scotia, Acadians resettled the Chéticamp area on Cape Breton Island (p441) and the French Shore north of Yarmouth (p419). New Brunswick has a large French population stretching up the east coast past the Acadian Peninsula at Caraquet (p522). New Brunswick Acadian writer Antonine Maillet captures the distinct Acadian language and culture in her novels and short stories, available in translation.

WOLFVILLE

The students and faculty of Acadia University, who represent some 3500 of Wolfville's 7000 residents, keep this charming town operating at full tilt all year. With easy access to the Acadian dykes, enjoyable hikes just north of town and fine dining, Wolfville is a great place to spend a few days.

Information

Odd Book (☎ 902-542-9491; 112 Front St) Secondhand books of all genres.

Tourist Office (☎ 902-542-7000; 11 Willow Ave; ◷ 9am-9pm Jul-Sep, 9am-5pm early May–June & Oct) A very helpful office at the east end of Main St.

Wolfville (www.wolfville.info) Information on Wolfville, Acadia University and exploring Nova Scotia.

Wolfville Memorial Library (☎ 902-542-5760; 21 Elm Ave; ◷ 11am-5pm & 6:30-8:30pm Tue-Thu, 11am-5pm Fri & Sat, 1-5pm Sun) Free Internet access.

Sights

Waterfront Park (cnr Gaspereau Ave & Front St) offers a stunning view of the tidal mudflats, Minas Basin and the red cliffs of Cape Blomidon (p424). Displays explain the tides, dykes, flora and fauna, and history of the area. This is an easy spot to start a walk or bike ride on top of the dykes.

Randall House Museum (☎ 902-542-9775; 171 Main St; admission by donation; ◷ 10am-5pm Mon-Sat, 2-5pm Sun mid-Jun–mid-Sep) relates the history of the New England planters and colonists who replaced the expelled Acadians. Tea ($3) is served on antique china at 2:30pm.

Activities

Locals fought to save the home of hundreds of chimney swifts, birds that migrate annually to Wolfville from Peru. As a result, the chimney of a now-demolished dairy has become the focal point of the **Robie Tufts Nature Centre** (Front St), opposite the public library. Drop by in the late evening in spring or summer to see the birds swooshing down for a night's rest.

When the water is high enough, **tubing** down the Gaspereau River is a unique experience. Locals such as Kevin Schofield and Joy Power (☎ 902-542-3002; 3498 Black River Rd, Gaspereau; rentals per day $3; ◷ Jun–mid-Jul or longer) rent inner tubes for this purpose.

Rent bikes at **Valley Stove & Cycle** (☎ 902-542-7280; 234 Main St; rentals half-/full-day $25/30).

Sleeping

Garden House B&B (☎ 902-542-1703; www.gardenhouse .ca; 220 Main St; s/d $60/70) This big old house 400m east of the tourist office has three rooms and a relaxing back garden overlooking the bay. The host will gladly give directions to local swimming holes and ice-cream parlors.

Carwarden B&B (☎ 902-678-7827, 888-763-3320; www.carwarden.com; 640 Church St, Port Williams; d with shared bathroom $75) About 7km from Wolfville, this heritage B&B with spacious rooms has a wide veranda overlooking dykelands and an orchard. It's a little too sedate for children.

Blue Shutters B&B (☎ 902-542-3363; www.bb canada.com/blueshutters; 7 Blomidon Tce; s/d from $80/90) Directly up the steep hill from the tourist office, this modern home is accessible to disabled guests.

Victoria's Historic Inn (☎ 902-542-5744, 800-556-5744; www.victoriashistoricinn.com; r incl breakfast $110-165) This elegant inn has 16 rooms with modern amenities and timeless charm.

Eating

Ivy Deck (☎ 902-542-1868; 8 Elm Ave; mains $9-14; ◷ lunch & dinner, closed Mon Nov-Jun) Try a salad with flowers intermingled among the lettuce or salmon and shrimp penne. There's a pleasant outside deck.

Tempest (☎ 902/866-542-0588; 117 Front St; lunch mains $8-15, dinner mains $22-30; ◷ lunch & dinner) Tasty fine dining that borrows from all sorts of cuisines, as in Mexican *poblanoa* (a chicken dish with a mole sauce), cornmeal-battered catfish and scallops with mango salsa.

Joe's Food Emporium (☎ 902-542-3033; 292 Main St; mains $5-10; ◷ 7:30am-midnight) A casual place claiming to specialize in Italian, Mediterranean and Canadian cuisine.

Drinking

JustUs Café (☎ 902-542-7731; 450 Main St; ◷ 7am-6pm Mon-Fri, 9:30am-5pm Sat & Sun) Sip a cup of fairtrade coffee, browse the community bulletin board, and enjoy the relaxed atmosphere and free newspapers.

Paddy's Brewpub (☎ 902-542-0059; 460 Main St) Paddy's microbrew is widely sought after, and there are popular Wednesday night traditional music sessions.

Shopping

Applewicks (☎ 902-542-9771; 10 Gaspereau Ave) carries candles and woven goods produced by

NOVA SCOTIA

adults with mental disabilities. The proceeds go to a good cause and you can tour the workshop.

Treasures (☎ 902-542-4404; 3 Elm Ave) has Nova Scotian crafts and unique gifts.

Weave Shed (☎ 902-542-5504; Ste 22, 360 Main St) sells works by many local artists and crafts-people.

A farmers' market is held on Saturday mornings in the spring and summer on Front St by the library.

Getting There & Away

Acadian Lines stops at Acadia University in front of Wheelock Hall off Highland Ave. Kings Transit buses run between Cornwallis and Wolfville and stop at 209 Main St.

NORTH OF HIGHWAY 1

The North Mountain, which ends at dramatic Cape Blomidon, defines one edge of the Annapolis Valley. On the other side of the mountain are fishing communities on the Bay of Fundy. The valley floor between Hwy 1 and the North Mountain is crisscrossed with small highways lined with farms and orchards. It's a great place to get out your road map – or throw it out – and explore. To start the adventure, turn north on Hwy 358 just west of Wolfville (at exit 11 of Hwy 101). The historic town of Canning is en route to Scots Bay, where Hwy 358 ends and a dramatic hiking trail leads to views of the Minas Basin and the Bay of Fundy.

Port Williams

Prescott House Museum (☎ 902-542-3984; http://prescott.museum.gov.ns.ca; 1633 Starr's Point Rd; adult/student $3/2; 9:30am-5:30pm Mon-Sat, 1-5:30pm Sun, Jun–mid-Oct), c 1814, is the finest example of Georgian architecture in Nova Scotia, and former home of the horticulturalist who introduced many of the apple varieties grown in the Annapolis Valley. To get to here, turn right on Starr's Point Rd at the flashing light in Port Williams, 2km north of Hwy 1, and follow it for 3.25km.

Canning

From November to March, hundreds of **bald eagles** gather in the Canning area, attracted by local chicken farms – a photographers' and nature-lovers' dream. Just west of Canning on Hwy 221 **Blomidon Estate Winery**

(☎ 902-582-7565; 101318 Hwy 221; 11am & 3pm, Jun-Sep) offers free tours and tastings. Further along Hwy 358, stop at the **Look-Off**. About 200m above the Annapolis Valley, this is the best view of its rows of fruit trees and picturesque farmhouses.

Farmhouse B&B (☎ 902-582-7900, 800-928-4346; www.farmhouseinn.ns.ca; 9757 Main St, Canning; d $105, ste $125-150) strives for superior service. Some suites have Jacuzzis.

Fireside Café (☎ 902-582-7270, 888-809-1555; 9819 Main St, Canning; mains $6-10; 7am-6pm Mon-Sat, 10am-6pm Sun, to 8pm Wed-Fri Jul & Aug) exhibits work by local artists. It has surprising selections (like carrot cashew curry) and great prices. Call ahead to order a picnic lunch or wait around while one is made up.

Scots Bay

The hike to the end of **Cape Split** starts in Scots Bay. This is probably the most popular hiking trail in Nova Scotia. It's about 15km return, taking 4½ hours with little elevation change if you follow the easier inland route. To do that, follow the trail along the fence as you leave the parking area, and then choose the trail on your right when you come to a fork. (The trail on the left leads to a coastal route, which is poorly marked and subject to erosion. Give yourself extra time – and consider carrying a compass – if you want to explore that route.) The hike ends in a grassy meadow on cliffs high above the Bay of Fundy. Here you can see the tides creating waves called tidal rips. The unique geography of the Bay of Fundy results in the most extreme tides in the world: at its peak, the flow of water between Cape Split and the Parrsboro shore is equal to the combined flow of all the rivers and streams in the world!

Take time before or after the hike to look for agates along the beach at **Scots Bay**.

Blomidon Provincial Park (☎ 902-582-7319; parks.gov.ns.ca; off Hwy 358; campsites $18) is on the opposite side of Cape Blomidon from Scots Bay. There are a number of routes to get here from Hwy 358, all well signed. One route begins 15km south of Scots Bay, and involves driving 10km along the Minas Basin. The campground is set atop high cliffs that overlook the basin. There's a beach and picnic area at the foot of the hill and a 14km system of hiking trails within the park.

Hall's Harbour

Further southeast on the Bay of Fundy (take any route west from Hwy 358 until you hit Hwy 359, then take it over the North Mountain), **Hall's Harbour** is a great spot to spend an afternoon hiking along the beach and in the surrounding hills. It's also the best place in Nova Scotia to eat lobster.

Pick your own lobster at **Hall's Harbour Lobster Pound** (☎ 902-679-5299; noon-8pm Jul & Aug, noon-7pm May, Jun, Sep & Oct). The price is determined by the market – a whole one will rarely cost below $25. Seafood baskets with scallops or clams cost $12.

KENTVILLE

Kentville is the county seat for the area, with a number of government offices along with stately old homes and some good pubs.

Information

Tourist Office (☎ 902-678-7170; 125 Park St; 9:30am-7pm Jul & Aug, 9:30am-5:30pm mid-May–Jun & Sep–early Oct) West of the town center.

Sights & Activities

Local artifacts, history and an art gallery can be seen at the **Old King's Courthouse Museum** (☎ 902-678-6237; 37 Cornwallis Ave; admission free; 9:30am-4:30pm Mon-Sat). At the eastern end of town, the **Agriculture Research Station** (☎ 902-678-1093; off Hwy 1; admission free; 8:30am-4:30pm Jun-Aug) includes a museum on the area's farming history and the apple industry in particular. Guided museum tours are offered during summer. The 4km-return **Ravine Trail** begins from the gravel parking lot immediately east of the entrance to the research station. No bicycles are allowed on this pleasant walking trail through the old-growth hemlock woods.

Sleeping & Eating

Grand Street Inn (☎ 902-679-1991, 877-245-4744; grandstreetinn@eastlink.ca; 160 Main St; s/d/ste & f incl breakfast from $65/75/85;) This attractive old three-story Queen Anne revival house 1km east of downtown Kentville offers great value, especially for families. Two suites in the carriage house have kitchens.

King's Arms Pub (☎ 902-678-0066; 390 Main St; mains $7-12; lunch & dinner) Meals at this classic pub include steak and kidney pie or a pot of mussels. Happy hour is from 4:30pm to 6:30pm daily. There's live music on weekends.

Paddy's Pub & Rosie's (☎ 902-678-3199; 30 Aberdeen St; mains $7-12; lunch & dinner, brunch) Paddy's and Rosie's share the same building and menu, but Rosie's is a family-friendly restaurant. Paddy's brews its own gems such as Annapolis Valley Ale. Try the Irish stew ($7.50) made with Paddy's Porter.

Getting There & Away

Acadian Lines (☎ 902-678-2000; 66 Cornwallis St) has an office in the old train station; buses run to Halifax ($18, two hours, twice daily). **Kings Transit** (☎ 888-546-4442; 66 Cornwallis St; flat fare $2.50; 6am-7pm Mon-Fri, 8am-3pm Sat) is an excellent regional bus service that runs between Cornwallis and Wolfville with free transfers between buses at Kentville and Greenwood. It could take five hours to do a one-hour trip by car, but the price is right.

ANNAPOLIS ROYAL

Annapolis Royal was the site of Canada's first permanent European settlement, Port Royal, founded by Samuel de Champlain in 1605. As the British and French battled (see p395), the settlement often changed hands. In 1710 the British had a decisive victory and changed the town's name to Annapolis Royal in honor of Queen Anne. Nowadays the permanent population is less than 600, though that number swells with seasonal residents and tourists in the summer.

Orientation & Information

Most sights are on or near long, curving St George St. A waterfront boardwalk behind King's Theatre on St George St provides views of the village of Granville Ferry across the Annapolis River.

Annapolis Royal (www.annapolisroyal.com) Links to history, festivals and everything else.

VIC (☎ 902-532-5769; 236 Prince Albert Rd; 10am-6pm mid-May–mid-Oct) At the Tidal Power Project site by the Annapolis River Causeway; pick up a historic walking tour pamphlet.

Sights & Activities

Fort Anne National Historic Site (☎ 902-532-2397; www.parkscanada.gc.ca/fortanne; Upper St George St; adult/child 6-16 yrs/family $3.50/1.75/8.75; 9am-6pm), in the town center, preserves the memory of the early Acadian settlement plus the remains of the 1635 French fort. Entry to the extensive grounds is free, but you'll also want to visit the museum where artifacts are contained in various period rooms. An extraordinary four-panel tapestry, crafted in needlepoint by more than 100 volunteers, depicts 400 years of history.

Annapolis Royal Historic Gardens (☎ 902-532-7018; www.historicgardens.com; 441 St George St; adult/student/family $6/5/15; ☽ 9am-5pm May-Oct, 8am-dusk Jul & Aug) has four gardens: an Acadian kitchen garden one might have seen in 1671; a 'Governor's' garden from when Annapolis Royal was the capital of British North America in 1740; a Victorian garden full of annuals; and an innovative, modern garden featuring edible plants and heirloom vegetables. The Secret Garden Café offers lunches and mid-afternoon snacks.

Tidal Power Project (☎ 902-532-5454; admission free; ☽ 10am-6pm mid-May–mid-Oct), a hydroelectric prototype at the Annapolis River Causeway, has been harnessing power from the Bay of Fundy tides since 1984. An interpretive center includes models, exhibits and a video.

ARTsPLACE (☎ 902-532-7069; 396 St George St; admission free; ☽ 10am-5pm Tue-Fri, 1-4pm Sat & Sun) is an artist-run center that hosts exhibits and workshops.

Tours

During the fort's nighttime **graveyard tours** (per person $5; ☽ 9:30pm Tue, Thu & Sun Jun-Sep) your undertaker-garbed guide will escort you by candlelight through the headstones. Starting from the lighthouse on St George St, **daytime tours** (per person $5; ☽ 2pm Mon-Fri) focus on the Acadian heritage of Annapolis Royal or the architecture of the historic district.

Festivals & Events

West of Jazz East (☎ 902-532-2741; www.tallships .ca/jazz; one-day tickets/festival passes $15/40; ☽ 3rd weekend in Jul) Three days of jazz.

Arts Festival (☎ 902-532-7069; www.arcac.ca; ☽ late Sep) Readings, exhibits and workshops.

Sleeping

Many fine B&Bs and inns line St George St.

Grange Cottage (☎ 902-532-7993; www.bbcanada .com/6225.html; 102 Ritchie St; s/d $55/70) This B&B offers good value and a quiet location just a block from St George St. Three rooms share a bathroom.

Croft House B&B (☎ 902-532-0584; www.bbcanada .com/crofthouse; 51 Riverview Lane; s/d $55/70) This farmhouse stands on about 40 hectares of land, across the river and about a five-minute drive from Annapolis Royal. One of the enthusiastic owners is a chef, and he whips up a fine breakfast with organic ingredients.

Helen's Cabins (☎ 902-532-5207; 106 Hwy 201; s/d $60/70) These five 1950s cabins 1km east of town have hot plates for cooking.

Waterfront Inn (☎ 902-532-0593, 800-565-0000; www.waterfrontinn.20m.com; Granville Ferry; r incl breakfast $90-120) Across the water from Annapolis Royal, guests here can enjoy the view from private balconies off unique rooms. One room is accessible to disabled guests.

Hillsdale House (☎ 902-532-2345, 877-839-2821; www.hillsdalehouse.ns.ca; 519 St George St; r incl breakfast $95-140) When he was still a prince, King George V slept in room No 2. Today this comfortable, relaxed inn welcomes families. It's also a fine place to eat – the three-course evening prix fixe costs $30 and is open to nonguests; call for reservations. The inn's four-hectare plot backs onto the Annapolis Royal Historic Gardens.

Eating

Leo's (☎ 902-532-7424; 222 St George St; mains $6-9; ☽ 9am-8pm Mon-Sat, noon-4pm Sun Jul-Sep, 9am-4pm Mon-Sat off-season) Very popular with locals; be prepared to wait for a delicious sandwich. Specials combine sandwiches with salad or soup.

Garrison House (☎ 902-532-5750; 350 George St; mains $15-20; ☽ dinner) This high-end B&B serves dishes like salmon poached with a maple-whiskey glaze, and Acadian jambalaya with farm-fresh garden vegetables.

Newman's (☎ 902-532-5502; 218 St George St; mains $18-27; ☽ lunch & dinner Tue-Sun Jun-Oct) This long-established restaurant offers mains with very fresh seafood, lamb and beef. Desserts feature local berries.

Entertainment

King's Theatre (☎ 902-532-7704; www.kingstheatre .ca; 209 St George St; movie ticket $6, live shows $14-22) Right on the waterfront, this theater presents musicals, dramas and concerts most evenings in July and August, and occasionally during the rest of the year. Hollywood films are screened on most weekends, and independent films most Tuesdays, year-round.

Shopping

Farmers & Traders Market (cnr St George & Church St; ☽ Sat am & Wed pm) Annapolis Royal's thriving community of artists and artisans offer their wares alongside local farmers at this popular market. There's live entertainment most Saturday mornings.

Lucky Rabbit Pottery (☎ 902-532-0928; 15 Church St) A husband-and-wife teams make fine but totally unstuffy porcelain: jars topped with chickadees, mugs decorated with frogs and so on.

Almost next door, **Far-Fetched Antiques & Art** (☎ 902-532-0179; 27 Church St; ⏰ 10am-6pm Mon-Fri, 9am- 6pm Sat, noon-6pm Sun Jun-Sep, 10am-5pm Mon-Fri, 9am-5pm Sat, noon-5pm Sun Oct) sells treasures gathered from southeast Asia.

Getting There & Away

Acadian Lines stops at the **Port Royal Wandlyn Inn** (☎ 902-532-2323; 3924 Hwy 1) from Halifax ($34, 3½ hours, daily), en route to Digby ($6, 30 minutes).

Around Annapolis Royal

North Hills Museum (☎ 902-532-2168; http://mu seum.gov.ns.ca/nhm; 5065 Granville Rd, Granville Ferry; adult/child $3/2; ⏰ 9:30am-5:30pm Mon-Sat, 1-5:30pm Sun Jun–mid-Oct), overlooking the Annapolis Basin, has a superb collection of Georgian antiques displayed in a farmhouse dating from 1764.

Some 14km northwest of Annapolis Royal, **Port Royal National Historic Site** (☎ 902-532-2898; 53 Historic Lane; adult/child $2.75/1.35; ⏰ 9am-6pm mid-May–mid-Oct) is the actual location of the first permanent European settlement north of Florida. It's a replica, reconstructed in the original manner of de Champlain's 1605 fur-trading habitation. Costumed workers help tell the story of this early settlement.

Over the North Mountain from Annapolis Royal, **Delap's Cove Wilderness Trail** lets you get out on the Fundy shore. It actually consists of two loop trails connected by an old inland road that used to serve a Black Loyalist community, now just old foundations and apple trees in the woods. With both loops, the trail is 9km return.

Fundy Trail Campground & Cottages (☎ 902-532-7711, 877-519-2267; www.fundytrail.com; 62 Delap's Cove; tent sites $24, RV sites $27-32; 🐾) caters mostly to RVs but it has 24 unserviced sites. Of these, Nos 70 to 77 are hidden in the woods next to a creek that runs down to the fishing wharf at Delap's Cove, just minutes from the trailhead for the hike.

BEAR RIVER

Historic homes nestle on the steep hills of the Bear River valley, a unique topography which has earned Bear River the hyperbolic nickname of the Switzerland of Nova Scotia. Some buildings near the river are on stilts. Just 400 people strong, Bear River attracts artists and quirky characters.

Information

VIC (☎ 902-467-3200; 109 Wharf Rd; ⏰ 9am-4pm mid-Jun–mid-Oct, to 6pm Jul & Aug) In a windmill beside the river, where there is also parking and several picnic tables.

Sights & Activities

DOWNTOWN BEAR RIVER

Up the hill from the VIC, the **Oakdene Centre** (1913 Clementsvale Rd) is a former elementary school now reborn as artists' studios. Wander the studios and check the bulletin board for details of performances, classes and other community happenings.

The founder of the **Riverview Ethnographic Museum** (☎ 902-467-4321; 18 Chute Rd; admission $2; ⏰ 10am-5pm Tue-Sat) is a retired costume designer who collected traditional clothing from around the world, now on display.

Bear River Heritage Museum (☎ 902-467-0902; 1890 Clementsvale Rd; admission free; ⏰ 10am-4pm Mon-Sat, 1-4pm Sun Jul–mid-Sep) has five rooms of exhibits on local history, including Mi'kmaw artifacts.

BEAR RIVER FIRST NATION

The Bear River First Nation is a five-minute drive from the heart of town: turn left after crossing the bridge from the VIC, then take a left where the road forks. In a beautiful new building, with a wigwam-shaped foyer, its **Heritage & Cultural Centre** (☎ 902-467-0301; 194 Reservation Rd; admission $2.50; ⏰ 10am-6pm mid-May–mid-Oct) offers demonstrations of traditional crafts and hands-on workshops. A 1km **trail** starts behind the center and highlights plants with traditional medicinal uses.

GREEN SEWAGE

Just past the windmill, check out the greenhouse that houses Bear River's award-winning **sewage treatment facility**. Beautiful, lush aquatic plants do the dirty work and thrive in the process. Ask at the VIC to see an explanatory video.

NOVA SCOTIA

Sleeping & Eating

House of Leaves B&B (☎ 902-467-0500, 866-644-0500; www.houseofleaves.ca; 52 Pleasant St; r incl breakfast $90–95) Run by a young British-Canadian couple who stumbled on Bear River on the Internet, this B&B is perched high on one of the hills overlooking the river. It offers fresh baked goods and generous, comfortable rooms.

Trading Post Café (☎ 902-467-3008; Main St, at the bridge; mains $5-8; ☼ 7:30am-8pm Jul & Aug, to 5pm rest of year) The only place to eat in town, this café offers good food (swiss cheese potato pancakes with two eggs and toast, $5.50) and views over the river.

Shopping

Flight of Fancy (☎ 902-467-4171; Main St, at the bridge; ☼ 9am-7pm Mon-Sat, 11am-7pm Sun Jul & Aug, 9am-5pm Mon-Sat, 11am-5pm Sun rest of year) An exquisitely curated craft store and gallery with work by more than 200 artists and craftspeople. If you want to buy one unique treasure to take away from Nova Scotia, this is a good place to find it.

Oddacity (☎ 902-467-0268) Next door to Flight of Fancy, this place sells original clothing designed by a Bob Dylan fan. Lyrics decorate the outside of the store.

Bear Town Baskets (☎ 902-467-3060; 44 Maple Ave, Bear River First Nation; ☼ 10am-10pm) Baskets sold here are made by a retired chief of the Bear River First Nation. Follow the signs to the studio in his front yard where he makes traditional ash baskets.

DIGBY

Digby is nestled in a protected inlet off the Bay of Fundy. Settled by United Empire Loyalists in 1783, it's home to the largest fleet of scallop boats in the world. The daily ferry (p397) to Saint John, New Brunswick, also squeezes through the small channel known as the Digby Gut.

Digby has been a tourist mecca for more than a century, despite few attractions other than a mild climate and the picturesque waterfront with an abundance of seafood restaurants and souvenir shops. Give it a pass if you don't enjoy crowds; Digby Neck (p429), Annapolis Royal and Bear River are more interesting destinations.

Information

Digby (www.klis.com/digby) Has a virtual tour of Digby as well as links to useful information.

Tourist Office (☎ 888-463-4429; 110 Montague Row; ☼ 8am-8pm Jul & Aug, 9am-5pm mid-May–Jun & Sep–mid-Oct)

Visitor Information Centre (VIC; ☎ 902-245-2201; Shore Rd; ☼ 8:30am-8:30pm mid-Jun–mid-Sep, 9am-5pm May–mid-Jun & mid-Sep–Oct) A large provincial tourist office, 2km from the ferry wharf, with hundreds of brochures.

Western Counties Regional Library (☎ 902-245-2163; 84 Warwick St; ☼ 12:30-5pm & 6-8pm Tue-Thu, 10am-5pm Fri, 10am-2pm Sat) Free Internet access.

Sights & Activities

Stroll the boardwalk and watch the scallop draggers come and go. The **Lady Vanessa** (☎ 902-245-4950; 34 Water St; admission $2; ☼ 9am-7pm Jul & Aug, 9am-5pm May, Jun, Sep & Oct), a 30m wooden dragger, is now permanently mounted on the sidewalk for visitors to tour. There are exhibits and a video on the scallop fishery inside.

A mid-19th century Georgian home is now the **Admiral Digby Museum** (☎ 902-245-6322; 95 Montague Row; admission by donation; ☼ 9am-5pm Tue-Sat, 1-5pm Sun mid-Jun–Aug, 9am-5pm Tue-Fri Sep–mid-Oct, 9am-5pm Wed & Fri mid-Oct–mid-May), which contains exhibits of the town's marine history and early settlement.

Sleeping & Eating

Thistle Down Country Inn (☎ 902-245-4490, 800-565-8081; www.thistledown.ns.ca/theinn; 98 Montague Row; r incl breakfast $95-120) Across from the Admiral Digby Museum and right on the water, this inn has six historic rooms in the main house, plus another six in a modern annex. Dine here on fresh local seafood (6:30pm by reservation; three courses $26.95 to $29.95).

Bayside Inn (☎ 888-754-0555, 902-245-2247; www.baysideinn.ca; 115 Montague Row; r incl breakfast $90; P ☐) A comfortable, older inn across from the harbor and the tourist office.

Fundy Restaurant (☎ 902-245-4950; 26 Water St; lunch $9-15; dinner $18-22; ☼ 7am-10pm mid-May–Oct, noon-8pm Nov–early May) This massive restaurant offers a great kids menu: $4.50 for any of seven choices. For adults, there are a variety of scallop and other seafood dishes.

Getting There & Away

Acadian Lines buses from Halifax ($40, four hours, daily) stop at the **Irving gas station** (☎ 902-245-2048; 77 Montague Row).

DIGBY NECK

The long, thin strip of land that protrudes into the Bay of Fundy is known as Digby Neck. At the far western end are Long and Brier Islands, connected by ferry with the rest of the peninsula.

People are drawn here by the sea life off the islands. Plankton stirred up by the strong Bay of Fundy tides attracts finback, minke and humpback whales. This is the best place in the world to see the endangered North Atlantic right whale.

The number of whale-watching operators here has exploded, from just one in the late 1980s to more than a dozen now, leading to some concern about impacts on the whales. Operators have agreed on a code of ethics: they won't chase whales that are trying to avoid them, won't force them toward fishing gear and won't converge on one area. That's good for travelers, too, as it's more pleasant to watch whales than other boats of whale-watchers. A number of the operators – including all those listed below – assist in whale research.

Bring plenty of warm clothing (regardless of how hot a day it seems), sunblock and binoculars. A motion-sickness pill taken before leaving the dock may not be a bad idea either.

Getting There & Away

Two ferries connect Long and Brier Islands to the rest of Digby Neck. The Petit Passage ferry leaves East Ferry (on Digby Neck) on the half hour and Tiverton on the hour; ferries are timed so that if you drive directly from Tiverton to Freeport (18km) there is no wait for the Grand Passage ferry to Westport. Both ferries operate hourly 24 hours a day year-round. Roundtrip passage is $4 for a car and all passengers. Pedestrians ride free.

Long Island

At the northeastern edge of Long Island, **Tiverton** is an active fishing community. The tourist information desk is found at the **Island Museum** (☎ 902-839-2853; 3083 Hwy 217; admission free; ☺ 9:30am-7:30pm Jul & Aug, 9:30am-4:30pm late May–Jun & Sep–mid-Oct), 2km west of the Tiverton ferry, which has exhibits on local history.

A 4km round-trip trail to the **Balancing Rock** starts 2km southwest of the museum. The trails features rope railings, boardwalks

and an extensive series of steps down a rock bluff to the bay. Be careful with children; it's very slippery. At the end there is a viewing platform where you can see a 7m-high stone column perched precariously just above the pounding surf of St Mary's Bay.

Near the center of Long Island, **Central Grove Provincial Park** has a 2km hiking trail to the Bay of Fundy. The family-operated **Pirate's Cove Whale & Seabird Cruises** (☎ 902-839-2242, 888-480-0004; www.piratescove.ca; adult/child 5-12 yrs/student incl tax $40/20/30), which depart from Tiverton Harbour, has new vessels and a great crew.

At the southwestern end of Long Island, **Freeport** is central for exploring both Brier Island and Long Island. The lovely old **Freeport House B&B** (☎ 902-839-2337; www.valleyweb.com/freeporthouse; d $60-80, f $130) has a huge wrap-around porch from which to watch the ocean. Bikes are available for guests to borrow.

Owned by a well-respected whale researcher, **Summer Solstice B&B** (☎ 902-839-2170; deb.tobin@ns.sympatico.ca; 325 Over Cove Rd; s/d $60/70) is a brand-new, gay-friendly, century-old house. Three rooms have views over the Bay of Fundy.

Lavena's Catch Café (☎ 902-839-2517; 15 Hwy 217; mains $7-10; ☺ lunch & dinner) is directly above the wharf at Freeport, perfect to enjoy a sunset. There are lots of seafood and a few vegetarian options on the menu. If you're staying in Westport on Brier Island, take the ferry over for dinner (passengers on foot travel free).

Brier Island

The only community on Brier Island, **Westport** was the home of Joshua Slocum, the first man to sail solo around the world. Westport is a quaint little fishing village and a good base to explore the numerous excellent, if rugged, hiking trails around the island. Columnar basalt rocks are seen all along the coast and agates can be found on the beaches.

Mariner Cruises (☎ 902-839-2346, 800-239-2189; www.marinercruises.ns.ca; adult/child under 12 $40/22; ☺ Jun-Oct) has a booking office just to the left of the ferry, but you board the boat a kilometer along the waterfront. The trips, complete with homemade muffins, can last anywhere from 2½ to five hours depending on where the whales are.

NOVA SCOTIA

The 12-bed **Brier Island Backpackers Hostel** (☎ 902-839-2273; www.brierislandhostel.com; 223 Water St; dm adult/child 6-12 yrs $15/7.50; 🖳) is to the left as you come off the ferry. It has squeaky-clean washrooms and a full kitchen.

Dock & Doze Motel (☎ 902-839-2601; dock.doze@ns.sympatio.ca; d $60), directly opposite the ferry landing at Westport, just to the right as you get off, has three units.

On top of cliffs 1km east of Westport, **Brier Island Lodge** (☎ 902-839-2300, 800-662-8355; www.brierisland.com; r $60-110) has 40 rooms, some wheelchair accessible. Its **restaurant** (mains $13-15; ☼ breakfast, dinner & boxed lunches) uses locally caught seafood.

ST BERNARD

The French shore, on the mainland directly across St Mary's Bay from Digby Neck, is the heart of Acadian Nova Scotia. This is where Acadians settled when, after trekking back to Nova Scotia following the deportation, they found their homesteads in the Annapolis Valley already occupied. Now linked by Hwy 1 – pretty much the only road in town – these are small fishing communities.

St Bernard's overwhelming attraction is **St Bernard Church** (☎ 902-837-5637; Hwy 1; ☼ tours Jun-Sep), a huge granite structure built by locals who added one row of blocks each year between 1910 and 1942. It has incredible acoustics which are showcased each summer through the **Musique Saint-Bernard** (http://wvcn.ns.ca/~msb; adult/under 18 $15/5) concert series.

BELLIVEAU COVE

Belliveau Beach, near the southern end of this community, is reached by turning right onto Major's Point. The beach is made up of masses of sea-polished stones broken only by small clumps of incredibly hardy fir trees. Just behind the beach, a cemetery and monument recall the struggles of the early Acadian settlers of the French shore.

Piau's trail, named for Pierre (Piau) Belliveau who led Acadians here during the deportation, starts here and wends 5km along the beach before ending up in the backyard of **Chez Jean Dairy Twirl** (☎ 902-837-5750; 3139 Hwy 1; meals $7-12; ☼ 11am-10pm Sun-Thu, to midnight Fri & Sat). This casual eatery with a great view serves ice cream as well as seafood.

Roadside Grill (☎ 902-837-5047; 3334 Hwy 1; meals $7-13; ☼ 8am-9pm Jul & Aug, 9am-7pm Sep-Jun) is a pleasantly old-fashioned local restaurant.

Try the steamed clams or the rappie pie (a type of meat pie topped with grated pastelike potato from which all the starch has been drawn). It also rents three small cabins (s/d $45/60) with cable TV and microwaves.

CHURCH POINT

Église Ste Marie (☎ 902-769-2808; Hwy 1; admission incl guide $2; ☼ 9am-5pm mid-May–mid-Oct) towers over the town, also commonly known as Pointe de l'Église. Built between 1903 and 1905, the church is said to be the tallest and biggest wooden church in North America. An informative guide will show you around. Adjacent is the **Université Ste Anne**, the only French university in the province and a center for Acadian culture, with 300 students.

The oldest of the annual Acadian cultural festivals, **Festival Acadien de Clare** is held during the second week of July. In July and August the musical *Évangéline*, based on Longfellow's romantic poem about the Acadian deportation, is presented in the **Théâtre Marc-Lescarbot** (☎ 902-769-2114; adult/child & student/senior $25/15/20) at Church Point. Performances are given in English on Saturday, in French with headset translation Tuesday and Friday, and outdoors in French only on Wednesday.

Rapure Acadienne (☎ 902-769-2172; 1443 Hwy 1; large pie $6; ☼ 8am-9pm Jul & Aug, 8am-5:30pm Sep-Jun), a bit over 1km south of the church toward Yarmouth, is where all the local establishments get their beef, chicken or clam rappie pie. Look for the Acadian flag outside.

METEGHAN

The largest community on the French shore is a busy fishing port. **Smuggler's Cove Provincial Park**, at the southern edge of town, is named for its popularity in 19th-century pirates. A hundred wooden stairs take you down to a rocky beach and a good cave for hiding treasure. There are picnic sites with barbecue pits at the top of the stairs, with a view across St Mary's Bay to Brier Island.

L'Auberge au Havre du Capitaine (☎ 902-769-2001; capitaine@auracom.com; 9118 Hwy 1; r $75-100) has one wheelchair-accessible room. From the cozy seating area to the handmade quilts, this inn says *bienvenue* (welcome). Try scrambled eggs with lobster ($12) for breakfast at the on-site **restaurant** (breakfast $5-7, lunch mains $7-8, dinner mains $12-15; ☼ 7am-9pm Jul & Aug, 7-9am & 5-7:30pm off-season). There's live Acadian entertainment on Friday evening.

CAPE ST MARY

A long, wide arc of fine sand, just 900m off Hwy 1, **Mavilette Beach** is great for collecting seashells, and the marsh behind it is good for bird-watching. The **Cape View Motel** (☎ 902-645-2258; http://nsonline.com/capeview; off Hwy 1; r/cottages incl breakfast $65/85), just above the beach, offers motel rooms and self-contained cottages with great views. Across the street, **Cape View Restaurant** (☎ 902-645-2519; lunch $5-8, dinner $12-20; ☻ lunch & dinner) serves seafood and Acadian dishes. The view of the beach and of Cape St Mary is spectacular. Come on a Wednesday night during the summer to enjoy live Acadian music.

CENTRAL NOVA SCOTIA

Essentially the corridor of land from Halifax up to the New Brunswick border, this region introduces Nova Scotia to those traveling overland from the rest of Canada. Don't turn against the province because of what you see from the Trans-Canada Hwy! Opt to follow the Bay of Fundy shore instead, thereby avoiding a $3 toll and negligible scenery. Both Advocate Harbour and Parrsboro are worthwhile stops and there is superb scenery between them. This area is called the 'Glooscap Trail' in provincial tourism literature, named for the figure in Mi'kmaw legend who created the unique geography of the Bay of Fundy region. Unfortunately, stories and representations of Glooscap are easier to come across than genuine acknowledgments of present-day Mik'mak people, some 5000 of whom live in this part of the province.

SHUBENACADIE

Shubenacadie, or simply 'Shube,' is best known for the **Shubenacadie Provincial Wildlife Park** (☎ 902-758-2040; http://wildlifepark.gov.ns.ca; 149 Creighton Rd; adult/child 6-17 yrs/family $4/$1.50/10; ☻ 9am-7pm mid-May–mid-Oct, 9am-3pm Sat & Sun rest of year), an unusual provincial park with Nova Scotian wildlife, including birds, waterfowl, foxes and deer, in large enclosures. The animals were either born in captivity or once kept as 'pets,' and as a result cannot be released into the wild. Turn off Hwy 102 at exit 11 and follow Hwy 2 to the park entrance.

TRURO

A quick look at the map explains why Truro is known as the hub of Nova Scotia. Several major highways converge here, along with a VIA Rail line. Truro is also a bus transfer point. While you can't avoid passing by, spend as little time here as possible. Despite some redevelopment of the older part of town around Prince and Inglis Sts, Truro most resembles an interminable mall.

It's reasonable to see the sights here in an afternoon – depending on the timing of high tide (see the boxed text on p432) – and then push on to Tatamagouche (p436) or Economy (p432). The best time to visit is the second weekend in August when Millbrook First Nation, on the outskirts of Truro, hosts a **powwow** (☎ 902-897-9199). Campsites and showers are available there; drugs and alcohol are prohibited.

Information
Tourist Office (☎ 902-893-2922; Victoria Sq, cnr Prince & Commercial Sts; ☻ 9am-5pm mid-May–Oct, 8:30am-7:30pm Jul & Aug) Offers Internet access.

Sights & Activities
Victoria Park (Park St off Brunswick St) is one pleasant way of escaping Truro. Explore 400 hectares of green space in the center of town, including a deep gorge and two waterfalls. The park attracts dozens of bird species.

Colchester Museum (☎ 902-895-6284; 29 Young St; adult/child $2/1; ☻ 10am-5pm Jul & Aug, 10am-noon & 2-5pm Tue-Fri, 2-5pm Sat Sep-Jun) has exhibits on the founding of Truro, the region's human history and Elizabeth Bishop, a noted poet who grew up in the area.

Jan van der Leest's large collection of melodeons, harmoniums and reed organs is in the **Organery** (☎ 902-893-4824; 53 Farnham Rd; admission by donation; ☻ 11am-4pm May-Oct). Ask for a performance.

Sleeping & Eating
Palliser Motel (☎ 902-893-8951; www.palliserrestaurant motelandgifts.ca; Tidal Bore Rd; r incl breakfast $65-75) This 42-room motel near exit 14 from Hwy 102 will give you a wake-up call to watch a nocturnal bore (see the boxed text on p432) lit by floodlights. In summer the Palliser is usually full by 5pm, so call ahead for a reservation. Some rooms are wheelchair-accessible.

NOVA SCOTIA

TIDAL BORE

The **tidal bore** is a unique phenomenon to witness. As a result of the extreme Bay of Fundy tides, a tidal bore or wave flows up the feeder rivers when high tide comes in. Sometimes the advancing wave is only a ripple, but with the right phase of the moon it can be a meter or so in height, giving the impression that the Salmon River is flowing backwards. See it from the lookout on Tidal Bore Rd, off Hwy 236 just west of exit 14 from Hwy 102 on the northwest side of Truro. The folks in the adjacent Palliser Motel **gift shop** (☎ 902-893-8951) can advise when the next tidal bore will arrive.

At the Organery (☎ 902-893-4824, 877-822-5655; www.organery.ca; 53 Farhham Rd; r/ste $75/95) Attached to the unusual museum there are four comfortable rooms in an older home.

Wooden Hog (☎ 902-895-0779; 627 Prince St; lunch $7, dinner mains $10-16; 🕒 9am-10pm Mon-Thu, 9am-11pm Fri, 11am-1pm Sat) Named for the huge, sculpted Harley that hangs off the back wall, this is a popular restaurant with healthy dishes and decadent desserts.

Murphy's Fish & Chips (☎ 902-895-1275; 88 Esplanade St; mains $5-9; 🕒 11am-7pm Mon-Thu & Sat, to 8pm Fri, noon-7pm Sun) Three doors down from the train station, this place is always packed with locals who rave about the fish and chips.

Getting There & Away

The **bus station** (☎ 902-895-3833; www.acadianbus.com; 280 Willow St; 🕒 8am-10:30pm) is busy with Acadian Lines buses en route to Amherst ($22, two hours, three times daily) and Sydney ($50, five hours, three times daily).

ECONOMY

Highway 2 hugs the shore of the Minas Basin, the northeast arm of the Bay of Fundy, and this is the first sizable community you'll hit. There's great hiking and several interesting sites around Economy.

Sights & Activities

Raspberry Bay Stone (☎ 902-647-2287; www.raspberrybaystone.com; Hwy 2, Bass River; 🕒 10am-5pm mid-May–Sep, call ahead rest of year), about 7km east of Economy, is a wonderful combination of an artist's studio, gallery, museum, garden and petting zoo. Heather Lawson was the first female stonemason in Canada; she manages to make stone feel light with inspired, highly skilled carving.

Get information about local hikes at the **Cobequid Interpretation Centre** (☎ 902-647-2600; 3248 Hwy 2, near River Phillip Rd; admission free; 🕒 9am-4:30pm Mon-Fri, to 6pm Sat & Sun Jul & Aug). It has good exhibits on the area's ecology and history. Climb a WWII observation tower for a bird's-eye view of the surrounding area.

The most challenging hikes are around Economy Falls. The **Devil's Bend Trail** begins 7km up River Phillip Rd toward the Cobequid Mountains. Turn right and park; the 6.5km (one-way) trail follows the river to the falls. The **Kenomee Canyon Trail** begins further up River Phillip Rd, at the top of the falls. A 20km loop, it takes you up the river to its headwaters in a protected wilderness area. Several streams have to be forded. There are designated campsites, making this a good two-day adventurous trek.

The **Thomas Cove Coastal Trail** is actually two 3.5km loops with great views across the Minas Basin and of the Cobequid Mountains. They begin down Economy Point Rd, 500m east of the Cobequid Interpretation Centre. Follow the signs to a parking area. Finally, just west of Economy, there are several hikes in **Five Islands Provincial Park** (☎ 902-254-2980; parks.gov.ns.ca), 7km past Economy. The 4.5km **Red Head Trail** is well developed with lookouts, benches and great views.

Sleeping & Eating

High Tide B&B (☎ 902-647-2788; www3.ns.sympatico.ca/hightide.bb; 2240 Hwy 2, Lower Economy; d $75-85). This friendly, modern bungalow has great views. Janet will have you down on the beach for a clam boil in no time.

Four Seasons Retreat (☎ 902-647-2628, 888-373-0339; 320 Cove Rd, Upper Economy; www.fourseasonsretreat.ns.ca; 1-/2-bedroom cottages $100/125; 🅿) Fully equipped cottages are surrounded by trees and face the Minas Basin. In summer there's a hot tub near the pool; in winter – or on a chilly night – there are woodstoves.

Five Islands Provincial Park (☎ 902-254-2980; http://parks.gov.ns.ca; Hwy 2; campsites $18) There are 90 sites here – from large grassy sites to smaller forested ones – plus showers, flush toilets and a playground. It's a good place to try clam digging.

Several take-away stands selling fried clams pop up along the highway near Five Islands Provincial Park in the summer. The café at **That Dutchman's Farm** (☎ 902-647-2751; 112 Brown Rd, Upper Economy; lunch $5; 🕐 11am-5pm late Jun–early Sep) offers sandwiches, soups and plates of the eccentric farmer's own gouda. You can tour the farm for a small fee.

PARRSBORO

Parrsboro, the largest of the small towns along the Minas Basin shore, is worth taking a couple days to explore. The Fundy Geological Museum has wonderful exhibits and good programs that take you to the beach areas known as Nova Scotia's 'Jurassic Park.' The annual **Gem & Mineral Show** is in mid-August.

Information

Tourist Office (☎ 902-254-3266; 69 Main St; 🕐 10am-7pm Jun-Oct) Has tide information and free Internet access.

Sights & Activities
FUNDY GEOLOGICAL MUSEUM

This award-winning **museum** (☎ 902-254-3814; www.museum.gov.ns.ca/fgm; 162 Two Islands Rd; adult/ child/student/family $5/3/4.25/12; 🕐 9:30am-5:30pm Jun–mid-Oct, 9am-5pm Tue-Sat mid-Oct–May) uses interactive exhibits to help its visitors 'time travel' to when the fossils littering Parrsboro's beaches were alive. You can see a lab where dinosaur bones are being cleaned and assembled. Two- to three-hour beach tours (adult/child $11.50/$5.75) focus on minerals or fossils; there are up to four tours daily. Check the website for full-day family programs.

PARTRIDGE ISLAND

Steeped in history, this is the most popular shoreline to search for gems. Samuel de Champlain landed here in 1607 and took away amethyst rocks from the beach. The island is 4km south of town on Whitehall Rd. Visitors search the pebbled shoreline or the bluffs for agate and other stones. From the end of the beach a 3km **hiking trail** with explanatory panels climbs to the top of Partridge Island (connected to the mainland by an isthmus) for superb views of Blomidon and Cape Split.

Just before the beach is **Ottawa House Museum** (☎ 902-254-2376; 1155 Whitehall Rd; admission $2; 🕐 10am-6pm Jun–mid-Sep), a 21-room mansion that was once the summer home of Sir Charles Tupper (1821–1915), who served as both premier of Nova Scotia and prime minister of Canada. The museum has exhibits on the former settlement on Partridge Island, shipbuilding and rum-running.

Sleeping & Eating

Riverview Cottages (☎ 902-254-2388; 3575 Eastern Ave; s/d $50/60; 🕐 Apr-Nov) Just east of town, some of these rustic cottages have woodstoves. Guests enjoy free use of the rowboats and canoes on the river behind the cottages.

Maple Inn (☎ 902-254-3735, 877-627-5346; www3 .ns.sympatico.ca/mapleinn; 17 Western Ave; s/d incl breakfast $75/90; 🕐 year-round) This place has nine comfortable rooms in two adjoining century-old homes, a short walk from the center of town.

Evangeline's Tower B&B (☎ 902-254-3383, 866-338-6937; www.evangelinestower.ca; 322 Main St; d incl breakfast $95-105; 🕐 year-round) This gay-friendly Victorian home has three rooms; one can be a two-room suite for families. Mountain bikes are available.

Glooscap Campground (☎ 902-254-2529; fax 902-254-2313; 1380 Two Island Rd; tent/RV sites $15/20; 🕐 mid-May–Sep) This very attractive municipally owned campground on the shore 5km south of town has some nice secluded tent sites.

John's Café (☎ 902-254-3255; 151 Main St; lunch $5-8, dinner mains $12-17; 🕐 8am-10pm Jun-Sep, 8am-4pm Mon-Fri rest of year) This attractive café serves breakfast all day, and also has quiche, soups and pasta. The dinner menu is only available in summer.

Berry's Restaurant (☎ 902-254-3040; 29 Two Island Rd; mains $8-12; 🕐 7am-10pm Jun-Sep, 7am-9pm rest of year) This is a dependable place for basics like fish chowder ($5.50) or a scallop dinner ($10).

Entertainment

Ship's Company Theatre (☎ 902-254-3000, 800-565-7469; www.shipscompany.com; 18 Lower Main St; adult $20-24, student/under 13 $15/10; 🕐 Jul–mid-Sep) This innovative theater company performs new Canadian and Maritime works 'on board' the MV *Kipawo*, the last of the Minas Basin ferries, now integrated into a new theater. There's high-quality theater for kids, improv comedy, readings and concerts.

NOVA SCOTIA

PORT GREVILLE

Port Greville is a lovely drive of about 20km to the west of Parrsboro on Rte 209. Stop for tea, baked goods and a tour at the **Age of Sail Heritage Centre** (☎ 902-348-2030; www.parrsboro .com/aos.htm; Rte 209; adult/family $2/5; ☺ 10am-6pm Jun-Sep). It captures the area's shipbuilding heritage. The site also includes a restored 1857 Methodist church and a working blacksmith shop.

ADVOCATE HARBOUR

This breathtaking place is wedged between Cape D'Or and Cape Chignecto. A 5km-long beach is piled high with driftwood. Behind it, salt marshes reclaimed with dykes by the Acadians are now replete with birds. The main attraction is Cape Chignecto Provincial Park, opened in 1998 and now the crown jewel of the park system. Spend an extra day in 'town' to recover from the exertions of exploring the park.

Reid's Century Farm Tourist Home (☎ 902-392-2592; www3.ns.sympatico.ca/reidadvocate/reids.htm; 1391 West Advocate Rd; d/cottages $55/100; ☺ Jun-Sep), close to Cape Chignecto Provincial Park, has three comfortable rooms. The cottage has a full kitchen and could sleep five comfortably.

Follow the signs off Hwy 209 to **Lightkeeper's Kitchen & Guest House** (☎ 902-670-0534; www.capedor.ca; Cape d'Or; s/d with ocean view $70/90; ☺ mid-May–mid-Oct). The lighthouse and foghorn warn vessels away from Cape d'Or, which juts out into the Bay of Fundy. The original lighthouse keeper's residence is now a four-room guesthouse. A small gourmet **restaurant** (lunch mains $7-8, dinner mains $16-18; ☺ 11am-4pm & 6-8pm mid-May–Aug, 11am-4pm & 6-8pm Thu-Mon Sep–mid Oct) serves original seafood, meat and vegetarian creations.

Fundy Tides Campground (☎ 902-392-2584; 95 Mills Rd; tent/RV sites $12/18) is a good alternative if you're camping with your car. The **canteen** (☺ 8am-9pm Jul & Aug, 11am-7pm rest of year) serves tasty fishburgers ($6.50) and other delicacies.

Around Advocate Harbour
CAPE CHIGNECTO PROVINCIAL PARK
The **Cape Chignecto Coastal Trail** is a rugged 60km loop with backcountry – nay, old-growth – campsites. Budget four days and three nights for the hike. The **Mill Brook Canyon Trail** (15km return) and the hike to **Refu-**

gee **Cove** (20km return) are other challenging overnight hikes. There are some easier hikes and more are being developed. Some hikers have tried to avoid the ups and downs of the trails by taking shortcuts along the beach at low tide and been cut off by the Bay of Fundy tides. Get a tide table and follow advice from park staff to avoid being trapped on the cliffs.

Park visitors must register and leave an itinerary at the **Visitor Centre** (☎ 902-392-2085; www.capechignecto.net; 1108 West Advocate Rd; hiking permits $3, backcountry sites $18; ☺ 8am-7pm Mon-Thu, 8am-8pm Fri & Sat, 8am-6pm Sun Jul & Aug, 8am-5pm Mon-Thu, 8am-7pm Fri & Sat, 8am-6pm Sun late May-Jun, Sep & Oct). Camping in the backcountry requires reservations. In addition to 51 wilderness campsites at six points along the coastal trail and 27 walk-in sites near the visitor center, there is also a 12-bed bunkhouse (dm $12) and a wilderness cabin ($50, up to four people).

AMHERST

Amherst is the geographic center of the Maritimes and a travel junction for travelers to Nova Scotia, PEI and New Brunswick. The historic downtown has some stately public buildings and it's conveniently located for bird-watching. Still, there's little reason to dawdle as you're just a short drive from either the Bay of Fundy shore or the Northumberland Strait (between Nova Scotia and PEI).

Information
VIC (☎ 902-667-8429; ☺ 8:30am-9pm Jul & Aug, to 8pm Jun & Sep, to 6pm May & Oct, to 5pm Nov-Apr) At exit 1 off Hwy 104, just as you cross the border from New Brunswick.

Sights
The **Cumberland County Museum** (☎ 902-667-2561; 150 Church St; adult/child under 16/family $3/free/5; ☺ 9am-5pm Mon-Sat May-Sep, closed Mon Oct-Apr) is in the erstwhile home of Father of Confederation RB Dickey. Exhibits include articles made by prisoners of war at the Amherst Internment Camp during WWI. Leon Trotsky was one of the prisoners of war.

The 490-hectare **Amherst Point Migratory Bird Sanctuary** has more than 200 bird species. From downtown Amherst, turn left off Church St onto Victoria and drive about 6km, crossing the Trans-Canada Hwy. (From the highway, take Exit 3 and turn toward Amherst Point.) A small parking lot, the trailhead for paths into the sanctuary, is on your left just after mailbox No 947.

Sleeping & Eating

Treen Mansion (☎ 902-667-2146; 113 Spring St; s/d incl breakfast $50/65) This large Victorian house has four comfortable rooms with private bathrooms and TVs.

Victorian Motel (☎ 902-667-7211; 150 E Victoria St; d $55-65) This 20-room motel is a few minutes' walk from the town center.

Hampton Diner Open Kitchen (☎ 902-667-3562; 21386 Fort Lawrence Rd; mains $7-10; ☽ 7am-9pm Tue-Sun May-Oct) This classic diner, 700m south of the Amherst VIC and 3km north of downtown Amherst, dates from 1956. Come here for seafood, steaks, burgers or pie.

Getting There & Away

Acadian Lines has bus services to Halifax ($36, three hours, twice daily) that leave from the **Irving Mainway gas station** (☎ 902-667-8435; 213 S Albion St).

The Trans-Canada Hwy east of Amherst charges a toll of $3. It's an incentive to use scenic Hwy 2 through Parrsboro instead of dull – but fast – Hwy 104. The Sunrise Trail (Hwy 6) through Pugwash and Tatamagouche to Pictou also avoids the toll.

SUNRISE TRAIL

The Northumberland Strait between Nova Scotia's north shore and PEI has some of the warmest waters north of the US Carolinas, with summer water temperatures averaging slightly over 20°C. It has beautiful beaches, plus some interesting small towns along Hwy 6, a reasonable highway for cycling.

PUGWASH

Pugwash is renowned for the events that took place at 247 Water St. In July 1957 industrialist Cyrus Eaton (1883–1979) brought together a group of 22 leading scientists from around the world to discuss disarmament issues and science. The meeting was sponsored by Bertrand Russell, Albert Einstein and others, though they did not attend. The Pugwash Conference laid the groundwork for the Partial Test Ban Treaty of 1963.

Built in 1888, the former Pugwash train station, one of the oldest in Nova Scotia, today serves as a **tourist office** (☎ 902-243-2449; 10222 Durham St; ☽ 9am-6pm late Jun–Sep). Wares by local craftspeople are sold along the main street and also at tables set up at the former train station on Saturdays. Pugwash hosts a colorful **Gathering of the Clans** festival each year on July 1. Street names in town are written in Scottish Gaelic as well as in English.

Pleasant **Shillelagh Sheila's Country Inn** (☎ 902-243-2885; 10340 Durham St; pages.ivillage.com/shillelaghsheilasinn; s/d $60/65) is in the heart of town.

WALLACE

Wallace is prime territory for birding and beachcombing. The tourist information center is at the **Wallace Museum** (☎ 902-257-2191; Hwy 6; ☽ 9am-5pm Mon-Sat, 1-4pm Sun). Granted to the community in 1990, this 1840 home was in one family for generations. With the house came collections of baskets woven by the Mi'kmaq, period dresses and shipbuilding memorabilia, which are now displayed. A section of the **Trans Canada Trail** (TCT; p56) runs behind the museum.

Wallace Bay Wildlife Bird Sanctuary (1km north of Hwy 6 on Aboiteau Rd) protects 585 hectares, including tidal and freshwater wetlands. A 4km walking trail is a nice way to explore some of it and observe the many bird species that flock here, particularly in spring and fall. In the spring, keep your eyes peeled for bald eagles nesting near the parking lot, which is on the left just before the causeway.

Dutch Mill Restaurant & Motel (☎ 902-257-2598; dutch@pchg.net; Hwy 6; r $45-60) is an older building offering basic accommodations and with friendly young owners. The **restaurant** (mains $7-12; ☽ breakfast, lunch & dinner) is an economical place to sample home-cooked seafood. A windmill is incorporated into the building.

WENTWORTH

The Wentworth Valley is a detour off the shore, 25km south of Wallace via Hwy 307. It's particularly pretty in the fall when the deciduous trees change color. The 24-bed **Wentworth Hostel** (☎ 902-548-2379; www.hihostels.ca; 249 Wentworth Station Rd; dm member/nonmember

NOVA SCOTIA

$15/20) is 1.3km west of Hwy 4 on Valley Rd, then straight up steep Wentworth Station Rd. The big rambling farmhouse, built in 1866, has been used as a hostel for half a century. There are two family rooms and a kitchen. It's central enough to be a base for both the Sunrise Trail and much of the Minas Bay shore. Trails for hiking and mountain biking start just outside the door. Downhill and cross-country skiing are practiced here in winter.

TATAMAGOUCHE

Tatamagouche is the largest of several small, charming towns around Tatamagouche Bay, a protected inlet off the Northumberland Strait. This area has a surprising number of attractions. The Malagash Peninsula is a great loop for a drive or bike ride, a local winery offers tastings, and there are beaches galore. Several interesting museums are a short drive inland.

Information

Fraser Cultural Centre (☎ 902-657-3285; 362 Main St; ◷ 10am-5pm Mon-Fri, 10am-4pm Sat, 11am-3pm Sun mid-Jun–Sep) Tourist information, Internet access ($2) and local history displays. One room is dedicated to local giantess Anna Swan, who achieved fame with Barnum & Bailey's circus in the early 20th century.

Village Florist & Hanna's Books (☎ 902-657-2024; 257 Main St) Books of local interest.

Sights & Activities

Sample the free wine that comes with a tour of the scenically located **Jost Winery** (☎ 902-257-2636; www.jostwine.com; off Hwy 6, Malagash; admission free; ◷ tours noon & 3pm mid-Jun–mid-Sep). Enjoy a snack and a glass of wine at the outdoor patio where there is often free music. Winery signs direct you about 5km off Hwy 6.

In a gorgeous setting on the stream that once provided it with power, the **Balmoral Grist Mill** (☎ 902-657-3016; http://gristmill.museum.gov.ns.ca; 660 Matheson Brook Rd; adult/child 6-16 yrs $3/2; ◷ 9:30am-5:30pm Mon-Sat, 1-5:30pm Sun Jun–mid-Oct) still grinds wheat in summer. Purchase some to take away or bring your own food for a picnic. From Tatamagouche, turn south on Hwy 311 (at the east edge of town) and then east on Hwy 256. There are plenty of signs along the way.

From the Balmoral Grist Mill, drive further east on Hwy 256, and then north on Hwy 326, to get to the **Sutherland Steam Mill** (☎ 902-657-3365; http://steammill.museum.gov.ns.ca; off Hwy 326 in Denmark; adult/child 6-17 yrs $3/2; ◷ 9:30am-5:30pm Mon-Sat, 1-5:30pm Sun Jun–mid-Oct). Built in 1894, it produced lumber, carriages, wagons and windows until 1958. Now it's a fully operational museum.

Blue Sea Beach on the Malagash Peninsula has warm water and fine sand, and a marsh area just inland that's ideal for bird-watching. There are picnic tables and shelters to change in. Small cottages crowd around **Rushton's Beach**, just east of Tatamagouche in Brule, but it's worth a visit to look for seals (turn left at the end of the boardwalk and walk toward the end of the beach) and birdlife in the adjoining saltmarsh.

The old railway from Tatamagouche to Oxford (50km) is now part of the **TCT** (p56), a great route to bike.

The gay-friendly **Tatamagouche Centre** (☎ 800-218-2220; www.tatacentre.ca; Loop 6), which is affiliated with the Uniting Church, offers retreats and short courses on everything from organic gardening to yoga (two-day course including lodging $250), plus guided excursions to First Nations powwows.

Festivals & Events

Oktoberfest (☎ 902-657-2380; tickets $10-20) Held the last weekend in September – yes, that's right! Tickets for Saturday night regularly sell out.

Read-by-the-Sea (www.sunrisetrail.ca/read-by-the-sea; admission free) Well-known Atlantic Canadian authors and a children's program.

Sleeping & Eating

Balmoral Motel (☎ 902-657-2000, 888-383-9357; www.balmoralmotel.ca; 131 Main St; r $70; ▣) This convenient 18-room motel is very well kept. Its restaurant offers German dishes like schnitzel and bratwurst and local seafood ($9 to $15) between 8am and 8pm.

Train Station Inn (☎ 902-657-3222, 888-724-5233; www.trainstation.ns.ca; 21 Station Rd; d/caboose incl breakfast $100/$130, extra person $10) Three rooms are in the old stationmaster's residence above the train station, and seven cabooses can comfortably sleep four. Breakfast is served in the men's waiting room. The dreamer behind the inn, Jim LeFresne, grew up across the tracks and saved the train station from demolition when he was just 18. A dining car serves a limited menu of chicken, steak and lobster dinners ($16 to

$25) from Thursday to Saturday mid-June to September.

Stone Garden Chalets (☎ 902-657-0024, 866-657-0024; www.stonegardenchalets.com; 1120 Sand Point Rd, Brule; 1-/2-bedroom cottages $130/160) Most cottages along this shore are rented by the week only. Not so these new log cabins, which have all the amenities but still feel rustic and private. The muddy beach is a drawback. One cabin is wheelchair-accessible.

Nelson Park Campground (☎ 902-657-2730; http://centralnovascotia.com/members/nelsonparkcamp/; 153 Loop 6; tent/RV sites $18/25; 🐾) Just 1.5km west of Tatamagouche and right on the bay, tent sites Nos 62 to 71 offer privacy near the water. You can walk or cycle to town on the TCT.

Sugar Moon Farm (☎ 902-657-3348, 866-816-2753; www.sugarmoon.ca; Alex Macdonald Rd, off Hwy 311, Earltown; mains $9-12, prix fixe $60-70; 🕐 9am-5pm Thu-Mon Jul & Aug, 9am-5pm Sat & Sun Sep-Jun) The food – simple, delicious pancakes and locally made sausages served with maple syrup – is the highlight of this working maple farm and woodlot. For an exquisite culinary treat, take in a 'Chef's Night': one Saturday night each month a different top chef creates a prix fixe meal. Check online for dates or call to reserve.

Chowder House (☎ 902-657-2223; 265 Main St; mains $8-14; 🕐 6:30am-9pm Mon-Sat, 7am-7pm Sun) This bright, pleasant restaurant offer three varieties of chowder, as well as seafood dinners, sandwiches and burgers.

Shopping

Lismore Sheep Farm (☎ 902-351-2889; 1389 Louisville Rd, off Hwy 6; 🕐 9am-5pm) A working farm with more than 300 sheep, this is a fun destination even if you don't buy a rug, blanket or socks. From May to October, the barn is open (adult/child $1/50¢) for visitors to pat the lambs and learn all about producing wool.

A vibrant **farmers' market** (end of Creamery Rd, off Main St) with wares from both farmers and artisans happens each Saturday morning all summer in the historic Tatamagouche Creamery.

PICTOU

Attractive Pictou (*pik*-toe) is unquestionably the brightest light on the Sunrise Trail, with several wonderful places to stay and some major attractions, including several festivals. It's also convenient for a side trip via ferry to PEI (p397).

The first Scottish immigrants to Nova Scotia landed here in 1773. Pictou's place as the 'Birthplace of New Scotland' is celebrated on the redeveloped waterfront. Water St, the main street, is lined with interesting shops and beautiful old stone buildings.

Information

Pictou Public Library (☎ 902-485-5021; 40 Water St; 🕐 noon-9pm Tue & Thu, to 5pm Wed, 10am-5pm Fri & Sat) Free Internet access.

Pictou Tourist Information Office (☎ 902-485-6151; 40 Water St; 🕐 8:30am-4:30pm Mon-Fri) In the library.

Town of Pictou (www.townofpictou.com) Links to sights and festivals.

VIC (☎ 902-485-6213; Pictou Rotary northwest of town; 🕐 8am-9:30pm Jul & Aug, 8am-7pm May, Jun & Sep–mid-Dec) A large center situated to meet travelers arriving from the PEI ferry.

Sights & Activities

The beautiful Pictou waterfront, with its ample boardwalks and interesting sights, is the result of a revitalization effort that began in 1989. A replica of the ship *Hector* that carried the first 200 Highland Scots to Nova Scotia is tied up for viewing during the summer.

Hector Heritage Quay (☎ 902-485-4371; 33 Caladh Ave; adult/student/senior/family $5/2/4/12; 🕐 9am-5pm Mon-Sat, noon-5pm Sun mid-May–early Oct) captures the experience of the first Scottish settlers through a re-created blacksmith shop, a collection of shipbuilding artifacts and varied displays about the *Hector* and its passengers. There are guided tours at 10am and 2pm.

You can picnic and swim at Caribou/Munroe's Island Provincial Park.

In the old train station, the **Northumberland Fisheries Museum** (☎ 902-485-4972; 71 Front St; adult/student/senior/family $4/2/3/9; 🕐 9am-6pm Mon-Sat, noon-6pm Sun, late-May–early Oct) explores the area's fishing heritage. Exhibits include strange sea creatures and the spiffy *Silver Bullet*, an early 1930s lobster boat.

A **monument** on the waterfront recognizes the 2nd Construction Battalion, a battalion of Black soldiers that left for Europe from Pictou and Truro during WWI.

NOVA SCOTIA

Festivals & Events

Pictou Landing First Nation Powwow (☎ 902-752-4912; ◷ 1st weekend of Jun) Across the Pictou Harbour (a 25-minute drive through New Glasgow), this annual powwow features sunrise ceremonies, drumming and craft demonstrations. Camping and food available on site, which is strictly alcohol- and drug-free.

Lobster Carnival (☎ 902-485-5150; www.townof pictou.com; ◷ 2nd week of Jul) Begun in 1934 as 'The Carnival of the Fisherfolk,' this four-day event now offers free entertainment, boat races and lots of chances to feast on lobster.

Hector Festival (☎ 902-485-8848; www.decostecentre .ca; ◷ mid-Aug) Free daily outdoor concerts, Highland dancing and piping competitions and a *Hector* landing re-enactment.

Bluegrass Festival (☎ 902-924-2604; www.townof pictou.com; ◷ last weekend of Aug)

New Scotland Days (☎ 902-485-6057; www.townof pictou.com; ◷ mid-Sep) Workshops on everything from knot-tying to Gaelic-speaking.

Sleeping

BUDGET

Hostel Pictou (☎ 902-485-8740; www.backpackers .ca; 14 Chapel St; dm $20) Reservations are recommended at this cozy, six-bed backpacker hostel a block from the Pictou waterfront.

Caribou/Munroe's Island Provincial Park (☎ 902-485-6101; http://parks.gov.ns.ca; 2119 Three Brooks Rd; campsites $18) This park is less than 5km from Pictou, set on a gorgeous beach. Site Nos 1 to 22 abut the day-use area and are less private; Nos 78 to 95 are gravel and suited for RVs. The rest are wooded and private.

MID-RANGE

Willow House Inn (☎ 902-485-5740; www.willow houseinn.com; 11 Willow St; r incl breakfast without/with private bathroom $65/80) This historic (c 1840) home is just a block from Water St. The generous, airy rooms are newly decorated, and the hosts are relaxed and personable. Families can rent two rooms with a shared bath for $110.

Auberge Walker Inn (☎ 902-485-1433, 800-370-5553; www.townofpictou.com/walkerinn; 34 Coleraine St; r incl breakfast $75-85, ste incl breakfast 145) This charming inn offers comfortable rooms in a historic (c 1865) three-story stone building right at the end of Water St. The ground-floor suite is fully wheelchair accessible.

Braeside Country Inn (☎ 902-485-5046, 800-613-7701; www.braesideinn.com; 126 Front St; s/d/f

$65/100/125) Set on two hectares overlooking Pictou Harbour, this older comfortable inn has a few small, single rooms.

TOP END

Pictou Lodge (☎ 902-485-4322, 888-662-7484; www .maritimeinns.com; 172 Lodge Rd, off Braeshore Rd; r/f/ cottages from $120/240/180; ◕) This atmospheric 1920s resort is on more than 60 hectares of wooded land between Caribou/Munroe's Island Provincial Park and Pictou. Beautifully renovated ocean-side log cabins have original stone fireplaces. Motel rooms are also available. There's a life-sized checker board, paddle boats, a private beach and a restaurant.

Customs House Inn (☎ 902-485-4546; www.customs houseinn.ca; 38 Depot St; r $120-140) Some rooms at this solid, imposing stone building on the waterfront have fireplaces and whirlpool baths. There's the cozy Old Stone Pub and two rooms are accessible for disabled guests.

Eating & Drinking

See opposite for other options in New Glasgow, a worthy side trip by water taxi or car for a good meal.

Carver's Coffeehouse & Studio (☎ 902-382-3332; 41 Coleraine St; $3-6; ◷ 8am-9pm Jun-Sep, 8am-6pm Mon-Sat, noon-5pm Sun rest of year) Opposite the waterfront, this bright and inviting café is also the carving studio for Keith Matheson, who did the detail work on the *Hector*. Anne, his partner, runs the café that specializes in decadent desserts, traditional Scottish oatcakes, and strong coffee with free refills.

Old Stone Pub (☎ 902-485-4546; 38 Depot St; mains $7-20; ◷ lunch & dinner) In the basement of the Customs House Inn, this cozy pub serves reasonably priced inventive sandwiches, pastas and seafood.

Pictou Lodge (☎ 902-485-4322, 888-662-7484; 172 Lodge Rd, off Braeshore Rd; mains $15-30; ◷ breakfast & dinner mid-May–mid-Oct) The decadent Sunday all-you-can-eat **brunch** (adult/child under 10 $20/5, ◷ mid-June–mid-Oct) is good value.

Fougere's Restaurant (☎ 902-485-1575; 89 Water St; lunch mains $5-12, dinner mains $15-24; ◷ lunch & dinner) This popular, well-located restaurant has a wide-ranging menu of pastas, steaks and schnitzels.

Pressroom Pub & Grill (☎ 902-485-4041; 50 Water St; mains $7-14; ◷ 11am-midnight) Eat standard salads, sandwiches, wraps or chowder on the big outdoor patio.

Entertainment

deCoste Entertainment Centre (☎ 902-485-8848; www.decostecentre.ca; 91 Water St; tickets about $16; ☻ box office 11:30am-5pm Mon-Fri, 1-5pm Sat & Sun) Opposite the waterfront, this impressive performing arts center stages a range of live shows. Experience some top-notch Scottish music during a summer series of ceilidhs (*kay*-lees) at 2pm from Tuesday to Thursday (adult/child $15/7).

Shopping

Water Street Studio (☎ 902-485-8398; 110 Water St) A cooperative begun more than 20 years ago by local craftswomen, this store sells beautiful clothing, jewelry and gifts.

Grohman's Knives (☎ 902-485-4224; 116 Water St). Take a tour of the factory where knives for every use are crafted in no less than 53 steps.

Whigmaleeries (☎ 902-485-2593; 27 Water St) Say your Scottish surname and the proprietor of this store will produce its tartan.

Getting There & Away

A **water taxi** (☎ 902-396-8855; one way/return $10/18) runs twice daily to and from New Glasgow in July and August. In Pictou it leaves from beside the Salt Water Café (opposite the *Hector*) at 1:30pm and 6:30pm; in New Glasgow it departs from the Riverfront Marina at noon and 5pm.

NEW GLASGOW

The largest town on the Northumberland Shore, New Glasgow has always been an industrial center. The first mine opened in neighboring Stellarton in 1807. An underground explosion in 1992 at the Westray Mine in Plymouth killed 26 men.

The few major local attractions are in Stellarton, a 5km drive away. Visit New Glasgow's old downtown for a couple of restaurants that offer something other than chowder.

Sights & Activities

Museum of Industry (☎ 902-755-5425; http://industry.museum.gov.ns.ca; Hwy 104 at Exit 24; adult/child 6-16 yrs/family $7/3/15; ☻ 9am-5pm Mon-Sat, 1-5pm Sun May & Jun, 9am-5pm Mon-Sat, 10am-5pm Sun Jul-Oct, 9am-5pm Mon-Fri Nov-Apr) This is a wonderful place for kids. There's a hands-on water power exhibit and an assembly line to try to keep up with.

Crombie Art Gallery (☎ 902-755-4440; 1780 Abercrombie Rd; admission free; ☻ tours on the hr, 9-11am & 1-4pm Wed Jul & Aug) This private gallery in the personal residence of the founder of the Sobey supermarket chain has an excellent collection of 19th- and early 20th-century Canadian art including works by Cornelius Krieghoff and the Group of Seven. It's near the paper mill between Pictou and New Glasgow.

Eating

Café Italia (☎ 902-928-2233; 62 Provost St; mains $8-13; ☻ 7:30am-10pm Mon-Thu, till midnight Fri, 11:30am-10pm Sat) Locals fill the booths at this small trattoria. Choose from salads, sandwiches, pasta and pizza. Open in the morning for coffee and snacks, but not breakfast. Pizzas are available for take-out.

Bistro (☎ 902-752-4988; 216 Archimedes St; mains $18-27; ☻ dinner Tue-Sat) The only constant on the menu is creativity in spicing and sauces. Try penne with beets and blue cheese or roast duck lasagne. Reservations are recommended.

Curry Point Take-Out (☎ 902-695-3303; 185 Archimedes St; meals $5-10; ☻ 11am-2pm & 4-7pm Mon-Wed, 11am-2pm & 4-8pm Thu-Sat) This humble Pakistani–East Indian take-out is just a short walk from the riverfront.

Dock (☎ 902-752-0884; 130 George St; mains $8-12; ☻ 11am-12:30am) This cozy pub near the marina has quality pub fare.

ANTIGONISH

Catholic Scots settled Antigonish (an-tee-guh-*nish*) and established St Francis Xavier University. Now Antigtonish is a pleasant university town with great places to eat. Beautiful beaches and hiking possibilities north of town could easily keep you busy for a couple of days. It's known for the Scottish Highland Games held each July since 1861.

Information

Antigonish Public Library (☎ 902-863-4276; 274 Main St; ☻ 10am-9pm Tue & Thu, 10am-5pm Wed, Fri & Sat) Free Internet access. Enter off College St.

Bookends Used Books (☎ 902-863-6922; 342 Main St) Trashy novels and erudite reading.

VIC (☎ 902-863-4921; 56 West St, at the junction of Hwy 104 & Hwy 7; ☻ 10am-8pm Jul & Aug, 10am-6pm mid-Jun–early Oct) Brochures, local calls and free Internet access.

NOVA SCOTIA

Sights & Activities

The **Heritage Museum** (☎ 902-863-6160; 20 E Main St; admission free; ⏲ 10am-5pm Mon-Sat July & Aug, 10am-noon & 1-5pm Mon-Fri Sep-Jun) has exhibits on customs and folklore.

A 4km hiking/cycling trail to the nature reserve at **Antigonish Landing** begins just across the train tracks from the museum, then 400m down Adam St. The landing's estuary is a good bird-watching area where you might see eagles, ducks and ospreys.

The attractive campus of 125-year-old **St Francis Xavier University** is behind the Romanesque **St Ninian's Cathedral** (www.antigonishdiocese.com/ninian1.htm; 120 St Ninian St; ⏲ 7:30am-8pm). The **Hall of the Clans** is on the 3rd floor of the old wing of the Angus L MacDonald Library, just beyond the St Ninian's Cathedral parking lot. In the hall, crests of all the Scottish clans that settled this area are displayed. Those clans gather each July for the Antigonish Highland Games.

Festivals & Events

Antigonish Highland Games (www.antigonishhighlandgames.com; ⏲ mid-Jul) An extravaganza of dancing, pipe-playing and heavy-lifting events involving hewn logs and iron balls.

Evolve (www.evolvefestival.com; ⏲ late Aug) Five stages of funk, bluegrass, hip-hop and more, plus workshops on everything from puppetry to media literacy.

Sleeping & Eating

Antigonish Highland Heart B&B (☎ 902-863-1858, 800-863-1858; www.bbcanada.com/3241.html; 135 Main St; r 75-85) Run by Shebby, a gracious and kind woman, this old (c 1854) home is well located.

Whidden's Campground & Trailer Court (☎ 902-863-3736; www.whiddens.com; 11 Hawthorne St; tent/RV sites $27/31, cottages $102, all incl taxes; 🅿) This unusual accommodation complex right in town offers campsites and two-bedroom mobile homes for rent.

Crindale Café (☎ 902-863-4682; Unit 2, 342 Main St; mains $5-7; ⏲ 8am-6pm Mon-Wed & Sat, to 9pm Thu & Fri) This relaxed bohemian café offers really good, fresh soup, grilled sandwiches and wraps.

Gabrieu's Bistro (☎ 902-863-1925; 350 Main St; lunch mains $8-13, dinner mains $20-26; ⏲ 8am-9:30pm Mon-Sat) Locals credit Chef Mark Gabrieu for setting the culinary high-water mark in Antigonish. This cozy bistro borrows from Mediterranean, Asian and other world cuisines.

Sunshine on Main Café (☎ 902-863-5851; 332 Main St; mains $8-13; ⏲ 7am-9pm Sun-Thu, 7am-9:30pm Fri & Sat) This local favorite serves salads, grilled sandwiches and thin-crust pizza.

Getting There & Away

Acadian Lines bus services stop at **Hollywood Video** (☎ 902-863-6900; 44 James St) near Hwy 104 (Trans-Canada Hwy).

Around Antigonish

CAPE GEORGE

Called the 'mini-Cabot Trail' (see opposite) for its beautiful views, this 72km route loops up Hwy 245 to Malignant Cove and around Cape George; you can easily spend a full day along it. From a well-marked picnic area near **Cape George Point Lighthouse**, a 1km walk leads to the lighthouse itself. It's automated and not that big, but there are views to Cape Breton Island and PEI. Signs at the picnic area also point to longer hikes through forests and coastal areas, including one 32km loop. Signs at all the trail junctions indicate how long it will take to follow alternate routes.

You can also start exploring these trails from the wharf at **Ballantyne's Cove**, one of the prettiest communities in Nova Scotia. To walk from the wharf to the lighthouse and back again is 8km. Also visit **Ballantyne's Cove Tuna Interpretive Centre** (☎ 902-863-8162; 57 Ballantyne's Cove Wharf Rd; admission free; ⏲ 10am-7:30pm Jul-Sep) for displays on both the fish and the fishery. A fish and chips van parks nearby.

There's nowhere to sleep in Ballantyne's Cove. Friendly **Fisherman Crossing B&B** (☎ 902-863-8022; theboyds@ns.sympatico.ca; 30 Fisherman Crossing; s/d $55/65; 🅿) is in a modern, lakefront home 11km further south.

Another 4km south, **Boyd's Seafood Galley** (☎ 902-867-1836; 304 Cribbons Point Rd; mains $8-12; ⏲ 11am-8pm, mid-Jun–mid-Sep) overlooks an active lobster wharf.

POMQUET

About 16km east of Antigonish, this tiny Acadian community is on a stunning **beach** with 13 dunes that keep growing; waves dump the equivalent of more than 4000 truckloads of sand on the beach each year. Many bird species frequent the salt marshes behind the dunes. Comfortable **Sunflower B&B** (☎ 902-386-2492; www.bbcanada.com/5382.html; 1572 Monk's Head Rd; r $80-90) has engaging Acadian hosts.

MONASTERY

The village of Monastery is 32km east of Antigonish. The Augustine Order now occupies a Trappist monastery established here by French monks in 1825. The access road to **Our Lady of Grace Monastery of the Monks of St Maron** is on the right after a small bridge just off the Trans-Canada Hwy at exit 37. Two kilometers up the valley, beyond the main monastery, a trail along a stream leads to the **Shrine of the Holy Spring**, a palpably spiritual place.

CAPE BRETON ISLAND

The 300km Cabot Trail around Cape Breton Highlands National Park is one of Canada's best-known scenic drives. It winds and climbs around and over coastal mountains, with gorgeous ocean views every couple of turns. It and Fortress Louisbourg in the southeastern corner of Cape Breton Island are two of the biggest tourist attractions in Nova Scotia. Thousands of visitors each year take a few days to cover both, often using Baddeck as a base.

Fans of music and dance will want to spend several days along the Ceilidh Trail taking in square dances in community halls; there are spectacular hikes near Mabou, in the national park and around Cape North; the French Acadian community of Chéticamp is rich in artistry and community spirit; and the region around the Bras d'Or lakes offers opportunities to explore the history and present of the Mi'kmaq First Nation.

The tourist season on Cape Breton Island is short and congested. Most tourists visit in July and August, and many restaurants, accommodations and VICs only open from mid-June to September. **Celtic Colours** (www .celtic-colours.com), a wonderful roving music festival each October that attracts top musicians from Scotland, Spain and other countries with Celtic connections, helps extend the season into the fall, a superb time to visit.

PORT HASTINGS

Cape Breton Island ceased to be a true island when the Canso Causeway was built across the Strait of Canso in 1955. A big and busy **VIC** (☎ 902-625-4201; 96 Hwy 4; ☼ 9am-6pm May, 8:30am-8:30pm Jun-Aug, 8:30am-7pm Sep, 9am-5pm Oct-Dec) is on your right as you drive onto Cape Breton Island. This is definitely worth a stop: there are few other centers on Cape Breton Island, especially outside of July and August; the staff is very well informed; and one wall is covered with posters advertising square dances and ceilidhs. Pick up a copy of the *Inverness Oran,* an excellent local weekly that lists most events in the northwest area of Cape Breton Island.

CEILIDH TRAIL

Take a hard left immediately after leaving the Port Hastings VIC to get on the Ceilidh Trail (Hwy 19), which snakes along the western coast of the island. Settled by Scotts with fiddles in hand, this area is renowned for its strong musical heritage. Local fiddlers have been recorded by the Smithsonian Museum and have played with Paul Simon.

For a great introduction to local culture, visit the **Celtic Music Interpretive Centre** (☎ 902-787-2708; www.celticmusicsite.com; 5473 Hwy 19; tours $4; ☼ 9am-5pm Mon-Fri Jun-Aug). Half-hour tours include some fiddle music and a dance step or two. The staff can tell you on which nights nearby communities have square dances – Cape Bretoners are very friendly and will help anyone to find their feet! Try a Saturday dance at the community hall in West Mabou or a Thursday evening dance in Glencoe Mills.

Creignish B&B (☎ 902-625-5709; 2154 Hwy 19; s/d/f incl taxes $45/55/75) is a 'recycled school house' that's been whimsically converted by its artist owner. She'll entertain kids with crafts and point you to the best hidden secrets of Cape Breton Island. Rooms are large and comfortable.

MABOU

Mabou is set among lush hills and quiet inlets. It's the heart of the Ceilidh Trail, and home to numerous musical families. It also offers some great hiking, single malt whiskey, and a choice of places to stay and eat.

Sights & Activities

In the **Cape Mabou Highlands**, an extensive network of hiking trails extends between Mabou and Inverness toward the coast west of Hwy 19. Hikes ranging from 4km to 12km start from three different trailheads. An excellent trail guide ($4) is available at the grocery store across from the Mull Café &

Deli. Maps are also posted at the trailheads. To reach the Mabou Post Rd trailhead, follow Mabou Harbour Rd 4.5km west from the large white St Mary's Church, then head 7.7km northwest on a gravel road signposted 'Mabou Coal Mines.' A spectacular hike (8km to 12km, depending on which return route you choose), including a dangerous section along high cliffs, starts here.

Glenora Inn & Distillery (☎ 902-258-2662, 800-839-0491; www.glenoradistillery.com; Hwy 19, 9km north of Mabou; guided tours incl tasting $5; ☼ tours on the hr 9am-5pm mid-Jun–mid-Oct) is the only distillery making single malt whiskey in Canada. After the tour enjoy free ceilidhs in the pub (open 1pm to 3pm and 8pm to 10pm); you can eat there or in the dining room (lunch $9 to $12, dinner prix fixe $40; open 8am to 10pm June to October).

Sleeping & Eating

Clayton Farm B&B (☎ 902-945-2719; fax 902-945-2078; 11247 Hwy 19; s/d $65/75) Four rooms share a bathroom in this very charming farmhouse. Artifacts of early Cape Breton Island life are casually scattered throughout the common areas and comfortable guest rooms.

Duncreigan Country Inn (☎ 902-945-2207, 800-840-2207; http://duncreigan.ca; Hwy 19; r incl breakfast $100-140) Just south of the Mabou River bridge, this very comfortable inn has enough trees between it and the highway to give an air of serenity. Several rooms have views over Mabou Harbour and one room is wheelchair accessible. The inn is open year-round with off-season rates. Its reputable restaurant opens for dinner from mid-June to mid-October (prix fixe $22 and $35).

Shining Waters Bakery & Eatery (☎ 902-945-2728; Hwy 19; light meals $5-8; ☼ 7am-7pm Mon-Sat, 8am-7pm Sun Jun-Sep, 7am-6pm Wed-Fri, 7am-3pm Sat & Sun rest of year) About 200m north of the Duncreigan, this bright, friendly bakery is a great choice for a healthy meal.

Mull Café & Deli (☎ 902-945-2244; Hwy 19; lunch mains $6-10, dinner mains $15-20; ☼ 11am-9pm) This popular restaurant serves unremarkable but generous portions of pasta, burgers and seafood.

INVERNESS

Row upon row of company housing betrays the history of coal mining in Inverness, the first town of any size on the coast. Its history and people are captured evocatively by writer Alistair MacLeod. His books are for sale at the **Bear Paw** (☎ 902-258-2528; Hwy 19), next to the Royal Bank. Proprietor Alice Freeman weaves at a loom at the back of the shop and will happily dispense information to travelers.

Beginning near the fishing harbor there are miles of sandy **beach** with comfortable water temperatures in late summer. A **boardwalk** runs 1km along the beach. In the old train station just back from the beach, the **Inverness Miners' Museum** (☎ 902-258-3822; 62 Lower Railway St; admission by donation; ☼ 9am-5pm Mon-Fri, noon-5pm Sat & Sun Jul & Aug) presents local history. **Inverness County Centre for the Arts** (☎ 902-258-2533; www.invernessarts.ca; 16080 Hwy 19; ☼ 10am-5pm Mon-Wed & Fri, to 7pm Thu, 1-5pm Sat & Sun Jun–mid-Sep, 10am-5pm Mon-Fri rest of year) is a beautiful new establishment with several galleries and an upmarket gift shop featuring work by local and regional artists. It's also a music venue with a floor built for dancing – of course!

Near the northern edge of town, **Inverness Beach Village** (☎ 902-258-2653; www.macleods.com; 56 Beach Village Rd, off Hwy 19; cottages $110-140) has 41 cottages, which look like boxes from the outside. Inside, the spacious cottages feature lots of natural wood and lovely cotton bedding. With a playground, laundromat and 3km-long beach just steps away, this is ideal for families.

Just south of Inverness Beach Village, the **Casual Gourmet & Bank Head Pub** (☎ 902-258-3839; Hwy 19; pub menu $8-13, dinner $15-20; ☼ 7am-9pm Jul & Aug, 11:30am-9pm rest of year) offers elegant and casual dining options. The pub kitchen is open all day, while upstairs the Casual Gourmet offers French-inspired evening meals.

CHÉTICAMP

Originally settled by fish merchants from Jersey, Chéticamp is now a vibrant Acadian community that has maintained its culture and language despite almost complete isolation from other French-speakers. It's a gateway to Cape Breton Highlands National Park (p444), and has several top-notch museums. The 1893 Church of St Pierre dominates the town with its silver spire and colorful frescoes.

Chéticamp is known for its crafts, particularly hooked rugs, and as a pioneer of the co-operative movement. Local fishermen organized themselves into a co-op in 1917 in order to secure better prices and more independence. It disbanded recently, a victim of the decline of the fishery. But there is still a Credit Union, a Co-op grocery store, and a Co-op Artisanale.

Information

A **tourist information kiosk** (☎ 902-224-3349; ☽ 8am-10pm Jul & Aug, 9am-5pm Mon-Fri Sep & Oct) is adjacent to a sizable parking lot and the waterfront boardwalk, directly across from the liquor store and post office.

Visitor information and Internet access ($2 per hour) are also available at Les Trois Pignons.

Sights & Activities

Les Trois Pignons (☎ 902-224-2642; www.lestrois pignons.com; 15584 Cabot Trail Hwy; adult/family $3.50/9; ☽ 8am-7pm Jul & Aug, 9am-5pm May-Jun & Sep–mid-Oct) is an excellent museum that explains how rug hooking went from being a simple, home-based activity aimed at preventing cold feet to an international business. Artifacts, including hooked rugs, illustrate early life and artisanship in Chéticamp. Almost everything artfully displayed here – from bottles to teacups to rugs – was collected by one eccentric local resident.

La Pirogue Fisheries Museum (☎ 902-224-3349; 15359 Cabot Trail Rd; admission $5; ☽ 9am-7pm May-Oct) tells the story of the local fish industry. The building that houses both this museum and the community development association incorporates green technologies like solar windows and geothermal heat pumps. In the basement, you can learn how to build a lobster trap or hook a rag rug.

Joe's Scarecrow Theatre (☎ 902-235-2108; 11842 Cabot Trail; admission free; ☽ 8:30am-9pm mid-Jun–early Oct), about 25km south of Chéticamp next to Ethel's Takeout restaurant, is a humorous, quasi-macabre outdoor collection of life-sized stuffed figures. Several other folk-art shops are along the highway between here and Chéticamp.

Whale Cruises (☎ 902-224-3376, 800-813-3376; www.whalecruises.com; Government Wharf; adult/child $29/12) Several operators sell tours from the Government Wharf, across and down from the church. Captain Cal is the most experienced and offers three-hour expeditions up to four times daily. It's wise to reserve your trip a day in advance in midsummer.

Sleeping & Eating

Accommodations are tight throughout July and August. It's advisable to call ahead or arrive early in the afternoon. If you're on a tight budget, the hostel at Pleasant Bay (p445) and the national park campgrounds (p444) are nearby.

Seashell Cabins (☎ 902-224-3569; 125 Chéticamp Island Rd; s/d $50/60) Just 700m off the Cabot Trail on the road that connects Chéticamp Island to the town itself, these three small and very rustic cabins are long on character but short on comfort. They do offer basic cooking facilities, a gay-friendly host and a beautiful view.

Laurence Guest House B&B (☎ 902-224-2184; 15408 Cabot Trail; s/d incl taxes $80/92) This gay-friendly, heritage B&B faces the waterfront and is within walking distance of most attractions. Four rooms furnished with antiques all have private bathrooms.

Parkview Motel (☎ 902-224-3232, 877-224-3232; www.parkviewresort.com; 16548 Cabot Trail Rd; r $90-110) This simple but comfortable motel is 5km north of Chéticamp at the entrance to the national park. Six newer units overlook the Chéticamp River and include fridges, microwaves and coffeemakers. The motel's restaurant is open for three meals (mains $7 to $18) a day during the peak tourist season.

Co-op Artisanale Restaurant (☎ 902-224-2170; 15067 Main St; mains $7-12; ☽ 9am-9pm) This restaurant specializes in Acadian dishes like a stewed chicken dinner ($11) and *pâté à la viande* (meat pie) for $5. Delicious potato pancakes ($6) with applesauce, molasses or sour cream are the only vegetarian option. The mark-up on local Jost wine – sold for $18 per liter – might be the lowest anywhere in Nova Scotia. **Seafood Stop** (☎ 902-224-1717; 14803 Main St; mains $7-14; ☽ 11am-9pm) is reputedly the best place in town to enjoy really fresh fish. A complete lobster dinner in the dining room will be $24 with dessert and coffee, or just have the fish and chips ($7 to $10). Take-away seafood is also available.

Entertainment

Doryman's Beverage Room (☎ 902-224-9909; 15528 Cabot Trail Rd) This no-nonsense drinking establishment hosts 'sessions' (cover $6) with a fiddler and piano players from Mabou each Saturday (2pm to 6pm); an acoustic Acadian group plays at 8pm Sunday, Tuesday, Wednesday and Friday.

NOVA SCOTIA

CAPE BRETON HIGHLANDS NATIONAL PARK

Established in 1936, this is one of Canada's most dramatic parks, with the famous **Cabot Trail** offering views of oceanside cliffs. The drive is at its best along the northwestern shore and then down to Pleasant Bay. Be sure to take advantage of the many pull-offs for scenic views and otherwise keep your eyes on this very circuitous road. Use a low gear to save your brakes – and lessen air pollution – when descending mountains.

Information

There are two park entrances; one at Chéticamp and one at Ingonish. Purchase an **entry permit** (adult/child under 17/up to 7 people in a vehicle $5/2.50/12.50) at either park entrance. A one-day pass is good until noon the next day.

Chéticamp Information Centre (☎ 902-224-2306; www.parkscanada.gc.ca; 16646 Cabot Trail; ☼ 8am-8pm Jul & Aug, 9am-5pm mid-May–Jun, Sep & Oct) Has displays and a relief map of the park, plus a bookstore. Ask the staff for advice on hiking or camping. It's usually staffed from 8am to 4pm, Monday to Friday, in winter.

Ingonish Information Centre (☎ 902-285-2535; 37677 Cabot Trail; ☼ 8am-8pm Jul & Aug, 9am-5pm mid-May–Jun, Sep & Oct) On the eastern edge of the park, this center is much smaller than the one at Chéticamp and has no bookstore. Wheelchair-accessible trails are indicated on the free park map available at either entrance.

Activities

HIKING

Two trails on the west coast of the park have spectacular ocean views. **Fishing Cove Trail** gently descends 330m over 8km to the mouth of rugged Fishing Cove River. You can opt for a steeper and shorter hike – 2.8km – from a second trailhead about 5km north of the first. Double the distances if you plan to return the same day. Otherwise, you must preregister for one of eight back-country sites ($20) at the Chéticamp Information Centre. Note that two hikes north of the park (p445 and p446) can also be overnight trips. Reviews of trails in and near the park are available at www.cabottrail.com. Most other trails are shorter and close to the road, many leading to ridge tops for impressive views of the coast. The best of these is **Skyline Trail**, a 7km loop that puts you on the edge of a headland cliff right above the water. The trailhead is about 5.5km north of Corney Brook Campground.

Just south of Neils Harbour (p446), on the eastern coast of the park, the **Coastal Trail** runs 11km round-trip and covers more gentle but still lovely coastline.

CYCLING

The park is a popular cycling destination. However, don't make this your inaugural trip. The riding is tough and there are no shoulders in many sections. You must be comfortable sharing the incredible scenery with RVs. Alternatively you can mountain bike on four inland trails in the park. Only **Branch Pond Lookoff Trail** offers ocean views.

Sea Spray Outdoor Adventures (☎ 902-383-2732; www.cabot-trail-outdoors.com; 1141 White Point Rd; half-/full-day $25/35; ☼ 9am-5pm Jun–mid-Oct) in Smelt Brook near Dingwall rents bikes and will do emergency repairs on the road. It also offers help planning trips and leads organized cycling, kayaking and hiking tours.

CROSS-COUNTRY SKIING

Best in March and April; there are groomed ski trails (day pass for adult/family $5/10) and possibilities for off-trail skiing. If you stay overnight there's a $10 fee for tenting. Two shelters at Black Brook, south of Neils Harbour, rent for $20 and $30.

Sleeping

Towns around the park offer a variety of accommodations. **Cape Breton Highlands National Park** (backcountry/tent/RV sites $20/21/27) has six drive-in campgrounds with discounts after three days. Most sites are first-come, first-served, but wheelchair-accessible sites, group campsites and backcountry sites can be reserved for $5. In the smaller campgrounds further from the park entrances, just pick a site and self-register. To camp at any of the three larger ones near the park entrances, register at the closest information center.

The 162-site **Chéticamp Campground** is behind the information center. Wheelchair-accessible sites are available. When the main campground is full, an overflow area is opened. There are no 'radio free' areas, so peace and quiet is not guaranteed.

Corney Brook (20 sites), 10km further north, is a particularly stunning campground high over the ocean. There's a small playground here, but it would be a nerve-racking place to camp with small kids. **MacIntosh Brook** (10 sites) is an open field 3km east of Pleasant Bay. It has wheelchair-accessible sites. **Big Intervale** (10 sites) is near a river 11km west of Cape North.

Near the eastern park entrance, you have a choice of the 256-site **Broad Cove Campground** at Ingonish and the 90-site **Ingonish Campground**, near Keltic Lodge at Ingonish Beach. Both have wheelchair-accessible sites. These large campgrounds near the beach are popular with local families in midsummer.

From late October to early May, you can camp at the Chéticamp and Ingonish campgrounds for $15, including firewood. In truly inclement weather, tenters can take refuge in cooking shelters with woodstoves. Bring your own food.

PLEASANT BAY

Pleasant Bay is aptly named: a carved-out bit of civilization hemmed in on all sides by the park and wilderness. It's an active fishing harbor known for its whale-watching tours and Tibetan monastery. If you are in the area on Canada Day (July 1), try to be in the stands for the annual monks vs townspeople baseball game.

Sights & Activities

Gampo Abbey (☎ 902-224-2752; www.gampoabbey .org), 8km north of Pleasant Bay past the village of Red River, is a monastery intended mostly for Western followers of Tibetan Buddhism. Students come from all across Canada and the USA for extended meditation programs in this beautiful place in the middle of nowhere. Ane Pema Chödrön, the founding director of the abbey and a noted Buddhist author, spends much of the year here.

Make a stop at the **Whale Interpretive Centre** (☎ 902-224-1411; www.whalecentre.ca; 104 Harbour Rd; adult/family $4.50/14; ☸ 9am-5pm Jun–mid-Oct) before taking a whale-watching tour – sightings guaranteed! They leave from the adjacent wharf. Park entrance permits are for sale here, and Internet access is available at the C@P site downstairs.

Captain Mark's Whale & Seal Cruise (☎ 902-224-1316, 888-754-5112; www.whaleandsealcruise.com; adult/child under 16 $25/12; ☸ mid-May–Sep) has three tours daily in the spring, five in the summer and fall. Captain Mark promises not only guaranteed whales but also time

to see seabirds, seals and Gampo Abbey. There's a discount of 25% if you reserve a spot on the earliest (9:30am) or latest (5pm) tour. Tours leave from the wharf next to the Whale Interpretive Center.

Wesley's Whale Watching (☎ 902-224-1919, 866-999-4253; adult/child $25/10; ☸ May–mid-Oct) offers a 25% discount if you reserve a spot on a Cape Island–style boat. Tours are also available on a Zodiac (adult/child $36/18) and leave from the wharf next to the Whale Interpretive Centre.

The popular, challenging 20km-return hiking trail to **Pollett's Cove** begins at the end of the road to Gampo Abbey. There are great views along the way and perfect spots to camp when you arrive at the abandoned fishing community. This is not a Parks Canada trail, so it can be rough underfoot. Several times each summer, **Scotia Sea Kayaking Tours** (☎ 902-224-1254, 800-564-2330; www.sco tiakayaking.com) of Chéticamp offers two-day tours (including meals $290) from Pleasant Bay to Pollett's Cove by kayak, with the return journey on foot.

Sleeping & Eating

Cabot Trail Hostel (☎ 902-224-1976; www.cabot trail.com/hostel; 23349 Cabot Trail; dm $24; ☐) Open year-round, this comfortable 18-bed hostel is a good base for exploring Cape Breton Highlands National Park and the beautiful area north of it.

Mid-Trail Motel & Inn (☎ 800-215-0411, 902-224-2529; www.midtrail.com; 23475 Cabot Trail; r $120) This comfortable motel offers great views and is walking distance to the harbor. Its restaurant is open for lunch and dinner (meals $12 to $20).

Andrea's Family Restaurant (☎ 902-224-2588; cnr Harbour Rd & Cabot Trail; mains $5-7; ☸ 11am-6pm May-Oct) Opposite the turnoff to Harbour Rd, this roadside take-out has a covered deck and a surprisingly broad menu.

BAY ST LAWRENCE

Bay St Lawrence is a picturesque little fishing village at the very north edge of Cape Breton Island.

Captain Cox (☎ 902-383-2981, 888-346-5556; Bay St Lawrence Wharf; adult/child $25/12) has been taking people to see whales aboard the 35-foot *Northern Gannet* since 1986. He does trips at 10:30am, 1:30pm and 4:30pm in July and August. Call for spring and fall schedules.

Jumping Mouse Campground (☎ 902-383-2914; 3360 Bay St Lawrence Rd; campsites $18, cabins for up to 4 people $30; ☺ Jun-Sep) has just 10 spacious oceanfront sites (no cars allowed). Reservations are accepted for multinight stays and for a beautifully built four-bunk cabin. There are hot showers and a cooking shelter, and frequent whale sightings.

South of Bay St Lawrence on protected and warm Aspy Bay, **Four Mile Beach Inn** (☎ 902-383-2282, 888-503-5551; www.fourmilebeach inn.com; 1530 Bay St Lawrence Rd; r $120, with kitchen $140) is awash in history and character. The building was a general store for decades and is still full of strange flotsam and jetsam. The rooms are all distinctly furnished with antiques. Three units have kitchen facilities. Kayaks, canoes and bicycles are available free for guests.

To enjoy Aspy Bay and its spectacular beach just for an afternoon, stop at nearby **Cabot's Landing Provincial Park**.

MEAT COVE

The northernmost road in Nova Scotia ends at unbelievably beautiful Meat Cove, 13km northwest of Bay St Lawrence (the last 7km of the road is gravel). Stop at the **Meat Cove Welcome Center** (☎ 902-383-2284; 2296 Meat Cove Rd; Internet per hr $2; ☺ 8am-8pm Jun-Sep) for information on hiking trails. Leave your car here, as there's no room at the trailhead.

From Meat Cove, a 16km **hiking trail** continues west to Cape St Lawrence lighthouse and Lowland Cove, an ideal spot for camping. Spend an hour gazing over the ocean, and you're guaranteed to see pods of pilot whales. They frolic here all spring, summer, and into the fall. Carry a compass and refrain from exploring side paths; locals have gotten lost in this area.

Meat Cove Campground (☎ 902-383-2379/2658; 2475 Meat Cove Rd; campsites $18; ☺ Jun-Oct) is spectacular, perched on a grassy bluff high above the ocean. There's room for small trailers, but no electricity. Bring some loose change with you: the showers are coin-operated ($1 for 12 minutes) and firewood is $3 for nine pieces.

Meat Cove Lodge (☎ 902-383-2672; 2305 Meat Cove Rd; d/f incl breakfast $40/50; ☺ Jun-mid-Sep) has three rooms in a rustic home at the entrance to Meat Cove, opposite the welcome center.

AROUND NEILS HARBOUR

On your way south to Ingonish, it's worth leaving the Cabot Trail and following the more scenic White Point Rd via Smelt Brook to the attractive fishing villages of White Point and Neils Harbour. You'll pass a number of gorgeous **beaches**.

Two Tittle B&B (☎ 902-383-2817, 866-231-4078; http://twotittle.com; 2119 White Point Village Rd; s/d incl breakfast $50/65), a simple bungalow directly above White Point harbor, has friendly, local hosts. The five rooms are directly off the living room and kitchen, but the location is unparalleled. A coastal hiking trail leaves from the backyard.

Chowder House (☎ 902-336-2463; meals $5-10; ☺ 11am-9pm Jul & Aug, 11am-6pm mid-Jun–late Jun & Sep), next to the lighthouse in Neils Harbour, serves to-die-for clam or seafood chowder for under $4 and a haddock platter ($9).

INGONISH

At the eastern entrance to the national park are Ingonish and Ingonish Beach, small towns lost in the background of motels and cottages. This is a long-standing popular destination, but there are few real attractions other than the **Highlands Links golf course** (☎ 902-285-2600, 800-441-1118; www .highlandslinksgolf.com; round $83), reputed to be one of the best in the world, and the beach. There are several hiking trails nearby in the national park (see p444).

Keltic Lodge, a theatrical Tudor-style resort erected in 1940, shares Middle Head Peninsula with the famous golf course and the Ingonish Campground (opposite). The lodge is worth visiting for its setting and the **hiking trail** to the tip of the peninsula just beyond the resort. You must have a valid entry permit (see p444) to the national park, as the lodge, the golf course and the hiking trail are all within park boundaries.

The beach at **Ingonish Beach** is lovely, a long, wide strip of sand tucked in a bay surrounded by green hills.

Sleeping & Eating

Knotty Pine Cottages (☎ 800-455-2058, 902-455-2058; www.ingonish.com/knotty; 39126 Cabot Trail, Ingonish Ferry; cottages $55-125) Ten cottages with varying levels of amenities overlook Ingonish Beach. All but one has cooking facilities; all have deck barbecues. It's open year-round and is near Smokey Mountain ski hill.

Driftwood Lodge (☎ 902-285-2558; www3.ns .sympatico.ca/driftwood.lodge; 36125 Cabot Trail, Ingonish; r $25-65, ste with kitchen $80-95) This ramshackle seaside establishment, 8km north of the Ingonish park entrance, offers a variety of accommodations. It's run by a great host who also works at the park. There's a fine-sand beach just below the lodge.

Castle Rock Country Inn (☎ 902-285-2700, 888-884-7625; www.ingonish.com/castlerock; 39339 Cabot Trail, Ingonish Ferry; r $90-140) This comfortable inn is perched high over Ingonish Harbour. The least expensive rooms in the basement still have an ocean view. The menu in its restaurant features creative seafood dishes.

Main Street Restaurant & Bakery (☎ 902-285-2225; 37764 Cabot Trail, Ingonish Beach; sandwiches $3-12, dinner mains $9-20; ☺ 7am-9pm Tue-Sat Jul & Aug, 7am-8pm Tue-Sat rest of year) This small, casual restaurant offers really fine meals.

Seagull Restaurant (☎ 902-285-2851; 35963 Cabot Trail, Ingonish; lunch $4-9, dinner mains $10-16; ☺ 11am-9pm Jul & Aug, 11am-7pm Jun & Sep) Locals pour into this long-established family restaurant on the first day of business each spring.

ST ANN'S LOOP

If you're running late en route to Louisbourg or the Newfoundland ferry, you can skip the drive around St Ann's Bay and take a $5 ferry to Englishtown. But you'll miss many artists' studios (this area is also known as the artists' loop) and pleasant vistas.

Gaelic College of Celtic Arts & Crafts (☎ 902-295-3411; www.gaeliccollege.edu; 51779 Cabot Trail; 5-day course incl lodging $680-715; ☺ 9am-5pm Jun–mid-Oct), at the end of St Ann's Bay, teaches Scottish Gaelic, bagpipe playing, Highland dancing, weaving, and more. The **Great Hall of the Clans Museum** (admission $3) traces Celtic history from ancient times to the Highland clearances.

Clucking Hen Deli & Bakery (☎ 902-929-2501; 45073 Cabot Trail; mains $4-10; ☺ 7am-7pm Jul-Sep, 7am-6pm May, Jun & Oct) is highly recommended. A full-lobster meal with soup and salad is only $20.

John C Roberts' studio, **Leather Works** (☎ 902-929-2414; 45808 Cabot Trail, Indian Brook; ☺ 9am-5pm Mon-Sat, 10am-5pm Sun) is full of stylish leather goods.

NORTH SYDNEY

North Sydney itself is nondescript, though there are some fine places to stay nearby.

Reserve accommodations if you're coming in on a late ferry or going out on an early one. Most North Sydney motels and B&Bs are open year-round, and it's understood that guests will arrive and leave at all hours.

Four rooms share two bathrooms in **Alexandra Shebib's B&B** (☎ 902-794-4876; 88 Queen St; s/d $45/60). It's convenient for backpackers who want to walk or take an inexpensive taxi ride to the ferry.

For something a little more elegant in the same area, **Heritage Home B&B** (☎ 902-794-4815, 866-601-9123; www.capebretonisland.com/northside/ heritagehome; 110 Queen St; d with private bathroom $80) is in a lovely Victorian home.

The very clean, family-run **Clansman Motel** (☎ 902-794-7226, 800-565-2668; www.clansmanmotel .com; King St at Hwy 125 exit 3; r $100-110; 🖳) is 2km from the ferry. The licensed restaurant is open 7am to 9pm.

Take a sharp right after you descend the ferry ramp and 10 minutes later you'll be at the gorgeous Georgian **Gowrie House** (☎ 902-544-1050, 800-372-1115; www.gowriehouse.com; 840 Shore Rd, Sydney Mines; s/d/ste incl breakfast $135/145/175; ☺ Apr-Dec) with its extensive gardens. Off-season discounts of up to 40% are available. Reservations are required for the inn's sumptuous evening feasts (prix fixe $45).

Robena's 2000 Family Restaurant (☎ 902-794-8040; 266 Commercial St; mains $6-10; ☺ 7am-9pm Jun-Sep, 8am-8pm Oct-May) serves breakfast until noon weekdays and 1pm weekends. Lunch and dinner specials are posted on boards in the window.

Acadian Lines buses to Halifax (adult/ student/child under 12 $60/50/28) and points in between can be picked up at the Best Western North Star Hotel opposite the Marine Atlantic ferry terminal. **Transit Cape Breton** (☎ 902-539-8124; adult/child 5-12 $3.25/$3) runs bus No 5 back and forth between North Sydney's Commercial St and Sydney at 8:40am, 12:40pm, 2:40pm and 5:40pm Monday to Saturday.

Around North Sydney

A 15km-drive northwest of North Sydney, **Bird Island Boat Tours** (☎ 902-674-2384, 800-661-6680; www.birdisland.net; 1672 Big Bras d'Or Rd; adult/ child under 13 $33/15) venture out to the cliff-edged islands of Hertford and Ciboux beyond St Ann's Bay. Depending on which month you take the tour, you'll see colonies of razorbills, kittiwakes, puffins or terns.

NOVA SCOTIA

SYDNEY

The second-biggest city in Nova Scotia and the only real city on Cape Breton Island, Sydney is the embattled core of the island's collapsed industrial belt. The now-closed steel mill and coal mines were the region's largest employers.

Orientation

Downtown, Charlotte St is lined with stores and restaurants and there's a pleasant boardwalk along Esplanade, while the North End historic district has a gritty charm. There are several nice places to stay if you want to use this as a base to explore Louisbourg.

Information

CB Island (www.cbisland.com) Virtual tour, trip planner etc.
McConnell Memorial Library (☎ 902-562-3279; cnr Falmouth & Charlotte Sts; ☺ 10am-9pm Tue-Fri, to 5:30pm Sat) Free Internet access.
VIC Sydney River (☎ 902-563-4636; 20 Keltic Dr; ☺ 8:30am-4:30pm Mon-Fri); Waterfront (☎ 902-539-9876; 74 Esplanade; ☺ 9am-7pm Jul & Aug, 9am-5pm Jun & Sep–late Oct)

Sights

There are eight buildings older than 1802 in a two-block radius in North End Sydney. Three are open to the public, including **St Patrick's Church Museum** (☎ 902-562-8237; 87 Esplanade; admission free; ☺ 9am-5pm Jun-Aug), in the oldest Catholic church on Cape Breton Island. Among artifacts housed here is a not-so-merciful whipping post from the mid-19th century.

The 1787 **Cossit House** (☎ 902-539-7973; http://cossit.museum.gov.ns.ca; 75 Charlotte St; adult/concession $2/1; ☺ 9am-5pm Mon-Sat, 1-5pm Sun Jun–mid-Oct) is the oldest house in Sydney. Just down the road, **Jost Heritage House** (☎ 902-539-0366; 54 Charlotte St; admission free; ☺ 9am-5pm Mon-Sat, 1-5:30pm Sun Jun–mid-Oct) features a collection of model ships as well as an assortment of medicines used by an early 20th-century apothecary.

Cape Breton Centre for Heritage & Science (☎ 902-539-1572; 225 George St; admission free; ☺ 9am-5pm Mon-Sat Jun-Aug, 10am-4pm Tue-Fri Sep-May) explores the social and natural history of Cape Breton Island. Upstairs the **Nova Scotia Centre for Craft & Design** (☎ 902-539-7491; ☺ 9am-4:30pm Mon-Thu, to 4pm Fri) showcases work by local craftspeople.

SYDNEY TAR PONDS

North America's largest toxic waste site lies just three blocks east of the Charlotte St museums, at the end of Ferry St. Since its founding in 1901, the Sydney steel mill has produced some 700,000 tons of toxic sludge, the by-product of burning dirty coal to produce coke for use in the steel plant. The 51-hectare coke-oven site is now a field of rubble contaminated to depths of 25m.

The immense scale and extreme toxicity of the site have thwarted several clean-up attempts. In 2004, the Canadian and Nova Scotian governments promised to spend $400 million over 10 years to completely reclaim the area. Local residents who put up with an incredible stench of tar in hot weather and suffer from elevated cancer rates (not proven to be linked to the waste site) are anxious to see progress.

Sleeping

Most establishments in Sydney are open year-round.

Gathering House B&B (☎ 902-539-7172, 866-539-7172; www.gatheringhouse.com; 148 Crescent St; s/d $50/65) This welcoming, ramshackle Victorian home is close to the heart of town.

Park Place B&B (☎ 902-562-3518; www.bbcanada.com/81.html; 169 Park St; s/d incl breakfast $50/65) This Victorian home is a few blocks from the Acadian Lines bus station.

Paul's Hotel (☎ 902/866-562-5747; www3.ns.sympatico.ca/candb.landry; cnr Pitt St & Esplanade; s/d/tw incl breakfast $60/65/70) This grand old hotel is run by a grand old dame in her 80s. The price is right for the waterfront location and private bathrooms.

Paradise Found B&B (☎ 902-539-9377, 877-539-9377; www3.ns.sympatico.ca/paradisefound; 62 Milton St; r $85-100) Knowledgeable and hospitable hosts take a lot of pride in this elegant B&B. They'll join you for a several-course breakfast and help plan your travels. The rooms are extra comfortable.

Eating

Bistro One Hundred (☎ 902-564-3200; 100 Townsend St; lunch $8-13, dinner mains $15-25; ☺ lunch & dinner, closed Mon) This restaurant on the edge of downtown has deluxe sandwiches and pastas, or in the evening, portobello mushrooms stuffed with olive tapanade ($17).

Joe's Warehouse Food Emporium (☎ 902-539-6686; 424 Charlotte St; lunch mains $7-10, dinner mains $14-25; ☺ 11:30am-11pm Mon-Sat, 4-11pm Sun Jul & Aug, 11:30am-10pm Mon-Sat, 4-10pm Sun rest of year) This popular restaurant has a cozy bar, a posh dining room and a casual family restaurant.

For nocturnal munchies try **Jasper's** (☎ 902-539-7109; 268 George St; meals $8-13; ☺ 24hr).

Entertainment

A lot of touring bands make the trek to Sydney. Fiddlers and other traditional musicians from the west coast of the island also perform here or at the Savoy in Glace Bay (below). Gigs are about $5.

Upstair's at French Club (☎ 902-371-0329; 44 Ferry St) This groovy little North End club features rock, celtic, jazz and movie nights.

Chandler's (☎ 902-539-3438; 76 Dorchester St) This standard, cavernous bar has top-end local and Canadian talent on stage.

Getting There & Away

The Sydney airport is none too busy. A $10 airport improvement fee must be paid at a separate counter by all departing passengers. Air Canada Jazz flies between Sydney and Halifax ($400 to $600, 45 minutes, four times daily). **Air St-Pierre** (☎ 902-562-3140, 877-277-7765; www.airsaintpierre.com in French) flies to Sydney from early July to early September, on Thursdays and Sundays.

The Acadian Lines bus depot is at 99 Terminal Dr. There are also a number of shuttle services to Halifax.

GLACE BAY

Glace Bay is 6km north of Sydney. For a rich insight into the history of industrial Cape Breton Island visit the **Cape Breton Miners' Museum** (☎ 902-849-4522; www.minersmuseum.com; 42 Birkley St; tour & mine visit adult/child $10/5; ☺ 10am-6pm Wed-Mon, 10am-7pm Tue Jun-Aug, 9am-4pm Mon-Fri Sep-May), off South St less than 2km east from the town center. A retired miner will guide you on an hour-long underground tour. There are also exhibits on the lives of early 20th-century miners and their families. The museum's **restaurant** (mains $8-14; ☺ noon-8pm) offers a good selection of seafood, sandwiches and burgers.

The town's grand 1920 **Savoy Theatre** (☎ 902-842-1577; www.savoytheatre.com; 116 Commercial St) is the region's premiere entertainment venue.

LOUISBOURG

Louisbourg, 37km south of Sydney, is famous for its historic fortress. The **tourist information office** (☎ 902-733-2720; 7336 Main St; ☺ 9am-7pm Jul & Aug, 9am-5pm Jun & Sep–mid-Oct) is inside the **Sydney & Louisbourg Railway Museum** (admission free) at the entrance to the town. Museum hours fluctuate, but some of the displays can be seen whenever the tourist office is open.

Sights & Activities

Starting from the trailhead at the lighthouse at the end of Havenside Rd, a rugged 6km **trail** follows the coast over bogs, barrens and pre-Cambrian polished granite. Bring your camera to capture the views back toward the fortress at the national historic site.

LOUISBOURG NATIONAL HISTORIC SITE

Budget a full day to explore this extraordinary **historic site** (☎ 902-733-2280; 259 Park Service Rd; adult/family $13.50/33.75 Jun-Sep, $5.50/13.50 May & late Oct; ☺ 9:30am-6pm Jul & Aug, 9:30am-5pm May, Jun, Sep & Oct) that faithfully re-creates Fortress Louisbourg as it was in 1744. Built to protect French interests in the region, it was also a base for cod fishing and an administrative capital. Louisbourg was worked on continually from 1719 to about 1745 as saltwater in the mortar led to corrosion. The British took it in a 46-day siege in 1745, exploiting intelligence from British soldiers who had been prisoners in the fortress. It would change hands twice more. In 1760, after British troops under the command of General James Wolfe took Québec City, the walls of Louisbourg were destroyed and the city was burned to the ground.

In 1961, with the closing of many Cape Breton Island coalmines, the federal government funded the largest historical reconstruction in Canadian history as a way to generate employment, resulting in 50 buildings open to visitors. Workers in period dress take on the lives of typical fort inhabitants.

Free guided tours around the site are offered throughout the day. Travelers with mobility problems can ask for a pass to drive their car up to the site; there are ramps available to access most buildings. Be prepared for lots of walking, and bring a sweater and raincoat even if it's sunny when you start out.

NOVA SCOTIA

Though the scale of the reconstruction is massive, three-quarters of Louisbourg is still in ruins. The 2.5km **Ruins Walk** guides you through the untouched terrain and out to the Atlantic coast. A short **interpretive walk** opposite the visitor center discusses the relationship between the French and the Mi'kmaq and offers some great views of the whole site.

Three restaurants serve food typical of the time. **L'Épée Royale** (3-course meal $16) is where sea captains and prosperous merchants would dine. Servers in period costume also dish out grub at **Grandchamps House** (meal $7-10), a favorite of sailors and soldiers. Wash down beans and sausage with a dark ale or hot buttered rum ($3.50). Otherwise buy a 1kg ration ($3.50) of soldiers' bread at the **Destouches Bakery**. It's delicious, and one piece with cheese makes a full meal.

Sleeping & Eating

Coal Captain B&B (☎ 902-733-2931; www.louisbourg tourism.com/coalcapt/coalcapt.html; 7524 Main St; s/d $55/60) This central and gay-friendly B&B is operated by two history buffs. There are two rooms, and a third may be opened. Enjoy smoked salmon for breakfast and a soak in the clawfoot tub in the shared bathroom.

Louisbourg Manse B&B (☎ 902-733-3155, 866-733-3155; www.bbcanada.com/lsbgmanse; 10 Strathcona St; r $70) A block off Main St, this friendly B&B has two rooms with big windows and harbor views.

Fortress View Suites (☎ 902-733-3131, 877-733-3131; www.fortressview.ca; 7513 Main St; 1-bedroom ste $80) These central suites with kitchen facilities are nicely decorated and sizable. It's a great choice for families. The hosts also rent a charming two-bedroom heritage cottage across the road for $110 per night.

Cranberry Cove Inn (☎ 902-733-2171, 800-929-0222; www.louisbourg.com/cranberrycove; 12 Wolfe St; r $130-150) Close to Fortress Louisbourg, this top-notch inn with lovely parlors is open year-round. Seven uniquely decorated rooms feature Jacuzzis and fireplaces. The chef at its new restaurant (open 5pm to 9pm) has a good reputation.

Grubstake (☎ 902-733-2308; 7499 Main St; lunch mains $7-10, dinner mains $16-25; ☽ lunch & dinner, mid-Jun–early Oct) This informal restaurant is the best place to eat in town. The menu features burger platters at lunch and pastas and fresh seafood for dinner.

Patriot Café (☎ 902-733-2606; 7535 Main St; meals $3-4; ☽ 7:30am-7pm Mon-Fri, 9am-6pm Sat) For all-day breakfast, lunch or a smoothie, try this casual spot.

Entertainment

Louisbourg Playhouse (☎ 902-733-2996; 11 Lower Warren St; tickets $12; ☽ 8pm late Jun–early Sep) A cast of young, local musicians entertain all summer long in this 17th-century-style theater.

BADDECK

An old resort town in a pastoral setting, Baddeck is on the north shore of the salt-water Bras d'Or Lake, halfway between Sydney and the Canso Causeway. It's the most popular place to stay for those who intend to 'do' the Cabot Trail as a one-day scenic drive.

Information

Baddeck Public Library (☎ 902-295-2055; 520 Chebucto St; ☽ 1-5pm Mon, 1-5pm & 6-8pm Tue & Fri, 5-8pm Thu, 10am-noon & 1-5pm Sat) Internet access by donation.

VIC (☎ 902-295-1911; 454 Chebucto St; ☽ 9am-7pm Jun-Sep)

Visit Baddeck (www.visitbaddeck.com) Maps, tour operators, golf courses etc.

Sights & Activities

The inventor of the telephone is buried near his summer home, Beinn Bhreagh, which is visible across the bay from Baddeck. The large museum of the **Alexander Graham Bell National Historic Site** (☎ 902-295-2069; www.parkscanada.gc.ca; 559 Chebucto St; adult/child/family $6/3/15; ☽ 9am-6pm Jun, 8:30am-6pm Jul–mid-Oct, 9am-5pm mid-Oct–May), at the eastern edge of town, covers all aspects of his inventions and innovations. See medical and electrical devices, telegraphs, telephones, kites and seaplanes.

Bras d'Or Lakes & Watershed Interpretive Centre (☎ 902-295-1675; www.brasdor-conservation.com; 532 Chebucto St; admission by donation; ☽ 11am-7pm Jun–mid-Oct) explores the unique ecology of the enormous saltwater lakes.

Sleeping & Eating

Mother Gaelic's (☎ 902-295-2885, 888-770-3970; mothergaelics@ns.sympatico.ca; 26 Water St; d $90, with shared bathroom $50-75) Named for the owner's great-grandmother, who was a bootlegger patronized by Alexander Graham Bell, this sweet cottage opposite the waterfront has the feel of an uncluttered summer home. Three rooms share a bathroom and one room has its own.

Tree Seat B&B (☎ 902-295-1996; baddeck.com/ treeseat; 555 Chebucto St; d $60-75) Next door to the Alexander Graham Bell National Historic Site, this charming B&B offers big breakfasts and comfy rooms, some with private bathrooms.

Broadwater Inn & Cottages (☎ 902-295-1101, 877-818-3474; www.broadwater.baddeck.com; Bay Rd; r incl breakfast $95-125, cottages $125-170) In a tranquil spot 1.5km east of Baddeck, this c 1830 home once belonged to JAD MacCurdy, who worked with Alexander Graham Bell on early aircraft designs and piloted one of their creations – for a full half-mile over a frozen Bras d'Or Lake – in 1909. Bell's friend Helen Keller also visited this home, and carved her initials in a doorframe. The rooms in the inn are full of character, while modern cottages are set in the woods. It's gay friendly.

Highwheeler Café/Deli/Bakery (☎ 902-295-3006; 486 Chebucto St; meals $6-9; ❂ 7am-9pm Jul & Aug, 7am-7pm May, Jun, Sep & Oct) An excellent eatery offering a mouthwatering selection of sandwiches, salads and bakery items. Get a packed lunch to go for $8.50.

Bell Buoy Restaurant (☎ 902-295-2581; lunch mains $8-10, dinner mains $16-20; 536 Chebucto St; ❂ dinner May & Jun, lunch & dinner Jul-Oct) This restaurant caters to families, seafood-lovers and just about everyone else with special children's, teen and even vegetarian menus.

Entertainment

Baddeck Gathering Ceilidhs (☎ 902-295-2794; www .baddeckgathering.com; St Michael's Parish Hall, 8 Old Margaree Rd; adult/child $7/3; ❂ 7:30pm) Nightly fiddling and dancing. The parish hall is just opposite the VIC right in the middle of town.

WAGMATCOOK

Stop in this Mi'kmaw community just west of Baddeck to visit the **Wagmatcook Culture & Heritage Centre** (☎ 902-295-2999/2492; www.wag matcook.com; Hwy 105; ❂ 9am-8pm May-Oct; call for hrs Nov-Apr). This new cultural attraction offers a rich entryway into Mi'kmaw culture and history. The small museum requires at least an hour. Photos from the 1930s show life in Mi'kmaw communities across Nova Scotia before government policies of centraliza-

tion and assimilation weakened their social fabric. Elders show the use of traditional games and craftspeople demonstrate beading and basket weaving. A craft shop in the museum sells high-quality traditional crafts. The adjoining **Clean Wave Restaurant** (mains $5-10; ❂ 8am-8pm May-Oct) serves hot venison sandwiches and excellent fish chowder.

WHYCOCOMAGH

Negemow Basket Shop (☎ 902-756-3491; 9217 Hwy 105; ❂ 8am-10pm Jul-Sep, 8am-8pm May-Oct) at the Waycobah First Nation just west of Whycocomagh sells Mi'kmaw crafts. Rod's One Stop next door pumps some of the cheapest gas on Cape Breton Island. **Whycocomagh Provincial Park** (☎ 902-756-2448; http://parks.gov .ns.ca; 9729 Hwy 105; campsites $18) usually has sites available even in midsummer. Starting just behind the park office, the 5km **Salt Mountain Trail** is a challenging climb that rewards you with views over Bras D'Or Lake. You're also almost guaranteed to see bald eagles.

EASTERN SHORE

Running from Cape Canso at the extreme eastern tip of the mainland to the outskirts of Dartmouth, the Eastern Shore is one of the least visited regions of the province. There are no large towns and the main road is almost as convoluted as the rugged shoreline it follows. If you want to experience wilderness and are willing to hike or kayak, this is ideal. Several good hiking trails take you to beautiful stretches of coastline and protected bays with lots of islands. Taking Hwy 7 from Antigonish – though it won't pass through every town on the Eastern Shore – is a scenic alternative for a return trip to Halifax and takes only an hour or so more than Hwy 102/104.

GUYSBOROUGH

Guysborough, 35km south of Monastery on Hwy 16, was settled by United Empire Loyalists after the American Revolution. The 26km Guysborough Trail, part of the TCT, is great for biking and hiking. **Old Court House Museum** (☎ 902-533-4008; 106 Church St; admission free; ❂ 9am-5pm Mon-Fri, 10am-4pm Sat & Sun Jun-Sep) displays artifacts related to early farming and housekeeping, and also offers tourist information and guides to hiking trails.

The 36 shaded sites at **Boylston Provincial Park** (☎ 902-533-3326; http://parks.gov.ns.ca; off Hwy 16; campsites $14) are never all taken. From the picnic area on the highway below the campground, a footbridge leads to a small island. A display near the park office relates the story that a Norwegian earl, Henry Sinclair of Orkney, visited Canada in 1398!

Carritt House B&B (☎ 902-533-3855; 20 Pleasant St; s/d $55/65), c 1810, has lovely hardwood floors and a big cast-iron tub in the shared bathroom.

Desbarres Manor (☎ 902-533-2099; www.desbarres manor.com; 90 Church St; r $140-180) offers opulent rooms in a tastefully renovated 1830 grand manor.

For homemade baked good, soups, sandwiches and seafood dinners, stop at the friendly **Days Gone By Bakery & Restaurant** (☎ 902-533-2762; 143 Hwy 16; mains $9-11; ☽ 7am-8pm).

CANSO

A further 55km down Hwy 16 from Guysborough and off the beaten track, Canso is one of the oldest towns in the province. Long dependent on the fishery, Canso has been decimated by emigration and unemployment since the northern cod stocks collapsed around 1990. The tourist office is at the 1885 **Whitman House Museum** (☎ 902-366-2170; 1297 Union St; admission free; ☽ 9am-5pm late May–Sep), which holds reminders of the town's history and offers a good view from the widow's walk on the roof.

An interpretive center on the waterfront tells the story of **Grassy Island National Historic Site** (☎ 902-366-3136; 1465 Union St; admission $2.50; ☽ 10am-6pm Jun–mid-Sep), which lies just offshore and can be visited by boat until 4pm. In 1720 the British built a small fort to offset the French who had their headquarters in Louisbourg. The outpost was extremely vulnerable to military attacks and was totally destroyed in 1744. Among the ruins today there's a self-guided hiking trail with eight interpretive stops explaining the history of the area. The boat to Grassy Island departs from the center upon demand, weather permitting.

Chapel Gully Trail is a 10km boardwalk and hiking trail along an estuary and out to the coast. It begins near the lighthouse on the hill behind the hospital at the eastern end of Canso. A large map is posted at the trailhead.

Most people come for the **Stan Rogers Folk Festival** (www.stanfest.com; ☽ 1st weekend Jul), the biggest festival in Nova Scotia, which quadruples Canso's population when six stages showcase amazing folk, blues and traditional musicians from around the world. Accommodations are pretty much impossible to get unless you reserve a year ahead. Locals set up 1000 campsites for the festival; check the website for details and try to get a site away from the festival site if sleep is a priority.

Last Port Motel (☎ 902-366-2400; hanhamsf@ns .sympatico.ca; Rte 16; r/with kitchen $60/80) is a friendly spot with clean rooms. It's 3km west of Canso. Its **restaurant** (mains $5-10; ☽ breakfast, lunch & dinner) serves basic fare.

In a quiet nearby fishing community is **Foxberry by the Sea B&B** (☎ 902-358-2605; www3 .ns.sympatico.ca/foxberry; RR2, Whitehead; d incl breakfast $70, cottages from $125).

SHERBROOKE

The pleasant little town of Sherbrooke, 123km west of Canso and 63km south of Antigonish, is overshadowed by its historic site, which is about the same size and a very popular attraction.

The local tourist office is at **Sherbrooke Village** (☎ 902-522-2400; http://museum.gov.ns.ca/sv; Hwy 7; adult/child/family $9/3.75/25; ☽ 9:30am-5:30pm Jun–mid-Oct), which re-creates everyday life from 125 years ago through buildings, demonstrations and costumed workers. There are 25 buildings to visit in this living museum that effectively helps its visitors step back in time.

On a quiet farm, **Days Ago B&B** (☎ 902-522-2811, 866-522-2811; www.bbcanada.com/daysago; 15 Cameron Rd; s/d incl breakfast $55/60) will lull you with its slower pace. There's a sun porch for sitting on, or take out a kayak if you feel energetic.

TAYLOR HEAD PROVINCIAL PARK

A little-known scenic highlight of Nova Scotia, this spectacular **park** (☎ 902-772-2218; 20140 Hwy 7; http://parks.gov.ns.ca; ☽ mid-May–mid-Oct) encompasses a peninsula jutting 6.5km into the Atlantic. On one side is a long, very fine, sandy beach fronting a protected bay. Some 17km of hiking trails cut through the spruce and fir forests. The **Headland Trail** is the longest at 8km round-trip and follows the rugged coastline to scenic views at Taylor

Head. The shorter **Bob Bluff Trail** is a 3km round-trip hike to a bluff with good views. In spring you'll see colorful wildflowers, and this is a great bird-watching venue. Pack the picnic cooler and plan on spending a full day hiking, lounging and (if you can brave the cool water) swimming here.

TANGIER

Southwest of Taylor Head Provincial Park, Tangier is one of the best settings for kayaking in the Maritimes. **Coastal Adventures Sea Kayaking** (☎ 902-772-2774, www.coastaladventures .com; off Hwy 7; ☯ mid-Jun–early Oct) offers introductions to sea-kayaking (half-/full-day $65/100), rentals (half-/full-day $35/50) and guided trips. One of the most established kayaking companies, it also has a small B&B, **Paddlers Retreat** (s/d/ste $45/55/75).

Murphy's Camping on the Ocean (☎ 902-772-2700; www.dunmac.com/murphys; 291 Murphy's Rd; tent/RV sites $20/25, trailer rental $65) offers some secluded tent sites, complimentary coffee and a cozy lounge area called 'Sailors Rest.' There's great kayaking among the small islands just offshore; canoes can be rented ($8/25 per hour/day). The owner, Brian Murphy, runs sunset boat tours ($15) most evenings.

JEDORE OYSTER POND

The tiny **Fisherman's Life Museum** (☎ 902-889-2053; http://museum.gov.ns.ca/flm; 58 Navy Pool Loop; adult/child $2/1; ☯ 9:30am-5:30pm Mon-Sat, 1-5:30pm Sun Jun–mid-Oct), 45km toward Halifax from Tangier, should really be renamed. The man of the house used to row 16km to get to his fishing grounds, leaving his wife and 13 daughters at home. The museum really captures women's domestic life of the early 20th century. Costumed local guides offer tea and hospitality.

Prince Edward Island

In the Gulf of St Lawrence, huddled close to the shores of New Brunswick and Nova Scotia, is Canada's smallest province. Golden beaches and dramatic dunes mark its shores, red cliffs rise from its waters and bucolic villages pepper its bright patchwork of fields and forests. It's obvious that Prince Edward Island (PEI) has been blessed with an unparalleled concentration of this country's beauty.

The crescent-shaped island's deep bays and incising tidal rivers have created a convoluted shoreline that naturally divides the province into three equal parts. Eastern PEI, known as Kings County, hosts secluded beaches and small fishing villages; its wealth of stunning routes is gaining it an international reputation as a cycling destination. Thanks to the 1908 novel *Anne of Green Gables,* Queens County, which comprises most of central PEI, cemented its reputation for remarkably verdant countryside; having some of Canada's finest beaches close at hand only increases the area's appeal. Prince County, which makes up western PEI, is a fascinating and gorgeous place to explore the cultures and history of the French Acadians and Mi'kmaq aboriginal peoples.

Despite the pervasive splendor of the province, the first thing most visitors notice, and fall in love with, is PEI's charm and relaxed atmosphere. You'll be hard-pressed not to follow cue. The peak tourism season is short, with most services shut between mid-September and mid-June. The margins of this season are great times to visit – the weather is still warm and the crowds of July and August are missing. The vibrant, changing colors of October make it the perfect time to hike or cycle the pastoral Confederation Trail.

HIGHLIGHTS

- Dance like nobody's watching while being serenaded by the sands of **Basin Head Beach** (p467)

- Stroll along the dramatic coast of **Prince Edward Island National Park** (p469)

- Send lobster juice skyward while savoring the island's most celebrated crustacean in **North Rustico** (p472)

- Absorb the charm of Canada's birthplace while wandering **Old Charlottetown** (p459)

- Forget that you're not Celtic while letting loose at a traditional ceilidh in **Summerside** (p474)

- Have your backside survive the amazing tip-to-tip 279km bike ride along the **Confederation Trail** (p478)

- Discover (but never, ever admit) that you like Anne Shirley (aka Anne of Green Gables) in **Cavendish** (p472)

Confederation Trail ★

Cavendish ★★
Summerside ★ North Rustico ★ Prince Edward Island National Park ★ Basin Head Beach ★
Old Charlottetown ★

PRINCE EDWARD ISLAND

| ▪ POPULATION: 137,800 | ▪ PROVINCIAL CAPITAL: CHARLOTTETOWN | ▪ AREA: 5700 SQ KM |

PRINCE EDWARD ISLAND

PRINCE EDWARD ISLAND

Ferry to Îles de la Madeleine

Confederation Trail

0   50 km
0   30 miles

Gulf of St Lawrence

Northumberland Strait

New Brunswick

Nova Scotia

History

Aboriginal inhabitancy in the region dates back almost 11,000 years, when the island was attached to the mainland. The Mi'kmaq, a branch of the Algonquin nation, arrived at about the time of Christ.

Although Jacques Cartier of France first recorded PEI's existence in 1534, settlement didn't begin until 1603. Initially small, the French colony grew only after Britain's expulsion of the Acadians from Nova Scotia in the 1750s. In 1758 the British took the island, known then as Île St Jean, and expelled the 3000 Acadians. Britain was officially granted the island in the Treaty of Paris of 1763.

To encourage settlement, the British divided the island into 67 lots and held a lottery to give away the land. Unfortunately most of the 'Great Giveaway' winners were speculators and did nothing to settle or develop the island. The questionable actions of these absentee landlords hindered population growth and caused incredible unrest among islanders.

One of the major reasons PEI did not become part of Canada in 1867 was because union did not offer a solution to the land problem. In 1873 the Compulsory Land Purchase Act forced the sale of absentee landlords' land and cleared the way for PEI to join Canada later that year. But foreign land-ownership is still a sensitive issue in the province. The population has remained stable, at around 140,000, since the 1930s.

In 1997, after much debate, PEI was linked to New Brunswick and the mainland by the Confederation Bridge – at almost 13km, it's the world's longest artificial bridge over ice-covered waters.

Climate

While July and August are the warmest and driest months, June and September are not far behind. During this four-month travel window, a typical 30-day period experiences 90mm of rain scattered over almost two weeks. Unique warm ocean currents mean the island has a milder climate than most of Canada; swimming in July and August is a pleasant proposition. In winter the snow can be meters deep, but it rarely hinders the major roadways. The last of the white stuff is usually gone by May.

National & Provincial Parks

Dunes and beaches take center stage in the deservedly celebrated Prince Edward Island National Park (p469) and its new eastern section, Greenwich (p468).

PEI's **provincial parks** (www.gov.pe.ca/visitorsguide/explore/parks) are abundant and spread out along the shores of the province. Their locations are marked on the provincial highway maps available at tourist offices. Along with an attractive shoreline, the parks typically have playgrounds, picnic areas and wheelchair-accessible toilets. Day use is free in all 27 parks and **camping** (campsites $19, with hookups $22-25) is possible in 13 of them. Opening dates vary, but the parks are typically open from mid-June to late September or October.

Kayaking is an increasingly popular activity in some of PEI's parks. Outside Expeditions (p472) operates trips into the national park from North Rustico, and Venture Out (p467) runs trips from Souris Beach Provincial Park. Both companies offer kayak trips at Brudenell River Provincial Park (p466).

Getting There & Away

AIR

Charlottetown's airport is 8km from town and serves all flights leaving the province. A $10 departure tax (not included in ticket prices) is charged to anyone over the age of two.

Air Canada has daily flights to Halifax ($129 to $243), Montréal ($220 to $280) and Toronto ($210 to $240). Jetsgo serves Toronto ($220) three times a week. **Prince Edward Air** (☎ 800-565-5359; www.peair.com) has seven weekly flights between Charlottetown and Halifax ($125).

BUS

Acadian Coach Lines (☎ 800-567-5151; 156 Belvedere Ave) only has direct services from Charlottetown to Moncton, New Brunswick ($36, three hours). For Halifax ($62, 4½ hours) you must change buses in New Brunswick. The company also operates services from Summerside.

Advanced Shuttle (☎ 877-886-3322; adult/student $50/45) has a convenient service from Charlottetown or Summerside to Halifax or any point along the way. An identical service is run by **Square One Shuttle** (☎ 877-675-3830). Reservations are necessary.

PRINCE EDWARD ISLAND IN...

Two Days

Relax and spend the better part of a day wandering through the historic, leafy streets of **Old Charlottetown** (opposite). Ascend the grand stairs of **Province House** (opposite) to see Canada's birthplace, then gawk at the harbor view from the veranda of **Beaconsfield House** (p461), before chilling out under some shade in Victoria Park's waterfront gardens. Hit the wharf before dinner, or head west to the idyllic village of **Victoria** (p468) for a seaside stroll and sumptuous meal at the **Victoria Village Inn** (p469).

Next morning, pack your beach gear and plop yourself on one of the exquisite beaches of **Prince Edward Island National Park** (p469).

Four Days

Spend a day exploring the magnificent dunes at **Greenwich** (p468) and the Anne-related sights near **Cavendish** (p472). Enjoy your last day exploring the coast by kayak from **North Rustico** (p472) or cycling the **Confederation Trail** (p478) around **Mt Stewart** (p468).

One Week

Allow a few days to tour **Kings County** (p465), with stops at **Orwell** (p466), **Montague** (p466) and the illustrious **Basin Head Beach** (p467).

Alternatively, delve into the Acadian and Mi'kmaq cultures of **Prince County** (p474) while en route from **Summerside** (p474) to the **North Cape** (p477).

CAR & MOTORCYCLE

The **Confederation Bridge** (☎ 902-437-7300; www .confederationbridge.com; car/motorcycle $39/16; ☼ 24hr) makes getting to the island faster, easier and cheaper than travel by ferry. Sadly, the 1.1m-high guardrails rob you of any hoped-for view. The toll is only charged on departure from PEI, and includes all passengers.

Cyclists and pedestrians are banned from the bridge and must use a free, demand-driven shuttle service. On the PEI side, go to the bridge operations building near the toll gates; on the New Brunswick side, look for the bridge facility building at the junction of Rtes 16 and 955. The operators guarantee you won't have to wait more than two hours for the shuttle at any time.

If you're planning to travel one way on the bridge and the other by ferry, it's cheaper to take the ferry to PEI and return via the bridge.

FERRY

Northumberland Ferries (☎ 902-566-3838, 888-249-7245; www.nfl-bay.com; pedestrian/motorcycle/car $12.50/34.50/53; ☼ May-Dec) runs the ferry service that links PEI's Wood Islands to Caribou, Nova Scotia. There are up to nine daily sailings in each direction during the summer, and five in the fall and spring. Note that vehicle fees include all passengers for the 1¼-hour trip. You only pay as you're leaving PEI; the trip over from Nova Scotia is free. The ferry operates on a first-come, first-served basis.

For information on the ferry service between Souris and Îles de la Madeleine, Québec, see p332.

Getting Around

Apart from the Beach Shuttle running between Charlottetown and Cavendish, there is no intra-island public transportation. While your easiest option is to get around by car, bicycle is also a good choice. You'll find the distances are short and the roads in good condition. In early spring it's wise to avoid any unpaved clay roads – their sticking power is legendary. See p465 for car-rental information.

CHARLOTTETOWN

☎ 902 / pop 32,200

Nestled at the confluence of the East Hillsborough and North Yorke Rivers is PEI's charming capital. As grand as it is diminutive, Charlottetown has quiet colonial and Victorian streets lined with gracious trees, elegant 19th-century mansions and the island's signature redbrick facades. Lurking under this pastoral skin are some contemporary buildings and hip eateries that give the city an intriguing mix of old and new. Charlottetown's history, natural beauty and short visiting season ensure that its streets are packed with visitors every July and August.

HISTORY

Charlottetown is named after the exotic consort of King George III. Her African roots, dating back to Margarita de Castro Y Sousa and the Portuguese royal house, are as legendary as they are controversial. The idea that this English queen had an African ancestry is still too much for many historians to handle.

While many believe the city's splendid harbor was the reason Charlottetown became the capital, the reality was less glamorous. In 1765 the surveyor-general decided on Charlottetown because he thought it prudent to bestow the poor side of the island with some privileges. Thanks to the celebrated 1864 conference, however, Charlottetown is etched in Canadian history as the country's birthplace.

ORIENTATION

University Ave is the city's largest street; its southern terminus is punctuated by historic Province House, which marks the entrance to **Old Charlottetown**. Befitting the transition is the stark juxtaposition of the house and the modern Confederation Centre of the Arts.

Parallel to University Ave is Queen St, which runs west of the Confederation Centre. Queen St and the adjacent blocks on Grafton, Richmond and Sydney Sts are home to Charlottetown's finest restaurants and shops.

Majestic Great George St runs south from Province House, past impressive St Dunstan's Basilica to Peake's Wharf and Confederation Landing Park. The waterfront is the hub of summer activity, hosting various festivals.

To the west of town, on the waterfront, is the verdant Victoria Park and its sweeping promenade.

INFORMATION
Bookstores
Bookman (☎ 902-892-8872; 177 Queen St) Huge selection of rare second-hand books.
Reading Well Bookstore (☎ 902-566-2703; 87 Water St) Features local authors.

Emergency
Police, Ambulance & Fire (☎ 911).
Royal Canadian Mounted Police (☎ 902-368-9300; 450 University Ave) For nonemergencies.

Internet Access
Confederation Centre Public Library (☎ 902-368-4642; cnr Queen & Grafton Sts; ☼ 10am-8pm Tue-Thu, 10am-5pm Fri & Sat, 1-5pm Sun) Free access.
Timothy's World Coffee (☎ 902-628-8503; 137B Kent St; per hr $5; ☼ 7am-7pm Mon-Fri, 9am-6pm Sat, 11:30am-5pm Sun)

Internet Resources
Visit Charlottetown (www.visitcharlottetown.com) A helpful website with upcoming festival information, city history and visitor information.

Medical Services
Polyclinic Professional Centre (☎ 902-629-8810; 199 Grafton St; ☼ 5:30-8pm Mon-Fri, 9:30am-noon Sat) Charlottetown's after-hours, walk-in medical clinic. Non-Canadians must pay a $40 fee.
Queen Elizabeth Hospital (☎ 902-894-2111; 60 Riverside Dr; ☼ 24hr) Emergency services.

Money
TD Canada Trust (☎ 902-629-2265; 192 Queen St; ☼ 8am-6pm Mon-Wed, 8am-8pm Thu & Fri, 9am-3pm Sat)

Post
Main post office (☎ 902-628-4400; 135 Kent St)

Tourist Information
Tourist Office (☎ 902-368-4444, 888-734-7529; www .peiplay.com; 178 Water St, PO Box 2000, Stn Central, Charlottetown, PE C1A 7N8; ☼ 9am-10pm Jul & Aug, 8.30am-6pm Sep–mid-Oct, 9am-4.30pm Mon-Fri mid-Oct–May) Located in the Stone Cottage near Founders' Hall, this is the island's main tourist office. It has all the answers and a plethora of brochures and maps, too.

SIGHTS & ACTIVITIES

All of the major sights are within the confines of Old Charlottetown, which makes wandering between them as rewarding as wandering through them.

Province House National Historic Site

Charlottetown's centerpiece is the imposing, yet welcoming, neoclassical **Province House** (☎ 902-566-7626; 165 Richmond St; admission free; ☼ 9am-5pm Jun-Sep, to 6pm Jul & Aug, 9am-5pm Mon-Fri Oct-May) The symmetry of design is carried throughout, including two brilliant

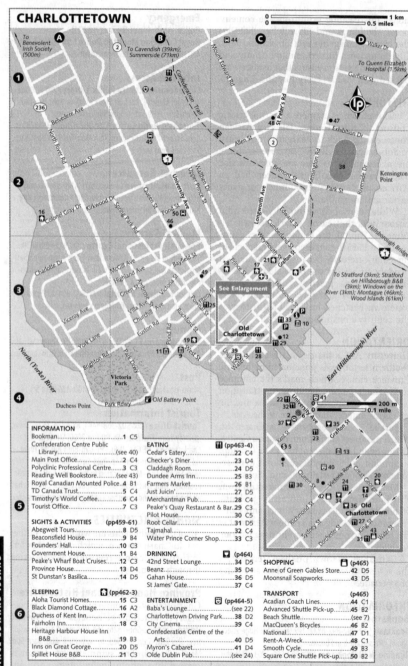

CHARLOTTETOWN

INFORMATION	
Bookman	1 C5
Confederation Centre Public Library	(see 40)
Main Post Office	2 C4
Polyclinic Professional Centre	3 C3
Reading Well Bookstore	(see 43)
Royal Canadian Mounted Police	4 B1
TD Canada Trust	5 C4
Timothy's World Coffee	6 C4
Tourist Office	7 C3

SIGHTS & ACTIVITIES	(pp459-61)
Abegweit Tours	8 D5
Beaconsfield House	9 B4
Founders' Hall	10 C4
Government House	11 B4
Peake's Wharf Boat Cruises	12 C3
Province House	13 D4
St Dunstan's Basilica	14 D5

SLEEPING	(pp462-3)
Aloha Tourist Homes	15 C3
Black Diamond Cottage	16 A2
Duchess of Kent Inn	17 C3
Fairholm Inn	18 C3
Heritage Harbour House Inn B&B	19 B3
Inns on Great George	20 D5
Spillet House B&B	21 C3

EATING	🍴 (pp463-4)
Cedar's Eatery	22 C4
Checker's Diner	23 C4
Claddagh Room	24 D5
Dundee Arms Inn	25 B3
Farmers Market	26 B1
Just Juicin'	27 C5
Merchantman Pub	28 C4
Peake's Quay Restaurant & Bar	29 C3
Pilot House	30 C5
Root Cellar	31 D5
Tajmahal	32 C4
Water Prince Corner Shop	33 C3

DRINKING	🍸 (p464)
42nd Street Lounge	34 D5
Beanz	35 D4
Gahan House	36 C4
St James' Gate	37 C3

ENTERTAINMENT	🎬 (pp464-5)
Baba's Lounge	(see 22)
Charlottetown Driving Park	38 C3
City Cinema	39 C4
Confederation Centre of the Arts	40 D5
Myron's Cabaret	41 D4
Olde Dublin Pub	(see 24)

SHOPPING	🛍 (p465)
Anne of Green Gables Store	42 D5
Moonsnail Soapworks	43 D5

TRANSPORT	(p465)
Acadian Coach Lines	44 C1
Advanced Shuttle Pick-up	45 B2
Beach Shuttle	(see 7)
MacQueen's Bicycles	46 B2
National	47 D1
Rent-A-Wreck	48 C1
Smooth Cycle	49 B3
Square One Shuttle Pick-up	50 B2

PRINCE EDWARD ISLAND

skylights reaching up through the massive sandstone structure. It was here in 1864, within the Confederation Chamber, that 23 representatives of Britain's North American colonies first discussed the creation of Canada (p27). Along with being the 'birthplace of Canada,' the site is home to Canada's second-oldest active legislature.

Several rooms have been restored, and in July and August you may find yourself face to face with Canada's first prime minister: actors in period garb wander the halls and regularly coalesce to perform reenactments of the famous conference. Enjoy the *Great Dream*, a 17-minute film about the monumental 1864 conference.

Founders' Hall

Opened in 2001, this high-tech multimedia **exhibit** (☎ 902-368-1864, 800-955-1864; 6 Prince St; adult/child 6-17 yrs/family $7/3.75/17; ☽ 9am-5pm Mon-Sat & 9am-4pm Sun mid-May–mid-Oct, to 8pm Mon-Sat Jul & Aug), housed in an old train station, deluges your senses with facts and fun about Canada's history since 1864. It's sure to entertain children, and the child in you.

Beaconsfield House

With its crowning belvedere, intricate gingerbread trim and elegant 19th-century furnishings, **Beaconsfield House** (☎ 902-368-6603; 2 Kent St; adult/student/family $4.25/3.25/14; ☽ 10am-5pm Jul & Aug, hours vary Sep-Jun) is the finest Victorian mansion in Charlottetown. Have a wander or sit on the veranda and be stunned by the view.

St Dunstan's Basilica

Rising from the ashes of a 1913 fire, the three towering stone spires of this neo-Gothic **basilica** (☎ 902-894-3486; 45 Great George St; admission free; ☽ 8am-5pm) are now a Charlottetown landmark. The marble floors, Italian carvings and decoratively embossed ribbed ceiling are surprisingly ornate.

Government House

Within the sprawling gardens of Victoria Park is **Government House** (☎ 902-368-5480; admission free; ☽ 10am-4pm Mon-Fri Jul & Aug). This striking colonial mansion, with its grand hall, Palladian window and Doric columns, has been home to PEI's lieutenant governors since 1835. In 2003 the Hon JL Bernard

---

LEFT OUT IN THE COLD

You may know that in the world of Western politics, it's tradition for the acting government to sit to the right of the speaker in the house, with the left being set aside for the opposition. The legislature of PEI was no different until 1847, when they moved into their new digs at the Confederation Building (then called the Colonial Building). It turned out that the coal stove heating the building sat to the left of the speaker, so the government quickly passed legislation sending the opposition into the cold. As the years went on, modern heating was installed but the government steadfastly maintained its position on the left. Is it nostalgia that's preventing them from moving back to the right, or is it the fact that the sun shines in the eyes of the opposition?

---

broke with an almost 170-year-old tradition and opened its doors to the public.

TOURS

Self-guided walking tours are available for just a loonie ($1) at the tourist office (p459).

Abegweit Tours (☎ 902-894-9966; adult/child under 11 $9.50/1; ☽ Jun-Oct) One-hour double-decker bus tours through Charlottetown leave from the Confederation Centre. The six-hour north shore tour ($65) will pick you up if you're staying in town.

Confederation Players (☎ 902-368-1864; 6 Prince St; adult $5; ☽ Jul & Aug, Tue-Sat mid-Jun–Sep). There is no better way to tour Charlottetown. Playing the fathers and ladies of Confederation, actors garbed in 19th-century dress educate and entertain through the town's historic streets. Tours leave from Founders' Hall, and there are Great George St, Merchants & Mansions and Waterfront storytelling tours.

Peake's Wharf Boat Cruises (☎ 902-566-4458; 1 Great George St; 70min cruise $16; ☽ 1pm, 6:30pm & 8pm Jun-Aug) Observe sea life, hear interesting stories and witness a wonderfully different perspective of Charlottetown from the waters of its harbor. An excellent seal-watching trip ($22) departs at 2:30pm, returning at 5pm.

FESTIVALS & EVENTS

Charlottetown Festival (☎ 902-566-1267; www .confederationcentre.com/festival.asp; ☽ mid-May–mid-Oct) This theatrical festival features free outdoor performances, a children's theater and dance programs.

PRINCE EDWARD ISLAND

THE AUTHOR'S CHOICE

Fairholm Inn (☎ 902-892-5022, 888-573-5022; www.fairholm.pe.ca; 230 Prince St; ste incl breakfast $150-275) This national historic inn was built in 1838 and is a superb example of the Picturesque movement in British architecture. Take tea while enjoying the morning sun in the beautiful conservatory, wander the gardens or hole up with a book in the library. Luxurious English fabrics, beautiful Prince Edward Island artwork and extravagant antiques, including grandiose beds, fill each of the five-star suites. Light a fire, soak in your tub and sink back into the elegant days of the 19th century.

Festival of Lights (☎ 902-368-1864, 800-955-1864; 🗓 Jun 30–Jul 3) Buskers roam the historic waterfront by day, while Canada's best musicians perform by night – all in celebration of their country's birthday. There's free entertainment and fireworks on July 1.

PEI's International Children's Theatre Festival (☎ 800-803-1421; 🗓 mid-Jul–Aug) Entertaining one-hour performances are held behind Beaconsfield House (p461) at 11am on weekdays.

Old Home Week (☎ 902-629-6623; www.peiprovincial exhibition.com; 🗓 mid-Aug) Held at the Provincial Exhibition grounds, this event features carnival rides, musical entertainment, games of chance, harness racing and traditional livestock shows.

Festival of the Fathers (☎ 902-368-1864, 800-955-1864; 🗓 weekend before Labour Day) On the waterfront, this three-day festival celebrates Charlottetown's history by recreating the enchanting events of the Victorian era. Expect musicians, dances, traditional food, carriage rides and humorous street games.

PEI International Shellfish Festival (☎ 866-955-2003; www.peishellfish.com; 🗓 3rd weekend in Sep) Now one of the island's largest festivals, this massive kitchen party, set on the Charlottetown waterfront, merges great traditional music with incredible seafood. Don't miss the oyster-shucking championships or the chowder challenge.

SLEEPING

Old Charlottetown's charms and proximity to major sights and restaurants makes it the most-enviable area to rest your head. There are numerous hotels, inns and B&Bs, with the last two offering the best value. Finding budget to mid-range choices is difficult, but a great option, if you have your own transport, is the nearby town of Stratford. It's 3km away on the opposite shore of the

East Hillsborough River, and offers cheaper accommodations in a fine country setting. During summer, Charlottetown hums with activity, so it's wise to book ahead. In the off-season accommodations are plentiful and most places reduce their rates. Parking is freely available at or close to all accommodations.

Budget

Spillett House B&B (☎ 902-892-5494; www.spillett house.pe.ca; 157 Weymouth St; s/d with shared bathroom $50/60; 🖳) This lovely heritage home with hardwood floors, spacious rooms and comfortable antique furnishings is perfectly located in Old Charlottetown. Kids are welcome and there are storage facilities for bicycles.

Aloha Tourist Homes (☎ 902-892-9944; www.aloha amigo.com; 234 Sydney St; s/d/tw with shared bathroom $35/55/55) These two old-fashioned homes are bright and clean, with large communal kitchens. Local calls are free, as is the coffee and tea.

Mid-Range

Heritage Harbour House Inn B&B (☎ 902-892-6633, 800-405-0066; hhhouse@attglobal.net; 9 Grafton St; d $115) A two-minute walk from Victoria Park is this family-friendly B&B-turned-inn. Country furnishings, modern amenities and balconies complete each of the large new rooms built onto this elegant old home. Spanish and Japanese are spoken.

Stratford on Hillsborough B&B (☎ 902-569-2462; 40 MacDonald Rd, Stratford; s with shared bathroom $25, d $75-100; 🖳 🐾) If the views, comfortable beds and Victorian veranda don't put a smile on your face, the enthusiasm of the owner, Betty, will. A pool, a games room and walking trails make this a perfect place for families.

Windows on the River (☎ 902-569-3327, 877-564-8925; www.stratfordwindowsontheriver.com; 58 East River Dr, Stratford; 1-/2-bedroom apt $85/130) Sit atop your private balcony, spark the barbecue and enjoy the perfect riverside view. The fireplace, angled ceilings and warm wooden interior of this coach house make it the best, and often the cheapest, choice.

Duchess of Kent Inn (☎ 902-566-5826; www.duchess ofkentinn.ca; 218 Kent St; d $95-125; 🗓 May-Nov) Set in Old Charlottetown, this restored 1875 heritage home, with its busy period decor, has several spacious rooms and a communal kitchen.

Black Diamond Cottage (☎ 902-566-9103; peiblack diamond.com; 1 Colonel Gray Dr; apt $100) The sparse decor gives each waterfront apartment the feel of a summer cottage. Steps lead down to the shore, where you can walk to Victoria Park. Each apartment has two bedrooms, a sofa bed and a full kitchen.

Top End
Inns on Great George (☎ 902-892-0606, 800-361-1118; www.innsongreatgeorge.com; 58 Great George St; d incl light breakfast $180-290) A colorful collage of celebrated buildings, built along Charlottetown's most famous street, has rooms ranging from plush and historic to bold and contemporary. It's both gay and family friendly. A babysitting service is available.

EATING
Radiating from Queen St, venerable restaurants pepper Old Charlottetown and prepare everything from fresh Atlantic seafood to mouthwatering Indian curries. The quality is high, as can be the price. Pubs dole out some great food and provide good value. During summer Victoria Row's pedestrian mall and the waterfront are also hot spots.

Budget
Just Juicin' (☎ 902-894-3104; 62 Queen St; wraps $5; breakfast & lunch) Although the smoothies star, the pita wraps here are the best quick eats in town. The smoothie concoctions are as refreshing as they are tasty. The imaginative fusion of carrot, ginger, pineapple and beet in the 'Aussie Experience' will put a serious bounce in your step.

Farmers Market (☎ 902-626-3373; 100 Belvedere Ave; 9am-2pm Sat, also Wed Jul & Aug) Come hungry and empty-handed. Enjoy some prepared island foods or peruse the cornucopia of fresh organic fruit and vegetables.

Root Cellar (☎ 902-892-6227; 34 Queen St) This grocer carries the essentials as well as specialty cheese, coffee and vegan selections.

Checker's Diner (☎ 902-892-4325; 41 University Ave; meals $5-8; 7am-7pm Mon-Sat, from 8am Sun) This checkerboard-floored diner serves all-day breakfasts and all-you-can-eat buffets ($8) from 11am to 2pm daily.

Mid-Range
Peake's Quay Restaurant & Bar (☎ 902-368-1330; 2 Great George St; lunch mains $8-12, dinner mains $15-20; 11-2am late May–Sep) The atmosphere here is

fantastic in summer. Patrons pack the huge balcony overlooking the historic waterfront to enjoy local seafood and nightly live Celtic music.

Cedar's Eatery (☎ 902-892-7377; 81 University Ave; meals $8-16; 11am-midnight Mon-Thu, 11-1am Fri & Sat, 11am-4pm Sun) This unassuming little place fills plates with great Lebanese dishes. The falafels, kabobs and hummus are popular, as are the vegetarian options such as *yabrak* (stuffed vine leaves with rice, onions, tomatoes and parsley) and *fool moudammas* (fava beans flavored with lemon juice and garlic).

Merchantman Pub (☎ 902-892-9150; 23 Queen St; mains $8-22; 11.30am-10pm Mon-Sat) In addition to great traditional pub grub, you can also dine on Asian-influenced creations such as Thai peanut curry or Madras chicken sauté.

Water Prince Corner Shop (☎ 902-368-3212; 141 Water St; meals $8-13; 9:30am-8pm May, Jun & Oct, 9am-10pm Jul-Sep) While the name and facade scream 'corner shop,' this rustic little place serves up amazing seafood. It is deservedly famous for its scallop burgers.

Tajmahal (☎ 902-892-4411; 67 University Ave; meals $8-13; lunch & dinner Apr-Nov) If you are craving a rich Indian curry, go no further. Try the shrimp *masala* or one of the many vegetarian selections.

Top End
Claddagh Room (☎ 902-892-9661; 131 Sydney St; mains $20-27; dinner) Locals herald the Claddagh Room as the best seafood restaurant in Charlottetown. Trust 'em! The Irish-inspired Galway Bay Delight features a coating of fresh cream and seasonings over scallops and shrimp that have been

---

THE AUTHOR'S CHOICE

Pilot House (☎ 902-894-4800; 70 Grafton St; mains $8-22; 11:30am-10:00pm Mon-Sat) The oversized wood beams and brick columns of the historic Roger's Hardware building provide a bold setting for fine dining or light pub fare. Chef Guy Leclair's signature dish of lobster-stuffed chicken with caramelized onions and white-wine cream sauce is sublime. Lunch specials are creative, delicious and a bargain at $10. Throw in some vegetarian selections and Pilot House has something for everyone.

sautéed with mushrooms and onions, then flambéed with Irish Mist liqueur.

Dundee Arms Inn (☎ 902-892-2496; 200 Pownal St; dinner mains $22-29; ◷ lunch & dinner, also breakfast Jun-Sep) The historic inn is home to chef Patrick Young and his imaginative dishes. The orange and ginger–glazed pork tenderloin with apple-cumin chutney is divine.

DRINKING

Charlottetown has an established and burgeoning drinking scene. Historic pubs dot the old part of town, while the budding café scene and newer bars are found around University Ave and Kent St. Most bars and pubs have a small cover charge (about $5) on weekends, or when there is live music. People spill into the streets at 2am when things wrap up.

Gahan House (☎ 902-626-2337; 126 Sydney St) Within these historic walls the pub owners brew PEI's only homegrown ales. Sir John A's Honey Wheat Ale is well worth introducing to your insides, as is the medium- to full-bodied Sydney Street Stout.

St James' Gate (☎ 902-892-4283; 129 Kent St) A trendy and lively atmosphere is found further north at this recent addition to the scene, which caters to a wide audience and presents bands on weekends.

Beanz (☎ 902-892-8797; 38 University Ave; ◷ 10am-5pm Sat-Thu, to 6pm Fri) It's a trendy spot with local artwork that blends, brews and steams the best hot beverages in Charlottetown.

Can't wait until 10am for your fix? A mean cup of coffee is also poured around the corner at Timothy's World Coffee (p459). If you answer their trivia question, it's free. Back on Queen St, Just Juicin' (p463) turns fruit's pain into your gain.

ENTERTAINMENT

From early evening to the morning hours, Charlottetown serves up a great mix of

---

THE AUTHOR'S CHOICE

42nd Street Lounge (☎ 902-566-4620; 125 Sydney St) Brick, velvet, warm shadows and the elegance of old make this hip place perfect for a drink and conversation. Slip in, sink into a comfy sofa and let the night begin. The gregarious bartender is known for his Jaeger Rita martinis.

---

theater, music, island culture and fun. To tap into the entertainment scene, pick up a free monthly copy of the *Buzz*.

Live Music

Throughout Charlottetown and PEI various venues host traditional ceilidhs (*kay*-lees). They are sometimes referred to as 'kitchen parties' and usually embrace gleeful Celtic music and dance. If you have the chance to attend one, don't miss it. The Friday edition of the *Guardian* newspaper lists times and locations of upcoming ceilidhs.

Benevolent Irish Society (☎ 902-963-3156; 582 North River Rd; admission $8; ◷ 8pm Fri mid-May–Oct) On the north side of town, this is a great place to catch a ceilidh. Come early, as seating is limited.

Olde Dublin Pub (☎ 902-892-6992; 131 Sydney St; cover $5) A traditional Irish pub with a jovial spirit and live entertainment nightly during the summer. Celtic bands and local notables take the stage and make for an engaging night out.

Baba's Lounge (☎ 902-892-7377; 81 University Ave; cover $5) Located above Cedar's Eatery (p463), this welcoming, intimate venue hosts great local bands playing their own tunes. Occasionally there are poetry readings.

Myron's Cabaret (☎ 902-892-4375; 151 Kent St; cover from $5) At the opposite end of the spectrum, Myron's believes that bigger is better. The line of stylish twenty-somethings strung out the door must agree. Three cavernous floors reverberate with heavy metal and alternative music pumped out by local bands and DJs.

Theater

Confederation Centre of the Arts (☎ 902-566-1267, 800-565-0278; www.confederationcentre.com; 145 Richmond St) This modern complex's large theater and outdoor amphitheater host concerts, comedic performances and elaborate musicals. *Anne of Green Gables – The Musical* has been entertaining audiences here as part of the Charlottetown Festival since 1964, making it Canada's longest-running musical. You'll enjoy it, and your friends will never have to know.

Cinemas

City Cinema (☎ 902-368-3669; 64 King St) A small independent theater featuring Canadian and foreign-language films.

Sports

Charlottetown Driving Park (☎ 902-892-6823; 46 Kensington Rd; admission free; ☙ Thu May-Dec, Thu & Sat Jun-Sep) Just north of the town center, this park allows you to witness human, horse and buggy in the spectacle of harness racing, a popular Maritime province pastime. A new grandstand is scheduled to be completed by August 2005.

SHOPPING

Local arts and crafts are an island institution. Shops abound along Victoria Row and the waterfront.

Moonsnail Soapworks (☎ 902-892-7627; 85 Water St) This little shop and artist's studio produces an amazing array of soaps, candles, jewelry and artwork. Lather up with their red-clay and kelp bar!

Anne of Green Gables Store (☎ 902-368-2663; 110 Queen St; ☙ 9am-9pm Mon-Sat, 11am-7pm Sun May-Sep, 10am-5pm Mon-Fri Oct-Apr) For those who haven't had their fill of LM Montgomery.

GETTING THERE & AWAY
Air

Charlottetown Airport is 8km north of the city center at Brackley Point and Sherwood Rds. A taxi to/from town costs $12, plus $4 for each additional person. See p457 for airport information and flight details.

Bus

The only intra-island bus transportation to and from Charlottetown is the **Beach Shuttle** (☎ 902-566-3243; one way/return $12/20), which makes stops between Charlottetown and Cavendish, leaving from the tourist office. For buses and shuttles traveling to the mainland, see p457.

Car & Motorcycle

With next to no public transportation available, rental cars are the preferred method for most travelers going to/from Charlottetown. During the summer cars are in short supply, so book ahead.

Nationwide companies such as Avis, Budget, National and Hertz have offices in town and at the airport. Note that the airport desks are strictly for people with reservations.

Your best option in Charlottetown is **National** (☎ 902-368-2228; cnr Kensington Rd & Exhibition Dr). New compact cars with unlimited kilometers and insurance rent for $60 per day. **Rent-A-Wreck** (☎ 902-566-9955; 57A St Peter's Rd) is another good option. It has compact used cars, including insurance, and 200 free kilometers per day, for the same price.

GETTING AROUND
Bicycle

Riding is a great way to get around this quaint town. **MacQueen's Bicycles** (☎ 902-368-2453; www .macqueens.com; 430 Queen St; per day/week $25/125) rents a variety of quality bikes. Children's models are half price. **Smooth Cycle** (☎ 902-566-5530; www .smoothcycle.com; 308 Queen St; per day/week $25/110) also provides super service. Both of these operators also offer excellent customized island-wide tours of the Confederation Trail.

Car & Motorcycle

During the summer, traffic snarls to a halt on University St and finding parking becomes an art form. That said, the municipal lots near the tourist office and Peak's Wharf charge $6 per day. One loonie gets you two hours at any of the town's parking meters, which operate between 8am and 6pm on weekdays.

Public Transportation

Trius Tours (☎ 902-566-5664; one-way fare $1.50) operates the anemic city transit within Charlottetown. One bus makes various loops through the city, stopping sporadically at Confederation Centre between 9:20am and 2:40pm.

Taxi

Fares are standardized and priced by zones. Between the waterfront and Hwy 1 there are three zones. Travel within this area is about $5, plus $1 per extra person. **City Taxi** (☎ 902-892-6567) and **Yellow Cab PEI** (☎ 902-566-6666) provide good service.

EASTERN PEI

Kings County, making up most of the eastern third of the province, is perhaps PEI's most underrated region. Its sinuous eastern shore possesses picturesque harbors and stunning beaches, both of which lack the crowds and winds found along the north shore. Majestic tree canopies seem to stretch endlessly over scenic heritage roads and the eastern sections of the Confederation Trail are some of the island's most beautiful. Moreover, the 374km King's Byway Scenic Drive winds circuitously through the hills and harbors of this beautiful county.

ORWELL

Found 28km east of Charlottetown, via Hwy 1, is **Orwell Corner Historic Village** (☎ 902-651-8510; off Hwy 1; adult/child under 12 $7.50/free; ☼ 9am-5pm Jul–early Sep, 9am-5pm Mon-Fri mid-May–Oct), a living re-creation of a 19th-century farming community. Painstaking restoration and workers in 19th-century dress bring everything from the schoolhouse to the shingle mill alive. Watch a smithy in action, or visit the massive draft horses that grace the barn. If possible, come on a Wednesday and take part in a traditional **ceilidh** (admission $10; ☼ 8pm). Ask here about visiting the **Sir Andrew MacPhail Homestead**, which is a further 1km down the road.

Rachel's Motel & Cottages (☎ 902-659-2874, 800-559-2874; www.holidayjunction.com/canada/pei/cpe0014 .html; 4827 Hwy 1; d/2-bedroom cottages $55/60; ☼ mid-May–mid-Oct), south of Orwell, just west of the Lord Selkirk Provincial Park turnoff, is a fine choice. There are well-kept rooms with small kitchenettes and two-bedroom cottages. It's set back from the highway and has a large playground.

Rainbow Lodge B&B (☎ 902-651-2202, 800-268-7005; 7521 Hwy 1; s/d $65/80) hails itself as the 'most out' accommodations west of Montréal; the spacious rooms here open onto a wonderful private garden. Straights are welcome, too.

WOOD ISLANDS

'Woods' is known for the PEI–Nova Scotia ferry terminal. A **tourist office** (☎ 902-962-7411; Plough Waves Centre, cnr Hwy 1 & Rte 4; ☼ 10:30am-6pm mid-May–late Oct, 8:30am-6pm late May–mid-Oct, to 9pm mid-Jun–Aug, closed Nov–mid-May) is up the hill from the terminal.

If you'll be waiting a while at the terminal, **Wood Islands Provincial Park** and its 1876 lighthouse are well worth the short walk.

MONTAGUE & AROUND

Perched on either side of the Montague River is the busy little town of Montague. As the service center for Kings County, its streets leading from the attractive marina are lined with shopping malls, supermarkets and fast-food outlets.

At Pooles Corner there is a large **tourist office** (☎ 902-838-0670; cnr Rtes 3 & 4; ☼ 9am-4:30pm late May–mid-Oct, 8am-7pm late Jun–late Aug). Along with the usual tourist office services, there are several museum-quality exhibits.

Back in town, the statuesque former post office and customs house (1888) overlooks the marina, and houses the **Garden of the Gulf Museum** (☎ 902-838-2467; 564 Main St S; adult/child under 12 $3/free; ☼ 9am-5pm Mon-Fri early Jun–late Sep). Inside are a few items of local significance, including an 18th-century PEI militia coat.

Across the marina is a restored train station, which marks a terminus on the Confederation Trail (see the boxed text on p478). The only things pulling up now are exhausted people – the trains stopped in 1984. The station contains a small information booth, an ice-cream stand and **Cruise Manada** (☎ 902-838-3444, 800-986-3444; adult/child under 14 $20/10; ☼ mid-May–Sep), which offers popular boat tours to PEI's largest seal colony, and takes a peek at mussel farms, too.

Just north of town, development meets nature at **Brudenell River Provincial Park** (☎ 902-652-8966; off Rte 3; tent sites $19, RV sites $22-5; ☼ late May–mid-Oct), which is a park and resort complex. Options range from kayaking (see p457) and nature walks to horseback riding and golf. The campground is nicely sheltered and close to the Confederation Trail.

Lane's Cottages & Suites (☎ 902-838-2433, 800-268-7532; 33 Brook St, Montague; apt $80, 2-bedroom cottages $100) is a simply furnished place on the hill above the marina. It has nice views, barbecues and a wee playground.

As famous for its chowder and mussels as it is for its scenic deck, **Windows on the Water Café** (☎ 902-838-2080; 106 Sackville St, Montague; dinner mains $15-22; ☼ lunch & dinner May-Oct) cooks up a tempting array of seafood, chicken and vegetarian dishes.

SOURIS

Embracing the waters of Colville Bay is the quaint town of Souris (*sur*-rey). It owes its name to the French Acadians and the gluttonous mice who repeatedly ravaged their crops. Thankfully it's now known more for its local musicians and fantastic music festivals than for the hungry field rodents of old.

This bustling fishing port makes a great base for your east coast adventures. The coast, Confederation Trail and nearby Scenic

Heritage Rd (The Glen) provide tremendous cycling options, and the waters are perfect for kayaking. This is also the launching point for ferries to the Îles de la Madeleine in Québec.

Information

Provincial Tourist Office (☎ 902-687-7030; Main St; ☽ 9am-4:30pm mid-Jun–early Oct, to 9pm Jul & Aug) In the Matthew & McLean building next to the CIBC Banking Centre.

Sights & Activities

Built of red island sandstone in 1901, the distinctive rounded tower of **St Mary's Catholic Church** (cnr Chapel & Longworth Sts) still looms over Souris. Another historic building that's worth a peak is the **Town Hall** on Main St.

Venture Out (☎ 902-687-1234, 877-473-4386; www .peisland.com/ventureout; Rte 2; tours $35-50, bicycle rentals per day/week $20/80; ☽ Jul-Sep), operating from the sweeping beach of **Souris Beach Provincial Park**, runs great kayak tours around the stunning Souris River estuary – you'll appreciate the third hour of the tour more than the extra $15 it costs. It also repairs and rents bicycles.

A Place to Stay Inn also rents bicycles ($4 per hour, $12/20 half-day/day).

Festivals & Events

The reputation of the **PEI Bluegrass & Oldtime Music Festival** (☎ 902-569-3153; www.bluegrasspei .com/rollobay.htm; Rte 2; ☽ early Jul) continues to grow. It's one of Atlantic Canada's top music festivals, with acts drawn from as far away as Nashville. Come for just a day, or camp out for all three.

Sleeping & Eating

A Place to Stay Inn (☎ 902-687-4626; apts1@pei.aibn .com; 9 Longworth St; dm $22, s/d $60/70) Located beside St Mary's Catholic Church, this absolutely superb facility includes dorm rooms and guest rooms. It has a full kitchen, laundry facilities, bicycle rental, a lounge and TV room. The owner is a treasure trove of information.

McLean House Inn (☎ 902-687-1875; www.mclean houseinn.com; 16 Washington St; tw/d incl light breakfast $95/110; ☽ late May–Sep) The view from, and atmosphere of, this beautiful mansard home make it perfect for a lazy afternoon. Head to the sunroom, grab some wicker and sink into a book. Ask for the Colville Bay room

(No 303). The house is a little hidden, down a side street opposite the tourist office.

Dockside B&B (☎ 902-687-2829, 877-687-2829; fax 902-687-4141; 37 Breakwater St; d with/without bathroom $55/50) Simple rooms are spread between two modern houses that sit above the ferry terminal, each with wonderful sea views.

Bluefin Restaurant (☎ 902-687-3271; 10 Federal Ave; meals $7-13; ☽ breakfast, lunch & dinner) Near McLean House Inn, this local favorite is known for its heaped servings of traditional island food. Its lunch special runs from 11am to 1pm.

BASIN HEAD PROVINCIAL PARK

While this **park** (off Rte 16; admission free) is home to the **Basin Head Fisheries Museum** (☎ 902-357-7233; adult/student $4.50/2; ☽ 9am-5pm Jun-Sep, to 6pm Jul & Aug), its star attraction is the sweeping sand of golden **Basin Head Beach**. Most islanders rank this as their favorite beach. The sand is also famous for its singing – well, squeaking. Five minutes of joyous 'musical' footsteps south from the museum and you have secluded bliss – enjoy! Atop the beach, the museum traces the island's fishing history and features an interpretive center and a coastal ecology exhibit.

EAST POINT & AROUND

Built the same year Canada was unified, the **East Point Lighthouse** (☎ 902-357-2106; adult/child $2.50/1; ☽ 10am-6pm mid-Jun–Aug) still stands guard over the northeastern shore of PEI. After being blamed for the 1882 wreck of the British *Phoenix*, the lighthouse was moved closer to shore. The eroding shoreline is now chasing it back. Teetering on the cliff, and soon to be moved, is the old assistant's house. It has a restored radio room and a gift shop.

The wooded coast and lilting accents of the north shore make for an interesting change of pace. **North Lake** and **Naufrage** harbors are intriguing places to stop and, if you feel so inclined, join a charter boat in search of a 450kg tuna.

ELMIRA

Ever expanding, the **Elmira Railway Museum** (☎ 902-357-7234; Rte 16A; adult/student/family $3/2/10; ☽ 10am-6pm Jul & Aug, 10am-5pm Fri-Wed mid-Jun–mid-Sep) includes a quirky **miniature-train ride** (adult/student/family $7/4/15) that winds through the surrounding forest. This magnificently restored station marks the eastern end of the Confederation Trail (see p478).

GREENWICH

Massive, dramatic and ever-shifting sand dunes epitomize the amazing area west of Greenwich. These rare parabolic giants are fronted by an awesome beach – a visit here is a must. Saved by Parks Canada in 1998, this 6km section of shore is now part of Prince Edward Island National Park (opposite).

Avant-garde meets barn at the **Greenwich Interpretation Centre** (☎ 902-961-2514; Hwy 13; ☾ 9:30am-4:30pm mid-May–mid-Oct, to 7pm late Jun–Aug), where pictorial and audiovisual exhibits detail the dune system and the vast archeological history of the site. While it's interesting inside, there's nothing better than wandering in the midst of the tree-eating sand dunes. The environment and flora are extremely sensitive, so be careful to stay on the trails.

ST PETERS TO MT STEWART

The region between these two small towns is a hotbed for cycling. The section of the Confederation Trail (p478) closest to St Peters flirts with the shoreline and rewards riders with an eyeful. In Mt Stewart three riverside sections of the Confederation Trail converge, giving riders and hikers plenty of attractive options within a relatively compact area. Both the Confederation Trail and a **provincial tourist office** (☎ 902-961-3540; Rte 2; ☾ 8am-7pm late Jun–late Aug, 9am-4:30pm mid-Jun–Oct) are found next to the bridge in St Peters.

Trailside Café & Inn (☎ 902-676-3130, 888-704-6595; www.trailside.ca; 109 Main St; d incl light breakfast $80-100; ☾ mid-May–mid-Oct) is smack dab in the middle of things and makes a great place to stay. You can also rent bicycles (2/4/12 hours $10/17/25) and the licensed **café** (mains $8-18; ☾ breakfast, lunch & dinner) serves up delectable desserts, chowder and other light fare.

TOP FIVE SUBTLE CHARMS OF PEI

- Flowering lupins taking over the roadsides in late June and July.
- The sound of locals saying 'yes' while quickly inhaling.
- Parking tickets costing just $5.
- The color of redbrick buildings at sunset.
- Never being more than a 15-minute drive from the beach.

On weekends, the intimate café hosts local musicians. Just to make things better, in 2005 the **Hillsborough River Eco-Centre** should open across the street.

Although designed for guests of the Christian center, the austere rooms of **Midgell Centre** (☎ 902-961-2963; 6553 Rte 2; dm & s with shared bathroom $20; ☾ mid-Jun–mid-Sep) are available to visitors. Depending on the set-up, you may be in a dorm or private room. Communal kitchens in each building add value to this great budget option – it's near St Peters and Greenwich.

CENTRAL PEI

Queens County covers most of central PEI, and nowhere on the island is the mix of nature and history more astounding. A beautiful mélange of colorful fields, quaint villages and forests undulates northward before meeting the dramatic coastal landscapes that form Prince Edward Island National Park. Throw in Anne, the island's most famous (albeit fictional) citizen, and you have a focal point of the province's tourism industry.

While tourism has spawned some unsightly development in the Cavendish area, it has led to a fine array of dining, lodging and activity options throughout the county. The 190km Blue Heron Scenic Drive skirts beautifully around this region of the province. A stretch of the Blue Heron on Rte 10, just west of Hwy 1, provides the island's best view of the Confederation Bridge.

For those entering central PEI via that bridge, it's worth stopping at the **Gateway Village Visitor Information Centre** (☎ 902-437-8570; Hwy 1; ☾ 8:30am-6pm mid-May–mid-Oct, to 8:30pm Jun–mid-Sep, 9am-4:30pm Wed-Sun mid-Oct–mid-May), near the PEI side of the bridge, for its free maps, brochures, restrooms and an excellent introductory exhibit called **Our Island Home** (☾ May-Nov). Staff can point you to the Confederation Trail (p478), which lurks nearby.

VICTORIA

Wandering the shaded tree-laden lanes of this charming little fishing village, you can't help but get a sense of the town's history and character. The entire village still fits neatly in the four blocks laid out when the town was formed in 1819. Colorful clapboard and shingled houses are home to more than one visitor who was so enthralled by the place they decided to stay. There's a profusion of art, cafés and eateries, as well as an excellent summer theater festival.

We dare you to just eat one of the sublime handmade Belgian chocolates at **Island Chocolates** (☎ 902-658-2320; 13 Main St; ⊙ 10am-8pm Mon-Sat, noon-8pm Sun Jun-Sep)!

Next to the theater, **Victoria Village Inn** (☎ 902-658-2483; 22 Howard St; tw/d/tr incl breakfast $90/90/140) has beautiful, relaxed rooms. You may even shed a tear saying goodbye to the plush sofas in the striking sitting room. Throw in the amazing cuisine of chef Stephen Hunter and you have a winner. His casual fine-dining **restaurant** (mains $14-19; ⊙ dinner) has a deceptively decadent menu. Vegetarian selections and theater packages are also available. Reservations are recommended.

Music, comedy and storytelling take center stage at **Victoria Playhouse** (☎ 902-658-2025, 800-925-2025; 20 Howard St; adult/youth & senior $20/18; ⊙ 8pm Jul-Sep) on Monday, with engaging theater productions on other days.

PRINCE EDWARD ISLAND NATIONAL PARK

Within this renowned **park** (☎ 902-672-6350; www.pc.gc.ca/pei; day pass adult/child under 17/family $5/2.50/12.50) heaving dunes and red sandstone bluffs provide startling backdrops for some of the island's finest stretches of sand. This dramatic coast, and the narrow sections of wetland and forests behind it, are home to diverse plants and animals, including the red fox and endangered piping plover.

The park is open year-round, but most services only operate between late June and the end of August. Entrance fees, which are charged between mid-June and mid-September, admit you to all park sites except the House of Green Gables (p473). If you are staying longer than five days, look into a seasonal pass. The park maintains an information desk at the Cavendish Visitor Centre (p473). Failing that, the provincial tourist office at Brackley Beach (p470) also provides information.

The following sights are organized from east to west, first covering the park-run facilities, then the private operations inside and out of the park.

Sights & Activities

Attractive beaches span almost the entire length of the park's 42km coastline. In most Canadians' minds, the park is almost synonymous with the beaches. **Dalvay Beach** sits to the east, and has some short hiking trails through the woods. The landscape flattens and the sand sprawls outward at **Stanhope Beach**. Here, a boardwalk leads from the campground to the shore. Backed by dunes, and slightly west, is the expansive and popular **Brackley Beach**. On the western side of the park, the sheer size of **Cavendish Beach** makes it the granddaddy of them all. During summer this beach sees copious numbers of visitors beneath its hefty dunes. If crowds aren't your thing, there are always the pristine sections of sand to the east.

A unique wrinkle in the Gulf Stream ensures the waters here are some of the warmest on the east coast north of Virginia. Lifeguards are on duty at Cavendish, Brackley and Stanhope beaches in midsummer, but take care, as undertows and rip currents are quite common. You may see small red jellyfish, known locally as bloodsuckers. Don't worry, they're not – at worst, they may irritate the skin. Last words of warning: don't forget the sunscreen!

Sleeping

Parks Canada operates three highly sought-after **campgrounds** (☎ 800-414-6765; tent sites $22, RV sites $25-27; ⊙ early Jun–late Aug), which are spread along its length. They all have kitchen shelters and showers. For an additional fee of $10, you can reserve a campsite, but you must do so at least three days in advance by phone or via the website www.canadian camping.ca. You can request a campground, but not a specific site; you must accept whatever is available when you arrive. While 80% of sites can be booked in advance, the remaining sites are first-come, first-served, so it's wise to arrive early.

Stanhope Campground, on Gulfshore East Parkway, is nestled nicely in the woods behind the beach of the same name. There is a well-stocked store on site.

Robinsons Island Campground, also on Gulfshore East Parkway, is open from late June. The most isolated of the three sites, it's set at the end of Brackley Point. It's not too much fun if the wind gets up.

The proximity of **Cavendish Campground**, off Rte 6, to the sights makes it the most popular. It has exposed oceanfront sites and ones

AROUND PEI NATIONAL PARK

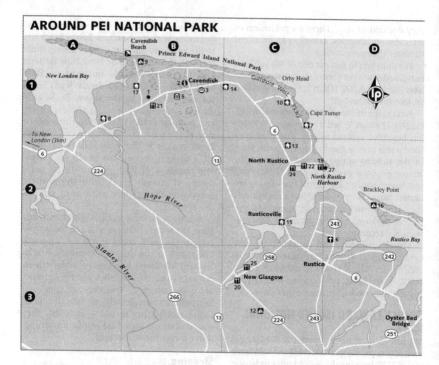

within the shelter and shade of the trees. Don't be lured by the view – it's nice, but sleep is better.

The communities listed below also provide excellent accommodation options in or around the park.

DALVAY BY THE SEA

Standing proudly near the east end of the park, and overlooking the beach named after it, is Dalvay, a historic mansion. Built in 1895 this majestic building is now owned by Parks Canada, and operated as an **inn** (☎ 902-672-2048; Gulfshore East Parkway; d incl breakfast & dinner $260-360; ☺ Jun-Oct). It's easily the most-luxurious and stunning accommodations on the north shore. Each plush room's view and antique furnishings are refreshingly unique. The majestic **dining room** (dinner mains $18-30; ☺ breakfast, lunch & dinner Jul & Aug) prepares remarkable dishes ranging from hazelnut and sage-crusted rack of lamb to fresh island lobster. It is open to nonguests, and both lunch and afternoon tea are reasonably priced. The inn also rents bicycles (per hour/half-day/day $5/12/20).

BRACKLEY BEACH

There's a **provincial tourist office** (☎ 902-672-7474; cnr Rtes 6 & 15; ☺ 8am-9pm Jul & Aug, 9am-4:30pm Jun–early Oct) 4km before the park entrance. Just north of the tourist office, **Paddy O'Malley's** (☎ 902-672-1217; Rte 15; ☺ noon-10pm Jun-Sep, noon-8pm Fri-Sun Oct-May) is a nice place to grab a pint and get away from the beach.

While over-the-top springs to mind, **Dunes Café & Gallery** (☎ 902-672-2586; Rte 15; dinner mains $16-25; ☺ 10am-6pm May & Oct, 11:30am-10pm Jun-Sep) is a nice change of pace. Honestly, where else on the island can you enjoy Vietnamese rice-noodle salad in the shade of a giant Buddha? Come in for a coffee, a meal or just to roam the eclectic mix of Asian and island art in the sprawling glass gallery and garden.

RUSTICO

The Acadian settlement at Rustico dates back to 1700, and several fine historic buildings speak of this tiny village's former importance. Most prominent is **St Augustine's Church** (1830), the oldest Catholic church on PEI. The old cemetery is on one side of the church, the solid red-stone **Farmer's Bank of**

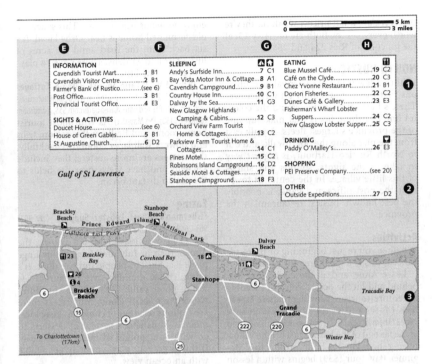

INFORMATION		
Cavendish Tourist Mart	1	B1
Cavendish Visitor Centre	2	B1
Farmer's Bank of Rustico	(see 6)	
Post Office	3	B1
Provincial Tourist Office	4	E3

SIGHTS & ACTIVITIES		
Doucet House	(see 6)	
House of Green Gables	5	B1
St Augustine Church	6	D2

SLEEPING		
Andy's Surfside Inn	7	C1
Bay Vista Motor Inn & Cottage	8	A1
Cavendish Campground	9	B1
Country House Inn	10	C1
Dalvay by the Sea	11	G3
New Glasgow Highlands Camping & Cabins	12	C3
Orchard View Farm Tourist Home & Cottages	13	C2
Parkview Farm Tourist Home & Cottages	14	C1
Pines Motel	15	C2
Robinsons Island Campground	16	D2
Seaside Motel & Cottages	17	B1
Stanhope Campground	18	F3

EATING		
Blue Mussel Café	19	C2
Café on the Clyde	20	C3
Chez Yvonne Restaurant	21	B1
Dorion Fisheries	22	C2
Dunes Café & Gallery	23	E3
Fisherman's Wharf Lobster Suppers	24	C2
New Glasgow Lobster Supper	25	C3

DRINKING		
Paddy O'Malley's	26	E3

SHOPPING		
PEI Preserve Company	(see 20)	

OTHER		
Outside Expeditions	27	D2

Gulf of St Lawrence

Stanhope Beach

Brackley Beach

Prince Edward Island National Park

Gulfshore East Pkwy

Brackley Bay

Covehead Bay

Stanhope

Dalvay Beach

Tracadie Bay

Brackley Beach

Grand Tracadie

To Charlottetown (17km)

Winter Bay

Rustico is on the other. The bank operated here from 1864 to 1894; it was a forerunner of the credit-union movement in Canada. Beside the bank is **Doucet House**, an old Acadian dwelling that was relocated here.

Resting on the shore of the New Glasgow River, just off Rte 6 in Rusticoville, the **Pines Motel** (☎ 902-963-2029, 800-878-5949; www.pinesmotel.pe.ca; 19 Snowy Rd; s/d $75/85, 1-/2-bedroom cottages $105/120; ⏲ Apr-Oct; 🖳) is a dated but well-kept choice. There's a playground and you can take a dip in the pool – or if you're brave, in the river. Feeling lazy? Find some shade and nap on all that riverside grass.

NEW GLASGOW

New Glasgow is a quiet town that's well known for its preserves and lobster suppers.

If there was ever a doctorate awarded in campsite planning, it would go to **New Glasgow Highlands Camping & Cabins** (☎ 902-964-3232; les.andrews@pei.sympatico.ca; Rte 224; tent/RV sites $26/29, cabins $50; ⏲ Apr-Oct; 🖳). The campground is likely the nicest on PEI, with 20-odd sites properly spaced in the forest, each with its own fire pit. For rainy days there are light

cooking facilities in the lodge. Add a laundromat, a small store, a heated swimming pool and a mystifying absence of bugs and you're laughing. There are also bright cabins, each with two bunks, a double bed, a sofa and a picnic table; bathrooms are shared. The word is out, so book ahead. Quiet campers are appreciated here, but rowdy folk should look elsewhere. The campgrounds are 1.7km east of PEI Preserve Co.

At **New Glasgow Lobster Supper** (☎ 902-964-2870; Rte 258; lobster dinners $26-32; ⏲ 4-8:30pm Jun–mid-Oct) you can make a right mess with the lobster, while also gorging on an endless supply of great chowder, mussels, salads, breads and homemade desserts.

Café on the Clyde (☎ 902-964-4300; dinner mains $13-17; ⏲ 9am-4pm late May–mid-Oct, to 8pm mid-Jun–late Sep) is perhaps the best casual dining option near the national park. Sun reflects in off the River Clyde and makes this place glow. The vegetarian wraps with a hint of feta truly hit the spot and the local fare is refreshing and creative. The café is a new addition to the famous **PEI Preserve Company** (⏲ 9am-5pm, to 9pm mid-Jun–late Sep). While the preserves are a tad pricey, we think they're worth every penny. Both are off Hwy 13, at the junction of Rtes 224 and 258.

NORTH RUSTICO

Within a few minutes of arrival, it is obvious that this is not simply a tourist town. There's bustling activity around the colorful line of fishing boats that make up one of the province's largest fleets. A walk east from the pier along the boardwalk, and out to North Rustico Harbour, is a great way to take in the sights, sounds and smells of this little village. In the center of town, near the post office and bank, is possibly the best-known, busiest restaurant in the province.

Activities

Whether you're just beginning or more advanced, this is a great area for **kayaking**.

Leave Anne, and all those who love her, behind and hit the ocean with PEI's leading adventure-tourism provider, **Outside Expeditions** (☎ 902-963-3366, 800-207-3899; www.getoutside.com; 374 Harbourview Dr; ☙ mid-Jun–mid-Oct), situated at the far end of the harbor in a bright-yellow fishing shed. The 1½-hour introductory 'Beginner Bay' tour ($39) begins with a lesson in kayaking techniques. The most-popular trip is the three-hour 'Harbour Passage' tour ($55), which operates three times daily (9am, 2pm and 6pm). Trips are run in the off-season, whenever at least four people want to go.

If your idea of ocean activity is reeling in a big one, look for the plethora of **deep-sea fishing operators** (2½hr trip adult/child $25/15; ☙ Jun–Aug) along Harbourview Dr.

Sleeping

Andy's Surfside Inn (☎ /fax 902-963-2405; Gulfshore W Pkwy; d incl light breakfast with/without bathroom $75/50; ☙ Jun–Oct) Inside the national park, 2.7km toward Orby Head from North Rustico, is this large, rambling house overlooking Doyle's Cove. It has been an inn since the 1930s, and the kitchen is open to those who want to bring home a few live lobsters. Sit back on the porch, put your feet up, and thank your lucky stars.

Country House Inn (☎ /fax 902-963-2055; Gulfshore W Pkwy; tw $50, d $60-90 both with shared bathroom & incl breakfast; ☙ Jun–Sep) If you're not blinded by the 1960s-colored bathroom fixtures, you'll

enjoy gorgeous ocean views. This spacious, old-fashioned home is near Orby Head. It's set back from the road amid 3½ acres of lush grass and gardens. There's even a playground for the little ones.

Orchard View Farm Tourist Home & Cottages (☎ 902-963-2302, 800-419-4468; www.peionline.com/al/orchard; 7602 Rte 6; d with shared bathroom $55, 2-bedroom cottages $150; ☙ May-Oct) As with most tourist home rooms and B&Bs in this region, frills and flowery wallpaper abound. Thankfully, the cottages are more austere; they include kitchens and have views over the fields to the not-so-distant ocean.

Eating

Fisherman's Wharf Lobster Suppers (☎ 902-963-2669; 7230 Main St; lobster dinners $27; ☙ lunch Jul–mid-Oct, dinner mid-May–mid-Oct) During the dinner rush in July and August this huge place has lines of people out the door. It's a fun, casual, holiday-style restaurant offering good value – that is if you don't wreck your shirt! Come hungry, as there are copious servings of chowder, tasty local mussels, rolls and a variety of desserts to go with your pound of messy crustacean. If things go your way, you may get a table with an ocean view.

Blue Mussel Café (☎ 902-963-2152; Harbourview Dr; dinner mains $14-22; ☙ lunch & dinner late Jun–late Sep) This place is relatively small, but its location, pan-fried scallops and steamed mussels will leave a big impression. It's en route to Outside Expeditions.

If you'd rather do the cooking and make a mess of your lobster in private, head straight to **Dorion Fisheries** (☎ 902-963-2442; Harbourview Dr; ☙ mid-May–mid-Oct). It has great seafood straight off the boat and at market prices.

CAVENDISH

Cavendish Beach and the House of Green Gables have lured tourists here for decades and still make this tiny village the most-visited community on PEI outside of Charlottetown. Many people are puzzled while trying to find the picturesque, historic town center. Understandable – no such place exists. At the junction of Rte 6 and Hwy 13 is the tourist center and the area's commercial hub. When you see the service station, wax museum, church, cemetery and assorted restaurants, you know you're there.

East of Cavendish is a large amusement park, and close by are go-cart tracks, water-slides, golf courses, miniature golf, fairy castles, petting farms, a palace of the bizarre, a planetarium, west-coast totem poles, a Ripley's Believe It or Not and other tacky diversions. The growing number of manufactured attractions is definitely an eyesore in this scenic region. On the bright side, it's a kiddie wonderland.

Information

Cavendish Visitor Centre (☎ 902-963-7830; ☒ 8am-8pm Jul–mid-Sep, 9am-4.30pm mid-May–Jun & mid-Sep–mid-Oct) Situated at the junction, near the police station, municipal offices and post office, this outlet has a wealth of information on the area, along with a craft shop, exhibits on the national park and a courtesy phone to make reservations. It's open until 9pm in July and August.

Laundromat (☎ 902-963-2370; 8934 Rte 6; ☒ 8am-9pm mid-May–Sep) At Cavendish Tourist Mart.

Sights

Cavendish is the home town of Lucy Maud Montgomery (1874–1942), author of *Anne of Green Gables*. Here she is simply known as Lucy Maud or LM. Owned by her grandfather's cousins, the now-famous **House of Green Gables** (☎ 902-672-7874; Rte 6; adult/youth under 17/family $5.75/3/14.50; ☒ 9am-5pm early May–Oct, to 8pm late Jun–late Aug, hours vary Nov-May) and its Victorian surrounds inspired the setting for her fictional tale. In 1937 the house became part of the national park and it's now administered as a national heritage site.

If you haven't read the 1908 novel, you really should try while you are on the island – not just to enjoy it, but to try to understand all the hype. The story revolves around Anne Shirley, a spirited eleven-year-old orphan with red pigtails and a creative wit, who was mistakenly sent from Nova Scotia to PEI. The aging Cuthberts (who were brother and sister) were expecting a strapping boy to help them with farm chores. In the end, Anne's strength of character wins over everyone in her path.

The site celebrates Lucy Maud and Anne with exhibits and audiovisual displays. The trails leading from the house through the green, gentle creek-crossed woods are worthwhile. The 'Haunted Wood' and 'Lover's Lane' have maintained their idealistic childhood ambience.

Tours

As one would suspect, most operators have an Anne-themed tour. **Cavendish Tours** (☎ 902-566-5466; half-/full day $50/60) offers a half-day tour that visits Green Gables and takes in North Rustico and New Glasgow; its departure follows the arrival of the Beach Shuttle (p465) from Charlottetown. The full-day tour adds the Lucy Maud Montgomery Birthplace and Silver Bush.

Sleeping & Eating

While accommodations are numerous, remember that this is the busiest and most-expensive area you can stay. There are more bargains east, toward North Rustico.

Seaside Motel & Cottages (☎ 902-963-2724, 888-351-2724; seasidemotel@auracom.com; Grahams Ln; d $80-100, 2-bedroom cottages $160; ☒ May–late Sep; ☒) This fine place, at the west entrance to Cavendish Beach, overlooks New London Bay. With all the buildings encircling a large grass field, it has a bit of an OK-Corral feel to it. Most of the motel rooms have small kitchens. A heated pool, a playground and nature trails add to its appeal.

Bay Vista Motor Inn & Cottage (☎ 902-963-2225, 800-846-0601; info@bayvistamotorinn.com; 9517 Rte 6; d $90-95; ☒ Jun–late Sep; ☒) This scenic choice, on a hillside sloping down to New London Bay, has barbecue areas, a heated pool and a playground. Its rooms are fairly standard.

Parkview Farm Tourist Home & Cottages (☎ 902-963-2027, 800-237-9890; www.peionline.com/al/parkview; 8214 Rte 6; s/d with shared bathroom incl light breakfast $50/60, 2-bedroom cottages $145) This fine choice is set on a working dairy farm, 2km east of Cavendish. Ocean views, bathrooms and the prerequisite flowered wallpaper and frills abound in this comfortable and roomy tourist home. Each of the seven cottages (available May to mid-October) has a kitchen and a barbecue, as well as a balcony to catch the dramatic comings and goings of the sun.

Chez Yvonne Restaurant (☎ 902-963-2070; 8947 Rte 6; mains $9-13; ☒ breakfast, lunch & dinner Jun-Sep) Opposite the Cavendish Tourist Mart, Chez Yvonne has been serving steak and seafood dinners to tourists since the 1970s. This place is well known for its home cooking, especially its bread and rolls, which are baked on the premises.

Cavendish Tourist Mart (☎ 902-963-2370; 8934 Rte 6; ☺ 8am-9pm mid-May–Sep) Stock up on essential supplies at this grocery store, 1.5km west of the House of Green Gables.

Getting Around
The Cavendish Red Trolley (all-day ticket $3; ☺ 10am-6pm late Jun–Aug) runs hourly along Hwy 13 and through Cavendish, making various stops, including the Cavendish Visitor Centre, Cavendish Beach and the House of Green Gables.

NEW LONDON & PARK CORNER
New London and Park Corner both have strong ties to Lucy Maud Montgomery, and are thus caught up in the everything-Anne pandemonium.

In New London, 10km southwest of Cavendish, is the Lucy Maud Montgomery Birthplace (☎ 902-886-2099; cnr Rtes 6 & 20; admission $2; ☺ 9am-5pm mid-May–mid-Oct, to 6pm Jul & Aug). The house is now a museum that contains some of her personal belongings, including her wedding dress.

Almost 10km northwest of New London is the village of Park Corner and the Lucy Maud Montgomery Heritage Museum (☎ 902-886-2807; 4605 Rte 20; adult/child $2.50/1; ☺ 9:30am-4:30pm mid-Jun–Labour Day, to 6pm Jul & Aug). It's believed to be the home of Lucy Maud's grandfather and there's a lot of Anne paraphernalia. Take a guided tour; there's a guarantee that if you're not absolutely fascinated, you don't pay the admission.

Almost 500m down the hill from here, surrounded by a luscious 110-acre property, is the charming home Lucy Maud liked to call Silver Bush. It was always dear to her and she chose the parlor for her 1911 wedding. Silver Bush hosts the Anne of Green Gables Museum (☎ 902-886-2884; 4542 Rte 20; adult/child under 17 $3/1; ☺ 9am-5pm mid-May–early Oct, to 6pm Jul & Aug). It contains such items as her writing desk and autographed first-edition books. Horse-drawn carriages roll past the alluring 'Lake of Shining Waters' ($3).

Blue Winds Tea Room (☎ 902-886-2860; 10746 Rte 6, New London; meals under $12; ☺ 11am-6pm mid-May–mid-Oct, to 8pm Fri-Sun Jul & Aug), just 500m southwest of Lucy Maud's birthplace, is a well-known café, with a nice view, which is a good choice for lunch or afternoon tea. The soup and salads, quiche and chicken dishes are well prepared, as are the rich desserts.

WESTERN PEI

Malpeque and Bedeque Bays converge to almost separate the western third of PEI from the rest of the province. This region sits entirely within the larger Prince County, and it combines the sparse pastoral scenery of Kings County's interior with some of Queens County's rugged coastal beauty.

The cultural history here stands out more than elsewhere on the island. On Lennox Island a proud Mi'kmaq community is working to foster knowledge of its past, while French Acadians are doing the same in the south, along Egmont and Bedeque Bays.

Named after the provincial flower, the 288km Lady Slipper Scenic Drive tours this region – its western coastal section is one of the province's most-rewarding drives.

SUMMERSIDE
Recessed deep within Bedeque Bay is PEI's second-largest city. A city in name only, this tiny seaside village possesses a lovely waterfront and quiet streets lined with leafy trees and grand old homes. The two largest economic booms in the province's history, shipbuilding and fox breeding, shaped the city's development in the 19th and early 20th centuries. Unfortunately, like Charlottetown, its outskirts are plagued by unsightly development. You'll find most of Summerside's interesting bits along, or near to, Water St, which runs parallel to the waterfront.

Information
Provincial Tourist Office (☎ 902-888-8364; Hwy 1A; ☺ 9am-4:30pm late May–mid-Oct, to 7pm late Jun–late Aug) About 4km east of Summerside. Grab the walking-tour pamphlet, which details the town's finer 19th-century buildings.
Rotary Regional Library (☎ 902-436-7323; 192 Water St; ☺ 10am-5pm Wed-Sat, to 9pm Tue, 1-5pm Sun) For free Internet access, visit the library in the city's old train station.

Sights & Activities
The Confederation Trail (p478) makes its way right through town and passes behind the library on Water St.

SPINNAKER'S LANDING
This redeveloped waterfront is the highlight of Summerside. A continually expanding

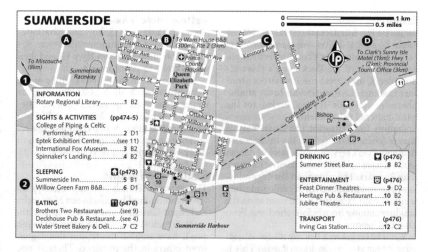

SUMMERSIDE

INFORMATION
Rotary Regional Library.............1 B2

SIGHTS & ACTIVITIES   (pp474–5)
College of Piping & Celtic
    Performing Arts......................2 D1
Eptek Exhibition Centre..........(see 11)
International Fox Museum.........3 B2
Spinnaker's Landing.................4 B2

SLEEPING   (p475)
Summerside Inn.......................5 B1
Willow Green Farm B&B...........6 D1

EATING   (p476)
Brothers Two Restaurant..........(see 9)
Deckhouse Pub & Restaurant...(see 4)
Water Street Bakery & Deli.......7 C2

DRINKING   (p476)
Summer Street Barz..................8 B2

ENTERTAINMENT   (p476)
Feast Dinner Theatres...............9 D2
Heritage Pub & Restaurant......10 B2
Jubilee Theatre......................11 B2

TRANSPORT   (p476)
Irving Gas Station...................12 C2

Summerside Harbour

boardwalk allows you to wander and enjoy the harbor and its scenic surrounds. There are some nice eateries, a stage for live music in the summer, and numerous shops. A mock lighthouse provides adults with a nice lookout and some local information, while a large model ship is a dream playground for kids. Backing all of this is the modern **Eptek Exhibition Centre** (☎ 902-888-8373; 130 Harbour Dr; admission by donation; ◷ 10am-4pm), which features local and traveling art exhibitions.

COLLEGE OF PIPING & CELTIC PERFORMING ARTS
In celebration of Celtic dance and music, this **school** (☎ 902-436-5377; 619 Water St E; ◷ 9am-9pm late Jun–Aug) provides visitors with free 20-minute mini-concerts Monday to Friday at 11:30am, 1:30pm and 3:30pm – expect bagpipes, singing and dancing. Inspired? Put on some warm clothes and enjoy the two-hour **ceilidhs** (adult/student $12/7; ◷ 7pm) that take place every night in the covered amphitheater.

INTERNATIONAL FOX MUSEUM
This tiny **museum** (☎ 902-436-2400; 286 Fitzroy St; admission by donation; ◷ 10am-5pm Jun-Sep) recounts the role of Summerside in the world's first successful captive breeding of the silver fox (1890) and the obscene flows of money and controversy that followed it. The museum is upstairs in the historic Holman Homestead (1855).

Sleeping
Warn House B&B (☎ 902-436-5242, 888-436-7512; www.warnhouse.com; 330 Central St; tw $85, d $95-115) Set in from the road, among trees in the old section of town, Warn House is extremely comfortable and welcoming. Lounge under a tree or on the lovely veranda. Original Canadian art adorns the walls and there's even a place to store bicycles.

Summerside Inn (☎ 902-436-1417, 877-477-1417; www.peisland.com/summersideinn; 98 Summer St; d incl light breakfast $85-95) This Victorian mansion, in the heart of town, has been home to an island premier and a chief justice. Antiques, hardwood floors and stained-glass windows make this a rather elegant stay. Try the Green Room, with its extra dressings and big windows.

Willow Green Farm B&B (☎ 902-436-4420; 117 Bishop Dr; d $50-100) With the Confederation Trail at its back door, and the College of Piping & Celtic Performing Arts out its front, this rambling farmhouse is a great place to stay. Rooms are bright and the bold country interior is a refreshing change from busy period decors. Read by the wood stove, or check out some of the more interesting farm animals.

Clark's Sunny Isle Motel (☎ 902-436-5665, 877-682-6824; myles@islandtelcom.com; 720 Water St E; d/tw $50/60; ◷ May-Oct) Clark's is the nicest of many motels spread east of town along Water St. While its rooms are fairly standard, its gardens and trail to the shore set it apart. Ask for a room out back.

Eating

Deckhouse Pub & Restaurant (☎ 902-436-0660; 150 Harbour Dr; mains $7-13; ☽ 11am-11pm Jun–mid-Sep) Step off the Spinnaker's Landing boardwalk and onto one of the Deckhouse's two outdoor decks, for a great meal in harbor-front surroundings. Live music adds to the atmosphere on weekends. It's well known for the hand-battered fish and chips.

Brothers Two Restaurant (☎ 902-436-9654; 618 Water St E; mains $10-15; ☽ lunch Mon-Fri, dinner daily) Brothers Two's service, pasta, steak and fresh seafood have made it a local favorite for more than 30 years. The vegetarian stir-fry and island blue mussels steamed in garlic and white wine are both excellent. If you want in on the laughter coming from below, check out Feast Dinner Theatres.

Water Street Bakery & Deli (☎ 902-536-5055; 605 Water St; lunch $4-6; ☽ 7am-6:30pm Mon-Sat) This is the best place in town for a quick and tasty sandwich or a slice of pizza.

Drinking & Entertainment

Jubilee Theatre (☎ 902-888-2500, 800-708-6505; www .jubileetheatre.com; 124 Harbour Dr) This modern theater is in the same complex as the Eptek Exhibition Centre and holds the **Summer on the Waterfront Festival** (☽ Jul–mid-Sep), which hosts local and well-known Canadian musical acts.

Feast Dinner Theatres (☎ 902-436-7674; 618 Water St; dinner & show $32; ☽ 6:30pm Mon-Sat Jun-Dec) Most locals start to giggle when they speak of their last time at Feast Dinner Theatres. It's found below Brothers Two Restaurant, and is the longest-running dinner theater in Atlantic Canada. Music, script and improvisation combine with audience participation to make a memorable evening. The food's not too shabby either.

Heritage Pub & Restaurant (☎ 902-436-8484; 250 Water St) This traditional pub is the only live-music venue (no cover charge) in town. Local bands play on Friday, and occasionally on Saturday.

Summer Street Barz (☎ 902-436-7400; 12 Summer St; cover $4) This is the only true nightclub in town, and it casts a pretty wide net. Thumping beats resonate from the basement, the cracks of pool cues echo from the core, and twangs of country ring from the rafters. Oh, and there's a sports bar too. Things don't pick up until after midnight on Friday and Saturday.

Getting There & Away

To reach Cavendish (36km) and Charlottetown (71km) from Summerside by car, it's quickest to head north on Hwy 1A and then follow Rte 2 to your turn-off.

Acadian Coach Lines (p457) stops at the **Irving gas station** (☎ 902-436-2420; 96 Water St) in the center of town and has services to Charlottetown ($11, one hour), Moncton ($30, two hours) and Halifax ($56, 3½ hours). On request, bus shuttles pick up at the Esso station on Hwy 1A at the end of Water St E.

RÉGION ÉVANGÉLINE

The strongest French Acadian ancestry on the island is found here, between Miscouche and Mont Carmel. Some 6000 residents still speak French as their first language, although you'll have trouble discerning this region from others in the province. There is one notable exception: the red, white, blue and yellow star of the Acadian flag hangs proudly from many homes. It was in Miscouche, on August 15, 1884, that the Acadian flag was unfurled for the very first time. The yellow star represents the patron saint of the Acadians, the Virgin Mary. Renewed efforts are underway to preserve the unique Acadian culture on the island. See the Nova Scotia (p422) and New Brunswick (p482) chapters for more information on Acadians.

The worthwhile **Acadian Museum** (☎ 902-432-2880; 23 Maine Dr E; adult/student/family $4.50/3.50/15; ☽ 9:30am-7pm Jul & Aug, 9:30am-5pm Mon-Fri & 1-4pm Sun Sep-Jun), in Miscouche, uses 18th-century Acadian artifacts, texts, visuals and music to enlighten visitors about the tragic and compelling history of the Acadians on PEI since 1720. The introspective video introduces a fascinating theory that the brutal treatment of the Acadians by the British may have backhandedly helped preserve a vestige of Acadian culture on PEI.

TYNE VALLEY

This area, famous for its Malpeque oysters, is one of the most scenic in the province. The village, with its cluster of ornate houses, gentle river and art studios, is definitely worth a visit.

Green Park Provincial Park, 6km north of the village along Rte 12, hosts the **Green Park Shipbuilding Museum & Historic Yeo House** (☎ 902-831-7947; Rte 12; adult/child under 13 $5/free; ☽ 9am-5pm mid-Jun–mid-Sep). The museum and restored Victorian home, along with a re-created shipyard and partially constructed 200-ton brigantine, combine to tell the story of the booming shipbuilding industry in the glory days of the 19th century.

The park has 58 **campsites** (☎ 902-831-7912; off Rte 12; campsites $19, with hookups $25, cabins with shared bathroom $35; ☼ mid-Jun–mid-Sep) spread within a mixed forest. The dozen cabins just beyond the campsite are a steal.

Doctor's Inn (☎ 902-831-3057; www.peisland.com/ doctorsinn; 32 Allen Rd; d with shared bathroom incl breakfast $60-75), an old country home, makes for a comfortable stay. One of the rooms has a small pullout bed to help accommodate children. Its **dining room** (3-course meal guests/ nonguests $50/55; ☼ by reservation) is known to prepare the finest meals in the region. Cooked over a wood stove, the *tournedos rossini* (beef tenderloin and liver pâté with a red-wine sauce), *sole almandine* (fillet of sole coated with white wine and toasted almonds) and organic vegetables from the garden are all superb.

Not surprisingly the specialty at **Landing Oyster House & Pub** (☎ 902-831-3138; 1327 Port Hill Station Rd; mains $8-13; ☼ lunch & dinner Tue-Sun Mar-Dec, also Mon in Jul) is 15 deep-fried oysters – definitely indulge. Live bands (cover $3 to $5) play here on Friday night, and also Saturday during July and August.

LENNOX ISLAND

Set in the mouth of Malpeque Bay, sheltered behind Hog Island, is Lennox Island and its 250 Mi'kmaq (mig–*maw*) aboriginal people. While working hard to promote awareness and understanding of their past, both in and out of their own community, they are also making renewed efforts to preserve their culture. New projects, like the Lennox Island Aboriginal Ecotourism Complex, are manifestations of this hard work. A trip to the island is rewarding and highly recommended. The island is connected by a causeway making it accessible from the town of East Bideford off Rte 12. There is a large celebration here at the end of June and another, for St Ann's day, on the last Sunday in July.

In June 2004 the new **Lennox Island Aboriginal Ecotourism Complex** (☎ 866-831-2702; 2 Eagle Feather Trail; adult/student $4/3; ☼ 10am-6pm Mon-Sat, noon-6pm late Jun–early Sep) opened its doors. Inside there is a worthwhile 15-minute audiovisual exhibit, and information about the

two excellent **interpretive trails** around the island. These trails consist of two loops, forming a total of 10km, with the shorter one (3km) being wheelchair-accessible. An on-site **restaurant** serves traditional Mi'kmaq food. In June 2005, a **hostel** will open on the top floor of this complex – the views should be spectacular.

Up the hill from the ecotourism complex, and across from **St Ann's Church** (1898), is the **Lennox Island Mi'kmaq Cultural Centre** (8 Eagle Feather Trail). It operates in unison with the ecotourism complex and houses artifacts along with displays about the history and culture of the Mi'kmaq.

Mi'kmaq Kayak Adventures (☎ 902-831-3131, 800-500-3131; 3hr tours $60; ☼ 9am, 1pm, 5pm & sunset Jul & Aug, by appointment May, Jun & Sep) operates from the ecotourism complex. It's also possible to organize a full-day or overnight kayaking trip.

TIGNISH

Tignish is a quiet town tucked up near the North Cape; it sees only a fraction of PEI's visitors. The towering **Church of St Simon and St Jude** (1859) was the first brick church built on the island. Have a peek inside – its ceiling has been restored to its gorgeous but humble beginnings, and the organ (1882) is of gargantuan proportions. Of its 1118 pipes, the shortest is 15cm, while the longest is nearly 5m!

The Confederation Trail begins (or ends!) two blocks south of the church on School St. The **Tignish Cultural Centre** (☎ 902-882-1999; 305 School St; admission free; ☼ 8am-4pm Mon-Fri), near the church, has a good exhibition of old maps and photos, tourist information and a library with Internet access.

NORTH CAPE

The drive toward North Cape seems stereotypically bucolic, until the moment your eyes rise above the quaint farmhouses to see the heavens being churned by dozens of sleek behemoth-sized white blades. Strangely, expecting the surreal sight takes nothing away from it.

The narrow, windblown North Cape is not only home to the **Atlantic Wind Test**, but also to the longest **natural rock reef** on the continent. At low tide, it's possible to walk out almost 800m – exploring tide pools and searching for seals along the way. The

CYCLING THE CONFEDERATION TRAIL

Like one of the province's many lighthouses, the 357km-long Confederation Trail acts as a beacon, calling North American and European cyclists. Thanks to its origins as the bed of Prince Edward Island's railway, the route is almost entirely flat, as it meanders around hills and valleys. There are some sections of the trail that are completely canopied in lush foliage, and in late June and the early weeks of July the trail is lined with bright, flowering lupins. There's perhaps no better way to enjoy the fall's change of colors on the island than by riding the trail.

The 279km tip-to-tip route from Tignish (p477), near North Cape, to Elmira (p467), near East Point, is extremely rewarding and passes through countless idyllic villages, where riders can stop for meals or rest for the night. Some of the most-popular sections are near Mt Stewart, St Peters (p468) and Harmony Junction. Note that the prevailing winds on PEI blow from the west and southwest, so cycling in this direction is easier. Branches connect the trail to the Confederation Bridge, Charlottetown (p458), Souris (p466) and Montague (p466).

Provincial tourist offices have excellent route maps and their **website** (www.gov.pe.ca/visitors guide/explore/trail.php3) offers a plethora of planning and trail information. The bicycle-rental shops in Charlottetown (p465) also run superb island-wide tours.

newly expanded **interpretive center** (☎ 902-882-2991; adult/student/family $5/3/13; ☺ 9:30am-6pm mid-May–early Oct, to 8pm Jul & Aug), at the northern end of Rte 12, provides high-tech displays dedicated to wind energy, and informative displays on the history of the area. The aquarium is always a hit with kids. The **Black Marsh Nature Trail** (2.7km) leaves the interpretive center and takes you to the west side of the cape – at sunset these crimson cliffs simply glow against the deep-blue waters.

For a bit of fun, check out **Captain Mitch's Boat Tours** (☎ 902-882-2883; Hwy 12; adult/child $20/10; ☺ Jul & Aug). The captain's a lively lobster fisherman who will take you out to his ocean playground of spray, seals and seabirds. Tours leave from Seacow Pond Harbour, 6.5km south of North Cape.

Sleeping & Eating

Tignish Heritage Inn (☎ 902-882-2491, 877-882-2491; www.tignish.com/inn; d $60-110; ☺ mid-May–mid-Oct) Behind the church, off Maple St, and hiding among the trees is this charming four-storey brick convent-turned-inn (1868). The high ceilings, spacious rooms and modern amenities make staying here a simple choice. The lower two floors are comfortable, if a little old-fashioned. The 3rd floor has a more-contemporary decor.

Island's End Motel (☎ 902-882-3554; Doyle Rd; d $65-75) Your closest option near North Cape, off Rte 12, and your only option if here in the off-season, is the friendly Island's End. The owner, Neil, takes a lot of pride in his place and it shows. It's simple and comfortable.

Wind & Reef Restaurant & Lounge (☎ 902-882-3535; mains $9-22; ☺ lunch & dinner) Located above the interpretive center, this atmospheric place attracts visitors and locals out for a treat. The menu and view are equally vast and pleasing.

Cousins Diner & Restaurant (☎ 902-882-5670; 276 Phillip St; mains $6-16; ☺ breakfast, lunch & dinner) Cousins is 1.5km south of the center of town on Rte 2. The diner side of this establishment is great for a cheap breakfast, burger or club sandwich. The charming restaurant is trying to be big-city, but its quaint roots show through – the seafood and quesadillas are good choices. **Gunner's Pub**, also at Cousins, is a good evening venue.

WEST COAST

Along the west coast, you may be puzzled at the sight of horse and rider dragging rakes in the shallows off shore. They are collecting Irish moss, a valuable purplish seaweed that gets uprooted and blown to shore in storms.

Along Rte 14, in the village of Miminegash, is the **Irish Moss Interpretative Centre** (☎ 902-882-4313; Rte 14; admission $2; ☺ 10am-7pm early Jun–late Sep), begun by local women long involved in the harvesting of Irish moss. Almost half the world's Irish moss supply comes from PEI, and goes into everything from ice cream and toothpaste to cough syrup and automobile tires! Still tempted? The **Seaweed Pie Cafe** (meals $5-12), at the center, serves a special seaweed pie.

Between Miminegash and West Point, Rte 14 hugs the shore and provides stunning vistas. It's perhaps the finest drive on the island.

Off Hwy 14, the striking black-and-white striped **West Point Lighthouse** (☎ 902-859-3605, 800-764-6854; www.peisland.com/westpoint/light.htm; ✆ mid-May–Sep), dating from 1875, has been restored. Between 1875 and 1955 there were only two lighthouse keepers. Today the staff are made up of their direct descendants. There's a small **museum** (adult/child/family $2.50/1.50/7; ✆ 9am-9pm mid-May–mid-Oct), where you can climb the tower for

a breathtaking view. Part of the former lighthouse keepers' quarters have been converted into a nine-room **inn** (d $85-130); the Tower Room ($130) is actually in the old lighthouse tower. The **restaurant** (meals $8-18; ✆ 8am-8pm mid-May–mid-Oct) is famous for its clam chowder.

Cedar Dunes Provincial Park (☎ 902-859-8785; tent/RV sites $19/22; ✆ late Jun–mid-Sep) has tent space in an open grassy field adjacent to West Point Lighthouse. Its red-sand beach is an island gem.

New Brunswick

New Brunswick's main characteristic may well be that it is little known. Even within Canada, its identity is barely on the radar. But visitors with a discriminating eye will discover a surprisingly varied province with more than enough memorable destinations to experience.

At 73,400 sq km, New Brunswick is the largest province in the Maritimes. Its attributes are markedly different from those of bucolic Prince Edward Island or sea-swept Nova Scotia. Forests and rivers are a major feature – and that means wildlife and hiking. The Appalachian Mountains extend across the pastoral Saint John River Valley, which flows to the stunning Bay of Fundy. There the world's largest tides have created majestic cliffs, sheltered coves and tidal flats rich with treasures to be discovered.

The Fundy Isles, ruled by the elements, are a tranquil world apart. Fredericton is a peaceful capital city, and Saint John raises eyebrows with its convoluted geography and historic character and architecture. Vibrant Acadian culture is alive and well along the province's eastern edge. Everywhere forts, historic sites and Loyalist graveyards reveal stories of the power struggles that raged over four centuries. With lobster a main catch and fishing wharves tucked around two sides of the province, succulent seafood is abundant.

When it's time to get active, there are outstanding outdoor possibilities. Whale-watching along the Eastern Fundy Shore and around the Fundy Isles is so good it comes with a sighting guarantee. Fundy National Park, the Fundy Trail Parkway, Mt Carleton Provincial Park and Grand Manan Island provide exceptional hiking trails. Bird-watching is so renowned across the southern shores and along the eastern coast it even lures birders from overseas. Sea-kayak outfitters, found around the province, offer a rigorous day out on the waves.

HIGHLIGHTS

- Step back in time at the Loyalist **King's Landing Historic Settlement** (p491)
- Explore the **Bay of Fundy** (p511) and its awesome tides
- Breathe deep along the cliff-side trails of **Grand Manan Island** (p501)
- Hike the wilderness and highest peaks in **Mt Carleton Provincial Park** (p492)
- Wade through the fog in atmospheric, well-preserved **Saint John** (p504)
- Cast a fly for salmon on the fabulous **Miramichi River** (p521)
- Absorb the resort ambience at long-established **St Andrews by-the-Sea** (p496)

Mt Carleton Provincial Park ★
Miramichi River ★
King's Landing Historic Settlement ★
St Andrews by-the-Sea ★
Saint John ★
Bay of Fundy ★
Grand Manan Island ★

■ POPULATION: 750,096　　■ PROVINCIAL CAPITAL: FREDERICTON　　■ AREA: 73,400 SQ KM

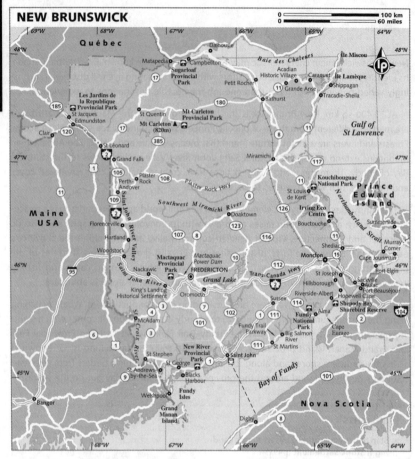

History

What is now New Brunswick was originally the land of the Mi'kmaq and, in the western and southern areas, the Maliseet First Nations. Small pockets remain inhabited by these peoples today.

The French first attempted settlement in the 1600s. The Acadians, as they came to be known, farmed the area around the Bay of Fundy using a system of dikes. In 1755 they were expelled by the English, whose numbers rose by some 14,000 with the arrival of the British Loyalists after the American Revolution. These refugees settled the valleys of the Saint John and St Croix Rivers and established Saint John. The majority of the population still has British roots. People with Irish ancestry form the biggest single group in Saint John and Miramichi.

Through the 1800s lumbering and shipbuilding boomed, and by the start of the 20th century, other industries, including fishing, had developed. That era of prosperity ended with the Depression. Today, lumber and pulp and paper operations are two of the main industries. Fishing and farming remain important. Newer ventures include high-tech businesses and nationwide telephone call centers.

Climate

Summers are generally mild with occasional hot days. The driest month of the year is August. Typically, there is more rain in the

NEW BRUNSWICK IN...

Five Days

Start your trip in **Saint John** (p504). Spend the morning uptown in the historic district. See the **museum** (p506), stroll the boardwalk and go to **Reversing Falls** (p506). The next day get a view from the **Martello Tower** (p506) and drive to **Irving Nature Park** (p507). Have dinner at the **Old City Market** (p508) and walk through the **Loyalist graveyard** (p506).

On the third day, leave town for the picturesque village of **St Martins** (p510). Spend the day at the beach, seeing the caves and driving along the spectacular **Fundy Trail Parkway** (p510). Next, stop at **Cape Enrage** (p513) for lunch on the way to **Fundy National Park** (p511). Spend the last two days in the park, hiking, wandering the tidal flats and eating seafood in **Alma** (p512).

One Week

Follow the five-day itinerary and add a trip to the capital, **Fredericton** (p484), where you can wander downtown. On the last day, drive to **King's Landing Historical Settlement** (p491).

Two Weeks

Spend the first two days in and around **Fredericton** (p484). Travel south to **St Andrews by-the-Sea** (p496) to explore the sites and possibly take a trip to **Deer Island** (p499) or **Campobello Island** (p500). Next, take the ferry to **Grand Manan** (p501) for a two-day stay including whale-watching and walking the fabulous trails. Then take two days to visit **Saint John** (p504). On the ninth day visit St Martins. Spend the next two days at **Fundy National Park** (p511). Finish up at Moncton's Magnetic Hill after stopping at **Hopewell Rocks** (p513).

south. The entire Fundy shore is very prone to fog, which sometimes burns off by noon and sometimes not at all. Spring and fall are good travel times although the tourist season (late July to early September), with all facilities open, is relatively short. Winters can be unbelievably snowy and cold.

National & Provincial Parks

New Brunswick has two national parks and six national historic sites. All are well worth visiting. Rugged, coastal Fundy National Park (p511) is the province's premier park, while Kouchibouguac National Park (p519) safeguards a stretch of the Northumberland coast. The national parks are larger sites and contain various attractions and accommodations, including camping. The historic sites are for day use. They are St Andrews Blockhouse in St Andrews by-the-Sea (p496), Carleton Martello Tower in Saint John (p506), Monument Lefebvre near St Joseph (p516), Fort Beauséjour near the Nova Scotia border (p517), Beaubears Island in Miramichi (p520) and Fort Gaspareaux near Port Elgin. For more details, call ☎ 888-773-8888 or go online at www.pc.gc.ca.

In addition, there are provincial parks scattered through the province. They pro-

tect a particularly significant environment and offer recreational activities, usually including camping. In this category, relatively unknown Mt Carleton (p492) in the Appalachian Mountain chain is most impressive.

Language

Surprisingly, New Brunswick is Canada's only officially bilingual province. Around 37% of the population has French ancestors. French is most often heard around Edmundston, the Acadian Peninsula (especially Caraquet), along the coast from Miramichi to Shediac and in Moncton. Almost all French speakers are bilingual in English.

Getting There & Away

The province has six primary visitor information centers at strategic entry points: St Jacques, Woodstock, St Stephen, Aulac, Cape Jourimain and Campbellton. These are open from mid-May to mid-October only.

AIR

Moncton, New Brunswick's busiest airport, is served by discount airlines CanJet and WestJet from cities across Canada. Flights to other parts of Canada tend to be cheaper here than those out of Halifax. Air Canada and its subsidiary Air Canada Jazz have flights from Montréal, Toronto, Halifax and Québec City. They also operate at least one nonstop flight daily to Fredericton from Montréal ($181), Ottawa ($212), Toronto ($187) and Halifax ($139). See p868 for airline contact details.

BOAT
The Bay Ferries' **Princess of Acadia** (☎ 506-649-7777, 888-249-7245; www.nfl-bay.com; adult/child under 10 $35/15 late Jun–mid-Oct, $20/10 mid-Oct–late Jun, car $70-80) sails between Saint John and Digby, Nova Scotia, year-round. The three-hour crossing can save a lot of driving. There's a passenger-only round-trip fare of $50 if you simply want a day cruise.

From Saint John between late June and mid-October, departure times are 12:45am, 9am and 4:45pm daily (there's no 12:45am trip on Sunday). During the rest of the year, ferries run once or twice daily. From Digby, departure times are 5am, 1pm and 8:45pm (except there's no 5am sailing Sunday).

Arrive early or call ahead for vehicle reservations (additional fee $5), as the ferry is very busy in July and August. Even with a reservation, arrive an hour before departure. Walk-ons and cyclists should be OK anytime. There's a restaurant and a bar.

BUS
Acadian Lines (p871), owners of SMT Bus Lines, is the largest Maritime bus company. Services operate as far as Rivière du Loup in Québec where they connect with Orléans Express (p871) buses for such destinations as Québec City and Montréal.

Acadian runs to Bangor, Maine, from Saint John ($28, three hours) and Moncton ($43, six hours) with onward service to Boston and New York. For information on the daily bus service between Bangor and Calais, see p496.

At the time of research, Salty Bear Adventure Travel (p875), a jump-on/jump-off backpacker bus service based in Nova Scotia, had plans for expansion into New Brunswick and through to Québec.

CAR & MOTORCYCLE
For drivers, the main access points into New Brunswick are through Edmundston, Maine or Nova Scotia. The opening of the Confederation Bridge at Cape Jourimain in

1997 meant the closing of the ferry terminal at nearby Cape Tormentine. These days most motorists zip straight onto the bridge from Hwy 16 and the nearby coast is relatively quiet. If you're going to Prince Edward Island, there's no charge to use the bridge eastbound – you pay on the way back. Nova Scotia–bound, there's a shortcut along Hwy 970 from Port Elgin to Tidnish Bridge, which is useful if you're going to Cape Breton.

Distances to Saint John include 678km from Boston, 424km from Halifax, 940km from Montréal and 1032km from New York City.

TRAIN
VIA Rail (p875) operates passenger services between Montréal and Halifax six times a week. Main New Brunswick stops are Campbellton, Miramichi and Moncton. The fare from Montréal to Campbellton is $125 (11 hours), to Miramichi $145 (14 hours) and to Moncton $176 (15½ hours).

Getting Around
Problems are few for drivers and traffic congestion is generally light to nil. At night, in rural or forest areas, be very cautious of wildlife – that is, deer and moose. Not much ends a holiday more abruptly.

Acadian Lines (p871) has a fairly exhaustive network throughout the province. It offers good senior, student and child discounts and same-day return specials. Route details are listed throughout this chapter.

VIA Rail (p875) links the eastern coastal area from Moncton to Campbellton through Miramichi.

For Fundy Isles ferries, see p501 and p503. Book ahead where possible and/or arrive early.

FREDERICTON

☎ 506 / pop 47,600
Fredericton is the queen of New Brunswick's towns. Unlike most of its counterparts, it is non-industrial and quickly reveals a very pretty, genteel, tranquil character. Here in the province's capital, about a fifth of its residents work for the government, and there's a major university. The small, tree-lined central area has visible history to explore, much of it alongside the gently arching Saint John

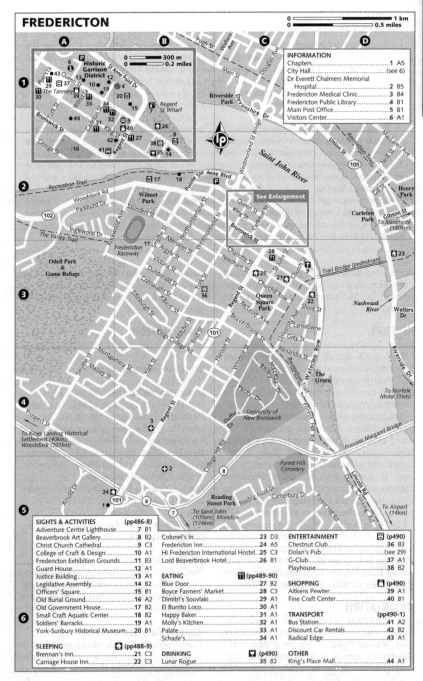

FREDERICTON

0 ————————— 1 km
0 ————————— 0.5 miles

Historic Garrison District

0 ———— 300 m
0 ———— 0.2 miles

The Tannery

Regent St Wharf

Riverside Park

Saint John River

See Enlargement

To Kings Landing Historical Settlement (40km); Woodstock (101km)

To Saint John (105km); Moncton (174km)

To Norfolk Motel (1km)

To Airport (14km)

To Miramichi (180km)

NEW BRUNSWICK

FREDERICTON'S FAMOUS FROG

Fredericton's most beloved character is not in the history texts. It's a legendary 19kg frog. The famous amphibian made its first appearance in 1885, when it literally leaped into the small boat of local innkeeper Fred Coleman while he was rowing on nearby Killarney Lake.

At the time, the frog weighed a mere 3.6kg but Coleman kept it at the inn by feeding it a steady (very steady) diet of buttermilk, cornmeal, June bugs and whiskey. Little wonder it became the world's largest. (And happiest too, no doubt.) It was even documented by *Ripley's Believe it or Not!*

Today the Coleman frog is forever enshrined in a glass case at the York-Sunbury Museum. But wait...there is major controversy and debate. Some say it is a fake! They claim this is not the real stuffed Coleman but rather an artificial likeness first used in a local drug store advertisement for a cough medicine said to clear the 'frog in your throat.' Later, they maintain, it ended up in the museum as the real 'ribbeter.' So take a close look. What do you think? Museum staff are keeping tight-lipped.

In the museum gift shop and around town, frog items from lawn ornaments to T-shirts are big sellers. The city's froggy infatuation manifests itself in other ways too. The Nature Trust of New Brunswick created the first park, Hayla Park Nature Preserve, to protect a frog (in this case, the vulnerable Gray Tree Frog) and they even have an ongoing adopt-a-frog campaign.

River. Abundant benches grace the streets of this welcoming city, one of the only major cities in the Maritimes not reached by tidal waters.

HISTORY

Three hundred years ago, Maliseet and Mi'kmaq Aboriginals lived and fished here. The French followed in 1732 but were eventually burned out by the British, who brought in 2000 Loyalists fleeing the United States after the American Revolution.

Fredericton really came into its own the next year when the British government decided to form a new province by splitting New Brunswick away from Nova Scotia. Lieutenant governor Thomas Carleton visited Ste Anne's Point and was impressed with its strategic location on the Saint John River, suitable for receiving large ships and practically in the center of the new province. In 1785, he not only made it the provincial capital and the base for a British garrison but renamed it Fredericstown in honor of Sir Frederick, Duke of York and the second son of King George III. The city has grown moderately in that capacity ever since.

ORIENTATION

The city center is on a small, rounded peninsula that juts into the Saint John River. The Westmorland St Bridge connects the downtown area with the north shore residential areas. Further east, Hwy 8 crosses the

river on the Princess Margaret Bridge. Coming into town from the Trans-Canada Hwy (Hwy 1), take Regent St straight down to the heart of town.

INFORMATION

Chapters (☎ 506-459-2616; 1381 Regent St) Megabookstore.

Dr Everett Chalmers Hospital (☎ 506-452-5400; 700 Priestman St)

Fredericton Medical Clinic (☎ 506-458-0200; 1015 Regent St; ✆ 6pm-10pm Mon-Fri, 1-5pm Sat & Sun)

Fredericton Public Library (☎ 506-460-2800; 4 Carleton St; ✆ 10am-5pm Mon-Sat, to 9pm Wed & Fri) Free Internet access is first-come, first-served.

Main Post Office (☎ 506-444-8602; 570 Queen St; ✆ 8am-5pm Mon-Fri) General delivery mail addressed to Fredericton, NB E3B 4Y1, is kept here.

Police, Ambulance & Fire (☎ 911) For emergencies.

Visitors Centre (☎ 506-460-2129, 888-888-4768; www.fredericton.ca; City Hall, 397 Queen St; ✆ 8am-4:15pm Mon-Fri Oct-May, 8am-8pm Jun-Sep) Free city parking passes provided here.

SIGHTS

Fredericton's attractions, nearly all conveniently in the central core, focus on the city's well-preserved history but in a light, entertaining way.

Historic Garrison District

The two-block strip along Queen St between York and Regent Sts, a national historic site, housed British soldiers for nearly 100 years commencing in 1784. It's now a lively, multi-use area utilizing the site's fine stone architecture.

At **Officers' Square** (btwn Carleton & Regent Sts), once the military parade ground, see the full-uniform changing of the guard ceremony at 11am and 7pm weekdays from mid-July to the third week in August. Also in summer the Outdoor Summer Theatre performs daily at 12:15pm weekdays and 2pm weekends. The free historical skits are laced with humor. On Tuesday and Thursday at 7:30pm, free band concerts attract crowds.

York-Sunbury Historical Museum (☎ 506-455-6041; Officers' Sq; adult/student/family $3/1/6; ☽ 10am-5pm mid-Jun-Aug, 1-4pm Tue-Sat Apr-mid-Dec), on the west side of the square, is in the old officers' quarters built between 1839 and 1851, an edifice typical of those designed by royal engineers during the colonial period. The older section has thicker walls of masonry and hand-hewn timbers. The other, newer end is made of sawn timber.

The museum has a collection from the city's past spread out in 12 rooms: military pieces used by local regiments and by British and German armies from the Boer and both world wars; furniture from a Loyalist sitting room and a Victorian bedroom; aboriginal and Acadian artifacts and archaeological finds. The prize exhibit, though, is a stuffed 19kg frog, the pet of a local innkeeper (see the boxed text opposite).

The **Soldiers' Barracks** (cnr Queen & Carleton Sts; admission free; ☽ Jun-Sep) gives you an idea of how the common soldier lived in the 1820s (lousy food, too much drink). The **Guard House** (15 Carleton St; admission free; ☽ Jul & Aug) from 1828 indicates more of the day-to-day hardships but the conditions for those held in cells were truly nasty. Threaten your kids. The lower section of the barracks is now used as artisan studios, and the **College of Craft & Design** (☎ 506-453-2305; ☽ tours 2pm Mon-Fri Jul & Aug), behind the Justice Building, presents the work of local artists.

Beaverbrook Art Gallery

This relatively small but excellent **gallery** (☎ 506-458-8545; www.beaverbrookartgallery.org; 703 Queen St; adult/student/senior/family $5/2/4/10; ☽ 9am-6pm Mon-Fri, 10am-5pm Sat & Sun Jun-Sep; 9am-5pm Tue-Fri, 10am-5pm Sat, noon-5pm Sun Oct-May) was one of Lord Beaverbrook's gifts to the town. The exceptional collection includes works by international heavyweights and is well worth an hour or so. Among others you may see Bacon, Constable, Dali, Gainsborough and Turner, as well as changing contemporary shows. There is also an enviable Kreighoff collection (see below).

Legislative Assembly

Built in 1880, this **government building** (☎ 506-453-2527; 706 Queen St; admission & tours free; ☽ 9am-7pm Mon-Fri, 10am-5pm Sat & Sun Jun-Aug; 9am-5pm Mon-Fri Sep-May; tours every 30min late May–late Aug & by appointment rest of year) is a marvel of craftsmanship and detailing. When the Legislative Assembly is not in session, guides show you around, pointing out things of particular merit, like the wooden speaker's chair and spiral staircase. When the assembly is in session (end of November to Christmas, March to June), visitors are welcome to observe.

Old Burial Ground

The Loyalist **cemetery** (Brunswick St, at Carleton St; ☽ 8am-9pm), dating back to 1784, is an

---

BEAVERBROOK DONNYBROOK

Max Aitken, the first Lord Beaverbrook, was one of New Brunswick's greatest benefactors and gave an art gallery to the province in 1959. It included a very impressive collection including works by internationally recognized masters such as Bacon, Dali, Gainsborough and Turner. Those 200 paintings have been the backbone of the Beaverbrook Art Gallery's exhibits for many years. In 2004 a couple of Beaverbrook's British descendents, and members of the UK Beaverbrook Foundation, decided those paintings were not a gift after all, but a loan. They thought the time had come for them to be sent across the pond. It wasn't the money (the paintings are now valued in the $100 million range) but the principle, they said, and the fact they were not being properly insured or presented. The art gallery board said to forget it. At press time, the matter was getting ugly and litigious. The Foundation had filed a suit to back its ownership claim and the gallery sued right back. The latter suggested that there should be no British case at all and that any differences should be sorted out in New Brunswick courts. Stay tuned...

atmospheric, thought-provoking history lesson of its own, revealing large families and kids dying tragically young. The Loyalists arrived from the 13 colonies after the American Revolution of 1776.

Old Government House

This magnificent stone **palace** (☎ 506-453-6440/2505; 51 Woodstock Rd; admission free; ☯ 10am-5pm mid-Jun–mid-Sep, 10am-4pm Mon-Fri mid-Sep–mid-Jun) was erected for the British governor in 1826. The representative of the queen moved out in 1893 after the province refused to continue paying his expenses, and during most of the 20th century the complex was a Royal Canadian Mounted Police (RCMP) headquarters. It now evocatively captures a moment in time with tours led by staff in period costume. New Brunswick's lieutenant governor lives on the 3rd floor and his limousine with a single crown for a license number is often parked outside.

Christ Church Cathedral

Built in 1853, this **cathedral** (off Queen St at Church St; tours free; ☯ tours on demand mid-Jun–Aug) is a fine early example of the 19th-century revival of decorated Gothic architecture and has exquisite stained glass. The cathedral is particularly notable because it's very compact – tall for the short length of the building, yet with a balance and proportion that make the interior seem both normal and spacious.

ACTIVITIES

For drifting away, the **Small Craft Aquatic Center** (☎ 506-460-2260; off Woodstock Rd; ☯ mid-May–early Oct), on the Saint John River beside Old Government House, rents out canoes, kayaks and rowboats at $10 an hour. On offer are good weekly passes, guided canoe tours, one-hour to three-day river ecology trips, and instruction in either canoeing or kayaking.

There are 12 recreational trails around town and along the river that either begin or intersect at **Adventure Center Lighthouse** (cnr Regent St & St Anne Pont Dr). They range from 700m to 10.2km. See the posted map/plaque/guide alongside the trails. For bike rentals, see p490.

TOURS

The tourist office (p486) has information on dozens of city and regional tours collectively called 'Tourrific Tours.' The suggested im-

pressive, thoughtful tours are of all types: walking and driving, free and ticketed.

From July to Labour Day, members of the Calithumpian actors' group wearing historic costumes lead good, free hour-long **Heritage Walking Tours** incorporating fun, folklore and history. Tours depart from City Hall at 10am, 1.30pm and 4pm daily. Ultra-popular **Haunted Hikes** (tours $13; ☯ 9.15pm Mon-Sat Jul-Sep) are given by the same, suddenly ghoulish, thespians.

To see Fredericton from the water, the **Carleton** (☎ 506-454-2628; Regent St Wharf; adult/child $7/3; ☯ Jun-Oct) has one-hour cruises on the Saint John River. Afternoon and evening departures are offered daily in July and August, and less frequently in June, September and October.

FESTIVALS & EVENTS

The following list features the major summer events and festivals.

New Brunswick Highland Games Festival (☎ 888-368-4444; www.highlandgames.ca; ☯ late Jul) Three-day Scottish festival with music, dancing and contests on the Old Government House grounds held each summer.

NotaBle Acts Summer Theatre Festival (☎ 506-452-0605; www.unbf.ca/nbacts; ☯ end Jul–early Aug) Showcases new and noted playwrights with street and theatre presentations.

New Brunswick Summer Music Festival (☎ 506-453-4697; www.unb.ca/nbsmf; ☯ mid-Aug) Two weeks of classical music at Memorial Hall at University of New Brunswick campus.

Fredericton Exhibition (☎ 506-458-9819; cnr Smythe & Saunders Sts; adult/child/student & senior $6/2/5; ☯ Sep) Known as Frex, this annual six-day affair is held from the first weekend of September. Held at the exhibition grounds, it includes animal competitions, a carnival, harness racing and stage shows.

Harvest Jazz & Blues Festival (☎ 888-622-5837; www.harvestjazzandblues.com; ☯ early Sep) Week-long event transforms the downtown area into the 'New Orleans of the North' when jazz, blues and Dixieland performers arrive from across North America.

SLEEPING
Budget

HI Fredericton International Hostel (☎ 506-450-4417; fredericton@hihostels.ca; 621 Churchill Row; members/nonmembers dm $16/20, s $20/24; ☯ office 7am-noon & 6-10pm; ℗ ▣) Set up in a capacious, older residence hall, this hostel welcomes a mix of students and visitors. Often travelers luxuriate in their own room.

Norfolk Motel (☎ 506-472-3278, 800-686-8555; 815 Riverside Dr; r $40-52; **P**) Go over Westmorland Bridge and follow Hwy 105 south to the door for 4km. The 20 air-conditioned rooms at this family-run motel are convenient and very clean.

Mid-Range

Carriage House Inn (☎ 506-452-9924, 800-267-6068; www.bbcanada.com/4658.html; 230 University Ave; s/d $95/105; **P**) This inn has been lovingly molded from an 1875 Victorian mansion, once belonging to the mayor. The rooms are spacious, with eight of 10 including a private bathroom. Noteworthy features are the New Brunswick paintings, antiques, high ceilings and the huge breakfasts served in a gorgeous dining/ballroom area.

Brennan's B&B (☎ 506-455-7346; www.bbcanada .com/3892.html; 221 Church St; r $75-85) The three tasteful rooms in this sizable, turreted Victorian house all have private bathrooms. It's close to the river in the quiet, historic district, a short walk from the main attractions. Wind down on the front porch swing.

Fredericton Inn (☎ 506-455-1430, 800-561-8777; www.frederictoninn.nb.ca; 1315 Regent St; d $80-120; **P** 🏊) Stepping forward into the modern age, this hotel/motel is often busy with conventions and seminars but appeals with its easy-access location and stress-busting amenities.

Top End

Lord Beaverbrook Hotel (☎ 506-455-3371, 866-444-1946; www.lordbeaverbrookhotel.com; 659 Queen St; r $110-155; **P** 🏊) Since 1946, the Beav has been the city's central, venerable, establishment hostelry. Back rooms look out on the river, as does the pub patio and dining room. It's good value given the amenities; ask about the frequent specials. Note that some rooms were renovated in 2004.

EATING

For a small city, Fredericton offers a wide, cosmopolitan cross-section of restaurants and most are in the walkable core. The city has fully embraced the patio culture with many places now offering laid-back alfresco seating. Many of these are clustered around the Tannery, also known as Piper's Lane, a courtyard of sorts between King and Queen Sts, west of York St. The alley

---

THE AUTHOR'S CHOICE

Colonel's In (☎ 506-452-2802; 877-455-3003; www.bbcanada.com/1749.html; 843 Union St; r $85-125; **P**) The name just hints at the playful minds at work here. Roger and Nancy, formerly in the military and nursing fields respectively, have infused their immaculate 1902 house with fun and puns to complement the antiques and pine floors. The mess hall offers breakfast choices and there's the best view in town to boot. You can walk right into the heart of town by crossing the pleasant old rail bridge spanning the river. The deluxe room, in the former garage, has its own balcony, fireplace and Jacuzzi.

---

between Nos 358 and 362 Queen St leads in. Most places there are primarily casual, popular pubs.

Budget

Boyce Farmers' Market (☎ 506-451-1815; 665 George St; 🕑 6am-1pm Sat) This Fredericton institution is great for picking up fresh fruit, vegetables, meat and cheese. Mixed in among the 150 or so stands are some selling handicrafts, homemade desserts and flowers. There is also a **restaurant** (🕑 breakfast & brunch).

Happy Baker (☎ 506-454-7200; 520 King St; dishes under $6; 🕑 7.30am-4.30pm Mon-Fri, 9am-4pm Sat) It's worth entering an office building even while on vacation for the tasty, fresh, cheap soups, salads, sandwiches and sweets turned out by this European bakery.

Molly's Kitchen (☎ 506-457-9305; 554 Queen St; mains under $7; 🕑 10am-11pm Mon-Fri, noon-midnight Sat & Sun) Half café, half pub, this arty place is filled with eclectic décor, graced with a quiet, green, backyard patio and serves up real food made onsite by Molly. In addition to soups and sandwiches, there are excellent salads and pastas, some of which are vegetarian. Specialties include baked lasagne and shepherd's pie from scratch.

Mid-Range

El Burrito Loco (☎ 506-459-5626; 304 King St; lunch $7-9, dinner $10-18; 🕑 11.30am-9pm Mon-Thu, 11.30am-11pm Fri & Sat, 4-9pm Sun) Feast your eyes as well as your stomach at this crazy cantina lit by sombreros. The largely authentic, south-of-the-border food, including tamales and enormous burritos, is savory, plentiful and never greasy. The Mexican drinks go down well with the Latin music, too.

Blue Door (☎ 506-455-2583; 100 Regent St; mains $8-20; ☒ 11:30am-10pm) Primary colors dominate the design inside and out at this local hotspot with an intriguingly varied menu. Dishes range from coconut curry with mussels and maple baked salmon to Uli's pasta incorporating local sausage and mushrooms. There's a kids' menu, too.

Dimitri's Souvlaki (☎ 506-452-8882; 349 King St; lunch $6-10, dinner $13-17; ☒ 11am-10pm Mon-Sat) Reliable Dimitri's has been presenting a broad menu of Greek taverna classics such as brochettes and moussaka since 1988. Some vegetarian options are available too. Enjoy your meal on the rooftop patio.

Schade's (☎ 506-450-3340; 536 Queen St; lunch $8-10, dinner $13-23; ☒ lunch & dinner Mon-Sat) Schnitzels dominate at this top-rate German spot, but Geschnetzeltes and Filettoepfchen help round out the authentic dishes available. Sample a Deutschland brew.

Top End
Palate (☎ 506-450-7911; 462 Queen St; mains $15-23; ☒ lunch & dinner Mon-Sat) For well-prepared fine continental dining with contemporary flair and a seasonally changing menu, this personable corner spot is recommended. The purple and yellow room is especially highly regarded for its seafood, but meats, pastas and chicken are also well represented. The Atlantic salmon is superb.

DRINKING
The Tannery, in and around Piper's Lane, has numerous bars and pubs popular with a young clientele.

Lunar Rogue Pub (☎ 506-450-2065; 625 King St; ☒ 11-1am) Lunar Rogue is (mostly) a quiet place with a good beer selection and a fine assortment of single malts. Enjoy summer under the umbrellas.

ENTERTAINMENT
The **Chestnut Club** (☎ 506-450-1222; 440 York St; cover under $5) is Fredericton's largest dance palace.

Dolan's Pub (☎ 506-454-7474; Piper's Ln; cover $5; ☒ closed Sun) Dolan's presents live Celtic/Maritime music Thursday to Saturday nights beginning around 10pm. Pub meals are served daily, too.

G-Club (☎ 506-455-7768; 377 King St, in Pipers Ln; ☒ 8pm-2am Wed-Sun) This is Fredericton's only gay/alternative club. Climb the metal stairs under the sign.

Playhouse (☎ 506-458-8344; www.theplayhouse.nb.ca; 686 Queen St) The Playhouse stages concerts, theater, ballet and shows.

SHOPPING
Aitkens Pewter (☎ 506-453-9474; 65 Regent St) With a workshop continuing the rare, ancient craft of working in pewter and unique products, this store is well worth a visit. Kitchenware, jewelry and other items are offered at reasonable prices. It's also great for souvenirs.

Fine Craft Center (☎ 506-450-8989; 87 Regent St) This new shop sells artistic local pottery and sculpture.

College of Craft & Design (☎ 506-453-2305; 457 Queen St; ☒ Jun-Sep) Nestled into the brick walls at the Soldiers Barracks, the booths here provide another chance to buy pottery and other works.

GETTING THERE & AWAY
Air
Fredericton Airport is on Hwy 102, 14km southeast of town, and gets a fair number of flights (see p483). A $12 'airport improvement fee' is not included in tickets and must be paid separately.

Bus
The **bus station** (☎ 506-458-6000; 101 Regent St; ☒ 7.30am-8.30pm Mon-Fri, 9am-8.30pm Sat & Sun) is very central. Schedules and fares to some destinations include: Moncton ($34, two hours, two daily); Charlottetown, Prince Edward Island ($67, five hours, two daily) and Bangor, Maine ($40, 6½ hours, one daily Friday and Saturday) via Saint John ($20, 1½ hours).

Car & Motorcycle
Avis, Budget, Hertz and National car rental agencies (see p873) all have desks at the airport. **Discount Car Rentals** (☎ 506-458-1118; 580 King St at Regent St) has compact cars starting at $40 a day including 200km. Staff will pick you up and drive you to the rental office. The $100 weekend special includes three days and unlimited mileage. In midsummer, prices could be higher.

GETTING AROUND
A taxi to the airport costs $16.

Bicycle rentals are available at **Radical Edge** (☎ 506-459-3478; 386 Queen St; per hr/day $5/25).

Check with Radical Edge staff or the tourist office for information on trails.

The city has a good bus system, **Fredericton Transit** (☎ 506-460-2200); tickets cost $1.60 and include free transfers. Service is halved on weekends. Most city bus routes begin at King's Place Mall, on King St between York and Carleton.

SAINT JOHN RIVER VALLEY

The Saint John River begins in the US state of Maine, then winds along the western border of the province past forests and beautiful lush farmland, drifts through Fredericton between tree-lined banks and flows around rolling hills before emptying into the Bay of Fundy 700km later.

It has been likened to the Rhine for its strong inexorable flow, the various industries within sight of its banks and the transportation corridors that follow its course. With a couple of noteworthy exceptions, the valley's soft, eye-pleasing landscape is more a thoroughfare than a destination. As such, it is surprisingly busy in summer, so beware that accommodations can get packed by late afternoon.

Two routes carve through the valley: the quicker Trans-Canada Hwy (Hwy 1), mostly on the west side of the river, and the more scenic old Hwy 105 on the east side, which meanders through many villages. Branching off from the valley are Hwy 17 (at St Leonard) and Rte 385 (at Perth-Andover), which cut northeast through the Appalachian highlands and lead to rugged Mt Carleton Provincial Park.

MACTAQUAC

The mega-sized **Mactaquac Power Dam** (☎ 506-462-3814; 451 Hwy 105; admission free; ☽ 9am-4pm May-Sep), 25km west of Fredericton on Hwy 102, is open for 45-minute tours of the generating station, including a peek at the roaring turbines and an explanation of how they work. Built in 1968, the concrete dam is 43m high, the tallest in the Maritimes. The six turbines can generate 600,000 kilowatts of electricity.

Busy, resort-like **Mactaquac Provincial Park** (day use per vehicle $5), the province's most de-

veloped, includes swimming, fishing, hiking, picnic sites, camping, boat rentals and a huge **campground** (☎ 506-363-4747; 1256 Hwy 105; ☽ mid-May-early Oct; tent/RV sites $23/26).

KING'S LANDING HISTORICAL SETTLEMENT

One of the province's best sites, the worthwhile re-creation of an early 19th-century **Loyalist village** (☎ 506-363-4999; www.kingslanding .nb.ca; adult/family $14/30; ☽ 10am-5pm Jun–mid-Oct) is 36km west of Fredericton. A community of 100 costumed staff create a living museum by role-playing in 11 houses, a school, church, store and sawmill typical of those used a century ago, providing a glimpse and taste of pioneer life in the Maritimes. Demonstrations and events are staged throughout the day and horse-drawn carts shunt visitors around. The prosperous Loyalist life reflected here can be tellingly compared to that at the Acadian Historic Village in Caraquet (p522). **The King's Head Inn**, a mid-1800s pub, serves traditional food and beverages, with a nice authentic touch – candlelight. The children's programs make King's Landing ideal for families, and special events occur regularly. It's not hard to while away a good half-day or more here.

HARTLAND

Hartland is a quaint, minute village with a pretty setting, and it's the granddaddy

---

IRISH FRIES ARE SMILIN'

The McCains came from Ireland in the early 1800s: poor, uneducated and desperate for a new chance. With few prospects they did what they knew and loved: growing potatoes. Man, did they grow potatoes. Their descendents now operate the largest farms in the province, concentrated in the Saint John River valley. The McCain production of frozen French fries began in Florenceville in 1957 and now leads the world. Internationally, they turn out hundreds of thousands of kilos of potato products an hour! The company has become a global leader in food production and has branched out into a wide variety of endeavors.

Another tasty fave, Humpty Dumpty potato chips, are made nearby in Hartland.

KISS ME QUICK

The picturesque, even symbolic, covered bridges dotted throughout the region were originally built in the 1800s, though most are now from the 1900s and are covered to protect the timber beams used in the construction. They are generally high and wide because cartloads of hay pulled by horses had to pass over them. But they also had a practical purpose of a different sort. They were long-known affectionately as kissing bridges because you could head your horse-drawn buggy into the darkness away from prying eyes and do what comes naturally.

As recently as 1944, there were 320 bridges in the area. Today, there remain 64 bridges across the province, more than anywhere else in Canada. Though traffic, age, fire and flooding have taken their tolls, most of the bridges are still part of the secondary road network, not idle relics.

About a quarter of these covered bridges are in Kings County, radiating from Sussex in southern New Brunswick. St Martins (p510), on the Bay of Fundy, is the only location where you can get two bridges in one photograph.

of New Brunswick's many wooden covered bridges. The photogenic 390m-long **Hartland Covered Bridge** over the Saint John River was erected in 1897 and is a national historic site.

Hatfield Heritage Inn (☎ 506-375-8000, 877-637-8200; www.premiercountryinns.com/hindex.html; 370 Main St; d $75-120), right by the famous bridge, is like walking into the past, complete with piano in the old-style parlor. The wonderful time-capsule **dining room** serves renowned meals (mains $12 to $21) from 5pm to 9pm; book ahead. Richard Hatfield, the former premier, lived here.

Ja-Sa-Le Motel (☎ 506-375-4419, 800-565-6433; khh@nb.aibn.com; Hwy 2; s/d mid-Jun–mid-Sep $50/75, mid-Sep–mid-Jun $46/50; 🐾), the only local motel, is about a century removed from Hatfield Heritage, but it is spotless and quiet and has a fine view. The name is taken from the first two letters of the names of the previous owner's three daughters. Can you guess what they are? Some rooms have kitchenettes.

GRAND FALLS

With a drop of around 25m and a 1.6km-long gorge with walls as high as 80m, the falls merit a stop in this one-street town. The **Grand Falls** are best in spring or after heavy rain. In summer, much of the water is diverted for generating hydroelectricity, yet the gorge appeals anytime.

In the middle of town, overlooking the falls, the **Malabeam Reception Centre** (☎ 877-475-7769; Madawaska Rd; admission free; ⏰ 10am-6pm Jun & Sep, 9am-9pm Jul & Aug) doubles as a tourist office. Among the displays is a scale model of the gorge showing its extensive trail system.

A 253-step stairway down into the gorge begins at **La Rochelle** (☎ 877-475-7769; 1 Chapel St; adult/family $4/8; ⏰ Jun-early Sep), across the bridge from the Malabeam Reception Center and left on Victoria St. Boats maneuver for 45-minute trips (adult/family $11/27) up the gorge. These run up to eight times a day but only in midsummer when water levels are low (it's too dangerous when the river is in full flood). Buy the boat ticket at La Rochelle first, as it includes the stairway to the base of the gorge.

Maple Tourist Home (☎ 506-473-1763; 888-840-8222; www.bbcanada.com/4029.html; 142 Main St; d incl breakfast $70-90) is the white, two-story house with the green shutters, which offers three rooms in the center of town.

Le Grand Salut (☎ 506-473-3876; 155 Broadway Blvd; breakfast $5, mains $8-15; ⏰ 6am-9pm Mon-Sat, 7am-9pm Sun), a popular, two-tiered spot with an inviting deck out front, serves up salads, pastas, brochettes and steaks.

The Acadian Lines bus stops at the **Irving gas station** (☎ 506-473-5704; 315 Broadway), right in the center of town. Highway 108, the Plaster Rock Hwy, cuts across the province to the east coast, slicing through forest for nearly its entirety. It's almost like driving in a tunnel and is most tedious, but fast. Watch out for deer and moose.

MT CARLETON PROVINCIAL PARK

If you're driving either Hwy 17 or Rte 385 from the Saint John River, be extremely cautious of moose and deer on the road. Collisions are very common and can be deadly. Driving at night is particularly dangerous. But this is the risk taken to access the Maritimes' only really remote, sizable nature park. The 17,427-hectare park offers visitors a wilderness of mountains, valleys, rivers and wildlife including moose, deer, bear and, potentially, the 'extinct' but regularly seen Eastern cougar. Partly because it's not a national park, Mt Carleton is little known and relatively unvisited, even in midsummer. It could be the province's best-kept secret.

The main feature of the park is a series of rounded glaciated peaks and ridges, including Mt Carleton, which at 820m is the Maritimes' highest. This range is actually an extension of the Appalachian Mountains, which begin in the US state of Georgia and end in Québec.

Orientation & Information

The park is open from mid-May to October; entry is free. Hunting and logging are prohibited in the park, and all roads are gravel-surfaced. The nearest town is 30km away, so bring all food and a full tank of gas.

At the entrance to the park is a **visitors center** (☎ 506-235-0793; www.gnb.ca/0078/Carleton; off Rte 385; ☿ 8am-8pm Mon-Fri, 10am-10pm Sat & Sun May-Oct) for maps and information. There is also another **office** (☎ 506-235-6040; dnr.Mt.carleton@gnb .ca; 11 Gagnon St), the park headquarters, in St Quentin.

Activities

HIKING

The best way to explore Mt Carleton is on foot. The park has a 62km network of trails, most of them loops winding to the handful of rocky knobs that are the peaks. The International Appalachian Trail (IAT; see p320) passes through here.

The easiest peak to climb is **Mt Bailey**; a 7.5km loop trail to the 564m hillock begins near the day-use area. Most hikers can walk this route in three hours. The highest peak is reached via the **Mt Carleton Trail**, a 10km route that skirts over the 820m knob, where there's a fire tower. Along the way is a backcountry campsite, located near three beaver ponds in full view of the mountain. Plan on three to four hours for the trek and pack your parka; the wind above the tree line can be brutal.

The most scenic hike is the **Sagamook Trail**, a 6km loop to a 777m peak with superlative vistas of Nictau Lake and the highlands area to the north of it; allow three hours for this trek. The **Mountain Head Trail** connects the Mt Carleton and Sagamook trails, making a long transit of the range possible.

All hikers intending to follow any long trails must register at the visitor center or park headquarters before hitting the trail. Outside the camping season (mid-May to mid-September), you should call ahead to make sure the main gate will be open, as the Mt Carleton trailhead is 13.5km from the park entrance. Otherwise park your car at the entrance and walk in – the Mt Bailey trailhead is only 2.5km from the gate.

CANOEING

Canoeing the chain of lakes and the Tobique and Nepisiguit Rivers winding through the landscape is excellent. Nictau and Nepisiguit Lakes, the two largest, are both glorious. For canoe rentals call **Guildo Martel** (☎ 506-235-2499).

Sleeping

With so few sites available, campgrounds can occasionally get full. Reservations are suggested, as space is very limited, by sending an email to the park office (see left) in St Quentin.

Armstrong Brook Campground (tent & RV sites Sun-Thu $11, Fri & Sat $14; ☿ mid-May-Sep) is an 88-site campground on the north side of Nictau Lake; Armstrong Brook is 3km from the park entrance. It has toilets, showers and a kitchen shelter, but no sites with hookups. RV drivers often have their noisy generators running, so tenters should check out the eight tent-only sites along Armstrong Brook on the north side of the campground.

Aside from Armstrong Brook, there are two walk-in campgrounds and one backcountry spot.

Williams Brook Campground (tent sites $9) A few kilometers beyond Armstrong Brook on the north side of Nictau Lake, Williams Brook has only eight walk-in sites, each with a wooden tent platform. It's great if you want to be alone.

Franquelin Campground (tent sites $9) On the south shore of the lake, Franquelin has nine walk-in campsites and is better situated for hiking as it's just 1.5km from the Mt Bailey trailhead (10km from Mt Carleton).

Headwaters Campsite (tent sites $5) Up on Mt Carleton itself, Headwaters has just three sites, and it's a good idea to call ahead and try to reserve one if you're sure you want to sleep there.

For those who prefer not to camp, **Nictau Lodge**, inside the park on the south side of Nictau Lake, was closed at time of writing, but there were plans for it to reopen in the future.

EDMUNDSTON

Working-class Edmundston, with a large paper mill and a mainly bilingual French citizenry, makes a convenient stopover, with Québec to the north and Maine, USA, just across the river. The Madawaska Maliseet First Nation has a large reserve along Queen St south of town and aboriginal craft shops by the road sell wallets, belts and moccasins.

Information

Provincial Tourist Office (☎ 506-735-2747; Hwy 2; ☉ 10am-6pm mid-May–early Oct, 8am-9pm Jul & Aug) About 20km north at the Québec border is this major stop.

Sights

The **Madawaska Museum** (☎ 506-737-5282; 195 Boul Hébert; admission $3.50; ☉ 7-10pm Wed & Thu, 1-5pm Sun Sep-Jun; 9am-8pm daily Jul & Aug) outlines regional human history, including the local timber trade, and presents local artists' work. The 1841 **Petit Salt Blockhouse** (☎ 506-735-7564; Rte 2), a replica of the one built during border conflicts with the USA, provides a fabulous view.

Festivals & Events

In August is the **Festival Foire Brayonne** (☎ 506-739-6608; www.foire-brayonne.nb.ca in French) when locals celebrate the whimsical, fictitious notion of their independent Republic of Madawaska, whose inhabitants are the Brayonnes. Evidently, the original blend of Acadians and Québecois were in a bit of a nationality vacuum in the 1700s when the British and Americans bickered over the border.

Sleeping & Eating

Le Fief Inn (☎ 506-735-0400; fax 506-735-0402; 87 Church St; d $100; ☉ Jun-Oct) This welcoming, friendly B&B in a central, substantial heritage house offers eight themed rooms with free movies or books from the expansive in-house library. The husband does the caricatures in the office.

University of Moncton (☎ 506-737-5016; www .cuslm.ca in French; 171 Boul Hébert; s/d $26/36; ☉ mid-Jun–late Aug) In summer, simple, institutional rooms are available at Residence Louis Cyr.

Several **motels** line the highway and old Hwy 2 (Boul Acadie).

Bel Air (☎ 506-735-3329; 174 Victoria St, cnr Boul Hébert; mains $6-14; ☉ 24hr) A city landmark since the 1950s, this is a total classic right down to the seasoned, uniformed waitresses. The you-name-it menu includes more-than-acceptable Italian, Chinese, seafood and basic Canadian fare. If you're putting on the dog, go next door to **Steak Seafood Paradise** (☎ 506-739-7822; 174 Victoria St; mains $15-25).

Getting There & Away

The **bus terminal** (☎ 506-739-8309; 169 Victoria) is across the street from the Bel Air restaurant.

ST JACQUES

Seven kilometers north of Edmonton, nearly halfway to the Québec border, is the small community of St Jacques and the pride of provincial horticulturists, the **New Brunswick Botanical Garden** (☎ 506-737-5383; off Rte 2; admission $4.75; ☉ 9am-6pm Jun-Sep, to 8pm Jul & Aug). Here there are 80,000 plants to brighten your day, all accompanied by classical music! Kids might prefer the insectarium. Adjacent **Les Jardins de la Republique Provincial Park** (☎ 506-735-2525; tent/RV sites $22/24) is not a bad stop for a cool, refreshing leg-stretch and picnic if you're in transit. It also has camping, but the highway makes for a noisy night.

WESTERN FUNDY SHORE

Almost the entire southern edge of New Brunswick is presided over by the ever-present, constantly rising and falling, always impressive waters of the Bay of Fundy.

The resort town of St Andrews, the serene Fundy Isles, fine seaside scenery and rich history make this easily one of the most appealing regions of the province. Whale-watching is a thrilling area activity. Most commonly seen are the fin, humpback and minke, and less so, the increasingly rare right whale. Porpoises and dolphins are plentiful. And let's not overlook the seafood – it's bountiful and delicious.

ST STEPHEN

Right on the US border across the river from Calais, Maine, St Stephen is a busy entry point with one tasty attraction. It is home to Ganong's, a family-run chocolate business operating since 1873, whose products are known around eastern Canada. The five-cent chocolate nut bar was invented by the Ganong brothers in 1910, and they are also credited with developing the heart-shaped box of chocolates seen everywhere on Valentine's Day.

Information

International Currency Exchange (☎ 506-466-3387; 128 Milltown Blvd; ⏰ 8am-6pm Dec-Apr, 8am-8pm May-Nov) Two blocks from Canada Customs.

Provincial Tourist Office (☎ 506-466-7390; cnr Milltown Blvd & King St; ⏰ 10am-6pm Jun & Sep, 8am-9pm Jul & Aug) In the former train station.

St Croix Public Library (☎ 506-466-7529; ⏰ 9am-5pm Wed, Thu & Sat, 1-5pm & 7-9pm Tue, 1-9pm Fri) Behind the tourist office, it has free Internet access.

Sights

The old chocolate factory on the town's main street is now **Ganong's Chocolate Museum** (☎ 506-466-7848; www.chocolatemuseum.ca; 73 Milltown Blvd; adult/child/family $5/3/15; ⏰ 9am-6:30pm Mon-Sat, 1-5pm Sun mid-Jun–Aug; 9am-5pm Mon-Fri Mar–mid-Jun & Sep-Dec), displaying everything from antique chocolate boxes to manufacturing equipment. The adjacent store (open daily year-round) sells boxes of chocolates

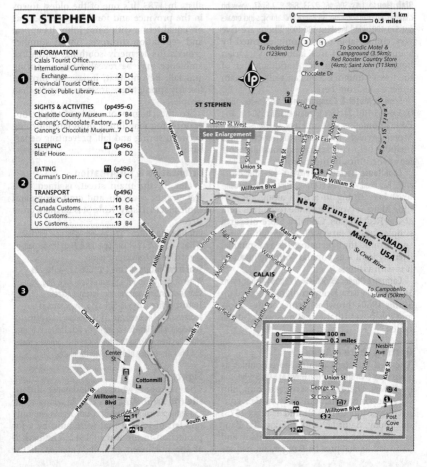

ST STEPHEN

and is free to visit; it also has Pal O'Mine, a very sweet little bar.

The **Charlotte County Museum** (☎ 506-466-3295; 443 Milltown Blvd; admission free; 9:30am-4:30pm Mon-Sat Jun-Aug), in an impressive mansion from 1864, stands among a stretch of substantial houses and mansions, and has displays on shipbuilding, lumbering and the area's connections to the USA.

Festivals & Events

Once a year during **Chocolate Fest** (☎ 506-465-5616; www.chocolate-fest.ca; 1st week Aug), the new chocolate factory (on Chocolate Dr, where else?) is open.

Sleeping & Eating

Blair House (☎ 506-466-2233, 888-972-5247; www.bbcanada.com/blairhouseinn; 38 Prince William St; s incl breakfast $75-100, d incl breakfast $80-100) There are five very comfortable rooms complemented by a quiet garden at this fabulous Victorian home belonging to the granddaughter of the town's founder. You can walk the main street easily from here.

Scoodic Motel & Campground (☎ 506-466-1540; fax 506-466-9103; 241 Hwy 1; tent sites $20, r $50-60;) Four kilometers east on Hwy 1, the Scoodic Motel is clean, has some kitchenettes and includes help-yourself cereal, toast and coffee at the office in the morning.

CookHouse Restaurant (☎ 506-466-0018; Hwy 1 at Old Bay Road, 4km east of town; mains $7-14; 6am-10pm) Like sitting in a barn alongside old-time Main St (you'll see), the restaurant here at the Red Rooster Country Store prepares simple, hearty fare well. Definitely take a sniff around the bakery too. It's a hospitable, friendly joint – as popular with the locals as it is with visitors.

Carman's Diner (☎ 506-466-3528; 164 King St; mains $4-12; 7am-10pm) Home cooking is served up at this 1960s throwback with counter stools and jukeboxes (that sometimes work) at the tables.

Getting There & Away

The Red Rooster Country Store doubles as a **bus stop** (☎ 506-466-2121; Hwy 1 at 5 Old Bay Rd, 4km east of town). There's a bus service to Saint John ($19) leaving at 4:10pm daily, which connects to Moncton ($38) and Halifax ($73) on Friday, Saturday and Sunday. To Bangor ($15), the bus only goes on Friday and Saturday at 3:30pm. In Bangor, immediate connections are available to Boston and New York.

Across the border in Calais, Maine, **West's Coastal Connection** (☎ 800-596-2823) buses connect to Bangor. They leave from the Angelhom restaurant, but call to confirm the location as this changes. In Bangor, buses use the Greyhound terminal and connect to Bangor Airport. Greyhound passes cannot be used from Calais.

ST ANDREWS BY-THE-SEA

As the name suggests, St Andrews is a summer resort of some tradition and gentility. Together with a fine climate and picturesque beauty, St Andrews has a long, charming and often visible history. Founded by Loyalists in 1783, it's one of the oldest towns in the province and for a long period was on equal terms with Saint John. Its appeal and reputation, however, mean summer crowds. Its formerly soothing, retreatlike ambience may be revealed best in spring and fall. Beyond that, in late fall through to early spring, there are more seagulls than people.

To the chagrin of whale-watching operators, fog may linger until late morning between spring and fall, preventing departures.

Orientation & Information

Water St, the main street, is lined with restaurants, souvenir and craft shops and some places to stay. King St is its main cross street.

Information Office (☎ 506-466-4858; near junction of Hwys 1 & 127; 10am-6pm Jul & Aug) The secondary tourist office is 17km north of town.

Seafarers' Internet Café (☎ 506-529-4610; 233 Water St; per 15min $2; 9am-10pm Jul & Aug, 9am-9pm Tue-Sun Sep-Jun) Provides Internet access.

Tourist Office (☎ 506-529-3555; www.town.standrews.nb.ca; 46 Reed Ave; 8am-8pm Jul & Aug 9am-5pm mid-May–Jun & Sep-early Oct) The main tourist office has free walking-tour brochures that include a map and brief description of 34 noteworthy places.

Sights

The restored wooden **Blockhouse Historic Site** (☎ 506-529-4270; Joe's Point Rd; admission free; 9am-8pm Jun-Aug, 9am-5pm early Sep) is the only one left of several that were built here for protection in the war of 1812. The park is at the northwest end of Water St. If the tide is out, there's a path that extends from the blockhouse out across the tidal flats. **Centennial Park**, opposite the blockhouse, has a picnic pavilion.

Huntsman Aquarium Museum (☎ 506-529-1202; www.huntsmanmarine.ca/aquapreview.htm; 1 Lower Campus Rd; adult/child $7.50/5; ۞ 10am-6pm Jul-Sep, noon-4:30pm Mon & Tue, 10am-4:30pm Wed-Sun late May-Jun & Oct), 2km northwest of the blockhouse, is part of the Federal Fisheries Research Centre – St Andrews' most important business, which employs some of Canada's leading marine biologists. The museum features most specimens found in local waters, including seals (feedings at 11am and 4pm). Kids also love the touch pool.

Minister's Island Historic Site (☎ 506-529-5081; adult/child $5/2.50; ۞ May-Oct) was first purchased and used as a summer retreat by William Cornelius van Horne, builder of the Canadian Pacific Railway. His former cottage of 50 rooms and the unusual bathhouse with its tidal swimming pool can be visited at low tide, even by car, when you can drive on the hard-packed sea floor. A few hours later it's 3m under water. Two-hour visits, by tour only, run once or twice a day, depending on the tides. You must use your own vehicle.

Sheriff Andrew House (☎ 506-529-5080; cnr King & Queen Sts; admission by donation; ۞ 9:30am-4:30pm Mon-Sat, 1-4:30pm Sun Jul-Sep), now a restored middle-class home dating from 1820, has been redecorated in period style and is attended by costumed guides.

Extensive, multi-hued **Kingsbrae Garden** (☎ 506-529-3335; 220 King St; adult/senior & student/family $8.50/7/23; ۞ 9am-6pm mid-May–mid-Oct) is considered one of the best horticultural displays in Canada.

Greenoch Presbyterian Church (cnr Edward & Montague Sts), one of many fine churches, stands out. Dating from 1824, it gets its name for the relief carving of a green oak on the steeple.

St Croix Island Viewpoint (Hwy 127 N, 9km off Hwy 1; admission free; ۞ 24hr), 8km from town, overlooks the tiny island in the St Croix River where in 1604 French explorer Samuel de Champlain spent his first winter in North America. The island itself is in Maine, but a series of panels explain the significance of this national historic site.

Sunbury Shores Arts & Nature Centre (☎ 506-529-3386; www.sunburyshores.org; 139 Water St; admission free; ۞ 9am-4:30pm Mon-Fri & noon-4pm Sat year-round, plus noon-4pm Sun May-Sep) is a nonprofit educational and cultural center offering instruction in painting, weaving, pottery and other crafts, as well as natural science courses. Various changing exhibits run through summer.

Activities
Eastern Outdoors (☎ 506-529-4662; www.eastern outdoors.com; 165 Water St; mountain bike rentals per hr/day $7/25, kayak rentals per ½ day/day $25/35 ۞ mid-May–Oct) is a St Andrews-based outfitter that offers three-hour kayak trips ($50). It also rents out kayaks and mountain bikes.

The 800m **Twin Meadows Walking Trail**, a boardwalk and footpath through fields and woodlands, begins opposite No 165 Joe's Point Road beyond the blockhouse.

Tours
Many companies offering **boat trips** and **whale-watching cruises** have offices at the Adventure Destinations complex beside Market Sq at the foot of King St. They're open from mid-June to early September. The $50 cruises do take in the lovely coast, sea birds are commonplace and seeing whales is the norm. The ideal waters for watching these beasts are further out in the bay, however, so if you're heading for the Fundy Isles, do your trip there.

There are also a couple of good land-based tours on offer:

Heritage Discovery Tours (☎ 506-529-4011) Offers a 'Magical History' walking tour (adult/family $16/42) with costumed guides at 10am daily from May to October. There's also a 'Mysteries of the Night Ghost Walk' (adult/family $12/34) at 8pm mid-June to November, which is great for families with children. All tours begin from the Algonquin Resort; they're often sold out a week in advance, especially during the 'bus tour months' of September and October.

HMS Transportation (☎ 506-529-4443; 260 Water St; adult/child $14/7; ۞ from 10am Jul & Aug) Has two-hour bus tours from the Algonquin Resort.

Sleeping
BUDGET
Salty Towers (☎ 506-529-4585; steeljm@nbnet.nb.ca; 340 Water St; s from $35, d $40-75; P) Jamie Steel, the proprietor and a local naturalist, dubs this 'Chateau Alternatato.' Although it has been an inn since 1921, Salty Towers is unlike anything else. The sprawling 1840s mansion, where Gothic intersects with funk,

is an offbeat, casual place for wanderers to call home. Musicians, kayakers, students and vacationers come and go. Hot Toddy, a wonderful rootsy band, even recorded their fourth album here. There are 16 rooms of every conceivable size and fashion, so take a browse. Five have private bathrooms and some have kitchenettes.

Kiwanis Oceanfront Camping (☎ 877-393-7070; www.kiwanisoceanfrontcamping.com; 550 Water St; tent/ RV sites $19/23; ⊙ mid-May–mid-Oct) At the far east end of town on Indian Point, this is mainly a gravel parking area for trailers, although some grassy spots do exist.

MID-RANGE

Mulberry B&B (☎ 506-529-4948; www.mulberrybb .com; 96 Water St; s/d $85/100; P) You can't lose at this delightful central place from 1820, with three comfortable rooms with ceiling fans. There are ocean views from the garden.

Eider Shore Guest house (☎ 506-529-4795; www .standrews.netfirms.com; 100 Queen St; s/d $95/105; ⊙ Apr-Nov; P) This central guest house is an appealing home that has been serving guests for many years. The center of town is just an amble away, and there's a three-day minimum stay.

Greenside Motel (☎ 506-529-3039; www.sn2000 .nb.ca/comp/greenside-motel; 242 Mowatt Drive; r $60-80; ⊙ May-Oct; P) Slightly away from the busy center, this small, modest place is quite suitable.

DO THE QUODDY LOOP

You won't need dance lessons for this, but it'll still make you light-footed. The loop is a circular two-nation tour of Passamaquoddy Bay, featuring the islands and bays of the western corner of the Bay of Fundy. This peaceful region, still dominated by the sea, was originally the home of the Aboriginal Passamaquoddy. British Loyalists later displaced them, but they remain on reserves in Maine. Wildlife in the region includes sea and shore birds, seals, porpoises and dolphins. Roads connect coastal Maine in the USA with St Stephen and St Andrews by-the-Sea, while Canadian ferries link the five main islands including Deer, Campobello and Grand Manan. The circuit can be completed using the bridge from Campobello back to Maine.

TOP END

Fairmont Algonquin Hotel (☎ 506-529-8823; www .fairmont.com; 184 Adolphus St; r $130-$190; ⧠ P) This classic 1889 hostelry, with its verandah, gardens, rooftop terrace and tennis courts, is worth a look even if you're not spending the night. There are a couple of places for a drink, be it tea or gin.

Eating

Market Sq downtown hosts a Thursday morning **farmer's market** (⊙ Jun–mid-Oct).

Sweet Harvest Market (☎ 506-529-6249; 182 Water St; all items under $9; ⊙ 9am-5pm, to 9pm Fri & Sat) In view, behind the counter, staff create soups, salads, sandwiches and sweets that are way beyond standard and chowder that is truly outstanding. The coffee's good too.

Harbourfront (☎ 506-529-4887; 225 Water St; lunch $7-11, dinner $15-22; ⊙ lunch & dinner) This seaside restaurant, built in 1840 and once a cinema, has a great deck and lots of fresh seafood and steak; there's also a kid's menu.

Gables (☎ 529-3440; 143 Water St; lunch $10, dinner $15-20; ⊙ lunch & dinner) Seafood and views of the ocean through a wall of glass dominate this comfortable place. To enter, head down the alley and through a gardenlike patio.

Windsor House (☎ 506-529-3330; 132 Water St; lunch $12, dinner $25-30; ⊙ lunch & dinner) The elegant dining room in this historic inn changes menus frequently but may suggest rack of lamb, pork tenderloin and two seafood entrees such as shrimp, mussels and scallops seared with vodka, tomato and green onions. Yum! But don't forget to save room for the mouth-watering desserts.

Niger Reef Teahouse (1 Joe's Point Rd; ⊙ Jun-Sep) The 1926 teahouse has a lovely deck and view, and serves teas and light meals.

Entertainment

Siren's Nest (☎ 506-529-8484; 248 Water St; ⊙ 7-1am) This is the only place in town with live music. There's blues and folk on weekends, and occasionally on weekdays.

Getting There & Around

Acadian Lines buses depart from **HMS Transportation** (☎ 506-529-3371; www.hmstrans.com; 260 Water St) once a day (schedule varies) for Saint John ($15). It goes the other way toward Bangor, Maine, from Thursday to Saturday at 3pm ($20). HMS Transportation also rents cars ($50 per day with 200 free kilometers).

FUNDY ISLES

The thinly populated, unspoiled Fundy Isles are ideal for a tranquil, nature-based escape. With grand scenery, colorful fishing wharves tucked into coves, supreme whale-watching, uncluttered walking trails and steaming dishes of seafood, everyday stresses fade away and blood pressure eases. The three main islands each have a distinct personality. Though none of these have knock-your-socks-off sites, they offer a memorable, gradually absorbed peace. Out of the summer season, all are nearly devoid of visitors and most services are shut.

Deer Island

Deer Island, the closest of the three main Fundy Isles, is a modest fishing settlement with a lived-in look. The 16km-by-5km island has been inhabited since 1770, and 1000 people live here year-round. It's well-forested and deer are still plentiful. Lobster is the main catch and there are half a dozen wharves around the island.

ORIENTATION & INFORMATION

Deer Island can be easily explored on a day trip. Narrow, winding roads run south down each side toward Campobello Island and the ferry (drive defensively). There's a summertime **tourist information kiosk** (☼ daily in summer) at the ferry landing.

SIGHTS & ACTIVITIES

At **Lamberts Cove** is a huge lobster pound used to hold live lobster (it could well be the world's largest). Another massive pound squirms at Northern Harbor.

At the other end of the island is the 16-hectare **Deer Island Point Park** where Old Sow, the world's second-largest natural tidal whirlpool, is seen offshore a few hours before high tide. Whales pass occasionally.

At the end of Cranberry Head Rd is a **deserted beach**. Most land on the island is privately owned, so there are no hiking trails.

TOURS

Whales usually arrive in mid-June and stay through October. There are several companies offering tours:

Cline Marine Inc (☎ 506-747-0114, 800-567-5880; www.clinemarine.com; 1745 Rte 772, Leonardville; 2½hr tours adult/child $45/30) Offers trips at 9:30am, 12:30pm and 3:30pm in July and August. The 12:30pm tour is most

likely to get booked out. Early and late in the season, only the midday trip goes. Boats depart from Richardson Wharf; from the Letete ferry, go 2.8km and turn left.

Eastern Outdoors (☎ 800-565-2925; www.eastern outdoors.com) Operates full-day kayak tours ($80) to see marine mammals, sea birds, islands and beaches. Participants meet at the northern ferry wharf.

Lambert's Outer Island Tours (☎ 506-747-2426; www.outerislandtours.com; adult/child/family $48/28/135) Offers whale-watching tours at 10am, 1pm and 4pm in July and August. It's a smaller operation than Cline Marine and uses a smaller boat. Tours leave from Lord's Cove, 2km from the Letete ferry.

SLEEPING & EATING

Gardner House B&B & Dining (☎ 506-747-2462; Lambert Rd; s/d $50/60; ☼ May-Sep) This large farmhouse at Lambert's Cove features three guest rooms on the second floor and a charming steak-and-seafood **restaurant** (☼ 11am-10pm in summer) on the first floor.

45th Parallel Motel & Restaurant (☎ 506-747-2231; parallel45th@hotmail.com; 941 Hwy 772, Fairhaven; mains $9-14; ☼ 11am-9pm early Jun–mid-Sep; noon-2pm Tue & Thu, 5pm-10pm Fri & Sat, noon-7pm Sun mid-Sep–May) The specialty is seafood at this small, rustic, country classic with a homey feel and great food. Ask to see Herman, the monster lobster. The motel rooms are a fine bargain, too.

Deer Island Point Park (☎ 506-747-2423; www .deerislandpointpark.com; 195 Deer Island Point Rd; tent sites $16; ☺ Jun–Sep) Set up your tent on the high bluff and spend an evening watching the Old Sow whirlpool. The campground is directly above the Campobello ferry landing.

GETTING THERE & AWAY

A free government-run ferry (25 minutes) runs to Deer Island from Letete, which is 14½km south of St George on Hwy 172 via Back Bay. The ferries run year-round every half hour from 7am to 7pm, and hourly from 7pm to 10pm. Get in line early on a busy day.

East Coast Ferries (☎ 506-747-2159, 877-747-2159; ☺ end Jun–mid-Sep), a private company, links Deer Island Point to Eastport, Maine, an attractive seaside town. It leaves for Eastport every hour on the hour from 9am to 6pm; it costs $10 per car and driver, plus $2 for each additional passenger.

For service to Campobello, see p501.

Campobello Island

The atmosphere on Campobello is remarkably different from that on Deer Island. It's a gentler and more prosperous island, with straight roads and better facilities. The wealthy have long been enjoyed Campobello as a summer retreat. Due to its accessibility and proximity to New England, it feels as much a part of the USA as of Canada, and most of the tourists here are Americans.

Like many moneyed families, the Roosevelts bought property in this peaceful coastal area at the end of the 1800s and it is for this that the island is best known. The southern half of Campobello is almost all park and a golf course occupies still more.

ORIENTATION & INFORMATION

There isn't even a gas station on the island; to fill their tanks, the 1200 residents of Campobello must cross the bridge to Lubec, Maine. They generally use the same bridge to go elsewhere in New Brunswick, as the Deer Island ferry only runs in summer (see opposite).

Tourist Office (☎ 506-752-7043; ☺ 9am-7pm Jul & Aug , 10am-6pm late May–Jun & Sep–early Oct) With currency exchange, it's 500m from the bridge.

SIGHTS & ACTIVITIES

The southernmost green area is the 1200-hectare **Roosevelt Campobello International Park** (☎ 506-752-2922; www.fdr.net; Hwy 774; admission free; ☺ 10am-6pm late-May–Oct), the site of the Roosevelt mansion and a visitor center. There are free guided tours of the 34-room 'cottage' where Franklin D Roosevelt grew up (between 1905 and 1921) and which he visited periodically throughout his time as US president (1933–45).

Adjacent **Hubbard House** (admission free), built in 1898, is open to visitors. The grounds around all of these buildings are open all the time, and you can peek through the windows when the doors are closed. The park is just 2.5km from the Lubec bridge, and from the Roosevelt mansion's front porch you can look directly across to Eastport, Maine. You'd hardly know you were in Canada.

Unlike the manicured museum area, most of the international park has been left in its natural state to preserve the flora and fauna that Roosevelt appreciated so much. A couple of gravel roads meander through it, leading to beaches and 7.5km of nature trails. It's a surprisingly wild, little-visited part of Campobello Island. Deer, moose and coyote call it home and seals can sometimes be seen offshore on the ledges near Lower Duck Pond, 6km from the visitor center. Look for eagles, ospreys and loons.

Along the international park's northern boundary is **Herring Cove Provincial Park** (admission free). This park has another 10km of walking trails as well as a campground and a picnic area on an arching 1.5km beach. It makes a fine, picturesque place for lunch.

Ten kilometers north of Roosevelt Park, **Wilson's Beach** has a large pier with fish for sale, and a sardine-processing plant with an adjacent store. There are various services and shops here in the island's biggest community.

Four kilometers north of Wilson's Beach, **East Quoddy Head** is the second busiest visitor spot with a lighthouse at the northern tip of the island. Whales browse offshore and many people sit along the rocky shoreline with a pair of binoculars enjoying the sea breezes.

TOURS

Island Cruises (☎ 506-752-1107, 888-249-4400; 62 Harbour Head Rd, Wilson's Beach; 2½hr tours adult/child

$45/28; ⏰ mid-Jun–Oct) offers 2½-hour whale-watching cruises.

Piskahegan River Company (☎ 506-755-6269, 800-640-8944; www.piskahegan.com; 2455 Hwy 774, Wilson's Beach; ⏰ Jun–mid-Sep) operates out of Pollock Cove Cottages. The company offers kayaking tours (three-hour/half-day $30/60) around Campobello, but you must call ahead for reservations.

SLEEPING
Lupine Lodge (☎ 506-752-2555; www.lupinelodge.com; 610 Hwy 774; s & d $50-125; ⏰ Jun–Oct) This unusual inn, 800m from Roosevelt Campobello International Park on the way from Welshpool, has 11 rooms in two large log cabin–style structures. The sunsets are mesmerizing.

Herring Cove Provincial Park (☎ 506-752-7010; fax 506-752-7012; www.tourismnewbrunswick.ca; 136 Herring Cove Rd; tent/RV sites $22/24; ⏰ mid-May–early Oct) This 76-site park on the east side of the island, 3km from the Deer Island ferry, has some nice secluded sites in a forest setting. It's preferable to Deer Island Point Park and makes a good base for visiting the adjacent international park, plus has a sandy beach and ample hiking.

EATING
Eating choices on the island are not abundant, but that doesn't mean you can't play gourmet.

Lupine Lodge (mains $15-20; ⏰ lunch & dinner). The best bet on the island. The dining room in the 1915 lodge (built by cousins of the Roosevelts) is lined with wood and features an immense stone fireplace. The specialty is seafood – fresh fish, scallops and lobster – but steaks are offered too. The deck is a fine place to have a drink and watch the sun sink.

Family Fisheries Restaurant (☎ 506-752-2470; Hwy 774, Wilson's Beach; mains $5-20; ⏰ lunch & dinner mid-Apr–late Oct) Complete with its own fish market, the specialty is seafood, especially fish and chips and chowders. This very casual spot also has sandwiches and burgers.

GETTING THERE & AWAY
East Coast Ferries (☎ 506-747-2159, 877-747-2159) connects Deer Island to Campobello Island, costing $13 per car and driver plus $2 per additional passenger. The ferry departs every half hour between 8:30am and 6:30pm (6pm in June and September). It's a scenic 25-minute trip from Deer Island past numerous islands, arriving at Welshpool, halfway up the 16km-long island.

Grand Manan Island
Grand Manan is the largest of the Fundy Isles and perhaps best typifies their allure. It's an idyllic, relaxed and engaging island of spectacular coastal topography, internationally renowned bird-watching, splendid hiking and sandy beaches. A series of small fishing villages are dotted along its 30km length.

In 1831, James Audubon first documented the many birds which frequented the island. About 312 species, including puffins and arctic terns, live here or pass by each year, so birders come in numbers too. Offshore from June onward it's not uncommon to see whales feeding on the abundant herring and mackerel.

The island's relative isolation and low-key development mean there are no crowds and little obvious commercialization. Some people make it a day trip, but lingering is recommended.

INFORMATION
Visitor Information Centre (VIC; ☎ 506-662-3442, 888-525-1655; www.grandmanannb.com; 130 Rte 772; ⏰ 10am-4pm Mon-Sat, 1-5pm Sun Jun-Oct) At the south edge of North Head.

SIGHTS
In North Head, across the street from the ferry terminal, the **Whale & Sea Bird Research Station** (☎ 506-662-3804; 24 Hwy 776; admission by donation; ⏰ 8:30am-5pm Jul & Aug, 10am-4pm mid-May–Jun & Sep) provides good information about the area's marine life. Exhibits include skeletons and photographs.

On the north side of Grand Harbour, the **Grand Manan Museum** (☎ 506-662-3524; 1141 Hwy 776; adult/student $4/2; ⏰ 10am-4:30pm Tue-Sat Jun-Sep) has a marine section, displays on the island's geology, antiques and reminders of the Loyalist days, but the highlight is the stuffed-bird collection with examples of species seen on the island. US writer Willa Cather spent summers here for years and some of her belongings, including a typewriter, remain. There's a good selection of books for sale, and birding checklists for the island.

Seal Cove flourished during the epoch of the smoked herring (1870–1930), and many wooden structures remain from that time including numerous smokehouses along the harbor. Purse seiners still fish for herring and Connors Brothers has a cannery here, but the biggest catch is lobster.

ACTIVITIES

Grand Manan features more than 18 marked and maintained paths covering 70km of some of the finest **hiking trails** in New Brunswick. The most extensive system is at the north end of the island, near Long Eddy Point Lighthouse, and several can be linked for an overnight trek. For details, buy *Heritage Trails and Foot Paths on Grand Manan* ($5) at the Grand Manan Museum.

Highly recommended is the somewhat pulse-quickening (especially in the fog) walk via a footbridge out to the lighthouse at Swallows Tail on a narrow cliff-edged promontory. The views of the coast and sea are great. To get to the lighthouse, turn right as you leave the ferry – it's only 1km. The walk around and beyond the **Southwest Head** lighthouse along the edge of the 180m cliffs should not be missed. Unlimited hiking possibilities extend in both directions.

South of Seal Cove, **Anchorage Provincial Park** (☎ 506-662-7022; btwn Grand Harbour & Seal Cove) is good for bird-watching – wild turkeys and pheasant are common.

TOURS

Several operators run whale-watching trips and guarantee results (see a whale or you get your money back) – this is one of the best places in Atlantic Canada to see the whales. Peak whale-watching begins in mid-July and continues through September.

Adventure High (☎ 506-662-3563; www.adventure high.com; 83 Hwy 776, North Head; ☺ mid-May–Oct) Around 600m to the left of the ferry wharf; offers sea kayak tours (half-/full-day $55/100). The two-hour sunset tour is $40. Adventure High also rents out bicycles (half-/full-day $16/22).

Sea Watch Tours (☎ 506-662-8552, 877-662-8552; www.seawatchtours.com; Seal Cove; adult/child/youth $46/26/36) Has been around since 1969 and knows these waters. Most of the company's wildlife-viewing tours are long (up to six hours), so take lunch, a motion sickness pill and a warm sweater. Whale sightings on these trips are almost certain and you often see the endangered northern right whale. In midsummer these tours are often booked out several days in advance.

SLEEPING

Swallowtail Inn (☎ 506-662-1100; www.swallowtail inn.com; 50 Lighthouse Rd, North Head; s/d incl breakfast from $70/85; ☺ May-Sep) For romantics, this inn with six guest rooms is awesome. It's not the prissiest place but that just adds to the remarkable ambience of the former lightkeeper's home beside the light above North Head. From the stoop, commanding views stretch in three directions. And what a walk to the front door! Beware the foghorn.

Manan Island Inn (☎ 506-662-8624; mananisland inn@nb.aibn.com; 22 Rte 776 North Head; d incl breakfast $90) Right by the ferry terminal, find this lovely Victorian house with eight rooms. Guests can use the fridge and microwave, as well as the sitting room that evokes another era.

Surfside Motel (☎ 506-662-8156, 877-662-8156; gmsurfsidemotel@yahoo.ca; 123 Hwy 776, North Head; s/d from $70/80) This is the only motel on Grand Manan Island, and while it isn't much to look at, it's clean and the location is perfect: close to town and on the water with a beach.

Shorecrest Lodge (☎ 506-662-3216; www.shore crestlodge.com; 100 Hwy 776, North Head; r $75-120) This cozy 10-room guest house, 700m to the left from the ferry, has just been bought by a couple from Cape Cod who plan to do numerous upgrades while maintaining the old charm. They also intend to uphold the dining room's impeccable reputation.

Harrington Cove Cottages (☎ 506-662-3868; Rte 776, Harrington Cove; r $90) Up the island, past Seal Cove, are these summery-looking cedar cabins, scattered on a hill and affording fine views from their own decks. Cheaper weekly rates are offered.

Anchorage Provincial Park (☎ 506-662-7022; btwn Grand Harbour & Seal Cove; tent/RV sites $22/25; ☺ mid-May–early Oct) The island's best camping is 16km from the ferry. There's a kitchen shelter for rainy days, a playground, laundromat and long sandy beach. It's possible to book ahead, but the staff never turn anyone away. Get down by the trees to block the wind. Anchorage adjoins some marshes, which comprise a migratory bird sanctuary, and there are several short hiking trails.

EATING

The never abundant options are nearly nonexistent in the off-season (from October to early June). That said, there is some fine eating on Grand Manan, often in lodging establishments' dining rooms, for which reservations are required. North Head has by far the widest selection.

Inn at Whale Cove (☎ 506-662-3181; 26 Whale Cove Cottage Rd; mains $15-22; ☾ dinner) Get out of town for a top-quality dinner in a fabulous setting. Look for the buoys hanging on a tree 1.2km from Rte 776 on the right hand side of Whale Cove Rd and turn down the lane. Call ahead to arrange one of the mouthwatering seafood meals.

Also noteworthy is the dining room at the blue **Compass Rose** (☎ 506-662-8570; 65 Rte 776; mains $14-20; ☾ lunch & dinner), in a bright little room overlooking the sea.

Fundy House Restaurant (☎ 506-662-8341; 1303 Hwy 776, Grand Harbour; meals $5-15; ☾ 7:30am-11pm Mon-Sat, noon-11pm Sun Jun-Sep; 11am-9pm Mon-Sat Oct-May) It's reliable and offers some seafood among the basic standards which include pizza. There's no sign, just 'Seafood' written on the roof.

North Head Bakery (☎ 506-662-8862; 199 Hwy 776, North Head) The seasonal bakery makes up quality bread along with rolls, pastries, cakes and pies. Coffee is served.

Something to sample on the island is the dulce, an edible seaweed for which the island is renowned. It's a very popular snack food around the Maritimes and connoisseurs say this is the best there is. It's sold mostly from people's homes; watch for signs.

GETTING THERE & AWAY
Coastal Transport Ltd (☎ 506-662-3724, 506-456-3842; www.coastaltransport.ca; North Head) operates the ferry service from Blacks Harbour to Grand Manan. Actually, there are two ferries – one old and one new. The MS *Grand Manan V*, built in 1990, is larger and quicker, knocking a half-hour off the two-hour trip. The older MV *Grand Manan* is used at peak periods or during the off-season. Both ferries have cafeterias. Seeing a whale during the trip is not uncommon.

The round-trip fare is $9.60/4.80 per adult/child and $28.75 for a car. The trip is free on the way over – just board and go. Pay on the way back. Advance-ticket sales are available at North Head and are *strongly* advised.

In July and August there are seven daily trips Monday through Saturday and six on Sunday, but there are still usually lines and there's no reservation system. Arrive (very)

early. For walk-ons and bicycles, there is never a problem. From September to the end of June the number of trips drops to three or four a day.

If the line of cars at Blacks Harbour is endless, consider doing Grand Manan as a day cruise (board the same boat, but leave the car behind). There's free parking and, depending on the season, you'll have between four and 10 hours on the island between ferries. Summer is the best time to do this as you'll be able to stand out on deck, whales will be in the area, everything in North Head will be open and you'll have a better choice of return ferries.

BLACKS HARBOUR
Sardine lovers will note this is home of Connor Brothers, one of the world's largest producers of that delectable little fish-in-a-can. Two thousand people work here. Connor Brothers' trademark brand is Brunswick Sardines and the company runs a **factory outlet store** (☎ 506-456-3897) behind Silver King Restaurant in the center of town. Load up!

Bayview B&B (☎ 506-456-1982; www.bbexpo.com/nb/bayview.htm; 391 Deadmans Harbour Rd; s/d with shared bathroom $45/50), a bayside family house about 4km from the Grand Manan ferry, offers three rooms (two with double beds and one with two single beds) in the renovated 18th-century house.

NEW RIVER PROVINCIAL PARK
Just off Hwy 1, about 35km west of Saint John on the way to St Stephen, this large **park** (☎ 506-755-4042) has one of the best beaches along the Fundy Shore, a wide stretch of sand bordered on one side by the rugged coastline of Barnaby Head. During camping season the park charges a $5 fee per vehicle for day use which includes parking at the beach and Barnaby Head trailhead.

You can spend an enjoyable few hours hiking Barnaby Head along a 6km network of nature trails. The **Chittick's Beach Trail** leads through coastal forest and past four coves, where you can check the catch in a herring weir or examine tidal pools for marine life. Extending from this loop is the 2.5km **Barnaby Head Trail**, which hugs the shoreline most of the way and rises to the edge of a cliff 15m above the Bay of Fundy.

The park's **campground** (☎ 506-755-4042; newriver@gnb.ca; 78 New River Beach Rd; tent/RV sites

$22/24; late May–early Oct) is across the road from the beach and features 100 secluded sites, both rustic and with hookups, in a wooded setting. Drawbacks are the gravel emplacements and traffic noise.

SAINT JOHN

The port city is an intriguing mix. It's a gritty working town steeped in visible history. It has an active sense of preservation and heritage, yet is not overly gentrified. The busy downtown is concentrated, walkable and offers plenty of culture yet retains an edge. When the sun shines, the city is physically appealing, with its hills and jagged bays and bridges; when it's foggy, it's thick with atmosphere. All told, it makes the province's best urban stop.

The protected downtown area reflects Saint John's proud past. It's known as the 'Loyalist City' for the thousands of late 18th-century refugees who settled here, and evidence of this background is plentiful. It has deservedly won honors for maintaining Canada's most intact collection of 19th-century commercial architecture.

Saint John (the name is always spelled out in full, never abbreviated, to avoid confusion with St John's, Newfoundland) is the province's largest city and main industrial center. Sitting on the bay at the mouth of the Saint John River, it is a major year-round port. The dry dock is one of the world's largest and the huge Irving conglomerate is headquartered here. The city has also become a major cruise-ship stopover, hosting dozens of ships annually.

HISTORY

The Maliseet Aboriginal people were here when the British and French began squabbling about furs. Though Samuel de Champlain had landed in 1604, the area remained pretty much a wilderness until 1783, when about 7000 people loyal to Britain arrived from republican America.

The Loyalists were the true founders of Saint John, turning a fort site into Canada's first legal city, incorporated in 1785. Between 1844 and 1848, some 35,000 Irish immigrants arrived, fleeing a famine in Ireland, and enough stayed that today they comprise the city's largest ethnic group.

By the mid-19th century Saint John had become a prosperous industrial town, important particularly for its wooden shipbuilding. Though it now uses iron and steel rather than wood, shipbuilding is still a major industry. In 1877, two-thirds of the city, including most of the mercantile district, was reduced to ashes by fire. It was soon rebuilt. Today, ethnic diversity is slowly emerging, with small but expanding communities from Latin America, the Caribbean, Lebanon and Asia. Despite this, economic growth is lethargic.

ORIENTATION

Downtown (known as Uptown) Saint John sits on a square peninsula between the mouth of the Saint John River and Courtenay Bay. Kings Sq marks the nucleus of town, and its pathways duplicate the pattern of the Union Jack. Water St borders the redeveloped waterfront area with Market Sq.

The district south of Kings Sq is known as the **South End** with Queens Sq at its heart. On Courtenay Bay, to the east, are the dry dock, shipbuilding yards and much heavy industry. North of town is Rockwood Park, a recreational area.

West over the Harbour Bridge (25¢ toll) is **Saint John West**. Many of the street names in this section of the city are identical to those of Saint John proper, and to avoid confusion, they end in a west designation, such as Charlotte St W. Saint John West has the ferries to Digby, Nova Scotia.

INFORMATION

Main Post Office (☎ 506-672-6704; 41 Church Ave West, Postal Station B, E2M 4X6; 8am-5pm Mon-Fri) In Saint John West. Send general delivery mail here.

Police, Fire & Ambulance (☎ 911) For emergencies.

Saint John Library (☎ 506-643-7220; 1 Market Sq; 9am-5pm Mon & Sat, 10am-5pm Tue & Wed, 10am-9pm Thu & Fri) Free Internet access.

Saint John Regional Hospital (☎ 506-648-6000; 400 University Ave; 24hr) Emergency room.

St Joseph's Hospital (☎ 506-632-5555; 130 Bayard Dr; emergency room 7am-10pm) On the north side of downtown.

Visitor & Convention Bureau (☎ 506-658-2990, 888-364-4444; www.tourismsaintjohn.com; Market Sq; 9:30am-8pm mid-Jun–Aug, to 6pm Sep–mid-Jun) Knowledgeable, friendly staff. Ask for the self-guided walking-tour pamphlets. Reversing Falls also has a seasonal visitors center (see p506).

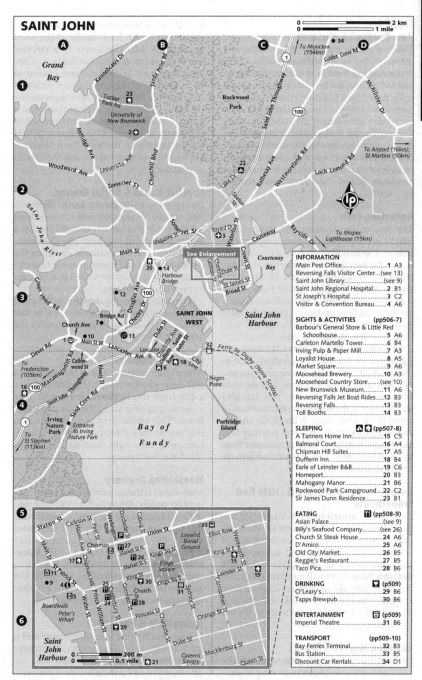

SIGHTS

New Brunswick Museum

This is a quality **museum** (☎ 506-643-2300; www .gnb.ca/0130; 1 Market Sq; adult/student/family $6/3.25/13; ❧ 9am-5pm Mon-Wed & Fri, to 9pm Thu, 10am-5pm Sat, noon-5pm Sun; closed Mon Nov–mid-May) with a varied collection. There's a captivating section on marine wildlife with an outstanding section on whales including a life-sized specimen. The provincial bird exhibit is comprehensive and the displays on the marine history of Saint John are good, with many excellent models of old sailing ships. There are also hands-on exhibits and worthwhile temporary shows.

Reversing Falls

The Bay of Fundy tides and their effects (p515) are a predominant regional characteristic. The falls here are part of that and are one of the best-known sites in the province. However, 'reversing falls' is a bit of a misnomer. When the high Bay of Fundy tides rise, the current in the river reverses, causing the water to flow upstream. When the tides go down, the water flows in the normal way. Generally, it looks like rapids.

Reversing Falls Visitors Centre (☎ 506-658-2937; 200 Bridge Rd; ❧ 8am-7pm mid-May–early Oct), next to the bridge over the falls, can supply a *Reversing Falls Tide Table* brochure that explains where in the cycle you are. You can also watch a film at the **observation deck** (admission $2) above the tourist office. With all the visitors and tour buses during summer you may find the people-watching more of an event than the flowing water. See opposite for a more involved experience.

Barbour's General Store & Little Red Schoolhouse

The fun old **general store** (☎ 506-658-2939; Market Sq; admission free; ❧ 9am-6pm mid-Jun–mid-Sep) is packed with the kind of merchandise sold 100 years ago, including old stoves, drugs, hardware and candy. Alongside it, the **Little Red Schoolhouse** is a small museum that's also bound to provoke memories. To get a peek through the Dutch door ask at Barbour's. They don't let people in anymore as it's full of hornets!

Carleton Martello Tower

In Saint John West, this **national historic site** (☎ 506-636-4011; 545 Whipple St, cnr Fundy Dr; adult/ family $3.50/8; ❧ 10am-6pm Jun-Oct) is just off Lancaster Ave, which leads to the Digby ferry terminal. A Martello tower is a circular two-story stone coastal fortification. They were first built in England and Ireland at the beginning of the 19th century. In North America, the British built 16 of them during the early 1800s. Inside, explore the restored powder magazine, barracks and the upper two levels that were added during WWII for the defense of the Saint John Harbour. Go when there's no fog because the view is outstanding.

Loyalist House & Burial Ground

Dating from 1810, **Loyalist House** (☎ 506-652-3590; 120 Union St; adult/child/family $3/1/7; ❧ 10am-5pm Mon-Fri Jun, 10am-5pm daily Jul-Aug) is the city's oldest unchanged building. The Georgian-style place is now a museum, depicting the Loyalist period and contains some fine carpentry. The monument to the Loyalists next to the house is striking.

The mood-inducing **cemetery**, with fading tombstones from as early as 1784, is just off Kings Sq, in a park-style setting in the center of town.

Mispec Lighthouse

After the 25-minute drive to the windswept cliff here you'll swear it was 100 miles to a city from this **lighthouse** (Red Head Rd). Take a picnic and stop along the way at Mispec Beach. This exhilarating excursion is not in the tourist information. Cross Courtenay Causeway, turn right, then right onto Red Head Rd. Keep going.

Moosehead Brewery

Moosehead is the country's oldest independent beer maker, dating back to 1867, the year of Confederation. At the time of research the free tours and tastings had been suspended due to the all-too familiar contemporary security and insurance fears. Call the **Moosehead Country Store** (☎ 506-635-7020; 49 Main St W; admission free; ❧ 9am-5pm Mon-Wed, 9am-9pm Thu & Fri, 10am-5pm Sat) for the latest news. The store has great logo attire for all you mooseheads.

Irving Pulp & Paper Mill

Seeing (and hearing) a modern paper mill is quite an educational experience. To arrange a free tour of **Irving Pulp & Paper Mill**, call ☎ 506-635-7749 during business hours.

ACTIVITIES

Beginning on a boardwalk at Market Sq (behind the Hilton hotel), **Harbour Passage** is a walk and cycle trail that leads around the harbor and naval facility across the toll bridge to Reversing Falls. Informative plaques line the route and it's about 45-minutes one-way right after Reversing Falls. In the other direction, it is to be continued along the revamped port lands downtown.

For those with vehicles and an apprecia-tion of nature, **Irving Nature Park** (☎ 506-653-7367; west end of Sand Cove Rd; admission free; ☷ 8am-dusk early May–early Nov) is a must for its rug-ged, unspoiled coastal topography. It's also a remarkable place for bird-watching, with hundreds of species regularly reported. Seals may be seen on rocks offshore. Though the park is said to be on Taylors Island, this is not an island at all but rather a 245-hectare mountainous peninsula protruding into the Bay of Fundy. Seven trails of varying lengths lead around beaches, cliffs, woods, mudflats, marsh and rocks. Good footwear is recom-mended. The perimeter can be driven on a 6.5km dirt road. It's well worth the 5km drive southwest from downtown to get here. Take Hwy 1 west from town and turn south at Exit 107, Bleury St. Then turn right on Sand Cove Rd and continue for 2km to the entrance.

TOURS

Many have asked, but whale-watching is not an attraction in Saint John, save for the very occasional, very wayward minke.

Gray Line (☎ 506-631-0172, 866-276-1111; www.gray line.com; ☷ mid-Jun–mid-Sep) From Barbour's General Store in Market Sq, there are guided walks around historic downtown ($13) at 10am and 2pm daily. Also two trips to St Andrews, one for general sight-seeing ($83) and one with a whale-watching cruise ($109).

Reversing Falls Jet Boat Rides (☎ 506-634-8987; www.jetboatrides.com; ☷ Jun–mid-Oct) Offers two types of trips. The one-hour slow boat trips (adult/child $32/25) to the Reversing Falls and around the harbor depart from Market Sq. There are also 20-minute jet-boat rides ($30) through the whitewater at Reversing Falls. Count on get-ting soaked. For extremists, there is also an open, plastic, bubble-cage for one that bobs through the turbulence ($100) – it was nice knowing you.

Saint John Transit Commission (☎ 506-658-4700) Runs 2½-hour bus tours (adult/child $16/5) around the city mid-June to early October. Departures and tickets from Reversing Falls Visitor Centre, Barbour's General Store at

Market Sq and Rockwood Park Campground. Two tours daily. At 9:30am the bus leaves Reversing Falls and takes 15 minutes to get to each of the other two stops. The trip is reversed from 12:30pm to 1pm.

FESTIVALS & EVENTS

Loyalist Days (☎ 888-364-4444; ☷ 3rd week of Jul) This eight-day event celebrates the city's Loyalist background with a re-creation of the first arrival, period costumes, parades, crafts, music, food, and fireworks on the last night.

Festival by the Sea (www.festivalbythesea.com; ☷ early Aug) For 10 days this very popular, highly regarded perform-ing arts event presents hundreds of singers, dancers and other performers from across Canada in concerts and shows put on throughout the city night and day. Many of the performances staged in parks and along the harborfront are free.

Grand Ole Atlantic National Exhibition (☎ 506-633-2020; ☷ end Aug) Held in Exhibition Park, this event includes stage shows, livestock judging, harness racing and a large midway (fairground).

SLEEPING
Budget

Saint John motels sit primarily along Mana-wagonish Rd, 7km west of the downtown, and its continuation Ocean West Way, the old Hwy 100 west of town. Rothesay Ave (Hwy 100 eastbound) has a few more, and though more expensive, they're closer to town.

Balmoral Court (☎ 506-672-3019; 1281 Manawag-onish Rd; s/d $52/57) Aside from the standard units, there are cute little individual cabins at this quiet, clean, low-cost, friendly choice.

Sir James Dunn Residence (☎ 506-648-5755; www
.unbsj.ca/hfs; off Sandy Point Rd near Rockwood Park; s/d
$29/42, students $21/32; P) The simple rooms of
Sir James Dunn Residence at the University of New Brunswick Saint John Campus,
6km north of the city center (take bus No
15 from Kings Sq), are available from May
to September.

Rockwood Park (☎ 506-652-4050; www.sn2000.nb
.ca/comp/rockwood-park-campground; Lake Drive South;
tent/RV sites $15/20; ☽ mid-May–early Oct) Just
north of Rothesay Ave, a couple of kilometers north of the downtown area, is huge
Rockwood Park, with small lakes and part
of the university campus. Too bad every city
doesn't have camping this fine so close to
the center – and with a view! Bus No 6 to
Mt Pleasant from Kings Sq comes within a
few blocks Monday to Saturday.

Mid-Range

Earle of Leinster B&B (☎ 506-652-3275; leinster@nbnet
.nb.ca; 96 Leinster St; s $45-80, d $65-90) Lauree and
Steve make this 1878 Victorian townhouse
and quiet annex a fine, amiable place, just
a short walk from Kings Sq. It has seven
rooms, each with a private bathroom. Rates
include laundry facilities, VCR with videos
and even popcorn! There's a $5 discount for
cash and off-season rates.

Mahogany Manor (☎ 506-636-8000, 800-796-7755;
www.sjnow.com/mm; 220 Germain St; d incl breakfast $95;
P) Get ready for comfort. This lovingly
restored, gay-friendly, antique-filled, early
20th-century home has it all, including
tasteful guest rooms. The expansive garden,
seemingly out in the countryside, comes
complete with a spot for massages. The upbeat owners know more about the city than
you'll absorb, even which meal to order at
which restaurant!

A Tanners Home Inn (☎ 506-634-8917, 877-634-
8917; www.tannershomeinn.com; 190 King St E; r $100-
110) Just blocks to downtown, the restored
former tanner's house from 1878 is a warm,
casual B&B that often puts up visiting performers in the three spacious rooms (one
with private bathroom). Never mind the dog
the size of a buffalo; he's a softy.

Chipman Hill Suites (☎ 506-693-1171; www.chip
manhill.com; 9 Chipman Hill; ste $70-130) What a great
concept! Chipman has taken 10 historic properties around downtown, renovated them
into mini-apartments with kitchens while
leaving all the character, and rents them out

by the day, week or month. Size and features
determine price, but all are a steal.

Top End

Homeport (☎ 506-672-7255; 888-678-7678; www
.homeport.nb.ca; 60 Douglas Ave; r incl breakfast $85-165;
P) Perched above grand, historic Douglas Ave, Homeport mansion offers a range
of well-appointed rooms, afternoon tea in
the traditional parlor, a great-start morning
meal and a flowering garden.

Also recommended is **Dufferin Inn** (☎ 506-
635-5968, 866-383-3466; www.dufferininn.com; 357 Dufferin Row; P), which has a highly regarded,
European-influenced dining room.

EATING

Budget

Old City Market (☎ 506-658-2820; 47 Charlotte St;
☽ 7:30am-6pm Mon-Thu, 7:30am-7pm Fri, 7:30am-5pm Sat)
Wedged between North and South Market
Sts is this sense-stunning, bustling market,
which has been home to wheeling and dealing since 1876. Apart from the fresh produce
stalls, which are at peak activity on Saturday
when local farmers arrive, there are numerous counters selling a range of delectable prepared meals and foods, even lobster.

Reggie's Restaurant (☎ 506-657-6270; 26 Germain
St; items under $7; ☽ 6am-5pm Mon-Sat, 7am-5pm Sun)
Since 1969, this classic, no-nonsense diner
downtown has fed the city. Great breakfasts
(Montréal-style bagels), soups, sandwiches
and the jovial environment are the draws.
The lobster roll, a Maritime specialty, is
chunks of the meat in a hotdog-like bun
eaten cold. Place your order at the counter.

Mid-Range

Taco Pica (☎ 506-633-8492; 96 Germain St; mains
$10-17; ☽ 10am-10pm Mon-Sat) Among the best
ethnic cuisine in Saint John is the fusion
of authentic Guatemalan and Mexican fare
served here. An economical introduction to
the cuisine is *pepian* ($9), a simple but spicy
beef stew that is as good as you'll find in
any Guatemalan household. The soft-shell
tacos served in this airy room are also noteworthy.

D'Amico (☎ 506-648-2377; 33 Canterbury St; mains
$15; ☽ lunch & dinner) A good place for a date
(especially on the second level), heralded
d'Amico's comes with a comfortable, contemporary design, does Italian favorites well
and also has specialty pizzas.

Asian Palace (☎ 506-642-4909; Market Sq; lunch specials $8, dinner mains $8-17; ☻ lunch & dinner) The Palace prepares exquisite Indian fare in a Western-style dining room. Specialties include tandoori (24-hour notice required for the exceptional mogul chicken), spicy curries and vindaloos. There are also a dozen vegetarian selections.

Top End

Church St Steak House (☎ 506-672-3463; 10 Church St; lunch $15, dinner $18-28; ☻ lunch Mon-Fri, dinner) To get to the best steakhouse in town, you have to go down the alley here and then up the fire-escape-like staircase. But there's nothing lowbrow about the historic room or the kitchen's output.

DRINKING & ENTERTAINMENT

Club action can be found in two main areas: in Market Sq, where the clubs have outdoor patios; and around the corner of Princess and Prince William Sts, where busy, noisy bars come and go.

Tapps Brewpub (☎ 506-634-1957; 78 King St; ☻ 11am-midnight Mon-Thu, 11-2am Fri & Sat, 4-10pm Sun) The House of Brews makes a half-dozen of its own beers on the premises. The Marco Polo is most popular, but consider the nut brown ale. There's also pub grub if you need something solid, and sometimes live music.

O'Leary's (☎ 506-634-7135; 46 Princess St; ☻ 11:30am-11pm Tue, 11:30-1:30am Wed-Fri, 11-1:30am Sat) This is a good old-fashioned, long-running Irish pub with plenty of British and Irish brews, as well as live music on Thursday to Saturday evenings. On Wednesday it's open-mic night.

Imperial Theatre (☎ 506-674-4100; 24 Kings Sq S; ☻ box office 10am-7pm Mon-Fri, noon-4pm Sat) Now restored to its original 1913 splendor, the Imperial is the city's premier venue for performances ranging from classical music to live theater. Call for schedule and ticket information.

GETTING THERE & AWAY
Air

The airport is east of town on Loch Lomond Rd toward St Martins. Air Canada and Air Canada Tango have flights to Montréal (one-way $180), Toronto ($190) and Halifax ($80) three or four times daily. A 'passenger facility charge' of $10 must be paid at the gate.

THE AUTHOR'S CHOICE

Billy's Seafood Company (☎ 506-672-3474; City Market, 47 Charlotte St, City Market; mains $17-22; ☻ 11am-10pm Mon-Sat, 4-10pm Sun) If the ocean fare was any fresher you'd be up to your waist in saltwater. Spanning the mid-range and top end categories, Billy's is a seafood outlet in the always vibrant market. The restaurant is attached to the counters of ice displaying the day's catch. It's a casual, friendly place that's all about the food and it's fabulous. For budgeters, get an appetizer and/or the chowder. For landlubbers, there is lamb and pasta and other delicious options.

Boat

There's a daily ferry service between Saint John and Digby, Nova Scotia (for more information, see p484).

Bus

The **bus station** (☎ 506-648-3500; 300 Union St; ☻ 7:30am-9pm Mon-Fri, 8am-9pm Sat & Sun) is a five-minute walk from downtown and served by Acadian Lines. There are services to Fredericton ($20, 1½ hours) and to Moncton ($26, two hours), with one morning and one afternoon trip in each direction. There's also a direct service to Bangor, Maine ($28, 3½ hours), on Friday and Saturday.

GETTING AROUND
To/From the Airport

City bus No 22 links the airport and Kings Sq. **Diamond Taxi** (☎ 506-648-0666) operates an airport shuttle costing $13. It leaves approximately 1½ hours before all flights, and runs to and from hotels like the Hilton on Market Sq and the Delta Brunswick on Brunswick Sq. For a taxi, call **Vets** (☎ 506-658-2020), which charges $27 for the first person plus $3 for each additional person.

Bus

Saint John Transit (☎ 506-658-4700) has 30 routes around the city; the fare is $2. The most important is the east–west bus service, which is either No 1 or 2 eastbound to McAllister Dr and No 3 or 4 westbound to Saint John West near the ferry terminal. It stops at Kings Sq in the city center. Another frequent bus service is No 15 or 16 to the university.

Car & Motorcycle

Discount Car Rentals (☎ 506-633-4440; 622 Rothesay Ave) is opposite the Park Plaza Motel. Avis, Budget, Hertz and National all have car-rental desks at the airport.

Parking meters in Saint John cost $1 an hour from 8am to 6pm weekdays only. You can park free at meters on weekends, holidays and in the evening. The parking meters on Sydney St south of Kings Sq allow up to 10 hours of free parking on weekends and holidays. Park free anytime on back streets such as Leinster and Princess Sts, east of Kings Sq. The **city parking lot** (11 Sydney St) is free on weekends.

EASTERN FUNDY SHORE

Much of the rugged, unspoiled Eastern Fundy Shore from Saint John to Hopewell Cape remains essentially untouched. Indeed, hikers, cyclists, kayakers and all nature lovers will be enchanted by this marvelous coast, edged by dramatic cliffs and tides. It's still not possible to drive directly along the coastline from St Martins to Fundy National Park; a detour inland by Sussex is necessary, unless you're prepared to hike.

ST MARTINS

A 40km drive east of Saint John, St Martins is a lovely, quintessential postcard village with a river, two covered bridges, fishing boats and red cliffs. Don't forget the camera. Once a somnolent wooden shipbuilding center, it's now garnering new attention due to the coastal recreational parkway, opened in 1998. For those with time, littoral Gardner Creek, en route on meandering Rte 825 from Saint John, has 8km of untouched beach.

Sights & Activities

The many fine, oversized homes reflect the wealth of the shipbuilding era (1803–1919). For details, visit the seasonal, unassuming **Quaco Museum** (☎ 506-833-4740; 236 Main St; ☿ noon-5pm Sat & Sun, May–mid-Jun, noon-5pm daily mid-June–Labour Day, noon-5pm Sat & Sun Labour Day–Oct).

Explore the **caves** at the far end of the vast expanse of beach.

FUNDY TRAIL PARKWAY

The **parkway** (☎ 506-833-2019; www.fundytrailparkway.com; adult/child/family $3/2/10; ☿ 6am-8pm mid-May–Oct) features a rugged section of what has been called the only remaining coastal wilderness between Florida and Newfoundland. The 11km-long parkway to Big Salmon River is a lovely stretch of pavement with numerous viewpoints and picnic areas. Eventually, it will extend to Fundy National Park. Nova Scotia is visible across the bay. A separate 16km-long hiking/biking trail also winds its way along.

Pedestrians and cyclists can enter free. In the off-season, the main gate is closed, but you can always park at the entrance and hike or pedal in. On Saturdays, Sundays and holidays an hourly shuttle bus operates from noon to 6pm ferrying hikers up and down the trail between the parkway entrance and Big Salmon River. The shuttle is $3, or free if you paid to enter.

At Big Salmon River is an **interpretive center** (☿ 8am-8pm mid-May–mid-Oct) with exhibits and a 10-minute video presentation. Remains of a sawmill that existed from the 1850s to the 1940s is visible at low tide directly below the interpretive center.

A suspension bridge leads to a vast wilderness hiking area beyond the end of the road. Hikers can make it from Big Salmon River to Goose River in Fundy National Park in three to five days. At last report, no permits or permissions were required to do so. But beyond Big Salmon River, be prepared for wilderness, rocky scree and even a rope ladder or two. Some beach sections are usable only at low tide and the cliffs are unsafe to climb.

Sleeping & Eating

Seaside B&B (☎ 506-833-2481; 48 West Quaco Rd; s $55-65, d $65-85) This central, very pretty, former sea captain's home overlooks the caves and ocean. There are four rooms at this home down the shore from Main St.

St Martin's Country Inn (☎ 506-833-4534, 800-566-5257; www.stmartinscountryinn.com; 303 Main St; r $95-145) The towering mansion overlooking the bay is the most deluxe place in town and also offers delectable meals in its delightful, caught-in-time dining room.

Century Farm Family Campground (☎ 506-833-2357; www.sn2000.nb.ca/comp/century-farm-campground; 67 Ocean Wave Dr; tent/RV sites $20/22, cabins s/d $45/50; ☿ May–mid-Oct) Century Farm hosts trailers but there are also grassy sites for tents. The rustic cabins are good for up to four people.

THE TIDES OF FUNDY

The tides of the Bay of Fundy are the highest in the world. This constant ebb and flow is a prime factor in the life of the bay, the appearance of the shoreline and even how residents set shipping and fishing schedules.

A Mi'kmaq legend explains the tide as the effect of a whale's thrashing tail sending the water forever sloshing back and forth. A more prosaic explanation is in the length, depth and gradual funnel shape of the bay itself.

The contrasts between the high and ebb tide are most pronounced at the eastern end of the bay and around the Minas Basin, with tides of 10 to 15m twice daily 12½ hours apart. The highest tide ever recorded anywhere was 16.6m, the height of a four-story building, at Burncoat Head near Noel, Nova Scotia.

All tides are caused by the rise and fall of the oceans due to the gravitational pull of the sun and the moon. When the moon is full or new, the gravitational forces of the sun and moon are working in concert, and the tides at these two times of the month are higher than average. When one of these periods coincides with the time when the moon is at its closest to earth (perigee, once every 27½ days) the tides are at their most dramatic.

Local schedules are available at regional tourist offices.

Seaside Restaurant (☎ 506-833-2394; 81 Macs Beach; mains $8-13; ⏲ 9:30am-8pm) Right on the beach, near the caves just east of the covered bridge, the resort-style Seaside serves fish and chips, scallops, seafood casserole and more. Now you know you are on holiday.

FUNDY NATIONAL PARK

This **national park** (☎ 506-887-6000; www.pc.gc.ca/fundy; daily permit adult/child/family $5/2.50/12.50, season pass $25/63) is one of the country's most popular. Highlights are the world's highest tides, the irregularly eroded sandstone cliffs and the wide beach at low tide that makes exploring the shore for small marine life and debris such a treat. The park features an extensive network of hiking trails.

Fundy is also home to one of the largest concentrations of wildlife in the Maritimes, including black bear, moose, beaver and peregrine falcons. In late 2004, DNA tests on a hair in the park found it to be that of a cougar, thought by many to be extinct in the region.

Information

Both visitor centers have bookstores and information counters, and sell entry permits and season passes.

Headquarters Visitors Centre (☎ 506-887-6000; ⏲ 10am-6pm mid-Jun–early Sep, 9am-4pm early Sep–mid-Jun) At the south entrance.

Wolfe Lake Information Centre (☎ 506-432-6026; Hwy 114; ⏲ 10am-6pm late Jun-early Sep) North entrance.

Activities

HIKING

Fundy features 120km of walking trails where it's possible to enjoy anything from a short stroll to a three-day trek. Several trails require hikers to ford rivers, so be prepared.

The most popular backpacking route is the **Fundy Circuit**, a three-day trek of 48km through the heart of the park. Hikers generally spend their first night at Marven Lake and their second at Bruin Lake, returning via the Upper Salmon River. First, stop at the visitors center to reserve your wilderness campsites ($4 per person per night; call ahead for reservations).

Another overnight trek is the **Goose River Trail**. It joins the Fundy Trail, accessible by road from St Martins. This undeveloped three-day trek is one of the most difficult in the province. While you can cycle to Goose River, the trail beyond can only be done on foot. For more information, see opposite.

Enjoyable day hikes in Fundy National Park include **Coppermine Trail**, a 4.4km loop which goes to an old mine site; and **Third Vault Falls Trail**, a challenging one-way hike of 3.7km to the park's tallest falls. On a lighter note, the three-hour, ranger-led **Fundy Night Life Hike** (adult/child/family $12/8/33) at 8pm Saturday in July and August is great, if spooky, fun. Book well in advance.

CYCLING

Mountain biking is permitted on six trails: Goose River, Marven Lake, Black Hole, East

Branch, Bennett Brook (partially open) and Maple Grove. Surprisingly, at last report there were no bicycle rentals in Fundy National Park or in nearby Alma. Call the visitor centers to find current information on this.

SWIMMING
The ocean is pretty bracing here; luckily, there's a heated saltwater **swimming pool** (☎ 506-887-6014; adult/child $3/1.50; ☼ 11am-6:30pm late Jun-early Sep) not far from the park's southern entrance.

Sleeping
Fundy Highlands Inn & Chalets (☎ 506-887-2930, 800-883-8639; www.fundyhighlandchalets.com; 8714 Hwy 114; cabins $65-85; ☼ May-Oct) Of the park's three roofed options, the well-maintained choices here are recommended. The simple but charming little cabins, all with decks and superlative views, are cheaper than the newly renovated motel-like units, but both options include kitchenettes. The property is green and quiet and the owners couldn't be more helpful.

The park has five campgrounds and 13 wilderness sites. **Camping reservations** (☎ 800-414-6765, 877-737-3783; reservation fee $7.50) must be

---

KEEPING A LIGHT ON FOR YOU
New Brunswick has about 100 lighthouses including replicas, decommissioned lights and privately owned ones. About 70 authentic ones remain in operation. One of those is still staffed, a rare case in all of Atlantic Canada. It sits on miniscule Machais Island and has a keeper for reasons of sovereignty as much as anything else. Another oddity is the string of inland lights beaming along the Saint John River Valley. The only other such river in the country is the St Lawrence. The **New Brunswick Lighthouse Preservation Society** (http://nblhs.nblighthouses.com) works hard to protect and promote these romantic, historic towers. Visitors appreciate them as great places to hike, photograph, kayak, see birds, and in a few cases have lunch (Cape Enrage) or even spend a night (Swallowtail). The Quoddy Loop (see the boxed text on p498) has 12 lights including two in Maine and two in Grand Manan.

---

made at least three days in advance. The park entry fee is extra and is paid upon arrival.

Wolfe Lake Campground (campsites $13) Just an open field at the northwest entrance to the park, Wolfe Lake has no showers. However, it has the advantages of a covered cooking area and few other campers.

In the interior are the two large **Chignecto Campgrounds** (tent/RV sites $21/25). The 131-site **Headquarters Campground** (tent/RV sites $21/27) is near the visitor center. Along the coast, 8km southwest of the visitor center, is **Point Wolfe Campground** (tent sites $21) and its 181 sites with sea breezes and cooler temperatures.

To reserve a backcountry site, call either of the visitor centers.

ALMA
The tiny village of Alma is a supply center for the park. It has accommodations, restaurants, a small grocery store plus a liquor outlet and laundromat. Most facilities close in winter, when it becomes a ghost town. Down on the beach is a statue of Molly Kool, the first female sea captain on the continent. Cool.

Fresh Air Adventure (☎ 800-545-0020; www.fresh airadventure.com; 16 Fundy View Dr; ☼ late May–mid-Sep) offers myriad kayaking tours in and around Fundy, from two-hour trips to multiday excursions.

Captains Inn B&B (☎ 506-887-2017; www.captains inn.ca; 8602 Main St; s/d $65/75; ☼ year-round) is a comely blue-and-white B&B that's central and bright.

Tides Restaurant (☎ 506-887-2313; 8601 Hwy 114; mains $12-21; ☼ lunch & dinner mid-May–Oct) is the dining room at Parkland Village Inn. It prepares top-rate seafood but the ribs aren't far behind. Between the beach, the village wharf and the hummingbirds out the window it's hard to concentrate on cracking a claw. The casual take-out patio has fish 'n' chips and cold beer.

Don't bypass **Kelly's Bake Shop** (☎ 506-887-2460; 8587 Hwy 114; ☼ 10am-5pm Mon-Fri, 9am-6pm Sat & Sun May-early Oct; 7am-8pm Jul & Aug) and its legendary $1 sticky buns; fill the trunk.

Collins Seafood Lobster Shop (☎ 506-887-2054; 20 Ocean Dr; ☼ 10am-5pm Mon-Sat), behind Kelly's, sells live or cooked lobsters, plus fresh scallops, shrimps and mussels and sometimes smoked salmon. Pig out back at your campsite.

CAPE ENRAGE & MARY'S POINT

From Alma, old Rte 915 yields two sensational, yet relatively isolated, promontories high over the bay.

See the lighthouse at windblown, suitably named Cape Enrage and wander the beach. **Cape Enrage Adventures** (☎ 506-887-2273; www .capenrage.com) offers kayaking and rappelling. Have some chowder at their tiny **Keeper's Lunchroom**.

At Mary's Point, 22km east, is the **Shepody Bay Shorebird Reserve** (Mary's Point Rd, off Hwy 915; admission free). From mid-July to mid-August literally hundreds of thousands of shorebirds, primarily sandpipers, gather here. Nature trails and boardwalks lead along the dikes and marsh. The interpretive center is open from late June to early September, but you can use the 6.5km of trails anytime.

For a restful night in the countryside, a fine choice is **Sandpipers Rest B&B** (☎ 506-882-2744; www.sandpipersrest.nb.ca; 15 Mary's Point Rd, Harvey; s/d with shared bathroom $45/50, d with bathroom $60; ☿ May-Oct), from the mid 1800s, with a nice garden. It's 4km south of Riverside-Albert via Hwy 915.

HOPEWELL ROCKS

At Hopewell Cape, where the Petitcodiac River meets the Fundy waters in Shepody Bay, is the **Hopewell Rocks Ocean Tidal Exploration Site** (☎ 877-734-3429; off Hwy 114; adult/child/ family $7/5/18, shuttle extra $2; ☿ 9am-5pm mid-May– late Jun & mid-Aug–early Oct, 8am-8pm late Jun–mid-Aug). The 'rocks' are unusual erosion formations known as 'flowerpots.' The shore here is lined with these irregular geological forms, as well as caves and tunnels, all of which have been created by erosion from the great tides.

With a parking lot the size of Fredericton, it can get extremely crowded. However, an exploratory walk along the beach at low tide is still worthwhile. Check the tide tables at any tourist office, and don't get stranded on the beach when the water rushes in; it's a long wait before you can reach the stairs again! You can't hit the beach at high tide, but the rock towers are visible from the trails above.

In either event, morning is the best time for shutterbugs and has fewer visitors. Note that the ticket is good for the next day too, so you may be able to see the site at various tide levels if you return later in the day. Admission includes the interpretation center. The expansive wooded property makes for pleasant strolling and has numerous places to picnic. The walk to Demoiselle Beach provides a good chance of spotting waterfowl and migratory birds. All told, a quick visit can cheerfully stretch into several hours.

From late June to early September **Baymount Adventures** (☎ 506-734-2660, 877-601-2660; www.baymountadventures.com; adult/child $55/45) offers two-hour kayak tours of the rocks with plenty of bird life as a bonus, and a cave tour near Hillsborough. The office is 100m beyond the café inside the Exploration Site.

HILLSBOROUGH

Fourteen kilometers north of Hopewell Rocks and 20km southeast of Moncton, Hillsborough is a small town overlooking the Petitcodiac River. From here, a restored steam engine of the **Salem-Hillsborough Railroad** (☎ 506-734-3195; www.shrr.ca/en/index.shtml; 2847 Main St (Hwy 114); 1hr trip adult/family $10/25) pulls antique coaches beside the river to Salem 8km away. The train departs at 2pm every Tuesday, Wednesday, Saturday and Sunday in July and August. Once or twice a month, dinner trips roll. For buffs, the adjacent museum has some coaches and displays.

SOUTHEASTERN NEW BRUNSWICK

This corner of New Brunswick is the geographical heart of the Maritimes and, though it's without major appeal, many visitors are bound to transit through at least once. Moncton, known as 'Hub City,' is a major crossroads with two well-known attractions where nature appears to defy gravity. Southeast, en route to Nova Scotia, are significant historical and bird life attractions.

MONCTON

As the province's second city and a major transportation and distribution center for Atlantic Canada, Moncton sees a lot of through traffic, especially in summer. Due to a couple of odd attractions – Magnetic Hill and a tidal bore – it's worth a pit stop on your way past. With a few good places to enjoy a meal and spend the night, it can be an accommodating, if fleeting host.

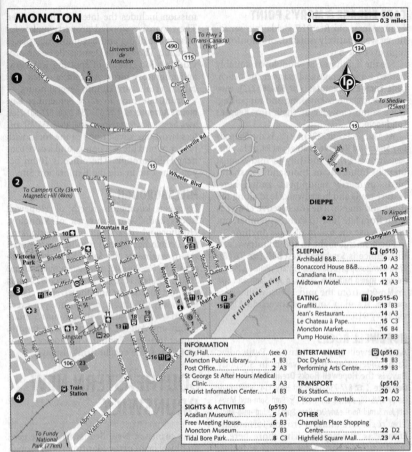

MONCTON

0 _____ 500 m
0 _____ 0.3 miles

To Hwy 2
(Trans-Canada)
(1km)

To Shediac
(25km)

Université
de
Moncton

DIEPPE

To Campers City (3km);
Magnetic Hill (4km)

To Airport
(6km)

To Fundy
National
Park (77km)

Train
Station

History

Moncton was originally on a Mi'kmaq portage route from Shediac. In the 1740s the first Acadians settled, to be followed in 1766 by Protestant German immigrants from Pennsylvania. In the mid-1800s, it became a major shipbuilding center, but falling demand for wooden ships led to the closure of Moncton's shipyards in the early 1860s. Later, it became a rail center and during WWII the city served as a transportation hub and training facility for pilots from many Allied countries. Moncton now thrives as a main service center for the Maritimes.

Today, nearly half the bilingual population has French as their mother tongue, thanks to the number of descendants of Acadians.

Orientation & Information

The small downtown area extends north and south of Main St. The river lies just to the south and the Trans-Canada Hwy (Hwy 2) runs east–west north of town. Lengthy Mountain Rd, leading west toward the Trans-Canada Hwy, is lined with service stations and chain restaurants.

Moncton Public Library (☎ 506-869-6000; 644 Main St; ⏰ 9am-8:30pm Tue-Thu, 9am-5pm Fri & Sat) Free Internet access.

St George St After Hours Medical Clinic (☎ 506-856-6122; 404 St George St; ⏰ 5:30-8pm Mon-Fri, noon-3pm Sat, Sun & holidays) No appointment is required to see a doctor. Adjacent to Jean Coutu Pharmacy.

Tourist Information Center (☎ 506-853-3590, 800-363-4558; www.gomoncton.com; Bore Park, Main

St E; 9am-8pm Jul & Aug, 9am-4:30pm late May & Sep–early-Oct, 9am-7pm Jun) From November to mid-May, find the office at City Hall, 2nd fl, 655 Main St.

Sights

At **Magnetic Hill** (☎ 506-858-8841; cnr Mountain Rd & Hwy 2; entry per car $5; 8am-8pm mid-May–mid-Sep), incredibly one of Canada's best-known (though not best-loved) attractions, gravity appears to work in reverse. Start at the bottom of the hill in a car and you'll drift upward. You figure it out. After hours and out of season, it's free. It's a goofy novelty, worth the head-scratching laugh, but all the money-generating, spin-off hoopla now surrounding the hill is nothing special. Family-oriented attractions include a zoo and water park.

Tidal Bore Park (east end of Main St; admission free; 24hr) features a twice-daily incoming wave caused by the tides of the Petitcodiac River, which are in turn related to the tides in the Bay of Fundy, the world's highest. As the tide advances up the narrowing bay it starts to build up on itself, forming a wave. The height of this oncoming rush can vary from just a few centimeters to about 1m. The size and height of the bore are determined by the tide, itself regulated by the moon. As with the tides, there are two bores a day, roughly 12 hours apart. While this is an interesting occurrence, especially in theory, the bores are often…boring.

The modest **Moncton Museum** (☎ 506-856-4382; 20 Mountain Rd, near Belleview St; admission $1.50; 10am-8pm Jul-Aug; 9am-4:30pm Mon-Sat & 1-5pm Sun Sep-Jun) outlines local history from the time of the Mi'kmaqs and early settlers to the present. Photos and artifacts show the influence of shipbuilding and the railway. Next door is the oldest building in town, the **Free Meeting House** (1821).

At the **Acadian Museum** (☎ 506-858-4088; www.umoncton.ca/maum; Clement Cormier Bldg; adult/student $3/2, all free on Sun; 10am-5pm Mon-Fri, 1-5pm Sat & Sun Jul & Aug; 1-4:30pm Tue-Fri, 1-4pm Sat & Sun Sep-Jun), on the university campus, displays offer a brief history of the Acadians, chronicling aspects of the day-to-day life of the first European settlers in the Maritimes.

Tours

Gray Line (☎ 866-276-1111; www.grayline.com) offers bus tours ($40) to Hopewell Rocks that includes kayaking around the formations.

Sleeping

Reservations are a good idea as the city often gets packed solid.

Canadiana Inn (☎ 506-382-1054; 46 Archibald St; r $75-135; P) It's almost worth visiting Moncton just to stay here. The gorgeous old place is steeped in time and character, and the breakfast nook won't be forgotten, guaranteed. The outdoor second-floor verandah is a perfect place to plan or review the day and the center of Main St is a very short walk.

Bonaccord House B&B (☎ 506-388-1535; www.bbcanada.com/4135.html; 250 Bonaccord St; s/d $45/55) Within walking distance of the center is the four-room ever-popular, bargain-priced Bonaccord House. It's the appealing yellow-and-white house with stately Doric columns on the porch and a yard surrounded by a white picket fence.

Archibald B&B (☎ 506-382-0123; www.archibald bed-breakfast.com; 194 Archibald St; s/d with shared bathroom incl breakfast $55-80, r with private bathroom incl breakfast $65-90; P) In the same historic neighborhood as Bonaccord House, this Swiss-run guest house is clean and quiet, and the owners are helpful. German is spoken.

Midtown Motel (☎ 506-388-5000, 800-463-1999; midtown@nbnet.nb.ca; 61 Weldon St; r $80-90) This mainstream, two-story motel is conveniently right in the center of town. The Magnetic Hill area has other motels.

Campers City (☎ 506-384-7867, 877-512-7868; www.sn2000.nb.ca/comp/camper_city; 138 Queensway Dr; tent/RV sites $25/30; Jun-Sep) This is the nearest campground to the city (around 3km west), at the Mapleton Rd exit from Hwy 2. It caters mostly to RVs but has some nice grassy sites for tents at the back.

Eating

Pump House (☎ 506-855-233; 5 Orange Lane; mains $7-13; 11-1am) Perhaps the busiest place in town, the Pump is where the locals unwind and you can get a good burger, steak-based meal or wood-fired pizza. Of the brews made on the premises, the Muddy River stout is tasty, or try the beer sample tray.

Le Chateau à Pape (☎ 506-855-7273; 2 Steadman St; mains $20-25; dinner from 4pm) For fresh seafood or a steak in a rambling wooden place with a Maritime setting, this is the spot. It's been serving top-rated meals for many years and is right beside Tidal Bore Park. After dinner, stroll along the adjoining Riverfront Promenade.

Graffiti (☎ 506-382-4299; 897 Main St; mains $9-13; ☺ 11am-11pm Sun-Thu, 11am-midnight Fri & Sat) Graffiti is upscale in everything but price. The kitchen prepares artfully presented dishes with a Mediterranean or 'new Greek' flair, including seafood, moussaka and a vegetarian couscous, and the room is understatedly refined.

Jean's Restaurant (☎ 506-855-1053; 371 St George St; meals under $9; ☺ 7am-10pm) Locals pack the stools and booths at this basic Moncton institution for cheap breakfasts.

Moncton Market (120 Westmorland St, ☺ 7am-1pm Sat) It's not really a farmer's market as most items are ready to eat, but the gastronomic array here is mind-boggling. Plan on having your breakfast or lunch here. It's a must if you're in Moncton on a Saturday morning.

Drinking & Entertainment

Free *Marque* or *Mascaret* magazines give rundowns on Moncton's vibrant (read: raucous) nightlife. Central Main St and side streets have several bars with a young crowd, live bands and dancing.

Doc Dylan's (☎ 506-382-3627; 841 Main St) A variety of live rock is a fixture at this casual beer parlor open to the street.

Performing Arts Centre (☎ 506-856-4379; 811 Main St; ☺ box office 9am-5pm Mon-Fri, 9am-1pm Sat) The impressive Capitol Theatre, a 1920s vaudeville house, has been restored and is now the city's Performing Arts Centre. It's home to Theatre New Brunswick and the Symphony New Brunswick, which give performances on a regular basis.

Getting There & Away

AIR

Greater Moncton Airport is about 6km east of Champlain Place Shopping Centre via Champlain St. Discount airline West Jet flies to and from Hamilton (one-way $159), Ontario with numerous onward connections to central and western Canada. Departing passengers must pay an 'airport improvement and reconstruction fee' of $10.

BUS

Acadian Lines stops at the **bus station** (☎ 506-859-5060; 961 Main St; ☺ 7:30am-8:30pm Mon-Fri, 9am-8:30pm Sat & Sun), right in the heart of town. Buses go to Fredericton ($34, two hours, two daily), Prince Edward Island ($39, three

hours, two to three daily) and Halifax ($48, four hours, three to four daily).

CAR & MOTORCYCLE

If you need wheels, Avis, Budget, Hertz and National all have car rental desks at the airport or try **Discount Car Rentals** (☎ 506-857-2323; 566 Paul St; ☺ 8am-6pm Mon-Fri, 9am-1pm Sat).

Parking can be a hassle in Moncton: the parking meters ($1 per hour) and 'no parking' signs extend far out from downtown. The municipal parking lot at Moncton Market on Westmorland St charges $1/7 per hour/day and is free on Saturday, Sunday and evenings after 6pm. Highfield Sq Mall on Main St provides free parking for its clients, and who's to say you aren't one?

TRAIN

The sparkling new **train station** (☎ 506-857-9830, 800-561-3952; 1240 Main St; ☺ 9am-6pm) is right in the heart of town. With VIA Rail, the *Ocean* goes through northern New Brunswick, including Miramichi and Campbellton, and into Québec, on its way to Montréal. It leaves at 5:40pm daily except Tuesday. The train to Halifax departs daily at 11:40am, except Wednesday. There are regular one-way services to Halifax ($56) and Montréal ($176).

Getting Around

The airport is served by bus No 20 Champlain from Champlain Place nine times on weekdays. A taxi to the center of town costs about $14.

Codiac Transit (☎ 506-857-2008) is the local bus system running daily, except Sunday. Single tickets are $1.75.

ST JOSEPH

In St Joseph, 25km southeast of Moncton, the **Monument-Lefebvre National Historic Site** (☎ 506-758-9783; 480 Central St; adult/child/senior/family $3.50/1.25/3/8.75; ☺ 9am-5pm Jun–mid-Oct) tells the enthralling but arduous story of the Acadians, the early French settlers of the region (most were expelled by the British in 1755). Exhibits such as paintings, crafts and life-sized models are well done and, unlike those at many similar sites, devote attention to the subjects' lives through to the present.

St Joseph is in the Memramcook Valley, the only area near the Bay of Fundy where some Acadians live on what was their forebears' land before the mass deportations.

SACKVILLE

Sackville is a small university town that's in the right place for a pit stop – for birds and people. The **Sackville Waterfowl Park**, across the road from the university off East Main St, is on a major bird migration route. Boardwalks with interpretive signs rise over portions of it. The **Wildlife Service** (☎ 506-364-5044; 17 Waterfowl Lane, off E Main St; admission free; ⊗ 8am-4pm Mon-Fri) has information and a wetlands display at one of the entrances. Enthusiasts should also see the **Tantramar Wetlands Centre** (☎ 506-364-4257; www.weted .com; 223 Main St, behind the high school; admission free; ⊗ 8am-4pm, Mon-Fri) with its walking trail and educational office.

Mel's Tea Room (☎ 506-536-1251; 17 Bridge St; mains $4-10; ⊗ 8am-midnight Mon-Sat, 10am-11pm Sun) is the favorite among locals. This tea room, operating in the center of town since 1919, has the charm of a 1950s diner, including a jukebox and prices to match.

FORT BEAUSÉJOUR NATIONAL HISTORIC SITE

Right by the Nova Scotia border, this **national historic site** (☎ 506-536-0720; www.pc.gc.ca/ fortbeausejour; 1.5km west of the visitor center; adult/ child/family $3.50/1.75/8.75; interpretive center ⊗ 9am-5pm Jun–mid-Oct) preserves the remains of a French fort built in 1751 to hold the British back. It didn't work. Later it was used as a stronghold during the American Revolution and the War of 1812. Only earthworks and stone foundations remain, but the view is excellent, vividly illustrating why this crossroads of the Maritimes was fortified by two empires.

To find out more, visit the **New Brunswick Visitor Centre** (☎ 506-364-4090; 158 Aulac Rd; ⊗ 9am-9pm Jul & Aug, 10am-6pm mid-May–early Oct), off Hwy 2 in Aulac, at the junction of roads leading to all three Maritime provinces.

NORTHUMBERLAND SHORE

New Brunswick's half of the Northumberland Shore stretches from the Confederation Bridge to Kouchibouguac National Park and makes up part of the tourist Acadian Coastal Drive. Folks here, like those further north on the Acadian Peninsula and in northern Prince Edward Island, claim their waters are the warmest north of either Virginia or the Carolinas in the USA, having been warmed by spin-off currents of the Gulf Stream. Regardless, it ain't Miami Beach by a long shot.

Coastal Shediac, on lobster lovers' itineraries, is a major resort town in a strip of summer seaside and beach playgrounds.

A good part of the population along this coast is French-speaking, and Bouctouche is an Acadian stronghold. Further north, Kouchibouguac National Park protects a variety of littoral environments and their natural flora and fauna.

CAPE JOURIMAIN

Near the bridge to Prince Edward Island, the **Cape Jourimain Nature Centre** (☎ 866-538-2220; Rte 16; admission free; ⊗ 8am-8pm May-Oct) sits in a 675-hectare national wildlife area that protects this undeveloped shoreline and its migratory birds. The center has exhibits on climate change, ecology and bird life. Seventeen kilometers of trails wind through salt marshes, dunes, woods and beach. A four-story lookout provides views of the surroundings and Confederation Bridge.

There's a **New Brunswick Visitor Centre** (☎ 506-538-2133; Hwy 16; ⊗ 8am-9pm Jul & Aug 9am-6pm mid-May–Jun & Sep–early-Oct) by the bridge.

For information on driving on the Confederation Bridge, see p484. If you're cycling or walking, you must pick up the free shuttle across the bridge at the Bridge Facility Building at the junction of Hwys 16 and 955. It leaves every two hours when required.

SHEDIAC

Shediac, a self-proclaimed lobster capital, is the focal point of the area's beach resorts and home of the annual July lobster fest. You can even enjoy it on pizza! The many white lights sprinkled around town all summer lend a festive air.

It seems on any hot weekend that half the province is flaked out on the sand at **Parlee Beach**, turning the color of cooked lobster. South at **Cap Pelé** are vast stretches of more sandy shorelines. Terrific **Aboiteau Beach** is over 5km of unsupervised sand, while others have all amenities and lifeguards.

Shediac Bay Cruises (☎ 506-532-2175, 888-894-2002; Pointe-du-Chene wharf) has a unique concept. They take passengers out on the water, pull up lobster traps, then show you how to cook and eat 'em – all for $65.

For a small town, accommodations are varied and generous, from camping to lovely old inns. **Le Coin Gretzky** (☎ 506-533-9626; cgretzky bnb@yahoo.com; 17 Cornwall Point Rd; r $70-95) is a beauty of a place with a wonderful porch and bright breakfast area. It's central but not right on the main drag.

For sucking a lobster leg, **Fisherman's Paradise** (☎ 506-532-6811; 640 Main St; mains $13-24; ⊗ 11am-10pm) has them lining up. The convivial atmosphere is perfect for a summer-holiday meal.

BOUCTOUCHE

This small, surprisingly busy town is an Acadian cultural focal point with several unique attractions. The **Visitor Information Centre** (☎ 506-743-8811; Hwy 134; ⊗ 9am-5pm Jun-Sep) at the town's south entrance features a boardwalk that explains the local oyster industry.

Sights & Activities

Le Pays de la Sagouine (☎ 800-561-9188; www .sagouine.com; 57 Acadie St; adult/student/senior/family $14/8/13/34; ⊗ 10am-6pm Jul & Aug, 10:30am-4pm mid-Jun–Sep) is an appealing attraction. Sitting on a small island in the Bouctouche River, it consists of a cluster of buildings made to appear like a fishing community. Dedicated to Acadian writer Antonine Maillet, Le Pays de la Sagouine is an immersion course in Acadian history and culture. It hosts live music and theatrical shows. In July and August there's a supper theater at 7pm Monday to Saturday with a variety of musical programs ($43 including dinner). In June and September, the dinner show is usually on Saturdays only (most programs are in French). Friday nights are given over to concerts.

Irving Eco Centre (☎ 506-743-2600; www.irvingeco center.com/main.htm; 1932 Hwy 475; admission free; interpretive center ⊗ 10am-8pm Jul & Aug; noon-5pm Mon-Thu, noon-6pm Fri, 10am-6pm Sat & Sun mid-May–Jun & Sep-Oct), on the coast 9km northeast of Bouctouche, protects and makes accessible 'La Dune de Bouctouche,' a beautiful, long sandspit jutting into the strait. The interpretive center has displays on the flora and fauna, but the highlight is the 2km boardwalk above the dune. The peninsula itself is 12km long, taking four to six hours to hike over the loose sand and back. Few visitors go beyond the boardwalk, so even a short walk means solitude.

To reduce the impact of the large numbers of visitors in July and August, only the first 2000 persons to arrive each day are admitted. It re-opens to everyone after 5pm. Otherwise the boardwalk is accessible anytime year-round. On Saturdays at 8am during July and August there's a free bird-watching tour. Bicycles are not allowed on the dune, but there's a separate 12km hiking/cycling trail through mixed forest to Bouctouche town, which begins at the Eco Centre parking lot.

At **Kent Museum** (☎ 506-743-5005; 150 Hwy 475; adult/child $3/1; ⊗ 9am-5pm Mon-Fri, noon-6pm Sat & Sun Jul & Aug; 9:30am-noon, 1-4pm Mon-Fri mid-Jun–end Jun & Sep–mid-Oct), in the former Convent of the Immaculate Conception (1880), 2km east of the center of Bouctouche, exhibits cover Acadian culture.

KayaBéCano (☎ 506-743-6265; 888-529-2232; www .kayabecano.nb.ca; 1465 Hwy 475; adult/child $30/15; ⊗ mid-May–early Sep), 2.5km south of Irving Eco Centre, runs two-hour kayak trips that explore the cultured oyster industry. It also rents out kayaks for self-guided trips along the dune.

KC Irving (1899–1992), founder of the Irving empire, was from Bouctouche, and there's a large bronze statue of him in the town park.

Sleeping & Eating

Aux P'tits Oiseaux B&B (☎ 506-743-8196; oiseau@ nbnet.nb.ca; 124 Hwy 475; r with shared bathroom $50-60) This friendly B&B near the Kent Museum features a collection of 500 carved birds mounted through the house. Call ahead as it's usually full all summer.

Bellevue Sur Mer (☎ 506-743-6575; bellebb@nbnet .nb.ca; 539 Rte 475; r $80) There are three guest rooms in this antique-filled 1870 home with a perfect view of the bay.

Restaurant Le Vieux Presbytère de Bouctouche (☎ 506-743-5568; opposite Kent Museum on Hwy 475; lobster dinner $35; ⊗ 5:30-8:30pm Jun-early Oct) This large restaurant in an old religious residence does casual, social PEI-style lobster suppers. Reservations are required.

ST LOUIS DE KENT

Blooming with visitors in summer, St Louis is ideal as a service base for visiting Kouchibouguac National Park (see opposite).

SLEEPING

Oasis Acadienne B&B (☎ 506-876-1199; www.kayak ouch.com; 10617 Hwy 134; s/d incl full breakfast $40-80; ☺ May-Oct) This congenial six-room B&B, 4km south of Kouchibouguac, is run by the Kayakouch people (see below) and has a dock astride the Kouchibouguac River right in the backyard!

Kouchibouguac Motel & Chalets (☎ 506-876-4317, 888-524-3200; www.kouch.com; 10983 Hwy 134; r $70, chalets & cottages $110) Just 400m south of the park, the very inviting, tree-shaded complex has motel units and comfortable, all-wood, self-contained chalets. The convenient **restaurant** specializes in seafood.

Daigle's Park (☎ 506-876-4540; www.campingdaig le.com; 10787 Hwy 134; tent sites $17, RV sites $20-26; ☺ mid-May–mid-Sep; ☒) If the national park, 2.5km north, is full, this is a good alternative. There are some nicely wooded sites for tenters.

KOUCHIBOUGUAC NATIONAL PARK

Coastal highlights – beaches, lagoons and offshore sand dunes extending for 25km – make this park. The sands invite strolling, bird-watching and clam-digging. At the south end of the main beach, seals are often seen offshore.

Kouchibouguac (*koosh*-e-boo-gwack), a Mi'kmaq word meaning 'river of long tides,' also has populations of moose, deer and black bear. Other features are the salt marsh and a bog where there's an observation platform.

Information

The **visitors center** (☎ 506-876-2443; www.pc.gc.ca/ kouchibouguac; 186 Hwy 117; daily park admission adult/ child/family $5/2.50/12.50, season pass child/adult $25/63; ☺ 8am-8pm July & Aug, 9am-5pm mid-May–mid-Oct) features interpretive displays and a small theater as well as an information counter and gift shop. Before buying a pass for just this park, ask about the full national parks season pass.

Activities

HIKING

The park has 10 trails, mostly short and flat. The excellent **Bog Trail** (1.9km) is a boardwalk beyond the observation tower, and only the first few hundred meters are crushed gravel. This trail tends to be crowded around the middle of the day and is best done early or late. The **Cedars Trail** (1.3km) is less used. The

Osprey Trail (5.1km) has a bit of everything. Maybe best is walking the **Kelly's Beach Boardwalk** (600m one-way), then turning right and going the 6km to the end of the dune. Take drinking water. The visitors center has a special all-terrain wheelchair with oversized wheels that park staff loan out free upon request. Otherwise, the boardwalk to Kelly's Beach is wheelchair-accessible.

CYCLING

Kouchibouguac features hiking trails and canoe routes, but what really sets it apart is the 40km of bikeways – crushed gravel paths that wind through the heart of the park's backcountry. **Ryan's Rental Center** (☎ 506-876-3733), near the South Kouchibouguac campground, rents out bicycles at $6/28 per hour/day and canoes/kayaks at $30/50 per day. From Ryan's it's possible to cycle a 23km loop and never be on the park road.

SWIMMING

For swimming, the lagoon area is shallow, warm and safe for children, while adults will find the deep water on the ocean side invigorating. There's also a 'gay beach' in the park, a 45-minute walk to the right from the end of the Kelly's Beach boardwalk.

KAYAKING

Kayakouch (☎ 506-876-1199; www.kayakouch.com; 10617 Hwy 134; ☺ mid-Jun–Aug), just 4km south of the national park, rents out kayaks and offers guided kayaking tours.

Sleeping

Kouchibouguac has two drive-in campgrounds and three primitive camping areas totaling 359 sites. The camping season is from mid-May to mid-October and the park is very busy throughout July and August, especially on weekends. **Camping reservations** (☎ 877-737-3783; www.pccamping.ca; reservation fee $8) are taken for 60% of the sites. Otherwise, get on the lengthy 'roll call' waiting list – it can take two or three days to get a site. The park entry fee is extra.

South Kouchibouguac (tent/RV sites $18/26 in summer), the largest campground, is located 13km inside the park near the beaches, with showers and a kitchen shelter.

Cote-a-Fabien (campsites $14), on the north side of Kouchibouguac River, is away from trails and beaches, and doesn't have showers.

The three **primitive campgrounds** have only vault toilets and a pump for water. These cost $8 per person per night, as does canoe camping.

THE MIRAMICHI

In New Brunswick, the word Miramichi connotes both the city and the river, but even more: an intangible, captivating mystique. The spell the region casts emanates partially from the Acadian and Irish mix of folklore, legends, superstitions and tales of ghosts. It also seeps from the dense forests and wilderness of the area and from the character of the residents who wrestle a livelihood from these natural resources. The fabled river adds its serpentine cross-country course, crystal tributaries and world-renowned salmon fishing. The region produces some wonderful rootsy music and inspires artists including noted writer David Adams Richards, whose work skillfully mines the temper of the region.

MIRAMICHI

The city of Miramichi is an amalgam of Chatham and Newcastle and the villages of Douglastown, Loggieville, Nelson and several others along a 12km stretch of the Miramichi River near its mouth. Miramichi City, with its Irish background, is an English-speaking enclave in the middle of a predominantly French-speaking region. The Mirimichi Folksong Festival is the oldest such festival in North America. It plays a considerable role in maintaining the region's ties to its history and unique culture.

Information

Books Inn (☎ 506-622-1185; 144 Newcastle Blvd) Great selection on the region (both fiction and nonfiction) and very helpful staff.

Chatham Tourist office (☎ 800-459-3131; www .miramichi.org; Hwy 11; ⏱ 9am-9pm late-May–early Oct, 9am-6pm at beginning and end of season) On the south side of the river.

Newcastle Public Library (☎ 506-623-2450; 100 Fountain Head Lane; ⏱ 1-8pm Tue & Wed, 10am-5pm Thu-Sat) Near Ritchie Wharf, free Internet access.

Newcastle Tourist office (☎ 506-623-2152; ⏱ Jun-Aug) Seasonal office downtown at Ritchie Wharf, on the river's north side.

Sights

Though surrounded by two paper mills and sawmills, central Newcastle is pleasant. In the central square is a **statue** to Lord Beaverbrook (1879–1964), one of the most powerful press barons in British history and a statesman and philanthropist of no small reputation (see the boxed text on p487). Among the many gifts he lavished on the province are the 17th-century English benches and the Italian gazebo here. His ashes lie under the statue presented as a memorial to him by the town.

Beaverbrook spent most of his growing years in Newcastle. **Beaverbrook House** (☎ 506-624-5474; 518 King George Hwy; admission free; ⏱ 9am-5pm Mon-Fri, 10am-5pm Sat, 1-5pm Sun mid-Jun–Aug), his boyhood home (erected 1879), is now a museum.

Ritchie Wharf, a riverfront boardwalk park nearby, has playgrounds, eateries, a lighthouse, an information center and also boat tours ($9) to **Beaubears Island** in the summer. The island has been a Mi'kmaq campsite, a refugee camp for Acadians during the expulsion, and a shipbuilding site. For all that, it is now a little-known national historic site.

The **Enclosure** (☎ 506-622-8638; 8 Enclosure Rd), 5km southwest of the city of Miramichi, was used as a refugee site in the 1700s by the Acadians. A small **museum** houses artifacts from area archaeological digs. Evidently, one of the ships that brought the Acadians was a sister to the famous *Bounty*. Now being developed is the **Scottish Interpretive Centre** at Wilson's Point, which is restoring an old Scottish cemetery and church from 1790. It was the first English settlement in the region.

Festivals & Events

Irish Festival (www.canadasirishfest.com; ⏱ mid-July)
Miramichi Folksong Festival (www.miramichifolk songfestival.com; ⏱ early Aug) Begun in 1957.

Sleeping & Eating

Governor's Mansion (☎ 506-622-3036, 877-647-2642; www.governorsmansion.ca; 62 St Patrick's St, Nelson; r incl breakfast & shared bathroom $49-99, d with private bathroom $75-99) On the south side of the river overlooking Beaubears Island is the Victorian Governor's Mansion (1860), onetime home of J Leonard O'Brien, the first Irish lieutenant governor of the province.

Fundy Line Motel (☎ 506-622-3650; fax 506-622-8723; 869 King George Hwy, Newcastle; r $40-50) These straightforward, no-frills rooms in three long rows are 2km east of central Newcastle.

Enclosure Campground (☎ 506-622-8638, 800-363-1733; www.sn2000.nb.ca/comp/enclosure-campground; 8 Enclosure Rd; tent/RV sites $21/27; ☒ May-Oct) Southwest of Newcastle off Hwy 8 is another of Lord Beaverbrook's gifts, a former provincial park called The Enclosure (also see opposite). This riverside park includes a nice wooded area with spacious quasi-wilderness sites for tenters.

Flo's Hide-A-Way (☎ 506-622-0680; 8 Enclosure Rd; mains $5-13; ☒ breakfast, lunch & dinner) Also at the multifaceted Enclosure site is this barn of a restaurant, a real 'down east' spot. Though good for a casual meal, staff also broil a mean Atlantic salmon. This fun, friendly place almost seems part community center, and at night, the beer and live music come out.

Getting There & Away

The **bus station** (☎ 506-622-0445; 60 Pleasant St; ☒ 8:30am-5pm Mon-Fri, 1-3pm Sat & Sun) is in downtown Newcastle. Daily buses leave for Fredericton ($19, 2½ hours), Saint John ($38, five hours) and Campbellton ($23, three hours).

The **VIA Rail station** (☎ 800-561-3952; on Station St at George St) is in Newcastle. Trains from Montréal and Halifax stop here.

MIRAMICHI RIVER VALLEY

The Miramichi is actually a complex web of rivers and tributaries draining much of central New Brunswick. The main branch, the 217km-long Southwest Miramichi River, flows from near Hartland through forest to Miramichi City where it meets the other main fork, the Northwest Miramichi. For over 100 years, the entire system has inspired reverent awe for its tranquil beauty and incredible Atlantic salmon fly-fishing. Famous business tycoons, international politicians, sports and entertainment stars and Prince Charles have all wet lines here. Even Marilyn Monroe is said to have dipped her legs. The legendary fishery has had some ups and downs with over-fishing, poaching and unknown causes (perhaps global warming) affecting stocks, but they now seem back at sustainable levels. The **tourist office** (☎ 506-365-7787, www.doaktown.com) is in the Salmon Museum.

Sights

Historic **Doaktown** is the river valley's main center and its unofficial fishing capital. See the **Atlantic Salmon Museum** (☎ 506-365-7787, 866-725-6662; www.atlanticsalmonmuseum.com; 263 Main St, adult/family $5/12; ☒ 9am-5pm Jun-mid-Oct) for its equipment, photos and an aquarium containing river life and, of course, salmon in various growth stages. **Doak Historic Site** (☎ 506-365-2026; 386 Main St; adult/family $5/15; ☒ 9am-6pm Jun-Sep) depicts the area through the mid-1800s with exhibits and demonstrations.

Activities

Sport fishing remains the main activity, but is tightly controlled for conservation. Licenses are required and all anglers must employ a registered guide. A three-day license for nonresidents is $40. All fish over 63cm must be released. For more, see www.gnb.ca/0078/fw/angling/summary.asp.

WW Doak & Sons (☎ 506-365-7828; www.doak.com; 331 Main St) is one of Canada's best fly-fishing shops. It sells a staggering number of flies annually, some made on the premises. A wander through here will certainly get an angler pumped.

Despite the presence of the king of freshwaters, there are other pastimes to enjoy. The **Miramichi Trail**, a walking and cycling path along an abandoned rail line, is now partially complete, with 75km of the projected 200km useable. At McNamee, the pedestrian **Priceville Suspension Bridge** spans the river. It's a popular put-in spot for canoeists and kayakers spending half a day paddling downriver to Doaktown. Several outfitters in Doaktown and Blackville offer equipment rentals, shuttle services and guided trips for leisurely canoe, kayak or even tubing trips along the river.

Sleeping & Eating

Beautiful rustic lodges and camps abound, many replicating the halcyon days of the 1930s and '40s. Click to www.doak.com for links to more accommodations choice.

O'Donnel's Cottages & Expeditions (☎ 506-365-7636, 800-563-8724; www.odonnellscottages.com; 439 Storeytown Rd; r $75-125) Among Doaktown's overnight options is O'Donnel's, with lodging rooms and new adventure activities seemingly every year. The dining room prepares meals on request.

Homestead B&B (☎ 506-365-7912; Hwy 8, nearby in Blissfield; r $70-125) This fifth-generation house, dating from 1877, has rooms in the main house and a couple of cabins, too.

In addition to sampling superb salmon from local menus, something to try is the fiddlehead, a green fern-like plant for which the province, and most notably this area, is celebrated.

NORTHEASTERN NEW BRUNSWICK

Almost the entire northern interior half of the province is inaccessible, rocky, river-filled forest. Inland, highways are lined with timberland, making for monotonous driving. The Acadian Peninsula, dividing Baie des Chaleurs (Chaleur Bay) from the Gulf of St Lawrence, is of most interest to visitors, with its strong, self-preserving Acadian culture. In 2004, the province celebrated 400 years of French settlement in North America. The northern edge of the peninsula is by far the most scenic and contains all the prime attractions. Campbellton provides access to Québec.

TRACADIE-SHEILA

Unmasking a little known but gripping story, the **Historical Museum of Tracadie** (☎ 506-393-6366; 399-222 Rue du Couvent; adult/child $3/1; ☑ 9am-6pm Mon-Fri, noon-6pm Sat & Sun) focuses on the leprosy colony, based here from 1868 to as late as 1965. It's the only place in Canada providing details on a leprosarium. The nearby cemetery has the graves of 60 victims of Hansen's Disease (leprosy).

CARAQUET

The Acadian Peninsula, extending from Miramichi and Bathurst out to two islands at the edge of the Baie des Chaleurs, was first settled by the unhappy Acadian victims of colonial battles between Britain and France in the 1700s. The descendants of Canada's earliest French settlers proudly fly the Acadian flag around the region, and many of the traditions live on in the music, food and language, which is different from that spoken in Québec.

The oldest of the Acadian villages, Caraquet, was founded in 1757 by refu-

gees from Nova Scotia. It's now the main center of the peninsula's French community. Caraquet's colorful, bustling fishing port, off Boul St Pierre Est, has an assortment of moored vessels splashing at the dock. East and west Boul St Pierre are divided at Rue le Portage.

Information

The **tourist office** (☎ 506-726-2676; 51 Boul St Pierre Est; ☑ 9am-5pm mid-Jun–mid-Sep) and all of the local tour operators are found at the **Callefour de la Mer** complex, with its Day Adventure Center, restaurant and views down on the waterfront near the fishing harbor.

Sights
ACADIAN MUSEUM

The **Acadian Museum** (☎ 506-726-2682; 15 Boul St Pierre Est; adult/student $3.50/2; ☑ 10am-6pm Mon-Sat, 1-6pm Sun Jun–mid-Sep; to 8pm Jul & Aug) is in the middle of town with views over the bay from the balcony. It has a neatly laid out collection of artifacts donated by local residents, including common household objects, tools, photographs and a fine wood stove. Most scary is the desk/bed, at which you could work all day and then fold down into a bed when exhaustion strikes! It belonged to a superior at the Caraquet Convent in 1880.

STE ANNE DU BOCAGE

Six kilometers west of town is **Ste Anne du Bocage** (☎ 506-727-3604; 579 Boul St Pierre Ouest; admission free; ☑ 8am-9pm May-Oct), one of the oldest religious shrines in the province. On this spot, Alexis Landry and other Acadians settled soon after the infamous expulsion and the graves of some of them are on the sanctuary grounds. Down a stairway by the sea is a sacred spring where the faithful come to fill their water bottles.

ACADIAN HISTORIC VILLAGE

Acadian Historic Village (☎ 506-726-2600, 877-721-2200; www.villagehistoriqueacadien.com; 14311 Hwy 11; adult/child/senior/family $14/9/12/34; ☑ 10am-6pm early–Jun-Sep), 15km west of Caraquet, is a major historic reconstruction set up like a village of old, with 33 buildings and workers in period costumes reflecting life from 1780 to 1880. The museum depicts daily routines in a typical, post-expulsion community and makes for an intriguing comparison to the obvious prosperity of the British King's Landing historic village (see below), west of Fredericton.

A good three to four hours is required to see the site, and you'll want to eat. For that, there are four choices: two snack bars; Dugas House, serving sit-down Acadian dishes; and the dining room at Château Albert, with a menu from 1910.

The site is on Hwy 11 between Bertrand and Grande Anse. The village has a program for kids ($35), which provides them with a costume and seven hours of supervised historical activities. If you don't have time to see everything, ask the receptionist to stamp your ticket for re-entry the next day. In September only five or six buildings are open and village admission is reduced to $7/4/17 per adult/student/family. Facing the village parking lot is a **wax museum**, which has an extra admission charge ($8 adult, audio guide included).

For accommodations for the Château Albert, see below.

Activities

Sea of Adventure (☎ 800-704-3966; ☽ Jul & Aug) offers three-hour whale-watching tours ($50) in rigid-hulled Hurricane zodiacs seating 12 passengers.

The boat **Île Caramer** (☎ 506-727-0813) runs deep-sea fishing trips ($25) from Caraquet three times daily from June to mid-October, leaving the fishing harbor at 5:45am, 1pm and 6pm. A minimum of six people is required to go, so call ahead. Another trip does whale-watching.

Festivals & Events

The largest annual Acadian cultural festival, **Festival Acadien** (☎ 506-727-2787; www.ville .caraquet.nb.ca in French) is held here the first two weeks of August. It draws 100,000 visitors; over 200 performers including singers, musicians, actors, dancers from Acadia and other French regions (some from overseas) entertain. The culminating Tintamarre Parade is a real blowout.

Sleeping & Eating

Gîte Le Poirier (☎ 506-727-4359, 888-748-9311; www .gitelepoirier.com; 98 Boul St Pierre Ouest; r $80-100) There are five rooms with all the comforts at this eye-catching, green and red place in the center of town.

Gîte à Rita (☎ 506-727-2841; 116 Boul St Pierre Est; d incl breakfast $50; ☽ Jun-Aug) More modest but welcoming, this typical Acadian house is only a few hundred meters from the fishing harbor.

Maison Touristique Dugas (☎ 506-727-3195; www.maisontouristiquedugas.ca; 683 Boul St Pierre Ouest; s/d with shared bathroom $40/45, d with private bathroom & cooking facilities $50-60, cabins d $50) This large red wooden house with a rear annex, 1.5km west of Ste Anne du Bocage, dates back to 1926. A variety of accommodations are available, from 11 rooms with shared bathrooms and two apartments with private cooking facilities in the main house to five cabins with private bathrooms and cooking facilities in the backyard. Breakfast costs extra.

Château Albert (Acadian Historic Village; www.village historiqueacadien.com/chateauanglais.htm; d $160) For complete immersion in the Acadian Historic Village, spend the night at Château Albert in early 20th-century style – no TV, no phone – but a comfortable, very quiet room. The fee of $160 per couple includes admission to the site and a tool around in a Model T Ford.

Camping Caraquet (☎ 506-726-2696; www.sn2000 .nb.ca/comp/camping-caraquet; 619 Boul St Pierre Ouest; tent/RV sites $19/25; ☽ mid-Jun–mid-Sep) This former provincial park overlooking the sea is just west of the Ste Anne du Bocage sanctuary. The core of the campground is a solid phalanx of RVs but there are plenty of tent sites around the perimeter.

Restaurant Le Caraquette (☎ 506-727-6009; 89 Boul St Pierre Est; mains $6-28; ☽ 6am-11pm Mon-Sat, 7am-11pm Sun) Next to the gas station directly above the port, La Caraquette is extremely popular with the locals. It's a good choice for breakfast, a simple lunch or more tantalizing seafood selections in the evening.

Carapro Fish Market (☎ 506-727-3462; 60 Boul St Pierre Est; ☽ 9am-9pm Jul & Aug, 10am-6pm Apr-Dec) Opposite the dock area is a big fish market with fresh, salted and frozen seafood for sale.

Getting There & Away

Public transportation around this part of the province is very limited as Acadian Lines buses don't pass this way. Local residents wishing to connect with the bus or train in Miramichi or Bathurst use a couple of van shuttles. Ask for details at the tourist office.

SHIPPAGAN

The intrepid may head further up the peninsula to the home of the province's largest fishing fleet with crab a main catch. The **Aquarium & Marine Centre** (☎ 506-336-3013; 100 Aquarium St; adult/family $7/14; ☺ 10am-6pm mid-May–Sep) is an educational and entertaining collection especially for kids, with its touch tanks and seals (fed at 11am and 4pm). Beyond here, there are few visitors.

GRANDE ANSE

Back along the shoreline west of Caraquet, this small town boasts the unique **Popes Museum** (☎ 506-732-3003; 184 Hwy 11; adult/family $5/10; ☺ 10am-6pm mid-Jun–Aug), which houses images of 262 popes from St Peter to the current one, as well as sundry religious articles. There is also a detailed model of the Basilica and St Peter's Square in Rome.

At the foot of the cliffs, behind the imposing church, is a beach and picnic spot. To get there, edge down Ave Portuaire toward the fishing wharf.

The road west to Bathurst skirts the rugged, scenic shoreline cliffs. Across Baie des Chaleurs, the outline of Québec's Gaspé Peninsula is clearly visible. Without doubt, stop at easily missed **Pokeshaw Community Park** (admission per car $1), 5.5km west of the Popes Museum (look carefully for signs). Just offshore atop an isolated sea stack created by coastal erosion, thousands of double-crested cormorants nest in summer. In late fall, the birds fly south to their winter home in Maryland. From the parking lot you can look straight across at the birds squawking and swirling. Other shore birds and gulls mingle with the cormorants. This wonderfully undeveloped park is a terrific place to photograph the coastal cliffs, and you can also picnic and swim.

PETIT ROCHER

Some 20km north of Bathurst in Petit Rocher is the **New Brunswick Mining & Mineral Interpretation Centre** (☎ 506-542-2672; 397 Hwy 134; admission $6; ☺ 10am-6pm late Jun-Aug). This mining museum has various exhibits on the local zinc industry. The tour includes a simulated descent in a mining shaft and takes about 45 minutes.

Auberge d'Anjou (☎ 506-783-0587, 866-783-0587; auberge.anjou@nb.aibn.com; 587 Hwy 134; r incl breakfast $65-85) is a fine place with immaculate spaces

that are well-furnished but minimalist. It was the first inn in the area and has been tastefully upgraded. The separate cottage is more expensive. The complex, which included an old convent, is near the large church, on the corner of the road to the wharf.

DALHOUSIE

Dalhousie is a small, industrial town with a huge pulp mill. William St and parallel Adelaide St near the dock are the two main streets.

On the corner of Adelaide St is the **Restigouche Regional Museum** (☎ 506-684-7490; 115 George St; admission free; ☺ 9am-5pm Mon-Fri, 9am-1pm Sat, 1-5pm Sun) with local artifacts and history.

From mid-May to September the cruise boat **Chaleur Phantom** (☎ 506-684-4722) departs from the marina at the west end of Adelaide St for a nature cruise in the bay at 9am ($16) in search of birds, seals and porpoises. Better are the afternoon scenic cruises along the Restigouche River at 2pm and 7pm ($16).

CAMPBELLTON

Campbellton, on the Québec border, is the second-biggest highway entry point to the Maritimes from the rest of Canada. It's in the midst of a scenic area on the edge of the Restigouche Highlands, a portion of the Appalachian Mountains. The lengthy Restigouche River which winds through northern New Brunswick and then forms the border with Québec empties to the sea here. The Baie des Chaleurs is on one side and rolling hills encompass the town on the remaining sides. Across the border is Matapédia and Hwy 132 leading to Mont Joli, 148km into Québec.

The last naval engagement of the Seven Years' War was fought in the waters off this coast in 1760. The Battle of Restigouche marked the conclusion of the long struggle for Canada by Britain and France.

Main streets in this town of about 9000 residents are Water St and Roseberry St, around which the commercial center is clustered. Campbellton is a truly bilingual town where store clerks say everything in both French and English.

Information

Campbellton Public Library (☎ 506-753-5253; 2 Aberdeen St at Andrew St; ☺ 10am-5pm Mon-Fri Jul & Aug, 10am-5pm Tue-Sat Sep-Jun) Free Internet access.

Provincial tourist office (☎ 506-789-2367; 56 Salmon Blvd; ☺ 10am-6pm mid-May–Jun & Sep–early Oct, 8am-9pm Jul & Aug) Next to City Center Mall, near the bridge from Québec. A park opposite features a huge statue of a salmon surrounded by man-made waterfalls.

Sights

Dominated by Sugarloaf Mountain, which rises nearly 400m above sea level and looks vaguely like one of its other namesakes in Rio, **Sugarloaf Provincial Park** (☎ 506-789-2366; 596 Val d'Amours Rd; admission free) is off Hwy 11 at exit 415. From the base, it's just a half-hour walk to the top – well worth the extensive views of town and part of the Restigouche River. Another trail leads around the bottom of the hill. Another attraction of Sugarloaf Provincial Park is the **Alpine Slide** (ride $4; late Jun–early Sep), which involves taking a chairlift up another hill and sliding back down a track on a small sled.

Sleeping

Campbellton Lighthouse Hostel (☎ 506-759-7044; campbellton@hihostels.ca; 1 Ritchie St; dm members/nonmembers $16/20; ☺ mid-Jun–Aug; Ⓟ) This distinctive, long-running HI hostel is in a converted lighthouse by the Restigouche River, just up from the provincial tourist office. There's ample parking and the Acadian bus stop is just 200m away.

Maison McKenzie House B&B (☎ 506-753-3133; www.bbcanada.com/4384.html; 31 Andrew St; d $60-90) This large two-story house from 1910,

with the impressive verandah, is four blocks south of the tourist office.

Sanfar Cottages (☎ 506-753-4287; www.sanfar.biz land.com; 35 Restigouche Dr, Tide Head; cottage d/tr/q $46/50/54, for 6 people $58; ☺ Jun-Sep) Sanfar is at Tide Head on Hwy 134, 7km west of Campbellton. The 11 neat, cozy little cottages vary in size and number of beds, with the larger ones including cooking facilities. There's also a **café** (☺ lunch Mon-Fri, dinner nightly from 5pm).

Sugarloaf Provincial Park (☎ 506-789-2366; 596 Val d'Amours Rd; tent sites $20, RV sites $22-25; ☺ mid-May–early-Oct) There are 76 sites in a pleasant wooded setting at this park 4km from downtown Campbellton.

Getting There & Away

The Acadian bus stop is at the **Pik-Quik convenience store** (☎ 506-753-3100; Water St, near Prince William St). The bus departs daily at 11am for Fredericton ($35, 3½ hours) and Moncton ($35, six hours). Twice a day (once in the morning and once in the afternoon), an Orléans Express bus leaves for Gaspé ($55) and Québec City ($66, seven hours).

The **VIA Rail station** (☎ 800-561-3952; 113 Roseberry St; ☺ 5:45-10:30am Wed-Mon & 5:45-10pm Thu-Tue) is conveniently central. There's one train daily, except Wednesday, going south to Moncton ($60, four hours) and Halifax ($83, nine hours), and one daily, except Tuesday, heading the other way to Montréal ($125, 11 hours).

Manitoba

Manitoba is a place of funny names and exciting places. Almost a 'mini Canada,' it's full of the things that make Canada what it is. Home to as varied geography as you'll find in the country, southern agricultural flatlands blend into the green woodlands embracing the nation's largest lakes. Glacial activity has left footprints behind in the potholed lakes, stubby vegetation and scraped-bare lands of the Canadian Shield in the north. If you're coming to Canada to see moose, beaver, polar bear and maple trees, complete your checklist in Manitoba.

Manitoba can also lay claim to some of Canada's oldest stories. Aboriginal settlements date back more than 6000 years and European discovery began up north in the 17th century. Isolation and often-forbidding circumstances forced the province to look within for inspiration, exploration, guile and ability. If you're coming to Canada to learn about cultural icons and unlikely heroes such as Louis Riel, Winnie the Pooh or Neil Young, Manitoba's the place to start.

As laid-back and friendly as Canada's other provinces, Manitoba is unlike any other place. Knowing full well what it has, it's unconcerned when other Canadians use 'Winnipeg' as a punch line. Able to take a joke – and even to take pride in being a secret garden – Manitoba casts its gaze across the landscape, daring you to follow, and laughs softly back. If you're coming to Canada for unflappable politeness, Manitoba is likely where you'll find it.

It's a place of life: nature, culture and spirit.

HIGHLIGHTS

- Experience Manitoba at its natural best in **Riding Mountain National Park** (p543)

- Meet polar bear and beluga whales in the expanse of the Great White North at **Churchill** (p548)

- Discover 6,000 year-old history at **The Forks National Historic Site** (p534) and take in metropolitan culture in a prairie atmosphere in **Winnipeg** (p530)

- Enjoy sandy beaches and summertime fun at **Lake Winnipeg** (p541), Manitoba's 'coast'

- Explore Canadian nature and Icelandic heritage at **Hecla/Grindstone Provincial Park** (p541)

★ Churchill

★ Lake Winnipeg

Riding Mountain National Park ★

★ Hecla/Grindstone Provincial Park

Winnipeg ★

▪ POPULATION: 1,119,583	▪ PROVINCIAL CAPITAL: WINNIPEG	▪ AREA: 551,937 SQ KM

MANITOBA

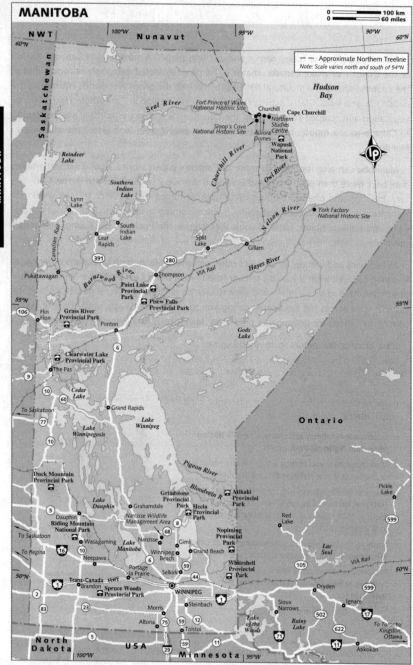

MANITOBA

0	100 km
0	60 miles

— — — Approximate Northern Treeline
Note: Scale varies north and south of 54°N

NWT · **Nunavut** · Hudson Bay

Saskatchewan

Seal River

Fort Prince of Wales
National Historic Site

Churchill · Cape Churchill

Sloop's Cove
National Historic Site

Northern
Studies
Centre

Aurora
Domes

Wapusk
National
Park

Reindeer
Lake

Owl River

Southern
Indian
Lake

Nelson River

Lynn
Lake

York Factory
National Historic Site

South Indian
Lake

Leaf
Rapids

Split
Lake

(280)

Gillam

Canadian Rail

(391)

Burntwood River

Thompson

VIA Rail

Hayes River

Pukatawagan

Paint Lake
Provincial
Park

Pisew Falls
Provincial Park

Flin
Flon

(106)

Grass River
Provincial Park

Ponton

(6)

Gods
Lake

Clearwater Lake
Provincial Park

(9)

The Pas

(10) (60)

Cedar
Lake

To Saskatoon

(77)

Grand Rapids

Lake
Winnipeg

Ontario

(10)

Lake
Winnipegosis

Duck Mountain
Provincial Park

Pigeon River

Pickle
Lake

Lake
Dauphin

Grindstone
Provincial
Park

Bloodvein R.

Atikaki
Provincial
Park

(599)

(5)

Grahamdale

Hecla
Provincial
Park

Red
Lake

Dauphin

Narcisse Wildlife
Management Area

(8)

Riding Mountain
National Park

Narcisse

(68)

Nopiming
Provincial
Park

Lac
Seul

To Saskatoon

(16) (10)

Wasagaming

Lake
Manitoba

Gimli

VIA Rail

To Regina

Neepawa

(6)

Winnipeg
Beach

Grand Beach

(105)

Whiteshell
Provincial
Park

Dryden

(599)

(2)

(1)

Trans-Canada Hwy

Brandon

Portage
la Prairie

Selkirk

(59)

(44)

WINNIPEG

(1)

Sioux
Narrows

Ignace

(17)

(83)

(23)

Spruce Woods
Provincial Park

Steinbach

Lake
of the
Woods

(502)

To Toronto;
Kingston;
Ottawa

Morris

(75) (59)

(12)

Rainy
Lake

(622)

(11)

Altona

Tolstoi

(11)

**North
Dakota**

(5)

USA

(29)

Minnesota

(59)

Atikokan

History

Early European exploration and settlement occurred not in the more hospitable south, but along the cold northern coast of Hudson Bay, where the indigenous Dene got involved in the fur trade soon after the Hudson's Bay Company (HBC) set up trading posts here in the 17th century (see p25).

Assiniboine, Cree and, to a lesser extent, Ojibwe and Algonquin Aboriginals inhabited the region when European exploration moved south. The Algonquin phrase *manito waba* indicates a strait *(waba)* in a huge lake, where water hitting the limestone edges makes an echoing sound associated with the Great Spirit *(manito)*. The lake is now known as Lake Manitoba.

Agricultural settlers moved to the future site of Winnipeg in 1811. Increasing numbers of Métis and an ever-growing government produced constant friction over land rights. When HBC sold parts of the land to the federal government, Métis leader Louis Riel launched a rebellion and formed his own provisional government for Manitoba (see p28). Negotiations between Riel and the federal government resulted in Manitoba joining the federation as Canada's fifth province in 1870.

That opened the door for waves of European settlers (mostly English, Scottish and Ukrainian) in the late 19th century, and established Winnipeg as the economic center for the surrounding farmland.

Climate

The climate in Manitoba is as variable as the geography. Average temperatures in the north range from -50°C to balmy summer highs of 11°C. In the southern areas 25°C is the average summer temperature. Manitoba is notorious for extreme winds all year long; they keep summer bugs away, but also create dust storms. Spring brings flooding to the southern areas.

Winter in the south averages -5°C to -15°C, but the winds can make it feel like -50°C – they don't call the capital 'Winterpeg' for nothing. There may not be a lot of snow coming from the sky, but there will always be lots of it on the ground.

National & Provincial Parks

Manitoba's two national and dozens of provincial parks are great ways to experience the province. Riding Mountain National Park (p543) is a microcosm of Manitoba ecology, while Spruce Woods Provincial Park (p542) is unlike any other place in the province.

Manitoba Provincial Parks Guide is published by **Manitoba Parks** (☎ 800-214-6497; www .manitobaparks.com; admission per day/year $5/20, tent sites

MANITOBA

MANITOBA IN...

Five Days

After two days in **Winnipeg** (p530) head north, stopping at **Lower Fort Garry** (p540) and then **Gimli** (p541) for an afternoon of fun in the sun. Continue north to **Hecla/Grindstone Provincial Park** (p541), grab a campsite or a room, and then take a nature walk at dusk to try and spot a moose, or head to the beach for an amazing sunset. Explore the area's Icelandic roots and return south to Rte 68, turn right and head west. Pause at the **Snake Pits** (p541) if you like, but your destination is **Riding Mountain National Park** (p543).

This park is at your disposal – you name it, you can do it: hiking, canoeing, fishing, biking, wildlife viewing. Spend the next day and night here, then head south in the morning, stopping for a day-hike in the sand dunes of **Spruce Woods Provincial Park** (p542) before returning to Winnipeg.

10 Days

From Rte 68, head north on Hwy 6 (after filling the gas tank) all the way to **Thompson** (p544) for the overnight train to **Churchill** (p545). Spend three days (and two nights) here and see the wildlife, the historic sites and the Eskimo Museum. Catch the overnight train back to Thompson and drive to **Clearwater Lake Provincial Park** (p544) for overnight camping. Drive through **The Pas** (p544) the following day, and hook up with the shorter itinerary at **Riding Mountain National Park** (p543).

NORTHERN WOODS & WATER ROUTE

Take the road less traveled from Manitoba to British Columbia on the series of roads running across northern portions of the four southwesterly provinces. Most of the roads are paved, though there are some stretches of gravel. There are no cities, but many small communities, parks, lakes and woods.

From Winnipeg, the route heads to The Pas, continues to Prince Albert, Saskatchewan, then through Alberta, north of Edmonton, ending at Dawson Creek, British Columbia. The road is marked on signs as 'NWWR.'

$7-14, RV sites $11-18) and available at information centers. An annual pass is a good deal if you'll be visiting parks for more than four days. Try to make reservations using the **Parks Reservation System** (☎ 888-482-2267; www .manitobaparks.com), as campsites often fill up.

Dangers & Annoyances
Mention 'Manitoba' and 'summer' in the same sentence enough times, and you'll hear about a trucker who hit a mosquito so big it blew a tire, or a horsefly that took a football-sized chunk out of someone's shoulder. You will encounter some very large, very nasty insects during the warm months. See p881 for information on avoiding and treating insect bites.

Bear can be a problem if you make them one. See the boxed text on p54 before you head into the woods.

Getting There & Away
Winnipeg is connected by air to several Canadian cities as well as to a few in the USA. Manitoba shares over a dozen US–Canada border crossings with North Dakota and Minnesota. By car, there are several routes into Saskatchewan, especially in the south, but only the Trans-Canada Hwy leads into Ontario (where it becomes Hwy 17). VIA Rail's *Canadian* (p876) passes through Winnipeg, Brandon and other southern communities three times a week.

Getting Around
Calm Air (p868) connects Winnipeg with communities in the north, and northern

communities with each other – some of which are otherwise unreachable.

Southern Manitoba has a fairly tight network of roads and services. If you're driving north, you've got two options: west of Lake Winnipegosis on Hwy 10, or east of Lake Winnipegosis on Hwy 6. Make sure you have a spare tire and a full tank. On Hwy 10 north of Dauphin services are few, and they're nonexistent (except for at Grand Rapids) on Hwy 6 between Grahamdale and Ponton.

VIA Rail (p875) runs the 36-hour, clickety-clack *Hudson Bay* train trip from Winnipeg at 10pm on Sunday, Tuesday and Thursday. It arrives at 8:30am two days later in Churchill, and returns at 8:30pm the same day. Sleepers sell out up to a year in advance and economy cars can fill up. The route jaunts into Saskatchewan and returns to Manitoba, west of The Pas. Round-trip prices range from $330 for a reclining seat to $1290 per person in a single or double room.

WINNIPEG

☎ 204 / pop 620,000

Winnipeg's skyscrapers rise from the surrounding prairies like a metropolitan crop of concrete, glass, history and culture. Though described as 'Canada's Chicago,' the affable and self-sufficient city prefers 'Canada's Winnipeg.' Alone in the southern section of the province, and hours from any other major center, Winnipeg has been getting it done for 200 years, and building its own industry, commerce, arts and culture. The result is an historically rich and profoundly contemporary city where you can catch world-class ballet, eat world flavors and visit world-famous sites all in the same place.

HISTORY
One look at the Assiniboine or Red Rivers and you won't question why the Cree called the area *win nipee* (muddy water). Originally used as an aboriginal camp, the confluence of these rivers was the center of fur-trading rivalry between the HBC and the North West Company in the early 19th century.

In 1812 Lord Selkirk led Scottish and Irish immigrants to the area to create the first permanent colonial settlement. Across the Red River, French settlers established the neighborhood of St Boniface, birthplace of the controversial Métis leader Louis Riel.

The arrival of the railroad in 1886 solidified Winnipeg's commercial importance and made it a natural choice as the provincial capital, which was capped by the HBC moving its headquarters here from London, England.

ORIENTATION

Winnipeg is almost at the longitudinal center of Canada. The Trans-Canada Hwy becomes Portage (*port*-idge) Ave as you arrive from the west. At the intersection with Main St, the Trans-Canada Hwy heads south, then east and out of town. 'Portage and Main' is nationally famous for incred-ibly strong winds and frigid temperatures – so much so that Randy Bachman and Neil Young wrote a song about it. It's also the center of downtown.

To the north is the warehouse-and-arts **Exchange District**, bordered to the north by **Chinatown**. South of downtown is **The Forks** and across the Red River is the French neighborhood of **St Boniface**. West of there is **Osborne Village**.

INFORMATION
Bookstores

McNally Robinson (Map p533; ☎ 204-943-8376; 393 Portage Ave) Large selection of Canadiana.

Red River Books (Map p533; ☎ 943-956-2195; 92 Arthur St) Piles of secondhand books.

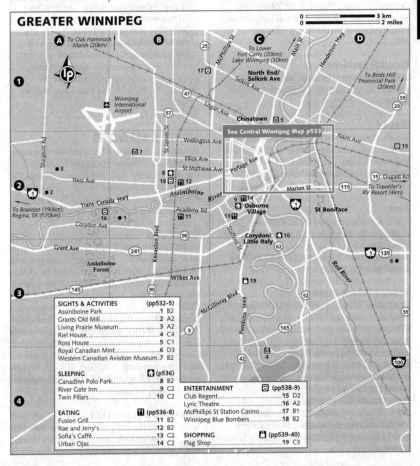

GREATER WINNIPEG

SIGHTS & ACTIVITIES	(pp532–5)
Assiniboine Park	1 B2
Grants Old Mill	2 A2
Living Prairie Museum	3 A2
Riel House	4 C4
Ross House	5 C1
Royal Canadian Mint	6 D3
Western Canadian Aviation Museum	7 B2

SLEEPING	(p536)
CanadInn Polo Park	8 B2
River Gate Inn	9 C2
Twin Pillars	10 C2

EATING	(pp536–8)
Fusion Grill	11 B2
Rae and Jerry's	12 B2
Sofia's Caffé	13 C2
Urban Ojas	14 C2

ENTERTAINMENT	(pp538–9)
Club Regent	15 D2
Lyric Theatre	16 A2
McPhillips St Station Casino	17 B1
Winnipeg Blue Bombers	18 B2

SHOPPING	(pp539–40)
Flag Shop	19 C3

MANITOBA

Cultural Centers

Centre Culturel Franco-Manitobain (Map p533; ☎ 204-233-8972; www.ccfm.mb.ca; 340 Boul Provencher; ☒ 9am-8pm Mon-Fri, noon-5pm Sat & Sun) Café, art gallery and theater in a French neighborhood.

Emergencies

Police, Ambulance & Fire (☎ 911)
Police Dispatch Line (☎ 204-986-6222) For non-emergencies.

Internet Access

The **main post office** (Map p533; ☎ 800-267-1177; 266 Graham Ave) has free 15-minute sessions of dial-up Internet access.

Libraries

Centennial Library (Map p533; ☎ 204-986-6450; www.millenniumlibrary.com; 251 Donald St) Undergoing a complete rebuild and modernization; will reopen summer 2005.

Medical Services

St Boniface General Hospital (Map p533; ☎ 204-233-8563; 409 Ave Taché; ☒ 24hr) Emergency medical services.

Money

There are numerous ATMs aroud town and all the major banks have branches at Portage and Main.

Custom House Currency Exchange (Map p533; ☎ 204-987-6000; 243 Portage Ave)

Post

Look for the red-and-blue signs for postal outlets with extended hours in drugstores around town.

Main Post Office (Map p533; ☎ 800-267-1177; 266 Graham Ave)

Tourist Information

Destination Winnipeg (☎ 800-665-0204; www .destinationwinnipeg.ca) Downtown (Map p533; ☎ 204-943-1970; 259 Portage Ave; ☒ 8:30am-4:30pm Mon-Fri); Airport (☎ 204-982-7543; Main level; ☒ 8am-9:45pm)

Explore Manitoba Centre (Map p533; ☎ 204-945-3777, 800-665-0040; 25 Forks Market Rd; ☒ 10am-6pm) In Johnstone Terminal at The Forks; information center for Winnipeg and Manitoba.

Parks Canada (Map p533; ☎ 204-983-6757, 888-748-2928; www.parkscanada.ca; 25 Forks Market Rd; ☒ 10am-6pm Victoria Day–Labour Day) Information kiosk for The Forks and other national sites. In the Explore Manitoba Centre.

WINNIPEG IN TWO DAYS

Browse the Market Building at **The Forks** (p534) for some breakfast on the banks of the Red River. Visit the **Manitoba Children's Museum** (p535), explore the grounds and walk along the Assiniboine River to the **Legislative Building** (below). Take a picture of Golden Boy and a tour of the building, and then walk west a few blocks for lunch at **Bistro Dansk** (p537). Visit the **Winnipeg Art Gallery** (below) on your way downtown for dinner and the ballet.

Day two is downtown. Face the wind at **Portage and Main** (p531) before or after breakfast in one of the food courts underground. Head into the **Exchange District** (p534), admire the architecture (try Destination Winnipeg's **walking tour**, left) and have dim sum in **Chinatown** (p537). Visit the **Manitoba Museum** (p534) before having dinner near **Old Market Square** (p534) and some theater; alternatively, catch a ballgame and have hotdogs. End the day with a nightcap in the **Exchange District** (p538).

SIGHTS & ACTIVITIES

Winnipeg is mostly concentrated around the walkable area north of the confluence of the Assiniboine and Red Rivers. Across the Red River is the French neighborhood of St Boniface; other sights around Winnipeg are reached most easily by vehicle.

Downtown

LEGISLATIVE BUILDING

The neoclassical beaux-arts design and marble and limestone construction of this **building** (Map p533; ☎ 204-945-5813; 450 Broadway Ave; admission free; ☒ 9am-6pm Mon-Fri, tours hourly Jul 1–Labour Day) flaunts its governmental importance from the cliff above the Red River. The remarkably green park on the south side has a huge monument to Louis Riel. Golden Boy – Winnipeg's oldest resident and city symbol – shines his 23½-carat gold–covered splendor from atop the oxidized copper dome.

WINNIPEG ART GALLERY

Shaped like the bow of a ship, the **WAG** (Map p533; ☎ 204-786-6641; www.wag.mb.ca; 300 Memorial Blvd; adult/child/youth/student/family $6/free/3/4/15;

CENTRAL WINNIPEG

MANITOBA

⊙ 11am-5pm Tue & Thu-Sun, to 9pm Wed) cuts through the waters of tradition and plots a course for contemporary Manitoban and Canadian artists. There's also an excellent collection of Inuit work and, oddly, Gothic and Renaissance altar paintings.

Exchange District
In this 20-block area, 100-year-old brick buildings wearing painted old advertisements house restaurants, nightclubs and art galleries. Destination Winnipeg has a brilliant walking tour booklet ($2) with a full history of most buildings.

Old Market Square (Map p533), at the corner of King St and Bannantyne Ave, is a focal point of the neighborhood; on summer weekends you may find a flea market or live music here.

MANITOBA MUSEUM
The galleries in this Manitoba-focused **museum** (Map p533; ☎ 204-956-2830; www.manitoba museum.mb.ca; 190 Rupert Ave; adult/child/family main galleries $8/6.50/26.50, science gallery $6.50/5/20, planetarium $6.50/5/20, combined ticket $18/12.50/60; ⊙ 10am-5pm) include dioramas that take you into the prairie fields for chores, or into a prairie forest for moose. Nineteen-twenties Winnipeg is recreated, and there is sincere pride in the HBC exhibit, with more than 10,000 pieces.

ARTSPACE
Across from Old Market Square, this massive **warehouse** (Map p533; ☎ 204-947-0984; 100 Arthur St; ⊙ 9am-6pm Tue-Sat) was renovated in order to provide studios for Winnipeg's talents. It houses a couple of galleries and the Cinémathèque (p539).

The Forks
Strategically important and visually fetching, the spot where the Assiniboine and Red Rivers meet has been attracting people for 6000 years. Technically a merging, joining, unification, amalgamation or confluence of two rivers, the area was hastily and fraudulently labeled 'Forks' by early explorers, and the name stuck.

FORKS NATIONAL HISTORIC SITE
Despite the historical gaffe, the **site** (Map p533; ☎ 204-983-6757, 888-748-2928; www.pc.gc.ca/lhn-nhs/ mb/forks) is one of Winnipeg's most popular draws.

The site is essentially a riverside park and recreation area. Excellent footpaths with historical markers in English, French and Cree line the riverbank and join the city's network of pathways. The Market Building and Johnston Terminal buzz with shoppers at produce stands, international art and craft shops, multiethnic food stalls and restaurants.

The rivers routinely overflow during spring runoff and it's not uncommon for some of the paths to be submerged under rising water levels in an event as exciting as it is dangerous. Flow the waterways (weather permitting) with a canoe from **Splash Dash Canoe Rentals** (☎ 204-783-6633; per 30min $7.50; ⊙ 11am-9pm summer). In winter there is skating on the river, cross-country skiing, and you can walk over the ice to St Boniface.

UPPER FORT GARRY GATE
The original oak, stone and mortar in the small **park** (Map p533; 130 Main St) mark the spot where four different forts have stood since 1738. Walk through restored ruins of the old stone gate of Fort Garry, built in 1835.

St Boniface
Across the Red River from The Forks is one of the oldest French communities in Canada outside of Québec. Historically, the river acted as a buffer between the English and French neighborhoods, but today there is a peaceful coexistence. You'll find French culture prominent after crossing the Provencher Bridge.

The tourist offices have an excellent historical self-guided walking map. **Taché Promenade** follows the Red River along Ave Taché, past many of St Boniface's historical sites.

ST BONIFACE BASILICA
The imposing facade is all that's left of the 1908 stone **basilica** (Map p533; 151 Ave de la Cathédrale), destroyed by fire in 1968; the current structure was rebuilt on the ruins. It's a massive place of worship that acted as a cultural beacon for the French neighborhood. Louis Riel rests in the cemetery.

ST BONIFACE MUSEUM
The huge, white mid-19th-century **convent** (Map p533; ☎ 204-237-4500, 494 Ave Taché; adult/child $2/1.50; ⊙ 9am-noon Mon-Fri, 10am-5pm Sat & Sun mid-May–Sep, 9am-noon Mon-Fri, noon-4pm Sun Oct–mid-May), next to the basilica, is the oldest building

in Winnipeg, and the largest oak-log construction on the continent. Its displays and artifacts focus on the establishment of the St Boniface neighborhood, the birth of the Métis nation, and the work and 3000km journey of the Grey Nuns. They also tell the story of the voyageurs (early French fur traders/explorers).

Greater Winnipeg

There are several attractions within the greater Winnipeg area. These include **Grants Old Mill** (Map p531; ☎ 204-986-5613; 2777 Portage Ave; admission free; ☺ 10am-6pm May–Labour Day), an 1829 log-and-stone water mill west of downtown, and the **Living Prairie Museum** (Map p531; ☎ 204-832-0167; 2795 Ness Ave; admission free; ☺ 10am-5pm Jul & Aug, Sun only Apr-Jun), a 12-hectare area protecting the original, unploughed, now-scarce, tall prairie grass. **Ross House** (Map p531; ☎ 204-943-3958; Joe Zuken Heritage Park, 140 Mead St N; admission free; ☺ 11am-6pm Wed-Sun Jun-Aug) is a small log cabin where William Ross ran the first post office in the west.

ROYAL CANADIAN MINT

Those much-beloved loonies and toonies weighing down your pockets were made at this **mint** (Map p531; ☎ 204-257-3359; 520 Boul Lagimodière; admission $2; ☺ 9am-5pm Mon-Fri, 10am-2pm Sat & Sun May-Aug, 10am-2pm Mon-Fri Sep-Apr). The pyramid-shaped glass facility also makes coins for many other countries, mainly Latin American ones, and the guided tours show how they crank out 15 million pieces a day.

RIEL HOUSE

After Louis Riel was executed for treason, his body was brought to his childhood **home** (Map p531; ☎ 204-257-1783; 330 River Rd; admission free; ☺ 10am-6pm mid-May–Labour Day) in St Vital before being buried in St Boniface (opposite). The plain cottage is set up in 1886 fashion, acting as a life-sized tribute. Costumed staff are knowledgeable on Riel and the Métis in general.

WESTERN CANADIAN AVIATION MUSEUM

In a hangar opposite the airport, the **museum** (WCAM; Map p531; ☎ 204-786-5503; 958 Ferry Rd; admission adult/child/family $5/3/12; ☺ 10am-4pm Mon-Sat, 1-4pm Sun) has a shiny collection of flying machines. Kids love the Skyways exhibit, with hands-on displays about the physics of

aerodynamics, and the chance to play pilot, navigator or air-traffic controller with actual equipment that grown-ups use.

WINNIPEG FOR CHILDREN

The words 'hands off' simply don't exist at the **Manitoba Children's Museum** (Map p533; ☎ 204-956-5437; www.childrensmuseum.com; 25 Forks Market Rd, Forks; adult/child/senior $6/5.50/5; ☺ 9:30am-4:30pm Sun-Thu, to 8pm Fri & Sat), where the best way of learning is by doing. The colorful, interactive exhibits encourage tykes to act as train conductors, astronauts and TV producers.

White snow leopards, white Bengal tigers and white polar bear are some of the 1800 animals at **Assiniboine Park** (Map p531; ☎ 204-986-6921; 460 Assiniboine Park Dr; adult/child/youth/senior/family $4/3.75/2.50/2/13.50; ☺ 10am-8pm Victoria Day–early Aug, 10am-7pm early Aug–Labour Day, hours vary in winter), a zoo that specializes in animals indigenous to harsher climates. Children love the close-up views. Kids of all ages will have a special fondness for the statue of Winnie the Bear, the inspiration for AA Milne's *Winnie the Pooh*.

The much-heralded Manitoba Theatre for Young People (p539) puts on performances for kids and teens, without being too patronizing for adults.

Kids also love the aviation gadgets at the Western Canadian Aviation Museum (p535) and the Science Gallery in the Manitoba Museum (p534).

TOURS

Beaver Tails and River Trails (☎ 204-983-6757, 888-748-2928; adult/child/youth $3/free/1.50; ☺ departs 11am Tue-Sun Jul & Aug) Costumed tour guides tell the 6000-year history of The Forks.

Ô Tours (☎ 204-254-3170; www.otours.net; 3hr tours $20-30) Themed city tours (some in French) visit Winnipeg neighborhoods by water taxi.

Paddlewheel River Rouge Tours (Map p533; ☎ 204-944-8000; www.paddlewheelcruises.com; 78 George Ave; boat tours adult/child/senior $13/7.50/12.75 ☺ May-Oct) Boat or double-decker bus tours.

FESTIVALS & EVENTS

February

Festival du Voyageur (☎ 204-237-7692; www.festival voyageur.mb.ca; ☺ mid-Feb) A 10-day festival celebrating fur traders and French voyageurs (boatmen employed by one of the early fur-trading companies). Concerts, dogsled races and a huge winter street party.

MANITOBA

June

Red River Exhibition (☎ 204-888-6990; www.red riverex.com; 3977 Portage Ave; ☿ late Jun) Ferris wheels, cotton candy and stage performances along the river banks.
Winnipeg Pride (www.gaypridewinnipeg.com; ☿ early Jun) A 10-day gay-and-lesbian celebration featuring baseball games, films and parties.

July

Winnipeg Folk Festival (☎ 204-231-0096; www.win nipegfolkfestival.ca; ☿ mid-Jul) More than 200 concerts on seven stages in Birds Hill Provincial Park (p540).
Winnipeg Fringe Festival (☎ 204-943-7464; www .winnipegfringe.com; ☿ mid-Jul) North America's second-largest fringe festival with international fringe theater, comedy, mime, music and cabaret.

August

Folklorama (☎ 204-982-6230; www.folklorama.ca; ☿ early Aug) Two-week fest celebrating Winnipeg's multiculturalism.

SLEEPING

The provincial **B&B Association** (☎ 204-661-5218; www.bedandbreakfast.mb.ca) or the information centers can help with B&B selection. The major routes in and out of the city are littered with standard motels.

Downtown

Guest House International Hostel (Map p533; ☎ 204-772-1272, 800-743-4423; www.backpackerswinnipeg.com; 168 Maryland St; s/d $22/42; ℗) The lived-in, cluttered but well-kept backpackers hostel has a variety of rooms; the street side is sunnier. There's a games room, a kitchen, a laundry and Internet access ($3 per 30 minutes).

Ivey House Hostel (Map p533; ☎ 204-772-3022, 866-762-4122; fax 204-784-1133; 210 Maryland St; s/d $24/42) This old, creaky turreted house has smallish rooms, but it's hip and super-friendly. It offers packages to Churchill during wildlife-watching seasons.

Gordon Downtowner Motor Hotel (Map p533; ☎ 204-943-5581; fax 204-943-5581; 330 Kennedy St; r $45-60) Purple on the outside, pink on the inside, this downtown hotel has rooms with new furniture in most. It's better than other downtown options.

Fort Garry Hotel (Map p533; ☎ 204-942-8251, 800-665-8088; www.fortgarryhotel.com; 222 Broadway Ave; s/d/ste incl buffet breakfast from $110/130/180; ☒) This 1913 grand hotel is a piece of Winnipeg history. The granite steps and wide, paisley hallways lead you to your spacious,

solid room. The duvets are overstuffed, and the light earth tones are comforting. Even-numbered rooms face the river.

The Forks

Inn at The Forks (Map p533; ☎ 204-942-6555, 877-377-4100; www.innforks.com; 75 Forks Market Rd; r $130-85, ste $200) Winnipeg's newest hotel is at Winnipeg's oldest location. Open since 2004, it was built with historical sensitivity and blends in well with the existing buildings. The stone- and wood-colored rooms range from standard to multiroom suites.

St Boniface

Norwood Hotel (Map p533; ☎ 204-233-4475; www .norwood-hotel.com; 112 Marion St; s/d $80/90; ℗) A friendly, family-owned boutique hotel, Norwood has clean, amazingly spacious rooms. The floral bedcovers are predictable, as is the standard furniture, but the staff will go out of their way to enhance your stay. It's close to downtown.

Greater Winnipeg

Traveller's RV Resort (☎ 204-864-2721; fax 204-253-9313; 870 Murdock Rd; tent/RV $17/25; ☿ May–mid-Oct; ☒) This grassy, family-friendly place is near town.

River Gate Inn (Map p531; ☎ 866-397-3345; www .rivergateinn.com; 186 West Gate; r $80-120; ℗ ☒) Shiny hardwood floors, four-poster beds and stone fireplaces create comfort at this huge mansion at Armstrong Point. The sleek billiard room adds a modern touch.

CanadInn Polo Park (Map p531; ☎ 204-775-8791; 1405 St Matthews Ave; www.canadinns.com; s/d from $90/100, ste $120-60; ℗ ☒) This regional chain, 2km west of downtown, has families in mind, especially those with restless children, who love the kid-themed suites. Themes for adults range from Old West to Japan.

Twin Pillars (Map p531; ☎ 204-284-7590; www.mts .net/~tls1; 235 Oakwood Ave; s $45-70, d $55-80) This red two-story Victorian is 2km south of The Forks, and walking distance to Osborne Village. It's an impeccably well-kept home with a big front balcony on the 2nd floor.

EATING

There's no shortage of diners, restaurants and take-out around downtown and The Forks, while the Exchange District to the north and Osborne Village to the south are home to funky cafés and chic bistros.

Downtown & The Forks
BUDGET
The Market Building at The Forks has multiethnic food stalls and small cafés. The walkways under Portage and Main are filled with food courts and decent diners and cafés.

Wagon Wheel (Map p533; ☎ 204-942-6695; 305 Hargrave St; mains $5-9; ☺ 6am-6pm) This narrow, easy-to-miss hole-in-the-wall has stools so close to the counter they're almost useless. It roasts its own turkey daily, and the soups are delicious, but the lunch crowd keeps coming back for the knockout club sandwiches.

Salisbury House (Map p533; ☎ 204-956-1714; 354 Portage Ave; mains $5-8; ☺ 7am-11pm) The downtown original of an expanding local chain, which is part-owned by Burton Cummings (see p538), is still the real thing. 'Nip and chips' is Sal's signature dish, a nip being a hamburger with a spiced beef patty served with fried onions.

VJ's Drive-In (Map p533; ☎ 204-943-2655; 170 Main St; mains $4-9; ☺ lunch & dinner) Across Main St from the train station, VJ's is the favorite spot for a take-out grease fix. It's a good place to get a burger to go while you wait for the train.

Wordsworth Building Cafeteria (Map p533; ☎ 204-944-8927; 405 Broadway Ave; items $2-7; ☺ breakfast & lunch) It seems half the downtown crowd comes here for lunch from the large salad bar in the open, airy lunchroom.

MID-RANGE
Bistro Dansk (Map p533; ☎ 204-775-5662; 63 Sherbrooke St; mains $6-10; ☺ 11am-2:30pm & 5-9pm Tue-Sat) This locally owned Danish and European café always has a light buzz of energy from the diners, who come for the hearty and delicious soups. Red and green vinyl chairs, wood paneling and newspaper article–covered walls add charm, and cheap wine prices, imported beers and homemade bread add to the dining experience.

One Night in Bangkok (Map p533; ☎ 204-777-0888; 207 Edmonton St; mains $6-14; ☺ lunch & dinner) Buddha statues now adorn this one-time Swiss chalet. Livelier colors have been added and chicken skewers and Thai curries have replaced the Wiener schnitzel. This can be a hopping little place some evenings.

Brio Restaurant (Map p533; ☎ 204-948-0085; Top fl, 300 Memorial Blvd; mains $7-12; ☺ 11:00am-4:30pm Tue-Fri, 10:00am-4:30pm Sat & Sun) Royal-blue linen and lots of windows are the setting for this semiformal restaurant above the art gallery. Seafood dishes such as lobster bisque and lemon-pepper pickerel stand out.

St Boniface
Step 'N Out (Map p533; ☎ 204-956-7837; 157 Boul Provencher; lunch $9-12, dinner $18-24; ☺ lunch & dinner) This romantic place has recently taken its soft colors and cozy tables to St Boniface. The eclectic food mixes Asian and Western cuisines; only organically grown vegetables are served.

Three Sisters Teahouse (Map p533; ☎ 204-885-2755; 271 Boul Provencher; mains $3-6; ☺ 8am-5pm) A quaint and proper place serving fluffy omelettes for breakfast, and delicious sandwiches and salads for lunch. Several varieties of loose tea are also available and steeped to your liking.

La Vielle Gare (Map p533; ☎ 204-237-7072; 630 Rue des Meurons; lunch mains $8-15, dinner mains $15-30; ☺ lunch & dinner) A former train station is now a fine French restaurant with dark wood and linens. Enjoy drinks in the 1914 passenger-car lounge before your foie gras and filet mignon.

Exchange District
Old brick warehouses have been reinvented as restaurants and bars in this district, north of downtown. The smells and tastes of Winnipeg's small Chinatown are further north of there.

Johnny G's (Map p533; ☎ 204-942-6656; 117 McDermot Ave; mains $6-13; ☺ lunch & dinner) Nothing says 'classic retro diner' like neon delight and the ass-end of an old Chevy sticking out of a brick building. Inside the Formica and chrome wonder, burgers, fries and shakes are served to the tunes of Buddy Holly.

Kum-Koon Garden (Map p533; ☎ 204-943-4655; 257 King St; mains $6-10; ☺ lunch & dinner) No matter how big your appetite, you won't leave Kum-Koon's hungry. Excellent dim sum is popular with downtown workers.

Tre Visi (Map p533; ☎ 204-949-9032; 173 McDermot Ave; mains $8-18; ☺ lunch & dinner) A stylish interior with white tables, yellow walls and textured pillars combines with excellent Italian food. Dishes such as *linguine adriatiche* (mussels and clams in white-wine and tomato sauce) fill the air with delightful aromas. Reservations are recommended.

MANITOBA

Osborne Village & Around

South of downtown, Osborne Village and Corydon Ave (the Italian area) are Winnipeg's funky neighborhoods.

Fusion Grill (Map p531; ☎ 204-489-6963; 550 Academy Rd; mains $8-17; ☺ lunch & dinner Tue-Sat) Simple booths and a hip young crowd have made this bistro a favorite. Foodsmiths use local fish, fowl and game, combined with more exotic techniques and spices, to bring Manitoba fusion to the culinary arena.

Urban Ojas (Map p531; ☎ 204-953-1812; 684 Osborne St; breakfast & lunch $6-12, dinner $12-23; ☺ 8am-11pm) Granite, brick, wood and glass back up an organic menu boasting dishes such as free-range chicken and crab risotto. Cornmeal and pine-nut pancakes for breakfast, or the crab fritters on the lunch/dinner menu, remind us how real food should taste.

Rae and Jerry's (Map p531; ☎ 204-775-8154; 1405 Portage Ave; mains $15-30; ☺ lunch & dinner) Winnipeg's long-serving steakhouse is known for its horseradish-spiked prime rib. The food on the fine-dining menu is taken seriously; the informal atmosphere is designed for fun.

Sofia's Caffé (Map p531; ☎ 204-452-3037; 635 Corydon Ave; mains $8-16; ☺ lunch & dinner) Quality pastas and chicken dishes in an informal atmosphere. Not only is the cream sauce on the fettuccine as smooth as velvet, but the portions are huge.

DRINKING

Shannon's Irish Pub (Map p533; ☎ 204-943-2302; 175 Carlton St) This new downtown pub has quickly become popular. The owners support Manchester United, but don't hold that against them, as they also have live Celtic music on weekends.

Royal Crown Building (Map p533; ☎ 204-947-1990; 83 Garry St) Thirty floors above The Forks, this is a nice place to sit and sip on a Manhattan or a martini.

King's Head Pub (Map p533; ☎ 204-957-7710; 120 King St) This busy British-style pub in the Exchange District is full of regulars; in an hour you'll make a bunch of new drinking buddies.

ENTERTAINMENT

Winnipeg has always had an arts scene, but it's really been on the rise in recent years. For events listings, check the *Winnipeg Free Press* on Thursday. For tickets contact **Ticketmaster** (☎ 204-780-3333; www.ticketmaster.ca) or venue box offices; student discounts are often available:

Burton Cummings Theatre (Map p533; ☎ 204-956-5656; 364 Smith St) Named in honor of the man who saved the 1907 former movie house, it now shows live theater and concerts.

Centre Culturel Franco-Manitobain (Map p533; ☎ 204-233-8972; www.ccfm.mb.ca; 340 Boul Provencher; tickets $26) The center puts on free jazz shows Tuesday evenings, acoustic shows on Friday and whimsical theater other nights. You don't have to *parler français* (speak French) to enjoy.

MTS Centre (Map p533; ☎ 204-987-7825; www.true northproject.mb.ca; cnr Portage Ave & Donald St) Winnipeg finally got a downtown arena when this one opened in November 2004. It hosts concerts and sporting events.

Nightclubs

Much of the dance scene is in the Exchange District; follow the crowds.

291 Bannatyne (Map p533; ☎ 204-987-3391; 291 Bannatyne Ave) It's a brick-and-concrete garage-turned-nightclub, but don't expect a blue-collar place; wear black.

Empire (Map p533; ☎ 204-943-3979; 436 Main St) Latin and European dance beats pulse the night away in this three-story concrete historic bank building, where you can escape into any of the many rooms or the outside courtyard.

There are other recommended bars:

Au Bar (Map p533; 65 Rorie St) Chic lounge that's good for martinis.

Coyote Cafe (Map p533; ☎ 204-957-7665; 171 McDermont) Young crowd and fun times.

Desire (Map p533; ☎ 204-956-5544; 441 Main St) Gay and lesbian club.

Phat Daddy's (Map p533; ☎ 204-284-7428; 165 McDermont) Hip-hop dance club and lounge with over-stuffed couches.

Live Music

Winnipeg is known for good blues. For folksy-acoustic fun, Osborne Village and Cordyon Ave have unfussy cafés and bar-restaurants.

Rogue's Gallery (Map p533; ☎ 204-947-0652; 432 Assiniboine Ave) Leave your shoes and attitude at the door; acoustic singer-songwriters play at this gay-friendly coffeehouse.

Times Change Café (Map p533; ☎ 204-957-0982; 234 Main St) This inexpensive café is good for jazz and blues, with live shows on weekend evenings.

Windsor Hotel (Map p533; ☎ 204-942-7528; 187 Garry St) The classic Windsor is the best place for live blues.

Centennial Concert Hall (Map p533; ☎ 204-956-1360; 555 Main St) is the home of the **Winnipeg Symphony Orchestra** (☎ 204-949-3999; www.wso .mb.ca; tickets $20-56) and the highly acclaimed **Manitoba Opera** (☎ 204-942-7479; www.manitoba opera.mb.ca; tickets $29-84; ☺ Nov-Apr) complete with subtitles, so you're not left guessing.

Theater & Cinema

Royal Winnipeg Ballet (Map p533; ☎ 204-956-2792, 800-667-4792; www.rwb.org; cnr Graham Ave & Edmonton St; tickets $12-35) A company with an excellent international reputation and a casual atmosphere.

Lyric Theatre (Map p531; ☎ 204-888-5466; 55 Pavilion Cres; admission free; ☺ summer) The theatre holds family-oriented (Pooh Friendship Day is in mid-August) shows in the Assiniboine Park bandstand. Ballet, symphony or jazz is performed; bring lawn chairs and a picnic and enjoy.

Manitoba Theatre Centre (Map p533; ☎ 204-942-6537; www.mtc.mb.ca; 174 Market Ave; tickets $20-40) This company stages mainstream Broadway on the main stage, and thought-provoking, independent dramas and comedies in a warehouse.

Pantages Playhouse (Map p533; ☎ 204-989-2889; www.pantagesplayhouse.com; 180 Market Ave) A 1913 luxury theater that puts on traditional theatrical and musical shows.

Manitoba Theatre for Young People (Map p533; ☎ 204-942-8898; www.mtyp.ca; 2 Forks Market Rd; tickets $10-12; ☺ Oct-May) Colorful sets and enthusiastic performances will appeal to children, but kids of all ages will enjoy themselves.

Cinémathèque (Map p533; ☎ 204-925-3457; 100 Arthur St) This cinema shows Canadian and international films, from art flicks to Monty Python comedies.

Raising Spirits (Map p533; ☎ 204-983-6757; Forks Amphitheatre; adult/youth $6/4; ☺ Jul & Aug) This outdoor theater at The Forks hosts live performances telling 6000-year-old and more recent stories.

Sports

Winnipeg Blue Bombers (Map p531; ☎ 204-784-2583, www.bluebombers.com; 1430 Maroons Rd; tickets $12-45; ☺ Jun-Oct) The Bombers chase their Canadian Football League Grey Cup championship dreams at CanadInns Stadium.

Manitoba Moose (Map p533; ☎ 204-780-7328; www.moosehockey.com; tickets $15-30; ☺ Sep-Mar) The American Hockey League (AHL) minor-league team for the National Hockey League's (NHL) Vancouver Canucks showcases future big-league talent in the new MTS Centre (p538).

Winnipeg Goldeyes (Map p533; ☎ 204-982-2273; www.goldeyes.com; Mill St; tickets $3-14; ☺ May-Sep) In a perfect spot for summer-evening ballgames by the river, the Goldeyes are inexpensive fun at CanWest Global Park.

Casinos

Winnipeg pioneered legal gambling houses in Canada, then the provincial government set up gambling-addiction programs. Both casinos have gaming tables (mainly blackjack and poker), huge bingo rooms and a zillion slot machines ranging from 5¢ to $20. There are smoking and nonsmoking gaming areas, but no entry for anyone under 18.

Club Regent (Map p531; ☎ 204-957-2700; 1425 Regent Ave; ☺ 24hr) A neon palm tree, walk-through aquarium and replicated Mayan ruins emulate the Caribbean theme.

McPhillips St Station Casino (Map p531; ☎ 204-957-3900; 484 McPhillips St; ☺ 24hr) The Old West train-station motif carries throughout the sprawling building.

SHOPPING

The huge indoor shopping mall, **Portage Place** (Map p533; ☎ 204-925-4636; Portage Ave, at Vaughn St) takes up three city blocks downtown and houses 160 stores. The area south of the Assiniboine River between Stradbrook Ave and Donald St, along Osborne St, is called Osborne Village and has funky, artistic shops.

United Army Surplus Sales (Map p533; ☎ 204-786-5421; 460 Portage Ave) has an exhaustive inventory. Charmingly disorganized, it's a great source for inexpensive camping equipment. Canada's favorite outdoor toy store, **MEC** (Map p533; ☎ 204-943-4202; www.mec.ca; 303 Portage Av) recently opened an impressive location downtown; they rent gear as well.

Bay (Map p533; ☎ 204-783-2112; cnr Portage Ave & Memorial Blvd) The world's oldest incorporated trading company has a modern department store above ground. In the basement are souvenirs, wool coats, and blankets reminiscent of when this was a trodden trading post (see the boxed text on p25).

Winnipeg is a good place to shop for northern aboriginal art, if you're not going up that way. **Northern Images** (Map p533; ☎ 204-942-5501; Portage Place; 393 Portage Ave) is a national chain selling authentic Dene and Inuit crafts, and **Upstairs Gallery** (Map p533; ☎ 204-943-2734; 266 Edmonton St) has stunningly detailed carvings of animals and humans.

Flag Shop (Map p533; ☎ 204-452-2689; 1195 Pembina Hwy) There's literally every kind of flag imaginable here, as well as pins, pennants and badges.

GETTING THERE & AWAY
Air
Winnipeg International Airport (Map p531; YWG; 2000 Wellington Ave) is 10km west of downtown. National carriers serve Canadian destinations, while Calm Air makes trips north. Northwest Airlines heads to US destinations, usually transferring in Minneapolis.

Bus
Greyhound uses the **Mall Centre Bus Depot** (Map p533; ☎ 204-783-8857; 487 Portage Ave) for three eastbound buses to Regina ($86, seven to eight hours), three westbound buses to Thunder Bay ($85, nine hours) and two northbound to Thompson ($90, nine hours) daily.

Train
VIA Rail's *Canadian* (see p876) passes through Winnipeg's **station** (Map p533; 123 Main St) at 4:55pm Wednesday, Friday and Sunday on its way west; the eastbound train arrives on Tuesday, Thursday and Sunday at 12:10pm. VIA Rail also sends the thrice-weekly *Hudson Bay* north to Churchill.

GETTING AROUND
Walking is easy and enjoyable from downtown to any of the surrounding neighborhoods. If the weather is crummy, a series of under- and above-ground walkways connect downtown buildings; Destination Winnipeg (p532) has a map.

To/From the Airport
A taxi from the airport to downtown costs $20. Winnipeg Transit's Sargent bus No 15 runs between the airport and downtown every 20 minutes (adult/child $1.80/1.50).

Car & Motorcycle
Parking at The Forks is free for patrons for three hours; for nonpatrons it's $1.25 per hour. Downtown car parks are plentiful,

though you'll have more luck and cheaper prices at Portage Place (p539; $3 per hour). Street parking is free after 6pm.

Don't leave your car at the Winnipeg train station while you're in Churchill: break-ins are common. The multilevel lot downtown on Edmonton St, near St Mary Ave, is a better option, or drive or take the bus to Thompson, then board the train from there.

Major car-rental agencies (p873) have counters at the airport, and in or near downtown.

Public Transportation
Winnipeg Transit (☎ 204-986-5700; www.winnipeg transit.com; adult/child $1.80/1.50) runs extensive bus routes around the Winnipeg area. Ask for a transfer and use exact change. Its free Downtown Spirit buses run on four downtown routes.

Water Taxi
See the city from a new perspective by taking **Splash Dash Water Taxi** (Map p533; ☎ 204-783-6633; one-way fare $2.50, day pass $15; ⊙ 10am-11pm May-Aug, noon-8pm Sep & Oct) between The Forks, the legislative building, St Boniface, Osborne Village and the Exchange District.

AROUND WINNIPEG
Birds Hill Provincial Park
Local families love this well laid out **park** (☎ 204-222-9151; Park Rd, off Hwy 59; admission $5; ⊙ dawn-dusk), 24km north of Winnipeg, with paths safe for cycling or roller-blading, sandy beaches and walking trails under canopies of trees, where deer and wild turkey are often spotted.

Lower Fort Garry
Surrounded by stone walls on the banks of the Red River is a restored HBC **fort** (☎ 204-785-6050; Hwy 9; adult/child/senior/family $5.50/3/5/16.50; ⊙ 9am-5pm mid-May–Labour Day). Impeccably neat, and recreated to reflect the 1830s, it's the only stone fort still intact from fur-trading days. Huge gates open onto the river.

Oak Hammock Marsh
Southern Manitoba's wetlands are critical homes and migration stopping points for hundreds of thousands of birds. In the middle of a field north of Winnipeg is **Oak Hammock Marsh** (☎ 204-467-3300; Rte 200, at Hwy 67; adult/child/family $4/3/14; ⊙ 10am-4:30pm, to 8pm

May-Oct), one of the best bird sanctuaries on the continent. Three hundred species of birds have been recorded here, and 250,000 to 450,000 geese show up in fall on their way south. Boardwalks, telescopes, remote-controlled cameras and canoes get you close to the birds. An excellent display center uses interactive exhibits and computer games to teach children about the local wildlife.

LAKE WINNIPEG

The southern end of Canada's fifth-largest lake has been a resort destination since the 1920s. The sandy white beaches, clear water and oceanlike size of the lake made a visit 'going to the coast' for all Winnipeggers. It's still a tremendously popular summer destination; in winter, when the lake is frozen and lined with snowy white beaches, the area is virtually deserted.

Most of the land around the lake is privately owned. Plenty of small towns and villages are lived in year-round, generally in the area between Lake Winnipeg and Lakes Manitoba and Winnipegosis, which is known as Interlake. North of here, it's just you and the wilderness.

GRAND BEACH

Sandy white beaches on Lake Winnipeg's eastern shore make Grand Beach the unofficial center of summer fun. Out of season it's a ghost town. Sand dunes pile up behind the beach and reach heights of 12m, and the lagoon behind accommodates hundreds of bird species. There is hiking in the area, but the main activity is sunning on the beach or walking the boardwalks along it. **Grand Beach Provincial Park & Campground** (☎ 204-754-2212; Hwy 12; tent/RV sites $12/15) is one of the busiest campgrounds in the province, which means that it does have a tendency to be quite loud. Book in advance. Grand Beach is 80km from Winnipeg.

GIMLI

Gimli (Icelandic for 'land of the Gods' and named long before *The Lord of the Rings*) is an Icelandic settlement 20km north of Winnipeg Beach, with beaches and a neat downtown, highlighted by the path along the harbor, the murals near the marina, and the Viking statue overlooking the lake.

New Iceland Heritage Museum (☎ 204-642-4001; 94 1st Ave; adult/child/youth/family $6/free/4/15; ☼ 10am-4pm May-Sep) outlines the little-known but fascinating history of an unlikely people settling in an even unlikelier part of Canada. It's a small building by the water, but packed with history and loads of artifacts. The Icelandic festival **Islendingadagurinn** (☎ 204-642-7417; www .icelandicfestival.com; ☼ late Jul) kicks off with Islendingadance, and hosts pancake breakfasts, rides, games and music, before wrapping up with an Iceland-themed parade.

There are several standard motels in Winnipeg Beach and along the way to Gimli and in between.

Lakeview Resort (☎ 204-642-8565; 877-355-3500; www.lakeviewhotels.com/li_gimli; 10 Centre St; s/d $100/110) is a modern, luxury resort with courteous staff and large, paisley-decorated and brightly lit rooms, right by the lake at the end of town.

Whitecap's Restaurant (☎ 204-642-9735; 72 1st Ave; mains $7-18) is a local institution located in a limestone building with blue-and-white linen. It's definitely a no-attitude kind of place. The menu is far reaching, and you can't go wrong with a juicy burger or grilled pickerel, the local catch.

HECLA/GRINDSTONE PROVINCIAL PARK

This collection of islands, marshes and forests is Manitoba at its natural best. It's breezy enough to almost keep all the bugs away, which makes it appealing to deer, moose, beaver and bear. Don't be surprised if you spot them on the causeway, or stop at **Grassy Narrows Marsh** and some of the other nature trails at the park's entrance leading to good viewing spots. There's a **park office** (☎ 204-378-2945; Hwy 8; tent/RV sites $12/15) for information.

Hecla Village was an Icelandic settlement in 1876. **Heritage Home Museum** (Village Rd; admission free; ☼ 10am-4pm mid-May–Labour Day) is an outdoor self-guided drive/walk of the settlement and the historically striking buildings that remain on the lakeshore.

SNAKE PITS

The **Narcisse Wildlife Management Area** (www.gov .mb.ca/conservation/wildlife/managing/snakes_narcisse .html; Hwy 17; admission free; ☼ dawn-dusk) protects the world's largest population of red-sided garter snakes. In late April and early May, tens of thousands of the harmless creatures emerge from their limestone lairs in a mating ritual for what are basically writhing, snake-orgy masses. They return to their dens in late September, but remain at the doors until cold weather forces them to crawl inside.

Along the 3km trail you'll hear the slithering funsters before you come across one of the three pits. There are interpretive signs that teach you all you ever needed to know. Take Hwy 17 6km north from Narcisse.

SOUTHEASTERN MANITOBA

The eastern border region of Manitoba has the same rugged woodland terrain as neighboring Ontario. Toward Winnipeg this begins to give way to the flatter expanse of the southern prairies.

MENNONITE HERITAGE VILLAGE

An 80km drive southeast of Winnipeg, through sunflower country, is the town of Steinbach, a Mennonite community. The recreated late-19th-century **Mennonite village** (☎ 204-326-9661; www.mennoniteheritagevillage .com; Hwy 12; adult/child/student/senior/family $8/2/4/6/20; ☸ 10am-4pm Mon-Fri Oct-Apr, to 5pm Mon-Sat & noon-5pm Sun May, Jun & Sep, to 9pm Mon-Sat & to 6pm Sun Jul & Aug) is 2km north of town. There's a replica windmill, and buildings ranging from farmhouses to modern businesses. A restaurant (mains $6 to $9) serves borscht and other Mennonite foods. The information center has information on their emigration from Europe, a quilting exhibit and a workshop.

WHITESHELL PROVINCIAL PARK

This 2590-sq-km park, 120km east of Winnipeg, gives a sneak peek at the green forests and clear lakes of northern Ontario. Trees pop out of the plains as soon as you cross the park border and the elevated topography allows rivers to rush down their slopes. There are numerous canoe routes, including a popular one through the tunnel on **Caddy Lake**, and trails good for hiking in summer and cross-country skiing in winter. The offices at summertime-only entrance gates have hiking information.

Most of the larger recreation areas have park offices, including one in the village of **Rennie** (☎ 204-369-5232, 800-214-6497; Hwy 44; ☸ 8am-noon & 1-4pm Mon-Fri).

The area around Falcon and West Hawk lakes has services and resorts, though a lot close during the winter. **Falcon Lake Resort Hotel** (☎ 204-349-8400; www.falcon-resort.mb.ca; Falcon Lake; s/d/ste from $60/70/90; ☒), open year-round, is near Rennie and has a sandy beach. The rooms are basic but the woodsy suites are pretty sweet. They have patios – with barbecue – and some have hot tubs. Also open year-round, **West Hawk Lake Resort** (☎ 204-349-2244; Hwy 44; cabins $75-90), 3km north of Hwy 1, offers clean, large two-bedroom cabins.

There are hundreds of **campsites** (tent sites $7-12, RV sites $12-15) in the park. **Lakeshore (Mohakan) Campground** (tent/RV sites $12/15) in Rennie has more trees and seclusion, and is only a short walk from Falcon Lake.

WESTERN MANITOBA

The agricultural lands dotted with parks, from Winnipeg westward toward the Saskatchewan border, are worth a visit.

SPRUCE WOODS PROVINCIAL PARK

South of the Hwy 1 is a place unlike any Manitoba you know. Shifting sand dunes and unlikely cacti at this 27,000-hectare **park** (☎ 204-827-8850; Hwy 5) provide a home for creatures such as Manitoba's only lizard: the northern prairie skink. Walking trails lead to some of the more interesting sections of the park, including the 1.6km trail to the dunes at Spirit Sands. At the park's entrance (parking $5), bikes can be rented ($5 per hour), and **Spirit Sands Wagon Outfitters** (☎ 204-827-2800; adult/child $8/5) take two-hour horsedrawn covered wagons around the park.

BRANDON

Brandon is an attractive residential city bisected by the Assiniboine River. The second-largest city in the province has a brick downtown and walking paths along the river. Tourist information is available at the **Riverbank Discovery Centre** (☎ 204-729-2141; 545 Conservation Dr; 8:30am-5pm Mon-Fri, noon-5pm Sat & Sun).

In a charming redbrick building named after Brandon's first mayor, the **Daly House Museum** (☎ 204-727-1722; 122 18th St; adult/child/family $3/2/7; ⊙ 10am-noon & 1-5pm Tue-Sun) is chock-full of Victoriana and local history including the whole Brandon pharmacy, c 1915.

Outside of town at the airport, the **Commonwealth Air Training Plan Museum** (☎ 204-727-2444; www.airmuseum.ca; Hwy 10; adult/child $5/3; ⊙ 10am-4pm May-Sep, 1-4pm Oct-Apr) tells the story of the thousands of recruits from around the British Commonwealth who trained for WWII before heading over to Europe. The 13 original training planes are only part of the exhibit.

Laugh all you will about Canada's military, but there's more at the **Royal Regiment of Canadian Artillery** (☎ 204-765-3000, Hwy 340; admission free; ⊙ 8am-4pm Mon-Fri & 1-4pm Sat & Sun Jun-Aug, 8am-4pm Tue-Fri Sep-May) than 12 BB-guns and an aluminum pot. More than 60 vehicles plus a collection of uniforms, guns and ammunition dating from 1796 through to the cold war are displayed. The museum is in Shilo, 20km east of Brandon; take Hwy 340 south from Hwy 1. Standard motels and restaurants line the exits from Hwy 1, and a few local eateries can be found downtown.

Greyhound Canada has five daily buses to Winnipeg from Brandon's downtown **depot** (☎ 204-727-0643; 141 6th St).

RIDING MOUNTAIN NATIONAL PARK

Due north of Brandon, **Riding Mountain National Park** (☎ 204-848-7275; www.parkscanada.ca/riding; Hwy 10; day pass adult/child/senior/family $5/2.50/4.25/12.50) is an escarpment rising above the plains and draped in brown fields, green forests and blue lakes. Elk, moose, beaver and bear can be seen from the road and Lake Audy has a fenced-in herd of 30 bison.

Most of the park is wilderness; the resort town of **Wasagaming**, on the south shore of Clear Lake, is inconspicuously and sensitively designed. The town can be peacefully quiet during the off-season, when most businesses close.

Just outside the park's northern border off Hwy 10, in the old Ukrainian village of Selo, **Canada's National Ukrainian Festival** (☎ 877-747-2683; www.cnuf.ca; ⊙ early Aug) features folk dancing, drinking, traditional costumes and cultural displays. Come for

the culture, stay for the food: stuff your face with pierogies, cabbage rolls and kielbasa. The festival **headquarters** (☎ 204-622-4600; 1550 Main St), with a gift shop and tea room, is open year-round in Dauphin, 12km north.

Information

Visitors Centre (☎ 204-848-7275; Wasagaming Rd; ⊙ 9:30am-5:30pm May-Thanksgiving, to 8pm Jun-Aug) Natural history displays, the invaluable *Visitor's Guide* and backcountry permits.

Sights & Activities

Highway 10 is pretty enough, but the park is at its best on any of the 400km of **walking**, **cycling** and **horseback-riding trails**. Hikes range from the 1km-long Lakeshore Trail to a 17km grind through forest and meadows to a cabin used by naturalist Grey Owl (see the boxed text on p570). Elkhorn Resort offers horseback riding (from $30).

Canoeing is good in parts, although Clear Lake is quite windy and allows motorboats. Rentals are available from **Clear Lake Marina** (☎ 204-867-7298; Wasagaming Rd; per day $25).

Sleeping & Eating

Backcountry camping is possible; check with the visitors center. Motels and cabins are plentiful in Wasagaming, but most close for winter.

Of the 600 campsites within the park, **Wasagaming Campground** (tent/RV sites $22/30) is the biggest and most accessible. Of the other **campgrounds** (sites $13), Lake Audy has abundant wildlife and Whirlpool Lake is a 50m hike, from parking lot to lakeshore, within thick forest.

Elkhorn Resort (☎ 204-848-2802; www.elkhornresort.mb.ca; Mooswa Dr W; s/d with fireplace $100/110, chalet from $250) is a place for those who want to feel like they're in the wilderness, but still have a bit of luxury. There's a country feel and rooms are big enough to throw gear about. The two- to four-bedroom chalets are bright and spacious, with views of the lake and open-beam construction.

Wasagaming is loaded with local and chain restaurants across from the beach.

Getting There & Away

Greyhound Canada connects Wasagaming to Winnipeg once daily, except Saturday, throughout the summer.

MANITOBA

NORTHERN MANITOBA

Two-thirds of the province lies north of The Pas, an area commonly referred to as 'North of 53' (the 53rd parallel). It's a place where convenience takes a backseat to rugged beauty as lake-filled timberland dissolves into the treeless tundra of the far north.

THE PAS

The northern community of The Pas (pronounced pah) was a traditional meeting place between Aboriginal and European fur traders. Today it's still an important trapping community and 'gateway to the North' gear-up spot for northbound treks. Highway 10 enters town as Gordon Ave from the south, becomes Fischer Ave, then 1st St through downtown, before crossing the Saskatchewan River on its way north.

The 1916 courthouse is now the small **Sam Waller Museum** (☎ 204-623-3802; 306 Fischer Ave; adult/child $2/1; ☼ 1-5pm), where Sam's passionate collection of eclectic items from around the world is on display.

Clearwater Lake Provincial Park (☎ 204-624-5525; www.gov.mb.ca/conservation/parks/popular_parks/clearwater_pp; tent/RV sites $12/15) is northeast of town, where boreal forests surround an amazingly clear lake in a pristine setting. Deep crevices and huge chunks of rock that have fallen from cliffs can be seen along the Caves Trail. There is camping on the south shore.

HIGHWAY 6

The drive up Hwy 6 doesn't have to be tedious; this is a spectacular environment. It's an area of forest, lakes, wildlife and wonder, so take a break to enjoy it. About 50km shy of Thompson, you'll see a sign pointing east toward Pisew Falls Provincial Park; follow it and the winding road to a trailhead. A short boardwalk leads to Pisew Falls (*pisew* is Cree for lynx), and whether it's winter, when the falls are frozen, or spring, when the water is gushing, the volume of water is amazing. Take the 500m walk to the bridge below the falls and, if you're particularly adventurous, continue on the 22km-backcountry detour to Kwasitchewan Falls – the highest in Manitoba.

The **Northern Manitoba Trappers' Festival** (☎ 204-623-2912; www.trappersfestival.com; ☼ mid-Feb) is The Pas' best-known party, involving dogsled races, snow sculptures, torchlight parades and trapping exhibits. The summertime festival is **Opaskwayak Indian Days** (☎ 204-623-6459; ☼ mid-Aug), when the local Cree celebrate their heritage through dance, hunting calls and traditional dress.

Motels are found at the entrances to town. **Kikiwak Inn** (☎ 204-623-1800, 888-545-4925; www.kikiwakinn.com; Hwy 10; r/ste $100/$150; 🖢) is just north of downtown across the river. The spacious lobby is woodsy and the rooms are clean and comfortable.

The Pas' **airport** (YQD; ☎ 204-624-5233) is connected to Manitoba by Calm Air, and to Ontario by Bearskin Airlines (p869). Greyhound Canada stops at the **bus depot** (☎ 204-23-3999; 352 Fischer Ave), and VIA Rail's *Hudson Bay* (p530) stops at the **train station** (380 Hazelwood Ave) here on its Winnipeg–Churchill run.

THOMPSON

The last stop on Hwy 6, and the northern edge of civilization, Thompson is a center for culture, commerce, recreation and industry. The town is on top of a significant belt of nickel, and mining is a major industry. For those lucky enough to head north, it's nothing but nature.

Just before town, the **Visitor Info Centre** (☎ 204-677-2216; www.thompson.ca; 162 Princeton Dr; ☼ 10am-5pm Jun-Sep, 1-5pm Mon-Fri Oct-May) can arrange two-hour tours of the refining and smelting operations at **Inco nickel mines** (☎ 204-778-2454; admission free; ☼ 10am Mon-Fri Jun-Aug, 10am Thu Sep-May).

In the same building, and with the same opening hours, is **Heritage North Museum** (adult/senior/child $3.35/1/2), a small but well laid-out museum with stuffed local wildlife, an actual caribou-hide tipi, displays on mining history, and the *Snowball Express* (used in the construction of the railroad). During the summer, witness blacksmithing and hide cleaning using traditional methods.

McReedy Campground (☎ 204-778-8810; fax 204-677-3567; 114 Manasan Dr; tent & RV sites $15; ☼ Victoria Day–Labour Day) is 2km off Hwy 6, on the north side of town, and caters mostly to recreational vehicles (RVs), although there are sites in the trees for tenters. It offers vehicle storage ($7 per day) and free shuttles to the train.

It's an unflattering-looking aluminum-sided box of a building when seen from the street, but ask for a room on the river side of **Interior Inn** (☎ 204-778-5535, 866-778-5535; fax 204-778-6658; 180 Thompson Dr; s/d $85/95) and you won't be disappointed. As Thompson's newest hotel, it has large windows and good-sized rooms with new furniture.

Thompson Airport (YTH; ☎ 204-778-5212) is 10km north of town on Hwy 6. Calm Air services the province. Greyhound Canada comes and goes twice a day from southern destinations like The Pas and Winnipeg ($90, nine hours), leaving from the **bus station** (☎ 204-677-0360; 81 Berens Rd) by the information center.

Thompson is the most northerly vehicle-accessible point for the VIA Rail (p530) train to Churchill. On Fridays, people living in northern communities spend the day here shopping for supplies before catching the train home. If you want to interact with locals, this is a good train to catch; if privacy or convenience is an issue for you, take a weekday train. The train station, on Station Rd in the industrial part of town, is not a recommended spot to leave your car. Instead, park it for free at **city hall** (226 Mystery Lake Rd) and catch a **Thompson Cab** (☎ 204-677-6262) or a McReedy Campground shuttle.

CHURCHILL

Way out on always-frozen ground, and far from everything at the northern end of the train tracks, on the shores of frigid Hudson Bay, Churchill defies logic. Presented with a list that includes barren, freezing, almost unreachable, expensive and small Canadian town, few people would pick this as a place to spend precious vacation time. Add to that the chance to see uncommon wildlife in their natural habitat and potential danger, and the polar-bear capital of the world has become Canada's worst-kept secret.

The remoteness of the town and vastness of the surrounding area instill a feeling that you're in an important place. Things like community, teamwork, values and neighbors take on a whole new meaning. The world that's so easily taken for granted means nothing when you consider that the same distance you'd travel to your grocery store back home could spell disaster if traveled out here. A visit to Churchill can teach a person a couple of things: the world is not small, and polar bear are very large.

History

In terms of European exploration, Churchill is one of the oldest places in the country. The first HBC outpost was set up here in 1717; it's been said HBC stands for 'Here Before Christ.' Churchill was also a stop in attempts to find the fabled Northwest Passage by explorers such as Samuel Hearne and Lord Churchill, former governor of HBC and the town's namesake.

The introduction of the railways in 1929 meant Churchill was a closer port to Europe than Montréal. Churchill was once the largest grain-handling port in the world, and is still Canada's only prairie seaport. After years of decline, grain handling is again increasing under new operations by Omni-Trax, which is based in Denver, Colorado.

Orientation

The train drops you at the southern side of town, on the 'commercial strip' of Kelsey Blvd. The big Town Centre Complex, two blocks north, holds the school, movie theater, and recreational and other town services; behind that is Hudson Bay. Just west of town is the Port of Churchill. The 30km road exiting town to the southeast goes to the airport and other sites, while the dirt road behind St Paul's Anglican Church leads 2km northwest to Cape Merry.

Information

EMERGENCIES
Ambulance/Hospital (☎ 204-675-8300, 204-675-8881)
Fire (☎ 204-675-2222)
Polar Bear Alert (☎ 204-675-2327)
Police (☎ 204-675-8821)
Police, Ambulance & Fire (☎ 911)

LIBRARIES
Library (☎ 204-675-2731; ☽ 1-5pm) Internet access.

MEDICAL SERVICES
Churchill Regional Health Authority (☎ 204-675-8318) Churchill's hospital.

MONEY
Royal Bank (☎ 204-675-8894; 203 La Verandrye Ave)

POST
Post Office (☎ 204-675-2696; 204 La Verandrye Ave; ☽ 8am-5pm Mon-Fri)

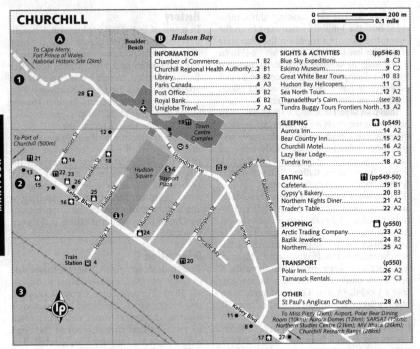

CHURCHILL

INFORMATION	
Chamber of Commerce	1 B2
Churchill Regional Health Authority	2 B1
Library	3 B2
Parks Canada	4 A3
Post Office	5 B2
Royal Bank	6 B2
Uniglobe Travel	7 A2

SIGHTS & ACTIVITIES	(pp546-8)
Blue Sky Expeditions	8 C3
Eskimo Museum	9 C2
Great White Bear Tours	10 B3
Hudson Bay Helicopers	11 C3
Sea North Tours	12 A2
Thanadelthur's Cairn	(see 28)
Tundra Buggy Tours Frontiers North	13 A2

SLEEPING	(p549)
Aurora Inn	14 A2
Bear Country Inn	15 A2
Churchill Motel	16 A2
Lazy Bear Lodge	17 C3
Tundra Inn	18 A2

EATING	(pp549-50)
Cafeteria	19 B1
Gypsy's Bakery	20 B3
Northern Nights Diner	21 A2
Trader's Table	22 A2

SHOPPING	(p550)
Arctic Trading Company	23 A2
Bazlik Jewelers	24 B2
Northern	25 A2

TRANSPORT	(p550)
Polar Inn	26 A2
Tamarack Rentals	27 C3

OTHER	
St Paul's Anglican Church	28 A1

To Miss Piggy (7km); Airport, Polar Bear Dining
Room (10km); Aurora Domes (12km); SARSAT (15km);
Northern Studies Centre (23km); MV Ithaca (26km);
Churchill Research Range (28km)

TOURIST INFORMATION

Chamber of Commerce (☎ 204-675-2022; cnr Kelsey
Blvd & Hudson St; www.churchillmb.net/~cccomm;
⏰ 8am-6pm Jun-Nov)

Parks Canada (☎ 204-675-8863; ⏰ 9am-noon &
1-4:30pm Mon-Fri) In the train station.

TRAVEL AGENCIES

Uniglobe Travel (☎ 204-675-2811; 140 Kelsey Blvd)

Dangers & Annoyances

During summer you'll wage full-on war
with the ferocious mosquitoes and blackflies. Repellent-saturated jackets and head-
nets are a wise investment but are often sold
out in town. The United Army Surplus Sales
(p539) store in Winnipeg sells this gear,
usually for less than you'll pay in Churchill.
Polar-bear season is in the cooler months,
when bugs aren't an issue (see the boxed
text on p549).

Sights

With a diverse natural and cultural history,
Churchill's main attraction is Churchill itself. It's possible to trace the roots of the

fur trade, and see a dozen unique kinds of
wildlife along the way.

ESKIMO MUSEUM

It's just a bunch of stuff in an unexciting
room with linoleum floors, but this little **museum** (☎ 204-675-2030; 242 La Verandrye Ave; suggested
donation $2; ⏰ 1-5pm Mon, 9am-noon & 1-5pm Tue-Sat
Jul-Oct, 1-4:30pm Mon-Sat Nov-Jun) will find a special
place in your heart. The obvious standouts –
stuffed polar bear, musk-ox, wolf and walrus – immediately get your attention, but
upon closer inspection you'll also find tiny
arrowheads, big harpoon blades and hundreds of carvings and other art. You'll have
a new appreciation for the people who not
only survived but prospered on such a desolate landscape.

THANADELTHUR'S CAIRN

A Chipewyan woman named Thanadelthur
assisted the HBC to arrange a treaty between
the rival Chipewyan and Cree, which allowed
the fort to be built in Churchill. This small
cairn (67 Bernier St) was erected in her honor behind St Paul's Anglican Church in 1967.

TIME OF THE SEASON

In climatological terms, Churchill has three seasons: July, August and winter. For visitors, it has four: bird and flower, beluga whale, polar bear and northern lights. Tours and other arrangements can – and should – be made for the best viewing of these natural attractions.

Bird
Peak season: mid-May to September

More than 200 species can be seen during the summer. Some, such as rare Ross's gulls, nest in Churchill; others simply pause on their way further north. Granary Ponds by the port, Cape Merry or Bird Cove are good viewing spots. About 40 species of rare tundra butterflies also decorate the air at this time of year.

Wildflower
Peak season: June to August

As the ice melts and the sun hits the soil for the first time in months, Churchill explodes in colors and aromas. Purple saxifrage comes into bloom, and boulders on the shore are covered in brilliant red lichen. Fireweed runs rampant at the fertile town dump.

Beluga Whale
Peak season: mid-June to August

Up to 3500 of these glossy white torpedoes follow the warm water into the Churchill River every summer. It's possible to see them from shore, but you'll probably hear them first; early whalers called them 'sea canaries.'

Polar Bear
Peak Season: late September to early November

No matter how many times you've seen these huge, intelligent, curious, playful and dangerous creatures in a zoo, nothing compares to seeing them in their natural setting.

Northern Lights
Peak season: October to March

The aqua-turquoise-yellow dance of the aurora borealis is nothing short of spectacular when you're hundreds of miles from urban lights. Anywhere is good for viewing. **Aurora Domes** (☎ 800-265-8563; 4-5hr per person $95), with its see-through roof, eliminates the need to bundle up.

FORT PRINCE OF WALES NATIONAL HISTORIC SITE

Parks Canada (☎ 204-675-8863; adult/child/senior $8/4/7.25; ☼ 1-5pm & 6-10pm Jun-Nov) administers three sites 2km northwest of town, documenting Churchill's varied history. Parks Canada won't take you to the sites, but interpreters will be there when you arrive. Tour operators include these sites in some tours.

Fort Prince of Wales, across the Churchill River from Cape Merry, is a star-shaped stone fort that stands prominently on rocky Eskimo Point. The site was selected for a military presence, as tensions with the French mounted in the early 1720s. It took 40 years to build, and today the never-used cannons point across the water from the reconstructed walls.

Sloop's Cove, about 4km south of the fort, was a harbor for European vessels during Churchill's harsh winters. The only indication of early explorers such as Samuel Hearn, a local 18th-century governor and the first person to make an overland trip to the Arctic Ocean, is their names inscribed in the seaside rocks.

A lone cannon behind a crumbling wall is all that's left of the battery built at **Cape Merry** in 1746 to protect the mouth of the Churchill River. It's about 2km northwest of town.

WAPUSK NATIONAL PARK

This unbelievably remote, 11,475-sq-km **park** (☎ 204-675-8863, 888-748-2928; www.pc.gc.ca/pn-np/mb/wapusk), extending along the shores of Hudson Bay 45km southeast of Churchill, was created in 1996. Established primarily to protect polar-bear breeding grounds (fittingly, *wapusk* is Cree for 'white bear'), it's also the habitat for other wildlife. Plans are underway to make it a little more accessible, but its ecological sensitivity has required a lot of proactive thinking and red tape. Right now it's hard to get to Wapusk without one of the approved tour operators.

YORK FACTORY NATIONAL HISTORIC SITE
Even more remote, 250km southeast of Churchill, this **site** (adult/child/senior $8/4/7; ⊙ hours vary Jun-Aug), near Hayes River, was an important gateway to the interior as an active HBC trading post for 273 years until 1957. Only two buildings remain standing among the visible ruins and artifacts of what was once a large complex. The site is accessible only by air, or (for the very determined and experienced) by canoe.

Courses
Northern Studies Centre (☎ 204-675-2307; www .churchillmb.net/~cnsc/; Launch Rd; courses $850-2000), on the old rocket range 29km east of town, is a base for researchers from around the world. It offers all-inclusive five-day courses on beluga whales, wildflowers, birds and polar bear, in addition to winter survival, the northern lights and astronomy lessons.

Quirky Churchill
If you can rent a truck or bum a ride, on the only road east out of town are some things that'll make you think, 'What the heck is that doing here?' Bear-tour shuttles drive (but won't stop) west to east along this road to their buggy depots, so you'll get glimpses of some of these sites:

Miss Piggy (8km from town) The 1979 wreckage of a massive C46 airplane.

Polar Bear Dining Room (11km) The town dump near the airport. Keep your distance.

SARSAT (16km) Satellite tracking station.

MV Ithaca (27km) Grounded supply ship in Bird Cove that's visible when the tide is out (or water is frozen). It's unsafe to go aboard.

Churchill Research Range (29km) Sporadically used rocket launching site built in 1957; now a national historic site.

There's a **boulder beach** behind Town Centre Complex where you can stick a toe in icy Hudson Bay.

Tours
Natural tours in Churchill offer the chance to see things you won't find anywhere else.

POLAR BEAR–WATCHING
Autumn polar-bear tours are Churchill's bread and butter. The 'buggies' have lightweight, aluminum frames that ride on huge, deeply treaded tires to protect the delicate tundra. They generally carry 30 to 40 passengers, and have lots of big windows (keep your hands inside) and viewing decks on the back (keep yourself inside). They even have heated bathrooms onboard. Hot coffee and sandwiches are part of the deal.

Both companies have built rolling 'tundra lodges' they drag out onto the frozen ground for better viewing and polar-bear sleepovers. Staying at the lodge isn't cheap, but two- to four-night packages include meals, day tours and transportation from Winnipeg. Both companies will pick you up and the offices have gift shops:

Great White Bear Tours (☎ 204-675-2781, 866-765-8344; www.greatwhitebeartours.com; cnr Kelsey Blvd & Thompson St; day-tours/lodge from $240/$2900) Continuously engineering and building new buggies to maximize viewing possibilities.

Tundra Buggy Tours/Frontiers North (☎ 204-949-2050, 800-663-9832; www.tundrabuggy.com; 124 Kelsey Blvd; day-tours/lodge from $195/3000) The only operator with a tundra lodge in Wapusk National Park.

SEA, AIR & LAND TOURS
Blue Sky Expeditions (☎ 204-675-2887, 204-675-2001; 321 Kelsey Blvd; half-day/overnight tours $50/110) Dogsled adventures and stories.

Hudson Bay Helicopters (☎ 204-675-2576; www .hudsonbayheli.com; Kelsey Blvd; tours from $210; ⊙ May-Nov) Offers a variety of sightseeing tours from the sky. Between Thompson St and James Ave.

Muncks Nature Tours (☎ 204-675-2350; www .churchillmb.net/~munck; tours from $225) Runs multiday walking/hiking/natural/cultural tours with experienced, fun locals who will never say 'no' to a martini.

Nature 1st (☎ 204-675-2147; www.nature1sttours .ca; half-/full-day tours May-Nov $60/110; ⊙ May-Nov) Believes in being part of nature, not just looking at it. Leads tours and nature hikes through four distinct ecozones. Tours held between January and April vary in length and costs.

Sea North Tours (☎ 204-675-2195; www.seanorth tours.com; 39 Franklin St; ⊙ Jun-Oct) Custom-built boat and enthusiastic, local guide for whale- and bear-spotting.

FLUFFY & DANGEROUS

Polar bear spend winters hunting on the frozen ocean, where they can smell seals through a meter of pack ice. As the ice melts, the bear are forced onto land, where they wait, and return north when the ice returns. Churchill happens to be smack in the middle of that migration path. Up to 300 bear have been seen migrating along the coast between Nelson River (200km south of Churchill) and Cape Churchill (40km east).

Recently, warmer and shorter winters mean the ice melts sooner, freezes later and the bear's hunting season doesn't last as long. Returning to land still hungry is not a good thing for the bear, or the people who live here.

These are not the same cuddly balls of fuzz you see in Coca-Cola commercials or wearing Santa hats in department stores. They are huge predators with razor-sharp claws and they can run up to 50km/h. That said, bear aren't in the habit of attacking people unless they feel threatened. Coming between a cub and mother is the worst thing you can do. Wandering from town without an experienced guide or inquiring about recent sightings is the second-worst. Read Parks Canada's *You Are in Polar Bear Country* guide and heed the Polar Bear Alert signs around town.

Local authorities maintain a 24-hour vigil from September to November; gunshots are fired at night to shoo off town-bound bear. If bear do break the perimeter, they're tranquilized and moved out of town by helicopter. The three-strikes rule applies; the third time a bear is caught, it's taken to the cinderblock jail cells of an old military base for the winter. There are no tours of 'Polar Bear Jail.'

Sleeping

Naturally, prices of accommodations increase dramatically in polar-bear season. Considering this is the only time of year when hotels are fully booked and people have to make a living somehow, just be happy you're seeing polar bear. Tour groups reserve most of the rooms in advance and then give back unsold rooms. In other words, a room booked now may become available later. Either book a year in advance (recommended) or try for cancellations just before your trip. It's also possible to sleep out with the bear.

Aurora Inn (☎ 204-675-2850, 888-840-1344; www .aurora-inn.mb.ca; 24 Bernier St; d off-season/summer $95/ 120, in bear season $150, each additional person $20) Expect to feel right at home in this former apartment building. Sleeping areas are in upstairs lofts, leaving plenty of room for the downstairs living rooms, which include pullout couches and complete kitchens.

Lazy Bear Lodge (☎ 204-675-2869, 866-687-2327; 313 Kelsey Blvd; s/d $80/90, in bear season $160/170) Anything at this two-story inn that could be made with logs, has been, from the walls to the furniture. The local whole-timber and the stone fireplace are rustically authentic. The rooms are only a little bit larger than the beds, but you'll still sleep comfortably here.

Tundra Inn (☎ 204-675-2850, 800-265-8563; www .tundrainn.com; 34 Franklin St; s/d $95/105, in bear season $175/185; ☐). Lacy curtains, floral bedcovers and comforting, homey rooms are like a relative's place. There's laundry, Internet access and a shared kitchen, and breakfast is included from December to September. The owners also run the Aurora Domes (p547).

Churchill also has a couple of no-frills options. **Churchill Motel** (☎ 204-675-8853; fax 204-675-8828; Kelsey Blvd, at Franklin St; s/d $75/85) has a wood-paneled greasy-spoon diner to compliment the wood-paneled hallways and rooms. **Bear Country Inn** (☎ 204-675-8299; fax 204-675-8803; 126 Kelsey Blvd; r from $40, in bear season from $120) is just up the road.

Eating

Most places in town know you came to experience Churchill, and will feature caribou and/or char (a local fish similar to salmon) on the menu.

Gypsy's Bakery (☎ 204-675-2322; 253 Kelsey Blvd; mains $7-23; ☼ 7am-9pm) This walk-up counter joint is as much a local hangout as it is a basic but good eatery. Everything from the cappuccino to the grilled char is made fresh. The brown vinyl chairs aren't flattering, but the food is…mmm…good.

Trader's Table (☎ 204-675-2141; 141 Kelsey Blvd; ☼ dinner) Intimate fine dining in the great white North. Open-beam construction, a stone fireplace and animal trophy heads ooze frontier country; white linen and juicy caribou roast bring luxury. Local berry desserts cap off a meal nicely, and the char chowder is delicious and creamy enough to hold it's own against any New England version.

Northern Nights Diner (☎ 204-675-2403; 101 Kelsey Blvd; mains $7-18; ☺ 8am-10pm Tue-Sun) This green-colored restaurant, at the northern end of the strip, has sectioned-off dining areas, including a nonsmoking section (an anomaly in Churchill). It's quiet, low key and unsurprising.

There's a **cafeteria** (items $2-6; ☺ lunch) in the Town Centre Complex serving burgers, hot dogs and the like.

Shopping
Kelsey Blvd is the commercial zone, with a collection of souvenir shops. **Northern** (☎ 204-675-8891; 171 Kelsey Blvd; ☺ closed Sun) is the town's grocery and department store.

Arctic Trading Company (☎ 204-675-8804; www .arctictradingco.com; 141 Kelsey Blvd) Locally made carvings, clothing and paintings; you may leave with a moose-antler cribbage board.

Bazlik Jewelers (☎ 204-675-2397; 219 Kelsey Blvd) Souvenirs of a different breed, such as gold polar-bear charms or almost-local diamonds, can be found in the display cases here.

Getting There & Away
There is no road to Churchill; access is by plane or train only.

AIR
Churchill Airport (YYQ; ☎ 204-675-8868) is 11km east of town. There are variances in schedules and fares, but generally a Winnipeg–Churchill return will cost between $700 and $1000, and Thompson–Churchill return is in the $200 to $400 range. The planes are modern but small, so luggage space is limited. Calm Air flies to/from Churchill throughout the province. **Kivalliq Air** (☎ 204-888-5619, 877-855-1500; www.kivalliqair.com) has flights from Winnipeg to Churchill and Nunavut three times a week.

TRAIN
Most people arrive in Churchill aboard VIA Rail's *Hudson Bay* (p530). The historically renovated **station** (☎ 204-675-2149; Hendry St) only opens for arrivals and departures. You can save time, and about half the fare, if you get on the train in Thompson or The Pas instead of Winnipeg.

Getting Around
Walking around Churchill is easy and enjoyable in summer, and invigorating in winter. **Polar Inn** (☎ 204-675-8878; 15 Franklin St; per day $15) rents bicycles as well as winter gear. If it gets too cold, **Big Bear Taxi** (☎ 204-675-2345) will drive you around. It's not impossible to get a ride from a local who's driving the road east, though getting back can sometimes be problematic. **Tamarack Rentals** (☎ 204-675-2192; 353 Kelsey Blvd) rents pick-up trucks ($65 per day). Gas will cost you dearly.

Saskatchewan

SASKATCHEWAN

Dispensing with all the clichés is the first order of business before visiting Canada's third-most westerly province. 'Flat,' 'Boring,' 'Is this it?' are for those who don't leave the Trans-Canada Hwy. Canada's cross-country route was designed as a path of least resistance to get a person across the country, not as a highlight reel. Intrepid travelers venturing north of Saskatoon find the boreal-forested swath running east–west across the midsection of the province, or glacial leftovers of 100,000 lakes north of that. The transition from north to south is a seemingly flat, undulating patchwork of crops and fields, yet gorgeous tree-lined valleys cut their way across the plains and can't be seen until you're on top of them. Distinct buttes and rock formations or dramatic forests suddenly appear as you round a hill or turn a corner.

The second thing is to prepare for a trip unlike any other you've ever had. Saskatchewan is not a thrill-a-minute, adrenaline-pumping place with a ton of major sights, but there are things here that you just can't see in any other part of the world. It's true that every stalk of wheat is just like the 40 million stalks of wheat you've seen before, and that slough isn't too inspiring, but Saskatchewan has more to show than that. Unless you've seen a herd of small deer sprinting – *sprinting* – across a field and kicking up dirt, rich yellow wheat or pale-blue flax rippling in the wind in a colorful dance, a sunset bleeding across the dome of the sky from orange in the west to violet in the east, or the steel-gray clouds of an approaching thunderstorm contrasted against golden fields, you haven't seen Saskatchewan the way it was meant to be seen.

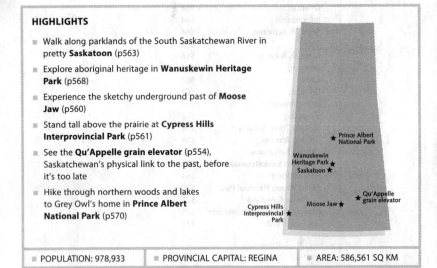

HIGHLIGHTS

- Walk along parklands of the South Saskatchewan River in pretty **Saskatoon** (p563)
- Explore aboriginal heritage in **Wanuskewin Heritage Park** (p568)
- Experience the sketchy underground past of **Moose Jaw** (p560)
- Stand tall above the prairie at **Cypress Hills Interprovincial Park** (p561)
- See the **Qu'Appelle grain elevator** (p554), Saskatchewan's physical link to the past, before it's too late
- Hike through northern woods and lakes to Grey Owl's home in **Prince Albert National Park** (p570)

★ Prince Albert National Park

Wanuskewin Heritage Park ★
Saskatoon ★

Qu'Appelle grain elevator ★

Moose Jaw ★

Cypress Hills Interprovincial Park ★

▓ POPULATION: 978,933	▓ PROVINCIAL CAPITAL: REGINA	▓ AREA: 586,561 SQ KM

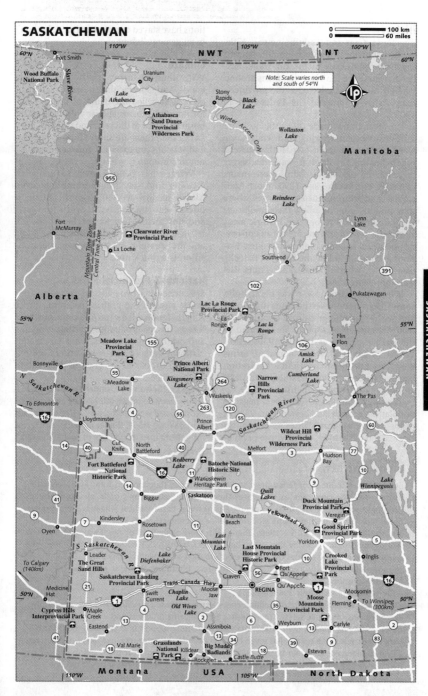

SASKATCHEWAN

History

The Dene, Cree and Assiniboine met 17th-century European settlers graciously, and involved themselves in the fur trade. Saskatchewan (Cree for 'river that turns around when it runs') was selected as the province's name when it entered the Federation in 1905.

However things were often sticky. More Europeans began arriving, and while some were content in their own little pockets, others, mainly the English, wanted a bigger piece of the pie. Land claims were made, or taken, and by the late 1890s most Aboriginals had been confined to reserves, where they couldn't hunt or follow their traditions. Several nationally recognized historic areas across the province were sites of major battles between federal soldiers and First Nations groups, including the Battle of Batoche (see p571), where Métis leader Louis Riel was apprehended (see p28).

While the railroad west was being built, some discovered the fertile lands in the area and word spread; agriculture boomed and nearly a million Europeans immigrated to the prairie provinces by the 1930s. After WWII wheat production increased, farms grew, more people arrived and urbanization began. The economy diversified as mineral and energy reserves were discovered.

These days, Saskatchewan has a negative population growth and fewer than 25% of residents live on farms; they're moving to Regina and Saskatoon, cities whose populations have stayed constant or (in Saskatoon's case) grown slightly.

Climate

With thunderstorms, puffy clouds, wild winds and spectacular sunsets, Saskatchewan isn't called the 'Land of Living Skies' for nothing. Storms appear with little warning at any time of the year, and disappear just as fast. Summers are short (June to August) and very hot (up to 35°C), and hailstorms are not uncommon.

Winter has been known to arrive in October and stay finger-numbingly cold (down as low as -40°C) until April; it doesn't snow a lot, but it will snow early and not melt. Most Saskatchewaners will tell you there isn't really a spring or a fall, and they're right; the summer–winter transition is a quick one.

National & Provincial Parks

Saskatchewan's two national parks are at opposite ends of the prairie spectrum. Prince Albert National Park (p570), in the northern forests, has loads of hiking, cycling, canoeing and fishing opportunities, while Grasslands National Park (p562) is an unserviced expanse of rocks and tall grass in the south of the province.

Saskatchewan's **provincial parks** (☎ 306-953-3751, within Saskatchewan 800-205-7070; www.saskparks .net; day/3-day/week/annual passes $7/17/25/50, tent sites $13-15, RV sites $18-24, campfire permits $3) are great for getting into the variety of Saskatchewan's

---

DISTINCT TO EXTINCT

Barn-red, tractor-green or faded-gray; striking yet simple; function and form as closely intertwined with the landscape as the wheat they hold; Saskatchewan's grain elevators are approaching extinction. Flagships of prairie architecture, these vertical wheat warehouses are being replaced by uncharismatic modern steel or concrete cylinders located near inland trucking routes. Introduced in the 1880s, there were more than 3200 of the 'Castles of the New World' lining train tracks by the 1930s. Built to last, with thick wooden walls, their presence was invaluable as the prairies became 'the breadbasket of the world.' They stood stoically; their strength and simplicity inspired Canadian painters, photographers and writers as they were given life and love.

By 1999 there were only 304 remaining.

Literally without warning, demolition crews arrive at unused elevators and tear them down, citing reasons of 'public safety.' Their destruction concerns residents and visitors who hope to prevent (not just lament) their disappearance. Community support in Inglis, Manitoba (north of Hwy 16 just across the border) has saved the last remaining elevator-row (five ratty but preserved elevators alongside the train tracks), built in the 1920s. Fleming, near the Manitoba border on Hwy 1, has one built in 1895. Qu'Appelle, on Hwy 1 east of Regina, has a bright-red one.

SASKATCHEWAN IN...

Five Days

Visit the Royal Saskatchewan Museum and RCMP Museum in **Regina** (p555), followed by dinner and drinks in the city's old warehouse district.

In the morning, head west on Hwy 1 to Moose Jaw and learn underground secrets at **Tunnels of Moose Jaw** (p561). Continue on to **Cypress Hills Interprovincial Park** (p561) to spend the night in Canada's highest elevations east of the Rockies. Do some hiking before heading east on Hwy 18, appreciating the vastness of big sky country and **Grasslands National Park** (p562). Spend the night in nearby Val Marie, waking up to drive through the **badlands** (p562) as the sun reflects off the valley walls.

Drive north to **Saskatoon** (p563) for a twilight walk along the river. Have an early breakfast and head to **Wanuskewin Heritage Park** (p568), then return to Saskatoon for **Shakespeare on the Saskatchewan** (p566).

One Week

Follow the five-day itinerary, then head north to **Batoche National Historic Site** (p571). Continue north to arrive at **Prince Albert National Park** (p570) in the evening. Hike to conservationist Grey Owl's cabin the next day and camp in the backcountry; alternatively, do some day hikes or canoe trips.

ecosystems. Camping is available in most parks, and some have backcountry sites. Some parks have a reservation system; check the website for details.

Getting There & Away

There are flights to/from other Canadian cities from Regina and Saskatoon as well to Minneapolis, Minnesota; see p868 for air travel within Canada and p868 for international routes.

Buses to Alberta or Winnipeg and beyond are handled by Greyhound Canada (p870). Saskatchewan roads cross into Montana and North Dakota in the USA. In the populated lower third of the province, plenty of roads lead east into Manitoba or west into Alberta. The Trans-Canada Hwy (Hwy 1) goes through Regina, the Yellowhead Hwy (Hwy 16) through Saskatoon.

VIA Rail's *Canadian* (p875) passes through Saskatoon three times weekly.

Getting Around

Transwest Air (p868) serves Prince Albert and various small northern towns from Saskatoon and Regina.

Saskatchewan Transportation Company (STC; ☎ 800-663-7181; www.stcbus.com) takes over Greyhound Canada's routes inside the provincial border, and runs services between more than 200 communities.

Driving is the best way to see the province. In the southern section service stations are plentiful, but don't trust that quarter tank to get you to the next town. Straight, vacant backroads are tempting, but be careful when close to main arteries; police aren't opposed to ticketing out-of-province drivers.

REGINA

☎ 306 / pop 178,200

Regina is Saskatchewan's commercial, financial, industrial and political capital. Though it's built-up with tall structures, it has still retained the sense of a quiet prairie town. Plunked on an unremarkable landscape, parks, tree-lined streets and lakes were created to provide comfortable insulation from the surrounding wheat fields. It's a real-people town with lots of nodding and waving, and every Mountie you've seen has lived and trained here. Two other interesting facts about the city: Regina is Canada's sunniest capital, and every single tree you see here was planted by hand.

HISTORY

The original Cree inhabitants left the remains of their buffalo hunts along the creek here and the area became known as Wascana, which means 'pile of bones.' European settlers chose this colorful English translation for Regina's original name. In 1882 the city was made the capital of the Northwest Territories, due to its central location, and its name was changed to Regina in honor of Queen Victoria. The North-West Mounted Police (NWMP) used the city as a base from the 1880s, and in 1905 it became the capital of the newly formed Saskatchewan.

ORIENTATION

The main commercial strips leading into the city are east–west Victoria Ave and north–south Albert St. Downtown Regina is an easily navigable grid centered on Victoria Park. At the park's northeastern corner is Scarth St pedestrian mall, with the large Cornwall Shopping Centre at its northern end. Most of Regina's main attractions are concentrated in Wascana Centre, a 1000-hectare park.

INFORMATION

Abstractions Café (☎ 306-352-5374; 2161 Rose St; per hr $5) Colorful and fun place to sip, eat and surf the web.

Book & Briar Patch (☎ 306-586-5814; 4065 Albert St) Independent shop and café with a large selection of Canadian literature. It's 1.6km south of Wascana Centre.

Central Library (☎ 306-777-6000; 2311 12th Ave; ⏰ 9:30am-9pm Mon-Thu, 9:30am-6pm Fri, 9:30am-5pm Sat, 1:30-5pm Sun) Small art gallery, huge children's section, and easy sign-in for free Internet access.

Main Post Office (☎ 800-267-1177; 2200 Saskatchewan Dr)

Police, Ambulance & Fire (☎ 911) For emergencies.

RCMP (☎ 306-780-5560) For nonemergencies.

Regina General Hospital (☎ 306-766-4444; 1440 14th Ave; ⏰ 24hr) Emergency room.

Regina Police (☎ 306-777-6500) For nonemergencies.

Tourism Regina (☎ 306-751-8781, 800-661-5099; www.tourismregina.com; Hwy 1; 8am-7pm Mon-Fri, 10am-6pm Sat & Sun Victoria Day–Labour Day, 8am-5pm Mon-Fri rest of year) On Hwy 1, 7 km east of downtown.

Tourism Saskatchewan (☎ 306-787-9600; www.sasktourism.com; 1922 Park St) Province-wide travel information.

SIGHTS & ACTIVITIES
Wascana Centre

Once the small 'Pile of Bones' Creek that ran through treeless prairie, Wascana Creek became artificial Wascana Lake in 1908. In the decades since, Wascana Centre has become Regina's favorite green space, and one of North America's largest urban parks. On the 4th floor of **Wascana Place** (☎ 306-522-3661;

www.wascana.sk.ca; 2900 Wascana Dr; ⏰ 8am-4pm Mon-Fri, art gallery 9:30am-5:30pm Mon-Sat) is the little Joe Moran art gallery and a balcony for great views of the river and the parliament buildings behind it. The park is pretty enough just to wander or you can pick up *Walks Through Wascana Centre*, a map book detailing eight different walks. **Marina Rentals** (☎ 306-780-9311; Wascana Marina; canoe/kayak rentals per hr $7/10; ⏰ noon-8pm May 15–Sep 18) rents canoes and kayaks. **Willow Island** is a good spot for picnics accessed via a passenger **ferry** (☎ 306-347-1810; cnr Wascana Dr & Broadway Ave; $3; ⏰ noon-9pm Victoria Day–Labour Day). **Spruce Island** is a bird sanctuary visible from the shore.

Royal Saskatchewan Museum

Step inside this **museum** (☎ 306-787-2815; www.royalsaskmuseum.ca; 2445 Albert St; suggested donation $2; ⏰ 9am-5:30pm May–Labour Day, 9am-4:30pm rest of year) for a mind-altering look at Saskatchewan's geological past. It might be prairie now, but the province was once mountain, ocean, meadow and glacier. The First Nations gallery presents thousands of years of history with interactive narration and life-sized scenes of sweatlodges and powwows. Forget glassed-in dioramas: the museum's wildlife displays bring Saskatchewan's native animals right up close.

Saskatchewan Science Centre

Science should be fun, and this **science center** (☎ 306-522-4629, 800-667-6300; www.sasksciencecentre.com; 2903 Powerhouse Dr; adult/child $6.50/4.75, with IMAX or planetarium $12/9; ⏰ 9am-6pm Mon-Thu, 9am-8:30pm Fri, 11am-6pm Sat & Sun), in the former Regina Power Plant, makes it so through hands-on displays and demonstrations of the planet, physical laws and life. An IMAX theater and the Kalium Observatory are also here.

MacKenzie Art Gallery

Specializing in Saskatchewan artists but with a host of international pieces, this impressive **gallery** (☎ 306-522-4242; www.mackenzieartgallery.sk.ca; 3475 Albert St; admission free; ⏰ 10am-5:30pm Sat-Wed, 10am-10pm Thu & Fri), 1km south of the Wascana Centre, focuses on contemporary art.

Provincial Legislature

Lost your marbles? You might find them at this **building** (☎ 306-787-5358; Legislative Dr;

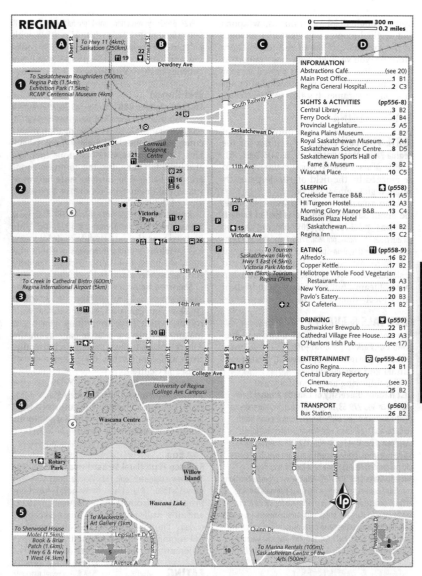

REGINA

To Hwy 11 (4km);
Saskatoon (250km)

Dewdney Ave

To Saskatchewan Roughriders (500m);
Regina Pats (1.5km);
Exhibition Park (1.5km);
RCMP Centennial Museum (4km)

South Railway St

Saskatchewan Dr

Cornwall
Shopping
Centre

11th Ave

12th Ave

Victoria
Park

Victoria Ave

To Tourism
Saskatchewan (4km);
Hwy 1 East (4.5km);
Victoria Park Motor
Inn (5km); Tourism
Regina (7km)

13th Ave

To Creek in Cathedral Bistro (600m);
Regina International Airport (5km)

14th Ave

15th Ave

College Ave

University of Regina
(College Ave Campus)

Wascana Centre

Broadway Ave

Rotary
Park

Willow
Island

Wascana Lake

To Mackenzie
Art Gallery (1km)

To Sherwood House
Motel (1.5km);
Book & Briar
Patch (1.6km);
Hwy 6 & Hwy
1 West (4.3km)

Legislative Dr

Avenue A

Quinn Dr

To Marina Rentals (100m);
Saskatchewan Centre of the
Arts (500m)

Rae St · Angus St · Albert St · McIntyre St · Smith St · Lorne St · Cornwall St · Scarth St · Hamilton St · Rose St · Broad St · Osler St · Halifax St · St John St

St Chads Cir · Ottawa St · Montreal Cir · Powerhouse Dr

0 ———— 300 m
0 ———— 0.2 miles

INFORMATION	
Abstractions Café	(see 20)
Main Post Office	1 B1
Regina General Hospital	2 C3

SIGHTS & ACTIVITIES	(pp556–8)
Central Library	3 B2
Ferry Dock	4 B4
Provincial Legislature	5 A5
Regina Plains Museum	6 B2
Royal Saskatchewan Museum	7 A4
Saskatchewan Science Centre	8 D5
Saskatchewan Sports Hall of	
Fame & Museum	9 B2
Wascana Place	10 C5

SLEEPING	(p558)
Creekside Terrace B&B	11 A5
HI Turgeon Hostel	12 A3
Morning Glory Manor B&B	13 C4
Radisson Plaza Hotel	
Saskatchewan	14 B2
Regina Inn	15 C2

EATING	(pp558–9)
Alfredo's	16 B2
Copper Kettle	17 B2
Heliotrope Whole Food Vegetarian	
Restaurant	18 A3
New York	19 B1
Pavlo's Eatery	20 B3
SGI Cafeteria	21 B2

DRINKING	(p559)
Bushwakker Brewpub	22 B1
Cathedral Village Free House	23 A3
O'Hanlons Irish Pub	(see 17)

ENTERTAINMENT	(pp559–60)
Casino Regina	24 B1
Central Library Repertory	
Cinema	(see 3)
Globe Theatre	25 B2

TRANSPORT	(p560)
Bus Station	26 B2

SASKATCHEWAN

admission free; 8am-9pm Victoria Day–Labour Day, 8am-5pm rest of year, tours every half hour), which features 34 types of marble sourced from Cyprus to Vermont. Built in 1908 on the western side of the park, it is a work of fine detail, from the stone carvings on the front to the carved oak in the Assembly Chamber.

RCMP Centennial Museum & Depot

Many of the 300 original NWMP couldn't ride horses – 'mounted' indeed – and this **museum** (☎ 306-780-5838; Dewdney Ave W; suggested donation $2; 8am-6:45pm Victoria Day–Labour Day, 10am-4:45pm rest of year) tells how they got from then to the patrol car–riding, and more horse-adept, RCMP of today. A chronological walk-through displays uniforms, weapons and original maps, and tells stories of some of the famous exploits of the force. Every Mountie you've ever seen has trained at these facilities, which can be viewed by tour (1:30pm Monday to Friday, included in admission) in summer. It's 4km west of town.

QUIRKY REGINA

While on the pedestrian-only section of Scarth St, take a couple of minutes for the **Regina Plains Museum** (☎ 306-780-9435; 2nd fl, 1835 Scarth St; admission free; ☽ 10am-4pm Mon-Fri) just to be amazed by the field of 10,000 patiently detailed glass wheat stalks.

In an amazing show of provincial pride, the small **Saskatchewan Sports Hall of Fame & Museum** (☎ 306-780-9232; 2205 Victoria Ave; suggested donation $2; ☽ 9am-5pm Mon-Fri, 1-5pm Sat & Sun Victoria Day–Labour Day, 9am-5pm rest of year) pays special tribute to 'Mr Hockey,' Gordie Howe, and Saskatchewan Roughriders championship football teams, but also honors hundreds of other local athletes and teams.

FESTIVALS & EVENTS

Just west of downtown off Dewdney Ave, **Exhibition Park** (☎ 306-781-9200, 888-734-3975; www .reginaexhibition.com; 1700 Elphinstone St) hosts most annual and special events.

The following are major festivals:
First Nations University of Canada Annual Pow Wow (☎ 306-779-6328; www.firstnationsuniversity.ca; ☽ 1st weekend Apr) With dancers from around North America, and traditional First Nations crafts and foods.
Children's Festival (☎ 306-352-7655; www.regina childrensfestival.com; ☽ early Jun) Face painting, crafts and performers let everyone be a kid for two days.
Buffalo Days (☎ 306-781-9200; www.reginaexhibition .com/buffalodays.html; ☽ early Aug) Regina's favorite festival; people dress up in pioneer garb for six days of country music, pancake breakfasts, amusement-park rides, a beard-growing contest and parades.
Regina Folk Festival (☎ 306-757-7684; www.regina folkfestival.com; ☽ mid-Aug) Three-day fest with fun and outdoor shows in Victoria Park.

SLEEPING

Victoria Ave, east of town, and Albert St, south of town, have chain motels with doubles for between $70 and $90.

Budget
HI Turgeon Hostel (☎ 306-791-8165; hihostels.sask@sk .sympatico.ca; 2310 McIntyre St; dm members/nonmembers

$19/24, d $52; ☽ reception 7am-11pm Jul & Aug, 7-10am & 5-10pm Sep-Jun; ℗) This white Victorian, with balconies everywhere, has 50 beds, cooking and laundry facilities, and 1950s-style couches in the TV room.

Mid-Range
Creekside Terrace B&B (☎ 306-569-2682; www.creek sideterrace.sk.ca; 2724 Angus Blvd; s/d incl breakfast $60/70, s/d ste incl breakfast $70/80; ℗) The location of this cottagelike home on Wascana Creek is fantastic. The hardwood floors, stone fireplace and breakfast served in the common room are even better. The upstairs suite has more space, the downstairs room has a peaceful view of the river.

Regina Inn (☎ 306-525-6767, 800-667-8162; www .reginainn.com; 1975 Broad Street; r $80-125; ℗) This high-rise, on the eastern side of downtown, has spacious standard rooms without the standard-hotel feel. Perks include friendly staff, great views and balconies.

Sherwood House Motel (☎ 306-586-3131; www .sherwoodhousemotel.com; 3915 Albert St; s/d $65/70; ℗ 🐾) You can park right outside your rooms, which have everything you need, making this place a relative bargain on the Albert St strip. It's well looked after, friendly, clean and comfortable. It's 1.5km south of Wascana Centre.

Morning Glory Manor B&B (☎ 306-525-2945; www .morningglorymanor.ca; 1718 College Ave; s $50-55, d $60-70; ℗) This 1923 home, with country décor, is near Wascana Park. The large South Room looks across the park.

Top End
Radisson Plaza Hotel Saskatchewan (☎ 306-522-7691; www.hotelsask.com; 2125 Victoria Ave; r $150-260, ste $250-1200; ℗) This provincial heritage property welcomed its first guest in 1927, and it's still pampering businesspeople today. Though a bit on the smallish side, the rooms are each decorated and colored differently; the bedcovers are overly fluffy.

EATING

Regina will never be considered a fine-dining town, but that's not to say it doesn't have a few good places for a bite.

BUDGET
Heliotrope Whole Food Vegetarian Restaurant (☎ 306-569-3373; 2204 McIntyre St; mains $5-12; ☽ lunch Mon-Fri, dinner Mon-Sat) This old brick building

with old home furnishings has seating on the veranda at the front, or in the garden at the back. Excellent vegetarian world cuisine is available, and the soups are delicious.

SGI Cafeteria (18th fl, 2260 11th Ave; mains $4-6; ⓨ breakfast & lunch) A great place to start the day (breakfast is $3 before 10am) is by the south-facing windows of this office building, which has views of downtown and the Provincial Legislature buildings.

Pavlo's Eatery (☎ 306-525-4489; 2100 15th Ave; mains $5-10; ⓨ breakfast & lunch) This neighborhood favorite doesn't offer anything fancy – and it doesn't have to. You get your honest breakfasts, sandwiches and burgers in an honest setting.

MID-RANGE
Creek in Cathedral Bistro (☎ 306-352-4448; 3414 13th Ave; lunch dishes $6-9, dinner mains $17-20; ⓨ lunch & dinner) It's got all the makings of a fine-dining restaurant with linen, jazz music and mood lighting, but avoids pretense and focuses on preparing exquisite meals. Dishes such as venison sirloin with sundried cranberries and spaetzle (dumplings) are as dramatic as they are delicious. It's 600m west of downtown.

Alfredo's (☎ 306-522-3366; 1801 Scarth St; mains $7-15; ⓨ lunch & dinner) This huge stone building, formerly Northern Bank, has a cavernous interior. The steak, seafood and pastas, served in either of the two dining rooms, lead to pure dining satisfaction. The wine bar has a street-facing patio, while the restaurant in the rear has more intimacy.

Copper Kettle (☎ 306-525-3673; 1953 Scarth St; mains $7-10; ⓨ lunch & dinner) The lunchtime sandwiches and wraps and huge dinnertime Greek and pasta dishes taste like they were made just for you. However the backbone of the menu has always been the pizzas, which are loaded with fresh toppings.

DRINKING
There are some favorite watering holes downtown, which can get pretty quiet on weekday nights. Dewdney St in the old warehouse district, just north of downtown, is establishing itself as a fun area of old warehouses converted to pubs and clubs.

Bushwakker Brewpub (☎ 306-359-7276; 2206 Dewdney Ave) It's easy to take an old brick warehouse and make it *look* like a brewpub, but Bushwakker takes beer craft very seri-

---

THE AUTHOR'S CHOICE

New Yorx (☎ 306-356-7771; 2300 Dewdney Ave; ⓨ 11am-late) Behind the big metal doors you'll find a multilevel chrome-and-black restaurant by day, nightclub by night. In the up-and-coming warehouse district, the awesome 3-D model of Manhattan sets this place apart from the ordinary. The pizzas and wraps here are delicious, and it's a cavernously and industriously hip place for a meal. Though the kitchen stays open late for appetizers and desserts, it's party time when the sun goes down. The chrome tables and chairs stay put, but the two dance floors and three bars open up.

---

ously, with a dozen permanent beers plus seasonal brews.

O'Hanlons Irish Pub (☎ 306-566-4094; 1943 Scarth St) O'Hanlon's has 74 beers on tap; if you need help deciding, the Irishness of downtown's favorite pub will put you in the mood for a Guinness.

Cathedral Village Free House (☎ 306-359-1661; 2062 Albert St) The Village is where people go just to relax, be loud and tell stories. Enjoy a microbrew in the creaky-chair pub, or out in the courtyard during summer.

ENTERTAINMENT
Prairie Dog is the free monthly entertainment newspaper listing what's happening around town. New Yorx (see the boxed text on above) is a can't-miss on weekends, with theme parties and frequent live bands. The band shell at the northern end of the park at Wascana Centre hosts **Sunday concerts** (admission free; ⓨ 2-4pm).

Theater & Cinemas
Globe Theatre (☎ 306-525-6400; www.globetheatre live.com; 1801 Scarth St; adult/child/senior $35/15/25; ⓨ Aug-Apr) The Globe kicks off its season with *Globe Theatricks*, an outdoor show in Victoria Park that is the product of a summer-long student workshop. During the rest of the season, classic plays and contemporary performances occur in the theater-in-the-round.

Saskatchewan Centre of the Arts (☎ 306-565-4500, box office 306-525-9999, 800-667-8497; www.centreofthearts.sk.ca; 200 Lakeshore Dr) Home to the symphony orchestra, the Centre also hosts

SASKATCHEWAN

the big acts, from Broadway shows to rock concerts and stand-up comedy. It's 500m southeast of Wascana Centre.

The **Central Library Repertory Cinema** (☎ 306-777-6000; 2311 12th Ave; adult/child/student $6/3/5), in the lower level of the library, shows art films. There's also an IMAX theater at the Saskatchewan Science Centre (p556).

Sports

Saskatchewan Roughriders (☎ 306-525-2181, 888-474-3377; www.saskriders.com; Taylor Field, 2940 10th Ave; ☽ Jun-Nov) The Riders have an amazing following and are one of the few professional sports teams – and the first Canadian Football (CFL) team – to sell shares to their fans. They play exciting, offensive-style football at their field 500m west of town.

Regina Pats (☎ 306-522-7287; www.reginapats.com; Agridome, Exhibition Park; ☽ Sep-Mar) The world's oldest junior hockey team, the Pats of the Western Hockey League (WHL) are archrivals of the Saskatoon Blades. They play 1.5km west of town.

Casinos

Casino Regina (☎ 306-565-3000, 800-555-3189; 1880 Saskatchewan Dr; ☽ 9-4am) The beautiful building of the grand old train station has been taken over by this house of chance, with poker tables, roulette, war and 1¢ slot machines.

GETTING THERE & AWAY

Regina International Airport (YQR; ☎ 306-761-7555; 5200 Regina Ave), 3km west of Wascana Centre, serves destinations throughout Canada plus a few US cities.

The **bus station** (☎ 306-787-3360; 2041 Hamilton St) is downtown, just south of Victoria Ave. Greyhound Canada runs eastbound to Winnipeg ($86, 11 hours) and westbound to Calgary ($99, 10 to 11 hours) four times daily. STC has three daily buses heading north to Saskatoon ($36, three hours).

All the major car-rental agencies (p873) have outlets at the airport and most have offices downtown.

GETTING AROUND

The airport is only 5km southwest of downtown. City buses don't go there, but a 10-minute cab ride with **Capital Cabs** (☎ 306-791-2225; $8) will get you there.

Regina Transit (☎ 306-777-7433, www.reginatransit .com; adult/child $1.90/$1.40) operates city buses.

Just about every route runs through downtown via 12th or 13th Aves.

Metered street parking ($1 to $2 per hour, from 8am to 6pm) downtown is limited to two-hour stays, but spots are plentiful. For all-day parking, try the city parking lots ($3 to $7 per day) on Victoria Ave or Impark ($3 to $6 per day) on Broad St, which are safe and cheaper than right downtown. Parking is free outside the downtown core.

AROUND REGINA
Qu'Appelle Valley

North and east of Regina, the Qu'Appelle Valley, along Hwy 10, isn't your stereotypical Saskatchewan landscape. A drive east along Rte 56, and then Rte 247, will take you through one of Saskatchewan's most visually stimulating areas: the glacier-formed valley is lined with velvety green slopes, and the sparkling blue Qu'Appelle River meanders along its floor. The valley is interspersed with provincial parks.

Kinsmen Rock'N the Valley (☎ 306-352-2300, 877-644-2300; www.rocknthevalley.sk.ca; adult/child $150/110; ☽ mid-Jul) is one big four-day-weekend-long rock 'n' roll party with recognizable bands from today and yesteryear. It's in Craven, 30km northwest of Regina. There are beach parties and beer gardens, and camping is available.

SOUTHERN SASKATCHEWAN

South of Regina, the prairie spreads out in every direction with distinct relief in only a few places. Welcome to Big Sky country, where the world doesn't seem that small, and black clouds on one horizon can be offset by brilliant sunshine on the other. Running across the south, the Red Coat Trail was a route traveled by the NWMP on their way west, as they discovered the diversity of Saksatchewan's southwest and left historical remnants behind. Further east, towards the Manitoba border, are a few notable historical sights and parks.

MOOSE JAW

Colonial butchering of the Cree language took *moosegaw* (meaning 'warm breezes') and turned it into the once-heard, never-forgotten, and always-confusing Moose Jaw. Halfway between Winnipeg and Calgary (and 71km west of Regina), the place became a major Canadian Pacific Railway terminal in the late 19th century; many downtown buildings date from this era. The boom days really hit Moose Jaw in the 1920s, when it served as 'Little Chicago,' a major whiskey-smuggling center during the days of US prohibition.

Orientation & Information

From Hwy 1, look for the statue of the huge moose beside **Tourism Moose Jaw** (☎ 306-693-8097; www.discovermoosejaw.com; 450 Diefenbaker Dr; ☽ 8am-6pm Mon-Fri, 10am-6pm Sat, noon-6pm Sun Jun-Sep, 9am-5pm Mon-Fri Oct-May).

Sights & Activities

The town's varied history and continued popularity blend old and new attractions.

Moose Jaw's branch of the **Western Development Museum** (WDM; ☎ 306-693-5989; 50 Diefenbaker Dr; adult/child/student/senior/family $7.25/2/5.25/6.25/16; ☽ 9am-5pm Apr-Dec, 9am-5pm Tue-Sun Jan-Mar) traces the history of transportation on the prairies with canoes and travois, c 1915 Harleys and steam trains. There's also a behind-the-scenes look at the Snowbirds (see right). Aside from the artifacts, there are also inspiring stories of guile in dealing with prairie climates and geography.

The heated mineral pool beside a huge wall of windows at **Temple Gardens Mineral Spa** (☎ 306-694-5055; 24 Fairford St E; adult/child under 6/youth under 17/senior/family $13.50/free/8.30/9.35/29.50; ☽ 9am-11pm, to midnight Fri & Sat) heals weary bones and souls. Health spa services, like a 90-minute hydrating seaweed body wrap ($90), are also available. Weekday evenings, prices are less than half price.

Quirky Moose Jaw

Urban myths come true at the **Tunnels of Moose Jaw** (☎ 306-693-5261; 108 Main St; adult/child tours $12/6, both tours $19/9; ☽ 10am-7pm Mon-Thu, 10am-9pm Fri-Sun summer, hr vary rest of year) underneath the town's buildings and streets. There are two different hour-long walks through the hallways of hidden history. The 'Chicago Connection' takes you through a 1920s underground world when gangster Al Capone used these spaces for running booze. Tommy gun–toting goons and brothel owners with Southern drawls lead

the way. The 'Passage to Fortune' tells the heart-wrenching tale of Chinese immigrants forced underground while they raised the money required to become citizens.

Tours

More than three-dozen murals of moments in Moose Jaw's history adorn the brick walls around town. The information center has a great walking tour map with descriptions. **Moose Jaw Trolley Company** (☎ 306-693-8537; adult/child under 6/youth under 18/senior $10/5/7/9; ☽ departs 1:15pm, 3:15pm, 4:30pm & 7pm) leads tours from Temple Gardens aboard its renovated streetcars.

Festivals & Events

Moose Jaw is home to the Snowbirds, Canada's famed aerial acrobatic squadron. They star, along with other air-borne craft, at the **Saskatchewan Air Show** (☎ 306-692-4411; www.saskatchewanairshow.com; ☽ mid-Jun), the largest on the prairies.

Sleeping & Eating

Many motels are found north of town on Hwy 1. There are plenty of chain restaurants around town.

Temple Gardens Resort Hotel (☎ 306-694-5055; www.templegardens.sk.ca; 24 Fairford St E; r $100-160, ste $180-250) The huge, modern structure downtown is juxtaposed against the boomtown architecture surrounding it, but it still has a soothing, resort feel. The rooms are spacious and simply colored; they may include a fireplace and big leather chairs. Access to the mineral pool is a perk; another is wearing the big fluffy bathrobes on the way down.

Getting There & Away

STC runs five daily trips to Regina ($13, one hour) and one to Saskatoon ($30, three hours) from the downtown **bus station** (☎ 306-692-2345; 63 High St E). **Hobo Express** (☎ 306-949-2121, 877-828-4626; adult/child/group $20/10/15) runs vans (even for nongamblers) between Temple Gardens and Casino Regina five times daily.

CYPRESS HILLS INTERPROVINCIAL PARK

Eastern Block

The eastern block of this **provincial park** (☎ 306-662-4411; www.cypresshills.com) straddling the Alberta border appears out of nowhere and hits you like a wall. The wheat fields and flatlands are replaced by a thick stand of thin trees. Before long, small lakes, streams, trees, green hills (real hills) and an abundance of wildlife make the farming landscape a distant memory.

Driving in from the east (watch for deer or sheep on the road), you'll arrive in the fairly developed center section of the park. While there are more restaurants, shacks, resorts and buildings than you might want in such a natural setting, an effort has been made to keep it natural-looking. **Campgrounds** (tent sites $13-15, RV sites $18-24, campfire permits $3) are here as well, from RV havens to unserviced wooded sites, and they all fill up in summer, especially on weekends. **Cypress Park Resort Inn** (☎ 306-662-4477; www .cypressresortinn.com; Park Rd; r $65-75, cabins $65-85) is a semifancy resort in the trees on the lake's shore.

Western Block

Standing on a stone precipice surrounded by pine trees in the western block of the park will allow you to really see across the prairies and seemingly to the edge of the world. Get here via 38km-long Gap Rd; the road is dicey when wet (officially 'impassable'). Also in the western section is **Fort Walsh National Historic Site** (☎ 306-662-3590; Park Rd; adult/child/ senior/family $7.75/4/6.50/17; ☯ 9:30am-5:30pm Victoria Day–Labour Day). This was a heavily traveled fur- and whiskey-trading area in the late 1800s. It was also the site of a brutal massacre of dozens of Cree over a misunderstanding (often the case when one mixes booze and money) about a missing horse. The buildings and stories in the living museum focus on the fort's colorful 1880s period.

EASTEND

The quiet and small town of Eastend is in the southwest part of the province on Hwy 13, about 50km south of Hwy 1. It's nestled in a valley of the badlands, which capture and give texture to the pinks and oranges of the sunsets. The **visitors center** (☎ 306-295-4144; Red Coat Dr; ☯ 9am-5pm Mon-Fri) has copies of the *Guide to the Valley of Hidden Secrets*, a self-guided driving tour of nearby geographical highlights.

One of the most complete *Tyrannosaurus rex* skeletons found anywhere was discovered in Saskatchewan in 1994. The **T Rex Discovery Centre** (☎ 306-295-4009; www.dinocountry .com; T-Rex Dr; adult/child $7.50/5; ☯ 9am-5pm Mon-Fri, 11am-4pm Sat & Sun) is a working lab carved into the hillside and available for hour-long tours. In summer, you can also tour active dig sites ($25, departs 9am and 1pm July and August) or do your own dig ($75, departs 9am July and August).

GRASSLANDS NATIONAL PARK

This **park** (www.pc.gc.ca/pn-np/sk/grasslands; per person $4, tent/RV sites $7/8), between the towns of Val Marie and Killdear, is for those who want to sleep with prairie dogs on a barren rock under the stars, and awaken to an orange sun reflecting off a red-rock butte above a carpet of tall grass.

Before going into the park, stop at its **information center** (☎ 306-298-2257; Hwy 4; ☯ 8am-

---

BADASS BADLANDS

Instead of taking a northbound route from Val Marie to Hwy 1, keep on Hwy 18 past Grasslands National Park all the way to Rockglen. About 18km later, rolling wheat fields suddenly disappear into the exposed hills, buttes and coulees of the Big Muddy Badlands. This is outlaw country, son, with the former hiding spots of train-robbin', whiskey-smugglin', horse-stealin' cowboys.

Keep on Hwy 18 through the valley and imagine Butch Cassidy finishing his Mexico-to-Canada outlaw trail journey here, or Sitting Bull making a home here after defeating Custer. Just before Hwy 34, follow the signs left and 25km later you'll be at the large rock formation of Castle Butte, which has no business being in Saskatchewan; stop and take photos. Follow the road east to Hwy 34 and turn left to head north. When you get to Hwy 13, going left takes you toward Moose Jaw (p560) and right into Regina (p555).

There is more to see in the badlands, such as the wolf-den-turned-hiding-cave of outlaw Sam Kelly and his posse, or rock effigies left by First Nations groups, but they're all on private land. The only way to view them legally is through four-hour tours organized by **Big Muddy Tours** (☎ 306-267-3312; adult/child $20/12) or day-long tours of southwestern Saskatchewan with **High View Tours** (☎ 306-478-2936; www.highviewtours.com; $95).

noon & 1-4:30pm Mon-Fri) in Val Marie. Excellent relief maps, a self-guided driving tour and the latest weather information and cautions are found here.

In Val Marie, the **Convent** (☎ 306-298-4515; conventinn@sasktel.net; Hwy 4; s/d incl breakfast $40/50), in a restored convent, has impressive rich oak woodwork complemented by white duvet covers. Exquisite dinners are available by reservation (available to nonguests). The huge lounge, with overstuffed furniture and a library, is a great place to relax after a hike.

MOOSE MOUNTAIN PROVINCIAL PARK

Moose Mountain is a massive plateau dotted with glacially created lakes, ponds and sloughs and topped with aspen; some of it is preserved in this **park** (☎ 306-577-2600, Hwy 9), 70km south of Hwy 1 and 150km southeast of Regina. For details on park accommodations, see p554.

Kennosee Inn Resort Hotel (☎ 306-577-2099; www .kenoseeinn.com; Hwy 9; s/d/ste $80/85/100, cabins $80-125) is the park lodge, situated above a sandy beach on the north shore of Kennosee Lake. The suites overlooking the lake are huge; the rooms on the lower floor have a nice back patio where you can walk right down to the lake. There are several configurations of semirustic cabins with small kitchens.

The park makes a unique Saskatchewan experience, where you can lie on a sandy beach, walk along aspen-lined trails, spot a beaver in a pond and scan a flat horizon in every direction.

YORKTON

Eastern European settlement makes Yorkton, 110km east of Regina along Hwy 10, a natural choice for a branch of the **Western Development Museum** (☎ 306-783-8361; Hwy 16 W; adult/child/student/senior/family $7.25/2/5.25/6.25/16; ☾ 9am-5pm Jul & Aug, 9am-5pm Mon-Fri, noon-5pm Sat & Sun May-Jun, 2-5pm Mon-Wed Sep-May). The Story of People accurately recreates pioneers' homes and farms with few details overlooked. As an indoor/outdoor museum, it depicts the struggles of early farm life and the triumphs of establishing new homes.

On the ceiling of the dome at **St Mary's Ukrainian Catholic Church** (☎ 306-783-4549; 155 Catherine St), Stephen Meuhsh painted a fresco that rivals the work of artists in Europe.

> ### VEREGIN & THE DOUKHOBOURS
>
> Veregin is a small town (population 90), in the middle of the plains, with an unexpectedly intriguing history. Leo Tolstoy sponsored the first wave of Doukhobours (an extraordinary religious sect fearing persecution for their unorthodox beliefs and searching for religious freedom) to emigrate from Russia. They settled this area at the turn of the 20th century and built a successful community under the leadership of Peter Veregin.
>
> Unable to leave their problems behind them, and known to resist mainstream authority, the Doukhobours again found themselves with unhappy neighbors and in trouble with the government. Whether true or false, tales of nude demonstrations and arson left a stigma on the group, and many either left to form communities in the Grand Forks area of British Columbia or returned home.

Canadian filmmakers and producers compete for Canada's Golden Sheaf Awards at the acclaimed **Yorkton Short Film & Video Festival** (☎ 306-782-7077; www.yorktonshortfilm.org; ☾ late May), the oldest continuously running short-film festival in North America.

VEREGIN

Northeast of Yorkton, near the Manitoba border, Veregin is home to the **National Doukhobour Heritage Village** (☎ 306-542-4441; Hwy 5; adult/child/youth $5/1/2; ☾ 10am-6pm mid-May–mid-Sep). The early-1900s Russian heritage building displays aspects of these immigrants' lives, and includes a brick oven (baked bread can be purchased), a bathhouse, a blacksmith shop and agricultural equipment.

SASKATOON

☎ 306 / pop 196,800

Saskatoon can use the term 'Pretty City' with authority. Welcome greenery and shade flanks both sides of the South Saskatchewan River and it's easy to forget that farmland surrounds the outskirts of town. The only city in the province with a positive population growth, it is also the slow-paced, laid-back cultural center.

SASKATCHEWAN

HISTORY

In 1883, 35 members of the Temperance Colonization Colony from Ontario founded a settlement on these Cree lands. The town stayed (though the ban on alcohol didn't), taking it's name from the Cree word, *misaskwatomin*, for one of the indigenous berries still enjoyed today in pies and jams. (The Saskatoon berry is similar to, but a little more fibrous than, a blueberry.) In 1890 the railway hit town and growth continued until the Depression. The city has had its ups and downs since then, but is now well established and diversified beyond its agricultural roots. Uranium mines and some of the world's largest potash deposits are found nearby.

ORIENTATION

The South Saskatchewan River cuts through the city from northeast to southwest. Downtown is on the west bank; the university and the old residential areas are on the east, with seven bridges joining them (thus, 'the City of Bridges').

Circle Dr circumnavigates the city's outskirts, acting as a bypass connecting all the highways. Idylwyld Dr divides the city's streets into east–west designations, and will be your north/south entrance to downtown. Twenty-second St splits the north–south designations and leads you downtown from the west. Entering town from the east, you'll take College Dr past the university (arguably Canada's most attractive campus, sitting high on a cliff overlooking the river) and over the University Bridge.

The southern end of the Broadway Bridge is known as **Five Corners**, the town's oldest shopping district, which runs south along Broadway Ave to Main St.

INFORMATION

Central Library (☎ 306-777-6000; 311 23rd St E) Free Internet access.

Main Post Office (☎ 800-267-1177; 202 4th Ave N)

Midtown Billiards (☎ 306-249-6691; 160 2nd Ave S; per hr $3) Internet access.

Royal University Hospital (☎ 306-665-1000; 103 Hospital Dr; ⊗ 24hr) On the university campus.

Saskatoon City Hospital (☎ 306-655-8000; 701 Queen St; ⊗ 24hr)

Tourism Saskatoon (☎ 306-242-1206, 800-567-2444; www.tourismsaskatoon.com) Idylwyld Dr (305 Idylwyld Dr N; ⊗ 8:30am-7pm Mon-Fri, 10am-7pm Sat & Sun Victoria Day–Labour Day, 8.30am-5pm rest of year); 47th St (cnr Ave C N & 47th St W; ⊗ 10am-7pm Victoria Day–Labour Day) The main office is in the old train station on Idylwyld Dr. There's a seasonal booth on 47th St.

SIGHTS & ACTIVITIES
Western Development Museum

Walk onto Main St in a 1910 boomtown at Saskatoon's branch of the **WDM** (☎ 306-931-1910, 800-363-6345; 2610 Lorne Ave S; adult/child/student/senior/family $7.25/2/5.25/6.25/16; ⊗ 9am-5pm). Although it's indoors, that doesn't really matter, as few details were overlooked in recreating authenticity. From the drugstore shelves lined with thousands of jars of 100-year-old remedies to the public bath in the barbershop, it's all here and it takes you there. Planned for a 2005 opening is the 'Winning the Prairie Gamble' exhibit, celebrating Saskatchewan's centennial by chronicling the risks and rewards of farm life over the previous 100 years. The museum is 4km south of town.

Automobile aficionados won't want to miss the **Transportation Gallery** next to Main St. Dozens of cars are on display, including a 1912 Peerless and a 1972 Cadillac.

Meewasin Valley & Centre

Deciduous trees cover the riverbanks and well-kept parks follow the South Saskatchewan River through the city. Meewasin Valley (*meewasin* is Cree for 'beautiful') is a 17km-long blend of urban creations and natural formations, making Saskatoon the beautiful city that it is.

On both sides of the river, the **Meewasin Valley Trail** is used for walking and cycling in the summer and cross-country skiing in the winter. Picnic tables scattered among the trees make good lunch spots, and **Rotary Park** (btwn Idylwyld & Victoria Bridges), south from downtown and across the river, is best for river and city views. You'll spot pelicans, and maybe beaver, on **Mendel Island** and the weir just north of University Dr Bridge.

The tiny but informative **Meewasin Centre** (☎ 306-665-6888; 402 3rd Ave S; admission free; ⊗ 9am-5pm Mon-Fri, 10:30am-5pm Sat & Sun) tells the history of the river and the city, and has maps and excellent self-guided walking tours.

Ukraina Museum

Expect a thorough in-your-face history lesson, and exhaustive displays on Ukrainian culture, from pre-history through to emigration to North America, when you step into

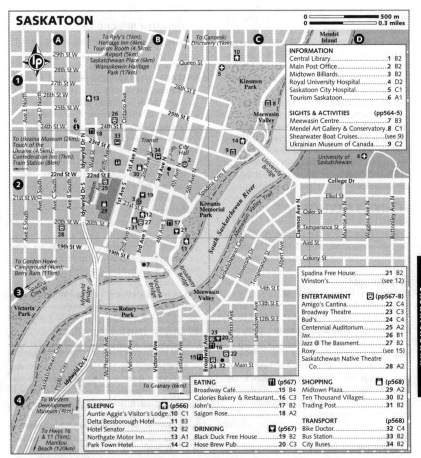

SASKATOON

0	500 m
0	0.3 miles

INFORMATION
Central Library	1 B2
Main Post Office	2 B2
Midtown Billiards	3 B2
Royal University Hospital	4 D2
Saskatoon City Hospital	5 C1
Tourism Saskatoon	6 A1

SIGHTS & ACTIVITIES (pp564-5)
Meewasin Centre	7 B3
Mendel Art Gallery & Conservatory	8 C1
Shearwater Boat Cruises	(see 9)
Ukrainian Museum of Canada	9 C2

Spadina Free House	21 B2
Winston's	(see 12)

ENTERTAINMENT (pp567-8)
Amigo's Cantina	22 C4
Broadway Theatre	23 C3
Bud's	24 C4
Centennial Auditorium	25 A2
Jax	26 B1
Jazz @ The Bassment	27 B2
Roxy	(see 15)
Saskatchewan Native Theatre Co	28 A2

EATING (p567)
Broadway Café	15 B4
Calories Bakery & Restaurant	16 C3
John's	17 B2
Saigon Rose	18 A2

SHOPPING (p568)
Midtown Plaza	29 A2
Ten Thousand Villages	30 B2
Trading Post	31 B2

DRINKING (p567)
Black Duck Free House	19 B2
Hose Brew Pub	20 C3

TRANSPORT (p568)
Bike Doctor	32 C4
Bus Station	33 B2
City Buses	34 B2

SLEEPING (p566)
Auntie Aggie's Visitor's Lodge	10 C1
Delta Bessborough Hotel	11 B3
Hotel Senator	12 B2
Northgate Motor Inn	13 A1
Park Town Hotel	14 C2

SASKATCHEWAN

this **museum** (☎ 306-244-4212; 202 Ave M S; adult/child $2/1; ◷ 11am-5pm Mon-Sat, 1-5pm Sun) 2km west of downtown. *Pysanka* (decorated wooden eggs), embroidered rugs, wedding displays, instruments and more are in one large room, and the extremely knowledgeable Ukrainian staff are never at a loss for words.

Ukrainian Museum of Canada
Recent renovations have given this **museum** (☎ 306-244-3800; 910 Spadina Cres E; adult/child $2/1; ◷ 10am-5pm Mon-Sat, 1-5pm Sun May–early Sep) a stunning new look. The permanent exhibit gives a history of the pioneers' arrival, and their attempts to adapt to a new life, while trying to maintain their culture and religion. It takes a more passive approach than the Ukrainia

Museum in exhibiting clothes, tools, money, wicker suitcases and original documents carried by Ukranian immigrants.

Mendel Art Gallery & Conservatory
A short walk northeast along the river from the downtown area brings you to this **gallery** (☎ 306-975-7610; 950 Spadina Cres E; admission free; ◷ 9am-9pm), which shows contemporary local art. There is also an annual school art exhibit, where high school students from around the city are given a theme and use it to create their masterpieces.

TOURS
Canoe Interpretive Tours (☎ 306-665-6887; 402 3rd Ave S; 1hr Wed evening tours $10, 4hr Sun morning tours

$35) Tours in 10-person voyageur canoes along the South Saskatchewan River; call for exact times.

Canoeski Discovery (☎ 306-653-5693; www.canoeski.com; 1618 9th Ave N; 2-day tours $175-290, 3- to 4-day tours $360-500) Multiday canoe trips when local rivers are flowing. Also offers cross-country skiing and dogsledding in winter.

Diefenbaker Canada Centre (☎ 306-966-8758; adult/child/family $3/2/7; ⓨ departs 10am Mon-Fri, 2pm Sun) University campus and history tours.

Shearwater Boat Cruises (☎ 306-549-2452, 888-747-7572; 950 Spadina Cres E; adult/child/senior $12/8/10; ⓨ departs 2:30pm, 4pm & 5:30pm Victoria Day–Labour Day) Hour-long sightseeing trips along the river. Departs from behind the Mendel Art Gallery.

FESTIVALS & EVENTS
June
Sasktel Saskatchewan Jazz Festival (☎ 306-652-1421; www.saskjazz.com; tickets $5-25; ⓨ late Jun–early Jul) Cool licks is the theme at various locations around town.

July–August
International Fringe Festival (☎ 306-664-2239; www.saskatoonfringe.org; tickets $9; ⓨ late Jul/early Aug) Week-long festival showcasing experimental theater.

Shakespeare on the Saskatchewan (☎ 306-652-9100; www.shakespeareonthesaskatchewan.com; adult/child/student evening shows $24.50/12.50/19.50, matinees $14.50/5/14.50; ⓨ Jul & Aug) Two plays by the Bard are performed in tents on the riverbank by the Mendel Art Gallery. Whether Elizabethan, contemporary or futuristic settings, even non-Shakespeare fans will enjoy. Advance tickets advised.

August
Exhibition (☎ 306-931-7149, 888-931-933; www.saskatoonex.com; adult/youth 11-15 $9/6; ⓨ mid-Aug) Livestock competitions, concerts, rides and fireworks at the Ex.

Saskatoon Folkfest (☎ 306-931-0100; www.folkfest.sk.ca; adult/child $12/free; ⓨ late Aug) Three-day festival of food, song, dance and folklore in pavilions around the city; free bus.

Ukraine Day in the Park (☎ 306-374-7675; admission free; ⓨ late Aug) Ukrainian dancing, clothing and food in Kiwanis Memorial Park, on the riverbank near downtown.

SLEEPING
The northern parts of Circle Dr are lined with motels and hotels.

Park Town Hotel (☎ 306-244-5564, 800-667-399; www.parktownhotel.com; 924 Spadina Cres E; s/d $80/90; 🏊) Across the street from the river, views from the standard-but-large rooms are out-

standing. It's on the quiet southeast edge of downtown, and you're only a short river-bank walk from the action. This place is a good deal.

Auntie Aggie's Visitor's Lodge (☎ 306-244-6300; auntieaggies@shaw.ca; 600 Queen St; s/d with bathroom $60/70) This 1912 Victorian, with a peaceful garden, has guestrooms with definite floral themes. It's four blocks from the river and within walking distance of downtown.

Hotel Senator (☎ 306-244-6141; www.hotelsenator.ca; 243 21st St E; s/d/ste $65/80/100) The Senator has been downtown since 1908; it's the oldest operating hotel in Saskatchewan. The granite steps leading up from the lobby have seen a million footsteps, but the majority of the rooms have been refurbished. It's not the pinnacle of luxury, but the rooms are good for those who appreciate a little character. There's also a bar here called Winston's (opposite).

Dependable motels include **Northgate Motor Inn** (☎ 306-664-4414, 866-664-4414; fax 306-652-7289; 706 Idylwyld Dr N; s/d $60/70; P), a short walk north of downtown, and **Heritage Inn** (☎ 306-665-8121, 888-888-4374; www.heritageinn.net; 102 Cardinal Cres; s/d $70/80, s/d ste $85/95; P), by the airport.

Gordon Howe Campground (☎ 306-975-3328; www.saskatoon.ca/org/leisure/facilities/ghc.asp; Ave P, south of 11th St; tent/RV sites $16/23; ⓨ mid-May–Oct) Tell your friends you spent the night at Gordie's place. The city-operated campground is more geared to RVs, but has lots of shady spots for tents. It's 4km southwest of downtown.

EATING

There are plenty of places to eat downtown, or you can venture further out to find a little character.

Broadway Café (☎ 306-652-8244; 818 Broadway Ave; mains $5-10; ⏰ 7am-9pm) This is Saskatoon's favorite diner, where the tables are close together and you don't necessarily need a menu to order. It is always packed for breakfast, and despite the fact that everyone seems to know everyone else, you won't feel out of place.

John's (☎ 306-244-6384; 401 21st Street E; lunch mains $7-15, dinner mains $25-50; ⏰ lunch & dinner) John takes meat very seriously. The burgers are ground sirloin, the sandwich meats are grilled or smoked to perfection, and there's patio seating outside on nice afternoons. All stops are pulled out in the evening as you pick your cut of beef (in true carnivore fashion, useless vegetables are considered extras); or go for a complete seafood, poultry or game dinner.

Saigon Rose (☎ 306-242-1351; 69 24th St E; mains $7-11; ⏰ lunch & dinner) This nondescript pink box of a building is a hidden gem. Happy eaters devour huge portions of noodles and soups amid green tablecloths and chrome chairs.

Calories Bakery & Restaurant (☎ 306-665-7991; 721 Broadway Ave; lunch mains $7-12, dinner mains $15-32; ⏰ 10am-11pm Mon-Sat, 10am-5pm Sun) Calories has gone from bakery to French bistro, yet maintained its prairie simplicity. The old plank floors and light earth tones compliment the chicken and seafood menu, which is tastefully creative without being overly inventive. It's still a good place to go for a morning coffee and pastry, or for a slice of cake or pie.

Touch of the Ukraine (☎ 306-382-7774; 2401 22nd St W; mains $6-12; ⏰ lunch & dinner) In true Ukrainian they're *varenyky*, but Canadian-Ukrainians say *pyrohy*. Whatever your pleasure, come and get your gluttonous fill of the real thing – peirogies – or *holubtsi* (cabbage rolls) and *kovbasa* (sausage) at this little restaurant 4.5km west of downtown.

Granary (☎ 306-373-6655; 2806 8th St E; mains $16-30; ⏰ dinner) Away from downtown on commercial 8th St, true – if a little overdone – prairie atmosphere can be experienced while chowing down on prime rib or a big steak. The former grain elevator and its creaky wooden floors, prairie colors and farming nostalgia is designed to give you a farmer's appetite.

DRINKING

Hose Brew Pub (☎ 306-477-3473; 612 11th St E) Fire Hall No 5 has recently been converted to this two-level watering hole that has daily specials on food and drinks, and especially its own well-crafted beer.

Winston's (☎ 306-244-6141; 243 21st St E) Winnie's, downtown in the lobby of the Hotel Senator (p566), is an English-style pub with the constant clamor of conversation and good times.

Black Duck Free House (☎ 306-244-8850; 154 2nd Ave S) There are 16 beers on tap and close to 40 scotches in this long, skinny tavern.

Spadina Free House (☎ 306-373-2346; 608 Spadina Cres E) This newcomer attracts a fair number of Saskatoon's happy-hour crowd. With the huge front patio across from the Delta Bessborough hotel, the park and the river, it's not hard to figure out why.

ENTERTAINMENT

From conventions to sporting events to rock concerts, **Saskatchewan Place** (☎ 306-975-3155; www.saskatchewanplace.com; 3535 Thatcher Ave), 12.5km north of downtown, is the largest venue in Saskatoon.

Saskatoon sports fans bleed blue for their **Saskatoon Blades** (☎ 306-938-7800; www.saskatoonblades.com; adult/child/student $14/7/11; ⏰ Sep-Mar). The Blades play WHL junior hockey at Saskatchewan Place.

Live Music & Nightclubs

The old warehouse area northwest of downtown has become a mini-nightlife district; the Broadway area has stood the test of time.

Amigo's Cantina (☎ 306-652-4912; 632 10th St E) Tex-Mex bar featuring alternative local and regional bands.

Bud's (☎ 306-244-4155; 817 Broadway Ave) Live rhythm and blues nightly, and a Saturday-afternoon jam.

Jazz @ The Bassment (☎ 306-683-2277; www.jazzbassment.com; 245 3rd Ave S) Passion for jazz and great sound.

Jax (☎ 306-934-4444; 302 Pacific Ave) Downtown nightclub with no cover charge before 9pm.

Roxy (☎ 306-665-7479; 834B Broadway Ave) Live music, of the rock-tribute-band variety, most nights. It's especially popular on Tuesday – must be the $1 draft beers.

Ryly's (☎ 306-664-0030; 1201 Alberta Ave) A fun bar that books smaller acts some nights, and acts as a rock 'n' roll nightclub on others. It's 1.5km north of downtown.

Theater & Cinemas

The **Saskatoon Symphony** (☎ 306-665-6414; www .saskatoonsymphony.org; adult/student/senior $26/19/25; ⏰ Sep–Jun) plays regularly at **Centennial Auditorium** (☎ 306-938-7800; www.saskcent.com; 35 22nd St E). On nonsymphony nights, the Centennial hosts large-scale theatrical productions, dance performances and concerts.

Persephone Theatre (☎ 306-384-7727; www.perse phonetheatre.org; 2802 Rusholme Rd; matinee/weeknight/ weekend tickets $16/21/25) Here since 1974, the theater's classic, contemporary and Canadiana performances have made audiences laugh and think. It's 7km west of downtown.

Broadway Theatre (☎ 306-652-6556; www.broad waytheatre.ca; 715 Broadway Ave; adult/child $9/4) This historic cinema shows cult classics, art films and occasional local live performances.

Saskatchewan Native Theatre Co (☎ 306-931-7682; www.sntc.ca; 228 20th St W; tickets $7.50-18.50; ⏰ Feb-Jun) Contemporary productions by Canadian Aboriginal artists put a different but entertaining spin on traditional theater.

SHOPPING

Broadway Ave has some cute and quirky little shops.

Trading Post (☎ 306-653-1769; 226 2nd Ave S) This shop specializes in crafts and souvenirs, with an emphasis on aboriginal goods, including fine Cowichan-style wool sweaters and British Columbian jade.

BERRY PICKER

If you're interested in berry picking, fruits such as blueberries, Saskatoons (similar to blueberries), raspberries, strawberries and chokecherries are only a few of those that can be culled at farms throughout Saskatchewan during the summer months. Signs along the highways direct you to these delicious stops (and tell you if the place is open). For a map of berry-picking farms, contact the **Saskatchewan Fruit Growers Association** (☎ 306-645-447, 877-973-7848; www.saskfruit.com).

Ten Thousand Villages (143 2nd Ave N) This is a nonprofit organization run by the Mennonite Central Committee, which hires aboriginal craftspeople from all over the world to create the pieces that are sold in these stores.

Berry Barn (☎ 306-978-9797; 830 Valley Rd; ⏰ Apr–mid-Dec) Saskatoon's own berry gets all the credit at this working farm 11km southwest of town. The barn-style country home, with a picturesque garden overlooking the river, sells jams, pies, teas and toppings made with the semi-tart Saskatoon berry, and in season (late June to early July) you can venture into the fields to pick your own Saskatoons.

GETTING THERE & AWAY

John G Diefenbaker International Airport (YXE; ☎ 306-975-8900; 2625 Airport Dr) is 5km northeast of the city, off Idylwyld Dr. Most flights serve regional destinations in Canada, but Northwest Airlines also flies to Minneapolis, Minnesota ($430, 4½ hours, daily).

STC covers the province extensively from the **bus station** (☎ 306-933-8000; 50 23rd St E); three daily buses head south to Regina ($36) and north to Prince Albert ($21). Greyhound Canada runs two buses to Winnipeg ($97), three to Calgary ($83) and four to Edmonton ($74) daily.

Unfortunately, not only is the **train station** (Chappell Dr) in the middle of nowhere (8km from downtown), the thrice-weekly VIA Rail trains pass through in the middle of the night, and are often delayed. Make accommodation arrangements before you arrive; belly-up at a pub before you leave.

GETTING AROUND

A taxi to the airport costs $14. A direct line to **Blueline Taxi** (☎ 306-653-3333) is available at the train station, with a trip to downtown costing $18. **City buses** (☎ 360-975-7500; www.city .saskatoon.sk.ca/org/transit; adult/child $2/1.20) take you from the bus-only section of 23rd St E (between 2nd and 3rd Aves N) around the city. Car-rental agencies (see p873) have outlets at the airport. Bicycles can be rented at the **Bike Doctor** (☎ 306-664-8555; 623 Main St; per day $15).

AROUND SASKATOON
Wanuskewin Heritage Park

Wanuskewin (wah-nus-*kay*-win, Cree for 'seeking peace of mind') is a fascinating cultural, historical and geographical center. You can walk past the statues and cairns of a re-created drive lane (used to herd hunted bison) towards the interpretive center of this **First Nations' heritage park** (☎ 306-931-6767; www .wanuskewin.com; Penner Rd, off Hwy 11; adult/child/ student/senior $8.50/free/6.50/7.50; ☺ 9am-9pm Victoria Day–Labour Day, 9am-5pm rest of year) and you're immediately involved in the beginning of a buffalo hunt. About 17km north of Saskatoon, alongside the South Saskatchewan River, this 100-hectare site presents and interprets the area's rich 7000-year-old aboriginal history.

The museum is a walk-through exhibit of re-created camps, tipis and buffalo jumps, which teaches about the people who used the land for spiritual and practical reasons. Kids enjoy touching buffalo furs and the hands-on computer games, while two dozen archeological sites attract researchers; active digs can be visited during summer.

Virtually invisible from the surrounding prairie, the Opamihaw ('the one who flies') Valley has been left untouched and it reveals why this was a spiritual and sacred place. It's worth walking the valley's trails amid wildflowers and songbirds to see park highlights like the old buffalo trail used by migrating herds, sites of buffalo jumps, where the animals were forced off cliffs in mass-hunting practices, and temporary hunting camps.

Cultural dance performances take place on summer afternoons, and the **café** (mains $5-12) has aboriginal dishes like buffalo, wild-rice bannock (unleavened fire-baked bread) and Saskatoon-berry desserts. In the summer, overnight tipi stays and full-day packages are offered; call for times and prices.

To see the site thoroughly (trails, performances and lunch), allow about four to six hours. Early morning, or off-season, is the best, most peaceful time to see the park, as there will be fewer people around, if any. Wear comfortable shoes on the trails, and bring plenty of fluids during the summer.

Manitou Beach

Underground springs have created the 'Lake of Healing Waters' (as it was called by the Cree), 120km southeast of Saskatoon, near the town of Watrous. **Manitou Lake** (www.watrous manitou.com), where you can take a healing, therapeutic swim for free, has a high concentration of minerals that makes it three times denser than the ocean.

If you're a little leery of the smelly lake, you can take a soak at the **Mineral Bath House** (☎ 306-946-4174; cnr Lake Ave & Unwin St; baths $8.50) in a single- to six-person tub (cleaned regularly) where you control the temperature. **Manitou Springs Resort & Mineral Spa** (☎ 306-946-2233, 800-667-7672; www.manitousprings.ca; cnr Lake Ave & Watrous St; baths $8, r $80-110) has three large indoor pools, heated to different temperatures, and large rooms overlooking the lake.

NORTHERN SASKATCHEWAN

North of Saskatoon, the geography changes dramatically. A belt of boreal forest crosses the province's midsection; north of that, glacially scoured rocks and potholes make up the landscape. Northern Saskatchewan is actually south of the center of the province; for all intents, the north begins at Saskatoon as accessibility beyond there becomes limited.

PRINCE ALBERT

Prince Albert (PA) has an old brick downtown in a pretty location beside the North

---

THERE'S DIAMONDS IN THEM THAR FLATLANDS

Prince Albert and northern Saskatchewan experienced a boom with fur trading in the 1770s, another with the growth of the west in the 1880s, and in keeping with the 110-year cycle, another as a result of unexpected diamond exploration in the 1990s. Small diamonds were first discovered near Prince Albert in the 1960s, and in 1988 the South African diamond company De Beers quietly staked a claim 40km north of Prince Albert. As history will tell, no discovery can ever truly be kept quiet, and millions of hectares nearby were staked for exploration. The company Dia Met (which was later bought by BHP) found the first kimberlite (geology-speak for 'diamond deposit') in 1991 in the Northwest Territories. Since then, Canada has become the sixth-largest diamond producer in the world, and Canadian diamonds are distinguished by the microscopic polar bear engraved onto each one.

Saskatchewan River. This is the gear-up spot for trips to the forested and lake-riddled north. Started as a 1776 fur-trading post, it became a real town and was named after Queen Victoria's husband in 1904.

The **Tourism & Convention Bureau** (☎ 306-953-4385; www.patourism.ca; 3700 2nd Ave W; ☯ 9am-8pm Victoria Day–Labour Day, 9am-5pm rest of year) has a lot of information on the town, the park and points north. The **Historical Museum** (☎ 306-764-2992; cnr Central Ave & River St E; admission $1; ☯ 10am-6pm Mon-Sat, 10am-9pm Sun), in the old fire station, displays the city's past.

Instead of a university, Prince Albert decided to build a major penitentiary. The small **Rotary Museum of Police & Corrections** (☎ 306-953-4385; 3700 2nd Ave W; admission free; ☯ 10am-6pm May-Aug) honors PA city police and RCMP through displays and stories. Of particular interest are the methods and tools used in discipline, and the inmate-fabricated weapons.

Amy's on Second (☎ 306-763-1515; 2990 2nd Ave W; lunch mains $7-13, dinner mains $10-25; ☯ lunch & dinner) is known throughout the area for its excellent food and top-notch cheesecake. It's a linen-and-candles place that's always busy and super-friendly. All dishes feature at least one local ingredient, like Saskatoon berries or grilled pickerel.

Catch excellent small-town hockey enthusiasm with almost-big-league talent at a **Prince Albert Raiders** (www.raiderhockey.com; adult/child $15/7) game at the **Comuniplex** (☎ 306-953-4848; 690 32nd St E).

Transwest Air has daily flights to Prince Albert from Saskatoon ($65, one hour) and Regina ($169, two hours). STC runs three daily trips to Saskatoon ($21, two hours) and one daily to places north from the downtown **bus station** (☎ 306-953-3700; 99 15th St E).

PRINCE ALBERT NATIONAL PARK

This **national park** (www.pc.gc.ca/pn-np/sk/princealbert; Rte 263 or Rte 264; adult/child/senior/family $5/2.50/4.25/12.50) is a huge tract of wilderness, where the southern waves of wheat fields hit the shores of northern boreal forests. Rolling forests, huge glacier potholes, spruce bogs and pockets of wildlife create winding, attractive, slow-paced hiking trails, bike routes, scenic drives and winter cross-country trails. No other place on earth has a white-pelican colony (at Lavallee Lake), a herd of wild bison (in the southwestern grassland) or controversial conservationist **Grey Owl's cabin** at Ajawaan Lake (see the boxed text below).

The resort village of **Waskesiu**, on the huge lake of the same name, is a lesson in how to build a town inside a national park. Amid log cabins and clean streets, with an obvious respect for the natural setting, you'll find the **information center** (☎ 306-663-4522; Waskesiu Dr; ☯ 8am-8pm mid-May–early Sep), motel-accommodation services and a sandy beach for swimming. It's a very busy place in the summer, but quiet out of season.

Waskesiu **marina** (☎ 306-663-5994) rents canoes, though Waskesiu Lake is way too big

---

GREY OWL AT HOME IN THE WILDERNESS

Conservationist, trapper, entertainer, boozer, Englishman, Mexican, best-selling author, worldwide fraudster; whatever the renowned naturalist Grey Owl *was*, he wasn't dull. Born Archibald Stansfield Belaney of Hastings, England in the early 1900s, he was enamored by stories of North American indigenous peoples and immigrated to Ontario at the age of 18. He quickly learned to trap and hunt, then married an Iroquois woman and was adopted as a brother by the Ojibwe tribe. With dyed skin, braided hair and speaking broken English, he gave up tracking animals; instead, he started a beaver colony and wrote about nature preservation.

Throughout the 1930s he lived and wrote in a small, one-room log cabin on Ajawaan Lake in the woodlands of Prince Albert National Park; he also toured North America and the UK, encouraging appreciation of the environment. His writings consistently sold out and his lectures were legendary. *Tales of an Empty Cabin,* published in 1936, is possibly his best-known work.

Heavy drinking caused poor health and he died in 1938 at his cabin. Research into his life discovered he was not the Apache-Mexican friend of Buffalo Bill Cody he had people convinced he was. In true celebrity fashion, this postmortem fall from grace only enhanced his reputation.

The cabin in which he lived has become a shrine among nature-lovers. It is a fairly inaccessible spot, but the 20km Grey Owl Trail along Kingsmere Lake will take you there. There is no camping at the cabin, but there is a backcountry site 3km away.

and rough for most paddlers. You can take the canoe to a smaller lake, or head out on a multiday trip.

There are many **campgrounds** (☎ reservations 877-737-3783; www.pccamping.ca; RV/backcountry/tent sites $27/5/13) in the park. The wooded **Beaver Glen**, in Waskesiu, accommodates RVs and fills up quickly. Throughout the park there are other secluded and quiet campgrounds designed for tenters, or there's backcountry camping for canoeists and hikers (pick up permits from the information center).

There are motel and resort accommodations around the town, as well as privately owned cottages available for rent. **Waskesiu Chamber of Commerce** (☎ 306-663-5410; www.waskesiulake.ca) is an excellent resource.

The park's natural expanse is hard to explore without a car, as the trailheads and marinas are outside of town. STC (p555) arrives here once a day on the way north to La Ronge ($30, two hours) and south to Prince Albert ($15, one hour).

LA RONGE & AROUND
Near the northern terminus of Hwy 2, on the western edge of huge Lac La Ronge, is the small village of **La Ronge**, busy with activity seekers come to hunt, fish, hike and ski.

For 20 years local proprietor, Alex Robertson, worked for Hudson's Bay Company as a fur grader; today he owns and operates **Robertson's Trading Post** (☎ 306-425-2080; 308 La Ronge Ave; ☾ Mon-Sat) as a fur trader. The scuffed-up, red-and-white-checkered linoleum floor has been walked on by many a wide-eyed tourist, grocery-buying local and fur-trapper. The shop is the local supply and grocery center, and the pelts and trophies at the back of the store are a commodity reminiscent of days gone by.

The geography changes drastically north of here, as the tall, skinny trees give way to shorter vegetation. The thousands of lakes and the scraped-clean rocks are evidence of the last glacial retreat. **Lac La Ronge Provincial Park** (☎ 306-425-4234, 800-772-4064; Hwy 2) surrounds huge, island-filled Lac La Ronge, which is great for fishing and canoeing. You can hike among stubby pines and over boardwalked marsh or barren rock. See the Tourism Saskatchewan brochure on fishing and hunting for a list of outfitters. The park has six year-round campgrounds and hundreds of hectares of backcountry camping.

For more information on accommodations, see p554. Services are only open from Victoria Day to Labour Day.

Transwest Air offers charter flights in floatplanes to points north from La Ronge. STC has a daily bus to Prince Albert ($40, three hours) and Saskatoon ($55, 6½ hours).

BATOCHE NATIONAL HISTORIC SITE
In the mid-1800s, after facing difficulties acquiring land in Manitoba, a group of Métis moved from the Red River and established this **village** (☎ 306-423-6227; Rte 225; adult/child/student $5.75/free/3; ☾ 9am-5pm May-Sep). Like a black cloud, their problems followed and a land-claim dispute incited the 1885 Battle of Batoche between 800 federal soldiers and 200 Métis, where Louis Riel (see p28) was finally captured. This realistic outdoor museum has re-created the village, including the mass grave and rifle pits, with artifacts, videos and storyboards on the lives, and deaths, of these pioneers. Plan on a two- or three-hour visit. Batoche is halfway between Saskatoon and PA (about 70km north of Saskatoon).

THE BATTLEFORDS
Linked by bridge across the North Saskatchewan River, the Battlefords are two towns and their adjacent districts, 140km northwest of Saskatoon on the Yellowhead Hwy.

If you think farming's tough today, visit North Battleford's branch of the **WDM** (☎ 306-445-8083, Hwy 16, at Hwy 40; adult/child/student/senior/family $7.25/2/5.25/6.25/16; ☾ 9am-5pm May-Sep, 12:30-4:30pm Wed-Sun Oct-Apr), where the Heritage Farm & Village shows how much harder it was in the 1920s. The boardwalked village includes a co-op store, the old gas station and fully outfitted residences; all are linked by an old-fashioned crank-telephone system.

Internationally acclaimed Cree artist Allen Sapp displays his incredibly realistic cultural and landscape paintings at the **Allen Sapp Gallery** (☎ 306-445-1760; www.allensapp.com; 1 Railway Ave; suggested donation $2; ☾ 10:30am-5pm May-Sep, 1-5pm Wed-Sun Oct-Apr).

Costumed guides and cannon firings give life to the NWMP fort, built in 1876. The walk-through **Fort Battleford National Historic Site** (☎ 306-937-2621; adult/child/senior/family $5.75/3/5/14.50; ☾ 9am-5pm Victoria Day–Labour Day) was also the site of an 1885 battle between police and the First Nations, who were frustrated at their presence.

SASKATCHEWAN

Alberta

If Alberta had a catchphrase it would have to be 'super size it.' And we're not just talking about the province's penchant for building giant replicas of sausages, ducks and dinosaurs. It's just that in the westernmost of the prairie provinces it seems everything is exceptionally big. Larger than life, you could say. There are wide, wide-open spaces with giant skies and seas of green and golden grasses. There are big mountains, the jagged, rugged-looking, wild kind that are full of glaciers and icefields and shimmering emerald lakes. There are big parks – Jasper, Canada's largest mountain park, is here, and so is Wood Buffalo National Park, Canada's largest park. There are big oil and gas reserves. And big cities: Edmonton and Calgary, two of Canada's largest. There is a big mall, supposedly the world's biggest. Even the bear are big – the mighty grizzly still roams in this province, where the prairies meet the Rocky Mountains.

Alberta's a bit of a magician, too – a master of illusions. Compared with other mountain ranges the Canadian Rockies are not actually that tall, but they look enormous when you see them up close, towering and majestic, thanks to a relatively low starting elevation. And don't even start on the glacier-fed mountain lakes. If you stare into one – crystal-clear emerald green or slightly opaque turquoise blue – without looking at the mountains behind it, you might just be convinced you've reached a tropical sea.

Wherever you venture in this vast and often sparsely inhabited province, we're pretty sure you'll leave not quite believing your eyes.

HIGHLIGHTS

- Explore the spectacular high-alpine trails and glacier lakes of **Banff** (p609) and **Jasper** (p622) **National Parks** by day and soak in one of the hot springs pools by night

- Admire the surreal turquoise waters of **Peyto Lake** (p607) in Banff; you'll have to see it to believe it's not an illusion

- Shop till you drop and then revive yourself with a pub crawl in Edmonton's vibrant **Old Strathcona** (p579) district

- Look for grizzly bear, elk and cougar without the crowds in stunning **Waterton Lakes National Park** (p634)

- Don your spurs and Stetson, pardner, and swagger down to the **Calgary Stampede** (p597), Canada's premier Wild West celebration

Jasper National Park ★
★ Edmonton
Peyto Lake ★
Banff National Park ★
★ Calgary
Waterton Lakes National Park ★

ALBERTA

| ▪ POPULATION: 3.2 MILLION | ▪ PROVINCIAL CAPITAL: EDMONTON | ▪ AREA: 661,185 SQ KM |

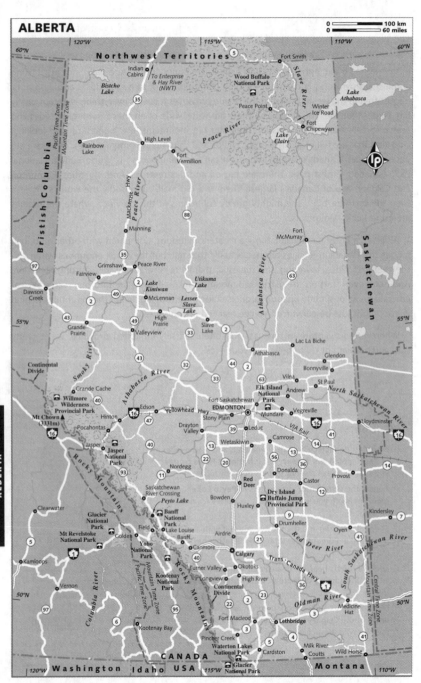

ALBERTA

0 — 100 km
0 — 60 miles

Northwest Territories

Fort Smith

Indian Cabins

To Enterprise & Hay River (NWT)

Wood Buffalo National Park

Bistcho Lake

Peace Point

Winter Ice Road

Lake Athabasca

Fort Chipewyan

Lake Claire

High Level

Fort Vermillion

Peace River

Rainbow Lake

Mackenzie Hwy

Peace River

Manning

Fort McMurray

Utikuma Lake

Athabasca River

Grimshaw

Peace River

Fairview

Dawson Creek

Lake Kimiwan

McLennan

Lesser Slave Lake

Grande Prairie

High Prairie

Slave Lake

Valleyview

Lac La Biche

Glendon

Athabasca

Bonnyville

Vilna

St Paul

Continental Divide

Smoky River

Grande Cache

Athabasca River

Willmore Wilderness Provincial Park

Edson

Yellowhead Hwy

Fort Saskatchewan

EDMONTON

Elk Island National Park

Andrew

Vegreville

Saskatchewan

North Saskatchewan River

Lloydminster

Mt Chown (3331m)

Hinton

Pocahontas

Stony Plain

Mundare

Jasper

Jasper National Park

Drayton Valley

Leduc

Camrose

VIA Rail

Brtistish Columbia

Wetaskiwin

Nordegg

Donalda

Castor

Provost

Saskatchewan River Crossing

Peyto Lake

Red Deer

Dry Island Buffalo Jump Provincial Park

Clearwater

Banff National Park

Bowden

Huxley

Glacier National Park

Mt Revelstoke National Park

Field

Lake Louise

Golden

Yoho National Park

Airdrie

Drumheller

Oyen

Kindersley

Kamloops

Banff

Canmore

Calgary

Rocky Mountains

Vernon

Turner Valley

Okotoks

Kootenay National Park

Longview

High River

Red Deer River

South Saskatchewan River

Columbia River

Continental Divide

Oldman River

Medicine Hat

Fort Macleod

Lethbridge

Pacific Time Zone

Mountain Time Zone

Kootenay Bay

Pincher Creek

Waterton Lakes National Park

Cardston

Coutts

Milk River

Wild Horse

CANADA

Washington Idaho USA

Glacier National Park

Montana

Rocky Mountains

History

The Blackfoot, Kainaiwa (Blood), Siksika, Peigan, Atsina (also called Gros Ventre), Cree, Tsuu T'ina (Sarcee) and Assiniboine Aboriginals occupied Alberta, particularly the southern portion, from 9500 to 5500 BC. For millennia they lived a nomadic life, walking great distances to hunt the vast herds of bison they used for food, clothing and shelter.

The first Europeans arrived in Alberta in the middle of the 17th century, seeking to trade fur. The Hudson's Bay Company and its main rival, the North-West Company, followed in the 18th century and set up trading posts throughout the region. The two companies amalgamated in 1821 when the territory became part of the Dominion of Canada. Settlers were then enticed to migrate to Alberta by the government's offers of cheap land.

The 1870s saw the establishment of the North-West Mounted Police (NWMP), later to become the Royal Canadian Mounted Police (RCMP), as a response to the lawlessness caused by the whiskey trade – Plains Indians were given cheap alcohol in exchange for bison hides.

The coming of the railway in the 1880s made access to the west easier and led to a rapid expansion of the population (see p28). Wheat farming and cattle ranching formed the basis of the economy, but coal mining and timber were also important. The discovery of natural gas and oil in the early 20th century added to Alberta's wealth.

In 1905 Alberta became a fully-fledged province of Canada, named after the fourth daughter of Queen Victoria, Princess Louise Caroline Alberta (1848–1939), who was married to Canada's fourth governor general, the Marquis of Lorne. Edmonton was named the capital.

The economy and immigration exploded in the early 1970s. Although large deposits of oil and natural gas were discovered in 1947, it wasn't until the 1970s oil crisis that people and money began to pour into the province from all parts of the country. Calgary and Edmonton became booming, modern cities – today the country's fifth and sixth largest, respectively.

In the mid-1980s, with the fall in oil and grain prices, the boom ended and hard times came quickly. Some Albertans left the province, but most of those leaving were easterners returning home. Oil and gas remain the biggest contributors to provincial coffers, but the manufacturing and service sectors have gained ground, leading to a healthier economic diversity. The province's per-capita gross domestic product grew by more than 27% from 1992 to 2000, and the provincial economy has now surpassed that of British Columbia (BC) as the country's third largest (after Ontario and Québec).

Climate

Alberta has about 2000 hours of sunshine per year – more than any other province. Summers are warm, with the southern areas reaching temperatures of around 25°C in July and August. The average annual rainfall is about 450mm, a good portion of which falls between June and early August. The generally dry, warm weather in August and September makes these months particularly good for traveling. In the mountains summers are short and it's always cool at night.

Snowstorms can sweep down from the north from early October. Temperatures can be in the subzero Celsius range for weeks, and you'll soon understand why cars have cords for engine block heaters poking through their grills. In the south the harshness of winter is reduced by the chinook winds – warm, dry southwesterlies that can quickly raise temperatures by as much as 20°C.

National & Provincial Parks

Alberta has five national parks, of which three – Banff, Jasper and Waterton Lakes – are in the Rocky Mountains. All three parks have excellent amenities and offer superb

---

THEY CALL THE WIND CHINOOK

The chinook is a warm, dry southwesterly wind that blows off the eastern slopes of the Rocky Mountains in winter. These winds can change the snowy streets of places such as Calgary to slush and puddles within hours. The name is derived from the Chinook Aboriginals, who lived along the northwest Pacific coast, mainly in what is now Washington State in the USA.

opportunities for outdoor activities and wildlife viewing. Jasper (p622) is the largest of the mountain national parks and is wilder and more remote than its southern neighbor, Banff (p609), which packs in serious crowds during the summer season. Waterton Lakes National Park (p634), an International Peace Park connected to the USA's Glacier National Park, sees fewer crowds and more opportunities to spot grizzly and black bear. Wood Buffalo National Park (p638), the least accessible, is in the far northeast, and is Canada's largest national park. Elk Island National Park (p589), the province's smallest, is just east of Edmonton. Camping in the parks operates on a first-come, first-served basis, and sites cost between $10 and $24, depending on facilities. For more on Canada's national parks and wildlife, see p51.

In addition, the province maintains scads of provincial parks and recreation areas – more than 500 sites in all. Many have campgrounds and opportunities for backcountry camping.

ALBERTA'S TOP WILDLIFE-VIEWING SPOTS

■ **Bow Valley Parkway** (Banff National Park, p619). Many consider this the best wildlife-viewing road in Canada. The parkway is the epicenter of wildlife viewing in the park and is the best place for any of the charismatic megafauna.

■ **Cave and Basin National Historic Site** (Banff National Park, p612). One of the many excellent wildlife sites around the town of Banff; perhaps the premier bird-watching site in the Canadian Rockies.

■ **Maligne Lake Rd** (Jasper National Park, p623). Hot spots for viewing bighorn sheep, harlequin ducks and trout are located along this road; this is one of the only sites where woodland caribou can reliably be found in winter.

■ **Red Rock Parkway** (Waterton Lakes National Park, p635). Visitors have opportunities to see moose, coyote, bear and bighorn sheep along this winding, scenic road.

Getting There & Away

Alberta is easily accessible by bus, car, train and air. The province shares a border with Montana, USA (for details about crossing the border, see p867).

AIR

The two major airports are in Edmonton and Calgary, and there are daily flights to both from major hubs across the world. Carriers serving the province include Air Canada, American Airlines, Continental, Delta, Horizon Air, Northwest Airlines, United Airlines and WestJet. For further details, see p863 and p868.

BUS

Greyhound Canada (p870) has bus services to Alberta from neighboring provinces and Greyhound (p870) has services from the USA. Fares from Edmonton include Winnipeg ($158, 20 hours, two daily), Vancouver ($143, 16 hours, three daily), Prince George ($104, 10 hours, two daily), Hay River ($137, 16 hours, one daily) and Whitehorse ($258, 29 hours, one daily). From Calgary, destinations include Kamloops ($86, nine hours, four daily), Regina ($99, 11 hours, four daily), Saskatoon ($85, nine hours, two daily), Vancouver ($120, 15 hours, five daily) and Winnipeg ($150, 20 hours, four daily).

Moose Travel Network (p875) runs two-to four-day trips in a tour bus between Banff and Vancouver, BC, stopping at great destinations along the way. The trips operate three times weekly between April and November and prices start at $95. You can book through local hostels.

TRAIN

VIA Rail's *Canadian* goes through Calgary and Banff, while the *Skeena* travels from Jasper to Prince Rupert, BC (see p876).

Getting Around

Roads are good in Alberta, although the further north you travel, the longer the distances are between towns. Make sure your petrol tank is filled before setting off. Alberta gets very cold in the winter; make sure your car is prepared. In the national parks certain roads become inaccessible (or are shut) during the snowy season. Check weather forecasts or chat with locals before venturing into an impending blizzard.

ALBERTA IN...

One Week

Spend one night exploring the friendly capital city of **Edmonton** (below). Stay at the very hip Met hotel, in the vibrant Old Strathcona neighborhood, and have a martini at the Savoy restaurant.

Next head west along the scenic Yellowhead Hwy to **Jasper National Park** (p622) for two nights. It's quieter and wilder than its southern sister, Banff. Hike around one of the famous emerald green lakes or soak in the **Miette Hot Springs** (p523). Keep your eyes peeled for wildlife – Jasper has plenty. Then drive the **Icefields Parkway** (p606) to Lake Louise, one of the Canadian Rockies' greatest assets. Also visit beautiful **Moraine Lake** (p619). Afterwards, head to lively **Banff Town** (p609). There are enough outdoor activities to keep you busy in Banff for days. It's essential to have a drink with a view at the Fairmont Banff Springs Hotel's Rundle Lounge. Finally, visit **Calgary** (p590) and gorge yourself on the city's famous steaks.

Two Weeks

Follow the above itinerary but spend more time in the national parks. Also visit **Dinosaur Provincial Park** (p631) and **Head-Smashed-In Buffalo Jump** (p632) in southern Alberta. Finish your trip in the rugged and remote **Waterton Lakes National Park** (p634), where seeing wildlife is almost guaranteed.

EDMONTON

☎ 780 / pop 824,000

Whether you're bar-hopping and browsing the funky shops of Old Strathcona, snorkeling around a lake in the self-proclaimed world's largest mall, eating a melt-in-your-mouth Alberta steak at a fine restaurant or taking the kids on an adventure in the futuristic Odyssium, Alberta's capital aims to please just about everyone.

Edmonton is a pleasant, low-key place filled with some of the friendliest folk around. Visitors are attracted to Canada's sixth-largest city for its proximity to Jasper and other national parks, its transportation links to the far north and its range of attractions.

Sitting astride the banks of the North Saskatchewan River, the city is easy on the eyes. As an early aviation center, Edmonton was once known as the 'Gateway to the North,' but that title changed to 'Oil Capital of Canada' in the 1970s, when the entire province boomed and shrugged off its cowboy image. The city experienced explosive growth, and the downtown area was totally modernized.

HISTORY

When European explorers and fur traders arrived in the late 18th century, the area had been populated by the Cree and Blackfoot nations for more than 5000 years.

In 1795 the Hudson's Bay Company built Fort Edmonton, which was as a fur-trading center until about 1870, when the Canadian government bought the land and opened up the area for pioneers. By 1891 the railway had arrived from Calgary, and in 1892 Edmonton was officially incorporated as a town. In 1905, with the creation of Alberta, Edmonton – then numbering 8000 residents – became the capital.

With the discovery of gold in the Yukon in 1897, Edmonton was the last outpost of civilization for many gold seekers heading north to the Klondike. In the gold-rush days, unscrupulous entrepreneurs lured gold seekers to the city with false tales of a trail from Edmonton to Dawson City in the Yukon. Many died trying to find the trail; others gave up and returned to settle in Edmonton.

WWII brought a large influx of people, many to work on the Alaska Hwy. Though the province's population is mainly of British descent, some residents have German and Ukrainian backgrounds.

ORIENTATION

The North Saskatchewan River drifts through the town center, separating downtown, on the north bank, from the lively and more interesting Old Strathcona district to the south. Between the two districts lies a

ALBERTA

EDMONTON

0 ———— 2 km
0 ———— 1 mile

INFORMATION
Royal Alexandria Hospital..........1 C2
Travel Shop.............................2 B3

SIGHTS & ACTIVITIES (pp579–82)
Alberta Government House.........3 B3
Fort Edmonton Park.................4 A4
Muttart Conservatory..............5 C3
Odyssium...............................6 A2
Out an' About Tours................7 D4
Provincial Museum of Alberta....8 B2
St Josaphat's Ukrainian Catholic
Cathedral.............................9 C2
Ukrainian Canadian Archives &
Museum of Alberta................10 C2
Ukrainian Museum of Canada..11 C2
Valley Zoo.............................12 A4

SLEEPING (pp583–6)
Glenora Bed & Breakfast Inn....13 B2
Inglewood House B&B..............14 B2
Rainbow Valley Campground & RV
Park.....................................15 A5

ENTERTAINMENT (pp587–8)
Buddy's Nite Club...................16 B3
Commonwealth Stadium...........17 C2
Jubilee Auditorium..................18 B3
Skyreach Centre.....................19 D1

SHOPPING (p588)
Old Strathcona Antique Mall...20 C4

To Alberta Railway Museum (9km)

To Carr's Streetside Garden B&B (600m)

To Peter's Edmonton Tours (4.5km)

To Driving Force & Hap's Hungry House (1km); Sandman Hotel West Edmonton (2km); Travelodge Edmonton West (2.5km); Glowing Embers Travel Centre & RV Park (6km)

To West Edmonton Mall & Fantasyland Hotel (2km)

To Derrick Motel (1km); Chateau Motel (3km); Half Moon Lake Resort (29km); Edmonton International Airport (30km); Calgary (35km)

To Alberta Craft Council Gallery and Shop (800m)

ALBERTA

---

series of beautiful parks. Note that many streets and avenues have both number designations and names, which are used interchangeably.

Downtown is bounded roughly by 104th Ave, 100th Ave, 109th St and 95th St. Filled with mirrored, 1970s high-rises, it bustles with office workers and shoppers during the day, but tends to be quiet at night and on weekends. Jasper Ave (101st Ave) is the main thoroughfare downtown.

Across the river, the historic **Old Strathcona** district runs along 82nd Ave (also called Whyte Ave) for several blocks east and west of 104th St. It's the hippest place to be in Edmonton.

INFORMATION
Bookstores
Audrey's Books (Map p580; ☎ 780-423-3487; 10702 Jasper Ave) Canadiana, travel guides and maps.

Map Town (Map p580; ☎ 780-429-2600; 10344 105th St; ☺ 10am-6pm Mon-Fri, 10am-5pm Sat) Great source for maps, travel books and atlases.

Orlando Books (Map p581; ☎ 780-432-7633; 10123 82nd Ave) Good selection of gay and lesbian titles. Readings on most Friday nights. Carries *Times.10*, Edmonton's free gay and lesbian monthly.

Travel Shop (Map p578; ☎ 780-439-3089; 10926 88th Ave) Stocks a wide range of travel books, maps and travel goods.

Emergency
Police, Ambulance & Fire (☎ 911)
Police Dispatch Line (☎ 780-423-4567) For non-emergencies.

Internet Access
Naked Cyber & Espresso Bar (Map p581; ☎ 780-433-9730; 10442 82nd Ave; per hr $5; ☺ 24hr)

Stanley A Milner Public Library (Map p580; ☎ 780-496-7000; 7 Sir Winston Churchill Sq; ☺ 9am-9pm Mon-Fri, 9am-6pm Sat, 1-5pm Sun) Lots of free Internet terminals.

Medical Services
Royal Alexandra Hospital (Map p578; ☎ 780-477-4111; 10240 Kingsway Ave) Has a 24-hour trauma center.

Money
American Express (Map p580; ☎ 780-421-0608; 10180 101st St) Foreign currency exchange.

Money Mart (Map p580; ☎ 780-425-2275; 10756 Jasper Ave) One of 16 Edmonton locations.

Post
Main post office (Map p580; ☎ 780-944-3271; 9808 103A Ave)

Tourist Information
Edmonton Tourism (Map p580; ☎ 780-426-4715, 800-463-4667; 9990 Jasper Ave; ☺ 8am-5pm) Friendly place with tons of flyers and brochures.

SIGHTS & ACTIVITIES
Provincial Museum of Alberta
Ever wondered about the forces and life forms that shaped Alberta? Wanted to get up close and personal with some creepy-crawlies in a room swarming with bugs? If so, this is the **museum** (Map p578; ☎ 780-453-9100; www.pma.edmonton.ab.ca; 12845 102nd Ave; adult/child $10/5; ☺ 9am-5pm) to see in Edmon-

ton. Don't miss the gallery of aboriginal culture that uses a multimedia display to document the lives of the Plains Indians. The museum also hosts frequent cultural shows, dance performances, films and special exhibits.

Alberta Government House
When you finish exploring the museum, head next door to **Government House** (Map p578; ☎ 780-427-2281; 12845 102nd Ave; tours free; ☺ 11am-4:30pm Sat & Sun Jun-Sep, 11am-4:30pm Sun Oct-May), the large and impressive former residence of provincial lieutenant governors. Built in 1913 at a cost of nearly $350,000 (quite a piece of change in those days), the Jacobean Revival residence is now used for government conferences.

Alberta Legislature
In a beautiful beaux-arts building completed in 1912 and surrounded by fountains and manicured lawns overlooking the river, the **Alberta Legislature** (Map p580; ☎ 780-427-7362; www.assembly.ab.ca; cnr 97th Ave & 107th St; admission free; ☺ 8:30am-5pm Mon-Fri, 9am-5pm Sat, Sun & holidays May–mid-Oct, 9am-4:30pm Mon-Fri, noon-5pm Sat, Sun & holidays mid-Oct–Apr) occupies the original Fort Edmonton site. Its dome has remained one of Edmonton's landmarks, and word has it that the expansive 57-acre grounds are favored by amorous locals for clandestine romantic activity. Free 30- to 40-minute tours are offered daily, starting from the interpretive center/gift shop in the pedway at 10820 98th Ave.

Muttart Conservatory
Four glass pyramids sheltering hundreds of plant species from seemingly endless winters are the highlight of the **Muttart Conservatory** (Map p578; ☎ reception 780-496-8735, recorded information 780-496-8755; www.edmonton.ca/muttart; 9626 96A St; adult/child $7/4; ☺ 9am-6pm Mon-Fri, 11am-6pm Sat, Sun & holidays, open longer in summer), south of the river off James MacDonald Bridge. One pyramid holds a tropical jungle, another the plants of arid desert regions, and a third showcases temperate-forest vegetation. The fourth pyramid is used for temporary exhibitions (Easter lily fans, take note!).

Old Strathcona
There's a buzz in this neighborhood not found elsewhere in the city. Funky shops, hip

ALBERTA

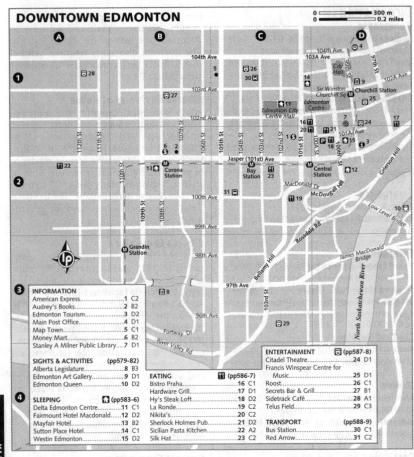

DOWNTOWN EDMONTON

bars, boutique hotels, theatres and nightclubs all give Old Strathcona a young, edgy, slightly artsy vibe. If you're into the bar scene, this strip is Edmonton's hottest. Even if you're not, the area south of the river along Whyte (82nd) Ave is still worth exploring for its rich historical buildings dating back to the 1890s, its old-style lampposts and its myriad of shops.

Anyone with a hang-up for telephones will enjoy the **Telephone Historical Centre** (Map p581; ☎ 780-433-1010; www.telephonehistoricalcentre .com; 10437 83rd Ave; adult/child/family $3/2/5; ☑ 10am-4pm Tue-Fri, noon-4pm Sat). The small museum holds a collection of antique telephones as well as several interesting and interactive exhibits.

West Edmonton Mall

When the snow won't stop falling and you just want to pretend it's summer, head to the **West Edmonton Mall** (☎ 780-444-5330, 800-661-8890; www.westedmontonmall.com; 170th St; snorkeling $50, scuba $75, submarine ride $10, admission to water park adult/child $25/19, bungee jump $60; ☑ 10am-9pm Mon-Fri, 10am-6pm Sat, noon-6pm Sun) for some indoor adventures. There's snorkeling – and believe it or not, even scuba diving – in the mall's giant lake. Swim past shipwrecked boats and fake coral, or ride the submarine. There's a massive water park with 20 waterslides (one that lets you reach speeds of 56km/h), a wave pool and even sun lounges to give the illusion of catching some rays. You can bungee jump from a height of 33m (suppos-

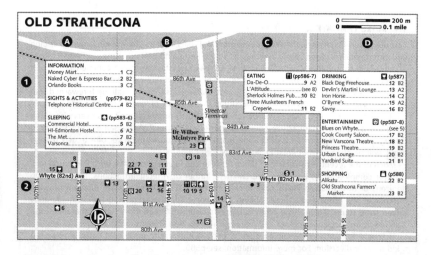

OLD STRATHCONA

INFORMATION	
Money Mart.........................1 C2	
Naked Cyber & Espresso Bar.....2 B2	
Orlando Books.....................3 C2	
SIGHTS & ACTIVITIES (pp579-82)	
Telephone Historical Centre......4 B2	
SLEEPING (pp583-6)	
Commercial Hotel..................5 B2	
HI-Edmonton Hostel................6 A2	
The Met............................7 B2	
Varsona............................8 A2	

EATING (pp586-7)	
Da-De-O............................9 A2	
L'Attitude........................(see 8)	
Sherlock Holmes Pub..............10 B2	
Three Musketeers French	
Creperie..........................11 B2	

DRINKING (p587)	
Black Dog Freehouse..............12 B2	
Devlin's Martini Lounge..........13 A2	
Iron Horse........................14 C2	
O'Byrne's.........................15 A2	
Savoy.............................16 B2	

ENTERTAINMENT (pp587-8)	
Blues on Whyte....................(see 5)	
Cook County Saloon...............17 B2	
New Varscona Theatre.............18 B2	
Princess Theatre.................19 B2	
Urban Lounge.....................20 B2	
Yardbird Suite...................21 B1	

SHOPPING (p588)	
Alikatu...........................22 B2	
Old Strathcona Farmers'	
Market............................23 B2	

edly an indoor record), walk with a camel in the petting zoo or flip round and round on the roller coaster in the amusement park. If you tire of all this, there's always shopping. For more on the mall, see p582.

Edmonton Art Gallery

This **art gallery** (Map p580; ☎ 780-422-6223; www .edmontonartgallery.com; 2 Sir Winston Churchill Sq, cnr 99th St & 102A Ave; adult/child $7/3, free after 4pm Thu; 10:30am-5pm Mon-Fri, to 8pm Thu, 11am-5pm Sat, Sun & holidays) has a collection of more than 5000 works of art by Canadian and international artists in all media, of which roughly 150 are on display at a time. The gallery also hosts regular traveling exhibitions.

Ukrainian Heritage Sites

Edmonton is rich in Ukrainian heritage sites, most of which are found north of downtown. The imposing **St Josaphat's Ukrainian Catholic Cathedral** (Map p578; ☎ 780-422-3181; 10825 97th St at 108th Ave; admission free; by appointment) has good examples of colorful Ukrainian decorative art.

Close by, the **Ukrainian Canadian Archives & Museum of Alberta** (Map p578; ☎ 780-424-7580; 9543 110th Ave; admission by donation; 10am-5pm Tue-Fri, noon-5pm Sat) has *pysanky* (Easter eggs) and other Ukrainian artifacts.

A small collection of costumes, *pysanky*, dolls and fine tapestries is found at the **Ukrainian Museum of Canada** (Map p578; ☎ 780-483-5932; 10611 110th Ave; admission free; 9:30am-4:30pm Mon-Fri May-Aug).

Alberta Railway Museum

This **museum** (☎ 780-472-6229; www.railwaymuseum .ab.ca; 24215 34th St; adult/child $4/1.25; 10am-5pm mid-May–early Sep), on the northeast edge of the city, has a collection of more than 50 railcars, including steam and diesel locomotives and rolling stock, built and used between 1877 and 1950. It also has a collection of railway equipment, old train stations and related buildings. On weekends, volunteers fire up some of the old engines and you can ride along for $3 (the diesel locomotives run every Sunday in season; the 1913 steam locomotive gets fired up only on holiday weekends). To get there, drive north on 97th St (Hwy 28) to Hwy 37, turn right and go east for 7km to 34th St, then turn right and go south about 2km.

Al Rashid Mosque

In 1938 North America's first mosque was built in Edmonton. Called the Al Rashid, it was built by the children of Muslim farmers and fur traders who came to Canada to seek their fortunes. It served the burgeoning Muslim population in Edmonton for 50 years, but eventually fell into disuse as newer, bigger mosques were built. The Al Rashid was tiny, measuring just 9m by 15m. Originally located at 101st St and 108th Ave, today the mosque is preserved in Fort Edmonton Park. Inside there are no pews and no altar, just Persian carpet and a Qiblah wall that shows the direction of Mecca. If it's sunny outside, streams of light flow in from six arched windows.

ALBERTA

THE MALL THAT ATE...

Sprawled over 48 hectares, the **West Edmonton Mall** bills itself as 'the world's largest shopping and entertainment centre.' Big it certainly is; how entertaining is another matter. From its roots as a humble suburban shopping mall, 'West Ed' has metastasized into a commercial monster that has sucked zillions of dollars out of the rest of Edmonton's retail life.

If you are drawn by the spectacle of the world's largest shopping mall, be forewarned that all is not what it seems. There's less diversity than the claim of 'over 800 stores and services' implies. The collection of stores will be familiar to North American mall rats everywhere; the numbers have been padded by counting numerous outlets of the same store scattered throughout the labyrinth. Fans of Orange Julius, the ubiquitous purveyor of a treacly orange drink, will be cheered that West Ed has many.

Much of the recent construction at the mall – like Canadian airports, the West Edmonton Mall is never complete – has been for entertainment, rather than retail, attractions. The frostbitten denizens of the Canadian Plains have flocked to West Ed's artificial climate, where a growing number of diversions await those looking for more in life than browsing the 30 moderately priced shoe stores. Again, hype often outpaces substance. 'Bourbon St' has all the allure of a watered-down Hurricane cocktail and features the non–New Orleans native Hooters.

That said, it's still an entertaining place, especially if it's really, really cold out or if you need a kid-friendly diversion! For more information, see p580.

North Saskatchewan River

You can get out on the river on the **Edmonton Queen** (Map p578; ☎ 780-424-2628; www.edmonton queen.com; 9734 98th Ave; 1hr cruise from $15, lunch/ dinner cruise $45/50; ☼ closed winter), a modern sternwheeler riverboat. The one-hour sightseeing cruises leave from Rafter's Landing, across from the Shaw Conference Centre, on the river's south bank, and cruise either up or down the river at the captain's discretion. Live onboard entertainment is often scheduled.

EDMONTON FOR CHILDREN

If you're traveling with the kids, there's no need for them to be bored. Edmonton has plenty of kid-friendly attractions. First check out the futuristic-looking **Odyssium** (Map p578; ☎ 780-451-3344; www.odyssium.com; 11211 142nd St; adult/child $10/8, admission plus IMAX adult/child $16/12; ☼ 10am-5pm, to 9pm Fri & Sat Sep-Jun, to 9pm daily Jul & Aug), Edmonton's space and science center. An entire gallery is dedicated especially to kids aged two to eight and features, among other exhibits, a 'construction zone' and a working beehive. The other galleries will hold older children's interest – they can walk through the human body, solve a mystery or explore the vast emptiness of space. Technologically inclined kids will enjoy the ham radio station and computer lab, while budding astronomers can check out the observatory and big planetarium,

where programs on the solar system and universe are presented.

If the weather is nice, head to **Fort Edmonton Park** (Map p578; ☎ 780-496-8787; www.edmonton .ca/fort; cnr Fox Dr & Whitemud Dr; adult/child $9/4.50; ☼ 10am-6pm Jul & Aug, reduced hrs mid-May–Jun & Sep), where history comes alive on the river's south side. Costumed interpreters help time slip away as you wander through a reconstruction of the old Hudson's Bay Company's Fort Edmonton and the surrounding town, c 1885. Kids can ride on the steam train or partake in pioneer children's games, while adults can check out the 1920s-style miniature golf course.

The **Valley Zoo** (Map p578; ☎ 780-496-8787; www .edmonton.ca/valleyzoo; 13315 Buena Vista Rd; adult/child $7/3.75; ☼ 9:30am-4pm, to 8pm Jul & Aug), with more than 100 exotic, endangered and native animals, is another option. Kids will enjoy the petting zoo, camel and pony rides, miniature train, carousel and paddleboats. If you want to brave the zoo in the frigid winter, admission costs are reduced.

If you do arrive in the middle of winter, there's always the West Edmonton Mall (p580). Older children can check out the amusement and water parks, while younger children try out the **Build-A-Bear-Workshop** (☎ 780-484-5343; ☼ 10am-9pm Mon-Fri, 10am-6pm Sat, noon-6pm Sun). Here you can pick up a teddy, help stuff it (and give it a heart), bathe it, name it and finally dress it before taking it home. Be aware it can become costly – fully dressed bears cost $40 to $70.

TOURS

Several companies offer half-day tours of Edmonton ($35 to $40) or longer tours that explore outlying areas.

Magic Times Tours (☎ 780-940-7479)

Out an' About (Map p578; ☎ 780-909-8687; www.out anabouttours.com)

Peter's Edmonton Tours (☎ 780-469-2641)

FESTIVALS & EVENTS

Edmonton has many festivals throughout the year. Some of the larger ones include the following:

June

Jazz City International Music Festival (☎ 780-433-4000; www.jazzcity.ca; ☉ late Jun) This week-long event at the end of June is marked by concerts all over town, many outside and free.

The Works: A Visual Arts Celebration (☎ 780-426-2122; www.theworks.ab.ca; ☉ late-Jun–early-Jul) This major arts celebration features two weeks of exhibits and events around town, including some in city parks.

July

International Street Performers Festival (☎ 780-425-5162; www.edmontonstreetfest.com; ☉ 2nd week of Jul) Amazing buskers bring the streets alive during this multiday event.

Klondike Days (☎ 780-423-2822; www.klondikedays .com; ☉ late Jul) A less than honorable period in Edmonton's history, the Klondike gold rush, is celebrated each year in late July. Festival events include locals in period costume, roadside stages alive with singers and dancers, parades through the streets and nightly concerts. Klondike Days is Edmonton's biggest festival.

August

Edmonton Heritage Festival (☎ 780-488-3378; www .heritage-festival.com; ☉ 1st week of Aug) This three-day Hawrelak Park festival celebrates the city's ethnic diversity.

Edmonton Folk Music Festival (☎ 780-429-1899; www.edmontonfolkfest.org; ☉ 2nd week of Aug) Gallagher Park, just east of the Muttart Conservatory, hosts four days of blues, jazz, country and western, bluegrass and traditional folk music.

Edmonton Fringe Theatre Festival (☎ 780-448-9000; www.fringetheatreadventures.ca; ☉ mid-Aug) Well worth catching, this event features an 11-day program of live alternative theater, with more than 1000 performances in 13 theaters on three outdoor stages in the parks and on the streets. Many shows are free and no ticket costs more

than $10; there's no booking – you choose a theater and stand in line. The festival draws half a million people each year to Old Strathcona.

Canadian Country Music Week (☎ 905-850-1144; www.ccma.org; ☉ 2nd week of Sep) A week of special events and appearances by Canadian country music stars lead up to the televised Canadian Country Music Awards ceremony.

November

Canadian Finals Rodeo (☎ 780-471-7210, 888-800-7275; www.canadianfinalsrodeo.ca; tickets $15-40; ☉ early Nov) Canada's major indoor rodeo boasts the biggest money prizes for roping, riding and the rest. The main event at Skyreach Centre is held concurrently with Farmfair International, a huge agricultural show at Agricom, next door. It all runs for 10 days.

SLEEPING

Old Strathcona is by far the best place to stay in Edmonton. Downtown hotels are plentiful but short on character. If the West Edmonton Mall is the reason for your visit, you can choose from a plethora of chain and independent motels near the mall on Stony Plain Rd. The Calgary Trail, south of the city, also has a slew of chain motels. Overall, lodging in Edmonton is quite cheap compared with other parts of the province and Canada. Expect to pay between $50 and $100 for a nice room at a mid-range property.

Budget

Commercial Hotel (Map p581; ☎ 780-439-3981; fax 780-439-5058; 10329 82nd Ave; s/d with shared bathroom $34/38, s/d $42/46; **P**) In Old Strathcona, this bare-bones place is friendly, decent and has live blues in the bar downstairs. It's good value for money in a very happening neighborhood.

Chateau Motel (☎ 780-988-6661; fax 780-988-8839; 1414 Calgary Trail SW; r $49; **P**) The friendly Chateau offers standard budget rooms with satellite TV and kitchenettes.

HI-Edmonton Hostel (Map p581; ☎ 780-988-6836, 877-467-8336; www.hihostels.ca; 10647 81st Ave; dm/d $18/40) Within easy walking distance of all the action in Old Strathcona, this hostel is slightly institutional-looking, but has a big lounge area with lots of couches and coin-operated Internet access. Nonmembers pay a few dollars extra.

Half Moon Lake Resort (☎ 780-922-3045; www .halfmoonlakeresort.com; 21524 Township Rd 520, Sherwood Park; tent/RV sites $21/30; ☉ May–early Oct; **P**) Lake swimming, paddleboat rentals, mini-golf, a

I'LL TAKE MY PIEROGY SUPER-SIZED, PLEASE

When you're a small town on a frozen prairie in the middle of nowhere you'll go to great lengths to attract tourists. And so you'll build something big, really big – like the world's largest pierogy. In tiny Glendon, 200km northeast of Edmonton, you'll find this 7.5m-tall, 3.5m-wide, 2720kg beige potato dumpling stabbed on the tines of a four-pronged fork. It even has its own monument in Pyrogy Park, which is of course off Pyrogy Dr, complete with a series of earnest plaques telling its tale: 'It originated as a boring dumpling and later people added whatever they desired inside.... Unveiled August 31, 1991 by the official pyrogy committee.' The village calls itself the 'Pierogy Capital of the World' and the dumplings are sold at restaurants throughout town.

Glendon is just one of many tiny outposts, and some not so tiny ones, sprinkled throughout Alberta's vast grasslands that have become obsessed with super-sizing anything and everything – from ducks to mushrooms to sausages. In fact, it seems the entire province has a penchant for claiming bragging rights to the world's biggest things, including parks, malls and glaciers.

■ Largest Ukrainian Sausage – Standing almost 13m high, this link in tiny Mundare, 92km northeast of Edmonton, commemorates local sausage-making. It cost about $120,000 and took four years to build, and can withstand winds of up to 160km per hour!

■ Largest Pysanky (Easter egg) – In Vegreville, 102km east of Edmonton, this massive Easter egg has an entire early-July festival dedicated to it. The 6½m-long, 5½m-wide brightly painted egg was made from 3500 pieces of aluminum, and tells the story of the area's settlers.

■ Largest Mushroom – Vilna, 150km northeast of Edmonton, has not one but three giant mushrooms. The fungi reach 6m into the sky. Mushroom hunting has been a local tradition in Vilna since Ukrainian settlers arrived in the early 1900s.

■ Largest Lamp – In Donalda, 140km southeast of Edmonton, the night skies glow every night with the light emitted by this 13m-tall lamp.

■ Largest Mallard Duck – Head to Andrew, 116km northeast of Edmonton, to pose with a 2300kg flying duck with a 7½m wingspan. The duck was built in 1992 with a grant from the provincial government.

■ Largest Dinosaur – In Drumheller there's the world's largest dinosaur (p629), standing 26m high. You can snap a picture from inside its mouth, which fits 12 people.

These are just a sampling. Wherever you travel in Alberta, you're bound to come across a super-sized monument.

But not all of Alberta's big attractions are made by humans. The province officially boasts that it's home to Canada's largest national park, remote Wood Buffalo National Park (p638), and within it the world's largest herd of free roaming buffalo. In addition, it claims it has the world's largest shopping mall in Edmonton (p582), which in turn has the world's highest indoor bungee jump. And then there's Canada's largest ski area, Lake Louise (p613).

So if you're looking for a common theme on your trip through the province, you could make an entire holiday out of just visiting the absurdly grandiose.

fish pond and horseback riding set this large resort, 29km southeast of Edmonton, apart. From Edmonton, follow 23rd Ave east, passing Hwy 21, and continuing another 10km (23rd Ave becomes Township Rd 520).

Rainbow Valley Campground & RV Park (Map p578; ☎ 780-434-5531, 888-434-3991; www.rainbow-valley.com; 13204 45th Ave; tent/RV sites $16/22; ⏰ mid-Apr–mid-Oct; P) Packed with amenities, including wood-burning stove cook shelters, horseshoe pits

and a playground, this campground also has a great location in central Whitemud Park. Take the 122nd St/119th St exit, go south on 119th and make the first right; the driveway starts a block down on the south side of Whitemud and goes under the freeway to the campground, on the north side.

Glowing Embers Travel Centre & RV Park (☎ 780-962-8100; fax 780-962-8162; 26309 Hwy 16A, Spruce Grove; tent & RV sites $24; P) A reasonable choice for

RVers heading to the West Edmonton Mall, this large west-side park at the junction of Hwys 16A and 60 has all the usual amenities and stays open year-round.

Mid-Range

Sutton Place Hotel (Map p580; ☎ 780-428-7111, 800-263-9030; www.suttonplace.com; 10235 101st St; s & d from $100; P ⚡) This is a classy, upmarket hotel with all the amenities – and a bit of glitz and glamor – that often has very cheap specials. The indoor water park is fantastic, and there are restaurants, cocktail lounges and a casino on the grounds.

Glenora Bed & Breakfast Inn (Map p578; ☎ 780-488-6766; www.glenorabnb.com; 12317 102nd Ave; s/d with shared bathroom $70/85, s/d $80/90; P) A cross between a traditional B&B and an inn, the Glenora is comfortable, with a large selection of rooms – from small ones with shared baths to studios and suites – all decorated in the Victorian style. There's an outdoor patio for warm days and an indoor parlor with fireplace and library for cold ones.

Travelodge Edmonton West (☎ 780-483-6031, 800-578-7878; www.travelodge.com; 18320 Stony Plain Rd; s/d $80/90; P ⚡) A good choice for mallsters with kids, the newish Travelodge is not only close to the West Edmonton Mall, it has in-room Super Nintendo and a gigantic water slide.

Inglewood House B&B (Map p578; ☎ 780-452-8679; www.bbcanada.com/2147.html; 11113 127th St; r from $60; P) Furnished with antiques, this spacious heritage home has three rooms for rent. There's a large private sitting area for guests with cable TV, a fireplace and a library.

Carr's Streetside Garden B&B (☎ 780-474-7046, 877-642-7884; www.bbcanada.com/streetsidegarden; 11318 63rd St; s/d from $60/65; P) Located in a quiet historic area 10 minutes from the city center, this B&B has two rooms and staff will cook breakfast to suit your taste, including vegetarian options. There's a garden area for relaxing after a day on the town.

Mayfair Hotel (Map p580; ☎ 780-423-1650, 800-463-7666; fax 780-425-6834; 10815 Jasper Ave; r from $60) Downtown, the Mayfair is a handsome older hotel that also holds residential apartments. It's good value and has friendly, professional staff.

Derrick Motel (☎ 780-438-6060, 866-303-6060; fax 780-461-5170; 3925 Calgary Trail North; s/d $55/60; P) Rooms are simple but clean, with mismatched furniture. The motel welcomes pets.

THE AUTHOR'S CHOICE

The Met (Map p581; ☎ 780-465-8150; www.methotel.com; 10454 82nd Ave; r from $125, ste from $245; P ⚡) Old Strathcona's newest boutique hotel, The Met is very chic, very modern and very easily the best place to stay in town. Rooms are uniquely decorated with African and Asian artwork hand-picked by the owners on their world travels. Guests will love the free nightly wine and cheese tasting, and private bar. The suites are good value for money and come with Aveda toiletries, a fireplace, beautiful martini glasses at the bar, and balconies. The Met's staff go beyond the call of duty to make your stay perfect.

Top End

Varscona (Map p581; ☎ 780-434-6111, 888-515-3355; www.varscona.com; 8208 106th St, cnr 82nd Ave; r from $115; P ⚡) This delightful little boutique hotel in the heart of Old Strathcona offers every plush amenity, including a business center, fitness center, morning paper, thick terry cloth robes, continental breakfast and evening wine and cheese tasting, as well as a perfect location for exploring the city's best neighborhood. It's fantastic value for money with exemplary staff ready to cater to your every whim and complimentary valet parking.

Fairmont Hotel Macdonald (Map p580; ☎ 780-424-5181, 800-441-1414; www.fairmont.com; 10065 100th St; r from $180, parking $20; P ⚡ ⚡) This regal establishment is Edmonton's oldest and most elegant hotel. Have your driver pull the carriage up to the grand entry and walk through the doors into a different era. Swanky through and through, the hotel commands a prime spot overlooking the river; enjoy the view while your diamond tiara is being polished. Rates fluctuate greatly; for a good deal, try prebooking on the hotel's website.

Fantasyland Hotel (☎ 780-444-3000; 800-737-3783; www.fantasylandhotel.com; 17700 87th Ave; r from $190; P ⚡) If you want to stay at the West Edmonton Mall, head to this hotel complete with theme suites such as the evocatively named 'Truck Room,' where you can bed down in the back of a pickup under the romantic glow of a stop light. The hotel can arrange babysitting services and also has themed rooms for kids with bunk beds and toys.

Sandman Hotel West Edmonton (☎ 780-483-1385, 800-726-3626; www.sandmanhotels.com/hotels/alberta/edmonton.asp; 17635 Stony Plain Rd; r from $120; P ☒) The Sandman makes up for a complete lack of charm with a large indoor pool that will keep the kids wet and wild for hours. A 24-hour Denny's restaurant is on site. There are often bed-and-breakfast specials.

Also recommended:

Delta Edmonton Centre (Map p580; ☎ 780-429-3900, 800-268-1133; www.deltahotels.com; 10222 102nd St; r from $130; P ☒) Rates constantly fluctuate.

Westin Edmonton (Map p580; ☎ 780-426-3636, 800-228-3000; www.westin.com; 10135 100th St; r from $110; P ☒) Top-dollar rooms at less than top-dollar rates.

EATING

Edmonton has restaurants for all budgets and all tastes. Alberta is known for its ranch-grown beef, and steaks here are generally thick and mouth-watering.

Budget

Silk Hat (Map p580; ☎ 780-425-1920; 10251 Jasper Ave; mains $6-10; ☽ breakfast & lunch) Established in 1912, this charismatic diner still has small wall jukeboxes at the booths and movie posters on the walls. It's fully licensed to sell booze and serves breakfast all day. Try the thick, tasty shakes.

Hap's Hungry House (☎ 780-483-2288; 16060 Stony Plain Rd; mains from $5; ☽ breakfast & lunch) Locals

---

> **THE AUTHOR'S CHOICE**
>
> **Hardware Grill** (Map p580; ☎ 780-423-0969; 9698 Jasper Ave; mains $25-40; ☽ dinner) Nationally recognized and widely regarded as Edmonton's finest restaurant, this smoke-free downtown dining room sits quietly behind huge windows in a restored historic building that once housed a hardware store. The menu changes regularly and features dishes with a Canadian flair – seafood, game, berries and whole grains. The signature cedar-plank cooked salmon ($23) is a perennial favorite. Adding to the draw is an outstanding wine list – a several-time honoree of the Wine Spectator Award of Excellence – that includes more than 500 top-quality selections at fair prices; many are available by the glass.

---

love this unadorned diner for its great breakfasts and lack of chain affiliation. It's also smoke-free.

Mid-Range

Da-De-O (Map p578; ☎ 780-433-0930; 10548A 82nd Ave; mains $10-12; ☽ lunch & dinner) A funky place with neon lights and a New Age diner decor, this Cajun restaurant is a local favorite serving spicy Louisiana fare to diners on plush red chairs at chrome-rimmed tables. Try the sweet potato fries.

Three Musketeers French Creperie (Map p578; ☎ 780-437-4239; 10416 82nd Ave; mains from $10; ☽ lunch & dinner) Murals on the walls, old-fashioned lampposts and twinkling lights hung from the ceiling make you think you've stepped onto a theater set. French specialties, including a long list of crepes, make up the menu.

Sicilian Pasta Kitchen (Map p580; ☎ 780-488-3838; 11239 Jasper Ave; mains from $12; ☽ lunch & dinner) The food is made from scratch and the menu has an impressive pasta and pizza selection at this comfortable Italian restaurant, making it another local favorite. Enormous meals are served piping hot.

Bistro Praha (Map p580; ☎ 780-424-4218; 10168 100A St; mains $15; ☽ lunch & dinner) This Eastern European–style spot has dark wood decor and a quiet clubby atmosphere. In the afternoon it's pleasant for a good coffee with cake or a pastry and a flip through a newspaper.

Nikita's (Map p580; ☎ 780-414-0606; 10162 100A St; burgers from $5, mains $8-14; ☽ lunch & dinner) Down a couple of doors from Bistro Praha is Nikita's, which has pub fare, pizza and more substantial items. It's cool and intimate with an Old-World flavor. There's a giant martini menu.

Sherlock Holmes Pub (Map p580; ☎ 780-433-9676; 10341 82nd Ave; mains from $10; ☽ lunch & dinner) Though part of a small chain, the Sherlock Holmes has not only a great selection of beers, but also offers some truly outstanding pub fare. The wide-ranging menu includes traditional English favorites such as steak and kidney pie, bangers and mash and fish and chips, as well as calamari, curries, quesadillas and chicken cordon bleu. A bright, spic-and-span interior and convivial atmosphere add to the experience. Look for the red British telephone booth out front.

Top End

L'Attitude (Map p578; ☎ 780-431-5343; 10454 82nd Ave; mains $14-30; ⏰ lunch & dinner) From attentive servers to beautifully prepared dishes, this restaurant will tease all your senses in just the way a top end establishment should. The menu is eclectic and features contemporary Canadian fare. The steaks are mouth-watering.

La Ronde (Map p580; ☎ 780-425-6564; 10111 Bellamy Hill; mains from $25; ⏰ dinner, Sun brunch) If you're looking for a romantic dinner spot you can't beat this restaurant at the top of the Crowne Plaza Hotel. It revolves once every 90 minutes and offers unparalleled city views. The restaurant, which serves a variety of local organic meats among other dishes, believes in using the whole animal and promoting the use of natural pastoral land.

Hy's Steak Loft (Map p580; ☎ 780-424-4444; 10013 101A Ave; mains from $26; ⏰ lunch & dinner) Locals praise this steakhouse, which serves a giant selection of steak in classic wooden decor. Vegetarians will be happier elsewhere.

DRINKING

Old Strathcona is the city's hottest nightlife area. Stroll down 82nd Ave and see what interests you – new bars and clubs are always opening.

Savoy (Map p581; ☎ 780-438-0373; 10401 82nd Ave) For swanky ambience you can't beat this martini bar with red walls, progressive artwork and shiny black and chrome tables. Candles and dimmed lights add to the atmosphere. The martini list is endless and includes an absinthe-flavored martini (delicious!). The bar serves a tempting array of tapas and some more substantial meals. Definitely a worthwhile experience.

Black Dog Freehouse (Map p581; ☎ 780-439-1082; 10425 82nd Ave) Friendly and popular, this pub features ancient wooden furniture, well-poured pints and occasional live rock. Check out the 'wooftop' patio.

Devlin's Martini Lounge (Map p581; ☎ 780-437-7489; 10507 82nd Ave) Another cool martini bar, Devlin's attracts a sophisticated, young professional crowd. Its big, open windows facing the sidewalk make for some of the best people-watching on Whyte.

O'Byrne's (Map p581; ☎ 780-414-6766; 10616 82nd Ave) A popular Irish pub, O'Byrne's offers the requisite Guinness on tap, along with superb Irish food and music. It's often packed.

Iron Horse (Map p581; ☎ 780-438-3710; 8101 103rd St) Occupying the cavernous former 1907 Canadian Pacific Railway (CPR) station, the Iron Horse has plenty of room for dancing (lots of live music), drinking, shooting pool and scoping the studs and studmuffins. But this place also has a fantastic side patio, where they fire up the barbecue when weather permits – a great place to hang out for lunch or a summer's eve dinner.

ENTERTAINMENT

See and *Vue* are free local alternative weekly papers with extensive arts and entertainment listings. For daily listings, see the entertainment section of the *Edmonton Journal* newspaper.

Live Music & Nightclubs

For concentrated club-hopping, Old Strathcona is the place.

Blues on Whyte (Map p581; ☎ 780-439-3981; 10329 82nd Ave) This 12-bar bastion presents live, hurts-so-good blues in the old Commercial Hotel, an appropriately world-weary venue that throughout its long history has no doubt inspired a blues lyric or two.

Cook County Saloon (Map p581; ☎ 780-432-2665; 8010 103rd St; ⏰ Wed-Sat) Visiting cowboys and cowgirls, urban or otherwise, stampede to Cook County Saloon for country music and dancing.

Yardbird Suite (Map p581; ☎ 780-432-0428; www .yardbirdsuite.com; 11 Tommy Banks Way, near 103rd St & 86th Ave) This large, low-key jazz club in Old Strathcona is the labor of love of the non-profit Edmonton Jazz Society. Big names play here when they're in town, and cover charges are always reasonable. Night owls, take note: shows often start and end early.

Also recommended:

Sidetrack Cafe (Map p580; ☎ 780-421-1326, 10333 112th St) This old roadhouse-style café, on downtown's west side, features blues as well as local rock groups.

Urban Lounge (Map p581; ☎ 780-439-3388; 8111 105th St) Live music and a slightly older crowd make this club a favorite with locals.

Gay & Lesbian Venues

Secrets Bar & Grill (Map p580; ☎ 780-990-1818; 10249 107th St) Locals rave about the warm and comfortable atmosphere at Edmonton's best lesbian bar. The staff is extremely friendly, and out-of-towners will be made to feel like regulars.

ALBERTA

Buddy's Nite Club (Map p578; ☎ 780-421-0992; 11725B Jasper Ave) A spot for a night out with the boys, this cozy pub caters mostly to men and features live entertainment.

Roost (Map p580; ☎ 780-426-3150, 10345 104th St) All genres of music play at this alternative-lifestyles hangout that accommodates both men and women.

Cinemas

Princess Theatre (Map p581; ☎ 780-433-0728; 10337 82nd Ave; tickets $5 Mon & weekend matinees, adult/student & child $8/6 rest of week) This is Edmonton's main outlet for good, varying films, including foreign and art flicks. The cinema itself is a historic site – it was the first marble-fronted building west of Winnipeg and at one time showed first runs of Mary Pickford films.

Theater

Edmonton offers a busy performing-arts calendar.

Citadel Theatre (Map p580; ☎ 780-425-1820, 888-425-1820; www.citadeltheatre.com; 9828 101A Ave; tickets from $35; Sep-May) Edmonton's foremost playhouse, the Citadel is actually a five-theater complex hosting mainstream drama, comedy, experimental productions, concerts, lectures and films.

New Varscona Theatre (Map p581; ☎ 780-433-3399; www.varsconatheatre.com; 10329 83rd Ave; tickets $15; Sep-May) The Varscona often stages edgy, fringe productions. Ask about specially priced matinees and two-for-one performances.

Jubilee Auditorium (Map p578; ☎ 780-451-8000; 1455 87th Ave) is the venue for the **Edmonton Opera** (☎ 780-429-1000; www.edmontonopera.com; tickets from $22; Oct-Apr). The Auditorium also hosts concerts and special performances.

Francis Winspear Centre for Music (Map p580; ☎ 780-428-1414, 800-563-5081; 4 Sir Winston Churchill Sq) is where the **Edmonton Symphony Orchestra** (☎ 780-428-1414, box office 800-563-5081; www.edmontonsymphony.com; tickets from $20; Sep-Jun) plays. Seniors and students receive discounts.

Sports

If you're here during ice hockey season (from October to April), try to see a home game of the National Hockey League's **Edmonton Oilers** (☎ 780-414-4625, 866-414-4625; www.edmontonoilers.com; tickets from $24) at **Skyreach Centre** (Map p578; 7424 118th Ave NW).

The **Edmonton Eskimos** (☎ 780-448-3757, 800-667-3757; www.esks.com; adult/child from $23/12.50) play in the Canadian Football League (CFL) from July to October at **Commonwealth Stadium** (Map p578; 11000 Stadium Rd).

The **Edmonton Trappers** (☎ 780-414-4450; www.trappersbaseball.com; tickets from $5) of the Pacific Coast Baseball League are affiliated with the Minnesota Twins. They play their home games at **Telus Field** (Map p580; 10233 96th Ave) from April to August.

SHOPPING

Old Strathcona is the best area for unique stores. If you're in search of more familiar brands head to the West Edmonton Mall (p580).

Old Strathcona Farmers' Market (Map p581; ☎ 780-439-1844; 10310 83rd Ave at 103rd St; 8am-3pm Sat, noon-5pm Tue Jul & Aug) This not-to-be-missed indoor market offers everything from organic food to vintage clothing to crafts and hosts some 130 vendors. Everyone comes here Saturday morning – it's quite the scene.

Alikatu (Map p581; ☎ 780-433-4116; 10464 82nd Ave) Need a miniature pool table for your desk? How about a jumping urban pet? A host of unnecessary, yet so 'essential,' objects can be found at this small shop in Old Strathcona.

Old Strathcona Antique Mall (Map p578; ☎ 780-433-0398; 7614 103rd St) Antiques aficionados can browse 22,000 sq ft occupied by more than 200 vendors.

Alberta Craft Council Gallery and Shop (☎ 780-436-8033; 5810 111th St) Features hand-crafted pottery, glassware, textiles and jewelry, among other things.

GETTING THERE & AWAY

Air

Edmonton International Airport (YEG; ☎ 780-890-8382) is about 30km south of the city along the Calgary Trail, about a 45-minute drive from downtown. For more information on flights into Edmonton, see p576.

Bus

The large **bus station** (Map p580; ☎ 780-413-8747; 10324 103rd St at 103rd Ave) has Greyhound Canada services to numerous destinations including Jasper ($56, five hours, four daily) and Calgary ($46, from 3½ hours, 11 daily). For more information on buses to other provinces in Canada, see p576.

Red Arrow (Map p580; ☎ 780-425-0820) buses stop at the Howard Johnson Plaza Hotel (10010 104th St) and serve Calgary ($46, 3½ hours, at least four daily). The deluxe buses have free soft drinks, power ports for laptop computers and other niceties.

Car

All the major car rental firms (p873) have offices at the airport and around town. **Driving Force** (☎ 780-483-1668; www.thedrivingforce.com; 16105 Stony Plain Rd) is a local agency that also sells and leases cars. One-way rentals are possible. Check the website for specials.

Train

The small **VIA Rail station** (Map p578; ☎ 780-448-2575; 12360 121st St) is on the west side of City Centre Airport. The *Canadian* (p877) travels three times a week east to Saskatoon, Winnipeg and Toronto and west to Jasper, Kamloops and Vancouver. At Jasper, you can connect to Prince George and Prince Rupert. VIA Rail services and fares are constantly in flux, so confirm details in advance.

GETTING AROUND
To/From the Airport

City buses don't go as far south as the international airport. The cheapest option is **Sky Shuttle Airport Service** (☎ 780-465-8515, 888-438-2342; adult/child $11/5.50), which runs vans on three routes serving hotels downtown, in the West End and in the university area. The downtown route operates at least every 30 minutes; the ride takes 35 minutes from the last downtown stop to the airport.

A cab fare to downtown will cost about $45.

Car & Motorcycle

There is metered parking throughout the city. If you're staying in Old Strathcona, most hotels offer complimentary parking to guests, and you can leave your car for the day and explore the neighborhood easily on foot. Edmonton also has public parking lots, which cost about $12 per day or $1.50 per half hour; after 6pm you can park for a flat fee of about $2.

Public Transportation

City buses and a 10-stop tram system known as the Light Rail Transit (LRT) cover most of the city. The fare is adult/child $1.75/1.25

(day passes $6). Buses operate at 30-minute intervals between 5:30am and 1:30am, but late-night service is limited. Travel between Churchill and Grandin stations on the LRT is free during the day.

Between mid-May and early October you can cross the High Level Bridge on a streetcar ($3 round-trip, every 30 minutes between 11am and 4pm). The vintage street cars leave from the river's north side next to the Grandin LRT Station (109th St between 98th and 99th Ave) and end in the heart of Old Strathcona (103rd St at 94th Ave).

Taxi

Two companies are **Yellow Cab** (☎ 780-462-3456) and **Alberta Co-Op Taxi** (☎ 780-425-8310). The fare from downtown to the West Edmonton Mall is about $20. Flagfall is $2.50, then it's $1.10 for every kilometer.

AROUND EDMONTON
East of Edmonton

Free-roaming herds of elk and plains bison, and a small herd of the threatened wood bison, can be found on a 194-sq-km tract of original aspen forest preserved as **Elk Island National Park** (☎ 780-922-5790; www.parks canada.gc.ca/elk; adult/child aged 6-16/senior $5/2.50/4.25; ☯ dawn–dusk), 45km east of Edmonton on the Yellowhead Hwy (Hwy 16). Bison can be seen from the road and will almost certainly be spied along the park's walking trails.

About 35 other mammal species also inhabit the park, and many can be seen on early morning or evening hikes. Fall is a particularly good time for wildlife viewing, as much of the vegetation has thinned out. Beaver are abundant in the many boggy areas, and the park holds large numbers of moose.

The park is a popular weekend spot, with camping, hiking, cycling and canoeing in summer and cross-country skiing and snowshoeing in winter. It can be reached in under an hour from Edmonton and makes a good day trip. The information office near the entrance off Hwy 16 distributes an excellent free guide to the park's features and wildlife. Read the guide to bison viewing, as these animals can be aggressive. The park's interpretive center schedules a variety of special programs and walks during the summer.

Some of the park's campsites close from early October to May. **Camping** (tent & RV sites $18, backcountry sites $6, campfire permits $4) is available.

The **Ukrainian Cultural Heritage Village** (☎ 780-662-3640; 8820 112th St; peak season adult/child aged 7-17/senior $6.50/3/5.50, half-price rest of the year; ☾ 10am-6pm mid-May–early-Sep, 10am-4pm early-Sep–mid-Oct, 10am-4pm Mon-Fri rest of the year), 50km east of Edmonton on Hwy 16 (3km east of Elk Island National Park), pays homage to the 250,000 Ukrainian immigrants who came to Canada in the late 19th and early 20th centuries. Many settled in central Alberta, where the landscape reminded them of the snowy steppes of home. Among the exhibits are a dozen or so structures, including a restored pioneer home and an impressive Ukrainian Greek Orthodox church. Docents in period costume add historical flavor.

South of Edmonton

Heading south toward Calgary, take Hwy 2A from Leduc to reach **Wetaskiwin**. It's home to the **Reynolds-Alberta Museum** (☎ 780-361-1351, 800-661-4726; Hwy 13; adult/child $9/5; ☾ 9am-5pm late-May–Jun, 9am-7pm Jul & Aug, 9am-5pm Tue-Sun & Mon holidays Sep–mid-May), an 83-acre complex 1km west of town devoted to celebrating the machine: in aviation, transportation, agriculture and industry. Among the collection highlights are a 1929 Duesenberg Phaeton Royale and a 1913 Chevy. The museum also houses **Canada's Aviation Hall of Fame**.

As you continue south, halfway between Edmonton and Calgary on Hwy 2, is **Red Deer**, a sprawling city in the heart of grain and cattle country. It's nothing special, but does have a string of motels and hotels that may come in handy during either Calgary's Stampede or Edmonton's Klondike Days, when hotel prices in both cities skyrocket and become hard to come by. Red Deer is about 1½ hours away from either city, and accommodations here will not be as tight or expensive. For more information, contact the **Red Deer Visitor & Convention Bureau** (☎ 403-346-0180, 800-215-8946; www.tourismreddeer.net; 30 Riverview Park) or just drive through the city – you'll have your pick of chain establishments.

Southeast of Red Deer on the way to Drumheller, **Dry Island Buffalo Jump Provincial Park** is an isolated park that begins on a dramatic bluff overlooking the Red River Valley, near the town of Huxley. The initial view is like that of a mini–Grand Canyon, whose multihued walls have been exposed by 63 million years of geological history. Among the many fossils that have been found here are those of

the enormous, carnivorous *Tyrannosaurus rex*. Some 2000 years ago, aboriginal tribes drove bison over the edge of the 45m bluffs. Today the park site is seldom crowded and is almost eerie when the wind howls down the river valley. To reach the park, which has no entrance gate or office, take the well-marked part-gravel road that runs 19km east of Hwy 21 just north of Huxley.

West of Edmonton

Heading west from Edmonton toward Jasper, Hwy 16 is a gorgeous drive through rolling wooded hills that are especially beautiful in fall. Accommodations are available along the way.

Hinton is the home of the Athabasca fire lookout tower, which offers a spectacular view of the Rockies. To get to the lookout tower, take Hwy 16 2km west from Hinton, then Hwy 40 18km north. Around the tower is a hang glider launch area and the 960-hectare **Athabasca Lookout Nordic Centre**, which offers winter visitors beautiful groomed ski trails up to 25km long. It also has lighted night skiing on a 1.5km trail, plus a 1km luge run. There's a use fee of $5. For more information, contact the **Hinton Ranger Station** (☎ 780-865-8264; 3rd fl, Government Centre, 131 Civic Centre Rd; ☾ 9am-5pm Mon-Fri).

CALGARY

☎ 403 / pop 943,000

Breathtaking expanses of big sky, prairie grass stretching in all directions, snow-capped peaks of the Rockies peeking out from the west – it's no wonder Calgary, and the land surrounding it, has become a favorite with Hollywood filmmakers hoping to recreate the Old West. Admired the scenery in films such as *Open Range*, *Unforgiven* and *Legends of the Fall*? Yes, that's greater Calgary standing in for US towns.

And just like a movie set, Calgary has more than one 'look.' Travel into town and you'll see slick streets lined with office towers. The city is young and modern and manages to fuse Old West clichés of cowboy boots and 10-gallon hats with hip boutiques, swanky restaurants, high heels and business suits. The city's residents are generally educated and well paid, and many work in high-tech, energy- and resource-based industries – yet

MAP MAKER, BIBLE READER & TIRELESS TREKKER

From 1784 to 1812 David Thompson mapped much of the Canadian Rockies and the surrounding region while leading four major expeditions for fur-trading companies. He discovered the source of the Columbia River in British Columbia (BC), helped map the border with the USA and found Athabasca Pass near Jasper, which for 40 years was the only route used by traders across the Rockies.

Though he was an energetic leader who covered about 130,000km by canoe, foot and horse, his daring exploits were not matched by an unbridled lifestyle. He extolled the virtues of soap in his meticulous journals, refused to use alcohol for trade with the Aboriginal peoples he met, and enjoyed reading the Bible to the crustier members of his parties around the evening campfire.

His relations with Aboriginal Canadians were generally good; he understood the value of their knowledge and readily adopted their advice for survival on his lengthy treks. His wife was part Cree, and he came to understand the Aboriginal's beliefs in the spirituality that was inherent in the land.

Thompson died at the age of 86 in 1857, and 59 years later material from his 77 notebooks was published in a volume simply titled *Narrative*. This caused a minor sensation, as Canadians and Americans began to realize the scope of Thompson's accomplishments. At the same time modern map-making techniques revealed the remarkable accuracy of the maps he had carefully drawn on his journeys 100 years before.

As you travel in Alberta, you'll often run into Thompson's name. One of the best books on Thompson is Jack Nisbet's *Sources of the River*. It places his accomplishments in the context of both historical and modern times.

the old life comes alive each summer when the cowboys come to town for the Calgary Stampede (p597), Canada's biggest rodeo.

HISTORY

Calgary's name, meaning 'clear, running water' in Gaelic, comes from Calgary Bay on Scotland's Isle of Mull. Initially home to the Blackfoot tribes, the 18th century saw the arrival of the Sarcee and the Stoney nations. In the 1800s, the NWMP arrived, sent in to cool down intertribal conflicts and troubles between the tribes and European trappers.

The late 1800s were busy times. The NWMP established Fort Calgary in 1875. The CPR arrived in 1883. Settlers were offered free land, and the population grew to 4000 by 1891. Soon, cattle herders from the USA were pushing north, looking for better grazing land. Calgary became a major meat-packing district and cowboy metropolis. Slowly, with moderate growth, it became a transportation and distribution hub, yet it still remains Canada's cattle center. The discovery of vast quantities of oil across Alberta in the late-1960s transformed Calgary from a fair-sized cattle cow town to a brand new city of steel and glass. The discovery of

'black gold,' coupled with the energy crisis of the 1970s, which bumped prices up sharply, saw an industry boom. The city took off, becoming the headquarters of 450 oil companies and home to more US citizens than any other place outside of the USA.

However, during the 1980s the bottom fell out of the oil market and, with 70% of the workforce dependent on that industry, times became tough. Calgary's fortunes and reputation were given a boost when it hosted the Winter Olympics in 1988. By 1993 the oil and gas industries had rebounded. The city now has a broader economic base, making it more prosperous.

ORIENTATION

Calgary lies on flat ground. It was first settled at the confluence of the Bow and Elbow Rivers and has spread equally in all directions; the city is the country's second largest in area. The downtown core is still bordered by the Bow River to the north. The Elbow River runs through the city's southern portions. The Trans-Canada Hwy (Hwy 1) cuts east–west across the city to the north along 16th Ave NE and 16th Ave NW. The international airport is to the northeast, off Barlow Trail; the University of Calgary is

ALBERTA

DOWNTOWN CALGARY

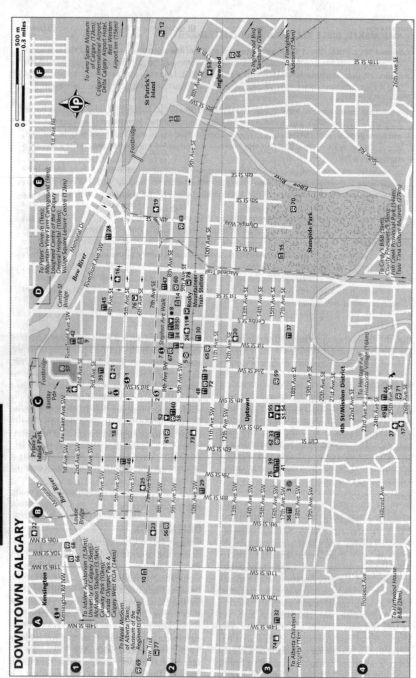

INFORMATION
Air Canada Office..................................1 C2
American Express.................................2 C2
Cyber Space...3 B3
Hostel Shop...4 A1
Main Post Office..................................5 C2
Map Town..6 C1
Tourism Calgary..................................7 C2

SIGHTS & ACTIVITIES   (pp594-6)
Brewster Gray Line...............................8 D2
Calgary Chinese Cultural Centre...........9 D1
Calgary Parks & Recreation Department
    Office...(see 60)
Calgary Science Centre.......................10 A2
Calgary Tower....................................11 D2
Calgary Zoo.......................................12 F2
Fort Calgary Historic Park...................13 F2
Glenbow Museum................................14 D2
Grain Academy...................................15 D3

SLEEPING   (pp597-9)
Delta Bow Valley................................16 D1
Elbow River Manor..............................17 C4
Hawthorn Hotel & Suites.....................18 C1
HI-Calgary..19 E2
Holiday Inn Calgary Downtown............20 D3
International Hotel...............................21 C1
Kensington Riverside Inn......................22 B1
Lord Nelson Inn..................................23 B2
Palliser...24 D2
Sandman Hotel....................................25 B2
Sheraton Suites Calgary Eau Claire.......26 C1
Twin Gables B&B.................................27 C4

EATING   (pp599-601)
Booker's BBQ Grill & Crabshack...........28 E1
Brewster's...29 B2
Buzzard's Cookshack & Watering Hole..30 D2
Cannery Row.......................................31 C2
Chianti...32 A3
Fiore Cantina Italiana...........................33 C3
Good Earth Coffeehouse & Bakery........34 D2
Hy's Steak House.................................35 C1
Jabulani..36 B3
La Chaumiere......................................37 D3
Latin Corner Cantina...........................38 D2
Melrose Cafe & Bar..............................39 B3
Nellie's Break the Fast Cafe..................40 C2
Nellie's Kitchen...................................41 B3
Pho Pasteur Saigon..............................42 D1
Piq Niq Cafe.......................................43 D2
Rajdoot...44 C4
Regency Palace....................................45 D1
Sushi Hiro..46 B1
Teatro..47 D2
Thai Sa-On...48 C2
Wildwood...49 C4

DRINKING   (p601)
Belvedere..50 D2
Bottlescrew Bill's Old English Pub....(see 30)
Bungalow..51 C3
Ceili's...52 C2
Hose & Hound.....................................53 F2
Lucky...54 C3
Ming...(see 54)
Rose & Crown......................................55 C3
Ship & Anchor.................................(see 51)

ENTERTAINMENT   (pp601-3)
Buckingham's......................................56 B2
Cineplex Odeon...................................57 C1
Cowboys...58 C2
Detour..59 C3
Epcor Centre for the Performing
    Arts..60 D2
Globe Cinema......................................61 C2
IMAX Theatre..................................(see 57)
Kaos...62 C3
King Edward Hotel..............................63 E2
Loose Moose Theatre Company............64 F3
Metro-Boyztown..................................65 C2
Mynt...(see 40)
Newt..66 B1
Palace Night Club................................67 C2
Plaza Theatre......................................68 B1
Pumphouse Theatres............................69 A2
Saddledome...70 E3
Verge..71 C4
Whiskey..72 C2

SHOPPING   (p603)
Alberta Boot Co...................................73 C2
Eau Claire Market.............................(see 57)
Naked...74 A3
Riley & McCormick...........................(see 7)
Rocket..75 B3

TRANSPORT   (pp603-4)
Budget Car Rental................................76 D2
Greyhound Bus Station.........................77 A2
Red Arrow...78 D2

located to the northwest, off Crowchild Trail (Hwy 1A).

The city is divided into four geographical quadrants: northwest (NW), northeast (NE), southwest (SW) and southeast (SE). These abbreviations are important, because they're marked on street signs and included in addresses. The Bow River and Memorial Dr divide the city between north and south. Centre St (in the north) and Macleod Trail (in the south) split the city into east and west. It's fairly easy to figure out where you're going, since most streets and avenues are numbered. Streets run north–south, and avenues run east–west.

Around the downtown center, a network of enclosed pedestrian bridges and over-the-street walkways connect buildings and shops. It's called the 'Plus 15' system, as the walkways are all at least 15ft (5m) above ground. Eighth Ave between 3rd St SW and 1st St SE is a long pedestrian mall called Stephen Ave Walk. It's lined with trees, benches, shops (including large department stores), restaurants and fast-food places. Vendors sell crafts and souvenirs.

The western downtown area mainly has offices and businesses. The eastern section was the last to undergo redevelopment. It used to be the savior of the impecunious with its cheap bars and tatty hotels, of which

there are a few remnants, but generally it's been cleaned up.

Stone lions guard each side of the Centre St Bridge over the Bow River, which has the grayish-green color of Rocky Mountain waters. The river marks the downtown area's northern edge. West of the bridge is Prince's Island Park, a pleasant natural area for strolling or dog-walking. On the north side of the bridge, stairs on both sides lead up to the cliff. A footpath along the cliff provides good city views, especially from atop the west-side stairs. Note that most points of interest downtown are within walking distance of each other.

Just northwest of downtown over the river, off Memorial Dr, is the agreeable older district of **Kensington**, which has restaurants, cafés and nightclubs. You can walk here from downtown, crossing the river at 10th St, or take the LRT to Sunnyside Station.

South of Calgary Tower, over the railway tracks, are **Uptown** and the **4th St/Mission** districts, vibrant areas popular with young people and single professionals. Uptown is focused on 17th Ave SW between Centre St and 10th St SW. The 4th St/Mission district is focused on 4th St SW south of 17th Ave SW. Both areas have pubs, clubs, boutiques, galleries and restaurants.

ALBERTA

Follow 17th Ave east to reach Stampede Park, east of which is the funky district of **Inglewood**, a cozy neighborhood with bookstores, antique shops and friendly pubs and restaurants.

INFORMATION
Bookstores
Map Town (☎ 403-215-4060; 400 5th Ave SW; ⊗ 10am-6pm Mon-Fri, 10am-5pm Sat) Travel guides and a wide range of maps.
Hostel Shop (☎ 403-283-8311; 1414 Kensington Rd NW) Travel, outdoor activity guides and maps.

Emergency
Police, Ambulance & Fire (☎ 911)
Police Dispatch Line (☎ 403-266-1234) For non-emergencies.

Internet Access
Cyber Space (☎ 403-802-6168; 817 17th Ave SW; per hr $4; ⊗ 9.30am-10pm Mon-Fri, 10am-9pm Sat, 11am-8pm Sun)

Medical Services
Alberta Children's Hospital (☎ 403-229-7211; 1820 Richmond Rd SW) Emergency room open 24 hours.
Lougheed Centre of the Calgary General Hospital (☎ 403-291-8555; 3500 26th Ave NE) Emergency room open 24 hours.

Money
Banks dot Stephen Ave Walk, and many are open Saturday. Most large branches will exchange foreign currency.
American Express (☎ 403-261-5982; 421 7th Ave SW) Currency exchange facilities.

Post
Main post office (☎ 403-974-2078; 207 9th Ave SW)

Tourist Information
Tourism Calgary (☎ 403-263-8510, 800-661-1678; www.tourismcalgary.com; 220 8th Ave SW; ⊗ 8am-5pm) Operates a visitors' center in the Riley & McCormick store on Stephen Ave Walk. It has city maps (including walking-tour maps that highlight various historic buildings) and lots of brochures. The staff will help you find accommodations. Information booths are also available at both the arrivals and departures levels of the airport.

SIGHTS
Canada Olympic Park
Calgary hosted the 15th Winter Olympics in 1988, a first for Canada. At **Canada Olympic Park** (☎ 403-247-5452; www.coda.ab.ca; 88 Canada Olympic Rd

SW; adult/family $15/40; ⊗ 8am-9pm Mon-Fri, 9am-5pm Sat & Sun), a 15-minute drive west of town on Hwy 1 to the Bowfort Rd exit, you can see the 70m and 90m ski jumps – from the top you realize how crazy those guys are – and the concrete bobsled and luge runs. The **Olympic Hall of Fame** has three floors of exhibits honoring athletic achievements, including an exhibit entitled 'Blood, Sweat and Cheers – a tribute to Canada's 2002 Olympic success.' Try the simulators that re-create the sensation of bobsledding and skiing.

Glenbow Museum
Western Canada's largest **museum** (☎ 403-777-5506; www.glenbow.org; 130 9th Ave SE; adult/student & youth/senior $12/8/9; ⊗ 9am-5pm Fri-Wed, to 9pm Thu) holds varied collections illustrating human history through artifacts and art. One permanent gallery is devoted to an in-depth look at the Blackfoot nations of the North American plains. In other galleries, exhibits spotlight different periods in history – everything from an Inuit kayak to a pioneer wagon to an exhibit of contemporary Canadian painters. The Canadian West is well represented, but the collections also include works from around the world.

Fort Calgary Historic Park
In 1875 the NWMP crossed the Bow River to build **Fort Calgary** (☎ 403-290-1875; www.fortcalgary .com; 750 9th Ave SE; adult/child/senior $9/5/7; ⊗ 9am-5pm May-Oct). Today this 16-hectare national and provincial historic site preserves the spot where Calgary's original settlement began. An interpretive center tells the story of Calgary's development, while streetscapes give you a feel for life in the city from 1875 to the 1940s. Good views, costumed interpreters and paths leading to the river make the site a pleasant place to spend an afternoon.

To the east, across the Elbow River, is **Hunt House**, built in 1876 for a Hudson's Bay Company employee, which is probably the oldest building on its original site in the Calgary area.

Calgary Zoo
More than 900 animals from around the world, many in enclosures simulating their natural habitats, make this **zoo** (☎ 403-232-9300, 800-588-9993; www.calgaryzoo.ab.ca; 1300 Zoo Rd NE; adult/child/senior $15/7.50/13; ⊗ 9am-5pm) one of Calgary's most popular attractions. Besides

the animals, the zoo has a **Botanical Garden** with changing garden displays, a tropical rain forest, a good butterfly enclosure and the 6½-hectare **Prehistoric Park**, featuring fossil displays and life-sized dinosaur replicas in natural settings. Picnic areas dot the zoo and island, and a café is on site. During winter, when neither you nor the animals will care to linger outdoors, the admission price is reduced. To get there, take C-Train east to the Zoo stop.

Heritage Park Historical Village

This 26-hectare living-history **park** (☎ 403-259-1900; www.heritagepark.ab.ca; 1900 Heritage Dr SW at 14th St SW; adult/child $13/8, plus $9 per person for train & boat ride; ☉ 9am-5pm mid-May–early-Sep, 9am-5pm Sat & Sun mid-Sep–mid-Oct) re-creates life in a western Canadian town during three different eras: the 1860s, the 1880s, and around 1910.

Highlights include a Hudson's Bay Company fort, a working grain mill, an 1896 church and many stores full of artifacts and antiques. Be sure to take a look in the two-storey outhouse, for which the phrase 'look out below!' has special meaning. There's an excellent collection of horse-drawn vehicles, including stage coaches, traps and surreys, as well as old cars, railway coaches and a working steam engine. But you won't be Huck Finn-ished until you hop aboard the SS *Moyie* sternwheeler for a cruise on the reservoir. Admission includes a pancake breakfast served between 9am and 10am in summer. To get there, take C-Train to Heritage station, then bus No 20.

Inglewood Bird Sanctuary

Home to at least 260 bird species and a resting spot for those on the migratory path, this 32-hectare **nature reserve** (☎ 403-269-6688; 2425 9th Ave SE; admission free; ☉ 9am-5pm, until 8pm Fri-Sun Jun-Aug) is a good resting spot for migrating humans as well – the serenity here makes a perfect antidote to city noise and traffic. Trails lead through the sanctuary; they're open during daylight hours year-round. A small **interpretive center** (admission free, donations appreciated; ☉ 10am-5pm May-Oct, 10am-4pm Tue-Sun rest of year) has kid-friendly interactive exhibits describing the local birdlife. The sanctuary is southeast of downtown at the end of 9th Ave. Bus No 411 goes within a few blocks of the sanctuary on weekdays only; weekends, you

can take bus No 1 from downtown, which stops a bit further away.

Calgary Chinese Cultural Centre

Inside this impressive **landmark building** (☎ 403-262-5071; 197 1st St SW; admission free; ☉ 9am-9pm), built by skilled Chinese artisans in 1993, you'll find a magnificent 21m-high dome ornately painted with 561 dragons and other imagery. Its design was inspired by Beijing's Temple of Heaven. The 2nd and 3rd floors frequently house changing art and cultural exhibitions. Downstairs, the **museum** (adult/senior & child $2/1; ☉ 11am-5pm) holds Chinese art and artifacts, including a collection of replica terracotta soldiers.

Prince's Island Park

This pretty park, on an island in the Bow River north of downtown, is connected to both sides of the river by pedestrian bridges. It's a cool, quiet spot with lots of trees and flowers, picnic tables and jogging and cycling paths – a good antidote to a hot summer's day in Calgary. As the signs say, the water in the Bow River is too swift and cold to be safe for swimming. The bridge to the island from downtown is at the north end of 3rd St SW.

Fish Creek Provincial Park

On Calgary's southwest edge, this huge **park** (☎ 403-297-5293; admission free; ☉ 8am-dark) protects Fish Creek, which flows into the Bow River, and its surrounding valley. It acts as a shelter for many animals and birds and is the country's largest urban park. Park interpreters present slide shows and lead walking tours to explain some of the local ecology. Dogs must be kept on a leash. There are numerous access points to the park, which stretches 20km between 37th St in the west and the Bow River in the east. From downtown, take bus No 3 via Elbow Dr.

Calgary Tower

This 1968 landmark **tower** (☎ 403-266-7171; www.calgarytower.com; 101 9th Ave SW; elevators adult/child aged 3-12/senior & youth aged 13-17 $10/5/7; ☉ observation gallery 7:30am-11:30pm in summer, 8am-10pm rest of the year), looming 191m over Centre St, may be a city symbol, but its aesthetics are questionable. The reinforced-concrete stem resembles a prison blockhouse or nuclear reactor cooling tower, while the top is '60s space age à la *The Jetsons*. Elevators take 62 seconds to reach the top, where you'll find a revolving restaurant, cocktail lounge, observation gallery, souvenir shop and, in summer, a coffee bar.

Other Museums

Visitors with an interest in airplanes and aviation will enjoy the **Aero Space Museum of Calgary** (☎ 403-250-3752; 4629 McCall Way NE; adult/child $6/2; ☼ 10am-5pm).

The growing, harvesting and processing of Alberta's amber waves of grain are detailed at the **Grain Academy** (☎ 403-263-4594; 2nd fl, Round-Up Centre, Stampede Park; admission free; ☼ 10am-4pm Mon-Fri year-round, also noon-4pm Sat Apr-Sep), while the history of the local Tsuu T'ina (Sarcee) people is shown at the **Tsuu T'ina Culture Museum** (☎ 403-238-2677; 3700 Anderson Rd SW; admission $3; ☼ 9am-4pm Mon-Fri).

Military-history buffs will appreciate the **Museum of the Regiments** (☎ 403-974-2850; 4520 Crowchild Trail SW; adult/student $5/3; ☼ 9:30am-9pm Mon-Thu, 9:30am-4pm Fri-Sun), which pays homage to Calgary's historic home military regiments, and the **Naval Museum of Alberta** (☎ 403-242-0002; 1820 24th St SW; adult/child under 12/student $5/2/3; ☼ 1-4pm Tue-Fri, 10am-4pm Sat & Sun), which holds three Royal Canadian Navy airplanes, ship models and historical exhibits.

ACTIVITIES

If you're searching for a winter adrenalin rush, try a **bobsled ride** ($45) down the actual track used in the 1988 Winter Olympics at Canada Olympic Park (p594).

In the summer the park becomes a haven for **mountain biking**. With 25km of trails services by lifts (day passes $14), it caters to all levels of riders – from hard-core enthusiasts looking to challenge their skills over jumps to families out for a leisurely cycle. Trails are marked from beginner to expert.

For more low-key activities, Calgary has an incredible 400km of **cycling** and **hiking** trails, many in the parks and nature areas. The city's excellent *Calgary Pathway and Bicycle Route Map* is available for $1 from the **Calgary Parks and Recreation Department office** (☎ 403-268-3888; 3rd fl, 205 8th Ave SE). The map is also sold at Canadian Tire stores and bike shops around town. Car rental company **Budget** (☎ 403-226-1550; 140 6th Ave SE) rents basic mountain bikes for $12 a day with a $200 deposit.

If you want to get wet in a giant wave pool, whip down a 6½-story-high waterslide, or relax in a hot tub, check out the **Village Square Leisure Centre** (☎ 403-280-9714; 2623 56th St NE; adult/child/student & senior $9/2/5; ☼ 6am-10pm Mon-Fri, 8am-10pm Sat, 8am-6pm Sun). It also has a kiddie pool for the little ones and a gym.

Looking to cast a line for trout? The 60km stretch of the Bow River from Calgary east to Carseland is considered one of North America's best **trout-fishing** rivers, thanks to its abundance of big brown and rainbow trout. Numerous fishing-guide services and sporting goods stores in town sell fishing tackle and provide information. One place that combines the two is **Country Pleasures** (☎ 403-271-1016; 10816 Macleod Trail S).

CALGARY FOR CHILDREN

With an amusement park, science center, kid-oriented museums and a large zoo, Calgary is a child-friendly city.

One of the best bets is the **Calgary Science Centre** (☎ 403-268-8300; www.calgaryscience.ca; 701 11th St SW; adult/child/senior & youth/family $11/8/9/32; ☼ 10am-4pm Tue-Thu, 10am-5pm Fri-Sun & holidays), just west of downtown at the junction of 7th Ave SW. A series of hands-on exhibits, both indoors and out, explore paleontology and natural phenomena. The Discovery Dome theater presents giant-screen shows on a wide variety of science and nature topics; one show is included in the admission price, and additional shows are $3. Also on the premises is a small observatory, open on some clear nights.

Children of all ages (and adults too) will enjoy **Calaway Park** (☎ 403-240-3822; www.calawaypark.com; adult/child/family $22/16/165; ☼ 10am-8pm Jul & Aug, 5-10pm Fri, 10am-8pm Sat & Sun late-May–Jun, 11am-6pm Sat & Sun early-Sep–early-Oct), Western Canada's largest outdoor family amusement park. It features 28 rides from wild to mild, live stage entertainment, 25 food vendors, a trout-fishing pond, a children's playground and an interactive maze.

Another option is the **Firefighters Museum** (☎ 403-246-3322; 4124 11th St SE; adult/child $2/free; ☼ 10am-5pm Mon & Wed-Sat, noon-5pm Sun May-Oct) with a large collection of fire trucks.

TOURS

The cheapest way to tour town is to take the No 10 bus ($1.75) from along 6th Ave.

This bus goes on a 2½-hour circular route past old and new areas and the city's highest point, with views to the foothills, the university and some wealthy districts in the northwest.

Brewster Gray Line (☎ 403-221-8242, 800-661-1152; www.brewster.ca; 808 Centre St S) runs traditional bus tours of Calgary. The Calgary tour (adult/child $46/23) takes about four hours and covers about 50km. The tour includes Fort Calgary, Canada Olympic Park and the downtown area, with admission prices included in the ticket. The guides provide an entertaining history of the city.

Hammerhead Tours (☎ 403-260-0940; www.hammerheadtours.com) runs full-day, small group trips to the Drumheller badlands and Royal Tyrrell Museum ($70) and to Head-Smashed-In Buffalo Jump ($70) between November and May. Trips take in various attractions along the way.

Working in conjunction with HI-Calgary hostel, **True North Tours** (☎ 403-912-0407; www.truenorthtours.com) operates the Rocky Express, a six-day trip to Banff, Lake Louise and Jasper with accommodations in various hostels along the way (around $215 plus hostel rates) and lots of hiking opportunities. Vans are used, and the optional group meals can really keep costs down. There is also a three-day trip with shorter hikes. Reservations should be made about two or three weeks in advance. Trips run from mid-May to early October.

FESTIVALS & EVENTS

For a year-round list of the city's events, go to www.tourismcalgary.com/festivals1.html. Calgary's two biggest events, the Calgary Stampede (p597) and the Calgary Folk Music Festival (p601), are held in July.

Other festivals include:

Calgary International Children's Festival (☎ 403-294-7414; www.calgarychildfest.org; Epcor Centre for the Performing Arts, 205 8th Ave SE; admission $8; 🕑 late May) This five-day event features child-oriented music, theater, storytelling and comedy from around the world.

Carifest (☎ 403-292-0310; www.carifest.ca; Stephen Ave & Prince's Island Park; 🕑 early Jun) The Caribbean comes to Calgary for eight days in June. The festival features dancing, storytelling, children's entertainment, food and arts and crafts.

Jazz Festival (☎ 403-249-1119; www.jazzfestivalcalgary.ca; 🕑 late Jun) More than 300 musicians perform for about 10 days throughout Calgary at this event.

WILD CALGARY

Calgary lets its hair down and shows it's Wild West roots during the 10-day **Calgary Stampede** (☎ 403-261-0101, 800-661-1260; www.calgarystampede.com; tickets from $24; 🕑 2nd week Jul). Dating back to 1912, the event starts with a huge parade in the second week of July. Most organized events take place in Stampede Park southeast of downtown, but many of the streets are full of activity, too. Stampede Park comes alive with concerts, shows, exhibitions, dancing and eating, attracting more than 100,000 people each day. An amusement area features rides, a gambling hall and lots of contests. Highlights are the chuck-wagon races and the rodeo, which is said to be North America's biggest and roughest. Events include calf-roping, branding and riding bucking broncos and bulls. At night the Stampede Stage Show takes over, with singers, bands, clowns, dancers and fireworks; tickets for the main events go early. The town and nearby countryside are packed for the duration of the celebrations, so it's a good idea to book accommodations well in advance or arrive early.

SLEEPING

The prices quoted in this section are normal for summer; some rise during the Stampede, while others fall during winter. Tourism Calgary (p594) makes bookings for free. Top-end places may not actually be out of your budget, as there are often specials, so it could be worth calling ahead. Most of the good, moderately priced accommodations lie outside the city center in motels and B&Bs. Calgary has dozens of them in all parts of the city, but there are some areas of heavy concentration, making it easy to shop around. One such area is south of the city along Macleod Trail, a commercial strip with service stations, fast-food restaurants, motels and furniture shops.

Budget

HI-Calgary (☎ 403-269-8239; www.hostellingintl.ca/Alberta; 520 7th Ave SE; dm from $24, r from $75; 🖳) This popular hostel is located on the east side of downtown, not far from Fort Calgary. It's a large place, complete with laundry, kitchen, Internet access and snack bar, but it still fills up in summer. Reservations are recommended. The hostel organizes a lot of events and activities and offers a variety of cost-saving ideas. Be careful in this area at night: some readers have said they didn't feel safe walking around.

Mountain View Farm Campground (☎ 403-293-6640; fax 403-293-4798; Hwy 1; tent & RV sites from $18; P) On a farm 3km east of the Calgary city limits. It has showers, laundry, a barbecue, mini-golf and even a petting zoo. German is spoken.

Calgary West KOA (☎ 403-288-0411, 800-562-0842; Hwy 1; tent/RV sites $25/30; P ☎) On the Trans-Canada's south side at the western city limits, near Canada Olympic Park, the KOA has 350 sites, a game room and shuttle service to downtown.

Mid-Range

Elbow River Manor (☎ 403-802-0799; www.elbowriver manor.com; 2511 5th St SW; s/d from $85/100; P ☐) The three rooms at Elbow River are elegantly decorated and feature Turkish rugs and designer linens. When you step out of the shower there will be a comfy robe and slippers waiting for you. The B&B is within walking distance of the city center.

Cindy's B&B (☎ 403-254-6698; www.cindysbedbreak fast.com; cnr Dunbow Rd & 44th St; s/d from $80/95; P) An outdoor hot tub, flower gardens, walking trails and a pond set this upmarket B&B, on the city's south side, apart. The four rooms are uniquely decorated with antique furnishings.

Twin Gables B&B (☎ 403-271-7754; www.twingables .ca; 611 25th Ave SW; r from $85; P ☐) In a lovely old home, this B&B features hardwood floors, stained-glass windows, Tiffany lamps and antique furnishings. The three rooms are tastefully decorated, and the location across from the Elbow River gives opportunities for serene walks.

Hartwood House B&B (☎ 403-287-0551; www.hart woodhouse.ca; 1727 47th Ave SW; r from $100; P ☐) In a restored home, this quaint place has a lovely veranda, beautiful gardens and a cozy conservatory. It's an eight-minute drive from downtown, and a short walk from the Elbow River.

Holiday Inn Calgary Downtown (☎ 403 266-4611, 800-661-9378; www.holiday-inn.com/calgary-dwntn; 119 12th Ave SW; r from $120) Though convenient to downtown, the Holiday Inn is a well-

kept secret. It sits quietly off by itself on the south side of the tracks, in a hip block of pubs and restaurants not far from the Uptown action.

Sandman Hotel (☎ 403-237-8626, 800-726-3626; www.sandmanhotels.com; 888 7th Ave SW; r from $110, parking $6; P ☐ ☎) The common area of this hotel is quite trendy (with a fun cocktail lounge featuring nightly drink specials and a restaurant) and is nicer than the rooms, which have a bland, chain hotel feel (although they are quite comfortable). Check out the cheap weekend specials.

Best Western Airport Inn (☎ 403-250-5015, 877-499-5015; www.bestwestern.com; 1947 18th Ave NE; r from $90; P ☎) Out near the airport, this Best Western is a straightforward place with decent rooms, a restaurant, bar, pool and free airport shuttle. It's not bad if you have to catch an early morning flight.

Lord Nelson Inn (☎ 403-269-8262, 800-661-6017; fax 403-269-4868; 1020 8th Ave SW; r from $115; P) On downtown's west side, the modest Lord Nelson has full facilities and clean rooms. Look into it if other places are full.

Top End

Palliser (☎ 403-262-1234, 800-441-1414; www.fairmont .com/palliser; 133 9th Ave SW; r from $200; P ☎ ☐) When Queen Elizabeth drops by Calgary she stays at this grand CPR hotel dating from 1914. Now a Fairmont, the hotel offers 405 elegantly updated rooms and suites varying greatly in size. Calgary's classiest sleeping establishment.

Kensington Riverside Inn (☎ 403-228-4442; www .kensingtonriversideinn.com; 1126 Memorial Dr NW; r from $260; P) A boutique hotel, rooms have such ritzy touches as heated towel rails, soaker tubs, high ceilings and French doors. In the morning you'll find a thermos of coffee and a newspaper outside your door. More expensive rooms have fireplaces. Rates include a yummy breakfast and free cookies. Check the website for packages and discounts.

Delta Bow Valley (☎ 403-266-1980; www.delta hotels.com; 209 4th Ave SE; r from $180, parking $15; P ☐ ☎) One of the city's finest hotels, the Delta has well-appointed rooms and a wonderful rooftop pool and deck. This is a family-friendly hotel; in the summer you can leave the kids at the activities center while you go out to dinner.

International Hotel (☎ 403-265-9600; www.inter nationalhotel.ca; 220 4th Ave SW; ste from $230, parking

$8; (P ⊠) An all-suites hotel with stunning city views from the upper balcony, this place has some of the most spacious rooms in town. It can also arrange childcare.

Sheraton Suites Calgary Eau Claire (☎ 403-266-7200, 800-325-3535; www.sheraton.com; 255 Barclay Pde SW; ste from $260; P ⊡ ⊠) The 325-suite Sheraton enjoys a great location right by Eau Claire Market. Its design, both inside and out, embodies a touch more class than most of the concrete corporate monstrosities downtown. Amenities are abundant for both the business and pleasure traveler.

Delta Calgary Airport Hotel (☎ 403-291-2600, 800-268-1133; www.deltahotels.com; 2001 Airport Rd NE; r from $155; P ⊠) In the airport itself, and connected to the terminals, this place is almost luxurious and features a health club, among other amenities. The rooms are suitably soundproofed. Should jet lag get you down, there's a masseuse on call.

Hawthorn Hotel & Suites (☎ 403-263-0520, 800-661-1592; www.hawthorncalgary.com; 618 5th Ave SW; ste from $210; P ⊠) All rooms have kitchenettes and come with a breakfast buffet at this modern all-suites hotel. Rates drop on weekends.

EATING

Alberta in general, and Calgary in particular, has long had a reputation for steak – this is the heart of cattle country after all. Several steak houses in town serve a mean hunk of cow, at a mean price. Carnivores on a budget can sample the local cattle less expensively, with a city lunch specialty known as beef dip. This consists of thinly sliced roast beef served in a long bun, usually with fries and a bowl of 'sauce' to dip the meat into. In the better places this dip is simply juice from the roast – it should not be like gravy. Beef dips typically costs from $5 to $7.

It's not all about beef, however. The city has restaurants to suit all tastes – from Asian to Indian to Italian.

Budget

Nellie's Break the Fast Café (☎ 403-265-5071; 516 9th Ave SW; mains $6.50-9; breakfast & lunch) A popular down-home breakfast place affiliated with the Nellie's empire, this upstairs café has tasty omelettes, pancakes and such, as well as Ukrainian-style breakfast and lunch specials. In fine weather you can read the paper on the rooftop deck.

Nellie's Kitchen (☎ 403-244-4616; 738B 17th Ave SW; mains $5-9; breakfast) This small, pleasant café, part of the Nellie's dynasty that includes Nellie's on 4th and Nellie's Cosmic Cafe, has fantastic breakfasts and a patio out back.

Pho Pasteur Saigon (☎ 403-233-0477; 207 1st St SE; soups $5; lunch & dinner) This rudimentary Vietnamese restaurant is famous for its 18 kinds of beef noodle soup. Toss in the plate of vegetation that comes with it, add some sauce and you have a great meal.

Good Earth Coffeehouse & Bakery (☎ 403-265-2636; 119 8th Ave SW; mains under $10; breakfast, lunch & dinner) A Calgary original, this citywide chain is just the place for a light and healthy lunch. Soups are made from scratch, and everything includes organic ingredients. There are options for vegetarians, and meat-eaters can try a fresh Alberta roast beef and Asiago cheese sandwich. There are eight other locations around town.

Peters' Drive-In (☎ 403-277-2747; 219 16th Ave NE; mains $2.50-5; 9am-midnight) Peters' is a Calgary institution that's been flipping out flame-broiled burgers since 1962. At dinnertime huge, hungry hordes pile up in front of the walk-up window, while a line of cars idles away in the extra-long drive-up lane. Look for the big lawn with picnic tables out front.

Mid-Range

Booker's BBQ Grill & Crabshack (☎ 403-264-6419; 316 3rd St SE; mains from $10; lunch Mon-Fri, dinner) The interior is rustic warehouse, and you eat with your hands – buckets of buffalo shrimp, apple brandy barbecue ribs and catfish po' boy sandwiches. Stop by on Mondays for all-you-can-eat specials. The restaurant stays open until midnight on Friday and Saturday, if you get a hankering after a night of boozing.

Piq Niq Cafe (☎ 403-263-1650; 811 1st St SW; mains $10-20; breakfast, lunch & dinner) This café with European flair packs in the customers for its gourmet breakfasts, panini sandwiches at lunch and its beef, seafood, chicken and pasta at dinner. After dinner on Thursday through Sunday head downstairs to the funky basement bar for live jazz.

Brewster's (☎ 403-263-2739; 834 11th Ave SW; mains $11-15; lunch & dinner) Brewpub lovers will be in heaven here. Brewster's brews a wide selection of fine beers on the premises, including some subtle fruit beers that even guys might drink. And the kitchen serves creative

ALBERTA

fare that's far too tasty to be labeled 'pub grub.' For lunch, try the pepper-seared tuna sandwich with *wasabi* mayo, sliced roma tomatoes, sweet pickled ginger and sunflower sprouts. For dinner, maybe it's the Irish ale salmon or cabernet sirloin. Yum.

Melrose Cafe & Bar (☎ 403-228-3566; 730 17th Ave SW; mains $9-15; ✆ lunch & dinner) Industrial meets faux-Venetian at this trendy spot in a trendy neighborhood. In fact the Melrose just might be the epitome of 17th Ave style. Readers of *Calgary Straight* voted its terraced patio best in town. The beer from the 16 taps is treated with TLC, including chilled lines and a special glass-rinser, and the menu offers gourmet pizzas from a wood-burning oven, as well as fresh and healthy sandwiches, salads, seafood and more. Come for dinner and stay for drinks.

Wildwood (☎ 403-228-0100; 2417 4th St SW; mains from $17; ✆ lunch & dinner) The beers are as carefully brewed as the food is prepared at this upmarket microbrewery/restaurant. Both the upstairs restaurant and downstairs pub offer gorgeous, casually elegant ambience. The innovative 'Canadian Rocky Mountain' cuisine features lots of meat, including caribou, elk, lamb and your basic beef. Tours of the brewery are available.

Buzzard's Cookshack & Watering Hole (☎ 403-264-6959; 140 10th Ave SW; mains $8-26; ✆ lunch & dinner) Next to (and affiliated with) Bottlescrew Bill's pub (p601), this thoroughly casual eatery with a busy Western decor offers sandwiches (including a good beef dip), burgers and wraps at lunch, plus steaks and other entrées at dinner. And you get the same great beer selection that's available in the pub. The patio is a nice place to hang out in summer.

Jabulani (☎ 403-228-4535; 907 17th Ave SW; mains from $18; ✆ lunch & dinner) Serving traditional South African dishes such as Boerewors sausage, Cape Malay *boboti* (a spiced beef dish) and ostrich carpaccio, this fine new restaurant features zebra-striped tablecloths and modern safari decor. The restaurant seats only 25 guests, so it's quite intimate.

Cannery Row (☎ 403-269-8889; 317 10th Ave SW; mains from $15; ✆ lunch & dinner) This is a very classy seafood and oyster bar with an Asian flair to its decor. Sit upstairs for sheer elegance, or downstairs where your bucket of steamers or platter of prawns comes with live R&B on Friday and Saturday nights.

Upstairs, the lobsters love jazz. Up or down, choose from the same excellent wine list.

Regency Palace (☎ 403-777-2288; 328 Centre St SE; mains $10-16; ✆ lunch & dinner) The cavernous but pleasant Regency Palace, in the Dragon City Shopping Centre, offers Chinese classics such as Peking duck and shark's fin soup on its extensive, 150-item menu. There are daily lunch buffets and dim sum, and even a children's menu.

Thai Sa-On (☎ 403-264-3526; 351 10th Ave SW; mains $7-13; ✆ lunch & dinner) The menu at this authentic Thai restaurant has a large vegetarian section with a couple of dozen different selections. A family restaurant, it serves consistently good food in a pleasant atmosphere with parquet floors and Thai art on the walls. Check out the lunch specials.

Latin Corner Cantina (☎ 403-262-7248; 109 8th Ave SW; mains $17; ✆ lunch & dinner) From Brazil to Argentina, Mexico City to Madrid – this small but stunning place celebrates Latin culture from around the world with an exciting menu and ambience to match. Pair a tapa or two with a glass of Rioja while you wait for your heavenly paella. Live Latin music (often big-name touring acts) is presented Thursday to Saturday nights year-round.

Fiore Cantina Italiana (☎ 403-244-6603; 638 17th Ave SW; mains $10; ✆ lunch & dinner) With a busy patio and an always-packed dining room, this place is a hub of activity in a lively neighborhood. The menu offers a long list of fresh pastas.

Chianti (☎ 403-229-1600; 1438 17th Ave SW; mains $8-16; ✆ lunch & dinner) Popular with families, this well-liked and modestly priced chain serves a wide menu of respectable pastas, seafood, chicken and, yes, veal dishes. There's a children's menu and daily specials.

Rajdoot (☎ 403-245-0181; 2424 4th St SW; mains $10-20; ✆ lunch & dinner) Sometimes you just get a hankering for a good *channa chandi chowk* or perhaps some scrumptious *methi chaman braham bhojan*. If you can't get to India, this award-winning restaurant is the next best place. Vegetarians will be pleased.

Top End

Teatro (☎ 403-290-1012; 200 8th Ave SE; mains from $20; ✆ lunch & dinner) Across from the performing arts center (hence the name), the stylish Teatro occupies a stately 1911 bank building complete with pillars and high ceilings. The menu is equally stunning, employing fresh regional ingredients in creative recipes. Try the seared sea bass served with slow-cooked fennel and leeks, olive tapenade and red-wine sauce ($29) or perhaps the whole roasted rack of lamb with mascarpone scalloped potatoes and gingered quince sauce ($37).

Hy's Steak House (☎ 403-263-2222; 316 4th Ave SW; mains from $25; ☼ lunch & dinner) Hy's has changed little from when it opened in 1955. It's a classic plush steak house where the carpets are as dark and thick as the prime Alberta beef.

La Chaumiere (☎ 403-228-5690; 139 17th Ave SW; mains from $16; ☼ lunch & dinner) You can start your meal with Beluga caviar on ice, or try the lobster bisque, at this very elegant French eatery. There's an extensive wine list. Jackets required for gents. Sit on the patio when it's warm.

DRINKING

For bars check out 17th Ave NW, with a slew of martini lounges and bustling pubs, and 4th St SW, with a lively after-work scene. Other notable areas include Kensington Rd NW and Stephen Ave (a six-block downtown stretch of 8th Ave).

Bungalow (☎ 403-209-5005; 524 17th Ave SW) A new favorite watering hotel, this urban place is packed on weekends when the city's beautiful people come out to play.

Ming (☎ 403-229-1986; 520 17th Ave) Blood red walls greet you at this intimate martini lounge popular with city hipsters. It's a great place to start an evening, sipping a cocktail and listening to house music. It draws a young crowd when school is in session.

Lucky (☎ 403-229-4036; 510 17th Ave SW) Cocktails are served at circular booths amidst a dark wood interior at this swanky lounge. Dress to impress.

Belvedere (☎ 403-265-9595; 107 8th Ave) On trendy Stephen Ave, this posh place is low-lit with potted palms. It's not a bad stop for a sedate upmarket drink.

Ceili's (☎ 403-508-9999; 126-513 8th Ave SW) Less an Irish pub than a place to see and be seen, this massive, trendy spot is a magnet for beautiful people, primarily downtown's movers and shakers. Fridays and Mondays get particularly jammed with the after-work crowd. Grab one of the tables outside if the weather's good.

Ship & Anchor (☎ 403-245-3333; 534 17th Ave SW) King of Calgary's English-pub scene, the Ship & Anchor is a neighborhood pub extraordi-

naire, drawing a mixed crowd for its good beer selection, food, music (both live and canned) and social ambience. Sit out on the patio and gape at the passersby, or stay inside and watch footy matches on the telly.

Bottlescrew Bill's Old English Pub (☎ 403-263-7900; 140 10th Ave SW) Just across the tracks from downtown, Bottlescrew Bill's boasts a selection of more than 150 beers from around the world.

Hose & Hound (☎ 403-234-0508; 1030 9th Ave SE) Cozy Inglewood's funky neighborhood pub occupies a converted firehouse and offers two patios, one of which is covered and heated. The kitchen serves good pub food – wings, salads, pasta, burgers, sandwiches, personal-sized pizzas and even substantial entrées (most $6 to $8).

Rose & Crown (☎ 403-244-7757; 1503 4th St SW) This huge British-style pub has an excellent beer selection, an outdoor patio and comfortable booths inside.

ENTERTAINMENT

For complete entertainment guides, pick up a copy of *ffwd*, the city's largest entertainment weekly, or the music-oriented *Calgary Straight*. Both are available free around town. The Friday edition of the *Calgary Herald* has a pull-out called 'What's Up' that does a good job of outlining the pleasures of the weekend and beyond.

Nightclubs

Cowboys (☎ 403-265-0699; 826 5th St SW; ☼ Wed-Sat) This big two-story club boasts bands and bevies of beautiful bodies boogying on the

ALBERTA

CALGARY FOLK MUSIC FESTIVAL

The main events of this **festival** (☎ 403-233-0904; www.calgaryfolkfest.com; tickets $40, four-day adult passes about $110; ☼ late Jul) take place on Prince's Island and include performances by big-name local, national and international artists. Past performers have included the Cowboy Junkies, David Byrne, Tom Cochrane, Kathy Mattea and Buckwheat Zydeco, among many, many others. The festival also brings free lunchtime performances on Stephen Ave Walk and evening performances in various venues around town. Four-day adult passes are available by advance purchase only.

large dance floor. If you don't have a Stetson, don't worry – the Western theme is only window dressing here; rock, country and dance music are all on the schedule.

Mynt (☎ 403-262-6968; www.mynt.ca; 516C 9th Ave SW) Calgary's newest hot spot attracts the beautiful party people. In fact if you have the cash you can order a helicopter to pick you up on the roof and take you home! Talk about VIP treatment.

Whiskey (☎ 403-770-2323; www.thewhiskeynight club.com; 341 10th Ave SW) Another newcomer to the Calgary club scene, the Whiskey is trendy club downstairs and relaxed pub upstairs. The place attracts an older crowd with a blend of retro hits and big name live bands.

Palace Night Club (☎ 403-263-9980; 219 8th Ave SW) This Stephen Ave Walk venue is great for live comedy, concerts and dancing to DJ beats.

Live Music
King Edward Hotel (☎ 403-262-1680; 438 9th Ave SE) Downtown, the King Eddy is the city's prime blues bar. A quintessential dive, it's been around as long as some of the ancient musicians who play here. Even the cigarette burns have cigarette burns. Lord have mercy, in the key of G.

Kaos (☎ 403-228-9997; 718 17th Ave SW) For nightly live jazz – and some blues for good measure – Kaos is the place.

Buckingham's (☎ 403-233-7550; 1000 9th Ave SW) Buckingham's is a big downstairs den with pool tables, dartboards, live rock and good bar-chow like burgers and fries.

Newt (☎ 403-283-1132; 107 10A St NW) North across the river in Kensington, this hip bar has a vast selection of martinis and live music that runs the gamut from folk to Latin to classic rock.

Gay & Lesbian Venues
For club and entertainment listings, pick up a copy of *Outlooks* (www.outlooks.ca), a gay-oriented monthly newspaper distributed throughout the province. The website offers an extensive gay resources guide to Calgary and beyond.

Detour (☎ 403-244-8537; 318 17th Ave SW) The Arena Coffee Bar by day, Detour by night; this place attracts a mixed crowd of gays and lesbians.

Metro-Boyztown (☎ 403-265-2028; 213 10th Ave SW) As the name suggests, this is a popular spot for boys, boys, boys. Talk about eye candy.

Verge (☎ 403-245-3344; 4A 2500 4th St SW) The Verge is predominantly a lesbian bar, although its clientele includes some gay men. It's a cozy, classy kind of place with a nice mahogany bar and occasional dancing, drag shows and live acoustic music.

Cinemas
Plaza Theatre (☎ 403-283-3636; 1113 Kensington Rd NW) The repertory Plaza Theatre has two different shows each night, plus midnight performances on Friday and Saturday. It presents offbeat US and foreign films.

Globe Cinema (☎ 403-262-3308; 617 8th Ave SW) The Globe screens an interesting schedule of foreign and revival movies.

IMAX Theatre (☎ 403-974-4629; 132-200 Barclay Parade SW) Calgary's IMAX is in the Eau Claire Market, just south of Bow River.

Cineplex Odeon (☎ 403-263-3166; 132-200 Barclay Parade SW) A multiplex cinema next door to the IMAX.

Theater
The city has several venues for drama, opera, symphony and major concerts.

Epcor Centre for the Performing Arts (☎ 403-294-7455; www.theartscentre.org; 205 8th Ave SE) Known as The Centre, this five-venue complex is home to six resident theater companies, including **Alberta Theatre Projects** (☎ 403-294-7402), **Theatre Calgary** (☎ 403-294-7440) and **One Yellow Rabbit Performance Theatre** (☎ 403-264-3224).

Loose Moose Theatre Company (☎ 403-265-5682; 1229 9th Ave SE) Loose Moose, in Inglewood just east of the downtown area, puts on comedy and drama, old and new.

Pumphouse Theatres (☎ 403-263-0079; www.pump housetheatres.ca; 2140 Pumphouse Ave SW) The Pumphouse stages experimental plays. To reach the theaters head west on Bow Trail, when you see the Greyhound Canada bus station on your left get into the far right lane and turn right at the Pumphouse Rd turn-off, then right again at Pumphouse Ave.

Jubilee Auditorium (☎ 403-297-8000; 1415 14th Ave NW; admission from $20) This is where the Alberta Ballet performs. Its performances are popular, and tickets often sell fast. Big-name concerts are also presented here.

Sports
Calgary Flames (☎ 403-777-0000; tickets from $12) Archrival of the Edmonton Oilers, the team plays ice hockey from October to April at the

Saddledome (Stampede Park). In 2004 the Flames made it to game seven of the Stanley Cup Finals before losing to Tampa Bay.

Calgary Stampeders (☎ 403-289-0258; tickets from $25; ☒ Jul-Sep) Part of the CFL, they play at **McMahon Stadium** (1817 Crowchild Trail NW) in northwest Calgary.

SHOPPING

Calgary has several shopping districts. Try 11th St SW, just off 17th Ave SW, for two blocks of art, home decor and clothing stores. Boutiques, trinket shops and other one-of-a-kind stores can be found on 4th St SW between 13th and 26th Aves SW. Stephen Ave Walk is an outdoor pedestrian mall with street-level boutiques. Galleries and other shops can be found on 17th Ave SW between Macleod Trail S and 14th St.

Alberta Boot Co (☎ 403-263-4605; www.albertaboot .com; 614 10th Ave SW; boots $235-1700) You can visit the factory and store run by the province's only Western boot manufacturer and pick up a pair of your choice made from kangaroo, ostrich, python, rattlesnake, lizard, alligator or boring old cowhide.

Naked (☎ 403 229 3013; 1510 17th Ave SW) Canadian and European designers are found at this women's clothing boutique. Here you will see the work of local jewelry designer Catherine Larose. Each piece of jewelry comes with a written statement explaining its symbolism and how it was made.

Rocket (☎ 403-244-2099; 738A 17th Ave; T-shirts about $30) Design your own unique T-shirt at this 17th Ave shop. Pick out a T-shirt type that suits your style and then choose from hundreds of logos to place on it.

Riley & McCormick (☎ 403-262-1556; 220 8th Ave SW) For cowboy hats, shirts, skirts, vests, spurs and other Western gear, check out this store, with locations on Stephen Ave Walk and elsewhere.

Eau Claire Market (☎ 403-264-6460; www.eauclaire market.com; cnr 2nd St & 2nd Ave SW). The town's most interesting shopping center is a large two-story enclosed mall with shops, restaurants, a produce market, nightspots, a multiplex theater and an IMAX theater.

GETTING THERE & AWAY
Air

Calgary International Airport (YYC; ☎ 403-735-1372; www.calgaryairport.com) is about 15km northeast of the center off Barlow Trail, a 25-minute drive away. For more information on flights into Calgary, see p576.

Bus

The Greyhound Canada **bus station** (☎ 403-265-9111; 850 16th St SW) is relatively close to the center and is served by a free city shuttle bus that departs from the C-Train 10th St SW stop. Fares include Banff ($26, two hours, six daily) and Edmonton ($46, from 3½ hours, 13 or more daily). For information on fares to other parts of Canada, see p576. **Red Arrow** (☎ 403-531-0350, 800-232-1958; www.redarrow.pwt.ca; 205 9th Ave SE) runs luxury buses to Edmonton ($46, 3½ hours, six daily).

Car

All the major car rental firms are represented at the airport and downtown. For more information on car hire, see p873.

Train

You can travel by train from Calgary to Vancouver via Banff with the privately owned **Rocky Mountaineer Railtours** (☎ 800-665-7245; www.rockymountaineer.com; cnr 9th Ave & Centre St). The peak season one-way fare to Vancouver is single $784, double $1458, including lunch and dinner and an overnight stop in a hotel in Kamloops. The service, which is like a cruise ship on rails, runs from May to mid-October. The station is underneath the Calgary Tower.

GETTING AROUND
To/From the Airport

The **Airporter** (☎ 403-531-3907/3909) runs every half hour from around 6:30am to 11:30pm between all the major downtown hotels and the airport, and charges $9/15 one-way/roundtrip. **Airport Shuttle Express** (☎ 403-509-4799, 888-438-2992; www.airportshuttleexpress.com) offers on-demand shared shuttle service for around $12 to any of the downtown hotels.

You can also go between the airport and downtown on public transportation. From the airport, take the No 57 bus to the Whitehorn stop (northeast of the city center) and transfer to the C-Train; or just reverse the process coming from downtown. This costs only $1.75, but takes about an hour.

A taxi to the airport costs about $25.

ALBERTA

Car & Motorcycle

Parking is generally free in Calgary, except downtown where you can expect to pay between $10 and $18 per day. In most cases parking is free on public streets after 6pm Monday to Saturday and all day Sunday. Public garages abound throughout downtown. Part of 7th Ave in downtown Calgary is closed to cars; this stretch of road is clearly marked.

Public Transportation

Public transport in Calgary is efficient and clean. You can choose from the Light Rapid Transit (LRT) rail system, known as the C-Train, and ordinary buses. One fare entitles you to transfer to other buses or another C-Train. The C-Train is free in the downtown area along 7th Ave between 10th St SW and 3rd St SE. If you're going further or need a transfer, buy your ticket from a machine on the C-Train platform. Most of the buses run at 15- to 30-minute intervals daily. There is no late-night service. The C-Train and bus fare per single/day is $2.60/5.

Taxi

For a cab, call **Alberta South Co-Op Taxi Lines** (☎ 403-531-8294) or **Yellow Cab** (☎ 403-974-1111). Fares are $2.50 for the first 160m, 20¢ for each additional 160m and 20¢ for each 30 seconds of elapsed time.

BANFF & JASPER NATIONAL PARKS

The mountains reach up and scrape the sky – a jumble of colors and shapes. Cerulean blue meets snowcapped majesty. The lakes are opaque emerald-green or milky-turquoise. They sparkle in the sunlight and you'll have to blink a few times because the color seems too intense, too out of place, to be real. The glaciers cling to rugged precipices, where intense ice blue merges with slate gray. Rivers rush by, fed on snowmelt and spring rains. Lush forests and high alpine meadows explode in a kaleidoscope of colors when the wildflowers bloom. A grizzly bear ambles past, swinging his big head from side to side, searching for food. A moose pauses at a fast-flowing river, stopping for a drink. It all almost seems too

surreal to be true, so picture perfect you're sure you're dreaming.

Welcome to Banff and Jasper National Parks, heart of the Canadian Rockies, and home to some of the most spectacular scenery on the continent. Much of the Rocky Mountains area of Alberta, running along the BC border, is contained and protected within these two huge, adjacent national parks: Banff to the south and Jasper to the north. The Icefields Parkway links the two, though there is no distinct boundary. Adjoining the southern boundary of Banff National Park is Kananaskis Country, a provincial recreation area.

Canada's first national park, Banff, was established in 1885 and named after Banffshire, Scotland, the home of two CPR financiers. Built around the thermal sulfur springs at what has become the Cave & Basin National Historic Site, Banff National Park today covers 6641 sq km and is by far the best known and most popular park in the Rockies. With 25 mountains 3000m or higher, Banff is world-famous for skiing and climbing, though most visitors just come to view the astonishing scenery. Jasper National Park is larger, wilder and less explored but, like Banff, offers excellent hiking trails.

The small townsites of Banff, Lake Louise, Jasper and Canmore act as focal points for orientation, supplies and information. In Banff National Park, accommodations during summer are expensive and hard to find. It's worth booking ahead or staying in one of the towns outside the park, such as Canmore in Alberta or Field, Golden, Radium Hot Springs, Windermere or Invermere in BC, and making day trips.

The one-day park entry fee is $7/6/3.50 adult/senior/child for entry to both parks; the passes are good until 4pm the following day. A day-pass for groups of two to seven costs just $14.

The backcountry hiking and wilderness camping fee is $6 per night, with a maximum charge of $30. Passes are available from all park visitors centers. Note that there may be a limit on the number of backcountry passes to some popular areas. Check with the relevant park visitors center for details.

KANANASKIS COUNTRY

Nestled next to each other over mountain ranges and through deep valleys, a string of Alberta's provincial parks and reserved multiuse areas create a 4000-sq-km rural playground. Bordering the southeastern corner of Banff National Park, Kananaskis Country is much quieter than its legendary neighbor yet provides excellent opportunities for heaps of outdoor pursuits. The area has its own look, and the carved sides and fashioned peaks of the mountains may leave you feeling like you've driven into a claymation cartoon starring a moose or two, nonchalantly munching by the roadside.

From Canmore in the northwest, Kananaskis Country stretches almost as far as the small town of Highwood House in the southeast. To fully take in the area, complete the loop from Canmore, driving down the Kananaskis Trail (Hwy 40) and up along the Smith-Dorrien Rd.

Near the northern end of the Kananaskis Trail the **Barrier Lake Information Centre** (☎ 403-673-3985; www.gov.ab.ca/env/parks/prov_parks/kananaskis; Hwy 40; ☻ 9am-4pm, to 5pm in summer) has loads of information and sells backcountry camping permits.

To see the area by horseback visit the **Boundary Ranch** (☎ 403-591-7171; www.boundaryranch.com; Hwy 40; per hr $30; ☻ mid-May–mid-Oct), which caters to all ages and abilities.

In winter skiing is top of the list. **Nakiska** (☎ 403-591-7777, 800-258-7669, snow report 403-244-6665; www.skinakiska.com; Hwy 40, 5min south of Kananaskis Village; day lift pass adult/youth/child $46/36/15) is where the alpine skiing events of the 1988 Winter Olympics were held. **Fortress Mountain** (☎ 403-591-7108, 800-258-7669, snow report 403-244-6665; www.skifortress.com; Hwy 40, 30min south of Kananaskis Village; day lift pass adult/youth/child $35/25/12; ☻ Wed-Sun & holidays) is home of the Canadian National Freestyle Team, and is better for snowboarders.

If you want to stay in a lodge with sweeping views across an alpine meadow, try the **Mount Engadine Lodge** (☎ 403-678-4090; www.mountengadine.com; full board per person from $105). There are snug lodge and cabin rooms. The included meals are hearty and they can be enjoyed outside on the big deck or inside in front of the fireplace. Service is very friendly. Kananaskis Country also has some stunning and peaceful campgrounds. For fabulous mountain and lake views try **Canyon Camping** (☎ 403-591-7226; www.kananaskicamping.com; Kananaskis Lakes Rd; tent sites $17; ☻ mid-Jun–Sep).

Kananaskis Country can be reached from Hwy 1 along the gravel Smith-Dorrien Rd from Canmore or the Kananaskis Trail (Hwy 40), just east of Canmore. From southern Alberta, you can reach the area in summer along Hwy 40.

CANMORE

Canmore's small downtown has yet to be buried under tacky tourism initiatives and remains a very pleasant place to stroll around. Unhindered by the growth limits imposed on the town of Banff, 26km to the west, fast-growing Canmore is a popular alternative to the resorts inside the national parks. Just off Hwy 1 and squeezed between Banff National Park and Kananaskis Country, Canmore is home to many outdoor enthusiasts who prefer its less chaotic pace. In the summer, when prices in Jasper and Banff Towns soar, Canmore may prove a cheaper alternative.

Information

Alberta Visitor Information Center (☎ 403-678-5277; www.discoveralberta.com; 2801 Bow Valley Trail; ☻ 8am-6pm, to 8pm in summer) Just off Hwy 1.
CyberWeb (☎ 403-609-2678; 717 10th St; per hr $6) Sip coffee and surf the Internet.

Sights & Activities

The town is a base for **Alpine Helicopters Ltd** (☎ 403-678-4802; www.alpinehelicopter.com; 91 Bow Valley Trail; heli-hike/alpine walk/flight tours from $375/250/145). The company gives you a bird's-eye view of the Rockies from the belly of a helicopter and then drops you onto a high alpine meadow for some middle-of-nowhere hiking. The helicopters are wheelchair-accessible.

If you'd rather explore the wonders under the mountains then try climbing through the narrow passageways and descending the shoots along 4km of an undeveloped cave system within Grotto Mountain. Both **Canmore Caves** (☎ 403-678-9918; www.canadianrockies.net/wildcavetours; full/half day $105/79) and **Canadian Rockies Cave Guiding** (☎ 403-678-3522; www.caveguiding.com; trips from $65) run tours year-round.

For something different you could try dogsledding. **Howling Dog Tours** (☎ 403-678-9588; www.howlingdogtours.com; 109 Bow Meadows Cres) is one of numerous companies around the parks. You can either drive your own sled under guide supervision or let someone else do the work and take in the scenery. There's a two-hour

---

SO MUCH TO SEE, SO LITTLE TIME

From paddling across a gem-colored lake to soaking in a natural hot spring to an early morning hike across an icefield, Banff and Jasper National Parks not only offer serene and majestic scenery, but a plethora of things to see and do. So how do you choose? We've picked a few of our favorite, absolutely-can't-miss highlights.

- Drive the Icefields Parkway for stunning views and stop at the **Columbia Icefield** (p608) for a walk on the Athabasca Glacier.
- Visit **Lake Louise** (p619), the gem of the Canadian Rockies. Meander along the flat Lakeshore Trail to enjoy spectacular scenery and to lose the crowds. Afterwards rent a boat and paddle atop the turquoise water.
- In **Banff Town** (p609) ride the gondola for panoramic views, take a soak in the Upper Hot Springs pool, have dinner at the novel Grizzly House and finish the night two-stepping away at the appropriately named Wild Bill's Legendary Saloon.
- Don't miss a late-afternoon drink in the **Rundle Lounge** (p618) of the historic Banff Springs Hotel. The glamor of this gothic castle is eclipsed by the million dollar views from the lounge's windows.
- Try **white-water rafting** (p613) in Horseshoe Canyon or on the Kicking Horse River for a wild day with magnificent views.
- Check out **Maligne Lake** (p623) in Jasper Park. Follow the driving tour and watch for wildlife.
- Hike along the **Valley of Five Lakes trail** (p624) in Jasper to see five different lakes, all varying shades of green and blue.
- In winter test your skiing and snowboarding skills at **Sunshine Village** (p613) or **Lake Louise** (p613); both offer mild to wild slopes.

---

trip, or a half-day one that includes a fireside trail lunch. Prices start at $70. Howling Dog Tours is 16km southeast of Canmore on the Smith-Dorian Rd. Call for prices.

Sleeping & Eating

Canmore Clubhouse (☎ 403-678-3200; www.alpine clubofcanada.ca; Indian Flats Rd; dm from $19) Just footsteps away from trailheads, the Alpine Club of Canada's beautiful hostel sits on a rise overlooking the valley. There are laundry facilities, a library, a kitchen, a sauna and an almost tangible aura of mountaineering history. The Alpine Club offers classes in mountaineering and maintains several backcountry huts. It is a good place to meet fellow mountaineers. The hostel is about 5km southeast of town (a 45-minute walk).

Georgetown Inn (☎ 403-678-3439; www.george towninn.ab.ca; 1101 Bow Valley Trail; d with breakfast from $129) Modern touches such as whirlpools and minikitchens mesh with antique furnishings at this inn decorated in Tudor style. It's full of character. Have a drink at its Miner's Lamp Pub to experience more authenticity.

Lady MacDonald Country Inn (☎ 800-567-3919; www.ladymacdonald.com; 1201 Bow Valley Trail; d with breakfast from $150) Sleigh or four-poster beds, warm-hued walls, plenty of cushions and down duvets make the 12 individually decorated rooms at this lodge a joy to stay in. The gourmet breakfast completes the experience.

Grizzly Paw Brewing Company (☎ 403-678-9983; 622 8th/Main St; mains $10-15; 🕑 lunch & dinner) How can you resist the names of the beers at this local microbrewery – Grumpy Bear Honey Wheat, Drooling Moose Pilsner? The wood and stone decor is bear-oriented: there's a climbing black bear teddy in thong panties and plenty of bear signs. The menu focuses on burgers, sandwiches and pastas.

Canmore is easily accessible from Banff Town and Calgary from Hwy 1. All buses en route between Banff Town and Calgary stop at the **Greyhound Bus Depot** (☎ 403-678-4465; cnr Main St & 7th Ave; 🕑 7:30am-midnight).

ICEFIELDS PARKWAY

This road curves around mountains, climbs high passes and follows three major river

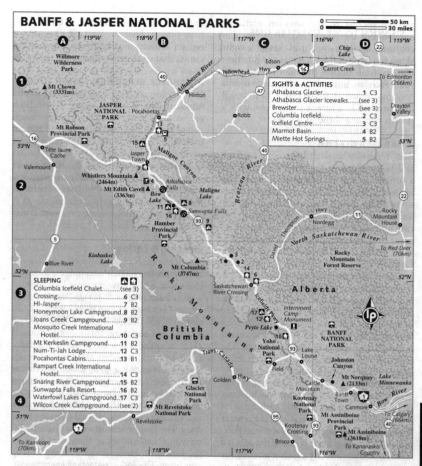

BANFF & JASPER NATIONAL PARKS

SIGHTS & ACTIVITIES
Athabasca Glacier................1	C3
Athabasca Glacier Icewalks......(see 3)	
Brewster..........................(see 3)	
Columbia Icefield................2	C3
Icefield Centre...................3	C3
Marmot Basin.....................4	B2
Miette Hot Springs...............5	B2

SLEEPING
Columbia Icefield Chalet.........(see 3)	
Crossing.........................6	C3
HI-Jasper........................7	B2
Honeymoon Lake Campground..8	B2
Joans Creek Campground..........9	B2
Mosquito Creek International	
Hostel.......................10	C3
Mt Kerkeslin Campground.......11	B2
Num-Ti-Jah Lodge................12	C3
Pocahontas Cabins...............13	B1
Rampart Creek International	
Hostel.......................14	C3
Snaring River Campground.......15	B2
Sunwapta Falls Resort............16	B2
Waterfowl Lakes Campground..17	C3
Wilcox Creek Campground......(see 2)	

ALBERTA

systems flowing through wide valleys. As the highest and most spectacular road in North America, the Icefields Parkway (Hwy 93) links Lake Louise village with Jasper Town and takes you about as close as you're going to get to the Rockies' craggy summits in your vehicle. If you get out and follow one of the many trailheads en route, you'll feel like you're on the top of the world within a matter of hours. Numerous roadside stops allow you to take in the Parkway's brilliantly colored glacial lakes, gushing waterfalls and exquisite viewpoints. While you can cover the 230km road in a few hours, it's worth spending a few days exploring the region; camp at one of the campgrounds along the parkway, stay in a rustic lodge, hike on an

icefield and keep your eyes peeled for grizzly bear, moose and bighorn sheep.

Sights

Every bend in the road reveals a view seemingly more stunning than the last. There are lakes and glaciers galore, too many to mention – so we'll focus on our favorites.

PEYTO LAKE

One of the world's most beautiful glacial lakes, with robin egg–blue water. The lake is best visited in early morning, between the time the sun first illuminates the water and the time the first tour bus arrives. From the bottom of the lake parking lot follow a paved trail for 15 minutes up a steady, gradual incline to the wooden platform overlooking the lake. From here you can continue up the paved trail, keeping right along the edge of the ridge. At the junction of three trails, follow the middle trail until you reach an unmarked dirt road; if you continue down it for about 2.5km you'll find yourself in a serene rocky bowl with a stream running through the center.

ATHABASCA GLACIER

About halfway between Lake Louise village and Jasper Town is the Athabasca Glacier, a tongue of the vast **Columbia Icefield**. The icefield contains about 30 glaciers and is up to 350m thick. This remnant of the last ice age covers 325 sq km on the plateau between Mt Columbia (3747m) and Mt Athabasca (3491m). It's the largest icefield in the Rockies and feeds the North Saskatchewan, Columbia, Athabasca, Mackenzie and Fraser River systems with its meltwaters.

The mountainous sides of this vast bowl of ice are some of the highest in the Rockies, with nine peaks higher than 3000m. One of its largest glaciers, the Athabasca, runs almost down to the road and can be visited on foot or in specially designed buses. The water you'll see at the toe of the glacier fell as snow on the icefield about 175 years ago.

Icefield Centre (☎ 780-852-6288; admission free; 🕙 9am-6pm May–mid-Oct) is across the highway from the glacier. It's a public/private joint venture between Parks Canada and Brewster Tours. It holds numerous well-designed displays explaining glaciers – one of the best is a time-lapse film showing a glacier altering the ground beneath it – and a Parks Canada information desk offering trail details, ecology information and backcountry trek planning.

You can walk or drive to the toe of the glacier from the Icefield Centre. To hike onto the glacier, you'll need a guide. **Athabasca Glacier Icewalks** (☎ 780-852-6550, 800-565-7547; www.telusplanet.net/public/iceman1; Icefield Center; 3hr hike adult/child $45/23, 6hr hike adult/child $50/25; 🕙 hikes 10:40am Jun-Sep) offers three-hour glacier hikes every day in the summer; on Sundays and Thursdays you can opt for a six-hour trip that takes in the icefalls of the glacier.

You'll find it impossible to miss the hype and hard sell for the 'snocoach' ice tours offered by **Brewster** (☎ 877-423-7433; www.brewster.ca; adult/child $30/15; 🕙 tours every 15min 9am-6pm May-Oct). It's touristy, that's for sure, but the 55-minute

tours are well worth the money if you don't have time to hike out yourself. Buses drive out on the ice and reach vast areas of the glacier that can't be seen from the road.

ATHABASCA GLACIER TO JASPER TOWN

Other points of interest are **Sunwapta Falls** and **Athabasca Falls**, closer to Jasper Town. Both are worth a stop, though you may be appalled by the bonehead decision to put an ugly utility road bridge over the most scenic part of Athabasca Falls.

At Athabasca Falls, Hwy 93A quietly sneaks off to the left. Take it. Literally the road less traveled, this old route into Jasper Town offers a blissfully traffic-free experience as it slips serenely through deep, dark woods and past small placid lakes and meadows.

Sleeping & Eating

The Icefields Parkway is lined with a good batch of rustic hostels and lodges. Most are close to the highway in scenic locations.

Num-Ti-Jah Lodge (☎ 403-522-2167; www.num-ti-jah.com; r with shared bathroom low/high season $115/210, r low/high season $150/230) Right on Bow Lake in a rustic log structure, this lodge is a lovely place to spend a few days. Inside it's decorated with old wooden skis, animal heads and furs. Winter is a great season to visit the lodge: rooms are cheaper and there are often specials that include breakfast, a three-course dinner and room (from $140 per person), and you can cross-country ski from the front door. The lounge area is a cozy place to curl up with a book and watch the snow falling. In the summer there is plenty of hiking to keep you busy. The lodge **restaurant** (mains from $14, 3-course dinner $45) has an extensive wine list.

Crossing (☎ 403-761-7000; www.thecrossingresort.com; s/d $95/100; 🖳) The crossing is quiet and serene. Rooms are in wooden chalets and there are mountain views in all directions. Sit outside on the pub's patio and stare into nothing. The hot tub will heal your aching limbs after a day of hiking.

Sunwapta Falls Resort (☎ 888-828-5777; info@sunwapta.com; d from $79; 🕙 May-Oct) There are numerous hiking trails around the resort. Some of the rooms come with stone fireplaces and patios, and staff are friendly.

Columbia Icefield Chalet (☎ 877-423-7433; icefield@brewster.ca; Icefields Center; r from $110; 🕙 May-Oct) Rooms are nothing special, although the views through the tiny windows are amaz-

THE ULTIMATE MOUNTAIN MAN

Entering Banff Town, you'll see the town's signs adorned with the image of a rugged-looking mountain man. It's Bill Peyto, a legendary character who explored much of the wilderness around Banff. Starting with his arrival from England in 1886, his exploits in the high peaks were matched by his hijinks around town. His cabin featured a set bear trap to thwart burglars. And once he brought a wild lynx into a bar, then sat back with a drink while chaos reigned. Generally regarded as the hardiest of the hardy breed that first settled high in the Rockies, he died in 1943 aged 75. Several local features are named in his honor, including one of the region's most beautiful lakes, a glacier and, perhaps most appropriately, Wild Bill's Legendary Saloon (p617).

ing. It's a rather chaotic place to stay, but you can't beat the location. There's a restaurant on site with fabulous glacier views.

Mosquito Creek International Hostel (☎ 403-670-7589; www.hihostels.ca; 26km north of Lake Louise; dm from $19; ☺ may close in winter) Next to Mosquito Creek, this basic hostel has cozy heated dorm cabins in a peaceful forest setting. There are also cooking facilities, a sauna and a campground.

Rampart Creek International Hostel (☎ 403-670-7589; www.hihostels.ca; 11km north of the Saskatchewan River Crossing; dm from $19; ☺ may close in winter) Popular with cyclists and climbers, these 12-bed cabins have rustic chic with decks, flower boxes and heaters. On a sunny site with a nice community campfire pit; there are good bouldering opportunities right behind the hostel. There's also a campground.

There are also numerous **campgrounds** (per night around $22) in the area. Some of our favorites are Honeymoon Lake, Joans Creek, Mt Kerkeslin, Waterfowl Lakes and Wilcox Creek Campgrounds.

BANFF TOWN

The small, rustic alpine-style village of Banff Town, 138km west of Calgary, is a destination in its own right. Filled with chic restaurants and bars, outdoor-oriented shops and even some worthwhile museums, the park's hub attracts several million visitors a year. In July and August the normal population swells by 25,000. Although this can cause problems, the many vacationers create a relaxed and festive atmosphere. The town makes a great base for exploring the area.

History

Banff Town was created solely as a tourist destination. The CPR wanted a health spa here to attract wealthy, well-traveled Victorians who would arrive – as paying passengers – on CPR trains. And come they did, ready to relax in the rejuvenating hot springs or hire one of the many outfitters to take them up the mountains.

In 1912, the decision to allow cars in Banff Town opened the area up to people other than rich Victorians, and the town began pushing its boundaries. The south side of the river, with the Banff Springs Hotel, catered to the wealthy crowd. The north side of the river resembled more of a prairie town, with small lots zoned in a grid system. This class-distinctive boundary is still evident today.

Banff Town continues to face conflicts over its growth. People complain that the townsite is too crowded and argue that more hotels and streets should be built to accommodate the camera-clicking tourists. Others think there's too much building already. To control growth, the federal government has decreed that only those who can demonstrate a valid need (such as owning a business) can live in town. But that doesn't solve the problem of what to do with all the tourists. Permits for the minimal new construction currently allowed by law are doled out under a lottery system, and a permanent building freeze is expected by 2006. With Banff's popularity continuing to grow, the debate will only intensify.

Orientation

Banff Ave, the main street, runs north–south through the whole length of town, then heads northeast to meet Hwy 1. The stretch of Banff Ave between Wolf and Buffalo Sts is lined with shops and restaurants. Toward the south end of Banff Ave is Central Park, where you can stroll or rent canoes to paddle on the mellow Bow River. Still further south over the Bow River Bridge is the Park Administration Building, a good place for a view and photo of town or the beautiful flower gardens around the building.

ALBERTA

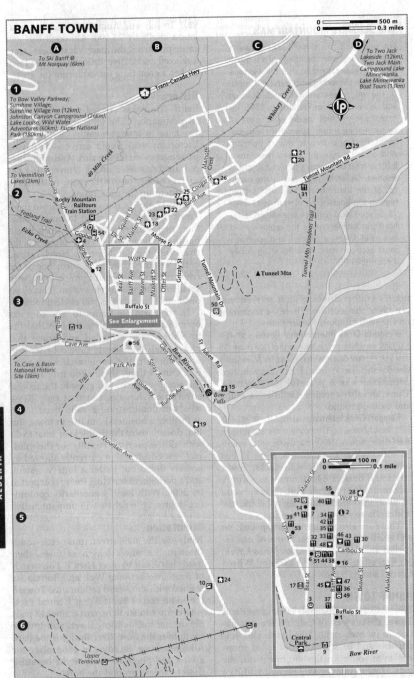

BANFF TOWN

0 _____ 500 m
0 _____ 0.3 miles

A To Ski Banff @ Mt Norquay (6km)

1

To Bow Valley Parkway; Sunshine Village, Sunshine Village Inn (12km); Johnston Canyon Campground (26km); Lake Louise, Wild Water Adventures (60km); Jasper National Park (180km)

Trans-Canada Hwy

B

C

D To Two Jack Lakeside (12km); Two Jack Main Campground Lake Minnewanka, Lake Minnewanka Boat Tours (13km)

Whiskey Creek

To Vermillion Lakes (2km)

Fenland Trail

Echo Creek

40 Mile Creek

Mt Norquay Rd

Rocky Mountain Railtours Train Station

Mammoth Crest

Cougar St

Squirrel St

Elk St

Marten St

Banff Ave

Moose St

Wolf St

Bear St

Banff Ave

Beaver St

Muskrat St

Otter St

Grizzly St

Gopher St

Bow Ave

Buffalo St

See Enlargement

Tunnel Mountain Dr

Tunnel Mtn Hoodoos Trail

Tunnel Mountain Rd

▲ Tunnel Mtn

2

3

To Cave & Basin National Historic Site (3km)

Trail

Park Ave

Spray Ave

Glen Ave

Cave Ave

Birch Ave

Bow River

St Julien Rd

Bow Falls

Mountain Ave

Kootenay Ave

Rundle Ave

4

5

6

Upper Terminal

0 _____ 100 m
0 _____ 0.1 mile

Marten St

Lynx St

Bear St

Banff Ave

Beaver St

Muskrat St

Wolf St

Caribou St

Buffalo St

Central Park

Bow River

Past the bridge, Mountain Ave leads south to the Banff Gondola and Upper Hot Springs, while Spray Ave leads to the Banff Springs Hotel, the town's most famous landmark. To the west, Cave Ave goes to the Cave & Basin National Historic Site, which preserves the first hot springs found in the area.

Information

BOOKSTORES

Banff Book & Art Den (☎ 403-762-3919; 94 Banff Ave; ☸ 9am-9pm) Features comfortable quarters and a good reading selection – including books on the mountains, history and local outdoor activities.

EMERGENCY

Banff Warden Office Dispatch Line (☎ 403-762-1470) Open 24 hours for nonemergency backcountry problems.

Mineral Springs Hospital (☎ 403-762-2222; 301 Lynx St; ☸ 24hr) Emergency medical treatment.

Police, ambulance, fire or backcountry emergencies (☎ 911)

INTERNET ACCESS

Underground (☎ 403-760-8776; 211 Banff Ave; per hr $6) Numerous terminals. There also are coin-fed terminals (per hour $6) in malls and hotels throughout town.

MONEY

Custom House Currency Exchange (☎ 403-760-6630; 211 Banff Ave; ☸ 9am-10pm) In the Park Ave Mall.

POST

Post office (☎ 403-762-2586; 204 Buffalo St; ☸ 9am-5:30pm Mon-Fri)

TOURIST INFORMATION

Banff Information Center (☎ 403-762-1550; www.parkscanada.gc.ca/banff; 224 Banff Ave; ☸ 8am-6pm, to 8pm in summer, 9am-noon & 1-5pm in winter) Offices for Parks Canada.

Banff/Lake Louise Tourism Bureau (☎ 403-762-8421; www.banfflakelouise.com; ☸ 8am-6pm, to 8pm in summer, 9am-noon & 1-5pm in winter) In the same building as the Banff Information Center; gives advice on services and activities in and around Banff Town.

Sights

WHYTE MUSEUM OF THE CANADIAN ROCKIES

The must-see **Whyte Museum** (☎ 403-762-2291; www.whyte.org; 111 Bear St; adult/senior & student $6/3.50; ☸ 10am-5pm) features an art gallery and a vast collection of photographs telling the history of early explorers, artists and the CPR. Special shows focus on particular aspects of mountain life around the world. The museum also hosts films, lectures and concerts and runs 90-minute **Historic Banff Walks** (admission $7; ☸ 3pm Jun-Sep).

BANFF GONDOLA

For spectacular views over the surrounding mountains, Bow River and Banff Town, ride up the **Banff Gondola** (☎ 403-762-2523; Mountain Ave; adult/child aged 6-15 $22/11; ☸ 7:30am-9pm summer, 10am-4pm winter, reduced hrs spring & fall, closed Jan 6-17). The gondola zips you to the 2285m summit of Sulphur Mountain in about eight minutes. An observation terrace, restaurants and a historic weather station are on top.

ALBERTA

Alternatively, you can hike up the mountain's steep east side – about two hours one way – and get a free gondola ride down (tickets are only needed going up). The trail starts from the Upper Hot Springs parking lot.

The gondola's lower terminal, adjacent to the Upper Hot Springs pool, is about 4km south of Banff on Mountain Ave. You can hitch a ride from town fairly easily, or take the Brewster shuttle bus (p618).

CAVE & BASIN NATIONAL HISTORIC SITE

Used therapeutically by Canada's Aboriginal people for more than 10,000 years, **Cave & Basin** (☎ 403-762-1566; Cave Ave; adult/child $4/3; ☉ 9am-6pm summer, 11am-4pm Mon-Fri & 9:30am-5pm Sat & Sun rest of year) has been attracting tourists to its eggy-smelling sulphur waters for more than 110 years. In fact, it was largely the spring's popularity that led to the establishment of the original nature reserve that later became Banff National Park. You can no longer bathe in the bubbling waters, but you can wander around the restored 1914 complex, as well as view exhibits and a 30-minute film.

BANFF UPPER HOT SPRINGS

You'll find a soothing hot pool, steam room, spa and excellent mountain views at these **hot springs** (☎ 403-762-1515; end of Mountain Ave; adult/student $7.50/6.50; ☉ 9am-11pm summer, 10am-10pm Sun-Thu, 10am-11pm Fri & Sat rest of year), near the Banff Gondola, 4km south of town. The water emerges from the spring at 47°C; in winter it has to be cooled before entering the pool, but in spring the snowmelt does that job. In addition to the pool, you can indulge in a massage or an aromatherapy wrap. Bathing suits, towels and lockers can be rented. At the time of research the springs had dried up and the pool was being filled with tap water (still hot, but kind of defeats the purpose). It was hoped the dry-up was a temporary result of a long drought in the province, but no one could be sure when the springs would flow again.

LAKE MINNEWANKA

Peaks and forests surround the park's largest reservoir, Lake Minnewanka, 13km east of Banff Town, making it a popular escape from downtown Banff. The scenic recreational area features plenty of hiking, swimming, sailing, boating and fishing opportunities.

Lake Minnewanka Boat Tours (☎ 403-762-3473; www.minnewankaboattours.com; adult/child $30/13; ☉ 4-5 departures 10:30am-7pm mid-May–Sep, 10:30am-5pm Sep–early-Oct) offers a 90-minute cruise on the lake to Devil's Gap that gives plenty of insight into the region's history and geology. You can also fish here or hike to the Alymer Lookout trail for spectacular lake and mountain views. There is no public transport to the lake.

BANFF PARK MUSEUM

Occupying an old wooden CPR building dating from 1903, this **museum** (☎ 403-762-1558; 93 Banff Ave; adult/child $3/2; ☉ 10am-6pm summer, 1-5pm rest of year) is a national historic site. Its exhibits – a taxidermal collection of animals found in the park, including grizzly and black bear, plus a tree carved with graffiti dating from 1841 – have changed little since the museum opened a century ago.

LUXTON MUSEUM OF THE PLAINS INDIANS

The **Luxton Museum** (☎ 403-762-2388; 1 Birch Ave; adult/senior & student/child 6-12 $8/6/2.50; ☉ 9am-6pm) illustrates the history of Alberta's indigenous peoples with life-sized displays, models and re-creations depicting various aspects of traditional cultures – from clothing to hunting equipment.

Activities

HIKING

You could spend months in Banff National Park and not hike all of the park's trails. Whether you are up for climbing a snow-capped peak or just taking a quiet stroll through the woods, hiking is the perfect way to really experience the park's sublime beauty.

Before doing any hiking, check in at the Banff Information Centre. Parks Canada staff will tell you about specific trail conditions and hazards. They can also provide you with a couple of excellent free brochures. Pick up *Day Hikes in Banff National Park* for an outline of hikes accessible from Banff Town.

You can take a pleasant, quiet stroll by **Bow River**, just three blocks west of Banff Ave beside Bow Ave. The trail runs from the corner of Wolf St along the river under the Bow River Bridge and ends shortly after on Buffalo St. If you cross the bridge, you can continue southeast through the woods along a trail to nearby **Bow Falls**.

For a good short climb to break in your legs and to view the area, walk up stubby **Tunnel Mountain**, east of downtown. A trail leads up from St Julien Rd; you can drive here, but it's not a long walk from downtown to the start of the path.

From the southern end of Buffalo St, a short interpretive trail between Bow River and Tunnel Mountain heads north and east to the **Tunnel Mountain hoodoos**. The term 'hoodoo' refers to the distinctive vertical pillar shapes carved into the rock face by rainfall and glacial erosion.

Just west of downtown, off Mt Norquay Rd, is the 2km **Fenland Trail** loop, which goes through marsh and forest and connects the town with First Vermilion Lake.

For longer, more remote hiking, get the *Backcountry Visitors' Guide,* which contains a simple map showing trails and backcountry campgrounds throughout the park, as well as recommended two- to five-day treks. Anybody hiking overnight in the backcountry must sign in and buy a wilderness permit ($6 per night per person).

If you can't make it to the Banff Information Center, get up-to-date trail reports in a recorded telephone message (☎ 403-760-1305) or on the park's website (www.parks canada.gc.ca/banff).

CANOEING & KAYAKING
Canoeing and kayaking are peaceful ways to experience the park and watch for wildlife. The season runs from about mid-May to early October. You can go canoeing on **Lake Minnewanka** and nearby **Two Jack Lake**, northeast of Banff. The **Vermilion Lakes**, three shallow lakes connected by narrow waterways, attract lots of wildlife and make excellent spots for canoeing. To get to the lakes, head northwest out of town along Lynx St and follow signs toward Hwy 1. Just before the highway, turn left onto Vermilion Lakes Dr and you'll soon come to small parking areas for the lakes.

You can rent a canoe from **Bow River Canoe Rentals** (☎ 403-762-3632; Cnr Bow Ave & Wolf St; per hr/day $16/40).

HORSEBACK RIDING
Horseback riding is the perfect way to reach backcountry trails with a minimal effort on your part (although more so on the horses). **Warner Guiding and Outfitting** (☎ 800-661-8352;

www.horseback.com; 132 Banff Ave) offers a variety of horseback-riding trips from covered-wagon cookouts ($66) to an hour-long ride along Spray River ($30) to a full-day ride up Sulphur Mountain, including a down-home barbecue ($135). The company also runs two- to six-day backcountry lodge and camping trips.

SKIING & SNOWBOARDING
Three excellent mountain resorts, all with spectacular scenery, are near Banff Town.

Sunshine Village (☎ 403-762-6500, 877-542-2633, snow conditions 403-277-7669; www.skibanff.com; lift ticket $60) straddles the continental divide and on one lift you'll cross into BC and then back into Alberta. The new super-fast gondola zips you quickly to the top, and the steeps at this resort are nothing short of awesome. Experts can show off their skills on a slew of shoots named after local legends, but you'll need an avalanche beacon, shovel, probe and partner to be allowed past the control gates.

Lake Louise Ski Area (☎ 403-522-3555, 800-258-7669; www.skilouise.com; lift ticket $59), 60km west of Banff Town near the Samson Mall, ranks among Canada's largest ski areas, with 17 sq km of skiable terrain spread over four mountain faces. Ski magazine ranked Lake Louise Ski Area the top resort in North America for scenery in their 2003 reader survey, and we can't really argue – you may spend more time staring at Lake Louise and Victoria Glacier than actually skiing the front side of the mountain. The back side is an endless, isolated, rugged, above-tree-line wilderness. Snowboarders should check out the Jungle, a massive terrain park with a 5.2m radius super-pipe.

Ski Banff @ Norquay (☎ 403-762-4421, 866-464-7669; www.banffnorquay.com; Mt Norquay Rd; lift ticket $46), just 6km north of downtown Banff, is the area's oldest resort. It has trails for all levels of skiers and a terrain park for boarders.

Local buses shuttle riders from Banff hotels to all three resorts (one-way/return from $6/10) every half hour during the season. A three-day ski pass, usable at all three resorts, is $199. Other multiday packages are also available.

WHITE-WATER RAFTING
Whether you're a novice, have the kids in tow or are after some serious adrenalin-pumping rapids, the companies in Banff

ALBERTA

have you covered. Trips run on the Bow River, which is good for floating and has some intermediate white water in Horseshoe Canyon, the Kananaskis River (which offers more novice excitement) and the more turbulent Kicking Horse (which includes some Class III-IV rapids).

The following companies offer tours starting at around $60:

Adventures Unlimited/Hydra River Guides (☎ 403-762-4554; www.raftbanff.com; 207 Caribou St)

Canadian Rockies Rafting Company (☎ 403-678-6535; www.rafting.ca) Includes the chance to go cliff-jumping and body surfing on all trips.

Wild Water Adventures (☎ 403-522-2211; www.wildwater.com; Fairmont Chateau Hotel, Lake Louise) Offers transport from Banff Town. Runs half-, one- and two-day rafting trips (from $64).

CYCLING

You can cycle on the highways and on some of the park trails. Popular routes around Banff Town include Sundance (7.4km roundtrip) and Spray River Loop (12.5km), both recommended for families. Spray River & Goat Creek (19km one way) is a moderate ride, while Rundle Riverside (14km one way) is more challenging, with ups-and-downs and rough root riding.

Snowtips/Bactrax (☎ 403-762-8177; 225 Bear St; tours per hr $15, rentals per hr/day from $10/36) runs excellent two- to four-hour mountain biking tours on popular trails, and rents a variety of bikes.

Parks Canada publishes the brochure *Mountain Biking & Cycling Guide – Banff National Park,* which describes trails and regulations.

ROCK CLIMBING

Banff National Park's rocky crags and limestone peaks present almost endless opportunities for good climbing. In fact, many of the world's best climbers live in nearby Canmore so that they can enjoy easy access to this mountain playground. This is not terrain for unguided novice climbers; even experienced climbers wanting to go it alone should first talk to locals, read books and get the weather lowdown before venturing out.

Inexperienced climbers will find quite a few companies offering climbing courses and organized tours into the mountains. **Banff Adventure Centre** (☎ 403-762-8536; www.mountainguide.com; 224 Bear St; 🕒 9am-6pm) is a good place to start. There are half-day trips ($69) for those with no previous climbing experience and multiday climbs (from $240) for those with a little to a lot of experience.

Tours

Brewster Gray Line (☎ 403-762-6767; www.brewster.ca; 100 Gopher St) offers a number of bus tours from Banff through the Rockies parks. The three-hour 'Discover Banff' tour (adult/child $43/22) goes to the hoodoos, Tunnel Mountain Dr, Sulphur Mountain (gondola ride not included in tour price) and Cave & Basin National Historic Site. Brewster also runs tours to Lake Louise, the Columbia Icefield and Jasper. Brewster Gray Line also runs a nine-hour 'Beautiful Banff' tour (adult/child $97/49).

A couple of companies offer budget-oriented tours, with overnight stays at HI hostels along the way. These tours are generally geared towards younger, backpacker types (usually ages 18 to 30), but are open to anyone. For more information see p576.

Bigfoot Adventure Tours (☎ 604-772-9905, 888-244-6673; www.bigfoottours.com) offers a two-day tour from Banff to Jasper and back again for $95, also not including accommodations and food.

The Whyte Museum of the Canadian Rockies organizes 90-minute Historic Banff Walks.

Festivals & Events

The town's biggest annual event is the dual **Banff Mountain Book Festival** and **Banff Mountain Film Festival** (☎ 800-413-8368; www.banffmountainfestivals.ca), held consecutively in late October and early November.

Sleeping

Compared with elsewhere in the province, accommodations in Banff Town is fairly costly and, in summer, often hard to find. The old adage of the early bird catching the worm really holds true here, and booking ahead is strongly recommended. The rates listed here apply to the high season (basically July and August) and low season (the rest of the year), although in the dead of winter rooms may be even cheaper. If you're not camping or staying at hostels, B&Bs and private tourist homes can be a reasonably priced alternative, and they're usually good sources of local information.

The Banff/Lake Louise Tourism Bureau tracks vacancies on a daily basis; check the listings at the Banff Information Centre. You might also try **Banff/Lake Louise Central Reservations** (☎ 403-705-4015, 877-542-2633; www.banff reservations.com), which books rooms for more than 75 different lodgings.

Some people stay in Canmore (p605) or Golden, BC (p756) just outside the park, where the rates are lower, then enter the park on a day-trip basis.

BUDGET

Samesun Banff (☎ 403-762-5521, 888-844-7875; www.samesun.com/banff_hostel.html; 449 Banff Ave; dm/ d $26/75; 🖵) This place is everything a hostel should be – brightly painted, lively and full of backpackers ready to party. It arranges different activities each night – from movie nights to pub-crawls to keg parties – and it draws a young international crowd. The Samesun fills quickly, so its wise to book ahead.

HI-Banff Alpine Centre (☎ 403-762-4122, 866-762-4122; www.hostellingintl.ca/alberta; 801 Coyote Dr; dm/d from $28/80) If organized activities galore is what you're searching for then this hostel may be the answer. Spacious buildings, fireplaces and big decks contribute to an alpine-meets-institutional atmosphere. There's a pub and restaurant on site as well as a self-catering kitchen. Located at the top of Tunnel Mountain, you can reach the hostel by taking a free shuttle from the bus depot or by hopping on the public bus from downtown.

Banff National Park contains 13 front-country campgrounds, most of which lie right around the townsite or along the Bow Valley Parkway. Most are open only between May or June and September. They are all busy in July and August, and availability is on a first-come, first-served basis, so check in by noon or you may be turned away. Campgrounds with showers always fill up first.

Johnston Canyon Campground (Bow Valley Parkway; tent sites from $22; 🌣 early-Jun–mid-Sep) One of Banff's finest campgrounds, this place is located next to Johnston Creek. Its 132 wooded sites are clean and well-maintained and a number of them are wheelchair-accessible. In the heart of Bow Valley, the campground is about 26km west of Banff. Facilities include flush toilets and showers.

Two Jack Lakeside (Minnewanka Loop Dr; tent sites from $17; 🌣 mid-May–mid-Sep) This campground

has showers and 80 sites set in the trees next to the lake, 12km northeast of Banff. It's close to lots of trails for day hikes and fills up quickly.

Two Jack Main Campground (Minnewanka Loop Dr; tent sites from $13; 🌣 mid-May–mid-Sep) If Two Jack Lakeside is full, try this much larger campground about 1km north. It features 381 sites, flush toilets and running water but no showers, and caters mostly to RVs.

Tunnel Mountain Village (Tunnel Mountain Rd; tent/RV sites $22/30) This complex, at the top of Tunnel Mountain Rd, includes three separate campgrounds with a whopping 618 tent sites. All are close to town and have flush toilets and showers. Another advantage is it remains open year-round.

MID-RANGE

Hidden Ridge Resort (☎ 403-762-3544; www.bestof banff.com/hrr/; 901 Coyote Dr; r low/high $124/204) This is a great place for families. Accommodations is in chalets with full kitchens, wood-burning stoves and barbecues. There's a giant hot tub nestled among the pine trees and a number of rooms have lofts for the kids to camp out in. Baby-sitting services are available.

Rundlestone Lodge (☎ 403-762-2201; www.rundle stone.com; 537 Banff Ave; r low/high from $105/187; 🖵) The loft suites come with whirlpools and wood-burning fireplaces, and you should try for one, especially in the winter. The standard rooms are pretty run-of-the-mill, but cheaper.

Treetops B&B (☎ 403-762-2809; www.banfftree tops.com; 336 Beaver St; r $125-145) In a wooden chalet with superb mountain views, this family-run B&B has cozy yet classy rooms and a rustic private lounge where the fire roars all winter long. Breakfast is a health-oriented buffet.

Banff Aspen Lodge (☎ 403-762-4401, 800-661-0227; www.banfftravellersinn.com; 401 Banff Ave; r low/high $90/190; 🖵) This place features friendly staff and a good location close to the center of town. The rooms have large balconies; other amenities include an outdoor hot tub and heated underground parking.

Red Carpet Inn (☎ 403-762-4184, 800-563-4609; 425 Banff Ave; r low/high $75/125) Rooms are motel standard at the Red Carpet, but it's close to town. Guests can use the pool next door at the High Country Inn, and it is quite good value for money.

ALBERTA

Irwin's Mountain Inn (☎ 403-762-4566, 800-661-1721; www.irwinsmountaininn.com; 429 Banff Ave; r low/high $75/165; 🚗) Amenities here include covered parking, a hot tub, sauna and fitness center; rooms are clean, but nothing special in the looks department.

TOP END

Fairmont Banff Springs (☎ 403-762-2211, 800-441-1414; www.fairmont.com/banffsprings; 405 Spray Ave; r low/high from $150/379; 🔲 🚗 P) Since it was completed in the 1920s, this 800-room baronial palace, about 2km south of downtown, has posed for thousands of postcards and millions of snapshots. The spectacular design includes towers, turrets and cornices, giving the impression that the hotel is full of hidden secrets. Within its thick granite walls are a myriad of public spaces, bars and restaurants. Even if you're not staying here, it's a fascinating place to wander around. If you visit in the off-season it's a very good deal and, regardless of season, it's *the* place to stay in Banff.

Rimrock Resort Hotel (☎ 403-762-3356, 800-661-1587; www.rimrockresort.com; 300 Mountain Ave; r low/high $255/365; 🚗) Classy with spectacular mountain views, this is one of Banff's top hotels. Rooms are large and luxurious with almost-too-comfortable beds. If the place is empty you just may score a very cheap walk-in rate.

Royal Canadian Lodge (☎ 403-762-3307; banff@charhonresorts.com; 459 Banff Ave; r low/high $240/500; 🚗 🔲) This place is luxurious, although you pay extra for the little things such as secure parking, high-speed Internet access and Nintendo. The digs are slightly small, but well appointed. The bathrooms are fabulous and rooms come with fluffy robes. Don't miss the grotto-style indoor pool and hot tub; it's mineral-water-fed and contains no chlorine.

Sunshine Village Inn (☎ 403-762-6500; Sunshine Village Ski Area; r from $270; 🌙 ski season) On the top of the gondola at Sunshine Village Ski Resort, this place has exceptional views and a bar and restaurant. If you're looking for that first fresh early-morning powder run, you can't beat the location. On the downside, the gondola closes at 9pm, so you'll have to be back by then. At night it's just you and a million stars, perfect for a romantic getaway. To reach the hotel you need to ride the gondola to the top of the resort.

Eating

Like any resort town, Banff has plenty of restaurants. Some of the better ones are listed below. The menu is always varied in Banff – you can choose from healthy wraps, Irish pub grub or elegant Canadian classics such as thick Alberta beef steaks.

BUDGET

Evelyn's Coffee Bar (☎ 403-762-0352; 201 Banff Ave; mains $6; 🌙 breakfast, lunch & dinner) The best local coffee place, this spot at the Park Ave Mall is packed at lunch when locals crowd in for the homemade sandwiches, wraps and soups, not to mention the freshly baked cookies and muffins.

Sunfood Café (☎ 403-760-3933; 215 Banff Ave; mains from $5; 🌙 lunch & dinner) On the upper level of Sundance Mall, this place offers a great vegetarian menu of organic soups, salads, sandwiches, hot dishes and desserts for lunch and dinner. It's also a quiet place to sit and write a postcard.

Sushi House Banff (☎ 403-762-4353; 304 Caribou St; sushi plates $2-5; 🌙 lunch & dinner) At Sushi House a minitrain chugs around the sushi counter and you take your pick from its cargo.

MID-RANGE

Coyote's Deli & Grill (☎ 403-762-3963; 206 Caribou St; breakfast $8, lunch mains $9-13, dinner mains $20; 🌙 breakfast, lunch & dinner) If you want inventive Southwestern cuisine, try Coyote's, where the open kitchen gives you a chance to see the chefs in action. The hip and lively setting is as refreshing as the menu. We especially liked the innovative breakfast options.

Cilantro Mountain Café (☎ 403-760-3008; Tunnel Mountain Rd; mains $20; 🌙 lunch & dinner, closed Mon & Tue) In a tiny wood cabin on top of Tunnel Mountain, the café's wood-burning oven churns out pizza, venison and duck prepared with fresh seasonal ingredients. Regulars pack the outdoor patio when it's warm.

Giorgio's Trattoria (☎ 403-762-5114; 219 Banff Ave; mains $12-26; 🌙 dinner) A perennial local favorite, the Trattoria serves homemade pasta and wood-fired pizza amidst twinkling candles, making this one of Banff's most romantic dining experiences.

Guido's Ristorante (☎ 403-762-4002; 116 Banff Ave; mains $11-25; 🌙 dinner) Another local favorite, Guido's has been serving Italian food to Banffonians for 30 years now. It's a low-key

JOHN McINNES

Polar bear–watching in Churchill
(p548), Manitoba

MARK LIGHTBODY

Hudson Bay coastline, Churchill (p545),
Manitoba

Cultural dance performance at Wanuskewin Heritage Park (p568), Saskatchewan

MARK LIGHTBODY

RICK RUDNICKI

Rodeo rider at the Calgary Stampede (p597), Calgary

MARK NEWMAN

Maligne Canyon (p623), Jasper National Park

RICHARD CUMMINS

Nigerian dancer at the Edmonton Heritage Festival (p583)

Moraine Lake (p619), Banff National Park

ANDREW BROWNBILL

place with a delicious dessert menu and a good wine list.

Typhoon (☎ 403-762-2000; 211 Caribou St; mains from $10; ☺ lunch & dinner) Eclectic Asian cuisine is served in a bright, colorful interior that still manages to remain intimate. The restaurant blends the tastes of India, Thailand and Indonesia with excellent results. Sample the curries and satays.

St James Gate Olde Irish Pub (☎ 403-762-9355; 205 Wolf St; mains from $10; ☺ lunch & dinner) This wonderful pub has great food and fun Irish music and atmosphere. But pub aficionados come for the 35 taps – with Guinness and many other European favorites – plus 55 Scotch and 10 Irish whiskeys. The pub is named after the Dublin address of the original (and still operational) Guinness Brewery, founded by 34-year-old Arthur Guinness in 1759.

Melissa's Restaurant (☎ 403-762-5511; 218 Lynx St; burgers $8, mains from $15; ☺ breakfast, lunch & dinner) A major local favorite (especially at breakfast), Melissa's occupies a log building from 1928 that looks like a wood cabin inside and an English cottage outside. The menu includes pizza, burgers, steak and more. Don your fleece vest and blend in with the locals on Tuesday, when highball cocktails are only $1.50.

Magpie & Stump (☎ 403-762-4067; 203 Caribou St; lunch mains $8, dinner mains $15; ☺ lunch & dinner) Decorated with saddles, guns and sombreros, Magpie serves absolutely huge portions of Tex-Mex cuisine in cozy surroundings. Order dishes mild or try them hot. It's a kid-friendly place with highchairs and a children's menu.

Bruno's Cafe & Grill (☎ 403-762-8115; 304 Caribou St; mains $6-20; ☺ breakfast, lunch & dinner) If you sleep late but still want breakfast, Bruno's is the place to go – it serves breakfast all day. Offering a wide-ranging menu including salads, burgers and vegetarian dishes, Bruno's is a fun place that packs in the crowds. There's occasional live music and a daily happy hour.

TOP END

Banffshire Club (☎ 403-762-6860; Banff Springs Hotel; 2/3/4 courses $100/110/120; ☺ dinner) With the flickering candlelight and harp music wafting through the room, the posh, award-winning Banffshire exudes intimacy. Elaborate mains include cedar-roasted sablefish, pecan-crusted caribou and roasted partridge

with truffles. The wine cellar overflows with more than 600 different labels. Jackets are required for the gents; ties are optional.

Grizzly House (☎ 403-762-4055; 207 Banff Ave; mains from $35; ☺ lunch & dinner) A local institution, the Grizzly House achieves a romantic atmosphere with soft lighting and secluded booths. The menu is fondue-oriented – everything from boring cheese, to beef and lobster, to the very exotic consisting of rattlesnake, shark, caribou and ostrich to name just a few.

Eden (☎ 403-762-1840; Rimrock Resort Hotel; 8/10 courses $110/150; ☺ dinner) An award-winning restaurant – for its food and its wine list – Eden presents delicately crafted mouthwatering multicourse French dinners to its discerning guests. The dining room is intimate, with plenty of mountain views to go around. Dress is smart casual.

Le Beaujolais (☎ 403-762-2712; Banff Ave at Buffalo St; mains from $30, 3-course dinner $55; ☺ dinner) The acclaimed Beaujolais employs regional ingredients in its gourmet French cuisine. The menu is as sophisticated as the decor and the food is perfectly presented.

Maple Leaf Grille & Spirits (☎ 403-760-7680; 137 Banff Ave; lunch mains $8-18, dinner mains $17-38; ☺ lunch & dinner) One of Banff's top restaurants, the Maple Leaf serves organic Canadian cuisine such as buffalo, beef, elk, venison and west coast oysters. The atmosphere is sedate with stone and wood, and there are mountain views out the big windows.

Saltlik (☎ 403-762-2467; 221 Bear St; mains $25; ☺ lunch & dinner) This upscale steak house has a trendy, elegant atmosphere with bright local artwork gracing the walls. The sauces set this place apart – top your steak with a citrus rosemary butter or blue cheese cream.

Drinking & Entertainment

Banff Town is the social and cultural center of the Rockies. You can find current entertainment listings in the 'Summit Up' section of the weekly *Banff Crag & Canyon* newspaper, or in the monthly *Wild Life*.

Wild Bill's Legendary Saloon (☎ 403-762-0333; 201 Banff Ave) A true cowboy hangout, this is the place to chug pints and two-step the night away. Dedicated to the memory of legendary Bill Peyto (see the boxed text on p609), Wild Bill's, upstairs in the Town Centre Mall, is Banff's hottest nightspot and is crammed any night of the week. Try the 'Rocky Mountain Bear Fuck' shooter.

ALBERTA

It's awful, but we couldn't resist the name, and if you drink enough of them you may just see that grizzly bear you've been hoping to spot wandering down Banff Ave. If all the drinking makes you hungry, the pub-grub is better than average.

Rundle Lounge (☎ 403-762-6860; Banff Springs Hotel, 405 Spray Ave) If you'd like to soak up a little glamour at Banff's ritziest hotel, the Rundle Lounge, upstairs in the Banff Springs Hotel, is the place to go. The chandeliers sparkle, the chairs are comfy and the views are worth a million dollars (or a million photographs). Everyone should have at least one late-afternoon cocktail here.

Barbary Coast (☎ 403-762-7673; 119 Banff Ave) A great place for happy hour. Grab a large basket of peanuts and chomp away leaving the shells on the floor – the later you arrive the more likely you'll be to trip over the escalating mounds of peanut shells. With a variety of beer on tap, locals flock to this low-key bar.

Lic Lounge (☎ 403-762-2467; 221 Bear St) The very hip Lic plays funky music and has big couches and a heated patio. DJs spin jazz and funk on Sunday evenings.

Tommy's Neighbourhood Pub (☎ 403-762-8888; 120 Banff Ave) A local crowd comes here for the sunken patio – perfect for Banff Ave people-watching. Tommy's gained notoriety when ZZ Top dropped in for ouzo shooters.

Rose & Crown (☎ 403-762-2121; 202 Banff Ave) This British-style pub is a smoky place with lots of beers on tap, a pool table and darts. Sunday evenings feature live bands and there's a rooftop patio when the weather cooperates.

Hoodoo Club (☎ 403-762-8434; 137 Banff Ave) Banff's club du jour at the time of research, Hoodoo is a packed basement nightclub filled with young people looking to hook up and dance. There is live music or a DJ nightly.

Aurora Nightclub (☎ 403-760-5300; 110 Banff Ave) Another place to groove and sweat is the Aurora, downstairs in the Clock Tower Village Mall. It has a state-of-the-art sound and light show and stays hopping well into the morning hours.

Banff Centre (☎ 403-762-6100, 800-413-8368; www .banffcentre.ca; 107 Tunnel Mountain Dr) Dance, theater, music and the visual arts are all on tap here. One of Canada's best-known art schools, the Centre regularly schedules public exhibits, concerts and other events throughout the year.

Lux Cinema Centre (☎ 403-762-8595; 229 Bear St) The local movie house screens first-run films.

Getting There & Away
AIR
The nearest airport is in Calgary.

BUS
Greyhound Canada (☎ 403-762-1092; 100 Gopher St) operates buses to Calgary ($25, 1¾ hours, five daily), Vancouver ($116, 14 hours, five daily) and points in-between.

Brewster Transportation (☎ 403-762-6767) operates from the Greyhound station and services Jasper ($51, four hours, daily) from April to October. It also runs buses to Lake Louise ($11, one hour, multiple buses daily).

In summer, **SunDog Tour Co** (☎ 780-852-4056; www.sundogtours.com) runs a shuttle between Banff and Jasper (adult/child $55/35, four hours, daily) stopping at all the hostels along the way. Fares to points in-between are based on length of trip. For an extra charge, you can arrange to take bikes on the shuttle.

CAR
All of the major car rental companies (p872) have branches in Banff Town. During summer all the cars might be reserved in advance, so call ahead. If you're flying into Calgary, reserving a car from the airport (where the fleets are huge) may yield a better deal than waiting to pick up a car when you reach Banff Town. **Banff Rent-A-Car** (☎ 403-762-3352; 204 Lynx St) is the local agent.

Getting Around
TO/FROM THE AIRPORT
Shuttle buses operate daily year-round between Calgary International Airport and Banff. Buses are less frequent in the spring and fall. Companies include **Rocky Mountain Sky Shuttle** (☎ 403-762-5200, 888-762-8754), **Brewster Transportation** (☎ 403-762-6767, 800-661-1152) and **Banff Airporter** (☎ 403-762-3330, 888-449-2901). The adult fare with all three companies is around $40 one way and $75 round trip.

BUS
Banff Transit (☎ 403-760-8294) operates two trolley bus routes through town. One route follows Spray and Banff Aves between the Banff Springs Hotel and the RV parking lot north of town; the other goes from the Luxton

Museum along Banff Ave, Wolf St, Otter St and Tunnel Mountain Rd to the hostel and Tunnel Mountain Village Campgrounds. Both stop at the Banff Information Centre. Buses operate every 30 minutes from 7am to midnight, mid-May to September, and from noon to midnight the rest of the year. The fare is $1/50¢ adult/child.

There's also a **Brewster shuttle bus** (☎ 403-762-6767; cnr Banff Ave & Caribou St; adult $5; ☺ hourly May-Oct) that operates in town.

TAXI

For cab service, try **Taxi Taxi & Tours** (☎ 403-762-3111) or **Mountain Taxi & Tours** (☎ 403-762-3351). Taxis are metered.

LAKE LOUISE

Known as the jewel of the Rockies, this stunning, emerald-green lake, about 57km north of Banff Town, sits in a small glacial valley surrounded by the tall, snowy peaks that hoist the hefty Victoria Glacier up for all to see. Depending on the stillness of the water and the angle of the sun, the lake's color will appear slightly different from each viewpoint and on each visit. On calm days, you may witness extraordinary reflections of the surrounding scenery.

Lake Louise is one of the park's busiest spots, and in summer you'll be greeted by wall-to-wall buses and camera-touting tourists. Despite the crowds and the humongous, out-of-place Chateau Lake Louise, which sits ostentatiously at the lake's north end, Lake Louise remains a magical place that should be a must-see on your park itinerary. A number of walks begin at the lakeshore and offer spectacular views, peaceful settings and even an alpine teahouse or two. These are a good way to escape the gawking crowds and shouldn't be missed. You can also rent boats and paddle into the middle of the lake for quieter views.

Before you get to the lake you'll come to the uninspiring village of Lake Louise, which is really nothing more than the small Samson Mall shopping center, a service station, and a few lodgings. The lake itself is 5km away. In summer, Parks Canada runs a shuttle bus from the village to Lake Louise and Moraine Lake. If you'd rather walk, it'll take you about 45 minutes on the footpath from the village to Lake Louise.

> ### TOP FIVE THINGS TO DO WHEN IT RAINS
>
> Just because the sky is practically black and the rain is pouring down doesn't mean your entire day in the park has to be a bust. Instead try one of these activities:
>
> - Visit a museum in Banff Town or Jasper Town.
> - Go rafting – you're bound to get wet anyway.
> - Head for the hot springs in Banff or Jasper (it's so warm in there the rain will feel good).
> - Take a driving tour and look for wildlife.
> - Ask at information centers about sheltered hikes that aren't all about mountain views (try Johnston Canyon in Banff).

The Bow Valley Parkway is a slightly slower but much more scenic drive than Hwy 1 between Banff Town and Lake Louise.

Information

The **Lake Louise Visitor Centre** (☎ 403-522-3833; beside Samson Mall, Lake Louise village; ☺ 9am-7pm summer, 9am-5pm spring & fall, 9am-4pm winter) doles out information on the park and on activities and services in the village.

Sights & Activities

MORAINE LAKE

The scenery will dazzle you long before you reach the spectacular deep-teal colored waters of Moraine Lake. The lake is set in the Valley of the Ten Peaks, and the narrow, winding road leading to it offers views of the distant, imposing Wenkchemna Peaks. With little hustle or bustle and lots of beauty, many people prefer the more rugged and remote setting of Moraine Lake to Lake Louise. There are some excellent day hikes from the lake, or rent a boat at the **Moraine Lake Boathouse** (per hr $27; ☺ 9am-4pm Jun-Oct) and paddle through the glacier-fed waters. You can stay at the Moraine Lake Lodge or just stop by for a coffee or lunch at the restaurant.

Moraine Lake Rd and its facilities are open from June to early October.

LAKE LOUISE SIGHTSEEING GONDOLA

In summer, the Lake Louise Ski Area will scoot you up Mt Whitehorn in its **gondola**

ALBERTA

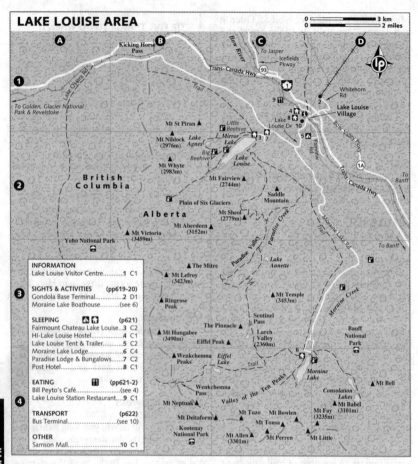

LAKE LOUISE AREA

INFORMATION	
Lake Louise Visitor Centre............1	C1

SIGHTS & ACTIVITIES	(pp619-20)
Gondola Base Terminal................2	D1
Moraine Lake Boathouse............(see 6)	

SLEEPING	(p621)
Fairmount Chateau Lake Louise...3	C2
HI-Lake Louise Hostel..................4	C1
Lake Louise Tent & Trailer...........5	C2
Moraine Lake Lodge....................6	C4
Paradise Lodge & Bungalows.......7	C2
Post Hotel.................................8	C1

EATING	(pp621-2)
Bill Peyto's Café.......................(see 4)	
Lake Louise Station Restaurant....9	C1

TRANSPORT	(p622)
Bus Terminal............................(see 10)	

OTHER	
Samson Mall.............................10	C1

ALBERTA

(☎ 403-522-3555; 1 Whitehorn Rd; round trip adult/child $20/10; ☼ 9am-4pm May, 8:30am-6pm Jun & Sep, 8am-6pm Jul & Aug). It's a 14-minute ride to the top station (2057m), where you'll have bird's-eye views of Lake Louise and Victoria Glacier, and access to hiking trails, a restaurant and snack bar. For skiing information, see p613.

OTHER HIKES

Note that trails may be snowbound beyond the 'normal' winter season; it has snowed here in July! The main Lake Louise trail follows the lake's northern banks west to the end of the lake and then beyond to the **Plain of Six Glaciers**. On the way is a teahouse. For a more rigorous venture, take the switchbacks up to **Mirror Lake**. There's an-

other teahouse here and good views from the **Little Beehive** and **Big Beehive** mountains. From there you can climb still higher to **Lake Agnes**, then around the long way to join the Plain of Six Glaciers trail and back along Lake Louise to the chateau. Alternatively, a popular two-hour hike takes you from Chateau Lake Louise to Lake Agnes. These trails can be followed for a couple of hours or turned into a good day's walk.

For a shorter stroll, there's a less-used path on the southern banks of Lake Louise; it begins by the boathouse and ascends through spruce forest, offering excellent views of the lake and the hotel.

The approximately 20km hike through the **Valley of the Ten Peaks**, between Moraine

Lake and Lake Louise, is highly recommended.

Take a quick detour to **Larch Valley**, where there's a stream and superb scenery. Before Larch Valley a trail heads west past **Eiffel Lake** into Yoho National Park (p757). Better still, hike to Moraine Lake from Lake Louise via **Paradise Creek** and **Sentinel Pass**. This is a full day's hike with some steep parts, but is an excellent route with great scenery. Getting up through Sentinel Pass is a long, scree-filled trek but well worth it. At the top, 2600m high, it's cool and breezy. Once at Moraine Lake you can hitchhike back to Lake Louise along Moraine Lake Rd.

It is common to see pikas (plump, furry animals also called conies) and the larger, more timid marmot along these trails. You often hear ice rumbling on the slopes, too.

There are other trails in the area as well. The free Parks Canada hiking guide lists and describes them.

ROCK CLIMBING

The **Back of the Lake**, a backwater crag, is a popular rock climbing spot. Access is easy, and there are lots of different climbing routes with interesting names such as Wicked Gravity and Chocolate Bunnies from Hell. Other places to climb, of varying degrees of difficulty, include **Mt Fairview**, **Mt Bell** and **Eiffel Peak**. Check with Parks Canada for more details. One locally recommended guide is Mark Klassen of **Corax Alpine** (☎ 403-760-0609; www.ascentguides.com).

Sleeping

Unless you camp or get a bed at the hostel, you'll have to pay a lot of loonies to stay in Lake Louise. Despite outrageous summer rates, places fill up months in advance, so booking ahead is advised.

HI-Lake Louise (☎ 403-522-2200; www.hostelling intl.ca/Alberta; Village Rd; dm/d from $24/75) Friendly and social, this large and popular hostel has a lot going on. In winter there are ski packages, in summer outdoor programs. The dorms are clean and bright, but the private rooms are rather plain and a little overpriced. A popular restaurant is on site.

Paradise Lodge & Bungalows (☎ 403-522-3595; www.paradiselodge.com; 105 Lake Louise Dr; r from $195) This cute choice, neat as a pin and very cozy, offers both lodge rooms and individual bungalows that sleep up to four people on flower-filled, manicured grounds. It's just a short walk from the lake. Try for cabin No 21, which has a very private deck overlooking endless forest.

Post Hotel (☎ 403-522-3989, 800-661-1586; www .posthotel.com; Village Rd; d from $305) In the village, this Relais & Chateaux lodging is the epitome of mountain elegance. The timber and stone conveys a warm and cozy lodge ambience, while dining and amenities – including goose-down duvets, fireplaces and hot tubs – are all first-rate. The rooms along the front are slightly cheaper, but face onto the parking lot. Those at the back have decks overlooking the river. Try for one of the suites or cabins, which have more character but fill up very quickly.

Moraine Lake Lodge (☎ 403-533-3733; www.mor rainelake.com; d from $395; ☼ Jun–Oct) On the Valley of the Ten Peaks, with lake and mountain views from every room, the cabins and lodge rooms here have a casual, relaxed air. Decor includes chunky log furniture, lots of cushions on the beds and, in most rooms, wood-burning fireplaces. These rooms fill up very quickly – book ahead.

Fairmont Chateau Lake Louise (☎ 403-522-3511, 800-441-1414; www.fairmont.com/lakelouise; Lake Louise Dr; d from $880; ☐ ☎) This gargantuan lakefront chateau doesn't have the classic charm of its sibling, the Banff Springs Hotel. Moreover, it seems unconscionable for a hotel of this size (or any size) to even be here. However, inside it's a very classy place and the rooms are plush, with small windows commanding brilliant views across the lake. The lake-facing bar is a pleasant place for an afternoon cocktail.

Lake Louise Tent & Trailer (☎ 403-522-3833; off Lake Louise Dr; tent & RV sites from $22; ☼ late-Jun–late-Sep) This is the closest campground to Lake Louise. Tent sites are pleasant and private, but a large electric fence divides you from the Bow River (and the bear!).

Eating

If you don't feel like chowing at your hotel, there are a few other eating options around town.

Bill Peyto's Café (☎ 403-670-7580; HI-Lake Louise, Village Rd; mains from $7; ☼ breakfast, lunch & dinner) Good music and good wine make this lively restaurant a popular hangout for hostel guests and locals alike. The food is tasty and filling and there's a children's

---

SILENT LEGACY

If you wandered upon the site today, deep in the Bow Valley forest, you'd find little to attest that it was once a prisoner of war camp. Nothing much remains – a rusted pot, a barbed wire fence, a few whitewashed stones – yet between 1915 and 1917 more than 600 prisoners were held here. Nevertheless, the prisoners left their mark in other ways – in the expansion of Banff Spring's Golf Course, in the building of the Cave and Basin pool and in the construction of the Bow Valley Parkway.

Few visitors to the park know that the infrastructure they enjoy was largely built by internees of WWI, the majority of them Ukrainian immigrants loyal to the British Crown and all settlers originally from enemy countries. Held in a camp beneath Castle Mountain during the summer and near Cave and Basin during the winter, prisoners suffered harsh conditions and brutal treatment. Separated from their families (women and children were imprisoned elsewhere), they were stripped of their possessions and property and forced to labor on public works. For most, their only crime was having left the Ukraine in search of a better life in Canada. It was wartime, and fear and xenophobia ran high.

In 1994, a small monument was finally erected along the Bow Valley Parkway, near the site of the camp. Take a moment to acknowledge the prisoners' unheralded contribution to the park.

---

menu. Check out the patio when the sun is shining.

Lake Louise Station Restaurant (☎ 403-522-2600; end of Sentinel Rd; lunch mains $9, dinner mains $25) Dine in the stationmaster's office surrounded by left luggage, opt for the elegant dining cars or sit outside on the patio overlooking the rails; whatever you choose you'll be glad you stopped by one of the most atmospheric places in the park. The food covers all the staples and families are welcome.

Getting There & Around

The **bus terminal** (☎ 403-522-3870) is at Samson Mall. See the Banff Town section (p618) for bus service details.

In summer, **Parks Canada** (☎ 403-762-1550; www.parkscanada.gc.ca/banff) runs the Vista shuttle bus from the village to both Moraine Lake and Lake Louise. The shuttles run to/from Lake Louise every half hour between around 8:15am and 7:30pm and to/from Moraine Lake every hour between 8:15am and 7pm, making several stops en route. At the time of research the service was free.

JASPER TOWN & AROUND

This is land of lush valleys and graceful peaks, where glaciers stretch across awe-inspiring mountains, waterfalls tumble into infinity, and rivers charge turbulently through wide-open meadows. Jasper National Park, Banff's northern counterpart, is a vast and remote wilderness of dense forests and alpine meadows and offers Banff's beauty without its crowds. The largest of Canada's Rocky Mountain parks, Jasper's greatest asset is its relative solitude. Wildlife abounds – moose, mountain lion, bear and wolves roam freely. Some of the most apparent Jasper residents are the elk, which hang out downtown during the fall rutting and spring calving seasons. They emit haunting cries and occasionally charge disrespectful tourists. Big horn sheep are also prominent; these camera-hogging animals like to pose for pictures on the side (and sometimes in the middle of) roads.

Covering a diverse 10,878 sq km, Jasper National Park is far from built up. While activities such as hiking and white-water rafting are well-established and popular, it's still easy to experience the park's serenity and remoteness. Take some time to wander off the beaten path. You may just stumble upon one of those sparkling green picture-perfect lakes, and, if you're lucky, your picture will be even more perfect when a grizzly bear lumbers up for a sip of glacier-fed water.

Orientation

Jasper Town makes a good base for exploring the park. The town is smaller and less chaotic than Banff, with a very pleasant resort-town atmosphere. The main street, Connaught Dr, has virtually everything, including the bus terminal, train station, banks, restaurants and souvenir shops. Outside the train station is a 21m totem pole carved by a Haida artisan from BC's Queen Charlotte Islands. Nearby is an old CN steam engine.

ALBERTA

Off the main street, small wooden houses bedecked with flower gardens brighten the alpine setting.

The address numbers throughout town, when posted at all, are difficult to follow.

Information

Jasper Information Centre (Map p624; ☎ 780-852-6176; www.parkscanada.gc.ca/jasper; 500 Connaught Dr; ☒ 9am-7pm summer, 9am-4pm rest of year) The Parks Canada info office. Easily one of Canada's most eye-pleasing tourist offices – it's a stone building covered in flowers and plants.

Post office (Map p624; ☎ 780-852-3041; 502 Patricia St, cnr Elm Ave; ☒ 9am-5pm Mon-Fri)

Seton General Hospital (Map p624; ☎ 780-852-3344; 518 Robson St)

Sierra Café & Internet (Map p624; ☎ 780-852-1199; 610 Connaught Dr; per hr $6) One of four Internet cafés in town.

Sights

JASPER TRAMWAY

The **tramway** (☎ 780-852-3093; www.jaspertramway .com; Whistlers Mountain Rd; adult/child $19/9; ☒ 8:30am-10:30pm Jul & Aug, 9:30am-6:30pm late-Apr–late-Jun & late-Aug–late-Sep) will zip you up 973m in just seven minutes to a boardwalk and lookout over the Rockies. On clear days you can see the Columbia Icefield, 75km south, and Mt Robson, 100km to the north in BC. You can get a bite to eat at the restaurant and then hit the hiking trails. It's a 45-minute walk to the summit, above the tree line, where it can be cool. The tramway is about 7km south of Jasper Town along Whistlers Mountain Rd off the Icefields Parkway.

MIETTE HOT SPRINGS

A good spot for a soak is the remote **Miette Hot Springs** (Map p607; ☎ 780-866-3939, 800-767-1611; www.parkscanada.gc.ca/hotsprings; Miette Rd; adult/senior & child/family $6/5/17, bathing suit rentals $1.50, towel rentals $1; ☒ 8:30am-10:30pm summer, 10:30am-9pm spring & fall), 61km northeast of Jasper off Hwy 16, near the park boundary. Miette has the hottest mineral waters in the Canadian Rockies, emerging from the ground at 54°C and cooled to around 40°C. The modern spa features two hot pools and a refreshing cool pool.

PATRICIA & PYRAMID LAKES

These lakes, about 7km northwest of town along Pyramid Lake Rd, are small and quiet.

They have hiking and horseback-riding trails, picnic sites, fishing and beaches; you can rent canoes, kayaks and windsurfers. In winter there's cross-country skiing and ice-skating. It's not uncommon to see deer, coyote or bear nearby.

LAKES ANNETTE & EDITH

Off Hwy 16, 3km northeast of town along Lodge Rd, Lake Annette and Lake Edith are at about 1000m in altitude and can be warm enough for a quick swim. The woodsy day-use area around them holds beaches, hiking and biking trails, and picnic areas. Boat rentals are available. This is a mellow, slightly-off-the-beaten-path place to kick back and soak in the beauty surrounding you.

JASPER TOWN TO MALIGNE LAKE

Maligne Lake Rd, between Jasper and Maligne (ma-*leen*) Lake, is a gorgeous drive that also provides some of the best opportunities in the park to view wildlife – with a little luck you'll spot wolf, bear or even moose on this scenic 48km stretch. About 11km east of Jasper, you pass **Maligne Canyon**, a limestone gorge about 50m deep at its deepest but just a couple of meters wide at its narrowest. From the teahouse, a trail leads down the canyon past views of waterfalls, springs, crystalline pools and interesting rock formations. Note that the tour-bus hordes all start at the teahouse, walk down the canyon a short distance and take the obligatory photo, then turn around and head directly back up for tea and scones. But you can park at the bottom and walk up toward the teahouse, through the equally spectacular and blissfully uncrowded lower canyon, until you run into them. Turn off the main road at the sign for 5th Bridge.

Continuing another 21km up the road to Maligne Lake, you'll come to **Medicine Lake**, whose level rises and falls due to the underground drainage system; sometimes the lake disappears completely.

MALIGNE LAKE

At the end of Maligne Lake Rd, 48km southeast of Jasper, is the largest of the glacier-fed lakes in the Rockies and the second largest in the world. The lake is promoted as one of the most scenic of mountain lakes, but this is perhaps unwarranted. It's a commercial, busy destination, and the classic view with

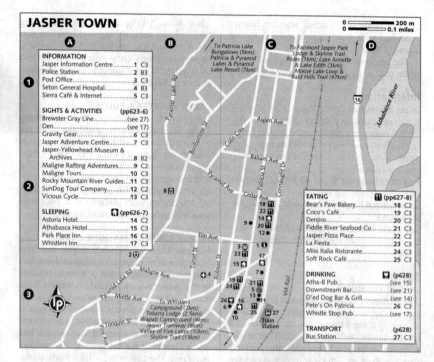

JASPER TOWN

0 —————— 200 m
0 —————— 0.1 miles

INFORMATION
Jasper Information Centre............1 C3
Police Station.................................2 B3
Post Office......................................3 C3
Seton General Hospital..................4 B3
Sierra Café & Internet....................5 C3

SIGHTS & ACTIVITIES (pp623–6)
Brewster Gray Line.....................(see 27)
Den..(see 17)
Gravity Gear...................................6 C3
Jasper Adventure Centre................7 C3
Jasper-Yellowhead Museum &
    Archives.....................................8 B2
Maligne Rafting Adventures...........9 C2
Maligne Tours...............................10 C3
Rocky Mountain River Guides......11 C3
SunDog Tour Company................12 C2
Vicious Cycle................................13 C3

SLEEPING (pp626–7)
Astoria Hotel.................................14 C2
Athabasca Hotel............................15 C3
Park Place Inn................................16 C3
Whistlers Inn..................................17 C3

To Patricia Lake
Bungalows (5km);
Patricia & Pyramid
Lakes & Pyramid
Lake Resort (7km)

To Fairmont Jasper Park
Lodge & Skyline Trail
Rides (1km); Lake Annette
& Lake Edith (3km);
Moose Lake Loop &
Bald Hills Trail (47km)

EATING (pp627–8)
Bear's Paw Bakery.........................18 C3
Coco's Café....................................19 C3
Denjiro...20 C2
Fiddle River Seafood Co................21 C3
Jasper Pizza Place..........................22 C2
La Fiesta...23 C3
Miss Italia Ristorante.....................24 C3
Soft Rock Café...............................25 C3

DRINKING (p628)
Atha-B Pub..................................(see 15)
Downstream Bar...........................(see 21)
D'ed Dog Bar & Grill....................(see 14)
Pete's On Patricia.........................26 C3
Whistle Stop Pub.........................(see 17)

TRANSPORT (p628)
Bus Station....................................27 C3

To Whistlers
Campground (2km);
Tekarra Lodge (2.5km);
Wapati Campground (4km);
Jasper Tramway (8km);
Valley of Five Lakes (10km);
Skyline Trail (13km)

Train
Station

---

the island is some kilometers out in the lake, accessible only by boat. That said, the lake is still a scenically beautiful destination.

The **Maligne Lake Boathouse** (☎ 780-852-3370; boat rentals per hr/day $15/70), on the lakeshore, rents canoes and rowboats for self-paddles around the lake. If you're not feeling quite so ambitious or are determined to see Spirit Island (where the classic views are) try **Maligne Tours** (☎ 780-852-3370; www.malignelake.com; 627 Patricia St; adult/child $35/10; ☽ 10am-5pm May-Oct). The company runs a 1½-hour boat tour to the island.

MUSEUMS

The small **Jasper-Yellowhead Museum & Archives** (Map p624; ☎ 780-852-3013; 400 Pyramid Lake Rd; adult/senior & student $4/3; ☽ 10am-9pm summer, 10am-5pm fall, 10am-5pm Tue-Sun rest of year) has some interesting displays on the town's history and development. One documents the story of the two Harragin sisters, the park's first women mountain guides (hired by Brewster in the 1920s).

Downstairs at the Whistlers Inn, a small wildlife museum called the **Den** (Map p624; ☎ 780-852-3361; cnr Connaught Dr & Miette Ave; adult/senior & student/family $3/2/6; ☽ 9am-10pm) houses a collection of taxidermied animals representing the park's wildlife in nature-like settings.

Activities
HIKING

Wildlife is more plentiful and hikers are generally fewer in Jasper National Park than in Banff. If the weather has been wet, you may want to avoid the lower trails, where horseback trips are run: they make the path a mud bath. Topographic maps are available at the Friends of Jasper shop in the Jasper Information Centre.

The leaflet *Day-Hikers' Guide to Jasper National Park* has descriptions of most of the park's easy walks, while the backcountry visitors' guide, *Jasper National Park*, details longer trails and backcountry campsites and suggests itineraries for hikes of two to 10 days. If you're hiking overnight, you must obtain a backcountry permit (per person per night $6, to a maximum of $30) from Parks Canada in the Jasper Information Centre. For detailed information and reservations for routes that have capacity restrictions, call the **Parks Canada Trail Office** (☎ 780-852-6177).

Off the Icefields Parkway, about 10km southeast of Jasper, is the small **Valley of the Five Lakes**. The 8km loop around the lakes is mostly flat and makes a pleasant two- to three-hour stroll. Alternatively, you can take the trail that heads north from the loop to **Old Fort Point**, about 2km from Jasper. The **Mt Edith Cavell** and **Miette Hot Springs** areas also have good day hikes. For a good two- or three-day hike, try the 45km **Skyline Trail**, which starts at the northwestern end of Maligne Lake and finishes on Maligne Lake Rd about 13km from Jasper. Approximately 26km of the trail is at or above the tree line and has great scenery. The trail has plenty of wildlife, too; watch out for grizzlies.

CYCLING

Cycling is permitted on the highways and on designated park trails. It's not allowed off the trails. Journeys of a few hours, a day or several days (with overnight stops at campgrounds, hostels or lodges) are all possible. For more information, get a copy of *Mountain Biking Guide, Jasper National Park* from the Jasper Information Centre.

A good cycling route that's close to town is along **Maligne Lake Rd** to Maligne Canyon or further to Medicine Lake. A popular, scenic but fairly tough trail ride goes through the Valley of the Five Lakes to Old Fort Point, a distance of about 23.5km.

If you didn't bring your bike, you can rent one from **Vicious Cycle** (Map p624; ☎ 780-852-1111; 630 Connaught Dr; per day from $20; ⊙ 9am-6pm).

ROCK CLIMBING

Jasper is a popular destination for rock climbers. Located up the trail from 5th Bridge off Maligne Lake Rd, **Rock Gardens** is the most popular crag and has the easiest approach. For climbers with experience, Mt Edith Cavell offers incredible vistas, while Ashlar's Ridge and Morro Ridge are off-limits to all but expert climbers. Climbing classes and guided climbs for all levels are available from **Paul Valiulis** (☎ 780-852-4161; www.icpeaks.com; per person $60). Or try **Peter Amann** (☎ 780-852-3237; www.incentre.net/pamann; two-day courses $160), who will introduce you to the sport with a two-day beginner course. If you just

need equipment, check out **Gravity Gear** (Map p624; ☎ 780-852-3155; 618 Patricia St).

HORSEBACK RIDING

Horseback riding always offers the chance to reach places not easily accessible by foot, and the trails around Jasper National Park do not disappoint. **Skyline Trail Rides** (☎ 780-852-4215; www.skylinetrail.com; Fairmont Jasper Park Lodge, Old Lodge Rd; rides from $35) offers short rides through the surrounding countryside, as well as overnight trips. In the winter they offer sleigh rides.

WHITE-WATER RAFTING

Calm to turbulent rafting can be found on the **Maligne**, **Sunwapta** and **Athabasca Rivers** near Athabasca Falls. Numerous companies offer trips of varying lengths. The season is from mid-May to the end of September.
Maligne Rafting Adventures (Map p624; ☎ 780-852-3370; www.mra.ab.ca; 627 Patricia St; trips from $44) Offers half-day, Class III white-water trips on the Sunwapta as well as float trips and overnight adventures.
Rocky Mountain River Guides (Map p624; ☎ 780-852-3777; www.rmriverguides.com; 626 Connaught Dr; trips from $45) Leads trips for all levels. Experienced rafters can sign up for Class IV multiday trips.

SKIING & SNOWBOARDING

Jasper National Park's only ski area is **Marmot Basin** (Map p607; ☎ 780-852-3816; www.skimarmot.com; Marmot Basin Rd; full-day pass adult/child $54/44), which lies 19km southwest of town off Hwy 93A. The 607-hectare area has 75 downhill runs, beginner through expert, served by six chairlifts and two T-bars. Marmot Basin also features plenty of scenic cross-country trails and a chalet. The season runs from December to May.

Near Maligne Lake, the **Moose Lake Loop** (8km) and the trail in the **Bald Hills** (11km) are easy introductions to the park's 200km of cross-country ski trails.

Tours

Three main companies in town book tickets for various tours and activities, including train rides, boat cruises, air tours, hiking, rafting, horseback riding, shuttle services and more. They are:
Brewster Gray Line (Map p624; ☎ 780-852-3332; 607 Connaught Dr; Discover Jasper tours adult/child $41/21, Icefields Parkway tours adult/child $70/35) This Canadian Rockies tour giant, in the train station, offers a four-hour

ALBERTA

Discover Jasper tour to some of the local sights, including Patricia and Pyramid Lakes and Maligne Canyon. It also runs 9½-hour Icefields Parkway tours.

Jasper Adventure Centre (Map p624; ☎ 780-852-5595, 800-565-7547; www.jasperadventurecentre.com; 604 Connaught Dr).

Maligne Tours (Map p624; ☎ 780-852-3370; www.malignelake.com; 627 Patricia St)

SunDog Tour Company (Map p624; ☎ 780-852-4056, 888-786-3641; www.sundogtours.com, 414 Connaught Dr)

Sleeping

In general, prices here are lower than in Banff Town.

BUDGET

HI-Jasper (Map p607; ☎ 780-852-3215, 877-852-0781; www.hostellingintl.ca/Alberta; Whistlers Mountain Rd; dm from $18; 🖳) Dorms are big here, sleeping about 40 people, but otherwise it's a comfortable place with a homey common area, Internet access, a kitchen and laundry facilities. The hostel is 7km southwest of Jasper near the Jasper Tramway; the last 2km are uphill.

Jasper's 10 park campgrounds are generally open from mid-May to late September or early October, although a few stay open until the first snowfall (which may not be that much later). All are first-come, first-served. For information, contact **Parks Canada** (☎ 780-852-6176; 500 Connaught Dr) at the Jasper Information Centre.

Whistlers Campground (Whistlers Rd; tent/RV sites $22/30; ☯ early-May–mid-Oct) This huge campground has showers, wheelchair access and an interpretive program. Sites are wooded, but not particularly private. It's the closest campground to town, about 3km south of the Icefields Parkway, and even with 781 sites it fills quickly.

Wapiti Campground (Hwy 98; tent/RV sites $22/30; ☯ late-Jun–early-Sep & mid-Oct–early-May) About 2km further south of Whistlers Campground, on the Icefields Parkway and beside the Athabasca River, Wapiti is the only campground in the park open during winter. It offers flush toilets and electricity year-round, but has showers only in the summer season. Try for a spot backing onto the river, it allows for more privacy.

Snaring River Campground (Map p607; Hwy 16, 17km north of Jasper Town; tent sites $13; ☯ mid-May–mid-Sep) A good argument could be made that this 66-site primitive campground enjoys

the most atmospheric setting in the park. It lies at the foot of the Palisades – a long, sheer cliff band. Across the highway, the Colin Range thrusts its pristine rock walls heavenward in an area that will have rock climbers salivating.

MID-RANGE

Numerous motels line Connaught Dr on the approaches to Jasper Town. Downtown holds more lodgings. A concentration of higher-end places is on Geikie St, within walking distance of downtown. And several places outside town proper offer bungalows (usually wooden cabins) that are only open in summer. The rates listed are for the summer high season; there are considerable discounts in other seasons, especially winter.

Park Place Inn (Map p624; ☎ 780-852-9970; www.parkplaceinn.com; 623 Patricia St; r from $200) You wouldn't expect it from the location (tucked away above a parade of downtown shops), but this is Jasper's best lodging option. Each of the 12 heritage-style rooms is luxurious and uniquely decorated with amazing attention to detail. Rooms come with king-sized beds, enormous tubs, thick fluffy robes and mountain views galore.

Tekarra Lodge (☎ 780-852-3058; www.maclabhotels.com/leisure_tekarralodge.com; Hwy 93A; d from $165; ☯ May-Oct) At the confluence of the Miette and Athabasca Rivers, the lodge has the most atmospheric cabins in town. Elegantly decorated with hardwood floors, wood-paneled walls and fireplaces, the cabins are set amidst the trees. You're only 1km south of Jasper, but you'll feel worlds away. A lovely option that's good value for money.

Patricia Lake Bungalows (☎ 780-852-3560, 888-499-6848; www.patricialakebungalows.com; Patricia Lake Rd off Pyramid Lake Rd; d from $80, cottage from $135; ☯ May–mid-Oct) A quiet family atmosphere pervades tidy Patricia Lake Bungalows, about 5km north of town and right on Patricia Lake. More parklike than rustic, the resort features manicured grounds, canoe and boat rentals, nature trails, a laundromat, outdoor hot tub and well-equipped cottages and motel rooms.

Pocahontas Cabins (Map p607; ☎ 780-866-3732; www.pocahontascabins.ca; cnr Hwy 16 & Miette Hot Springs Rd; cabins from $115; 🖳) Full of nostalgia, these wooden cabins come with wood-burning stoves, old black-and-white photos of the area and a fully equipped kitchen. There's a playground for the kids and the cabins are close to the hot springs and in a scenically beautiful location.

Whistlers Inn (Map p624; ☎ 780-852-9919; www .whistlersinn.com; cnr Connaught Dr & Miette Ave; r $205) We loved the rooftop hot tub at this place. The rooms are quite decent with sturdy furniture and rustic decor.

Athabasca Hotel (Map p624; ☎ 780-852-3386, 877-542-8422; www.athabascahotel.com; 510 Patricia St; r $145) Although it looks rather dismal on the outside, on the inside it's been renovated and rooms have an old-fashioned, European feel about them with dark wooden furniture. Stay away from the east wing, it's over the town's most popular nightclub and can be a little loud (although the rooms are usually cheaper).

Astoria Hotel (Map p624; ☎ 780-852-3351, 800-661-7343; www.astoriahotel.com; 404 Connaught Dr; r $180) The comfortable Astoria has nicely appointed rooms with floral bedspreads, TVs, VCRs and fridges. It's attached to D'ed Dog Bar & Grill, a popular pub and restaurant. Note: room Nos 114 to 117 and 132 to 135 face a noisy back alley and are best avoided.

TOP END

Fairmont Jasper Park Lodge (☎ 780-852-3301, 800-441-1414; www.fairmont.com/jasper; 1 Old Lodge Rd; r from $500) Once the haunt of royalty, artists and members of the jet set, such as Bing Crosby and Marilyn Monroe, this famous lodge sprawls across acres of green lawn on the shores of turquoise-blue Lake Beauvert. With a country-club-meets-1950s-holiday-camp air, the amenity-filled cabins and chalets are classy. The lodge's gem is its main lounge, open to the public, with stupendous lake views. It's filled with log furniture, chandeliers and fireplaces and is the best place in town to write a postcard over a quiet cocktail. There are often off-season discounts.

Pyramid Lake Resort (☎ 780-852-4900, 888-852-4900; www.maclabhotels.com/leisure_pyramidlake.htm; Pyramid Lake Rd; d from $270) This bustling place is a large, fancy resort with a licensed dining room, stunning mountain views and boats, canoes and kayaks to take out on the gorgeous lake. It's been tastefully renovated and rooms are comfy with lake views. It's slightly lacking in remote tranquility though, and seems just a tad overpriced. There are often really cheap off-season specials.

Eating

There's no shortage of restaurants in Jasper. In addition, many of the hotels and lodges have their own dining rooms.

BUDGET

Bear's Paw Bakery (Map p624; ☎ 780-852-3233; 4 Cedar Ave; mains $3; ☽ breakfast & lunch) Wholesome homemade baked goods are the specialty at this welcoming little bakery. The aromas of delicious croissants, muffins and wholegrain breads waft out onto nearby Connaught Dr; follow your nose.

Coco's Café (Map p624; ☎ 780-852-4550; 608 Patricia St; mains $4-7; ☽ breakfast, lunch & dinner) For breakfast, this small, hip café offers eggs, waffles, muesli, muffins and more. Lunch brings delicious sandwiches and burritos. Vegetarians will appreciate the menu's many vegan items, and solo travelers will find plenty of essential reading material, such as old copies of *Climbing* magazine. Save room for the heavenly peanut butter Nanaimo bar.

Sierra Café & Internet (Map p624; ☎ 780-852-1199; 610 Connaught Dr; mains $5-7; ☽ breakfast & lunch) A great place to start the day, Sierra Café offers affable proprietor Dieter's homemade touch on fresh-baked scones, granola and more. Breakfast is served all day. The atmosphere is mellow and jovial, and you can check your email, too.

Soft Rock Café (Map p624; ☎ 780-852-5850; 622 Connaught Dr; mains $8; ☽ breakfast & lunch) Breakfast is served all day at this small, often packed, place with a giant omelette selection. For lunch try one of the hot, stuffed baguettes. On sunny days there's an outdoor patio for lounging.

MID-RANGE & TOP END

Fiddle River Seafood Co (Map p624; ☎ 780-852-3032; 620 Connaught Dr; mains from $14; ☽ lunch & dinner) The town's best seafood place has a fine view from its 2nd-floor location. The salmon and trout ($19 to $24) couldn't be any fresher if they flopped right onto your plate, and for vegetarians there are innovative choices like pistachio- and sunflower seed–crusted tofu ($19). The dining room is a casual place with wooden tables and big windows.

La Fiesta (Map p624; ☎ 780-852-0404; 504 Patricia St; mains from $10; ☽ lunch & dinner) Mediterranean casual decor and a huge tapas menu greet you at this lovely place. The offerings are

ALBERTA

innovative – spinach and goat cheese frittata appetizers and cinnamon- and chili-rubbed paella mains.

Denjiro (Map p624; ☎ 780-852-3780; 410 Connaught Dr; mains from $10; ☽ lunch & dinner) Japanese dishes are prepared with fresh ingredients and served at low tables in traditional, private booths. You can cook your own sukiyaki, *shabu shabu* and *nabe* hot pot at your table.

Jasper Pizza Place (Map p624; ☎ 780-852-3225; 402 Connaught Dr; mains $8-12; ☽ lunch & dinner) Locals love Jasper's, which has a rooftop patio and excellent pizza, as well as burgers, salads and pasta. The family-friendly restaurant features bright yellow and purple chairs and black-and-white photos of the region.

Miss Italia Ristorante (Map p624; ☎ 780-852-4004; 610 Patricia St; mains from $10; ☽ lunch & dinner) The decor is slightly kitsch, but still atmospheric, with twinkle lights and hanging garlic. Huge portions of fresh pasta and Italian sausage are served to boisterous patrons by extremely friendly staff.

Drinking

Pete's on Patricia (Map p624; ☎ 780-852-6262; 614 Patricia St) Locals say this is the late-night hot spot. There's nightly DJs and a hip-hop night with drink specials. Thursday is ladies night. The club gets going after 10pm.

Whistle Stop Pub (Map p624; ☎ 780-852-3361; cnr Connaught Dr & Miette Ave) Pool tables, 10 ales on tap and big-screen TVs showing sports make this a popular local dive. There are pool tournaments and chicken-wing specials certain nights.

De'd Dog Bar & Grill (Map p624; ☎ 780-852-3351; Astoria Hotel, 404 Connaught Dr) This venue is famous for its imported draft beers. You can play pool and darts with the colorful locals who like to hang out here.

Downstream Bar (Map p624; ☎ 780-852-3032; downstairs at 620 Connaught Dr) Smokers are confined to one room, so if you don't inhale you can breathe at this basement bar featuring daily happy hours, a good beer selection and open mike nights.

Atha-B Pub (Map p624; ☎ 780-852-3386; Athabasca Hotel, 510 Patricia St) Another late-night hot spot, this club has a variety of theme nights – from ladies night to karaoke sing-along. It also showcases live rock bands.

Getting There & Around

BUS

The **bus station** (Map p624; ☎ 780-852-3926; www .greyhound.ca; 607 Connaught Dr) is in the train station. Greyhound buses serve Edmonton ($52, from 4½ hours, four daily), Prince George ($52, five hours, two daily), Kamloops ($60, six hours, two daily) and Vancouver ($105, from 11½ hours, two daily).

Brewster Transportation (☎ 780-852-3332; www .brewster.ca), departing from the same station, operates express buses to Lake Louise village ($49, 4½ hours, at least one daily) and Banff Town ($57, 5½ hours, at least one daily).

CAR

International car-rental agencies (p873) have offices in Jasper Town.

TAXI

If you're in need of a taxi, call **Heritage Cabs** (☎ 780-852-5558), which has metered cabs.

JASPER TAXI : 01 - 780 - 852 - 3600

TRAIN

VIA Rail offers tri-weekly train services west to Vancouver and east to Toronto. In addition, there is a tri-weekly service to Prince George, where the train continues to Prince Rupert after an overnight stay. Basic fares are usually a bit more than the bus, although the train is more comfortable, if slower. With the gutting of rail funding by the Canadian government, these trains are geared mostly toward sightseeing tourists. Call or check at the **train station** (607 Connaught Dr) for exact schedule and fare details or see p875 for general information on rail travel in Canada.

SOUTHERN ALBERTA

The roads stretch out endlessly in Southern Alberta, snaking past cattle ranches and wheat fields, through yellow prairies and under big, vacant skies. Wide-open spaces are punctuated with a smattering of towns and historic sites. In the southern part of the province you'll come across evocatively named places such as Head-Smashed-In Buffalo Jump, where the Blackfoot used to hunt herds of buffalo, and Writing-On-Stone Provincial Park, where you can see hoodoos and ancient petroglyphs. There are badlands in this part of the province, where almost eerie rock formations loom, and where the dinosaurs used to roam.

The region is also home to not one, but two, Unesco world heritage sites. Both Dinosaur Provincial Park and Head-Smashed-In Buffalo Jump have earned the special designation.

The Rockies are here too, extending south across the border into the USA. You'll also find the awesome beauty of the Waterton Lakes National Park, a gorgeous mountain realm offering stunning scenery and as much opportunity to see bear and elk as in Banff and Jasper National Parks, but without the crowds.

DRUMHELLER

Dinosaurs still reign supreme in Drumheller, a small city about 150km northeast of Calgary in the Red Deer River Valley. You'll see them on street corners and attached to lampposts. Stores and restaurants use their names, and you can even climb 106 stairs to stand in the mouth of one that's 26m tall. It's all a little over-the-top, but Drumheller is one of those towns that charms a little more with each extra hour spent there.

Don't let a first drive-through deter you. There's a tiny, but historic, old town hidden amidst the chain motels and car dealerships, and even if it comes off as a little kitschy, the surrounding scenery and archaeological importance make a stop worthwhile.

Driving in, the badlands greet you – small, humped and craggy hills and steep-walled canyons eroded out of the prairie revealing millions of years of the earth's geological history. The area is renowned for its dinosaur fossils. More complete dinosaur skeletons of the Cretaceous period (from 64 to 140 million years ago) have been found in this region than anywhere else on the planet. The outstanding Royal Tyrrell Museum, reason enough to come here on a day trip from Calgary, sits a short distance outside town, as if a wee bit embarrassed to be seen with all the dino-schlock.

Information

The **tourist information center** (☎ 403-823-1331; 60 1st Ave W; ☉ 10am-6pm) is marked by a huge *T rex*. If you're driving, tune into 94.5, the local radio station, which provides up-to-date information about what's happening in town.

Sights & Activities

DINOSAUR TRAIL, HORSESHOE CANYON & HOODOO DRIVE

Drumheller is on the Dinosaur Trail, a 48km loop that runs northwest from town and includes Hwys 837 and 838; the scenery is quite worth the drive. Badlands and river views await you at every turn. The loop takes you past **Midland Provincial Park** (no camping), where you can take a self-guided hike; across the Red Deer River on the free, cable-operated **Bleriot Ferry**, which has been running since 1913; and to vista points overlooking the area's impressive canyons.

Horseshoe Canyon, the most spectacular area chasm, is best seen on a short drive west of Drumheller on Hwy 9. A large sign in the parking lot explains the geology of the area, while trails lead down into the canyon for further exploration.

The 25km **Hoodoo Drive** starts about 18km southeast of Drumheller on Hwy 10; the road only goes one way so you must return by the same route. Along this drive you'll find the best examples of hoodoos: weird, eroded, mushroom-like columns of sandstone rock. This area was the site of a once-prosperous coal-mining community, and the Atlas Mine is now preserved as a provincial historic site. Take the side trip on Hwy 10X (which includes 11 bridges in 6km) from Rosedale to the small community of Wayne, where you can stop for a beer at the fabled **Last Chance Saloon** (☎ 405-823-9189; ☉ lunch & dinner), an old-fashioned bar decorated with period antiques.

ROYAL TYRRELL MUSEUM OF PALAEONTOLOGY

This excellent **museum** (☎ 403-823-7707, 888-440-4240; www.tyrrellmuseum.com; adult/youth/senior/family $8.50/4.50/6.50/20, fossil dig adult/youth $85/55, guided hike adult/youth $12/8; ☉ 9am-9pm Tue-Sun mid-May–Sep, 10am-5pm Tue-Sun rest of year) is set in a fossil-rich valley along Hwy 838, 6km northwest of town. Displays, videos, films and computers outline the study of early life on earth. Fossils of ancient creatures, including flying reptiles, prehistoric mammals and amphibious animals, help trace the story of evolution; best of all is the extensive display of more than 35 complete dinosaur skeletons. A Burgess Shale exhibit shows the many wild and weird creatures that died and became part of the shale. In

ALBERTA

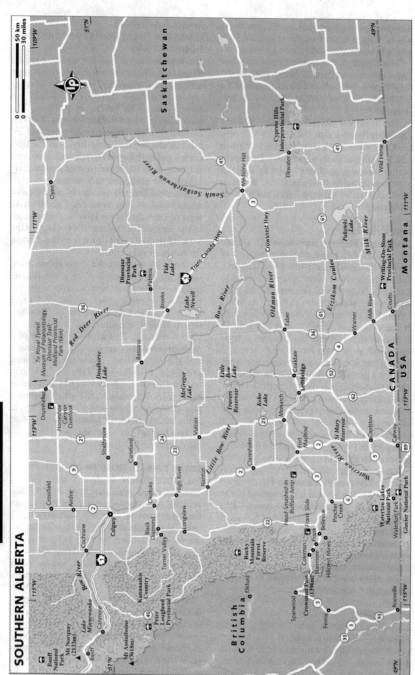

SOUTHERN ALBERTA

summer, with advance reservations, you can participate in a fossil dig or join an expert-led guided hike to a dig site.

WORLD'S LARGEST DINOSAUR

We admit this 26m-high **dinosaur** (☎ 866-823-8100; 60 1st Ave W; admission $2; ⏰ 10am-6pm) in front of the tourist information center is a rather cheesy novelty attraction, but they do say it's the largest in the world. Kids will love climbing 106 stairs to stand in the *T rex*'s mouth, which can fit 12 people at once. The dinosaur is 46m long and 4.5 times bigger than its extinct counterpart.

Sleeping

For some reason (which hotel proprietors explain with a shrug and the retort 'lots is always going on here') hotels can fill up even on odd days in the off season; it might be best to call ahead.

Heartwood Manor (☎ 403-823-6495, 888-823-6495; www.discoveralberta.com/heartwoodmanor; 320 N Railway Ave E; r from $110) This small, friendly inn offers luxuriously appointed rooms, each one unique, with whirlpools. If you're looking for a little romance, try one of the larger rooms (from $140) with elaborate beds – they're raised a few feet off the floor – huge tubs, big-screen TVs and couches. The only downside might be the inn's proximity to the railroad tracks and main road.

Badlands Motel (☎ 403-823-5155; fax 403-823-7653; 801 N Dinosaur Trail; r summer/rest of year $44/80) Small front porches offer scenic views at this friendly motel. Rooms are tidy and standard with fresh coats of paint.

Super 8 Motel (☎ 403-823-8887, 888-823-8882; fax 403-823-8884; 680 2nd St SE; s/d from $99/110; 🖭) If you're traveling with kids, try this very up-market Super 8 for its two-story waterslide and indoor pool. A continental breakfast is included.

River Grove Campground & Cabins (☎ 403-823-6655; www.virtuallydrumheller.com/rivergrove; 25 Poplar St; campsites from $20, cabins from $60; ⏰ May-Sep) In town, this campground enjoys a pleasant shady spot on the river's north bank. It has showers, a laundromat, a store, fishing, beach access and a playground.

Eating

Whif's Flapjack House (☎ 403-823-7595; 801 N Dinosaur Trail; mains $4-7; ⏰ breakfast & lunch) At the Badlands Motel, Whif's is a good bet for a homemade breakfast or lunch. It specializes in flapjacks and waffles.

Sizzling House (☎ 403-823-8098; 160 Centre St; mains $8; ⏰ lunch & dinner) A perennial local favorite serving much better Chinese and Thai food than you'd expect in a small town. Don't let the outside turn you away, inside there's a newly renovated dining room and giant menu. The kids can enjoy chicken fingers and fries while you chow on salt-and-pepper squid or Singapore noodles.

Stavros (☎ 403-823-6362; 1103A Hwy 9; mains $10-20; ⏰ breakfast, lunch & dinner) When locals want something upmarket, many go to Stavros in the Best Western Jurassic Inn. The dinner menu, which is wide-ranging, offers Greek specialties, calzones, pizzas and pastas, steak, seafood and more.

Molly Brown's Caffe (☎ 403-823-7481; 233 Centre St; mains $6-8; ⏰ breakfast & lunch) This tiny, serene café has classical music playing in the background and a menu featuring three types of homemade sandwiches – chicken, tuna and seafood – prepared either cold, melted or wrapped – and served with soup or salad. There are also Asian soups.

Getting There & Away

Greyhound Canada runs buses from the **bus station** (☎ 403-823-7566; 308 Centre St) to Calgary ($25, two hours, daily) and Edmonton ($50, 5½ hours, twice weekly).

Hammerhead Tours (p576) runs a full-day tour ($60) from Calgary to the Drumheller badlands and Royal Tyrrell Museum from May to November.

DINOSAUR PROVINCIAL PARK

This isn't Jurassic Park but, as a Unesco world heritage site, it's the next best thing. **Dinosaur Provincial Park** (☎ 403-378-4342; www3.gov.ab.ca/env/parks/prov_parks/dinosaur; off Hwy 544; admission free; ⏰ 9am-6pm mid-May–mid-Sep, 10am-5pm mid-Sep–mid-May) is a 76½-million-year-old dinosaur graveyard about halfway between Calgary and Medicine Hat, some 48km northeast of Brooks. From Hwy 1, take Hwy 36 or Secondary Hwy 873 to Hwy 544.

The park's dry, convoluted lunar landscape was once a tropical rain forest on the shores of an inland sea. Dinosaurs thrived here; archaeologists have uncovered more than 300 complete skeletons, many of which now reside in museums around the world.

ALBERTA

A full day can easily be spent exploring the 73-sq-km park, which is full of wildlife, wildflowers and hoodoos – photographers will have a field day here. In summer, take plenty of water (walking in the valley can be as hot as hell), a hat, sunscreen and insect repellent.

Five interpretive hiking trails and a driving loop run through part of the park, but to preserve the fossils, access to 70% of the park is restricted. The off-limits areas may be seen only on guided hikes (adult/child $4.50/2.25) or bus tours (adult/child $4.50/2.25), which operate from late May to October. The hikes and tours are popular, and you should reserve a place by calling ☎ 403-378-4344 or toll-free in Alberta ☎ 310-0000 ext 403-378-4344 after May 1 for the following season.

The park's **Royal Tyrrell Museum Field Station** (☎ 403-378-4342; adult/child $2.50/1.50; ✆ 8:30am-9pm mid-May–early-Sep, reduced hrs early-Sep–early-Oct, 9am-4pm Mon-Fri early-Oct–mid-May) has four display areas where nearly complete skeletons have been encased in glass. Archaeologists are on hand to answer questions during summer.

The park's two good **campgrounds** (☎ 403-378-3700; reservation fee $6, tent/RV sites $15/$18) lie by a creek, which makes a small, green oasis in this stark place. Laundry facilities and hot showers are available. These sites fill up regularly, so you should phone for reservations.

HEAD-SMASHED-IN BUFFALO JUMP

For thousands of years, Blackfoot peoples stampeded bison over the cliff at the world heritage–listed **Head-Smashed-In Buffalo Jump** (☎ 403-553-2731; www.head-smashed-in.com; Spring Point Rd/Secondary Hwy 785; interpretive center mid-Sep–mid-May adult/child $6.50/3, mid-May–mid-Sep adult/child $8.50/4; ✆ 9am-6pm mid-May–mid-Sep, 10am-5pm mid-Sep–mid-May), then used the meat, hide, bone, horns and nearly everything else for their supplies and materials. The area was used for this practice until the early 19th century. According to legend, a young brave (Aboriginal warrior) wanted to view a killing from beneath the cliff but became trapped and was crushed by the falling bison, hence the name Head-Smashed-In.

The excellent interpretive center, built into the hillside, provides explanations of how the Blackfoot hunters used the site. A 10-minute film dramatization of the buffalo hunt is shown regularly during the day, and sometimes Aboriginal people give lectures on the lives of their ancestors. Outside are nearly 2km of outdoor trails; allow an hour for the trails and 1½ hours for the indoor displays.

A snack bar serves bison, chicken and sandwiches. The site, located about 18km northwest of Fort Macleod and 16km west of Hwy 2, gets busy by late morning, so arriving early is advisable; also you may see deer and more birds on the trails before the sun gets too hot.

LETHBRIDGE

Straddling the beautiful, undeveloped Oldman River Valley (known here simply as 'the coulee') is Lethbridge, southern Alberta's largest town. Located on the Crowsnest Hwy, it's a center for the local agricultural communities. Lethbridge is very spread out, and there's nothing particular to draw you to it, but it doesn't make for a bad stopping point on a long day's drive.

The small downtown and most commercial businesses are on the coulee's east side, while the University of Lethbridge and residential districts are on the west. Linking the two sides is the High Level Bridge, supposedly the world's longest (1.6km) and highest (96m) railway trestle. It's easily visible from Hwy 3. Down in the coulee, the parkland along the Oldman River holds 62km of walking and cycling trails.

West of downtown the appropriately named Scenic Dr runs along the Coulee rim. To its east, busy Mayor Mcgrath Dr (Hwy 5) is a chain-store-infested drag that could be Anywhere, North America. Here you'll find many places to stay and eat.

Information

Esquire's Coffeehouse (☎ 403-380-6747; 621 4th Ave S; per hr $12) Internet access.

Main post office (☎ 403-382-4604; 704 4th Ave S)

Main tourist office (☎ 403-320-1222, 800-661-1222; www.chinookcountry.com; 2805 Scenic Dr S at Mayor Mcgrath Dr S; ✆ 9am-5pm) Can help with car hire.

Sights & Activities

The **Nikka Yuko Japanese Garden** (☎ 403-328-3511; www.japanesegarden.ab.ca; 7th Ave S at Hwy 5; adult/child $5/3; ✆ 9am-9pm Jun 1-Sep 6, 9am-5pm May 8-Jun 10 & Sep 7-Oct 11), in Henderson Park, was built to honor Japanese–Canadian friendship. Its authentically designed Japanese gardens consist of ponds, rocks and shrubs. The buildings and bridges were built in Japan and reassembled here on the 1.6-hectare site. Young women in traditional Japanese kimonos greet you and provide background information, while weekend special events offer insight into Japanese culture.

In the coulee between the east and west sides of the city, beside Oldman River, is **Indian Battle Park** (3rd Ave S, west of Scenic Dr), named after a famous 1870 battle between the Blackfoot and the Cree. Within the park is **Fort Whoop-Up** (☎ 403-329-0444; www .fortwhoopup.com; adult/child $5/3; ☽ 10am-6pm Mon-Sat, noon-5pm Sun Victoria Day–Labour day; 1-4pm Tue-Fri & Sun rest of year), a replica of Alberta's first and most notorious illegal whiskey-trading post. Around 25 of these outposts were set up in the province between 1869 and 1874 to trade whiskey, guns, ammunition and blankets for buffalo hides and furs from the Blackfoot tribes. Their existence led directly to the formation of the NWMP, who arrived in 1874 at Fort Macleod to bring law and order to the Canadian west.

Nearby, on the north side of the High Level Bridge, is the **Helen Schuler Coulee Centre and Lethbridge Nature Reserve** (☎ 403-320-3064; admission free; ☽ dawn-dusk), which contains a small interpretive center and nature trails on the reserve's 80 wooded hectares along the river. It's quiet and cool in the coulee, and you'll see a range of flora and fauna.

Well-documented exhibits of artifacts and art focusing on various aspects of southern Alberta history can be found at the small but well-run **Sir Alexander Galt Museum** (☎ 403-320-4258/3898; 320 Galt St; admission by donation; ☽ 10am-4pm). Exhibits rotate regularly, and the museum often hosts impressive visiting exhibitions. In the back a fantastic observation gallery overlooks the coulee.

Sleeping & Eating

A huge selection of hotels can be found on Hwy 5. Most bars and restaurants are also located here.

Lethbridge Lodge (☎ 403-328-1123, 800-661-1232; www.lethbridgelodge.com; 320 Scenic Dr S; r from $99) The best thing about this full-service business hotel is the absolutely awesome Cotton Blossom Lounge, which is done up like a tropical jungle. There are streams, fountains and pathways, a safari-themed bar and live piano music (the piano is on an island in the stream). Of course it's artificial, but not bad for the middle of the prairie. And the rooms are quite satisfactory.

Ramada Hotel & Suites (☎ 403-380-5050; www .ramada.ca; 2375 Hwy 5 S; s/d/family ste $145/155/195; ☒) The fabulous indoor water park sets this chain option apart, and makes it the best choice if you're traveling with kids. There's a wave pool, a giant waterslide wrapping around the outside of the building and even a splash pool for the toddlers. Rooms have all the creature comforts expected at such a classy place, and there's a restaurant, lounge and small store as well. Non-guests can pay to use the water park (adult $15, child $10).

South Country Inn (☎ 403-380-6677; www.south countryinn.ca; 2225 Hwy 5 S; r with continental breakfast $65) A soothing and modern interior and friendly staff make for a pleasant stay. There's a hot tub and small fitness center. Rooms are large with all the amenities.

Parkside Inn (☎ 403-328-2366, 800-240-1471; fax 403-328-5933; 1009 Hwy 5 S; r $40) Surprisingly nicer on the inside than it appears on the outside, it's not bad value for money. The attached lounge features daily specials such as chicken wings for 20c, and there are pool tables and slot machines. Nonsmokers beware – a smoky smell permeates the place.

Bridgeview Campground (☎ 403-381-2357; 1501 2nd Ave W; tent & RV sites from $22; ☒) This 100-site park enjoys a beautiful location on the river bottom, 'underlooking' the High Level Bridge. Amenities include showers, a laundromat, a general store and a heated pool.

Treat's Eatery (☎ 403-380-4880; 1104 Hwy 5 S; mains $9-11; ☽ lunch & dinner) Hugely popular with locals, Treat's has a giant menu – listing everything from sandwiches and quesadillas to burgers, pasta and steak. And as with most establishments in Lethbridge there is a designated 'cheap wing night'; at Treat's it's on Sundays, when happy hour runs all day and night.

Tank House Alberta Neighbourhood Pub (☎ 403-328-9000; 1814 Hwy 5 S; mains $7-10; ☽ lunch & dinner) Good beer and decent food in a casual atmosphere make this a popular choice for university students. There's a variety of Alberta beers on tap, and a different special each night. Meals are mostly meaty (the Tank House takes pride in serving Alberta beef) and there are pool tables and sometimes live music.

ALBERTA

Getting There & Around

The **Lethbridge airport** (☎ 403-329-4474; 417 Stubb Ross Rd), a short drive south of town on Hwy 5, is served by commuter affiliates of Air Canada. Six or seven flights a day go to Calgary.

Greyhound Canada (☎ 403-327-1551; 411 5th St S) has services to Calgary ($32, three hours, at least one daily) and Regina ($75, from 13 hours, daily).

For detailed information about local bus services, call the **Lethbridge Transit Infoline** (☎ 403-320-4978/3885). The downtown bus terminal is on 4th Ave at 6th St. Local bus fare is $1.85.

WRITING-ON-STONE PROVINCIAL PARK

Named for the extensive carvings and paintings made by the Plains Indians more than 3000 years ago on the sandstone cliffs along the banks of Milk River, this **park** (☎ 403-647-2364; admission and tours free; ☼ tours 9am-6pm mid-May–mid-Sep, 10am-5pm mid-Sep–mid-May) offers a variety of activities. The highlights are the petroglyphs and pictographs, some of which can be seen along a 2km trail open to self-guided hiking. The best art is found in a restricted area (to protect it from vandalism), which you can only visit on a guided tour with the park ranger. Other activities possible here include canoeing and swimming in the river in summer and cross-country skiing in winter. Park wildlife amounts to more than 160 bird species, 30 kinds of mammals, four kinds of amphibians and three kinds of reptiles, not to mention the fish in the river. Pick up tickets for tours from the naturalist's office at the park entrance one hour before tour time.

The park's **campground** (☎ 403-647-2877; tent & RV sites from $16; ☼ Apr-Sep) by the river has sites with running water, showers and flush toilets and is popular on weekends.

Writing-On-Stone Provincial Park is southeast of Lethbridge and close to the US border; the Sweetgrass Hills of northern Montana are visible to the south. To get to the park, take Hwy 501 42km east of Hwy 4 from the town of Milk River.

On the way to the park from Lethbridge, dinosaur enthusiasts may want to stop at **Devil's Coulee**, near Warner, where dinosaur nests and eggs were uncovered in 1987. Here you can visit a **museum** (☎ 403-642-2118; admission free; ☼ 9am-5pm May-Sep, by appointment rest of year) and an active dig (tours available).

WATERTON LAKES NATIONAL PARK

Mountains and prairie collide with dramatically beautiful results in **Waterton Lakes National Park** (per day adult/senior/child $7/6/3.5). Here the flat land rises into a rugged, desolate alpine terrain full of lush valleys, crystal-clear lakes and rushing waterfalls. Wildlife enthusiasts will have a field day in this park, as it's common to spot animals – cougar, grizzly and black bear and elk all roam freely. In addition, more than 800 wildflower species grow here. Take some time to explore this off-the-beaten-path gem.

Established in 1895 and now part of a Unesco world heritage site, the 525-sq-km Waterton Lakes lies in Alberta's southwestern corner, 130km from Lethbridge.

The park's spectacular landscape continues uninterrupted across the 49th Parallel into the USA, where it is protected in Glacier National Park. Together the two parks comprise Waterton–Glacier International Peace Park. Although the name evokes images of bi-national harmony, in reality each park is operated separately, and entry to one does not entitle you to entry to the other.

Glacier National Park was created in 1910 and comprises more than 400,000 hectares. The park is open year-round; however, most services are only open from mid-May to September. From Waterton Lakes, take Hwy 6 22km south to the US border, where the road becomes US Hwy 17. Follow this 23km south to US Hwy 89 and continue 21km south to the park entrance at St Mary, Montana. The road into the park here is sometimes closed in winter. The main services for the park are on the southwestern side at West Glacier, Montana.

For more information on Glacier National Park, contact the **US National Park Service** (☎ general information 406-888-7800, campground reservations 800-365-2267, hotel reservations 406-892-2525; www.nps.gov/glac).

Orientation & Information

Waterton makes for a convenient national park experience once you've reached it. From your hotel or campground within the Waterton townsite, which is well inside the park, you can walk to several trailheads. Everything you might need for your trip – from equipment to a packed lunch – is available in the townsite. The park is open year-round and gets considerably fewer visitors than Banff and Jasper; it's blissfully low on tour buses. Spring and fall are great for storm-watching, as high winds regularly kick up whitecaps and even full-on waves on the lake.

Waterton Visitor Centre (☎ 403-859-5133; www .parkscanada.gc.ca/waterton; ☷ 8am-7pm early-May–early-Oct) is across the road from the Prince of Wales Hotel. It is the central stop for information.

Sights & Activities

Though backpackers get to savor Waterton's best scenery, even those who don't venture far from the RV can marvel at **Upper Waterton Lake**, the deepest lake (146m) in the Canadian Rockies. A highlight for many visitors is a boat ride across its shimmering waters to the far shore of Goat Haunt, Montana, USA. **Waterton Shoreline Cruises** (☎ 403-859-2362; round trip adult/child $25/13; ☷ May-Aug) operates boats holding up to 200 passengers. A limited operation begins in May; the full schedule starts in July. It takes 45-minutes to cross the lake and boat guides tend to be knowledgeable and amusing. Boats usually dock for a half-hour on the US shore. Bring your passport just in case. For a great half-day hike, take the boat one way and walk the 13km trail back. Or join rangers in the not-to-be-missed **International Peace Park Hike** (hike free; ☷ 10am Sat end Jun–Aug), an eight-hour guided hike (which includes a lunch stop) from Waterton Village to Goat Haunt. Hikers must pay for their boat ride back.

The park is laced with 255km of hiking trails, some of which are also good for cycling and horseback riding. In winter many become cross-country skiing/snowshoeing trails. Among the many hikes, the 8.7km **Crypt Lake Trail** is one of the most interesting in Canada. The route is both challenging and exhilarating – hikers negotiate a ladder, a precipitous ledge and a tunnel. The only way to reach the trailhead is by boat. The **Waterton Shoreline Cruises** (round trip $13; ☷ from townsite marina 9am & 10am Jul & Aug, 10am only rest of year, from Crypt Lake Trailhead 4pm & 5pm) boat leaves the townsite marina in the morning and picks up the weary at the Crypt Lake Trailhead in the afternoon. Most hikers will find these timings allow time for a relaxed lunch break at Crypt Lake.

If you're looking for a great drive, check out **Red Rock Parkway** between Hwy 5 and Red Rock Canyon. The 15km drive starts about 8km south of the park entrance at Hwy 5 and runs alongside Blakiston Creek for much of its route. Full of wildflower-speckled prairie that spills into incredible mountain vistas, the parkway also offers some of the best opportunities in the area to view wildlife.

Sleeping

BUDGET

HI-Waterton (☎ 403-859-2151, 888-985-6343; www .hostellingintl.ca/Alberta; Cameron Falls Dr at Windflower Ave; dm from $30, r from $95, ☷ mid-May–Nov) This spotless hostel is just about the only budget accommodations in the park and is thus busy with travelers staying in small but comfy dorms. It has a well-equipped kitchen, lounge and laundry.

The park has three Parks Canada vehicle-accessible campgrounds, none of which take reservations. Backcountry campsites are limited and should be reserved through the visitor center.

Waterton Townsite Campground (Hwy 5 at the southern end of town; tent & RV sites from $19; ☷ mid-May–mid-Oct) The park's largest campground has full facilities on grassy grounds. Though largely unshaded, it is near the waterfront and the townsite center. In the summer it can be full by late morning.

Crandell Mountain Campground (Red Rock Pkwy; tent & RV sites $17; ☷ mid-May–Sep) A tranquil campground loaded with trees. If aspens are your favorites try loops K and L, otherwise lodgepole pines dominate. The campground is northeast of town.

Belly River Campground (Chief Mountain Hwy; tent & RV sites $13; ☷ mid-May–early-Sep) Aspen trees and far-off mountain views are found at this primitive campground in the southeast corner of the park, outside the park's pay area.

MID-RANGE & TOP END

Aspen Village Inn (☎ 403-859-2255; www.waterton info.ab.ca/aspen; Windflower Ave; r from $100; ☷ May-Oct) A good pick for families: there's a small playground, hot tub and grill for barbecuing. A couple of ground-floor rooms are wheelchair-accessible.

Northland Lodge (☎ 403-859-2353; www.northland lodgecanada.com; 408 Evergreen Ave; r with continental breakfast from $100; ☷ mid-May–mid-Oct) Just a

ALBERTA

half-mile from the main street and within howling distance of Cameron Falls, this lodge has nine appealing rooms, an outdoor grill and a self-catering kitchen . Continental breakfast is included.

Kilmorey Lodge (☎ 403-859-2334; www.kilmorey lodge.com; 117 Evergreen Ave; r from $110) The historic lakefront Kilmorey dates from the late 1920s and has a comfortable, home-away-from-home feel to it. The lodge's ambience is upscale-rustic; the 23 rooms are nicely furnished with antiques and down comforters but without TVs or phones. Think quiet. The restaurant is excellent. The lodge is one of only a few places that stay open year-round, with cheaper rates in the winter.

Bayshore Inn (☎ 403-859-2211, 888-527-9555; www .bayshoreinn.com; 111 Waterton Ave; r $140; ☼ Apr–mid-Oct) The Bayshore elevates itself from basic motel monotony by having a prime lake-front location right in town. All rooms are spacious with balconies. Try for a ground-floor room with immediate lake access. Rooms are slightly cheaper at the beginning and end of the season.

Waterton Glacier Suites (☎ 403-859-2004, 866-621-3330; www.watertonsuites.com; Windflower Ave; r from $170) The owners of this polished place know how to make their guests happy. It offers spacious, sparkling rooms, all with porch or balcony, microwave, fridge and at least one fireplace. It's one of the few places that remains open year-round.

Waterton Lakes Lodge (☎ 403-859-2150, 888-985-6343; www.watertonlakeslodge.com; 101 Clematis Ave; r $195; ☼ mid-May–late-Oct; ☒) New and glitzy, the nine two-story lodging units here look like modern suburban condos. Amenities include a restaurant and pool/health club/ recreation center. Rates are lower in May and October.

Prince of Wales Hotel (☎ in season 403-859-2231, other times 406-756-2444; www.princeofwaleswaterton .com; Prince of Wales Rd; r from $260; ☼ mid-May–Sep) The most venerable Prince of Wales Hotel, a national historic site, perches on a rise overlooking the lake. Though incredibly photogenic from a distance (we're talking cover-model material), up close the hotel looks smaller and much more genteel. Nevertheless, the views alone could be worth the price. If you're looking for ghosts, the 5th- and 6th-floor rooms are rumored to be haunted. To get there, turn in across the road from the park visitor center.

Eating

Lamp Post (☎ 403-859-2334; 117 Evergreen Ave; mains $6-12; ☼ breakfast, lunch & dinner) Rustically elegant and slightly charming, this restaurant has a large menu sure to please the whole family – everything from pasta to Alberta beef to seafood.

Pizza of Waterton (☎ 403-859-2660; 103 Fountain Ave; mains $7-12; ☼ lunch & dinner) Not surprisingly, pizza is what to order at this inviting eatery with a cozy interior and outdoor patio. Salads, sandwiches and wraps are in close competition for deliciousness.

Big Scoop Ice Cream (☎ 403-859-2346; Main St; ice cream $3-5; ☼ 10am-10pm) If you've coaxed your children down the mountain with promises of ice cream, head to this very popular stop. There's a tempting menu of sundaes and milkshakes and 32 hand-dipped ice cream flavors.

Drinking & Entertainment

Thirsty Bear Saloon (☎ 403-859-2111; Main St) To down a few cold ones and play some pool or dance to DJ driven music head on down to this bar. Popular with seasonal workers and tourists alike, it gets crowded after 10pm.

Getting There & Away

Waterton lies in Alberta's southwestern corner, 130km from Lethbridge and 156km from Calgary. The one road entrance into the park is in its northeast corner along Hwy 5. Most visitors coming from Glacier and the USA reach the junction with Hwy 5 via Hwy 6 (Chief Mountain International Hwy) from the southeast. From Calgary, to the north, Hwy 6 shoots south towards Hwy 5 into the park. From the east, Hwy 5, through Cardston heads west and then south into the park.

CROWSNEST PASS

West of Fort Macleod the Crowsnest Hwy (Hwy 3) heads through the prairies and into the Rocky Mountains to Crowsnest Pass (1396m) and the BC border. At the beginning of the 20th century this was a rich coal-producing region, which gave rise to a series of small mining towns. In 1903 one of these, Frank, was almost completely buried when 30 million cubic meters (some 82 million tons worth) of nearby Turtle Mountain collapsed and killed around 70 people. This and other mining disasters, plus a fall in demand for coal, eventually led to the demise of the coal industry. Today the Pincher Creek area is a center for a different form of energy: wind farms are a growing presence.

Frank Slide Interpretive Centre (☎ 403-562-7388; www.frankslide.com; adult/child $6.50/3; ⊙ 9am-5pm), 1.5km off Hwy 3 and 27km east of the BC border, overlooks the Crowsnest Valley. As well as displays on the slide's cause and effects, it has exhibits on the coming of the railway and on late 19th- and early 20th-century life and mining technology.

NORTHERN ALBERTA

If you're looking to lose yourself in one of those vast and isolated landscapes not quite touched by modern times then head north of Edmonton into the great unknown. Here you'll find a place where the buffalo still roam, where the northern lights put on dazzling winter displays nightly and where you'll feel really small amid all the empty space.

That said, there's not a lot to do up here – it's really a solitary, sparsely populated region of farms, forests, wilderness areas, lakes, open prairies and oilfields. The Cree, Slavey and Dene were the first peoples to inhabit the region, and many of them still depend on fishing, hunting and trapping for survival. The northeast has virtually no roads and is dominated by Wood Buffalo National Park, the Athabasca River and Lake Athabasca. The northwest is more accessible, with a network of highways connecting Alberta with northern BC and the Northwest Territories.

PEACE RIVER & AROUND

From Edmonton, Hwy 43 heads northwest to Dawson Creek, BC (a distance of 590km). It's really only of interest if you're trying to reach the official starting point of the Alaska Hwy (p778). Numerous campgrounds and several provincial parks line the route. The scenery is generally flat or gently undulating, with dairy and cereal farms and grain silos in nearly every town. **Grande Prairie**, a large, sprawling community, is an administrative, commercial and agricultural center. Most of the accommodations are centered on 100th St and 100th Ave.

Highway 2, heading north directly out of Edmonton, is a more interesting route

than Hwy 43; it follows the southern shore of **Lesser Slave Lake** part of the way. On the northern edge of the town of McLennan, the **Kimiwan Birdwalk and Interpretive Centre** (☎ 780-324-2004; admission free; ⊙ 10am-5:30pm May-Aug) is a special place for birders. The lake and surrounding marsh stand in the middle of three migratory routes, and nearly 300,000 birds pass through each year. The interpretive center is open only during the summer, but the paths remain open year-round.

The Peace River is so named because the warring Cree and Beaver Indians made peace along its banks. The town of **Peace River** sits at the confluence of the Heart, Peace and Smoky Rivers. It has several motels and two campgrounds. Greyhound Canada buses leave daily for the Yukon and Northwest Territories. West out of town, Hwy 2 leads to the Mackenzie Hwy.

MACKENZIE HIGHWAY

The small town of **Grimshaw** is the official starting point of the Mackenzie Hwy (Hwy 35) north to the Northwest Territories (p806). The relatively flat and straight road is paved for the most part, though there are stretches of loose gravel or earth where the road is being reconstructed.

The mainly agricultural landscape between Grimshaw and Manning gives way to endless stretches of spruce and pine forest. Come prepared, as this is frontier territory and services become fewer (and more expensive) as the road cuts northward through the wilderness. A good basic rule is to fill your tank any time you see a gas station from here north.

High Level, the last settlement of any size before the Northwest Territories border, is a center for the timber industry. Workers often stay in the motels in town during the week. The only service station between High Level and Enterprise (in the Northwest Territories) is at Indian Cabins.

LAKE DISTRICT

From St Paul, more than 200km northeast of Edmonton, to the Northwest Territories border lies Alberta's immense lake district. Fishing is popular (even in winter, when there is ice-fishing) but many of the lakes, especially further north, have no road access and you have to fly in.

ALBERTA

St Paul, the gateway to the lake district, is a trading center, with a **flying-saucer landing pad** (which is still awaiting its first customer). Residents built the 12m-high circular landing pad in 1967 as part of a centennial project and as a stunt to try to generate tourism (it's billed as the world's largest, and only, UFO landing pad) to the remote region. It worked: UFO enthusiasts have been visiting ever since.

Highway 63 is the main route into the province's northeastern wilderness interior. The highway, with a few small settlements and campgrounds on the way, leads to **Fort McMurray**, which is 439km north of Edmonton. Originally a fur-trading outpost, it is now home to one of the world's largest oilfields. The story of how crude oil is extracted from the vast tracts of sand is told at the **Oil Sands Discovery Centre** (☎ 780-743-7167; junction of Hwy 63 & MacKenzie Blvd; adult/child $3/2; ☀ 9am-5pm mid-May–early-Sep; 10am-4pm Tue-Sun rest of year).

WOOD BUFFALO NATIONAL PARK

This huge park is best accessed from Fort Smith in the Northwest Territories. For more information, see p820.

In Alberta, the only access is via air to Fort Chipewyan. In winter, an ice road leads north to Peace Point (which connects to Fort Smith), and another road links the park to Fort McMurray.

British Columbia

CONTENTS

'Beautiful British Columbia' has been the license-plate legend on vehicles in British Columbia (BC) for decades, but there's never been a single recorded complaint from visitors about this bold assertion. Of course, it's hard to argue against the evidence. In a nation known for its uncommonly attractive scenery, BC can lay a strong claim to being the home to some of Canada's most outstanding natural treasures.

Four times the size of the UK, this province is the giant, largely untouched home of snow-crowned mountains, shimmering lakes, sparkling waterfalls, breathtaking glaciers, slender fjords, lush rain forests, tree-covered islands, crenulated coastlines and even a small desert. For city dwellers, the province's vast, variegated tracts of jaw-dropping wilderness often act like a tonic to remind them what mother nature is all about.

Many of these areas are accessible to visitors. There are dozens of activities available, providing some great ways to interact with the outdoors, whatever the season. Whistler is BC's world-renowned winter center for skiing, snowboarding, snowshoeing and all manner of snowbound activities. Vancouver Island's west coast, with its kilometers of white-sand beaches and Pacific Ocean exposure, is the region's surfing capital. And hikers, cyclists, kayakers and campers can all be kept blissfully occupied in BC for months without a struggle.

BC isn't just about the outdoors. The region's aboriginal heritage is on prominent display. Victoria, the picturesque capital on Vancouver Island, wears its colonial ties on its sleeve, but also has a lively restaurant scene and an excellent provincial museum. Vancouver is a cosmopolitan mainland metropolis of fine shops, galleries, museums, restaurants, parks and some of the best sea-to-sky vistas of any city in the world.

HIGHLIGHTS

- Explore cosmopolitan **Vancouver** (p647), reserving time for a stroll along Stanley Park's stunning seawall, a delve into Granville Island's colorful market and a taste-tripping trawl through some of its excellent restaurants
- Hit the slopes at **Whistler** (p687), a world-class ski resort with pulsating nightlife
- Kayak through the rugged **Broken Islands** (p716), off Vancouver Island's wild western coast
- Hit the outdoors with a rip-roaring rafting trip along the Kicking Horse River at **Golden** (p757)
- Discover aboriginal culture and its ancient origins at the remote **Queen Charlotte Islands** (p768)

| ■ POPULATION: 4.168 MILLION | ■ PROVINCIAL CAPITAL: VICTORIA | ■ AREA: 947,796 SQ KM |

History

The ancestors of BC's modern Aboriginal people arrived in North America at least 15,000 years ago, possibly via a land bridge across the Bering Strait between Asia and Alaska. Some settled along the mild Pacific coast, while others found their way into the interior.

The coastal tribes included the Bella Coola, Cowichan, Gitksan, Haida, Kwakiutl, Nisga'a, Nootka, Salish, Sechelt and Tsimshian. With abundant animal, marine and plant life available, they developed a sophisticated, structured culture and an intricate trade network, dwelling as extended families in large, single-roofed cedar lodges.

Inland, with its more extreme climate, the people led a nomadic, subsistence life. In the north they followed migratory herds of caribou and moose; in the south they pursued bison and salmon. Most of these people were Athapaskans, including groups such as Beaver, Chilcotin, Carrier, Sekani and Tahltan. Other important groups were the Interior Salish (divided into the Lillooet, Okanagan, Shuswap and Thompson) and the Kootenay.

During the 18th century, European explorers in search of new sources of wealth appeared off the west coast. The Russians and Spanish arrived first, followed in 1778 by Britain's Captain James Cook. His return home with tales of untold riches to be had from fur trading encouraged a rush of 'fur prospectors.' By the 1820s the Hudson's Bay Company controlled a network of trading posts across the region, and a few years later Britain declared Vancouver Island a crown colony – much to the annoyance of the Americans.

The discovery of gold along the Fraser River in 1858 resulted in an economic boom in the region, with thousands arriving to seek their instant fortunes. The British swiftly claimed the rest of the province, and named New Westminster as the capital. A second wave of fortune hunters arrived when gold was discovered further north in the Cariboo region. Although the gold rush only lasted a few years, many of those who came remained behind, forming permanent settlements.

Mainland BC and Vancouver Island were united in 1866, with Victoria named the new capital in 1868. The province united with much of the rest of Canada under confederation in 1871, on the condition that a transcontinental railroad be extended to the west coast. This was finally achieved, several years later, in 1886.

The Panama Canal, completed in 1914, allowed BC to exploit markets for its products – especially lumber – in Europe and eastern North America. But after WWI and the 1929 Wall St crash, the region entered a prolonged economic downturn that led to depression and unemployment. Prosperity only returned with the advent of WWII, when both shipbuilding and armaments manufacturing bolstered the region's traditional economic base of resource exploitation, and was sustained after the war with the discovery of new ways to exploit resources and the development of a manufacturing base.

At the start of the 1990s, BC experienced another economic upsurge, led by Vancouver, which enjoyed its links to then-booming Asia. The area welcomed a large influx of moneyed immigrants from Hong Kong who spearheaded a development surge in the city.

However the crash of Asian economies in the late 1990s sent a chill through Vancouver. The rest of the province was affected by a devastating drop in world demand for premium lumber and the collapse of regional fishing stocks. BC's once-dominant resource sectors will likely never return to their earlier peaks. Small towns that once relied on natural resources have, in recent years, been faced with the difficult issue of how to adapt and survive.

Politically the province has recently moved to a right-leaning Liberal government, which has committed itself to BC's economic survival. Painful cuts to health and welfare programs have ensued, with the government hinging many of its business sector hopes on the 2010 Winter Olympic Games, to be hosted in Vancouver and Whistler.

Climate

BC's varied climate is influenced by each area's latitude, mountainous terrain and proximity to the Pacific Ocean. It's generally warmer in the south and cooler in the north. Winters are mild in Greater Vancouver and Greater Victoria, with only brief snowfalls, while other regions – especially the north and the interior – are subject to

BRITISH COLUMBIA

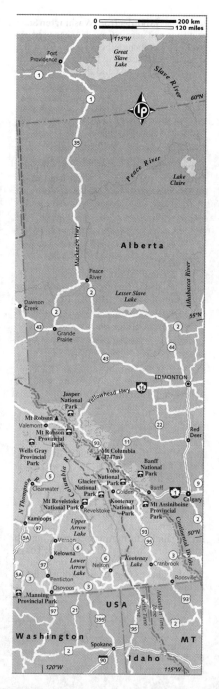

freezing temperatures and heavy snow from November to March.

Spring and fall are often warm and pleasant in BC but rainfall can be heavy, particularly on the coast. Summers (June to September) are mostly dry and sunny with warm temperatures, but the province's interior region can become very hot in July and August, when temperatures routinely surpass 30°C. For daily weather forecasts and alerts for all BC regions visit www.weatheroffice.pyr.ec.gc.ca.

National & Provincial Parks

BC has seven national parks and 817 provincial parks, recreation areas and ecological reserves, together offering a myriad of outdoor activities, wilderness camping and wonderful opportunities to commune with nature.

Four of the national parks – Yoho National Park (p757), Kootenay National Park (p758), Glacier National Park (p756) and Mt Revelstoke National Park (p756) – are in the southeast region and fairly close to each other. Yoho and Kootenay adjoin Alberta's Banff National Park (p604) in the Rockies, while Glacier and Mt Revelstoke are further west in the Columbia Mountains. Pacific Rim National Park Reserve (p716) arches along Vancouver Island's wet and craggy west coast, offering visitors a kaleidoscope of elemental ocean vistas. The Kootenay and Pacific Rim parks are Unesco world heritage sites.

The remote Gwaii Haanas National Park Reserve (p768) occupies a rugged coastal rain-forest locale in the Queen Charlotte Islands. This remote region offers an opportunity to experience both the wilderness and the area's rich aboriginal heritage. In May 2003 the Gulf Islands National Park Reserve became Canada's 40th national park. It protects a representative area of this maritime region, which is busy and increasingly developed, for future generations. For visitor information and individual phone numbers for all of BC's national parks, visit the website of **Parks Canada** (☎ 888-773-8888; www.parkscanada.ca).

BC's provincial parks, recreation areas and ecological reserves, which range in size up to the 989,000-hectare Tweedsmuir Provincial Park (p773), cover almost 12% of the province. They provide a combined 3000km of hiking trails and 234 of them have good facilities for disabled visitors. Among the most notable, Khutzeymateen Provincial

Park (p767) is Canada's only grizzly-bear sanctuary and is home to about 50 grizzlies, Kitlope Heritage Conservancy houses the world's largest intact coastal temperate rain forest, and Anne Vallee (Triangle Island) Ecological Reserve protects BC's largest seabird colony and Canada's largest Stellar's sea-lion rookery in Canada. For more information, visit the province's official parks website (http://wlapwww.gov.bc.ca/bcparks).

While visits to provincial parks are free, there are one-day parking charges ($3 to $5) at 41 sites in the Lower Mainland, Southern Vancouver Island, Okanagan and Thompson areas. A $50 parking pass, allowing unlimited vehicle access to these designated parks for one year, is also available.

Provincial-park camping fees range from $9 to $22 per party, per vehicle, per night, with stopovers limited to a maximum annual stay of 14 days per park. For additional camping information, contact **Discover Camping** (☎ 604-689-9025; www.discovercamping.ca).

Dangers & Annoyances
FIRES
Forest fires are a major issue in BC every summer, with the interior region around the Okanagan Valley particularly at risk. Do not travel into an area you have been warned to avoid; at their height, these fires can spread rapidly and unpredictably. Forest fires often force temporary campfire bans in the summer in BC, even far from the burning areas, so make sure you obey any posted signs.

BEAR
Bear are quite common in BC's wilderness areas in summer. Visit the BC government's provincial-parks website (wlapwww.gov.bc.ca/bcparks) and see the boxed text on p54 for detailed information on bear attacks.

INSECTS
Blackflies and mosquitoes can be a nightmare in spring and summer in BC, especially in the interior and in the north. Wood ticks are at their most annoying from March to June. For more information on insects, see p850; see p881 for information on avoiding and treating bites.

Getting There & Away
Most travelers arrive in Vancouver via domestic or international flights, or by vehicle across the US border from Washington State or points east across Canada. Less-used arrival options include boat routes from the USA, as well as bus and train services from elsewhere in Canada and the USA.

AIR
Most BC-bound travelers fly into Vancouver, but those interested in the Rockies may prefer to alight in Calgary, Alberta (p603) and make their way through the spectacular mountains to the coast. Aside from Vancouver, there are many smaller airports throughout the province. **Abbotsford** (☎ 604-855-1135; www.abbotsfordairport.ca) is a small airport in the Fraser Valley, a one-hour drive southeast of Vancouver. Other regional airports include Victoria (p706), Nanaimo (p713), Kamloops (p738), Kelowna (p750), Prince George (p775), Dawson Creek, Fort Nelson and Fort St John.

For a complete list of domestic air carriers, see p868. Among the many regular cross-Canada services to BC are Calgary–Abbotsford (WestJet; $200, 1½ hours), Halifax–Vancouver (Air Canada; $700, 10 hours), Edmonton–Vancouver (Air Canada and WestJet; $175, 1½ hours), Montréal–Vancouver (Air Canada and WestJet; $450, five hours), Toronto–Vancouver (Air Canada, WestJet, Jetsgo and Harmony; $300, 4½ hours) and Toronto–Victoria (Air Canada and West Jet; $300, 5½ hours).

Flights to/from the USA include San Francisco ($150, two hours), Los Angeles ($200, 2½ hours), Chicago ($200, four hours) and New York ($300, 5½ hours). **Alaska Airlines** (☎ 800-252-7522; www.alaskaair.com) flies from Seattle to Vancouver, ($130, one hour), Victoria ($180, 45 minutes) and other destinations. Its Horizon Air subsidiary goes to Kelowna ($250, one hour). Other international services to Vancouver include flights from Amsterdam or London (nine hours), Sydney (20 hours), and Tokyo (10 hours). For more details on international flights to Canada, including a list of airlines, see p863.

BOAT
Ferries to the state of Washington depart from Vancouver Island's Belleville Ferry Terminal in Victoria:
Black Ball Transport (☎ 250-386-2202; www.cohoferry.com; adult/child US$9/4.50, car US$36; ⏱ 6:10am,

10:30am, 3pm & 7:30pm) Operates the MV *Coho* to Port Angeles, 90 minutes across the Strait of Juan de Fuca. Check the website for extra holiday sailings.

Clipper Navigation (☎ 250-382-8100, 800-555-2535; www.victoriaclipper.com; adult/child US$86/80; ☻ 11:30am & 7pm mid-May–Jun, also 5:30pm Jun-Sep) *Victoria Clipper* and *Victoria Clipper II* make the three-hour journey to Seattle in water-jet-propelled catamarans.

Victoria Express (☎ 250-361-9144; www.victoria express.com; per person US$10, bicycle US$5; ☻ 9:45am & 6:15pm mid-May–mid-Jul & Sep, also 2pm Jul 19-Sep 1) One-hour passenger-only journey to Port Angeles. Advance bookings recommended during peak season.

Victoria-San Juan Cruises (☎ 250-443-4552; www .whales.com; adult/child US$50/45; ☻ 5pm) The pedestrian-only *Victoria Star* goes to Bellingham.

The BC coast is one of the world's most popular cruise routes for large boats en route to Alaska, with Vancouver, and to a lesser extent Victoria and Prince Rupert, included in many itineraries. Among the major operators are **Norwegian Cruise Lines** (☎ 800-327-7030; www.ncl.com) and **Princess Cruises** (☎ 800-774-6377; www.princess.com).

BUS
Greyhound Canada (p870) operates dozens of cross-Canada services to/from BC, including Calgary–Prince George ($147, 14½ hours, twice daily), Toronto–Kelowna ($342, 65 hours, four daily) and Winnipeg–Vancouver ($207, 35 hours, four daily). For details on routes to/from Vancouver, see p681. In the USA, Greyhound (p867) has many connecting services to BC, all of which travel via Vancouver.

CAR & MOTORCYCLE
The US highway system connects directly with Canadian highways at several points along the BC border. Major points of entry are open 24 hours, although weekends and holidays, particularly in summer, can be especially busy with long line-ups a common problem. For more information on border crossings, see p867.

The main cross-Canada highways into BC include Hwy 3 (via Sparwood), Hwys 1 and 5 (from Banff and Jasper), and Hwys 2 and 97 (via Dawson Creek). The provincial border is a two-hour (180km) drive from Seattle, a two-hour (160km) drive from Calgary and a five-hour (380km) drive from Edmonton.

TRAIN
VIA Rail (p875) runs cross-Canada services into Vancouver's Pacific Central Station and from Jasper, Alberta (p628), to Prince George and Prince Rupert. Amtrak (p867) has services from Seattle that also arrive at Pacific Central Station; see p682 for more information.

Rocky Mountaineer Railtours (☎ 604-606-7245; www.rockymountaineer.com) operates several luxury vacation packages that alight in Vancouver. These seasonal rail journeys are a very popular way to explore the Rockies and the breathtaking BC wilderness. Packages include the seven-day Vancouver and the Rockies tour that travels from Calgary via Banff and Kamloops (from $1200) between April and October.

Getting Around
Driving is the most common method of getting around for visitors traveling in BC. But the province is also well served by air and ferry networks and, to a lesser extent, bus and train services.

AIR
Along with Air Canada's domestic services, BC is teeming with small propeller, seaplane and helicopter operators servicing more than 30 destinations throughout the province. Sample intra-BC routes, fares and operators include Victoria–Vancouver (Air Canada; $100, 25 minutes), Vancouver–Whistler (Whistler Air; $149, 30 minutes) and Kamloops–Kelowna (Central Mountain Air; $76, 25 minutes).

BOAT
BC Ferries (☎ 250-386-3431; www.bcferries.com) operates one of the world's largest and busiest passenger ferry systems, with 25 routes and 46 ports of call. Main routes link Vancouver Island with the mainland, but there are additional links to the Gulf Islands, Sechelt Peninsula and Queen Charlotte Islands.

The company offers several passes for those with the time to really enjoy BC's spectacular coastal waters. Options include the new Summer Sail Vacation Pass (see the boxed text on p696). Also check the BC Ferries website for additional package deals. Vehicle reservations ($15 per car) are recommended for weekend travel in summer and on holidays

---

BRITISH COLUMBIA IN...

Five Days

Start your tour with a three-night stay in **Vancouver** (opposite), delving into the city's richly cosmopolitan neighborhoods. Enjoy self-guided explorations of **Gastown** (p655), **Chinatown** (p656), **Yaletown** (p657) and **Kitsilano** (p658), stopping off for dim sum, coffee or a local beer wherever takes your fancy. Make sure you check out some of Vancouver's fine dining options in the evening.

On day four, take the ferry to **Vancouver Island** (p692), checking in at the **Fairmont Empress Hotel** (p703) for a two-night pampering in **Victoria** (p693), the provincial capital. Take in sites such as the **Royal British Columbia Museum** (p694) and make sure you check out a restaurant or two featuring some of the city's emerging young chefs (see the boxed text on p61).

One Week

Follow the five-day itinerary, then drive from Victoria to Vancouver Island's west coast. Spend two nights exploring the **Pacific Rim National Park Reserve** (p716), especially around **Long Beach** (p716) between **Tofino** (p718) and **Ucluelet** (p721).

Two Weeks

Follow the one-week itinerary, then drive to **Nanaimo** (p710) for the mainland-bound ferry. Alighting in Horseshoe Bay, drive up to **Whistler** (p687) for a couple of nights. From here, you can launch your exploration of BC's interior. Take your time winding into **Kamloops** (p737), then branch out to **Glacier** (p756), **Yoho** (p757) or **Kootenay** (p758) **National Parks**. On your way back to Vancouver, drive though the Okanagan Valley towns of **Kelowna** (p746) and **Vernon** (p750) to explore the vineyards and pick up some local ice wine.

---

on the main routes, including Tsawwassen–Swartz Bay, Horseshoe Bay–Departure Bay and Tsawwassen–Duke Point.

There are also a few private operators serving smaller routes; check individual destinations in this chapter for details.

BUS

Greyhound Canada (p870) covers most of BC. Sample services, fares and durations include Vancouver–Prince Rupert ($193, 25 hours, twice daily), Victoria–Nanaimo ($19, 2½ hours, six daily) and Kamloops–Kelowna ($27, three hours, three daily).

CAR & MOTORCYCLE

Tourists are allowed to drive in BC for up to six months with a valid driver's license from another province or country, or up to 12 months with an International Driving Permit (p872) issued outside Canada. International car rental firms, such as Hertz and Budget, have offices at major BC airports and in towns and cities across the province. See p873 for information about car rentals.

Driving in BC, especially outside Vancouver and Victoria, can make for some very long journeys; for example, it takes 10 hours to cover the 780km between Vancouver and Prince George, and 19 hours to drive 1500km from Vancouver to Prince Rupert. Service stations can be few and far between so make sure your car is up to the drive, keep an eye on the gas gauge and bring along some tools, spare parts, water and food. Driving in areas with heavy snow is not recommended, especially if you're not used to the conditions. See p874 for more advice on driving in Canada.

The provincial government's Ministry of Transport home page (www.gov.bc.ca/tran) contains some excellent resources for drivers, including daily road condition reports, border traffic wait times, seasonal driving tips and a road trip distance calculator.

The **British Columbia Automobile Association** (BCAA; ☎ 877-325-8888; www.bcaa.com) is affiliated with the Canadian Automobile Association (p872) and membership offers all of the same benefits.

TRAIN

VIA Rail (p875) runs the *Skeena* from Jasper, Alberta, to Prince Rupert, BC, with stops in

Prince George and other points along the route by prior arrangement. You can be picked up at 'request stops'– large signposts alongside the track that have a drop-down flap to signal oncoming drivers. See p867 for further information. On Vancouver Island, VIA Rail's *Malahat* links communities between Victoria and Courtenay. See p707 for details.

VANCOUVER

☎ 604 / pop 2.1 million

'When you're tired of Vancouver, you're tired of life,' a time-traveling Dr Johnson might have said about this western Canadian city that routinely tops international surveys of the best places to live. However despite a laid-back vibe, and cosmopolitan flair framed by a spectacular mountain backdrop, Vancouverites love to understate the qualities of their region.

Perhaps they're just embarrassed about the rain. While Vancouver's summers are long and sunny and tourism reps claim there's less annual precipitation here than on the average Caribbean island, October to May sees days of unrelenting rainfall: this is not called the 'Wet Coast' for nothing. Oblivious locals stroll around in shorts and T-shirts on the rainiest afternoons, but since denial is rarely contagious, savvy visitors come armed with rain jackets and umbrellas.

The damp, though, is simply a symptom of Vancouver's unique location. Cradled between the craggy Coast Mountains and twinkling calm of the Pacific Ocean, the city's natural vistas are its most obvious asset. But the area doesn't just rely on its looks. Although Victoria is the provincial capital, downtown Vancouver is the region's unrivaled economic and cultural center.

Fascinating aboriginal heritage is showcased in the area's museums; colorful pioneer history is preserved in its older neighborhoods; colonial influences are echoed in Stanley Park cricket matches; and its quirky art scene, multicultural restaurants and doorstep access to outdoor adventure makes this an active, modern city where there's something exciting worth doing every day.

HISTORY

The Aboriginal peoples thrived for thousands of years before British James Cook, following Russian and Spa explorers, turned up to cause trouble in 177 Mistaking his ragged crew for a boat full of transformed salmon, the Nootka Sound locals were no match for the interlopers' unexpected firepower, which ended years of relatively peaceful living in the region.

The adventurers put the region on the world map, paving the way for waves of European settlers.

A burgeoning fur trade quickly emerged, accompanied by a gold rush that forever changed the region. By the 1850s, thousands of fortune seekers had arrived, prompting the Brits to claim the area as a colony, and one talkative entrepreneur to cleverly seize the initiative. When 'Gassy' Jack Deighton opened his first bar on the forested shores of Burrard Inlet in 1867, he triggered a rash of development that was soon nicknamed 'Gastown,' the forerunner of Vancouver.

However not everything went to plan for the fledgling city. While Vancouver's population soon reached 1000, and the city was linked to the rest of Canada by the Canadian Pacific Railway in 1886, it was almost completely destroyed in a blaze quickly dubbed the Great Fire – even though it lasted only 20 minutes. A prompt rebuild followed, and the modern-day downtown core soon began taking shape. Buildings from this era still survive, as does Stanley Park; originally the town's military reserve, it was opened as a public recreation space in 1891. By 1895 Vancouver's rapidly rising population had outpaced its regional rival, Victoria, the island-based provincial capital.

Relying on its port, Vancouver soon became a hub of industry, importing thousands of immigrant workers to fuel its growth. The Chinatown that was built at this time is one of the largest and most historic in North America. However WWI and the 1929 Wall St crash brought economic depression to Canada, and Vancouver saw mass unemployment, which quickly turned into demonstrations and rioting. The economy only recovered during WWII, when both shipbuilding and armaments manufacturing increased.

Growing steadily throughout the 1950s and '60s, Vancouver gained a National Hockey

...st at the **Templeton** (p671) before hitting the **Vancouver Art Gallery** ... a tranquility break at **Christ Church Cathedral** (p655) then continue ... the waterfront. Head to **Canada Place** (p655) for some panoramic ... ollow the seawall towards **Stanley Park** (p656), stopping for coffee at ... p674). Spend the afternoon exploring the attractions of Canada's largest urban park. M... enman St at dinnertime, perhaps to the **Denman St Freehouse** (p675) overlooking English Bay.

Two Days

Follow the itinerary for day one, then strike out for **Chinatown** (p656), one of North America's largest. Wander the colorful streets and partake of dim sum, before heading to the fascinating **Dr Sun Yat-Sen Classical Chinese Garden** (p656). Change the pace at nearby **Science World** (p656). Reflect on your day over dinner in **Kitsilano** (p673), before hitting a bar or two in **Yaletown** (p675).

Three Days

After your two-day city trek, hit the nature trails at **Lighthouse Park** (p660) in West Vancouver. Park the car and explore the rocky waterfront and forest hideaways, then continue your drive to North Vancouver where you can lunch and check out **Lynn Canyon Park** (p660), with its suspension bridge and ecology center. Head next to nearby **Grouse Mountain** (p660) for a Skyride to the peak and some spectacular vistas. Drive back downtown for dinner at **Cin Cin Ristorante & Bar** (p671).

League (NHL) team and other accoutrements of a midsized North American city. Vancouver finally recognized its heritage, and Gastown – by now a slum area – was designated for gentrification. And in 1986, the city hosted a highly successful world's fair, Expo '86, which sparked a massive wave of modern development, adding the first of the mirrored skyscrapers that now define the downtown core.

Now Canada's third-largest city, and routinely designated as one of the world's best places to live, Vancouver is preparing for another global event that it hopes will kick-start what has become a lackluster BC economy. The 2010 Winter Olympic Games are seen by local politicians as a golden opportunity to showcase the city (and Whistler, p687) to the world.

ORIENTATION

Greater Vancouver is built on a series of peninsulas, and bound on the north by Burrard Inlet and on the south by Fraser River and Boundary Bay. The Coast Mountains rise directly behind the city to the north, while to the west, the Strait of Georgia is cluttered with islands. The many bays, inlets and river branches, as well as the Pacific coastline, are major features of the city.

Downtown Vancouver occupies a narrow peninsula bounded on three sides by Burrard Inlet, English Bay and False Creek, with **Stanley Park** at the tip. Key attractions and neighborhoods are all easily accessible on foot, and streets are organized on a grid system. Robson St and Georgia St are the main downtown east–west thoroughfares, while Granville St is the main north–south artery. If you get lost, red-suited 'Downtown Ambassadors' walk the streets to assist visiting tourists, when they're not moving on panhandlers or naughty sidewalk skateboarders.

Three prominent neighborhoods are just a few steps from the downtown core: **Yaletown** is on Hamilton and Mainland Sts; **Gastown** is centered on Water St; and **Chinatown** is in the area around Pender St, between Abbott St and Gore Ave. You'll need to be on wheels if you want to quickly get to **Kitsilano** or **Richmond**; they're south of downtown via bridges. Over Lions Gate Bridge and Second Narrows Bridge respectively reside **West Vancouver** and **North Vancouver** (which together comprise the North Shore).

ROSS BARNETT

An in-line skater on the seawall in Stanley Park (p656), Vancouver

Pacific Rim National Park Reserve
(p716), Vancouver Island

FRANK CARTER

MARY L PEACHIN

Parliament Buildings (p696),
Victoria

GLENN VAN DER KNIJFF

Whistler Mountain, Whistler-Blackcomb (p688)

GRANT DIXON

Auyuittuq National Park (p838), Nunavut

SUSAN RIMERMAN

Dawson City Bunkhouse (p802),
Dawson City, Yukon

Iqaluit (p834), Nunavut

GRANT DIXON

Dempster Highway (p803), Yukon

SUSAN RIMERMAN

Vancouver International Airport is about 23km south of downtown, while Pacific Central Station, the combined bus and train terminus, is just across from the Main St SkyTrain station.

Maps

Tourism Vancouver's Touristinfo Centre (TIC; p651) provides a useful free map of the grid-like downtown core. The much more comprehensive *Greater Vancouver Streetwise Map Book* ($5.95) is in an easy-to-follow A-to-Z style and is widely available in newsagents, bookstores and convenience stores. Rand McNally also produces a popular fold-out city map ($3.95). TransLink publishes the useful *Regional Vancouver Cycling Map & Guide* ($3.95), which details cycle routes and amenities throughout the Lower Mainland.

INFORMATION

Bookstores

Banyen Books & Sound (Map pp650-1; ☎ 604-732-7912; 3608 W 4th Ave; ⌚ 10am-9pm Mon-Fri, 10am-8pm Sat, 11am-7pm Sun) New-age megastore.

Barbara-Jo's Books to Cooks (Map pp652-4; ☎ 604-688-6755; 1128 Mainland St; ⌚ 10am-6pm Mon-Fri, 10:30am-5:30pm Sat, noon-5pm Sun) Foodie bookstore with cooking demonstrations and classes.

Granville Book Company (Map pp652-4; ☎ 604-687-2213; 850 Granville St; ⌚ 9:30am-midnight Mon-Sat, noon-midnight Sun) Independent bookstore with quirky magazine section.

International Travel Maps & Books (Map pp650-1; ☎ 604-879-3621; 530 W Broadway; ⌚ 9am-6pm Mon-Fri, 10am-6pm Sat, noon-6pm Sun) Best map shop in western Canada.

Kidsbooks (Map pp650-1; ☎ 604-738-5335; 3083 W Broadway; ⌚ 9:30am-6pm Mon-Sat, to 9pm Fri, noon-5pm Sun) Giant selection of children's titles.

Pulp Fiction Books (Map pp650-1; ☎ 604-876-4311; 2422 Main St; ⌚ 10am-8pm Mon-Wed, 10am-9pm Thu-Sat, 11am-7pm Sun) Excellent secondhand selection, specializing in paperbacks.

Travel Bug (Map pp650-1; ☎ 604-737-1122; 3065 W Broadway; ⌚ 10am-6pm Mon-Sat, to 7pm Thu, to 5pm Fri) Extensive selection of guides, maps and accessories for travel around the world.

Emergency

Crisis Centre (☎ 604-872-3311) Emotional-crisis counseling.

Police, Fire & Ambulance (☎ 911)

Rape Crisis Centre (☎ 604-255-6344; ⌚ 24hr) Sexual-assault crisis line.

Vancouver Police Department (Map pp652-4; ☎ 604-717-3321; 2120 Cambie St) For nonemergencies.

Internet Access

Cyber Madness (Map pp652-4; ☎ 604-633-9389; 779 Denman St; per 30min $1.75; ⌚ 10am-midnight)

Electric Internet Café (Map pp652-4; ☎ 604-681-0667; 605 W Pender St; per 30min $1.50; ⌚ 7-3am Mon-Fri, 8-3am Sat & Sun) Thirty-six terminals, good food specials.

Georgia Post Plus (Map pp652-4; ☎ 604-632-4226; 1358 W Georgia St; per 30min $2; ⌚ 9:30am-6pm Mon-Fri, 10am-4pm Sat)

Vancouver Public Library (Map pp652-4; ☎ 604-331-3600; 350 W Georgia St; 30min free; ⌚ 10am-9pm Mon-Thu, 10am-6pm Fri & Sat, 1-5pm Sun) Over 25 terminals for nonmembers, no ID required, busy at peak times.

Internet Resources

Discover Vancouver (www.discovervancouver.com) General visitors' guide to the city.

Preview (www.preview-art.com) Online version of guide with listings and links for art galleries in the city and beyond.

Vancouver 2010 (www.vancouver2010.com) Official tourism site for 2010 Winter Olympics build-up.

Vancouver Plus (www.vancouverplus.ca) Local news and listings resource with useful map location feature.

Visit Vancouver (www.visitvancouver.com) Overview of the city for visitors.

Visitors Choice Vancouver (www.visitorschoice.com) Good searchable maps and an overview of attractions and accommodations in the region.

Media

Georgia Straight (www.straight.com) Must-get free listings newspaper with some two-for-one restaurant coupons.

Province (www.vancouverprovince.com) Daily tabloid.

Terminal City (www.terminalcity.ca) Indie-scene guide.

Vancouver Magazine (www.vanmag.com) Monthly glossy covering local mainstream trends.

Vancouver Sun (www.vancouversun.com) Main daily.

Westender (www.westender.com) Quirky downtown community newspaper.

Xtra! West (www.xtra.ca) Free gay and lesbian newspaper.

Medical Services

BC Nurse Line (☎ 604-215-4700) One-on-one phone guidance on health issues.

St Paul's Hospital (Map pp652-4; ☎ 604-682-2344; 1081 Burrard St; ⌚ 24hr) Accident and emergency services.

Shoppers Drug Mart (Map pp652-4; ☎ 604-669-2424; 1125 Davie St; ⌚ 24hr) Pharmacy chain.

Travel Medicine & Vaccination Centre (Map pp652-4; ☎ 604-681-5656; 314-1030 W Georgia St) Shots and medical advice for onward travel.

VANCOUVER

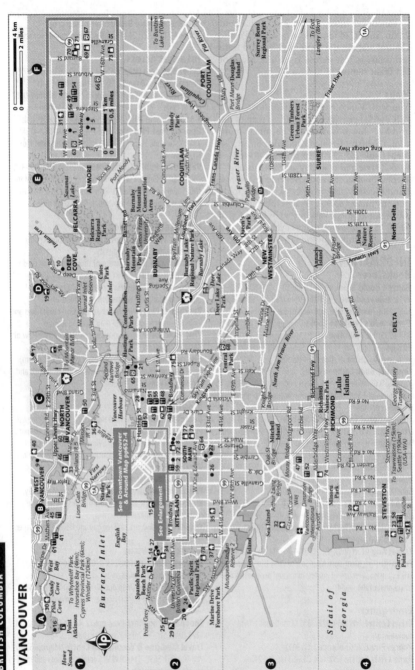

See Downtown Vancouver
& Around Map pp652–4

See Enlargement

INFORMATION
Banyen Books & Sound ... 1 E1
International Travel Maps & Books ... 2 B2
Kidsbooks ... 3 E1
Pulp Fiction Books ... 4 C2
Travel Bug ... 5 F1

SIGHTS & ACTIVITIES (pp654-64)
Bloedel Floral Conservatory ... 6 B2
Burnaby Village Museum ... 7 D2
Canada West Mountain School ... 8 C2
Capilano Suspension Bridge & Park ... 9 B1
Deep Cove Canoe & Kayak Centre ... 10 D1
Ecomarine Ocean Kayak Centre (Jericho Beach) ... 11 B2
Gulf of Georgia Cannery National Historic Site ... 12 B4
Hastings Racecourse ... 13 C2
Jericho Beach Park ... 14 B2
Kitsilano Beach Park ... 15 B2
Lighthouse Park ... 16 A1
Lynn Canyon Ecology Centre ... 17 C1
Lynn Canyon Park ... 18 C1
Mt Seymour Provincial Park ... 19 D1
Nitobe Memorial Gardens ... 20 A2
Playland ... 21 C2
Queen Elizabeth Park ... 22 B2
Steveston Museum ... 23 B4
UBC Botanical Gardens ... 24 A2
UBC Museum of Anthropology ... 25 A2
VanDusen Botanical Gardens ... 26 B2
Windsure Windsurfing School ... 27 B2
WISE Hall ... 28 C2
Wreck Beach ... 29 A2

SLEEPING (pp666-70)
Beachside B&B ... 30 A1
Corkscrew Inn ... 31 F1
Fairmont Vancouver Airport ... 32 B3
Grouse Inn ... 33 B1
HI Vancouver Jericho Beach ... 34 B2
Johnson's Heritage House B&B ... 35 B2
Lonsdale Quay Hotel ... 36 C1
Pacific Spirit Guest House ... 37 B2
Steveston Hotel ... 38 B4
Stone Hedge B&B ... 39 B4
ThistleDown House ... 40 C1

EATING (pp670-4)
Beach House at Dundarave Pier ... 41 B1
Belgian Fries ... 42 C2
Bukowski's ... 43 C2
Capers Community Markets ... 44 F1
Capers Community Markets ... 45 B1
Caspian ... 46 B1
Chiu Chow Garden ... 47 B3
Clove ... 48 C2
Feenies ... 49 F1
Gusto di Quattro ... 50 C1
Havana ... 51 C2
Kelong Singapore Cuisine ... 52 B3
La Casa Gelato ... 53 C2
Lumière ... 54 F1
Mekong House ... 55 C2
Naam ... 56 F1
Papi's ... 57 B4
Steveston Seafood House ... 58 B4
Tojo's ... 59 B2
Tomahawk Barbecue ... 60 C1
Vera's Burger Shack ... 61 B1

DRINKING (pp674-6)
Calabria Coffee Bar ... 62 C2

ENTERTAINMENT (pp676-8)
Cellar Restaurant & Jazz Club ... 63 E1
Nat Bailey Stadium ... 64 C2
Pacific Coliseum ... 65 C2
Ridge Theatre ... 66 F1
Stanley Theatre ... 67 F1
Swangard Stadium ... 68 C3

SHOPPING (pp678-80)
Bau-xi Gallery ... 69 F1
Diane Farris Gallery ... 70 F1
La Grotta del Formaggio ... (see 62)
Lonsdale Quay Market ... (see 36)
Meinhardt Fine Foods ... 71 F1
Mountain Equipment Co-op ... 72 C2
Paperhaus ... 73 F1
Richmond Night Market ... 74 B4
Roots Factory Outlet ... 75 C2
Simple ... 76 C2
Smoking Lily ... 77 C2
UBC Farm Market ... 78 B2

Traveller's Medicentre (Map pp652-4; ☎ 604-683-8138; Bentall Centre Mall, 1055 Dunsmuir St; ⏰ 8am-4:30pm Mon-Fri) Walk-in clinic for visitors.

Money

Banks and ATMs are located throughout the city, with main bank branches congregating around the business district bordered by Burrard St, Georgia St, Pender St and Granville St.

American Express (Map pp652-4; ☎ 604-669-2813 2501; 666 Burrard St; ⏰ 8:30am-5:30pm Mon-Fri, 10am-4pm Sat)

Thomas Cook Foreign Exchange (Map pp652-4; ☎ 604-689-3116; 777 Dunsmuir St; ⏰ 10am-6pm Mon-Sat, noon-6pm Sun)

Post

Georgia Post Plus (Map pp652-4; ☎ 604-632-4226; 1358 W Georgia St; ⏰ 9:30am-6pm Mon-Fri, 10am-4pm Sat) Full-service postal outlet, plus computer terminals and stationery store.

Howe St Postal Outlet (Map pp652-4; ☎ 604-688-2068; 732 Davie St; ⏰ 8am-8pm Mon-Fri, 9am-5pm Sat)

Main Post Office (Map pp652-4; ☎ 604-662-5723; 349 W Georgia St; ⏰ 8am-5:30pm Mon-Fri)

Tourist Information

Tourism Vancouver Tourist Info Centre (Map pp652-4; TIC; ☎ 604-683-2000; www.tourismvancouver.com; 200 Burrard St; ⏰ 8am-6pm mid-May–Sep, 8:30am-5pm Mon-Fri, 9am-5pm Sat Oct–mid-May) Free map, visitor guide, half-price theater tickets and 24-hour automated currency exchange. There are also two airport branches covering destinations throughout BC.

DANGERS & ANNOYANCES

Overall, Vancouver is a safe city for visitors. Purse-snatching and pick-pocketing does take place, however, so you should be vigilant with your personal possessions, especially in crowded areas such as Robson St, downtown shopping malls, and at festivals that attract large crowds. Theft from unattended cars is also common, so never leave valuables in vehicles.

The downtown eastside, between Chinatown and Gastown, is a depressing ghetto of lives wasted by drug abuse and prostitution. Crime against visitors is not common here, but you are advised to be vigilant and stick to the area's main streets, especially at night. You may be discretely offered drugs by small-fry pushers in this part of town, but just walk on and they won't bother you again.

Street begging across the city has become an issue for visitors, with a small assortment of hardcore scam artists – known by locals as the 'usual suspects' – targeting gullible tourists with their made-up tales of woe. One professional beggar has been requesting help for the ferry fare back to Vancouver Island for at least five years. Unfortunately, these individuals have hardened many

DOWNTOWN VANCOUVER & AROUND

To Third
Beach (500m)

Stanley Park Dr

To Rose
Garden (200m)

To Lumberman's
Arch (300m)

To Totem
Poles (200m)

A 41 **B** **C** **D**

Lost Lagoon

Coal Harbour

1

Second
Beach

Stanley Park

Devonian
Harbour Park 147

Royal Vancouver
Yacht Club

62

99
1A

81 34

52 Chilco St Haro St
Gilford St

Lagoon Dr

5 96
38 Georgia St
Alberni St

Coal Harbour
Quay

Barclay St

Comox St

54

85
103

Robson St
Haro St

77

Pender St

Coal Harbour
Park

Melville St

2

Pendrell St

Barclay St

83

7

88 69
75

Bidwell St Nelson St Cardero St

101
84 80

Barclay
Heritage Sq

61 50
138
78 93

99
104

Comox St

60
Nicola St

35
Broughton St

Jervis St

Bute St Haro St

3

English Bay

Inukshuk

Pendrell St

Davie St

Burnaby St

Harwood St

West End

Thurlow St

4 Nelson
Park

Burrard St

137
111

12

11

48
73 149
122

Hornby St
51

4

False Creek Ferry

Hadden
Park

Seaside Trail

False Creek

Sunset
Beach
Park

Pacific St

Beach Ave

Burrard St Drake St

121
9 124
116

Howe St

Granville St

Kitsilano Point

45

Ogden Ave

Vanier
Park

144

42

129

Seymour St

Richards St

Pacific Blvd

McNicoll Ave
Whyte Ave

46
31

Burrard St

Burrard Bridge

False Creek
Ferry

142

Seabreeze
Walk

Seawall

5

Kitsilano
Beach Park

Creelman Ave

Cornwall Ave

Laburnum St
Walnut St
Chestnut St

87

False Creek
Ferry

76
26
133
120
98 127
89

Granville
Island

Granville Bridge

Promenade

108

York Ave

64

28

30
32

Broker's
Bay

148

Cartwright St

Johnston St

27

29

56

Sutcliffe Park

6

100 90

49
131

Yew St
Arbutus St
Maple St
Cypress St

Cornwall Ave

W 1st Ave

W 2nd Ave

W 3rd Ave

Fir St

19

99

117

W 4th Ave

W 5th Ave

W 6th Ave

The Mound

Alder Bay

Lamey's Mill Rd

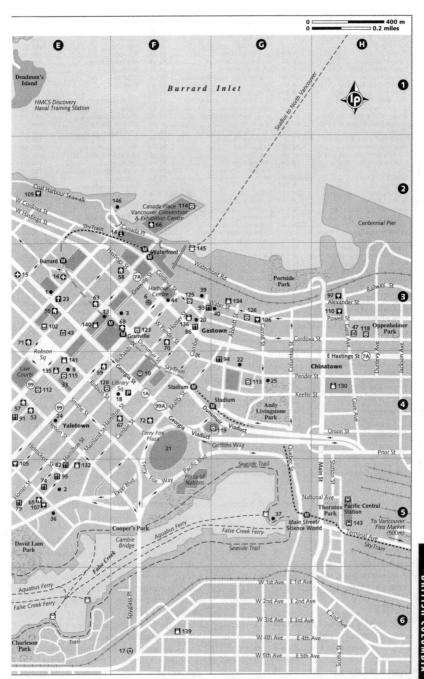

locals against those who live on the streets and genuinely need help.

With its proximity to the West End, Stanley Park is a casual nighttime pick-up spot for local gay men. There have been some violent assaults by homophobic out-of-towners here, so it's becoming an increasingly risky proposition.

SIGHTS

Vancouver's primary attractions are spread among the key neighborhoods around the city, with some hot spots – in particular Gastown, Chinatown, Stanley Park and Granville Island – drawing those visitors who simply like to wander around the city and explore.

Downtown   Map pp652-4

Downtown Vancouver is bordered on two sides by water, and on one side by the enormous Stanley Park. This constraint has forced the city upward. While none of the business towers is startlingly high, the cumulative effect of so many skyscrapers makes the city center seem *über*-modern – it has been used as a sci-fi movie set on more than one occasion. The center of downtown is where Granville St meets Georgia St and Robson St.

VANCOUVER ART GALLERY

Housed in a former colonial courthouse that's often used for movie shoots, this **art gallery** (VAG; ☎ 604-662-4719; 750 Hornby St; adult/child/concession $15/free/$11, by donation after 5pm Thu; ⏱ 10am-5:30pm, to 9pm Thu, closed Mon Oct-Easter) showcases the natural heart of west-coast culture. Start on the 4th floor for the swirling, stylized canvasses of BC legend Emily Carr, a pioneering painter of mountain, forest and aboriginal scenes. The rest is a changing mélange of temporary exhibitions mixing contemporary artists (photographic art is a regional specialty) with traveling shows. There are frequent artist-led gallery talks and the VAG's **Young Associates** (ya@vanartgallery.bc.ca) arm hosts regular social events. Membership is not required and these events offer visiting under-40s a great way to meet like-minded locals.

VANCOUVER LOOKOUT!

The 1970s-style **Vancouver Lookout! Harbour Centre Tower** (☎ 604-689-0421; www.vancouverlookout.com; 555 W Hastings St; adult/child/concession $10/4/7; ⏱ 8:30am-10:30pm May–mid-Oct, 9am-9pm mid-Oct–Apr) is a pricey way to check out the inlet's floating gas stations and the downtown sprawl from on high, but the ticket to the observation deck includes a guided tour of the sights from the top and is valid all day, so you can return for a nighttime view. The website has a $1 discount coupon.

CHRIST CHURCH CATHEDRAL

Completed in 1895, this **cathedral** (☎ 604-682-3848; 690 Burrard St; admission free; ⏱ 10am-4pm, services Sat & Sun) is the biggest and best neo-Gothic church in the city, and nestles incongruously amidst the glass towers of the business district. Head down to the basement for a little-known treat: a William Morris stained-glass window.

CANADA PLACE

Check Vancouver's most distinctive landmark building over at **Canada Place** (☎ 604-647-7390; 999 Canada Place Way). Built for Expo '86, this iconic waterfront structure is shaped like a series of sails and is a major cruiseship terminal and convention center. It's well worth a visit for its panoramic views of Stanley Park and the mountains, punctuated by the regular splash of seaplanes out front.

ROEDDE HOUSE MUSEUM

It's hard to remember that Vancouver was a new pioneering town, nestled among virgin rain forest, less than 150 years ago. The idea of heritage preservation didn't really take off until the 1970s, when it was too late to save many of the timber-framed houses that launched the city. Bucking the trend, **Roedde House Museum** (☎ 604-684-7040; 1415 Barclay St; adult/concession $4/3; ⏱ 2-4pm Wed-Fri & Sun), an 1893 mansion packed with period antiques, is a superb re-creation of how well-heeled Vancouverites used to live. Sunday entry includes tea and costs $1 more.

BC PLACE STADIUM

Home of the BC Lions Canadian Football League (CFL) team (see p678), **BC Place** (777 Pacific Blvd) is a little past its prime compared to the nearby NHL hockey venue, GM Place, but there are a couple of good off-the-beaten-track attractions here for visiting sports fans. The excellent **BC Sports Hall of Fame & Museum** (☎ 604-687-5520; adult/child/family $6/4/15; ⏱ 10am-5pm) is where you can check out a giant selection of historic sporting ephemera from the region's various teams and sporting heroes. And there's a guided **stadium tour** (☎ 604-661-7362; Gate H; adult/child/concession $5/3/4; ⏱ 11am & 1pm Tue & Fri mid-Jun–early Sep) providing a fascinating behind-the-scenes glimpse of the locker rooms and celebrity suites outside game hours.

WALL CENTRE

The church of capitalism is celebrated at the 138m-high **Wall Centre** (1008 Burrard St), where a ludicrous dispute with the City has left Vancouver's highest tower block with two clashing window finishes.

Gastown   Map pp652–4

While it's hardly an auspicious name, this is where Vancouver began after 'Gassy' Jack Deighton, an English sailor, forsook the sea, in 1867, to open a bar servicing the region's developing timber mills. When a village sprang up around his establishment, the area became known as Gassy's Town. Look out for the jocular bronze of Gassy Jack perched atop a beer barrel at the juncture of Cordova St and Water St.

Seeking a fresh start after a devastating fire in 1893, the city relocated itself and

Gastown quickly became Vancouver's skid row, only to be restored as a cobbled thoroughfare of souvenir shops, buskers and restaurants in the 1970s. The heritage buildings are still here – just look up and you'll see many have been restored as offices and live-work spaces.

Vancouver's most photographed attraction, the noisy **steam clock**, is halfway along Water St. Join the throng waiting for it to sound the quarter-hours like a train whistle and keep one of the city's best-kept secrets to yourself: the 'steam clock' is actually powered by electricity.

For a walking tour of Gastown, see p664.

VANCOUVER POLICE CENTENNIAL MUSEUM

This may be Vancouver's best **museum** (☎ 604-665-3346; 240 E Cordova St; adult/child $6/4; ⏰ 9am-3pm Mon-Fri Nov-Apr, 9am-3pm Mon-Fri, 10am-3pm Sat May-Oct). Housed in the city's former morgue and coroner's court, the atmosphere is suitably chilling to tell the story of the city's most famous crimes and criminals. A lethal armory of weapons, counterfeit money, forensic autopsy tools and a century's worth of drug paraphernalia help to illustrate the fascinating story of law enforcement in Vancouver.

STORYEUM

Vancouver's newest attraction, **Storyeum** (☎ 604-687-8142, 800-687-8142; www.storyeum.ca; 142 Water St; adult/child/concession $22/16/19; ⏰ 9am-7pm May-Oct, 10am-6pm Nov-Apr) offers an unusual, 70-minute trawl through the region's history. An antidote to the stuffy display cases of most museums, visitors here move through a series of live-action theaters, where they find out how the Aboriginal people lived, what the gold rush was all about and how BC began. The whole 70-minute show takes place underground. Opening hours change often, so call ahead.

Chinatown   Map pp652–4

North America's third-largest Chinatown is one of Vancouver's most enticing areas. A sensory explosion of sights, sounds and aromas, it's also a richly historic neighborhood. Look above shop level, and you'll see the paint-peeled evidence of decades of history, along with the occasional year marker showing the true age of many of the buildings.

While many younger Chinese have moved out to Richmond, this bustling downtown area is still teeming with shops hawking exotic fruits, ancient remedies, and the occasional bucket of live frogs. Don't miss the lively summer night market (p679) and consider stopping for the best dim sum in town: there's nowhere better to sample Chinese food than at a place where all the customers are Chinese. Among the sites you'll find while wandering the streets here is the three-story-high **Chinatown Millennium Gate** (cnr W Pender & Taylor Sts), a giant new entry point for the area.

DR SUN YAT-SEN CLASSICAL CHINESE GARDEN

A tranquil break from clamorous Chinatown, this intimate **garden** (☎ 604-662-3207; www.vancouverchinesegarden.com; 578 Carrall St; adult/child/senior/family $8.25/5.75/6.75/18; ⏰ 10am-4:30pm Oct-Apr, to 6pm May–mid-Jun & Sep, 9:30am-7pm mid-Jun–Aug) reveals the Taoist symbolism behind the placing of gnarled pine trees, winding covered pathways and ancient limestone formations. The only full-scale classical Chinese garden outside China, entry includes an excellent guided tour; look out for lazy turtles bobbing in the water on sunny days. There's a less impressive free-entry garden immediately next door.

SCIENCE WORLD

The landmark silver geodesic dome looks like a spaceship but it actually houses **Science World** (☎ 604-443-7443; www.scienceworld.bc.ca; 1455 Quebec St; adult/child/family $12.75/8.50/42.50; ⏰ 10am-5pm Mon-Fri, 10am-6pm Sat & Sun), a science, technology and natural-history center with interactive exhibits. Aimed primarily at children, hands-on experiments help explain scientific and physical phenomena. There's also an **Omnimax Theatre** (an additional charge applies), where movies are guaranteed to have you swaying in your seat. For the streetcar between Science World and Granville Island, see p657.

Stanley Park   Map pp652–4

One of North America's largest urban parks, **Stanley Park** (☎ 604-257-8400) is the highlight of any Vancouver visit because of its combination of natural and human-built attractions. Don't miss a jog, stroll or cycle (rentals are available near the entrance on W Georgia St; see p662) around the 9km-long and 5.5m-wide **seawall**, with its dramatic sea-to-sky vistas and smattering of sandy beaches. The **Rose Garden** and **Rhododendron Garden** will satisfy flora lovers, and this is also a good spot to photograph the **totem poles**. There are eight clustered just past Deadman's Island but you'll have to elbow the tour groups aside to see them in the summer. Bring a picnic lunch and watch the cruise ships slip by at **Lumberman's Arch**, or hit one of the four restaurants. If you've got kids in tow, check out the miniature railway or the summer outdoor swimming pool. There's a free around-the-park shuttle bus with commentary from June to September.

VANCOUVER AQUARIUM MARINE SCIENCE CENTRE

The park's biggest draw, the **Vancouver Aquarium Marine Science Centre** (☎ 604-659-3474; adult/child/concession $17.25/10/13; ◷ 10am-5:30pm Sep-Jun, 9:30am-7pm Jul & Aug) is home to 9000 sea creatures, including sharks, dolphins, beluga whales and an octopus. Look out for the iridescent-jellyfish tank and the two sea otters that eat the way everyone should: lying on their backs using their chests as plates. The aquarium has worked hard to reposition itself as a conservation center but not all environmentalists agree with its claims.

Yaletown Map pp652–4

A former redbrick warehouse district which was transformed into chichi apartments, loungy restaurants and bling-bling boutiques in the 1990s, pedestrian-friendly Yaletown – Vancouver's 'little Soho' – is where the city's beautiful people come to be seen.

Roughly bordered by Nelson, Homer, Drake and Pacific Sts, Yaletown has not completely abandoned its past: old railway tracks are still embedded in the roads, and the **Roundhouse Community Centre** (☎ 604-713-1800; www.roundhouse.ca; theater tickets $10-25), the home of some innovative theater productions, is situated in a revamped train shed that is complete with a restored steam locomotive.

Drop by the recently relocated **Contemporary Art Gallery** (☎ 604-681-2700; 555 Nelson St; admission free; ◷ 11am-5pm Wed-Sat, noon-5pm Sun)

for a glimpse [...] are up to. Ph[...] represented [...] accessible sp[...]

Granville I[...]

You can w[...] downtown, bu[...] ninsula (it's not actuall[...] Granville Bridge is best reached via a [...] sized ferry (see p682) from the north bank of False Creek. Successfully redeveloped in the 1970s into a highly popular blend of restaurants, theaters, buskers, artisan businesses and boutique shops, it's always crowded on hot summer weekends.

Get your bearings at the **Granville Island Information Centre** (☎ 604-666-5784; 1398 Cartwright St; ◷ 9am-6pm) before heading inside to the **Public Market** (☎ 604-666-6477; Johnson St; ◷ 9am-6pm, closed Mon in Jan). Like a vast multicountered deli, the market specializes in gourmet meat, fish, cheese and other delectables. There's also an excellent international food court (eat early or late to avoid the crush) and some superb craft stands and artisan bakeries.

For beer fans, this is the spiritual home of **Granville Island Brewing** (☎ 604-687-2739; 1441 Cartwright St) and there's a recommended **brewery tour** (adult/child/concession $9.75/2/8.75; ◷ noon, 2pm & 4pm) here to convert the naysayers. Guides walk and talk you through the tiny brewing room (production has mostly shifted to a larger industrial facility) before depositing you in the bar for some generous sampling. The Maple Cream Ale is recommended and don't forget to ask for your souvenir glass. Kids receive a soda pop.

If you have time, a visit to the public galleries at the highly regarded **Emily Carr Institute of Art & Design** (☎ 604-844-3800; 1399 Johnson St; admission free; ◷ noon-5pm Mon-Fri, 10am-5pm Sat & Sun) is an eye-opening glimpse into the minds of some great up-and-coming artists.

This area is also home to two transportation modes at opposite ends of the technology scale. **Downtown Historic Railway** (adult/child $2/1; ◷ 12:30-4:30pm Sat, Sun & holidays mid-May–mid-Oct) runs two beautifully restored streetcars between Granville Island and Science World, while **Future Human Transport Solutions** (☎ 604-734-9280; 1524 Duranleau St; per hr $21.88) rents Segways, the two-wheeled stand-up people movers, for private use.

nville Island, 'Kits' is a neigh-
here 1960s hippies have settled
bly into their mortgages and high-
professions, creating pleasant streets
ll-maintained heritage homes, cozy cof-
bars, good restaurants and excellent one-
of-a-kind shops. Young artsy types still live
here, but mostly with their parents: it's now
one of the priciest parts of town for accommodations. This area is great for a summer's
day of street strolling, window shopping and
coffee-bar hopping. If it's really hot, grab an
organic smoothie and head to **Jericho Beach
Park** (Map pp650–1) or **Kitsilano Beach Park**
(Map pp650–1), both great sunset spots.

VANIER PARK   Map pp652–4
The closest Kitsilano point to downtown
is Vanier Park (it's virtually adjacent to the
Burrard Bridge), site of the annual Bard on
the Beach Shakespeare festival (p665) and
home to a veritable nest of old-school family-
friendly Vancouver museums. Pick up an
Explorepass (adult/child $25/20) for all three of
these attractions.

   Vancouver Museum (☎ 604-736-4431; 1100 Chestnut
St; adult/child/concession $10/6/8; ☽ 10am-5pm Tue-Sun,
to 9pm Thu) attracts most visitors with its traditional re-creations of the region's ancient
and recent history. There are some unique
aboriginal artifacts – although they're not
nearly as well-presented as those at the UBC
Museum of Anthropology (see right) – but
the emphasis is on recent social history
with plenty of nostalgic items donated from
grandparents' attics.

   The adjacent **HR MacMillan Space Centre**
(☎ 604-738-7827; 1100 Chestnut St; adult/child/concession
$13.50/9.50/10.50; ☽ 10am-5pm Tue-Sun) is popular
with school groups, whose students always
hit the hands-on exhibits with maximum
force. There's an additional free-entry,
stand-alone **observatory** (☽ weekend nights,
weather permitting) and a **planetarium**, which also
runs the occasional nighttime laser-show
celebration of bands like Radiohead.

   The final member of the Vanier Park trio,
the **Vancouver Maritime Museum** (☎ 604-257-
8300; 1905 Ogden Ave; adult/concession/family $8/5.50/18;
☽ 10am-5pm Tue-Sat, noon-5pm Sun) combines
dozens of intricate model ships with some
detailed re-created boat sections and a few
historic vessels. There are plenty of kid-
friendly exhibits along with the *St Roch*, the

legendary arctic patrol vessel that was the
first to navigate the Northwest Passage in
both directions.

South Main (SoMa)
One of the city's roughest neighborhoods not
too long ago, South Main (SoMa) – in the
area where Broadway and Main St collide – is
being successfully re-created as one of Vancouver's hippest new hot spots, despite its
still-grungy appearance. Plenty of bohemian
coffee bars, vegetarian-friendly eateries, one-
of-a-kind boutiques and bold little artist-run
galleries punctuate the area, which is populated increasingly by the art-student-turned-
film-producer set with their brick-loft-loving
ways. This is among the city's best areas for
an afternoon of exploring on foot.

Commercial Drive
Adventurers should also consider trekking
along East Vancouver's Commercial Dr,
where decades of European immigrants –
especially Italians, Greeks and Portuguese –
have created a UN of well-priced restaurants,
coffee bars, ice-cream parlors and exotic
delis. This is the perfect spot for watching
World Cup soccer games among the city's
most passionate fans. See p673 for restaurant
recommendations in this area.

University of British Columbia   Map pp652–4
Located west of Kits, on a forested peninsula,
the University of British Columbia (UBC) is
the province's largest university. The concrete campus is surrounded by University
Endowment Lands with accessible beach
and forest wilderness sites, and some excellent visitor attractions. Naturists should
check out Wreck Beach (p662).

MUSEUM OF ANTHROPOLOGY
The **Museum of Anthropology** (☎ 604-822-3825;
6393 NW Marine Dr; adult/concession $9/7, free Tue after
5pm; ☽ 10am-5pm Wed-Mon, to 9pm Tue mid-May–Aug,
11am-5pm Wed-Sun, to 9pm Tue Sep–mid-May) offers
perhaps the best displays of northwest-coast
aboriginal heritage in Canada. The totem
poles alone – displayed against a wall of
glass overlooking a stunning cliff-top promontory – are worth the admission. Spend
some extra time here reading up on the
area's often forgotten ancient past; the next
time someone in Vancouver moans about

their lack of history, remind them of the thousands of years' worth on display here.

NITOBE MEMORIAL GARDENS

The nearby **Nitobe Memorial Gardens** (☎ 604-822-6038; 1903 West Mall, Point Grey; adult/child/concession $3/1.50/2, reduced in winter; ⌚ 10am-6pm mid-Mar–mid-Oct, 10am-2:30pm mid-Oct–mid-Mar) were designed by a leading Japanese landscape architect, and they're a perfect example of the symbolic horticultural art form. Aside from some traffic noise and summer bus tours, they're a tranquil retreat, ideal for quiet meditation. Combined entry with the UBC Botanical Garden is $6 per adult.

UBC BOTANICAL GARDEN

Another nearby gem, the **UBC Botanical Garden** (☎ 604-822-9666; 6804 SW Marine Dr; adult/child/concession $5/2/3, reduced in winter; ⌚ 10am-6pm mid-Mar–mid-Oct, 10am-3pm mid-Oct–mid-Mar) is an internationally renowned 28-hectare complex of several themed gardens, including Canada's largest collection of rhododendrons, an apothecary garden and a winter garden of plants that bloom outside spring and summer. Combined entry with the Nitobe Memorial Gardens is $6 per adult.

Queen Elizabeth Park   Map pp652–4

Located between Cambie and Ontario Sts near 33rd Ave, this 53-hectare park has some of the best views of the city. The park features a mix of sports fields, manicured lawns and formal botanical gardens. The well-designed sunken garden houses some impressive seasonal displays. Nat Bailey Stadium resides on the park's east side, and is a popular summer-afternoon destination for fans of the Vancouver Canadians (p678) baseball team.

Crowning the hill at Queen Elizabeth Park is the triodetic dome of the **Bloedel Floral Conservatory** (☎ 604-257-8584; 2099 Beach Ave; adult/child/concession $4.10/2/2.90; ⌚ 10am-5:30pm), where 500 species and varieties of plants and more than 100 tropical birds populate a lush climate-controlled jungle environment.

If your green thumb's still itchy, four blocks west of Queen Elizabeth Park is **VanDusen Botanical Garden** (☎ 604-878-9274; 5251 Oak St; adult/child/senior $7.50/3.90/5.20, reduced in fall & winter; ⌚ 10am-4pm Oct-Mar, 10am-9pm Jun–mid-Aug, 10am-8pm May & mid-Aug–Labour Day, 10am-6pm Apr & Sep), a highly ornamental confection of sculptures, Canadian heritage flowers, rare

---

TOP FIVE VIEWS

- **Grouse Mountain** (p660) Unrivaled mountain-top promontory overlooking the city and its spectacular natural setting.

- **C-9 Live Lounge** (p674) Revolving restaurant bar with panoramic views 42 storeys above the city.

- **Stanley Park seawall** (p656) Sparkling sea-to-sky vistas interrupted only by inline skaters and cyclists.

- **Bard on the Beach tent** (p665) The main-stage tent flap, behind the stage, is opened during performances, providing a sunset mountain backdrop for Shakespeare's finest.

- **Third Beach** (p662) Bring a blanket, recline against a beach log, and enjoy the city's most romantic sunset views from Stanley Park.

---

plants from around the world, and a popular Elizabethan hedge maze. There's a giant flower and garden show every June, and it's one of the city's top Christmastime destinations when thousands of fairy lights illuminate the plants. It's wheelchair-accessible.

Richmond

Close to the airport, and built on 17 islands of silt where the Fraser River meets the Pacific, Richmond is Vancouver's modern-day Chinatown. Heavily populated by free-spending young Asian immigrants, the area has become a hotbed of boy racers, ethnic restaurants, bubble tea (tapioca pearl tea) shops and ultracool stores in several large shopping malls. The vibrancy of the area, compared with the region's traditional Chinatown, is illustrated by the two summer **night markets** (p679); Richmond's are much larger than Vancouver's.

However Richmond isn't just about *manga* (Japanese comic books) and Hello Kitty backpacks. The area was once the center of the region's fishing trade and, on the waterfront, it wears its maritime heritage with pride.

STEVESTON

In Richmond's southwestern corner, this old fishing village is a great day out from the city. The old part of town that fronts the Fraser River is quite charming, with several good pubs and restaurants, and some highly browse-worthy shops. There's lots of activity in the harbor, where the sights and smells of the fishing vessels still permeate the air – you'll come across plenty of fisherfolk hawking their fresh catches direct from the boat.

Stop by **Steveston Museum** (☎ 604-271-6868; 3811 Moncton St; admission free; ⊙ 10am-5pm), which relates the colorful story of the town's fishing past, but don't miss the **Gulf of Georgia Cannery** (Map pp650-1; ☎ 604-664-9009; 12138 4th Ave; adult/child/concession $6.50/5/3.25; ⊙ 10am-5pm Thu-Mon Apr-May & Oct, 10am-6pm Jul–Labour Day, 10am-5pm Jun, Sep & Nov-Mar). Housed in a former fish cannery, which operated from 1894 until 1979, you can learn about the fate of sockeye salmon in the region, amid the clatter of tin cans and the rhythmic hum of the still-working machinery.

North Vancouver   Map p650-1

Extending west from the Indian Arm waterway to West Vancouver, with the Capilano River approximating a western boundary, 'North Van' is a predominantly residential area with some great views of the Vancouver skyline twinkling across the water.

CAPILANO SUSPENSION BRIDGE

Capilano Suspension Bridge & Park (☎ 604-985-7474; 3735 Capilano Rd; adult/child/concession $21.95/10.95/$16.50; ⊙ 9am-5pm Nov-Apr, to 6pm or 6:30pm Oct, to 7:30pm May & Sep, 8pm Jun-Aug) is a well-developed tourist magnet that continually draws busloads of eager happy snappers to its 170m cabled walkway, which sways dramatically over the fast-running waters of tree-lined Capilano Canyon. A nifty network of bridges was also recently strung between eight trees in the park, providing a squirrel's-eye view of the forest.

LYNN CANYON PARK

If you want to sway for free, the nearby **Lynn Canyon Park**, set in the heart of the temperate rain forest, has a no-cost, less-showy suspension bridge that's slightly smaller than Capilano's. There are also plenty of excellent hiking trails here and some good picnic spots. Find time to check out the park's **Ecology Centre** (☎ 604-981-3103; www.dnv .org/ecology; admission free; ⊙ 10am-5pm Mon-Fri, 10am-5pm Sat & Sun Jun-Sep, noon-4pm Sat & Sun Oct-

May), which has displays, films and slide shows about the area's rich biodiversity.

GROUSE MOUNTAIN

With unrivalled views of the distant city (if the weather's fine), **Grouse Mountain** (☎ 604-980-9311; 6400 Nancy Greene Way; adult/child/concession $26.95/9.95/24.95; ⊙ 9am-10pm) touts itself as the 'peak of Vancouver.' It's a great winter activity destination (see opposite), but it's also a popular summer spot, and the **Grouse Grind** (☎ 604-432-6200; www.gvrd.bc.ca) hike is a favorite local pursuit (see opposite). Admission includes a Skyride ticket, plus mountaintop access to lumberjack shows, walking tours, a grizzly-bear refuge and a movie presentation. In winter, those who don't want to ski can take family-friendly sleigh rides, or partake of outdoor ice-skating. There's a variety of good restaurants and cafés here, too. Grouse is a 20-minute drive from downtown in North Vancouver.

MT SEYMOUR PROVINCIAL PARK

A quick nature escape from the city, **Mt Seymour Provincial Park** is also a great spot to hug 500-year-old Douglas firs. There's a road most of the way up, and the park has many good hiking trails (see opposite): the views of Vancouver's surroundings are beautiful. Some areas are rugged, so hikers should register at the park office, where trail maps are also available. There's also a wide array of activities here in winter (see opposite).

West Vancouver

West of the Capilano River, and north of Burrard Inlet, is West Van, one of the wealthiest municipalities in Canada. Marine Dr passes by Park Royal Shopping Centre (Canada's first mall, for all you retail historians) and on the hillsides are some of the city's priciest houses, with views to match. Marine Dr follows the coast to Horseshoe Bay, where you can wander around the marina or catch a ferry.

One of the city's prettiest picnic spots is **Lighthouse Park**, about 10km west of Lion's Gate Bridge. This 75-hectare park offers easy access to the rain forest via 13km of hiking trails. The most popular of these lead to the lighthouse at **Point Atkinson**, which commands the inlet from its rocky perch. Park maps are available in the parking lot.

More-rugged terrain is part of the attraction at **Cypress Mountain**, where the provincial-park setting includes summer hiking trails, a cozy pub lodge, and a packed roster of winter activities (right), making this a popular spot for locals.

The small community of **Horseshoe Bay** enjoys great views across the Pacific and up Howe Sound to distant glacial peaks. Several places to eat and shop line the waterfront but the area is all about the BC Ferries terminal, where you can travel to Bowen Island, Vancouver Island and along the picturesque Sunshine Coast. For more information about the ferries, see p681.

ACTIVITIES

Vancouver is the gateway to a veritable cornucopia of outdoor west-coast activities. However just because locals boast about skiing in the morning and hitting the beach to sunbathe in the afternoon, doesn't mean you should try to – it makes for a very tiring day. Recommended activities include hiking, biking, kayaking, skiing and snowboarding.

Hiking

The **Grouse Grind** (☎ 604-432-6200; www.gvrd.bc.ca) is a rite of passage for fit locals, many of whom dutifully tramp up Grouse Mountain (opposite) at least once every summer. It's not a walk in the park though, so hiking boots and bottled water are recommended for the steep 2.9km wilderness trail, which takes most people about 90 minutes. If you're feeling sprightly, try for the world record of 27 minutes.

Other hiking opportunities include **Cypress Provincial Park** (above), 8km north of West Vancouver off Hwy 99. It has eight hiking trails, including the Baden-Powell, Yew Lake and Howe Sound Crest trails. **Mt Seymour Provincial Park** (opposite), 13km northeast of the city off Mount Seymour Rd in North Vancouver, has 10 trails varying in difficulty and length. At both parks you should be prepared for continually changing mountain weather conditions. On clear days both parks offer magnificent views.

For gentle hikes, try **Stanley Park** (p656), which has dozens of hidden forest trails, or **Lighthouse Park** (opposite) in West Vancouver, which combines flattish forest hikes with some craggy seafront vistas.

Winter Sports

With the 2010 Winter Olympics on the way, Vancouver's already excellent menu of highly accessible snowbound activities will only get better, and so will Whistler's (see p688). There are several close-by ski runs, which also offer a tempting combination of snowboarding, snowshoeing and cross-country skiing.

Grouse Mountain (☎ 604-984-0661; 6400 Nancy Greene Way, North Vancouver; day pass adult/child/concession $42/18/30) has 25 ski and snowboard runs, five snowshoeing trails, tremendous summit views, good restaurants and excellent facilities. It's notable for its night skiing, when 13 downhill runs are illuminated and open till 10pm.

Cypress Mountain (☎ 604-926-5612; Cypress Bowl Rd, West Vancouver; day pass adult/child/youth $45/22/38), at Cypress Provincial Park, has the city's best vertical drop (512m) among its 36 runs, and a superb track-set for cross-country skiing. There's also a snow-tubing course (rental $13, two hours) and several snowshoeing trails. It's the future site of the 2010 Olympic freestyle-skiing and freestyle-snowboarding events.

Also on the North Shore, **Mt Seymour** (☎ 604-986-2261; 1700 Mt Seymour Rd, North Vancouver; day pass adult/child/concession $34/18/24) has three chairlifts and a 318m vertical drop. Snowshoeing is popular here and there's a family-oriented toboggan area and a snow-tubing course (rental $13, two hours), where you can whiz along dedicated paths on top of a squashy rubber ring.

Canoeing, Kayaking & Windsurfing

If you've got the energy for canoeing or kayaking, Vancouver is a hotbed of opportunity for everyone from nervous beginners to paddle-driven water nuts.

Located on Granville Island, **Ecomarine Ocean Kayak Centre** (Map pp650-1; ☎ 604-689-7575; 1668 Duranleau St) rents singles ($33 per two hours) and doubles ($45); it also offers excellent 2½-hour guided tours ($49). From the **Jericho Beach branch** (Map pp650-1; ☎ 604-222-3565; 1300 Discovery St) in Kitsilano, it organizes popular Wednesday-evening races ($2 per entry plus half-price rentals). It's a great way to meet local kayakers, especially when everyone heads to the pub afterwards.

In North Vancouver, **Deep Cove Canoe & Kayak Centre** (Map pp650-1; ☎ 604-929-2268; 2156 Banbury Rd) is the ideal place for beginners.

The waters here are calm and the setting, around North America's southernmost fjord, couldn't be more tranquil. Single rentals ($28 per two hours) and doubles ($40) are available but the three-hour introductory course ($65) is highly recommended for first-timers.

Windsure Windsurfing School (Map pp650-1; ☎ 604-224-0615; 1300 Discovery St) rents boards and wetsuits (combo fee $20 per hour) for those who want to hit the waters off Jericho Beach. It also has kite-surfing and skimboarding rentals, and offers good-value lessons for all abilities.

Cycling

Bike-friendly Vancouver's most popular trail is the 10.5km **Stanley Park seawall**, which uses dual lanes to avoid messy collisions between walkers, cyclists and inline skaters. The sea-to-sky vistas are breathtaking, but the exposed route can be hit with crashing waves and icy winds in winter. Crowds hog the lanes in summer, when it's best to come early in the morning or late at night. **Spokes** (Map pp652-4; ☎ 604-688-5141; 1798 W Georgia St; rentals per hr from $6), a block from the park entrance, rents bikes and blades.

Another popular seaside route is the 15km jaunt that begins in English Bay and takes you along both sides of False Creek, past Science World, Granville Island, Vanier Park and Jericho Beach, to the forested peninsula occupied by UBC. It's a good day trip if you want to stop off at some of the interesting attractions along the way and dip into a Kitsilano café for lunch or a coffee break.

Running

Vancouver is a joggers paradise, with the gentle, paved pathways of the **Stanley Park seawall** drawing most locals and visitors with fitness on their minds. On hot summer days the ocean breeze and shade of the Lions Gate Bridge and towering Douglas firs are always welcome. There are also several marked internal trails in the park, including the 4km trek around **Lost Lagoon**, if you want to get away from the tourists. **UBC** is also a great spot for running, with trails marked through endowment lands.

For those who like company on their jogs, **Pacific Running Guides** (☎ 604-684-6464; www.pacificrunningguides.com) offers several guided jogging treks in the city, as well as tours and packages

further afield. Their Stanley Park service ($40) includes a seawall run tailored to your personal fitness level. Marvel silently at the effortless ability of your guide to jog and tell you about the city at the same time.

Swimming

Several city beaches are crowded with swimmers in summer, including **English Bay**, **Kitsilano Beach**, **Jericho Beach** and Stanley's family-oriented **Second Beach** and **Third Beach**.

Naturists find a comfortable, though often busy, haven at **Wreck Beach** (Map pp650-1; www.wreckbeach.org), where a dedicated community of counterculture locals, independent vendors and in-the-know visitors share the sand. From UBC, follow the trails marked 4, 5 or 6 into the woods, then head down the steep steps to the water.

There's an excellent, but often crowded, outdoor **swimming pool** (☎ 604-257-8371; Stanley Park Dr; ⓨ 10am-8:45pm Mon-Fri, noon-8:45pm Sat & Sun, late May–late Aug) at Second Beach in Stanley Park, while the **Vancouver Aquatic Centre** (Map pp652-4; ☎ 604-665-3424; 1050 Beach Ave; ⓨ 10am-8:45pm Mon-Fri, noon-8:45pm Sat & Sun, late May–late Aug) has an indoor heated pool, along with a whirlpool, a diving tank and a sauna. Kitsilano Beach has a giant outdoor heated **saltwater pool** (☎ 604-731-0011; 2305 Cornwall Ave). Rates for the city's nine indoor and six outdoor public pools are standardized (adult/child/concession $4.40/3.30/2.25). Visit www.vancouverparks.ca for information.

Scuba Diving

Vancouver's beauty extends beneath the waves, where divers can get up close and personal with rare coral, wolf eel and giant octopuses. Popular diving areas include **Cates Park** in North Vancouver and **Whytecliffe Park** in West Vancouver. The **International Diving Centre** (☎ 604-736-2541; 2572 Arbutus St) in Kits can help with information and gear rentals.

COURSES

There are dozens of opportunities for taking a more educational approach to your Vancouver trip.

See p65 for information on popular cooking classes run by top city chefs at **Barbara-Jos Books to Cooks** (Map pp652-4; ☎ 604-688-6755; 1128 Mainland St) in Yaletown. Gourmands should also consider the casual, hands-on classes (typically $50 to $100 per class) aimed at nonprofessionals offered by the **Pacific Culinary Institute** (Map pp652-4; ☎ 604-734-4488; www.picachef .com; 1505 W 2nd Ave).

Those who want to explore BC's spectacular outdoors but lack some of the required skills should check in with the city's **Canada West Mountain School** (Map pp650-1; ☎ 604-878-7007; http://themountainschool.com; 47 W Broadway). This established and well-respected institution offers dozens of training and guided excursion programs, including snow camping ($185 plus GST) and rock climbing (from $95 plus GST). Beginners should consider joining the excellent outdoor rock-skills class ($225 plus GST), aimed at first-timers who want to learn how to climb.

If acting is your thing, Vancouver offers a unique opportunity to study at the **William Davis Centre for Actors Study** (Map pp652-4; ☎ 604-687-8115; www.williamdaviscentre.com; 1102 Hornby St), named after its founder, a film and TV character actor who had a recurring role as CGB Spender, aka 'The Cigarette-Smoking Man,' in *The X-Files*. Short-term classes include Acting for Commercials ($175) and Audition Technique ($180). Considering recent blockbuster movies like *Catwoman* and *I, Robot* were filmed here in Vancouver, you might even be discovered.

VANCOUVER FOR CHILDREN

Family-friendly Vancouver is filled with things to do with kids. Get a copy of the free *Kids' Guide Vancouver* flyer from the TIC, or visit www.kidfriendly.org for information on local child-friendly places. If you're traveling without a car, make sure you hop on the SkyTrain, SeaBus or miniferry to Granville Island: kids love 'em.

The top attractions for families are Science World (p656) and the Vancouver Aquarium Marine Science Centre (p657). Stay on at Stanley Park (p656) after an aquarium visit to check out the miniature railway, beaches and outdoor swimming pool nestled on the waterfront. Rainy days should include a visit to the CN IMAX Theatre (p677) at Canada Place or the HR MacMillan Space Centre (p658) in Vanier Park. If the weather's fine, the Capilano Suspension Bridge & Park (p660) or the free-entry Lynn Canyon Suspension Bridge and Ecology Centre (p660) are recommended.

On long summer days there's nothing better for kids than hitting a water park.

Vancouver has three great free options: near Lumberman's Arch in Stanley Park (p657), along the seawall near Mill Marine Bistro (p674) and behind the Kids Market on Granville Island (p657), which is touted as the largest free water park in North America. Once you've dried off the kids, head over to the nearby **Kids Market** (Map pp652-4; ☎ 604-689-8447; 1496 Cartwright St, Granville Island).

Older children might prefer to visit **Playland** (Map pp650-1; ☎ 604-253-2311; Hastings Park), an amusement park with dozens of fairground rides, including an excellent old wooden roller coaster.

Plan your visit to coincide with the Pacific National Exhibition (p666) or drop by one of the city's other family-friendly festivals, including the Vancouver International Children's Festival (p665), Alcan Dragon Boat Festival (p665) and the Celebration of Light (p666). If you're looking for a bedtime read at the end of the day, visit **Kidsbooks** (Map pp650-1; ☎ 604-738-5335; 3083 W Broadway; ☒ 9:30am-6pm Mon-Sat, to 9pm Fri, noon-5pm Sun) on W Broadway for a gargantuan selection of children's titles.

QUIRKY VANCOUVER

For some visitors, Vancouver's most surprising feature is its mini-strip of stoner-friendly businesses around the 300-block of W Hastings St. It's no secret that BC Bud is a particularly favored commodity, but many are still mildly shocked to see pot cafés, hemp shops and hydroponics stores openly

---

COUPLAND'S VANCOUVER

In *City of Glass*, his affectionate and highly recommended homage to Vancouver, hometown *Generation X*–author Douglas Coupland gives readers his offbeat take on what makes this place tick. He explores the big questions that are part of everyday life for locals: What was Expo '86 all about? Why is there so much fleece here? What's the deal with BC Bud? What are all the young Japanese kids doing? How come there are so many 8s in street addresses? What are the giant yellow mounds on the North Shore bank of Burrard Inlet? It's a guidebook of off-the-wall trivia that nevertheless speaks eloquently of the peculiarities bubbling under the surface of the city.

BRITISH COLUMBIA

selling the required paraphernalia. For arguments in support of the weed, duck into the **BC Marijuana Party Bookshop** (Map pp652-4; ☎ 604-682-1172; 307 W Hastings St; ☯ 10am-6pm Mon-Sat, noon-6pm Sun). It doubles as the headquarters for a political party that is increasingly influential in regional and national elections.

The city's most historic playhouse, the baroque-themed **Orpheum Theatre** (Map pp652-4; ☎ 604-665-3050; 884 Granville St; ☯ 10am Jul-Sep), offers a highly entertaining but little-known 90-minute backstage tour ($5) that walks visitors through some haunted nooks, past some colorful characters, and to some on-location *The X-Files* sets.

Much smaller than the city's sprawling Chinatown, the **Punjabi Market** (Map pp650-1) area, on Fraser and Main Sts above 49th Ave, is a colorful Little India of sari shops, Bangra record stores, gaudy jewelry boutiques and low-key, great-value restaurants. Make sure you leave room for an all-you-can eat lunch here, usually priced at $6 to $8.

The **Art of Loving** (Map pp652-4; ☎ 604-742-9988; www.theartofloving.ca; 1819 W 5th Ave; ☯ 11am-7pm Mon-Thu, 11am-8pm Friday, 11am-6pm Sat, noon-6pm Sun) is a tasteful sex shop for those not in the dirty-mac brigade, but it was recently in the news for staging a play involving sexual acts. The police threatened closure but backed down at the last minute, allowing the show to play to a not-surprisingly packed house. The store also hosts regular classes with titles like the Joy of Flirting and the Art of Kissing.

Vancouver has several small performance venues, but the **WISE Hall** (Map pp650-1; ☎ 604-254-5858; www.wisehall.ca; 1882 Adananc St) is one of the best. A comfortably grungy former church, it's a friendly, neighborhood gem that's close to the heart of in-the-know locals, who flock here to catch folk, ska and dances that remind them of youth-club discos. The bouncy dance floor brings out the latent mosh-pit desires in the most reluctant of dancers.

Hastings Racecourse (Map pp650-1; ☎ 604-254-1631; www.hastingspark.com; cnr Hastings & Renfrew Sts; ☯ Apr-Sep), established in 1889, offers a recipe for a fun day out, just 15 minutes from downtown. Novice betters are welcome and, when you're not watching the horses, there are some great views of the North Shore mountains and the harbor, although this probably won't console you when you lose your shirt.

Illuminares (☎ 604-879-8611; www.publicdreams.org) is a magical festival with a loyal local following held on the last Saturday in July at Trout Lake. The family-friendly event includes paper-lantern making, a procession of illuminated lanterns, roving musical performers and a nighttime fireworks display.

TOURS

While downtown is best explored on foot, time-pressed travelers, or those who want to see more than the central attractions, should consider a guided tour. Each of these companies operates a wide range of tours, so make sure you check out their full selection before committing to one.

Gray Line (☎ 604-879-3363; www.grayline.ca/vancouver) Offers an array of bus sightseeing excursions ranging from downtown explorers to trips throughout the west coast region. Recommended is the Vancouver Double Decker Attraction Tour (adult/child/concession $28/$15.90/$27.10). Valid for two consecutive days, it allows passengers to hop on and off and take in the sights around the city.

Harbour Cruises (Map pp652-4; ☎ 604-688-7246; www.boatcruises.com) See the city in a different light from the water: this company's best trip is the 75-minute Harbour Tour (adult/child/concession $19/7/16), where you'll learn more than you need to know about the history, industry and development of the region. Watch for seals bobbing curiously offshore.

Historic Vancouver: Gastown and Old Civic Centre Walking Tour (☎ 604-683-8588; tours $5; ☯ 1:30pm Jun-Sep) To learn more about this area's rich history, take this tour. It starts at 440 Cambie St.

Sewell's Sea Safari (☎ 604-921-3474; www.sewellsmarina.com) Grab a seat on a rigid-hull inflatable for a two-hour, high-speed ride (adult/child/senior $55/25/50) out to sea. With the spray in your face and the wind threatening to whip off your sunglasses, keep your eyes open for possible whale pod sightings. Barking seals and soaring eagles are a more likely proposition on most trips.

Vancouver Trolley Company (☎ 604-801-5515; www.vancouvertrolley.com) Operates the city's familiar fleet of red replica trolleybuses. The City Attractions Tour (adult/child $28/14) allows you a full day of transport between 23 different stops, or you can hop on one of its free tours around Stanley Park. Its website has a $1 discount coupon.

Watershed Tours (☎ 604-432-6430; www.gvrd.bc.ca/watershed; ☯ 8am & 12:30pm Thu-Sun mid-Jun–mid-Sep) Unusual but highly recommended free bus and walking tours of the forested Capilano and Coquitlam watersheds are offered annually by the Greater Vancouver

Regional District (GVRD). The tours, which provide unique cultural and natural insights into the area's ecosystem and water supply, are very popular, so you have to book ahead.
West Coast Air (☎ 604-606-6888; www.westcoastair .com) For a little more money, a seaplane tour is the ultimate way to see just how spectacular Vancouver's natural setting really is. The 30-minute Vancouver Scenic flight ($95) takes off from the floating terminal near Canada Place and takes in the city's best mountain, park and seafront vistas.
West Coast Sightseeing (☎ 604-451-1600; www .vancouversightseeing.com) Those who prefer to tour in comfort on a hot summer's day will like the air-conditioned minibuses used by this operator. Its popular five-hour City Highlights tour (adult/child/concession $51/32/47) is a group-tour experience, so you'll be herded around each attraction as if you couldn't find it on your own even if you tried.

FESTIVALS & EVENTS

The summer is a popular time for large festivals in Vancouver, but there are dozens of smaller events throughout the year, often running for just one or two days. Check the free listings guide *Georgia Straight* (www .straight.com) for up-to-date information about many of these smaller cultural happenings, or visit www.tourismvancouver .com for a roundup of major events.

January & February
Dine Out Vancouver (☎ 604-683-2000; ❧ last week Jan) Dozens of Vancouver restaurants offer superb-value two-course ($15) or three-course ($25) sample menus during this popular new annual event. Head to Tourism Vancouver's website (www.tourismvancouver.com) to check out the list of participants – including some of Vancouver's best eateries – and book as early as possible.
Chinese New Year (☎ 604-415-6322; www.sunbrite festival.com) Depending on the calendar, this celebration can take place in January or February, but it always includes plenty of color, dancing, parades and great food.

March
Vancouver Playhouse International Wine Festival (☎ 604-873-3311; www.playhousewinefest.com; events from $40; ❧ mid-Mar) In a region where wine festivals are sprouting like mushrooms, this older weeklong event still rules the roost. There's a strong educational element and several events for neophytes, with hundreds of wines from more than a dozen countries typically on the table.

April
Vancouver Sun Run (☎ 604-689-9441; www.sunrun .com; ❧ mid-Apr) One of the world's largest 10km races

---

TOP FIVE FESTIVALS

▪ **Vancouver International Film Festival** (p666) Canadian and international movies celebrated at perhaps the city's best festival.

▪ **Vancouver International Jazz Festival** (below) Giant annual summer fixture with a refreshing number of free events.

▪ **Vancouver Fringe Festival** (p666) Entertaining and eclectic array of local and international short plays and performances.

▪ **Bard on the Beach** (below) City institution presenting professional Shakespeare performances in a tented beachfront setting.

▪ **Dine Out Vancouver** (left) Dip into the city's burgeoning fine-dining scene via tasting menus at Vancouver's best restaurants.

---

attracts around 50,000 runners (and walkers and wheelchair racers) from around the world, to a picturesque route that includes Stanley Park.

May
Vancouver International Children's Festival (☎ 604-708-5655; www.vancouverchildrensfestival.com; tickets 2 performances $22, 3 performances $30) The last week of the month brings kid-friendly performers and hundreds of families to the multitented Vanier Park complex. Face painting is almost expected here.

June
Bard on the Beach (☎ 604-739-0559; www.bardon thebeach.org; evening tickets $27; ❧ Jun-Sep) The perfect way to see Shakespeare, this professional repertory company performs three plays per season at its giant tented complex in Vanier Park. Bring a sweater and watch the show in comfort, while the sun sets over the mountains behind the stage.
Vancouver International Jazz Festival (☎ 604-872-5200; www.jazzvancouver.com; ❧ late Jun) Into its second decade, Vancouver's biggest music festival takes places at an eclectic array of venues over 10 days. There are always a few superstar performances (Oscar Peterson and Diana Krall are past masters) and there are plenty of free outdoor shows, especially in Gastown and Granville Island.
Alcan Dragon Boat Festival (☎ 604-683-4707; www .adbf.com; False Creek) An epic splashathon for teams from around the world, this popular weekend event, held

around the third week of June, has grown to include an excellent live world-music stage.

July

Canada Day (☎ 604-775-8025; www.canadadayat canadaplace.com; ☺ Jul 1) Traditionally held around the be-sailed Canada Place, music, food and fireworks combine to help Canadians celebrate the birth of their nation. There's also a smaller event at Granville Island.

Vancouver Early Music Festival (☎ 604-732-1610; www.earlymusic.bc.ca; tickets $20-45) Stretching over three weeks, the lute and harpsichord players emerge for this gem of a festival, combining complex and more-accessible performances of some of the world's lesser-known music.

Vancouver Folk Music Festival (☎ 604-602-9798; www.thefestival.bc.ca; Jericho Beach; tickets $90-130, per day $55) A long weekend in mid-July is the spot for the west coast's best live folk event. Eight stages cover the gamut from local favorites to world-music artists and headliners like Billy Bragg and Bruce Cockburn.

Pride Week (☎ 604-687-0955; www.vanpride.bc.ca) A giant weeklong kaleidoscope of gay, lesbian and bisexual events including fashion shows, gala parties and concerts culminating in western Canada's largest pride parade – Vancouver's only official parade. Starts last week of July.

Celebration of Light (☎ 604-641-1193; www.cele bration-of-light.com) Hundreds of thousands of specta-tors flock to English Bay on several late July/early August evenings for this free international fireworks festival. With the rockets launched from barges in the water, the views can be better and far less crowded from vantage points along the Kitsilano beachfront.

Molson Indy Vancouver (☎ 604-280-4639; www .molsonindy.com; general admission 3 days $60, per day $19-50) The city's loudest long weekend takes place around Science World and False Creek. Hang out with the race nerds salivating over the cars, or soak up some beer and sun in the stands.

August

Festival Vancouver (☎ 604-688-8441; www.festival vancouver.bc.ca; tickets $20-50) Choral, opera, classical, jazz and world-music sounds performed by local and international artists at venues around the city in the first two weeks of August.

Pacific National Exhibition (☎ 604-253-2311; www .pne.bc.ca; adult/child $10/8) This three-week old-school country fair, known locally as the PNE, has evolved into consumer product exhibitions, a fairground with a kicking wooden rollercoaster and an extensive program of music concerts. There are farm-animal displays and piglet racing for the traditionalists, and don't leave without downing a bag of minidoughnuts.

September

Vancouver Fringe Festival (☎ 604-257-0350; www .vancouverfringe.com) Now in its second decade, the lively fringe takes over venues large, small and unconventional on Granville Island for 10 days of wild, wacky and sometimes downright weird live theater. Most shows last around 60 minutes and cost about $10; hang around the 'festival HQ' at Granville Island Brewing and catch the buzz on the best shows to see.

Vancouver International Film Festival (☎ 604-685-0260; www.viff.org; adult/senior $9/7) Traditionally more ac-cessible than its starry brother in Toronto, the VIFF has grown to become one of the city's favorite festivals. Held for two weeks at mainstream and art-house cinemas across the city, advance booking is recommended. If you're a true devotee, check out some of the scheduled workshops and gala events.

October

Vancouver International Writers & Readers Festi-val (☎ 604-681-6330; www.writersfest.bc.ca; per event $12-20) Popular premier literary event, where famed local and international scribblers turn up for seminars, galas and a host of public forums. Past guests have included Salman Rushdie, Irving Welsh and Douglas Coupland.

December

Christmas Carol Ship Parade (☎ 604-878-8999; www.carolships.org) Cheesy but ever-popular yuletide tradition, where dozens of local boats cover themselves in fairy lights and parade along Vancouver's waterfronts to recorded or live carol music. Throughout December.

SLEEPING

Vancouver has a wide array of accommo-dation options spread throughout the city, with plenty of first-class, boutique, B&B and budget choices available. Among the most popular areas, and those where the options are widest, are downtown and the areas around Stanley Park and Yaletown.

Prices can be high in the downtown core during the peak summer months, but there are some real bargains to be had off-season and in outlying areas. Tourism Vancouver (p651) lists many accommodation options, as well as the latest package deals from local hotels. For free Vancouver accommodation information and reservations, contact the province's **Hello BC** (☎ 604-663-6000; www.hellobc .com) booking service.

Downtown   Map pp652–4
BUDGET
HI Vancouver Central (☎ 604-685-5335, 888-203-8333; www.hihostels.ca/vancouvercentral; 1025 Granville

St; dm incl breakfast from $20; ⏰ 24hr) In a city saturated with so-so hostels, the newest HI location also happens to be the best. Small rooms, private bathrooms (with the occasional claw-foot tub), free laptop Internet hook-up, and a great location in a former heritage hotel, right in the heart of the action on Granville St, make it a hot backpackers destination. There's also a lively bar with good drinks specials. Reservations are recommended.

Jolly Taxpayer Hotel (☎ 604-681-3550; www.jollytax payerhotel.com; 828 W Hastings St; s/d with shared bathroom incl breakfast $70/80) This is a family-run B&B above a popular downtown British-style pub. Located in the business district, some rooms have balconies, but it can be a bit noisy until the bar below shuts up for the night.

MID-RANGE

Listel (☎ 604-684-8461, 800-663-5491; www.listel-vancouver.com; 1300 Robson St; s/d from $125/150; Ⓟ $19) Excellent service and a liberal sprinkling of artworks in suites and corridors make the Listel one of Vancouver's most popular hotels for credit-card-wielding bohemians. Stay here during the Van-

couver International Jazz Festival (p665) and you'll be rubbing shoulders with visiting performers.

Blue Horizon Hotel (☎ 604-688-1411, 800-663-1333; www.bluehorizonhotel.com; 1225 Robson St; s/d from $125/150; Ⓟ $10 🐾) Once Vancouver's tallest building, this blue-tiled tower is right in the heart of the action. Head to the 31st floor for great views of the nighttime cityscape. There's a giant neighborhood pub on the ground floor where you can play drunken darts.

Bosman's Vancouver Hotel (☎ 604-682-3171, 888-267-6267; www.bosmanshotel.com; 1060 Howe St; s/d/ste from $100/110/150; Ⓟ 🐾) A 1970s-style motel in the heart of the city, Bosman's offers well-maintained. comfortable if basic facilities. There's an outdoor pool and an unintentionally kitschy restaurant serving a mean rib-sticking breakfast. It's kid-friendly and wheelchair-accessible.

St Regis Hotel (☎ 604-681-1135; www.stregishotel .com; 602 Dunsmuir St; s/d incl breakfast from $110/130) Superb location with clean, comfortable rooms. It's an older building, so some of the suites are a little small. The staff is attentive, though, and you have your pick of a Starbucks or the lively pub on the ground floor.

GAY & LESBIAN VANCOUVER

Vancouver has had western Canada's largest gay population for decades, centered on the West End and, to a lesser extent, Commercial Dr. Pick up a free copy of *Xtra! West* (www.xtra.ca) at streetboxes and businesses in these areas for event listings and an overview of the scene.

Replete with rainbow flags and shop-window decals, the West End's Davie St is the heart of Vancouver's gay culture. It's scattered with gay-friendly cafés, bars, stores, and the city's best resource center for gay and lesbian locals and visitors, **Little Sisters Book & Art Emporium** (Map pp652-4; ☎ 604-669-1753; 1238 Davie St; ⏰ 10am-11pm). With one of North America's widest selection of specialist literature, an active bulletin board and a hyper-knowledgeable staff, it's a good first stop for visitors. Pick up a free copy of the glossy *Gay & Lesbian Business Directory* while you're there for an exhaustive list of other pertinent local enterprises, then head down to Denman St and read it at **Delany's** (Map pp652-4; ☎ 604-662-3344; 1105 Denman St; ⏰ 6am-11pm Mon-Fri, 6:30am-11pm Sat & Sun), a laid-back neighborhood coffee bar that's a popular hangout of the local scene. If you arrive early enough, this is a great spot to catch the giant **Pride Week** (opposite) parade, held every July. Along with this family-friendly street fiesta, there are dozens of pre- and post-parade events for all kinds of interests.

Among the city's most popular gay-friendly nightlife options are **Pump Jack** (Map pp652-4; ☎ 604-685-3417; 1167 Davie St; ⏰ 1pm-midnight Mon-Thu, 1pm-3am Fri & Sat, 1pm-1am Sun), a loud and proud pub hangout with a great patio, and **Odyssey** (Map pp652-4; 604-689-5256; 1251 Howe St), the city's number-one gay nightclub, with a host of ever-changing special events. For support of all kinds, the **Centre** (Map pp652-4; ☎ 604-684-5307; www.lgbtcentrevancouver.com; 1170 Bute St) provides a smorgasbord of discussion groups, a library, a health clinic and legal advice for lesbians, gays, bisexuals and the transgendered. These friendly folk also staff the **Prideline** (☎ 604-684-6869; ⏰ 7-10pm), a telephone peer-support information and referral service.

TOP END

Wedgewood Hotel (☎ 604-689-7777, 800-663-0666; www.wedgewoodhotel.com; 845 Hornby St; s/d/ste from $250/200/260; P $19) The antithesis of the modern minimalist hotel, the boutique Wedgewood combines classic European luxury with a North American flair for good service. The ground-floor Bacchus Lounge, with its roaring fireplace and overstuffed leather chairs, is the best place to be on long winter evenings.

Fairmont Hotel Vancouver (☎ 604-684-3131; www.fairmont.com/hotelvancouver; 900 W Georgia St; s/d/ste from $175/250/350; P $26 ⚓) The grand dame of Vancouver hotels was one of the original chateau-style properties strung like pearls along Canada's national rail network. Today's well-heeled guests enjoy deluxe rooms, a health club with a spa, and even a dog they can take for walkies. It's also kid-friendly.

Metropolitan Hotel (☎ 604-687-1122, 800-667-2300; www.metropolitan.com; 645 Howe St; s/d from $175/250; P $25 ⚓) A discreet, luxurious boutique hotel with a contemporary European sophistication that includes indulgent marble bathrooms. Adult and stylish, with a popular lounge and one floor dedicated to smokers.

Pan Pacific Hotel Vancouver (☎ 604-662-8111; www.panpacific.com; 300-999 Canada Pl; s/d/ste from $200/300/450; P $27 ⚓) Spectacular sea-to-sky views on the waterfront at Canada Place, this 'five diamond' award-winning hotel is at the top of the tree for many city visitors. There's a popular spa and a sauna, and the restaurants and bars here have some of the best outdoor scenery of any in the region. It's kid-friendly.

Stanley Park/West End   Map pp652–4
BUDGET

Buchan Hotel (☎ 604-685-5354, 800-668-6654; www.buchanhotel.com; 1906 Haro St; s/d from $45/70) A great-value heritage property, the Buchan may lack an elevator, but it has bags of charm (love the old radiators), and its bike-storage facilities make this an ideal stopover for cyclists. There are laundry facilities and some shared bathrooms. It's family-friendly.

MID-RANGE

Sylvia Hotel (☎ 604-681-9321; www.sylviahotel.com; 1154 Gilford St; s/d/tr from $65/65/110; P $7) The most charming city hotel is also the coziest. The heritage-designated, ivy-covered Sylvia, built in 1912, and named after the owner's daughter, has some great rooms with panoramic views across English Bay. The decor is a bit worn – some would say comfortable – but its candlelit bar is a seafront neighborhood favorite.

English Bay Inn (☎ 604-683-8002, 866-683-8002; www.englishbayinn.com; 1968 Comox St; s/d incl breakfast from $120/140) One of the city's best B&Bs, housed in a mock Tudor confection. The gourmet breakfast here often includes poached eggs with smoked salmon or chicken, and asparagus crepes. The warm welcome includes complimentary port or sherry throughout the day.

Langtry (☎ 604-687-7892, 800-699-7892; www.thelangtry.com; 968 Nicola St; ste from $80) Distinctive, comfortable and self-contained suites, each with their own garden, make up the Langtry. It's close to the park and Robson St but is located on a quiet, leafy backstreet.

TOP END

Lord Stanley Suites on the Park (☎ 604-688-9299, 888-767-7829; www.lordstanley.com; 1889 Alberni St; ste incl breakfast from $150; P $12) In a superb location for park-lovers, suites here are Vancouver's most comfortable accommodation option, with their sitting rooms, bedrooms, office nooks and sunrooms.

THE AUTHOR'S CHOICE

Opus Hotel (Map pp652-4; ☎ 604-642-6787, 866-642-6787; www.opushotel.com; 322 Davie St; s/d/ste from $125/150/250; P $25) Vancouver's trendiest boutique hotel has worked hard to cultivate an image of postmodern sophistication. However its designer rooms – including some with bathrooms exposed to the outside – are not just about magazine-quality good looks. Surprisingly comfortable, with an air of understated tranquility, the hotel's corner-situated executive suites, with their mod-lounges and diagonally placed beds, are the city's coziest home-from-home rooms. The bathrooms, with heated floors, acres of white tile and a clutch of high-end French toiletries, make dragging yourself from the bath a real chore. With a great lobby bar that's known to occasionally attract the likes of Halle Berry and Michael Stipe, it's worth making a quick trip down in the elevators.

BRITISH COLUMBIA

Yaletown
Map pp652–4

BUDGET

YWCA Hotel/Residence Vancouver (☎ 604-895-5830, 800-663-1424; www.ywcahotel.com; 733 Beatty St; s/d/tr from $51/56/73; **P** $8 **묘**) One of North America's best YWCAs, the purpose-built, modern Vancouver branch, on the edge of Yaletown, is packed with facilities and is especially welcoming to kids, families and groups; the five-bedded 'quint rooms' are always popular and cost from $105 per night. Ask for student, senior and weekly discounts.

MID-RANGE

Victorian Hotel (☎ 604-681-6369, 877-681-6369; www.victorianhotel.ca; 514 Homer St; s/d/tr incl breakfast from $60/90/100; **P** $10) Close to Yaletown, Gastown and the downtown core, this large family-run B&B gem in an 1898 heritage building features hardwood floors and an *über*-cozy ambience. Some rooms have shared bathrooms. Parking is available for an additional charge.

Kingston Hotel Bed & Breakfast (☎ 604-684-9024, 888-713-3304; www.kingstonhotelvancouver.com; 757 Richards St; s/d/tw incl breakfast from $50/60/100; **P** $15) Rooms at the good-value Kingston, on the edge of Yaletown, are a bit dated, and some walls are thin, but they're clean and, surprisingly, there's a sauna. Close to Yaletown restaurants and the Granville St entertainment district.

Comfort Inn Downtown (☎ 604-605-4333; 654 Nelson St; www.comfortinndowntown.com; s/d/ste incl breakfast from $90/120/170; **P** $11) The old heritage building Hotel Dakota, brilliantly located between Yaletown and Granville St, has been restored and rebranded as the Comfort Inn Downtown. The result is a boutique hotel without the high prices, and some rooms even have Jacuzzis and fireplaces. There is monitored parking nearby at reduced rates for guests.

Rosedale on Robson (☎ 604-689-8033, 800-661-8870; 838 Hamilton St; s/d/ste from $100/125/145; **P**) The Yaletown end of Robson St is home to this discreet but well-located tower block. Rooms are spacious and comfortable, and some with kitchenettes are available.

Granville Island

Granville Island Hotel (Map pp652–4; ☎ 604-683-7373, 800-663-1840; www.granvilleislandhotel.com; 1253 Johnston St; s/d from $120/140) Located on the end of Granville Island, this hotel enjoys great cityscape views. Rooms are comfortable with a modern European feel, but the facilities are superior: check out the health club and the restaurant. There's even one of Vancouver's best brewpubs, Dockside Restaurant & Pub (p672), on site.

Kitsilano

BUDGET

HI Vancouver Jericho Beach (Map pp650–1; ☎ 604-224-3208, 888-203-4303; www.hihostels.ca/vancouverjericho beach; 1515 Discovery St; dm from $18.50; ☷ 24hr May-Sep) One of Canada's largest hostels is perfectly located for beach-lovers, and the city center is just a 20-minute free shuttle-bus ride away. There are some private rooms, as well as a roster of daily guest activities.

MID-RANGE

Corkscrew Inn (Map pp650–1; ☎ 604-733-7276, 877-737-7276; www.corkscrewinn.com; 2735 W 2nd Ave; s/d incl breakfast from $110/130; **P**) Wine-lovers can't believe their luck when they turn up here; there's a mini wine museum and corkscrew-themed stained-glass windows, all housed in a beautiful 1912 heritage home. Some rooms have fireplaces and soaker tubs. The giant gourmet breakfast is sans wine.

Mickey's Kits Beach Chalet (Map pp652–4; ☎ 604-739-3342, 888-739-3342; www.mickeysbandb.com; 2142 W 1st Ave; s/d from $95/135; **P** 묘) The private balconies and decks are the main draw at this B&B. It's kid-friendly and perfect for those who want to combine easy access to the city center with proximity to a great beach.

Between Friends B&B (Map pp652–4; ☎ 604-734-5082; www.betweenfriends-vancouver.com; 1916 Arbutus St; s/d incl breakfast from $65/115; **P**) Welcoming owners, and a location close to Kits Beach and the trendy coffee shops of W 4th Ave, await visitors to this charming 1912 heritage home.

University of British Columbia
Map pp650–1

MID-RANGE

Johnson's Heritage House B&B (☎ 604-266-4175; www.johnsons-inn-vancouver.com; 2278 West 34th Ave; s/d incl breakfast from $85/125; **P** 묘) A charming 1920s Craftsman home with a large porch, rhododendron garden and a quiet, residential Kerrisdale locale. Hosts are happy to help plan your day in the city, which should be executed on foot, so that you can work off what may be the largest breakfast in town. This is an adult-oriented, romantic getaway spot.

Pacific Spirit Guest House (☎ 604-261-6837, 866-768-6837; www.vanbb.com; 4080 W 35th Ave; s/d incl breakfast from $75/90; P) Tiny and unassuming B&B with a warm welcome and excellent proximity to beaches and UBC attractions. It's also good value with the kind of amenities – robes, gourmet breakfasts and in-room flowers – usually reserved for pricier operations. It's both kid- and pet-friendly ($20 per stay for pets, includes bed and a biscuit).

Richmond
Map pp650–1

MID-RANGE
Stone Hedge B&B (☎ 604-274-1070; www.thestone hedge.com; 5511 Cathay Rd; s/d from $110/125; P 🛋) In a surprisingly peaceful location is this Richmond B&B, named after the privacy-enhancing 2m stone wall surrounding it. The best feature is the lounge – it opens onto a large, secluded swimming pool.

Steveston Hotel (☎ 604-277-9511; www.steveston hotel.com; 1211 3rd Ave; s/d/tr from $55/60/65; P) Basic but comfortable motel-style accommodations that should attract fans of 1980s kitsch. Some rooms have shared bathrooms, and there's a Jacuzzi and a steam room for guests. The bar downstairs can be noisy on weekends, so ask for an upper-floor or back room if you want to get to sleep early.

TOP END
Fairmont Vancouver Airport (☎ 604-207-5200; www .fairmont.com/vancouverairport; Vancouver International Airport; s/d/ste from $150/175/250) At this luxurious airport hotel guests can partake of a day spa and a health club before hopping on their plane. Rooms are spacious and effectively soundproofed, and the bar, with its plane-spotter views over the adjacent runways, is worth a visit even if you're not a guest.

North Vancouver
Map pp650–1

MID-RANGE
Mountainside Manor B&B (☎ 604-990-9772, 877-779-7888; www.mtnsidemanor.com; 5909 Nancy Greene Way; s/d incl breakfast from $90/110; P) In a superb location for ski and snowboard fans, at the foot of Grouse Mountain, this small contemporary home has three rooms, so book well ahead in winter. Rooms have fireplaces and hot tubs, and the breakfast is hearty.

Lonsdale Quay Hotel (☎ 604-986-6111; www.lons dalequayhotel.com; 123 Carrie Cates Ct; s/d from $100/110; P $7) Easy access to the mountains but also close to the SeaBus terminal for swift

downtown trips. Some of the rooms at this older boutique hotel have great views of the Vancouver skyline.

Grouse Inn (☎ 604-988-1701, 800-779-7888; www .grouseinn.com; 1633 Capilano Rd; s/d incl breakfast from $90/100; P 🛋) Facilities abound at this popular modern motel favored by winter skiers and summer wilderness explorers. There's a playground, free movie channel and free continental breakfast. It's kid-friendly and there's a senior's discount.

TOP END
ThistleDown House (☎ 604-986-7173, 888-633-7173; www.thistle-down.com; 3910 Capilano Rd; s/d incl breakfast from $125/145; P) A restored 1920s Arts and Crafts house packed with antiques is the location for this romantic, adult-oriented B&B situated among its own large gardens. There's a resident dog to welcome guests, as well as cozy hearths in all the rooms. In addition to the four-course breakfast, rates include afternoon tea.

West Vancouver
Beachside B&B (Map pp650–1; ☎ 604-922-7773, 800-563-3311; www.beach.bc.ca; 4208 Evergreen Ave; s/d incl breakfast from $150/175) Superb views of the waterfront and downtown make this luxurious B&B a popular romantic getaway. Of course the Jacuzzis and proximity to hiking, fishing and golfing also help.

EATING
Every conceivable cuisine is available in Vancouver, especially on Denman St, Davie St and parts of W Broadway and Commercial Dr. Pick up a copy of the free *City Food* magazine at restaurants and liquor stores for a taste of the Vancouver food scene. For budget travelers, Vancouver's shopping-mall food courts are excellent value, especially with their varied Asian offerings.

Downtown
Map pp652–4

BUDGET
Mouse and the Bean Café (☎ 604-633-1781; 207 W Hastings St; meals $4-7; ☯ breakfast & lunch) Excellent off-the-beaten-track family-run Mexican joint, where everything, including the refried beans, is made in house. There are plenty of vegetarian options. Favorites include bulging enchiladas and giant quesadillas.

Copper Onion (☎ 604-642-0755; 1313 Robson St; meals $6-7; ☯ lunch & dinner) A great-value Japanese curry bar, where you'll receive a heaping plate of meat or vegetable curry and sticky rice, garnished with tangy pickled radish.

MID-RANGE

Templeton (☎ 604-685-4612; 1087 Granville St; meals $6-10; ⊙ 9am-11pm Mon-Thu, 9-1am Fri & Sat) An authentic chrome-and-vinyl diner with a twist: organic burgers, vegetarian sausages and the best breakfast in town (served until 3pm). Drop by on Monday night for the free movie screening.

Hon's Wun-Tun House (☎ 604-685-0871; 1339 Robson St; meals $8-14; ⊙ lunch & dinner) A legendary local Chinese-food minichain, the Robson St location has 'em queuing out the doors on many weekend nights. The giant menu is executed in several open-plan kitchens dotted around the dining area, and the main draws are the delectable pot stickers and heaping noodle soups. Expect to leave with a doggy bag.

Bin 941 Tapas Parlour (☎ 604-683-1246; 941 Davie St; meals $12-18; ⊙ 5pm-2am) Funky, noisy and ever-popular (come early or late to ensure a table), this tiny sliver of a restaurant specializes in perfect tasting plates of seafood, poultry and meat, showcasing the region's culinary treats.

Hapa Izakaya (☎ 604-689-4272; 1479 Robson St; meals $15-20; ⊙ dinner) A midpriced reinvention of the Japanese *izakaya* (tapas bar), this cozy new haunt is already one of the hottest spots in town, due to its combination of comfort foods, highly welcoming service and Sapporo beer. Reservations are recommended.

Tropika (☎ 604-737-6002; 1128 Robson St; meals $12-20; ⊙ lunch & dinner) Sophisticated and modern reinvention of cuisines from Indonesia, Thailand and Malaysia, with some surprising fish dishes – check out the chili clams – and a great range of satay sticks are found here.

Wild Rice (☎ 604-642-2882; 117 W Pender; meals $8-18; ⊙ brunch, lunch & dinner) Loungy reinvention of the Chinese restaurant, fusing traditional dishes with influences from around the world. Wild boar with jasmine rice and plantain chips is particularly recommended, and the comprehensive martini list is too.

Water St Café (☎ 604-689-2832; 300 Water St; meals $14-22; ⊙ lunch & dinner) Perfectly prepared pasta is the mainstay of the menu, but the street-café ambience – you can sit on the cobbled streets of historic Gastown – is the best

reason to dine here. Check out the *Georgia Straight* before you come in; there's often a two-for-one coupon lurking in its restaurant pages.

TOP END

Cin Cin Ristorante & Bar (☎ 604-688-7338; 1154 Robson St; meals $20-50; ⊙ lunch Mon-Fri, dinner daily) Tuscan ambience fused with west-coast sophistication means a host of homesick Hollywood movie stars keep on coming back to this excellent restaurant. If they're not gorging on alder-smoked wild salmon pizza, they're salivating over local fish and game produced in a simple, yet always elegant, manner. Reservations are recommended.

Stanley Park/West End   Map pp652–4

While the park has four restaurants of its own, nearby Denman St contains dozens of eateries of every conceivable flavor.

BUDGET

Hot Dog Johnny's (☎ 604-913-3647; 1061 Denman St; meals $4-6; ⊙ lunch & dinner) Hot dogs never

---

THE AUTHOR'S CHOICE

Tojo's (Map pp650-1; ☎ 604-872-8050; 202-777 W Broadway; meals $30-60; ⊙ dinner Mon-Sat) If you only have one sushi meal in Vancouver (and that's quite a challenge in a city that has more sushi bars per head than most cities outside Tokyo), make sure it's at Tojo's. Expect to spend a few dollars more for the opportunity to sample a Japanese feast of supreme seafood – and sushi is only a part of what goes on here – prepared by the multiaward-winning, legendary Hidekazu Tojo. Tojo has been sharpening his knives in Vancouver for 30 years and has an encyclopedic mastery of 2000 recipes. Among his exquisite, beautifully presented dishes are favorites such as lightly fried red tuna wrapped with seaweed and served with a Japanese plum sauce, lightly steamed monkfish and sautéed halibut cheeks. It's the shrimp dumplings with hot mustard sauce that can stir the taste buds of even the most jaded diners, though. The sushi-bar seats here are more sought after than a couple of front-row Stanley Cup tickets, so reserve as early as possible.

TOP FIVE VANCOUVER EATS

- **Bin 941 Tapas Parlour** (p671)
- **Cin Cin Ristorante & Bar** (p671)
- **Feenies** (p673)
- **Raincity Grill** (below)
- **Tojo's** (p671)

---

tasted like this before: no hidden hoofs in the meat, a clutch of gourmet varieties, tasty vegetarian options and more toppings than you can balance on a giant bun.

MID-RANGE

Brass Monkey (☎ 604-685-7626; 1072 Denman St; meals $10-18; ☯ brunch Sun, dinner daily) The city's coziest home-from-home eatery is a funky mélange of velvet curtains and mismatched lampshades. There's an eclectic menu including Dijon-crusted wild salmon, pan-seared with bok choy and served in a banana leaf.

Yoshi (☎ 604-738-8226; 689 Denman St; meals $12-18; ☯ dinner) With great upper-floor views of the marina and Stanley Park, this Japanese favorite is a testament to the high quality of Vancouver's sushi and sashimi scene.

TOP END

Raincity Grill (☎ 604-685-7337; 1193 Denman St; meals $20-50; ☯ dinner) Great showcase for fine west coast cuisine, this laid-back venue has superb English Bay views and one of the city's best wine selections. Reservations recommended, or you could order a $10 sampler picnic box from the take-out window – one of the best deals in town.

Fish House in Stanley Park (☎ 604-681-7275; 8901 Stanley Park Dr; meals $18-30; ☯ brunch, lunch & dinner) A local legend, this is one of the city's best spots to explore seasonal local seafood at its best. The simply prepared grilled swordfish is recommended, as are reservations.

Yaletown Map pp652–4

MID-RANGE

Glowbal Grill & Satay Bar (☎ 604-602-0835; 1079 Mainland St; meals $12-20; ☯ brunch, lunch & dinner) Hip but unpretentious Yaletown hangout where the finger-licking satay sticks are just the start of a menu that includes beautifully presented fish and meat entrees fusing South Asian and Western influences.

Yaletown Brewing Company (☎ 604-681-2739; 1111 Mainland St; meals $12-18; ☯ lunch & dinner) As you walk in, there's a brick-lined pub on the left and a giant dining room on the right; both serve pints of beer brewed on site, but the restaurant adds a menu of great comfort foods. The gourmet thin-crust pizzas are recommended, as is dropping by on Sunday for beer and pizza specials.

Coast (☎ 604-685-5010; 1257 Hamilton St; meals $16-26; ☯ dinner) Good patio and a swish, airy interior enhance the ambience at this new Yaletown spot where seafood dominates. There are plenty of sophisticated options, but the simply grilled Chilean sea bass is a winner.

TOP END

Blue Water Café & Raw Bar (☎ 604-688-8078; 1095 Hamilton St; meals $20-50; ☯ brunch, lunch & dinner) Sushi and shellfish fans love this attractive Yaletown haunt but local catches also make regular appearances and there's a good selection of wine accompaniments. Reservations are recommended.

Granville Island Map pp652–4

BUDGET

Food Court at Granville Island Public Market (1689 Johnston St; meals $5-8; ☯ lunch) Aside from the cornucopia of bakeries and deli stalls, the compact food court here is one of the city's best, combining an international array of quality fajitas, pierogies, pizzas, curries and fish and chips. Eat during off-peak hours to avoid the crowds.

MID-RANGE

Bridges Restaurant (☎ 604-687-4400; 1696 Duranleau St; meals $10-18; ☯ lunch & dinner) At this casual thirtysomethings' bistro pub, with views of Yaletown skyscrapers and the Burrard Bridge, the menu ranges from fish faves to chicken quesadillas.

Dockside Restaurant & Pub (☎ 604-685-7070; 1253 Johnston St; meals $10-18; ☯ breakfast, brunch, lunch & dinner) Well-prepared pub comfort food, including thin-crust pizzas and rotisserie-chicken dishes, accompany some of the city's best house-made microbrews and patio views.

TOP END

Sandbar (☎ 604-669-9030; 1535 Johnston St; meals $18-35; ☯ brunch, lunch & dinner) It's almost all about west-coast seafood at this restaurant with a view, tucked under Granville Bridge. The oysters here rock, and they're best sampled on the fireplace-warmed rooftop deck. Reservations are recommended.

Kitsilano
BUDGET
Capers Community Markets (Map pp650–1; ☎ 604-739-6676; 2285 W 4th Ave; meals $4-8; ⏰ 8am-10pm) Health-minded, mostly organic supermarket with a great café-take-out section. The quality salad bar and glutinous fruit smoothies are popular but the hearty wraps ($4) are highly recommended for those on the run. There's also a branch **downtown** (Map pp652-4; ☎ 604-687-5288; 1675 Robson St; ⏰ 8am-10pm Mon-Sat, 8am-9pm Sun) and in **West Vancouver** (Map pp650-1; ⏰ 604-925-3316; 2496 Marine Dr; ⏰ 7am-7pm Mon-Thu, 7am-9pm Fri & Sat, 8am-7pm Sun).

Planet Veg (Map pp652-41; ☎ 604-734-1001; 1941 Cornwall Ave; meals $4-7; ⏰ breakfast, lunch & dinner) Great value Indian-fusion vegetarian spot where meat-eaters will be more than satisfied. The hot pots with rice are great value, and the homemade samosas are perfectly portable.

MID-RANGE
Feenies (Map pp650-1; ☎ 604-739-7115; 2563 W Broadway; meals $12-20; ⏰ lunch & dinner) Vancouver's favorite chef Rob Feenie (see Lumière, below) recently opened this modern diner, where comfort food receives the high-end treatment. The hamburgers and hot dogs are revelatory, while the duck shepherd's pie is a winner.

Naam (Map pp650-1; ☎ 604-738-7151; 2724 W 4th Ave; meals $8-16; ⏰ 24hr) Legendary Kits vegetarian eatery that attracts nonvegetarians by the droves. Breakfast is well worth the trek, and there's a patio for summertime eating.

Sophie's Cosmic Café (Map pp652-4; ☎ 604-732-6810; 2095 West 4th Ave; meals $6-12; ⏰ breakfast, brunch, lunch & dinner) A local institution, Sophie's is one of the best breakfast/weekend brunch spots in town. The 1950s-diner ambience only adds to the taste of the great eggs Benedict.

TOP END
Lumière (Map pp650-1; ☎ 604-739-8185; 2551 W Broadway; meals from $40; ⏰ dinner) Vancouver's best restaurant, and one of the best in Canada, Rob Feenie's French-inspired Lumière is best sampled via the tasting menu, which includes a nine-course vegetarian option. Reservations are recommended.

Commercial Drive
Map pp650–1
A kaleidoscope of immigrants has made 'The Drive' the city's best strip for ethnic and fusion food adventuring. Prices are fab – you won't find any top-end joints here – and the area is vegetarian-friendly.

BUDGET
Belgian Fries (☎ 604-253-4220; 1885 Commercial Dr; meals $5-8; ⏰ lunch & dinner) The best fries in town are best accompanied by a Montréal-style smoked-meat sandwich. For heart-attack lovers the *poutine* (fries served under gravy and cheese curds) is highly regarded, and you can then suck down a deep-fried Mars bar to push you right over the edge. The excellent beer selection includes Québec favorites with satanic-looking labels and Storm, a rare BC brew.

La Casa Gelato (604-251-3211; 1033 Venables St; cones from $2) It's worth a detour a few blocks from Commercial Dr for Vancouver's favorite ice-cream parlor. Along with every flavor you might desire (there's usually around 200 to choose from), there are always a few weird and wonderful concoctions. Anyone for the salmon-and-fudge combo?

MID-RANGE
Havana (☎ 604-253-9119; 1212 Commercial Dr; meals $8-18; ⏰ lunch & dinner) The granddaddy of Commercial Dr, the funky Havana combines a live theater and gallery with a roster of satisfying Afro-Cuban-Southern comfort dishes. The rib-sticking Cajun stews should not be missed.

Bukowski's (☎ 604-253-4770; 1447 Commercial Dr; meals $8-14; ⏰ lunch & dinner) Bohemian poetry readings and live music accompany a superb and well-priced menu that fuses Asian, Moroccan and Indian influences. Favorites include chicken, prawn or tofu-noodle bowls.

Mekong House (☎ 604-253-7088; 1414 Commercial Dr; meals $8-14; ⏰ lunch & dinner) Thai, Vietnamese and French cuisines combine effortlessly here on an impressive menu featuring meat, seafood and vegetarian options, along with possibly the best pumpkin soup you'll ever taste.

Clove (☎ 604-255-5550; 2054 Commercial Dr; mains $8-16) The city's best *chai* tea is just one of the attractions on the menu here, where Thai, Indonesian and Indian cuisines collide. Reservations are recommended.

Richmond
Map pp650–1

MID-RANGE

Papi's (☎ 604-275-8355; 12551 No 1 Rd; meals $12-18; ☾ lunch & dinner) Richmond's best Italian restaurant serves delicate seafood ravioli and hearty fine-beef pastas. There are good desserts and an interesting, mostly Italian, wine list too.

Kelong Singapore Cuisine (☎ 604-821-9883; 130-4800 No 3 Rd; meals $10-18; ☾ lunch & dinner) Spicy Malaysian and Singaporean approaches combine in this bright restaurant, where vegetarians are also well served.

TOP END

Steveston Seafood House (☎ 604-271-5252; 3951 Moncton St; meals $25-40; ☾ dinner) A great way to celebrate Steveston's historic fishing industry is to stroll past the fish-and-chip shops, and make for this classy eatery, where local catches are expertly prepared. Reservations are recommended.

North & West Vancouver
Map pp650–1

BUDGET

Vera's Burger Shack (☎ 604-836-8372; 2506 Bellevue Ave; meals $5-7; ☾ lunch & dinner) A local favorite, Vera's epic burgers are among Vancouver's best. Dare to try the double-patty, double-cheese and double-onion special, and see if you can still stand.

MID-RANGE

Tomahawk Barbecue (☎ 604-988-2612; 1550 Phillip Ave; meals $6-14; ☾ breakfast, brunch, lunch & dinner) A blast from Vancouver's past, the Tomahawk Barbecue has been cooking up comfort food since 1926. It's an excellent weekend-breakfast spot; favorites include oysters on toast, the fried chicken and heaping hamburgers.

Gusto di Quattro (☎ 604-924-4444; 1 Lonsdale Ave; meals $12-18; ☾ lunch Mon-Fri, dinner daily) A good-value gourmet Italian restaurant serving quality pastas alongside specialties such as grilled Cornish hen. The wine selection is determinedly Italian.

Caspian (☎ 604-921-1311; 1495 Marine Dr; meals $12-18; ☾ dinner) Authentic Iranian restaurant serving a wide array of fish and meat kebabs, along with hearty stews.

TOP END

Beach House at Dundarave Pier (☎ 604-922-1414; 150 25th St; meals $30-50; ☾ lunch & dinner) Dramatic West Vancouver waterfront views are as good a reason for eating here as the menu, which relies on west coast–style seafood and meat dishes. Reservations are recommended.

DRINKING

Vancouver's drinking scene has moved on from the days of stinking neighborhood bars already full of red-nosed drunks by 10am (you can still find them on the eastern side of downtown, if you really miss them) and into an era of scrubbed character pubs and cool lounges with bewildering martini lists. Wherever you end up for the evening, check out some of BC's excellent craft beers, including ales and lagers from Nelson, Granville Island and Crannóg breweries. There's also a ubiquity of coffee shops, including the chains. Dive into the more rewarding hangouts in areas like Kitsilano and Commercial Dr; mismatched tables, homemade cookies and the best organic java are what real Vancouver coffee bars are all about.

Downtown

O'Douls (Map pp652-4; ☎ 604-661-1400; 1300 Robson St) A good bar, an excellent wine selection and live jazz every night attracts the over-30s set here. It's also the center of the action during the Vancouver International Jazz Festival (p665).

Mill Marine Bistro (Map pp652-4; ☎ 604-687-6455; 1199 W Cordova St) Overpriced food but good beer and spectacular panoramic views of Stanley Park, North Shore mountains and seaplanes descending on Burrard Inlet.

C-9 Live Lounge (Map pp652-4; ☎ 604-687-0511; 1400 Robson St) It's all about the view here at this revolving eatery on the 42nd floor of the Empire Landmark Hotel. Bypass the restaurant and head straight to the bar for cocktails, live weekend jazz and an unrivalled 360-degree view of the city.

Caffe Artigiano (Map pp652-4; ☎ 604-696-9222; 763 Hornby St) The best coffee in town is served in rustic painted cups with a leafy motif decorating the froth on top. These fellas have won awards around the world, and not just for presentation.

Jugo Juice (Map pp652-4; ☎ 604-899-9237; 202 Davie St) This homegrown independent juice chain has branches throughout the city and its smoothies are a meal unto themselves. Try the luscious, hangover-battling Power-zone with an Energy Boost.

Gastown

Alibi Room (Map pp652-4; ☎ 604-623-3383; 157 Alexander St) It's all about great conversation here, where the design crowd and film industries congregate at long tables, or hunker down in the low-ceilinged basement to bitch about work. A quality comfort-food menu perfectly matches the fortifying martinis on offer.

Irish Heather (Map pp652-4; ☎ 604-688-9779; 217 Carrall St) There's a European gastropub feel to this unpretentious labyrinth of brick-lined nooks. Warm up in winter with the restorative 'Hot Irish,' a concoction of whisky, lemon, cloves, sugar and boiling water, or head straight for the hidden Shebeen Whisky House back room, where 140 varieties await.

DV8 (Map pp652-4; ☎ 604-682-4388; 515 Davie St) A bar by day and a late-blooming loungy hangout by night, the grungy DV8 is a comfortable alternative to the stresses of the noisy Granville scene. There's local art on the walls, live comedy on Sunday, and a wide variety of turntable tunes from old-school funk to new wave.

Mo'Butta (Map pp652-4; ☎ 604-688-6439; 52 Powell St) A comfortable new Gastown haunt spread over two brick-lined floors, with a jazz/blues live-music space. There are well-priced local beers, no cover for bands and good service.

Stanley Park/West End

Denman St Freehouse (Map pp652-4; ☎ 604-801-6681; 1780 Davie St) A cool reinvention of the neighborhood pub, the recently opened Freehouse has a great array of worldwide boutique beers, a good menu and some breathtaking views of English Bay from its covered patio.

Bayside Lounge (Map pp652-4; ☎ 604-682-1831; 2nd fl, 1755 Davie St) A local loyal clientele keeps on coming back to this somewhat hidden gem overlooking English Bay. With its comfortable 1980s decor and circular bar, it's the perfect spot for a late-night drink on your way home.

Yaletown

Afterglow (Map pp652-4; ☎ 604-602-0835; 1082 Hamilton St) The city's most intimate lounge is tucked at the back of Yaletown's Glow-

---

TOP FIVE PUB PATIOS

- **Mill Marine Bistro** (opposite) Drink in the local brews and uninterrupted panoramic vistas of Stanley Park, the North Shore mountains and dramatic seaplane landings.
- **Malones** (below) Laid-back sports bar overlooking the beautiful people hanging out at Kitsilano Beach.
- **Denman St Freehouse** (left) International boutique beers and a covered patio overlooking picturesque English Bay.
- **Yaletown Brewing Company** (p672) Popular urban patio for quaffing beer that's brewed on site and watching the great and good of Yaletown sidle past.
- **Backstage Lounge** (below) Cast an eye at the busy miniferries and public market rabble while knocking back the nightly beer special at this place nestled under Granville Bridge.

---

ball Grill & Satay Bar (p672). Its sexy pink interior features giant silhouettes of naked women à la James Bond, and a flirty cocktail list includes You Glow Girl and Pink Pussycat – perfect for washing down the finger-licking satay sticks.

Granville Island

Backstage Lounge (Map pp652-4; ☎ 604-687-1354; 1585 Johnston St) Gotta love this lively grunge hangout on Granville Island, where local live bands and a patio with a great view are topped only by Tuesday night's $2.50 beer specials. A popular hangout for 'cougars' – local slang for fun-loving ladies looking to pick up younger men.

Kitsilano

Bimini's Tap House (Map pp652-4; ☎ 604-732-9232; 2010 W 4th Ave) A Kitsilano institution that's been reinvigorated in recent years, Bimini's is a pub-restaurant during the week, and a happening nightclub venue on weekends. When you're tired of moshing, you can cool down with darts or pool.

Malones (Map pp652-4; ☎ 604-737-7777; 2210 Cornwall Ave) An unpretentious Kitsilano sports bar where the beer is cold and the nachos are always nicely cheesy. The patio is good for people-watching, and is always packed in the summer.

Commercial Drive

Calabria Coffee Bar (Map pp650-1; ☎ 604-253-7017; 1745 Commercial Dr) Commercial Dr is the main drag for Vancouver coffee bars with character; you could go on a coffee crawl here and not sleep for a week. Among the best, the Calabria's high-kitsch decor perfectly complements some serious grinding.

ENTERTAINMENT

Vancouver's entertainment and cultural scene is divided into pockets around the city, so you have to hunt down the best options. Check the *Georgia Straight*, *Westender* and *Terminal City* for listings and pick up the *Vancouver Sun* on Thursday for its tabloid-sized *Queue* section, which lists most major local happenings.

Live Music

Commodore (Map pp652-4; ☎ 604-739-4550; www.hob .com/venues/concerts/commodore; 868 Granville St; most shows $20-35) Legendary midsized venue with a bouncy ballroom dance floor and a great mosh pit. This is where nonstadium visiting bands play and it's also a showcase for the best in local talent.

Cellar Restaurant & Jazz Club (Map pp650-1; ☎ 604-738-1959; www.cellarjazz.com; 3611 W Broadway; cover incl meal weeknights $5-10, weekends $25-45; ☑ 7pm-midnight Wed-Sun) A serious jazz venue where you're required to keep the noise down and respect the performances on the tiny corner stage, the Cellar is a windowless, subterranean gem.

TOP FIVE LATE-NIGHT SPOTS

- **Railway Club** (opposite) Eclectic nightly live-music roster in a pub-like setting.

- **Cellar Restaurant & Jazz Club** (above) Classy live venue for serious jazz musos.

- **Afterglow** (p675) Small, sexy and intimate Yaletown lounge.

- **DV8** (p675) Artsy, bohemian old-school lounge with a great dance floor.

- **Naam** (p673) A 24-hour vegetarian eatery that's perfect for 3am tofu binges.

You could be in a smoky 1950s New York club (if smoking were allowed here, that is).

Yale (Map pp652-4; ☎ 604-681-9253; www.theyale.ca; 1300 Granville St; most shows $10-25) Blowsy, unpretentious R&B joint with a large stage and a devoted clientele of hard-drinking music-lovers. Beer-sticky dance floor.

Nightclubs

The Granville entertainment district, between Robson and Davie Sts, is nightclub central for the young, mainstream good-looking set, but there are also other options slightly off the beaten track.

Shine (Map pp652-4; ☎ 604-408-4321; 364 Water St) With music from electro to funky house and hip-hop, Shine is divided into a main room and an intimate cozy cave, with a 12m chill-out sofa. Saturday's Big Sexy Funk is recommended.

Sonar (Map pp652-4; ☎ 604-683-6695; 66 Water St) Top DJs from around the world sometimes spin their stuff here, but most nights revolve around house in the main space, and hip-hop, reggae and R&B in the lounge.

Crush (Map pp652-4; ☎ 604-684-0355; 1180 Granville St) Attracting a smartly dressed over-25s crowd, Crush has a sultry lounge bar and its dance floor gently rocks to R&B, soul and jazz while customers sip champagne cocktails.

Voda (Map pp652-4; ☎ 604-684-3003; 783 Homer St) There's a laid-back loungey vibe and a dash of 1970s Scandinavian aesthetic to this small downtown club, which routinely attracts the city's beautiful people. Dress up or you'll feel out of place in the line-up.

Caprice (Map pp652-4; ☎ 604-681-2114; 967 Granville St) Among the best of the Granville clubs, Caprice has a large dance floor and bars on two levels. There's a dress code, an over-21s age policy and queues on weekends. The adjacent Caprice Lounge serves drinks and food till late.

Theater

Vancouver has an eclectic array of performance options for visitors. Pick up local listings publications like the *Georgia Straight* for upcoming events and check **Tickets Tonight** (Map pp652-4; ☎ 604-684-2787; www.tickets tonight.ca; Touristinfo Centre, Plaza Level, 200 Burrard St; ☑ Tue-Sat 10am-5pm) for half-price, day-of-performance tickets. **Ticketmaster** (☎ 604-280-4444; www.ticketmaster.ca) is the main local hawker for most Vancouver shows.

THE AUTHOR'S CHOICE

Railway Club (Map pp652-4; ☎ 604-681-1625; www.therailwayclub.com; 579 Dunsmuir St; cover $4-10) The city's best live-music venue, 'the Rail' has been upstairs at the corner of Dunsmuir and Seymour Sts since the 1930s. It still feels like a well-kept secret, though – especially to those new arrivals who 'discover' it for the first time. Combining the ambience of a grungy British pub with an eclectic nightly roster of indie, folk, punk, new wave, soul and everything in between, the clientele is a cheery mix of end-of-day office workers, turtleneck-wearing musos and homework-avoiding students. They gather around the tiny stages to catch performances that range from obscure names to some that have ultimately become household names, including the Bare Naked Ladies, kd lang and iconic Canadian rockers the Tragically Hip. It's not just about the music here, though. While the club has steadily improved its selection of wines and spirits, the Rail will always be a favorite haunt for local beer-tipplers. West-coast drafts from Granville Island and Okanagan Spring breweries feature heavily, and there's even room for Crannóg, a lip-smacking organic BC ale. With drafts served in traditional dimpled glasses – these may be the only real pints in town – there's an alternating $4.35 beer special every day.

Arts Club Theatre Company (☎ 604-687-1644; www.artsclub.com; tickets $25-45) The city's leading theater company performs at the **Granville Island Stage** (Map pp652-4; 1585 Johnston St) and the **Stanley Theatre** (Map pp650-1; 2750 Granville St; tickets $25-45) and mixes works by favorite regional playwrights like Morris Panych with popular classics from around the world.

Vancouver Symphony Orchestra (Map pp652-4; ☎ 604-876-3343; www.vancouversymphony.ca; Orpheum Theatre; tickets $25-45) Under avuncular maestro Bramwell Tovey, the VSO has grown into a popular night out for Vancouverites, fusing complex and stirring recitals with crossover shows of movie music, opera and even Shakespearean sonnets.

Scotiabank Dance Centre (Map pp652-4; ☎ 604-606-6400; www.thedancecentre.ca; 677 Davie St; tickets from $10) Entertaining and often challenging recitals by professional and student dancers in this dynamic new space, which is the resource center of dance in BC. The innovative **Ballet BC** (☎ 604-732-5003; www.balletbc.com) is headquartered here and frequently performs when not on tour locally, nationally or internationally.

Vancouver TheatreSports League (Map pp652-4; ☎ 604-738-7013; www.vtsl.com; New Revue Stage, 1601 Johnston St; tickets $10-16.50) Performing their comedy improv high jinks at their Granville Island base for more than 15 years, local favorite TheatreSports offers a safe bet for a gut-busting night out. Check the *Georgia Straight* for regular two-for-one coupons.

Firehall Arts Centre (Map pp652-4; ☎ 604-689-0926; www.firehallartscentre.ca; 280 E Cordova St; tickets $15-30)

Intimate fringe-style theater venue, where more challenging plays and performances are usually presented to an artsy, local crowd.

Cinemas

There are two chain cinemas almost facing each other on Granville St, between Robson and Smithe Sts, with a new multiplex set to open on Smithe in 2005.

Cinemark Tinseltown (Map pp652-4; ☎ 604-806-0799; www.cinemark.com; 88 W Pender St) A Vancouver favorite, combining blockbusters and art-house offerings.

Pacific Cinematheque (Map pp652-4; ☎ 604-688-3456; www.cinematheque.bc.ca; 1131 Howe St) For art-house films only. This is like an ongoing film festival, but membership is required ($3) before you can sit in the stalls and stroke your chin.

Fifth Avenue Cinemas (Map pp652-4; ☎ 604-734-7469; 2110 Burrard St) is also a popular indie and foreign movie screener, as is Kitsilano's long-established **Ridge Theatre** (Map pp650-1; ☎ 604-738-6311; 3131 Arbutus St).

CN IMAX Theatre (Map pp652-4; ☎ 604-682-4629; www.imax.com/vancouver; 201-999 Canada Place) This IMAX screens mostly worthy documentaries, but the occasional rejigged *Matrix* or *Star Wars* movie sometimes makes it through the net.

Sports
HOCKEY
Vancouver has two hockey venues.

GM Place (Map pp652-4; ☎ 604-899-4625; www.canucks.com; 800 Griffiths Way; tickets from $45) Since losing its NBA basketball franchise in 2002, Vancouver's top sporting attraction is the Vancouver Canucks NHL hockey team, who play at GM Place. Aim to book your ticket way in advance – most games are sold to capacity – and expect local sports bars to fill up on game night.

Pacific Coliseum (Map pp650-1; ☎ 604-444-2687; www.vancouvergiants.com; Hastings Park; tickets $10-25) If you're itching to see a hockey game, but can't get your hands on a Canucks ticket, the Vancouver Giants are an excellent alternative. The World Hockey League (WHL) side holds its home games at Pacific Coliseum, and they're often lively affairs with enough brawls to please the 5000-plus crowds.

FOOTBALL

The cavernous **BC Place stadium** (Map pp652-4; ☎ 604-589-7627; www.bclions.com; tickets $20-60) is home to the BC Lions, members of the Canadian Football League, who play from June to November. Tickets are usually easy to come by, so don't bother with the parasitic scalpers outside. See p655 for information about the sports hall of fame and the stadium tour.

SOCCER

Soccer is a highly popular participatory sport here. but only a few thousand turn up for Vancouver Whitecaps games at **Swangard Stadium** (Map pp650-1; ☎ 604-669-9283; www.white capssoccer.com; Burnaby; tickets $12-22). The ground is not well shielded from the cold, so dress warmly or plan to run around the pitch a lot. You can get to Swangard Stadium by SkyTrain (p683).

BASEBALL

Nat Bailey Stadium (Map pp650-1; ☎ 604-872-5332; www.canadiansbaseball.com; 4601 Ontario St; tickets $7.50-20) A sunny afternoon at Nat Bailey Stadium with the Vancouver Canadians is less about watching great baseball, and more about cold beer in plastic cups, a fistful of salty pretzels and a great family atmosphere.

SHOPPING

Robson St is the city's main shopping thoroughfare. Department stores such as Sears, The Bay and the high-end Holt Renfrew are nearby, and the **Pacific Centre** (Map pp652-4; ☎ 604-688-7236; Main entrance, cnr Georgia St & Howe St; ☼ 10am-7pm Mon-Wed, 10am-9pm Thu & Fri, 11am-6pm Sun) shopping mall is just a credit-card-throw away. Souvenir shopping can be taken care of in minutes along Gastown's Water St.

For more intrepid shoppers, there are some pockets of great independent stores in Yaletown, where upscale designer boutiques are de rigeur, and in the SoMa, Kitsilano and Commercial Dr areas, where galleries and one-of-a-kind clothing stores showcase local artists and designers. The area currently being marketed as South Granville Rise (the strip on Granville St that extends a few blocks from W 2nd Ave) is also a good spot for some leisurely afternoon window-shopping. It combines small galleries with clothes boutiques, old established delis and some one-of-a-kind design stores. It's also close to Granville Island, a shoppers paradise for art and crafts.

Art Galleries

Coastal Peoples Fine Arts Gallery (Map pp652-4; ☎ 604-685-9298; 1024 Mainland St; ☼ 10am-7pm Mon-Sat, 11am-5pm Sun) A sumptuous gallery-style setting for a fine selection of locally produced aboriginal jewelry, carvings and prints.

Hill's Native Art (Map pp652-4; ☎ 604-685-4249; 165 Water St; ☼ 9am-9pm) Specializing in Pacific Northwest coast aboriginal arts and crafts, including 4.6m totem poles and more portable silver jewelry, this store has been a Gastown favorite for years.

Bau-xi Gallery (Map pp650-1; ☎ 604-733-7011; 3045 Granville St) Pronounced 'bow-she,' the oldest contemporary art gallery in western Canada concentrates on bringing Canadian artists to audiences on the west coast. Many of the region's finest young painters, sculptors and conceptual artists are exhibited here.

Diane Farris Gallery (Map pp650-1; ☎ 604-737-2629; 1590 W 7th Ave) This small but perfectly formed private gallery, showcasing contemporary Canadian and international art, has a reputation for unearthing new talent. Make sure you check out its sculpture garden before heading inside. It's located a block from the main strip of South Granville Rise.

Clothing

Lululemon Athletica (Map pp652-4; ☎ 604-681-3118; 1148 Robson St; ☼ 10am-7pm Mon-Wed, 10am-9pm Thu-Sat, 11am-7pm Sun) Doing for yoga gear what Gap did for cargo pants, Lululemon is a fast-growing fashion phenomenon. There are no statistics on how many customers actually practice yoga, but the widespread

---

MARKETS TO MEANDER

▪ **Granville Island Public Market** (Map pp652-4; ☎ 604-666-6477; Johnson St; ⏲ 9am-6pm, closed Mon in Jan) Colorful mountains of fruit and veg dominate at the city's leading covered market. This is also a great spot for more eclectic purchases: take home some exotic loose tea, a bottle of Okanagan ice wine or some of Oyama Sausage Co's finest.

▪ **Lonsdale Quay Market** (Map pp650-1; ☎ 604-985-6261; 123 Carrie Cates Court; ⏲ 9:30am-6:30pm) A popular half-day excursion via a 15-minute SeaBus trip from downtown, Lonsdale Quay offers a more touristy market than Granville Island. The product mix ranges from books to salmon, and the upper floors contain some clothing stores. There's a good food court, and some spectacular views of the city's waterfront skyline.

▪ **Richmond Night Market** (Map pp650-1; Lansdowne Centre, 5300 No 3 Rd, Richmond; ⏲ 7pm-midnight Fri & Sat, 7-11pm Sun, Jun-Sep) It will take you several hours to properly trawl Richmond's 250-plus vendors. Save your appetite till you arrive so that you can sample the take-out, while perusing the Pokemon cards and fake designer kitsch. There's also a smaller **Chinatown night market** (Map pp652-4; Pender St & Keefer St; ⏲ 6:30-11pm Fri-Sun Jun-Sep) downtown that's also popular with visitors.

▪ **UBC Farm Market** (Map pp650-1; ☎ 604-822-5092; 6182 South Campus Rd; ⏲ 9:30am-4:30pm Tue-Sat May-Aug) A tasty cornucopia of local farm produce hits the stalls here throughout the summer. Among the highlights are the lush apricots and peaches, while seasonal berries including strawberries, blueberries and blackberries are much sought-after. Artisan breads, hearty cakes and handmade soaps are often added to the product mix that's available. Arrive early in the day for the best selection.

▪ **Vancouver Flea Market** (Map pp652-4; ☎ 604-685-0666; 703 Terminal Ave) If sifting through boxes of dusty LPs or trying on authentic 1970s trucker baseball caps is your thing, the rough-and-ready Vancouver Flea Market is the place to be. Its giant, barnlike location houses dozens of semiprofessional and amateur hawkers: it's like a huge indoor garage sale.

---

appeal of this laid-back, sporty clothing range is undisputed.

John Fluevog Shoes (Map pp652-4; ☎ 604-688-2828; 837 Granville St; ⏲ Mon-Wed 11am-7pm, Thu & Fri 11am-8pm, Sat 11am-7pm, Sun noon-5pm) While Madonna reportedly struts her stuff in Day-Glo Fluevog footwear, you don't have to be a Material Girl to shop here. Looking like Doc Martens on acid, these funky, chunky shoes, sandals and thigh-hugging boots have been a Vancouver fashion legend since 1970.

Smoking Lily (Map pp650-1; ☎ 604-873-5459; 3634 Main St; ⏲ 11am-6pm Mon-Sat, noon-5pm Sun) Art-student hippie cool is the style here; cute skirts and halter tops are tastefully accented with prints of ants, skulls or squid, making their wearers appear interesting and complex.

Kawabata-ya (Map pp652-4; ☎ 604-806-0020; 437 Hastings St; ⏲ 11am-7pm Mon-Sat, noon-5pm Sun) Perhaps Vancouver's hottest vintage store, Kawabata-ya has been featured in fashion magazines across North America. Regular items include Japanese denim jeans, 1970s wraparound sunglasses and a range of old

garments cleverly redesigned into new items.

Roots Factory Outlet (Map pp650-1; ☎ 604-433-4337; 3695 Grandview Hwy; ⏲ 10am-6pm Mon-Wed, 10am-9pm Thu-Sat, 11am-6pm Sun) Canada's favorite sports and casual-wear outfitter has a factory outlet and periodic sales, where sweatpants, T-shirts, footwear and kids clothing are almost given away. It's the official outfitter for the Canadian, US and UK Olympic teams.

Maynards (Map pp652-4; ☎ 604-675-2236; 415 W 2nd Ave; ⏲ 9:30am-5:30pm Mon-Fri, 9:30am-5pm Sat, noon-5pm Sun) An upmarket liquidation store with designer clothes (Diesel, Calvin Klein etc), high-end bedding and home decor. Worth checking out for a pair of cheap Ray-Ban sunglasses, before you head to the beach.

True Value Vintage (Map pp652-4; ☎ 604-685-5403; 710 Robson St; ⏲ 10am-9pm Mon-Thu, 10am-10pm Fri & Sat, 10am-8pm Sun) The city's largest vintage store, this musty, subterranean Aladdin's cave will have you hunting (probably successfully) for that all-important *Battlestar Galactica* T-shirt you had when you were nine.

TOP FIVE SHOPPING AREAS

▪ **Granville Island** (p657) The region's best public market (see the boxed text on p679) is joined by dozens of artisan workshops and some fascinating small galleries.

▪ **4th Ave, Kitsilano** (p658) A street-shopper's haven of bookstores, cafés and boutiques awaits between Burrard and Balsam Sts.

▪ **Richmond Night Market** (p679) Modern-day Chinese market that's also a walkable feast of food stands.

▪ **Robson St** The city's main shopping thoroughfare is a great place to check out members of the opposite sex: if Vancouver had a promenade, this would be it.

▪ **Granville St** Small galleries, bookstores, top restaurants and home-decor joints crowd around the intersection with Broadway – a great area for an afternoon of window shopping.

Outdoor Gear

Mountain Equipment Co-op (MEC; Map pp650-1; ☎ 604-872-7858; 130 W Broadway; ✆ 10am-7pm Mon-Wed, 10am-9pm Thu & Fri, 9am-6pm Sat, 11am-5pm Sun) If you've come to Vancouver, chances are you're an outdoorsy person, which means you shouldn't leave town without checking out the granddaddy of local gear stores. The giant MEC superstore is surrounded by a ghetto of smaller outdoor supply stores looking for some spin-off action.

Coast Mountain Sports (Map pp652-4; ☎ 604-731-6181; 2201 W 4th Ave; ✆ 9:30am-9pm) A popular, more mainstream alternative to MEC, this outdoor-oriented superstore has some regular sales and combines utilitarian gear with more fashionable outfits for those who want to look like they're hikers, even when they're not.

Specialty Items

Simple (Map pp650-1; ☎ 604-877-0323; 3638 Main St; ✆ 11am-6pm Mon-Sat, noon-5pm Sun) This eponymous ministore stocks a range of highly design-conscious, yet surprisingly inexpensive, knickknacks for the home, including silk pillows that are handmade on site, slender white vases and lots of shiny stainless steel must-haves.

Paperhaus (Map pp650-1; ☎ 604-737-2225; 3057 Granville St; ✆ 10am-6pm Mon-Sat, noon-5pm Sun) A stationery store for the postmodern set, this clinical-looking space hawks all manner of small, cool items you'd like to leave lying around your apartment for people to notice.

Meinhardt Fine Foods (Map pp650-1; ☎ 604-732-4405; 3002 Granville St; ✆ 8am-9pm Mon-Sat, 9am-9pm Sun) Great deli, excellent take-out but for most visitors it's all about condiments at this bustling upmarket corner store. If you're looking for the very best in aged balsamic vinegar to take back home and secretly sniff, this may be your favorite spot in town.

La Grotta del Formaggio (Map pp650-1; ☎ 604-255-3911; 1791 Commercial Dr; ✆ 9am-6pm Sat-Thu, 9am-7pm Sun) Dozens of international cheeses are the backbone of this food-lovers paradise, but there are plenty of high-end Italian staples to keep you nipping back, including olives, oils and excellent panini.

GETTING THERE & AWAY
Air

Vancouver International Airport (☎ 604-207-7077; www.yvr.ca) is on Sea Island in Richmond, a 13km (30-minute) drive from downtown Vancouver. It's one of the most attractive airports in North America – check out the aboriginal artworks liberally sprinkled throughout the two main terminals – and it's the key west-coast hub for major airlines from the rest of Canada, the United States and international destinations, including Europe and Asia.

The airport's separate south terminal is linked to the main airport by a free shuttle bus. The south terminal receives smaller internal flights, seaplanes and helicopter services from domestic destinations, mostly within BC. Regular arrivals here include Hawkair (p869) with services to/from Victoria ($109, 25 minutes, daily) and Prince Rupert ($242, two hours, Sunday to Friday), and Pacific Coastal Airlines (p869) with services from Campbell River ($95, 20 minutes, nine daily) and Powell River ($85, 30 minutes, four daily).

There are also several highly convenient services that fly directly to Vancouver's downtown waterfront, near Canada Place. **Harbour Air** (☎ 604-274-1277; www.harbour-air.com) and **West Coast Air** (☎ 604-606-6888; www.west

coastair.com) operate similar seaplane services only during daylight hours from Victoria ($99, 25 minutes, half-hourly). Harbour Air's additional services arrive from Nanaimo ($54, 20 minutes, hourly) and the Gulf Islands ($74, four daily).

Helijet (☎ 604-273-4688; www.helijet.com) helicopter services from Victoria arrive at the south terminal ($159, 30 minutes, four daily Monday to Friday) and Vancouver waterfront area near Canada Place ($159, 35 minutes, hourly Monday to Friday plus limited weekend service).

Boat

BC Ferries (☎ 888-223-3779; www.bcferries.com) operates several services for Vancouver-bound passengers via its terminals at Tsawwassen, an hour's drive from the city center, and Horseshoe Bay, 30 minutes from downtown.

In summer, services to Tsawwassen arrive from Swartz Bay (90 minutes, hourly until 10pm) and Nanaimo (two hours, eight daily); fares are $10 per passenger and $36 per car. Summer services to Horseshoe Bay arrive from Nanaimo ($10/36 per person/car, 95 minutes, 14 daily until 10pm), Bowen Island ($6/20, 20 minutes, 14 to 16 daily) and Langdale ($8.50/30, 40 minutes, every two hours until 10pm). Reduced fares and schedules apply for most services during the rest of the year.

A new scheduled service, **HarbourLynx** (☎ 604-688-5465; www.harbourlynx.com) operates high-speed ferries ($25 per person, 80 minutes, three daily) between Nanaimo and downtown Vancouver, delivering passengers to a purpose-built terminal near Canada Place.

Bus

Vancouver's **bus station** (Map pp652-4; 1150 Station St) is part of Pacific Central Station, the colonial-style railway terminus between Chinatown and Science World. It's right on the SkyTrain transit line (Main St/Science World station).

Greyhound operates buses from the USA, including Seattle (US$24.50, four hours, five daily), Portland (US$47, eight to 11 hours, five daily) and San Francisco (US$85.50, 30 hours, three daily). Greyhound Canada has regular buses to Canadian destinations across the country, including Banff ($116, 12 to 15 hours, four daily), Calgary ($133,

14 to 16 hours, four daily) and Whitehorse ($250, 40 hours, three weekly). BC-specific arrivals include Nanaimo ($22, 2¾ hours, eight daily), Kamloops ($56, four to five hours, eight daily), Kelowna ($60, six hours, six daily) and Whistler ($17, 2½ hours, six daily).

Quick Coach Lines (☎ 604-940-4428; www.quick coach.com) operates an express shuttle service to Vancouver from Seattle, with departures from both downtown (US$33, four hours, six daily) and that city's Sea-Tac International airport (US$41, 4½ hours, six daily).

Pacific Coach Lines (☎ 604-662-7575; www.pacific coach.com) services arrive from downtown Victoria ($30.75, 3½ hours, hourly) via the BC Ferry route between Vancouver Island's Swartz Bay and Tsawwassen on the mainland. Bus reservations are required, particularly in the summer when this service is packed with tourists. Schedules and fares are reduced outside the peak season. You can also pick up the bus to downtown Vancouver on the ferry ($10.50, one hour).

Perimeter (☎ 604-717-6600; www.perimeterbus .com) runs a Whistler Express service from the resort's main hotels to Vancouver International Airport (adult/child $65/45, 2½ hours, eight to 11 daily). It'll also drop off at downtown Vancouver hotels on specific schedules, if requested at the time of booking.

Malaspina Coach Lines (☎ 877-227-8287) services arrive from Powell River ($37, 5¼ hours, two daily), Gibsons ($7, 1¾ hours, two daily) and Sechelt ($13, 2¼ hours, two daily) on the Sunshine Coast. Service is reduced to one per day in winter.

Car & Motorcycle

If you're coming from Washington state in the USA, you'll be on the US I-5 until you hit the border town of Blaine, then you'll be on Hwy 99 in Canada. It's about an hour's drive from there to downtown Vancouver, or around three hours total from Seattle to Vancouver. Highway 99 continues through downtown, across the Lions Gate Bridge to Horseshoe Bay, Squamish and Whistler.

If you're coming from the east, you'll probably be on the Trans-Canada Hwy (Hwy 1), which snakes through the city's eastern end, eventually meeting with Hastings St. It continues over the Iron Workers Memorial Second Narrows Bridge (known to locals simply as the Second Narrows Bridge) to

North Vancouver, and eventually on to West Vancouver (where it also becomes Hwy 99) and Horseshoe Bay. If you want to go downtown, turn left onto Hastings St and follow it into the city center.

If you're coming from Horseshoe Bay in the north, Hwy 1 heads through West Vancouver and North Vancouver before going over the Second Narrows Bridge into Burnaby. If you're heading downtown, leave the highway at the Taylor Way exit in West Vancouver (it's also a part of Hwy 99) and follow it over the Lions Gate Bridge into Stanley Park and the city center.

All the national car-rental chains have branches around the city. The Avis, Budget, Hertz and Thrifty agencies also have airport branches.

Train

Trains from across Canada and the USA arrive at Vancouver's Pacific Central Station (Map pp652-4), located by the bus station.

Vancouver is the western terminus for VIA Rail with services from Kamloops ($102, nine hours, three weekly), Jasper ($215, 17 hours, three weekly), Edmonton ($288, 24 hours, three weekly) and Toronto ($700, three days, three weekly), and additional connections across the country.

Amtrak rail services also arrive at Pacific Central Station. Amtrak's *Cascades* trains arrive from Eugene (US$57, 13½ hours, two daily), Portland (US$52, eight hours, three daily) and Seattle (US$31, 3½ hours, five daily), with connections available across the USA. Buses are used on many of the services, so call ahead if you want to ensure you're on a train.

GETTING AROUND
To/From the Airport

It takes around 30 minutes to drive downtown from Vancouver International Airport. Taxis charge $25 to $30, or you can arrive in style for just a few dollars more – limos are $42 for a maximum of six passengers.

Green-painted **Vancouver Airporter** (☎ 604-946-8866; www.yvrairporter.com) shuttle buses run from the airport (adult/child/senior $12/5/9) to more than 20 downtown hotels and Pacific Central Station. Services run every 15 to 30 minutes from 6:20am to 10:50pm in summer, with a reduced service the rest of the year. Reservations are not required – just

pay the driver or buy a ticket at the desk inside the airport. Return fares are available (adult/child/senior $18/10/17).

TransLink (p683) offers three bus services from the airport (fares from $2): route 100 connects to Vancouver and points east; route 404 travels to Richmond and Delta (Ladner) connecting to points south; and the 98 B-Line route is an express service that connects to downtown Vancouver. Information on these buses is available at Visitor Information Centres (VICs) on the arrivals level of both domestic and international terminals.

Boat

Aquabus Ferries (☎ 604-689-5858; www.aquabus .bc.ca) runs mini pedestrian-only vessels between the foot of Hornby St and Granville Island (adult/child $2/1, five minutes, every five minutes from 6:45am to 10:30pm, reduced service in winter). It also services routes from Science World, Stamps Landing and Yaletown (adult $2 to $5, child $1 to $3 depending on route) and can take bikes on some vessels (50¢). If you're making multiple trips, consider a $10 all-day pass.

False Creek Ferries (☎ 604-684-7781; www.granville islandferries.bc.ca) operates a similar service to Granville Island (adult/child $2/1, five minutes, every five minutes from 7am to 10:30pm, reduced service in winter), this time from the Aquatic Centre. It also services additional routes from Vanier Park, Yaletown, Science World and Stamps Landing (adult $2 to $5, child $1 to $3 depending on route). A day pass is $12.

TransLink operates the popular SeaBus shuttle service between Waterfront Station and Lonsdale Quay (see p683).

Car & Motorcycle

The city's rush-hour traffic can be a nightmare, especially in the evening when enormous lines of cars snaking along Georgia St, waiting to cross the Lions Gate Bridge, are a common sight between 4pm and 6pm. Try the alternative Second Narrows Bridge if you need to get across to the North Shore in a relative hurry. Other peak-time traffic-jam hot spots to avoid include the George Massey Tunnel and Hwy 1 to Surrey.

Parking is at a premium downtown: there are few free spots available on residential side streets (parking permits are often required) and traffic wardens, along with their associates in the private vehicle-towing business, are predatory. There is metered parking on some streets, but parking lots (from $2 per hour) are a more accessible proposition. Arrive before 9am at some lots for an early-bird, all-day discount. The **Pacific Centre** (Map pp652–4) parking lot is centrally located and close to many downtown attractions, as is the underground parking at the **Central Library** (Map pp652–4), a few blocks away.

Public Transportation

Vancouver's public transportation authority, **TransLink** (☎ 604-953-3333; www.translink.bc.ca), oversees bus, SkyTrain light rail and SeaBus boat services. Visit the TransLink website for a useful trip-planner tool, or pick up a copy of its *Transportation Map & Guide for the Greater Vancouver Area* ($1.95) from stores where maps are sold.

A ticket bought on any one of the three systems is valid for up to 90 minutes of transfer travel across the entire network, depending on the zone you intend to travel in. There are three zones, which become progressively more expensive the further you intend to journey. Tickets are $2 (one zone only), $3 (two zones) or $4 (three zones), with concessions available for children under 14 and seniors. All travel after 6:30pm, or on weekends and holidays, costs $2, and an all-day pass costs $8/6 per adult/concession. Fare-Saver tickets are also a good idea if you plan to use the system regularly during your stay. Available from newsagents and convenience stores, they come in books of 10 and cost $18 (one zone), $27 (two zones) and $36 (three zones). FareSaver tickets must be inserted in station validating machines for SkyTrain or SeaBus travel.

BUS

Buses use on-board fare machines and drivers do not handle the money, so the exact change (or more) is required.

The bus and trolleybus network is very extensive in the downtown core, with buses on many routes – especially along major corridors like Granville St, Broadway, Hastings St, Main St and Burrard St – arriving every few minutes. Many buses are wheelchair accessible and some also have front-mounted bike racks. Call the customer service line to make sure these are offered on your route.

B-Line express buses operate on routes between Richmond, the airport and Vancouver (98 B-Line) and between UBC and Broadway and Commercial SkyTrain stations (99 B-Line). These buses have their own limited arrival and departure points, and do not use regular bus stops.

TransLink also operates several night buses every 30 minutes on Saturday and Sunday between 2am and 4:10am to and from downtown Vancouver, the West End, UBC, Burnaby's Simon Fraser University and Scott Rd SkyTrain station. Look for the special night-bus signs on designated bus stops.

SEABUS

SeaBus shuttle services operate every 15 to 30 minutes throughout the day, taking 15 minutes to cross the Burrard Inlet between Waterfront Station and Lonsdale Quay in North Vancouver. At Lonsdale there's a bus terminal servicing routes throughout North Vancouver and West Vancouver, including buses to the Capilano Suspension Bridge (p660) and Grouse Mountain (p660). SeaBus tickets must be purchased in advance from vending machines on either side of the route. SeaBuses are wheelchair-accessible and bikes are also welcome.

SKYTRAIN

SkyTrain tickets must be purchased from station vending machines prior to boarding (change is given for bills up to $20). Spot checks from fare inspectors are frequent and they can issue an on-the-spot fine if you don't have the correct ticket. Avoid buying transfers from the 'SkyTrain scalpers' at many downtown stations since they are usually expired or close to expiration (the transfers not the scalpers).

The SkyTrain network consists of two routes, with services operating every few minutes. The 40-minute Expo Line takes passengers to and from downtown Vancouver and Surrey, via stops in Burnaby (for Swangard soccer stadium and Metrotown shopping center) and New Westminster (for the public market and a boat-mounted casino). The new Millennium Line alights near shopping malls and suburban residential districts in Coquitlam and Burnaby. Both lines share the tracks from Waterfront Station before going their separate ways at

Columbia in New Westminster. For downtown travelers, the SkyTrain stops are Waterfront, Burrard, Granville, Stadium and Main St/Science World, but these areas are almost as easily reached on foot. All SkyTrain services are wheelchair-accessible; however, there is no lift at downtown's Granville station. A free taxi service is available for wheelchair travelers between Granville and Burrard stations by calling ☎ 604-255-5111. Bikes are welcome on most SkyTrain services during off-peak hours, but bicyclists are permanently prohibited from using Granville or Metrotown stations to alight or depart.

Taxi

If you want to hail a cab downtown, it's best to make for Robson, Georgia or Granville Sts or head to one of the major hotels. Meters start at $2.30, and add $1.25 per kilometer. Main operators include **Yellow Cab** (☎ 604-681-1111) and **Black Top** (☎ 604-681-3201). **Vancouver Taxi** (☎ 604-871-1111) has a large fleet of wheelchair-accessible vehicles. For the environmentally savvy, Yellow Cab also has a couple of Honda Prius low-emission taxis.

AROUND VANCOUVER

There are several major provincial parks a short bus ride or car journey from downtown Vancouver. Among the city's other accessible day-trip escapes are several natural beauty spots and a couple of worthwhile historical towns.

Buntzen Lake

A true natural gem that's been attracting locals for decades, **Buntzen Lake** (☎ 604-469-9679; Coquitlam) is a perfect example of how BC has struck the ideal balance between environmental stewardship and access for visitors. This incredibly beautiful oasis of tranquility is a giant, naturally occurring BC Hydro reservoir, surrounded on three sides by steep, tree-covered mountains, and on its fourth side by a gently curving sun-kissed beach, with picnic tables, old-growth trees and an ever-present gaggle of Canada geese. There are well-marked hiking and mountain-biking trails through the forest, and, if you don't bring your own canoe, there's a rental operation near the park entrance called the **Anmore Store** (☎ 604-469-9928; Sunnyside Rd).

If you're driving to Buntzen Lake from Vancouver, follow Hastings St (Hwy 7A) through the city to Burnaby and Coquitlam, where it becomes the Barnet Hwy. Take the Ioco exit and follow Ioco Rd to the left. Turn right on First Ave and continue to Sunnyside Rd. Turn right again and continue to Buntzen Lake's recreation-area entrance gate. The journey should take less than an hour. The family-friendly lake can also be reached by public transit; call **TransLink** (☎ 604-953-3333) for connection information. It can get crowded in summer, so arrive early if you want a picnic table.

Burnaby Village Museum

If you're hankering for a little local history, a visit to the evocative **Burnaby Village Museum** (Map pp650-1; ☎ 604-293-6501; 6501 Deer Lake Ave, Burnaby; adult/child/senior $8/4.85/5.70; ⏰ 11am-4:30pm May–mid-Sep, closed mid-Sep–mid-Nov, open occasional weekends mid-Nov–Apr) can be a highly rewarding day out. A large living snapshot of Burnaby as it might have looked in 1925, it features costumed locals, historic buildings, hands-on activities and demonstrations of old jobs and pastimes. There are more than 30 re-created shops and homes, including a one-room schoolhouse, a Chinese herbalist and a blacksmith. The highlight, though, is a trip on the beautifully restored 1912 CW Parker carousel. This family-friendly outdoor museum complex also stages special events to coincide with public holidays.

If you need a swift return to the present, drive the short distance to **Metrotown** (Map pp650-1; ☎ 604-438-4700; 4800 Kingsway, Burnaby) BC's largest shopping center, which should satiate your every shopping whim. The center is also conveniently located on the SkyTrain line, 20 minutes from downtown Vancouver.

Fort Langley

Built in 1827, the **fort** (☎ 604-513-4777; 23433 Mavis Av, Fort Langley; adult/child/family $5.75/3/14.50; ⏰ 10am-5pm Mar-Oct, Nov-Feb by appointment only) is now a fascinating national historic site. The wood-walled complex at Fort Langley was part of the Hudson's Bay Company network of fur-trading posts, and is regarded as the birthplace of BC. At the forefront of the gold rush, it became a British crown colony in 1858, and is now an evocative reminder of the region's pioneer history. One original building and several re-created structures, along with costumed interpreters, historic artifacts and temporary exhibitions, make up most of the attractions. Kids will also enjoy panning for gold here, and the surrounding town is great for strolling and browsing in old-school ice-cream shops and boutiques.

If you're driving from Vancouver to Fort Langley, a one-hour drive, follow Hwy 1 east to the 232nd St north exit. Follow 232nd St to the stop sign on Glover Rd. Turn right. Follow Glover Rd into the village of Fort Langley. At Mavis Av, just before the railway tracks, turn right. The fort is at the end of the street.

THE SUNSHINE COAST & WHISTLER

From Horseshoe Bay north to the mountain town of Whistler, the Sea to Sky Hwy (Hwy 99) affords mountain scenery to rival the Rockies. Alas, the area's blessing (its proximity to the Vancouver metro area) is also its curse – it can get damned crowded up here. However if you're a climber, skier, snowboarder or hiker, the rewards are well worth the effort. The moniker 'Sunshine Coast' refers to a narrow strip of land north of Horseshoe Bay, accessible only via ferries.

SUNSHINE COAST

Stretching from Langdale to Lund, the Sunshine Coast is a geographical orphan, separated from the rest of the Lower Mainland by the formidable Coast Mountains and the waters of Howe Sound. Vancouverites have filled the area with summer homes, and the area gets crazily busy during school holidays and long weekends. At other times, however, it can be a pretty peaceful and welcoming place. The main draws are the fine scuba diving, cruises into the majestic Princess Louisa Inlet, and kayaking around the islands to the north.

Langdale to Earls Cove

To reach these good bits you've got to jump past the holiday towns of **Gibsons** and **Roberts Creek**, although they'll do the trick if you just want a swim and some fish and chips.

Sechelt isn't much different to other towns on land, but offshore there are a dozen dive sites, including the wreck of the HMCS *Chaudiere* and Tuwanek Point Marine Park. **Suncoast Diving & Watersports** (☎ 604-740-8006; www.suncoastdiving.com; 5643 Wharf St; rentals $75, dives from $135; ❤ 9am-5:30pm Mon-Sat, 9am-4:30pm Sun) can advise you. Drop into the **VIC** (☎ 604-885-0662; Trail Bay Mall, 5755 Cowrie St; ❤ 8:30am-5pm Mon-Fri, 8:30am-12:30pm Sat) for recommendations on kayaking companies to take you up the tranquil waters of the Sechelt Inlet.

From the twin communities of **Egmont** and **Earls Cove** you can take a cruise through the stunning fjord landscapes and sheer granite gorges of **Princess Louisa Inlet** and **Chatterbox Falls**. Contact **Egmont Water Taxi** (☎ 604-883-2092; www.sunshinecoasttours.bc.ca; day tours from $100). For a good hike to a natural wonder, the 4km trail in **Skookumchuck Narrows Provincial Park** (❤ 604-885-3714; wlapwww.gov.bc.ca/bcparks), near Egmont, leads to an inlet so narrow that water forced through during tides can cause rapids as fast as 30km/h.

GETTING THERE & AWAY

BC Ferries (☎ 604-886-2242, 888-223-3779; www.bcferries.com; adult/child $8.50/4.25, bike/car $2.50/30) travels eight to 11 times daily, between 6:20am and 10:10pm, from Horseshoe Bay to Langdale. The fare covers either a round-trip between Horseshoe Bay and Langdale, or a one-way trip from Horseshoe Bay through to Saltery Bay, via Earls Cove.

There are eight daily sailings between Earls Cove and Saltery Bay; again, the fare covers either a round-trip between Earls Cove and Saltery Bay or a through-trip from Saltery Bay to Horseshoe Bay. A 30km drive from Saltery takes you to Powell River.

Powell River

This plain little town is surrounded by lots of natural beauty, and is also the jumping-off point for ferries to Vancouver Island. The **VIC** (☎ 604-485-4701; 4690 Marine Ave; ❤ 9am-5:30pm) stays open year-round and has good information on the local attractions.

You can hike all or part of the 180km **Sunshine Coast Trail** (www.sunshinecoast-trail.com) that wanders through the forests and marine environments from Saltery Bay to Sarah Point. Or you can paddle the 57km **Powell Forest Canoe Route**, which connects 12 lakes via easily portaged trails. **Scuba diving** is also an option, as is **mountain biking**. Beautiful **Desolation Sound** can be explored for a couple

TOP 10 ADRENALINE RUSHES

British Columbia is simply bursting with wonderful adventure activities. The island-rich Strait of Georgia offers an array of outstanding sea-kayak routes, and there's also a superb multiday hike, a classic 10-lake canoe odyssey, and as much skiing and snowboarding as you can take. Add in world-class surfing, caving, white-water rafting, climbing and diving, and you'll be wondering what to leave out as you journey through the province. Here's just a selection of the things you can do:

- Take in 10 lakes, three rivers and breathtaking mountain views along a 116km-long canoe route at **Bowron Lake Provincial Park** (p776), southeast of Prince George.
- Surf the pounding Pacific waves at **Long Beach** (p716), south of Tofino.
- Sea kayak through the still beauty of the **Broken Group Islands** (p716) near Ucluelet.
- Suit up for some amazing cold-water diving off the coast of **Sechelt** (p685).
- White-water raft the raging waters of the Kicking Horse River at **Golden** (p756).
- Plunge underground and explore the caves around **Port Hardy** (p728).
- Ski the slopes of the 2010 Winter Olympics and party down in **Whistler** (p687).
- Slog your way along the taxing but stunning 75km **West Coast Trail** (p717).
- Climb the 200-plus routes of the Stawamus Chief monolith looming over **Squamish** (below).
- Roar down the mountain-bike trails of **Rossland** (p764), southwest of Nelson.

of hours or several days with **Powell River Sea Kayak** (☎ 604-483-2160, 866-617-4444; www.bc seakayak.com; 6812E Alberni Pl; tours from $110, s/d kayak rentals from $26/35, lessons $60-110).

SLEEPING & EATING

While there's plenty of accommodation and food options, it's still a good idea to book in advance.

Old Courthouse Inn & Hostel (☎ 604-483-4000, 877-483-4777; oldcourthouseinn@armourtech.com; 6243 Walnut St; r $20-75) This beautifully restored courthouse and police station is very cool. In keeping with the historic theme, each of the rooms is nicely decorated with antique furnishings.

Westview Centre Motel (☎ 604-485-4023, 877-485-4023; fax 604-485-7736; 4534 Marine Ave; r $65-80) These bungalow motel rooms have amazing ocean views.

Willingdon Beach Campsite (☎ 604-485-2242; 4845 Marine Ave; tent/RV sites $15/20) Right on the water, the facilities here include showers and a laundry. There's also a large plastic Popeye.

Captain Billy's Old Fashioned Fish & Chips (☎ 604-485-2252; mains $6-8; ☾ lunch & dinner Apr-Nov) This place has been dishing the fish at the ferry terminal for more than 25 years.

Chiang Mai (☎ 604-485-0883; 4463 Marine Ave; mains $7-13; ☾ lunch & dinner) The linoleum floors and light wooden tables and chairs

are nothing special to look at, but this Thai place is about the food, not image. The *pad thai* (Thai-style fried noodles) and seafood dishes are tasty and spicy.

Shinglemill Pub (☎ 604-483-2001; 6233 Powell Pl; mains $7-12; ☾ lunch & dinner) On Powell Lake, north of town, this woodsy pub offers good pub grub accompanied by great views.

GETTING THERE & AWAY

Malaspina Coach Lines (☎ 604-485-5030, 877-227-8287) runs buses to Vancouver (adult/child $40/20, 6½ hours).

For details of the Powell River–Comox ferry, see p697.

SQUAMISH

Some 48km from Horseshoe Bay, Squamish enjoys a spectacular natural setting at the confluence of ocean, river and alpine forest. The imposing monolith of the Stawamus Chief looms over the town center, and is the town's premier attraction – its sheer flanks attract climbing junkies from across the globe. Walking, windsurfing and mountain biking also bring in fair numbers of visitors, while bird-watchers bliss out on the thousands of bald eagles that winter here.

If you're coming from Vancouver, turn left off Hwy 99 at the signal to reach Cleveland Ave and Squamish's small, plain downtown

area. The well-stocked **VIC** (☎ 604-892-9244; www
.squamishchamber.bc.ca; 37950 Cleveland Ave; ☻ 9am-5pm
Mon-Fri, 10am-2pm Sat & Sun Oct-May, 9am-6pm daily Jun-
Sep) is near the far end of the street.

West Coast Railway Heritage Park (☎ 604-898-
9336; www.wcra.org/heritage; 39645 Government Rd;
adult/concession $10/8.50; ☻ 10am-5pm, trains 11am-
4pm) is the final resting place of the world-
famous *Royal Hudson* steam engine, and
has a large collection of historic railroad
cars that serve as a walk-through museum
of rail history.

Just northeast of Squamish is the immense **Garibaldi Provincial Park** (wlapwww.gov.bc
.ca/bcparks), a rugged, undeveloped 195-sq-
km mountain wilderness known mainly for
its excellent hiking. It's covered by more
than 67km of developed trails, which become cross-country ski runs in winter. Five
park access roads lie along Hwy 99 between
Squamish and Pemberton.

Activities

Stawamus Chief has more than 200 climbing routes, from the simple to the death
defying. For information, guides or instruction, call **Squamish Rock Guides** (☎ 604-815-1750;
www.squamishrockguides.com). Be sure to respect
the space and nests of the peregrine falcon
population.

Winds up to 60km/h blow up Howe Sound
and into Squamish Harbour, creating great
conditions for windsurfing. For information
on weather and water conditions, call the
Squamish Windsurfing Society (☎ 604-926-9463;
www.squamishwindsurfing.org).

Garibaldi's trails draw a lot of mountain-
biking enthusiasts. Stop at **Tantalus Bike Shop**
(☎ 604-898-2588; www.tantalusbikeshop.com; 40446
Government Rd; half-/full-day rentals $15/35; ☻ 9:30am-
5:30pm Mon-Sat, 9:30am-5pm Jun-Aug, shorter hours rest
of year) for bike hire and information on the
best routes.

Sleeping & Eating

Squamish International Hostel (☎ 604-892-9240,
800-449-8614; www.squamishhostel.com; 38220 Hwy 99;
dm/r $20/40) Completely rebuilt in 2003, yet
still casual and friendly, this place is bright,
colorful and well appointed. The hostel of
choice for climbers, it offers rock-climbing
and rafting trips, and has free bikes, a small
climbing wall, a good kitchen and a rooftop
deck. It's just across the highway from
downtown.

Howe Sound Inn & Brewing Company (☎ 604-
892-2603, 800-919-2537; www.howesound.com; 37801
Cleveland Ave; s & d $105; P) In a town with
several nondescript motels, this one stands
out from the pack. Away from the noise of
downtown, it has inviting character-filled
rooms, and the attached brewpub offers
several specialties of the house, which you
can enjoy on the patio while watching the
antlike antics of climbers on the Chief.

Camping is available at **Stawamus Chief
Provincial Park** (wlapwww.gov.bc.ca/bcparks; tent sites
$9), and attracts the climbing fraternity.
Garibaldi Provincial Park (wlapwww.gov.bc.ca/bc
parks; campsites $5) has nine separate walk-in
camping areas. **Dryden Creek Resorts** (☎ 604-
898-9726, 877-237-9336; cnr Hwy
99 & Depot Rd; tent/RV sites $20/26, d $80-90) has comfortable sites by the creek and also offers
basic doubles.

Sunflower Bakery Cafe (☎ 604-892-2231; 38086
Cleveland Ave; light meals $2-7; ☻ breakfast & lunch)
Among a handful of good eateries in town,
the mellow yellow Sunflower is notable for
its flaky pastries, hearty soups and good coffee – all at great prices.

Yiannis Taverna (☎ 604-892-9696; 38043 Cleveland
Ave; mains $8-14; ☻ lunch & dinner) This little Greek
place can't really be called a hidden gem,
since it's always crowded and obviously
popular. Its plain furnishings belie the quality of its meals, which include good-value
specials that change nightly.

Getting There & Away

Greyhound Canada has services from Vancouver ($8, 45 minutes, five daily).

WHISTLER

One of North America's best and most
popular resorts (and the principle venue for
the 2010 Winter Olympics), Whistler gets
insanely busy over winter and is merely busy
the rest of the time. It is worth all the jostling:
year-round skiing and snowboarding, great
hiking, loads of accommodation options
and a central village crammed with quality stores, cafés and restaurants make this a
place for everyone, from grungy backpackers and too-cool-for-school snowboarders to
young families and starchy couples sporting
the latest high-end gear.

While the Whistler region stretches to the
north and south, Whistler Village is where
most of the action is. Built almost entirely

from scratch from the early 1980s, the resorts, hotels and stores here blend together like one big ultramodern outdoor mall, mountain-style – but done with at least a modicum of taste and an eye for low-rise urban design. Despite the crowds both on and off the slopes, everyone seems to be having a good time, which lends the place a light yet energetic atmosphere.

Information
Pick up a copy of *Pique Newsmagazine* for news and entertainment listings.

Activity & Information Centre (☎ 604-938-2769, 877-991-9988; www.mywhistler.com; 4010 Whistler Way; ☼ 8am-6pm) There are also two other VICs: Village North Info Kiosk and Upper Village Info Kiosk.

Custom House Currency Exchange (☎ 604-938-6658; 4227 Village Stroll)

Electric Daisy (☎ 604-938-9961; 9-4308 Main St; per 15min $3.50) Internet access.

HotBox (☎ 604-932-6773; 109-4369 Main St; per 15min $4) Internet access.

Post Office (☎ 604-932-5012; 106-4360 Lorimer Rd; ☼ 8am-5pm Mon-Fri, 8am-noon Sat)

Town Plaza Medical Clinic (☎ 604-905-7089; 40-4314 Main St)

Activities
Whistler and Blackcomb Mountains are highly developed resort areas with world-class facilities. The mild Pacific air flowing around the mile-high peaks provides reliable snowfall to the areas, without getting the truly frigid conditions of inland resorts.

You can also bungee jump, dogsled, play tennis, fish, ice-climb, fly over a glacier or hop on a horse or snowmobile. Contact the Activity & Information Centre for details on year-round activities and operators.

SKIING & SNOWBOARDING
Whistler-Blackcomb (☎ 604-932-3434, 800-766-0449; www.whistlerblackcomb.com; all-day lift pass adult/child $70/35; ☼ 8:30am-3pm Nov–late Jan, 8:30am-3:30pm late Jan–Mar, 9am-4pm Mar–season end) has more than 7000 acres of terrain suitable for skiing and 200 longer-than-average trails, and that doesn't include the backcountry. The typical season runs from mid-November until late April on Blackcomb, and until June on Whistler, with the bulk of the crowds showing up from December through to late March. High-speed lifts make long lines

move relatively quickly, but prepare yourself for half-hour waits on weekends.

Mountain Adventure Centres (www.whistlerblackcomb.com/rentals; adult/child from $32/21) has offices at **Whistler** (☎ 604-905-2252) and **Blackcomb** (☎ 604-938-7737) bases. Fourteen locations scattered around the Whistler area rent gear, and there are even more pick-up locations if you reserve equipment online.

TLH Heliskiing (☎ 250-558-5379, 800-667-4854; www.tlhheliskiing.com; from $2300) and **Whistler Heli-Skiing** (☎ 604-932-4105, 888-435-4754; www.heliskiwhistler.com; 3-4241 Village Stroll; from $640) offer trips in helicopters to the untouched powder of backcountry peaks.

Amazingly, the **Horstman Glacier** (adult/child $45/36; ☼ noon-3pm Jun 7–Aug 1, lift opens 11am) on the top of Blackcomb (1609m) is open until August, although there obviously won't be any powder.

CROSS-COUNTRY SKIING & SNOWSHOEING
Whistler Municipality (☎ 604-935-8300; www.whistler.ca; Lot 4A off Lorimer Rd; day/night pass $10/4; ☼ 8am-9pm Nov-Mar) grooms more than 30km of cross-country ski trails through serene Lost Lake Park and the valley. **Lost Lake Cross-Country Connection** (☎ 604-905-0071; www.crosscountryconnection.bc.ca; adult/child ski-rental packages with skis, boots, bindings & poles from $24/16, tours from $60; ☼ 9am-8pm Mon-Sat, 9am-5pm Sun Nov-Mar), beside the cross-country skiing ticket booth, rents equipment and operates tours.

Several outfits offer all-inclusive snowshoeing tours. Try **Outdoor Adventures at Whistler** (☎ 604-932-0647; www.adventureswhistler.com; 4205 Village Square; tours from $55; ☼ 7am-2pm).

HIKING
To experience some alpine hiking the easy way, take the lifts to the top of **Whistler** (all-day lift pass adult/child $24/20; ☼ 8am-5pm late Jun–Aug) and the 48km of trails – the views go forever.

MOUNTAIN BIKING
It doesn't get any easier than taking a lift to **Whistler Mountain Bike Park** (all-day lift pass adult/child $40/18, bike rentals $60/30; ☼ 10am-5pm Jun-Sep) and enjoying a gravity-fed adrenaline rush down again. Opportunities range from easy trails for recreational riders to hard-core mountain descents for experienced cyclists.

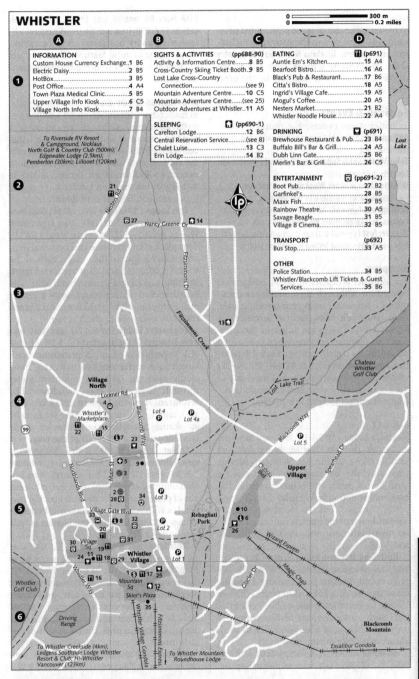

WHISTLER

INFORMATION
Custom House Currency Exchange...**1** B6
Electric Daisy.................................**2** B5
HotBox..**3** B5
Post Office...................................**4** A4
Town Plaza Medical Clinic...........**5** B5
Upper Village Info Kiosk..............**6** C5
Village North Info Kiosk..............**7** B4

SIGHTS & ACTIVITIES (pp688-90)
Activity & Information Centre........**8** B5
Cross-Country Skiing Ticket Booth..**9** B5
Lost Lake Cross-Country
  Connection...........................(see 9)
Mountain Adventure Centre........**10** C5
Mountain Adventure Centre......(see 25)
Outdoor Adventures at Whistler...**11** A5

SLEEPING (pp690-1)
Carelton Lodge..........................**12** B6
Central Reservation Service.........(see 8)
Chalet Luise..............................**13** C3
Erin Lodge................................**14** B2

EATING (p691)
Auntie Em's Kitchen...................**15** A4
Bearfoot Bistro..........................**16** A6
Black's Pub & Restaurant............**17** B6
Citta's Bistro.............................**18** A5
Ingrid's Village Cafe...................**19** A5
Mogul's Coffee..........................**20** A5
Nesters Market..........................**21** B2
Whistler Noodle House................**22** A4

DRINKING (p691)
Brewhouse Restaurant & Pub......**23** B4
Buffalo Bill's Bar & Grill..............**24** A5
Dubh Linn Gate.........................**25** B6
Merlin's Bar & Grill.....................**26** C5

ENTERTAINMENT (pp691-2)
Boot Pub..................................**27** B2
Garfinkel's................................**28** B5
Maxx Fish.................................**29** B5
Rainbow Theatre.......................**30** A5
Savage Beagle..........................**31** B5
Village 8 Cinema.......................**32** B5

TRANSPORT (p692)
Bus Stop..................................**33** A5

OTHER
Police Station............................**34** B5
Whistler/Blackcomb Lift Tickets & Guest
  Services...............................**35** B6

To Riverside RV Resort
& Campground, Nicklaus
North Golf & Country Club (500m);
Edgewater Lodge (2.5km);
Pemberton (30km); Lillooet (120km)

Nesters Rd

Nancy Greene Dr

Fitzsimmons Dr

Fitzsimmons Creek

Lost Lake

Lost Lake Trail

Chateau
Whistler
Golf Club

Village
North

Lorimer Rd

Blackcomb Way

Whistler's
Marketplace

Lot 4

Lot 4a

Lot 5

Blackcomb Way

Upper
Village

Chateau
Blvd

Spearhead Dr

Main St

Northlands Blvd

Village Gate Blvd

Lot 3

Lot 2

Rebagliati
Park

Wizard Express

Village
Sq

Whistler
Village

Lot 1

Magic Chair

Glacier Dr

Mountain
Sq

Skier's Plaza

Whistler Way

Whistler
Golf Club

Driving
Range

Whistler Village Gondola

Fitzsimmons Express

Blackcomb
Mountain

Excalibur Gondola

To Whistler Creekside (4km);
Ledgens Southside Lodge Whistler
Resort & Club; Hi-Whistler
Vancouver (123km)

To Whistler Mountain;
Roundhouse Lodge

0 — 300 m
0 — 0.2 miles

GOLF

Whistler is the site of some of the most prestigious golf courses in the province, including the superb **Nicklaus North Golf & Country Club** (☎ 604-938-9898, 800-386-9898; 8080 Nicklaus North Blvd; green fees $165), designed by the great man himself.

Festivals & Events

Whistler stages events year-round:
Altitude (☼ early Feb) Gay and lesbian skiing and snowboard fest.
Telus World Ski & Snowboard Festival (☼ mid-Apr) Concerts and sports.
Whistler Jazz & Blues Weekend (☼ mid-Jun) Provincial & national artists play into the night.
ArtRageous (☼ early Jul) Multidisciplinary event with exhibits, performances and fun interactive crafts.
Oktoberfest (☼ mid-Oct) Can it get any more perfect than a beer and sausage festival in an alpine setting?

Sleeping

Yes, Whistler is expensive, but all budgets are catered for, although there are fewer cheap options. No matter what your traveling style, make sure you book well in advance for winter visits. Things are easier in the summer and shoulder seasons, when substantial discounts are usually offered. **Central Reservation Service** (☎ 604-664-5625, 800-944-7857; www.my whistler.com) can book a room at almost any of the area's hotels, lodges and condominiums (but not budget lodgings or B&Bs).

BUDGET

Southside Lodge (☎ 604-932-3644; www.snowboard whistler.com; 2102 Lake Placid Rd; dm per night/week $30/200) Close to the Mt Whistler lifts at Creekside, this old stager has been given a fresh lick of paint, and is now probably the best budget option in Whistler. Everything's pretty cramped, but the location's unbeatable and each of the bunk rooms comes with its own bathroom and shower, cable TV and VCR.

Hostelling International-Whistler (☎ 604-932-5492; www.hihostels.ca; 5678 Alta Lake Rd; dm $25) It's remote, but this fine hostel enjoys a beautiful setting on Alta Lake, 4km from Whistler Village (a 45-minute walk, or hop on a local bus) and awesome views of Blackcomb. It only has 32 beds, so it's a good idea to book ahead, especially during ski season.

Riverside RV Resort & Campground (☎ 604-905-5533, 877-905-5533; www.whistlercamping.com;

8018 Mons Rd; tent/RV sites $30/45, cabins winter/summer $175/150) Just north of Whistler Village, this 'resort' has grassy sites, log cabins, plus a range of good features like a hot tub, putting greens and well-maintained amenity blocks.

MID-RANGE & TOP END

Whistler has dozens of stone-and-log resorts and condos, but if you're after a double room that doesn't break the bank, consider a B&B, which generally offers better value than a condo (not to mention a decent cooked breakfast thrown in). The Activity & Information Centre has a useful brochure that lists most of them.

Erin Lodge (☎ 604-932-3641, 800-665-2003; www .pensionedelweiss.com; 7162 Nancy Greene Dr; d summer $95-125, winter $125-285, tr summer/winter $120/185) This place offers genuine and personal Irish hospitality. Close to the village, each of the rooms is different, and all of them are bright, inviting and have a private bathroom. The sun-drenched dining room hosts a generous European-style breakfast, and there's room for everyone in the hot tub.

Edgewater Lodge (☎ 604-932-0688; www.edge water-lodge.com; 8030 Alpine Way; d $125-185, ste $150-215) Superbly sited on a promontory on Green Lake, each room here makes the most of the awesome lake and mountain views through large plate-glass windows. The restaurant is among the best in the Whistler area, and there's kayaking in the summer or ice-skating when the lake freezes up. A car is needed as it's a little out of the way.

Chalet Luise (☎ 604-932-4187, 800-665-1998; www.chaletluise.com; 7461 Ambassador Cres; r summer $125-160, winter $170-220) This country-style inn with country-style hospitality doesn't seem out of place among the mountains of Whistler. It's within walking distance of Whistler Village and the lifts, and the Jacuzzi is welcome after a day on the hills.

Whistler Resort & Club (☎ 604-932-2343; www .rainbowretreats.com; 2129 Lake Placid Rd; summer/winter d $70/105, ste $85/135) In Whistler Creekside, this is a genuine 1970s resort, with redbrick fireplaces, wood paneling and pull-down beds in some rooms. The bargain prices include a hot tub and a sauna, and free use of canoes, tennis courts and bicycles in summer.

Legends (☎ 604-689-8816, 800-649-9243; www .clubintrawest.com; 2036 London Lane; ste $145-235; ☒)

For the ultimate in convenience, this resort has the Creekside Gondola right next to the lobby. Ski-in/ski-out access allows you to spend more time on the slopes or relaxing in the hot tub and in your modern suite.

Carleton Lodge (☎ 604-932-2343; reserve@rainbow retreats.com; 4290 Mountain Lane; ste summer $85-155 winter $300-450) The Carleton is a suite-only complex that sits at the nadir where Whistler meets Blackcomb, and gives easy access to both mountains. The rooms are fully furnished and they are equipped with kitchens and have plenty of space to throw your gear about.

Eating

Whistler is a gourmet's paradise, with more than 90 eateries covering all bases – budget cafés, honest steakhouses and top-shelf international dining.

BUDGET

Ingrid's Village Cafe (☎ 604-932-7000; 4305 Skiers Approach; light meals $4-9; ☺ breakfast & lunch) This friendly and compact little eatery offers the best value in town. The cooked breakfasts are standouts, but there are also inviting salads and quiches, espresso coffee that doesn't spare the caffeine, and plenty for hungry vegetarians.

Other options for a quick bite include **Auntie Em's Kitchen** (☎ 604-932-1163; 4340 Lorimer Rd; light meals $5-8; ☺ breakfast & lunch) and **Mogul's Coffee** (☎ 604-932-4845; 203-4204 Village Square; snacks $2-6; ☺ breakfast, lunch & dinner), and there are a number of pizza places around to tackle your hunger.

Self-caterers can head to **Nesters Market** (☎ 604-932-3545; 7019 Nesters Rd). Bigger is **Marketplace IGA** (☎ 604-938-2850; 4330 Northlands Blvd).

MID-RANGE & TOP END

Black's Pub & Restaurant (☎ 604-932-6408; 4270 Mountain Square; mains $8-15; ☺ lunch & dinner) Known for its pizzas and extraordinary selection of beers (almost 100), this is a popular spot among Whistlerites, and you can catch some rays in summer at the upstairs patio.

Whistler Noodle House (☎ 604-932-2228; 9-4330 Northlands Rd; mains $8-12; ☺ lunch & dinner) Nothing delivers comfort like a hearty bowl of hot soup after playing in the snow. This place gives you that in a relaxed and casual setting. The bowls are huge and there are plenty of vegetarian options.

Citta's Bistro (☎ 604-932-4177; 4217 Village Stroll; mains $8-22; ☺ lunch & dinner) The patio right on the edge of Village Square means there's no shortage of activity. This place is always lively and serves better-than-average pub grub.

Roundhouse Lodge (☎ 604-932-3434; Whistler Mountain; mains $5-20) The complex at the top of the Whistler Village Gondola is a great place for nonskiers to meet their skiing travel partners for lunch. Aside from an outdoor grill, it houses cafeteria-style Pika's; an open-air market with a selection of international dishes at the Marketplace; the casual, full-service restaurant Steeps; and the semiformal Italian restaurant Paloma's.

Bearfoot Bistro (☎ 604-932-3433; 4121 Village Green; mains $15-30; ☺ dinner) This place attracts attention with wild-game specialties like moose and venison. It's got a solid and woodsy feeling on the inside, and the atmosphere is casual.

Drinking

After a day on the slopes, what the body needs is some quality R and R, and Whistler caters for all tastes.

Brewhouse Restaurant & Pub (☎ 604-905-2739; 4355 Blackcomb Way) This place makes its own beer on the premises, including some inspired by the magnificent surrounds – kick back and take a long draught of Twin Peaks Pale Ale or Lifty Lager. It's a great pub, away from the huge crowds, and the place to go to just have fun.

Dubh Linn Gate (☎ 604-905-4047; 4320 Sundial Crescent) A more than competent Guinness is pulled at this popular pub at the base of Whistler. There's a vibrant social scene with folksy Gaelic songs resounding through the stone-and-wood dining room.

There are other popular watering holes: **Buffalo Bill's Bar & Grill** (☎ 604-932-6613; 4122 Village Green) The 30-and-older crowd gathers here for hot toddies.

Merlin's Bar & Grill (☎ 604-938-7700; Upper Village) Sit out on the patio and watch other skiers hurtle down Blackcomb.

Entertainment

A lot of eateries also have live music after the sun goes down. Stroll around the village and trust your ears.

NIGHTCLUBS

Garfinkel's (☎ 604-932-2323; 1-4308 Main St) This club of choice among residents and regular visitors is a good place to hang out. It's the usual stop for touring musical acts, and on other nights people dance to hip-hop and dance music, with a little old-fashioned rock 'n' roll thrown in.

Other places worth checking out:

Boot Pub (☎ 604-932-3338; 7124 Nancy Greene Dr) A good live venue; strippers also feature regularly.

Maxx Fish (☎ 604-932-1904; 4232 Village Stroll) College crowds and wild parties.

Savage Beagle (☎ 604-938-3337; 4222 Village Square) Top 40 and younger crowds.

CINEMAS

Rainbow Theatre (☎ 604-932-2422; 4010 Whistler Way; admission $5) Has discount screenings for second-run movies.

Village 8 Cinema (☎ 604-932-5833; Whistler Village; admission $8) For new-release flicks.

Getting There & Away

From Vancouver, Whistler is convenient with a capital 'C', but the sinuous curves of the 123km trip on the Sea to Sky Hwy can get seriously clogged, so leave plenty of time if you're driving. Land transport is your only option during winter. To get to Whistler Village, turn off the highway at Village Gate Blvd.

Whistler Air (☎ 888-806-2299; www.whistlerair.ca; $135) offers daily float-plane services between Green Lake and Vancouver from June to September. **Helijet** (☎ 800-665-4354; www.helijet .com; $185) does the same route by chopper.

Greyhound Canada operates six daily trips from Vancouver to Whistler ($18, 2½ hours).

Bigfoot Adventure Tours (☎ 888-244-6673; www .bigfoottours.com; one way/return $27/49; ⏱ 6:30am-5pm) runs a shuttle between central Vancouver and Whistler between December and mid-April.

Getting Around

The **WAVE** (☎ 604-932-4020; www.whistler.net/transit; adult/child/concession $1.50/free/1.25) is the Whistler area's public transit; buses are equipped with outside ski and bicycle racks. The shuttle between Whistler Village, Village North and Upper Village is free.

For a taxi, call **Sea to Sky Taxi** (☎ 604-932-3333).

VANCOUVER ISLAND

Beautiful Vancouver Island is at last claiming its rightful place near the top of Canada's list of traveler destinations. There really is something for everybody here: fine restaurants and stately colonial architecture in Victoria; skiing and snowboarding at Mt Washington, whale-watching and sea kayaking along the desolate yet stunning west coast; and superb backcountry hiking in the island's northern tip. When you factor in the good road system, hospitable locals, rare and captivating wildlife, outstanding fishing and crabbing, and convenient access to the Southern Gulf Islands, it's easy to see why more and more people are crossing the strait to check it out.

This was not always the case, however. For decades Vancouver Island was seen as little more than a provincial backwater, useful only for exploiting mineral, fishing and, especially, timber resources – as the countless bleak and blasted hillsides across the island eloquently attest. Harsh economic realities have meant that tourism is now the number-one focus, and many small towns are reinventing themselves to take full advantage. The mild climate helps, along with diverse ecologies that range from the rocky and tempestuous west coast to the gentle and protected sandy bays on the east, divided by the central Vancouver Island mountains, home to some of the island's last remaining old-growth forests.

Today the island is a thriving and modern place that's home to nearly 700,000 souls, most of whom live along the southeastern coast. It can get very busy in summer, but it's easy enough to escape the madding crowds by heading inland or up the coast. The drive up to Port Hardy displays yet another face of this large, complex island, and also serves as the jumping-off point for traveling by ferry to Prince Rupert, in the province's remote north, via the magnificent Inside Passage, which is an absolute must-see if you have the time.

The information in this section is presented roughly south to north, following the major east-coast highway, which is the fastest and most efficient way of exploring the island. It does, however, include four significant detours west to the island's mountainous center and wild Pacific coast:

* from Victoria, west along the southern coast to Port Renfrew
* from Duncan, inland to the Cowichan Valley, with dirt-road access to the Carmanah Walbran Provincial Park
* from Parksville via Port Alberni to Ucluelet, Tofino and the Pacific Rim National Park Reserve
* from Campbell River inland to Gold River.

VICTORIA
☎ 250 / pop 325,000

British Columbia's stately provincial capital, Victoria lies at the southeastern end of Vancouver Island and enjoys a mild climate thanks to the shelter afforded by the Olympic Peninsula, which looms across the Strait of Juan de Fuca from Washington State.

Today Victoria remains the most English of Canadian cities, graced by the province's finest colonial architecture and making good use of its attractive harbor setting, with a host of pubs, restaurants and minor attractions overlooking the water.

Hanging flower baskets on the lampposts, impeccable public and private gardens, and year-round flowering trees and shrubs make a compelling case for the title of 'Garden City.' This gentility is reinforced by a quality restaurant scene, great shopping, and a cosmopolitan and easy-going populace. Victoria also makes a great springboard for adventure travelers, who can kayak the Inner Harbour, dive the clear waters along the southern coast, and hike the West Coast Trail.

History

Originally the home of Salish Indians, Victoria was colonized in 1843 when James Douglas, acting for the Hudson's Bay Company, founded Fort Victoria as a fur-trading post; Vancouver Island was declared a crown colony of Britain in 1849. Merging with the mainland in 1866 to form British Columbia, its citizens were soon faced with a critical choice – consolidate their historical and cultural ties with Washington and Oregon by joining the USA, or throw in their lot with the new Dominion of Canada,

far to the east. Eventually, Ottawa's commitment to a railroad link to the east won the day, and in 1871 BC delegates voted to join Canada, with Victoria declared capital of the new province.

Orientation

The Inner Harbour is the heart of Victoria, and is watched over by the nonidentical twins of the Fairmont Empress Hotel and the Parliament Buildings. From the harbor, Wharf St leads northwest to James Bay, paralleled by the main shopping strip of Government St. A block to the east, Douglas St (Hwy 1) is downtown's main north–south thoroughfare and the usual entrance to the city. It heads north to Nanaimo – keep going and roughly 8000km later you'll be in Newfoundland! Blanshard St is the other northern access to/from the city, and leads to Hwy 17, the airport and the Swartz Bay BC Ferries terminal. Crossing these streets is the one-way Fort St, which heads east up the hill, then along Oak Bay Ave, through the 'tweed curtain' to the wealthier, very British area of Oak Bay, 3km from downtown.

With the exception of Craigdarroch Castle, the art gallery and Government House, Victoria's main attractions are easily accessed by foot or by bicycle – just perfect on a warm summer's day.

Information
BOOKSTORES

Victoria is the place to stock up on books, both new and old, for your travels. There are several excellent stores on Johnson St, between Douglas and Wharf:

Lamplight Books (Map pp700-1; ☎ 250-381-1430; 551A Johnson St) First-rate selection of soft- and hardcover fiction.

Munro's Books (Map pp700-1; ☎ 250-382-2464; 1108 Government St) Distinguished shop, boasting magnificent interiors.

INTERNET ACCESS

James Bay Coffee & Books (Map p698; ☎ 250-386-4700; 143 Menzies St; per hr $4; ⏰ 7:30am-9pm)

Stain Internet (Map pp700-1; ☎ 250-382-3352; www.staincafe.com; 609 Yates St; per hr $3; ⏰ 10am-2am)

MEDIA

The *Times Colonist* is the daily island newspaper. Weekly freebie *Monday Magazine*

BRITISH COLUMBIA

VANCOUVER ISLAND

[Map of Vancouver Island showing locations including Rivers Inlet, Knight Inlet, Queen Charlotte Sound, Queen Charlotte Strait, Malcolm Island, Cormorant Island, Alert Bay, Telegraph Cove, Sointula, Port McNeill, Port Hardy, Quatsino, Holberg, Cape Scott Provincial Park, Winter Harbour, Raft Cove Provincial Park, Scott Islands, Quatsino Sound, Brooks Bay, Brooks Peninsula Provincial Recreation Area, Port Alice, Fair Harbour, Kyuquot, Kyuquot Sound, Brooks Peninsula, Esperanza Inlet, Nootka Island, Friendly Cove, Nootka Sound, Yuquot, Maquinna Provincial Marine Park, Hot Springs Cove, Fair Harbour, Zeballos, Tahsis, Gold River, Mt Golden Hinde (2200m), Vancouver Island, Schoen Lake Provincial Park, Woss, Nimpkish Lake, Johnstone Strait, Sayward, Quadra Island, Heriot Bay, Seymour Narrows, PACIFIC OCEAN. To Prince Rupert (440km); Bella Coola]

(www.mondaymag.com) has arts and entertainment listings.

MEDICAL SERVICES
Downtown Medical Centre (Map pp700-1; ☎ 250-380-2210; 622 Courtney St; ☽ 9am-6pm)
Royal Jubilee Hospital (Map pp700-1; ☎ 250-370-8000; 1952 Bay St; ☽ 24hr)

MONEY
There are ATMs downtown, and major banks have branches on Douglas St. There are a couple of places to change currency:
American Express (Map pp700-1; ☎ 250-385-8731; www.americanexpress.com; 1213 Douglas St; ☽ 8:30am-4:30pm Mon-Fri, 10am-4pm Sat)
Custom House Currency Exchange (Map pp700-1; ☎ 250-389-6007; www.customhouse.com; 815 Wharf St; ☽ 9am-7pm Mon-Fri, 9am-5pm Sat & Sun Oct-May, 9am-9pm daily Jun-Sep)

POST
Look for the red-and-blue signs of postal outlets in businesses around town.
Main Post Office (Map pp700-1; ☎ 250-953-1352; 706 Yates St)

TOURIST INFORMATION
BC Ferries Information Office (Map pp700-1; ☎ 250-386-3431; 1112 Fort St; ☽ 7am-10pm)
VIC (Map pp700-1; ☎ 250-953-2033; www.tourism victoria.com; 812 Wharf St; ☽ 8:30am-6pm) At the Inner Harbour.

Dangers & Annoyances
Victoria is a safe city – even at night there's rarely any kind of disturbance. There are plenty of panhandlers, and some homeless people hang out near the water by the Johnson St Bridge, but it's unlikely you'll feel threatened by anyone.

Sights
The majority of Victoria's sights are clustered around the Inner Harbour.

ROYAL BRITISH COLUMBIA MUSEUM
The remarkable First Nations exhibit is the headline-grabber at this acclaimed **museum** (Map pp700-1; ☎ 250-356-7226, 888-447-7977; http://rbcm1.rbcm.gov.bc.ca; 675 Belleville St; adult/concession $11/8; ☽ 9am-6:30pm mid-Jul–Oct, 9am-5pm Nov–mid-Jul). Dominating the 3rd floor, it's packed with

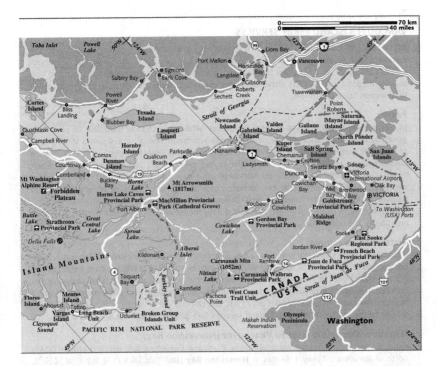

carvings, canoes, beadwork, tools, weapons and basketry, supplemented by good notes. Even more enlightening and poignant are the early black-and-white movies that show real interactions between settlers and Aboriginal peoples from yesteryear. There are also displays of totem poles, a model of the 19th-century Haida village of Skedans, and a re-creation of Nawalagwatsi, 'the cave of supernatural power.'

Other displays are not as captivating, unless you're into lifeless dioramas featuring stuffed animals, which you'll find in spades at the 'Living Land, Living Sea' gallery (although the mammoth is worth a look, and kids will enjoy the tide pool). Elsewhere, exhibits cover the gold rush, coal mining and early 20th century, and there's a walk-through tour of Captain Vancouver's *Discovery*.

ART GALLERY OF GREATER VICTORIA

East of downtown, the best feature of this fine **gallery** (Map pp700-1; ☎ 250-384-4101; www.aggv.bc.ca; 1040 Moss St; adult/child $6/4; ☑ 10am-5pm, to 9pm Thu) is the permanent collection of

Emily Carr artworks, which are illuminated by brutally honest writings from the journal of this pioneering west-coast artist (see boxed text on p699). There are also reasonable collections of Asian, pre-Columbian and Latin American art, as well as contemporary Canadian paintings and Inuit pieces. Bus Nos 10, 11 and 14 will get you there.

BASTION SQUARE

On the site of old Fort Victoria, between Government and Wharf Sts, Bastion Square once held the courthouse, jail, gallows and a brothel, but the square's old buildings have since turned into restaurants, nightclubs, boutiques, galleries and offices.

In the 1889 building that was BC's first provincial law court, the **Maritime Museum** (Map pp700-1; ☎ 250-385-4222; www.mmbc.bc.ca; 28 Bastion Square; adult/concession $8/5; ☑ 9am-4:30pm) explores Vancouver Island's seafaring past and present. Exhibits include more than 400 model ships dating back to 1810, displays on piracy, shipwrecks and navigation, and the

---

VANCOUVER ISLAND FERRY SERVICES

BC Ferries (☎ 250-386-3431, 888-223-3779; www.bcferries.com) connects Vancouver Island with the mainland from several points on each side of the Strait of Georgia. It also services the Southern Gulf Islands (p729) and Northern Gulf Islands. Pick up timetables from ferry terminals and Visitor Information Centres (VICs). Other operators connect Victoria with cities across the border in Washington State (see p644).

Passes

BC Ferries also offers a range of multiday passes. While they change from year to year, they generally offer steep discounts for people wanting to travel several routes over a short period of time. The Summer Sail Pass (available June to October) is especially popular, and provides a hassle-free way to explore many of the islands and towns of the Strait of Georgia. In a recent incarnation, for $200 it offered eight nonconsecutive days of travel within a 15-day period for two adults with a normal-sized car, including one round-trip on each of 20 southern routes (ie everything except the Inside Passage, Discovery Passage and the Queen Charlotte Islands). Similar, but more limited deals are available during the other seasons; check out the BC Ferries website for the latest offers.

Victoria to Vancouver

Victoria's BC Ferries terminal is at Swartz Bay, 27km north of Victoria via Hwy 17. Services to **Vancouver** (adult/child $10.50/5.50, car/bicycle $36/2.50, 95 minutes, hourly 7am to 9pm in summer, reduced services in the off-season) dock at Tsawwassen in southern Vancouver. Reservations ($15) are highly recommended in summer, especially on Friday and Sunday afternoons; it's not uncommon to arrive for the 4pm ferry and not get on a boat until 7pm. You can also get between Victoria and Vancouver on one of the many Southern Gulf Island services (see p729) if you're not in a hurry.

Nanaimo (Departure Bay) to Vancouver (Horseshoe Bay)

Nanaimo has two BC Ferries terminals, Duke Point and Departure Bay, which is around 3.5km north of Nanaimo off Hwy 1. Ferries to **Horseshoe Bay** (adult/child $10.50/5.50, bicycle/car $2.50/36, reservation fees $15; 🕑 6:30am-9pm), in West Vancouver, leave Departure Bay eight times daily (1½ hours). A similar number come the other way.

Tilikum, a converted dugout canoe in which John Voss sailed almost completely around the world (1901–04).

PARLIAMENT BUILDINGS

The stately stone-and-copper **Parliament Buildings** (Map pp700-1; ☎ 250-387-1400; www.leg is.gov.bc.ca; 501 Belleville St; admission & tours free; 🕑 8:30am-5pm, tours Jun-Sep) keep a watchful eye on the harbor and dominate the southern area of the city center. Designed by Francis Rattenbury (who was also responsible for Victoria's Fairmont Empress Hotel) and finished in 1898, the main dome is topped by a statue of Captain George Vancouver, who was the first white man to circumnavigate the island. Inside, marble floors and brass trim are complemented by paintings of Canadian history and industries. If you're in the mood, you can watch the debates of the provincial legislature when it's in session.

CHINATOWN

Small but charismatic, this area has all the inexpensive restaurants and authentic Asian markets you'd expect to find in a **Chinatown** (Map pp700-1). Set on the northern edge of downtown, it's the oldest in Canada. Look for **Fan Tan Alley** (a narrow passageway between Fisgard St and Pandora Ave), which was the place to buy opium in the 1800s.

FISHERMAN'S WHARF

Though overrun by colossal condominium complexes of impossible geometric shapes, **Fisherman's Wharf** (Map p698) hasn't lost its identity. Just west of the Inner Harbour, it bustles with fishing boats and pleasure craft. Buy fresh seafood from the boats, or stop by Barb's Place (p704) for fish and chips.

Starting from Fisherman's Wharf, the **Scenic Marine Drive** skirts the coast along Dallas Rd and Beach Dr. Plenty of parks and

Nanaimo (Duke Point) to Vancouver (Tsawwassen)

Duke Point ferry terminal is 12.5km south of Nanaimo off Hwy 1, and is the departure point for ferries to **Tsawwassen** (adult/child $10.50/5.50, car/bicycle $36/2.50, reservation fee $15; ☒ 5:15am-10:45pm). They run eight times daily (two hours, six on Sunday) each way.

Comox to Powell River

Little River ferry terminal, 8km north of Comox, is the departure point for ferries to **Powell Rover** (adult/child $4/4, car/bicycle $27/2.50) on the Sunshine Coast north of Vancouver. There are four daily sailings each way (80 minutes).

Port Hardy to Prince Rupert

The *Queen of the North* makes one of the great ferry journeys of the world as it sails up the spectacular Inside Passage to **Prince Rupert** (adult/child $103/52, cabin $60, car $242, bike $6.50) for 15-hour daylight sailings every second day between May and October. You'll pass small villages, islands and inlets; keep your eyes peeled for the wealth of wildlife, which can include seals, and killer, humpback and gray whales. At other times sailings are weekly, with stops along the way (including Bella Bella – a drop-off point for kayakers). This overnight route can take up to 24 hours, so it's worth considering a cabin for these trips (adult/child $76/38 car/bicycle $180/6.50, cabins from $50).

Port Hardy to Prince Rupert, via Bella Coola

A scaled-down version of the Inside Passage, this route heads up the 'Discovery Coast' then heads far inland to **Bella Coola** (adult/child $107/54, car/bicycle $213/6.50), via Dean Channel, on its way to Prince Rupert. Again, the setting is stunning, and you can access Hwy 97 from Bella Coola, via Tweedsmuir Provincial Park and Williams Lake (see p776), 460km to the east – a longish but useful shortcut when compared with the drive south from Prince Rupert.

Other Vancouver Island Routes

BC Ferries also operates several routes to the Northern Gulf Islands from towns on Vancouver Island. Routes include Mill Bay to Brentwood Bay (p708), Chemainus to Thetis and Kuper Islands (p709), Nanaimo to Newcastle and Gabriola Islands (p710), Buckley Bay to Denman and Hornby Islands (p723), and Campbell River to Quadra and Cortes Islands (p725).

---

beaches dot the coastline along the way, though access to the shore is restricted in places because of private homes. You can also begin the drive at Beacon Hill Park.

THUNDERBIRD PARK

Right next door to the museum, this **park** (Map pp700-1; admission free) is chock full of totem poles, and is one of Victoria's most popular landmarks. Famed carver Mungo Martin oversaw the initial plans for the park and the restoration of many of the poles. In summer, it's possible to watch First Nations artists do their thing in the carving shed.

Sharing the grounds are the unassuming **Helmcken House** (Map pp700-1; ☎ 250-361-0021; 10 Elliot Sq; adult/concession $5/4; ☒ 10am-5pm May-Oct), dating from 1852 and the oldest unchanged house in the province; and **St Anne's Pioneer Schoolhouse** (Map pp700-1), one of the oldest buildings in Victoria still in use.

BEACON HILL PARK

An easy walk south from downtown via Douglas St, this 61-hectare park offers gardens, ponds and playing fields. You'll find the world's second-tallest totem pole, a 100-year-old cricket pitch, a wildfowl sanctuary and a children's petting zoo. The southern edge overlooks the ocean, which you can reach via steps down to the beach across Dallas Rd. The intersection of Dallas Rd and Douglas St marks **Mile 0** (Map p698) of Hwy 1.

OTHER ATTRACTIONS

East of the city center, the aptly named **Government House** (Map p698; ☎ 250-387-2080; 1401 Rockland Ave) is the official residence of the province's lieutenant governor (the representative of the Queen). The building is closed to the public, but visitors are welcome to stroll the extensive gardens, which are open from dawn to dusk, and play host

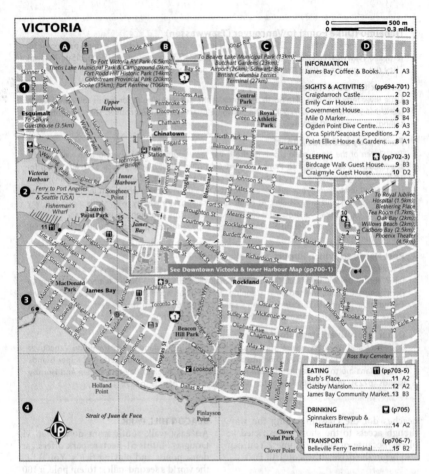

VICTORIA

0 ————— 500 m
0 ————— 0.3 miles

to live music in the summer. Bus Nos 11 or 14 will get you there and to Craigdarrock Castle.

Just around the corner, **Craigdarroch Castle** (Map p698; ☎ 250-592-5323; www.craigdarroch castle.com; 1050 Joan Cres; adult/concession $10/6.50; ☼ 10am-4:30pm) was the brainchild of millionaire coal-mogul Robert Dunsmuir. The house was finished in 1889, just a scant few months after he died, so he never got to see his grandiose vision realized. The castle-like, 2400-sq-meter house has 39 rooms and 17 fireplaces. It has been completely restored, with late-Victorian furniture and fittings.

The social elite of the gold-rush days used to hobnob in the beautiful 1861

Italianate **Point Ellice House & Gardens** (Map p698; ☎ 250-380-6506; 2616 Pleasant St; adult/child $7/5; afternoon tea & tours $20; ☼ noon-5pm mid-May–mid-Sep). Situated close to the Point Ellice Bridge, the house retains a wonderful collection of Victorian furnishings and decorations.

Sadly, the 1925 **Crystal Garden** (Map pp700-1; 713 Douglas St) no longer delights citizens and visitors with its butterflies, monkeys and tropical gardens, after the provincial government decided to close it in 2004. A casino proposal has come and gone, and the future of this lovely neo-Victorian greenhouse remained uncertain at the time of research (for the latest information, see www.bcpcc .com/crystal/).

THE LIFE & WORK OF EMILY CARR

Born to English parents, Emily Carr (1871–1945) was raised in a traditional household in Victoria, and her rebellious and independent nature became quickly evident, with tales of tomboy pranks and wild episodes – like her frequent solo horse rides deep into the surrounding forests. Her conservative family was hardly impressed, and sent Carr to drawing classes when she was eight years old. However these were meant to lend refinement to her character, not to launch her career as a controversial and pioneering artist.

After the death of both parents in her teens, Carr was blocked from traveling to Europe to study by her elder sister, but convinced the family's trustee that the costs of studying in San Francisco were supportable, and she moved to the California School of Design. When the money ran out in 1893, she was forced to return to the colonial backwater of Victoria, where she taught art to local children for several years.

Paradoxically, it was here that Carr found the muse that would define her career, after she accompanied a cleric on his mission to Ucluelet on Vancouver Island's western coast. The life and arts of the First Nations village had a profound effect on Carr, and the artist began using both the area's landscape and its people as her subject matter – an unheard-of practice at the time.

In 1910 she headed to Paris for further study, and returned with a more mature technique and greater confidence. However her new paintings scandalized the staid values of the time, and she became something of a pariah. It wasn't until the late 1920s, when her scorned paintings were shown in eastern Canada, that she began to get a measure of respect. Carr returned to painting with renewed energy, and until the late 1930s painted some of her best-known works, with her signature rich colors, emotive content and stylized depiction of nature well to the fore.

In all truth, Carr's works are hardly the most accomplished paintings you'll ever encounter, but her willingness to challenge gender roles, to portray indigenous cultures, and to remain true to her own artistic vision has assured her legacy as one of western Canada's most respected artists.

Her family home, **Emily Carr House** (Map p698; ☎ 250-383-5843; www.emilycarr.com; 207 Government St; admission by donation; ⏰ 10am-5pm mid-May–mid-Oct) can be visited, and features displays on her life and work, including pieces from across her creative career.

Activities

Victoria offers a host of great adventure activities, from whale-watching and diving to windsurfing and sea kayaking.

Inner Harbour Adventure Centre (Map pp700-1; ☎ 250-995-2211; www.marine-adventures.com; 950 Wharf St; ⏰ 9am-6pm) On the docks at the foot of Broughton St, this is a good place to start; it also houses several other charter and tour companies.

Sports Rent (Map pp700-1; ☎ 250-385-7368; www .sportsrentbc.com; 1950 Government St) An excellent place for all activity-equipment rentals.

SCUBA DIVING

Victoria's nutrient-rich waters support diverse underwater ecosystems and are amazingly clear. Good shore dives include 10 Mile Point, Ogden Point Breakwater, Race Rocks and Saanich Inlet.

Frank White's Scuba Shop (Map pp700-1; ☎ 250-385-4713; 1855 Blanshard St; ⏰ 9am-6pm)

Ogden Point Dive Centre (Map p698; ☎ 250-380-9119; www.divevictoria.com; 199 Dallas Rd; ⏰ 9am-6pm)

WHALE-WATCHING

Around 90 orcas (killer whales) hang out south of the island between April and October, and are accessible from Victoria. The popularity of these tours has prompted around a dozen companies to set up shop; each has its own territory, so it's worth checking out a few to see what their prices and success rates are:

Five Star Whale Watching (Map pp700-1; ☎ 250-388-7223, 800-634-9617; www.5starwhales.com; 706 Douglas St; adult/child $90/60; ⏰ 10am, 2pm & 5:30pm Apr-Oct)

Orca Spirit/Seacoast Expeditions (Map p698; ☎ 250-383-8411, 888-672-6722; www.orcaspirit.com; 146 Kingston Rd; adult/child $90/60; ⏰ 9am, 1pm & 5pm Apr-Oct, 1pm Nov-Mar)

SpringTide Victoria Whale Watching (Map pp700-1; ☎ 250-386-6016, 800-470-3474; www.springtidecharters

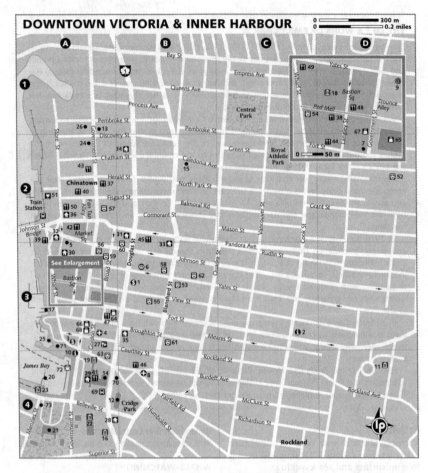

DOWNTOWN VICTORIA & INNER HARBOUR

.com; 950 Wharf St; adult/child $90/60; � 9 departures daily Apr-Sep)

KAYAKING

A paddle in the protected waters off the coast gives a fresh perspective on Victoria's beauty. Companies offer tours ranging from one- to seven-day trips with varying prices.

Sports Rent (Map pp700-1; ☎ 250-385-7368; www .sportsrentbc.com; 1950 Government St; kayak/canoe rentals $45/35) No tours are offered, but this is the best deal if you want to paddle solo.

Vancouver Island Canoe & Kayak Centre (Map pp700-1; ☎ 250-361-9365, 877-921-9365; www.canoe andkayakcentre.com; 575 Pembroke St; kayak/canoe rentals $50/30; � 9am-5:30pm Mon-Sat) Local experts with good-quality gear and tours.

OTHER ACTIVITIES

The **windsurfing** is much better on the west coast, but if you're itching to jump some waves (and you have your own gear), head to Cadboro Bay, northeast of downtown, or Willows Beach, to the east at Oak Bay. **Excel Watersports** (Map pp700-1; ☎ 250-383-8667; www .excel-sports.com; 2001 Douglas St; � 9am-5:30pm) can advise on local conditions.

If you just want a cooling dip, there's good **swimming** at Willows Beach, or you can head to the waterholes at Thetis Lake Municipal Park and Beaver Lake Municipal Park, both north of town.

Deep-sea fishing is also popular in the waters around Victoria; ask the VIC (p694) for a list of operators.

INFORMATION			SLEEPING 🏠 (pp702-3)			ENTERTAINMENT 🎭 (pp705-6)		
American Express	1	B3	Crystal Court Motel	28	A4	Belfry	52	D2
BC Ferries Information Office	2	C3	Fairmont Empress Hotel	29	A4	Capitol 6 Cinema	53	B3
Custom House Currency Exchange	3	A3	HI Victoria Hostel	30	A3	Darcy's Wharf Pub	54	C1
Downtown Medical Centre	4	A3	Hotel Douglas	31	B2	Hermann's Jazz	55	B3
Lamplight Books	5	A3	Isabella's Guest Suites	32	A2	Hush	56	A3
Main Post Office	6	B3	Ocean Island Backpackers Inn	33	B3	IMAX Theatre	(see 22)	
Munro's Books	7	D2	Paul's Motor Inn	34	B2	Legends	(see 35)	
Royal Jubilee Hospital	8	B4	Strathcona Hotel	35	B3	McPherson Playhouse	57	A2
Stain Internet	9	D1	Swans Suite Hotel	36	A2	Odeon Theatre	58	B3
Visitor Info Centre	10	A4				One Lounge	59	A3
			EATING 🍴 (pp703-5)			Prism Lounge	60	B3
SIGHTS & ACTIVITIES (pp694-701)			Brasserie L'ecole	37	A2	Royal Theatre	61	B3
Art Gallery of Greater Victoria	11	D4	Camille's Fine Westcoast Dining	38	D1	Sugar	62	B3
Crystal Garden	12	A4	Chandler's Seafood Restaurant	39	A2	Vic Theatre	63	A4
Excel Watersports	13	A1	Don Mee	40	A2			
Five Star Whale Watching	14	A4	Empress Room	41	A4	SHOPPING 🛍 (p706)		
Frank White's Scuba Shop	15	B2	Green Cuisine	42	A2	Alcheringa Gallery	64	A3
Helmcken House	16	A4	Herald St Caffe	43	A2	Bay Centre	65	D2
Inner Harbour Adventure Centre	17	A3	India Curry House	44	D2	Edinburgh Tartan Shop	66	A3
Maritime Museum	18	D1	John's Place	45	B2	Old Morris Tobacconists	67	D1
Miniature World	19	A4	Milos	46	B4	Rogers' Chocolates	68	A3
Pacific Undersea Gardens	20	A4	Pagliacci's	47	A3			
Parliament Buildings	21	A4	Re-Bar	48	D1	TRANSPORT (pp706-7)		
Royal British Columbia Museum	22	A4	Suze Lounge & Restaurant	49	C1	Bus Station	69	A4
Royal London Wax Museum	23	A4	Wild Saffron Bistro	50	A2	Cycle BC Rentals	70	A4
St Anne's Pioneer Schoolhouse	(see 16)		Willie's Bakery	(see 32)		Cycle BC Rentals (Summer Office)	71	A3
Sports Rent	24	A2				Victoria Harbour Ferry	72	A4
SpringTide Victoria Whale Watching	25	A4	DRINKING 🍷 (p705)					
Thunderbird Park	(see 16)		Canoe Brewpub & Restaurant	51	A2	OTHER		
Vancouver Island Canoe and Kayak Centre	26	A1	Sticky Wicket Pub	(see 35)		Gray Line	(see 29)	
Victoria Bug Zoo	27	A3	Swans Brewpub	(see 36)		Victoria Carriage Tours	73	A4

Victoria for Children

There are some seriously cheesy attractions in Victoria, but your kids will get a real kick out of some of them, and so might you. **Victoria Bug Zoo** (Map pp700-1; ☎ 250-384-2847; www.bugzoo.bc.ca; 631 Courtney St; adult/child $6/4; ☻ 9am-5:30pm, to 9pm Jul & Aug) is the coolest of the bunch. From hairy tarantulas and giant scorpions to the perpetually pregnant Australian stick insect, there are loads of critters to check out, and plenty of info for young enquiring minds. The leaf-cutter ants going about their business inside the Plexiglas tubes are mesmerizing.

There are other places that are also worth a look:

Miniature World (Map pp700-1; ☎ 250-385-9731; www.miniatureworld.com; 649 Humboldt St; adult/child $8/7; ☻ 9am-5pm Sep-May, 8:30am-9pm Jun-Aug) Features space stations, fairy tales and the world of Dickens.

Pacific Undersea Gardens (Map pp700-1; ☎ 250-382-5717; www.pacificunderseagardens.com; 490 Belleville St; adult/child $8.50/4.50; ☻ 9am-5pm, to 8:30pm Jul & Aug) It's pretty small, but there are fish, eels and crabs to gawp at, while the octopus, with its rubbery antics, tops the bill.

Royal London Wax Museum (Map pp700-1; ☎ 250-388-4461; www.waxworld.com; 470 Belleville St; adult/child $9/4.50; ☻ 9am-7:30pm mid-May–Sep, 9:30am-5pm Sep–mid-May) Older kids will squeal in delicious horror at the dungeon.

Tours

There are plenty of sightseeing options if you want to save on shoe leather, or wear it out. **Gray Line** (Map pp700-1; ☎ 250-388-6539, 800-663-8390; www.grayline.ca; adult/child from $20/10) A broad range of double-decker bus tours start in front of the Fairmont Empress Hotel (p703).

Victoria Bobby Walking Tours (☎ 250-995-0233; 75min tours $15; ☻ 11am May–mid-Sep) A daily city walk led by a retired, uniformed London Bobby (police officer), who is also a history buff.

Victoria Carriage Tours (Map pp700-1; ☎ 250-383-2207, 877-663-2207; www.victoriacarriage.com; trolley tours adult/child $12/6, 30/60/90min carriage tours $80/120/160) Tours board from Menzies St near Belleville St.

Victoria Harbour Ferry (☎ 250-708-0201; harbor tours adult/child/senior $14/12/7) Little bathtublike boats that bounce around the Inner Harbour. Offers tours plus scheduled ferry services (see p707).

Festivals & Events

Major events in Victoria happen year-round, but the bulk of the activity is from May to September. Check the VIC or *Monday Magazine* for a calendar of events.

Victoria Flower & Garden Festival (www.flowerandgarden.net; ☻ mid-Jun) Seas of blooms in private and public gardens.

Folkfest (www.icafolkfest.com; ☻ late Jun) Victoria's longest-running multicultural arts festival.

Jazzfest International (www.vicjazz.bc.ca; ☻ late Jun) International and local acts in venues around town.

BRITISH COLUMBIA

First People's Festival (www.vnfc.ca/culturecomm relation.html; ![] 1st weekend of Aug) Three days of cultural celebrations.

Victoria Fringe Theatre Festival (www.victoriafringe .com; ![] late Aug) Four venues staging new and experimental works.

Great Canadian Beer Festival (www.gcbf.com; ![] early Sep) Microbreweries and ales, lagers, porters and pilsners galore over the Labour Day weekend.

Sleeping

Victoria is a busy place, especially in summer, so make reservations as soon as you know your travel plans. **Tourism Victoria** (☎ 250-663-3883, 800-663-3883; www.tourismvictoria .com) has a useful room-reservation service.

BUDGET

Ocean Island Backpackers Inn (Map pp700-1; ☎ 250-385-1785, 888-888-4180; www.oceanisland.com; 791 Pandora Ave; dm $17-23, s/d/f $30/40/60; ![] 24hr; ![]) This bright and cheery four-floor veteran is still packing travelers into rooms of all shapes and sizes. Spacious facilities (including a great kitchen) plus fridges in all rooms, and a location handy to everything, is boosted by the truly friendly atmosphere they've got going here.

HI Victoria Hostel (Map pp700-1; ☎ 250-385-4511, 888-883-0099; www.hihostels.ca; 516 Yates St; dm $17-24; ![] 24hr) This old converted warehouse near the Inner Harbour offers bunks in barracks-style dorm rooms. There are all the usual facilities, and reservations are a must.

The best camping is at Goldstream Provincial Park (p708), but it's a fair distance from town. Closer in are two reasonable options:

Fort Victoria RV Park (☎ 250-479-8112; info@fortvicrv .com; 340 Island Hwy; RV/tent sites $29/23) The closest campground (6.5km from downtown), although it's mainly set up for RVs.

Thetis Lake Campground (☎ 250-478-3845; thetis lake@shaw.ca; 1938 W Park Lane; RV/tent sites $8/6) A fully serviced park 10km northwest of the city center, with great swimming in the lake.

MID-RANGE

Most of cheaper motels are found in the Gorge Rd area northwest of downtown, but there are good options closer in. Victoria also abounds with guesthouses and B&Bs – contact the VIC (p694) for a full list. Peak-season (summer) rates are quoted here, but prices drop substantially during the rest of the year, sometimes by 40% or more.

Hotel Douglas (Map pp700-1; ☎ 250-383-4157, 800-332-9981; www.hoteldouglas.com; 1450 Douglas St; d with/without bathroom from $70/50) A long-time budget favorite, this central hotel dates from 1911, but is going a little more upmarket with a program of renovations. Happily the prices are not shifting too much with the new comfort levels, and the rooms with shared facilities are among the best value in town. Downstairs there's a bar, a bottle shop and Cafe de la Lune, which stays open until the wee hours.

Strathcona Hotel (Map pp700-1; ☎ 250-383-7137, 800-663-7476; www.strathconahotel.com; 919 Douglas St; d $90-120; ![]) Simple but comfortable rooms in dark cherry timber are a good reason to stay at this historic hotel in the heart of town, but better excuses are the attached bar, Sticky Wicket Pub (p705) and restaurant, not to mention the two roof-top beach-volleyball courts. This place is one of a kind.

Selkirk Guest House (Map p698; ☎ 250-389-1213, 800-974-6638; www.selkirkguesthouse.com; 934 Selkirk Ave; dm $22, d $80-105) Part hostel, part B&B, this lovely old home is just over the Johnson St Bridge in Esquimalt (a half-hour walk from the centre), and has a tree house, a trampoline, a waterfront hot tub, and a dock on the Gorge Waterway with boats for use.

Craigmyle Guest House (Map p698; ☎ 250-595-5411; www.bctravel.com/craigmyle; 1037 Craigdarroch Rd; s/d/tw/f/ste $65/90/100/155/170; ![]) Around the corner from Craigdarroch Castle, it was originally built on the castle grounds as a guesthouse, and remains a stylish and comfortable place.

Birdcage Walk Guest House (Map p698; ☎ 250-389-0804, 877-389-0804; birdcagebnb@hotmail.com; 505 Government St; s/d incl breakfast $85/105; ![]) Probably Victoria's most conveniently located B&B (Inner Harbour to the north, ocean to the south, Beacon Hill Park to the east), the rooms are nicely, if fussily, decorated with antiques, and breakfast is delivered to your room.

Crystal Court Motel (Map pp700-1; ☎ 250-384-0551; martin.scott@crystalcourt.ca; 701 Belleville St; s/d $80/90; ![]) Nothing much has changed at the Crystal Court for a long time – witness the shag-pile carpet and the heavy ceramic bath tiles – but its location across from the BC Museum is first rate, and the budget prices offer genuine value, particularly outside of high season.

Paul's Motor Inn (Map pp700-1; ☎ 250-382-9231, 866-333-7285; www.paulsmotorinn.com; 1900 Douglas St; r/ste $95/115; ℗) Rather extraordinary copper cladding conceals similar 1970s features like paneled walls and an enormous metal sun, but the location is great and the rooms are spacious. Popular with businesspeople, this is a solid performer.

TOP END

Swans Suite Hotel (Map pp700-1; ☎ 250-361-3310, 800-668-7926; www.swanshotel.com; 506 Pandora Ave; studio/1-/2-bedroom ste $160/190/260) This former ugly duckling of an old warehouse has been converted into a beautiful swan, and is now one of the city's finest boutique hotels. Most of the two-story suites have high ceilings and exposed-beam interiors, bolstered by all the modern luxuries you'll need. The attached Swans Brewpub (p705) and restaurant are an added bonus.

Isabella's Guest Suites (Map pp700-1; ☎ 250-381-8414; www.isabellasbb.com; 537 Johnson St; ste per night/week from $150/800) In an excellent off-street location down Waddington Alley, Isabella's two gorgeous self-contained suites are in the heart of Victoria's bar-hopping and dining district, and include huge beds, full kitchens, claw-foot tubs and chic furnishings. Weeklong stays are encouraged.

Eating

Victoria's eating scene is simply terrific, taking in everything from greasy spoons to the finest of west-coast cuisine, and leavened by vegetarian, Asian, seafood and European specialty restaurants. Dive in and let your taste buds roam.

BUDGET

Willie's Bakery (Map pp700-1; ☎ 250-381-8414; 537 Johnson St; mains $6-10; ☺ breakfast & lunch) This cool coffeehouse and bakery has an inviting breakfast and lunch menu, but there are plenty of cheap pastries and sandwiches to fill you up – plus a good cup of coffee – and it can all be enjoyed on the cobblestone patio.

Green Cuisine (Map pp700-1; ☎ 250-385-1809; 560 Johnson St; buffet per 100g $2; ☺ breakfast, lunch & dinner) Inside Market Square, this vegetarian buffet has a great selection of meals (pay by weight). There are also fresh juices and smoothies with plenty of extras, including spirulina for that protein hit, and many dishes are suitable for vegans.

Self-caterers can head to **James Bay Community Market** (Map p698; ☎ 250-381-5323; 547 Michigan St; ☺ breakfast & lunch Sat), an excellent farmers' market.

MID-RANGE

John's Place (Map pp700-1; ☎ 250-389-0799; 723 Pandora Ave; mains $7-11; ☺ breakfast, lunch & dinner) John's is everything a greasy spoon should be – fast and rowdy, but welcoming and generous with the portions. This place is an absolute institution, attracting patrons from across the social spectrum, and you shouldn't leave town without trying to finish one of their breakfasts. You may have to queue, but not for long.

Pagliacci's (Map pp700-1; ☎ 250-386-1662; 1011 Broad St; mains $8-12; ☺ lunch & dinner) One of the great-value places in town, Pagliacci's fine Italian dishes and boisterous atmosphere draws repeat business from visitors and locals alike. The elbow room can be in short supply, but a couple of glasses of rough Italian red and you'll no longer notice or care.

THE AUTHOR'S CHOICE

Camille's Fine Westcoast Dining (Map pp700-1; ☎ 250-381-3433; 45 Bastion Sq; mains $18-20; dinner) Head underground to one of Victoria's favorite restaurants. Run by dedicated foodies, the menu is highly and commendably seasonal, and makes great use of island produce and game; it also includes a rolling weekly exploration of a particular international cuisine. It's all complemented by an enormous and well-priced wine list, with particular attention paid to BC tipples. Soft jazz music and warm service complete a gourmet package.

Brasserie L'ecole (Map pp700-1; ☎ 250-475-6260; 1715 Government St; mains $18; dinner Tue-Sat) High ceilings, warm colors and sleek fittings announce this fashionable little place. An inviting menu gently mixes classic flavors and ingredients – how about Sooke trout with Le Puy lentils in hazelnut butter? – and makes the prices look very good indeed.

Barb's Place (Map p698; ☎ 250-384-6515; 310 St Lawrence St; mains $7-9; lunch & dinner) Authentic fish and chips so fresh you can still smell the brine. The harborside location, among a forest of masts at Fisherman's Wharf, is perfect on a warm day.

Suze Lounge & Restaurant (Map pp700-1; ☎ 250-383-2829; 515 Yates St; mains $11-15; dinner-late) The architecture is old and the walls distressed, but the place is hip. The lively kitchen serves good pizza and pasta, but the majority of the glam crowd have an appetizer in front of them and a martini in hand.

Re-Bar (Map pp700-1; ☎ 250-360-2401; 50 Bastion Sq; mains $7-12; breakfast, lunch & dinner) A happening spot with an eclectic, international menu that's heavy on the vegetarian options, this place attracts a young and interesting crowd (although you're just as likely to see office workers at lunchtime). It also has a juice bar and a decent bakery.

Don Mee (Map pp700-1; ☎ 250-383-1032; 538 Fisgard St; mains $11-15; dim sum $9-15; lunch & dinner) In the heart of Chinatown, this place has been here forever, and is still churning out top-shelf seafood and duck dishes in an enormous and occasionally deafening upstairs eating area. Fans of dim sum will have a great time here.

Millos (Map pp700-1; ☎ 250-382-5544; 716 Burdett Ave; mains $11-16; lunch & dinner) Of Victoria's many Greek restaurants, this is among the most popular. Typically white-walled with blue trimming, it serves a full list of Hellenic standards and is a good place to bring the kids, who can select from their own menu.

India Curry House (Map pp700-1; ☎ 250-361-9000; 506 Fort St; mains $9-17; lunch Mon-Sat, dinner) Down an alarmingly bright corridor, the lights soon dim to a romantic level as you enter this formal-yet-affordable East Indian restaurant. The menu at Victoria's favorite curry house is packed with classics, and the vegetarian dishes are an absolute steal. You can get a delivery to your room as well.

TOP END

Victoria's fine-dining scene is the equal of any on the west coast. Hold yourself to a light lunch, pull out the credit card, and prepare to tantalize your taste buds.

Empress Room (Map pp700-1; ☎ 250-348-8111, 800-441-1414; Empress Hotel, 721 Government St; 3-course $60, prix fixe $58; dinner) Appropriately enough, the Fairmont Empress Hotel is home to three of Victoria's finest restaurants. This is probably the pick, thanks to its stunning setting: a grand dining room of mahogany, tapestries, crisp linen and soothing music. The food is classic and fairly orthodox, but undoubtedly of the highest quality. It may be a bit stuffy for some, but it certainly is an experience – especially if you start to explore the 800-strong wine list.

Herald St Caffe (Map pp700-1; ☎ 250-381-1441; 546 Herald St; mains $17-30; lunch & dinner) A stalwart of the local fine-dining scene, the Herald features cozy booths, well-spaced tables and renowned Italian cuisine, with an emphasis on the use of local seafood. Be sure to try the excellent fresh pasta. Attracting a generally older crowd, it's another one for fans of fine wine: there's more than 400 available here, with a good selection available by the glass.

Wild Saffron Bistro (Map pp700-1; ☎ 250-361-3150; 1605 Store St; mains $17-32; dinner Tue-Sun) A bustling little place kitted out in warm Tuscan and timber tones, Wild Saffron has made its name by its deft handling of potentially disparate tastes. A typical example: mustard-seared halibut and salmon fillet in a maple and citrus reduction served with a grilled vegetable and mascarpone flan.

Attentive service and a terrific international wine list round out the experience.

Chandler's Seafood Restaurant (Map pp700-1; ☎ 250-385-3474; 1250 Wharf St; lunch $10-14, dinner $18-28; Ⓥ lunch & dinner) Great food, outstanding views, good service and a pleasant nautical atmosphere pretty much sums up what this restaurant has been doing since 1862. There's a variety of tasty sauces, but if you want to know what good fish tastes like, just order it sautéed.

Drinking

Mmmm, beer. Victoria has several very fine brewpubs, each cranking out a personal take on everything from pale pilsners to somber stouts.

Spinnakers Brewpub & Restaurant (Map p698; ☎ 250-386-2739; 308 Catherine St) A little out of the way in Esquimalt, Spinnakers is the pioneer of Victoria brewpubs with more than a dozen beers on tap, killer views of the harbor, a gourmet deli and an ever-popular restaurant. Get here by Victoria Harbour Ferry (p707).

Sticky Wicket Pub (Map pp700-1; ☎ 250-383-7137; 919 Douglas St) It doesn't make its own beer, but the Sticky Wicket, in the Strathcona Hotel, has a rooftop patio, two games rooms, four dining areas, several hundred feet of bar, and enough cricket and other sporting memorabilia to start a museum.

Canoe Brewpub & Restaurant (Map pp700-1; ☎ 250-361-1940; 450 Swift St) It's a huge brick warehouse but surprisingly intimate, though on a nice day you'll want to sit on the patio. It serves a limited selection of signature brews, including the lip-smacking Beaver Brown Ale.

Swans Brewpub (Map pp700-1; ☎ 250-361-3310; 506 Pandora Ave) Takes up half the main floor of Swans Suite Hotel. Only the oatmeal stout has anything in it other than hops, yeast and water.

Entertainment

Check out the calendar of weekly freebie *Monday Magazine* (www.mondaymag.com) to see what's happening.

LIVE MUSIC

Hermann's Jazz Bar & Grill (Map pp700-1; ☎ 250-388-9166; 753 View St) Excellent acoustics and cool tunes for just a $5 cover most nights. Hermann's attracts the best of the visiting

---

> ## HIGH TEA AT THE EMPRESS (AND ELSEWHERE)
>
> The traditional English high tea is an irresistible and artery-hardening assortment of scones, clotted cream, berries, sandwiches and pastries – and tea of course – taken at one's leisure at around 3pm. The **Fairmont Empress Hotel** (Map pp700-1; ☎ 250-348-8111, 800-441-1414; www.fairmont.com/empress; 721 Government St; afternoon tea $50; Ⓥ noon-5pm) is Victoria's undisputed High Tea Champion. Its combination of gorgeous formal tearooms, fluffy scones, delicate pastries and top-quality blended tea making it an almost mandatory experience for well-heeled tourists. The price is pretty hefty though, and you need to book two weeks in advance during summer.
>
> A couple of other places offer good alternatives at a fraction of the price. **Blethering Place Tea Room** (☎ 250-598-1413; 2250 Oak Bay Ave; $17; Ⓥ lunch) is a very floral place in an Oak Bay mock Tudor building, but the high tea is generous and good value. At **The Gatsby Mansion** (Map p698; ☎ 250-663-7557; 309 Belleville St; $22; Ⓥ lunch), right on the harbor in a lovely old Victorian building, you can take your tea on the verandah in sunny weather.

jazz masters, and the first set (5:30pm to 7:30pm) is usually free. The expertly mixed martinis also go down a treat.

Darcy's Wharf St Pub (Map pp700-1; ☎ 250-380-1322; 1127 Wharf St) With a welcoming and casual atmosphere, this is the kind of place where you can just hang out. Crowds line up Thursday to Saturday nights to see the cover band.

Legends (Map pp700-1; ☎ 250-383-7137; 919 Douglas St) This long-standing nightclub in the Strathcona Hotel books an eclectic mix of good live bands several times a month – otherwise it's Top 40 dancing.

NIGHTCLUBS

Clubs in Victoria change as often as the drink specials and cover charges. Check www.clubvibes.com or follow your ears and the crowds around Bastion Square. The following are some Victoria standards.

Hush (Map pp700-1; ☎ 250-385-0566; 1325 Government St) Now firmly part of the club scene, this gay-friendly place has great music and isn't self-important.

Prism Lounge (Map pp700-1; ☎ 250-388-0505; 642 Johnson St) BJ's re-badged, it's still the main gay and lesbian spot in town. It's open nightly with DJs spinning on the weekend.

Sugar (Map pp700-1; ☎ 250-920-9950; 858 Yates St; ☽ Fri & Sat) An old stager that gets packed in the wee hours.

One Lounge (Map pp700-1; ☎ 250-384-3557; 1318 Broad St) Fun early-20s crowds, Top 40, R&B and hip-hop; the illuminated bars are pretty cool.

THEATER

McPherson Playhouse (Map pp700-1; ☎ 250-386-6121; www.rmts.bc.ca; 3 Centennial Sq) This place and the Royal Theatre are the elegant main stages of Victoria – think velvet ropes and curtains, marble floors and wood carvings.

The **Royal Theatre** (Map pp700-1; ☎ 250-386-6121; 805 Broughton St) is the home of the **Victoria Symphony** (☎ 250-385-6515; www.victoriasymphony.bc.ca; tickets $20-57) and **Pacific Opera Victoria** (☎ 250-386-6121; www.pov.bc.ca; tickets $28-90).

For independent theater, head to the **Belfry** (Map pp700-1; ☎ 250-385-6815; www.belfry.bc.ca; 1291 Gladstone Ave) or the **Phoenix Theatre** (☎ 250-721-8000; University of Victoria campus, 3800 Finnerty Rd). Friday- and Saturday-night tickets start from $20, but prices drop on weekday evenings and Saturday matinees, and both theaters offer generous student discounts.

CINEMAS

There are plenty of silver screens around.

The **IMAX Theatre** (Map pp700-1; ☎ 250-953-4629; www.imaxvictoria.com; 675 Belleville St; adult/child $9.75/3.50; ☽ 10am-6pm) is at the Royal British Columbia Museum; discounts are available for joint IMAX-museum admission.

Vic Theatre (Map pp700-1; ☎ 250-383-1998; 808 Douglas St; adult/child $8.50/5) is a stylish old cinema that shows lesser-known first-run movies in its single theater.

The first-run cinemas downtown are **Capitol 6 Cinema** (Map pp700-1; ☎ 250-384-6811; 805 Yates St; tickets $8) and **Odeon Theatre** (Map pp700-1; ☎ 250-383-0513; 780 Yates St; tickets $8.50).

Shopping

There's some satisfying retail therapy to be had in Victoria. Many of the finest shops are found along, or just off, Government St, but other strips to check out include: Trounce Alley, between Yates and View Sts, which is lined with fashion shops; Johnson St, for new and used books; and Fort St east of Blanshard St, which is also known as 'Antique Row.'

Alcheringa Gallery (Map pp700-1; ☎ 250-383-8224; 665 Fort St) An excellent upmarket collection of northwestern First Nations art, plus pieces from Papua New Guinea, Australia and Africa.

Rogers' Chocolates (Map pp700-1; ☎ 250-384-7021; 913 Government St) A fabulous old-fashioned little chocolate shop.

Bastion Sq Festival of the Arts (Bastion Sq; ☽ 10:30am-5:30pm Wed-Sun & holidays) For handcrafted pieces, head to this open-air market.

Old Morris Tobacconists (Map pp700-1; ☎ 250-382-4811; 1116 Government St) This grand place has been purveying gentleman's accessories and smoking paraphernalia for 111 years.

Edinburgh Tartan Shop (Map pp700-1; ☎ 250-953-7788; 909 Government St) For that indispensable sporran or Fair Isle knit.

Bay Centre (Map pp700-1; ☎ 250-382-7141) This is a large, central, modern mall stocked with chain stores.

Getting There & Away

AIR

Victoria International Airport (☎ 250-953-7500; www.cyyj.ca), about 26km north of Victoria, is Vancouver Island's main airport, although there are also airfields at Nanaimo, Campbell River and Tofino, as well as several ports for floatplane services.

Airlines in Canada that offer direct services to Victoria include Air Canada from Vancouver ($145, 25 minutes), Calgary ($235, 2½ hours) and Toronto ($355, 7¼ hours); Air Canada Jazz from Vancouver; and WestJet from Vancouver and other major Canadian cities. Horizon Air also has flights from Vancouver and Seattle.

West Coast Air (☎ 250-388-4521, 800-347-2222; www.westcoastair.com) and **Harbour Air Seaplanes** (☎ 250-384-2215, 800-665-0212; www.harbour-air.com) both offer seaplane flights ($99, 25 minutes, half-hourly) from Victoria to Vancouver's downtown waterfront. **Kenmore Air** (☎ 800-543-9595; www.kenmoreair.com) flies seaplanes to Seattle daily.

BOAT

For details of ferry services between Victoria and the mainland, see the boxed text on pp696–7. For information on ferries that depart from Victoria's Belleville Ferry Terminal and go to the state of Washington, see p644.

BUS

Long and short-range bus trips depart from the **bus station** (Map pp700-1; 700 Douglas St). From here, **Vancouver Island Coach Lines** (☎ 250-475-3339, 800-318-0818) operates services up the coast to Port Hardy. Greyhound Canada doesn't serve Vancouver Island, but there's an office in the station to purchase tickets for Vancouver buses.

TRAIN

VIA Rail runs the *Malahat* up-island to Courtenay daily ($58, 4½ hours). Victoria's **train station** (Map pp700-1; ☎ 250-842-7245; 450 Pandora Ave) is only open when trains are arriving or departing.

Getting Around

Since Victoria is concentrated around the Inner Harbour, it's a walking or cycling town.

TO/FROM THE AIRPORT

A taxi to the airport from downtown costs about $45. **AKAL Airport Shuttle Bus** (☎ 250-386-2525; adult/child $14/7; ⌚ 4:30am-midnight) provides service between the airport and all area hotels and B&Bs.

BICYCLE

Cycle BC Rentals (☎ 250-385-2453, 866-380-2453; www.cyclebc.ca; Main office Map pp700-1; 747 Douglas St; Summer office Map pp700-1; 950 Wharf St; bicycle/scooter/motorcycle rentals per day from $20/50/90) and **Sports Rent** (Map pp700-1; ☎ 250-385-7368; www.sportsrentbc.com; 1950 Government St; road/mountain bike per day from $25/20) are both central.

BOAT

Victoria Harbour Ferry (Map pp700-1; ☎ 250-708-0201; www.harbourferry.com; adult/child from $3.50/1.75) provides scheduled services to the Inner Harbour, Songhees Park (Spinnakers Brewpub), Fisherman's Wharf and other stops up the Gorge waterway. The ferry is a great way to get around. Fares vary with distance traveled.

CAR

All major car-rental companies have offices at the airport and also in the downtown area.

PUBLIC TRANSPORTATION

BC Transit (☎ 250-382-6161; www.bctransit.com; 1-/2-zone fare $1.75/2.50, day pass $5.50) buses run frequently and cover a wide area; two-zone travel will take you into suburbs such as Colwood or Sidney. You must have the exact change. Day passes aren't sold on buses, but are available from convenience stores and the VIC.

TAXI

The two-seater pedicabs of **Kabuki Kabs** (☎ 250-385-4243; per min $1) are fun, if only to hear the 'driver' spin a yarn. For a traditional (motorized) cab, contact **Blue Bird Cabs** (☎ 250-382-3611) or **Empress Taxi** (☎ 250-381-2222).

SOUTHERN VANCOUVER ISLAND

There are plenty of interesting sights around Victoria. Of the areas listed in the following section, Fort Rodd, Butchart Gardens, Goldstread and Mill Bay are all north of Victoria.

SOUTHWESTERN SHORE

West of Victoria, Hwy 14 takes you from the city's manicured parks and gardens to the pristine wilderness of Vancouver Island's west coast. The highway runs through Sooke (36km west of Victoria), then along the coast overlooking the Strait of Juan de Fuca to terminate at the hiking center of Port Renfrew. Along the way are parks and beaches for walking, beachcombing and picnicking. Note that you cannot reach Ucluelet or Tofino along this road.

Before you reach **Sooke**, follow the signs from Milnes Landing up Sooke River Rd to the **Sooke Potholes**, where you can swim, picnic and hike. The **Sooke VIC** (☎ 250-642-6351; www.sookenet.com; 2070 Phillips Rd; ⌚ 9am-5pm), which also houses the local museum, can give you more information.

Starting north of Sooke, the **Galloping Goose Trail**, named for a noisy gas railcar that ran between Victoria and Sooke in the 1920s, is a 55km bike-and-walking path to Victoria on abandoned railway beds. For a brochure with maps, ask at the area VICs, or go online at www.crd.bc.ca/parks/galloping_goose.htm.

East Sooke Regional Park (☎ 250-478-3344; www.eastsookepark.com; ⌚ dawn-dusk) makes a great day trip from Victoria for its 50km of hiking trails crisscrossing 1400 hectares of beautiful coastal scenery. It features one of the

BRITISH COLUMBIA

best and most accessible hikes on the island: the **East Sooke Coastal Trail** is a rugged 10km one-way hike that takes you along bluffs and cliffs and through stands of pine, spruce and rain forest. You'll need to allow around six hours, and arrange transport from the finishing point. From Hwy 14 westbound, turn left on Gillespie Rd and right onto E Sooke Rd.

Further along Hwy 14, the windswept **French Beach Provincial Park** offers hiking trails and swimming, and a little further along in **Juan de Fuca Provincial Park** (☎ 250-391-2300; wlap-www.gov.bc.ca/bcparks) you can begin the 47km **Juan de Fuca Marine Trail**. It doesn't require hiking reservations and features several access points, so you can tramp for a day without having to go all the way. From east to west, access points from Hwy 14 are China Beach (the start of the trail), Sombrio Beach, Parkinson Creek and Botanical Beach (the trail's end). There are six established campsites ($5, payable at trailheads), and most hikers take four days to make the complete trek. **West Coast Trail Express** (☎ 250-477-8700; www.trailbus.com; China Beach/Port Renfrew $30/35) runs shuttle services between Victoria and the trailheads. It departs Victoria at 6:40am and returns at 4:30pm.

The highway ends at sleepy **Port Renfrew**, a start/finish point for the renowned West Coast Trail (p717). Port Renfew gets packed with hikers during summer, but otherwise its main attraction is **Botanical Beach**, a sandstone shelf with fabulous rock pools. Accommodations are limited and you'll need to book well in advance during hiking season.

On the waterfront, **Arbutus Beach Lodge** (☎ 250-647-5458, 866-772-8887; 5 Questo Dr; s/d from $70/80) is a basic but comfy lodge with a hot tub and good sea views.

The **West Coast Trail Motel** (☎ 250-647-5565, 877-299-2288; www.westcoasttrailmotel.com; Parkinson Rd; d $75 with kitchenette $90) has clean and basic motel-style rooms and an outdoor hot tub.

On the beach at the trailhead of the West Coast Trail, **Pacheedaht First Nations Campground** (☎ 250-647-0090; www.portrenfrew.com/pachee daht; campsites $10) is popular with hikers.

FORT RODD HILL NATIONAL HISTORIC SITE

The job of protecting Esquimalt Harbour and the Royal Navy yards rested squarely on the sturdy, concrete shoulders of Fort Rod

Hill in the late 19th to mid-20th century. Now you can tour the gun batteries and barracks at the **Fort Rodd Hill National Historic Site** (☎ 250-478-5849; 603 Fort Rodd Hill Rd; www.fortroddhill .com; adult/child $4/2; ⊙ 10am-5:30pm Mar-Nov, 9am-4:30pm Apr-Oct), 14km northwest of the city, off Ocean Blvd. The site also contains western Canada's first lighthouse, **Fisgard Lighthouse**, in continuous use since 1860.

BUTCHART GARDENS

These manicured and very formal **flower gardens** (☎ 250-652-5256, 866-652-4422; www.butch artgardens.com; 800 Benvenuto Ave; adult/child/youth $21/2/10.50; ⊙ 9am-10:30pm Jun 15–Aug 31, closing time varies seasonally), in Brentwood Bay on the Saanich Peninsula, are one of the province's top tourism draws. Over 20 hectares have been painstakingly laid out, with the Sunken Gardens and the peaceful Japanese Garden the best of the themed areas. Though the visual spectacle of color and texture is quite pleasing, this is definitely not one for avant-gardeners. Also, the entry price is pretty hefty and it's easy to tire of the overwhelming flood of tour-bus visitors, particularly in spring when the gardens are in their full pomp.

The gardens are 23km north of Victoria via Patricia Bay Hwy (Hwy 17) and can be reached via bus No 75 ($2.75, 45 minutes) from downtown Victoria, though it's a slow trek. It's better to go with **Gray Line** (☎ 250-388-0818; www.grayline.ca/victoria; express bus fare incl gardens admission $28, tours adult/child $43/13).

GOLDSTREAM PROVINCIAL PARK

About 20km west of Victoria on the Island Hwy, this park, at the base of Malahat Mountain, makes a scenic day trip from Victoria. Best known for its chum salmon spawning season (late October to December), and the bald eagles attracted to the fish, its stands of enormous cedar are equally captivating. You'll also find good fishing and hiking, along with human- and natural-history exhibits at the park's **Freeman King Visitor Centre** (☎ 250-478-9414; wlapwww.gov.bc.ca/bcparks; ⊙ 9am-4:30pm). The **campground** (☎ 250-391-2300; tent sites $18.50) is always busy, but it's the nicest camping spot in the area.

MILL BAY

About 27km north of Goldstream, the village of **Mill Bay** is the departure point for **BC Ferries** (☎ 250-223-3779; www.bcferries.com; adult/

child $4.75/2.50, car $12, 9 daily) to Brentwood Bay, which is a useful shortcut to the Swartz Bay BC Ferries Terminal (see the boxed text on pp696–7), if you're coming from the north.

DUNCAN & COWICHAN VALLEY

About 60km northwest of Victoria, along Hwy 1, is the small town of **Duncan**. It marks the beginning of the Cowichan Valley, which runs west towards the island's center and contains large Cowichan Lake. This is the land of the Cowichan people, BC's largest First Nations group. Duncan itself is of little interest, but its **VIC** (☎ 250-746-4636; www.duncancc.bc.ca; 381 Trans-Canada Hwy; ⏰ 9am-5pm mid-Apr–mid-Oct) has details of the surrounding attractions.

Around 5km south of Duncan is the turn-off to the village of **Cowichan Bay**, 3.5km to the east of the highway. It's worth a brief detour because it has somehow escaped the relentless modernization of the rest of the area, and features several historic fishing homes that sit over the water on stilts. The ice cream at **Udder Guys Ice Cream Parlour** (☎ 250-746-8981; 1759 Cowichan Bay Rd) has been voted the best on the island.

About 22km west of Duncan is the township of **Lake Cowichan**, which is good for camping, swimming, fishing, canoeing and hiking, including the **Cowichan River Footpath**, an 18km trail with a good variety of scenery along the way. Lake Cowichan is also the departure point for trips to Carmanah Walbran Provincial Park.

About 16km north of Duncan is the small town of **Crofton**, from where you can catch ferries to Vesuvius Bay, north of Salt Spring Island (p729).

Carmanah Walbran Provincial Park

Some of the island's last remaining old-growth forest can be found in this superb 16,450-hectare **park** (☎ 250-474-1336; backcountry camping per person $5). Proclaimed in 1990 and expanded in 1995, it's home to the world's tallest spruce trees (some hitting 95m) and 1000-year-old cedars, and its wild beauty is absolutely compelling. Despite its position on the island's western coast, the best access is from Lake Cowichan, but it still requires around 45km of driving on private logging roads, making it almost a mandatory overnight trip: pick up a map from Duncan's VIC before you go. Once you're there, it's a half-hour walk down the valley into the

tallest trees. Campsites with tent pads, tables and water are provided at the trailhead, and dedicated campsites with food stashes (to deter bears) are found up the trail. The closest phone and gas station are on the Didtidaht Reserve, at Nitinat Lake.

Chemainus

This small logging village, 10km north of Crofton, was on the brink of collapse in 1983, when the local mill closed down. Rather than submit to a slow death, town officials commissioned a large outdoor mural of local history. People took notice, and 33 murals, some of them remarkably good, now bring in the tourists. The mill has since reopened, and these days Chemainus is a bustling little community.

The **VIC** (☎ 250-246-3944; 9796 Willow St; ⏰ 9am-5pm May-Oct, 10am-5pm Mon-Fri Nov-Apr) can fill you in on the town's other attraction – a pair of islands just off the coast. **Kuper Island** is a First Nations reserve for which you need permission from the chief to visit. **Thetis Island** is primarily geared to boaters, and has a nice pub, plus some interesting sandstone formations on the beach at Pilkey Point. **BC Ferries** (☎ 250-223-3779; www.bcferries.com; adult/child $6/3, car/bicycle $15/2) leave from Oak St and loop to both islands every 90 minutes or so from 7:10am to 10pm.

Ladysmith & Yellow Point

A postcard-pretty small town about 26km north of Duncan, Ladysmith's main claim to fame is the seawater at **Transfer Beach Park**, said to be the warmest north of San Francisco; it certainly attracts its share of swimmers. First Ave's restored 19th- and 20th-century buildings are also worth a stroll. Stop in at the **VIC** (☎ 250-245-2112; www.town.ladysmith.bc.ca; 26 Gatacre St; ⏰ 9am-5pm Jun-Aug, 9am-5pm Mon-Fri Sep-May) for details of other minor attractions around town.

North of town, you can turn off onto **Yellow Point Rd**, a beautiful bucolic route to Nanaimo that passes a couple of places of interest. **Roberts Memorial Provincial Park** (wlapwww.gov.bc.ca/bcparks; Yellowpoint Rd) is a good place to stretch your legs; there's a 700m walk down to the peaceful shoreline, where you can have a dip if the weather's good and maybe spot some basking sea lions. The park is about 5km north of the excellent beachfront **Yellow Point Lodge** (☎ 250-245-7422;

www.yellowpointlodge.com; 3700 Yellow Point Rd; cottages from $90, s/d from $100/180), which is backed by 66 hectares of woods and offers kayaking, tennis, swimming and mountain biking. Further north along the road you come to the **Crow & Gate** (☎ 250-722-3731; 2313 Yellow Point Rd; mains $8-11; ☺ 11am-midnight), an authentic British-style pub where you can kick back with a properly poured pint of Guinness, or tuck into steak-and-kidney pud.

NANAIMO

Vancouver Island's second-largest city, 110km northwest of Victoria, Nanaimo may be a pale shadow of the province's illustrious capital, but town officials are doing their best to smarten the place up. The development of the harbor into a shopping and café precinct was a good start, and there's enough other attractions – in town and offshore – to keep you engaged for a day or so.

A number of First Nations bands once shared Sne-Ny-Mos, a Salish word meaning 'meeting place.' Today, Nanaimo's more recent coal-mining heritage remains evident in its down-to-earth atmosphere and utilitarian architecture. It's also a transportation hub for BC Ferries.

Orientation

For visitors, the focus is the inner harbor, which extends from the Boat Basin Marina area near Harbour Park Mall to Departure Bay. The city center is behind the harbor, with most shops on Commercial St and Terminal Ave. Old City Quarter, a small section up the hill from downtown, bordered by Fitzwilliam, Selby and Wesley Sts, has been spruced up to reflect old-city charm.

Information

Major banks and ATMs are located on Commercial St. Nanaimo is a treasure trove for book-lovers, with several excellent shops on Commercial St.

Bygone Books (☎ 250-741-1766; 99 Commercial St) Great selection of quality used fiction and nonfiction books.
Literacy Nanaimo Bookstore (☎ 250-754-8982; 19 Commercial St) Cheap used books, and the profits help people learn to read. Also has Internet access ($3 per hour).
Money Mart (☎ 250-753-1440; 164 Nicol St) Exchanges currency.
Nanaimo Regional General Hospital (☎ 250-755-7618; 1200 Dufferin Cres; ☺ 24hr emergency room) Northwest of downtown.

Post Office (☎ 250-267-1177; Harbour Park Mall; ☺ 8:30am-5pm Mon-Fri)
Vancouver Island Regional Library (☎ 250-753-1154; 90 Commercial St; per hr $2) You may need to book in advance for Internet access.
VIC (www.tourismnanaimo.com); Bowen Rd (☎ 250-756-0106, 800-663-7337; 2290 Bowen Rd; ☺ 8am-7pm May-Sep, 9am-5pm Mon-Fri & 10am-4pm Sat & Sun Oct-Apr); Bastion (cnr Front & Bastion Sts; ☺ 9am-6pm summer) The main VIC office on Bowen Rd is curiously located away from downtown, but it's extremely helpful; the Bastion is a seasonal outlet.

Sights

Nearby Newcastle and Gabriola Islands are Nanaimo's best attractions; otherwise the central sights are modest.

NEWCASTLE & GABRIOLA ISLANDS
Just across the inlet, car-free **Newcastle Island Provincial Marine Park** (☎ 250-753-5141; wlapwww.gov.bc.ca/bcparks) offers picnicking, cycling, hiking and beaches unpolluted by engine noise or smell. Walks range from a 1km stroll to the 7.5km perimeter hike. There's also a great **campground** (☎ 250-753-3481; tent sites summer/winter $14/9). It has only 18 walk-in sites, no reservations and no services, but there's often a few to share with, and no traffic, so you'll sleep soundly. Catch a ferry (adult/child $7/6, 10 minutes, hourly, 10am to 7pm May to mid-October) here from near Mafeo-Sutton Park.

Further out into the strait is **Gabriola Island**, the most northerly of the Southern Gulf Islands. Known for its large community of artists, it makes for a fun day trip, although you'll need a bicycle or car to get around. It has several beaches and three lovely provincial parks offering swimming, shoreline walks and tidal-pool examination. A fair range of accommodations and camping are available on the island; for details contact the island's **VIC** (☎ 250-247-9332, 888-284-9332; www.gabriolaisland.org; 575 North Rd; ☺ 9am-5pm May-Sep); it's the second on the left after you leave the ferry. **BC Ferries** (☎ 250-223-3779; www.bcferries.com; passenger/bicycle/car $6/free/14.50) travels to Gabriola from the Nanaimo dock north of Harbour Park Mall (16 daily, 5:45am to 10:25pm).

CENTRAL NANAIMO
Get your map at the VIC or follow the color-coded walks to see the remarkable **Jeff King's Murals** on building walls around town.

NANAIMO

Marina
(Boat Basin
Marina)

Old City
Quarter

To Galaxy Cinemas (3km);
Avalon Cinema Centre (4.5km);
Whitehouse on Long Lake B&B (5km)

Northfield Rd

To Visitor Info
Centre (1km);
Hwy 19 (2km)

Woodlands St
Strathmore St
Nelson St
Crescent View Dr
Dufferin St
Oakley St
Chelsea St
St George St
Cadogan St
St Andrews St
Hunter St
Eberts St

Townsite Rd
Bowen Rd

Millstone River

Bowen
Park

Rosehill St
Bradley St

Pimbury
Point

Newcastle
Island

Brechin Rd

Drake St
Chestnut St
Poplar St
Larch St
Hemlock St
Juniper St

Walnut St
Cypress St

Newcastle
Island
Provincial
Marine Park

Newcastle Island Channel

Mt Benson
St

Queen Elizabeth
Promenade

Protection
Island

Mark
Bay

Swy-A-
Lana
Lagoon

Comox Rd

Georgia
Park

Nanaimo
Cemetery

Bowen Rd
1st St

2nd St

Campbell St
Wentworth St

See Enlargement

Nanaimo
Harbour

To Port Alberni (80km);
Campbell River (151km)

Nanaimo Pkwy

Train
Station

3rd St

Department
of National
Defense

To Victoria (110km)

4th St

To Living Forest Oceanside
Campground (2km); Petroglyph
Provincial Park (3km); Duke
Point Ferry Terminal (7km);
Bungy Zone (10km);
Airport (18km)

Crace St

0   500 m
0   0.3 miles

0   200 m
0   0.1 mile

Mafeo-Sutton Park, just north of downtown, is a great place for kids with its artificial tidal pool and playground.

Overlooking downtown, the **Nanaimo District Museum** (☎ 250-753-1821; www.nanaimo.museum .bc.ca/ndm; 100 Cameron Rd; adult/child $2/0.75; ✆ 10am-5pm mid-May–early Sep, 10am-5pm Tue-Sat Sep–mid-May) traces the growth of the city, from its First Nations heritage to coal mining and then the Hudson's Bay Company days.

Bastion (cnr Front & Bastion Sts; admission $1; ✆ 9am-5pm Wed-Sun summer) was built by the Hudson's Bay Company in 1853 for protection from First Nations locals, though it was never used, save for the odd cannon firing to quell disturbances. It still fires daily at noon.

Three kilometers south of town, on Hwy 1, is **Petroglyph Provincial Park**, which has important but faded First Nations carvings in sandstone, although replicas nearby help you to interpret the petroglyphs.

Activities

Nanaimo and its nearby islands offer some of the best scuba diving in BC. In 2001 dive enthusiasts sunk the WWII supply ship *Cape Breton* northwest of Gabriola Island, creating the area's largest artificial reef. For information on dive sites, or guides, lessons and equipment, visit **Ocean Explorers Diving** (☎ 250-753-2055, 800-233-4145; www.oceanexplorersdiving.com; 1690 Stewart Ave; dives from $50).

Kayak Shack (☎ 250-753-3234; dives from $30; ✆ 9am-6pm) offers sea-kayaking lessons, rentals and tours from its headquarters near the Departure Bay terminal.

Parkway Trail extends 20km along Hwy 19, and offers opportunities for cycling, in-line skating, jogging and walking. The trail accesses many parks, including **Buttertubs Marsh Sanctuary**, a rare urban marshland where great blue herons, American bitterns, Bohemian waxwings and many wintering waterfowl species can be seen.

Bungy Zone (☎ 250-753-5867, 800-668-7771; www .bungyzone.com; 35 Nanaimo River Rd; jumps from $50), set on a bridge spanning the Nanaimo River (10km south of town), will keep adrenaline junkies happy. There's free pick-up from either of the local BC Ferry terminals if someone pays for a jump.

Festivals & Events

The top annual event is the **Nanaimo Bathtub Race**, a 58km motor down the Strait of Georgia to Vancouver, held each July as part of **Nanaimo's Marine Festival**. There's also a busy calendar of events for culture vultures; ask at the VIC for a list.

Sleeping

BUDGET

Cambie International Hostel (☎ 250-754-5323, 877-754-5323; www.cambiehostels.com/nanaimo; 63 Victoria Cres; dm/r incl breakfast $22.50/45) The small dorms at this popular hostel have good-sized bunks, plus a private toilet. There are no cooking facilities, but breakfast is served at the street-level bakery-café.

There are other budget places that are recommended:

Living Forest Oceanside Campground & RV Park (☎ 250-755-1755; www.campingbc.com; 6 Maki Rd; tent/RV sites $20/30) A large place on the water, it's the closest campground to town.

Nicol St Hostel (☎ 250-753-1188; www.nanaimohostel .com; 65 Nicol St; campsites/dm/r $10/17/45) This friendly, family-run hostel is a five-minute walk from downtown. With an outdoor shower, camping in the backyard and barbecue facilities, it's great for families.

MID-RANGE

Nanaimo's mid-range accommodations are dominated by the motels that line Nicol St and Terminal Ave north and south of town. Most offer a $10 discount if you present a flyer from the VIC. It's worth spending a little more to stay in the nicer places around the town center.

Whitehouse on Long Lake B&B (☎ 250-756-1185, 877-956-1185; www.nanaimobandb.com; 231 Ferntree Pl; d $80-105; 🖳) As the name would suggest, it's on Long Lake, north of Nanaimo via Hwy 19A. Huge south-facing windows face the lake but if you'd rather do more than look, take the complimentary canoe, kayak or paddleboat out there. The fireplace beside the Jacuzzi tub adds a romantic touch.

Buccaneer Inn (☎ 250-753-1246; www.thebuccaneer inn.com; 1577 Stewart Ave; s/d $75/80; 🖳) The closest motel to Departure Bay terminal welcomes divers to its comfortable rooms. Up on a hill, it has sweeping views of Newcastle Island and staff are more than happy to help you arrange any activities in the area.

Tourist Inn Motel (☎ 250-716-1671; 250 Terminal Ave North; www.tourist-inn.com; s/d from $70/90; 🐾) Of Nanaimo's abundant standard motels, the Tourist's huge central pool and the motel's location relatively close to town make it worth seeking out. The rooms are unremarkable but comfortable.

TOP END

Coast Bastion Inn (☎ 250-753-6601, 800-663-1144; www.coasthotels.com; 11 Bastion St; r/ste $130/200) Nanaimo's high-end option has several floors of renovated and well-presented rooms that attract plenty of businesspeople, but it's the panoramic water views that are the real payoff.

Eating

Thanks to cheap beer, live music on weekends and an international crowd, **Cambie International Hostel** (☎ 250-754-5323, 877-754-5323; www.cambiehostels.com/nanaimo; 63 Victoria Cres) transforms into the most happening bar and grill in town at night.

BUDGET

Roxy's Diner (☎ 250-753-5333; 187 Commercial St; mains $6-10; ☒ breakfast & lunch) A compact little diner with shiny red booths and a classic Formica counter, this sassy place offers the usual enormous, artery-hardening fare, and gets its fair share of patrons throughout the day.

Trollers Fish & Chips (☎ 250-741-7994; 104 Front St; mains $7-10; ☒ lunch & dinner) Nothing beats the ambience of Troller's when it comes to chowing down on some fish and chips. This shack on the docks cooks fish fresh off the boat, and you can watch the harbor traffic come and go as you eat.

Charlie's (☎ 250-753-7044; 123 Commercial St; breakfast dishes $3-6) A rather large and soulless place on Commercial St, it compensates by offering the cheapest breakfasts in town. How can you go wrong with eggs, toast and bacon or sausage for $2.95?

The **Nanaimo Farmers' Market** (Pioneer Waterfront Plaza; ☒ 10am-2pm Fri May-Oct) is held near the Bastion.

MID-RANGE

Dinghy Dock Floating Pub (☎ 250-753-2373; 8 Pirates Lane, Protection Island; mains $8-14; ☒ lunch & dinner) This long-standing pub really does float off the eastern edge of Protection Island, and offers views of the city center that are especially pretty at night. Popular with visitors and locals alike, it puts on live music on weekends, and can get fairly raucous at times. The food sticks to seafood, steak and pasta standards, and is capable enough. A 10-minute **ferry**

(☎ 250-753-8244; round-trip adult/concession $4/3) runs hourly between 11am and 11pm in summer, from Nanaimo harbor.

Acme Food Company (☎ 250-753-0042; 14 Commercial St; mains $8-18 ☒ lunch & dinner) A cool, low-lit place on a central corner, Acme serves up plenty of choices, from build-your-own pizzas to steak and sushi, with jazzy strains in the background. The bar mixes a mean martini and keeps the place hopping.

Drinking

As a general rule, **Club Malibu** (☎ 250-716-0030; 150 Skinner St) is the most happening nightclub, but **Jungle Cabaret** (☎ 250-754-1775; 241 Skinner St), just across the road, pulls its fair share of the party crowd. A quieter drink can be had at the neighboring local **Palace Hotel** (☎ 250-754-9041; 275 Skinner St), which has a pool table, or you can dabble in some cocktails at **Katz Lounge** (☎ 250-753-5280; 121 Bastion St).

Entertainment

Port Theatre (☎ 250-754-8550; www.porttheatre.nisa .com; 125 Front St) This modern theater presents local and touring fine-arts performances.

New-release flicks are screened at **Avalon Cinema Centre** (☎ 250-390-5021; Woodgrove Centre, 6631 N Island Hwy) and **Galaxy Cinemas** (☎ 250-741-9000; Rutherford Village Mall, 4750 Rutherford Rd), both in the suburbs northwest of town.

Getting There & Away

AIR

Nanaimo Airport (☎ 250-245-2157) is 18km south of town on Hwy 1. **Baxter Aviation** (☎ 250-754-1066) and **Harbour Air** (☎ 250-714-0900) fly to Vancouver ($54, 20 minutes, hourly) and other regional destinations. **Canadian Western Airlines** (☎ 866-835-9292) and Air Canada offer scheduled flights to/from Vancouver ($155, 15 minutes). Nanaimo also has a seaplane terminal right on the harbor.

BOAT

Nanaimo is linked via two BC Ferries (p696) terminals (Duke Point and Departure Bay) with Horseshoe Bay and Tsawwassen on the mainland.

BUS

Vancouver Island Coach Lines (☎ 250-475-3339, 800-318-0818; 1 N Terminal Ave; www.grayline.ca/victoria) connects south to Victoria and north to Port Hardy.

BRITISH COLUMBIA

TRAIN

VIA Rail (☎ 250-842-7245; www.viarail.ca) operates the *Malahat*, with daily links to Courtenay ($16, two hours) and Victoria ($16, 2½ hours). Tickets can be purchased from the conductor.

Getting Around

Downtown is easily accessed on foot, but after that the city spreads out and your own vehicle or strong cycling legs will make things easier.

BC Transit (☎ 250-390-4531; one-way trip/day pass $1.75/4.50) buses stop along Gordon St, west of Harbour Park Mall. No 2 goes to the Departure Bay ferry terminal; no city buses run to Duke Point. Pick up a transit guide at the VIC.

Nanaimo Seaporter (☎ 250-753-2118; Departure Bay/Duke Point $6/14) provides door-to-door bus services between downtown and the BC Ferries terminals. For a cab, call **AC Taxi** (☎ 250-753-1231; to Departure Bay/Duke Point $9/25).

Chain Reaction (☎ 250-754-3309; 12 Lois Lane), down the steps between Victoria Cres and the Harbour Park Mall, rents bicycles (from $20 per day) and offers good information on local cycling. The two hostels (see p712) also rent out bikes.

PORT ALBERNI

Just outside Parksville, Hwy 4 splits off from Hwy 19 and heads west towards the natural wonders of the Pacific coast. Halfway across the island, at the head of Alberni Inlet, a 35km-long fjord, is the old-fashioned and scenic town of Port Alberni.

Built on the declining industries of forestry and fishing, the town is now re-inventing itself to attract tourists, heavily promoting its local provincial parks, salmon fishing and tours of the inlet. The revitalized waterfront offers a nice mix of working docks and tourist development, and there's enough to keep you occupied for an overnight stay if you fancy.

Information

On the highway, the **Alberni Valley VIC** (☎ 250-724-6535; www.avcoc.com; 2533 Redford St; ☉ 8am-6pm) is a great facility with helpful information on the area. There are plenty of banks along Johnson St (the main highway as it heads through town). There's Internet access at the **Web Grind Café** (☎ 250-720-0358; 3131 3rd Ave;

per hr $4; ☉ 7am-5pm), a welcoming little neighborhood coffee shop. For medical help, go to **West Coast General Hospital** (☎ 250-723-2135; 3841 8th Ave).

Sights & Activities

Just east of town, must-see **Cathedral Grove** is the highlight of **MacMillan Provincial Park** (☎ 250-248-9460; wlapwww.gov.bc.ca/bcparks). This delicate, ancient ecosystem, unsurprisingly regarded by local First Nations people as a sacred place, is a tract of virgin forest featuring towering Douglas firs and red cedars, some more than 800 years old. It's a popular spot, and the roadside parking can be horrendous.

Tour boats leave from **Harbour Quay**, at the foot of Argyle St, a tourist area with shops, restaurants, an observation-clock tower and a farmers' market on Saturday year-round. On the quay's southern side (look for the red-and-white lighthouse) is the **Maritime Discovery Centre** (☎ 250-723-6164; Industrial Rd; adult/child $5/3; ☉ 10am-5pm mid-Jun–Sep), which exhibits maritime history.

Other minor heritage attractions include a local **museum**, a **steam train** and an historic steam-powered **mill**; ask at the VIC for details.

There are also a couple of good regional parks around Port Alberni with nice campgrounds that can be reserved. **Stamp River Provincial Park** (☎ 250-248-9460; wlapwww.gov.bc .ca/bcparks; Beaver Creek Rd), 15km northwest of town, has a large fish ladder, where you can watch salmon thrash at your feet between August and December. **Sproat Lake Provincial Park** (☎ 250-248-9460; wlapwww.gov.bc.ca/bcparks; Hwy 4), 13km west of town on the north shore of massive Sproat Lake, attracts plenty of water enthusiasts, and also features some prehistoric petroglyphs.

Tours

Lady Rose Marine Services (☎ 250-723-8313, 800-663-7192; www.ladyrosemarine.com; 5425 Argyle St) offers day trips down Alberni Inlet to the west coast. This trip is an enjoyable, scenic way to spend a day, as well as a practical means of returning from the northern end of the West Coast Trail (p717) or a kayaking trip in the Broken Group Islands (p716).

Passengers ride on the 100-passenger MV *Lady Rose* (1937) or the 200-passenger

MV *Frances Barkley* (1958), both historic working freighters that stop en route to deliver mail and supplies. Boats head to Bamfield ($25, departures at 8am Tuesday, Thursday and Saturday year-round, also Sunday July to September) and Ucluelet ($28, departures at 8am Monday, Wednesday and Friday, June to October). Most services between October and May will stop on request at the Broken Group Islands to pick up or drop off kayakers.

Sleeping

Esta Villa Motel (☎ 250-724-1261, 800-724-0844; www .alberni.net/estavilla; 4014 Johnston Rd; s/d from $75/90) It's not much to look at from outside, but the refurbished rooms, large TVs and competitive rates make Esta Villa the standout among the clutch of motels lining the route into town. The woods out the back are good for the kids to run off their energy, too.

Cedar Wood Lodge (☎ 250-724-6800, 877-314-6800; www.cedarwood.bc.ca; 5895 River Rd; s/d incl breakfast $125/135) You immediately feel relaxed upon entering this B&B, nestled under the canopy of trees in a garden by the Somass River. The colors are soft, the furnishings are comfortable and the breakfasts are delicious.

Somass Motel (☎ 250-724-3236, 800-927-2217; www.somass-motel.ca; 5279 River Rd; d with/without kitchenette $90/75, ste $115; 🖴 🐾) The rooms are nice, bright and comforting in this little motel across from the inlet. It also has a private garden to enjoy, if the sun's shining. The two-bedroom suites are great value for small groups.

Tsunami Backpacker Guesthouse (☎ 250-724-9936; tsunamiguesthouse@shaw.ca; 5779 River Rd; dm $17) This large converted family home is a little ramshackle, and the decor doesn't seem to have changed much since the 1970s, but the common areas are generous, and there's a full kitchen and a pool table to keep you occupied on a cold winter's night.

Arrowvale Campground (☎ 250-723-7948; www .arrowvalecottages.com; 5955 Hector Rd; tent sites $17, cottages $150) Situated on the Somass River, 6km west of Port Alberni, the Arrowvale has showers and a laundry, as well as swimming, a playground and farm tours. The two deluxe river-view cottages feature vaulted wooden timber-trussed ceilings, fireplaces and full kitchens.

DOING DELLA FALLS

At 440m, Della Falls is the highest in Canada, and getting there can be a tall task in itself. Though set deep within Strathcona Provincial Park (p725), the 'easiest' way to reach Della is from Port Alberni. Take Hwy 4 and drive 13km west of town to Great Central Lake Rd. You'll then need to cross the Great Central Lake. It's a 35km trip and will take from seven to 12 hours in a canoe, although **Ark Resort** (☎ 250-723-2657; www.arkresort.com; 11000 Great Central Lake Rd, Port Alberni; campsites $23, r $70) offers a water-taxi service ($95) to the trailhead. Once there, it's a 16km, five- to eight-hour, 510m-elevation-gain scramble through the woods and up steep slopes to the falls. Set aside a minimum of two days for the trip (four for canoeists), but once you're there, prepare to be amazed. Backcountry camping (campsites $5) is permitted at a designated place on the trail.

You can also camp at **Stamp River Provincial Park** (tent sites $14) and **Sproat Lake Provincial Park** (tent sites $17-20); see p714 for details.

Eating

Clam Bucket (☎ 250-723-1315; 4479 Victoria Quay; mains $8-18; 😋 lunch & dinner) Known more for its seafood, the Clam Bucket also makes huge sandwiches and gourmet burgers. Funky oranges and blues provide a casual atmosphere indoors, or you can eat on the patio with a view of the inlet. It fills up quickly at both lunch and dinnertime.

H_2O-4 (☎ 250-723-4274; 3044 4th Ave; meals $4-16; 😋 breakfast, lunch & dinner) This buzzing local diner serves up the usual enormous portions to hungry locals and has regular specials like all-you-can-eat ribs for $10.

Blue Door Café (☎ 250-723-8811; 5415 Argyle St; mains $3-8; 😋 breakfast & lunch) This hole-in-the-wall café opens at 5am and draws an early-morning crowd of fisherfolk. It's a handy spot to grab breakfast before boarding the *Lady Rose*.

Getting There & Away

Vancouver Island Coach Lines (☎ 250-388-0818; www .grayline.ca/victoria) runs a daily bus from Victoria to Port Alberni ($34, 2½ hours) and on to Ucluelet and Tofino ($51, 2½ hours).

PACIFIC RIM NATIONAL PARK RESERVE

With extensive fir and cedar forests, rocky islets, wild weather, crashing waves, abundant wildlife and long remote beaches, it's little wonder that Pacific Rim National Park Reserve has become one of BC's top attractions. Divided into three sections, this 50,000-hectare park stretches from Tofino in the north down to Port Renfrew in the south, and takes in both land and marine environments.

The first of the three 'units,' **Long Beach**, hugs the coastline between Ucluelet and Tofino, and is the park's most-visited and most-accessible section. The other units are the **Broken Group Islands**, offshore from Ucluelet, and the famous **West Coast Trail**, further south between Bamfield and Port Renfrew.

For casual visits to Long Beach, stop in at the **Park Information Centre** (☎ 250-726-4212; www.parkscanada.pch.gc.ca; Hwy 4; ⏰ 10am-5pm mid-Mar–mid-Oct), just inside the southern boundary of the Long Beach Unit. For trips to the Broken Group Islands or the West Coast Trail, do your research ahead of time and get detailed information from **Parks Canada** (☎ 250-726-7721; www.parkscanada.pch.gc.ca).

Long Beach Unit

Easily accessed by Hwy 4, the Long Beach Unit attracts the largest number of visitors in the park, and features some beautiful beaches, great swimming and superb short walks that showcase the park's biodiversity.

A good way to start is to check out the interpretive exhibits on the park's cultural and natural history at **Wickaninnish Centre** (Wick Rd; ⏰ 9am-6pm mid-Mar–mid-Oct), named for a chief of the Nuu-chah-nulth tribe, which has lived in the Long Beach area for centuries. Then hit the walking trails. The following are three of the best:

Nuu-chah-nulth Trail (5km round-trip) A beautiful shoreline and forest trail from Wickaninnish Beach to Florencia Bay. It features interpretive signs that reflect the knowledge and culture of this First Nations tribe.

Rainforest Trail (1km) Actually two interpretive loops, which take you through magnificent old-growth forest dominated by western red cedar and hemlock, and provide excellent information about the flora and fauna around you.

Shorepine Bog Trail (800m round-trip) A completely different experience, this trail takes you through a low-lying area of 2m-deep sphagnum moss supporting a stunted shorepine forest, sedges and carnivorous sundew plants. This ancient and fragile area has little permanent wildlife, but bear, cougar, deer and boar use it as a corridor to feeding areas.

There are other walking trails at Long Beach Unit:

Long Beach Easy walking at low tide.

Radar Hill A 100m climb to a former WWII installation.

Schooner Cove A 2km walk through second-growth forests to the beach.

South Beach A 1km walk through forest to a pebble beach.

Spruce Fringe A 1.5km loop trail featuring hardy Sitka spruce trees.

The safest place to **swim** is the northern end of Long Beach, where surf guards patrol the beach during July and August.

SLEEPING & EATING

Green Point Campground (☎ 250-689-9025; tent/RV sites $14/20) On Hwy 4, this is the only park-run campground. The 94 RV sites can be reserved three months ahead; it's first come, first served for the 20 tent sites.

Also within the park is the privately run **Long Beach Golf Course Campground** (☎ 250-725-3314; www.longbeachgolfcourse.com; tent & RV sites $25), near Grice Bay and with a heavily wooded camping area.

Wickaninnish Restaurant (☎ 250-726-7706; Wickaninnish Centre; mains $10-15; ⏰ lunch & dinner Mar-Oct) Not to be confused with Tofino's upmarket Wickaninnish Inn, this lauded restaurant offers a fine changing menu of Pacific Northwest cuisine, which you can enjoy while the surf crashes onto Long Beach below you.

GETTING THERE & AWAY

Long Beach Link (☎ 250-726-7779, 877-954-3556; one way/round-trip $9/12) shuttles passengers between Tofino and Ucluelet (one hour) several times a day, with stops at the Tofino Airport and within Pacific Rim National Park (Long Beach, Green Point and Wickaninnish Centre).

Broken Group Islands Unit

Broken Group is a fascinating collection of about 100 rugged forested islets and rocky outcrops scattered about the entrance to Barkley Sound, just south of Ucluelet. A part of traditional Nuu-chah-nulth territories, the islands' sheltered bays provide protection for sea otter, sea lions, killer whales and migratory gray whales; whale-watching cruises (p721) and sea kayaking are the main activities here, although bird-watchers will be in heaven too.

If you fancy a paddle, the distances and conditions involved are such that, unless you're really experienced, you should sign on with a guided trip. Several operators head out there:

Majestic Ocean Kayaking (☎ 250-726-2868; www .oceankayaking.com; 1167 Helen Rd, Ucluelet; 4-day trip $800)

Wildheart Adventures (☎ 250-722-3683, 877-722-3683; www.kayakbc.com; 4-day trip $675)

SLEEPING

A water-taxi service, **Lady Rose Marine Services** (☎ 250-723-8313, 800-663-7192; www.ladyrosemarine .com; Sechart; s/d $110/150) has a base in the archipelago, and you can stay in one of its historic rooms. They also hire kayaks (single/double per day $40/55).

Designated **campgrounds** (tent sites $8) are located on eight islands: Hand, Turret, Gibraltar, Willis, Dodd, Clarks, Benson and Gilbert. They're very basic and you'll need to be completely self-sufficient. The maximum stay in Broken Group is 14 nights, with no more than four nights at the same site.

There's a BC Forest Service campground at Toquart Bay, the principal launching spot.

GETTING THERE & AROUND

Toquart Bay is accessed via 16km of gravel logging road off Hwy 4, 12km northeast of the Pacific Rim Hwy junction.

Lady Rose Marine Services (☎ 250-723-8313, 800-663-7192; www.ladyrosemarine.com; 5425 Argyle St, Port Alberni; per person $30-45) runs a water taxi from Toquart Bay and Sechart (an old whaling station) to several of the Broken Group Islands. They also run regular services inland to Port Alberni (see p714).

Parking fees ($10 per car per day, annual pass $45) apply within the unit, and can be purchased from machines at each of the trailheads. Note that you don't need to pay if you're simply driving through to Tofino.

West Coast Trail Unit

The third and most southerly section of the park contains the 75km **West Coast Trail** (WCT), one of North America's best-known and toughest hiking routes. There are two things you need to know before you think about attempting this hike: it's one of the most demanding experiences you'll ever endure; and doing it once probably won't be enough. This magnificent region never puts on the same show twice, and people return time after time to pit their strength and skills against its challenges.

Originally constructed as an escape route for shipwreck survivors, following a century of horrific maritime accidents, the trail is open from May 1 to September 30 only, and takes between five and seven days to hike. It runs between the WCT Information Centres at **Pachena Bay** (☎ 250-728-3234), near Bamfield on the northern end, and **Gordon River** (☎ 250-647-5434), near Port Renfrew on the southern end.

The trail itself is simply breathtaking, passing through virgin spruce, cedar and hemlock forests; across cliff tops and over suspension bridges; along stretches of deserted beaches punctuated by clear tidal pools; and up and down steep gullies and waterways. And every kilometer must be earned. Toting a heavy pack, you'll climb hundreds of rocky steps, cross streams on slippery logs, scale cliffs on rock-face ladders, plough through knee-deep mud, and pick your way along narrow and treacherous pathways. Heavy fog and torrential rain are de rigueur (as are chance encounters with bear and even cougars), and you'll need to be able to read and use topographical maps and tide charts.

Needless to say, this is one for experienced hikers only. Camping is at designated backcountry sites along the route, most of which have solar-composting toilets, but otherwise you'll need to be completely self-sufficient. Apart from good boots, a tent, a stove, sleeping gear, waterproofs, fuel and food, you'll need a comprehensive first-aid kit, and someone in your party who knows how to use it. Accidents are common, and help can be literally days away. You'll also need to either boil or purify all your drinking water.

All of that aside, the payoffs of this magnificent region are so great that more than 8000 people each year attempt the trail – so many, in fact, that a permit system is in place to limit the number of hikers on the trail. You'll cough up $90 for an overnight trail permit, plus another $28 for the two ferries along the trail. The permits limit the number of hikers starting the trail to 52 per day (26 in each direction, with a maximum group size of 10), and you can either reserve your spot or simply turn up and register for one of the daily standby spaces. Reservations are only taken (and needed) in July and August, and are made through **Super Natural British Columbia Reservation Service** (☎ 250-435-5622, 800-435-5622; www.snbc-res.com; reservation fee $25) from the first day of the month, two months prior to your desired departure date. If you're going to arrive at your trailhead later than 1pm on your day of departure, call ahead or your place will go to the standby list. Ten standby spaces are allocated at 1pm each day on a first-come, first-served basis. You may have to wait a couple of days in summer, so register at either of the WCT Information Centres upon arrival.

All overnight hikers must attend a one-hour **orientation session** (☉ 9:30am, 1:30pm & 3:30pm, also noon at Gordon River) at one of the WCT Information Centres before hiking. While you're there, pick up two essential documents: *The West Coast Trail Map* and *Canadian Tide and Current Tables 2003 (Vol 6 Tofino)*.

It is possible to do a day hike from either trailhead, although Pachena Bay is considered the easier end of the route. You'll need to get a day-use permit (free) from a WCT Information Centre before you head out.

GETTING THERE & AWAY
West Coast Trail Express (☎ 250-477-8700; www.trailbus.com; shuttle $35-55; ☉ 6:40am-4:30pm) can take you to either trailhead from Victoria, Nanaimo or Port Alberni.

TOFINO
At the northern terminus of Hwy 4, 122km west of Port Alberni, Tofino is definitely not a dead-end town. Activity-packed and ecologically friendly, its setting on Clayoquot Sound (a Unesco world-biosphere reserve) is both serene and spectacular, and the surrounding waters are dotted with gorgeous islands and flanked by crescent beaches. An increasingly fashionable and expensive place to visit, it boasts some first-class accommodations and terrific restaurants, plus the healing waters of Hot Springs Cove. Wildlife-watching is another draw card, with gray whales, orcas (killer whales), sea lions and sea otter all found in the surrounding waters, and the forests,

islands and beaches are rich with endemic and migratory birdlife.

Information
The **VIC** (☎ 250-725-3414; www.island.net/~tofino; 1426 Pacific Rim Hwy; ☉ 10am-6pm May-Sep) is 6km south of town and has detailed listings and photos of area accommodations, although finding last-minute places can be difficult. Pick up a copy of the local newspaper, *Tofino Time*, and the helpful *Long Beach Maps* brochure, or buy the encyclopedic *Tofino Insider's Guide* ($6), if you're going to hang around for a while.

The main **post office** (☎ 250-267-1177; 161 First St) is half a block north of the **Tofino Hospital** (☎ 250-725-3204; 261 Neill St).

Sights
A lot of Tofino's sights are north of Tofino, in Clayoquot Sound; see p719 for details on how to reach them.

HOT SPRINGS COVE
One of the more sought-out day-trip destinations, Hot Springs Cove is the central attraction of **Maquinna Provincial Marine Park** (☎ 250-248-9460; wlapwww.gov.bc.ca/bcparks), 37km north of Tofino. Sojourners travel by Zodiac boat or seaplane, watching for whales and other sea critters en route. From the boat landing, 2km of boardwalks lead to a series of natural hot pools that rejuvenate the soul.

MEARES ISLAND
Visible from Tofino, **Meares Island** is home to the Big Tree Trail, a 400m-boardwalk through old-growth forest, including a 1500-year-old red cedar. The island was the site of the key 1984 anti-logging protest that kicked off the modern environmental movement in Clayoquot Sound. **Tom's Water Taxi** (☎ 250-725-3747; per person $20) can take you there.

AHOUSAT
Located on remote Flores Island, **Ahousat** is home to a Nuu-chah-nulth community and the spectacular Wild Side Heritage Trail (see p719), a moderately difficult path that traverses 10km of forests, beaches and headlands between Ahousat and Cow Bay.

TOFINO BOTANICAL GARDENS
Cleverly and artistically laid out – even borderline abstract – these **gardens** (☎ 250-

725-1237; www.tofinobotanicalgardens.com; 1084 Pacific Rim Hwy; adult/child $10/2, without vehicle $9/1; 8am-dusk) display the unique plants of Clayoquot Sound and other rain forests from around the world. Kids will enjoy the playground, and grown-ups will enjoy the tree house and several themed gardens and bird-watching blinds. Admission is valid for three consecutive days.

Activities

KAYAKING

The island system means that the kayaking around Tofino is superb, and several companies can take you onto the water:

Rainforest Kayak Adventures (250-725-3117, 877-422-9453; www.rainforestkayak.com; 316 Main St; tours from $460) Specializes in four- to six-day guided tours and courses for beginners and intermediates.

Tla-ook (250-725-2656, 877-942-2663; www.tlaook.com; 2/4/6hr tours $45/60/140) Learn about First Nations culture while paddling an authentic dugout canoe.

Tofino Sea Kayaking Co (250-725-4222; www.tofino-kayaking.com; 320 Main St; day tours $55-100) Paddles to Meares Island, runs multiday tours, and offers rentals (half-/full-day $35/50).

SURFING

With nothing between Japan and Vancouver Island's west coast to slow the waves down, the sandy beaches south of Tofino make excellent surfing spots, and there are plenty of shops that hire out gear:

Live to Surf (250-725-4464; www.livetosurf.com; 1180 Pacific Rim Hwy; board/wetsuit $25/20) Tofino's first surf shop, its website has good info on the local conditions.

Surf Sister (250-725-4456, 877-724-7873; www.surfsister.com; 1180 Pacific Rim Hwy) All-female surf school offers daily lessons ($75) to boys and girls, but no dudes are allowed in multiday courses (from $195).

WHALE-WATCHING

You might spot a whale on any trip to Hot Springs Cove or Flores Island, but there are trips devoted solely to whale-watching. Gray whales migrate through the area from March to May, though many linger through summer.

Remote Passages (250-725-3330, 800-666-9833; 71 Wharf St; www.remotepassages.com; adult/child $65/50) Also offers tours to Hot Springs.

Whale Centre (250-725-2132, 800-474-2288; www.island.net/~whales; 411 Campbell St; adult/child $60/40, museum free) Its headquarters has a small museum displaying gray-whale skeletal pieces.

You can also go storm-watching, diving, sailing, fishing, horse riding, mountain biking or bird-watching; ask at the VIC for recommendations.

Tours

Tofino teems with tours and operators. Here's a selection:

Just Birding (250-725-8018; www.justbirding.com; half-/full-day $75/160) Specialist tours (eg pelagic, seabird, shorebird) offered by a passionate ornithologist.

Remote Passages (250-725-3330, 800-666-9833; www.remotepassages.com; 71 Wharf St; adult/child $100/70) Seven-hour Hot Springs tours with guides well versed in the natural history of Clayoquot Sound.

Tofino Air Lines (250-725-4454, 866-486-3247; www.tofinoair.ca; 3 people from $385) Scenic tours over beautiful Clayoquot Sound.

Walk the Wild Side (250-670-9586, 888-670-9586; adult/child $75/50) Guided hikes of Ahousat, with the option of hiring a First Nations guide ($45 to $150).

Sleeping

Tofino's ever-increasing popularity means you'll want to book way ahead, especially over summer. Most accommodations offer package deals with area activities, and discount heavily outside of summer.

BUDGET

Whalers on the Point Guesthouse (250-725-3443; www.tofinohostel.com; 81 West St; dm/d/tr/q $26/75/85/115) Purpose-built in 1999, this HI affiliate is the Cadillac of hostels. In a secluded waterfront location, its huge windows offer sweeping water views, and there are airy common rooms, a sauna, surfboard lockers and cable TV.

Hummingbird Hostel (250-670-9679; www.hummingbird-hostel.com; dm $20; Mar-Sep) In a restored 1904 house on the waterfront in Ahousat, Flores Island, the Hummingbird is accessible by water taxi twice a day from Tofino ($15 each way), and the tariff includes the permit to hike the Wild Side Heritage Trail. And yes, you'll see hummingbirds – and possibly a bear or wolf, too.

Bella Pacifica Resort & Campground (250-725-3400; www.bellapacifica.com; 400 Mackenzie Beach Rd; tent & RV sites Jun-Sep $29-41, Feb-May & Oct $20-25) Right on the ocean's edge, this campground has some superb beachfront sites that are well worth booking in advance. The other sites are reasonably spaced and sit in heavily wooded areas, which include some nature trails.

See p716 for information about camping within the Pacific Rim National Park Reserve.

MID-RANGE & TOP END

Paddler's Inn B&B (☎ 250-725-4222; www.tofino-kayaking.com; 320 Main St; s/d $60/70, with ocean view $70/80) This excellent little place has sweet, whitewashed timber rooms in an historic building right on the bay. Run by the Tofino Sea Kayaking Co, the B&B rooms are perched above its shop. Bathrooms are shared, but the tariff includes a continental breakfast.

Middle Beach Lodge (☎ 250-725-2900; www.middlebeach.com; Mackenzie Beach; r/ste/cabins from $115/215/260) On the highway 3km south of Tofino, this contemporary resort sits on 16 magnificent oceanfront hectares. The twin lodges (family and adults only) have a huge range of rooms, make extensive use of recycled timber and have all the luxurious touches you need. Off-season rates are particularly good value.

Inn at Tough City (☎ 250-725-2021; 877-725-2021; www.toughcity.com; 350 Main St; d $130-175) Big beds, soft quilts, antique furniture and a large oceanfront verandah place this two-story timber-and-brick boutique hotel a cut above the average mid-ranger.

Maquinna Lodge (☎ 250-725-3261, 800-665-3199; www.maquinnalodge.com; 120 First St; d with/without view $130/110) An older place just above the docks, Maquinna Lodge offers good bay views; the rooms are large and well equipped, if not especially inspiring. There's a pub downstairs too.

InnChanter (☎ 250-670-1149; www.innchanter.com; d cabins incl breakfast & dinner $200-220) A heritage vessel moored near Hot Springs Cove has been restored and refitted to include luxurious sleeping cabins. It's a short walk to the springs.

There are a couple of other places that are recommended:

Dolphin Motel (☎ 250-725-3377; www.dolphinmotel.ca; 1190 Pacific Rim Hwy; d $85-110) A small and tidy motel about 3km south of town near Chesterman Beach. Off-season rates are very good.

Schooner Motel (☎ 250-725-3478; www.schoonermotel.net; 315-321 Campbell St; d from $120) A better than average motel (with rates to match) overlooking the bay.

Eating

Pointe Restaurant (☎ 250-725-3100; Wickaninnish Inn, 500 Osprey Lane; mains $25-40, prix fixe $70; ☿ lunch & dinner) Wraparound windows in this award-winning cliff-top restaurant provide uninterrupted ocean views, but they won't distract you from the superb west coast and classic European cuisine. The extensive wine list emphasizes BC's best tipples.

So Bo (☎ 250-725-2341; 1180 Pacific Rim Hwy; lunch $4-5; ☿ lunch Wed-Mon) This isn't your typical roach coach. Local chefs Lisa and Aaron prepare and serve gourmet salads, soups and tacos in their construction-site lunch wagon behind Beaches Grocery.

Alley Way Café/Costa Azul (☎ 250-725-3105; Rear 305 Campbell St; mains $8-10; ☿ lunch & dinner) This schizophrenic eatery, tucked behind the intersection of First and Campbell Sts, serves all-day breakfasts, vegetarian and nonvegetarian lunches by day, and Mexican dinners by night. It's a colorful spot in a gardenlike setting with a very, very casual vibe.

Shelter (☎ 250-725-3353; 601 Campbell St; mains $24-28; ☿ dinner) Locals say this new kid on the block has the best seafood in town, and the seasonal menu is dominated by clams, halibut, mussels and Dungeness crab. Low light, flickering flames and timber fittings provide a cozy ambience in the main dining room.

Coffee Pod (☎ 250-725-4246; 151 Fourth St; mains $4-7; ☿ breakfast & lunch) The huge deck outside is always full of locals scoffing good pastries and a small selection of full breakfasts, although the coffee's only fair. Beware the marauding ravens.

For self-catering, **Beaches Grocery** (☎ 250-725-2270; 1184 Pacific Rim Hwy) is a grocer with organic products.

Getting There & Away

Tofino Airport (☎ 250-725-2006) is south of town off the Pacific Rim Hwy. **Canadian Western Airlines** (☎ 866-835-9292) flies to Vancouver year-round, while **Northwest Seaplanes** (☎ 250-690-0086) runs high-season floatplane services between Seattle and Tofino.

Vancouver Island Coach Lines (☎ 250-388-0818; www.grayline.ca/victoria) runs a daily bus to Victoria ($51, five hours) via Port Alberni ($17, 2½ hours), as does **Tofino Bus** (☎ 250-725-2871, 866-986-3466; www.tofinobus.com; 564 Campbell St) during summer.

You can get to the Pacific Rim National Park Reserve (Long Beach, Greenpoint and Wickaninnish Centre) and Ucluelet with **Long Beach Link** (☎ 250-726-7779; one way/round-trip $9/12). It also stops at the airport.

For taxis, call **Tofino Taxi** (☎ 250-725-3333). Water taxis that take you up the sound and to offshore islands can be flagged down at the government dock; there's also a regular sea bus ($12, 40 minutes, 10:30am to 4pm) to Ahousat.

UCLUELET

Ucluelet (yew-*klew*-let, or just plain 'Yewkie') has for a long time stood in the shadow of chic Tofino – much to the locals' quiet annoyance – but it has some real advantages over its sister town. Far less affected than Tofino, it has a greater sense of community, and generally charges less for its food, tours and accommodations. When you add in lower visitor numbers, and the town's proximity to the wild and rugged beauty of the Broken Islands, not to mention the best walking trails in the Long Island Unit, you have an alternative base that's well worth investigating, particularly for adventure travelers and those on a budget.

The **VIC** (☎ 250-726-4641; www.uclueletinfo.com; 100 Main St; ⏰ 9am-5pm) is near the government wharf. There's Internet access (and good coffee) at **Blue Raven Coffee House** (☎ 250-726-7110; 1627 Peninsula Rd; per hr $8; ⏰ breakfast & lunch).

Sights & Activities

The tide pools, seashells and kelp beds make **Big Beach** a great spot to discover and wonder what else is out there. The 8.5km **Wild Pacific Trail** winds through rain forests and along the wild coastline, with views of the Broken Islands and Barkley Sound, or nothing but the Pacific Ocean as far as the eye can see.

Whale-watching tours from Ucluelet have a significant advantage over those from Tofino: the bleak beauty of the Broken Group Islands (p716). Most will take a spin through the archipelago on request, and it's also likely you'll be sharing the boat with fewer people. You might even see bear and sea otter. There's a noted surf school here as well. Check out the following local operators:

Inner Rhythm Surf Camp (☎ 250-726-2211; www .innerrhythm.net; 2490 Pacific Rim Hwy; lessons $80, 2-day camp $350) Learn how to master the Pacific surf.

Jamie's Whaling Station (☎ 250-725-3919, 800-667-9913; www.jamies.com; 606 Campbell St; adult/child $65/50) A good outfit that runs tours from Tofino.

Long Beach Nature Tours (☎ 250-726-7099; www .oceansedge.bc.ca; 855 Barkley Cres; half-day tours for up to five people $180) Guided walks of the area led by the

former chief naturalist of the Pacific Rim National Park Reserve, Bill McIntyre.

Subtidal Adventures (☎ 250-726-7336; www.subtidal adventures.com; 1950 Peninsula Rd adult/child $65/50) Well-regarded outfit that also offers kayaking and tours of the Broken Group.

Sleeping

Surf's Inn (☎ 250 726 4426; www.surfsinn.ca; 1874 Peninsula Rd; dm/d $20/45) This attractive timber home is right on the waterfront. It has a couple of nice bright rooms and owners with a true love of surfing. Beds are limited, so book in advance.

Snug Harbour Inn (☎ 250-726-2686, 888-936-5222; www.awesomeview.com; 460 Marine Dr; d $245-315) This upmarket and romantic waterfront inn perches on a cliff high above the ocean, and the views are indeed spectacular. Each luxurious room has a deck, a hot tub and heated floors in the bathroom.

Thornton Motel (☎ 250-726-7725; www.thornton motel.com; 1861 Peninsula Rd; s with/without kitchenette $105/90, ste $165) The rooms in this nicely turned-out place are spacious and the suites have two bedrooms, which are great for families and small groups. Rates drop markedly out of season.

Ucluelet Hotel (☎ 250-726-4324; www.ucluelet hotel.com; 250 Main St; d with shared bathroom $45-60, d $60-75). Above the pub, the rooms here are very basic and most share facilities. In those that don't, the bathrooms, rather bizarrely, have baths rather than showers. Still, the rooms are the cheapest in town. Bands play on weekends in the pub, which may disturb your rest.

Ucluelet Campground (☎ 250-726-4355; www .uclueletcampground.com; 260 Seaplane Base Rd; tent/RV sites $27/32) A very basic place with hot showers and flush toilets.

Eating

Blueberries Café (☎ 250-726-7707; 1627 Peninsula Rd; mains $11-20; ⏰ breakfast, lunch & dinner) A great little outdoor deck overlooks the harbor at this café-cum-restaurant. The menu ranges from soups and light lunches to seafood and steak dishes. The breakfasts get good reports too.

Matterson Restaurant (☎ 250-726-6600; 1682 Peninsula Rd; mains $15-28; ⏰ breakfast, lunch & dinner) This cute little 1931 farmhouse-turned-restaurant has a tidy little dining room, where good steak and seafood mains are supported by excellent desserts. In nice weather, you can hang out on the porch.

Gray Whale Ice Cream & Delicatessen (☎ 250-726-2113; 1950 Peninsula Rd; mains $5-8; ☺ breakfast & lunch) Sandwiches, salads, pastries and everything you'd expect from a deli is here. They also do a fishermen's picnic, available for pick-up as early as 5:30am.

Getting There & Away
Vancouver Island Coach Lines (☎ 250-388-0818; www .grayline.ca/victoria) runs a daily bus to Victoria ($51, five hours) via Port Alberni ($17, 1½ hours).

PARKSVILLE TO CAMPBELL RIVER
Back on the island's east coast, this 117km stretch takes you past the towns of Parksville, Qualicum Beach, Comox and Courtenay, which have some decent beaches and are surrounded by several small provincial parks.

You can easily bypass these towns if you're in a hurry, but there are some other good attractions in the area: two pleasant islands to visit and Vancouver Island's premier ski resort. The Comox Valley's **VIC** (☎ 250-334-3234, 888-357-4471; www.comox-valley -tourism.ca; 2040 Cliffe Ave; ☺ 9am-6pm) can fill you in on other regional attractions.

Comox is also the departure point for ferries to Powell River (see p697) on the mainland.

Denman & Hornby Islands
Part of the Northern Gulf Islands, both Denman and Hornby are pretty chilled sorts of places that don't attract the same hordes of visitors as islands further south. Outdoor activities are the go here, with some lovely provincial parks and good swimming spots, so if that's your scene, consider an overnight stop. Both islands publish annual map brochures, available at VICs or on the ferry. Visit www.denmanisland.com and www .hornbyisland.com for more details.

SIGHTS & ACTIVITIES
Denman has three provincial parks: **Fillongley**, with easy hiking and beachcombing; **Boyle Point**, with a beautiful walk to the lighthouse; and **Sandy Island**, only accessible by water from Denman's northern tip.

Of Hornby's provincial parks, **Tribune Bay** features a long sandy beach with safe swimming, while **Helliwell** offers notable hiking.

Ford's Cove, on Hornby's south coast, offers the chance for divers to swim with six-gill sharks.

For kayak rentals, contact **Denman Hornby Canoes & Kayaks** (☎ 250-335-0079; rentals per hr from $12). **Hornby Ocean Kayaks** (☎ 250-335-2726; hikayak@telus.net; rentals per 3hr $35) will come to where you are.

SLEEPING
Ships Point Inn (☎ 250-335-1004, 877-742-1004; www .shipspointinn.com; 7584 Ships Point Rd, Fanny Bay, Denman Island; tw $155, d $135-185 both incl breakfast) This seaside home occupies a happy place between forest and ocean. However the beauty doesn't stop there; the rooms and common areas are colorfully and tastefully decorated.

Denman Island Guest House (☎ 250-335-2688; www.earthclubfactory.com/guesthouse; 3806 Denman Rd, Denman Island; dm/s/d $20/40/50) Up the hill, and on the left from the ferry landing, you'll find this 1912 farmhouse, a combination hostel-B&B. You can rent bikes, including one with a trailer to put kids in.

Sea Breeze Lodge (☎ 250-335-2321; www.sea breezelodge.com; Tralee Point, Hornby Island; adult/child $180/65) This 12-acre resort features cottages overlooking the ocean. It's got the feel of a Spanish villa with a Pacific Rim twist, and few things are more peaceful than sitting on the patio or in the hot tub with the sea breeze in your face.

You can camp by the beach on Denman Island at **Fillongley Provincial Park** (☎ 250-689-9025; wlapwww.gov.bc.ca/bcparks; campsites $17). On the east side of Hornby Island is **Tribune Bay Campsite** (☎ 250-2359; www.tribunebay.com; 5200 Shields St, Ford's Cove; tent & RV sites $25; ☺ May-Sep).

EATING
Denman Island Bakery & Pizza (☎ 250-335-1310; Northwest Rd, Denman Island; mains $7-11; ☺ breakfast, lunch & dinner, closed Sun) This little café in the village is the local hangout. Talk to some of the local artists over a cuppa and a muffin, or try one of the excellent slices of pizza.

Wheelhouse Restaurant (☎ 250-335-0136; Hornby Island; mains $6-12; ☺ dinner) Near the ferry landing, this place has its boardwalk patio on ground level, among gardens and hanging baskets, with no need for annoying railings to get in the way of the incredible view. Summer evenings feature a BBQ buffet and the ambience is supercasual.

GETTING THERE & AWAY

Between 7am and 11pm **BC Ferries** (☎ 250-223-3779; www.bcferries.com; adult/child $6/3, car $13) makes 17 daily sailings from Buckley Bay terminal, 75km north of Nanaimo, to Denman (10 minutes). It makes 12 trips daily from the other side of Denman to Hornby (10 minutes, 7:45am to 6:35pm Sunday to Thursday and Saturday, 7:45am to 10:35pm Friday).

Mount Washington Alpine Resort

Vancouver Island's best and most popular ski resort, **Mount Washington Alpine Resort** (☎ 250-338-1386, 888-231-1499; www.mtwashington.ca; adult/child lift ticket $50/25, in summer $19/16) features 50 alpine ski runs, a snowboard park, cross-country and snowshoe trails and a snow-tubing park ($16). Mt Washington stays open year-round, and summer activities include horseback riding, fly-fishing, hiking and mountain biking. Even if you're not up for an adrenaline rush, the views of the Gulf Islands from the resort are amazing.

Lodgings, restaurants and cafés are open year-round on the mountain. The resort is 25km northwest of Courtenay, off Hwy 19. The road is extremely steep and chains are required during ski season. It's also the access road for the Forbidden Plateau section of Strathcona Provincial Park (p725).

CAMPBELL RIVER

The appealing town of Campbell River is the self-proclaimed 'Salmon Capital of the World.' Sportfishing is king here, along with scuba diving, and the town is also the main departure point for the vast wilderness of Strathcona Provincial Park and the nearby Quadra and Cortes Islands, which both make great day trips.

Information

For local information, stop at the **VIC** (☎ 250-287-4636; www.campbellrivertourism.bc.ca; 1235 Shoppers Row; ☟ 9am-7pm). You can access the Internet at **Bee Hive Café** (☎ 250-286-6812; 921 Island Hwy) or the **library** (☎ 250-287-3655; 1240 Shoppers Row; per 30min $1; ☟ 10am-8pm Mon-Fri, 10am-5pm Sat).

Sights

The excellent **Museum at Campbell River** (☎ 250-287-3103; www.crmuseum.ca; 470 Island Hwy; adult/student & senior $5/3.75; ☟ 10am-5pm Mon-Sat, noon-5pm Sun mid-May–Sep, noon-5pm Tue-Sun rest of year) examines the town's triple historical pillars of First Nations heritage, logging and fishing. The First Nations story chamber presents an absorbing local legend, while the trials and tribulations of settlers and their families are brought to life in photographs, models and personal anecdotes. Check out the short film on the 1958 Ripple Rock explosion that tore apart this submerged mountain in the Seymour Narrows, which had wrecked more than 100 ships. A lookout on Hwy 19 shows what's left of it.

Activities

Most visitors come here to fish for one or more of five salmon species – coho, Chinook, sockeye, humpback (or pink) and chum. You can either wet a line right off the downtown Discovery Pier or contact the VIC, which has a list of deep-sea outfitters and can match something to your requirements. For a different perspective, **Paradise Found Adventure Tours** (☎ 250-923-0848, 800-897-2872; www.paradisefound.bc.ca; tours $95; ☟ Jul-Oct) leads snorkeling trips to see migrating salmon in the shallow pools and slow-running waters of the Campbell River.

The artificial reef provided by HMCS *Columbia*, sunk near Campbell River, is a major draw for scuba diving, along with the reefs and walls around Quadra Island. **DynaMike Dive Charters** (☎ 250-285-2891; www.divedynamike .com; per day from $150) can take you to the plum spots, while **Beaver Aquatics Limited** (☎ 250-287-7652; www.connected.bc.ca/~baquatics; 760 Island Hwy; lessons from $200; ☟ 9:30am-5pm Mon-Sat) offers information, gear and lessons.

Other outfitters can take you whale-watching, sea kayaking, white-water rafting and wilderness camping; ask at the VIC for recommendations.

There are also good walking trails within **Beaver Lodge Forest Lands** and **Elk Falls Provincial Park**, which abut the western and northern fringe of town respectively.

Sleeping

Highway 19's southern entrance to town is lined with motels that have views of the Strait of Georgia, and they all get booked up in summer (prices drop out of season). There's no hostel, but the camping is good in surrounding provincial parks.

Hotel Bachmair (☎ 250-923-2848, 888-923-2849; www.hotelbachmair.com; 492 Sth Island Hwy; s/d/ste from $90/100/110) Beautifully appointed rooms and suites in this boutique hotel include comfy couches, crisp linen, deep baths, artworks and fully equipped kitchens. The penthouse suite is the size of a small house and has an enormous outside area to cavort in. Out of season, rates drop substantially, placing a touch of luxury within the means of mid-range travelers.

Above Tide Motel (☎ 250-286-6231; fax 250-286-0290; 361 Sth Island Hwy; d $65-85) All rooms here front the Strait of Georgia, with those in the upper stories featuring narrow balconies, which are perfect for a tranquil evening drink while watching the passing parade of boats and ships. Prices are also the most competitive, making it the pick of the crop south of town.

Rustic Motel (☎ 250-286-6295, 800-567-2007; www.rusticmotel.com; 2140 Nth Island Hwy; s/d $90/110) North of downtown, on the main highway, this place boasts spacious, if standard, rooms and sits quietly in the trees by the Campbell River. Some rooms include microwaves and drip-filter coffee machines.

Camping is available at **Elk Falls Provincial Park** (☎ 250-248-9460; wlapwww.gov.bc.ca/bcparks; campsites $14), 10km west of Campbell River on Hwy 28; **Loveland Bay Provincial Park**, 19km northeast at Campbell Lake; and **Morton Lake Provincial Park** (☎ 250-337-8550), 19km north on Hwy 19.

Eating

Bee Hive Café (☎ 250-286-6812; 921 Island Hwy; mains $8-16; ☯ breakfast, lunch & dinner) In business since 1929, this waterfront eatery, in the heart of downtown, has an inviting outside deck overlooking the Strait of Georgia. The Bee Hive is licensed and blends modern food and contemporary decor with historical photos of Campbell River.

Riptide (☎ 250-830-0044; 1340 Island Hwy; mains $10-23; ☯ lunch & dinner) A large and popular local that overlooks the water, Riptide has a standard selection of steak and seafood offerings, plus cheaper pizzas and burgers. There's also a good selection of beer on tap, and fine water views through the large, plate windows.

Dick's Fish & Chips (☎ 250-287-3336; 1003 G Coast Marina; mains $6-10; ☯ lunch & dinner) A fish-and-chips place on the dock can't get away with being a fraud, and Dick's isn't. It also serves burgers and has indoor seating, but you'll want to eat the specialty outside.

Getting There & Around

Campbell River Airport (☎ 250-923-5012) is south of town, off the Pacific Rim Hwy. Pacific Coastal Airlines (p869) provides scheduled air services to/from Vancouver ($95, 20 minutes, nine daily). **Kenmore Air** (☎ 250-543-9595; www.kenmoreair.com) operates floatplanes to/from Seattle (from $185). **Vancouver Island Coach Lines** (☎ 250-388-0818; www.grayline.ca/victoria) runs regular buses up and down the coast.

QUADRA & CORTES ISLANDS

Quadra Island is a quick hop from Campbell River, while Cortes Island is actually closer to the mainland than Vancouver Island, but together they're the biggest of the 'Discovery Islands' and offer some beautiful parks, hiking and sea kayaking.

Information

Visit Quadra's **visitor-information booth** (☎ 250-286-1616; www.quadraisland.ca; Harper Rd; ☯ 9am-4:30pm Jun-Sep), near the shopping center and eastern ferry terminal, and pick up the *Quadra Island* brochure, which details the best of the island's many walking trails. Pick up the *Cortes Island* brochure at the information centers on Quadra Island, or at Port Campbell, before you arrive.

Sights & Activities
QUADRA ISLAND

Beautiful **Rebecca Spit Provincial Park**, on the western coast, has sandy beaches and great swimming. Several outfits can take you sea kayaking around the island's rugged coast, including **Coastal Spirits Sea Kayak Tours** (☎ 250-285-2895; www.kayakbritishcolumbia.com; 1069 Topcliff Rd; day trips $40-60), while **Abyssal Diving Charters & Lodge** (☎ 250-285-2420, 800-499-2297; www.abyssal.com), just up the hill from the Quathiaski Cove ferry dock, is Quadra's source for scuba diving.

The island's other big draw card is the acclaimed **Kwagiulth Museum & Cultural Centre** (☎ 250-285-3733; adult/child $3/1; ☯ 10am-4:30pm Mon-Sat, noon-4:30pm Sun Jun-Sep), at Cape Mudge, which features a fascinating collection of items used in potlatches, along with early photographs of traditional Kwakwaka'wakw villages.

CORTES ISLAND

About an hour's ferry ride east of Quadra Island, quiet Cortes has plenty of deserted beaches and lots of wildlife to check out. **Manson's Landing Provincial Park** boasts abundant shorebirds and shellfish, and **Smelt Bay Provincial Park** is a great place to watch sunsets. Nearby **Mittlenatch Island Nature Park**, called the 'Galapagos of Strait of Georgia' for its natural diversity, can be seen on guided walks led by long-time area guide and ornithologist **George Sirk** (☎ 250-935-6926).

Sleeping & Eating

Tsa-Kwa-Luten Lodge & RV Park (☎ 250-285-2042, 800-665-7745; www.takuresort.com; 1 Lighthouse Rd, Quadra Island; tent & RV sites $25, d from $105) Near the museum is the standout accommodation choice on Quadra Island. A First Nations–owned resort on the island's southern tip, it's superbly set among 1100 acres of lush green forest, with views of Discovery Passage. It also features aboriginal art and architecture, and rents out sea kayaks.

Great places for a beer or meal on Quadra Island, while you wait for your ferry, are **Heriot Bay Inn & Marina** (☎ 250-285-3322; mains $8-14; ⏰ lunch & dinner) and the **Landing Pub** (☎ 250-285-3713; mains $7-15; ☎ lunch & dinner) at the Quathiaski Cove and Heriot Bay ferry ports respectively.

Each of the island brochures (see Information on p724) have lists of other eating and accommodation choices.

Getting There & Around

From 6:15am to 11pm **BC Ferries** (☎ 250-286-1412, 888-223-3779; www.bcferries.com) runs 17 times daily from Quathiaski Cove, on Quadra (adult/child $5.50/3, car/bicycle $13/free), to Campbell River, and five times from Heriot Bay (adult/child $6.50/3.50, car/bicycle $16/free), on the other side of Quadra, to Whaletown on Cortes.

The **Cortes Connection** (☎ 250-935-6911; www.cortesconnection.com; adult/child $14/9, plus ferry fare; ⏰ Mon-Sat summer, Mon-Fri spring & autumn, Mon, Wed & Fri winter) uses the ferries to provide a shuttle-bus service from Campbell River to points on Cortes Island, crossing Quadra on the way. Reservations are advised.

Both Quadra and Cortes are fairly large islands, so it's something of a challenge to get around without a car. Check if your accommodations offer pick-up from the ferry. **Island Cycle** (☎ 250-285-3627; Heriot Bay; per day/week $25/90) has bike rentals.

STRATHCONA PROVINCIAL PARK

By far the largest provincial park on Vancouver Island, 250,000-hectare **Strathcona Provincial Park** (☎ 250-337-2400; wlapwww.gov.bc.ca/bcparks) is BC's oldest protected area, and dominates the centre of the island, peaking at the 2200m Mt Golden Hinde. It includes large tracts of wilderness, but has two main public areas: Buttle Lake, a 35km-long, narrow lake that's accessed by car from Campbell River via Hwy 28; and Forbidden Plateau, reached from Courtenay via the Mt Washington Ski Resort (p722).

Activities

Buttle Lake is hugely popular with the **fishing** crowd, and is best explored by boat (many campgrounds and hikes are accessible by water only), but there are still plenty of good walks with trailheads along Hwy 28 and the Buttle Lake road:

Flower Ridge Trail (Buttle Lake Rd) A steep and challenging 6km round-trip, five-hour hike with great alpine scenery.

Karst Creek (Buttle Lake Rd) A 2km, 45-minute walk winds past sinkholes, disappearing streams and beautiful waterfalls carved from limestone.

Lady Falls (Hwy 28) An easy 900m, 20-minute walk through old-growth stands of hemlock, fir and cedar to a platform where you can view the waterfalls.

The Forbidden Plateau area is best accessed from the parking lot of the Mt Washington cross-country ski zone. There are some notable trails:

Lake Helen Mackenzie A few different walks (8km to 14km, taking three to six hours) depart from this subalpine lake and showcase rolling hills, mountain lakes, pockets of forest and great views.

Paradise Meadows Loop An easy 2.2km, 45-minute walk through subalpine meadows that are carpeted in flowers during spring and early summer.

In the southern part of the park is **Della Falls**, Canada's highest waterfall (440m), but it's better accessed from Port Alberni (p715).

Sleeping & Eating

Strathcona has two campgrounds in the Buttle Lake area.

Buttle Lake Campground (campsites $14) Offers both first-come, first-served and reservable sites. The swimming area and the nearby playground make this a good choice for families. There are also some campsites accessible by water only ($8).

Ralph River Campground (campsites $14) Has first-come, first-served sites. Backcountry sites ($5) are available throughout the park. It's 26km south of the Hwy 28 junction.

Strathcona Park Lodge (☎ 250-286-3122; Hwy 28; www.strathcona.bc.ca; r $120-145, 1-/2-/3-bedroom cabins $170/195/255), on the shores of Upper Campbell Lake, is a private resort and education centre that offers accommodations, meals, tours and activities.

GOLD RIVER

In the centre of the island, 89km west of Campbell River, at the end of Hwy 28, this small town is a relative newcomer to Vancouver Island. Built in the 1960s for workers in the now-defunct pulp mill, it's a gem of a launching spot for sportfishing, a base camp for outdoor activities, and is surrounded by natural beauty – a combination that's bringing in more visitors every year.

Information

The **VIC** (☎ 250-283-2418; ☼ 9am-6pm mid-May–Labour Day) is at the corner of Hwy 28 and Scout Lake Rd.

Sights & Activities

Gold River is one of Canada's caving capitals – ask at the VIC about organized and self-guided caving tours to the 450m of passages and 16 known entrances of **Upana Caves**, northwest of town on the gravel road toward Tahsis.

Fishing in the beautiful Nookta Sound is legendary, and **Nootka Sound Sports Fishing** (☎ 877-283-7194; www.nootkasoundfish.com) is one of the outfits that can take you out for bass, halibut, cod and salmon.

Tours

If you just want to check out the scenery, **Nootka Sound Service** (☎ 250-283-2325; www.mv uchuck.com) uses the *Uchuck III*, a converted WWII minesweeper, to deliver supplies and packages to remote villages and settlements up-island. Year-round, passengers can go on overnight trips up Nootka Sound to Zeballos (single/double/child $185/295/65, departs 9am Monday, returns 4pm Tuesday), or further up the coast through the open waters of the Pacific to Kyuquot (single/double/child/ transportation only $245/385/95/55, departs 7am Thursday, returns 5pm Friday). Overnight accommodations and breakfast are included, and this is a great way to see some otherwise inaccessible territory.

Sleeping & Eating

Ridgeview Motor Inn (☎ 250-283-2277, 800-989-3393; www.ridgeview-inn.com; 395 Donner Court; d from $95) This hotel-lodge, up on the hill, has impressive views of the inlet. It features upmarket rooms and a hospitality room, where guests can do some light cooking. The attached **Ridge Neighborhood Pub** (☎ 250-283-2600; mains $8-14) has better-than-average pub food and excellent seafood.

Manila Grill (☎ 250-283-7779; mains $6-12; ☼ breakfast, lunch & dinner) In all respects this place is a diner, until you look at the menu. Vegetarian dishes and stir-fries are listed right along with traditional breakfasts, sandwiches and burgers.

Camping is available alongside the river at **Lions Club Campground** (per person $10, pay at gate) on the south side of town.

NORTH VANCOUVER ISLAND

North of Campbell River, about 5% of Vancouver Island's population occupies about 40% of its landmass. However that doesn't mean there's nothing here – far from it, in fact. Some of the island's best wildlife-watching can be done around Port McNeill and Telegraph Cove, and there's the remote and spectacularly beautiful Cape Scott Provincial Park to explore. Exploration of a different nature is possible within the First Nations community at Alert Bay.

It's a scenic 238km drive from Campbell River to Port Hardy, which takes you through forests and past lakes and mountains, punctuated by a handful of no-nonsense, no-frills towns filled with independently minded people. Sophisticated it ain't, but it does offer a study in contrasts with the 'pampered southerners,' and a further insight into the character of the whole island.

Telegraph Cove

About 8km south of Port McNeill, a road heads east off Hwy 19 for 10km to this small community, known as one of the best of the west coast's boardwalk villages, where most of the buildings are built over the water on wooden pilings. Formerly a sawmill village, today killer whales are its main attraction, along with sea-kayaking trips up the lovely Knight's Inlet. Johnstone Strait, between Sayward and Alert Bay, is a migration route for hundreds of orcas every year.

Stubbs Island Whale Watching (☎ 250-928-3185/17, 800-665-3066; www.stubbs-island.com; Beaver Cove Rd; adult/child under 13 $70/60; ☺ daily trips Jun-Sep, reduced schedule late May & early Oct) runs three-hour whale-watching tours. Reservations are required. **Discovery Expeditions** (☎ 250-758-2488, 800-567-3611; www.orcaseakayaking.com; from $750) offers four- to six-day sea-kayaking tours in and around Johnstone Strait, with camping or lodge accommodations.

Accommodation and meals are available at **Telegraph Cove Resorts** (☎ 250-928-3105, 800-200-4665; www.telegraphcoveresort.com; tent/RV sites $20/25, d $145, cabins from $150; ☺ May–mid-Oct), which uses historic cabins and an old grand residence to house its guests. Rates almost halve outside of summer. The resort also has a large campground.

Port McNeill

McNeill is a small, straightforward logging town, and the departure point for the engaging town of Alert Bay on Cormorant Island. Whale-watching, diving and fishing also bring visitors in. The **VIC** (☎ 250-956-3131; www.portmcneill.net; 351 Shelley Crest; ☺ 9am-5pm summer, 9am-5pm Sat, Sun & Mon rest of year) can direct you to local tour operators.

The downtown **Haida-Way Motor Inn** (☎ 250-956-3373; www.portmcneillhotels.com; 1817 Campbell Way; s/d/q $85/100/110; ▣) is the biggest place in town. Amenities include a good pub and restaurant.

The town also has a few private campgrounds, B&Bs and modest motels. Reservations are essential in summer.

Alert Bay

On Cormorant Island, the village of Alert Bay (population 580) has an aura that seems mythical, ancient and well used. Alert Bay's First Nations community and traditions are prevalent, and its blend with an old fishing settlement makes the place a fascinating day trip.

INFORMATION

Alert Bay's **VIC** (☎ 250-974-5024; www.alertbay.ca; 116 Fir St; ☺ 9am-4:30pm Mon-Fri) has enthusiastic and knowledgeable staff.

HAVING A WHALE OF A TIME

Using sonar to track the fish, more than a dozen pods of killer whales (each pod containing about 20 members) come to Johnstone Strait in summer to feed on the migrating salmon. Many of the whales swim along one of the beaches in Robson Bight, rubbing their sides and stomachs on the pebbles and rocks that have been smoothed and rounded by the actions of the water. No one knows quite why the killer whales do this, but they obviously get a lot of pleasure from it, and perhaps that's reason enough. After all, who would want to tangle with a pleasure-seeking killer whale?

SIGHTS & ACTIVITIES

The **U'Mista Cultural Centre** (☎ 250-974-5403; www.umista.org; adult/child $5/1; ☺ 9am-5pm Jun-Aug, 9am-5pm Mon-Fri Sep-May) immaculately presents its impressive collection of Kwakwaka'wakw masks and other potlatch items originally confiscated by the federal government in the 1920s. Modern-day totem-pole carvers can usually be seen working out the front. At 53m, the **world's tallest totem pole** is appropriately placed on the front lawn of the enormous **Big House**, which hosts traditional **dances** (☎ 250-974-5403; ☺ 1pm Thu-Sun; admission $15); ask if it's possible to pop your head inside, as the construction is truly impressive.

Amazing tranquility is the difference between other nature walks and a mossy walk through giant cedar trees at **Alert Bay Ecological Park** (also known as Gator Gardens); an excellent interpretive guide is available at the VIC.

Seasmoke Whale Watching (☎ 250-974-5225, 800-668-6722; www.seaorca.com; adult/child $75/60) offers whale-watching aboard its classic yacht – so there are no engines to distract the orcas or you.

GETTING THERE & AWAY

BC Ferries (☎ 250-956-4533, 888-223-3779; www.bcferries.com; adult/child $6.50/3.50, bicycle/car free/$16; ☺ 6:45am-9:25pm) runs services between Port McNeill, Alert Bay and Sointula on nearby Malcolm Island, but check the schedule carefully as sailings generally alternate between the islands.

Port Hardy

'The highway ends and the adventure begins' in this small town at the northern end of Vancouver Island, best known as the gear-up spot for Cape Scott, and the departure point for ferry trips through the famed Inside Passage to Prince Rupert, aboard the *Queen of the North* (see p697).

INFORMATION

VIC (☎ 250-949-7622; www.ph-chamber.bc.ca; 7250 Market St; ☺ 9am-5pm)

SIGHTS & ACTIVITIES

The VIC operates the town's small **museum** (7110 Market St; admission free ☺ 10am-5pm Mon-Sat). The caves under the area around Port Hardy draw international attention among spelunkers. Reappearing rivers, sinkholes and land bridges are examples of what to expect at sites like **Eternal Fountain** and **Disappearing River**. Contact **Vancouver Island Nature Exploration** (☎ 250-902-2662; www.nature-exploration .com; half-/full-day trips from $90/65) or the VIC for details.

The area around Port Hardy has good salmon fishing, kayaking and scuba diving. **North Island Diving & Water Sports** (☎ 250-949-2664; 8665 Hastings St; canoe/kayak rentals per day $40/55) rents and sells equipment and runs courses. You can also rent canoes and kayaks at the end of the jetty.

SLEEPING & EATING

Port Hardy fills up most nights from June through September – particularly on the eve of ferry departures – so book ahead.

Glen Lyon Inn (☎ 250-949-7115, 877-949-7115; www.glenlyoninn.com; 6435 Hardy Bay Rd; s/d/ste from $95/105/120) The best place in town, Glen Lyon's rooms here are decked out with quality fittings and plenty of extras, and the waterfront views from the upper floors are an even bigger bonus. The suites are worth the extra bucks.

Quarterdeck Inn (☎ 250-902-0455; www.quarter deckresort.net; 6555 Hardy Bay Rd; s/d/ste $95/115/125) Right next door to the Glen Lyon, this fine hotel comes a close second, and boasts a hot tub and a fitness center, although its views are not quite as good.

The budget motels in town look like they've been worn out by decades of hard-living loggers, but the best is **North Shore Inn** (☎ 250-949-8500; north_shore_inn@hotmail.com; 7370 Market St; s/d/tw from $70/80/100). The poo-brown carpet is not the best first impression, but there's plenty of elbow room, it's central and the large enclosed balconies overlook the bay. Generous discounts apply in the off-season.

You can camp at **Quatse River Campground** (☎ 250-949-2395; 5050 Hardy Bay Rd; tent/RV sites $14/18).

IV's Quarterdeck Pub (☎ 250-949-6922; Quarterdeck Inn; mains $8-13), at the hotel of the same name, and **High Tide Restaurant** (☎ 250-949-7122; Glen Lyon Inn; mains $6-11) both offer standard fish, steak and chicken menus. Otherwise, there's pizza, Chinese or fish and chips available in the center of town.

GETTING THERE & AROUND

Pacific Coastal Airlines (p869) offers air services to/from Vancouver (from $185).

BC Ferries (p696) has services to Prince Rupert and Bella Coola on the mainland. **North Island Transportation** (☎ 250-949-6300; nit@ island.net; $5.25) runs a shuttle to/from the ferry terminal.

Vancouver Island Coach Lines (☎ 250-388-0818, 800-318-0818; www.grayline.ca/victoria) runs a daily bus to/from Victoria.

Cape Scott Provincial Park

Pristine beaches and challenging hikes await in **Cape Scott Provincial Park** (wlapwww.gov.bc.ca/ bcparks; camping per person $5), 70km west of Port Hardy, over an active logging gravel road. From the trailhead, a well-maintained path leads 2.5km through attractive forest to **San Josef Bay**. This is a lovely and accessible walk that requires no special preparations.

The 24km slog to remote **Cape Scott**, however, is a different kettle of fish. Cape Scott is an old Danish settlement at the park's northwestern tip, and the grueling trail features knee-high mud and is open to unpredictable storms, with strong winds and freezing rain. Wildlife is abundant, including stable populations of bear and cougar. This all adds up to low numbers of hikers, and the chance to experience some of the best backcountry camping on the island. Waking up on the fine, white sand of Nels Bight Beach, and the endless views at Cape Scott, will leave you awestruck, and ease the aches in your muscles. You must be totally self-sufficient, and don't forget to boil all water.

SOUTHERN GULF ISLANDS

While the west coast of Vancouver Island is storm-tossed, wild and rugged, the protected southeast coast creates a tranquil oasis and mild climate that's home to a series of green, forested islands rising from the Strait of Georgia. People on the Southern Gulf Islands are seemingly always on vacation and best characterized as open, artsy and stress-free. The relaxed, unhurried pace is easy to get used to, yet a glut of activities make the islands a popular destination for kayaking, cycling, hiking, scuba diving and gallery hopping.

Even just getting to the Southern Gulf Islands is a treat: you must either take a plane or ride one of the wonderful ferries that ply the waters between the islands. The routes are premier voyages, each through channels and passages that seem impossibly narrow for such large vessels sailing just a stone's throw from forested and rocky shorelines.

Lodging is tight, so reservations are mandatory, especially in peak summer season. There's little budget accommodations to be found at any time, so be prepared to carry your tent and cooking stove if you're on a budget.

Getting There & Around

BC Ferries (☎ 250-386-3431, 888-223-3779; www.bc ferries.com) runs regular services to, from and between the islands.

There's a dizzying range of permutations within the schedules of boats from Vancouver Island to the Southern Gulf Islands of Saturna, Mayne, Galiano, North and South Pender, and Salt Spring. The stops alter depending on the service, but you can connect to any island on any given day, allowing you to island-hop through the region over the course of a few days (see the boxed text on p696 for information about the Summer Sail Pass).

In general terms, each island is serviced by several sailings; just take the time to study the timetables properly and plan your route. This is particularly important if you have a vehicle, as missing the last service could consign you an overnight stay – not so hot on a long weekend when all the accommoda-

tions are booked out – so make reservations if possible. Similarly, Gulf Island commuters make Friday-evening and Sunday-afternoon ferries from Tsawwassen particularly busy.

One thing that is uniform on these routes is the prices (not including taxes): Swartz Bay to Outer Gulf Islands (Galiano, Mayne, Pender and Saturna; adult/child $7/3.50, car/bicycle $24/1.50), Swartz Bay to Salt Spring Island (adult/child $6.50/3.50, car/ bicycle $21/1.50), Tsawwassen to all Gulf Islands (adult/child $10.50/5.50, car/bicycle $38/3.50); interisland fares are adult/child $3.75/1.25, car/bicycle $7.75/1.50.

Bicycle and scooter rental is usually available near the ferry terminals, marinas or main towns. Cycling the quiet island roads is a very popular pastime, but check out a topographic map first. On Salt Spring, for example, the roads are narrow, winding and sometimes almost impossibly steep!

SALT SPRING ISLAND

Salt Spring Island is the largest and most-populous island in the Southern Gulf Islands. It has about 12,000 permanent residents and about three times that number of people in summer. Originally settled by the Salish First Nation over a thousand years ago, it became a place where African Americans fled to escape racial tensions in the USA. Local farms produce everything from apples to organic cheese to some of Canada's best lamb and wool. There's also a robust and engaging alternative culture here, reflected in the markets, cafés and artists' studios.

Orientation

The village of Ganges is the heart of the island. There are three BC Ferries terminals, each with a road leading to Ganges: Fulford-Ganges Rd from Fulford Harbour (via Swartz Bay) in the south; Long Harbour Rd from Long Harbour (via Tsawwassen or Southern Gulf Islands) in the east; and Vesuvius Bay Rd from Vesuvius Bay (via Crofton) in the west. Beaver Point Rd, near Fulford Harbour, leads to Ruckle Provincial Park on Salt Spring's southeastern reach, while North End Rd winds past St Mary's Lake toward the island's northern tip.

Information

The helpful staff at the Ganges **VIC** (☎ 250-537-5252; 121 Lower Ganges Rd; ☺ 10am-4pm) have loads

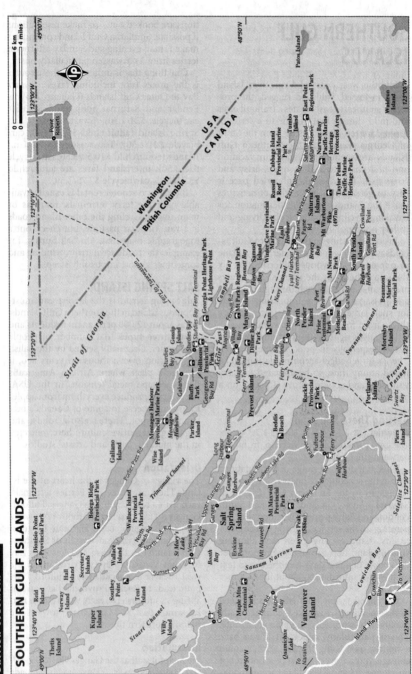

SOUTHERN GULF ISLANDS

of information, including hiking guides, a beach-access map and extensive accommodation listings. **Salt Spring Books** (☎ 250-537-2812; 104 McPhillips, Ganges; per min 10¢) offers Internet access. Major banks have branches and ATMS in Ganges, and there are two **post offices** (☎ 800-267-1177; Ganges 109 Purvis Lane; Fulford Harbour 101 Morningside Rd).

Sights & Activities

Salt Spring Out Of Doors ($3.95), available from the VIC, details hiking trails, beach-access points, historic sites and more.

Mt Maxwell Provincial Park (☎ 250-248-9460; wlapwww.gov.bc.ca/bcparks), just south of Ganges, protects the largest dogwoods and Garry oaks in BC, and features stands of old-growth Douglas fir. It also offers mind-blowing views of the Gulf Islands from its viewpoint. The route includes 5km of steep, rough roads, so go carefully if you're in a conventional vehicle.

Ruckle Provincial Park (☎ 250-539-2115; wlapwww .gov.bc.ca/bcparks; **P** $3) is home to BC's oldest farm (1872), but it also has fascinating rock pools, great diving and a network of attractive walking trails. It's 10km east of Fulford Harbour.

Popular beaches include **Southey Point** at the island's north end, and **Beddis Beach** on the island's east side, noted for good swimming and sunbathing. Head to **Erskine Bay** or **Vesuvius Bay** for vivid sunsets.

Kayaking the calm waters and beautiful shorelines of the island can be done through **Salt Spring Kayaking** (☎ 250-653-9111; www.salt springkayaking.com; 2923 Fulford-Ganges Rd, Fulford Wharf; tours from $38, rentals per 2hr/day $35/50), which offers two-hour to multiday tours; it also rents bicycles ($15/30 per two hours/day) if you want to punish yourself in the hilly terrain. **Salt Spring Guided Rides** (☎ 250-537-5761; per hr $35) leads horseback riding on Mt Maxwell.

Sleeping

There are literally dozens of B&Bs, which span the $90 to $500 range; contact the VIC for details.

Salt Spring Island Hostel (☎ 250-537-4149; www .beacom.com/ssihostel; 640 Cusheon Lake Rd; dm/tipis/d/ tree houses/caravans $21/50/70/80/80; 🕙 mid-Mar–mid-Oct) Hidden away on four hectares of woodlands, on the shores of Cusheon Lake, this is not your standard hostel. Regular dorms are complemented by quirky tree houses,

caravans and tipis, while the large private rooms are a great mid-range option for couples. In the grounds there's a gorgeous little waterfall, woodpeckers and swimming in the lake. A terrific place – advance reservations are essential.

Salt Spring Spa Resort (☎ 250-537-4111, 800-665-0039; www.saltspringspa.com; 1460 North Beach Rd; d $250-300) A luxurious collection of cedar cottages, each with mineral spa and uninterrupted views of Galiano Island, here you can indulge in some serious self-pampering with Austrian mud baths, massages, reflexology, facials and back scrubs among the à la carte services on offer. Rates drop nicely mid-week and off-season.

Seabreeze Inne (☎ 250-537-4145, 800-434-4112; www.seabreezeinne.com; 101 Bittancourt Rd; d $95-125, with kitchenette $120-160) A better-than-average motel with smallish rooms decorated in warm yellows and greens, plus good-sized baths and an outdoor hot tub to soak your cares away. There's also a convivial barbecue area and free bikes – all just a short walk from Ganges.

Lakeside Gardens (☎ 250-537-5773; www.saltspring .com/lakesidegardens; 1450 North End Rd; tent & RV sites/cabanas/cottages $25/65/125) and **St Mary Lake Resort** (☎ 250-537-2832, 888-329-5651; www.stmary lakeresort.com; 1170 North End Rd; cottages $110-130), both on St Mary's Lake, are away from the hustle and bustle, packed with water-based activities, and perennially popular with families. The cabins are nicer at St Mary, but the Lakeside Garden's position by the water is unbeatable.

Ruckle Provincial Park (☎ 250-539-2115; wlapwww .gov.bc.ca/bcparks; campsites $14) has walk-in campsites right on the beach, where you can wake up to sunrises of unbelievable colors.

Eating

Most restaurants are found in and around Ganges and make use of its serene harbor setting.

Treehouse Café (☎ 250-537-5379; 106 Purvis Lane; mains $5-11; 🕙 breakfast & lunch) In an almost comically undersized building (once the town's generator house), Ganges' hippest and hippiest café serves a fine selection of wholesome breakfasts, most accompanied by the café's moreish homemade berry sauce. Try the excellent granola or a vegetarian delight – a tasty tofu scramble. They also know what to do with an espresso machine.

Moby's Marine Pub (☎ 250-537-5559; 124 Upper Ganges Rd; mains $10-20; ☺ lunch & dinner, brunch Sun) Tall plate-glass windows maximize the harbor views, and the food is well prepared and good value. Pizza and beer on a warm summer night is just perfect, although you'll be fighting for a table in this very popular place. On Sunday, come for brunch in the morning or live jazz in the evening.

Embe Bakery (☎ 250-537-5611; 174 Fulford-Ganges Rd; snacks $3-5; ☺ breakfast & lunch) A no-nonsense country bakery with a huge range of delectable crusty pies, both meat and fruit, plus a great range of cakes and bread – all well priced and delicious.

Salt Spring, like most islands, is a pub kind of place. **Fulford Inn** (☎ 250-653-4432; 2661 Fulford-Ganges Rd; mains $7-13; ☺ lunch & dinner), on the south end, and **Vesuvius Inn Pub** (☎ 250-537-2312; 805 Vesuvius Bay Rd; mains $8-14; ☺ lunch & dinner), on the west coast, attract locals and visitors alike.

Getting There & Around

For details on getting to Salt Spring Island, see p729.

It's best to have a car on Salt Spring, but **Silver Shadow Taxi** (☎ 250-537-3030) offers cab service. **Ganges Faerie** (☎ 250-537-6758; www.ganges faerie.com) shuttles between ferry terminals, the hostel, Ganges and Ruckle, and anywhere en route. **Marine Drive Car & Truck Rentals** (☎ 250-537-5464; 122A Upper Ganges Rd; per day $50), at the Ganges Marina, rents cars and has free pickup from the ferry.

GALIANO ISLAND

Long, narrow Galiano Island has an uncrowded feel, although it's the closest island to the mainland and the most often visited. With more than 75% of the island protected by parks and reserves, it has the most ecological diversity of the Southern Gulf Islands, and offers a bounty of activities for marine enthusiasts and landlubbers alike.

Orientation & Information

Ferries dock at Sturdies Bay, on Galiano's eastern end. As always, grab the island map brochure on the ferry; the **Galiano Chamber of Commerce** (☎ 250-539-2233; www.galianoisland.com) has an information shack on your right-hand side as you leave the ferry. Galiano Island has no banks, but there's an ATM at the Hummingbird Pub.

Sights & Activities

The sheltered peninsula of **Montague Harbour Provincial Marine Park** (☎ 250-539-2115; wlapwww .gov.bc.ca/bcparks; P $3) allows you to enjoy relaxing sunrises and sunsets. A trail leads through the ecological hodgepodge of white-shell beaches, middens, open meadows, tidal lagoons, towering forests and a cliff carved by glacial movements.

Bluffs Park boasts great views of Active Pass, along with 5km of hiking paths. Known for its abundant and colorful bird life, **Bodega Ridge Provincial Park** (☎ 250-539-2115; wlapwww .gov.bc.ca/bcparks) contains the sheer drop-off Lovers' Leap viewpoint. **Bellhouse Provincial Park** (☎ 250-539-2115; wlapwww.gov.bc.ca/bcparks), the island's easternmost point, looks on Active Pass from the shallow granite slope at sea level.

Galiano is a good spot for scuba diving, thanks to Alcala Point and its friendly wolf eels, Race Point and Baines Bay's anemone walls, and the sunken Point Grey tugboat. For gear and tours, contact **Galiano Island Diving** (☎ 250-539-3109; 1005 Devina Dr; rentals $49).

Galiano's sandstone cliffs can really only be appreciated from offshore; the protected waters of Trincomali Channel and the chaotic waters of Active Pass appease paddlers of all kayaking skill levels. **Gulf Island Kayaking** (☎ 250-539-2442; www.seakayak.ca; Montague Marina; 3hr/full-day rentals from $28/50, tours from $40) will help with rentals and specializes in multiday tours.

Cycling the island's narrow, hilly roads is thrilling and **Galiano Bicycle Rental & Repair** (☎ 250-539-9906; 36 Burrill Rd; 4hr/full-day $23/28), near Sturdies Bay, has rentals.

Sleeping

Bodega Resort (☎ 250-539-2677; 120 Cook Rd; r/cabins $80/100) This pastoral farmland, sitting up on the ridge, has incredible views onto Trincomali Channel. The fully equipped, two-story log cottages are furnished in rustic country fashion, as are the two B&B rooms in the lodge.

Island Time B&B (☎ 250-539-3506, 877-588-3506; www.galianoaccommodation.com; 952 Sticks Allison Rd; r incl 4-course breakfast $135-215) This place enjoys a spectacular setting of wooded seclusion right on the west coast, and the tariff includes an outdoor hot tub. You may spend much of your time mesmerized by the views and scenery.

Montague Harbour Provincial Marine Park
(☎ 800-689-9025; www.discovercamping.ca; tent sites
$17) has drive-in and walk-in campsites; site
Nos 34 to 38 are on a cliff above the harbor. Kayakers and hikers appreciate **Dionisio
Point Provincial Park** (☎ 250-539-2115; wlapwww.gov
.bc.ca/bcparks; backcountry sites/campsites $5/14) at the
island's far northwestern end; the park can
only be reached by boat or via a hiking trail
from Devina Dr.

Eating

Max & Moritz Spicy Island Food House (☎ 250-539-
5888; mains $3.50-8; ☺ breakfast, lunch & dinner) From
this trailer at the Sturdies Bay ferry terminal, the most unlikely of settings, you can
grab some delicious Indonesian and German food.

Hummingbird Pub (☎ 250-539-5472; 47 Sturdies
Bay Rd; mains $8-12; ☺ lunch & dinner) This is where
locals and regular visitors come to hang out
and enjoy a beer or an honest meal. The
huge log columns and well-used outdoor
deck lend the pub an earthy feel, and the
play area makes it a favorite with families.

Harbour Grill (☎ 250-539-5733; Montague Marina;
mains $8-20; ☺ breakfast, lunch & dinner) This restau-
rant on the deck of Montague Marina makes
standard breakfasts and pick-your-meat
(ribs, steak or coho salmon) dinners.

Getting There & Around

For details on getting to Galiano Island, see
p729.

Go Galiano Island Shuttle (☎ 250-539-0202; rides
$4; ☺ daily in summer, Fri-Sun May, Jun & Sep) meets the
ferries for island transport and also makes
evening runs to the Hummingbird Pub.

MAYNE ISLAND

Once a stopover for gold rushers moving
between Vancouver Island and the Fraser
River, Mayne is home to artists, musicians,
writers and professionals. It does lack the
wildness of other Gulf Islands, but there
are a couple of nice parks to explore and
some good, well-priced accommodations.

Orientation & Information

Ferries dock at Village Bay, a couple of
kilometers from Miner's Bay, where most
amenities are found. The ferry has free
copies of the *Mayne Island* brochure, which
contains a useful map and listings of places
to stay, eat and play. There are no ATMs on

Mayne Island. The **post office** (☎ 800-267-1177;
472 Village Bay Rd; ☺ 9am-6pm Mon-Fri, 9am-noon Sat) is
at Tru Value Foods in Miner's Bay.

Sights & Activities

About two dozen **artists' studios** operate
on Mayne and there are some late 19th-
century **heritage buildings** at Miners Bay, including the **Plumper Pass Lock-up** (☎ 250-539-
5286; ☺ 11am-3pm Fri-Mon late Jun–early Sep), a tiny
museum that once served as a jailhouse for
late 19th-century rowdies.

There's a great hike up the forested flanks
of **Mt Parke**, in the regional park of the same
name. The loop takes about an hour from
the trailhead at Montrose Dr, and rewards
you with sweeping views of the surrounding islands.

There are plenty of **beaches**, and Mayne's
rolling back roads offer some of the best
cycling in the Gulf Islands. **Mayne Island Canoe
& Kayak Rentals** (☎ 250-539-5599; www.maynekayak
.com; 411 Fernhill Rd; kayaks half-/full-day from $26/45, bikes
$15/20) can get you paddling and cycling.

Sleeping & Eating

Oceanwood Country Inn (☎ 250-539-5074; www
.oceanwood.com; 630 Dinner Bay Rd; d incl breakfast &
afternoon tea from $170) Hidden behind tall trees
and nestled against the rocky coast sits this
unassuming yet luxurious inn. All rooms
are plush and spacious, and the views of
Navy Channel are incredible. Breakfast and
afternoon tea are in the downstairs restaurant, which is also open to nonguests for
dinner ($48).

Springwater Lodge (☎ 250-539-5521; www.spring
waterlodge.com; d/cabins $40/95) This white pioneer-
days hotel (established in 1890) at Miners
Bay could possibly be the oldest continuously operating hotel in BC. The wainscoted
rooms in the lodge share a bathroom and
are pretty basic, but the cottages are better,
with sun decks perfect for evening lounging.
There's a fair restaurant here, too (mains
$8 to $15).

Mayne Inn Hotel (☎ 250-539-3122; www3.telus.net/
mayne_inn; 494 Arbutus Dr; d $70-80) This waterfront
hotel on Bennett Bay has eight bright and
spacious rooms with outstanding eastward
views, and the huge deck outside has possibly one of the calmest views on the island.

Mayne Island Eco Camping Tours & Charters
(☎ 250-539-2667; www.mayneisle.com; 359 Maple Dr;
campsites per person $12), at Miners Bay, offers

BRITISH COLUMBIA

forested sites on the coast and a hot tub and showers.

Miners Bay Café (☎ 250-539-9888; 417 Fernhill Rd; mains $4-10) This earthy café features lots of vegetarian options and excellent pizzas; kick back on the couches on the front deck under birch trees.

Getting There & Around

For details on getting to Mayne Island, see p729.

Mayne is a fairly large island and getting around on foot will take a while if you want to go much beyond Miner's Bay. **MIDAS Taxi Company** (☎ 250-539-3132, 250-539-0181) offers taxi service.

SATURNA ISLAND

The least accessible of the major Southern Gulf Islands, Saturna (population 350) is also among the most beautiful. Much of the island is protected by national or provincial parks, and there are white-sand beaches, thick forests and rocky coasts waiting to be explored.

Orientation & Information

Ferries dock at Lyall Harbor on the west coast, and usually run via Mayne Island. Pick up a couple of the *Saturna Island* map brochures on the ferry, or click to www.saturna tourism.com. The **post office** (☎ 800-267-1177; 101 Navarez Bay Rd; ☺ 9am-3pm Tue-Sat) is in the Saturna General Store. Get some cash before you come to the island as there are no ATMs here.

Sights & Activities

Winter Cove Provincial Marine Park (www.pc.gc.ca/ pn-np/bc/gulf) on the island's northern side has a fine white, sandy beach with access to fishing, boating and swimming. The hiking trail that wanders between forest and coastline is especially nice in the spring, when wildflowers bloom and cover the ground in pinks and golds. You can walk to the top of **Mt Warburton Pike** (497m), where you'll find a wildlife reserve with goats and pleasant views of the Strait of Georgia.

Narvaez Bay, on the southern coast, is a dramatic and windswept promontory that's worth a wander. Nearby, some of the area's best (and cheapest!) whale-watching can be enjoyed from the shores of **East Point Regional Park**.

Saturna Island Vineyards (☎ 250-539-5139, 877-918-3388; www.saturnavineyards.com; 8 Quarry Rd; ☺ 11:30am-4:30pm May-Oct) offers tastings and tours for wine-lovers through its four beautiful vineyards and post-and-beam built winery.

Near the ferry, **Saturna Sea Kayaking** (☎ 250-539-5553; http://saturna.gulfislands.com/saturnasea kayaking; 121 Boot Cove Rd; half-/full-day rentals $35/45, tours from $50) offers kayaking lessons and rentals, along with good paddling advice for Saturna and surrounding islands.

Sleeping & Eating

There are no campgrounds on Saturna Island and it's not the kind of place where you can just show up and get a room, so book ahead. All eateries on Saturna close by 8pm, so be prepared if you're the midnight-snack kind of person.

East Point Resort (☎ 250-539-2975; http://saturna .gulfislands.com/eastpointresort; 187 East Point Rd; cottages $90-130) Six individual cottages sit on these 80 acres of forested land on the east coast of the island. Private sandy beaches or patios facing the water are excellent places for watching whales. There's a seven-day minimum in high season and two days in the low season.

Breezy Bay B&B (☎ 250-539-5957; 131 Payne Rd; d from $70) Much more affordable is this nice old farmhouse, which is among the cheapest of the island's B&Bs; most others charge in excess of $120 per night.

Saturna Lodge & Restaurant (☎ 250-539-2254; 130 Payne Rd; dinner $33; ☺ dinner) The restaurant at this upmarket lodge offers fixed-price dinners that blend fresh seafood with locally grown produce and locally raised lamb.

Pick up picnic goodies at **Saturna General Store** (☎ 250-539-2936; 101 Navarez Bay Rd; snacks $4-7), which stocks locally made Haggis Farm baked goods, fresh produce and deli items, or grab some soup or a wrap at the small café nearby. The **Lighthouse Pub** (☎ 250-539-5725; 102 East Point Rd; mains $7-10) at the Saturna Point Store is another popular spot for a quick bite.

Getting There & Around

For details on getting to Saturna Island, see p729.

A car will come in handy here as there is no taxi or bus service.

NORTH & SOUTH PENDER ISLANDS

Appealingly unpretentious, the Pender Islands (population 1900) offer the simple pleasures of sun, sky, forest and beach without going too crazy on the Chablis and caviar side of tourism. There are a couple of good walks and some nice beaches to check out, but otherwise they're pretty quiet places.

Orientation & Information

Ferries dock at Otter Bay on the northwestern coast. The **VIC** (☎ 250-629-6541; 2332 Otter Bay Rd; ☷ 9am-5pm Jun-Sep, 9am-5pm Thu-Sun Oct-May) has a useful brochure on the island. At **Driftwood Centre** (4605 Bedwell Harbour Rd) shopping center you'll find an ATM and the **post office** (☎ 800-267-1177; ☷ 8:30am-4pm Mon-Fri, 8:30am-noon Sat).

Sights & Activities

The islands, which are connected by a small bridge, have several nice beaches, including **Medicine Beach** and **Clam Bay** on North Pender, and **Gowlland Point** on the east coast of South Pender.

Just over the bridge to South Pender is **Mt Norman Park**, and the hike up its namesake (255m) rewards you with grand views of the San Juan and Gulf Islands. North Pender's **Prior Centennial Park** has several walking trails and the best camping on the island.

Kayak Pender Island (☎ 250-629-6939, 877-683-1746; www.kayakpenderisland.com; 2319 MacKinnon Rd; lessons from $54, tours adult/child from $39/25), at Otter Bay Marina on North Pender, offers guided kayaking tours around the many harbors and inlets of the islands.

Sleeping

A lot of accommodations have bikes available for guests to cycle the winding, narrow roads of the islands.

Betty's Bed & Breakfast (☎ 250-629-6599; www.gulfislands-accom.com; 4711 Buccaneer Rd; d incl breakfast $100) This pink B&B is in a wonderful garden setting on the shores of Magic Lake. Take the rowboat for a paddle on the lake, or the bikes for a pedal around the islands after you've devoured your full breakfast.

Inn on Pender Island (☎ 250-629-3353, 800-550-0172; www.innonpender.com; 4709 Canal Rd; s/d/cabins $80/90/140) This small motel is located on 7 acres of wooded property. Rooms in the lodge are bright and comfortable, and the log cabins are fully appointed and popular with cyclists. There's an outdoor hot tub for lodgers, and the cabins get their very own private tub.

Prior Centennial Park (☎ 604-689-9025; www.pc.gc.ca/pn-np/bc/gulf; campsites $14) has campsites set in thick forest close to Medicine Beach.

Eating

Islanders Restaurant (☎ 250-629-6811; 1325 MacKinnon Rd; mains $17-30; ☷ dinner) Everything about this place is local: the art on the walls; the music from the speakers; the chef in the kitchen; and most of the ingredients on the menu. The small and refined dining room takes full advantage of the water views.

Memories at the Inn (☎ 250-629-3353; Inn on Pender Island, 4709 Canal Rd; mains $8-13; ☷ dinner) This restaurant specializes in pizza, but is also successful at creating seafood dishes like wild spring salmon or crab cakes. The dining room is small but inviting, and there are tables on the patio.

If you're waiting for your BC Ferries ship to come in, grab a sandwich or hamburger at the **Stand** (☎ 250-629-3292; 1371 Otter Bay Rd; mains $5-9) at the terminal.

Getting There & Around

For details on getting to North and South Pender Islands, see p729.

Having a car isn't crucial since there are several lodgings close to the ferry. If you don't have wheels, and your host can't pick you up, catch a ride with **Pender Island Taxi** (☎ 250-629-6516).

FRASER & THOMPSON VALLEYS

For many travelers, the heavily populated farming area east and northeast of Vancouver is just an area to be negotiated on the way to the Okanagan, the Rockies or the northern reaches of the province. This is probably fair comment, but there are a few nice attractions to check out if time is not of the essence.

The usual route through this region is the broad, multilane Hwy 5 (toll $10), which, under most circumstances, will quickly whisk you between Vancouver and the main regional town of Kamloops; note that evening peak-hour and long-weekend traffic entering Vancouver can slow to a crawl. However

BRITISH COLUMBIA

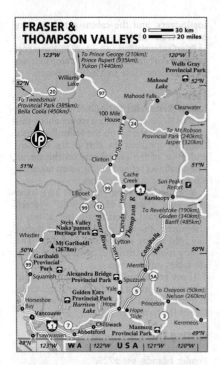

there are two good alternative routes from the small town of Hope, at about the halfway mark of the drive: the Crowsnest Hwy (Hwy 3) heads east through the gorgeous Manning Provincial Park to Osoyoos and the southern reaches of the Okanagan Valley; and Hwy 1 goes north to Cache Creek via the spectacular scenery of the Fraser River Canyon. From here you can continue north to Prince George, Prince Rupert or even Alaska.

About 150km east of Vancouver, Hope itself has little to divert you, but its good **VIC** (☎ 604-869-2021; 919 Water Ave; ☼ 9am-5pm) has helpful staff and plenty of information about the local provincial parks, plus information kiosks outside for if you arrive after hours.

MANNING PROVINCIAL PARK

One of Vancouverites' favorite playgrounds, this 70,844-hectare **provincial park** (☎ 604-795-6169; wlapwww.gov.bc.ca/bcparks), 30km southeast of Hope, is a model of diversity, and home to more than 200 species of birds and 60 species of mammals. Its climate zones range from arid valleys to alpine high country, and it's notable for its excellent collection of

long-distance hikes. Day-trippers will find it hard to lose the crowds though; there are extensive facilities, loads of year-round visitors and large campgrounds that fill up quickly.

The **VIC** (☼ 8:30am-4:30pm Jun-Oct, 8:30am-4pm Mon-Fri Oct-May) is 30km inside the western boundary and has detailed hiking descriptions and a 3-D relief model of the park. The following are good hiking choices:

Dry Ridge Trail (3km round-trip, 45 minutes) Crosses from dry interior to alpine climate; excellent views and wildflowers.

Heather Trail (21km each way, two long days) Usually an overnight hike through premier alpine country and lupine meadows; the first half makes a great day hike (bring the bug spray).

Lightning Lake Loop (9km, 2½ hours) An easy amble around this central lake.

Rhododendron Flats (500m, 20 minutes) An easy loop through masses of flowering bushes that put on a spectacular show in June.

Rather than hibernate, Manning puts on its parka and stares winter in the face. **Manning Park Resort** (☎ 250-840-8822, 800-330-3321; www.manningparkresort.com) offers downhill skiing and snowboarding (adult/child lift-ticket $34/22) and 100km of groomed trails for cross-country skiing and snowshoeing.

You can pitch your tent at **Coldspring**, **Hampton** or **Mule campgrounds** (☎ reservations 800-689-9025; www.discovercamping.ca; campsites $14) or the more-popular **Lightning Lake campground** (campsites $22). There are 10 **backcountry campgrounds** (campsites per person $5) for overnight hikers.

Manning Park Resort (☎ 250-840-8822, 800-330-3321; www.manningparkresort.com; r from $70, cabins/chalets from $115/190) is the only indoor lodging in the park, and the rooms and cabins are comfortable enough, if not outstanding value.

Greyhound Canada has buses from Vancouver (adult/child $35/17.50, 3½ hours, five daily).

FRASER RIVER CANYON

From Hope, Hwy 1 heads north through the small towns of Yale, Spuzzum and Lytton on its way to Cache Creek, 85km west of Kamloops. It shadows the swiftly flowing Fraser River and offers some of the province's more impressive scenery, plus decent provincial parks, and excellent and very accessible white-water rafting.

Just north of Spuzzum, **Alexandra Bridge Provincial Park** (☎ 604-795-6169; wlapwww.gov.bc.ca/

bcparks) makes a good picnic stop; you can munch your sandwiches while gazing at the historic 1861 span. Further north, near Lytton, the ecologically diverse and relatively unlogged **Stein Valley Nlaka'pamux Heritage Park** (wlapwww.gov.bc.ca/bcparks) offers some truly superb hiking through semidesert valleys and across alpine glaciers, but it's mostly long-distance stuff.

White-water rafting down the Fraser and its tributaries' fast-flowing rapids is popular, and a number of companies offer trips. One-day trips cost $80 to $120 per adult and most places offer discounts on Sundays:

Fraser River Raft Expeditions (☎ 800-363-7238; www.fraserraft.com) Runs the lesser-known but very fast Nahatlatch River.

Hyak River Rafting (☎ 800-663-7238; www.hyak.com) Covers all the main waterways.

REO Rafting Adventure Resort (☎ 800-736-7238; www.reorafting.com) Also runs the Nahatlatch River.

KAMLOOPS

Sitting in the valley where the North Thompson, South Thompson and Thompson Rivers meet, Kamloops has always been a service and transport crossroads. The Shuswap First Nation used the rivers and many lakes for transportation and salmon fishing before fur traders set up camp in 1811. The city is surrounded by some 200 lakes, making it a good water-sports area, and there's a couple of decent provincial parks nearby. Otherwise, this pleasant small city has only moderate attractions for the traveler, although it's a good point at which to break your journey to the Rockies (p752).

Orientation & Information

Highway 1 cuts east–west through town, linking Vancouver with the Rockies, while Yellowhead Hwy (Hwy 5) heads northeast to Jasper and southwest to Vancouver via Merritt (this stretch is called the Coquihalla Hwy). The focus of the attractive and compact downtown area is Victoria St, the main shopping strip. One block south is Seymour St, which also has its share of shops and services, while Lansdowne St shadows the very busy train tracks that separate the Thompson River from the downtown area.

The **VIC** (☎ 250-374-3377, 800-662-1994; www.adventurekamloops.com; 1290 W Trans-Canada Hwy, exit 368; ☽ 8am-6pm summer, 9am-6pm Mon-Fri rest of year) is high above the downtown center. Major

banks have branches on Victoria St. The **post office** (☎ 250-374-2444; cnr Seymour St & 3rd Ave; ☽ 8:30am-5pm Mon-Fri) is a block south. Fast Internet connections are available at **PC Doctor's Digital Café** (☎ 250-372-5723; 463 Lansdowne St; per hr $6; ☽ 9am-9pm Mon-Fri, 11am-7pm Sat).

Sights & Activities

North of downtown, the **Secwepemc Museum & Heritage Park** (☎ 250-828-9801; www.secwepemc .org/museum.html; 355 Yellowhead Hwy; adult/child $6/4; ☽ 8:30-8pm Mon-Fri, from 10am weekends summer, 8:30-4:30pm Mon-Fri rest of year) holds re-created traditional Secwepemc (Shuswap) winter and summer houses, and has an indoor museum that outlines the history and the culture of the Secwepemc Nation.

Kamloops Museum (☎ 250-828-3576; www.city .kamloops.bc.ca/museum; cnr Seymour St & 2nd Ave; admission by donation; ☽ 9am-4:30pm Tue-Sat) is better than the average town museum. It explores the area's history, and includes an excellent collection of historical photographs.

The exhibition space at **Kamloops Art Gallery** (☎ 250-828-3543; www.kag.bc.ca; 465 Victoria St; adult/concession $5/3; ☽ 10am-5pm Mon-Wed & Fri, to 9pm Thu, noon-4pm Sat & Sun) is small but thoroughly modern and thoughtfully lit, and showcases rolling exhibitions, with an emphasis on contemporary Western and First Nations art.

The kids may enjoy the caged critters at **British Columbia Wildlife Park** (☎ 250-573-3242; www.kamloopswildlife.org; adult/child $9/6; ☽ 8am-4:30pm, to 8:30pm Jul & Aug), 17km east of Kamloops on Hwy 1, but you can try for more satisfying sightings in the wild at **Paul Lake Provincial Park** (☎ 250-819-7376; wlapwww .gov.bc.ca/bcparks), which is a protected zone for falcons, bald eagles, coyote and mule deer. It's 24km north of Kamloops via Hwy 5.

Sleeping

Plaza Heritage Hotel (☎ 250-377-8075, 877-977-5292; www.plazaheritagehotel.com; 405 Victoria St; d $140-240) The twee floral decor here may be a bit much for some, but this grand old hotel (1927), smack dab in the middle of town, is still the pick of Kamloops' lodgings. There are great views from the upper stories and the rooms are beautifully maintained; tariffs are much cheaper out of season.

HI Kamloops (☎ 250-828-7991, 866-782-9526; www.hihostels.ca; 7 W Seymour St; dm/d $20/50; ☽ 8am-noon & 5-10pm; ☐) The stern Victorian lines of this former courthouse conceal a terrific and atmospheric hostel, only a couple of blocks from town. The old judges' chambers have been converted into dorms, and the huge common areas in the original dark-timbered courtroom are a great place to kick back with a book. It fills up very quickly in summer, so book as early as you can.

The two main areas for motels are Columbia St, west of the downtown area, and on Hwy 1, east of town, and there's plenty to select from. A notable standout is the **Grandview Motel** (☎ 250-372-1312, 800-210-6088; www.grandviewmotel.com; 463 Grandview Terrace; s/d $72/80), which does indeed feature fine views from some rooms, plus a large patio with outdoor barbecues.

The closest site for camping is the quiet, shady and plain **Silver Sage Tent & Trailer Park** (☎ 250-828-2077, 877-828-2077; http://silversage.kam loops.com; 771 Athabasca St; campsites $20-25) across the river from downtown in the city's industrial area. The facilities include a coin laundry and showers. You can also camp at **Paul Lake Provincial Park** (☎ reservations 250-554-0720; wlapwww .gov.bc.ca/bcparks; campsites $14).

Eating & Drinking

Numerous places along and around Victoria St offer meals or just coffee.

Zach's (☎ 250-347-6487; 377 Victoria St; light meals $4-8; ❀ 7am-11pm) A local hub, the perennially busy Zach's has sidewalk tables where you can enjoy gourmet sandwiches and bagels, plus a damn fine cup of coffee.

Sanbiki (☎ 250-377-8857; 476 Victoria St; meals $12; ❀ lunch & dinner Tue-Sun) A bright and refreshing little Japanese restaurant, it is also known for its good sushi, which is brought in daily from Vancouver. The patio is heated.

Kelly O'Bryan's (☎ 250-828-1559; 244 Victoria St; ❀ noon-late) This old-fashioned British-style pub-restaurant offers well-poured pints of Guinness as well as good burgers and hearty Irish stew (mains $8 to $21).

Magnum's (☎ 250-377-7700; 357 Victoria St; ❀ noon-late) The buzzing place in town, Magnum's spans several high-concept floors and offers a mix of acid jazz, deep house and hip-hop.

Getting There & Around

Seven kilometers northwest of town, on Kamloops' north shore, is **Kamloops Airport** (YKA; ☎ 250-376-3613). Air Canada Jazz flies

to/from Vancouver ($160, one hour) several times daily.

The **bus depot** (☎ 250-374-1212; 725 Notre Dame Dr) is southwest of the downtown area off Columbia St W. Greyhound Canada buses leave daily for Vancouver ($56, four to five hours, eight daily), Calgary ($86, nine hours, four daily), Jasper ($60, six hours, twice daily), Prince George ($75, seven hours) and Kelowna ($28, four hours).

The **train station** (☎ 800-561-8630), located 11km north of town off the Yellowhead Hwy, is only open 30 minutes prior to departures. With VIA Rail, three weekly trains go to Vancouver ($102, nine hours), and three others head east to Jasper ($105, 7½ hours), Edmonton ($160, 14 hours) and beyond.

For information about local bus routes, call **Kamloops Transit Service** (☎ 250-376-1216; www.city.kamloops.bc.ca/transportation/transit; one-way fare adult/child $1.50/free). For a taxi, try **Yellow Cabs** (☎ 250-374-3333).

NORTH OF KAMLOOPS

Highway 5 heads north out of Kamloops, passing a ski resort and a beautiful provincial park on the way to Valemont, and the turn-off to Alberta's Jasper National Park (p604), a journey of 440km in total. Northwest of Kamloops, Hwy 97 (which is joined at Cache Creek) heads to Prince George; see p775 for details.

Sun Peaks Resort

A year-round recreation spot, **Sun Peaks Resort** (☎ 250-578-5474, 800-807-3257; www.sunpeaks resort.com; lift tickets adult/child $55/29) is built on Tod Mountain, 53km northeast of Kamloops. The mountain boasts 117 runs (including some long powder trails), 10 lifts, a snowboard park, 881m of vertical rise and a good base-area village. In summer, the **quad chair** (adult/child $12/9) keeps running to take hikers and mountain bikers up top to play around on the snowless runs.

Accommodations run from the **Sun Peaks International Hostel** (☎ 250-578-0057; www.sun peakshostel.com; 1140 Sun Peaks Rd; dm from $20) to top-end condos. Contact the resort for details.

Wells Gray Provincial Park

In the Cariboo Mountains, about halfway between Kamloops and Jasper, and off the Yellowhead Hwy (Hwy 5), lies this enormous

541,000-hectare **wilderness park** (☎ 250-674-2194; wlapwww.gov.bc.ca/bcparks), a seldom-visited jewel filled with incredible waterfalls.

Most people enter the park via the town of Clearwater on Hwy 5, where the **VIC** (☎ 250-674-2646; www.ntvalley.com/clearwater chamber; 425 E Yellowhead Hwy, at Clearwater Valley Rd; ☺ 9am-5pm Jul & Aug, 9am-5pm Mon-Fri Apr-Jun & Sep-Dec) has useful information and maps of the park.

From Clearwater the Wells Gray Corridor takes you into the heart of the park and the major walking trails and waterfalls, including the incredible **Helmcken Falls**, where the Murtle River plunges 137m into a misty abyss. You'll also find opportunities for **hiking**, **cross-country skiing** or **horseback riding** along more than 20 trails of varying lengths.

Another great way to explore the park is by canoeing on Clearwater, Azure, Murtle and Mahood Lakes. To rent canoes, contact **Clearwater Lake Tours** (☎ 250-674-2121; www.clearwaterlaketours.com; rentals per day $40). The Clearwater River also makes for some excellent, adrenaline-pumping white-water rafting. **Interior Whitewater Expeditions** (☎ 250-674-3727, 800-661-7238; www.interiorwhitewater.bc.ca; 3hr trip adult/child $85/64) runs the river with a variety of trips.

SLEEPING

Wells Gray Guest Ranch (☎ 250-674-2792, 866-467-4346; www.wellsgrayranch.com; campsites/tipis $14/30, d $85-120) Just outside of the south gate you'll find this ranch, which has no end of guided activities for guests, including horse riding, hiking, mountain biking, fishing, dogsledding and snowshoeing.

Wells Gray has four designated **campgrounds** (campsites $14) available on a first-come, first-served basis, plus plenty of **backcountry camping** (per person $5) along the shores of the larger lakes.

GETTING THERE & AWAY

There are three access points to the park. The most popular entrance is the south gate, 36km north of Clearwater on Clearwater Valley Rd. You can also reach the park from 100 Mile House via an 86km gravel road that leads to Mahood Falls and the west end of Mahood Lake. From Blue River, north of Clearwater, a 24km gravel road and 2.5km track lead to Murtle Lake in the southeast part of the park.

OKANAGAN VALLEY

The Okanagan, a beautiful and unique area of Canada, is a series of valleys running about 180km north–south in southern central BC. This fertile valley, dominated by orchards, wineries and warm lakes, gets more than 2000 hours of sunshine a year. Summer travelers coming to this region from the Lower Mainland marvel at the seemingly impossible shift in climate; it brings the sunseekers here in droves, not to mention a vast and continuing stream of well-heeled retirees settling here to avoid the bitter cold of other parts of the country.

Near Osoyoos, close to the US border, cactuses grow on desert slopes that receive only 200mm of rain a year and provide a pocket of desert environment unique in Canada. Just to the north, three 'sister cities' – Penticton, Kelowna and Vernon – attract the majority of visitors, who sip wine, play golf, hike or mountain bike in the dry hills, or simply flake out on one of the many sandy lakeside beaches. During winter, when dry, fluffy snow falls, the climate stays mild, the sun

---

OKANAGAN FRUIT ORCHARDS

The hot, dry summers, in combination with the fertile soil and heavy irrigation, has made the Okanagan Valley region the country's top fruit-growing area. About 100 sq km of orchards bear fruit in the region, which contains 85% of Canada's orchards.

During April and May the entire valley springs to life with blossoms from thousands of fruit trees. In late summer and autumn the orchards drip with delicious fresh fruit. Stands dotting the roads sell Canada's best and cheapest produce. Grapes are the last fruit of summer to ripen, but one of the most important; the valley has a national reputation for its high-quality wine, and several of the area's 30-odd vineyards offer tasting rooms (see p745).

The drive north along Hwy 97 from Osoyoos is an almost endless succession of orchards, farms, fruit stands and the like. Slow-moving tourists and retirees on this route will give you plenty of time to smell the apples, peaches and, yes, the roses.

BRITISH COLUMBIA

OKANAGAN VALLEY

0 _____ 30 km
0 _____ 20 miles

To Kamloops (20km) | 120°W | To Kamloops (30km)
119°W

Enderby

To Revelstoke (103km);
Golden (251km);
Banff (385km)

Shuswap R

Mabel
Lake

Trapp
Lake

Roche
Lake

Westwold

97

Mt Tuktakamin
(1771m)

Armstrong

Silver Star
Provincial
Park

Spallumcheen

Silver Star
Mountain Resort

Stump
Lake

5A

To Merritt (40km);
Vancouver (311km)

Chapperon
Lake

Mt Tahaetkun
(2039m)

Swan
Lake

Vernon

Coldstream

Lumby

6

To Naskup
(via ferry; 152km)

Kalamalka Lake
Provincial Park

Ellison
Provincial Park

Kekuli Bay
Provincial Park

Douglas
Lake

50°N

Thompson
Plateau

Fintry
Provincial Park

Kalamalka
Lake

Oyama

Wood
Lake

Swalwell
Lake

Okanagan
Centre

50°N

Monashee Mountains

To Merritt (37km);
Vancouver (308km)

Okanagan Lake

97

Postill
Lake

Bear Creek
Provincial Park

97C

Kelowna

Westbank

Big White Mtn
(2317m)

Peachland

Big White
Ski Resort

97

Okanagan Mountain
Provincial Park

Okanagan
Mtn

Okanagan Lake
Provincial Park

Interior
Plateau

Summerland

Okanagan Lake

Naramata

33

To Princeton (10km);
Hope (136km);
Vancouver (286km)

Penticton

Beaverdell

Apex
Mountain
Resort

Skaha
Lake

Apex
Mountain
Recreation
Area

Kaleden

Crowsnest Hwy

Similkameen R

Okanagan Falls
Provincial Park

Okanagan Falls

Vaseux Lake

3

3A

Vaseux Lake
Provincial Park

Keremeos

Baldy Mtn
(2301m)

Westbridge

Cawston

Mt Baldy
Ski Area

Cathedral
Provincial
Park

Mt Kobau

Oliver

To Nelson (209km);
Cranbrook (430km);
Fernie (523km)

Okanagan R

Osoyoos
Lake

Anarchist
Mtn Pass
(1234m)

Crowsnest Hwy

3

49°N

Osoyoos

Haynes Point
Provincial Park

49°N

BRITISH COLUMBIA

WASHINGTON (U S A)

120°W

97

To Yakima, USA (390km);

119°W

still shines and snow sports take over. The region remains incredibly scenic, however, with rolling, scrubby hills, narrow blue lakes and clear skies. In July and August expect all types of accommodations to be tight.

OSOYOOS

At the southern end of the Okanagan Valley, small Osoyoos sits at the edge of dark blue Osoyoos Lake, surrounded by stark, dry rolling hills. The skies are sunny and the waters warm, and with its hot, dry weather, the Osoyoos region produces Canada's earliest and most-varied fruit and vegetable crops. Look for roadside stands selling cherries, apricots, peaches, apples and other fruit.

On the lake's eastern side lies a small desert, known as a 'pocket desert,' that runs about 50km north to Skaha Lake and is about 20km across at its widest point. Averaging less than 200mm of rain a year, the area has flora and fauna uncharacteristic for Canada, including the calliope hummingbird (Canada's smallest bird), rattlesnakes, painted turtles, coyote, numerous species of mice, and various cacti, desert brushes and grasses. You can see it all at one of two desert parks. Otherwise, just kick back and enjoy the swimming, boating and sunshine.

Orientation & Information

Osoyoos is at the crossroads of Hwy 97, heading north to Penticton (past several provincial parks where you can camp), and the Crowsnest Hwy (Hwy 3), which runs east to the Kootenay region and west to Hope. The US border, cutting through Osoyoos Lake, is just 5km to the south. Most of the town is strung out along several kilometers of Hwy 3, known locally as Main St, with the majority of accommodations found on the narrow strip of land that splits Osoyoos Lake, offering water views both north and south. The **VIC** (☎ 250-495-7142, 888-676-9667; cnr Hwys 3 & 97; ⏰ 9am-5pm summer, 9am-5pm Mon-Fri rest of year) has free Internet access, and excellent hiking maps and recommendations.

Sights & Activities

The mild climate makes **Osoyoos Lake** the warmest in the country. That, together with the sandy beaches, means great swimming. Many motels and campgrounds hire out kayaks, canoes and small boats.

The excellent **Nk'Mip Desert & Heritage Centre** (☎ 250-495-7901, 888-495-8555; www.nkmipdesert .com; 1000 Rancher Creek Rd; adult/child $7/4; ⏰ 9am-7pm Jul & Aug, 10am-4pm May, Jun, Sep & Oct) has been developed by the Osoyoos Indian Band and takes you on an hour-long walk through the Antelope Brush ecosystem, a fragile extension of the Sonora and Mojave Deserts. It also includes a reconstructed Indian village of summer and winter homes. The presence of rattlesnakes adds a certain focus to the walk. It's off 45th St, north of Hwy 3.

Along similar lines, the **Desert Centre** (☎ 250-495-2470; www.desert.org; adult/child $6/3; ⏰ 9am-7pm May-Sep), 3km north of Osoyoos off Hwy 97, sits on 27 hectares and features interpretive kiosks along raised boardwalks that meander through the dry terrain. Guided tours are mandatory, and run less frequently outside of summer, so call ahead for times.

If you're sunburnt, or just plain sick of the hot sun, the small **Osoyoos Museum** (☎ 250-495-2582; Gyro Community Park, off Hwy 3; adult/child $3/1; ⏰ 10am-3:30pm Jun-Sep) will fill a shady hour with its displays on natural and local history, orchards and irrigation.

Sleeping & Eating

The eastern edge of the lake is lined with campgrounds, which all feature nice grassy campsites, and there's a slew of motels and resorts along Main St (Hwy 3), but no hostel. Everything fills up in summer – it's wise to book well in advance.

Sun Beach Motel (☎ 250-495-7766; sunbeachmotel@ otvcablelan.net; 7303 Main St; d from $85) Probably the pick of the 'cheapies' along Main St, Sun Beach has no-frills but roomy quarters, plus barbecues, boat docks and patios, and generally undercuts the competition in price.

Poplars Motel (☎ 250-495-6035; www.poplarsmotel the.supersites.ca; 6404 Cottonwood Dr; d from $90) Consider this older beachfront place if you're traveling in a group or with kids. All rooms have very functional kitchenettes (including a stove and an oven) and many four-berth rooms have one double in a separate room.

Holiday Inn Sunspree Resort (☎ 250-495-7223, 877-786-7773; www.holidayinosoyoos.com; 7906 Main St; d from $180; 🖳) OK, so it's a big chain motel, but its lakefront location is unbeatable, there's loads of water-based activities, and rooms have private balconies from which you can take in the views. Rates almost halve outside of summer.

BRITISH COLUMBIA

Haynes Point Provincial Park (☎ 250-494-0321, 800-689-9025; www.discovercamping.ca; tent sites $22) Jutting into the lake, 2km south of downtown off Hwy 97, this lovely spot is the most sought-after campground in town. Reservations are essential.

Wildfire Grill (☎ 250-495-2215; 8526 Main St; meals $15-20; ☾ lunch & dinner, brunch Sun) A range of global cuisines is produced in the bustling open kitchen at this excellent restaurant, right in the center of town. The ingredients are mostly local and the menu changes often. The decor is warm and romantic, and the courtyard is a treat.

Grab a beer and pub food at the **Owl Pub** (☎ 250-495-3274; 7603 Spartan Ave; meals $7-15; ☾ noon-late), a large and friendly watering hole with a patio overlooking the lake.

Getting There & Away
The **bus station** (☎ 250-495-7252; Chuckers Convenience Store; 6615 Lakeshore Dr) is at the east end of the motel strip. Greyhound Canada buses run daily to Vancouver and Calgary, and north up the valley to Penticton ($13, one hour) and Kelowna ($23, three hours).

Around Osoyoos
West of Osoyoos, Hwy 3 runs up the Similkameen Valley to **Keremeos**, a little town surrounded by orchards.

About 30km west of Keremeos is **Cathedral Provincial Park** (☎ 604-795-6169; wlapwww.gov .bc.ca/bcparks), a 33-sq-km mountain wilderness characterized by unusual rock formations and the beautiful Cathedral Lakes. The park offers excellent backcountry camping and hiking around wildflower meadows and turquoise lakes. Two steep and long trails, the **Lakeview Trail** (16km) and **Ewart Creek Trail** (28km), lead from the park's boundary to the core area around Quiniscoe Lake and the gorgeous **Cathedral Lakes Lodge** (☎ 250-492-1606, 888-255-4453; www.cathedral-lakes-lodge.com; r & cabins per 2 nights from $320). Private vehicles aren't permitted within the park, but the lodge operates a shuttle service for wilderness campers (a whopping $75 round-trip in summer) for the 16km journey from Ashnola River Rd. **Backcountry camping** (per person $5) is available along the Lakeview Trail and around Quiniscoe Lake, Lake of the Woods and Pyramid Lake. To reach the park, take Hwy 3 via Keremeos to Ashnola River Rd, then continue for another 21km.

NORTH OF OSOYOOS
North of Osoyoos, on the way to Penticton, watch for the small sign for **Vaseux Wildlife Centre** (☎ 250-494-6500; admission free; ☾ dawn-dusk) at the northern end of Vaseux Lake, off Hwy 97. Part of the Vaseux Lake Provincial Park, it's a haven for rare and endangered birds, and you might catch a glimpse of bighorn sheep or the northern Pacific rattlesnake. From the center, you can hike to the **Bighorn National Wildlife Area** and the **Vaseux Lake Migratory Bird Sanctuary**, where more than 160 bird species nest. There are also nature trails of varying lengths.

You can camp at one of the provincial park's 12 year-round **campsites** (sites $14) on the east side of the lake, which is popular for bass fishing, swimming and canoeing in summer. In winter, people head to the lake for skating and ice fishing.

PENTICTON
Smaller than Kelowna and buzzier than Osoyoos, Penticton is just about the perfect size for a beach town. Set scenically on Okanagan Lake, it's grown-up enough to boast plenty of quality restaurants, shops, pubs and accommodations, yet small enough to navigate on foot. Though popular with retirees, the town still exudes a young, sporty feel, thanks to a diverse cycle of annual festivals, excellent mountain biking and world-class climbing on Skaha Bluffs. The long, sunny, lakeside days don't hurt either – in Penticton the sun shines for an average of 600 hours in July and August (about 10 hours a day) – that's more than it shines in Honolulu! All in all, it's a great spot to cool your heels for a day or three.

Orientation
Highway 97 splits the town, running south to Osoyoos and north to Kelowna. The attractive downtown area extends for about 10 blocks southward from Okanagan Lake along Main St, and has a full range of restaurants, shops, banks and services. Go further south, however, and you'll encounter strip malls, sprawl and the like, which are best avoided.

Information
ATMs and banks abound along Main St. **BC Wine Information Centre** (☎ 250-493-4055,

800-663-5052; 888 Westminster Ave W; 8am-8pm summer, 9am-5pm Mon-Fri 11am-5pm Sat & Sun rest of year) At the VIC; offers sales, information and tastings of the region's finest.

Book Shop (☎ 250-492-6661; 242 Main St) Massive collection of secondhand books.

Mouse Pad (☎ 250-493-2050; 320 Martin St; per hr $6; 7am-10pm Mon-Sat, 8am-8pm Sun) Internet access.

Gallop's Flowers (☎ 250-492-0615; 187 Westminster Ave W; 9am-6pm Mon-Sat) A central and convenient Canada Post sub-branch.

VIC (☎ 250-493-4055, 800-663-5052; 888 Westminster Ave W; 8am-8pm summer, 9am-5pm Mon-Fri 11am-5pm Sat & Sun rest of year) Has one free Internet terminal.

Sights

Penticton is mostly about fun in the sun, but there are a few minor attractions, if the rain sweeps in.

The **Penticton Museum** (☎ 250-490-2451; 785 Main St; suggested donation $2; 10am-5pm Tue-Sat) is a fine small-town museum where you can pick up excellent brochures for historic walks.

The **Art Gallery of Southern Okanagan** (☎ 250-493-2928; www.galleries.bc.ca/agso; 199 Front St; admission $2; 10am-5pm Tue-Sat) displays a reasonable collection of regional, provincial and national artists. Exhibits change regularly.

SS Sicamous (☎ 250-492-0403; 1099 Lakeshore Dr W; adult/child $5/1; 9am-9pm summer, 9am-4pm Mon-Fri rest of year) is a nicely restored old paddle-wheeler that hauled passengers and freight on Okanagan Lake from 1914 to 1936.

Activities

The paved **Okanagan River Channel Biking & Jogging Path** follows the channel from Okanagan Lake to Skana Lake. It's great for running, walking, cycling or in-line skating.

WATER SPORTS

When the mercury climbs, the beaches start looking pretty good. Close to the downtown area, **Okanagan Beach** is about 1300m long. It's sandy, and in summer the water temperature is about 22°C. At the town's south end, **Skaha Beach** is about 1.5km long and has sand, trees and picnic areas.

Both Okanagan and Skaha Lakes enjoy some of the best windsurfing and boating conditions in the Okanagan Valley. **Castaways** (☎ 250-490-2033; http://parasailcanada.com/castaways; Penticton Lakeside Resort, 21 Lakeshore Dr; paddleboats/kayaks/ski boats per hr $16/19/80; 9am-9pm) rents just about anything that floats.

Coyote Cruises (☎ 250-492-2115; 215 Riverside Dr; rentals & shuttle $13) rents out inner tubes that you can float on all the way down the Okanagan River Channel to Skaha Lake. The trip takes nearly two hours; Coyote Cruises buses you back.

MOUNTAIN BIKING

The dry climate and rolling hills around the city combine to offer some excellent mountain-biking terrain. Get to popular rides by heading east out of town, towards Naramata. Follow signs to the city dump and Campbell's Mountain, where you'll find lots of single-track trails and a dual-slalom course, both of which aren't too technical. In summer, the fast quad **chairlift** (adult/child $10/5) at Apex Mountain Resort zips riders and their bikes to the top of the mountain. **Freedom – The Bike Shop** (☎ 250-493-0686; 533 Main St) rents out bikes for $35 per day.

ROCK CLIMBING

Propelled by the dry weather and compact gneiss rock, climbers from all over the world come to the Skaha Bluffs to enjoy a seven-month climbing season on more than 400 bolted routes. **Skaha Rock Adventures** (☎ 250-493-1765; www.skaharockclimbing.com; 1-day courses from $125) offers advanced, technical instruction and introductory courses for anyone venturing into a harness for the first time.

SKIING & SNOWBOARDING

Apex Mountain Resort (☎ 877-777-2739, conditions 250-487-4848; www.apexresort.com; lift tickets adult/child $50/30, in summer $10/7), 37km west of Penticton off Green Mountain Rd is one of Canada's best small ski resorts. It has more than 60 downhill runs for all ability levels, but the mountain is known for its plethora of double-black-diamond and technical runs (the drop is over 600m). There's also 30km of cross-country trails that can be used for hiking, mountain biking and horseback riding in summer.

Festivals & Events

Penticton is the city of festivals, which happen almost nonstop throughout the summer.

Beach Blanket Film Festival (www.beachblanketfilmfest.ca; tickets $8, 3-day pass $20; Jul) Bring a deck chair or blanket and kick back to watch the movie screen floating offshore on Skaha Lake.

Peach Festival (☎ 800-663-5052; www.peachfest.com; ☼ early Aug) The city's premier event: a weeklong party of sports, street music and a major parade.

Ironman Triathlon (☎ 250-490-8787; www.ironman .ca; ☼ late Aug) Watch almost 2000 masochists swim 3.9km, cycle 180km and then, just for the hell of it, run a full marathon (42km).

Pentastic Jazz Festival (☎ 250-770-3494; www .pentasticjazz.com; ☼ early Sep) Fills the city venues with cool beats and rhythms.

Sleeping

The nicest accommodations overlook the lake just north of the city center, but the cheaper motels line Skaha Lake Rd far to the south. The VIC has complete lists of all types of lodging, including many area B&Bs.

BUDGET

HI Penticton Hostel (☎ 250-492-3992; www.hihos tels.ca; 464 Ellis St; dm $22-24; ☼ 8am-noon & 5-10pm; ☐) This slightly worn but nonetheless fine hostel occupies a venerable 1901 house and has a brilliant downtown location. Facilities include private rooms, a kitchen, a laundry and a decent patio, and there are various discounts on activities and meals, plus tours of the local wineries.

There are several tent and trailer parks south of town, around Skaha Lake.

Waterworld RV & Campground (☎ 250-492-4255; www.pentictonwaterslides.com; 185 Yorkton Ave; tent/RV sites $28/39) Kids will love this campground, which is part of a big water-slide park near Skaha Lake. Tent sites and full-hookup sites are available, and the park has all the usual amenities.

MID-RANGE & TOP END

Lakeshore Dr W and S Main St/Skaha Lake Rd contain most of the local motels.

Tiki Shores Beach Resort (☎ 250-492-8769, 866-492-8769; www.tikishores.com; 914 Lakeshore Dr; condos from $110; ☢) A good option for groups or families, all the units have separate bedrooms and kitchens, and you're next to the beach and close to the restaurants.

Club Paradise Motel (☎ 250-493-8400; http://club paradise.penticton.com; 1000 Lakeshore Dr; d from $65) Just behind Salty's, most rooms here don't have beach views, but you're not paying for the privilege either. A clean, central and affordable option for couples.

Log Cabin Motel (☎ 250-492-3155, 800-342-5678; www.logcabinmotel.penticton.com; 3287 Skaha Lake Rd; s/d from $80/90; ☢) One of the better places at the Skaha Lake end of town, the Log Cabin has very nice grounds, a pool and some units with kitchenettes. You'll need a car to get to town.

Penticton Lakeside Resort (☎ 250-493-8221, 800-663-9400; www.pentictonlakesideresort.com; 21 Lakeshore Dr W; s/d from $150/160; ☢) A newish high-rise complex that somehow got permission to completely block the lake views from downtown. Still, it has well-turned-out rooms and extensive facilities, which include a restaurant and a bar that enjoy (surprise, surprise) some great lake views.

Eating

Penticton has a great dining scene. Stroll around Main St and Lakeshore Dr and you will find a wide range of cuisines from around the globe.

Il Vecchio Deli (☎ 250-492-7610; 317 Robinson St; sandwiches $4; ☼ lunch Mon-Sat) The best sandwiches in town are served at this popular old Italian deli, one block back from Main St. Europeans just might find that favorite food they've been craving among the imported deli items.

Voodoo's (☎ 250-770-8867; 67 E Nanaimo Ave; meals $8-12; ☼ 5pm-late) You can while away your night in this stylish space, which is known for its interesting and inventive cuisine. There's live music nightly, with liberal doses of blues and folk.

Elite Restaurant (☎ 250-492-3051; 340 Main St; meals $6-18; ☼ breakfast & lunch) The classic old 1950s sign ushers you into an equally authentic tan-and-brown diner setting, where there's plenty of elbowroom. The brekkie specials (before 11am) are an economical way to prepare for a day of beachside lounging.

Front St Pasta Factory (☎ 250-493-5666; 75 Front St; meals $11-18; ☼ lunch & dinner) On colorful Front St, this place serves excellent Italian food, which you can take on the patio to watch the passing parade. This is a good place to bring the kids.

Salty's Beachouse Seafood Restaurant (☎ 250-493-5001; 1000 Lakeshore Dr; mains $13-25; ☼ dinner Apr-Oct) Ropes, lanterns and other nautical paraphernalia reflect a seasonal seafood menu that includes excellent fresh halibut. However, the real draw is the courtyard directly opposite the beach – perfect for a languid meal on a warm evening.

Drinking & Entertainment

Barking Parrot (☎ 250-493-8221; Penticton Lakeside Resort, 21 Lakeshore Dr W; ☺ noon–late summer) Attracts a local crowd that lounges around at the outdoor tables overlooking the lake. There's frequent live music and comedy.

Element (☎ 250-493-1023; 535 Main St; cover $5; ☺ 7pm-late) A stayer that still packs the dancers in for hip-hop, house and touring musical acts.

Blue Mule (☎ 250-493-1819; 218 Martin St; cover varies; ☺ 8pm-late Sat & Sun) Located near the corner of Westminster Ave, the Mule features country music, classic rock and dancing.

OKANAGAN VALLEY WINERIES

If you're into slow walks through lush vineyards and long lazy lunches complemented by fine regional wines, then you're going to have a splendid time in the Okanagan Valley. With ample sunshine and fertile soil, the Okanagan Valley is BC's largest, oldest and best wine-growing district.

While the region is particularly known for its Chardonnay, Pinot Grigio, Merlot and Burgundy varietals, its signature tipple is ice wine (see the boxed text on p133). Expect to pay between $55 and $70 for a bottle of decent quality.

Information

Both of these places offer guidance on styles and vintages, and can recommend wineries that specialize in your favorite style:

BC Wine Information Centre (☎ 250-493-4055, 800-663-5052; 888 Westminster Ave W, Penticton; ☺ 8am-8pm summer, 9am-5pm Mon-Fri, 11am-5pm Sat & Sun rest of year)

Wine Museum (☎ 250-868-0441; 1304 Ellis St, Kelowna; ☺ 10am-5pm Mon-Sat, noon-5pm Sun)

Festivals & Tours

A great way to get inside the local scene is to visit during one of the four seasonal festivals held each year. The wineries know how to put on a party and use the festivals to launch new and premier wines, conduct tastings of rare wines, host special tasting dinners and more. Check up on the seasonal happenings with a visit to the very good website of **Okanagan Wine Festivals** (www.owfs.com). The festivals are held in spring (early May), summer (early August), fall (early October) and winter (late January).

There are several tour companies that let you do the sipping while they do the driving; others include winery visits in cycling or walking tours. See p748 for details.

Visiting the Wineries

At all the wineries open to visitors you can expect to taste wine, but the quality of the experience varies widely, from a couple of bottles sitting on a table to a fully blown tasting centre with attached restaurant and sweeping valley views.

At last count, there were more than 50 wineries in the Okanagan Valley. The following are just a few that are worth a visit – others you'll have to discover yourself.

CedarCreek Estate Winery (☎ 250-764-8866; www.cedarcreek.bc.ca; 5445 Lakeshore Rd, Kelowna; ☺ 10am-6pm May-Oct, 11am-5pm Mon-Apr, tours at 11am, 2pm & 3pm May-Oct) Known for excellent tours, as well as its Pinot Blanc.

Inniskillin Okanagan Vineyards (☎ 250-498-6663; www.inniskillin.com; Rd 11 W, Oliver; ☺ 10am-5pm, until 3pm winter) Renowned for its ice wines; includes the Vidal and Riesling varietals.

Quails' Gate Estate Winery (☎ 250-769-4451; www.quailsgate.com; 3303 Boucherie Rd, Kelowna; ☺ 10am-5pm) A small winery with a huge reputation; known for its Pinot Noir, Sauvignon Blanc and its superb botrytis dessert wine. One of the best places for a visit.

Sumac Ridge Estate Winery (☎ 250-494-0451; www.sumacridge.com; 17403 Hwy 97, Summerland; ☺ 9am-9pm, to 5pm Jan & Feb) A family-run winery with good personal tours ($5 per person, redeemable on wine purchase); try the Cabernet Merlot, unoaked Chardonnay and Okanagan Blush.

Getting There & Around

Penticton Regional Airport (YYF; ☎ 250-492-6042; www.cyyf.org) is served by Air Canada Jazz, which has daily flights to Vancouver ($140, one hour).

The **bus depot** (☎ 250-493-4101; 307 Ellis St) has Greyhound Canada services within the Okanagan Valley, as well as routes to Vancouver ($60, six hours), Prince George ($110, 13 hours) and Calgary ($96, 12 hours).

The lake-to-lake shuttle bus of **Penticton Transit** (☎ 250-492-5602; www.busonline.ca/regions/pen/; one-way fare $1.75, day pass $4; ☼ 9am-6:50pm Sun only) runs hourly along both waterfronts.

KELOWNA

pop 150,000

The Okanagan's major city, Kelowna is an excellent base for exploration. It has an attractive lakefront, thriving downtown nightlife and numerous cultural institutions – not to forget a junior hockey team that's the pride of the city. The rounded, scrubby hills typical of the valley encircle Kelowna, but the city center is bursting with gardens and parks, the green hues contrasting beautifully with the clear blue waters of the lake. Beneath skies that are almost always clear, scores of summer tourists come through to sip wine, play in the lake, visit wineries, hike the hills or simply laze around in the sunshine. Summer days are usually dry and hot, and the nights pleasantly cool. Winters are snowy but dry, making nearby Big White a big attraction for skiers and snowboarders. It's a terrific place, and you could happily while away several days here exploring the city and region.

Orientation

Kelowna sits midway between Vernon and Penticton, along the east side of 136km-long Okanagan Lake. Starting from City Park, Bernard Ave runs east and is the city's main drag. Ellis St, running north–south, is also an important thoroughfare and parallels the Cultural District.

Highway 97, called Harvey Ave in Kelowna, marks the southern edge of the downtown area and heads west over the bridge towards Penticton. East of downtown, Harvey Ave degenerates into a 10km strip lined with service stations, shopping malls, motels and fast-food restaurants. Past the sprawl, Harvey Ave is again called Hwy 97 and heads northeast toward Vernon.

Information

Most of the town's banks (with ATMs) are on Bernard Ave, between Water and Ellis Sts.

Kelowna General Hospital (☎ 250-862-4000; cnr Pandosy St & Royal Ave; ☼ 24hr) Emergency medical services.

Kelowna Library (☎ 250-762-2800; 1380 Ellis St; ☼ 10am-5:30pm Mon, Fri & Sat, 10am-9pm Tue-Thu Apr-Sep, 1-5pm Sun Oct-Mar) Internet access is free with registration.

Mosaic Books (☎ 250-763-4418; 411 Bernard Ave) A huge range of quality fiction and nonfiction here, plus a popular coffee bar.

Post office (☎ 250-868-8480; 591 Bernard Ave; ☼ 8:30am-5:30pm Mon-Sat)

Ted's Paperbacks & Comics (☎ 250-763-1258; 269 Leon Ave) Used books and an eclectic mix of collector comics.

VIC (☎ 250-861-1515, 800-663-4345; www.tourism kelowna.org; 544 Harvey Ave; ☼ 8am-7pm summer, 8am-5pm Mon-Fri, 10am-3pm Sat & Sun winter) Near the corner of Ellis St; pick up the impressive brochure for a self-guided tour of the Cultural District.

Sights

CITY PARK & PROMENADE

The focal point of the city's shoreline, this lovely downtown park is home to manicured gardens, water features and **Hot Sands Beach**, where the water is just slightly cooler than the summer air. Restaurants and pubs take advantage of the uninterrupted views of the lake and forested shore opposite. North of the marina, **Waterfront Park** offers similar relaxed charms.

The beach runs from the marina to the **Okanagan Lake Floating Bridge**, west of City Park. This long floating bridge is supported by 12 pontoons and has a lift span in the middle, so boats can pass through. From Bernard Ave, the lakeside promenade extends north past the marina and is good for a stroll or jog in the morning or evening.

CULTURAL DISTRICT

This revamped arts district lies around the intersection of Water St and Cawston Ave, and is good for an afternoon stroll. The **Kelowna Art Gallery** (☎ 250-762-2226; www .kelownaartgallery.com; 1315 Water St; adult/concession $4/3; ☼ 10am-5pm Tue, Wed, Fri & Sat, to 9pm Thu, 1-5pm Sun) is a light, airy gallery that features changing exhibitions of local and regional artists. Nearby, **Turtle Island Gallery** (☎ 250-717-

KELOWNA

0 — 300 m
0 — 0.2 miles

To Knox Mountain (750m)→

To Farmers' Market (1km);
Greyhound Canada Bus Depot (2km);
Safari Inn (3km); Airport (20km);
Vernon (45km); Big White Ski Resort (55km)→

To Kelowna General Hospital (100m);
Kelowna International Hostel (400m);
Mission Creek Greenway (2.5km);
Okanagan Mountain
Provincial Park (15km)→

To Bear Creek
Provincial Park (9km);
Penticton (68km);
Vancouver (395km)→

8235; 1295 Cannery Lane; 🕙 10am-5:30pm Mon-Sat, also 11am-4pm Sun May–mid-Oct) sells works by First Nations artists.

In the old Laurel Orchards packinghouse, the **BC Orchard Industry Museum** (☎ 250-763-0433; www.kelownamuseum.ca; 1304 Ellis St; admission by donation; 🕙 10am-5pm Tue-Sat) recounts the conversion of the Okanagan Valley from cattle range to orchards; a highlight is the brilliant colors and designs of old packing-crate labels. In the same building, the **Wine Museum** (☎ 250-868-0441; www.kelownamuseum.ca; admission free; 🕙 10am-5pm Tue-Sat) can advise on the best of the regional vineyards, or just fill your car with the local product.

Not far away, the **Kelowna Museum** (☎ 250-763-2417; www.kelownamuseum.ca; cnr Queensway Ave &

Ellis St; admission by donation; 🕙 10am-5pm Tue-Sat), in the civic-center complex, has mildly interesting displays on Kelowna's ethnographic and natural history. The Japanese **Kasugai Gardens** (admission free; 🕙 9am-6pm), just west of the museum and where you can meditate in the peaceful ambience, are better.

The cultural district is also home to a couple of theaters and the large venue of Skyreach Place.

Activities

The weather makes Kelowna a great spot for outdoor activities. Lots of them are centered on the district's 200 lakes, particularly fishing, boating and windsurfing. You can rent speedboats (starting at $55 per hour), arrange fishing trips and cruises, or rent windsurfing gear from **Kelowna Marina** (☎ 250-861-8001) at the lake end of Queensway Ave. Windsurfers take to the water from the old seaplane terminal, near the corner of Water St and Cawston Ave. Parasailing is offered daily in summer by **Kelowna Parasail Adventures** (☎ 250-868-4838; www.parasailcanada.com; 1310 Water St; flights from $50), in front of the Grand Okanagan hotel.

You'll find great walking, hiking and mountain biking all around town. To get started, pick up the excellent *Heritage Walking Tour* brochure from the VIC. While you're there, ask for directions to **Mission Creek Greenway**, a meandering, wooded path following the creek from the coast south of downtown, and 18km inland to Layer Cake Mountain; it makes for a nice, mellow bike ride. You can also hike or ride up **Knox Mountain**, which sits at the north end of the city. Along with bobcats and snakes, the mountain has good trails, and rewards you with excellent views from the top. Sadly, devastating fires in 2003 destroyed much of the **Kettle Valley Railway Trail**, but plans are afoot to rebuild it; check with the VIC.

Bear Creek Provincial Park (☎ 250-494-6500; wlapwww.gov.bc.ca/bcparks), located approximately 8.5km northwest of Kelowna, offers opportunities for hiking as well as windsurfing, fishing, swimming and backcountry camping. To get there from downtown, cross the floating bridge and go north on Westside Rd.

Almost completely burnt out in 2003, **Okanagan Mountain Provincial Park** (☎ 250-494-6500; wlapwww.gov.bc.ca/bcparks) usually offers great horse riding, hiking, canoeing and camping, but was still closed at the time of research. Contact the park rangers to get the latest news.

Tours

Numerous Kelowna companies offer tours to many of the region's wineries, ranging in length from a few hours to a full day, with various eating options as well. Tour prices usually include a pick-up at hotels and motels. See also p745 for an overview of the region's wineries.

Monashee Adventure Tours (☎ 250-762-9253, 888-762-9253; www.monasheeadventuretours.com; tours from $100) Cycling specialists that tie in winery visits with their tours.

Okanagan Wine Country Tours (☎ 250-868-9463; www.okwinetours.com; 4hr tours $52) All-day tours include a gourmet lunch ($110).

Tasteful Tours (☎ 250-769-1929; www.homestead.com/tastefulwinetours; 3hr tours $35) Visits four local wineries.

Wildflower Trails and Wine Tours (☎ 250-979-1211, 866-979-1211; www.wildflowersandwine.com; day tours $95) Combines a lovely hike through the wildflower-covered hills of the valley with lunch and an afternoon of wine tasting.

Sleeping

As in the rest of the Okanagan Valley, accommodations here can be difficult to find in summer; it's best to book ahead or arrive early in the day.

BUDGET

Kelowna has two good, but very different, hostels. If you wish to camp, you'll end up a long way from downtown; either on the western side of the lake or south along Lakeshore Rd.

Kelowna SameSun International Hostel (☎ 250-763-9814, 877-562-2783; www.samesun.com; 245 Harvey Ave; dm $22, d from $40; P ☐) A large, modern and fairly institutional hostel, it's perfectly located on the edge of downtown and has a huge range of amenities, including volleyball courts, pool tables, Internet access, a barbecue area and bike rentals. The hostel also offers packages to its Big White and Silver Star ski-resort hostels.

Kelowna International Hostel (☎ 250-763-6024; www.kelowna-hostel.bc.ca; 2343 Pandosy St; dm from $13; P ☐) A short walk from the beach, and 12 blocks from downtown, this is a far more relaxed place in a small old house, although it still has all the facilities you need.

Bear Creek Provincial Park (☎ 250-494-0321; wlapwww.gov.bc.ca/bcparks; campsites $22; P) On the western side of the lake, 9km north of Kelowna off Westside Rd, this is the best camping option, with 122 shady sites close to the park's 400m-long beachfront area.

MID-RANGE & TOP END

Grand Okanagan (☎ 250-763-4500, 800-465-4651; www.grandokanagan.com; 1310 Water St; d from $180; P ☒) The town's finest, the ever-growing Grand boasts a premier position on the lake in the Cultural District, and throws in a spa, excellent pool area, a gym and restaurants, plus a casino for those with more money than sense.

Safari Inn (☎ 250-860-8122, 800-989-9399; www .safariinn.kelowna.com; 1651 Powick St; d from $65; P ☺) One of the better outlying motels, the Safari is set back from the noise of the highway and has large clean rooms. Its finest feature is the generous private lawn that surrounds a very big pool (by motel standards anyway).

Royal Anne Hotel (☎ 250-763-2277, 888-811-3400; www.royalannehotel.com; 348 Bernard Ave; s/d from $90/100; P) Offering the best value for money among the central hotels, the Anne's rooms are functional if unexciting, but the location puts you right in the thick of things.

Prestige Inn (☎ 250-860-7900, 877-737-8443; www .prestigeinn.com; 1675 Abbott St; d from $150; P ☐ ☺) Another place with a super location, just across from City Park; the rooms have free high-speed Internet access, and there's also a restaurant, a pool, a hot tub and a fitness center.

Kelowna Motor Inn (☎ 250-762-2533, 800-667-6133; www.kminn.bc.ca; 1070 Harvey Ave; s/d/ste from $85/100/150; P ☺) Popular with families, thanks to its large indoor pool and small spa, this place has good rates on two-bedroom suites with kitchens.

Also recommended:

Accent Inn (☎ 250-862-8888, 800-663-0298; www .accentinns.com; 1140 Harvey Ave; r from $100; P ☺) A well-run place near Kelowna Motor Inn and with comfortable rooms.

Traveler's Choice Motor Inn (☎ 250-762-3221, 800-665-2610; www.travellerschoice.org; 1780 Gordon Dr; r from $70; P ☺) Not too far from town, this good chain motel has spacious rooms with balconies.

Eating

Kelowna makes good use of its access to fine fresh produce to offer an excellent selection of restaurants.

Fresco (☎ 250-868-8805; 1560 Water St; mains $35; ☽ dinner Tue-Sat) Noted BC chef Ron Butters has entrenched this restaurant as Kelowna's finest. Seasonal and regional ingredients are used to superb effect in the dramatic open kitchen, while the linen is crisp, the cutlery heavy and the wine list long and inviting. You'll need to book well in advance, especially during summer.

Verve (☎ 250-860-8086; 345 Lawrence Ave; meals $10; ☽ breakfast, lunch & dinner) This hip café-bistro drags in everyone from young mums and students to businesspeople dodging the office politics. An ever-changing menu and

fine coffee are served in a long, stylish room with well-spaced tables; or you can take in the sun on the pavement.

Tripke Bakery & Café (☎ 250-763-7666; 567 Bernard Ave; light meals $5; ☽ breakfast & lunch) A classic German bakery with pan-European cakes and pastries, plus a little café area for a light lunch.

La Bussola (☎ 250-763-3110; 234 Leon Ave; mains $25; ☽ dinner Tue-Sat) The backstreet location is a bit skanky, but the elegant decor and fine Italian food is anything but. Fresh pasta is complemented by seasonal ingredients, deferential service and an international wine list.

Coyote's Waterfront Bar & Grill (☎ 250-860-1226; 1352 Water St; steaks $24; ☽ lunch & dinner) The best thing about this place on the waterfront is the great lake view. That said, the enormous steaks and dripping ribs are perennially popular, and the place is packed out in summer.

Grateful Fed Psyche Deli (☎ 250-862-8621; 509 Bernard Ave; sandwiches $5; ☽ breakfast, lunch & dinner) This dark and friendly little place hangs its hat on the Montréal smoked meats it serves, along with celebrity visitors and as much ambient Garcia as you can take.

Kelowna boasts some damn fine pubs that also serve good pub grub of the burger, pizza, chicken-wings and chowder variety.

Self-caterers can head to the well-stocked **Safeway Supermarket** (☎ 250-860-0332; 697 Bernard Ave) or, during summer, out of town to the **farmers' market** (☎ 250-878-5029; cnr Springfield Rd & Dilworth Dr, off Hwy 97; ☽ 8am-1pm Wed & Sat May-Oct), which has more than 100 stands, including many with prepared foods.

Drinking

Sturgeon Hall (☎ 250-860-4664; 1481 Water St) Home to the fanatical fans of the Kelowna Rockets hockey team, the Sturgeon's twin levels drip with NHL, WHL and Memorial Cup memorabilia. It's the best place in town to catch a TV game, especially when the Rockets take the points.

Rose's Waterfront Pub (☎ 250-860-1141; 1352 Water St) A more relaxed beer-swilling spot, Rose's is popular with locals and has a terrific lakefront patio, with heaters overhead to extend the season.

Kelly O'Bryan's (☎ 250-861-1338; 262 Bernard Ave) This is a fun place. Its upstairs 'paddy-o' fills quickly on warm summer nights, and the well-drawn Guinness attracts expats and Brit travelers.

Entertainment

Downtown Kelowna boasts several ever-changing clubs.

Flashbacks Nite Club (☎ 250-861-3039; 1268 Ellis St; cover varies; ⏰ 7pm-late Wed-Sun), in a former cigar factory, brings back the halcyon days of the 1980s. You can play pool, take in a live band or get into one of the regular theme nights.

Gotcha (☎ 250-860-0800; 238 Leon Ave; cover varies; ⏰ 7pm-late Tue-Sat) is one of three clubs on this stretch of Leon. A two-story place with three bars and plenty of room for dancing, it often fills up late.

If you haven't caught a hockey game yet, the much-loved **Kelowna Rockets** (☎ 250-860-7825; www.kelownarockets.com; tickets from $10) play in 6000-seat **Skyreach Place** (☎ 250-979-0888; www.skyreachplace.com; cnr Water St & Cawston Ave), which also hosts touring bands.

You can catch a new-release flick at **Paramount Theatre** (☎ 250-869-3939; 261 Bernard Ave). Kelowna also has two good live theaters, playing everything from community shows to musicals and traveling national acts: **Kelowna Community Theatre** (☎ 250-762-2471; 1375 Water St) **Rotary Centre for the Performing Arts** (☎ 250-717-5304, box office 250-763-1849; 421 Cawston Ave)

Getting There & Away

Kelowna Airport (YLW; ☎ 250-765-5125; www.kelowna airport.com) is 20km north on Hwy 97. WestJet serves Vancouver ($70, one hour), Victoria ($80, 50 minutes), Edmonton ($85, two hours) and Calgary ($80, 1½ hours) with nonstop cheap flights, while Air Canada Jazz serves Vancouver ($115, one hour) and Calgary ($140, two hours), and Horizon Air provides international service and connections to Seattle ($250, one hour).

The **Greyhound Canada bus depot** (☎ 250-860-3835; www.greyhound.ca; 2366 Leckie Rd) is north of the downtown area, off Hwy 97; take city bus No 10 from Queensway Station in downtown. Daily buses travel to other points in the Okanagan Valley, as well as Kamloops ($27, three hours, three daily), Vancouver ($60, six hours, six daily), Calgary and Prince George.

All the major car-rental companies (see p873) operate from the airport.

Getting Around

Kelowna Airport Shuttle (☎ 250-765-0182; one-way fare $20) connects the city with the airport.

A taxi costs about $28 each way. If you're heading north, **Vernon Airporter** (☎ 250-542-7574) can take you to that town ($22).

For bicycle hire, contact **Monashee Adventure Tours** (☎ 250-762-9253; www.monasheeadventure tours.com; 470 Cawston Ave; rentals from $25), which has good-quality hybrids and fully sprung mountain bikes.

Pick up a copy of *Kelowna Regional Rider's Guide* from the VIC, or try **Kelowna Regional Transit Systems** (☎ 250-860-8121; www.busonline.ca/regions/kel). There are three zones for bus travel; the one-way fare in the central zone is $1.75, while a day pass for all three zones costs $5. All the city buses pass through Queensway Station in downtown.

Taxi companies include **Kelowna Cabs** (☎ 250-762-4444) and **Checkmate Cabs** (☎ 250-861-1111).

BIG WHITE SKI RESORT

Known for its incredible powder, **Big White Ski Resort** (☎ 250-765-8888, 800-663-2772; www.big white.com; lift pass adult/child $60/32), 55km east of Kelowna off Hwy 33, is one of BC's best ski resorts. With a vertical drop of 777m, it features 840 hectares of runs that offer excellent downhill and backcountry skiing, while deep gullies make for killer snowboarding. Because of Big White's distance from Kelowna, most people stay up here. The resort includes numerous restaurants, bars, hotels, condos, rental homes and a hostel. Contact **central reservations** (☎ 800-663-2772; www.bigwhite .com) for full details and rates.

VERNON

Vernon, the most northerly of Okanagan's 'Big Three,' lies in a scenic valley encircled by three lakes and several provincial parks. It's a blue-collar logging town with few attractions of its own, but the swimming, fishing and camping in the surrounding provincial parks bring in the visitors. If that's not your scene, keep on trucking up the highway.

Orientation & Information

Downtown Vernon is a clean, neat place that's spilt by Hwy 97. Most of the shops are found along 30th Ave (known as Main St) on the eastern side, while restaurants and pubs are found both there and along the highway. Confusingly, 30th Ave (Main St) is intersected by 30th St in the middle of downtown, so check addresses before heading out.

Vernon has twin **VICs** (☎ 250-542-1415, 800-665-0795; www.vernontourism.com; 6326 Hwy 97 N & 701 Hwy 97 S; ☺ 8:30am-6pm summer; 8:30am-4:30pm Mon-Fri, 10am-4pm Sat & Sun rest of year) that cover the main entrances and exits to town.

Vernon Public Library (☎ 250-542-7610; 3001 32nd Ave; ☺ 10am-5:30pm Mon & Thu-Sat, 10am-4pm Tue & Wed) has free Internet access, and there's a **post office** (☎ 250-545-8239; 3101 32nd Ave) on the corner of 31st St.

Sights & Activities

The beautiful 9-sq-km **Kalamalka Lake Provincial Park** (☎ 250-545-1560; wlapwww.gov.bc.ca/bcparks) south of town lies on the eastern side of this warm, shallow lake. The park offers great swimming at Jade and Kalamalka Beaches, good fishing and a network of mountain-biking and hiking trails. There's also excellent rock climbing at Cougar Canyon.

Ellison Provincial Park, 16km southwest of Vernon on Okanagan Lake, is western Canada's only freshwater marine park; scuba diving is popular here and gear can be rented from **Innerspace Dive & Kayak** (☎ 250-549-2910; 3103 32nd St). Ellison also has an excellent campground and hiking and biking trails. North of town is Silver Star Mountain Resort, a provincial park with winter skiing and summer hiking and biking.

If the weather's poor, the **Vernon Museum** (☎ 250-542-3142; www.vernonmuseum.ca; cnr 32nd Ave & 31st St; admission free; ☺ 10am-5pm Tue-Sat) and **Vernon Art Gallery** (☎ 250-545-3173; www.galleries.bc.ca/vernon; 3228 31st Ave; admission by donation; ☺ 10am-5pm Mon-Fri, 11am-4pm Sat) are modest, but will help kill a couple of hours.

Sleeping

Accommodations are available in all price ranges. The twin VICs have information on local B&Bs.

Tiki Village Motel (☎ 250-503-5566, 800-661-8454; www.tikivillagevernon.com; 2408 34th St; d $90-145) This likeable, retro motel boasts lovely grounds and a fair-sized outdoor pool, while the large rooms throw the standard motel decor out the window, featuring cane furniture and timber-and-paper screens. All rooms have balconies.

HI Lodged Inn (☎ 250-549-3742, 888-737-9427; www .hihostels.ca; 3201 Pleasant Alley Rd; dm $20; ☺ 5-10pm; 🖳) Just a few minutes' walk from downtown, this lovely hostel works with local organizations to arrange paragliding, skydiving, climbing and hiking trips, plus winery tours and interpretive tours of the area's flora and fauna.

Ellison Provincial Park (☎ 800-689-9025; wlapwww .gov.bc.ca/bcparks; Okanagan Landing Rd; campsites $17) Located 16km southwest of Vernon, this is by far the best campground, with a lovely beach, and good hiking and biking trails nearby. Its campsites fill up early, so book in advance.

Silver Star Motel (☎ 250-545-0501; silverstar.vernon .bcnetwork.com; 3700 32nd St; d from $65) A high-quality budget motel, the rooms here are big, spotlessly clean and quite well-baffled against the highway noise. It also has discounts for meals at nearby restaurants and take-out places.

Eating & Drinking

Eclectic Med (☎ 250-558-4646; 3117 32nd St; meals $12-25; ☺ lunch Mon-Fri, dinner) A long-standing local favorite, this place is heavy on the Med (plenty of Italian and North African flavors), while the judicious use of Thai, Chinese and Vietnamese tastes takes care of the 'eclectic' bit. There's a good wine list to wash it all down.

Amarin Thai (☎ 250-542-9300; 2903 31st St; meals $9-15; ☺ lunch Mon-Fri, dinner Mon-Sat) A fairly formal setting conceals a relaxed and stylish eatery, with all the mouthwatering spices and textures of this alluring cuisine.

Sir Winston's Pub (☎ 250-549-3485; 2705 32nd St; pizza $10; ☺ noon-late) There's a lively pub atmosphere here, with fine beer choices and a cool patio. The pub menu is long and the food is a cut above the norm.

Getting There & Around

Buses stop at the **Greyhound Canada depot** (☎ 250-545-0527; cnr 30th St & 31st Ave). To get to the lakes, **local buses** (☎ 250-545-7221; one-way fare $1.50) leave infrequently from downtown at the corner of 31st St and 30th Ave. For Kalamalka Lake, catch bus Nos 1 or 6; for Okanagan Lake, take bus No 7.

NORTH OF VERNON

There are only a couple of attractions in this area, which is more notable for its major highway connections. Just north of Vernon, Hwy 97 heads northwest to Kamloops (and eventually to Prince Rupert), while Hwy 97A continues northeast to Sicamous and Hwy 1. From Sicamous, this major artery can take you west to Shuswap Lake, Salmon Arm and Kamloops, and east to Revelstoke and past a trio of excellent national parks to Lake Louise (p619) in Alberta.

Silver Star Mountain Resort

A provincial park 22km northeast of Vernon (take 48th St), **Silver Star Mountain Resort** (☎ 250-542-0224, 800-663-4431, snow report ☎ 250-542-1745; www.silverstarmtn.com; 1-day lift pass adult/child $56/30) offers both winter and summer activities. Boasting more than 1100 hectares of snowy terrain (with a vertical drop of 760m), it attracts all levels of skier and snowboarder from late October to early April. The summer season starts in late June and the ski runs become excellent hiking and mountain-biking trails. There is all manner of accommodations at the resort, with its built-up Victorian-style village of hotels and great restaurants, including the fine **SameSun Budget Lodge** (☎ 250-545-8933, 877-562-2783; www .samesun.com; 9898 Pinnacles Rd; dm/d $25/60). Contact the resort directly for other options.

Shuswap Region

The district around **Shuswap Lake** is picturesque, with green, wooded hills, farms and two small towns, Sicamous and Salmon Arm. The latter has the area's main **VIC** (☎ 250-832-2230, 877-725-6667; www.sachamber.bc.ca; 200 Trans-Canada Hwy; ☻ 9am-7pm summer, 9am-5pm Mon-Fri rest of year).

The area is home to several lake-based provincial parks and is a popular destination for family holidays. The main attraction, though, is the annual spawning of sockeye salmon at **Roderick Haig-Brown Provincial Park** (☎ 250-851-3000), just off the highway via Squilax. This 1059-hectare park protects both sides of the Adams River between Shuswap Lake and Adams Lake, a natural bottleneck for the bright-red sockeye when they run upriver every October. The fish population peaks every four years, when as many as four million fish crowd the Adams' shallow riverbeds – the next big spawns are due in 2006 and 2010.

Houseboating can be a fun way to explore the Shuswap, especially during the height of summer, when the lake resembles a floating village. Most rent by the week (from $2000) and can sleep about 10 people. Contact the

VIC for a list of houseboat operators and other accommodations in the district.

THE KOOTENAYS & THE ROCKIES

The picturesque Kootenay region of BC is dominated by four mountain ranges – the Selkirks and Monashees in the west and the Rockies and Purcells in the east – and almost anywhere you look, you'll see snow-covered peaks. Wedged between the parallel mountain chains is an incredibly scenic series of lakes, rivers and thinly populated valleys. Dense populations of grizzly and black bear, elk, moose and deer thrive here, so you stand a good chance of seeing wildlife, particularly within the network of excellent national and provincial parks.

The Kootenays can be divided into western and eastern sections, with the 150km-long north–south Kootenay Lake providing a rough line of delineation. The West Kootenays run in and around the Selkirk Mountains west of Creston to Grand Forks and include Nelson, Nakusp and Rossland. The East Kootenays covers the Purcell Mountain region below Golden, taking in Radium Hot Springs, Kimberley and Fernie. Further east, BC's Rocky Mountains parks (Mt Revelstoke, Glacier, Yoho and Kootenay) do not get the raves of their Alberta neighbors, Banff and Jasper National Parks, but don't be too quick to pass them by; they are fine, self-contained parks in their own right, protecting different

---

CHECK YOUR WATCH

Like Alberta and Idaho, the East Kootenays and the Rockies lie in the Mountain Time Zone, unlike the West Kootenays and the rest of BC, which fall within the Pacific Time Zone. If you're heading west on the Trans-Canada Hwy (Hwy 1) from Golden, the time changes at the east gate of Glacier National Park. As you travel west on the Crowsnest Hwy (Hwy 3), the time changes between Cranbrook and Creston. Mountain Time is always an hour ahead of Pacific Time. So when it's noon in Golden and Cranbrook, it's 11am in Glacier National Park and Creston.

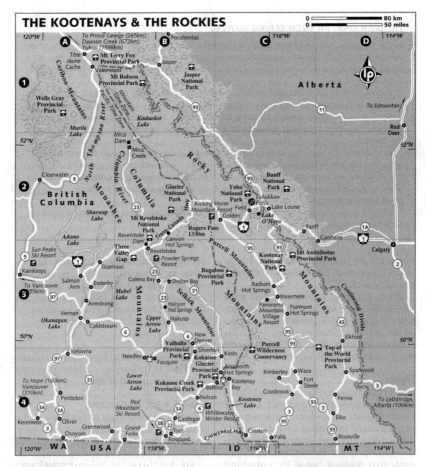

THE KOOTENAYS & THE ROCKIES

ecosystems and providing their own special experiences.

This section heads east from Revelstoke to the Rockies (where you can link up with Banff and Jasper), then swings back into BC and west through the Kootenays. Note that the southeastern corner of BC is on Mountain Standard Time, while most of the province is on Pacific Standard Time, which is one hour earlier (see opposite).

REVELSTOKE

On Hwy 1, 70km east of Sicamous, this small town is a picturesque, outdoorsy place. Its quiet streets are lined with neat wooden houses and tidy gardens, and snowcapped peaks pierce the sky in every direction. Mt

Revelstoke National Park is just outside town, and Glacier National Park is a short drive down the highway. Revelstoke is also a busy railway center – you may eventually stop twitching at the ear-splitting blasts of trains passing through town.

Orientation & Information

Revelstoke is south of Hwy 1. Victoria Rd runs parallel to the very busy railway tracks that run along the northeastern end of town. The main streets include 1st St and Mackenzie Ave.

The **VIC** (☎ 250-837-5345, 800-487-1493; www.see revelstoke.com; 206 Campbell Ave; ♥ 8:30am-4:30pm Mon-Fri) also has a **summer office** (111 Mackenzie St; ♥ 8:30am-6pm). **Parks Canada** (☎ 250-837-7500;

THE IRON LINK: AN ENGINEERING MARVEL

British Columbia had an almost separate existence from the rest of Canada until 1885, when the Canadian Pacific Railway across the Rockies was completed. These rails for the first time linked the disparate territories of the west and east, and were instrumental in cementing the unity of the nation.

Running the rails through the Rockies was an enormous challenge that was accomplished by the labor of thousands of immigrant workers, who endured harsh conditions to complete the dangerous work. Hundreds were killed by disease and accidents, including horrific avalanches in Rogers Pass. Eventually huge tunnels and snow sheds were laboriously constructed to protect the trains.

East of Field, the gradients were so steep that any braking problem caused trains to run away down the hill, where they would eventually fly off the tracks with terrible loss of life. To solve this problem, two huge spiraling tunnels were built inside the granite mountains, reducing the grade to a much more manageable 2.2%. These remain in use and are an internationally recognized engineering marvel.

Want to know more? Revelstoke's railway museum (p654) documents the history of the entire Canadian Pacific Railway line.

---

www.pc.gc.ca; 301 3rd St; ☯ 8am-4:30pm Mon-Fri) has lots of information about the town and surrounding parks.

Other facilities include the **post office** (☎ 250-837-3228; 313 3rd St) and **Queen Victoria Hospital** (☎ 250-837-2131; 6622 Newlands Rd; ☯ doctor on call 24hr), while free Internet access is available at **Revelstoke Library** (☎ 250-837-5095; 605 Campbell Ave; ☯ noon-8pm Tue, 10am-5pm Wed-Sat).

Sights

Grizzly Plaza, between Mackenzie and Orton Aves, is a pedestrian precinct and the heart of downtown, where free live-music performances take place in the evenings throughout July and August. While outdoor activities are Revelstoke's real draw card, there is also a pair of local museums you can check out.

Revelstoke Railway Museum (☎ 250-837-6060, 877-837-6060; www.railwaymuseum.com; 719 Track St W; adult/child $6/3.50; ☯ 9am-8pm summer, 9am-5pm Mon-Fri winter), in an attractive building across the tracks from the town center, contains restored steam locomotives, including one of the largest steam engines ever used on Canadian Pacific Railway lines. Photographs and artifacts document the construction of the CPR, which was instrumental – if not essential – in linking eastern and western Canada (see the boxed text above).

Revelstoke Museum (☎ 250-837-3067; 315 1st St; adult/child $2.50/1; ☯ 10am-5pm Mon-Sat summer, 1-4pm Mon-Fri winter) holds a permanent collection of furniture and historical odds and ends, including mining, logging and railway artifacts that date back to the town's establishment in the 1880s. Also look for the many historical plaques mounted on buildings around town.

Activities

The paved Revelstoke River Trail (an excellent place to walk or jog) runs along the river at the southern end of town.

SKIING & SNOWBOARDING

Whether you ski, board or just like to romp around in the snow, Revelstoke's long, snowy winter season and experienced tour operators give you plenty of options.

For downhill skiing, head to **Powder Springs Resort** (☎ 250-837-5151, 877-991-4455; www.catpowder .com/indexsprings.html; 1-day lift tickets adult/child $28/ free) on Mt Mackenzie, 4km southeast of Revelstoke. It lacks the multiple chairlifts of bigger resorts, but its heavy snowfall (up to 1.2m), access to backcountry slopes and small crowds make it a spectacular spot. You can get great deals if you stay at the Powder Springs Inn.

A popular but expensive way to find fresh powder is by heli-skiing, where a helicopter takes you into the high mountains to ski or snowboard steep slopes, deep powder and even glaciers. **Selkirk Tangiers Helicopter Skiing** (☎ 250-837-5378, 800-663-7080; www.selkirk-tangiers.com) runs three-day trips for $2100.

Though sometimes called the poor man's heli-skiing, **snowcats** can take you to some pristine areas, but they aren't exactly cheap. **CAT Powder Skiing** (☎ 250-837-5151, 800-991-4455; www.catpowder.com) offers packages starting at $1100 for two days.

Free Spirit Sports (☎ 250-837-9453; 203 1st St W) rents a wide variety of winter gear, including essential avalanche-protection equipment.

MOUNTAIN BIKING
Once the snow melts, ski runs become excellent mountain-biking trails. Pick up a copy of the *Biking Trail Map* from the VIC or at **High Country Cycle & Sports** (☎ 250-814-0090; 118 Mackenzie Ave), where you can also rent bikes from $20 per day.

WHITE-WATER RAFTING
Apex Rafting Company (☎ 250-837-6376, 888-232-6666; www.apexrafting.com; adult/child $75/63) With an office at Canyon Hot Springs, Apex runs mellow, four-hour guided trips on the Illecillewaet River in spring and summer.

Sleeping
Revelstoke has a good selection of places to stay in all price ranges. The downtown motels are great value and generally fill up first.

BUDGET
SameSun Budget Lodge (☎ 250-837-4050, 877-562-2783; www.samesun.ca; 400 2nd St W; dm/d $22/45) A small, neat place in a restored but somewhat labyrinthine building, it has two kitchens and a nice outdoor deck. It also offers various deals for local activities.

Martha Creek Provincial Park (☎ 250-825-4421; campsites $14), 16km north of town on Hwy 23, has flush toilets and running water but no showers.

MID-RANGE & TOP END
Powder Springs Inn (☎ 250-837-5151, 800-991-4455; www.catpowder.com; 200 3rd St W; d incl breakfast $60-80) Part of the empire that includes the ski resort and the snow-cat skiing operation, this excellent little motel has large rooms and a hot tub and spa, and has become a hub for skiers and snowboarders. There's also a convivial bar.

Regent Inn (☎ 250-837-2107, 888-245-5523; www.regentinn.com; 112 1st St W; d $110-180) With some of the nicest rooms in town, this is where a lot of

the heli-skiers stay in winter. The renovated and historic hotel contains a spa, a sauna, a restaurant and a lively bar.

Monashee Lodge (☎ 250-837-6778, 800-668-3139; www.monasheelodge.com; 1601 3rd St W; d from $50) This is a terrific budget hotel that's particularly good for groups (a five-person room goes for $90). The rooms are pretty plain, but are in good shape.

There are plenty of other motels in town and on the highway:

Canyon Motor Inn (☎ 250-837-5221, 877-837-5221; www.revelstokecc.bc.ca/; 1911 Fraser Dr; d from $75; 🖳). This older but well-maintained property on the highway has large rooms and free high-speed Internet access.

Swiss Chalet Motel (☎ 250-837-4650, 888-272-4538; www.swisschaletmotel.com; 1101 Victoria Rd; d $70-80) Features newly renovated rooms and is close to town.

Eating & Drinking
Frisby Ridge Teriyaki (☎ 250-837-5449; 201 1st St W; mains $6-14; ☺ lunch & dinner) In this simple little restaurant the bulk of the menu is Japanese but the best dishes have the clear, sour and spicy flavors of Korean cuisine, including excellent *bulgogi* (Korean barbecued beef) and kimchi.

Woolsey Creek (☎ 250-837-5500; 212 MacKenzie Ave; meals $6-12; ☺ breakfast, lunch & dinner) A great choice for a meal with everything from omelets to oatmeal in the morning, followed by great salads and sandwiches at lunch, and at night an interesting and changing fusion menu with lots of seafood and pasta. It's also licensed, so you can enjoy a beer on one of the comfy chairs out front.

Manning's Restaurant (☎ 250-837-3200; 302 Mackenzie Ave; meals $9; ☺ noon-9pm) Manning's is a throwback to the 1950s, right down to its classic neon sign out front. It's pretty popular, so the Chinese chow they serve must be OK.

Grizzly Sports Bar & Grill (☎ 250-837-5576; 314 1st St W; meals $8; ☺ lunch & dinner) Here you'll find a fun sports bar with good pub food. The fish and chips are excellent. It has the full line of the very fine locally brewed Mt Begbie beers on tap as well.

Getting There & Away
The **bus depot** (☎ 250-837-5874; 1899 Fraser Dr) is west of town, just off Hwy 1. Greyhound Canada buses go east to Banff ($46, 4½ hours) and Calgary ($62, six hours), and west to Kamloops ($36, three hours), Kelowna ($28, four hours) and beyond.

MT REVELSTOKE NATIONAL PARK

This 260-sq-km **park** (☎ 250-837-7500; www.pc .gc.ca/pn-np/bc/revelstoke; adult/child day pass $5/2.50), just northeast of Revelstoke in the Selkirk Mountains, comes alive with blankets of wildflowers in summer. The Selkirks are known for their jagged, rugged peaks and steep valleys. From the 2223m summit of Mt Revelstoke, the views of the mountains and the Columbia River valley are excellent.

To get to the summit, take the 26km **Meadows in the Sky Parkway**, 1.5km east of Revelstoke off Hwy 1. Open July to September, this paved road winds through lush cedar forests and alpine meadows, and ends at Balsam Lake, within 2km of the peak. From here walk to the top or take the free shuttle, which runs from 10am to 4:20pm daily.

There are several good hiking trails from the summit. You can camp only in designated backcountry campsites, and you must have an $8 Wilderness Pass camping permit (in addition to your park pass), which is available from **Parks Canada** (☎ 250-837-7500) in Revelstoke, or from the Rogers Pass Centre inside Glacier National Park (p756).

Another good walk is the **Skunk Cabbage Trail**, 28km east of Revelstoke on Hwy 1. Umbrella-sized leaves are just some of the highlights of a 1.2km boardwalk along the Illecillewaet River, giving an up-close view of the eponymous skunk cabbage, the marshes and myriad birds.

The entry fee is also good for Glacier National Park.

CANYON HOT SPRINGS

Around 35km east of Revelstoke, **Canyon Hot Springs** (☎ 250-837-2420; www.canyonhotsprings.com; adult/child day pass $8.50/7; ☾ 9am-9pm May, Jun & Sep, 9am-10pm Jul & Aug) is great for a quick visit. The site consists of a hot pool (42°C) and a larger, cooler swimming pool (32°C). You can rent a bathing suit and towel here. There's also a grocery store and a range of **accommodations** (tent/RV sites $22/30, cabins $95), with pool passes included in the cabin tariff.

GLACIER NATIONAL PARK

In the Columbia Mountains, about halfway between Revelstoke and Golden, lies this 1350-sq-km **park** (☎ 250-837-7500; www.parks canada.gc.ca/glacier; adult/child $7/3.50), which contains more than 430 glaciers. If you thought the other mountain parks were wet, then you'll like this place. It only rains twice a week here – once for three days and then again for four. It's the same in winter; it snows nearly every day, and the annual snowfall can be as much as 23m. Because of the sheer mountain slopes, this is one of the world's most-active avalanche areas. For this reason skiing, caving and mountaineering are closely regulated; you must register before you head out.

The hiking here is spectacular but hardcore, with extremely steep trails constructed mainly as access points for climbing. However, you're rewarded with simply stunning views. Contact the informative **Rogers Pass Centre** (☎ 250-814-5233; ☾ 8am-7pm summer, 9am-5pm spring & fall, 9am-7pm winter), 72km east of Revelstoke. The center also shows films on the park, organizes guided walks in summer, and sells Wilderness Pass camping permits ($8) for backcountry campers.

Not far from here are the park's two campgrounds: **Illecillewaet Campground** (tent & RV sites $17) and **Loop Brook Campground** (tent & RV sites $17). Both have running water and flush toilets. If a little more luxury is your style, then the **Best Western Glacier Park Lodge** (☎ 250-837-2126; www .glacierparklodge.ca; d from $135; ☒) will oblige.

GOLDEN

Sandwiched between the Purcell and Rocky Mountains, near the confluence of the Columbia and Kicking Horse Rivers, Golden is within striking distance of six major national parks, including the wildly popular Japser and Banff reserves, across the border in Alberta. The slew of hotels and fast-food franchises on the highway puts many people off, but across the railway line you'll find a neat little town that's starting to take real advantage of its serendipitous position. White-water rafting is hugely popular and the area's mountains beckon skiers, boarders, hikers and mountain bikers, while other brave souls launch hang gliders off nearby peaks. Golden is only accessible by car.

Orientation & Information

The center of town lies 2km south of the highway. On the way in you'll pass the helpful **VIC** (☎ 250-344-7125, 800-622-4653; www.golden chamber.bc.ca; 500 10th Ave N; ☾ 9am-5pm Jul & Aug, 9am-5pm Mon-Fri rest of year).

Activities

Golden is the center for white-water rafting trips on the turbulent and chilly Kicking Horse River. Powerful Class III and IV rapids and breathtaking scenery along the sheer valley walls make this rafting experience one of North America's best. **Glacier Raft Company** (☎ 250-344-6521; www.glacierraft.com) and **Wet 'n' Wild** (☎ 250-344-6546, 800-668-9119; www.wetnwild .bc.ca) both offer a range of trips from $55.

At Whitetooth Mountain, 14km northwest of Golden on Kicking Horse Trail, **Kicking Horse Mountain Resort** (☎ 250-439-5400, 866-754-5425; www.kickinghorseresort.com; 1-day lift pass adult/child $55/25) has three lifts, 1260 vertical meters and a relatively snow-heavy, wind-free position for skiing and snowboarding between the Rockies and the Purcells. A challenging 60% of its 96 runs are rated advanced or expert.

Sleeping & Eating

Mary's Motel (☎ 250-344-7111, 866-234-6279; www .marysmotel.com; 603 8th Ave N; r $60-90; ☒) In town right along the river, Mary's is tidy inside and out, and its quiet location makes it the town's best option. There are indoor and outdoor pools, two hot tubs, and some nice walks nearby.

Sportsman Lodge (☎ 250-344-2915, 888-989-5566; www.sportsmanlodge.ca; 1200 12th St N; d from $75; ☒) Back on the highway, you can kick back in the lodge's indoor pool or hot tub. The kids will love the water slide.

Sander Lake Campground (☎ 250-344-6517; www .rockies.net/~bsander; tent sites $12-15, 2-person cabins $75) Around 12km southwest of Golden, off Hwy 95, this place has a very pretty location amid trees and hills.

Kicking Horse Grill (☎ 250-344-2330; 1105 9th St S; meals $20-30; ☸ lunch & dinner Tue-Sat) Golden's best place for a fun yet very fine meal. The ever-changing menu concentrates on simple foods prepared well, although it branches out with offerings like Madagascar pork in a peppercorn sauce.

The **Kicking Horse Mountain Resort** (☎ 250-439-5400, 866-754-5425; www.kickinghorseresort.com) has a small range of accommodations that you'll need to book; contact the resort for details.

YOHO NATIONAL PARK

Established in 1886, waterfall-filled **Yoho National Park** (☎ 250-343-6783; www.pc.gc.ca/pn-np/bc/ yoho; day pass adult/child $7/3.50) is the smallest of the four national parks in the Rockies, with

an area of merely 1310 sq km. Still, with its mountain peaks, river valleys, glacial lakes and beautiful meadows, it's a truly awe-inspiring place, as befits its name (the Cree word *yoho* means 'awe'). The park is adjacent to the Alberta border and Banff National Park to the east, and Kootenay National Park to the south. Not as busy as Banff, Yoho often has campsite vacancies when Banff is full, though its position on the west side of the Rockies means that Yoho experiences more wet or cloudy days than Banff. The rushing Kicking Horse River flows through the park.

Orientation & Information

Yoho National Park Information Centre (☎ 250-343-6783; ☸ 9am-4pm Oct-Apr, 9am-5pm May, Jun & Sep, 9am-7pm Jul & Aug) is in the tiny town of Field, which is the focal point of the park's facilities. Tourism BC and Alberta Tourism staff their own desks here in summer. The center also contains an interesting display on the Burgess Shale world heritage site (see p758). While you're there, pick up the free *Backcountry Visitors' Guide*; its map and trail descriptions make it an excellent resource for exploring the park.

Sights & Activities

LAKE O'HARA

Nestled high in the mountains, this somewhat exclusive beauty spot more than lives up to its exalted reputation, and is definitely worth the sizable hassle to reach. Compact wooded hillsides, alpine meadows, snow-covered passes, mountain vistas and glaciers are all concentrated around the stunning lake, and a web of trails that are perfect for daylong and half-day hikes, most fairly rigorous, makes it all accessible. A simple day trip is well worthwhile, but overnighting makes hiking more trails possible. The fine Alpine Circuit trail (12km) offers a bit of everything.

To reach the lake, you can take the **shuttle bus** (☎ reservations 250-343-6433; adult/child $15/7.50; ☸ mid-Jun–early Oct) from the Lake O'Hara parking lot, 15km east of Field, but numbers are limited to reduce human pressure on the trails. Alternatively, you can walk the 13km from the parking area. Reservations for the bus and backcountry sites (permits $8) are all but mandatory in summer. If you don't have reservations, six day-use seats on the bus and three to five campsites are set aside for 'standby' users, but you need to register at the Field information center the day before you want to go.

BURGESS SHALE WORLD HERITAGE SITE
This world heritage site protects the amazing Cambrian-age fossil beds on Mt Stephen and Mt Field. These 515-million-year-old fossils preserve the remains of marine creatures that were some of the earliest forms of life on earth. You can only get to the fossil beds by guided hikes, which are led by naturalists from the **Yoho-Burgess Shale Foundation** (☎ 800-343-3006; www.burgess-shale.bc.ca; tours from $65). Reservations are essential.

WATERFALLS & LAKES
East of Field on Hwy 1, the Takakkaw Falls road is open from late June to early October. At 254m, **Takakkaw Falls** is one of the highest waterfalls in Canada. From here, the **Iceline**, a 20km hiking loop, passes many glaciers and spectacular scenery.

The beautiful green **Emerald Lake**, 10km north of Field off Hwy 1, features a flat 5.2km loop trail with other trails radiating from it. The lake gets its incredible color from light reflecting off the fine glacial rock particles, deposited into the lake over time by grinding glaciers.

Back near the south gate of Yoho National Park, you can reach pretty **Wapta Falls** via a 2.4km trail. The easy walk takes about 45 minutes in each direction.

Sleeping & Eating
The town of Field contains several B&Bs and a lodge; for details, ask at the park information center.

Cathedral Mountain Lodge & Chalets (☎ 250-343-6442; www.cathedralmountain.com; d $250-400) This place, 4km east of Field on Yoho Valley Rd, is highly recommended and pleasantly rustic. It offers luxurious cabins at the base of Cathedral Mountain and alongside the river.

HI Whiskey Jack Hostel (☎ 403-762-4122, 866-762-4122; www.hihostels.ca; dm $23; ☻ Jun-Sep) Fifteen kilometers off Hwy 1 on Yoho Valley Rd, just before the Takakkaw Falls Campground, this hostel offers 27 dorm-style beds. The daily shuttle bus between Banff and Jasper takes a detour off the Icefields Parkway to pick up and drop off people at the hostel.

Yoho contains four campgrounds, all of which close in winter and don't take reservations. Only the **Kicking Horse Campground** (tent & RV sites $22) has showers, making its 92 sites the most popular. **Hoodoo Creek** (tent & RV sites $17), **Monarch** (tent sites $14) and **Takakkaw Falls** (tent sites $14) are the others.

In Field, the cool little **Truffle Pigs Café** (☎ 250-343-6462; 318 Stephen Ave; meals $5-11; ☎ breakfast, lunch & dinner) is a good place for a cup of coffee or a light bite, and the adjacent store sells supplies and booze.

Getting There & Away
The Greyhound Canada bus also stops in Field, coming west from Lake Louise ($10, 40 minutes) and east from Golden ($15, one hour) along Hwy 1.

MT ASSINIBOINE PROVINCIAL PARK
Between Kootenay and Banff National Parks lies this lesser-known and smaller (39-sq-km) **provincial park** (wlapwww.gov.bc.ca/bcparks), part of the Rockies' Unesco world heritage site. The craggy summits of Mt Assiniboine (3618m), often referred to as Canada's Matterhorn, and its near neighbors, have become a magnet for experienced rock climbers and mountaineers. The park also attracts lots of backcountry hikers to its meadows, lake and glaciers.

The park's main focus is Lake Magog, which is reachable by foot, although there are trails coming in from all directions. At the lake there's the commercially operated **Mt Assiniboine Lodge** (☎ 403-678-2883; s incl all meals from $180), a **campground** (tent sites $5) and some **alpine huts** (per person $30), which may be reserved through the lodge. There's backcountry camping in other parts of the park.

From Hwy 93, two hiking trails start near the road at Vermilion Crossing in Kootenay National Park; both are close to 30km from Magog Lake. Another hiking trail begins at Sunshine Village Ski Resort in Banff National Park; allow a good eight hours to make this 27km trek.

KOOTENAY NATIONAL PARK
Kootenay National Park, which is in BC but adjacent to Alberta's Banff National Park, runs south from Yoho National Park. Encompassing 1406 sq km, Kootenay has a more moderate climate than the

other Rocky Mountains parks, and in the southern regions especially, summers can be hot and dry. It's the only national park in Canada to contain both glaciers and cacti.

Information

Kootenay National Park Information Centre
(☎ 250-347-9505, 800-347-9704; 7556 Main St, Radium Hot Springs; ☺ 9am-5pm Jul & Aug, shorter hours rest of year) Inside the VIC in the town of Radium Hot Springs.
Kootenay Park Lodge Visitor Centre (☎ 403-762-9196; ☺ 10am-7pm summer, 11am-6pm Fri-Sun spring & fall) At Vermillion Crossing, 63km from Radium.

Sights & Activities

Between the northern entrance at Vermillion Crossing, and the park's southern end at Radium Hot Springs, there are six campgrounds, plenty of points of interest, hiking trails and views of the valley along the Kootenay River.

Stop at **Marble Canyon** for the 30-minute walk – it is a real adrenaline rush. The trail follows the rushing Tokumm Creek, crisscrossing it frequently on small wooden bridges with longer and longer drops below as you head up to the waterfall.

Some 2km further south on the main road is the short, easy trail through forest to ochre pools known as the **Paint Pots**, where first the Kootenay people and then European settlers collected this orange- and red-colored earth to make paint.

RADIUM HOT SPRINGS

Lying just outside the southwest corner of Kootenay National Park, Radium Hot Springs is a major gateway to the whole Rocky Mountains national park area.
Kootenay National Park & Radium Hot Springs VIC (☎ 250-347-9331, 800-347-9704; www.rhs.bc.ca; 7556 Main St E; ☺ 9am-7pm summer, 9am-5pm Mon-Sat winter) carries useful Parks Canada information and lists of local accommodations.

Radium boasts a large resident population of **bighorn sheep**, which often wander through town, but the big attraction is the **hot springs** (☎ 250-347-9485; adult/child $6.50/5.50; ☺ 9am-11pm summer, noon-9pm winter), 3km out of town. Even though they are the largest hot-springs pools in Canada, the pools can get very busy in summer. The water comes from the ground at 44°C, enters the first pool at 39°C and hits the final one at 29°C.

INVERMERE & AROUND

South from Radium Hot Springs, Hwy 93/95 follows the Columbia River between the Purcell and Rocky Mountains. It's a fairly undistinguished area, apart from a couple of ski resorts and some decent provincial parks.

From Invermere you can head 18km up a winding road to **Panorama Mountain Village Resort** (☎ 250-342-6941, 800-663-2929; www.panorama resort.com; 1-day lift pass adult/child $65/30), which has lately been developed into a major, full-service resort. Boasting a 1220m vertical drop, the resort has over 100 immaculately groomed runs, plus a gondola that shuttles people from the upper to lower villages. With an endless array of new services and condos, Panorama is fast becoming a built-up and exclusive resort.

Around 20km south of Invermere, **Fairmont Hot Springs** is another resort town with hot springs as its focus. At Skookumchuk, another 55km south, a gravel road heads eastwards to **Top of the World Provincial Park** (☎ 250-422-4200; wlapwww.gov.bc.ca/bcparks), which has hiking trails and backcountry camping ($5). Heading south from Skookumchuk, the road forks. If you go left, you'll head southeast to Fort Steele. Bearing right will take you to Kimberley.

KIMBERLEY

At 1113m, Kimberley is one of Canada's highest cities. In 1973, the small mountain mining town was revamped to look like a Bavarian alpine village, complete with piped oompah music and timber-shingled buildings – it's hokey as hell, but has a quirky charm nonetheless.

Downtown is centered on the Platzl, a small pedestrian mall with a gigantic yodeling cuckoo clock (truly), and plenty of restaurants and cafés. The **VIC** (☎ 250-427-3666; 350 Ross St; ☺ 9am-4:30pm Mon-Sat summer, 1-4pm Mon-Fri rest of year) may have moved to the Platzl by the time you read this.

The biggest attraction here is **Kimberley Alpine Resort** (☎ 250-427-4881, 877-754-5462; www .skikimberley.com; 1-day lift pass adult/child $48/16), which boasts 728 hectares of skiable terrain, mild weather and 67 runs. A high-speed quad lift serves the 8200m Main Run, which has a 609m vertical drop and is fully lit for night skiing. Ski-package rentals start at $30 per day.

BRITISH COLUMBIA

Cute little rooms are available above **Chef Bernard's Platzl Inn** (☎ 250-427-4820, 800-905-8338; www.cyberlink.bc.ca/~chefbernards; 170 Spokane St; d from $60), famed for its bratwurst and strudel, on the Platzl. Room prices vary wildly depending on demand.

Right in the middle of the Platzl, the excellent location and modern, clean rooms make **Kimberley SameSun Budget Lodge** (☎ 250-427-7191, 877-562-2783; www.samesun.com; 275 Spokane St; dm $22, d from $60) a good place to stay, especially in the ski season. The hostel runs a shuttle to the ski hill in winter.

Below SameSun, **Ozone Pub** (☎ 250-427-7744; 275 Spokane St; ☺ noon-late) is big with travelers, and ski bums who play pool and await the occasional live band.

There are plenty of other eating and sleeping options; visit the VIC for a list.

FERNIE

A beautiful little town with active preservation and arts movements, Fernie was once a mining town, but those days are long gone. Today, it's known for its attractive late-Victorian architecture and the constant winter storms that travel over the Rockies and dump vast amounts of snow on the area. In winter it's a powdery paradise for skiers and snowboarders, while in summer the run-off means great rafting on local rivers.

Orientation & Information

Downtown Fernie lies southeast of Hwy 3. Many shops and services can be found on 7th Ave, which runs parallel to the highway. The **VIC** (☎ 250-423-6868; www.ferniechamber.com; 102 Commerce Rd; ☺ 9am-7pm summer, 9am-5pm Mon-Fri winter) is just past the Elk River crossing.

Sights & Activities

Fernie experienced a devastating fire in 1908, which resulted in a brick-and-stone building code. Thus, today you'll see numerous fine **buildings** dating from that period, many of which are built out of local yellow brick. Grab the free *Heritage Walking Tour* brochure from the VIC and go for a stroll.

Otherwise, Fernie is all about the great outdoors, starting with the white stuff. **Fernie Alpine Resort** (☎ 250-423-4655, 877-333-2339; snow conditions 250-423-3555; www.skifernie.com; 1-day lift pass adult/child $60/20), a five-minute drive from downtown off Ski Hill Rd, gets a whopping 8.75m of snow per year on its 107 runs and

five bowls. Now a year-round resort, it's grown like crazy in recent years, and development continues apace. You can rent ski or snowboard gear in town at **Fernie Sports** (☎ 250-423-3611; www.ferniesports.com; 1191 7th Ave; rentals from $25; ☺ 8am-7pm Mon-Fri, 8am-6pm Sat & Sun winter).

A couple of outfits can take you rafting on the Bull and Elk Rivers: **Canyon Raft Company** (☎ 250-423-7226, 888-423-7226; www.canyonraft.com) and **Mountain High River Adventures** (☎ 250-423-5008, 877-423-4555; www.raftfernie.com); trips start at $90. **Hiking** is also popular, with great trails radiating in all directions from Fernie, with the excellent and challenging **Three Sisters Hike** a local favorite; check with the VIC for directions.

Fernie's variety of terrain makes it a great place for mountain biking, with something for every level of interest and ability. *The Secret of Single Track*, available at the VIC, is a good local map with trail descriptions. Fernie Sports also rents bikes from $30 per day.

Sleeping & Eating

Being a big ski town, Fernie's high season is winter.

Snow Valley Motel (☎ 250-423-4421, 877-696-7669; www.snowvalleymotel.com; 1041 7th Ave; d from $70) This great little motel has actually been decorated by someone with an eye for color, and is set up for the skiing crowd with deep baths, a good spa, microwaves and decent-sized fridges to keep your post-snow beer in. Rooms are discounted heavily in the off-season.

Royal Hotel (☎ 250-423-7750; 501 1st St; d from $110) Built in 1909, this hotel was run for many years by the Quail family, and their spooky family photos still line the walls. The rooms have been freshened and are comfortable though basic, but you stay here for the goofy atmosphere and the attached **Saloon** (meals from $8; ☺ lunch & dinner), one of the best bars in town.

HI-Fernie Raging Elk Hostel (☎ 250-423-6811; www.hihostels.ca; 892 6th Ave; dm $22) This is a fairly basic hostel with the usual facilities, but it can arrange snowfield packages and has an excellent central location.

Three kilometers west of town, **Mt Fernie Provincial Park** (☎ 250-422-3003, reservations 800-689-9025; wlapwww.gov.bc.ca/bcparks; tent sites $14) offers 38 sites, flush toilets, waterfalls, a self-guided interpretive trail and access to mountain-biking trails.

Rip 'n' Richards Eatery (☎ 250-423-3002; 301 Hwy 3; meals $9; ☯ lunch & dinner) The quesadillas draw raves from local aficionados. You'll agree, but you'll also probably rave about the view of the river from the deck. The varied menu also has pizza, jambalaya, burgers and more.

Getting There & Around

From the **bus stop** (Park Place Lodge, 742 Hwy 3), Greyhound Canada buses run in each direction to Vancouver ($130, 17 hours) and Calgary ($57, seven hours).

CRANBROOK & CRESTON

The area's main center, 31km southeast of Kimberley, **Cranbrook** is a large and unattractive place that's best skipped, unless you're into trains. The **Canadian Museum of Rail Travel** (☎ 250-489-3918; www.crowsnest.bc.ca/cmrt/; adult/child $8/3.50; ☯ 10am-6pm Easter–mid-Oct, noon-5pm Tue-Sat mid-Oct–Easter) has some fine examples of classic Canadian trains, including the luxurious 1929 edition of the *Trans-Canada Limited*, a legendary train that ran from Montréal to Vancouver.

Near the US border, **Creston** is the center of a green, fruit-growing district. Again there's not much to drag you here, apart from the nearby **Creston Valley Wildlife Management Area** (☎ 250-428-3259; www.crestonwildlife .ca; adult/child $3/2; ☯ dawn-dusk), 11km west of Creston along Hwy 3. These lush, attractive 6900 hectares are home to more than 100,000 migrating birds each year, including the province's largest populations of black terns, white-fronted geese and blue herons. You can walk along a 1km boardwalk to a watchtower or cruise around silently in a canoe as part of a guided tour ($5).

NELSON

Nelson, surrounded by the Selkirk Mountains and snug up against the west arm of Kootenay Lake, is both the highlight and the heart of the Kootenays. Regardless of what activity you're after, be it kayaking on the lake, skiing at Whitewater or checking out the local arts, Nelson makes a great base for exploring the region.

Born as a mining town in the late 1800s, in 1977 Nelson was chosen for the government's project on heritage conservation, and today this picturesque town boasts more than 350 carefully preserved and restored period buildings. The town's charm and

location lure many creative types who are seeking city culture but small-town lifestyle. The renowned Kootenay School of the Arts, the Selkirk School of Music and a school of Chinese medicine draw an interesting and eclectic mix.

Orientation & Information

Nelson sits on the west arm of Kootenay Lake. As it travels down from the north, Hwy 3A becomes a series of local streets before heading west to Castlegar. Highway 6, which skirts the west side of downtown, also goes to Castlegar, or south to the small lumber town of Salmo, before connecting with Hwy 3 and heading to Creston and the East Kootenays. Baker St is the main drag and has many shops and restaurants.

The **VIC** (☎ 250-352-3433, 877-663-5706; www.dis covernelson.com; 225 Hall St; ☯ 8:30am-8pm summer, 8:30am-5pm Mon-Fri rest of year) is on an outlandishly steep hill. Other facilities in town include **Nelson Library** (☎ 250-352-6333; 602 Stanley St; ☯ 1-8pm Mon, Wed & Fri, 10am-6pm Tue & Thu, 11am-6pm Sat), which has free Internet access, **Kootenay Lake District Hospital** (☎ 250-352-3111; 3 View St; ☯ 24hr) and the **post office** (☎ 250-352-3538; 514 Vernon St).

Sights

Almost a third of Nelson's **historic buildings** have been restored to their high- and late-Victorian architectural splendor, so you may want to pick up the superb *Heritage Walking Tour* leaflet from the VIC. It gives details on 26 buildings in the center and offers a good lesson in Victorian architecture.

Lakeside Park is a popular spot where you can hang out or walk along the trail that runs through the park. **Streetcar No 23** (adult/child $3/2; noon-6pm summer, noon-6pm Sat & Sun spring & fall), one of the town's originals, has been restored and now follows a 2km track from under the bridge (at the north end of Lakeside Park) to the wharf at the foot of Hall St.

Beer-lovers will want to check out the **Nelson Brewing Company** (☎ 250-352-3582; 402 Anderson St; 512 Latimer St). Call to find out about the frequent tours and tastings. Their many top-notch brews are served all over town.

Activities
KAYAKING

All that lake water is just waiting to be rippled by a kayak. **ROAM** (☎ 250-354-2056, 877-229-

BRITISH COLUMBIA

4959; www.roamthekootenays.com; 579 Baker St; rentals per day $60, tours from $60) is a large outfit that also arranges rafting and white-water kayaking expeditions around the province.

HIKING

The two-hour climb to Pulpit Rock, practically in town, affords fine views of Nelson and Kootenay Lake, while excellent hikes abound in two nearby parks. **Kokanee Creek Provincial Park** (☎ 250-825-4212; wlapwww.gov.bc.ca/bcparks), 20km northeast of town off Hwy 3A, has several trails heading away from the visitor center. Lake-filled **Kokanee Glacier Provincial Park** (trail conditions ☎ 250-825-3500; wlapwww.gov.bc.ca/bcparks) boasts 85km of some of the area's most superb hiking trails. The 4km (two-hour) hike to Kokanee Lake is wonderful and can be continued to the glacier.

MOUNTAIN BIKING

Mountain bikers can pick up a copy of *Your Ticket to Ride* ($10), an extensive trail map, from **Gerick Cycle & Sports** (☎ 250-354-4622, 877-437-4251; 702 Baker St; rentals from $20), which also rents out machines. Most of the trails wind up from Kootenay Lake along steep and rather challenging hills, followed by stomach-swooping downhills.

SKIING & SNOWBOARDING

Known for its heavy powdery snowfall, **Whitewater Winter Resort** (☎ 250-354-4944, 800-666-9420; www.skiwhitewater.com; 1-day lift pass adult/child $42/26), 12km south of Nelson off Hwy 6, features good skiing and boarding via two double chairs and a rope tow. There are 11 groomed cross-country trails as well.

Sleeping

BUDGET

HI Dancing Bear Inn (☎ 250-352-7573, 877-352-7573; www.dancingbearinn.com; 171 Baker St; dm/d $20/40) This is a beautifully renovated hostel with quiet, immaculate rooms. The comfortable living room makes a great place to read a book or find out about local happenings.

Flying Squirrel International Hostel (☎ 250-352-7285; www.flyingsquirrelhostel.com; 198 Baker St; dm/r $20/49) Nearby, this is a decent choice with a lively bar filled with lively locals on its ground floor.

The Redfish and Sandspit Campgrounds at **Kokanee Creek Provincial Park** (☎ reservations 800-689-9025; campsites $22) contain wooded sites with toilets and showers.

MID-RANGE & TOP END

Heritage Inn (☎ 250-352-5331, 877-568-0888; www.heritageinn.org; 422 Vernon St; d from $80) With a pub, Mike's Place, a restaurant and a nightclub, this hotel is something of a hub, whether you stay here or not. As in most heritage buildings – this one dates from 1898 – the rooms are small, but they're clean and full of character.

Best Western Baker St Inn (☎ 250-352-3525, 888-255-3525; www.bwbakerstreetinn.com; 153 Baker St; d from $125; ☐) A typical business-class hotel, it offers free high-speed Internet in the rooms, which are comfortable enough.

Alpine Motel (☎ 250-352-5501, 888-356-2233; www.alpine-motel.com; 1120 Hall Mines Rd; d from $65) South of town, near Observatory St, the grounds here are lovely and there is a fine view of the lake from the hot tub.

Inn the Garden B&B (☎ 250-352-3226, 800-596-2337; www.innthegarden.com; 408 Victoria St; d $85-200) Right downtown, this B&B offers guest rooms in a lovingly restored Victorian home. The yard and patio are bedecked with flowers and the rooms feature comfy wicker furniture.

Eating

For its size, Nelson has a fine restaurant scene, but don't leave your run too late – most still close up around 8:30pm.

All Seasons Café (☎ 250-352-0101; 620 Herridge Lane; meals $20-30; ☽ dinner Mon-Sat) One of the finest spots in town, it features a heated patio on a quiet tree-lined alley. The menu features local ingredients and seasonal flavors, and the wine list is worth exploring.

Redfish Grill (☎ 250-352-3456; 491 Baker St; meals $4-15; ☽ breakfast, lunch & dinner) Always bustling, Redfish serves, throughout the day, its menu including good-value brekkies, tasty soups and salads, and fusion cuisine in the evening.

Stanley's on Baker (☎ 250-354-4458; 402 Baker St; meals $5-10; ☽ breakfast & lunch) Enjoy omelettes made with organic free-range eggs at this high-quality breakfast spot.

Drinking

Mike's Place (Heritage Inn, 422 Vernon St; ☽ 11am-late) Mike's is a classic, with dark paneling and a good mix of visitors and locals. Good pub

---

KOOTENAY FERRIES

There are free car-ferry services on the long Kootenay, Upper Arrow and Lower Arrow lakes, and they provide a gentle and enjoyable way to get around this pretty area, while you save yourself tens or hundreds of kilometers of driving. You also get to see some nice little lakeside communities and some lovely countryside. Not all of the communities mentioned here are covered in this chapter, but this is a great region to explore.

Log on to **Inland Ferries** (www.th.gov.bc.ca/bchighways/inlandferryschedule/ferryschedule.htm) to plan your route (note that sailings may be less frequent in winter).

■ **Kootenay Lake Ferry** (☎ 250-229-4215; 45min, every 50min 6:40am-9:40pm) Sails between Balfour on the west arm of Kootenay Lake (34km northeast of Nelson) and Kootenay Bay.

■ **Needles Ferry** (☎ 250-837-8418; 5min, half-hourly 5am-10pm, on demand other times) Crosses Lower Arrow Lake between Fauquier (57km south of Nakusp) and Needles (135km east of Vernon).

■ **Upper Arrow Lake Ferry** (☎ 250-837-8418; 20min, hourly 6am-11pm) Travels between Galena Bay (49km south of Revelstoke) and Shelter Bay (49km north of Nakusp).

---

food ($10) can be washed down by the full complement of Nelson Brewing Company beers.

Uptown Tavern (☎ 250-352-7211; New Grand Hotel, 616 Vernon St; ☻ noon-late) This tavern has DJs some nights, hockey other nights and a good vibe most nights.

Getting There & Around

The **long-distance bus depot** (☎ 250-352-3939; 1112A Lakeside Dr) can be found in the Chahko-Mika Mall. Greyhound Canada buses depart for Calgary ($96, 12 hours) via Fernie, and for Vancouver ($105, 12 hours) via Kelowna. Local services are run by **Nelson Transit System Buses** (☎ 250-352-8228). The VIC has routes and timetables.

NORTH OF NELSON

Across the water from downtown Nelson, you can catch a free ferry across scenic Kootenay Lake to **Kootenay Bay** (see the boxed text above). An interesting alternative is the scenic drive up the western shore of the lake to the quiet and attractive little holiday town of **Kaslo**. It holds many Victorian-style buildings, plus the old stern-wheeler, the SS *Moyie*. Kaslo's **VIC** (☎ 250-353-2525; www.klhs.bc.ca; 324 Front St; ☻ 9am-5pm mid-May–mid-Sep) can give you information on swimming, hiking and mountain-biking trails in the area. Accommodations are limited during school holidays, so reserve in advance.

From here you can head west to **New Denver**, via a slow tortuous road, and south back to Nelson, via the gorgeous and rugged

Valhalla Provincial Park (wlapwww.gov.bc.ca/bcparks), which offers hiking trails and wilderness camping mainly accessed by boat (canoes can be rented). If you head north, it's another 48km to Nakusp and its relaxing hot springs.

Nakusp

Charmingly frayed around the edges, quiet Nakusp sits about midway up the long Upper Arrow Lake and is the main town in the valley, south of Revelstoke. This very attractive portion of the province enjoys a relatively low profile and, refreshingly, is not overrun with tourists. Good camping and hiking areas, pleasant travel roads and nearby hot springs make Nakusp a fine place to spend a day or two. **Nakusp VIC** (☎ 250-265-4234, 800-909-8819; www.nakusphotsprings.com; 92 W 6th Ave; ☻ 9am-5pm summer, 11am-5pm Mon-Fri winter) has good hiking information for the area.

The **hot springs** (☎ 250-265-4528; www.nakusphotsprings.com; adult/child $9/free; ☻ 9:30am-10pm summer, 10am-9:30pm rest of year), 12km northeast of Nakusp off Hwy 23, are a mere 2km from the spring's source. Though the squeaky-clean pools tend to ruin some of the natural vibe, the tranquil atmosphere and gorgeous scenery remind you that you are steeping deep in nature.

By Upper Arrow Lake, 32km north of Nakusp, **Halcyon Hot Springs** (☎ 250-265-3554; http://halcyon-hotsprings.com; day pass adult/child $9.50/6.50; ☻ 8am-10pm, to 11pm in summer) has three pools, and doubles as a resort with a good range of **accommodations** (tent/RV sites $18/27, cabins $76, cottages/chalets from $140/190). Otherwise try **Nakusp International Hostel** (☎ 250-265-3069; www.nakusphostel.com; 1950 Hwy 23 N; dm $20 s & d $45), a newish, neat hostel with a killer location on the lake just across from Hot Springs Rd.

One of the friendliest places in town, **Broadway Deli & Bistro** (☎ 250-265-3767; 408 Broadway St; meals $6; ☺ breakfast & lunch) serves good breakfasts, plus salads, sandwiches and burritos. **Wylie's Pub** (☎ 250-265-4944; 401 Broadway St; meals $8; ☺ lunch & dinner) is the place for beer and burgers.

WEST OF NELSON

From Nelson there are 291km of meandering roads to Osoyoos (p741) at the southern end of the Okanagan Valley. You'll pass several small towns along the way, including sprawling **Castlegar**, industrial **Trail** and enigmatic **Grand Forks**, but the only jewel in this crown is the attractive little mountain hamlet of Rossland, 74km southwest of Nelson.

Rossland

If you take Fleeing Trail upcanyon on Hwy 3B/22, you'll eventually ascend to the beautiful former mining town of Rossland. Born in the 1890s after the discovery of massive deposits of gold, it was once the province's wildest and roughest town. These days, however, it's a young, hip ski town, perched in the Monashee Mountains.

The **VIC** (☎ 250-362-7722, 888-448-7444; www.rossland.com; cnr Hwys 22 & 3B; ☺ 9am-5pm mid-May–mid-Sep) shares space with the local museum. Staff can advise on accommodations and food options around town.

Red Mountain Ski Resort (☎ 250-362-7384, 800-663-0105, snow report 250-362-5500; www.ski-red .com; 1-day lift pass adult/child $50/25), 5km up Hwy 3B from town, is the big draw card. Apart from some of the best technical trails in the world, it has 480 hectares of skiable terrain, with a vertical drop of 880m, and five lifts serving 83 runs.

Rossland also has some of BC's best mountain biking, with a well-developed and extensive trail system that radiates right from downtown. **Powderhound** (☎ 250-362-5311; 2044 Columbia Ave; per day from $35) offers bike rentals and copies of *Trails of the Rossland Range* ($8).

PACIFIC NORTHWEST

Northwestern BC is a little-developed, huge but lightly populated region, whose remoteness is one of its main attractions. This largely inaccessible area is one of North America's last true wilderness regions. Various First Nations peoples have long inhabited the area and to this day they make up a considerable percentage of the permanent residents. The land is dominated by forests, several mountain ranges, and scores of lakes and swift rivers. Don't be in a hurry and you'll have a most-rewarding time indeed.

PRINCE RUPERT

Set within a stunning natural harbor – the world's deepest natural ice-free port, in fact – Prince Rupert is the largest coastal city north of Vancouver, and the jumping-off point to the desolate and beautiful Queen Charlotte Islands. Once home to more than 20 distinct First Nations cultures, 'Rupert' developed as a fishing center for the Pacific Northwest, and became famous as the halibut capital of the world. The fishing trade being a touch precarious these days, the town has adopted a new title, the 'City of Rainbows,' which is a euphemistic way of saying that it rains more often than not – about 220 days each year. If the weather clears, however, Rupert's setting, on the mouth of the Skeena River and flanked by mountains and rugged coastlines, will take your breath away.

While most travelers stop in here on their way to the Charlottes, or as part of an Alaskan cruise, Prince Rupert is more than just a mere staging post: a historic wharf precinct, some good restaurants and an excellent museum can all be added to a list that includes beautiful clean air, some of BC's best wildlife-watching, and superb natural surroundings, which can explored by boat, kayak, or on foot.

Orientation

Prince Rupert is on Kaien Island and is connected to the mainland by a bridge. The Yellowhead Hwy passes right through downtown on its way to the BC Ferries terminal at Fairview Bay, 3km southwest of the town center. Just northeast of downtown is Cow Bay, named for a dairy farm that used

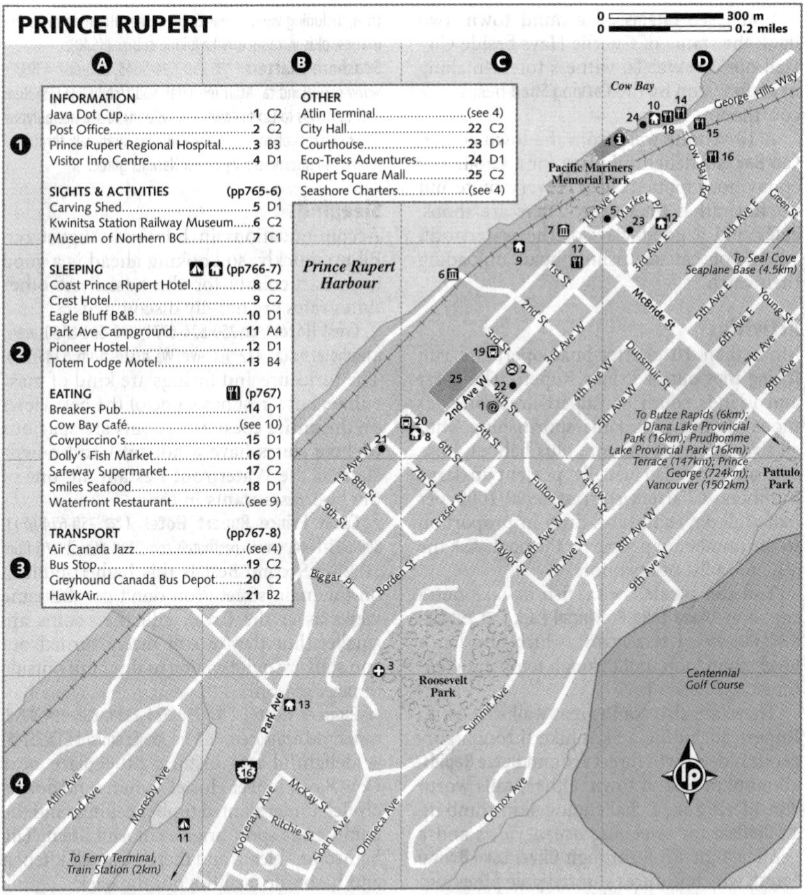
PRINCE RUPERT
0 300 m
0 0.2 miles
A
B
C
D
1
2
3
4
INFORMATION
Java Dot Cup 1 C2
Post Office 2 C2
Prince Rupert Regional Hospital 3 B3
Visitor Info Centre 4 D1
SIGHTS & ACTIVITIES (pp765-6)
Carving Shed 5 D1
Kwinitsa Station Railway Museum 6 C2
Museum of Northern BC 7 C1
SLEEPING (pp766-7)
Coast Prince Rupert Hotel 8 C2
Crest Hotel 9 C2
Eagle Bluff B&B 10 D1
Park Ave Campground 11 A4
Pioneer Hostel 12 D1
Totem Lodge Motel 13 B4
EATING (p767)
Breakers Pub 14 D1
Cow Bay Café (see 10)
Cowpuccino's 15 D1
Dolly's Fish Market 16 D1
Safeway Supermarket 17 C2
Smiles Seafood 18 D1
Waterfront Restaurant (see 9)
TRANSPORT (pp767-8)
Air Canada Jazz (see 4)
Bus Stop 19 C2
Greyhound Canada Bus Depot 20 C2
HawkAir 21 B2
OTHER
Atlin Terminal (see 4)
City Hall 22 C2
Courthouse 23 D1
Eco-Treks Adventures 24 D1
Rupert Square Mall 25 C2
Seashore Charters (see 4)
Cow Bay
George Hills Way
Pacific Mariners Memorial Park
Prince Rupert Harbour
Cow Bay Rd
Market Pl
1st Ave E
3rd Ave E
4th Ave E
5th Ave E
6th Ave E
7th Ave
8th Ave
Green St
Young St
McBride St
Dunsmuir St
To Seal Cove Seaplane Base (4.5km)
To Butze Rapids (6km); Diana Lake Provincial Park (16km); Prudhomme Lake Provincial Park (16km); Terrace (147km); Prince George (724km); Vancouver (1502km)
Pattulo Park
1st St
2nd St
3rd St
4th St
5th St
6th St
7th St
8th St
9th St
1st Ave W
2nd Ave W
3rd Ave W
4th Ave W
5th Ave W
6th Ave W
7th Ave W
8th Ave W
9th Ave W
Fraser St
Fulton St
Tatlow St
Taylor St
Borden St
Biggar Pl
Roosevelt Park
Summit Ave
Comox Ave
Centennial Golf Course
Park Ave
McKay St
Ritchie St
Kootenay Ave
Sloan Ave
Omineca Ave
Atlin Ave
2nd Ave
Moresby Ave
16
To Ferry Terminal, Train Station (2km)

to be located there, and now a historic waterfront area full of shops and restaurants.

Information

Java Dot Cup (☎ 250-622-2822; 516 3rd Ave W; per 15min $2; 🕑 7am-9pm) Plenty of terminals and a café.

Post office (☎ 250-624-2353; 500 2nd Ave W; 🕑 8:30am-5pm Mon-Fri)

Prince Rupert Regional Hospital (☎ 250-624-2171; 1305 Summit Ave; 🕑 24hr) In Roosevelt Park.

VIC (☎ 250-624-5637, 800-667-1994; www.tourismprince rupert.com; Atlin Terminal, Cow Bay; 🕑 8am-9pm summer, 9am-5pm rest of year)

Sights

The **Museum of Northern BC** (☎ 250-624-3207; www.museumofnorthernbc.com; 100 1st Ave W; adult/child $5/1; 🕑 9am-8pm Mon-Sat, to 5pm Sun Jun-Aug, 9am-5pm Mon-Sat Sep-May) is located inside a striking post-and-beam building which is styled after a First Nation longhouse. This is something not to be missed. Through excellent exhibits and superb documentation, the museum shows how local civilizations enjoyed sustainable ways of life that lasted for thousands of years. The interesting displays include a wealth of excellent Haida, Gitksan and Tsimshian art. Included with the price of admission is the **Kwinitsa Station Railway Museum** (🕑 9am-5pm summer), down the hill on Bill Murray Dr. Housed in an old train station, it documents the drama surrounding the building of the railway to Rupert.

You'll see **totems** all around town; two flank the statue of Charlie Hays beside City Hall on 3rd Ave. To witness totem-making in action, stop by the **Carving Shed** beside the courthouse.

A 10-minute walk from the town center, **Cow Bay** is a delightful place for a stroll. The eponymous spotted decor is everywhere, but it's fun rather than twee. There are shops, cafés and a good view of the waterfront, where you can see fishing boats unloading their catch.

Activities

More than 70 charter-boat operators run **fishing trips** out of Prince Rupert. The coast and islands south of Rupert are world famous for their awesome sportfishing, with all five species of salmon, plus halibut, lingcod and rockfish usually present in large numbers. Charters start at $500/1000 per half-/full day, and rates drop in proportion to the number of people on the boat. Ask the VIC for a list of operators.

You can picnic, swim, fish or take out a canoe at **Diana Lake Provincial Park** (☎ 250-638-8490; wlapwww.gov.bc.ca/bcparks), which also has a lovely 3km loop trail through temperate rain forest.

There are also some great walks closer to Rupert, including a 5km hike through gorgeous old-growth forest around **Butze Rapids**, about 6km east of town. Other trails worth considering are a challenging 4km climb up **Mt Oldfield** for sweeping ocean views and a gentler 4km stroll through **Oliver Lake Bonsai Forest**, which features stunted pole pines and carnivorous sundew plants. Again, the VIC can help you out with the details.

Tours

In summer, the Museum of Northern BC offers guided heritage and totem **walking tours** (free with museum admission) around town; call for times.

The spectacular untouched scenery north and south of Rupert can be explored on a range of good ecotours. The best is a trip to **Khutzeymateen Grizzly Bear Sanctuary** (see the boxed text on p767), but you can also visit offshore islands by boat or kayak, go hiking, take a cruise or go whale-watching.

Eco-Treks Adventures (☎ 250-624-8311; www.citytel .net/ecotreks; 203 Cow Bay Rd; tours from $60, kayak rentals per half-/full day $35/50) Offers a variety of guided trips, including wildlife-watching and exploration of harbor islands, plus introductory kayaking courses ($40).

Seashore Charters (☎ 250-624-5645, 800-667-4393; www.pikeisland.ca; Atlin Terminal; adult/child $45/35) Runs half-day trips to Laxspa'aws (Pike Island) to see petroglyphs and remnants of ancient native villages, and walk through forests, all interpreted by a First Nations guide.

Sleeping

Accommodations in July and August can fill up quickly, so booking ahead is a good idea, particularly for the hostel. At other times rates are heavily discounted.

Crest Hotel (☎ 250-624-6771, 800-663-8150; www .cresthotel.bc.ca; 222 1st Ave W; d/ste from $145/200) The furniture and fittings are kind of masculine, but Crest has some of the best views on the entire coast, the rooms are spacious (deluxe suites have a hot tub) and downstairs is the Waterfront Restaurant, one of the best restaurants in town.

Coast Prince Rupert Hotel (☎ 250-624-6711, 800-663-1144; www.coasthotels.com; 118 6th St; s/d from $110/120) Second best is this high-rise block on the main street. You don't get the same views as at the Crest, and the rooms are smaller, but they're still nicely turned out and staff are quite willing to discount outside of peak season.

Pioneer Hostel (☎ 250-624-2334, 888-794-9998; www.citytel.net/pioneer; 167 3rd Ave E; dm/s/d $17/35/45) A delightful and historic little place near Cow Bay, Pioneer Hostel's rooms and dorms crouch under slanted timber ceilings and the comfy beds sport bright, colorful linen. The bathrooms gleam and there's a small kitchen and barbecue facilities out the back.

Totem Lodge Motel (☎ 250-624-6761, 800-550-1078; www.tkp-biz.com/totemlodgemotel; 1335 Park Ave; s/d from $80/95) This reasonable, friendly motel generally undercuts opposition rates. Its proximity to the ferry terminal ensures it fills quickly. It is a fair walk into town, though.

Eagle Bluff B&B (☎ 250-627-4955, 800-833-1550; www.citytel.net/eaglebluff; 201 Cow Bay Rd; s with/without bathroom $60/45, d $95/65) Eagle Bluff offers five comfortable rooms in a heritage building, right by the marina in Cow Bay.

Ask at the VIC for details of the town's other B&Bs.

Camping is available at **Park Ave Campground** (☎ 250-624-5861, 800-667-1994; campgrd@citytel.net; 1750 Park Ave; tent sites $12-20), near the ferry terminal, or further out at **Prudhomme Lake Provincial Park** (☎ 250-847-7320; wlapwww.gov.bc.ca/

bcparks; tent sites $14; mid-May–mid-Sep), 16km east of Prince Rupert on Hwy 16 (neighboring Diana Lake Provincial Park). It has campsites within a conifer forest.

Eating

With fishing still a major local industry, it's not surprising to find seafood on almost every menu. Salmon and halibut feature.

Smiles Seafood (250-624-3072; 113 Cow Bay Rd; meals $8-20; lunch & dinner) Top billing goes to this long-standing joint on the waterfront at Cow Bay. Since 1934 it has served fresh ocean fare, as well as steaks and sandwiches. Flip over the placemat for a look at the menu from 1945, when a sardine sandwich cost 25¢.

Waterfront Restaurant (250-624-6771; Crest Hotel, 222 1st Ave; meals $15-30; breakfast, lunch & dinner) Arguably Rupert's best restaurant, the paneled walls, club furniture and sweeping views are complemented by a long and varied meat and seafood menu, and a decent wine list.

Cowpuccino's (250-627-1395; 25 Cow Bay Rd; mains $8-18; breakfast, lunch & dinner) The blue skies and fluffy clouds painted on the ceiling may be wishful thinking, but this perennially popular place does have a sunny disposition, and the fresh seafood, delectable cakes and fine coffee will put a spring in your step – no matter what the weather.

Cow Bay Café (250-627-1212; 205 Cow Bay Rd; meals $10-15; lunch & dinner Mon-Sat) Right on the waterfront, the creative menu here changes daily, but there are always a half-dozen mains and some amazing desserts to choose from. Enjoy your meal from one of the deck tables overlooking the harbor.

Breakers Pub (250-624-5990; 117 George Hills Way; mains $8-19; lunch & dinner) A haven of warmth and cheer on a cold evening, this waterside pub has plenty of good seafaring chow, including generous servings of fresh halibut and plump oysters.

Self-caterers can head to **Safeway supermarket** (250-624-5125; 200 2nd Ave W; 7am-10pm) or **Dolly's Fish Market** (250-624-6099; 7 Cow Bay Rd; 10am-7pm), where you can buy seafood fresh from the boat.

Getting There & Away

For flights to Sandspit on the Queen Charlotte Islands, see p771.

Prince Rupert Airport (250-622-2222; www.ypr .ca) is on Digby Island, across the harbor from town and accessible by a bus/ferry combo (adult/child $11/8), which means you must check in at your airline's downtown terminal two hours before flight time, as this is where you ultimately arrive and depart. Air Canada Jazz services Vancouver from $230, while Hawkair charges from $265.

BC Ferries from Prince Rupert service Port Hardy (see p696) on Vancouver Island, the Queen Charlotte Islands and Alaska. Bookings are essential on all services. Boats depart from the harbor southwest of town,

---

THE GREAT GRIZZLY

The 45,000-hectare Khutzeymateen Grizzly Bear Sanctuary is one of the few remaining pristine grizzly habitats in the world.

Located 45km northeast of Prince Rupert, the park sits in the remote Khutzeymateen River Valley, the traditional territory of the Gitsees people, who used the valley for fishing, hunting, trapping and growing food such as berries, crab apples and potatoes. When Europeans arrived in North America, an estimated 200,000 grizzlies lived on the continent. Today, that estimate hovers at only 25,000, and 50 of those bears live in the Khutzeymateen sanctuary.

Khutzeymateen (koot-sa-ma-teen) Provincial Park became permanently protected as parkland in 1992. In 1994, the area became officially designated as a 'grizzly-bear sanctuary' and is jointly managed by the provincial government and the Tsimshian nation. Because grizzlies are reclusive and do better when left alone, human presence in the park is heavily restricted, though you can join a boat tour or take a floatplane for a peek if you book early. While many outfits seem keen to take you there, only two tour guides are licensed to lead groups into the sanctuary:

■ **Dan Wakeman, Sun Chaser Charters** (250-624-5472; www.citytel.net/sunchaser; 4-day trip $1600)

■ **Tom Ellison, Ocean Light II Adventures** (604-328-5339; www.oceanlight2.bc.ca; 4-day trip $1500 plus GST)

BRITISH COLUMBIA

although the Alaska Marine Highway terminal is behind large fences, as it is considered a US border crossing. **Alaska Marine Highway ferries** (☎ 250-627-1744, 800-642-0066; www.alaska .gov/ferry; adult/child $160/80, cabins from $100, bicycle $30, car from $395) run to Skagway, Alaska, via Ketchikan, Wrangell, Petersburg, Juneau and Haines, three times a week in summer and twice weekly in winter.

The **Greyhound Canada bus depot** (☎ 250-624-5090; 112 6th St) has services to Prince George ($105, 11 hours) and points beyond.

VIA Rail operates the thrice-weekly *Skeena* from Jasper and Prince George from the BC Ferries Terminal. See p876 for details.

Getting Around

Prince Rupert Transit (☎ 250-624-3343; www.busonline .ca; adult/child $1.25/1) has regular downtown bus services, plus infrequent services to the ferry port on route No 55 ($1.25) three or four times daily. The main downtown bus stop is at Rupert Square Mall on 2nd Ave. A one-way trip to the ferry with **Skeena Taxi** (☎ 250-624-5318) is about $10. Most major car-rental companies are represented in Rupert.

QUEEN CHARLOTTE ISLANDS (HAIDA GWAII)

The Queen Charlotte Islands (or Haida Gwaii, as they are called by the Haida nation) are a dagger-shaped archipelago of some 154 islands lying 80km west of the BC coast, and about 50km from the southern tip of Alaska. Sometimes known as the Canadian Galapagos, this sparsely populated, wild, rainy and almost magical place teems with bald eagles and other birdlife, and features superb old-growth forests and historical Haida cultural artifacts.

Believed to be the only part of Canada that escaped the last Ice Age, the islands abound with flora and fauna that are markedly different from those of the mainland. A warm ocean current rolls in to the Charlottes from Japan, which means the islands get hit with 1.3m of rain annually, creating a landscape filled with thousand-year-old spruce and cedar rain forests and waters teeming with marine life.

A visit to the Charlottes rewards those who invest time to get caught up in their allure, their culture and their people – don't be in too much of a hurry to get in and out. The number one attraction here is Gwaii

Haanas National Park Reserve, which makes up the bottom third of the archipelago. Having made the effort to get all the way here, you'd be crazy to miss this beautiful and remote region, but it does take time and effort to organize and visit. If you are limited to a day or two, there are enough other attractions – natural and cultural – to keep you occupied and happy. You can always arrange a one-day paddle or boat trip, and there's lots to see by car or bicycle.

Orientation

Mainland ferries dock at Skidegate on Graham Island. It's the main island in terms of both population (80%) and commerce. It's also the site of the principal town, Queen Charlotte City (QCC), which is a very grand name for a very small place. Around 7km from Skidegate, it sits prettily on a wide bay that's dotted with small, rugged islets; most of the island's accommodations and eateries are found here.

Other attractions range along Hwy 16, which links QCC via Skidegate with Masset, 101km away, passing the small towns of Tlell and Port Clements on the way. Tow Hill in Naikoon Provincial Park is 26km along the coast east of Masset. You really need your own transport to get around easily.

Graham Island is linked to Moresby Island to the south by a small and frequent ferry from Skidegate. The airport is in Sandspit on Moresby Island, 22km east of the ferry landing at Aliford Bay. The only way to get to Gwaii Haanas National Park Reserve is by boat or plane.

Information

All of the following services and offices are found in QCC. ATMs are found in QCC, Masset and Sandspit; occasionally communication to the mainland is lost, however, so bring a few extra days' cash with you.

Isabel Creek Store (☎ 250-559-8623; 3219 Wharf St; ⊙ 10am-5:30pm Mon-Sat) Has a large selection of used paperbacks upstairs.

Post office (☎ 250-559-8349; 117 3rd Ave; ⊙ 9am-5pm Mon-Fri, noon-4pm Sat)

Queen Charlotte Islands General Hospital (☎ 250-559-4300; 3209 3rd Ave; ⊙ 24hr) For major emergencies patients are generally sent to Prince Rupert by air ambulance.

Queen Charlotte Library (☎ 250-559-4518; 138 Bay St; ⊙ 10:30am-12:30pm, 1:30-5:30pm & 6:30-8:30pm

CANADIAN GALAPAGOS

The distinctive ecosystems of the Queen Charlotte Islands are a dream come true for naturalists, bird-watchers, botanists and everyday fans of natural beauty. The islands are home to several unique subspecies, including the pine marten, deer mouse, black bear (the largest type of bear extant) and short-tailed weasel. Sadly, another singular beast, the Dawson caribou, has been hunted to extinction.

The Charlottes support 15% of all nesting seabirds in BC, as well as the only confirmed nesting site of horned puffins in Canada. A whopping 30% of the world's population of ancient murrelets nest here, as do most of the province's Peales peregrine falcons, which are easy to spot swooping and wheeling through the skies. From late April through late June, it's common to see gray whales cruising by on their 16,000km annual migration route along the west coast. The Queen Charlotte Islands also include the largest sea-lion rookery in BC.

Onshore, the islands are dominated by mighty stands of western hemlock, Sitka spruce and western red cedar, and support a wonderful array of forest birds. Four unique species of moss, one liverwort and six species of flowering plants grow here, along with *Senecio newcombi*, a yellow flowering daisy. The northern end of Graham Island is quite different from the rest, with poor drainage producing low-lying tracts of sphagnum moss and gentian, surrounded by lodgepole pine and yellow cedar. This area attracts huge numbers of migratory bird species, which can be viewed at the Delkatla Wildlife Sanctuary (p770).

Mon & Wed, 10:30am-12:30pm & 1:30-5:30pm Sat) Free Internet access.

VIC (☎ 250-559-8316; www.qcinfo.com; 3220 Wharf St; ☒ 8am-noon May 1-14 & Sep 16–Sep 30, 10am-7pm May 15–Sep 15)

Sights & Activities

GWAII HAANAS NATIONAL PARK RESERVE

Protected since 1988, this huge park encompasses Moresby and 137 smaller islands at the southern end of the Charlottes. This 640km stretch of rugged coastline is true wilderness at its best. If you take out a kayak, you can paddle for hours without seeing another human being (though you'll see lots of wildlife).

Recent archaeological finds have documented more than 500 ancient Haida sites, including villages and burial caves dotted throughout the islands. The most famous (and photographed) village is **SG̲aang Gwaii (Ninstints)** on Anthony Island, where rows of totem poles stare eerily out to sea. This ancient village was declared a Unesco world heritage site in 1981. Other major sights include the ancient village of **Skedans**, on Louise Island, and **Hotspring Island**, where you can soak away the bone-chilling cold in natural springs. These ancient sites are protected by Haida Gwaii watchmen, who live on the islands during summer.

Access to the park is by boat or plane only. A visit demands a decent amount of

advance planning and usually requires several days. If you want to travel independently, you need to reserve in advance, as only a limited number of people can be in the park at any given time. Once on the Charlottes, you must attend an orientation session before you enter the park. Contact Parks Canada's **Gwaii Haanas office** (☎ 250-559-8818; www.pc.gc.ca/pn-np/bc/gwaiihaanas/; Box 37, QCC, BC, V0T 1S0) with queries and to obtain the essential information pack.

Beginning each February 1, you can make **reservations** (☎ 250-387-1642, 800-435-5622; fee $15) to enter the park between May 1 and September 30. Fees are $10 per person per night for the first five nights, $60 for anything up to 14 days, and $80 for a longer period. Each day, six standby spaces are made available at the QCC VIC at 8am; demand for these can be fierce. From October to April there is no need for reservations or to pay fees.

The easiest way to get into the park is with a tour company. The VIC can provide you with lists of operators:

Gwaii Eco Tours (☎ 250-559-8333, 877-559-8333; www.gwaiiecotours.com; 602 1st Ave, QCC; tours from $150) Haida-owned and -led tours of the region that get good reviews and book out quickly.

Queen Charlotte Adventures (☎ 250-559-8990, 800-668-4288; http://queencharlotteadventures.com; tours from $125) Offers one- to 10-day trips using power boats, kayaks or sailboats.

HAIDA GWAII MUSEUM

Near the ferry terminal in Skidegate is the excellent **Haida Gwaii Museum at Qay'llnagaay** (☎ 250-559-4643; muse@qcislands.net; adult/child $3/1.50; ☺ 10am-5pm Mon-Sat summer) at Sealion Point. It holds a fine collection of Haida art, including button blankets (woolen blankets traditionally decorated with shells, and later pearl buttons, that usually feature the family crest), silver and gold jewelry, and argillite totems. Here you can learn about Bill Reid, one of the best-known, prolific Haida artists. The good displays on the area's natural history include an extensive bird collection.

SPIRIT LAKE TRAIL

Nearby the museum, this beautiful 3km, 1½-hour round-trip **trail** climbs into the foothills to loop around these small twin lakes. It starts with a steepish climb through lush temperate forest before flattening out a little at the well-named lakes: the skeletal white trunks of dead trees that clog sections of the lakes lend it a spooky air. The trail is rougher here, but there's birdlife aplenty and lots of large hemlock, Sitka spruce and cedar trees. You can extend your walk by 30 minutes if you tackle the loop that links the two lakes; follow the colored markers.

NAIKOON PROVINCIAL PARK

The Yellowhead Hwy (Hwy 16) heads 110km north from Queen Charlotte past Tlell and Port Clements – the famous golden spruce tree on the banks of the Yakoun River was cut down by a deranged forester in 1997 – to Masset. There's good bird-watching at **Delkatla Wildlife Sanctuary**, off Tow Rd north of town.

Much of the island's northeastern side, between Port Clements and Masset, is devoted to the beautiful 72,640-hectare **Naikoon Provincial Park** (☎ 250-626-5115; wlapwww.gov .bc.ca/bcparks), which combines sand dunes and low sphagnum bogs, surrounded by stunted and gnarled lodgepole pine, and red and yellow cedar. East of Masset, a 21km loop trail traverses a good bit of the park to/from Fife Beach from the end of Tow Hill Rd. The beaches in this area feature strong winds, pounding surf and driftwood from across the Pacific. Another 10km trail (five hours round-trip) departs from the Tlell River bridge at the park's southern end. It starts with a serene riverside stretch before leading along windswept beaches to the wreck of the barge *Pesuta*.

Sleeping

Most of the island's accommodations are found in QCC.

Premier Creek Lodging (☎ 250-559-8415, 888-322-3388; www.qcislands.net/premier; 3101 3rd Ave; dm $19, r $30-75) One of the best places to stay on the islands, it has a great range of accommodations that range from dorms to individual rooms complete with balconies and ocean views. The charge for dorm beds includes the use of a communal kitchen and a barbecue. The lodge rooms are in a refurbished 1910 building and range from small singles with shared bath to suites with kitchens and fabulous views of Bearskin Bay.

Gracie's Place (☎ 250-559-4262, 888-244-4262; 3113 3rd Ave; www.graciesplace.ca; d from $100) This attractive timber house in the middle of town has views to the water, and character-filled rooms stocked with antiques. Some have kitchen and laundry facilities.

Sea Raven Motel (☎ 250-559-4423, 800-665-9606; www.searaven.com; 3301 3rd Ave; r $45-95) This modern motel contains 29 standard rooms, with the best ones overlooking the bay. There are private balconies and kitchenettes in some rooms, and downstairs is a restaurant and bar.

Hayden Turner Campground (tent sites $10) Just west of QCC follow 3rd Ave to this community campground located in a lovely, heavily wooded setting. There are also three **beach campsites** (sites $5) accessed via a short trail, but they're very exposed.

The other towns on Graham Island also offer some accommodations, and backcountry camping is possible in the forests and on the beaches throughout the archipelago. Contact the VIC for details.

Eating

The islands' few restaurants are clustered in QCC. Many are closed from October to April.

Lam's Cafe (☎ 250-559-4204; 3223 Wharf St; breakfast $6-9; ☺ breakfast & lunch) This plain café serves up a spread in the morning and light meals throughout the day, with nice views of the bay thrown in.

Howler's Bistro (☎ 250-559-8602; 2600 3rd Ave; mains $7-18; ☺ lunch & dinner) In an old timber place, with verandahs facing the bay, Howler's has a large menu of burgers, pasta, steak and fish. Downstairs, join others for beer and a game of pool at the pub, the only place in town that stays open late.

Summerland Pizza & Steakhouse (☎ 250-559-4588; 233 3rd Ave; meals $7-25; ☺ lunch & dinner) A little way west of town, this friendly spot has a large patio that is great when the sun's shining. The pizza isn't bad either.

Isabel Creek Store (☎ 250-559-8623; 3219 Wharf St; ☺ 10am-5:30pm Mon-Sat) For self-caterers, this shop stocks natural and organic foods.

Getting There & Away

AIR

Flying is a good option as the sea crossing can be rough. Planes land on Moresby Island at **Sandspit Airport** (YZP; ☎ 250-559-0052), which is connected to Skidegate on Graham Island by ferry. Airline services include Air Canada Jazz with flights to Vancouver (from $200) several times weekly and Hawkair, which flies daily to Prince Rupert (from $180) and Vancouver (from $230). Harbour Air (p869) flies to/from Prince Rupert (from $125) using the Seal Cove seaplane base at 7th Ave E in Prince Rupert.

BOAT

BC Ferries (☎ 250-386-3431, 888-223-3779; www.bc ferries.com; one-way adult/child $25/12.50, bicycle/car $6/90) sails between Prince Rupert and Skidegate six times weekly in summer, and three times a week the rest of the year. Bookings are essential in summer as the seats and cabins fill quickly. The crossing,

---

STILL STANDING

Inhabited continuously for 10,000 years, the Queen Charlotte Islands are the traditional homelands (Haida Gwaii) of the Haida nation, generally acknowledged as the dominant regional culture at the time Europeans arrived. When Captain Cook swung past in 1778, he found a large community of formidable warriors who periodically terrorized the nearby mainland communities.

However, in a microcosm of colonial practice occurring across the world, the arrival of European explorers and settlers forced the Haida into a centuries-long struggle to maintain their population, lands and cultural practices. Typically, they had few defenses against the diseases that were introduced by European explorers. In 1835 the Haida population was estimated at 6000 people; by 1915 that number had dropped below 600.

Paradoxically this period of population decline coincided with the flowering of one of northwestern BC's most enduring symbols – the totem pole. Carved since ancient times by the Tlingit, Tsimshian and Kwakiutl tribes, as well as the Haida, totem poles became popular during the mid-19th century as a way of displaying family wealth acquired through the fur trade. They often recorded a group's lineage (much like an English quartered family crest) and featured several carved ancestral beings and animal spirits, stacked one upon another.

Totem poles were often raised at potlatch ceremonies, and the Canadian Government's decision to outlaw these ceremonies in 1884 (see the boxed text on p772) resulted in a decline in totem carving. The law was abolished in 1951, and these days new totem poles are carved, although they tend to be employed more as public art, honoring the broader culture rather than depicting a familial history. Several fine examples of older poles still stand at Gwaii Haanas National Park Reserve (p769). You can see modern versions outside the Haida Gwaii Museum (p770) near Skidegate.

Also still standing are the Haida themselves. A politically active people, they make up around 40% of the Charlottes' population and have won some significant victories in recent times. In the 1980s they led an internationally publicized fight to preserve the islands from further logging. A bitter debate raged, but finally the federal government decided to save southern Moresby Island and create Gwaii Haanas National Park Reserve. In 2002 the BC Court of Appeals ruled that companies and governments must consult with the Haida before renewing licenses (such as forestry, mining and fishing) that affect lands and waters over which the Haida have a potential claim for native title. The Haida responded by lodging just such a claim, taking in the archipelago and surrounding waters, which have massive oil and gas reserves. This claim was still before the courts at the time of research.

which takes at least six hours, can be very rough; bring pills if you're prone to seasickness.

Getting Around

Eagle Transit (☎ 250-559-4461; $15-25) provides a shuttle service from the airport to the ferry terminal at Skidegate and QCC. It's also the local taxi service.

Local ferries (adult/child $5/2.50, car $12.50) run several times a day between Alliford Bay (Moresby Island, 11km west of Sandspit) and Skidegate (Graham Island).

There is no public transportation, although hitchhiking is common and the paved roads on Graham Island are good for cycling. Most other roads are gravel logging roads, many of them still active. If you plan to go on these, contact **Weyerhauser** (☎ 250-557-6810; ⊗ 6:30am-5:30pm Mon-Fri) to check traffic and conditions.

If you want a car, you'll have to weigh the cost of local car rental (from $50 a day) against the cost of bringing a vehicle on the ferry.

Budget (☎ 250-637-5688, 800-268-8900; www.budget .com; 3113 3rd Ave, QCC) Also at the airport.

Rustic Car Rentals (☎ 250-559-4641, 877-559-4641; citires@qcislands.net)

FORBIDDEN FEAST

The potlatch (a Chinook jargon word derived from the Nootka word *patschmatl*, meaning 'to give' or 'gift') is a feast or ceremony common among the First Nations people of the Pacific Northwest coast, especially the Kwakiutl. The potlatch traditionally involved the public exchange of gifts and destruction of property in a competitive display of affluence. Its main purpose was to validate the status of the chief or clan, although individuals also used it to try to enhance their social ranking. A significant social event such as a wedding or funeral was used as an occasion for a potlatch. The potlatch was prohibited by the federal government in 1884, when the Kwakiutl, at the cost of their own impoverishment, used it to shame and humble their former enemies. However, the practice continued in secret. The ban was eventually lifted in 1951 and small-scale potlatches again take place today.

YELLOWHEAD HIGHWAY TO PRINCE GEORGE

With the exception of a couple of interesting provincial parks, this 725km stretch of the Yellowhead Hwy (Hwy 16) from Prince Rupert to Prince George is fairly uneventful, passing a string of small, undistinguished towns along the way. Most of these have a VIC on the highway and the usual run of campgrounds and motels.

Prince Rupert to Smithers

It starts promisingly enough, as the road out of Prince Rupert hugs the Skeena River for 150km to **Terrace**, passing some of the province's most-breathtaking lake, forest and mountain scenery on the way.

From Terrace you can head 80km north to **Nisga'a Memorial Lava Bed Provincial Park** (☎ 250-798-2277; wlapwww.gov.bc.ca/bcparks; campsites $14; ⊗ mid-May–Oct), which preserves a huge, 260-year-old lava flow that killed more than 2000 of the local Nisga'a people. Several short trails take you through the eerie, lunarlike landscape.

From Terrace, the Yellowhead Hwy continues east to Kitwanga, where the **Stewart-Cassiar Hwy** (Hwy 37) strikes north towards the Yukon and Alaska (see p777).

Just east of Kitwanga you reach the **Hazelton** area (comprising New Hazelton, Hazelton and South Hazelton), the center of some interesting First Nations sites, including **'Ksan Historical Village & Museum** (☎ 250-842-5544; www .ksan.org; admission $2; tours adult/child $10/8.50; ⊗ 9am-6pm mid-Apr–mid-Oct, reduced hr Mon-Fri rest of year). This re-created village of the Gitksan people features longhouses, a museum, various outbuildings and totem poles.

Almost 70km further on you reach **Smithers**, the largest town on the route and a centre for adventure activities. The **VIC** (☎ 250-847-5072, 800-542-6673; www.tourismsmithers.com; 1411 Court St; ⊗ 9am-6pm summer, 9am-5pm Mon-Fri rest of year) has plenty of good information on mountain biking, white-water rafting and climbing in the area. Particularly good hiking is found at nearby **Babine Mountains Provincial Park** (☎ 250-847-7329; wlapwww.gov.bc.ca/bcparks; backcountry sites per person $5), a 32,400-hectare park with trails to glacier-fed lakes and subalpine meadows.

Smithers to Prince George

South of Smithers, you pass through Houston on the way to **Burns Lake**, the center of a popular fishing district. One of the best spots for canoeing, kayaking and fishing is 177km-long **Babine Lake**, 34km north of Burns Lake on Babine Lake Rd.

Burns Lake is also the northern gateway to the remote northern section of **Tweedsmuir Provincial Park** (wlapwww.gov.bc.ca/bcparks), an enormous and exceptional wilderness area to the south that's rich in wildlife; see the website for details. The southern section is accessible from Williams Lake (p776).

Just before you reach **Vanderhof**, Hwy 27 heads 66km north to **Fort St James National Historic Site** (☎ 250-996-7191; adult/child $6/3; May-Sep), a former Hudson's Bay Company trading post that's on the southeastern shore of Stuart Lake and has been renovated to its 1896 glory. From Vanderhof it's an uneventful 100km to Prince George.

NORTHEASTERN BRITISH COLUMBIA

Northeastern BC is a largely undeveloped, sparsely populated region dominated by the Rocky Mountains to the west and by the interior plains to the east. The region's attractions are relatively modest, and most travelers you'll encounter here are going to (or coming from) Prince Rupert or Alaska. Prince George is the area's main town, and sits at the crossroads of two major highways. The Yellowhead (Hwy 16) runs east–west between Prince Rupert and the Alberta border, while Hwy 97 heads north to the Yukon and Alaska, and south to Kamloops.

PRINCE GEORGE

A logging town since 1807, when Simon Fraser's men cut the first spruce trees down to build Fort George for the North West Company, Prince George is the largest town in northern BC and remains dominated by pulp mills. Apparently spurned by architects for 200 years, its downtown area has been neglected and it fails to make much of its riverside location. Still, it's a major regional center and many travelers will find themselves killing some time here. There are a few minor attractions to keep you occupied, but the best advice is to stock up on supplies and move on.

Orientation

Highway 97 from Cache Creek cuts through the center of town on its way north to Dawson Creek (406km) and the Alaska Hwy. The Yellowhead Hwy (Hwy 16) becomes Victoria St as it runs through town on its way west to Prince Rupert (724km), and east through Jasper (377km) to Edmonton. The downtown area is small, with little character. Victoria St is the main road, crossed by the east–west 2nd, 3rd and 4th Aves.

Information

Banks and ATMs can be found along Victoria St.

Books & Company (☎ 250-563-6637; 1685 3rd Ave; 8am-6pm Mon-Wed & Sat, to 9pm Thu, to 10pm Fri, 10am-5pm Sun) In a beautiful building downtown.

London Drugs (☎ 250-561-0011; Parkwood Place, 11th Ave; per 15min $1; 9am-10pm Mon-Sat, 10am-8pm Sun) Offers Internet access.

Post office (☎ 250-561-2568; 1323 5th Ave; 8:30am-5pm Mon-Fri)

Prince George Library (☎ 250-563-9251; Civic Centre, 887 Dominion St; 10am-9pm Mon-Thu, to 5:30pm Fri & Sat, 1-5pm Sun Sep-May) Free Internet access.

Prince George Regional Hospital (☎ 250-565-2000; 1547 Edmonton St; 24hr)

VIC (www.tourismpg.com); Train station (☎ 250-562-3700, 800-668-7646; VIA Rail, 1300 1st Ave; 8:30am-5pm Mon-Sat, closed Sat winter); Hwy (☎ 250-563-5493; cnr Hwy 97 & Hwy 16; 9am-7pm Jun-Sep) There's a summer outlet at the highway intersection.

Sights & Activities

Exploration Place (☎ 250-562-1612; www.theexplorationplace.com; Fort George Park; adult/concession $11/9; 10am-5pm summer, 10am-5pm Wed-Sun rest of year), southeast of downtown (follow 20th Ave east of Gorse St), has various large kid-friendly galleries devoted to science, natural history and cultural history. Other highlights include an Internet café and a SimEX full-motion ride simulator.

Prince George Railway & Forest Industry Museum (☎ 250-563-7351; www.pgrfm.bc.ca; 850 River Rd; adult/concession $6/5; 9am-5pm mid-May–mid-Oct), at Cottonwood Island Nature Park, has a mildly interesting collection of trains and railway memorabilia, plus an antique chainsaw display.

Prince George is full of parks. Right downtown, **Connaught Hill Park** sits atop the city and provides a good vantage point. North of downtown, between the railway tracks and

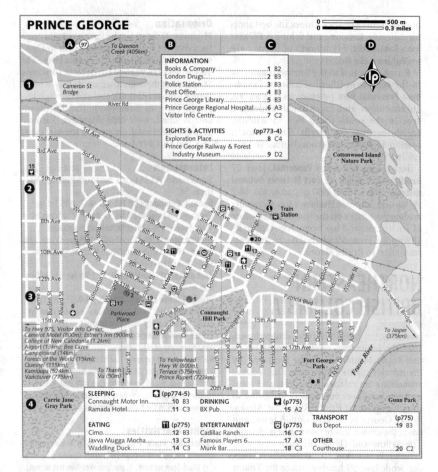

PRINCE GEORGE

INFORMATION		
Books & Company	1	B2
London Drugs	2	B3
Police Station	3	B3
Post Office	4	B3
Prince George Library	5	B3
Prince George Regional Hospital	6	A3
Visitor Info Centre	7	C2

SIGHTS & ACTIVITIES	(pp773-4)	
Exploration Place	8	C4
Prince George Railway & Forest Industry Museum	9	D2

SLEEPING	(pp774-5)	
Connaught Motor Inn	10	B3
Ramada Hotel	11	C3

EATING	(p775)	
Cimo	12	B3
Javva Mugga Mocha	13	C3
Waddling Duck	14	C3

DRINKING	(p775)	
BX Pub	15	A2

ENTERTAINMENT	(p775)	
Cadillac Ranch	16	C2
Famous Players 6	17	A3
Munk Bar	18	C3

TRANSPORT	(p775)	
Bus Depot	19	B3

OTHER		
Courthouse	20	C2

the river, 33-hectare **Cottonwood Island Nature Park** is a protected riparian forest with a good network of trails.

The 130-hectare **Forests of the World** features 15km of easily navigable interpretive trails with plaques that describe local flora and fauna. The forests lie at the north end of the University of Northern British Columbia campus, west of town.

Sleeping

Other than motels, accommodations are limited. There's no hostel and most campgrounds cater for RVs, so tent sites are generally not great. For B&B rooms, contact the **Bed & Breakfast Hotline** (☎ 250-562-2222, 877-562-2626; www.princegeorgebnb.com).

Connaught Motor Inn (☎ /fax 250-562-4441, 800-663-6620; 1550 Victoria St; d from $60; ☑) An older but well-maintained property in the center of town, this tidy motel offers three good ways to relax – an indoor pool, a hot tub and a sauna – and is popular with business travelers.

Camelot Motel (☎ 250-563-0661; http://camelot .prince-george.com; cnr Central St & 15th Ave; s/d $60/65; ☑) Of the many budget motels on the Hwy 97 strip, west of the center, this one gets the nod thanks to its friendly staff, larger rooms, microwave ovens and indoor pool.

College of New Caledonia (☎ 250-561-5849; www .cnc.bc.ca/res; 3330 22nd Ave; r from $25) The student residences here are the best bet for budget travelers in summer. Rooms share bathrooms and it's about a 20-minute walk into town.

Bee Lazee Campground (☎ 250-963-7263, 866-679-6699; drone@pgonline.com; 15910 Hwy 97S; campsites $15; 🛒) About 15km south of town, this place has all the facilities, including a pool, a laundry, a small shop and reasonable tent sites.

Also recommended:

Esther's Inn (☎ 250-562-4131, 800-663-6844; www .esthersinn.bc.ca; 1151 Commercial Dr; s/d from $60/70) Just out of the center, this place has a Polynesian-themed restaurant and lounge, plus a small attractive garden.

Ramada Hotel (☎ 250-563-0055, 800-830-8833; www .ramadaprincegeorge.com; 444 George St; r $140-200; 🖥 🛒) A good choice for those looking for a touch more class than that found at a standard motel.

Eating & Drinking

Cimo (☎ 250-564-7975; 601 Victoria St; meals $10-25; ⏱ lunch Mon-Fri, dinner Mon-Sat) One of the town's nicest places, the stylish decor here is complemented by a long list of Mediterranean dishes, with pasta, veal and chicken combos prominent.

Thanh Vu (☎ 250-564-2255; cnr 20th Ave & Spruce St; meals $8-12; ⏱ lunch Mon-Fri, dinner) Authentic, fresh Vietnamese flavors make this place a favorite with locals, and a welcome respite from rural Canadian fare. The price is right, too.

Waddling Duck (☎ 250-561-5550; 1157 5th Ave; meals $6-20; ⏱ dinner Mon-Sat) This pub offers steak and pasta standards plus a great range of British and local beers. Head for one of the pavement tables if the sun is shining.

Javva Mugga Mocha (☎ 250-562-3338; 304 George St; light meals $4-9; ⏱ breakfast & lunch) Across from the courthouse, this relaxed café has a limited but satisfying range of sandwiches, soups and pies, which can be enjoyed in the cozy sunroom if the wind's a bit chilly outside.

BX Pub (☎ 250-561-2900; cnr Carnie St & 5th Ave; ⏱ 11am-late) A large and friendly neighborhood joint that attracts a regular student crowd.

Entertainment

For clubbing, head to **Munk Bar** (☎ 250-564-3773; 1192 5th Ave; cover $5; ⏱ till late Wed-Sun). Fans fo boot-scooting can get their country-and-western fix at **Cadillac Ranch** (☎ 250-563-7720; 1380 2nd Ave; cover varies; ⏱ 3pm-2am). Meanwhile, **Famous Players 6** (☎ 250-612-3993; Parkwood Pl, 15th Ave) shows new-release films.

Getting There & Away

Prince George Airport (☎ 250-963-2400; www.pg airport.ca; Airport Rd) is 14km southeast of downtown, off Hwy 97. Air Canada Jazz serves Vancouver ($170, 1½ hours); WestJet serves Calgary ($135, five hours) and Vancouver ($130, 1½ hours).

From the **bus depot** (☎ 250-564-5454; 1566 12th Ave), Greyhound Canada buses run to Kamloops ($75, eight hours), Prince Rupert ($105, 11 hours) and Vancouver ($110, 12 hours).

Run by VIA Rail, the *Skeena* passes through Prince George's **train station** (1300 1st Ave) between Prince Rupert and Jasper three times a week in both directions.

Getting Around

To get to downtown hotels and motels from the airport, take the **Airporter bus** (☎ 250-563-2220; $10). **Prince George Taxi** (☎ 250-564-4444) will do the journey for around $18. Major car-rental agencies have offices at the airport. **Prince George Transit** (☎ 250-563-0011; www.buson line.ca) operates local buses; the one-way fare in the central zone is $1.50.

HIGHWAY 16 EAST OF PRINCE GEORGE

An unexciting, 380km stretch of highway links Prince George with Jasper, just over the Alberta border. The only attraction along the route actually abuts Jasper National Park, but on the BC side of the border. **Mt Robson Provincial Park** (☎ 250-964-2243; wlapwww.gov.bc.ca/ bcparks; campsites $17) may not get the rave reviews of its illustrious neighbor, but its steep glaciers, prolific wildlife and backcountry hiking should not be underestimated. One of the highlights of the park is the popular trip to **Berg Lake**, a 23km (two-day) hike to the base of Mt Robson, which passes numerous glaciers. You need to register and pay at the **visitor center** (☎ 800-689-9025; www.discovercamping .ca; backcountry fee $5) before you head out.

HIGHWAY 97 SOUTH OF PRINCE GEORGE

From Prince George, Hwy 97 follows the old Goldrush Trail south through 'Cariboo Country,' passing a series of small towns on the way, notably Quesnel, Williams Lake and Cache Creek. The route does contain a couple of minor attractions (plus one of the world's best canoeing routes), but mostly it's just a long drive of 525km to Kamloops, or 780km to Vancouver.

BRITISH COLUMBIA

BARKING UP THE RIGHT TREE

Between 1858 and 1861 the Cariboo Trail (now Hwy 97) was pushed north from Kamloops to Quesnel. It was lined with ramshackle towns that were hastily built by gold prospectors from around the world. In 1862 a Cornishman, Billy Barker, hit the jackpot, making $1000 in the first two days of his claim. Soon Barkerville sprang up to become the largest city west of Chicago and north of San Francisco. The big boom was instrumental in the creation of British Columbia in 1866, when Vancouver and the mainland were united.

Barkerville Historic Park

This restored **gold rush town** (☎ 250-994-3332; www.heritage.gov.bc.ca; adult/child $12.50/3.50; ☼ 8am-8pm) is 89km east of Quesnel at the end of Hwy 26. More than 125 buildings have been restored, and in summer people dressed in period garb roam through town. It's quite well done, but an extremely long detour is required. A bonus is that there's a good chance of seeing bear and deer along the road. The nearby town of Wells has accommodations, restaurants and a general store. Visit the **VIC** (☎ 250-994-2323, 877-451-9355; www.wellsbc.com; ☼ 9am-6pm summer) for details.

Bowron Lake Provincial Park

Surrounded by snowy peaks, this 149,207-hectare **park** boasts one of the best canoe trips in the world. The 116km circular canoe route passes through 10 lakes (Bowron, Kibbee, Indianpoint, Isaac, McLeary, Lanezi, Sandy, Babcock, Skoi and Swan) and over sections of the Isaac, Cariboo and Bowron Rivers, with the surrounding Cariboo and Mowdish Ranges affording spectacular views in every direction. In between are eight portages, with the longest (2km) over well-defined trails. There's usually plenty of wildlife to spot, with moose, bear, caribou mountain goat joined by abundant birdlife.

The whole circuit takes between six and 10 days, and you'll need to be completely self-sufficient. You can paddle the circuit any time from mid-May to October. Most people do it in July and August, but September is an excellent choice, since that's when the tree leaves change color. Mosquitoes are at their worst in the spring.

Numbers are limited: the park service only allows 27 canoes to start the circuit each day. Find Bowron Lake at **BC Parks** (wlapwww.gov.bc.ca/bcparks.htm) to download the essential *Bowron Lake Canoe Circuit Pre-Trip Information* documentation. You will then need to reserve your circuit with **BC Parks** (☎ 250-387-1642, 800-435-5622; per person $60, plus reservation fee $18), which can be done around January 2. Once you get to the park, you must go to the registration center to check in and undergo an orientation session.

If this sounds hard-core, you can do day trips on Bowron Lake, which require no advance registration or fee. Guided paddles of Bowron Lake are offered by **Whitegold Adventures** (☎ 250-994-2345, 866-994-2345; www.whitegold.ca; Hwy 26, Wells; day trips from $50, 4-/8-day trips $550/1300). Bowron Lake Lodge and Becker's Lodge both offer long- and short-term canoe rentals ($10/40 per hour/day, 10 days $125).

SLEEPING

Becker's Lodge (☎ 250-992-8864, 800-808-4761; www.beckers.bc.ca; Bowron Lake via Barkerville; campsites $20, d cabin/chalet from $80/200) The attractive Becker's features a cozy restaurant and nice log chalets and cabins. Tent sites include firewood and use of the facilities.

Bowron Lake Lodge (☎ 250-992-2733, 800-519-3399; www.bowronlakelodge.com; campsites $20, d from $65; ☼ May-Nov) Just up the road, this friendly lodge on the lake, at the end of Bowron Lake Rd, offers different types of accommodations. You can also camp right by the lake.

Bowron Lake Provincial Park Campground (campsites $14) has 25 nonreservable sites with pit toilets.

GETTING THERE & AWAY

By car, turn off Hwy 26 just before Barkerville and follow the 28km gravel Bowron Lake Rd.

Williams Lake & Around

Williams Lake, 120km south of Quesnel, is a large logging center that's also the access point to the southern section of **Tweedsmuir South Provincial Park** (☎ 250-398-4414; wlapwww.gov.bc.ca/bcparks; campsites $20), which is known for its excellent canoeing and beautiful waterfalls. It's 360km to the park from Williams Lake, then a further 100km to Bella Coola on the coast. (From there you can catch a ferry north to Prince Rupert or south to Port Hardy; see p697 for details.) South of Williams Lake, the forested hills gradually give way to dry, scrub-covered hills as you approach Cache Creek, where you can head east to Kamloops or continue south to Hope.

THE FAR NORTH

This section details the two main routes that head north out of BC: the Stewart-Cassiar Hwy (Hwy 37) from New Hazelton, and the Alaska Hwy (Hwy 97) from Prince George. Both take you into the Yukon Territory and they meet up just west of Watson Lake, a few kilometers over the border, from where you can head to Whitehorse (p783) and the Alaskan border at Beaver Creek.

STEWART-CASSIAR HIGHWAY

This remote stretch of highway splits off the Yellowhead Hwy (Hwy 16), about 43km west of New Hazelton, and meanders 570km north to the Yukon border, passing through scenery spectacular enough to rival that of the Alaska Hwy. It officially becomes the Stewart-Cassiar Hwy at Meziadin Junction, 150km along the way.

Once considered something of an adventure, these days only 15% of the route remains unsealed and it's generally a safe road. Do check your spare tire and take some drinking water with you in case of a breakdown, but don't get stressed – the longest distance between service stations is under 150km (note, however, that they don't keep extended hours). Traffic is generally light, but includes long logging trucks and the occasional maniac. It's best to grant them the right of way, while you enjoy the ride and the views. For road conditions, call ☎ 250-771-4511 or log on to www.th.gov.bc.ca/road reports.htm.

Stewart & Hyder

The rough-and-ready twin border towns of Stewart, BC (population 600), and Hyder, Alaska (population 95), are quite the eye-opener and worth the 65km detour west from Meziadin Junction. On the way, you pass by breathtaking scenery, including waterfalls and the stunning Bear Glacier, the largest ice tongue of the Cambria Icefields.

The **VIC** (☎ 250-636-9224, 888-366-5999; 222 5th Ave; ⊙ 9am-7pm summer, reduced hr rest of year) in Stewart represents both towns, and can help with accommodations, while border formalities are conducted in a little booth between the communities.

If you're visiting between late July and September, take Salmon Glacier Rd to **Fish Creek**, about 3km past Hyder, where you can stand on a viewing platform, see the salmon swimming upstream to spawn, and watch bears hungrily feeding on them. Afterwards, you can get 'Hyderized' by slamming back a shot of 190-proof alcohol at the **Glacier Inn** (☎ 250-636-9248), whose walls are covered in signed dollar bills.

Also in Hyder, **Grand View Inn** (☎ 250-636-9174; www.grandviewinn.net; r from $60) has modern rooms, some with kitchenettes. There are good views of the bears wandering the streets. In Stewart, **King Edward Motel/Hotel** (☎ 250-636-2244, 800-663-3126; www.kingedwardhotel .com; d $70-110) is a standard motel downtown on 5th Ave. **Rainey Creek Municipal Campground** (☎ 250-636-2537; 8th Ave; campsites $12), also in Stewart, has showers and flush toilets.

Meziadin Junction to Watson Lake

Vast **Spatsizi Plateau Provincial Wilderness Park** (☎ 250-771-4591; wlapwww.gov.bc.ca/bcparks) is accessed by a rough, 28km gravel road from Tatogga, about 150km north of Meziadin Junction. The park is undeveloped and isolated, and supports large populations of Stone's sheep, mountain goat, moose, grizzly and black bear, caribou and wolves. The trails are often little more than vague notions across the untouched landscape. You'll need to be both highly experienced and self-sufficient to tackle this one.

Back on the highway, **Red Goat Lodge** (☎ 250-234-3261, 888-733-4628; www.karo-ent.com/ redgoat.htm; campsites $13, dm $20, r $55-95) sits on the shores of Eddontenajon Lake. It's a haven for travelers, with a coin-op laundry and communal kitchen facilities. You can camp alongside the lake or stay in one of the cabins. The lodge rents canoes and organizes trips into the parks.

In the same region, **Mt Edziza Provincial Park** (☎ 250-771-4591; wlapwww.gov.bc.ca/bcparks) is a 230,000-hectare wilderness park that protects a volcanic landscape featuring lava flows, basalt plateaus and cinder cones surrounding an extinct shield volcano. Though it's inaccessible by car, you can hike, horseback ride or fly into the park by making arrangements in Telegraph Creek or Dease Lake.

Less than 90km from the provincial border, **Boya Lake Provincial Park** (☎ 250-771-4591; wlapwww.gov.bc.ca/bcparks; campsites $12) is more accessible. This stunning little park surrounds the shockingly turquoise Boya Lake, which is dotted with small tree-covered islets. You can camp right on the shore.

ALASKA HIGHWAY

As you travel north from Prince George, the mountains and forests give way to gentle rolling hills and farmland, until near Dawson Creek the landscape resembles the prairies of Alberta. There's no real need to dawdle on this stretch, although the road passes **Summit Lake**, **Bear Lake** and **MacLeod Lake**, which offer good canoeing and fishing, and camping in the surrounding provincial parks.

From **Chetwynd** you can take Hwy 29 north past Hudson's Hope (a 20-minute drive from the eastern arm of Williston Lake) to join the Alaska Hwy north of Fort St John, or continue straight ahead to **Dawson Creek**. This small town is notable as the starting point (Mile 0) for the Alaska Hwy (which heads 2451km northwest to Fairbanks), but not much else. However, it has a fair range of accommodations and is a convenient stopping point for long-distance travelers. The **VIC** (☎ 250-782-9595, 866-645-3022; 8am-7pm summer, 9am-5pm Mon-Sat spring & fall, Tue-Sat winter) can help with accommodations, which include the **George Dawson Inn** (☎ 250-782-9151, 800-663-2745; www.georgedawsoninn.bc.ca; 11705 8th St; r $75-90) and the **Alaska Hotel** (☎ 250-782-7998; www.alaskahotel.com; 10209 10th St; r with shared bathroom $30-45), a classic old hotel with an atmospheric bar and restaurant. There are several RV parks on the approaches to town.

Heading northwest from Dawson Creek, the landscape again changes, as the prairies are left behind, and the Alaska Hwy crosses the Peace River on its way into the foothills of the Rocky Mountains. Except for Fort St John and Fort Nelson, most of the towns on the highway usually have little more than one or two service stations, campgrounds or lodgings. The real attraction here is the scenery and ever-present wildlife. You won't regret allowing time to explore a couple of provincial parks on the way.

The 390km drive from Fort St John to Fort Nelson passes several small reserves, **Buckinghorse River**, **Prophet River** and **Andy Bailey**, which all are nice spots to camp, but the better parks are still ahead of you. Fort Nelson's **VIC** (☎ 250-774-2541; www.northernrockies.org; 5500 50th Ave N; 8am-8pm summer, 8:30am-4:30pm Mon-Fri rest of year) can supply park information and local accommodation options.

Around 140km northwest of Fort Nelson **Stone Mountain Provincial Park** (☎ 250-427-5452; wlapwww.gov.bc.ca/bcparks; campsites $14) has hiking trails with backcountry camping and a campground. The moose in the park can often be seen eating nonchalantly by the side of the road.

A further 75km brings you to **Muncho Lake Provincial Park**, centered on the emerald-green lake of the same name, and boasting spruce forests, vast rolling mountains and some truly breathtaking scenery. There are two **campgrounds** (campsites $14) by the lake, plus a few lodges scattered along the highway through the park, including **Northern Rockies Lodge** (☎ 250-776-3481, 800-663-5269; www.northern-rockies-lodge.com; tent sites $20, r $60-80), which also has a restaurant.

Finally, you can soothe any stiff legs at **Liard River Hot Springs Provincial Park** (☎ 250-427-5452; wlapwww.gov.bc.ca/bcparks), where underground springs create a unique ecosystem that's home to an incredible 250 species of plants, including 14 different varieties of orchid. Rangers run interpretive programs throughout the summer. The park's **campground** (☎ 800-689-9025; www.discovercamping.ca; campsites $17) has 52 campsites. From here it's 220km to Watson Lake (p790) and the Yukon.

Yukon Territory

Every year visitors discover the Yukon's rugged charm during its short summer, or arrive later to ski or snowshoe and experience the harsh winter landscape. Like the hardy locals, they take on the often challenging environment which has rewards that match its extremes.

Whitehorse, the capital, has a thriving cultural life, while Dawson City is simply a fun place to be during the summer. With good road access, transportation and services, costs in the Yukon are reasonable compared with other remote areas of Canada. It's also a great place for kids.

And then there's the land. What land! From the Unesco-recognized Kluane National Park in the southwest, with the world's largest nonpolar icefields, to the tundra of Ivvavik National Park in the Arctic, the landscape is wild and offers endless opportunities to explore. Stand on a bluff overlooking the surging Yukon River and you see a vista unchanged in eons.

The Yukon offers an abundance of outdoor opportunities amid the scenic splendor of mountains, forests, fast-flowing rivers and tundra. Mountain ranges almost cover the territory, which is 80% wilderness. There are large populations of moose, caribou, bear, sheep, beaver, porcupines, coyote and wolves, which far outnumber the humans.

The best-known hiking route is the Chilkoot Trail, which begins in Skagway, but Kluane National Park in the territory's southwest corner also has excellent hikes, from short and easy to long and demanding. Canoeists have many choices, from easy float trips down the waters of the Yukon River and its tributaries to challenging white water. The Alsek and Tatshenshini Rivers ranked among the best and wildest in North America. They're found in British Columbia, south of Kluane, and are accessible from Haines Junction.

A trip to the Yukon is an adventure of a lifetime – unless, like many, you return often.

HIGHLIGHTS

- Paddle the fast-flowing **Yukon River** (p786) or its tributaries
- Hike the greenbelt or fly over the icy heart of **Kluane National Park** (p791)
- Follow the gold-seekers on the **Gold Rush Trail** (p795)
- Amble down the gold rush–era streets of **Dawson City** (p798)
- Experience the 747km **Dempster Hwy** (p803), the last great adventure road, with wide-open tundra and a chance to cross the Arctic Circle

★ Dempster Hwy
★ Dawson City
★ Yukon River
★ Kluane National Park
★ Gold Rush Trail

■ POPULATION: 32,000 | ■ TERRITORIAL CAPITAL: WHITEHORSE | ■ AREA: 483,450 SQ KM

YUKON TERRITORY

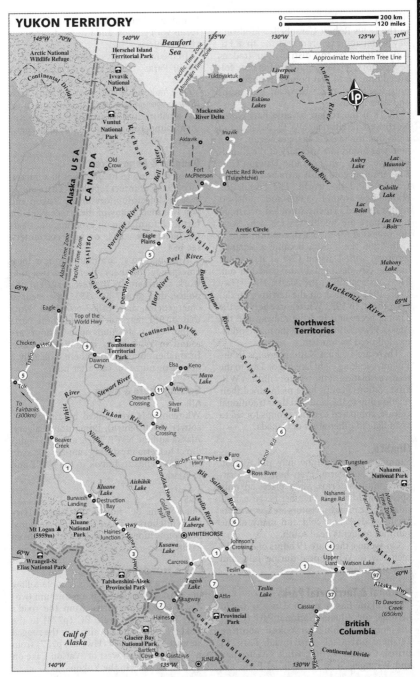

0 ___ 200 km
0 ___ 120 miles

– – – Approximate Northern Tree Line

Beaufort Sea

Arctic National Wildlife Refuge

Herschel Island Territorial Park

Ivvavik National Park

Vuntut National Park

Continental Divide

Old Crow

Richardson

Bell River

Porcupine River

Tuktoyaktuk

Mackenzie River Delta

Aklavik

Inuvik

Fort McPherson

Arctic Red River (Tsiigehtchie)

Liverpool Bay

Eskimo Lakes

Anderson River

Carnwath River

Aubry Lake

Lac Maunoir

Colville Lake

Lac Belot

Lac Des Bois

Mahony Lake

Arctic Circle

Eagle Plains

Peel River

Mountains

Dempster Hwy

Hart River

Bonnet Plume River

Mackenzie River

Northwest Territories

Eagle

Top of the World Hwy

Continental Divide

Tombstone Territorial Park

Dawson City

Chicken

Hwy

Taylor Hwy

Tok

To Fairbanks (300km)

White River

Stewart River

Yukon River

Elsa

Keno

Mayo Lake

Mayo

Stewart Crossing

Silver Trail

Pelly Crossing

Selwyn Mountains

Carmacks

Robert Campbell Hwy

Faro

Carol Rd

Ross River

Tungsten

Nahanni National Park

Beaver Creek

Nisling River

Kluane Lake

Aishihik Lake

Klondike Hwy

Big Salmon River

Nahanni Range Rd

Logan Mtns

Burwash Landing

Destruction Bay

Mt Logan (5959m)

Kluane National Park

Haines Junction

Alaska Hwy

Gold Rush Trail

Teslin River

Lake Laberge

●WHITEHORSE

Johnson's Crossing

Wrangell–St Elias National Park

Haines Hwy

Kusawa Lake

Carcross

Upper Liard

Watson Lake

Tatshenshini-Alsek Provincial Park

Tagish Lake

Atlin

Teslin

Teslin Lake

Alaska Hwy

Skagway

Atlin Provincial Park

Cassiar

To Dawson Creek (650km)

Haines

Coast Mountains

Stewart-Cassiar Hwy

British Columbia

Gulf of Alaska

Glacier Bay National Park

Bartlett Cove

Gustavus

JUNEAU

Continental Divide

Alaska USA / CANADA

Alaska Time Zone / Pacific Time Zone

Pacific Time Zone / Mountain Time Zone

Mountain Time Zone

Pacific Time Zone

History

In the 1840s Robert Campbell, a Hudson's Bay Company explorer, was the first European to travel the district. Fur traders, prospectors, whalers and missionaries followed him. Until that point there had been only limited contact between Europeans and Aboriginals.

In 1870 the region became part of the Northwest Territories (NWT). But it was in 1896 that the biggest changes began, when gold was found in a tributary of the Klondike River near what became Dawson City. The ensuing gold rush attracted hopefuls from around the world. The population boomed to around 38,000 and transport routes opened. Towns sprouted overnight to support the wealth-seekers, who were not prepared for the harsh conditions.

In 1898 the Yukon became a separate territory, with Dawson City as its capital, but the city declined as the gold ran out. The construction of the Alaska Hwy (Hwy 1) in 1942 opened up the territory to development. In 1953 Whitehorse became the capital, because it had the railway and the Alaska Hwy. Mining is still the main industry, followed by tourism.

There are 14 First Nations groups in the Yukon, speaking eight languages. Due to the relative isolation of the territory until WWII, First Nations groups have maintained their relationship to the land and their traditional culture, compared to other groups forced to assimilate in other areas of Canada.

Climate

Summers, spanning June, July and August, are short but warm, even hot, with occasional thunderstorms. Many places are only open from May to September because, outside of these months, visitors are few, winters are long, dark and cold and many of the summer residents head south.

On average there are 19 hours of daylight each day in Whitehorse during July, and only six in January.

National & Territorial Parks

The Yukon has a major Unesco world heritage site. Kluane National Park (p791) sits solidly within the Yukon abutting Tatshenshini-Alsek Provincial Park in British Columbia (BC), while Glacier Bay and Wrangell-St Elias National Parks are found in adjoining Alaska, USA. This area teems with glaciers and raw landscape over two countries.

In the far north, Ivvavik and Vuntut National Parks (p804) are wild and remote places.

The Yukon has only four **territorial parks** (www.environmentyukon.gov.yk.ca), but much of the territory itself is parklike and government campgrounds can be found in many places.

Dangers & Annoyances

If you're going to be outdoors in summer, take plenty of insect repellent. There are 25 varieties of mosquitoes in the Yukon and you will meet many of them (see p881 for further information on avoiding and treating bites). For advice on bear encounters, see p54.

Although most communities have local emergency numbers, there are two that work anywhere in the territory. For the police, dial ☎ 867-667-5555; for medical emergencies, dial ☎ 867-667-3333. Note that ☎ 911 may not work in some parts of the Yukon. Hospitals open 24 hours are found in Whitehorse and Watson Lake. In smaller communities there is usually a doctor or nurse on call after hours.

Getting There & Away

AIR

Whitehorse is well linked by air to Vancouver ($300 return), Edmonton, Calgary, Alaska and the NWT. There are even flights direct to Germany during summer. Dawson City has flights to Inuvik in the NWT and to Alaska.

BUS

Buses from BC follow the Alaska Hwy to Whitehorse. There are also seasonal bus connections to towns in Alaska from Whitehorse.

CAR & MOTORCYCLE

Driving to the Yukon, most people follow the Alaska Hwy, which is a minimum two-day, 1426km-long drive from the road's start in Dawson Creek, BC (p778) to the Yukon border. You can also take the rugged Stewart-Cassiar Hwy (Hwy 37; p777) from BC to a point just west of Watson Lake on the Alaska Hwy in the Yukon.

FERRY

An excellent way to reach the Yukon from the south is via ferry to Skagway or Haines in Alaska, from where you can drive into the Yukon.

Alaska Marine Hwy (☎ 800-642-0066; www.alaska.gov/ferry) ferries run from Prince Rupert in BC to Skagway via Ketchikan, Wrangell, Petersburg, Juneau and Haines.

From Prince Rupert to Skagway the 35-hour trip costs adult/child US$159/80, with cabins/cars from US$116/333).

From Prince Rupert to Haines it is 32 hours and costs adult/child US$150/75, cabin from US$116, car from US$316.

There are three sailings per week in summer and two in winter. Book vehicles and cabins well in advance.

Getting Around

The major towns in the Yukon are connected by air and bus.

Driving your own vehicle is the best way to get around, and there are car and RV rental outlets in Whitehorse and car rental available in Dawson City. See p873 for a list of national car-rental agencies.

The road system in the Yukon is fairly extensive, if rough. Many roads are gravel. Most of the Alaska Hwy and the Klondike Hwy (Hwy 2) are paved, but not necessarily smooth, and some parts may be gravel, especially where the never-ending maintenance is taking place. Make certain you can change a tire and that you have at least one full-sized spare in good condition. Headlights are required to be on at all times on all roads.

Gasoline prices along the highways can be high, so plan your budget accordingly. Generally, along the main routes there's a service station every 100km, but in some areas there may be nothing for 200km or more.

For information on road conditions, call ☎ 867-456-7623. For Dempster Hwy (Hwy 5) information, call ☎ 800-661-0752.

WHITEHORSE

Spread along the banks of the Yukon River, Whitehorse is the largest town in the territory and is its capital. It is a pleasant place that makes a good base to start a Yukon trip. If you have traveled by land from the south, Whitehorse is a good place to stop and gather your wits. There are good restaurants, an active artistic community and a few things to do. Artists and writers escaping the big city mix well with government workers and grizzled old-timers. If you're planning a wilderness adventure, this is where you can get fully outfitted.

HISTORY

Whitehorse has always been a transportation hub, initially as a terminus for the White Pass & Yukon Route railway from Skagway. During WWII it was a major center for work on the Alaska Hwy and its airport played an important strategic role. In 1953 Whitehorse was made the capital of the territory, to the continuing regret of the much smaller and more isolated Dawson City.

YUKON TERRITORY

WHITEHORSE

0 ————— 300 m
0 ————— 0.2 miles

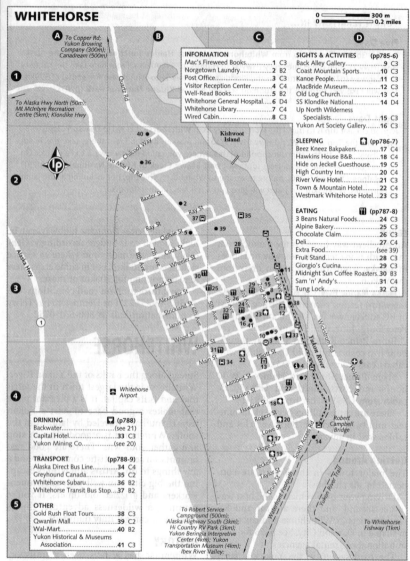

INFORMATION
Mac's Fireweed Books............**1** C3
Norgetown Laundry................**2** B2
Post Office.............................**3** C3
Visitor Reception Center.........**4** C4
Well-Read Books....................**5** B2
Whitehorse General Hospital....**6** D4
Whitehorse Library.................**7** C3
Wired Cabin..........................**8** C3

SIGHTS & ACTIVITIES (pp785–6)
Back Alley Gallery...................**9** C3
Coast Mountain Sports...........**10** C3
Kanoe People........................**11** C3
MacBride Museum..................**12** C3
Old Log Church......................**13** C3
SS Klondike National...............**14** D4
Up North Wilderness
  Specialists.........................**15** C3
Yukon Art Society Gallery.......**16** C3

SLEEPING (pp786–7)
Beez Kneez Bakpakers............**17** C4
Hawkins House B&B................**18** C4
Hide on Jeckell Guesthouse....**19** C5
High Country Inn...................**20** C4
River View Hotel....................**21** C4
Town & Mountain Hotel..........**22** C4
Westmark Whitehorse Hotel....**23** C3

EATING (pp787–8)
3 Beans Natural Foods............**24** C3
Alpine Bakery.......................**25** C3
Chocolate Claim....................**26** C3
Deli.....................................**27** C4
Extra Food.......................(see 39)
Fruit Stand...........................**28** C3
Giorgio's Cucina....................**29** C3
Midnight Sun Coffee Roasters.**30** B3
Sam 'n' Andy's......................**31** C4
Tung Lock.............................**32** C3

DRINKING (p788)
Backwater.........................(see 21)
Capital Hotel........................**33** C3
Yukon Mining Co.................(see 20)

TRANSPORT (pp788–9)
Alaska Direct Bus Line............**34** C4
Greyhound Canada.................**35** C2
Whitehorse Subaru.................**36** B2
Whitehorse Transit Bus Stop....**37** B2

OTHER
Gold Rush Float Tours.............**38** C3
Qwanlin Mall........................**39** C2
Wal-Mart.............................**40** B2
Yukon Historical & Museums
  Association.........................**41** C3

ORIENTATION

The town sits just off the Alaska Hwy between Dawson Creek in BC (1430km to the east), where the highway starts, and Fairbanks in Alaska (970km west).

The official city limits cover 421 sq km, making it one of the largest urban-designated areas in Canada. Despite its growth, Whitehorse still has something of a frontier feel, even if it is home to two-thirds of the Yukon's population.

The central core of Whitehorse is quite small and it is easy to walk around on foot. Downtown is designed on a grid system, and the main traffic routes are 2nd and 4th Aves.

INFORMATION

There is one Internet terminal at Midnight Sun Coffee Roasters (p787; per hour $3).

Mac's Fireweed Books (☎ 867-668-2434; www.yukon books.com; 203 Main St; ☺ 8am-midnight summer, 9am-6pm rest of year) Has a superb selection of history, geography and wildlife titles plus a section on First Nations culture. It also carries topographical maps, road maps, magazines and newspapers.

Norgetown Laundry (☎ 867-667-6113; 4213 4th Ave; ☺ 8am-9:30pm)

Post office (☎ 867-667-2485; 211 Main St; ☺ 9am-6pm Mon-Fri, 11am-4pm Sat) In the basement of Shoppers Drug Mart.

Visitor Reception Center (VRC; ☎ 867-667-3084; 100 Hanson St; ☺ 8am-8pm mid-May–mid-Sep, 9am-4:30pm Mon-Fri rest of year)

Well-Read Books (☎ 867-393-2987; www.wellread books.yk.net; 4194B 4th Ave; ☺ 10am-6pm Mon-Sat, noon-5pm Sun) Has a large and varied selection of used books. Here's a chance to buy that trashy novel guilt-free.

Whitehorse General Hospital (☎ 867-393-8700; 5 Hospital Rd; ☺ 24hr) Emergency services.

Whitehorse Library (☎ 867-667-5239; 2071 2nd Ave; ☺ 10am-9pm Mon-Fri, 10am-6pm Sat, 1-9pm Sun) Free Internet access for 15 minutes.

Wired Cabin (☎ 867-393-3597; 107 Jarvis St; per 15min $2; ☺ 9am-midnight) Internet access.

SIGHTS

Whitehorse's sights provide visitors with a good base of knowledge about the territory.

Yukon Beringia Interpretive Centre (☎ 867-667-8855; www.beringia.com; Km 1473 Alaska Hwy; adult/child $6/4; ☺ 8:30am-7pm mid-May–mid-Sep) focuses on Beringia, an area that, during the last Ice Age, encompassed the Yukon, Alaska and eastern Siberia yet was untouched by glaciers. Interactive displays re-create the time. This museum is the most interesting local sight, and it's just south of the airport. From downtown, take the airport bus from Ogilvie St to the airport and then walk south for five minutes. This is a good way to occupy yourself if you're stuck waiting at the airport for connecting flights.

The perfectly restored **SS Klondike** (☎ 867-667-4511; cnr South Access Rd & 2nd Ave; adult/child $5/3; ☺ 9am-5:30pm mid-May–mid-Sep) was one of the last and largest sternwheelers used on the Yukon. Built in 1937, it made its final run upriver in 1955 and is now a museum and national historic site. Admission includes a guided tour.

MacBride Museum (☎ 867-667-2709; cnr 1st Ave & Wood St; adult/child $5/3.50; ☺ 10am-9pm Mon-Fri, 10am-7pm Sat & Sun mid-May–Sep) looks like a log cabin with a turf roof. It has a collection from First Nations cultures, the fur trade, gold-rush days and the construction of the Alaska Hwy. There's the requisite collection of stuffed critters and a mixed bag of old mining equipment. Check out the good shot of the old Whitehorse waterfront at the entrance. In summer there are lectures on the collections at 7pm most nights.

Built by the town's first priest in 1900, the **old log church** (☎ 867-668-2555; 303 Elliott St; adult/child $2.50/1; ☺ 10am-6pm mid-May–Aug) is the only wooden cathedral in the world and the oldest building in town. Try to imagine looking for forgiveness here.

Yukon Brewing Company (☎ 867-668-4183; 102 Copper Rd; ☺ 11am-6pm, tours 11am & 4pm), the maker of the popular and excellent Yukon Gold, Arctic Red, Winter Lead Dog Porter and Sourdough Ale (the owner's favorite), is based in Whitehorse.

Located close to the Yukon Beringia Interpretive Centre, the **Yukon Transportation Museum** (☎ 867-668-4792; 30 Electra Circle; adult/child $6/4; ☺ 10am-6pm May-Aug) covers the perils and adventures of getting around the Yukon by plane, train, truck and dog sled. Check out the crashes in the bush pilot room. If you have a mud fetish, you'll love the Alaska Hwy exhibit.

Whitehorse Fishway (☎ 867-633-5965; Nisultin Dr; admission free; ☺ 8am-8pm summer) is one of the coolest sights in Whitehorse. The fishway is a 366m-long wooden fish ladder (the world's longest!) that gives fish a route past the hydroelectric plant just south of town. The real attraction here is the large viewing window that lets you look eye to eye with returning salmon. If they look pooped it's because they've been swimming 2792km since they entered the Yukon River in west Alaska and they still have another 208km to go before finally reaching their spawning grounds. There's an excellent free booklet available. The fishway is off 2nd Ave after it crosses the Robert Campbell Bridge.

At the **Yukon Art Society Gallery** (☎ 867-667-4080; 305 Wood St; admission free; ☺ 11am-5:30pm Mon-Sat) you can get an answer to 'Why have all the hippie artists come to the Yukon?' Answer: 'It's cheap, the people are laid-back and the air and water are clean.' This small space shows and sells works by local artists. You can also get good leads on the dozens of artists in the area whose galleries you can visit. In summer, lunchtime concerts are held in the small adjoining park.

Back Alley Gallery (☎ 867-667-2002; 204A Main St; ✆ noon-5pm Tue-Sat) is located just where the name implies; it's a sleek space that exhibits and sells works by noted Yukon artists.

ACTIVITIES

Whitehorse has no shortage of ways to get your feet wet (even literally) in the myriad of Yukon activities. **Coast Mountain Sports** (☎ 867-667-4074; 208A Main St; ✆ 9:30am-6pm Mon-Sat, to 9pm Thu & Fri, noon-4pm Sun) has a large selection of outdoor clothing and equipment, including stove fuel.

Hiking, Cycling & Skiing

You can **walk** a scenic 15km loop around Whitehorse's waters that includes a stop at the fishway. From the SS *Klondike* head south on the Waterfront Footpath until you reach the footbridge across the Miles Canyon and the Yukon River. Then head north along the east side of the water that includes Schwatka Lake. The Yukon River Trail will take you past the fishway. Cross the Robert Campbell Bridge and you are back in the town center. You may see coyote, beaver and mule deer.

Around Whitehorse you can go **hiking** and **cycling**, particularly at Mt McIntyre Recreation Center, up Two Mile Hill Rd, and at Grey Mountain, east of town. All along the Ibex River Valley west of Whitehorse is good for cycling. The hiking trails there become **cross-country skiing** trails in winter.

Canoeing & Kayaking

Whitehorse is the starting place for popular canoe and kayak trips to Carmacks or on to Dawson City. It's an average of eight days to the former and 16 days to the latter.

Kanoe People (☎ 867-668-4899; www.kanoepeople .com; cnr 1st Ave & Strickland St), at the river's edge, can arrange any type of trip (to Carmacks in canoe/kayak $195/275, to Dawson City $325/475). These prices for unguided trips include an orientation session and drop-off. Bicycle rentals are also available. The store has a great – and inspirational – view of the river. Vast amounts of gear, maps

and guides are for sale. In addition you can book trips to the increasingly popular Big Salmon River. The staff are patient, helpful and just plain friendly.

Up North Wilderness Specialists (☎ 867-667-7035; www.upnorth.yk.ca; 103 Strickland St) offers similar services and competitive prices. Its staff speak German.

TOURS

You can ride a piece of history on a restored **trolley** (adult/child $1/free; ✆ 10am-5pm summer) that runs along the river. It doesn't go anywhere special, but it's fun for kids.

Yukon Historical & Museums Association (☎ 867-667-4704; 3126 3rd Ave; tours $2; ✆ 10am-4pm Mon-Sat summer) This organization offers downtown walking tours four times daily. Meet at its office in the 1904 Donneworth House.

Gold Rush Float Tours (☎ 867-668-4836; cnr 1st Ave & Wood St; adult/child $58/32; ✆ summer) For something adventurous, take 2½-hour trips on re-created gold-rush rafts down the Yukon River.

FESTIVALS & EVENTS

In early 2007 the **Canadian Winter Games** will be held in and around Whitehorse. Annual festivals and events include:

International Storytelling Festival (☎ 867-633-7550; ✆ Jun) Features First Nations participants. In odd years there is a potlatch, a large gathering of northern Aboriginal people.

Yukon Quest (www.yukonquest.org; ✆ Feb) A 1600km dogsled race between Whitehorse and Fairbanks, Alaska.

SLEEPING
Budget
HOSTELS

There are two good hostels in Whitehorse, both in a quiet residential area close to the center.

Beez Kneez Bakpakers (☎ 867-456-2333; www .bzkneez.com; 408 Hoge St; dm/r $20/40; Ⓟ 🖳) This hostel offers a kitchen and free use of bicycles.

Hide on Jeckell Guesthouse (☎ 867-633-4933; www.hide-on-jeckell.com; 410 Jeckell St; dm $20; Ⓟ 🖳) Rates include kitchen facilities, a fireplace and strong morning coffee. There's a 10% discount for those arriving by bicycle (tandem 20%).

An International Whitehorse Hostel across from the VRC has been in the planning stage for years. Like the mother lode, its opening date is elusive.

CAMPING

As if Wal-Mart didn't pose a big enough threat to local shop-owners, its policy of allowing RVs to park in its dusty and barren parking lot overnight for free has severely hurt local campgrounds. Scores of people in $150,000 RVs prefer the charms of Wal-Mart to the pretty spots listed below. Locals also report that there has been a worrisome increase in campers simply dumping their tanks along Whitehorse roads, as Wal-Mart offers no services.

Robert Service Campground (☎ 867-668-3721; sercamp@hotmail.com; Robert Service Way; tent sites $14) This popular tent-only campground along the river is just 1km south of town on the South Access Rd, with showers, firepits and a small store.

Hi Country RV Park (☎ 867-667-7445; hicountryrv@ polarcom.com; 91374 Alaska Hwy; campsites $14, RV sites from $20; 🖳) At the top of Robert Service Way, this campground in a wooded setting offers hookups, showers, laundry and modem access.

Yukon Government Campgrounds (☎ 867-667-5648; tent & RV sites $12) South of Whitehorse on the Alaska Hwy are two campgrounds: Wolf Creek (16km from town), set in a wooded area, and Marsh Lake (50km), with nearby beach access. Sites include firewood.

Mid-Range

There are scores of B&Bs around Whitehorse; many are mere rooms in houses. The VRC has a list. There are also many fairly charmless but serviceable motels.

Hawkins House B&B (☎ 867-668-7638; www .hawkinshouse.yk.ca; 303 Hawkins St; r $100-175; 🖳) This lovely Victorian-style establishment has four distinct rooms, each with private bath and balcony. The second 'B' comes at a price: $7.

Town & Mountain Hotel (☎ 867-668-7644, 800-661-0522; www.townmountain.com; 401 Main St; r $70-110) This is a good mid-range choice with newer, comfortable rooms with air-conditioning.

River View Hotel (☎ 867-667-7801; www.river view.ca; 102 Wood St; r $110-140; 🖳) The big rooms here are much brighter and nicer than the dreary hallways would suggest.

Top End

High Country Inn (☎ 867-667-4471, 800-554-4471; www.highcountryinn.yk.ca; 4051 4th Ave; r $90-210; 🖳)

Modern and friendly, this is the best high-end place to stay. Rooms – some with large whirlpools – have free high-speed Internet access.

Westmark Whitehorse Hotel (☎ 867-668-9700, 800-544-0970; www.westmarkhotels.com; 201 Wood St; r $89-159; 🖳) Rooms, with air-conditioning, are nice but unexceptional, although the service is good. Here's your chance to find out what's going on with the bus-tour set.

EATING

Whitehorse eateries can be found to suit every budget.

Budget

Midnight Sun Coffee Roasters (☎ 867-633-4563; 4168 4th Ave; coffee $2; ☯ 7am-10pm) Tables inside and outside are always hopping (is it the caffeine?). The coffee roasting happens right by the door. The baked goods and sandwiches are also good.

Chocolate Claim (☎ 867-667-2202; 305 Strickland St; light meals $4-8; ☯ 7am-6pm Mon-Fri, 8am-6pm Sat, 10am-3pm Sun) This inviting place has its own bakery with pastries, soups and sandwiches and, as the name implies, fine chocolates. There's a collection of local art on the walls.

Deli (☎ 867-667-6077; 203 Hanson St; sandwiches $5; ☯ 9am-5:30pm Mon-Sat) A classic deli that makes good sandwiches to eat in or take out. The grocery section, known as Yukon Meat & Sausage, has lots of unusual items.

Alpine Bakery (☎ 867-668-6871; 411 Alexander St; meals $4-10; ☯ 8am-6pm Mon-Sat) This bakery in a log building has great bread, rolls and pizza from organic ingredients. The preserves made with Yukon berries are a treat, as is the patio.

Fruit Stand (☎ 867-393-3994; 208 Black St; ☯ 10am-7pm summer) A cross between a stand and a store that sells fresh foods, many organic and many from the Yukon. Buy some berries and try the fireweed honey. Yum.

3 Beans Natural Foods (☎ 867-668-4908; 308 Wood St; ☯ 10am-6pm Mon-Sat) For good organic and bulk food, vitamins and juice, try 3 Beans.

Extra Food (☎ 867-667-6251; 303 Ogilvie St; ☯ 8:30am-7pm Mon-Sat, to 9pm Thu & Fri, 10am-6pm Sun) With backcountry and paddling provisions, Extra Food in the Qwanlin Mall is the largest supermarket and has a huge bulk-foods section.

Mid-Range

Sam 'n' Andy's (☎ 867-668-6994; 506 Main St; meals $10-15; ⏰ 11am-11pm) Busy Sam 'n' Andy's specializes in Mexican food and big portions. Although the food loses some authenticity crossing two national borders, it's a fun place. You can have a beer or margarita with your meal in the garden out front.

Tung Lock (☎ 867-668-3298; 404 Wood St; meals $7-20; ⏰ 11am-11pm) Of several Chinese restaurants, this one is recommended. Seafood is emphasized, but there is a wide selection of Chinese and a few Western dishes. All the usual standards make an appearance on the popular $9 lunch buffet.

Top End

Giorgio's Cucina (☎ 867-668-4050; 206 Jarvis St; meals $15-30; ⏰ dinner) Popular with discerning locals, Giorgio's has an open kitchen where you can see the excellent steak, seafood and fresh pasta being put through their paces.

DRINKING

There are a lot of local bands playing in Whitehorse – maybe because it's too far away for touring acts. To find out who's playing where, check out the posters that appear on trashcans all over town.

Capital Hotel (☎ 867-667-2565; 103 Main St; ⏰ 3pm-late) This place has a lively bar scene and live music almost every night. It draws a large, mostly young crowd who appreciate the many drink specials.

Backwater (☎ 867-667-2250; 102 Wood St; ⏰ 4pm-late) The secluded booths are good for tête-à-têtes; whispered entreaties are muffled by the live jazz and other music. In the River View Hotel, the bar has happy hour from 4pm to 7pm.

Yukon Mining Co (☎ 867-667-6457; 4051 4th Ave; ⏰ 11am-midnight summer) A lively pub located in the High Country Inn, Yukon Mining Co has a huge outdoor deck, good barbecued fresh fish (meals $7 to $15) and lots of TVs for watching games. There's an excellent selection of beers.

GETTING THERE & AWAY

In addition to the options below, you can take a combination train and bus trip to/from Skagway along the historic **White Pass & Yukon Route** (☎ 867-668-7245); see p797 for details.

Air

Whitehorse Airport is a five-minute drive west of downtown off the Alaska Hwy. Air North serves Dawson City and Old Crow in the Yukon, Inuvik in the NWT, Juneau and Fairbanks in Alaska, plus Vancouver, Edmonton and Calgary. Air Canada serves Vancouver.

In summer, **Condor (Thomas Cook)** (☎ 800-524-6975, in Germany 01803-333 130; www.condor.com) operates a weekly service to/from Frankfurt.

Bus

Whitehorse is the northern end of the line for **Greyhound Canada** (☎ 867-667-2223; www.greyhound.ca; 2191 2nd Ave), which has services south along the Alaska Hwy to Dawson Creek and beyond including Vancouver (41 hours).

Alaska Direct Bus Line (☎ 867-668-4833, 800-770-6652; 509 Main St) has services to Anchorage (US$165, 18 hours) and Fairbanks (US$140, 14 hours) in Alaska, and points en route such as Haines Junction (US$40, three hours), Beaver Creek ($70, seven hours, three weekly in summer) and Skagway (US$50, three hours, four weekly).

Dawson City Courier (☎ 867-393-3334) has daily summer service to/from Dawson City ($90, eight hours). Call to arrange pick-up.

GETTING AROUND
To/From the Airport

Yellow Cab (☎ 867-668-4811) charges $15 to/from the airport. Whitehorse Transit buses also serve the airport.

Bus

The main **Whitehorse Transit** (☎ 867-668-7433; tickets $2; ⏰ Mon-Sat, every 70 min) bus stop is at Qwanlin Mall. Route 2 serves the airport, the city center and the Robert Service Campground.

Car & RV

Hertz, Budget and National/NorCan can be found at the airport; see p873 for details. **Whitehorse Subaru** (☎ 867-393-6550; raman@yt.sim patico.ca; 17 Chilkoot Way) can usually beat the large firms on price. **Canadream** (☎ 867-668-3610; www.canadream.com; 110 Copper Rd) rents all shapes and sizes of RVs at rates that average about $200 per day.

Check your rate very carefully, as it is common for a mileage charge to be added after the first 100km, which will get you next to nowhere in the Yukon. Also fully understand your insurance coverage and who pays for a cracked windshield and other damage that can easily occur on gravel roads.

ALASKA HIGHWAY

The Alaska Hwy, the main road in the Yukon, is 2451km long and starts in Dawson Creek, BC. It enters the Yukon in the southeast and passes through Watson Lake, Whitehorse, Haines Junction and Beaver Creek en route to Fairbanks, Alaska. The road is Hwy 97 in BC, Hwy 1 in the Yukon and Hwy 2 in Alaska.

Except for areas where maintenance is being done, the highway is paved for its entire length and is generally in excellent shape. Each summer the Alaska Hwy is busy with visitors driving RVs. At times there are 10 of these homes-on-wheels for every car or truck. Services for gasoline, food and lodging can be found at regular intervals.

Along with the mythic lure of the Alaska Hwy is the tangible sense of adventure that comes from going on a real road trip. The Yukon will really make you feel as if you're going somewhere. It has no choice – sometimes towns are separated by hundreds of kilometers. The scenery is dramatic and you can't help but be charmed by the

---

THE ALASKA HIGHWAY

The construction of the Alaska Hwy in 1942 is considered one of the major engineering feats of the 20th century. Canada and the USA had originally agreed to build an all-weather highway to Fairbanks from the south as early as 1930, but nothing serious was done until WWII. Japan's attack on Pearl Harbor, then its bombing of Dutch Harbor in the Aleutians and occupation of the Aleutian islands of Attu and Kiska increased Alaska's strategic importance.

Thousands of US soldiers and Canadian civilians, including First Nations people, built the 2450km gravel highway between Dawson Creek in British Columbia (BC) and Fairbanks in Alaska. The route chosen for the highway followed a series of existing airfields – Fort St John, Fort Nelson, Watson Lake and Whitehorse – known as the Northwest Staging Route.

Work began on March 9, 1942 and was completed before falling temperatures (in what was to be one of the worst winters in recorded history) could halt the work. Conditions were harsh: sheets of ice rammed the timber pilings; floods during the spring thaw tore down bridges; and bogs swallowed trucks, tractors and other heavy machinery.

In April 1946 the Canadian section of the road (1965km) was officially handed over to Canada. In the meantime private contractors were busy widening, graveling and straightening the highway, leveling its steep grades and replacing temporary bridges with permanent steel ones. In 1949 the Alaska Hwy was opened to full-time civilian traffic. The completion of the highway opened the northwest to exploitation of its natural resources, changed settlement patterns and altered the First Nations' way of life forever.

The name of the highway has gone through several incarnations. It has been called the Alaskan International Hwy, the Alaska Military Hwy and the Alcan (short for Alaska–Canada) Hwy. Officially, it is now called the Alaska Hwy, but many people still affectionately refer to it simply as the Alcan.

The Alaska Hwy begins at 'Mile 0' in Dawson Creek in northeastern BC and goes to Fairbanks, Alaska, although the official end is at Delta Junction (Mile 1422) about 155km southeast of Fairbanks (Mile 1523).

Milepost signs were set up in the 1940s to help drivers calculate how far they had traveled along the road. Since then improvements, including the straightening of the road, mean that its length has been shortened and the mileposts can't be used literally. On the Canadian side the distance markers are in kilometers. Mileposts are still much in evidence in Alaska, and communities on both sides of the border still use the original mileposts for postal addresses and as reference points.

You can get a sense of what building the road entailed (and why everybody took boats before 1942) at the Visitor Reception Center in Watson Lake and the Yukon Transportation Museum (p785) in Whitehorse.

idiosyncrasies of the people in some of the more remote towns along the way. Then, between the RVs, are the cars piled with household goods. College students off to school? Pioneers in search of a new life? Refugees from an old life? As the miles roll past, you can make up your own answers.

EAST OF WHITEHORSE
Watson Lake

Originally named after Frank Watson, a British trapper, Watson Lake is the first town in the Yukon as you head northwest on the Alaska Hwy from BC. It's a good rest stop, but otherwise skippable.

The **VRC** (☎ 867-536-7469; Km 1021 Alaska Hwy; ⏰ 8am-8pm summer), at the junction of the Alaska and Robert Campbell Hwys, has a fun little museum on the history of the territory and the Alaska Hwy. The town offers campgrounds, motels, gas, ATMs and a Greyhound Canada station.

The town is famous for its **Signpost Forest** just outside the VRC. The first signpost, 'Danville, Illinois,' was nailed up in 1942. Others added their own signs and now there are more than 50,000. You can have your own sign made on the spot or find a way to bring one from home…

From Watson Lake, the 588km gravel **Robert Campbell Hwy** (Hwy 4) is an alternative route north to Dawson City; it meets the Klondike Hwy near Carmacks. Named after Robert Campbell, a 19th-century explorer and trader with the Hudson's Bay Company, it's a scenic and less-traveled route that parallels several major rivers and has few services.

Ross River, 373km from Watson Lake at the junction with the Canol Rd (Hwy 6; see p790), is home to the Kaska First Nation and is a supply center for the local mining industry. There's a campground and motels in town, and a government campground at Lapie Canyon.

Faro, 10km off the Robert Campbell Hwy on the Pelly River, was created in 1968 to support the huge copper, lead and zinc mine in the Anvil Mountains. There are motels, a campground nearby, an interpretive center and some trails around town.

Twenty-six kilometers west of Watson Lake is the junction with the Stewart-Cassiar Hwy (Hwy 37), which heads south into BC (see p777).

Teslin

Teslin, on the Nisutlin River 272km west of Watson Lake, began as a trading post in 1903 to serve the Tlingits (lin-*kits*). The Alaska Hwy brought both prosperity and rapid change for this First Nations population. The good **George Johnston Museum** (☎ 867-390-2550; Km 1294 Alaska Hwy; adult/child $5/3; ⏰ 9am-5pm mid-May–early Sep) has photographs, displays and artifacts on the Tlingits and the gold-rush days. There's canoeing and camping at nearby Teslin Lake.

Just west of Teslin, the new **Tlingit Heritage Centre** (☎ 867-390-2526; ⏰ 9am-5pm) has a pleasant lakeside spot with dramatic carved masks setting off the light-filled building. Displays introduce you to First Nations culture.

Johnson's Crossing

About 53km north of Teslin is Johnson's Crossing, at the junction of the Alaska Hwy and Canol Rd (Hwy 6). During WWII the US army built the Canol pipeline at tremendous human and financial expense to pump oil from Norman Wells in the NWT to Whitehorse. The only services on Canol Rd are in Ross River (see left) at the Robert Campbell Hwy junction. Canol Rd ends near the NWT border; to go any further you have to hike the demanding Canol Heritage Trail (p825).

See p797 for a detour to Carcross.

WEST OF WHITEHORSE
Haines Junction

Small on the map but large in appeal, Haines Junction makes an excellent base for exploring Kluane National Park or to launch a serious mountaineering, backcountry or river trip. Edged by the Kluane Range and surrounding greenbelt, the views are dramatic and access is easy via the Alaska Hwy from Whitehorse (158km) or Tok, Alaska (498km); also via the Haines Hwy (Hwy 3) from Haines, Alaska (238km).

INFORMATION

The **VRC** (☎ 867-634-2345; Logan St; ⏰ 8am-8pm) is in the Kluane National Park headquarters building and has good displays. **Parks Canada** (☎ 867-634-7250; www.parkscanada.gc.ca/kluane; ⏰ 9am-5pm) is in the same building.

The post office, bank and ATM are inside **Madley's Store** (☎ 867-634-2200; Hwy 3; ⏰ 8am-9pm), which carries everything from fresh berries and never-fresh doughnuts to spark plugs and fishing tackle. All shops, lodging and services, including a **Shell station** (☎ 867-634-2246), are clustered around the junction of the Alaska and Haines Hwys.

Village Bakery & Deli has free Internet access.

SIGHTS & ACTIVITIES

You'll know you've reached Haines Junction when you see a huge **sculpture** that looks like a nightmare cupcake at the junction of the Alaska and Haines Hwys. In a blow to unattractive public art everywhere, critics have taken literal potshots at the critters depicted on the flanks of the work.

The ridges looming over Haines Junction don't begin to hint at the beauty of Kluane National Park (see right). Although the park should be your focus, there are some good activities in and around Haines Junction.

For a good way to stretch your legs after hours of driving, there's a pretty 5.5km **nature walk** along Dezadeash River where Hwy 3 crosses it at the south end of town. At Pine Lake campground, 6km east of town on the Alaska Hwy, there's good **swimming**, picnic tables and a sandy beach with firepits.

Paddlewheel Adventures (☎ 867-634-2683; www.paddlewheeladventures.com; Logan St), opposite the VRC, arranges Tatshenshini rafting trips ($100 per person including lunch), Kluane helicopter hikes and fishing trips at a range of prices. It rents mountain bikes or canoes ($25 per day).

TOURS

On a sunny day, consider an inspiring 40- to 120-minute flight over the icy heart of Kluane National Park with **Kluane Glacier Tours** (☎ 867-634-2916; Km 1632 Alaska Hwy), which charges $115 to $325 per person with three passengers. Call for schedules. Paddlewheel Adventures arranges other types of tours.

SLEEPING & EATING

There's a little thicket of motels in Haines Junction.

Raven Motel (☎ 867-634-2500; www.yukonweb.com/tourism/raven; 181 Alaska Hwy; s/d $110/125) The Raven has deluxe motel rooms with air-conditioning and a well-known **restaurant** (meals $35-50; ☺ dinner). It's the latter that has brought the Raven acclaim. The menu has French and Italian inspirations, but the

ingredients are Canadian, many of them organic. Wonderfully composed salads and house-made desserts are recommended.

Alcan Motor Inn (☎ 867-634-2371, 888-265-1018; www.yukonweb.com/tourism/alcan; r incl breakfast $90-125; ▢) Alcan has large, modern, air-conditioned rooms with great views of Kluane. There's dozens of channels on the large TVs, continental breakfast and a coin laundry.

On the Alaska Hwy 6km from town, **Pine Lake Campground** is a good choice, with wooded sites ($12) and a day-use area. In town, **Kluane RV Campground** (☎ 867-634-2709, 866-634-6789; kluanerv@yknet.yk.ca; Km 1635 Alaska Hwy; tent & RV sites from $14) has wooded grounds, public showers and a laundromat.

Village Bakery & Deli (☎ 867-634-2867; Logan St; sandwiches $6; ☺ 7am-9pm) Opposite the VRC, this laid-back place with an outdoor deck has delicious pizza, soup and sandwiches. Don't miss the salmon barbecue ($15) with live music at 7pm on summer Fridays.

GETTING THERE & AROUND

Alaska Direct Bus Line (☎ 800-770-6652) runs a service to Haines, Whitehorse and west to Alaska. Make sure you reserve a seat.

Kluane National Park

This rugged and magnificent wilderness covers 22,015 sq km in the southwest corner of the Yukon. With BC's Tatshenshini-Alsek Provincial Park to the south and Alaska's Wrangell-St Elias National Park to the west, this is one of the largest protected wilderness areas in the world. Kluane (*kloo*-wah-neee), which is a Unesco world heritage site, gets its name from the Southern Tutchone word for 'lake with many fish.'

INFORMATION

There are two information centers operated by Parks Canada. One is in Haines Junction (see opposite) and the other at **Tachal Dhal** (Sheep Mountain; Km 1706.8 Alaska Hwy; ☺ 9am-5pm). The latter caters to visitors arriving from the west and is the starting point for hikes at the northern end. Get a copy of the *Recreation Guide*, which shows the scope of the park (and how little is actually easily accessible). The map also shows hiking opportunities, which range from 10 minutes to 11 days.

Winters are long and can be harsh. Summers are short, and generally temperatures are comfortable between mid-June and mid-September, the best time to visit. Note that freezing temperatures can occur at any time, especially in the high country.

SIGHTS

The park consists primarily of the **St Elias Mountains** and the world's largest nonpolar **icefields**. Two-thirds of the park is glacier interspersed with valleys, glacial lakes, alpine forest, meadows and tundra. The **Kluane Ranges** (averaging a height of 2500m) are seen along the western edge of the Alaska Hwy. A greenbelt wraps around the base where most of the animals and vegetation live. Turquoise **Kluane Lake** is the Yukon's largest. Hidden are the immense icefields and towering peaks, including **Mt Logan** (5959m), Canada's highest mountain, and **Mt St Elias** (5488m), the second highest. Partial glimpses of the interior peaks can be found at the Kilometer 1622 viewpoint on the Alaska Hwy from Whitehorse and also around the Donjek River Bridge, but the best views are from the air (see p791). When you climb over the ridge and see that Kluane is literally a sea of glaciers stretching over the horizon you'll understand what all the fuss is about.

Just 18km past Haines Junction on the Alaska Hwy, Parks Canada has a **Spruce Beetle Walk**. This 1.7km loop trail into the dead and dying forest has good explanatory signs on the phenomenon that is destroying spruce forests from BC to Alaska (see the boxed text below).

ACTIVITIES

Parks Canada runs a range of **interpretive programs** through the summer from both visitors' centers. Guided walks (free, one to two hours) and the more ambitious guided hikes ($20, four to six hours) are recommended.

The greenbelt area of the park is a great place for **hiking**, along either marked trails or less defined routes. There are about a dozen in each category, some following old mining roads, others traditional First Nations paths. There is a Parks Canada hiking leaflet with a map and lists of trails with distances and starting points, including limited possibilities for **mountain biking**. Detailed trail guides and topographical maps are available at the information centers. Talk to the rangers before setting out. They will help select a hike and can provide updates on areas that may be closed due to bear activity. Overnight hikes require backcountry permits ($8 per person per night) and you must have a bear-proof food canister ($5 per day, deposit $150).

The Tachal Dhal information center is the starting point for **Slims West**, a popular 60km round-trip trek to **Kaskawulsh Glacier** – one of the few that can be reached on foot. This is a difficult, world-class route that takes from three to five days to complete. An easy overnight trip is the 5.8km (each way) **Bullion Creek** trail. **Sheep Creek** is a moderate 10km day hike. From Kathleen Lake,

---

BEETLE-MANIA

Global warning has struck again – this time through the agency of some harmless-looking borer beetles. Throughout the Yukon, especially Kluane National Park, in British Columbia and west to the Kenai Peninsula in Alaska, the numbers of spruce beetle, mountain pine beetle and (to a lesser extent) Douglas fir beetle have exploded in recent years, killing massive tracts of forest, and alarming environmentalists, forestry companies and average citizens alike.

The affected stands are easily spotted by the reddish-brown color of the dying foliage, brought about by infestations of the beetles, which bore into the trunks of trees to lay their eggs. Worse, it's all happened shockingly fast, with the first signs of trouble only apparent in the mid-90s. Today, millions of acres have died, leaving devastated rangers just as worried about the scale of the inferno if these tinder-dry sections catch alight.

And the culprit? Officially, the jury is still out, but a favored theory is that several years of warm winters, brought on by global warming, has meant the loss of the frigid temperatures required to keep the beetle numbers in check. And so people stare uneasily at the brown hillsides and recall with some nostalgia the bitterly cold winters of yesteryear.

The hundreds of thousands of acres of dead trees are fuel waiting for what will be the mother of all forest fires. That huge fire will create a huge amount of smoke, and that smoke will further add to global warming.

King's Throne is a 5km one-way route with a steep 1220m elevation gain. Great views of the Alsek Valley are waiting at the top.

Fishing is good and **wildlife-watching** plentiful. Most noteworthy are the thousands of Dall sheep that can be seen on Sheep Mountain in April, May and September. There's a large and diverse population of grizzly bear, as well as black bear, moose, caribou, goats and 150 varieties of birds, among them eagles and the rare peregrine falcon.

Some start to venture out **skiing** or **snowshoeing** in February.

SLEEPING

The only campground technically within the park is at Kathleen Lake (sites $10), 24km south of Haines Junction off the Haines Hwy.

Destruction Bay

This small village on the shore of Kluane Lake is 107km north of Haines Junction. Like Haines Junction and Beaver Creek, it started off as a camp and supply depot during the construction of the Alaska Hwy. It was given its present name after a storm tore through the area. There's **boating** and **fishing** on Kluane Lake and the village has a gas station and government campground at **Congdon Creek** (Km 1723 Alaska Hwy). Note any bear warnings as the area's abundant ripe berries are a principal food source for bears.

Burwash Landing

Burwash Landing, 19km north of Destruction Bay, predates the Alaska Hwy with a brief gold strike on nearby 4th of July Creek. It's also home to the Kluane First Nation and noted for the excellent **Kluane Museum** (☎ 867-841-5561; Km 1759 Alaska Hwy; adult/child $4/2; ☽ 9am-9pm mid-May–early Sep). The museum features intriguing animal exhibits (note the stunning moose) and displays on natural and First Nations history. The tiny town has a gas station, too.

Beaver Creek

Tiny Beaver Creek, Canada's westernmost town, is on the Alaska Hwy 457km northwest of Whitehorse and close to the Alaska border. The **VRC** (☎ 867-862-7321; Km 1202 Alaska Hwy; ☽ 8am-8pm) has a wildflower exhibit and information on the Yukon and Alaska.

Just past the VRC is a goofy life-sized **sculpture park** where you can get friendly with a Mountie or up close to a beaver.

Of the four motels, the **Westmark Inn Beaver Creek** (☎ 867-862-7501, 800-544-0920; www .westmarkhotels.com; 1202 Alaska Hwy; dm $20, r $90-110; ☽ May-Sep) is notable for having hostel rooms. It also has an evening show that features staff pressed into service. Helping drive show attendance is the fact that the spartan rooms lack TVs. The pub is nice, however, the food in the restaurant is tasty, and there are good beers in both.

The Canadian customs checkpoint is just north of town; the US customs checkpoint is 27km further west. The border is open 24 hours.

Into Alaska

You'll soon note that the incredible scenery of the Alaska Hwy dims a bit once you cross into its namesake state. The Alaska Hwy Department seems to have a 'bulldoze it and leave' philosophy, so the route is much more torn up and despoiled than the pristine conditions in the Yukon.

From the US border, it's 39 miles to **Tetlin National Wildlife Refuge** on the Alaska Hwy; it makes an interesting stop after you've passed the border. The **visitor center** (☎ 867-883-5321; ☽ 9am-4pm) has good displays on the refuge and its myriad species. The views are good as well.

The turnoff for the Taylor Hwy (US Hwy 5), which connects with the Top of the World Hwy (Hwy 9) to Dawson City, is 73 miles past Tetlin Junction. Another 12 miles past the junction is **Tok** (population 1400), which has a slew of motels, restaurants and services.

HAINES HIGHWAY

In a mere 259km you get to visit Alaska, BC and the Yukon, as well as going from sea level to wind-blown passes high above the treeline where June snow is common. All this and more is between Haines, Alaska and Haines Junction on the Alaska Hwy in the Yukon.

The route is popular with cyclists, many of whom compete here in the annual Kluane Chilkat International Bike Relay along the length of the highway in June. There

GLACIER BAY NATIONAL PARK (ALASKA)

Sixteen tidewater glaciers spill out from the mountains to the sea, making this unusual icy preserve one of the most renowned in the world. The glaciers here are in retreat, revealing plants and animals that fascinate naturalists. The humpback whales are by far the most impressive residents, but there are also harbor seals, porpoises, orcas and sea otters. Above the waterline are brown and black bear, wolves, moose and 200 species of birds. Most people prefer to kayak the small inlets and bays, particularly Muir, where cruise ships are not allowed. There are few trails except around the **park headquarters** (☎ 907-697-2627; www.nps.gov/glba) in Bartlett Cove. Free ranger-led **walks** (☼ 2:30pm Jun-Aug) of the rainforest are highly recommended.

There are a number of inns and cabins in **Gustavus**, the small village adjacent to the park, or you can stay in the free campground near park headquarters.

The only boat connections to Glacier Bay are from Juneau, Alaska, but it's a quick flight to Gustavus. From Haines and Skagway, **Skagway Air** (☎ in Skagway 907-983-2218, in Haines 907-766-3233; www.skagwayair.com) has daily flights, as well as flightseeing (adult/child US$130/90, 90 minutes) over Glacier Bay.

are innumerable places to pull over and admire the beauty. One not to miss near the Yukon border is **Million Dollar Falls**. Thundering through a narrow chasm, the surging water is just super.

HAINES (ALASKA)

This pretty harbor town sits on the Lynn Canal at the end of Hwy 3 from Haines Junction. Surrounded by mountains and with the salty smell of the sea, Haines is wonderfully quiet compared to other southeastern Alaskan towns such as Skagway, as few cruise ships dock here in the summer (although you can watch them elephant-walk their way to Skagway across the water). Haines is also the departure point for longer raft trips on the Tatshenshini or Alsek Rivers in BC, flights to Alaska's Glacier Bay National Park (see the boxed text above) and boats on the Inside Passage (p697) of the Alaska Marine Hwy.

For detailed coverage of Haines and Skagway, see Lonely Planet's *Alaska*.

Information

Haines is on Alaska time, which is one hour earlier than the Yukon. Trail maps are available from **Haines Visitor Bureau** (☎ 907-766-2234, 800-458-3579; www.haines.ak.us; 122 2nd Ave; ☼ 8am-7pm Mon-Fri, 9am-6pm Sat & Sun).

Sights & Activities

The **American Bald Eagle Foundation** (☎ 907-766-3094; http://baldeagles.org; cnr Haines Hwy & 2nd Ave; adult/child US$3/1; ☼ 9am-5pm) has a center featuring an impressive display of more than 100 spe-

cies of eagles and a video of the massive annual gathering of bald eagles at Chilkat River. Better yet is the live video feed of an eagle's nest (April to September).

If you need more American icons, say a few thousand, the **Alaska Chilkat Bald Eagle Preserve**, from Mile 9 to Mile 32 along the Haines Hwy, has a local population of eagles that congregate by the thousands in November for the late salmon run.

Sheldon Museum (☎ 907-766-2366; 11 Main St; admission US$3; ☼ 10am-5pm Mon, Tue & Fri, 10am-5pm & 7-9:30pm Wed & Thu, 1-5pm Sat & Sun) houses a collection of indigenous artifacts and relics from Haines' pioneer and gold-rush days.

Fort Seward, the first and for a time the only army post in Alaska, was established in the early 1900s and designated a national historical site in 1972. The **Alaska Indian Arts Center** (☎ 907-766-2160; 13 Fort Seward Dr; ☼ 9am-5pm Mon-Fri), in the former post hospital, features resident artists working in the Tlingit manner. A small gallery sells their work.

There are three Alaskan state parks and good hiking.

Sleeping & Eating

Keep your eyes peeled and gullet open for anything by Haines Brewing. And if you have some of its wonderful Spruce Bud Ale (made with just that) you might just start checking real estate prices.

Captain's Choice Motel (☎ 907-766-3111, 800-478-2345; www.capchoice.com; 108 2nd Ave N; r US$75-100) The captain offers the town's nicest lodging, especially the rooms with private balconies and air-conditioning. The motel's big flower-ringed sundeck overlooking Lynn Canal is a nice place to while away the day watching boats and whales plying the waters.

Chilkat State Park (Mud Bay Rd; campsites US$6) On the scenic Chilkat Peninsula seven miles southeast of Haines, this park with water, privies and firepits has good views of Lynn Canal and of the Davidson and Rainbow Glaciers.

Fireweed (☎ 907-766-3838; Bldg 37, Blacksmith Rd; meals US$4-16; ⏰ 11am-10pm) In Fort Seward, Fireweed has a great deck where you can happily munch away on pizza, seafood, salads, lovely desserts and more, much of it organic. Sip fresh juices or quaff Haines Brewing beers.

Getting There & Away
Haines is linked to Haines Junction in the Yukon by, you guessed it, the scenic Haines Hwy. **Alaska Direct Bus Line** (☎ 800-770-6652) has services to Haines Junction, Tok and beyond. Make reservations.

Haines–Skagway Fast Ferry (☎ 907-766-2100, 888-766-2103; www.chilkatcruises.com; adult/child US$25/12.50) links Haines with Skagway (35 minutes, three daily). Be sure to book ahead.

See p783 for ferries along the Alaska Marine Hwy route.

KLONDIKE HIGHWAY

The 716km Klondike Hwy, from Skagway in Alaska through the northwestern corner of BC to Whitehorse and Dawson City, more or less follows the **Gold Rush Trail**, the route some 40,000 gold seekers took in 1898 (see the boxed text below). The highway, open year-round, is paved most of the way but there are some long stretches of gravel where construction is taking place. Smoke and forest fires (or scorched remains) may be seen through the summer, but the road is rarely closed. The stretch from Skagway to Carcross is a scenic marvel of lakes and mountains.

THE TOUGHEST PEOPLE YOU'D EVER MEET

Some 40,000 dreamers traveled from Skagway to Dawson City in 1897–98 in search of gold. Most didn't strike it rich, and in fact the majority left the Yukon poorer than when they arrived – a consequence of overly optimistic claims, bad luck and the highly efficient apparatus in place to fleece even those few who did strike it rich.

It started in the summer of 1897 when ships docked in Seattle and San Francisco crammed with gold from the Yukon. Word that there was lots more spread quickly, and the fact that Canada would allow non-Canadians to stake claims and that the gold around Dawson City was placer gold – fairly easily mined without special tools – fueled the fire. Boats poured into Skagway that fall, turning it into a boomtown.

That winter (could there have been a worse time for this?) thousands made their way up the Chilkoot Trail to the Canadian border. Only those with at least 1000lb of supplies were allowed into Canada; the country had enough problems without a bunch of starving miners dying all over the place. Consider this: the average miner had to walk back and forth in the snow the equivalent of 1800 miles to pack their supplies (few could afford animals or help) to cover the 30 miles between Dyea and Bennett. And that was going uphill, loaded.

Once in Bennett, the prospective prospectors built boats out of whatever they could find. When the ice broke at the end of May, one of the motliest flotillas ever assembled set sail for Dawson on the Yukon River. Of course few of these people knew what to expect or had any experience with white-water rafting. Although the number is not known, it is thought that far more people drowned during the summer of 1898 on the Yukon River and its tributaries than perished on the Chilkoot Trail. Those who made it to Dawson faced lawlessness, claim-jumpers, deprivation and a myriad of other hardships. Those who survived – whether they struck it rich or not – are the toughest people you'd ever meet.

The Klondike Hwy generally follows the Gold Rush Trail (as Parks Canada calls it) past White-horse as far north as Minto. If you want to stay on the route of the prospectors to Dawson City, you'll need a canoe from one of the outfitters in Whitehorse (p783) and it'll take several days to navigate the Yukon River.

SKAGWAY (ALASKA)

Skagway is a little town that most travelers either love or hate. Although it's in the USA, it can only be reached by road using the Klondike Hwy from the Yukon through BC. It's the starting point for the famed Chilkoot Trail and the White Pass & Yukon Route narrow gauge railroad, and the departure point for flights to Alaska's Glacier Bay National Park (see the boxed text on p794). It's also the most popular stop for Alaska cruise lines. John Muir described Skagway during the gold-rush era as 'an anthill stirred with a stick.' You'll recall this quote on summer afternoons when cruise ships disembark as many as 7500 day-tripping passengers on the narrow streets.

From the ferry terminal, the foot and vehicle traffic spills onto Broadway and the center of town. There's a post office, banks, campgrounds, hotels, restaurants and shops, some selling furs and diamonds. Most of the buildings have been restored. The Klondike Hwy runs into the center from the opposite end. If you are coming by ferry, you may wish to head into the Yukon via the much more mellow Haines Hwy (p793).

Information

Skagway is on Alaska time, which is one hour earlier than the Yukon.

Skagway Convention & Visitors Bureau (☎ 907-983-2854, 888-762-1898; www.skagway.com; 245 Broadway; ☿ 8am-5pm) Complete area details.

Skagway News Depot & Books (☎ 907-983-3354; 264 Broadway; ☿ 8:30am-8:30pm Mon-Fri, 8:30am-7:30pm Sat & Sun) Good selection of regional titles and topographical maps.

Trail Centre (☎ 907-983-3655, 800-661-0486; www .nps.gov/klgo; cnr Broadway & 2nd; ☿ 8am-6pm May-Sep, 8am-5pm Oct-Apr) Run by Parks Canada and the US National Park Service; provides advice, permits, maps and a list of transportation options to/from the Chilkoot Trail.

US National Park Service (☎ 907-983-2921; cnr Broadway & 2nd St; ☿ 8am-8pm Jun-Aug, 8am-6pm Sep-May) Offers free daily walking tours and the *Skagway Trail Map* for area hikes.

Sights

Skagway is a delightful place to arrive aboard the ferry. You step off the boat right into a bustling town.

A seven-block corridor along Broadway, part of the **historic district**, is home to the restored buildings, false fronts and wooden sidewalks of Skagway's golden era. The **Arctic Brotherhood Hall**, which houses the Skagway Convention & Visitors Bureau, is hard to miss, as there are 20,000 pieces of driftwood tacked to its front.

Near the corner of 3rd Ave and Broadway is the **Mascot Saloon Museum** (admission free; ☿ 9am-5pm early May–late Sep), a renovation project of the US National Park Service. Built in 1898, the Mascot was one of 70 saloons during Skagway's heyday as 'the roughest place in the world.'

Moore's Cabin (5th Ave at Spring St) is Skagway's oldest building, dating from 1887. At the southeastern end of 7th Ave is a 1900 granite building housing the **Skagway Museum** (☎ 907-983-2420; 7th Ave at Spring St; adult/student US$2/1; ☿ 9am-5pm). The museum has sections devoted to various aspects of local history, including aboriginal heritage and the Klondike Gold Rush.

Sleeping & Eating

Reservations are strongly recommended during July and August.

Gold Rush Lodge (☎ 907-983-2831, 877-983-3509; www.goldrushlodge.com; 611 Alaska St; r US$95-115) A short walk from town, this place manages to avoid most of the hubbub. An older motel with a mountain-lodge motif, the Gold Rush has comfortable rooms with TV/VCRs and friendly service.

Sergeant Preston's Lodge (☎ 907-983-2521; sgt -prestons@usa.net; 370 6th Ave; r US$75-95; 💻) This tidy motel offers 30 rooms right in the center of things. The good sergeant – well, actually a surrogate – will pick you up at the ferry.

There's free camping, but no water at **Dyea Campground** (Dyea Rd), 14km from town at the start of the Chilkoot Trail. Near the ferry, try **Pullen Creek RV Park** (☎ 907-983-2768, 800-936-3731; 501 Congress St; campsites from US$18).

Haven Café (☎ 907-983-3553; cnr 9th Ave & State St; light meals US$4-8; ☿ 6am-10pm) A great place for breakfast (*panini*s, granola, yogurt) or a light lunch or dinner. The aptly named coffeehouse is removed from the heart of the hurly-burly and makes a great place to kick back and plan your next move.

Bonanza Bar & Grill (☎ 907-983-6214; Broadway btw 3rd & 4th Aves; sandwiches US$7-11; ☿ 10am-midnight) A spacious restaurant/sports pub with a number of good microbrew beers on tap.

Getting There & Away

It's 177km from Skagway to Whitehorse on the Klondike Hwy (Hwy 2). The road is modern and paved, and customs at the border usually moves fairly quickly. **Alaska Direct Bus Line** (☎ 800-770-6652) has services to Whitehorse.

White Pass & Yukon Route (☎ 907-983-2217, 800-343-7373; www.wpyr.com; cnr 2nd Ave & Spring St; ☼ mid-May–mid-Sep) offers a rail and bus connection to/from Whitehorse (adult/child US$95/47.50). Primarily a tourist train, the White Pass & Yukon offers round-trip daily sightseeing tours of this truly gorgeous route into Canada that parallels the original White Pass trail. The trains were once the only link to Whitehorse, but now they mostly terminate in Fraser, BC, just over the Canadian border.

Haines–Skagway Fast Ferry (☎ 907-766-2100, 888-766-2103; www.chilkatcruises.com; adult/child US$25/12.50) connects Skagway with Haines (35 minutes, three daily). Make reservations.

See p783 for ferries along the Alaska Marine Hwy route.

CHILKOOT TRAIL

Skagway was the landing point for many in the gold-rush days of the late 1890s. From there began the long, slow, arduous and often deadly haul inland to the Klondike goldfields near Dawson City. One of the main routes from Skagway, the Chilkoot Trail over the Chilkoot Pass is now extremely popular with hikers.

The well-marked 53km trail begins near Dyea, 14km northwest of Skagway, then heads northeast following the Taiya River to Lake Bennett in BC, and takes three to five days to hike. It's considered a difficult route in good weather and can be treacherous in bad. You must be in good physical condition and come fully equipped. Layers of warm clothes and rain gear are essential. Solo hikers will not have a problem finding company.

Along the trail you'll see hardware, tools and supplies dumped by the gold seekers. At several places there are wooden shacks where you can put up for the night, but these are usually full so a tent and sleeping bag are required. There are 10 designated campgrounds along the route, each with bear caches. The most strenuous part of the trail is over the Chilkoot Pass. The elevation gain on the trail is 1110m.

At the Canadian end you can either take the White Pass & Yukon Rte train from Bennett back to Skagway or further up the line to Fraser in BC, where you can connect with a bus for Whitehorse.

The Chilkoot Trail is a primary feature of the **Klondike Gold Rush International Historic Park**, a series of sites managed by both Parks Canada and the US National Park Service that stretches from Seattle, Washington to Dawson City. See p796 for details on contacting both service agencies, which issue a free preparation guide for the trail and an all-but-mandatory trail map (US$2).

Each hiker must obtain one of the 50 permits available each day. It's vital to reserve in advance. **Parks Canada/US National Park Service** (☎ 867-667-3910, 800-661-0486) charges $50 for a permit plus $10 for a reservation. The permits must be picked up from the Trail Centre (p796) in Skagway. Each day eight of the permits are issued on a first-come, first-served basis.

CARCROSS

Carcross, 74km southeast of Whitehorse, is the first settlement you reach in the Yukon coming from Skagway on the Klondike Hwy. The site was once a major seasonal hunting camp of the Tagish people, who called the area Todezzane (meaning 'blowing all the time'). The present town name is an abbreviation of Caribou Crossing and refers to the local woodland caribou herds.

The **VRC** (☎ 867-821-4431; ☼ 8am-8pm summer) is in the old train station and provides a top-notch walking tour booklet of the area buildings, many removed from Bennett by boat when the White Pass & Yukon Route railway extended north and that town was abandoned in 1900. The station also has good displays on the local history.

Two kilometers north of town, **Carcross Desert**, the world's smallest, is the exposed sandy bed of a glacial lake that retreated after the last Ice Age. Strong winds allow little vegetation to grow.

With its old buildings, picturesque railroad bridge over Lake Bennett and overall feel, Carcross is worth the extra 45km you'll drive detouring off the stretch of the Alaska Hwy (p790) between Whitehorse and Jakes Corner.

WHITEHORSE TO CARMACKS

North of Whitehorse, between the Takhini Hot Springs Rd and Carmacks, the land is dry and scrubby, although there are some farms with cattle and horses. The Klondike Hwy skirts several lakes where you can go swimming, boating and fishing. The largest is lovely **Lake Laberge**, with a beach, 40km north of Whitehorse, followed by **Fox Lake**, 24km further north, and **Twin Lakes**, 23km south of Carmacks. Each has a government campground with shelters and pump water. Near Carmacks the mountains become lower, the hills more rounded and the land more forested. On the way to Dawson City, gas stations have taken to selling gargantuan cinnamon buns better called dough bombs.

CARMACKS

Perched on the banks of the Yukon River, Carmacks was once a fueling station for riverboats and a stopover on the overland trail from Whitehorse to Dawson City. Originally known as Tantalus, the town name was changed to Carmacks to honor George Washington Carmack who, along with Skookum Jim and Tagish Charley, discovered gold at Bonanza Creek in 1896 and sparked the Klondike gold rush.

There are gas stations, a campground and motels here, as well as a junction for the Robert Campbell Hwy (p790). Otherwise there's little reason to linger.

About 25km north of town, the **Five Finger Recreation Site** has excellent views of the treacherous stretch of the rapids that tested the wits of riverboat captains. There's a steep 1.5km walk down to the rapids.

Look for **Penny's Place** (burgers $7; 9am-6pm), further along the road in **Pelly Crossing**. The milkshakes are real and the burgers are real good. The fun-filled washrooms have a collection of dog photos.

STEWART CROSSING

Once a supply center between Dawson City and Whitehorse, Stewart Crossing sits at the junction of the Klondike Hwy (Hwy 2) and the Silver Trail (Hwy 11), another route taken by prospectors in search of silver.

Canoeists can put in here for the very good five-day **float trip** down the Stewart River to the Yukon River and on to Dawson City. Though you travel through wilderness, and wildlife is commonly seen, it is a trip suitable for the inexperienced. Canoeists should organize and outfit in Whitehorse or Dawson City.

The tiny town has a café and gas station. At times there's a roadside visitor hut that can supply useful information on the Silver Trail and towns.

SILVER TRAIL

The Silver Trail heads northeast to three old mining and fur-trading towns: **Mayo**, **Elsa** and **Keno**. The road is paved as far as Mayo. Almost ghost towns, these are fascinating places to wander around.

Yukon Tourism publishes excellent walking tours to all three which can be found at VRCs. In Keno City, 60km past Mayo and near Elsa, **Mooseberry Bakery** (☎ 867-995-2383; meals $6; lunch) is in a 1922 log cabin and has great homemade food. There's also a small **museum** (☎ 867-995-3103; 10am-6pm). At each of these towns you'll really feel like you're at the end of the road. And if you want to be sure something will be open, call first.

There are some outdoor possibilities near to all three towns as well as campgrounds and other lodgings, although there are no services in Elsa. **Keno Hill**, with its signposts and distances to cities all over the world, offers views of the mountains and valleys. There are hiking trails in the vicinity, ranging from 2km to 20km long, providing access to old mining areas and alpine meadows.

DAWSON CITY

Dawson City, a compact town at the confluence of the Yukon and Klondike Rivers just 240km south of the Arctic Circle, became the heart of the Klondike gold rush. Once known as 'the Paris of the North' with a population in the west second only to San Francisco, it had deluxe hotels and restaurants, plush river steamers and stores with luxury goods.

Many attractions remain from its fleeting but vibrant fling with world fame, and some of the original buildings are still standing. Parks Canada is involved in restoring or preserving those considered historically significant, and regulations ensure that new buildings are built in sympathy with the old. With unpaved streets and board sidewalks, the town still has a gritty, edge-of-the-world feel.

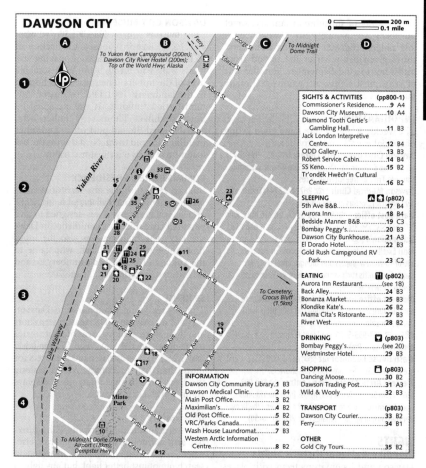

DAWSON CITY

0 —————— 200 m
0 —————— 0.1 mile

| **SIGHTS & ACTIVITIES** | **(pp800-1)** |
| Commissioner's Residence........9 A4 |
| Dawson City Museum............10 A4 |
| Diamond Tooth Gertie's |
| Gambling Hall................11 B3 |
| Jack London Interpretive |
| Centre....................12 B4 |
| ODD Gallery.................13 B3 |
| Robert Service Cabin..........14 B4 |
| SS Keno...................15 B2 |
| Tr'ondëk Hwëch'in Cultural |
| Center...................16 B2 |

| **SLEEPING** | **(p802)** |
| 5th Ave B&B.................17 B4 |
| Aurora Inn..................18 B4 |
| Bedside Manner B&B..........19 C3 |
| Bombay Peggy's..............20 B3 |
| Dawson City Bunkhouse.........21 A3 |
| El Dorado Hotel..............22 B3 |
| Gold Rush Campground RV |
| Park....................23 C2 |

| **EATING** | **(p802)** |
| Aurora Inn Restaurant..........(see 18) |
| Back Alley..................24 B3 |
| Bonanza Market..............25 B3 |
| Klondike Kate's..............26 B2 |
| Mama Cita's Ristorante........27 B3 |
| River West.................28 B2 |

| **DRINKING** | **(p803)** |
| Bombay Peggy's..............(see 20) |
| Westminster Hotel............29 B3 |

| **SHOPPING** | **(p803)** |
| Dancing Moose..............30 B2 |
| Dawson Trading Post..........31 A3 |
| Wild & Wooly...............32 B3 |

| **TRANSPORT** | **(p803)** |
| Dawson City Courier...........33 B2 |
| Ferry....................34 B1 |

| **OTHER** |
| Gold City Tours..............35 B2 |

| **INFORMATION** |
| Dawson City Community Library.1 B3 |
| Dawson Medical Clinic..........2 B4 |
| Main Post Office...............3 B2 |
| Maximilian's.................4 B2 |
| Old Post Office...............5 B2 |
| VRC/Parks Canada.............6 B2 |
| Wash House Laundromat........7 B3 |
| Western Arctic Information |
| Centre....................8 B2 |

The town is built on permafrost, which begins just a few centimeters down. Buildings have foundations of planks resting on gravel and many show the seasonal effects of heaving. Outside of town are the eerie piles of tailings, which look like the work of mammoth gophers. These huge mounds are actually from gold dredges that sucked up the swampy earth at one end and left it behind, sans gold, at the other. Some 100 years after the original gold rush, dozens of enterprises are still mining for gold in the region around Dawson City.

Summer sees a large influx of tourists and seasonal workers; RVs roam the streets like caribou. But by September, 'flee sale' signs begin to appear all over town as seasonal residents head south. For those remaining, Dawson is a cold and quiet place.

For many travelers, a summer visit to Dawson will be the highlight of their Yukon trip. Plan on staying at least two or three days.

ORIENTATION

Dawson City, 527km from Whitehorse, is small enough to walk around in a few hours. The Klondike Hwy leads into Front St (also called 1st Ave) along the Yukon River. Just north of town, a free ferry crosses the Yukon River to the Top of the World Hwy and onward to Alaska. Lately, talk of replacing the ferry with a bridge has sparked much debate.

Like a ray of sunshine in January, street numbers are a rarity in Dawson. Unless noted otherwise, opening hours and times given below cover the period from mid-May to mid-September. For the rest of year, most sights, attractions and many businesses are closed.

INFORMATION

The weekly *Klondike Sun* has a good listing of special events and activities.

Dawson City Community Library (☎ 867-993-5571; cnr 5th Ave & Queen St; ☾ 10am-5pm Mon & Sat, until 8pm Tue-Fri) Has free Internet access.

Dawson Medical Clinic (☎ 867-993-5744; Church St near 6th Ave) Doctors always on call.

Main post office (☎ 867-993-5342; 3rd Ave btwn King & Queen Sts; ☾ 8:30am-5:30pm Mon-Fri, 9am-noon Sat)

Maximilian's (☎ 867-993-6537; Front St; ☾ 8am-8pm) Excellent selection of regional books, magazines, out-of-town newspapers and topographical and river maps. Goofy gifts such as the fund-raising 'Women of Dawson' calendar ($20).

Old post office (cnr King St & 3rd Ave; ☾ noon to 6pm) Beautiful restored building has mail drop and stamps for sale.

VRC (☎ 867-993-5566; cnr Front & King Sts; ☾ 8am-8pm) Also has a Parks Canada desk.

Wash House Laundromat (☎ 867-993-6555; cnr 2nd Ave & Queen St; ☾ 9am-8pm) Has showers.

Western Arctic Information Centre (☎ 867-993-6167; Front St; ☾ 9am-8pm) Across from the VRC, this place has maps and information on the NWT and the Dempster Hwy including road updates (☎ 800-661-0750).

SIGHTS
Klondike National Historic Sights

Dawson and its environs teem with places of historic interest. Parks Canada does an excellent job of providing information and tours. In addition to the individual sight fees listed below, there is a good-value pass (adult/child $28/14) valid for all the Parks Canada sites and tours. For information, go to the Parks Canada desk in the VRC.

ROBERT SERVICE CABIN

Called the 'Bard of the Yukon,' Robert W Service lived in this typical gold rush–era **cabin** (cnr 8th Ave & Hanson St; admission free; ☾ 10am-4pm) from 1909 to 1912. Don't miss the **readings** (adult/child $5/2.50; ☾ 10am & 3pm) of Service's poems by a Parks Canada employee. Long-time reader Tom Byrne has decamped to the Westmark Inn (see opposite).

DAWSON CITY MUSEUM

This **museum** (☎ 867-993-5291; 5th Ave; adult/child $7/5; ☾ 10am-6pm) houses a collection of 25,000 gold-rush artifacts. Engaging exhibits walk you through the hard-scrabble lives of the miners. The museum is housed in the landmark 1901 Old Territorial Administration Building. It was designed by noted architect Thomas W Fuller, who also designed the old post office and other buildings around town. Next door is the old locomotive barn with historic trains.

COMMISSIONER'S RESIDENCE

Built in 1901 to house the territorial commissioner, this proud **building** (adult/child $5/2.50; ☾ 10am-5pm, tour times vary) was designed to give potential civic investors confidence in Dawson city. The building was also the long-time home of Martha Black, who came to the Yukon in 1898, owned a lumberyard and was elected to parliament at age 70.

SS KENO

The voyage from Whitehorse to Dawson was not an easy one. The season was short and there were perilous areas of white water to navigate on the way. The **SS Keno** (adult/child $5/2.50; ☾ 10am-6pm) worked the rivers for more than half a century. Moored along the river, the boat has many good displays about travel a century ago.

ODD Gallery

Dawson is another northern city with a thriving arts community – although like elsewhere, most artists head south in winter in search of not just better light, but any light at all. The **ODD Gallery** (☎ 867-993-5005; cnr 2nd Ave & Princess St; ☾ 10am-8pm) is a small but bright and open space that shows local works. It shares space with the **Klondike Institute for Art & Culture** (www.kiac.org), a local artists group.

Tr'ondëk Hwëch'in Cultural Center

Inside this beautiful wood **building** (☎ 867-993-6768; www.trondek.com; Front St; admission $5; ☾ 10:30am-6pm) on the riverfront there's a slide show and interpretative talks on the Hän Hwëch'in (river people), who were the first to inhabit the area. The collection includes traditional artifacts and First Nations regalia. Locally made crafts are for sale. Check on the schedule for cultural tours; there are also frequent performances of authentic dances.

Jack London Interpretive Centre

In 1898 Jack London lived in the Yukon, the setting for his most popular animal stories, including *Call of the Wild* and *White Fang*. Talks are given at 11:30am and 2:15pm daily at the writer's **cabin** (8th Ave at Grant St; admission $2; ☺ 10am-1pm & 2-6pm). A labor of love by historian Dick North, Dawne Mitchell and others, this place is a treasure trove. Read the stories about 'Jack,' a local dog which Jack, the noted author, used as a model for Buck in *Call of the Wild,* and how North was able to locate a photo of London working in the Klondike.

Diamond Tooth Gertie's Gambling Hall

This is a re-creation of an 1898 **saloon** (☎ 867-993-5575; cnr Queen St & 4th Ave; admission $8; ☺ 7pm-2am), complete with small-time gambling, honky-tonk piano and dancing girls. The casino's winnings go toward town restoration, so go ahead, lose a bundle. On weekends it can become packed as locals jostle with tourists to support preservation. The enjoyable floor shows are a model for the town's oft- or perhaps over-used logo of a dancehall girl.

Robert Service Show

Longtime Robert Service re-enactor Tom Byrne gives his captivating **readings** (☎ 867-993-5543; Westmark Inn, 5th Ave; admission $10; ☺ 3pm) of the works of Robert Service. The fun, educational readings are in an atrium, although you sorta wish he and Parks Canada would sort things out so he can return to the cabin (see opposite). This is definitely worth the time for those in the thrall of Service's poetry.

Midnight Dome

The Midnight Dome, at 880m above sea level, provides great views of the Ogilvie Mountains, Klondike Valley, Yukon River and Dawson City. From here on summer solstice, the midnight sun barely sinks below the Ogilvie Mountains to the north before rising again.

The quarried face of this hill overlooks the town to the north, but to reach the top you must travel south of town about 1km, turn left off the Klondike Hwy onto New Dome Rd, and continue for about 7km. There's also a steep **trail** from Judge St in town; maps available at the VRC.

Crocus Bluff

Less of a slog than marching to the Midnight Dome, a 15-minute walk up King St behind town leads to historic **cemeteries**. Look for the parking area and the short path out to pretty **Crocus Bluff**, which has excellent views of Dawson and the Klondike and Yukon Rivers.

Ship Graveyard

When the Klondike Hwy was completed, the paddlewheel ferries were abandoned. Several were sailed just downstream from town and left to rot on the bank. Now overgrown, the remains are a fascinating destination for a short hike. Take the ferry across the river, walk north through the Yukon River Campground for 10 minutes and then another 10 minutes north along the beach.

ACTIVITIES

One of the main do-it-yourself canoe float trips goes from Dawson three days downstream to Eagle City, Alaska. This popular trip is good for inexperienced canoeists.

Dawson Trading Post rents out canoes ($30 per day), with longer trips and transportation arranged.

Dawson City River Hostel, across the river, can also rent you a canoe and help make arrangements.

TOURS

Parks Canada docents, often in period garb, lead excellent **walking tours** (adult/child $5/2.50; ☺ 9:30am, extra tours some days) of Dawson. You can also rent a player for an audio **self-guided tour** (adult/child $5/2.50; ☺ 9:30am-4:30pm).

Gold City Tours (☎ 867-993-5175; Front St), opposite the SS *Keno*, has a daily city tour (adult/child $40/20) and a trip to the Bonanza Creek gold mine, where you can do some panning. Vans go to Midnight Dome ($12 per person) at 11pm daily.

FESTIVALS & EVENTS

Dawson City Music Festival (☎ 867-993-5384; www .dcmf.com; ☺ late Jul) Features well-known Canadian musicians. It's very popular – tickets sell out two months in advance and the city fills up – so reservations are a good idea.

Discovery Day (☺ Aug) The premier annual event in Dawson City celebrates the you-know-what of 1896. On the third Monday in August there are parades and picnics. Events begin days before, including the very good **Riverside Art Festival** (☎ 867-993-5005).

SLEEPING

Most places fill up in July and August. The VRC will tirelessly search for vacant rooms on busy weekends if you arrive without a reservation. Many places will pick you up at the airport, a not inconsiderable distance; ask in advance. Unless otherwise stated, the following are open year-round.

Budget

Dawson City River Hostel (☎ 867-993-6823; www.yukonhostels.com; dm member/non-member $15/19, r $39; ☾ mid-May–late Sep; ℗) This fun hostel is across the river from town and five minutes up the hill from the ferry landing. It's a rustic and funky spot with good views, cabins, a wooded area for tents, cooking shelter and communal bathhouse. There's no electricity and lockers are recommended for your gear. Owner Dieter Reinmuth is a character and a charmer.

Yukon River Campground (campsites $12; ☾ summer) On the western side of the river about 250m up the road to the right after you get off the ferry. It's the pleasant destination of smart campers.

Gold Rush Campground RV Park (☎ 867-993-5247; goldrush@yukon.net; cnr 5th Ave & York St; RV sites $17-26; ☾ summer) is literally one big parking lot downtown for RVs.

Mid-Range

Bedside Manner B&B (☎ 867-993-6948; cnr 8th Ave & Princess St; s/d $80/90; ☐) The small Bedside Manner is comfortable, and the owner can give lots of good advice on local events and activities.

5th Ave B&B (☎ 867-993-5941; www.5thavebandb.com; 702 5th Ave; r $75-135; ☐) This is another homey place in a neighborhood of historic homes near the museum.

Dawson City Bunkhouse (☎ 867-993-6164; www.bunkhouse.ca; Princess St; r $50-110; ☾ May–mid-Sep) This is a good frontier-style place with clean, basic rooms, some of which share a bathroom. Note that the solid wood construction means it can get noisy as guests liquored up at nearby saloons go clomping about.

Top End

Bombay Peggy's (☎ 867-993-6969; www.bombaypeggys.com; cnr 2nd Ave & Princess St; r $75-190; ☐) Located in a renovated old brothel, Peggy's is the best and most stylish place to stay in town. Rooms range from 'snugs' with shared bath to suites. There's a great pub downstairs.

Aurora Inn (☎ 867-993-6860; www.aurorainn.ca; 5th Ave; r $120-180; ☐) The Aurora has bright, large and nicely decorated rooms with friendly service. Breakfast ($10) is fresh and good; there's an excellent restaurant as well.

El Dorado Hotel (☎ 867-993-5451, 800-661-0518; www.eldoradohotel.ca; cnr 3rd Ave & Princess St; s/d $130/150) The El Dorado has good, large, modern rooms. The hotel offers good services for business travelers – there are some in Dawson.

EATING

Klondike Kate's (☎ 867-993-6527; cnr King St & 3rd Ave; meals $6-20; ☾ breakfast, lunch & dinner) Everybody likes Kate's and with good reason: the smoked King salmon is killer, and there's a long list of other dishes and great desserts. Locally a favorite, it's a fun spot out on the covered patio.

Mama Cita's Ristorante (☎ 867-993-2370; 2nd Ave; meals $8-22; ☾ lunch & dinner) Portions of the excellent pasta dishes are insanely large. The pizzas are popular as are the sandwiches. Good service.

Aurora Inn Restaurant (☎ 867-993-6860; 5th Ave; meals $9-25; ☾ lunch & dinner) Excellent, hearty meals are served in a bright and cheery space at the Aurora Inn Restaurant. The menu leans toward German, but there is food for all tastes available. The steaks at dinner, replete with fresh mushrooms, are tops.

Back Alley (☎ 867-993-5800; 2nd Ave; meals $7-14; ☾ lunch & dinner) Behind the Westminster Hotel, the Back Alley serves great souvlaki sandwiches and pizza, making it a top choice. There are tables outside where you can eat or you can get free delivery in town.

River West (☎ 867-993-6339; cnr Front & Queen Sts; snacks $2-5; ☾ 7am-7pm) The best of several places along Front St, this café has excellent coffee, bagels, soup and sandwiches on delicious bread. The tables outside are a local meeting spot.

Bonanza Market (☎ 867-993-6567; 2nd Ave; sandwiches $5; ☾ 8am-6pm) A good market with interesting, organic fresh foods. The deli makes scrumptious sandwiches.

DRINKING

Bombay Peggy's (☎ 867-993-6969; www.bombay peggys.com; cnr 2nd Ave & Princess St; ☒ 11am-11pm) In the inn of the same name, Bombay Peggy's is a delightful place for a drink with good beers on tap and a fine wine selection. There are some nice, quiet tables out the back.

Westminster Hotel (3rd Ave; ☒ noon-late) The Westminster's two bars are variously known as the 'Snakepit' or 'Armpit,' or simply the 'Pit.' The one to your left as you face the pink building has a great old tin roof which matches the age of some of the timeless characters hanging out by the bar. The bar to the right has more of a '70s motif, and hosts live music many nights. Both can get lively.

SHOPPING

Dawson Trading Post (☎ 867-993-5316; Front St; ☒ 9am-7pm) Sells interesting old mining gadgets, antiques and books, and stones and old mammoth tusks so you can take up carving.

Wild & Wooly (☎ 867-993-5170; cnr 3rd Ave & Princess St; ☒ 10am-7pm) This shop stocks all sorts of tempting, lovely locally made jewelry, as well as some quite fashionable men's and women's clothing (surprise!). Look out for the items made from mammoth-tusk ivory.

Dancing Moose (☎ 867-993-5549; cnr 2nd Ave & King St; ☒ 10am-7pm) has a range of items produced by local artists.

GETTING THERE & AROUND

Dawson City Airport is 19km east of town off the Klondike Hwy. Air North serves Whitehorse and Old Crow in the Yukon, Inuvik in the NWT and Juneau in Alaska.

Dawson City Courier (☎ 867-993-6688) operates daily summer bus service to Whitehorse ($91, eight hours). Be sure to reserve in advance; the stop is on the corner of 2nd Ave and York St. **Alaska Trails & Tours** (☎ 888-600-6001) has a van service to/from Anchorage, Fairbanks and Tok ($95, eight hours, three weekly).

Gold City Tours (p801) also books airline tickets and airport shuttles.

The **ferry** (☎ 867-993-5441) runs 24 hours a day when the Yukon River isn't frozen. It's free.

AROUND DAWSON CITY
Top of the World Hwy

At the northern end of Dawson City's Front St, the ferry crosses the Yukon River to the scenic Top of the World Hwy (Hwy 9). Only open in summer, the 106km-long ridge-top road to the US border is paved most of the way.

As you cross the border you'll really feel on top of the world: the area is alpine and treeless. Note the border crossing has very strict hours (9am to 9pm Yukon time/8am to 8pm Alaska time, May 15 to September 15); don't be one minute late or you'll have to turn back and try the next day.

On the US side the road becomes all gravel. After 12 miles you reach the Taylor Hwy (Hwy 5). The old gold-mining town of **Eagle** on the Yukon River is 65 miles north. South 29 miles, you encounter **Chicken**, a small, idiosyncratic community of 37 which has a couple of shops and a bar that even at 11am is filled with a good percentage of the local population commenting on the 'goddamn government.' Another 77 miles south and you reach the Alaska Hwy (p789) and **Tok**, a town with a range of services and motels. From there you can return to the Yukon.

DEMPSTER HIGHWAY

The Dempster Hwy (Hwy 5 in the Yukon, Hwy 8 in the NWT) starts 40km southeast of Dawson City off the Klondike Hwy. It heads north over the Ogilvie and Richardson Mountains beyond the Arctic Circle and on to Inuvik in the NWT, near the shores of the Beaufort Sea.

The highway, which celebrated its 25th anniversary in 2004, makes road travel along the full length of North America possible. Inuvik is a long way from Dawson City – 747km of gravel road – but the scenery is remarkable: mountains, valleys, rivers and vast open tundra. The highway is open most of the year, but the best time to travel is between June and early September when the ferries over the Peel and Mackenzie Rivers operate. In the winter, ice forms a natural bridge over the rivers, which become ice roads. The Dempster is closed during the spring thaw and the winter freeze-up; the timing of these vary by the year and can occur from mid-April to June and mid-October to December respectively.

Accommodations and vehicle services along the route are scarce. There is a gas station at the southern start of the highway at **Klondike River Lodge** (☎ 867-993-6892). The lodge will rent jerry cans of gas that you can take north with you and return on the way back. From there it's 370km to Eagle Plains and the next services. The **Eagle Plains Hotel** (☎ 867-993-2453; eagleplains@yknet.yk.ca; r $112-135) is open year-round and offers 26 rooms. The next service station on the highway is 180km further north at Fort McPherson in the NWT. From there it's 216km to Inuvik.

The Yukon government has three campgrounds (sites $12) – at Tombstone Territorial Park, **Engineer Creek** (194km) and **Rock River** (447km) – and there's an NWT government campground at **Nitainlaii Territorial Park**, 9km south of Fort McPherson. For maps and information on the road, ask at the Western Arctic Information Centre (p800) in Dawson City.

The road is a test for drivers and cars. Travel with extra gas and tires and expect to use them. Road and ferry **reports** (☎ 800-661-0750) are available. It takes 10 to 12 hours to drive to Inuvik without stopping for a break.

TOMBSTONE TERRITORIAL PARK

The Yukon's newest territorial park, Tombstone is 73km up the Dempster Hwy, with the good **Dempster Hwy Interpretive Centre** (🕙 9am-5pm summer). The pointed shape of the prominent peak was a distinctive landmark on First Nations routes and is now an aerial guide for pilots.

There are several good **day hikes** leading from the center, as well as longer, more rigorous **backcountry trips** for experienced wilderness hikers. In mid-June there's hiking with some snow pack still around; July is best for wildflowers, balancing the annoyance of bug season.

It's possible to visit Tombstone as a day trip from Dawson City or to spend the night at the campground (pit toilets, river water, firewood) adjoining the interpretive center to experience a bit of the Dempster and see the headwaters of the Klondike River.

ARCTIC PARKS

VUNTUT NATIONAL PARK

Vuntut, a Gwich'in word meaning 'among the lakes,' was declared a national park in 1993. It's north of the isolated village of Old Crow, the most northerly settlement in the Yukon. Each spring a herd of 160,000 porcupine caribou follows a migration route north across the plain to calving grounds near the Beaufort Sea. In Canada these calving grounds are protected within Ivvavik National Park and extend into Alaska where they are part of the Arctic National Wildlife Refuge.

With its many lakes and ponds, Vuntut National Park is visited by around 500,000 waterbirds each autumn. Archaeological sites contain fossils of ancient animals such as the mammoth, plus evidence of early humans. The only access to the 4345-sq-km park is by chartered plane from Old Crow, which itself is reachable only by air. The park has no services or facilities.

IVVAVIK NATIONAL PARK

Ivvavik, meaning 'a place for giving birth to and raising the young,' is situated along the Beaufort Sea and adjoining Alaska and covers 10,170 sq km. The park is dominated by the British Mountains and its vegetation is mainly tundra. It's on the migration route of the porcupine caribou and is also a major waterfowl habitat.

The park holds one of the world's great white-water rivers, the **Frith River**, which can be navigated for 130km from Margaret Lake near the Alaskan border north to the Beaufort Sea. When the river meets Joe Creek, the valley narrows to a canyon and there are numerous areas of white-water rated Class II and III+.

Access is by charter plane from either Old Crow or Inuvik where there is also an office for the park. There are no facilities or services in the park.

HERSCHEL ISLAND TERRITORIAL PARK

Off the coast of Ivvavik is Herschel Island in the Beaufort Sea, below the Arctic Ocean and about 90km south of the packed ice. Rich in plant, bird and marine life, particularly ringed seal and bowhead whales, it was an important area for the Thule people. There have been several waves of people through the area, but the Thule, expert whale hunters, were thought to be the first to make a permanent settlement here about 1000 years ago. They called it Qikiqtaruk (meaning 'it is an island').

Pauline Cove is deep enough for ocean vessels and is protected from the northerly winds and drifting pack ice. As a haven for ships, it became a key port during the last days of the whaling industry when the whales were hunted first for lamp oil and then for baleen. Bowhead whales had the longest bones and were the most desirable for women's corsets. Fashion nearly drove them to extinction. Following the whalers and their families, who numbered about 1500, was an Anglican missionary party in 1897, whose members tried to win converts among the Thule. The whaling station was abandoned around 1907, though the Canadian police continued to use the island as a post until 1964.

The flight across the MacKenzie Delta to reach the island is spectacular. At Pauline Cove, park rangers provide a tour of the historical buildings and in July they lead a hike above the harbor to a hill carpeted with tiny wildflowers. The rangers are wonderful hosts and some have family connections to the island. Backcountry camping during the short summer season (from late June to August) is possible. There are fire rings, wind shelters, pit toilets and limited water. Access is by chartered plane, usually from Inuvik, 250km southeast. Most visitors spend half a day.

Northwest Territories

The Northwest Territories (NWT) is a huge and humbling wilderness – a thinly peopled expanse of lakes and stunted forests, fringed to the west by weather-worn peaks and to the north by barren islands reaching toward the top of the world.

This is the North you *don't* know, because it lacks the polar exoticism of Nunavut and the lore and grandeur of the Yukon. But in ways, it's an ideal compromise. The NWT is rugged, accessible and largely Aboriginal – a potent combo found nowhere else in Canada.

With 32 sq km for every resident, there's enough room to disappear for a while. Canoeing, kayaking, fishing and hiking are all top-notch, and high-quality tours abound. The more-intrepid traveler can go it alone in the hinterlands, following epic paddling routes such as the Nahanni, Mackenzie, Slave or Thelon, or trekking the 372km Canol Heritage Trail. In winter, the air turns icy – but the bugs disappear, the northern lights rev up and skiers and dogsledders slip through the silent, surreal backcountry.

Even within communities, the NWT is refreshingly wild. Mass culture hasn't benumbed this place. The Euro-Canadian population displays a colorful streak of pioneer iconoclasm, and as for the other half of residents, who are indigenous, ancestral traditions are alive and kicking. Most Aboriginals belong to one of several First Nations bands collectively called the Dene (*deh*-nay) and they, along with the few thousand Inuvialuit (Western Arctic Inuit), keep one foot in the precontact world by hunting and harvesting as the season dictates.

Wildlife is rife. Bison herds are found around Great Slave Lake and Wood Buffalo National Park, and there are great numbers of moose, bear and caribou, plus rare birds such as white pelicans and whooping cranes. As you drive the desolate highways, many of these creatures amble unfazed along the roadsides, as if to say, 'Here, *we* are still in charge.'

NORTHWEST TERRITORIES

HIGHLIGHTS

- Tempt fate with a flightseeing trip over Deadmen Valley, Death Lake and Crash Lake, en route to **Virginia Falls** (p823)

- Paddle past rainbow-hued houseboats on **Great Slave Lake** (p814), then down fresh-caught trout at a gourmet fish shack.

- Peruse caribou-antler carvings and avant-garde paintings at the Great Northern Arts Festival in **Inuvik** (p827)

- Shout 'Hike! Gee! Haw!' as you drive a dog team under the aurora borealis near **Yellowknife** (p814)

- Get a whiff – and an unbeatable view – of the continent's biggest land animal in **Wood Buffalo National Park** (p821)

★ Inuvik

Yellowknife ★
★ Great Slave Lake
Virginia Falls ★

★ Wood Buffalo National Park

| ▦ POPULATION: 42,180 | ▦ TERRITORIAL CAPITAL: YELLOWKNIFE | ▦ AREA: 1,346,106 SQ KM |

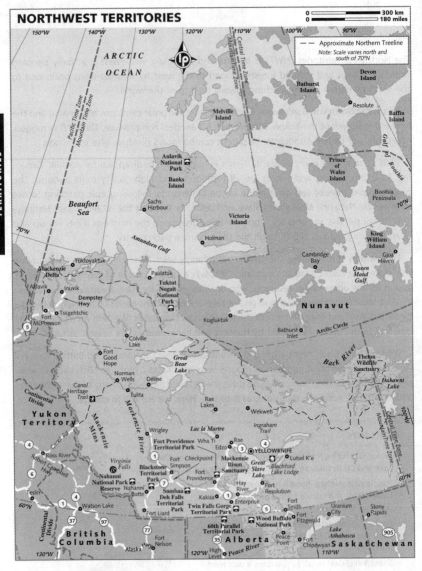

NORTHWEST TERRITORIES

0 ——— 300 km
0 ——— 180 miles

- - - Approximate Northern Treeline
Note: Scale varies north and south of 70°N

ARCTIC OCEAN

Devon Island

Bathurst Island

Resolute

Baffin Island

Melville Island

Prince of Wales Island

Gulf of Boothia

Aulavik National Park

Banks Island

Boothia Peninsula

Beaufort Sea

Sachs Harbour

Victoria Island

King William Island

Holman

Gjoa Haven

Amundsen Gulf

Cambridge Bay

Queen Maud Gulf

Tuktoyaktuk

Mackenzie Delta

Paulatuk

Aklavik

Inuvik

Tuktut Nogait National Park

Nunavut

Dempster Hwy

Tsiigehtchic

Fort McPherson

Kugluktuk

Colville Lake

Bathurst Inlet

Arctic Circle

Fort Good Hope

Great Bear Lake

Back River

Norman Wells

Déline

Thelon Wildlife Sanctuary

Canol Heritage Trail

Tulita

Dubawnt Lake

Continental Divide

Rae Lakes

Wekweti

Yukon Territory

Mackenzie Mtns

Mackenzie River

Wrigley

Lac la Martre

Ingraham Trail

Fort Providence Territorial Park

Wha Ti

Rae

Edzo

YELLOWKNIFE

Lutsel K'e

Virginia Falls

Fort Simpson

Checkpoint

Mackenzie Bison Sanctuary

Great Slave Lake

Blachford Lake Lodge

Ross River

Robert Campbell Hwy

Nahanni National Park Reserve

Blackstone Territorial Park

Fort Providence

Hay River

Fort Resolution

Teslin

Nahanni Butte

Sambaa Deh Falls Territorial Park

Kakisa

Enterprise

Fort Smith

Uranium City

Stony Rapids

Watson Lake

Twin Falls Gorge Territorial Park

Fort Liard

60th Parallel Territorial Park

Wood Buffalo National Park

Fort Fitzgerald

Lake Athabasca

Continental Divide

British Columbia

Fort Nelson

Alberta

Peace Point

Fort Chipewyan

Saskatchewan

Alaska Hwy

High Level

Peace River

History

Archeologists say the earliest NWT residents – ancestors of today's Dene – came here from Asia about 14,000 years ago. The Inuvialuit, who migrated from Alaska, showed up more recently.

With the prospect of wealth from the fur trade, Europeans penetrated Northern Canada in the 18th and 19th centuries, and on their heels were missionaries. Even well into the 1900s the region was largely administered by competing churches and the Hudson's Bay Company.

After oil was discovered near Tulita in the 1920s, a territorial government was formed. In the '30s, gold near Yellowknife and radium near Great Bear Lake brought an influx of non-Aboriginals. Federal health, welfare and education programs began in earnest in the 1950s and '60s. In the 1970s the Dene and Inuvialuit emerged as a political force, demanding a say in – and benefits from – resource extraction in their land.

In 1999 the territory was halved, with the eastern and central Arctic becoming Nunavut. The remaining population is evenly divided between Aboriginals and non-Aboriginals. The latter group, and to some extent the former, have benefited from recent oil, gas and diamond development, which have thrown the territorial economy into hyperdrive.

Climate

Summer weather can range from miserable to stupendous. In Yellowknife and Inuvik, midsummer highs average 20°C, but on any given day you could find yourself sweltering or shivering. One sure thing is the daylight: from May through July there's no night. June is the driest summer month, but lake ice often lingers until the month's end. Most visitors come in July and August.

Winters are long, dark and excruciating. In January, average lows in Yellowknife sink to -35°C and daylight is feeble and fleeting. If you're keen on visiting in the snowy season, try March or April, when the sun begins to climb and the mercury follows suit.

National & Territorial Parks

The NWT has four national parks. Nahanni National Park Reserve (p823), near the Yukon border, is legendary for canoeing and contains the jaw-dropping Virginia Falls. Wood Buffalo National Park (p821), more of a wildlife preserve, straddles the border with Alberta, and is the only road-accessible park. Aulavik National Park (p829), on northern Banks Island, and Tuktut Nogait National Park (p829), near the arctic coast, are among the newest, least-visited Canadian parks.

The NWT also has numerous roadside territorial parks. Most *claim* to be open May 15 to September 15, but the actual dates depend on the weather, so check ahead with **NWT Parks & Tourism** (☎ 867-920-8974; parksandtourism@gov.nt.ca). For day-use you need a one-time $10 vehicle pass. Due to the absence of hostels or other cheap digs, overnighting in these parks is your best budget option. Camping usually costs $15 per night for tent sites and $20 for sites with RV hook-ups.

THE NORTHWEST TERRITORIES IN...

Two Days

After flying to **Yellowknife** (p811), spend the morning getting the scoop on the Northwest Territories (NWT) at the **Prince of Wales Northern Heritage Centre** (p813). Then amble down to **Old Town** (p814), grab lunch at the famous **Wildcat Café** (p815) and summit **Bush Pilot's Monument** (p814). The lake looks inviting, eh? Rent a **canoe** (p814) and circumnavigate Latham Island leisurely, gawking at the shacks, mansions, floatplanes and houseboats. Righteously fatigued, repair to **Bullock's Bistro** (p815) to sip beer, sup on whitefish, and watch the sun not set.

Next morning, rent a car, pack hiking boots and a fishing rod, and explore lake-lined **Ingraham Trail** (p817). At Cameron Falls, break out the picnic basket.

One Week

Now motor west toward the **Mackenzie Bison Sanctuary** (p818) and get close-up snapshots of these wooly behemoths. Car-camp your way along the **Waterfalls Route** (p818), then backtrack to **Fort Simpson** (p822). Join a flightseeing tour into **Nahanni National Park Reserve** (p823) and lunch euphorically at the legendary Virginia Falls.

Two weeks

Skip the road trip. Fly from Yellowknife to Fort Simpson, meet your outfitter and spend 10 days paddling the paradisiacal **South Nahanni River** (p824).

WHAT'S IN A NAME?

Explore Canada's Arctic: Bob.

That's what the Northwest Territories' distinctive polar-bear license plates *could* have read, had the wags won the Great NWT Name Debate.

The debate arose as Nunavut's independence loomed in the late 1990s. The about-to-be-jilted west was having an identity crisis. 'The Northwest Territories is not a name,' said Stephen Kakfwi, who was then territorial premier. 'Rather, it's a direction – a geographic label in relation to Ottawa.' Moreover, it's not even accurate. The NWT is *east* of the Yukon. And it's a territory – not 'territories.'

More than a century ago, the name made sense. In 1870, after the Hudson's Bay Company sold its empire to Canada, the Northwest Territories comprised almost everything north and west of southern Ontario and Québec. Slowly, provinces and the Yukon Territory were carved away. The 1999 separation of Nunavut would be just the latest indignity.

Rather than continuing as a rump state, many First Nations leaders wanted to re-brand the territory 'Denendeh,' meaning land of the Dene. This didn't sit well with non-Aboriginals, or with Inuvialuit, who feared their own identity would be subsumed.

Then, jokers launched the 'Bob' campaign, which spread like wildfire. The territory's official sport could be bobsledding, they said. Its animal could be the bobcat, and its police, bobbies. A 1996 poll showed 'Bob' running second, behind sticking with 'NWT.' 'Denendeh' trailed in third – and the renaming effort was scrapped.

So, 'Northwest Territories' remains the name, still emblazoned on the NWT's polar bear–shaped license plates. Which, it must be noted, Nunavut also wanted to take away, because *they* have almost all the polar bears. But that's a different story entirely.

Language

The NWT has a whopping 11 official languages: English, French, and nine aboriginal tongues, from Cree in the south to Inuvialuktun in the Arctic. Though the aboriginal languages have been eroded by cultural change and past government policies, they remain in daily use. There are still elders who speak no English. The aboriginal phrase you'll most likely hear is *mahsi cho* – Dene for 'thank you very much.' Don't hesitate to use it.

Dangers & Annoyances

Few places on earth have more-bloodthirsty bugs. Mosquitoes appear first and peak in late June; blackflies reach their maximum in July. If you're not prepared, they'll drive you mad. For ways to preserve your flesh and sanity, see p881.

Getting There & Away

AIR

For air travelers, Edmonton is the main gateway to the NWT. Both First Air (p869) and Canadian North (p869) fly daily from there to Yellowknife, starting at around $700 return. Canadian North also flies from Edmonton to Hay River (about $640 return).

Northwestern Air Lease (☎ 877-872-2216; www.nwal .ca) serves Fort Smith direct from Edmonton (around $836 return).

From Whitehorse, Yukon Territory, First Air flies to Yellowknife (about $1100 return, via Fort Simpson), while Air North (p869) goes to Inuvik ($525 return).

From Iqaluit, Nunavut, both First Air and Canadian North depart for Yellowknife (about $1400 return).

BUS

The sole bus link to the southern NWT is provided by Greyhound Canada (p870), which runs year-round from Edmonton to Hay River for $145 one-way. From there, a regional carrier connects to other communities (see opposite).

In summer, **Dawson City Courier** (☎ 867-993-6688) offers a shuttle service from Dawson City, Yukon, to Inuvik ($261, one-way) and Whitehorse ($91, one-way).

CAR & MOTORCYCLE

There are two road-trip routes to the southern NWT. From Edmonton, Alberta, a long (and, frankly, monotonous) day's drive up Hwy 35 brings you to the NWT border, 84km shy of Enterprise. Alternatively, from

Fort Nelson, British Columbia (on the Alaska Hwy) the Liard Trail runs 137 potholed-but-paved kilometers to the border. Fort Liard is another 38km north.

If you're heading up to the Mackenzie Delta, you can set out from Dawson City, Yukon, on the shockingly scenic Dempster Hwy, which reaches the NWT boundary after 465km.

Getting Around

AIR

Half of the NWT's 32 communities are fly-in only, accessed from hub airports in Yellowknife, Norman Wells and Inuvik. Service in the North Slave region is provided by **Air Tindi** (☎ 867-669-8260; www.airtindi .com), in the Mackenzie Valley by **North-Wright Air** (☎ 867-587-2962; www.north-wrightair ways.com), and in the Mackenzie Delta by **Aklak Air** (☎ 867-777-3777). Various charter carriers offer flightseeing trips or flights to backcountry destinations; see p822 and p824 for more information.

BUS

Frontier Coachlines (☎ 867-874-2566) meets Greyhound Canada in Hay River, and offers connecting buses to Yellowknife (five times a week), Fort Smith (twice a week) and Fort Simpson (twice a week).

CAR & MOTORCYCLE

To best appreciate the NWT, you need wheels. Automobiles can be rented in major communities. For Yellowknife car-rental agencies, see p817; for other towns, contact the local tourism office for information.

The territory has two highway networks: a southern system, linking most of the communities in the North Slave, South Slave and Deh Cho regions; and the Dempster Hwy, which winds through the Mackenzie Delta. Getting to the Delta from southern NWT requires a three-day detour through BC and the Yukon.

In the south, the Mackenzie Hwy (Hwy 1) and Hwy 2 are paved from the border to Hay River. Highway 5 is partially paved east to Fort Smith, and the Mackenzie Hwy and Hwy 3 are paved to Rae/Edzo. The surfacing of the final 98km of road to Yellowknife should be complete by late 2005. The rest of the NWT's roads are gravel, dirt or muck.

In summer, free ferries cross several rivers; in winter, vehicles drive across on 4ft-thick ice. Travel is interrupted for several weeks during 'break-up' (April and May) and 'freeze-up' (December or January). For ferry information, call ☎ 800-661-0750. The major crossing, at the Mackenzie River on Hwy 3, may soon be obviated by construction of a $60-million bridge.

Northern driving isn't easy. The Dempster Hwy, in particular, is notorious for shredding tires. In heavy rains, the Liard Trail turns to dough. On all unpaved roads, other vehicles create dusty smokescreens and hurl windshield-cracking rocks. Even paved highways can be taxing, due to repetitive scenery and long distances between gas stations. Bring a full-size spare and know how to change it. Also carry a first-aid kit, flares, water and food. In winter, add a shovel, jumper cables, sleeping bags and matches. Before traveling, call ☎ 800-661-0750 for highway reports.

See also p874 for general information about driving safely in Canada.

YELLOWKNIFE

Rising from the wilderness, Yellowknife is a subarctic boomtown. In the local Dogrib language, this is Somba K'e: place of money. It's the territorial capital, the business and transport nucleus, and the biggest community by far, with nearly 18,000 residents.

It's also a Northern crossroads, meaning that townsfolk are a fairly comfortable mix: Dene and Métis from across the territory, Inuit and Inuvialuit from further north, grizzled non-Aboriginal pioneers, get-rich-quick newcomers from southern Canada, plus Armenians, Somalis and other more recent immigrants.

The dark, super-cold winters can be claustrophobic and alienating, but in the quick, frenzied summer, Yellowknife becomes the territory's must-visit community. Not surprisingly, the greatest diversity of shops and restaurants are here. Conveniently, this is also one of the most scenic towns in the NWT, with unbeatable access to wilderness playgrounds. On hot, sunny days, innumerable lakes and rivers beckon, making this back-of-beyond metropolis a bit like paradise.

HISTORY

When the first Europeans reached Great Slave Lake in 1771, the north shore was home to the Tetsot'ine who, due to their penchant for copper blades, were dubbed the Yellowknives. Wars and foreign diseases eradicated them, but on the map the moniker remained.

More than a century later, Klondike-bound prospectors on Yellowknife Bay unearthed a different yellow metal: hard-rock gold. By the mid-1930s, bush planes had made the area accessible to commercial mining. Yellowknife became a boomtown.

In 1967 when Ottawa decided to devolve management of the NWT, Yellowknife, as the most populous town, was picked as the capital. The culture of the community began to shift from that of a hardscrabble outpost to a buttoned-down bureaucratic hub. That shift accelerated horrifically in 1992, when a bitter labor dispute at Giant Mine led to the underground-bombing death of nine strikebreakers. Roger Warren, an unemployed miner, went to jail for life.

Since then, gold mining has effectively ceased in Yellowknife. Three kimberlite mines, north of town, are now fueling a new boom, making diamonds the city's new best friend.

ORIENTATION

Appropriately, Yellowknife is like a knife pointing northward, with its tip – peninsular Old Town – impaling Great Slave Lake, and its hilt – downtown – reaching back from the rocky shore. Linking the two is Franklin Ave (50th Ave), the main drag. At its south end, Franklin joins Old Airport Rd, which winds several kilometers through the commercial district.

Downtown has the shops, businesses, services and hotels, but its corrugated-metal architecture and ho-hum landscape hold little appeal. More interesting is hilly Old Town, wedged between Back and Yellowknife Bays, where funky cabins and subarctic-style mansions share the views with B&Bs, houseboats and floatplane bases. At the tip of Old Town, N'Dilo (*dee*-lo, meaning 'end of the road') is Yellowknife's aboriginal village.

From the airport to downtown is about 5km via Hwy 3 and 48th St. From the bus station downtown is 3.5km up Kam Lake Rd and Franklin Ave.

INFORMATION

Bookstores

Map Place (☎ 867-873-8448; 2nd fl, 5016 Franklin Ave; ☽ 9am-5pm Mon-Fri, 10am-4pm Sat) Topographical and nautical maps.

Yellowknife Book Cellar (☎ 867-920-2220; 48th St entrance, Panda II Mall; ☽ 9:30am-8pm Mon-Fri, 9:30am-6pm Sat, noon-5pm Sun) Best selection of Northern and aboriginal titles.

Emergencies

Note that ☎ 911 is not the emergency number in the NWT.

Ambulance & Fire (☎ 867-873-2222) For emergencies.

Police (☎ emergencies 867-669-1111, nonemergencies 867-669-5100; 5010 49th Ave)

Libraries

Yellowknife Public Library (☎ 867-920-5642; 2nd fl, Centre Square Mall; ☽ 10am-9pm Mon-Thu, 10am-6pm Fri, 10am-5pm Sat) An ample Northern book collection; there's also free Internet access.

Medical

Stanton Territorial Hospital (☎ 867-669-4111; off Old Airport Rd; ☽ 24hr) Large, full-service facility located behind Extra Foods.

Money

American Express (☎ 867-873-2121; Key West Travel, 5014 Franklin Ave; ☽ 9am-6pm Mon-Fri, 11am-3pm Sat)

CIBC (☎ 867-873-4452; 5001 Franklin Ave)

Royal Bank of Canada (☎ 867-873-5961; 4920 52nd St)

Scotia Bank (☎ 867-669-6000; 5102 50th Ave)

TD Bank (☎ 867-873-5891; 4910 50th Ave)

Post

Main post office (☎ 867-873-2500; 4902 Franklin Ave)

Tourist Information

Northern Frontier Visitors Centre (☎ 867-873-4262, 877-881-4262; www.northernfrontier.com; 4807 49th St; Internet access per 15min $1; ☽ 8:30am-6pm Jun-Aug, 8:30am-5pm Mon-Fri, noon-4pm Sat & Sun Sep-May) The Visitors Centre has knowledgeable staff and scads of maps and brochures, as well as interesting displays on NWT culture and natural history. You can pick up the indispensable *Explorers' Guide*, published annually by NWT Arctic Tourism, here.

DANGERS & ANNOYANCES

At night, booze and some bad attitudes can make for an unsavory scene on 50th St between Franklin and 52nd Aves.

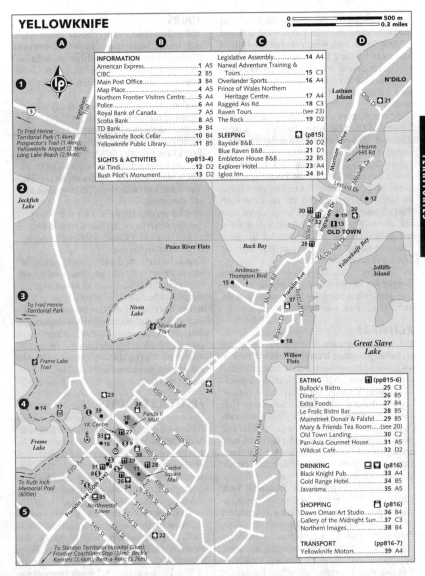

YELLOWKNIFE

0 — 500 m
0 — 0.3 miles

INFORMATION
American Express.....................................1 A5
CIBC..2 B5
Main Post Office..3 B4
Map Place..4 A5
Northern Frontier Visitors Centre.......5 A4
Police..6 A5
Royal Bank of Canada.............................7 A5
Scotia Bank...8 A5
TD Bank..9 B4
Yellowknife Book Cellar........................10 B4
Yellowknife Public Library....................11 B5

SIGHTS & ACTIVITIES   (pp813-4)
Air Tindi..12 D2
Bush Pilot's Monument.........................13 D2

Legislative Assembly..............................14 A4
Narwal Adventure Training &
  Tours...15 C3
Overlander Sports...................................16 A4
Prince of Wales Northern
  Heritage Centre...................................17 A4
Ragged Ass Rd...18 C3
Raven Tours....................................(see 23)
The Rock..19 D2

SLEEPING   (p815)
Bayside B&B..20 D2
Blue Raven B&B..21 D1
Embleton House B&B.............................22 B5
Explorer Hotel..23 A4
Igloo Inn..24 B4

EATING   (pp815-6)
Bullock's Bistro..25 C3
Diner..26 B5
Extra Foods...27 B4
Le Frolic Bistro Bar.................................28 B5
Mainstreet Donair & Falafel.....29 B5
Mary & Friends Tea Room..........(see 20)
Old Town Landing....................................30 C2
Pan-Asia Gourmet House.....................31 A5
Wildcat Café..32 D2

DRINKING   (p816)
Black Knight Pub.....................................33 A4
Gold Range Hotel....................................34 B5
Javaroma..35 A5

SHOPPING   (p816)
Dawn Oman Art Studio..........................36 B4
Gallery of the Midnight Sun.....37 C3
Northern Images......................................38 B4

TRANSPORT   (pp816-7)
Yellowknife Motors..................................39 A4

NORTHWEST TERRITORIES

SIGHTS

A fine introduction to the NWT can be found at **Prince of Wales Northern Heritage Centre** (☎ 867-873-7551; www.pwnhc.ca; admission free; 🕙 10:30am-5pm Mon-Fri, noon-5pm Sat & Sun Sep-May, 10:30am-5:30pm Jun-Aug), off 48th St and near Frame Lake. Here, displays address Dene and Inuit ways of life, as well as natural his-

tory, European exploration and Northern aviation. Extensive renovations will close certain galleries until 2006, but will result in more display space.

In 1993, the NWT government coughed up $25 million to build the impressive, igloo-shaped **Legislative Assembly** (☎ 867-669-2230, 800-661-0784; www.assembly.gov.nt.ca; admission free; ☀ 7am-6pm Mon-Fri, 10am-6pm Sat & Sun, tours given at 10:30am Mon-Fri, also 1:30pm & 3:30pm Mon-Fri & 1:30pm Sun Jun-Aug), which is also off 48th St and near Frame Lake. You can learn about the territory's aboriginal-style government by joining a free hour-long tour. There's also excellent Northern art throughout the building.

At the visitors' center, arm yourself with a copy of the *Old Town Heritage Walking Tour of Yellowknife*, a superlative illustrated booklet showing the town's many interesting old buildings, and then head down Franklin Ave to **Old Town**. The **Rock** is the large outcrop right before the bridge to Latham Island. Climb the stairs to **Bush Pilot's Monument**, from which you can watch the floatplane traffic, and envy the folks on polychromatic houseboats in the bay. Summer sunsets – if you can stay up that late – are often stunning.

Close by is the city's most famous lane, **Ragged Ass Rd**, which some say is becoming gentrified, despite the sagging gold rush–era cabins and antique trucks.

ACTIVITIES

On hot, buggy days, the water's where it's at. **Narwal Adventure Training & Tours** (☎ 867-873-6443; www.ssimicro.com/~narwal; canoe rentals per evening/day/weekend/week $20/30/50/150), on Anderson-Thompson Blvd on Back Bay, rents canoes and kayaks, and offers tours and lessons. Call ahead. **Overlander Sports** (☎ 867-873-2474; www.overlandersports.com; 4909 50th St; canoe rentals per day/weekend/week $30/50/160, cross-country skis, poles & boots per day/weekend $30/50; ☀ 9am-6pm Mon-Sat) rents canoes and kayaks in summer and cross-country skis in winter.

In popular **Fred Henne Territorial Park** (☎ 867-920-2472; ☀ mid-May–Sep 15), opposite the airport off Hwy 3, there's swimming at **Long Lake Beach** and hiking on the 4km **Prospector's Trail**. This path leads through a microcosm of Northern topography: over rocky outcrops, through muskeg, to a lake. Get the map from the park office, because it can be easy to lose the trail. The 7km **Frame Lake Trail**, and the shorter **Niven Lake Trail**, are nice in-town hikes.

Smelly backpackers can shower at **Ruth Inch Memorial Pool** (☎ 867-920-5683, 6001 Franklin Ave; showers $2.75; ☀ 6am-11pm Mon-Thu, 6am-10:30pm Fri, noon-9:30pm Sat, noon-11pm Sun). There's also a whirlpool and steam room.

TOURS

Yellowknife has lots to choose from: walking tours, boat trips, kayak adventures, photography safaris, fishing expeditions and more. Check out the *Explorers' Guide*, available from the Northern Frontier Visitors Centre for options:

Air Tindi (☎ 867-669-8218; www.airtindi.com; 35 Mitchell Rd; tours for 1-3 people $175, 4-7 $350) Offers excellent floatplane tours (30 minutes) over Yellowknife, the Ingraham Trail and Great Slave Lake.

Beck's Kennels (☎ 867-873-5603; fax 867-873-2593; 124 Curry Dr) The Becks have the biggest dog yard in the NWT. In winter, go for an 8km guided dogsled tour ($40) or learn to drive your own team ($55). In summer, the dogs pull wheeled sleds.

Bluefish Services (☎ 867-873-4818; bluefishservices@ssimicro.com; per person $85) Bluefish takes fisherfolk out on Great Slave Lake (4½ hours) to battle arctic grayling, northern pike and lake trout.

Cygnus Ecotours (☎ /fax 867-873-4782; cygnus@the edge.ca; per person $50-60, 4-person minimum) Irrepressible ecologist Jamie Bastedo leads nature walks (four hours) near Yellowknife.

Raven Tours (☎ 867-873-4776; www.raventours.yk .com; 4908 50th St) With a tour desk in the Explorer Hotel, Raven offers a daily two-hour boat tour on Great Slave Lake ($30-40); a basic, 2½-hour bus tour of the city ($30); a weekly trip down Ingraham Trail to Cameron Falls ($45); and, in winter, aurora borealis–viewing tours ($90).

FESTIVALS & EVENTS

For a capital city, Yellowknife has few quality festivals. A notable exception is **Folk on the Rocks** (☎ 867-920-7806; www.folkontherocks.com; day/weekend pass $30/50; ☀ 3 days mid-Jul), a groovefest on Long Lake. No mere hoedown, the event features everything from hip-hop to Dene drumming, and draws musicians from northern and southern Canada.

The **Summer Solstice Festival** (☀ 1 week late Jun), is actually a series of unrelated events, including cultural performances on National Aboriginal Day (June 21), and Raven Mad Daze, a downtown street fair.

The big winter bash, **Caribou Carnival** (www .cariboucarnival.com; ☀ Mar), nearly expired a few years ago, but has apparently been revived. Held on frozen Frame Lake, it involves cabin-feverish locals competing in contests like moose calling and tea boiling. Happening simultaneously, but officially unrelated, is the **Canadian Championship Dog Derby**, a 240km sled-dog race on Great Slave Lake.

SLEEPING

Yellowknife has no hostels and, unless you want to camp, no other real budget accommodations. In general, B&Bs are the best deals; Old Town seems to have dozens of them.

Budget

Those with their own transport can also camp along the Ingraham Trail (p817). **Fred Henne Territorial Park** (☎ 867-920-2472; off Hwy 3; tent/RV sites $15/20; ☼ mid-May–mid-Sep) is the closest campground to town. Opposite the airport, it has full facilities, including showers and toilets. You can walk to downtown in under 40 minutes using the Jackfish and Frame Lake trails.

Mid-Range

Bayside B&B (☎ 867-920-4686; bryant@ssimicro.com; 3505 McDonald Dr; s/d incl breakfast $70/80) On the Rock by the floatplane terminal, this B&B has terrific views of Yellowknife Bay.

Blue Raven B&B (☎ 867-873-6328; tmfoto@inter north.com; 37 Otto Dr; s/d incl breakfast $65/80) Perched on a hill on Latham Island, Blue Raven has a great sundeck overlooking Yellowknife Bay and serves up one of the best breakfasts in town.

Igloo Inn (☎ 867-873-8511; iglooinn@theedge.ca; 4115 Franklin Ave; r $95) Somewhat contorted by permafrost, this basic motel is halfway between downtown and Old Town. Most of its rooms have kitchenettes.

Embleton House B&B (☎ 867-873-2892; www.bb canada.com/embletonhouse; 5203 52nd St; s/d incl breakfast $70/80; 🖳) Convenient to downtown, this subterranean B&B has a stocked kitchen for preparing your own breakfast.

Top End

Explorer Hotel (☎ 867-873-3531, 800-661-0892; www .explorerhotel.nt.ca; 4825 49th Ave; s/d $125/140) Looming over downtown, this high-rise has comfortable modern rooms, great views, a restaurant and a lounge. A shuttle is available from the airport.

EATING

Yellowknife has a wider range of restaurants than elsewhere in the territory. A few are quite good, and some offer Northern cuisine, like caribou, musk ox and arctic char. Vegetarians will eat better here than elsewhere in the NWT.

Budget

Diner (☎ 867-920-7770; 5008 50th St; meals under $10; ☼ 5:45am-9pm Mon-Sat, 6:45am-9pm Sun) Around rickety tables, old-time prospectors and bush pilots shoot the bull. Breakfasts and lunchtime burgers are greasy, but the flavor here is all in the patrons.

Mainstreet Donair & Falafel (☎ 867-766-3910; 4905 Franklin Ave; mains $7-12; ☼ 11am-6pm Mon-Fri, 11am-5pm Sat) The best place for a fast, take-out lunch. The chicken shwarmas ($7.25), smothered in garlic sauce, are addictive, and vegetarian options abound.

Pan-Asia Gourmet House (☎ 867-669-7878; 5014 Franklin Ave; mains $7-12; ☼ 4-10pm Tue-Thu, 4pm-midnight Fri, 4-11pm Sat & Sun) This restaurant is Chinese, not pan-Asian. It's above a strip club, not in a house. And gourmet? Well, it's good enough for the lunch crowd to throng the place.

Extra Foods (☎ 867-669-9100; 48th St entrance, YK Centre; ☼ 9am-9pm Mon-Sat, 10am-6pm Sun) The sole downtown supermarket.

Mid-Range

Wildcat Café (☎ 867-873-8850; cnr Wiley Rd & Doornbos Ln; ☼ Jun-Sep) You'll get cozy with your tablemates at this well-known Old Town café, where the seating is communal and the setting – a 1937 log cabin – is rustic. A different vendor runs it each summer, so the menu, prices and opening hours vary.

Le Frolic Bistro Bar (☎ 867-669-9852; 5019 49th St; mains $12-35; ☼ 11am-11pm Mon-Sat) This cheery establishment and the L'Héritage Restaurant upstairs are the token French eateries in Les Territories du Nord-Ouest. The usually delectable meals range from sandwiches on a baguette ($12) to rack of lamb ($31) to various fondues ($21 to $33).

Mary & Friends Tea Room (☎ 867-920-4686; bryant@ssimicro.com; 3505 McDonald Dr; meals $10; ☼ noon-4.30pm Wed-Sun) Located by the Bayside B&B, Mary's offers waterfront views, affordable soup-and-sandwich combos, and a dainty dollhouse atmosphere.

Top End

Bullock's Bistro (☎ 867-873-3474; cnr Ingraham Dr & Wiley Rd; mains $16-28; ☼ noon-9pm Mon-Sat, 2-9pm Sun, often closed Oct) This fish shack is the city's most-revered eatery, despite (or perhaps because of) the irascible service. Only fresh local cod, trout and whitefish make the menu. The atmosphere is ultra-informal, the deck has bay views, and kitsch and countless photos bedeck the walls. Reservations are recommended.

Old Town Landing (☎ 867-873-3531; 3506 Wiley Rd; mains $20-40; ⊗ 11am-4pm & 5-10pm Mon-Fri, 10am-3pm & 5-10pm Sat & Sun) In a candlelit dining room, almost overhanging Back Bay, enjoy the grilled arctic char ($29), baked musk-ox medallions with mango chutney ($37), or other Northern delicacies.

DRINKING

Maybe it's the cold, the wintertime dark, or the fact that nearby villages and mines restrict liquor. Whatever the reason, when folks visit Yellowknife they flock to the bars. There are lots of 'em, from swank to foul, and most are on Franklin Ave or 50th St downtown.

Gold Range Hotel (☎ 867-873-4441; 5010 50th St; ⊗ 10am-2am) In this huge, dim, infamous landmark, Northerners have been hooking up, breaking up, dancing up a storm, getting beat up, throwing up and just generally whooping it up since 1958. Predominantly an aboriginal country-rock saloon, the so-called Strange Range has such notoriety that it's a must-see for visitors; some, it seems, never leave.

Black Knight Pub (☎ 867-920-4041; 4910 49th St; ⊗ 11am-2am) Among the more straight-laced drinkeries, the local favorite is the Black Knight, which has an English-Irish-Scottish theme to its brews and decor. The **Top Knight** dance club is upstairs.

Javaroma (☎ 867-669-0725; 5201 Franklin Ave; ⊗ 7am-10pm Mon-Fri, 9am-10pm Sat, 10am-10pm Sun) For the city's best joe, join the legions of coffee-lovers on the comfy couches here.

SHOPPING

Yellowknife is the best place in Canada to buy Northern art, crafts and clothing. Shops and galleries are numerous. If you can't find what you want (say, a size XL moosehide vest), request contact information for artisans, who often work on commission. Note that not all art for sale is actually made by Aboriginal people. For the lowdown on how to distinguish the real thing from fakes, see the boxed text on p859. If high-end art doesn't empty your wallet, consider decorating yourself with local jewelry. Most Yellowknife jewelers sell the real deal: authentic NWT diamonds, laser-etched with a microscopic polar-bear logo.

Northern Images (☎ 867-873-5944; 4801 Franklin Ave; ⊗ 10am-6pm Mon-Sat) This place is jointly owned by aboriginal art-and-crafts cooperatives in the NWT and Nunavut. It's particularly strong in Inuit carvings and tapestries, but also carries Dene paintings and clothing.

Gallery of the Midnight Sun (☎ 867-873-8064; www.gallerymidnightsun.com; 5005 Bryson Dr) This gallery has an ample supply of aboriginal art, including ornately decorated Dene moccasins and jackets. It also stocks souvenirs made in southern Canada.

Dawn Oman Art Studio (☎ 867-920-4681; www.dawnoman.com; 4911 47th St; ⊗ noon-6pm) Dawn Oman, a nationally lauded Métis painter, renders Northern themes in vivid primary colors. Her work appears on canvas, silk, mouse pads etc at her at-home gallery.

GETTING THERE & AWAY
Air
Yellowknife is the NWT's air hub. Most flights from outside the territory land here, and most headed to smaller NWT communities depart from here; brace yourself for high prices. First Air serves Hay River ($284 one way, 45 minutes, daily), Fort Simpson ($352 one way, one hour, Sunday to Friday) and Inuvik ($663 one way, 1¾ hours, Sunday, Monday, Wednesday and Friday), while Canadian North flies to Hay River ($209 one way, 35 minutes, three times a week), Inuvik ($411 one way, 2½ hours, daily) and Norman Wells ($344 one way, one hour, daily). Smaller airlines sometimes offer good special fares. Northwestern Air Lease goes to Fort Smith ($262 one way, one hour, daily), **Buffalo Airways** (☎ 867-873-6112; www.buffaloairways.com) flies to Hay River ($175 one way, 45 minutes, six times a week), North-Wright Air will deliver you to Norman Wells via Deline and Tulita ($495 one way, four hours, five times a week) and Air Tindi lands in Fort Simpson ($281 one way, 80 minutes, daily) and the small Dogrib and Chipewyan communities around Great Slave Lake.

Bus
Inconveniently, Frontier Coachlines is at 113 Kam Lake Rd, in Yellowknife's industrial boondocks. Buses depart Tuesday through Saturday, stopping in Rae ($29, 80 minutes), Fort Providence ($64, four hours) and

Enterprise ($71, seven hours) en route to Hay River ($77, eight hours). From there, connections can be made to Edmonton, Fort Smith or Fort Simpson.

Car

Renting a car in Yellowknife isn't cheap. Mileage charges rapidly wipe out seemingly reasonable daily rates. A small car typically costs about $60/340 per day/week, *plus* 30¢ per kilometer, with 250 free kilometers thrown in with weekly rentals only. Some companies prohibit taking rentals on rugged Hwy 3. For those that permit it, take care to determine your liability, given the high likelihood of windshield and other flying-rock damage.

Rent-a-Relic (☎ 867-873-3400; 356 Old Airport Rd; ⊙ 8am-5:30pm Mon-Fri, 9am-noon Sat) is dirt cheap, but you pretty much need a car just to get there. Downtown, try **Yellowknife Motors** (☎ 867-766-5000; cnr 49th Ave & 48th St). National car-rental agencies (see p873) like Budget and National are at the airport.

GETTING AROUND

Much of Yellowknife is easily walkable. From downtown to Old Town is about 2km, or a 25-minute walk.

To/From the Airport

Yellowknife's airport is opposite Long Lake, a couple of kilometers west of downtown. On weekdays during the daytime, buses depart for the city center every half hour. Taxis operate around the clock, charging about $13 for a ride downtown.

Car

With its prominent landmarks, Yellowknife is easy to navigate. Parking around Franklin Ave is metered; free spots are a few blocks away on side streets. Ask at the visitors center about the three-day parking pass for tourists.

Public Transportation

Yellowknife City Transit (☎ 867-873-4693; adult/child $2/1.50) runs three routes. Route 1 serves the airport, Old Airport Rd and downtown. Route 2 connects downtown and Old Town. The summer-only Rte 3 links the airport, downtown and Old Town. Most buses run every half hour, roughly 7am to 7pm Monday to Friday, and for just a few hours on Saturday.

Taxi

Cabs are plentiful. Fares are $3.25 plus $1.30 per kilometer. The biggest company is **City Cab** (☎ 867-873-4444).

AROUND YELLOWKNIFE
Ingraham Trail

The Ingraham Trail (Hwy 4), winding 69km northeast of Yellowknife, is where locals go to play. The route reveals scenic, lake-dotted, jack pine–lined Canadian Shield topography, and offers good fishing, hiking, camping, paddling, picnicking and, in winter, skiing and snowmobiling. *Blue Lake and Rocky Shore*, by naturalist Jamie Bastedo (see Cygnus Ecotours on p814), is an excellent guide to the area.

The trail begins inauspiciously, weaving past the rotting infrastructure of **Giant Mine**. A few kilometers later is the 11km access road to **Dettah**, a tiny, quiet Dene settlement.

Prelude Lake, 30km from Yellowknife, is a busy, family-oriented weekend spot. There's a vast **campground** (tent sites $15; ⊙ mid-May–Sep 15), a boat launch and nature trails.

At **Hidden Lake Territorial Park**, 47km from Yellowknife, a 1.2km trail leads to popular **Cameron Falls**. You can cross the upstream footbridge and crawl to the brink of this marvelous cascade. Another 9km down the Ingraham Trail, just before the highway bridge, a 400m trail goes to Cameron River Ramparts, a small but pretty cousin of Cameron Falls.

At **Reid Lake**, 59km from Yellowknife, you can swim, canoe or fish for pike, whitefish and trout. The **campground** (tent sites $15; ⊙ mid-May–Sep 15) is busy on weekends; otherwise it's quiet. There's a good beach and walking trail, and campsites on the ridge with views of Pickerel Lake.

WILDERNESS LODGES

Numerous remote lodges dot the Northwest Territory (NWT), and several are a short floatplane ride from Yellowknife. They're not cheap, but they're among the best ways to experience the backcountry. Particularly popular is the year-round **Blachford Lake Lodge** (☎ 867-873-3303; www.blachfordlakelodge.com), east of Yellowknife, which offers activities from fishing to dog-mushing. Consult the *Explorers' Guide* (p812) for other lodges.

In summer, the trail ends at **Tibbitt Lake** where, fittingly, there's a stop sign. The lake has good fishing and is the start of some fine canoe routes – ask for details at the North Frontier Visitors Centre (p812). In winter, this is the beginning of the 570km ice road to the diamond mines.

NORTH SLAVE

This region, between Great Slave and Great Bear lakes, is rocky, lake-strewn and rich in minerals. Save for the folks in Yellowknife, most people here are Dogrib, living traditional (and nontourist-oriented) lives.

HIGHWAY 3

From Yellowknife, Hwy 3 runs 98km northwest to Rae, rounds the North Arm of Great Slave Lake, and dives 214km to Fort Providence.

The Yellowknife–Rae stretch is like motocross: absurdly rutted and twisty (though final paving may happen by late 2005). On this section, the roadsides feature bogs, taiga and pinkish Canadian Shield outcrops.

There's little to see in **Rae** (population 1831), 10km north of Hwy 3 on an access road. Though it's among the NWT's largest communities – and by far the biggest aboriginal settlement – it's very insular, and tourists may feel out of place. There's a basic service station, a café, a motel and a convenience store.

Across the Hwy 3 bridge, the outcrops vanish and the land becomes flat boreal forest, which is ubiquitous in southern NWT. The road also changes, becoming wide, straight and smooth. If you're tempted to gun it, beware: the **Mackenzie Bison Sanctuary**, with the world's largest herd of free-ranging, pure wood bison, is just east of here. The animals graze along the road, outweigh your car, and have tempers. There are no trails or visitor facilities in the sanctuary.

On the south side of the sanctuary, a 5km access road leads to Fort Providence. Bypassing that, you'll come to a service station, a sometimes-open visitor information booth and, a few kilometers beyond, the free car-ferry **MV Merv Hardie** (☎ 800-661-0750; ☼ 6am–midnight). In winter there's an ice bridge. Work on a controversial, expensive, permanent bridge should begin in 2005.

FORT PROVIDENCE

This low-key Slavey community (population 750), near the head of the Mackenzie River, was settled in 1861 with the establishment of a Roman Catholic mission. Halfway along the access road to the community is the pretty (though apparently theft-prone) **Fort Providence Territorial Park** (tent sites $15; ☼ mid-May–Sep 15). It has pit toilets and riverfront sites.

In Fort Providence proper there are good picnic benches atop the 10m riverbanks. Past the beautiful wooden church is a boat launch. The fishing is good, and pike, walleye and sometimes grayling can be caught from shore. If nothing is biting, outfitters can take you on the water.

At the entrance to town, the **Snowshoe Inn** (☎ 867-699-3511; www.ssimicro.com/snowshoe; s/d $115/135) has decent, modern, waterfront rooms. Across the road, the short-order **Snowshoe Inn Restaurant** (☎ 867-699-3511; dishes $6-10 ☼ 7am-8pm Mon-Sat, 10am-8pm Sun) whips up sandwiches and smooth milkshakes ($4). Photos on the wall depict local history. A fine craft shop featuring the area's specialty, moose-hair tufting, is beside the Snowshoe Inn Restaurant.

SOUTH SLAVE

The South Slave Region, encompassing the area south of Great Slave Lake, is mostly flat forestland, cut through by big rivers and numerous spectacular waterfalls. The communities here feel more 'southern' – and aboriginal culture is less evident – than elsewhere in the territory.

MACKENZIE HIGHWAY

From the Hwy 3 junction, 23km south of the Mackenzie River, the Mackenzie Hwy (Hwy 1) branches west into the Deh Cho region and southeast into the South Slave. This latter branch is well traveled and well paved. It runs 186km to the Alberta border (and thence to Edmonton) and is dubbed the **Waterfalls Route**, due to some stunning roadside cascades.

First up along this route is **Lady Evelyn Falls Territorial Park** (tent sites $15; ☼ mid-May–Sep 15), 7km off the Mackenzie Hwy on the Kakisa access road. There's a short path to the 17m falls, which pour over an ancient,

NORTHWEST TERRITORIES

crescent-shaped coral reef. Another trail leads to the Kakisa River beneath the falls, which is a good whitefish fishing spot. The campground has showers, towering pines and, on weekends, lots of fishermen. Another 6km down the access road, on scenic Kakisa Lake, is the tiny Slavey settlement of **Kakisa** (population 40).

From the Kakisa access road it's 83km to the service-station hodge-podge of **Enterprise** (population 61). **Twin Falls Inn** (☎ 867-984-3711; r $90), at the junction of Hwys 1 and 2, offers gas, snacks and utilitarian rooms, but you need to get there before the 10pm closing time. Around the bend is **Winnie's** (☎ 867-984-3211; meals $5-10; ⏰ 7am-7pm Mon-Sat, 8am-6pm Sun), where the breakfasts are greasily good and the customers are a cross-section from the region.

South on the Mackenzie Hwy the road parallels impressive **Twin Falls Gorge Territorial Park** (⏰ mid-May–Sep 15). Despite the name, the park has three falls, linked by a 6km trail, which makes an ideal day-hike. The first, where **Escarpment Creek** spills into the Hay River, can be accessed from the Escarpment Creek Group Campsite just south of Enterprise. The second, 3km down the highway, is the tiered, 15m **Louise Falls**, on the Hay River itself. There's an extensive **campground** (tent/RV sites $15/20) with toilets and showers here. Another 2km south is the most impressive cascade, 33m **Alexandra Falls**, with a lookout and stairs down to the lip of the spillover.

At the Alberta border, 72km south, is the **60th Parallel Territorial Park**, which has a **visitors' center** (⏰ 8:30am-8:30pm mid-May–Sep 15) and **campground** (tent sites $15). The center displays aboriginal arts and crafts; the campground has toilets and showers.

HAY RIVER

On the shores of Great Slave Lake, scrubby, grubby Hay River is hard to love. Arriving from Enterprise, the first thing you'll see is the 16-story high-rise looming over the flatness. Then you'll see the sprawl – kilometers of motels (ranging in appearance from dilapidated to devastated), hulking tank farms, creaking railcars, and scores of boats and trucks decomposing in weed-choked lots. This is the NWT's third-largest community (population 3570) and the North's freight distribution center; it's the terminus of

Canada's northernmost railroad, the depot for Arctic-bound barges and the port of the Great Slave commercial fishery.

Orientation & Information
There are two distinct areas. The harbor is at the north end on Vale Island; the newer section, with the restaurants and stores, is south and will be seen first on arrival by road.

The **Visitor Information Centre** (☎ 867-874-3180; cnr Mackenzie Hwy & McBryan Dr; ⏰ 9am-9pm mid-May–mid-Sep) is packed with pamphlets. In the off-season, stop by the town hall, a block north on Commercial Dr. The library next door has free Internet access.

Sights & Activities
If it's hot and sunny, hit the Vale Island **beach** – probably the best north of the 60th parallel. Otherwise, the visitor center can provide information on hiking, flightseeing, fishing, harbor tours and canoe rentals. Frankly, though, just about anything here is available elsewhere in the NWT, and in a more appealing setting.

Sleeping
Hay River Territorial Park Campground (☎ 867-874-3772; tent/RV sites $15/20; ⏰ mid-May–Sep 15) A Frisbee's throw from the beach, this densely wooded campground has hot showers and a barbecue area. The flush toilets get two thumbs up. It's off 104th St on Vale Island.

Harbour House B&B (☎ 867-874-2233; 2 Lakeshore Dr; s/d $65/85) On pilings above a beachfront lot, this sunny, eight-room B&B is packed with arctic and nautical artifacts. Guests cook in the communal kitchen.

Ptarmigan Inn (☎ 867-874-6781, 800-661-0842; www.ptarmiganinn.com; 10J Gagnier St; s/d $120/135) In the heart of downtown, Hay River's only true hotel has clean, well-appointed rooms.

Eating
Back Eddy Cocktail Lounge & Restaurant (☎ 867-874-6680; 6 Courtoreille St; mains $15-20; ⏰ lunch & dinner Mon-Sat) This low-lit dining room is probably the NWT's finest outside of Yellowknife. Featured is fresh-caught Great Slave Lake fish, including whitefish almondine ($18).

Hay River Bakery (☎ 867-874-2322; 2-4 Courtoreille St; ⏰ 8am-6pm Mon-Fri, 9am-6pm Sat) This busy downtown lunch counter and coffee shop draws a diversity of locals. There are inexpensive doughnuts and muffins, and a soup-and-sandwich special for $6.25.

Fisherman's Wharf (cnr 101st St & 100th Ave; 🕙 10am-2pm Sat Jun 15–Sep 15) A weekly outdoor market with fresh fish and Northern-grown produce.

Design Elements (☎ 867-874-3760; 2-6 Courtoreille St; 🕙 9am-6pm Mon-Fri, 10am-6pm Sat) An oddly elegant nook, offering decent specialty coffees ($4 to $5), fruit smoothies – and tanning.

Getting There & Away

AIR
Flying to Yellowknife nearly daily (just under $200 one way, 45 minutes) are Buffalo Airways, First Air and Canadian North. Canadian North also operates direct flights to Edmonton ($320 one way, 1½ hours, three a week).

BUS
Greyhound Canada has nearly daily service to Edmonton ($145 one way, 16 hours). Frontier Coachlines goes to Yellowknife ($77, eight hours), Fort Smith ($37, three hours) and Fort Simpson ($53, six hours). The depot is just north of the Vale Island bridge.

CAR & MOTORCYCLE
By road, it's 38km to Enterprise. Along the way is the Paradise Garden farming settlement and the turnoff to Hwy 5, leading 267 km to Fort Smith.

Getting Around
Once Hwy 2 enters town it's called the Mackenzie Hwy and becomes the main drag. On Vale Island it changes names again, to 100th Ave. Both Vale Island and downtown are walkable, but they're a couple of kilometers apart, making wheels desirable. You can pick up a street map at the visitor-information centre at the entrance to town. **Reliable Cabs** (☎ 867-974-4444) provides a taxi service.

FORT SMITH
On a high bluff above the Slave River, Fort Smith feels strangely un-Northern. Maybe it's the brick homes, ball fields and water tower, or the fact that the town abuts Alberta. For years though, this spot, situated

at the end of a portage route around the Slave River Rapids, was the gateway to the North. The Hudson's Bay Company set up shop here in 1874, and until Yellowknife became the territorial capital in 1967, Fort Smith was the NWT's administrative center. Today the town remains a government hub and the headquarters of Wood Buffalo National Park. Two-thirds of the 2650 residents are Cree, Chipewyan or Métis.

Information
The **Visitor Information Centre** (☎ 867-872-3065; 108 King St; 🕙 9am-10pm) is in the recreation complex (with the bison statue in front), where the $1 showers make up for the hit-or-miss help. McDougal Rd and Portage Ave have most of the eateries, hotels and shops, including **North of 60 Books** (☎ 867-872-2606; 66 Portage Ave; 🕙 noon-6pm Tue-Sat). While you're in town, you may also want to visit the Visitors Reception Centre for Wood Buffalo National Park (see opposite).

Sights
The **Northern Life Museum** (☎ 867-872-2859; cnr King St & McDougal Rd; admission free; 🕙 10am-noon & 1-7pm Mon-Fri, 10am-noon & 1-5pm Sat-Sun Jun-Aug, 10am-5pm Mon-Fri Sep-May) highlights the region's history and culture, and displays the corpse of Canus, a whooping crane sire whose… um, efforts…helped save his species from extinction.

Fort Smith Mission Historic Park (cnr Breynat St & Mercredi Ave; admission free) commemorates the days when this was Roman Catholicism's beachhead into the North. Self-guided tour maps are available from the visitors' center.

Activities
In addition to Wood Buffalo National Park (see opposite), there are several worthwhile activities. The **rapids** in the area are famous for two things: the northernmost nesting colony of white pelicans, which can be seen fishing from midriver islands; and world-class **paddling** (see the boxed text opposite).

The Rapids of the Drowned, in front of the town, are accessible from a stairway off Wolf Ave. Upriver, the Mountain, Pelican and Cassette rapids can be viewed by **hiking** the 30km Trans Canada Trail, or by shorter **walks** beginning along the 24km road to Fort Fitzgerald.

SLAVE TO THE WAVES

Q: What do the White Nile, the Zambezi and the Slave have in common?

A: On each, the world's hardest-core kayakers get chewed up. But on the Slave, it's not by crocs.

More than a century after putting Fort Smith on the map, the Slave River Rapids are doing it again. With the worldwide boom in white-water 'playboating,' professional paddlers have begun caravanning north, lured by rumors of monster waters, where the Slave slams into the Canadian Shield.

The rapids here have six times the volume of the Grand Canyon and go on for miles, frothing with Oahu-sized whitecaps and seething with Class VI holes. There are hundreds of routes and play spots, and boaters could spend weeks without surfing the same wave twice.

However, even pros don't paddle the Slave unguided. Keith Morrison, therefore, is a good man to know. He runs **Slave Kayak Lodge** (☎ 250-318-3278, 866-588-3278; www.slavekayaklodge.com) which, for $2000, offers airfare from Edmonton, eight days of paddling, tipi accommodations, meals, and a wood-fired hot-tub to unwind in at day's end. He also rents boats and gear for $150 per week.

And lest it be thought that the Slave is the NWT's sole spot for white-water madness, think again. In 2003, pro boater Ed Lucero set a world record, plunging his kayak off 33m Alexandra Falls (p819). He is still alive.

Sleeping & Eating

Thebacha B&B (☎ 867-872-2060; taigatour@auroranet .nt.ca; 53 Portage Ave; s/d $80/95; 🖳) Thebacha offers clean, wood-paneled rooms in a pine tree–shaded home near the heart of town. The proprietors also run Taiga Tour Company (p822) and rent outdoor gear.

Pelican Rapids Inn (☎ 867-872-2789; fax 867-872-4727; 152 McDougal Rd; s/d $134/150) Across from the park visitors center, the town's best hotel has standard rooms and a **restaurant** (☎ 867-872-2729; mains $7-13; 🕙 7am-10pm Mon-Fri, 9am-10pm Sat, 9am-9pm Sun) with laughably curt service.

Gallery (☎ 867-872-5005; 195 McDougal Rd; mains $6-13; 🕙 8:30am-9pm) This Chinese, pizza, pasta and burger joint is probably Fort Smith's best eatery – but that's not saying much.

Queen Elizabeth Territorial Park (☎ 867-872-2607; tent sites $15; 🕙 mid-May–Sep 15) At the end of Tipi Trail, 4km west of the town center, this campground lies near the river bluff. Showers and firewood are available.

Getting There & Around

Northwestern Air Lease offers flights to Yellowknife ($256, one hour, daily) and Edmonton ($418, two hours, six weekly). Frontier Coachlines runs buses to Hay River ($37, three hours, three weekly). In the winter, an ice road runs to Fort MacMurray, Alberta.

From Hay River, partially paved Hwy 5 cuts through the top of Wood Buffalo National Park; for more on this drive see p822. In the winter, an ice road runs from Fort Smith to Fort McMurray, Alberta. Fort Smith proper is walkable, and McDougal Rd is the main drag. For a taxi service, try **Portage Cabs** (☎ 867-872-3333).

WOOD BUFFALO NATIONAL PARK

Straddling the Alberta-NWT border, Canada's biggest national park isn't spectacular, but it *is* weird. In this Switzerland-sized boreal flatland are salt-springs that encrust the landscape, rivers that disappear underground, and balls of mating snakes.

Another strange thing: there are no wood buffalo here. Though the park was established in 1922 to protect this larger Northern subspecies, plains bison were later imported, meaning most of the park's 4300 buffalo are mongrels. Pure wood buffalo were *removed* from the park, and now flourish along Hwy 3, the Mackenzie Hwy and the Liard Trail.

Preservation worked better with the park's whooping cranes – the last wild migratory flock on Earth. These giant birds nearly disappeared, but are rebounding thanks to international protection. They, along with millions of ducks and geese, avail themselves of park wetlands, including the enormous Peace-Athabasca Delta. Moose, caribou, bear, lynx and wolves are also residents, along with countless mosquitoes and horseflies. Come prepared for battle.

Orientation & Information

There are two main roads. One of them, Hwy 5, is the 267km partially paved route linking Hay River to Fort Smith. For much of its length it cuts through the park's northeast corner, where bison are a traffic hazard. South from Fort Smith there's a dusty 121km road to Peace Point, in the heart of the park.

Park entry is free. The park headquarters are in Fort Smith where there's an excellent **Visitors Reception Centre** (☎ 867-872-7960; www .pc.gc.ca/buffalo; 149 McDougal Rd; ⏰ 9am-noon & 1-5pm Mon-Fri, 1-5pm Sat-Sun mid-Jun–early Sep, 9am-noon & 1-5pm Mon-Fri early Sep–mid-Jun). It offers a slide show, exhibits and hiking maps.

Sights & Activities

Along Hwy 5, roadside points of interest include the karst topography at **Angus Sinkhole**, the disappearing **Nyarling River** and, just outside the park boundary, sudsy **Little Buffalo River Falls**. Further on, there's a 13km dirt side road to the **Salt Plains Lookout**, where a half-kilometer walk leads to a vast white field formed by saltwater burbling from an ancient seabed.

Along the Peace Point road is the **Salt River Day-Use Area**, home to the continent's northernmost snake hibernaculum (alas, they only have group sex in late April), and the trailhead for excellent **day hikes** to salt flats and sinkholes. Down the road 36km, at popular **Pine Lake Campground** (tent sites $10; ⏰ late May–mid-Sep), you can **swim** and bask on white-sand beaches. This is the only roadside campground in the park.

For the adventurous, there are **backcountry hiking** trails, plus **paddling** on the historical fur-trade routes along the Athabasca, Peace and Slave rivers. Contact the park well ahead of time for details and permits.

Tours

Taiga Tour Company (☎ 867-872-2060; taigatour@ auroranet.nt.ca; 53 Portage Ave) is the park's only licensed outfitter, offering wildlife-watching, dog-sledding and fishing. **Big River Air** (☎ 867-872-3030; www.bigriverair.com), located in Hanger 1 at the airport, does flightseeing, including a park tour ($95 per person, one hour).

DEH CHO

Deh cho means 'big river' in the local Slavey tongue, and this region in the southwestern NWT is awash in waterways – most notably the Mackenzie, Liard and Nahanni. The area is also blessed with mountains, comparatively warm temperatures and rich aboriginal culture.

MACKENZIE HIGHWAY

From the Hwy 3 junction, 30km south of Fort Providence, the gravel Mackenzie Hwy (Hwy 1) cuts west through 288km of flat boreal forest to Fort Simpson. This is the NWT's dullest drive, with few views or points of interest.

The blessed exception is **Sambaa Deh Falls Territorial Park** (tent sites $15; ⏰ mid-May–Sep 15), halfway to Fort Simpson. It features a marvelous roadside waterfall, a fishing spot 10 minutes' walk downstream, through multihued muskeg (look for the hidden waterfall), and the smaller Coral Falls. The pleasant, clean campground also has showers.

Another 90km further on, at the junction of the Mackenzie Hwy and Hwy 7, is the **Checkpoint**, with less-than-friendly service, expensive gas, a restaurant and a **motel** (☎ 867-695-2953; r $90; ⏰ 8am-midnight) in a mobile home.

Here, the Mackenzie Hwy becomes paved. A free car-ferry, the **MV Lafferty** (☎ 800-661-0750; ⏰ 8am-11:45pm mid-May–late Oct), crosses the Liard River just south of Fort Simpson. In winter there's an ice bridge. Traffic halts during freeze-up and thaw.

From Fort Simpson, the Mackenzie Hwy continues 222km north along the Mackenzie River to the Dene settlement of **Wrigley** (population 165). Hunting, fishing and trapping remain the basis of this mainly log-cabin village. A winter ice road continues to Tulita.

FORT SIMPSON

In Slavey, this is Liidlii Kue – where two rivers meet. The voluminous Liard and Mackenzie converge here, and for thousands of years so have the people of the southwestern NWT. Permanent settlement began with a fur-trading post in 1803, and Fort Simpson was soon the Hudson's Bay

Company's district headquarters. Today, with an easygoing blend of Slavey, Métis and European cultures, it's the administrative and transport hub of the region (population 1240) and the gateway to nearby Nahanni National Park Reserve (right).

Information

The **Visitors Information Centre** (☎ 867-695-3182; vofsvic@cancom.net; ☺ 9am-9pm Mon-Fri, 10am-7pm Sat & Sun May-Sep), at the entrance to town, has helpful staff and brochures. There's a grocery store, a gas station, a craft shop, ATMs and a bank in town, too.

Sights & Activities

There's a **walk** along the Mackenzie riverfront with views of the water and of Papal Flats, where thousands gathered to welcome the Pope in 1987. Historic **McPherson House** and the **cabin** of eccentric trapper Albert Faille are also nearby. Ask at the visitors' center for details on **historical tours**.

Sleeping & Eating

Bannockland Inn (☎ 867-695-3337; bbcanada.com/ 1831.html; s/d $135/145) This posh B&B, located 4.6km east of town, overlooks the sweeping intersection of the rivers. It's a prime choice if you have a car or another way into town.

Nahanni Inn (☎ 867-695-2201; nahanmar@cancom .net; s/d $125/150) This basic, worn hotel is on the main street at the heart of town.

Nahanni Inn Restaurant (☎ 867-695-2201; meals $10; ☺ 7am-7pm Mon-Fri, 8am-5pm Sat, 9am-5pm Sun) Downstairs from the hotel, the town's main eatery fries up standard fare like bacon and eggs and burgers.

Fort Simpson Territorial Campground (tent/RV sites $15/20; ☺ mid-May–Sep 15) In the woods between the visitors' center and Papal Flats, the campground has showers, pit toilets and pleasant campsites.

Getting There & Around

Air Tindi ($281 one way, 80 minutes, daily) and First Air ($352 one way, one hour, six weekly) operate services from Yellowknife. The latter also flies from Whitehorse ($643 one way, two hours, three a week). Frontier Coachlines operates buses from Hay River ($53 one way, six hours, twice a week). Once in Fort Simpson, the town is easily walkable.

NAHANNI NATIONAL PARK RESERVE

To many, Nahanni means wilderness. Situated in the southwestern NWT, near the Yukon border, this 4766-sq-km park embraces its namesake, the epic South Nahanni River. Untamed and pure-blooded, the river tumbles more than 500km through the jagged Mackenzie Mountains.

Dene stories of giants in the area go back thousands of years. Since the early 1900s outsiders have added their own tales about wild tribes, lost gold and mysterious deaths, including the legendary decapitation of two treasure-seeking brothers. Place names such as the Headless Range and Deadmen Valley underscore this mythology.

Appropriately, the Nahanni is a Canadian Heritage river, and the park is a Unesco world heritage site – the first place given that designation in Canada. To further protect the region, environmentalists and downstream Aboriginals are pushing to expand the park boundaries to encompass the whole watershed. Mining companies – eyeing the area's tungsten, lead, zinc and silver – don't like the idea.

Orientation & Information

You can't get here by road, yet each year about 1000 people visit. Half are paddlers on epic white-water expeditions; the others are mostly with fly-in day tours to the falls and hot springs. Admission quotas are strict: 12 guided and 12 unguided visitors per night at the Virginia Falls campground, with a maximum two-night stay. For unguided visitors (particularly in big groups), it's wise to reserve months in advance.

You can obtain park information and permits in Fort Simpson at **Parks Canada** (☎ 867-695-3151; www.parkscanada.gc.ca/nahanni; ☺ 8:30am-noon & 1-5pm Jun 15–Sep 15, 8:30am-noon & 1-5pm Mon-Fri Sep 16–Jun 14). The day-use fee is $15; longer-term visitors pay a flat fee of $100.

Sights & Activities

Near its midpoint, the Nahanni River drops 30 stories over Canada's premier cascade, **Virginia Falls**; elsewhere it's framed by canyons, flanked by caves and warmed by **Rabbitkettle Hot Springs**. Moose, wolves, grizzly bear, Dall sheep and mountain goats patrol the landscape.

Paddling is one of the most-popular activities with visitors to Nahanni National Park

Reserve. If you plan to do this independently, you should be a capable white-water paddler (in Class IV rapids). This is no pleasure float; people have died here. Consult with the park office for advice, warnings and recommendations on good maps and books. Contact the tour companies for assistance with renting canoes or rafts.

Tours

FLIGHTSEEING

The cheapest, easiest way to see the park is to join a flightseeing tour. A typical six-hour excursion departs Fort Simpson aboard a floatplane, follows the Nahanni upriver through steep-walled canyons, and then lands just above Virginia Falls. Two hours of hiking and picnicking ensue. On these tours, you pay for the plane: about $975 for a three-passenger craft, and $1200 for four. To find fellow travelers to split the cost, phone the air companies in advance, or ask around at the campground, visitors' center, hotels and restaurants in town. Flightseeing companies based in Fort Simpson are all located on Antoine Drive near the in-town airstrip:

Simpson Air (☎ 867-695-2505; www.cancom.net/~simpair)

South Nahanni Airways (☎ 867-695-2007; www.cancom.net/~snasimp)

Wolverine Air (☎ 867-695-2263; www.wolverineair.com)

PADDLING

Raft, canoe or kayak trips can be arranged with a licensed outfitter. Prices range from $3100 to $5200 depending on distance. Trips should be prebooked, preferably months in advance. Canoes are best for people with basic experience; rafts are more relaxing and are suitable for all ages.

Black Feather (☎ 705-746-1372, 888-849-7668; www.blackfeather.com)

Nahanni River Adventures (☎ 867-668-3180, 800-297-6927; www.nahanni.com)

Nahanni Wilderness Adventures (☎ 403-678-3374, 888-897-5223; www.nahanniwild.com)

Within the park, trips begin at either Rabbitkettle Lake or Virginia Falls, because that's where planes can land. For the 118km from Rabbitkettle to the falls, the river meanders placidly through broad valleys. Once the falls are portaged, it's another 252km to Blackstone Territorial Park, first through

steep-sided, turbulent canyons, and then along the broad Liard River. The lower-river trip requires seven to 10 days. From Rabbitkettle it's around 14 days.

Sleeping

Camping is allowed along the river banks. There are only four designated campgrounds; the one at Virginia Falls is staffed and has a dock for canoes and floatplanes, as well as composting toilets exposed to the grandeur of nature. The campground at Rabbitkettle Lake is also staffed.

Getting There & Away

If you're traveling independently, you'll need to charter an airplane into the park by contacting a flightseeing company.

LIARD TRAIL

At the Checkpoint, 63km south of Fort Simpson, the dirt Liard Trail (Hwy 7) branches off the Mackenzie Hwy (Hwy 1) and heads south through the Liard Valley, with the Mackenzie Mountains appearing to the west. Black bear and bison abound. The only gas station is at Fort Liard. South of there, at the British Columbia border, pavement starts. The trail links with the Alaska Hwy near Fort Nelson, making a loop through British Columbia, the NWT and Alberta possible. From Fort Simpson to Fort Nelson is 487km. Beware: in wet weather, this route can be treacherous.

Halfway between Checkpoint and Fort Liard is **Blackstone Territorial Park** (tent sites $15; ⓨ mid-May–Sep 15) with information, a campground, short hiking trails and terrific views of the mountains and the confluence of the Liard and Nahanni. Most trips down the South Nahanni end here.

Across the Liard from Blackstone is **Nahanni Butte** (population 107), a Slavey village accessible only by air charter or boat, or by ice road in winter. There's a general store, a motel and river-taxi services.

Fort Liard

Fort Liard has lush forests, prim log homes, and an economy buzzing with gas exploration. But this Dene village still values its traditions, such as weaving birch-bark baskets, which are ornately decorated with porcupine quills. These can be bought at one of the NWT's finest craft shops, **Acho Dene Native**

Crafts (☎ 867-770-4161; cnr Main St & Poplar Rd; ⏰ 9am-5pm Mon-Fri, 9am-8pm Thu, 1-5pm Sat), in the middle of town. It doubles as the visitors' center.

Before you reach the village of nearly 600 souls, the free **Hay Lake Community Campground** has drinking water, an outhouse and, if the dung heaps are any indication, a resident bison population. The **Liard Valley General Store & Motel** (☎ 867-770-4441; fax 867-770-4442; cnr Main St & Black Water Rd; s/d $95/115) is on the far side of town. It and the other motel are often full, so make reservations.

There's also a café and a service station across the road from Acho Dene Native Crafts. The British Columbia border is 38km south.

SAHTU

The northwestern region of the NWT is wide and flat. The Mackenzie River, swollen by water draining from one-fifth of Canada, wends its way across the countryside; in places it is more than 3km wide. This is popular canoe and kayak country, with some hearty souls taking advantage of the long summer days to paddle from Fort Providence to Tuktoyaktuk on the Arctic Ocean – a distance of 1800km.

NORMAN WELLS

This historic oil town lies on the northern shore of the Mackenzie River halfway between Fort Simpson and Inuvik. The town itself is primarily of interest for its links to parks such as Nahanni National Park Reserve and the Canol Heritage Trail. You can only reach the town by vehicle over winter ice roads.

Information
Norman Wells Historical Centre (☎ 867-587-2416; Mackenzie Dr; admission free; ⏰ noon-6pm Jul & Aug) Displays and videos on regional geology, arts and crafts, rivers and the Canol Heritage Trail, plus an art gallery.
Village Office (☎ 867-587-3700; www.normanwells .com) Provides general information on the area.

Sights & Activities
The **Great Norman Wells Fossil Hunt** is a week-long series of activities each August that focuses on searching for fossils along the river and canyons. Hikers can also explore fossil-laden areas such as **Fossil Canyon** by themselves. Picnicking and canoeing are possible at **Jackfish Lake**. If that doesn't keep you busy, you can make a trip to the town dump at dusk to watch the black bear.

The town is used as a jumping-off point for several canoeable rivers, including the Mountain, Keele and Natla. Some of the guide companies listed in the Nahanni National Park Reserve section (p824) lead trips here. The friendly folks at **Mountain River Outfitters** (☎ 867-587-2698; www .mountainriver.nt.ca) rent canoes, provide transportation back from the rivers, and carry Canol Heritage Trail hikers by boat across the Mackenzie River to the start of the trail.

CANOL HERITAGE TRAIL
Norman Well's main attraction is the national historic site, **Canol Heritage Trail**, which leads 372km southwest to the Yukon border. From there, a road leads to Ross River and the Yukon highway system. The trail was built at enormous monetary and human cost during WWII to transport oil to Whitehorse; Canol is shorthand for 'Canadian Oil.' However the huge project was abandoned in 1945 because the war was almost over and there were cheaper sources of oil. Today the trail is lined with derelict army camps and equipment, and should really be designated as a monument to American taxpayers, who forked out more than $300 million for its construction.

The route traverses peaks, canyons and barrens. Wildlife is abundant, and there are numerous deep river crossings along the trail. There are no facilities, although you can get a little shelter in some of the old Quonset huts. Canol Rd (Hwy 6) from Whitehorse, Yukon Territory, meets the trail on the NWT border. Hiking the whole length takes three to four weeks, and most people need to arrange food drops along the way. The beginning of the trail is flat and swampy, so day hikes from Norman Wells are not recommended. Some visitors use helicopters (available in Norman Wells, ask at the **Village Office** (☎ 867-587-3700; www.normanwells.com) or **Mountain River Outfitters** (☎ 867-587-2698; www.mountainriver.nt.ca)) to reach the most interesting parts of the trail. A couple of dozen stout souls hike the entire trail each year.

Sleeping & Eating

Mackenzie Valley Hotel (☎ 867-587-3035; www.mac
kenzievalleyhotel.com; r $120-160; ☯ year-round) This
decent place has 40 rooms with cable TV
and some feature vivid decor to counteract
the long and dim winters. There is a good
restaurant and a bar.

The other two hotels are the small **Ray-
uka Inn** (☎ 867-587-2354; rayukainn@nt.simpatico.ca;
r $115-120; ☯ year-round), which has a restau-
rant and is in the center of town, and the
Yamouri Inn (☎ 867-587-2262, 800-661-0841; r $160;
☯ year-round).

The **campground** (sites free) is inconveniently
located a few kilometers west of town.
Campers often just pitch their tents on the
riverbanks in front of the town proper. No
one seems to mind.

Getting There & Around

The only road access to Norman Wells is
by ice road in the winter. Canadian North
stops on daily flights between Yellowknife
and Inuvik. North-Wright Airways serves
Yellowknife and Inuvik (indirectly), as well
as the more isolated communities along the
river.

WESTERN ARCTIC

Inuvik, with its road link to the Yukon and
busy airport, is the base for exploring the
tiny villages and remote and wild expanses
of the Western Arctic. In comparison with
these sparsely settled areas, Inuvik seems
like a metropolis.

INUVIK

Inuvik (population 3500) lies on the East
Channel of the Mackenzie River, 97km
south of the arctic coast. It's the NWT's
second-largest town, and the tourism and
supply center for the Western Arctic.
Founded in 1955 as a government administrative post, Inuvik is a feat of engineering
considering the permanently frozen subsoil
on which it was built. The population is
equally divided between Inuit, Dene and
non-Aboriginal people.

For 56 days each year, from late June,
Inuvik has 24 hours of daylight. The first
snow falls in September. In early December the sun sets and does not rise until
January.

Inuvik has the shabby appearance typical of Northern towns, but it's a fascinating
place and worth the effort and expense to
visit, especially if you can use it as a jumping-
off point for journeys into the Arctic.

For many, just reaching the town on the
rugged and much-vaunted 747km Dempster Hwy from the Yukon is reason enough
to visit. The drive traverses vast swaths of
undisturbed wilderness and includes two
river crossings by ferry in summer. During winter, until about mid-April, you can
also try your hand on the many ice roads
around town. The one north on the Mackenzie River is like a superhighway, and it
is both a thrill and a good way to quickly
get out into the wilderness.

Information

Boreal Books (☎ 867-777-2198; 75 Mackenzie Rd;
☯ 9am-6pm Mon-Fri, 1-5pm Sat & Sun) This store has
a big selection of Northern books and topographical
and river maps. It also offers photocopying and business
services.

CIBC Bank (☎ 867-777-2848; 134 Mackenzie Rd) Has
an ATM.

Inuvik Centennial Library (☎ 867-777-8620;
100 Mackenzie Rd; ☯ 10am-6pm & 7-9pm Mon-Thu,
10am-6pm Fri, 2-5pm Sat & Sun) Free Internet access, a
used-book exchange and an excellent selection of Northern
books.

Inuvik Regional Hospital (☎ 867-777-8000; 285
Mackenzie Rd; ☯ 24hr) Large new facility across from the
visitors center.

Parks Canada (☎ 867-777-8800; 187 Mackenzie Rd;
☯ 8:30am-5pm Jun-Aug, call ahead at other times) Information on Northern national parks such as Tuktut Nogait,
Ivvavik and Aulavik. Maps for sale, and information and
videos available. Register here for trips into the parks.

Post office (☎ 867-777-2252; 187 Mackenzie Rd)

Western Arctic Visitors Centre (☎ 867-777-4727;
Dec-Feb 867-777-7237; www.inuvik.ca; 284 Mackenzie Rd;
☯ 9am-7pm Jun–mid-Sep) Has numerous displays about
the area and its ecology.

Sights

The town landmark is **Our Lady of Victory
Church** (☎ 867-777-2236; Mackenzie Rd), or Igloo
Church, with a lovely interior created by
local artists. **Jàk Park**, 6km south of town,
has a good lookout tower for viewing the
subarctic terrain.

Northern Images (☎ 867-777-2786; 115 Mackenzie Rd; ☯ Mon-Sat) is a store and gallery with
a huge range of work by Northern artists.

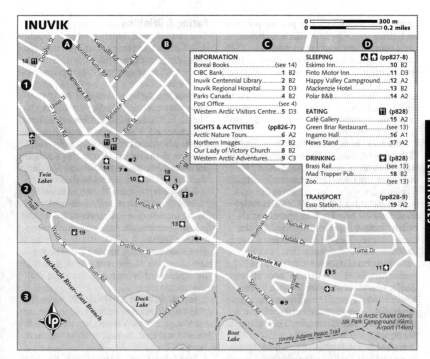

INUVIK

INFORMATION	
Boreal Books.....................(see 14)	
CIBC Bank........................1 B2	
Inuvik Centennial Library........2 B2	
Inuvik Regional Hospital.........3 D3	
Parks Canada....................4 B2	
Post Office......................(see 4)	
Western Arctic Visitors Centre...5 D3	

SIGHTS & ACTIVITIES	(pp826-7)
Arctic Nature Tours..............6 A2	
Northern Images.................7 B2	
Our Lady of Victory Church......8 B2	
Western Arctic Adventures......9 C3	

SLEEPING	(pp827-8)
Eskimo Inn.....................10 B2	
Finto Motor Inn.................11 D3	
Happy Valley Campground.....12 A2	
Mackenzie Hotel................13 B2	
Polar B&B.......................14 A2	

EATING	(p828)
Café Gallery....................15 A2	
Green Briar Restaurant..........(see 13)	
Ingamo Hall....................16 A1	
News Stand....................17 A2	

DRINKING	(p828)
Brass Rail......................(see 13)	
Mad Trapper Pub...............18 B2	
Zoo............................(see 13)	

TRANSPORT	(pp828-9)
Esso Station...................19 A2	

NORTHWEST TERRITORIES

Many of the works are created in remote aboriginal villages and are quite stunning. Stone carvings are a specialty.

Tours

The best reason to come to Inuvik is to get out of town on an arctic tour. Most involve flights over the **Mackenzie Delta**, a spectacular place of water, squalls (sudden, violent winds often with rain or snow), pingos (huge earth-covered ice hills formed by the upward expansion of underground ice), wildlife and abandoned trapper's huts on emerald-green banks. Photographers should try for a seat at the rear of the plane.

Arctic Chalet (☎ 867-777-3535; www.arcticchalet.com; 25 Carn St) Provides year-round adventure services in addition to their comfy cabins. Canoes and kayaks are available for rent during the summer, and they can help with plans. In winter, dogsled tours are run daily ($98). Participants are given the opportunity of commanding the teams of snow-white huskies over the trails.

Arctic Nature Tours (☎ 867-777-3300; www.arctic naturetours.com; 65 Mackenzie Rd) Offers a range of tours to the Mackenzie Delta and to untouched places like

Herschel Island (p804; $480 per person) Another popular day or overnight trip is to the small village of Tuktoyaktuk ($225/395 half-/full day).

Western Arctic Adventures (☎ 867-777-2594; www .inuvik.net/canoenwt; 38 Spruce Hill Dr) Rents canoes and kayaks for about $200 per week, depending on the destination, and makes logistical arrangements for independent travelers.

Festivals & Events

Sunrise Festival (☎ 867-777-2607; ☼ early Jan) Brings the locals together for fireworks on the ice to greet the first sunrise after 30 days of darkness.

Great Northern Arts Festival (☎ 867-777-3536; www.greatart.nt.ca; ☼ 3rd week of Jul) This is a major show of aboriginal art. Most of the more than 100 artists travel from remote villages to display and sell their high-quality work. There are evening dance and drumming performances, as well as workshops and demonstrations during the day.

Sleeping

Arctic Chalet (☎ 867-777-3535; www.arcticchalet.com; 25 Carn St; r $110) The Arctic Chalet, with its bright cabin-style rooms situated in a pretty setting, is the best place to stay in

Inuvik. Each building has private porches and there are simple kitchen facilities in each unit. The energetic owners also rent canoes, kayaks and cars, run dogsledding tours and are also good sources of local info. The Chalet is about 3km from town towards the airport (or about a 20-minute walk). There is a rustic cabin sans facilities ($40) for travelers who want a true pioneering experience.

Polar B&B (☎ 867-777-2554; www.inuvik.net/polar; 75 Mackenzie Rd; r from $95) This centrally located B&B has four large rooms with shared bath, common area and kitchen, and includes free laundry.

Finto Motor Inn (☎ 867-777-2647; 288 Mackenzie Rd; s/d $160/175) The Finto is one of the three hotels in town operated by the Mackenzie Delta Hotel Group (www.inuvikhotels .com), a local corporation that has enjoyed an unfortunate lack of competition. The motor inn is at the eastern end of town and has good views to the south. The rooms have enjoyed a recent revamp and now have large TVs, some kitchenettes and, most importantly, new furniture. The lounge is pleasant.

Mackenzie Hotel (☎ 867-777-2861; 185 Mackenzie Rd; s/d $150/165) Right in the center of town, the Mackenzie has little to boast about beyond its typically cheery employees. Rooms are aged and the hallways will quickly inspire a sense of gloom that only 24 hours of sunshine can possibly chase away. The hotel is home to the popular Green Briar Restaurant.

Eskimo Inn (☎ 867-777-2801; 133 Mackenzie Rd; s/d $150/165) Just up the street from the Mackenzie, the Eskimo has much in common with its nearby sibling. The warren of corridors lead to uninspired rooms. The restaurant and lounge are not places you'll want to linger in.

Jàk Park Campground (☎ 867-777-3613; tent/RV sites $10/20; ☼ Jun-Sep) This pretty government-run campground, about 6km south of town on the Dempster Hwy, provides hot showers and firewood. There's a good view of the delta and the breeze keeps the mosquitoes down a bit.

Happy Valley Campground (☎ 867-777-3652; Franklin Road; tent/RV sites $10/20; ☼ Jun-Sep) Offering the same services as Jàk Park Campground, Happy Valley has nice views and a coin laundry.

Eating & Drinking

You can get good, hearty food in Inuvik but don't expect anything that will have you clamoring for the recipe. Various Northern critters such as caribou turn up on most local menus.

Green Briar Restaurant (☎ 867-777-4671; 185 Mackenzie Rd; meals $10-25; ☼ lunch & dinner) In the Mackenzie Hotel, Green Briar has arctic foods like char and musk ox, and a very popular prime-rib special on Thursday nights, which sells out to the locals. There's also a pub, the **Brass Rail** (☼ 11am-2am Mon-Sat) and the dance club **Zoo** (☼ 9pm-2am Fri & Sat) in the hotel.

Café Gallery (☎ 867-777-2888; 90 Mackenzie Rd; meals $4-10; ☼ 8am-8pm Mon-Fri, noon-8pm Sat & Sun) This pleasant café has espresso, fresh sandwiches, homemade soup and muffins.

News Stand (☎ 867-777-4822; 90 Mackenzie Rd; ☼ 8:30am-midnight) This well-stocked grocery lives up to its name with same-day newspapers arriving every day from major Canadian cities.

Ingamo Hall (☎ 867-777-2166; 20 Mackenzie Rd; meals free; ☼ lunch every 2nd Thu) This is primarily for village elders. Visitors are welcome but should call first. Expect to hear wonderful stories.

Mad Trapper Pub (☎ 867-777-3825; 124 Mackenzie Rd; ☼ 11am-2am Mon-Sat) This raucous pub snares locals and visitors alike. Pool tables add to the fun.

Getting There & Away
AIR
Mike Zubko Airport (YEV) is 14km south of town. It has a decent café. **Town Cab** (☎ 867-777-4777) charges $25 to/from the airport.

Air North operates flights to Dawson City, Old Crow and Whitehorse. Aklak Air has scheduled services to Aklavik, Tuktoyaktuk and Sachs Harbour. It also offers charter service to the smaller arctic communities and the national parks. Canadian North services Norman Wells (daily) and Yellowknife (daily), where you can make connecting flights to Calgary and Edmonton. First Air operates flights to Yellowknife, where there are connections throughout the North.

BUS
In summer, **Dawson City Courier** (☎ 867-993-6688) offers a shuttle service from Dawson City, Yukon, to Inuvik ($261 one way).

CAR

Arctic Chalet Car Rental (☎ 867-777-3535; www .arcticchalet.com; 25 Carn St) rents a range of vehicles and has a counter at the airport. **NorCan/ National Car & Truck Rental** (☎ 867-777-2346, 800-227-7368; norcan@permafrost.com) also has an airport counter.

If you are driving, it's vital that you check Dempster Hwy road and ferry conditions (☎ 800-661-0750). In town, there's an **Esso Gas Station** (☎ 867-777-3974; 17 Distributor St; ☽ 8am-9pm).

Getting Around

Inuvik has a compact centre that is easily walked.

AKLAVIK

Aklavik, 113km north of the Arctic Circle and about 50km west of Inuvik, is home to the Inuvialuit and the Gwich'in, who have, over the centuries, traded and sometimes fought each other in this region. Aklavik was, for a time, the administrative center of the area, but serious flooding and erosion from the Mackenzie Delta prompted the Canadian government to select a new site at Inuvik in the 1950s. Many residents have remained in town, refusing to move to drier land. For local information contact the **hamlet office** (☎ 867-978-2351). Inuvik tour companies (see p814) visit Aklavik, and it is reachable by ice road in winter.

TUKTOYAKTUK

About 137km northeast of Inuvik, in Kugmallit Bay on the arctic coast, is Tuktoyaktuk, commonly known as Tuk. Originally the home of the whale-hunting Inuit, it's a land base for some of the Beaufort Sea oil and gas explorations.

Pods of beluga whales can be seen in July and early August. The Tuk peninsula has the world's highest concentration of pingos. Some 1400 of these huge mounds of earth and ice made by frost heaves dot the landscape and have been designated the **Pingo National Monument**. The **hamlet office** (☎ 867-977-2286) can provide more information on the area and services.

There is an old **military base** here, dating from the cold war, as well as old **whaling buildings**, and two charming little **churches** dating from the time when the Catholic and Anglican churches battled to proselytize the Aboriginal people. Land access is limited to a winter ice road, and most tourists arrive by air in the summer as part of half-day trips from Inuvik.

PAULATUK

This small Karngmalit community of 300 residents is on the arctic coast near the mouth of the Hornaday River, about 400km east of Inuvik. The town's name means 'soot of coal'; one of the main attractions is the **Smoking Hills**, which contain smoldering sulfide-rich slate and seams of coal. For more information, contact the **hamlet office** (☎ 867-580-3531).

Paulatuk is the closest settlement to **Tuktut Nogait National Park**, a wild and untouched place about 45km east that is a major calving ground for Bluenose caribou. There are no services or facilities here, however a small **visitors' center** for the park is open for inspection in town during the summer. For information, contact **Parks Canada** (☎ 867-777-8800; 187 Mackenzie Rd; ☽ 8:30am-5pm Jun-Aug, call ahead at other times) in Inuvik.

BANKS ISLAND

Lying in the Arctic Ocean to the north of Paulatuk, Banks Island may have been first inhabited 3500 years ago. Wildlife is abundant, and this is one of the best places to see musk ox. The island has two bird sanctuaries where you can see flocks of snowgeese and seabirds in the summer. **Sachs Harbour**, also known as Kiaahuk, an Inuvialuit community of about 150, is the only settlement on the island. Contact the **hamlet office** (☎ 867-690-4351) for information.

Kuptana's Guest House (☎ /fax 867-690-4151; r $180) has rooms that include all meals in their price. It organizes nature tours of the island.

Aulavik National Park, on the north of the island, covers 12,275 sq km. It has the world's largest concentration of musk ox as well as badlands, tundra and archaeological sites. The name means 'place where people travel' and that's what you'll have to do to get there. Contact **Parks Canada** (☎ 867-777-8800; 187 Mackenzie Rd; ☽ 8:30am-5pm Jun-Aug, call ahead at other times) in Inuvik for details on visiting the park.

There is a scheduled air service to Sachs Harbour from Inuvik.

Nunavut

CONTENTS

NUNAVUT

Nunavut is the arctic archetype: an unfathomable vastness of glaciers, sea ice, craggy mountains and boundless tundra, patrolled by polar bear, lashed by winds and locked solid by cold. This is harsh country, and consequently it's almost unpopulated. There are fewer humans here than in Monaco, in a million times the space.

But for the folks who *are* here – the Inuit – that harshness is heaven-sent. It means they, unlike other Aboriginals in the hemisphere, hold sway over their indigenous territory. They've thrived for eons in a land that even today rebuffs pavement, lacks Big Macs and drives Euro-Canadian folks bananas. And despite dysfunction aplenty – everything from litter to suicide – the Inuit remain optimistic.

Appropriately, in Inuktitut, *nunavut* means 'our land.' Inuit form 85% of the population, and enjoy democratic control of the government and legal title to millions of acres. But Nunavut governs them too. Natural rhythms prevail, and if you visit when caribou are in the hills, or whales are in the bay, you may find everyone has closed up shop and gone hunting.

For travelers, Nunavut is a paradox: it's so bizarre and imposing that you'll never grow complacent, but unless you have sacks of cash, you'll quickly run out of affordable things to do. You'll also need patience. Polar weather plays havoc with itineraries. Moreover, people here – even those who work with visitors – can seem maddeningly unhelpful and uninterested.

The cheapest prices and best tourism infrastructure are on southern Baffin Island, which has several intriguing communities and some stellar, primeval parks for hiking, paddling and wildlife-viewing. The more adventuresome can head to even-less-visited areas, such as the Kivalliq region on the Hudson Bay coast, the Kitikmeot on the Arctic shore, or the end-of-the-Earth islands of the High Arctic.

NUNAVUT

HIGHLIGHTS

- Hike past a kilometer-high cliff and across the Arctic Circle on **Akshayuk Pass** (p838)
- Float by caribou, waterfalls and a miniature polar forest on the Eden-like **Soper River** (p837)
- Watch a carver conjure spirits out of soapstone in the Inuit art capital of **Cape Dorset** (p838)
- Tuck into a meal of *maktaaq* (rubbery chunks of whale skin and blubber) at one of the many eateries in **Iqaluit** (p834)
- Observe the sun spiral in the sky without setting in desolate **Resolute** (p839)

Resolute ★
Akshayuk ★ Pass
★ Iqaluit
Cape Dorset ★   Soper River

POPULATION: 29, 384 ▪ TERRITORIAL CAPITAL: IQALUIT ▪ AREA: 2,093,190 KM

NUNAVUT

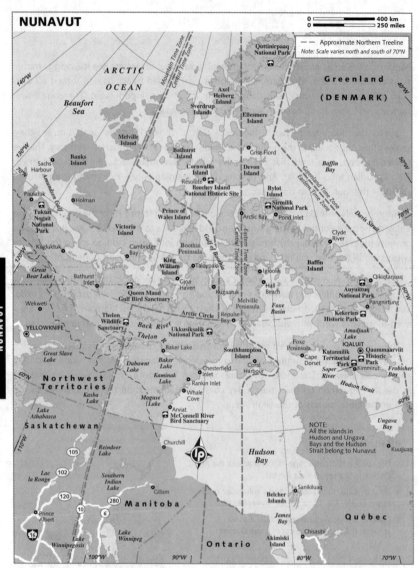

NUNAVUT

	0	400 km
	0	250 miles

- - - Approximate Northern Treeline
Note: Scale varies north and south of 70°N

History

Nunavut has been peopled for about 4000 years, though the Inuit arrived just a millennium ago, migrating from Alaska. For countless generations they lived here nomadically, pursuing game as the season dictated and devising an ingenious material culture to cope with the conditions.

Though Vikings may have visited Baffin Island – Helluland, in the sagas – the first definitive European arrival was in 1576, when Martin Frobisher came seeking the Northwest Passage. For the next 375 years the Arctic saw more explorers (including Sir John Franklin, who disappeared here in 1845), whalers, traders and missionaries. In a vast land, these visits had comparatively little impact on the Inuit.

Then, after WWII, Nunavut's history went supersonic. Canada finally took interest in the Arctic, recognizing its strategic importance. In the 1950s and '60s Inuit were settled into villages and, in some cases, relocated to the High Arctic to bolster national sovereignty.

In the 1960s and '70s rising political awareness among the Inuit inspired dreams of self-government. After years of negotiations, in 1999 Canada's map was redrawn. Nunavut split from the Northwest Territories and became a separate territory. Many of the Inuit who now govern here were born in igloos and raised nomadically. They've experienced more change in their lifetimes than Europe has in a thousand years.

Climate
Unsurprisingly, it's chilly here. Even in summer snowdrifts linger, the sea stays frozen until July, and the tundra turns red and yellow in August. Midsummer highs average 12°C in Iqaluit and 7°C farther north in Resolute. This isn't to say it never warms up: the community of Baker Lake once baked at 33.6°C. Also on the upside, because the Arctic is technically a desert, there's little rain. And from May to mid-August, you'll enjoy perpetual daylight.

Winter – from September to May – can be excruciating. Though ambient winter temperatures are sometimes warmer here than south of the tree line, relentless winds create hard-to-fathom chill factors, such as the -92°C reading once recorded at Kugaaruk.

The prime visitor season is July and August. For dogsledding and other snow sports, come in late April or May.

National & Territorial Parks
Of Nunavut's three national parks, the most accessible is Auyuittuq National Park (p838), amid the glaciers, fjords and sky-high cliffs of eastern Baffin Island. Similarly rugged – but bankrupting to get to – is Quttinirpaaq National Park (p840), Canada's northernmost park, on far-flung Ellesmere Island. There are two new parks: Sirmilik National Park (p839), on the north coast of Baffin Island, is home to sprawling glaciers, sky-scraping peaks and sea-bird colonies. A still-in-the-works fourth park,

Ukkusiksalik, will soon provide a haven for the whales and bear of Wager Bay in the northern Kivalliq region. For information, contact the Iqaluit branch of **Parks Canada** (☎ 867-975-4673; nunavut.info@pc.gc.ca).

Nunavut also has several territorial parks. Some are mere campgrounds, others are historic sites, and a few – like Katannilik Territorial Park (p837), near Iqaluit – are sizable, spectacular national treasures. All are free.

In parks, and everywhere else in Nunavut, wildlife rules. Breeding ground–bound waterfowl fill the sky by the millions; caribou, musk ox, wolves and snowshoe hare inhabit the tundra, while the oceans are home to seals, walruses, three kinds of whales – beluga, bowhead and narwhal – and the arctic icon, the polar bear.

Because of the short summers, plants are tough, tiny and delicate. Flowers endure 10 months of ice before exploding into bloom. Other plants grow slowly: shrubs the diameter of a thumb might be 400 years old.

Dangers & Annoyances
Polar bear aren't just on Nunavut's license plates. Nanuq is an inveterate wanderer and can turn up just about anywhere, any time

---

LANGUAGE

Forget English versus French: here, Inuktitut is king. It's the primary tongue of 70% of Nunavummiut, and the only language for many elders and children. It's not easy to grasp, being guttural as well as polysynthetic (meaning words morph together to form paragraph-sized monsters), and it's also hard to read, because it's mostly written in syllabics (an inscrutable orthographic system based on syllables instead of letters).

You'll get by fine if you combine English, hand gestures and a sense of humor. Still, a few local words will help bridge the cultural divide:

How are you?	Qanuippit?	ka-nwee-peet?
I am fine	Qanuingi	ka-nweeng-ee
Thank you	Qujannamiik	coy-ahn-nah-meek
You're welcome	Ilaali	ee-lah-lee
Yes	Ii	ee
No	Aakka	ah-kah
Good morning	Ullaakkut	ood-lahk-kut
Good afternoon	Unnusakkut	oo-noo-sahk-koot

of year. Worse, unlike grizzlies and black bear, they actively prey on people. Inquire about bear sightings before trudging out of town, or go with a shotgun-toting guide.

Getting There & Away

Flights are the only way to get here, and they cost a king's ransom. Iqaluit has nearly daily arrivals from Montréal and Ottawa aboard First Air and Canadian North for about $1300 return. Both airlines serve Iqaluit from Yellowknife for about $1400 return. See p869 for airline contact details.

Rankin Inlet is linked to Winnipeg by Calm Air (p869), **Kivalliq Air** (☎ 877-855-1500; www.kivalliqair.com) and First Air for between $1300 and $1500 return. Cambridge Bay is accessible from Yellowknife on First Air and Canadian North for about $900 return.

Getting Around

With only 21km of highway (linking Arctic Bay to a mine), Nunavut isn't exactly road-accessible. Smaller communities are reached by air from three hubs. From Iqaluit, First Air and **Kenn Borek Air** (☎ 867-252-3845; www .borekair.com) serve the High Arctic and Baffin Island. From Rankin Inlet, Calm Air and Kivalliq Air cover the Kivalliq region. From Cambridge Bay, First Air covers the Kitikmeot region.

Even hardened travelers may be daunted by Nunavut's logistical complexities. Thankfully, scores of organized tours and packages are available. There's a list of international and local tour providers in the *Nunavut Travel Planner* (see the boxed text below).

NUNAVUT: BREAKING THE ICE

Nunavut isn't a place to visit on a whim; do your homework. **Nunavut Tourism** (☎ 866-686-2888, 867-979-6551; www.nunavut tourism.com) produces the annual *Nunavut Travel Planner*, with lots of practical information. More detailed is the *Nunavut Handbook*, an encyclopedic guide written by longtime residents. It can be ordered from **Nortext Multimedia** (☎ 613-727-5466, 800-263-1452; www.arctic-travel.com) or purchased in Iqaluit. **Parks Nunavut** (☎ 867-975-5900; www.nunavutparks.com) has a great website with details on territorial parks and visitors centers.

IQALUIT

Nunavut's capital, Iqaluit (ee-*kal*-oo-eet), is the unlikeliest of Canadian cities, at once ancient and space-age, ramshackle and chic, exotic and all too familiar. Unlike the territory's insular villages, this boomtown throngs with newcomers: Ottawa technocrats and Québecois cabbies, plus Inuit professionals and politicians from around the Arctic. Many of these Inuit walk in two worlds (as the cliché goes), wearing sealskin parkas over Montréal fashions and – in at least one case – monitoring choice hunting spots via webcam.

The dusty, debris-strewn townscape of Iqaluit, with its moon-base buildings and tangle of above-ground pipes, is perversely fascinating for a while, and there are some sights, restaurants and shops worth a stop. However, real life here takes place on the land, and most visitors head out there, hiking along the Sylvia Grinnell River or taking a boat tour to Qaummaarviit Historic Park.

HISTORY

Each summer, for centuries, nomadic Inuit trekked to Sylvia Grinnell River to spear char in the roiling waters. They called the area Iqaluit (place of fish).

In 1576, Martin Frobisher showed up. The English naval captain, on a quest for the fabled Northwest Passage, had made a wrong turn into what's now Frobisher Bay. There he unearthed glittering yellow ore, mined it, and sailed home with a million-plus pounds of worthless iron pyrite.

For another 350 years local Inuit kept fishing, interrupted occasionally by whalers, explorers and missionaries. Then, during WWII, American servicemen established an airbase. After the war, Canadian forces stayed on, and the outpost, named Frobisher Bay, became the administrative center of the eastern Arctic.

In 1987 the community officially changed its name to Iqaluit, and in 1995 voters picked it (over Rankin Inlet) to be Nunavut's capital.

ORIENTATION

Set amid high, rocky hills overlooking Koojesse Inlet, Iqaluit is a city planner's

NUNAVUT IN...

Two Days

After arriving in **Iqaluit** (opposite), get your bearings via a guided **city historical tour** (p836). Then revel in contemporary Inuit art at the **Nunatta Sunakkutaangit Museum** (below), **Legislative Assembly** (below) and **galleries** (p837). By now parched and famished, join half of Iqaluit for beer and a burger at the **Storehouse Bar & Grill** (p837).

On the second day, get out of town – first, aboard a boat tour to **Qaummaarviit Historic Park** (p836), and then by stalking fox and snowy owls in **Sylvia Grinnell Territorial Park** (p836).

One Week

On the third day, make a splash in **Katannilik Territorial Park** (p837): rent a canoe from an Iqaluit outfitter and fly to the **Soper River** (p837). For the next five days, float through a polar paradise, bathing under waterfalls and slipping silently past caribou on the riverbank.

Two Weeks

After exercising your arms on the Soper, it's time to work those legs. Fly to **Pangnirtung** (p838), check out the **Uqqurmiut Centre for Arts & Crafts** (p838) then catch a boat ride to **Auyuittuq National Park** (p838). Hike pristine, surreal **Akshayuk Pass** (p838) beneath icy spires and the tallest cliffs you'll ever see.

nightmare. In the past decade the population has doubled (to nearly 6000), causing sprawl and traffic snarls – obviously unusual in the Arctic. The erection of street signs has been an ongoing ordeal, so most homes go by unique numbers, while major buildings are identified by name. Cabbies know where everything is, but if you're walking, get a tourist map from the visitors center.

The heart of Iqaluit is the 'Four Corners' – the intersection of Queen Elizabeth Way and Niaqunngusiaq Rd. These two streets loop around to form what is colloquially called the Ring Rd, encircling the city's jumbled core. Within the ring is the most prominent landmark, the towering Astro Hill complex.

A few kilometers east of town by road is Apex, where Inuit lived during WWII.

INFORMATION

Ambulance & Fire (☎ 867-979-4422) For emergencies. Note that ☎ 911 is not the emergency number in Nunavut.

Arctic Ventures (☎ 867-979-5992; Queen Elizabeth Way; ⏰ 10am-10pm Mon-Sat, noon-5pm Sun) Tucked away upstairs is an excellent, eclectic selection of Arctic books and CDs.

Baffin Regional Hospital (☎ 867-979-7300; Niaqunngusiaq Rd; ⏰ 24hr) Nunavut's only hospital is undergoing a major expansion.

Iqaluit Centennial Library (☎ 867-979-5400; Sinaa St; ⏰ 1-6pm Mon & Wed, 3-8pm Tue & Thu, 3-6pm Fri, 1-4pm Sat & Sun) In the visitors center building, with free Internet.

Police (☎ emergencies 867-979-1111, nonemergencies 867-975-0123) Note that ☎ 911 is not the emergency number in Nunavut.

Royal Bank of Canada (☎ 867-979-8700; cnr Queen Elizabeth Way & Niaqunngusiaq Rd) This bank is at the Four Corners intersection. Nearby is the CIBC.

Unikkaarvik Visitors Centre (☎ 867-979-4636; Sinaa St; ⏰ 10am-6pm Mon-Fri, 1-4pm Sat & Sun) Has ample pamphlets, an informative mini-museum and a reference collection of Nunavut books and videos. Topographical maps can also be purchased here.

SIGHTS

Nunavut's prefab **Legislative Assembly** (☎ 867-975-5000, 877-334-7266; Federal Rd; admission free; ⏰ 9am-5pm Mon-Fri, tours 1:30pm Mon-Fri Jun-Aug or by appointment) is no marble-columned parliament, but has touches such as sealskin benches and a narwhal-tusk ceremonial mace. Local art is displayed in the foyer.

Nunatta Sunakkutaangit Museum (☎ 867-979-5537; Sinaa St; admission free; ⏰ 1-5pm Tue-Sun), though itty-bitty, is worth a look. It permanently displays traditional Inuit garments, tools and carvings, and has a more interesting gallery with ever-changing exhibits of contemporary northern art.

The **waterfront**, between the breakwater and Coast Guard Station, is the locus of traditional Inuit activity. Amid the old snowmobiles and fuel cans, hunters butcher seals and build boats and sleds. Ask before taking photos.

Since you can't go inside, and there's not much signage outside, the old red-and-white **Hudson Bay Trading Post** (Bill Mackenzie Rd) is interesting mainly for its plum location on sandy **Apex Beach**.

ACTIVITIES

Hiking on spongy, hummocky tundra can be wearisome, but the lack of trees makes route-finding a snap. There are often caribou and fox at **Sylvia Grinnell Territorial Park** (Iqaluit Rd; admission free) where paths lead to a waterfall, rapids and escarpments. The park is 2km out of town; head toward the airport, then follow the signs. Other excellent hikes include tracing the waterfront from downtown to Apex or, at low tide, exploring Tarr Inlet beyond Apex.

Not keen on perambulating? Four-wheelers are available from **C&C Rentals** (☎ 867-975-1514, 867-979-4008; per hr/12hr $25/120). In winter, several companies rent **snowmobiles**; ask for details at the **visitors center** (☎ 867-979-4636; Sinaa St; ◷ 10am-6pm Mon-Fri, 1-4pm Sat & Sun).

Alas, no one currently rents **kayaks**, but this may change. It's worth asking around, because Koojesse and Tarr inlets have great paddling.

Blueberry picking is a tasty way to get familiar with the exquisite, delicate tundra. Berries flourish near the river and above Apex. Take a container, or gobble as you go.

TOURS

Though outfitters vary from year to year, there's usually a range of tours available, from helicopter flights to dogsled journeys. Consult the *Nunavut Travel Planner* or the staff at the visitors center for specifics. Most tours require minimum numbers, so bring friends or reserve early so other visitors can be rounded up.

Polynya Adventure (☎ 867-979-6260, 866-366-6784; www.polynya.ca) acts as an intermediary for several tour providers. Among their offerings are: 1½-hour city historical tours ($40), guided 1½-hour nature hikes along the Sylvia Grinnell River ($40), two-hour jet-boat rides upriver ($125), hour-long flightseeing trips ($125), or the recommended two-hour boat excursions ($125) to Qaummaarviit Historic Park, 12km from town. The park preserves a 750-year-old Inuit winter camp. Sod houses – and human bones – are still there.

SLEEPING

Camping is the only cheap option. For everything else, book ahead and prepare to hemorrhage cash.

Accommodations By The Sea (☎ 867-979-6074; www.accommodationsbythesea.ca; Bldg 2536, Paurngaq Rd; s/d incl breakfast $120/140) About 2km from downtown, this spacious house has excellent views of the bay. Guests prepare their own breakfasts with food provided.

Crazy Caribou Bed and Breakfast (☎ 867-979-2449, 866-341-4441; www.crazycariboubedandbreakfast.com; Bldg 490, Atungauyait St; s/d incl breakfast $120/140) This cozy Inuit-owned place has comfortable rooms, a sauna and free rides from the airport.

Frobisher Inn (☎ 867-979-2222, 877-422-9422; www.frobisherinn.com; Astro Hill; s & d $210) Up on the hill, the 'Frobe' has modern bayside rooms with marvelous views. There's a good restaurant, and the Astro Hill complex has a coffee shop, a pool, a bar and a movie theater.

Sylvia Grinnell Territorial Park (Iqaluit Rd; tent sites free) There are no facilities here except pit toilets.

EATING

For eons, Inuit survived on almost nothing but meat. Vegetarians may feel Iqaluit's restaurants are upholding that tradition.

Snack (☎ 867-979-6767; Nipisa St; breakfasts $9-11, sandwiches $6-15; ◷ 6am-8pm) A Francophone-run diner bedecked with 1950s kitsch which serves cheap, decent, mainstream meals (on paper plates).

Wizard's Bistro (☎ 867-979-4726; Bldg 1107, Ikaluktuutiak St; lunches $8-16; ◷ 11am-9pm Mon-Thu, 11am-10pm Fri & 6-10pm Sat) Wizard's conjures up good pastries, wraps and lunch specials, like Reuben with mulligatawny soup ($14). Sadly, the service is far from magical.

Kamotiq Inn (☎ 867-979-5937; Cnr Queen Elizabeth Way & Four Corners; most dishes $14-22; ◷ 11:30am-10pm) This geodesic igloo has a dubious history of health violations. It offers pizza, burgers and (we dare you) raw, frozen *maktaaq* – rubbery chunks of whale skin and blubber ($27).

Discovery Lodge Hotel (☎ 867-979-4433; Niurai-vik St; mains $30-45; ⏰ 6-9am, noon-2pm & 6-9pm) Nunavut's top dining room has an extensive wine list and luscious local cuisine, like poached arctic char ($38) and caribou steak in peppercorn sauce ($39).

Frobisher Inn (☎ 867-979-2222; Astro Hill; mains $25-40; ⏰ 7am-2pm & 5-9pm Mon-Fri, 8am-2pm & 5-9pm Sat & Sun) A close second to the Discovery, offering caribou, char, pasta and steak. In the evening, artists hawk their wares in the dining room.

DRINKING

In Iqaluit, almost all crimes, as well as the astronomical suicide rate, are linked to drinking. To combat this, the town clamps down on alcohol. Beer and wine can be had with a meal at several restaurants, but there's no liquor store and only one public bar.

Storehouse Bar & Grill (☎ 867-979-2222; Astro Hill; ⏰ 5pm-12:30am) This big, new, well-appointed watering hole is less of a madhouse than the former saloon, although this writer *was* knocked from his stool by drunken brawlers. The food (pizza and burgers) here is yummy.

Fantasy Palace (☎ 867-979-3963; Bldg 1085E, Mivvik St; ⏰ 8am-6pm Mon-Fri, 10am-5pm Sat, 11am-5pm Sun) Also called the 'Belly Button,' due to the fashions of a former proprietor, Iqaluit's upscale coffeehouse offers cappuccinos and lattes (large $4.25), plus ice cream and pastries.

SHOPPING

Inuit prints, carvings and tapestries are world renowned, and there are a couple of high-end galleries in Iqaluit. For deals on less-refined pieces, have dinner at the Frobisher Inn, where artists circulate through the dining room offering their works for sale.

Northern Country Arts (☎ 867-979-0067; www .northerncountryarts.ca; Bldg 1555, Federal Rd; ⏰ 8:30am-5:30pm Mon-Fri, 1-4pm Sat) This well-established place has a middle-of-nowhere location, but also a decent selection of quality antler, whalebone and soapstone carvings, plus tapestries, prints, Pangnirtung hats and a few Northern books and CDs.

Coman Arctic Galleries (☎ 867-979-6300; Bldg 1127, Mivvik St; ⏰ 9am-5pm Mon-Fri) Right across from the airport terminal, this gallery usually has a large selection of carvings.

For details on how to distinguish genuine art from fakes, see the boxed text on p859.

GETTING THERE & AROUND

Most flights from outside the territory land here (p834) and flights to the smaller Baffin communities depart from here. First Air serves all communities on the island, plus Resolute and Rankin Inlet. Kenn Borek Air operates services to fewer destinations but is often cheaper. Canadian North goes to Rankin.

Iqaluit is compact and, despite the dearth of sidewalks, thoroughly walkable. Even the airport is an easy stroll from downtown, about half a kilometer along Mivvik St. The city is also awash with cabs that charge $5 to anywhere. Expect to share: drivers often load to capacity before making drop-offs. Try **Pai-Pa Taxi** (☎ 867-979-5222).

BAFFIN REGION

The Baffin region comprises Nunavut's constellation of eastern and High Arctic islands. It reaches from the swampy, forested isles of James Bay to the jagged peaks of Ellesmere Island, 3000km north. Half of Nunavut's population lives in this region, and visitors will find the best scenery, outdoor opportunities and tourism infrastructure here.

KATANNILIK TERRITORIAL PARK

One of the finest parks in Nunavut is just a few dozen kilometers – by foot, flight or snowmobile – from Iqaluit. *Katannilik* means 'place of waterfalls,' and comprises two main features: the Soper River and the Itijjagiaq Trail.

A Canadian Heritage waterway, the aquamarine **Soper River** splashes 50 navigable kilometers through a deep, fertile valley, past cascades, caribou, gemstone deposits and dwarf-willow forests, to the community of Kimmirut (population 433). Paddlers usually spend three days to a week floating and exploring.

Hikers and skiers can opt for the **Itijjagiaq Trail**, a traditional 120km route over the tablelands of the Meta Incognita Peninsula and through the Soper valley. The hike usually takes 10 or 12 days. The trailhead is on Frobisher Bay, about 10km west of Iqaluit.

NUNAVUT

For more details, contact **Parks Nunavut** (☎ 867-975-5900; www.nunavutparks.com).

Most paddlers charter a plane from Iqaluit to the riverside airstrip at Mt Joy, float from the put-in to Kimmirut, and then fly back to Iqaluit. Kenn Borek Air charges $1634 from Iqaluit to Mt Joy and can carry 1090kg of people and gear. For hikers, you can hire an Iqaluit outfitter to take you to the trailhead by boat; ask for names at the **Unikkaarvik Visitors Centre** (☎ 867-979-4636; Sinaa St; ☽ 10am-6pm Mon-Fri, 1-4pm Sat & Sun) in Iqaluit.

First Air (p869) flies from Kimmirut to Iqaluit four times weekly ($143 one way).

PANGNIRTUNG

Among Nunavut's outlying communities, Pangnirtung, or 'Pang,' is the best destination, with art and outdoor opportunities galore. The community of 1400, 40km south of the Arctic Circle, hugs a stunning fjord and is the gateway to Auyuittuq National Park.

Information

Angmarlik Interpretive Centre (☎ 867-473-8737; fax 867-473-8685; ☽ 8:30am-9pm Jul & Aug, 8:30am-5pm Mon-Fri Sep-Jun) Has displays on Inuit life and information on local guides and outfitters.

Parks Canada (☎ 867-473-8828; www.parkscanada .gc.ca; ☽ 8:30am-5pm Jul & Aug, 8:30am-5pm Mon-Fri Sep-Jun) Next door to the interpretive center.

Sights & Activities

The town is famous for tapestries, prints and woven hats, all available at the **Uqqurmiut Centre for Arts & Crafts** (☎ 867-473-8669; inuitart@nunanet.com; ☽ 9am-noon, 1-5pm & 6-9pm Mon-Sat Jul & Aug, 9am-noon & 1-5pm Mon-Fri Sep-Jun).

Two hiking paths begin in Pang. The 6km **Ukama Trail** follows the Duval River and takes three hours. The highly recommended 13km **Ikuvik Trail** summits Mt Duval (671m), about a six-hour round-trip. Though not always well marked, it offers superb views of the town and the fjord. Get a map at the interpretive center.

About 50km south of town is **Kekerten Historic Park**, an old whaling station on an island. A trail leads past the remains of 19th-century houses, tools and graves. A boat tour ($160 per person, minimum four people) takes 12 hours. Outfitters can also take you wildlife-watching or fishing. The

Angmarlik Interpretive Centre can put you in touch with the best ones.

Sleeping & Eating

The only hotel is **Auyuittuq Lodge** (☎ 867-473-8955; fax 867-473-8611; s/d $150/300, incl meals $215/430), just down the street from the interpretive centre, with rudimentary, shared rooms and shared bathrooms. Book early. If you opt not to eat here, you can self-cater from the **Northern Store** (☎ 867-473-8935; ☽ 10am-6pm Mon-Sat, noon-5pm Sun), which is just down the road. **Pitsutinu Tugavik Territorial Park** (tent sites $5) is at the edge of town and is, alas, theft-prone.

Contact the interpretive centre for **homestays** (s/d $80/125, with meals $120/175), where you bunk with a local Inuit family.

Getting There & Away

From Iqaluit, First Air and Kenn Borek Air run daily flights to Pangnirtung ($288 return).

AUYUITTUQ NATIONAL PARK

Auyuittuq (ah-you-*ee*-tuk) means 'the land that never melts.' Appropriately, there are plenty of glaciers in this 19,500-sq-km park, plus jagged peaks, vertiginous cliffs and deep valleys. Hikers trek along the 97km **Akshayuk Pass** (crossing the Arctic Circle), between late June and early September, when it's snow-free. Nearby, climbers scale Mt Thor (1500m), the earth's highest sheer cliff. Camp wherever you can find a safe and ecologically appropriate spot. Nine emergency shelters dot the pass.

Parks Canada (☎ 867-473-8828; www.parkscanada .gc.ca; ☽ 8:30am-5pm Jul & Aug, 8:30am-5pm Mon-Fri Sep-Jun) is in Pangnirtung, next to the Angmarlik Interpretive Centre (see left). You must register here and pay the park entry fee ($15 per day trip, $40 up to three nights).

The south end of the pass is 30km from Pangnirtung. In summer you can hike there in two days, or have an outfitter take you by boat ($85 to $95). For about $200, through-hikers can arrange to be picked up at the other end by an outfitter from Qikiqtarjuaq, which is served by First Air and Kenn Borek Air.

CAPE DORSET

Cape Dorset (population 1300), on the rocky shore of Baffin Island's Foxe Peninsula, is the epicenter of Inuit art. A half-century ago the residents here pioneered modern arctic carving and printmaking, marketing it to the world with remarkable success. Though many Inuit communities now generate world-class artworks, Cape Dorset's remain the most revered. The **West Baffin Eskimo Cooperative** (☎ 867-897-8944; ☻ Sep-May) has studios and a gallery, but – in maddening Nunavut fashion – is technically closed in summer. Call ahead and someone might let you in. The Kingnait Inn also sells sculptures, and you can often find artists carving outside their homes.

You can hike to **Mallikjuaq Historic Park** in about 45 minutes, but only at low tide. Otherwise, hire an outfitter to take you there by boat. The park features ruins of thousand-year-old pre-Inuit stone houses, hiking trails, wildlife and tundra flowers. Ask at the hotel about other **hiking** routes near town.

Kingnait Inn (☎ 867-897-8907; s/d with meals $250/$300), around the bend from the Eskimo Cooperative, is the local hotel, offering meals and spartan rooms. You may have to share a room if the place fills up. The waterfront **Beach House** (☎ 867-897-8806; www .capedorsettours.com; s/d $175/350) is a guest home with two bedrooms and a kitchen for preparing meals.

First Air and Kenn Borek Air both operate services from Iqaluit for about $450 return.

POND INLET

On Baffin Island's north coast, Pond Inlet (population 1290) is in Tununiq – 'the place facing away from the sun.' Non-Inuit people originally arrived here for whaling and trading opportunities; now they come to kayak, hunt and gaze slack-jawed at the mountainous landscape.

Information

Nattinnak Centre (☎ 867-899-8225; fax 867-899-8246; ☻ 9am-noon & 1:30-5pm Mon-Fri Jun-Aug) has information on area activities and outfitters and, with advance notice, might arrange cultural activities, Inuktitut lessons or walking tours.

Activities

For a short hike, head a few kilometers out of town to Salmon Creek and the remains of an old Inuit village. The more ambitious trek is to **Mt Herodier** (765m), 15km east of town. Along the coast, there's fishing for arctic char in July and August.

Polar Sea Adventures (☎ 867-899-8870; www .polarseaadventures.com) rents kayaks and paddling gear ($50/$315 per day/week). It and other outfitters, including **Tununiq Travel & Adventure** (☎ 867-899-8194; www.tununiq.com), guide summer kayaking and whale-watching expeditions, and late-spring wildlife-viewing adventures to the floe edge, the biologically rich area where the sea ice meets the open water. Durations and costs vary; expect to pay up to $4000 for a week at the floe edge.

Near Pond Inlet is the new **Sirmilik National Park**, strewn with spires, glaciers and hoodoos, and providing breeding grounds for countless seabirds. There's no entrance fee, though this may change. Experiencing Sirmilik on your own is a challenge; most people go on package tours. **Parks Canada** (☎ 867-899-8092; sirmilik.info@pc.gc.ca; ☻ 1-5pm Mon-Fri) has a list of outfitters.

Sleeping & Eating

The main lodge is the **Sauniq Hotel** (☎ 867-899-8928; s/d $185/370, incl meals $260/520). There's also a guest room at **Sirmilik Inn B&B** (☎ 867-899-8688; s/d incl breakfast $135/220, incl all meals $180/310). Camping is available at **Qilaluqat Park** (tent sites free).

Getting There & Away

First Air flies to/from Iqaluit ($1130 return), and Kenn Borek Air serves Resolute ($622 return).

RESOLUTE

Godforsaken Resolute (population 215), on Cornwallis Island, was founded when the federal government lured Inuit here to shore up Canadian sovereignty. The land is downright lunar, and most visitors are just passing through to Quttinirpaaq National Park, the North Pole, or Canada's only more-northerly community, scenic Grise Fiord.

If you have time in Resolute, try local hiking, or fly to the national historic site, **Beechey Island**, about 80km east; charter flights for up to 10 people cost $1660. This desolate place was where the ill-fated Franklin expedition wintered in 1845–46 before vanishing forever. Traces of the 128 men and their unsuccessful rescuers remain. Ask at Resolute's hotels for information on tours and outfitters.

Qausuittuq Inns North (☎ 867-252-3900; www .resolutebay.com; s/d $165/330, incl meals $215/430) is a delightful family-style lodge that offers good home cooking. **South Camp Inn** (☎ 867-252-3737; www.southcampinn.com; s/d $240/480; 🖥) may be expensive, but there's Internet access, hot tubs and free use of the snowmobiles.

First Air flies to/from Iqaluit twice weekly ($1793 return), while Kenn Borek Air serves small High Arctic towns and does charters.

QUTTINIRPAAQ NATIONAL PARK

If you have a fortune to squander, a fun way would be to visit Canada's second-biggest park, way up on northern Ellesmere Island. A chartered plane from Resolute costs $32,000 round-trip for up to six people.

Highlights include **Cape Columbia**, the continent's northernmost point, **Mt Barbeau**, which at 2616m is the highest peak in eastern North America, and **Lake Hazen Basin**, a thermal oasis where animals, due to their unfamiliarity with humans, appear strangely tame. For park information, contact **Parks Canada** (☎ 867-473-8828; www .parkscanada.gc.ca/quttinirpaaq) in Pangnirtung (p838).

KIVALLIQ REGION

The Kivalliq region takes in the Hudson Bay coast and the barren lands west of there. This is a flat, windswept area, thick with caribou and waterfowl, and cut through by such wilderness rivers as the Back, Kazan and Thelon.

RANKIN INLET

Founded in 1955 as a mining center, Rankin is the Kivalliq's largest community (population 2300) and the regional government and transport center. From here you can go fishing in the bay or in the many rivers and lakes.

The **Kivalliq Regional Visitors Centre** (☎ 867-645-3838; fax 867-645-3904; ⏰ 8:30am-10pm, staffed Jul & Aug), located at the airport, has area information and historical displays.

Ijiraliq Territorial Park, 10km from town, is popular for hiking and berry-picking. Near the Meliadine River's mouth are archeological sites where Dorset people, who preceded the Inuit, used to live.

In Hudson Bay, 50km east of Rankin, is **Marble Island**, a graveyard for James Knight and his crew, who sought the Northwest Passage in the 18th century. Some 19th-century whaling ships are there too.

Tara's Bed & Breakfast (☎ 867-645-3478; taras bb@arctic.ca; r $160) has two twin rooms and a double. The big **Siniktarvik Hotel** (☎ 867-645-

---

IS POSSESSION NINE-TENTHS OF THE THAW?

The chilly Arctic is becoming a geopolitical hot zone, smoldering with disputes over who owns what.

In Canada, the main flashpoint is the Northwest Passage, weaving tortuously through Nunavut's polar archipelago. For centuries this ice-choked route rebuffed ships, but now, with global temperatures rising, it's predicted to become dependably navigable within a generation.

The USA is tantalized by this prospect. They deem the passage an international waterway and have been known to cruise icebreakers through it. This sends Canada into apoplexies. Ottawa insists the passage is Canada's, and fears shipwrecks, oil spills and the defense implications posed by ships skirting the arctic coast. The problem is that Canada has little capacity to monitor or defend the passage. For now, it pays Inuit 'rangers' – armed with WWII-era rifles – to keep an eye on the 2000-plus-km waterway.

Americans aren't Canada's only antagonists up north. Denmark, too, recently provoked Ottawa by hoisting the Danish flag on Hans Island. This 1.3-sq-km nub of barren rock lies between Greenland and Nunavut and – like the Northwest Passage – can be accessed by ship only when the ice is thin. Apparently, the big deal isn't the island *per se*, but its role in determining who owns the surrounding (fish-filled) seas.

2807; www.siniktarvik.ca; s/d $195/240) also offers meals for about $80 per day.

Canadian North and First Air operate services to/from Yellowknife and Iqaluit, and First Air, Calm Air and Kivalliq Air run flights to Winnipeg. Calm Air and Kivalliq Air run services to the region's smaller communities.

KITIKMEOT REGION

The Kitikmeot is Nunavut's least-populous and probably least-visited region, occupying the mainland arctic coast and the islands north of there. Between them runs the fabled – and usually frozen – Northwest Passage.

CAMBRIDGE BAY

Say 'Cambridge Bay' and even Nunavut residents shiver. This wind-wracked settlement (population 1500) on southeast Victoria Island is the regional administrative and transport center.

Explorers seeking the Northwest Passage often took shelter here; you can see what remains of Roald Amundsen's schooner *Maud* in the harbor. **Uvajuq Territorial Park**, a 15km walk from town, is a prime place to see musk ox and offers good views from **Mt Pelly** (200m). South across the passage is **Queen Maud Bird Sanctuary**, the world's largest migratory bird refuge.

Arctic Coast Visitors Centre (☎ 867-983-2842; fax 867-983-2302; ☒ 9am-5pm Mon-Fri) organizes tours, has displays about exploration, and offers showers. **Arctic Island Lodge** (☎ 867-983-2345; ailodge@polarnet.ca; s/d $185/260) is swanky by Nunavut standards. Meals cost an extra $30 to $60 per day.

Canadian North and First Air fly to/from Yellowknife for about $900 return. First Air flies from Cambridge Bay to the Kitikmeot's other communities, while Kenn Borek Air goes north to Resolute.

NUNAVUT

Directory

CONTENTS

PRACTICALITIES

- Electrical supply is 110V AC, 50/60 Hz.
- The most widely-read newspaper is the Toronto-based *Globe and Mail*. Other principal dailies are the *Montréal Gazette*, *Ottawa Citizen*, *Toronto Star* and *Vancouver Sun*.
- *Maclean's* is Canada's weekly news magazine.
- The Canadian Broadcasting Corporation (CBC) is the dominant nationwide network for both radio and TV. The Canadian Television Network (CTN) is the major competition.
- The NTSC system (not compatible with PAL or Secam) is used for videos.
- Canada officially uses the metric system, but imperial measurements are used for many day-to-day purposes. To convert between the two systems, see the chart on the inside front cover.

ACCOMMODATIONS

Accommodations in Canada are generally comfortable and well organized. Depending on your destination, you'll usually be able to take your pick of a range of B&Bs, chain motels, hotels and hostels. If you're traveling in the busy summer season, we recommend that you book your rooms as far in advance as possible. The same goes for ski resorts in winter. Rooms can also be scarce and prices high during holidays (p854), major festivals and special events, which are mentioned throughout this book and on p852. If you aren't able to make advance bookings, local or provincial tourist offices may be able to help you find a place to unpack.

In this book we list accommodation options in all price categories. The budget category comprises campgrounds, hostels and simple hotels where you may have to share bathrooms. Rates rarely exceed $70 for a double, although the budget threshold may be slightly higher in cities and at tourist resorts.

Mid-range accommodations, such as most B&Bs, inns (*auberges* in French), motels and some hotels, generally offer the best value for money. Expect to pay between $70 and $125 for a clean, comfortable, decent-sized double with at least a modicum of style, a private bathroom, TV and, sometimes, a telephone.

Accommodations at the top end (more than $125 per double, on average) offer an international standard of amenities and perhaps a scenic location, special decor or historical ambience. Some may also have pools, saunas, business centers or other upmarket facilities. Unless you're going to use these, though, it's rarely worth the extra cost compared to mid-range hotels. Hotels in this top category are most likely to have rooms equipped for wheelchair users.

Most properties have rooms set aside for nonsmokers, and some smaller ones, especially B&Bs, ban smoking altogether. Air-conditioning is not a standard amenity at most budget and mid-range places. Sometimes a property has upgraded some rooms but not others. If you can't do without air-conditioning, be sure to ask about it when you book. Accommodations offering guests free Internet access are identified in this book with an Internet icon (🖳).

Prices listed in this book are for peak-season travel (usually summer, normally from Victoria Day in late May to Labour Day in early September) and, unless stated otherwise, do not include taxes. These rates do not take into account seasonal or promotional discounts. Big city business hotels, for instance, often drop prices on weekends. In winter, prices everywhere can plummet by as much as 50%. Membership of the American Automobile Association (AAA) or an associated automobile association, American Association of Retired Persons (AARP) or other organizations may yield modest savings (usually 10%) at any time of year.

Online agencies such as www.orbitz.com, www.expedia.com, www.travelocity.com and www.hotels.com may get you a better rate than you'd get if booking directly with the hotel. A handy Web resource is **Tripadvisor** (www.tripadvisor.com), which features reader and published reviews and which simultaneously searches for rates offered by all of the above-mentioned agencies for some of the properties listed. For an even more exhaustive rate comparison, try **Travelaxe** (www.travelaxe.com), a website which has several filters to help you narrow down your search (eg distance, price, comfort level). It requires a free software download (spyware-free, or so they say). Also check hotel websites (listed throughout this book) for special online rates or packages.

For details about how to get your lodging taxes refunded, see p857.

B&Bs

If you like waking up to the smell of fresh coffee, staying at a B&B may be your kind of thing. B&Bs (*gîtes* in French) are essentially converted private homes – sometimes lovely old Victorians or other heritage buildings –

whose owners live on the premises. Many take great pride in decorating the guest rooms and common areas and a personal interest in ensuring that you enjoy your stay. People in need of lots of privacy may find B&Bs a bit too intimate, as walls are rarely soundproof and it's usual to mingle with your hosts and other guests.

Standards vary widely, sometimes even within a single B&B. Breakfast can be anything from light and continental to multi-course gourmet meals that can take up the better part of your morning. The cheapest rooms tend to be small with few amenities (maybe a clock radio) and a shared bathroom. Nicer ones have added features such as a TV, a balcony, a fireplace and your own facilities. Top-end rooms have all of this plus maybe a spa bath, plush terry robes and small fridge. Almost none have in-room phones and few provide guest computer terminals with Internet access. However, if you ask nicely, most owners will let you make short local or calling-card calls from their phones or allow you check email on their office computers.

Some hosts impose strict house rules, such as having to take your shoes off or refraining from showering after a certain hour. Many also have a strict nonsmoking policy. Not all accept children. Minimum stays (usually two nights) are common at certain times, especially holiday weekends. Some B&Bs are only open seasonally.

Camping

Camping in Canada is much more than a cheap way to spend the night. While some campgrounds are in or near cities, the nicest ones are in national and provincial parks, at wildlife reserves or along river banks.

Facilities vary widely. Backcountry sites offer little more than pit toilets and fire rings, and have no potable water. Unserviced (tent) campgrounds come with access to drinking water and a washroom with toilets and sometimes showers. The best-equipped sites feature flush toilets and hot showers, and water, electrical and sewer hookups for recreational vehicles (RVs). Private campgrounds sometimes cater only to trailers (caravans) and RVs, and may feature convenience stores, playgrounds and swimming pools. It is a good idea to phone ahead to make sure the size of sites and the services provided at a particular campground are suitable for your vehicle.

Most government-run sites are available on a first-come first-served basis and fill up quickly, especially in July and August. In 2004, Parks Canada launched a pilot **camping reservation program** (☎ 877-737-3788; www.pccamping.ca) in eight national parks, including Gros Morne and Jasper. It is expected to include all Parks Canada–operated parks soon.

Nightly camping fees in national and provincial parks range from $10 to $24 for tents up to $33 for full hookup sites. Backcountry camping costs $5 to $9. Private campgrounds tend to be a bit pricier.

In parks, the official camping season runs from May to September, but exact dates vary by location. Some campgrounds remain open for maintenance year-round and may let you camp at a reduced rate in the off-season. This can be great in late autumn or early spring when there's hardly a soul tramping about. Winter camping, though, is only for the hardy.

Farm Vacations

A holiday on a working farm is a great way for city slickers to get close to nature in relative comfort. This type of vacation is also a big hit with families. Kids get to meet their favorite barnyard animals up close and personal and to help with everyday chores. Each province has a farm or ranch vacation program. Stays can range from a day to a week or longer. The size and type of farm vary considerably, as do the activities offered. Rates range from about $50 to $60 for singles and $60 to $90 for doubles, including meals. Family rates and discounts for children are available. For further details, contact the provincial tourist boards (see p860).

Hostels

Canada has independent hostels as well as those affiliated with Hostelling International (HI). Some are in unique locations such as converted train cars, rustic cabins, ancient prisons and dairy barns. All have dorms sleeping two to 10 people, and many have private rooms for couples and families. Rooms in HI hostels are gender-segregated and alcohol and smoking are prohibited.

Bathrooms are usually shared, although there are a growing number of rooms with private facilities. Other features include a kitchen, lockers, Internet access, a laundry room and a common room with a TV, games and books.

Most hostels, especially those in big cities, are open 24 hours. Some HI affiliates in rural areas still cling to curfews, but even then you should be able to make arrangements with the host if you're going to be out late.

Dorm beds cost $8 to $50, with most around $22. At HI hostels, nonmembers pay a surcharge of $2 to $5 for up to six nights. Private rooms start at $30/40 per single/double. Quoted rates usually include all taxes.

Reservations are always a good idea, especially during peak travel periods (late spring through summer). Most hostels take bookings by phone, fax, mail or email. HI accommodations can also be reserved online at www.hihostels.ca. For independent hostels, try www.hostels.com or www.backpackers.ca, though you may get a better price and more choice by contacting the hostel directly.

Hotels & Motels

Hotels range from luxurious international chains to comfortable mid-range options and small family-run establishments. Rooms usually have a TV, often with cable or satellite reception, and direct-dial phones are common in all but budget places. Rooms in newer or recently renovated hotels often feature minibars, hairdryers and alarm clocks; the most luxurious also have swimming pools, saunas and fitness centers.

In many older, privately run hotels, rooms vary dramatically in terms of size, decor and amenities. In the cheapest ones you must share facilities. If possible, ask to see several rooms before committing.

Rooms with two double or queen-sized beds sleep up to four people, although there is usually a small surcharge for the third and fourth person. Many places advertise that 'kids stay free' but sometimes you have to pay extra for a crib or a rollaway (portable bed).

In Canada, like the USA (both lands of the automobile), motels are ubiquitous. They dot the highways and cluster in groups on the outskirts of towns and cities. Although rooms may not win style awards, they're usually clean and comfortable and offer good value for money. Many motels remain 'mom and pop' operations, but plenty of North American chains have also opened up (see the boxed text right).

Reservations at chain hotels or motels can be made by booking online or calling a central toll-free number, although it may be better to call an individual property directly to find out about specific amenities and local promotions.

University Accommodations
In the lecture-free summer months, some universities and colleges rent beds in their student dormitories to travelers of all ages. Most rooms are quite basic, but with rates ranging from $25 to $40 a night, often including breakfast, you know you're not getting the Ritz. Students usually qualify for small discounts.

ACTIVITIES
For outdoor enthusiasts Canada offers the mother lode of possibilities. No matter what kind of activity gets you off the couch, you'll be able to pursue it in this vast land of lakes, rivers, mountains, islands, forests and prairies. Everywhere you go you'll find outfitters and tour operators eager to set you up.

Canoeing & Kayaking
Laced with rivers, dotted with lakes and surrounded by pristine shoreline, Canada is tailor-made for canoeing and kayaking. The possibilities are practically limitless, whether you're up for an easy paddle or a battle with roiling white water. The government parks are good places to start if you've never dipped an oar in the water. Maps and equipment rentals are usually available from the information centers, where the staff can also give route recommendations. Canoe camping – essentially a water-based exploration of the backcountry – is a perfect way to find solitude away from the madding crowds.

With more than 100,000km of routes, Ontario has the world's largest canoe network, with some of the most spectacular routes leading through the Algonquin (p166) and Killarney (p171) Provincial Parks. Other popular canoeing areas:

Bowron Lake Provincial Park (p776) British Columbia.
Kejimkujik National Park (p415) Nova Scotia.
Nahanni National Park (p823) Northwest Territories.
Parc National du Canada de la Mauricie (p277) Québec.

THE CHAIN GANG
Budget
Days Inn (☎ 800-329-7466; www.daysinn.com)
Econo Lodge (☎ 877-424-6423; www.econo lodge.com)
Super 8 (☎ 800-800-8000; www.super8.com)

Mid-Range
Best Western (☎ 800-780-7234; www.bestwestern.com)
Clarion Hotel (☎ 877-424-6423; www.clarionhotel.com)
Comfort Inn (☎ 877-424-6423; www.comfortinn.com
Fairfield Inn (☎ 800-228-2800; www.fairfieldinn.com)
Hampton Inn (☎ 800-426-7866; www.hamptoninn.com)
Holiday Inn (☎ 800-465-4329; www.holiday-inn.com)
Howard Johnson (☎ 800-446-4656; www.hojo.com)
Quality Inn & Suites (☎ 877-424-6423; www.qualityinn.com)
Travelodge/Thriftlodge (☎ 800-578-7878; www.travelodge.com)

Top End
Delta (☎ 877-814-7706; www.deltahotels.com)
Fairmont (☎ 800-257-7544; www.fairmont.com)
Hilton (☎ 800-445-8667; www.hilton.com)
Hyatt (☎ 888-591-1234; www.hyatt.com)
Marriott (☎ 888-236-2427; www.marriott.com)
Radisson (☎ 888-201-1718; www.radisson.com)
Ramada (☎ 800-272-6232; www.ramada.com)
Sheraton (☎ 888-625-5144; www.sheraton.com)
Westin (☎ 800-228-3000; www.westin.com)

Prince Albert National Park (p570) Saskatchewan.
Wells Gray Provincial Park (p738) British Columbia.
Yukon River (p786) Yukon Territory.

Both white-water and sea kayaking are finding new fans every day. Recommended areas:
Bay Bulls (p356) Newfoundland.
Bay of Fundy (p512) New Brunswick.
Gulf Islands (p731) British Columbia.
Lake Superior (p192) Ontario.
Mingan Archipelago National Park (p311) Québec.
Ottawa River (p229) Ontario.
Percé (p326) Québec.
Vancouver Island (p700) British Columbia.

The **Canadian Recreational Canoeing Association** (☎ 613-269-2910, 888-252-6292; www.paddlingcanada .com) publishes *Kanawa* paddling magazine and has an extensive online bookstore.

Cycling & Mountain Biking

Canada is a great place for cycling, no matter whether you want to take a leisurely spin around the countryside, experience an adrenaline rush while chasing down a mountain or test your stamina on multiday wilderness explorations.

In eastern Canada, popular pedaling terrain includes:

Bay of Fundy (p511) New Brunswick.
Bruce Peninsula (p157) Ontario.
Cape Breton Highlands National Park (p444) Nova Scotia.
Confederation Trail (p478) Price Edward Island.
Gaspé Peninsula (p319) Québec.
Niagara wine region (p131) Ontario.

Even the cities don't have to be off-limits; Montréal (p251), for instance, has been crowned the best cycling city in North America by *Bicycle* magazine.

Mountain biking is best in the west, although it's also a popular activity in the Laurentians (p265) in Québec. In BC and Alberta, mountain-bike paths often follow old railway lines and mining trails through breathtaking mountain terrain. In summer, ski slopes offer hair-raising downhill challenges to mountain bikers. There are classic routes around Banff Town (p614), and Revelstoke (p755), Nelson (p762) and Rossland (p764) in the Kootenays also offer lots of exciting terrain.

For specific ideas, see the Activities sections of individual destinations in the regional chapters. For day tours, staff at the local tourist offices are usually fonts of information. They often sell route maps and can refer you to local bicycle rental outfits, many of which you'll find listed in this book. **Cycle Canada** (www.cyclecanada .com) operates a website packed with route ideas, club and events directories and lists of bicycle-friendly lodging options. The **Canadian Cycling Association** (☎ 613-248-1353; www .canadian-cycling.com) is another good resource. *Canadian Cyclist* (www.canadiancyclist .com) and *Pedal* (www.pedalmag.com) are cycling magazines available at many newsagents.

Fishing

Salmon, cod, haddock, mackerel, trout, muskellunge – it's easy to get hooked on fishing in Canada. Casting a line in one of the many fertile lakes, rivers and coastal waters is pretty much a national pastime. Visitors can join in the fun provided they buy a nonresident fishing license. Each provincial government has its own set of regulations and there may be bait restrictions or quotas and closed seasons for certain fish species. Staff at any tourist office should be able to tell you where to obtain licenses and information on the latest regulations.

Hiking

There's great hiking all throughout Canada, no matter whether you've got your heart set on rambling along rugged coastal trails, going peak-bagging in the Rockies or simply taking a walk in the park. Practically all of the country's trails, and certainly the best ones, lead through the beautiful scenery of national and provincial parks, conservation areas and wildlife reserves. You'll usually find a range of well-marked trails, from short and easy strolls to multiday wilderness treks. The most popular paths may have quotas and require reservations. Some require backcountry permits. Maps are available at park information centers, although for extended hikes you may need topographic maps (see p855).

Some of Canada's prime spots for hiking:
Banff National Park (p612) Alberta.
Bruce Trail (p156) Ontario.
Chilkoot Trail (p797) Yukon Territory.
Fundy Trail Parkway (p510) New Brunswick.
Gros Morne National Park (p374) Newfoundland.
Jasper National Park (p624) Alberta.
Killarney Provincial Park (p171) Ontario.
Kluane National Park (p792) Yukon Territory.
Parc de la Gaspésie (p323) Québec.
Parc du Mont Tremblant (p269) Québec.
Pukaskwa National Park (p193) Ontario.
West Coast Trail (p717) Pacific Rim National Park, British Columbia.
Yoho National Park (p757) British Columbia.

Canada is also home to one of the most ambitious trails ever conceived, the **Trans Canada Trail** (p56). Upon completion it will traverse every province and territory on its 18,078km journey across the country and north to the Arctic Ocean.

Canada Trails (www.canadatrails.ca) has lots of hiking information, although some of it is outdated.

Rock Climbing & Mountaineering

Rock climbing and mountaineering have come out from under their, well…rock, and are attracting a growing following. Group climbs, with instructors and equipment, are available across the country. Some areas to look into:

Banff (p614) Alberta.
Collingwood (p160) Ontario.
Jasper (p625) Alberta.
Squamish (p687) British Columbia.

The **Alpine Club of Canada** (☎ 403-678-3200; www.alpineclubofcanada.ca) may be able to help with additional information.

Scuba Diving

Most of Canada's coastal waters are too frigid to make underwater exploration a pleasant experience. The main exception is southern BC, where you can swim with wolf eels and octopuses in such places as Vancouver (p662), and Victoria (p699) and Nanaimo (p712) on Vancouver Island. Another good place to take the plunge is in Tobermory, Ontario (p157).

Skiing & Snowboarding

Modern ski lifts, trails from 'Sesame Street' to 'Death Wish', breathtaking scenery, crisp mountain air, hearty dinners by a crackling fire – all of these are the hallmarks of a skiing vacation in Canada.

The country's best skiing can be found in the Rocky Mountains, which offer world-class resorts at Banff (p613) and Lake Louise (p619), both in Alberta, with mile-high vertical drops and longer runs than in the European Alps. Just as famous is Whistler-Blackcomb (p688) in BC, which frequently hosts international competitions. There's also good skiing in British Columbia near Penticton (p743) in the Okanagan Valley, and in Revelstoke (p754) in the Kootenays.

The mountains may not soar as high in eastern Canada, but there's still good skiing, most notably in Québec where several resorts beckon in the Laurentians (p265) and Eastern Townships (p270). Efficient snowmaking equipment ensures winter fun even in years when nature doesn't play along.

Each of these alpine regions also offers cross-country skiing, although there are good Nordic trails and conditions all across Canada.

The provincial tourist boards (see p860) produce guides to skiing, and travel agents and many hotels/resorts can arrange full-package tours that include transportation, accommodations and lift tickets. Many resorts are close to cities, making it easy to head to the slopes just for the day.

For further information contact the **Canadian Ski Council** (☎ 905-212-9040; www.canadianskicouncil.org).

BUSINESS HOURS

Standard business hours, including for most government offices, are 9am to 5pm Monday to Friday. Bank hours vary but are generally 10am to 4pm Monday to Thursday, until 6pm Friday and sometimes 9am to noon on Saturday. Post offices are generally open 9am to 5pm on weekdays, but outlets in retail stores (eg pharmacies, grocery stores) may stay open later and on weekends.

Most restaurants serve lunch between 11:30am and 2:30pm Monday to Friday and dinner from 5pm to 9:30pm daily, later on weekends. Some are closed on Monday. A few serve breakfast from 7am to 10am on weekdays and brunch from 10am to 2pm on Saturday and/or Sunday.

Pubs are generally open from 11am to 2am daily, although exact times vary by province. Bars welcome patrons from around 5pm until 2am nightly, while music and dance clubs in cities open their doors at 8pm or 9pm, though often on Friday and Saturday only. Most close at 2am, but if they're busy they may stay open until 3am or 4am.

Shops are generally open from 10am to 6pm Monday to Saturday. In shopping malls and districts, stores often stay open until 8pm or 9pm on Thursday and Friday evenings. Many shops also open on Sunday from noon to 5pm, although less so on Prince Edward Island and in New Brunswick and not at all in Nova Scotia, which remains closed up tight by law on the 'Lord's day'.

CHILDREN
Practicalities

Traveling around Canada with the tots can be child's play, especially if you don't over-pack the schedule and do involve the little ones in day-to-day trip planning. Lonely Planet's *Travel with Children* offers a wealth of tips and tricks on the subject. The website www.travelwithyourkids.com is another good, general resource.

Children who are traveling to Canada without both of their parents need authorization from the nonaccompanying parent (see p863).

Once in Canada, children (or more specifically, their parents) enjoy a wide range of discounts for everything from museum admissions to bus fares and hotel stays. The definition of a 'child' varies, however. Some places consider anyone under 18 eligible for discounts, while others put the cut-off age at six.

Airlines usually allow infants (up to two years old) to fly for free, while older children requiring a seat of their own qualify for reduced fares. Many, such as Air Canada, also offer special kids' meals, although you need to pre-order them.

Hotels and motels commonly have rooms with two double beds or a double and a sofa bed, which are ideal for families. Even those that don't can bring in rollaways or cots, usually for a small extra charge. Some properties offer 'kids stay free' promotions, although this may apply only if the children don't need their own bedding.

Baby food, infant formula, milk (including soy), disposable diapers (nappies) and the like are widely available in drugstores and supermarkets. Breastfeeding in public is legal in all communities, and tolerated in most, although most women are discrete about it. If someone complains, point out politely but firmly that you're not doing anything illegal.

Most facilities can accommodate a child's needs. You'll find that nearly all restaurants have high chairs, and if they don't have a specific children's menu, most can make a kid-tailored meal. See p64 for more information on dining out with kids. Public toilets in airports, stores, malls, cinemas etc usually have diaper-changing tables.

In all vehicles, children under 18kg must be restrained in a child-booster seat, while infants need a rear-facing infant safety seat. Most car-rental firms rent these for about $5 per day, but it is essential that you book them in advance.

Sights & Activities

It's easy to keep kids entertained no matter where you travel in Canada. The great outdoors yields endless possibilities. A day spent wildlife-watching, swimming, walking, horseback riding, canoeing or otherwise engaging in physical activity is sure to leave the little ones ready for sleep by the day's end. Many national parks offer nature walks or other programs specially geared to children. Many outfitters also offer dedicated kids' tours. To be fully immersed in the outdoors, you might even consider a farm holiday (see p844).

Even in the cities there's usually no shortage of entertaining options for children. Take 'em to parks, playgrounds, public swimming pools, ice-skating rinks, zoos or kid-friendly museums. For specific suggestions, see the 'for Children' sections throughout the regional chapters of this book. In addition, most tourist offices can lead you to resources for children's programs, childcare facilities and pediatricians in their area.

TOP FIVE CANADIAN BOOKS FOR CHILDREN

Get your children in the mood for their trip with these fun books:

- *Only in Canada! From the Colossal to the Kooky* by Vivian Bowers – illustrated and jam-packed with quirky, humorous yet educational facts.
- *The Kids Book of Canada* by Barbara Greenwood – fun-filled facts about all the provinces and territories.
- *The Broken Blade* by William Durbin – gripping adventure about a brave teen who joins fur traders on their 3000km journey across Lake Superior in 1800.
- *Call of the Wild* by Jack London – classic story about a kidnapped dog and his survival during the Yukon gold rush.
- *Sea Gift* by John Ashby – fast-paced hunt for Mi'kmaq treasure off the coast of Cape Breton.

CLIMATE CHARTS

For general advice on climate and when to travel in Canada, see p9. Each regional chapter also has its own Climate section filled with useful details. The climate charts below provide a snapshot of Canada's weather patterns.

CUSTOMS

Canadian customs allows each person over the age of 18 (entering Alberta, Manitoba and Québec) or 19 (everywhere else) to import duty-free either 1.5L of wine, 1.14L of liquor or 24 12oz beers, as well as up to 200 cigarettes, 50 cigars or cigarillos, 200g of tobacco and 200 tobacco sticks. You can also bring in gifts valued at up to $60 in total. If you spend at least 48 hours outside Canada you again become eligible for these allowances.

Personal effects – including camping gear, sports equipment, cameras, laptop computers and the like – can be brought into Canada

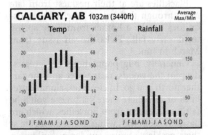

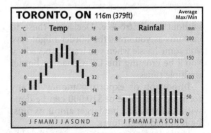

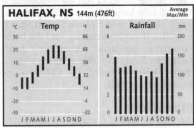

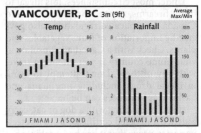

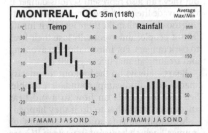

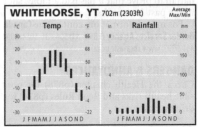

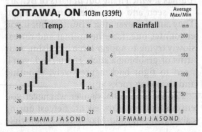

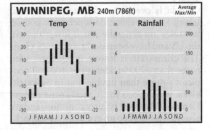

TRAVEL ADVISORIES

▪ **Australia** (☎ 1300 139 281; www.smart raveler.gov.au)

▪ **Germany** (www.auswaertiges-amt.de)

▪ **New Zealand** (☎ 04-439-8000; www .mft.govt.nz/travel)

▪ **UK** (☎ 0870-606 0290; www.fco.gov.uk)

▪ **USA** (☎ 202-647-5225; www.travel. state.gov)

without much trouble. Declaring these to customs as you cross the border might save you some hassle when you leave, especially if you'll be crossing the US–Canadian border multiple times.

Importing or exporting money in any form up to a value of $10,000 can be done without formality, but larger amounts must be reported to customs.

Under most circumstances, it is illegal to bring firearms, pepper spray or mace into Canada. Complicated regulations also govern the importation of fruit, vegetables and plants. Check with a Canadian consulate in your home country if you intend to travel with any of these. Don't attempt to bring in illegal drugs, including marijuana and hashish, as sentences can be harsh.

If you're traveling with a dog or cat, carry a signed and dated certificate from a veterinarian to prove that it has had a rabies shot in the past 36 months.

For more information, contact the **Canada Border Services Agency** (CBSA; ☎ 506-636-5064, 800-461-9999; www.cbsa-asfc.gc.ca).

DANGERS & ANNOYANCES

Check the Health chapter (p878) for possible health risks and Road Rules (p874) for driving tips.

Crime

Canada is overall a safe place to live and travel. Violent crime does occur, of course, but rates are generally much lower than in the US and have been declining for 25 years. The crime rate is lowest in Québec, with fewer than 5700 incidents per 100,000 people; it's more than double that in Saskatchewan, which posts the highest crime rates in Canada. Petty theft is fairly common, and it's always wise to keep an eye out for pickpock-

ets in crowded places. Leaving valuables on view in your parked car may invite smash-and-grab thefts, especially in the cities.

Insects

Bugs are the creatures most likely to torture you while you're in the woods. You might hear tales of lost hikers going insane from being incessantly swarmed by blackflies and mosquitoes. This is no joke – they can make you miserable.

Blackflies are at their peskiest from late May through the end of June, while mosquitoes can be a bother from early spring until early fall. Ticks are an issue from March to June.

Generally, bug populations are greatest deep in the woods, near water and the farther north you go. In clearings, along shorelines or anywhere there's a breeze you'll be fairly safe, except from horseflies, which are basically teeth with wings. Mosquitoes are at their peskiest around sundown; building a fire will help keep them away. For campers, a tent with a zippered screen is pretty much essential. If you're venturing into the backcountry, a 'bug jacket' (essentially a mesh jacket/head-net), available at most camping stores, is recommended. For additional information, see p881.

Other Wildlife

Animals are among Canada's greatest assets, but they can also represent serious danger if you invade their turf. Feeding animals or getting too close will make them lose their innate fear of people, and eventually lose their lives to park rangers. For information on avoiding and treating animal bites, see p881.

Bears – always on the lookout for an easy snack – can find campgrounds irresistible. See p54 for details on how to avoid bear encounters and what to do if they happen.

Mountain lions (also called 'cougars' or 'pumas'), which hang out in parts of BC, are rarely seen and are active mainly at night. They almost never attack humans but if you encounter one, face the animal and retreat slowly trying to appear large by raising your arms or grabbing a stick. If attacked, you'll need to fight back aggressively, shouting and throwing rocks at it.

Elk are a potential danger whenever you encounter them. Cow elk are fiercest during calving season (mid-May to late June) while bull elk are most aggressive during mating season (mid-September to late October). Elk, deer and moose also represent a problem when driving, especially at night in rural areas. Be extra cautious, as hitting one of these creatures can be fatal to both of you.

Weather

On winter days, you'll need to bundle up against frostbite, which is especially likely when the wind-chill factor is dangerously high. Everyone discusses the freezing cold, and radio stations broadcast warnings about how many minutes it's safe to expose your skin. For information on avoiding and treating hypothermia, see p880.

DISABLED TRAVELERS

Canada is making progress when it comes to easing the everyday challenges facing the disabled, especially the mobility-impaired. Naturally, there is always room for improvement and numerous lobby groups are working hard to ensure that governments and others are not resting on their laurels.

You'll find access ramps and/or lifts in many public buildings, including museums, tourist offices, train stations, shopping malls and cinemas. Most public restrooms feature extra-wide stalls equipped with hand rails. Many pedestrian crossings have sloping curbs. Newer and recently remodeled hotels, especially chain hotels, have rooms with extra-wide doors and spacious bathrooms.

Interpretive centers at national and provincial parks should be accessible and many parks have trails that can be navigated in wheelchairs. In parking lots and garages, look for designated disabled spots marked with a painted wheelchair symbol. Some car-rental agencies offer hand-controlled vehicles and vans with wheelchair lifts at no additional charge, but you must reserve them well in advance.

Getting around on public transport is possible but requires some planning. The best place to start is **Access to Travel** (www.accesstotravel.gc.ca), a centralized source of information on accessible air, bus, rail and ferry transportation throughout Canada. The site's 'travel resources' link leads to other useful websites sorted by province. In general, most transportation agencies can accommodate people with disabilities if you make your specific needs known when booking your ticket.

Other organizations and tour operators that specialize in the needs of disabled travelers:

Access-Able Travel Source (in the USA ☎ 303-232-2979; www.access-able.com) Operates a useful website with many links.

Canadian Parapalegic Association (☎ 416-422-5640, 800-720-4933; www.canparaplegic.org) Excellent resource for information about facilities for mobility-impaired travelers in Canada.

Flying Wheels Travel (☎ 507-451-5005 in the USA; www.flyingwheelstravel.com) Escorted tours, customized itineraries and cruises.

Mobility International (in the USA ☎ 541-343-1284, in the UK ☎ 020-7403-5688; www.miusa.org) Advises disabled travelers on mobility issues and runs an educational exchange program.

Society for Accessible Travel & Hospitality (SATH; in the USA ☎ 212-447-7284; www.sath.org) Lots of useful links and information for disabled travelers.

DISCOUNT CARDS

If you're a student, never leave home without an **International Student Identity Card** (ISIC; www.isiccard.com), which entitles you to discounts on movie and theater tickets, travel insurance and admission to museums and other sights. If you're under 26 but not a student, get an International Youth Travel Card (IYTC), which offers many of the same savings and benefits. All these cards are issued by student unions, hosteling organizations and youth-oriented travel agencies.

Discounts are also common for seniors, children, families and the disabled, although no special discount cards are available for people from these groups. In some cases you may be asked to show identification to prove your age.

EMBASSIES & CONSULATES
Canadian Embassies

Canada has diplomatic representation in almost every country in the world. The embassy or high commission is always located in the capital city but consulates, which handle visas and other travel-related services, are located in other major cities. Contact the relevant embassy or high commission for a referral to the consulate closest to you or check the website of **Foreign Affairs Canada** (www.fac.gc.ca), which has links to all Canadian embassies and consulates abroad.

DIRECTORY

Australia (☎ 02-6270-4000; www.dfait-maeci.gc.ca/australia/contact-en.asp; Commonwealth Ave, Canberra, ACT 2600)

France (☎ 01-44-43-29-00; www.dfait-maeci.gc.ca/canadaeuropa/france; 35 Ave Montaigne, 75008 Paris)

Germany (☎ 030-203120; www.dfait-maeci.gc.ca/canadaeuropa/germany; Friedrichstrasse 95, 10117 Berlin)

Ireland (☎ 01-417-4100; www.dfait-maeci.gc.ca/canadaeuropa/Ireland; 65 St Stephen's Green, Dublin 2)

Italy (☎ 06-44-59-81; www.dfait-maeci.gc.ca/canada europa/italy; Via G B de Rossi 27, Rome 00161)

Japan (☎ 03-5412-6200; www.canada.or.jp; 3-38 Akasaka 7-chome, Minato-ku, Tokyo 107-8503)

Mexico (☎ 55-247 900; www.dfait-maeci.gc.ca/mexico-city; Schiller 529, Col Polanco, Rincón del Bosque, 11580 México, DF)

Netherlands (☎ 070-311-1600; www.dfait-maeci.gc.ca/canadaeuropa/Netherlands; Sophialaan 7, 2514 JP The Hague)

New Zealand (☎ 04-473-9577; www.dfait-maeci.gc.ca/newzealand; 61 Molesworth St, Thorndon, Wellington)

UK (☎ 020-7258-6600; www.dfait-maeci.gc.ca/canada europa/united_kingdom; 1 Grosvenor Square, London W1K 4AB)

USA (☎ 212-682-1740; www.canadianembassy.org; 501 Pennsylvania Ave NW; Washington DC 20001)

Embassies & Consulates in Canada

All countries have their embassies in Ottawa and maintain consulates in such cities as Montréal, Vancouver, Calgary and Toronto. Contact the relevant embassy to find out which consulate is closest to you.

Australia (☎ 613-236-0841; www.ahc-ottawa.org; 50 O'Connor St, Ste 710, Ottawa, ON K1P 6L2)

France (☎ 613-562-3735; www.ambafrance-ca.org; 42 Sussex Dr, Ottawa, ON K1M 2C9)

Germany (☎ 613-232-1101; www.ottawa.diplo.de/en/Startseite.html; 1 Waverley St, Ottawa, ON K2P 0T8)

Ireland (☎ 613-233-6281; emb.ireland@sympatico.ca; 130 Albert St, Ottawa, ON K1P 5G4)

Italy (☎ 613-232-2401; www.italyincanada.com; 275 Slater St, 21st fl, Ottawa, ON K1P 5H9)

Japan (☎ 613-241-8541; www.ca.emb-japan.go.jp; 255 Sussex Dr, Ottawa, ON K1N 9E6)

Mexico (☎ 613-233-8988; www.embamexican.com; 45 O'Connor St, Suite 1500, Ottawa, ON K1P 1A4)

Netherlands (☎ 613-237-5030; www.netherlands embassy.ca; 350 Albert St, Suite 2020, Ottawa, ON K1R 1A4)

New Zealand (☎ 613-238-5991; www.nzembassy.com; 99 Bank St, Suite 727, Ottawa, ON K1P 6G3)

Sweden (☎ 613-241-8553; www.swedishembassy.ca; 377 Dalhousie St, Ottawa, ON K1N 9N8)

Switzerland (☎ 613-235-1837; www.eda.admin.ch/canada; 5 Marlborough Ave, Ottawa, ON K1N 8E6)

UK (☎ 613-237-2008; www.britainincanada.org; 80 Elgin St, Ottawa, ON K1P 5K7)

USA (☎ 613-238-5335; www.usembassycanada.gov; 490 Sussex Dr, Ottawa, ON K1N 1G8)

FESTIVALS & EVENTS

Canada has a packed schedule of festivals and special events, the bulk of them taking place in the summer. The following list is an overview of major festivities throughout the country, each of which is detailed in the Festivals & Events sections for individual destinations in the regional chapters. For information on holidays in Canada, see p854.

JANUARY & FEBRUARY
Fête des Neiges (p253) Montréal, Québec.
Festival du Voyageur (p535) Winnipeg, Manitoba.
Winter Carnival (p287) Québec City, Québec.
Winterlude (p220) Ottawa, Ontario.
Yukon Quest (p786) Whitehorse, Yukon.

MARCH–MAY
Stratford Festival (p142) Through November, Stratford, Ontario.

JUNE
Toronto Downtown Jazz Festival (p95) Toronto, Ontario.
Grand Prix of Canada (p253) Montréal, Québec.
International Storytelling Festival (p786) Whitehorse, Yukon.
Le Mondial SAQ (p253) Montréal, Québec.
Pride Week (p95) Toronto, Ontario.
Vancouver International Jazz Festival (p665) Vancouver, British Columbia.

JULY
Atlantic Jazz Festival (p404) Halifax, Nova Scotia.
Calgary Folk Music Festival (p601) Calgary, Alberta.
Calgary Stampede (p597) Calgary, Alberta.
Caribana (p93) Toronto, Ontario
Celebration of Light (p666) Vancouver, British Columbia.
Dawson City Music Festival (p801) Dawson City, Yukon.
Festival International de Jazz (p253) Montréal, Québec.
Festival International du Blues (p269) Mont-Tremblant, Québec.
Great Northern Arts Festival (p827) Inuvik, Northwest Territories.
Klondike Days (p583) Edmonton, Alberta.
Loyalist Days (p507) Saint John, New Brunswick.
New Brunswick Highland Games Festivals (p488) Fredericton, New Brunswick.
Shakespeare on the Saskatchewan (p566) Saskatoon, Saskatchewan.

UNIQUELY CANADIAN CELEBRATIONS

- **National Flag Day** (Feb 15) Commemorates the first time the maple leaf flag was raised above Parliament Hill in Ottawa, at the stroke of noon on February 15, 1965.

- **Victoria Day** (late May) This day was established in 1845 to observe the birthday of Queen Victoria and now celebrates the birthday of the British sovereign who's still Canada's titular head of state. Victoria Day marks the official beginning of the summer season (which ends with Labour Day on the first Monday of September). Some communities hold fireworks.

- **National Aboriginal Day** (Jun 21) Created in 1996, it celebrates the contributions of Aboriginal peoples to Canada. Coinciding with the summer solstice, festivities are organized locally and may include traditional dancing, singing and drumming; storytelling; arts and crafts shows; canoe races; and lots more.

- **Canada Day** (Jul 1) Known as Dominion Day until 1982, Canada Day was created in 1869 to commemorate the creation of Canada two years earlier. All over the country, people celebrate with barbecues, parades, concerts and fireworks.

- **Thanksgiving Day** (late Oct) First celebrated in 1578 in what is now Newfoundland by explorer Martin Frobisher to give thanks for surviving his Atlantic crossing, Thanksgiving became an official Canadian holiday in 1872 to celebrate the recovery of the Prince of Wales from a long illness. These days, it's essentially a harvest festival involving a special family dinner of roast turkey and pumpkin, very much as is it is practiced in the US.

Summer Festival (p287) Québec City, Québec.
Winnipeg Folk Festival (p536) Winnipeg, Manitoba.
Winnipeg Fringe Festival (p536) Winnipeg, Manitoba.

AUGUST
Buffalo Days (p558) Regina, Saskatchewan.
Canadian National Exhibition (p96) Toronto, Ontario.
Edmonton Fringe Theatre Festival (p583) Edmonton, Alberta.
Festival Acadien (p523) Caraquet, New Brunswick.
Festival by the Sea (p507) Saint John, New Brunswick.
Festival des Films du Monde (p253) Montréal, Québec.
Halifax International Busker Festival (p404) Halifax, Nova Scotia.
Royal St John's Regatta (p351) St John's, Newfoundland.

SEPTEMBER
Harvest Jazz & Blues Festival (p488) Fredericton, New Brunswick.
Niagara Wine Festival (p133) Niagara Peninsula Wine Country, Ontario.
PEI International Shellfish Festival (p462) Charlottetown, Prince Edward Island.
Toronto International Film Festival (p96) Toronto, Ontario.

OCTOBER–DECEMBER
Canadian Finals Rodeo (p583) Edmonton, Alberta.
International Festival of Authors (p96) Toronto, Ontario.
Oktoberfest (p137) Kitchener, Ontario.

Vancouver International Writers & Readers Festival (p666) Vancouver, British Columbia.

FOOD
In this guide we've included eating options to match all tastes and travel budgets. Budget eateries include takeouts, delis, cafés, snack bars, markets and basic restaurants where you can fill up for less than $10 including taxes. At mid-range establishments you get tablecloths, full menus, beer and wine lists and a bill that shouldn't exceed $30 per person for an appetizer, main course and one drink, not including tax and tip. Top-end places are usually gourmet affairs with fussy service, creative and freshly prepared food and matching wine lists. Main courses alone can cost $25 or more. The best deals are usually set menus (called *table d'hôte* in Québec) which include three or four courses and coffee starting at around $20.

Most restaurants in urban Canada have nonsmoking sections (and in many cities they are required by law to do so) and an increasing number prohibit smoking altogether. Not all places have air-conditioning during the summer months. If air-conditioning is important to you, enquire ahead to avoid disappointment.

For the full run-down on cuisine, customs and even where to find cooking classes in Canada, see p65.

GAY & LESBIAN TRAVELERS

Much of Canada is tolerant when it comes to gays and lesbians. In June 2003, Ontario became the first province to legalize same-sex marriage. BC followed suit in July 2003 and Québec and the Yukon in 2004. In July 2004, an Ontario lesbian couple became the first to file for divorce, sparking a round of legal wrangling. Stay tuned.

Montréal, Toronto and Vancouver are by far Canada's gayest cities, each with a humming nightlife scene, magazines, and lots of associations and support groups. All have sizeable Pride celebrations, too, which attract big crowds. For more details, see the boxed texts on p95, p254 and p667.

Attitudes remain more conservative in the northern regions. In fact, in the March 2004 Nunavut territorial election, the protection of gays and lesbians under the Nunavut Human Rights Act was *the* seminal campaign issue. The forces of tolerance won out – but only just. Throughout Nunavut, and to a lesser extent in the aboriginal communities of the Northwest Territories, there's a strain of religious zealotry that includes retrogressive attitudes toward homosexuality. The Yukon, in contrast, is more like British Columbia, with a live-and-let-live West Coast attitude.

The leading online resource for all things gay in Canada is www.gaycanada.com; also worth checking out are www.queercanada.ca and www.outandabout.com. The latter publishes downloadable gay travel guides, including one to Canada, for $12.95. **Gay Line** (☎ 888-505-1010; www.gayline.qc.ca; ☺ 7-11pm) provides information, counseling and referrals to organizations within the gay community.

HOLIDAYS
Public Holidays

Canada observes 11 national public holidays and several more at the provincial level. Banks, schools and government offices remain closed on these days. For some important festivals and major events, see p852.

NATIONAL HOLIDAYS
New Year's Day January 1
Good Friday March or April
Easter March or April
Victoria Day Monday before May 25
Civic Holiday (first Monday of August) Also known as Simcoe Day, Heritage Day or Natal Day. All provinces except Québec and the Yukon Territory.

Canada Day (July 1) Called Memorial Day in Newfoundland.
Labour Day First Monday of September
Thanksgiving Second Monday of October
Remembrance Day November 11
Christmas Day December 25
Boxing Day December 26

PROVINCIAL HOLIDAYS
Some provinces also observe local holidays, with Newfoundland leading the pack.
Family Day (Third Monday of February) Alberta.
St Patrick's Day (Monday nearest March 17) Newfoundland.
St George's Day (Monday nearest April 23) Newfoundland.
National Day (June 24) Québec; also called St-Jean-Baptiste Day.
Discovery Day (Monday nearest Jun 24) Newfoundland.
Orangemen's Day (Monday nearest July 12) Newfoundland.
Discovery Day (Third Monday of August) Yukon Territory.

School Holidays

Kids break for summer holidays in late June and don't return to school until early September. University students get even more time off, usually from sometime in May to early or mid-September. Most people take their big annual vacation during these months. Traveling is also at a peak during the week-long March Break holiday.

INSURANCE

No matter how long or short your trip, make sure you have adequate travel insurance. At a minimum, you need coverage for medical emergencies and treatment, including hospital stays and an emergency flight home. Medical treatment for non-Canadians is exorbitant; simply visiting an emergency room can set you back a whopping $500, and that's before you've received any treatment or medication. For more on health insurance, see p878.

You should also consider insurance for luggage theft or loss. If you already have a home owners or renters policy, check what it will cover and only get supplemental insurance to protect against the rest. If you have prepaid a large portion of your vacation, trip cancellation insurance is worthwhile.

Several agencies offer comprehensive travel insurance:

Insure.com (☎ 800-556-9393; www.insure.com) An independent site that compares quotes from 200 US-based insurance companies.

Quoteline Direct (☎ 0870-444 0870; www.quoteline
direct.co.uk) Compares quotes from 30 UK-based insurance
companies.
Travel Guard (☎ 877-370-4742; www.travelguard.com)
A big company.
Travelex (☎ 800-228-9792; www.travelex.com)
Another major insurer with offices worldwide.

For information about what type of vehicle
insurance you need while driving in Canada,
see p872.

INTERNET ACCESS
Surfing the Web and checking email is
rarely a problem while traveling in most
parts of Canada. Internet access is usually
free at public libraries, but downsides may
include time limits, reservation requirements, long lines and slow connections. In
smaller towns, though, this may be your
only choice. Otherwise, Internet cafés are
plentiful; they are listed in the Information
sections for individual destinations in the
regional chapters. Online access generally
costs $3 to $8 per hour. Hostels, B&Bs and
hotels offering guest terminals with free Internet access are identified in this book with
an Internet icon (🖳).

If you're traveling with your own laptop,
you'll find that in many of the newer and
recently renovated hotels you can plug in
from the comfort of your own room. High-
speed access is becoming increasingly common, especially in hotels courting a business
clientele.

Beware of digital phones without built-
in data ports, which may fry your modem
unless you're using a digital-to-analog con-
verter. Depending on where you bought your
laptop, you may need adapters for Canadian
electrical outlets and telephone sockets. Both
are available in larger electronics stores.

For more information on traveling with
a laptop and the gadgets you might need to
help you get online, see www.roadwarrior
.com or www.teleadapt.com. For information on finding wireless hotspots in Canada,
see www.wi-fihotspotlist.com/browse/ca/ or
www.hotspot-locations.com.

See p10 for a list of websites about traveling in Canada.

LEGAL MATTERS
Should you be arrested or charged with an
offense, you have the right to keep your

LEGAL AGE

- Driving a car: 16
- Smoking tobacco: 18
- Homosexual consent (for males): 18
- Consent for other sexual activity: 14
- Voting in an election: 18
- Drinking alcoholic beverages: 19 (18 in Alberta, Manitoba and Québec)

---

mouth shut and to hire any lawyer you wish
(contact your embassy for a referral, if necessary). If you cannot afford one, ask to be
represented by public counsel. There is a
presumption of innocence.

If driving in Canada, you need to carry
your driver's license (p872) and carefully
obey road rules (p874). The highest permissible blood-alcohol limit is 0.08% and
driving cars, motorcycles, boats and snowmobiles while drunk is a criminal offense.
If you are caught, you may face stiff fines,
have your license suspended, be charged
higher insurance premiums and other nasty
consequences. Consuming alcohol anywhere other than at a residence or licensed
premises is also a no-no, which puts parks,
beaches and the rest of the great outdoors
off limits, at least officially.

When it comes to illegal drugs, the sensible
thing to do is to avoid them entirely, as penalties may entail heavy fines, possible jail time
and a criminal record. The only exception is
the use of marijuana for medical purposes,
which became legal in 2001. Meanwhile, the
decriminalization of pot possession for personal use remains a subject of intense and
ongoing debate among the general public
and in parliament. Statistically, less than 0.5%
of marijuana users are caught by police and
over 50% of them get off with a warning.

Abortion is legal.

MAPS
Most tourist offices distribute free (often
very basic) city maps, but if you're driving around Canada, you can't do without a detailed road map or atlas, such as
those published by Rand McNally. If you
are a member of the Canadian Automobile Association (CAA; p872) or one of its
international affiliates, you can get CAA's

high-quality maps for free from any local office. Bookshops usually stock a good assortment of maps, while newsagents and gas stations have more limited selections. For downloadable maps and driving directions, try **Mapquest** (www.mapquest.com) or **Yahoo! Maps** (http://maps.yahoo.com).

If you're going on an extended hike or multiday backcountry trek, it's a good idea to carry a topographic map. The best are the series of 1:50,000 scale maps published by the government's **Centre for Topographic Information** (http://maps.nrcan.gc.ca) These are sold by around 900 map dealers around the country; check the website, or the Yellow Pages under 'maps', for the one nearest you. You can also download and print maps from www.geobase.ca.

MONEY

All prices quoted in this book are in Canadian dollars ($), unless stated otherwise.

Canadian coins come in 1¢ (penny), 5¢ (nickel), 10¢ (dime), 25¢ (quarter), $1 (loonie) and $2 (toonie or twoonie) denominations. The gold-colored loonie features the loon, a common Canadian water bird, while the two-toned toonie is decorated with a polar bear.

Paper currency comes in $5 (blue), $10 (purple), $20 (green) and $50 (red) denominations. The $100 (brown) and larger bills are less common, and they can be tough to change.

Thanks to an unstable world economy, wars and other destabilizing factors, the Canadian dollar has seen some fluctuation in recent years, bottoming out in January 2002 when one loonie was worth a mere US$0.62. By late 2004 it had rebounded to about US$0.83, thanks in large part to a weak US economy. Good websites to check for the latest rates are www.xe.com/ucc and www.oanda.com.

When changing money, compare rates and fees. In the larger cities, currency exchange offices may offer better conditions than banks. Conditions are likely to be less favorable at counters in airports, train stations and tourist centers than in larger city centers. Some businesses near the US–Canadian border and in big cities accept payment in US dollars, with change usually given in Canadian dollars. Don't expect the exchange rate to be in your favor.

For an overview of how much things cost in Canada, see p9.

ATMs

Many grocery stores, shopping centers, airports, bus and train stations and convenience stores have ATMs. Most are linked to several international networks, the most common being Cirrus, Plus, Star and Maestro.

Most ATMs also spit out cash if you use a major credit card. This method tends to be more expensive because, in addition to a service fee, you'll be charged interest immediately (in other words, there's no interest-free period as with purchases). For exact fees, check with your own bank or credit-card company.

Cash & Personal Checks

Most Canadians don't carry large amounts of cash for everyday use, relying instead on credit and debit cards. Still, carrying some cash, say $100 or less, comes in handy when making small purchases. Unlike in the USA, shops and businesses rarely accept personal checks.

Credit Cards

Major credit cards such as MasterCard, Visa and American Express are widely accepted in Canada, except in remote, rural communities where cash is king. Still, you'll find it hard or impossible to rent a car, book a room or order tickets over the phone without having a piece of plastic. Even if you prefer ATMs and/or traveler's checks, a credit card may be vital in emergencies. Carry copies of your credit card numbers separately from the cards and immediately report lost or stolen cards:

American Express (☎ 866-296-5198; www.american express.com)

MasterCard (☎ 800-307-7309; www.mastercard.com)

Visa (☎ 800-847-2911; www.visa.com)

Taxes & Refunds

Canada's federal goods and services tax (GST), variously known as the 'gouge and screw' or 'grab and steal' tax, adds 7% to just about every transaction. To make matters worse, most provinces also charge a provincial sales tax (PST) ranging from 7% to 10%. Only the Yukon, Northwest Territories and Nunavut do not levy PST. The Atlantic provinces – New Brunswick, Nova Scotia,

Newfoundland and Labrador – have combined the GST and PST into a harmonized sales tax (HST) of 15%.

If you've spent at least $200 on short-term accommodations and nonconsumable goods, you can have the GST and HST refunded if you leave Canada within 60 days from the date of purchase. The only other hitch is that each eligible receipt must be for at least $50 before taxes.

At the airport or land border crossing have your original receipts (credit-card slips alone are not sufficient) stamped by a customs agent, then mail them along with a tax-rebate application (widely available at tourist offices, shops, hotels and on the Internet) to the address listed on the form. Allow a couple of months for processing. Don't be misled by private companies that distribute 'official tax refund' booklets at visitor centers and duty-free shops. These companies offer to obtain your refund for you and then take up to 20% for their 'services'. It's usually just as fast and easy to do it on your own.

For full details, check with the **Visitor Rebate Program** (☎ 902-432-5608, 800-668-4748; www .ccra-adrc.gc.ca/visitors).

Tipping
In restaurants, leaving a tip of about 15% of the pretax bill is standard. Tipping is expected for bar service too. For more on tipping in restaurants, see p65.

At hotels, tip bellhops about $1 to $2 per bag. Leaving a few dollars for the room cleaners is always a welcome gesture. Cab drivers, hairdressers and barbers also expect a tip, usually 10% to 15%.

Traveler's Checks
Once a popular alternative to carrying large wads of cash, traveler's checks are becoming increasingly obsolete in the age of ATMs. Still, they may come in handy as a backup, especially when traveling in remote regions where ATMs may be thin on the ground, or in case your bank card isn't affiliated with any of the international networks.

Traveler's checks issued in Canadian dollars are generally treated like cash in hotels, restaurants and stores. Some vendors may be reluctant to accept large checks for small purchases, so be sure to get at least some in denominations of $20 or $50. Traveler's

checks in most other currencies must be exchanged for Canadian dollars at a bank or foreign-currency office.

Traveler's checks issued by American Express, Citibank, Visa and MasterCard are widely accepted and quickly replaced if lost or stolen, usually within 24 hours. Keeping a record of the check numbers separate from the checks themselves will greatly expedite the replacement process.

American Express (☎ 866-296-5198)
MasterCard (☎ 800-223-9920)
Visa (☎ 800-227-6811)

POST
Canada's national postal service, known as Canada Post/Postes Canada, is neither quick nor cheap, but it is fairly reliable. Stamps are available at post offices, drugstores, convenience stores and hotels.

Postcards or standard 1st-class airmail letters up to 30g cost 50¢ within Canada, 85¢ to the USA and $1.45 to all other countries. For other rates, postal codes and general information, ask at any post office, call the toll-free **helpline** (☎ 800-267-1177; ☯ 8am-6pm Mon-Fri) or visit www.canadapost.ca.

Poste restante mail is held for collection at the local main post office or, in the case of big cities, a designated branch. It is kept for 15 days before being returned to the sender. There is no charge, but you need to bring a passport or other photo ID when collecting it. Call the helpline for the postal codes of specific post offices where general delivery mail is accepted.

POSTAL ABBREVIATIONS	
Provinces & Territories	**Abbreviations**
Alberta	AB
British Columbia	BC
Manitoba	MB
New Brunswick	NB
Newfoundland & Labrador	NL
Northwest Territories	NT
Nova Scotia	NS
Nunavut	NU
Ontario	ON
Prince Edward Island	PE
Québec	QC
Saskatchewan	SK
Yukon Territory	YT

Sometimes Canadian customs may hold up packages being sent from other countries, especially the USA. Travelers often find they have to pay high duties on items sent to them while in Canada.

SHOPPING

Canada is a great place to shop, with a big selection of everyday and unique items. Much shopping these days is done in malls, with the West Edmonton Mall (p582) and its over 800 stores clearly the mother of them all. As elsewhere, more unusual and interesting items are typically found in smaller establishments and galleries. Everything you buy is subject to tax, but some of your purchases may qualify for a refund (see p857).

Art & Jewelry

While Yellowknife (p816) is North America's diamond capital and Dawson City (p798) is still capitalizing on its Klondike gold-rush days, the north is great for buying shiny baubles. Yellowknife (p816) is the best place in Canada for buying aboriginal art and crafts. There are paintings and prints, but the most stunning items are carved sculptures representing various animals and spirits, made from soapstone, antler, wood, bone and jade. The Inuit in Nunavut (p837) also make stunning embroidered tapestries that would brighten up any room. The Dene in Fort Liard (p824) are famous for their birch-bark baskets adorned with porcupine quills.

Art-lovers can pick up works by Canadian artists in just about every province. Woodcarving has enjoyed a long tradition, notably in St Jean Port Joli (p313) in Québec and along the French Shore of Nova Scotia. Chéticamp (p442), also in Nova Scotia, is famous for its handmade hooked rugs. You'll also find a wealth of First Nations art across the country; in BC it includes handmade jewelry, ceremonial masks, carved cedar sculptures and even totem poles (see p678).

Edibles

If you're shopping for edible souvenirs, BC's smoked salmon is a real treat. West Coast purveyors will also pack fresh salmon to take on flights home. In Québec, maple syrup and maple sugar make inexpensive gifts. Wine grown in Ontario's Niagara region or British Columbia's Okanagan Valley can be very good. Rye whiskey is a Canadian specialty.

Fashion

Montréal is one of the best places for cool fashions by local designers such as Jean-Claude Poitras, Marie Saint-Pierre, Michel Desjardin and Maurice Ferland. Across the country, in Vancouver, John Fluevog's shoes and Yumi Eto's glamour gowns have fans that include Madonna, Sarah McLachlan and Susan Sarandon.

BC is also home-base for Roots, a fine outdoor clothing company which has outlets across the country. It catapulted to international fame during the 2002 Winter Olympics when both the US and Canadian teams flaunted their comfy outfits. Alberta and Saskatchewan are both great for discovering your inner cowboy. There are plenty of stores selling quality Stetsons, neck ties and big belt-buckles.

Further north, in the Yukon and Northwest Territories, you'll be able to stock up on such unique items as hand-sewn hide moccasins, gloves and vests. Nunavut has a wide selection of Arctic clothing made from caribou, sea wolf and even polar bear.

SOLO TRAVELERS

There are no particular problems or difficulties traveling alone in Canada. Although it is not for everybody, a major advantage is the freedom to do anything and go anywhere you want, whenever you want.

Canadians are generally friendly and easy to talk to. Women don't need to be afraid of initiating a conversation, even with men. Unless you're overtly coquettish, it most likely won't be interpreted as a sexual advance. Going alone to cafés and restaurants is perfectly acceptable, although how comfortable you feel doing so depends entirely on you. Hostels are among the best places for hooking up with other travelers. Unless you're a total loner, you'll soon meet people with whom to share travel tips or go sightseeing, bar-hopping or out to a movie. Guided walking tours, major tourist attractions and Internet cafés are also good places to run into other travelers.

If you're going for a long hike, be sure to let someone – anyone, but preferably a park ranger – know about your intended where-

CAVEAT EMPTOR! A PRIMER ON BUYING ABORIGINAL ART

Authentic aboriginal sculpture is exquisite, highly prized and expensive. A small soapstone carving can cost up to $500, depending on the detail. Jade and ivory are pricier still, and large sculptures can run into the thousands of dollars.

Unfortunately, such precious artwork has generated a roaring business in fakes. Mass-produced items, sometimes from places as far away as Bali, are often passed off as handmade in Canada – and priced accordingly. These imitations may look like the real thing, but they have no real value and are not endorsed by the artists or the Canadian government. Purchasing them robs Aboriginal people of their intellectual property and undercuts their economies.

If you're coveting that dancing polar bear or reclining walrus for your mantelpiece, take a few cautionary steps to make sure it's the real thing before handing over your credit card. To protect consumers and artists, the Canadian government has registered the symbol of the igloo as a trademark. Sculptures bearing this 'igloo tag' or sticker are government-certified to be handmade by an Inuit. In addition, some artists carve their names or initials on their work either in Roman or Inuktikut script.

Be especially conscious of from whom you are purchasing the art. Ask lots of questions: Is the product made in Canada? Is it made by an Aboriginal artist? What is the artist's name and where is he or she from? A reputable dealer will happily talk about the artists, their cultural background and the material used. Watch out for the wiggle words: carvings may be labeled 'Canadian soapstone' but just because the raw material is from Canada, it doesn't mean that an Aboriginal artist did the work.

Take time to shop around and learn about the item you want to buy. Check out art books, museums or other collections for information. Ask the staff at tourist offices or museums for reputable dealers. Purchasing handmade Aboriginal art is an investment that should not be made lightly.

abouts in case something should happen to you. Carrying a cell phone can be a lifesaver in such emergencies.

Other issues of safety are slightly different for women than they are for men; see p861 for more specific advice.

TELEPHONE

Canada has an excellent telephone system. Public pay phones are ubiquitous and generally coin operated, although many also accept prepaid phonecards and credit cards. Local calls cost 25¢. Dialing the operator (☎ 0), directory assistance (☎ 411) or the emergency number (☎ 911) is free of charge from both public and private phones. Note that ☎ 911 is not the emergency number in the Yukon, Northwest Territories or Nunavut (see those chapters for emergency numbers). For long-distance directory assistance, dial ☎ 1 + area code + 555-1212, which is also a free call. Calls made from hotel rooms are usually charged at a premium, but you may be able to get around this by using a phonecard (see right). That is, unless your hotel (or motel) applies an access fee for every call, even for local or toll-free numbers.

Mobile Phones

Canadians are increasingly becoming as cell-phone-addicted as people in the USA and Europe. This is especially true in major urban centers and populous provinces. The GSM/GPRS network is sparse, so reception may be poor outside urban areas. The only foreign phones that will work in North America are tri-band models, operating on GSM 1900 and other frequencies. If you don't have such a phone, your best bet may be to buy a prepaid one at a consumer electronics store. Most cost less than $100, including some prepaid minutes and a rechargeable SIM card for buying additional call time. Most throw in free voicemail as well. There are no contracts or billing hassles and you don't have to be a resident to buy one. On the downside, per-minute rates are relatively high, but a plan may be available to suit your particular needs.

Phone Codes

Canadian phone numbers consist of a three-number area code followed by a seven-digit local number. When dialing a number within the same area code, just dial the seven-digit number. Long-distance calls must be preceded by ☎ 1.

For direct international calls, dial ☎ 011 + country code + area code + local phone number. The country code for Canada is ☎ 1 (the same as for the USA, although international rates still apply for all calls made between the two countries).

Toll-free numbers begin with ☎ 800, ☎ 877 or ☎ 866 and must be preceded by 1. Some of these numbers are good throughout Canada and the USA, others only work within Canada, and some work in just one province.

Phonecards

Prepaid phonecards usually offer the best per-minute rates for long-distance and international calling. They come in denominations of $5, $10 or $20 and are widely sold in drugstores, supermarkets and convenience stores. Beware of cards with hidden charges such as 'activation fees' or a per-call connection fee. A surcharge ranging from 30¢ to 85¢ for calls made from public pay phones is common.

If you're staying at upmarket hotels, fax transmissions are generally not a problem. There's usually no fee for receiving faxes, though sending them can cost a bundle. If you carry a laptop with a fax modem, you only pay for the cost of the telephone call (but do keep in mind that hotel phone rates are often exorbitant). Faxes can also be sent from Internet cafes (p855) and copy shops.

TIME

Canada spans six of the world's 24 time zones. The Eastern zone in Newfoundland is unusual in that it's only 30 minutes different from the adjacent zone. The time difference from coast to coast is 4½ hours. Refer to the World Time Zones map on p883 for additional data.

Canada observes daylight saving time, which comes into effect on the first Sunday in April, when clocks are put forward one hour, and ends on the last Sunday in October. Saskatchewan and small pockets of Québec, Ontario and BC are the only areas that do not switch to daylight saving time.

For detailed time-zone information, see the website of the **Institute for National Measurement Standards** (www.nrc.ca/inms).

In Québec especially, times for shop hours, train schedules, film screenings etc are usually indicated by the 24 hour clock.

TOURIST INFORMATION

The Internet site maintained by the **Canadian Tourism Commission** (www.travelcanada.ca) is loaded with general information, packages and links. Provincial tourist offices all maintain comprehensive websites packed with information helpful in planning your trip. Staff also field telephone enquiries and, on request, will happily mail out free maps and brochures about accommodations, attractions and events. Some offices can also help with making hotel, tour or other reservations.

For detailed information about a specific area, you'll need to contact a local tourist office. Just about every city and town has at least a seasonal branch with helpful staff, racks of free pamphlets and books and maps for sale. Their addresses are listed in the Information sections for individual destinations in the regional chapters of this book.

Provincial tourist offices:

Travel Alberta (☎ 780-427-4321, 800-252-3782; www.travelalberta.com; PO Box 2500, Edmonton, AB T5J 2Z4)

Tourism British Columbia (☎ 250-356-6363, 604-435-5622, 800-435-5622; www.hellobc.com; PO Box 9860, Stn Prov Govt/3rd fl, 1803 Douglas St, Victoria, BC V8W 9W5)

Travel Manitoba (☎ 204-945-3777, 800-665-0040; www.travelmanitoba.com; Travel Manitoba, Dept SM5, 7th fl, 155 Carlton St, Winnipeg, MB R3C 3H8)

Tourism New Brunswick (☎ 506-753-3876, 800-561-0123; www.tourismnbcanada.com; PO Box 12345, Campbellton, NB E3N 3T6)

Newfoundland & Labrador Tourism (☎ 800-563-6353; www.gov.nf.ca/tourism; PO Box 8700, St John's, NL A1B 4J6)

Northwest Territories (NWT) Arctic Tourism (☎ 867-873-7200, 800-661-0788; www.nwttravel.nt.ca; PO Box 610, Yellowknife, NT X1A 2N5)

Tourism Nova Scotia (☎ 902-425-5781, 800-565-0000; www.novascotia.com; PO Box 456, Halifax, NS B3J 2R5)

Nunavut Tourism (☎ 867-979-4636, 866-686-2888; www.nunatour.nt.ca; PO Box 1450, Iqaluit, NU X0A 0H0)

Ontario Tourism (☎ 800-668-2746; www.ontariotravel.net; 10th fl, Hearst Block, 900 Bay St, Toronto, ON M7A 2E1)

Prince Edward Island (PEI) Tourism (☎ 902-368-4444, 888-734-7529; www.peiplay.com; PO Box 2000, Stn Central, Charlottetown, PE C1A 7N8)

Tourisme Québec (☎ 514-873-2015, 877-266-5687; www.bonjourquebec.com; PO Box 979, Montréal, QC H3C 2W3)

Tourism Saskatchewan (☎ 306-787-9600, 877-237-2273; www.sasktourism.com; 1922 Park St, Regina, SK S4P 3V7)

Yukon Department of Tourism (☎ 867-667-5036, 800-789-8566; www.touryukon.com; PO Box 2703, Whitehorse, YT Y1A 2C6)

VISAS

For information about passport requirements, see p863.

Citizens of dozens of countries – including the USA, most Western European and Commonwealth countries, as well as Mexico, Japan, South Korea and Israel – don't need visas to enter Canada for stays up to 180 days. US permanent residents are also exempt from obtaining visas regardless of their nationality.

Nationals of around 150 other countries, including South Africa, China (including Hong Kong) and Poland, need to apply to the Canadian visa office in their home country (usually at the embassy, high commission or consulate) for a temporary resident visa (TRV). The website maintained by **Citizenship and Immigration Canada** (CIC; www.cic.gc.ca) has full details, including office addresses and the latest requirements. A separate visa is required if you plan to study or work in Canada (see p862).

Single-entry TRVs ($75) are usually valid for a maximum stay of six months from the date of your arrival in Canada, unless the immigration officer enters a different date on your visa at the time of entry. Multiple-entry TRVs ($150) allow you to enter Canada from all other countries multiple times while the visa is valid (usually two or three years), provided no single stay exceeds six months.

Visa extensions ($75) need to be filed with the **CIC Visitor Case Processing Centre** (☎ 888-242-2100; ◷ 8am-4pm Mon-Fri) in Alberta at least one month before your current visa expires.

A passport and/or visa do not guarantee entry. The admission and duration of a permitted stay is based on various factors, including good health, being law abiding, having sufficient money and, possibly, having a return ticket out of the country.

Visiting the USA

Visitors to Canada who also plan to spend time in the USA should know that admission requirements are subject to rapid change. Check with a US consulate in your home country or the visa website maintained by the **US Department of State** (www.unitedstatesvisas.gov) for the latest eligibility requirements.

Under the US visa-waiver program, visas are not currently required for citizens of 27 countries – including most EU members, Australia and New Zealand – for visits of up to 90 days (no extensions allowed), although visitors must present a valid, machine-readable passport. Starting on October 26, 2005, however, only citizens from visa-waiver countries who can present a passport containing biometric information (such as a fingerprint or face scan) may enter the USA without a visa. If you don't have such a passport, you will need to apply for a US visa in your home country.

Canadian citizens are exempt from visa and passport requirements but must show proof of citizenship. Citizens of all other countries need to apply for a US visa in their home country before arriving in Canada.

All visitors, regardless of their country of origin, are subject to a US$6 entry fee at land border crossings. Note that you don't need a Canadian multiple-entry TRV (see left) for repeated entries into Canada from the USA, unless you have visited a third country.

In 2004, the US Department of Homeland Security introduced a new set of security measures called US-VISIT. When you arrive by air or sea, you will be photographed and have your two index fingers scanned. Eventually this biometric data will be matched when you leave the USA. The goal is to ensure that the person who entered the USA is the same as the one leaving it and to catch people who've overstayed the terms of their admission.

At the time of writing, this procedure was also being implemented at the busiest land border crossings, including many with Canada, with the goal of extending it to all entry points by the end of 2005. Visitors from visa-waiver countries are currently exempt from being finger-scanned and photographed at land borders, although this could change at any time. For full details about US-VISIT, check with a US consulate in your country or see www.dhs.gov/us-visit.

WOMEN TRAVELERS

Canada is generally a safe place for women to travel, even alone and even in the cities.

Of course, this doesn't mean you can let your guard down and blindly entrust your life to every stranger. Simply use the same common sense you would at home.

In bars and nightclubs, solo women are likely to attract a lot of attention, but if you don't want company, most men will respect a firm 'no thank you.' If you feel threatened, protesting loudly will often make the offender slink away with embarrassment – or will at least spur other people to come to your defense. Note that carrying mace or pepper spray is illegal in Canada.

Although physical attack is unlikely it does, of course, happen. If you are assaulted, call the police immediately (☎ 911) or contact a women's or rape crisis center. The latter can also help you in dealing with all kinds of emotional and physical issues surrounding an assault and make referrals to useful organizations and support groups. Centers exist in all major and many smaller Canadian cities. For a complete list, contact the **Canadian Association of Sexual Assault Centres** (☎ 604-876-2622; www.casac.ca). Hotlines in some of the major cities:

Calgary (☎ 403-237-5888)
Montréal (☎ 514-934-4504)
Toronto (☎ 416-597-8808)
Vancouver (☎ 604-255-6344)

Good online resources for women travelers include **Journeywoman** (www.journeywoman.com) and **Her Own Way** (www.voyage.gc.ca/main/pubs/PDF/her_own_way-en.pdf). The latter is published by the Canadian government for Canadian travelers, but it contains lots of good general advice.

WORK

In almost all cases, you need a valid work permit if you wish to work in Canada. Depending on your skills, obtaining one may be difficult, as employment opportunities go to Canadians first. Before you can even apply, you need a specific job offer from an employer who in turn must have been granted permission from the government to give the position to a foreign national. Applications must be filed at a visa office of a Canadian embassy, consulate or high commission in your home country. Some jobs are exempt from the requirement for a work permit. For full details, see www.cic.gc.ca/english/work.

Employers hiring temporary service workers (hotel, bar, restaurant, resort) and construction, farm or forestry workers often don't ask for a permit. If you get caught, however, you can kiss Canada goodbye.

Students aged 18 to 25 from over a dozen countries, including the UK, Australia, New Zealand, Ireland and South Africa, are eligible to apply for a spot in the **Student Work Abroad Program** (SWAP; www.swap.ca). If successful, you get a one-year, nonextendable visa that allows you to work anywhere you wish in Canada in any job you can get. Most 'SWAPpers' find work in the service industry as servers, hotel porters, bartenders or as farmhands. The program is administered by different agencies in each country.

Even if you're not a student, you may be able to spend up to a year in Canada on a **Working Holiday Program** (WHP; www.dfait-maeci.gc.ca/123go/workholiday-en.asp). You must be between 18 and 30 years old and a citizen of Australia, France, Germany, Ireland, Japan, the Netherlands, New Zealand, South Korea, Sweden or the UK. There are quotas for each country and spaces are filled on a first-come, first-served basis. Competition is stiff, so apply as early as possible. It takes about 12 weeks to process an application.

Transportation

THINGS CHANGE...

The information in this chapter is particularly vulnerable to change. Check directly with the airline or a travel agent to make sure you understand how a fare (and ticket you may buy) works, and be aware of the security requirements for international travel. Shop carefully. The details given in this chapter should be regarded as pointers and are not a substitute for your own careful, up-to-date research.

GETTING THERE & AWAY

ENTERING THE COUNTRY

Passengers arriving in Canada by plane are given the standard immigration and customs forms to fill out during the flight. After landing you first go through immigration, then through customs. In the post-9/11 world, officials can be very strict and you may be asked a series of questions. Questioning may be more intense at land border crossings (especially ones that are not very busy) and your car may be searched as well.

Having a criminal record of any kind, including a DUI (driving under the influence) charge, may keep you out of Canada. If this affects you, you should apply for a 'waiver of exclusion' at a Canadian consulate in your country. The process costs $200, takes several weeks and approval is not guaranteed. If your conviction dates back 10 years or more, you're automatically considered 'rehabilitated,' at least as long as you haven't broken the law since.

Like many countries, Canada is very concerned about child abduction. This is why single parents, grandparents or guardians traveling with anyone under 18 should carry proof of legal custody, or a notarized letter from the nonaccompanying parent or parents authorizing the trip. Not having such documentation may cause delays when entering the country. Unaccompanied children need a notarized letter of consent from both parents or legal guardians. This is in addition to a passport or proof of citizenship.

Passport

Visitors from all countries except the USA need a passport to enter Canada. US citizens must show either a US passport or proof of US citizenship – such as a certified copy of their birth certificate or certificate of naturalization – plus photo identification, preferably a current valid driver's license. Permanent US residents don't need passports, but do need to bring their green cards. A US citizen or permanent resident entering Canada from a third country must have a valid passport.

Some visitors require visas in order to enter Canada (see p861).

AIR
Airports & Airlines

Canada has about 500 airports and 800 unpaved landing strips, but you're most likely to arrive at one of the following international gateways:

Calgary (YYX; ☎ 403-735-1200; www.calgaryairport.com)
Edmonton (YEG; ☎ 780-890-8382, 800-268-7134; www.edmontonairports.com)

Halifax (YHZ; ☎ 902-873-4422; www.hiaa.ca)
Montréal (Pierre Elliott Trudeau; YUL; ☎ 514-394-7377, 800-465-1213; www.admtl.com)
Ottawa (YOW; ☎ 613-248-2000; www.ottawa-airport.ca)
Toronto (Pearson; YYZ; ☎ 416-776-3000; www.gtaa.com)
Vancouver (YVR; ☎ 604-207-7077; www.yvr.ca)
Winnipeg (YWG; ☎ 204-987-9402; www.waa.ca)

Air Canada, the national flagship carrier, is considered one of the world's safest airlines. Other companies based in Canada and serving international destinations are the charter airline Air Transat and the discount airlines CanJet, WestJet and JetsGo. In addition, numerous US airlines and national carriers of other countries serve Canada.

The following list contains airlines' telephone numbers in Canada for reservations, flight changes and information. For contact information in your home country, see the websites.

Air Canada (AC; ☎ 888-247-2262; www.aircanada.ca)
Air France (AF; ☎ 800-667-2747; www.airfrance.com/ca)
Air New Zealand (NZ; ☎ 800-663-5494; www.airnewzealand.com)
Air Transat (TSC; ☎ 866-847-1919; www.airtransat.com)
Alaska Air (AS; ☎ 800-252-7522; www.alaskaair.com)
Alitalia (AZ; ☎ 800-268-9277; www.alitalia.ca)
America West Airlines (HP; ☎ 800-327-7810; www.americawest.com)
American Airlines (AA; ☎ 800-433-7300; www.aa.com)
ANA (☎ 800-235-9262; www.anaskyweb.com)
British Airways (BA; ☎ 800-247-9297; www.britishairways.com)
CanJet (C6; ☎ 800-809-7777; www.canjet.com)
Cathay Pacific (CX; ☎ 800-268-6868; www.cathay.ca)
China Airlines (CI; ☎ 800-227-5118; www.china-airlines.com)
Continental Airlines (CO; ☎ 800-231-0856; www.continental.com)
Czech Airlines (OK; ☎ 416-363-3174; www.czech-Airlines.com)
Delta (DL; ☎ 800-241-4141; www.delta.com)
Eva Air (BR; ☎ 800-695-1188; www.evaair.com)
Japan Airlines (JL; ☎ 800-525-3663; www.japanair.com)
JetsGo (SG; ☎ 866-440-0441; www.jetsgo.com)
Horizon Air (QX; ☎ 80-547-9308; www.horizonair.com)
KLM (KL; ☎ 800-225-2525; www.klm.com)
Lufthansa (LH; ☎ 800-563-5954; www.lufthansa.com)
Northwest Airlines (NWA; ☎ 800-225-2525; www.nwa.com)
Philippine Airlines (PR; ☎ 800-235-9262; www.philippineairlines.com)
Qantas (QF; ☎ 800-227-4500; www.quantas.com)

Singapore Airlines (SQ; ☎ 800-387-0038; www.singaporeair.com)
Swiss Air (LX; ☎ 877-359-7947; www.swiss.com)
United Airlines (UA; ☎ 800-621-5647; www.united.ca)
US Airways (US; ☎ 800-428-4322; www.usairways.com)
WestJet (WS; ☎ 888-937-8538; www.westjet.com)

Tickets

Since the airplane ticket eats the single biggest chunk out of most travel budgets, it's wise to spend a little time shopping around. Basically, timing is key when it comes to snapping up cheap fares. As a rule of thumb, you can save a bundle by booking as early as possible (at least three weeks in advance, more for summer dates) and by traveling midweek (Tuesday to Thursday) and in the off-season (October to mid-May, except for winter-sports destinations). Departures in the late evening or early morning may also be less costly than the daytime flights popular with suits. Some airlines offer lower fares, if you stay over a Saturday.

Your best friend in ferreting out bargain fares is the Internet. Online agencies, such as the ones listed below, are good places to start, but they are best when used in conjunction with other search engines. One of these is ITA Software (www.itasoftware.com), a search matrix that sorts results by price, while also alerting you to potential downsides such as long layovers, tight connections or overnight travel. The cheapest flight may not be the best flight. An extra $20 may be money well spent, if it gets you to your destination in the afternoon instead of at midnight. You can even search for the cheapest fare during any 30-day period. No software download is required. Note this site does not actually sell tickets, which must be bought from a travel agent or the airline.

Another handy tool is Sidestep (www.sidestep.com, requires a free software download that may contain spyware), which searches multiple airlines simultaneously, including low-cost carriers, which are not covered by companies such as Expedia and Orbitz.

One way to learn about late-breaking bargain fares is by signing on to airlines' free weekly email newsletters. Even the old-fashioned newspaper can yield deals, especially in times of fare wars, when airlines plaster the travel sections with giant ads. And don't forget about travel agents, who can be especially helpful when planning extensive trips or complicated routes.

Tickets for flights departing from Canada, whether purchased in Canada or abroad, should include departure taxes. Some airports also charge departing passengers a so-called 'airport improvement tax,' usually $10 or $15.

Atevo Travel (www.atevo.com)
Cheap Tickets (www.cheaptickets.com)
Expedia (www.expedia.com)
Hotwire (www.hotwire.com)
Info-Hub Specialty Travel Guide (www.biztravel.com)
LowestFare (www.lowestfare.com)
Orbitz (www.orbitz.com)
Priceline (www.priceline.com)
STA Travel (www.sta.com)
Travelocity (www.travelocity.com)
Yahoo! Travel (www.travel.yahoo.com)

COURIER FLIGHTS
If you're on a flexible schedule and traveling solo, flying as a courier might save you a bundle. Couriers accompany freight to its destination, in exchange for a discounted ticket. You don't have to handle any shipment personally; you simply deliver the freight papers to a representative of the courier company at your destination. Your luggage is limited to carry-on and there may be other restrictions, such as the length of stay.

International Association of Air Travel Couriers (IAATC; ☎ 352-475-1584; www.courier.org) and **Air Courier Association** (ACA; ☎ 800-282-1202; www.air courier.org) are both US-based central clearing houses that keep track of routes offered by courier companies; membership is required. IAATC also has an office in the **UK** (☎ 0800-0746-481; www.aircourier.co.uk).

INTERCONTINENTAL (RTW) TICKETS
Round-the-world (RTW) tickets are great, if you want to visit other countries besides Canada. They're usually more expensive than a simple round-trip ticket, but the extra stops are good value. They're of most value for trips that combine Canada with Europe, Asia or Australasia. RTW itineraries that include South America or Africa, as well as North America, are substantially more expensive.

Official RTW tickets are usually put together by a combination of airlines, or an entire alliance, and permit you to fly to a specified number of stops and/or a maximum mileage, so long as you don't back-track. They are usually valid for one year. An alternative type of RTW ticket is one put together by a travel agent using a combination of discounted tickets.

Most RTW fares restrict the number of stops within Canada and the USA. The cheapest fares permit only one stop; others allow two or more. Some airlines 'black out' a few heavily traveled routes (such as Honolulu to Tokyo). In most cases a 14-day advance purchase is required. After the ticket is purchased, dates can usually be changed without penalty, and tickets can be rewritten to add or delete stops for an extra charge.

Air Brokers (www.airbrokers.com)
Air Treks (www.airtreks.com)
Circle the Planet (www.circletheplanet.com)
Just Fares (www.justfares.com)

Asia
The main Canadian gateway for flights originating in Asia is Vancouver. Air Canada operates nonstop services from Hong Kong, Osaka, Seoul, Shanghai, Taipei and Tokyo. Japan Airlines and ANA fly in from Tokyo, Philippine Airlines from Manila, China Airlines and Eva Air from Taipei and Cathay Pacific from Hong Kong. In addition, Air Canada operates direct flights to Toronto from New Delhi, Tokyo and Hong Kong.

Traveling to other Canadian cities requires a stopover or transfer, often in a US gateway city such as Los Angeles or Chicago.

Four Seas Tours Hong Kong (☎ 2200-7760; www.four seastravel.com/english)
No 1 Travel Tokyo (☎ 3205-6073; www.no1-travel.com)
STA Travel Bangkok (☎ 236-0262; www.statravel.co.th); Singapore (☎ 6737-7188; www.statravel.com.sg); Hong Kong (☎ 2736-1618; www.statravel.com.hk); Tokyo (☎ 5391-2922; www.statravel.co.jp)

Australia & New Zealand
There are no nonstop flights from Australia or New Zealand to Canada. The best route is from Sydney to Los Angeles, with onward service to your Canadian destination. Air Canada, Air New Zealand and Qantas are the dominant airlines on this route, but United Airlines and American Airlines also offer flights. Some flights stop in Honolulu.

AUSTRALIA
Flight Centre (☎ 133-133; www.flightcentre.com.au)
STA Travel (☎ 1300-733-035; www.statravel.com.au)
Travel.com (www.travel.com.au)

NEW ZEALAND

Flight Centre (☎ 0800-243-544; www.flightcentre.co.nz)
STA Travel (☎ 0508-782-872; www.statravel.co.nz)
Travel.co.nz (www.travel.co.nz)

Continental Europe

Toronto is the main gateway for European flights. Air Canada is the primary carrier, with services from Amsterdam, Copenhagen, Frankfurt, Munich, Paris, Vienna and Zurich. European airlines flying to Toronto include Alitalia, Czech Airlines and Lufthansa.

If you're headed for Montréal, you'll find direct flights from Amsterdam (KLM), Athens (Olympic Airways), Frankfurt (Air Canada), Paris (Air France, Air Canada), Prague (Czech Airlines) and Zurich (Swiss Air). Air Canada also operates a direct flight from Frankfurt to Calgary, while KLM and Lufthansa fly nonstop to Vancouver. In summer, the charter airline Air Transat has flights from nine European countries to all major cities, including Edmonton and Halifax.

FRANCE

Anyway (☎ 0892-893-892; www.anyway.fr)
Lastminute (☎ 0892-705-000; www.fr.lastminute.com)
Nouvelles Frontières (☎ 0825-000-747; www.nouvelles-frontieres.fr)
OTU Voyages (www.otu.fr) Specializes in student and youth travelers.
Voyageurs du Monde (☎ 01-40-15-11-15; www.vdm.com)

GERMANY

Expedia (www.expedia.de)
Just Travel (☎ 089-747-3330; www.justtravel.de)
Lastminute (☎ 01805-284-366; www.lastminute.de)
STA Travel (☎ 01805-456-422; www.statravel.de)

ITALY

A recommended travel agency is **CTS Viaggi** (☎ 06-462-0431; www.cts.it).

NETHERLANDS

The travel agency **Airfair** (☎ 020-620-5121; www.airfair.nl) is recommended.

SPAIN

A recommended travel agency is **Barceló Viajes** (☎ 902-116-226; www.barceloviajes.com).

The UK & Ireland

The UK is especially well connected to major Canadian cities. Air Canada, British Airways and Air Transat together operate some 40 daily flights from London to Toronto alone. There are also direct connections on Air Canada from London to Calgary, Halifax, St John's, Montréal and Vancouver. British Airways also serves Montréal and Vancouver.

Besides the travel agencies listed in this section, look for special deals in the travel pages of the weekend broadsheet newspapers or in *Time Out,* the *Evening Standard* and the free magazine *TNT.* Whatever agency you book with, make sure it's registered with the Association of British Travel Agents (ABTA), which will guarantee a refund or an alternative ticket, if you've paid money to an agent who ends up going out of business.

Bridge the World (☎ 0870-444-7474; www.b-t-w.co.uk)
Ebookers (☎ 0870-010-7000; www.ebookers.com)
Flight Centre (☎ 0870-890-8099; www.flightcentre.co.uk)
North-South Travel (☎ 01245-608-291; www.northsouthtravel.co.uk) Donates part of its profit to projects in the developing world.
Quest Travel (☎ 0870-442-3542; www.questtravel.com)
STA Travel (☎ 0870-160-0599; www.statravel.co.uk)
Trailfinders (www.trailfinders.co.uk)
Travel Bag (☎ 0870-890-1456; www.travelbag.co.uk)

The USA

Flights to Canada from the USA abound. Air Canada and its subsidiary Air Canada Jazz connect numerous major US cities with Vancouver, Calgary, Montréal, Toronto and Ottawa. Practically all other US carriers, including US Airways, United Airlines, American Airlines, Continental, Delta and Northwest Airlines, also head to numerous north-of-the-border destinations. Alaska Air and Horizon Air have flights to western Canada, with most originating in Seattle, except for Calgary, which is also served from Los Angeles. America West has flights to British Columbia, Alberta and Toronto from Phoenix, Las Vegas and Los Angeles.

Bargain hounds should also consider low-cost carriers CanJet, which connects eastern Canada with New York and Florida, and JetsGo, which serves numerous Canadian destinations from 10 US cities, including Los Angeles, Las Vegas and Orlando. Air Transat has seasonal flights to Toronto and Montréal from Las Vegas, St Petersburg, Orlando and Fort Lauderdale. Another discount airline, WestJet, flies to Calgary and Toronto from several cities in Florida, California and Arizona.

FlightCentre (☎ 866-967-5351; www.flightcentre.us)
STA Travel (☎ 800-781-4000; www.statravel.com)

LAND
Border Crossings

There are 22 official border crossings along the US–Canadian border, from New Brunswick to British Columbia. The Canadian Border Services Agency maintains a handy website (www.cbsa-asfc.gc.ca/general/times/menu-e.html) showing current wait times at any of them. Wait times rarely exceed 30 minutes, except during the peak summer season, and on Friday and Sunday afternoon, especially on holiday weekends, when you might get stuck at the border for several hours. Some entry points are especially busy:

- Windsor, Ontario, to Detroit, Michigan
- Fort Erie, Ontario, to Buffalo, New York State
- Niagara Falls, Ontario, to Niagara Falls, New York State
- Québec to Rouse's Point, New York State
- Surrey, British Columbia, to Blaine, Washington State

Other border points tend to be quieter, sometimes so quiet that the officers have nothing to do except tear apart your luggage. When approaching the border, turn off any music, take off your sunglasses and be exceptionally polite. Most officers do not welcome casual conversation, jokes or clever remarks.

When returning to the USA, check http://apps.cbp.gov/bwt, maintained by the US Department for Homeland Security, for border wait times.

For information on entering the country see p863, and p861 for information about visa requirements.

Bus

Greyhound (☎ 800-229-9424; www.greyhound.com) and its Canadian equivalent, **Greyhound Canada** (☎ 800-661-8747; www.greyhound.ca), operate the largest bus network in North America, with services to about 3600 destinations. There are direct connections between main cities in the USA and Canada, but

you usually have to transfer to a different bus at the border. See the table below for sample fares and durations.

Route	Standard Fare (US$)	Duration	Frequency
Boston-Montréal	68	from 6¼hr	up to 6 daily
Detroit-Toronto	44	5½hr	up to 5 daily
New York-Montréal	73	8hr	up to 8 daily
Seattle-Vancouver	28	from 3½hr	up to 5 daily

Call or consult Greyhound websites for additional fare and schedule information. Tickets may be bought by phone (a US$4/C$10.70 transaction fee applies), at Greyhound terminals or online. For information on discounts, see p871. For information on making reservations, see p872.

For those planning on making buses their main method of travel to, from and around Canada, Greyhound offers a variety of passes (see p871).

Car & Motorcycle

The highway system of the continental USA connects directly with the Canadian highway system at numerous points along the border. These Canadian highways then meet up with the east–west Trans-Canada Hwy further north. Between the Yukon Territory and Alaska, the main routes are the Alaska and Klondike Hwys and Haines Rd.

If you're driving into Canada, you'll need the vehicle's registration papers, proof of liability insurance and your home driver's license. Cars rented in the USA may usually be driven into Canada and back, but make sure your rental agreement says so in case you are questioned by border officials. If you're driving a car registered in someone else's name, bring a letter from the owner authorizing use of the vehicle in Canada. For general information about border crossings see left. For tips and details about driving in Canada, see p872.

Train

Amtrak (☎ 800-872-7245; www.amtrak.com) runs four routes between the USA and Canada. In the east, one train daily connects New York City with Montréal and Toronto (p114). Another runs from Buffalo-Depew, New York State, to Toronto. On the west coast, one train daily chugs from Seattle to Vancouver. The North

America Rail Pass (p877) is valid on Amtrak and Canada's VIA Rail.

SEA
Ferry
On the east coast, there are ferry services between Bar Harbor, Maine, and Yarmouth in southwestern Nova Scotia, which is also served by ferry from Portland, Maine (p397). Another ferry runs from Deer Island Point, New Brunswick, to Eastport, Maine (p500).

On the west coast, ferries travel between Washington State and Victoria on Vancouver Island (p644). From Port Hardy on northern Vancouver Island, ferries also head north along the Inside Passage to Alaska (p697). Travelers bound for the Yukon should consider the ferry service to Skagway, Alaska, from Prince Rupert, British Columbia (p795).

Freighters
An adventurous, though not necessarily inexpensive, way to travel to or from Canada is aboard a cargo ship. Freighters carry between three and 12 passengers and, though considerably less luxurious than cruise ships, they give a salty taste of life at sea. A 20-day trip from Montréal to the UK typically costs between $1600 and $1900. Your best sources of information are **Cruise & Freighter Travel Association** (in USA ☎ 800-872-8584; www.travltips.com) and **Freighter World Cruises** (☎ 626-449-3106, in USA 800-531-7774; www.freighter world.com).

TOURS
Group travel can be an enjoyable way to go, especially for single travelers. Try to pick a tour that will suit you in terms of age, interest and activity level. The best source for organized travel may be your travel agent back home. Choose a company that has been around for a while and enjoys a good reputation:

Arctic Odysseys (☎ 206-325-1977 in the US; www .arcticodysseys.com) Experience Arctic Canada close up on tours chasing the northern lights in the Northwest Territories, heli-skiing on Baffin Island or polar-bear spotting on Hudson Bay.

Backroads (☎ 510-527-1555, 800-462-2848; www .backroads.com) Guided and self-guided bicycle tours in the Rockies, the Gulf Islands, British Columbia, Nova Scotia and Prince Edward Island.

Canadian River Expeditions (☎ 250-392-9195, 800-898-7238; www.canriver.com) Operates rafting expeditions in the Yukon, British Columbia and Alaska, including trips on the Firth, Alsek and Babine Rivers, as well as down the Tatshenshini-Alsek watershed.

Elderhostel (in USA ☎ 877-426-8056; www.elder hostel.org) Nonprofit organization offers study tours in nearly all provinces for active people over 55, including train trips, cruises, bus and walking tours.

Routes to Learning (☎ 613-530-2222, 866-745-1690; www.routestolearning.ca) From bird-watching in the Rockies to trekking around Québec City to walking in the footsteps of Vikings on Newfoundland, this nonprofit has dozens of educational tours throughout Canada.

Trek America (in USA ☎ 800-221-0596, in UK ☎ 0870-444-8735; www.trekamerica.com) Active camping, hiking and canoeing tours in small groups, geared primarily for people between 18 and 38, although some are open to all ages. The 21-day Frontier Canada tour takes you cross-country from British Columbia to Québec.

GETTING AROUND

AIR
Airlines in Canada
The Canadian airline industry has experienced great turbulence in recent years. Even Air Canada, the country's largest carrier and a Star Alliance member, got into trouble for a while but finally emerged from bankruptcy protection in October 2004 following major financial restructuring. Despite such woes the company still operates the largest domestic-flight network serving some 150 destinations together with its regional subsidiary, Air Canada Jazz.

Low-cost, low-frills carriers are chasing Air Canada's wings. The biggest is Calgary-based WestJet, but start-ups like Jetsgo and CanJet are further adding to the competition. In response, Air Canada entered the discount game by introducing inexpensive 'Tango' fares, which sometimes undercut even the discount carriers, on its regular flights.

The Canadian aviation arena also includes many independent regional and local airlines, which tend to focus on small, often-remote regions, mostly in the North. Depending on the destination, fares in such noncompetitive markets can be rather high.

See the Getting There & Away and Getting Around sections of the regional chapters for specific route and fare information. The following is a list of the main domestic carriers.

Air Canada (☎ 888-247-2262; www.aircanada.ca) Nationwide flights.

Air Canada Jazz (☎ 888-247-2262; www.flyjazz.ca) Regional flights throughout western and eastern Canada.

Air Creebec (☎ 800-567-6567; www.aircreebec.ca) Serves northern Québec and Ontario, including Chisasibi and Chibougamau from Montréal and other cities.

Air Inuit (☎ 888-247-2262; www.airinuit.com) Flies from Montréal to all 14 Inuit communities in Nunavik, including Kuujjuaq and Puvirnituq.

Air Labrador (☎ 709-758-0002; www.airlabrador.com) Flights within Newfoundland and Labrador.

Air North (in Canada ☎ 867-668-2228, 800-661-0407, in USA ☎ 800-764-0407; www.flyairnorth.com) Flights within British Columbia, Alberta, Yukon, Northwest Territories and Alaska.

Bearskin Airlines (☎ 800-465-2327; www.bearskin airlines.com) Serves almost 40 destinations throughout Ontario and eastern Manitoba.

Calm Air (☎ 204-778-6471, 800-839-2256; www.calm air.com) Flights throughout Manitoba and Nunavut.

Canadian North (☎ 800-661-1505; www.canadian north.com) Flights to, from and within the Northwest Territories.

CanJet (☎ 800-809-7777; www.canjet.com) Low-cost carrier serving eastern Canada, including Montréal, Toronto, Halifax, Deer Lake and St John's, plus US destinations.

Central Mountain Air (☎ 888-865-8585; www.cmair .bc.ca) Destinations throughout British Columbia and Alberta.

First Air (☎ 800-267-1247; www.firstair.ca) Flies from Ottawa, Montréal, Winnipeg and Edmonton to 24 Arctic destinations, including Whitehorse and Nunavik.

Harbour Air (☎ 800-665-0212; www.harbour-air.com) Seaplane service from the city of Vancouver to Vancouver Island and the Gulf Islands.

Hawkair (☎ 800-487-1216; www.hawkair.net) Serves northern British Columbia from Vancouver and Victoria.

Jetsgo (☎ 800-665-0212; www.jetsgo.net) Low-cost airline serving all major Canadian cities.

Pacific Coastal Airlines (☎ 800-663-2872; www .pacific-coastal.com) Vancouver-based airline with service to many British Columbia locales.

Provincial Airlines (☎ 800-563-2800; www.provincial airlines.ca) St John's–based airline with service throughout Newfoundland and to Labrador.

Québecair Express (☎ 877-871-6500; www.quebecair express.com) Intra-Québec.

Transwest Air (☎ 800-667-9356; www.transwestair .com) Service within Saskatchewan.

WestJet (☎ 888-937-8538; www.westjet.com) Calgary-based low-cost carrier serving destinations throughout Canada.

Air Passes

Overseas travelers planning to do a lot of flying within Canada, or around the USA and Canada, might save some money by buying an air pass. Star Alliance (www.staralliance .com) members Air Canada, United Airlines and US Airways have teamed up to offer the North American Airpass, which is available to anyone not residing in the USA, Canada, Mexico, Bermuda or the Caribbean. It's sold only in conjunction with an international flight operated by any Star Alliance–member airline. You can buy as few as three coupons (US$399) or as many as 10 (US$1099). Each is good for one trip in economy class and must be used within 60 days from the date of the international flight. Besides the international trip, only the first coupon leg must be booked. Seats for the other coupons can be reserved up to 24 hours before departure. In peak season, though, it's best to book flights as early as possible to guarantee a seat. There's no penalty for date changes, but a fee applies, if you wish to change a destination.

BICYCLE

Cycling across Canada would be an enormous, though not-impossible undertaking, but touring regions is easier to do and popular. Long-distance trips can be done entirely on quiet back roads, and many cities – Edmonton, Montréal, Ottawa, Toronto and Vancouver among them – have designated bike routes (see p846).

Cyclists must follow the same rules of the road as vehicles, but don't expect drivers to always respect your right of way. Helmets may give you a bad hair day, but they are mandatory for all cyclists in British Columbia, New Brunswick, Prince Edward Island and Nova Scotia, as well as for anyone under 18 in Alberta and Ontario.

Emergency roadside assistance is available from the **Better World Club** (☎ 866-238-1137; www .betterworldclub.com). Membership costs $40 per year, plus a $10 enrolment fee, and entitles you to two free pick-ups, and transport to the nearest repair shop, or home, within a 50km radius of where you're picked up.

Most airlines will carry bikes as checked luggage without charge on international flights, as long as they're in a box. On domestic flights they usually charge between $30 and $65. Always check details before you buy the ticket.

If you're traveling on Greyhound Canada, you must ship your bike as freight. In addition to a bike box ($12), you'll be charged according to the weight of the bike, plus a 35% oversize charge and GST. Shipping a 30lb bike from Vancouver to Calgary, for instance, would cost about $47. Bikes only travel on the same bus as the passenger if there's enough space. To ensure that yours arrives at the same time as (or before) you do, ship it a day early.

For $15, VIA Rail will transport your bicycle, but only on trains offering checked-baggage service, including all long-distance and many regional trains.

Purchase

Buying a bike is easy, as is reselling it before you leave. Specialist bike shops have the best selection and advice, but general sporting-goods stores may have lower prices. Some bicycle stores and rental outfitters also sell used bicycles. To sniff out the best bargains, scour flea markets, garage sales and thrift shops, or study the notice boards in hostels and universities. These are also the best places to sell your bike, although stores selling used bikes may also buy it.

Rental

Outfitters renting bicycles from an hour to several weeks exist in practically all towns and cities; many are listed throughout this book. Rentals start at about $10 per day for touring bikes and $20 for mountain bikes; this usually includes a helmet and a lock. Most companies require a security deposit of $20 to $200.

BOAT

With oceans at both ends of the country and a lake- and river-filled interior, don't be surprised to find yourself in a boat at some point. Extensive ferry services between islands and the mainland exist throughout the Maritime provinces and in British Columbia. For route details, see the Getting There & Away and Getting Around sections of the respective regional chapters. The following is a list of main operators.

Bay Ferries (☎ 506-649-7777, 888-249-7245; www .nfl-bay.com) Year-round service between St John's, New Brunswick and Digby, Nova Scotia.

BC Ferries (☎ 250-386-3431; www.bcferries.com) Huge passenger-ferry systems with 25 routes and 46 ports

of call, including Vancouver Island, the Gulf Islands, the Sechelt Peninsula along the Sunshine Coast and the Queen Charlotte Islands, all in British Columbia.

Coastal Transport (☎ 506-662-3724, 506-456-3842; www.coastaltransport.ca) Ferry service from Blacks Harbour to Grand Manan in the Fundy Isles, New Brunswick.

CTMA Ferries (☎ 418-986-3278, 888-986-3278; www .ctma.ca) Runs daily ferries to Québec's Îles de la Madeleine from Souris, Prince Edward Island (PEI), and also a weekly service between the islands and Montréal.

Labrador Marine (☎ 866-535-2567) Connects Newfoundland to Labrador.

Marine Atlantic (☎ 800-341-7981; www.marine -atlantic.ca) Connects Port aux Basques and Argentia in Newfoundland with North Sydney, Nova Scotia.

Northumberland Ferries (☎ 902-566-3838, 888-249-7245; www.nfl-bay.com) Service between Wood Islands, PEI, and Caribou, Nova Scotia.

Private East Coast Ferries (☎ 506-747-2159, 877-747-2159) Connects Deer Island to Campobello Island, both in the Fundy Isles of New Brunswick.

BUS

Greyhound Canada (☎ 800-661-8747; www.greyhound .ca) is the king of the bus world, plowing along an extensive network in central and western Canada (as well as to/from the USA – see p867). In eastern Canada, it is part of an alliance of regional carriers, including Orléans Express, in Québec, and Acadian Lines, in the Atlantic provinces. You can transfer from one carrier to another on a single ticket. Tickets may be bought at bus terminals and by phone (plus $10.70 transaction fee). One-way tickets are generally valid for 60 days and round-trip tickets for a year, though this may vary by company and ticket type.

The frequency of bus services ranges from 'rarely' to 'constantly,' but even the least-popular routes usually have one bus per day. Main routes will have a service every hour or so. Buses travel mostly on highways, but trips can still be very long because of the great distances. Express buses operate on busy routes.

By most standards, bus services are really quite good. Buses are generally clean, comfortable and reliable. Amenities may include onboard toilets, air-conditioning (bring a sweater), reclining seats and onboard movies. Smoking is not permitted. On long journeys, buses make meal stops every few hours, usually at highway service stations, where the food tends to be bad and overpriced.

Acadian Lines (☎ 800-567-5151; www.acadianbus .com) Service throughout New Brunswick, Nova Scotia and Prince Edward Island.

Coach Canada (☎ 800-461-7661; www.coachcanada .com) Scheduled service within Ontario and from Toronto to Montréal.

Dawson City Courier (☎ 867-993-6688) Connects Whitehorse and Dawson City, Yukon, with Inuvik, Northwest Territories.

DRL Coachlines (☎ 709-738-8088; www.drlgroup.com/ Coachlines/coachlines_new.html) Service throughout Newfoundland and Nova Scotia.

Laidlaw Transit (☎ 519-376-5712, 519-376-5375) Operates within Ontario.

Limocar (☎ 866-700-8899; www.limocar.com) Regional service in Québec.

Malaspina Coach Lines (☎ 877-227-8287) Operates within British Columbia.

Ontario Northland (☎ 800-461-8558; www.ontc.on .ca) Operates train and bus routes throughout northern Ontario.

Orléans Express (☎ 888-999-3977; www.orleansexpress .com) Service to eastern Québec.

Pacific Coach Lines (☎ 604-662-7575; www.pacific coach.com) Service between Vancouver Island and mainland British Columbia.

Saskatchewan Transportation Company (STC; ☎ 800-663-7181; www.stcbus.com) Service within Saskatchewan.

Voyageur (☎ 800-661-8747; www.greyhound.ca) Operates within Ontario and Québec.

For information about traveling on buses operated by Moose Travel Network, see p875.

Bus Passes

If you want to cover a lot of ground in a short period, Greyhound Canada's Canada Pass might be more economical than individual tickets – just make sure you're not spending all your time on the bus. The pass ($309 to $719, plus GST) allows unlimited travel from coast to coast, within periods ranging from seven to 60 days.

Passes are valid on all routes operated by Greyhound Canada and affiliated companies, such as Orléans Express and Acadian Lines. You can also use them for VIA Rail travel on the Toronto–Montréal and Ottawa–Montréal routes; for the ferry between Vancouver Island and Vancouver; and for travel to the USA on certain direct routes (Toronto to Buffalo, Detroit

and New York; Montréal to New York; and Vancouver to Seattle).

If your travel itinerary includes both Canada and the USA, consider the CanAm Pass, which is good for unlimited travel within the USA and Canada on all Greyhound routes, plus scores of affiliated regional carriers, such as Orléans Express and Acadian Lines in eastern Canada. It's available for periods ranging from 15 to 60 consecutive days, and costs between US$439 and US$719. If you're going to limit your explorations to either western or eastern Canada and the USA, you may be better served by the West CanAm Pass or East CanAm Pass (10-/21-days for US$299/399).

Passes can be purchased in person at any Greyhound terminal, and online at least 14 days prior to departure. Overseas travelers qualify for the slightly cheaper international versions of these passes, which are sold through selected agents around the world and online at least 21 days before your first Greyhound trip. Check the websites for the nearest agent in your home country.

Costs

Bus travel is cheaper than other means of transport, and there are many ways you can avoid paying the full fare. Some minor variations aside, Greyhound and other bus operators generally lop 10% off regular fares for seniors, students and soldiers, while children under 12 pay half price. Advance purchases (seven or 14 days) also save quite a bit, as do 'companion fares' (the second person travels for $15 on the same itinerary) and 'family fares' (one child under 16 travels free on the same trip, if accompanied by an adult). Alas, special fares do come with restrictions and blackout periods, which are usually around major holidays. It's also worth checking Greyhound's website for the latest promotions. For specific route and fare information, see the Getting There & Away sections of the regional chapters.

The following table shows sample long-distance fares with Greyhound.

Route	Standard Fare	7-day Fare	Duration
Vancouver–Calgary	$134	$62	15hr
Montréal–Toronto	$88	$53	8hr
Toronto–Vancouver	$360	$160	68hr

Reservations

Greyhound and most other bus lines don't take reservations, and even buying tickets in advance does not guarantee you a seat on any particular bus. Show up at least 45 minutes to one hour prior to the scheduled departure time, and chances are pretty good you'll get on. Allow more time on Friday and Sunday afternoons and around holidays.

CAR & MOTORCYCLE
Automobile Associations

For long road trips in your own vehicle or a rental car, an auto-club membership is an excellent thing to have. The main motoring organization is the **Canadian Automobile Association** (CAA; ☎ 800-268-3750; www.caa.ca), which has offices in all major cities and many smaller ones. CAA's services, including 24-hour emergency roadside assistance, are also available to members of its international affiliates such as AAA in the USA, AA in the UK and ADAC in Germany. The club also offers trip-planning advice, free maps, travel-agency services and a range of discounts on hotels, car rentals etc.

In recent years, Better World Club (p869), which donates 1% of its annual revenue to environmental cleanup efforts, has emerged as an alternative. It offers service throughout the USA and Canada, and also has a roadside-assistance program for bicycles.

Bring Your Own Vehicle

Requirements for bringing your car into Canada overland from the USA are discussed on p867. Forget about shipping your car from overseas, unless you're actually moving to Canada. It simply doesn't make economic sense and you'll be better off renting a car in Canada (see opposite).

Drivers' License

In most provinces visitors can legally drive for up to three months with their home driver's license. In some, such as British Columbia, this is extended to six months. However, the easiest thing to do, especially if you're spending considerable time in the country, is to get an International Driving Permit (IDP), which is valid for one year. Just grab a passport photo and your home license, and stop by your local automobile association, which will issue you one for a small fee. IDPs may give you greater credibility with traffic police and ease the car-rental process, especially if your home license doesn't have a photograph or is not written in English or French.

Fuel & Spare Parts

Most gas stations are self-service and finding one is generally not a problem, except in sparsely populated areas such as the Yukon or northern Québec. In those regions, it's a good idea to fill your tank every time you pass a gas station, and to carry a canister filled with gasoline as a backup. Some gas stations are closed on Sunday.

Depending on the age and model of your car, finding spare parts can be a tall order away from the big cities. When traveling in remote regions, always bring some tools and at least a spare tire. Be sure to have some sort of roadside emergency assistance (left) in case your car breaks down.

Gas is sold in liters (see the inside front cover for a metric conversion chart). At the time of writing, the national average for mid-grade fuel was 84¢ (about C$3.17 per US gallon). Prices are higher in remote areas, with Yellowknife usually setting the national record; drivers in Winnipeg pay the least for gas.

Insurance

Canadian law requires liability insurance for all vehicles, to cover you for damage caused to property and people. The minimum requirement is $200,000 in all provinces except Québec, where it is $50,000. If you already have auto insurance at home, or if you have purchased travel insurance, make sure that the policy has adequate liability cover for where you'll be driving. Americans traveling to Canada in their own car should ask their insurance company for a Nonresident Interprovince Motor Vehicle Liability Insurance Card, which is accepted as evidence of financial responsibility anywhere in Canada. Although not mandatory, it may come in handy in an accident.

Car-rental agencies will provide liability insurance. Sometimes adequate cover is already included in the base rental rate, but always ask to be sure. Insurance against damage to the car itself, called Collision Damage Waiver (CDW), reduces or eliminates the amount you'll have to reimburse the rental company. It's optional but, although it's expensive ($12 to $15 per day), it's unwise to drive without it. Certain credit cards, especially the gold and platinum versions, cover CDW for a certain rental period, if you use the card to pay for the entire rental, and decline the policy offered by the rental company. Always check with your card issuer to see what coverage they offer in Canada.

Personal accident insurance (PAI) covers you and any passengers for medical costs incurred as a result of an accident. If your travel insurance or your health-insurance policy at home does this as well (and most do, but check), then this is one expense you can do without.

Rental

As anywhere, rates for car rentals vary considerably by model and pick-up location, but you should be able to get an economy-sized vehicle for about $30 to $45 per day. Expect surcharges for rentals originating at airports and train stations, additional drivers and one-way rentals. Child safety seats are compulsory (reserve them when you book) and cost about $5 per day.

In order to rent your own wheels in Canada you generally need to be at least 25 years old and hold a valid driver's license (an international one may be required, if you're not from an English- or French-speaking country – see opposite) and a major credit card. American Express, Diners, Visa and MasterCard are widely accepted, and JCB (Japan Credit Bank) and Discover are usually fine as well, but it's best to check in advance. Some companies may rent to drivers between the ages of 21 and 24 for an additional charge (about $15 to $25 per day). Those under 21, or not in possession of a credit card, are usually out of luck.

Major international car-rental companies usually have branches at airports, train stations and in city centers:

Alamo (☎ 800-462-5266; www.alamo.com)
Avis (☎ 800-437-0358; www.avis.com)
Budget (☎ 800-268-8900; www.budget.com)
Dollar (☎ 800-800-4000; www.dollar.com)
Enterprise (☎ 800-736-8222; www.enterprise.com)
Hertz (☎ 800-263-0600; www.hertz.com)
National (☎ 800-227-7368; www.nationalcar.com)
Thrifty (☎ 800-847-4389; www.thrifty.com)

Local agencies may offer lower rates, so it's worth checking with them as well. In-

dependents are also more likely to rent to drivers under 25, and may even accept cash or travelers-check deposits. About 300 independent agencies are represented by **Car Rental Express** (☎ 604-714-5911, 888-557-8188; www.carrentalexpress.com), which may yield savings of up to 25% off rates charged by the national chains.

Prebooked and prepaid packages arranged in your home country often work out to be cheaper than on-the-spot rentals. The same is true of fly-drive packages. Search the car-rental agency and airline websites, as well as online travel agencies for deals.

MOTORCYCLE

Several companies offer motorcycle rentals and tours, but rates can be steep, especially if you've got 'Harley hunger.' A Heritage Softail Classic, for instance, starts at about $175 per day, including liability insurance and 200km to 250km mileage. Smaller models, such as a Kawasaki KLR 650, start at around $75 per day. Some companies have minimum rental periods, which are sometimes as much as seven days. Riding a hog is especially popular in British Columbia:

Coastline Motorcycle Tours & Rentals (☎ 250-335-1837, 866-338-0344; www.coastlinemc.com) Out of Courtenay on Vancouver Island, British Columbia.

Great Canadian Motor Corporation (☎ 250-837-6500, 800-667-8865; www.gcmc.com) Rents bikes out of Vancouver and Calgary.

McScoots Motorcycle & Scooter Rentals (☎ 250-763-4668; www.mcscoots.com) Big selection of Harleys, also operates motorcycle tours, based in Kelowna, British Columbia.

Okanagan Motorcycle Rentals & Tours (☎ 250-860-5270, 866-810-8687; www.okanaganmotorcycle.com) Also out of Kelowna.

RECREATIONAL VEHICLES

The RV market is big in the west, with specialized agencies in Calgary, Edmonton, Whitehorse, Vancouver and other cities (see the *Yellow Pages* under 'Recreational Vehicles'). But RVs and camper vans can also be rented in Toronto, and other central and eastern cities. For summer travel, book as early as possible, as the most-popular models rent quickly. The base cost is roughly $160 to $250 per day in high season for mid-sized vehicles, although insurance, fees and taxes add a hefty chunk to the final bill. Diesel-fueled RVs have considerably lower running costs. Your travel agency back home may have the best deals, or check out some recommended companies:

Canadream Campers (☎ 403-291-1000, 800-461-7368; www.canadream.com) Based in Calgary with rentals (including one-ways), in 10 cities, including Vancouver, Whitehorse and Halifax.

Go West Campers (☎ 403-240-1814, 800-240-1814; www.gowestcampers.com) Calgary-based, but arranges rentals from Vancouver and Toronto, too. Also rents motorcycles.

Road Conditions & Hazards

Most roadway dangers in Canada can be avoided with simple common sense and courteous driving. But there are a few points to bear in mind – bear among them. Fierce winters can leave potholes the size of landmine craters, so be prepared to swerve. Winter travel in general can be hazardous due to heavy snow and ice, which may cause some roads and bridges to close periodically. The website maintained by the CAA (www.caa.ca) has lots of useful tips on winter driving. In general, make sure your vehicle is in top shape, and equipped with four-seasonal radial or snow tires, and emergency supplies in case you're stranded. Distances between services can be long, so keep your gas topped up whenever possible. Remember that much of Canada is wilderness. This means that moose, deer and elk may insist on sharing the road with you – especially at night. There's just no contest between an 1800lb bull moose and a Subaru, so keep your eyes peeled. And don't roll down your windows to share your Cheetos with bear (see p54). Words to live by…

Road Rules

Canadians drive on the right-hand side of the road. Seat belt use is compulsory at all times. Children under 40lb must be strapped in child-booster seats, except infants, who must be in a rear-facing safety seat. Motorcyclists must wear helmets and drive with their headlights on.

Distances and speed limits are posted in kilometers. The speed limit is generally 40km/h to 50km/h in cities, and 90km/h to 110km/h outside town. You must slow down to 60km/h when passing emergency vehicles (such as police cars and ambulances) stopped on the roadside with their lights flashing. Traffic in both directions must stop when stationary school buses flash their red lights – this means that children are getting off and on.

Turning right at red lights after coming to a full stop is permitted in all provinces. The only exceptions are at intersections where road signs prohibit such turns, and on the island of Montréal, where turning right without a green light is always a no-no. There seems to be a national propensity for running red lights, however, so don't take your 'right of way' at intersections for granted. Tailgating is also a frequent annoyance; always exercise discretion and try not to provoke road rage.

Driving while talking on a cell phone is (still) legal anywhere but in Newfoundland and Labrador. Radar detectors are not allowed in Québec, Ontario, Manitoba, and the Yukon and Northwest Territories. If you're caught driving with a radar detector, even one that isn't being operated, you could receive a fine of $1000 and your device may be confiscated.

The highest permissible blood-alcohol level for drivers is 0.08%.

HITCHING & RIDE-SHARING

Hitching is never entirely safe in any country and we don't recommend it. That said, in remote and rural areas in Canada it is not uncommon to see people thumbing for a ride. If you do decide to hitch, understand that you are taking a small but potentially serious risk. Remember that it's safer to travel in pairs and be sure to let someone know where you are planning to go.

If you're in a big city, use public transport to get you out to a major highway. Not only do your chances for pick-up increase, but you also avoid running into trouble with the police (hitchhiking is illegal in some cities). Roadside stops, smaller roads and the beginning of highway on-ramps are the best places stick out that thumb. Start early in the day, especially when hoping to log long distances, and avoid getting stranded at all costs; Canadian nights are cold at most times of the year, and bugs can drive you mad. Finally, when a car stops, ask the driver where he or she is headed and use the time to look over the car and get a sense of the person. If your gut tells you that you've met a potential weirdo, decline the ride (pretending that you're actually headed in the opposite direction and were mistakenly standing on the wrong side of the road is a good excuse).

Ride-share services offer an alternative to hitching. **Autotaxi** (www.autotaxi.com) is a free web-based bulletin board for ride-sharing within Canada and to the USA. You can advertise a ride yourself or make arrangements with drivers going to your destinations. In Québec, **Allô Stop** (www.allostop.com) does much the same (see p235).

LOCAL TRANSPORTATION
Bicycle

Cycling is a popular means of getting around during the warmer months and many cities have hundreds of kilometers of dedicated bike paths. Bicycles may often be taken on public transportation at certain times of day. Rental companies are listed throughout this book. See p869 and p846 for more on cycling in Canada.

Bus

Buses are the most-ubiquitous form of public transportation and practically all towns have their own systems. Most are commuter oriented, and offer only limited or no services in the evenings and on weekends.

Metro

Toronto, Montréal and Edmonton are the only Canadian cities which have subway systems. Vancouver's version is mostly an above-ground monorail. Route maps are posted in all stations, and you can pick up a printed copy from the stationmaster or ticket office. The frequency of services fluctuates with demand, with more trains during commuter hours than, say, in the middle of the day.

Taxi

Taxis are metered and fares comprise a base fee, called a flag fall ($2.50 or so), and a per-kilometer charge (around $1.20). If you have a lot of luggage, there may be an extra handling fee. Drivers expect a tip of between 10% and 15%. In most cities, taxis can be flagged down or ordered by phone.

TOURS

All across Canada, local companies offer guided tours of various lengths. Many of these are listed in the regional chapters throughout this book.

Moose Travel Network (in eastern Canada ☎ 416-504-7514, 888-816-6673, in western Canada 604-777-9905, 888-244-6673; www.moosenetwork.com) is a backpacker-oriented company that operates various tours in small buses throughout British Columbia, Alberta, Québec and Ontario. Tours last from two to 10 days, and include transportation and some activities. Accommodations cost extra; the company pre-books dorm beds or private rooms at participating hostels, although you are free to make your own arrangements as well. Moose also offers a variety of passes valid during the entire season (usually May to mid-October) on selected routes. You can either stay onboard for the entire circuit, or customize your itinerary by taking advantage of the hop-on, hop-off nature of the pass. The popular West Pass ($449), for instance, is a 10-day loop starting in Vancouver and taking in Whistler, Jasper, Banff and other destinations. In winter, various skiing and snowboarding packages are available.

Salty Bear Adventure Tours (☎ 902-446-3866, 866-458-2327; www.saltybear.ca) is a smaller but similar outfit operating out of Halifax. It operates a two-day circuit around Nova Scotia ($99/109 with/without International Student Identity Card (ISIC) card) and a four-day route that also takes in Cape Breton, Prince Edward Island and New Brunswick ($239/249). You can combining the two tours ($299/319), which gives you jump-on, jump-off flexibility.

TRAIN

VIA Rail (☎ 888-842-7245; www.viarail.ca) operates most of Canada's intercity and transcontinental passenger trains, linking most of the major cities and about 450 smaller communities along 14,000km of track. The network does not extend to Newfoundland, Prince Edward Island and Canada's Northern territories. In some remote parts of the country, such as Churchill in Manitoba, trains provide the only overland access.

Rail service is most efficient in southern Ontario and southern Québec. Many trains connect Montréal and Toronto, which are both major hubs with service to many other communities. From Montréal, there are trains bound for Ottawa, Québec City, Jonquière and the Gaspé Peninsula. Communities served from Toronto include

TRANSPORTATION

Windsor, London, Kingston, Niagara Falls, Sarnia and White River. Overnight service is provided on the Toronto–Montréal, Montréal–Halifax and Montréal–Gaspésie routes.

For a complete train schedule, check the website or pick up the *National Timetable* booklet at any VIA Rail station. Most train stations have left-luggage offices. Smoking is prohibited on many trains, and is restricted to designated areas on others. There are snack services on most routes, and some trains also have dining cars; some tickets include meals.

Classes

On VIA Rail, fares are lowest in comfort class, which is offered on all trains, and buys you a fairly basic, if indeed quite comfortable, reclining seat with a headrest. Blankets and pillows are provided for overnight travel.

On trains operating in southern Ontario and Québec, you can upgrade to the VIA 1 class, where seats are more spacious and have outlets for plugging in laptops or other devices; tickets also include a meal. On some routes, wireless high-speed Internet access is available.

For overnight travel, VIA offers various sleeping-car classes, including compartments with upper or lower pullout berths, and private single, double or triple roomettes. Fares usually include access to a shower and the sightseeing car, and sometimes meals as well.

Costs

Taking the train is more expensive than the bus, but most people find it a more comfortable way to travel. Thanks to numerous special deals, you rarely have to pay full fare. Round-trip tickets are cheaper than one-way fares, and buying tickets five or seven days in advance can yield savings of between 30% and 40%. No advance purchase is needed for infants to travel for free, or for children to receive from 35% to 50% off regular fares. Full-time students of any age save 35% but must show an ISIC card (p851). Seniors over 60 can shave 10% off the price of regular tickets. Predictably, certain restrictions and blackout periods apply. Also see VIA Rail's website for special promotions and vacation packages.

Long-Distance Routes

VIA Rail's longest continuous route travels between Toronto and Vancouver, a stretch covered by the *Canadian,* so named in memory of Canadian Pacific Railway's original route. It even looks like the 1950s stainless-steel classic, complete with the two-story windowed 'dome' car – prime for sightseeing. On its three-day journey, the train crosses the northern Ontario lake country, and ploughs through the western plains via Winnipeg and Saskatoon, before reaching Jasper in the craggy Rockies, and then on to Vancouver. There are three departures weekly in both directions year-round. Fares vary widely by season and comfort level. In July, one-way tickets start at $710 for a reclining seat, but zoom to $1850 for a single room; an upper berth costs about $1230, including taxes. For the same trip in November, prices drop to $460, $770 and $1160 respectively.

If you want to cross the entire country, hop on the overnight *Ocean* in Halifax, then change in Montréal for the train bound for Toronto, where you can catch the *Canadian.* Of course, you can also start your trip in Vancouver and work your way east. In either direction, a cross-country trip can be very pleasant and relaxing, particularly if you have your own room. For travel during the summer months you should book well ahead.

Other long-distance trains include the *Hudson Bay,* which travels from the prairie to the subarctic – Winnipeg to the polar-bear hangout of Churchill on the Hudson Bay. See p530 for details.

In the west, the *Skeena* is an all-daylight route chugging from Jasper, Alberta, to coastal Prince Rupert, British Columbia, in two days, with an overnight stop in Prince George (you must make your own hotel reservations). Seats cost about $230 in comfort class. From May to October only, you can travel in Totem Class ($1040), which includes meals and access to the glass-domed sightseeing car.

On Vancouver Island, British Columbia, the *Malahat* carves through magnificent countryside from Victoria to Courtenay once daily in each direction. The entire trip lasts 4½ hours, but you're free to get off and back on as many times as you'd like. The cheapest fare is $31.

The *Bras D'Or* is a tourist-oriented service offering an introduction to Cape Breton culture, with meals and onboard entertainment on its daylong journey from Halifax to Sydney ($275). There's one train weekly in either direction, operating from June to mid-October. Most people travel one way, returning by bus or rental car. Train buffs should also check out Canada by Rail (www.canadabyrail.ca), an excellent portal packed with information and all sorts of train-related links, including to regional excursion trains, railroad museums and historical train stations.'

There are several privately run regional train companies that offer additional rail-touring opportunities:

Algoma Central Railway (p187) Access to northern Ontario wilderness areas.

Ontario Northland (p72) Operates the *Northlander* from Toronto to Cochrane in northern Ontario and the seasonal *Polar Bear Express* from Cochrane to Moosonee on Hudson Bay.

QNS&L Railway (p310) Scenic journey through forest, gorges and valleys from Sept Îles, Québec to Labrador City.

Rocky Mountaineer Railtours (p603) Spectacular Canadian Rockies scenery on trips between Vancouver, Kamloops and Calgary.

White Pass & Yukon Route (p797) Gorgeous route paralleling the original White Pass trail from Whitehorse, Yukon to Fraser, British Columbia.

Reservations

Tickets and train passes are available for purchase online, by phone, at VIA Rail stations and from many travel agents. Seat reservations are highly recommended, especially in summer, on weekends and around holidays. During peak season, some of the most popular sleeping arrangements sell out months in advance, especially on long-distance trains

such as the *Canadian*. The *Hudson Bay* often books solid during polar-bear season (late September to early November). Booking early gives you the best chance of snagging fare discounts.

Train Passes

If you're going to ride the rails a lot, a train pass may be the ticket to savings. As a passholder, you must still obtain a ticket for each leg of your trip. Make seat reservations early, since only a limited number of seats are set aside for passholders on each train. Prices quoted are for travel in comfort class, but upgrades are available for a surcharge.

The Canrailpass buys 12 days of travel within a 30-day period beginning with the first day of travel. During peak season (June to mid-October), passes cost about $740/670 per adult/child, ISIC cardholder, or senior over 60. You can also buy up to three extra days at $63/57 per day. The rest of the year prices drop to $460/415, with extensions costing $40/36 per day.

If you'll be limiting your exploration to southern Ontario and Québec, the Corridorpass may come in handy. It offers unlimited travel between Québec City and Windsor during 10 consecutive days and costs $242/218 in comfort class. and $631/568 in VIA 1 class.

For those who have built their itinerary around Canada and the USA, the North America Rail Pass may be a good buy. It allows unlimited travel in both countries for 30 consecutive days and costs $1000/900 from June to mid-October and $710/640 at all other times. Amtrak is the US equivalent of VIA Rail; many Canadian train stations sell Amtrak passes and offer information on its routes (see also p867).

Health

CONTENTS

Canada encompasses an extraordinary range of climates and terrains, from the freezing heights of the Rockies to the sweltering summers of the prairies. Because of the high level of hygiene here, infectious diseases will not be a significant concern for most travelers.

BEFORE YOU GO

INSURANCE

Canada offers some of the finest health care in the world. The problem is that, unless you are a Canadian citizen, it can be prohibitively expensive. It's essential to purchase travel health insurance if your regular policy doesn't cover you when you're abroad.

Bring any medications you may need clearly labeled in their original containers. A signed, dated letter from your physician that describes all your medical conditions and medications, including generic names, is also a good idea.

If your health insurance does not cover you for medical expenses incurred abroad, it is worth considering taking out supplemental insurance. Check the Subwwway section of the **Lonely Planet website** (www.lonelyplanet .com/subwwway) for more information. Find out in advance if your insurance plan will make payments directly to providers or reimburse you later for overseas health expenditures. For additional information, see p854.

RECOMMENDED VACCINATIONS

No special vaccines are required or recommended for travel to Canada. All travelers should be up-to-date on routine immunizations, listed below.

INTERNET RESOURCES

There is a wealth of travel health advice available on the Internet. The World Health Organization publishes a superb book, called *International Travel and Health*, which is revised annually and is available online at no cost at www .who.int/ith. Another website of general interest is **MD Travel Health** (www.mdtravel health.com). The website provides complete travel health recommendations for every country, updated daily, also at no cost.

It's usually a good idea to consult your government's travel health website before departure, if one is available:
Australia (www.dfat.gov.au/travel)
United Kingdom (www.doh.gov.uk/traveladvice)
United States (www.cdc.gov/travel)

Vaccine	Recommended for	Dosage	Side effects
tetanus-diphtheria	all travelers who haven't had booster within 10 years	one dose lasts 10 years	soreness at injection site
measles	travelers born after 1956 who've had only one measles vaccination	one dose	fever, rash, joint pains, allergic reactions
chicken pox	travelers who've never had chicken pox	two doses a month apart	fever, mild case of chicken pox
influenza	all travelers during flu season (November through March)	one dose	soreness at the injection site, fever

MEDICAL CHECKLIST

- acetaminophen (eg Tylenol) or aspirin
- anti-inflammatory drugs (eg ibuprofen)
- antihistamines (for hay fever and allergic reactions)
- antibacterial ointment (eg Neosporin) for cuts and abrasions
- steroid cream or cortisone (for poison ivy and other allergic rashes)
- bandages, gauze, gauze rolls
- adhesive or paper tape
- scissors, safety pins, tweezers
- thermometer
- pocket knife
- DEET-containing insect repellent for the skin
- permethrin-containing insect spray for clothing, tents and bed nets
- sunblock

IN CANADA

AVAILABILITY & COST OF HEALTH CARE

For immediate medical assistance in most provinces and territories, call ☎ 911. In general, if you have a medical emergency, the best bet is to find the nearest hospital and go to its emergency room. If the problem isn't urgent, you can call a nearby hospital and ask for a referral to a local physician, which is usually cheaper than a trip to the emergency room.

Pharmacies are abundant, but you may find that some medications which are available over the counter in your home country require a prescription in Canada, and if you don't have insurance to cover the cost of prescriptions, they can be shockingly expensive.

INFECTIOUS DISEASES

In addition to more common ailments, there are several infectious diseases that are unknown or uncommon outside North America. Most are acquired by mosquito or tick bites, or environmental exposure.

Severe Acute Respiratory Syndrome (SARS)

In 2003 the world's attention was drawn to the outbreak of a new and serious respiratory illness that became known as SARS. Since the outbreak, there have been just over 300 probable or suspect cases of SARS reported in Canada, resulting in 24 confirmed deaths. The majority of these cases were reported in Ontario, mostly in the Greater Toronto Area. At the time of writing, SARS appeared to have been brought under control in Canada, and the World Health Organization did not recommend any travel restrictions, as the risk of contracting SARS was extremely low. For the latest updates on SARS, go to the **Health Canada website** (www .sars.gc.ca).

The symptoms of SARS are identical to many other respiratory infections, namely influenza. Symptoms include a high fever over 38°C and a cough, often accompanied by chills, headaches, muscle aches, a sore throat and diarrhea. The case definition of SARS is a person with fever, cough, and travel to an infected area or close contact with an infected person within the previous 10 days. There is no specific quick test for SARS, but certain blood test and chest X-ray results offer support for the diagnosis. There is no specific treatment available and death from respiratory failure occurs in around 10% of patients. Fortunately it appears that it is not as easy to catch SARS as was initially thought. The disease is spread through close personal contact with someone already infected with the SARS coronavirus. Wearing masks has a limited effect and is not generally recommended.

West Nile Virus

Cases of West Nile virus were unknown in Canada until a few years ago, but have now been reported in many provinces, including Ontario, Québec, Nova Scotia, New Brunswick, Saskatchewan, Manitoba and Alberta. The virus is transmitted by Culex mosquitoes, which are active in late summer and early fall and generally bite after dusk (also see p881). Most infections are mild or asymptomatic, but the virus may infect the central nervous system leading to fever, headache, confusion, lethargy, coma and sometimes death. There is no treatment for West Nile virus. For the latest update on the areas affected by West Nile, go to the **Health Canada website** (www.hc-sc.gc.ca/english/ westnile/index.html).

Lyme Disease

Most documented cases of Lyme Disease occur in the southern parts of Canada, especially in areas bordering the USA. Lyme disease is transmitted by deer ticks, which are only 1mm to 2mm long. Most cases occur in late spring and summer. The first symptom is usually an expanding red rash that is often pale in the center, known as a bull's-eye rash. However, in many cases, no rash is observed. Flu-like symptoms are common, including fever, headache, joint pain, body aches and malaise. When the infection is treated promptly with an appropriate antibiotic, usually doxycycline or amoxicillin, the cure rate is high. Luckily, since the tick must be attached for 36 hours or more to transmit Lyme disease, most cases can be prevented by performing a thorough tick check after you've been outdoors (see opposite). The US-based Centers for Disease Control and Prevention has an informative **Lyme disease website** (www.cdc.gov/ncidod/dvbid/lyme).

Rabies

Rabies is a viral infection of the brain and spinal cord that is almost always fatal. The rabies virus is carried in the saliva of infected animals and is typically transmitted through an animal bite (see opposite), though contamination of any break in the skin with infected saliva may result in rabies. In Canada, most cases of human rabies are related to exposure to bats. Rabies may also be contracted from raccoons, skunks, foxes and unvaccinated cats and dogs.

If there is any possibility, however small, that you have been exposed to rabies, you should seek preventative treatment, which consists of rabies immune globulin and rabies vaccine and is quite safe. In particular, any contact with a bat should be discussed with health authorities, because bats have small teeth and may not leave obvious bite marks.

Giardiasis

This parasitic infection of the small intestine occurs throughout North America and the rest of the world. Symptoms may include nausea, bloating, cramps and diarrhea, and may last for weeks. To protect yourself from giardia, you should avoid drinking directly from lakes, ponds, streams and rivers, which may be contaminated by animal or human feces. The infection can also be transmitted from person to person if proper hand washing is not performed. Giardiasis is easily diagnosed by a stool test and is readily treated with antibiotics.

ENVIRONMENTAL HAZARDS
Heat

Dehydration is the main contributor to heat exhaustion. Symptoms include feeling weak, headache, irritability, nausea or vomiting, sweaty skin, a fast, weak pulse and a normal or slightly elevated body temperature. Treatment involves getting out of the heat and/or sun, fanning the victim and applying cool, wet cloths to the skin, laying the victim flat with their legs raised and rehydrating with water containing a quarter of a teaspoon of salt per liter. Recovery is usually rapid but it's common to feel weak for some days afterwards.

Heatstroke is a serious medical emergency. Symptoms come on suddenly and include weakness, nausea, a hot, dry body with a temperature over 41°C, dizziness, confusion, loss of coordination, fits and eventually collapse and loss of consciousness. Seek medical help and commence cooling by getting the person out of the heat, removing their clothes, fanning them and applying cool wet cloths or ice to their body, especially to the groin and armpits.

Cold

Cold exposure may be a significant problem, especially in the northern regions of the country. To prevent hypothermia, keep all body surfaces covered, including the head and neck. Synthetic materials such as Gore-Tex and Thinsulate provide excellent insulation. Because the body loses heat faster when wet, stay dry at all times. Change inner garments promptly when they become moist. Keep active, but get enough rest. Consume plenty of food and water. Be especially sure not to have any alcohol. Caffeine and tobacco should also be avoided.

Watch out for the 'Umbles' – stumbles, mumbles, fumbles and grumbles – which are important signs of impending hypothermia. If someone appears to be developing hypothermia, you should insulate them from the ground, protect them from the wind, remove wet clothing or cover them with a vapor barrier such as a plastic bag, and transport them immediately to a warm environment and a medical facility. Warm fluids (but not coffee or tea – noncaffeinated herbal teas are OK) may be given if the person is alert enough to swallow.

Altitude Sickness

Acute Mountain Sickness (AMS), aka 'Altitude Sickness,' may develop in those who ascend rapidly to altitudes greater than 2500m. Being physically fit offers no protection. Those who have experienced AMS in the past are prone to future episodes. The risk increases with faster ascents, higher altitudes and greater exertion. Symptoms may include headaches, nausea, vomiting, dizziness, malaise, insomnia and loss of appetite. Severe cases may be complicated by fluid in the lungs (high-altitude pulmonary edema) or swelling of the brain (high-altitude cerebral edema).

The best treatment for AMS is descent. If you are exhibiting symptoms, do not ascend. If symptoms are severe or persistent, descend immediately. When traveling to high altitudes, it's also important to avoid overexertion, eat light meals and abstain from alcohol. If your symptoms are more than mild or don't resolve promptly, see a doctor. Altitude sickness should be taken seriously; it can be life-threatening when severe.

Bites & Stings
MOSQUITO BITES

When traveling in areas where West Nile Virus (p879) or other mosquito-borne illnesses have been reported, keep covered (wear long sleeves, long pants, hats, and shoes rather than sandals) and apply a good insect repellent, preferably one containing DEET, to exposed skin and clothing. In general, adults and children over 12 should use preparations containing 25% to 35% DEET, which usually lasts about six hours. Children between two and 12 years of age should use preparations containing no more than 10% DEET, applied sparingly, which will usually last about three hours. Neurologic toxicity has been reported from DEET, especially in children, but appears to be extremely uncommon and is generally related to overuse. DEET-containing compounds should not be used on children under age two.

Insect repellents containing certain botanical products, including oil of eucalyptus and soybean oil, are effective but last only 1½ to two hours. Products based on citronella

are not effective. For additional protection, you can apply permethrin to clothing, shoes, tents and bed nets. Permethrin treatments are safe and remain effective for at least two weeks, even when items are laundered. Permethrin should not be applied directly to the skin.

TICK BITES

Ticks are parasitic arachnids that may be present in brush, forest and grasslands, where hikers often get them on their legs or in their boots. Adult ticks suck blood from hosts by burrowing into the skin and can carry infections such as Lyme disease (p879). To protect yourself from tick bites, follow the same precautions as for mosquitoes (see left), except that boots are preferable to shoes and pants should be tucked in.

Always check your body for ticks after walking through high grass or thickly forested areas. If ticks are found unattached, they can simply be brushed off. If a tick is found attached, press down around the tick's head with tweezers, grab the head and gently pull upwards – do not twist it. (If no tweezers are available, use your fingers, but protect them from contamination with a piece of tissue or paper.) Do not rub oil, alcohol or petroleum jelly on it. If you get sick in the following couple of weeks, consult a doctor.

MAMMAL BITES

Do not attempt to pet, handle or feed any mammal, with the exception of domestic animals known to be free of any infectious disease. Most animal injuries are directly related to a person's attempt to touch or feed the animal.

ALTERNATIVE MEDICINE

Canadian health food stores and many regular groceries abound with so-called 'natural' remedies. These are a few of the more successful ones, in our opinion. They're not guaranteed, of course, but they may work. You never know...

Problem	Treatment
jet lag	melatonin
motion sickness	ginger
mosquito bite	oil of eucalyptus

Any bite or scratch by a mammal, including bats, should be promptly and thoroughly cleansed with large amounts of soap and water, followed by the application of an antiseptic such as iodine or alcohol. The local health authorities should be contacted immediately for possible post-exposure rabies treatment, whether or not you've been immunized against rabies (p880). It may also be advisable to start an antibiotic, since wounds caused by animal bites and scratches frequently become infected.

SNAKE BITES

There are several varieties of venomous snakes in Canada, but unlike those in other countries they do not cause instantaneous death, and antivenins are available. First aid is to place a light constricting bandage over the bite, keep the wounded part below the level of the heart and move it as little as possible. Stay calm and get to a medical facility as soon as possible. Bring the dead snake for identification if you can, but don't risk being bitten again. Do not use the mythic 'cut an X and suck out the venom' trick; this

causes more damage to snakebite victims than the bites themselves.

SPIDER & SCORPION BITES

Although there are many species of spiders in Canada, the only ones that cause significant human illness are the black widow and hobo spiders. The black widow is black or brown in color, measuring about 15mm in body length, with a shiny top, fat body, and distinctive red or orange hourglass figure on its underside. It's found throughout Canada, usually in barns, woodpiles, sheds, harvested crops and the bowls of outdoor toilets. Hobo spiders are found chiefly in western Canada.

If bitten by a black widow, you should apply ice or cold packs and go immediately to the nearest emergency room. Complications of a black widow bite may include muscle spasms, breathing difficulties and high blood pressure. The milder bite of a hobo spider typically causes a large, inflamed wound, sometimes associated with fever and chills. If bitten, apply ice and see a physician.

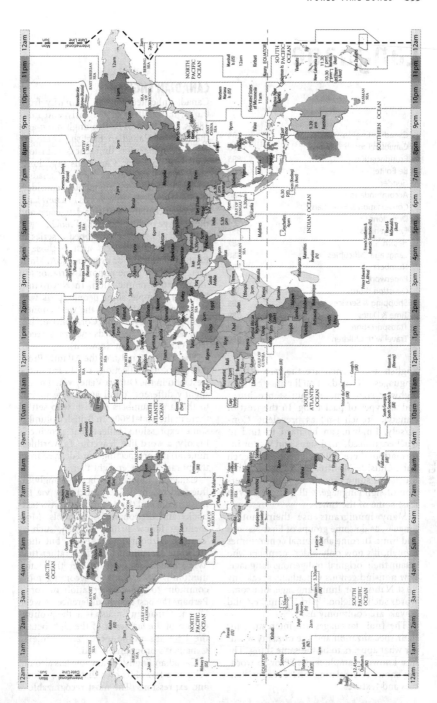

Language

English and French are the two official languages of Canada. You'll notice both on highway signs, maps, tourist brochures and all types of packaging. In the west of Canada, French isn't as prevalent. Conversely, English can be hard to find in Québec. Indeed, road signs and visitor information there will often be in French only. Outside Montréal and Québec City, the use of some French, or your own version of sign language, will be necessary at least some of the time.

Many immigrants use their mother tongues, as do some groups of First Nations and Inuit. In some aboriginal communities though, it's now only older members who retain their original indigenous language. Few non-indigenous Canadians speak any First Nations or Inuit language, but some words such as 'igloo,' 'parka,' 'muskeg' and 'kayak' are commonly used.

The Inuit languages are interesting for their specialization and use of many words for what appears to be the same thing. The best known example is the 20 or so words for 'snow,' each relating different consistencies and textures.

CANADIAN ENGLISH

Canada inherited English primarily from the British settlers of the early and mid-1800s. This form of British English remains the basis of Canadian English. There are some pronunciation differences – Britons say 'clark' for clerk, Canadians say 'clurk.' Grammatical differences are few. Canadian vocabulary has been augmented considerably by the need for new words in a new land, the influence of the aboriginal languages and the heritage of the pioneering French.

Canada has never developed a series of easily detectable dialects such as those of England, Germany or even the USA. However, there are some regional variations in idiom and pronunciation. In Newfoundland, for example, some people speak with an accent reminiscent of the west country of England (Devon and Cornwall) or Ireland, and some use words such as 'screech' (rum) and 'shooneen' (coward).

The spoken English of the Atlantic Provinces, too, has inflections not heard in the west, and in the Ottawa Valley you'll hear a slightly different sound again, due mainly to the large numbers of Irish who settled there in the mid-1800s. In British Columbia some expressions reflect that province's history; a word like 'leaverite' (a worthless mineral) is a prospecting word derived from the phrase 'Leave 'er right there.'

Canadian English has been strongly influenced by the USA, particularly via the mass media and the historic use of US textbooks and dictionaries in schools. Most spellings follow British English, such as 'centre,' 'harbour' and 'cheque,' but there are some exceptions like 'tire' (rather than 'tyre') and 'aluminum' (rather than 'aluminium'). US spelling is becoming more common, to the consternation of some. Perhaps the best known difference between US and Canadian English is in the pronunciation of the last letter of the alphabet. In the USA it's pronounced 'zee,' while in Canada it's pronounced 'zed.'

Canadian English as a whole has also developed a few of its own distinctive idioms and expressions. The most recognizable is the interrogative 'eh?,' which sometimes seems to appear at the end of every spoken sentence. Although to many non–North Americans, Canadians and Americans may sound the same, there are real differences. Canadian pronunciation of 'ou' is the most notable of these – 'out' and 'about' sound more like 'oat' and 'aboat.'

Canadian English has also added to the richness of the global English language, with words like 'kerosene' (paraffin), 'puck' (from ice hockey) and 'bushed' (exhausted). 'Moose' and 'muskeg' come from anglicised aboriginal words.

For those wishing to delve deeper into the topic, try the excellent *Oxford Dictionary of Canadian English*.

CANADIAN FRENCH

The French spoken in Canada is essentially the same as what you'd hear in France. There are differences, however, just as there are between the English of New Zealand and the English of Australia. Although many English (and most French) students in Québec are still taught the French of France, the local tongue is known as 'Québecois' or *joual*. While many around the world schooled in Parisian French would say *Quelle heure est-il?* for 'What time is it?,' on the streets of Québec you're likely to hear *Y'est quelle heure?* Québecois people will have no problem understanding more formal French.

Other differences between European French and the Québec version worth remembering (because you don't want to go hungry!) are the terms for breakfast, lunch and dinner. Rather than *petit déjeuner*, *déjeuner* and *diner* you're likely to see and hear *déjeuner*, *diner* and *souper*.

If you have any car trouble, you'll be happy to know that English terms are generally used for parts. Indeed, the word *char* (pronounced 'shar') for car may be heard. Hitchhiking is known not as *auto stop* but as *le pousse* (the thumb).

Announcers and broadcasters on Québec TV and radio tend to speak a more refined, European style of French, as does the upper class. Visitors to the country without much everyday French-speaking experience will have the most luck understanding them. Despite all this, the preservation of French

in Québec is a primary concern and fuels the separatist movement.

New Brunswick is, perhaps surprisingly, the only officially bilingual province. French is widely spoken, particularly in the north and east. Again, it is somewhat different from the French of Québec. Nova Scotia and Manitoba also have significant French-speaking populations, and there are pockets in most other provinces.

The following is a short guide to some French words and phrases that may be useful for the traveler. Québec French employs a lot of English words; this may make understanding and speaking the language a little easier.

For words and phrases related to food and dining, see p66. For a far more comprehensive guide to the language, get a copy of Lonely Planet's *French Phrasebook*.

PRONUNCIATION

Most letters in the French alphabet are pronounced more or less the same as their English counterparts; a few that may cause confusion are listed below. The combinations **un** and **on** in the pronunciation guides are nasal sounds – the 'n' is not pronounced; *zh* is pronounced as the 's' in 'measure.'

c	before **e** and **i**, as the 's' in 'sit'
	before **a**, **o** and **u** it's pronounced as English 'k'
ç	always the 's' in 'sit'
h	always silent
j	as the 's' in 'leisure'
r	from the back of the throat while constricting the muscles to restrict the flow of air
n, m	where a syllable ends in a single **n** or **m**, these letters are not pronounced, but the preceding vowel is given a nasal pronunciation
s	often not pronounced in plurals or at the end of words

BE POLITE!

You'll find that any attempt to communicate in French will be very much appreciated. Even if the only sentence you can muster is *Pardon, madame/monsieur/mademoiselle, parlez-vous anglais?* (Excuse me, madam/sir/miss, do you speak English?), you're sure to be more warmly received than if you blindly address a stranger in English.

An important distinction is made in French between *tu* and *vous*, which both mean 'you'; *tu* is only used when addressing people you know well, children or animals. If you're addressing an adult who isn't a personal friend, *vous* should be used unless the person invites you to use *tu*. In general, younger people insist less on this distinction between polite and informal, and you will find that in many cases they use *tu* from the beginning of an acquaintance.

GENDER

All nouns in French are either masculine or feminine and adjectives reflect the gender of the noun they modify. The feminine form of many nouns and adjectives is indicated by a silent **e** added to the masculine form, as in *ami* and *amie* (the masculine and feminine for 'friend').

In the following phrases both masculine and feminine forms have been indicated where necessary. The masculine form comes first and is separated from the feminine by a slash. The gender of a noun is often indicated by a preceding article: 'the/a/some,' *le/un/du* (m), *la/une/de la* (f); or one of the possessive adjectives, 'my/your/his/her,' *mon/ton/son* (m), *ma/ta/sa* (f). With French, unlike English, the possessive adjective agrees in number and gender with the thing in question: 'his/her mother' is *sa mère*.

ACCOMMODATIONS

I'm looking for a ...
Je cherche ...   zher shersh ...
  camping ground
  un camping   un kom·peeng
  guesthouse
  une pension (de famille)   ewn pon·syon (der fa·mee·yer)
  hotel
  un hôtel   un o·tel
  youth hostel
  une auberge de jeunesse   ewn o·berzh der zher·nes

Where is a cheap hotel?
Où est-ce qu'on peut trouver un hôtel pas cher?
oo es·kon per troo·vay un o·tel pa shair
What is the address?
Quelle est l'adresse?
kel e la·dres
Could you write the address, please?
Est-ce que vous pourriez écrire l'adresse, s'il vous plaît?
e·sker voo poo·ryay e·kreer la·dres seel voo play

Do you have any rooms available?
Est-ce que vous avez des chambres libres?
e·sker voo·za·vay day shom·brer lee·brer
I'd like (a) ...
Je voudrais ...   zher voo·dray ...
  single room
  une chambre à un lit   ewn shom·brer a un lee
  double-bed room
  une chambre avec un   ewn shom·brer a·vek un
    grand lit   gron lee
  twin room with two beds
  une chambre avec des lits   ewn shom·brer a·vek day lee
    jumeaux   zhew·mo
  room with a bathroom
  une chambre avec une   ewn shom·brer a·vek ewn
    salle de bains   sal der bun
  to share a dorm
  me coucher dans   me koo·sher don
  un dortoir   zun dor·twa

How much is it ...? Quel est le prix ...? kel e ler pree ...
  per night   par nuit   par nwee
  per person   par personne   par per·son

May I see it?
Est-ce que je peux voir   es·ker zher per vwa
  la chambre?   la shom·brer
Where is the bathroom?
Où est la salle de bains? oo e la sal der bun
Where is the toilet?
Où sont les toilettes?   oo·son lay twa·let
I'm leaving today.
Je pars aujourd'hui.   zher par o·zhoor·dwee
We're leaving today.
On part aujourd'hui.   on par o·zhoor·dwee

CONVERSATION & ESSENTIALS

Hello.   Bonjour.   bon·zhoor
Goodbye.   Au revoir.   o·rer·vwa
Yes.   Oui.   wee
No.   Non.   no
Please.   S'il vous plaît. seel voo play
Thank you.   Merci.   mair·see
You're welcome. Je vous en prie. zher voo·zon pree
                    De rien. (inf) der ree·en
Excuse me.   Excusez-moi.   ek·skew·zay·mwa
Sorry. (forgive me) Pardon.   par·don

What's your name?
Comment vous appelez-vous? (pol)
ko·mon voo·za·pay·lay voo
Comment tu t'appelles? (inf)
ko·mon tew ta·pel

My name is ...
Je m'appelle ...
zher ma·pel ...
Where are you from?
De quel pays êtes-vous? (pol)
der kel pay·ee et·voo
De quel pays es-tu? (inf)
der kel pay·ee e·tew
I'm from ...
Je viens de ...
zher vyen der ...
I like ...
J'aime ...
zhem ...
I don't like ...
Je n'aime pas ...
zher nem pa ...
Just a minute.
Une minute.
ewn mee·newt

DIRECTIONS

Where is ...?
Où est ...? oo e ...
Go straight ahead.
Continuez tout droit. kon·teen·way too drwa
Turn left.
Tournez à gauche. toor·nay a gosh
Turn right.
Tournez à droite. toor·nay a drwat
at the corner
au coin o kwun
at the traffic lights
aux feux o fer

behind	*derrière*	dair·ryair
in front of	*devant*	der·von
far (from)	*loin (de)*	lwun (der)
near (to)	*près (de)*	pray (der)
opposite	*en face de*	on fas der

SIGNS	
Entrée	Entrance
Sortie	Exit
Renseignements	Information
Ouvert	Open
Fermé	Closed
Interdit	Prohibited
(Commissariat de)	Police Station
Police	
Toilettes/WC	Toilets
Hommes	Men
Femmes	Women

beach	*la plage*	la plazh
bridge	*le pont*	ler pon
church	*l'église*	le·gleez
island	*l'île*	leel
lake	*le lac*	ler lak
museum	*le musée*	ler mew·zay
quay	*le quai*	ler kay
riverbank	*la rive*	la reev
sea	*la mer*	la mair
tourist office	*l'office de*	lo·fees der
	tourisme	too·rees·mer

EMERGENCIES

Help!
Au secours! o skoor
There's been an accident!
Il y a eu un accident! eel ya ew un ak·see·don
I'm lost.
Je me suis égaré/e. (m/f) zhe me swee·zay·ga·ray
Leave me alone!
Fichez-moi la paix! fee·shay·mwa la pay

Call ...!	*Appelez ...!*	a·play ...
a doctor	*un médecin*	un med·sun
the police	*la police*	la po·lees

HEALTH

I'm ill.
Je suis malade. zher swee ma·lad
It hurts here.
J'ai une douleur ici. zhay ewn doo·ler ee·see

I'm ...	*Je suis ...*	zher swee ...
asthmatic	*asthmatique*	(z)as·ma·teek
diabetic	*diabétique*	dee·a·be·teek
epileptic	*épileptique*	(z)e·pee·lep·teek

I'm allergic	*Je suis*	zher swee
to ...	*allergique ...*	za·lair·zheek ...
antibiotics	*aux antibiotiques*	o zon·tee·byo·teek
bees	*aux abeilles*	o za·bay·yer
nuts	*aux noix*	o nwa
peanuts	*aux cacahuètes*	o ka·ka·wet
penicillin	*à la pénicilline*	a la pay·nee·see·leen

antiseptic	*l'antiseptique*	lon·tee·sep·teek
condoms	*des préservatifs*	day pray·zair·va·teef
contraceptive	*le contraceptif*	ler kon·tra·sep·teef
diarrhoea	*la diarrhée*	la dee·ya·ray
medicine	*le médicament*	ler me·dee·ka·mon
nausea	*la nausée*	la no·zay
sunblock cream	*la crème solaire*	la krem so·lair

| tampons | des tampons | day tom·pon |
| | hygiéniques | ee·zhen·eek |

LANGUAGE DIFFICULTIES
Do you speak English?
Parlez-vous anglais?
par·lay·voo ong·lay
Does anyone here speak English?
Y a-t-il quelqu'un qui parle anglais?
ya·teel kel·kung kee par long·glay
How do you say ... in French?
Comment est-ce qu'on dit ... en français?
ko·mon es·kon dee ... on fron·say
What does ... mean?
Que veut dire ...?
ker ver deer ...
I understand.
Je comprends.
zher kom·pron
I don't understand.
Je ne comprends pas.
zher ner kom·pron pa
Could you write it down, please?
Est-ce que vous pourriez l'écrire, s'il vous plaît?
es·ker voo poo·ryay le·kreer seel voo play
Can you show me (on the map)?
Pouvez-vous m'indiquer (sur la carte)?
poo·vay·voo mun·dee·kay (sewr la kart)

NUMBERS
0	zero	ze·ro
1	un	un
2	deux	der
3	trois	twa
4	quatre	ka·trer
5	cinq	sungk
6	six	sees
7	sept	set
8	huit	weet
9	neuf	nerf
10	dix	dees
11	onze	onz
12	douze	dooz
13	treize	trez
14	quatorze	ka·torz
15	quinze	kunz
16	seize	sez
17	dix-sept	dee·set
18	dix-huit	dee·zweet
19	dix-neuf	deez·nerf
20	vingt	vung
21	vingt et un	vung tay un
22	vingt-deux	vung·der
30	trente	tront

40	quarante	ka·ront
50	cinquante	sung·kont
60	soixante	swa·sont
70	soixante-dix	swa·son·dees
80	quatre-vingts	ka·trer·vung
90	quatre-vingt-dix	ka·trer·vung·dees
100	cent	son
1000	mille	meel

PAPERWORK
name	nom	nom
nationality	nationalité	na·syo·na·lee·tay
date/place	date/place	dat/plas
of birth	de naissance	der nay·sons
sex/gender	sexe	seks
passport	passeport	pas·por
visa	visa	vee·za

QUESTION WORDS
Who?	Qui?	kee
What?	Quoi?	kwa
What is it?	Qu'est-ce que c'est?	kes·ker say
When?	Quand?	kon
Where?	Où?	oo
Which?	Quel/Quelle?	kel
Why?	Pourquoi?	poor·kwa
How?	Comment?	ko·mon

SHOPPING & SERVICES
I'd like to buy ...
Je voudrais acheter ... zher voo·dray zash·tay ...
How much is it?
C'est combien? say kom·byun
I don't like it.
Cela ne me plaît pas. ser·la ner mer play pa
May I look at it?
Est-ce que je peux le voir? es·ker zher per ler vwar
I'm just looking.
Je regarde. zher rer·gard
It's cheap.
Ce n'est pas cher. ser nay pa shair
It's too expensive.
C'est trop cher. say tro shair
I'll take it.
Je le prends. zher ler pron

Can I pay by ...?
Est-ce que je peux payer avec ...?
es·ker zher per pay·yay a·vek ...
  credit card
  ma carte de crédit ma kart der kre·dee
  traveler's checks
  des chèques de voyage day shek der vwa·yazh

more	plus	plew
less	moins	mwa
smaller	plus petit	plew per·tee
bigger	plus grand	plew gron

I'm looking for ...	Je cherche ...	zhe shersh ...
a bank	une banque	ewn bonk
the ... embassy	l'ambassade de ...	lam·ba·sahd der ...
the hospital	l'hôpital	lo·pee·tal
the market	le marché	ler mar·shay
the police	la police	la po·lees
the post office	le bureau de poste	ler bew·ro der post
a public phone	une cabine téléphonique	ewn ka·been te·le·fo·neek
a public toilet	les toilettes	lay twa·let

TIME & DATES

What time is it?	Quelle heure est-il?	kel er e til
It's (8) o'clock.	Il est (huit) heures.	il e (weet) er
It's half past ...	Il est (...) heures et demie.	il e (...) er e der·mee
It's quarter to ...	Il est (...) heures moins le quart.	il e (...) er mwun ler kar

in the morning	du matin	dew ma·tun
in the afternoon	de l'après-midi	der la·pray·mee·dee
in the evening	du soir	dew swar
today	aujourd'hui	o·zhoor·dwee
tomorrow	demain	der·mun
yesterday	hier	yair

Monday	lundi	lun·dee
Tuesday	mardi	mar·dee
Wednesday	mercredi	mair·krer·dee
Thursday	jeudi	zher·dee
Friday	vendredi	von·drer·dee
Saturday	samedi	sam·dee
Sunday	dimanche	dee·monsh

January	janvier	zhon·vyay
February	février	fev·ryay
March	mars	mars
April	avril	a·vreel
May	mai	may
June	juin	zhwun
July	juillet	zhwee·yay
August	août	oot
September	septembre	sep·tom·brer
October	octobre	ok·to·brer
November	novembre	no·vom·brer
December	décembre	day·som·brer

TRANSPORTATION
Public Transportation

What time does ... leave/arrive?	À quelle heure part/arrive ...?	a kel er par/a·reev ...
boat	le bateau	ler ba·to
bus	le bus	ler bews
plane	l'avion	la·vyon
train	le train	ler trun

I'd like a ... ticket.	Je voudrais un billet ...	zher voo·dray un bee·yay ...
one-way	simple	sum·pler
return	aller-retour	a·lay rer·toor
1st class	de première classe	der prem·yair klas
2nd class	de deuxième classe	der der·zyem klas

I want to go to ...
Je voudrais aller à ...   zher voo·dray a·lay a ...
The train has been delayed.
Le train est en retard.   ler trun et on rer·tar
The train has been cancelled.
Le train a été annulé.   ler trun a e·te a·new·lay

the first	le premier (m)	ler prer·myay
	la première (f)	la prer·myair
the last	le dernier (m)	ler dair·nyay
	la dernière (f)	la dair·nyair
platform number	le numéro de quai	ler new·may·ro der kay
ticket office	le guichet	ler gee·shay
timetable	l'horaire	lo·rair
train station	la gare	la gar

Private Transportation

I'd like to hire a/an...	Je voudrais louer ...	zher voo·dray loo·way ...
bicycle	un vélo	un vay·lo
car	une voiture	ewn vwa·tewr
4WD	un quatre-quatre	un kat·kat
motorbike	une moto	ewn mo·to

Is this the road to ...?
C'est la route pour ...?   say la root poor ...
Where's a service station?
Où est-ce qu'il y a
une station-service?   oo es·keel ya ewn sta·syon·ser·vees
Please fill it up.
Le plein, s'il vous plaît.   ler plun seel voo play
I'd like ... litres.
Je voudrais ... litres.   zher voo·dray ... lee·trer

petrol/gas	essence	ay·sons
unleaded	sans plomb	son plom
leaded	au plomb	o plom
diesel	diesel	dyay·zel

ROAD SIGNS

Cédez la Priorité	Give Way
Danger	Danger
Défense de Stationner	No Parking
Entrée	Entrance
Interdiction de Doubler	No Overtaking
Péage	Toll
Ralentissez	Slow Down
Sens Interdit	No Entry
Sens Unique	One-Way
Sortie	Exit

(How long) Can I park here?
(Combien de temps) Est-ce que je peux stationner ici?
(kom·byun der tom) es·ker zher per sta·syo·nay ee·see

I've run out of petrol.
Je suis en panne d'essence.
zher swee zon pan day·sons

I need a mechanic.
J'ai besoin d'un mécanicien.
zhay ber·zwun dun me·ka·nee·syun

The car/motorbike has broken down (at ...)
La voiture/moto est tombée en panne (à ...)
la vwa·tewr/mo·to ay tom·bay on pan (a ...)

The car/motorbike won't start.
La voiture/moto ne veut pas démarrer.
la vwa·tewr/mo·to ner ver pa day·ma·ray

I had an accident.
J'ai eu un accident.
zhay ew un ak·see·don

I have a flat tyre.
Mon pneu est à plat.
mom pner ay ta pla

TRAVEL WITH CHILDREN

Is there a/an ...?
Y a-t-il ...?   ya teel ...

I need a/an ...
J'ai besoin ...   zhay ber·zwun ...

baby change room
d'un endroit pour   dun on·drwa poor
  changer le bébé   shon·zhay ler be·be
car baby seat
d'un siège-enfant   dun syezh·on·fon
child-minding service
d'une garderie   dewn gar·dree
children's menu
d'un menu pour enfant   dun mer·new poor on·fon
disposable nappies/diapers
de couches-culottes   der koosh·kew·lot
formula
de lait maternisé   de lay ma·ter·nee·zay
(English-speaking) babysitter
d'une babysitter (qui   dewn ba·bee·see·ter (kee
  parle anglais)   parl ong·glay)
highchair
d'une chaise haute   dewn shay zot
potty
d'un pot de bébé   dun po der be·be
pusher/stroller
d'une poussette   dewn poo·set

Do you mind if I breastfeed here?
Cela vous dérange si j'allaite mon bébé ici?
ser·la voo day·ron·zhe see zha·lay·ter mon bay·bay ee·see

Are children allowed?
Les enfants sont permis?
lay zon·fon son pair·mee

Also available from Lonely Planet:
French Phrasebook

Glossary

Aboriginal – peoples living in Canada before European colonization (*First Nations* and *Inuit*) and the *Métis*

Acadians – the first settlers from France who lived in Nova Scotia

allophones – people living in Québec whose first language is neither French nor English

Anglophones –people who speak English as their first or only language

Atlantic Provinces – a region that includes Newfoundland, Nova Scotia, Prince Edward Island and New Brunswick

ATV – All-terrain vehicle, or four-wheel drive vehicle

aurora borealis – charged particles from the sun that are trapped in the earth's magnetic field and appear as other-worldly, colored, waving beams; also called the *northern lights*

B&B – bed-and-breakfast

backcountry site – a primitive campsite with few facilities, often found in national or provincial parks

badlands – a barren, arid region of southern Alberta with unusual features caused by erosion; the rocks in such areas often contain prehistoric fossils

BC – British Columbia

Black Loyalists – slaves of African origin freed by the British to fight against the USA during the American Revolution, many of whom later settled in Nova Scotia

boreal – refers to the Canadian North and its character, as in the boreal forest or the boreal wind

BYOW – bring your own wine

calèche – horse-drawn carriages that can be taken around parts of Montréal and Québec City

Canadian Shield – a plateau of rock formed 2.5 billion years ago that covers much of the Northern region of Canada; also known as the Precambrian or Laurentian Shield

ceilidh (*kay*-lee) – a Gaelic word meaning an informal gathering for song, dance and story; it's sometimes known as a house party; may refer to any public performance where music is played and is especially popular in Prince Edward Island and Nova Scotia

CFL – Canadian Football League

coulees – gulches, usually dry

Cowichan – an indigenous people originally from the Lake Cowichan area on Vancouver Island; also the name of the hand-knitted, 100% wool sweaters they produce

CPR – Canadian Pacific Railway

Cree – an *Aboriginal* people, and their language

Dominion of Canada – historical name of Canada assumed at the time of Confederation in 1867

Doukhobours – an unorthodox Russian Christian sect, some of whom settled in Saskatchewan and BC during the 19th century

First Nations – most groups of *Aboriginal* peoples in Canada, except *Inuit* and *Métis*

Francophones – people who speak French as their first or only language

gasoline – petrol, known as gas or fuel; mostly sold unleaded in Canada

gîte du passant – a term often used in Québec for B&Bs

Group of Seven – a group of celebrated Canadian landscape painters from the 1920s

GST – 7% goods and services tax levied on most purchases throughout Canada

hoodoo – distinctive vertical pillar shape carved into a rock face by rainfall and glacial erosion, mainly found in the *badlands* regions of southern Alberta

hookup – at campgrounds; refers to *RV* connections for electricity, water and sewage

Hudson's Bay Company (Compagnie de la Baie d'Hudson) – an English enterprise created in 1670 to exploit the commercial potential of the Hudson Bay and its waterways

icefield – a large, level expanse of floating ice

Innu – *First Nations* people living in eastern Québec and Labrador and comprising the Montagnais and Naskapi subgroups

Inside Passage – sea route from the Alaskan Panhandle to Washington state that runs between mainland *BC* and the chain of islands off the coast

Inuit – *Aboriginal* people descended from the Thule and residing primarily in Nunavut and Arctic Québec

Inukshuk – stone cairn mimicking the human form, originally built by *Inuit* as landmarks or to herd prey toward waiting hunters

Inuktitut – language of the *Inuit* people

Inuvialuit – Western Artic *Inuit* people

Inuvialuktun – language of the *Inuvialuit*

Klondike – region along the Klondike River in the Yukon Territory where the discovery of gold in 1897 led to the Klondike Gold Rush

Labour Day – public holiday on the first Monday in September; end of the summer holiday season

Left Coast – sometimes applied to coastal *BC* for the perceived left-wing, eccentric nature of its residents

l'Estrie – *Québecois* term for the Cantons de l'Est (Eastern Townships), a former *Loyalist* region southeast of Montréal toward the US border

loonie – Canada's one-dollar coin, which depicts a loon on one side

Lower Mainland – common term for the southwestern part of *BC*, including metropolitan Vancouver

Loyalists – British North American colonists who remained loyal to the British crown during the American Revolution; many settled in Ontario and Québec; also known as United Empire Loyalists

Lunenberg bump – a five-sided dormer window on the 2nd floor that overhangs the 1st floor, a common architectural feature in Lunenberg, Nova Scotia

Maritime provinces – also known as the Maritimes, this group includes three provinces: New Brunswick, Nova Scotia and Prince Edward Island

Métis – Canadians of mixed French and *First Nations* ancestry

midden – archaeological term for mound or heap containing domestic refuse and thus indicating human settlement

Mi'kmaq – *First Nations* people living throughout the *Maritime provinces*, especially Nova Scotia. Also spelled micmac

Mounties – Royal Canadian Mounted Police *(RCMP)*

muskeg – undrained boggy land most often found in Northern Canada

névé – compacted, accumulated snow that forms the surface of the upper part of a glacier

NHL – National Hockey League

northern lights – see *aurora borealis*

Northwest Passage – sea route from the Atlantic to the Pacific Ocean via the Canadian Arctic

NWMP – North-West Mounted Police

Ogopogo –similar to the Loch Ness monster, thought to reside in Okanagan Lake; has never been photographed

Ojibwe – *Aboriginal* people living in southern Canada, primarily west of Lake Superior; also known as Ojibway or Chippewa

Old World – of European origin

outfitter – a business or store supplying outdoor/adventure equipment, often for rent

outports – small, isolated coastal villages of Newfoundland, connected with the rest of the province by boat

permafrost – permanently frozen subsoil that covers the far northern regions of Canada

petroglyphs – ancient paintings or carvings on rock

piastre – *Québecois* term for a Canadian dollar

pingo – in the far North, a huge earth-covered ice hill formed by the upward expansion of underground ice

portage – process of transporting boats and supplies overland between navigable waterways; can also refer to the overland route used

potlatch – competitive ceremonial activity among some *First Nations* people (usually coastal), traditionally involving the giving of lavish gifts in order to emphasize the wealth and status of a chief or clan; now often just refers to a wild party or revel

powwow – a festive social gathering of *Aboriginal* people, often involving singing, dancing and general merriment

PST – Provincial Sales Tax; ranges from 7% to 10%

pysanky – decorated wooden Easter egg

Québecois – the local tongue of Québec, where the vast majority of the population is of French descent; the term also refers to the residents of Québec, although it is applied only to *Francophones*, not English-speaking Quebecers

RCMP – Royal Canadian Mounted Police, the main law-enforcement agency throughout Canada

RV – recreational vehicle (commonly a motor home), used for traveling or camping; 'caravan' in British English

screech – a particularly strong rum once available only in Newfoundland, now widely available across Canada (but only in diluted form)

spelunking – exploration and study of caves

sugar shack – the place where collected sap from maple trees is distilled in large kettles and boiled as part of the production process for maple syrup

table d'hôte – set-price meal

taiga – coniferous forests extending across much of subarctic North America and Eurasia

terrasse – patio

toonie – slang name for a Canadian two-dollar coin

trailer – in Canada and the US, a caravan or a mobile home

tundra – vast, treeless Arctic plains north of the tree line with perpetually frozen subsoil

two-four – a case of beer containing 24 bottles

United Empire Loyalists – see *Loyalist*

VIC – visitor information center

Victoria Day – public holiday held on the Monday before May 25; start of the summer holiday season

voyageur – a boatman employed by one of the early fur-trading companies; he could also perform the functions of a woodsman, guide, trapper or explorer

VRC – visitor reception center

Behind the Scenes

THIS BOOK

The 9th edition of *Canada* was written by a team of authors led by Andrea Schulte-Peevers. Andrea wrote all of the front and back chapters, with the exceptions of The Culture and Food & Drink. She also wrote part of the Québec chapter (Montréal, North of Montréal and Montréal to Québec City). Coauthors Becca Blond (Alberta and the 'Bear Necessities' boxed text in The Environment), Kerryn Burgess (Georgian Bay & Lakelands and Northern Ontario), Pete Cruttenden (all of British Columbia except the chapter introduction and Vancouver), John Lee (British Columbia chapter introduction and Vancouver), Mark Lightbody (New Brunswick, Eastern Ontario and Ottawa, and all of the Québec chapter except Montréal, North of Montréal and Montréal to Québec City), Graham Neale (Manitoba, Saskatchewan, and Southwest Ontario except Stratford and the Niagara region), Matt Phillips (Newfoundland & Labrador, Prince Edward Island), Lisa Roberts (Nova Scotia), Aaron Spitzer (all of the Northwest Territories except Mackenzie River Valley and Arctic Region), Justine Vaisutis (Ontario chapter introduction, Toronto, the Niagara region and Stratford) and Ryan Ver Berkmoes (Yukon Territory, the Sahtu and Western Arctic regions of the Northwest Territories) contributed tirelessly to this title. John Lee wrote Food & Drink; Dr David Goldberg wrote Health; Bruce Dowbiggin, Will Ferguson, Margo Pfeiff and Jennie Punter wrote The Culture, with boxed text contributions from Sam Benson ('The Oracle of the Electronic Age'), Cleo Paskal ('The Whole World Loves a Québecois Accordion Player') and Aaron Spitzer

('Throatsinging'). Some text and maps for the Ontario chapter were updated and adapted from the second edition of *Toronto* by Sam Benson; for the British Columbia and Yukon Territory chapters, from the second edition of *British Columbia* by Ryan Ver Berkmoes and Graham Neale; and for the Québec chapter, from the second edition of *Montréal* by Jeremy Gray and the first edition of *Québec* by Steve Kokker. Mark Lightbody was the coordinating author on the previous two editions of this book.

THANKS from the Authors

Andrea Schulte-Peevers Marie José Pinsonnault of Tourisme Montréal and Bard Nordby of Tourisme Québec deserve gold medals for their generous and tireless help. A great big thank you also to Monica Campbell of the Canadian Tourism Commission for making all the introductions. The irrepressible Ruby Roy shall forever be remembered for her limitless knowledge and excellent company. Big thanks also to Jeremy Gray for clueing me about Montréal and for so generously sharing his favorite places. Erin Corrigan – thanks for trusting me with this gig. Sam Benson – you're all an author could wish for in a commissioning editor. Charlotte Harrison deserves thanks for her sensitive editing and kind and professional attitude. Thanks also to this great team of authors, with a special nod to Mark Lightbody for going the extra mile. And finally, David – you're my rock.

Becca Blond Thanks to Lani for agreeing to join me on my research sojourn in Alberta. Big thanks also to all those Canadians who offered helpful

THE LONELY PLANET STORY

The story begins with a classic travel adventure: Tony and Maureen Wheeler's 1972 journey across Europe and Asia to Australia. There was no useful information about the overland trail then, so Tony and Maureen published the first Lonely Planet guidebook to meet a growing need.

From a kitchen table, Lonely Planet has grown to become the largest independent travel publisher in the world, with offices in Melbourne (Australia), Oakland (USA) and London (UK). Today Lonely Planet guidebooks cover the globe. There is an ever-growing list of books and information in a variety of media. Some things haven't changed. The main aim is still to make it possible for adventurous travelers to get out there – to explore and better understand the world.

At Lonely Planet we believe travelers can make a positive contribution to the countries they visit – if they respect their host communities and spend their money wisely. Every year 5% of company profit is donated to charities around the world.

advice along the way. To my family, David, Patricia, Jessica, Jennie & Vera, thanks for the constant love and support. To Sam Benson at Lonely Planet and all the other authors on the Canada book, it was great working with y'all. Finally, to Aaron, thanks for putting up with me being away so much of the time, and always being there for me when I need a shoulder to lean on. I couldn't have done it without you.

Kerryn Burgess Most of all, I'm grateful to Sam Benson, Erin Corrigan and Michelle Glynn for making it possible for me to research my favorite places. I'm also grateful to Charlotte Harrison for her insightful, sensitive editing. Of the many kind, generous souls who helped me so much in northern Ontario and beyond, Caryn Colman, Jungle Jane, Katherine Kitching, Beth Mairs, Jane McDonald and David Wells really went out of their way – thank you. Jane Thompson, Alison Lyall and Nikki Parker were always there to lend an ear, and the whole experience was such a blast thanks to Pippa Beck, Peter Czerny, Yoav Farkash, Alex Fayle, Carolyn Foster, Daniel Hudon, Mike Matisko and the spirit of Moosemeat.

Pete Cruttenden Thanks firstly to Ryan Ver Berkmoes and Graham Neale for their fine work on *British Columbia*. Thanks also to Bruce Baird in Vancouver, Des and Jo Hutchinson in Cobble Hill, Paul, Holly and Poppy Kirwan in LA, Sam Benson at Lonely Planet USA, Rebecca Cole back home, and the good folk of BC whose paths I crossed.

John Lee Credit is due to Tourism Vancouver and Tourism BC for their assistance on this and other projects. Thanks also to my friends in Vancouver for enduring my frequent moans of exhaustion toward the end of the write-up period, and to my local Tim Hortons for being open 24 hours a day: Maple Cream doughnuts may look good but at 5am toasted bagels always taste better. Thanks also to my nephew Andrew and his enthusiasm for making me attend the city's annual Bard on the Beach Shakespeare festival.

Mark Lightbody Much thanks to all the travelers and residents met during research and to those who wrote with their experiences. In Tadoussac, thanks go to Georges Monfré for warm hospitality and information and wishes for a speedy recovery to André. Thanks to Patricia Stewart for her observations on Québec and New Brunswick. Thanks as always to Lloyd Jones for ongoing backpacking news. In Ottawa, thanks to Jill and Konrad Sechley.

A big thanks also to Andrea Schulte-Peevers for her blend of camaraderie and professionalism. A nod goes to Steve Kokker for his fine research and writing in Québec and the same for Jim Dufresne in New Brunswick. Thanks, too, to Lonely Planet staff, in particular Sam Benson, for editorial and technical help. Lastly, thanks to Colleen for nourishment and a watchful eye.

Graham Neale Travel 12,000 kilometers throughout Canada and you meet a lot of people. It's impossible to thank them all. I do this: Sarah Williams from Cardiff, Wales, kept me moving through her inspiration. The Mayhews (five and counting) fed me and gave me the world's most comfortable chesterfield. Steak dinner and catching up with the Dacks was enjoyable. Penny, Daryl, Nadine and Michelle gave invaluable help. The Surrey Public Library gave me an office. My dad and Annie passive-aggressively tolerated the mess on the dining-room table. Of course I thank you, yes you; writing this book would be useless without you reading it.

Matt Phillips Thanks to: Sam Benson 'speaking' for your help, enthusiasm and the chance to have some fun on the east coast; the beautiful woman who let me hole up in her home for three mad weeks of keyboard crushing – thanks, Mum; Dad for always believing; Pam for being my most ardent supporter; Lara, Hamish and Laura, for always giving more than you should; my loved ones for loving; Donalda Doucette for her help and smiles in PEI; Bonnie Gaudy for her support in Labrador; and to all the wonderful people who helped me out along the way.

Lisa Roberts Kathryn Anderson and Wilf Bean shared travel tips and inaugurated my adventure with a comfortable bed and good company. Thanks to Sarah Roberts and L'Arche Homefires, Jo-Ann Citrigno and Doug MacKinlay, Hermina and Ted van Zutphen, and Margrit Gahlinger for breaking up my solo travels with their company and hospitality. Denise Morley shared detailed knowledge of Cape Breton. Thanks also to Jen Graham, Dave Redwood, Louise Van Wart, Ross McLaren, Dan Frid, Kermit de Gooyer, Deborah Tobin and Al Keith for various forms of assistance. Many thanks to commissioning editor Sam Benson for answering my questions with patience and grace.

Aaron Spitzer *Qujannamiik* and *mahsi cho* to Don Jaque and Jessica Book for the inside scoop on – and tour of – Fort Smith; to Sean Percy and Pieta

Goudron for their noble (though, alas, fruitless) efforts to sell me on Hay River; to Derek Neary for the low-down on Fort Simpson; to Denie Olmstead of the Northern Frontier Visitors Centre for the up-to-the-minute skinny on Yellowknife; to Amy Elgersma and Sharla Mulley for food, lodging and great good fun in Iqaluit; to Lonely Planet honchos Sam Benson and Andrea Schulte-Peevers for guiding me through my first Lonely Planet effort and tolerating countless dumb questions; and most of all to Ally, for everything.

Justine Vaisutis This job was made immensely more enjoyable thanks to the support, patience and culinary skills of my partner in crime and fellow Lonely Planet author Alan Murphy. I'd also like to extend a huge thanks to Sam Benson, not only for her excellent text, but also for opening the doors of communication wide. Andrea, thanks for your flexible coordinating and lastly thanks to the folks at Tourism Toronto for being such a great resource.

Ryan Ver Berkmoes Thanks to my many friends in the North, who include Jim Kemshead, the effervescent Wendy Burns and Debra Ryan. Thanks as well to the LPers like Sam Benson and Maria Donohoe (who I will always miss) for giving me the chance to work on this book about a place I love. And of course extra warm thoughts for the ever-inspirational Erin Corrigan. And there's further gratitude for the travel gods who timed my visit to the NWT before the thaw so that I could finally try my hand driving the oh-so-fun ice roads. Doughnuts in snow-covered parking lots were never like this.

CREDITS

The 9th edition of *Canada* was commissioned and developed in Lonely Planet's Oakland office. Erin Corrigan began contracting and briefing this title; Sam Benson took over from there. Maria Donohoe and David Zingarelli provided invaluable assistance along the way. Charlotte Harrison and Kate Evans were the coordinating editors. Susie Ashworth, Michelle Coxall, Tony Davidson, Victoria Harrison, Sarah Hassall, Brooke Lyons, Charlotte Orr and Jane Thompson helped with editing and proofing. Laurie Mikkelsen and Kusnandar were the coordinating cartographers, assisted by Tim Lohnes, Anthony Phelan and Lyndell Stringer. Yvonne Bischofberger was the layout designer and also did the colour pages. Laura Jane assisted with layout and cross-referencing, Brooke Lyons also helped with cross-referencing, and Gerard Walker helped with the images. Julie Rovis and Sally Darmody worked on

the cover. Wayne Murphy designed the back cover map and Quentin Frayne coordinated the language content. Glenn van der Knijff was the project manager, Martin Heng was the managing editor and Alison Lyall was the managing cartographer.

THANKS from Lonely Planet
Many thanks to the travelers who used the last edition and wrote to us with helpful hints, useful advice and interesting anecdotes:

A Daniel Abbott, Z Abdullah, Nerea Achutegui, Andrea Adams, Julie Adamson, Amy Agorastos, Richel Aguirre, Sheetal Aiyer, Marc Alarie, Max Alavi, Claire Albrecht, Richard Alderton, Glenn Alger, Helen & Dave Allan, Janet & Dave Allan, Pierre Allard, Christy Allen, Nicole Allen, Richard Allen, John Allenby, Myles Anderson, Nils F Anderson, Riley Anderson, Trygve Anderson, Luc Andre, Nicole Andrews, Eduardo Angel, Kate Angel, Wolfgang Angerer, Gill Ankers, John Annabell, Thierry Antoine, Vanesa Aparicio, Stephanie Appert, Eileen Arandiga, Rosalind Archer, Jarkko Arjatsalo, S Arnold, Terry Aspinall, Sue Asquith, John Atkin, BH Atkins, Katherine Austin **B** Brian Back, Idelberto Badell, Heather Badenoch, Hans Bahlmann, Ace Bailey, Steve Bailey, Grace Ann Baker, Helen Baker, Jason Baker, Nick Baldwin, Georgia Banks, Kelly Banks, Bruno P Baratta, Michele Barber, Nina Barnaby, Craig Barrack, Greg Barry, Carmen Barteaux, Anke Bartels, Cathy Bartlett, Maria Basaraba, Ian Batt, Janet Beale, Andrea Beal-Oetterli, Shayne Beard, Adam Becalski, Phil Beicken, Michel Belec, Piet Bels, Melanie Benoit, Tracey B Berger, Verena Berger, Brian & Caryl Bergeron, Shirley Bergert, Jesse Bergman, Andrea Berreth, David Berridge, W J Best, Sjaak Beukers, Jen Bibeau, Alison Bibra, Luke Biggs, Jude A Billard, PR Birch, Jim Bird, Stephane Eric Bisson, Frida Caroline Bjerkan, Julia Black, Sarah Blackwell, Rachel Blair, Bob & Joan Blanchard, Jorge Blanco, John Blatz, Heather Blois, Nicole Boelens, Barbie Bojcun, Maria Bolano, Stephanie Bolduc, Claire Bolin, Phil Munter Bond, David Bonham, Christopher Booth, Michael Borger, Mike Borger, Jack Bornstein, Chris Borthwick, Carmen Boudreau-Kiviaho, Sarah P Bourque, Simon Bower, James Bown, Kim Boyce, Kevin Boyle, Bas & Bertrand Braam, Willard Bradley, Matthew Brady, Amy Brandon, Michael Brasier, Dan Brennan, Kathleen Brient, Michael Briggs, Ashley Bristowe, Joan Brittain, Jack Brondum, Amy Brooks, Sean Brooks, Michael Brothers, JF Brouillette, B Gavin Brown, Eliza C Brown, Gerald Brown, Maxine Brown, John & Eileen Browne, Anton Brugman, Claire Brutails, Annette Buckley, Sandra Buhlmann, Larry Buickel, Terrilee Bulger, MD Bullen, Leigh Burbidge, Dwight Burditt, Ron Burdo, Lesley Burgon, Kat Burns, Taodhg Burns, Carl Burrett, Eugenia Bursey, Marianne Busch, Jonathan Butchard, Claire Butler, Jean Butler, Donna Buxton, Kelly Byrnes **C** Nicole Caissey, Noel & Rosemary Callow, Cory Camilleri, Blaine Campbell, Kate Campbell, Jonathan Campton, Mark A Canning, Tony & Lena Cansdale, Elisabete Cardoso, Lilia Cardoso-Gould, Sharyn Carey, Chris Carlisle, Zahavit Carmel, Colleen Carroll, T Carter Ross, Ernest Carwithen, Edson Castilho, Vagner Castilho, Robert Catto, Jacky Chalk, Madeline & John Chambers, Sally Chambers, Joanna

Champion, Chan Wan Soi, RK Chaplin, Craig Chapman, Lisa Chapman, Don Charlton, Julian Chen, Eve Chenu, DeWayne Chiasson, Ian Chiclo, Chungwah Chow, KM Chow, Chow Kai Ming, Natalie Chow, Ton Christiaanse, Niall GF Christie, Steven Christie, Claudia Chritl, Isabel Chudleigh, Pierre Chum, Wendy & Steve Churchill, Florence Ciavatta, Marlene Cirillo, Charles Citroen, Antoni Cladera, Guido Claessen, Carrie Clark, Dean Clark, Phil Clark, Steve Clark, Anna Clarke, Martin Clarke, Neville Clarke, Peter Clough, Mike Clyne, Mike Coburn, Juliet Coe, Celine Cogneau, M Cohen, David Colburn, Elizabeth Cole, Don Coleman, Sarah & David Coleopy, Berna Collier, Thea Collin, Paul Collins, Rachel Collis, Maurice Conklin, Victoria Conlin, Philip Coo, Laurence Coogan, Katherine Cook, Nathan Cook, Angela Cookson, Jeremy Copeland, Lenior Corbeau, Max Corbeil, Leanne Cormack, Tosja Coronell, Sonja Corradini, Rebecca Cory, Agustin Cot, Linda Cotton, Lynda Cotton, Elsa Coudon, Marney Coulter, Peter Court-Hampton, Catrin Cousins, Callum Couston, Catherine Cowan, Michael Cowie, Sara & Brian Cox, Simon Cox, Dean Cracknell, Cilla Craig, Steve Craig, Kevin Crampton, Brian Crawford, Yvette Creighton, Phil Crew, Brad Crockett, William & Norma Cross, Ken Crossman, Dany Cuello, Daniel Cunningham, Valentina Cusnir, Cathy Ann Cwycyshyn, Krystyna Cynar **D** Rod Daldry, Edward Dale, Mary-Camillus Dale, Leonne Damson, Leonne & Alan Damson, Barbara Danin, Margaret Darby, Martina d'Ascola, Huw Davies, Louise Davies, Chuck Davis, Max Davis, Leanne & Alan Dawson, Nicky & Murray Sayers Dawson, Richard Dawson, M de Souza, Wendela de Vos, Ron Deacon, Bjorn Debaillie, Leroy W Demery, Petra Dengl, Yves Desrichard, Pierre Devinat, Dominique Devoucoux, Adri di Nobile, Lara Diamond, Julia Dickinson, M Digel, Liza Dilley, Louise Dillon, Martin Dinn, Kerry T Diotte, Tilman Dnrbeck, Alexandra Dodd, Monique Dodinet, Sarah Dodson, Allan Doig, Nikki Dolbaczuk, Sandra Dollar, Clare Dominguez, Megan Donald, Robert Dorin, Matt Doughty, Allan Douglas, Guy Douglas, Jean Dragushan, Shannon Draper, Tilman Duerbeck, P Duffy, Judy & Roger Dumm, Jayleen Duncan, Traci Dunlop, Geoff Durham, Mieke Dusseldorp **E** Jackie Early, Phillip East, Rebecca Easterly, Nadja Eberhardt, Donna Ebert, Hermann Ebsen, Peter Eden, Chris Edwards, Jay Edwards, Martin Edwards, Mike Edwards, David Egan, Henning Eifler, Reinhart Eisenberg, Frank Eisenhuth, Krispen Elder, Laura Ell, Adriana Ellis-Fragoso, Ben Elliston, Tom Elvin, Nicholas A Enright, Chris Enting, Emily Evans, Nancy Evelyn Bikaunieks **F** Tore Fagervold, Keith Fairbairn, Paul Falvo, Alan Farleigh, Sandra Farley, Nicole Faubert, Gabriele Faust, Peter Fennick, Annette Ferguson, Joseph Ferigno, Gina Field, Elizabeth & Alan Fieldus, Nadine Fillipoff, Raymond Finan, Shaun Finch, Alaric Fish, Sarah Fisher, Mandy Fletcher, Michael Fletcher, Richard Foltz, Selena Sung Li Foong, Andrew Forbes, Graham Ford, Doreen Forney, Peter Forte, Marian Fortner, Jamie Foster, Jonathan Foster, Timothy Fowkes, Mark Frankel, Justin Fraser, Suzan Fraser, Jen Frederickson, Anders Frederiksen, Magnus Fredrikson, Ben Freeman, Kevin Freer, Constance Frey, Ingo Friese, Donna Fruin, Becky Fryer, Boris Funke **G** Eric Gagnon, Jason Galea, Derek Galon, Fabiana Gamberini, Christina Gamouras, Juan Garbajosa, Abraham Garcia, Jennifer Gardner, William Gardner, Alex Garic, Pam Gaskin, Richard Gavey, Costanza Gechter, Verstrepen Geert, Dominic Geisler, Mathieu Georges, Samira Ghazi, Ferdinando Emilio

Giammichele, Marg Gibson, Jemma Gilbert, Philip Gilbert, Sandra Gilis, James Gill, James Gilmour, BR Giri, Brad Gledhill, Mike Gleeson, Michele Glover, Javeen Godbeer, Cathy Godfrey, Barbara Goldflam, Shelley Goldschlager, Lisa Goldsworthy, Claudia Gomes, Nigel Goodall, Kristy Goodchild, Hilary Gooding, George Goracz, Katherine Gordon, Dayna Gorman, Ivan Gorman, Paul Goudreau, Peter Gourley, CBT Grace, Kim Graham, Eileen Grant, Anthea Grasty, John Gray, Toni Gray, Andrew Graybill, Dylan Green, Ronalie Green, Ray Greenwood, Ian A Griffin, Andrea Grill, Sabine Groener, Wellum & Nonna Gross, Bob Grubb, Judy Grubb, Ken Guappone, Gilbert Guinard, Lisa Guiton, Maria Gulliern, Rob & Annemieke Gulmans, Joseph Gumino, Gavin Guthrie, Jim Guthrie, Lise Guyot, Valerie Gwinner **H** Alison Hahn, Natalie Haines, Daryl Hal, Justine Hall, Nancy Hall, David & Hannah Halliday, Ruth Halsall, Jean-Lou Hamelin, Andrew & Kirsty Hamilton-Wright, Gill Hamson, Lydia Han, Lutz Hankewitz, Ralf Hansen, Mabel Haourt, Deborah Hardoon, Natalie Hardwicke, Janelle Hardy, Kate Hare, Brian Harland, Tony Harminc, John Harper, Roger Harris, Barbara Harrison, Alan Hart, Lorraine Hart, Christopher Harte, Bernice Hartley, Catherine Hartung, John Harvie, Jeff Haslam, Sharn Hassall, Rob Haub, Lilly Haupt, Jessica Hauser, Beatriz Hausner, Andy Hay, M Hayden, Nick Hayward, Sendy Van & Jeroen Heel, Roland Heere, Deb Heighes, Sally Helm, Martin Helmantel, Saskia Helmantel, Reuben Helms, Laura Henderson, David Henry, Robert Herritt, Moritz Herrmann, Marian Van den Heuvel, Roger B Hicks, Amy Higgenbotham, Dave Higgs, Jennifer Hildebrand, Tim Hildebrandt, Jackie Hill, Neil Hill, TE Hillman, Chris & Sheila Hills, Derrick & Ann Hilton, Jim Hilton, Abigail Hine, Joan Hirons, Kelley Hishon, Charity Hobbs, Chris Hocking, Pettina Hodgson, Axel Hofer, Fabienne Hoffmann, Kristi Hofman, Clare Holder, Martin Holder, James Holgate, Greg Holland, Samantha Hollier, Sarah Hollingham, John Holman, Henry Hon, Muei Hoon Tan, JP Hope, Rebecca Hope, Meg Horn, Margaret Hothi, John Hough, Alison Howard, Janet & Casey Howell, Simon Huang, Paul Hubbard, Keith Hughes, Alan Humphries, Graham Hunt, Jane Hunt, Malcolm Hunt, Martin Hunt, Quentin & Ann Hunter, Paul Hutt, John Hyslop **I** Jose Igartua, Heidi Ilhren, Jeroen Immerzeel, Ingrid Indermaur, Cristina Infante, Brent Irvine, Carolyn Irvine, Keith Isherwood **J** Louis Jacobs, Nick Jacobs, Ed Jager, Marian Jago, Dafydd James, Darlene James, John Jansen, Elfneede Jauelter, Rommary Jenkins, Viv Jenkins, Esther M Jensen, Henrik C Jessen, Maxwell Jitney, Geoffrey Joachim, Diana Johns, Bob Johnson, Buffy Johnson, Carolyn Johnson, Catriona Johnson, KR Johnson, Margaret Johnson, Pam Johnson, Paul Johnson, Alan Jones, Anita Jones, Cliff Jones, Lloyd Jones, Margaret Jorstead, Vincent Joumel, Stephan Jurak, Karen Jury **K** Steven Kabanuk, Junko Kajino, Jill Kasner, David Kaye, Grant Keddie, Innes Keighren, Steve Kelleher, Stroud Kelley, Marina Kelly, Mary Kelly, Pat Kelly, Kieran Kelmar, Madeline Kemna, John Kemp, Dwight Kenney, Don Kerr, Judy Kerr, Steven Kerr, Roger Kershaw, Tarik Khelifi, Barbara Kiepenheuer, Bernard Kiernan, Pauline Kiernan, Concetta Kincaid, Brian King, Simone Kingston, Mike & Gill Kirkbride, Tyler Kirsh, Darren Kiziak, Hanne Kjeldehl, Wim Klasen, Linda Klauke, Frank Klimt, Jennifer Klinec, Eberhard Kloeber, Dayalh Kmeta, Christopher M Knapp, Jill Knoechel, Carla Knoll, Janet Komars, Tim Kong, Tom Korecki, Airi

& George Krause, Tobias Krause, David Kreindler, Vikram Krishnan, Andreas Krueger, Daniel Kruse, Dave Kruse, Pierre Kruse, Marion Kuehl, M Kulowski, Sr, Shiv Kumar **L** Michelle Labelle, Maxime Lachance, Johannes & Tobias Laengle, Marie-Helene Lagace, Bart Lam, Emmanuel Lambert, Stuart Lamble, Micky Lampe, Denise Lamy, Robyn Land, Stephen Lane, Judy Lang, Katrina Lange, Guenter Langergraber, Dany LaRochelle, Kim Latendresse, Hans Latour, Lee Lau, Hans Laue, Kimberlee Lauer, Ron Laufer, Sylvie Laurenty, Etienne Laverdiere, Mélanie Lavoie-Fulop, Al Lawrence, David Lawrence, Denise Le Gal, Gilles Le Pouesard, Patricia Leah, Julie Leatherland, Pierre L'Ecuyer, Angela Lee, Jessica Lee, Lech Lee, Derek Leebosh, Belinda Lees, Peter Lehrke, Aimee Leidich, Caroilne Lemieux, Deborah Leo, Sarah Leonard, Stacie Leptick, Stephen Leslie, Mike B Leussink, James LeVesconte, Lise Levesque, Fabienne Levy, Bill & Daphne Lewis, Adam Liard, DM Lightfoot, Charles Wei Siong Lim, Tan Shuh Lin, Morten Lindow, Kim Linekin, Kim Lipscomb, Paul Littlefair, Wai-Ping Lo, Andreas Lober, Edgar H Locke, Raffaella Loi, Mun Kwong Loke, Clive Long, Robin Longley, Karl Lorenz, Helen Lorimer, Helen Lowe, James Lowenthal, Anne Lozier, Kris Ludwig, Marcel Luginbuehl, Mark Lunn, Peter Lunt, Derek Lutz, Fiona Lyle, Nick Lynch, Joanna Lyon, Kim Lyons **M** Carol MacDonald, Krista MacDonald, Peta MacDonald, Peta & Stirling MacDonald, Stanley Macdonald, Laurie MacDougall, Dave Macmeekin, Mike MacMillan, Amy Madycki, Leen Maes, Eddie Magnussen, Eddie Magnusson, Jens Mahlow, Carol Maier, Andrew Mair, Leslie Maldonado, Maya Malik, Mike Mannion, John Marett, Hilary Marrinan, Edward Marriott, Anne Marsh, Vickie Marsh, Clive & Jean Marshall, C Marston, Donna Martin, James Martin, Alex Matskevich, Alexander Matskevich, Brent Matsuda, Linda Mattern, Jenny Matthews, Nancy Matthews, Angela May, Carolyn May, Duncan May, Sarah May, Stuart Mazza, Riccardo Mazzoni, Hilary McCully, Ian Mccahon, Susan McCain, JR McDermott, Emma McDonald, Pat McDonald, Irma M McDougall, Laura McEachern, Jeremy McElrea, Dudley McFadden, David McFarlane, Paul McFarlane, Megan McGlynn, Fiona B McIntyre, Steve McKay, Liam McKeever, DS Mckinley, Sue McKinley, Craig McKinnie, Nancie McKinnon, Tom McKown, Margaret McLean, Raymond McLean, Wallace McLean, Sarah McMullin, Gerard McNamee, Bronwyn McNaughton, Meagan McNaughton, Fran McQuail, Neil McRae, Judith McRostie, Angela McSweeney, Ryan Medd, Sheila Meehan, Inaki Mendieta, Marc Mentzer, N Merrin, Michael Mersereau, Neal Michael, Lynnell Mickelsen, Nicole Middleton, Sarah Middleton, David Mifsud, Alain Miguelez, Andy Miller, Betty Jean Miller, Katie Miller, Simon Miller, Gillian Millett, Karen Mistilis, Ian Mitchinson, Stephanie Monaghan, Massimo Mondani, Peter W Monteath, Tanya Montebello, Heather Montgomery, Keith Montgomery, Gordon A Moodie, Marcel Moonen, Philip Mooney, Kevin Morai, Yvonne Morgan, Dan Morris, Stuart Morris, Tom Morrow, Ian Mortimer, Ian Moseley, Renate Moser, Dorothy Moszynski, Dominique Mouttet, Mary Movic, Johan Muit, James Mules, Mary Mullane, Andrea Mullin, Meaghan Mulvany, Lily Mungti, Liane Munro, Moira Munro, Gary Murphy, Anne Murray, Peter Murray **N** Shioko Nagaoka, Jed Nancarrow, B Nanser, Jessica Nash, Liz Nash, Daniel Neale, Don Nelson, Steve Newcomer, Darlene Newman, Tom Newman, Andrew Newman-

Martin, Brian P Nicholas, Brian P Nichols, Alex & Diane Nikolic, Andrew Noblet, Martin Noellenburg, Michael Nold, Luca Nonato, Adrien Noordhof, Bianca Noordhuizen, Jody Nunn **O** John O'Brien, Etain O'Carroll, Fidelma O'Connor, Keith Odlin, Geni Ogihara, Melinda O'Gorman, Kate O'Hara, Karen Olch, Janke Olsson, O'Rourk Swinney **P** Jean Yves Paille, Bruce & Ann Palmer, Rose Pantalone, Christine Paquette, Dennis Paradine, Craig Park, Ed Parker, Greg Parker, Laura Parker, Dick Parson, Dick Parsons, Anthony Pasko, Lori Pasko, Tony Pastachak, Jayde Patching, Neil Pattemore, Jo Patterson, Graeme Paul Hamilton, Jo Payne, Mary Peachin, Andree Peacock, Jonathon Pease, Richard Pedder, Daiana Pellizzon, Chris Penny, Kara Penny, Sophie Percival, Chritopher Perraton, Patrick Perrault, Laure Perrier, Wendy Persoon, Piergiorgio Pescali, Brent Peters, Marc Peverini, Uli Pfeiffer, Chris Phillips, Jackey Phillips, Yoan Piché, Andrew Pilliar, Jean-Frantois Pin, Blaine Pinch, Sonia Pinkney, Gabriel Pinkstone, Lucy Platt, Helen Pleasance, Dan Plomish, Vanessa Pocock, Adri Pols, Dwight Poole, Jackie Poole, Paul Poole, Tony & Jill Porco, Lesley Porter, Erhard Poser, Jocelyn Potter, Yves Potvin, Nanda Poulisse, Nina & Tyrone Power, Tyrone Power, Marcelo Horacio Pozzo, Antonella Precoma, Mike Preece, Sheila Preece, Simon Preece, Annette Prelle, Martin Prestage, Nichola & Kevin Prested, Meredith Preston, Howard Prior, Nancy Prober, Greg Proctor, Marc Prokosch, Martine Proulx, Aljaz & Urska Prusnik, Cindy Puijk, Aart Pyl **Q** Phillip Qin, Paul Quayle, Merissa Quek, Sylrre Quellet, Helen Quigley, David Quinn, Michel Quintas **R** Bjorn Anders Radstrom, Anita Rafidi, Claudia Raichle, Glen Rajaram, Linda Rammage, Roger Randall, Shirley Randall, Thomas Rau, Jenny Raven,

SEND US YOUR FEEDBACK

We love to hear from travelers – your comments keep us on our toes and help make our books better. Our well-traveled team reads every word on what you loved or loathed about this book. Although we cannot reply individually to postal submissions, we always guarantee that your feedback goes straight to the appropriate authors, in time for the next edition. Each person who sends us information is thanked in the next edition – and the most useful submissions are rewarded with a free book.

To send us your updates – and find out about Lonely Planet events, newsletters and travel news – visit our award-winning website: **www.lonelyplanet.com/feedback**

Note: we may edit, reproduce and incorporate your comments in Lonely Planet products such as guidebooks, websites and digital products, so let us know if you don't want your comments reproduced or your name acknowledged. For a copy of our privacy policy visit www.lonelyplanet.com/privacy

Reinhard Reading, Mike Reams, Lynette Reed, Margaret Reed, Thomas Regel, Michael Reine, Pierre Renault, Jane Rennie, Janice G Richards, Emma Richardson, Jeremy Richardson, Rachel Richardson, John Riley, Barbara Robb, Judy Roberts, Karen Roberts, Al Robinson, Jane Robinson, Janet Robinson, Yetta Robinson, Bernhard Rock, Adolfo Rodriguez, Scott Rogers, Andrea Rogge, Hans-Peter Roggensack, Alex Rooke, Marco Roos, Sarah Rose Werner, Candace Ross, Derek Ross, Joanne Ross, Susan Ross, Petra Rossback, Louison Rousseau, Duncan Routledge, Shelagh M Rowan-Legg, Michael Rowe, Sandrine Ruaux, Nele Rubart, Gladys Rubatto, Karl Rubin, Con Ruddock, Mark Rudman, Claudia Rudolph, Carol Rudram, Danielle Ruppert, David Rusk, Oxy Rynchus **S** Isabella Sabelli Nadeau, Ayaka Sakata, Dieter & Sheila Salden, Karlie Salmon, Arnaud Samson, Richard Samuelson, Miguel Sanchez, Paul Sands, Andrew Sansbury, Carol & Rick Sarchet, Gwyn Sarkar, Robin Sarkar, Andre J Sauve, Colin Savage, Maria Scandore, Penny Scheenhouwer, Marc Schlichtner, Neil Schlipalius, Simon Schlosser, Erich Schmitt, Sebastian Schmitz, Martina Schoefberger, Anisha Schubert, Bruce Schultz, Ruth Schulze, Oliver Schusser, Florian Schweiger, James Scott, Martin Scott, Maik G Seewald, Lyne Seguin, Anthony Sell, Richard Semple, Andy Serra, Anne Sevriuk, Anna Shah, Ruth Shannon, Stuart Sharp, Sarah Shaughnessy, Hilary Shaw, SW Shekvadod, Mike Sheldrick, Ed Shepard, Edmund Shepard, Ed Shephard, Kerren Sherry, SW Sherwood, Maureen Shipton, Denis Shor, Peggy Shyns, Shreen Sidhu, Constanze Siefarth, Linda & Jason Sim, Michel Simard, Melissa Simmons, Anna & Chris Simon, Massimo Simoncini, Jocelyne Simoneau, Andrew Sinclair, Norm Singer, Sujee Sivasubramaniyam, Bronwyn Sivour, Valerie Slade, Thomas R Sluberski, David Smallwood, Jeroen Smeets, Ivo Smit, Alan Smith, Barney Smith, Heather Smith, Heidi Smith, Inga Smith, Jonathan Smith, Peter Smith, Rachel & Trevor Smith, Rob Smith, Stephen Smith, Mary Smyth, Elisa Snel, Luis Ducla Soares, Kathleen Solose, Ann Soper, Tina Spangler, David & Jill Spear, Kent Spencer, Patrick Spink, Mike St John, Kaz Stafford, Robert JH Stagg, Jane Stalker, Sheila Stam, Jenn Stanley, Michael Stanley, Gavin Staton, Joe Stead, Bryun Stedman, Andrew Steele, Mary Steer, John Steinbachs, Rebecca Stevens, N Stevenson, Mrs JMW & Prof Stewart, John Stigant, Ellie Stirling, Maxime St-Laurent, Stephy Stoker, Cheryl Stonehouse, Jason Strauss, Stephen Streich, Tim Stubbs, John Sturley, Aruna Subramamian, Sue Summers, Arden Sutherland, Peter Sutton, Anders Svensson, Fabio Sverzut, Eric Swan, **T** Sharona Eliahou Taieb, Dorinda Talbot, Calvin Tam, Kat Tancock, Michel Tanguay, Roy Tanner, Christine Tarrach, David Taylor, Bobby Tehranian, Mike Telford, Rachael Templeton, Reinier ten Veen, Cyrus Teng, Paul Terbasket, Ulrik Terreni, Rowena Thakore, Frank Theissen, Marcelle Thibodeau, Pia Thiemann,

Aaron Thom, Alan & Jo Thomas, Catherine Thomas, Lyndon Thomas, Peter Thomas, Carolyn Thompson, Judy & Gary Thompson, Nicole Thorpe, Matt Thrower, Donna Tidey, Glen Timpson, Kerry Tobin, Larissa Tomlinson, Veronique Torche, Pierre Tremblay, Rhiannon Elizabeth Trevethan, Cathy Tuck, Steven Turner, Richard Twigg **U** F Ubliani, Rosemary & Philip Ulyett, Sam Unruth, Dennis Urbonas **V** Sarah Valair, Joe Valcourt, Maurice Valentine, Jos van den Akker, Luc Van den Dorpel, Marga van den Ham, Jeroen & Sendy Van Heel, Marim & Rob van den Heuvel, Annerieke van Hoek, Madelon van Luijk, Lies Van Nieuwenhove, Hulya van Tangeren, Vanessa Vanclief, Nicole VandenBerg, Sabrina Vandierendonck, Ferenc Vanhoutte, Stewart Vanns, Elizabeth E Vans, Oliver Vanzon, Desmond Vas, Isabelle Vassot, Angele Vautour, Vincent Verdult, S & J Veringer, Rene Vermaire, Herma & Otto Vermeulan, John Verri, Salvatore Vespa, James Vieland, Veronica Villa, Theo Vlachos, Nichy Vyce **W** Maddy W, Sally Wade, Janet Wagner, Aron Wahl, Lary Waldman, Cheryl Walk, Alan Walker, Neil Walker, Keith Walkerdine, Naomi Wall, Gerry Wallace, Ron Wallace, Ron W Wallace, Virginia Wan, Chenya Wang, Helen Wardle, Helen & John Wardle, Julia Warner, Sylvia Warner, Alastair Warner-Green, Klaus Wartenberg, V A Waters, Lorna Watkins, Linda M Watsham, Pauline Watson, Tara Watt, Jayne Weber, Patrick Weeding, Bert Weissbach, Claudia Werger, Sandra West, Ling Weston, Susan Westwood, Mark Wettlaufer, Michael & Sarah Weyburne, Heather Wharton, Chris Whatley, Christopher Wheeler, Mark Whiffin, Andrea White, Jennifer Whitman, Mattias Wick, Daniel Wickie, Andrew Wicks, Roma Wiemer, Roy Wiesner, Leonore Wigger, Diederik JD Wijnmalen, Andrew Willers, Edith William, Edith & Bernard William, Amanda Williams, Guylaine Williams, Katheen Williams, Olugbala Williams, Pauline Williams, Scott Williams, Paul Williamson, Kim Willoughby, Jeremy Wills, Mary Wills, Alex Wilson, Alison Wilson, Chris Wilson, Elsbeth Wilson, Ryan Wilson, Karin Winkelmann, Peter Winter, Katherine Wisborg, Andrew Witham, Rhonda Witt, Katrin Wohlleben, Sandra Wolf, Nora & Rick Wolff, Clinton Wong, Jenn Wood, Wendy Worley, A Wright, Andrew Wright, Colin & Robyn Wright, Douglas Wright, Mark Wright, Chandi Wyant, Ingrid Wyles, Scott Wylie **Y** Yildiz Yanmaz, Mary Yearsley, GK Yeoh, Y Yerbury-Nodgron, Andrew Young, Paul Young, So Young, Victoria Young, Wanieta Young, Jay Wan Yu **Z** Natacha Zana, Mijke Zengerink, Arlene Zimmerman, Harold & Joyce Zuberman, Wanda Zyla

ACKNOWLEDGEMENTS
Many thanks to the following for the use of their content:

Globe on back cover © Mountain High Maps 1993 Digital Wisdom, Inc.

Index

INDEX

MAP LEGEND

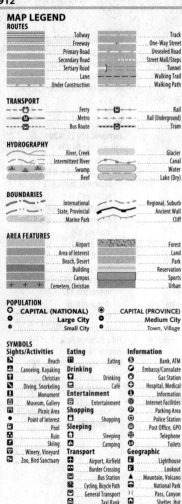

ROUTES

Tollway	Track
Freeway	One-Way Street
Primary Road	Unsealed Road
Secondary Road	Street Mall/Steps
Tertiary Road	Tunnel
Lane	Walking Trail
Under Construction	Walking Path

TRANSPORT

Ferry	Rail
Metro	Rail (Underground)
Bus Route	Tram

HYDROGRAPHY

River, Creek	Glacier
Intermittent River	Canal
Swamp	Water
Reef	Lake (Dry)

BOUNDARIES

International	Regional, Suburb
State, Provincial	Ancient Wall
Marine Park	Cliff

AREA FEATURES

Airport	Forest
Area of Interest	Land
Beach, Desert	Park
Building	Reservation
Campus	Sports
Cemetery, Christian	Urban

POPULATION

○ **CAPITAL (NATIONAL)**	◉ CAPITAL (PROVINCE)
● **Large City**	● Medium City
○ Small City	○ Town, Village

SYMBOLS

Sights/Activities
- Beach
- Canoeing, Kayaking
- Christian
- Diving, Snorkeling
- Monument
- Museum, Gallery
- Picnic Area
- Point of Interest
- Pool
- Ruin
- Skiing
- Winery, Vineyard
- Zoo, Bird Sanctuary

Eating
- Eating

Drinking
- Drinking
- Café

Entertainment
- Entertainment

Shopping
- Shopping

Sleeping
- Sleeping
- Camping

Transport
- Airport, Airfield
- Border Crossing
- Bus Station
- Cycling, Bicycle Path
- General Transport
- Taxi Rank
- Trail Head

Information
- Bank, ATM
- Embassy/Consulate
- Gas Station
- Hospital, Medical
- Information
- Internet Facilities
- Parking Area
- Police Station
- Post Office, GPO
- Telephone
- Toilets

Geographic
- Lighthouse
- Lookout
- Mountain, Volcano
- National Park
- Pass, Canyon
- Shelter, Hut
- Waterfall

LONELY PLANET OFFICES

Australia
Head Office
Locked Bag 1, Footscray, Victoria 3011
☎ 03 8379 8000, fax 03 8379 8111
talk2us@lonelyplanet.com.au

USA
150 Linden St, Oakland, CA 94607
☎ 510 893 8555, toll free 800 275 8555
fax 510 893 8572, info@lonelyplanet.com

UK
72–82 Rosebery Ave,
Clerkenwell, London EC1R 4RW
☎ 020 7841 9000, fax 020 7841 9001
go@lonelyplanet.co.uk

Published by Lonely Planet Publications Pty Ltd
ABN 36 005 607 983

© Lonely Planet 2005

© photographers as indicated 2005

Cover photographs: Canadian Rockies, Alberta, Jacob Taposchaner/
Getty Images (front); autumn foliage in Montréal, Alain Evrard/
Lonely Planet Images (back). Many of the images in this guide are
available for licensing from Lonely Planet Images: www.lonelyplanet
images.com

Printed through SNP Security Printing Pte Ltd at
KHL Printing Co Sdn Bhd, Malaysia